Contents

Acknowledgements

With *Football League Players' Records* now in its fourth edition, the editor would once again like to thank the many experts without whose help this book would not have been updated as effectively.

The assistant editor, Alan Platt, is by profession a freelance transport planner whose most recent assignments have been abroad. He first introduced himself to me as long ago as 1981, following the release of the first edition. His help on the ever continuing project has been invaluable, especially in the area of current players, which he researches diligently. Unlike many schoolboys he did not take an interest in soccer until reaching the age of 14, but from that moment he was hooked. From 1960 onwards he has kept detailed records on all Football League clubs and their players. During 1985 to 1986 he contributed to the Chesterfield (where he resides when in England) match programme, but more recently he has thrown himself wholeheartedly into the tremendous amount of research that is required to make FLPRs the "Bible" that it has hopefully become.

Another important member of the production team is Michael Featherstone. Michael was a willing helper when I first perceived the idea for such a book way back in 1975. His speciality is in researching births and deaths, something he also does for the various cricketing societies and the new wave of soccer histories that have begun to be produced over the last ten years or so, with Tony Matthews and Anton Rippon of Breedon Books, leading the way. He started out by collecting both cricket and football information, often topping up with visits to the Colindale National Newspaper Library. Eventually, he joined Ray Spiller's Association of Football Statisticians after being introduced by his good friend, the late Morley Farror. He has also contributed to the *British Boxing Yearbook*, *The Olympic Games: Complete Track & Field Results 1896-1988*, *Cricket Who's Who*, *The Official Football League Yearbook* and many other publications.

More recently, I have received invaluable help from Mike Davage, the editor of *Canary Citizens, The Official History of Norwich City FC*. Mike has been involved in football for a good many years now and is currently compiling a Football League Players' Records covering the period between the two wars. With his vast pre-war expertise, I asked him for help when it came to producing complete career records for men who had played prior to 1946. He responded brilliantly, so much so, that after much research between us, I have managed to include these records in FLPRs. At the same time, I would like to think that we have helped Mike in no little way, proving the point that without a great deal of teamwork a major football publication, such as this, would just not be possible.

Also, I would like to place on record my appreciation of the willing and enthusiastic co-operation of the following in researching individual club details:- Steve Adamson (Scarborough), Tony Ambrosen (Newport County), Chris Ashton & Don Nannestad (Lincoln City), David Batters (York City), Mike Blackstone (Exeter City), Tony Bluff (Doncaster Rovers), Wallace Chadwick (Burnley), Clive Childs (Chesterfield), John Crooks (Cardiff City), Mike Davage (Norwich City), David Downs (Reading), Garth Dykes (Oldham Athletic), John Eastwood (Ipswich Town), Colin Faiers (Cambridge United), Harold Finch (Crewe Alexandra), Terry Frost (Bradford City), Brian Gosney (Bristol Rovers), John Hughes (Chester City), Bernard Jones (Tranmere Rovers), Doug Lamming (Hull City), Ian Mills (Notts County), Tony Matthews (West Bromwich Albion), Gerald Mortimer (Derby County), Dave Roberts (Wrexham), Bill Rodgers (Carlisle United), Roger Triggs (Gillingham), Paul Truscott (Plymouth Argyle), Tony White (Fulham), Frank Tweddle (Darlington), Peter Wyatt (Stoke City) and the editors of all the various club histories that I mentioned earlier.

The photographs, as in my recent publication, *Premier League: The Players*, were supplied by Neal Simpson of Empics Photo Agency, 26 Musters Road, West Bridgford, Nottingham (0602 455885). Yet again they reached the high standard demanded in production and were also able to supply many shots that go back to those early post-war days which have been invaluable in the make up of a book of this nature.

I would like to once again show my appreciation for the support given by Gordon Taylor, the Chief Executive of the Professional Footballers' Association, who has helped to make this book possible and who has always recognised that FLPRs is a testament to his members, both past and present. And, as in previous years, I would like to thank the Football League, who through Sheila Murphy, once again kindly made their records available to myself and my team.

Finally, I must thank Tony Williams, the publisher, for his blinding faith in FLPRs; Jean Bastin, the typesetter, for her many months of patient and time consuming work which would drive the average person into the ground; Jennifer Hugman, my wife, for reading and correcting many hours worth of galleys; George Brown, who designed the layouts; and Character Graphics for producing the picture spreads and film origination.

Barry J. Hugman

Introduction

This is the fourth edition of this now well-established work of reference on post-war footballers. Since the first edition appeared in 1980, published by Rothmans, we have striven to improve its accuracy, not only by updating the statistics and listing new entries for players who made their Football League debuts since the last edition, but also correcting, where necessary, the details of players long since retired.

When Barry Hugman first started this compendium in the late 1970s, the only source of data were the hardy football perennials – the *News of the World* and *News Chronicle (later Playfair) Football Annuals* – which listed each player's appearances and goals for the previous season. During the 1980s, a number of football statisticians began to chronicle the detailed history of their favourite clubs, match by match, with reference to Football League archives and local newspapers. Much of their research has been published by Breedon Books in their "Complete Record" series under the editorship of Anton Rippon. To date, approximately 35 such club histories have been published by Breedon Books, but other club historians have published their work either independently, or with other publishers such as Tony Matthews for the West Midlands clubs, John Eastwood (Ipswich Town and Norwich City), Dave Smith (Leicester City), Tony Ambrosen (Newport County) and Roger Triggs (Gillingham).

All their researches have been cross-referenced with the data contained in previous editions of this book and many discrepancies in appearances and goals have been noted. In most cases the discrepancies were trival, a question of one or two appearances or goals difference. In a few cases they were significant, usually when players with the same (or similar) surname played in the same season for the same club. If we are satisfied that the research has been done correctly and that the statistics continued in these books are more reliable than the figures in by-gone football annuals, we have corrected our records accordingly.

It should be noted, however, that while an appearance in a particular match is a matter of fact, goalscorers are often a matter of opinions. In a goalmouth scramble, a goal may be credited to one player by the assembled journalists sitting 100 yards from the action and reported as such by the press the following day, whilst the club, following a post-mortem, credits the goal to another of its players. In such cases we accept the opinion of the club rather than the press. However, there are other cases where the club is anxious to credit a goal to one of its own players when it is quite manifestly an own goal. For example the misjudged back pass, the misdirected shot deflected into goal by an opposing defender, or the goalkeeper stepping over the line after safely catching a high ball. Such examples we consider as "own goals" and not credited to any player. As a result of these differences of interpretation, there are inevitably some small discrepancies between the goalscoring figures of some players in this book and those logged by other sources.

Regular purchasers of *Football League Players' Records* will note a change of format. As the number of players listed has increased we have been forced to conserve space by creating two columns per page with seperate lines for players' names and bio-data details, plus international honours.

Players Names: As far as is humanly possible, we have listed players in alphabetic order, firstly by surname and then by first christian name. However, in cases where players are better known by their second or third christian name, we have listed them under their commonly used name. For example Mark Hughes of Manchester United was christened "Leslie Mark" but will be found under "Mark". Philip Lee Jones of Liverpool will be found under "Lee". To do otherwise could cause confusion to the reader searching for the entry of a player with a very common surname. Other players are not recorded under the family surname. For example, the Brazilian, Mirandinha, of Newcastle United, is in fact "Francisco da Silva", but is listed under his adopted moniker rather than his family name. In the case of double-barrelled surnames we have taken a pragmatic view, according to the name most commonly used by themselves or the media. Thus, Ian Storey-Moore and Forbes Phillipson-Masters will be found under their full names while the Martin-Chambers brothers, Derek and Philip, will be found under "Chambers" and the recent Spurs debutant, Jeffrey Thompson-Minton, under "Minton". In many cases players were known by a corruption of their christian names or by a totally different nickname, such as the Brentford goalkeeper "Sonny" Feehan, christened Ignatius. In such cases, players are listed under their christened name with their familiar moniker shown in brackets afterwards.

Birthplaces: The purpose of showing birthplaces is to indicate the area of the British Isles a player originates from. However, this is frequently misleading. Many players were born overseas, either as sons of fathers serving in the armed forces stationed in West Germany, or in further flung former colonies. Their birthplace does not, however, indicate their nationality, which is conferred on them by their parentage. A player may be born in one area, but grow up in another. In such cases the place of education is more meaningful than place of birth. Some players were born while their parents were on holiday, such as the Kimble brothers, Alan and Garry, in Poole (Dorset). In their particular case, as it was known to us, the birthplace is shown as the family home of Dagenham. Birthplaces are taken from birth certificates, copies of which are deposited with the Football League when the player is registered by a club. However, birth certificates may only indicate an area of the county, such as a county or the birth registration district with an antiquated name, often not stating the town or village of birth. All persons born in the counties of Gloucestershire and

Worcestershire are registered as born in the county town. Those born in County Durham are shown by obscure registration districts such as "Central South-East" and "North-West", which do not indicate the town of origin. Most players shown with their birthplace as "Ormskirk" were almost certainly born in the neighbouring new town of Skelmersdale. Some players were born in maternity hospitals located in different administrative areas from the parential home, such as Rochford (for Southend) and Orsett (for Grays and Thurrock). In cases where the actual birthplace is known to the authors, the original information as shown in earlier editions has been corrected. In some cases where the birthplace was an obscure country village, or suburb of a large city, the name of the nearest market town or city has been substituted. However, in the case of mining villages which produced many fine players, we have taken care to preserve their identity. For players born outside the British Isles and Ireland, only the name of the country is given. Irishmen born outside of Dublin and Belfast are indicated by (Ire) and (NI), respectively, while players from the numerous Caribbean islands are indicated by (WI) for the West Indies. In some cases the following code is used to determine the county of origin: (Cam) Cambridgeshire; (Dm) Durham; (Dst) Dorset; (Dy) Derbyshire; (Ex) Essex; (Kt) Kent; (Lei) Leicestershire; (Lk) Lanarkshire; (Nd) Northumberland; (Nk) Norfolk; (Nts) Nottinghamshire; (Sf) Suffolk; (Sx) Sussex; (IoW) Isle of Wight.

Birthdate: Since these are taken from the Football League's records, which copy the birth certificate of every professional, this evidence is regarded as incontrovertible, although some discrepancies with clubs histories have been noted, mainly in the year of birth. However, when we are satisfied that a transcribing error has occurred we have corrected the original birthdate.

League Clubs: Self explanatory.

Source (or Previous Club): This column indicates a player's origins, whether from outside the FL or within the ranks of the League. For the latter the following code is used:
Jnrs = Junior players signed from school/college, without serving an apprenticeship or trainee period.
App = Apprentice signing prior to 1986.
YTS = Trainee. This rank was introduced in 1986 and includes players sponsored by the Government's Youth Training Scheme.
Tr = Transfers (including free transfers).
L = Loan signing, or temporary transfer, shown only when the player made an appearance.
For players signed from overseas clubs, the following code for countries is employed:
(Arg) Argentina; (Aus) Australia; (Bel) Belgium; (Br) Brazil; (Can) Canada; (Den) Denmark; (Fin) Finland; (Fr) France; (Gr) Greece; (HK) Hong Kong; (It) Italy; (Neth) Netherlands; (NZ) New Zealand; (Nor) Norway; (Pol) Poland; (Port) Portugal; (SA) South Africa; (Sp) Spain; (Swe) Sweden; (Switz) Switzerland; (WG) West Germany; (Yug) Yugoslavia.

Date Signed: The date given by month/year is when the player signed professional forms, or as in the case of non-contract, apprentices and amateurs, the date of signing is that of the status indicated. Occasionally, there were players who made their FL debuts before signing professional forms and in those cases we have recorded the date that they first joined the club. For players first signed on loan, before a permanent transfer was arranged, the date of signing is that of the loan transfer, except when the player returned to his former club and made further appearances. Non-League (N/L) is only shown where the compilers have not been able to find the necessary date in question.

Seasons Played: The year shown is the first year of the season played. Thus, 1979 indicates the season 1979-80, "1979-85" means that the player made his debut in 1979-80 and his last appearance in 1985-86, but does not mean necessarily that he played in every intervening season.

Appearances, Subs and Goals: The statistics shown are for Football League matches only. Cup games and end of season play-offs are not included, nor are appearances made for League clubs before they entered the FL or in temporary absence (e.g. Lincoln City 1987-88 and Darlington 1989-90). Whilst other sources have aggregated full and substitute appearances into a single total, we consider it important to maintain the distinction. Most substitutions occur in the final quarter of the game and we feel that one full appearance, plus 17 substitute appearances, is not the same as 18 full appearances.

Positions:

(G)	Goalkeeper	(LH)	Left-half
(D)	Defender - general	(M)	Central midfield
(RB)	Right full-back	(RM)	Right side midfield
(LB)	Left full-back	(LM)	Left side midfield
(FB)	Both full-back positions	(OR) (RW)	Outside-right/Right-wing
(CD)	Central defender	(OL) (LW)	Outside-left/Left-wing
(HB)	Half-back - wing and centre	(W)	Winger - either flank
(CH)	Centre-half	(IF)	Inside-forward
(WH)	Wing-half - left or right	(CF)	Centre-forward
(RH)	Right-half	(F)	Forward

The position shown for each player is that in which he played most frequently, or is most commonly associated. However, today, many players frequently switch between defence and midfield, or between defence and attack. In such cases their two most common positions are shown e.g. (FB/M), (CD/F), (M/F). The nomenclature of playing positions has changed considerably since the last war. From 1946 to the early 1960s it was widely assumed that teams played a 2-3-5 formation with two full-backs, three half-backs and five forwards. In fact, the true formation was 3-3-4, since the change in the off-side law in the 1930s when the centre-half was converted to centre-back and one inside-forward was withdrawn into a deeper position. Despite all the changes, the term "centre-half" still persists up to the present day, whilst, until the invention of the term "midfield" in the mid 1960s, inside-forwards could be either deep lying schemers such as Johnny Haynes (Fulham), or lethal goalscorers such as Ted Phillips (Ipswich Town). In 1958 Brazil introduced 4-2-4 to the world, when winning the World Cup in Sweden. Under this system, one wing-half was converted to twin centre-back, while the other wing-half, plus an inside-forward, patrolled the middle of the park. Although this system was copied by many English clubs, it was not entirely successful since it required two talented and hard working players in the central positions. After Alf Ransey won the 1966 World Cup for England with a 4-3-3 system, with one winger withdrawn to augment the midfield, most English clubs adopted the same system and when Ramsey dispensed with wingers altogether with a 4-4-2 system for the 1970 World Cup in Mexico, the orthodox attacking winger disappeared for several years from the English game, to be replaced by workaholic midfielders. By 1970 the terms "centre-half", "wing-half", "inside-forward" and "centre-forward", "outside-right" and "outside-left" were virtually obsolescent, to be replaced by "centre backs" (or defenders), "midfield", "twin strikers" and occasionally "wingers". Happily, the orthodox winger returned to favour in the 1980s with a corresponding increase in the goal rate, as some clubs reverted to 4-3-3 instead of 4-4-2. Since the late 1980s many teams have played with three central defenders, with one deployed behind the other two as a "sweeper" and the two full-backs pushed forward into midfield as auxiliary wingers. The result has been the emergence of a 3-5-2 formation, with overcrowded midfield areas, or a more fluid 3-4-3 system with one winger deployed as an auxiliary forward.

Finally, one major change we have implemented for the very first time within this edition, is that of listing the complete career record of all players who played in the Football League, prior to the last war. This takes into account famous players like Sir Stanley Matthews, who played for eight seasons before the outbreak of war and for nearly 20 after and also many other stars whose careers ran parallel with a man such as Stan Cullis. These are the players who had lost the best years of their football life because of hostilities and retired early into the post-war period. Previous editions showed Cullis as having played only 37 games for "Wolves", whereas in fact he played 152 times between 1934-35 and 1946-47.

As we have stated in previous editions, one thing is for sure . . . if they have played in the post-war Football League, they are included within the pages of this book and somebody, somewhere, sometime, will look them up. *Football League Players' Records* is a testament to all of the men who have donned the colours of their specific FL side since 1946-47 and to the Professional Footballers' Association who have magnificently supported their members throughout that period.

Foreword

by Gordon Taylor (Chief Executive, Professional Footballers' Association)

THE IDEA of compiling a list of every footballer to have played in the Football League since the Second World War would be enough to drive most journalists into an early grave, or a football statistician into Seventh Heaven! So, where exactly do you start on such a project? How many years of research are needed to complete the job? On the face of it, the task would seem an impossible one!

However, Barry Hugman and his team of enthusiasts, have, without question, given us the definitive record of all our professional (and a few amateur) players who have graced the Football League.

To be good enough to be selected for a Football League club's first team is proof enough of a players ability. You only have to ask all those who didn't make the grade! So, here then is the official list of all those who actually wore their club colours in League battle. And, of course, this book also shows the transfers, plus the career records of every single player. All of these men have been members of 'The Professional Footballers' Association' and we at 'The PFA' are proud to see such a magnificently produced record of the careers of so many members past and present.

In my opinion, this book will give hours and hours of pleasure to ex-players reminiscing, present day players comparing records, plus supporters of all ages, who can check on players they saw years and years ago, or even only last season. The statistics, the photos and those long lost names from the distant past provide a remarkable cast list.

We are delighted to be involved with this publication and anticipate referring to it time and time again and our thanks go to Barry and his team for all their dedicated hard work and to Tony Williams for organising the publishing of such a marvellous book.

The Professional Footballers' Association

Organised professional football began in 1888 with the formation of the Football League. Unsuccessful attempts were made to form a players union, but it was not until December 2nd 1907 that there took place in Manchester the first meeting of the Professional Footballers' Association. It was chaired by the famous Welsh International, William Meredith. From that early beginning of players joining together to improve their working conditions, the PFA has grown to become the highly respected professional body it is today. Those men would have been proud of the advances the PFA have made to improve the lot of the professional player. The PFA represent all full-time professional players, plus a number of semi-professionals outside of the League and have 1,200 Youth Trainees on two year courses, combining football with college learning, intended to help them when their playing days are over.

The aim of the PFA has always been to systematically protect and improve the conditions and status of its members. This involves many different aspects, including enforcement of contracts, providing insurance against death and disability, being trustees of contributory and non-contributory pension funds, representing players negotiating contracts, or at disciplinary hearings with the Football League or the FA, or in dispute with their clubs over fines or other disciplinary problems. They are represented on the ultimate appeals body for disciplinary measures and are directly involved with matters relating to penalties imposed on players who receive cautions or are sent off.

The PFA work with the governing bodies with regard to work permit criteria for players outside the Common Market. They are part of the decision making process that ensures the criteria are observed, thus protecting national players and ensuring that foreign players enjoy wages commensurate with their ability and have a standard of skill that will enable them to be successful in our very competitive leagues.

The PFA has been involved in various disputes during its history. Two of the milestones were the removal of the maximum wage in 1961 and the court ruling that football's retain and transfer system was illegal in 1963. In the 1970s, a commission on industrial relations eventually brought in all the present day procedures that footballers enjoy today. The most important decision was the establishment in 1978 of a player's right to change clubs at the end of his contract. Now, if a player wishes to leave a club to play for another, he can go and a transfer tribunal, which has an independent chairman, will set a fee. The PFA make up one member of the tribunal. Approximately 30 such cases are dealt with each year.

The PFA have an Education Fund to provide training courses for players wanting to prepare for a career after their playing days are over. Last year 544 grants were made, costing £150,000, on a myriad of various programmes, including FA coaching, business management, journalism, HGV licences and even Christian Ministry. They are also responsible for formulating the Football Club and Community Programme, which was set up to establish a better relationship between clubs and their local community, following the crowd problems of the '80s. The 1986 pilot scheme of six North-West clubs has now grown to involve well over 80 and employs some 60 former players full-time and has allowed over 800 to train for re-employment.

The PFA is involved with the welfare of players through three schemes. The first ensures every player has a lump sum upon retirement from the game, funded by a 5% levy on all transfer fees. Some four million pounds has been paid out to players in all divisions since 1980. There is also an Accident Insurance Fund, which covers medical costs through grants to present and former members suffering from football related conditions such as osteoarthritis. It also provides private medical insurance cover for all current members, to ensure quick treatment of injuries. The Benevolent Fund exists to help members and ex-members and dependants who fall upon hard times. They have also made loans of over £250,000 to various clubs struggling to survive in recent years. The English Football Leagues provide international players for England, Wales, Scotland, Northern Ireland and Eire and so the PFA feels it must play a role in making sure that home grown talent is encouraged and allowed to develop.

Last season there were over 30 players transferred for more than a million pounds. This does not give a true impression of the financial state of the game, or make it easy for football to present a credible case for government help to implement the Taylor report. However, the redeeming feature of the transfer system is that money can filter through to the lower divisions, as many transfers involve players developed by the smaller clubs being snapped up for large sums by the big clubs. For this reason, the PFA has never tried to obtain total freedom of movement for players, as it feels it would be counter-productive and adversely affect similar clubs and thereby members' jobs.

In Europe, EUFA has a rigid system for when a player's contract ends, dependent on a maximum fee, his age and previous years' wages. In England, there is probably a more flexible system, involving arbitration. A panel made up of an independent Chairman and representatives of various footballing bodies, including the PFA, decide upon the fee when the buying and selling clubs cannot agree, making possible the player's move and their decision is binding.

Unfortunately, many politicians in the European Parliament believe there should be no restraint whatsoever on the movement of players, which could have catastrophic results for football if implemented as law.

The PFA firmly believes that the future of professional football can only be guaranteed if the various bodies involved in the administration of the game work together to achieve government by consent. The days of government by dictat are gone. The Premier League tried to steam roller the players, but found that they were prepared to support their union to the tune of over 90% in its attempt to ensure their voice is not just heard but listened to and that the interests of players are understood to be of paramount importance in all decisions made about football. After all, FA Committees, League officials, Club Chairmen and Directors, Bankers or Accountants, cannot actually play the game and keep the fans piling through the turnstiles and the TV companies panting to bring their cameras to the match.

PFA OFFICE BEARERS 1907-1985

Secretaries

H. C. Bloomfield	1907-1910
A. J. Owen	1910-1913
N. J. Newbould	1913-1929
J. A. Fay	1929-1953
C. Lloyd, O.B.E.	1953-1981
G. Taylor, M.A., B.Sc (Econ)	1981-

Chairmen

H. L. Mainman	1907-1910
E. H. Lintott	1910-1911
C. Veitch	1911-1918
C. Roberts	1919-1921
J. Lawrence	1921-1922
J. A. Fay	1922-1929
H. Matthews	1929-1930
A. Wood	1930-1936
A. F. Barrett	1936-1937
S. D. Crooks	1937-1946
J. C. Guthrie	1946-1957
J. W. T. Hill	1957-1961
T. S. Cummings	1961-1963
M. C. Musgrove	1963-1966
N. Cantwell	1966-1967
J. W. T. Neill	1967-1970
A. D. Dougan	1970-1978
G. Taylor	1978-1980
A. Gowling	1980-1982
S. J. Coppell	1982-1984
B. Talbot	1984-1988
G. Crooks	1988-1990
B. Marwood	1990-

THE PFA AWARDS

Player of the Year: 1974 Norman Hunter (Leeds U); 1975 Colin Todd (Derby Co); 1976 Pat Jennings (Tottenham H); 1977 Andy Gray (Aston Villa); 1978 Peter Shilton (Nottingham F); 1979 Liam Brady (Arsenal); 1980 Terry McDermott (Liverpool); 1981 John Wark (Ipswich T); 1982 Kevin Keegan (Southampton); 1983 Kenny Dalglish (Liverpool); 1984 Ian Rush (Liverpool); 1985 Peter Reid (Everton); 1986 Gary Lineker (Everton); 1987 Clive Allen (Tottenham H); 1988 John Barnes (Liverpool); 1989 Mark Hughes (Manchester U); 1990 David Platt (Aston Villa); 1991 Mark Hughes (Manchester U); 1992 Gary Pallister (Manchester U).

Young Player of the Year: 1974 Kevin Beattie (Ipswich T); 1975 Mervyn Day (West Ham U); 1976 Peter Barnes (Manchester C); 1977 Andy Gray (Aston Villa); 1978 Tony Woodcock (Nottingham F); 1979 Cyrille Regis (West Bromwich A); 1980 Glenn Hoddle (Tottenham H); 1981 Gary Shaw (Aston Villa); 1982 Steve Moran (Southampton); 1983 Ian Rush (Liverpool); 1984 Paul Walsh (Luton T); 1985 Mark Hughes (Manchester U); 1986 Tony Cottee (West Ham U); 1987 Tony Adams (Arsenal); 1988 Paul Gascoigne (Tottenham H); 1989 Paul Merson (Arsenal); 1990 Matthew Le Tissier (Southampton); 1991 Lee Sharpe (Manchester U); 1992 Ryan Giggs (Manchester U).

Merit Award: 1974 Bobby Charlton OBE, Cliff Lloyd OBE; 1975 Denis Law; 1976 George Eastham OBE; 1977 Jack Taylor OBE; 1978 Bill Shankly OBE; 1979 Tom Finney OBE; 1980 Sir Matt Busby CBE; 1981 John Trollope MBE; 1982 Joe Mercer OBE; 1983 Bob Paisley OBE; 1984 Bill Nicholson; 1985 Ron Greenwood CBE; 1986 The 1966 England World Cup team, Sir Alf Ramsey, Harold Shepherdson; 1987 Sir Stanley Matthews CBE; 1988 Billy Bonds MBE; 1989 Nat Lofthouse; 1990 Peter Shilton OBE, MBE; 1991 Tommy Hutchison; 1992 Brian Clough.

PFA DIVISIONAL AWARD WINNERS: 1992

Division One: Tony Coton (Manchester C); Rob Jones (Liverpool); Stuart Pearce (Nottingham F); Gary Pallister (Manchester U); Des Walker (Nottingham F); Ray Houghton (Liverpool); Gary McAllister (Leeds U); Andy Townsend (Chelsea); Gary Lineker (Tottenham H); Alan Shearer (Southampton); Mark Hughes (Manchester U).

Division Two: David James (Watford); David Kerslake (Swindon T); John Beresford (Portsmouth); David Linighan (Ipswich T); Colin Calderwood (Swindon T); Mike Hazard (Swindon T); Gordon Cowans (Blackburn Rov); Scott Sellars (Blackburn Rov); Duncan Shearer (Swindon T); John Aldridge (Tranmere Rov); David Speedie (Blackburn Rov).

Division Three: Chris Turner (Leyton Orient); Scott Hiley (Exeter C); Simon Charlton (Huddersfield T); Terry Evans (Brentford); Vince Overson (Stoke C); Chris Marsden (Huddersfield T); Tony Kelly (Bolton W); Nigel Gleghorn (Birmingham C); Wayne Biggins (Stoke C); Dean Holdsworth (Brentford); Iwan Roberts (Huddersfield T).

Division Four: Kelham O'Hanlon (Carlisle U); Paul Fleming (Mansfield T); Phil Hardy (Wrexham); Steve Davis (Burnley); Alan Walker (Gillingham); Shaun Goodwin (Rotherham U); Paul Groves (Blackpool); Kenny Lowe (Barnet); Gary Bull (Barnet); Dave Bamber (Blackpool); Phil Stant (Mansfield T).

Tony Adams (Arsenal & England)
Current Arsenal captain, having led the "Gunners" to two League Championship wins

League Club	Source	Date Signed	Seasons Played	Career Record Apps	Subs	Gls
AAS, Einar J.						
Norway, 12 October, 1955 Norwegian Int						(CD)
Nottingham F.	Bayem Munich	03.81	80-81	20	1	1
ABBISS, Keith D.						
Hatfield, 26 April, 1932						(IF)
Brighton & H.A.	Hitchin T.	10.57	59-60	19	-	3
ABBLEY, Stephen G.						
Liverpool, 10 March, 1957						(W)
Swindon T.	Parks	10.79	79-81	14	9	0
ABBOTT, Gregory S.						
Coventry, 14 December, 1963						(M/RB)
Coventry C.	App	12.81				
Bradford C.	Tr	09.82	82-90	256	25	38
Halifax T.	Tr	07.91	91	24	4	1
ABBOTT, John						
Winsford, 25 May, 1943						(CH)
Crewe Alex.	Winsford U.	06.61	61-64	4	-	0
ABBOTT, Peter A.						
Rotherham, 1 October, 1953						(F)
Manchester U.	App	10.70				
Swansea C.	Tr	02.74	73-75	34	7	3
Crewe Alex.	Hartford (USA)	08.76	76	27	4	8
Southend U.	Tr	07.77	77-78	26	1	4
ABBOTT, Ronald F.						
Lambeth, 2 August, 1953						(CD)
Queens Park R.	App	07.71	73-78	32	14	4
ABBOTTS, John						
Stoke, 10 October, 1924						
Port Vale		05.49	50	3	-	0
ABEL, Graham						
Runcorn, 17 September, 1960						(CD)
Chester C.	Northwich Vic.	10.85	85-91	259	4	29
ABLETT, Gary I.						
Liverpool, 19 November, 1965 Eu21-1/E 'B'						(D)
Liverpool	App	11.83	86-91	103	6	1
Derby Co.	L	01.85	84	3	3	0
Hull C.	L	09.86	86	5	0	0
Everton	Tr	01.92	91	17	0	1

Gary Ablett (Liverpool & Everton)

League Club	Source	Date Signed	Seasons Played	Career Record Apps	Subs	Gls
ABRAHAM, Gareth J.						
Merthyr Tydfil, 13 February, 1969						(CD)
Cardiff C.	YT	07.87	87-91	82	5	4
ABRAHAMS, Lawrence A. M.						
Stepney, 3 April, 1953						(F)
Charlton Ath.	Barking	05.77	77	12	4	2
ABREY, Brian A.						
Hendon, 25 April, 1939						(CH)
Chelsea	Jnrs	10.56				
Colchester U.	Tr	05.61	61	38	-	2
ABRUZZESE, David						
Aberdare, 8 October, 1969 W Yth						(D)
Newport Co.	YT	08.86	86-87	24	1	0
ABTHORPE, John						
Nottingham, 19 January, 1933						(CF)
Notts Co. (Am)	Wolverhampton W. (Am)	09.55	55	5	-	3
ACHAMPONG Kenneth						
Kilburn, 26 June, 1966						(F)
Fulham	App	06.84	84-87	68	13	15
Charlton Ath.	Tr	08.89	89	2	8	0
Leyton Orient	Tr	08.90	90-91	45	13	6
ACKERLEY, Ernest N.						
Manchester 23 September, 1943						(CF)
Manchester U.	Jnrs	10.60				
Barrow	Tr	04.63	62-63	53	-	12
ACKERLEY, Stanley						
Manchester, 12 July, 1942						(FB)
Manchester U.	Jnrs	11.59				
Oldham Ath.	Tr	06.61	61	2	-	0
ACKERMAN, Alfred A. E.						
South Africa, 5 January, 1929 Died 1988						(CF)
Hull C.	Clyde	07.50	50	34	-	21
Norwich C.	Tr	08.51	51-53	66	-	31
Hull C.	Tr	10.53	53-54	58	-	28
Derby Co.	Tr	03.55	54-56	36	-	21
Carlisle U.	Tr	11.56	56-58	96	-	62
Millwall	Tr	01.59	58-60	81	-	35
ACKERMAN, Antony A.						
Islington, 20 February, 1948						(CH)
Leyton Orient	West Ham U. (Am)	10.66	66-67	4	0	0

Tony Ackerman (Leyton Orient)

ACKLAND, Michael E.
Sidcup, 4 June, 1935 (IF)

League Club	Source	Date Signed	Seasons Played	Apps	Subs	Gls
Gillingham	Harland Social	08.55	56	2	-	0

A'COURT Alan
Rainhill, 30 September, 1934 Eu23-7/EF Lge/E-5 (OL)

League Club	Source	Date Signed	Seasons Played	Apps	Subs	Gls
Liverpool	Prescot Cables	09.52	52-62	355	-	61
Tranmere Rov.	Tr	10.64	64-65	50	0	11

ACRES, Basil D. J.
Brantham, 27 October, 1926 (FB)

League Club	Source	Date Signed	Seasons Played	Apps	Subs	Gls
Ipswich T.	Brantham	09.50	51-59	217	-	6

ACTON, Alec E.
Leicester, 12 November, 1938 (HB)

League Club	Source	Date Signed	Seasons Played	Apps	Subs	Gls
Stoke C.	Leicester C. (Am)	01.56				
Stockport Co.	Brush Sports	08.58	58-59	9	-	0

ADAM, Charles
Glasgow, 22 March, 1919 (W)

League Club	Source	Date Signed	Seasons Played	Apps	Subs	Gls
Leicester C.	Strathclyde	09.38	46-50	158	-	22
Mansfield T.	Tr	07.52	52-54	93	-	6

Charlie Adam (Leicester City & Mansfield Town)

ADAM, James
Glasgow, 13 May, 1931 (OL)

League Club	Source	Date Signed	Seasons Played	Apps	Subs	Gls
Aldershot (Am)		08.50	50	1	-	0
Luton T.	Spennymoor U.	07.53	53-58	137	-	22
Aston Villa	Tr	08.59	59-60	24	-	3
Stoke C.	Tr	07.61	61	22	-	7

ADAM, James
Palsley, 22 April, 1931 (IF)

League Club	Source	Date Signed	Seasons Played	Apps	Subs	Gls
Leeds U.	Penilee U.	06.51				
Mansfield T.	Tr	08.54	54	39	-	12

ADAMS, Anthony A.
Romford, 10 October, 1966 E Yth/Eu21-5/E'B'/E-19 (CD)

League Club	Source	Date Signed	Seasons Played	Apps	Subs	Gls
Arsenal	App	01.84	83-91	248	1	20

ADAMS, Brian T.
Tottenham, 18 May, 1947 (WH)

League Club	Source	Date Signed	Seasons Played	Apps	Subs	Gls
Millwall	Chelsea (App)	08.64	64-65	15	0	0

ADAMS, Christopher J.
Hornchurch, 6 September, 1927 (OL)

League Club	Source	Date Signed	Seasons Played	Apps	Subs	Gls
Tottenham H.	Romford	11.48	51-52	6	-	1
Norwich C.	Tr	12.52	52-54	29	-	3
Watford	Tr	03.54	53-55	75	-	5

ADAMS, Craig J.
Northampton, 9 November, 1974

League Club	Source	Date Signed	Seasons Played	Apps	Subs	Gls
Northampton T.	YT	07.91	91	0	1	0

ADAMS, Donald F.
Northampton, 15 February, 1931 (CF)

League Club	Source	Date Signed	Seasons Played	Apps	Subs	Gls
Northampton T.		05.51	51-55	24	-	7

ADAMS, Ernest R.
Dagenham, 17 January, 1948 (G)

League Club	Source	Date Signed	Seasons Played	Apps	Subs	Gls
Arsenal	App	01.65				
Colchester U.	Tr	07.67	67-68	48	0	0
Crewe Alex.	Tr	07.69	69-71	112	0	0
Darlington	Tr	07.72	72	25	0	0

ADAMS, Ernest W.
Willesden, 3 April, 1922 (F)

League Club	Source	Date Signed	Seasons Played	Apps	Subs	Gls
Preston N.E.		01.45				
Queens Park R.	Tr	09.47	47-49	5	-	0

ADAMS, Francis N.
Liverpool, 8 February, 1933 (G)

League Club	Source	Date Signed	Seasons Played	Apps	Subs	Gls
Bury	Bury Amats	01.56	56-61	169	-	0
Chester C.	Tr	07.63	63	8	-	0
Tranmere Rov.	Tr	02.64				

ADAMS, George
Falkirk, 16 October, 1926 (W)

League Club	Source	Date Signed	Seasons Played	Apps	Subs	Gls
Leyton Orient	Chelmsford C.	05.49	49	4	-	0

ADAMS, George R.
Hackney, 28 September, 1947 (WH)

League Club	Source	Date Signed	Seasons Played	Apps	Subs	Gls
Chelsea	Jnrs	09.65				
Peterborough U.	Tr	07.66	66-67	13	3	2

ADAMS, Graham W.
Torrington, 1 March, 1933 (FB)

League Club	Source	Date Signed	Seasons Played	Apps	Subs	Gls
Plymouth Arg.		01.58	57	1	-	0

ADAMS, James A.
Stoke, 2 August, 1937 (HB)

League Club	Source	Date Signed	Seasons Played	Apps	Subs	Gls
Port Vale		06.56	57	1	-	0

ADAMS, Lawrence
Barnet, 14 February, 1931 (IF)

League Club	Source	Date Signed	Seasons Played	Apps	Subs	Gls
Watford (Am)		01.52	51	1	-	0

ADAMS, Michael A.
Banwell (Avon), 20 February, 1965 (M)

League Club	Source	Date Signed	Seasons Played	Apps	Subs	Gls
Bristol Rov.	App	02.83	82	0	1	0

ADAMS, Michael R.
Sheffield, 8 November, 1961 E Yth (LB)

League Club	Source	Date Signed	Seasons Played	Apps	Subs	Gls
Gillingham	App	11.79	79-82	85	7	5
Coventry C.	Tr	07.83	83-86	85	5	9
Leeds U.	Tr	01.87	86-88	72	1	2
Southampton	Tr	03.89	88-91	86	1	3

ADAMS, Neil J.
Stoke, 23 November, 1965 Eu21-1 (W)

League Club	Source	Date Signed	Seasons Played	Apps	Subs	Gls
Stoke C.		06.85	85	31	1	4
Everton	Tr	06.86	86-87	17	3	0
Oldham Ath.	L	01.89	88	9	0	0
Oldham Ath.	Tr	06.89	89-91	60	24	14

ADAMS, Rex M.
Oxford, 13 February, 1928 (OR)

League Club	Source	Date Signed	Seasons Played	Apps	Subs	Gls
Blackpool	Oxford C.	06.48	48-50	16	-	0
Oldham Ath.	Tr	06.53	53	23	-	1

ADAMS, Rodney L.
Bath, 15 September, 1945 (W)

League Club	Source	Date Signed	Seasons Played	Apps	Subs	Gls
Bournemouth	Frome T.	06.66	66-68	15	2	4

ADAMS, Stephen
Sheffield, 7 September, 1959 (W)

League Club	Source	Date Signed	Seasons Played	Apps	Subs	Gls
Scarborough	Worksop T.	09.87	87-88	25	23	5
Doncaster Rov.	Tr	10.89	89-90	25	10	2

ADAMS, Stephen T.
Windsor, 18 June, 1958 (M)

League Club	Source	Date Signed	Seasons Played	Apps	Subs	Gls
Queens Park R.	App	07.75				
Millwall	Tr	07.77	77	1	0	0
Cambridge U.	Windsor & Eton	03.78	77-78	1	2	0

ADAMS, Vincent
Chesterfield, 16 October, 1946 E Sch (WH)

League Club	Source	Date Signed	Seasons Played	Apps	Subs	Gls
Arsenal	App	10.63				
Chesterfield	Tr	11.65	65-66	15	2	1

ADAMS, William H.
Arlecdon, 8 January, 1919 (RB)

League Club	Source	Date Signed	Seasons Played	Apps	Subs	Gls
Tottenham H.	Hartlepool U. (Am)	05.39				
Carlisle U.	Tr	06.46	46	33	-	1
Workington	Cheltenham T.	(N/L)	51	3	-	0

ADAMS, William V.
Plymouth, 10 May, 1921 (FB)

League Club	Source	Date Signed	Seasons Played	Apps	Subs	Gls
Plymouth Arg.	Plymouth U.	04.45	46	1	-	0

ADAMSON, David H.
Chester-le-Street, 7 May, 1951 E Semi Pro (FB)

League Club	Source	Date Signed	Seasons Played	Apps	Subs	Gls
Doncaster Rov.	Durham C.	07.70	70-71	28	0	0

ADAMSON, Henry
Kelty, 27 June, 1924 (WH)

League Club	Source	Date Signed	Seasons Played	Apps	Subs	Gls
Notts Co.	Jeanfield Swifts	08.46	47-55	233	-	5

ADAMSON, James
Ashington, 4 April, 1929 EF Lge (WH)

League Club	Source	Date Signed	Seasons Played	Apps	Subs	Gls
Burnley	Ashington	01.47	50-63	426	-	17

Jimmy Adamson (Burnley)

ADAMSON, Keith B.
Houghton-le-Spring, 3 July, 1945 (F)

League Club	Source	Date Signed	Seasons Played	Apps	Subs	Gls
Barnsley	Tow Law T.	03.66	65-66	7	0	0

ADAMSON, Terence
Houghton-le-Spring, 15 October, 1948 (FB)

League Club	Source	Date Signed	Seasons Played	Apps	Subs	Gls
Sunderland	App	11.65				
Luton T.	Tr	07.66	66	2	0	0
Hartlepool U.	Tr	07.67	67	1	0	0

ADCOCK, Anthony C.
Bethnal Green, 27 February, 1963 (F)

League Club	Source	Date Signed	Seasons Played	Apps	Subs	Gls
Colchester U.	App	02.81	80-86	192	18	98
Manchester C.	Tr	06.87	87	12	3	5
Northampton T.	Tr	01.88	87-89	72	0	30
Bradford C.	Tr	10.89	89-90	33	5	6
Northampton T.	Tr	01.91	90-91	34	1	10
Peterborough U.	Tr	12.91	91	23	1	7

ADCOCK, Paul M.
Ilminster, 2 May, 1972 (F)

League Club	Source	Date Signed	Seasons Played	Apps	Subs	Gls
Plymouth Arg.	YT	07.90	90	9	3	0

ADDINALL, Albert W.
Paddington, 31 January, 1921 (CF)

League Club	Source	Date Signed	Seasons Played	Apps	Subs	Gls
Queens Park R.		04.45	46-52	149	-	59
Brighton & H.A.	Tr	01.53	52-53	60	-	31
Crystal Palace	Tr	07.54	54	12	-	2

ADDISON, Colin
Taunton, 18 May, 1940 (IF)

League Club	Source	Date Signed	Seasons Played	Apps	Subs	Gls
York C.	Jnrs	05.57	57-60	87	-	27
Nottingham F.	Tr	01.61	60-66	160	0	62
Arsenal	Tr	09.66	66-67	27	1	9
Sheffield U.	Tr	12.67	67-70	93	1	22
Hereford U.	Tr	10.71	72-73	23	0	1

ADDY, Michael
Knottingley, 20 February, 1943 (WH)

League Club	Source	Date Signed	Seasons Played	Apps	Subs	Gls
Leeds U.	Jnrs	05.62	62	2	-	0
Barnsley	Tr	06.64	64-66	49	1	5

ADEY, Arthur
Glasgow, 1 March, 1930 (CF)

League Club	Source	Date Signed	Seasons Played	Apps	Subs	Gls
Doncaster Rov	Bishop Auckland	09.50	50-53	48	-	10
Gillingham	Tr	07.54	54	7	-	1
Bradford P.A.	Tr	10.54	54	13	-	4

ADKINS, Nigel H.
Birkenhead, 11 March, 1965 E Sch (G)

League Club	Source	Date Signed	Seasons Played	Apps	Subs	Gls
Tranmere Rov.	App	03.83	82-85	86	0	0
Wigan Ath.	Tr	07.86	86-91	117	0	0

ADLINGTON, Terence
Blackwell, 21 November, 1935 (G)

League Club	Source	Date Signed	Seasons Played	Apps	Subs	Gls
Derby Co.	Blackwell Colly	12.55	56-61	36	-	0
Torquay U.	Tr	06.62	62-65	148	0	0

AGANA, P. Anthony
Bromley, 2 October, 1963 E Semi Pro (F)

League Club	Source	Date Signed	Seasons Played	Apps	Subs	Gls
Watford	Weymouth	08.87	87	12	3	1
Sheffield U.	Tr	02.88	87-91	105	13	42
Notts Co.	Tr	11.91	91	11	2	1
Leeds U.	L	02.92	91	1	1	0

AGAR, Roy F.
Islington, 1 April, 1936 E Amat (IF)

League Club	Source	Date Signed	Seasons Played	Apps	Subs	Gls
Swindon T. (Am)	Barnet	12.55	55-56	12	-	0

AGBOOLA, Reuben O. F.
Camden, 30 May, 1962 (LB)

League Club	Source	Date Signed	Seasons Played	Apps	Subs	Gls
Southampton	App	04.80	80-84	89	1	0
Sunderland	Tr	01.85	84-91	129	11	0
Charlton Ath.	L	10.86	86	1	0	0
Port Vale	L	11.90	90	9	0	0
Swansea C.	Tr	11.91	91	20	1	0

AGNEW, David G.
Belfast, 31 March, 1925 NI Amat (G)

League Club	Source	Date Signed	Seasons Played	Apps	Subs	Gls
Sunderland	Crusaders	01.50	50	1	-	0

AGNEW, David Y.
Kilwinning, 4 August, 1939 (FB)

League Club	Source	Date Signed	Seasons Played	Apps	Subs	Gls
Leicester C.	Jnrs	08.58				
Scunthorpe U.	Tr	06.61	61	1	-	0
Notts Co.	Tr	06.62	62-66	85	0	1

AGNEW, John
Stockton, 27 June, 1935 (OL)

League Club	Source	Date Signed	Seasons Played	Apps	Subs	Gls
Sheffield Wed.		11.53				
Darlington	Tr	08.54	54-55	24	-	4

AGNEW, Paul
Lisburn NI, 15 August, 1965 NI Sch/NI Yth/NIu21-1 (LB)

League Club	Source	Date Signed	Seasons Played	Apps	Subs	Gls
Grimsby T.	Cliftonville	02.84	83-91	171	14	3

AGNEW, Stephen M.
Shipley, 9 November, 1965 (M)

League Club	Source	Date Signed	Seasons Played	Apps	Subs	Gls
Barnsley	App	11.83	83-90	186	8	30
Blackburn Rov.	Tr	06.91	91	2	0	0

League Club	Source	Date Signed	Seasons Played	Career Record Apps	Subs	Gls
AHERNE, Thomas						
Limerick (Ire), 26 January, 1919 NI-4/IR-16						(FB)
Luton T.	Belfast Celtic	03.49	48-56	267	-	0
AIKEN, Thomas						
Ballymena (NI), 18 March, 1946 NI Amat						(OR)
Doncaster Rov.	Ballymena	11.67	67-68	12	1	1
AIMSON, Paul E.						
Macclesfield, 3 August, 1943						(CF)
Manchester C.	Jnrs	08.60	61-63	16	-	4
York C.	Tr	07.64	64-65	77	0	43
Bury	Tr	03.66	65-66	30	1	11
Bradford C.	Tr	09.67	67	23	0	11
Huddersfield T.	Tr	03.68	67-68	34	4	13
York C.	Tr	08.69	69-72	133	9	55
Bournemouth	Tr	03.73	72	7	2	2
Colchester U.	Tr	08.73	73	3	1	2
AINDOW, Roger						
Liverpool, 23 October, 1946						(D)
Southport	Blackpool (Am)	10.67	68-70	52	6	4
AINGE, Ronald P.						
Pontardawe, 5 August, 1920						(W)
Newport Co.	Llanelli	10.46	46	5	-	0
AINSCOUGH, John						
Adlington, 26 March, 1926						(CH)
Blackpool	Astley Bridge	08.49	50-53	7	-	0
AINSCOW, Alan						
Bolton, 15 July, 1953 E Yth						(M)
Blackpool	App	07.71	71-77	178	14	28
Birmingham C.	Tr	07.78	78-80	104	4	16
Everton	Tr	08.81	81-82	24	4	3
Barnsley	L	11.82	82	2	0	0
Wolverhampton W.	Hong Kong	08.84	84-85	56	2	5
Blackburn Rov.	Tr	12.85	85-88	42	23	5
Rochdale	Tr	07.89	89	19	1	0
AINSCOW, Andrew P.						
Orrell, 1 October, 1968 E Yth						(F)
Wigan Ath.	App	10.86	87-88	14	8	4
Rotherham U.	Tr	08.89	89	0	1	0
AINSLEY, George E.						
South Shields, 15 April, 1915 Died 1985						(CF)
Sunderland	South Shields St A.	04.32	32-33	4	-	0
Bolton W.	Tr	08.36	36	7	-	0
Leeds U.	Tr	12.36	36-47	91	-	30
Bradford P.A.	Tr	11.47	47-48	44	-	29
AINSWORTH, Alphonso						
Manchester, 31 July, 1913 Died 1975						(IF)
Manchester U.	Ashton Ath.	02.34	33	2	-	0
New Brighton	Tr	09.35	35-47	180	-	48
AINSWORTH, David						
Bolton, 28 January, 1958						(F)
Rochdale	App	01.76	75	0	2	0
AINSWORTH, Gareth						
Blackburn, 10 May, 1973						(W)
Preston N.E.	Blackburn Rov. (YT)	08.91	91	2	3	0
AINSWORTH, John						
Wallasey						(CF)
New Brighton (Am)		03.47	46-47	14	-	3
AIRD, John (Jock)						
Glencraig (Fife), 18 February, 1926 S-4						(FB)
Burnley	Jeanfield Swifts	08.48	49-54	132	-	0
AIREY, Carl						
Wakefield, 6 February, 1965						(F)
Barnsley	App	02.83	82-83	30	8	5
Bradford C.	L	10.83	83	4	1	0
Darlington	Tr	08.84	84-85	72	3	28
Chesterfield (L)	Charleroi (Bel)	12.86	86	24	2	4
Rotherham U.	Tr	08.87	87	25	7	11
Torquay U.	Charleroi (Bel)	01.89	88-89	21	8	11
AIREY, John (Jack)						
Blackburn, 28 November, 1937						(W)
Blackburn Rov.		01.59	58-59	3	-	1

League Club	Source	Date Signed	Seasons Played	Career Record Apps	Subs	Gls
AITCHISON, Barry G.						
Colchester, 15 November, 1937						(W)
Tottenham H.	Jnrs	01.55				
Colchester U.	Tr	08.64	64-65	49	1	7
AITCHISON, Peter M.						
Harlow, 19 September, 1931						(W)
Colchester U.		10.51	51-54	18	-	2
AITKEN, Andrew F. S.						
Edinburgh, 21 August, 1934						(W)
West Bromwich A.	Hibernian	09.59	59-60	22	-	2
AITKEN, Charles A.						
Edinburgh, 1 May, 1942 Su23-3						(LB)
Aston Villa	Edinburgh Th.	08.59	60-75	559	2	14

Charlie Aitken (Aston Villa)

League Club	Source	Date Signed	Seasons Played	Career Record Apps	Subs	Gls
AITKEN, George B.						
Dalkeith, 13 August, 1928						(CH)
Middlesbrough	Edinburgh Th.	06.46	51-52	17	-	0
Workington	Tr	07.53	53-59	262	-	3
AITKEN, George C.						
Lochgelly, 28 May, 1925 S-8						(WH)
Sunderland	Third Lanark	11.51	51-58	245	-	3
Gateshead	Tr	03.59	58-59	58	-	0
AITKEN, Glenn L.						
Woolwich, 30 September, 1952 E Yth						(FB)
Gillingham	Chelsea (Am)	12.72	72-74	19	4	0
Wimbledon	Tr	09.74	77	11	0	1
AITKEN, Peter G.						
Cardiff, 30 June, 1954						(D)
Bristol Rov.	App	07.72	72-79	230	4	3
Bristol C.	Tr	11.80	80-81	41	0	1
York C.	Tr	02.82	81	18	0	2
Bournemouth (N/C)	Hong Kong	11.82	82	1	0	0
AITKEN, Robert S. (Roy)						
Irvine, 24 November, 1958 S Sch/Su21-16/S-57						(M)
Newcastle U.	Glasgow Celtic	01.90	89-90	54	0	1
AITKEN, William R. C.						
Dumfries, 11 January, 1951						(IF)
Oldham Ath.	App	01.68	68	1	0	0

AIZLEWOOD, Mark
Newport, 1 October, 1959 W Sch/Wu21-1/W-33 (M/CD)

League Club	Source	Date Signed	Seasons Played	Apps	Subs	Gls
Newport Co.	App	10.77	75-77	35	3	2
Luton T.	Tr	04.78	78-81	90	8	3
Charlton Ath.	Tr	11.82	82-86	152	0	9
Leeds U.	Tr	02.87	86-88	65	5	3
Bradford C.	Tr	08.89	89	39	0	1
Bristol C.	Tr	08.90	90-91	75	1	3

AIZLEWOOD, Steven
Newport, 9 October, 1952 W Sch (CD)

League Club	Source	Date Signed	Seasons Played	Apps	Subs	Gls
Newport Co.	Jnrs	01.70	68-75	191	6	18
Swindon T.	Tr	03.76	75-78	111	1	10
Portsmouth	Tr	07.79	79-83	175	0	13

AKERS, Victor D.
Islington, 24 August, 1946 (FB)

League Club	Source	Date Signed	Seasons Played	Apps	Subs	Gls
Cambridge U.	Bexley U.	07.71	71-74	122	7	5
Watford	Tooting & Mitcham	07.75	75	22	0	0

ALBERRY, William E.
Doncaster, 21 July, 1922 Died 1978 (CH)

League Club	Source	Date Signed	Seasons Played	Apps	Subs	Gls
Leeds U.	Doncaster Rov. (Am)	05.46				
Hull C.	Tr	04.47	46	1	-	0

ALBESON, Brian
Oldham, 14 December, 1946 E Yth (CD)

League Club	Source	Date Signed	Seasons Played	Apps	Subs	Gls
Bury	Jnrs	05.65	65	0	1	0
Darlington	Tr	07.67	67-70	135	2	2
Southend U.	Tr	07.71	71-73	109	1	9
Stockport Co.	Tr	03.74	73-74	54	0	1

ALBISTON, Arthur R.
Edinburgh, 14 July, 1957 S Sch/Su21-5/S-14 (LB)

League Club	Source	Date Signed	Seasons Played	Apps	Subs	Gls
Manchester U.	App	07.74	74-87	364	15	6
West Bromwich A.	Tr	08.88	88	43	0	2
Chesterfield (L)	Dundee	11.90	90	3	0	1
Chester C.	Tr	08.91	91	44	0	0

ALBURY, William F.
Portsmouth, 10 August, 1933 (WH)

League Club	Source	Date Signed	Seasons Played	Apps	Subs	Gls
Portsmouth	Jnrs	10.51	56-57	23	-	0
Gillingham	Tr	07.59	59	38	-	12

ALCOCK, Terence
Hanley, 9 December, 1946 (D)

League Club	Source	Date Signed	Seasons Played	Apps	Subs	Gls
Port Vale	App	09.64	63-66	112	0	0
Blackpool	Tr	08.67	67-75	190	6	21
Bury	L	02.72	71	6	0	1
Blackburn Rov.	L	12.76	76	3	0	1
Port Vale	Tr	02.77	76-77	4	0	0
Halifax T.	Portland (USA)	09.77	77	14	0	2

ALDECOA, Emilio G.
Spain, 30 November, 1922 Spanish Int (W)

League Club	Source	Date Signed	Seasons Played	Apps	Subs	Gls
Wolverhampton W.		12.43				
Coventry C.	Tr	12.45	46	29	-	0

ALDERSON, Brian R.
Dundee, 5 May, 1950 Su23-1 (W)

League Club	Source	Date Signed	Seasons Played	Apps	Subs	Gls
Coventry C.	Lochee Harp	07.70	70-74	116	11	29
Leicester C.	Tr	07.75	75-77	87	3	9

ALDERSON, Kevin
Shildon, 21 August, 1953 (W)

League Club	Source	Date Signed	Seasons Played	Apps	Subs	Gls
Darlington (App)	App	05.69	70	1	0	0

ALDERSON, Stuart
Bishop Auckland, 15 August, 1948 (OR)

League Club	Source	Date Signed	Seasons Played	Apps	Subs	Gls
Newcastle U.	Evenwood T.	08.65	66	3	0	0
York C.	Tr	06.67	67	17	2	5

ALDERTON, James H.
Wingate, 6 December, 1924 (WH)

League Club	Source	Date Signed	Seasons Played	Apps	Subs	Gls
Wolverhampton W.	Jnrs	12.41	46	11	-	0
Coventry C.	Tr	10.47	47-51	62	-	0

ALDIS, Peter B.
Birmingham, 11 April, 1927 (FB)

League Club	Source	Date Signed	Seasons Played	Apps	Subs	Gls
Aston Villa	Hay Green	05.49	50-58	262	-	1

ALDOUS, Stanley E. R.
Northfleet, 10 February, 1923 (CH)

League Club	Source	Date Signed	Seasons Played	Apps	Subs	Gls
Leyton Orient	Gravesend & Nft	07.50	50-57	302	-	3

ALDREAD, Paul
Mansfield, 6 November, 1946 (CF)

League Club	Source	Date Signed	Seasons Played	Apps	Subs	Gls
Mansfield T.	Jnrs	12.63	65-66	11	1	3

ALDRED, Arthur
Atherton, 27 August, 1919

League Club	Source	Date Signed	Seasons Played	Apps	Subs	Gls
Aston Villa		07.46				
Walsall	Tr	05.48	48	11	-	1

ALDRED, Graeme
Ferryhill, 11 September, 1966 Died 1987 (D)

League Club	Source	Date Signed	Seasons Played	Apps	Subs	Gls
Darlington	Newcastle U. (YT)	09.84	84-85	31	13	1

ALDRIDGE, John W.
Liverpool, 18 September, 1958 IR-47 (F)

League Club	Source	Date Signed	Seasons Played	Apps	Subs	Gls
Newport Co.	South Liverpool	04.79	79-83	159	11	69
Oxford U.	Tr	03.84	83-86	111	3	72
Liverpool	Tr	01.87	86-89	69	14	50
Tranmere Rov.	Real Sociedad (Sp)	07.91	91	43	0	22

John Aldridge (Newport County, Oxford United, Liverpool, Real Sociedad, Tranmere Rovers & Republic of Ireland)

ALDRIDGE, Martin J.
Northampton, 6 December, 1974 (F)

League Club	Source	Date Signed	Seasons Played	Apps	Subs	Gls
Northampton T.	YT	07.91	91	2	3	0

ALDRIDGE, Neil R.
Manchester, 10 January, 1966 E Yth (LB)

League Club	Source	Date Signed	Seasons Played	Apps	Subs	Gls
Manchester C.	App	11.83				
Crewe Alex.	Tr	07.84	84	12	3	0

ALDRIDGE, Norman H.
Walsall, 23 February, 1921 (FB)

League Club	Source	Date Signed	Seasons Played	Apps	Subs	Gls
West Bromwich A.	Foxford	05.46	46	1	-	0
Northampton T.	Tr	06.48	48	2	-	0

ALDRIDGE, Stephen P.
Armthorpe, 2 November, 1957 (F)

League Club	Source	Date Signed	Seasons Played	Apps	Subs	Gls
Sheffield U.	App	12.75				
Doncaster Rov.		02.81	80	1	0	0

ALEKSIC, Milija
Newcastle-u-Lyme, 14 April, 1951 (G)

League Club	Source	Date Signed	Seasons Played	Apps	Subs	Gls
Plymouth Arg.	Stafford R.	02.73	73-75	32	0	0
Luton T.	Tr	12.76	76-78	77	0	0
Tottenham H.	Tr	12.78	78-81	25	0	0
Luton T.	L	11.81	81	4	0	0

ALESINOYE, Martin
Middlesbrough, 1 October, 1955 (M)

League Club	Source	Date Signed	Seasons Played	Apps	Subs	Gls
Doncaster Rov.	Barnsley (Am)	10.75	75	13	1	1

ALEXANDER, Alan
Cumbernauld, 1 November, 1941 (G)

League Club	Source	Date Signed	Seasons Played	Apps	Subs	Gls
Bradford P.A.		07.59	61	5	-	0

ALEXANDER, Alexander
Glasgow, 28 September, 1924

League Club	Source	Date Signed	Seasons Played	Apps	Subs	Gls
Tranmere Rov.	New Brighton (Am)	10.47	46-48	23	-	3

ALEXANDER, Angus C.
Arbroath, 10 January, 1934 (IF)

League Club	Source	Date Signed	Seasons Played	Apps	Subs	Gls
Burnley	Jnrs	01.51				
Southport	Tr	07.57	57	14	-	1
Workington	Tr	02.58	57-58	49	-	4
York C.	Tr	06.59	59	7	-	0

ALEXANDER, Anthony A.
Reading, 8 February, 1935 (F)

League Club	Source	Date Signed	Seasons Played	Apps	Subs	Gls
Reading	Jnrs	08.52	52-55	11	-	2

ALEXANDER, Dennis L.
Nottingham, 19 February, 1935 (IF)

League Club	Source	Date Signed	Seasons Played	Apps	Subs	Gls
Nottingham F.	Jnrs	06.55	55-56	20	-	4
Brighton & H.A.	Tr	03.58				
Gateshead	Tr	10.58	58	18	-	1

ALEXANDER, Graham
Coventry, 10 October, 1971 (RW)

League Club	Source	Date Signed	Seasons Played	Apps	Subs	Gls
Scunthorpe U.	YT	03.90	90-91	30	7	5

ALEXANDER, Ian
Glasgow, 26 January, 1963 (RB)

League Club	Source	Date Signed	Seasons Played	Apps	Subs	Gls
Rotherham U.	Leicester Juveniles	10.81	81-82	5	6	0
Bristol Rov.	Pezoporikos Larnaca (Cyp.)	08.86	86-91	228	4	5

ALEXANDER, John E.
Liverpool, 3 October, 1955 (F)

League Club	Source	Date Signed	Seasons Played	Apps	Subs	Gls
Millwall	Ulysses	07.77	76-77	10	5	2
Reading	Tr	10.78	78-80	22	3	9
Northampton T.	Tr	08.81	81	21	1	4

ALEXANDER, Keith
Nottingham, 14 November, 1958 (W/F)

League Club	Source	Date Signed	Seasons Played	Apps	Subs	Gls
Grimsby T.	Barnet	07.88	88-90	64	19	26
Stockport Co.	Tr	09.90	90	9	2	0
Lincoln C.	Tr	12.90	90-91	26	12	4

ALEXANDER, Philip J.
Slough, 4 September, 1962 (D)

League Club	Source	Date Signed	Seasons Played	Apps	Subs	Gls
Norwich C.	Wokingham T.	08.81	82	0	1	0

ALEXANDER, Rowan S.
Ayr, 28 January, 1961 (F)

League Club	Source	Date Signed	Seasons Played	Apps	Subs	Gls
Brentford	St Mirren	09.84	84-85	41	6	6

ALFORD, Carl P.
Manchester, 11 February, 1972 (M)

League Club	Source	Date Signed	Seasons Played	Apps	Subs	Gls
Rochdale (YT)	YT	11.88	88	0	4	0

ALISON, James
Peebles, 11 October, 1923 (OR)

League Club	Source	Date Signed	Seasons Played	Apps	Subs	Gls
Manchester C.	Falkirk	12.49	49-50	19	-	0
Aldershot	Tr	07.52	52-56	171	-	9

ALLAN, Alexander B. (Sandy)
Forfar, 29 October, 1947 (CF)

League Club	Source	Date Signed	Seasons Played	Apps	Subs	Gls
Cardiff C.	Rhyl	03.67	67-69	8	0	1
Bristol Rov.	Tr	03.70	69-72	52	7	18
Swansea	L	03.73	72	6	2	1

ALLAN, James
Inverness, 10 November, 1953 (G)

League Club	Source	Date Signed	Seasons Played	Apps	Subs	Gls
Swindon T.	App	07.71	71-83	371	0	0

ALLAN, John
Stirling, 23 March, 1931 (CF)

League Club	Source	Date Signed	Seasons Played	Apps	Subs	Gls
Bradford P.A.	Third Lanark	02.59	58-60	70	-	51
Halifax T.	Tr	03.61	60	10	-	1

ALLAN, John
Amble, 26 September, 1931 (G)

League Club	Source	Date Signed	Seasons Played	Apps	Subs	Gls
Barnsley	Amble W.	01.49	51-52	11	-	0

ALLANSON, Gary E.
Hull, 6 March, 1965 (RB)

League Club	Source	Date Signed	Seasons Played	Apps	Subs	Gls
Doncaster Rov.	App	03.83	81-82	11	2	0

ALLARDYCE, Samuel
Dudley, 19 October, 1954 (CD)

League Club	Source	Date Signed	Seasons Played	Apps	Subs	Gls
Bolton W.	App	11.71	73-79	180	4	21
Sunderland	Tr	07.80	80	24	1	2
Millwall	Tr	09.81	81-82	63	0	2
Coventry C.	Tampa Bay (USA)	09.83	83	28	0	1
Huddersfield T.	Tr	07.84	84	37	0	0
Bolton W.	Tr	07.85	85	14	0	0
Preston N.E.	Tr	08.86	86-88	88	2	2
West Bromwich A.	Tr	06.89	89	0	1	0

ALLATT, Vernon
Hednesford, 28 May, 1959 (F)

League Club	Source	Date Signed	Seasons Played	Apps	Subs	Gls
Halifax T.	Hednesford T.	11.79	79-82	93	5	14
Rochdale	Tr	08.83	83	40	0	8
Crewe Alex.	Tr	06.84	84-85	36	3	8
Preston N.E.	Tr	11.85	85	17	2	3
Stockport Co.	Tr	10.86	86	23	1	10
Crewe Alex. (N/C)	Hednesford T.	12.87	87	4	1	2

ALLAWAY, James
Bristol, 23 April, 1922 (IF)

League Club	Source	Date Signed	Seasons Played	Apps	Subs	Gls
Bristol Rov.		12.46	46	4	-	0
Bristol C.	Tr	09.47				

ALLCHURCH, Ivor J.
Swansea, 16 October, 1929 W-68 (IF)

League Club	Source	Date Signed	Seasons Played	Apps	Subs	Gls
Swansea C.	Plasmarl	05.47	49-58	330	-	123
Newcastle U.	Tr	10.58	58-61	143	-	46
Cardiff C.	Tr	08.62	62-64	103	-	39
Swansea C.	Tr	07.65	65-67	116	2	42

Ivor Allchurch (Swansea City, Newcastle United, Cardiff City, Swansea City & Wales)

ALLCHURCH, Leonard
Swansea, 12 September, 1933 W Sch/W-11 (OR)

League Club	Source	Date Signed	Seasons Played	Apps	Subs	Gls
Swansea C.	Jnrs	10.50	51-60	272	-	49
Sheffield U.	Tr	03.61	60-64	123	-	32
Stockport Co.	Tr	09.65	65-68	131	0	16
Swansea C.	Tr	07.69	69-70	70	3	11

ALLCOCK, Frank E.
Nottingham, 7 September, 1925 (FB)

League Club	Source	Date Signed	Seasons Played	Apps	Subs	Gls
Nottingham F.	Beeston B.C.	03.45				
Aston Villa	Tr	08.46				
Bristol Rov.	Cheltenham T.	06.52	53-55	59	-	0

ALLCOCK, Kenneth
Kirkby-in-Ashfield, 24 April, 1921 (CF)

League Club	Source	Date Signed	Seasons Played	Apps	Subs	Gls
Mansfield T.	Notts Co. (Am)	04.47	47	1	-	0

ALLCOCK, Terence
Leeds, 10 December, 1935 (IF)

League Club	Source	Date Signed	Seasons Played	Apps	Subs	Gls
Bolton W.	Jnrs	12.52	53-57	31	-	9
Norwich C.	Tr	03.58	57-68	334	5	106

ALLDER, Douglas S.
Hammersmith, 30 December, 1951 E Yth (M)

League Club	Source	Date Signed	Seasons Played	Apps	Subs	Gls
Millwall	App	10.69	69-74	191	11	10
Leyton Orient	Tr	07.75	75-76	34	7	0
Watford	Torquay U. (N/C)	09.77	77	1	0	0
Brentford	Tr	10.77	77-79	68	20	2

ALLDIS, Gilbert J.
Birkenhead, 26 January, 1920 (WH)

League Club	Source	Date Signed	Seasons Played	Apps	Subs	Gls
Tranmere Rov.		10.38	38-48	74	-	4
New Brighton	Tr	07.50	50	12	-	0

ALLEN, Adrian
Preston , 23 March, 1934 (OR)

League Club	Source	Date Signed	Seasons Played	Apps	Subs	Gls
Southport (Am)	Preston N.E. (Am)	05.54	54	6	-	0

ALLEN, Andrew
Liverpool, 4 September, 1974

League Club	Source	Date Signed	Seasons Played	Apps	Subs	Gls
Chester C.	YT	07.91	91	0	1	0

ALLEN, Anthony
Stoke, 27 November, 1939 E Yth/Eu23-7/EF Lge/E-3 (LB)

League Club	Source	Date Signed	Seasons Played	Apps	Subs	Gls
Stoke C.	Jnrs	11.56	57-69	414	3	2
Bury	Tr	10.70	70-71	29	0	0

ALLEN, H. Anthony (Tanner)
Nottingham, 27 October, 1924 (FB)

League Club	Source	Date Signed	Seasons Played	Apps	Subs	Gls
Nottingham F.	Beeston B.C.	01.46	47	1	-	0
Notts Co.	Tr	08.49	51-53	30	-	0

ALLEN, Bradley J.
Romford, 13 September, 1971 E Yth/Eu21-4 (F)

League Club	Source	Date Signed	Seasons Played	Apps	Subs	Gls
Queens Park R.	Jnrs	09.88	88-91	14	8	7

ALLEN, Brynley W.
Gilfach Goch, 28 March, 1921 W-2 (IF)

League Club	Source	Date Signed	Seasons Played	Apps	Subs	Gls
Swansea C.	Gilfach Welfare	03.39				
Cardiff C.	Tr	12.45	46-47	41	-	18
Newport Co.	Tr	10.47	47	26	-	7
Cardiff C.	Tr	08.48	48	17	-	4
Reading	Tr	05.49	49	26	-	12
Coventry C.	Tr	02.50	49-52	88	-	26

ALLEN, Christopher A.
Oxford, 18 November, 1972 (LW)

League Club	Source	Date Signed	Seasons Played	Apps	Subs	Gls
Oxford U.	YT	05.91	91	13	1	1

ALLEN, Clive D.
Stepney, 20 May, 1961 E Sch/E Yth/Eu21-3/E-5 (F)

League Club	Source	Date Signed	Seasons Played	Apps	Subs	Gls
Queens Park R.	App	09.78	78-79	43	6	32
Arsenal	Tr	06.80				
Crystal Palace	Tr	08.80	80	25	0	9
Queens Park R.	Tr	06.81	81-83	83	4	40
Tottenham H.	Tr	08.84	84-87	97	8	60
Manchester C.	Bordeaux	08.89	89-91	31	22	16
Chelsea	Tr	12.91	91	15	1	7
West Ham U.	Tr	03.92	91	4	0	1

ALLEN, Dennis J.
Dagenham, 2 March, 1939 (IF)

League Club	Source	Date Signed	Seasons Played	Apps	Subs	Gls
Charlton Ath.	Jnrs	08.56	57-60	5	-	1
Reading	Tr	06.61	61-69	332	4	85
Bournemouth	Tr	08.70	70	17	0	3

ALLEN, Derek
Wombwell, 14 July, 1946 (HB)

League Club	Source	Date Signed	Seasons Played	Apps	Subs	Gls
Rotherham U.	Jnrs	11.65	65	1	0	0

ALLEN, Derrick S.
Luton, 8 April, 1930 Died 1978 (F)

League Club	Source	Date Signed	Seasons Played	Apps	Subs	Gls
Luton T.	Alton T.	01.52	54	1	-	0
Watford	Tr	06.56	56	6	-	1

ALLEN, Frank
Shirebrook, 28 June, 1927 (FB)

League Club	Source	Date Signed	Seasons Played	Apps	Subs	Gls
Chesterfield		03.51	51-52	3	-	0
Mansfield T.	Tr	07.53	53-54	7	-	0

ALLEN, Geoffrey B.
Newcastle, 10 November, 1946 E Yth (OL)

League Club	Source	Date Signed	Seasons Played	Apps	Subs	Gls
Newcastle U.	Jnrs	02.64	63-68	22	0	1

ALLEN, George H.
Birmingham, 23 January, 1932 (FB)

League Club	Source	Date Signed	Seasons Played	Apps	Subs	Gls
Birmingham C.	Coventry C. (Am)	11.52	53-61	134	-	0
Torquay U.	Tr	01.62	61-64	133	-	0

ALLEN, Graham F.
Walsall, 30 August, 1932 (F)

League Club	Source	Date Signed	Seasons Played	Apps	Subs	Gls
Walsall (Am)		04.54	53	1	-	1

ALLEN, Gregory F.
West Ham, 18 October, 1967 (M)

League Club	Source	Date Signed	Seasons Played	Apps	Subs	Gls
Arsenal	App	07.85				
Cambridge U. (N/C)	Dagenham	08.88	88	4	0	0

ALLEN, John
Deeside, 14 November, 1964 W Sch/W Yth (M)

League Club	Source	Date Signed	Seasons Played	Apps	Subs	Gls
Chester C.	App	11.81	81-83	67	12	5
Mansfield T.	Tr	08.84	84	1	1	0

ALLEN, John
Coventry, 24 April, 1955 (F)

League Club	Source	Date Signed	Seasons Played	Apps	Subs	Gls
Leicester C.	Hinckley Ath.	08.78				
Port Vale	Tr	06.80	80	18	0	4

ALLEN, John C. (Ian)
Paisley, 27 January, 1932 (F)

League Club	Source	Date Signed	Seasons Played	Apps	Subs	Gls
Queens Park R.	Beith Jnrs	09.52	53	1	-	1
Bournemouth	Tr	07.54	54-55	52	-	11

ALLEN, Keith
Newport (IOW), 9 November, 1943 (IF)

League Club	Source	Date Signed	Seasons Played	Apps	Subs	Gls
Portsmouth	Ryde	12.62				
Grimsby T.	Tr	05.64	64	6	-	1
Stockport Co.	Tr	06.65	65-66	49	0	16
Luton T.	Tr	03.67	66-69	128	9	36
Plymouth Arg.	Tr	07.70	70-72	74	5	10

Clive Allen (Queens Park Rangers, Arsenal, Crystal Palace, Queens Park Rangers, Tottenham Hotspur, Bordeaux, Manchester City, Chelsea, West Ham United & England)

ALLEN, Kenneth R.
Thornaby, 12 January, 1949 (G)

League Club	Source	Date Signed	Seasons Played	Apps	Subs	Gls
Hartlepool U. (Am)	Jnrs	08.68	68	7	0	0
West Bromwich A.	South Africa	12.72				
Bournemouth	Bath C.	08.78	78-82	152	0	0
Peterborough U. (N/C)	Bury (N/C)	12.83				
Torquay U.	Tr	03.84	83-85	58	0	0
Swindon T.	Tr	09.85	85-86	45	0	0
Torquay U.	Tr	12.86	86-87	74	0	0
Torquay U.	Bath C.	03.89				

ALLEN, Kevin
Ryde (IOW), 22 March, 1961 (FB)

League Club	Source	Date Signed	Seasons Played	Apps	Subs	Gls
Bournemouth	Jnrs	08.79	79	1	0	0

ALLEN, Leslie W.
Dagenham, 4 September, 1937 E-u23-1/EF Lge (CF)

League Club	Source	Date Signed	Seasons Played	Apps	Subs	Gls
Chelsea	Briggs Sports	09.54	56-59	44	-	11
Tottenham H.	Tr	12.59	59-64	119	-	47
Queens Park R.	Tr	07.65	65-68	123	5	54

ALLEN, Malcolm
Caernarfon, 21 March, 1967 W Yth/W 'B'/W-12 (F)

League Club	Source	Date Signed	Seasons Played	Apps	Subs	Gls
Watford	App	03.85	85-87	27	12	5
Aston Villa	L	09.87	87	4	0	0
Norwich C.	Tr	08.88	88-89	24	11	8
Millwall	Tr	03.90	89-91	34	6	14

ALLEN, Mark S.
Newcastle, 18 December, 1963 (F)

League Club	Source	Date Signed	Seasons Played	Apps	Subs	Gls
Burnley	App	12.81	81	0	2	1
Tranmere Rov.	Tr	08.83	83	6	4	0

ALLEN, Martin J.
Reading, 14 August, 1965 E Yth/Eu21-2 (M)

League Club	Source	Date Signed	Seasons Played	Apps	Subs	Gls
Queens Park R.	App	05.83	84-89	128	8	16
West Ham U.	Tr	08.89	89-91	81	17	12

ALLEN, Michael
South Shields, 30 March, 1949 (D)

League Club	Source	Date Signed	Seasons Played	Apps	Subs	Gls
Middlesbrough	App	05.66	67-71	32	2	0
Brentford	Tr	10.71	71-78	223	10	11

ALLEN, Paul K.
Aveley, 28 August, 1962 E Yth/Eu21-3/E'B' (RM)

League Club	Source	Date Signed	Seasons Played	Apps	Subs	Gls
West Ham U.	App	08.79	79-84	149	3	6
Tottenham H.	Tr	06.85	85-91	238	15	20

ALLEN, Paul M.
Leeds, 30 July, 1967 (G)

League Club	Source	Date Signed	Seasons Played	Apps	Subs	Gls
Doncaster Rov. (N/C)	Bradford C. (YT)	10.84	84-85	4	0	0

ALLEN, Paul R.
Bury, 13 March, 1968 (M)

League Club	Source	Date Signed	Seasons Played	Apps	Subs	Gls
Bolton W.	YT	07.86	86	0	1	0

ALLEN, Peter C.
Hove, 1 November, 1946 (M)

League Club	Source	Date Signed	Seasons Played	Apps	Subs	Gls
Leyton Orient	Tottenham H. (Am)	07.65	65-77	424	8	28
Millwall	Tr	03.78	77-78	16	2	0

ALLEN, Peter M.
Bristol, 8 October, 1934 (CH)

League Club	Source	Date Signed	Seasons Played	Apps	Subs	Gls
Bristol C.		07.53	54	1	-	0

ALLEN, A. Reginald
Marylebone, 3 May, 1919 EF Lge (G)

League Club	Source	Date Signed	Seasons Played	Apps	Subs	Gls
Queens Park R.	Corona	05.38	38-49	179	-	0
Manchester U.	Tr	06.50	50-52	75	-	0

ALLEN, A. Robert
Bromley, 11 October, 1916 E Sch (FB)

League Club	Source	Date Signed	Seasons Played	Apps	Subs	Gls
Leyton Orient (Am)	Tottenham H. (Am)	12.33	33	1	-	0
Fulham	Leytonstone	05.34	34-36	11	-	0
Doncaster Rov.	Tr	06.37	37	31	-	6
Brentford	Tr	06.38				
Northampton T.		09.45	46	5	-	0
Colchester U.	Tr	(N/L)	50	29	-	1

ALLEN, Robert
Belfast, 16 January, 1939 (WH)

League Club	Source	Date Signed	Seasons Played	Apps	Subs	Gls
Wolverhampton W.	Denbigh T.	09.57				
Coventry C.	Tr	06.59	60-61	25	-	2

ALLEN, Robert H. A.
Shepton Mallet, 5 December, 1916 (FB)

League Club	Source	Date Signed	Seasons Played	Apps	Subs	Gls
Notts Co.		02.45	46	1	-	0
Bristol C.	Tr	11.46	46	1	-	0

ALLEN, Ronald
Fenton, 15 January, 1929 EF Lge/E'B'-2/E-5 (CF)

League Club	Source	Date Signed	Seasons Played	Apps	Subs	Gls
Port Vale	Jnrs	04.46	46-49	123	-	34
West Bromwich A.	Tr	03.50	49-60	415	-	208
Crystal Palace	Tr	05.61	61-64	100	-	34

ALLEN, Ronald L.
Birmingham, 22 April, 1935 (RB)

League Club	Source	Date Signed	Seasons Played	Apps	Subs	Gls
Birmingham C.	Jnrs	05.53				
Lincoln C.	Tr	07.58	58-60	60	-	1

ALLEN, Russell P.
Birmingham, 9 January, 1954 (F)

League Club	Source	Date Signed	Seasons Played	Apps	Subs	Gls
West Bromwich A.	Arsenal (App)	05.71				
Tranmere Rov.	Tr	07.73	73-77	137	19	44
Mansfield T.	Tr	07.78	78-80	99	17	18

ALLEN, William
Newburn, 22 October, 1917 (IF)

League Club	Source	Date Signed	Seasons Played	Apps	Subs	Gls
Chesterfield		11.37	38	2	-	0
York C.	Tr	05.39	46-49	129	-	23
Scunthorpe U.	Tr	06.50	50-51	64	-	1

ALLEYNE, Andrew M.
Barbados, 19 May, 1951 (FB)

League Club	Source	Date Signed	Seasons Played	Apps	Subs	Gls
Reading	Newbury T.	11.72	72-75	46	2	2

ALLEYNE, Robert A.
Dudley, 27 September, 1968 (F)

League Club	Source	Date Signed	Seasons Played	Apps	Subs	Gls
Leicester C.	Jnrs	01.87	86	1	2	0
Wrexham	L	10.87	87	7	3	2
Chesterfield	Tr	03.88	87-88	32	8	5

ALLINSON, Ian J. R.
Stevenage, 1 October, 1957 (W)

League Club	Source	Date Signed	Seasons Played	Apps	Subs	Gls
Colchester U.	App	10.75	74-82	291	17	69
Arsenal	Tr	08.83	83-86	60	23	16
Stoke C.	Tr	06.87	87	6	3	0
Luton T.	Tr	10.87	87-88	24	8	3
Colchester U.	Tr	12.88	88-89	36	2	10

ALLISON, John
Stannington (Nd), 31 July, 1922 (OL)

League Club	Source	Date Signed	Seasons Played	Apps	Subs	Gls
Chesterfield	West Sleekburn	04.47				
Reading	Blyth Spartans	01.49	48-49	29	-	4
Walsall	Tr	06.50	50-51	47	-	1

ALLISON, John A.
Cramlington, 9 August, 1932 (CH)

League Club	Source	Date Signed	Seasons Played	Apps	Subs	Gls
Chesterfield	Blyth Spartans	05.55	57-60	32	-	0

ALLISON, John J.
Consett, 17 November, 1913 Died 1971

League Club	Source	Date Signed	Seasons Played	Apps	Subs	Gls
Barnsley	Workington	05.39				
Hartlepool U.	Tr	09.46	46	13	-	0

ALLISON, Kenneth
Edinburgh, 6 January, 1937 (IF)

League Club	Source	Date Signed	Seasons Played	Apps	Subs	Gls
Darlington	Cowdenbeath	07.63	63-65	75	0	39
Lincoln C.	Tr	02.66	65-66	41	1	12

ALLISON, Malcolm A.
Dartford, 5 September, 1927 (CH)

League Club	Source	Date Signed	Seasons Played	Apps	Subs	Gls
Charlton Ath.	Erith & Belvedere	12.45	49	2	-	0
West Ham U.	Tr	02.51	50-57	238	-	10

ALLISON, Michael
Johnstone, 17 March, 1966 (G)

League Club	Source	Date Signed	Seasons Played	Apps	Subs	Gls
Chesterfield	Horwich R.M.I.	07.89	90	16	0	0

ALLISON, Neil J.
Hull, 20 October, 1973 (CD)

League Club	Source	Date Signed	Seasons Played	Apps	Subs	Gls
Hull C.	YT	07.90	90-91	6	2	0

ALLISON, Thomas
Fencehouses (Dm), 20 February, 1921 (IF)

League Club	Source	Date Signed	Seasons Played	Apps	Subs	Gls
Darlington	South Hetton	09.46	46	6	-	0

ALLISON, Wayne A.
Huddersfield, 16 October, 1968 (F)

League Club	Source	Date Signed	Seasons Played	Apps	Subs	Gls
Halifax T.	YT	06.87	86-88	74	10	21
Watford	Tr	07.89	89	6	1	0
Bristol C.	Tr	07.90	90-91	55	25	16

ALLISTER, John G.
Edinburgh, 30 June, 1927 (IF)

League Club	Source	Date Signed	Seasons Played	Apps	Subs	Gls
Chelsea	Tranent Jnrs	07.49	51-52	4	-	1
Chesterfield	Aberdeen	06.58				

ALLMAN, George
Stockport, 23 July, 1930 (F)

League Club	Source	Date Signed	Seasons Played	Apps	Subs	Gls
Stockport Co.		05.50	50-51	7	-	1
Chester C.		07.55	55-56	49	-	13

ALLON, Joseph B.
Gateshead, 12 November, 1966 E Yth (F)

League Club	Source	Date Signed	Seasons Played	Apps	Subs	Gls
Newcastle U.	YT	11.84	84-86	9	0	2
Swansea C.	Tr	07.87	87-88	27	7	12
Hartlepool U.	Tr	10.88	88-90	112	0	51
Chelsea	Tr	08.91	91	2	9	2
Port Vale	L	02.92	91	2	4	0

ALLPRESS, Timothy J.
Hitchin, 27 January, 1971 (CD)

League Club	Source	Date Signed	Seasons Played	Apps	Subs	Gls
Luton T.	YT	07.89	89	1	0	0
Preston N.E.	L	10.91	91	7	2	0

ALLSOP, Norman
West Bromwich, 1 November, 1930 (IF)

League Club	Source	Date Signed	Seasons Played	Apps	Subs	Gls
West Bromwich A.	Hednesford T.	05.48				
Walsall	Tr	10.53	53	9	-	0

ALLSOP, William H.
Ripley, 29 January, 1912 (FB)

League Club	Source	Date Signed	Seasons Played	Apps	Subs	Gls
Port Vale	Bolton W. (Am)	08.31	31-32	6	-	0
Halifax T.	Tr	05.34	34-46	203	-	0

ALLUM, Albert
Notting Hill, 15 October, 1930 (F)

League Club	Source	Date Signed	Seasons Played	Apps	Subs	Gls
Queens Park R.		06.57	57	1	-	0

ALSOP, Gilbert
Bristol, 10 September, 1908 Died 1992 (CF)

League Club	Source	Date Signed	Seasons Played	Apps	Subs	Gls
Coventry C.	Bath C.	12.29	29-30	16	-	4
Walsall	Tr	10.31	31-35	159	-	126
West Bromwich A.	Tr	11.35	35	1	-	0
Ipswich T.	Tr	06.37	38	9	-	2
Walsall	Tr	11.38	38-46	35	-	26

ALSTON, Adrian
Preston, 6 February, 1949 Australian Int (F)

League Club	Source	Date Signed	Seasons Played	Apps	Subs	Gls
Luton T.	Safeways (Aus)	08.74	74-75	26	3	8
Cardiff C.	Tr	10.75	75-76	44	4	16

ALSTON, Alec
Preston, 26 February, 1937 (F)

League Club	Source	Date Signed	Seasons Played	Apps	Subs	Gls
Preston N.E.	Netherfield	05.55	57-62	102	-	26
Bury	Tr	03.63	62-65	86	0	22
Barrow	Tr	09.65	65-66	46	1	14

ALTY, Colin
Preston, 23 October, 1944 (D)

League Club	Source	Date Signed	Seasons Played	Apps	Subs	Gls
Preston N.E.	Jnrs	10.61	62	1	-	0
Southport	Tr	06.64	64-69	184	6	22

AMBLER, Roy
Wakefield, 2 December, 1937 (IF)

League Club	Source	Date Signed	Seasons Played	Apps	Subs	Gls
Leeds U.	Jnrs	12.54				
Shrewsbury T.	Tr	01.59	58-60	29	-	8
Wrexham	Tr	05.61	61-62	21	-	13
York C.	Tr	11.62	62	12	-	3
Southport	Tr	07.63	63	11	-	0

AMBROSE, A. Leroy
St Vincent (WI), 22 June, 1960 (M)

League Club	Source	Date Signed	Seasons Played	Apps	Subs	Gls
Charlton Ath.	Croydon	08.79	79-81	28	5	1

AMES, Kenneth
Poole, 17 September, 1933 E Sch (CF)

League Club	Source	Date Signed	Seasons Played	Apps	Subs	Gls
Portsmouth	Jnrs	09.50	53	2	-	0

AMES, Percy T.
Bedford, 13 December, 1931 (G)

League Club	Source	Date Signed	Seasons Played	Apps	Subs	Gls
Tottenham H.	Bedford Ave.	05.51				
Colchester U.	Tr	05.55	55-64	397	-	0

AMES, Trevor
Poole, 14 December, 1962 (F)

League Club	Source	Date Signed	Seasons Played	Apps	Subs	Gls
Hereford U.	Aston Villa (App)	10.80	80-81	5	3	0
Crystal Palace	Tr	10.81				

AMOR, William
Pewsey, 6 November, 1919 Died 1988 E Amat (OR)

League Club	Source	Date Signed	Seasons Played	Apps	Subs	Gls
Reading (Am)	Huntley & Palmers	12.47	47-51	66	-	12

AMOS, Keith
Walton-on-Thames, 13 January, 1932 (G)

League Club	Source	Date Signed	Seasons Played	Apps	Subs	Gls
Arsenal	Jnrs	05.52				
Aldershot	Tr	08.54	55-57	77	-	0

AMPADU, Kwame
Bradford, 20 December, 1970 IR Yth/IRu21-2 (W)

League Club	Source	Date Signed	Seasons Played	Apps	Subs	Gls
Arsenal	YT	11.88	89	0	2	0
Plymouth Arg.	L	10.90	90	6	0	1
West Bromwich A.	L	03.91	90	3	4	0
West Bromwich A.	Tr	06.91	91	15	6	3

AMPHLET, T. Raymond
Manchester, 25 September, 1922 (LB)

League Club	Source	Date Signed	Seasons Played	Apps	Subs	Gls
Cardiff C.	Guildford C.	04.48				
Newport Co.	Tr	04.49	49	13	-	0

AMPOFO, Christopher J. K.
Paddington, 6 October, 1963 (D)

League Club	Source	Date Signed	Seasons Played	Apps	Subs	Gls
West Ham U.	App	10.81				
Aldershot	Tr	08.83	83	4	0	0

ANDERS, Harry
St Helens, 28 November, 1926 (OR)

League Club	Source	Date Signed	Seasons Played	Apps	Subs	Gls
Preston N.E.	St Helens	08.45	47-52	69	-	4
Manchester C.	Tr	03.53	52-54	32	-	4
Port Vale	Tr	07.56	56	3	-	0
Accrington St.	Tr	06.57	57-59	114	-	18
Workington	Tr	07.60	60	7	-	1

ANDERS, James
St Helens, 8 March, 1928 (OL)

League Club	Source	Date Signed	Seasons Played	Apps	Subs	Gls
Preston N.E.	St Helens	08.45				
Brentford	Tr	09.48	49-50	12	-	0
Bradford C.	Tr	06.51	51-52	51	-	11
Rochdale	Tr	07.53	53-56	123	-	28
Bradford P.A.	Tr	09.56	56	20	-	4
Accrington St.	Tr	01.57	56-59	129	-	29
Bradford P.A.	Buxton	09.60	60-61	39	-	8
Tranmere Rov.	Tr	11.61	61	8	-	1

ANDERS, Jason S.
Littleborough, 13 March, 1974 (F)

League Club	Source	Date Signed	Seasons Played	Apps	Subs	Gls
Rochdale (YT)	YT	07.90	90	0	2	0

ANDERSEN, Vetle
Norway, 20 April, 1964 (D)

League Club	Source	Date Signed	Seasons Played	Apps	Subs	Gls
West Bromwich A.	Lyngby (Den)	12.89	89	0	1	0

ANDERSON, Alan A.
Edinburgh, 21 December, 1939 (WH)

League Club	Source	Date Signed	Seasons Played	Apps	Subs	Gls
Millwall	Falkirk	09.59	60-61	74	-	0
Scunthorpe U.	Tr	07.62	62	6	-	0

ANDERSON, Alexander
Glasgow, 8 January, 1922 Died 1984 LOI (G)

League Club	Source	Date Signed	Seasons Played	Apps	Subs	Gls
Rochdale	Hearts	02.48	47	4	-	0
Southport	Dundalk	11.49	49-50	21	-	0

ANDERSON, Alexander F.
Monifieth, 15 November, 1921 (FB)

League Club	Source	Date Signed	Seasons Played	Apps	Subs	Gls
Southampton	Forfar Ath.	11.49	49-51	20	-	0
Exeter C.	Tr	06.52	52	6	-	0

ANDERSON, Alexander O. W. (Sandy)
Auchtermuchty, 20 February, 1930 (FB)

League Club	Source	Date Signed	Seasons Played	Apps	Subs	Gls
Southend U.	Newburgh Jnrs	04.50	50-62	451	-	6

ANDERSON, Benjamin C.
Aberdeen, 18 February, 1946 (HB)

League Club	Source	Date Signed	Seasons Played	Apps	Subs	Gls
Blackburn Rov.	Peterlee	03.64	64-67	21	7	7
Bury	Tr	07.68	68-69	51	2	4
Crystal Palace	Cape Town C. (SA)	11.73	73	11	0	1

ANDERSON, Christopher
Aberdeen, 30 August, 1925 (RH)

League Club	Source	Date Signed	Seasons Played	Apps	Subs	Gls
Hartlepool U.	Aberdeen	09.46	46	2	-	0

ANDERSON, Christopher S.
East Wemyss, 28 November, 1928 (OR)

League Club	Source	Date Signed	Seasons Played	Apps	Subs	Gls
Blackburn Rov.	Lochore Welfare	08.50	50-51	13	-	1
Stockport Co.	Tr	06.53	53	34	-	0
Southport	Tr	07.54	54	28	-	0

ANDERSON, Colin R.
Newcastle, 26 April, 1962 (LW)

League Club	Source	Date Signed	Seasons Played	Apps	Subs	Gls
Burnley	App	04.80	80-81	3	3	0

League Club	Source	Date Signed	Seasons Played	Apps	Subs	Gls
Torquay	North Shields	09.82	82-84	107	2	11
West Bromwich A.	Tr	03.85	85-90	131	9	10
Walsall	Tr	08.91	91	25	1	2

ANDERSON, Dale
Newton Ayclyffe, 23 August, 1970 (F)

League Club	Source	Date Signed	Seasons Played	Apps	Subs	Gls
Darlington	YT	09.88	86-88	4	11	0
Middlesbrough	Tr	07.90				

ANDERSON, Darren I.
Merton, 6 September, 1966 E Yth (CD)

League Club	Source	Date Signed	Seasons Played	Apps	Subs	Gls
Charlton Ath.	Coventry C. (App)	03.84	83-84	10	0	1
Crewe Alex.	L	10.85	85	5	0	0
Aldershot	Tr	07.86	86-89	69	29	4

ANDERSON, Desmond
Edinburgh, 9 January, 1938 S Sch (WH)

League Club	Source	Date Signed	Seasons Played	Apps	Subs	Gls
Millwall	Hibernian	06.61	61-63	46	-	1

ANDERSON, Douglas E.
Hong Kong, 29 August, 1963 (LW)

League Club	Source	Date Signed	Seasons Played	Apps	Subs	Gls
Oldham Ath.	Port Glasgow	09.80	81-83	4	5	0
Tranmere Rov.	Tr	08.84	84-86	125	1	15
Plymouth Arg.	Tr	08.87	87	17	2	1
Cambridge U.	L	09.88	88	8	0	2
Northampton T.	L	12.88	88	4	1	0

ANDERSON, Edward
Glasgow, 23 September, 1917 (FB)

League Club	Source	Date Signed	Seasons Played	Apps	Subs	Gls
Rochdale	Stirling A.	03.48	47	1	-	0

ANDERSON, Edward W.
Newcastle, 17 July, 1911 (FB)

League Club	Source	Date Signed	Seasons Played	Apps	Subs	Gls
Wolverhampton W.	Worksop T.	12.29	30	3	-	0
Torquay U.	Tr	12.31	31-32	61	-	2
West Ham U.	Tr	06.33	33-34	26	-	2
Chester C.	Tr	06.35	35-36	23	-	0
Tranmere Rov.	Tr	07.37	37-47	74	-	0

ANDERSON, Eric
Manchester, 12 July, 1931 (IF)

League Club	Source	Date Signed	Seasons Played	Apps	Subs	Gls
Liverpool		12.51	52-56	73	-	21
Barnsley	Tr	07.57	57	9	-	1

ANDERSON, Gary L.
Bow, 20 November, 1955 (FB)

League Club	Source	Date Signed	Seasons Played	Apps	Subs	Gls
Tottenham H.	App	12.72				
Northampton T.	Tr	03.75	74-75	14	0	0

ANDERSON, Geoffrey T.
Sheerness, 26 November, 1944 (W)

League Club	Source	Date Signed	Seasons Played	Apps	Subs	Gls
Birmingham C.	App.	12.62	63	1	-	0
Mansfield T.	Tr	05.64	64-65	43	0	13
Lincoln C.	Tr	07.66	66	44	0	6

ANDERSON, J. Desmond
Templepatrick (NI), 11 September, 1940 NI Amat/NI-5 (HB)

League Club	Source	Date Signed	Seasons Played	Apps	Subs	Gls
Exeter C.	Glenavon	08.62	62-65	142	2	1
Chesterfield	Tr	07.66	66-67	8	0	0

ANDERSON, James
Felling, 26 May, 1913 (LB)

League Club	Source	Date Signed	Seasons Played	Apps	Subs	Gls
Brentford	Blyth Spartans	07.39				
Carlisle U.	Tr	09.46	46	10	-	0

ANDERSON, James M.
Glasgow, 25 September, 1932 (HB)

League Club	Source	Date Signed	Seasons Played	Apps	Subs	Gls
Bristol Rov.		04.53	54-56	24	-	0
Chester C.	Tr	06.57	57-59	62	-	0

ANDERSON, John
Barrhead, 8 September, 1929 S-1/S'B'-1 (G)

League Club	Source	Date Signed	Seasons Played	Apps	Subs	Gls
Leicester C.	Arthurlie	12.48	48-58	261	-	0
Peterborough U.	Tr	07.60				

ANDERSON, John
Salford, 11 October, 1921 (WH)

League Club	Source	Date Signed	Seasons Played	Apps	Subs	Gls
Manchester U.	Jnrs	11.38	47-48	33	-	1
Nottingham F.	Tr	10.49	49-50	40	-	1

ANDERSON, John C.
Dundee, 8 May, 1915 (CF)

League Club	Source	Date Signed	Seasons Played	Apps	Subs	Gls
Portsmouth	Stobswell	01.33	33-38	80	-	36
Aldershot	Tr	06.46	46	4	-	1

ANDERSON, John C. P.
Dublin, 7 November, 1959 IR Yth/IRu21-1/IR-16 (D)

League Club	Source	Date Signed	Seasons Played	Apps	Subs	Gls
West Bromwich A.	App.	11.77				
Preston N.E.	Tr	08.79	79-81	47	4	0
Newcastle U.	Tr	09.82	82-90	283	16	14

ANDERSON, John E.
Bellingham, 7 June, 1931 (FB)

League Club	Source	Date Signed	Seasons Played	Apps	Subs	Gls
Grimsby T.	Langold Colly	05.54	55	3	-	0

ANDERSON John H.
Renfrew, 11 January, 1937 (W)

League Club	Source	Date Signed	Seasons Played	Apps	Subs	Gls
Stoke C.	Johnstone Burgh	01.57	57-60	24	-	2

ANDERSON John L.
Glasgow, 5 April, 1928 (IF)

League Club	Source	Date Signed	Seasons Played	Apps	Subs	Gls
Northampton T.	Partick Th.	06.53	53	14	-	3
Exeter C.	Tr	07.54	54	7	-	0
Wrexham	Dundee	06.56	56-58	98	-	27
Rochdale	Tr	07.59	59	28	-	5
Chester C.	Tr	07.60	60	17	-	2
Wrexham	Tr	08.61	61	1	-	0

ANDERSON, Lee C.
Tottington, 4 October, 1973 (RB)

League Club	Source	Date Signed	Seasons Played	Apps	Subs	Gls
Bury	YT	10.91	91	3	2	0

ANDERSON, Nicholas J.
Lincoln, 29 March, 1969 (M/RB)

League Club	Source	Date Signed	Seasons Played	Apps	Subs	Gls
Mansfield T.	YT	01.87	86-88	9	11	0
Lincoln C. (N/C)	Tr	08.89	89	1	0	0

ANDERSON, Norman
Hebburn, 30 November, 1930 (F)

League Club	Source	Date Signed	Seasons Played	Apps	Subs	Gls
Gateshead	Reyrolles	03.51	53-55	19	-	2

ANDERSON, Percy
Cambridge, 22 September, 1930 (IF)

League Club	Source	Date Signed	Seasons Played	Apps	Subs	Gls
West Bromwich A.	Cambridge U.	09.51				
Stockport Co.	Tr	07.53	53	1	-	0

ANDERSON, Peter D.
Plymouth, 11 September, 1932 (W)

League Club	Source	Date Signed	Seasons Played	Apps	Subs	Gls
Plymouth Arg.	Oak Villa	07.50	52-62	241	-	41
Torquay U.	Tr	12.62	62-64	77	-	18

ANDERSON, Peter T.
Hendon, 31 May, 1949 (M)

League Club	Source	Date Signed	Seasons Played	Apps	Subs	Gls
Luton T.	Hendon	02.71	70-75	178	3	34
Sheffield U.	Tampa Bay (USA)	09.78	78	28	2	12
Millwall	Tampa Bay (USA)	12.80	80-82	30	2	4

ANDERSON, Philip O.
Portadown (NI), 5 January, 1948 (IF)

League Club	Source	Date Signed	Seasons Played	Apps	Subs	Gls
Bury	Portadown	05.66	66-69	5	4	1

ANDERSON, Robert
Newton Mearns, 11 August, 1928 (W)

League Club	Source	Date Signed	Seasons Played	Apps	Subs	Gls
Leicester C.	Jnrs	01.46	46-47	19	-	2

ANDERSON, Robert
Aberdeen, 21 January, 1937 (OR)

League Club	Source	Date Signed	Seasons Played	Apps	Subs	Gls
Chesterfield	Partick Th.	08.59	59	4	-	0

ANDERSON, J. Robert
Newcastle, 9 November, 1924 (G)

League Club	Source	Date Signed	Seasons Played	Apps	Subs	Gls
Middlesbrough		11.45	47	1	-	0
Crystal Palace	Blackhall Colly	10.51	51-52	38	-	0
Bristol Rov.	Tr	03.53	52-53	10	-	0
Bristol C.	Tr	04.54	54-58	106	-	0

ANDERSON, Robert J.
Portsmouth, 23 February, 1936 (W)

League Club	Source	Date Signed	Seasons Played	Apps	Subs	Gls
Mansfield T.	Chesterfield Tube	09.56	56-59	40	-	4

ANDERSON, Robert L.
Derry (NI), 23 April, 1926 (FB)

League Club	Source	Date Signed	Seasons Played	Apps	Subs	Gls
Doncaster Rov.	Ulsterville	11.49	50-51	3	-	0

ANDERSON, Ronald J.
Gateshead, 3 July, 1922 (IF)

League Club	Source	Date Signed	Seasons Played	Apps	Subs	Gls
Bury		08.39	46	2	-	0
Crystal Palace	Tr	05.47				

ANDERSON, Samuel
Manchester, 11 January, 1936 (FB)

League Club	Source	Date Signed	Seasons Played	Apps	Subs	Gls
Oldham Ath.	Oldham Amats	08.54	55-56	6	-	0

ANDERSON, Stanley
Horden, 27 February, 1934 E Sch/Eu23-4/E-2 (WH)

League Club	Source	Date Signed	Seasons Played	Apps	Subs	Gls
Sunderland	Jnrs	03.51	52-63	402	-	31
Newcastle U.	Tr	11.63	63-65	81	0	13
Middlesbrough	Tr	11.65	65	21	0	1

ANDERSON, Terence K.
Woking, 11 March, 1944 Died 1980 E Yth (W)

League Club	Source	Date Signed	Seasons Played	Apps	Subs	Gls
Arsenal	App	08.61	62-64	25	-	6
Norwich C.	Tr	02.65	64-73	218	18	16
Colchester U.	L	02.74	73	4	0	0
Scunthorpe U.	Baltimore (USA)	09.74	74	10	0	0
Crewe Alex.	Tr	11.74	74	4	0	0
Colchester U.	Baltimore (USA)	08.75	75	13	3	0

ANDERSON, Thomas C.
Edinburgh, 24 September, 1934 S Sch (IF)

League Club	Source	Date Signed	Seasons Played	Apps	Subs	Gls
Watford	Queen of South	12.56	56-57	52	-	12
Bournemouth	Tr	06.58	58	5	-	1
Queens Park R.	Tr	11.58	58	11	-	3
Torquay U.	Tr	07.59	59	9	-	4
Stockport Co.	Tr	06.60	60-61	60	-	17
Doncaster Rov.	Tr	11.61	61	16	-	3
Wrexham	Tr	03.62	61-62	12	-	3
Barrow	Hellas (Aus)	12.63	63	11	-	3
Watford	Hellas (Aus)	12.64	64-65	21	0	2
Leyton Orient	Australia	07.67	67	8	1	0

ANDERSON, Trevor
Belfast, 3 March, 1951 NIu21-1/NI-22 (W)

League Club	Source	Date Signed	Seasons Played	Apps	Subs	Gls
Manchester U.	Portadown	10.72	72-73	13	6	2
Swindon T.	Tr	11.74	74-77	128	3	35
Peterborough U.	Tr	12.77	77-78	49	0	6

ANDERSON, Vivian A.
Nottingham, 29 August, 1956 Eu21-1/E-'B'/EF Lge/E-30 (RB)

League Club	Source	Date Signed	Seasons Played	Apps	Subs	Gls
Nottingham F.	App	08.74	74-83	323	5	15
Arsenal	Tr	07.84	84-86	120	0	9
Manchester U.	Tr	05.87	87-90	50	4	3
Sheffield Wed.	Tr	01.91	90-91	36	8	5

ANDERSON, William
Lochore (Fife), 6 November, 1926 (IF)

League Club	Source	Date Signed	Seasons Played	Apps	Subs	Gls
Southend U.	Hibernian	05.54	54-55	16	-	1

ANDERSON, William B.
Sunderland, 28 March, 1935 (WH)

League Club	Source	Date Signed	Seasons Played	Apps	Subs	Gls
Barnsley	Silksworth Jnrs	09.52	55	6	-	0
Hartlepool U.	Tr	02.56	55-60	179	-	11

ANDERSON, William J.
Liverpool, 24 January, 1947 (W)

League Club	Source	Date Signed	Seasons Played	Apps	Subs	Gls
Manchester U.	App	02.64	63-66	7	2	0
Aston Villa	Tr	01.67	66-72	229	2	36
Cardiff C.	Tr	02.73	72-76	122	4	12

ANDERSON, William R.
Kilmarnock, 13 November, 1919 Died 1981 (F)

League Club	Source	Date Signed	Seasons Played	Apps	Subs	Gls
Millwall	Dundee	07.44	46-47	32	-	6

ANDERSON, William R.
Ponteland, 20 September, 1927 (G)

League Club	Source	Date Signed	Seasons Played	Apps	Subs	Gls
Newcastle U.	Throckley Welfare	02.47	46	1	-	0

ANDERTON, Darren R.
Southampton, 3 March, 1972 E Yth (W)

League Club	Source	Date Signed	Seasons Played	Apps	Subs	Gls
Portsmouth	YT	02.90	90-91	53	9	7

ANDERTON, John
Skelmersdale, 7 February, 1933 (FB)

League Club	Source	Date Signed	Seasons Played	Apps	Subs	Gls
Everton	Jnrs	03.51				
Torquay U.	Tr	07.54	54-57	40	-	2

ANDERTON, Steven D.
Lancaster, 2 October, 1969 (M)

League Club	Source	Date Signed	Seasons Played	Apps	Subs	Gls
Preston N.E.	YT	07.88	89	0	1	0

ANDERTON, Sylvan J.
Reading, 23 November, 1934 (WH)

League Club	Source	Date Signed	Seasons Played	Apps	Subs	Gls
Reading	Jnrs	06.52	52-58	155	-	18
Chelsea	Tr	03.59	58-61	76	-	2
Queens Park R.	Tr	01.62	61	4	-	0

ANDREW, George
Glasgow, 24 November, 1945 (CH)

League Club	Source	Date Signed	Seasons Played	Apps	Subs	Gls
West Ham U.	Possilpark Jnrs	09.63	66	2	0	0
Crystal Palace	Tr	07.67				

ANDREW, Matthew
Johnstone, 5 January, 1922 (HB)

League Club	Source	Date Signed	Seasons Played	Apps	Subs	Gls
Bristol C.		10.47				
Swansea C.	Tr	08.48	48-50	4	-	0
Workington	Tr	06.51	51	22	-	0

ANDREW, Ronald E. H.
Ellesmere Port, 5 January, 1936 (CH)

League Club	Source	Date Signed	Seasons Played	Apps	Subs	Gls
Stoke C.	Ellesmere Port	05.54	57-63	115	-	1
Port Vale	Tr	06.64	64	8	-	1

ANDREWS, Cecil J.
Alton, 1 November, 1930 (WH)

League Club	Source	Date Signed	Seasons Played	Apps	Subs	Gls
Portsmouth		01.49				
Crystal Palace	Tr	06.52	52-55	104	-	12
Queens Park R.	Tr	06.56	56-57	58	-	1

ANDREWS, Derek
Bury, 14 December, 1934 (IF)

League Club	Source	Date Signed	Seasons Played	Apps	Subs	Gls
Rochdale		03.55	55	22	-	4

ANDREWS, Gary M.
Nottingham, 12 May, 1968 (FB)

League Club	Source	Date Signed	Seasons Played	Apps	Subs	Gls
Nottingham F.	App	09.85				
Peterborough U.	Tr	08.88	88-89	42	1	0

ANDREWS, George
Dudley, 23 April, 1942 (CF)

League Club	Source	Date Signed	Seasons Played	Apps	Subs	Gls
Luton T.		01.60				
Cardiff C.	Lower Gornal Ath.	10.65	65-66	43	0	21
Southport	Tr	02.67	66-69	115	2	41
Shrewsbury T.	Tr	11.69	69-72	123	1	50
Walsall	Tr	01.73	72-76	156	3	38

ANDREWS, Glen
Dudley, 11 February, 1945 (FB)

League Club	Source	Date Signed	Seasons Played	Apps	Subs	Gls
Manchester U.	Jnrs	09.63				
Wolverhampton W.	Tr	07.66				
Bradford P.A.	Tr	09.67	67-68	47	1	6

ANDREWS, Ian E.
Nottingham, 1 December, 1964 E Yth/Eu21-1 (G)

League Club	Source	Date Signed	Seasons Played	Apps	Subs	Gls
Leicester C.	App	12.82	83-87	126	0	0

Darren Anderton (Portsmouth)

League Club	Source	Date Signed	Seasons Played	Career Record Apps	Subs	Gls
Swindon T.	L	01.84	83	1	0	0
Leeds U. (L)	Glasgow Celtic	12.88	88	1	0	0
Southampton	Glasgow Celtic	12.89	89-91	5	0	0

ANDREWS, James P.
Invergordon, 1 February, 1927 (OL)

League Club	Source	Date Signed	Seasons Played	Apps	Subs	Gls
West Ham U.	Dundee	11.51	51-55	114	-	21
Leyton Orient	Tr	06.56	56-58	36	-	8
Queens Park R.	Tr	06.59	59-61	82	-	15

ANDREWS, John E.
York, 3 February, 1950 (G)

League Club	Source	Date Signed	Seasons Played	Apps	Subs	Gls
York C. (Am)	Moor Lane Y.C.	08.68	68	11	0	0

ANDREWS, Keri A.
Swansea, 28 April, 1968 W Yth (W)

League Club	Source	Date Signed	Seasons Played	Apps	Subs	Gls
Swansea C.	App	04.86	84-87	32	9	3

ANDREWS, Leslie L.
Dudley, 29 October, 1953 (CF)

League Club	Source	Date Signed	Seasons Played	Apps	Subs	Gls
Wolverhampton W.	Jnrs	09.72				
Scunthorpe U.	L	03.74	73	7	2	1

ANDREWS, Percy
Alton, 12 June, 1922 Died 1985 (LB)

League Club	Source	Date Signed	Seasons Played	Apps	Subs	Gls
York C.	Portsmouth (Am)	09.47	47-54	176	-	0

ANDRUSZEWSKI, Emanuel F. (Manny)
Eastleigh, 4 October, 1955 (FB)

League Club	Source	Date Signed	Seasons Played	Apps	Subs	Gls
Southampton	App	10.73	74-79	82	1	3
Aldershot	Tampa Bay (USA)	08.82	82	25	2	0

ANGELL, Brett A. M.
Marlborough, 20 August, 1968 (F)

League Club	Source	Date Signed	Seasons Played	Apps	Subs	Gls
Portsmouth (N/C)	YT	08.86				
Derby Co.	Cheltenham T.	02.88				
Stockport Co.	Tr	10.88	88-89	60	10	28
Southend U.	Tr	07.90	90-91	79	6	36

ANGELL, Darren J.
Marlborough, 19 January, 1967 (D)

League Club	Source	Date Signed	Seasons Played	Apps	Subs	Gls
Portsmouth	Newbury T.	06.85				
Colchester U.	L	12.87	87	1	0	0
Lincoln C.	Cheltenham T.	07.88				

ANGELL, Peter F.
Slough, 11 January, 1932 Died 1979 (WH)

League Club	Source	Date Signed	Seasons Played	Apps	Subs	Gls
Queens Park R.	Slough T.	07.53	53-64	418	-	37

ANGUS, John
Newcastle, 12 March, 1909 Died 1965 (FB)

League Club	Source	Date Signed	Seasons Played	Apps	Subs	Gls
Wolverhampton W.	Amble W.	09.28				
Exeter C.	Scunthorpe U.	05.30	30-47	246	-	1

ANGUS, John
Amble, 2 September, 1938 E Yth/EF Lge/Eu23-7/E-1 (RB)

League Club	Source	Date Signed	Seasons Played	Apps	Subs	Gls
Burnley	Jnrs	09.55	56-71	438	1	4

ANGUS, Michael A.
Middlesbrough, 28 October, 1960 (M)

League Club	Source	Date Signed	Seasons Played	Apps	Subs	Gls
Middlesbrough	Jnrs	08.78	79-81	35	2	1
Scunthorpe U.	L	09.82	82	20	0	2
Southend U.	Tr	08.83				
Darlington	Tr	03.84	83-84	18	0	7

ANGUS, Terence N.
Coventry, 14 January, 1966 (CD)

League Club	Source	Date Signed	Seasons Played	Apps	Subs	Gls
Northampton T.	V. S. Rugby	08.90	90-91	79	0	4

ANSAH, Andrew
Lewisham, 19 March, 1969 (W)

League Club	Source	Date Signed	Seasons Played	Apps	Subs	Gls
Brentford	Dorking	03.89	88-89	3	5	2
Southend U.	Tr	03.90	89-91	83	4	19

ANSELL, Barry
Birmingham, 29 September, 1947 (FB)

League Club	Source	Date Signed	Seasons Played	Apps	Subs	Gls
Aston Villa		10.67	67	1	0	0

ANSELL, William (Jack)
Bletchley, 4 August, 1921 (G)

League Club	Source	Date Signed	Seasons Played	Apps	Subs	Gls
Northampton T.		03.48	47-51	131	-	0

ANSLOW, Stanley T.
Hackney, 5 May, 1931 (LB)

League Club	Source	Date Signed	Seasons Played	Apps	Subs	Gls
Millwall	Eton Manor	03.51	51-58	131	-	13

ANTHONY, Thomas H.
Hounslow, 16 August, 1943 (FB)

League Club	Source	Date Signed	Seasons Played	Apps	Subs	Gls
Brentford	Jnrs	12.61	62	33	-	1
Millwall	Coventry C. (trial)	11.65				

ANTHROBUS, Stephen A.
Lewisham, 10 November, 1968 (W)

League Club	Source	Date Signed	Seasons Played	Apps	Subs	Gls
Millwall	YT	08.86	87-89	19	2	4
Wimbledon	Tr	02.90	89-91	23	0	0

ANTIC, Radomir (Raddy)
Yugoslavia, 22 November, 1949 Yugoslav Int (M)

League Club	Source	Date Signed	Seasons Played	Apps	Subs	Gls
Luton T.	Real Zaragoza (Sp)	07.80	80-83	54	46	9

ANTONIO George R.
Whitchurch, 20 October, 1914 (WH)

League Club	Source	Date Signed	Seasons Played	Apps	Subs	Gls
Stoke C.	Oswestry T.	02.36	35-46	84	-	13
Derby Co.	Tr	03.47	46-47	18	-	2
Doncaster Rov.	Tr	10.48	48-49	34	-	7
Mansfield T.	Tr	10.49	49-50	67	-	2

APPLEBY, James P.
Shotton (Dm), 15 June, 1934 (CH)

League Club	Source	Date Signed	Seasons Played	Apps	Subs	Gls
Burnley	Wingate W.	02.53	56	1	-	0
Blackburn Rov.	Tr	02.58	58-61	2	-	0
Southport	Tr	10.61	61	13	-	0
Chester C.	Tr	06.62	62	1	-	0

APPLEBY, Matthew W.
Middlesbrough, 16 April, 1972 (CD)

League Club	Source	Date Signed	Seasons Played	Apps	Subs	Gls
Newcastle U.	YT	05.90	90-91	17	2	0

APPLEBY, Robert
Warkworth, 15 January, 1940 (G)

League Club	Source	Date Signed	Seasons Played	Apps	Subs	Gls
Middlesbrough	Amble W.	05.57	59-66	99	0	0

APPLETON, Colin H.
Scarborough, 7 March, 1936 EF Lge (WH)

League Club	Source	Date Signed	Seasons Played	Apps	Subs	Gls
Leicester C.	Scarborough	03.54	54-65	277	0	19
Charlton Ath.	Tr	06.66	66	28	0	1
Barrow	Tr	08.67	67-68	40	4	1

APPLETON, Ronald
Cleator Moor, 24 September, 1932 (W)

League Club	Source	Date Signed	Seasons Played	Apps	Subs	Gls
Workington		02.53	52	3	-	0

APPLETON, Stephen
Liverpool, 27 July, 1973 (CD)

League Club	Source	Date Signed	Seasons Played	Apps	Subs	Gls
Wigan Ath.	YT	09.90	90-91	7	12	0

APPLETON, Thomas H.
Stanley, 9 June, 1936 (HB)

League Club	Source	Date Signed	Seasons Played	Apps	Subs	Gls
Burnley	Annfield Plain	08.54				
Gateshead	Tr	08.58	58	26	-	0

ARBER, Robert L.
Poplar, 13 January, 1951 (FB)

League Club	Source	Date Signed	Seasons Played	Apps	Subs	Gls
Arsenal	App	03.68				
Leyton Orient		07.70	71-72	31	0	0

ARBLASTER, Brian M.
Kensington, 6 June, 1943 (G)

League Club	Source	Date Signed	Seasons Played	Apps	Subs	Gls
Sheffield U.	Jnrs	07.62				
Chesterfield	Tr	12.64	64-66	55	0	0
Scunthorpe U.	Tr	06.67	67	10	0	0
Barnsley	Tr	05.68	67-73	111	0	0

ARCHDEACON, Owen D.
Greenock, 4 March, 1966 (W)

League Club	Source	Date Signed	Seasons Played	Apps	Subs	Gls
Barnsley	Glasgow Celtic	07.89	89-91	102	4	12

ARCHELL, Graham L.
Islington, 8 February, 1950 (M)

League Club	Source	Date Signed	Seasons Played	Apps	Subs	Gls
Leyton Orient	Jnrs	11.67	67-68	5	2	0

ARCHER, John
Biddulph, 18 June, 1941 (IF)

League Club	Source	Date Signed	Seasons Played	Apps	Subs	Gls
Port Vale	Jnrs	07.58	59-60	10	-	3
Bournemouth	Tr	07.61	61-65	139	0	37
Crewe Alex.	Tr	09.66	66-67	59	0	14
Huddersfield T.	Tr	01.68	67	7	2	0
Chesterfield	Tr	05.69	69-71	116	0	22

ARCHER, John C
Whitstable, 9 April, 1936 (G)

League Club	Source	Date Signed	Seasons Played	Apps	Subs	Gls
Grimsby T.	Whitstable T.	04.54	54	10	-	0

League Club	Source	Date Signed	Seasons Played	Apps	Subs	Gls
ARCHER, Lee						
Bristol, 6 November, 1972						(M)
Bristol Rov.	YT	05.91	91	3	2	0
ARCHER, Philip						
Rotherham, 25 August, 1952						(FB)
Reading	Sheffield U. (App)	09.70	71	12	5	0
ARCHER, Ronald						
Barnsley, 3 September, 1933 E Sch						(WH)
Barnsley	Jnrs	09.50	51-55	28	-	0
ARCHER, William H.						
Scunthorpe, 5 February, 1914						(CH)
Lincoln C.		06.39				
Doncaster Rov.	Tr	10.45	46-47	14	-	0
ARCHIBALD, Murray J.						
Carron, 19 March, 1917						
Wrexham		03.46	46	1	-	0
ARCHIBALD, Steven						
Glasgow, 27 September, 1956 Su21-5/S-27						(F)
Tottenham H.	Aberdeen	05.80	80-83	128	3	58
Blackburn Rov.	Barcelona (Sp)	12.87	87	20	0	6
Reading (N/C)	St Mirren	01.92	91	1	0	0
ARDILES, Osvaldo C.						
Argentina, 3 August, 1952 Argentine Int						(M)
Tottenham H.	Huracan (Arg)	07.78	78-87	221	16	16
Blackburn Rov.	L	03.88	87	5	0	0
Queens Park R.	Tr	08.88	88	4	4	0
Swindon T. (N/C)	Tr	07.89	89	0	2	0
ARDLEY, Neal C.						
Epsom, 1 September, 1972						(M)
Wimbledon	YT	07.91	90-91	8	1	0
ARDRON, Walter						
Swinton on Dearne, 19 September, 1918 Died 1978						(CF)
Rotherham U.	Denaby U.	12.38	38-48	123	-	94
Nottingham F.	Tr	07.49	49-55	182	-	123

League Club	Source	Date Signed	Seasons Played	Apps	Subs	Gls
ARENTOFT, Preben						
Denmark, 1 November, 1942						(M)
Newcastle U.	Morton	03.69	68-70	46	4	2
Blackburn Rov.	Tr	09.71	71-73	94	0	3
ARGUE, James						
Glasgow, 27 November, 1911 Died 1978						(IF)
Birmingham C.	St Rocks	12.31				
Chelsea	Tr	05.33	33-46	118	-	30
ARINS, Anthony F.						
Chesterfield, 26 October, 1958						(D)
Burnley	App	07.76	78-79	29	0	2
Leeds U.	Tr	05.80	81	0	1	0
Scunthorpe U.	Tr	11.81	81	20	0	1
ARKWRIGHT, Ian						
Shafton, 18 September, 1959						(W)
Wolverhampton W.	App	09.77	78	3	1	0
Wrexham	Tr	03.80	79-83	102	2	10
Torquay U.	L	03.84	83	2	0	0
ARMES, Ivan W.						
Lowestoft, 6 April, 1924						(WH)
Norwich C.	Brooke Marine	11.46	46-49	61	-	1
Exeter C.	Tr	12.51	51-52	14	-	2
ARMFIELD, James C.						
Blackpool, 21 September, 1935 Eu23-9/EF Lge/E-43						(RB)
Blackpool	Jnrs	09.54	54-70	568	0	6
ARMITAGE, Andrew M.						
Leeds, 17 October, 1968						(LB)
Leeds U. (N/C)	YT	08.87				
Rochdale	Tr	07.88	88	33	3	0
ARMITAGE, Kenneth J.						
Sheffield, 23 October, 1920 Died 1952						(CH)
Barnsley	Jnrs	12.37				
Leyton Orient	Gainsborough Trin.	04.46	46	7	-	0
Oldham Ath.	Tr	07.47	47	5	-	0

Ossie Ardiles (Huracan, Tottenham Hotspur, Queens Park Rangers, Swindon Town & Argentina)

ARMITAGE, Louis C.
Hull, 15 December, 1921 (F)

League Club	Source	Date Signed	Seasons Played	Apps	Subs	Gls
Rotherham U.		12.40	46-47	15	-	9
Grimsby T.	Tr	01.48	47	8	-	2

ARMITAGE, Stanley
Woolwich, 5 June, 1919

League Club	Source	Date Signed	Seasons Played	Apps	Subs	Gls
Queens Park R.		06.46	46	2	-	0

ARMSTRONG, Adam
Blackpool, 6 June, 1925 (OL)

League Club	Source	Date Signed	Seasons Played	Apps	Subs	Gls
Chesterfield	Petershill	09.49	49	1	-	0

ARMSTRONG, Christopher P.
Newcastle, 19 June, 1971 (F)

League Club	Source	Date Signed	Seasons Played	Apps	Subs	Gls
Wrexham	Jnrs	10.88	89-90	40	20	13
Millwall	Tr	08.91	91	8	17	4

ARMSTRONG, David
Durham, 26 December, 1954 Eu23-4/E' B'/E-3 (M)

League Club	Source	Date Signed	Seasons Played	Apps	Subs	Gls
Middlesbrough	App	01.72	71-80	357	2	59
Southampton	Tr	08.81	81-86	222	0	59
Bournemouth	Tr	07.87	87	6	3	2

ARMSTRONG, David T.
Mile End, 9 November, 1942 (W)

League Club	Source	Date Signed	Seasons Played	Apps	Subs	Gls
Millwall	Hornchurch	12.65	65-67	14	6	1
Brighton & H.A.	Tr	09.68	68-69	38	6	6

ARMSTRONG, Derek
Carlisle, 16 March, 1939 (OL)

League Club	Source	Date Signed	Seasons Played	Apps	Subs	Gls
Blackpool		08.58	58	1	-	0
Carlisle U.	Morecambe	08.61	61	1	-	0

ARMSTRONG, Eric
Hebburn, 25 May, 1921 Died 1975 (WH)

League Club	Source	Date Signed	Seasons Played	Apps	Subs	Gls
West Ham U.	Cramlington W.	01.47	47	1	-	0

ARMSTRONG, Gary S.
West Ham, 2 January, 1958 (FB)

League Club	Source	Date Signed	Seasons Played	Apps	Subs	Gls
Gillingham	Jnrs	01.76	75-79	82	4	2
Wimbledon	Tr	03.80	79-81	71	0	0
Gillingham	Barnet	11.83	83	7	1	0
Crewe Alex.	Tr	08.84	84	31	0	0

ARMSTRONG, George
Hebburn, 9 August, 1944 E Yth/Eu23-5 (W)

League Club	Source	Date Signed	Seasons Played	Apps	Subs	Gls
Arsenal	Jnrs	08.61	61-76	490	10	53
Leicester C.	Tr	09.77	77-78	14	1	0
Stockport Co.	Tr	09.78	78	34	0	0

ARMSTRONG, Gerard J.
Belfast, 23 May, 1954 NI-63 (F)

League Club	Source	Date Signed	Seasons Played	Apps	Subs	Gls
Tottenham H.	Bangor (NI)	11.75	76-80	65	19	10
Watford	Tr	11.80	80-82	50	26	12
West Bromwich A.	Real Mallorca (Sp)	08.85	85	7	1	0
Chesterfield	L	01.86	85	12	0	1
Brighton & H.A.	Tr	07.86	86-88	30	17	6
Millwall	L	01.87	86	7	0	0

ARMSTRONG, Gordon I.
Newcastle, 15 July, 1967 (M)

League Club	Source	Date Signed	Seasons Played	Apps	Subs	Gls
Sunderland	App	07.85	84-91	258	4	44

ARMSTRONG, James
Ulverston, 14 September, 1943 (F)

League Club	Source	Date Signed	Seasons Played	Apps	Subs	Gls
Barrow	App	01.61	60-62	17	-	2
Chesterfield	Tr	07.63	63	7	-	0

ARMSTRONG, John
Airdrie, 5 September, 1936 (G)

League Club	Source	Date Signed	Seasons Played	Apps	Subs	Gls
Barrow	Bellshill	03.58	57-58	21	-	0
Nottingham F.	Tr	11.58	58-62	20	-	0
Portsmouth	Tr	02.63	62-66	79	0	0
Southport	Tr	08.67	67-70	86	0	0

ARMSTRONG, Joseph
Brighton, 16 November, 1931 Died 1986 (IF)

League Club	Source	Date Signed	Seasons Played	Apps	Subs	Gls
Southend U.		11.52				
Barrow	Tr	07.53	53-57	104	-	33
Workington	Tr	03.58	57-58	25	-	10

ARMSTRONG, Joseph M.
Newcastle, 29 January, 1939 (IF)

League Club	Source	Date Signed	Seasons Played	Apps	Subs	Gls
Leeds U.	Leslie B.C.	05.57				
Gateshead	Tr	07.59	59	22	-	9

ARMSTRONG, Keith T.
Corbridge, 11 October, 1957 (W)

League Club	Source	Date Signed	Seasons Played	Apps	Subs	Gls
Sunderland	Jnrs	01.75	77	7	4	0
Newport Co.	L	08.78	78	3	1	0
Scunthorpe U.	L	10.78	78	0	1	0
Newcastle U.	Oulu (Finland)	06.79				

ARMSTRONG, Kenneth
Bradford, 3 June, 1924 Died 1984 EF Lge/E'B'-3/E-1 (WH)

League Club	Source	Date Signed	Seasons Played	Apps	Subs	Gls
Chelsea	Bradford Rov.	12.46	47-56	362	-	25

ARMSTRONG, Kenneth C.
Bridgnorth, 31 January, 1959 (CD)

League Club	Source	Date Signed	Seasons Played	Apps	Subs	Gls
Southampton	Kilmarnock	06.83	83	26	0	0
Notts Co.	L	03.84	83	10	0	0
Birmingham C.	Tr	08.84	84-85	58	0	1
Walsall	Tr	02.86				

ARMSTRONG, Lee W.
Cockermouth, 19 October, 1972 (RB)

League Club	Source	Date Signed	Seasons Played	Apps	Subs	Gls
Carlisle U.	YT	01.79	90-91	12	8	0

ARMSTRONG, Robert
Newcastle, 1 July, 1938 (F)

League Club	Source	Date Signed	Seasons Played	Apps	Subs	Gls
Darlington		07.59	59	1	-	0

ARMSTRONG, Terence
Barnsley, 10 July, 1958 (M)

League Club	Source	Date Signed	Seasons Played	Apps	Subs	Gls
Huddersfield T.	App	07.76	76-78	36	4	2
Port Vale	Tr	02.81	80-84	113	3	12

ARMSTRONG, Thomas
Carlisle, 27 February, 1920 (FB)

League Club	Source	Date Signed	Seasons Played	Apps	Subs	Gls
Carlisle U.	Holme Head	08.46	46	3	-	0

ARNELL, Alan J.
Chichester, 25 November, 1933 (CF)

League Club	Source	Date Signed	Seasons Played	Apps	Subs	Gls
Liverpool	Worthing	03.54	53-60	69	-	33
Tranmere Rov.	Tr	02.61	60-62	68	-	34
Halifax T.	Tr	07.63	63	14	-	6

ARNISON, Joseph
South Africa, 27 June, 1924 (CF)

League Club	Source	Date Signed	Seasons Played	Apps	Subs	Gls
Luton T.	Glasgow Rangers	08.48	48-50	44	-	19

ARNOLD, Eric A.
Lowestoft, 13 September, 1922 (FB)

League Club	Source	Date Signed	Seasons Played	Apps	Subs	Gls
Norwich C.	Lowestoft T.	09.47	47-51	13	-	0

ARNOLD, Ian
Durham City, 4 July, 1972 (F)

League Club	Source	Date Signed	Seasons Played	Apps	Subs	Gls
Middlesbrough	YT	01.90	90-91	0	3	0

ARNOLD, James A.
Stafford, 6 August, 1950 E Semi-Pro (G)

League Club	Source	Date Signed	Seasons Played	Apps	Subs	Gls
Blackburn Rov.	Stafford R.	06.79	79-80	58	0	0
Everton	Tr	08.81	81-83	48	0	0
Preston N.E.	L	10.82	82	6	0	0
Port Vale	Tr	08.85	85-86	53	0	0

ARNOLD, John W.L.
Southwark, 6 December, 1954 (F)

League Club	Source	Date Signed	Seasons Played	Apps	Subs	Gls
Charlton Ath.	App	12.72	72-73	1	4	0

ARNOLD, Rodney J.
Wolverhampton, 3 June, 1952 (G)

League Club	Source	Date Signed	Seasons Played	Apps	Subs	Gls
Wolverhampton W.	App	06.70				
Mansfield T.	L	02.71	70	17	0	0
Mansfield T.	Tr	03.73	72-83	423	0	0

ARNOLD, Stephen F.
Crewe, 5 January, 1951 (M)

League Club	Source	Date Signed	Seasons Played	Apps	Subs	Gls
Crewe Alex.	App	01.69	68-70	13	2	0
Liverpool	Tr	09.70	70	1	1	0
Southport	L	01.72	71	16	0	3
Torquay U.	L	09.72	72	2	1	1
Rochdale	Tr	06.73	73	37	3	1

ARNOTT, Andrew J.
Chatham, 18 October, 1973 (F)

League Club	Source	Date Signed	Seasons Played	Apps	Subs	Gls
Gillingham	YT	05.91	91	7	12	2

ARNOTT, John H.
Sydenham, 6 September, 1932 (WH)

League Club	Source	Date Signed	Seasons Played	Apps	Subs	Gls
West Ham U.	Beckenham	07.54	53-54	6	-	2
Shrewsbury T.	Tr	08.55	55	30	-	6
Bournemouth	Tr	07.56	56-61	173	-	21
Gillingham	Tr	08.62	62-67	184	2	2

ARNOTT, Kevin W.
Gateshead, 28 September, 1958 (M)

League Club	Source	Date Signed	Seasons Played	Apps	Subs	Gls
Sunderland	App	09.76	76-81	132	1	16
Blackburn Rov.	L	11.81	81	17	0	2
Sheffield U.	Tr	06.82	82-86	120	1	11
Blackburn Rov.	L	11.82	82	11	1	1
Rotherham U.	L	03.83	82	9	0	2
Chesterfield	Vasalund (Swe)	11.87	87-89	67	4	4

ARNOTT, William
Edinburgh, 29 May, 1935

League Club	Source	Date Signed	Seasons Played	Apps	Subs	Gls
Crewe Alex.		12.57	57	7	-	0

ARROWSMITH, Alfred W.
Manchester, 11 December, 1942 (CF)

League Club	Source	Date Signed	Seasons Played	Apps	Subs	Gls
Liverpool	Ashton U.	09.60	61-67	43	4	20
Bury	Tr	12.68	68-69	45	3	11
Rochdale	Tr	06.70	70-71	40	6	14

ARROWSMITH, Brian W.
Barrow, 2 July, 1940 (D)

League Club	Source	Date Signed	Seasons Played	Apps	Subs	Gls
Barrow	Vickers Sports	10.61	61-70	376	2	2

ARTHUR, David R.
Wolverhampton, 9 March, 1960 (FB)

League Club	Source	Date Signed	Seasons Played	Apps	Subs	Gls
West Bromwich A.	App	03.78	81	2	1	0
Walsall	Tr	08.82	82	8	1	0

ARTHUR, John (Jackie)
Edenfield, 14 December, 1917 (OR)

League Club	Source	Date Signed	Seasons Played	Apps	Subs	Gls
Stockport Co.	Blackburn Rov. (Am)	05.38	38	2	-	0
Everton	Tr	11.40				
Chester C.	Tr	05.46	46	24	-	3
Rochdale	Tr	04.47	46-53	170	-	25

ARUNDEL, Frank W.
Plymouth, 20 February, 1939 (W)

League Club	Source	Date Signed	Seasons Played	Apps	Subs	Gls
Plymouth Arg.	Oak Villa	08.56	56	4	-	0
Torquay U.	Tr	07.59	59-60	6	-	0

ASH, Mark C.
Sheffield, 22 January, 1968 (RB)

League Club	Source	Date Signed	Seasons Played	Apps	Subs	Gls
Rotherham U.	App	01.86	86-88	14	6	0
Scarborough	Tr	08.89	89-91	32	7	0

ASH, Michael
Sheffield, 4 September, 1943 E Sch/E Yth (IF)

League Club	Source	Date Signed	Seasons Played	Apps	Subs	Gls
Sheffield U.	App	11.60	63	3	-	1
Scunthorpe U.	Tr	09.65	65-66	48	2	7

ASHALL, George H.
Killamarsh, 29 September, 1911 EF Lge (OL)

League Club	Source	Date Signed	Seasons Played	Apps	Subs	Gls
Wolverhampton W.	Frickley Colly	02.36	35-37	94	-	19
Coventry C.	Tr	07.38	38-47	62	-	10

ASHALL, James
Chesterfield, 13 December, 1933 (FB)

League Club	Source	Date Signed	Seasons Played	Apps	Subs	Gls
Leeds U.	Hasland O.B.	10.51	55-60	89	-	0

ASHBY, Barry J.
Brent, 21 November, 1970 (CD)

League Club	Source	Date Signed	Seasons Played	Apps	Subs	Gls
Watford	YT	12.88	89-91	52	10	1

ASHCROFT, Charles T.
Chorley, 3 July, 1926 E 'B'-1 (G)

League Club	Source	Date Signed	Seasons Played	Apps	Subs	Gls
Liverpool	Chorley	05.46	46-54	87	-	0
Ipswich T.	Tr	06.55	55	7	-	0
Coventry C.	Tr	06.57	57	19	-	0

ASHCROFT, Lee
Preston, 7 September, 1972 Eu21-1 (F)

League Club	Source	Date Signed	Seasons Played	Apps	Subs	Gls
Preston N.E.	YT	07.91	90-91	41	11	6

ASHCROFT, Llewellyn L.
Flint, 10 July, 1921 (OR)

League Club	Source	Date Signed	Seasons Played	Apps	Subs	Gls
Tranmere Rov.	Flint T.	08.45	46	20	-	4

ASHCROFT, William
Liverpool, 1 October, 1952 (F/CD)

League Club	Source	Date Signed	Seasons Played	Apps	Subs	Gls
Wrexham	Jnrs	10.70	70-77	196	23	72
Middlesbrough	Tr	09.77	77-81	139	20	21
Tranmere Rov.	T. Enschede (Neth)	08.85	85	16	7	2

ASHDJIAN, John A.
Hackney, 13 September, 1972 (W)

League Club	Source	Date Signed	Seasons Played	Apps	Subs	Gls
Scarborough	Northampton T. (YT)	07.91	91	18	14	9

ASHE, Armour D.
Palsley, 14 October, 1925 Died 1968 (FB)

League Club	Source	Date Signed	Seasons Played	Apps	Subs	Gls
Stockport Co.	St Mirren	06.53	53	2	-	0
Accrington St.	Tr	09.53	53-57	162	-	0
Gateshead	Tr	11.57	57-58	54	-	1
Southport	Tr	07.59	59	14	-	2

ASHE, Norman J.
Bloxwich, 16 November, 1943 E Sch/E Yth (OR)

League Club	Source	Date Signed	Seasons Played	Apps	Subs	Gls
Aston Villa	App	05.61	59-60	5	-	0
Rotherham U.	Tr	03.63	62	6	-	1

ASHENDEN, Russell H.
South Ockenden, 4 February, 1961 (M)

League Club	Source	Date Signed	Seasons Played	Apps	Subs	Gls
Northampton T.	App	02.79	78-79	6	12	0

ASHER, Sidney J.
Portsmouth, 24 December, 1930 (CF)

League Club	Source	Date Signed	Seasons Played	Apps	Subs	Gls
Portsmouth	Jnrs	08.48				
Northampton T.	Hastings U.	11.56	56	21	-	11

ASHER, Thomas
York, 21 December, 1936 E Sch (F)

League Club	Source	Date Signed	Seasons Played	Apps	Subs	Gls
Notts Co.	Wolverhampton W. (Am)	07.54	57-58	31	-	4

ASHFIELD, George O.
Manchester, 7 April, 1934 (CH)

League Club	Source	Date Signed	Seasons Played	Apps	Subs	Gls
Stockport Co.	Jnrs	09.51				
Aston Villa	Tr	03.54	55-57	9	-	0
Chester C.	Tr	02.59	58	5	-	0

ASHLEY, Joseph
Clowne, 10 June, 1931 (G)

League Club	Source	Date Signed	Seasons Played	Apps	Subs	Gls
York C.	Frickley Colly	10.50	50	9	-	0

ASHLEY, Kevin M.
Birmingham, 31 December, 1968 (RB)

League Club	Source	Date Signed	Seasons Played	Apps	Subs	Gls
Birmingham C.	App	12.86	86-90	56	1	1
Wolverhampton W.	Tr	09.90	90-91	59	1	1

ASHMAN, G. Allan
Rotherham, 30 May, 1928 (CF)

League Club	Source	Date Signed	Seasons Played	Apps	Subs	Gls
Nottingham F.	Sheffield U. (Am)	04.46	48-49	13	-	3
Carlisle U.	Tr	06.51	51-57	207	-	98

ASHMAN, Ronald G.
Whittlesey, 19 May, 1926 (D)

League Club	Source	Date Signed	Seasons Played	Apps	Subs	Gls
Norwich C.	Whittlesey	05.44	47-63	592	-	55

ASHMORE, Arthur G.
Goldthorpe, 11 August, 1946 (HB)

League Club	Source	Date Signed	Seasons Played	Apps	Subs	Gls
Doncaster Rov.	Frickley Colly	11.66	66-67	3	0	0

ASHMORE, A. Michael
Sheffield, 11 September, 1937 (G)

League Club	Source	Date Signed	Seasons Played	Apps	Subs	Gls
Sheffield U.		08.57	57	1	-	0
Bradford C.	Tr	07.61	61	9	-	0
Chesterfield	Tr	10.62	62	2	-	0

ASHTON, Derek O.
Worksop, 4 July, 1922 (FB)

League Club	Source	Date Signed	Seasons Played	Apps	Subs	Gls
Wolverhampton W.		09.41				
Aston Villa	Tr	05.46	46-48	8	-	0

ASHTON, John
Reading, 4 July, 1954 (F)

League Club	Source	Date Signed	Seasons Played	Apps	Subs	Gls
Reading	Jnrs	04.72	71-74	10	3	1

ASHTON, Kenneth J.
Irlam, 12 December, 1936 (FB)

League Club	Source	Date Signed	Seasons Played	Apps	Subs	Gls
Stockport Co.	Bolton W. (Am)	09.56	57-61	39	-	0

ASHTON, Roy W.
Llanidloes, 16 August, 1921 (G)

League Club	Source	Date Signed	Seasons Played	Apps	Subs	Gls
Wrexham		12.45				
Cardiff C.		04.48	47	1	-	0
Newport Co.	Bath C.	12.49	49-50	11	-	0

ASHURST, John (Jack)
Coatbridge, 12 October, 1954 (CD)

League Club	Source	Date Signed	Seasons Played	Apps	Subs	Gls
Sunderland	App	10.71	72-79	129	11	4
Blackpool	Tr	10.79	79-80	53	0	3
Carlisle U.	Tr	08.81	81-85	194	0	2
Leeds U.	Tr	07.86	86-88	88	1	1
Doncaster Rov.	Tr	11.88	88-89	73	0	1
Doncaster Rov.	Bridlington T.	11.90	90-91	66	0	1

ASHURST, Leonard
Liverpool, 10 March, 1939 E Yth/Eu23-1 (LB)

League Club	Source	Date Signed	Seasons Played	Apps	Subs	Gls
Sunderland	Prescot Cables	12.57	58-69	403	6	4
Hartlepool U.	Tr	03.71	70-72	42	4	2

ASHWORTH, Alec
Southport, 1 October, 1939 (IF)

League Club	Source	Date Signed	Seasons Played	Apps	Subs	Gls
Everton	Jnrs	05.57	57-59	12	-	3
Luton T.	Tr	10.60	60-61	63	-	20
Northampton T.	Tr	07.62	62	30	-	25
Preston N.E.	Tr	06.63	63-65	42	1	14

ASHWORTH, Barry
Stockport, 18 August, 1942 (WH)

League Club	Source	Date Signed	Seasons Played	Apps	Subs	Gls
Southend U.	Bangor C.	07.63	63-64	31	-	5
Hartlepool U.	Tr	03.65	64-65	45	0	4
Tranmere Rov.	Tr	07.66	66	21	0	3
Chester C.	Tr	08.67	67-69	117	2	11

ASHWORTH, Frederick
Oldham, 26 January, 1928

League Club	Source	Date Signed	Seasons Played	Apps	Subs	Gls
Blackburn Rov.		10.48				
Shrewsbury T.	Tr	11.51	51-52	56	-	1

ASHWORTH, Ian
Blackburn, 17 December, 1958 (OL)

League Club	Source	Date Signed	Seasons Played	Apps	Subs	Gls
Manchester U.	App	12.75				
Crewe Alex.	Tr	07.79	79	7	6	0

ASHWORTH, John
Nottingham, 4 July, 1937 E Amat (CH)

League Club	Source	Date Signed	Seasons Played	Apps	Subs	Gls
Portsmouth (Am)	Wealdstone	08.62	62	1	-	0

ASHWORTH, Joseph M.
Huddersfield, 6 January, 1943 (WH)

League Club	Source	Date Signed	Seasons Played	Apps	Subs	Gls
Bradford P.A.	Jnrs	01.60	61	3	-	0
York C.	Tr	05.62	62-64	57	-	0
Bournemouth	Tr	06.65	65-66	60	0	2
Southend U.	Tr	07.67	67	36	0	2
Rochdale	Tr	07.68	68-71	133	0	3
Chester C.	Tr	12.71	71	5	0	0
Stockport Co.	Tr	06.72	72	14	0	0

ASHWORTH, Neil
Southend, 16 January, 1968 (M)

League Club	Source	Date Signed	Seasons Played	Apps	Subs	Gls
Rochdale	YT	07.85	84	1	0	0

ASHWORTH, Philip A.
Burnley, 14 April, 1953 (F)

League Club	Source	Date Signed	Seasons Played	Apps	Subs	Gls
Blackburn Rov.	Nelson	01.75				
Bournemouth	Tr	09.75	75	30	1	2
Workington	Tr	07.76	76	38	1	7
Southport	Tr	08.77	77	22	2	9
Rochdale	Tr	07.78	78	9	2	0
Portsmouth	Tr	09.79	79	3	1	4
Scunthorpe U.	Tr	07.80	80	14	9	3

ASKEW, William
Lumley, 2 October, 1959 (LM)

League Club	Source	Date Signed	Seasons Played	Apps	Subs	Gls
Middlesbrough	App	10.77	79-81	10	2	0
Hull C.	Gateshead	09.82	82-89	247	6	19
Newcastle U.	Tr	03.90	89-90	5	1	0
Shrewsbury T.	L	01.91	90	5	0	0

ASKEY, Colin
Stoke, 3 October, 1932 (OR)

League Club	Source	Date Signed	Seasons Played	Apps	Subs	Gls
Port Vale	Jnrs	10.49	49-57	200	-	23
Walsall	Tr	07.58	58-61	83	-	12
Mansfield T.	Tr	06.62	62-63	30	-	2

ASPDEN, Raymond J.
Horwich, 6 February, 1938 (CH)

League Club	Source	Date Signed	Seasons Played	Apps	Subs	Gls
Rochdale	Bolton W. (Am)	05.55	55-65	297	0	2

ASPIN, Neil
Gateshead, 12 April, 1965 (CD)

League Club	Source	Date Signed	Seasons Played	Apps	Subs	Gls
Leeds U.	App	10.82	81-88	203	4	5
Port Vale	Tr	07.89	89-91	123	2	1

ASPINALL, John
Aston-under-Lyne, 27 April, 1916 (HB)

League Club	Source	Date Signed	Seasons Played	Apps	Subs	Gls
Oldham Ath.	Stalybridge Celtic	05.36	36-38	11	-	0
Bolton W.	Ashton Nat.	09.45	46-49	14	-	0

ASPINALL, John J.
Birkenhead, 15 March, 1959 (W)

League Club	Source	Date Signed	Seasons Played	Apps	Subs	Gls
Tranmere Rov.		10.82	82-84	100	7	25
Tranmere Rov.	Bangor C.	07.87	87	11	1	1

ASPINALL, Warren G.
Wigan, 13 September, 1967 E Yth (F)

League Club	Source	Date Signed	Seasons Played	Apps	Subs	Gls
Wigan Ath.	App	08.85	84-85	39	12	22
Everton	Tr	05.86	85-86	0	7	0
Aston Villa	Tr	02.87	86-87	40	4	14
Portsmouth	Tr	08.88	88-91	78	22	19

ASPINALL, Wayne
Wigan, 10 December, 1964 (FB)

League Club	Source	Date Signed	Seasons Played	Apps	Subs	Gls
Wigan Ath.	Atherton	06.83	83-84	8	0	0

ASPREY, William
Wolverhampton, 11 September, 1936 (D)

League Club	Source	Date Signed	Seasons Played	Apps	Subs	Gls
Stoke C.	Jnrs	09.53	53-65	304	0	23
Oldham Ath.	Tr	01.66	65-67	80	0	3
Port Vale	Tr	12.67	67-68	30	1	0

ASQUITH, Beaumont
Wakefield, 16 September, 1910 Died 1977 (WH)

League Club	Source	Date Signed	Seasons Played	Apps	Subs	Gls
Barnsley	Painthorpe A.	07.33	34-38	105	-	40
Manchester U.	Tr	05.39				
Barnsley	Tr	07.42	46-47	38	-	5
Bradford C.	Tr	09.48	48-49	31	-	4

ASTALL, Gordon
Horwich, 22 September, 1927 E'B'-1/EF Lge/E-2 (OR)

League Club	Source	Date Signed	Seasons Played	Apps	Subs	Gls
Plymouth Arg.	Southampton (Am)	11.47	47-53	188	-	42
Birmingham C.	Tr	10.53	53-60	235	-	60
Torquay U.	Tr	07.61	61-62	33	-	10

ASTBURY, Michael J.
Leeds, 22 January, 1964 (G)

League Club	Source	Date Signed	Seasons Played	Apps	Subs	Gls
York C.	App	01.82	80-85	48	0	0
Peterborough U.	L	01.86	85	4	0	0
Darlington	Tr	03.86	85-86	38	0	0
Chester C.	Tr	07.87	87	5	0	0
Chesterfield	Tr	07.88	88	8	0	0

ASTBURY, Thomas A.
Buckley, 9 February, 1920 (RH)

League Club	Source	Date Signed	Seasons Played	Apps	Subs	Gls
Chester C.	Mold Alex.	05.38	46-54	301	-	37

ASTLE, Jeffrey
Eastwood, 13 June, 1942 EF Lge/E-5 (CF)

League Club	Source	Date Signed	Seasons Played	Apps	Subs	Gls
Notts Co.	Jnrs	10.59	61-64	103	-	32
West Bromwich A.	Tr	09.64	64-73	290	2	137

Jeff Astle (Notts County, West Bromwich Albion & England)

League Club	Source	Date Signed	Seasons Played	Career Record Apps	Subs	Gls
ASTON, A. John						
Newport, 29 July, 1930						(OL)
Newport Co.	Jnrs	04.48	47-50	6	-	1
ASTON, John						
Manchester, 3 September, 1921 EF Lge/E-17						(FB)
Manchester U.	Jnrs	04.46	46-53	253	-	29
ASTON, John						
Manchester, 28 June, 1947 Eu23-1						(OL)
Manchester U.	App	06.63	64-71	139	16	25
Luton T.	Tr	07.72	72-77	171	3	31
Mansfield T.	Tr	09.77	77	24	7	4
Blackburn Rov.	Tr	07.78	78-79	12	3	2
ASTON, Philip						
Measham, 13 May, 1924 E Amat						(WH)
Walsall	Measham Imperial	12.51	51	10	-	0
ASTON, Stanley						
Nuneaton, 10 May, 1940						(CH)
Hartlepool U.	Burton A.	12.66	66-67	20	1	0
ASTON, Vivien W.						
Coseley, 16 October, 1918						(D)
Bury		12.36	38-47	23	-	0
Oldham Ath.	Tr	07.48	48-51	30	-	1
Chester C.	Tr	01.52				
ATHERSYCH, Russell						
Sheffield, 21 September, 1962						(M)
Chesterfield	App	09.80	81-82	11	9	0
ATHERTON, Dewi L.						
Bangor, 6 July, 1951						(M)
Blackburn Rov.	Jnrs	07.68	68-70	9	1	0
ATHERTON, F. Gordon						
Horwich, 18 June, 1934						(WH)
Bury	Bury Amats	09.55	55-64	327	-	13
Swindon T.	Tr	12.64	64-65	31	0	0
Bury	Tr	01.66	65	7	0	0
ATHERTON, James G.						
Queensferry, 2 April, 1923 W Amat						(G)
Wrexham (Am)		07.47	47-48	18	-	0
ATHERTON, Peter						
Orrell, 6 April, 1970 E Sch/Eu21-1						(CD)
Wigan Ath.	YT	02.88	87-91	145	4	1
Coventry C.	Tr	08.91	91	35	0	0
ATKIN, John M.						
Scunthorpe, 14 February, 1948						(CD)
Scunthorpe U.		09.69	69-74	116	5	0
ATKIN, Paul A.						
Nottingham, 3 September, 1969 E Yth						(CD/M)
Notts Co.	YT	07.87				
Bury	Tr	03.89	88-90	14	7	1
York C.	Tr	07.91	91	29	4	1
ATKINS, Arthur W.						
Tokyo (Japan), 21 February, 1925 Died 1988						(CH)
Birmingham C.	Paget R.	11.48	49-53	97	-	0
Shrewsbury T.	Tr	06.54	54	16	-	0
ATKINS, Dennis						
Bradford, 8 November, 1938						(FB)
Huddersfield T.	Jnrs	12.55	59-66	194	0	0
Bradford C.	Tr	03.68	67-70	108	0	0
ATKINS, Ian L.						
Birmingham, 16 January, 1957						(D/M)
Shrewsbury T.	App	01.75	75-81	273	5	58
Sunderland	Tr	08.82	82-83	76	1	6
Everton	Tr	11.84	84-85	6	1	1
Ipswich T.	Tr	09.85	85-87	73	4	4
Birmingham C.	Tr	03.88	87-89	93	0	6
Birmingham C.	Colchester U.	09.91	91	5	3	0
ATKINS, Mark N.						
Doncaster, 14 August, 1968 E Sch						(M/RB)
Scunthorpe U.	Jnrs	07.86	84-87	45	5	2
Blackburn Rov.	Tr	06.88	88-91	162	11	22

League Club	Source	Date Signed	Seasons Played	Career Record Apps	Subs	Gls
ATKINS, Robert G.						
Leicester, 16 October, 1962						(CD)
Sheffield U.	Enderby T.	07.82	82-84	36	4	3
Preston N.E.	Tr	02.85	84-89	198	2	5
ATKINS, Trevor A. J.						
Exeter, 17 August, 1941						(OR)
Exeter C.	Jnrs	08.58	57-59	3	-	3
ATKINS, William M.						
Bingley, 9 May, 1939						(F)
Aston Villa	Birmingham G.P.O.	05.58				
Swindon T.	Tr	06.59	59-64	75	-	28
Halifax T.	Tr	08.65	65-66	74	0	34
Stockport Co.	Tr	03.67	66-68	92	0	37
Portsmouth	Tr	04.69	68-69	11	0	2
Halifax T.	Tr	11.69	69-72	123	2	37
Rochdale	Tr	12.72	72-73	25	0	7
Darlington	Tr	09.73	73-74	41	3	12
ATKINSON, Brian						
Sheffield, 16 November, 1934						(HB)
Sheffield U.		06.53				
Halifax T.	Tr	06.56	56-58	67	-	0
ATKINSON, Brian						
Darlington, 19 January, 1971 Eu21-6						(M)
Sunderland	YT	07.89	88-91	46	6	2
ATKINSON, Bryan H.						
Saffron Walden, 15 April, 1934						(HB)
Watford	Bishops Stortford	06.54	55-56	20	-	0
ATKINSON, Charles						
Hull, 17 December, 1932						(WH)
Hull C.	Marist O.B.	05.50	53-55	37	-	2
Bradford P.A.	Tr	07.56	56-63	339	-	50
Bradford C.	Tr	06.64	64	16	-	1
ATKINSON, Charles B. C.						
Haswell (Dm), 5 May, 1938						(HB)
Hartlepool U.		12.58	59-63	47	-	0
ATKINSON, Dalian R.						
Shrewsbury, 21 March, 1968 E 'B'						(F)
Ipswich T.	App	06.85	85-88	49	11	18
Sheffield Wed.	Tr	07.89	89	38	0	10
Aston Villa	Real Sociedad (Sp)	07.91	91	11	3	1
ATKINSON, David J.						
Hull, 3 April, 1951						(OR)
Hartlepool U. (App)	App	01.68	68	8	0	1
Charlton Ath.	Tr	05.69				
ATKINSON, Frederick						
Newcastle, 24 August, 1919						
Gateshead		12.45	46-48	32	-	6
ATKINSON, Graeme						
Hull, 11 November, 1971						(W)
Hull C.	YT	05.90	89-91	42	12	9
ATKINSON, Graham G.						
Liverpool, 17 May, 1943						(IF)
Oxford U.	Aston Villa (Am)	02.60	62	18	-	4
Oxford U.	Cambridge U.	12.64	64-73	303	4	73
ATKINSON, Harold						
Liverpool, 28 July, 1925						(CF)
Tranmere Rov.	Carlton	03.45	46-54	185	-	95
Chesterfield	Tr	07.55				
ATKINSON, Hugh A.						
Dublin, 8 November, 1960						(M/D)
Wolverhampton W.	App	11.78	79-81	38	8	3
Exeter C.		10.83	83	28	0	1
York C.	Tr	07.84	84	3	4	0
Darlington	L	03.85	84	7	0	0
ATKINSON, Ian						
Carlisle, 19 December, 1932						(IF)
Carlisle U.		06.51	52-56	122	-	52
Exeter C.	Tr	07.57	57	8	-	2
ATKINSON, John E.						
Washington, 20 December, 1913 E Sch						(CH)
Bolton W.	Washington Colly	09.31	32-47	240	-	4
New Brighton	Tr	05.48	48-49	52	-	0

ATKINSON, Patrick D. (Paddy)
Singapore, 22 May, 1970 (F)

League Club	Source	Date Signed	Seasons Played	Apps	Subs	Gls
Hartlepool U.	Sheffield U. (YT)	08.88	88-89	9	12	3

ATKINSON, Paul
Chester-le-Street, 19 January, 1966 E Yth (W)

League Club	Source	Date Signed	Seasons Played	Apps	Subs	Gls
Sunderland	App	11.83	83-87	46	14	5
Port Vale	Tr	06.88	88	4	0	3
Hartlepool U.	L	03.90	89	5	6	1

ATKINSON, Paul G.
Pudsey, 14 August, 1961 (W)

League Club	Source	Date Signed	Seasons Played	Apps	Subs	Gls
Oldham Ath.	App	08.79	79-82	139	4	11
Watford	Tr	07.83	83	8	3	0
Oldham Ath.	Tr	08.85	85-87	29	4	1
Swansea C.	L	12.86	86	6	0	1
Bolton W.	L	02.87	86	2	1	0
Swansea C.	L	03.87	86	12	0	2
Burnley	Tr	07.88	88-89	18	4	1

ATKINSON, Peter
Middlesbrough, 13 September, 1924 Died 1972 (G)

League Club	Source	Date Signed	Seasons Played	Apps	Subs	Gls
Hull C.	Billingham Synth.	04.47	46-47	6	-	0

ATKINSON, Peter
Gainsborough, 14 December, 1949 (FB)

League Club	Source	Date Signed	Seasons Played	Apps	Subs	Gls
Rotherham U.		05.69	69	3	0	0

ATKINSON, Peter
Spilsby, 20 September, 1929 (G)

League Club	Source	Date Signed	Seasons Played	Apps	Subs	Gls
Walsall	Walsall Y.M.C.A.	11.49	49-51	2	-	0

ATKINSON, Ronald F.
Liverpool, 18 March, 1939 (WH)

League Club	Source	Date Signed	Seasons Played	Apps	Subs	Gls
Aston Villa	B.S.A. Tools	05.56				
Oxford U.	Tr	07.59	62-71	383	1	14

ATKINSON, Trevor
Barnsley, 19 November, 1928 (OL)

League Club	Source	Date Signed	Seasons Played	Apps	Subs	Gls
Hull C.	Hull Amats	05.46	46	2	-	0
Barnsley	Tr	08.48				

ATKINSON, Trevor J.
Bishop Auckland, 23 November, 1942 (WH)

League Club	Source	Date Signed	Seasons Played	Apps	Subs	Gls
Darlington	Spennymoor U.	11.63	63-68	137	4	3
Bradford P.A.	Tr	01.69	68-69	59	1	6

ATKINSON, Walter
Gateshead, 31 August, 1920 (WH)

League Club	Source	Date Signed	Seasons Played	Apps	Subs	Gls
Norwich C.	Hexham Hearts	01.49	51	1	-	0

ATKINSON, William
Sunderland, 21 December, 1944 (W)

League Club	Source	Date Signed	Seasons Played	Apps	Subs	Gls
Birmingham C.	App	03.62				
Torquay U.	Tr	06.64	64	19	-	7

ATTEVELD, Raymond
Amsterdam, Holland, 8 September, 1966 (FB/M)

League Club	Source	Date Signed	Seasons Played	Apps	Subs	Gls
Everton	Haarlem (Neth)	08.89	89-91	41	10	1
West Ham U.	L	02.92	91	1	0	0
Bristol C.	Tr	03.92	91	4	3	1

ATTHEY, Nicholas
Newcastle, 8 May, 1946 (M/D)

League Club	Source	Date Signed	Seasons Played	Apps	Subs	Gls
Walsall	App	07.63	63-76	431	10	17

ATTLEY, Brian R.
Cardiff, 27 August, 1955 (D/M)

League Club	Source	Date Signed	Seasons Played	Apps	Subs	Gls
Cardiff C.	App	08.73	74-78	73	6	1
Swansea C.	Tr	02.79	78-81	83	6	6
Derby Co.	Tr	02.82	81-83	54	1	1
Oxford U.	L	03.83	82	5	0	0

Ron Atkinson (Aston Villa & Oxford United)

ATTWELL, Reginald F.
Oakengates, 23 March, 1920 Died 1986 EF Lge (WH)

League Club	Source	Date Signed	Seasons Played	Apps	Subs	Gls
West Ham U.	Denaby U.	04.38	37-46	5	-	0
Burnley	Tr	10.46	46-54	244	-	9
Bradford C.	Tr	10.54	54	24	-	0

ATYEO, P. John W.
Westbury, 7 February, 1932 E Yth/Eu23-2/EF Lge/E' B'-3/E-6 (CF)

League Club	Source	Date Signed	Seasons Played	Apps	Subs	Gls
Portsmouth (Am)	Westbury U.	09.50	50	1	-	0
Bristol C.	Tr	06.51	51-65	597	0	315

AUGUSTE, Joseph
Trinidad (WI), 24 November, 1965 (F)

League Club	Source	Date Signed	Seasons Played	Apps	Subs	Gls
Exeter C. (N/C)	Hounslow	09.83	83	7	3	0

AULD, Robert (Bertie)
Glasgow, 23 March, 1938 S Lge/S-3 (OL)

League Club	Source	Date Signed	Seasons Played	Apps	Subs	Gls
Birmingham C.	Glasgow Celtic	05.61	61-64	125	-	26

AULD, Walter B.
Bellshill, 9 July, 1929 (OL)

League Club	Source	Date Signed	Seasons Played	Apps	Subs	Gls
Middlesbrough	Bellshill Ath.	12.50	50	2	-	1

AUSTIN, Dean B.
Hemel Hempstead, 26 April, 1970 (RB)

League Club	Source	Date Signed	Seasons Played	Apps	Subs	Gls
Southend U.	St Albans C.	03.90	89-91	96	0	2

AUSTIN, J. Frank
Stoke, 6 July, 1933 E Sch (FB)

League Club	Source	Date Signed	Seasons Played	Apps	Subs	Gls
Coventry C.	Jnrs	07.50	52-62	302	-	2
Torquay U.	Tr	01.63	62-63	24	-	0

AUSTIN, Karl
Stoke, 7 August, 1961 (G)

League Club	Source	Date Signed	Seasons Played	Apps	Subs	Gls
Port Vale (N/C)	Stafford R.	02.85	84	1	0	0

AUSTIN, Roy L.
Islington, 26 March, 1960 (F)

League Club	Source	Date Signed	Seasons Played	Apps	Subs	Gls
Doncaster Rov.	Millwall (App)	08.78	78	3	0	0

AUSTIN, Terence W.
Isleworth, 1 February, 1954 (F)

League Club	Source	Date Signed	Seasons Played	Apps	Subs	Gls
Crystal Palace	Jnrs	06.72				
Ipswich T.	Tr	05.73	74-75	10	9	1
Plymouth Arg.	Tr	10.76	76-77	58	0	18
Walsall	Tr	03.78	77-78	44	3	19
Mansfield T.	Tr	03.79	78-80	84	0	31
Huddersfield T.	Tr	12.80	80-82	39	3	10
Doncaster Rov.	Tr	09.82	82	30	4	5
Northampton T.	Tr	08.83	83	42	1	10

AVERY, Roger J.
Cambridge, 17 February, 1961 (F)

League Club	Source	Date Signed	Seasons Played	Apps	Subs	Gls
Cambridge U.	App	02.79	77	0	1	0

AVEYARD, Walter
Hemsworth, 11 June, 1918 (IF)

League Club	Source	Date Signed	Seasons Played	Apps	Subs	Gls
Sheffield Wed.	Denaby U.	10.38	46	4	-	3
Birmingham C.	Tr	04.47	47	7	-	3
Port Vale	Tr	06.48	48-51	103	-	26
Accrington St.	Tr	03.52	51-52	24	-	4

AVIS, Vernon C.S.
Marylebone, 24 October, 1935 (FB)

League Club	Source	Date Signed	Seasons Played	Apps	Subs	Gls
Brentford	Jnrs	11.52	53-60	19	-	0

AVRAMOVIC, Radojko (Raddy)
Yugoslavia, 29 November, 1949 Yugoslav Int (G)

League Club	Source	Date Signed	Seasons Played	Apps	Subs	Gls
Notts Co.	N.K.Rijeka (Yug)	08.79	79-82	149	0	0
Coventry C.	Montreal (USA)	09.83	83	18	0	0

AWFORD, Andrew T.
Worcester, 14 July, 1972 E Yth (D)

League Club	Source	Date Signed	Seasons Played	Apps	Subs	Gls
Portsmouth	YT	07.89	88-91	56	7	0

AYLOTT, Stephen J.
Ilford, 3 September, 1951 (M)

League Club	Source	Date Signed	Seasons Played	Apps	Subs	Gls
West Ham U.	App	08.69				
Oxford U.	Tr	04.71	71-75	143	11	8
Brentford	Tr	07.76	76-77	6	1	0

AYLOTT, Trevor K. C.
Bermondsey, 26 November, 1957 (F)

League Club	Source	Date Signed	Seasons Played	Apps	Subs	Gls
Chelsea	App	11.75	77-79	26	3	2
Barnsley	Tr	11.79	79-81	93	3	26
Millwall	Tr	08.82	82	32	0	5
Luton T.	Tr	03.83	82-83	32	0	10
Crystal Palace	Tr	07.84	84-85	50	3	12
Barnsley	L	02.86	85	9	0	0
Bournemouth	Tr	08.86	86-90	137	10	27
Birmingham C.	Tr	10.90	90-91	25	2	0
Oxford U.	Tr	09.91	91	35	2	6

AYRE, Colin
Ashington, 14 March, 1956 (W)

League Club	Source	Date Signed	Seasons Played	Apps	Subs	Gls
Newcastle U.	App	09.73				
Torquay U.		09.76	76	2	0	0

AYRE, Robert W.
Berwick, 26 March, 1932 Eu23-2 (OR)

League Club	Source	Date Signed	Seasons Played	Apps	Subs	Gls
Charlton Ath.	Chippenham T.	07.52	52-57	109	-	48
Reading	Tr	05.58	58-59	57	-	24

AYRE, William
Consett, 7 May, 1952 (CD)

League Club	Source	Date Signed	Seasons Played	Apps	Subs	Gls
Hartlepool U.	Scarborough	08.77	77-80	141	0	27
Halifax T.	Tr	01.81	80-81	63	0	5
Mansfield T.	Tr	08.82	82-83	67	0	7
Halifax T.	Tr	07.84	84-85	32	0	2

AYRES, Frederick
Stoke, 17 July, 1926 (CF)

League Club	Source	Date Signed	Seasons Played	Apps	Subs	Gls
Crewe Alex.		11.48	48	2	-	0

AYRES, Harold
Redcar, 10 March, 1920 (WH)

League Club	Source	Date Signed	Seasons Played	Apps	Subs	Gls
Fulham	Clapton	07.46	46-48	38	-	8
Gillingham	Tr	06.50	50-54	136	-	2

AYRES, Kenneth E.
Oxford, 15 May, 1956 E Sch (F)

League Club	Source	Date Signed	Seasons Played	Apps	Subs	Gls
Manchester U.	App	06.73				
Crystal Palace	Tr	11.73	74	3	3	0

AYRIS, John P.
Wapping, 8 January, 1953 E Yth (W)

League Club	Source	Date Signed	Seasons Played	Apps	Subs	Gls
West Ham U.	App	10.70	70-76	41	16	1

AYRTON, Neil J.
Lewisham, 11 February, 1962 (F)

League Club	Source	Date Signed	Seasons Played	Apps	Subs	Gls
Portsmouth	Maidstone U.	12.79	80	1	1	0

AYTON, James
Barrhead, 15 October, 1923 Died 1988 (IF)

League Club	Source	Date Signed	Seasons Played	Apps	Subs	Gls
Leicester C.	Third Lanark	10.48	48-50	8	-	1
Shrewsbury T.	Tr	06.51	51	25	-	1

Andy Awford (Portsmouth)

B

George Best (Manchester United, Fulham, Bournemouth & Northern Ireland)
Mercurial Irishman who was the outstanding
player of his generation

League Club	Source	Date Signed	Seasons Played	Apps	Subs	Gls
BAAH, Peter H.						
Littleborough, 1 May, 1973						(M)
Blackburn Rov.	YT	06.91	91	1	0	0
BABB, Philip A.						
Lambeth, 30 November, 1970						(CD/F)
Millwall	YT	04.89				
Bradford C.	Tr	07.90	90-91	73	7	14
BABER, John M.						
Lambeth, 10 October, 1947						(W)
Southend U.	Charlton Ath. (App)	09.66	66-70	72	10	18
BABES, John						
Lurgan (NI), 20 November, 1929						(RB)
Arsenal	Glentoran	01.48				
Scunthorpe U.	Tr	09.50	50-51	9	-	0
BACCI, Alfred						
Bedlington, 15 July, 1922						(IF)
Chesterfield	West Sleekburn	08.50	50-51	6	-	2
BACKOS, Desmond P.						
South Africa, 13 November, 1950						(F)
Stoke C.	Los Angeles (USA)	10.77	77	1	1	0
BACON, Cyril W.						
Hammersmith, 9 November, 1919						(WH)
Leyton Orient	Hayes	06.46	46-49	118	-	3
BACON, Paul D.						
Newham, 20 December, 1970						(M)
Charlton Ath	YT	01.89	90-91	11	4	0
BACON, Ronald A. S.						
Fakenham, 4 March, 1935						(W)
Norwich C.	Holt	12.55	55-57	42	-	6
Gillingham	Tr	05.58	58-60	128	-	15
BACUZZI, David R.						
Islington, 12 October, 1940 E Yth						(FB)
Arsenal	Eastbourne	05.59	60-63	46	-	0
Manchester C.	Tr	04.64	64-65	56	1	0
Reading	Tr	09.66	66-69	107	0	1
BACUZZI, Giuseppe (Joe)						
Holborn, 25 September, 1916						(FB)
Fulham	Tufnell Park	04.36	36-55	283	-	2
BADDELEY, Kevin						
Swindon, 12 March, 1962						(FB)
Bristol C.	App	03.80	80	1	0	0
Swindon T.	Tr	06.81	81-84	94	1	2
BADDELEY, Lee M.						
Cardiff, 12 July, 1974						(CD)
Cardiff C.	YT	08.91	90-91	16	4	0
BADES, Brian						
Blackburn, 3 July, 1939						(W)
Accrington St.		02.60				
Chester C.		08.63	63	16	-	1
BADGER, Colin A.						
Rotherham, 16 June, 1930						(F)
Rotherham U.		11.50	50	2	-	0
BADGER, Leonard						
Sheffield, 8 June, 1945 E Sch/E Yth/Eu23-13/EF Lge						(RB)
Sheffield U.	App	08.62	62-75	457	1	7
Chesterfield	Tr	01.76	75-77	46	0	0
BADHAM, John (Jack)						
Birmingham, 31 January, 1919 Died 1992						(D)
Birmingham C.	Muntz Street Y.C.	05.46	47-56	173	-	4
BADMINTON, Roger G.						
Portsmouth, 15 September, 1947						(WH)
Brighton & H.A.		07.66	66	1	0	0
BADOCK, Stephen W.						
Kensington, 10 September, 1958						(W)
Bristol Rov.	Bristol Portway	07.85	85	14	3	3

League Club	Source	Date Signed	Seasons Played	Apps	Subs	Gls
BAGNALL, Reginald						
Brinsworth, 22 November, 1926						
Notts Co.	Rotherham U. (Am)	06.45	46-47	8	-	0
BAILEY, Alfred						
Walsall (Am)	Darwen	09.53	53	1	-	0
BAILEY, Anthony D.						
Burton, 23 September, 1946						(CD)
Derby Co.	Burton A.	09.70	71	1	0	0
Oldham Ath.	Tr	01.74	73-74	26	0	1
Bury	Tr	12.74	74-78	124	7	1
BAILEY, W. Craig						
Airdrie, 6 July, 1944						(CF)
Brighton & H.A.	Kirkintilloch Rob Roy	12.61	62	4	-	1
BAILEY, Danny S.						
Leyton, 21 May, 1964						(M)
Bournemouth (App)	App	08.80	80	1	1	0
Torquay U. (N/C)	Walthamstow Ave.	03.84	83	1	0	0
Exeter C.	Wealdstone	08.89	89-90	63	1	2
Reading	Tr	12.90	90-91	49	1	2
BAILEY, David						
Worksop, 11 January, 1957						(F)
Chesterfield	Jnrs	01.76	75	1	0	1
BAILEY, Dennis						
Biddulph, 24 September, 1935						(OL)
Bolton W.	Jnrs	09.53	56	1	-	0
Port Vale	Tr	08.58	58	1	-	0
BAILEY, Dennis L.						
Lambeth, 13 November, 1965						(F)
Fulham (N/C)	Barking	11.86				
Crystal Palace	Farnborough T.	12.87	87	0	5	1
Bristol Rov.	L	02.89	88	17	0	9
Birmingham C.	Tr	08.89	89-90	65	10	23
Bristol Rov.	L	03.91	90	6	0	1
Queens Park R.	Tr	06.91	91	19	5	9
BAILEY, Gary R.						
Ipswich, 9 August, 1958 Eu21-14/E 'B'/E-2						(G)
Manchester U.	Witts Univ. (SA)	01.78	78-86	294	0	0
BAILEY, George E.						
Doncaster, 31 October, 1958 E Sch						(D)
Manchester U.	App	11.75				
Doncaster Rov.	L	02.78	77	3	0	0
BAILEY, Graham						
Stoke, 8 December, 1934						
Port Vale		03.55	55	2	-	0
BAILEY Graham T.						
Dawley, 22 March, 1920						(FB)
Huddersfield T.	Jnrs	03.37	46	33	-	0
Sheffield U.	Tr	03.48	47-48	20	-	0
BAILEY, Ian C.						
Middlesbrough, 20 October, 1956						(LB)
Middlesbrough	App	10.74	75-81	140	4	1
Doncaster Rov.	L	11.76	76	9	0	0
Carlisle U.	L	02.77	76	7	0	1
Bolton W.	L	11.81	81	5	0	0
Sheffield Wed.	Tr	08.82	82	35	0	0
Blackpool	L	10.84	84	3	0	0
Bolton W.	L	03.85	84	10	0	0
BAILEY, E. John (Jack)						
Bristol, 17 June, 1921 Died 1987						(LB)
Bristol C.	B.A.C.	05.45	46-57	348	-	0
BAILEY, John A.						
Liverpool, 1 April, 1957						(LB)
Blackburn Rov.	App	04.75	75-78	115	5	1
Everton	Tr	07.79	79-85	171	0	3
Newcastle U.	Tr	10.85	85-87	39	1	0
Bristol C.	Tr	09.88	88-90	79	1	1
BAILEY, John S.						
Oxford, 30 July, 1950						(WH)
Swindon T.	App	08.68	67	0	2	0

League Club	Source	Date Signed	Seasons Played	Career Record Apps	Subs	Gls
BAILEY, Malcolm						
Halifax, 7 May, 1937						(W)
Bradford P.A.	Luddendenfoot	04.58	57-58	10	-	1
Accrington St.	Tr	10.60	60	2	-	0
BAILEY, Malcolm R.						
Biddulph, 14 April, 1950						(WH)
Port Vale	Jnrs	05.67	68	2	0	0
BAILEY, Michael A.						
Wisbech, 27 February, 1942 Eu23-5/EF Lge/E-2						(M)
Charlton Ath	Jnrs	03.59	60-65	151	0	20
Wolverhampton W.	Tr	03.66	65-76	360	1	19
Hereford U.	Minnesota (USA)	08.78	78	13	3	1
BAILEY, Neil						
Billinge, 26 September, 1958						(LM)
Burnley	App	07.76				
Newport Co.	Tr	09.78	78-83	129	5	7
Wigan Ath.	Tr	10.83	83-85	31	10	2
Stockport Co.	Tr	07.86	86-87	50	1	0
Newport Co.	L	03.87	86	8	1	1
BAILEY, Raymond R.						
St Neots, 16 May, 1944						(WH)
Gillingham	Bedford T.	05.66	66-70	154	6	7
Northampton T.	L	10.71	71	1	0	0
BAILEY, Roy N.						
Epsom, 26 May, 1932						(G)
Crystal Palace	Jnrs	06.49	49-55	118	-	0
Ipswich T.	Tr	03.56	55-64	315	-	0
BAILEY, Steven J.						
Bristol, 12 March, 1964						(M)
Bristol Rov.	App	03.82	81	15	1	1
BAILEY, Terence						
Stoke, 18 September, 1947						(M)
Port Vale	Stafford R.	08.74	74-77	161	4	26

John Bailey (Blackburn Rovers, Everton, Newcastle United & Bristol City)

League Club	Source	Date Signed	Seasons Played	Career Record Apps	Subs	Gls
BAILIE, Colin J.						
Belfast, 31 March, 1964						(FB/M)
Swindon T.	App	03.82	81-84	105	2	4
Reading	Tr	07.85	85-87	83	1	1
Cambridge U.	Tr	08.88	88-91	104	15	3
BAILLIE, Douglas						
Drycross, 27 January, 1937 S Sch/Su23-2						(CH)
Swindon T.	Airdrieonians	03.56	55	1	-	0
BAILLIE, Joseph						
Dumfries, 26 February 1929 SF Lge/S' B'						(FB)
Wolverhampton W.	Gasgow Celtic	12.54	54	1	-	0
Bristol C.	Tr	06.56	56	10	-	0
Leicester C.	Tr	06.57	57-59	75	-	0
Bradford P.A.	Tr	06.60	60	7	-	1
BAILY, Edward F.						
Clapton, 6 August, 1925 EF Lge/E 'B'-3/E-9						(IL)
Tottenham H.	Jnrs	02.46	46-55	296	-	64
Port Vale	Tr	01.56	55-56	24	-	8
Nottingham F.	Tr	10.56	56-58	68	-	14
Leyton Orient	Tr	12.58	58-59	29	-	3
BAIN, Alexander E.						
Edinburgh, 22 January, 1936						(CF)
Huddersfield T.	Motherwell	08.57	57-58	29	-	11
Chesterfield	Tr	02.60	59	18	-	9
Bournemouth	Falkirk	08.61	61	8	-	4
BAIN, James A.						
Blairgowrie, 14 December, 1919						(OL)
Chelsea	Gillingham	05.45	46	9	-	1
Swindon T.	Tr	05.47	47-53	235	-	40
BAIN, John						
Glasgow, 23 June, 1957						(M)
Bristol C.	App	07.74	76-78	5	1	0
Brentford	L	02.77	76	17	1	1
BAIN, John S.						
Airdrie, 20 July, 1946						(FB)
Bury	Clarkston	07.63	64-66	9	2	0
BAIN, William C.						
Alloa, 16 November, 1924						(F)
Hartlepool U.	Dunfermline Ath.	08.50	50	2	-	0
BAINBRIDGE, Kenneth V.						
Barking, 15 January, 1921						(OL)
West Ham U.	Leyton	11.44	46-49	80	-	16
Reading	Tr	06.50	50-52	89	-	32
Southend U.	Tr	02.53	52-54	78	-	24
BAINBRIDGE, Peter E.						
York, 30 January, 1958						(CD)
York C.	Middlesbrough (App)	11.77	77-78	9	0	0
Darlington	Tr	08.79	79	16	0	0
BAINBRIDGE, Robert E.						
York, 22 February, 1931						(CF)
York C.		04.54	53-54	4	-	0
BAINBRIDGE, Terence						
Hartlepool, 23 December, 1962						(D)
Hartlepool U.	Henry Smith Y.C.	12.81	81-83	34	3	1
BAINBRIDGE, William						
Gateshead, 9 March, 1922						(IR)
Manchester U.	Ashington	12.45				
Bury	Tr	05.46	46	2	-	1
Tranmere Rov.	Tr	11.48	48-53	168	-	63
BAINES, John R.						
Colchester, 25 September, 1937						(CF)
Colchester U.	Colchester Casuals	01.60	60-62	4	-	0
BAINES, Paul						
Burton, 15 January, 1972						(W)
Stoke C.	YT	07.90	90	1	1	0
BAINES, Peter C.						
Australia						(IF)
Wrexham	Oldham Ath. (Am)	04.43	46	6	-	2
Crewe Alex.	Tr	11.46	46	7	-	0
Hartlepool U.	Tr	06.47	47	9	-	1
New Brighton	Tr	10.47	47	2	-	0

BAINES, Stanley N.
Leicester, 28 July, 1920 (OL)

League Club	Source	Date Signed	Seasons Played	Apps	Subs	Gls
Leicester C.	Coalville T.	11.37	38	7	-	1
Northampton T.		07.46	46	1	-	0

BAINES, Stephen J.
Newark, 23 June, 1954 (CD)

League Club	Source	Date Signed	Seasons Played	Apps	Subs	Gls
Nottingham F.	App	06.72	72	2	0	0
Huddersfield T.	Tr	07.75	75-77	113	1	10
Bradford C.	Tr	03.78	77-79	98	1	17
Walsall	Tr	07.80	80-81	47	1	5
Bury	L	12.81	81	7	0	0
Scunthorpe U.	Tr	08.82	82	37	1	1
Chesterfield	Tr	07.83	83-86	132	1	9

BAIRD, Douglas H.
Falkirk, 26 November, 1935 Su23-1/SF Lge (RB)

League Club	Source	Date Signed	Seasons Played	Apps	Subs	Gls
Nottingham F.	Partick Th.	09.60	60-62	32	-	0
Plymouth Arg.	Tr	10.63	63-67	147	1	1

BAIRD, J. A. Gordon
Nottingham, 14 January, 1924 (WH)

League Club	Source	Date Signed	Seasons Played	Apps	Subs	Gls
Mansfield T.	New Houghton	11.46	46-47	9	-	0

BAIRD, Henry H. C.
Belfast, 17 August, 1913 Died 1973 NI Lge/NI-1 (WH)

League Club	Source	Date Signed	Seasons Played	Apps	Subs	Gls
Manchester U.	Linfield	01.37	36-37	49	-	15
Huddersfield T.	Tr	09.38	38	19	-	4
Ipswich T.	Tr	06.46	46-51	216	-	6

BAIRD, Hugh
Airdrie, 14 March, 1930 S-1 (CF)

League Club	Source	Date Signed	Seasons Played	Apps	Subs	Gls
Leeds U.	Airdrieonians	06.57	57-58	46	-	22

BAIRD, Ian J.
Rotherham, 1 April, 1964 E Sch (F)

League Club	Source	Date Signed	Seasons Played	Apps	Subs	Gls
Southampton	App	04.82	82-84	20	2	5
Cardiff C.	L	11.83	83	12	0	6
Newcastle U.	L	12.84	84	4	1	1
Leeds U.	Tr	03.85	84-86	84	1	33
Portsmouth	Tr	06.87	87	20	0	1
Leeds U.	Tr	03.88	87-89	76	1	17
Middlesbrough	Tr	01.90	89-90	60	3	18

BAIRD, Samuel
Denny, 13 May, 1930 SF Lge/S-7 (IF)

League Club	Source	Date Signed	Seasons Played	Apps	Subs	Gls
Preston N.E.	Clyde	06.54	54	15	-	2

BAIRSTOW, David L.
Bradford, 1 September, 1951 (F)

League Club	Source	Date Signed	Seasons Played	Apps	Subs	Gls
Bradford C.	Jnrs	12.71	71-72	10	7	1

BAKER, Alan R.
Tipton, 22 June, 1944 E Sch/E Yth (IF)

League Club	Source	Date Signed	Seasons Played	Apps	Subs	Gls
Aston Villa	App	07.61	60-65	92	1	13
Walsall	Tr	07.66	66-70	128	8	31

BAKER, Charles J.
Turners Hill, 6 January, 1936 (G)

League Club	Source	Date Signed	Seasons Played	Apps	Subs	Gls
Brighton & H.A.		05.60	60-62	81	-	0
Aldershot	Tr	07.64	64-65	28	0	0

BAKER, Christopher
Maltby, 2 February, 1952 (F)

League Club	Source	Date Signed	Seasons Played	Apps	Subs	Gls
Barnsley (Am)		11.70	71	0	1	0

BAKER, Clifford H.
Bristol, 11 January, 1924 (IF)

League Club	Source	Date Signed	Seasons Played	Apps	Subs	Gls
Bristol Rov.	Coalpit Heath	01.47	46	5	-	2

BAKER, Clive
Doncaster, 5 July, 1934 (F)

League Club	Source	Date Signed	Seasons Played	Apps	Subs	Gls
Doncaster Rov.		08.52				
Halifax T.	Tr	08.55	55-58	58	-	22

BAKER, Clive E.
North Walsham, 14 March, 1959 (G)

League Club	Source	Date Signed	Seasons Played	Apps	Subs	Gls
Norwich C.	Jnrs	07.77	77-80	14	0	0
Barnsley	Tr	08.84	84-90	291	0	0
Coventry C.	Tr	08.91				

BAKER, Colin W.
Cardiff, 18 December, 1934 Wu23-1/W-7 (WH)

League Club	Source	Date Signed	Seasons Played	Apps	Subs	Gls
Cardiff C.	Cardiff Nomads	03.53	53-65	293	1	18

BAKER, Darren S.
Wednesbury, 28 June, 1965 W Sch (M)

League Club	Source	Date Signed	Seasons Played	Apps	Subs	Gls
Wrexham	Jnrs	08.83	82-83	18	6	1

BAKER, David H.
Penzance, 21 October, 1928 (CH)

League Club	Source	Date Signed	Seasons Played	Apps	Subs	Gls
Nottingham F.	Brush Sports	10.49	49	3	-	0

BAKER, Douglas G.
Lewisham, 8 April, 1947 (F)

League Club	Source	Date Signed	Seasons Played	Apps	Subs	Gls
Arsenal	App	05.64				
Millwall	Tr	06.66	66	4	1	1

BAKER, Frank
Stoke, 22 October, 1918 Died 1989 (IF)

League Club	Source	Date Signed	Seasons Played	Apps	Subs	Gls
Stoke C.	Jnrs	05.36	36-49	162	-	32

BAKER, T. George
Maerdy, 6 April, 1936 Wu23-2 (W)

League Club	Source	Date Signed	Seasons Played	Apps	Subs	Gls
Plymouth Arg.	Jnrs	10.53	54-59	78	-	16
Shrewsbury T.	Tr	06.60	60-61	52	-	5

BAKER, Gerald
South Hiendley, 22 April, 1939 (FB)

League Club	Source	Date Signed	Seasons Played	Apps	Subs	Gls
Bradford P.A.	Jnrs	01.57	57-60	16	-	0

BAKER, Gerrard
Wigan, 16 September, 1938 (FB)

League Club	Source	Date Signed	Seasons Played	Apps	Subs	Gls
Nottingham F.	Wigan Ath.	12.59				
York C.	Tr	07.63	63-68	214	0	7

BAKER, Gerard A.
USA, 11 April, 1938 (CF)

League Club	Source	Date Signed	Seasons Played	Apps	Subs	Gls
Chelsea	Larkhall Th.	06.55				
Manchester C.	St Mirren	11.60	60-61	37	0	14
Ipswich T.	Hibernian	12.63	63-67	135	0	58
Coventry C.	Tr	11.67	67-69	27	4	5
Brentford	L	10.69	69	8	0	2

BAKER, Graham E.
Southampton, 3 December, 1958 Eu21-2 (M)

League Club	Source	Date Signed	Seasons Played	Apps	Subs	Gls
Southampton	App	12.76	77-81	111	2	22
Manchester C.	Tr	08.82	82-86	114	3	19
Southampton	Tr	06.87	87-89	57	3	8
Aldershot	L	03.90	89	7	0	2
Fulham	Tr	07.90	90-91	8	2	1

Joe Baker (Hibernian, Torino, Arsenal, Nottingham Forest, Sunderland & England)

BAKER, Joseph H.
Liverpool, 17 July, 1940 S Sch/Eu23-6/E-8 (CF)

League Club	Source	Date Signed	Seasons Played	Apps	Subs	Gls
Arsenal	Torino (It)	08.62	62-65	144	0	93
Nottingham F.	Tr	03.66	65-68	117	1	41
Sunderland	Tr	07.69	69-70	39	1	12

BAKER, Keith
Oxford, 15 October, 1956 E Sch (G)

League Club	Source	Date Signed	Seasons Played	Apps	Subs	Gls
Oxford U.	App	11.74				
Grimsby T.	L	08.75	75	1	0	0

BAKER, Kieron R.
Isle of Wight, 29 October, 1949 (G)

League Club	Source	Date Signed	Seasons Played	Apps	Subs	Gls
Bournemouth	Fulham (Am)	07.67	69-77	217	0	0
Brentford	L	02.73	72	6	0	0
Ipswich T.	Tr	08.78				

BAKER, Mark
Swansea, 26 April, 1961 (F)

League Club	Source	Date Signed	Seasons Played	Apps	Subs	Gls
Swansea C.	Jnrs	09.78	78-79	3	8	2

BAKER, D. Paul
Newcastle, 5 January, 1963 (F/CD)

League Club	Source	Date Signed	Seasons Played	Apps	Subs	Gls
Southampton	Bishop Auckland	06.84				
Carlisle U.	Tr	06.85	85-86	66	5	11
Hartlepool U.	Tr	07.87	87-91	192	5	65

BAKER, Peter R.
Walthamstow, 24 August, 1934 (FB)

League Club	Source	Date Signed	Seasons Played	Apps	Subs	Gls
Sheffield Wed.	Tottenham H. (Am)	11.54	57	11	-	0
Queens Park R.	Tr	03.61	60-62	27	-	0

BAKER, Peter R. B.
Hampstead, 10 December, 1931 (FB)

League Club	Source	Date Signed	Seasons Played	Apps	Subs	Gls
Tottenham H.	Enfield	10.52	52-64	299	-	3

BAKER, Roy V.
Bradford, 8 June, 1954 (F)

League Club	Source	Date Signed	Seasons Played	Apps	Subs	Gls
Bradford C.		07.72	72-74	39	7	11

BAKER, Stephen,
Wallsend, 2 December, 1961 (FB/M)

League Club	Source	Date Signed	Seasons Played	Apps	Subs	Gls
Southampton	App	12.79	80-87	61	12	0
Burnley	L	02.84	83	10	0	0
Leyton Orient	Tr	03.88	87-90	105	7	6
Bournemouth (N/C)	Tr	08.91	91	5	1	0

BAKER, Terence B.
Rochford, 13 November, 1965 (CD)

League Club	Source	Date Signed	Seasons Played	Apps	Subs	Gls
West Ham U.	App	11.83				
Colchester U.	Billericay T.	11.85	85-87	55	0	2

BAKER, Thomas A.
Charlton, 9 August, 1939 (WH)

League Club	Source	Date Signed	Seasons Played	Apps	Subs	Gls
Bristol Rov.		10.56	62	1	-	0

BAKER, Wayne R.
Leeds, 4 December, 1965 (G)

League Club	Source	Date Signed	Seasons Played	Apps	Subs	Gls
Sheffield Wed.	App	12.83				
Darlington (N/C)	Whitby T.	11.86	86	5	0	0

BAKER, William G.
Penrhiwceiber, 3 October, 1920 W Sch/W-1 (LH)

League Club	Source	Date Signed	Seasons Played	Apps	Subs	Gls
Cardiff C.	Troedrhiw	01.38	38-54	293	-	5
Ipswich T.	Tr	06.55	55	20	-	0

BAKES, Martin S.
Bradford, 8 February, 1937 (OL)

League Club	Source	Date Signed	Seasons Played	Apps	Subs	Gls
Bradford C.	Jnrs	02.54	53-58	72	-	7
Scunthorpe U.	Tr	06.59	59-62	77	-	5

BAKEWELL, Herbert
Barnsley, 8 March, 1921 (G)

League Club	Source	Date Signed	Seasons Played	Apps	Subs	Gls
Barnsley	Jnrs	02.39				
Newport Co.	Tr	09.46	46	8	-	0

BAKHOLT, Kurt
Denmark 12 August, 1963 (M)

League Club	Source	Date Signed	Seasons Played	Apps	Subs	Gls
Queens Park R.	Vejie (Den)	01.86	85	0	1	0

B'ALAC, Peta J.
Exeter, 9 December, 1953 (G)

League Club	Source	Date Signed	Seasons Played	Apps	Subs	Gls
Plymouth Arg.	App	12.71	71-72	40	0	0
Hereford U.	L	08.73	73	2	0	0
Swansea C.	L	09.73	73	4	0	0

BALCOMBE, Stephen W.
Bangor, 2 September, 1961 Wu21-1 (F)

League Club	Source	Date Signed	Seasons Played	Apps	Subs	Gls
Leeds U.	App	06.79	81	1	0	1

BALDERSTONE, J. Christopher
Huddersfield, 16 November, 1940 (IF)

League Club	Source	Date Signed	Seasons Played	Apps	Subs	Gls
Huddersfield T.	Jnrs	05.58	59-64	117	-	24
Carlisle U.	Tr	06.65	65-74	369	7	68
Doncaster Rov.	Tr	07.75	75	38	1	1

BALDIE, Douglas W.
Scoon, 16 April, 1921 (IF)

League Club	Source	Date Signed	Seasons Played	Apps	Subs	Gls
Bristol Rov.		04.46	46-47	8	-	4

BALDRIDGE, Robert
Sunderland, 26 November, 1932 (F)

League Club	Source	Date Signed	Seasons Played	Apps	Subs	Gls
Gateshead	Hendon Social	02.57	56-59	59	-	22

BALDRY, William J.
Luton, 9 July, 1956 (LB)

League Club	Source	Date Signed	Seasons Played	Apps	Subs	Gls
Cambridge U.	Luton T. (Am)	03.76	75-77	27	0	0

BALDWIN, George
Islington, 26 July, 1921 (WH)

League Club	Source	Date Signed	Seasons Played	Apps	Subs	Gls
Gillingham	Dartford	08.51	51	1	-	0

BALDWIN, Harold
Birmingham, 17 July, 1920 (G)

League Club	Source	Date Signed	Seasons Played	Apps	Subs	Gls
West Bromwich A.	Sutton T.	04.38	37	5	-	0
Brighton & H.A.	Tr	05.39	46-51	164	-	0
Walsall	Kettering T.	12.53	53-54	37	-	0

BALDWIN, James J.
Blackburn, 12 January, 1922 Died 1985 (WH)

League Club	Source	Date Signed	Seasons Played	Apps	Subs	Gls
Blackburn Rov.	Mill Hill St Peter	12.45	46-49	88	-	0
Leicester C.	Tr	02.50	49-55	180	-	4

BALDWIN, Thomas
Gateshead, 10 June, 1945 Eu23-2 (F)

League Club	Source	Date Signed	Seasons Played	Apps	Subs	Gls
Arsenal	Wrekenton Jnrs	12.62	64-66	17	0	7
Chelsea	Tr	09.66	66-74	182	5	74
Millwall	L	11.74	74	6	0	1
Manchester U.	L	01.75	74	2	0	0
Brentford (N/C)	Gravesend & Nft	10.77	77	4	0	1

BALL, Alan J.
Farnworth, 12 May, 1945 Eu23-8/EF Lge/E-72 (M)

League Club	Source	Date Signed	Seasons Played	Apps	Subs	Gls
Blackpool	App	05.62	62-65	116	0	41
Everton	Tr	08.66	66-71	208	0	66
Arsenal	Tr	12.71	71-76	177	0	45
Southampton	Tr	12.76	76-79	132	0	9
Blackpool	Vancouver (Can)	07.80	80	30	0	5
Southampton	Tr	03.81	80-82	63	0	2
Bristol Rov.	Hong Kong	01.83	82	17	0	2

BALL, J. Alan
Farnworth, 23 September, 1924 Died 1982

League Club	Source	Date Signed	Seasons Played	Apps	Subs	Gls
Southport	Bolton B.F.	03.46	46	2	-	0
Birmingham C.	Tr	05.47				
Southport	Tr	02.48	47-49	39	-	9
Oldham Ath.	Tr	07.50	50	7	-	1
Rochdale	Tr	02.52	51	5	-	1

BALL, Donald
Barnard Castle, 14 June, 1962 (CD)

League Club	Source	Date Signed	Seasons Played	Apps	Subs	Gls
Darlington	App	06.80	79-81	57	3	2

BALL, S, Gary
St Austell, 15 December, 1959 (M)

League Club	Source	Date Signed	Seasons Played	Apps	Subs	Gls
Plymouth Arg.	App	12.77	79	0	1	0
Lincoln C.	Tr	10.79	79	3	0	0

BALL, Geoffrey H.
Nottingham, 2 November, 1944 (FB)

League Club	Source	Date Signed	Seasons Played	Apps	Subs	Gls
Nottingham F.	Jnrs	02.63	64-65	3	0	0
Notts Co.	Tr	11.67	67-71	111	1	0

BALL, John
Wigan, 13 March, 1925 EF Lge (RB)

League Club	Source	Date Signed	Seasons Played	Apps	Subs	Gls
Manchester U.	Wigan Ath.	03.48	47-49	22	-	0
Bolton W.	Tr	09.50	50-57	200	-	2

BALL, John A.
Brighton, 16 July, 1923 (G)

League Club	Source	Date Signed	Seasons Played	Apps	Subs	Gls
Brighton & H.A.	Vernon Ath.	02.43	46-52	113	-	0

League Club	Source	Date Signed	Seasons Played	Career Record Apps	Subs	Gls

BALL, Joseph H.
Walsall, 4 April, 1931 Died 1974 (W)

League Club	Source	Date Signed	Seasons Played	Apps	Subs	Gls
Ipswich T.	Banbury Spencer	08.51	51-52	32	-	2
Aldershot	Tr	06.54	54-55	31	-	6

BALL, Keith
Walsall, 26 October, 1940 (G)

League Club	Source	Date Signed	Seasons Played	Apps	Subs	Gls
Walsall		01.59	58-61	11	-	0
Walsall	Worcester C.	05.65	66-67	35	0	0
Port Vale	Tr	11.68	68-71	130	0	0
Walsall	Stourbridge	11.72	72	2	0	0

BALL, Kevin A.
Hastings, 12 November, 1964 (CD)

League Club	Source	Date Signed	Seasons Played	Apps	Subs	Gls
Portsmouth	Coventry C. (App)	10.82	83-89	96	9	4
Sunderland	Tr	08.90	90-91	64	2	4

BALL, Steven J.
Colchester, 2 September, 1969 (M)

League Club	Source	Date Signed	Seasons Played	Apps	Subs	Gls
Arsenal	YT	09.87				
Colchester U. (N/C)		12.89	89	3	1	0
Norwich C.		09.90	91	0	2	0

Alan Ball (Blackpool, Everton, Arsenal, Southampton, Blackpool, Southampton, Bristol Rovers & England)

BALLAGHER, John
Ashton-u-Lyne, 21 March, 1936 (IF)

League Club	Source	Date Signed	Seasons Played	Apps	Subs	Gls
Sheffield Wed.	Stalybridge Celtic	02.57	58	3	-	0
Doncaster Rov.	Tr	02.61	60-61	41	-	13
Gillingham	Tr	08.62	62-63	41	-	10

BALLANTYNE, John D.
Newburn, 16 September, 1927

League Club	Source	Date Signed	Seasons Played	Apps	Subs	Gls
West Ham U.		05.46				
Hartlepool U.	Tr	07.50	50-51	13	-	0

BALLARD, Edgar A. (Ted)
Brentford, 16 June, 1920 (FB)

League Club	Source	Date Signed	Seasons Played	Apps	Subs	Gls
Leyton Orient	Brentford (Am)	04.46	46	26	-	1
Southampton	Tr	06.47	47-50	45	-	0
Leyton Orient	Tr	08.52				

BALMER, John (Jack)
Liverpool, 6 February, 1916 Died 1984 (IF)

League Club	Source	Date Signed	Seasons Played	Apps	Subs	Gls
Liverpool	Everton (Am)	08.35	35-51	292	-	99

BALMER, J. Michael
Hexham, 25 May, 1946 (CF)

League Club	Source	Date Signed	Seasons Played	Apps	Subs	Gls
Leicester C.	App	01.64				
Halifax T.	Tr	05.65	65-66	28	0	9

BALMER, Stuart M.
Falkirk, 20 September, 1969 (CD)

League Club	Source	Date Signed	Seasons Played	Apps	Subs	Gls
Charlton Ath.	Glasgow Celtic	08.90	90-91	35	7	0

BALOGUN, Jesilimi
Nigeria, 27 March, 1931 (F)

League Club	Source	Date Signed	Seasons Played	Apps	Subs	Gls
Queens Park R.	Skegness	09.56	56	13	-	3

BALSOM, Clifford G.
Torquay, 25 March, 1946 (FB)

League Club	Source	Date Signed	Seasons Played	Apps	Subs	Gls
Torquay U.	App	03.64	63	4	-	0
Swindon T.	Tr	06.64				

Kevin Ball (Portsmouth & Sunderland)

BALSON, Michael J. C.
Bridport, 9 September, 1947 (D)

League Club	Source	Date Signed	Seasons Played	Apps	Subs	Gls
Exeter C.	Jnrs	08.65	66-73	273	3	9

BALTACHA, Sergei P.
Ukraine, 17 February, 1958 USSR Int (M)

League Club	Source	Date Signed	Seasons Played	Apps	Subs	Gls
Ipswich T. (N/C)	Dinamo Kiev (USSR)	01.89	88-89	22	6	1

BAMBER, J. David
St Helens, 1 February, 1959 (F)

League Club	Source	Date Signed	Seasons Played	Apps	Subs	Gls
Blackpool	Manchester Univ.	09.79	79-82	81	5	29
Coventry C.	Tr	06.83	83	18	1	3
Walsall	Tr	03.84	83-84	17	3	7
Portsmouth	Tr	12.84	84	4	0	1
Swindon T.	Tr	11.85	85-87	103	3	31
Watford	Tr	06.88	88	16	2	3
Stoke C.	Tr	12.88	88-89	43	0	8
Hull C.	Tr	02.90	89-90	25	3	5
Blackpool	Tr	11.90	90-91	65	0	42

David Bamber (Blackpool, Coventry City, Walsall, Portsmouth, Swindon Town, Watford, Stoke City, Hull City & Blackpool)

BAMBRIDGE, Keith G.
Rawmarsh, 1 September, 1935 (OL)

League Club	Source	Date Signed	Seasons Played	Apps	Subs	Gls
Rotherham U.	Masborough St Pauls	02.55	55-62	161	-	16
Darlington	Tr	12.64	64	6	-	0
Halifax T.	Tr	03.65	64-65	8	1	1

BAMBRIDGE, Stephen M.
Marylebone, 27 May, 1960 (F)

League Club	Source	Date Signed	Seasons Played	Apps	Subs	Gls
Aldershot	App	05.78	76	0	2	0

BAMFORD, Harold C.
Bristol, 8 February, 1920 Died 1958 (FB)

League Club	Source	Date Signed	Seasons Played	Apps	Subs	Gls
Bristol Rov.	Ipswich T. (Am)	01.46	46-58	486	-	5

BAMFORD, Harold F. E.
Kingston, 8 April, 1914 Died 1949

League Club	Source	Date Signed	Seasons Played	Apps	Subs	Gls
Brentford	Ealing Y.C.	05.39				
Brighton & H.A.	Tr	06.46	46	8	-	0

BANCROFT, Paul A.
Derby, 10 September, 1964 (M)

League Club	Source	Date Signed	Seasons Played	Apps	Subs	Gls
Derby Co.	App	09.82				
Crewe Alex.	L	01.83	82	21	0	3
Northampton T.	Tr	07.84	84	15	1	0

BANFIELD, Neil A.
Poplar, 20 January, 1962 E Sch/E Yth (CD)

League Club	Source	Date Signed	Seasons Played	Apps	Subs	Gls
Crystal Palace	App	08.79	80	2	1	0
Leyton Orient	Adelaide C. (Aus.)	12.83	83-84	30	1	0

BANGER, Nicholas L.
Southampton, 25 February, 1971 (F)

League Club	Source	Date Signed	Seasons Played	Apps	Subs	Gls
Southampton	YT	04.89	90-91	0	10	0

BANHAM, Roy
Nottingham, 30 October, 1936 (CH)

League Club	Source	Date Signed	Seasons Played	Apps	Subs	Gls
Nottingham F.	Jnrs	11.53	55-56	2	-	0
Peterborough U.	Tr	07.58	60-61	16	-	0

BANJO, Tunji
Kennington, 19 February, 1960 Nigerian Int (M)

League Club	Source	Date Signed	Seasons Played	Apps	Subs	Gls
Leyton Orient	App	03.77	77-81	20	7	1

BANKS, Alan
Liverpool, 5 October, 1938 (CF)

League Club	Source	Date Signed	Seasons Played	Apps	Subs	Gls
Liverpool	Rankin Boys	05.58	58-60	8	-	6
Exeter C.	Cambridge C.	10.63	63-65	85	0	43
Plymouth Arg.	Tr	06.66	66-67	19	0	5
Exeter C.	Tr	11.67	67-72	160	13	58

BANKS, Christopher
Stone, 12 November, 1965 (FB)

League Club	Source	Date Signed	Seasons Played	Apps	Subs	Gls
Port Vale	Jnrs	12.82	84-87	50	15	1
Exeter C.	Tr	06.88	88	43	2	1

BANKS, Eric
Workington, 7 April, 1950 (W)

League Club	Source	Date Signed	Seasons Played	Apps	Subs	Gls
Workington	Jnrs	09.68	67-72	26	3	1

BANKS, Francis S.
Hull, 21 August, 1945 (FB)

League Club	Source	Date Signed	Seasons Played	Apps	Subs	Gls
Southend U.	Jnrs	10.62	63-65	4	0	0
Hull C.	Tr	09.66	67-75	284	4	7
Southend U.	Tr	03.76	75-77	75	0	0

BANKS, George E.
Wednesbury, 28 March, 1919 (CF)

League Club	Source	Date Signed	Seasons Played	Apps	Subs	Gls
West Bromwich A.	Brownhills Ath.	06.38	38	1	-	2
Mansfield T.	Tr	11.47	47-48	63	-	21

BANKS, Gordon
Sheffield, 20 December, 1937 Eu23-2/EF Lge/E-73 (G)

League Club	Source	Date Signed	Seasons Played	Apps	Subs	Gls
Chesterfield	Rawmarsh Welfare	09.55	58	23	-	0
Leicester C.	Tr	05.59	59-66	293	0	0
Stoke C.	Tr	04.67	66-72	194	0	0

Gordon Banks (Chesterfield, Leicester City, Stoke City & England)

BANKS, Ian F.
Mexborough, 9 January, 1961 (M)

League Club	Source	Date Signed	Seasons Played	Apps	Subs	Gls
Barnsley	App	01.79	78-82	158	6	37
Leicester C.	Tr	06.83	83-86	78	15	14
Huddersfield T.	Tr	09.86	86-87	78	0	17
Bradford C.	Tr	07.88	88	26	4	3
West Bromwich A.	Tr	03.89	88	2	2	0
Barnsley	Tr	07.89	89-91	87	9	7

BANKS, Jason M.
Farnworth, 16 November, 1968 (D)

League Club	Source	Date Signed	Seasons Played	Apps	Subs	Gls
Wigan Ath.	App	11.86				
Chester C.		10.87	87	1	1	0

BANKS, Kenneth
Wigan, 19 October, 1923 (WH)

League Club	Source	Date Signed	Seasons Played	Apps	Subs	Gls
Southport	Wigan Ath.	08.45	46-51	118	-	5

BANKS, Ralph
Farnworth, 28 June, 1920 (FB)

League Club	Source	Date Signed	Seasons Played	Apps	Subs	Gls
Bolton W.	South Liverpool	12.40	46-52	104	-	0
Aldershot	Tr	01.54	53-54	43	-	1

BANKS, Thomas
Farnworth, 10 November, 1929 EF Lge/E-6 (FB)

League Club	Source	Date Signed	Seasons Played	Apps	Subs	Gls
Bolton W.	Jnrs	10.47	47-60	233	-	2

BANNAN, Thomas N.
Lanark, 13 April, 1930 (CF)

League Club	Source	Date Signed	Seasons Played	Apps	Subs	Gls
Wrexham	Airdrieonians	06.51	51-54	158	-	55
Lincoln C.	Tr	06.55	55-56	67	-	19
Wrexham	Tr	08.57	57-58	68	-	23
Barrow	Tr	08.59	59-60	45	-	15

BANNER, Arthur
Sheffield, 28 June, 1918 Died 1980 (FB)

League Club	Source	Date Signed	Seasons Played	Apps	Subs	Gls
Doncaster Rov.	Lopham Street	03.37				
West Ham U.	Tr	05.38	38-47	27	-	0
Leyton Orient	Tr	02.48	47-52	164	-	1

BANNERMAN, Telford G.
Coupar Angus, 17 September, 1924 (W)

League Club	Source	Date Signed	Seasons Played	Apps	Subs	Gls
New Brighton	Blairgowrie Jnrs	01.49	48-50	35	-	3

BANNISTER, Bruce I.
Bradford, 14 April, 1947 (F)

League Club	Source	Date Signed	Seasons Played	Apps	Subs	Gls
Bradford C.	Jnrs	08.65	65-71	199	9	60
Bristol Rov.	Tr	11.71	71-76	202	4	80
Plymouth Arg.	Tr	12.76	76	24	0	7
Hull C.	Tr	06.77	77-79	79	6	20

BANNISTER, Edward
Leyland, 2 June, 1920 (FB)

League Club	Source	Date Signed	Seasons Played	Apps	Subs	Gls
Leeds U.	Oaks Fold	05.46	46-49	44	-	1
Barnsley	Tr	07.50	50	32	-	0

BANNISTER, Gary
Warrington, 22 July, 1960 Eu21-1 (F)

League Club	Source	Date Signed	Seasons Played	Apps	Subs	Gls
Coventry C.	App	05.78	78-80	17	5	3
Sheffield Wed.	Tr	08.81	81-83	117	1	55
Queens Park R.	Tr	08.84	84-87	136	0	56
Coventry C.	Tr	03.88	87-89	39	4	11
West Bromwich A.	Tr	03.90	89-91	62	10	18
Oxford U.	L	03.92	91	7	3	2

BANNISTER, Jack
Chesterfield, 26 January, 1942 (WH)

League Club	Source	Date Signed	Seasons Played	Apps	Subs	Gls
West Bromwich A.	Jnrs	08.59	59-62	9	-	0
Scunthorpe U.	Tr	06.64	64	9	-	0
Crystal Palace	Tr	07.65	65-68	117	3	7
Luton T.	Tr	10.68	68-70	79	3	0
Cambridge U.	Tr	05.71	71-73	28	4	0

BANNISTER, James H.
Chesterfield, 1 February, 1929 (FB)

League Club	Source	Date Signed	Seasons Played	Apps	Subs	Gls
Chesterfield		12.50				
Shrewsbury T.	Tr	06.52	52-57	238	-	2
Northampton T.	Tr	07.58	58	24	-	0
Aldershot	Tr	08.59	59-60	85	-	0

BANNISTER, Keith
Sheffield, 13 November, 1930 E Yth (WH)

League Club	Source	Date Signed	Seasons Played	Apps	Subs	Gls
Sheffield U.	Jnrs	05.48				
Birmingham C.	Tr	08.50	52-53	22	-	0
Wrexham	Tr	07.55	55	14	-	0
Chesterfield	Tr	12.55	55	21	-	1
Norwich C.	Tr	07.56	56	7	-	0

BANNISTER, Keith
Sheffield, 27 January, 1923 (FB)

League Club	Source	Date Signed	Seasons Played	Apps	Subs	Gls
Sheffield Wed.	Sheffield Y.M.C.A.	02.45	46-52	75	-	0
Chesterfield	Tr	06.53	53	17	-	0

BANNISTER, Neville
Burnley, 21 July, 1937 (OR)

League Club	Source	Date Signed	Seasons Played	Apps	Subs	Gls
Bolton W.	Jnrs	07.54	55-60	26	-	4
Lincoln C.	Tr	03.61	60-63	68	-	16
Hartlepool U.	Tr	08.64	64	41	-	8
Rochdale	Tr	07.65	65	18	1	2

BANNISTER, Paul
Stoke, 11 October, 1947 (F)

League Club	Source	Date Signed	Seasons Played	Apps	Subs	Gls
Port Vale	Jnrs	04.65	64-67	12	0	2

BANNON, Eamonn J. P.
Edinburgh, 18 April, 1958 S Sch/Su21-7/S Lge/S-6 (M)

League Club	Source	Date Signed	Seasons Played	Apps	Subs	Gls
Chelsea	Hearts	01.79	78-79	25	0	1

BANNON, Ian
Bury, 3 September, 1959 (CD)

League Club	Source	Date Signed	Seasons Played	Apps	Subs	Gls
Rochdale	App	09.77	76-79	112	10	0

BANNON, Paul A.
Dublin, 15 November, 1956 (F)

League Club	Source	Date Signed	Seasons Played	Apps	Subs	Gls
Nottingham F.	Jnrs	06.75				
Carlisle U.	Bridgend T.	02.79	78-83	127	12	45
Darlington	L	10.83	83	2	0	0
Bristol Rov.	Tr	01.84	83-84	27	2	8
Cardiff C.	L	08.84	84	3	1	0
Plymouth Arg.	L	11.84	84	0	2	0

BANOVIC, Yakka
Yugoslavia, 12 November, 1956 Yugoslav Int (G)

League Club	Source	Date Signed	Seasons Played	Apps	Subs	Gls
Derby Co.	Heidelberg (Aus)	09.80	81-83	35	0	0

BANTON, Dale C.
Kensington, 15 May, 1961 (F)

League Club	Source	Date Signed	Seasons Played	Apps	Subs	Gls
West Ham U.	App	05.79	79-81	2	3	0
Aldershot	Tr	08.82	82-84	105	1	47
York C.	Tr	11.84	84-88	129	9	49
Walsall	Tr	10.88	88	9	1	0
Grimsby T.	Tr	03.89	88	3	5	1
Aldershot	Tr	08.89	89-90	29	15	3

BANTON, Geoffrey
Ashton-u-Lyne, 16 March, 1957 (CD)

League Club	Source	Date Signed	Seasons Played	Apps	Subs	Gls
Plymouth Arg.	Bolton W. (App)	05.75	76-77	6	1	0
Fulham	Tr	07.78	78-81	37	1	3

BARACLOUGH, Ian R.
Leicester, 4 December, 1970 (F)

League Club	Source	Date Signed	Seasons Played	Apps	Subs	Gls
Leicester C.	YT	12.88				
Wigan Ath.	L	03.90	89	8	1	2
Grimsby T.	L	12.90	90	1	3	0
Grimsby T.	Tr	08.91				

BARBER, David E.
Wombwell, 6 December, 1939 E Yth (WH)

League Club	Source	Date Signed	Seasons Played	Apps	Subs	Gls
Barnsley	Jnrs	06.58	57-60	82	-	4
Preston N.E.	Tr	06.61	61-63	38	-	2

BARBER, Eric
Stockport, 25 March, 1926 (W)

League Club	Source	Date Signed	Seasons Played	Apps	Subs	Gls
Sheffield U.		02.47				
Bolton W.	Macclesfield T.	03.50				
Rochdale	Tr	04.51	50-51	17	-	2

BARBER, Eric
Dublin, 18 January, 1942 NI-2 (F)

League Club	Source	Date Signed	Seasons Played	Apps	Subs	Gls
Birmingham C.	Shelbourne	03.66	65-66	3	1	1

BARBER, Frederick
Ferryhill, 26 August, 1963 (G)

League Club	Source	Date Signed	Seasons Played	Apps	Subs	Gls
Darlington	App	08.81	82-85	135	0	0
Everton	Tr	03.86				
Walsall	Tr	10.86	86-90	153	0	0
Peterborough U.	L	10.89	89	6	0	0
Chester C.	L	10.90	90	3	0	0
Blackpool	L	11.90	90	2	0	0
Chester C.	L	03.91	90	5	0	0
Peterborough U.	Tr	08.91	91	39	0	0

League Club	Source	Date Signed	Seasons Played	Career Record Apps	Subs	Gls

BARBER, John M.
Lichfield, 9 October, 1929 (OL)

Swansea C.	Arsenal	08.50	50	4	-	0
Walsall	Tr	07.51	51	6	-	0

BARBER, Keith
Luton, 21 September, 1947 (G)

Luton T.	Dunstable T.	04.71	70-76	142	0	0
Swansea C.	Tr	07.77	77	42	0	0
Cardiff C.	L	09.78	78	2	0	0

BARBER, Leonard
Stoke, 3 July, 1929 (CF)

Port Vale	Bury (Am)	06.47	49-54	47	-	12

BARBER, Michael J.
Kensington, 24 August, 1941 (OL)

Queens Park R.	Arsenal (Am)	12.59	60-62	63	-	11
Notts Co.	Tr	07.63	63-64	33	-	3

BARBER, Philip A.
Tring, 10 June, 1965 (M/F)

Crystal Palace	Aylesbury U.	02.84	83-90	207	27	35
Millwall	Tr	07.91	91	26	3	4

BARBER, William
Watford, 9 September, 1939 (WH)

Watford	Jnrs	03.57	56-59	25	-	0
Aldershot	Tr	08.62	62	1	-	0

BARCLAY, John M.
Mid Calder, 8 September, 1921 (CF)

Bournemouth	Haddington	12.47	47-48	5	-	2

BARCLAY, Robert
Perth, 3 November, 1922

Preston N.E.		10.45				
Stockport Co.		08.48	48	1	-	0

BARCLAY, William
Larkhall, 11 July, 1924 (OL)

Bury	Motherwell	03.49	48-49	17	-	0

BARDSLEY, David J.
Manchester, 11 September, 1964 E Yth (RB)

Blackpool	App	09.82	81-83	45	0	0
Watford	Tr	11.83	83-87	97	3	7
Oxford U.	Tr	09.87	87-89	74	0	7
Queens Park R.	Tr	09.89	89-91	110	0	1

BARDSLEY, Leslie
Stockport, 8 August, 1925 (WH)

Manchester C.	Jnrs	01.45				
Bury	Linfield	04.48	47-54	200	-	2
Barrow	Tr	09.55	55	21	-	0

BARGH, George W.
Garstang, 27 May, 1910 Died 1980 (IF)

Preston N.E.	Garstang	02.28	28-34	141	-	43
Sheffield Wed.	Tr	09.35	35	5	-	0
Bury	Tr	05.36	36-38	89	-	13
Chesterfield	Tr	06.39				
Bury		09.46	46	1	-	0

BARHAM, Mark F.
Folkestone, 12 July, 1962 E Yth/E-2 (RW)

Norwich C.	App	04.80	79-86	169	8	23
Huddersfield T.	Tr	07.87	87-88	25	2	1
Middlesbrough	Tr	11.88	88	3	1	0
West Bromwich A.	Tr	09.89	89	4	0	0
Brighton & H.A.	Millwall (N/C)	12.89	89-91	70	3	8

BARK, Robert
Stranraer, 27 January, 1926

Barrow	Queen of South	04.48	48	1	-	0

BARKAS, Samuel
Wardley, 29 December, 1909 EF Lge/E-5 (FB)

Bradford C.	Middle Dock	08.27	27-33	202	-	8
Manchester C.	Tr	04.34	33-46	175	-	1

BARKAS, Thomas
South Shields, 27 March, 1912 (IF)

Bradford C.	Washington Colly	09.32	32-34	16	-	2
Halifax T.	Tr	12.34	34-38	168	-	36
Rochdale	Tr	09.46	46-47	44	-	17
Stockport Co.	Tr	11.47	47-48	44	-	18
Carlisle U.	Tr	02.49	48	14	-	5

League Club	Source	Date Signed	Seasons Played	Career Record Apps	Subs	Gls

BARKE, J. Lloyd
Nuncargate, 16 December, 1912 (CH)

Sheffield U.	Scunthorpe U.	05.33	34-36	6	-	0
Mansfield T.	Tr	06.37	37-46	114	-	0

BARKER, Donald
Long Eaton, 17 June, 1911 Died 1979 (IF)

Bradford P.A.	Notts Co. (Am)	01.34	33-36	55	-	15
Millwall	Tr	01.37	36-38	62	-	18
Brighton & H.A.	Tr	07.46	46	14	-	4

BARKER, Geoffrey A.
Hull, 7 February, 1949 (CD)

Hull C.	Jnrs	03.67	68-70	29	1	2
Southend U.	L	12.70	70	25	0	0
Darlington	Tr	07.71	71-74	151	0	6
Reading	Tr	02.75	74-76	51	1	2
Grimsby T.	Tr	07.77	77-78	66	0	1

BARKER, Gordon
Leeds, 6 July, 1931 (F)

Southend U.	Bishop Auckland	12.54	54-58	57	-	9

BARKER, Jeffrey
Scunthorpe, 16 October, 1915 Died 1985 (FB)

Aston Villa	Scunthorpe U.	11.36	37	3	-	0
Huddersfield T.	Tr	11.45	46-47	67	-	0
Scunthorpe U.	Tr	08.48	50-51	73	-	1

BARKER, John
Huddersfield, 4 July, 1948 (FB)

Scunthorpe U.	App	07.66	65-74	261	2	6

BARKER, Keith
Stoke, 22 February, 1949 (G)

Cambridge U.		(N/L)				
Barnsley	Tr	03.71	71	9	0	0

BARKER, Leonard
Salford, 26 March, 1924 (F)

Stockport Co.		01.48	48-50	39	-	12

BARKER, A. Michael
Bishop Auckland, 23 February, 1956 (LB)

Newcastle U.	App	03.73	74-78	21	2	0
Gillingham	Tr	01.79	78-79	64	0	2
Hartlepool U.	Bishop Auckland	09.82	82-83	59	1	1

BARKER, Richard
Derby, 23 November, 1939 (IF)

Derby Co.	Burton A.	10.67	67-68	30	8	12
Notts Co.	Tr	12.68	68-70	99	13	37
Peterborough U.	Tr	09.71	71	36	0	9

BARKER, Robert C.
Kinglassie (Fife), 1 December, 1927 (OL)

West Bromwich A.	Kelty R.	09.45	48	14	-	2
Shrewsbury T.	Tr	08.50	50	25	-	1

BARKER, Simon
Farnworth, 4 November, 1964 Eu21-4 (M)

Blackburn Rov.	App	11.82	83-87	180	2	35
Queens Park R.	Tr	07.88	88-91	107	15	11

BARKER, Thomas H.
Tyldesley, 12 January, 1936 (F)

Southport	Boothstown	12.57	57-58	35	-	4

BARKER, William
Stoke, 31 May, 1924 (F)

Stoke C.		10.48	49	1	-	0

BARKS, Edwin
Ilkeston, 1 September, 1921 (WH)

Nottingham F.	Heanor T.	04.39	46-48	66	-	5
Mansfield T.	Tr	01.49	48-54	213	-	6

BARKUS, Lea P.
Reading, 7 December, 1974 (F)

Reading (YT)	YT	07.91	91	4	2	1

BARLEY, Derek C. (Jack)
Highbury, 20 March, 1932 E Yth (HB)

Arsenal	Maidenhead U.	12.51				
Queens Park R.	Tr	05.53	53	4	-	0
Aldershot	Tr	07.54	54	2	-	0

BARLEY, Peter J.
Scunthorpe, 25 April, 1936 (G)

League Club	Source	Date Signed	Seasons Played	Apps	Subs	Gls
Scunthorpe U.	Leeds U. (Am)	10.53	53	5	-	0

BARLOW, Andrew J.
Oldham, 24 November, 1965 (LB)

League Club	Source	Date Signed	Seasons Played	Apps	Subs	Gls
Oldham Ath.	Jnrs	07.84	84-91	234	13	5

BARLOW, Colin J.
Manchester, 14 November, 1935 (OR)

League Club	Source	Date Signed	Seasons Played	Apps	Subs	Gls
Manchester C.	Tarporley	12.56	57-62	179	-	78
Oldham Ath.	Tr	08.63	63	6	-	1
Doncaster Rov.	Tr	08.64	64	3	-	0

BARLOW, Frank
Mexborough, 15 October, 1946 E Sch (WH)

League Club	Source	Date Signed	Seasons Played	Apps	Subs	Gls
Sheffield U	Jnrs	09.65	65-71	116	5	2
Chesterfield	Tr	08.72	72-75	140	1	3

BARLOW, Harold
Manchester, 28 October, 1923 (CH)

League Club	Source	Date Signed	Seasons Played	Apps	Subs	Gls
Crewe Alex.	Manchester C. (Am)	02.46	46-50	29	-	1

BARLOW, Herbert
Kilnhurst, 22 July, 1916 (IF)

League Club	Source	Date Signed	Seasons Played	Apps	Subs	Gls
Barnsley	Silverwood Colly	07.35	35-37	58	-	13
Wolverhampton W.	Tr	06.38	38	3	-	1
Portsmouth	Tr	02.39	38-49	104	-	34
Leicester C.	Tr	12.49	49-51	42	-	9
Colchester U.	Tr	07.52	52-53	60	-	16

BARLOW, Martin D.
Plymouth, 25 June, 1971 (W)

League Club	Source	Date Signed	Seasons Played	Apps	Subs	Gls
Plymouth Arg	YT	07.89	88-91	48	12	4

BARLOW, Peter
Colchester, 9 January, 1950 (F)

League Club	Source	Date Signed	Seasons Played	Apps	Subs	Gls
Colchester U.	App	01.68	66-68	18	3	4
Workington	Tr	02.69	68-69	41	1	11
Hartlepool U.	Tr	07.70	70	8	3	0

BARLOW, Philip D.
Shipley, 19 December, 1946 (HB)

League Club	Source	Date Signed	Seasons Played	Apps	Subs	Gls
Bradford C.	Guiseley	07.66	66	15	1	0
Lincoln C.	Tr	08.67	67	5	0	0

BARLOW, Raymond J.
Swindon, 17 August, 1926 E-1 (WH)

League Club	Source	Date Signed	Seasons Played	Apps	Subs	Gls
West Bromwich A.	Garrards	06.44	46-59	403	-	31
Birmingham C.	Tr	08.60	60	5	-	0

BARLOW, Stuart
Liverpool, 16 July, 1968 (F)

League Club	Source	Date Signed	Seasons Played	Apps	Subs	Gls
Everton	Sherwood Park	06.90	90-91	3	6	0

BARMBY, Jeffrey
Hull, 15 January, 1943 (CF)

League Club	Source	Date Signed	Seasons Played	Apps	Subs	Gls
York C. (Am)	Selby T.	03.63	62-63	2	-	0

BARNARD, Arthur
Mossley, 20 June, 1932 (G)

League Club	Source	Date Signed	Seasons Played	Apps	Subs	Gls
Bolton W.	Astley Colly	11.51	54-55	2	-	0
Stockport Co.	Tr	07.56	56-58	53	-	0
Southport	Tr	09.59	59	42	-	0

BARNARD, Christopher L.
Cardiff, 1 August, 1947 (M)

League Club	Source	Date Signed	Seasons Played	Apps	Subs	Gls
Southend U.	App	08.65	65	4	4	0
Ipswich T.	Tr	07.66	66-70	18	3	0
Torquay U.	Tr	10.70	70-71	29	4	2
Charlton Ath.	Tr	01.72	71	0	1	0

BARNARD, Darren S.
Rinteln (Ger), 30 November, 1971 E Sch (M)

League Club	Source	Date Signed	Seasons Played	Apps	Subs	Gls
Chelsea	Wokingham T.	07.90	91	1	3	0

BARNARD, Geoffrey
Southend, 23 March, 1946 (G)

League Club	Source	Date Signed	Seasons Played	Apps	Subs	Gls
Norwich C.	Jnrs	09.63	64-66	6	0	0
Scunthorpe U.	Tr	07.68	68-74	265	0	0
Scunthorpe U	Scarborough	09.76	76	6	0	0

BARNARD, Leigh K.
Worsley, 29 October, 1958 (M)

League Club	Source	Date Signed	Seasons Played	Apps	Subs	Gls
Portsmouth	App	10.76	77-81	71	8	8
Peterborough U.	L	03.82	81	1	3	0
Swindon T.	Tr	07.82	82-89	212	5	21
Exeter C.	L	02.85	84	6	0	2
Cardiff C.	Tr	10.89	89-90	61	2	8

BARNARD, H. Michael
Portsmouth, 8 July, 1933 (IF)

League Club	Source	Date Signed	Seasons Played	Apps	Subs	Gls
Portsmouth	Gosport Bor.	08.51	53-58	116	-	24

BARNARD, Raymond S.
Middlesbrough, 16 April, 1933 E Sch (FB)

League Club	Source	Date Signed	Seasons Played	Apps	Subs	Gls
Middlesbrough	Jnrs	04.50	51-59	113	-	0
Lincoln C.	Tr	06.60	60-62	43	-	0

BARNES, Andrew J.
Croydon, 31 March, 1967 (F)

League Club	Source	Date Signed	Seasons Played	Apps	Subs	Gls
Crystal Palace	Sutton U.	09.91	91	0	1	0

BARNES, Bernard
Plymouth, 25 December, 1937 (CF)

League Club	Source	Date Signed	Seasons Played	Apps	Subs	Gls
Plymouth Arg.	Bideford	01.55	56-57	4	-	1

BARNES, Colin
Notting Hill, 28 May, 1957 (F)

League Club	Source	Date Signed	Seasons Played	Apps	Subs	Gls
Torquay U.	Adelaide C. (Aus)	08.83	83-84	42	1	11

BARNES, David
Paddington, 16 November, 1961 E Yth (LB)

League Club	Source	Date Signed	Seasons Played	Apps	Subs	Gls
Coventry C.	App	05.79	79-81	9	0	0
Ipswich T.	Tr	05.82	82-83	16	1	0
Wolverhampton W.	Tr	10.84	84-87	86	2	4
Aldershot	Tr	08.87	87-88	68	1	1
Sheffield U.	Tr	07.89	89-91	67	0	1

Bobby Barnes (West Ham United, Aldershot, Swindon Town, Bournemouth, Northampton Town & Peterborough United)

BARNES, David O. (Bobby)
Kingston, 17 December, 1962 (F)

League Club	Source	Date Signed	Seasons Played	Apps	Subs	Gls
West Ham U.	App	09.80	80-85	31	12	5
Scunthorpe U.	L	11.85	85	6	0	0
Aldershot	Tr	03.86	85-87	49	0	26
Swindon T.	Tr	10.87	87-88	43	2	13

League Club	Source	Date Signed	Seasons Played	Career Record Apps	Subs	Gls
Bournemouth	Tr	03.89	88-89	11	3	0
Northampton T.	Tr	10.89	89-91	97	1	37
Peterborough U.	Tr	02.92	91	15	0	5

BARNES, Eric
Wythenshawe, 29 November, 1937 (CH)

League Club	Source	Date Signed	Seasons Played	Apps	Subs	Gls
Crewe Alex.		01.58	57-69	347	2	1

BARNES, John C. B.
Jamaica, 7 November, 1963 Eu21-2/EF Lge/E-67 (F)

League Club	Source	Date Signed	Seasons Played	Apps	Subs	Gls
Watford	Sudbury Court	07.81	81-86	232	1	65
Liverpool	Tr	07.87	87-91	152	0	62

John Barnes (Watford, Liverpool & England)

BARNES, Kenneth H.
Birmingham, 6 March, 1929 EF Lge (WH)

League Club	Source	Date Signed	Seasons Played	Apps	Subs	Gls
Manchester C.	Stafford R.	05.50	51-60	258	-	18
Wrexham	Tr	05.61	61-64	132	-	24

BARNES, Michael F.
Reading, 17 September, 1963 (CD)

League Club	Source	Date Signed	Seasons Played	Apps	Subs	Gls
Reading	App	09.81	80-83	29	5	2
Northampton T.	Tr	08.84	84	19	0	1

BARNES, Paul L.
Leicester, 16 November, 1967 (F)

League Club	Source	Date Signed	Seasons Played	Apps	Subs	Gls
Notts Co.	App	11.85	85-89	36	17	14
Stoke C.	Tr	03.90	89-91	10	14	3
Chesterfield	L	11.90	90	1	0	0

BARNES, Peter
St Albans, 29 June, 1938 (WH)

League Club	Source	Date Signed	Seasons Played	Apps	Subs	Gls
Watford	Jnrs	03.57	60-61	10	-	0

BARNES, Peter S.
Manchester, 10 June, 1957 E Yth/Eu21-9/EF Lge/E-22 (W)

League Club	Source	Date Signed	Seasons Played	Apps	Subs	Gls
Manchester C.	App	08.74	74-78	108	7	15
West Bromwich A.	Tr	07.79	79-80	76	1	23
Leeds U.	Tr	08.81	81	31	0	1
Leeds U.	Real Betis (SP)	08.83	83	25	2	4
Coventry C.	Tr	10.84	84	18	0	2
Manchester U.	Tr	07.85	85-86	19	1	2
Manchester C.	Tr	01.87	86	8	0	0
Bolton W.	L	10.87	87	2	0	0
Port Vale	L	12.87	87	3	0	0
Hull C.	Tr	03.88	87	11	0	0
Bolton W.	Farense (Port)	11.88	88	2	1	0
Sunderland	Tr	02.89	88	1	0	0

Peter Barnes (Manchester City, West Bromwich Albion, Leeds United, Real Betis, Leeds United, Coventry City, Manchester United, Manchester City, Hull City, Farense, Bolton Wanderers, Sunderland & England)

BARNES, Robert A.
Stoke, 26 November, 1969 (FB)

League Club	Source	Date Signed	Seasons Played	Apps	Subs	Gls
Manchester C.	YT					
Wrexham	Tr	06.89	89-90	8	1	0

BARNES, C. Ronald
Bolton, 21 February, 1936 (OR)

League Club	Source	Date Signed	Seasons Played	Apps	Subs	Gls
Blackpool	Jnrs	05.54	56-58	9	-	0
Rochdale	Tr	06.59	59-60	91	-	7
Wrexham	Tr	07.61	61-63	88	-	24
Norwich C.	Tr	08.63	63	21	-	1
Peterborough U.	Tr	07.64	64-65	39	0	6
Torquay U.	Tr	01.66	65-68	110	4	25

BARNES, Walter
Brecon, 16 January, 1920 Died 1975 W-22 (FB)

League Club	Source	Date Signed	Seasons Played	Apps	Subs	Gls
Arsenal	Southampton (Am)	09.43	46-55	267	-	11

BARNES, William
Dumbarton, 16 March, 1939 (FB)

League Club	Source	Date Signed	Seasons Played	Apps	Subs	Gls
Bradford C.	Glencairn	04.58	58-60	59	-	0
Bradford P.A.	Scarborough	09.66	66-67	53	0	0

BARNESS, Anthony
Lewisham, 25 March, 1973 (LB)

League Club	Source	Date Signed	Seasons Played	Apps	Subs	Gls
Charlton Ath.	YT	03.91	91	16	6	1

BARNETT, Alan G.
Croydon, 4 November, 1934 (G)

League Club	Source	Date Signed	Seasons Played	Apps	Subs	Gls
Portsmouth	Croydon Amats	09.55	55-57	25	-	0
Grimsby T.	Tr	12.58	58-62	116	-	0
Exeter C.	Tr	07.63	63-65	57	0	0
Torquay U.	Tr	06.66				

BARNETT, David
Lambeth, 24 September, 1951 (D)

League Club	Source	Date Signed	Seasons Played	Apps	Subs	Gls
Southend U.	App	09.69	68-72	48	9	0

BARNETT, David K.
Birmingham, 16 April, 1967 (CD/M)

League Club	Source	Date Signed	Seasons Played	Apps	Subs	Gls
Colchester U. (N/C)	Windsor & Eton	08.88	88	19	1	0
West Bromwich A.	Edmonton (Can)	10.89				
Walsall	Tr	07.90	90	4	1	0
Barnet	Kidderminster H.	02.92	91	3	1	0

BARNETT, Gary L.
Stratford, 11 March, 1963 (W)

League Club	Source	Date Signed	Seasons Played	Apps	Subs	Gls
Coventry C.	App	01.81				
Oxford U.	Tr	07.82	82-85	37	8	9
Wimbledon	L	02.83	82	5	0	1
Fulham	L	12.84	84	0	2	1
Fulham	Tr	09.85	85-89	167	13	30
Huddersfield T.	Tr	07.90	90-91	46	7	4

BARNETT, Geoffrey C.
Northwich, 16 October, 1946 E Sch/E Yth (G)

League Club	Source	Date Signed	Seasons Played	Apps	Subs	Gls
Everton	App	05.64	65-67	10	0	0
Arsenal	Tr	10.69	69-75	39	0	0

BARNETT, Graham
Stoke, 17 May, 1936 (F)

League Club	Source	Date Signed	Seasons Played	Apps	Subs	Gls
Port Vale		06.56	58-59	49	-	35
Tranmere Rov.	Tr	03.60	59-60	32	-	11
Halifax T.	Tr	08.61	61	32	-	9

BARNETT, Thomas
Muswell Hill, 12 October, 1936 (F)

League Club	Source	Date Signed	Seasons Played	Apps	Subs	Gls
Crystal Palace	Chatham	12.58	58-60	14	-	2

BARNEY, Victor C.
Stepney, 3 April, 1922 (IF)

League Club	Source	Date Signed	Seasons Played	Apps	Subs	Gls
Reading	Oxford C.	09.46	46-48	45	-	12
Bristol C.	Tr	10.48	48	28	-	4
Grimsby T.	Tr	06.49	49	7	-	0

BARNEY, Victor R.
Oxford, 18 November, 1947 (WH)

League Club	Source	Date Signed	Seasons Played	Apps	Subs	Gls
Bristol Rov.	App	12.65	66-69	30	1	3

BARNHOUSE, David J.
Swansea, 19 March, 1975 (M)

League Club	Source	Date Signed	Seasons Played	Apps	Subs	Gls
Swansea C. (YT)	YT	07.91	91	0	1	0

BARNSLEY, Andrew
Sheffield, 9 June, 1962 (D)

League Club	Source	Date Signed	Seasons Played	Apps	Subs	Gls
Rotherham U.	Denaby U.	06.85	85	28	0	0
Sheffield U.	Tr	07.86	86-88	73	4	0
Rotherham U.	Tr	12.88	88-90	77	6	3
Carlisle U.	Tr	08.91	91	28	0	3

BARNSLEY, Geoffrey R. T.
Bilston, 9 December, 1935 (G)

League Club	Source	Date Signed	Seasons Played	Apps	Subs	Gls
West Bromwich A.	Jnrs	12.52	54	1	-	0
Plymouth Arg.	Tr	06.57	57-60	132	-	0
Norwich C.	Tr	05.61	61	8	-	0
Torquay U.	Tr	12.62	63	6	-	0

BARNWELL, John
Newcastle, 24 December, 1938 E Yth/Eu23-1 (WH)

League Club	Source	Date Signed	Seasons Played	Apps	Subs	Gls
Arsenal	Bishop Auckland	11.56	56-63	138	-	23
Nottingham F.	Tr	03.64	63-69	172	8	22
Sheffield U.	Tr	04.70	70	9	0	2

BARON, Kevin P.
Preston, 19 July, 1926 Died 1971 (IF)

League Club	Source	Date Signed	Seasons Played	Apps	Subs	Gls
Liverpool	Preston N.E. (Am)	08.45	47-53	140	-	32
Southend U.	Tr	05.54	54-58	138	-	47
Northampton T.	Tr	09.58	58	25	-	4
Aldershot	Gravesend & Nft	07.60	60	6	-	0

BARR, Hugh H.
Ballymena (NI), 17 May, 1935 NI Sch/NI-3 (IF)

League Club	Source	Date Signed	Seasons Played	Apps	Subs	Gls
Coventry C.	Linfield	07.62	62-63	47	-	15

BARR, John M.
Bridge of Weir, 9 September, 1917 (CH)

League Club	Source	Date Signed	Seasons Played	Apps	Subs	Gls
Queens Park R.	Third Lanark	05.39	46	4	-	0

BARR, Robert A.
Halifax, 5 December, 1969 (CD)

League Club	Source	Date Signed	Seasons Played	Apps	Subs	Gls
Halifax T.	YT	06.88	86-88	4	1	0

BARR, William J.
Halifax, 21 January, 1969 (LB/M)

League Club	Source	Date Signed	Seasons Played	Apps	Subs	Gls
Halifax T.	YT	07.87	87-91	150	18	10

BARRAS, Anthony
Billingham, 29 March, 1971 (CD)

League Club	Source	Date Signed	Seasons Played	Apps	Subs	Gls
Hartlepool U.	YT	07.89	88-89	9	3	0
Stockport Co.	Tr	07.90	90-91	79	3	5

BARRASS, Malcolm W.
Blackpool, 13 December, 1924 EF Lge/E-3 (CH)

League Club	Source	Date Signed	Seasons Played	Apps	Subs	Gls
Bolton W.	Ford Motors	11.44	46-56	329	-	25
Sheffield U.	Tr	09.56	56	18	-	0

BARRATT, Alfred G.
Corby, 13 April, 1920 (CH)

League Club	Source	Date Signed	Seasons Played	Apps	Subs	Gls
Northampton T.	Kettering T.	07.38	38	1	-	0
Leicester C.	Stewart & Lloyds	09.46	47-48	4	-	0
Grimsby T.	Tr	07.50	50	23	-	0
Southport	Tr	07.51	51-55	198	-	0

BARRATT, Anthony
Salford, 18 October, 1965 (RB/M)

League Club	Source	Date Signed	Seasons Played	Apps	Subs	Gls
Grimsby T.	Billingham T.	08.85	85	20	2	0
Hartlepool U.	Billingham T.	12.86	86-88	93	5	4
York C.	Tr	03.89	88-91	100	8	9

BARRATT, Harold
Oxford, 25 December, 1918 Died 1990 (D)

League Club	Source	Date Signed	Seasons Played	Apps	Subs	Gls
Coventry C.	Herberts Ath.	12.35	37-51	170	-	12

BARRATT, Leslie E.
Windermere, 13 August, 1945 (WH)

League Club	Source	Date Signed	Seasons Played	Apps	Subs	Gls
Barrow	App	08.62	62-63	10	-	0
Grimsby T.	Tr	07.64	64	4	-	1
Southport	Tr	07.65	65	9	1	0

BARRELL, Leslie
Colchester, 30 August, 1932 (F)

League Club	Source	Date Signed	Seasons Played	Apps	Subs	Gls
Colchester U.		12.56	56	4	-	1

BARRETT, Arthur H.
Liverpool, 21 December, 1927 (CH)

League Club	Source	Date Signed	Seasons Played	Apps	Subs	Gls
Tranmere Rov.	Jnrs	03.45	46	1	-	0

BARRETT, Colin
Stockport, 3 August, 1952 (FB)

League Club	Source	Date Signed	Seasons Played	Apps	Subs	Gls
Manchester C.	Cheadle Heath	05.70	72-75	50	3	0
Nottingham F.	Tr	03.76	75-78	64	5	4
Swindon T.	Tr	06.80	80	3	0	0

BARRETT, Earl D.
Rochdale, 28 April, 1967 Eu21-4/E 'B'/E FL/E-1 (CD)

League Club	Source	Date Signed	Seasons Played	Apps	Subs	Gls
Manchester C.	YT	04.85	85-86	2	1	0
Chester C.	L	03.86	85	12	0	0
Oldham Ath.	Tr	11.87	87-91	181	2	7
Aston Villa	Tr	02.92	91	13	0	0

BARRETT, James G.
West Ham, 5 November, 1930 (IF)

League Club	Source	Date Signed	Seasons Played	Apps	Subs	Gls
West Ham U.	Jnrs	02.49	49-54	85	-	24
Nottingham F.	Tr	12.54	54-58	105	-	64
Birmingham C.	Tr	10.59	59	10	-	4

BARRETT, John
Birmingham, 26 March, 1931 E Yth (HB)

League Club	Source	Date Signed	Seasons Played	Apps	Subs	Gls
Aston Villa	Jnrs	07.49				
Scunthorpe U.	Tr	06.54	54-55	17	-	0

BARRETT, Kenneth B.
Bromsgrove, 5 May, 1938 (OL)

League Club	Source	Date Signed	Seasons Played	Apps	Subs	Gls
Aston Villa	Stoke Wks	02.57	58	5	-	3
Lincoln C.	Tr	06.59	59-62	17	-	4

BARRETT, Leslie
Chelsea, 22 October, 1947 Eu23-1 (OL)

League Club	Source	Date Signed	Seasons Played	Apps	Subs	Gls
Fulham	Jnrs	10.65	65-76	420	3	74
Millwall	Tr	10.77	77	8	0	1

BARRETT, Michael J.
Bristol, 12 September, 1959 Died 1984 (W)

League Club	Source	Date Signed	Seasons Played	Apps	Subs	Gls
Bristol Rov.	Shirehampton	10.79	79-83	119	10	18

BARRETT, C. Roger
Doncaster, 19 October, 1946 (IF)

League Club	Source	Date Signed	Seasons Played	Apps	Subs	Gls
Doncaster Rov.	Doncaster U.	10.68	68	1	0	0

BARRETT, Ronald H.
Maidenhead, 22 July, 1939 (CF)

League Club	Source	Date Signed	Seasons Played	Apps	Subs	Gls
Grimsby T.	Maidenhead U.	08.58	58	3	-	0

BARRETT, Scott
Ilkeston, 2 April, 1963 (G)

League Club	Source	Date Signed	Seasons Played	Apps	Subs	Gls
Wolverhampton W.	Ilkeston T.	09.84	84-86	30	0	0
Stoke C.	Tr	07.87	87-89	51	0	0
Colchester U.	L	01.90	89	13	0	0
Stockport Co.	L	03.90	89	10	0	0

BARRETT, Thomas G.
Salford, 16 March, 1934 (WH)

League Club	Source	Date Signed	Seasons Played	Apps	Subs	Gls
Manchester U.	Jnrs	08.52				
Plymouth Arg.	Tr	07.57	57-58	26	-	1
Chester C.	Tr	07.60	60-61	41	-	2

BARRICK, Dean
Hemsworth, 30 September, 1969 (M)

League Club	Source	Date Signed	Seasons Played	Apps	Subs	Gls
Sheffield Wed.	YT	05.88	88-89	11	0	2
Rotherham U.	Tr	02.91	90-91	51	2	2

BARRIE, John
Hamilton, 17 May, 1925

League Club	Source	Date Signed	Seasons Played	Apps	Subs	Gls
Cardiff C.	Thorniewood Ath.	07.48				
Tranmere Rov.	Tr	11.48	48-50	14	-	3

BARRITT, Ronald
Huddersfield, 15 April, 1919 (CF)

League Club	Source	Date Signed	Seasons Played	Apps	Subs	Gls
Doncaster Rov.	Wombwell	01.49	48-49	13	-	6
Leeds U.	Frickley Colly	04.51	51	6	-	1
York C.	Tr	07.52	52	5	-	0

BARRON, James
Blyth, 19 July, 1913 Died 1969 (G)

League Club	Source	Date Signed	Seasons Played	Apps	Subs	Gls
Blackburn Rov.	Blyth Spartans	03.35	35-38	76	-	0
Darlington		06.46	46	23	-	0

BARRON, James
Tantobie, 19 October, 1943 (G)

League Club	Source	Date Signed	Seasons Played	Apps	Subs	Gls
Wolverhampton W.	Newcastle W.E.	11.61	63-64	8	-	0
Chelsea	Tr	04.65	65	1	0	0
Oxford U.	Tr	03.66	65-69	152	0	0
Nottingham F.	Tr	07.70	70-73	155	0	0
Swindon T.	Tr	08.74	74-76	79	0	0
Peterborough U.	Connecticut (USA)	08.77	77-80	21	0	0

BARRON, Paul G.
Woolwich, 16 September, 1953 (G)

League Club	Source	Date Signed	Seasons Played	Apps	Subs	Gls
Plymouth Arg.	Slough T.	07.76	76-77	44	0	0
Arsenal	Tr	07.78	78-79	8	0	0
Crystal Palace	Tr	08.80	80-82	90	0	0
West Bromwich A.	Tr	12.82	82-84	63	0	0
Stoke C.	L	01.85	84	1	0	0
Queens Park R.	Tr	03.85	85-86	32	0	0
Reading	L	12.86	86	4	0	0

BARRON, Roger W.
Northampton, 30 June, 1947 (G)

League Club	Source	Date Signed	Seasons Played	Apps	Subs	Gls
Northampton T.	App	07.65	67-68	17	0	0

BARRON, William
Houghton-le-Spring, 26 October, 1917 (FB)

League Club	Source	Date Signed	Seasons Played	Apps	Subs	Gls
Charlton Ath.	Annfield Plain	10.37	37	3	-	2
Northampton T.	Tr	05.38	38-50	167	-	3

BARROW, Graham
Chorley, 13 June, 1954 (M)

League Club	Source	Date Signed	Seasons Played	Apps	Subs	Gls
Wigan Ath.	Altrincham	07.81	81-85	173	6	36
Chester C.	Tr	07.86	86-91	202	0	15

BARROWCLIFFE, Geoffrey
Ilkeston, 18 October, 1931 (FB)

League Club	Source	Date Signed	Seasons Played	Apps	Subs	Gls
Derby Co.	Ilkeston T.	10.50	51-65	475	0	37

BARROWCLOUGH, Stewart J.
Barnsley, 29 October, 1951 Eu23-5 (W)

League Club	Source	Date Signed	Seasons Played	Apps	Subs	Gls
Barnsley	App	11.69	69	9	0	0
Newcastle U.	Tr	08.70	70-77	201	18	21
Birmingham C.	Tr	05.78	78	26	3	2
Bristol Rov.	Tr	07.79	79-80	60	1	14
Barnsley	Tr	02.81	80-82	46	6	1
Mansfield T.	Tr	08.83	83-84	50	4	10

BARRY, Kevin
Newcastle, 9 January, 1961 (G)

League Club	Source	Date Signed	Seasons Played	Apps	Subs	Gls
Darlington	Nottingham F. (App)	09.79	79-80	18	0	0

BARRY, Kevin A.
Woolwich, 13 September, 1930 (OL)

League Club	Source	Date Signed	Seasons Played	Apps	Subs	Gls
Charlton Ath.	Jnrs	12.47	52	3	-	0

BARRY, Michael J.
Hull, 22 May, 1953 Wu23-1 (M)

League Club	Source	Date Signed	Seasons Played	Apps	Subs	Gls
Huddersfield T.	App	06.70	70-72	21	5	0
Carlisle U.	Tr	05.73	73-76	73	8	10
Bristol Rov.	Tr	09.77	77-78	46	1	3

BARRY, Patrick P.
Southampton, 25 October, 1920 (FB)

League Club	Source	Date Signed	Seasons Played	Apps	Subs	Gls
Southampton		02.40				
Blackburn Rov.	Hyde U.	05.48				
Bournemouth	Tr	05.50	50	4	-	0

BARRY, Roy A.
Edinburgh, 19 September, 1942 (CH)

League Club	Source	Date Signed	Seasons Played	Apps	Subs	Gls
Coventry C.	Dunfermline Ath.	10.69	69-72	82	1	2
Crystal Palace	Tr	09.73	73-74	41	1	1

BART-WILLIAMS Christopher G.
Sierra Leone, 16 June, 1974 E Yth (M)

League Club	Source	Date Signed	Seasons Played	Apps	Subs	Gls
Leyton Orient	YT	07.91	90-91	34	2	2
Sheffield Wed.	Tr	11.91	91	12	3	0

BARTHOLOMEW, Henry
Motherwell, 18 January, 1920 (WH)

League Club	Source	Date Signed	Seasons Played	Apps	Subs	Gls
Exeter C.	Motherwell	05.47	47-48	66	-	6
Bournemouth	Tr	08.49				
Newport Co.	Tr	06.50	50	3	-	0

BARTLETT, Frank
Chester-le-Street, 8 November, 1930 (IF)

League Club	Source	Date Signed	Seasons Played	Apps	Subs	Gls
Barnsley	Blackhall Colly	08.50	52-62	296	-	65
Halifax T.	Tr	07.63	63	21	-	4

BARTLETT, Frederick L.
Reading, 5 March, 1913 (CH)

League Club	Source	Date Signed	Seasons Played	Apps	Subs	Gls
Queens Park R.		10.32	34-36	48	-	0
Leyton Orient	Tr	05.37	37-47	96	-	0

BARTLETT, Gordon
Chiswick, 3 December, 1955 (F)

League Club	Source	Date Signed	Seasons Played	Apps	Subs	Gls
Portsmouth	App	12.73	74	0	2	1

BARTLETT, Kevin F.
Portsmouth, 12 October, 1962 (F)

League Club	Source	Date Signed	Seasons Played	Apps	Subs	Gls
Portsmouth	App	10.80	80-81	0	3	0
Cardiff C.	Fareham T.	09.86	86-88	60	22	25
West Bromwich A.	Tr	02.89	88-89	25	12	10
Notts Co.	Tr	03.90	89-91	75	8	27

BARTLETT, Paul J.
Grimsby, 17 January, 1960 (W)

League Club	Source	Date Signed	Seasons Played	Apps	Subs	Gls
Derby Co.	App	12.77	77-79	7	6	0

BARTLETT, Terence R.
Cleethorpes, 28 August, 1948 (OR)

League Club	Source	Date Signed	Seasons Played	Apps	Subs	Gls
Grimsby T. (Am)	Jnrs	08.67	67	1	0	0

BARTLEY, Anthony
Stalybridge, 8 March, 1938 (OL)

League Club	Source	Date Signed	Seasons Played	Apps	Subs	Gls
Bolton W.	Stalybridge Celtic	09.56				
Bury	Stalybridge Celtic	11.58	58-64	116	-	24
Oldham Ath.	Tr	09.64	64-65	48	2	13
Chesterfield	Tr	07.66	66	12	0	2

BARTLEY, Daniel R.
Paulton, 3 October, 1947 E Yth (OL)

League Club	Source	Date Signed	Seasons Played	Apps	Subs	Gls
Bristol C.	App	10.64	65-72	92	8	7
Swansea C.	Tr	08.73	73-79	195	4	8
Hereford U.	Tr	03.80	79-82	112	2	6

BARTLEY, John R.
Camberwell, 15 September, 1958 (F)

League Club	Source	Date Signed	Seasons Played	Apps	Subs	Gls
Millwall	Welling U.	10.80	80-81	39	1	8

League Club	Source	Date Signed	Seasons Played	Apps	Subs	Gls
BARTON, Anthony E.						
Sutton, 8 April, 1937 E Sch						(OR)
Fulham	Jnrs	05.54	53-58	49	-	8
Nottingham F.	Tr	12.59	59-61	22	-	1
Portsmouth	Tr	12.61	61-66	129	1	34
BARTON, David						
Bishop Auckland, 9 May, 1959						(CD)
Newcastle U.	App	05.77	77-81	101	1	5
Blackburn Rov.	L	08.82	82	8	0	1
Darlington	Tr	02.83	82-83	49	0	3
BARTON, Douglas J.						
Ilsington, 31 July, 1927						(FB)
Reading	Ford Sports	02.49	50-52	10	-	1
Newport Co.	Tr	01.53	52-53	23	-	0
BARTON, Frank						
Barton-on-Humber, 22 October, 1947 E Yth						(M)
Scunthorpe U.	App	08.65	64-67	93	0	26
Carlisle U.	Tr	01.68	67-71	161	4	22
Blackpool	Tr	07.72	72	18	0	1
Grimsby T.	Tr	06.73	73-75	123	0	15
Bournemouth	Tr	06.76	76-77	66	0	13
Hereford U.	Tr	01.78	77-78	22	0	3
Bournemouth	Tr	09.78	78	22	0	2
BARTON, John B.						
Wigan, 27 April, 1942						(G)
Preston N.E.	Jnrs	05.59	58-65	48	0	0
Blackburn Rov.	Tr	06.66	66-71	68	0	0
BARTON, John S.						
Birmingham, 24 October, 1953						(RB)
Everton	Worcester C.	12.78	78-80	18	2	0
Derby Co.	Tr	03.82	81-83	68	1	1

Kevin Bartlett (Portsmouth, Cardiff City, West Bromwich Albion & Notts County)

League Club	Source	Date Signed	Seasons Played	Apps	Subs	Gls
BARTON, Kenneth R.						
Caernarfon, 20 September, 1937 Died 1982 W Sch						(FB)
Tottenham H.	Jnrs	10.56	60-63	4	-	0
Millwall	Tr	09.64				
Luton T.	Tr	12.64	64	11	-	0
BARTON, Leslie						
Rochdale, 20 March, 1920						(D)
Bolton W.		09.46				
New Brighton	Tr	08.49	49-50	64	-	1
BARTON, Michael G.						
Gainsborough, 23 September, 1973						(G)
Shrewsbury T.	YT	07.90	91	1	0	0
BARTON, Peter						
Barrow, 3 April, 1951						(G)
Barrow	App	04.69	68	2	0	0
BARTON, Reginald						
Chester, 4 March, 1942						(G)
Chester C.		06.61	61-64	14	-	0
BARTON, Roger						
Hoyland, 25 September, 1946						(W)
Wolverhampton W.	App	10.63				
Lincoln C.	Tr	07.64	64-65	28	0	0
Barnsley	Tr	07.66	66-68	52	3	3
BARTON, Warren D.						
Stoke Newington, 19 March, 1969						(D/M)
Maidstone U.	Leytonstone & Ilford	07.89	89	41	1	0
Wimbledon	Tr	06.90	90-91	79	0	4
BARTRAM, Per						
Denmark, 8 January, 1944						(CF)
Crystal Palace	Morton	08.69	69	8	2	2
BARTRAM, Samuel						
Jarrow, 22 January, 1914 Died 1981						(G)
Charlton Ath.	Boldon Villa	09.34	34-55	579	-	0

Sam Bartram (Charlton Athletic)

League Club	Source	Date Signed	Seasons Played	Career Record Apps	Subs	Gls
BARTRAM, Vincent L.						
Birmingham, 7 August, 1968						(G)
Wolverhampton W.	Jnrs	08.85	86-90	5	0	0
Blackpool	L	10.89	89	9	0	0
Bournemouth	Tr	07.91	91	46	0	0
BASEY, Philip						
Cardiff, 27 August, 1948						(OL)
Brentford	Jnrs	06.66	66	2	0	0
BASFORD, John						
Crewe, 24 July, 1925						(IF)
Crewe Alex.		04.48	48-53	146	-	52
Chester C.	Tr	01.54	53	10	-	1
BASHIR, Naseem						
Amersham, 12 September, 1969						(M)
Reading	Jnrs	06.88	89	1	2	1
BASON, Brian						
Epsom, 3 September, 1955 E Sch						(M)
Chelsea	App	09.72	72-76	18	1	1
Plymouth Arg.	Tr	09.77	77-80	126	3	10
Crystal Palace	Tr	03.81	80-81	25	2	0
Portsmouth	L	01.82	81	9	0	0
Reading	Tr	08.82	82	41	0	0
BASS, David						
Camberley, 29 November, 1974						(CD)
Reading (YT)	YT	07.91	91	2	1	0
BASSETT, David						
Hendon, 4 September, 1944 E Amat						(D)
Wimbledon	Walton & Hersham	08.74	77	35	0	0
BASSETT, George R.						
Birmingham, 12 May, 1943						(OL)
Coventry C.	Jnrs	08.61	61	1	-	0
BASSETT, Graham R.						
Sunderland, 6 October, 1964						(F)
Hartlepool U.	Sunderland (App)	08.83	83	4	3	0
Burnley	Tr	03.84				
BASSETT, William						
Brithdir, 8 June, 1912						(CH)
Cardiff C.	Aberaman	08.34	34-38	154	-	2
Crystal Palace	Tr	09.42	46-48	70	-	0
BASSHAM, Alan J.						
Kensington, 3 October, 1933 E Sch						(FB)
Brentford	Jnrs	10.51	53-57	43	-	0
BASTIN, Clifford S.						
Exeter, 14 March, 1912 Died 1991 E Sch/EF Lge/E-21						(OL)
Exeter C.	Jnrs	03.29	27-28	17	-	6
Arsenal	Tr	05.29	29-46	350	-	150
BASTOCK, Paul A.						
Leamington, 19 May, 1970						(G)
Cambridge U.	Coventry C. (YT)	03.88	87-88	12	0	0
BASTOW, Ian J.						
Torquay, 12 August, 1971						(W)
Torquay U.	YT	03.89	88-89	7	4	0
BATCH, Nigel A.						
Huddersfield, 9 November, 1957						(G)
Grimsby T.	Derby Co. (App)	07.76	76-86	348	0	0
Lincoln C.	Tr	07.87				
Darlington	Tr	09.88	88	30	0	0
Stockport Co.	L	03.89	88	12	0	0
Scunthorpe U.	(Retired)	08.91	91	1	0	0
BATCHELOR, Edward						
Rugby, 4 August, 1930						(HB)
Wolverhampton W.	Jnrs	10.47				
Swindon T.	Tr	08.50	50-54	91	-	0
BATEMAN, Albert						
Stocksbridge, 13 June, 1924						(OR)
Huddersfield T.	Yorkshire I. & S. Wks	09.43	46-48	73	-	14
BATEMAN, Arthur						
Audley, 12 June, 1918						
Crewe Alex.		11.42	46	3	-	0

League Club	Source	Date Signed	Seasons Played	Career Record Apps	Subs	Gls
BATEMAN, Colin						
Hemel Hempstead, 22 October, 1930						(FB)
Watford	Hemel Hempstead	03.53	54-57	50	-	0
BATEMAN, Ernest						
Hemel Hempstead, 5 April, 1929						(CH)
Watford	Hemel Hempstead	03.52	55-56	23	-	0
BATER, Philip T.						
Cardiff, 26 October, 1955 Wu21-2						(FB)
Bristol Rov.	App	10.73	74-80	211	1	2
Wrexham	Tr	09.81	81-82	73	0	1
Bristol Rov.	Tr	09.83	83-85	90	8	1
Brentford	Tr	05.86	86	19	0	2
Cardiff C.	Tr	07.87	87-88	67	9	0
BATES, Anthony N.						
Blidworth, 6 April, 1938						(CF)
Notts Co.	Blidworth Colly	07.59	58	1	-	0
BATES, Brian F.						
Stapleford, 4 December, 1944						(W)
Notts Co.	Loughborough Colly	07.63	63-68	125	3	15
Mansfield T.	Tr	07.69	69	20	0	3
BATES, Donald L.						
Brighton, 10 May, 1933						(WH)
Brighton & H.A.	Lewes	11.50	57	20	-	1
BATES, Edric T. (Ted)						
Thetford, 3 May, 1918						(IF)
Norwich C.	Thetford T.	09.36				
Southampton	Tr	05.37	37-52	202	-	64
BATES, Ernest						
Huddersfield, 10 June, 1935						(FB)
Huddersfield T.	Deighton Y.M.C.A.	08.55				
Bradford P.A.	Tr	05.57	57-58	44	-	0
BATES, George R.						
Sheffield, 21 November, 1923						(OR)
Sheffield Wed.	Shardlows	03.45				
Darlington	Tr	07.46	46	3	-	0
BATES, Jamie A.						
Croydon, 24 February, 1968						(D)
Brentford	YT	08.86	86-91	152	20	6
BATES, John W.						
Newcastle, 28 April, 1942						(OR)
Hartlepool U.	Consett	03.66	65	11	0	0
BATES, Keith						
Huddersfield, 1 September, 1933						(IL)
Halifax T. (Am)	Bradley R.	11.56	56	1	-	0
BATES, Mark						
Walsall, 25 April, 1965						(FB)
Walsall	App	04.83	82-83	6	0	0
Shrewsbury T.	Tr	07.84	84	7	1	0
BATES, Michael J.						
Doncaster, 19 September, 1947						(M)
Leeds U.	App	09.64	66-75	106	16	4
Walsall	Tr	06.76	76-77	84	1	4
Bradford C.	Tr	06.78	78-79	54	2	1
Doncaster Rov.	Tr	06.80	80	3	1	0
BATES, Philip D. (Chic)						
West Bromwich, 28 November, 1949						(F)
Shrewsbury T.	Stourbridge	05.74	74-77	160	0	45
Swindon T.	Tr	01.78	77-79	50	13	15
Bristol Rov.	Tr	03.80	79-80	26	3	4
Shrewsbury T.	Tr	12.80	80-85	114	20	19
BATES, William H.						
Eaton Bray, 13 January, 1922						(OR)
Luton T.	Waterlows	09.41	46	1	-	0
Watford		07.48	48	13	-	1
BATEY, N. Robert						
Greenhead, 18 October, 1912 Died 1988						(WH)
Carlisle U.		09.32	32-33	23	-	0
Preston N.E.	Tr	03.34	34-38	78	-	0
Leeds U.	Tr	04.46	46	8	-	0
Southport	Tr	06.47	47	29	-	0

BATHGATE, Sydney
Aberdeen, 20 December, 1919 Died 1962 (FB)

League Club	Source	Date Signed	Seasons Played	Apps	Subs	Gls
Chelsea	Parkvale	09.46	46-52	135	-	0

BATSON, Brendon M.
Grenada (WI), 6 February, 1953 E 'B' (RB)

League Club	Source	Date Signed	Seasons Played	Apps	Subs	Gls
Arsenal	App	06.71	71-73	6	4	0
Cambridge U.	Tr	01.74	73-77	162	1	6
West Bromwich A.	Tr	02.78	77-82	172	0	1

BATT, Victor T.
Dorking, 13 March, 1943 (W)

League Club	Source	Date Signed	Seasons Played	Apps	Subs	Gls
Reading	Jnrs	08.61	61-62	15	-	0

BATTY, David
Leeds, 2 December, 1968 Eu21-7/E 'B'/E-10 (M)

League Club	Source	Date Signed	Seasons Played	Apps	Subs	Gls
Leeds U.	YT	07.87	87-91	163	9	3

David Batty (Leeds United & England)

BATTY, Frederick R.
Stanley, 20 December, 1934 (CH)

League Club	Source	Date Signed	Seasons Played	Apps	Subs	Gls
Bradford P.A.	Stanley U.	01.56	55-58	56	-	0

BATTY, Lawrence W.
Westminster, 15 February, 1964 (G)

League Club	Source	Date Signed	Seasons Played	Apps	Subs	Gls
Fulham	Maidenhead U.	08.84	85-90	9	0	0
Brentford	Tr	02.91				

BATTY, Michael
Manchester, 10 July, 1944 (CH)

League Club	Source	Date Signed	Seasons Played	Apps	Subs	Gls
Manchester C.	App	07.61	62-64	13	-	0

BATTY, Paul W.
Doncaster, 9 January, 1964 (M)

League Club	Source	Date Signed	Seasons Played	Apps	Subs	Gls
Swindon T.	App	01.82	82-84	102	6	7
Chesterfield	Tr	07.85	85	24	2	0
Exeter C.	Tr	07.86	86-90	98	13	11

BATTY, Ronald R.
Lanchester, 5 October, 1925 Died 1971 (FB)

League Club	Source	Date Signed	Seasons Played	Apps	Subs	Gls
Newcastle U.	East Tanfield Colly	10.45	48-57	161	-	1
Gateshead	Tr	03.58	57-58	40	-	0

BATTY, Stanley G.
Tottenham, 14 February, 1917 (WH)

League Club	Source	Date Signed	Seasons Played	Apps	Subs	Gls
Aston Villa	Finchley	11.37				
Newport Co.	Tr	12.45	46-47	60	-	3

BATTYE, John E.
Scissett, 19 May, 1926 (WH)

League Club	Source	Date Signed	Seasons Played	Apps	Subs	Gls
Huddersfield T.	Jnrs	12.43	49-57	71	-	1
York C.	Tr	07.59	59	17	-	0

BAUGH, John R.
Uganda, 23 February, 1956 (G)

League Club	Source	Date Signed	Seasons Played	Apps	Subs	Gls
Exeter C.	St Lukes College	02.77	76-77	20	0	0

BAULD, Philip
Glasgow, 20 September, 1929 (HB)

League Club	Source	Date Signed	Seasons Played	Apps	Subs	Gls
Plymouth Arg.	Clyde	06.53				
Aldershot	Tr	07.54	54	3	-	0

BAURESS, Gary J.
Liverpool, 19 January, 1971 (D)

League Club	Source	Date Signed	Seasons Played	Apps	Subs	Gls
Tranmere Rov.	YT	08.89	89	1	0	0

BAVERSTOCK, Raymond
Southall, 3 December 1963 (FB)

League Club	Source	Date Signed	Seasons Played	Apps	Subs	Gls
Swindon T.	App	12.81	82	17	0	0

BAVIN, John
Ferriby, 25 May, 1921 (FB)

League Club	Source	Date Signed	Seasons Played	Apps	Subs	Gls
Tranmere Rov.	Arbroath	04.49	48	2	-	0

BAXTER, James
Cowdenbeath, 29 September, 1939 Su23-1/SF Lge/S-34 (M)

League Club	Source	Date Signed	Seasons Played	Apps	Subs	Gls
Sunderland	Glasgow Rangers	05.65	65-67	87	0	10
Nottingham F.	Tr	12.67	67-68	47	1	3

Jim Baxter (Raith Rovers, Glasgow Rangers, Sunderland, Nottingham Forest & Scotland)

League Club	Source	Date Signed	Seasons Played	Career Record Apps	Subs	Gls

BAXTER, James C.
Cowdenbeath, 8 November, 1925 (IF)

Barnsley	Dunfermline Ath.	08.45	46-51	224	-	56
Preston N.E.	Tr	07.52	52-58	245	-	65
Barnsley	Tr	07.59	59	26	-	4

BAXTER, Lawrence R.
Leicester, 24 November, 1931 (OR)

Northampton T.		03.52	52-53	18	-	1
Norwich C.	Tr	11.54	54	5	-	0
Gillingham	Tr	10.55	55-56	61	-	7
Torquay U.	Tr	09.57	57-61	164	-	22

BAXTER, Michael J.
Birmingham, 30 December, 1956 Died 1989

Preston N.E.	App	12.74	74-80	209	1	17
Middlesbrough	Tr	08.81	81-83	122	0	7
Portsmouth	Tr	06.84				

BAXTER, Paul A.
Hackney, 22 April, 1964 (D)

Crystal Palace	Tottenham H. (App)	09.81	81	1	0	0

BAXTER, Robert D.
Redcar, 4 February, 1937 (LB)

Darlington	Bo'ness	11.59	59-60	64	-	30
Brighton & H.A.	Tr	06.61	61-66	195	0	6
Torquay U.	Tr	07.67	67-68	58	4	6
Darlington	Tr	07.69	69	41	1	1

BAXTER, Stuart W.
Wolverhampton, 16 August, 1953 (CD)

Preston N.E.	App	10.71	72-74	34	7	1
Stockport Co.	Dundee	12.76	76	4	0	0

BAXTER, William
Methil, 21 September, 1924 (WH)

Wolverhampton W.	Jnrs	03.45	48-53	43	-	1
Aston Villa	Tr	11.53	53-56	98	-	6

BAXTER, William A.
Edinburgh, 23 April, 1939 (CH)

Ipswich T.	Broxburn Ath.	06.60	60-70	409	0	21
Hull C.	Tr	03.71	70-71	20	1	0
Watford	L	10.71	71	11	0	0
Northampton T.	Tr	06.72	72	41	0	4

BAXTER, William E.
Nottingham, 6 September, 1917 (CH)

Nottingham F.	Berridge Rd Inst.	12.36	37-46	15	-	0
Notts Co.	Tr	10.46	46-53	140	-	0

BAYES, Ashley J.
Lincoln, 19 April, 1972 (G)

Brentford	YT	07.90	89-91	2	0	0

BAYLEY, Thomas K.
Wednesbury, 25 June, 1921 (G)

Wrexham	Walsall (Am)	08.47	47	6	-	0

BAYLISS, Ronald
Belfast, 20 September, 1944 (D)

Reading		02.65	64-67	35	3	1
Bradford C.	Tr	07.68	68-69	35	4	0

BAYLY, Martin J.
Dublin, 14 September, 1966 IR Yth (M)

Wolverhampton W.	App	07.84	83-84	9	1	0

BAYNHAM, John
Rhondda, 21 April, 1918 (W)

Leyton Orient	Brentford (Am)	03.46	46-47	60	-	7
Swindon T.	Tr	08.48	48	4	-	1

BAYNHAM, Ronald L.
Birmingham, 10 June, 1929 E'B'-1/EF Lge/E-3 (G)

Luton T.	Worcester C.	11.51	52-64	388	-	0

BAZELEY, Darren S.
Northampton, 5 October, 1972 Eu21-1 (W)

Watford	YT	05.91	89-91	26	16	6

BAZLEY, John A.
Runcorn, 4 October, 1936 (OR)

Oldham Ath.	Bangor Univ.	10.56	56-61	130	-	19

League Club	Source	Date Signed	Seasons Played	Career Record Apps	Subs	Gls

BEACH, Douglas F.
Watford, 2 February, 1920 (FB)

Luton T.	Sheffield Wed. (Am)	08.45	46	23	-	0
Southend U.	Tr	07.47	47-48	41	-	0

BEACOCK, Gary C.
Scunthorpe, 22 January, 1960 (M)

Grimsby T.	Netherlands	05.80	80-82	10	7	0
Hereford U.	Tr	08.83	83-85	22	5	4

BEADLE, Peter C.
Lambeth, 13 May, 1972 (F)

Gillingham	YT	05.90	88-91	42	25	14

BEADNELL, William
Sunderland, 25 January, 1933 (CF)

Chesterfield	Burnley (Am)	06.50				
Middlesbrough		05.53				
Southport	Tr	05.54	54-55	63	-	19

BEAGRIE, Peter S.
Middlesbrough, 29 November, 1965 Eu21-2/E'B' (LW)

Mddlesbrough	Jnrs	09.83	84-85	24	8	2
Sheffield U.	Tr	08.86	86-87	81	3	11
Stoke C.	Tr	06.88	88-89	54	0	7
Everton	Tr	11.89	89-91	48	15	5
Sunderland	L	09.91	91	5	0	1

Peter Beagrie (Middlesbrough, Sheffield United, Stoke City & Everton)

BEAL, Philip
Godstone, 8 January, 1945 EYth (D)

Tottenham H.	App	01.62	63-74	330	3	1
Brighton & H.A.	Tr	07.75	75-76	9	1	0
Crewe Alex.	Memphis (USA)	08.79	79	4	0	0

BEALE, John M.
Portsmouth, 16 October, 1930 (WH)

Portsmouth	Jnrs	08.48	51-52	14	-	1

BEAMAN, Ralph W.
Willenhall, 14 January, 1943 (F)

Walsall		12.60	61	1	-	0

League Club	Source	Date Signed	Seasons Played	Apps	Subs	Gls

BEAMENT, Roger
Croxley, 28 September, 1937 (G)

League Club	Source	Date Signed	Seasons Played	Apps	Subs	Gls
Watford (Am)	Croxley B.C.	07.56	56	1	-	0

BEAMISH, Kenneth G.
Bebington, 25 August, 1947 (F)

League Club	Source	Date Signed	Seasons Played	Apps	Subs	Gls
Tranmere Rov.	Jnrs	07.66	65-71	176	1	49
Brighton & H.A.	Tr	03.72	71-73	86	10	27
Blackburn Rov.	Tr	05.74	74-76	86	0	19
Port Vale	Tr	09.76	76-78	84	1	29
Bury	Tr	09.78	78-79	49	0	20
Tranmere Rov.	Tr	11.79	79-80	57	2	15
Swindon T.	Tr	08.81	81	1	1	0

BEAN, Alan
Doncaster, 17 January, 1935 (CH)

League Club	Source	Date Signed	Seasons Played	Apps	Subs	Gls
Blackburn Rov.	Jnrs	04.52	52-54	2	-	0

BEAN, Alfred S.
Lincoln, 25 August, 1915 (LB)

League Club	Source	Date Signed	Seasons Played	Apps	Subs	Gls
Lincoln C.	Lincoln Corries	05.35	34-48	171	-	10

BEAN, Ronald E.
Crayford, 10 April, 1926 (G)

League Club	Source	Date Signed	Seasons Played	Apps	Subs	Gls
Gillingham	Gravesend & Nft	06.51	51	3	-	0

BEANEY, William R.
Southampton, 29 May, 1954 (FB)

League Club	Source	Date Signed	Seasons Played	Apps	Subs	Gls
Southampton	App	06.72	72-74	2	1	0

BEANLAND, Anthony
Bradford, 11 January, 1944 (WH)

League Club	Source	Date Signed	Seasons Played	Apps	Subs	Gls
Blackpool	App	01.62				
Southport	Tr	07.62	62-65	143	0	3
Southend U.	Tr	03.66	65-66	57	0	3
Wrexham	Tr	07.67	67-68	84	0	5
Bradford P.A.	Tr	06.69	69	29	2	1

BEARD, Malcolm
Cannock, 3 May, 1942 E Yth (WH)

League Club	Source	Date Signed	Seasons Played	Apps	Subs	Gls
Birmingham C.	Jnrs	05.59	60-70	350	1	27
Aston Villa	Tr	07.71	71-72	5	1	0

BEARDALL, James T.
Whitefield, 18 October, 1946 (CF)

League Club	Source	Date Signed	Seasons Played	Apps	Subs	Gls
Blackburn Rov.	Bury (Am)	03.68	67-68	4	2	1
Oldham Ath.	Tr	05.69	69	21	1	10

BEARDS, Alan
Normanton, 19 October, 1932 (OL)

League Club	Source	Date Signed	Seasons Played	Apps	Subs	Gls
Bolton W.	Whitewood Jnrs	10.50	50-53	14	-	2
Swindon T.	Tr	03.54	53-54	21	-	4
Stockport Co.	Tr	07.55	55	5	-	0

BEARDSHAW, E. Colin
South Hetton, 26 November, 1912 Died 1977 (FB)

League Club	Source	Date Signed	Seasons Played	Apps	Subs	Gls
Gateshead		02.36	35	12	-	0
Stockport Co.	Tr	05.36	37	18	-	0
Bradford C.	Tr	07.38	38	42	-	0
Southport	Cork U.	10.48	48-50	61	-	0

BEARDSLEY, Donald T.
Alyth, 23 October, 1946 (FB)

League Club	Source	Date Signed	Seasons Played	Apps	Subs	Gls
Hull C.	App	11.64	66-72	128	2	0
Doncaster Rov.	L	03.72	71	10	0	0
Grimsby T.	Tr	08.73	73-74	66	0	0

BEARDSLEY, Peter A.
Newcastle, 18 January, 1961 EF Lge/E'B'/E-49 (F)

League Club	Source	Date Signed	Seasons Played	Apps	Subs	Gls
Carlisle U.	Wallsend B.C.	08.79	79-81	93	11	22
Manchester U.	Vancouver (Can)	09.82				
Newcastle U.	Vancouver (Can)	09.83	83-86	146	1	61
Liverpool	Tr	07.87	87-90	120	11	46
Everton	Tr	08.91	91	42	0	15

BEARDSMORE, Russell P.
Wigan, 28 September, 1968 Eu21-5 (M)

League Club	Source	Date Signed	Seasons Played	Apps	Subs	Gls
Manchester U.	App	09.86	88-90	30	26	4
Blackburn Rov.	L	12.91	91	1	1	0

BEARPARK, Ian H.
Stonehouse (Lk), 13 January, 1939 (G)

League Club	Source	Date Signed	Seasons Played	Apps	Subs	Gls
Bristol Rov.	Stonehouse Violet	08.60	60	2	-	0

BEARRYMAN, Henry W.
Wandsworth, 26 September, 1924 (WH)

League Club	Source	Date Signed	Seasons Played	Apps	Subs	Gls
Chelsea	Jnrs	09.41				
Colchester U.	Tr	(N/L)	50-53	174	-	3

BEASANT, David J.
Willesden, 20 March, 1959 E-'B'/E-2 (G)

League Club	Source	Date Signed	Seasons Played	Apps	Subs	Gls
Wimbledon	Edgware T.	08.79	79-87	340	0	0
Newcastle U.	Tr	06.88	88	20	0	0
Chelsea	Tr	01.89	88-91	116	0	0

BEASLEY, Albert E. (Pat)
Stourbridge, 27 July, 1913 Died 1986 E-1 (WH)

League Club	Source	Date Signed	Seasons Played	Apps	Subs	Gls
Arsenal	Stourbridge	05.31	31-36	79	-	19
Huddersfield T.	Tr	10.36	36-38	108	-	24
Fulham	Tr	12.45	46-49	153	-	13
Bristol C.	Tr	08.50	50-51	66	-	5

BEASLEY, Andrew
Sedgley, 5 February, 1964 (G)

League Club	Source	Date Signed	Seasons Played	Apps	Subs	Gls
Luton T.	App	02.82				
Mansfield T.	Tr	07.84	84-91	94	0	0
Peterborough U.	L	07.86	86	7	0	0
Scarborough	L	03.88	87	4	0	0

BEASON, Malcolm L.
Dulwich, 1 December, 1955 (M)

League Club	Source	Date Signed	Seasons Played	Apps	Subs	Gls
Crystal Palace	App	08.73				
Leyton Orient	Tr	09.75	75	0	1	0

BEATON, William
Dunfermline, 30 September, 1935 (G)

League Club	Source	Date Signed	Seasons Played	Apps	Subs	Gls
Aston Villa	Dunfermline Ath.	10.58	58	1	-	0

BEATTIE, Andrew
Aberdeen, 11 August, 1913 Died 1938 S-7 (FB)

League Club	Source	Date Signed	Seasons Played	Apps	Subs	Gls
Preston N.E.	Inverurie Loco	05.35	34-46	125	-	5

BEATTIE, Andrew H.
Liverpool, 9 February, 1964 (CD)

League Club	Source	Date Signed	Seasons Played	Apps	Subs	Gls
Cambridge U.	App	02.82	83-87	94	3	2

Peter Beardsley (Carlisle United, Manchester United, Newcastle United, Liverpool, Everton & England)

BEATTIE, Bradley
Torquay, 20 August, 1957 (IF)

League Club	Source	Date Signed	Seasons Played	Apps	Subs	Gls
Torquay U. (App)	App	11.73	73-74	2	2	0

BEATTIE, George
Aberdeen, 16 June, 1925 (IF)

League Club	Source	Date Signed	Seasons Played	Apps	Subs	Gls
Southampton	Rosslyn Rosemount	08.47	47	1	-	0
Newport Co.	Gloucester C.	09.50	50-52	113	-	26
Bradford P.A.	Tr	07.53	53-54	53	-	16

BEATTIE, T. Kevin
Carlisle, 18 December, 1953 E Yth/E-9 (CD)

League Club	Source	Date Signed	Seasons Played	Apps	Subs	Gls
Ipswich T.	App	07.71	72-80	225	3	24
Colchester U. (N/C)	Tr	07.82	82	3	1	0
Middlesbrough	Tr	11.82	82	3	1	0

Kevin Beattie (Ipswich Town, Colchester United, Middlesbrough & England)

BEATTIE, Richard S.
Glasgow, 24 October, 1936 Su23-3/SF Lge (G)

League Club	Source	Date Signed	Seasons Played	Apps	Subs	Gls
Portsmouth	Glasgow Celtic	08.59	59-61	122	-	0
Peterborough U.	Tr	06.62	62	10	-	0

BEATTIE, Robert
Kilmarnock, 24 January, 1916 Died 1984 S-1 (IF)

League Club	Source	Date Signed	Seasons Played	Apps	Subs	Gls
Preston N.E.	Kilmarnock	09.37	37-53	264	-	49

BEATTIE, Stuart R.
Stevenston, 10 July, 1967 (CD)

League Club	Source	Date Signed	Seasons Played	Apps	Subs	Gls
Doncaster Rov.	Glasgow Rangers	01.87	86-88	26	0	1

BEATTIE, Thomas
Sheepwash, 12 March, 1921 (CF)

League Club	Source	Date Signed	Seasons Played	Apps	Subs	Gls
Gateshead	Morpeth T.	01.47	46-47	20	-	4

BEAUCHAMP, Joseph D.
Oxford, 13 March, 1971 (W)

League Club	Source	Date Signed	Seasons Played	Apps	Subs	Gls
Oxford U.	YT	05.89	88-91	30	5	7
Swansea C.	L	10.91	91	5	0	2

BEAUMONT, Alan
Liverpool, 9 January, 1927 (FB)

League Club	Source	Date Signed	Seasons Played	Apps	Subs	Gls
Chester C.		04.49	48	5	-	0

BEAUMONT, Christopher P.
Sheffield, 5 December, 1965 (W)

League Club	Source	Date Signed	Seasons Played	Apps	Subs	Gls
Rochdale	Denaby U.	07.88	88	31	3	7
Stockport Co.	Tr	07.89	89-91	97	4	22

BEAUMONT, David A.
Edinburgh, 10 December, 1963 S Yth/Su21-1 CD)

League Club	Source	Date Signed	Seasons Played	Apps	Subs	Gls
Luton T.	Dundee U.	01.89	88-91	66	10	0

BEAUMONT, Frank
Hoyland, 22 December, 1939 E Yth (IF)

League Club	Source	Date Signed	Seasons Played	Apps	Subs	Gls
Barnsley	Jnrs	12.57	57-61	107	-	37
Bury	Tr	09.61	61-63	68	-	12
Stockport Co.	Tr	09.64	64-65	52	3	4

BEAUMONT, Nigel
Hemsworth, 11 February, 1967 (CD)

League Club	Source	Date Signed	Seasons Played	Apps	Subs	Gls
Bradford C.	YT	07.85	85	2	0	0
Wrexham	Tr	07.88	88-91	112	3	4

BEAVEN, Kenneth H.
Bovingdon, 26 December, 1949 (F)

League Club	Source	Date Signed	Seasons Played	Apps	Subs	Gls
Luton T. (App)	App	12.66	67	1	0	0

BEAVER, David
Kirkby-in-Ashfield, 4 April, 1966 (M)

League Club	Source	Date Signed	Seasons Played	Apps	Subs	Gls
Notts Co.	App	04.84	84	1	0	0

BEAVON, Cyril
Barnsley, 27 September, 1937 E Yth (RB)

League Club	Source	Date Signed	Seasons Played	Apps	Subs	Gls
Wolverhampton W.	Jnrs	12.54				
Oxford U.	Tr	01.59	62-68	271	2	7

BEAVON, David G.
Nottingham, 8 December, 1961 (D)

League Club	Source	Date Signed	Seasons Played	Apps	Subs	Gls
Notts Co.	App	12.79	80	5	0	0
Lincoln C.	Tr	11.81	81-82	7	1	0
Northampton T.	Tr	03.83	82	2	0	0

BEAVON, M. Stuart
Wolverhampton, 30 November, 1958 (M)

League Club	Source	Date Signed	Seasons Played	Apps	Subs	Gls
Tottenham H.	App	07.76	78-79	3	1	0
Notts Co.	L	12.79	79	6	0	0
Reading	Tr	07.80	80-89	380	16	44
Northampton T.	Tr	08.90	90-91	74	0	13

BEBBINGTON, R. Keith
Nantwich, 4 August, 1943 (W)

League Club	Source	Date Signed	Seasons Played	Apps	Subs	Gls
Stoke C.	Jnrs	08.60	62-65	99	2	17
Oldham Ath.	Tr	08.66	66-71	237	0	38
Rochdale	Tr	07.72	72-73	57	3	6

BEBBINGTON, Peter A.
Oswestry, 13 October, 1946 (FB)

League Club	Source	Date Signed	Seasons Played	Apps	Subs	Gls
Leicester C.	Oswestry T.	10.65				
Barrow	Tr	11.67	67-68	51	1	3
Stockport Co.	Tr	07.69	69	16	1	1

BECK, John A.
Edmonton, 25 May, 1954 (M)

League Club	Source	Date Signed	Seasons Played	Apps	Subs	Gls
Queens Park R.	App	05.72	72-75	32	8	1
Coventry C.	Tr	06.76	76-78	60	9	6
Fulham	Tr	10.78	78-81	113	1	12
Bournemouth	Tr	09.82	82-85	132	5	13
Cambridge U.	Tr	07.86	86-89	105	7	11

BECKERS, Peter
Dundee, 3 October, 1947 (OL)

League Club	Source	Date Signed	Seasons Played	Apps	Subs	Gls
Grimsby T.	Craigmore Th.	11.64	64	1	-	0

BECKETT, Roy W.
Stoke, 20 March, 1928 (HB)

League Club	Source	Date Signed	Seasons Played	Apps	Subs	Gls
Stoke C.	Jnrs	04.45	50-53	14	-	1

BECKETT, William
Liverpool, 4 July, 1915 (OL)

League Club	Source	Date Signed	Seasons Played	Apps	Subs	Gls
New Brighton	Litherland	11.34	34-35	25	-	4
Tranmere Rov.	Tr	07.36				
Blackpool	South Liverpool	04.37				
Bradford C.	Tr	07.38	38	5	-	1
Watford	Tr	05.39	46	7	-	1
Northampton T.	Tr	06.47				

BECKFORD, Darren R.
Manchester, 12 May, 1967 E Sch/E Yth (F)

League Club	Source	Date Signed	Seasons Played	Apps	Subs	Gls
Manchester C.	App	08.84	84-86	7	4	0
Bury	L	10.85	85	12	0	5
Port Vale	Tr	03.87	86-90	169	9	71
Norwich C.	Tr	07.91	91	25	5	7

BECKFORD, Jason N.
Manchester, 14 February, 1970 E Yth (W)

League Club	Source	Date Signed	Seasons Played	Apps	Subs	Gls
Manchester C.	YT	08.87	87-90	8	12	0
Blackburn Rov.	L	03.91	90	3	1	0
Port Vale	L	09.91	91	4	1	1
Birmingham C.	Tr	01.92	91	2	2	1

League Club	Source	Date Signed	Seasons Played	Apps	Subs	Gls
BEDFORD, N. Brian						
Ferndale, 24 December, 1933						(CF)
Reading		04.54	54	3	-	1
Southampton	Tr	07.55	55	5	-	2
Bournemouth	Tr	08.56	56-58	75	-	32
Queens Park R.	Tr	07.59	59-64	258	-	163
Scunthorpe U.	Tr	09.65	65-66	37	0	23
Brentford	Tr	09.66	66	21	0	10
BEDFORD, Kevin E.						
Carshalton, 26 December, 1968						(LB)
Wimbledon	App	11.86	87	4	0	0
Aldershot	L	02.88	87	16	0	0
Colchester U.	Tr	07.88	88	24	2	0
BEDSON, Raymond A.						
Newcastle-u-Lyme, 4 February, 1929						(HB)
Crewe Alex.		08.52	53	2	-	0
BEE, Frank E.						
Nottingham, 23 January, 1927						(IF)
Sunderland	Nottingham F. (Am)	06.47	47	5	-	1
Blackburn Rov.	Tr	03.49	48	4	-	0
BEEBY, Oliver						
Leicester, 2 October, 1934 E Yth						(FB)
Leicester C.		05.53	55	1	-	0
Notts Co.	Tr	06.59	59	13	-	0
BEECH, Cyril						
Tamworth, 12 March, 1925						(OL)
Swansea C.	Merthyr Tydfil	08.49	49-53	133	-	29
Newport Co.	Worcester C.	07.55	55-56	39	-	8
BEECH, Gilbert						
Tamworth, 9 January, 1922						(FB)
Swansea C.	Merthyr Tydfil	11.49	49-57	157	-	2
BEECH, Harold W.						
Kearsley, 7 January, 1946						(WH)
Bolton W.	Jnrs	06.64	65-66	14	1	0
Stockport Co.	Tr	07.67	67	2	2	0
BEECH, Kenneth						
Stoke, 18 March, 1958						(M)

League Club	Source	Date Signed	Seasons Played	Apps	Subs	Gls
Port Vale	App	01.76	74-80	169	6	17
Walsall	Tr	08.81	81-82	78	1	5
Peterborough U.	Tr	08.83	83-84	58	2	5
BEEKS, Stephen J.						
Staines, 10 April, 1971						(M)
Aldershot	YT	07.89	89-90	0	3	0
BEEL, William J. L.						
Leominster, 23 August, 1945						(G)
Shrewsbury T.	App	07.63	62-63	3	-	0
Birmingham C.		01.65	64	1	-	0
BEENEY, Mark R.						
Tunbridge Wells, 30 December, 1967						(G)
Gillingham	YT	08.86	86	2	0	0
Maidstone U.	Tr	02.87	89-90	50	0	0
Aldershot	L	03.90	89	7	0	0
Brighton & H.A.	Tr	03.91	90-91	27	0	0
BEER, Alan D.						
Swansea, 11 March, 1950 W Amat						(F)
Swansea C.	West End	02.71	70-71	9	5	3
Exeter C.	Weymouth	11.74	74-77	114	0	52
BEER, Colin						
Exeter, 15 August, 1936						(OR)
Exeter C.	Exbourne	05.56	56-57	5	-	2
BEESLEY, Colin						
Stockton, 6 October, 1951						(W)
Sunderland	App	01.69	68	0	3	0
BEESLEY, Michael A.						
Epping Forest, 10 June, 1942						(IF)
West Ham U.	Jnrs	10.59	60	2	-	1
Southend U.	Tr	08.62	62-64	79	-	34
Peterborough U.	Tr	07.65	65-66	23	2	3
Southend U.	Tr	08.67	67-70	121	14	11
BEESLEY, Paul						
Liverpool, 21 July, 1965						(CD)
Wigan Ath.	Marine	09.84	84-89	153	2	3
Leyton Orient	Tr	10.89	89	32	0	1
Sheffield U.	Tr	07.90	90-91	75	2	3

Darren Beckford (Manchester City, Port Vale & Norwich City)

League Club	Source	Date Signed	Seasons Played	Career Record Apps	Subs	Gls

BEESTON, Carl F.
Stoke, 30 June, 1967 Eu21-1 (M)

League Club	Source	Date Signed	Seasons Played	Apps	Subs	Gls
Stoke C.	App	06.85	84-91	154	5	9

BEESTON, Thomas
Gateshead, 26 April, 1933 (G)

League Club	Source	Date Signed	Seasons Played	Apps	Subs	Gls
Gateshead (Am)		09.56	56	1	-	0

BEGG, James A.
Dumfries, 14 February, 1930 (G)

League Club	Source	Date Signed	Seasons Played	Apps	Subs	Gls
Liverpool	Auchinleck T.	04.52				
Bradford P.A.	Tr	08.53	53-54	10	-	0

BEGLIN, James M.
Waterford, 29 July, 1963 IR'B'/IR-15 (LB)

League Club	Source	Date Signed	Seasons Played	Apps	Subs	Gls
Liverpool	Shamrock Rov.	05.83	84-86	64	0	2
Leeds U.	Tr	07.89	89	18	1	0
Plymouth Arg.	L	11.89	89	5	0	0
Blackburn Rov.	L	10.90	90	6	0	0

BEIGHTON, Graham
Sheffield, 1 July, 1939 (G)

League Club	Source	Date Signed	Seasons Played	Apps	Subs	Gls
Sheffield Wed.	Firthbrown Tools	03.59				
Stockport Co.	Tr	06.61	61-65	137	0	0
Wrexham	Tr	01.66	65	23	0	0

BEINLICH, Stefan
Berlin (Germany), 13 January, 1972 (F)

League Club	Source	Date Signed	Seasons Played	Apps	Subs	Gls
Aston Villa	Bergman Bosnig	10.91	91	0	2	0

BEKKER, Jan F.
Cardiff, 24 December, 1951 (F)

League Club	Source	Date Signed	Seasons Played	Apps	Subs	Gls
Swansea C.	Bridgend T.	02.75	74-75	16	6	4

BELCHER, James A.
Stepney, 31 October, 1932 (WH)

League Club	Source	Date Signed	Seasons Played	Apps	Subs	Gls
Leyton Orient	Jnrs	03.50				
West Ham U.	Snowdown Colly	08.52				
Crystal Palace	Tr	06.54	54-57	128	-	22
Ipswich T.	Tr	05.58	58-59	27	-	0
Brentford	Tr	07.61	61	30	-	1

BELFIELD, Michael R.
Wandsworth, 10 June, 1961 (F)

League Club	Source	Date Signed	Seasons Played	Apps	Subs	Gls
Wimbledon		03.80	79-82	16	8	4

BELFITT, Rodney M.
Doncaster, 30 October, 1945 (CF)

League Club	Source	Date Signed	Seasons Played	Apps	Subs	Gls
Leeds U.	Retford T.	07.63	64-71	57	16	17
Ipswich T.	Tr	11.71	71-72	40	0	13
Everton	Tr	11.72	72	14	2	2
Sunderland	Tr	10.73	73-74	36	3	4
Fulham	L	11.74	74	6	0	1
Huddersfield T.	Tr	02.75	74-75	34	0	8

BELFON, Frank
Wellingborough, 18 February, 1965 (W)

League Club	Source	Date Signed	Seasons Played	Apps	Subs	Gls
Northampton T.	Jnrs	04.82	81-84	64	15	15

BELFORD, Dale
Burton-on-Trent, 11 July, 1967 (G)

League Club	Source	Date Signed	Seasons Played	Apps	Subs	Gls
Aston Villa	App	07.85				
Notts Co.	Sutton Coldfield T.	03.87	87	1	0	0

BELL, Alexander S.
Ayr, 13 March, 1931 (G)

League Club	Source	Date Signed	Seasons Played	Apps	Subs	Gls
Exeter C.	Partick Th.	08.54	54-57	40	-	0
Grimsby T.	Tr	07.58	58	8	-	0

BELL, Andrew D.
Taunton, 6 May, 1956 (CF)

League Club	Source	Date Signed	Seasons Played	Apps	Subs	Gls
Exeter C.	Taunton T.	07.79	79	2	1	0

BELL, Anthony W.
North Shields, 27 February, 1955 (G)

League Club	Source	Date Signed	Seasons Played	Apps	Subs	Gls
Newcastle U.	App	03.73	74	1	0	0

BELL, Arthur
Sedgefield, 5 March, 1931

League Club	Source	Date Signed	Seasons Played	Apps	Subs	Gls
Barrow	Hylton Colly	08.50	50	1	-	0

BELL, Barry R.
Woolwich, 9 April, 1941 (CF)

League Club	Source	Date Signed	Seasons Played	Apps	Subs	Gls
Millwall	Jnrs	10.58	58	1	-	0

BELL, Charles T.
Sheffield, 21 March, 1945 (CH)

League Club	Source	Date Signed	Seasons Played	Apps	Subs	Gls
Sheffield U.	Jnrs	01.64	66	3	0	1
Chesterfield	Tr	06.68	68-72	149	3	11

BELL, Colin
Horsley, 24 March, 1926 (WH)

League Club	Source	Date Signed	Seasons Played	Apps	Subs	Gls
Derby Co.	Holbrook	09.46	50-54	77	-	2

BELL, Colin
Hesleden (Dm), 26 February, 1946 Eu23-2/EF Lge/E-48 (M)

League Club	Source	Date Signed	Seasons Played	Apps	Subs	Gls
Bury	Horden Colly	07.63	63-65	82	0	25
Manchester C.	Tr	03.66	65-78	393	1	117

Colin Bell (Bury, Manchester City & England)

BELL, David
Corbridge, 24 December, 1909 (FB)

League Club	Source	Date Signed	Seasons Played	Apps	Subs	Gls
Newcastle U.	Wallyford Bluebell	05.30	31-33	21	-	1
Derby Co.	Tr	06.34	34-38	52	-	0
Ipswich T.	Tr	10.38	38-49	171	-	3

BELL, David J.
Carlisle, 13 September, 1939 (OR)

League Club	Source	Date Signed	Seasons Played	Apps	Subs	Gls
Carlisle U.	Jnrs	03.57	58	1	-	1

BELL, Derek M.
Boston, 30 October, 1956 (F)

League Club	Source	Date Signed	Seasons Played	Apps	Subs	Gls
Derby Co.	App	10.74				
Halifax T.	Tr	05.75	75-78	104	8	21
Sheffield Wed.	L	03.76	75	5	0	1
Barnsley	Tr	10.78	78-79	46	1	21
Lincoln C.	Tr	11.79	79-82	69	14	33
Chesterfield	Tr	08.83	83	15	2	3
Scunthorpe U.	Tr	01.84	83-84	22	0	7

BELL, Derek S.
Newcastle, 19 December, 1963 (M)

League Club	Source	Date Signed	Seasons Played	Apps	Subs	Gls
Newcastle U.	App	12.81	81-82	3	1	0

League Club	Source	Date Signed	Seasons Played	Apps	Subs	Gls
BELL, Douglas K.						
Paisley, 5 September, 1959 Su21-2						(M)
Shrewsbury T.	Hibernian	12.87	87-89	47	3	6
Hull C.	L	03.89	88	4	0	0
Birmingham C.	Tr	10.89	89-90	15	1	0
BELL, Eric						
Manchester, 27 November, 1929 E'B'-2/EF Lge						(WH)
Bolton W.		11.49	50-57	102	-	1
BELL, Eric J.						
Bedlington, 13 February, 1922 EF Lge						(WH)
Blackburn Rov.	Blyth Spartans	05.45	46-56	323	-	9
BELL, Ernest						
Hull, 22 July, 1918 Died 1968						(IF)
Hull C.	Blundell S.O.B.	03.36	36-37	27	-	5
Mansfield T.	Tr	05.38	38	28	-	1
Aldershot	Tr	07.39				
Hull C.	Tr	08.46	46	5	-	1
BELL, Gary						
Halesowen, 4 April, 1947						(LB)
Cardiff C.	Lower Gornal Ath.	02.66	66-73	222	2	10
Hereford U.	L	03.74	73	8	0	0
Newport Co.	Tr	08.74	74-77	126	0	5
BELL, George W.						
South Shields, 26 March, 1937						(F)
Doncaster Rov.	St Marys B.C.	05.55	55	1	-	0
Cardiff C.	Frickley Colly	03.59				
BELL, Graham T. A.						
Middleton, 30 March, 1955 E Yth						(M)
Oldham Ath.	Chadderton	12.73	74-78	166	4	9
Preston N.E.	Tr	03.79	78-82	140	3	9
Huddersfield T.	L	11.81	81	2	0	0
Carlisle U.	Tr	08.83	83	11	3	0
Bolton W.	Tr	02.84	83-85	86	6	3
Tranmere Rov.	Tr	08.86	86	41	1	4
BELL, Harold						
Liverpool, 22 November, 1924						(CH)
Tranmere Rov.	Jnrs	11.41	46-59	595	-	11
BELL, Harold D.						
Sunderland, 14 October, 1924						(WH)
Middlesbrough	Hylton Colly	09.45	46-54	290	-	9
Darlington	Tr	09.55	55-58	125	-	19
BELL, Ian C.						
Middlesbrough, 14 November, 1958						(M)
Middlesbrough	App	12.76	77-80	10	0	1
Mansfield T.	Tr	07.81	81-82	82	2	12
BELL, John A.						
Edinburgh, 25 April, 1936						(WH)
Swindon T.	Stirling A.	07.60	60-61	29	-	2
BELL, John H.						
Morpeth, 29 August, 1919						(LB)
Gateshead		01.45	46-49	50	-	0
BELL, John R. (Jackie)						
Evenwood, 17 October, 1939						(WH)
Newcastle U.	Jnrs	10.56	57-61	111	-	8
Norwich C.	Tr	07.62	62-63	48	-	3
Colchester U.	Tr	06.65	65	7	0	0
BELL, Joseph						
Sunderland, 28 July, 1924						(FB)
Sunderland		01.44				
Chesterfield	Stockton	05.46	47-48	37	-	0
Coventry C.	Tr	06.49	49-51	10	-	0
BELL, Michael						
Newcastle, 15 November, 1971						(W)
Northampton T.	YT	07.90	89-91	50	14	4
BELL, Norman						
Sunderland, 16 November, 1955						(CF)
Wolverhampton W.	App	11.73	75-81	58	22	17
Blackburn Rov.	Tr	11.81	81-83	57	4	10
BELL, Peter						
Grangemouth, 10 April, 1935						(HB)
Plymouth Arg.	Gairdoch Jnrs	07.54	55	1	-	0

League Club	Source	Date Signed	Seasons Played	Apps	Subs	Gls
BELL, Robert						
Glasgow, 23 March, 1935 S Sch						(IF)
Plymouth Arg.	Partick Th.	11.55	55	2	-	1
Carlisle U.	Partick Th.	06.59	59	1	-	0
BELL, Robert C.						
Cambridge, 26 October, 1950						(CD)
Ipswich T.	Tottenham H. (App)	10.68	68-71	32	0	1
Blackburn Rov.	Tr	09.71	71	2	0	0
Crystal Palace	Tr	09.71	71-73	31	0	0
Norwich C.	L	02.72	71	3	0	0
York C.	South Africa	02.77	76	5	0	0
BELL, Robert Mc.						
Ayr, 16 September, 1934						(FB)
Watford	Ayr U.	05.57	57-64	268	-	2
BELL, Stanley W. G.						
West Ham, 28 October, 1923						
Southend U.		07.48	48	3	-	0
BELL, Stephen						
Middlesbrough, 13 March, 1965 E Yth						(LW)
Middlesbrough	App	05.82	81-84	79	6	12
Darlington	Whitby T.	03.87	86-87	28	12	3
BELL, Sydney E.						
Stepney, 8 January, 1920						(LB)
Southend U.	Monarchs	11.45	46-47	15	-	0
BELL, Terence J.						
Nottingham, 1 August, 1944						(F)
Nottingham F.	Burton A.	08.64				
Manchester C.	Tr	10.64				
Portsmouth	Tr	11.64				
Hartlepool U.	Nuneaton Bor.	07.66	66-69	111	6	34
Reading	Tr	03.73	69-72	82	5	20
Aldershot	Tr	07.73	73-77	112	12	49
BELL, Thomas A.						
Crompton, 30 December, 1923						(FB)
Oldham Ath.	Mossley	12.46	46-51	170	-	0
Stockport Co.	Tr	08.52	52	31	-	0
Halifax T.	Tr	07.53	53-55	117	-	1
BELL, Thomas H.						
Stanley, 14 June, 1924						(CH)
Millwall (Am)	Hammersmith U.	03.49	48	1	-	0
BELL, William G.						
Manchester, 16 June, 1953						(M)
Rochdale (N/C)	Hyde U.	05.74	74	5	1	0
BELL, William J.						
Johnstone, 3 September, 1937 S Amat/S-2						(LB)
Leeds U.	Queens Park	07.60	60-67	204	0	15
Leicester C.	Tr	09.67	67-68	49	0	0
Brighton & H.A.	Tr	07.69	69	44	0	1
BELLAMY, Arthur						
Consett, 5 April, 1942						(M)
Burnley	Jnrs	06.59	62-71	204	13	29
Chesterfield	Tr	07.72	72-75	133	0	12
BELLAMY, Gary						
Worksop, 4 July, 1962						(D)
Chesterfield	App	06.80	80-86	181	3	7
Wolverhampton W.	Tr	07.87	87-91	133	3	9
Cardiff C.	L	03.92	91	9	0	0
BELLAS, William J.						
Liverpool, 21 May, 1925						(CH)
Notts Co.		04.45				
Nottingham F.	Tr	05.46				
Southport	Tr	10.48	48-50	88	-	0
Grimsby T.	Tr	07.51	51	5	-	0
BELLETT, Walter R.						
Stratford, 14 November, 1933 E Yth						(FB)
Chelsea	Barking	09.54	55-58	35	-	1
Plymouth Arg.	Tr	12.58	58-59	41	-	1
Leyton Orient	Chelmsford C.	01.61				
Chester C.	Tr	07.61	61	12	-	1
Wrexham	Tr	07.62	62	2	-	0
Tranmere Rov.	Tr	07.63				

BELLIS, Alfred
Liverpool, 8 October, 1920 (OL)

League Club	Source	Date Signed	Seasons Played	Apps	Subs	Gls
Port Vale	Burnells Iron Wks	03.38	37-47	82	-	18
Bury	Tr	01.48	47-50	95	-	18
Swansea C.	Tr	08.51	51-52	43	-	12
Chesterfield	Tr	08.53	53	13	-	3

BELLIS, Thomas, G.
Mold, 21 April, 1919 (D)

League Club	Source	Date Signed	Seasons Played	Apps	Subs	Gls
Wrexham		05.38	38-48	95	-	1

BELLOTTI, Derek C.
West Ham, 25 December, 1946 (G)

League Club	Source	Date Signed	Seasons Played	Apps	Subs	Gls
Gillingham	Bedford T.	07.66	66-69	35	0	0
Charlton Ath.	Tr	10.70	70-71	14	0	0
Southend U.	Tr	12.71	71-73	77	0	0
Swansea C.	Tr	05.74	74	19	0	0

BEMROSE, Frank E.
Caistor, 20 October, 1935 (OL)

League Club	Source	Date Signed	Seasons Played	Apps	Subs	Gls
Grimsby T. (Am)	Caistor	08.58	58-60	2	-	0

BENALI, Francis V.
Southampton, 30 December, 1968 E Sch (LB)

League Club	Source	Date Signed	Seasons Played	Apps	Subs	Gls
Southampton	App	12.86	88-91	54	14	0

Francis Benali (Southampton)

BENBOW, Ian R.
Hereford, 9 January, 1969 (M)

League Club	Source	Date Signed	Seasons Played	Apps	Subs	Gls
Hereford U.	YT	07.87	87-90	60	23	4

BENCE, Paul I.
Littlehampton, 21 December, 1948 (D)

League Club	Source	Date Signed	Seasons Played	Apps	Subs	Gls
Brighton & H.A.	App	05.67	67	0	1	0
Reading	Tr	06.68	68-69	12	2	2
Brentford	Tr	07.70	70-76	238	6	6
Torquay U.	L	11.76	76	5	0	0

BENJAFIELD, Brian J.
Barton-on-Sea, 2 August, 1960 (M)

League Club	Source	Date Signed	Seasons Played	Apps	Subs	Gls
Bournemouth	Jnrs	01.79	78	2	0	0

BENJAMIN, Christopher
Sheffield, 5 December, 1972 (F)

League Club	Source	Date Signed	Seasons Played	Apps	Subs	Gls
Chesterfield	YT	07.91	90-91	5	10	1

BENJAMIN, Ian T.
Nottingham, 11 December, 1961 E Yth (F)

League Club	Source	Date Signed	Seasons Played	Apps	Subs	Gls
Sheffield U.	App	05.79	78-79	4	1	3
West Bromwich A.	Tr	08.79	80	1	1	0
Notts Co.	Tr	02.82				
Peterborough U.	Tr	08.82	82-83	77	3	14
Northampton T.	Tr	08.84	84-87	147	3	58
Cambridge U.	Tr	10.87	87	20	5	2
Chester C.	Tr	07.88	88	18	4	3
Exeter C.	Tr	02.89	88-89	30	2	4
Southend U.	Tr	03.90	89-91	106	0	26

BENJAMIN, Tristam L.
St Kitts (WI), 1 April, 1957 (D)

League Club	Source	Date Signed	Seasons Played	Apps	Subs	Gls
Notts Co.	App	03.75	74-86	296	15	4
Chesterfield	Tr	07.87	87	32	2	0

BENN, Alfred
Leeds, 26 January, 1926

League Club	Source	Date Signed	Seasons Played	Apps	Subs	Gls
Leeds U.		01.47				
Southport	Tr	07.48	48	3	-	0

BENNELLICK, James A.
Torquay, 9 September, 1974

League Club	Source	Date Signed	Seasons Played	Apps	Subs	Gls
Torquay U. (YT)	YT	07.91	91	0	1	0

BENNETT, Albert
Durham, 16 July, 1944 E Yth/Eu23-1 (CF)

League Club	Source	Date Signed	Seasons Played	Apps	Subs	Gls
Rotherham U.	Chester Moor Jnrs	10.61	61-64	108	-	64
Newcastle U.	Tr	07.65	65-68	85	0	22
Norwich C.	Tr	02.69	68-70	54	1	15

BENNETT, Allan
Stoke, 5 November, 1931 E Yth (OL)

League Club	Source	Date Signed	Seasons Played	Apps	Subs	Gls
Port Vale	Jnrs	05.49	48-56	123	-	9
Crewe Alex.	Tr	09.57	57	10	-	0

BENNETT, Craig
Doncaster, 29 August, 1973 (F)

League Club	Source	Date Signed	Seasons Played	Apps	Subs	Gls
Doncaster Rov.	YT	07.91	90-91	4	3	0

BENNETT, David A.
Manchester, 11 July, 1959 (W)

League Club	Source	Date Signed	Seasons Played	Apps	Subs	Gls
Manchester C.	Jnrs	06.77	78-80	43	9	9
Cardiff C.	Tr	09.81	81-82	75	2	18
Coventry C.	Tr	07.83	83-88	157	15	25
Sheffield Wed.	Tr	03.89	88-89	20	8	0
Swindon T.	Tr	09.90	90	1	0	0
Shrewsbury T.	L	11.91	91	2	0	2

BENNETT, David M.
Southampton, 5 March, 1939 E Sch (W)

League Club	Source	Date Signed	Seasons Played	Apps	Subs	Gls
Arsenal	Jnrs	05.56				
Portsmouth	Tr	06.58				
Bournemouth	Tr	12.60	60-61	12	-	2

BENNETT, David P.
Oldham, 26 April, 1960 (W)

League Club	Source	Date Signed	Seasons Played	Apps	Subs	Gls
Norwich C.	Manchester C. (App)	08.78	78-83	64	7	9

BENNETT, Desmond A.
Doncaster, 30 October, 1963

League Club	Source	Date Signed	Seasons Played	Apps	Subs	Gls
Doncaster Rov.	App	06.80	80-81	0	2	0

BENNETT, Donald
Wakefield, 18 December, 1933 E Yth (FB)

League Club	Source	Date Signed	Seasons Played	Apps	Subs	Gls
Arsenal	Jnrs	08.51				
Coventry C.	Tr	09.59	59-61	73	-	0

BENNETT, Edgar W.
Stoke, 29 March, 1929 (OR)

League Club	Source	Date Signed	Seasons Played	Apps	Subs	Gls
Luton T.	Vauxhall Motors	09.52	53	1	-	0

BENNETT, Edward E.
Kilburn, 22 August, 1925 E Amat (G)

League Club	Source	Date Signed	Seasons Played	Apps	Subs	Gls
Queens Park R. (Am)	Southall	02.49	48	2	-	0
Watford	Southall	12.53	53-55	81	-	0

BENNETT, Gary
Enfield, 13 November, 1970 (W)

League Club	Source	Date Signed	Seasons Played	Apps	Subs	Gls
Colchester U.	YT	11.88	88-89	32	13	5

BENNETT, Gary E.
Manchester, 4 December, 1961 (CD)

League Club	Source	Date Signed	Seasons Played	Apps	Subs	Gls
Manchester C.	Ashton U.	09.79				
Cardiff C.	Tr	09.81	81-83	85	2	11
Sunderland	Tr	07.84	84-91	292	4	23

BENNETT, Gary M.
Liverpool, 20 September, 1962 (W/F)

League Club	Source	Date Signed	Seasons Played	Apps	Subs	Gls
Wigan Ath. (N/C)	Kirkby T.	10.84	84	10	10	3
Chester C.	Tr	08.85	85-88	109	17	36
Southend U.	Tr	11.88	88-89	36	6	6
Chester C.	Tr	03.90	89-91	71	9	15

BENNETT, George F.
South Shields, 16 March, 1938 (FB)

League Club	Source	Date Signed	Seasons Played	Apps	Subs	Gls
Burnley	Jnrs	04.55				
Barnsley	Tr	01.60	59-60	24	-	0

BENNETT, Harold
Liverpool, 16 May, 1949 (WH)

League Club	Source	Date Signed	Seasons Played	Apps	Subs	Gls
Everton	Jnrs	03.67	67	2	1	0
Aldershot	Tr	01.71	70-72	77	12	7
Crewe Alex.	Tr	07.73	73	28	2	1

BENNETT, Ian M.
Worksop, 10 October, 1970 (G)

League Club	Source	Date Signed	Seasons Played	Apps	Subs	Gls
Newcastle U. (N/C)	Queens Park R. (YT)	03.89				
Peterborough U.	Tr	03.91	91	7	0	0

BENNETT, John
Rotherham, 15 May, 1949 (OL)

League Club	Source	Date Signed	Seasons Played	Apps	Subs	Gls
Rotherham U. (App)	App	11.65	65	1	0	0

BENNETT, John G.
Liverpool, 21 March, 1946 (LB)

League Club	Source	Date Signed	Seasons Played	Apps	Subs	Gls
Liverpool	App	04.63				
Chester C.	Tr	06.66	66-68	72	4	0

BENNETT, Kenneth E.
Wood Green, 2 October, 1921 (IF)

League Club	Source	Date Signed	Seasons Played	Apps	Subs	Gls
Tottenham H.		10.40				
Southend U.	Tr	06.46	46-47	50	-	10
Bournemouth	Tr	06.48	48	19	-	1
Brighton & H.A.	Tr	06.50	50-52	101	-	37
Crystal Palace	Tr	07.53	53	17	-	2

BENNETT, Lawson H.
Darwen, 28 August, 1938 (OR)

League Club	Source	Date Signed	Seasons Played	Apps	Subs	Gls
Accrington St.	Darwen	05.58	58-60	29	-	2

BENNETT, Leslie D.
Wood Green, 10 January, 1918 (IF)

League Club	Source	Date Signed	Seasons Played	Apps	Subs	Gls
Tottenham H.	Jnrs	05.39	46-54	272	-	104
West Ham U.	Tr	12.54	54-55	26	-	3

BENNETT, Martyn
Birmingham, 4 August, 1961 E Sch (CD)

League Club	Source	Date Signed	Seasons Played	Apps	Subs	Gls
West Bromwich A.	App	08.78	78-89	181	1	9

BENNETT, Michael
Bolton, 24 December, 1962 E Yth (LB)

League Club	Source	Date Signed	Seasons Played	Apps	Subs	Gls
Bolton W.	App	01.80	79-82	62	3	1
Wolverhampton W.	Tr	06.83	83	6	0	0
Cambridge U.	Tr	03.84	83-85	76	0	0
Preston N.E.	Bradford C. (N/C)	09.86	86-89	85	1	1
Carlisle U.	Tr	07.90	90-91	21	3	0

BENNETT, Michael R.
Camberwell, 27 July, 1969 E Yth (W)

League Club	Source	Date Signed	Seasons Played	Apps	Subs	Gls
Charlton Ath.	App	04.87	86-89	24	11	2
Wimbledon	Tr	01.90	89-91	12	6	2

BENNETT, Paul
Liverpool, 30 January, 1961 (M)

League Club	Source	Date Signed	Seasons Played	Apps	Subs	Gls
Port Vale	Everton (App)	09.78	80-81	28	2	1

BENNETT, Paul R.
Southampton, 4 February, 1952 (CD)

League Club	Source	Date Signed	Seasons Played	Apps	Subs	Gls
Southampton	App	11.69	71-75	116	0	1
Reading	Tr	07.76	76-78	105	0	3
Aldershot	Tr	08.79	79-81	112	1	2

BENNETT, Peter
Plymouth, 29 November, 1939 (CF)

League Club	Source	Date Signed	Seasons Played	Apps	Subs	Gls
Exeter C.	Plymstock	08.59	59-60	6	-	5

BENNETT, Peter L.
Hillingdon, 24 June, 1946 E Sch (M)

League Club	Source	Date Signed	Seasons Played	Apps	Subs	Gls
West Ham U.	App	07.63	63-70	38	4	3
Leyton Orient	Tr	10.70	70-78	195	4	13

BENNETT, Richard
Northampton, 16 February, 1945 E Yth (WH)

League Club	Source	Date Signed	Seasons Played	Apps	Subs	Gls
Peterborough U.	Wellingborough	08.63	63-64	4	-	0

BENNETT, Robert
Harrow, 29 December, 1951 (CF)

League Club	Source	Date Signed	Seasons Played	Apps	Subs	Gls
Southend U.	Staines T.	06.72	72	1	0	0
Scunthorpe U.	L	10.73	73	2	1	0

BENNETT, Ronald
Hinckley, 8 May, 1927 (OL)

League Club	Source	Date Signed	Seasons Played	Apps	Subs	Gls
Wolverhampton W.		01.45				
Portsmouth	Tr	07.48	49-51	8	-	1
Crystal Palace	Tr	01.52	51-52	27	-	5
Brighton & H.A.	Tr	07.53	53	3	-	0

BENNETT, Sean
Newport, 3 September, 1970 (LB)

League Club	Source	Date Signed	Seasons Played	Apps	Subs	Gls
Newport Co. (YT)	Leeds U. (YT)	01.88	87	4	1	0

BENNETT, Stanley T.
Birmingham, 18 September, 1944 (CH)

League Club	Source	Date Signed	Seasons Played	Apps	Subs	Gls
Walsall	App	09.62	63-74	377	8	12

BENNETT, Thomas M.
Falkirk, 12 December, 1969 (D)

League Club	Source	Date Signed	Seasons Played	Apps	Subs	Gls
Aston Villa	App	12.87				
Wolverhampton W.	Tr	07.88	88-91	91	5	2

BENNETT, Walter H.
Mexborough, 15 December, 1918 (CF)

League Club	Source	Date Signed	Seasons Played	Apps	Subs	Gls
Barnsley	Mexborough	04.38	46-47	37	-	23
Doncaster Rov.	Tr	01.48	47-49	39	-	14
Halifax T.	Tr	01.50	49	7	-	1

BENNING, Michael D.
Watford, 3 February, 1938 (OR)

League Club	Source	Date Signed	Seasons Played	Apps	Subs	Gls
Watford	Jnrs	09.56	58-61	103	-	14

BENNING, Paul M.
Watford, 7 June, 1963 (D)

League Club	Source	Date Signed	Seasons Played	Apps	Subs	Gls
Peterborough U.	Hayes	12.87	87	2	0	0

BENNION, John R.
Burnley, 2 April, 1934 (WH)

League Club	Source	Date Signed	Seasons Played	Apps	Subs	Gls
Burnley		01.52				
Hull C.	Tr	06.57	57-59	35	-	1
Stockport Co.	Tr	07.60	60	26	-	1
Barrow	Tr	07.61	61-62	16	-	0

BENNION, Stanley
Chester, 9 February, 1938 (IF)

League Club	Source	Date Signed	Seasons Played	Apps	Subs	Gls
Wrexham		10.59	59-62	52	-	18
Chester C.	Tr	06.63	63	19	-	3

BENNYWORTH, Ian R.
Hull, 15 January, 1962 (CD)

League Club	Source	Date Signed	Seasons Played	Apps	Subs	Gls
Hull C.	App	01.80	79	1	0	0
Scarborough	Nuneaton Bor.	(N/L)	87-89	88	1	3
Hartlepool U.	Tr	12.89	89-91	81	1	3

BENSKIN, Dennis W.
Nottingham, 28 May, 1947 (OL)

League Club	Source	Date Signed	Seasons Played	Apps	Subs	Gls
Notts Co. (Am)	Jnrs	05.65	65	4	0	1

BENSON, John H.
Arbroath, 23 December, 1942 (FB)

League Club	Source	Date Signed	Seasons Played	Apps	Subs	Gls
Manchester C.	Jnrs	07.61	61-63	44	-	0
Torquay U.	Tr	06.64	64-70	233	7	7
Bournemouth	Tr	10.70	70-73	85	8	0
Exeter C.	L	03.73	72	4	0	0
Norwich C.	Tr	12.73	73-74	29	1	1
Bournemouth	Tr	01.75	74-78	56	1	0

BENSON, Joseph R.
Misterton, 7 January, 1933

League Club	Source	Date Signed	Seasons Played	Apps	Subs	Gls
Scunthorpe U.		09.55	55	2	-	0

BENSON, Ronald
York, 26 March, 1925 (OR)

League Club	Source	Date Signed	Seasons Played	Apps	Subs	Gls
York C.		10.47	49	21	-	3

League Club	Source	Date Signed	Seasons Played	Apps	Subs	Gls
BENSTEAD, Graham M.						
Aldershot, 20 August, 1963 E Yth						(G)
Queens Park R.	App	07.81				
Norwich C.	Tr	03.85	84-87	16	0	0
Colchester U.	L	08.87	87	18	0	0
Sheffield U.	Tr	03.88	87-88	47	0	0
Brentford	Tr	07.90	90-91	82	0	0
BENT, Geoffrey						
Salford, 27 September, 1932 Died 1958						(FB)
Manchester U.	Jnrs	04.51	54-56	12	-	0
BENT, Graham W.						
Ruabon, 6 October, 1945 W Sch						(W)
Wrexham	Aston Villa (App)	12.63	63-64	10	-	2
BENT, Junior A.						
Huddersfield, 1 March, 1970						(W)
Huddersfield T.	YT	12.87	87-89	25	11	6
Burnley	L	11.89	89	7	2	3
Bristol C.	Tr	03.90	89-91	22	16	4
Stoke C.	L	03.92	91	1	0	0
BENTALL, Charles E.						
Helmsley, 28 January, 1922 Died 1947						(CH)
York C.		10.45	46	1	-	0
BENTHAM, Alan						
Liverpool, 12 September, 1940 E Sch						(FB)
Everton	Jnrs	11.57				
Southport	Tr	06.60	60-61	25	-	1
BENTHAM, John J.						
Pontefract, 3 March, 1963						(W)
York C.	App	03.81	81	22	1	0
BENTHAM, Stanley J.						
Leigh, 17 March, 1915						(WH)
Everton	Wigan Ath.	01.34	35-48	110	-	17
BENTLEY, Alfred						
Aylesham, 28 October, 1931						(G)
Coventry C.	Snowdown Colly	10.55	55-56	29	-	0
Gillingham	Margate	08.58	58-61	13	-	0
BENTLEY, Anthony						
Stoke, 20 December, 1939						(FB)
Stoke C.	Jnrs	12.56	58-60	44	-	17
Southend U.	Tr	05.61	61-70	378	3	14
BENTLEY, David A.						
Edwinstowe, 30 May, 1950						(M)
Rotherham U.	App	07.67	66-73	243	7	13
Mansfield T.	L	09.72	72	1	3	1
Chesterfield	Tr	06.74	74-76	53	2	1
Doncaster Rov.	Tr	08.77	77-79	87	2	4
BENTLEY, John (Jack)						
Liverpool, 17 February, 1942						(OR)
Everton	Jnrs	11.59	60	1	-	0
Stockport Co.	Tr	05.61	61-62	49	-	5
BENTLEY, Keith J.						
Hull, 27 July, 1936						(IF)
Hull C.		11.57	57	4	-	0
BENTLEY, Roy T. F.						
Bristol, 17 May, 1924 EF Lge/E'B'-1/E-12						(CF)
Bristol C.	Jnrs	09.41				
Newcastle U.	Tr	06.46	46-47	48	-	22
Chelsea	Tr	01.48	47-56	324	-	128
Fulham	Tr	09.56	56-60	143	-	23
Queens Park R.	Tr	06.61	61-62	45	-	0
BENTLEY, William J.						
Stoke, 21 October, 1947 E Sch/E Yth						(LB)
Stoke C.	App	10.64	65-68	44	4	1
Blackpool	Tr	01.69	68-76	289	7	10
Port Vale	Tr	07.77	77-79	92	3	0
BENTON, James						
Wexford (IR), 9 April, 1975						(CD)
Northampton T. (YT)	YT	07.91	91	4	1	1

League Club	Source	Date Signed	Seasons Played	Apps	Subs	Gls
BERESFORD, John						
Sheffield, 4 September, 1966 E Sch/E Yth						(LB)
Manchester C.	App	09.83				
Barnsley	Tr	07.86	86-88	79	9	5
Portsmouth	Tr	03.89	88-91	102	5	8
BERESFORD, John T.						
Sunderland, 2 January, 1943						(WH)
Hartlepool U. (Am)		08.66	66	3	0	0
BERESFORD, John W.						
Sheffield, 25 January, 1946						(IF)
Chesterfield	App	01.63	62-64	52	-	10
Notts Co.	Tr	05.65	65-66	49	1	13
BERESFORD, Marlon						
Lincoln, 2 September, 1969						(G)
Sheffield Wed.	YT	09.87				
Bury	L	08.89	89	1	0	0
Northampton T.	L	09.90	90	13	0	0
Crewe Alex.	L	03.91	90	3	0	0
Northampton T.	L	08.91	91	15	0	0
BERESFORD, Philip						
Chesterfield, 30 November, 1944						(CF)
Chesterfield		01.64	63	7	-	3
BERESFORD, Reginald						
Chesterfield, 29 June, 1925						(OR)
Notts Co.	Hardwick Colly	09.45	46	10	-	1
BERESFORD, Reginald H.						
Walsall, 3 June, 1921						(IF)
Aston Villa	Jnrs	10.38				
Birmingham C.	Tr	09.46				
Crystal Palace	Tr	08.48	48	7	-	1
BERGSSON, Gudni						
Iceland, 21 July, 1965 Iceland Int						(RB)
Tottenham H.	Valur (Iceland)	12.88	88-91	51	15	3
BERKLEY, Austin J.						
Dartford, 28 January, 1973						(M)
Gillingham	YT	05.91	91	0	3	0

Roy Bentley (Bristol City, Newcastle United, Chelsea, Fulham, Queens Park Rangers & England)

BERMINGHAM, Alan
Liverpool, 11 September, 1944 (FB)

League Club	Source	Date Signed	Seasons Played	Apps	Subs	Gls
Wrexham	Skelmersdale U.	06.67	67-70	115	3	2

BERNAL, Andrew
Australia, 16 May, 1966 (D)

League Club	Source	Date Signed	Seasons Played	Apps	Subs	Gls
Ipswich T.	Sporting Gijon (Sp)	09.87	87	4	5	0

BERNARD, Michael P.
Shrewsbury, 10 January, 1948 E Yth/Eu23-3 (M)

League Club	Source	Date Signed	Seasons Played	Apps	Subs	Gls
Stoke C.	App	01.65	65-71	124	12	6
Everton	Tr	04.72	72-76	139	8	8
Oldham Ath.	Tr	07.77	77-78	6	0	0

BERNARD, Paul R. J.
Edinburgh, 30 December, 1972 Su21-4 (M)

League Club	Source	Date Signed	Seasons Played	Apps	Subs	Gls
Oldham Ath.	YT	07.91	90-91	18	5	6

Paul Bernard (Oldham Athletic)

BERNARDEAU, Oliver
France, 19 August, 1962 (W)

League Club	Source	Date Signed	Seasons Played	Apps	Subs	Gls
Chesterfield	Leeds U. (N/C)	08.86	86	5	4	0

BERRY, David
Newton-le-Willows, 1 June, 1945 (CH)

League Club	Source	Date Signed	Seasons Played	Apps	Subs	Gls
Blackpool	Jnrs	09.63				
Chester C.	Tr	07.64	66	0	1	0

BERRY, George F.
West Germany, 19 November, 1957 W-5 (CD)

League Club	Source	Date Signed	Seasons Played	Apps	Subs	Gls
Wolverhampton W.	App	11.75	76-81	124	0	4
Stoke C.	Tr	08.82	82-89	229	8	27
Doncaster Rov.	L	08.84	84	1	0	0
Peterborough U.	Tr	07.90	90	28	4	5
Preston N.E.	Tr	08.91	91	4	0	0

BERRY, Gregory J.
Grays, 5 March, 1971 (LW)

League Club	Source	Date Signed	Seasons Played	Apps	Subs	Gls
Leyton Orient	East Thurrock U.	07.89	89-91	68	12	14

BERRY, John A.
Manchester, 27 August, 1965 (D)

League Club	Source	Date Signed	Seasons Played	Apps	Subs	Gls
Torquay U. (N/C)		01.84	83	1	0	0

BERRY, John J.
Aldershot, 1 June, 1926 EF Lge/E'B'-1/ E-4 (OR)

League Club	Source	Date Signed	Seasons Played	Apps	Subs	Gls
Birmingham C.	Aldershot Y.M.C.A.	12.44	47-51	104	-	6
Manchester U.	Tr	08.51	51-57	247	-	37

BERRY, Leslie D.
Plumstead, 4 May, 1956 (CD)

League Club	Source	Date Signed	Seasons Played	Apps	Subs	Gls
Charlton Ath.	App	03.74	75-85	352	6	11
Brighton & H.A.	Tr	08.86	86	22	1	0
Gillingham	Tr	03.87	86-87	26	5	0
Maidstone U.	Tr	07.88	89-90	62	1	2

BERRY, Michael J.
Newbury, 14 February, 1955 (FB)

League Club	Source	Date Signed	Seasons Played	Apps	Subs	Gls
Southampton	App	02.73	74	2	0	0

BERRY, Neil
Edinburgh, 6 April, 1963 S Yth (D)

League Club	Source	Date Signed	Seasons Played	Apps	Subs	Gls
Bolton W.	App	03.81	81-84	25	7	0

BERRY, Norman
Bury, 15 August, 1922

League Club	Source	Date Signed	Seasons Played	Apps	Subs	Gls
Bury (Am)		05.46	46-47	23	-	6

BERRY, Paul
Grays, 15 November, 1935 (CH)

League Club	Source	Date Signed	Seasons Played	Apps	Subs	Gls
Chelsea	Jnrs	04.53	56-57	3	-	0

BERRY, Paul A.
Oxford, 8 April, 1958 (F)

League Club	Source	Date Signed	Seasons Played	Apps	Subs	Gls
Oxford U.	App	04.76	76-81	98	12	20

BERRY, Peter
Aldershot, 20 September, 1933 (OR)

League Club	Source	Date Signed	Seasons Played	Apps	Subs	Gls
Crystal Palace	Jnrs	08.51	53-57	151	-	27
Ipswich T.	Tr	05.58	58-59	38	-	6

BERRY, Stephen A.
Gosport, 4 April, 1963 (M)

League Club	Source	Date Signed	Seasons Played	Apps	Subs	Gls
Portsmouth	App	01.81	81-82	26	2	2
Aldershot	L	03.84	83	5	2	0
Sunderland	Tr	07.84	84-85	32	3	2
Newport Co.	Tr	12.85	85-86	60	0	6
Swindon T.	Tr	03.87	86-87	4	0	0
Aldershot	Tr	10.87	87-88	48	0	6
Northampton T.	Tr	10.88	88-90	95	7	7

BERRY, Thomas
Clayton-le-Moors, 31 March, 1922 (CH)

League Club	Source	Date Signed	Seasons Played	Apps	Subs	Gls
Hull C.	Great Harwood	05.47	47-57	275	-	1

BERRY, William
Mansfield, 4 April, 1934 (IF)

League Club	Source	Date Signed	Seasons Played	Apps	Subs	Gls
Mansfield T.	Langwith Colly	03.56	56	10	-	1

BERRYMAN, Stephen C.
Blackburn, 26 December, 1966 (G)

League Club	Source	Date Signed	Seasons Played	Apps	Subs	Gls
Hartlepool U. (N/C)	Leyland Motors	03.90	89	1	0	0
Exeter C.	Tr	08.90				
Cambridge U.	Tr	03.91	90	1	0	0
Barnet (N/C)	Tr	08.91				

BERTOLINI, John (Jack)
Stirling, 21 March, 1934 (WH)

League Club	Source	Date Signed	Seasons Played	Apps	Subs	Gls
Workington	Stirling A.	01.53	52-57	181	-	35
Brighton & H.A.	Tr	07.58	58-65	158	0	12

BERTRAM, James T.
Whitehaven, 3 February, 1953

League Club	Source	Date Signed	Seasons Played	Apps	Subs	Gls
Workington (Am)	Carlisle U. (App)	02.72	71	0	1	0

BERTSCHIN, Christian
Kensington, 7 September, 1924

League Club	Source	Date Signed	Seasons Played	Apps	Subs	Gls
Reading	Ilford	08.47	47-48	12	-	1

BERTSCHIN, Keith E.
Enfield, 25 August, 1956 E Yth/Eu21-3 (F)

League Club	Source	Date Signed	Seasons Played	Apps	Subs	Gls
Ipswich T.	Barnet	10.73	75-76	19	13	8
Birmingham C.	Tr	07.77	77-80	113	5	29
Norwich C.	Tr	08.81	81-84	112	2	29
Stoke C.	Tr	11.84	84-86	82	6	29
Sunderland	Tr	03.87	86-87	25	11	7
Walsall	Tr	08.88	88-89	40	15	9
Chester C.	Tr	11.90	90	14	5	0

BESAGNI, Remo
Italy, 22 April, 1935 (CF)

League Club	Source	Date Signed	Seasons Played	Apps	Subs	Gls
Crystal Palace	Jnrs	10.52	52	2	-	0

BEST, Andrew K.
Dorchester, 5 January, 1959 (M)

League Club	Source	Date Signed	Seasons Played	Apps	Subs	Gls
Torquay U.	Teignmouth	11.84	84	15	4	2

BEST, Clyde C.
Bermuda, 24 February, 1951 (CF)

League Club	Source	Date Signed	Seasons Played	Apps	Subs	Gls
West Ham U.	Bermuda	03.69	69-75	178	8	47

Clyde Best (West Ham United)

BEST, David
Wareham, 6 September, 1943 (G)

League Club	Source	Date Signed	Seasons Played	Apps	Subs	Gls
Bournemouth	Jnrs	10.60	60-66	230	0	0
Oldham Ath.	Tr	09.66	66-68	98	0	0
Ipswich T.	Tr	10.68	68-73	168	0	0
Portsmouth	Tr	02.74	73-74	53	0	0
Bournemouth	Tr	07.75	75	2	0	0

BEST, George
Belfast, 22 May, 1946 NI-37 (F)

League Club	Source	Date Signed	Seasons Played	Apps	Subs	Gls
Manchester U.	Jnrs	05.63	63-73	361	0	137
Stockport Co.	L	11.75	75	3	0	2
Fulham	Los Angeles (USA)	09.76	76-77	42	0	8
Bournemouth	Golden Bay (USA)	03.83	82	5	0	0

BEST, John B.
Liverpool, 11 July, 1940 (WH)

League Club	Source	Date Signed	Seasons Played	Apps	Subs	Gls
Liverpool	Jnrs	05.58				
Tranmere Rov.	Tr	08.60	60	7	-	0

BEST, Thomas H.
Milford Haven, 23 December, 1920 (F)

League Club	Source	Date Signed	Seasons Played	Apps	Subs	Gls
Chester C.	Merthyr Tydfil	07.47	47-48	40	-	14
Cardiff C.	Tr	10.48	48-49	28	-	10
Queens Park R.	Tr	12.49	49	12	-	3

BEST, William J. B.
Glasgow, 7 September, 1943 (F)

League Club	Source	Date Signed	Seasons Played	Apps	Subs	Gls
Northampton T.	Pollok	07.62	63-67	38	2	11

League Club	Source	Date Signed	Seasons Played	Apps	Subs	Gls
Southend U.	Tr	01.68	67-72	225	1	106
Northampton T.	Tr	09.73	73-77	201	2	37

BESWICK, Ivan
Manchester, 2 January, 1936 (FB)

League Club	Source	Date Signed	Seasons Played	Apps	Subs	Gls
Manchester U.		10.54				
Oldham Ath.	Tr	08.58	58-60	46	-	0

BESWICK, Keith
Cardiff, 3 February, 1943 (G)

League Club	Source	Date Signed	Seasons Played	Apps	Subs	Gls
Millwall	Cardiff Corries	01.62	62	12	-	0
Newport Co.	Tr	08.64	64-66	58	0	0

BETMEAD, Harold A.
Grimsby, 11 April, 1912 Died 1984 E-1 (CH)

League Club	Source	Date Signed	Seasons Played	Apps	Subs	Gls
Grimsby T.	Hay Cross	10.30	31-46	296	-	10

BETT, Frederick
Scunthorpe, 5 December, 1920 (IF)

League Club	Source	Date Signed	Seasons Played	Apps	Subs	Gls
Sunderland	Scunthorpe U.	12.37	37-38	3	-	0
Coventry C.	Tr	05.46	46-48	27	-	11
Lincoln C.	Tr	09.48	48	14	-	2

BETTANY, Colin D.
Leicester, 15 June, 1932 (FB)

League Club	Source	Date Signed	Seasons Played	Apps	Subs	Gls
Crewe Alex.	Leicester C. (Am)	08.53	53-54	29	-	6
Birmingham C.	Tr	06.55				
Torquay U.	Tr	04.57	57-65	335	0	4

BETTANY, John W.
Laughton, 16 December, 1937 (WH)

League Club	Source	Date Signed	Seasons Played	Apps	Subs	Gls
Huddersfield T.	Thurcroft	09.60	60-64	59	-	6
Barnsley	Tr	03.65	64-69	194	3	24
Rotherham U.	Tr	06.70	70	16	0	1

BETTERIDGE, R. Michael
Alcester, 11 August, 1924 (IF)

League Club	Source	Date Signed	Seasons Played	Apps	Subs	Gls
West Bromwich A.	Warslow Celtic	11.48	49-50	5	-	0
Swindon T.	Tr	07.51	51-53	108	-	23
Chester C.	Tr	03.54	53	8	-	1

BETTS, Anthony
Derby, 31 October, 1953 E Yth (F)

League Club	Source	Date Signed	Seasons Played	Apps	Subs	Gls
Aston Villa	Jnrs	03.72	74	1	3	0
Southport	L	12.74	74	8	0	1
Port Vale	Tr	10.75	75	1	0	0

BETTS, J. Barry
Barnsley, 18 September, 1932 (FB)

League Club	Source	Date Signed	Seasons Played	Apps	Subs	Gls
Barnsley	Jnrs	11.50	52-56	55	-	0
Stockport Co.	Tr	11.57	57-59	112	-	3
Manchester C.	Tr	06.60	60-63	101	-	5
Scunthorpe U.	Tr	08.64	64	7	-	0

BETTS, Eric
Coventry, 27 July, 1925 (OL)

League Club	Source	Date Signed	Seasons Played	Apps	Subs	Gls
Mansfield T.	Mansfield Villa	02.46	46	19	-	5
Coventry C.	Tr	08.47	47	1	-	0
Walsall	Nuneaton Bor.	05.49	49	30	-	3
West Ham U.	Tr	04.50	50	3	-	1
Rochdale	Nuneaton Bor.	10.51	51-52	52	-	8
Crewe Alex.	Tr	02.53	52-53	25	-	5
Wrexham	Tr	10.53	53-55	53	-	21
Oldham Ath.	Tr	02.56	55-56	26	-	5

BETTS, Michael J.
Barnsley, 21 September, 1956 (D)

League Club	Source	Date Signed	Seasons Played	Apps	Subs	Gls
Blackpool	App	10.73	75	4	3	0
Bury (N/C)	Northwich Vic.	11.80	80	1	0	0

BETTS, Stuart
Barnsley, 21 September, 1956 (F)

League Club	Source	Date Signed	Seasons Played	Apps	Subs	Gls
Blackpool	App	10.73				
Halifax T.		09.76				
Crewe Alex. (N/C)	Tr	08.77	77	2	0	0

BEVAN, Brian E.
Exeter, 20 March, 1937 (OL)

League Club	Source	Date Signed	Seasons Played	Apps	Subs	Gls
Bristol C.	Bridgwater T.	02.56	57-59	2	-	0
Carlisle U.	Tr	03.60	59-60	27	-	2
Millwall	Tr	02.61	60	3	-	0

BEVAN, Paul P.
Shrewsbury, 20 October, 1952 (D)

League Club	Source	Date Signed	Seasons Played	Apps	Subs	Gls
Shrewsbury T.	App	10.70	70-72	67	5	1
Swansea C.	Tr	08.73	73-74	77	2	5
Crewe Alex.	Tr	07.75	75-79	170	2	7

League Club	Source	Date Signed	Seasons Played	Career Record Apps	Subs	Gls

BEVANS, Stanley
Kingsley, 16 April, 1934 (F)

Stoke C.	Jnrs	04.51	50-54	15	-	1

BEVIS, David R.
Southampton, 27 June, 1942 (G)

Ipswich T.	Jnrs	08.59	63-65	6	0	0

BEVIS, William
Warsash, 29 September, 1918 (OR)

Portsmouth		07.36				
Southampton	Gosport Bor.	06.37	37-46	82	-	17

BEWLEY, David G.
Bournemouth, 22 September, 1920 E Sch (WH)

Fulham	Gravesend & Nft	05.45	46-48	17	-	1
Reading	Tr	03.50	49-50	11	-	1
Fulham	Tr	11.50				
Watford	Tr	05.53	53-55	113	-	1

BEYNON, Edgar R.
Swansea, 3 May, 1940 (FB)

Wrexham		07.59	59	1	-	0

BEYNON, Edwin R.
Aberdare, 17 November, 1924 W Sch (FB)

Wrexham		01.47	46-51	72	-	22
Shrewsbury T.	Tr	10.51	51-54	91	-	6

BICKERSTAFFE, John
St Helens, 8 November, 1918

Bury	Peasley Cross	05.39	46-48	27	-	0
Lincoln C.	Tr	12.48	48-50	12	-	0
Halifax T.	Tr	09.51	51-52	37	-	0

BICKLE, Michael J.
Plymouth, 25 January, 1944 (CF)

Plymouth Arg.	St Austell	12.65	65-71	171	10	71
Gillingham	Tr	11.71	71-72	32	0	7

BICKLES, David
West Ham, 6 April, 1944 E Yth (CH)

West Ham U.	App	07.61	63-66	24	1	0
Crystal Palace	Tr	10.67				
Colchester U.	Tr	09.68	68-69	68	0	3

BICKNELL, Charles
Alfreton, 6 November, 1905 (FB)

Chesterfield	New Tupton Ivenhoe	10.27	28-30	79	-	0
Bradford C.	Tr	03.30	30-35	240	-	2
West Ham U.	Tr	03.36	35-46	137	-	1

BICKNELL, John (Jack)
Edlington, 16 December, 1931 (IL)

Walsall	Retford T.	02.54	53	3	-	0

BICKNELL, Roy
Doncaster, 19 February, 1926 (CH)

Wolverhampton W.	Jnrs	09.43				
Charlton Ath.	Tr	05.47	47-48	7	-	0
Bristol C.	Tr	06.49	49-50	21	-	0
Colchester U.	Gravesend & Nft	06.52	52-53	25	-	0

BICKNELL, Stephen J.
Rugby, 28 November, 1958 (W)

Leicester C.	App	12.76	76	6	1	0
Torquay U.	Tr	08.78	78	0	3	0

BIELBY, Paul A.
Darlington, 24 November, 1956 E Yth (W)

Manchester U.	App	11.73	73	2	2	0
Hartlepool U.	Tr	11.75	75-77	74	19	8
Huddersfield T.	Tr	08.78	78	29	2	5

BIELBY, Terence
Doncaster, 24 November, 1943 (FB)

Doncaster Rov.	Jnrs	01.61	60	1	-	0

BIGGINS, Brian
Ellesmere Port, 19 May, 1940 (G)

Chester C.	Jnrs	06.57	57-58	5	-	0

BIGGINS, Graham W.
Chapeltown, 10 March, 1958 (G)

Doncaster Rov.	Rotherham U. (Am)	07.77	77	2	0	0

League Club	Source	Date Signed	Seasons Played	Career Record Apps	Subs	Gls

BIGGINS, Stephen J.
Walsall, 20 June, 1954 (F)

Shrewsbury T.	Hednesford T.	12.77	77-81	140	6	41
Oxford U.	Tr	07.82	82-84	44	15	22
Derby Co.	Tr	10.84	84	8	2	1
Wolverhampton W.	L	03.85	84	4	0	0
Port Vale	L	03.86	85	1	3	0
Exeter C. (N/C)	Trelleberg (Swe)	10.86	86	14	0	2

BIGGINS, Wayne
Sheffield, 20 November, 1961 (F)

Lincoln C.	App	11.79	80	8	0	1
Burnley	Matlock T.	02.84	83-85	78	0	29
Norwich C.	Tr	10.85	85-87	66	13	16
Manchester C.	Tr	07.88	88	29	3	9
Stoke C.	Tr	08.89	89-91	112	2	44

Wayne Biggins (Lincoln City, Burnley, Norwich City, Manchester City & Stoke City)

BIGGS, Alfred G.
Bristol, 8 February, 1936 (CF)

Bristol Rov.	Jnrs	02.53	53-60	214	-	77
Preston N.E.	Tr	07.61	61-62	49	-	22
Bristol Rov.	Tr	10.62	62-67	210	0	101
Walsall	Tr	03.68	67-68	23	1	9
Swansea C.	Tr	11.68	68	16	0	4

BIGGS, Anthony
Greenford, 17 April, 1936 E Amat (CF)

Arsenal	Hounslow T.	08.56	57-58	4	-	1
Leyton Orient	Tr	12.58	58-59	4	-	1

BILCLIFF, Raymond
Blaydon, 24 May, 1931 (FB)

Middlesbrough	Spen Jnrs	05.49	51-60	182	-	0
Hartlepool U.	Tr	01.61	60-63	118	-	0

BILEY, Alan P.
Leighton Buzzard, 26 February, 1957 (F)

Cambridge U.	Luton T. (App)	07.75	75-79	160	5	74
Derby Co.	Tr	01.80	79-80	47	0	19

League Club	Source	Date Signed	Seasons Played	Apps	Subs	Gls
Everton	Tr	07.81	81	16	3	3
Stoke C.	L	03.82	81	8	0	1
Portsmouth	Tr	08.82	82-84	101	4	51
Brighton & H.A.	Tr	03.85	84-85	34	1	8
Cambridge U. (N/C)	New York (USA)	11.86	86	0	3	0

BILL, Roger J.
Creswell, 17 May, 1944 (OR)

League Club	Source	Date Signed	Seasons Played	Apps	Subs	Gls
Reading	Chelsea (Am)	09.62	62	4	-	0

BILLING, Peter G.
Liverpool, 24 October, 1964 (CD)

League Club	Source	Date Signed	Seasons Played	Apps	Subs	Gls
Everton	South Liverpool	01.86	85	1	0	0
Crewe Alex.	Tr	12.86	86-88	83	5	1
Coventry C.	Tr	06.89	89-91	48	7	1

BILLINGHAM, John
Daventry, 3 December, 1914 Died 1981 (CF)

League Club	Source	Date Signed	Seasons Played	Apps	Subs	Gls
Northampton T.		09.35	35	3	-	0
Bristol C.	Tr	07.37	37	7	-	0
Burnley	Tr	05.38	38-48	91	-	35
Carlisle U.	Tr	09.49	49-50	64	-	17
Southport	Tr	03.51	50-54	150	-	37

BILLINGHAM, Peter A.
Pensnett, 8 October, 1938 (WH)

League Club	Source	Date Signed	Seasons Played	Apps	Subs	Gls
Walsall	Jnrs	10.55	55-59	98	-	9
West Bromwich A.	Tr	05.60	60	7	-	0

BILLINGS, John
Doncaster, 30 March, 1944 (F)

League Club	Source	Date Signed	Seasons Played	Apps	Subs	Gls
Doncaster Rov.	Jnrs	05.61	62-64	18	-	4

BILLINGTON, Brian
Leicester, 28 April, 1951 (F)

League Club	Source	Date Signed	Seasons Played	Apps	Subs	Gls
Notts Co.	Leicester C. (Am)	10.69	69	4	3	0

BILLINGTON, Charles R.
Chesterfield, 8 November, 1927 (CH)

League Club	Source	Date Signed	Seasons Played	Apps	Subs	Gls
Aldershot		12.46	46-55	210	-	11
Norwich C.	Tr	01.56	55-56	22	-	0
Watford	Tr	07.57	57	14	-	0
Mansfield T.	Tr	06.58	58	1	-	0

BILLINGTON, Hugh J. R.
Ampthill, 24 February, 1916 Died 1988 (CF)

League Club	Source	Date Signed	Seasons Played	Apps	Subs	Gls
Luton T.	Waterlows	05.38	38-47	87	-	63
Chelsea	Tr	03.48	47-50	83	-	28

BILLINGTON, Stanley
Wallasey, 23 February, 1937 E Yth (RB)

League Club	Source	Date Signed	Seasons Played	Apps	Subs	Gls
Everton	Jnrs	06.55				
Tranmere Rov.	Tr	07.60	60-63	93	-	0

BILLINGTON, Wilfred F.
Blackburn, 28 January, 1930 (G)

League Club	Source	Date Signed	Seasons Played	Apps	Subs	Gls
Blackburn Rov.		04.48				
Workington	Tr	07.54	54-57	52	-	0

BILLY, Christopher A.
Huddersfield, 2 January, 1973 (W)

League Club	Source	Date Signed	Seasons Played	Apps	Subs	Gls
Huddersfield T.	YT	05.91	91	8	2	2

BIMPSON, J. Louis
Rainford, 14 May, 1929 (CF)

League Club	Source	Date Signed	Seasons Played	Apps	Subs	Gls
Liverpool	Burscough	01.53	52-59	94	-	39
Blackburn Rov.	Tr	11.59	59-60	22	-	5
Bournemouth	Tr	02.61	60	11	-	1
Rochdale	Tr	08.61	61-62	54	-	16

BINCH, David
Doncaster, 10 February, 1956 (M)

League Club	Source	Date Signed	Seasons Played	Apps	Subs	Gls
Doncaster Rov.		02.76	75-76	3	2	0

BINES, Henry M.
Cardiff, 17 April, 1930 (WH)

League Club	Source	Date Signed	Seasons Played	Apps	Subs	Gls
Swindon T.		08.50	51-52	6	-	0

BING, Douglas
Broadstairs, 27 October, 1928 (OR)

League Club	Source	Date Signed	Seasons Played	Apps	Subs	Gls
West Ham U.	Margate	01.51	51-54	29	-	3

BING, Thomas
Broadstairs, 24 November, 1931 (F)

League Club	Source	Date Signed	Seasons Played	Apps	Subs	Gls
Tottenham H.	Margate	09.54	57	1	-	0

BINGHAM, John G.
Ripley, 23 September, 1949 (OL)

League Club	Source	Date Signed	Seasons Played	Apps	Subs	Gls
Manchester C.	Charlton Ath. (App)	10.67				
Oldham Ath.	Tr	07.69	69	16	1	3
Mansfield T.	Tr	08.70	70-71	18	3	0
Chester C.	L	03.72	71	7	0	1
Stockport Co.	Tr	07.72	72	16	4	3

BINGHAM, William L.
Belfast, 5 August, 1931 IR Lge/NI-56 (OR)

League Club	Source	Date Signed	Seasons Played	Apps	Subs	Gls
Sunderland	Glentoran	11.50	50-57	206	-	45
Luton T.	Tr	07.58	58-60	87	-	27
Everton	Tr	10.60	60-62	86	-	23
Port Vale	Tr	08.63	63-64	40	-	6

BINGHAM, William P.
Swindon, 12 July, 1922 (HB)

League Club	Source	Date Signed	Seasons Played	Apps	Subs	Gls
Swindon T.		08.46	46-47	20	-	0

BINGLEY, Walter
Sheffield, 17 April, 1930 (FB)

League Club	Source	Date Signed	Seasons Played	Apps	Subs	Gls
Bolton W.	Eccleshall M.W.	04.48	49-54	6	-	0
Sheffield Wed.	Tr	05.55	55-57	38	-	0
Swindon T.	Tr	01.58	57-59	101	-	0
York C.	Tr	08.60	60-62	130	-	5
Halifax T.	Tr	07.63	63-64	63	-	1

BINKS, Martin J.
Romford, 15 September, 1953 (CD)

League Club	Source	Date Signed	Seasons Played	Apps	Subs	Gls
Colchester U.	Leyton Orient (App)	05.72	72	10	0	0
Cambridge U.	Tr	01.73	72	1	0	0

BINNEY, Frederick E.
Plymouth, 12 August, 1946 (F)

League Club	Source	Date Signed	Seasons Played	Apps	Subs	Gls
Torquay U.	Launceston	10.66	67-69	24	10	10
Exeter C.	Tr	02.69	68-73	177	0	90
Brighton & H.A.	Tr	05.74	74-76	68	2	35
Plymouth Arg.	St Louis (USA)	10.77	77-79	67	4	39
Hereford U.	Tr	01.80	79-81	21	6	6

BINNIE, Laurence
Falkirk, 17 December, 1917 (HB)

League Club	Source	Date Signed	Seasons Played	Apps	Subs	Gls
Chesterfield	Camelon Jnrs	05.39				
Mansfield T.	Tr	11.46	46	20	-	0

BINNS, Eric
Halifax, 13 August, 1924 (CH)

League Club	Source	Date Signed	Seasons Played	Apps	Subs	Gls
Halifax T.	Huddersfield T. (Am)	05.46	46	6	-	1
Burnley	Goole T.	03.49	52-54	15	-	0
Blackburn Rov.	Tr	05.55	55-56	23	-	0

BIRBECK, John D.
Lincoln, 1 October, 1932 (FB)

League Club	Source	Date Signed	Seasons Played	Apps	Subs	Gls
Lincoln C.	Spilsby	01.52	54	2	-	0

BIRBECK, Joseph
Gateshead, 15 April, 1932 (LH)

League Club	Source	Date Signed	Seasons Played	Apps	Subs	Gls
Middlesbrough	Evenwood T.	04.53	53-58	38	-	0
Grimsby T.	Tr	07.59	59	18	-	0

BIRCH, Alan
West Bromwich, 12 August, 1956 (W)

League Club	Source	Date Signed	Seasons Played	Apps	Subs	Gls
Walsall	App	08.73	72-78	158	13	23
Chesterfield	Tr	07.79	79-80	90	0	35
Wolverhampton W.	Tr	08.81	81	13	2	0
Barnsley	Tr	02.82	81-82	43	1	11
Chesterfield	Tr	08.83	83	30	2	5
Rotherham U.	Tr	03.84	83-85	99	2	28
Scunthorpe U.	Tr	06.86	86-87	19	4	2
Stockport Co.	Tr	10.87	87	18	2	3

BIRCH, Brian
Southport, 9 April, 1938 E Sch/E Yth (OR)

League Club	Source	Date Signed	Seasons Played	Apps	Subs	Gls
Bolton W.	Jnrs	04.55	54-63	165	-	23
Rochdale	Tr	07.64	64-65	60	1	6

BIRCH, Brian
Salford, 18 November, 1931 E Yth (IF)

League Club	Source	Date Signed	Seasons Played	Apps	Subs	Gls
Manchester U.	Jnrs	05.49	49-51	11	-	4
Wolverhampton W.	Tr	03.52	51	3	-	1
Lincoln C.	Tr	12.52	52-54	56	-	15
Barrow	Tr	06.56	56-58	60	-	27
Exeter C.	Tr	09.58	58-59	19	-	2
Oldham Ath.	Tr	01.60	59-60	35	-	10
Rochdale	Tr	03.61	60-61	11	-	0

League Club	Source	Date Signed	Seasons Played	Apps	Subs	Gls

BIRCH, Clifford
Crumlin, 1 September, 1928 (OR)

League Club	Source	Date Signed	Seasons Played	Apps	Subs	Gls
Norwich C.	Ebbw Vale	12.46	49	5	-	3
Newport Co.	Tr	10.50	50-53	142	-	28
Colchester U.	Tr	06.54	54	12	-	3

BIRCH, Harold
Crieff, 11 January, 1914 (WH)

League Club	Source	Date Signed	Seasons Played	Apps	Subs	Gls
Barrow	Bangor (NI)	09.45	46	26	-	2

BIRCH, James V.
Ashover, 25 October, 1927

League Club	Source	Date Signed	Seasons Played	Apps	Subs	Gls
Huddersfield T.	Grenoside	05.45				
Halifax T.		08.48	48	3	-	1

BIRCH, Jeffrey
Sheffield, 21 October, 1927 (OL)

League Club	Source	Date Signed	Seasons Played	Apps	Subs	Gls
Sheffield U.	Scarborough	09.47				
York C.	Tr	10.49	49	7	-	1

BIRCH, Kenneth J.
Birkenhead, 31 December, 1933 (WH)

League Club	Source	Date Signed	Seasons Played	Apps	Subs	Gls
Everton	Jnrs	08.51	55-57	43	-	1
Southampton	Tr	03.58	57-58	34	-	3

BIRCH, Paul
Birmingham, 20 November, 1962 (M)

League Club	Source	Date Signed	Seasons Played	Apps	Subs	Gls
Aston Villa	App	07.80	83-90	153	20	16
Wolverhampton W.	Tr	02.91	90-91	63	2	10

BIRCH, Paul A.
Reading, 3 December, 1968 (F)

League Club	Source	Date Signed	Seasons Played	Apps	Subs	Gls
Portsmouth	Arsenal (App)	01.87				
Brentford	Tr	12.87	87-88	13	5	2

BIRCH, Trevor
West Bromwich, 20 November, 1933 (WH)

League Club	Source	Date Signed	Seasons Played	Apps	Subs	Gls
Aston Villa	Accles & Pollock	01.52	54-59	22	-	0
Stockport Co.	Tr	11.60	60-61	43	-	0

BIRCH, Trevor N.
Ormskirk, 16 February, 1958 (M)

League Club	Source	Date Signed	Seasons Played	Apps	Subs	Gls
Liverpool	App	12.75				
Shrewsbury T.	Tr	03.79	78-79	23	2	4
Chester C.	Tr	07.80	80	30	1	0

BIRCH, J. Walter
Ecclesfield, 5 October, 1917 (CH)

League Club	Source	Date Signed	Seasons Played	Apps	Subs	Gls
Huddersfield T.		05.39				
Rochdale	Tr	03.46	46-52	246	-	10

BIRCH, William
Southport, 20 October, 1944 (F)

League Club	Source	Date Signed	Seasons Played	Apps	Subs	Gls
West Bromwich A.	App	10.62				
Crystal Palace	Tr	06.63	63-64	6	-	0

BIRCHALL, Paul
Liverpool, 3 September, 1957 (M)

League Club	Source	Date Signed	Seasons Played	Apps	Subs	Gls
Southport	Everton (Am)	03.77	76-77	16	3	1

BIRCHAM, Bernard
Philadelphia (Dm), 31 August, 1924 (G)

League Club	Source	Date Signed	Seasons Played	Apps	Subs	Gls
Sunderland	Jnrs	07.43				
Chesterfield	Tr	11.46				
Grimsby T.	Tr	06.48	49	8	-	0
Colchester U.	Tr	07.50	50	7	-	0

BIRCHAM, W. Clive
Herrington (Dm), 7 September, 1939 (W)

League Club	Source	Date Signed	Seasons Played	Apps	Subs	Gls
Sunderland	Jnrs	09.56	58-59	28	-	2
Hartlepool U.	Tr	02.60	59-62	105	-	15

BIRCHENALL, Alan J.
East Ham, 22 August, 1945 Eu23-4 (M)

League Club	Source	Date Signed	Seasons Played	Apps	Subs	Gls
Sheffield U.	Thorniewood Ath.	06.63	64-67	106	1	31
Chelsea	Tr	11.67	67-69	74	1	20
Crystal Palace	Tr	06.70	70-71	41	0	11
Leicester C.	Tr	09.71	71-76	156	7	12
Notts Co.	L	03.76	75	5	0	0
Notts Co.	San Jose (USA)	09.77	77	28	0	0
Blackburn Rov.	Memphis (USA)	07.78	78	17	1	0
Luton T.	Tr	03.79	78-79	9	1	0
Hereford U.	Tr	10.79	79	11	0	0

BIRCUMSHAW, Anthony
Mansfield, 8 February, 1945 (FB)

League Club	Source	Date Signed	Seasons Played	Apps	Subs	Gls
Notts Co.	App	02.62	60-65	148	0	1
Hartlepool U.	Tr	07.66	66-70	182	3	11

BIRCUMSHAW, Peter B.
Mansfield, 29 August, 1938 (OL)

League Club	Source	Date Signed	Seasons Played	Apps	Subs	Gls
Notts Co.	Jnrs	07.56	56-61	72	-	40
Bradford C.	Tr	06.62	62	27	-	7
Stockport Co.	Tr	06.63	63	17	-	4

BIRD, Adrian L.
Bristol, 8 July, 1969 (CD)

League Club	Source	Date Signed	Seasons Played	Apps	Subs	Gls
Birmingham C.	App	07.87	86-88	23	4	0

BIRD, John C.
Doncaster, 9 June, 1948 (CD)

League Club	Source	Date Signed	Seasons Played	Apps	Subs	Gls
Doncaster Rov.	Doncaster U.	03.67	67-70	48	2	3
Preston N.E.	Tr	03.71	70-75	166	0	9
Newcastle U.	Tr	08.75	75-79	84	3	5
Hartlepool U.	Tr	07.80	80-84	139	2	15

BIRD, John F.
Cardiff, 21 November, 1940 W Sch (FB)

League Club	Source	Date Signed	Seasons Played	Apps	Subs	Gls
Newport Co.	Jnrs	11.57	57-66	276	0	3
Swansea Co.	Tr	07.67	67	7	0	0

BIRD, Kenneth
Norwich, 25 September, 1918 E Sch (G)

League Club	Source	Date Signed	Seasons Played	Apps	Subs	Gls
Wolverhampton W.	Willenhall Rov.	05.37				
Bournemouth	Tr	10.38	38-52	249	-	0

BIRD, Kevin
Doncaster, 7 August, 1952 (CD)

League Club	Source	Date Signed	Seasons Played	Apps	Subs	Gls
Mansfield T.	Doncaster Rov. (Am)	07.72	72-82	372	5	55
Huddersfield T.	Tr	08.83	83	1	0	0

BIRD, Ronald P.
Birmingham, 27 December, 1941 E Yth (OL)

League Club	Source	Date Signed	Seasons Played	Apps	Subs	Gls
Birmingham C.	Jnrs	01.59				
Bradford P.A.	Tr	06.61	61-65	129	0	39
Bury	Tr	10.65	65	13	0	3
Cardiff C.	Tr	02.66	65-70	97	10	24
Crewe Alex.	Tr	07.71	71	19	1	0

BIRKETT, Clifford
Newton-le-Willows, 17 September, 1933 E Sch (OR)

League Club	Source	Date Signed	Seasons Played	Apps	Subs	Gls
Manchester U.	Jnrs	10.50	50	9	-	2
Southport	Tr	06.56	56	14	-	4

BIRKETT, Ronald
Warrington, 21 July, 1927 (OL)

League Club	Source	Date Signed	Seasons Played	Apps	Subs	Gls
Manchester C.	Crompton Rec.	01.46				
New Brighton	Tr	01.47	46-47	8	-	0
Oldham Ath.	Tr	08.48	48	4	-	0
Accrington St.	Tr	07.49	49	14	-	2

BIRKETT, Wilfred
Warrington, 26 June, 1922 (G)

League Club	Source	Date Signed	Seasons Played	Apps	Subs	Gls
Everton	Haydock	02.44				
Southport	Tr	11.46	46-51	162	-	0
Shrewsbury T.	Tr	07.52	52	20	-	0
Southport	Tr	07.53	53	15	-	0

BIRKS, Graham
Sheffield, 25 January, 1942 (FB)

League Club	Source	Date Signed	Seasons Played	Apps	Subs	Gls
Sheffield Wed.	Jnrs	01.60	62	4	-	0
Peterborough U.	Tr	05.64	64-65	34	0	0
Southend U.	Tr	01.66	65-69	138	1	1
Chester C.	Tr	10.69	69-71	71	2	0

BIRMINGHAM, Charles
Liverpool, 24 August, 1922 (IF)

League Club	Source	Date Signed	Seasons Played	Apps	Subs	Gls
Tranmere Rov.	Everton (Am)	08.46	46	2	-	1

BIRSE, Charles D. V.
Dundee, 26 October, 1916 (WH)

League Club	Source	Date Signed	Seasons Played	Apps	Subs	Gls
Watford	Hibernian	05.46	46	7	-	0
Northampton T.		07.47				

BIRTLES, Garry
Nottingham, 27 July, 1956 Eu21-2/E'B'/E-3 (F)

League Club	Source	Date Signed	Seasons Played	Apps	Subs	Gls
Nottingham F.	Long Eaton U.	12.76	76-80	87	0	32
Manchester U.	Tr	10.80	80-81	57	1	11
Nottingham F.	Tr	09.82	82-86	122	3	38
Notts Co.	Tr	06.87	87-88	62	1	9
Grimsby T.	Tr	07.89	89-91	54	15	9

BISHOP, Charles D.
Nottingham, 16 February, 1968 (LB)

League Club	Source	Date Signed	Seasons Played	Apps	Subs	Gls
Watford	Stoke C. (App)	04.86				
Bury	Tr	08.87	87-90	104	10	6
Barnsley	Tr	07.91	91	25	3	0

BISHOP, Edward M.
Liverpool, 28 November, 1962 (M)

League Club	Source	Date Signed	Seasons Played	Apps	Subs	Gls
Tranmere Rov.	Runcorn	03.88	87-90	46	30	19
Chester C.	Tr	12.90	90-91	40	0	11
Crewe Alex.	L	03.92	91	3	0	0

BISHOP, Ian W.
Liverpool, 29 May, 1965 (M)

League Club	Source	Date Signed	Seasons Played	Apps	Subs	Gls
Everton	App	05.83	83	0	1	0
Crewe Alex.	L	03.84	83	4	0	0
Carlisle U.	Tr	10.84	84-87	131	1	14
Bournemouth	Tr	07.88	88	44	0	2
Manchester C.	Tr	07.89	89	18	1	2
West Ham U.	Tr	12.89	89-91	94	4	7

Ian Bishop (Everton, Carlisle United, Bournemouth, Manchester City & West Ham United)

BISHOP, Peter J.
Sheffield, 4 January, 1944 E Yth (OL)

League Club	Source	Date Signed	Seasons Played	Apps	Subs	Gls
Sheffield U.	Jnrs	04.63				
Chesterfield	Tr	05.65	65-70	78	3	7

BISHOP, Raymond J.
Hengoed, 24 November, 1955 (F)

League Club	Source	Date Signed	Seasons Played	Apps	Subs	Gls
Cardiff C.	Cheltenham T.	01.77	77-80	92	10	25
Newport Co.	Tr	02.81	80-81	8	10	2
Torquay U.	Tr	08.82	82-83	33	7	8

BISHOP, Sydney H. R.
Tooting, 8 April, 1934 (CH)

League Club	Source	Date Signed	Seasons Played	Apps	Subs	Gls
Leyton Orient	Chertsey	06.52	53-64	296	-	4

BISHTON, Dennis R.
Windsor, 22 September, 1950 (RB)

League Club	Source	Date Signed	Seasons Played	Apps	Subs	Gls
Reading	App	09.68	68	2	0	0

BISSELL, Steven J.
Birmingham, 8 October, 1958 (W)

League Club	Source	Date Signed	Seasons Played	Apps	Subs	Gls
Nottingham F.	App	10.76				
Blackpool	Tr	09.78	78	1	0	0

BISSET, Thomas A.
Croydon, 21 March, 1932 (FB)

League Club	Source	Date Signed	Seasons Played	Apps	Subs	Gls
Brighton & H.A.	Redhill	01.53	52-60	115	-	5

BISSETT, Nicholas
Fulham, 5 April, 1964 (CD)

League Club	Source	Date Signed	Seasons Played	Apps	Subs	Gls
Brighton & H.A.	Barnet	09.88	88-91	58	3	6

BITHELL, Brian
Winsford, 5 October, 1956 (D)

League Club	Source	Date Signed	Seasons Played	Apps	Subs	Gls
Stoke C.	App	10.73	76	16	1	0
Port Vale	L	09.77	77	2	0	0
Wimbledon	Tr	12.77	77	6	0	0

BLACK, Alan D.
Dumbarton, 4 June, 1943 (FB)

League Club	Source	Date Signed	Seasons Played	Apps	Subs	Gls
Sunderland	Dumbarton	08.64	64-65	4	2	0
Norwich C.	Tr	09.66	66-73	172	4	1

BLACK, Andrew
Stirling, 23 September, 1917 SF Lge/S-3 (CF)

League Club	Source	Date Signed	Seasons Played	Apps	Subs	Gls
Manchester C.	Hearts	06.46	46-49	139	-	47
Stockport Co.	Tr	08.50	50-52	94	-	38

BLACK, Ian H.
Aberdeen, 27 March, 1924 S-1 (G)

League Club	Source	Date Signed	Seasons Played	Apps	Subs	Gls
Southampton	Aberdeen	12.47	47-49	97	-	0
Fulham	Tr	08.50	50-57	263	-	1

BLACK, John
Blackburn, 4 November, 1945 W Sch (G)

League Club	Source	Date Signed	Seasons Played	Apps	Subs	Gls
Arsenal	App	02.63				
Swansea C.	App	12.64	64-65	15	0	0

BLACK, John
Helensburgh, 10 November, 1957 (W)

League Club	Source	Date Signed	Seasons Played	Apps	Subs	Gls
Wolverhampton W.	App	12.75	77-78	5	1	0
Bradford C.	Tr	01.80	79-82	50	5	13
Hereford U.	Tr	08.83	83	8	1	0

BLACK, Kenneth G.
Stenhousemuir, 29 November, 1963 S Sch/S Yth (M)

League Club	Source	Date Signed	Seasons Played	Apps	Subs	Gls
Portsmouth	Hearts	07.89	89-90	50	12	3

BLACK, Kingsley
Luton, 22 June, 1968 E Sch/NIu23-1/NI-22 (LW)

League Club	Source	Date Signed	Seasons Played	Apps	Subs	Gls
Luton T.	Jnrs	07.86	87-91	123	4	25
Nottingham F.	Tr	09.91	91	25	0	4

BLACK, Neville
Ashington, 19 June, 1931 (IF)

League Club	Source	Date Signed	Seasons Played	Apps	Subs	Gls
Newcastle U.	Pegswood	09.49				
Exeter C.	Tr	01.53	52	4	-	0
Rochdale	Tr	07.53	53-55	62	-	13

BLACK, Russell P.
Dumfries, 29 July, 1960 (F)

League Club	Source	Date Signed	Seasons Played	Apps	Subs	Gls
Sheffield U.	Gretna	08.84	84-85	10	4	0
Halifax T.	Tr	08.86	86-87	63	9	14

BLACKADDER, Frederick
Carlisle, 13 January, 1916 (CH)

League Club	Source	Date Signed	Seasons Played	Apps	Subs	Gls
Carlisle U. (Am)	Queens Park	05.37	37-46	3	-	0

BLACKBURN, Alan
Mansfield, 4 August, 1935 (OL)

League Club	Source	Date Signed	Seasons Played	Apps	Subs	Gls
West Ham U.	Jnrs	08.53	54-57	15	-	3
Halifax T.	Tr	11.57	57-60	124	-	35

BLACKBURN, Colin
Richmond (Yorks), 16 January, 1961 (W)

League Club	Source	Date Signed	Seasons Played	Apps	Subs	Gls
Middlesbrough	Jnrs	12.79	80	1	0	0

BLACKBURN, Derek
Wakefield, 5 July, 1931 (HB)

League Club	Source	Date Signed	Seasons Played	Apps	Subs	Gls
Burnley		06.53				
Chesterfield	Tr	06.54				
Swansea C.	Ossett T.	01.57	57	2	-	0

League Club	Source	Date Signed	Seasons Played	Apps	Subs	Gls
BLACKBURN, Edwin H.						
Houghton-le-Spring, 18 April, 1957						(G)
Hull C.	App	09.74	74-79	68	0	0
York C.	Tr	04.80	80-81	76	0	0
Hartlepool U.	Tr	01.83	82-86	161	0	0
BLACKBURN, Keith						
Manchester, 17 July, 1940						(IF)
Portsmouth	Bolton W. (Am)	07.59	60-63	34	-	8
BLACKBURN, Kenneth A.						
Wembley, 13 May, 1951						(F)
Brighton & H.A.	App	05.69	68	1	0	1
BLACKER, James A.						
Leeds, 10 August, 1945						(CH)
Bradford C.	Jnrs	01.63	63-64	21	-	0
BLACKFORD, Gary J.						
Redhill, 25 September, 1968						(RB)
Barnet (N/C)	Fisher Ath.	07.91	91	2	4	0
BLACKHALL, Mark C.						
Barking, 17 November, 1960						(F)
Leyton Orient	App	11.78	81-82	12	6	1
BLACKHALL, Raymond						
Ashington, 19 February, 1957						(FB)
Newcastle U.	App	08.74	74-77	25	12	0
Sheffield Wed.	Tr	08.78	78-81	115	0	1
Mansfield T.	I.K. Tord (Swe)	11.82	82	15	0	0
BLACKHALL, Sidney						
Ashington, 25 September, 1945						(F)
Bradford P.A.	App	10.62	63	1	-	0
BLACKLAW, Adam S.						
Aberdeen, 2 September, 1937 S Sch/Su23-2/S-3						(G)
Burnley	Jnrs	10.54	56-66	318	0	0
Blackburn Rov.	Tr	07.67	67-69	96	0	0
Blackpool	Tr	06.70	70	1	0	0
BLACKLER, Martin J.						
Swindon, 14 March, 1963						(M)
Swindon T.	App	03.81	82	8	1	0
BLACKLEY, Arthur						
Carlisle, 31 January, 1939						(IF)
Chelsea	Jnrs	10.56				
Carlisle U.	Tr	11.60	60-61	38	-	7
BLACKLEY, John H.						
Falkirk, 12 May, 1948 Su23-4/S-7						(CD)
Newcastle U.	Hibernian	10.77	77-78	46	0	0
Preston N.E.	Tr	07.79	79-81	51	2	0
BLACKMAN, Ronald H.						
Portsmouth, 2 April, 1925						(CF)
Reading	Gosport Bor.	03.47	46-53	218	-	158
Nottingham F.	Tr	06.54	54	11	-	3
Ipswich T.	Tr	07.55	55-57	27	-	12
BLACKMORE, Clayton G.						
Neath, 23 September, 1964 W Sch/W Yth/Wu21-3/W-33						(M/FB)
Manchester U.	App	09.82	83-91	138	34	19
BLACKSHAW, William						
Ashton-u-Lyne, 6 September, 1920						(OR)
Manchester C.	Audenshaw U.	05.38	38	3	-	0
Oldham Ath.	Tr	07.46	46-48	67	-	22
Crystal Palace	Tr	07.49	49-50	32	-	5
Rochdale	Tr	02.51				
BLACKSTONE, Ian K.						
Harrogate, 7 August, 1964						(F)
York C.	Harrogate T.	09.90	90-91	46	12	14
BLACKWELL, Dean R.						
Camden, 5 December, 1969 Eu21-6						(CD)
Wimbledon	YT	07.88	89-91	32	10	1
Plymouth Arg.	L	03.90	89	5	2	0
BLACKWELL, Kevin P.						
Luton, 21 December, 1958						(G)
Scarborough	Barnet	(N/L)	87-89	44	0	0
Notts Co.	Tr	11.89				

League Club	Source	Date Signed	Seasons Played	Apps	Subs	Gls
BLACKWELL, Paul						
Deeside, 13 January, 1963						(M)
Chester C.	Jnrs	09.81	81-84	89	5	3
BLACKWELL, Stephen G.						
Wolverhampton, 8 June, 1967						
Wolverhampton W.	YT	11.84	84	0	1	0
BLACKWELL, Wilfred						
Maltby, 19 November, 1926 Died 1959						(OL)
Portsmouth		10.47				
Mansfield T.	Tr	08.48				
Aldershot	Tr	06.50	50	1	-	0
BLACKWOOD, John S. D.						
Cumnock, 25 January, 1935						(IF)
Accrington St. (Am)	Girvan Jnrs	10.58	58-59	4	-	1
BLACKWOOD, Robert R.						
Edinburgh, 20 August, 1934 SF Lge						(WH)
Ipswich T.	Hearts	06.62	62-64	62	-	12
Colchester U.	Tr	05.65	65-67	104	1	6
BLADES, Paul A.						
Peterborough, 5 January, 1965 E Yth						(D)
Derby Co.	App	12.82	82-89	157	9	1
Norwich C.	Tr	07.90	90-91	47	0	0
BLAGG, Edward A.						
Worksop, 9 February, 1918 Died 1976						(CH)
Nottingham F.	Netherton U.	02.38	46-47	54	-	0
Southport	Tr	11.48	48	11	-	0
BLAIN, Colin A.						
Urmston, 7 March, 1970						(M)
Halifax T.	YT	06.88	87-88	18	5	0
BLAIN, James D.						
Liverpool, 9 April, 1940						(M)
Everton	Jnrs	05.59				
Southport	Tr	02.60	59-62	127	-	40
Rotherham U.	Tr	12.62	62-63	23	-	2
Carlisle U.	Tr	04.64	64-65	41	0	7
Exeter C.	Tr	10.65	65-73	310	10	14
BLAIR, Andrew						
Kirkcaldy, 18 December, 1959 Su21-5						(M)
Coventry C.	App	10.77	78-80	90	3	6
Aston Villa	Tr	08.81	81-83	24	9	0
Wolverhampton W.	L	10.83	83	10	0	0
Sheffield Wed.	Tr	08.84	84-85	58	0	3
Aston Villa	Tr	03.86	85-87	19	2	1
Barnsley	L	03.88	87	6	0	0
Northampton T.	Tr	10.88	88	1	2	0
BLAIR, Douglas						
Sheffield, 26 June, 1921						(IF)
Blackpool		05.39				
Cardiff C.	Tr	08.47	48-53	201	-	28
BLAIR, James						
Airdrie, 13 January, 1947						(F)
Norwich C.	St Mirren	09.72	72-73	3	3	0
BLAIR, James A.						
Glasgow, 6 January, 1918 S-1						(IF)
Blackpool	Cardiff C. (Am)	06.35	37-46	50	-	7
Bournemouth	Tr	10.47	47-49	80	-	8
Leyton Orient	Tr	12.49	49-52	104	-	26
BLAIR, Kenneth G.						
Dublin, 28 September, 1952						(M)
Derby Co.	Jnrs	06.70				
Halifax T.	Tr	10.74	74-75	42	1	4
Stockport Co.	L	02.76	75	7	0	0
Southport	Tr	08.76	76	17	0	0
BLAIR, Ronald V.						
Coleraine (NI), 26 September, 1949 NI Sch/NI-5						(D)
Oldham Ath.	Coleraine	10.66	66-69	74	2	1
Rochdale	Tr	03.70	69-71	66	5	3
Oldham Ath.	Tr	08.72	72-80	285	10	22
Blackpool	Tr	08.81	81	35	1	3
Rochdale	Tr	08.82	82	3	0	0

League Club	Source	Date Signed	Seasons Played	Career Record Apps	Subs	Gls

BLAKE, Anthony J.
Rednal, 26 February, 1927 (FB)

Birmingham C.	Rubery Owen	01.49	49	2	-	0
Gillingham	Tr	07.52	52	10	-	1

BLAKE, James B.
Manchester, 5 May, 1966 (D)

Rochdale (N/C)	Jnrs	09.83	83	2	0	0

BLAKE, Mark A.
Nottingham, 16 December, 1970 E Sch/E Yth/Eu21-8 (M)

Aston Villa	YT	07.89	89-91	26	4	2
Wolverhampton W.	L	01.91	90	2	0	0

BLAKE, Mark C.
Portsmouth, 19 December, 1967 E Yth (CD)

Southampton	App	12.85	85-88	18	0	2
Colchester U.	L	09.89	89	4	0	1
Shrewsbury T.	L	03.90	89	10	0	0
Shrewsbury T.	Tr	07.90	90-91	85	0	2

BLAKE, Nathan A.
Cardiff, 27 January, 1972 Wu21-1/W'B' (M)

Cardiff C.	Chelsea (YT)	03.90	89-91	63	14	10

BLAKE, Noel L. G.
Jamaica, 12 January, 1962 (CD)

Aston Villa	Sutton Coldfield	08.79	79-81	4	0	0
Shrewsbury T.	L	03.82	81	6	0	0
Birmingham C.	Tr	09.82	82-83	76	0	5
Portsmouth	Tr	08.84	84-87	144	0	10
Leeds U.	Tr	07.88	88-89	51	0	4
Stoke C.	Tr	02.90	89-91	74	1	3
Bradford C.	L	02.92	91	6	0	0

BLAKE, Russell T.
Colchester, 24 July, 1935 (W)

Colchester U.		04.56	55-60	57	-	8

BLAKEMAN, Alec G.
Oxford, 11 June, 1918 (IF)

Brentford	Oxford C.	05.46	46-48	42	-	7
Sheffield U.	Tr	11.48	48	5	-	0
Bournemouth	Tr	02.49	48-49	25	-	8

BLAKEMAN, Allan
Oldham, 2 November, 1937 (F)

Rotherham U.	Ashton U.	05.58	58	2	-	0
Workington	Tr	01.59	58	14	-	8

BLAKEY, David
Newburn, 22 August, 1929 (CH)

Chesterfield	Chevington Drift	05.47	48-66	617	0	20

BLAKIE, James S.
Reston, 9 December, 1926 (F)

Barrow		08.50	50	9	-	1

BLAMPEY, Stuart L.
North Ferriby, 13 June, 1951 (M)

Hull C.	Jnrs	08.68	69-74	61	11	1

BLANCHFLOWER, R. Daniel
Belfast, 10 February, 1926 EF Lge/NI-56 (WH)

Barnsley	Glentoran	04.49	48-50	68	-	2
Aston Villa	Tr	03.51	50-54	148	-	10
Tottenham H.	Tr	12.54	54-63	337	-	15

BLANCHFLOWER, John (Jackie)
Belfast, 7 March, 1933 NI Sch/NI-12 (CH)

Manchester U.	Jnrs	03.50	51-57	105	-	26

BLANKLEY, Barry S.
Aldershot, 27 October, 1964 (RB)

Southampton	App	10.82				
Aldershot	Tr	12.84	84-86	90	0	0

BLANT, Colin
Rawtenstall, 7 October, 1946 (CD)

Burnley	Rossendale U.	08.64	66-69	46	7	7
Portsmouth	Tr	04.70	70-71	64	0	1
Rochdale	Tr	07.72	72-73	51	0	0
Darlington	Tr	01.74	73-75	89	0	0
Grimsby T.	Tr	08.76	76	9	0	0
Workington	Tr	11.76	76	21	0	0

League Club	Source	Date Signed	Seasons Played	Career Record Apps	Subs	Gls

BLATCHFORD, Patrick J.
Plymouth, 28 December, 1925 (OL)

Plymouth Arg.	Saltash U.	11.48	48-50	19	-	2
Leyton Orient	Tr	08.51	51-52	60	-	8

BLEANCH, W. Norman
Heddon, 19 August, 1940 (CF)

West Ham U.	Willington	02.60				
Southend U.	Tr	07.61	61	3	-	0
Bradford P.A.	Tr	11.61	61	9	-	3

BLEARS, Brian T.
Prestatyn, 18 November, 1933 (FB)

Chester C.		07.54	54-55	2	-	0

BLEASDALE, David G.
St Helens, 23 March, 1965 (M)

Preston N.E.	Liverpool (App)	08.83	83	4	1	0

BLEASE, Rory W.
Bebington, 16 August, 1960 (M)

Chester C. (N/C)	Pwllheli	12.84	84	4	0	0

BLENKINSOPP, Thomas W.
Blyth, 13 May, 1920 EF Lge (D)

Grimsby T.	West Auckland	03.39	46-47	74	-	10
Middlesbrough	Tr	05.48	48-52	98	-	0
Barnsley	Tr	11.52	52	8	-	0

BLICK, Michael R.
Berkeley, 20 September, 1948 (CH)

Swindon T.	App	09.66	67-70	6	0	0

BLINCOW, Ernest
Walsall, 9 September, 1921

Walsall (Am)	West Bromwich A.	01.47	46	1	-	0

BLISSETT, Gary P.
Manchester, 29 June, 1964 (F)

Crewe Alex.	Altrincham	08.83	83-86	112	10	38
Brentford	Tr	03.87	86-91	174	13	58

BLISSETT, Luther L
Jamaica, 1 February, 1958 Eu21-4/E'B'/E-14 (F)

Watford	Jnrs	07.75	75-82	222	24	95
Watford	A.C. Milan (It)	08.84	84-88	113	14	44
Bournemouth	Tr	11.88	88-90	121	0	56
Watford	Tr	08.91	91	34	8	9

BLIZZARD, Leslie W. B.
Acton, 13 March, 1923 (WH)

Queens Park R.		07.41	46	4	-	0
Bournemouth	Tr	05.47	47	1	-	0
Leyton Orient	Yeovil T.	07.50	50-56	222	-	12

BLOCHEL, Joseph E.
Charlton St Giles, 3 March, 1962 (F)

Southampton	App	03.80				
Wimbledon	L	01.82	81	6	0	1

BLOCK, Michael J.
Ipswich, 28 January, 1940 E Yth (OR)

Chelsea	Jnrs	02.57	57-61	37	-	6
Brentford	Tr	01.62	61-65	146	0	30
Watford	Tr	10.66	66	11	2	2

BLOCKLEY, Jeffrey P.
Leicester, 12 September, 1949 Eu23-10/EF Lge/E-1 (CD)

Coventry C.	App	06.67	68-72	144	2	6
Arsenal	Tr	10.72	72-74	52	0	1
Leicester C.	Tr	01.75	74-77	75	1	2
Notts Co.	Tr	06.78	78-79	57	2	5

BLONDEL, Frederick
Lancaster, 31 October, 1923 (IF)

Bury	Morecambe	07.46	46	1	-	0

BLOOD, John F.
Nottingham, 2 October, 1914 Died 1992 (FB)

Notts Co	Johnson & Barnes	06.38	38	8	-	0
Exeter C.	Tr	05.39	46-47	39	-	1

BLOOMER, Brian Mc.
Cleethorpes, 3 May, 1952 (F)

Scunthorpe U.	Brigg T.	08.78	78	3	4	1

Danny Blanchflower (Glentoran, Barnsley, Aston Villa, Tottenham Hotspur & Northern Ireland)

BLOOMER, James
Rutherglen, 10 April, 1926 (IF)

League Club	Source	Date Signed	Seasons Played	Apps	Subs	Gls
Hull C.	Strathclyde	02.48	47	4	-	2
Grimsby T.	Tr	07.49	49-54	109	-	42

BLOOMER, James M.
Glasgow, 22 August, 1947 (FB)

League Club	Source	Date Signed	Seasons Played	Apps	Subs	Gls
Grimsby T.	Jnrs	11.64	65-68	48	4	0

BLOOMER, Robert
Sheffield, 21 June, 1966 (FB/M)

League Club	Source	Date Signed	Seasons Played	Apps	Subs	Gls
Chesterfield	Jnrs	08.85	85-89	120	21	15
Bristol Rov.	Tr	03.90	90-91	11	11	0

BLOOMFIELD, Edward
Wisbech, 28 June, 1932 (OR)

League Club	Source	Date Signed	Seasons Played	Apps	Subs	Gls
Carlisle U.		08.53	53-55	5	-	1
Southport	Tr	07.56	56	2	-	0

BLOOMFIELD, James H.
Kensington, 15 February, 1934 Died 1983 Eu23-2/EF Lge (IF)

League Club	Source	Date Signed	Seasons Played	Apps	Subs	Gls
Brentford	Walthamstow Ave.	10.52	52-53	42	-	5
Arsenal	Tr	07.54	54-60	210	-	54
Birmingham C.	Tr	11.60	60-63	123	-	28
Brentford	Tr	06.64	64-65	44	0	4
West Ham U.	Tr	10.65	65	9	1	0
Plymouth Arg.	Tr	09.66	66-67	25	0	1
Leyton Orient	Tr	03.68	67-68	43	2	3

BLOOMFIELD, Raymond
Kensington, 15 October, 1944 E Sch/E Yth (W)

League Club	Source	Date Signed	Seasons Played	Apps	Subs	Gls
Arsenal	Jnrs	11.61				
Aston Villa	Tr	08.64	64-65	3	0	0

BLOOMFIELD, William
Kensington, 25 August, 1939 (F)

League Club	Source	Date Signed	Seasons Played	Apps	Subs	Gls
Brentford	Jnrs	08.56	56-57	3	-	0

BLOOR, Alan
Stoke, 16 March, 1943 E Yth (D)

League Club	Source	Date Signed	Seasons Played	Apps	Subs	Gls
Stoke C.	Jnrs	03.60	61-76	384	4	17
Port Vale	Tr	06.78	78	5	1	1

BLOOR, Michael B.
Wrexham, 25 March, 1949 (FB)

League Club	Source	Date Signed	Seasons Played	Apps	Subs	Gls
Stoke C.	Newport (Salop)	04.67				
Lincoln C.	Tr	05.71	71-72	71	2	0
Darlington	Tr	08.73	73	7	0	0

BLOOR, Robert
Stoke, 8 July, 1932

League Club	Source	Date Signed	Seasons Played	Apps	Subs	Gls
Crewe Alex.		01.54	53-54	25	-	1

BLORE, Reginald
Wrexham, 18 March, 1942 Wu23-4 (W)

League Club	Source	Date Signed	Seasons Played	Apps	Subs	Gls
Liverpool	Jnrs	05.59	59	1	-	0
Southport	Tr	07.60	60-63	139	-	55
Blackburn Rov.	Tr	11.63	63-65	11	0	0
Oldham Ath.	Tr	12.65	65-69	182	5	20

BLOSS, Philip K.
Colchester, 16 January, 1953 (M)

League Club	Source	Date Signed	Seasons Played	Apps	Subs	Gls
Colchester U.	App	01.71	70-72	32	2	2

BLOTT, John P.
Middlesbrough, 26 February, 1965 (G)

League Club	Source	Date Signed	Seasons Played	Apps	Subs	Gls
Manchester C.	Jnrs	09.82				
Carlisle U.		11.84	84	2	0	0
Newport Co. (N/C)	Mansfield T. (N/C)	03.87	86	1	0	0

BLOWMAN, Peter
Billingham, 12 December, 1949 (F)

League Club	Source	Date Signed	Seasons Played	Apps	Subs	Gls
Hartlepool U.		11.67	67-69	56	7	15

BLOXHAM, James A.
New Houghton, 2 July, 1923 (W)

League Club	Source	Date Signed	Seasons Played	Apps	Subs	Gls
Hull C.	Ollerton Colly.	10.47	47-49	33	-	2

BLUCK, David
India, 31 January, 1930 (LH)

League Club	Source	Date Signed	Seasons Played	Apps	Subs	Gls
Aldershot (Am)		08.51	51	1	-	0

BLUE, Archibald
Glasgow, 8 April, 1940 (CF)

League Club	Source	Date Signed	Seasons Played	Apps	Subs	Gls
Exeter C.	Hearts	07.61	61	34	-	6
Carlisle U.	Tr	07.62	62	2	-	1

BLUNDELL, Alan
Birkenhead, 18 August, 1947 (WH)

League Club	Source	Date Signed	Seasons Played	Apps	Subs	Gls
Tranmere Rov	App	08.65	65-66	3	0	0

BLUNDELL, Christopher K.
Billinge, 7 December, 1969 (CD)

League Club	Source	Date Signed	Seasons Played	Apps	Subs	Gls
Oldham Ath.	YT	07.88	87-88	2	1	0
Rochdale	Tr	09.90	90	10	4	0

BLUNSTONE, Frank
Crewe, 17 October, 1934 E Yth/Eu23-5/EF Lge/E-5 (OL)

League Club	Source	Date Signed	Seasons Played	Apps	Subs	Gls
Crewe Alex.	Jnrs	01.52	51-52	48	-	12
Chelsea	Tr	03.53	52-63	317	-	47

BLUNT, David
Goldthorpe, 29 April, 1949 (IF)

League Club	Source	Date Signed	Seasons Played	Apps	Subs	Gls
Bradford P.A. (Am)		03.68	67	2	0	0
Chester C.	Tr	06.68				

BLUNT, Edwin
Tunstall, 21 May, 1918 (WH)

League Club	Source	Date Signed	Seasons Played	Apps	Subs	Gls
Northampton T.	Port Vale (Am)	05.37	37-48	87	-	2
Accrington St.	Tr	07.49	49	9	-	1

BLY, Terence G.
Fincham (Nk), 22 October, 1935 (CF)

League Club	Source	Date Signed	Seasons Played	Apps	Subs	Gls
Norwich C.	Bury Town	08.56	56-59	57	-	31
Peterborough U.	Tr	06.60	60-61	88	-	81
Coventry C.	Tr	07.62	62-63	32	-	26
Notts Co.	Tr	08.63	63-64	29	-	4

BLY, William
Newcastle, 15 May, 1920 Died 1982 (G)

League Club	Source	Date Signed	Seasons Played	Apps	Subs	Gls
Hull C.	Walkers Temp.	08.37	38-59	403	-	0

Billy Bly (Hull City)

BLYTH, James A.
Perth, 2 February, 1955 S-2 (G)

League Club	Source	Date Signed	Seasons Played	Apps	Subs	Gls
Preston N.E.	App	10.72	71	1	0	0
Coventry C.	Tr	10.72	75-81	151	0	0
Hereford U.	L	03.75	74	7	0	0
Birmingham C.	Tr	08.82	82	14	0	0

BLYTH, John W.
Edinburgh, 26 May, 1947 (WH)

League Club	Source	Date Signed	Seasons Played	Apps	Subs	Gls
Halifax T.		05.67	66-67	5	0	0

BLYTH, Melvyn B.
Norwich, 28 July, 1944 (CD)

League Club	Source	Date Signed	Seasons Played	Apps	Subs	Gls
Scunthorpe U.	Great Yarmouth	11.67	67	27	0	3
Crystal Palace	Tr	07.68	68-74	213	3	9
Southampton	Tr	09.74	74-76	104	1	6
Crystal Palace	L	11.77	77	6	0	0
Millwall	Margate	11.78	78-80	75	0	0

BLYTHE, John A.
Darlington, 31 October, 1924 (CH)

League Club	Source	Date Signed	Seasons Played	Apps	Subs	Gls
Darlington		06.46	46-48	17	-	0

BLYTHE, John D.
Huddersfield, 21 July, 1947 (CF)

League Club	Source	Date Signed	Seasons Played	Apps	Subs	Gls
Hartlepool U. (Am)		01.70	69	1	1	0

BOAG, James
Blairhall, 12 November, 1937 (G)

League Club	Source	Date Signed	Seasons Played	Apps	Subs	Gls
Exeter C.	Bath C.	10.62	62	2	-	0

BOAM, Stuart W.
Kirkby-in-Ashfield, 28 January, 1948 (CD)

League Club	Source	Date Signed	Seasons Played	Apps	Subs	Gls
Mansfield T.	Kirkby B.C.	07.66	66-70	175	0	3
Middlesbrough	Tr	06.71	71-78	322	0	14
Newcastle U.	Tr	08.79	79-80	69	0	1
Mansfield T.	Tr	07.81	81-82	11	4	1
Hartlepool U. (N/C)	Tr	03.83	82	1	0	0

BOARDMAN, George
Glasgow, 14 August, 1943 S Amat (IF)

League Club	Source	Date Signed	Seasons Played	Apps	Subs	Gls
Shrewsbury T.	Queens Park	06.63	63-68	173	4	49
Barnsley	Tr	06.69	69-72	123	2	14

BODAK, Peter J.
Birmingham, 12 August, 1961 (M)

League Club	Source	Date Signed	Seasons Played	Apps	Subs	Gls
Coventry C.	App	05.79	80-81	30	2	5
Manchester U.	Tr	08.82				
Manchester C.	Tr	12.82	82	12	2	1
Crewe Alex.	Antwerp (Bel)	12.86	86-87	49	4	7
Swansea C.	Tr	03.88	87-88	25	6	4
Walsall (N/C)	Happy Valley (HK)	08.90	90	3	1	1

BODEL, Andrew C.
Clydebank, 12 February, 1957 (CD)

League Club	Source	Date Signed	Seasons Played	Apps	Subs	Gls
Oxford U.	App	02.75	75-79	128	0	11

BODELL, Norman
Manchester, 29 January, 1938 (D)

League Club	Source	Date Signed	Seasons Played	Apps	Subs	Gls
Rochdale		09.56	58-62	79	-	1
Crewe Alex.	Tr	05.63	63-66	108	1	2
Halifax T.	Tr	10.66	66-67	36	0	0

BODEN, John G.
Grimsby, 4 October, 1926 (OR)

League Club	Source	Date Signed	Seasons Played	Apps	Subs	Gls
Lincoln C.	Skegness T.	04.50	49-50	3	-	2

BODEN, Kenneth
Thrybergh, 5 July, 1950 (M)

League Club	Source	Date Signed	Seasons Played	Apps	Subs	Gls
Doncaster Rov.	Bridlington T.	03.77	76	1	0	0

BODIN, Paul J.
Cardiff, 13 September, 1964 WYth/Wu21-1/W-15 (LB)

League Club	Source	Date Signed	Seasons Played	Apps	Subs	Gls
Newport Co.	Chelsea (Jnrs)	01.82				
Cardiff C.	Tr	08.82	82-84	68	7	4
Newport Co.	Bath C.	01.88	87	6	0	1
Swindon T.	Tr	03.88	87-90	87	6	9
Crystal Palace	Tr	03.91	90-91	8	1	0
Newcastle U.	L	12.91	91	6	0	0
Swindon T.	Tr	01.92	91	21	0	2

BODLE, Harold
Doncaster, 4 October, 1920 (IF)

League Club	Source	Date Signed	Seasons Played	Apps	Subs	Gls
Rotherham U.	Ridgehill Ath.	05.38	38	9	-	0
Birmingham C.	Tr	12.38	38-48	95	-	32
Bury	Tr	03.49	48-51	119	-	40
Stockport Co.	Tr	10.52	52	29	-	6
Accrington St.	Tr	08.53	53-56	94	-	13

BODLEY, Michael J.
Hayes, 14 September, 1967 (CD)

League Club	Source	Date Signed	Seasons Played	Apps	Subs	Gls
Chelsea	App	09.85	87	6	0	1
Northampton T.	Tr	01.89	88	20	0	0
Barnet	Tr	09.89	91	36	0	1

BOERSMA, Philip
Liverpool, 24 September, 1949 (F)

League Club	Source	Date Signed	Seasons Played	Apps	Subs	Gls
Liverpool	Jnrs	09.68	69-75	73	9	17
Wrexham	L	03.70	69	3	2	0
Middlesbrough	Tr	12.75	75-76	41	6	3
Luton T.	Tr	08.77	77-78	35	1	8
Swansea C.	Tr	09.78	78	15	3	1

BOGAN, Thomas
Glasgow, 18 May, 1920 SF Lge (IF)

League Club	Source	Date Signed	Seasons Played	Apps	Subs	Gls
Preston N.E.	Glasgow Celtic	10.48	48	11	-	0
Manchester U.	Tr	08.49	49-50	29	-	7
Southampton	Aberdeen	12.51	51-52	8	-	2
Blackburn Rov.	Tr	08.53	53	1	-	0

BOGIE, Ian
Newcastle, 6 December, 1967 E Sch (M)

League Club	Source	Date Signed	Seasons Played	Apps	Subs	Gls
Newcastle U.	App	12.85	86-88	7	7	0
Preston N.E.	Tr	02.89	88-90	67	12	12
Millwall	Tr	08.91	91	20	5	0

BOGIE, Malcolm
Edinburgh, 26 December, 1939 S Sch (W)

League Club	Source	Date Signed	Seasons Played	Apps	Subs	Gls
Grimsby T.	Hibernian	07.63	63	1	-	0
Aldershot	Tr	07.64	64	2	-	1

BOLAM, Thomas E.
Newcastle, 8 July, 1924 (CH)

League Club	Source	Date Signed	Seasons Played	Apps	Subs	Gls
Barrow		08.50	50-51	35	-	0

BOLDER, Robert J.
Dover, 2 October, 1958 (G)

League Club	Source	Date Signed	Seasons Played	Apps	Subs	Gls
Sheffield Wed.	Dover T.	03.77	77-82	196	0	0
Liverpool	Tr	08.83				
Sunderland	Tr	09.85	85	22	0	0
Charlton Ath.	Tr	08.86	86-91	222	0	0

BOLLAND, Gordon E.
Boston, 12 August, 1943 (IF)

League Club	Source	Date Signed	Seasons Played	Apps	Subs	Gls
Chelsea	Jnrs	08.60	61	2	-	0
Leyton Orient	Tr	03.62	61-63	63	-	19
Norwich C.	Tr	03.64	63-67	104	1	29
Charlton Ath.	Tr	11.67	67-68	9	2	2
Millwall	Tr	10.68	68-74	239	5	62

BOLLANDS, John F.
Middlesbrough, 11 July, 1935 (G)

League Club	Source	Date Signed	Seasons Played	Apps	Subs	Gls
Oldham Ath.	South Bank	05.53	54-55	23	-	0
Sunderland	Tr	03.56	55-59	61	-	0
Bolton W,	Tr	02.60	59	13	-	0
Oldham Ath.	Tr	09.61	61-65	131	0	0

BOLTON, Anthony G.
Newport, 15 January, 1968 (W)

League Club	Source	Date Signed	Seasons Played	Apps	Subs	Gls
Charlton Ath.		01.85				
Newport Co.	Tr	08.86	86	6	2	0

BOLTON, Ian R.
Leicester, 13 July, 1953 (CD)

League Club	Source	Date Signed	Seasons Played	Apps	Subs	Gls
Notts Co.	Birmingham C. (App)	03.72	71-76	61	9	4
Lincoln C.	L	08.76	76	1	0	0
Watford	Tr	08.77	77-83	233	1	28
Brentford	Tr	12.83	83	14	0	1

BOLTON, John M.
Lesmahagow, 26 October, 1941 (HB)

League Club	Source	Date Signed	Seasons Played	Apps	Subs	Gls
Ipswich T.	Raith Rov.	07.63	63-65	69	0	2

BOLTON, Joseph
Birtley, 2 February, 1955 (LB)

League Club	Source	Date Signed	Seasons Played	Apps	Subs	Gls
Sunderland	App	02.72	71-80	264	9	11
Middlesbrough	Tr	07.81	81-82	59	0	1
Sheffield U.	Tr	08.83	83-85	109	0	2

BOLTON, Lyall
Gateshead, 11 July, 1932 (WH)

League Club	Source	Date Signed	Seasons Played	Apps	Subs	Gls
Sunderland	Windy Nook Jnrs	08.50	55-56	3	-	0

BOLTON, Ronald (Danny)
Rotherham, 1 September, 1921 (G)

League Club	Source	Date Signed	Seasons Played	Apps	Subs	Gls
Bolton W.		05.39				
Rotherham U.	Owen & Dyson	06.48	48-54	150	-	0

BOLTON, Ronald
Golborne, 21 January, 1938 (M)

League Club	Source	Date Signed	Seasons Played	Apps	Subs	Gls
Bournemouth	Crompton Rov.	04.58	58-65	199	0	31
Ipswich T.	Tr	10.65	65-67	21	1	0
Bournemouth	Tr	09.67	67-68	61	4	17

BOND, Anthony
Preston, 27 December, 1913 (OR)

League Club	Source	Date Signed	Seasons Played	Apps	Subs	Gls
Blackburn Rov.	Dick Kerr's	04.32				
Wolverhampton W.	Chorley	11.36				
Torquay U.	Tr	06.37	37	15	-	0
Southport	Tr	08.45				
Accrington St.	Tr	05.46	46	29	-	4

BOND, Dennis J. T.
Walthamstow, 17 March, 1947 E Sch/E Yth (M)

League Club	Source	Date Signed	Seasons Played	Apps	Subs	Gls
Watford	App	03.64	64-66	93	0	17
Tottenham H.	Tr	03.67	66-70	20	3	1
Charlton Ath.	Tr	10.70	70-72	70	5	3
Watford	Tr	02.73	72-77	178	1	20

BOND, J. Ernest
Preston, 4 May, 1929 (OL)

League Club	Source	Date Signed	Seasons Played	Apps	Subs	Gls
Manchester U.	Leyland Motors	12.50	51-52	20	-	4
Carlisle U.	Tr	09.52	52-58	191	-	24

BOND, Graham C.
Torquay, 30 December, 1932 (IF)

League Club	Source	Date Signed	Seasons Played	Apps	Subs	Gls
Torquay U.		09.51	53-60	129	-	46
Exeter C.	Tr	10.60	60	10	-	4
Torquay U.	Weymouth	10.61	61	5	-	1

BOND, John F.
Colchester, 17 December, 1932 EF Lge (FB)

League Club	Source	Date Signed	Seasons Played	Apps	Subs	Gls
West Ham U.	Colchester Casuals	03.50	51-64	381	-	32
Torquay U.	Tr	01.66	65-68	129	1	12

BOND, Kevin J.
West Ham, 22 June, 1957 (CD)

League Club	Source	Date Signed	Seasons Played	Apps	Subs	Gls
Norwich C.	Bournemouth (App)	07.74	75-80	137	5	12
Manchester C.	Seattle (USA)	09.81	81-84	108	2	11
Southampton	Tr	09.84	84-87	139	1	6
Bournemouth	Tr	08.88	88-91	121	5	4

BOND, Leonard A.
Ilminster (Som), 12 February, 1954 (G)

League Club	Source	Date Signed	Seasons Played	Apps	Subs	Gls
Bristol C.	App	09.71	70-76	30	0	0
Exeter C.	L	11.74	74	30	0	0
Torquay U.	L	10.75	75	3	0	0
Scunthorpe U.	L	12.75	75	8	0	0
Colchester U.	L	01.76	75	3	0	0
Brentford	Tr	08.77	77-79	122	0	0
Exeter C.	Tr	10.80	80-83	138	0	0

BONDS, William A.
Woolwich, 17 September, 1946 Eu23-2 (CD)

League Club	Source	Date Signed	Seasons Played	Apps	Subs	Gls
Charlton Ath.	App	09.64	64-66	95	0	1
West Ham U.	Tr	05.67	67-87	655	8	48

BONE, James
Bridge of Allan, 22 September, 1949 Su23-3/S-2 (CF)

League Club	Source	Date Signed	Seasons Played	Apps	Subs	Gls
Norwich C.	Partick Th.	02.72	71-72	39	0	9
Sheffield U.	Tr	02.73	72-73	30	1	9

BONE, John
Hartlepool, 19 December, 1930 (CH)

League Club	Source	Date Signed	Seasons Played	Apps	Subs	Gls
Sunderland	Wingate	05.51	54-56	11	-	0

BONER, David
Queensferry, 12 October, 1941 S Sch (OR)

League Club	Source	Date Signed	Seasons Played	Apps	Subs	Gls
Everton	Jnrs	10.58				
Mansfield T.	Raith Rov.	07.63	63	12	-	1

BONETTI, Peter P.
Putney, 27 September, 1941 Eu23-12/EF Lge/E-7 (G)

League Club	Source	Date Signed	Seasons Played	Apps	Subs	Gls
Chelsea	Jnrs	05.59	59-78	600	0	0

BONNAR, Patrick
Ballymena (NI), 27 November, 1920 LOI (OL)

League Club	Source	Date Signed	Seasons Played	Apps	Subs	Gls
Barnsley	Belfast Celtic	08.49	49	5	-	1
Aldershot	Tr	06.50	50-52	62	-	20

BONNELL, Arnold
Barnsley, 23 March, 1921 (FB)

League Club	Source	Date Signed	Seasons Played	Apps	Subs	Gls
Barnsley	Jnrs	04.38	46-47	7	-	0
Rochdale	Tr	07.48	48	5	-	0

BONNER, Bernard
Motherwell 22 July, 1927 (CF)

League Club	Source	Date Signed	Seasons Played	Apps	Subs	Gls
Wrexham	Airdrieonians	02.52	51	1	-	0

BONNER, Mark
Ormskirk, 7 June, 1974 (M)

League Club	Source	Date Signed	Seasons Played	Apps	Subs	Gls
Blackpool	YT	06.92	91	2	1	0

BONNYMAN, Philip
Glasgow, 6 February, 1954 (M)

League Club	Source	Date Signed	Seasons Played	Apps	Subs	Gls
Carlisle U.	Hamilton Acad.	03.76	75-79	149	3	26
Chesterfield	Tr	03.80	79-81	98	1	25
Grimsby T.	Tr	08.82	82-86	146	5	15
Stoke C.	L	03.86	85	7	0	0
Darlington	Tr	07.87	87-88	49	1	5

BONSON, Joseph
Barnsley, 19 June, 1936 (CF)

League Club	Source	Date Signed	Seasons Played	Apps	Subs	Gls
Wolverhampton W.	Jnrs	07.53	56	10	-	3
Cardiff C.	Tr	11.57	57-59	72	-	37
Scunthorpe U.	Tr	06.60	60-61	52	-	11
Doncaster Rov.	Tr	02.62	61	14	-	4
Newport Co.	Tr	06.62	62-63	83	-	47
Brentford	Tr	06.64	64-65	35	0	13
Lincoln C.	Tr	01.66	65-66	46	1	16

BOOK, Anthony K.
Bath, 4 September, 1935 (FB)

League Club	Source	Date Signed	Seasons Played	Apps	Subs	Gls
Plymouth Arg.	Bath C.	08.64	64-65	81	0	3
Manchester C.	Tr	07.66	66-73	242	2	4

BOOK, Kim
Bath, 12 February, 1946 (G)

League Club	Source	Date Signed	Seasons Played	Apps	Subs	Gls
Bournemouth	Frome T.	07.67	67-68	2	0	0
Northampton T.	Tr	10.69	69-71	78	0	0
Mansfield T.	L	09.71	71	4	0	0
Doncaster Rov.	Tr	12.71	71-73	84	0	0

BOOKER, Kenneth
Sheffield, 3 March, 1918 (CH)

League Club	Source	Date Signed	Seasons Played	Apps	Subs	Gls
Chesterfield	Dronfield	04.36	38-51	183	-	4
Shrewsbury T.	Tr	07.52	52	9	-	0

BOOKER, Michael
Barnsley, 22 October, 1947 E Sch (FB)

League Club	Source	Date Signed	Seasons Played	Apps	Subs	Gls
Barnsley	App	10.65	66	0	2	0
Bradford P.A.	Tr	06.68	68	11	2	0

Peter Bonetti (Chelsea & England)

BOOKER, Robert
Watford, 25 January, 1958 (M)

League Club	Source	Date Signed	Seasons Played	Apps	Subs	Gls
Brentford	Bedmond Social	10.78	78-88	207	44	42
Sheffield U.	Tr	11.88	88-91	91	18	13
Brentford	Tr	11.91	91	14	2	2

BOOKER, Trevor C.
Lambeth, 26 February, 1969 (F)

League Club	Source	Date Signed	Seasons Played	Apps	Subs	Gls
Millwall (N/C)	Jnrs	07.86	86	1	2	0

BOORN, Alan
Folkestone, 11 April, 1953 E Yth (M)

League Club	Source	Date Signed	Seasons Played	Apps	Subs	Gls
Brighton & H.A.	Coventry C. (Am)	08.71	72	2	0	0

BOOT, Edward
Laughton, 13 October, 1915 (WH)

League Club	Source	Date Signed	Seasons Played	Apps	Subs	Gls
Sheffield U.	Denaby U.	10.35	35-36	41	-	0
Huddersfield T.	Tr	03.37	36-51	305	-	5

BOOT, Michael C.
Leicester, 17 December, 1947 E Sch (F)

League Club	Source	Date Signed	Seasons Played	Apps	Subs	Gls
Arsenal	App	12.64	66	3	1	2

BOOTH, Andrew D.
Huddersfield, 6 December, 1973 (F)

League Club	Source	Date Signed	Seasons Played	Apps	Subs	Gls
Huddersfield T.	YT	06.92	91	0	3	0

BOOTH, Anthony J.
Biggin Hill, 20 June, 1961 (M)

League Club	Source	Date Signed	Seasons Played	Apps	Subs	Gls
Charlton Ath.	Jnrs	06.78	78-79	2	6	0

BOOTH, Colin
Manchester, 30 December, 1934 Eu23-1 (IF)

League Club	Source	Date Signed	Seasons Played	Apps	Subs	Gls
Wolverhampton W.	Jnrs	01.52	54-59	78	-	26
Nottingham F.	Tr	10.59	59-61	87	-	39
Doncaster Rov.	Tr	08.62	62-63	88	-	57
Oxford U.	Tr	07.64	64-65	48	0	23

BOOTH, David
Barnsley, 2 October, 1948 (FB)

League Club	Source	Date Signed	Seasons Played	Apps	Subs	Gls
Barnsley	Jnrs	05.67	67-71	161	2	8
Grimsby T.	Tr	06.72	72-77	199	1	7

BOOTH, David C.
Manchester, 25 October, 1962 (M)

League Club	Source	Date Signed	Seasons Played	Apps	Subs	Gls
Stockport Co.	Jnrs	04.80	79-80	20	8	4

BOOTH, Dennis
Ilkeston, 9 April, 1949 (M)

League Club	Source	Date Signed	Seasons Played	Apps	Subs	Gls
Charlton Ath.	App	04.66	66-70	67	10	5
Blackpool	Tr	07.71	71	12	0	0
Southend U.	Tr	03.72	71-73	77	1	1
Lincoln C.	Tr	02.74	73-77	162	0	9
Watford	Tr	10.77	77-79	97	3	2
Hull C.	Tr	05.80	80-84	121	2	2

BOOTH, Grenville V.
Chester, 2 April, 1925 (LH)

League Club	Source	Date Signed	Seasons Played	Apps	Subs	Gls
Chester C.		08.48	48	8	-	0

BOOTH, Kenneth K.
Blackpool, 22 November, 1934 (IF)

League Club	Source	Date Signed	Seasons Played	Apps	Subs	Gls
Blackpool	Jnrs	01.52	54-56	2	-	1
Bradford P.A.	Tr	05.57	57-58	45	-	14
Workington	Tr	06.59	59	30	-	13
Southport	Tr	07.60	60	26	-	7

BOOTH, Paul
Bolton, 7 December, 1965 (FB)

League Club	Source	Date Signed	Seasons Played	Apps	Subs	Gls
Bolton W.	App	12.83	84	1	0	0
Crewe Alex.	Tr	07.85	85	23	4	0

BOOTH, Raymond
Wrexham, 5 September, 1949 (W)

League Club	Source	Date Signed	Seasons Played	Apps	Subs	Gls
Wrexham	Jnrs	10.67	66-68	5	0	0

BOOTH, Samuel
Shotts, 20 April, 1926 (WH)

League Club	Source	Date Signed	Seasons Played	Apps	Subs	Gls
Exeter C.	Derry C.	08.51	51-53	62	-	0
Bradford C.	Tr	07.54	54	15	-	0

BOOTH, W. Samuel
Hove, 7 July, 1920

League Club	Source	Date Signed	Seasons Played	Apps	Subs	Gls
Port Vale		02.39	38	9	-	0
Cardiff C.	Tr	05.39				
Brighton & H.A.	Tr	08.47	47-48	28	-	6

BOOTH, Thomas A.
Manchester, 9 November, 1949 Eu23-4 (CD)

League Club	Source	Date Signed	Seasons Played	Apps	Subs	Gls
Manchester C.	Jnrs	08.67	68-81	380	2	25
Preston N.E.	Tr	10.81	81-84	84	0	2

BOOTH, Wilfred
Mapplewell, 26 December, 1918 (F)

League Club	Source	Date Signed	Seasons Played	Apps	Subs	Gls
Halifax T.	Wombwell Ath.	12.47	47	5	-	2

BOOTHMAN, James
Great Harwood, 2 December, 1920 (FB)

League Club	Source	Date Signed	Seasons Played	Apps	Subs	Gls
Oldham Ath.	R.A.F.	01.46	46-47	44	-	0

BOOTHROYD, Adrian N.
Bradford, 8 February, 1971 (FB)

League Club	Source	Date Signed	Seasons Played	Apps	Subs	Gls
Huddersfield T.	YT	07.89	89	9	1	0
Bristol Rov.	Tr	06.90	90-91	10	6	0

BOOTHWAY, John
Manchester, 4 February, 1919 (CF)

League Club	Source	Date Signed	Seasons Played	Apps	Subs	Gls
Manchester C.		07.41				
Crewe Alex.	Tr	07.44	46	11	-	5
Wrexham	Tr	10.46	46-49	95	-	55

BOOTLE, William
Ashton-u-Lyne, 9 January, 1926 (W)

League Club	Source	Date Signed	Seasons Played	Apps	Subs	Gls
Manchester C.		06.43	48-49	5	-	0
Crewe Alex.	Wigan Ath.	03.54	53-54	14	-	4

BOOTY, Martyn J.
Kirby Muxloe, 30 May, 1971 (RB)

League Club	Source	Date Signed	Seasons Played	Apps	Subs	Gls
Coventry C.	YT	06.89	91	2	1	0

BOROTA, Petar
Yugoslavia, 5 March, 1952 Yugoslav Int (G)

League Club	Source	Date Signed	Seasons Played	Apps	Subs	Gls
Chelsea	Partizan Belgrade (Yug)	03.79	78-81	107	0	0

BORROWS, Brian
Liverpool, 20 December, 1960 E'B' (RB)

League Club	Source	Date Signed	Seasons Played	Apps	Subs	Gls
Everton	Jnrs	04.80	81-82	27	0	0
Bolton W.	Tr	03.83	82-84	95	0	0
Coventry C.	Tr	06.85	85-91	261	2	9

Brian Borrows (Everton, Bolton Wanderers & Coventry City)

BORTHWICK, Gary M.
Slough, 30 November, 1955 (M)

League Club	Source	Date Signed	Seasons Played	Apps	Subs	Gls
Bournemouth	Barnet	03.78	77-79	66	8	4

BORTHWICK, John R.
Hartlepool, 24 March, 1964 (F)

League Club	Source	Date Signed	Seasons Played	Apps	Subs	Gls
Hartlepool U.	Owton Social	12.82	82-88	96	21	15
Darlington	Tr	(N/L)	90-91	57	18	15

BORTHWICK, Walter
Edinburgh, 4 April, 1948 (IF)

League Club	Source	Date Signed	Seasons Played	Apps	Subs	Gls
Brighton & H.A.	Morton	05.67	66	1	0	0

BOSLEM, William
Manchester, 11 January, 1958 (CD)

League Club	Source	Date Signed	Seasons Played	Apps	Subs	Gls
Rochdale	Jnrs	11.75	75-77	42	3	1

BOSNICH, Mark J.
Sydney (Australia), 13 January, 1972 (G)

League Club	Source	Date Signed	Seasons Played	Apps	Subs	Gls
Manchester U.	Jnrs	06.89	89-90	3	0	0
Aston Villa	Sydney Croatia (Austr)	02.92	91	1	0	0

BOSSONS, Percy L.
Crewe, 10 January, 1924 Died 1950 (LB)

League Club	Source	Date Signed	Seasons Played	Apps	Subs	Gls
Crewe Alex.	West Ham U. (Am)	06.46	46-48	34	-	2

BOSTOCK, Benjamin R.
Mansfield, 19 April, 1929 (OR)

League Club	Source	Date Signed	Seasons Played	Apps	Subs	Gls
Crystal Palace	Jnrs	05.46	48	4	-	0

BOSWELL, Alan H.
Walsall, 8 August, 1943 (G)

League Club	Source	Date Signed	Seasons Played	Apps	Subs	Gls
Walsall	Jnrs	08.60	61-62	66	-	0
Shrewsbury T.	Tr	08.63	63-68	222	0	0
Wolverhampton W.	Tr	09.68	68	10	0	0
Bolton W.	Tr	10.69	69-70	51	0	0
Port Vale	Tr	08.72	72-73	86	0	0

BOSWELL, James
Chester, 13 March, 1922 (WH)

League Club	Source	Date Signed	Seasons Played	Apps	Subs	Gls
Gillingham		07.46	50-57	342	-	6

BOTHAM, Ian T.
Heswall, 24 November, 1955 (D)

League Club	Source	Date Signed	Seasons Played	Apps	Subs	Gls
Scunthorpe U. (N/C)		03.80	79-84	7	4	0

BOTTIGLIERI, Antonio (Tony)
Chatham, 29 May, 1962 (M)

League Club	Source	Date Signed	Seasons Played	Apps	Subs	Gls
Gillingham	App	04.80	79-81	5	3	0

BOTTOM, Arthur E.
Sheffield, 28 February, 1930 (CF)

League Club	Source	Date Signed	Seasons Played	Apps	Subs	Gls
Sheffield U.	Jnrs	04.47	48-53	24	-	7
York C.	Tr	06.54	54-57	137	-	92
Newcastle U.	Tr	01.58	57-58	11	-	10
Chesterfield	Tr	11.58	58-59	33	-	6

BOTTOMS, Michael C.
Harrow, 11 January, 1939 (F)

League Club	Source	Date Signed	Seasons Played	Apps	Subs	Gls
Queens Park R.	Harrow T.	07.60	60	2	-	0
Oxford U.	Tr	02.62				

BOUGHEN, Dean
Hemsworth, 25 July, 1971 (D)

League Club	Source	Date Signed	Seasons Played	Apps	Subs	Gls
Newport Co. (YT)	YT	08.87	87	1	0	0

BOUGHEN, Paul
South Kirkby, 17 September, 1949 (CH)

League Club	Source	Date Signed	Seasons Played	Apps	Subs	Gls
Barnsley	App	10.67	70	3	5	0

BOUGHEY, Darren J.
Stoke, 30 November, 1970 (RW)

League Club	Source	Date Signed	Seasons Played	Apps	Subs	Gls
Stoke C.	YT	07.89	89	4	3	0
Wigan Ath.	L	01.91	90	2	0	2
Exeter C.	L	03.91	90	8	0	1

BOULD, Stephen A.
Stoke, 16 November, 1962 (CD)

League Club	Source	Date Signed	Seasons Played	Apps	Subs	Gls
Stoke C.	App	11.80	81-87	179	4	6
Torquay U.	L	10.82	82	9	0	0
Arsenal	Tr	06.88	88-91	107	5	3

BOULTER, David A. M.
Stepney, 5 October, 1962 (FB)

League Club	Source	Date Signed	Seasons Played	Apps	Subs	Gls
Crystal Palace	App	07.80	81	16	0	0

BOULTON, Clinton W.
Stoke, 6 January, 1948 (D)

League Club	Source	Date Signed	Seasons Played	Apps	Subs	Gls
Port Vale	App	08.65	64-71	244	0	11
Torquay U.	Tr	11.71	71-78	260	2	35

BOULTON, Colin D.
Cheltenham, 12 September, 1945 (G)

League Club	Source	Date Signed	Seasons Played	Apps	Subs	Gls
Derby Co.	Cheltenham P.C.	08.64	64-77	272	0	0
Southampton	L	09.76	76	5	0	0
Lincoln C.	New York (USA)	07.80	80	4	0	0

BOULTON, Frank P.
Chipping Sodbury, 12 August, 1917 Died 1987 (G)

League Club	Source	Date Signed	Seasons Played	Apps	Subs	Gls
Arsenal	Bath C.	10.36	36-37	36	-	0
Derby Co.	Tr	08.38	38	39	-	0
Swindon T.	Tr	08.46	46-49	97	-	0

BOULTON, Ralph
Grimsby, 22 July, 1923 (IF)

League Club	Source	Date Signed	Seasons Played	Apps	Subs	Gls
Grimsby T.		04.48	47-48	3	-	0

BOUND, Matthew T.
Melksham, 9 November, 1972 (CD)

League Club	Source	Date Signed	Seasons Played	Apps	Subs	Gls
Southampton	YT	05.91	91	0	1	0

BOURNE, Albert
Golborne, 30 September, 1934 (F)

League Club	Source	Date Signed	Seasons Played	Apps	Subs	Gls
Manchester C.		08.52				
Oldham Ath.	Tr	06.58	58-59	35	-	9

BOURNE, George F.
Stoke, 5 March, 1932 (FB)

League Club	Source	Date Signed	Seasons Played	Apps	Subs	Gls
Stoke C.		06.50	52-55	100	-	1

BOURNE, Jeffrey A.
Burton, 19 June, 1948 (W)

League Club	Source	Date Signed	Seasons Played	Apps	Subs	Gls
Derby Co.	Burton A.	06.69	70-76	35	14	9
Crystal Palace	Tr	03.77	76-77	32	0	10
Sheffield U.	Atlanta (USA)	09.79	79	25	1	11

BOURNE, Richard A.
Colchester, 9 December, 1954 (CD)

League Club	Source	Date Signed	Seasons Played	Apps	Subs	Gls
Colchester U.	Jnrs	04.73	71-72	3	1	0
Torquay U.	Bath C.	06.79	79-81	64	4	7

BOUSTON, Bryan J.
Hereford, 3 October, 1960 (FB)

League Club	Source	Date Signed	Seasons Played	Apps	Subs	Gls
Hereford U.	App	10.78	77	4	2	0

BOVINGTON, Edward E. P.
Edmonton, 23 April, 1941 (WH)

League Club	Source	Date Signed	Seasons Played	Apps	Subs	Gls
West Ham U.	Jnrs	05.59	59-67	138	0	1

BOWDEN, John (Jack)
Manchester, 25 August, 1921 (WH)

League Club	Source	Date Signed	Seasons Played	Apps	Subs	Gls
Oldham Ath.	Jnrs	09.45	46-48	72	-	1

BOWDEN, Jonathan L.
Stockport, 21 January, 1963 (M)

League Club	Source	Date Signed	Seasons Played	Apps	Subs	Gls
Oldham Ath.	Jnrs	01.80	81-84	73	9	5
Port Vale	Tr	09.85	85-86	64	6	7
Wrexham	Tr	07.87	87-91	137	10	20
Rochdale	Tr	09.91	91	25	6	6

BOWDEN, Peter W.
Liverpool, 23 July, 1959 (M)

League Club	Source	Date Signed	Seasons Played	Apps	Subs	Gls
Doncaster Rov.	Jnrs	08.77	76-78	22	6	1

BOWEN, Daniel
Ynysybwl 16 November, 1921 (F)

League Club	Source	Date Signed	Seasons Played	Apps	Subs	Gls
Scunthorpe U.	Treharris	07.50	50	5	-	0

BOWEN, David L.
Maesteg, 7 June, 1928 W-19 (WH)

League Club	Source	Date Signed	Seasons Played	Apps	Subs	Gls
Northampton T.		07.47	47-48	12	-	0
Arsenal	Tr	07.50	50-58	146	-	2
Northampton T.	Tr	07.59	59	22	-	1

BOWEN, Jason P.
Merthyr Tydfil, 24 August, 1972 W Yth (F)

League Club	Source	Date Signed	Seasons Played	Apps	Subs	Gls
Swansea C.	YT	07.90	90-91	6	8	0

BOWEN, Keith B.
Northampton, 26 February, 1958 W Sch (F)

League Club	Source	Date Signed	Seasons Played	Apps	Subs	Gls
Northampton T. (N/C)	Jnrs	08.76	76-81	61	4	25
Brentford	Tr	09.81	81-82	42	9	9
Colchester U.	Tr	03.83	82-85	115	1	38

BOWEN, R. Mark
Neath, 7 December, 1963 W Sch/W Yth/Wu21-3/W-19 (LB)

League Club	Source	Date Signed	Seasons Played	Apps	Subs	Gls
Tottenham H.	App	12.81	83-86	14	3	2
Norwich C.	Tr	07.87	87-91	168	2	14

BOWEN, Stewart A.
West Bromwich, 12 December, 1972 (LB)

League Club	Source	Date Signed	Seasons Played	Apps	Subs	Gls
West Bromwich A.	YT	07.91	91	8	0	1

BOWEN, Thomas H.
West Bromwich, 21 August, 1924 (OR)

League Club	Source	Date Signed	Seasons Played	Apps	Subs	Gls
West Bromwich A.	West Bromwich A.	04.44				
Newport Co.	Tr	07.46	46-49	37	-	6
Walsall	Tr	07.50	50-52	94	-	7

BOWER, Kenneth
Huddersfield, 18 March, 1926 (CF)

League Club	Source	Date Signed	Seasons Played	Apps	Subs	Gls
Darlington		01.47	46-48	75	-	35
Rotherham U.	Tr	07.49	49	27	-	11

BOWERING, Michael
Hull, 15 November, 1936 (W)

League Club	Source	Date Signed	Seasons Played	Apps	Subs	Gls
Hull C.		09.58	58-59	45	-	7
Chesterfield	Tr	06.60	60	16	-	1

BOWERS, Ian (Danny)
Stoke, 16 January, 1955 (LB)

League Club	Source	Date Signed	Seasons Played	Apps	Subs	Gls
Stoke C.	Jnrs	06.73	74-77	35	4	2
Shrewsbury T.	L	03.78	77	6	0	0
Crewe Alex.	Tr	07.79	79-83	170	5	2

BOWERS, John A.
Leicester, 14 November, 1939 (W)

League Club	Source	Date Signed	Seasons Played	Apps	Subs	Gls
Derby Co.	Derby Corries	02.57	59-65	65	0	19
Notts Co.	Tr	06.66	66	5	0	0

BOWERY, Herbert N.
St Kitts (WI), 29 October, 1954 (F)

League Club	Source	Date Signed	Seasons Played	Apps	Subs	Gls
Nottingham F.	Worksop T.	01.75	75-76	2	0	2
Lincoln C.	L	02.76	75	2	2	1

BOWEY, Keith A.
Newcastle, 9 May, 1960 (M)

League Club	Source	Date Signed	Seasons Played	Apps	Subs	Gls
Blackpool	App	03.78	78-79	3	0	1

BOWGETT, Paul
Stevenage, 17 June, 1955 (CD)

League Club	Source	Date Signed	Seasons Played	Apps	Subs	Gls
Tottenham H.	Letchworth G.C.	02.78				
Wimbledon	Tr	03.79	78-79	41	0	0

BOWIE, James D.
Aberdeen, 9 August, 1924 (IF)

League Club	Source	Date Signed	Seasons Played	Apps	Subs	Gls
Chelsea	Park Vale	01.44	47-50	76	-	18
Fulham	Tr	01.51	50-51	33	-	7
Brentford	Tr	03.52	51	9	-	0
Watford	Tr	07.52	52-55	125	-	39

BOWIE, James M.
Johnstone, 11 October, 1941 (M)

League Club	Source	Date Signed	Seasons Played	Apps	Subs	Gls
Oldham Ath.	Arthurlie Jnrs	07.62	62-71	331	2	37
Rochdale	Tr	10.72	72	1	2	0

BOWKER, Keith
West Bromwich, 18 April, 1951 (F)

League Club	Source	Date Signed	Seasons Played	Apps	Subs	Gls
Birmingham C.	App	08.68	70-72	19	2	5
Exeter C.	Tr	12.73	73-75	110	0	38
Cambridge U.	Tr	05.76	76	12	5	1
Northampton T.	L	12.76	76	4	0	0
Exeter C.	Tr	08.77	77-79	93	9	28
Torquay U.	Tr	08.80	80-81	50	3	9

BOWLER, Gerard C.
Derry (NI), 8 June, 1919 NI-3 (CH)

League Club	Source	Date Signed	Seasons Played	Apps	Subs	Gls
Portsmouth	Distillery	08.46	46-48	8	-	0
Hull C.	Tr	08.49	49	38	-	0
Millwall	Tr	06.50	50-54	165	-	0

BOWLES, John C.
Cheltenham, 4 August, 1914 (G)

League Club	Source	Date Signed	Seasons Played	Apps	Subs	Gls
Newport Co.	Cheltenham T.	05.36	36	4	-	0
Accrington St.	Tr	06.37	37	12	-	0
Stockport Co.	Tr	07.38	38-52	276	-	0

BOWLES, Paul M. A.
Manchester, 31 May, 1957 (CD)

League Club	Source	Date Signed	Seasons Played	Apps	Subs	Gls
Crewe Alex.	App	05.75	74-79	174	4	20
Port Vale	Tr	10.79	79-81	98	0	8
Stockport Co.	Tr	06.82	82-84	67	3	0

BOWLES, Stanley
Manchester, 24 December, 1948 EF Lge/E-5 (M)

League Club	Source	Date Signed	Seasons Played	Apps	Subs	Gls
Manchester C.	App	01.67	67-69	15	2	2
Bury	L	07.70	70	5	0	0
Crewe Alex.	Tr	09.70	70-71	51	0	18
Carlisle U.	Tr	10.71	71-72	33	0	12
Queens Park R.	Tr	09.72	72-79	255	0	70
Nottingham F.	Tr	12.79	79	19	0	2
Leyton Orient	Tr	07.80	80-81	46	0	7
Brentford	Tr	10.81	81-83	80	1	16

Stan Bowles (Manchester City, Crewe Alexandra, Carlisle United, Queens Park Rangers, Nottingham Forest, Leyton Orient, Brentford & England)

BOWLING, Ian
Sheffield, 27 July, 1965 (G)

League Club	Source	Date Signed	Seasons Played	Apps	Subs	Gls
Lincoln C.	Gainsborough Trin.	10.88	88-91	44	0	0
Hartlepool U.	L	08.89	89	1	0	0

BOWMAN, Andrew
Pittenweem (Fife), 7 March, 1934 S Sch (WH)

League Club	Source	Date Signed	Seasons Played	Apps	Subs	Gls
Chelsea	Jnrs	06.51	53	1	-	0
Newport Co.	Hearts	08.61	61-62	69	-	7

BOWMAN, David
Tonbridge, 10 March, 1960 Su21-1 (M)

League Club	Source	Date Signed	Seasons Played	Apps	Subs	Gls
Coventry C.	Hearts	12.84	84-85	38	2	2

BOWMAN, David M.
Scarborough, 16 December, 1960 (F)

League Club	Source	Date Signed	Seasons Played	Apps	Subs	Gls
Scarborough (N/C)	Bridlington T.	08.87	87	4	0	2

BOWMAN, Richard D.
Lewisham, 25 September, 1954 (M)

League Club	Source	Date Signed	Seasons Played	Apps	Subs	Gls
Charlton Ath.	App	03.73	72-76	93	3	7
Reading	Tr	12.76	76-80	194	0	30
Gillingham	Tr	08.81	81-82	26	0	6

BOWMAN, Robert C. C.
Motherwell, 21 October, 1920 (RB)

League Club	Source	Date Signed	Seasons Played	Apps	Subs	Gls
New Brighton	Kilmarnock	01.49	48	18	-	0

League Club	Source	Date Signed	Seasons Played	Apps	Subs	Gls

BOWRON, Kenneth
Newcastle, 10 April, 1939 (F)

League Club	Source	Date Signed	Seasons Played	Apps	Subs	Gls
Workington	Berwick R.	12.65	65-66	8	1	2

BOWSTEAD, Peter E.
Cambridge, 10 May, 1944 (F)

League Club	Source	Date Signed	Seasons Played	Apps	Subs	Gls
Oxford U.	Cambridge U.	10.62	62-63	8	-	2

BOWTELL, Stephen J.
Bethnal Green, 2 December, 1950 E Sch/E Yth (G)

League Club	Source	Date Signed	Seasons Played	Apps	Subs	Gls
Leyton Orient	App	01.68	67-71	8	0	0

BOWYER, Frank
Chesterton, 10 April, 1922 (IF)

League Club	Source	Date Signed	Seasons Played	Apps	Subs	Gls
Stoke C.	Jnrs	04.39	47-59	398	-	138

BOWYER, Gary D.
Manchester, 22 June, 1971 (LB/W)

League Club	Source	Date Signed	Seasons Played	Apps	Subs	Gls
Hereford U. (N/C)	Westfields	12.89	89	12	2	2
Nottingham F.	Tr	09.90				

BOWYER, Ian
Ellesmere Port, 6 June, 1951 (M)

League Club	Source	Date Signed	Seasons Played	Apps	Subs	Gls
Manchester C.	App	08.68	68-70	42	8	13
Leyton Orient	Tr	06.71	71-72	75	3	19
Nottingham F.	Tr	10.73	73-80	222	17	49
Sunderland	Tr	01.81	80-81	15	0	1
Nottingham F.	Tr	01.82	81-86	203	3	19
Hereford U.	Tr	07.87	87-89	33	7	1

BOXALL, Alan R.
Woolwich, 11 May, 1953 (CD)

League Club	Source	Date Signed	Seasons Played	Apps	Subs	Gls
Scunthorpe U.	Barton T.	08.80	80-83	50	4	1
Chesterfield	Tr	11.83	83	4	1	0

BOXLEY, John (Jack)
Cradley, 31 May, 1931 (OL)

League Club	Source	Date Signed	Seasons Played	Apps	Subs	Gls
Bristol C.	Stourbridge	10.50	50-56	193	-	34
Coventry C.	Tr	12.56	56-59	92	-	17
Bristol C.	Tr	08.60	60	12	-	0

BOXSHALL, Daniel
Bradford, 2 April, 1920 (W)

League Club	Source	Date Signed	Seasons Played	Apps	Subs	Gls
Queens Park R.	Salem Ath.	01.46	46-47	30	-	14
Bristol C.	Tr	05.48	48-49	52	-	10
Bournemouth	Tr	07.50	50-51	51	-	8
Rochdale	Tr	07.52	52-53	11	-	3

BOYCE, Ronald W.
West Ham, 6 January, 1943 E Sch/E Yth (M)

League Club	Source	Date Signed	Seasons Played	Apps	Subs	Gls
West Ham U.	Jnrs	05.60	60-72	275	7	21

BOYD, Brian G.
Carlisle, 4 January, 1938 (OL)

League Club	Source	Date Signed	Seasons Played	Apps	Subs	Gls
Carlisle U.	Raffles Rov.	08.55	55-58	6	-	0

BOYD, Charles M.
Liverpool, 20 September, 1969 (M)

League Club	Source	Date Signed	Seasons Played	Apps	Subs	Gls
Liverpool	YT	05.87				
Chesterfield (N/C)	Bristol Rov. (N/C)	11.90	90	0	1	0

BOYD, Gordon
Glasgow, 27 March, 1958 S Sch (M)

League Club	Source	Date Signed	Seasons Played	Apps	Subs	Gls
Fulham	Glasgow Rangers	05.78	78	1	2	0
Barnsley	Glasgow Rangers	06.80	80	1	1	0
Scunthorpe U.	Tr	03.82	81	10	1	0

BOYD, John (Jack)
Consett, 10 April, 1925 (FB)

League Club	Source	Date Signed	Seasons Played	Apps	Subs	Gls
Sunderland	Medomsley B.C.	05.45				
West Bromwich A.	Tr	06.48	48	1	-	0

BOYD, John
USA, 10 September, 1926 (OR)

League Club	Source	Date Signed	Seasons Played	Apps	Subs	Gls
Bristol C.	Gloucester C.	12.50	50-51	31	-	6

BOYD, John R.
Bo'ness, 7 March, 1926 (CH)

League Club	Source	Date Signed	Seasons Played	Apps	Subs	Gls
Newport Co.	Bo'ness Jnrs	03.47	47	1	-	0

BOYD, Leonard A.
Plaistow, 11 November, 1923 E'B'-1 (WH)

League Club	Source	Date Signed	Seasons Played	Apps	Subs	Gls
Plymouth Arg.	Ilford	12.45	46-48	78	-	5
Birmingham C.	Tr	01.49	48-55	255	-	14

BOYD, Stuart
Workington, 22 December, 1954 (RB)

League Club	Source	Date Signed	Seasons Played	Apps	Subs	Gls
Workington (Am)	Jnrs	08.73	73	1	2	0

BOYD, Thomas
Glasgow, 24 November, 1965 S Yth/Su21-5/S'B'/S-10 (LB)

League Club	Source	Date Signed	Seasons Played	Apps	Subs	Gls
Chelsea	Motherwell	06.91	91	22	1	0

BOYD, William
Bellshill, 18 October, 1958 S Yth (G)

League Club	Source	Date Signed	Seasons Played	Apps	Subs	Gls
Hull C.	App	10.77				
Doncaster Rov.	Tr	02.80	79-83	104	0	0

BOYDEN, Joseph
Willenhall, 12 February, 1929

League Club	Source	Date Signed	Seasons Played	Apps	Subs	Gls
Walsall	Jnrs	12.48	52	4	-	0

BOYER, Philip J.
Nottingham, 25 January, 1949 Eu23-2/E-1 (F)

League Club	Source	Date Signed	Seasons Played	Apps	Subs	Gls
Derby Co.	App	11.66				
York C.	Tr	07.68	68-70	108	1	27
Bournemouth	Tr	12.70	70-73	140	1	46
Norwich C.	Tr	12.74	73-76	115	1	34
Southampton	Tr	08.77	77-80	138	0	49
Manchester C.	Tr	11.80	80-82	17	3	3

BOYES, Kenneth
York, 4 February, 1935 (CH)

League Club	Source	Date Signed	Seasons Played	Apps	Subs	Gls
York C.	Scarborough	10.55	57-65	53	0	2

BOYES, Walter E.
Sheffield, 5 January, 1913 Died 1960 EF Lge/E-3 (OL)

League Club	Source	Date Signed	Seasons Played	Apps	Subs	Gls
West Bromwich A.	Woodhouse M.U.	02.31	31-37	151	-	35
Everton	Tr	02.38	37-48	66	-	11
Notts Co.	Tr	08.49	49	3	-	1
Scunthorpe U.	Tr	08.50	50	13	-	2

BOYLAN, Anthony
Hartlepool, 19 February, 1950 (M)

League Club	Source	Date Signed	Seasons Played	Apps	Subs	Gls
Hartlepool U. (Am)	Bishop Auckland	09.68	69-71	11	1	0

BOYLE, David W.
North Shields, 24 April, 1929 (IF)

League Club	Source	Date Signed	Seasons Played	Apps	Subs	Gls
Newcastle U.		10.47				
Barnsley	Berwick R.	03.51				
Crewe Alex.	Tr	06.52	52-53	25	-	3
Chesterfield	Tr	07.54	54-55	42	-	10
Bradford C.	Tr	07.56	56-60	92	-	13

BOYLE, Henry
Glasgow, 22 April, 1924 (FB)

League Club	Source	Date Signed	Seasons Played	Apps	Subs	Gls
Southport	Murton Colly	07.47	47-49	88	-	0
Rochdale	Tr	06.50	50-55	175	-	0

BOYLE, Ian R.
Barnsley, 7 December, 1953 (CD)

League Club	Source	Date Signed	Seasons Played	Apps	Subs	Gls
Barnsley	App	12.71	72-73	19	2	0

BOYLE, John
Motherwell, 25 December, 1946 (M)

League Club	Source	Date Signed	Seasons Played	Apps	Subs	Gls
Chelsea	Jnrs	08.64	64-73	188	10	10
Brighton & H.A.	L	09.73	73	10	0	0
Leyton Orient	Tr	12.73	73-74	18	0	0

BOYLE, Lee D.
North Shields, 22 January, 1972 (D)

League Club	Source	Date Signed	Seasons Played	Apps	Subs	Gls
Doncaster Rov.	Ipswich T. (YT)	07.90	91	2	1	0

BOYLE, Terence D. J.
Ammanford, 29 October, 1958 W Sch/Wu21-1/W-2 (CD)

League Club	Source	Date Signed	Seasons Played	Apps	Subs	Gls
Tottenham H.	App	11.75				
Crystal Palace	Tr	01.78	77-80	24	2	1
Wimbledon	L	09.81	81	5	0	1
Bristol City	Tr	10.81	81-82	36	1	0
Newport Co.	Tr	11.82	82-85	165	1	11
Cardiff C.	Tr	08.86	86-88	126	2	7
Swansea C.	Tr	08.89	89	27	0	1

BOYLEN, David
Manchester, 26 October, 1947 (M)

League Club	Source	Date Signed	Seasons Played	Apps	Subs	Gls
Grimsby T.	Ryder Brow B.C.	07.65	66-77	370	14	34

BRABIN, Gary
Liverpool, 9 December, 1970 (M)

League Club	Source	Date Signed	Seasons Played	Apps	Subs	Gls
Stockport Co.	YT	12.89	89-90	1	1	0

BRABROOK, Peter
Greenwich, 8 November, 1937 *E Yth/Eu23-9/EF Lge/E-3* (OR)

League Club	Source	Date Signed	Seasons Played	Apps	Subs	Gls
Chelsea	Jnrs	03.55	54-61	251	-	47
West Ham U.	Tr	10.62	62-67	167	0	33
Leyton Orient	Tr	07.68	68-70	70	2	6

BRACE, Robert L.
Edmonton, 19 December, 1964 (F)

League Club	Source	Date Signed	Seasons Played	Apps	Subs	Gls
Tottenham H.	App	12.82	83	0	1	0

BRACE, Stuart C.
Taunton, 21 September, 1942 (W)

League Club	Source	Date Signed	Seasons Played	Apps	Subs	Gls
Plymouth Arg.	Taunton T.	11.60	62-65	9	0	0
Watford	Tr	09.65	65	16	0	4
Mansfield T.	Tr	07.66	66-67	55	2	25
Peterborough U.	Tr	11.67	67-68	22	1	6
Grimsby T.	Tr	10.68	68-73	205	1	81
Southend U.	Tr	10.73	73-75	106	6	37

BRACEWELL, Kenneth
Colne, 5 October, 1936 (FB)

League Club	Source	Date Signed	Seasons Played	Apps	Subs	Gls
Burnley		04.57				
Tranmere Rov.	Tr	05.59	59-60	28	-	1
Lincoln C.	Canada	11.63	63-64	23	-	1
Bury	Margate	12.66	66	1	0	0
Rochdale	Toronto (Can)	03.68	67	5	0	0

BRACEWELL, Paul W.
Heswall, 19 July, 1962 *Eu21-13/E-3* (M)

League Club	Source	Date Signed	Seasons Played	Apps	Subs	Gls
Stoke C.	App	02.80	79-82	123	6	5
Sunderland	Tr	07.83	83	38	0	4
Everton	Tr	05.84	84-88	95	0	7
Sunderland	Tr	08.89	89-91	112	1	2

BRACEY, Lee M. I.
Barking, 11 September, 1968 (G)

League Club	Source	Date Signed	Seasons Played	Apps	Subs	Gls
West Ham U.	YT	07.87				
Swansea C.	Tr	08.88	88-91	99	0	0
Halifax T.	Tr	10.91	91	32	0	0

BRACK, Alistair H.
Aberdeen, 27 January, 1940 (FB)

League Club	Source	Date Signed	Seasons Played	Apps	Subs	Gls
Cardiff C.		09.61	62	1	-	0

BRADBURY, Allen
Barnsley, 23 January, 1947 (WH)

League Club	Source	Date Signed	Seasons Played	Apps	Subs	Gls
Barnsley	App	01.65	64-69	68	1	9
Hartlepool U.	Tr	01.71	70	7	0	0

BRADBURY, Barry
Rochdale, 5 August, 1952 (FB)

League Club	Source	Date Signed	Seasons Played	Apps	Subs	Gls
Rochdale	Matthew Moss	08.72	72-73	12	2	0

BRADBURY, Terence E.
Paddington, 15 November, 1939 *E Sch* (WH)

League Club	Source	Date Signed	Seasons Played	Apps	Subs	Gls
Chelsea	Jnrs	07.57	60-61	29	-	1
Southend U.	Tr	09.62	62-65	160	1	19
Leyton Orient	Tr	06.66	66	25	2	0
Wrexham	Tr	06.67	67-68	77	1	4
Chester C.	Tr	06.69	69-70	90	0	2

BRADBURY, William
Matlock, 3 April, 1933 (IF)

League Club	Source	Date Signed	Seasons Played	Apps	Subs	Gls
Coventry C.	Jnrs	05.50	51-54	24	-	7
Birmingham C.	Tr	11.54	54-55	3	-	2
Hull C.	Tr	10.55	55-59	178	-	82
Bury	Tr	02.60	59-60	18	-	4
Workington	Tr	11.60	60	23	-	5
Southport	Tr	08.61	61	11	-	2

BRADD, Leslie J.
Buxton, 6 November, 1947 (CF)

League Club	Source	Date Signed	Seasons Played	Apps	Subs	Gls
Rotherham U.	Earl Sterndale	03.66	67	3	0	0
Notts Co.	Tr	10.67	67-77	381	17	125
Stockport Co.	Tr	08.78	78-80	116	1	31
Wigan Ath.	Tr	07.81	81-82	57	6	25
Bristol Rov.	L	12.82	82	1	0	1

BRADER, Alec
Horncastle, 6 October, 1942 (IF)

League Club	Source	Date Signed	Seasons Played	Apps	Subs	Gls
Grimsby T.	Horncastle U.	05.60	60	2	-	0

BRADFORD, David W.
Manchester, 22 February, 1953 (M)

League Club	Source	Date Signed	Seasons Played	Apps	Subs	Gls
Blackburn Rov.	App	08.71	71-73	58	6	3
Sheffield U.	Tr	07.74	74-76	54	6	3
Peterborough U.	L	10.76	76	4	0	0
West Bromwich A.	Tr	02.77				
Coventry C.	Washington (USA)	10.81	81	6	0	1

BRADFORD, Geoffrey R. W.
Bristol, 18 July, 1927 *E-1* (CF)

League Club	Source	Date Signed	Seasons Played	Apps	Subs	Gls
Bristol Rov.	Soundwell	05.49	49-63	461	-	242

BRADFORD, Lewis
Swadlincote, 24 November, 1916 (FB)

League Club	Source	Date Signed	Seasons Played	Apps	Subs	Gls
Preston N.E.		12.34				
Bradford C.	Kilmarnock	10.46	46-48	68	-	1
Newport Co.	Tr	11.48	48	24	-	0

BRADLEY, Brendan
Derry (NI), 7 June, 1950 (IF)

League Club	Source	Date Signed	Seasons Played	Apps	Subs	Gls
Lincoln C.	Finn Harps	07.72	72	31	0	12

BRADLEY, Charles
York, 15 May, 1922 (IF)

League Club	Source	Date Signed	Seasons Played	Apps	Subs	Gls
York C.		10.41	46	10	-	2

BRADLEY, Darren M.
Birmingham, 24 November, 1965 *E Yth* (D)

League Club	Source	Date Signed	Seasons Played	Apps	Subs	Gls
Aston Villa	App	11.83	84-85	16	4	0
West Bromwich A.	Tr	03.86	85-91	160	12	6

BRADLEY, David
Manchester, 16 January, 1958 *E Sch* (CD)

League Club	Source	Date Signed	Seasons Played	Apps	Subs	Gls
Manchester U.	App	01.75				
Wimbledon	L	03.78	77	7	0	0
Doncaster Rov.	Tr	08.78	78-79	67	0	5
Bury	Tr	08.80	80	8	0	0

BRADLEY, David H.
Bolton, 6 December, 1953 (F)

League Club	Source	Date Signed	Seasons Played	Apps	Subs	Gls
Workington	Silcoms	09.75	75	8	0	1

BRADLEY, Donald J.
Annesley, 11 September, 1924 (FB)

League Club	Source	Date Signed	Seasons Played	Apps	Subs	Gls
West Bromwich A.	Clipstone Colly	09.43				
Mansfield T.	Tr	08.49	49-61	384	-	6

BRADLEY, George T.
Maltby, 7 November, 1917 (D)

League Club	Source	Date Signed	Seasons Played	Apps	Subs	Gls
Rotherham U.	Maltby Hall O.B.	03.37	37-38	28	-	0
Newcastle U.	Tr	11.38	38	1	-	0
Millwall	Tr	09.46	46-49	74	-	2

BRADLEY, Gordon
Easington, 23 November, 1933 (WH)

League Club	Source	Date Signed	Seasons Played	Apps	Subs	Gls
Bradford P.A.	Stanley U.	01.56	55-56	18	-	1
Carlisle U.	Tr	09.57	57-60	129	-	3

BRADLEY, Gordon
Scunthorpe, 20 May, 1925 (G)

League Club	Source	Date Signed	Seasons Played	Apps	Subs	Gls
Leicester C.	Scunthorpe U.	11.42	46-49	69	-	0
Notts Co.	Tr	02.50	50-57	192	-	1

BRADLEY, James
Greenock, 21 March, 1927 (W)

League Club	Source	Date Signed	Seasons Played	Apps	Subs	Gls
Shrewsbury T.	Third Lanark	07.52	52	1	-	0

BRADLEY, John
Hemsworth, 27 November, 1916 (IF)

League Club	Source	Date Signed	Seasons Played	Apps	Subs	Gls
Swindon T.	Huddersfield T. (Am)	08.36	36-37	24	-	5
Chelsea	Tr	06.38				
Southampton	Tr	05.39	46-47	49	-	22
Bolton W.	Tr	10.47	47-50	92	-	19
Norwich C.	Tr	11.50	50-51	6	-	0

BRADLEY, Keith
Ellesmere Port, 31 January, 1946 (D)

League Club	Source	Date Signed	Seasons Played	Apps	Subs	Gls
Aston Villa	App	06.63	64-71	115	7	2
Peterborough U.	Tr	11.72	72-75	106	3	0

BRADLEY, Lee H.
Manchester, 27 May, 1957 (D)

League Club	Source	Date Signed	Seasons Played	Apps	Subs	Gls
Stockport Co.	App	08.75	75	39	1	4
Halifax T.	Tr	10.76	76-78	62	10	4

BRADLEY, Noel B.
Manchester, 17 December, 1957 (D)

League Club	Source	Date Signed	Seasons Played	Apps	Subs	Gls
Manchester C.	St Roberts B.C.	11.78				
Bury	L	03.80	79	9	0	0
Bury	Tr	08.81	81	15	3	1
Chester C.	Tr	08.82	82	27	4	0

BRADLEY, Patrick
Sydney (Australia), 27 April, 1972 E Yth (FB)

League Club	Source	Date Signed	Seasons Played	Apps	Subs	Gls
Bury	YT	07.90	90	0	1	0

BRADLEY, Peter K.
Donnington, 18 March, 1955 (D)

League Club	Source	Date Signed	Seasons Played	Apps	Subs	Gls
Shrewsbury T.	App	07.73	73	3	0	0

BRADLEY, Ronald
Wolverhampton, 24 April, 1939 E Yth (WH)

League Club	Source	Date Signed	Seasons Played	Apps	Subs	Gls
West Bromwich A.	Jnrs	06.56	62	13	-	0
Norwich C.	Tr	07.64	64-65	4	0	0

BRADLEY, Russell
Birmingham, 28 March, 1966 (CD)

League Club	Source	Date Signed	Seasons Played	Apps	Subs	Gls
Nottingham F.	Dudley T.	05.88				
Hereford U.	L	11.88	88	5	0	0
Hereford U.	L	03.89	88	7	0	1
Hereford U.	Tr	07.89	89-91	75	2	3
Halifax T.	Tr	09.91	91	25	1	2

BRADLEY, Warren
Hyde, 20 June, 1933 E Amat/E-3 (OR)

League Club	Source	Date Signed	Seasons Played	Apps	Subs	Gls
Manchester U.	Bishop Auckland	11.58	58-61	63	-	20
Bury	Tr	03.62	61-62	13	-	1

BRADLEY, William
Glasgow, 26 June, 1937 (IF)

League Club	Source	Date Signed	Seasons Played	Apps	Subs	Gls
Hartlepool U.	Ayr U.	07.63	63-65	100	0	15

BRADSHAW, Alan
Blackburn, 14 September, 1941 (M)

League Club	Source	Date Signed	Seasons Played	Apps	Subs	Gls
Blackburn Rov.	Jnrs	07.63	62-64	11	-	2
Crewe Alex.	Tr	05.65	65-72	287	7	50

BRADSHAW, Carl
Sheffield, 2 October, 1968 E Yth (F)

League Club	Source	Date Signed	Seasons Played	Apps	Subs	Gls
Sheffield Wed.	App	08.86	86-88	16	16	4
Barnsley	L	08.86	86	6	0	1
Manchester C.	Tr	09.88	88	1	4	0
Sheffield U.	Tr	09.89	89-91	59	16	5

BRADSHAW, Darren S.
Sheffield, 19 March, 1967 E Yth (RB/M)

League Club	Source	Date Signed	Seasons Played	Apps	Subs	Gls
Chesterfield	Matlock T.	08.87	87	18	0	0
York C.	Matlock T.	11.87	87-88	58	1	3
Newcastle U.	Tr	08.89	89-91	32	6	0

BRADSHAW, George F.
Southport, 10 March, 1913 Died 1989 (G)

League Club	Source	Date Signed	Seasons Played	Apps	Subs	Gls
New Brighton	High Park Villa	09.33	33-34	83	-	0
Everton	Tr	11.34	34	2	-	0
Arsenal	Tr	03.35				
Doncaster Rov.	Tr	05.36	36-37	53	-	0
Bury	Tr	06.38	38-49	118	-	0
Oldham Ath.	Tr	07.50	50	1	-	0

BRADSHAW, George H.
Clay Cross, 24 March, 1920 (CF)

League Club	Source	Date Signed	Seasons Played	Apps	Subs	Gls
Chesterfield	Newstead Colly	04.46	47	7	-	1

BRADSHAW, Mark
Ashton-u-Lyne, 7 June, 1969 (FB)

League Club	Source	Date Signed	Seasons Played	Apps	Subs	Gls
Blackpool	YT	12.87	86-90	34	8	1
York C.	L	04.91	90	0	1	0

BRADSHAW, Paul
Sheffield, 2 October, 1953 E Sch/E Yth (W)

League Club	Source	Date Signed	Seasons Played	Apps	Subs	Gls
Burnley	App	10.70	74-76	11	2	2
Sheffield Wed.	Tr	09.76	76-77	62	2	9

BRADSHAW, Paul W.
Altrincham, 28 April, 1956 E Yth/Eu21-4 (G)

League Club	Source	Date Signed	Seasons Played	Apps	Subs	Gls
Blackburn Rov.	App	07.73	73-77	78	0	0
Wolverhampton W.	Tr	09.77	77-83	200	0	0
West Bromwich A.	Vancouver (Can)	04.85	85	8	0	0
Bristol Rov. (N/C)	Walsall (Coach)	03.87	86	5	0	0
Newport Co. (N/C)	Tr	07.87	87	23	0	0
West Bromwich A.	Tr	08.88	88-89	6	0	0
Peterborough U.	Tr	06.90	90	39	0	0

BRADY, Kieron
Glasgow, 17 September, 1971 IRu21-1 (W)

League Club	Source	Date Signed	Seasons Played	Apps	Subs	Gls
Sunderland	YT	07.89	89-91	17	16	7

BRADY, Patrick J.
Dublin, 11 March, 1936 (LB)

League Club	Source	Date Signed	Seasons Played	Apps	Subs	Gls
Millwall	Home Farm	01.59	58-62	148	-	1
Queens Park R.	Tr	07.63	63-64	61	-	0

BRADY, Paul J.
Birmingham, 26 March, 1961 (FB)

League Club	Source	Date Signed	Seasons Played	Apps	Subs	Gls
Birmingham C.	App	08.78				
Northampton T.	Tr	08.81	81-82	49	2	3
Crewe Alex.	Tr	02.83	82-83	42	1	1

BRADY, T. Raymond
Dublin, 3 June, 1937 IR-6 (D)

League Club	Source	Date Signed	Seasons Played	Apps	Subs	Gls
Millwall	Home Farm	07.57	57-62	165	-	4
Queens Park R.	Tr	07.63	63-65	89	0	0

BRADY, William (Liam)
Dublin, 13 February, 1956 IR-72 (M)

League Club	Source	Date Signed	Seasons Played	Apps	Subs	Gls
Arsenal	App	08.73	73-79	227	8	43
West Ham U.	Ascoli (It)	03.87	86-89	79	10	8

BRAGG, Walter L.
London, 8 July, 1929 (D)

League Club	Source	Date Signed	Seasons Played	Apps	Subs	Gls
Brentford	Jnrs	01.47	46-56	161	-	6

BRAHAN, Marcel E. L. (Lou)
Stepney, 3 December, 1926 (CH)

League Club	Source	Date Signed	Seasons Played	Apps	Subs	Gls
Leyton Orient (Am)	Walthamstow Ave.	07.55	55	1	-	0

BRAIN, Simon, A. J.
Evesham, 31 March, 1966 (F)

League Club	Source	Date Signed	Seasons Played	Apps	Subs	Gls
Hereford U.	Cheltenham T.	12.90	90-91	60	3	18

BRAITHWAITE, Robert M.
Belfast, 24 February, 1937 NI Sch/NI-10 (W)

League Club	Source	Date Signed	Seasons Played	Apps	Subs	Gls
Middlesbrough	Linfield	06.63	63-66	67	1	12

BRAITHWAITE, J. Rodney
Isleworth, 19 December, 1965 (F)

League Club	Source	Date Signed	Seasons Played	Apps	Subs	Gls
Fulham	Jnrs	07.84	85-86	7	5	2

BRAITHWAITE, Ronald S.
Ash Vale, 9 April, 1931 (CH)

League Club	Source	Date Signed	Seasons Played	Apps	Subs	Gls
Crystal Palace		08.49	52	3	-	0

BRAMHALL, John
Warrington, 20 November, 1956 (CD)

League Club	Source	Date Signed	Seasons Played	Apps	Subs	Gls
Tranmere Rov.	Stockton Heath	07.76	76-81	164	6	7
Bury	Tr	03.82	81-85	165	2	17
Chester C.	L	11.85	85	4	0	0
Rochdale	Tr	08.86	86-87	86	0	13
Halifax T.	Tr	08.88	88-89	62	0	5
Scunthorpe U.	Tr	01.90	89-90	32	0	0

BRAMHALL, Neil
Blackpool, 16 October, 1965 (F)

League Club	Source	Date Signed	Seasons Played	Apps	Subs	Gls
Blackpool	App	10.83	82	0	3	0

BRAMLEY, Arthur
Mansfield, 25 March, 1929 (G)

League Club	Source	Date Signed	Seasons Played	Apps	Subs	Gls
Mansfield T.	Bentinck Colly	10.49	49-52	19	-	0

BRAMLEY, Ernest
Mansfield, 29 August, 1920 (RB)

League Club	Source	Date Signed	Seasons Played	Apps	Subs	Gls
Mansfield T.	Bolsover Colly	12.38	38-47	45	-	1

BRAMLEY, J. Stuart
Scunthorpe, 19 April, 1946 (F)

League Club	Source	Date Signed	Seasons Played	Apps	Subs	Gls
Scunthorpe U.	App	04.64	64-66	35	0	3

BRAMWELL, John
Ashton-in-Makerfield, 1 March, 1937 (FB)

League Club	Source	Date Signed	Seasons Played	Apps	Subs	Gls
Everton	Wigan Ath.	04.58	58-59	52	-	0
Luton T.	Tr	10.60	60-64	187	-	1

BRAMWELL, Steven
Stockport, 9 October, 1970 (M)

League Club	Source	Date Signed	Seasons Played	Apps	Subs	Gls
Oldham Ath.	YT	07.89	88	0	1	0
Crewe Alex.	Tr	05.90				

BRANAGAN, James P. S.
Urmston, 3 July, 1955 (FB)

League Club	Source	Date Signed	Seasons Played	Apps	Subs	Gls
Oldham Ath.	Jnrs	07.73	74-76	24	3	0
Huddersfield T.	Cape Town C. (SA)	11.77	77-78	37	1	0
Blackburn Rov.	Tr	10.79	79-86	290	4	5
Preston N.E.	Tr	05.87	87	3	0	0
York C.	Tr	10.87	87-88	40	2	1

BRANAGAN, Keith G.
Fulham, 10 July, 1966 (G)

League Club	Source	Date Signed	Seasons Played	Apps	Subs	Gls
Cambridge U.	Jnrs	08.83	83-87	110	0	0
Millwall	Tr	03.88	89-91	46	0	0
Brentford	L	11.89	89	2	0	0
Gillingham	L	10.91	91	1	0	0

BRANAGAN, Kenneth F.
Salford, 27 July, 1930 (FB)

League Club	Source	Date Signed	Seasons Played	Apps	Subs	Gls
Manchester C.	N.Salford B.C.	11.48	50-59	196	-	3
Oldham Ath.	Tr	10.60	60-65	177	0	5

BRANCH, Graham
Liverpool, 12 February, 1972 (W)

League Club	Source	Date Signed	Seasons Played	Apps	Subs	Gls
Tranmere Rov.	Heswall	05.91	91	0	4	0

BRAND, Andrew S. (Drew)
Edinburgh, 8 November, 1957 (G)

League Club	Source	Date Signed	Seasons Played	Apps	Subs	Gls
Everton	App	11.75	75-76	2	0	0
Crewe Alex.	L	02.77	76	14	0	0
Crewe Alex.	L	08.78	78	1	0	0
Hereford U.	Tr	05.80	80-81	54	0	0
Wrexham	L	11.82	82	1	0	0
Blackpool (N/C)	Witton A.	03.84	83	3	0	0

BRAND, Kenneth R.
Whitechapel, 28 April, 1938 (LB)

League Club	Source	Date Signed	Seasons Played	Apps	Subs	Gls
Millwall	Eton Manor	09.56	56-57	13	-	0

BRAND, Ralph L.
Edinburgh, 18 December, 1936 S Sch/Su23-1/SF Lge/S-8 (CF)

League Club	Source	Date Signed	Seasons Played	Apps	Subs	Gls
Manchester C.	Glasgow Rangers	08.65	65-66	20	0	2
Sunderland	Tr	08.67	67-68	31	0	7

BRAND, Raymond E.
Islington, 2 October, 1934 (CH)

League Club	Source	Date Signed	Seasons Played	Apps	Subs	Gls
Millwall	Hatfield	10.51	55-60	150	-	8
Southend U.	Tr	08.61	61-62	22	-	9

BRANDER, George M.
Aberdeen, 1 November, 1929 (W)

League Club	Source	Date Signed	Seasons Played	Apps	Subs	Gls
Newcastle U.	Raith Rov.	03.52	52	5	-	2

BRANDON, Kenneth, A.
Birmingham, 8 February, 1934 (OL)

League Club	Source	Date Signed	Seasons Played	Apps	Subs	Gls
Swindon T. (Am)	Kingstanding B.C.	01.53	52	5	-	0
Chester C.	Tr	06.53	53-55	36	-	6
Leicester C.	Tr	07.56				
Darlington	Tr	06.58	58	16	-	1

BRANFOOT, Ian G.
Gateshead, 26 January, 1947 (RB)

League Club	Source	Date Signed	Seasons Played	Apps	Subs	Gls
Sheffield Wed.	Gateshead	07.65	66-69	33	3	0
Doncaster Rov.	Tr	12.69	69-72	156	0	5
Lincoln C.	Tr	07.73	73-77	166	0	11

BRANNAN, Gerard D.
Prescot, 15 January, 1972 (FB)

League Club	Source	Date Signed	Seasons Played	Apps	Subs	Gls
Tranmere Rov.	YT	07.90	90-91	32	4	2

BRANNAN, Peter
Bradford, 7 April, 1947 (F)

League Club	Source	Date Signed	Seasons Played	Apps	Subs	Gls
Bradford P.A.		02.69	68-69	38	4	2

BRANNAN, Robert
Bradford, 27 August, 1924 (OR)

League Club	Source	Date Signed	Seasons Played	Apps	Subs	Gls
Bradford C.		09.47	47-48	11	-	2

BRANNIGAN, Kenneth
Glasgow, 8 July, 1965 (CD)

League Club	Source	Date Signed	Seasons Played	Apps	Subs	Gls
Sheffield Wed.	Queens Park	08.86	86	1	0	0
Stockport Co.	L	08.86	86	8	0	0
Doncaster Rov.	L	12.87	87	15	0	1

BRANSTON, Terence G.
Rugby, 25 July, 1938 (CH)

League Club	Source	Date Signed	Seasons Played	Apps	Subs	Gls
Northampton T.		10.58	60-66	244	2	2
Luton T.	Tr	06.67	67-70	101	2	9
Lincoln C.	Tr	09.70	70-72	99	1	1

BRASS, Robert A.
Middlesbrough, 9 November, 1943 (HB)

League Club	Source	Date Signed	Seasons Played	Apps	Subs	Gls
Middlesbrough	Jnrs	06.62				
Hartlepool U.	Tr	10.64	64-65	27	1	0

BRASTED, Gordon A.
Burnham (Ex), 30 June, 1933 (CF)

League Club	Source	Date Signed	Seasons Played	Apps	Subs	Gls
Arsenal	Burnham Ramblers	12.53				
Gillingham	Tr	07.56	56	5	-	4

BRATLEY, Anthony C.
Spalding, 30 April, 1939 (FB)

League Club	Source	Date Signed	Seasons Played	Apps	Subs	Gls
Grimsby T.		08.57	58	2	-	0

BRATT, Harold
Salford, 8 October, 1939 E Sch (WH)

League Club	Source	Date Signed	Seasons Played	Apps	Subs	Gls
Manchester U.	Jnrs	11.57				
Doncaster Rov.	Tr	05.61	61-62	54	-	0

BRATTAN, Gary
Hull, 1 January, 1960 (M)

League Club	Source	Date Signed	Seasons Played	Apps	Subs	Gls
Hull C.	App	01.78				
Cambridge U. (N/C)	North Ferriby U.	08.87	87	7	1	0

BRAY, Geoffrey C.
Chatham, 30 May, 1951 (F)

League Club	Source	Date Signed	Seasons Played	Apps	Subs	Gls
Oxford U.	Erith & Belvedere	07.71	72-74	22	11	6
Swansea C.	Tr	07.75	75-76	43	3	20
Torquay U.	Tr	11.76	76	7	0	2

BRAY, George
Oswaldtwistle, 11 November, 1918 (WH)

League Club	Source	Date Signed	Seasons Played	Apps	Subs	Gls
Burnley	Great Harwood T.	10.37	38-51	241	-	8

BRAY, Ian M.
Neath, 6 December, 1962 (LB)

League Club	Source	Date Signed	Seasons Played	Apps	Subs	Gls
Hereford U.	App	12.80	81-84	105	3	4
Huddersfield T.	Tr	07.85	85-89	87	2	1
Burnley	Tr	07.90	90-91	15	2	0

BRAY, John
Rishton, 16 March, 1937 (FB)

League Club	Source	Date Signed	Seasons Played	Apps	Subs	Gls
Blackburn Rov.	Jnrs	03.54	59-64	153	-	2
Bury	Tr	04.65	65	32	0	0

BRAY, Wayne
Bristol, 17 November, 1964 (M)

League Club	Source	Date Signed	Seasons Played	Apps	Subs	Gls
Bristol C.	App	11.81	81-82	28	1	2

BRAYTON, Barry J.
Carlisle, 29 September, 1938 (OR)

League Club	Source	Date Signed	Seasons Played	Apps	Subs	Gls
Carlisle U.		01.60	59-66	158	1	34
Workington	Tr	02.67	66-67	43	0	8

BRAZIER, Colin J.
Solihull, 6 June, 1957 E Semi-Pro (CD)

League Club	Source	Date Signed	Seasons Played	Apps	Subs	Gls
Wolverhampton W.	Alvechurch	08.75	76-81	69	9	2
Birmingham C.	Jacksonville (USA)	09.82	82	10	1	1
Lincoln C.	A.P. Leamington	04.83	82	9	0	0
Walsall	Tr	08.83	83-86	114	1	4

BRAZIL, Alan B.
Glasgow, 15 June, 1959 Su21-8/S-13 (F)

League Club	Source	Date Signed	Seasons Played	Apps	Subs	Gls
Ipswich T.	App	05.77	77-82	143	11	70
Tottenham H.	Tr	03.83	82-83	29	2	9
Manchester U.	Tr	06.84	84-85	18	13	8
Coventry C.	Tr	01.86	85	15	0	2
Queens Park R.	Tr	06.86	86	1	3	0

BRAZIL, Derek M.
Dublin, 14 December, 1968 IR Yth/IRu21-3/IR'B' (CD)

League Club	Source	Date Signed	Seasons Played	Apps	Subs	Gls
Manchester U.	Rivermount B.C.	03.86	88-89	0	2	0
Oldham Ath.	L	11.90	90	1	0	0
Swansea C.	L	09.91	91	12	0	1

BRAZIL, Gary N.
Tunbridge Wells, 19 September, 1962 (F)

League Club	Source	Date Signed	Seasons Played	Apps	Subs	Gls
Sheffield U.	Crystal Palace (App)	08.80	80-84	39	23	9
Port Vale	L	08.84	84	6	0	3
Preston N.E.	Tr	02.85	84-88	163	3	56
Newcastle U.	Tr	02.89	88-89	7	16	2
Fulham	Tr	09.90	90-91	87	1	18

BREACKER, Timothy S.
Bicester, 2 July, 1965 Eu21-2 (RB)

League Club	Source	Date Signed	Seasons Played	Apps	Subs	Gls
Luton T.	App	05.83	83-90	204	6	3
West Ham U.	Tr	10.90	90-91	56	2	3

BREAKS, Edward
Halifax, 29 December, 1919 (FB)

League Club	Source	Date Signed	Seasons Played	Apps	Subs	Gls
Halifax T.		07.48	48-54	179	-	1

League Club	Source	Date Signed	Seasons Played	Career Record Apps	Subs	Gls

BREARS, Paul
Oldham, 25 September, 1954 (M)

League Club	Source	Date Signed	Seasons Played	Apps	Subs	Gls
Rochdale	Oldham Ath. (Am)	08.73	73-75	26	1	0

BRECKIN, John
Sheffield, 27 July, 1953 (FB)

League Club	Source	Date Signed	Seasons Played	Apps	Subs	Gls
Rotherham U.	App	11.71	71-82	405	4	8
Darlington	L	10.72	72	4	0	0
Bury	Tr	02.83	82	17	0	0
Doncaster Rov.	Tr	08.83	83	17	1	0

BREEN, Gary
Hendon, 12 December, 1973 (CD)

League Club	Source	Date Signed	Seasons Played	Apps	Subs	Gls
Maidstone U.	Jnrs	03.91	91	19	0	0

BREITKREUTZ, Matthias
Berlin (Ger), 12 May, 1971 (M)

League Club	Source	Date Signed	Seasons Played	Apps	Subs	Gls
Aston Villa	Bergman Bosnig	10.91	91	7	1	0

BREMNER, Desmond G.
Banff, 7 September, 1952 Su23-9/S-1 (M)

League Club	Source	Date Signed	Seasons Played	Apps	Subs	Gls
Aston Villa	Hibernian	09.79	79-84	170	4	9
Birmingham C.	Tr	09.84	84-88	167	1	5
Fulham	Tr	08.89	89	7	9	0
Walsall (N/C)	Tr	03.90	89	2	4	0

BREMNER, Kevin J.
Banff, 7 October, 1957 (F)

League Club	Source	Date Signed	Seasons Played	Apps	Subs	Gls
Colchester U.	Keith	10.80	80-82	89	6	31
Birmingham C.	L	10.82	82	3	1	1
Wrexham	L	12.82	82	4	0	1
Plymouth Arg.	L	01.83	82	5	0	1
Millwall	Tr	02.83	82-84	87	9	32
Reading	Tr	08.85	85-86	60	4	21
Brighton & H.A.	Tr	07.87	87-89	125	3	36
Peterborough U.	Tr	07.90	90	13	4	3
Shrewsbury T. (L)	Dundee	03.92	91	7	0	2

BREMNER, William J.
Stirling, 9 December, 1942 S Sch/Su23-4/S-54 (M)

League Club	Source	Date Signed	Seasons Played	Apps	Subs	Gls
Leeds U.	Jnrs	12.59	59-76	585	1	90
Hull C.	Tr	09.76	76-77	61	0	6
Doncaster Rov.	Tr	09.79	79-81	2	3	0

BRENEN, Albert
South Shields, 5 October, 1915 (HB)

League Club	Source	Date Signed	Seasons Played	Apps	Subs	Gls
York C.	South Shields	08.38	38-50	206	-	13

BRENNAN, Bryan
Halifax, 25 May, 1933 E Sch

League Club	Source	Date Signed	Seasons Played	Apps	Subs	Gls
Stockport Co.	Jnrs	06.50	50	4	-	0

BRENNAN, Frank
Glenboig, 23 April, 1924 S-7 (CH)

League Club	Source	Date Signed	Seasons Played	Apps	Subs	Gls
Newcastle U.	Airdrieonians	05.46	46-55	318	-	3

BRENNAN, Harold
Derby, 17 November, 1930

League Club	Source	Date Signed	Seasons Played	Apps	Subs	Gls
Shrewsbury T.		12.53	53-54	19	-	3

BRENNAN, Ian
Easington, 25 March, 1953 (LB)

League Club	Source	Date Signed	Seasons Played	Apps	Subs	Gls
Burnley	App	10.70	74-79	173	2	11
Bolton W.	Tr	12.80	80-81	16	1	0

BRENNAN, James
Downpatrick (NI), 29 February, 1932 (OL)

League Club	Source	Date Signed	Seasons Played	Apps	Subs	Gls
Birmingham C.	Glentoran	06.52				
Swindon T.	Tr	06.54	54-55	16	-	1

BRENNAN, Malcolm
Manchester, 11 November, 1934

League Club	Source	Date Signed	Seasons Played	Apps	Subs	Gls
Crewe Alex.		12.52	56	1	-	0

BRENNAN, Mark R.
Rossendale, 4 October, 1965 E Yth/Eu21-5 (M)

League Club	Source	Date Signed	Seasons Played	Apps	Subs	Gls
Ipswich T.	App	04.83	83-87	165	3	19
Middlesbrough	Tr	07.88	88-89	61	4	6
Manchester C.	Tr	07.90	90-91	25	4	6

BRENNAN, Matthew
Glasgow, 3 January, 1943 (IF)

League Club	Source	Date Signed	Seasons Played	Apps	Subs	Gls
Luton T.	St Rochs	06.62	62	4	-	1

BRENNAN, Michael
Salford, 17 May, 1952 (F)

League Club	Source	Date Signed	Seasons Played	Apps	Subs	Gls
Manchester C.	App	12.69	70-72	1	3	0
Stockport Co.	L	02.72	71	18	0	3
Rochdale	Tr	10.73	73-74	35	2	4

BRENNAN, Patrick J.
Dublin, 1 March, 1924 Died 1991 (HB)

League Club	Source	Date Signed	Seasons Played	Apps	Subs	Gls
Brighton & H.A.	Shelbourne	08.48	48-50	45	-	0

BRENNAN, Raymond J.
Blackpool, 13 November, 1944 (F)

League Club	Source	Date Signed	Seasons Played	Apps	Subs	Gls
Blackburn Rov.	Wolverhampton W. (Am)	07.62				
Barrow	Tr	03.64	63-64	46	-	10

BRENNAN, Robert A.
Belfast, 14 March, 1925 IR Lge/NI-5 (IF)

League Club	Source	Date Signed	Seasons Played	Apps	Subs	Gls
Luton T.	Distillery	10.47	47-48	69	-	22
Birmingham C.	Tr	07.49	49	39	-	7
Fulham	Tr	06.50	50-52	73	-	13
Norwich C.	Tr	07.53	53-59	223	-	44

BRENNAN, Seamus
Manchester, 6 May, 1937 IR-19 (FB)

League Club	Source	Date Signed	Seasons Played	Apps	Subs	Gls
Manchester U.	Jnrs	04.55	57-69	291	1	3

BRENNAN, Stephen A.
Mile End, 3 September, 1958 (M)

League Club	Source	Date Signed	Seasons Played	Apps	Subs	Gls
Crystal Palace	App	02.76	76-77	2	1	1
Plymouth Arg.	Tr	08.78	78	6	0	0

BRENT, Peter
Staveley, 18 November, 1937 Died 1988 (HB)

League Club	Source	Date Signed	Seasons Played	Apps	Subs	Gls
Chesterfield	Jnrs	01.55	59	2	-	0

BRENTANO, Stephen R.
Hull, 9 November, 1961 (FB)

League Club	Source	Date Signed	Seasons Played	Apps	Subs	Gls
Hull C.	North Ferriby U.	03.82	84-86	11	1	0

BRESSINGTON, Graham
Eton, 8 July, 1966 (M/CD)

League Club	Source	Date Signed	Seasons Played	Apps	Subs	Gls
Lincoln C.	Wycombe W.	10.87	88-91	111	2	3

BRETHERTON, Thomas
Chorley, 9 April, 1920 (IR)

League Club	Source	Date Signed	Seasons Played	Apps	Subs	Gls
Accrington St.	Leyland Motors	02.47	46	4	-	0

BRETT, David S.
Chester, 8 April, 1961 (M)

League Club	Source	Date Signed	Seasons Played	Apps	Subs	Gls
Chester C.	Colwyn Bay	08.83	83-85	52	15	6

BRETT, Ronald A.
Stanford-le-Hope, 4 September, 1937 Died 1962 (CF)

League Club	Source	Date Signed	Seasons Played	Apps	Subs	Gls
Crystal Palace	Jnrs	09.54	55-58	36	-	12
West Ham U.	Tr	06.59	59-60	12	-	4
Crystal Palace	Tr	03.62	61	8	-	1

BRETTELL, Raymond L.
Strood, 22 August, 1935 (IF)

League Club	Source	Date Signed	Seasons Played	Apps	Subs	Gls
Doncaster Rov. (Am)		01.61	60	8	-	1

BREVETT, Rufus E.
Derby, 24 September, 1969 (LB)

League Club	Source	Date Signed	Seasons Played	Apps	Subs	Gls
Doncaster Rov.	YT	06.88	87-90	106	3	3
Queens Park R.	Tr	02.91	90-91	16	1	0

BREWER, Anthony P.
Edmonton, 20 May, 1932 (G)

League Club	Source	Date Signed	Seasons Played	Apps	Subs	Gls
Millwall	Jnrs	10.49	50-57	47	-	0
Northampton T.	Tr	12.57	58-60	87	-	0

BREWSTER, George W.
Barlborough, 19 October, 1925 (F)

League Club	Source	Date Signed	Seasons Played	Apps	Subs	Gls
Bristol C.	Retford T.	09.49	49-50	13	-	3

BREWSTER, John R.
Creswell, 19 August, 1942 (WH)

League Club	Source	Date Signed	Seasons Played	Apps	Subs	Gls
Sheffield U.	Jnrs	04.60				
Torquay U.	Tr	08.64	64-65	21	0	2

BREWSTER, William C.
Kinglassie (Fife), 4 August, 1933 (G)

League Club	Source	Date Signed	Seasons Played	Apps	Subs	Gls
Chelsea	Dundonald Bluebell	08.51				
Southend U.	Tr	08.55	55	2	-	0

BRICE, Gordon H.J.
Bedford, 4 May, 1924 (CH)

League Club	Source	Date Signed	Seasons Played	Apps	Subs	Gls
Luton T.	Jnrs	10.44	46	13	-	0
Wolverhampton W.	Tr	05.47	47	12	-	0
Reading	Tr	03.48	47-52	198	-	9
Fulham	Tr	12.52	52-55	87	-	1

BRICKLEY, Dennis
Bradford, 9 September, 1929 E Yth (OR)

League Club	Source	Date Signed	Seasons Played	Apps	Subs	Gls
Bradford P.A.	Huddersfield T. (Am)	08.49	50-56	169	-	24

BRIDDON, Samuel
Alfreton, 26 July, 1915 Died 1975 (LH)

League Club	Source	Date Signed	Seasons Played	Apps	Subs	Gls
Brentford	Port Vale (Am)	08.35	38	6	-	0
Swindon T.	Tr	07.39				
Swansea C.	Tr	01.46	46	18	-	0

BRIDGE, M. John (Jack)
Great Wakering, 30 May, 1932 (HB)

League Club	Source	Date Signed	Seasons Played	Apps	Subs	Gls
Southend U.	Jnrs	08.50	52-55	54	-	3

BRIDGER, David J.
Hartley Witney, 8 November, 1941 (CH)

League Club	Source	Date Signed	Seasons Played	Apps	Subs	Gls
Reading		03.62	62-64	10	-	0

BRIDGES, Barry J.
Norwich, 29 April, 1941 E Sch/E Yth/EF Lge/E-4 (CF)

League Club	Source	Date Signed	Seasons Played	Apps	Subs	Gls
Chelsea	Jnrs	05.58	58-65	174	2	80
Birmingham C.	Tr	05.66	66-68	83	0	37
Queens Park R.	Tr	08.68	68-70	72	0	32
Millwall	Tr	09.70	70-71	77	0	27
Brighton & H.A.	Tr	09.72	72-73	56	10	14

BRIDGES, Benjamin
Hull, 3 February, 1937 (IF)

League Club	Source	Date Signed	Seasons Played	Apps	Subs	Gls
Hull C.	Jnrs	08.55	57	1	-	0

BRIDGES, Bernard
Doncaster, 28 February, 1959 (CD)

League Club	Source	Date Signed	Seasons Played	Apps	Subs	Gls
Scunthorpe U.	Jnrs	07.76	76-77	22	1	0

BRIDGES, Harold
Burton, 30 June, 1915 (IL)

League Club	Source	Date Signed	Seasons Played	Apps	Subs	Gls
Manchester C.		04.37				
Tranmere Rov.	Tr	07.39	46-47	33	-	9

BRIDGETT, John
Walsall, 10 April, 1929 (F)

League Club	Source	Date Signed	Seasons Played	Apps	Subs	Gls
West Bromwich A.	Jnrs	05.46				
Walsall	Tr	08.50	50-54	108	-	18

BRIDGETT, Raymond
Nottingham, 5 April, 1947 (FB)

League Club	Source	Date Signed	Seasons Played	Apps	Subs	Gls
Nottingham F.	Jnrs	05.64	67-69	2	2	0

BRIDGWOOD, Gerald
Stoke, 17 October, 1944 (M)

League Club	Source	Date Signed	Seasons Played	Apps	Subs	Gls
Stoke C.	App	10.61	60-68	90	4	6
Shrewsbury T.	Tr	02.69	68-72	112	3	7

BRIEN, Anthony J.
Dublin, 10 February, 1969 (CD)

League Club	Source	Date Signed	Seasons Played	Apps	Subs	Gls
Leicester C.	App	02.87	87-88	12	4	1
Chesterfield	Tr	12.88	88-91	153	3	7

BRIEN, William R.
Stoke, 11 November, 1930 (HB)

League Club	Source	Date Signed	Seasons Played	Apps	Subs	Gls
Port Vale		05.51	53	1	-	0

BRIER, John D.
Halifax, 3 April, 1941 (WH)

League Club	Source	Date Signed	Seasons Played	Apps	Subs	Gls
Burnley	Jnrs	06.58				
Halifax T.	Tr	08.61	61-65	78	2	0

BRIERLEY, Keith
Dewsbury, 14 December, 1951 (CF)

League Club	Source	Date Signed	Seasons Played	Apps	Subs	Gls
Halifax T.	Jnrs	12.69	69-72	54	4	11

BRIERLEY, Kenneth
Ashton-u-Lyne, 3 April, 1926 (OL)

League Club	Source	Date Signed	Seasons Played	Apps	Subs	Gls
Oldham Ath.	Range Boilers	04.45	46-47	58	-	5
Liverpool	Tr	02.48	47-52	58	-	8
Oldham Ath.	Tr	03.53	52-54	67	-	5

BRIGGS, Alec M.
Sheffiield, 21 June, 1939 (FB)

League Club	Source	Date Signed	Seasons Played	Apps	Subs	Gls
Bristol C.	Jnrs	04.57	57-69	349	2	1

BRIGGS, Charles E.
Newtown, 4 April, 1911 (G)

League Club	Source	Date Signed	Seasons Played	Apps	Subs	Gls
Fulham	Guildford C.	12.35				
Crystal Palace	Guildford C.	05.36				
Bradford P.A.	Guildford C.	05.37				
Halifax T.	Tr	03.38	37-38	52	-	0
Rochdale	Clyde	05.47	46-47	12	-	0
Chesterfield	Tr	12.47				

BRIGGS, Gary
Leeds, 21 June, 1959 (CD)

League Club	Source	Date Signed	Seasons Played	Apps	Subs	Gls
Middlesbrough	App	05.77				
Oxford U.	Tr	01.78	77-88	418	2	18
Blackpool	Tr	06.89	89-91	71	0	2

BRIGGS, George H.
Shotton, 27 February, 1923 (CH)

League Club	Source	Date Signed	Seasons Played	Apps	Subs	Gls
Crystal Palace	Shotton Colly	11.47	48-54	146	-	4

BRIGGS, John (Jackie)
Barnsley, 27 October, 1924 (IF)

League Club	Source	Date Signed	Seasons Played	Apps	Subs	Gls
Gillingham	Huddersfield T. (Am)	10.46	50-52	52	-	14

BRIGGS, John C.
Salford, 24 November, 1918 E Sch (CH)

League Club	Source	Date Signed	Seasons Played	Apps	Subs	Gls
Manchester U.	Darwen	10.44				
Accrington St.	Tr	08.45	46-49	135	-	1
Southport	Tr	03.50	49	3	-	0

BRIGGS, Malcolm D.
Sunderland, 14 September, 1961 (M)

League Club	Source	Date Signed	Seasons Played	Apps	Subs	Gls
Birmingham C.	App	08.79	78	0	1	0

BRIGGS, Maxwell F.
Norwich, 9 September, 1948 (M)

League Club	Source	Date Signed	Seasons Played	Apps	Subs	Gls
Norwich C.	Jnrs	12.67	68-73	127	8	1
Oxford U.	Tr	02.74	73-77	94	3	1

BRIGGS, W. Ronald
Belfast, 29 March, 1943 (G)

League Club	Source	Date Signed	Seasons Played	Apps	Subs	Gls
Manchester U.	Jnrs	03.60	60-61	9	-	0
Swansea C.	Tr	05.64	64	27	-	0
Bristol Rov.	Tr	06.65	65-67	35	0	0

BRIGGS, Stephen
Leeds, 2 December, 1946 (CF)

League Club	Source	Date Signed	Seasons Played	Apps	Subs	Gls
Leeds U.	Jnrs	10.65				
Doncaster Rov.	Tr	02.69	68-72	114	7	34

BRIGGS, Thomas H.
Chesterfield, 27 November, 1923 Died 1984 E'B'-1 (CF)

League Club	Source	Date Signed	Seasons Played	Apps	Subs	Gls
Plymouth Arg.		03.46				
Grimsby T.	Tr	05.47	47-50	116	-	78
Coventry C.	Tr	01.51	50-51	11	-	7
Birmingham C.	Tr	09.51	51-52	50	-	22
Blackburn Rov.	Tr	12.52	52-57	194	-	140
Grimsby T.	Tr	03.58	57-58	19	-	9

BRIGGS, Thomas R.
Rotherham, 11 May, 1919 (CH)

League Club	Source	Date Signed	Seasons Played	Apps	Subs	Gls
Huddersfield T.		02.46	46-49	45	-	0
Crewe Alex.	Tr	12.49	49-55	202	-	2

BRIGGS, Walter
Middlesbrough, 29 November, 1922 (G)

League Club	Source	Date Signed	Seasons Played	Apps	Subs	Gls
Middlesbrough	Cochranes	05.47	46-47	2	-	0
Southport	Tr	06.48	48	4	-	0
Hartlepool U.	Tr	09.49	49-51	45	-	0

BRIGGS, Wilson W.
Gorebridge, 15 May, 1942 (FB)

League Club	Source	Date Signed	Seasons Played	Apps	Subs	Gls
Aston Villa	Arniston Rov.	08.59	61-62	2	-	0

BRIGHAM, Harold
Selby, 19 November, 1914 (RB)

League Club	Source	Date Signed	Seasons Played	Apps	Subs	Gls
Stoke C.	Frickley Colly	05.36	36-46	92	-	0
Nottingham F.	Tr	11.46	46-47	35	-	2
York C.	Tr	07.48	48-49	56	-	5

BRIGHT, David
Prudhoe, 24 December, 1946 (FB)

League Club	Source	Date Signed	Seasons Played	Apps	Subs	Gls
Sunderland	West Wylan Jnrs	08.65				

League Club	Source	Date Signed	Seasons Played	Career Record Apps	Subs	Gls
Preston N.E.	Tr	08.67	68	1	0	0
Oldham Ath.	Tr	03.69	68-69	19	0	0

BRIGHT, David J.
Bath, 5 September, 1972 (F)

Stoke C.	YT	07.91	90	0	1	0

BRIGHT, Gerald
Northampton, 2 December, 1934

Northampton T.		02.57	56-57	4	-	0

BRIGHT, Mark A.
Stoke, 6 June, 1962 (F)

Port Vale	Leek T.	10.81	81-83	18	11	10
Leicester C.	Tr	07.84	84-86	26	16	6
Crystal Palace	Tr	11.86	86-91	219	3	89

Mark Bright (Port Vale, Leicester City & Crystal Palace)

BRIGHT, Stewart L.
Colchester, 13 October, 1957 (RB)

Colchester U.	App	10.75	75-76	23	2	0

BRIGHTWELL, David J.
Lutterworth, 7 January, 1971 (CD)

Manchester C.	Jnrs	04.88	91	3	1	0
Chester C.	L	03.91	90	6	0	0

BRIGHTWELL, Ian R.
Lutterworth, 9 April, 1968 E Sch/E Yth/Eu21-4 (M/RB)

Manchester C.	Congleton T.	05.86	86-91	148	28	15

BRIGNALL, Stephen J.C.
Tenterden, 12 June, 1960 (D)

Arsenal	App	05.78	78	0	1	0

BRIGNULL, Philip A.
Stratford, 2 October, 1960 ESch

West Ham U.	App	09.78	78	0	1	0
Bournemouth	Tr	08.81	81-84	128	1	11

League Club	Source	Date Signed	Seasons Played	Career Record Apps	Subs	Gls
Wrexham	L	12.85	85	5	0	1
Cardiff C.	Tr	02.86	85-86	49	0	0
Newport Co.	Tr	08.87	87	3	0	0

BRILEY, Leslie
Lambeth, 2 October, 1956 (M)

Chelsea	App	06.74				
Hereford U.	Tr	05.76	76-77	60	1	2
Wimbledon	Tr	02.78	77-79	59	2	2
Aldershot	Tr	03.80	79-83	157	0	3
Millwall	Tr	05.84	84-90	225	2	13
Brighton & H.A.	Tr	08.91	91	11	4	0

BRIMACOMBE, Anthony
Plymouth, 6 August, 1939 (IF)

Plymouth Arg. (Am)	Barnet	12.65	65-67	15	2	0

BRIMACOMBE, John F.
Plymouth, 25 November, 1958 (RB/M)

Plymouth Arg.	Saltash U.	08.85	85-89	93	5	3

BRIMS, Donald
Auchendinny, 8 January, 1934 (WH)

Bradford P.A.	Motherwell	05.58	58-59	76	-	3

BRINDLE, John J.
Blackburn, 12 July, 1917 Died 1975 (IF)

Rochdale	Howard & Bullough	09.45				
Chelsea	Tr	03.46				
Rochdale	Tr	08.47	47	1	-	0
New Brighton	Tr	03.48	47	9	-	3

BRINDLE, William
Liverpool, 29 January, 1950 (M)

Everton	App	08.67	67	1	0	0
Barnsley	Tr	05.70	70	0	1	0

BRINDLEY, Christopher P.
Stoke, 5 July, 1969 (CD)

Wolverhampton W.	Hednesford T.	11.86	86	7	0	0

BRINDLEY, John
Ashbourne, 2 May, 1931 (IF)

Chesterfield	Buxton	12.53	53	1	-	0

BRINDLEY, John C.
Nottingham, 29 January, 1947 E Sch/E Yth (RB)

Nottingham F.	Jnrs	02.64	65-69	7	8	1
Notts Co.	Tr	05.70	70-75	221	2	0
Gillingham	Tr	07.76	76	19	1	1

BRINE, Peter K.
Greenwich, 18 July, 1953 (M)

Middlesbrough	App	09.70	72-77	59	20	6

BRINTON, Ernest J.
Bristol, 26 May, 1908 d1981 (LH)

Bristol C.	Avonmouth T.	02.30	29-36	249	-	7
Newport Co.	Tr	06.37	37-38	75	-	3
Aldershot	Tr	08.46	46	12	-	0

BRINTON, John V.
Avonmouth, 11 July, 1916 (W)

Bristol C.	Avonmouth T.	08.35	35-36	12	-	1
Newport Co.	Tr	07.37	37	6	-	0
Derby Co.	Tr	01.38	37	8	-	2
Stockport Co.	Tr	07.46	46-47	58	-	9
Leyton Orient	Tr	08.48	48	4	-	1

BRISCOE, James E. R.
St Helens, 23 April, 1917 Died 1981 (OR)

Preston N.E.	St Helens T.	05.34	36	5	-	0
Northampton T.	Hearts	09.46	46-48	53	-	17

BRISCOE, James P.
Swinton-on-Dearne, 14 October, 1923 (CF)

Sheffield Wed.	Jnrs	08.46	46	5	-	3

BRISCOE, John
Huddersfield, 31 May, 1947 (CF)

Barnsley	Jnrs	10.66	66-67	11	0	5

BRISCOE, Robert D.
Derby, 4 September, 1969 (LB)

Derby Co.	YT	09.87	89-90	10	3	1

BRISLEY, Terence W.
Stepney, 4 July, 1950 (M)

League Club	Source	Date Signed	Seasons Played	Apps	Subs	Gls
Leyton Orient	App	07.68	67-74	133	9	9
Southend U.	L	03.75	74	8	0	0
Millwall	Tr	07.75	75-77	106	1	14
Charlton Ath.	Tr	01.78	77-78	44	4	5
Portsmouth	Tr	07.79	79-80	55	0	13

BRISSETT, Trevor A.
Stoke, 2 January, 1961 (FB)

League Club	Source	Date Signed	Seasons Played	Apps	Subs	Gls
Stoke C.	Jnrs	04.78				
Port Vale	Tr	05.80	80-81	47	8	0
Darlington	Tr	08.82	82	10	2	0

BRISTOW, George A.
Chiswick, 25 June, 1933 (WH)

League Club	Source	Date Signed	Seasons Played	Apps	Subs	Gls
Brentford	Jnrs	07.50	50-60	244	-	9
Queens Park R.	Tr	05.61				

BRISTOW, Guy A.
Kingsbury, 23 October, 1955 (CD)

League Club	Source	Date Signed	Seasons Played	Apps	Subs	Gls
Watford	App	07.73	74-76	18	5	0

BRITT, Martin C.
Leigh-on-Sea, 17 January, 1946 E Yth (CF)

League Club	Source	Date Signed	Seasons Played	Apps	Subs	Gls
West Ham U.	App	01.63	62-65	20	0	6
Blackburn Rov.	Tr	03.66	65	8	0	0

BRITTAN, Colin
Bristol, 2 June, 1927 (WH)

League Club	Source	Date Signed	Seasons Played	Apps	Subs	Gls
Tottenham H.	Bristol O.B.	10.48	50-57	41	-	1

BRITTEN, Martyn E. W.
Bristol, 1 May, 1955 (W)

League Club	Source	Date Signed	Seasons Played	Apps	Subs	Gls
Bristol Rov.	App	05.73	74-76	17	3	2
Reading	Tr	08.77	77-78	6	2	0

BRITTON, Gerard J.
Glasgow, 20 October, 1970 (F)

League Club	Source	Date Signed	Seasons Played	Apps	Subs	Gls
Reading (L)	Glasgow Celtic	11.91	91	0	2	0

BRITTON, Ian
Dundee, 19 May, 1954 (W)

League Club	Source	Date Signed	Seasons Played	Apps	Subs	Gls
Chelsea	App	07.71	72-81	253	10	33
Blackpool	Dundee U.	12.83	83-85	100	6	15
Burnley	Tr	08.86	86-88	102	6	10

BRITTON, James
Salford, 27 May, 1920 (WH)

League Club	Source	Date Signed	Seasons Played	Apps	Subs	Gls
Bradford P.A.	Lowestoft	01.46	46	1	-	0
Rochdale	Tr	12.47	47-48	20	-	0

BROAD, Ronald
Sandbach, 18 August, 1933 (OL)

League Club	Source	Date Signed	Seasons Played	Apps	Subs	Gls
Crewe Alex. (Am)	Congleton T.	12.55	55	6	-	0

BROADBENT, Albert H.
Dudley, 20 August, 1934 (OL)

League Club	Source	Date Signed	Seasons Played	Apps	Subs	Gls
Notts Co.	Dudley T.	03.52	53-54	31	-	11
Sheffield Wed.	Tr	07.55	55-57	81	-	17
Rotherham U.	Tr	12.57	57-58	48	-	13
Doncaster Rov.	Tr	06.59	59-61	100	-	20
Lincoln C.	Tr	11.61	61-62	38	-	4
Doncaster Rov.	Tr	01.63	62-65	106	0	19
Bradford P.A.	Tr	10.65	65-66	56	0	11
Hartlepool U.	Tr	02.67	66-67	25	0	3

BROADBENT, Graham R.
Halifax, 20 December, 1958 (F)

League Club	Source	Date Signed	Seasons Played	Apps	Subs	Gls
Halifax T.	Emley	09.88	88-90	13	19	3

BROADBENT, Peter F.
Dover, 15 May, 1933 Eu23-1/E'B'-1/EF Lge/E-7 (IF)

League Club	Source	Date Signed	Seasons Played	Apps	Subs	Gls
Brentford	Jnrs	05.50	50	16	-	1
Wolverhampton W.	Tr	02.51	50-64	452	-	127
Shrewsbury T.	Tr	01.65	64-66	68	0	7
Aston Villa	Tr	10.66	66-68	60	4	2
Stockport Co.	Tr	10.69	69	31	0	1

BROADFOOT, Joseph
Lewisham, 4 March, 1940 (OR)

League Club	Source	Date Signed	Seasons Played	Apps	Subs	Gls
Millwall	Jnrs	01.58	58-63	225	-	60
Ipswich T.	Tr	10.63	63-65	81	0	17
Northampton T.	Tr	11.65	65	17	0	1
Millwall	Tr	07.66	66	26	0	5
Ipswich T.	Tr	02.67	66-67	19	1	2

BROADHURST, Brian W.
Sheffield, 24 November, 1938 (F)

League Club	Source	Date Signed	Seasons Played	Apps	Subs	Gls
Chesterfield	Hallam	10.61	61	7	-	0

BROADHURST, Kevin
Dewsbury, 3 June, 1959 (D)

League Club	Source	Date Signed	Seasons Played	Apps	Subs	Gls
Birmingham C.	App	03.77	76-83	147	6	10
Walsall	L	11.79	79	3	0	0

BROADIS, Ivor A.
Poplar, 18 December, 1922 EF Lge/E-14 (IF)

League Club	Source	Date Signed	Seasons Played	Apps	Subs	Gls
Carlisle U.	Tottenham H. (Am)	08.46	46-48	91	-	52
Sunderland	Tr	02.49	48-51	79	-	25
Manchester C.	Tr	10.51	51-53	74	-	10
Newcastle U.	Tr	10.53	53-54	42	-	15
Carlisle U.	Tr	07.55	55-58	159	-	32

BROADLEY, Leslie
Goole, 10 August, 1930 (CF)

League Club	Source	Date Signed	Seasons Played	Apps	Subs	Gls
Scunthorpe U.	Goole T.	08.52	52	5	-	2

BROADLEY, Patrick J.
Croy, 13 May, 1926 (LH)

League Club	Source	Date Signed	Seasons Played	Apps	Subs	Gls
Oldham Ath.	Sligo Rov.	06.51	51	4	-	0

BROCK, Kevin S.
Bicester, 9 September, 1962 E Sch/Eu21-4 (M)

League Club	Source	Date Signed	Seasons Played	Apps	Subs	Gls
Oxford U.	App	09.79	79-86	229	17	26
Queens Park R.	Tr	08.87	87-88	38	2	2
Newcastle U.	Tr	12.88	88-91	131	7	13

BROCKBANK, Andrew
Millom, 23 September, 1961 (LB)

League Club	Source	Date Signed	Seasons Played	Apps	Subs	Gls
Blackpool	App	12.79	79-82	32	4	1

BROCKEN, Budde J. P.
Netherlands, 12 September, 1957 (M)

League Club	Source	Date Signed	Seasons Played	Apps	Subs	Gls
Birmingham C.	Willem Tilburg (Neth)	08.81	81	17	0	

Peter Broadbent (Brentford, Wolverhampton Wanderers, Shrewsbury Town, Aston Villa, Stockport County & England)

League Club	Source	Date Signed	Seasons Played	Career Record Apps	Subs	Gls

BROCKIE, Vincent
Greenock, 2 February, 1969 (RB)

League Club	Source	Date Signed	Seasons Played	Apps	Subs	Gls
Leeds U.	YT	07.87	87	2	0	0
Doncaster Rov.	Tr	12.88	88-90	43	11	7

BROCKLEHURST, John F.
Horwich, 15 December, 1927 (WH)

League Club	Source	Date Signed	Seasons Played	Apps	Subs	Gls
Accrington St.	Stalybridge Celtic	05.52	52	34	-	0
Bradford P.A.	Stalybridge Celtic	08.54	54-55	47	-	1

BRODDLE, Julian R.
Laughton, 1 November, 1964 (W/FB)

League Club	Source	Date Signed	Seasons Played	Apps	Subs	Gls
Sheffield U.	App	11.82	81	1	0	0
Scunthorpe U.	Tr	08.83	83-87	126	18	32
Barnsley	Tr	09.87	87-89	63	14	4
Plymouth Arg.	Tr	01.90	89	9	0	0

BRODERICK, Mortimer
Cork (Ire) 1 September, 1923 IR F Lge

League Club	Source	Date Signed	Seasons Played	Apps	Subs	Gls
Sheffield U.	Cork	08.50	50	2	-	0

BRODIE, Charles T. G. (Chic)
Duntocher, 22 February, 1937 S Sch (G)

League Club	Source	Date Signed	Seasons Played	Apps	Subs	Gls
Manchester C.	Partick Avondale	03.54				
Gillingham	Tr	07.57	57	18	-	0
Aldershot	Tr	07.58	58-60	95	-	0
Wolverhampton W.	Tr	02.61	60	1	-	0
Northampton T.	Tr	09.61	61-63	87	-	0
Brentford	Tr	11.63	63-70	201	0	0

BRODIE, Eric
Blairgowrie, 8 November, 1940 (WH)

League Club	Source	Date Signed	Seasons Played	Apps	Subs	Gls
Shrewsbury T.	Dundee U.	06.63	63-67	181	4	24
Chester C.	Tr	05.68	68-69	43	0	4
Tranmere Rov.	Tr	10.69	69-71	80	3	4

BRODIE, John
Ashington, 8 September, 1947 (FB)

League Club	Source	Date Signed	Seasons Played	Apps	Subs	Gls
Carlisle U.	Whitley Bay	12.67	67-68	8	1	0
Bradford P.A.	Tr	06.69	69	43	0	0
Port Vale	Tr	01.71	70-76	175	4	2

BRODIE, Murray
Glasgow, 26 September, 1950 (M)

League Club	Source	Date Signed	Seasons Played	Apps	Subs	Gls
Leicester C.	Cumbernauld U.	10.69	69	3	0	2
Aldershot	Tr	09.70	70-82	450	11	84

BROGAN, David
Glasgow, 11 January, 1939 (F)

League Club	Source	Date Signed	Seasons Played	Apps	Subs	Gls
Luton T.	St Anthonys	09.60	60	4	-	0

BROGAN, Frank A.
Glasgow, 3 August, 1942 (W)

League Club	Source	Date Signed	Seasons Played	Apps	Subs	Gls
Ipswich T.	Glasgow Celtic	06.64	64-69	201	2	58
Halifax T.	Tr	11.71	71-72	25	2	6

BROGAN, James
Glasgow, 5 June, 1944 SF Lge/S-4 (FB)

League Club	Source	Date Signed	Seasons Played	Apps	Subs	Gls
Coventry C.	Glasgow Celtic	08.75	75	28	0	0

BROGDEN, Lee
Leeds, 18 October, 1949 (W)

League Club	Source	Date Signed	Seasons Played	Apps	Subs	Gls
Rotherham U.	Ashley Road	12.67	67-71	79	8	16
Rochdale	Tr	03.72	71-73	48	9	7

BROLLS, Norman
Wigtown, 26 September, 1933 (OR)

League Club	Source	Date Signed	Seasons Played	Apps	Subs	Gls
Bradford P.A.	Third Lanark	06.56	56	11	-	0

BROLLY, Michael J.
Galston, 6 October, 1954 S Sch (W)

League Club	Source	Date Signed	Seasons Played	Apps	Subs	Gls
Chelsea	Jnrs	10.71	72-73	7	1	1
Bristol C.	Tr	06.74	74-75	27	3	2
Grimsby T.	Tr	09.76	76-81	246	8	27
Derby Co.	Tr	08.82	82	41	1	4
Scunthorpe U.	Tr	08.83	83-85	92	3	15

BROLLY, Thomas H.
Belfast, 1 June, 1912 NI-4 (D)

League Club	Source	Date Signed	Seasons Played	Apps	Subs	Gls
Sheffield Wed.	Glenavon	05.33	33	2	-	0
Millwall	Tr	07.35	35-49	229	-	8

BROMAGE, Russell
Stoke, 9 November, 1959 (LB)

League Club	Source	Date Signed	Seasons Played	Apps	Subs	Gls
Port Vale	App	11.77	77-86	339	8	13
Oldham Ath.	L	10.83	83	2	0	0
Bristol C.	Tr	08.87	87-89	44	2	1
Brighton & H.A.	Tr	08.90	90	1	0	0
Maidstone U.	L	01.91	90	3	0	0

BROMILOW, Geoffrey W.
Farnworth, 14 September, 1945 (IF)

League Club	Source	Date Signed	Seasons Played	Apps	Subs	Gls
Bolton W. (Am)		10.68	68	3	2	0

BROMILOW, George J.
Southport, 4 December, 1931 E Yth/E Amat (IF)

League Club	Source	Date Signed	Seasons Played	Apps	Subs	Gls
Southport (Am)	Northern Nomads	06.55	55-58	84	-	37

BROMLEY, Brian
Burnley, 20 March, 1946 E Yth (M)

League Club	Source	Date Signed	Seasons Played	Apps	Subs	Gls
Bolton W.	App	03.63	62-68	165	1	25
Portsmouth	Tr	11.68	68-71	88	1	3
Brighton & H.A.	Tr	11.71	71-73	47	3	3
Reading	Tr	09.73	73-74	13	1	2
Darlington	L	02.75	74	3	0	0

BROMLEY, Thomas C.
West Bromwich, 30 April, 1933 (IF)

League Club	Source	Date Signed	Seasons Played	Apps	Subs	Gls
Walsall (Am)	Swan Village	07.53	53	13	-	1

BROOK, Daryl
Holmfirth, 19 November, 1960 (M)

League Club	Source	Date Signed	Seasons Played	Apps	Subs	Gls
Huddersfield T.	App	11.78	78	1	0	0

BROOK, Gary
Dewsbury, 9 May, 1964 (F)

League Club	Source	Date Signed	Seasons Played	Apps	Subs	Gls
Newport Co.	Frickley Ath.	12.87	87	14	0	2
Scarborough	Tr	03.88	87-89	59	5	16
Blackpool	Tr	11.89	89-91	27	3	6
Notts Co.	L	09.90	90	0	1	0
Scarborough	L	10.90	90	8	0	0

BROOK, Harold
Sheffield, 15 October, 1921 (CF)

League Club	Source	Date Signed	Seasons Played	Apps	Subs	Gls
Sheffield U.	Hallam	04.43	46-53	229	-	89
Leeds U.	Tr	07.54	54-57	102	-	46
Lincoln C.	Tr	03.58	57	4	-	1

BROOK, Lewis
Northowram, 27 July, 1918 (FB)

League Club	Source	Date Signed	Seasons Played	Apps	Subs	Gls
Huddersfield T.	Halifax T. (Am)	05.36	37-46	18	-	6
Oldham Ath.	Tr	03.48	47-56	189	-	14

BROOKE, Garry J.
Bethnal Green, 24 November, 1960 (W)

League Club	Source	Date Signed	Seasons Played	Apps	Subs	Gls
Tottenham H.	App	10.78	80-84	49	24	15
Norwich C.	Tr	07.85	85-86	8	6	2
Wimbledon	Groningen (Neth)	08.88	88-89	5	7	0
Stoke C.	L	03.90	89	6	2	0
Brentford	Tr	08.90	90	8	3	1
Reading (N/C)	Tr	03.91	90	1	3	0

BROOKE, Maurice
Thurcroft, 4 June, 1925 (F)

League Club	Source	Date Signed	Seasons Played	Apps	Subs	Gls
Stockport Co.	Buxton	01.51	50	1	-	0

BROOKES, Colin
Barnsley, 2 January, 1942 E Sch (OL)

League Club	Source	Date Signed	Seasons Played	Apps	Subs	Gls
Barnsley	Jnrs	05.59	59-60	46	-	5
West Bromwich A.	Tr	06.61				
Peterborough U.	Tr	06.62				
Southport	Tr	07.63	63	20	-	2

BROOKES, Eric
Mapplewell, 3 February, 1944 E Sch/E Yth (LB)

League Club	Source	Date Signed	Seasons Played	Apps	Subs	Gls
Barnsley	Jnrs	04.61	60-68	324	1	1
Northampton T.	Tr	07.69	69-70	81	0	1
Peterborough U.	Tr	06.71	71-72	41	1	1

BROOKES, John V.
Stalybridge, 18 October, 1944 (IF)

League Club	Source	Date Signed	Seasons Played	Apps	Subs	Gls
Sheffield Wed.	Sheffield U. (Am)	09.64				
Southport	Tr	07.65	65	14	0	5
York C.	Tr	08.66	66	1	0	0
Stockport Co.	Cleveland (USA)	08.70	70	18	2	3

BROOKES, Stanley K.
Doncaster, 2 February, 1953 (CD)

League Club	Source	Date Signed	Seasons Played	Apps	Subs	Gls
Doncaster Rov.	App	02.71	71-76	230	5	7

BROOKES, William A.
Dudley, 19 April, 1931 (WH)

League Club	Source	Date Signed	Seasons Played	Apps	Subs	Gls
West Bromwich A.	Churchfield	05.49	53-56	19	-	0

BROOKFIELD, Anthony J.
Southport, 11 April, 1959 (F)

League Club	Source	Date Signed	Seasons Played	Apps	Subs	Gls
Southport (N/C)	Jnrs	07.76	76-77	14	5	1

BROOKIN, William J.
Reading, 14 June, 1919 (G)

League Club	Source	Date Signed	Seasons Played	Apps	Subs	Gls
Newport Co.	R.A.F.	08.46	46	2	-	0

BROOKING, Trevor D.
Barking, 2 October, 1948 E Sch/E Yth/Eu23-1/EF Lge/E-47 (M)

League Club	Source	Date Signed	Seasons Played	Apps	Subs	Gls
West Ham U.	App	05.66	67-83	521	7	88

BROOKMAN, Nicholas A.
Manchester, 28 October, 1968 (M)

League Club	Source	Date Signed	Seasons Played	Apps	Subs	Gls
Bolton W.	Wrexham (N/C)	11.86	86-89	47	10	10
Stockport Co.	Tr	03.90	89	4	2	0

BROOKS, Anthony
Wigan, 12 March, 1944 (F)

League Club	Source	Date Signed	Seasons Played	Apps	Subs	Gls
Blackpool	App	03.62				
Bury		08.63	63	1	-	0
Stockport Co.	Tr	06.64	64	2	-	0

BROOKS, Harold
Tibshelf, 2 June, 1915 (CF)

League Club	Source	Date Signed	Seasons Played	Apps	Subs	Gls
Doncaster Rov.	Heanor T.	01.37	36-38	5	-	0
Aldershot	Tr	06.39	46-47	23	-	14

BROOKS, John
Stoke, 8 February, 1927 (HB)

League Club	Source	Date Signed	Seasons Played	Apps	Subs	Gls
Stoke C.		12.46	50	2	-	0

BROOKS, John
Reading, 23 December, 1931 E-3 (IF)

League Club	Source	Date Signed	Seasons Played	Apps	Subs	Gls
Reading	Jnrs	04.49	49-52	46	-	5
Tottenham H.	Tr	02.53	52-59	166	-	46
Chelsea	Tr	12.59	59-60	46	-	6
Brentford	Tr	09.61	61-63	83	-	36
Crystal Palace	Tr	01.64	63	7	-	0

BROOKS, John T.
Paddington, 23 August, 1947 (G)

League Club	Source	Date Signed	Seasons Played	Apps	Subs	Gls
Queens Park R.	App	08.65				
Ipswich T.	Tr	12.66				
Northampton T.	Tr	10.67	67	1	0	0

BROOKS, Norman H.
Reading, 28 May, 1920 Died 1973

League Club	Source	Date Signed	Seasons Played	Apps	Subs	Gls
Reading (Am)	Huntley & Palmer	11.46	46	1	-	0

BROOKS, Shaun
Reading, 9 October, 1962 E Sch/E Yth (M)

League Club	Source	Date Signed	Seasons Played	Apps	Subs	Gls
Crystal Palace	App	10.79	79-83	47	7	4
Leyton Orient	Tr	10.83	83-86	140	8	26
Bournemouth	Tr	06.87	87-91	114	14	13

BROOKS, Stephen M.
Liverpool, 18 June, 1955 (CD)

League Club	Source	Date Signed	Seasons Played	Apps	Subs	Gls
Southport	Marine	02.77	76-77	65	0	3
Hartlepool U.	Tr	07.78	78-79	62	1	2
Halifax T. (N/C)	Barrow	03.85	84	16	0	0

BROOKS, Thomas W.
Wallsend, 2 February, 1948 (D)

League Club	Source	Date Signed	Seasons Played	Apps	Subs	Gls
Lincoln C.	App	02.65	64-70	102	9	1

BROOME, Frank H.
Berkhamsted, 11 June, 1915 E-7 (CF)

League Club	Source	Date Signed	Seasons Played	Apps	Subs	Gls
Aston Villa	Berkhamsted	11.34	34-46	133	-	77
Derby Co.	Tr	09.46	46-49	112	-	45
Notts Co.	Tr	10.49	49-52	105	-	35
Brentford	Tr	07.53	53	6	-	1
Crewe Alex.	Tr	10.53	53-54	36	-	16

BROOMFIELD, Desmond
Hove, 6 October, 1921 (HB)

League Club	Source	Date Signed	Seasons Played	Apps	Subs	Gls
Brighton & H.A.		01.47	46-47	20	-	0

BROOMFIELD, Ian L.
Bristol, 17 December, 1950 (F)

League Club	Source	Date Signed	Seasons Played	Apps	Subs	Gls
Bristol C.	App	08.68	68-72	18	3	2
Stockport Co.	Tr	12.72	72-74	22	5	1
Workington	South Africa	10.75	75	3	0	0

BROOMFIELD, John
Crewe, 6 June, 1934

League Club	Source	Date Signed	Seasons Played	Apps	Subs	Gls
Crewe Alex. (Am)		10.56	56	1	-	0

BROOMHALL, Keith L.
Stoke, 21 May, 1951 (FB)

League Club	Source	Date Signed	Seasons Played	Apps	Subs	Gls
Port Vale (App)	App	10.67	68	1	1	0

BROPHY, Hubert
Dublin, 2 September, 1948 NI Amat (F)

League Club	Source	Date Signed	Seasons Played	Apps	Subs	Gls
Crystal Palace	Shamrock Rov.	07.66	66	0	1	0

BROTHERSTON, Noel
Belfast, 18 November, 1956 NIu21-1/NI-27 (W)

League Club	Source	Date Signed	Seasons Played	Apps	Subs	Gls
Tottenham H.	App	04.74	75	1	0	0
Blackburn Rov.	Tr	07.77	77-86	307	10	40
Bury	Tr	06.87	87-88	32	6	4
Scarborough	L	10.88	88	5	0	0

BROUGH, Neil K.
Daventry, 22 December, 1965 (W)

League Club	Source	Date Signed	Seasons Played	Apps	Subs	Gls
Northampton T.	App	12.83	83-84	6	6	0

BROUGH, Paul D.
York, 24 January, 1965 (F)

League Club	Source	Date Signed	Seasons Played	Apps	Subs	Gls
York C. (N/C)	York R.I.	08.87	87	0	1	0

BROUGHTON, Edward
Bradford, 9 February, 1925 (OR)

League Club	Source	Date Signed	Seasons Played	Apps	Subs	Gls
Bradford C.		09.45				
New Brighton	Tr	07.47	47	4	-	0
Crystal Palace	Tr	08.48	48-52	96	-	6

BROWN, Alan
Lewes, 11 December, 1937 (CF)

League Club	Source	Date Signed	Seasons Played	Apps	Subs	Gls
Brighton & H.A.	Portslade	09.58	61	7	-	2
Exeter C.	Tr	01.62	61	11	-	3

BROWN, Alan
Easington, 22 May, 1959 (F)

League Club	Source	Date Signed	Seasons Played	Apps	Subs	Gls
Sunderland	App	07.76	76-81	87	26	21
Newcastle U.	L	11.81	81	5	0	3
Shrewsbury T.	Tr	08.82	82-83	65	0	15
Doncaster Rov.	Tr	03.84	83-85	15	0	6

BROWN, Allan D.
Leven, 12 October, 1926 SF Lge/S-14 (IF)

League Club	Source	Date Signed	Seasons Played	Apps	Subs	Gls
Blackpool	East Fife	12.50	50-56	157	-	68
Luton T.	Tr	02.57	56-60	151	-	52
Portsmouth	Tr	03.61	60-62	69	-	8

BROWN, Allan W.
Corbridge, 26 August, 1914 EF Lge (CH)

League Club	Source	Date Signed	Seasons Played	Apps	Subs	Gls
Huddersfield T.	Spen Black	03.33	34-38	57	-	0
Burnley	Tr	02.46	46-48	88	-	0
Notts Co.	Tr	10.48	48	13	-	0

BROWN, Albert E.
Bristol, 4 March, 1934 (WH)

League Club	Source	Date Signed	Seasons Played	Apps	Subs	Gls
Crystal Palace	Exeter Univ.	08.56	57	3	-	0
Queens Park R.	Tr	07.59				

BROWN, Albert R.
Nottingham, 14 August, 1917 (OR)

League Club	Source	Date Signed	Seasons Played	Apps	Subs	Gls
Nottingham F.	Sneinton	02.36	35-38	51	-	7
Wrexham	Tr	06.39	46	24	-	3
Mansfield T.	Tr	07.47	47	17	-	2

BROWN, Alexander
Glasgow, 15 August, 1930 (FB)

League Club	Source	Date Signed	Seasons Played	Apps	Subs	Gls
Preston N.E.	Partick Th.	06.57				
Carlisle U.	Tr	06.58	58-60	104	-	0

BROWN, Alexander
Seaton Delaval, 21 November, 1914 (IF)

League Club	Source	Date Signed	Seasons Played	Apps	Subs	Gls
Chesterfield		12.33	34	10	-	0
Darlington	Tr	06.35	35	5	-	0
Mansfield T.	Shrewsbury T.	11.46	46	5	-	0

BROWN, Alexander D. (Sandy)
Grangemouth, 24 March, 1939 SF Lge (FB)

League Club	Source	Date Signed	Seasons Played	Apps	Subs	Gls
Everton	Partick Th.	09.63	63-70	176	33	9
Shrewsbury T.	Tr	05.71	71	21	0	0
Southport	Tr	07.72	72	17	2	0

BROWN, Allistair
Musselburgh, 12 April, 1951 (F)

League Club	Source	Date Signed	Seasons Played	Apps	Subs	Gls
Leicester C.	Jnrs	04.68	68-71	93	8	32
West Bromwich A.	Tr	03.72	71-82	254	25	72
Crystal Palace	Tr	03.83	82	11	0	2
Walsall	Tr	08.83	83	37	1	13
Port Vale	Tr	07.84	84-85	62	5	22

BROWN, Andrew L.
Liverpool, 17 August, 1963 (D)

League Club	Source	Date Signed	Seasons Played	Apps	Subs	Gls
Tranmere Rov. (N/C)	Jnrs	08.82	82	1	0	0

BROWN, Andrew R.
Coatbridge, 20 February, 1915 Died 1973 (LB)

League Club	Source	Date Signed	Seasons Played	Apps	Subs	Gls
Cardiff C.	Cumbernauld Th.	12.36	36-37	2	-	0
Torquay U.	Tr	06.38	38-46	34	-	5

BROWN, Anthony J.
Oldham, 3 October, 1945 EF Lge/E-1 (M)

League Club	Source	Date Signed	Seasons Played	Apps	Subs	Gls
West Bromwich A.	App	10.63	63-79	561	13	218
Torquay U.	Jacksonville (USA)	10.81	81-82	38	7	11

Tony Brown (West Bromwich Albion, Torquay United & England)

BROWN, Anthony J.
Bradford, 17 September, 1958 (CD)

League Club	Source	Date Signed	Seasons Played	Apps	Subs	Gls
Leeds U.	Thackley	03.83	82-84	24	0	1
Doncaster Rov.	L	11.84	84	5	0	0
Doncaster Rov.	Tr	03.85	84-86	80	2	2
Scunthorpe U.	Tr	07.87	87-88	46	8	2
Rochdale	Tr	08.89	89-91	107	2	0

BROWN, R. Berry
Hartlepool, 6 September, 1927 (G)

League Club	Source	Date Signed	Seasons Played	Apps	Subs	Gls
Manchester U.		08.46	47-48	4	-	0
Doncaster Rov.	Tr	01.49	48	4	-	0
Hartlepool U.		08.51	51-55	125	-	0

BROWN, Brian D.
Shoreditch, 10 September, 1949 (FB)

League Club	Source	Date Signed	Seasons Played	Apps	Subs	Gls
Chelsea	App	11.66				
Millwall	Tr	03.68	68-74	186	4	5

BROWN, Cyril
Ashington, 25 May, 1918 (WH)

League Club	Source	Date Signed	Seasons Played	Apps	Subs	Gls
Brentford	Felixstowe	01.39				
Sunderland	Tr	04.45				
Notts Co.	Tr	08.46	46	13	-	5
Rochdale	Tr	08.48	48-50	61	-	11

BROWN, David
Wallasey, 21 October, 1963 (D)

League Club	Source	Date Signed	Seasons Played	Apps	Subs	Gls
Tranmere Rov. (N/C)		08.82	82	1	0	0

BROWN, David J.
Hartlepool, 28 January, 1957 (G)

League Club	Source	Date Signed	Seasons Played	Apps	Subs	Gls
Middlesbrough	Horden Colly	02.77	77	10	0	0
Plymouth Arg.	L	08.79	79	5	0	0
Oxford U.	Tr	10.79	79-80	21	0	0
Bury	Tr	09.81	81-84	146	0	0
Preston N.E.	Tr	06.86	86-88	74	0	0
Scunthorpe U.	L	01.89	88	5	0	0
Halifax T.	Tr	07.89	89-90	38	0	0

BROWN, Dennis J.
Reading, 8 February, 1944 (IF)

League Club	Source	Date Signed	Seasons Played	Apps	Subs	Gls
Chelsea	Jnrs	06.62	63	10	-	1
Swindon T.	Tr	11.64	64-66	92	0	38
Northampton T.	Tr	02.67	66-68	41	5	10
Aldershot	Tr	07.69	69-74	237	8	56

BROWN, W. Dewis
Rotherham, 4 June, 1919 (IF)

League Club	Source	Date Signed	Seasons Played	Apps	Subs	Gls
Stockport Co.		08.45	46-49	65	-	15
Rotherham U.	Tr	08.50	51	1	-	0

BROWN, Douglas A.
Airdrie, 21 March, 1958 (F)

League Club	Source	Date Signed	Seasons Played	Apps	Subs	Gls
Sheffield U.	Clydebank	03.79	78-79	17	8	2

BROWN, Edward A. C.
Camden, 4 October, 1927

League Club	Source	Date Signed	Seasons Played	Apps	Subs	Gls
Brentford		02.50				
Aldershot		08.53	53	3	-	0

BROWN, Edwin
Preston, 28 February, 1926 (CF)

League Club	Source	Date Signed	Seasons Played	Apps	Subs	Gls
Preston N.E.		08.48	48-50	36	-	6
Southampton	Tr	09.50	50-51	57	-	32
Coventry C.	Tr	03.52	51-54	85	-	50
Birmingham C.	Tr	10.54	54-58	158	-	74
Leyton Orient	Tr	01.59	58-60	63	-	28

BROWN, Ernest
Stockport, 30 May, 1923 (LH)

League Club	Source	Date Signed	Seasons Played	Apps	Subs	Gls
Manchester C.		04.44				
Aldershot	Tr	06.46	46	12	-	0
Accrington St.	Tr	08.49	49	2	-	0

BROWN, Ernest C.
South Shields, 3 February, 1921

League Club	Source	Date Signed	Seasons Played	Apps	Subs	Gls
Newcastle U.	South Shields	12.45				
Southend U.	Tr	02.47	46-47	5	-	0

BROWN, Frederick
Leyton, 6 December, 1931 (G)

League Club	Source	Date Signed	Seasons Played	Apps	Subs	Gls
Aldershot	Leytonstone	06.52	52-54	107	-	0
West Bromwich A.	Tr	05.55	55-57	11	-	0
Portsmouth	Tr	06.58	58-59	18	-	0

BROWN, George
Bonnybridge, 12 January, 1932 (G)

League Club	Source	Date Signed	Seasons Played	Apps	Subs	Gls
Crewe Alex.	Stenhousemuir	06.57	57	38	-	0

BROWN, George
Sheffield, 18 October, 1934 E Sch (RH)

League Club	Source	Date Signed	Seasons Played	Apps	Subs	Gls
Liverpool	Jnrs	10.51				
Chesterfield	Tr	05.53	53-54	66	-	5

BROWN, George D.
Airdrie, 8 May, 1928 (IF)

League Club	Source	Date Signed	Seasons Played	Apps	Subs	Gls
Southport	Airdrieonians	04.51	50	1	-	0
Bradford P.A.	Clyde	07.56	56	17	-	2

BROWN, Gordon
Ellesmere Port, 30 June, 1933 (IF)

League Club	Source	Date Signed	Seasons Played	Apps	Subs	Gls
Wolverhampton W.	Jnrs	09.51				
Scunthorpe U.	Tr	12.52	52-56	154	-	71
Derby Co.	Tr	01.57	56-59	53	-	20
Southampton	Tr	03.60	59-60	8	-	2
Barrow	Tr	07.61	61-63	39	-	16
Southport	Tr	01.64	63	4	-	1

League Club	Source	Date Signed	Seasons Played	Apps	Subs	Gls

BROWN, Gordon
Dunfermline, 4 February, 1932 (OL)

League Club	Source	Date Signed	Seasons Played	Apps	Subs	Gls
Blackburn Rov.	Blairhall Colly	04.51				
Newport Co.	Tr	08.55	55-58	137	-	14
Gillingham	Tr	06.59	59-60	67	-	13

BROWN, Gordon A.
East Kilbride, 7 December, 1965 (D)

League Club	Source	Date Signed	Seasons Played	Apps	Subs	Gls
Rotherham U.	App	12.83	83	1	0	0

BROWN, Gordon S.
Worksop, 21 March, 1929 (WH)

League Club	Source	Date Signed	Seasons Played	Apps	Subs	Gls
Nottingham F.	Jnrs	12.46				
York C.	Tr	06.50	50-57	322	-	25

BROWN, Graham C.
Matlock, 21 March, 1944 (G)

League Club	Source	Date Signed	Seasons Played	Apps	Subs	Gls
Millwall		12.64				
Mansfield T.	Crawley T.	08.69	69-73	142	0	0
Doncaster Rov.	Tr	07.74	74-75	53	0	0
Swansea C.	Portland (USA)	09.76	76	4	0	0
York C.	Portland (USA)	08.77	77-79	69	0	0
Rotherham U.	Tr	02.80	79-80	31	0	0
Mansfield T. (N/C)	Tr	01.82	81	1	0	0

BROWN, Graham F.
Leicester, 5 November, 1950 (F)

League Club	Source	Date Signed	Seasons Played	Apps	Subs	Gls
Leicester C.	App	11.68	69	0	1	0

BROWN, Grant A.
Sunderland, 19 November, 1969 (CD)

League Club	Source	Date Signed	Seasons Played	Apps	Subs	Gls
Leicester C.	YT	06.88	87-88	14	0	0
Lincoln C.	L	08.89	89	14	0	1
Lincoln C.	Tr	01.90	89-91	89	0	3

BROWN, Harold T.
Kingsbury, 9 April, 1924 Died 1982 (G)

League Club	Source	Date Signed	Seasons Played	Apps	Subs	Gls
Queens Park R.	Jnrs	04.41				
Notts Co.	Tr	04.46	46-48	93	-	0
Derby Co.	Tr	10.49	49-50	37	-	0
Queens Park R.	Tr	08.51	51-55	187	-	0
Plymouth Arg.	Tr	08.56	56-57	66	-	0

BROWN, Henry S.
Workington, 23 May, 1918 Died 1963 (CH)

League Club	Source	Date Signed	Seasons Played	Apps	Subs	Gls
Wolverhampton W.	Workington T.	02.37	38	2	-	0
Hull C.	Tr	05.46	46	22	-	0

BROWN, Hugh
Carnyle, 7 December, 1921 SF Lge/S-3 (WH)

League Club	Source	Date Signed	Seasons Played	Apps	Subs	Gls
Torquay U.	Partick Th.	11.50	50-51	55	-	0

BROWN, Irvin
Lewes, 20 September, 1935 (CH)

League Club	Source	Date Signed	Seasons Played	Apps	Subs	Gls
Brighton & H.A.	Jnrs	10.52	57	3	-	0
Bournemouth	Tr	09.58	58-62	65	-	2

BROWN, James
Cumnock, 16 February, 1924 (CF)

League Club	Source	Date Signed	Seasons Played	Apps	Subs	Gls
Chesterfield	Motherwell	05.48	48	5	-	2
Bradford C.	Tr	11.48	48	20	-	11
Carlisle U.	Queen of South	09.50	50-51	15	-	9

BROWN, James
Manchester, 5 October, 1935 (OR)

League Club	Source	Date Signed	Seasons Played	Apps	Subs	Gls
Rochdale		04.57	56-60	52	-	4

BROWN, James B.
Stirling, 7 June, 1939 (WH)

League Club	Source	Date Signed	Seasons Played	Apps	Subs	Gls
Darlington	Dumbarton	09.60	60-62	14	-	0

BROWN, James G.
Coatbridge, 11 May, 1952 Su23-4/S-1 (G)

League Club	Source	Date Signed	Seasons Played	Apps	Subs	Gls
Chesterfield	Albion Rov.	12.72	72-73	47	0	0
Sheffield U.	Tr	03.74	73-77	170	0	0
Cardiff C.	Chicago Stings (USA)	12.82	82	3	0	0
Chesterfield	Kettering T.	07.83	83-88	135	0	1

BROWN, James K.
Musselburgh, 3 October, 1953 (M)

League Club	Source	Date Signed	Seasons Played	Apps	Subs	Gls
Aston Villa	App	10.70	69-74	73	2	1
Preston N.E.	Tr	10.75	75-77	64	0	3
Portsmouth	Ethnikos (Gre)	02.80	79	5	0	0

BROWN, Jeremy
Newport, 13 June, 1961 (F)

League Club	Source	Date Signed	Seasons Played	Apps	Subs	Gls
Newport Co.	App	06.78	78	2	1	0

BROWN, John
Edinburgh, 6 March, 1940 (HB)

League Club	Source	Date Signed	Seasons Played	Apps	Subs	Gls
Colchester U.	Dunbar	09.61	62	1	-	0

BROWN, John
Wadebridge, 29 July, 1940 (IF)

League Club	Source	Date Signed	Seasons Played	Apps	Subs	Gls
Plymouth Arg.	Wadebridge	10.60	60-62	9	-	2
Bristol Rov.	Tr	07.63	63-67	156	0	32

BROWN, John C.
Bradford, 30 December, 1947 (G)

League Club	Source	Date Signed	Seasons Played	Apps	Subs	Gls
Preston N.E.	App	03.65	66-74	67	0	0
Stockport Co.	L	11.70	70	26	0	0
Stockport Co.	Tr	07.75	75	15	0	0
Wigan Ath.	Tr	07.76	78-81	93	0	0

BROWN, John (Jackie)
Belfast, 8 November, 1914 NI-10 (OR)

League Club	Source	Date Signed	Seasons Played	Apps	Subs	Gls
Wolverhampton W.	Belfast Celtic	12.34	34-36	27	-	6
Coventry C.	Tr	10.36	36-37	69	-	26
Birmingham C.	Tr	09.38	38	34	-	6
Ipswich T.	Barry T.	05.48	48-50	98	-	25

BROWN, John L.
Crook, 23 March, 1921 (RB)

League Club	Source	Date Signed	Seasons Played	Apps	Subs	Gls
York C.	Stanley U.	02.48	47-49	22	-	0

BROWN, John M.
(CF)

League Club	Source	Date Signed	Seasons Played	Apps	Subs	Gls
Shrewsbury T. (Am)	Queens Park	05.53	53	5	-	3

BROWN, John T.
Edinburgh, 2 April, 1935 S Sch (FB)

League Club	Source	Date Signed	Seasons Played	Apps	Subs	Gls
Tranmere Rov.	Third Lanark	01.61	60-61	33	-	0
Hartlepool U.	Tr	07.62	62-63	68	-	10

BROWN, Jonathan
Barnsley, 8 September, 1966 (FB)

League Club	Source	Date Signed	Seasons Played	Apps	Subs	Gls
Exeter C.	Denaby U.	06.90	90-91	59	5	0

BROWN, Joseph
Cramlington, 26 April, 1929 (WH)

League Club	Source	Date Signed	Seasons Played	Apps	Subs	Gls
Middlesbrough	Jnrs	04.46	49-50	11	-	0
Burnley	Tr	08.52	52	6	-	0
Bournemouth	Tr	06.54	54-59	215	-	5
Aldershot	Tr	07.60	60	5	-	0

BROWN, Joseph S.
Bebington, 7 May, 1920 (OL)

League Club	Source	Date Signed	Seasons Played	Apps	Subs	Gls
Chester C.	Port Sunlight	09.47	46-47	15	-	2

BROWN, Keith
Grimsby, 23 September, 1954 (OL)

League Club	Source	Date Signed	Seasons Played	Apps	Subs	Gls
Nottingham F.	App	09.72				
Grimsby T.	Tr	10.73	73-75	32	7	5

BROWN Keith
Hucknall, 1 January, 1942 E Sch (F)

League Club	Source	Date Signed	Seasons Played	Apps	Subs	Gls
Notts Co.	Jnrs	01.59	58	8	-	4
Rotherham U.	Tr	07.59				

BROWN, Keith
Liverpool, 19 October, 1957 (FB)

League Club	Source	Date Signed	Seasons Played	Apps	Subs	Gls
Southport (N/C)	East Villa	11.76	76	4	0	0

BROWN, Keith G.
Coseley, 16 July, 1954 (FB)

League Club	Source	Date Signed	Seasons Played	Apps	Subs	Gls
Walsall	Jnrs	07.73	73-74	8	2	0

BROWN, Keith J.
Bournemouth, 29 January, 1942 (FB)

League Club	Source	Date Signed	Seasons Played	Apps	Subs	Gls
Bournemouth	Pokesdown	09.60	63-64	15	-	0

BROWN, Keith T.
Bristol, 28 September, 1959 (F)

League Club	Source	Date Signed	Seasons Played	Apps	Subs	Gls
Bristol Rov.	Bristol St Georges	10.77	78-80	4	3	0

BROWN, Kenneth
Forest Gate, 16 February, 1934 E-1 (CH)

League Club	Source	Date Signed	Seasons Played	Apps	Subs	Gls
West Ham U.	Neville U.	10.51	52-66	386	0	4
Torquay U.	Tr	05.67	67-68	40	2	1

BROWN, Kenneth G.
Barnsley, 21 March, 1952 (M)

League Club	Source	Date Signed	Seasons Played	Apps	Subs	Gls
Barnsley	App	04.70	69-77	267	11	24
Bournemouth	Tr	06.78	78-79	29	3	4

BROWN, Kenneth J.
Upminster, 11 July, 1967 (RB)

League Club	Source	Date Signed	Seasons Played	Apps	Subs	Gls
Norwich C.	App	07.85	86-87	24	1	0
Plymouth Arg.	Tr	08.88	88-90	126	0	4
West Ham U.	Tr	08.91	91	25	2	3

BROWN, Kenneth J.
Coventry, 18 October, 1933 (IF)

League Club	Source	Date Signed	Seasons Played	Apps	Subs	Gls
Coventry C.		01.56				
Nottingham F.	Corby T.	11.56				
Bournemouth	Tr	07.57	57	6	-	1
Torquay U.	Tr	07.58	58	8	-	1

BROWN, Kevan B.
Andover, 2 January, 1966 (RB)

League Club	Source	Date Signed	Seasons Played	Apps	Subs	Gls
Southampton	Jnrs	07.84				
Brighton & H.A.	Tr	02.87	86-88	52	1	0
Aldershot	Tr	11.88	88-90	108	2	2

BROWN, Laurence
Shildon, 22 August, 1937 E Amat (CH)

League Club	Source	Date Signed	Seasons Played	Apps	Subs	Gls
Darlington (Am)	Bishop Auckland	03.59	58	3	-	0
Northampton T.	Bishop Auckland	10.60	60	33	-	21
Arsenal	Tr	08.61	61-63	101	-	2
Tottenham H.	Tr	04.63	63-65	62	0	3
Norwich C.	Tr	09.66	66-68	80	1	2
Bradford P.A.	Tr	12.68	68-69	36	0	1

BROWN, Malcolm
Salford, 13 December, 1956 (RB)

League Club	Source	Date Signed	Seasons Played	Apps	Subs	Gls
Bury	App	12.74	73-76	10	1	0
Huddersfield T.	Tr	05.77	77-82	256	0	16
Newcastle U.	Tr	08.83	84	39	0	0
Huddersfield T.	Tr	06.85	85-88	93	3	1
Rochdale (N/C)	Tr	02.89	88	11	0	0
Stockport Co.	Tr	07.89	89-90	71	0	3
Rochdale	Tr	08.91	91	18	0	1

BROWN, Michael
Walsall, 11 July, 1939 (FB)

League Club	Source	Date Signed	Seasons Played	Apps	Subs	Gls
Hull C.	Jnrs	10.58	59-65	8	0	0
Lincoln C.	Tr	07.67	67	39	0	0

BROWN, Michael A.
Birmingham, 8 February, 1968 (W)

League Club	Source	Date Signed	Seasons Played	Apps	Subs	Gls
Shrewsbury T.	App	02.86	86-90	174	16	9
Bolton W.	Tr	08.91	91	23	4	3

BROWN, Michael J.
Slough, 11 April, 1944 (F)

League Club	Source	Date Signed	Seasons Played	Apps	Subs	Gls
Fulham	App	09.61	61-62	4	-	0
Millwall	Tr	02.65	64-66	47	5	11
Luton T.	Tr	07.67	67-68	9	5	2
Colchester U.	Tr	10.68	68-69	47	5	12

BROWN, Michael J. L.
Swansea, 27 September, 1951 W Sch (CD)

League Club	Source	Date Signed	Seasons Played	Apps	Subs	Gls
Crystal Palace	App	09.69				
Brighton & H.A.	Tr	06.73	73	5	3	1
Brentford	L	09.73	73	3	0	0

BROWN, Monty R.
Grimsby, 7 September, 1943 (OR)

League Club	Source	Date Signed	Seasons Played	Apps	Subs	Gls
Scunthorpe U.	Jnrs	07.63	64-65	19	0	6

BROWN, Neil R.
Sheffiield, 16 January, 1966 (LB)

League Club	Source	Date Signed	Seasons Played	Apps	Subs	Gls
Chesterfield	App	11.83	83	5	0	0

BROWN, Nicholas J.
Northampton, 25 January, 1973 (G)

League Club	Source	Date Signed	Seasons Played	Apps	Subs	Gls
Halifax T.	Norwich C. (YT)	07.91	91	1	0	0

BROWN, Nicholas L.
Hull, 16 October, 1966 (FB)

League Club	Source	Date Signed	Seasons Played	Apps	Subs	Gls
Hull C.	YT	08.85	85-91	80	6	3

BROWN, Owen J.
Liverpool, 4 September, 1960 (F)

League Club	Source	Date Signed	Seasons Played	Apps	Subs	Gls
Liverpool	Jnrs	11.78				
Carlisle U.	Tr	06.80	80	4	0	2

League Club	Source	Date Signed	Seasons Played	Apps	Subs	Gls
Tranmere Rov.	Tr	08.81	81	29	8	8
Crewe Alex.	Tr	08.82	82	1	0	0
Tranmere Rov.	Tr	10.82	82-83	47	9	12
Chester C.	Tr	08.84	84	9	1	3

BROWN, Peter B.
Andover, 13 July, 1934 (OR)

League Club	Source	Date Signed	Seasons Played	Apps	Subs	Gls
Southampton	Jnrs	01.52	53-57	16	-	3
Wrexham	Tr	07.58	58-59	33	-	9

BROWN, Peter R.
Hemel Hempstead, 1 September, 1961 (FB)

League Club	Source	Date Signed	Seasons Played	Apps	Subs	Gls
Wimbledon	Chelsea (App)	08.80	80-81	53	2	3

BROWN, Philip
South Shields, 30 May, 1959 (RB)

League Club	Source	Date Signed	Seasons Played	Apps	Subs	Gls
Hartlepool U.		07.78	79-84	210	7	8
Halifax T.	Tr	07.85	85-87	135	0	19
Bolton W.	Tr	06.88	88-91	172	2	7

BROWN, Philip J.
Sheffield, 16 January, 1966 (W)

League Club	Source	Date Signed	Seasons Played	Apps	Subs	Gls
Chesterfield	App	10.83	82-86	82	5	19
Stockport Co.	Tr	(N/L)	86	23	0	1
Lincoln C.	Tr	08.87	88-89	32	11	3

BROWN, Ralph
Ilkeston, 26 February, 1944 (F)

League Club	Source	Date Signed	Seasons Played	Apps	Subs	Gls
Aston Villa	App	03.61				
Notts Co.	Tr	05.62	62	18	-	3

BROWN, Raymond M.
Carlisle, 11 February, 1928

League Club	Source	Date Signed	Seasons Played	Apps	Subs	Gls
Notts Co.	Queens Park	08.51	51	7	-	0

BROWN, Richard A.
Nottingham, 13 January, 1967 (FB)

League Club	Source	Date Signed	Seasons Played	Apps	Subs	Gls
Sheffield Wed.	Ilkeston T.	12.84				
Blackburn Rov.	Kettering T.	09.90	91	24	2	0
Maidstone U.	L	02.91	90	3	0	0

BROWN, Richard C.
Sutton Coldfield, 25 December, 1973 (D)

League Club	Source	Date Signed	Seasons Played	Apps	Subs	Gls
Walsall	YT	03.92	91	6	3	0

BROWN, Robert
Glasgow, 9 August, 1924 (IF)

League Club	Source	Date Signed	Seasons Played	Apps	Subs	Gls
Derby Co.	Camerons	10.47				
Southend U.	Tr	07.48	48-49	12	-	0
Shrewsbury T.	Tr	07.50	50-52	104	-	41
Barnsley	Tr	07.53	53-56	121	-	55
Rotherham U.	Tr	09.56	56-57	41	-	13

BROWN, Robert
Workington, 23 November, 1955 (D)

League Club	Source	Date Signed	Seasons Played	Apps	Subs	Gls
Workington	Jnrs	08.74	74-76	44	0	0

BROWN, Robert
Motherwell, 2 December, 1931 (FB)

League Club	Source	Date Signed	Seasons Played	Apps	Subs	Gls
Workington	Motherwell	05.56	56-67	418	1	2

BROWN, Robert
Bristol, 14 May, 1949 (IF)

League Club	Source	Date Signed	Seasons Played	Apps	Subs	Gls
Bristol Rov.	App	06.67	68-71	28	7	4
Newport Co.	L	03.70	69	8	1	0

BROWN, Robert A. J. ("Sailor")
Great Yarmouth, 7 November, 1915 (IF)

League Club	Source	Date Signed	Seasons Played	Apps	Subs	Gls
Charlton Ath.	Gorleston	08.34	37-38	47	-	21
Nottingham F.	Tr	05.46	46-47	46	-	17
Aston Villa	Tr	10.47	47-48	30	-	9

BROWN, Robert C.
Plymouth, 24 November, 1953 (M)

League Club	Source	Date Signed	Seasons Played	Apps	Subs	Gls
Chelsea	Jnrs	08.72				
Sheffield Wed.	Tr	08.74	74-75	17	4	3
Aldershot	L	02.76	75	3	2	0

BROWN, Robert H.
Streatham, 2 May, 1940 E Amat (CF)

League Club	Source	Date Signed	Seasons Played	Apps	Subs	Gls
Fulham (Am)	Barnet	09.60	60-61	8	-	4
Watford	Tr	11.61	61-62	28	-	10
Northampton T.	Tr	12.63	63-66	51	0	22
Cardiff C.	Tr	10.66	66-67	50	0	24

League Club	Source	Date Signed	Seasons Played	Career Record Apps	Subs	Gls
BROWN, Roger W.						
Tamworth, 12 December, 1952						(CD)
Bournemouth	A.P. Leamington	02.78	77-78	63	0	3
Norwich C.	Tr	07.79	79	16	0	0
Fulham	Tr	03.80	79-83	141	0	18
Bournemouth	Tr	12.83	83-86	83	1	5
BROWN, Ronald						
Ballymoney (NI), 20 March, 1923						(CF)
Plymouth Arg.	Linfield	04.45				
Hull C.	Tr	03.47	46	7	-	3
BROWN, Ronald E.						
Sunderland, 26 December, 1944						(OR)
Blackpool	Whitley Bay	11.65	65-70	54	7	13
Plymouth Arg.	Tr	02.71	70-72	31	5	3
Bradford C.	Tr	09.72	72-74	90	7	11
BROWN, Roy						
Stockton, 10 June, 1925						(FB)
Darlington	Stockton W.E.	01.47	46-55	159	-	20
Hartlepool U.	Tr	08.56				
BROWN, Roy						
Bradford, 17 June, 1932						(F)
Doncaster Rov.	Gainsborough Trin.	05.53	53-56	26	-	6
BROWN, Roy E.						
Hove, 5 October, 1945						(G)
Tottenham H.	App	10.62	66	1	0	0
Reading	Tr	07.68	68-69	63	0	0
Notts Co.	Tr	07.70	70-74	113	0	0
Mansfield T. (N/C)		11.75	75	1	0	0
BROWN, Roy H.						
Stoke, 20 December, 1923						(CF)
Stoke C.	Jnrs	08.42	46-52	70	-	14
Watford	Tr	07.53	53-57	142	-	40
BROWN, Stanley						
Lewes, 15 September, 1941						(WH)
Fulham	Jnrs	05.59	60-72	348	5	16
Brighton & H.A.	L	10.72	72	9	0	0
Colchester U.	Tr	12.72	72	23	0	0
BROWN, Stephen F.						
Northampton, 6 July, 1966						(W)
Northampton T.	Jnrs	06.85	83-84	14	1	3
Northampton T.	Irthlingborough Diam.	07.89	89-91	83	13	6
BROWN, Steven A. J.						
Peckham, 13 July, 1952						(W)
Millwall	App	06.70	69-74	47	23	5
BROWN, Steven B.						
Brighton, 13 May, 1972						(CD)
Charlton Ath.	YT	07.90	91	0	1	0
BROWN, Thomas						
Galashiels, 7 June, 1929						(IF)
Ipswich T.	Annbanks Jnrs	07.52	52-55	84	-	17
Walsall	Tr	06.56	56-57	39	-	8
BROWN, Thomas						
Leven, 17 November, 1933						(HB)
Lincoln C.	Newburgh Jnrs	04.56	57	3	-	0
BROWN, Thomas						
Troon, 26 October, 1919						(G)
Ipswich T.	Glenathon Jnrs	10.38	46-50	111	-	0
BROWN, Thomas E.						
Throckley, 8 September, 1935						(FB)
Middlesbrough	Jnrs	04.53	54-57	44	-	0
BROWN, Thomas G.						
Cowdenbeath, 11 August, 1924						(IF)
Portsmouth	Worcester C.	10.46	47	17	-	1
Watford	Tr	08.49	49-53	108	-	11
BROWN, Thomas H.						
Liverpool, 8 May, 1930 E Yth						(HB)
Doncaster Rov.	South Liverpool	02.51	51-53	86	-	1
Swansea C.	Tr	12.55	55-58	69	-	0

League Club	Source	Date Signed	Seasons Played	Career Record Apps	Subs	Gls
BROWN, Thomas L.						
Glenbuck, 17 April, 1921 Died 1966						(WH)
Millwall	Hearts	01.45	46-48	68	-	7
Charlton Ath.	Tr	10.48	48-49	34	-	1
Leyton Orient	Tr	08.50	50-52	99	-	5
BROWN, Walter S.						
Oakengates, 8 February, 1921						(IF)
Walsall	Oakengates T.	10.40	46-47	19	-	4
BROWN, William						
						(CF)
Accrington St.	Forfar Ath.	08.53	53	6	-	2
BROWN, William						
Falkirk, 5 February, 1950						(F)
Burnley	Jnrs	02.67	68	0	1	0
Carlisle U.	Tr	07.69	69	16	3	8
Barrow	L	09.69	69	6	0	1
Newport Co.	Tr	08.70	70-74	166	2	50
Hereford U.	L	03.74	73	9	0	6
Brentford	Tr	11.74	74	16	0	9
Torquay U.	Tr	03.75	74-77	137	2	46
BROWN, William						
Murton, 27 March, 1928						(HB)
Gateshead	Murton Colly	09.50	50-57	214	-	7
BROWN, William						
Kilsyth, 21 February, 1929						(F)
Reading	Bridgeton Waverley	02.50				
Exeter C.	Tr	08.51	51	7	-	0
BROWN, William C.						
Barking, 24 April, 1920 Died 1982						(CF)
Leyton Orient	Romford	08.46	46	2	-	1
BROWN, William D. F.						
Dundee, 8 October, 1931 SF Lge/S'B'-1/S-28						(G)
Tottenham H.	Dundee	06.59	59-65	222	0	0
Northampton T.	Tr	10.66	66	17	0	0
BROWN, William F.						
Larkhall, 20 October, 1922 Died 1979						(FB)
Preston N.E.	Larkhall Th.	01.42	46-49	40	-	0
Grimsby T.	Queen of South	06.51	51-57	265	-	1
BROWN, William H.						
Choppington, 11 March, 1909						(FB)
Middlesbrough	West Stanley	12.28	31-38	256	-	2
Hartlepool U.	Tr	06.46	46-47	80	-	0
BROWN, William I.						
Silvertown, 6 September, 1909						(RB)
Luton T.	Silvertown	03.30	30-34	49	-	4
Huddersfield T.	Tr	03.35	34-35	20	-	2
Brentford	Tr	03.37	36-46	92	-	2
Leyton Orient	Tr	05.47	46-47	26	-	0
BROWN, William I.						
Clydebank, 25 November, 1938						(G)
Accrington St.	St Mirren	08.59	59	29	-	0
Chester C.	Tr	06.60	60	41	-	0
BROWN, William T.						
Croydon, 7 February, 1943						(CF)
Southampton		09.60				
Charlton Ath.	Tr	07.61				
Gillingham	Bedford T.	02.66	65-67	104	1	33
Portsmouth	Tr	06.68	68	8	0	2
Brentford	Tr	07.69	69	4	0	0
BROWNBILL, Derek A.						
Liverpool, 4 February, 1954						(M)
Liverpool	Jnrs	02.72	73	1	0	0
Port Vale	Tr	02.75	74-77	84	8	13
Wigan Ath.	Tr	09.78	78-79	32	16	8
BROWNE, Corey A.						
Enfield, 2 July, 1970						(W)
Fulham		08.91	91	1	0	0
BROWNE, Robert J.						
Derry (NI), 9 February, 1912 Irish Lge/NI-6						(WH)
Leeds U.	Derry C.	10.35	35-46	107	-	0
York C.	Tr	08.47	47	5	-	0

League Club	Source	Date Signed	Seasons Played	Career Record Apps	Subs	Gls
BROWNE, Stephen L.						
Hackney, 21 June, 1964						(F)
Charlton Ath.	App	06.82	81	0	1	0
BROWNING, Leonard J.						
Leeds, 30 March, 1928						(CF)
Leeds U.	Headingley R.	08.46	46-51	97	-	42
Sheffield U.	Tr	11.51	51-53	65	-	25
BROWNING, Marcus T.						
Bristol, 22 April, 1971						(F)
Bristol Rov.	YT	07.89	89-91	5	7	0
BROWNLEE, Thomas C.						
Carnwath, 21 May, 1935						(CF)
Walsall	Broxburn	09.56	57-58	30	-	14
York C.	Tr	12.58	58	9	-	2
Workington	Tr	06.59	59-60	25	-	2
Bradford C.	Netherfield	01.65	64-65	25	0	15
BROWNLIE, John J.						
Caldercruix, 11 March, 1952 Su23-5/S-7						(RB)
Newcastle U.	Hibernian	08.78	78-81	124	0	2
Middlesbrough	Tr	08.82	82	12	0	0
Hartlepool U.	Tr	08.84	84	19	0	1
BROWNLOW, John M. (Jackie)						
Belfast, 18 June, 1916						(W)
Ipswich T.	Gravesend & Nft	05.46	46	1	-	0
Hartlepool U.	Tr	10.48	48	3	-	0
BROWNSWORD N. John (Jack)						
Campsall, 15 May, 1923						(FB)
Hull C.	Frickley Colly	09.46	46	10	-	0
Scunthorpe U.	Tr	07.47	50-64	595	-	50
BRUCE, Alexander R.						
Dundee, 23 December, 1952 Su23-1						(F)
Preston N.E.	App	05.70	71-73	55	7	22
Newcastle U.	Tr	01.74	73-75	16	4	3
Preston N.E.	Tr	08.75	75-82	288	13	135
Wigan Ath.	Tr	08.83	83-84	35	8	7
BRUCE, Marcelle E.						
Detroit (USA), 15 March, 1971						(RB)
Colchester U.	YT	07.89	89	28	1	1
BRUCE, Robert						
Belfast, 14 October, 1928						(OL)
Leicester C.	Larne T.	03.50				
Leyton Orient		11.51	51	1	-	0
BRUCE, Stephen R.						
Corbridge, 31 December, 1960 E Yth/E'B'						(CD)
Gillingham	App	10.78	79-83	203	2	29
Norwich C.	Tr	08.84	84-87	141	0	14
Manchester U.	Tr	12.87	87-91	161	0	26
BRUCK, Dietmar J.						
Germany, 19 April, 1944						(FB)
Coventry C.	App	05.62	60-70	181	8	7
Charlton Ath.	Tr	10.70	70-71	54	2	0
Northampton T.	Tr	06.72	72-73	41	0	0
BRUNFIELD, Peter						
Treeton, 5 September, 1944						(HB)
Chesterfield		07.64	64	1	-	0
BRUNSKILL, Joseph						
Carlton, 22 April, 1932						(F)
Sunderland	Newcastle U. (Am)	04.50				
Oldham Ath.	Tr	05.54	54	12	-	2
BRUNT, Geoffrey R.						
Nottingham, 24 November, 1926						(WH)
Notts Co.	Jnrs	09.49	49-53	29	-	1
BRUNT, Malcolm E.						
Sheffield, 5 December, 1946						(G)
Chesterfield	Sheffield Wed. (Am)	07.66	66	7	0	0
BRUSH, Paul						
Plaistow, 22 February, 1958						(FB)
West Ham U.	App	02.76	77-84	144	7	1
Crystal Palace	Tr	09.85	85-87	50	0	3
Southend U.	Tr	01.88	87-89	69	4	1

League Club	Source	Date Signed	Seasons Played	Career Record Apps	Subs	Gls
BRUTON, David E.						
Dursley, 31 October, 1952						(CD)
Bristol C.	App	07.71	71-72	16	1	0
Swansea C.	Tr	08.73	73-78	185	8	19
Newport Co.	L	02.77	76	6	0	1
Newport Co.	Tr	10.78	78-80	79	3	9
BRUTON, Michael						
Gloucester, 6 May, 1958						(F)
Newport Co.	Gloucester C.	08.79	79	3	6	1
BRYAN, Ernest N.						
Hawarden, 6 June, 1926						(RB)
Chester C.	Jnrs	11.45	48	1	-	0
BRYAN, Peter						
Oxford, 30 April, 1944						(FB)
Oxford U.	Botley Minors	07.61	62-65	18	0	0
BRYAN, Peter A.						
Birmingham, 22 June, 1943						(FB)
Middlesbrough		08.61	64	4	-	0
Oldham Ath.	Tr	07.65	65	5	1	0
BRYANT, Eric						
Birmingham, 18 November, 1921						(CF)
Mansfield T.		05.46	46-47	35	-	17
Plymouth Arg.	Yeovil T.	10.49	49-50	11	-	4
Leyton Orient	Tr	07.51	51	12	-	1
BRYANT, Jeffrey S.						
Redhill, 27 November, 1953 E Yth						(D)
Wimbledon	Walton & Hersham	(N/L)	77-78	70	3	9
Bournemouth	Tr	06.79	79	16	0	2
BRYANT, Matthew						
Bristol, 21 September, 1970						(CD)
Bristol C.	YT	07.89	90-91	65	0	3
Walsall	L	08.90	90	13	0	0

Steve Bruce (Gillingham, Norwich City & Manchester United)

League Club	Source	Date Signed	Seasons Played	Career Record Apps	Subs	Gls

BRYANT, Richard J.
Bristol, 20 June, 1963 (CD)

League Club	Source	Date Signed	Seasons Played	Apps	Subs	Gls
Bristol C.	D.R.G.	12.85	85	2	0	1

BRYANT, Steven P.
Islington, 5 September, 1953 (LB)

League Club	Source	Date Signed	Seasons Played	Apps	Subs	Gls
Birmingham C.	App	07.71	74-75	34	2	1
Sheffield Wed.	L	08.76	76	2	1	0
Northampton T.	Tr	12.76	76-78	95	2	5
Portsmouth	Tr	03.79	78-81	111	0	5
Northampton T.	Tr	03.82	81	10	0	0

BRYCELAND, Thomas
Greenock, 1 March, 1939 S Sch (IF)

League Club	Source	Date Signed	Seasons Played	Apps	Subs	Gls
Norwich C.	St Mirren	09.62	62-69	253	1	49
Oldham Ath.	Tr	03.70	69-71	66	1	10

BRYDON, Ian F.
Edinburgh, 22 March, 1927 Died 1973 (CF)

League Club	Source	Date Signed	Seasons Played	Apps	Subs	Gls
Darlington	St Johnstone	09.53	53	1	-	0
Accrington St.	Tr	11.53	53-54	27	-	19
Bradford P.A.	Tr	06.55	55	12	-	3

BRYSON, J. Ian C.
Kilmarnock, 26 November, 1962 (W)

League Club	Source	Date Signed	Seasons Played	Apps	Subs	Gls
Sheffield U.	Kilmarnock	08.88	88-91	129	10	33

BUCHAN, Alistair R.
Aberdeen, 27 May, 1926 (WH)

League Club	Source	Date Signed	Seasons Played	Apps	Subs	Gls
Rochdale	Huntly	02.51	50-53	106	-	2

BUCHAN, George
Aberdeen, 2 May, 1950 (W)

League Club	Source	Date Signed	Seasons Played	Apps	Subs	Gls
Manchester U.	Aberdeen	05.73	73	0	3	0
Bury	Tr	08.74	74-75	57	8	6

BUCHAN, Martin M.
Aberdeen, 6 March, 1949 Su23-3/S-34 (CD)

League Club	Source	Date Signed	Seasons Played	Apps	Subs	Gls
Manchester U.	Aberdeen	03.72	71-82	376	0	4
Oldham Ath.	Tr	08.83	83-84	28	0	0

Martin Buchan (Aberdeen, Manchester United, Oldham Athletic & Scotland)

BUCHAN, Thomas
Edinburgh, 6 December, 1915 (WH)

League Club	Source	Date Signed	Seasons Played	Apps	Subs	Gls
Blackpool	Woodhall Th.	05.38	46-47	12	-	0
Carlisle U.	Tr	08.49	49	30	-	0

BUCHAN, William R. M.
Grangemouth, 17 October, 1914 SF Lge (IF)

League Club	Source	Date Signed	Seasons Played	Apps	Subs	Gls
Blackpool	Glasgow Celtic	11.37	37-47	90	-	34
Hull C.	Tr	01.48	47-48	40	-	12
Gateshead	Tr	11.49	49-51	88	-	16

BUCHANAN, Cameron C.
Airdrie, 31 July, 1928 (IF)

League Club	Source	Date Signed	Seasons Played	Apps	Subs	Gls
Wolverhampton W.	Jnrs	09.45				
Bournemouth	Tr	08.49	49-54	83	-	19
Norwich C.	Tr	10.56	56	3	-	0

BUCHANAN, David
Newcastle, 23 June, 1962 E Yth/E Semi-Pro (F)

League Club	Source	Date Signed	Seasons Played	Apps	Subs	Gls
Leicester C.	App	06.79	78-82	24	9	7
Northampton T.	L	10.82	82	3	2	0
Peterborough U.	Tr	08.83	83	13	3	4
Sunderland	Blyth Spartans	08.86	86-87	25	9	8
York C.	L	09.87	87	7	0	2

BUCHANAN, John
Dingwall, 19 September, 1951 (M)

League Club	Source	Date Signed	Seasons Played	Apps	Subs	Gls
Northampton T.	Ross Co.	11.70	70-74	104	10	25
Cardiff C.	Tr	10.74	74-81	217	14	54
Northampton T.	Tr	09.81	81-82	66	3	6

BUCHANAN, John
Falkirk, 9 June, 1928 (CF)

League Club	Source	Date Signed	Seasons Played	Apps	Subs	Gls
Derby Co.	Clyde	02.55	54-56	32	-	12
Bradford P.A.	Tr	12.57	57-62	164	-	67

BUCHANAN, John (Jock)
Cumbernauld, 3 January, 1935 (CF)

League Club	Source	Date Signed	Seasons Played	Apps	Subs	Gls
Newport Co.	Raith Rov.	08.61	61	31	-	7

BUCHANAN, Peter S.
Glasgow, 13 October, 1915 S-1 (IF)

League Club	Source	Date Signed	Seasons Played	Apps	Subs	Gls
Chelsea	Wishaw Jnrs	11.35	36-38	39	-	6
Fulham	Tr	03.46	46	19	-	1
Brentford	Tr	08.47	47-48	74	-	13

BUCHANAN, William
Glasgow, 29 July, 1924 (FB)

League Club	Source	Date Signed	Seasons Played	Apps	Subs	Gls
Carlisle U.	Motherwell	07.49	49	9	-	0
Barrow	Tr	10.49	49-55	242	-	0

BUCK, Alan M.
Colchester, 25 August, 1946 (G)

League Club	Source	Date Signed	Seasons Played	Apps	Subs	Gls
Colchester U.	Jnrs	07.64	64-68	38	0	0

BUCK, Anthony R.
Whitwell, 18 August, 1944 (CF)

League Club	Source	Date Signed	Seasons Played	Apps	Subs	Gls
Oxford U.	Eastbourne	08.62	62-67	30	5	6
Newport Co.	Tr	12.67	67-68	49	0	17
Rochdale	Tr	02.69	68-72	73	12	29
Bradford C.	L	01.72	71	3	0	0
Northampton T.	Tr	01.73	72-73	16	1	3

BUCK, David C.
Colchester, 25 August, 1946 (WH)

League Club	Source	Date Signed	Seasons Played	Apps	Subs	Gls
Colchester U.	Jnrs	05.65	65	0	1	0

BUCK, George W.
Abingdon, 25 January, 1941 (W)

League Club	Source	Date Signed	Seasons Played	Apps	Subs	Gls
Reading	Jnrs	01.58	58-60	31	-	4
Stockport Co.	Tr	07.62	62	3	-	0

BUCKINGHAM, Colin M. E.
Plymouth, 12 August, 1943 (WH)

League Club	Source	Date Signed	Seasons Played	Apps	Subs	Gls
Plymouth Arg.	App	08.61	62-65	16	0	0
Exeter C.	Tr	09.65	65-66	29	0	0

BUCKINGHAM, Victor F.
Greenwich, 23 October, 1915 (LB)

League Club	Source	Date Signed	Seasons Played	Apps	Subs	Gls
Tottenham H.	Jnrs	05.35	35-48	205	-	1

BUCKLAND, Mark C.
Cheltenham, 18 August, 1961 (M)

League Club	Source	Date Signed	Seasons Played	Apps	Subs	Gls
Wolverhampton W.	A.P. Leamington	02.84	83-84	44	6	5

BUCKLE, Edward W.
Southwark, 28 October, 1924 (W)

League Club	Source	Date Signed	Seasons Played	Apps	Subs	Gls
Manchester U.		11.45	46-49	20	-	6
Everton	Tr	11.49	49-54	97	-	31
Exeter C.	Tr	07.55	55-56	65	-	12

BUCKLE, Paul J.
Hatfield, 16 December, 1970 (W)

League Club	Source	Date Signed	Seasons Played	Apps	Subs	Gls
Brentford	YT	07.89	87-91	38	14	1

BUCKLEY, Alan P.
Eastwood, 20 April, 1951 (F)

League Club	Source	Date Signed	Seasons Played	Apps	Subs	Gls
Nottingham F.	App	04.68	71-72	16	2	1
Walsall	Tr	08.73	73-78	241	0	125
Birmingham C.	Tr	10.78	78	24	4	8
Walsall	Tr	07.79	79-84	161	17	49

BUCKLEY, Ambrose
Brinsley, 31 January, 1909 Died 1968 (LB)

League Club	Source	Date Signed	Seasons Played	Apps	Subs	Gls
Fulham	Sherwood Forest	03.33	34-38	6	-	0
Doncaster Rov.	Tr	05.39				
Stockport Co.	Dartford	11.45	46	11	-	0

BUCKLEY, Frank L.
Lichfield, 11 May, 1922 (WH)

League Club	Source	Date Signed	Seasons Played	Apps	Subs	Gls
Notts Co.		08.39				
Crystal Palace	Tr	11.46	47-50	69	-	0

BUCKLEY, Gary
Manchester, 3 March, 1961 (M)

League Club	Source	Date Signed	Seasons Played	Apps	Subs	Gls
Manchester C.	App	04.78	80	4	2	0
Preston N.E.	Tr	10.81	81-82	27	7	2
Bury	Chorley	03.84	83-85	23	8	1

BUCKLEY, Glen
Wigan, 31 August, 1960 (F)

League Club	Source	Date Signed	Seasons Played	Apps	Subs	Gls
Wigan Ath. (N/C)	Preston N.E. (N/C)	10.79	79	1	0	0

BUCKLEY, Ian
Oldham, 8 October, 1953 E Yth (LB)

League Club	Source	Date Signed	Seasons Played	Apps	Subs	Gls
Oldham Ath.	App	12.71	71	5	0	0
Rochdale	L	02.74	73	6	0	0
Stockport Co.	Tr	08.75	75-76	55	10	2
Cambridge U.	Durban C. (SA)	11.77	77-80	51	6	2

BUCKLEY, John W.
East Kilbride, 10 May, 1962 (W)

League Club	Source	Date Signed	Seasons Played	Apps	Subs	Gls
Doncaster Rov.	Partick Th.	07.84	84-85	79	5	11
Leeds U.	Tr	06.86	86-87	6	4	1
Leicester C.	L	03.87	86	1	4	0
Doncaster Rov.	L	10.87	87	6	0	0
Rotherham U.	Tr	11.87	87-90	85	20	13
Scunthorpe U.	Partick Th.	08.91	91	26	2	6

BUCKLEY, Michael J.
Manchester, 4 November, 1953 E Yth/Eu23-1 (M)

League Club	Source	Date Signed	Seasons Played	Apps	Subs	Gls
Everton	App	06.71	71-77	128	7	10
Sunderland	Tr	08.78	78-82	117	4	7
Hartlepool U. (N/C)	Tr	08.83	83	6	0	0
Carlisle U.	Tr	09.83	83	24	1	2
Middlesbrough	Tr	06.84	84	27	0	0

BUCKLEY, Neil A.
Hull, 25 September, 1968 (CD)

League Club	Source	Date Signed	Seasons Played	Apps	Subs	Gls
Hull C.	YT	12.86	86-91	55	5	3
Burnley	L	03.90	89	5	0	0

BUCKLEY, Patrick M.
Leith, 12 August, 1946 (OL)

League Club	Source	Date Signed	Seasons Played	Apps	Subs	Gls
Wolverhampton W.	Third Lanark	02.64	64-67	28	1	8
Sheffield U.	Tr	01.68	67-70	9	6	2
Rotherham U.	Tr	06.72	72	1	2	0

BUCKLEY, Steven
Eastwood, 16 October, 1953 (LB)

League Club	Source	Date Signed	Seasons Played	Apps	Subs	Gls
Luton T.	Burton A.	04.74	74-77	123	0	9
Derby Co.	Tr	01.78	77-85	323	0	21
Lincoln C.	Tr	08.86	86	36	0	2

BUDD, Kevin J.
Hillingdon, 20 March, 1962 (D)

League Club	Source	Date Signed	Seasons Played	Apps	Subs	Gls
Norwich C.	Bournemouth (App)	10.79				
Manchester C.	Tr	02.81				
Swansea C. (N/C)		11.85	85	1	0	0

BUGG, Alec A.
Needham Market, 27 November, 1948 (G)

League Club	Source	Date Signed	Seasons Played	Apps	Subs	Gls
Ipswich T.	Jnrs	06.67	68-69	4	0	0
Bournemouth	L	02.70	69	4	0	0

BUICK, Joseph L.
Broughty Ferry, 1 July, 1933 (WH)

League Club	Source	Date Signed	Seasons Played	Apps	Subs	Gls
Lincoln C.	Broughty Ath.	10.55	55-61	31	-	3

BUIST, James G.
Falkirk, 19 June, 1918 (W)

League Club	Source	Date Signed	Seasons Played	Apps	Subs	Gls
New Brighton	Dundee	08.46	46	21	-	6
Plymouth Arg.	Tr	06.47	48	1	-	0

BUKOVINA, John F.
Barnsley, 2 February, 1964 (F)

League Club	Source	Date Signed	Seasons Played	Apps	Subs	Gls
Barnsley	App	02.82				
Doncaster Rov.	Tr	08.83	83	1	0	0

BUKOWSKI, David J.
Northampton, 2 November, 1952 (CD)

League Club	Source	Date Signed	Seasons Played	Apps	Subs	Gls
Northampton T.	App	11.70	71-72	10	1	0

BULCH, Robert S.
Newcastle, 1 January, 1933 (WH)

League Club	Source	Date Signed	Seasons Played	Apps	Subs	Gls
Notts Co.	Washington	03.53	55-57	27	-	1
Darlington	Tr	06.58	58-59	44	-	1

BULL, Gary W.
Tipton, 12 June, 1966 (F)

League Club	Source	Date Signed	Seasons Played	Apps	Subs	Gls
Southampton	Paget R.	10.86				
Cambridge U.	Tr	03.88	87-88	13	6	4
Barnet	Tr	03.89	91	42	0	20

BULL, Michael F.
Twickenham, 3 April, 1930 (W)

League Club	Source	Date Signed	Seasons Played	Apps	Subs	Gls
Brentford		09.48	52	3	-	0
Swindon T.	Tr	06.53	53-54	69	-	15

BULL, Stephen G.
Tipton, 28 March, 1965 Eu21-/E-'B'/E-13 (F)

League Club	Source	Date Signed	Seasons Played	Apps	Subs	Gls
West Bromwich A.	Tipton T.	08.85	85-86	2	2	2
Wolverhampton W.	Tr	11.86	86-91	247	0	155

BULL, William H.
Birmingham, 1 April, 1926 (CF)

League Club	Source	Date Signed	Seasons Played	Apps	Subs	Gls
Coventry C.		03.48	48	1	-	0

BULLESS, Brian
Hull, 4 September, 1933 (D)

League Club	Source	Date Signed	Seasons Played	Apps	Subs	Gls
Hull C.	Jnrs	10.50	52-63	326	-	30

BULLIMORE, Alwyn A.
Norwich, 22 October, 1933 (WH)

League Club	Source	Date Signed	Seasons Played	Apps	Subs	Gls
Norwich C.	Jnrs	10.53	56	1	-	0

BULLIMORE, Wayne A.
Sutton-in-Ashfield, 12 September, 1970 E Yth (M)

League Club	Source	Date Signed	Seasons Played	Apps	Subs	Gls
Manchester U.	YT	09.88				
Barnsley	Tr	03.91	91	17	1	1

BULLIONS, James L.
Stirling, 12 March, 1924 (WH)

League Club	Source	Date Signed	Seasons Played	Apps	Subs	Gls
Derby Co.	Clowne	10.44	46-47	17	-	0
Leeds U.	Tr	11.47	47-49	35	-	0
Shrewsbury T.	Tr	09.50	50-53	131	-	2

BULLIVANT, Terence P.
Lambeth, 23 September, 1956 (M)

League Club	Source	Date Signed	Seasons Played	Apps	Subs	Gls
Fulham	App	05.74	74-79	94	7	2
Aston Villa	Tr	11.79	79-81	10	3	0
Charlton Ath.	Tr	07.82	82	30	0	3
Brentford	Tr	07.83	83-85	36	1	2

BULLOCK, Michael E.
Stoke, 2 October, 1946 (CF)

League Club	Source	Date Signed	Seasons Played	Apps	Subs	Gls
Birmingham C.	App	10.63	63-66	27	0	10
Oxford U.	Tr	06.67	67-68	58	1	15
Leyton Orient	Tr	10.68	68-75	267	10	65
Halifax T.	Tr	02.76	75-78	98	8	19

BULLOCK, Norman
Nuneaton, 26 March, 1932 (F)

League Club	Source	Date Signed	Seasons Played	Apps	Subs	Gls
Aston Villa	Coton Villa	09.49				
Chester C.	Tr	07.52	52-59	190	-	41

BULLOCK, Peter L.
Stoke, 17 November, 1941 E Sch/E Yth (IF)

League Club	Source	Date Signed	Seasons Played	Apps	Subs	Gls
Stoke C.	Jnrs	11.58	57-61	44	-	14
Birmingham C.	Tr	03.62	61-64	27	-	3
Southend U.	Tr	02.65	64-65	11	0	2
Colchester U.	Tr	10.65	65-67	94	1	33
Exeter C.	Tr	07.68	68	14	0	2
Walsall	Tr	12.68	68	7	0	0

League Club	Source	Date Signed	Seasons Played	Career Record Apps	Subs	Gls
BULLOCK, Simon J.						
Stoke, 28 September, 1962						(F)
Halifax T.	Stoke C. (App)	09.80	80-81	15	2	1
BULLOCK, Steven						
Stockport, 5 October, 1966						(D)
Oldham Ath.	Jnrs	07.84	84-85	10	8	0
Tranmere Rov.	Tr	08.86	86	25	5	1
Stockport Co.	Tr	08.87	87-90	106	14	0
BULMER, Peter						
Liverpool, 31 August, 1965						(FB)
Chester C.	App	08.83	82-84	56	15	2
Preston N.E.	Rhyl	07.86	86	4	0	0
BULZIS, Riccardo R. B.						
Bedford, 22 November, 1974						(F)
Northampton T.	YT	07.91	91	1	3	0
BUMPSTEAD, David J.						
Rainham, 6 November, 1935 E Amat						(WH)
Millwall	Tooting & Mitcham	06.58	57-61	84	-	8
Bristol Rov.	Tr	12.61	61-63	40	-	0
BUMSTEAD, Charles H.						
Croydon, 8 January, 1922						(G)
Millwall		03.43	46-47	12	-	0
Crystal Palace	Tr	08.48	48-51	53	-	0
BUMSTEAD, John						
Rotherhithe, 27 November, 1958						(M)
Chelsea	App	11.76	78-90	314	25	38
Charlton Ath.	Tr	07.91	91	36	0	0
BUMSTEAD, Raymond G.						
Ringwood, 27 January, 1936						(OR)
Bournemouth	Ringwood	05.58	58-59	412	2	55
BUNCE, Frederick						
Watford, 16 February, 1938 E Yth						(OL)
Watford	Jnrs	10.55	55-62	150	-	34
BUNCE, Paul E.						
Coalville, 7 January, 196/						(W)
Leicester C.	App	01.85	86	5	1	0
Northampton T.	Tr	03.87	86-87	6	6	2
BUNCLARK, Cyril						
Rotherham, 27 March, 1931						(F)
Rotherham U.		11.53	54	2	-	1
BUNKELL, Raymond K.						
Edmonton, 18 September, 1949 E Yth						(M)
Tottenham H.	App	06.67				
Swindon T.	Tr	06.71	71-73	52	4	3
Colchester U.	Tr	12.73	73-79	117	12	9
BUNN, Frank S.						
Birmingham, 6 November, 1962						(F)
Luton T.	App	05.80	80-84	52	7	9
Hull C.	Tr	07.85	85-87	89	6	23
Oldham Ath.	Tr	12.87	87-89	75	3	26
BUNNER, Harold						
Manchester, 18 September, 1936						(CH)
Bury	Bury Amats	04.57	57-64	106	-	0
Stockport Co.	Tr	04.65	65	3	0	0
BUNTING, Benjamin						
Rochdale, 14 February, 1923						(FB)
Oldham Ath.	Rochdale (Am)	08.46	46-47	32	-	0
BURBANKS, W. Edward						
Bentley, 1 April, 1913 Died 1983						(OL)
Sunderland	Denaby U.	02.35	34-47	131	-	26
Hull C.	Tr	06.48	48-52	143	-	21
Leeds U.	Tr	07.53	53	13	-	1
BURBECK, Ronald T.						
Leicester, 27 February, 1934 E Yth						(W)
Leicester C.	Jnrs	05.52	52-55	3	-	0
Middlesbrough	Tr	10.56	56-62	139	-	24
Darlington	Tr	08.63	63	18	-	1
BURCKITT, John D.						
Coventry, 16 December, 1946 E Yth						(FB)

League Club	Source	Date Signed	Seasons Played	Career Record Apps	Subs	Gls
Coventry C.	Jnrs	07.64	64	5	-	0
Bradford C.	L	03.67	66	9	-	0
Walsall	Tr	06.68				
BURDEN, Brian						
Gainsborough, 26 November, 1939						(G)
Lincoln C.		03.61	60	1	-	0
BURDEN, Ian						
Bradford, 27 May, 1944						(CF)
York C. (Am)	Poppleton Road	10.65	65	3	0	2
BURDEN, Thomas D.						
Andover, 21 February, 1924						(WH)
Wolverhampton W.	Jnrs	08.41				
Chester C.	Tr	11.45	46-47	82	-	39
Leeds U.	Tr	07.48	48-54	243	-	13
Bristol C.	Tr	10.54	54-60	231	-	20
BURDESS, John						
East Rainton (Dm), 10 April, 1946						(IF)
Oldham Ath.	App	04.64	63-64	3	-	0
BURGESS, Albert C. (Cam)						
Birkenhead, 21 September, 1919						(IF)
Bolton W.	Bromborough	02.38	46-47	5	-	3
Chester C.	Tr	10.48	48-51	111	-	64
Crystal Palace	Tr	09.51	51-52	47	-	40
York C.	Tr	07.53	53	32	-	14
BURGESS, Daryl						
Birmingham, 24 January, 1971						(CD)
West Bromwich A.	YT	07.89	89-91	91	4	2
BURGESS, David J.						
Liverpool, 20 January, 1960						(FB)
Tranmere Rov.		08.81	81-85	217	1	1
Grimsby T.	Tr	08.86	86-87	66	3	0
Blackpool	Tr	07.88	88-91	81	0	1
BURGESS, Eric R. C.						
Edgware, 27 October, 1944						(FB)
Watford	App	07.62	63-64	3	-	0
Torquay U.	Tr	07.65	65-67	73	2	0
Plymouth Arg.	Tr	07.68	68-69	14	1	0
Colchester U.	Plymouth C.	12.70	70-71	46	1	9
BURGESS, Michael R.						
Canada, 17 April, 1932						(CH/IF)
Bradford P.A.		08.52				
Leyton Orient	Tr	07.53	53-55	31	-	12
Newport Co.	Tr	02.56	55-56	23	-	7
Bournemouth	Tr	06.57	57-60	109	-	34
Halifax T.	Tr	07.61	61-62	34	-	3
Gillingham	Tr	03.63	62-65	109	1	2
Aldershot	Tr	11.65	65	6	0	0
BURGESS, Robert B.						
Glasgow, 1 April, 1927						
Walsall (Am)	Third Lanark	09.53	53	2	-	1
BURGESS, W. A. Ronald						
Rhondda, 9 April, 1917 W-32/EF Lge						(WH)
Tottenham H.	Cwm Villa	05.36	38-53	298	-	15
Swansea C.	Tr	08.54	54-55	47	-	1
BURGESS, Walter						
Golborne, 19 June, 1921						(IF)
Halifax T.	Coleraine	11.46	46	13	-	2
BURGHER, Symon G.						
Birmingham, 29 October, 1966						(M)
Exeter C.	YT	02.85	84	11	3	0
BURGIN, Andrew						
Sheffield, 6 March, 1947						(FB)
Sheffield Wed.	App	03.64	64	1	-	0
Rotherham U.	Tr	08.67	67	9	0	0
Halifax T.	Detroit (USA)	12.68	68-74	243	0	9
Blackburn Rov.	Tr	09.74	74-75	45	0	1
BURGIN, Edward (Ted)						
Sheffield, 29 April, 1927 E'B'-2						(G)
Sheffield U.	Alford T.	03.49	49-56	281	-	0
Doncaster Rov.	Tr	12.57	57	5	-	0
Leeds U.	Tr	03.58	58-60	58	-	0
Rochdale	Tr	01.61	60-65	207	0	0

BURGIN, Eric
Sheffield, 4 January, 1924 (CH)

League Club	Source	Date Signed	Seasons Played	Apps	Subs	Gls
Sheffield U.		12.46				
York C.	Tr	05.49	49-50	23	-	0

BURGIN, Terence
Nottingham, 9 October, 1938 (CF)

League Club	Source	Date Signed	Seasons Played	Apps	Subs	Gls
Reading		11.59	60	2	-	0

BURGIN, Trevor
Darfield, 28 August, 1943 (HB)

League Club	Source	Date Signed	Seasons Played	Apps	Subs	Gls
Bradford P.A.	Wombwell	07.67	67	12	5	0

BURKE, Charles
Arran, 13 September, 1921 CF)

League Club	Source	Date Signed	Seasons Played	Apps	Subs	Gls
Bournemouth	Ardeer Rec.	06.39	46	25	-	6

BURKE, David I.
Liverpool, 6 August, 1960 E Yth (LB)

League Club	Source	Date Signed	Seasons Played	Apps	Subs	Gls
Bolton W.	App	08.77	78-80	65	4	1
Huddersfield T.	Tr	06.81	81-87	189	0	3
Crystal Palace	Tr	10.87	87-89	80	1	0
Bolton W.	Tr	07.90	90-91	50	1	0

BURKE, John
Motherwell, 10 August, 1962 S Sch (W)

League Club	Source	Date Signed	Seasons Played	Apps	Subs	Gls
Sheffield U.	Motherwell	07.80				
Exeter C. (N/C)	Tr	03.83	82	3	0	0
Chester C. (N/C)	Tr	08.83	83	3	0	0

BURKE, John J.
Dublin, 28 June, 1911 (G)

League Club	Source	Date Signed	Seasons Played	Apps	Subs	Gls
Chester C.	Shelbourne	07.31	31-35	80	-	0
Millwall	Tr	06.36	36-46	24	-	0
Gillingham	Tr	09.47	50	5	-	0

BURKE, Mark S.
Solihull, 12 February, 1969 E Yth (W)

League Club	Source	Date Signed	Seasons Played	Apps	Subs	Gls
Aston Villa	App	02.87	86-87	5	2	0
Middlesbrough	Tr	12.87	87-89	32	25	6
Darlington	L	10.90	90	5	0	1
Wolverhampton W.	Tr	03.91	90-91	16	8	2

BURKE, Marshall
Glasgow, 26 March, 1959 S Sch (M)

League Club	Source	Date Signed	Seasons Played	Apps	Subs	Gls
Burnley	App	03.77	77-79	22	2	5
Leeds U.	Tr	05.80				
Blackburn Rov.	Tr	12.80	80-81	34	5	7
Lincoln C.	Tr	10.82	82-83	49	1	7
Cardiff C.	L	12.83	83	3	0	0
Tranmere Rov.	Scarborough	09.84	84	3	0	0

BURKE, Peter
Rotherham, 26 April, 1957 (CD)

League Club	Source	Date Signed	Seasons Played	Apps	Subs	Gls
Barnsley	App	04.75	74-76	36	0	1
Halifax T.	Tr	03.78	77-79	79	6	9
Rochdale	Tr	07.80	80-81	68	0	2

BURKE, Peter J.
Fazakerley, 1 February, 1912 (CH)

League Club	Source	Date Signed	Seasons Played	Apps	Subs	Gls
Oldham Ath.	Prescot Cables	05.33	33-35	93	-	6
Norwich C.	Tr	12.35	35-38	114	-	0
Luton T.	Tr	06.39				
Southport	Tr	07.46	46	1	-	0

BURKE, Richard
Ashton-u-Lyne, 28 October, 1920 (FB)

League Club	Source	Date Signed	Seasons Played	Apps	Subs	Gls
Blackpool	Jnrs	07.38	38	1	-	0
Newcastle U.	Tr	12.46	46	15	-	0
Carlisle U.	Tr	08.47	47-48	78	-	8

BURKE, Robert G.
Ballymena (NI), 5 November, 1934 (IF)

League Club	Source	Date Signed	Seasons Played	Apps	Subs	Gls
Burnley	Albertville U.	09.55	55	19	-	5
Chester C.	Tr	06.58				

BURKE, Ronald S.
Redcar, 13 August, 1921 (CF)

League Club	Source	Date Signed	Seasons Played	Apps	Subs	Gls
Manchester U.	St Albans C.	08.46	46-48	28	-	16
Huddersfield T.	Tr	06.49	49-51	27	-	6
Rotherham U.	Tr	03.53	52-54	73	-	54
Exeter C.	Tr	06.55	55-56	42	-	14

BURKE, Steven J.
Nottingham, 29 September, 1960 E Yth (W)

League Club	Source	Date Signed	Seasons Played	Apps	Subs	Gls
Nottingham F.	App	03.78				
Queens Park R.	Tr	09.79	79-83	43	24	5
Millwall	L	10.83	83	7	0	1
Notts Co.	L	10.84	84	4	1	0
Lincoln C.	L	08.85	85	4	1	0
Brentford	L	03.86	85	10	0	1
Doncaster Rov.	Tr	08.86	86-87	50	7	8
Stockport Co.	L	10.87	87	5	0	0

BURKE, Thomas
Greenock, 18 October, 1939 (F)

League Club	Source	Date Signed	Seasons Played	Apps	Subs	Gls
Barnsley	Clyde	02.63	62	1	-	0

BURKETT, John W. (Jack)
Edmonton, 21 August, 1942 (FB)

League Club	Source	Date Signed	Seasons Played	Apps	Subs	Gls
West Ham U.	Jnrs	10.59	61-67	141	1	4
Charlton Ath.	Tr	06.68	68-69	8	0	0

BURKINSHAW, George A.
Barnsley, 1 October, 1922 Died 1982 (CH)

League Club	Source	Date Signed	Seasons Played	Apps	Subs	Gls
Barnsley	Woolley Colly	03.42				
Carlisle U.	Tr	09.46	46	25	-	0
Barnsley	Tr	06.47				
Bradford C.	Tr	11.48	48	12	-	0

BURKINSHAW, Keith H.
Barnsley, 23 June, 1935 (WH)

League Club	Source	Date Signed	Seasons Played	Apps	Subs	Gls
Liverpool	Denaby U.	11.53	54	1	-	0
Workington	Tr	12.57	57-64	293	-	9
Scunthorpe U.	Tr	05.65	65-67	107	1	3

BURKITT, John O. (Jack)
Wednesbury, 19 January, 1926 (WH)

League Club	Source	Date Signed	Seasons Played	Apps	Subs	Gls
Nottingham F.	Darlaston	05.47	48-61	464	-	14

BURLEIGH, Martin S.
Newcastle, 2 February, 1951 (G)

League Club	Source	Date Signed	Seasons Played	Apps	Subs	Gls
Newcastle U.	Willington	12.68	70-73	11	0	0
Darlington	Tr	10.74	74	30	0	0
Carlisle U.	Tr	06.75	75-76	26	0	0
Darlington	Tr	08.77	77-78	71	0	0
Hartlepool U.	Tr	10.79	79-81	84	0	0

BURLEY, Craig W.
Irvine, 24 September, 1971 S Sch/S Yth/Su21-1 (M)

League Club	Source	Date Signed	Seasons Played	Apps	Subs	Gls
Chelsea	YT	09.89	90-91	6	3	0

BURLEY, George E.
Cumnock, 3 June, 1956 S Sch/Su21-5/S-11 (RB)

League Club	Source	Date Signed	Seasons Played	Apps	Subs	Gls
Ipswich T.	App	06.73	73-85	394	0	6
Sunderland	Tr	09.85	85-86	54	0	0
Gillingham	Tr	07.88	88	46	0	2

BURLISON, Robert L.
Newcastle, 29 March, 1920 Died 1987 (F)

League Club	Source	Date Signed	Seasons Played	Apps	Subs	Gls
Charlton Ath.	Horden Colly	09.39	46	1	-	0

BURLISON, Thomas H.
Edmondsley (Dm), 23 May, 1936 (WH)

League Club	Source	Date Signed	Seasons Played	Apps	Subs	Gls
Lincoln C.	Jnrs	12.53				
Hartlepool U.	Tr	07.57	57-63	148	-	5
Darlington	Tr	08.64	64	26	-	2

BURLURAUX, Donald S.
Skelton, 8 June, 1951 (W)

League Club	Source	Date Signed	Seasons Played	Apps	Subs	Gls
Middlesbrough	Jnrs	07.68	70-71	4	1	0
York C.	L	12.71	71	3	0	1
Darlington	Tr	07.72	72-74	105	7	13

BURMAN, Anthony P.
Stockwell, 3 June, 1958 (F)

League Club	Source	Date Signed	Seasons Played	Apps	Subs	Gls
Charlton Ath.	Queens Park R. (App)	08.76	76-77	16	3	3

BURMAN, Simon J.
Ipswich, 26 November, 1965 (W)

League Club	Source	Date Signed	Seasons Played	Apps	Subs	Gls
Colchester U.	App	11.83	84-86	28	4	3

BURN, John H.
South Shields, 21 January, 1930 (G)

League Club	Source	Date Signed	Seasons Played	Apps	Subs	Gls
Chelsea		10.48				
Chesterfield	Tr	08.50				
Carlisle U.	Tr	06.55	55	26	-	0

BURN, Ralph G.
Alnwick, 9 November, 1931 (WH)

League Club	Source	Date Signed	Seasons Played	Apps	Subs	Gls
Northampton T.		08.50	50	1	-	0
Crewe Alex.	Tr	07.54	54	1	-	0

League Club	Source	Date Signed	Seasons Played	Apps	Subs	Gls
BURNETT, Alfred P.						
Aberdeen, 23 July, 1922						(CF)
Barrow	Dundee	12.46	46-49	87	-	32
Lincoln C.	Tr	11.49	49	4	-	1
BURNETT, Dennis H.						
Bermondsey, 27 September, 1944						(D)
West Ham U.	Jnrs	10.62	65-66	48	2	0
Millwall	Tr	08.67	67-73	257	0	3
Hull C.	Tr	10.73	73-74	46	0	2
Millwall	L	03.75	74	6	0	2
Brighton & H.A.	St Louis (USA)	09.75	75-76	41	3	1
BURNETT, George G.						
Liverpool, 11 February, 1920						(G)
Everton	Jnrs	09.38	46-50	47	-	0
Oldham Ath.	Tr	10.51	51-54	100	-	0
BURNETT, John						
Market Rasen, 24 June, 1939						(LB)
Grimsby T.	Gainsborough Trin.	07.58	58	1	-	0
BURNETT, Wayne						
Lambeth, 4 September 1971 E Yth						(M)
Leyton Orient	YT	11.89	89-91	34	6	1
BURNETT, William J.						
Pelaw, 1 March, 1926						(OR)
Grimsby T.	Wardley Welfare	07.46	47	10	-	0
Hartlepool U.	Tr	11.48	48-53	193	-	17
BURNHAM, Jason J.						
Mansfield, 8 May, 1973						(CD)
Northampton T.	YT	07.91	91	36	4	2
BURNS, Anthony J.						
Edenbridge, 27 March, 1944						(G)
Arsenal	Tonbridge	03.63	64-65	31	0	0
Brighton & H.A.	Tr	07.66	66-68	54	0	0
Charlton Ath.	Tr	03.69	68-69	10	0	0
Crystal Palace	Durban U. (SA)	10.73	74-77	90	0	0
Brentford	L	01.77	76	6	0	0
Plymouth Arg.	Memphis (USA)	08.78	78	8	0	0
BURNS, Barry						
Doncaster, 19 June, 1937						(F)
Rotherham U.	Dunscroft	10.54	57	5	-	4
BURNS, Christopher						
Manchester, 9 November, 1967						(M)
Portsmouth	Cheltenham T.	03.91	91	42	4	8
BURNS, David						
Ellesmere Port, 12 November, 1958						(LB)
Chester C.	App	10.76	76-81	66	12	1
BURNS, Derek G.						
Bournemouth, 23 January, 1950						(M)
Bournemouth	App	01.68	68	3	1	0
BURNS, Eric O.						
Newton Stewart, 8 March, 1945						(W)
Bradford P.A.	App	03.62	63-65	26	2	3
Barnsley	Tr	08.66	66	3	0	0
BURNS, Francis J.						
Workington, 11 November, 1924						(WH)
Swansea C.	Wolverhampton W. (Am)	08.44	46-51	172	-	9
Southend U.	Tr	07.52	52-54	88	-	14
Crewe Alex.	Tr	11.56	56-57	30	-	7
BURNS, Francis S.						
Glenboig, 17 October, 1948 S Sch/Su23-1/S-1						(LB)
Manchester U.	Jnrs	10.65	67-71	111	10	6
Southampton	Tr	06.72	72	20	1	0
Preston N.E.	Tr	08.73	73-80	271	2	9
BURNS, Hugh						
Lanarkshire, 13 December, 1965						(LB)
Fulham (L)	Dunfermline Ath.	12.89	89	6	0	0
BURNS, Kenneth						
Glasgow, 23 September, 1953 Su23-2/S-20						(CD)
Birmingham C.	App	07.71	71-76	163	7	45
Nottingham F.	Tr	07.77	77-81	137	0	13
Leeds U.	Tr	10.81	81-83	54	2	2

League Club	Source	Date Signed	Seasons Played	Apps	Subs	Gls
Derby Co.	L	03.83	82	6	1	1
Derby Co.	Tr	02.84	83-84	30	1	1
Notts Co.	L	02.85	84	2	0	0
Barnsley (N/C)	Tr	08.85	85	19	2	0
BURNS, Kinear						
Isle of Man, 24 September, 1923						(OR)
Tranmere Rov.		09.46	46	14	-	4
Southport	Tr	11.47	47	5	-	0
BURNS, Leo F.						
Manchester, 3 August, 1932						(WH)
Oldham Ath.	Manchester C. (Am)	09.53	55	4	-	0
BURNS, Leslie G. H.						
Shepherds Bush, 22 June, 1944						(CH)
Charlton Ath.	Carshalton Ath.	03.67	66-67	8	0	0
BURNS, Michael E.						
Blackpool, 21 December, 1946 E Amat						(F)
Blackpool	Skelmersdale U.	05.69	69-73	174	5	53
Newcastle U.	Tr	07.74	74-77	143	2	39
Cardiff C.	Tr	08.78	78	6	0	0
Middlesbrough	Tr	10.78	78-80	58	3	24
BURNS, Michael T.						
Coundon (Dm), 7 June, 1908 Died 1982						(G)
Newcastle U.	Chilton Colly	09.27	27-35	104	-	0
Preston N.E.	Tr	07.36	36-37	12	-	0
Ipswich T.	Tr	05.38	38-51	157	-	0
BURNS, Neil J.						
Bellshill, 11 June, 1945						(F)
Mansfield T.	Bethesda	11.65	65-66	7	3	0
BURNS, Oliver H.						
Larkhall, 16 May, 1914						(IF)
Burnley	Glenavon	03.39				
Oldham Ath.	Tr	10.46	46	25	-	5
Halifax T.	Tr	09.47	47	27	-	5
BURNS, Peter						
Ulverston, 17 April, 1931						(CF)
Barrow	Askam U.	02.52	51	8	-	2
BURNS, Philip M.						
Stockport, 18 December, 1966						(G)
Reading	Army	03.89	90	12	0	0
BURNS, William						
Motherwell, 10 December, 1969						(D)
Manchester C.	YT	01.88				
Rochdale	Tr	07.89	89-90	68	4	2
BURNSIDE, David G.						
Bristol, 10 December, 1939 E Yth/Eu23-1						(IF)
West Bromwich A.	Jnrs	02.57	57-62	127	-	39
Southampton	Tr	10.62	62-64	61	-	22
Crystal Palace	Tr	12.64	64-66	52	4	8
Wolverhampton W.	Tr	09.66	66-67	38	2	5
Plymouth Arg.	Tr	03.68	67-70	105	0	15
Bristol C.	Tr	12.71	71	1	0	0
Colchester U.	Tr	03.72	71	13	0	0
BURRELL, Gerald M.						
Belfast, 6 September, 1926						(OR)
Huddersfield T.	St Mirren	12.53	53-55	59	-	10
Chesterfield	Tr	07.56	56-57	51	-	4
BURRELL, Leslie F.						
Brighton, 8 August, 1917						(IF)
Crystal Palace	Margate	02.46	46-47	19	-	5
Ipswich T.	Tr	05.48				
BURRIDGE, John						
Workington, 3 December, 1951						(G)
Workington	App	12.69	68-70	27	0	0
Blackpool	Tr	04.71	70-75	134	0	0
Aston Villa	Tr	09.75	75-76	65	0	0
Southend U.	L	01.78	77	6	0	0
Crystal Palace	Tr	03.78	77-79	88	0	0
Queens Park R.	Tr	12.80	80-81	39	0	0
Wolverhampton W.	Tr	08.82	82-83	74	0	0
Derby Co.	L	09.84	84	6	0	0
Sheffield U.	Tr	10.84	84-86	109	0	0
Southampton	Tr	08.87	87-88	62	0	0
Newcastle U.	Tr	10.89	89-90	67	0	0

League Club	Source	Date Signed	Seasons Played	Apps	Subs	Gls
BURRIDGE, Peter J.						
Harlow, 30 December, 1933						(IF)
Leyton Orient	Barnet	04.58	58-59	6	-	2
Millwall	Tr	08.60	60-61	87	-	58
Crystal Palace	Tr	06.62	62-65	114	0	42
Charlton Ath.	Tr	11.65	65-66	42	2	4
BURROWS, Adrian M.						
Sutton-in-Ashfield, 16 January, 1959						(CD)
Mansfield T.		05.79	79-81	77	1	6
Northampton T.	Tr	08.82	82-83	88	0	4
Plymouth Arg.	Tr	07.84	84-91	232	3	13
Southend U.	L	09.87	87	6	0	0
BURROWS, Alan						
Thorne, 20 October, 1941						(HB)
Blackpool	Stockport Co. (Am)	05.59	59	1	-	0
BURROWS, Arthur						
Stockport, 4 December, 1919						(WH)
Stockport Co.	Jnrs	11.37	38-46	5	-	1
Accrington St.	Ashton U.	03.48	48	9	-	0
BURROWS, David						
Dudley, 25 October, 1968 Eu21-7/E'B'/EF Lge						(LB)
West Bromwich A.	App	10.86	85-88	37	9	1
Liverpool	Tr	10.88	88-91	103	9	1
BURROWS, David W.						
Bilsthorpe (Nts), 7 April, 1961						(FB)
Lincoln C.	App	04.79	78	1	0	0
BURROWS, Frank						
Larkhall, 30 January, 1944						(CD)
Scunthorpe U.	Raith Rov.	06.65	65-67	106	0	4
Swindon T.	Tr	07.68	68-76	293	4	9
Mansfield T.	L	03.74	73	6	0	0

John Burridge (Workington, Blackpool, Aston Villa, Crystal Palace, Queens Park Rangers, Wolverhampton Wanderers, Sheffield United, Southampton & Newcastle United)

League Club	Source	Date Signed	Seasons Played	Apps	Subs	Gls
BURROWS, Harold						
St Helens, 17 March, 1941 Eu23-1						(OL)
Aston Villa	Jnrs	03.58	59-64	147	-	53
Stoke C.	Tr	03.65	64-72	239	6	69
Plymouth Arg.	Tr	08.73	73-74	18	1	3
BURROWS, Paul S.						
Swansea, 2 October, 1967 W Yth						(F)
Swansea C.	App	10.85	85	1	2	0
BURROWS, Philip A.						
Stockport, 8 April, 1946						(LB)
Manchester C.	Jnrs	07.64				
York C.	Tr	06.66	66-73	333	4	14
Plymouth Arg.	Tr	07.74	74-75	81	0	2
Hereford U.	Tr	08.76	76-79	110	0	2
Gillingham	L	10.77	77	5	0	0
BURSELL, J. Clifford						
Hull, 16 January, 1935 Died 1973						(IF)
Hull C.	Jnrs	11.52	52	2	-	2
BURT, James H. L.						
Harthill, 5 April, 1950						(FB)
Leicester C.	Whitburn Jnrs	06.67				
Aldershot	Tr	09.70	70-71	22	2	0
Northampton T.	Tr	07.72	72	16	5	0
Rochdale	Tr	09.73	73	4	0	0
BURTENSHAW, Charles E.						
Hove, 16 October, 1922						(OR)
Luton T.	Southwick	01.48	48-49	10	-	1
Gillingham	Tr	10.49	50-51	28	-	5
BURTENSHAW, Stephen						
Hove, 23 November, 1935						(WH)
Brighton & H.A.	Jnrs	11.52	52-66	237	0	3
BURTENSHAW, William F.						
Hove, 13 December, 1925						(IR)
Luton T.	Southwick	08.48	48-49	2	-	0
Gillingham	Tr	10.49	50-51	39	-	7
BURTON, Alan R,						
Aldershot, 11 January, 1939						(W)
Aldershot	Wimbledon	01.61	60-69	225	5	44
BURTON, Alwyn D. (Ollie)						
Chepstow, 11 November, 1941 W Sch/Wu23-5/W-9						(WH)
Newport Co.	Jnrs	12.58	58-60	53	-	8
Norwich C.	Tr	03.61	60-62	57	-	8
Newcastle U.	Tr	06.63	63-71	181	7	6
BURTON, Brian B.						
Nottingham, 28 December, 1932						(OL)
Nottingham F.		07.51	54	1	-	0
BURTON, Ernest						
Sheffield, 2 September, 1921						(OR)
Sheffield Wed.		11.47				
York C.	Tr	08.48	48	3	-	0
BURTON, Kenneth O.						
Sheffield, 11 February, 1950						(FB)
Sheffield Wed.	App	05.67	68-71	55	2	2
Peterborough U.	L	03.73	72	3	1	0
Chesterfield	Tr	07.73	73-78	234	3	6
Halifax T.	Tr	08.80	80	26	1	1
BURTON, Michael J.						
Birmingham, 5 November, 1969						(W)
Birmingham C.	YT	07.88	88	0	4	0
Shrewsbury T.	Sheffield Wed. (N/C)	03.91	90	3	3	0
BURTON, Paul S.						
Hereford, 6 August, 1973						(F)
Hereford U.	YT	07.91	89-91	1	4	1
BURTON, Royston						
Wantage, 13 March, 1951						(G)
Oxford U.	Jnrs	09.70	71-82	397	0	0
BURTON, Samuel						
Swindon, 10 November, 1926						(G)
Swindon T.	Jnrs	06.45	46-61	463	-	0

BURVILL, Glen
Canning Town, 26 October, 1962 (M)

League Club	Source	Date Signed	Seasons Played	Apps	Subs	Gls
West Ham U.	App	09.80				
Aldershot	Tr	08.83	83-84	57	8	15
Reading	Tr	03.85	84-85	24	6	0
Fulham	L	03.86	85	9	0	2
Aldershot	Tr	07.86	86-90	176	19	23

BUSBY, David E.
Paddington, 27 July, 1956 (F)

League Club	Source	Date Signed	Seasons Played	Apps	Subs	Gls
Brighton & H.A.	App	08.74	73-74	1	2	0

BUSBY, Martin G.
Slough, 24 March, 1953 E Yth (M)

League Club	Source	Date Signed	Seasons Played	Apps	Subs	Gls
Queens Park R.	App	07.70	70-76	71	7	6
Portsmouth	L	02.76	75	6	0	1
Notts Co.	Tr	10.76	76-77	37	0	4
Queens Park R.	Tr	09.77	77-79	56	10	11
Burnley	L	02.80	79	4	0	1

BUSBY, Vivian D.
Slough, 19 June, 1949 (F)

League Club	Source	Date Signed	Seasons Played	Apps	Subs	Gls
Luton T.	Wycombe W.	01.70	69-72	64	13	16
Newcastle U.	L	12.71	71	4	0	2
Fulham	Tr	08.73	73-76	114	4	29
Norwich C.	Tr	09.76	76-77	22	0	11
Stoke C.	Tr	11.77	77-79	33	17	9
Sheffield U.	L	01.80	79	3	0	1
Blackburn Rov.	Tulsa (USA)	02.81	80	8	0	1
York C. (N/C)	Tulsa (USA)	08.82	82-83	9	10	4

BUSH, Brian
Bristol, 25 April, 1925 (W)

League Club	Source	Date Signed	Seasons Played	Apps	Subs	Gls
Bristol Rov.	Soundwell	10.47	47-54	114	-	19

BUSH, Terence D.
Kings Lynn, 29 January, 1943 (F)

League Club	Source	Date Signed	Seasons Played	Apps	Subs	Gls
Bristol C.	Jnrs	02.60	60-69	147	15	43

BUSH, W. Thomas
Shirpheel, 22 February, 1914 Died 1969 (CH)

League Club	Source	Date Signed	Seasons Played	Apps	Subs	Gls
Liverpool	Shrewsbury T.	03.33	33-46	64	-	1

BUSHBY, Alan
Doncaster, 15 January, 1932 Died 1967 (WH)

League Club	Source	Date Signed	Seasons Played	Apps	Subs	Gls
Scunthorpe U.		08.52	52-58	218	-	10
Rochdale	Tr	07.59	59-60	66	-	0

BUSHBY, Dennis
Bournemouth, 25 December, 1933 (WH)

League Club	Source	Date Signed	Seasons Played	Apps	Subs	Gls
Bournemouth		11.57	57	6	-	0

BUSHBY Thomas W.
Shildon, 21 August, 1914 (CH)

League Club	Source	Date Signed	Seasons Played	Apps	Subs	Gls
Southend U.	Wolverhampton W. (Am)	10.34	34-38	40	-	13
Portsmouth	Tr	06.39				
Southampton	Tr	09.46	46	2	-	0

BUSHELL, Alan
Burnley, 4 September, 1932 (W)

League Club	Source	Date Signed	Seasons Played	Apps	Subs	Gls
Accrington St. (Am)	Wood Top	05.52	52	8	-	1

BUSHELL, Mark J.
Northampton, 5 June, 1968 (FB)

League Club	Source	Date Signed	Seasons Played	Apps	Subs	Gls
Northampton T.	YT	09.85	84	1	0	0

BUSHELL, Stephen P.
Manchester, 28 December, 1972 (M)

League Club	Source	Date Signed	Seasons Played	Apps	Subs	Gls
York C.	YT	02.91	90-91	25	6	0

BUTCHER, John M.
Newcastle, 27 May, 1956 (G)

League Club	Source	Date Signed	Seasons Played	Apps	Subs	Gls
Blackburn Rov.		03.76	76-81	104	0	0
Oxford U.	Tr	07.82	82	16	0	0
Halifax T.	L	09.82	82	5	0	0
Bury	L	12.83	83	11	0	0
Chester C.	Tr	08.84	84-86	84	0	0
Bury	L	10.85	85	5	0	0

BUTCHER, Reginald
Liverpool, 13 February, 1916 (FB)

League Club	Source	Date Signed	Seasons Played	Apps	Subs	Gls
Aston Villa	Shrewsbury T.	06.33	34	2	-	0
Reading	Tr	05.36	36-38	18	-	0
Chester C.	Tr	11.38	38-49	155	-	1

BUTCHER, Terence I.
Singapore, 28 December, 1958 Eu21-7/E-77 (CD)

League Club	Source	Date Signed	Seasons Played	Apps	Subs	Gls
Ipswich T.	Jnrs	08.76	77-85	271	0	16
Coventry C. (N/C)	Glasgow Rangers	11.90	90	6	0	0

BUTLER, P. Anthony
Stockport, 28 September, 1972 (CD)

League Club	Source	Date Signed	Seasons Played	Apps	Subs	Gls
Gillingham	YT	05.91	90-91	11	0	0

BUTLER, Barry
Stockton, 30 July, 1934 Died 1966 (CH)

League Club	Source	Date Signed	Seasons Played	Apps	Subs	Gls
Sheffield Wed.	South Bank	09.52	53-54	26	-	1
Norwich C.	Tr	07.57	57-65	303	0	3

BUTLER, Barry
Farnworth, 4 June, 1962 (M/D)

League Club	Source	Date Signed	Seasons Played	Apps	Subs	Gls
Chester C.	Atherton L.R.	12.85	85-91	225	12	16

BUTLER, Brian F.
Salford, 4 July, 1966 (M/LB)

League Club	Source	Date Signed	Seasons Played	Apps	Subs	Gls
Blackpool	App	07.84	85-87	58	16	5
Stockport Co.	Tr	07.88	88	32	0	2
Halifax T.	Tr	07.89	89-90	44	12	4

BUTLER, David
Stockton, 23 March, 1945 (FB)

League Club	Source	Date Signed	Seasons Played	Apps	Subs	Gls
Workington	Stockton	11.64	64-70	195	4	7
Watford	Tr	11.70	70-75	168	0	2

BUTLER, David J.
Wednesbury, 30 March, 1953 (W)

League Club	Source	Date Signed	Seasons Played	Apps	Subs	Gls
West Bromwich A.	App	04.71				
Shrewsbury T.	Tr	06.73	73	5	5	0
Workington	L	03.74	73	10	0	0

BUTLER, David J.
Wolverhampton, 1 September, 1962 (W)

League Club	Source	Date Signed	Seasons Played	Apps	Subs	Gls
Wolverhampton W.	App	04.80				
Torquay U.	Tr	12.81	81	5	1	0

BUTLER, Dennis A.
Macclesfield, 24 April, 1944 (W)

League Club	Source	Date Signed	Seasons Played	Apps	Subs	Gls
Bolton W.	Jnrs	06.61	62-67	62	3	11
Rochdale	Tr	02.68	67-72	152	4	34

BUTLER, Dennis G.
Compton, 4 August, 1952 (WH)

League Club	Source	Date Signed	Seasons Played	Apps	Subs	Gls
Reading	App	05.70	69-70	7	3	1

BUTLER, Dennis M.
Fulham, 7 March, 1943 (FB)

League Club	Source	Date Signed	Seasons Played	Apps	Subs	Gls
Chelsea	Jnrs	06.60	61-62	18	-	0
Hull C.	Tr	06.63	63-69	215	2	0
Reading	Tr	12.69	69-73	170	0	0

BUTLER, Ernest
Middlesbrough, 28 August, 1924 (OR)

League Club	Source	Date Signed	Seasons Played	Apps	Subs	Gls
Southend U.	Stockton	08.48	48-51	36	-	3
Darlington	Tr	06.53	53	6	-	0

BUTLER, Ernest A.
Box, 13 May, 1919 (G)

League Club	Source	Date Signed	Seasons Played	Apps	Subs	Gls
Portsmouth	Bath C.	05.38	46-52	222	-	0

BUTLER, Geoffrey
Middlesbrough, 29 September, 1946 (FB)

League Club	Source	Date Signed	Seasons Played	Apps	Subs	Gls
Middlesbrough	App	05.64	65-67	54	1	1
Chelsea	Tr	09.67	67	8	1	0
Sunderland	Tr	01.68	67-68	1	2	0
Norwich C.	Tr	10.68	68-75	151	2	1
Bournemouth	Tr	03.76	75-80	118	1	1
Peterborough U. (N/C)	Tr	08.81	81	39	0	0

BUTLER, Ian
Darton, 1 February, 1944 E Yth (OL)

League Club	Source	Date Signed	Seasons Played	Apps	Subs	Gls
Rotherham U.	App	08.61	60-64	101	-	28
Hull C.	Tr	01.65	64-72	300	5	66
York C.	Tr	08.73	73-74	43	3	2
Barnsley	L	10.75	75	5	0	1

BUTLER, John
Dawley, 16 October, 1920 (OL)

League Club	Source	Date Signed	Seasons Played	Apps	Subs	Gls
Shrewsbury T.	Dawley	08.50	50-53	58	-	8

BUTLER, John E.
Liverpool, 7 February, 1962 (RB/M)

League Club	Source	Date Signed	Seasons Played	Apps	Subs	Gls
Wigan Ath.	Prescot Cables	01.82	81-88	238	7	15
Stoke C.	Tr	12.88	88-91	142	0	6

BUTLER, John H.
Birmingham, 10 March, 1937 (CH)

League Club	Source	Date Signed	Seasons Played	Apps	Subs	Gls
Notts Co.	Eastwood Colly	10.57	58-61	111	-	0
Chester C.	Tr	05.62	62-67	220	2	0

BUTLER, John P.
Salford, 7 September, 1964 (M)

League Club	Source	Date Signed	Seasons Played	Apps	Subs	Gls
Blackpool	App	09.82	81-82	4	1	0

BUTLER, Joseph W.
Newcastle, 7 February, 1943 (M)

League Club	Source	Date Signed	Seasons Played	Apps	Subs	Gls
Newcastle U.	Jnrs	09.60	63	3	-	0
Swindon T.	Tr	08.65	65-75	355	7	18
Aldershot	Tr	08.76	76-77	31	8	0

BUTLER, Kenneth
Whitburn, 23 August, 1936 (OL)

League Club	Source	Date Signed	Seasons Played	Apps	Subs	Gls
Hartlepool U.		01.60	59-60	20	-	1

BUTLER, Lee S.
Sheffield, 30 June, 1966 (G)

League Club	Source	Date Signed	Seasons Played	Apps	Subs	Gls
Lincoln C.	Harworth C.I.	06.86	86	30	0	0
Aston Villa	Tr	08.87	88-90	8	0	0
Hull C.	L	03.91	90	4	0	0
Barnsley	Tr	07.91	91	43	0	0

BUTLER, Malcolm P.
Belfast, 6 August, 1913 NI-1 (FB)

League Club	Source	Date Signed	Seasons Played	Apps	Subs	Gls
Blackpool	Belfast Celtic	01.35	35-38	25	-	0
Accrington St.	Tr	07.47	47	32	-	0

BUTLER, Martin C.
Hull, 3 March, 1966 (W)

League Club	Source	Date Signed	Seasons Played	Apps	Subs	Gls
York C.	YT	10.84	84-88	40	25	9
Aldershot	L	12.85	85	2	0	1
Exeter C.	L	02.87	86	4	0	1
Carlisle U.	L	12.88	88	1	0	0
Scunthorpe U.	Tr	08.89	89	2	0	0
Scarborough (N/C)	Macclesfield T.	11.89	89	1	5	0

BUTLER, Michael A.
Barnsley, 27 January, 1951 (F)

League Club	Source	Date Signed	Seasons Played	Apps	Subs	Gls
Barnsley	Worsboro' Bridge	07.73	72-75	118	2	57
Huddersfield T.	Tr	03.76	75-77	73	6	22
Bournemouth	Tr	07.78	78-79	68	1	19
Bury	Tr	08.80	80-81	80	2	15

BUTLER, Paul J.
Manchester, 2 November, 1972 (D)

League Club	Source	Date Signed	Seasons Played	Apps	Subs	Gls
Rochdale	YT	07.91	90-91	22	5	0

BUTLER, Paul J.
Stockton, 9 June, 1964 (W)

League Club	Source	Date Signed	Seasons Played	Apps	Subs	Gls
Wolverhampton W.	App	06.82	82-84	18	11	2
Hereford U.	L	01.84	83	16	0	2
Hereford U.	Tr	02.85	84-86	49	15	2
Hartlepool U.	Tr	07.87	87	6	3	0

BUTLER, Peter J. F.
Halifax, 27 August, 1966 (W)

League Club	Source	Date Signed	Seasons Played	Apps	Subs	Gls
Huddersfield T.	App	08.84	84-85	0	5	0
Cambridge U.	L	01.86	85	14	0	1
Bury	Tr	07.86	86	9	2	0
Cambridge U.	Tr	12.86	86-87	55	0	9
Southend U.	Tr	02.88	87-91	135	7	9
Huddersfield T.	L	03.92	91	7	0	0

BUTLER, Peter L.
Nottingham, 3 October, 1942 (G)

League Club	Source	Date Signed	Seasons Played	Apps	Subs	Gls
Notts Co.	Jnrs	11.60	61-65	44	0	0
Bradford C.	Tr	08.66	66	17	0	0

BUTLER, Stanley
Stellington, 7 January, 1919 d1969 (OL)

League Club	Source	Date Signed	Seasons Played	Apps	Subs	Gls
West Bromwich A.	Scunthorpe U.	05.38	38-46	4	-	0
Southport	Tr	07.47	47	4	-	1

BUTLER, Stephen
Birmingham, 27 January, 1962 (F)

League Club	Source	Date Signed	Seasons Played	Apps	Subs	Gls
Brentford	Wokingham T.	12.84	84-85	18	3	3
Maidstone U.	Tr	(N/L)	89-90	76	0	41
Watford	Tr	03.91	90-91	38	15	9

BUTLER, Thomas
Atherton, 28 April, 1918 (OR)

League Club	Source	Date Signed	Seasons Played	Apps	Subs	Gls
Bolton W.	Astley	09.36				
Oldham Ath.	Macclesfield T.	02.38	37-38	45	-	9

League Club	Source	Date Signed	Seasons Played	Apps	Subs	Gls
Middlesbrough	Tr	03.39	38	2	-	0
Oldham Ath.	Tr	08.46	46	30	-	3
Accrington St.	Tr	07.47	47-52	218	-	26

BUTLER, Walter G.
Birmingham, 7 February, 1923 (FB)

League Club	Source	Date Signed	Seasons Played	Apps	Subs	Gls
Derby Co.		11.42				
Port Vale		06.46	46-50	128	-	0

BUTLIN, Barry D.
Roliston (Dy), 9 November, 1949 (F)

League Club	Source	Date Signed	Seasons Played	Apps	Subs	Gls
Derby Co.	Jnrs	01.67	67-72	4	0	0
Notts Co.	L	01.69	68-69	29	1	13
Luton T.	Tr	11.72	72-74	56	1	24
Nottingham F.	Tr	10.74	74-76	71	3	17
Brighton & H.A.	L	09.75	75	5	0	2
Reading	L	01.77	76	5	0	1
Peterborough U.	Tr	08.77	77-78	64	0	12
Sheffield U.	Tr	08.79	79-80	50	3	12

BUTT, Leonard
Wilmslow, 26 August, 1910 (IF)

League Club	Source	Date Signed	Seasons Played	Apps	Subs	Gls
Stockport Co.	Ashton Nat.	08.28	29-30	8	-	1
Huddersfield T.	Macclesfield T.	05.35	35-36	67	-	11
Blackburn Rov.	Tr	01.37	36-46	110	-	44
York C.	Tr	01.47	46-47	25	-	2
Mansfield T.	Tr	10.47	47	15	-	4

BUTT, Robert
Chester, 27 March, 1946 (W)

League Club	Source	Date Signed	Seasons Played	Apps	Subs	Gls
Wrexham (Am)	Jnrs	01.65	64	3	-	0

BUTTERFIELD, John (Jack)
Barnsley, 30 August, 1922 (RB)

League Club	Source	Date Signed	Seasons Played	Apps	Subs	Gls
Burnley	Tamworth	02.46	47	3	-	0

BUTTERS, Guy
Hillingdon, 30 October, 1969 Eu21-3 (CD)

League Club	Source	Date Signed	Seasons Played	Apps	Subs	Gls
Tottenham H.	YT	07.88	88-89	34	1	1
Southend U.	L	01.90	89	16	0	3
Portsmouth	Tr	09.90	90-91	55	1	3

BUTTERWORTH, Aidan J.
Leeds, 7 November, 1961 E Sch (F)

League Club	Source	Date Signed	Seasons Played	Apps	Subs	Gls
Leeds U.	Jnrs	05.80	80-83	54	10	15
Doncaster Rov.	Tr	08.84	84-85	35	15	5

BUTTERWORTH, David
Bristol, 5 May, 1937 (WH)

League Club	Source	Date Signed	Seasons Played	Apps	Subs	Gls
Exeter C.	Guildford C.	12.57	57-59	26	-	0

BUTTERWORTH, Gary J.
Whittlesey, 8 September, 1969 (LB)

League Club	Source	Date Signed	Seasons Played	Apps	Subs	Gls
Peterborough U.	YT	06.88	86-91	101	23	4

BUTTERWORTH, Ian S.
Crewe, 25 January, 1964 Eu21-8 (CD)

League Club	Source	Date Signed	Seasons Played	Apps	Subs	Gls
Coventry C.	App	08.81	81-84	80	10	0
Nottingham F.	Tr	06.85	85-86	26	1	0
Norwich C.	L	09.86	86	4	0	0
Norwich C.	Tr	12.86	86-91	177	3	3

BUTTIGIEG, John
Malta, 15 October, 1963 Maltese Int (D)

League Club	Source	Date Signed	Seasons Played	Apps	Subs	Gls
Brentford	Sliema W. (Malta)	11.88	88-89	24	16	0
Swindon T.	L	09.90	90	2	1	0

BUTTLE, Stephen A.
Norwich, 1 January, 1953 (M)

League Club	Source	Date Signed	Seasons Played	Apps	Subs	Gls
Ipswich T.	App	01.71				
Bournemouth	Tr	08.73	73-76	136	3	12

BUTTRESS, Michael D.
Peterborough, 23 March, 1958 (FB)

League Club	Source	Date Signed	Seasons Played	Apps	Subs	Gls
Aston Villa	App	02.76	76-77	1	2	0
Gillingham	Tr	03.78	77-78	5	2	0

BUXTON, Ian R.
Cromford, 17 April, 1938 (IF)

League Club	Source	Date Signed	Seasons Played	Apps	Subs	Gls
Derby Co.	Jnrs	03.59	59-67	144	1	41
Luton T.	Tr	09.67	67-68	46	1	14
Notts Co.	Tr	07.69	69	4	1	1
Port Vale	Tr	12.69	69	16	2	6

BUXTON, Michael J.
Corbridge, 29 May, 1943 (FB)

League Club	Source	Date Signed	Seasons Played	Apps	Subs	Gls
Burnley	Jnrs	06.60	62-67	16	2	0
Halifax T.	Tr	06.68	68-70	35	0	0

BUXTON, Stephen C.
Birmingham, 13 March, 1960 (F)

League Club	Source	Date Signed	Seasons Played	Apps	Subs	Gls
Wrexham	Jnrs	07.78	77-83	93	16	21
Stockport Co.	Tr	07.84	84	12	6	1
Wrexham	Altrincham	10.85	85-89	86	35	25

BYATT, Dennis J.
Hillingdon, 8 August, 1958 (CD)

League Club	Source	Date Signed	Seasons Played	Apps	Subs	Gls
Fulham	App	05.76				
Peterborough U.	Tr	07.78	78	2	1	0
Northampton T.	Tr	06.79	79-80	46	1	3

BYCROFT, Sydney
Lincoln, 19 February, 1912 (CH)

League Club	Source	Date Signed	Seasons Played	Apps	Subs	Gls
Doncaster Rov.	Newark T.	01.36	35-51	333	-	2

BYERS, Richard
Haltwhistle, 19 November, 1951 (CF)

League Club	Source	Date Signed	Seasons Played	Apps	Subs	Gls
Workington (Am)	Hadrian Paints	10.71	71	1	0	0

BYRNE, Anthony B.
Rathdowney (IR), 2 February, 1946 IR-14 (D)

League Club	Source	Date Signed	Seasons Played	Apps	Subs	Gls
Millwall	Jnrs	08.63	63	1	-	0
Southampton	Tr	08.64	66-73	81	12	3
Hereford U.	Tr	08.74	74-76	54	1	0
Newport Co.	Tr	03.77	76-78	80	0	10

BYRNE, David S.
Hammersmith, 5 March, 1961 (RW)

League Club	Source	Date Signed	Seasons Played	Apps	Subs	Gls
Gillingham	Kingstonian	07.85	85	18	5	3
Millwall	Tr	07.86	86-87	52	11	6
Cambridge U.	L	09.88	88	4	0	0
Blackburn Rov.	L	02.89	88	4	0	0
Plymouth Arg.	Tr	03.89	88-90	52	7	2
Bristol Rov.	L	02.90	89	0	2	0
Watford	Tr	11.90	90	16	1	2
Reading	L	08.91	91	7	0	2
Fulham	L	01.92	91	5	0	0

BYRNE, Gerald
Glasgow, 10 April, 1957 (M)

League Club	Source	Date Signed	Seasons Played	Apps	Subs	Gls
Cardiff C.	App	04.75	77-78	11	4	0

BYRNE, Gerald
Liverpool, 29 August, 1938 Eu23-1/E-2 (LB)

League Club	Source	Date Signed	Seasons Played	Apps	Subs	Gls
Liverpool	Jnrs	08.55	57-68	273	1	2

BYRNE, John
Cambuslang, 25 May, 1939 (IF)

League Club	Source	Date Signed	Seasons Played	Apps	Subs	Gls
Preston N.E.	Pollok Jnrs	03.58				
Tranmere Rov.	Queen of South	05.61	61	27	-	4
Barnsley	Hibernian	11.63	63-64	69	-	12
Peterborough U.	Tr	07.65	65-67	106	1	28
Northampton T.	Tr	12.67	67-68	40	0	4

BYRNE, John F.
Manchester, 1 February, 1961 IR-22 (F)

League Club	Source	Date Signed	Seasons Played	Apps	Subs	Gls
York C.	App	01.79	79-84	167	8	55
Queens Park R.	Tr	10.84	84-87	108	18	30
Brighton & H.A.	Le Havre (Fr)	09.90	90-91	47	4	14
Sunderland	Tr	10.91	91	27	0	7

BYRNE, John J.
West Horsley, 13 May, 1939 E Yth/Eu23-7/E-11 (CF)

League Club	Source	Date Signed	Seasons Played	Apps	Subs	Gls
Crystal Palace	Jnrs	05.56	56-61	203	-	85
West Ham U.	Tr	03.62	61-66	156	0	79
Crystal Palace	Tr	02.67	66-67	36	0	5
Fulham	Tr	03.68	67-68	16	3	2

BYRNE, John J. A.
Wallasey, 24 March, 1949 (OR)

League Club	Source	Date Signed	Seasons Played	Apps	Subs	Gls
Tranmere Rov. (Am)	Cammell Laird	11.68	68	1	0	0

BYRNE, Joseph
Workington, 24 April, 1929 (G)

League Club	Source	Date Signed	Seasons Played	Apps	Subs	Gls
Workington (Am)	Frizington	09.52	52	2	-	0

BYRNE, Michael
Dublin, 14 January, 1960 (F)

League Club	Source	Date Signed	Seasons Played	Apps	Subs	Gls
Huddersfield T.	Shamrock Rov.	09.88	88-89	46	10	11

BYRNE, Patrick J.
Dublin, 15 May, 1956 (M)

League Club	Source	Date Signed	Seasons Played	Apps	Subs	Gls
Leicester C.	Shelbourne	07.79	79-80	31	5	3

BYRNE, Paul P.
Dublin, 30 June, 1972 (M)

League Club	Source	Date Signed	Seasons Played	Apps	Subs	Gls
Oxford U.	YT	07.89	89-91	4	2	0

BYRNE, Roger W.
Manchester, 8 February, 1929 Died 1958 E'B'-3/EF Lge/E-33 (FB)

League Club	Source	Date Signed	Seasons Played	Apps	Subs	Gls
Manchester U.	Ryder Brow B.C.	03.49	51-57	245	-	17

BYRNE, William
Newcastle, 22 October, 1918

League Club	Source	Date Signed	Seasons Played	Apps	Subs	Gls
Port Vale		05.46	46	15	-	2
Crewe Alex.	Tr	07.47	47-48	18	-	1

BYROM, David J.
Padham, 6 January, 1965 (D)

League Club	Source	Date Signed	Seasons Played	Apps	Subs	Gls
Blackburn Rov.	App	01.83				
Stockport Co.	Tr	10.84	84	3	0	0

BYROM, John
Blackburn, 28 July, 1944 E Yth (F)

League Club	Source	Date Signed	Seasons Played	Apps	Subs	Gls
Blackburn Rov.	Jnrs	08.61	61-65	106	2	45
Bolton W.	Tr	06.66	66-75	296	8	113
Blackburn Rov.	Tr	09.76	76	15	1	5

BYROM, Raymond
Blackburn, 2 January, 1935 (OL)

League Club	Source	Date Signed	Seasons Played	Apps	Subs	Gls
Accrington St.		01.56	57-58	9	-	1
Bradford P.A.	Tr	12.58	58-60	70	-	14

BYROM, Thomas
Upton, 17 March, 1920 (WH)

League Club	Source	Date Signed	Seasons Played	Apps	Subs	Gls
Tranmere Rov.	Heswall	05.39	46	3	-	0

BYROM, William
Blackburn, 30 March, 1915 (FB)

League Club	Source	Date Signed	Seasons Played	Apps	Subs	Gls
Burnley		08.37				
Queens Park R.	Tr	05.39				
Rochdale	Tr	06.46	46-47	30	-	0

BYRON, Gordon F.
Prescot, 4 September, 1953 (M)

League Club	Source	Date Signed	Seasons Played	Apps	Subs	Gls
Sheffield Wed.	App	07.71				
Lincoln C.	Tr	08.74	74	3	3	0

BYRON, Paul B.
Preston, 9 May, 1965 (D)

League Club	Source	Date Signed	Seasons Played	Apps	Subs	Gls
Hartlepool U.	Blackburn Rov. (N/C)	08.86	86	1	0	0

BYWATER, N. Leslie
Lichfield, 8 February, 1920 (G)

League Club	Source	Date Signed	Seasons Played	Apps	Subs	Gls
Huddersfield T.		03.45				
Luton T.	Tr	09.46	46	19	-	0
Rochdale	Tr	12.47	47-48	34	-	0

Johnny Byrne (Crystal Palace, West Ham United, Crystal Palace, Fulham & England)

Bobby Charlton (Manchester United, Preston North End & England)
Survived the Munich air crash to play over 100 games for England and to collect a World Cup winners medal in 1966

League Club	Source	Date Signed	Seasons Played	Career Record Apps	Subs	Gls
CABRIE, David						
Port Glasgow, 3 June, 1918						(WH)
Newport Co.	St Mirren	05.46	46	9	-	0
CADDEN, Joseph Y.						
Glasgow, 13 April, 1920						(CH)
Liverpool	Brooklyn (USA)	07.48	50	4	-	0
Grimsby T.	Tr	02.52	52	1	-	0
Accrington St.	Tr	06.53	53	17	-	0
CADE, David						
Hemsworth, 29 September, 1938 E Sch						(F)
Barnsley	Doncaster R. (Am)	05.57				
Bradford P.A.	Tr	07.59	59	1	-	0
CADETTE, Richard R.						
Hammersmith, 21 March, 1965						(F)
Leyton Orient	Wembley	08.84	84	19	2	4
Southend U.	Tr	08.85	85-86	90	0	49
Sheffield U.	Tr	07.87	87	26	2	7
Brentford	Tr	07.88	88-91	67	20	20
Bournemouth	L	03.90	89	4	4	1
CAESAR, Gus C.						
Tottenham, 5 March, 1966 Eu21-3						(CD)
Arsenal	App	02.84	85-89	27	17	0
Queens Park R	L	11.90	90	5	0	0
Cambridge U.	Tr	07.91				
Bristol C.	Tr	09.91	91	9	1	0
CAFFREY, Henry						
Paisley, 15 February, 1966						(W)
Hereford U.	Clydebank	07.91	91	12	5	2
CAHILL, Paul G.						
Liverpool, 29 September, 1955 E Yth						(D)
Coventry C.	App	01.73				
Portsmouth	Tr	02.75	74-77	95	2	2
Aldershot	L	01.78	77	2	0	0
Tranmere Rov.	California (USA)	10.78	78	5	0	0
Stockport Co.	Tr	02.79	78	3	0	0
CAHILL,Thomas						
Glasgow, 14 June, 1931						(LB)
Newcastle U.	Vale of Leven	12.51	52-53	4	-	0
Barrow	Tr	08.55	55-64	283	-	3
CAIN, James P.						
Fishburn (Dm), 29 December, 1933						(WH)
Bristol C.	Stockton	05.57				
Hartlepool U.	South Shields	08.60	60-61	30	-	0
CAINE, Brian						
Nelson, 20 June, 1936						(G)
Blackpool	Accrington St. (Am)	02.57	57	1	-	0
Coventry C.	Tr	09.59	60	1	-	0
Northampton T.	Tr	07.61				
Barrow	Tr	10.61	61-63	109	-	0
CAINE, William G.						
Barrow, 1 July, 1927						(CH)
Barrow	Barrow R.C.	07.52	51-54	12	-	0
CAIRNEY, Charles						
Blantyre, 21 September, 1926						(RH)
Leyton Orient	Glasgow Celtic	10.50	50	4	-	0
Bristol Rov.	Barry T.	07.53	53-54	14	-	1
CAIRNEY, James						
Glasgow, 13 July, 1931						(HB)
Portsmouth	Shawfield Jnrs	09.49		-	-	-
York C.	Tr	07.56	56-57	53	-	0
CAIRNS, Colin						
Alloa, 17 September, 1936						(F)
Southend U.	Camelon Jnrs	02.58	58	2	-	0
CAIRNS, John G.						
Newcastle, 13 April, 1922						
Hartlepool U.		03.48	47-49	16	-	2
CAIRNS, Kevin W.						
Preston, 29 June, 1937						(LB)
Southport	Dundee U.	08.62	62-67	204	2	1

League Club	Source	Date Signed	Seasons Played	Career Record Apps	Subs	Gls
CAIRNS, Robert L.						
Choppington, 25 December, 1927 Died 1958						(FB)
Gateshead	Sunderland (Am)	09.48	48-56	141	-	0
CAIRNS, Robert S.						
Glenboig, 27 May, 1929						(WH)
Stoke C.	Ayr U.	12.53	53-60	175	-	9
CAIRNS, Ronald						
Chopwell, 4 April, 1934						(IF)
Blackburn Rov.	Consett	09.53	55-58	26	-	7
Rochdale	Tr	06.59	59-63	195	-	66
Southport	Tr	07.64	64	34	-	13
CAIRNS, William H.						
Newcastle, 7 October, 1912 Died 1988						(IF)
Newcastle U.	Stargate Rov.	05.33	34-38	79	-	51
Gateshead	Tr	11.44		-	-	-
Grimsby T.	Tr	05.46	46-53	221	-	120
CAIZLEY, Kevin						
Jarrow, 2 December, 1968						(M)
Newcastle U.	YT	08.87				
Darlington	Tr	07.88	88	8	4	1
CAKEBREAD, Gerald						
Acton, 1 April, 1936 E Yth						(G)
Brentford	Jnrs	06.55	54-63	348	-	0
CALDER, William C.						
Glasgow, 28 September, 1934						(CF)
Leicester C.	Port Glasgow	08.55	58	3	-	0
Bury	Tr	05.59	59-63	174	-	67
Oxford U.	Tr	11.63	63-66	66	1	28
Rochdale	Tr	11.66	66	7	1	1
CALDERBANK, G. Raymond						
Manchester, 8 February, 1936						
Rochdale (Am)	Hyde U.	08.53	53	1	-	0
CALDERWOOD, Colin						
Stranraer, 20 January, 1965						(CD)
Mansfield T.	Jnrs	03.82	81-84	97	3	1
Swindon T.	Tr	06.85	85-91	282	2	18
CALDERWOOD, James						
Glasgow, 28 February, 1955 Su23-1						(FB/M)
Birmingham C.	App	07.72	72-79	135	10	4
Cambridge U.	L	11.79	79	8	0	0
CALDWELL, Anthony						
Salford, 21 March, 1958						(F)
Bolton W.	Horwich R.M.I.	06.83	83-86	131	8	58
Bristol C.	Tr	07.87	87-88	9	8	3
Chester C.	L	01.88	87	4	0	0
Grimsby T.	Tr	09.88	88	2	1	0
Stockport Co.	Tr	10.88	88-89	23	3	6
CALDWELL, David L.						
Clydebank, 7 May, 1932						(FB)
Rotherham U.	Aberdeen	05.60	60	1	-	0
CALDWELL, David W.						
Aberdeen, 31 July, 1960						(F)
Mansfield T.	Inverness Caledonians	06.79	79-84	145	12	57
Carlisle U.	L	12.84	84	4	0	0
Swindon T.	L	02.85	84	5	0	0
Chesterfield	Tr	07.85	85-87	64	4	17
Torquay U.	Tr	11.87	87	24	0	4
Torquay U. (L)	KW Overpelt (Bel)	12.89	89	17	0	6
Chesterfield	KW Overpelt (Bel)	10.90	90-91	27	5	4
CALDWELL, Terence						
Sharlston, 5 December, 1938 E Yth						(LB)
Huddersfield T.	Jnrs	06.57	59	4	-	0
Leeds U.	Tr	12.59	59-60	20	-	0
Carlisle U.	Tr	07.61	61-69	340	4	1
Barrow	Tr	07.70	70-71	29	1	0
CALEB, Graham S.						
Oxford, 25 May, 1945						(CH)
Luton T.	App	05.63	63-64	20	-	0
CALLACHAN, Ralph						
Edinburgh, 29 April, 1955						(M)
Newcastle U.	Hearts	02.77	77	9	0	0

League Club	Source	Date Signed	Seasons Played	Apps	Subs	Gls

CALLAGHAN, Aaron J.
Dublin, 8 October, 1966 IR Yth/IRu21 (CD)

League Club	Source	Date Signed	Seasons Played	Apps	Subs	Gls
Stoke C.	App	10.84	84-86	10	5	0
Crewe Alex.	L	11.85	85	8	0	0
Oldham Ath.	Tr	10.86	86-87	11	5	2
Crewe Alex.	Tr	05.88	88-91	148	10	6

CALLAGHAN, Christopher
Sandbach, 25 August, 1930 (FB)

League Club	Source	Date Signed	Seasons Played	Apps	Subs	Gls
Crewe Alex.		12.52	53-56	45	-	0

CALLAGHAN, Ernest
Birmingham, 21 January, 1910 Died 1972 (RB)

League Club	Source	Date Signed	Seasons Played	Apps	Subs	Gls
Aston Villa	Atherstone T.	09.30	32-46	125	-	0

CALLAGHAN, Frederick J.
Fulham, 19 December, 1944 (LB)

League Club	Source	Date Signed	Seasons Played	Apps	Subs	Gls
Fulham	App	08.62	63-73	291	4	9

CALLAGHAN, Henry
Glasgow, 20 March, 1929 (OL)

League Club	Source	Date Signed	Seasons Played	Apps	Subs	Gls
Ipswich T.	Kirkintilloch Rob Roy	09.54	54	1	-	0

CALLAGHAN, Ian M.
Prescot, 5 August, 1969 (M)

League Club	Source	Date Signed	Seasons Played	Apps	Subs	Gls
Bolton W.	YT	07.87	87	1	0	0

CALLAGHAN, Ian R.
Liverpool, 10 April, 1942 Eu23-4/EF Lge/E-4 (OR)

League Club	Source	Date Signed	Seasons Played	Apps	Subs	Gls
Liverpool	Jnrs	03.60	59-77	637	3	50
Swansea C.	Fort Lauderdale (USA)	09.78	78-79	76	0	1
Crewe Alex.	Cork Hibs.	10.81	81	15	0	0

CALLAGHAN, Nigel C.
Singapore, 12 September, 1962 Eu21-9 (W)

League Club	Source	Date Signed	Seasons Played	Apps	Subs	Gls
Watford	App	07.80	80-86	209	13	41
Derby Co.	Tr	02.87	86-88	76	0	10
Aston Villa	Tr	02.89	88-90	24	2	1
Derby Co.	L	09.90	90	12	0	1
Watford	L	03.91	90	6	6	1
Huddersfield T.	L	01.92	91	8	0	0

CALLAGHAN, Robert
Glasgow, 5 October, 1931 (F)

League Club	Source	Date Signed	Seasons Played	Apps	Subs	Gls
Scunthorpe U.	Duntocher H.	08.55	55	19	-	6
Barrow	Tr	10.56	56-57	40	-	10

CALLAGHAN, William
Glasgow, 7 February, 1930 (IR)

League Club	Source	Date Signed	Seasons Played	Apps	Subs	Gls
Ipswich T.	Great Perth Jnrs	07.52	52-54	21	-	7

CALLAGHAN, William A.
Glasgow, 9 December, 1941 (OR)

League Club	Source	Date Signed	Seasons Played	Apps	Subs	Gls
Barnsley	Dumbarton	08.64	64	16	-	0

CALLAGHAN, William F.
Ebbw Vale, 26 February, 1924

League Club	Source	Date Signed	Seasons Played	Apps	Subs	Gls
Aldershot	Frickley Colly	06.49	49	1	-	0

CALLAGHAN, William T.
Dunfermline, 23 March, 1967 (F)

League Club	Source	Date Signed	Seasons Played	Apps	Subs	Gls
Walsall (L)	Dunfermline Ath. (L)	09.88	88	2	0	1

CALLAN, Dennis
Merthyr Tydfil, 27 July, 1932 (WH)

League Club	Source	Date Signed	Seasons Played	Apps	Subs	Gls
Cardiff C.	Troedyrhiw	07.52	55	1	-	0
Exeter C.	L	05.54	54	10	-	1

CALLAN, Francis T. M.
Belfast, 24 May, 1935 (F)

League Club	Source	Date Signed	Seasons Played	Apps	Subs	Gls
Doncaster Rov.	Dundalk	11.57	57-58	28	-	6

CALLAND, Albert
Lanchester, 10 September, 1929

League Club	Source	Date Signed	Seasons Played	Apps	Subs	Gls
Torquay U.		03.50	51-53	24	-	11

CALLAND, Edward (Ted)
Lanchester, 15 June, 1932 (CF)

League Club	Source	Date Signed	Seasons Played	Apps	Subs	Gls
Torquay U.		09.52	52-56	47	-	22
Exeter C.	Tr	07.57	57-59	105	-	49
Port Vale	Tr	08.60	60	12	-	3
Lincoln C.	Tr	07.61	61	7	-	3

CALLAND, Ralph
Lanchester, 5 July, 1916 (FB)

League Club	Source	Date Signed	Seasons Played	Apps	Subs	Gls
Charlton Ath.		05.37				
Torquay U.		05.39	46-53	207	-	14

CALLENDER, John (Jack)
West Wylam, 2 April, 1923 (WH)

League Club	Source	Date Signed	Seasons Played	Apps	Subs	Gls
Gateshead	Jnrs	05.39	46-57	470	-	41

CALLENDER, Norman
Newburn, 9 June, 1924 (RH)

League Club	Source	Date Signed	Seasons Played	Apps	Subs	Gls
Darlington		06.46	46-48	27	-	1

CALLENDER, Thomas S.
West Wylam, 20 September, 1920 E Sch (CH)

League Club	Source	Date Signed	Seasons Played	Apps	Subs	Gls
Lincoln C.		09.37	38	23	-	0
Gateshead	Tr	11.45	46-56	439	-	61

CALLOWAY, Laurence J.
Birmingham, 17 June, 1945 (LB/M)

League Club	Source	Date Signed	Seasons Played	Apps	Subs	Gls
Wolverhampton W.	App	10.62				
Rochdale	Tr	07.64	64-67	161	1	4
Blackburn Rov.	Tr	03.68	67-69	17	8	1
Southport	Tr	08.70	70	45	0	7
York C.	Tr	06.71	71-72	54	1	3
Shrewsbury T.	Tr	12.72	72-74	77	5	3

CALOW, Charles J.
Belfast, 30 September, 1931 NI Amat (G)

League Club	Source	Date Signed	Seasons Played	Apps	Subs	Gls
Bradford P.A.	Cliftonville	06.52	52	1	-	0

CALVER, R. John
Glasgow, 22 September, 1938 (WH)

League Club	Source	Date Signed	Seasons Played	Apps	Subs	Gls
Burnley	Jnrs	09.55				
Southport	Tr	07.61	61	2	-	0

CALVERLEY, Alfred
Huddersfield, 24 November, 1917 (W)

League Club	Source	Date Signed	Seasons Played	Apps	Subs	Gls
Huddersfield T.		11.43				
Mansfield T.	Tr	06.46	46	30	-	1
Arsenal	Tr	03.47	46	11	-	0
Preston N. E.	Tr	07.47	47	13	-	0
Doncaster Rov.	Tr	12.47	47-52	142	-	11

CALVERT, Clifford A.
York, 21 April, 1954 E Yth (FB/M)

League Club	Source	Date Signed	Seasons Played	Apps	Subs	Gls
York C.	Jnrs	07.72	72-75	62	5	0
Sheffield U.	Tr	09.75	75-78	78	3	5

CALVERT, Joseph W.
Bullcroft, 3 February, 1907 (G)

League Club	Source	Date Signed	Seasons Played	Apps	Subs	Gls
Bristol Rov.	Frickley Colly	05.31	31	42	-	0
Leicester C.	Tr	05.32	32-47	72	-	0
Watford	Tr	02.48	47	5	-	0

CALVERT, Mark R.
Consett, 11 September, 1970 (W)

League Club	Source	Date Signed	Seasons Played	Apps	Subs	Gls
Hull C.	YT	07.89	88-91	19	4	1

CALVERT, Steven
Barrow, 2 April, 1952 (M)

League Club	Source	Date Signed	Seasons Played	Apps	Subs	Gls
Barrow (Am)	Jnrs	08.70	71	22	0	4

CAMDEN, Christopher E.
Birkenhead, 28 May, 1963 (F)

League Club	Source	Date Signed	Seasons Played	Apps	Subs	Gls
Chester C.	Poulton Vic.	12.83	83	9	0	2
Tranmere R. (N/C)	Oswestry T.	03.87	86	2	1	1

CAME, Mark R.
Exeter, 14 September, 1961 (CD)

League Club	Source	Date Signed	Seasons Played	Apps	Subs	Gls
Bolton W.	Winsford U.	04.84	84-91	185	6	7

CAMERON, Alexander
Leith, 5 October, 1943 (RB)

League Club	Source	Date Signed	Seasons Played	Apps	Subs	Gls
Oldham Ath.	Hibernian	05.64	64	15	-	0

CAMERON, Daniel
Dundee, 9 November, 1953 (FB)

League Club	Source	Date Signed	Seasons Played	Apps	Subs	Gls
Sheffield Wed.	App	07.71	73-75	31	0	1
Colchester U.	L	02.75	74	5	0	0
Preston N. E.	Tr	04.76	75-80	120	2	0

CAMERON, Daniel P.
Dublin, 16 June, 1922 (CH)

League Club	Source	Date Signed	Seasons Played	Apps	Subs	Gls
Everton	Shelbourne	07.48	48	1	-	0

CAMERON, David
Glasgow, 10 March, 1936 (IF)

League Club	Source	Date Signed	Seasons Played	Apps	Subs	Gls
Bradford C.	Glencairn	04.58	58	7	-	2

CAMERON, Duncan
Lanark, 1 February, 1936 (OR)

League Club	Source	Date Signed	Seasons Played	Apps	Subs	Gls
Swindon T.		09.56	56-57	2	-	0

CAMERON, Hugh G.
Hamilton, 1 February, 1927 (OR)

League Club	Source	Date Signed	Seasons Played	Apps	Subs	Gls
Torquay U.	Clyde	05.48	48-50	120	-	17
Newcastle U.	Tr	04.51	51	2	-	0
Bury	Tr	03.52	51-53	29	-	1
Workington	Tr	11.53	53-55	54	-	4

CAMERON, John (Jack)
Dumbarton, 7 March, 1931 (FB)

League Club	Source	Date Signed	Seasons Played	Apps	Subs	Gls
Hartlepool U.	Dumbarton	11.53	53-59	175	-	0

CAMERON, John
Greenock, 29 November, 1929 (WH)

League Club	Source	Date Signed	Seasons Played	Apps	Subs	Gls
Bradford P.A.	Motherwell	07.56	56	3	-	0

CAMERON, Robert
Greenock, 23 November, 1932 S Sch (IF)

League Club	Source	Date Signed	Seasons Played	Apps	Subs	Gls
Queens Park R	Port Glasgow	06.50	50-58	254	-	56
Leeds U.	Tr	07.59	59-61	57	-	9
Southend U.	Gravesend & Nft	10.63	63	3	-	0

CAMERON, Rodney P.
Newcastle, 11 April, 1939 (FB)

League Club	Source	Date Signed	Seasons Played	Apps	Subs	Gls
Bradford C.	Newcastle W.E.	08.57	58	1	-	0

CAMERON, Stuart J.
Liverpool, 28 November, 1966 (G)

League Club	Source	Date Signed	Seasons Played	Apps	Subs	Gls
Preston N.E.	YT	08.83	83	1	0	0

CAMMACK, Stephen R.
Sheffield, 20 March, 1954 E Yth (F)

League Club	Source	Date Signed	Seasons Played	Apps	Subs	Gls
Sheffield U.	App	05.71	71-75	21	15	5
Chesterfield	Tr	01.76	75-78	95	18	21
Scunthorpe U.	Tr	09.79	79-80	84	0	27
Lincoln C.	Tr	07.81	81	18	0	6
Scunthorpe U.	Tr	03.82	81-86	159	2	83
Port Vale	L	12.85	85	1	2	0
Stockport Co.	L	01.86	85	3	1	1

CAMP, Stephen G.
Manchester, 8 February, 1954 (F)

League Club	Source	Date Signed	Seasons Played	Apps	Subs	Gls
Fulham	Leatherhead	09.75	75-76	4	1	0
Peterborough U.	Tr	08.77	77	6	1	1

CAMPBELL, Alan J.
Arbroath, 21 January, 1948 S Yth/Su23-1 (M)

League Club	Source	Date Signed	Seasons Played	Apps	Subs	Gls
Charlton Ath.	Jnrs	02.65	65-70	196	2	28
Birmingham C.	Tr	10.70	70-75	169	6	11
Cardiff C.	Tr	03.76	75-80	165	2	2
Carlisle U.	Tr	11.80	80-81	29	2	2

CAMPBELL, Alan T.
Belfast, 11 September, 1944 (FB)

League Club	Source	Date Signed	Seasons Played	Apps	Subs	Gls
Grimsby T.	Coleraine	10.70	70-72	84	1	0

CAMPBELL, Charles
Oban, 27 February, 1928 (WH)

League Club	Source	Date Signed	Seasons Played	Apps	Subs	Gls
Oldham Ath.	Rutherglen Glencairn	11.49	49	2	-	0

CAMPBELL, Daniel
Manchester, 3 February, 1944 (CH)

League Club	Source	Date Signed	Seasons Played	Apps	Subs	Gls
West Bromwich A.	Droylsden	11.62	65-67	8	0	0
Stockport Co.	Los Angeles (USA)	01.69	68-69	31	0	3
Bradford P.A.	Tr	03.70	69	10	0	1

CAMPBELL, David
Wrexham, 18 February, 1947 (W)

League Club	Source	Date Signed	Seasons Played	Apps	Subs	Gls
Wrexham	Jnrs	07.65	64-66	41	2	7

CAMPBELL, David A.
Edinburgh, 2 November, 1958 (CD)

League Club	Source	Date Signed	Seasons Played	Apps	Subs	Gls
Charlton Ath.	Jnrs	06.77	75-79	71	5	3

CAMPBELL, David A.
Derry (NI), 2 June, 1965 NI-10 (M)

League Club	Source	Date Signed	Seasons Played	Apps	Subs	Gls
Nottingham F.	App	06.83	84-87	35	6	3
Notts Co.	L	02.87	86	18	0	2
Charlton Ath.	Tr	10.87	87-88	26	4	1
Plymouth Arg.	L	03.89	88	1	0	0
Bradford C.	Tr	03.89	88-89	27	8	4

CAMPBELL, David M.
Dublin, 13 September, 1969 (CD)

League Club	Source	Date Signed	Seasons Played	Apps	Subs	Gls
Huddersfield T.	Bohemians	08.90	90-91	4	0	0

CAMPBELL, Donald
Bootle, 19 October, 1932 E Yth (FB)

League Club	Source	Date Signed	Seasons Played	Apps	Subs	Gls
Liverpool	Jnrs	11.50	53-57	47	-	2
Crewe Alex.	Tr	07.58	58-61	149	-	1
Gillingham	Tr	09.62	62-63	29	-	0

CAMPBELL, Dougald
Kirkintilloch, 14 December, 1922 (OR)

League Club	Source	Date Signed	Seasons Played	Apps	Subs	Gls
Queens Park R		03.48				
Crewe Alex.	Tr	07.49	49	34	-	0
Barrow	Tr	08.50	50-51	30	-	3
Grimsby T.	Tr	10.51	51	6	-	0

CAMPBELL, Frank
Dunkeld, 23 December, 1950 (WH)

League Club	Source	Date Signed	Seasons Played	Apps	Subs	Gls
Grimsby T.	Jnrs	03.68	68	4	0	0

CAMPBELL, Gary
Belfast, 4 April, 1966 (M)

League Club	Source	Date Signed	Seasons Played	Apps	Subs	Gls
Arsenal	App	01.84				
Leyton Orient (N/C)	Leyton-Wingate	01.90	89	4	4	0

CAMPBELL, A. Glen
Leyland, 26 February, 1965 (G)

League Club	Source	Date Signed	Seasons Played	Apps	Subs	Gls
Preston N. E.	App	02.83	82-84	18	0	0

CAMPBELL, Gregory R.
Portsmouth, 13 July, 1965 (F)

League Club	Source	Date Signed	Seasons Played	Apps	Subs	Gls
West Ham U.	App	10.82	84-85	3	2	0
Brighton & H. A.	L	02.87	86	0	2	0
Plymouth Arg.	Sparta Rotterdam (Neth)	11.88	88-89	21	14	6
Northampton T.	Tr	07.90	90-91	32	15	7

CAMPBELL, James
Glasgow, 25 November, 1918 (OL)

League Club	Source	Date Signed	Seasons Played	Apps	Subs	Gls
Leicester C.		10.43				
Walsall	Tr	10.46	46-47	15	-	1

CAMPBELL, James (Jock)
East Kilbride, 11 November, 1922 Died 1983 (FB)

League Club	Source	Date Signed	Seasons Played	Apps	Subs	Gls
Charlton Ath.	R.A.F. Brize Norton	01.45	46-57	255	-	1

CAMPBELL, James C.
Camden, 11 April, 1937 (OR)

League Club	Source	Date Signed	Seasons Played	Apps	Subs	Gls
West Bromwich A.	Maidenhead U.	10.55	57-58	31	-	9
Portsmouth	Tr	07.59	59-61	50	-	13
Lincoln C.	Tr	05.62	62-63	63	-	15

CAMPBELL, Jamie
Birmingham, 21 October, 1972 (F)

League Club	Source	Date Signed	Seasons Played	Apps	Subs	Gls
Luton T.	YT	07.91	91	4	7	0

CAMPBELL, John
West Wylam, 23 July, 1928 (OL)

League Club	Source	Date Signed	Seasons Played	Apps	Subs	Gls
Gateshead		11.49	49-55	183	-	48

CAMPBELL, John
Dumbarton, 22 September, 1934 (FB)

League Club	Source	Date Signed	Seasons Played	Apps	Subs	Gls
Chesterfield	Motherwell	08.59	59	1	-	0

CAMPBELL, John J.
Liverpool, 17 March, 1922 (WH)

League Club	Source	Date Signed	Seasons Played	Apps	Subs	Gls
Liverpool		04.43				
Blackburn Rov.	Tr	12.45	46-55	224	-	19
Oldham Ath.	Tr	07.56	56	26	-	5

CAMPBELL, John P.
Belfast, 28 June, 1923 Died 1968 Irish Lge/NI-2 (OL)

League Club	Source	Date Signed	Seasons Played	Apps	Subs	Gls
Fulham	Belfast Celtic	03.49	49-52	62	-	4

CAMPBELL, Joseph
Glasgow, 28 March, 1925 (IF)

League Club	Source	Date Signed	Seasons Played	Apps	Subs	Gls
Leyton Orient	Glasgow Celtic	07.49	49	5	-	1
Gillingham	Tr	09.50	50	12	-	2

CAMPBELL, Kevin J.
Lambeth, 4 February, 1970 Eu21-4 (F)

League Club	Source	Date Signed	Seasons Played	Apps	Subs	Gls
Arsenal	YT	02.88	87-91	45	24	24
Leyton Orient	L	01.89	88	16	0	9
Leicester C.	L	11.89	89	11	0	5

CAMPBELL, Leslie G.
Wigan, 26 July, 1935 (OL)

League Club	Source	Date Signed	Seasons Played	Apps	Subs	Gls
Preston N. E.	Wigan Ath.	06.53	53-59	64	-	6
Blackpool	Tr	07.60	60	11	-	0
Tranmere Rov.	Tr	06.61	61-63	99	-	9

CAMPBELL, Michael J.
Oban, 19 November, 1966 (M)

League Club	Source	Date Signed	Seasons Played	Apps	Subs	Gls
Hereford U. (N/C)	Army	08.88	88	1	0	0

CAMPBELL, Paul J.
Newcastle, 7 October, 1964 (M)

League Club	Source	Date Signed	Seasons Played	Apps	Subs	Gls
Hartlepool U.	Gateshead	10.83	83	1	2	0
Burnley	Tr	03.84				

CAMPBELL, Philip A.
Barnsley, 16 October, 1961 (W)

League Club	Source	Date Signed	Seasons Played	Apps	Subs	Gls
Sheffield Wed.	App	10.79	80	0	1	0

CAMPBELL, Raymond M. J.
Downpatrick (NI), 3 October, 1968 (W)

League Club	Source	Date Signed	Seasons Played	Apps	Subs	Gls
Nottingham F.	App	10.86				
Hereford U.	L	01.88	87	4	0	0

CAMPBELL, Robert
Liverpool, 23 April, 1937 EYth (WH)

League Club	Source	Date Signed	Seasons Played	Apps	Subs	Gls
Liverpool	Jnrs	05.54	58-60	24	-	2
Portsmouth	Wigan Ath.	11.61	61-65	60	1	2
Aldershot	Tr	07.66	66	2	3	0

CAMPBELL, Robert
Glasgow, 28 June, 1922 S-5 (OR)

League Club	Source	Date Signed	Seasons Played	Apps	Subs	Gls
Chelsea	Falkirk	05.47	47-53	188	-	36
Reading	Tr	08.54	54-57	94	-	12

CAMPBELL, Robert M.
Belfast, 13 September, 1956 NI Yth/NI-2 (F)

League Club	Source	Date Signed	Seasons Played	Apps	Subs	Gls
Aston Villa	App	01.74	73-74	7	3	1
Halifax T.	L	02.75	74	14	1	0
Huddersfield T.	Tr	04.75	75-76	30	1	9
Sheffield U.	Tr	07.77	77	35	2	11
Huddersfield T.	Vancouver (USA)	09.78	78	7	0	3
Halifax T.	Tr	10.78	78	19	3	3
Bradford C.	Brisbane C. (Aus)	12.79	79-82	147	1	76
Derby Co.	Tr	08.83	83	11	0	4
Bradford C.	Tr	11.83	83-86	126	0	45
Wigan Ath.	Tr	10.86	86-87	61	8	27

CAMPBELL, Roy
Congleton, 19 October, 1934 (HB)

League Club	Source	Date Signed	Seasons Played	Apps	Subs	Gls
Crewe Alex.		12.55	55-56	14	-	0

CAMPBELL, Thomas
Glasgow, 20 February, 1935 (CF)

League Club	Source	Date Signed	Seasons Played	Apps	Subs	Gls
Tranmere Rov.	Dundee U.	06.61	61	4	-	0

CAMPBELL, William
Belfast, 2 July, 1944 NIu23-3/NI-6 (W)

League Club	Source	Date Signed	Seasons Played	Apps	Subs	Gls
Sunderland	Distillery	09.64	64-65	5	0	0

CAMPBELL, Winston R.
Sheffield, 9 October, 1962 (W)

League Club	Source	Date Signed	Seasons Played	Apps	Subs	Gls
Barnsley	App	10.80	79-86	121	7	9
Doncaster Rov.	L	01.83	82	3	0	0
Rotherham U.	Tr	09.86	86-87	67	2	9

CANDLIN, Maurice H.
Jarrow, 11 November, 1921 (CH)

League Club	Source	Date Signed	Seasons Played	Apps	Subs	Gls
Northampton T.	Partick Th.	02.49	49-52	138	-	1
Shrewsbury T.	Tr	07.53	53-54	69	-	2

CANHAM, Anthony
Leeds, 8 June, 1960 (LW)

League Club	Source	Date Signed	Seasons Played	Apps	Subs	Gls
York C.	Harrogate R.I.	01.85	84-91	227	20	47

CANN, Darren J.
Torquay, 17 June, 1969 (CD)

League Club	Source	Date Signed	Seasons Played	Apps	Subs	Gls
Torquay U.	YT	06.87	86-87	12	1	0

CANN, Ralph G.
Sheffield, 17 November, 1934 (CH)

League Club	Source	Date Signed	Seasons Played	Apps	Subs	Gls
Mansfield T.		05.57	57	1	-	0

CANNELL, Paul A.
Newcastle, 2 September, 1953 (F)

League Club	Source	Date Signed	Seasons Played	Apps	Subs	Gls
Newcastle U.	Jnrs	07.72	73-77	48	1	13
Mansfield T.	Washington (USA)	01.82	81-82	29	1	4

CANNELL, Stuart
Doncaster, 31 December, 1958 (CD)

League Club	Source	Date Signed	Seasons Played	Apps	Subs	Gls
Doncaster Rov.	Bentley Vic.	03.78	77-78	22	4	0

CANNING, L. Daniel
Pontypridd, 21 February, 1926 (G)

League Club	Source	Date Signed	Seasons Played	Apps	Subs	Gls
Cardiff C.	Abercynon	07.45	46-47	80	-	0
Swansea C.	Tr	01.49	48-50	47	-	0
Nottingham F.	Tr	07.51	51	5	-	0

CANNING, Lawrence (Larry)
Cowdenbeath, 1 November, 1925 (RH)

League Club	Source	Date Signed	Seasons Played	Apps	Subs	Gls
Aston Villa	Paget R.	10.47	48-53	39	-	3
Northampton T.	Kettering T.	06.56	56	2	-	0

CANNON, James
Coatbridge, 19 March, 1927 (IF)

League Club	Source	Date Signed	Seasons Played	Apps	Subs	Gls
Darlington	Third Lanark	06.56	56	12	-	1

CANNON, James A.
Glasgow, 2 October, 1953 (CD)

League Club	Source	Date Signed	Seasons Played	Apps	Subs	Gls
Crystal Palace	App	05.71	72-87	568	3	30

CANOVILLE, Paul K.
Hillingdon, 4 March, 1962 (W)

League Club	Source	Date Signed	Seasons Played	Apps	Subs	Gls
Chelsea	Hillingdon Bor.	12.81	81-85	53	26	11
Reading	Tr	08.86	86-87	16	0	4

CANTELLO, Leonard
Manchester, 11 September, 1951 E Yth/Eu23-8 (M)

League Club	Source	Date Signed	Seasons Played	Apps	Subs	Gls
West Bromwich A.	App	10.68	68-78	297	4	13
Bolton W.	Tr	06.79	79-81	89	1	3
Hereford U. (N/C)	Altrincham	01.83	82	1	0	0
Bury (N/C)	Tr	02.83	82	8	1	1

CANTONA, Eric
Paris (France), 24 May, 1966 French Int (F)

League Club	Source	Date Signed	Seasons Played	Apps	Subs	Gls
Leeds U.	Nimes (Fr)	02.92	91	6	9	3

Eric Cantona (Auxerre, Bordeaux, Montpellier, Marseille, Nimes, Leeds United & France)

CANTWELL, Noel
Cork (Ire), 28 February, 1932 IR-36 (LB)

League Club	Source	Date Signed	Seasons Played	Apps	Subs	Gls
West Ham U.	Cork Celtic	09.52	52-60	248	-	11
Manchester U.	Tr	11.60	60-66	123	-	6

CANVIN, Cyril E.
Hemel Hempstead, 23 January, 1924 Died 1950 (IL)

League Club	Source	Date Signed	Seasons Played	Apps	Subs	Gls
Leyton Orient	Apsley	03.47	46	3	-	0

CAPE, John P.
Carlisle, 16 November, 1910 (OR)

League Club	Source	Date Signed	Seasons Played	Apps	Subs	Gls
Carlisle U.	Penrith	05.29	29	15	-	2
Newcastle U.	Tr	01.30	29-33	51	-	18
Manchester U.	Tr	01.34	33-36	59	-	18
Queens Park R	Tr	06.37	37-38	61	-	13
Carlisle U.	Scarborough	10.46	46	3	-	0

CAPEL, Frederick J.
Manchester, 14 January, 1927 (FB)

League Club	Source	Date Signed	Seasons Played	Apps	Subs	Gls
Chesterfield	Goslings	06.48	49-56	285	-	16

CAPEL, John E.
Newport, 31 March, 1937 W Sch (OR)

League Club	Source	Date Signed	Seasons Played	Apps	Subs	Gls
Newport Co.	Jnrs	12.55	55	3	-	0

CAPEL, Maurice J.
Crewe, 15 February, 1935

League Club	Source	Date Signed	Seasons Played	Apps	Subs	Gls
Crewe Alex.		07.56	55-56	6	-	0

CAPEL, Thomas A.
Manchester, 27 June, 1922 (IF)

League Club	Source	Date Signed	Seasons Played	Apps	Subs	Gls
Manchester C.	Droylsden	11.41	46-47	9	-	2
Chesterfield	Tr	10.47	47-48	62	-	27
Birmingham C.	Tr	06.49	49	8	-	1
Nottingham F.	Tr	11.49	49-53	154	-	69
Coventry C.	Tr	06.54	54-55	36	-	19
Halifax T.	Tr	10.55	55	7	-	1

CAPEWELL, Ronald
Sheffield, 26 July, 1929 (G)

League Club	Source	Date Signed	Seasons Played	Apps	Subs	Gls
Sheffield Wed.		03.50	52-53	29	-	0
Hull C.	Tr	07.54	54	1	-	0

CAPPER, John
Wrexham, 23 July, 1931 (CH)

League Club	Source	Date Signed	Seasons Played	Apps	Subs	Gls
Wrexham	Jnrs	11.49	52-54	48	-	0
Lincoln C.	Headington U.	01.56	55-58	21	-	0
Chester C.	Tr	09.59	59-60	36	-	0

CAPSTICK, Albert L.
South Kirkby, 2 January, 1928 (IF)

League Club	Source	Date Signed	Seasons Played	Apps	Subs	Gls
Accrington St.	Fleetwood	08.48	1948	1	-	0

CARBERRY, Albert (Bert)
Glasgow, 16 January, 1931 (WH)

League Club	Source	Date Signed	Seasons Played	Apps	Subs	Gls
Norwich C.	Avondale	01.49	53-54	5	-	0
Gillingham	Bedford T.	07.56	56	1	-	0
Port Vale	Tr	07.57	57	29	-	0
Exeter C.	Tr	08.58				

CARBERRY, James
Liverpool, 13 October, 1969 (W)

League Club	Source	Date Signed	Seasons Played	Apps	Subs	Gls
Everton	YT	06.88				
Wigan Ath.	Tr	06.89	89-91	30	35	6

CARBERRY, Lawrence J.
Liverpool, 18 January, 1936 (RB)

League Club	Source	Date Signed	Seasons Played	Apps	Subs	Gls
Ipswich T.	Bootle	05.56	56-64	257	-	0
Barrow	Tr	07.65	65-66	17	0	0

CARDEW, Norman
South Shields, 7 November, 1938 (IF)

League Club	Source	Date Signed	Seasons Played	Apps	Subs	Gls
Darlington (Am)	South Shields	07.65	65	6	0	0

CARDWELL, Louis
Blackpool, 20 August, 1912 Died 1986 (CH)

League Club	Source	Date Signed	Seasons Played	Apps	Subs	Gls
Blackpool	Whitegate Jnrs	04.30	30-37	133	-	6
Manchester C.	Tr	09.38	38-46	39	-	0
Crewe Alex.	Netherfield	10.47	47-48	25	-	0

CAREY, Brian P.
Cork, 31 May, 1968 IR-1 (CD)

League Club	Source	Date Signed	Seasons Played	Apps	Subs	Gls
Manchester U.	Cork C.	09.89				
Wrexham	L	01.91	90	3	0	0
Wrexham	L	12.91	91	13	0	1

CAREY, John J.
Dublin, 23 February, 1919 IR-29/NI-7 (FB)

League Club	Source	Date Signed	Seasons Played	Apps	Subs	Gls
Manchester U.	St James Gate	11.36	37-52	304	-	16

CAREY, Peter R.
Barking, 14 April, 1933 (WH)

League Club	Source	Date Signed	Seasons Played	Apps	Subs	Gls
Leyton Orient	Barking	10.57	56-59	34	-	2
Queens Park R	Tr	07.60	60	15	-	1
Colchester U.	Tr	11.60	60	10	-	0
Aldershot	Tr	08.61	61-62	48	-	0

CAREY, Richard
Palsley, 19 November, 1927 (WH)

League Club	Source	Date Signed	Seasons Played	Apps	Subs	Gls
Southport	Cowdenbeath	07.49	49	1	-	0

CARGILL, David A.
Arbroath, 21 July, 1936 (OL)

League Club	Source	Date Signed	Seasons Played	Apps	Subs	Gls
Burnley	Jnrs	07.53	53-55	5	-	0
Sheffield Wed.	Tr	09.56	56-57	10	-	0
Derby Co.	Tr	04.58	58-60	56	-	8
Lincoln C.	Tr	12.60	60	9	-	0

CARGILL, James G.
Alyth, 22 September, 1945 S Sch (G)

League Club	Source	Date Signed	Seasons Played	Apps	Subs	Gls
Nottingham F.	Jnrs	09.62	64-65	2	0	0
Notts Co.	Tr	07.66	66	10	0	0

CARLESS, Ernest F.
Barry, 9 September, 1912 Died 1987 (IF)

League Club	Source	Date Signed	Seasons Played	Apps	Subs	Gls
Cardiff C. (Am)	Wolverhampton W.(Am)	10.32	32	2	-	0
Plymouth Arg.	Barry T.	12.46	46	4	-	0

CARLIN, Patrick
Dunscroft, 17 December, 1929 (RB)

League Club	Source	Date Signed	Seasons Played	Apps	Subs	Gls
Bradford P. A.	Dunscroft	07.53	53	6	-	0

CARLIN, William
Liverpool, 6 October, 1940 E Sch/E Yth (M)

League Club	Source	Date Signed	Seasons Played	Apps	Subs	Gls
Liverpool	Jnrs	05.58	59	1	-	0
Halifax T.	Tr	08.62	62-64	95	-	32
Carlisle U.	Tr	10.64	64-67	92	1	21
Sheffield U.	Tr	09.67	67-68	36	0	3
Derby Co.	Tr	08.68	68-70	89	0	14
Leicester C.	Tr	10.70	70-71	31	0	1
Notts Co.	Tr	09.71	71-73	57	3	2
Cardiff C.	Tr	11.73	73	22	0	1

CARLINE, Peter
Chesterfield, 2 March, 1951 (WH)

League Club	Source	Date Signed	Seasons Played	Apps	Subs	Gls
Chesterfield	Jnrs	09.70	70	2	0	0

CARLING, Terence P.
Otley, 26 February, 1939 (G)

League Club	Source	Date Signed	Seasons Played	Apps	Subs	Gls
Leeds U.	Dawsons	11.56	60-61	5	-	0
Lincoln C.	Tr	07.62	62-63	84	-	0
Walsall	Tr	06.64	64-66	101	0	0
Chester C.	Tr	12.66	66-70	199	0	0

CARLSON, George E.
Liverpool, 27 July, 1925

League Club	Source	Date Signed	Seasons Played	Apps	Subs	Gls
Tranmere Rov.		09.47	47-48	2	-	0

CARLTON, David G.
Stepney, 24 November, 1952 (M)

League Club	Source	Date Signed	Seasons Played	Apps	Subs	Gls
Fulham	App	12.69	71-72	5	4	0
Northampton T.	Tr	10.73	73-76	99	5	6
Brentford	Tr	10.76	76-79	138	2	7
Northampton T.	Tr	09.80	80-81	76	0	1

CARMICHAEL, John (Jack)
Newcastle, 11 November, 1948 (CD)

League Club	Source	Date Signed	Seasons Played	Apps	Subs	Gls
Arsenal	Possilpark Jnrs	11.66				
Peterborough U.	Tr	01.71	70-79	331	21	5
Swindon T.	New England (USA)	09.80				
Peterborough U.(N/C)	Jacksonville (USA)	01.83	82	5	1	0

CARMICHAEL, Matthew
Singapore, 13 May, 1964 (CD/F)

League Club	Source	Date Signed	Seasons Played	Apps	Subs	Gls
Lincoln C.	Basingstoke T.	08.89	89-91	72	20	14

CARMODY, Michael J.
Huddersfield, 9 February, 1966 (LB)

League Club	Source	Date Signed	Seasons Played	Apps	Subs	Gls
Huddersfield T.	Emley	12.84	84	8	0	0
Tranmere R. (N/C)	Emley	09.86	86	2	0	0

CARNABY, Brian J.
Plymouth, 14 December, 1947 (M)

League Club	Source	Date Signed	Seasons Played	Apps	Subs	Gls
Reading	Bexley U.	07.72	72-76	136	9	10

CARNEY, Leonard F.
Liverpool, 30 May, 1915 (IF)

League Club	Source	Date Signed	Seasons Played	Apps	Subs	Gls
Liverpool (Am)	Collegiate O.B.	07.46	46-47	6	-	1

CARNEY, Stephen
Wallsend, 22 September, 1957 (D)

League Club	Source	Date Signed	Seasons Played	Apps	Subs	Gls
Newcastle U.	Blyth Spartans	10.79	79-84	125	9	1
Carlisle U.	L	03.85	84	6	0	0
Darlington	Tr	08.85	85	10	2	0
Rochdale	L	01.86	85	4	0	0
Hartlepool U.	Tr	03.86	85	7	0	0

CAROLAN, Joseph F.
Dublin, 8 September, 1937 IR-2 (FB)

League Club	Source	Date Signed	Seasons Played	Apps	Subs	Gls
Manchester U.	Home Farm	02.56	58-60	66	-	0
Brighton & H. A.	Tr	12.60	60-61	33	-	0

CAROLIN, Brian
Ashington, 6 December, 1939 (HB)

League Club	Source	Date Signed	Seasons Played	Apps	Subs	Gls
Gateshead		08.57	57-59	17	-	0

CARPENTER, Richard
Sheerness, 30 September, 1972 (M)

League Club	Source	Date Signed	Seasons Played	Apps	Subs	Gls
Gillingham	YT	05.91	90-91	8	4	1

CARPENTER, Stephen
Torquay, 23 September, 1960 (M)

League Club	Source	Date Signed	Seasons Played	Apps	Subs	Gls
Torquay U. (N/C)		04.86	85	2	0	0

CARPENTER, Thomas A.
Carshalton, 11 March, 1925 (G)

League Club	Source	Date Signed	Seasons Played	Apps	Subs	Gls
Watford	Harrow T.	11.50	50	4	-	0

CARR, Ashley
Crowland, 15 August, 1968 (M)

League Club	Source	Date Signed	Seasons Played	Apps	Subs	Gls
Peterborough U.	Jnrs	08.86	86-88	9	6	0

CARR, Clifford P.
Hackney, 19 June, 1964 Eu21-1 (LB)

League Club	Source	Date Signed	Seasons Played	Apps	Subs	Gls
Fulham	App	06.82	82-86	136	9	14
Stoke C.	Tr	07.87	87-90	116	8	1
Shrewsbury T.	Tr	08.91	91	1	0	1
Mansfield T.	Telford U.	10.91	91	20	0	0

CARR, Darren J.
Bristol, 4 September, 1968 (CD)

League Club	Source	Date Signed	Seasons Played	Apps	Subs	Gls
Bristol Rov.	YT	08.86	85-87	26	4	0
Newport Co.	L	10.87	87	4	0	0
Newport Co.	Tr	01.88	87	5	0	0
Sheffield U.	Tr	03.88	87-88	12	1	1
Crewe Alex.	Tr	09.90	90-91	65	7	3

CARR, David
Wheatley Hill (Dm), 19 January, 1937 (IF)

League Club	Source	Date Signed	Seasons Played	Apps	Subs	Gls
Darlington	Spennymoor U.	05.57	57-61	132	-	42
Workington	Tr	07.62	62-64	108	-	47
Watford	Tr	02.65	64-65	10	0	3

CARR, David
Aylesham (Kt), 31 January, 1957 (D)

League Club	Source	Date Signed	Seasons Played	Apps	Subs	Gls
Luton T.	App	01.75	76-78	39	4	0
Lincoln C.	Tr	07.79	79-82	165	3	4
Torquay U.	Tr	08.83	83	34	0	0

CARR, Derek H.
Blidworth, 1 September, 1927 (RH)

League Club	Source	Date Signed	Seasons Played	Apps	Subs	Gls
Birmingham C.	Lockheed Leamington	02.48	49	3	-	0

CARR, Edward M.
Wheatley Hill (Dm), 3 October, 1917 (CF)

League Club	Source	Date Signed	Seasons Played	Apps	Subs	Gls
Arsenal	Margate	05.35	37-38	12	-	7
Huddersfield T.	Tr	10.45	46	2	-	0
Newport Co.	Tr	10.46	46-49	98	-	48
Bradford C.	Tr	10.49	49-52	94	-	49
Darlington	Tr	08.53	53	7	-	0

CARR, Everton D.
Antigua (WI), 11 January, 1961 (FB)

League Club	Source	Date Signed	Seasons Played	Apps	Subs	Gls
Leicester C.	App	01.79	78-80	11	1	0
Halifax T.	Tr	08.81	81-82	49	4	0
Rochdale	Tr	03.83	82	9	0	0

CARR, Francis J.
Maltby, 21 April, 1919 (IF)

League Club	Source	Date Signed	Seasons Played	Apps	Subs	Gls
Rotherham U.		09.41				
York C.	Tr	08.46	46	7	-	3

CARR, Franz A.
Preston, 24 September, 1966 E Yth/Eu21-9 (W)

League Club	Source	Date Signed	Seasons Played	Apps	Subs	Gls
Blackburn Rov.	App	07.84				
Nottingham F.	Tr	08.84	85-90	122	9	17
Sheffield Wed.	L	12.89	89	9	3	0
West Ham U.	L	03.91	90	1	2	0
Newcastle U.	Tr	06.91	91	12	3	2

Franz Carr (Blackburn Rovers, Nottingham Forest & Newcastle United)

CARR, W. Graham
Newcastle, 25 October, 1944 E Yth (CH)

League Club	Source	Date Signed	Seasons Played	Apps	Subs	Gls
Northampton T.	Jnrs	08.62	62-67	84	1	0
York C.	Tr	06.68	68	32	1	1
Bradford P. A.	Tr	07.69	69	42	0	2

CARR, Graham G. J.
Darlington, 8 December, 1970 (G)

League Club	Source	Date Signed	Seasons Played	Apps	Subs	Gls
Hartlepool U. (N/C)	YT	08.89	89	1	0	0

CARR, John (Jackie)
Lanark, 12 January, 1924 (IF)

League Club	Source	Date Signed	Seasons Played	Apps	Subs	Gls
Gillingham	Alloa Ath.	06.48	50	11	-	2

CARR, John W.
Durban (South Africa), 10 June, 1926 (OL)

League Club	Source	Date Signed	Seasons Played	Apps	Subs	Gls
Huddersfield T.	Durban Railways (SA)	10.50	50	1	-	0

CARR, Kevin
Ashington, 6 November, 1958 (G)

League Club	Source	Date Signed	Seasons Played	Apps	Subs	Gls
Newcastle U.	Burnley (App)	07.76	77-84	173	0	0
Carlisle U.	Tr	08.85	85-86	17	0	0
Darlington	L	11.86	86	3	0	0
Hartlepool U.	Middlesbrough (N/C)	07.87	87	31	0	0

CARR, Lance L.
South Africa, 18 February, 1910 (OL)

League Club	Source	Date Signed	Seasons Played	Apps	Subs	Gls
Liverpool	Boksburg (SA)	08.33	33-35	31	-	8
Newport Co.	Tr	10.36	36-38	25	-	0
Bristol Rov.	Tr	08.46	46	42	-	8

League Club	Source	Date Signed	Seasons Played	Apps	Subs	Gls
CARR, Peter						
Darlington, 25 August, 1951 (FB)						
Darlington	App	08.69	67-72	131	4	1
Carlisle U.	Tr	11.72	72-77	202	2	1
Hartlepool U.	New England (USA)	10.79	79	22	0	0
CARR, Peter						
Rawmarsh, 16 November, 1960 (M)						
Rotherham U.	App	11.78	78-81	31	5	3
CARR, Stanley R.						
Southport, 1 June, 1926 (FB)						
Southport	Brockhouse	10.45				
New Brighton	Tr	08.48	48	1	-	0
CARR, William M.						
Glasgow, 6 January, 1950 Su23-4/S-6 (M)						
Coventry C.	App	07.67	67-74	245	7	33
Wolverhampton W.	Tr	03.75	74-81	231	6	21
Millwall	Tr	08.82	82	8	0	1
CARRICK, M. David						
Evenwood, 5 December, 1946 Died 1989 (W)						
Wolverhampton W.	App	12.64				
Wrexham	Tr	07.66	66-67	20	4	3
Port Vale	Altrincham	01.69	68	14	2	0
Preston N. E.	Witton A.	11.73	73	0	2	0
Rochdale	Tr	03.74	73-74	25	1	4
CARRICK, William F.						
Dublin, 26 September, 1952 (G)						
Manchester U.	App	09.70				
Luton T.	Tr	07.72	72	4	0	0
CARRINGTON, Andrew S.						
Grimsby, 14 November, 1936 (CH)						
Grimsby T.	Jnrs	09.55	59-60	4	-	0
CARRODUS, Francis						
Manchester, 31 May, 1949 (W)						
Manchester C.	Altrincham	11.69	69-73	33	9	1
Aston Villa	Tr	08.74	74-78	150	0	7
Wrexham	Tr	12.79	79-81	97	0	6
Birmingham C.	Tr	08.82	82	7	1	0
Bury	Tr	10.83	83	31	3	1
CARROLL, Alfred						
Bradford, 6 March, 1920 (CH)						
Bradford C.	Metallic Packing	03.48	48-49	28	-	0
CARROLL, John						
Limerick (IR) (CF)						
West Ham U.	Limerick	05.48	48	5	-	0
CARROLL, Joseph						
Radcliffe, 6 January, 1957 (F)						
Oldham Ath.	Jnrs	07.75	75	3	1	0
Halifax T.	Tr	09.76	76-78	76	6	14
CARROLL, Michael						
Aberdeen, 10 September, 1952 S Sch (F)						
Grimsby T.	Liverpool (App)	03.71	70	0	1	0
CARROLL, Michael						
Blaydon, 4 October, 1961 (W)						
Chesterfield	Whickham	09.81	81-82	5	1	1
CARROLL, Robert (Robbie)						
Greenford, 15 February, 1968 (F)						
Southampton	App	02.86				
Brentford	Gosport Bor.	09.86	86-87	24	10	8
CARROLL, Thomas R.						
Dublin, 18 August, 1942 R Amat/IR-17 (RB)						
Ipswich T.	Cambridge C.	07.66	66-71	115	2	2
Birmingham C.	Tr	10.71	71-72	38	0	0
CARRUTHERS, Alexander N.						
Loganlea, 12 May, 1915 Died 1977 (OR)						
Bolton W.	Falkirk	02.37	36-37	26	-	4
Rochdale	Falkirk	05.46	46	13	-	4
CARRUTHERS, Eric						
Edinburgh, 22 February, 1953 (F)						
Derby Co.	Hearts	01.75	76	0	1	0

League Club	Source	Date Signed	Seasons Played	Apps	Subs	Gls
CARRUTHERS, John P.						
Dumfries, 2 August, 1926 (W)						
Carlisle U.		07.49	49	2	-	0
Workington	Tr	07.51	51	3	-	0
CARRUTHERS, Martin G.						
Nottingham, 7 August, 1972 (F)						
Aston Villa	YT	07.90	91	2	1	0
CARSON, Alexander M.						
Glasgow, 12 November, 1942 (CH)						
Northampton T.	Jnrs	11.59	60-61	8	-	0
Aldershot	Tr	05.63	63-64	5	-	0
CARSON, Thomas						
Dumbarton, 26 March, 1959 (G)						
Ipswich T. (L)	Dundee	01.88	87	1	0	0
CARSTAIRS, James W.						
St Andrews (Fife), 29 January, 1971 (LB)						
Arsenal	YT	03.89				
Brentford	L	02.91	90	8	0	0
Cambridge U.	Tr	07.91				
Stockport Co.	Tr	11.91	91	20	0	0
CARTER, Brian						
Weymouth, 17 November, 1938 (WH)						
Portsmouth	Weymouth	01.56	57-60	45	-	0
Bristol Rov.	Tr	07.61	61	4	-	0
CARTER, Darren S.						
Hackney, 29 June, 1969 (LW)						
Leyton Orient	Billericay T.	07.88	88-91	82	12	12
CARTER, Donald F.						
Midsomer Norton, 11 September, 1921 (W)						
Bury	Stourbridge	01.39	46-47	56	-	27
Blackburn Rov.	Tr	06.48	48	2	-	0
New Brighton	Tr	11.48	48-50	105	-	19
CARTER, Geoffrey						
Northwich, 14 February, 1943 (OL)						
West Bromwich A.	Jnrs	02.60	59-64	25	-	3
Bury	Tr	07.66	66	4	0	0
Bradford C.	Tr	08.67	67	1	0	0
CARTER, Horatio S. (Raich)						
Sunderland, 21 December, 1913 E Sch/E F Lge/E-13 (IF)						
Sunderland	Jnrs	11.31	32-38	246	-	118
Derby Co.	Tr	12.45	46-47	63	-	34
Hull C.	Tr	04.48	47-51	136	-	57

Raich Carter (Sunderland, Derby County, Hull City & England)

League Club	Source	Date Signed	Seasons Played	Apps	Subs	Gls
CARTER, James W. C.						
Hammersmith, 9 November, 1965 (RW)						
Crystal Palace	App	11.83				
Queens Park R	Tr	09.85				

League Club	Source	Date Signed	Seasons Played	Apps	Subs	Gls
Millwall	Tr	03.87	86-90	99	11	11
Liverpool	Tr	01.91	90	2	3	0
Arsenal	Tr	10.91	91	5	1	0

CARTER, Joseph
Bingley, 23 April, 1920 (G)

League Club	Source	Date Signed	Seasons Played	Apps	Subs	Gls
Walsall		11.36				
Notts Co.		09.44				
Hull C.	Tr	06.46	46	5	-	0
Bournemouth	Tr	03.47				

CARTER, Lee R.
Dartford, 22 March, 1970 (CD)

League Club	Source	Date Signed	Seasons Played	Apps	Subs	Gls
Northampton T. (N/C)	YT	07.88	87	0	1	0

CARTER, Leslie A.
Farnborough, 24 October, 1960 E Sch (F)

League Club	Source	Date Signed	Seasons Played	Apps	Subs	Gls
Crystal Palace	App	11.77	80	1	1	0
Bristol C.	Tr	02.82	81	16	0	0

CARTER, Mark C.
Liverpool, 17 December, 1960 E Semi-Pro (F)

League Club	Source	Date Signed	Seasons Played	Apps	Subs	Gls
Barnet	Runcorn	02.91	91	32	4	19

CARTER, Michael
Warrington, 18 April, 1960 (W)

League Club	Source	Date Signed	Seasons Played	Apps	Subs	Gls
Bolton W.	App	07.77	79-81	37	12	8
Mansfield T.	L	03.79	78	18	0	4
Swindon T.	L	03.82	81	4	1	0
Plymouth Arg.	Tr	08.82	82	6	6	1
Hereford U.	Tr	03.83	82-86	91	6	11
Wrexham	Tr	07.87	87-88	25	9	7

CARTER, Raymond
Chester, 1 May, 1951 (M)

League Club	Source	Date Signed	Seasons Played	Apps	Subs	Gls
Chester C.	Jnrs	09.71	71-73	56	6	0
Crewe Alex.	Tr	07.74	74	26	0	3

CARTER, Raymond H.
East Grinstead, 1 June, 1933 (IF)

League Club	Source	Date Signed	Seasons Played	Apps	Subs	Gls
Torquay U.	Brixham	08.58	58-59	3	-	1
Exeter C.	Tr	10.60	60-62	105	-	50

CARTER, Roger F.
Great Yarmouth, 11 October, 1937 (WH)

League Club	Source	Date Signed	Seasons Played	Apps	Subs	Gls
Aston Villa	Gorleston	12.55				
Torquay U.	Tr	07.60	60	5	-	0

CARTER, Roy W.
Torpoint, 19 February, 1954 (M)

League Club	Source	Date Signed	Seasons Played	Apps	Subs	Gls
Hereford U.	Falmouth	04.75	74-77	64	7	9
Swindon T.	Tr	12.77	77-82	193	7	34
Torquay U.	Tr	10.82	82-83	27	0	8
Bristol Rov.	L	12.82	82	4	0	1
Newport Co.	Tr	09.83	83-86	150	2	21
Exeter C.	Tr	06.87	87	37	4	2

CARTER, Stanley A.
Exeter, 6 September, 1928 (CH)

League Club	Source	Date Signed	Seasons Played	Apps	Subs	Gls
Exeter C.	Heavitree U.	11.49	50-51	2	-	0

CARTER, Stephen C.
Great Yarmouth, 23 April, 1953 (W)

League Club	Source	Date Signed	Seasons Played	Apps	Subs	Gls
Manchester C.	App	08.70	70-71	4	2	2
Notts Co.	Tr	02.72	71-78	172	16	21
Derby Co.	Tr	08.78	78-79	32	1	1
Bournemouth	Notts Co. (N/C)	03.82	81-83	42	4	1
Torquay U.	Tr	07.84	84	16	0	1

CARTER, Stephen G.
Sunderland, 13 April, 1972 (LW)

League Club	Source	Date Signed	Seasons Played	Apps	Subs	Gls
Scarborough	Manchester U. (YT)	07.90	90-91	33	4	3

CARTER, Sydney Y.
Chesterfield, 28 July, 1916 (CF)

League Club	Source	Date Signed	Seasons Played	Apps	Subs	Gls
Mansfield T.	Macclesfield	05.38	38-46	39	-	10

CARTER, Timothy D.
Bristol, 5 October, 1967 E Yth (G)

League Club	Source	Date Signed	Seasons Played	Apps	Subs	Gls
Bristol Rov.	App	10.85	85-87	47	0	0
Newport Co.	L	12.87	87	1	0	0
Sunderland	Tr	12.87	87-91	24	0	0
Carlisle U.	L	03.88	87	4	0	0
Bristol C.	L	09.88	88	3	0	0
Birmingham C.	L	11.91	91	2	0	0

CARTER, Wilfred
Wednesbury, 4 October, 1933 (IF)

League Club	Source	Date Signed	Seasons Played	Apps	Subs	Gls
West Bromwich A.	Jnrs	01.51	51-56	57	-	12
Plymouth Arg.	Tr	03.57	57-63	253	-	134
Exeter C.	Tr	05.64	64-65	48	0	6

CARTER, William J.
Woking, 14 September, 1945 (WH)

League Club	Source	Date Signed	Seasons Played	Apps	Subs	Gls
Leyton Orient	Jnrs	10.64	65-66	26	3	3

CARTLIDGE, David T.
Leicester, 9 April, 1940 (WH)

League Club	Source	Date Signed	Seasons Played	Apps	Subs	Gls
Leicester C.	Jnrs	10.57				
Bradford C.	Tr	06.61	61	6	-	3
Chester C.	Tr	11.61	61-62	19	-	0

CARTWRIGHT, Ian J.
Brierley Hill, 13 November, 1964 (M)

League Club	Source	Date Signed	Seasons Played	Apps	Subs	Gls
Wolverhampton W.	App	09.82	82-85	59	2	3

CARTWRIGHT, John W.
Northampton, 5 November, 1940 E Yth (IF)

League Club	Source	Date Signed	Seasons Played	Apps	Subs	Gls
West Ham U.	Jnrs	11.57	59-60	4	-	0
Crystal Palace	Tr	05.61	61-62	11	-	1

CARTWRIGHT, Lee
Rawtenstall, 19 September, 1972 (M)

League Club	Source	Date Signed	Seasons Played	Apps	Subs	Gls
Preston N. E.	YT	07.91	90-91	44	3	5

CARTWRIGHT, Leslie
Aberdare, 4 April, 1952 Wu23-4/W-7 (M)

League Club	Source	Date Signed	Seasons Played	Apps	Subs	Gls
Coventry C.	Jnrs	05.70	73-76	50	18	4
Wrexham	Tr	06.77	77-81	111	4	6
Cambridge U.	Tr	03.82	81-84	52	8	1
Southend U.	L	09.83	83	2	2	0

CARTWRIGHT, Michael
Birmingham, 9 October, 1946 (FB)

League Club	Source	Date Signed	Seasons Played	Apps	Subs	Gls
Coventry C.		08.65				
Notts Co.	Tr	06.67	67-68	15	1	0
Bradford C.	L	11.67	67	1	-	0

CARTWRIGHT, Neil A.
Stourbridge, 20 February, 1971 (M)

League Club	Source	Date Signed	Seasons Played	Apps	Subs	Gls
West Bromwich A.	YT	07.89	88-91	5	6	0

CARTWRIGHT, Peter
Newcastle, 23 August, 1957 (M)

League Club	Source	Date Signed	Seasons Played	Apps	Subs	Gls
Newcastle U.	North Shields	06.79	79-82	57	8	3
Scunthorpe U.	L	12.82	82	2	2	1
Darlington	Tr	03.83	82-83	48	2	5

CARTWRIGHT, Stephen R.
Tamworth, 8 January, 1965 (FB)

League Club	Source	Date Signed	Seasons Played	Apps	Subs	Gls
Colchester U.	Tamworth	08.88	88	10	0	0

CARTWRIGHT, William
Malpas, 11 June, 1922

League Club	Source	Date Signed	Seasons Played	Apps	Subs	Gls
Tranmere Rov.		02.41	46-47	9	-	1

CARTY, Stephen F.
Dunfermline, 12 January, 1934 (FB)

League Club	Source	Date Signed	Seasons Played	Apps	Subs	Gls
Crewe Alex.	Blair Hall	05.57	56-59	37	-	0

CARVER, David F.
Rotherham, 16 April, 1944 (FB)

League Club	Source	Date Signed	Seasons Played	Apps	Subs	Gls
Rotherham U.	App	01.62	61-64	83	-	0
Cardiff C.	Tr	01.66	65-72	210	1	1
Swansea C.	L	12.72	72	3	0	0
Hereford U.	Tr	08.73	73	14	0	0
Doncaster Rov.	Tr	03.74	73-74	29	1	0

CARVER, Gerald F.
Worcester, 27 June, 1935 (WH)

League Club	Source	Date Signed	Seasons Played	Apps	Subs	Gls
Notts Co.	Jnrs	08.52	53-65	279	1	10

CARVER, John W.
Newcastle, 16 January, 1965 (FB)

League Club	Source	Date Signed	Seasons Played	Apps	Subs	Gls
Newcastle U.	App	01.83				
Cardiff C.	Tr	07.85	85	13	0	0

CASCARINO, Anthony G.
Orpington, 1 September, 1962 IR-38 (F)

League Club	Source	Date Signed	Seasons Played	Apps	Subs	Gls
Gillingham	Crockenhill	01.82	81-86	209	10	78
Millwall	Tr	06.87	87-89	105	0	42
Aston Villa	Tr	03.90	89-90	43	3	11
Chelsea	Glasgow Celtic	02.92	91	11	0	2

League Club	Source	Date Signed	Seasons Played	Career Record Apps	Subs	Gls
CASE, James R.						
Liverpool, 18 May, 1954 *Eu23-1*						(M)
Liverpool	South Liverpool	05.73	74-80	170	16	23
Brighton & H. A.	Tr	08.81	81-84	124	3	10
Southampton	Tr	03.85	84-90	213	2	10
Bournemouth	Tr	07.91	91	38	2	1
CASE, Norman						
Prescot, 1 September, 1925 *IR Lge*						(CF)
Sunderland	Ards	09.49	49-50	4	-	2
Watford	Tr	12.50	50	10	-	4
Rochdale	Tr	02.52	51	2	-	0
CASEY, Gerald H.						
Birkenhead, 25 August, 1941						(M)
Tranmere Rov.	Holyhead T.	08.67	67-69	49	3	5
CASEY, Leonard J.						
Brentford, 24 May, 1931						(WH)
Chelsea	Leyton	02.54	55-58	34	-	0
Plymouth Arg.	Tr	12.58	58-59	44	-	0
CASEY, Paul						
Worksop, 6 October, 1961						(M/RB)
Sheffield U.	App	06.79	79-81	23	2	1
Lincoln C.	Boston U.	03.88	88-90	44	5	4
CASEY, Paul						
Great Yarmouth, 29 July, 1969						(G)
Cambridge U. (N/C)	YT	07.87	87	1	0	0
CASEY, Terence D.						
Swansea, 5 September, 1943						(WH)
Leeds U.	Jnrs	10.60	61	3	-	0
CASEY, Thomas						
Belfast, 11 March, 1930 *NI-12*						(WH)
Leeds U.	Bangor (NI)	05.49	49	4	-	0
Bournemouth	Tr	08.50	50-51	66	-	1
Newcastle U.	Tr	08.52	52-57	116	-	8
Portsmouth	Tr	07.58	58	24	-	1
Bristol C.	Tr	03.59	58-62	122	-	9
CASH, Stuart P.						
Tipton, 5 September, 1965						(LB)
Nottingham F.	Halesowen T.	09.89				
Rotherham U.	L	03.90	89	8	0	1
Brentford	L	09.90	90	11	0	0
Shrewsbury T.	L	09.91	91	8	0	1
CASHLEY, A. Raymond						
Bristol, 23 October, 1951						(G)
Bristol C.	Jnr	09.70	70-80	227	0	1
Hereford U.	L	01.81	80	20	0	0
Bristol Rov.	(Retired)	08.82	83-84	53	0	0
Chester C. (N/C)	Trowbridge T.	10.85	85	9	0	0
CASHMORE, Norman						
Aldershot, 24 March, 1939						(WH)
Aldershot	Woking	07.63	64	7	-	0
CASKEY, William T.						
Belfast, 12 October, 1953 *NI-7*						(F)
Derby Co.	Glentoran	09.78	78-79	26	2	3
CASLEY, John E.						
Torquay, 27 April, 1926						(G)
Torquay U.		06.47	47	1	-	0
CASPER, Frank						
Barnsley, 9 December, 1944 *EF Lge*						(F)
Rotherham U.	App	07.62	62-66	101	1	26
Burnley	Tr	06.67	67-75	230	7	74
CASS, David W. R.						
Forest Gate, 27 March, 1962						(G)
Leyton Orient (N/C)	Billericay T.	03.87	86	7	0	0
Leyton Orient	Billericay T.	02.88				
CASSELL, James						
Manchester, 23 April, 1947						(IF)
Bury		07.70	70	2	1	0
CASSELLS, Keith B.						
Islington, 10 July, 1957						(F)
Watford	Wembley	11.77	78-80	6	6	0

League Club	Source	Date Signed	Seasons Played	Career Record Apps	Subs	Gls
Peterborough U.	L	01.80	79	8	0	0
Oxford U.	Tr	11.80	80-81	43	2	13
Southampton	Tr	03.82	81-82	13	6	4
Brentford	Tr	02.83	82-84	80	6	28
Mansfield T.	Tr	08.85	85-88	162	1	52
CASSIDY, Andrew D.						
Leeds, 1 March, 1959						(G)
Stockport Co.		02.77	77-78	5	0	0
CASSIDY, Francis J. A.						
Watford, 20 August, 1964						(M)
Watford	App	08.82				
Plymouth Arg.	L	02.84	83	1	0	0
Peterborough U.	Tr	08.84	84-85	44	2	9
CASSIDY, James T.						
Glasgow, 1 December, 1943						(FB/W)
Oxford U.	East Stirling	07.63	63	5	-	0
Barrow	Tr	03.65	64	5	-	0
CASSIDY, Laurence						
Manchester, 10 March, 1923						(F)
Manchester U.		02.47	47-51	4	-	0
Oldham Ath.	Tr	07.56	56	4	-	1
CASSIDY, Nigel						
Sudbury, 7 December, 1945						(CF)
Norwich C.	Lowestoft	07.67	67-68	2	1	0
Scunthorpe U.	Tr	12.68	68-70	88	0	35
Oxford U.	Tr	11.70	70-73	113	3	33
Cambridge U.	Tr	03.74	73-75	52	2	13
CASSIDY, Thomas						
Belfast, 18 November, 1950 *NI-24*						(M)
Newcastle U.	Coleraine	10.70	70-79	170	10	22
Burnley	Tr	07.80	80-82	70	2	4
CASSIDY, William						
Gateshead, 30 June, 1917						(WH)
Gateshead	Close Wks	01.36	35-52	132	-	6
CASSIDY, William P.						
Hamilton, 4 October, 1940						(IF)
Rotherham U.	Glasgow Rangers	08.61	61-62	28	-	1
Brighton & H. A.	Tr	11.62	62-66	113	5	26
Cambridge U.	Detroit (USA)	07.70	70	27	4	6
CASTLE, Stephen C.						
Barkingside, 17 May, 1966						(M)
Leyton Orient	App	05.84	84-91	232	11	55
CASTLEDINE, Gary J.						
Dumfries, 27 March, 1970						(M)
Mansfield T.	Shirebrook Colly	01.91	91	3	4	0
CASTLEDINE, Stewart M.						
Wandsworth, 22 January, 1973						(M)
Wimbledon	YT	07.91	91	0	2	0
CASWELL, Brian L.						
Wednesbury, 14 February, 1956						(FB)
Walsall	App	09.73	72-84	388	12	17
Doncaster Rov.	Tr	08.85	85	15	0	2
Leeds U.	Tr	11.85	85-86	10	0	0
Wolverhampton W.	L	01.87	86	1	0	0
CASWELL, Peter D.						
Leatherhead, 16 January, 1957						(G)
Crystal Palace	App	08.75	76-77	3	0	0
Crewe Alex.	Tr	08.78	78	22	0	0
CATER, Ronald						
Fulham, 2 February, 1922						(WH)
West Ham U.	Leytonstone	01.44	46-49	63	-	0
Leyton Orient	Tr	06.51	51	13	-	0
CATERER, Brian						
Hayes, 23 January, 1943						(CH)
Brentford (Am)	Chesham U.	05.68	68	1	0	0
CATLEUGH, George C.						
Horden, 11 June, 1932						(WH)
Watford	Nuneaton Bor.	05.54	54-64	293	-	15

CATLEY, John W.
Grimsby, 16 March, 1945 (OR)

League Club	Source	Date Signed	Seasons Played	Apps	Subs	Gls
Grimsby T.	Jnrs	07.62	62	2	-	0

CATON, Thomas S.
Liverpool, 6 October, 1962 E Sch/E Yth/Eu21-14 (CD)

League Club	Source	Date Signed	Seasons Played	Apps	Subs	Gls
Manchester C.	App	10.79	79-83	164	1	8
Arsenal	Tr	12.83	83-85	81	0	2
Oxford U.	Tr	02.87	86-87	50	3	3
Charlton Ath.	Tr	11.88	88-90	56	1	5

CATON, William C.
Stoke, 11 September, 1924 (IF)

League Club	Source	Date Signed	Seasons Played	Apps	Subs	Gls
Stoke C.	Jnrs	09.41	47-49	22	-	2
Carlisle U.	Tr	04.50	49-51	64	-	16
Chesterfield	Tr	10.52	52	7	-	0
Crewe Alex.	Worcester C.	07.54	54	38	-	8

CATTERICK, Harold
Darlington, 26 November, 1919 Died 1985 (CF)

League Club	Source	Date Signed	Seasons Played	Apps	Subs	Gls
Everton	Cheadle Heath	03.37	46-51	59	-	19
Crewe Alex.	Tr	12.51	51-52	24	-	11

CATTLIN, Christopher J.
Milnrow, 25 June, 1946 Eu23-1 (LB)

League Club	Source	Date Signed	Seasons Played	Apps	Subs	Gls
Huddersfield T.	Burnley (Am)	08.64	64-67	59	2	1
Coventry C.	Tr	03.68	67-75	213	4	0
Brighton & H. A.	Tr	06.76	76-78	95	1	1

CATTRELL, Gordon W.
Sunderland, 18 December, 1954 E Sch (M)

League Club	Source	Date Signed	Seasons Played	Apps	Subs	Gls
Leeds U.	App	01.72				
Darlington	Tr	08.73	73-75	96	6	5

CAUGHEY, Mark
Belfast, 27 August, 1960 (F)

League Club	Source	Date Signed	Seasons Played	Apps	Subs	Gls
Burnley (L)	Hibernian	02.87	86	8	0	0

CAUGHTER, Alan
Bangor, 19 February, 1946 (FB)

League Club	Source	Date Signed	Seasons Played	Apps	Subs	Gls
Chester C.		08.69	69	1	0	0

CAULFIELD, Graham W.
Leeds, 18 July, 1943 (CF)

League Club	Source	Date Signed	Seasons Played	Apps	Subs	Gls
York C. (Am)	Frickley Colly	02.67	66	9	0	2
Bradford C. (Am)	Tr	07.67	67	1	0	0

CAVANAGH, Irvin
Rochdale, 31 July, 1924

League Club	Source	Date Signed	Seasons Played	Apps	Subs	Gls
Bury		05.48	49	1	-	0

CAVANAGH, Thomas H.
Liverpool, 29 June, 1928 (WH)

League Club	Source	Date Signed	Seasons Played	Apps	Subs	Gls
Preston N. E.		08.49				
Stockport Co.	Tr	01.50	49-51	32	-	2
Huddersfield T.	Tr	05.52	52-55	93	-	29
Doncaster Rov.	Tr	05.56	56-58	119	-	16
Bristol C.	Tr	07.59	59	24	-	6
Carlisle U.	Tr	06.60	60	34	-	4

CAVANAH, John L.
Salford, 4 August, 1961 (RB)

League Club	Source	Date Signed	Seasons Played	Apps	Subs	Gls
Rochdale (N/C)	Barrow	09.84	84	14	3	0

CAVE, Michael J.
Weymouth, 28 January, 1949 Died 1984 (M)

League Club	Source	Date Signed	Seasons Played	Apps	Subs	Gls
Torquay U.	Weymouth	07.68	68-70	106	8	17
Bournemouth	Tr	07.71	71-73	91	8	17
Plymouth Arg.	L	03.72	71	8	0	4
York C.	Tr	08.74	74-76	94	2	13
Bournemouth	Tr	02.77	76-77	42	0	3

CAVEN, John B.
Kirkintilloch, 6 July, 1934 (CF)

League Club	Source	Date Signed	Seasons Played	Apps	Subs	Gls
Brentford	Kilmarnock	10.57	57-58	7	-	1
Brighton & H. A.	Airdrieonians	03.62	61-62	10	-	0

CAVENER, Philip
Tynemouth, 2 June, 1961 (W)

League Club	Source	Date Signed	Seasons Played	Apps	Subs	Gls
Burnley	App	05.79	79-82	55	14	4
Bradford C.	L	03.83	82	9	0	2
Gillingham		10.83	83	4	6	1
Northampton T.	Tr	08.84	84-85	41	4	11
Peterborough U.	Tr	03.86	85	9	1	0

CAWLEY, Peter E.
Walton-on-Thames, 15 September, 1965 (CD)

League Club	Source	Date Signed	Seasons Played	Apps	Subs	Gls
Wimbledon	Chertsey T.	01.87	88	1	0	0
Bristol Rov.	L	02.87	86	9	1	0
Fulham	L	12.88	88	3	2	0
Bristol Rov.	Tr	07.89	89	1	2	0
Southend U.	Tr	07.90	90	6	1	1
Exeter C.	Tr	11.90	90	7	0	0
Barnet (N/C)	Tr	11.91	91	3	0	0

CAWSTON, Mervyn W.
Diss, 4 February, 1952 E Sch (G)

League Club	Source	Date Signed	Seasons Played	Apps	Subs	Gls
Norwich C.	App	07.69	70	4	0	0
Southend U.	L	08.74	74	10	0	0
Newport Co.	L	01.76	75	4	0	0
Gillingham	Tr	05.76	76	19	0	0
Southend U.	Chicago (USA)	08.78	78-83	189	0	0
Stoke C.	Tr	03.84				
Southend U. (N/C)	Chelmsford C.	11.84	84	9	0	0

CAWTHORNE, Graham J.
Doncaster, 30 September, 1958 (CD)

League Club	Source	Date Signed	Seasons Played	Apps	Subs	Gls
Grimsby T.	Harworth Colly	11.79	79	1	0	0
Doncaster Rov.	Tr	03.82	81-82	33	0	1

CECERE, Michele J.
Chester, 4 January, 1968 (F)

League Club	Source	Date Signed	Seasons Played	Apps	Subs	Gls
Oldham Ath.	App	01.86	86-88	35	17	8
Huddersfield T.	Tr	11.88	88-89	50	4	8
Stockport Co.	L	03.90	89	0	1	0
Walsall	Tr	08.90	90-91	55	12	14

CEGIELSKI, Wayne
Blackwood, 11 January, 1956 Wu21-2 (CD)

League Club	Source	Date Signed	Seasons Played	Apps	Subs	Gls
Tottenham H.	App	05.73				
Northampton T.	L	03.75	74	11	0	0
Wrexham	Schalke 04 (WG)	09.76	76-81	112	11	0
Port Vale	Tr	08.82	82-84	91	1	5
Hereford U.	Tr	07.85	85-86	46	4	2

CHADBOURNE, William
Mansfield, 29 October, 1922 (IF)

League Club	Source	Date Signed	Seasons Played	Apps	Subs	Gls
Mansfield T.		04.47	46-47	9	-	3

CHADWICK, Clifton
Bolton, 26 January, 1914 (OR)

League Club	Source	Date Signed	Seasons Played	Apps	Subs	Gls
Oldham Ath.	Fleetwood	10.33	33	18	-	6
Middlesbrough	Tr	02.34	33-38	93	-	27
Hull C.	Tr	09.46	46	23	-	7
Darlington	Tr	07.47	47	37	-	5

CHADWICK, David E.
India, 19 August, 1943 (W)

League Club	Source	Date Signed	Seasons Played	Apps	Subs	Gls
Southampton	Jnrs	10.60	61-65	25	0	1
Middlesbrough	Tr	07.66	66-69	100	2	3
Halifax T.	Tr	01.70	69-71	95	0	15
Bournemouth	Tr	02.72	71-73	29	7	4
Torquay U.	L	12.72	72	10	0	0
Gillingham	Tr	09.74	74	35	0	3

CHADWICK, Frank R.
Blackburn, 9 November, 1927 (WH)

League Club	Source	Date Signed	Seasons Played	Apps	Subs	Gls
Blackburn Rov.	Jnrs	06.46	48-52	11	-	1
York C.	Tr	07.55				

CHADWICK, Frederick W.
Manchester, 8 September, 1913 (CF)

League Club	Source	Date Signed	Seasons Played	Apps	Subs	Gls
Wolverhampton W.	British Dyes	05.35				
Newport Co.	Tr	09.36	36-37	40	-	18
Ipswich T.	Tr	06.38	38-46	40	-	20
Bristol Rov.	Tr	07.47	47	6	-	1

CHADWICK, Graham
Oldham, 8 April, 1942 (WH)

League Club	Source	Date Signed	Seasons Played	Apps	Subs	Gls
Manchester C.	Jnrs	03.62	62-63	12	-	0
Walsall	Tr	08.64	64	9	-	0
Chester C.	Tr	07.65	65-66	11	1	0

CHADWICK, Harold

League Club	Source	Date Signed	Seasons Played	Apps	Subs	Gls
Grimsby T.		05.45				
Tranmere Rov.		03.48	47-48	9	-	0

CHADWICK, Keith M.
Stoke, 10 March, 1953 (F)

League Club	Source	Date Signed	Seasons Played	Apps	Subs	Gls
Port Vale	Jnrs	09.73	73-75	29	12	7

League Club	Source	Date Signed	Seasons Played	Career Record Apps	Subs	Gls

CHADWICK, Simon L.
Liverpool, 15 March, 1968 (F)

League Club	Source	Date Signed	Seasons Played	Apps	Subs	Gls
Wrexham	Jnrs	08.85	85	1	1	0

CHALK, Martyn P. G.
Swindon, 30 August, 1969 (W)

League Club	Source	Date Signed	Seasons Played	Apps	Subs	Gls
Derby Co.	Louth U.	01.90	91	4	3	1

CHALK, Stephen R.
Southampton, 15 October, 1957 (G)

League Club	Source	Date Signed	Seasons Played	Apps	Subs	Gls
Bournemouth	App	10.75	75-77	11	0	0
Charlton Ath.	Tr	06.78				

CHALKLIN, Geoffrey
Swindon, 1 October, 1956 E Sch (D)

League Club	Source	Date Signed	Seasons Played	Apps	Subs	Gls
Swindon T.	App	10.74	75	3	0	0

CHALLIS, Roger L. A.
Rochester, 3 August, 1943 E Yth (FB)

League Club	Source	Date Signed	Seasons Played	Apps	Subs	Gls
Gillingham	Jnrs	07.61	60-62	10	-	0
Crewe Alex.	Tr	08.64	64	3	-	0

CHALLIS, Stanley M.
Lympstone, 22 April, 1918 (OL)

League Club	Source	Date Signed	Seasons Played	Apps	Subs	Gls
Exeter C.	Lympstone	09.45	46	4	-	1

CHALMERS, Leonard
Corby, 4 September, 1936 (RB)

League Club	Source	Date Signed	Seasons Played	Apps	Subs	Gls
Leicester C.	Corby T.	01.56	57-65	171	0	4
Notts Co.	Tr	07.66	66-67	51	0	1

CHALMERS, Paul
Glasgow, 31 October, 1963 S Yth (F)

League Club	Source	Date Signed	Seasons Played	Apps	Subs	Gls
Bradford C. (L)	Glasgow Celtic	01.86	85	2	0	0
Swansea C.	St Mirren	11.89	89-91	39	19	13

CHAMBERLAIN, Alec F. R.
March, 20 June, 1964 (G)

League Club	Source	Date Signed	Seasons Played	Apps	Subs	Gls
Ipswich T.	Ramsey T.	07.81				
Colchester U.	Tr	08.82	82-86	188	0	0
Everton	Tr	07.87				
Tranmere Rov.	L	11.87	87	15	0	0
Luton T.	Tr	07.88	88-91	106	0	0

CHAMBERLAIN, Derek C.
Nottingham, 6 January, 1933 (FB)

League Club	Source	Date Signed	Seasons Played	Apps	Subs	Gls
Aston Villa	Parliament St M.	11.53				
Mansfield T.	Tr	11.56	56-57	43	-	0
York C.	Tr	07.58				

CHAMBERLAIN, Glyn
Chesterfield, 29 July, 1957 (D)

League Club	Source	Date Signed	Seasons Played	Apps	Subs	Gls
Burnley	App	11.74				
Chesterfield	Tr	12.76	76-78	17	1	0
Halifax T.	Tr	08.81	81	35	0	0

CHAMBERLAIN, Kenneth R.
South Africa, 30 June, 1926 (CH)

League Club	Source	Date Signed	Seasons Played	Apps	Subs	Gls
Charlton Ath.	Parkhill (SA)	10.51	52-56	42	-	0

CHAMBERLAIN, Mark V.
Stoke, 19 November, 1961 E Sch/Eu21-4/E-8 (W)

League Club	Source	Date Signed	Seasons Played	Apps	Subs	Gls
Port Vale	App	04.79	78-81	90	6	17
Stoke C.	Tr	08.82	82-85	110	2	17
Sheffield Wed.	Tr	09.85	85-87	32	34	8
Portsmouth	Tr	08.88	88-91	94	13	15

CHAMBERLAIN, Neville P.
Stoke, 22 January, 1960 (F)

League Club	Source	Date Signed	Seasons Played	Apps	Subs	Gls
Port Vale	App	01.78	77-82	133	8	33
Stoke C.	Tr	09.82	82-83	6	0	0
Newport Co.	L	11.83	83	6	0	2
Plymouth Arg.	L	03.84	83	7	4	3
Newport Co.	Tr	07.84	84	39	2	13
Mansfield T.	Tr	07.85	85-86	56	5	19
Doncaster Rov.	Tr	08.87	87	22	7	4

CHAMBERLAIN, Peter M.
Liverpool, 30 June, 1935 (CH)

League Club	Source	Date Signed	Seasons Played	Apps	Subs	Gls
Leicester C.		09.56				
Swindon T.	Tr	06.57	57-62	80	-	6
Aldershot	Tr	10.62	62-64	46	-	1

CHAMBERLAIN, Trevor C. (Tosh)
Camden Town, 11 July, 1934 E Sch/E Yth (OL)

League Club	Source	Date Signed	Seasons Played	Apps	Subs	Gls
Fulham	Jnrs	07.51	54-64	183	-	59

CHAMBERS, Brian M.
Newcastle, 31 October, 1949 E Sch (M)

League Club	Source	Date Signed	Seasons Played	Apps	Subs	Gls
Sunderland	Jnrs	08.67	70-72	53	10	5
Arsenal	Tr	06.73	73	1	0	0
Luton T.	Tr	02.74	74-76	73	3	9
Millwall	Tr	07.77	77-78	54	5	9
Bournemouth	Tr	07.79	79-80	39	3	7
Halifax T.	Tr	03.81	80	10	0	1

CHAMBERS, David M.
Barnsley, 6 June, 1947 (W)

League Club	Source	Date Signed	Seasons Played	Apps	Subs	Gls
Rotherham U.	App	06.65	65-67	21	5	4
Southend U.	Cambridge U.	10.68	68-70	51	6	5
York C.	Tr	03.71	70-71	8	8	1

CHAMBERS, John F.
Birmingham, 7 October, 1949 (WH)

League Club	Source	Date Signed	Seasons Played	Apps	Subs	Gls
Aston Villa	App	10.66	68	1	1	0
Southend U.	Tr	07.69	69	6	1	0

CHAMBERS, Paul A.
Wolverhampton, 14 January, 1965 (D)

League Club	Source	Date Signed	Seasons Played	Apps	Subs	Gls
Plymouth Arg.	App	01.83				
Torquay U. (N/C)	Saltash U.	10.84	84	1	1	0

CHAMBERS, Philip M.
Barnsley, 10 November, 1953 E Sch (LB)

League Club	Source	Date Signed	Seasons Played	Apps	Subs	Gls
Barnsley	App	11.71	70-84	442	1	7
Rochdale (N/C)	Tr	08.85	85	9	1	0
Hartlepool U.	Tr	11.85	85	29	0	0

CHAMBERS, Stephen
Worksop, 20 July, 1968 (M/RB)

League Club	Source	Date Signed	Seasons Played	Apps	Subs	Gls
Mansfield T.	Sheffield Wed. (App)	11.86	86-90	42	15	0

CHAMPELOVIER, Leslie
Kensington, 23 April, 1933 E Amat (IF)

League Club	Source	Date Signed	Seasons Played	Apps	Subs	Gls
Brighton & H. A. (Am)	Hayes	05.57	57	1	-	0

CHANDLER, Frederick E. J.
Hythe, 2 August, 1912 (IL)

League Club	Source	Date Signed	Seasons Played	Apps	Subs	Gls
Reading	Portsmouth (Am)	05.32	32-35	41	-	13
Blackpool	Tr	10.35	35	15	-	3
Swindon T.	Tr	05.36	36	22	-	7
Crewe Alex.	Tr	05.37	37-46	80	-	22

CHANDLER, Ian
Sunderland, 20 March, 1968 E Sch (F)

League Club	Source	Date Signed	Seasons Played	Apps	Subs	Gls
Barnsley	Jnrs	08.86	86	8	4	4
Stockport Co.	L	08.87	87	4	1	0
Aldershot	Tr	08.88	88	5	4	2

CHANDLER, Jeffrey G.
Hammersmith, 19 June, 1959 IRu21-1/IR-2 (W)

League Club	Source	Date Signed	Seasons Played	Apps	Subs	Gls
Blackpool	App	08.76	77-78	31	6	7
Leeds U.	Tr	09.79	79-80	21	5	2
Bolton W.	Tr	10.81	81-84	152	5	36
Derby Co.	Tr	07.85	85-86	45	1	9
Mansfield T.	L	11.86	86	6	0	0
Bolton W.	Tr	07.87	87-89	18	6	4
Cardiff C.	Tr	11.89	89-90	21	4	1

CHANDLER, Raymond E. J.
Bath, 14 August, 1931 (G)

League Club	Source	Date Signed	Seasons Played	Apps	Subs	Gls
Bristol Rov.	Bristol C. (Am)	06.53	53-54	12	-	0
Swindon T.	Tr	06.56	56-58	35	-	0

CHANDLER, Richard D. (Ricky)
Bristol, 26 September, 1961 E Sch (F)

League Club	Source	Date Signed	Seasons Played	Apps	Subs	Gls
Bristol C.	App	10.78	80-82	57	4	13

CHANDLER, Robin A. S.
Luton, 19 December, 1942 E Sch (CF)

League Club	Source	Date Signed	Seasons Played	Apps	Subs	Gls
Luton T.	Jnrs	12.61	60-64	13	-	0

CHANNING, Justin A.
Reading, 19 November, 1968 E Yth (D/M)

League Club	Source	Date Signed	Seasons Played	Apps	Subs	Gls
Queens Park R	App	08.86	86-90	40	13	4

CHANNON, Michael R.
Salisbury Plain, 28 November, 1948 Eu23-9/EF Lge/E-46 (F)

League Club	Source	Date Signed	Seasons Played	Apps	Subs	Gls
Southampton	App	12.65	65-76	388	4	157
Manchester C.	Tr	07.77	77-79	71	1	24
Southampton	Tr	09.79	79-81	119	0	28
Newcastle U.	Tr	09.82	82	4	0	1
Bristol Rov.	Tr	10.82	82	4	5	0
Norwich C.	Tr	12.82	82-84	84	4	16
Portsmouth	Tr	08.85	85	34	0	6

CHAPMAN, Campbell
Sutton-in-Ashfield, 28 June, 1963 (M)

League Club	Source	Date Signed	Seasons Played	Apps	Subs	Gls
Peterborough U.	App	06.81				
Wolverhampton W.	Bilston	12.84	84-85	47	6	4
Crewe Alex. (N/C)		11.86	86	0	1	0

CHAPMAN, Cavan
Emsworth, 11 September, 1967 (F)

League Club	Source	Date Signed	Seasons Played	Apps	Subs	Gls
Wolverhampton W.	YT	07.84	84	1	0	0

CHAPMAN, Daren P.
Lincoln, 15 November, 1974

League Club	Source	Date Signed	Seasons Played	Apps	Subs	Gls
Lincoln C. (YT)	YT	07.91	91	0	1	0

CHAPMAN, Daryl M.
Kenilworth, 17 September, 1963 (F)

League Club	Source	Date Signed	Seasons Played	Apps	Subs	Gls
Derby Co.	Jnrs	07.82				
Crewe Alex.(N/C)	Tr	03.83	82	3	3	2

CHAPMAN, Edward
East Ham, 3 August, 1923 (IF)

League Club	Source	Date Signed	Seasons Played	Apps	Subs	Gls
West Ham U.	Romford	09.42	48	7	-	3

CHAPMAN, Edwin
Blackburn, 2 May, 1919 Died 1977 (CF)

League Club	Source	Date Signed	Seasons Played	Apps	Subs	Gls
Blackburn Rov.	Darwen	05.36				
Accrington St.	Tr	07.38	38	4	-	1
Oldham Ath.	Tr	06.39				
Stockport Co.	Tr	08.46	46	9	-	3

CHAPMAN, Gary A.
Leeds, 1 May, 1964 (F)

League Club	Source	Date Signed	Seasons Played	Apps	Subs	Gls
Bradford C.	Ossett A.	08.88	88-89	2	3	0
Notts Co.	L	09.89	89	10	0	4
Notts Co.	Tr	02.90	89-90	3	12	0
Mansfield T.	L	10.90	90	6	0	0
Exeter C.	Tr	09.91	91	17	3	4

Mike Channon (Southampton, Manchester City, Southampton, Newcastle United, Bristol Rovers, Norwich City, Portsmouth & England)

CHAPMAN, George
Burton, 8 October, 1920 (IL)

League Club	Source	Date Signed	Seasons Played	Apps	Subs	Gls
West Bromwich A.	Donisthorpe	12.38				
Brighton & H. A.	Tr	07.46	46-47	43	-	12

CHAPMAN, Harold
Liverpool, 4 March, 1921 (WH)

League Club	Source	Date Signed	Seasons Played	Apps	Subs	Gls
Aston Villa	Ellesmere Port	02.47	47	6	-	0
Notts Co.	Tr	03.49	48-50	53	-	1

CHAPMAN, Ian R.
Brighton, 31 May, 1970 (LB/M)

League Club	Source	Date Signed	Seasons Played	Apps	Subs	Gls
Brighton & H. A.	YT	06.87	86-91	114	12	2

CHAPMAN, John
Sacriston (Dm), 24 May, 1945 (D)

League Club	Source	Date Signed	Seasons Played	Apps	Subs	Gls
Workington	Stockton	02.63	63-65	28	0	1
Reading	Tr	06.66	66-68	102	1	2
Stockport Co.	Tr	07.69	69-71	89	3	5

CHAPMAN, Kenneth A.
Coventry, 25 April, 1932 (F)

League Club	Source	Date Signed	Seasons Played	Apps	Subs	Gls
Blackpool	Jnrs	08.49				
Crewe Alex.	Tr	07.53	53	24	-	8
Bradford C.	Tr	07.54	54	26	-	4

CHAPMAN, Kenneth F. R.
Grimsby, 16 November, 1948 (OL)

League Club	Source	Date Signed	Seasons Played	Apps	Subs	Gls
Grimsby T. (Am)	Louth U.	06.68	69	6	1	0

CHAPMAN, Lee R.
Lincoln, 5 December, 1959 Eu21-1/E'B' (F)

League Club	Source	Date Signed	Seasons Played	Apps	Subs	Gls
Stoke C.	Jnrs	06.78	79-81	95	4	34
Plymouth Arg.	L	12.78	78	3	1	0
Arsenal	Tr	08.82	82-83	15	8	4
Sunderland	Tr	12.83	83	14	1	3
Sheffield Wed.	Tr	08.84	84-87	147	2	63
Nottingham F.	Niort (Fr)	10.88	88-89	48	0	15
Leeds U.	Tr	01.90	89-91	97	0	49

Lee Chapman (Stoke City, Arsenal, Sunderland, Sheffield Wednesday, Niort, Nottingham Forest & Leeds United)

CHAPMAN, Leslie
Oldham, 27 September, 1948 (M)

League Club	Source	Date Signed	Seasons Played	Apps	Subs	Gls
Oldham Ath.	Huddersfield T. (Am)	01.67	66-69	75	1	9
Huddersfield T.	Tr	09.69	69-74	120	14	8
Oldham Ath.	Tr	12.74	74-78	186	1	11
Stockport Co.	Tr	05.79	79	32	0	1
Bradford C.	Tr	02.80	79-82	137	2	3
Rochdale	Tr	06.83	83-84	87	1	0
Stockport Co.	Tr	07.85	85	38	0	3
Preston N. E.	Tr	07.86	86-87	50	3	1

CHAPMAN, Neville
Cockfield (Dm), 15 September, 1941 (RB)

League Club	Source	Date Signed	Seasons Played	Apps	Subs	Gls
Middlesbrough	Jnrs	11.58	61-66	51	2	0
Darlington	Tr	09.67	67-68	31	1	0

CHAPMAN, Paul C.
Cardiff, 28 September, 1951 (D)

League Club	Source	Date Signed	Seasons Played	Apps	Subs	Gls
Plymouth Arg.	App	10.69	69	2	1	0

CHAPMAN, Philip E.
Chasetown, 27 November, 1925 (CF)

League Club	Source	Date Signed	Seasons Played	Apps	Subs	Gls
Walsall	Cannock T.	09.48	48-50	62	-	36

CHAPMAN, Reginald
Eccles, 14 June, 1928 (F)

League Club	Source	Date Signed	Seasons Played	Apps	Subs	Gls
Crewe Alex.	Hereford U.	05.50	50-51	21	-	1

CHAPMAN, Reginald F. J.
Shepherds Bush, 7 September, 1921 (CH)

League Club	Source	Date Signed	Seasons Played	Apps	Subs	Gls
Queens Park R		08.44	46-52	98	-	2

CHAPMAN, Robert D. (Sammy)
Wednesbury, 18 August, 1946 (CD)

League Club	Source	Date Signed	Seasons Played	Apps	Subs	Gls
Nottingham F.	Jnrs	08.63	63-76	347	12	17
Notts Co.	Tr	08.77	77	42	0	0
Shrewsbury T.	Tr	07.78	78-79	36	1	6

CHAPMAN, Roger A.
Doncaster, 20 November, 1944 (G)

League Club	Source	Date Signed	Seasons Played	Apps	Subs	Gls
Rotherham U.		07.65	64	2	-	0
Doncaster Rov.	Tr	12.65	65	5	0	0

CHAPMAN, Roy C.
Birmingham, 18 March, 1934 Died 1983 (IF)

League Club	Source	Date Signed	Seasons Played	Apps	Subs	Gls
Aston Villa	Kynoch Wks	02.52	53-57	19	-	7
Lincoln C.	Tr	11.57	57-61	105	-	45
Mansfield T.	Tr	08.61	61-64	136	-	78
Lincoln C.	Tr	01.65	64-66	69	1	31
Port Vale	Tr	08.67	67-68	77	1	38
Chester C.	Tr	06.69	69	9	0	3

CHAPMAN, Samuel E. C.
Belfast, 16 February, 1938 NI 'B'-1 (IF)

League Club	Source	Date Signed	Seasons Played	Apps	Subs	Gls
Mansfield T.	Shamrock Rov.	10.56	56-57	50	-	25
Portsmouth	Tr	02.58	57-61	48	-	10
Mansfield T.	Tr	12.61	61-63	105	-	15

CHAPMAN, Stuart
Lynemouth, 6 May, 1951 (IF)

League Club	Source	Date Signed	Seasons Played	Apps	Subs	Gls
Port Vale	App	07.69	66-69	4	2	0

CHAPMAN, Vernon W.
Leicester, 9 May, 1921 (OR)

League Club	Source	Date Signed	Seasons Played	Apps	Subs	Gls
Leicester C.		01.42	46	1	-	0
Leyton Orient	Tr	07.47	47-48	31	-	7

CHAPMAN, Vincent J.
Newcastle, 5 December, 1967 (LB)

League Club	Source	Date Signed	Seasons Played	Apps	Subs	Gls
Huddersfield T.	Tow Law T.	01.88	87	4	2	0
Rochdale	Tr	07.89	89-90	23	1	1

CHAPPELL, Larratt (Lol)
Sheffield, 19 December, 1930 Died 1988 (CF)

League Club	Source	Date Signed	Seasons Played	Apps	Subs	Gls
Barnsley	Jnrs	05.49	52-58	218	-	94
Doncaster Rov.	Tr	08.59	59-60	34	-	5

CHAPPELL, Leslie A.
Nottingham, 6 February, 1947 (M)

League Club	Source	Date Signed	Seasons Played	Apps	Subs	Gls
Rotherham U.	App	02.65	65-67	109	2	36
Blackburn Rov.	Tr	05.68	68	7	0	0
Reading	Tr	07.69	69-74	193	8	78
Doncaster Rov.	Tr	12.74	74-75	57	1	10
Swansea C.	Tr	07.76	76-77	65	2	5

CHAPPELL, Shaun R.
Swansea, 14 February, 1973 Wu21-1 (M)

League Club	Source	Date Signed	Seasons Played	Apps	Subs	Gls
Swansea C.	YT	07.91	91	17	4	2

CHAPPLE, Philip R.
Norwich, 26 November, 1966 (CD)

League Club	Source	Date Signed	Seasons Played	Apps	Subs	Gls
Norwich C.	YT	07.85				
Cambridge U.	Tr	03.88	87-91	167	2	17

CHARD, Philip J.
Corby, 16 October, 1960 (M/FB)

League Club	Source	Date Signed	Seasons Played	Apps	Subs	Gls
Peterborough U.	Corby T.	01.79	78-84	153	19	18
Northampton T.	Tr	08.85	85-87	113	2	27
Wolverhampton W.	Tr	03.88	87-89	26	8	5
Northampton T.	Tr	10.89	89-91	101	0	12

CHARLERY, Kenneth L.
Stepney, 28 November, 1964 (F)

League Club	Source	Date Signed	Seasons Played	Apps	Subs	Gls
Maidstone U.	Fisher Ath.	03.89	89-90	41	18	11
Peterborough U.	Tr	03.91	90-91	35	6	16

CHARLES, Clive M.
Bow, 3 October, 1951 EYth (FB)

League Club	Source	Date Signed	Seasons Played	Apps	Subs	Gls
West Ham U.	App	08.69	71-73	12	2	0
Cardiff C.	Tr	03.74	73-76	75	2	5

CHARLES, Gary A.
Newham, 13 April, 1970 Eu21-4/E-2 (FB)

League Club	Source	Date Signed	Seasons Played	Apps	Subs	Gls
Nottingham F.	YT	11.87	88-91	40	2	1
Leicester C.	L	03.89	88	5	3	0

CHARLES, Jeremy M.
Swansea, 26 September, 1959 Wu21-2/W-19 (F)

League Club	Source	Date Signed	Seasons Played	Apps	Subs	Gls
Swansea C.	App	01.77	76-83	224	23	53
Queens Park R	Tr	11.83	83	10	2	5
Oxford U.	Tr	02.85	84-86	41	5	13

CHARLES, W. John
Swansea, 27 December, 1931 W-38 (CF)

League Club	Source	Date Signed	Seasons Played	Apps	Subs	Gls
Leeds U.	Jnrs	01.49	48-56	297	-	150
Leeds U.	Juventus (It)	08.62	62	11	-	3
Cardiff C.	Roma (It)	08.63	63-65	65	1	19

John Charles (Leeds United, Juventus, Leeds United, Roma, Cardiff City & Wales)

CHARLES, John W.
Canning Town, 20 September, 1944 E Yth (FB)

League Club	Source	Date Signed	Seasons Played	Apps	Subs	Gls
West Ham U.	App	05.62	62-69	117	1	1

CHARLES, Melvyn
Swansea, 14 May, 1935 Wu23-1/W-31 (CF)

League Club	Source	Date Signed	Seasons Played	Apps	Subs	Gls
Swansea C.	Leeds U. (Am.)	05.52	52-58	233	-	69
Arsenal	Tr	04.59	59-61	60	-	26
Cardiff C.	Tr	02.62	61-64	81	-	24
Port Vale	Portmadoc	02.67	66	7	0	0

Mel Charles (Swansea City, Arsenal, Cardiff City, Port Vale & Wales)

CHARLES, Stephen
Sheffield, 10 May, 1960 (M)

League Club	Source	Date Signed	Seasons Played	Apps	Subs	Gls
Sheffield U.	Sheffield Univ.	01.80	79-84	112	11	10
Wrexham	Tr	10.84	84-86	111	2	37
Mansfield T.	Tr	07.87	87-91	209	5	36

CHARLES, Robert
Southampton, 26 December, 1941 E Sch/E Yth (G)

League Club	Source	Date Signed	Seasons Played	Apps	Subs	Gls
Southampton	Jnrs	04.59	59-60	26	-	0

CHARLESWORTH, Arnold
Sheffield, 6 July, 1930 (IF)

League Club	Source	Date Signed	Seasons Played	Apps	Subs	Gls
West Bromwich A.	Boston U.	03.52				
Rotherham U.	Tr	08.53				
York C.	Tr	04.54	54	1	-	0

CHARLESWORTH, Stanley F.
Conisborough, 10 March, 1920 (CH)

League Club	Source	Date Signed	Seasons Played	Apps	Subs	Gls
Grimsby T.	Wath W.	12.37	38-46	2	-	0
Barnsley	Tr	12.46	46	7	-	0

CHARLESWORTH, Terence
Scunthorpe, 13 July, 1933 (G)

League Club	Source	Date Signed	Seasons Played	Apps	Subs	Gls
Scunthorpe U.		06.52	52-56	19	-	0

CHARLTON, Harold
Gateshead, 22 June, 1951 (M)

League Club	Source	Date Signed	Seasons Played	Apps	Subs	Gls
Middlesbrough	App	07.68	70-74	8	2	0
Hartlepool U.	L	01.76	75	2	1	0
Chesterfield	Tr	03.76	75-76	17	4	0
Darlington	Buxton	08.79	79-81	69	3	4

CHARLTON, John (Jack)
Ashington, 8 May, 1935 EF Lge/E-35 (CH)

League Club	Source	Date Signed	Seasons Played	Apps	Subs	Gls
Leeds U.	Jnrs	05.52	52-72	628	0	70

CHARLTON, John A.
(G)

League Club	Source	Date Signed	Seasons Played	Apps	Subs	Gls
Gateshead (Am.)		08.49	49	1	-	0

CHARLTON, Kevin P.
Tamworth, 12 September, 1954 E Semi-Pro (G)

League Club	Source	Date Signed	Seasons Played	Apps	Subs	Gls
Wolverhampton W.	App	09.72				
Bournemouth	Tr	12.73	73-74	21	0	0
Hereford U.	Tr	06.75	75-77	52	0	0
Scarborough (N/C)	Telford U.	09.88	88	3	0	0

CHARLTON, Robert
Ashington, 11 October, 1937 E Sch/E Yth/Eu23-6/EF Lge/E-106 (IF)

League Club	Source	Date Signed	Seasons Played	Apps	Subs	Gls
Manchester U.	Jnrs	10.54	56-72	604	2	198
Preston N. E.	Tr	05.74	74	38	0	8

CHARLTON, Simon T.
Huddersfield, 25 October, 1971 (LB)

League Club	Source	Date Signed	Seasons Played	Apps	Subs	Gls
Huddersfield T.	YT	07.89	89-91	75	3	0

CHARLTON, Stanley
Exeter, 28 June, 1929 E Amat (FB)

League Club	Source	Date Signed	Seasons Played	Apps	Subs	Gls
Leyton Orient	Bromley	11.52	52-55	151	-	1
Arsenal	Tr	11.55	55-58	99	-	0
Leyton Orient	Tr	12.58	58-64	216	-	1

CHARLTON, Wilfred S.
Blyth, 12 September, 1933 (WH)

League Club	Source	Date Signed	Seasons Played	Apps	Subs	Gls
Huddersfield T.	Jnrs	11.50				
Southport	Tr	07.54	54-56	109	-	8
Tranmere Rov.	Tr	06.57	57-60	92	0	4

CHARNLEY, Derek L.
Doncaster, 7 May, 1954 (F)

League Club	Source	Date Signed	Seasons Played	Apps	Subs	Gls
Scunthorpe U.		02.73	72-75	28	10	3

CHARNLEY, James C. (Chic)
Glasgow, 11 June, 1963 (M)

League Club	Source	Date Signed	Seasons Played	Apps	Subs	Gls
Bolton W. (L)	St Mirren	03.92	91	3	0	0

CHARNLEY, Raymond O.
Lancaster, 29 May, 1935 E-1 (CF)

League Club	Source	Date Signed	Seasons Played	Apps	Subs	Gls
Blackpool	Morecambe	05.57	57-67	363	0	193
Preston N. E.	Tr	12.67	67	23	0	4
Wrexham	Tr	07.68	68	19	1	5
Bradford P. A.	Tr	01.69	68-69	59	0	15

CHARTER, Raymond
Ashton-u-Lyne, 10 January, 1950 (FB)

League Club	Source	Date Signed	Seasons Played	Apps	Subs	Gls
Blackburn Rov.	App	01.68	69-70	13	5	0
Stockport Co.	Tr	07.71	71-73	87	4	2

CHASE, Charles T.
Steyning, 31 January, 1924 (HB)

League Club	Source	Date Signed	Seasons Played	Apps	Subs	Gls
Watford	Brighton & H.A.(Am)	09.46	46-47	16	-	1
Crystal Palace	Tr	07.48	48-49	55	-	2

CHATHAM, Alexander
Glasgow, 7 July, 1936 (G)

League Club	Source	Date Signed	Seasons Played	Apps	Subs	Gls
Barrow		12.58	58	1	-	0

CHATHAM, Raymond H.
Wolverhampton, 20 July, 1924 (CH)

League Club	Source	Date Signed	Seasons Played	Apps	Subs	Gls
Wolverhampton W.	Jnrs	06.45	46-53	76	-	0
Notts Co.	Tr	01.54	53-58	128	-	4

CHATTERLEY, Lawson C. (Lew)
Birmingham, 15 February, 1945 E Yth (M)

League Club	Source	Date Signed	Seasons Played	Apps	Subs	Gls
Aston Villa	App	02.62	62-70	149	4	26
Doncaster Rov.	L	03.71	70	9	0	0
Northampton T.	Tr	09.71	71	23	0	2
Grimsby T.	Tr	02.72	71-73	72	1	16
Southampton	Tr	03.74	73-74	7	2	0
Torquay U.	Tr	02.75	74-76	55	2	10

League Club	Source	Date Signed	Seasons Played	Apps	Subs	Gls

CHATTERTON, Nicholas J.
Norwood, 18 May, 1954 (M)

League Club	Source	Date Signed	Seasons Played	Apps	Subs	Gls
Crystal Palace	Jnrs	03.72	73-78	142	9	31
Millwall	Tr	11.78	78-85	258	6	56
Colchester U.	Tr	09.86	86-88	47	2	8

CHAYTOR, Kenneth
Trimdon (Dm), 18 November, 1937 (IF)

League Club	Source	Date Signed	Seasons Played	Apps	Subs	Gls
Oldham Ath.	Jnrs	11.54	54-59	77	-	20

CHEADLE, Reginald G.
Stoke, 17 October, 1929

League Club	Source	Date Signed	Seasons Played	Apps	Subs	Gls
Port Vale	Jnrs	11.46	47	1	-	0

CHEADLE, Thomas
Stoke, 8 April, 1919 (CH)

League Club	Source	Date Signed	Seasons Played	Apps	Subs	Gls
Port Vale		05.46	46-56	332	-	14
Crewe Alex.	Tr	07.57	57-58	37	-	0

CHEESEBROUGH, Albert
Burnley, 17 January, 1935 Eu23-1 (IF)

League Club	Source	Date Signed	Seasons Played	Apps	Subs	Gls
Burnley	Jnrs	01.52	51-58	142	-	35
Leicester C.	Tr	06.59	59-62	122	-	40
Port Vale	Tr	07.63	63-64	57	-	13
Mansfield T.	Tr	07.65	65-66	24	0	0

CHEESEWRIGHT, John A.
Romford, 12 January, 1973 (G)

League Club	Source	Date Signed	Seasons Played	Apps	Subs	Gls
Southend U. (N/C)	Tottenham H. (YT)	03.91				
Birmingham C. (N/C)	Tr	11.91	91	1	0	0

CHEESLEY, Paul M.
Bristol, 20 October, 1953 (F)

League Club	Source	Date Signed	Seasons Played	Apps	Subs	Gls
Norwich C.	App	10.71	72-73	10	3	1
Bristol C.	Tr	12.73	73-76	61	3	20

CHEETHAM, Hugh D.
Manchester, 3 February, 1958 (M)

League Club	Source	Date Signed	Seasons Played	Apps	Subs	Gls
Crewe Alex.	App	01.76	75-78	90	6	0
Reading	Tr	07.79	79-80	10	2	0

CHEETHAM, Michael M.
Amsterdam (Neth), 30 June, 1967 (M)

League Club	Source	Date Signed	Seasons Played	Apps	Subs	Gls
Ipswich T.	Basingstoke T.	10.88	88-89	1	3	0
Cambridge U.	Tr	10.89	89-91	99	3	20

CHEETHAM, Roy A. J.
Eccles, 2 December, 1939 (WH)

League Club	Source	Date Signed	Seasons Played	Apps	Subs	Gls
Manchester C.	Jnrs	12.56	57-67	127	5	4
Charlton Ath.	Detroit (USA)	10.68				
Chester C.	Tr	12.68	68-71	122	2	8

CHEETHAM, Thomas
Liverpool, 8 December, 1950 (F)

League Club	Source	Date Signed	Seasons Played	Apps	Subs	Gls
Southport		12.69	69-70	24	2	4

CHEETHAM, Thomas M.
Newcastle, 11 October, 1910 (CF)

League Club	Source	Date Signed	Seasons Played	Apps	Subs	Gls
Queens Park R		08.35	36-38	116	-	80
Brentford	Tr	02.39	38	17	-	8
Lincoln C.	Tr	10.45	46-47	47	-	31

CHENEY, Dennis
Coalville, 30 June, 1924 (CF)

League Club	Source	Date Signed	Seasons Played	Apps	Subs	Gls
Leicester C.	Jnrs	11.41	47-48	2	-	0
Watford	L	02.48	47	18	-	5
Bournemouth	Tr	10.48	48-53	157	-	47
Aldershot	Tr	06.54	54-55	53	-	19

CHENHALL, John C.
Bristol, 23 July, 1927 (FB)

League Club	Source	Date Signed	Seasons Played	Apps	Subs	Gls
Arsenal	Maidenhead U.	11.45	51-52	16	-	0
Fulham	Tr	07.53	53-57	91	-	0

CHEREDNIK, Alexei
USSR, 12 December, 1960 USSR Int (RB)

League Club	Source	Date Signed	Seasons Played	Apps	Subs	Gls
Southampton	Dnepr (USSR)	02.90	89-90	19	4	0

CHERRY, Rex A.
Sheffield, 11 November, 1933 (CF)

League Club	Source	Date Signed	Seasons Played	Apps	Subs	Gls
Gillingham	Army	03.53	52-53	10	-	4

CHERRY, Steven R.
Nottingham, 5 August, 1960 EYth (G)

League Club	Source	Date Signed	Seasons Played	Apps	Subs	Gls
Derby Co.	App	03.78	79-83	77	0	0
Port Vale	L	11.80	80	4	0	0
Walsall	Tr	08.84	84-85	71	0	0
Plymouth Arg.	Tr	10.86	86-88	73	0	0
Chesterfield	L	12.88	88	10	0	0
Notts Co.	Tr	02.89	88-91	152	0	0

CHERRY, Trevor J.
Huddersfield, 23 February, 1948 EF Lge/E-27 (D)

League Club	Source	Date Signed	Seasons Played	Apps	Subs	Gls
Huddersfield T.	Jnrs	07.65	66-71	185	3	12
Leeds U.	Tr	06.72	72-82	393	6	24
Bradford C.	Tr	12.82	82-84	92	0	0

CHESSELL, Samuel
Shirebrook, 9 July, 1921 (FB)

League Club	Source	Date Signed	Seasons Played	Apps	Subs	Gls
Mansfield T.	Welbeck Colly	09.45	46-53	258	-	7

CHESTERS, Colin W.
Crewe, 21 November, 1959 (F)

League Club	Source	Date Signed	Seasons Played	Apps	Subs	Gls
Derby Co.	App	11.77	77-78	6	3	1
Crewe Alex.	Tr	09.79	79-81	52	9	6

CHETTLE, Stephen
Nottingham, 27 September, 1968 Eu21-12 (CD)

League Club	Source	Date Signed	Seasons Played	Apps	Subs	Gls
Nottingham F.	App	08.86	87-91	126	13	6

CHEUNG, Chi-Doy
Hong Kong, 30 July, 1941 (F)

League Club	Source	Date Signed	Seasons Played	Apps	Subs	Gls
Blackpool	Hong Kong	10.60	60-61	2	-	1

CHEW, John (Jackie)
Blackburn, 13 May, 1920 (OR)

League Club	Source	Date Signed	Seasons Played	Apps	Subs	Gls
Burnley	Blackburn Rov. (Am.)	05.45	46-53	225	-	39
Bradford C.	Tr	06.54	54	36	-	4

CHEW, John
Longton, 21 November, 1915

League Club	Source	Date Signed	Seasons Played	Apps	Subs	Gls
Luton T.		11.42				
Port Vale	Tr	03.46	46	9	-	0

CHIEDOZIE, John O.
Nigeria, 18 April, 1960 Nigerian Int (W)

League Club	Source	Date Signed	Seasons Played	Apps	Subs	Gls
Leyton Orient	App	04.77	76-80	131	14	20
Notts Co.	Tr	08.81	81-83	110	1	15
Tottenham H.	Tr	08.84	84-86	45	8	12
Derby Co.	Tr	08.88	88	2	0	0
Notts Co. (N/C)	Tr	01.90	89	0	1	0
Chesterfield (N/C)	Tr	03.90	89	5	2	0

Alexei Cherednik (Dnepr, Southampton & Russia)

CHILCOTT, Kenneth
Rhondda, 17 March, 1920 (OR)

League Club	Source	Date Signed	Seasons Played	Apps	Subs	Gls
Bristol C.	Eastville U.	10.37	37-48	46	-	6

CHILDS, Albert R. (Bert)
Liverpool, 25 September, 1930 E Amat (FB)

League Club	Source	Date Signed	Seasons Played	Apps	Subs	Gls
Liverpool (Am.)	Northern Nomads	09.53	53	2	-	0

CHILDS, Gary P. C.
Birmingham, 19 April, 1964 E Yth (W)

League Club	Source	Date Signed	Seasons Played	Apps	Subs	Gls
West Bromwich A.	App	02.82	81-83	2	1	0
Walsall	Tr	10.83	83-86	120	11	17
Birmingham C.	Tr	07.87	87-88	39	16	2
Grimsby T.	Tr	07.89	89-91	93	5	12

CHILTON, Allenby C.
Sunderland, 16 September, 1918 E-2 (CH)

League Club	Source	Date Signed	Seasons Played	Apps	Subs	Gls
Manchester U.	Seaham Colly	11.38	46-54	352	-	3
Grimsby T.	Tr	03.55	54-56	63	-	0

CHILTON, Anthony J. T.
Maryport, 7 September, 1965 (FB)

League Club	Source	Date Signed	Seasons Played	Apps	Subs	Gls
Sunderland	App	09.83				
Burnley (N/C)	Tr	02.85	84	1	0	0
Hartlepool U. (N/C)	Tr	10.85	85	3	0	0

CHILTON, Christopher R.
Hull, 25 June, 1943 (CF)

League Club	Source	Date Signed	Seasons Played	Apps	Subs	Gls
Hull C.	Jnrs	07.60	60-71	415	0	193
Coventry C.	Tr	09.71	71	26	1	3

Chris Chilton (Hull City & Coventry City)

CHILTON, Frederick
Washington, 10 July, 1935 (FB)

League Club	Source	Date Signed	Seasons Played	Apps	Subs	Gls
Sunderland	Usworth Colly	05.53	56-57	3	-	0

CHILVERS, Geoffrey T.
Sutton, 31 January, 1925 E Sch (WH)

League Club	Source	Date Signed	Seasons Played	Apps	Subs	Gls
Crystal Palace	Sutton U.	03.45	48-53	118	-	1

CHILVERS, Gordon M.
Norwich, 15 November, 1933 (G)

League Club	Source	Date Signed	Seasons Played	Apps	Subs	Gls
Walsall	Fordhouses B.C.	04.52	51-57	123	-	0

CHINAGLIA, Giorgio
Italy, 24 January, 1947 Italian Int (CF)

League Club	Source	Date Signed	Seasons Played	Apps	Subs	Gls
Swansea C.	App	04.65	64-65	4	1	1

CHINE, Athumani Khamiss
Tanzania, 12 March, 1967 (M)

League Club	Source	Date Signed	Seasons Played	Apps	Subs	Gls
Walsall		03.92	91	4	1	0

CHIPPENDALE, Brian A.
Bradford, 29 October, 1964 (M)

League Club	Source	Date Signed	Seasons Played	Apps	Subs	Gls
York C.	Bradford C. (App)	10.83	83-84	2	6	0
Halifax T.	L	11.84	84	1	1	0
Burnley (N/C)	Tr	08.85	85	6	2	0
Preston N. E. (N/C)	Tr	10.85	85	5	1	0

CHISHOLM, Gordon W.
Glasgow, 8 April, 1960 (CD)

League Club	Source	Date Signed	Seasons Played	Apps	Subs	Gls
Sunderland	App	04.78	78-85	192	5	10

CHISHOLM, Jack R.
Edmonton, 9 October, 1924 Died 1977 (CH)

League Club	Source	Date Signed	Seasons Played	Apps	Subs	Gls
Tottenham H.	Jnrs	10.42	47	2	-	0
Brentford	Tr	10.47	47-48	49	-	1
Sheffield U.	Tr	03.49	48-49	21	-	1
Plymouth Arg.	Tr	12.49	49-53	175	-	2

Jack Chisholm Tottenham Hotspur, Brentford, Sheffield United & Plymouth Argyle)

CHISHOLM, Kenneth M.
Glasgow, 12 April, 1925 Died 1990 (IF)

League Club	Source	Date Signed	Seasons Played	Apps	Subs	Gls
Leeds U.	Partick Th.	01.48	47-48	40	-	17
Leicester C.	Tr	01.49	48-49	42	-	17
Coventry C.	Tr	03.50	49-51	68	-	34
Cardiff C.	Tr	03.52	51-53	63	-	13
Sunderland	Tr	01.54	53-55	78	-	33
Workington	Tr	08.56	56-57	39	-	15

CHISHOLM, Wilfred
Hebburn, 23 May, 1921 (G)

League Club	Source	Date Signed	Seasons Played	Apps	Subs	Gls
Grimsby T.	Newcastle U. (Am.)	09.46	46-50	92	-	0

League Club	Source	Date Signed	Seasons Played	Apps	Subs	Gls
CHISNALL, J. Philip						
Manchester, 27 October, 1942 E Sch/Eu23-1						(M)
Manchester U.	Jnrs	11.59	61-63	35	-	8
Liverpool	Tr	04.64	64	6	-	1
Southend U.	Tr	08.67	67-70	137	5	28
Stockport Co.	Tr	09.71	71	30	0	2
CHISWICK, Peter J. H.						
Plaistow, 19 September, 1929 Died 1962						(G)
West Ham U.	Jnrs	07.47	53-54	19	-	0
Gillingham	Tr	07.56	56	14	-	0
CHITTY, Wilfred S.						
Walton-on-Thames, 10 July, 1912						(OL)
Chelsea	Woking	03.30	31-37	45	-	16
Plymouth Arg.	Tr	12.38	38	3	-	1
Reading	Tr	08.39	46-47	23	-	7
CHIVERS, Gary P. S.						
Stockwell, 15 May, 1960						(D)
Chelsea	App	07.78	78-82	128	5	4
Swansea C.	Tr	08.83	83	10	0	0
Queens Park R	Tr	02.84	84-86	58	2	0
Watford	Tr	09.87	87	14	0	0
Brighton & H.A.	Tr	03.88	87-91	172	2	13

Gary Chivers (Chelsea, Swansea City, Queens Park Rangers, Watford & Brighton & Hove Albion)

League Club	Source	Date Signed	Seasons Played	Apps	Subs	Gls
CHIVERS, Martin H.						
Southampton, 27 April, 1945 Eu23-17/EF Lge/E-24						(F)
Southampton	Jnrs	09.62	62-67	174	1	97
Tottenham H.	Tr	01.68	67-75	268	10	118
Norwich C.	Servette (Swi)	07.78	78	11	0	4
Brighton & H. A.	Tr	03.79	78-79	4	1	1
CHMILOWSKY, Roman						
Bradford, 19 April, 1959						(G)
Halifax T. (Am.)	Jnrs	04.77	76	1	0	0
CHOLERTON, William						
Derby, 1 January, 1949						(FB)
Derby Co.	App	12.66	66	1	0	0
CHOULES, Leonard G.						
Orpington, 29 January, 1932						(CH)
Crystal Palace	Sutton U.	05.51	52-61	258	-	2

League Club	Source	Date Signed	Seasons Played	Apps	Subs	Gls
CHRISTENSEN, Thomas A.						
Aarhus (Denmark), 20 July, 1961						(F)
Leicester C. (N/C)	Elche (Sp)	11.85	85	1	1	0
Portsmouth (N/C)	Tr	11.85	85	3	0	2
CHRISTIE, David						
Salford, 26 February, 1973						(F)
Preston N.E.	YT	07.91	91	0	2	0
CHRISTIE, Derrick H. M.						
Bletchley, 15 March, 1957						(W)
Northampton T.	App	03.75	73-78	116	22	18
Cambridge U.	Tr	11.78	78-83	132	6	19
Reading	Tr	07.84	84	8	6	1
Cardiff C.	Tr	10.85	85	18	1	2
Peterborough U.	Tr	08.86	86	6	2	0
CHRISTIE, Frank						
Perth, 17 February, 1927						(WH)
Liverpool	Forfar Ath.	03.49	49	4	-	0
CHRISTIE, John A.						
Fraserburgh, 26 September, 1929						(G)
Southampton	Ayr U.	01.51	50-58	197	-	0
Walsall	Tr	06.59	59-62	102	-	0
CHRISTIE, Trevor						
Newcastle, 28 February, 1959						(F)
Leicester C.	App	12.76	77-78	28	3	8
Notts Co.	Tr	06.79	79-83	158	29	64
Nottingham F.	Tr	07.84	84	14	0	5
Derby Co.	Tr	02.85	84-85	65	0	22
Manchester C.	Tr	08.86	86	9	0	3
Walsall	Tr	10.86	86-88	91	8	22
Mansfield T.	Tr	03.89	88-90	88	4	24
CHRISTOPHER, Paul A.						
Poole, 19 June, 1954						(F)
Bournemouth	App	11.71				
Mansfield T.	Tr	07.73	73	7	1	1
CHUNG, Cyril (Sammy)						
Abingdon, 16 July, 1932						(WH)
Reading	Headington U.	11.51	53-54	22	-	12
Norwich C.	Tr	01.55	54-56	47	-	9
Watford	Tr	06.57	57-64	220	-	22
CHURCH, Gary						
Pontefract, 20 September, 1944						(HB)
Bradford P. A.	Great Preston Jnrs	07.62	63	4		0
CHURCH, John						
Lowestoft, 17 September, 1919						(OL)
Norwich C.	Lowestoft	09.36	37-49	110	-	16
Colchester U.	Tr	07.50	50-53	118	-	20
CHURCHILL, Trevor						
Barnsley, 20 November, 1923						(G)
Reading	Sheffield U. (Am)	09.46	46	10	-	0
Leicester C.	Tr	08.47				
Rochdale	Tr	01.49	48-52	110	-	0
Swindon T.	Tr	05.53	53	11	-	0
CHURCHOUSE, Gary						
Wembley, 1 February, 1957						(M)
Charlton Ath.	Windsor & Eton	03.79	78-79	13	5	0
CHURMS, Dennis J.						
Rotherham, 8 May, 1931						(IF)
Rotherham U.	Spurley Hey	04.50	53-55	15	-	0
Coventry C.	Tr	06.56	56	10	-	2
Exeter C.	Tr	03.57	56-57	44	-	8
CINI, Joseph						
Malta Maltese Int						(OR)
Queens Park R (Am.)	Floriana (Malta)	08.59	59	7	-	1
CITRON, Gerald C.						
Manchester, 8 April, 1935						(IF)
Chester C. (Am.)	Corinthian Casuals	10.59	59	2	-	0
CLACK, Frank E.						
Witney, 30 March, 1912						(G)
Birmingham C.	Witney T.	05.33	33-38	60	-	0
Brentford	Tr	07.39				
Bristol C.	Tr	05.47	46-48	67	-	0

CLAESEN, Nico P. J.
Belgium, 1 October, 1962 Belgian Int (F)

League Club	Source	Date Signed	Seasons Played	Apps	Subs	Gls
Tottenham H.	Standard Léige (Bel)	10.86	86-87	37	13	18

CLAMP, Edward
Coalville, 14 September, 1934 E Sch/EF Lge/E-4 (WH)

League Club	Source	Date Signed	Seasons Played	Apps	Subs	Gls
Wolverhampton W.	Jnrs	04.52	53-61	214	-	23
Arsenal	Tr	11.61	61-62	22	-	1
Stoke C.	Tr	09.62	62-63	50	-	2
Peterborough U.	Tr	10.64	64	8	-	0

CLAMP, Edward
Burton, 13 November, 1922 Died 1990 (G)

League Club	Source	Date Signed	Seasons Played	Apps	Subs	Gls
Derby Co.	Gresley Rov.	11.47	48	1	-	0
Oldham Ath.	Tr	07.49	49	3	-	0

CLAMP, Martin
Coventry, 31 January, 1948 (G)

League Club	Source	Date Signed	Seasons Played	Apps	Subs	Gls
Coventry C.	Jnrs	01.66				
Plymouth Arg.	Tr	07.68	69	8	0	0

CLANCY, John P.
Perivale, 5 July, 1949 (W)

League Club	Source	Date Signed	Seasons Played	Apps	Subs	Gls
Bristol C.	Tottenham H. (App)	03.67				
Bradford P. A.	Tr	07.67	67-68	52	4	2

CLAPHAM, Graham L.
Lincoln, 23 September, 1947 (M)

League Club	Source	Date Signed	Seasons Played	Apps	Subs	Gls
Newcastle U.	App	09.65				
Shrewsbury T.	Tr	08.67	67-71	73	15	5
Chester C.	Tr	01.72	71-72	37	4	7

CLAPHAM, Keith
Fareham, 9 September, 1952 (CD)

League Club	Source	Date Signed	Seasons Played	Apps	Subs	Gls
Bournemouth	App	09.70				
Exeter C.	Tr	07.72	72-76	79	12	0

CLAPTON, Daniel R.
Stepney, 22 July, 1934 Died 1986 EF Lge/E-1 (OR)

League Club	Source	Date Signed	Seasons Played	Apps	Subs	Gls
Arsenal	Leytonstone	08.53	54-61	207	-	25
Luton T.	Tr	09.62	62	10	-	0

CLAPTON, Dennis P.
Hackney, 12 October, 1939 E Yth (CF)

League Club	Source	Date Signed	Seasons Played	Apps	Subs	Gls
Arsenal	Jnrs	08.58	59-60	4	-	0
Northampton T.	Tr	08.61	61	1	-	0

CLARE, James E.
Islington, 6 November, 1959 (F)

League Club	Source	Date Signed	Seasons Played	Apps	Subs	Gls
Chelsea	App	08.78	80	0	1	0
Charlton Ath	Tr	08.81				

CLARIDGE, Stephen E.
Portsmouth, 10 April, 1966 (F)

League Club	Source	Date Signed	Seasons Played	Apps	Subs	Gls
Bournemouth	Fareham T.	09.84	84-85	3	4	1
Crystal Palace	Weymouth	08.88				
Aldershot	Tr	10.88	88-89	58	4	19
Cambridge U.	Tr	02.90	89-91	56	23	28

CLARK, Albert H.
Ashington, 24 July, 1921 (WH)

League Club	Source	Date Signed	Seasons Played	Apps	Subs	Gls
Newcastle U.	North Shields	01.48	48	1	-	0

CLARK, Alexander (Sandy)
Airdrie, 28 October, 1956 (F)

League Club	Source	Date Signed	Seasons Played	Apps	Subs	Gls
West Ham U.	Airdrieonians	06.82	82	26	0	7

CLARK, Benjamin
North Shields, 14 April, 1933 (WH)

League Club	Source	Date Signed	Seasons Played	Apps	Subs	Gls
Sunderland	North Shields	08.50				
Derby Co.	Yeovil T.	05.54	54-57	16	-	0
Barrow	Tr	02.59	58-63	202	-	7

CLARK, Brian D.
Bristol, 13 January, 1943 (F)

League Club	Source	Date Signed	Seasons Played	Apps	Subs	Gls
Bristol C.	Jnrs	03.60	60-66	195	0	83
Huddersfield T.	Tr	10.66	66-67	28	4	11
Cardiff C.	Tr	02.68	67-72	178	4	75
Bournemouth	Tr	10.72	72-73	28	2	12
Millwall	Tr	09.73	73-74	66	5	17
Cardiff C.	Tr	05.75	75	19	2	1
Newport Co.	Tr	08.76	76-78	72	8	18

CLARK, Clive
Leeds, 14 December, 1940 Eu23-1 (OL)

League Club	Source	Date Signed	Seasons Played	Apps	Subs	Gls
Leeds U.	Jnrs	01.58				
Queens Park R	Tr	08.58	58-60	58	-	7
West Bromwich A.	Tr	01.61	60-68	300	1	80
Queens Park R	Tr	06.69	69	7	1	1
Preston N. E.	Tr	01.70	69-72	71	1	9
Southport	Tr	07.73	73	7	1	1

CLARK, David G.
Ilford, 19 January, 1938 (CH)

League Club	Source	Date Signed	Seasons Played	Apps	Subs	Gls
Leyton Orient	Leyton	12.61	61-62	4	-	0

CLARK, Derek
Newcastle, 10 August, 1931 (IR)

League Club	Source	Date Signed	Seasons Played	Apps	Subs	Gls
Lincoln C.	Durham C.	12.51	51	4	-	1

CLARK, Derek B.
Leyburn, 27 December, 1935 (F)

League Club	Source	Date Signed	Seasons Played	Apps	Subs	Gls
Darlington		03.55	54-55	5	-	1

CLARK, Donald F.
Bristol, 25 October, 1917 (CF)

League Club	Source	Date Signed	Seasons Played	Apps	Subs	Gls
Bristol C.	North Bristol O.B.	05.37	38-50	117	-	67

CLARK, Frank A.
Rowlands Gill, 9 September, 1943 E Yth/E Amat/EF Lge (LB)

League Club	Source	Date Signed	Seasons Played	Apps	Subs	Gls
Newcastle U.	Crook T.	11.62	63-74	388	1	0
Nottingham F.	Tr	07.75	75-78	116	1	1

CLARK, Graham J.
Aberdeen, 20 January, 1961 S Sch (M)

League Club	Source	Date Signed	Seasons Played	Apps	Subs	Gls
Sheffield U.	App	10.78				
Darlington	Tr	08.79	79	6	0	0

CLARK, Harold
Cloughdene, 30 March, 1913 (OL)

League Club	Source	Date Signed	Seasons Played	Apps	Subs	Gls
Accrington St.	Manchester C. (Am.)	12.44				
Gateshead	Tr	06.46	46	23	-	1

CLARK, Harold
Sunderland, 11 September, 1934 (IF)

League Club	Source	Date Signed	Seasons Played	Apps	Subs	Gls
Sunderland	St Benets	05.56	56	6	-	0

CLARK, Harold M.
Newcastle, 29 December, 1932 (IF)

League Club	Source	Date Signed	Seasons Played	Apps	Subs	Gls
Darlington		07.51	50-56	142	-	20
Sheffield Wed.	Tr	10.57	57	1	-	0
Hartlepool U.	Tr	08.58	58-60	118	-	43

Steve Claridge Bournemouth, Crystal Palace, Aldershot & Cambridge United)

CLARK, Howard W.
Coventry, 19 September, 1968 (M/CD)

League Club	Source	Date Signed	Seasons Played	Apps	Subs	Gls
Coventry C.	App	09.86	88-90	9	11	1
Darlington	L	09.91	91	5	0	0
Shrewsbury T.	Tr	12.91	91	21	2	0

CLARK, James D.
Dornoch, 1 May, 1923 (FB)

League Club	Source	Date Signed	Seasons Played	Apps	Subs	Gls
Exeter C.	Aberdeen	08.48	48-52	95	-	5
Bradford C.	L	09.52	52	6	-	0

CLARK, Jonathan
Swansea, 12 November, 1958 W Sch/Wu21-2 (M)

League Club	Source	Date Signed	Seasons Played	Apps	Subs	Gls
Manchester U.	App	11.75	76	0	1	0
Derby Co.	Tr	09.78	78-80	48	5	3
Preston N. E.	Tr	08.81	81-86	107	3	10
Bury	Tr	12.86	86	13	1	1
Carlisle U.	Tr	08.87	87-88	48	1	2

CLARK, Joseph T.
Bermondsey, 2 March, 1920 (FB)

League Club	Source	Date Signed	Seasons Played	Apps	Subs	Gls
Leyton Orient	Gravesend & Nft	02.46	46	18	-	0

CLARK, Lee R.
Wallsend, 27 October, 1972 E Yth/E-u21-2 (M)

League Club	Source	Date Signed	Seasons Played	Apps	Subs	Gls
Newcastle U.	YT	12.89	90-91	38	10	7

CLARK, Martin J.
Holytown, 13 October, 1968 (M)

League Club	Source	Date Signed	Seasons Played	Apps	Subs	Gls
Nottingham F.	Clyde	02.89				
Mansfield T.	L	03.90	89	14	0	1
Mansfield T.	Tr	08.90	90-91	31	2	0

CLARK, Neville
Gateshead, 9 October, 1930 (RH)

League Club	Source	Date Signed	Seasons Played	Apps	Subs	Gls
Grimsby T.	Chilton Colly	12.48				
Sunderland		12.49				
Hartlepool U.	Tr	08.53	53	2	-	0

CLARK, Paul P.
Benfleet, 14 September, 1958 E Sch/E Yth (CD)

League Club	Source	Date Signed	Seasons Played	Apps	Subs	Gls
Southend U.	App	07.76	76-77	29	4	1
Brighton & H. A.	Tr	11.77	77-80	69	10	9
Reading	L	10.81	81	2	0	0
Southend U.	Tr	08.82	82-90	269	7	3
Gillingham	Tr	07.91	91	42	0	0

CLARK, Peter J.
Doncaster, 22 January, 1938 (WH)

League Club	Source	Date Signed	Seasons Played	Apps	Subs	Gls
Wolverhampton W.	Jnrs	03.55				
Doncaster Rov.	Tr	07.59	59	14	-	8
Mansfield T.	Tr	06.60	60	2	-	0
Stockport Co.	Stourbridge	08.65	65	21	0	2
Crewe Alex.	Tr	07.66	66	2	0	0

CLARK, Ronald
Clarkston, 21 May, 1932 (OL)

League Club	Source	Date Signed	Seasons Played	Apps	Subs	Gls
Gillingham	Kilmarnock	07.56	56-57	33	-	6
Oldham Ath.	Tr	06.58	58	4	-	0

CLARK, Steven
Baldock, 20 September, 1964 (FB)

League Club	Source	Date Signed	Seasons Played	Apps	Subs	Gls
Cambridge U.	App	09.82	83-85	63	3	0

CLARK, Thomas H.
Luton, 5 October, 1924 Died 1981 (IF)

League Club	Source	Date Signed	Seasons Played	Apps	Subs	Gls
Aston Villa	Vauxhall Motors	04.47				
Walsall	Tr	05.48	48	9	-	2

CLARK, William R.
Christchurch, 19 May, 1967 (CD)

League Club	Source	Date Signed	Seasons Played	Apps	Subs	Gls
Bournemouth	YT	09.84	84-87	4	0	0
Bristol Rov.	Tr	10.87	87-91	76	4	3

CLARK, William
Larkhall, 25 February, 1932 (CF)

League Club	Source	Date Signed	Seasons Played	Apps	Subs	Gls
Queens Park R	Petershill	02.54	53-55	95	-	32

CLARKE, Alan
Houghton Regis, 10 April, 1942 (OR)

League Club	Source	Date Signed	Seasons Played	Apps	Subs	Gls
Luton T.	Jnrs	10.61	61-62	9	-	0

CLARKE, Alfred
Oldham, 23 August, 1926 (CF)

League Club	Source	Date Signed	Seasons Played	Apps	Subs	Gls
Crewe Alex.	Stalybridge Celtic	02.48	47-48	22	-	12
Burnley	Tr	12.48	48-51	24	-	6
Oldham Ath.	Tr	08.52	52-53	43	-	12
Halifax T.	Tr	03.54	53-55	71	-	22

CLARKE, Allan J.
Willenhall, 31 July, 1946 Eu23-6/E-19 (F)

League Club	Source	Date Signed	Seasons Played	Apps	Subs	Gls
Walsall	App	08.63	63-65	72	0	41
Fulham	Tr	03.66	65-67	85	1	45
Leicester C.	Tr	06.68	68	36	0	12
Leeds U.	Tr	07.69	69-77	270	3	110
Barnsley	Tr	06.78	78-79	47	0	15

Allan Clarke (Walsall, Fulham, Leicester City, Leeds United, Barnsley & England)

CLARKE, Allen F.
Crayford, 2 December, 1952 (G)

League Club	Source	Date Signed	Seasons Played	Apps	Subs	Gls
Charlton Ath.	App	07.71	71	2	0	0
Bristol Rov.	L	09.71	71	1	0	0
Exeter C.	Tr	02.73	72-73	16	0	0

CLARKE, Ambrose
Liverpool, 10 September, 1945 (WH)

League Club	Source	Date Signed	Seasons Played	Apps	Subs	Gls
Everton		06.64				
Southport	Tr	01.66	65-70	193	4	4
Barrow	Tr	07.71	71	45	1	0

CLARKE, Andrew W.
Islington, 22 July, 1967 E Semi-Pro (F)

League Club	Source	Date Signed	Seasons Played	Apps	Subs	Gls
Wimbledon	Barnet	02.91	90-91	20	26	6

CLARKE, Brian R.
Eastbourne, 10 October, 1968 (CD)

League Club	Source	Date Signed	Seasons Played	Apps	Subs	Gls
Gillingham	YT	06.87	88-91	42	2	0

CLARKE, Christopher E.
Battersea, 11 December, 1946 (OL)

League Club	Source	Date Signed	Seasons Played	Apps	Subs	Gls
Millwall	Chelsea (App)	12.63	64-65	19	0	4
Watford	Tr	08.66	66	1	1	0

CLARKE, Colin
Penilee, 4 April, 1946 (CD)

League Club	Source	Date Signed	Seasons Played	Apps	Subs	Gls
Arsenal	Arthurlie Jnrs	10.63				
Oxford U.	Tr	07.65	65-77	443	1	23
Plymouth Arg.	Los Angeles (USA)	09.78	78	35	0	3

CLARKE, Colin J.
Newry (NI), 30 October, 1962 NI-35 (F)

League Club	Source	Date Signed	Seasons Played	Apps	Subs	Gls
Ipswich T.	App	10.80				
Peterborough U.	Tr	07.81	81-83	76	6	18
Gillingham	L	03.84	83	8	0	1
Tranmere Rov.	Tr	07.84	84	45	0	22
Bournemouth	Tr	06.85	85	46	0	26
Southampton	Tr	06.86	86-88	82	0	36
Bournemouth	L	12.88	88	3	1	2
Queens Park R	Tr	03.89	88-89	39	7	11
Portsmouth	Tr	06.90	90-91	57	9	17

CLARKE, David A.
Derby, 25 September, 1946 (W)

League Club	Source	Date Signed	Seasons Played	Apps	Subs	Gls
Nottingham F.	Derby Co. (Am)	05.64				
Notts Co.	Tr	07.66	66	23	1	0

CLARKE, David A.
Nottingham, 3 December, 1964 E Yth (LB)

League Club	Source	Date Signed	Seasons Played	Apps	Subs	Gls
Notts Co.	App	12.82	82-86	113	10	7
Lincoln C.	Tr	07.87	88-91	104	5	6

CLARKE, Dennis
Stockton, 18 January, 1948 (FB)

League Club	Source	Date Signed	Seasons Played	Apps	Subs	Gls
West Bromwich A.	App	02.65	66-68	19	2	0
Huddersfield T.	Tr	01.69	68-73	172	0	3
Birmingham C.	Tr	09.73	73-74	14	0	0

CLARKE, Derek
Willenhall, 19 February, 1950 (F)

League Club	Source	Date Signed	Seasons Played	Apps	Subs	Gls
Walsall	App	12.67	67	6	0	2
Wolverhampton W.	Tr	05.68	68-69	2	3	0
Oxford U.	Tr	10.70	70-75	172	6	35
Leyton Orient	Tr	08.76	76-78	30	6	6
Carlisle U.	L	10.78	78	0	1	0

CLARKE, Donald L.
Poole, 29 June, 1931 (F)

League Club	Source	Date Signed	Seasons Played	Apps	Subs	Gls
Cardiff C.		08.54				
Brighton & H. A.	Tr	06.55	55	2	-	0

CLARKE, Douglas
Bolton, 19 January, 1934 (OR)

League Club	Source	Date Signed	Seasons Played	Apps	Subs	Gls
Bury	Darwen	02.52	53-55	37	-	16
Hull C.	Tr	11.55	55-64	368	-	79
Torquay	Tr	07.65	65-67	116	4	21

CLARKE, Frank J.
Willenhall, 15 July, 1942 (F)

League Club	Source	Date Signed	Seasons Played	Apps	Subs	Gls
Shrewsbury T.	Willenhall	11.61	61-67	189	0	77
Queens Park R	Tr	02.68	67-69	67	0	17
Ipswich T.	Tr	03.70	69-72	62	4	15
Carlisle U.	Tr	08.73	73-77	121	5	30

CLARKE, Frederick J.
Crewe, 3 January, 1931 (HB)

League Club	Source	Date Signed	Seasons Played	Apps	Subs	Gls
Crewe Alex.		11.51	53-54	3	-	0

CLARKE, Frederick R. G.
Banbridge (NI), 4 November, 1941 (FB)

League Club	Source	Date Signed	Seasons Played	Apps	Subs	Gls
Arsenal	Glenavon	11.60	61-64	26	-	0

CLARKE, Gary
Boston, 6 November, 1960 (W)

League Club	Source	Date Signed	Seasons Played	Apps	Subs	Gls
Bristol Rov.	App	11.78	78-79	6	5	0

CLARKE, George E.
Ipswich, 25 April, 1921 (CH)

League Club	Source	Date Signed	Seasons Played	Apps	Subs	Gls
Ipswich T.		11.46	46-52	34	-	1

CLARKE, Gerald
Barrow Hill, 4 January, 1936 (RB)

League Club	Source	Date Signed	Seasons Played	Apps	Subs	Gls
Chesterfield	Oaks Fold	03.55	54-67	383	0	20

CLARKE, Graham P.
Nottingham, 11 August, 1935 (FB)

League Club	Source	Date Signed	Seasons Played	Apps	Subs	Gls
Southampton		06.53	57-58	3	-	0

CLARKE, Harold
Sunderland, 26 November, 1960 (M)

League Club	Source	Date Signed	Seasons Played	Apps	Subs	Gls
Hartlepool U.	Middlesbrough (N/C)	08.79	81	5	2	1

CLARKE, Harold A.
Woodford, 23 February, 1923 E 'B'-1/E-1 (CH)

League Club	Source	Date Signed	Seasons Played	Apps	Subs	Gls
Tottenham H.	Lovells Ath.	03.49	48-56	295	-	4

CLARKE, J. Henry
Sheffield, 27 March, 1921 (CF)

League Club	Source	Date Signed	Seasons Played	Apps	Subs	Gls
Rotherham U.	Goole T.	05.37	37-38	54	-	12
Darlington	Tr	04.46	46	19	-	17
Leeds U.	Tr	02.47	46	14	-	1
Darlington	Tr	11.47	47-48	37	-	25
Hartlepool U.	Tr	11.49	49	6	-	1
Darlington	Stockton	09.52	52	14	-	12

CLARKE, Isaac (Ike)
Tipton, 9 January, 1915 (IF)

League Club	Source	Date Signed	Seasons Played	Apps	Subs	Gls
West Bromwich A.	T. E. Wesley	01.37	37-47	108	-	39
Portsmouth	Tr	11.47	47-52	116	-	49

CLARKE, James
West Bromwich, 7 December, 1923 (LB)

League Club	Source	Date Signed	Seasons Played	Apps	Subs	Gls
Nottingham F.		05.47	47-53	18	-	0

CLARKE, Jeffrey D.
Pontefract, 18 January, 1954 (CD)

League Club	Source	Date Signed	Seasons Played	Apps	Subs	Gls
Manchester C.	Jnrs	01.72	74	13	0	0
Sunderland	Tr	06.75	75-81	178	3	6
Newcastle U.	Tr	08.82	82-86	124	0	4
Brighton & H. A.	L	08.84	84	4	0	0

CLARKE, John L.
Northampton, 23 October, 1946 E Yth (CD)

League Club	Source	Date Signed	Seasons Played	Apps	Subs	Gls
Northampton T.	Jnrs	07.65	66-74	228	5	1

CLARKE, W. John
Bargoed, 26 December, 1940 (G)

League Club	Source	Date Signed	Seasons Played	Apps	Subs	Gls
Newport Co.	Bargoed Y.M.C.A.	05.59	59-61	12	-	0

CLARKE, Kelvin L.
Wolverhampton, 16 July, 1957 (D)

League Club	Source	Date Signed	Seasons Played	Apps	Subs	Gls
Walsall	App	07.75	74-78	4	5	0

CLARKE, Kevin
Drogheda (IR), 29 April, 1923

League Club	Source	Date Signed	Seasons Played	Apps	Subs	Gls
Barrow	Drogheda	12.45	46	13	-	1

CLARKE, Kevin N.
Santry, 3 December, 1921 LOI/IR-2 (HB)

League Club	Source	Date Signed	Seasons Played	Apps	Subs	Gls
Swansea C.	Drumcondra	11.48	48-51	10	-	0

CLARKE, Malcolm M. G.
Clydebank, 29 June, 1944 (M)

League Club	Source	Date Signed	Seasons Played	Apps	Subs	Gls
Leicester C.	Johnstone Burgh	07.65	65	0	1	0
Cardiff C.	Tr	08.67	67-68	43	2	5
Bristol C.	Tr	07.69	69	2	1	0
Hartlepool U.	Tr	07.70	70-71	29	4	0

CLARKE, Michael
Sheffield, 28 November, 1944 (LB)

League Club	Source	Date Signed	Seasons Played	Apps	Subs	Gls
Sheffield U.	App	01.62				
Aldershot	Tr	06.64	64	5	-	0
Halifax T.	Tr	07.65	65-66	50	1	1

CLARKE, Michael D.
Birmingham, 22 December, 1967 (LB/W)

League Club	Source	Date Signed	Seasons Played	Apps	Subs	Gls
Barnsley	Birmingham C. (App)	11.86	86-88	37	3	3
Scarborough	Tr	08.89	89-90	31	6	1

CLARKE, Nicholas J.
Walsall, 20 August, 1967 (CD)

League Club	Source	Date Signed	Seasons Played	Apps	Subs	Gls
Wolverhampton W.	Jnrs	02.85	85-91	73	8	1
Mansfield T.	Tr	12.91	91	16	0	1

CLARKE, Norman F. (Nobby)
Birmingham, 31 October, 1934 E Yth (WH)

League Club	Source	Date Signed	Seasons Played	Apps	Subs	Gls
Aston Villa	Jnrs	07.53	54	1	-	0
Torquay U.	Tr	07.56	56-58	55	-	0

CLARKE, Norman S.
Antrim (NI), 1 April, 1942 NIu23-2 (W)

League Club	Source	Date Signed	Seasons Played	Apps	Subs	Gls
Sunderland	Ballymena	02.62	62	4	-	0

CLARKE, Paul S.
Chesterfield, 25 September, 1950 E Sch (CD)

League Club	Source	Date Signed	Seasons Played	Apps	Subs	Gls
Liverpool	App	10.67				
Rochdale	Tr	08.69	69-71	10	1	0

CLARKE, Peter A.
Bolton, 6 July, 1949 (G)

League Club	Source	Date Signed	Seasons Played	Apps	Subs	Gls
Bolton W.	Jnrs	06.69	70	13	0	0
Stockport Co.	Tr	07.71	71-74	49	0	0

CLARKE, Raymond C.
Hackney, 25 September, 1952 E Yth (F)

League Club	Source	Date Signed	Seasons Played	Apps	Subs	Gls
Tottenham H.	App	10.69	72	0	1	0
Swindon T.	Tr	06.73	73	11	3	2
Mansfield T.	Tr	08.74	74-75	91	0	52
Brighton & H. A.	Bruges (Bel)	10.79	79	30	0	8
Newcastle U.	Tr	07.80	80	14	0	2

League Club	Source	Date Signed	Seasons Played	Apps	Subs	Gls
CLARKE, A. Robert						
Liverpool, 13 October, 1941						(IF)
Chester C.		10.61	61-62	29	-	2
CLARKE, Royston J.						
Newport, 1 June, 1925 W-22						(OL)
Cardiff C.	Jnrs	12.42	46	39	-	11
Manchester C.	Tr	04.47	46-57	349	-	73
Stockport Co.	Tr	09.58	58	25	-	5
CLARKE, Simon N.						
Chelmsford, 23 September, 1971						(LM)
West Ham U.	YT	03.90	90-91	0	2	0
CLARKE, Stephen						
Saltcoats, 29 August, 1963 S Yth/Su21-8/S-5						(RB)
Chelsea	St Mirren	01.87	86-91	161	2	6
CLARKE, Stuart A.						
Torquay, 25 January, 1961						(M)
Torquay U.	Jnrs	02.78	78	4	1	0
CLARKE, Thomas						
Ardrossan, 12 April, 1946						(G)
Carlisle U.	Airdrieonians	07.70	71-74	23	0	0
Preston N. E.	Tr	07.75	75	3	0	0
CLARKE, Timothy J.						
Stourbridge, 16 May, 1965						(G)
Coventry C.	Halesowen T.	10.90				
Huddersfield T.	Tr	07.91	91	39	0	0
CLARKE, Wayne						
Wolverhampton, 28 February, 1961 E Sch/E Yth						(F)
Wolverhampton W.	App	03.78	77-83	129	19	30
Birmingham C.	Tr	08.84	84-86	92	0	38
Everton	Tr	03.87	86-88	46	11	17
Leicester C.	Tr	07.89	89	10	1	1
Manchester C.	Tr	01.90	89-91	7	14	2
Shrewsbury T.	L	10.90	90	7	0	6
Stoke C.	L	03.91	90	9	0	3
Wolverhampton W.	L	09.91	91	1	0	0
CLARKE, William A.						
Newport, 17 April, 1923 W Amat						(WH)
Ipswich T. (Am.)		02.47	46	3	-	0
CLARKSON, David J.						
Preston, 1 February, 1968						(M)
Brighton & H.A.	Sunshine G.C. (Aus)	09.91	91	4	9	0
CLARKSON, Ian S.						
Solihull, 4 December, 1970						(RB)
Birmingham C.	YT	12.88	88-91	100	8	0
CLARKSON, Philip I.						
Garstang, 13 November, 1968						(F)
Crewe Alex.	Fleetwood T.	10.91	91	18	10	6
CLAXTON, Thomas						
Rochdale, 17 October, 1944						(W)
Bury	Burnley (Am)	03.63	63-68	97	4	3
CLAY, John H.						
Stockport, 22 November, 1946						(IF)
Manchester C.	App	05.64	67	1	1	0
CLAYPOLE, Anthony W.						
Weldon, 13 February, 1937						(FB)
Northampton T.	Jnrs	03.54	56-61	116	-	1
CLAYTON, Edward						
Bethnal Green, 7 May, 1937						(IF)
Tottenham H.	Eton Manor	12.57	57-67	88	4	20
Southend U.	Tr	03.68	67-69	70	3	16
CLAYTON, Gary						
Sheffield, 2 February, 1963 E Semi Pro						(M/RB)
Doncaster Rov.	Burton A.	08.86	86	34	1	5
Cambridge U.	Tr	06.87	87-91	112	6	7
Peterborough U.	L	01.91	90	4	0	0
CLAYTON, Gordon						
Wednesbury, 3 November, 1936 Died 1991 E Sch/E Yth						(G)
Manchester U.	Jnrs	11.53	56	2	-	0
Tranmere Rov.	Tr	11.59	59-60	4	-	0

League Club	Source	Date Signed	Seasons Played	Apps	Subs	Gls
CLAYTON, John						
Elgin, 20 August, 1961						(F)
Derby Co.	App	12.78	78-81	21	3	4
Chesterfield	Hong Kong	06.83	83	25	8	5
Tranmere Rov.	Tr	07.84	84-85	47	0	35
Plymouth Arg.	Tr	08.85	85-87	68	9	21
CLAYTON, John M.						
St Asaph, 28 March, 1937						(WH)
Everton	Jnrs	06.55				
Southport	Tr	07.59	59-60	32	-	3
CLAYTON, Kenneth						
Preston, 6 April, 1933						(WH)
Blackburn Rov.	Jnrs	05.50	52-58	72	-	0
CLAYTON, Lewis						
Royston, 7 June, 1924						(WH)
Barnsley	Monkton Ath.	03.42				
Carlisle U.	Tr	09.46	46	24	-	0
Barnsley	Tr	06.47	48-49	15	-	0
Queens Park R	Tr	08.50	50-53	90	-	5
Bournemouth	Tr	05.55	55-56	40	-	1
Swindon T.	Tr	06.57	57-58	35	-	2
CLAYTON, Paul S.						
Dunstable, 4 January, 1965						(F)
Norwich C.	App	01.83	83-85	8	5	0
Darlington	Tr	03.88	87-88	20	2	3
Crewe Alex.	Tr	01.89	88-90	51	9	12
CLAYTON, Ronald						
Hull, 18 January, 1937						(F)
Arsenal	Hereford U.	01.58				
Brighton & H. A.	Tr	09.58	58-59	14	-	3
CLAYTON, Ronald						
Preston, 5 August, 1934 Eu23-6/EF Lge/E'B'-1/E-35						(WH)
Blackburn Rov.	Jnrs	08.51	50-68	579	2	15

Ronnie Clayton (Blackburn Rovers & England)

CLAYTON, Roy
Dudley, 18 February, 1950 (F)

League Club	Source	Date Signed	Seasons Played	Apps	Subs	Gls
Oxford U.	Warley Bor.	08.69	69-72	49	4	8

CLEARY, George
Bedford, 14 May, 1948 (F)

League Club	Source	Date Signed	Seasons Played	Apps	Subs	Gls
Cambridge U.	Kettering T.	12.75	75	5	3	0

CLEARY, William
Middlesbrough, 20 April, 1931 (WH)

League Club	Source	Date Signed	Seasons Played	Apps	Subs	Gls
Sunderland	South Bank East End	05.49				
Norwich C.	Tr	05.52	53-55	18	-	0
Port Vale	Wisbech T.	11.57	57	8	-	0

CLEEVELY, Nigel
Cheltenham, 23 December, 1945 (OL)

League Club	Source	Date Signed	Seasons Played	Apps	Subs	Gls
Derby Co.	Jnrs	07.64	64-66	15	1	3

CLEGG, Anthony
Keighley, 8 November, 1965 (D)

League Club	Source	Date Signed	Seasons Played	Apps	Subs	Gls
Bradford C.	App	11.83	83-86	41	7	2
York C.	Tr	08.87	87-88	38	3	0

CLEGG, Donald
Huddersfield, 2 June, 1921 (G)

League Club	Source	Date Signed	Seasons Played	Apps	Subs	Gls
Huddersfield T.	I.C.I.	05.40	46-47	3	-	0
Bury	Tr	07.48	48-49	15	-	0
Stoke C.	Tr	06.50	50	2	-	0

CLEGG, Malcolm B.
Leeds, 9 April, 1936 (CF)

League Club	Source	Date Signed	Seasons Played	Apps	Subs	Gls
Bradford P.A.(Am.)	Bradford Rov.	01.58	57	6	-	0

CLELAND, Peter M.
Glasgow, 8 May, 1932 (F)

League Club	Source	Date Signed	Seasons Played	Apps	Subs	Gls
Norwich C.	Cheltenham T.	08.58	58	3	-	0

CLELLAND, Crawford
USA, 3 December, 1930 (IF)

League Club	Source	Date Signed	Seasons Played	Apps	Subs	Gls
Plymouth Arg.	Aberdeen	06.55	55	2	-	0

CLELLAND, David
Larkhall, 18 March, 1924 (OR)

League Club	Source	Date Signed	Seasons Played	Apps	Subs	Gls
Arsenal		08.46				
Brighton & H. A.	Tr	01.48	47	8	-	1
Crystal Palace	Tr	09.49	49	2	-	0
Scunthorpe U.	Weymouth	07.50	50	16	-	8

CLEMENCE, Raymond N.
Skegness, 5 August, 1948 Eu23-4/EF Lge/E-61 (G)

League Club	Source	Date Signed	Seasons Played	Apps	Subs	Gls
Scunthorpe U.	Notts Co. (Jnr)	08.65	65-66	48	0	0
Liverpool	Tr	06.67	69-80	470	0	0
Tottenham H.	Tr	08.81	81-87	240	0	0

Ray Clemence (Scunthorpe United, Liverpool, Tottenham Hotspur & England)

CLEMENT, Andrew D.
Cardiff, 12 November, 1967 W Yth (FB/M)

League Club	Source	Date Signed	Seasons Played	Apps	Subs	Gls
Wimbledon	App	10.85	86-88	14	12	0
Bristol Rov.	L	03.87	86	5	1	0
Newport Co.	L	12.87	87	5	0	1
Plymouth Arg.	Woking	12.90	90-91	28	14	0

CLEMENT, David T.
Battersea, 2 February, 1948 Died 1982 E Yth/E-5 (RB)

League Club	Source	Date Signed	Seasons Played	Apps	Subs	Gls
Queens Park R	Jnrs	07.65	66-78	402	3	22
Bolton W.	Tr	06.79	79-80	33	0	0
Fulham	Tr	10.80	80	17	1	0
Wimbledon	Tr	10.81	81	9	0	2

CLEMENTS, Andrew P.
Swindon, 11 October, 1955 (CD)

League Club	Source	Date Signed	Seasons Played	Apps	Subs	Gls
Bolton W.	App	10.73	77	1	0	0
Port Vale	L	02.77	76	2	1	0
York C.	Tr	11.77	77-80	146	2	6

CLEMENTS, David
Lame (NI), 15 September, 1945 NI Amat/NIu23-3/NI-48 (LB)

League Club	Source	Date Signed	Seasons Played	Apps	Subs	Gls
Wolverhampton W.	Portadown	01.63				
Coventry C.	Tr	07.64	64-71	228	2	26
Sheffield Wed.	Tr	08.71	71-73	78	0	0
Everton	Tr	09.73	73-75	81	2	6

Dave Clements (Portadown, Wolverhampton Wanderers, Coventry City, Sheffield Wednesday, Everton & Northern Ireland)

CLEMENTS, Kenneth H.
Manchester, 9 April, 1955 (CD)

League Club	Source	Date Signed	Seasons Played	Apps	Subs	Gls
Manchester C.	Jnrs	07.75	75-78	116	3	0
Oldham Ath.	Tr	09.79	79-84	204	2	2
Manchester C.	Tr	03.85	84-87	104	2	1
Bury	Tr	03.88	87-89	66	15	1
Shrewsbury T.		10.90	90	19	1	0

CLEMENTS, Paul R.
Greenwich, 7 November, 1946 E Amat (M)

League Club	Source	Date Signed	Seasons Played	Apps	Subs	Gls
Oldham Ath.	Skelmersdale U.	06.71	71-72	32	3	0

CLEMENTS, Stanley F.
Portsmouth, 25 June, 1923 (CH)

League Club	Source	Date Signed	Seasons Played	Apps	Subs	Gls
Southampton	Gosport Bor.	07.44	46-54	116	-	1

League Club	Source	Date Signed	Seasons Played	Career Record Apps	Subs	Gls

CLEMPSON, Frank
Salford, 27 May, 1930 (IF)

League Club	Source	Date Signed	Seasons Played	Apps	Subs	Gls
Manchester U.		09.48	49-52	15	-	2
Stockport Co.	Tr	02.53	52-58	246	-	36
Chester C.	Tr	07.59	59-60	69	-	7

CLEWLOW, Sidney J.
Wallasey, 8 November, 1919 (WH)

League Club	Source	Date Signed	Seasons Played	Apps	Subs	Gls
New Brighton	Poulton Vic.	02.39				
Wolverhampton W.	Tr	05.39				
New Brighton	Tr	08.46	46	1	-	0

CLEWS, Malcolm D.
Tipton, 12 March, 1931 (OL)

League Club	Source	Date Signed	Seasons Played	Apps	Subs	Gls
Wolverhampton W.	Jnrs	03.48	51	1	-	0
Lincoln C.	Tr	02.54	53-54	7	-	0

CLIFF, Edward
Liverpool, 30 September, 1951 (FB)

League Club	Source	Date Signed	Seasons Played	Apps	Subs	Gls
Burnley	App	10.68	70-72	21	0	0
Notts Co.	Tr	09.73	73	5	0	0
Lincoln C.	L	10.74	74	3	0	0
Tranmere Rov.	Chicago (USA)	09.76	76-78	44	6	4
Rochdale	Tr	09.79	79-80	25	1	0

CLIFF, John G.
Middlesbrough, 7 November, 1946 (F)

League Club	Source	Date Signed	Seasons Played	Apps	Subs	Gls
Middlesbrough	App	11.63				
Halifax T.	Tr	07.66	66	1	0	0

CLIFF, Philip R.
Rotherham, 20 November, 1947 (W)

League Club	Source	Date Signed	Seasons Played	Apps	Subs	Gls
Sheffield U.	Jnrs	11.65	66-69	16	6	5
Chesterfield	Tr	02.71	70-72	30	1	2

CLIFFORD, Darren R.
Bristol, 2 November, 1966

League Club	Source	Date Signed	Seasons Played	Apps	Subs	Gls
Exeter C.	App	11.84	84	0	1	0

CLIFTON, Brian
Whitchurch (Hants), 15 March, 1934 (WH)

League Club	Source	Date Signed	Seasons Played	Apps	Subs	Gls
Southampton	Whitchurch	02.53	57-62	111	-	35
Grimsby T.	Tr	10.62	62-65	104	0	5

CLIFTON, Bryan
Doncaster, 13 February, 1939 (WH)

League Club	Source	Date Signed	Seasons Played	Apps	Subs	Gls
Doncaster Rov.		10.58	58	2	-	0

CLIFTON, Henry
Newburn, 28 May, 1914 (IF)

League Club	Source	Date Signed	Seasons Played	Apps	Subs	Gls
Chesterfield	Scotswood	08.33	33-37	122	-	66
Newcastle U.	Tr	06.38	38	29	-	15
Grimsby T.	Tr	02.46	46-48	69	-	23

CLINCH, Peter
Coventry, 15 October, 1950 (CH)

League Club	Source	Date Signed	Seasons Played	Apps	Subs	Gls
Oxford U.	App	08.69	69	2	0	0

CLINTON, Thomas J.
Dublin, 13 April, 1926 IR-3 (FB)

League Club	Source	Date Signed	Seasons Played	Apps	Subs	Gls
Everton	Dundalk	03.48	48-53	73	-	4
Blackburn Rov.	Tr	04.55	55	6	-	0
Tranmere Rov.	Tr	06.56	56	9	-	0

CLISH, Colin
Newcastle, 14 January, 1944 (LB)

League Club	Source	Date Signed	Seasons Played	Apps	Subs	Gls
Newcastle U.	Jnrs	01.61	61-63	20	-	0
Rothetham U.	Tr	12.63	63-67	130	0	4
Doncaster Rov.	Tr	02.68	67-71	99	1	4

CLISH, Thomas P.
Wheatley Hill (Dm), 19 October, 1932 (G)

League Club	Source	Date Signed	Seasons Played	Apps	Subs	Gls
West Ham U.	Wheatley Hill	09.53				
Darlington	Tr	07.55	55-57	52	-	0

CLISS, Anthony
March, 22 September, 1959 (W)

League Club	Source	Date Signed	Seasons Played	Apps	Subs	Gls
Peterborough U.	Jnrs	08.77	77-82	65	20	11
Crewe Alex.	Tr	12.82	82-86	109	4	11

CLISS, David L.
Enfield, 15 November, 1939 E Yth (IF)

League Club	Source	Date Signed	Seasons Played	Apps	Subs	Gls
Chelsea	Jnrs	11.56	57-61	24	-	1

CLOSE, D. Brian
Rawdon, 24 February, 1931 E Yth (CF)

League Club	Source	Date Signed	Seasons Played	Apps	Subs	Gls
Leeds U.	Jnrs	02.49				
Arsenal	Tr	08.50				
Bradford C.	Tr	10.52	52	6	-	2

CLOSE, Shaun C.
Islington, 8 September, 1966 (F)

League Club	Source	Date Signed	Seasons Played	Apps	Subs	Gls
Tottenham H.	YT	08.84	86-87	3	6	0
Bournemouth	Tr	01.88	87-88	28	11	8
Swindon T.	Tr	09.89	89-91	12	25	1

CLOUGH, Brian H.
Middlesbrough, 21 March, 1935 Eu23-3/E'B'-1/EF Lge/E-2 (CF)

League Club	Source	Date Signed	Seasons Played	Apps	Subs	Gls
Middlesbrough	Great Broughton Jnrs	05.53	55-60	213	-	197
Sunderland	Tr	07.61	61-64	61	-	54

CLOUGH, James
Hazlerigg, 30 August, 1918 (OL)

League Club	Source	Date Signed	Seasons Played	Apps	Subs	Gls
Southport	Seaton Bum	02.39	38-46	45	-	11
Crystal Palace	Tr	09.47	47-48	67	-	12
Southend U.	Tr	05.49	49	34	-	7
Barrow	Tr	07.50	50	17	-	3

CLOUGH, Nigel H.
Sunderland, 19 March, 1966 Eu21-15/E'B'/EF Lge/E-7 (F)

League Club	Source	Date Signed	Seasons Played	Apps	Subs	Gls
Nottingham F.	Heanor T.	09.84	84-91	265	4	91

CLOVER, William
Bracknell, 19 February, 1920 (FB)

League Club	Source	Date Signed	Seasons Played	Apps	Subs	Gls
Reading		02.46	46-49	44	-	4

CLOWES, John A.
Alton (Staffs), 5 November, 1929 (F)

League Club	Source	Date Signed	Seasons Played	Apps	Subs	Gls
Stoke C.		06.59	50	2	-	2
Shrewsbury T.	Tr	06.52	52-53	11	-	2
Stoke C.	Wellington T.	08.55	55	2	-	0

CLUGSTON, James E.
Belfast, 30 October, 1934 NISch (F)

League Club	Source	Date Signed	Seasons Played	Apps	Subs	Gls
Liverpool	Distillery	01.52				
Portsmouth	Glentoran	01.57	56	1	-	0

CLUNIE, James R.
Kirkcaldy, 4 September, 1933 (CH)

League Club	Source	Date Signed	Seasons Played	Apps	Subs	Gls
Bury	St Mirren	07.65	65	10	0	0

CLUROE, Malcolm
Nottingham, 6 February, 1935 (IF)

League Club	Source	Date Signed	Seasons Played	Apps	Subs	Gls
Nottingham F.		11.54	54	1	-	0

CLUTTON, Nigel K.
Chester, 12 February, 1954 (F)

League Club	Source	Date Signed	Seasons Played	Apps	Subs	Gls
Chester C. (N/C)		12.77	77	1	0	0

CLYDESDALE, William
Stirling, 14 September, 1935 (FB)

League Club	Source	Date Signed	Seasons Played	Apps	Subs	Gls
Hartlepool U.	Aberdeen	08.60	60	14	-	0

COADY, John
Dublin, 25 August, 1960 (M)

League Club	Source	Date Signed	Seasons Played	Apps	Subs	Gls
Chelsea	Shamrock Rov.	12.86	86-87	9	7	2

COADY, Michael L.
Dipton (Dm), 1 October, 1958 (D)

League Club	Source	Date Signed	Seasons Played	Apps	Subs	Gls
Sunderland	App	07.76	76-79	4	2	0
Carlisle U.	Tr	07.80	80-81	48	3	1
Wolverhampton W.	Sydney Olympics	01.85	84-85	14	1	1

COAK, Timothy D. T.
Southampton, 16 January, 1958 (LB)

League Club	Source	Date Signed	Seasons Played	Apps	Subs	Gls
Southampton	App	01.76	76-77	4	0	0

COAKLEY, Thomas
Bellshill, 2 May, 1947 (OR)

League Club	Source	Date Signed	Seasons Played	Apps	Subs	Gls
Arsenal	Motherwell	05.66	66	9	0	1

COATES, David P.
Newcastle, 11 April, 1935 (WH)

League Club	Source	Date Signed	Seasons Played	Apps	Subs	Gls
Hull C.	Shiney Row	10.52	56-59	62	-	13
Mansfield T.	Tr	03.60	59-63	159	-	17
Notts Co.	Tr	07.64	64-66	66	0	1

Brian Clough Middlesbrough, Sunderland & England)

COATES, Frank
Farrington, 16 April, 1922 (OR)

League Club	Source	Date Signed	Seasons Played	Apps	Subs	Gls
Blackburn Rov.	Leyland Motors	01.43				
Accrington St.	Leyland Motors	01.48	47	4	-	0

COATES, John A.
Limehouse, 13 May, 1920 (OR)

League Club	Source	Date Signed	Seasons Played	Apps	Subs	Gls
Crystal Palace (Am.)		08.46	46	4	-	0

COATES, John A.
Southport, 3 June, 1944 (G)

League Club	Source	Date Signed	Seasons Played	Apps	Subs	Gls
Southport	Burscough	02.65	64	5	-	0
Chester C.	Tr	08.66	66	1	0	0
Southport (N/C)	Morecambe	07.76	76	16	0	0

COATES, Ralph
Hetton-le-Hole, 26 April, 1946 Eu23-8/EF Lge/E-4 (M/W)

League Club	Source	Date Signed	Seasons Played	Apps	Subs	Gls
Burnley	App	06.63	64-70	214	2	26
Tottenham H.	Tr	05.71	71-77	173	15	14
Leyton Orient	St Georges (Aus)	10.78	78-80	76	0	12

COATSWORTH, Frederick W.
Lincoln, 5 July, 1948 (F)

League Club	Source	Date Signed	Seasons Played	Apps	Subs	Gls
Scunthorpe U.	Jnrs	07.65	65-66	15	0	2

COATSWORTH, Gary
Sunderland, 7 October, 1968 (M/FB)

League Club	Source	Date Signed	Seasons Played	Apps	Subs	Gls
Barnsley	Jnrs	02.87	87	3	3	0
Darlington	Tr	08.89	90-91	15	7	2
Leicester C.	Tr	10.91	91	2	1	0

COATSWORTH, John
Newcastle, 21 May, 1933

League Club	Source	Date Signed	Seasons Played	Apps	Subs	Gls
Gateshead	Crook T.	03.57	56	16	-	4

COBB, Gary E.
Luton, 6 August, 1968 (W)

League Club	Source	Date Signed	Seasons Played	Apps	Subs	Gls
Luton T.	App	08.86	86-87	6	3	0
Northampton T.	L	10.88	88	1	0	0
Swansea C.	L	08.89	89	5	0	0
Fulham	Tr	08.90	90-91	8	14	0

COBB, Paul M.
Aveley, 13 December, 1972 (F)

League Club	Source	Date Signed	Seasons Played	Apps	Subs	Gls
Leyton Orient	Purfleet	11.90	90-91	3	2	0

COBB, William W.
Newark, 29 September, 1940 (IF)

League Club	Source	Date Signed	Seasons Played	Apps	Subs	Gls
Nottingham F.	Ransome & Marles	09.59	60-62	30	-	5
Plymouth Arg.	Tr	10.63	63-64	31	-	0
Brentford	Tr	10.64	64-66	69	2	23
Lincoln C.	Tr	11.66	66-67	67	0	10

COCHRAN, Albert G.
Ebbw Vale, 26 November, 1939 (G)

League Club	Source	Date Signed	Seasons Played	Apps	Subs	Gls
Plymouth Arg.	Ilford	09.59				
Leyton Orient	Tr	07.60	60	1	-	0

COCHRANE, Alan
Belfast, 16 March, 1956 (W)

League Club	Source	Date Signed	Seasons Played	Apps	Subs	Gls
Shrewsbury T.	App	03.74	73-74	3	0	0

COCHRANE, Colin
Sutton-in-Ashfield, 26 August, 1921 (IF)

League Club	Source	Date Signed	Seasons Played	Apps	Subs	Gls
Mansfield T.		09.47	47	1	-	0

COCHRANE, David
Portadown (NI), 14 August, 1920 NI-12 (OR)

League Club	Source	Date Signed	Seasons Played	Apps	Subs	Gls
Leeds U.	Portadown	08.37	37-50	172	-	28

COCHRANE, George N.
Glasgow, 27 February, 1931 (IF)

League Club	Source	Date Signed	Seasons Played	Apps	Subs	Gls
New Brighton	Arthurlie	07.50	50	2	-	0

COCHRANE, Hugh
Glasgow, 9 February, 1943 (IF)

League Club	Source	Date Signed	Seasons Played	Apps	Subs	Gls
Barnsley	Dundee U.	08.63	63	5	-	0

COCHRANE, James
Brierley Hill, 26 October, 1935 (IF)

League Club	Source	Date Signed	Seasons Played	Apps	Subs	Gls
Birmingham C.	Jnrs	10.52	52-53	3	-	1
Walsall	Tr	06.58	58	6	-	1

COCHRANE, James K.
Glasgow, 14 January, 1954 (LB)

League Club	Source	Date Signed	Seasons Played	Apps	Subs	Gls
Middlesbrough	Drumchapel	05.71	73	3	0	0
Darlington	Tr	02.75	74-79	222	1	5
Torquay U.	Tr	08.80	80	16	0	0

COCHRANE, John
Bellshill, 27 April, 1959 (F)

League Club	Source	Date Signed	Seasons Played	Apps	Subs	Gls
Preston N. E.	App	02.77	76-78	3	2	2

COCHRANE, John J.
Belfast, 11 May, 1944 (W)

League Club	Source	Date Signed	Seasons Played	Apps	Subs	Gls
Brighton & H. A.	Jnrs	10.61	61-62	14	-	3
Exeter C.	Tr	08.63	63	2	-	0

COCHRANE, G. Terence
Killyleagh (NI), 23 January, 1953 NI-26 (W)

League Club	Source	Date Signed	Seasons Played	Apps	Subs	Gls
Burnley	Coleraine	10.76	76-78	62	5	13
Middlesbrough	Tr	10.78	78-82	96	15	7
Gillingham	Tr	10.83	83-85	105	2	17
Millwall (N/C)	Dallas (USA)	11.86	86	1	0	0
Hartlepool U. (N/C)	Tr	01.87	86	2	0	0

COCKBURN, Henry
Ashton-u-Lyne, 14 September, 1923 E'B'-1/EF Lge/E-13 (WH)

League Club	Source	Date Signed	Seasons Played	Apps	Subs	Gls
Manchester U.	Goslings	08.44	46-54	243	-	4
Bury	Tr	10.54	54-55	35	-	0

COCKBURN, Keith
Barnsley, 2 September, 1942 (OL)

League Club	Source	Date Signed	Seasons Played	Apps	Subs	Gls
Barnsley	Jnrs	11.66	66	1	0	0
Bradford P. A.	Tr	07.68	68	16	0	1
Grimsby T.	Tr	01.69	68-69	15	4	2

COCKBURN, William R.
Shotton, 3 May, 1937 (WH)

League Club	Source	Date Signed	Seasons Played	Apps	Subs	Gls
Burnley	Murton Jnrs	08.55				
Gillingham	Tr	06.60	60-61	62	-	1

COCKCROFT, Victor H.
Birmingham, 25 February, 1941 E Yth (FB)

League Club	Source	Date Signed	Seasons Played	Apps	Subs	Gls
Wolverhampton W.	Jnrs	12.59				
Northampton T.	Tr	07.62	62-66	45	1	1
Rochdale	Tr	06.67	67	42	0	0

COCKELL, David J.
Ashford, 1 February, 1939 (WH)

League Club	Source	Date Signed	Seasons Played	Apps	Subs	Gls
Queens Park R	Hounslow	08.60	60-61	9	-	0

COCKER, Leslie
Stockport, 13 March, 1924 Died 1979 (F)

League Club	Source	Date Signed	Seasons Played	Apps	Subs	Gls
Stockport Co.		08.47	46-52	173	-	42
Accrington St.	Tr	08.53	53-57	122	-	48

COCKER, Leslie J.
Wolverhampton, 18 September, 1939 E Yth (WH)

League Club	Source	Date Signed	Seasons Played	Apps	Subs	Gls
Wolverhampton W.	Jnrs	06.58	60	1	-	0

COCKERILL, Glenn
Grimsby, 25 August, 1959 (M)

League Club	Source	Date Signed	Seasons Played	Apps	Subs	Gls
Lincoln C.	Louth U.	11.76	76-79	65	6	10
Swindon T.	Tr	12.79	79-80	23	3	1
Lincoln C.	Tr	08.81	81-83	114	1	25
Sheffield U.	Tr	03.84	83-85	62	0	10
Southampton	Tr	10.85	85-91	239	11	32

COCKERILL, John
Grimsby, 12 July, 1961 (M)

League Club	Source	Date Signed	Seasons Played	Apps	Subs	Gls
Grimsby T.	Stafford R.	08.88	88-91	99	8	19

COCKERILL, Ronald
Sheffield, 28 February, 1935 (WH)

League Club	Source	Date Signed	Seasons Played	Apps	Subs	Gls
Huddersfield T.	Jnrs	05.52	55-57	40	-	1
Grimsby T.	Tr	08.58	58-67	293	1	28

COCKHILL, Andrew J.
Altrincham, 11 October, 1967 (F)

League Club	Source	Date Signed	Seasons Played	Apps	Subs	Gls
Stockport Co.	Derby Co. (YT)	08.86	86	3	0	0

COCKRAM, Allan C.
Kensington, 8 October, 1963 (W)

League Club	Source	Date Signed	Seasons Played	Apps	Subs	Gls
Tottenham H.	App	01.81	83	2	0	0
Bristol Rov. (N/C)	Tr	08.85	85	1	0	0
Brentford	St Albans C.	03.88	87-90	66	24	14
Reading (N/C)	Woking	10.91	91	2	4	1

COCKROFT, Hubert
Barnsley, 21 November, 1918 (LH)

League Club	Source	Date Signed	Seasons Played	Apps	Subs	Gls
Barnsley		06.38				
Bradford C.		05.46	46	27	-	0
Halifax T.	Tr	07.47	47	10	-	1
Bradford C.	Peterborough U.	05.50				

COCKROFT, Joseph
Barnsley, 20 June, 1911 (WH)

League Club	Source	Date Signed	Seasons Played	Apps	Subs	Gls
Rotherham U.	Wombwell	02.31	30-31	3	-	1
West Ham U.	Gainsborough Trin.	03.33	32-38	251	-	3
Sheffield Wed.	Dartford	11.45	46-48	87	-	2
Sheffield U.	Tr	11.48	48	12	-	0

COCKS, Alan W.
Burscough, 7 May, 1951 (CF)

League Club	Source	Date Signed	Seasons Played	Apps	Subs	Gls
Chelsea	App	04.69				
Brentford	L	01.70	69	11	0	2
Southport	Tr	07.70	70	24	1	7

CODD, Ronald W.
Sheffield, 3 December, 1928 (OR)

League Club	Source	Date Signed	Seasons Played	Apps	Subs	Gls
Bolton W.	Meynell Y.C.	03.50	50-53	31	-	5
Sheffield Wed.	L	03.53	52	2	-	0
Barrow	Tr	10.54	54-55	45	-	11

CODDINGTON, John W.
Worksop, 16 December, 1937 (CH)

League Club	Source	Date Signed	Seasons Played	Apps	Subs	Gls
Huddersfield T.	Jnrs	01.55	55-66	332	0	17
Blackburn Rov.	Tr	06.67	67-69	72	1	3
Stockport Co.	Tr	01.70	69-70	52	0	0

CODNER, Robert A. G.
Walthamstow, 23 January, 1965 (M)

League Club	Source	Date Signed	Seasons Played	Apps	Subs	Gls
Leicester C.	Tottenham H. (Jnrs)	09.83				
Brighton & H. A.	Barnet	09.88	88-91	153	7	24

COE, Norman C.
Swansea, 6 December, 1940 (G)

League Club	Source	Date Signed	Seasons Played	Apps	Subs	Gls
Arsenal	Jnrs	08.58				
Northampton T.	Tr	07.60	60-65	58	0	0

COEN, R. W. Lawrence
Lowestoft, 4 December, 1914 Died 1972 E Sch (LB)

League Club	Source	Date Signed	Seasons Played	Apps	Subs	Gls
West Bromwich A.	Milford Haven	10.32	36	7	-	4
Coventry C.	Tr	06.38	38-47	20	-	3

COFFEY, Michael J. J.
Liverpool, 29 September, 1958 (M)

League Club	Source	Date Signed	Seasons Played	Apps	Subs	Gls
Everton	App	07.76				
Mansfield T.	Tr	07.78	78	2	1	0

COFFILL, Peter T.
Romford, 14 February, 1957 (W)

League Club	Source	Date Signed	Seasons Played	Apps	Subs	Gls
Watford	App	02.75	75-77	56	7	6
Torquay U.	Tr	11.77	77-80	101	21	11
Northampton T.	Tr	07.81	81-82	64	5	3

COFFIN, Geoffrey W.
Chester, 17 August, 1924 (CF)

League Club	Source	Date Signed	Seasons Played	Apps	Subs	Gls
Chester C.		05.47	47-54	150	-	35

COGGINS, Philip R.
Bristol, 10 July, 1940 (OR)

League Club	Source	Date Signed	Seasons Played	Apps	Subs	Gls
Bristol C.		10.58	59	4	-	0
Bristol Rov.	Tr	07.60	60	4	-	0

COGLAN, Alan
Barrow, 14 December, 1936 Died 1987 (G)

League Club	Source	Date Signed	Seasons Played	Apps	Subs	Gls
Barrow	Jnrs	04.54	53-61	51	-	0

COHEN, Avi
Israel, 14 November, 1956 Israel Int (LB)

League Club	Source	Date Signed	Seasons Played	Apps	Subs	Gls
Liverpool	Macabbi Tel Aviv (Isr)	07.79	79-80	16	2	1

COHEN, George R.
Kensington, 22 October, 1939 Eu23-8/EF Lge/E-37 (RB)

League Club	Source	Date Signed	Seasons Played	Apps	Subs	Gls
Fulham	Jnrs	10.56	56-68	408	0	6

COHEN, Jacob
Israel, 25 September, 1956 Israel Int (LB)

League Club	Source	Date Signed	Seasons Played	Apps	Subs	Gls
Brighton & H. A.	Macabbi Tel Aviv (Isr)	10.80	80	3	3	0

COKER, Ade O.
Nigeria, 19 May, 1954 (F)

League Club	Source	Date Signed	Seasons Played	Apps	Subs	Gls
West Ham U.	App	12.71	71-73	9	1	3
Lincoln C.	L	12.74	74	6	0	1

COLBOURNE, Neil
Swinton, 25 August, 1956 (G)

League Club	Source	Date Signed	Seasons Played	Apps	Subs	Gls
Rochdale (N/C)	Hyde U.	03.80	79	1	0	0

COLBRIDGE, Clive
Hull, 27 April, 1934 (OL)

League Club	Source	Date Signed	Seasons Played	Apps	Subs	Gls
Leeds U.	Hull C. (Am)	05.52				
York C.	Tr	05.55	55-57	37	-	14
Workington	Tr	09.57	57-58	46	-	8
Crewe Alex.	Tr	10.58	58	29	-	8
Manchester C.	Tr	05.59	59-61	62	-	12
Wrexham	Tr	02.62	61-64	108	-	33

COLCOMBE, Scott
West Bromwich, 15 December, 1971 (W)

League Club	Source	Date Signed	Seasons Played	Apps	Subs	Gls
West Bromwich A.	YT	07.90				
Torquay U.	Tr	08.91	91	21	7	0

COLDRICK, Graham G.
Newport, 6 November, 1945 W Sch/Wu23-2 (D)

League Club	Source	Date Signed	Seasons Played	Apps	Subs	Gls
Cardiff C.	App	11.62	63-69	91	5	2
Newport Co.	Tr	03.70	69-74	156	1	10

COLDWELL, G. Cecil
Sheffield, 16 January, 1929 (RB)

League Club	Source	Date Signed	Seasons Played	Apps	Subs	Gls
Sheffield U.	Norton Woodseats	09.51	51-66	409	1	2

COLE, Andrew A.
Nottingham, 15 October, 1971 E Sch/E Yth/Eu21-3 (F)

League Club	Source	Date Signed	Seasons Played	Apps	Subs	Gls
Arsenal	YT	10.89	90	0	1	0
Fulham	L	09.91	91	13	0	3
Bristol C.	L	03.92	91	12	0	8

COLE, David A.
Barnsley, 28 September, 1962 (CD)

League Club	Source	Date Signed	Seasons Played	Apps	Subs	Gls
Sunderland		10.83				
Swansea C.	Tr	09.84	84	7	1	0
Swindon T.	Tr	02.85	84-86	69	0	3
Torquay U.	Tr	11.86	86-88	107	3	6
Rochdale	Tr	07.89	89-90	73	11	6
Exeter C.	Tr	08.91	91	0	2	0

COLE, G. Douglas
Heswall, 2 July, 1916 Died 1959 (D)

League Club	Source	Date Signed	Seasons Played	Apps	Subs	Gls
Sheffield U.		05.37	37	1	-	0
Chester C.	Tr	05.39	46-47	21	-	0

COLE, James E.
Wrexham, 14 August, 1925 (RB)

League Club	Source	Date Signed	Seasons Played	Apps	Subs	Gls
Bolton W.	Wrexham (Am)	05.47				
Chester C.	Tr	08.49	49	1	-	0

COLE, Michael E.
Ilford, 9 June, 1937 (FB)

League Club	Source	Date Signed	Seasons Played	Apps	Subs	Gls
Norwich C.	Harwich & Parkeston	08.56	55-57	3	-	0

COLE, Michael W.
Stepney, 3 September, 1966 (F)

League Club	Source	Date Signed	Seasons Played	Apps	Subs	Gls
Ipswich T.	App	11.83	84-87	24	14	3
Port Vale	L	01.88	87	4	0	1
Fulham	Tr	03.88	87-90	45	3	4

COLE, Roy
Barnsley, 8 December, 1953 (CD)

League Club	Source	Date Signed	Seasons Played	Apps	Subs	Gls
Barnsley	App	12.71	71-73	6	0	0

COLEMAN, Anthony G.
Liverpool, 2 May, 1945 (OL)

League Club	Source	Date Signed	Seasons Played	Apps	Subs	Gls
Tranmere Rov.	Stoke C. (App)	10.62	62-63	8	-	0
Preston N. E.	Tr	05.64	64	5	-	1
Doncaster Rov.	Bangor C.	11.65	65-66	58	0	11
Manchester C.	Tr	03.67	66-69	82	1	12
Sheffield Wed.	Tr	10.69	69	25	1	2
Blackpool	Tr	08.70	70	17	0	0
Southport	Durban C. (SA)	11.73	73	22	1	1
Stockport Co.	Tr	06.74	74-75	28	2	3

COLEMAN, Christopher
Swansea, 10 June, 1970 W Sch/W Yth/Wu21-3/W-1 (LB)

League Club	Source	Date Signed	Seasons Played	Apps	Subs	Gls
Swansea C.	Manchester C. (Jnrs)	08.87	87-90	159	1	2
Crystal Palace	Tr	07.91	91	14	4	4

COLEMAN, David H.
Salisbury, 8 April, 1967 (LB)

League Club	Source	Date Signed	Seasons Played	Apps	Subs	Gls
Bournemouth	Jnrs	09.84	85-90	40	10	2
Colchester U.	L	02.88	87	6	0	1

League Club	Source	Date Signed	Seasons Played	Apps	Subs	Gls

COLEMAN, David J.
Colchester, 27 March, 1942 (F)

League Club	Source	Date Signed	Seasons Played	Apps	Subs	Gls
Colchester U.	Harwich & Parkeston	11.61	61-62	2	-	1

COLEMAN, Edward P.
Middlesbrough, 23 September, 1957 (F)

League Club	Source	Date Signed	Seasons Played	Apps	Subs	Gls
Middlesbrough	App	09.75	75	1	0	0
Workington	L	03.77	76	10	2	1

COLEMAN, Geoffrey J.
Bedworth, 13 May, 1936 (FB)

League Club	Source	Date Signed	Seasons Played	Apps	Subs	Gls
Northampton T.	Bedworth T.	05.55	55-58	18	-	0

COLEMAN, Gordon M.
Nottingham, 11 February, 1954 (M)

League Club	Source	Date Signed	Seasons Played	Apps	Subs	Gls
Preston N. E.	Padstow Y.C.	09.73	73-82	248	21	25
Bury	Tr	08.83	83	24	5	0

COLEMAN, John H.
Nottingham, 3 March, 1946 (WH)

League Club	Source	Date Signed	Seasons Played	Apps	Subs	Gls
Nottingham F.	Jnrs	03.63				
Mansfield T.	Tr	08.66	66-67	43	0	1
York C.	Tr	07.68	68	8	3	3

COLEMAN, Keith
Washington, 24 May, 1951 (FB)

League Club	Source	Date Signed	Seasons Played	Apps	Subs	Gls
Sunderland	App	06.68	71-72	49	0	2
West Ham U.	Tr	09.73	73-76	96	5	0
Darlington	K.V. Mechelen (Bel)	07.79	79	25	0	0

COLEMAN, Neville J.
Baschurch, 29 January, 1930 (OR)

League Club	Source	Date Signed	Seasons Played	Apps	Subs	Gls
Stoke C.	Gorleston	01.55	53-58	114	-	46
Crewe Alex.	Tr	02.59	58-60	73	-	16

COLEMAN, Nicholas
Crayford, 6 May, 1966 (LB)

League Club	Source	Date Signed	Seasons Played	Apps	Subs	Gls
Millwall	App	01.84	84-89	87	1	0
Swindon T.	L	09.85	85	13	0	4

COLEMAN, Philip
Woolwich, 8 September, 1960 (D)

League Club	Source	Date Signed	Seasons Played	Apps	Subs	Gls
Millwall	App	08.78	78-80	23	13	1
Colchester U.	Tr	02.81	80-83	82	4	6
Wrexham	L	09.83	83	17	0	2
Exeter C. (N/C)	Chelmsford C.	12.84	84	6	0	0
Aldershot	Tr	02.85	84-85	45	0	5
Millwall	Dulwich Hamlet	09.86	86	8	2	0
Colchester U. (N/C)	Finland	12.88	88	6	4	0

COLEMAN, Simon
Worksop, 13 March, 1968 (CD)

League Club	Source	Date Signed	Seasons Played	Apps	Subs	Gls
Mansfield T.	Jnrs	07.85	86-89	96	0	7
Middlesbrough	Tr	09.89	89-90	51	4	2
Derby Co.	Tr	08.91	91	43	0	2

COLES, Arthur
Crediton, 28 January, 1914 (D)

League Club	Source	Date Signed	Seasons Played	Apps	Subs	Gls
Exeter C.	Copplestone	06.37	37-48	16	-	0

COLES, David A.
Wandsworth, 15 June, 1964 (G)

League Club	Source	Date Signed	Seasons Played	Apps	Subs	Gls
Birmingham C.	App	04.82				
Mansfield T.	Tr	03.83	82	3	0	0
Aldershot	Tr	08.83	83-87	120	0	0
Newport Co.	L	01.88	87	14	0	0
Brighton & H.A. (N/C)	H.J.K. Helsinki (Fin)	02.89	88	1	0	0
Aldershot	Tr	07.89	89-90	30	0	0
Fulham	Tr	08.91				

COLES, James E.
(RB)

League Club	Source	Date Signed	Seasons Played	Apps	Subs	Gls
Chester C.		08.49	49	1	-	0

COLEY, William E.
Wolverhampton, 17 September, 1916 (WH)

League Club	Source	Date Signed	Seasons Played	Apps	Subs	Gls
Wolverhampton W.	Jnrs	09.33	36	2	-	0
Bournemouth	Tr	09.37	37	13	-	0
Torquay U.	Tr	07.38	38-46	61	-	2
Northampton T.	Tr	08.47	47-50	105	-	7
Exeter C.	Tr	07.51	51	8	-	0

COLFAR, Raymond J.
Liverpool, 4 December, 1935 (OL)

League Club	Source	Date Signed	Seasons Played	Apps	Subs	Gls
Crystal Palace	Sutton U.	11.58	58-60	41	-	6
Oxford U.	Cambridge U.	08.62	62-63	18	-	4

COLGAN, Walter
Castleford, 3 April, 1937 (FB)

League Club	Source	Date Signed	Seasons Played	Apps	Subs	Gls
Queens Park R	Ashley Road	07.54	57-58	3	-	0

COLKIN, Lee
Nuneaton, 15 July, 1974 (CD)

League Club	Source	Date Signed	Seasons Played	Apps	Subs	Gls
Northampton T.	YT	07.90	91	2	1	0

COLL, William S. (Liam)
Carrick, 16 December, 1929 (OR)

League Club	Source	Date Signed	Seasons Played	Apps	Subs	Gls
Accrington St.		08.49	49-50	13	-	0

COLLARD, J. Bruce
Hetton-le-Hole, 21 August, 1953 (CD)

League Club	Source	Date Signed	Seasons Played	Apps	Subs	Gls
West Bromwich A.	App	05.71				
Scunthorpe U.	Tr	07.73	73	21	1	0

COLLARD, Ian
Hetton-le-Hole, 31 August, 1947 (M)

League Club	Source	Date Signed	Seasons Played	Apps	Subs	Gls
West Bromwich A.	App	11.64	64-68	63	6	7
Ipswich T.	Tr	05.69	69-74	83	9	5
Portsmouth	L	09.75	75	1	0	0

COLLETON, Anthony
Manchester, 17 January, 1974

League Club	Source	Date Signed	Seasons Played	Apps	Subs	Gls
Rochdale (YT)	YT	07.90	90	0	1	0

COLLETT, Ernest
Sheffield, 17 November, 1914 Died 1980 (WH)

League Club	Source	Date Signed	Seasons Played	Apps	Subs	Gls
Arsenal	Oughtbridge W.M.C.	04.33	37-46	20	-	0

COLLIER, Alan S.
Markyate, 24 March, 1938 E Sch/E Yth (G)

League Club	Source	Date Signed	Seasons Played	Apps	Subs	Gls
Luton T.	Jnrs	05.55	58-60	10	-	0

COLLIER, Austin
Dewsbury, 24 July, 1914 (WH)

League Club	Source	Date Signed	Seasons Played	Apps	Subs	Gls
Mansfield T.	Frickley Colly	05.38	38	21	-	0
York C.	Tr	05.39	46	10	-	0
Rochdale	Queen of South	04.47	46-47	6	-	0
Halifax T.	Tr	11.47	47	1	-	0

COLLIER, Darren
Stockton, 1 December, 1967 (G)

League Club	Source	Date Signed	Seasons Played	Apps	Subs	Gls
Blackburn Rov.	Middlesbrough (N/C)	12.87	88-90	27	0	0

COLLIER, David
Colwyn Bay, 2 October, 1957 (FB)

League Club	Source	Date Signed	Seasons Played	Apps	Subs	Gls
Shrewsbury T.	App	10.75	74-76	20	0	4
Crewe Alex.	Tr	08.77	77	24	2	1

COLLIER, Gary B.
Bristol, 4 February, 1955 (CD)

League Club	Source	Date Signed	Seasons Played	Apps	Subs	Gls
Bristol C.	App	11.72	72-78	193	0	3
Coventry C.	Tr	07.79	79	2	0	0

COLLIER, Geoffrey
Blackpool, 25 July, 1950 (F)

League Club	Source	Date Signed	Seasons Played	Apps	Subs	Gls
Notts Co.	Macclesfield T.	07.73	73	0	3	0

COLLIER, Graham R.
Nottingham, 12 September, 1951 (M)

League Club	Source	Date Signed	Seasons Played	Apps	Subs	Gls
Nottingham F.	App	03.69	69-70	13	2	2
Scunthorpe U.	Tr	07.72	72-76	155	6	19
Barnsley	Tr	08.77	77	22	2	2
York C.	Buxton	09.78	78	5	0	0

COLLIER, James R.
Stockport, 24 August, 1952 (M)

League Club	Source	Date Signed	Seasons Played	Apps	Subs	Gls
Stockport Co.	App	03.70	68-73	99	5	11

COLLINDRIDGE, Colin
Barnsley, 15 November, 1920 (OL)

League Club	Source	Date Signed	Seasons Played	Apps	Subs	Gls
Sheffield U.	Barugh Green	01.39	46-49	142	-	52
Nottingham F.	Tr	08.50	50-53	151	-	45
Coventry C.	Tr	06.54	54-55	34	-	6

COLLINGS, Paul W.
Liverpool, 30 September, 1968 (G)

League Club	Source	Date Signed	Seasons Played	Apps	Subs	Gls
Tranmere Rov.	Ellesmere Port	08.88	88-90	4	0	0

COLLINGWOOD, Graham
South Kirkby, 8 December, 1954 (M)

League Club	Source	Date Signed	Seasons Played	Apps	Subs	Gls
Barnsley	App	12.72	73-74	12	2	0

COLLINS, Albert D.
Chesterfield, 15 April, 1923 (W)

League Club	Source	Date Signed	Seasons Played	Apps	Subs	Gls
Chesterfield	Jnrs	01.41	46	8	-	0
Halifax T.	Tr	11.46	46-47	44	-	10
Carlisle U.	Tr	02.48	47-48	20	-	3
Barrow	Tr	12.48	48-49	55	-	7
Bournemouth	Tr	08.50	50	5	-	1
Shrewsbury T.	Tr	08.51	51	9	-	2
Accrington St.	Tr	07.52	52	17	-	2

COLLINS, Andrew B.
Carlisle, 20 October, 1958 (FB)

League Club	Source	Date Signed	Seasons Played	Apps	Subs	Gls
Carlisle U.	Carlisle Spartans	09.77	77-81	47	7	1

COLLINS, Anthony N.
Kensington, 19 March, 1926 (IF)

League Club	Source	Date Signed	Seasons Played	Apps	Subs	Gls
Sheffield Wed.	Brentford (Am)	11.47				
York C.	Tr	07.49	49	10	-	1
Watford	Tr	08.50	50-52	90	-	8
Norwich C.	Tr	07.53	53-54	29	-	2
Torquay U.	Tr	07.55	55-56	89	-	17
Watford	Tr	07.57	57	17	-	1
Crystal Palace	Tr	11.57	57-58	55	-	14
Rochdale	Tr	06.59	59-60	47	-	5

COLLINS, Benjamin V.
Kislingbury, 9 March, 1928 (CH)

League Club	Source	Date Signed	Seasons Played	Apps	Subs	Gls
Northampton T.	Jnrs	04.48	48-58	213	-	0

COLLINS, Darren
Winchester, 24 May, 1967 (F)

League Club	Source	Date Signed	Seasons Played	Apps	Subs	Gls
Northampton T.	Petersfield U.	01.89	88-90	40	11	9

COLLINS, David D.
Dublin, 30 October, 1971 (M)

League Club	Source	Date Signed	Seasons Played	Apps	Subs	Gls
Liverpool	YT	11.88				
Wigan Ath.	L	01.92	91	9	0	0

COLLINS, J. Douglas
Doncaster, 28 August, 1945 (M)

League Club	Source	Date Signed	Seasons Played	Apps	Subs	Gls
Grimsby T.	Rotherham U. (App)	06.63	63-68	96	7	9
Burnley	Tr	09.68	68-75	172	15	18
Plymouth Arg.	Tr	05.76	76	22	1	2
Sunderland	Tr	03.77	76-77	4	2	0
Rochdale	Tulsa (USA)	01.79	78	6	2	0

COLLINS, Eamonn A. S.
Dublin, 22 October, 1965 IR Yth (M)

League Club	Source	Date Signed	Seasons Played	Apps	Subs	Gls
Southampton	App	10.83	84	1	2	0
Portsmouth	Tr	05.86	86	4	1	0
Exeter C.	L	11.87	87	8	1	0
Colchester U.	Tr	05.89	89	39	0	2

COLLINS, George G.
Barry, 6 August, 1935 (CF)

League Club	Source	Date Signed	Seasons Played	Apps	Subs	Gls
Bristol Rov.	Ton Pentre	06.60	60	2	-	1

COLLINS, Glyn
Hereford, 18 January, 1946 (G)

League Club	Source	Date Signed	Seasons Played	Apps	Subs	Gls
Brighton & H.A.(Am)		03.66	65	2	0	0

COLLINS, Graham F.
Bury, 5 February, 1947 (HB)

League Club	Source	Date Signed	Seasons Played	Apps	Subs	Gls
Rochdale	Jnrs	09.65	65-66	7	1	0

COLLINS, James
Ayr, 21 December, 1937 (IF)

League Club	Source	Date Signed	Seasons Played	Apps	Subs	Gls
Tottenham H.	Lugar Boswell Th.	06.56	61	2	-	0
Brighton & H. A.	Tr	10.62	62-66	199	2	44

COLLINS, James K.
Colne, 7 November, 1923 (WH)

League Club	Source	Date Signed	Seasons Played	Apps	Subs	Gls
Barrow	Derby Co. (Am)	09.47	47-54	295	-	52
Chester C.	Tr	07.55	55-56	48	-	11

COLLINS, James P.
Urmston, 27 December, 1966 (RB)

League Club	Source	Date Signed	Seasons Played	Apps	Subs	Gls
Oldham Ath.	YT	08.84	83	0	1	0
Bury	Tr	10.86	86-87	10	1	0

COLLINS, Jeremy D.
Plymouth, 21 December, 1961 (M)

League Club	Source	Date Signed	Seasons Played	Apps	Subs	Gls
Plymouth Arg.	App	01.80	80-81	4	0	0
Torquay U.	Falmouth	08.83	83	6	0	0

COLLINS, John J.
Manchester, 30 January, 1945 (FB)

League Club	Source	Date Signed	Seasons Played	Apps	Subs	Gls
Blackburn Rov.	Jnrs	02.63				
Stockport Co.	Tr	01.64	63-65	83	0	1

COLLINS, John L.
Rhymney, 21 January, 1949 W Sch/Wu23-7 (FB)

League Club	Source	Date Signed	Seasons Played	Apps	Subs	Gls
Tottenham H.	App	03.66	65-67	2	0	0
Portsmouth	Tr	05.71	71-73	71	3	0
Halifax T.	Tr	08.74	74-75	82	0	1
Sheffield Wed.	Tr	07.76	76	7	0	0
Barnsley	Tr	12.76	76-79	128	1	1

COLLINS, John W.
Chiswick, 10 August, 1942 (IF)

League Club	Source	Date Signed	Seasons Played	Apps	Subs	Gls
Queens Park R	Jnrs	08.59	59-66	174	1	43
Oldham Ath.	Tr	10.66	66	20	1	8
Reading	Tr	08.67	67-68	82	3	28
Luton T.	Tr	08.69	69-70	40	2	10
Cambridge U.	Tr	02.71	70-72	93	4	16

COLLINS, Kenneth
Pontypridd, 11 October, 1933 (FB)

League Club	Source	Date Signed	Seasons Played	Apps	Subs	Gls
Fulham	Ynysybwl	05.52	55-58	32	-	0

COLLINS, Kevin
Birmingham, 21 July, 1964 (D)

League Club	Source	Date Signed	Seasons Played	Apps	Subs	Gls
Shrewsbury T.	Boldmere St Michael	01.84	83	1	0	0

COLLINS, Lyn
Neath, 30 April, 1948 (FB)

League Club	Source	Date Signed	Seasons Played	Apps	Subs	Gls
Newport Co.		06.66	66-67	17	0	0

COLLINS, R. Michael
Redcar, 8 June, 1933 (G)

League Club	Source	Date Signed	Seasons Played	Apps	Subs	Gls
Chelsea	Redcar	11.51	53	1	-	0
Watford	Tr	07.57	57-58	43	-	0

COLLINS, Michael A.
South Africa, 27 July, 1953 (F)

League Club	Source	Date Signed	Seasons Played	Apps	Subs	Gls
Wolverhampton W.	Jnrs	08.71				
Swindon T.	Stafford R.	07.73	73	2	4	0

COLLINS, Michael J. A.
Bermondsey, 1 February, 1938 (CH)

League Club	Source	Date Signed	Seasons Played	Apps	Subs	Gls
Luton T.	Jnrs	03.55	59-61	8	-	0

COLLINS, Paul
West Ham, 11 August, 1966 E Yth (M)

League Club	Source	Date Signed	Seasons Played	Apps	Subs	Gls
Gillingham	App	08.84	84-86	30	7	3

COLLINS, Peter J.
Chelmsford, 29 November, 1948 (CH)

League Club	Source	Date Signed	Seasons Played	Apps	Subs	Gls
Tottenham H.	Chelmsford C.	01.68	68-72	77	6	4

COLLINS, Robert L.
Winchester, 12 August, 1939 (G)

League Club	Source	Date Signed	Seasons Played	Apps	Subs	Gls
Newport Co. (Am)	Winchester C.	03.63	62	1	-	0

COLLINS, Robert Y.
Glasgow, 16 February, 1931 SF Lge/S-31 (IF)

League Club	Source	Date Signed	Seasons Played	Apps	Subs	Gls
Everton	Glasgow Celtic	09.58	58-61	133	-	42
Leeds U.	Tr	03.62	61-66	149	0	24
Bury	Tr	02.67	66-68	74	1	5
Oldham Ath.	Morton	10.72	72	6	1	0

COLLINS, Roderick
Dublin, 7 August, 1962 (F)

League Club	Source	Date Signed	Seasons Played	Apps	Subs	Gls
Mansfield T.	Dundalk	12.85	85-86	11	5	1
Newport Co.	Tr	08.87	87	5	2	1

COLLINS, Ronald D. (Sam)
Bristol, 13 January, 1923 (IF)

League Club	Source	Date Signed	Seasons Played	Apps	Subs	Gls
Bristol C.		11.44	46-47	14	-	2
Torquay U.	Tr	06.48	48-57	355	-	203

COLLINS, Stephen M.
Stamford, 21 March, 1962 (LB)

League Club	Source	Date Signed	Seasons Played	Apps	Subs	Gls
Peterborough U.	App	08.79	78-82	92	2	1
Southend U.	Tr	08.83	83-84	51	0	0
Lincoln C.	Tr	03.85	84-85	24	0	0
Peterborough U.	Tr	12.85	85-88	114	8	2

COLLINS, Terence J.
Penrhiwceiber, 8 January, 1943 (IF)

League Club	Source	Date Signed	Seasons Played	Apps	Subs	Gls
Swansea C.	Ton Pentre	03.67	67	1	0	0

COLLINS, William H.
Belfast, 15 February, 1920 (WH)

League Club	Source	Date Signed	Seasons Played	Apps	Subs	Gls
Luton T.	Distillery	02.48	47-48	7	-	0
Gillingham	Tr	10.49	50	13	-	0

COLLINSON, Clifford
Middlesbrough, 3 March, 1920 (G)

League Club	Source	Date Signed	Seasons Played	Apps	Subs	Gls
Manchester U.	Urmston B.C.	09.46	46	7	-	0

COLLINSON, Leslie
Hull, 2 December, 1935 (WH)

League Club	Source	Date Signed	Seasons Played	Apps	Subs	Gls
Hull C.	Jnrs	09.56	56-66	296	1	14
York C.	Tr	02.67	66-67	35	0	2

COLLINSON, Roger
Rawmarsh, 5 December, 1940 E Sch/E Yth (FB)

League Club	Source	Date Signed	Seasons Played	Apps	Subs	Gls
Bristol C.	Doncaster Rov. (Am)	10.58	59-60	50	-	1
Stockport Co.	Tr	0761	61	2	-	0

COLLYMORE, Stanley V.
Stone, 22 January, 1971 (F)

League Club	Source	Date Signed	Seasons Played	Apps	Subs	Gls
Wolverhampton W.	YT	07.89				
Crystal Palace	Stafford R.	12.90	90-91	4	14	1

COLMAN, Edward
Salford, 1 November, 1936 Died 1958 (WH)

League Club	Source	Date Signed	Seasons Played	Apps	Subs	Gls
Manchester U.	Jnrs	11.53	55-57	85	-	1

COLOMBO, Donald
Poplar, 26 October, 1928 (OL)

League Club	Source	Date Signed	Seasons Played	Apps	Subs	Gls
Portsmouth	Barking	03.53				
Walsall	Tr	12.53	53	20	-	1

COLQUHOUN, Edward P.
Prestonpans, 29 March, 1945 S-9 (CD)

League Club	Source	Date Signed	Seasons Played	Apps	Subs	Gls
Bury	Jnrs	03.62	63-66	81	0	2
West Bromwich A.	Tr	02.67	66-68	46	0	1
Sheffield U.	Tr	10.68	68-77	360	3	21

Eddie Colquhoun (Bury, West Bromwich Albion, Sheffield United & Scotland)

COLQUHOUN, John
Stirling, 3 June, 1940 (M)

League Club	Source	Date Signed	Seasons Played	Apps	Subs	Gls
Oldham Ath.	Stirling A.	08.61	61-64	163	-	33
Scunthorpe U.	Tr	06.65	65-68	149	0	25
Oldham Ath.	Tr	11.68	68-69	68	2	6

COLQUHOUN, John M.
Stirling, 14 July, 1963 (W)

League Club	Source	Date Signed	Seasons Played	Apps	Subs	Gls
Millwall	Hearts	08.91	91	27	0	3

COLRAIN, John J.
Glasgow, 4 February, 1937 Su23-1 (F)

League Club	Source	Date Signed	Seasons Played	Apps	Subs	Gls
Ipswich T.	Clyde	06.63	63-65	55	1	17

COLVAN, Hugh
Port Glasgow, 24 September, 1925 (IL)

League Club	Source	Date Signed	Seasons Played	Apps	Subs	Gls
Rochdale	Hibernian	02.48	47	1	-	0

COLVILLE, Henry
Kirkcaldy, 12 February, 1924 (OL)

League Club	Source	Date Signed	Seasons Played	Apps	Subs	Gls
Chester C.	East Fife	08.47	47	4	-	1

COLVILLE, Robert J.
Nuneaton, 27 April, 1963 W Semi-Pro (F)

League Club	Source	Date Signed	Seasons Played	Apps	Subs	Gls
Oldham Ath.	Rhos U.	02.84	83-86	22	10	4
Bury	Tr	10.86	86-87	5	6	1
Stockport Co.	Tr	09.87	87-88	67	4	18
York C.	Tr	06.89	89	17	7	0

COMERFORD, Patrick
Chester-le-Street, 30 November, 1925 (WH)

League Club	Source	Date Signed	Seasons Played	Apps	Subs	Gls
Shrewsbury T.		07.52	52	7	-	0

COMFORT, Alan
Aldershot, 8 December, 1964 E Yth (LW)

League Club	Source	Date Signed	Seasons Played	Apps	Subs	Gls
Queens Park R	App	10.82				
Cambridge U.	Tr	09.84	84-85	16	2	5
Leyton Orient	Tr	03.86	85-88	145	5	46
Middlesbrough	Tr	07.89	89	15	0	2

COMLEY, Leonard G.
Swansea, 25 January, 1922 (F)

League Club	Source	Date Signed	Seasons Played	Apps	Subs	Gls
Swansea C.		10.45	46-47	28	-	7
Newport Co.	Tr	10.48	48-50	76	-	29
Scunthorpe U.	Tr	03.51	50	12	-	5

COMMON, Alan R.
Ashington, 16 December, 1954 (FB)

League Club	Source	Date Signed	Seasons Played	Apps	Subs	Gls
West Bromwich A.	App	12.72				
Stockport Co.	Tr	07.73	73	2	1	0

COMMONS, Michael
Doncaster, 18 April, 1940 (CF)

League Club	Source	Date Signed	Seasons Played	Apps	Subs	Gls
Lincoln C.	Wath W.	05.58	59-60	2	-	1
Workington	Tr	07.61	61-63	74	-	36
Chesterfield	Tr	07.64	64	10	-	1

COMPTON, Denis C. S.
Hendon, 23 April, 1918 (OL)

League Club	Source	Date Signed	Seasons Played	Apps	Subs	Gls
Arsenal	Nunhead	05.35	36-49	54	-	15

COMPTON, John F.
Poplar, 27 August, 1937 (LB)

League Club	Source	Date Signed	Seasons Played	Apps	Subs	Gls
Chelsea	Jnrs	02.55	55-59	12	-	0
Ipswich T.	Tr	07.60	60-63	111	-	0
Bournemouth		07.64	64	27	-	1

COMPTON, Leslie H.
Woodford, 12 September, 1912 EF Lge/E-2 (CH)

League Club	Source	Date Signed	Seasons Played	Apps	Subs	Gls
Arsenal	Hampstead T.	02.32	31-51	253	-	5

COMPTON, Paul D.
Stroud, 6 June, 1961 (CD)

League Club	Source	Date Signed	Seasons Played	Apps	Subs	Gls
Bournemouth	Trowbridge T.	10.80	80-82	64	0	0
Aldershot (N/C)	Tr	12.83	83	13	0	0
Torquay U.	Tr	02.84	83-86	95	0	4
Newport Co.	Tr	12.86	86	27	0	2
Torquay U. (N/C)	Bashley	08.91	91	19	0	0

COMPTON, Roy
Lambeth, 8 November, 1954 (F)

League Club	Source	Date Signed	Seasons Played	Apps	Subs	Gls
Swindon T.	Millwall (App)	11.72	73	4	0	2

COMPTON, Terence
Bristol, 28 November, 1931 Died 1991 (CH)

League Club	Source	Date Signed	Seasons Played	Apps	Subs	Gls
Bristol C.	Jnrs	12.48	51-57	44	-	0

COMSTIVE, Paul T.
Southport, 25 November, 1961 (M)

League Club	Source	Date Signed	Seasons Played	Apps	Subs	Gls
Blackburn Rov.	Jnrs	10.79	80-82	3	3	0
Rochdale	L	09.82	82	9	0	2
Wigan Ath.	Tr	08.83	83-84	35	0	2

League Club	Source	Date Signed	Seasons Played	Apps	Subs	Gls
Wrexham	Tr	11.84	84-86	95	4	8
Burnley	Tr	07.87	87-88	81	1	17
Bolton W.	Tr	09.89	89-90	42	7	3
Chester C.	Tr	11.91	91	28	0	3

COMYN, Andrew J.
Wakefield, 2 August, 1968 (CD)

League Club	Source	Date Signed	Seasons Played	Apps	Subs	Gls
Aston Villa	Alvechurch	08.89	89-90	12	3	0
Derby Co.	Tr	08.91	91	46	0	1

CONBOY, Francis J. A.
Marylebone, 5 September, 1947 (WH)

League Club	Source	Date Signed	Seasons Played	Apps	Subs	Gls
Chelsea	App	07.65				
Luton T.	Tr	10.66	66	19	0	1

CONDE, James P.
Creswell, 19 July, 1944 (CF)

League Club	Source	Date Signed	Seasons Played	Apps	Subs	Gls
Wolverhampton W.	Jnrs	05.62				
Scunthorpe U.	Tr	06.63	63	4	-	1

CONDIE, James
Hamilton, 24 July, 1926 (W)

League Club	Source	Date Signed	Seasons Played	Apps	Subs	Gls
Walsall	Kilsyth R.	12.47	47-49	49	-	2

CONEY, Dean H.
Dagenham, 18 September, 1963 Eu21-9 (F)

League Club	Source	Date Signed	Seasons Played	Apps	Subs	Gls
Fulham	App	05.81	80-86	209	2	56
Queens Park R	Tr	06.87	87-88	36	12	7
Norwich C.	Tr	03.89	88-89	12	5	1

CONLEY, Brian J.
Thurnscoe, 21 November, 1948 (WH)

League Club	Source	Date Signed	Seasons Played	Apps	Subs	Gls
Sheffield U.	App	01.66				
Bradford P. A.	Tr	12.68	68-69	11	2	0

CONLEY, Joseph J.
Whitstable, 27 September, 1920 (F)

League Club	Source	Date Signed	Seasons Played	Apps	Subs	Gls
Torquay U.		05.39	46-50	156	-	72

CONLON, Bryan
Shildon, 14 January, 1943 (F)

League Club	Source	Date Signed	Seasons Played	Apps	Subs	Gls
Newcastle U.	Jnrs	05.61				
Darlington	South Shields	08.64	64-67	71	3	27
Millwall	Tr	11.67	67-68	40	1	13
Norwich C.	Tr	12.68	68-69	29	0	8
Blackburn Rov.	Tr	05.70	70-71	43	2	7
Crewe Alex.	L	01.72	71	4	0	1
Cambridge U.	Tr	03.72	71-72	17	1	3
Hartlepool U.	Tr	09.72	72-73	38	3	3

Les Compton (Arsenal & England)

CONMY, Oliver M.
Mulrany (Ire), 13 November, 1939 IR-5 (W)

League Club	Source	Date Signed	Seasons Played	Apps	Subs	Gls
Huddersfield T.	St Paulinus Y.C.	05.59	60-62	3	-	0
Peterborough U.	Tr	05.64	64-71	251	11	34

CONN, Alfred J.
Edinburgh, 5 April, 1952 Su23-3/S-2 (M)

League Club	Source	Date Signed	Seasons Played	Apps	Subs	Gls
Tottenham H.	Glasgow R.	07.74	74-76	35	3	6
Blackpool	Hearts	03.81	80	3	0	0

CONNACHAN, Edward D.
Prestonpans, 27 August, 1935 SF Lge/S-2 (G)

League Club	Source	Date Signed	Seasons Played	Apps	Subs	Gls
Middlesbrough	Dunfermline Ath.	08.63	63-65	95	0	0

CONNAUGHTON, John P.
Wigan, 23 September, 1949 E Yth (G)

League Club	Source	Date Signed	Seasons Played	Apps	Subs	Gls
Manchester U.	App	10.66	71	3	0	0
Halifax T.	L	09.69	69	3	0	0
Torquay U.	L	10.71	71	22	0	0
Sheffield U.	Tr	10.72	73	12	0	0
Port Vale	Tr	06.74	74-79	191	0	0

CONNEALLY, Martin P.
Lichfield, 2 February, 1962 (G)

League Club	Source	Date Signed	Seasons Played	Apps	Subs	Gls
Walsall	App	02.80	80	3	0	0

CONNELL, James D.
Blackburn, 24 May, 1951 (OL)

League Club	Source	Date Signed	Seasons Played	Apps	Subs	Gls
Bury	Blackburn Rov. (App)	02.68	69	9	0	2

CONNELL, Peter M.
East Kilbride, 26 November, 1927 (FB)

League Club	Source	Date Signed	Seasons Played	Apps	Subs	Gls
Northampton T.	Morton	05.51	51	13	-	0

CONNELL, Roger
Seaford, 8 September, 1946 E Amat (F)

League Club	Source	Date Signed	Seasons Played	Apps	Subs	Gls
Wimbledon	Walton & Hersham	08.74	77-78	30	2	14

CONNELL, Thomas E.
Newry (NI), 25 November, 1957 (CD)

League Club	Source	Date Signed	Seasons Played	Apps	Subs	Gls
Manchester U.	Coleraine	08.78	78	2	0	0

CONNELLY, Dean
Glasgow, 6 January, 1970 (M)

League Club	Source	Date Signed	Seasons Played	Apps	Subs	Gls
Arsenal	YT	02.88				
Barnsley	Tr	06.90	90-91	7	5	0
Wigan Ath.	L	10.91	91	12	0	2

CONNELLY, Edward
Dumbarton, 9 December, 1916 Died 1990 (IF)

League Club	Source	Date Signed	Seasons Played	Apps	Subs	Gls
Newcastle U.	Rosslyn Pk	03.35	35-37	25	-	8
Luton T.	Tr	03.38	37-38	50	-	16
West Bromwich A.	Tr	08.39				
Luton T.	Tr	04.46	46-47	38	-	8
Leyton Orient	Tr	06.48	48-49	32	-	5
Brighton & H.A.	Tr	10.49	49	6	-	1

CONNELLY, John M.
St Helens, 18 July, 1938 Eu23-1/EF Lge/E-20 (OR)

League Club	Source	Date Signed	Seasons Played	Apps	Subs	Gls
Burnley	St Helens T.	11.56	56-63	215	-	86
Manchester U.	Tr	04.64	64-66	79	1	22
Blackburn Rov.	Tr	09.66	66-69	148	1	36
Bury	Tr	06.70	70-72	128	0	37

CONNELLY, Michael
Stainforth, 8 September, 1938 (W)

League Club	Source	Date Signed	Seasons Played	Apps	Subs	Gls
Doncaster Rov. (Am)	Jnrs	03.57	56	3	-	0
Stockport Co.	Halifax T. (Am)	11.60	59-60	6	-	0

CONNER, Richard J.
Jarrow, 13 August, 1931 (WH)

League Club	Source	Date Signed	Seasons Played	Apps	Subs	Gls
Newcastle U.	Jnrs	01.50				
Grimsby T.	South Shields	08.52	53-58	185	-	8
Southampton	Tr	07.59	59-60	78	-	2
Tranmere Rov.	Tr	07.61	61	4	-	0
Aldershot	Tr	07.62	62	6	-	0

CONNING, T. Peter
Liverpool, 18 October, 1964 (W)

League Club	Source	Date Signed	Seasons Played	Apps	Subs	Gls
Rochdale	Altrincham	08.86	86	40	0	1

CONNOLLY, John
Barrhead, 13 June, 1950 Su23-2/S-1 (W)

League Club	Source	Date Signed	Seasons Played	Apps	Subs	Gls
Everton	St Johnstone	03.72	71-75	105	3	16
Birmingham C.	Tr	09.76	76-77	49	8	9
Newcastle U.	Tr	05.78	78-79	42	7	10

League Club	Source	Date Signed	Seasons Played	Apps	Subs	Gls
CONNOLLY, Karl						
Prescot, 9 February, 1970						(F)
Wrexham	Juventus (Liverpool)	07.91	91	33	3	8
CONNOLLY, Patrick J.						
Newcastle-u-Lyme, 27 July, 1941						(CF)
Crewe Alex.		01.61	60-62	9	-	3
Colchester U.	Macclesfield	07.64	64	21	-	6
CONNOR, David R.						
Wythenshawe, 27 October, 1945						(FB)
Manchester C.	Jnrs	11.62	64-71	130	11	10
Preston N. E.	Tr	01.72	71-72	29	0	0
CONNOR, Harold						
Liverpool, 26 December, 1929						(F)
Stoke C. (Am)	Marine	03.53	52-53	3	-	2
CONNOR, James						
Sunderland, 28 November, 1938						(OL)
Darlington (Am)	Stanley U.	09.65	65	3	0	0
CONNOR, James T.						
Stockport, 31 January, 1959						(D)
Stockport Co.	Jnrs	02.79	78	1	1	0
CONNOR, John						
Stockport, 15 May, 1965						(G)
Stockport Co. (N/C)	Jnrs	09.81	81	1	0	0
CONNOR, John						
Ashton-u-Lyne, 1 February, 1914						(FB)
Bolton W.	Mossley	10.34	34-38	29	-	0
Tranmere Rov.	Tr	06.47	47-48	46	-	3
CONNOR, John F. (Jack)						
Maryport, 25 July, 1934						(CH)
Huddersfield T.	Jnrs	10.52	54-60	85	-	10
Bristol C.	Tr	10.60	60-70	354	1	10
CONNOR, John T. (Jack)						
Todmorden, 21 December, 1919						(CF)
Ipswich T.	Albion Rov.	11.44	46	12	-	4
Carlisle U.	Tr	12.46	46-47	39	-	12
Rochdale	Ards	12.48	48-50	82	-	42
Bradford C.	Tr	04.51	50-51	14	-	7
Stockport Co.	Tr	10.51	51-56	206	-	132
Crewe Alex.	Tr	09.56	56	27	-	4
CONNOR, Kevin H.						
Radcliffe, 12 January, 1945						(RB)
Rochdale		01.66	65-66	21	4	1
CONNOR, Robert						
Bradford, 13 October, 1925						(G)
Bradford C.	Salts	11.49	49-50	28	-	0
Wrexham	Tr	07.51	51-53	77	-	0
CONNOR, Terence F.						
Leeds, 9 November, 1962 E Yth/Eu21-1						(F)
Leeds U.	App	11.79	79-82	83	13	19
Brighton & H. A.	Tr	03.83	82-86	153	3	51
Portsmouth	Tr	06.87	87-89	42	6	12
Swansea C.	Tr	08.90	90-91	39	0	6
Bristol C.	Tr	09.91	91	9	2	1
CONNORS, John J.						
Stockton, 21 August, 1927						(HB)
Darlington		03.48	47-51	65	-	0
CONROY, Gerard A. (Terry)						
Dublin, 2 October, 1946 IR-26						(F)
Stoke C.	Glentoran	03.67	67-78	244	27	49
Crewe Alex.	Hong Kong	01.80	79-80	37	0	5
CONROY, Michael G.						
Johnstone, 31 July, 1957						(M)
Blackpool	Hibernian	08.84	84-85	66	0	2
Wrexham	Tr	07.86	86	23	2	2
Leyton Orient	Tr	07.87	87	2	1	0
CONROY, Michael K.						
Glasgow, 31 December, 1965						(F/CD)
Reading	St Mirren	09.88	88-90	65	15	7
Burnley	Tr	07.91	91	38	0	24
CONROY, M. Richard						
Bradford, 26 April, 1919						(D)
Fulham		05.37				
Accrington St.	Tr	09.44	46-48	87	-	1
Scunthorpe U.	Tr	09.50	50	1	-	0
CONROY, Richard						
Bradford, 29 July, 1927						(CH)
Bradford C.	Swain House	02.48	48-52	158	-	0
Bradford P.A.	Tr	10.53	53-55	57	-	0
CONROY, Robert B.						
Kilsyth, 20 June, 1929 Died 1978						(LB)
Bury	Ashfield Jnrs	10.51	55-61	217	-	2
Tranmere Rov.	Tr	07.62	62-64	103	-	1
CONROY, Steven H.						
Chesterfield, 19 December, 1956						(G)
Sheffield U.	App	06.74	77-82	104	0	0
Rotherham U. (N/C)	Tr	02.83	82	5	0	0
Rochdale	Tr	06.83	83-84	49	0	0
Rotherham U.	Tr	01.85				
CONSTANTINE, David						
Dukinfield, 2 February, 1957 E Semi-Pro						(FB)
Bury	Hyde U.	02.79	78-81	67	3	2
CONSTANTINE, James						
Ashton-u-Lyne, 16 February, 1920						(CF)
Rochdale	Ashton Nat.	01.45				
Manchester C.	Tr	04.45	46	18	-	12
Bury	Tr	08.47	47	32	-	14
Millwall	Tr	05.48	48-51	141	-	74
CONWAY, Andrew						
South Shields, 17 February, 1923						(CF)
Hull C.	North Shields	06.47	47-48	6	-	5
Stockport Co.	Dartford	07.50				
CONWAY, Christopher						
Dundee, 23 July, 1928						(G)
Bury	Ayr U.	09.54	54-55	44	-	0
CONWAY, James						
Motherwell, 27 August, 1940 S Sch						(CF)
Norwich C.	Glasgow Celtic	05.61	61-63	42	-	13
Southend U.	Tr	10.63	63-64	32	-	9
CONWAY, James P.						
Dublin, 10 August, 1946 IR Amat/IR-19						(OR)
Fulham	Bohemians	05.66	66-75	312	4	67
Manchester C.	Tr	08.76	76	11	2	1
CONWAY, John						
Dublin, 11 July, 1951						(W)
Fulham	Bohemians	08.71	71-74	30	8	6
CONWAY, John G.						
Gateshead, 24 January, 1931						(F)
Gateshead		05.53	53-54	4	-	0
CONWAY, Michael D.						
Sheffield, 11 March, 1956						(W)
Brighton & H. A.	App	03.74	72-73	1	1	1
Swansea C.	Tr	12.75	75-77	56	5	11
CONWAY, Patrick						
Newcastle, 19 September, 1968						(M)
Cambridge U. (N/C)	YT	10.85	85-86	2	0	0
CONWAY, Thomas						
Stoke, 7 November, 1933						(F)
Port Vale	Jnrs	05.51	55	15	-	4
CONWELL, Anthony						
Bradford, 17 January, 1932						(FB)
Sheffield Wed.	Jnrs	02.49	53-54	44	-	0
Huddersfield T.	Tr	07.55	55-58	106	-	2
Derby Co.	Tr	06.59	59-61	98	-	1
Doncaster Rov.	Tr	07.62	62-63	35	-	0
COOK, Andrew C.						
Romsey, 10 August, 1969						(LB)
Southampton	App	06.87	87-90	11	5	1
Exeter C.	Tr	09.91	91	38	0	0

League Club	Source	Date Signed	Seasons Played	Career Record Apps	Subs	Gls
COOK, Anthony						
Bristol, 8 October, 1929						(G)
Bristol C.	Clifton St Vincent	01.50	52-63	320	-	0
COOK, Anthony J.						
Crewe, 26 December, 1961						(M)
Crewe Alex. (N/C)		05.81	81	2	1	0
COOK, Charles I.						
Cheltenham, 28 January, 1937						(FB)
Bristol C.	Gloucester C.	02.57	56-57	2	-	0
COOK, Jason P.						
Edmonton, 29 December, 1969						(M)
Tottenham H.	YT	07.88				
Southend U.	Tr	07.89	89-90	29	1	1
COOK, Jeffrey W.						
Hartlepool, 14 March, 1953						(F)
Stoke C.	Hellenic (SA)	10.77	77-81	22	8	5
Bradford C.	L	02.79	78	8	0	1
Plymouth Arg.	L	12.79	79	4	3	5
Plymouth Arg.	Tr	10.81	81-82	54	1	21
Halifax T.	Tr	08.83	83-84	49	7	9
COOK, John A.						
Iron Acton, 27 June, 1929						(IF)
Bristol Rov.	Jnrs	09.46	46	2	-	0
COOK, Leslie						
Blackburn, 11 November, 1924 E Sch						(WH)
Blackburn Rov.	Jnrs	11.41	46-48	76	-	0
Coventry C.	Tr	07.49	49-53	88	-	0
COOK, Malcolm I.						
Glasgow, 24 May, 1943						(WH)
Bradford P. A.	Motherwell	07.63	63-64	45	-	2
Newport Co.	Tr	07.65	65	30	2	0
COOK, Mark R.						
Boston, 7 August, 1970						(M)
Lincoln C.	YT	08.88	88-89	7	0	0
COOK, Maurice						
Berkhamsted, 10 December, 1931						(CF)
Watford	Berkhamsted	05.53	53-57	208	-	68
Fulham	Tr	02.58	57-64	221	-	89
Reading	Tr	05.65	65	12	0	2
COOK, Michael						
Enfield, 9 April, 1951						(FB)
Colchester U.	Leyton Orient (Am)	07.69	69-83	609	4	21
COOK, Michael J.						
Stroud, 18 October, 1968						(M)
Coventry C.	YT	03.87				
York C.	L	08.87	87	6	0	1
Cambridge U.	Tr	06.89	89-90	12	5	1
York C.	L	11.90	90	3	3	0
COOK, Michael J.						
Sutton, 25 January, 1950						(CF)
Crystal Palace	App	02.68	67	1	0	0
Brentford	Tr	08.69	69	16	4	4
COOK, Mitchell C.						
Scarborough, 15 October, 1961						(M/LB)
Darlington	Scarborough	08.84	84-85	34	0	4
Middlesbrough	Tr	09.85	85	3	3	0
Scarborough	Tr	08.86	87-88	61	20	10
Halifax T.	Tr	07.89	89-90	52	2	2
Scarborough	L	10.90	90	9	0	1
Darlington	Tr	03.91	90-91	35	1	4
Blackpool	Tr	03.92	91	8	0	0
COOK, Paul A.						
Liverpool, 22 February, 1967						(M)
Wigan Ath.	Jnrs	07.84	84-87	77	6	14
Norwich C.	Tr	05.88	88-89	3	3	0
Wolverhampton W.	Tr	11.89	89-91	113	0	16
COOK, Peter H.						
Hull, 1 February, 1927 Died 1960						(W)
Hull C.	Kingston Wolves	06.46	46-47	5	-	0
Bradford C.	Scarborough	05.49	49	1	-	0
Crewe Alex.	Tr	08.50	50-52	45	-	7
COOK, Reuben						
Gateshead, 9 March, 1933						(WH)
Arsenal	Tow Law T.	11.51				
Leyton Orient	Tr	01.56	56	2	-	0
COOK, Robert K.						
Letchworth, 13 June, 1924						(W)
Reading	Letchworth T.	03.48				
Tottenham H.	Tr	07.49	49	3	-	0
Watford	Tr	08.51	51-52	53	-	8
COOK, Trevor						
Blidworth, 2 July, 1956						(F)
Mansfield T.	App	07.74	73	1	0	0
COOKE, Alan						
Crewe Alex.		08.55	55	8	-	0
COOKE, Barry A.						
Wolverhampton, 22 January, 1938 EYth						(WH)
West Bromwich A.	Erdington	05.55				
Northampton T.	Tr	07.59	59-61	58	-	1

Charlie Cooke (Aberdeen, Dundee, Chelsea, Crystal Palace, Chelsea & Scotland)

League Club	Source	Date Signed	Seasons Played	Career Record Apps	Subs	Gls
COOKE, Charles						
St Monance (Fife), 14 October, 1942 Su23-4/SF Lge/S-16						(M)
Chelsea	Dundee	04.66	66-72	204	8	15
Crystal Palace	Tr	10.72	72-73	42	2	0
Chelsea	Tr	01.74	73-77	85	2	7
COOKE, David F.						
Birmingham, 29 November, 1946						(FB)
Wolverhampton W.	Jnrs	07.65				
Stockport Co.	Tr	07.68	68	3	0	0
COOKE, Edward J.						
Barnsley, 18 March, 1942						(G)
Port Vale	Jnrs	06.60	60-63	7	-	0
COOKE, Gordon C.						
Crewe, 31 May, 1928						
Crewe Alex.	Jnrs	05.48	48	2	-	0

COOKE, John
Salford, 25 April, 1962 E Yth (W)

League Club	Source	Date Signed	Seasons Played	Apps	Subs	Gls
Sunderland	App	11.79	79-84	42	13	4
Carlisle U.	L	11.84	84	5	1	2
Sheffield Wed.	Tr	06.85				
Carlisle U.	Tr	10.85	85-87	105	1	11
Stockport Co.	Tr	07.88	88-89	54	4	7
Chesterfield	Tr	07.90	90-91	48	5	8

COOKE, Joseph
Dominica (WI), 15 February, 1955 (CD/F)

League Club	Source	Date Signed	Seasons Played	Apps	Subs	Gls
Bradford C.	App	05.72	71-78	184	20	62
Peterborough U.	Tr	01.79	78	18	0	5
Oxford U.	Tr	08.79	79-80	71	1	13
Exeter C.	T	06.81	81	17	0	3
Bradford C.	Tr	01.82	81-83	61	1	6
Rochdale	Tr	07.84	84-85	75	0	4
Wrexham	Tr	07.86	86-87	49	2	4

COOKE, Peter C.
Northampton, 15 January, 1962 (M)

League Club	Source	Date Signed	Seasons Played	Apps	Subs	Gls
Northampton T.	Jnrs	07.80	80	4	1	1

COOKE, Richard E.
Islington, 4 September, 1965 E Yth/Eu21-1 (W)

League Club	Source	Date Signed	Seasons Played	Apps	Subs	Gls
Tottenham H.	App	05.83	83-85	9	2	2
Birmingham C.	L	09.86	86	5	0	0
Bournemouth	Tr	01.87	86-88	63	9	15
Luton T.	Tr	03.89	88-89	3	14	1
Bournemouth	Tr	03.91	90-91	30	11	2

COOKE, Robert L. (Robbie)
Rotherham, 16 February, 1957 (F)

League Club	Source	Date Signed	Seasons Played	Apps	Subs	Gls
Mansfield T.	App	02.75	76-77	7	8	1
Peterborough U.	Grantham	05.80	80-82	115	0	51
Cambridge U.	Tr	02.83	82-84	62	3	14
Brentford	Tr	12.84	84-87	122	1	53
Millwall	Tr	12.87	87	4	0	1

COOKE, Terence A.
Wrexham, 21 February, 1962 (F)

League Club	Source	Date Signed	Seasons Played	Apps	Subs	Gls
Chester C.	App	02.80	80-82	37	12	11

COOKE, Wilfred H.
Crewe, 10 October, 1915 (IF)

League Club	Source	Date Signed	Seasons Played	Apps	Subs	Gls
Bradford C.	Leeds U. (Am)	08.35	36-37	21	-	2
Leeds U.	Tr	07.38				
Fulham	Tr	07.39				
Crewe Alex.	Tr	02.46	46	12		2

COOKE, William H.
Whittington, 7 March, 1919 (FB)

League Club	Source	Date Signed	Seasons Played	Apps	Subs	Gls
Bournemouth		04.38				
Luton T.	Tr	01.46	46-52	211	-	4
Shrewsbury T.	Tr	07.53	53	4	-	0
Watford	Tr	07.54	54	10	-	0

COOKSON, James
Liverpool, 22 August, 1927 (FB)

League Club	Source	Date Signed	Seasons Played	Apps	Subs	Gls
Everton		10.45				
Southport	Tr	08.49	49-51	55	-	1

COOKSON, Steven J.
Wolverhampton, 19 February, 1972 (F)

League Club	Source	Date Signed	Seasons Played	Apps	Subs	Gls
Torquay U.	YT	07.90	89-90	7	5	1

COOLE, William
Manchester, 27 January, 1925 (OR)

League Club	Source	Date Signed	Seasons Played	Apps	Subs	Gls
Mansfield T.	Royal Navy	01.48	47-53	182	-	35
Notts Co.	Tr	10.53	53-55	42	-	5
Barrow	Tr	07.56	56-58	56	-	3

COOLING, Roy
Barnsley, 9 December, 1921 (IF)

League Club	Source	Date Signed	Seasons Played	Apps	Subs	Gls
Barnsley	Mitchell M.W.	03.42	46	6	-	3
Mansfield T.	Tr	09.47	47-49	65	-	14

COOMBE, Mark A.
Torquay, 17 September, 1968 (G)

League Club	Source	Date Signed	Seasons Played	Apps	Subs	Gls
Bristol C.	Bournemouth (YT)	08.87				
Colchester U. (N/C)	Carlisle U. (N/C)	10.88	88	3	0	0
Torquay U.	Tr	12.88	88	8	0	0

COOMBES, Jeffrey
Rhondda, 1 April, 1954 W Sch (M)

League Club	Source	Date Signed	Seasons Played	Apps	Subs	Gls
Bristol Rov.	App	04.72	72-74	10	1	1

COOMBES, Lee E.
Dinnington, 5 July, 1966 (D)

League Club	Source	Date Signed	Seasons Played	Apps	Subs	Gls
Sheffield Wed.	App	07.84				
Scunthorpe U.	Tr	08.85				
Chesterfield	Tr	07.86	86	1	2	0

COOMBS, Frank H.
East Ham, 24 April, 1925 (G)

League Club	Source	Date Signed	Seasons Played	Apps	Subs	Gls
Bristol C.	Dartford	06.49	49	24	-	0
Southend U.	Tr	06.50	50	20	-	0
Colchester U.	Tr	07.51	51-53	38	-	0

COOMBS, Paul A.
Bristol, 4 September, 1970 (F)

League Club	Source	Date Signed	Seasons Played	Apps	Subs	Gls
Aldershot	YT	07.89	88-90	9	7	1

COOP, James
Horwich, 17 September, 1927 (OL)

League Club	Source	Date Signed	Seasons Played	Apps	Subs	Gls
Sheffield U.		05.46	47-48	9	-	1
York C.	Tr	07.49	49-50	12	-	4

COOP, Michael A.
Leamington, 10 July, 1948 (RB)

League Club	Source	Date Signed	Seasons Played	Apps	Subs	Gls
Coventry C.	App	01.66	66-80	413	12	18
York C.	L	11.74	74	4	0	0
Derby Co.	Tr	07.81	81	17	1	0

COOPER, Adrian S. J.
Reading, 16 January, 1957 E Sch (M)

League Club	Source	Date Signed	Seasons Played	Apps	Subs	Gls
Reading	App	01.75	73-75	14	0	2

COOPER, Arthur
Eturia, 16 March, 1921 (LH)

League Club	Source	Date Signed	Seasons Played	Apps	Subs	Gls
Port Vale	Shelton St Marks	08.41	46	4	-	0

COOPER, Charles
Farnworth, 14 June, 1941 (FB)

League Club	Source	Date Signed	Seasons Played	Apps	Subs	Gls
Bolton W.	Jnrs	05.59	60-68	79	4	0
Barrow	Tr	07.69	69-70	54	0	0

COOPER, Colin T.
Sedgefield, 28 February, 1967 Eu21-8 (FB)

League Club	Source	Date Signed	Seasons Played	Apps	Subs	Gls
Middlesbrough	Jnrs	06.84	85-90	183	5	6
Millwall	Tr	07.91	91	36	0	2

COOPER, David A.
Lambeth, 25 June, 1971 (F)

League Club	Source	Date Signed	Seasons Played	Apps	Subs	Gls
Wimbledon	YT	07.89				
Plymouth Arg.	Tr	03.91	90	0	3	0

COOPER, David B. E.
Hatfield, 7 March, 1973 (FB)

League Club	Source	Date Signed	Seasons Played	Apps	Subs	Gls
Exeter C.	Luton T. (YT)	08.91	91	9	4	0

COOPER, Douglas
Middlesbrough, 18 October, 1936 (F)

League Club	Source	Date Signed	Seasons Played	Apps	Subs	Gls
Middlesbrough	Jnrs	10.53	54-56	5	-	0
Rotherham U.	Tr	01.59	58	13	-	5
Hartlepool U.	Tr	08.60	60	16	-	6

COOPER, Frederick J.
West Ham, 18 November, 1934 E Sch (FB)

League Club	Source	Date Signed	Seasons Played	Apps	Subs	Gls
West Ham U.	Jnrs	12.51	56-57	4	-	0

COOPER, Gary J.
Hammersmith, 20 November, 1965 E Sch/E Yth (M)

League Club	Source	Date Signed	Seasons Played	Apps	Subs	Gls
Queens Park R	App	06.83	84	1	0	0
Brentford	L	09.85	85	9	1	0
Maidstone U.	Fisher Ath.	03.89	89-90	53	7	7
Peterborough U.	Tr	03.91	90-91	35	4	5

COOPER, Gary S.
Horwich, 15 February, 1955 (F)

League Club	Source	Date Signed	Seasons Played	Apps	Subs	Gls
Rochdale	Horwich R.M.I.	12.73	73-76	81	11	14
Southport	Tr	08.77	77	13	7	5

COOPER, Geoffrey V.
Kingston, 27 December, 1960 (LB)

League Club	Source	Date Signed	Seasons Played	Apps	Subs	Gls
Brighton & H.A.	Bognor Regis T.	12.87	87-88	2	5	0
Barnet	Tr	07.89	91	13	1	1

COOPER, George
Kingswinford, 1 October, 1932 (F)

League Club	Source	Date Signed	Seasons Played	Apps	Subs	Gls
Crystal Palace	Brierley Hill Alliance	01.55	54-58	69	-	27
Rochdale	Tr	01.59	58-59	32	-	9

COOPER, Graham
Huddersfield, 22 May, 1962 (W)

League Club	Source	Date Signed	Seasons Played	Apps	Subs	Gls
Huddersfield T.	Emley	03.84	83-87	61	13	13
Wrexham	Tr	08.88	88-90	50	13	16
York C.	L	11.90	90	2	0	0
Halifax T.	Tr	01.91	90-91	32	7	4

COOPER, Ian L.
Bradford, 21 September, 1946 (LB)

League Club	Source	Date Signed	Seasons Played	Apps	Subs	Gls
Bradford C.	Jnrs	08.66	65-76	442	1	4

COOPER, James E.
Blackpool, 13 January, 1928 (F)

League Club	Source	Date Signed	Seasons Played	Apps	Subs	Gls
Accrington St.	Fleetwood	06.52	52	7	-	1

COOPER, James E.
Chester, 19 January, 1942 (W)

League Club	Source	Date Signed	Seasons Played	Apps	Subs	Gls
Chester C.	Jnrs	09.59	59-61	91	-	17
Southport	Tr	06.62	62	28	-	7
Blackpool	Tr	07.63	63	4	-	0
Mansfield T.	Tr	05.64	64	7	-	4
Crewe Alex.	Tr	07.65	65	6	0	0

COOPER, James T.
Glasgow, 28 December, 1939 (OR)

League Club	Source	Date Signed	Seasons Played	Apps	Subs	Gls
Brighton & H. A.	Airdrieonians	08.62	62-63	41	-	6
Hartlepool U.	Tr	07.65	65	19	0	1

COOPER, Joseph
Reddish, 16 February, 1918 (LB)

League Club	Source	Date Signed	Seasons Played	Apps	Subs	Gls
Blackpool		01.38				
Crewe Alex.	Tr	07.39	46	3	-	0

COOPER, Joseph
Gateshead, 15 October, 1934 (HB)

League Club	Source	Date Signed	Seasons Played	Apps	Subs	Gls
Newcastle U.	Winlaton Mill	09.52	53-57	6	-	0

COOPER, Leigh V.
Reading, 7 May, 1961 (LB)

League Club	Source	Date Signed	Seasons Played	Apps	Subs	Gls
Plymouth Arg.	App	05.79	79-89	316	7	15
Aldershot	Tr	08.90	90	33	0	2

COOPER, Leonard A.
Lower Gornal, 11 May, 1936 E Yth (OL)

League Club	Source	Date Signed	Seasons Played	Apps	Subs	Gls
Wolverhampton W.	Jnrs	05.53				
Walsall		02.56	55	5	-	2

COOPER, Mark D.
Watford, 5 April, 1967 (F)

League Club	Source	Date Signed	Seasons Played	Apps	Subs	Gls
Cambridge U.	App	10.84	83-86	62	9	17
Tottenham H.	Tr	03.87				
Shrewsbury T.	L	09.87	87	6	0	2
Gillingham	Tr	10.87	87	38	11	11
Leyton Orient	Tr	02.89	88-91	77	16	30

COOPER, Mark N.
Wakefield, 18 December, 1968 (M)

League Club	Source	Date Signed	Seasons Played	Apps	Subs	Gls
Bristol C.	YT	09.87				
Exeter C.		10.89	89-91	46	4	12
Southend U.	L	03.90	89	4	1	0
Birmingham C.	Tr	09.91	91	27	6	4

COOPER, Neale J.
India, 24 November, 1963 S Yth/Su21-13 (CD)

League Club	Source	Date Signed	Seasons Played	Apps	Subs	Gls
Aston Villa	Aberdeen	07.86	86-87	19	1	0
Reading	Glasgow Rangers	07.91	91	6	1	0

COOPER, Neil
Aberdeen, 12 August, 1959 S Sch (CD)

League Club	Source	Date Signed	Seasons Played	Apps	Subs	Gls
Barnsley	Aberdeen	01.80	79-81	57	3	6
Grimsby T.	Tr	03.82	81-83	47	0	2

COOPER, Paul D.
Brierley Hill, 21 December, 1953 (G)

League Club	Source	Date Signed	Seasons Played	Apps	Subs	Gls
Birmingham C.	App	07.71	71-73	17	0	0
Ipswich T.	Tr	03.74	73-86	447	0	0
Leicester C.	Tr	06.87	87-88	56	0	0
Manchester C.	Tr	03.89	88-89	15	0	0
Stockport Co.	Tr	08.90	90	22	0	0

COOPER, Paul T.
Birmingham, 12 July, 1957 (FB)

League Club	Source	Date Signed	Seasons Played	Apps	Subs	Gls
Huddersfield T.	App	08.75	76	2	0	0
Grimsby T.	Tr	07.77	77	3	0	0

COOPER, Richard D.
Brent, 7 May, 1965 (M)

League Club	Source	Date Signed	Seasons Played	Apps	Subs	Gls
Sheffield U.	App	05.83	82-84	2	4	0
Lincoln C.	Tr	08.85	85-86	57	4	2
Exeter C.	Tr	07.87	87-88	55	7	2

COOPER, Robert C.
Sutton Coldfield, 3 September, 1966 (M)

League Club	Source	Date Signed	Seasons Played	Apps	Subs	Gls
Leicester C.	YT	05.85				
Tranmere Rov.	L	12.85	85	3	2	0

COOPER, Ronald
Peterborough, 28 August, 1938 (FB)

League Club	Source	Date Signed	Seasons Played	Apps	Subs	Gls
Peterborough U.	Jnrs	(N/L)	63-67	132	0	1

COOPER, Stephen B.
Birmingham, 22 June, 1964 (F)

League Club	Source	Date Signed	Seasons Played	Apps	Subs	Gls
Birmingham C.	Moor Green	11.83				
Halifax T.	L	12.83	83	7	0	1
Newport Co.	Tr	09.84	84	38	0	11
Plymouth Arg.	Tr	08.85	85-87	58	15	15
Barnsley	Tr	08.88	88-90	62	15	13
Tranmere Rov.	Tr	12.90	90-91	13	13	3
Peterborough U.	L	03.92	91	2	7	0

COOPER, Stephen M.
Basingstoke, 14 December, 1955 E Yth (F)

League Club	Source	Date Signed	Seasons Played	Apps	Subs	Gls
Torquay U.	Stourbridge	03.78	77-83	219	15	77

COOPER, Terence
Castleford, 12 July, 1944 E-20 (LB)

League Club	Source	Date Signed	Seasons Played	Apps	Subs	Gls
Leeds U.	App	07.62	63-74	240	10	7
Middlesbrough	Tr	03.75	74-77	105	0	1
Bristol C.	Tr	07.78	78	11	0	0
Bristol Rov.	Tr	08.79	79-81	53	6	0
Doncaster Rov.	Tr	11.81	81	20	0	0
Bristol C.	Tr	08.82	82-84	38	22	1

COOPER, Terence
Cwmbran, 11 March, 1950 (CD)

League Club	Source	Date Signed	Seasons Played	Apps	Subs	Gls
Newport Co.	Jnrs	07.68	67-69	64	4	1
Notts Co.	Tr	07.70	71-72	3	6	0
Lincoln C.	L	12.71	71	3	0	0
Lincoln C.	Tr	08.72	72-78	265	2	12
Scunthorpe U.	L	11.77	77	4	0	0
Bradford C.	Tr	06.79	79-80	47	1	2
Rochdale	Tr	08.81	81	35	0	2

COOPER, William G. E.
York, 2 November, 1917 Died 1978 (F)

League Club	Source	Date Signed	Seasons Played	Apps	Subs	Gls
Bradford C.	Halifax T. (Am)	09.46	46-47	7	-	4

COOTE, Kenneth A.
Paddington, 19 May, 1928 (D)

League Club	Source	Date Signed	Seasons Played	Apps	Subs	Gls
Brentford	Wembley T.	05.49	49-63	513	-	14

COPE, Anthony
Doncaster, 17 January, 1941 (WH)

League Club	Source	Date Signed	Seasons Played	Apps	Subs	Gls
Doncaster Rov.	Jnrs	09.58	58-59	8	-	0

COPE, Ronald
Crewe, 5 October, 1934 E Sch (CH)

League Club	Source	Date Signed	Seasons Played	Apps	Subs	Gls
Manchester U.	Jnrs	10.51	56-60	93	-	2
Luton T.	Tr	08.61	61-62	28	-	0

COPELAND, Edward
Hetton-le-Hole, 19 May, 1921 (OR)

League Club	Source	Date Signed	Seasons Played	Apps	Subs	Gls
Hartlepool U.	Easington Colly	06.44	46-47	38	-	9

COPELAND, Michael W.
Cardiff, 31 December, 1954 (FB)

League Club	Source	Date Signed	Seasons Played	Apps	Subs	Gls
Newport Co.	Jnrs	07.73	73	3	1	0

COPELAND, Philip
Workington, 16 September, 1936 (CH)

League Club	Source	Date Signed	Seasons Played	Apps	Subs	Gls
Workington		02.57	60-62	11	-	0

COPELAND, Simon D.
Sheffield, 10 October, 1968 (RB)

League Club	Source	Date Signed	Seasons Played	Apps	Subs	Gls
Sheffield U.	YT	06.87				
Rochdale	Tr	07.88	88	27	1	0

COPESTAKE, Oliver F. P.
Mansfield, 1 September, 1921 Died 1953 (F)

League Club	Source	Date Signed	Seasons Played	Apps	Subs	Gls
Mansfield T.	Church Warsop	01.46	46	33	-	7

League Club	Source	Date Signed	Seasons Played	Apps	Subs	Gls

COPLEY, Dennis I.
Misterton (Nts), 21 December, 1921 (IF)

League Club	Source	Date Signed	Seasons Played	Apps	Subs	Gls
Lincoln C.	Norwich C. (Am)	09.46	46	1	-	0

COPLEY, Gary
Rotherham, 30 December, 1960 (G)

League Club	Source	Date Signed	Seasons Played	Apps	Subs	Gls
Barnsley (N/C)	App	01.79	78	1	0	0

COPP, Leonard J. H.
Aberystwyth, 7 October, 1940 (IF)

League Club	Source	Date Signed	Seasons Played	Apps	Subs	Gls
Leeds U.	Jnrs	10.57				
Shrewsbury T.	Tr	07.58	60	2	-	1

COPPELL, Stephen J.
Liverpool, 9 July, 1955 Eu23-1/EF Lge/E-42 (W)

League Club	Source	Date Signed	Seasons Played	Apps	Subs	Gls
Tranmere Rov.	Liverpool Univ.	01.74	73-74	35	3	10
Manchester U.	Tr	02.75	74-82	320	2	54

CORBETT, Alexander M.
Saltcoats, 20 April, 1921 (G)

League Club	Source	Date Signed	Seasons Played	Apps	Subs	Gls
New Brighton	Ayr U.	07.46	46-47	58	-	0
Hull C.	Tr	01.48	47	8	-	0
Hartlepool U.	Weymouth	07.53	53	7	-	0

CORBETT, Anthony
Wolverhampton, 28 April, 1940 E Yth (FB)

League Club	Source	Date Signed	Seasons Played	Apps	Subs	Gls
Woverhampton W.	Jnrs	05.59				
Shrewsbury T.	Tr	07.60	60-61	8	-	0

CORBETT, Arthur B.
Birmingham, 17 August, 1928 (WH)

League Club	Source	Date Signed	Seasons Played	Apps	Subs	Gls
Walsall	Sutton T.	12.49	49-50	24	-	5

CORBETT, David F.
Marshfield, 15 May, 1940 (OR)

League Club	Source	Date Signed	Seasons Played	Apps	Subs	Gls
Swindon T.	Jnrs	08.58	58-61	68	-	3
Plymouth Arg.	Tr	02.62	61-66	84	0	8

CORBETT, George
Newburn, 11 May, 1925 (FB)

League Club	Source	Date Signed	Seasons Played	Apps	Subs	Gls
Sheffield Wed.		05.45				
West Bromwich A.	Spennymoor U.	03.51	51	1	-	0
Workington	Tr	07.53	53	9	-	0

CORBETT, John T.
Bow, 9 January, 1920 Died 1990 (F)

League Club	Source	Date Signed	Seasons Played	Apps	Subs	Gls
Hartlepool U.		09.43				
Swansea C.		08.45				
Crystal Palace		09.46	46	1	-	1

CORBETT, Norman G.
Falkirk, 23 June, 1919 Died 1990 (WH)

League Club	Source	Date Signed	Seasons Played	Apps	Subs	Gls
West Ham U.	Hearts	04.37	36-49	166	-	3

CORBETT, Patrick A.
Hackney, 12 February, 1963 EYth (CD)

League Club	Source	Date Signed	Seasons Played	Apps	Subs	Gls
Tottenham H.	App	10.80	81-82	3	2	1
Leyton Orient	Tr	08.83	83-85	77	0	2

CORBETT, Peter
Preston, 5 March, 1934 (G)

League Club	Source	Date Signed	Seasons Played	Apps	Subs	Gls
Preston N. E.		06.56				
Workington	Tr	08.57	57-58	11	-	0
Oldham Ath.	Tr	07.59	59	10	-	0

CORBETT, Robert
Newburn, 16 March, 1922 (FB)

League Club	Source	Date Signed	Seasons Played	Apps	Subs	Gls
Newcastle U.	Throckley Welfare	08.43	46-51	46	-	1
Middlesbrough	Tr	12.51	51-56	92	-	0
Northampton T.	Tr	08.57	57	8	-	1

CORBETT, William
Wolverhampton, 29 July, 1920 (LB)

League Club	Source	Date Signed	Seasons Played	Apps	Subs	Gls
Doncaster Rov.		01.42	46-47	37	-	0
Bristol C.	Tr	06.48	48	1	-	0

CORBETT, William R.
Falkirk, 31 August, 1922 (CH)

League Club	Source	Date Signed	Seasons Played	Apps	Subs	Gls
Preston N. E.	Glasgow Celtic	06.48	48	19	-	0
Leicester C.	Tr	08.49	49	16	-	0

CORBIN, Kirk D.
West Indies, 12 March, 1955 (FB)

League Club	Source	Date Signed	Seasons Played	Apps	Subs	Gls
Cambridge U.	Wokingham T.	01.78	78	3	0	0

CORBISHLEY, Colin
Stoke, 13 June, 1939 (WH)

League Club	Source	Date Signed	Seasons Played	Apps	Subs	Gls
Port Vale		10.59	60-61	11	-	0
Chester C.	Tr	08.62	62-64	83	-	11

CORDELL, John G.
Walsall, 6 December, 1928 (G)

League Club	Source	Date Signed	Seasons Played	Apps	Subs	Gls
Aston Villa	Walsall Star	09.49	51-52	5	-	0
Rochdale	Tr	05.53	53-54	15	-	0

CORDEN, Stephen
Eston, 9 January, 1967 (M)

League Club	Source	Date Signed	Seasons Played	Apps	Subs	Gls
Middlesbrough	YT	06.84	85	1	0	0

CORDER, Peter R.
Loughton, 12 December, 1966 (G)

League Club	Source	Date Signed	Seasons Played	Apps	Subs	Gls
Tottenham H.	App	10.84				
Peterborough U.	L	10.85	85	2	0	0

CORDICE, Neil A.
Amersham, 7 April, 1960 (F)

League Club	Source	Date Signed	Seasons Played	Apps	Subs	Gls
Northampton T.	Wycombe W.	07.78	78	4	4	1

CORDJOHN, Barry R.
Oxford, 5 September, 1942 (FB)

League Club	Source	Date Signed	Seasons Played	Apps	Subs	Gls
Charlton Ath.	Jnrs	06.60				
Aldershot	Tr	07.63				
Portsmouth	Tr	07.64	64	14	-	0

CORDNER, Scott
Derby, 3 August, 1972 (M)

League Club	Source	Date Signed	Seasons Played	Apps	Subs	Gls
Chesterfield (YT)	YT	07.89	90	1	3	1

CORE, John
Ripponden, 29 March, 1929 (CF)

League Club	Source	Date Signed	Seasons Played	Apps	Subs	Gls
Halifax T. (Am)		09.49	49-53	29	-	14

CORFIELD, Ernest
Wigan, 18 January, 1931 (IF)

League Club	Source	Date Signed	Seasons Played	Apps	Subs	Gls
Bolton W.	Jnrs	04.48	49-51	6	-	0
Stockport Co.	Tr	07.53	53	2	-	0

CORISH, Robert
Liverpool, 13 September, 1958 (FB)

League Club	Source	Date Signed	Seasons Played	Apps	Subs	Gls
Derby Co.	Jnrs	08.76	77	0	1	0

Alan Cork (Derby County, Wimbledon & Sheffield United)

CORK, Alan G.
Derby, 4 March, 1959 (F)

League Club	Source	Date Signed	Seasons Played	Apps	Subs	Gls
Derby Co.	Jnrs	07.77				
Lincoln C.	L	09.77	77	5	0	0
Wimbledon	Tr	02.78	78-91	352	78	145
Sheffield U.	Tr	03.92	91	7	1	2

CORK, David
Doncaster, 28 October, 1962 (F)

League Club	Source	Date Signed	Seasons Played	Apps	Subs	Gls
Arsenal	App	06.80	83	5	2	1
Huddersfield T.	Tr	07.85	85-87	104	6	25
West Bromwich A.	L	09.88	88	1	3	0
Scunthorpe U. (N/C)	Tr	02.89	88	8	7	0
Darlington	Tr	07.89	90-91	53	11	11

CORK, David
Doncaster, 8 October, 1959 (M)

League Club	Source	Date Signed	Seasons Played	Apps	Subs	Gls
Manchester U.	App	10.76				
Doncaster Rov.	Tr	08.78	78-79	9	0	1

CORKAIN, Stephen
Stockton, 25 February, 1967 (M)

League Club	Source	Date Signed	Seasons Played	Apps	Subs	Gls
Hull C.	Jnrs	06.85	86	5	0	1

CORKHILL, Robert
Barrow, 20 November, 1943 (OL)

League Club	Source	Date Signed	Seasons Played	Apps	Subs	Gls
Barrow	Holker C.O.B.	08.63	63-64	8	-	1

CORKHILL, William
Belfast, 23 April, 1910 (WH)

League Club	Source	Date Signed	Seasons Played	Apps	Subs	Gls
Notts Co.	Marine	05.31	31-37	166	-	8
Cardiff C.	Tr	05.38	38	23	-	0
Notts Co.	Tr	11.45	46-51	99	-	0

CORMACK, Peter B.
Edinburgh, 17 July, 1946 S Amat/Su23-5/SF Lge/S-9 (M)

League Club	Source	Date Signed	Seasons Played	Apps	Subs	Gls
Nottingham F.	Hibernian	03.70	69-71	74	0	15
Liverpool	Tr	07.72	72-75	119	6	21
Bristol C.	Tr	11.76	76-79	59	8	15

CORNER, Brian
Glasgow, 6 January, 1961 (M)

League Club	Source	Date Signed	Seasons Played	Apps	Subs	Gls
Fulham	App	01.79	80	1	2	0

CORNER, David E.
Sunderland, 15 May, 1966 EYth (CD)

League Club	Source	Date Signed	Seasons Played	Apps	Subs	Gls
Sunderland	App	04.84	84-87	33	0	1
Cardiff C.	L	09.85	85	6	0	0
Peterborough U.	L	03.88	87	9	0	0
Leyton Orient	Tr	07.88	88	4	0	0
Darlington	Tr	07.89	90	13	2	0

CORNER, Norman J.
Horden, 16 February, 1943 (CH/CF)

League Club	Source	Date Signed	Seasons Played	Apps	Subs	Gls
Hull C.	Horden Colly	08.62	63-66	5	0	4
Lincoln C.	Tr	10.67	67-68	44	1	12
Bradford C.	Tr	01.69	68-71	105	5	16

CORNES, J. Stuart
Usk, 4 March, 1960 (CD)

League Club	Source	Date Signed	Seasons Played	Apps	Subs	Gls
Hereford U.	App	01.78	77-81	91	2	3

CORNFIELD, Allen H.
Dudley, 19 December, 1940 (OL)

League Club	Source	Date Signed	Seasons Played	Apps	Subs	Gls
Shrewsbury T.	Lower Gornal Ath.	11.59	59-61	9	-	0

CORNFORTH, John M.
Whitley Bay, 7 October, 1967 (M)

League Club	Source	Date Signed	Seasons Played	Apps	Subs	Gls
Sunderland	App	10.85	84-90	21	11	2
Doncaster Rov.	L	11.86	86	6	1	3
Shrewsbury T.	L	11.89	89	3	0	0
Lincoln C.	L	01.90	89	9	0	1
Swansea C.	Tr	07.91	91	17	0	0

CORNISH, Richard G. (Ricky)
Newham, 1 December, 1970 (LB)

League Club	Source	Date Signed	Seasons Played	Apps	Subs	Gls
Aldershot	Cornard U.	11.90	90	7	2	0

CORNOCK, Walter B.
Australia, 1 January, 1921 (G)

League Club	Source	Date Signed	Seasons Played	Apps	Subs	Gls
Oldham Ath.		01.41				
Rochdale	Hereford U.	11.47	47	1	-	0

CORNWELL, Ellis
Coppull, 14 November, 1913 (FB)

League Club	Source	Date Signed	Seasons Played	Apps	Subs	Gls
Accrington St.	Chorley	11.45	46	5	-	0

CORNWELL, John A.
Bethnal Green, 13 October, 1964 (M/CD)

League Club	Source	Date Signed	Seasons Played	Apps	Subs	Gls
Leyton Orient	App	10.82	81-86	194	9	35
Newcastle U.	Tr	07.87	87-88	28	5	1
Swindon T.	Tr	12.88	88-89	7	18	0
Southend U.	Tr	08.90	90-91	56	6	2

CORNWELL, Kevin J.
Birmingham, 10 December,1941 (F)

League Club	Source	Date Signed	Seasons Played	Apps	Subs	Gls
Oxford U.	Banbury Spencer	07.62	62-63	26	-	10

CORR, John J.
Glasgow, 18 December, 1946 (W)

League Club	Source	Date Signed	Seasons Played	Apps	Subs	Gls
Arsenal	Possilpark Jnrs	07.65				
Exeter C.	Tr	07.67	67-70	73	6	19

CORR, Patrick M.
Derry (NI), 31 March, 1927 NI Amat/IRF Lge (WH)

League Club	Source	Date Signed	Seasons Played	Apps	Subs	Gls
Burnley	Coleraine	10.51	51	1	-	0

CORR, Peter J.
Dundalk (Ire), 26 June, 1923 IR-4 (OR)

League Club	Source	Date Signed	Seasons Played	Apps	Subs	Gls
Preston N. E.	Dundalk	04.47	46	3	-	0
Everton	Tr	08.48	48-49	24	-	2

CORRIGAN, Frank J.
Liverpool, 13 November, 1952 (M)

League Club	Source	Date Signed	Seasons Played	Apps	Subs	Gls
Blackpool	Ormskirk	08.72				
Walsall	Tr	07.73	73	1	0	0
Wigan Ath.	Northwich Vic.	(N/L)	78-80	113	3	12

CORRIGAN, Joseph T.
Manchester, 18 November, 1948 Eu21-3/EF Lge/E'B'/E-9 (G)

League Club	Source	Date Signed	Seasons Played	Apps	Subs	Gls
Manchester C.	Sale	01.67	68-82	476	0	0
Brighton & H. A.	Seattle (USA)	09.83	83	36	0	0
Norwich C.	L	09.84	84	3	0	0
Stoke C.	L	10.84	84	9	0	0

CORTHINE, Peter A.
Highbury, 19 July, 1937 (IF)

League Club	Source	Date Signed	Seasons Played	Apps	Subs	Gls
Chelsea	Leytonstone	12.57	59	2	-	0
Southend U.	Tr	03.60	59-61	73	-	24

COSSLETT, Michael P.
Barry, 17 April, 1957 (CD)

League Club	Source	Date Signed	Seasons Played	Apps	Subs	Gls
Newport Co.	Barry T.	02.78	77-78	2	0	0

COSTELLO, John
Prestonpans, 23 May, 1920 (FB)

League Club	Source	Date Signed	Seasons Played	Apps	Subs	Gls
Southend U.		08.52				
Barrow	Tr	07.53	53	6	-	0

COSTELLO, Matthew B.
Airdrie, 4 August, 1924 (OR)

League Club	Source	Date Signed	Seasons Played	Apps	Subs	Gls
Chesterfield	New Stevenston	05.49	49-51	18	-	2
Chester C.	Tr	07.52	52	9	-	2

COSTELLO, Mortimer D.
Dagenham, 8 July, 1936 (WH)

League Club	Source	Date Signed	Seasons Played	Apps	Subs	Gls
Aldershot (Am)	Leyton	05.56	56	28	-	7
Southend U.	Tr	05.57	57-64	250	-	15

COSTELLO, Nigel G.
Catterick, 22 November, 1968 (W)

League Club	Source	Date Signed	Seasons Played	Apps	Subs	Gls
York C. (N/C)	YT	07.87	86-87	2	2	0

COSTELLO, Peter
Halifax, 31 October, 1969 (F)

League Club	Source	Date Signed	Seasons Played	Apps	Subs	Gls
Bradford C.	YT	07.88	88-89	11	9	2
Rochdale	Tr	07.90	90	31	3	10
Peterborough U.	Tr	03.91	90-91	3	3	0
Lincoln C.	L	09.91	91	3	0	0

COTHLIFF, Harold
Liverpool, 24 March, 1916 (RH)

League Club	Source	Date Signed	Seasons Played	Apps	Subs	Gls
Manchester C.	Prestcot Cables	04.36				
Nottingham F.	Tr	05.37				
Torquay U.	Tr	06.38	38-47	65	-	1

COTON, Anthony P.
Tamworth, 19 May, 1961 E'B' (G)

League Club	Source	Date Signed	Seasons Played	Apps	Subs	Gls
Birmingham C.	Mile Oak Rov.	10.78	80-84	94	0	0
Watford	Tr	09.84	84-89	233	0	0
Manchester C.	Tr	07.90	90-91	70	0	0

League Club	Source	Date Signed	Seasons Played	Apps	Subs	Gls
COTON, Paul S.						
Birmingham, 9 February, 1949						(FB)
Walsall	App	02.67	66	1	0	0
COTTAM, John E.						
Worksop, 5 June, 1950						(CD)
Nottingham F.	App	04.68	70-75	92	3	4
Mansfield T.	L	11.72	72	2	0	1
Lincoln C.	L	03.73	72	1	0	0
Chesterfield	Tr	08.76	76-78	120	0	7
Chester C.	Tr	07.79	79-81	117	3	1
COTTEE, Anthony R.						
West Ham, 11 July, 1965 EYth/Eu21-8/E-7						(F)
West Ham U.	App	09.82	82-87	203	9	92
Everton	Tr	08.88	88-91	97	19	44
COTTERILL, Stephen						
Cheltenham, 20 July, 1964						(F)
Wimbledon	Burton A.	02.89	88-90	6	4	3
COTTEY, Philip A.						
Swansea, 2 June, 1966						(M)
Swansea C.	App	06.84	84	2	1	0
COTTINGTON, Brian A.						
Hammersmith, 14 February, 1965						(D)
Fulham	App	02.83	83-86	67	6	1
COTTON, Frederick						
Halesowen, 12 March, 1932						(IF)
Crystal Palace		08.56	56	4	-	0
COTTON, John						
Stoke, 2 March, 1930						(FB)
Stoke C.		05.52	52-53	3	-	0
Crewe Alex.	Tr	10.55	55	14	-	0
COTTON, Perry						
Chislehurst, 11 November, 1965						(F)
Scunthorpe U.	Nelson U. (NZ)	12.88	88-90	24	9	2
COTTON, Roy W. L.						
Fulham, 14 November, 1955 E Yth						(F)
Brentford (Am)	Jnrs	09.73	73	1	1	0
Leyton Orient	Tr	07.74	75	0	3	0
Aldershot	Tr	07.76	77	5	0	0
COTTON, Russell A.						
Wellington, 4 April, 1960						(M)
Colchester U.	App	04.78	77-81	33	4	1
COTTON, Terence						
Swansea, 25 January, 1946 W Amat						(CF)
Swansea C.	Ammanford	06.68	68-70	12	1	1
COUCH, Alan						
Neath, 15 March, 1953						(M)
Cardiff C.	Jnrs	08.70	71-72	7	4	0
COUCH, Geoffrey R.						
Crowle, 3 April, 1953						(F)
Scunthorpe U.	Crowle	03.78	77-79	22	4	5
COUGHLIN, Dennis M.						
Houghton-le-Spring, 26 November, 1937						(CF)
Barnsley	Durham C.	10.57				
Bournemouth	Yeovil T.	03.63	62-65	86	2	41
Swansea C.	Tr	08.66	66-67	38	1	11
Exeter C.	L	03.68	67	13	0	2
COUGHLIN, James						
Cheltenham, 26 July, 1953						(F)
Hereford U.	Albion Rov.	03.77	76	1	1	1
COUGHLIN, Russell J.						
Swansea, 15 February, 1960						(M)
Manchester C.	App	02.78				
Blackburn Rov.	Tr	03.79	78-80	22	2	0
Carlisle U.	Tr	10.80	80-83	114	16	13
Plymouth Arg.	Tr	07.84	84-87	128	3	18
Blackpool	Tr	12.87	87-89	100	2	8
Shrewsbury T.	L	09.90	90	4	1	0
Swansea C.	Tr	10.90	90-91	61	1	1
COULL, George						
Dundee, 10 August, 1935						(IF)
Millwall	Dundee Downfield	08.56	56	6	-	1
COULSON, William J.						
North Shields, 14 January, 1950						(W)
Newcastle U.	Consett	09.71				
Southend U.	Tr	10.73	73-75	51	1	4
Aldershot	L	02.75	74	3	0	0
Huddersfield T.	L	11.75	75	2	0	0
Darlington	L	01.76	75	11	2	1
COUPE, Joseph N.						
Carlisle, 15 July, 1924						(FB)
Carlisle U.	Swift Rov.	09.47	48-50	31	-	0
Rochdale	Tr	10.51	51	8	-	0
Workington	Tr	10.52	52	6	-	0
COUPLAND, Joseph						
Glasgow, 10 April, 1920						(FB)
Bradford C.	Ayr U.	08.50	50-51	18	-	0
Carlisle U.	Tr	07.52	52-53	3	-	0
COURT, Colin C.						
Winchester, 25 March, 1964						(G)
Reading (N/C)	Andover T.	07.81	81	1	0	0
COURT, Colin R.						
Ebbw Vale, 3 September, 1937 W Sch						(W)
Chelsea	Jnrs	09.54				
Torquay U.	Tr	05.59	59-60	27	-	5
COURT, David J.						
Mitcham, 1 March, 1944						(M)
Arsenal	App	01.62	62-69	168	7	17
Luton T.	Tr	07.70	70-71	50	2	0
Brentford	Tr	08.72	72	8	4	1
COURT, Harold J.						
Tirphil, 13 June, 1917						(IF)
Cardiff C.	Llanbradach	03.39	38	1	-	0
Swindon T.	Dundee	06.50	50	16	-	2
COUSANS, W. Eric						
Doncaster, 10 September, 1929						(W)
Walsall	Goole T.	08.54	54	4	-	1
Gillingham	Tr	09.55	55	2	-	0
COUSINS, Harold						
Chesterfield, 25 Sepember, 1907 Died 1981						(WH)
Chesterfield	North Wingfield	10.26	26-31	85	-	0
Swindon T.	Tr	08.32	32-46	240	-	1
COUSINS, Jason M.						
Hayes, 14 October, 1970						(CD)
Brentford	YT	07.89	89-90	20	1	0
COUSINS, Kenneth F.						
Bristol, 6 August, 1922						(G)
Bristol C.	Brislington	03.46	46	3	-	0
COUTTS, Roger						
Barrow, 18 December, 1944						(OR)
Barrow	Walney Rov.	08.64	64	2	-	0
COVERDALE, Andrew (Drew)						
Middlesbrough, 20 September, 1969						(FB)
Middlesbrough	YT	07.88				
Darlington	Tr	07.89	90-91	24	6	3
COWAN, Donald						
Durham, 17 August, 1931						(G)
Darlington		11.52	52-53	17	-	0
COWAN, Ian						
Falkirk, 27 November, 1944						(OR)
Southend U.	Dunfermline Ath.	07.70	70	3	0	0
COWAN, James C.						
Paisley, 16 June, 1926 Died 1968 SF Lge/S-25						(G)
Sunderland	Morton	06.53	53	28	-	0
COWAN, John						
Belfast, 8 January, 1949 NI-1						(M)
Newcastle U.	Crusaders	02.67	69-72	6	3	0
Darlington	Drogheda	08.75	75	10	0	0

COWAN, Thomas
Bellshill, 28 August, 1969 (LB)

League Club	Source	Date Signed	Seasons Played	Apps	Subs	Gls
Sheffield U.	Glasgow Rangers	07.91	91	20	0	0

COWANS, Gordon S.
Cornforth (Dm), 27 October, 1958 EYth/Eu21-5/E'B'/E-10 (M)

League Club	Source	Date Signed	Seasons Played	Apps	Subs	Gls
Aston Villa	App	09.76	75-84	276	10	42
Aston Villa	Bari (It)	07.88	88-91	114	3	7
Blackburn Rov.	Tr	11.91	91	26	0	1

COWDRILL, Barry J.
Birmingham, 3 January, 1957 (FB)

League Club	Source	Date Signed	Seasons Played	Apps	Subs	Gls
West Bromwich A.	Sutton Coldfield T.	04.79	79-87	127	4	0
Rotherham U.	L	10.85	85	2	0	0
Bolton W.	Tr	07.88	88-91	117	2	4
Rochdale	Tr	02.92	91	15	0	1

Barry Cowdrill (West Bromwich Albion, Bolton Wanderers & Rochdale)

COWELL, G. Robert
Trimdon, 5 December, 1922 (FB)

League Club	Source	Date Signed	Seasons Played	Apps	Subs	Gls
Newcastle U.	Blackhall Colly	10.43	46-54	289	-	0

COWEN, John M.
Lewisham, 1 December, 1944 EYth (G)

League Club	Source	Date Signed	Seasons Played	Apps	Subs	Gls
Chelsea	App	10.62				
Watford	Tr	10.64	64-66	17	0	0

COWIE, Andrew D.
Motherwell, 11 March, 1913 (WH)

League Club	Source	Date Signed	Seasons Played	Apps	Subs	Gls
Swindon T.	Aberdeen	07.48	48-50	89	-	4

COWIE, George A.
Buckie, 9 May, 1961 (M)

League Club	Source	Date Signed	Seasons Played	Apps	Subs	Gls
West Ham U.	App	08.78	81-82	6	2	0

COWLEY, Carl C.
Stepney, 10 July, 1965 (CD)

League Club	Source	Date Signed	Seasons Played	Apps	Subs	Gls
Millwall	App	10.82	83	2	1	0

COWLEY, Francis W.
Stepney, 28 November, 1957 (W)

League Club	Source	Date Signed	Seasons Played	Apps	Subs	Gls
Derby Co.	Sutton U.	08.77				
Wimbledon	Tr	02.78	77-78	5	3	0

COWLING, Christopher
Scunthorpe, 19 September, 1962 (F)

League Club	Source	Date Signed	Seasons Played	Apps	Subs	Gls
Scunthorpe U.	App	12.79	79-84	117	17	27

COWLING, David R.
Doncaster, 27 November, 1958 (LW)

League Club	Source	Date Signed	Seasons Played	Apps	Subs	Gls
Mansfield T.	App	11.76				
Huddersfield T.	Tr	08.77	78-87	331	9	43
Scunthorpe U.	L	11.87	87	1	0	0
Reading	L	12.87	87	2	0	0
Reading	Tr	03.88	87	7	1	1
Scunthorpe U.	Tr	08.88	88-90	85	4	5

COWLING, Jason P.
Cambridge, 12 August, 1969 (M)

League Club	Source	Date Signed	Seasons Played	Apps	Subs	Gls
Cambridge U. (N/C)	Jnrs	07.87	86	0	2	0

COWSILL, Charles
Farnworth, 5 May, 1929

League Club	Source	Date Signed	Seasons Played	Apps	Subs	Gls
Bury		05.50				
Workington		11.51	51	1	-	0

COX, Alan W.
Liverpool, 4 September, 1920 (OR)

League Club	Source	Date Signed	Seasons Played	Apps	Subs	Gls
Tranmere Rov.		03.41	46-47	8	-	1

COX, Albert E. H.
Treeton, 24 June, 1917 (FB)

League Club	Source	Date Signed	Seasons Played	Apps	Subs	Gls
Sheffield U.	Woodhouse Mill	04.35	35-51	267	-	5
Halifax T.	Tr	07.52	52-53	53	-	1

COX, Brian R.
Sheffield, 7 May, 1961 (G)

League Club	Source	Date Signed	Seasons Played	Apps	Subs	Gls
Sheffield Wed.	App	02.79	78-80	22	0	0
Huddersfield T.	Tr	03.82	81-87	213	0	0
Mansfield T.	Tr	08.88	88-89	54	0	0
Hartlepool U.	Tr	08.90	90	34	0	0

COX, David
Dukinfield, 16 September, 1936 (F)

League Club	Source	Date Signed	Seasons Played	Apps	Subs	Gls
Stockport Co.	Oldham Ath. (Am)	10.55	56-57	8	-	4

COX, Frederick J. A.
Reading, 1 November, 1920 Died 1973 (OR)

League Club	Source	Date Signed	Seasons Played	Apps	Subs	Gls
Tottenham H.	Jnrs	08.38	38-48	99	-	15
Arsenal	Tr	09.49	49-52	79	-	9
West Bromwich A.	Tr	07.53	53	4	-	1

COX, Geoffrey
Arley, 30 November, 1934 (IF)

League Club	Source	Date Signed	Seasons Played	Apps	Subs	Gls
Birmingham C.	Jnrs	12.51	52-56	35	-	3
Torquay U.	Tr	12.57	57-66	260	1	62

COX, Graham P.
Willesden, 30 April, 1959 (G)

League Club	Source	Date Signed	Seasons Played	Apps	Subs	Gls
Brentford	App	04.77	76-77	4	0	0
Aldershot (N/C)	Hillingdon Bor.	01.85	84-85	13	0	0

COX, Keith
Heanor, 26 January, 1936 (FB)

League Club	Source	Date Signed	Seasons Played	Apps	Subs	Gls
Charlton Ath.	Heanor T.	04.54	56-58	14	-	0

COX, Mark L.
Birmingham, 4 October, 1959 (F)

League Club	Source	Date Signed	Seasons Played	Apps	Subs	Gls
Lincoln C.	App	09.77	76-77	3	2	0
Doncaster Rov.	Tr	09.78	78	10	5	3

COX, Maurice
Torquay, 1 October, 1959 (F)

League Club	Source	Date Signed	Seasons Played	Apps	Subs	Gls
Torquay U.	Jnrs	01.80	78-81	49	13	13
Huddersfield T. (N/C)	Tr	08.82	82	3	1	1

COX, Neil J.
Scunthorpe, 8 October, 1971 (RB)

League Club	Source	Date Signed	Seasons Played	Apps	Subs	Gls
Scunthorpe U.	YT	03.90	90	17	0	1
Aston Villa	Tr	02.91	91	4	3	0

COX, Paul R.
Nottingham, 6 January, 1972 (M)

League Club	Source	Date Signed	Seasons Played	Apps	Subs	Gls
Notts Co.	YT	08.89	91	0	1	0

COX, Ronald B.
Coventry, 2 May, 1919 (CH)

League Club	Source	Date Signed	Seasons Played	Apps	Subs	Gls
Coventry C.	Wyken Pippin	10.45	46-51	29	-	0

COX, Samuel
Mexborough, 30 October, 1920 (FB)

League Club	Source	Date Signed	Seasons Played	Apps	Subs	Gls
West Bromwich A.	Denaby U.	05.48	48	2	-	0
Accrington St.	Tr	07.51	51	43	-	0
Scunthorpe U.	Tr	07.52	52	3	-	0

COXHILL, David
Aberdeen, 10 April, 1952 (M)

League Club	Source	Date Signed	Seasons Played	Apps	Subs	Gls
Millwall	Jnrs	06.70	70-71	6	2	0
Gillingham	Tr	07.73	73-74	32	2	1

COXON, E. Gary
Liverpool, 31 May, 1946 (FB)

League Club	Source	Date Signed	Seasons Played	Apps	Subs	Gls
Blackburn Rov.	Everton (App)	12.63	66-67	10	0	0

COXON, John
Old Hartley, 7 April, 1922 (FB)

League Club	Source	Date Signed	Seasons Played	Apps	Subs	Gls
Darlington (Am)	Hartley	05.46	46	1	-	0

COXON, William G.
Derby, 28 April, 1933 (OL)

League Club	Source	Date Signed	Seasons Played	Apps	Subs	Gls
Derby Co.	Jnrs	05.50				
Norwich C.	Ilkeston T.	05.52	52-57	98	-	24
Lincoln C.	Tr	03.58	57-58	11	-	6
Bournemouth	Tr	11.58	58-65	199	1	37

COY, Robert A.
Birmingham, 30 November, 1961 (CD)

League Club	Source	Date Signed	Seasons Played	Apps	Subs	Gls
Wolverhampton W.	App	11.79	81-83	40	3	0
Chester C.	Tr	03.84	83-85	93	0	2
Northampton T.	Tr	08.86	86	15	2	0

COYLE, Anthony
Glasgow, 17 January, 1960 (W)

League Club	Source	Date Signed	Seasons Played	Apps	Subs	Gls
Stockport Co.	Albion Rov.	12.79	79-85	215	4	28
Chesterfield	Tr	06.86	86-87	71	5	4
Stockport Co.	Tr	08.88	88	23	0	3
Exeter C. (N/C)	Northwich Vic.	11.89	89	1	0	0

COYLE, Francis (Fay)
Derry (NI), 1 April, 1924 NI Amat/NI-4 (CF)

League Club	Source	Date Signed	Seasons Played	Apps	Subs	Gls
Nottingham F.	Coleraine	03.58	57	3	-	0

COYLE, Robert I.
Belfast, 31 January, 1948 NI-5 (M)

League Club	Source	Date Signed	Seasons Played	Apps	Subs	Gls
Sheffield Wed.	Glentoran	03.72	72-73	38	2	2
Grimsby T.	Tr	10.74	74	24	0	1

COYLE, Ronald P.
Glasgow, 19 August, 1961 (M)

League Club	Source	Date Signed	Seasons Played	Apps	Subs	Gls
Middlesbrough	Glasgow Celtic	12.86	86	1	2	0
Rochdale	Tr	08.87	87	23	1	1

COYLE, William
Newcastle, 24 October, 1926 (CH)

League Club	Source	Date Signed	Seasons Played	Apps	Subs	Gls
Darlington (Am)	West Auckland	05.49	49	16	-	0

COYNE, Brian
Glasgow, 13 December, 1959 (M)

League Club	Source	Date Signed	Seasons Played	Apps	Subs	Gls
Shrewsbury T.	Glasgow Celtic	06.79	79	1	0	0

COYNE, Cyril
Barnsley, 2 May, 1924 Died 1981

League Club	Source	Date Signed	Seasons Played	Apps	Subs	Gls
Leeds U.	Barnsley Main Colly	10.44				
Halifax T.	Stalybridge Celtic	06.51	51	4	-	0

COYNE, Gerard A.
Hebburn, 9 August, 1948 (CF)

League Club	Source	Date Signed	Seasons Played	Apps	Subs	Gls
York C.		08.66	66	2	0	0

COYNE, John D.
Liverpool, 18 July, 1951 (F)

League Club	Source	Date Signed	Seasons Played	Apps	Subs	Gls
Tranmere Rov.		08.71	71	12	3	3
Hartlepool U.	Tr	07.72	72-73	47	8	9
Stockport Co.	Wigan Ath.	11.75	75	3	1	0

COYNE, Peter D.
Hartlepool, 13 November, 1958 (F)

League Club	Source	Date Signed	Seasons Played	Apps	Subs	Gls
Manchester U.	App	11.75	75	1	1	1
Crewe Alex.	Ashton U.	08.77	77-80	113	21	47
Swindon T.	Hyde U.	08.84	84-88	99	11	30
Aldershot	L	08.89	89	3	0	0

COZENS, John W.
Hammersmith, 14 May, 1946 (F)

League Club	Source	Date Signed	Seasons Played	Apps	Subs	Gls
Notts Co.	Hillingdon Bor.	08.70	70-72	41	5	13
Peterborough U.	Tr	11.72	72-77	127	5	41
Cambridge U.	Tr	12.77	77-79	52	9	3

CRABBE, S. A. John (Buster)
Weymouth, 20 October, 1954 (M)

League Club	Source	Date Signed	Seasons Played	Apps	Subs	Gls
Southampton	App	10.72	74-76	8	4	0
Gillingham	Tr	01.76	76-80	181	0	13
Carlisle U.	Tr	08.81	81	26	0	4
Hereford U.	Tr	08.82	82	15	1	2
Crewe Alex.	Tr	08.83	83-85	75	0	7
Torquay U.	Tr	09.85	85	27	2	2

CRABTREE, Richard E.
Exeter, 6 February, 1955 (G)

League Club	Source	Date Signed	Seasons Played	Apps	Subs	Gls
Bristol Rov.	App	02.73	71	7	0	0
Doncaster Rov.	L	10.74	74	1	0	0
Torquay U. (N/C)	Tr	08.75	75	1	0	0
Exeter C. (N/C)	Dawlish	07.83	83	1	0	0

CRADDOCK, L. Miller
Newent, 21 September, 1926 Died 1960 (F)

League Club	Source	Date Signed	Seasons Played	Apps	Subs	Gls
Newport Co.	Chelsea (Am)	05.46	46	7	-	0
Aston Villa	Hereford U.	09.48	48-50	34	-	10

CRAGGS, John E.
Flint Hill (Dm), 31 October, 1948 E Yth (RB)

League Club	Source	Date Signed	Seasons Played	Apps	Subs	Gls
Newcastle U.	App	12.65	66-70	50	2	1
Middlesbrough	Tr	08.71	71-81	408	1	12
Newcastle U.	Tr	08.82	82	10	2	0
Darlington	Tr	08.83	83-84	53	1	0

CRAIG, Albert H.
Glasgow, 3 January, 1962 (W)

League Club	Source	Date Signed	Seasons Played	Apps	Subs	Gls
Newcastle U.	Hamilton Acad.	02.87	86-88	6	4	0
Northampton T.	L	01.89	88	2	0	1

CRAIG, Benjamin
Leadgate, 6 December, 1915 (FB)

League Club	Source	Date Signed	Seasons Played	Apps	Subs	Gls
Huddersfield T.	Eden Colly	01.34	33-38	99	-	0
Newcastle U.	Tr	11.38	38-49	66	-	0

CRAIG, David J.
Belfast, 8 June, 1944 NI Yth/NIu23-1/NI-25 (RB)

League Club	Source	Date Signed	Seasons Played	Apps	Subs	Gls
Newcastle U.	App	04.62	63-77	346	5	8

CRAIG, Derek M.
Hexham, 28 July, 1952 (CD)

League Club	Source	Date Signed	Seasons Played	Apps	Subs	Gls
Newcastle U.	Jnrs	08.69				
Darlington	San Jose (USA)	09.75	75-79	186	1	10
York C.	Tr	05.80	80-81	53	0	1

CRAIG, James P.
Glasgow, 30 April, 1943 S-1 (FB)

League Club	Source	Date Signed	Seasons Played	Apps	Subs	Gls
Sheffield Wed.	Hellenic (SA)	12.72	72-73	5	1	0

CRAIG, Joseph
Alloa, 14 May, 1954 Su23-4/S-1 (F)

League Club	Source	Date Signed	Seasons Played	Apps	Subs	Gls
Blackburn Rov.	Glasgow Celtic	09.78	78-80	44	4	8

CRAIG, Robert
Consett, 16 June, 1928 (FB)

League Club	Source	Date Signed	Seasons Played	Apps	Subs	Gls
Sunderland	Jnrs	11.45	49	1	-	0

CRAIG, Robert M.
Airdrie, 8 April, 1935 (IF)

League Club	Source	Date Signed	Seasons Played	Apps	Subs	Gls
Sheffield Wed.	Third Lanark	11.59	59-61	84	-	25
Blackburn Rov.	Tr	04.62	61-62	8	-	3
Oldham Ath.	St Johnstone	03.64	63-64	18	-	4

CRAIG, Thomas B.
Glasgow, 21 November,1950 S Sch/Su21-1/Su23-9/S-1 (M)

League Club	Source	Date Signed	Seasons Played	Apps	Subs	Gls
Sheffield Wed.	Aberdeen	05.69	68-74	210	4	38
Newcastle U.	Tr	12.74	74-77	122	2	22
Aston Villa	Tr	01.78	77-78	27	0	2
Swansea C.	Tr	07.78	79-80	47	5	9
Carlisle U.	Tr	03.82	81-84	92	6	10

CRAIG, William D.
Liverpool, 27 December, 1921 (OR)

League Club	Source	Date Signed	Seasons Played	Apps	Subs	Gls
Blackpool		05.46				
Southport	Tr	08.48	48	5	-	2

CRAIG, William J.
Aberdeen, 11 September, 1929 (D)

League Club	Source	Date Signed	Seasons Played	Apps	Subs	Gls
Millwall	Dundee	08.56	56-58	21	-	1

CRAINIE, Daniel
Kilsyth, 24 May, 1962 Su21-1 (W)

League Club	Source	Date Signed	Seasons Played	Apps	Subs	Gls
Wolverhampton W.	Glasgow Celtic	12.83	83-85	63	1	4
Blackpool	L	03.85	84	6	0	0

CRAKER, Laurence D.
Aylesbury, 1 March, 1953 (M)

League Club	Source	Date Signed	Seasons Played	Apps	Subs	Gls
Chelsea	App	08.70				
Watford	Jewish Guild	11.72	72-76	60	6	4

CRAM, Robert
Hetton-le-Hole, 19 November, 1939 (RB)

League Club	Source	Date Signed	Seasons Played	Apps	Subs	Gls
West Bromwich A.	Jnrs	01.57	59-66	141	0	25
Colchester U.	Vancouver (Can)	01.70	69-71	99	1	4

CRAMPTON, David W.
Bearpark (Dm), 9 June, 1944 (G)

League Club	Source	Date Signed	Seasons Played	Apps	Subs	Gls
Blackburn Rov.	Spennymoor U.	03.68				
Darlington	Tr	07.69	69	14	0	0

CRAMPTON, Paul
Cleethorpes, 28 January, 1953 (FB)

League Club	Source	Date Signed	Seasons Played	Apps	Subs	Gls
Grimsby T. (App)	App	04.68	70	0	1	0

CRANE, Andrew D.
Ipswich, 3 January, 1967 (LB)

League Club	Source	Date Signed	Seasons Played	Apps	Subs	Gls
Ipswich T.	App	04.84				
Shrewsbury T.	Tr	06.87				
Hereford U.	Tr	07.88	88	30	2	0

CRANFIELD, Harold R.
Chesterton, 25 December, 1917 (OL)

League Club	Source	Date Signed	Seasons Played	Apps	Subs	Gls
Fulham	Cambridge T.	12.37	46	1	-	0
Bristol Rov.	Tr	06.47	47	24	-	2

CRANGLE, James P.
Glasgow, 4 April, 1953 (W)

League Club	Source	Date Signed	Seasons Played	Apps	Subs	Gls
York C.	Campsie B.W.	08.72	72	4	0	0

CRANSON, Ian
Easington, 2 July, 1964 Eu21-5 (CD)

League Club	Source	Date Signed	Seasons Played	Apps	Subs	Gls
Ipswich T.	App	07.82	83-87	130	1	4
Sheffield Wed.	Tr	03.88	87-88	29	1	0
Stoke C.	Tr	07.89	89-91	24	2	4

CRANSTON, Nicholas G.
Carlisle, 20 October, 1972 (M)

League Club	Source	Date Signed	Seasons Played	Apps	Subs	Gls
Carlisle U.	YT	01.92	91	0	2	0

CRANSTON, William
Kilmarnock, 18 January, 1942 (WH)

League Club	Source	Date Signed	Seasons Played	Apps	Subs	Gls
Blackpool	Saxone Y.C.	08.60	61-64	33	-	0
Preston N. E.	Tr	12.64	64-69	80	7	1
Oldham Ath.	Tr	07.70	69-72	98	2	2

CRAVEN, John R.
St Annes, 15 May, 1947 (M)

League Club	Source	Date Signed	Seasons Played	Apps	Subs	Gls
Blackpool	App	01.65	65-70	154	9	24
Crystal Palace	Tr	09.71	71-72	56	7	14
Coventry C.	Tr	05.73	73-76	86	3	8
Plymouth Arg.	Tr	01.77	76-77	45	0	3

CRAVEN, Michael
Birkenhead, 20 November, 1957 (G)

League Club	Source	Date Signed	Seasons Played	Apps	Subs	Gls
Chester C.	Jnrs	09.75	76	4	0	0

CRAVEN, Stephen J.
Birkenhead, 17 September, 1957 (M)

League Club	Source	Date Signed	Seasons Played	Apps	Subs	Gls
Tranmere Rov.		03.78	77-81	106	8	17
Crewe Alex.	Tr	08.82	82	26	3	3
Tranmere Rov.	Caernarfon T.	07.87	87	6	7	0

CRAVEN, Terence
Barnsley, 27 November, 1944 E Yth (WH)

League Club	Source	Date Signed	Seasons Played	Apps	Subs	Gls
Barnsley	Jnrs	06.63	64	3	-	0

CRAWFORD, Alan P.
Rotherham, 30 October, 1953 (W)

League Club	Source	Date Signed	Seasons Played	Apps	Subs	Gls
Rotherham U.	App	10.71	73-78	233	4	49
Mansfield T.	L	01.73	72	1	1	0
Chesterfield	Tr	08.79	79-81	88	6	20
Bristol C.	Tr	08.82	82-84	85	7	26
Exeter C.	Tr	07.85	85	33	0	3

CRAWFORD, Andrew
Filey, 30 January, 1959 (F)

League Club	Source	Date Signed	Seasons Played	Apps	Subs	Gls
Derby Co.	App	01.77	77-79	16	5	4
Blackburn Rov.	Tr	10.79	79-81	56	0	21
Bournemouth	Tr	11.81	81-82	31	2	10
Cardiff C.	Tr	08.83	83	6	0	1
Middlesbrough	Tr	10.83	83	8	1	1
Stockport Co. (N/C)		12.84	84	6	0	2
Torquay U. (N/C)		02.85	84	3	0	0

CRAWFORD, J. R. Bruce
Preston, 10 October, 1938 Eu23-1 (WH)

League Club	Source	Date Signed	Seasons Played	Apps	Subs	Gls
Blackpool	Jnrs	05.56	59-64	98	-	7
Tranmere Rov.	Tr	09.65	65-66	24	2	5

CRAWFORD, Campbell H. R.
Dumbarton, 1 December, 1943 S Sch (FB)

League Club	Source	Date Signed	Seasons Played	Apps	Subs	Gls
West Bromwich A.	Jnrs	12.60	63-66	10	0	0
Exeter C.	Tr	07.67	67-73	224	10	3

CRAWFORD, P. Graeme
Falkirk, 7 August, 1947 (G)

League Club	Source	Date Signed	Seasons Played	Apps	Subs	Gls
Sheffield U.	East Stirling	09.68	69-70	2	0	0
Mansfield T.	L	07.71	71	2	0	0
York C.	Tr	10.71	71-76	235	0	0
Scunthorpe U.	Tr	08.77	77-79	104	0	0
York C.	Tr	01.80	79	17	0	0
Rochdale	Tr	09.80	80-82	70	0	0

CRAWFORD, Ian
Edinburgh, 14 July, 1934 Su23-1 (OL)

League Club	Source	Date Signed	Seasons Played	Apps	Subs	Gls
West Ham U.	Hearts	07.61	61-62	24	-	5
Scunthorpe U.	Tr	02.63	62-63	35	-	2
Peterborough U.	Tr	07.64	64-68	172	0	6

CRAWFORD, James C.
Belshill, 27 September, 1930 (IF)

League Club	Source	Date Signed	Seasons Played	Apps	Subs	Gls
Leicester C.	Jnrs	10.47	50-53	10	-	2
Plymouth Arg.	Tr	03.54	53-55	25	-	4

CRAWFORD, John C. (Ian)
Falkirk, 27 June, 1922 (F)

League Club	Source	Date Signed	Seasons Played	Apps	Subs	Gls
Oldham Ath.	Ayr U.	07.52	52-53	24	-	8
Halifax T.	Tr	07.54	54	11	-	2

CRAWFORD, Raymond
Portsmouth, 13 July, 1936 EF Lge/E-2 (CF)

League Club	Source	Date Signed	Seasons Played	Apps	Subs	Gls
Portsmouth	Jnrs	12.54	57-58	19	-	9
Ipswich T.	Tr	09.58	58-63	197	-	143
Wolverhampton W.	Tr	09.63	63-64	57	-	39
West Bromwich A.	Tr	02.65	64-65	14	0	6
Ipswich T.	Tr	03.66	65-68	123	0	61
Charlton Ath.	Tr	03.69	68-69	21	0	7
Colchester U.	Kettering T.	06.70	70	45	0	25

Ray Crawford (Portsmouth, Ipswich Town, Wolverhampton Wanderers, West Bromwich Albion, Ipswich Town, Charlton Athletic, Colchester United & England)

League Club	Source	Date Signed	Seasons Played	Career Record Apps	Subs	Gls
CRAWLEY, Thomas						
Hamilton, 10 November, 1911 Died 1977						(CH)
Preston N. E.	Motherwell	05.35	35	2	-	0
Coventry C.	Tr	02.36	35-46	42	-	16
CRAWSHAW, Cyril B.						
Eccles, 2 March, 1916						(IF)
Exeter C.	Queen of South	07.39				
Hull C.	Stalybridge Celtic	06.46	46	2	-	1
CREAMER, Peter A.						
Hartlepool, 20 September, 1953 E Sch						(D)
Middlesbrough	App	10.70	72-73	9	0	0
York C.	L	11.75	75	4	0	0
Doncaster Rov.	Tr	12.75	75-76	31	1	0
Hartlepool U.	Tr	10.76	76-77	63	0	3
Rochdale (N/C)	Gateshead	12.78	78	18	2	0
CREANE, Gerard M.						
Lincoln, 2 February, 1962						(CD)
Lincoln C.	App	02.80	78-82	6	1	0
CRELLIN, Andrew						
Gainsborough, 11 October, 1954						(FB)
Doncaster Rov.	Ashby Inst.	03.74	74	4	0	0
CRERAND, Daniel P.						
Manchester, 5 May, 1969						(M)
Rochdale (N/C)	Chapel Villa	02.88	87	3	0	0
CRERAND, Patrick T.						
Glasgow, 19 February, 1939 Su23-1/SF Lge/S-16						(RH)
Manchester U.	Glasgow Celtic	02.63	62-70	304	0	10

League Club	Source	Date Signed	Seasons Played	Career Record Apps	Subs	Gls
CRESSWELL, Corbett E.						
Sunderland, 3 August, 1932 E Amat						(CH)
Carlisle U.	Bishop Auckland	03.58	57-58	14	-	2
CRESSWELL, Peter F.						
Linby (Nts), 9 November, 1935						(OR)
Derby Co.	Heanor T.	04.54	54-56	12	-	2
CRESSWELL, Philip						
Hucknall, 11 May, 1933						(OR)
Coventry C.	Jnrs	05.50	54	2	-	0
CRIBLEY, Alexander						
Liverpool, 1 April, 1957						(CD)
Liverpool		06.78				
Wigan Ath.	Tr	10.80	80-87	268	3	16
CRICHTON, George						
Leslie (Fife), 11 December, 1925						(FB)
Workington	Loughborough Col.	(N/L)	51	4	-	0
CRICHTON, Paul A.						
Pontefract, 3 October, 1965						(G)
Nottingham F.	Jnrs	05.86				
Notts Co.	L	09.86	86	5	0	0
Darlington	L	01.87	86	5	0	0
Peterborough U.	L	03.87	86	4	0	0
Darlington	L	09.87	87	3	0	0
Swindon T.	L	12.87	87	4	0	0
Rotherham U.	L	03.88	87	6	0	0
Torquay U.	L	08.88	88	13	0	0
Peterborough U.	Tr	11.88	88-89	47	0	0
Doncaster Rov.	Tr	08.90	90-91	36	0	0

Paddy Crerand (Glasgow Celtic, Manchester United & Scotland)

CRICKETT, Norman
Carlisle, 13 October, 1932 (OR)

League Club	Source	Date Signed	Seasons Played	Apps	Subs	Gls
Carlisle U.		11.52	55	1	-	0

CRICKMORE, Charles A.
Hull, 11 February, 1942 (OL)

League Club	Source	Date Signed	Seasons Played	Apps	Subs	Gls
Hull C.	Jnrs	02.59	59-61	53	-	13
Bournemouth	Tr	07.62	62-65	128	0	17
Gillingham	Tr	06.66	66-67	53	0	13
Rotherham U.	Tr	11.67	67	7	1	1
Norwich C.	Tr	01.68	67-69	54	2	9
Notts Co.	Tr	03.70	69-71	59	0	11

CRICKSON, George E. (Gerry)
Dover, 21 September, 1934 E Sch/ E Yth (WH)

League Club	Source	Date Signed	Seasons Played	Apps	Subs	Gls
Queens Park R	Jnrs	09.51	52-55	5	-	0

CRIPPS, Harold R.
East Dereham, 29 April, 1941 (LB)

League Club	Source	Date Signed	Seasons Played	Apps	Subs	Gls
West Ham U.	Jnrs	09.58				
Millwall	Tr	06.61	61-74	390	10	37
Charlton Ath.	Tr	10.74	74-75	17	3	4

Harry Cripps (West Ham United, Millwall & Charlton Athletic)

CRIPSEY, Brian
Hull, 26 June, 1931 (OL)

League Club	Source	Date Signed	Seasons Played	Apps	Subs	Gls
Hull C.	Brunswick Inst.	11.51	52-58	145	-	19
Wrexham	Tr	09.58	58-59	27	-	3

CRISP, Ronald J.
Slough, 24 September, 1938 (WH)

League Club	Source	Date Signed	Seasons Played	Apps	Subs	Gls
Watford	Dulwich Hamlet	01.61	60-64	89	-	14
Brentford	Tr	08.65	65-66	17	0	0

CRISPIN, Timothy
Leicester, 7 June, 1948 (FB)

League Club	Source	Date Signed	Seasons Played	Apps	Subs	Gls
Notts Co.	Jnrs	07.66	66-67	8	0	0

CROFT, Alexander R.
Chester, 17 June, 1937 (W)

League Club	Source	Date Signed	Seasons Played	Apps	Subs	Gls
Chester C.		08.58	58-60	53	-	3

CROFT, Brian G. A.
Chester, 27 September, 1967 (W)

League Club	Source	Date Signed	Seasons Played	Apps	Subs	Gls
Chester C.	YT	07.86	85-87	36	23	3
Cambridge U.	Tr	10.88	88	12	5	2
Chester C.	Tr	08.89	89-91	90	24	3

CROFT, Charles
Dewsbury, 26 November, 1918 (LH)

League Club	Source	Date Signed	Seasons Played	Apps	Subs	Gls
Huddersfield T.		05.39				
Mansfield T.	Tr	05.47	47-49	85	-	5

CROFT, Gary
Burton, 17 February, 1974

League Club	Source	Date Signed	Seasons Played	Apps	Subs	Gls
Grimsby T. (YT)	YT	07.90	90	0	1	0

CROFT, Stuart D.
Ashington, 12 April, 1954 (CD)

League Club	Source	Date Signed	Seasons Played	Apps	Subs	Gls
Hull C.	App	04.72	72-80	187	3	4
Portsmouth	Tr	03.81	80	6	0	1
York C.	Tr	08.81	81	14	0	0

CROKER, Edgar A. (Ted)
Kingston, 13 February, 1924 (LB)

League Club	Source	Date Signed	Seasons Played	Apps	Subs	Gls
Charlton Ath.	Kingstonian	07.48	50	8	-	0

CROKER, Peter H.
Kingston, 21 December, 1921 (RB)

League Club	Source	Date Signed	Seasons Played	Apps	Subs	Gls
Charlton Ath.	Bromley	11.45	46-50	59	-	0
Watford	Tr	06.52	52	23	-	0

CROMACK, David C.
Leeds, 22 December, 1948 (G)

League Club	Source	Date Signed	Seasons Played	Apps	Subs	Gls
Doncaster Rov.	Hull C. (Am)	11.66	66	8	0	0

CROMACK, Victor
Mansfield, 17 March, 1920 (G)

League Club	Source	Date Signed	Seasons Played	Apps	Subs	Gls
Mansfield T.		01.46	46	10	-	0

CROMBIE, Dean M.
Lincoln, 9 August, 1957 (D)

League Club	Source	Date Signed	Seasons Played	Apps	Subs	Gls
Lincoln C.	Ruston Sports	02.77	76-77	33	0	0
Grimsby T.	Tr	08.78	78-86	316	4	3
Reading	L	11.86	86	4	0	0
Bolton W.	Tr	08.87	87-90	90	5	1
Lincoln C.	Tr	01.91	90	0	1	0

CROMBIE, Thomas R.
Kirkcaldy, 3 June, 1930 (LB)

League Club	Source	Date Signed	Seasons Played	Apps	Subs	Gls
Blackpool	Jeanfield Swifts	08.51				
Gillingham	Tr	07.55	55-56	17	-	0

CROMPTON, Alan
Manchester, 6 March, 1958 (M)

League Club	Source	Date Signed	Seasons Played	Apps	Subs	Gls
Sunderland	App	03.75				
Blackburn Rov.	Tr	07.76	76	2	2	0
Wigan Ath.	Tr	(N/L)	78-79	7	7	0

CROMPTON, David G.
Wigan, 6 March, 1945 (WH)

League Club	Source	Date Signed	Seasons Played	Apps	Subs	Gls
Rochdale (Am)		11.66	66-67	15	2	0

CROMPTON, Dennis
Bolton, 12 March, 1942 (WH)

League Club	Source	Date Signed	Seasons Played	Apps	Subs	Gls
Burnley	Wigan Ath.	12.59				
Doncaster Rov.	Tr	06.63	63	23	-	0

CROMPTON, John (Jack)
Manchester, 18 December, 1921 (G)

League Club	Source	Date Signed	Seasons Played	Apps	Subs	Gls
Manchester U.	Goslings	01.45	46-55	191	-	0

CROMPTON, Jonathan D.
Orrell, 25 January, 1970 (F)

League Club	Source	Date Signed	Seasons Played	Apps	Subs	Gls
Wigan Ath.	YT	07.88	89	1	0	0

CROMPTON, Stephen W.
Wrexham, 3 December, 1958 (F)

League Club	Source	Date Signed	Seasons Played	Apps	Subs	Gls
Hereford U.	Wolverhampton W.(App)	02.77	76-78	30	4	6

CROMPTON, Steven G.
Partington, 20 April, 1968 (G)

League Club	Source	Date Signed	Seasons Played	Apps	Subs	Gls
Manchester C.	Jnrs	05.86				
Carlisle U.	Tr	07.87	87	10	0	0
Stockport Co.(N/C)	Tr	02.88	87	2	0	0

CRONIN, Dennis
Manchester, 30 October, 1967 (F)

League Club	Source	Date Signed	Seasons Played	Apps	Subs	Gls
Manchester U.	App	10.85				
Stockport Co.	Tr	08.87	87	11	4	1
Crewe Alex.	Tr	08.88	88	12	3	2

CRONIN, Thomas P.
Richmond, 17 December, 1932 (WH)

League Club	Source	Date Signed	Seasons Played	Apps	Subs	Gls
Fulham	East Sheen Ath.	09.50	53-54	2	-	0
Reading	Tr	06.56	56-57	30	-	4

CROOK, Alfred R.
Brewood, 13 August, 1923 (FB)

League Club	Source	Date Signed	Seasons Played	Apps	Subs	Gls
Wolverhampton W.	Boulton Paul	05.45	48	1	-	0

CROOK, George
Easington, 30 January, 1935 (IF)

League Club	Source	Date Signed	Seasons Played	Apps	Subs	Gls
Oldham Ath.		02.53	53-57	57	-	13
Middlesbrough	Tr	11.58				

CROOK, Ian S.
Romford, 18 January, 1963 E'B' (M)

League Club	Source	Date Signed	Seasons Played	Apps	Subs	Gls
Tottenham H.	App	08.80	81-85	10	10	1
Norwich C.	Tr	06.86	86-91	151	19	11

Ian Crook (Tottenham Hotspur & Norwich City)

CROOK, Leslie R.
Manchester, 26 June, 1949 (M)

League Club	Source	Date Signed	Seasons Played	Apps	Subs	Gls
Oxford U.	Manchester Amats	10.68	68	1	0	0
Hartlepool U.	Tr	07.70	70	23	2	3

CROOK, Walter
Chorley, 28 April, 1913 Died 1988 (FB)

League Club	Source	Date Signed	Seasons Played	Apps	Subs	Gls
Blackburn Rov.	Jnrs	01.31	31-46	218	-	2
Bolton W.	Tr	05.47	47	28	-	0

CROOK, William C.
Wolverhampton, 7 June, 1926 (WH)

League Club	Source	Date Signed	Seasons Played	Apps	Subs	Gls
Wolverhampton W.	Jnrs	08.45	46-52	196	-	1
Walsall	Tr	10.54	54-55	46	-	2

CROOKES, Robert E.
Retford, 29 February, 1924 (IF)

League Club	Source	Date Signed	Seasons Played	Apps	Subs	Gls
Notts Co.	Retford T.	06.49	49-55	177	-	45

CROOKS, Garth A.
Stoke, 10 March, 1958 Eu21-4 (F)

League Club	Source	Date Signed	Seasons Played	Apps	Subs	Gls
Stoke C.	App	03.76	75-79	141	6	48
Tottenham H.	Tr	07.80	80-84	121	4	48
Manchester U.	L	11.83	83	6	1	2
West Bromwich A.	Tr	08.85	85-86	39	1	16
Charlton Ath.	Tr	03.87	86-90	41	15	15

CROOKS, Paul
Durham, 12 October, 1966 (F)

League Club	Source	Date Signed	Seasons Played	Apps	Subs	Gls
Stoke C.	Caernarfon T.	08.86	86	0	1	0

CROOKS, Samuel D.
Bearpark, 16 January, 1908 Died 1981 EF Lge/E-26 (OR)

League Club	Source	Date Signed	Seasons Played	Apps	Subs	Gls
Durham C.	Tow Law	06.26	26	15	-	4
Derby Co.	Tr	04.27	27-46	408	-	101

CROPLEY, Alexander J.
Aldershot, 16 January, 1951 Su23-3/S-2 (M)

League Club	Source	Date Signed	Seasons Played	Apps	Subs	Gls
Arsenal	Hibernian	12.74	74-76	29	1	5
Aston Villa	Tr	09.78	76-79	65	2	7
Newcastle U.	L	02.80	79	3	0	0
Portsmouth	Toronto (USA)	09.81	81	8	2	2

CROPLEY, John T.
Edinburgh, 27 September, 1924 (WH)

League Club	Source	Date Signed	Seasons Played	Apps	Subs	Gls
Aldershot	Tranent Jnrs	10.46	47-53	162	-	3

CROSBIE, Robert C.
Glasgow, 2 September, 1925 (CF)

League Club	Source	Date Signed	Seasons Played	Apps	Subs	Gls
Bury		05.47	47-48	9	-	5
Bradford P. A.	Tr	05.49	49-53	139	-	72
Hull C.	Tr	10.53	53-54	61	-	22
Grimsby T.	Tr	07.55	55-56	65	-	45

CROSBY, Andrew K.
Rotherham, 3 March, 1973 (D)

League Club	Source	Date Signed	Seasons Played	Apps	Subs	Gls
Doncaster Rov.	Leeds U. (YT)	07.91	91	15	7	0

CROSBY, Gary
Sleaford, 8 May, 1964 (W)

League Club	Source	Date Signed	Seasons Played	Apps	Subs	Gls
Lincoln C. (N/C)	Lincoln U.	08.86	86	6	1	0
Nottingham F.	Grantham	12.87	87-91	115	8	11

Gary Crosby (Lincoln City & Nottingham Forest)

League Club	Source	Date Signed	Seasons Played	Apps	Subs	Gls
CROSBY, Geoffrey J.						
Stoke, 24 August, 1931						(F)
Stockport Co.	Leek T.	09.52	52-53	5	-	1
CROSBY, Malcolm						
South Shields, 4 July, 1954						(M)
Aldershot	App	07.72	71-81	272	22	23
York C.	Tr	11.81	81-84	99	4	4
Wrexham	L	09.84	84	5	1	0
CROSBY, Philip A.						
Leeds, 9 November, 1962 E Yth						(LB)
Grimsby T.	App	09.80	79-82	34	5	1
Rotherham U.	Tr	08.83	83-88	181	2	2
Peterborough U.	Tr	08.89	89-90	85	2	0
York C.	Tr	07.91	91	25	0	0
CROSLAND, John R.						
St Annes, 10 November, 1922 E 'B'-2						(FB)
Blackpool	Ansdell Rov.	05.46	46-53	68	-	0
Bournemouth	Tr	06.54	54-56	106	-	0
CROSS, David						
Heywood, 8 December, 1950						(F)
Rochdale	Jnrs	08.69	69-71	50	9	21
Norwich C.	Tr	10.71	71-73	83	1	21
Coventry C.	Tr	11.73	73-76	90	1	30
West Bromwich A.	Tr	11.76	76-77	38	0	18
West Ham U.	Tr	12.77	77-81	178	1	77
Manchester C.	Tr	08.82	82	31	0	12
Oldham Ath.	Vancouver (Can)	10.83	83	18	4	6
West Bromwich A.	Vancouver (Can)	10.84	84	16	0	2
Bolton W.	Tr	06.85	85	19	1	8
Bury	L	01.86	85	12	1	0
CROSS, Graham F.						
Leicester, 15 November, 1943						(CD)
Leicester C.	App	11.60	60-75	495	3	29
Chesterfield	L	03.76	75	12	0	0
Brighton & H. A.	Tr	06.76	76	46	0	3
Preston N. E.	Tr	07.77	77-78	45	0	1
Lincoln C.	Enderby T.	03.79	78	19	0	0
CROSS, James K.						
Liverpool, 3 December, 1926						(RH)
Everton		10.50				
Swindon T.	Tr	07.53	53-57	154	-	5
CROSS, John (Jack)						
Bury, 5 February, 1927						(CF)
Bournemouth	Guildford C.	06.47	47-53	137	-	64
Northampton T.	Tr	10.53	53	10	-	10
Sheffield U.	Tr	02.54	53-55	44	-	16
Reading	Tr	10.55	55	15	-	6
CROSS, Jonathan N.						
Wallasey, 2 March, 1975						(M)
Wrexham (YT)	YT	07.91	91	3	3	0
CROSS, Michael J.						
Walkden, 25 April, 1956						(LB)
Bolton W.	App	04.74				
Stockport Co.	Tr	07.75	75	27	0	2
CROSS, Nicholas J. R.						
Birmingham, 7 February, 1961						(F)
West Bromwich A.	App	02.79	80-84	68	37	15
Walsall	Tr	08.85	85-87	107	2	45
Leicester C.	Tr	01.88	87-88	54	4	15
Port Vale	Tr	06.89	89-91	58	11	16
CROSS, Paul						
Barnsley, 31 October, 1965						(LB)
Barnsley	App	10.83	82-91	115	4	0
Preston N.E.	L	09.91	91	5	0	0
Hartlepool U.	Tr	01.92	91	21	0	0
CROSS, Roger G.						
East Ham, 20 October, 1948						(F)
West Ham U.	App	07.64	68-69	5	2	1
Leyton Orient	L	10.68	68	4	2	2
Brentford	Tr	03.70	69-71	62	0	18
Fulham	Tr	09.71	71-72	39	1	8
Brentford	Tr	12.72	72-76	141	4	52
Millwall	Tr	01.77	76-78	14	4	0

League Club	Source	Date Signed	Seasons Played	Apps	Subs	Gls
CROSS, Roy						
Walsall, 4 December, 1947						(CH)
Walsall	Jnrs	07.66	66-69	11	1	0
Port Vale	Tr	07.70	70-74	135	0	0
CROSS, Ryan						
Plymouth, 11 October, 1972						(D)
Plymouth Arg.	YT	03.91	90-91	18	1	0
CROSS, Stephen C.						
Wolverhampton, 22 December, 1959						(M/FB)
Shrewsbury T.	App	12.77	76-85	240	22	34
Derby Co.	Tr	06.86	86-91	42	31	3
Bristol Rov.	Tr	09.91	91	31	1	2
CROSSAN, Edward						
Derry (NI), 17 November, 1925 NI-3						(IF)
Blackburn Rov.	Derry C.	11.47	47-56	287	-	73
Tranmere Rov.	Tr	08.57	57	39	-	6
CROSSAN, Errol G.						
Canada, 6 October, 1930						(OR)
Manchester C.	Isle of Man	01.54				
Gillingham	Tr	07.55	55-56	76	-	16
Southend U.	Tr	08.57	57-58	40	-	11
Norwich C.	Tr	09.58	58-60	102	-	28
Leyton Orient	Tr	01.61	60	8	-	2
CROSSAN, John A.						
Derry (NI), 29 November, 1938 NI-23						(IF)
Sunderland	Standard Liége (Bel)	10.62	62-64	82	-	39
Manchester C.	Tr	01.65	64-66	94	0	24
Middlesbrough	Tr	08.67	67-69	54	2	7
CROSSLEY, James						
Belfast, 19 July, 1922						(LB)
Portsmouth	Cliftonville	04.45				
Reading	Tr	07.46	46	1	-	0
CROSSLEY, Mark G.						
Barnsley, 16 June, 1969 Eu21-3						(G)
Nottingham F.	YT	07.87	88-91	84	0	0
CROSSLEY, Paul						
Rochdale, 14 July, 1948						(W)
Rochdale	Jnrs	09.65	65-66	17	0	2
Preston N. E.	Tr	11.66	66-67	3	0	0
Southport	L	09.68	68	10	0	2
Tranmere Rov.	Tr	06.69	69-75	186	17	37
Chester C.	Tr	09.75	75-77	93	6	26
CROSSLEY, Richard M.						
Huddersfield, 5 September, 1970						(CD)
York C.	Northwich Vic.	10.89	89-90	6	0	0
CROSSLEY, Roy						
Hebden Bridge, 16 October, 1923						(CF)
Huddersfield T.		05.46				
Halifax T.		09.48	48-50	41	-	15
CROSSLEY, Russell						
Hebden Bridge, 25 June, 1927						(G)
Liverpool	Jnrs	06.47	50-53	68	-	0
Shrewsbury T.	Tr	07.54	54-59	173	-	0
CROSSLEY, Terence G.						
Birkenhead, 24 February, 1936						(OL)
Oldham Ath.	Bangor Univ.	08.57	57	2	-	1
CROSSON, David J.						
Bishop Auckland, 24 November, 1952						(RB)
Newcastle U.	Jnrs	11.70	73-74	6	0	0
Darlington	Tr	08.75	75-79	115	13	2
CROTTY, Colin						
Aberfan, 12 February, 1951						(F)
Swansea C. (Am)	Jnrs	08.68	68	1	1	1
CROUCH, Nigel J.						
Ardleigh, 24 November, 1958						(FB)
Ipswich T.	App	11.76				
Lincoln C.	L	08.79	79	7	0	0
Colchester U.	Tr	07.80	80	9	1	0

CROWE, Alexander A.
Motherwell, 24 November, 1924 (IF)

League Club	Source	Date Signed	Seasons Played	Apps	Subs	Gls
Ipswich T.	St Mirren	05.53	53-54	50	-	9

CROWE, Charles A.
Newcastle, 30 October, 1924 (WH)

League Club	Source	Date Signed	Seasons Played	Apps	Subs	Gls
Newcastle U.	Wallsend St Luke	10.44	46-56	178	-	5
Mansfield T.	Tr	02.57	56-57	37	-	0

CROWE, Christopher
Newcastle, 11 June, 1939 S Sch/E Yth/Eu23-4/E-1 (IF)

League Club	Source	Date Signed	Seasons Played	Apps	Subs	Gls
Leeds U.	Jnrs	06.56	56-59	97	-	27
Blackburn Rov.	Tr	03.60	59-61	51	-	6
Wolverhampton W.	Tr	02.62	61-63	83	-	24
Nottingham F.	Tr	08.64	64-66	73	0	12
Bristol C.	Tr	01.67	66-68	66	1	13
Walsall	Tr	09.69	69	10	3	1

CROWE, Mark A.
Southwold, 21 January, 1965 (CD)

League Club	Source	Date Signed	Seasons Played	Apps	Subs	Gls
Norwich C.	App	01.83	82	1	-	0
Torquay U.	Tr	07.85	85-86	57	0	2
Cambridge U.	Tr	12.86	86-87	51	0	0

CROWE, Matthew J.
Bathgate, 4 July, 1932 (WH)

League Club	Source	Date Signed	Seasons Played	Apps	Subs	Gls
Bradford P. A.	Bathgate Th.	07.49	52	1	-	0
Norwich C.	Partick Th.	05.57	57-61	186	-	14
Brentford	Tr	07.62	62-63	73	-	0

CROWE, Michael
Ulverston, 13 August, 1942 (IF)

League Club	Source	Date Signed	Seasons Played	Apps	Subs	Gls
Barrow	Ulverston Ath.	08.60	60-62	15	-	1

CROWE, Victor H.
Abercynon, 31 January, 1932 W-16 (WH)

League Club	Source	Date Signed	Seasons Played	Apps	Subs	Gls
Aston Villa	West Bromwich A.(Am)	06.52	54-63	294	-	10
Peterborough U.	Tr	07.64	64-66	56	0	0

CROWN, David I.
Enfield, 16 February, 1958 (F)

League Club	Source	Date Signed	Seasons Played	Apps	Subs	Gls
Brentford	Walthamstow Ave.	07.80	80-81	44	2	8
Portsmouth	Tr	10.81	81-82	25	3	2
Exeter C.	L	03.83	82	6	1	3
Reading	Tr	08.83	83-84	87	1	15
Cambridge U.	Tr	07.85	85-87	106	0	44
Southend U.	Tr	11.87	87-89	113	0	61
Gillingham	Tr	06.90	90-91	64	2	32

CROWSHAW, Alan A.
Willenhall, 12 December, 1932 (OL)

League Club	Source	Date Signed	Seasons Played	Apps	Subs	Gls
West Bromwich A.	Bloxwich Strollers	05.50	54-55	11	-	2
Derby Co.	Tr	06.56	56-57	18	-	6
Millwall	Tr	05.58	58-59	49	-	10

CROWTHER, Kenneth
Halifax, 17 December, 1924 (IF)

League Club	Source	Date Signed	Seasons Played	Apps	Subs	Gls
Burnley	Halifax T. (Am)	09.45				
Bradford P. A.	Tr	07.48	48	6	-	1
Rochdale	Tr	08.50	50	2	-	0

CROWTHER, Stanley
Bilston, 3 September, 1935 Eu23-3 (WH)

League Club	Source	Date Signed	Seasons Played	Apps	Subs	Gls
Aston Villa	Bilston	08.55	56-57	50	-	4
Manchester U.	Tr	02.58	57-58	13	-	0
Chelsea	Tr	12.58	58-59	51	-	0
Brighton & H. A.	Tr	03.61	60	4	-	0

CROWTHER, Stephen J.
Romiley, 16 January, 1955 (FB)

League Club	Source	Date Signed	Seasons Played	Apps	Subs	Gls
Stockport Co.		01.74	73-74	42	2	4
Hartlepool U.	Tr	07.75	75	3	0	0

CROY, John
Falkirk, 23 February, 1925 (FB)

League Club	Source	Date Signed	Seasons Played	Apps	Subs	Gls
Northampton T.	Third Lanark	07.50	51-54	24	-	0

CROZIER, Joseph
Coatbridge, 2 December, 1914 Died 1985 (G)

League Club	Source	Date Signed	Seasons Played	Apps	Subs	Gls
Brentford	East Fife	05.37	37-48	200	-	0

CRUDGINGTON, Geoffrey
Wolverhampton, 14 February, 1952 E Sch (G)

League Club	Source	Date Signed	Seasons Played	Apps	Subs	Gls
Aston Villa	Wolverhampton W. (Jnr)	09.69	70-71	4	0	0
Bradford C.	L	03.71	70	1	0	0
Crewe Alex.	Tr	03.72	71-77	250	0	0
Swansea C.	Tr	07.78	78-79	52	0	0
Plymouth Arg.	Tr	10.79	79-87	326	0	0

CRUICKSHANK, Frank J.
Falkirk, 20 November,1931 (FB)

League Club	Source	Date Signed	Seasons Played	Apps	Subs	Gls
Notts Co.	Nuneaton Bor.	01.50	53-59	151	-	5

CRUICKSHANK, George
Malaya, 22 July, 1931 (IF)

League Club	Source	Date Signed	Seasons Played	Apps	Subs	Gls
Carlisle U.	Queen of South	08.57	57	14	-	0

CRUICKSHANK, J. Paul
Oldham, 18 January, 1960 (M)

League Club	Source	Date Signed	Seasons Played	Apps	Subs	Gls
Blackpool	App	08.77				
Bury	Tr	07.79	79-82	65	17	4

CRUMBLEHULME, Kevin
Manchester, 17 June, 1952 (M)

League Club	Source	Date Signed	Seasons Played	Apps	Subs	Gls
Oldham Ath.	App	07.70	71	2	0	0

CRUMPLIN, Ian
Newburn, 12 September, 1954 (F)

League Club	Source	Date Signed	Seasons Played	Apps	Subs	Gls
Hartlepool U.	Blue Star	06.78	78	25	4	5

CRUMPLIN, John L.
Bath, 26 May, 1967 (W/FB)

League Club	Source	Date Signed	Seasons Played	Apps	Subs	Gls
Brighton & H. A.	Bognor Regis T.	02.87	86-91	117	26	4

CRUSE, Peter L.
Camden, 10 January, 1951 E Amat (M)

League Club	Source	Date Signed	Seasons Played	Apps	Subs	Gls
Arsenal	Slough T.	04.72				
Luton T.	Tr	07.73	73	3	1	0
Shrewsbury T.	L	02.74	73	2	0	0

CRUTCHLEY, W. Ronald
Walsall, 20 June, 1922 (WH)

League Club	Source	Date Signed	Seasons Played	Apps	Subs	Gls
Walsall		03.45	46-49	62	-	4
Shrewsbury T.	Tr	09.50	50-53	146	-	1

CRYLE, George
Aberdeen, 10 April, 1928 (WH)

League Club	Source	Date Signed	Seasons Played	Apps	Subs	Gls
Wolverhampton W.	Jnrs	02.46				
Reading	Tr	06.48	48-50	8	-	2
Swindon T.	Ayr U.	08.52	52	12	-	0

CUBIE, Neil G.
South Africa, 3 November, 1932 (WH)

League Club	Source	Date Signed	Seasons Played	Apps	Subs	Gls
Bury	Clyde (SA)	10.56				
Hull C.	Tr	07.57	57	4	-	0

CUDDIHEY, Russell
Rawtenstall, 8 September, 1939 (WH)

League Club	Source	Date Signed	Seasons Played	Apps	Subs	Gls
Accrington St.		09.60	60	10	-	0

CUDDY, Paul
Kendal, 21 February, 1959 E Semi-Pro (D)

League Club	Source	Date Signed	Seasons Played	Apps	Subs	Gls
Rochdale (N/C)	Jnrs	08.77	77	0	1	0

CUFF, Patrick J.
Middlesbrough, 19 March, 1952 E Sch (G)

League Club	Source	Date Signed	Seasons Played	Apps	Subs	Gls
Middlesbrough	App	05.69	73-77	31	0	0
Grimsby T.	L	09.71	71	2	0	0
Millwall	Tr	08.78	78	42	0	0
Darlington	Tr	06.80	80-82	110	0	0

CUGGY, M. Stephen
Wallsend, 18 March, 1971 (F)

League Club	Source	Date Signed	Seasons Played	Apps	Subs	Gls
Maidstone U.	Blyth Spartans	06.91	91	1	12	1

CULLEN, Anthony
Gateshead, 30 September, 1969 (W)

League Club	Source	Date Signed	Seasons Played	Apps	Subs	Gls
Sunderland	Newcastle U. (YT)	09.88	88-91	11	18	0
Carlisle U.	L	12.89	89	2	0	1
Rotherham U.	L	01.91	90	3	0	1
Bury	L	10.91	91	4	0	0

CULLEN, D. John
Durham, 10 January, 1973 (M)

League Club	Source	Date Signed	Seasons Played	Apps	Subs	Gls
Doncaster Rov.	YT	09.91	90-91	8	1	0

CULLEN, S. John R.
Oxford, 9 October, 1962 (FB)

League Club	Source	Date Signed	Seasons Played	Apps	Subs	Gls
Reading	App	10.80	79-81	14	5	0

CULLEN, Michael J.
Glasgow, 3 July, 1931 S'B'-1/S-1 (IF)

League Club	Source	Date Signed	Seasons Played	Apps	Subs	Gls
Luton T.	Douglasdale Jnrs	08.49	51-57	111	-	16
Grimsby T.	Tr	04.58	58-62	178	-	35
Derby Co.	Tr	12.62	62-64	24	-	5

CULLEN, Patrick J.
Mexborough, 9 August, 1949 IR Amat (F)

League Club	Source	Date Signed	Seasons Played	Apps	Subs	Gls
Halifax T.	Mexborough	05.68	67-73	1	5	0

CULLERTON, Michael J.
Edinburgh, 25 November, 1948 (M)

League Club	Source	Date Signed	Seasons Played	Apps	Subs	Gls
Port Vale		01.66	65-68	95	2	22
Chester C.	L	03.69	68	5	2	0
Derby Co.	Tr	07.69				
Port Vale	Stafford R.	07.75	75-77	67	16	28

CULLINGFORD, Robert
Bradford, 3 December, 1953 (D)

League Club	Source	Date Signed	Seasons Played	Apps	Subs	Gls
Bradford C. (Am)	Jnrs	10.69	69-71	1	1	0

CULLIS, Stanley
Ellesmere Port, 25 October, 1915 EF Lge/E-12 (CH)

League Club	Source	Date Signed	Seasons Played	Apps	Subs	Gls
Wolverhampton W.	Ellesmere Port	02.34	34-46	152	-	0

CULLUM, Arthur R.
Colchester, 28 January, 1931 (F)

League Club	Source	Date Signed	Seasons Played	Apps	Subs	Gls
Colchester U.		01.51	50-53	2	-	1

CULLUM, Riley G.
West Ham, 2 April, 1923 (IF)

League Club	Source	Date Signed	Seasons Played	Apps	Subs	Gls
Charlton Ath.	Dartford	10.47	49-52	32	-	6

CULPIN, Paul
Kirby Muxloe, 8 February, 1962 E Semi-Pro (F)

League Club	Source	Date Signed	Seasons Played	Apps	Subs	Gls
Leicester C.		05.81				
Coventry C.	Nuneaton Bor.	06.85	85-86	5	4	2
Northampton T.	Tr	10.87	87-89	52	11	24
Peterborough U.	Tr	10.89	89-91	30	17	15
Hereford U. (N/C)	Tr	02.92	91	1	1	0

CULVERHOUSE, Ian B.
Bishops Stortford, 22 September, 1964 E Yth (RB)

League Club	Source	Date Signed	Seasons Played	Apps	Subs	Gls
Tottenham H.	App	09.82	83	1	1	0
Norwich C.	Tr	10.85	85-91	212	1	0

CUMBES, James
Manchester, 4 May, 1944 (G)

League Club	Source	Date Signed	Seasons Played	Apps	Subs	Gls
Tranmere Rov.	Runcorn	09.65	66-69	137	0	0
West Bromwich A.	Tr	08.69	69-71	64	0	0
Aston Villa	Tr	10.71	71-75	157	0	0
Southport (N/C)	Portland (USA)	01.78	77	19	0	0

CUMMING, David S.
Aberdeen, 6 May, 1910 S-1 (G)

League Club	Source	Date Signed	Seasons Played	Apps	Subs	Gls
Middlesbrough	Aberdeen	10.36	36-46	135	-	0

CUMMING, Gordon R. R.
Johnstone, 23 January, 1948 (M)

League Club	Source	Date Signed	Seasons Played	Apps	Subs	Gls
Arsenal	Glasgow U.	01.65				
Reading	Tr	12.69	69-77	277	18	51

CUMMING, Robert
Airdrie, 7 December, 1955 (W/FB)

League Club	Source	Date Signed	Seasons Played	Apps	Subs	Gls
Grimsby T.	Baillieston Jnrs	03.74	74-86	338	27	58
Lincoln C.	Tr	07.87	88-89	40	1	5

CUMMINGS, George W.
Falkirk, 5 June, 1913 Died 1987 SF Lge/S-9 (FB)

League Club	Source	Date Signed	Seasons Played	Apps	Subs	Gls
Aston Villa	Partick Th.	11.35	35-48	210	-	0

CUMMINGS, John
Greenock, 5 May, 1944 (CF)

League Club	Source	Date Signed	Seasons Played	Apps	Subs	Gls
Port Vale	Aberdeen	08.65	65	2	1	0

CUMMINGS, Robert D.
Ashington, 17 November, 1935 (CF)

League Club	Source	Date Signed	Seasons Played	Apps	Subs	Gls
Newcastle U.	New Hartley Jnrs	05.54				
Newcastle U.	Aberdeen	10.63	63-65	43	1	14
Darlington	Tr	10.65	65-67	73	1	43
Hartlepool U.	Tr	02.68	67-68	48	4	12

CUMMINGS, Thomas S.
Sunderland, 12 September, 1928 E'B-3/EF Lge (CH)

League Club	Source	Date Signed	Seasons Played	Apps	Subs	Gls
Burnley	Stanley U.	10.47	48-62	434	-	3
Mansfield T.	Tr	03.63	62-63	10	-	0

CUMMINS, George P.
Dublin, 12 March, 1931 IR-19 (IF)

League Club	Source	Date Signed	Seasons Played	Apps	Subs	Gls
Everton	St Patricks Ath.	11.50	51-52	24	-	0
Luton T.	Tr	08.53	53-60	186	-	21
Hull C.	Cambridge C.	11.62	62-63	21	-	2

CUMMINS, James W. H.
Hebburn, 15 February, 1925 Died 1981 (CF)

League Club	Source	Date Signed	Seasons Played	Apps	Subs	Gls
Southport	Horden Colly	09.49	49	9	-	1

CUMMINS, Stanley
Ferryhill, 6 December, 1958 (M)

League Club	Source	Date Signed	Seasons Played	Apps	Subs	Gls
Middlesbrough	App	12.76	76-79	39	5	9
Sunderland	Tr	11.79	79-82	132	1	29
Crystal Palace	Tr	08.83	83-84	27	1	7
Sunderland	Tr	10.84	84	13	4	0

CUMNER, R. Horace
Aberdare, 31 March, 1918 (OL)

League Club	Source	Date Signed	Seasons Played	Apps	Subs	Gls
Hull C.	Margate	01.38	37	12	-	4
Arsenal	Tr	05.38	38	12	-	2
Notts Co.	Tr	08.46	46-47	66	-	10
Watford	Tr	07.48	48-50	62	-	7
Scunthorpe U.	Tr	09.50	50-52	104	-	22
Bradford C.	Tr	08.53				

CUNDY, Jason V.
Wandsworth, 12 November, 1969 E Yth/Eu21-3 (CD)

League Club	Source	Date Signed	Seasons Played	Apps	Subs	Gls
Chelsea	YT	08.88	90-91	40	1	2
Tottenham H.	Tr	03.92	91	10	0	0

CUNLIFFE, Arthur
Blackrod, 5 February, 1909 (OL)

League Club	Source	Date Signed	Seasons Played	Apps	Subs	Gls
Blackburn Rov.	Chorley	01.28	29-32	129	-	47
Aston Villa	Tr	05.33	32-35	69	-	11
Middlesbrough	Tr	12.35	35-36	27	-	5
Burnley	Tr	04.37	37	9	-	0
Hull C.	Tr	06.38	38	42	-	20
Rochdale	Tr	08.45	46	23	-	5

CUNLIFFE, J. Graham
Hindley, 16 June, 1936 (WH)

League Club	Source	Date Signed	Seasons Played	Apps	Subs	Gls
Bolton W.		01.55	57-62	25	-	0
Rochdale	Tr	07.64	64	36	-	0

CUNLIFFE, James N.
Blackrod, 5 July, 1912 E-1 (IF)

League Club	Source	Date Signed	Seasons Played	Apps	Subs	Gls
Everton	Adlington	05.30	32-38	174	-	73
Rochdale	Tr	09.46	46	2	-	0

CUNLIFFE, James W.
Adlington, 4 October, 1941 (CF)

League Club	Source	Date Signed	Seasons Played	Apps	Subs	Gls
Stockport Co. (Am)	Horwich R.M.I.	11.60	60	1	-	0

CUNLIFFE, John (Jack)
Wigan, 4 February, 1930 (OL)

League Club	Source	Date Signed	Seasons Played	Apps	Subs	Gls
Port Vale		12.50	50-59	283	-	51
Stoke C.	Tr	09.59	59	26	-	3

CUNLIFFE, Reginald
Wigan, 4 December, 1920 (LB)

League Club	Source	Date Signed	Seasons Played	Apps	Subs	Gls
Swansea C.	Wigan Ath.	06.46	46-47	2	-	0

CUNLIFFE, Robert
Manchester, 17 May, 1945 (IF)

League Club	Source	Date Signed	Seasons Played	Apps	Subs	Gls
Manchester C.	App	08.62	63	3	-	1
York C.	Tr	06.65	65	11	1	2

CUNLIFFE, Robert A.
Bryn, 27 December, 1928 (OL)

League Club	Source	Date Signed	Seasons Played	Apps	Subs	Gls
Manchester C.	Jnrs.	01.46	49-55	44	-	9
Chesterfield	Tr	06.56	56-57	62	-	19
Southport	Tr	07.58	58	17	-	2

CUNNING, Robert R.
Dunfermline, 12 February, 1930 (OL)

League Club	Source	Date Signed	Seasons Played	Apps	Subs	Gls
Sunderland	Port Glasgow	06.50	50	5	-	0

CUNNINGHAM, Anthony E.
Jamaica, 12 November, 1959 (F)

League Club	Source	Date Signed	Seasons Played	Apps	Subs	Gls
Lincoln C.	Stourbridge	05.79	79-82	111	12	32
Barnsley	Tr	09.82	82-83	40	2	11
Sheffield Wed.	Tr	11.83	83	26	2	5
Manchester C.	Tr	07.84	84	16	2	1
Newcastle U.	Tr	02.85	84-86	37	10	4
Blackpool	Tr	07.87	87-88	71	0	17
Bury	Tr	07.89	89-90	55	3	17
Bolton W.	Tr	03.91	90	9	0	4
Rotherham U.	Tr	08.91	91	34	2	17

CUNNINGHAM, David
Kirkcaldy, 10 August, 1953 (W)

League Club	Source	Date Signed	Seasons Played	Apps	Subs	Gls
Southend U.	Brechin C.	04.73	73-76	56	4	4
Hartlepool U.	L	03.77	76	10	2	1
Swindon T.	Tr	06.77	77-78	18	5	3
Peterborough U.	L	11.78	78	4	0	1
Aston Villa	Tr	12.78				
Hereford U.	Tr	08.79	79	28	2	2
Newport Co.	Tr	08.80				

CUNNINGHAM, Edward
South Shields, 20 March, 1928 (WH)

League Club	Source	Date Signed	Seasons Played	Apps	Subs	Gls
Blackburn Rov.		09.49				
Chesterfield	North Shields	08.52	52-54	56	-	0

CUNNINGHAM, Edwin
Jarrow, 20 September, 1919 (W)

League Club	Source	Date Signed	Seasons Played	Apps	Subs	Gls
Bristol C.		05.39	46	1	-	0

CUNNINGHAM, Hugh
Kirkintilloch, 5 April, 1947 (HB)

League Club	Source	Date Signed	Seasons Played	Apps	Subs	Gls
Fulham	Glasgow Celtic	05.66	67	0	1	0

CUNNINGHAM, Ian
Glasgow, 6 September, 1956 (RB)

League Club	Source	Date Signed	Seasons Played	Apps	Subs	Gls
Bournemouth	App	08.74	74-80	180	8	4

CUNNINGHAM, John
Derry (NI), 30 November, 1966 NI Yth (W)

League Club	Source	Date Signed	Seasons Played	Apps	Subs	Gls
Mansfield T.	Jnrs	08.84	84	3	1	0

CUNNINGHAM, Kenneth E.
Dublin, 28 June, 1971 IRu21-1 (RB)

League Club	Source	Date Signed	Seasons Played	Apps	Subs	Gls
Millwall	Tolka Rov.	09.89	89-91	41	4	0

CUNNINGHAM, Kenneth H.
Glasgow, 26 October, 1941 (CF)

League Club	Source	Date Signed	Seasons Played	Apps	Subs	Gls
Hartlepool U.	Falkirk	07.63	63	2	-	0

CUNNINGHAM, Laurence
Consett, 20 October, 1921 (FB)

League Club	Source	Date Signed	Seasons Played	Apps	Subs	Gls
Barnsley	Consett U.	11.45	46-47	52	-	1
Bournemouth	Tr	06.48	48-56	273	-	0

CUNNINGHAM, Lawrence P.
Holloway, 8 March, 1956 Died 1989 Eu21-6/E-6 (W)

League Club	Source	Date Signed	Seasons Played	Apps	Subs	Gls
Leyton Orient	App	07.74	74-76	72	3	15
West Bromwich A.	Tr	03.77	76-78	81	5	21
Manchester U.	Real Madrid (Sp)	03.83	82	3	2	1
Leicester C. (N/C)	Marseille (Fr)	10.85	85	13	2	0
Wimbledon (N/C)	Charleroi (Bel)	02.88	87	6	0	2

CUNNINGHAM, Thomas E.
Bethnal Green, 7 December, 1955 (CD)

League Club	Source	Date Signed	Seasons Played	Apps	Subs	Gls
Chelsea	App	10.73				
Queens Park R	Tr	05.75	76-78	27	3	2
Wimbledon	Tr	03.79	78-81	99	0	12
Leyton Orient	Tr	09.81	81-86	162	0	17

CUNNINGHAM, William C.
Cowdenbeath, 22 February, 1925 S-8 (FB)

League Club	Source	Date Signed	Seasons Played	Apps	Subs	Gls
Preston N. E.	Airdrieonians	07.49	49-62	440	-	3
Southport	Tr	03.64	64	12	-	0

CUNNINGHAM, William E.
Belfast, 20 February, 1930 NI-30 (FB)

League Club	Source	Date Signed	Seasons Played	Apps	Subs	Gls
Leicester C.	St Mirren	12.54	54-59	127	-	4

CUNNINGHAM, William L.
Paisley, 11 July, 1938 (WH)

League Club	Source	Date Signed	Seasons Played	Apps	Subs	Gls
Barnsley	Third Lanark	07.64	64	24	-	0

CUNNINGTON, Shaun G.
Bourne, 4 January, 1966 (M/LB)

League Club	Source	Date Signed	Seasons Played	Apps	Subs	Gls
Wrexham	Jnrs	01.84	82-87	196	3	12
Grimsby T.	Tr	02.88	87-91	182	0	13

CURBISHLEY, Llewellyn C. (Alan)
Forest Gate, 8 November, 1957 EYth/Eu21-1/E Sch (M)

League Club	Source	Date Signed	Seasons Played	Apps	Subs	Gls
West Ham U.	App	08.75	74-78	78	7	5
Birmingham C.	Tr	07.79	79-82	128	2	11
Aston Villa	Tr	03.83	82-84	34	2	1
Charlton Ath.	Tr	12.84	84-86	62	1	6
Brighton & H. A.	Tr	08.87	87-89	111	5	13
Charlton Ath.	Tr	07.90	90-91	21	5	0

CURLE, Keith
Bristol, 14 November, 1963 E'B'/EF Lge/E-3 (CD)

League Club	Source	Date Signed	Seasons Played	Apps	Subs	Gls
Bristol Rov.	App	11.81	81-82	21	11	4
Torquay U.	Tr	11.83	83	16	0	5
Bristol C.	Tr	03.84	83-87	113	8	1
Reading	Tr	10.87	87-88	40	0	0
Wimbledon	Tr	10.88	88-90	91	2	3
Manchester C.	Tr	08.91	91	40	0	5

CURLEY, Thomas
Glasgow, 11 June, 1945 (OR)

League Club	Source	Date Signed	Seasons Played	Apps	Subs	Gls
Brentford	Glasgow Celtic	08.65	65-66	40	0	6
Crewe Alex.	Tr	08.67	67-68	48	4	7

CURLEY, William
Trimdon, 20 November, 1945 (FB)

League Club	Source	Date Signed	Seasons Played	Apps	Subs	Gls
Darlington	App	11.63	62-64	29	0	1

CURRAN, Christopher J.
Birmingham, 17 September, 1971 (D)

League Club	Source	Date Signed	Seasons Played	Apps	Subs	Gls
Torquay U.	YT	07.90	89-91	26	5	0

CURRAN, Christopher P.
Heywood, 6 January, 1971 (D)

League Club	Source	Date Signed	Seasons Played	Apps	Subs	Gls
Crewe Alex.	YT	09.89	89-90	2	3	0
Scarborough	Tr	03.92	91	8	0	2

CURRAN, Edward (Terry)
Kinsley, 20 March, 1955 (W)

League Club	Source	Date Signed	Seasons Played	Apps	Subs	Gls
Doncaster Rov.	Jnrs	07.73	73-75	67	1	11
Nottingham F.	Tr	08.75	75-76	46	2	12
Bury	L	10.77	77	2	0	0
Derby Co.	Tr	11.77	77	26	0	2
Southampton	Tr	08.78	78	25	1	0
Sheffield Wed.	Tr	03.79	78-81	122	3	35
Sheffield U.	Tr	08.82	82	31	2	3
Everton	L	12.82	82	7	0	1
Everton	Tr	09.83	83-84	12	5	0
Huddersfield T.	Tr	07.85	85	33	1	7
Hull C.	Panionis (Gre)	10.86	86	4	0	0
Sunderland	Tr	11.86	86	9	0	1
Grimsby T.	Grantham	11.87	87	10	2	0
Chesterfield (N/C)	Tr	03.88	87	0	1	0

Laurie Cunningham (Leyton Orient, West Bromwich Albion, Real Madrid, Manchester United, Marseille, Leicester City, Charleroi, Wimbledon & England)

League Club	Source	Date Signed	Seasons Played	Apps	Subs	Gls
CURRAN, Frank						
Royton, 31 May, 1917						(IF)
Southport	Washington Colly	08.35	35-36	16	-	3
Accrington St.	Tr	02.37	36-37	34	-	14
Bristol Rov.	Tr	06.38	38	27	-	21
Bristol C.	Tr	05.39				
Bristol Rov.	Tr	05.46	46	11	-	3
Tranmere Rov.	Shrewsbury T.	06.47	47	17	-	7
CURRAN, Hugh P.						
Glasgow, 25 September, 1943 S-5						(F)
Millwall	Corby T.	03.64	63-65	57	0	26
Norwich C.	Tr	01.66	65-68	112	0	46
Wolverhampton W.	Tr	01.69	68-71	77	5	40
Oxford U.	Tr	09.72	72-74	69	1	28
Bolton W.	Tr	09.74	74-76	40	7	13
Oxford U.	Tr	07.77	77-78	30	5	11
CURRAN, James						
Macclesfield, 24 September, 1947						(G)
Newcastle U.	Jnrs	10.64				
Oldham Ath.		12.66	66	3	0	0
Crewe Alex.	Tr	04.67	68	3	0	0
CURRAN, John						
Glasgow, 22 June, 1924						(G)
Shrewsbury T.	East Fife	08.56	56	24	-	0
Watford	Tr	06.57	57	30	-	0
CURRAN, Patrick J.						
Sunderland, 14 September, 1918						(IF)
Sunderland	Sunderland St Patrick	10.36	37	1	-	0
Ipswich T.	Tr	10.38	38	7	-	1
Watford	Tr	06.39				
Bradford C.	Tr	06.47	47	5	-	1
CURRAN, Terence W.						
Staines, 29 June, 1940						(IF)
Brentford	Tottenham H. (Am)	09.57	60	5	-	0
CURRIE, Anthony W.						
Edgware, 1 January, 1950 E Yth/Eu23-13/EF Lge/E-17						(M)
Watford	App	05.67	67	17	1	9
Sheffield U.	Tr	02.68	67-75	313	0	55
Leeds U.	Tr	06.76	76-78	102	0	11
Queens Park R	Tr	08.79	79-82	79	2	5
Torquay U. (N/C)	Chesham U.	02.84	83-84	14	0	1
CURRIE, Charles J.						
Belfast, 17 April, 1920 IR Lge						(WH)
Bradford P. A.	Belfast Celtic	06.49	49-53	118	-	2
CURRIE, David N.						
Stockton, 27 November, 1962						(F)
Middlesbrough		02.82	81-85	94	19	31
Darlington	Tr	06.86	86-87	76	0	33
Barnsley	Tr	02.88	87-89	80	0	30
Nottingham F.	Tr	01.90	89	4	4	1
Oldham Ath.	Tr	08.90	90-91	17	14	3
Barnsley	Tr	09.91	91	30	7	7
CURRIE, James A. C.						
Glasgow, 25 April, 1932						(F)
Exeter C.	Falkirk	06.56	56-57	54	-	19
Workington	Tr	10.57	57-59	23	-	8
CURRIE, James T.						
Stirling, 6 August, 1948						(WH)
Scunthorpe U.		09.68	68-69	4	2	0
CURRIE, John						
Motherwell, 19 March, 1935						(IR)
Accrington St.	Cleland Jnrs	11.53	53-54	16	-	3
CURRIE, John E.						
Liverpool, 18 March, 1921						(OR)
Bournemouth (Am)	Stafford R.	10.46	46	8	-	2
Port Vale	Tr	06.47	47	9	-	0
CURRIE, John G.						
Dumfries, 7 April, 1939 S Sch						(WH)
Leicester C.	Jnrs	04.57				
Workington	Tr	07.61	61-62	55	-	2
Chester C.	Tr	07.63	63	2	-	0

League Club	Source	Date Signed	Seasons Played	Apps	Subs	Gls
CURRIE, Malcolm						
Rutherglen, 5 February, 1932						(D)
Bradford C.	Rutherglen Glencairn	07.56	56-60	136	-	1
CURRY, Robert						
Gateshead, 2 November, 1918						(IR)
Sheffield W.		10.37	37	1	-	0
Colchester U.	Gainsborough Trin.	(N/L)	50	32	-	13
CURRY, Sean P.						
Liverpool, 13 November, 1966						(F)
Liverpool	App	07.84				
Blackburn Rov.	Tr	01.87	86-88	25	13	6
Hartlepool U.	Tr	08.89	89	0	1	0
Preston N. E.	Tr	09.89				

Tony Currie (Watford, Sheffield United, Leeds United, Queens Park Rangers, Torquay United & England)

League Club	Source	Date Signed	Seasons Played	Career Record Apps	Subs	Gls

CURRY, William M.
Newcastle, 12 October, 1935 Died 1990 E-u23-1 (CF)

League Club	Source	Date Signed	Seasons Played	Apps	Subs	Gls
Newcastle U.	Jnrs	10.53	54-58	80	-	36
Brighton & H. A.	Tr	07.59	59-60	49	-	26
Derby Co.	Tr	10.60	60-64	148	-	67
Mansfield T.	Tr	02.65	64-67	102	0	53
Chesterfield	Tr	01.68	67-68	14	0	2

CURTIN, Douglas J.
Cardiff, 15 September, 1947 W Sch (OL)

League Club	Source	Date Signed	Seasons Played	Apps	Subs	Gls
Mansfield T.	Cardiff C. (App)	11.65	65	3	0	0

CURTIS, Alan T.
Rhondda, 16 April, 1954 Wu21-1/Wu23-1/W-35 (F/M)

League Club	Source	Date Signed	Seasons Played	Apps	Subs	Gls
Swansea C.	Jnrs	07.72	72-78	244	4	72
Leeds U.	Tr	06.79	79-80	28	0	5
Swansea C.	Tr	12.80	80-83	82	8	21
Southampton	Tr	11.83	83-85	43	7	5
Stoke C.	L	03.86	85	3	0	0
Cardiff C.	Tr	07.86	86-89	122	3	10
Swansea C.	Tr	10.89	89	21	5	3

CURTIS, Andrew
Rotherham, 2 December, 1972 (W)

League Club	Source	Date Signed	Seasons Played	Apps	Subs	Gls
York C.	YT	05.91	90-91	6	6	0

CURTIS, Dermot P.
Dublin, 26 August, 1932 IR-17 (CF)

League Club	Source	Date Signed	Seasons Played	Apps	Subs	Gls
Bristol C.	Shelbourne	12.56	56-57	26	-	16
Ipswich T.	Tr	09.58	58-62	41	-	17
Exeter C.	Tr	08.63	63-65	91	0	23
Torquay U.	Tr	08.66	66	12	0	1
Exeter C.	Tr	06.67	67-68	64	2	10

CURTIS, George F.
Grays, 3 December, 1919 (WH)

League Club	Source	Date Signed	Seasons Played	Apps	Subs	Gls
Arsenal	Anglo Purfleet	04.37	38-46	13	-	0
Southampton	Tr	08.47	47-51	174	-	11

CURTIS, George W.
Dover, 5 May, 1939 EYth (CH)

League Club	Source	Date Signed	Seasons Played	Apps	Subs	Gls
Coventry C.	Snowdown Colly	05.56	55-69	483	4	11
Aston Villa	Tr	12.69	69-71	51	0	3

CURTIS, John
Poulton-le-Fylde, 2 September, 1934 (FB)

League Club	Source	Date Signed	Seasons Played	Apps	Subs	Gls
Blackpool	App	09.72	73-76	96	6	0
Blackburn Rov.	Tr	07.77	77-78	9	1	0
Wigan Ath.	Tr	03.79	78-80	32	0	0

CURTIS, Norman W.
Dinnington, 10 September, 1924 (FB)

League Club	Source	Date Signed	Seasons Played	Apps	Subs	Gls
Sheffield Wed.	Gainsborough Trin.	01.50	50-59	310	-	21
Doncaster Rov.	Tr	08.60	60	39	-	3

CURTIS, Paul A. E.
Woolwich, 1 July, 1963 (FB)

League Club	Source	Date Signed	Seasons Played	Apps	Subs	Gls
Charlton Ath.	App	07.81	82-84	69	3	5
Northampton T.	Tr	07.85	85	27	0	1

CURTIS, Robert D.
Langwith, 25 January, 1950 (RB)

League Club	Source	Date Signed	Seasons Played	Apps	Subs	Gls
Charlton Ath.	App	02.67	66-67	324	13	34
Mansfield T.	Tr	02.78	77-79	69	4	7

CURTIS, M. Wayne
Neath, 22 February, 1967 (RB)

League Club	Source	Date Signed	Seasons Played	Apps	Subs	Gls
Cardiff C.	Swansea C. (Jnr)	10.84	85	24	3	2

CURWEN, Eric
Blackpool, 16 September, 1947 E Sch (FB)

League Club	Source	Date Signed	Seasons Played	Apps	Subs	Gls
Everton	App	05.65				
Southport	Tr	12.66	66-68	89	0	0

CURZON, Terence
Winsford, 26 May, 1936 (OL)

League Club	Source	Date Signed	Seasons Played	Apps	Subs	Gls
Crewe Alex.	Bolton W. (Am)	10.53	53-56	11	-	1

CUSACK, David S.
Thurcroft, 6 June, 1956 (CD)

League Club	Source	Date Signed	Seasons Played	Apps	Subs	Gls
Sheffield Wed.	App	06.74	75-77	92	3	1
Southend U.	Tr	09.78	78-82	186	0	17
Millwall	Tr	03.83	82-84	98	0	9
Doncaster Rov.	Tr	07.85	85-87	100	0	4
Rotherham U.	Tr	12.87	87	18	0	0
Doncaster Rov. (N/C)	Boston U.	08.89	89	1	0	0

CUSACK, Nicholas J.
Maltby, 24 December, 1965 (F)

League Club	Source	Date Signed	Seasons Played	Apps	Subs	Gls
Leicester C.	Alvechurch	06.87	87	5	11	1
Peterborough U.	Tr	07.88	88	44	0	10
Darlington	Motherwell	01.92	91	21	0	6

CUSH, Wilbur
Lurgan (NI), 10 June, 1928 Died 1981 IR Lge/NI-26 (WH)

League Club	Source	Date Signed	Seasons Played	Apps	Subs	Gls
Leeds U.	Glenavon	11.57	57-59	89	-	9

CUSHIN, Edward
Whitehaven, 27 January, 1927 (FB)

League Club	Source	Date Signed	Seasons Played	Apps	Subs	Gls
Workington	Lowca	(N/L)	51-55	119	-	4

CUSHLEY, John W.
Hamilton, 21 January, 1943 (CH)

League Club	Source	Date Signed	Seasons Played	Apps	Subs	Gls
West Ham U.	Glasgow Celtic	07.67	67-69	38	0	0

CUSHLOW, Richard
Shotton (Dm), 15 June, 1920 (CH)

League Club	Source	Date Signed	Seasons Played	Apps	Subs	Gls
Chesterfield	Murton Colly	05.46	46-47	34	-	0
Sheffield U.	Tr	12.47				
Derby Co.	Tr	03.48	48-49	2	-	0
Crystal Palace	Tr	02.51	50-51	28	-	0

CUTBUSH, W. John
Malta, 28 June, 1949 (RB)

League Club	Source	Date Signed	Seasons Played	Apps	Subs	Gls
Tottenham H.	App	09.66				
Fulham	Tr	07.72	72-76	131	3	3
Sheffield U.	Tr	03.77	76-80	126	3	1

CUTHBERT, Ean R.
Ayr, 5 February, 1942 (FB)

League Club	Source	Date Signed	Seasons Played	Apps	Subs	Gls
Blackpool	Alyth U.	07.59				
Stockport Co.	Tr	07.63	63-65	94	0	0
Crewe Alex.	Bangor C.	11.66	66	1	0	0

CUTHBERTSON, James
Sunderland, 7 December, 1947 (W)

League Club	Source	Date Signed	Seasons Played	Apps	Subs	Gls
Bradford C.	App	07.66	66-67	25	3	7

CUTHBERTSON, John
Glasgow, 10 March, 1932 (IF)

League Club	Source	Date Signed	Seasons Played	Apps	Subs	Gls
Mansfield T.		10.53	53	3	-	0

CUTLER, Christopher P.
Manchester, 7 April, 1964 (M/F)

League Club	Source	Date Signed	Seasons Played	Apps	Subs	Gls
Bury	Jnrs	08.81	81-84	8	15	3
Crewe Alex.	Tr	08.85	85-89	116	24	24

CUTLER, Paul
Welwyn, 18 June, 1946 (OL)

League Club	Source	Date Signed	Seasons Played	Apps	Subs	Gls
Crystal Palace	App	04.64	64-65	10	0	1

CUTLER, Reginald V.
Blackheath, 17 February, 1935 (W)

League Club	Source	Date Signed	Seasons Played	Apps	Subs	Gls
West Bromwich A.	Jnrs	02.52	51-54	5	-	0
Bournemouth	Tr	06.56	56-58	96	-	21
Portsmouth	Tr	09.58	58-61	100	-	13
Stockport Co.	Tr	07.62	62	34	-	0

CUTTING, Frederick C.
North Walsham, 4 December, 1921 (IF)

League Club	Source	Date Signed	Seasons Played	Apps	Subs	Gls
Leicester C.		01.46				
Norwich C.	Tr	09.46				
Colchester U.	Tr	(N/L)	50-51	29	-	12

CUTTING, John A.
Fleetwood, 15 April, 1924 (IF)

League Club	Source	Date Signed	Seasons Played	Apps	Subs	Gls
Oldham Ath.		11.46	46	4	-	1
Accrington St.	Fleetwood	06.48	48	23	-	5

CUTTING, Stanley W.
St Faiths (Nk), 21 September, 1914 (RH)

League Club	Source	Date Signed	Seasons Played	Apps	Subs	Gls
Southampton	Norwich C. (Am)	05.37	38	3	-	0
Exeter C.	Tr	07.39	46-47	38	-	2

CYGAN, Paul
Doncaster, 4 March, 1972 (D)

League Club	Source	Date Signed	Seasons Played	Apps	Subs	Gls
Doncaster Rov. (YT)	YT	07.88	89	0	1	0

CZUCZMAN, Michael
Carlisle, 27 May, 1953 (D)

League Club	Source	Date Signed	Seasons Played	Apps	Subs	Gls
Grimsby T.	Preston N.E. (App)	08.71	71-75	107	6	6
Scunthorpe U.	Tr	08.76	76-78	115	1	1
Stockport Co.	Tr	05.79	79	36	0	7
Grimsby T.	San Jose (USA)	09.80	80-81	9	0	0
York C.	Tr	11.81	81	17	0	0

Kenny Dalglish (Glasgow Celtic, Liverpool & Scotland)
Great Scot who performed wonders on the pitch during his heyday and now performs them from the touchline as manager of the rapidly improving Blackburn Rovers

DADLEY, Peter R.
Farnham, 10 December, 1948 (OR)

League Club	Source	Date Signed	Seasons Played	Apps	Subs	Gls
Aldershot	App	12.66	66	1	0	1

DAGG, Henry C.
Sunderland, 4 March, 1924 (F)

League Club	Source	Date Signed	Seasons Played	Apps	Subs	Gls
Lincoln C. (Am)	Boston U.	12.46	46	1	-	1

DAGGER, J. Leslie
Preston, 25 April, 1933 (OR)

League Club	Source	Date Signed	Seasons Played	Apps	Subs	Gls
Preston N.E.	West Auckland	05.56	56-60	61	-	8
Carlisle U.	Tr	06.61	61-62	74	-	9
Southport	Tr	07.63	63-64	81	-	9

DAILEY, James
Airdrie, 8 September, 1927 (CF)

League Club	Source	Date Signed	Seasons Played	Apps	Subs	Gls
Sheffield Wed.	Third Lanark	10.46	46-48	37	-	24
Birmingham C.	Tr	02.49	48-51	41	-	14
Exeter C.	Tr	08.52	52-53	45	-	13
Workington	Tr	12.53	53-57	176	-	74
Rochdale	Tr	10.57	57-58	53	-	25

DAINES, Barry R.
Witham, 30 September, 1951 E Yth (G)

League Club	Source	Date Signed	Seasons Played	Apps	Subs	Gls
Tottenham H.	App	09.69	71-80	146	0	0
Mansfield T. (N/C)	Hong Kong	10.83	83	21	0	0

DAINTY, Albert
Lancaster, 4 December, 1923 Died 1979 (CF)

League Club	Source	Date Signed	Seasons Played	Apps	Subs	Gls
Preston N.E.		10.42	46	1	-	1
Stockport Co.	Tr	04.47	46-48	36	-	16
Southport	Tr	02.49	48-50	48	-	11

DAINTY, James A.
Coleshill, 21 January, 1954 (W)

League Club	Source	Date Signed	Seasons Played	Apps	Subs	Gls
Walsall	Jnrs	10.71	71-72	4	1	0

DAISH, William S. (Liam)
Portsmouth, 23 September, 1968 IRu21-4/IR-1 (CD)

League Club	Source	Date Signed	Seasons Played	Apps	Subs	Gls
Portsmouth	App	09.86	86	1	0	0
Cambridge U.	Tr	07.88	88-91	105	0	2

DALE, Alan G.
Thorne, 20 September, 1958 (F)

League Club	Source	Date Signed	Seasons Played	Apps	Subs	Gls
Scunthorpe U.	App	09.76	75-76	1	2	0

DALE, Carl
Colwyn Bay, 24 September, 1966 (F)

League Club	Source	Date Signed	Seasons Played	Apps	Subs	Gls
Chester C.	Bangor C.	05.88	88-90	106	10	41
Cardiff C.	Tr	08.91	91	41	0	22

DALE, Christopher
York, 16 April, 1950 (OL)

League Club	Source	Date Signed	Seasons Played	Apps	Subs	Gls
York C. (Am)	Hull C. (Am)	05.68	68	5	0	0

DALE, Eric
Manchester, 6 July, 1924 (F)

League Club	Source	Date Signed	Seasons Played	Apps	Subs	Gls
Shrewsbury T.		(N/L)	50	1	-	0

DALE, Gordon
Worksop, 20 May, 1928 (OL)

League Club	Source	Date Signed	Seasons Played	Apps	Subs	Gls
Chesterfield	Worksop T.	02.48	48-50	92	-	3
Portsmouth	Tr	07.51	51-56	114	-	18
Exeter C.	Tr	10.57	57-60	124	-	8

DALE, Joseph
Northwich, 3 July, 1921 (OR)

League Club	Source	Date Signed	Seasons Played	Apps	Subs	Gls
Manchester U.	Witton A.	06.47	47	2	-	0
Port Vale	Tr	04.48	47-48	9	-	1

DALE, Leonard
Esh Winning, 11 October, 1933 (W)

League Club	Source	Date Signed	Seasons Played	Apps	Subs	Gls
Doncaster Rov.	Durham C.	02.54	54	1	-	0

DALE, Robert J.
Irlam, 31 October, 1931 (IF)

League Club	Source	Date Signed	Seasons Played	Apps	Subs	Gls
Bury	Altrincham	09.51	52-53	15	-	2
Colchester U.	Tr	12.53	53-56	127	-	11

DALE, F. William
Doncaster, 26 October, 1925 (F)

League Club	Source	Date Signed	Seasons Played	Apps	Subs	Gls
Halifax T.	Scunthorpe U.	08.49	49-51	69	-	16
Southport	Tr	07.52	52-53	47	-	5
Accrington St.	Tr	07.54	54	1	-	0
Crewe Alex.	Tr	10.54	54	4	-	3

DALEY, Alan J.
Mansfield, 11 October, 1927 Died 1975 (OL)

League Club	Source	Date Signed	Seasons Played	Apps	Subs	Gls
Mansfield T.	Pleasley B.C.	09.46				
Hull C.	Tr	07.47	47	7	-	0
Doncaster Rov.	Worksop T.	03.50	49	1	-	1
Scunthorpe U.	Boston U.	07.52	52	35	-	9
Mansfield T.	Corby T.	11.53	53-55	97	-	25
Stockport Co.	Tr	02.56	55-57	73	-	17
Crewe Alex.	Tr	06.58	58	14	-	1
Coventry C.	Tr	11.58	58-60	56	-	10

DALEY, Anthony M.
Birmingham, 18 November, 1967 E Yth/E-7 (RW)

League Club	Source	Date Signed	Seasons Played	Apps	Subs	Gls
Aston Villa	App	05.85	84-91	162	31	28

Tony Daley (Aston Villa & England)

DALEY, Peter J.
Liverpool, 14 February, 1970 (W)

League Club	Source	Date Signed	Seasons Played	Apps	Subs	Gls
Southend U.	Knowsley U.	09.89	89	0	5	1

DALEY, Phillip
Liverpool, 12 April, 1967 (F)

League Club	Source	Date Signed	Seasons Played	Apps	Subs	Gls
Wigan Ath.	Newton	10.89	89-91	110	2	30

DALEY, Stephen J.
Barnsley, 15 April, 1953 E Yth/E'B' (M)

League Club	Source	Date Signed	Seasons Played	Apps	Subs	Gls
Wolverhampton W.	App	06.71	71-78	191	1	38
Manchester C.	Tr	09.79	79-80	47	1	4
Burnley	Seattle (USA)	11.83	83	20	3	4
Walsall	San Diego (USA)	08.85	85	28	0	1

DALEY, Thomas E.
Grimsby, 15 November, 1933 (G)

League Club	Source	Date Signed	Seasons Played	Apps	Subs	Gls
Grimsby T.	Jnrs	08.51	51-56	14	-	0
Huddersfield T.	Tr	03.57	56	1	-	0
West Bromwich A.	Tr	08.58				

DALGLISH, Kenneth M.
Glasgow, 4 March, 1951 Su23-4/S-102 (F)

League Club	Source	Date Signed	Seasons Played	Apps	Subs	Gls
Liverpool	Glasgow Celtic	08.77	77-89	342	13	118

DALL, David G.
St Andrews, 10 October, 1957 (CD)

League Club	Source	Date Signed	Seasons Played	Apps	Subs	Gls
Scunthorpe U.	Grantham	10.79	79-81	77	0	2

League Club	Source	Date Signed	Seasons Played	Apps	Subs	Gls
DALLAS, William R. D.						
Glasgow, 6 March, 1931						(CH)
Luton T.		09.52				
Wrexham	St Mirren	07.57	57	8	-	0
DALLING, Nigel A.						
Swansea, 20 February, 1959						(M)
Swansea C.	App	02.77	74-77	3	5	0
DALLMAN, William						
Mansfield, 8 August, 1918						(CH)
Mansfield T.		03.47	46-47	5	-	0
DALRYMPLE, Malcolm O.						
Bedford, 8 October, 1951 E Yth						(G)
Luton T.	Jnrs	07.70				
Bristol Rov.	Cambridge U.	10.71	71-72	7	0	0
Watford	Tr	07.73	73	5	0	0
DALTON, George						
Newcastle, 4 September, 1941						(FB)
Newcastle U.	Jnrs	11.58	60-66	85	0	2
Brighton & H.A.	Tr	06.67	67	24	0	0
DALTON, Paul						
Middlesbrough, 25 April, 1967						(LW)
Manchester U.	Brandon U.	05.88				
Hartlepool U.	Tr	03.89	88-91	140	11	37
DALTON, R. Timothy						
Waterford, 14 October, 1965						(G)
Coventry C.	App	09.83				
Notts Co.	Tr	07.84	85	1	0	0
Bradford C.	Boston U.	09.86				
Tranmere Rov.	L	12.86	86	1	0	0
DALY, Gerard A.						
Dublin, 30 April, 1954 IRu21-1/IR-46						(M)
Manchester U.	Bohemians	04.73	73-76	107	4	23
Derby Co.	Tr	03.77	76-79	111	1	31
Coventry C.	Tr	08.80	80-83	82	2	19
Leicester C.	L	01.83	82	17	0	1
Birmingham C.	Tr	08.84	84-85	31	1	1
Shrewsbury T.	Tr	10.85	85-86	55	0	8
Stoke C.	Tr	03.87	86-87	17	5	1
Doncaster Rov.	Tr	07.88	88	37	2	4
DALY, Maurice						
Dublin, 28 November, 1955 IR-2						(FB)
Wolverhampton W.	Home Farm	07.73	75-77	28	4	0
DALY, Patrick						
Dublin, 4 December, 1927 LOI/IR-1						(FB)
Aston Villa	Shamrock Rov.	11.49	49	3	-	0
DALY, Patrick						
Manchester, 3 January, 1941						(OL)
Blackburn Rov.	Jnrs	01.58	59-60	3	-	0
Southport	Tr	02.62	61	10	-	0
DALY, Ronald G.						
Clerkenwell, 22 July, 1930						(IF)
Watford		10.50	50	3	-	0
DALZIEL, Gordon						
Motherwell, 16 March, 1962						(M)
Manchester C.	Glasgow Rangers	12.83	83	4	1	0
DALZIEL Ian						
South Shields, 24 October, 1962						(D)
Derby Co.	App	10.79	81-82	22	0	4
Hereford U.	Tr	05.83	83-87	137	13	8
Carlisle U.	Tr	07.88	88-90	79	0	2
DAMERELL, Mark A.						
Plymouth, 31 July, 1965						(W)
Plymouth Arg.	St Blazey	11.89	89-91	0	6	0
Exeter C. (N/C)	Tr	12.91	91	1	0	0
DANCE, Trevor						
Hetton-le-Hole, 31 July, 1958						(G)
Port Vale	App	07.76	76-80	84	0	0
DANDO, Philip						
Liverpool, 8 June, 1952						(G)
Liverpool	Jnrs	09.69				
Barrow	L	10.70	70	9	0	0

League Club	Source	Date Signed	Seasons Played	Apps	Subs	Gls
DANGERFIELD, Christopher G.						
Birmingham, 9 August, 1955						(F)
Wolverhampton W.	App	08.73				
Port Vale	Portland (USA)	09.76	76	0	2	0
DANGERFIELD, David A.						
Tetbury, 27 September, 1951 E Sch						(M)
Swindon T.	App	08.69	68-72	16	4	0
DANIEL, Alan W.						
Ashford, 5 April, 1940						(FB)
Luton T.	Bexleyheath & Welling	01.58	58-63	50	-	3
DANIEL Melvyn J.						
Llanelli, 26 January, 1916						(IF)
Luton T.	Ashford T.	09.44	46-48	53	-	20
Aldershot	Tr	06.49	49	28	-	1
DANIEL, Peter A.						
Ripley, 22 December, 1946						(D)
Derby Co.	App	12.64	65-78	188	7	7
DANIEL, Peter W.						
Hull, 12 December, 1955 Eu21-7/Eu23-3						(M/RB)
Hull C.	Jnrs	09.73	74-77	113	0	9
Wolverhampton W.	Tr	05.78	78-83	157	0	13
Sunderland	Tr	08.84	84-85	33	1	0
Lincoln C.	Tr	11.85	85-86	55	0	2
Burnley	Tr	07.87	87-88	40	1	0
DANIEL, Raymond C.						
Luton, 10 December, 1964						(LB)
Luton T.	App	09.82	82-85	14	8	4
Gillingham	L	09.83	83	5	0	0
Hull C.	Tr	06.86	86-88	55	3	3
Cardiff C.	Tr	08.89	89-90	56	0	1
Portsmouth	Tr	11.90	90-91	20	2	0
DANIEL Raymond W.						
Swansea, 2 November, 1928 W-21						(CH)
Arsenal	Swansea C. (Am)	10.46	48-52	87	-	5
Sunderland	Tr	06.53	53-56	136	-	6
Cardiff C.	Tr	10.57	57	6	-	0
Swansea C.	Tr	03.58	57-59	45	-	7
DANIEL, Thomas						
Middleton, 14 April, 1923						(IF)
Bury	Castleton Gabriel	12.46	47-57	276	-	58
DANIELS, Bernard (Barney)						
Salford, 24 November, 1950						(F)
Manchester U.	Jnrs	04.69				
Manchester C.	Ashton U.	04.73	73-74	9	4	2
Chester C.	Tr	07.75	75	8	1	1
Stockport Co.	Tr	07.76	76-77	45	2	17
DANIELS, Douglas						
Manchester, 21 August, 1924						(G)
New Brighton	Manchester C. (Am)	08.47	47	25	-	0
Chesterfield	Tr	07.48				
Accrington St.	Tr	10.49	49-52	112	-	0
DANIELS, D. Graham						
Farnborough, 9 April, 1962						(W)
Cambridge U.	Cardiff Corries	11.83	83-84	37	2	4
DANIELS, Harold, A. G.						
Kensington, 25 June, 1920						(LH)
Queens Park R.		10.44	46-47	14	-	0
Brighton & H.A.	Tr	08.48	48-49	32	-	0
York C.	Tr	08.50	50	4	-	2
DANIELS, John F.						
St Helens, 8 January, 1925						(G)
Lincoln C.	British Cider	05.46	46	17	-	0
New Brighton		03.48	48	3	-	0
DANIELS, Scott C.						
Benfleet, 22 November, 1969						(CD)
Colchester U.	YT	06.88	87-89	64	9	0
Exeter C.	Tr	08.91	91	43	0	3
DANIELS, Stephen R.						
Leeds, 17 December, 1961						(LB)
Doncaster Rov.	App	10.79	79	0	1	0

League Club	Source	Date Signed	Seasons Played	Career Record Apps	Subs	Gls
DANKS, P. Derek						
Cheadle, 15 February, 1931						
Northampton T.		11.53	54	1	-	0
DANN, Terence E.						
Shoreditch, 6 July, 1936 (F)						
Plymouth Arg.	Penzance	07.59	59	8	-	0
Torquay U.	Sittingbourne	07.62	62	1	-	0
DANSKIN, Jason						
Winsford, 28 December, 1967 (M)						
Everton	YT	07.85	84	1	0	0
Mansfield T.	Tr	03.87	86	10	0	0
Hartlepool U.	L	01.88	87	3	0	0
DANSKIN, Robert						
Newcastle, 28 May, 1908 Died 1985 (CH)						
Leeds U.	Wallsend U.	05.29	30-31	5	-	1
Bradford P.A.	Tr	12.32	32-47	261	-	6
DANZEY, Michael J.						
Widnes, 8 February, 1971 (F)						
Nottingham F.	YT	05.89				
Chester C.	L	02.90	89	0	2	0
Peterborough U. (N/C)		01.91	90	0	1	0
DARBY, Alan						
Sheffield, 3 June, 1942 (G)						
Doncaster Rov.	Goole T.	06.59	60	1	-	0
DARBY, Douglas						
Bolton-on-Dearne, 26 December, 1919 Died 1963 (F)						
Wolverhampton W.	Wath W.	09.41				
Walsall	Tr	05.46	46	15	-	4
DARBY, Duane A.						
Birmingham, 17 October, 1973 (F)						
Torquay U.	YT	07.92	91	6	8	2
DARBY, Julian T.						
Bolton, 3 October, 1967 E Sch (M)						
Bolton W.	YT	07.86	85-91	237	7	32
DARBY, Lee A.						
Salford, 20 September, 1969 (M)						
Portsmouth	YT	10.86	87	1	0	0
DARBYSHIRE, Harold						
Leeds, 22 October, 1931 (IF)						
Leeds U.		02.50				
Halifax T.	Tr	07.52	52-56	161	-	32
Bury	Tr	08.57	57-58	29	-	12
Darlington	Tr	06.59	59	15	-	2
D'ARCY, Arnold J.						
Blackburn, 13 January, 1933 (OL)						
Accrington St.	St Matthews Y.C.	03.52	51-52	39	-	7
Swindon T.	Wigan Ath.	11.56	56-63	223	-	29
D'ARCY, Colin R.						
Greasby, 5 August, 1954 (G)						
Everton		04.73				
Bury	Tr	01.75	74	4	0	0
Wigan Ath.	Tr	01.79				
D'ARCY, Frank A.						
Liverpool, 8 December, 1946 (FB)						
Everton	App	08.64	65-70	8	8	0
Tranmere Rov.	Tr	07.72	72	7	1	1
D'ARCY, Michael E.						
Dublin, 8 March, 1933 (G)						
Oldham Ath.	Dundalk	09.54	54-55	45	-	0
D'ARCY, Seamus D. (Jimmy)						
Newry (NI), 14 December, 1921 Died 1985 NI-5 (F)						
Charlton Ath.	Ballymena	03.48	47-50	13	-	1
Chelsea	Tr	10.51	51-52	23	-	12
Brentford	Tr	10.52	52	13	-	3
D'ARCY, Thomas M.						
Edinburgh, 22 June, 1932 Died 1985 (F)						
Bournemouth	Hibernian	09.54				
Southend U.	Hibernian	05.56	56-57	3	-	0

League Club	Source	Date Signed	Seasons Played	Career Record Apps	Subs	Gls
DARE, Kevin J.						
Finchley, 15 November, 1959 (FB)						
Crystal Palace	App	02.77	80-81	6	0	0
DARE, Reginald A.						
Blandford, 26 November, 1921 (CF)						
Southampton	Windsor & Eton	06.49				
Exeter C.	Tr	08.50	50	6	-	0
DARE, William T.						
Willesden, 14 February, 1927 (CF)						
Brentford	Hendon	11.48	48-54	208	-	61
West Ham U.	Tr	01.55	54-58	111	-	44
DAREY, Jeffrey A.						
Hammersmith, 26 February, 1934 E Amat (CF)						
Brighton & H.A.	Hendon	03.57	56-60	10	-	2
DARFIELD, Stuart C.						
Leeds, 12 April, 1950 (WH)						
Bradford P.A.	Wolverhampton W. (App)	07.68	68	15	2	0
DARGIE, Ian C.						
Camberwell, 3 October, 1931 (CH)						
Brentford	Tonbridge	02.52	51-62	263	-	2
DARK, Trevor C.						
St Helier, 29 January, 1961 (W)						
Birmingham C.	App	01.79	78	2	3	1
DARKE, Peter G.						
Exeter, 21 December, 1953 (D)						
Plymouth Arg.	App	12.71	71-76	94	7	2
Exeter C.	L	10.76	76	5	0	0
Torquay U.	Tr	07.77	77-78	58	1	0
DARLING, H. Leonard						
Gillingham, 9 August, 1911 Died 1958 (CH)						
Gillingham	Chatham T.	05.32	32	14	-	0
Brighton & H.A.	Tr	08.33	33-47	199	-	5
DARLING, Malcolm						
Arbroath, 4 July, 1947 (F)						
Blackburn Rov.	Luncarty Jnrs	10.64	65-69	114	14	30
Norwich C.	Tr	05.70	70-71	16	0	5
Rochdale	Tr	10.71	71-73	82	4	16
Bolton W.	Tr	09.73	73	6	2	0
Chesterfield	Tr	08.74	74-76	100	4	33
Stockport Co.	L	03.77	76	11	0	2
Sheffield Wed.	Tr	08.77	77	1	1	0
Hartlepool U.	Tr	09.77	77	2	2	0
Bury (N/C)	Morecambe	03.78	77	1	1	0
DARLINGTON, Jermaine C.						
Hackney, 11 April, 1974 (W)						
Charlton Ath.	YT	06.92	91	1	1	0
DARMODY, Aubrey						
Swansea, 17 May, 1921 (FB)						
Norwich C.	Cardiff Nomads	10.46	46	2	-	0
DARRACOTT, Terence M.						
Liverpool, 6 December, 1950 (FB)						
Everton	App	07.68	67-78	138	10	0
Wrexham	Tulsa (USA)	09.79	79	22	0	0
DARRELL, Michael A.						
Bilston, 14 January, 1947 (M)						
Birmingham C.	App	01.65	65-68	10	3	2
Newport Co.	L	10.70	70	8	0	0
Gillingham	L	12.70	70	19	2	1
Peterborough U.	Tr	05.71	71-72	32	10	6
DARVELL, Roger D.						
Watford, 10 February, 1931 (CH)						
Charlton Ath.	Rickmansworth	12.53				
Gillingham	Tr	07.57	57	3	-	0
Southport	Tr	07.58	58-64	256	-	1
DARWIN, George H.						
Chester-le-Street, 16 May, 1932 (IF)						
Huddersfield T.	Kimblesworth Jnrs	05.50				
Mansfield T.	Tr	11.53	53-56	126	-	63
Derby Co.	Tr	05.57	57-60	94	-	32
Rotherham U.	Tr	10.60	60	2	-	2
Barrow	Tr	07.61	61-63	92	-	28

DAUBNEY, Raymond
Oldham, 7 December, 1946 (OR)

League Club	Source	Date Signed	Seasons Played	Apps	Subs	Gls
Rochdale		12.66	66-67	12	0	2

D'AURIA, David A.
Swansea, 26 March, 1970 (M)

League Club	Source	Date Signed	Seasons Played	Apps	Subs	Gls
Swansea C.	YT	07.88	87-90	27	18	6

DAVENPORT, Carl
Bolton, 30 May, 1944 (CF)

League Club	Source	Date Signed	Seasons Played	Apps	Subs	Gls
Preston N.E.	App	05.62				
Stockport Co.	Tr	03.63	62-63	16	-	4

DAVENPORT, Peter
Birkenhead, 24 March, 1961 E'B'/E-1 (F)

League Club	Source	Date Signed	Seasons Played	Apps	Subs	Gls
Nottingham F.	Cammell Laird	01.82	81-85	114	4	54
Manchester U.	Tr	03.86	85-88	73	19	22
Middlesbrough	Tr	11.88	88-89	53	6	7
Sunderland	Tr	07.90	90-91	52	13	11

Peter Davenport (Nottingham Forest, Manchester United, Middlesbrough, Sunderland & England)

DAVEY, Frederick
Crediton, 13 April, 1924 (HB)

League Club	Source	Date Signed	Seasons Played	Apps	Subs	Gls
Exeter C.	Crediton T.	08.47	47-55	276	-	3

DAVEY, Nigel G.
Garforth, 20 June, 1946 (FB)

League Club	Source	Date Signed	Seasons Played	Apps	Subs	Gls
Leeds U.	Jnrs	02.64	67-70	13	1	0
Rotherham U.	Tr	07.74				

DAVEY, Simon
Swansea, 1 October, 1970 (W)

League Club	Source	Date Signed	Seasons Played	Apps	Subs	Gls
Swansea C.	YT	07.89	86-91	37	12	4

DAVEY, Stephen R.
Plymouth, 5 September, 1948 E Yth (W)

League Club	Source	Date Signed	Seasons Played	Apps	Subs	Gls
Plymouth Arg.	App	07.66	66-74	213	11	47
Hereford U.	Tr	08.75	75-77	104	3	32
Portsmouth	Tr	06.78	78-80	82	10	8
Exeter C.	Tr	08.81	81	15	0	0

DAVEY, Stuart
Crewe, 4 January, 1938 (FB)

League Club	Source	Date Signed	Seasons Played	Apps	Subs	Gls
Crewe Alex.		08.56	56	1	-	0

DAVIDS, Neil G.
Bingley, 22 September, 1955 E Yth (CD)

League Club	Source	Date Signed	Seasons Played	Apps	Subs	Gls
Leeds U.	App	08.73				
Norwich C.	Tr	04.75	75	2	0	0
Northampton T.	L	09.75	75	9	0	0
Stockport Co.	L	01.76	75	5	0	1
Swansea C.	Tr	07.77	77	9	0	0
Wigan Ath.	Tr	07.78	78-80	66	2	1

DAVIDSON, Adam R.
Invergowrie, 28 November, 1929 (OR)

League Club	Source	Date Signed	Seasons Played	Apps	Subs	Gls
Sheffield Wed.		03.48				
Colchester U.	Tr	08.51	51	19	-	0

DAVIDSON, Alan E.
Australia, 1 June, 1960 Australian Int (FB)

League Club	Source	Date Signed	Seasons Played	Apps	Subs	Gls
Nottingham F.	South Melbourne (Aus)	11.84	84	3	0	0

DAVIDSON, Alexander M.
Langholm, 6 June, 1920 (IF)

League Club	Source	Date Signed	Seasons Played	Apps	Subs	Gls
Chelsea	Hibernian	08.46	46	2	-	0
Crystal Palace	Tr	08.48	48	10	-	2

DAVIDSON, Andrew
Douglas Water, 13 July, 1932 (RB)

League Club	Source	Date Signed	Seasons Played	Apps	Subs	Gls
Hull C.	Jnrs	09.49	52-67	520	0	18

DAVIDSON, Angus G.
Dundee, 2 October, 1948 (M)

League Club	Source	Date Signed	Seasons Played	Apps	Subs	Gls
Grimsby T.	Dundee	11.65	65-68	46	5	1
Scunthorpe U.	Tr	07.69	69-76	304	17	44

DAVIDSON, Brian W.
Workington, 23 August, 1951 (OL)

League Club	Source	Date Signed	Seasons Played	Apps	Subs	Gls
Workington (Am)	Jnrs	08.72	72	1	0	0

DAVIDSON, David
Govan Hill, 28 August, 1934 (HB)

League Club	Source	Date Signed	Seasons Played	Apps	Subs	Gls
Manchester C.	Jnrs	08.51	53	1	-	0
Workington	Tr	07.58	58	3	-	0

DAVIDSON, David B. L.
Lanark, 25 March, 1920 Died 1954 (WH)

League Club	Source	Date Signed	Seasons Played	Apps	Subs	Gls
Bradford P.A.	Douglas Water Th.	05.38	46	13	-	0
Leyton Orient	Tr	01.47	46-49	84	-	1

DAVIDSON, David C.
Douglas Water, 19 March, 1926 (W)

League Club	Source	Date Signed	Seasons Played	Apps	Subs	Gls
Hull C.	Douglas Water Th.	10.46	46-47	22	-	4

DAVIDSON, Dennis
Aberdeen, 18 May, 1937 (WH)

League Club	Source	Date Signed	Seasons Played	Apps	Subs	Gls
Portsmouth	Jnrs	05.54	59	1	-	0

DAVIDSON, Douglas B.
Dundee, 2 December, 1918 Died 1968 (IF)

League Club	Source	Date Signed	Seasons Played	Apps	Subs	Gls
Blackpool	East Fife	10.48	48-49	14	-	0
Reading	Tr	04.50	49-50	11	-	1

DAVIDSON, Duncan
Elgin, 5 July, 1954 (F)

League Club	Source	Date Signed	Seasons Played	Apps	Subs	Gls
Manchester C.	See Bee (HK)	09.83	83	2	4	1

DAVIDSON, Ian
Goole, 31 January, 1947 (M)

League Club	Source	Date Signed	Seasons Played	Apps	Subs	Gls
Hull C.	Jnrs	02.65	66-67	5	1	1
Scunthorpe U.	L	09.68	68	32	3	0
York C.	Tr	06.69	69-70	82	4	4
Bournemouth	Tr	07.71	71	7	2	0
Stockport Co.	Tr	05.72	72-73	74	4	6

DAVIDSON, Ian
East Lothian, 8 September, 1937 (WH)

League Club	Source	Date Signed	Seasons Played	Apps	Subs	Gls
Preston N.E.	Kilmarnock	12.62	62-64	67	-	1
Middlesbrough	Tr	02.65	64-66	46	0	0
Darlington	Tr	09.67	67	27	0	0

DAVIDSON, John S.
Lanark, 6 November, 1931 (F)

League Club	Source	Date Signed	Seasons Played	Apps	Subs	Gls
Walsall	Alloa Ath.	08.55	55	5	-	0

League Club	Source	Date Signed	Seasons Played	Apps	Subs	Gls
DAVIDSON, Jonathan S.						
Cheadle, 1 March, 1970						(CD)
Derby Co.	YT	07.88	89-91	7	5	0
DAVIDSON, Peter E.						
Newcastle, 31 October, 1956						(W)
Queens Park R.	Berwick R.	07.79	79	0	1	0
DAVIDSON, Robert T.						
Lochgelly (Fife), 27 April, 1913						(IF)
Arsenal	St Johnstone	02.35	34-37	57	-	13
Coventry C.	Tr	11.37	37-47	47	-	9
DAVIDSON, Roger						
Islington, 27 October, 1948 E Sch						
Arsenal	App	11.65	67	0	1	0
Portsmouth	Tr	06.69	69	3	0	0
Fulham	Tr	08.70	70	1	0	0
Lincoln C.	Tr	10.71	71	6	0	0
Aldershot	L	02.72	71	12	0	2
DAVIDSON, Victor F.						
Glasgow, 8 November, 1950						(M)
Blackpool	Motherwell	07.78	78	23	2	3
DAVIE, Alexander G. (Sandy)						
Dundee, 10 June, 1945						(G)
Luton T.	Dundee	09.68	68-69	58	0	0
Southampton	Tr	05.70	70	1	0	0
DAVIE, James G.						
Newton, 7 September, 1922						(WH)
Preston N.E.	Kilmarnock	06.48	48-49	28	-	0
Northampton T.	Tr	07.50	50-52	75	-	1
Shrewsbury T.	Tr	07.53				
DAVIE, John						
Dunfermline, 19 February, 1913						(CF)
Brighton & H.A.	Margate	05.36	36-38	89	-	39
Barnsley	Stockton	12.46	46	6	-	0
DAVIE, William C.						
Paisley, 7 January, 1925						(IF)
Luton T.	St Mirren	12.50	50-51	42	-	11
Huddersfield T.	Tr	12.51	51-56	113	-	16
Walsall	Tr	07.57	57	7	-	0
DAVIES, Alan						
Manchester, 5 December, 1961 Died 1992 Wu21-3/W-11						(W)
Manchester U.	App	12.78	81-83	6	1	0
Newcastle U.	Tr	08.85	85-86	20	1	1
Charlton Ath.	L	03.86	85	1	0	0
Carlisle U.	L	11.86	86	4	0	1
Swansea C.	Tr	07.87	87-88	84	0	8
Bradford C.	Tr	06.89	89	24	2	1
Swansea C.	Tr	08.90	90-91	41	2	4
DAVIES, Albert J.						
Greenwich, 19 April, 1935						(G)
Millwall		10.56	57	1	-	0
DAVIES, Albert L.						
Pontypridd, 11 March, 1933						(OR)
Newport Co.	Merthyr Tydfil	04.51	50	1	-	0
DAVIES, Alexander M.						
Dundonald, 21 May, 1920 Died 1964						(OR)
Sheffield Wed.		04.45				
Lincoln C.	Tr	07.45	46-48	37	-	9
DAVIES, Andrew J.						
Wolverhampton, 6 June, 1972						(CD)
Torquay U. (YT)	YT	07.88	88-89	9	4	0
Hartlepool U.	Tr	06.90	90-91	4	3	0
DAVIES, Brian W.						
Doncaster, 21 August, 1947						(F)
Sheffield Wed.	App	08.64	65	3	0	1
DAVIES, Byron						
Llanelli, 5 February, 1932						(HB)
Leeds U.	Llanelli	05.52	53	1	-	0
Newport Co.	Tr	06.56				

League Club	Source	Date Signed	Seasons Played	Apps	Subs	Gls
DAVIES, Cecil J.						
Aberbargoed, 26 March, 1918 W Sch						(WH)
Charlton Ath.	Lovells Ath.	03.35				
Barrow	Tr	06.38	38-46	76	-	3
Millwall	Tr	07.47	47-48	31	-	0
DAVIES, Colin F.						
Shrewsbury, 12 April, 1936						(CH)
Port Vale		06.59	59-60	13	-	0
DAVIES, Cyril J.						
Swansea, 7 September, 1948 W Sch/Wu23-4/W-1						(M)
Swansea C.	App	09.66				
Carlisle U.	Tr	06.68	68	1	1	0
Charlton Ath.	Yeovil T.	05.70	70-72	70	6	6
DAVIES, W. David (Dai)						
Ammanford, 1 April, 1948 Wu23-3/W-52						(G)
Swansea C.	Ammanford	08.69	69-70	9	0	0
Everton	Tr	12.70	70-76	82	0	0
Swansea C.	L	02.74	73	6	0	0
Wrexham	Tr	09.77	77-80	144	0	0
Swansea C.	Tr	07.81	81-82	71	0	0
Tranmere Rov.	Tr	06.83	83	42	0	0
DAVIES, David D. (Dai)						
Aberdare, 5 December, 1914 Died 1984						(IF)
Hull C.	Aberaman Ath.	08.35	35-46	141	-	30
DAVIES, David I.						
Bridgend, 21 July, 1932						(CF)
Leyton Orient	Harwich & Parkeston	04.53	53	4	-	0
DAVIES, David J.						
Port Talbot, 21 May, 1952						(CD)
Swansea C.	Afan Lido	07.73	73-74	27	1	0
DAVIES, David L.						
Port Talbot, 11 July, 1956						(W)
Swansea C.	App	07.74	72	0	1	0
Crewe Alex.	Tr	03.75	74-80	196	13	26

Alan Davies (Manchester United, Newcastle United, Swansea City, Bradford City, Swansea City & Wales)

DAVIES, Dudley
Shoreham, 27 December, 1924 (OR)

League Club	Source	Date Signed	Seasons Played	Apps	Subs	Gls
Charlton Ath.	Lancing T.	01.58				
Leyton Orient	Tr	05.50	50-51	17	-	2

DAVIES, Edmund
Oswestry, 5 June, 1927 (CF)

League Club	Source	Date Signed	Seasons Played	Apps	Subs	Gls
Arsenal	Liverpool (Am)	08.48				
Queens Park R.	Tr	04.50	50	1	-	1
Crewe Alex.	Tr	07.51	51	7	-	0

DAVIES, Edward

League Club	Source	Date Signed	Seasons Played	Apps	Subs	Gls
Port Vale		01.43	46	3	-	0

DAVIES, Edward K.
Birkenhead, 19 February, 1934

League Club	Source	Date Signed	Seasons Played	Apps	Subs	Gls
Tranmere Rov.		07.53	53	1	-	0

DAVIES, Eric
Manchester, 20 February, 1943 Died 1988 (CF)

League Club	Source	Date Signed	Seasons Played	Apps	Subs	Gls
Southport	Southport Trin.	03.62	61-64	3	-	0

DAVIES, Frederick
Liverpool, 22 August, 1939 (G)

League Club	Source	Date Signed	Seasons Played	Apps	Subs	Gls
Wolverhampton W.	Llandudno	04.57	61-67	156	0	0
Cardiff C.	Tr	01.68	67-69	99	0	0
Bournemouth	Tr	07.70	70-73	134	0	0

DAVIES, Gareth M.
Hereford, 11 December, 1973 (D)

League Club	Source	Date Signed	Seasons Played	Apps	Subs	Gls
Hereford U.	YT	04.92	91	4	0	0

DAVIES, Gareth R.
Cardiff, 6 October, 1959 (M)

League Club	Source	Date Signed	Seasons Played	Apps	Subs	Gls
Cardiff C. (N/C)	Sully	11.86	86	1	1	0

DAVIES, Geoffrey P.
Ellesmere Port, 1 July, 1947 (M)

League Club	Source	Date Signed	Seasons Played	Apps	Subs	Gls
Chester C.	Wigan Ath.	08.72	72-73	18	14	5
Wrexham	Tr	10.73	73-75	64	3	15
Port Vale	Tr	08.76	76	7	0	0
Hartlepool U.	L	11.76	76	5	0	1
Wimbledon	San Jose (USA)	08.77	77	23	0	1

DAVIES, George
Oswestry, 1 March, 1927 (WH)

League Club	Source	Date Signed	Seasons Played	Apps	Subs	Gls
Sheffield Wed.	Oswestry T.	06.50	50-54	98	-	1
Chester C.	Tr	07.56	56-57	35	-	4

DAVIES, E. Glen G.
Swansea, 30 June, 1950 (CD)

League Club	Source	Date Signed	Seasons Played	Apps	Subs	Gls
Swansea C.	Jnrs	07.70	70-75	138	12	14

DAVIES, Glyn
Swansea, 31 May, 1932 (WH)

League Club	Source	Date Signed	Seasons Played	Apps	Subs	Gls
Derby Co.	Jnrs	07.49	53-61	200	-	5
Swansea C.	Tr	07.62	62	17	-	1

DAVIES, Gordon E.
Manchester, 4 September, 1932 (IF)

League Club	Source	Date Signed	Seasons Played	Apps	Subs	Gls
Manchester C.	Ashton U.	12.51	51-54	13	-	5
Chester C.	Tr	06.57	57	22	-	5
Southport	Tr	08.58	58	11	-	1

DAVIES, Gordon J.
Merthyr Tydfil, 8 August, 1955 W Sch/W-18 (F)

League Club	Source	Date Signed	Seasons Played	Apps	Subs	Gls
Fulham	Merthyr Tydfil	03.78	77-84	244	3	114
Chelsea	Tr	11.84	84-85	11	2	6
Manchester C.	Tr	10.85	85-86	31	0	9
Fulham	Tr	10.86	86-90	120	27	45
Wrexham	Tr	08.91	91	21	1	4

DAVIES, Graham G.
Swansea, 3 October, 1921 W Sch (G)

League Club	Source	Date Signed	Seasons Played	Apps	Subs	Gls
Swansea C.		02.42	46	22	-	0
Watford	Tr	06.47	47-48	9	-	0

DAVIES, Grant
Barrow, 13 October, 1959 (CD)

League Club	Source	Date Signed	Seasons Played	Apps	Subs	Gls
Preston N.E.	App	10.77				
Newport Co.	Tr	07.78	78-82	147	3	1
Exeter C.	L	02.83	82	7	0	0

DAVIES, Ian C.
Bristol, 29 March, 1957 Wu21-1 (LB)

League Club	Source	Date Signed	Seasons Played	Apps	Subs	Gls
Norwich C.	App	03.75	73-78	29	3	2
Newcastle U.	Tr	06.79	79-81	74	1	3
Manchester C.	Tr	08.82	82-83	7	0	0
Bury	L	11.82	82	14	0	0
Brentford	L	11.83	83	2	0	0
Cambridge U.	L	02.84	83	5	0	0
Carlisle U.	Tr	08.84	84	4	0	0
Exeter C.	Tr	12.84	84	5	0	0
Bristol Rov.(N/C)	Yeovil T.	08.85	85	13	1	1
Swansea C.(N/C)	Tr	11.85	85	11	0	0

DAVIES, John G.
Llandysul, 18 November, 1959 (G)

League Club	Source	Date Signed	Seasons Played	Apps	Subs	Gls
Cardiff C.	App	11.77	78-79	7	0	0
Hull C.	Tr	07.80	80-82	24	0	0
Notts Co.	L	03.86	85	10	0	0

DAVIES, John R.
Portsmouth, 26 September, 1933 (OR)

League Club	Source	Date Signed	Seasons Played	Apps	Subs	Gls
Portsmouth	Jnrs	05.52	53-54	2	-	0
Scunthorpe U.	Tr	07.55	55-57	68	-	10
Walsall	Tr	01.59	58-60	65	-	16

DAVIES, John W.
Denbigh, 14 November, 1916 W Sch (WH)

League Club	Source	Date Signed	Seasons Played	Apps	Subs	Gls
Chester C.	Troedyhiw	12.34	35-36	18	-	1
Everton	Tr	07.37	46	1	-	0
Plymouth Arg.	Tr	02.47	46-47	33	-	0
Bristol C.	Tr	05.48	48	30	-	1

DAVIES, Joseph
Birkenhead, 30 January, 1926 (F)

League Club	Source	Date Signed	Seasons Played	Apps	Subs	Gls
Chester C.		05.48	47-51	55	-	10

DAVIES, Kenneth
Doncaster, 20 September, 1923 (F)

League Club	Source	Date Signed	Seasons Played	Apps	Subs	Gls
Wolverhampton W.		01.44				
Walsall	Tr	06.46	46-47	28	-	5
Brighton & H.A.	Tr	05.48	48-49	36	-	5

DAVIES, Kenneth F.
Stockton, 22 December, 1970 (M)

League Club	Source	Date Signed	Seasons Played	Apps	Subs	Gls
Hartlepool U.	YT	07.89	89-90	4	2	0

DAVIES, Kevin P.
Hereford, 1 April, 1963 (M)

League Club	Source	Date Signed	Seasons Played	Apps	Subs	Gls
Hereford U. (N/C)	Westfields	07.85	85	0	1	0

DAVIES, Leonard
(G)

League Club	Source	Date Signed	Seasons Played	Apps	Subs	Gls
Southend U.		11.45	46	3	-	0

DAVIES, D. Lyn
Neath, 29 September, 1947 W Sch/Wu23-1 (G)

League Club	Source	Date Signed	Seasons Played	Apps	Subs	Gls
Cardiff C.	App	10.65	65-66	16	0	0
Swansea C.	Llanelli	07.72	72	3	0	0

DAVIES, Malcolm
Aberdare, 26 June, 1931 (OR)

League Club	Source	Date Signed	Seasons Played	Apps	Subs	Gls
Plymouth Arg.	Aberaman	04.49	52-56	84	-	15

DAVIES, Mark
Swansea, 9 August, 1972 (D)

League Club	Source	Date Signed	Seasons Played	Apps	Subs	Gls
Swansea C.	YT	07.91	91	1	0	0

DAVIES, Michael J.
Stretford, 19 January, 1966 (RB/M)

League Club	Source	Date Signed	Seasons Played	Apps	Subs	Gls
Blackpool	App	01.84	83-91	221	34	15

DAVIES, Paul
St Asaph, 10 October, 1952 W Sch (CF)

League Club	Source	Date Signed	Seasons Played	Apps	Subs	Gls
Arsenal	App	11.69	71	0	1	0
Charlton Ath.	Tr	08.72	72-74	51	6	9

DAVIES, Paul A.
Kidderminster, 9 October, 1960 E Semi-Pro (F)

League Club	Source	Date Signed	Seasons Played	Apps	Subs	Gls
Cardiff C.	Oldswinford	10.78	79-80	1	1	0

DAVIES, Peter
Llanelli, 8 March, 1936 (WH)

League Club	Source	Date Signed	Seasons Played	Apps	Subs	Gls
Arsenal	Llanelli	11.57				
Swansea C.	Tr	03.59	58-64	134	-	4
Brighton & H.A.	Tr	07.65	65	6	0	0

League Club	Source	Date Signed	Seasons Played	Apps	Subs	Gls
DAVIES, Peter						
Merthyr Tydfil, 1 July, 1942 W Amat (IF)						
Newport Co. (Am)	Merthyr Tydfil	05.64	64	1	-	0
DAVIES, L. Raymond						
Birkenhead, 3 October, 1931 (IF)						
Tranmere Rov.		10.49	51-57	121	-	27
DAVIES, E. Reginald						
Cymmer, 27 May, 1929 W-6 (IF)						
Southend U.	Southampton (Am)	07.49	49-50	41	-	18
Newcastle U.	Tr	04.51	51-58	157	-	49
Swansea C.	Tr	10.58	58-61	108	-	29
Carlisle U.	Tr	06.62	62-63	65	-	13
DAVIES, Reginald W.						
Tipton, 10 October, 1933 (G)						
West Bromwich A.	Jnrs	01.51	53-54	4	-	0
Walsall	Tr	07.55	55-56	53	-	0
Millwall	Tr	05.58	58-62	199	-	0
Leyton Orient	Tr	07.63	63	11	-	0
Port Vale	Tr	07.64	64	13	-	0
Leyton Orient	Tr	03.65	64-65	16	0	0
DAVIES, Robert G.						
Blaenau Ffestiniog, 19 October, 1913 Died 1978 (CH)						
Nottingham F.	Blaenau Ffestiniog	11.36	36-46	55	-	0
DAVIES, Roger						
Wolverhampton, 25 October, 1950 Eu23-1 (F)						
Derby Co.	Worcester C.	09.71	72-75	98	16	31
Preston N.E.	L	08.72	72	2	0	0
Leicester C.	Bruges (Bel)	12.77	77-78	22	4	6
Derby Co.	Tulsa (USA)	09.79	79	22	0	3
Darlington	Fort Lauderdale (USA)	11.83	83	10	0	1
DAVIES, Ronald G.						
Swansea, 13 November, 1935 (WH)						
Swansea C.	Tower U.	05.58	58	2	-	0
Plymouth Arg.	Tr	06.59				
DAVIES, Ronald T.						
Merthyr Tydfil, 21 September, 1932 (FB)						
Cardiff C.	Merthyr Tydfil	10.52	55-57	32	-	3
Southampton	Tr	03.58	57-63	161	-	0
Aldershot	Tr	08.64	64-66	83	1	1
DAVIES, Ronald T.						
Holywell, 25 May, 1942 Wu23-3/W-29 (CF)						
Chester C.	Jnrs	07.59	59-62	94	-	44
Luton T.	Tr	10.62	62-63	32	-	21
Norwich C.	Tr	09.63	63-65	113	0	58
Southampton	Tr	08.66	66-72	239	1	134
Portsmouth	Tr	04.73	73-74	59	0	18
Manchester U.	Tr	11.74	74	0	8	0
Millwall	L	11.75	75	3	0	0
DAVIES, Roy						
Ealing, 25 October, 1953 (M)						
Reading	Slough T.	09.77	77	37	0	2
Torquay U.	Tr	08.78	78-79	65	5	6
Wimbledon	Tr	08.80	80	6	3	0
DAVIES, Roy A.						
South Africa, 23 August, 1924 (W)						
Luton T.	Clyde	05.51	51-56	150	-	24
DAVIES, Roy M.						
Cardiff, 19 August, 1971 W Yth (RB)						
Newport Co.(YT)	YT	08.87	87	0	2	0
Chelsea	YT	07.89				
DAVIES, Steven E.						
Liverpool, 16 July, 1960 (W)						
Port Vale	Congleton T.	12.87	87	1	5	0
DAVIES, William						
Middlesbrough, 16 May, 1930 (CH)						
Hull C.	St. Mary's C.O.B.	04.49				
Leeds U.	Tr	08.50				
Reading	Scarborough	12.52	54-60	202	-	0
DAVIES, William						
Troedyrhiw, 24 June, 1910 (OL)						
Watford	New Tredegar	07.30	30-49	284	-	69

League Club	Source	Date Signed	Seasons Played	Apps	Subs	Gls
DAVIES, William E.						
(OR)						
Crewe Alex.	Droylsden	02.47	46	11	-	3
DAVIES, William M.						
Glasgow, 31 May, 1964 (M)						
Leicester C.	St Mirren	08.90	90	5	1	0
DAVIES, R. Wyn						
Caernarfon, 20 March, 1942 Wu23-4/W-34 (F)						
Wrexham	Caernarfon	04.60	60-61	55	-	22
Bolton W.	Tr	03.62	61-66	155	0	66
Newcastle U.	Tr	10.66	66-70	181	0	40
Manchester C.	Tr	08.71	71-72	45	0	8
Manchester U.	Tr	09.72	72	15	1	4
Blackpool	Tr	06.73	73-74	34	2	5
Crystal Palace	L	08.74	74	3	0	0
Stockport Co.	Tr	08.75	75	28	2	7
Crewe Alex.	Tr	08.76	76-77	50	5	13
DAVIN, Joseph						
Dumbarton, 13 February, 1942 S Sch (FB)						
Ipswich T.	Hibernian	07.63	63-65	77	0	0
DAVIS, Arron S.						
Wanstead, 11 February, 1972 (FB)						
Torquay U.	YT	07.90	91	9	3	0
DAVIS, Cyril						
Walsall (Am)		05.48	48	1	-	0
DAVIS, Darren J.						
Sutton-in-Ashfield, 5 February, 1967 E Yth (D)						
Notts Co.	App	02.85	83-87	90	2	1
Lincoln C.	Tr	08.88	88-90	97	5	4
Maidstone U.	Tr	03.91	90-91	31	0	2
DAVIS, Derek E. C.						
Colwyn Bay, 19 June, 1922 Died 1985 (G)						
Norwich C.	Plymouth Arg. (Am)	10.45	46-47	26	-	0
Torquay U.	Tr	08.48	48-50	89	-	0
DAVIS, Edward						
Brackley, 8 March, 1922 (F)						
Newport Co.	R.A.F.	10.46	46	3	-	1
DAVIS, Eric W.C.						
Plymouth, 26 February, 1932 (CF)						
Plymouth Arg.	Tavistock	08.52	52-56	63	-	29
Scunthorpe U.	Tr	07.57	57-58	40	-	20
Chester C.	Tr	02.59	58-59	32	-	11
Oldham Ath.	Tr	09.60	60	2	-	1
DAVIS, J. Frederick						
Walsall, 23 May, 1929 (WH)						
Reading	Bloxwich Strollers	12.52	53-54	63	-	1
Wrexham	Tr	07.55	55-60	230	-	12
DAVIS, Gareth						
Bangor, 11 July, 1949 Wu23-4/W-3 (CD)						
Wrexham	Colwyn Bay	10.67	67-82	482	7	9
DAVIS, Gordon						
Newcastle, 14 December, 1930 (HB)						
Gateshead	Everton (Am)	11.49	51-56	87	-	0
DAVIS, Ian						
Hull, 1 February, 1965 (M)						
Hull C.	App	02.83	81-82	25	3	1
DAVIS, John L.						
Hackney, 31 March, 1957 (FB)						
Gillingham	Arsenal (App)	07.75	75	2	1	1
Sheffield Wed.	Tr	10.76	76	1	0	0
DAVIS, Joseph						
Glasgow, 22 May, 1941 (LB)						
Carlisle U.	Hibernian	12.69	69-71	75	4	0
DAVIS, Joseph T.						
Bristol, 24 August, 1938 (CH)						
Bristol Rov.	Jnrs	03.56	60-66	210	1	4
Swansea C.	Tr	03.67	66-67	38	0	0

League Club	Source	Date Signed	Seasons Played	Career Record Apps	Subs	Gls
DAVIS, Kenneth E.						
Romsey, 6 February, 1933						(F)
Bristol C.	Jnrs	05.52	52	1	-	0
DAVIS, Leonard P.						
Cork, 31 July, 1931						(CF)
Arsenal		11.49				
Walsall	Tr	02.54	53-54	25	-	5
DAVIS, Mark R.						
Wallsend, 12 October, 1969						(M)
Darlington (YT)	YT	08.86	86	0	2	0
DAVIS, Paul E.						
Newham, 31 January, 1968						(D)
Queens Park R.	App	12.85				
Aldershot	Tr	08.87	87	1	0	0
DAVIS, Paul V.						
Dulwich, 9 December, 1961 Eu21-11/E'B'/EF Lge						(M)
Arsenal	App	07.79	79-91	301	18	29
DAVIS, Richard D.						
Birmingham, 22 January, 1922 E Sch						(CF)
Sunderland	Morris & J.	02.39	46-53	144	-	72
Darlington	Tr	05.54	54-56	93	-	32
DAVIS, Richard F.						
Plymouth, 14 November, 1943						(FB)
Plymouth Arg.	App	11.61	62-63	23	-	0
Southampton	Tr	07.64	64	1	-	0
Bristol C.	Tr	07.65	67-68	8	0	0
Barrow	Tr	03.69	68-69	50	0	0
DAVIS, Stephen M.						
Hexham, 30 October, 1968						(M)
Southampton	YT	07.87	89-90	5	1	0
Burnley	L	11.89	89	7	2	0
Notts Co.	L	03.91	90	0	2	0
Burnley	Tr	08.91	91	40	0	6
DAVIS, Steven P.						
Birmingham, 26 July, 1965 E Yth						(CD)
Crewe Alex.	Stoke C. (App)	08.83	83-87	140	5	1
Burnley	Tr	10.87	87-90	147	0	11
Barnsley	Tr	07.91	91	8	1	0
DAVISON, Aidan J.						
Sedgefield, 11 May, 1968						(G)
Notts Co.	Billingham Synth.	03.88	88	1	0	0
Bury	Tr	10.89				
Millwall	Tr	08.91	91	33	0	0
DAVISON, Alan						
Sunderland, 8 September, 1931						(FB)
Norwich C.		09.49				
Darlington		08.51	51	1	-	0
DAVISON, Arthur E.						
Hackney, 21 December, 1915						
Stockport Co.		09.45				
Torquay U.		11.46	46	1	-	0
DAVISON, Daniel						
Newcastle, 11 November, 1947						(FB)
Barrow	Newcastle U. (Am)	09.65	66-69	7	0	0
DAVISON, Edward						
Seaham, 15 April, 1933						(CH)
Hartlepool U.	Seaham Jnrs	08.53	53	1	-	0
DAVISON, James H.						
Sunderland, 1 November, 1942						(OR)
Sunderland	Jnrs	11.59	59-62	62	-	10
Bolton W.	Tr	11.63	63	21	-	1
DAVISON, Joseph H.						
Newcastle, 29 July, 1919						(RB)
Darlington	Throckley Welfare	01.47	46-53	239	-	7
DAVISON, Robert						
South Shields, 17 July, 1959						(F)
Huddersfield T.	Seaham Colly	07.80	80	1	1	0
Halifax T.	Tr	08.81	81-82	63	0	29
Derby Co.	Tr	12.82	82-87	203	3	83
Leeds U.	Tr	11.87	87-91	79	12	32

League Club	Source	Date Signed	Seasons Played	Career Record Apps	Subs	Gls
Derby Co.	L	09.91	91	10	0	8
Sheffield U.	L	03.92	91	6	5	4
DAVOCK, Michael						
St Helens, 27 April, 1935						(OL)
Stockport Co.	St Helens	01.57	56-63	235	-	37
D'AVRAY, J. Michael (Mich)						
Johannesburg (SA), 19 February, 1962 Eu21-2						(F)
Ipswich T.	App	05.79	79-89	170	41	37
Leicester C.	L	02.87	86	3	0	0
DAVY, Stephen J.						
Norwich, 9 April, 1955						(FB)
Scunthorpe U.	West Ham U. (N/C)	08.77	77-81	126	8	1
DAWES, Derek M.						
Dawley, 23 June, 1944						(IF)
Shrewsbury T.	App	06.62	61-62	9	-	0
DAWES, Frederick W.						
Frimley Green, 2 May, 1911 Died 1989						(LB)
Northampton T.	Frimley Green	03.30	29-35	161	-	1
Crystal Palace	Tr	02.36	35-49	222	-	2
DAWES, Ian M.						
Aldershot, 5 January, 1965 E Sch						(D)
Newcastle U.	Jnrs	06.83				
Northampton T.	Tr	06.85	85	3	2	0
DAWES, Ian R.						
Croydon, 22 February, 1963 E Sch						(LB)
Queens Park R.	App	12.80	81-87	229	0	3
Millwall	Tr	08.88	88-91	141	3	5
DAWES, Malcolm						
Trimdon, 3 March, 1944						(D)
Darlington		03.62				
Aldershot	Horden Colly	08.65	65-69	160	3	2
Hartlepool U.	Tr	07.70	70-75	193	2	12
Workington	Tr	11.75	75-76	49	2	1
DAWKINS, Derek A.						
Edmonton, 29 November, 1959						(FB/M)
Leicester C.	App	11.77	77	3	0	0
Mansfield T.	Tr	12.78	78-80	73	0	0
Bournemouth	Tr	08.81	81-82	4	4	0
Torquay U.	Weymouth	02.84	83-88	153	22	7
DAWKINS, Trevor A.						
Southend, 7 October, 1945 E Sch/E Yth						(M)
West Ham U.	App	10.62	64-66	5	1	0
Crystal Palace	Tr	10.67	67-70	24	1	3
Brentford	L	09.71	71	3	1	0
DAWS, Anthony						
Sheffield, 10 September, 1966 E Yth						(F)
Notts Co.	App	09.84	84-85	6	2	1
Sheffield U.	Tr	08.86	86	7	4	3
Scunthorpe U.	Tr	06.87	87-91	145	14	59
DAWSON, Alexander						
Glasgow, 23 October, 1933						(W)
Queens Park R.	Gourock Jnrs	02.57	56-58	58	-	5
DAWSON, Alexander D.						
Aberdeen, 21 February, 1940 S Sch						(CF)
Manchester U.	Jnrs	04.57	56-61	80	-	45
Preston N.E.	Tr	10.61	61-66	197	0	114
Bury	Tr	03.67	66-68	49	1	21
Brighton & H.A.	Tr	12.68	68-70	53	4	26
Brentford	L	09.70	70	10	0	6
DAWSON, Alistair J.						
Glasgow, 25 February, 1958 S Yth/Su21-8/S-5						(CD)
Blackburn Rov.	Glasgow Rangers	08.87	87-89	32	8	0
DAWSON, Carl M.						
Harwich, 24 June, 1934						
Lincoln C. (Am)	Jnrs	05.50	50	1	-	0
DAWSON, Edward						
Chester-le-Street, 16 January, 1913						(G)
Manchester C.	Blyth Spartans	12.34				
Bristol C.	Tr	05.36	36-38	66	-	0
Gateshead	Tr	08.46	46-48	83	-	0

DAWSON, George
Glasgow, 13 September, 1930

League Club	Source	Date Signed	Seasons Played	Apps	Subs	Gls
Queens Park R.	Motherwell	05.55	55	1	-	0

DAWSON, James E. I. B.
Stoneyburn, 21 December, 1927 (OL)

League Club	Source	Date Signed	Seasons Played	Apps	Subs	Gls
Leicester C.	Polkemmet	05.46	46-48	5	-	0
Portsmouth	Tr	06.49	49	1	-	0

DAWSON, Jason
Burslem, 9 February, 1971 (F)

League Club	Source	Date Signed	Seasons Played	Apps	Subs	Gls
Rochdale	Port Vale (YT)	07.89	89-90	37	18	7

DAWSON, Owen J.
Christchurch, 7 March, 1943 E Yth (FB)

League Club	Source	Date Signed	Seasons Played	Apps	Subs	Gls
Portsmouth	Jnrs	06.60				
Swindon T.	Tr	06.62	62-70	196	7	4

DAWSON, Peter
Crewe, 19 January, 1933

League Club	Source	Date Signed	Seasons Played	Apps	Subs	Gls
Crewe Alex.		01.54	55	2	-	0

DAWSON, J. Reginald
Sheffield, 4 October, 1914 (OL)

League Club	Source	Date Signed	Seasons Played	Apps	Subs	Gls
Rotherham U.		01.39	38-46	52	-	3

DAWSON, Richard
Sheffield, 12 April, 1967 (G)

League Club	Source	Date Signed	Seasons Played	Apps	Subs	Gls
Grimsby T.	Stoke C. (Jnrs)	08.84	84	1	0	0

DAWSON, Richard
Chesterfield, 19 January, 1960 (F)

League Club	Source	Date Signed	Seasons Played	Apps	Subs	Gls
Rotherham U.	App	01.78	77-79	21	3	3
Doncaster Rov.	Tr	02.81	80-81	39	4	14
Chesterfield	Tr	08.82	82	6	6	0

DAWSON, Richard
York, 6 July, 1962 (D)

League Club	Source	Date Signed	Seasons Played	Apps	Subs	Gls
York C.		07.80	81-82	45	0	0

DAWSON, Robert
South Shields, 31 January, 1935 (FB)

League Club	Source	Date Signed	Seasons Played	Apps	Subs	Gls
Leeds U.	South Shields	11.53	53	1	-	0
Gateshead	Tr	11.55	55-59	118	-	1

DAWSON, Robert A.
Doncaster, 21 June, 1944 (G)

League Club	Source	Date Signed	Seasons Played	Apps	Subs	Gls
Doncaster Rov.		12.64	65-66	28	0	0

DAWSON, Thomas
Middlesbrough, 6 February, 1915 Died 1972 (IF)

League Club	Source	Date Signed	Seasons Played	Apps	Subs	Gls
Darlington	Whitby T.	12.36	36-37	20	-	4
Charlton Ath.	Spennymoor U.	02.39	38-46	23	-	2
Brentford	Tr	08.47	47	36	-	10
Swindon T.	Tr	05.48	48-49	65	-	15

DAWSON, William
Glasgow, 5 February, 1931 (CF)

League Club	Source	Date Signed	Seasons Played	Apps	Subs	Gls
Northampton T.	Ashfield Jnrs	03.55	54-55	14	-	6

DAWTRY, Kevin A.
Hythe, 15 June, 1958 (M)

League Club	Source	Date Signed	Seasons Played	Apps	Subs	Gls
Southampton	App	06.76	78	0	1	0
Crystal Palace	Tr	05.80				
Bournemouth	Tr	03.81	80-83	58	7	11
Reading	L	09.82	82	4	0	0

DAY, Albert
Camberwell, 7 March, 1918 (F)

League Club	Source	Date Signed	Seasons Played	Apps	Subs	Gls
Brighton & H.A.		08.38				
Ipswich T.	Tr	05.46	46-48	63	-	25
Watford	Tr	08.49	49	4	-	1

DAY, Clive A.
Grays, 27 January, 1961 (FB)

League Club	Source	Date Signed	Seasons Played	Apps	Subs	Gls
Fulham	App	08.78	80-81	2	8	0
Mansfield T.	L	08.82	82	10	2	1
Aldershot	Tr	08.83	83-84	53	7	0

DAY, Eric C.
Dartford, 6 November, 1921 (OR)

League Club	Source	Date Signed	Seasons Played	Apps	Subs	Gls
Southampton		04.45	46-56	398	-	145

DAY, Graham G.
Bristol, 22 November, 1953 (CD)

League Club	Source	Date Signed	Seasons Played	Apps	Subs	Gls
Bristol Rov.		05.73	74-78	129	1	1

DAY, B. James
Watford, 9 May, 1931

League Club	Source	Date Signed	Seasons Played	Apps	Subs	Gls
Watford	Berkhamsted T.	12.51	51	3	-	0

DAY, John N. (Jack)
Northfleet, 21 January, 1924 (G)

League Club	Source	Date Signed	Seasons Played	Apps	Subs	Gls
Gillingham	Brighton & H.A. (Am)	07.50	50	1	-	0

DAY, Keith D.
Grays, 29 November, 1962 (CD)

League Club	Source	Date Signed	Seasons Played	Apps	Subs	Gls
Colchester U.	Aveley	08.84	84-86	113	0	12
Leyton Orient	Tr	07.87	87-91	177	5	8

DAY, Mervyn R.
Chelmsford, 26 June, 1955 E Yth/Eu23-5 (G)

League Club	Source	Date Signed	Seasons Played	Apps	Subs	Gls
West Ham U.	App	03.73	73-78	194	0	0
Leyton Orient	Tr	07.79	79-82	170	0	0
Aston Villa	Tr	08.83	83-84	30	0	0
Leeds U.	Tr	01.85	84-89	225	0	0
Luton T.	L	03.92	91	4	0	0
Sheffield U.	L	04.92	91	1	0	0

Mervyn Day (West Ham United, Leyton Orient, Aston Villa & Leeds United)

DAY, Roger
Romford, 3 December, 1939 E Amat (F)

League Club	Source	Date Signed	Seasons Played	Apps	Subs	Gls
Watford (Am)	Enfield	12.61	61	1	-	0

DAY, William
Middlesbrough, 27 December, 1936 (OR)

League Club	Source	Date Signed	Seasons Played	Apps	Subs	Gls
Middlesbrough	South Bank	05.55	55-61	120	-	18
Newcastle U.	Tr	03.62	61-62	13	-	1
Peterborough U.	Tr	04.63	62-63	18	-	2

DAYKIN, Brian R.
Long Eaton, 4 August, 1937 (WH)

League Club	Source	Date Signed	Seasons Played	Apps	Subs	Gls
Derby Co.	Long Eaton U.	11.55	59-61	4	-	1
Notts Co.	Tr	07.62	62	3	-	0

DeGARIS, James F.
Worcester, 9 October, 1952 (M)

League Club	Source	Date Signed	Seasons Played	Apps	Subs	Gls
Arsenal	App	06.70				
Bournemouth	Tr	09.71	71-73	8	4	0
Torquay U.	Tr	03.74	73	7	2	0

DeGOEY, Leendert
Netherlands, 29 February, 1952 (M)

League Club	Source	Date Signed	Seasons Played	Apps	Subs	Gls
Sheffield U.	Sparta Rotterdam (Neth)	08.79	79	33	0	5

DeGRUCHY, Raymond P.
Guernsey, 18 May, 1932 (FB)

League Club	Source	Date Signed	Seasons Played	Apps	Subs	Gls
Nottingham F.		08.53				
Grimsby T.	Tr	05.54	54-57	74	-	2
Chesterfield	Tr	06.58	58	1	-	0

DeMANGE, Kenneth J. P.
Dublin, 3 September, 1964 IR Yth/IRu21-1/IR-2 (M)

League Club	Source	Date Signed	Seasons Played	Apps	Subs	Gls
Liverpool	Home Farm	08.83				
Scunthorpe U.	L	12.86	86	3	0	2
Leeds U.	Tr	09.87	87	14	1	1
Hull C.	Tr	03.88	87-90	48	20	1
Cardiff C.	L	11.90	90	5	0	0
Cardiff C.	L	03.91	90	10	0	0

DePLACIDO, Michael S.
Scarborough, 9 March, 1954 E Yth (W)

League Club	Source	Date Signed	Seasons Played	Apps	Subs	Gls
York C.	Jnrs	03.72	71-72	4	7	0

DeVRIES, Roger S.
Hull, 25 October, 1950 (LB)

League Club	Source	Date Signed	Seasons Played	Apps	Subs	Gls
Hull C.	Jnrs	09.67	70-79	314	4	0
Blackburn Rov.	Tr	07.80	80	13	0	0
Scunthorpe U.		10.81	81	6	0	1

DEACON, David B.
Broome, 10 March, 1929 (FB)

League Club	Source	Date Signed	Seasons Played	Apps	Subs	Gls
Ipswich T.	Bungay	11.50	50-59	66	-	0

DEACY, Eamonn S.
Galway (Ire), 1 October, 1958 IR-4 (FB)

League Club	Source	Date Signed	Seasons Played	Apps	Subs	Gls
Aston Villa	Galway Rov.	03.79	79-83	27	6	1
Derby Co.	L	10.83	83	5	0	0

DEACY, Michael
Cardiff, 29 November, 1943 (CH)

League Club	Source	Date Signed	Seasons Played	Apps	Subs	Gls
Newport Co.		08.66	66-69	46	1	2

DEACY, Nicholas S.
Cardiff, 19 July, 1953 Wu21-1/Wu23-1/W-12 (D)

League Club	Source	Date Signed	Seasons Played	Apps	Subs	Gls
Hereford U.	Merthyr Tydfill	09.74	74	13	4	2
Workington	L	12.74	74	5	0	2
Hull C.	Vitesse Arnhem (Neth)	02.80	79-81	80	7	7
Bury	Happy Valley (HK)	10.83	83	30	1	0

DEAKIN, Alan R.
Birmingham, 27 November, 1941 Eu23-6 (WH)

League Club	Source	Date Signed	Seasons Played	Apps	Subs	Gls
Aston Villa	Jnrs	12.58	59-69	230	1	9
Walsall	Tr	10.69	69-71	46	4	0

DEAKIN, Frederick A.
Birmingham, 5 February, 1920 (FB)

League Club	Source	Date Signed	Seasons Played	Apps	Subs	Gls
Birmingham C.		01.38				
Crystal Palace	Tr	09.46	46-47	6	-	0

DEAKIN, John
Stocksbridge, 29 September, 1966 (M)

League Club	Source	Date Signed	Seasons Played	Apps	Subs	Gls
Doncaster Rov.	Barnsley (YT)	08.85	85-86	21	2	0
Birmingham C.	Shepshed Charterhouse	09.89	89	3	4	0
Carlisle U.	Tr	08.91	91	3	0	0

DEAKIN, Michael R. F.
Birmingham, 25 October, 1933 (CF)

League Club	Source	Date Signed	Seasons Played	Apps	Subs	Gls
Crystal Palace	Bromsgrove Rov.	11.54	54-59	143	-	56
Northampton T.	Tr	10.59	59-60	45	-	31
Aldershot	Tr	01.61	60-61	17	-	5

DEAKIN, Peter
Normanton, 25 March, 1938 (IF)

League Club	Source	Date Signed	Seasons Played	Apps	Subs	Gls
Bolton W.	Jnrs	05.55	57-63	63	-	13
Peterborough U.	Tr	06.64	64-66	74	1	34
Bradford P.A.	Tr	09.66	66-67	36	0	9
Peterborough U.	Tr	09.67	67	16	0	1
Brentford	Tr	07.68	68	7	1	2

DEAKIN, Raymond J.
Liverpool, 19 June, 1959 (LB)

League Club	Source	Date Signed	Seasons Played	Apps	Subs	Gls
Everton	App	06.77				
Port Vale	Tr	08.81	81	21	2	6
Bolton W.	Tr	08.82	82-84	104	1	2
Burnley	Tr	07.85	85-90	212	1	6

DEAKIN, William E.
Maltby, 19 January, 1925 (OL)

League Club	Source	Date Signed	Seasons Played	Apps	Subs	Gls
Barnsley	Sunnyside W.M.C.	05.49	49-51	26	-	3
Chester C.	Tr	07.52	52	27	-	5

DEAN, Alan J.
Aldershot, 20 January, 1950 (FB)

League Club	Source	Date Signed	Seasons Played	Apps	Subs	Gls
Aldershot	App	01.68	66-67	3	0	0

DEAN, Andrew G.
Salford, 27 November, 1966 (D)

League Club	Source	Date Signed	Seasons Played	Apps	Subs	Gls
Rochdale (N/C)	Burnley (Jnrs)	10.83	83	1	0	0

DEAN, Brian R.
Stockport, 10 September, 1947 (FB)

League Club	Source	Date Signed	Seasons Played	Apps	Subs	Gls
Blackpool	Jnrs	09.64	67	0	1	0
Barrow	Tr	07.69	69-70	44	2	0

DEAN, George C.
Walsall, 22 February, 1930 (HB)

League Club	Source	Date Signed	Seasons Played	Apps	Subs	Gls
Walsall	Hillery Street O.B.	05.50	50-53	73	-	13

DEAN, Joby
Chesterfield, 25 November, 1934 (HB)

League Club	Source	Date Signed	Seasons Played	Apps	Subs	Gls
Queens Park R.	Thoresby Colly	11.52	55-56	15	-	0
Bradford P.A.	Sutton T.	12.57	57-58	53	-	1

DEAN, Joseph
Manchester, 4 April, 1939 E Sch/E Yth (G)

League Club	Source	Date Signed	Seasons Played	Apps	Subs	Gls
Bolton W.	Jnrs	04.56	55-59	17	-	0
Carlisle U.	Tr	07.62	62-69	137	0	0
Barrow	Tr	07.70	70-71	41	0	0

DEAN, Mark C.
Northwich, 18 November, 1964 (D)

League Club	Source	Date Signed	Seasons Played	Apps	Subs	Gls
Chester C.	App	10.82	81-82	23	2	0

DEAN, Norman
Corby, 13 September, 1944 (F)

League Club	Source	Date Signed	Seasons Played	Apps	Subs	Gls
Southampton	Corby T.	04.63	65	18	0	11
Cardiff C.	Tr	03.67	66-68	20	1	3
Barnsley	Tr	09.68	68-72	58	2	18

DEAN, Raymond G.
Steventon, 15 December, 1945 (CH)

League Club	Source	Date Signed	Seasons Played	Apps	Subs	Gls
Reading		05.66	66-68	50	4	0
Aldershot	Tr	07.69	69-74	256	0	6

DEANE, Brian C.
Leeds, 7 February, 1968 E'B'/E-2 (F)

League Club	Source	Date Signed	Seasons Played	Apps	Subs	Gls
Doncaster Rov.	Jnrs	12.85	85-87	59	7	12
Sheffield U.	Tr	07.88	88-91	156	0	68

Brian Deane (Doncaster Rovers, Sheffield United & England)

DEANS, John (Dixie)
Johnstone, 30 July, 1946 S-2 (F)

League Club	Source	Date Signed	Seasons Played	Apps	Subs	Gls
Luton T.	Glasgow Celtic	06.76	76	13	1	6
Carlisle U.	L	02.77	76	4	0	2

DEANS, Raymond
Lanarkshire, 24 January, 1966 S Yth (F)

League Club	Source	Date Signed	Seasons Played	Apps	Subs	Gls
Doncaster Rov.	Clyde	02.85	84-85	18	1	5

DEANS, Thomas
Shieldhill, 7 January, 1922 SF Lge (FB)

League Club	Source	Date Signed	Seasons Played	Apps	Subs	Gls
Notts Co.	Clyde	10.49	49-55	239	-	0

DEAR, Brian C.
Plaistow, 18 September, 1943 E Sch (CF)

League Club	Source	Date Signed	Seasons Played	Apps	Subs	Gls
West Ham U.	App	11.60	62-68	63	2	33
Brighton & H.A.	L	03.67	66	7	0	5
Fulham	Tr	02.69	68	13	0	7
Millwall	Tr	07.69	69	5	1	0
West Ham U.	Woodford T.	10.70	70	4	0	0

Brian Dear (West Ham United, Fulham, Millwall & West Ham United)

DEAR, Gerald A.
Kensington, 5 January, 1937 (D)

League Club	Source	Date Signed	Seasons Played	Apps	Subs	Gls
Swindon T.		07.56	56	4	-	0

DEARDEN, Kevin C.
Luton, 8 March, 1970 (G)

League Club	Source	Date Signed	Seasons Played	Apps	Subs	Gls
Tottenham H.	YT	07.88				
Cambridge U.	L	03.89	88	15	0	0
Hartlepool U.	L	08.89	89	10	0	0
Swindon T.	L	03.90	89	1	0	0
Peterborough U.	L	08.90	90	7	0	0
Hull C.	L	01.91	90	3	0	0
Rochdale	L	08.91	91	2	0	0
Birmingham C.	L	03.92	91	12	0	0

DEARDEN, William
Oldham, 11 February, 1944 (F)

League Club	Source	Date Signed	Seasons Played	Apps	Subs	Gls
Oldham Ath.	Jnrs	09.63	64-66	32	2	2
Crewe Alex.	Tr	12.66	66-67	44	3	7
Chester C.	Tr	06.68	68-69	85	0	22
Sheffield U.	Tr	04.70	70-75	170	5	61
Chester C.	Tr	02.76	75-76	35	1	7
Chesterfield	Tr	08.77	77-78	18	9	2

DEARSON, Donald J.
Ynysybwl, 13 May, 1914 Died 1990 W Amat/W-3 (IF)

League Club	Source	Date Signed	Seasons Played	Apps	Subs	Gls
Birmingham C.	Barry T.	04.34	34-46	131	-	17
Coventry C.	Tr	02.47	46-49	84	-	10
Walsall	Tr	03.50	49-50	51	-	13

DEARY, John S.
Ormskirk, 18 October, 1962 (M)

League Club	Source	Date Signed	Seasons Played	Apps	Subs	Gls
Blackpool	App	03.80	80-88	285	18	43
Burnley	Tr	07.89	89-91	122	2	15

DEATH, Stephen V.
Elmswell (Sk), 19 September, 1949 S Sch (G)

League Club	Source	Date Signed	Seasons Played	Apps	Subs	Gls
West Ham U.	App	06.67	68	1	0	0
Reading	Tr	11.69	69-81	471	0	0

DEEHAN, John M.
Birmingham, 6 August, 1957 E Yth/Eu21-7 (F)

League Club	Source	Date Signed	Seasons Played	Apps	Subs	Gls
Aston Villa	App	04.75	75-79	107	3	41
West Bromwich A.	Tr	09.79	79-81	44	3	5
Norwich C.	Tr	12.81	81-85	158	4	62
Ipswich T.	Tr	06.86	86-87	45	4	11
Manchester C.	Tr	07.88				
Barnsley	Tr	01.90	90	3	8	2

DEELEY, Norman V.
Wednesbury, 30 November, 1933 E Sch/E-2 (OR)

League Club	Source	Date Signed	Seasons Played	Apps	Subs	Gls
Wolverhampton W.	Jnrs	12.50	51-61	206	-	66
Leyton Orient	Tr	02.62	61-63	73	-	9

DEERE, Stephen H.
Burnham Market, 31 March, 1948 (CD)

League Club	Source	Date Signed	Seasons Played	Apps	Subs	Gls
Scunthorpe U.	Norwich C. (Am)	11.67	67-72	232	6	21
Hull C.	Tr	06.73	73-74	65	1	2
Barnsley	L	10.75	75	4	0	0
Stockport Co.	L	12.75	75	6	0	0
Scunthorpe U.	Scarborough	02.78	77-79	105	0	2

DELANEY, James
Stoneyburn, 3 September, 1914 Died 1989 SF Lge/S-13 (W)

League Club	Source	Date Signed	Seasons Played	Apps	Subs	Gls
Manchester U.	Glasgow Celtic	02.46	46-50	164	-	25

DELANEY, James C.
London, 22 July, 1945 (CF)

League Club	Source	Date Signed	Seasons Played	Apps	Subs	Gls
Newport Co. (Am)	Port Talbot	07.69	69	1	0	0

Billy Dearden (OldhamAthletic, Crewe Alexandra, Chester City, Sheffield United, Chester City & Chesterfield)

DELANEY, John J.
Slough, 3 February, 1942 E Amat (CD)

League Club	Source	Date Signed	Seasons Played	Apps	Subs	Gls
Bournemouth	Wycombe W.	08.73	73-74	25	0	0

DELANEY, Louis P.
Bothwell, 28 February, 1921 (FB)

League Club	Source	Date Signed	Seasons Played	Apps	Subs	Gls
Arsenal	Nunhead	05.43				
Crystal Palace	Tr	11.49	49	3	-	0

DELAPENHA, Lloyd L. (Lindy)
Jamaica, 25 May, 1927 (F)

League Club	Source	Date Signed	Seasons Played	Apps	Subs	Gls
Portsmouth	Arsenal (Am)	04.48	48-49	7	-	0
Middlesbrough	Tr	04.50	49-57	260	-	90
Mansfield T.	Tr	06.58	58-60	115	-	27

DELF, Barrie S.
Southend, 5 June, 1961 (G)

League Club	Source	Date Signed	Seasons Played	Apps	Subs	Gls
Southend U. (N/C)		03.83	82	1	0	0

DELGADO Robert A.
Cardiff, 29 January, 1949 (CD)

League Club	Source	Date Signed	Seasons Played	Apps	Subs	Gls
Luton T.	Barry T.	02.70				
Carlisle U.	Tr	07.71	72-73	25	10	3
Workington	L	10.73	73	7	0	0
Rotherham U.	Tr	12.73	73-75	69	1	5
Chester C.	Tr	10.75	75-78	125	3	8
Port Vale	Tr	12.78	78-79	41	0	0

DELLOW, Ronald W.
Crosby, 13 July, 1914 (OR)

League Club	Source	Date Signed	Seasons Played	Apps	Subs	Gls
Blackburn Rov.	Liverpool (Am)	08.33				
Mansfield T.	Tr	06.34	34	24	-	10
Manchester C.	Tr	01.35	34	10	-	4
Tranmere Rov.	Tr	03.36	35-38	105	-	29
Carlisle U.	Tr	08.39	46	16	-	5

DELVE, John F.
Isleworth, 27 September, 1953 (M)

League Club	Source	Date Signed	Seasons Played	Apps	Subs	Gls
Queens Park R.	App	07.71	72-73	9	6	0
Plymouth Arg.	Tr	07.74	74-77	127	5	6
Exeter C.	Tr	03.78	77-82	215	0	20
Hereford U.	Tr	06.83	83-86	116	2	11
Exeter C. (N/C)	Gloucester C.	10.87	87	12	1	1

DEMAINE, David J.
Cleveleys, 7 May, 1942 (W)

League Club	Source	Date Signed	Seasons Played	Apps	Subs	Gls
Blackpool	Jnrs	07.60				
Tranmere Rov.	Tr	08.61	61	2	-	0
Southport	Tr	07.62	62	5	-	0

DEMPSEY, John
Cumbernauld, 22 June, 1913 (IF)

League Club	Source	Date Signed	Seasons Played	Apps	Subs	Gls
Ipswich T.	Queen of South	06.48	48	22	-	5

DEMPSEY, John T.
Hampstead, 15 March, 1946 IR-19 (CD)

League Club	Source	Date Signed	Seasons Played	Apps	Subs	Gls
Fulham	App	03.64	64-68	149	0	4
Chelsea	Tr	01.69	68-75	161	4	4

DEMPSEY, John W.
Birkenhead, 2 April, 1951 (FB)

League Club	Source	Date Signed	Seasons Played	Apps	Subs	Gls
Tranmere Rov.	App	04.69	67-71	52	1	1

DEMPSEY, Mark A. P.
Dublin, 10 December, 1972 IR Yth/IRu21-2 (M)

League Club	Source	Date Signed	Seasons Played	Apps	Subs	Gls
Gillingham	YT	08.90	90-91	18	14	2

DEMPSEY, Mark J.
Manchester, 14 January, 1964 (M)

League Club	Source	Date Signed	Seasons Played	Apps	Subs	Gls
Manchester U.	App	01.82	85	1	0	0
Swindon T.	L	01.85	84	5	0	0
Sheffield U.	Tr	08.86	86-87	60	3	8
Chesterfield	L	09.88	88	3	0	0
Rotherham U.	Tr	10.88	88-90	71	4	7

DENHAM, Charles H.
Hartlepool, 28 April, 1937 (CF)

League Club	Source	Date Signed	Seasons Played	Apps	Subs	Gls
Hartlepool U. (Am)	West Amats	11.58	58	5	-	3

DENHAM, John W.
Middleton, 6 November, 1925 (LH)

League Club	Source	Date Signed	Seasons Played	Apps	Subs	Gls
Hull C.	Yorkshire Amats	06.48				
Hartlepool U.	Tr	08.49	49	1	-	0

DENIAL, Geoffrey
Sheffield, 3 January, 1932 (WH)

League Club	Source	Date Signed	Seasons Played	Apps	Subs	Gls
Sheffield U.		01.52	52-54	10	-	0
Oxford U.	Tr	09.56	62	6	-	0

DENNEHY, Jeremiah (Miah)
Cork (Ire), 29 March, 1950 IR-11 (W)

League Club	Source	Date Signed	Seasons Played	Apps	Subs	Gls
Nottingham F.	Cork Hibs	01.73	72-74	37	4	4
Walsall	Tr	07.75	75-77	123	5	22
Bristol Rov.	Tr	07.78	78-79	47	5	6

DENNIS, Alan G.
Colchester, 22 December, 1951 (CH)

League Club	Source	Date Signed	Seasons Played	Apps	Subs	Gls
Colchester U.	Jnrs	08.70	69-70	2	3	0

DENNIS, J. Anthony
Maidenhead, 1 December, 1963 (W)

League Club	Source	Date Signed	Seasons Played	Apps	Subs	Gls
Plymouth Arg.	App	12.81	81-82	7	2	0
Exeter C.	Tr	08.83	83	3	1	0
Cambridge U.	Slough T.	02.89	88-91	77	18	9

DENNIS, Mark E.
Streatham, 2 May, 1961 E Yth/Eu21-3 (LB)

League Club	Source	Date Signed	Seasons Played	Apps	Subs	Gls
Birmingham C.	App	08.78	78-82	130	0	1
Southampton	Tr	11.83	83-86	95	0	2
Queens Park R.	Tr	05.87	87-88	26	2	0
Crystal Palace	Tr	08.89	89-90	8	1	0

Mark Dennis (Birmingham City, Southampton, Queens Park Rangers & Crystal Palace)

DENNISON, Charles R.
Hull, 12 September, 1932 (FB)

League Club	Source	Date Signed	Seasons Played	Apps	Subs	Gls
Hull C.	Jnrs	07.54	54-57	24	-	1

DENNISON, Robert (Robbie)
Banbridge (NI), 30 April, 1963 NI-15 (W)

League Club	Source	Date Signed	Seasons Played	Apps	Subs	Gls
West Bromwich A.	Glenavon	09.85	85-86	9	7	1
Wolverhampton W.	Tr	03.87	86-91	193	13	29

DENNISON, Robert S.
Ambleside, 6 March, 1912 (CH)

League Club	Source	Date Signed	Seasons Played	Apps	Subs	Gls
Newcastle U.	Radcliffe U.	05.29	32-33	11	-	2
Nottingham F.	Tr	05.34	34	15	-	5
Fulham	Tr	06.35	35-38	31	-	0
Northampton T.	Tr	09.45	46-47	55	-	0

DENNY, Paul N.
Croydon, 5 September, 1957 (M)

League Club	Source	Date Signed	Seasons Played	Apps	Subs	Gls
Southend U.	App	09.75	76	8	1	2
Wimbledon	Tr	08.77	77-80	87	16	11

DENTON, Edward J.
Oxford, 18 May, 1970 (M)

League Club	Source	Date Signed	Seasons Played	Apps	Subs	Gls
Oxford U.	YT	07.88	87	0	2	0
Watford	Witney T.	02.91	90	0	2	0

DENTON, Peter R.
Gorleston, 1 March, 1946 (OR)

League Club	Source	Date Signed	Seasons Played	Apps	Subs	Gls
Coventry C.	App	03.64	65-67	10	0	1
Luton T.	Tr	01.68	67-68	4	1	0

DENTON, Roger W.
Stretford, 6 January, 1953 (FB)

League Club	Source	Date Signed	Seasons Played	Apps	Subs	Gls
Bolton W.	Jnrs	05.71	71	3	1	0
Bradford C.	Tr	07.72	72-73	25	5	0
Rochdale	L	02.74	73	2	0	0

DENYER, Albert F. T.
Swindon, 6 December, 1924 (OR)

League Club	Source	Date Signed	Seasons Played	Apps	Subs	Gls
Swindon T.		10.45	46	7	-	1
Cardiff C.	Tr	05.48				

DENYER, Peter R.
Chiddingfold, 26 November, 1957 (M)

League Club	Source	Date Signed	Seasons Played	Apps	Subs	Gls
Portsmouth	App	12.75	75-78	123	8	15
Northampton T.	Tr	07.79	79-82	138	9	28

DEPEAR, E. Roland (Roly)
Spalding, 10 December, 1923 (CH)

League Club	Source	Date Signed	Seasons Played	Apps	Subs	Gls
Leeds U.	Boston U.	05.48	48	4	-	0
Newport Co.	Tr	06.49	49	16	-	0
Shrewsbury T.	Tr	07.50	50-51	74	-	5

DEPLIDGE, William
Bradford, 12 November, 1924 (IF)

League Club	Source	Date Signed	Seasons Played	Apps	Subs	Gls
Bradford P.A.	Jnrs	08.42	46-55	274	-	62

DERBYSHIRE, Thomas
Manchester, 10 December, 1930

League Club	Source	Date Signed	Seasons Played	Apps	Subs	Gls
Hartlepool U. (Am)		08.50	50	1	-	0

DERKO, T. Franco
Italy, 22 December, 1946 (FB)

League Club	Source	Date Signed	Seasons Played	Apps	Subs	Gls
Mansfield T.	App	01.65	66	1	0	0

DERRETT, Stephen C.
Cardiff, 16 October, 1947 W Sch/Wu23-3/W-4 (FB)

League Club	Source	Date Signed	Seasons Played	Apps	Subs	Gls
Cardiff C.	App	10.65	66-71	61	5	0
Carlisle U.	Tr	04.72	72	13	0	0
Aldershot	L	10.73	73	4	0	0
Rotherham U.	Tr	12.73	73-75	79	2	2
Newport Co.	Tr	06.76	76-77	61	0	0

DERRICK, E. Albert
Newport, 6 August, 1939 (IF)

League Club	Source	Date Signed	Seasons Played	Apps	Subs	Gls
Newport Co.		12.60	60	3	-	1
Newport Co.	Hereford U.	07.69	69	25	2	8

DERRICK, Albert E.
Newport, 8 September, 1908 Died 1975 (OR)

League Club	Source	Date Signed	Seasons Played	Apps	Subs	Gls
Newport Co.		10.35	35-38	125	-	48
Swindon T.	Tr	01.46	46	1	-	0

DERRICK, Jantzen S.
Bristol, 10 January, 1943 E Sch (W)

League Club	Source	Date Signed	Seasons Played	Apps	Subs	Gls
Bristol C.	Jnrs	01.60	59-70	254	6	32
Mansfield T.	L	03.71	70	2	1	0

DESMEULES, Rodney L.
Newbury, 23 September, 1948 (WH)

League Club	Source	Date Signed	Seasons Played	Apps	Subs	Gls
Swindon T.	App	10.66	66-67	4	0	0

DESMOND, Peter
Cork (Ire), 23 November, 1926 Died 1990 LOI/IR-4 (IF)

League Club	Source	Date Signed	Seasons Played	Apps	Subs	Gls
Middlesbrough	Shelbourne	05.49	49	2	-	0
Southport	Tr	08.50	50	12	-	2
York C.	Tr	12.51	51	1	-	0
Hartlepool U.		08.53	53	1	-	0

DEVANEY, Philip C.
Huyton, 12 February, 1969 (F)

League Club	Source	Date Signed	Seasons Played	Apps	Subs	Gls
Burnley	App	02.87	86-87	8	5	1

DEVANNEY, Alan
Otley, 5 September, 1941 (CF)

League Club	Source	Date Signed	Seasons Played	Apps	Subs	Gls
Bradford C.	Jnrs	02.59	59-61	12	-	4

DEVERALL, Harold R. (Jackie)
Reading, 5 May, 1916 E Sch (WH)

League Club	Source	Date Signed	Seasons Played	Apps	Subs	Gls
Reading	Maidenhead U.	11.37	38-47	74	-	9
Leyton Orient	Tr	08.48	48-52	115	-	2

DEVEREUX, Anthony W. J.
Gibraltar, 6 January, 1940 (FB)

League Club	Source	Date Signed	Seasons Played	Apps	Subs	Gls
Aldershot	Chelsea (Am)	11.58	59-65	133	0	0

DEVEREUX, James A.
Fleet, 20 February, 1970 (D)

League Club	Source	Date Signed	Seasons Played	Apps	Subs	Gls
Aldershot	YT	07.88	88-89	0	2	0

DEVEREUX, Robert
Sudbury, 31 January, 1971 (M)

League Club	Source	Date Signed	Seasons Played	Apps	Subs	Gls
Colchester U.	Ipswich T. (YT)	05.89	89	1	1	0

DEVEY, Raymond
Birmingham, 19 December, 1917 (HB)

League Club	Source	Date Signed	Seasons Played	Apps	Subs	Gls
Birmingham C.	Shirley Jnrs	08.37	46	1	-	0
Mansfield T.	Tr	08.47	47-49	76	-	4

DEVINE, J. Henry
Liverpool, 9 July, 1933 (OR)

League Club	Source	Date Signed	Seasons Played	Apps	Subs	Gls
Chester C.	Rhyl	07.55	55	1	-	0

DEVINE, John A.
Dublin, 11 November, 1958 IRu21-2/IR-12 (M)

League Club	Source	Date Signed	Seasons Played	Apps	Subs	Gls
Arsenal	App	10.76	77-82	86	3	0
Norwich C.	Tr	08.83	83-84	51	2	3
Stoke C.	Tr	11.85	85	15	0	1

DEVINE, Peter
Blackburn, 25 May, 1960 (W)

League Club	Source	Date Signed	Seasons Played	Apps	Subs	Gls
Bristol C.	Vancouver (Can)	07.81	81	19	2	1
Blackburn Rov. (N/C)	Tr	09.82	82-83	8	0	2
Burnley	Tr	06.84	84-85	46	10	4

DEVINE, Stephen B.
Strabane (NI), 11 December, 1964 NI Yth (D)

League Club	Source	Date Signed	Seasons Played	Apps	Subs	Gls
Wolverhampton W.	App	12.82				
Derby Co.	Tr	03.83	83-84	10	1	0
Stockport Co.	Tr	08.85	85	2	0	0
Hereford U.	Tr	10.85	85-91	235	10	4

DEVINE, William
Paisley, 22 August, 1933 (OL)

League Club	Source	Date Signed	Seasons Played	Apps	Subs	Gls
Watford	St Mirren	03.58	57-58	30	-	6
Accrington St.	Partick Th.	05.60	60	46	-	6

DEVITT, Malcolm B.
Bradford, 26 January, 1937 (IF)

League Club	Source	Date Signed	Seasons Played	Apps	Subs	Gls
Bradford C.	Bradford Rov.	03.59	58-62	100	-	13

DEVLIN, Alan T.
Edinburgh, 10 October, 1953 (F)

League Club	Source	Date Signed	Seasons Played	Apps	Subs	Gls
Exeter C.	Dundee U.	11.73	73	1	0	0

DEVLIN, Douglas K.
Glasgow, 17 March, 1953 (M)

League Club	Source	Date Signed	Seasons Played	Apps	Subs	Gls
Wolverhampton W.	App	06.71				
Walsall	Tr	07.72	72	15	3	0

DEVLIN, Ernest
Gateshead, 6 March, 1920 Died 1976 (FB)

League Club	Source	Date Signed	Seasons Played	Apps	Subs	Gls
Gateshead		08.42				
West Ham U.	Tr	06.46	46-52	70	-	0
Darlington	Tr	02.54	53-56	115	-	1

DEVLIN, John
Airdrie, 11 December, 1917 (IF)

League Club	Source	Date Signed	Seasons Played	Apps	Subs	Gls
Walsall	Kilmarnock	12.47	47-51	159	-	50

DEVLIN, Joseph
Cleland, 12 March, 1931 (OR)

League Club	Source	Date Signed	Seasons Played	Apps	Subs	Gls
Accrington St.	Falkirk	07.53	53-56	114	-	18
Rochdale	Tr	09.56	56-57	38	-	7
Bradford P.A.	Tr	11.57	57-58	34	-	3
Carlisle U.	Tr	07.59	59	5	-	0

DEVLIN, Mark A.
Irvine, 18 January, 1973 (M)

League Club	Source	Date Signed	Seasons Played	Apps	Subs	Gls
Stoke C.	YT	04.91	90	18	3	2

DEVLIN, Paul J.
Birmingham, 14 April, 1972 (W)

League Club	Source	Date Signed	Seasons Played	Apps	Subs	Gls
Notts Co.	Stafford R.	02.92	91	1	1	0

DEVLIN, William
Glasgow, 30 May, 1931 (W)

League Club	Source	Date Signed	Seasons Played	Apps	Subs	Gls
Carlisle U.	Peterborough U.	08.56	56	28	-	6

DEVONSHIRE, Alan E.
Park Royal, 13 April, 1956 E-8 (M)

League Club	Source	Date Signed	Seasons Played	Apps	Subs	Gls
West Ham U.	Southall	10.76	76-89	345	13	29
Watford	Tr	07.90	90-91	23	2	1

DEVONSHIRE, Leslie E.
Acton, 13 June, 1926 (W)

League Club	Source	Date Signed	Seasons Played	Apps	Subs	Gls
Brentford	Queens Park R. (Am)	05.48				
Chester C.	Tr	06.50	50	44	-	4
Crystal Palace	Tr	08.51	51-54	83	-	12

DEWHURST, Robert M.
Keighley, 10 September, 1971 (CD)

League Club	Source	Date Signed	Seasons Played	Apps	Subs	Gls
Blackburn Rov.	YT	10.90	90	13	0	0
Darlington	L	12.91	91	11	0	1

DEWICK, John A.
Rotherham, 28 November, 1919 (G)

League Club	Source	Date Signed	Seasons Played	Apps	Subs	Gls
Notts Co.		10.46	46	1	-	0

DEWIS, George
Burbage, 22 January, 1913 (F)

League Club	Source	Date Signed	Seasons Played	Apps	Subs	Gls
Leicester C.	Nuneaton T.	10.33	33-49	116	-	45

DEWS, George
Ossett, 5 June, 1921 (IF)

League Club	Source	Date Signed	Seasons Played	Apps	Subs	Gls
Middlesbrough		08.46	46-47	33	-	8
Plymouth Arg.	Tr	10.47	47-54	257	-	76
Walsall	Tr	06.55	55	10	-	1

DEWSBURY, John
Swansea, 16 February, 1932 (FB)

League Club	Source	Date Signed	Seasons Played	Apps	Subs	Gls
Swansea C.	Jnrs	07.50	52	9	-	0
Newport Co.	Tr	08.55	55	2	-	0

DEWSNIP, George E.
Salford, 6 May, 1956 (W)

League Club	Source	Date Signed	Seasons Played	Apps	Subs	Gls
Southport	Preston N.E. (App)	06.74	74-76	83	4	11

DEY, Geoffrey
Chesterfield, 11 January, 1964 E Yth (M)

League Club	Source	Date Signed	Seasons Played	Apps	Subs	Gls
Sheffield U.	App	01.82				
Scunthorpe U.	Tr	08.83	83-84	17	0	1

DEYNA, Kazimierz
Poland, 23 October, 1947 Died 1989 Polish Int (F)

League Club	Source	Date Signed	Seasons Played	Apps	Subs	Gls
Manchester C.	Legia Warsaw (Pol)	11.78	78-80	34	4	12

DIAMOND, Anthony J.
Rochdale, 23 August, 1968 NIu23-1 (F)

League Club	Source	Date Signed	Seasons Played	Apps	Subs	Gls
Blackburn Rov.	YT	06.86	86-88	9	17	3
Wigan Ath.	L	10.88	88	6	0	2
Blackpool	Tr	08.89	89	2	1	1

DIAMOND, Barry
Dumbarton, 20 February, 1960 (F)

League Club	Source	Date Signed	Seasons Played	Apps	Subs	Gls
Rochdale	Barrow	07.84	84-85	50	2	16
Stockport Co.	L	12.85	85	6	0	0
Halifax T.	Tr	02.86	85-86	17	5	3
Wrexham	L	01.87	86	2	2	0

DIBBLE, Andrew G.
Cwmbran, 8 May, 1965 W Yth/Wu21-2/W-3 (G)

League Club	Source	Date Signed	Seasons Played	Apps	Subs	Gls
Cardiff C.	App	08.82	81-83	62	0	0
Luton T.	Tr	07.84	84-87	30	0	0
Sunderland	L	02.86	85	12	0	0
Huddersfield T.	L	03.87	86	5	0	0
Manchester C.	Tr	06.88	88-91	74	0	0
Middlesbrough	L	02.91	90	19	0	0
Bolton W.	L	09.91	91	13	0	0
West Bromwich A.	L	02.92	91	9	0	0

DIBBLE, Christopher
Morden, 10 October, 1960 E Sch (M)

League Club	Source	Date Signed	Seasons Played	Apps	Subs	Gls
Millwall	App	11.77	77-81	49	14	5
Wimbledon	Tr	07.82	82-83	7	2	0

DIBDEN, Keith
Southampton, 17 December, 1933 (F)

League Club	Source	Date Signed	Seasons Played	Apps	Subs	Gls
Southampton	Jnrs	01.52				
Gillingham	Tr	07.57	57	1	-	0

DICK, Alistair J.
Stirling, 25 April, 1965 S Sch/S Yth (W)

League Club	Source	Date Signed	Seasons Played	Apps	Subs	Gls
Tottenham H.	App	05.82	81-85	16	1	2

DICK, George W.
Torphichen, 12 June, 1921 Died 1960 (IF)

League Club	Source	Date Signed	Seasons Played	Apps	Subs	Gls
Blackpool		08.46	46-47	46	-	13
West Ham U.	Tr	10.48	48	14	-	1
Carlisle U.	Tr	07.49	49-50	52	-	23
Stockport Co.	Tr	10.50	50	25	-	12
Workington	Tr	10.51	51-52	56	-	16

DICK, John
Glasgow, 19 March, 1930 S'B'-1/S-1 (IF)

League Club	Source	Date Signed	Seasons Played	Apps	Subs	Gls
West Ham U.	Crittalls Ath.	06.53	53-62	326	-	153
Brentford	Tr	09.62	62-64	72	-	45

DICK, Thomas W.
Glasgow, 19 July, 1936 (CF)

League Club	Source	Date Signed	Seasons Played	Apps	Subs	Gls
Bradford P.A.	Third Lanark	06.60	60	4	-	0

DICK, P. Watt (Wattie)
Glasgow, 28 August, 1927 (WH)

League Club	Source	Date Signed	Seasons Played	Apps	Subs	Gls
Accrington St.	Third Lanark	06.55	55-58	125	-	37
Bradford P.A.	Tr	12.58	58-62	155	-	2

DICKENS, Alan W.
Plaistow, 3 September, 1964 E Yth/Eu21-1 (M)

League Club	Source	Date Signed	Seasons Played	Apps	Subs	Gls
West Ham U.	App	08.82	82-88	173	19	23
Chelsea	Tr	08.89	89-91	39	9	1

DICKENS, Leo
Hemsworth, 16 March, 1927 (HB)

League Club	Source	Date Signed	Seasons Played	Apps	Subs	Gls
Rotherham U.	Frickley Colly	07.50				
Chester C.	Tr	07.52	52	7	-	0

Andy Dibble (Cardiff City, Luton Town, Manchester City & Wales)

League Club	Source	Date Signed	Seasons Played	Career Record Apps	Subs	Gls

DICKENSON, Kevin J.
Hackney, 24 November, 1962 (LB)

League Club	Source	Date Signed	Seasons Played	Apps	Subs	Gls
Charlton Ath.	Tottenham H. (App)	04.80	79-84	72	3	1
Leyton Orient	Tr	07.85	85-91	190	2	3

DICKER, Leslie R.
Stockwell, 20 December, 1926 (OL)

League Club	Source	Date Signed	Seasons Played	Apps	Subs	Gls
Tottenham H.	Chelmsford C.	06.51	52	10	-	2
Southend U.	Tr	07.53	53-54	18	-	7

DICKIE, Alan L.
Charlton, 30 January, 1944 (G)

League Club	Source	Date Signed	Seasons Played	Apps	Subs	Gls
West Ham U.	App	02.62	61-65	12	0	0
Coventry C.	Tr	03.67	67	2	0	0
Aldershot	Tr	07.68	68	6	0	0

DICKIE, Murdoch M.
Dumbarton, 28 December, 1919 (OR)

League Club	Source	Date Signed	Seasons Played	Apps	Subs	Gls
Port Vale		10.44				
Chelsea	Guildford C.	04.45	46	1	-	0
Bournemouth	Tr	02.47	46-47	16	-	2

DICKINS, Matthew J.
Sheffield, 3 September, 1970 (G)

League Club	Source	Date Signed	Seasons Played	Apps	Subs	Gls
Sheffield U.	YT	07.89				
Lincoln C.	Tr	02.91	90-91	27	0	0
Blackburn Rov.	Tr	03.92	91	1	0	0

DICKINSON, James A.
South Elmsall, 26 September, 1931 (FB)

League Club	Source	Date Signed	Seasons Played	Apps	Subs	Gls
Barrow	Pontefract	08.51	51-57	67	-	0

DICKINSON, James W.
Alton, 24 April, 1925 Died 1982 EF Lge/E'B'-3/E-48 (WH)

League Club	Source	Date Signed	Seasons Played	Apps	Subs	Gls
Portsmouth	Jnrs	01.44	46-64	764	-	9

Jimmy Dickinson (Portsmouth & England)

DICKINSON, Leonard
South Elmsall, 6 March, 1942 (IF)

League Club	Source	Date Signed	Seasons Played	Apps	Subs	Gls
Sheffield Wed.	Jnrs	02.60				
Oldham Ath.	Tr	06.61	61	5	-	2

DICKINSON, Martin J.
Leeds, 14 March, 1963 (CD)

League Club	Source	Date Signed	Seasons Played	Apps	Subs	Gls
Leeds U.	App	05.80	79-85	100	3	2
West Bromwich A.	Tr	02.86	85-87	46	4	2
Sheffield U.	Tr	07.88	88	0	1	0

DICKINSON, Ronald A.
Coventry, 29 June, 1930 (HB)

League Club	Source	Date Signed	Seasons Played	Apps	Subs	Gls
Shrewsbury T.(Am)	Nuneaton Bor.	05.53	53	11	-	0
Coventry C.	Tr	06.54				

DICKS, Alan V.
Kennington, 29 August, 1934 (WH)

League Club	Source	Date Signed	Seasons Played	Apps	Subs	Gls
Chelsea	Jnrs	09.51	52-57	33	-	1
Southend U.	Tr	11.58	58-61	85	-	2
Coventry C.	Tr	02.62				

DICKS, Julian A.
Bristol, 8 August, 1968 Eu21-4 (LB)

League Club	Source	Date Signed	Seasons Played	Apps	Subs	Gls
Birmingham C.	App	03.86	85-87	83	6	1
West Ham U.	Tr	03.88	87-91	118	0	18

Julian Dicks (Birmingham City & West Ham United)

DICKS, Ronald W.
Kennington, 13 April, 1924 (WH)

League Club	Source	Date Signed	Seasons Played	Apps	Subs	Gls
Middlesbrough	Dulwich Hamlet	05.43	47-58	316	-	10

DICKSON, Adam
Hamilton, 4 January, 1929 (G)

League Club	Source	Date Signed	Seasons Played	Apps	Subs	Gls
Leicester C.	Thorniewood Ath.	06.51	51-54	16	-	0

DICKSON, Joseph J.
Liverpool, 31 January, 1934 Died 1990 E Yth (F)

League Club	Source	Date Signed	Seasons Played	Apps	Subs	Gls
Liverpool	Jnrs	06.52	55	6	-	3

DICKSON, William
Lurgan (NI), 15 April, 1923 NI-12 (WH)

League Club	Source	Date Signed	Seasons Played	Apps	Subs	Gls
Notts Co.	Glenavon	11.45	46-47	21	-	2
Chelsea	Tr	11.47	47-52	101	-	4
Arsenal	Tr	10.53	53-55	29	-	1
Mansfield T.	Tr	07.56	56	19	-	0

DIGBY, Derek F.
Teignmouth, 14 May, 1931 (W)

League Club	Source	Date Signed	Seasons Played	Apps	Subs	Gls
Exeter C.	Dawlish	08.49	51-52	31	-	2
Southampton	Tr	09.53	53-54	15	-	2

DIGBY, Fraser C.
Sheffield, 23 April, 1967 E Yth/Eu21-5 (G)

League Club	Source	Date Signed	Seasons Played	Apps	Subs	Gls
Manchester U.	App	04.85				
Swindon T.	Tr	09.86	86-91	223	0	0

DIGHTON, Richard A.
Corby, 26 July, 1951 (G)

League Club	Source	Date Signed	Seasons Played	Apps	Subs	Gls
Peterborough U.	Coventry C. (App)	11.69	70-71	8	0	0
Stockport Co.	L	10.70	70	1	0	0

DIGNAM, Joseph
Glasgow, 10 January, 1931

League Club	Source	Date Signed	Seasons Played	Apps	Subs	Gls
Wrexham	Alloa Ath.	07.57	57	8	-	0

DIGWEED, Perry M.
Westminster, 26 October, 1959 (G)

League Club	Source	Date Signed	Seasons Played	Apps	Subs	Gls
Fulham	App	08.77	76-80	15	0	0
Brighton & H.A.	Tr	01.81	80-91	175	0	0
Chelsea	L	02.88	87	3	0	0

DILLON, Andrew
Caerphilly, 20 January, 1969 (G)

League Club	Source	Date Signed	Seasons Played	Apps	Subs	Gls
Newport Co.	YT	07.87	86-87	15	0	0

DILLON, John
Coatbridge, 9 November, 1942 (OL)

League Club	Source	Date Signed	Seasons Played	Apps	Subs	Gls
Sunderland	Jnrs	11.59	60-61	18	-	1
Brighton & H.A.	Tr	07.62	62	21	-	3
Crewe Alex.	Tr	07.63	63	5	-	1

DILLON, Kevin P.
Sunderland, 18 December, 1959 E Yth/Eu21-1 (M)

League Club	Source	Date Signed	Seasons Played	Apps	Subs	Gls
Birmingham C.	App	07.77	77-82	181	5	15
Portsmouth	Tr	03.83	82-88	206	9	45
Newcastle U.	Tr	07.89	89-90	62	0	0
Reading	Tr	07.91	91	29	0	3

DILLON, Michael L.
Highgate, 29 September, 1952 E Sch/E Yth (CD)

League Club	Source	Date Signed	Seasons Played	Apps	Subs	Gls
Tottenham H.	App	12.69	72-73	21	3	1
Millwall	L	12.74	74	4	0	0
Swindon T.	L	03.75	74	7	2	0

DILLON, Vincent
Manchester, 2 October, 1923 (CF)

League Club	Source	Date Signed	Seasons Played	Apps	Subs	Gls
Bolton W.		04.48	47-50	17	-	2
Tranmere Rov.	Tr	02.51	50-52	33	-	17

DILLSWORTH, Edward
Sierra Leone, 16 April, 1946 (WH)

League Club	Source	Date Signed	Seasons Played	Apps	Subs	Gls
Lincoln C. (Am)	Wealdstone	03.67	66	2	0	0

DIMMER, Hyam
Scotstown, 14 March, 1914 (IF)

League Club	Source	Date Signed	Seasons Played	Apps	Subs	Gls
Aldershot	Ayr U.	08.46	46	7	-	1
Bristol C.	Tr	05.47	47	1	-	0

DIMOND, Stuart
Manchester, 3 January, 1920 (CF)

League Club	Source	Date Signed	Seasons Played	Apps	Subs	Gls
Manchester U.		12.42				
Bradford C.	Tr	11.45	46	9	-	1

DINE, John
Newton Stewart, 3 May, 1940 (G)

League Club	Source	Date Signed	Seasons Played	Apps	Subs	Gls
Bradford P.A.	Bulford U.	08.62	62-64	32	-	0

DINGWALL, W. Norman
Gateshead, 29 July, 1923 (F)

League Club	Source	Date Signed	Seasons Played	Apps	Subs	Gls
Sheffield U.		03.46				
Halifax T.	Tr	07.47	47	9	-	0

DINSDALE, Peter
Bradford, 19 October, 1938 (WH)

League Club	Source	Date Signed	Seasons Played	Apps	Subs	Gls
Huddersfield T.	Yorkshire Amats	01.56	59-66	213	1	8
Bradford P.A.	Tr	08.67	67	9	0	0

DISLEY, Martin
Ormskirk, 24 June, 1971 (F)

League Club	Source	Date Signed	Seasons Played	Apps	Subs	Gls
Crewe Alex.	YT	09.89	89-91	0	2	0

DITCHBURN, Edward G. (Ted)
Gillingham, 24 October, 1921 E'B'-2/EF Lge/E-6 (G)

League Club	Source	Date Signed	Seasons Played	Apps	Subs	Gls
Tottenham H.	Jnrs	05.39	46-58	418	-	0

DIVERS, John
Clydebank, 6 August, 1911 S-1 (IF)

League Club	Source	Date Signed	Seasons Played	Apps	Subs	Gls
Oldham Ath.	Morton	08.47	47	1	-	0

DIVERS, John R.
Glasgow, 24 November, 1931 (F)

League Club	Source	Date Signed	Seasons Played	Apps	Subs	Gls
Exeter C.	Clyde	05.56	56	12	-	1

DIX, Richard
South Shields, 17 January, 1924 (OL)

League Club	Source	Date Signed	Seasons Played	Apps	Subs	Gls
Bradford P.A.	Jnrs	08.44	46-47	18	-	5
Bradford C.	North Shields	08.52	52	8	-	1

DIX, Ronald W.
Bristol, 5 September, 1912 E Sch/EF Lge/E-1 (IF)

League Club	Source	Date Signed	Seasons Played	Apps	Subs	Gls
Bristol Rov.	Jnrs	02.28	27-31	101	-	33
Blackburn Rov.	Tr	05.32	32	38	-	14
Aston Villa	Tr	05.33	32-36	97	-	30
Derby Co.	Tr	02.37	36-38	94	-	35
Tottenham H.	Tr	06.39	46-47	36	-	5
Reading	Tr	11.47	47-48	44	-	13

DIXEY, Richard
Leicester, 2 September, 1956 (CD)

League Club	Source	Date Signed	Seasons Played	Apps	Subs	Gls
Burnley	Enderby T.	12.74	74	3	0	0
Stockport Co.	L	02.76	75	14	0	1

DIXON, Andrew
Louth, 19 April, 1968 (FB)

League Club	Source	Date Signed	Seasons Played	Apps	Subs	Gls
Grimsby T.	YT	05.86	86-88	35	3	0
Southend U.	Tr	08.89	89	24	0	0

DIXON, Andrew P.
Hartlepool, 5 August, 1968 (F)

League Club	Source	Date Signed	Seasons Played	Apps	Subs	Gls
Hartlepool U.	Jnrs	07.87	86-87	7	7	1

DIXON, Arthur
Middleton, 17 November, 1921 (IF)

League Club	Source	Date Signed	Seasons Played	Apps	Subs	Gls
Northampton T.	Hearts	11.49	49-51	68	-	23
Leicester C.	Tr	10.51	51-52	11	-	0

DIXON, Benjamin
Lincoln, 16 September, 1974

League Club	Source	Date Signed	Seasons Played	Apps	Subs	Gls
Lincoln C. (YT)		07.91	91	0	3	0

DIXON, Cecil H.
Trowbridge, 28 March, 1935 (OR)

League Club	Source	Date Signed	Seasons Played	Apps	Subs	Gls
Cardiff C.	Trowbridge T.	07.54	54-56	21	-	1
Newport Co.	Tr	07.57	57-60	107	-	15
Northampton T.	Tr	08.61	61	15	-	4

DIXON, Colin
Newcastle, 24 September, 1963 (D)

League Club	Source	Date Signed	Seasons Played	Apps	Subs	Gls
Southampton	App	09.81				
Hartlepool U.		11.83	83	1	0	0

DIXON, David
Seaham, 3 November, 1951 (FB)

League Club	Source	Date Signed	Seasons Played	Apps	Subs	Gls
Middlesbrough	App	11.68	69	1	0	0

DIXON, John T.
Hebburn, 10 December, 1923 (IF)

League Club	Source	Date Signed	Seasons Played	Apps	Subs	Gls
Aston Villa	Spennymoor U.	01.46	46-60	392	-	132

DIXON, John W.
Hartlepool, 12 March, 1934 (FB)

League Club	Source	Date Signed	Seasons Played	Apps	Subs	Gls
Hartlepool U.		10.57	58-60	35	-	2

DIXON Joseph
Newcastle-u-Lyme, 24 September, 1916

League Club	Source	Date Signed	Seasons Played	Apps	Subs	Gls
Northampton T.	Audley U.	04.45				
Port Vale	Tr	10.46	46	1	-	0

DIXON, Kerry M.
Luton, 24 July, 1961 Eu21-1/E-8 (F)

League Club	Source	Date Signed	Seasons Played	Apps	Subs	Gls
Tottenham H.	Chesham U.	07.78				
Reading	Dunstable T.	07.80	80-82	110	6	51
Chelsea	Tr	08.83	83-91	331	4	147

League Club	Source	Date Signed	Seasons Played	Apps	Subs	Gls
DIXON, Kevin L.						
Consett, 27 July, 1960						(W)
Carlisle U.	Tow Law T.	08.83	83	5	4	0
Hartlepool U.	L	10.83	83	6	0	3
Hartlepool U.	Tr	08.84	84-86	103	4	26
Scunthorpe U.	L	01.86	85	14	0	2
Scunthorpe U.	Tr	08.87	87	37	4	4
Hartlepool U.	Tr	06.88	88	14	0	4
York C.	Tr	11.88	88-89	33	5	8
Scarborough	L	02.90	89	3	0	0
DIXON, Lee M.						
Manchester, 17 March, 1964 EF Lge/E'B'/E-12						(RB)
Burnley	Jnrs	07.82	82-83	4	0	0
Chester C.	Tr	02.84	83-84	56	1	1
Bury	Tr	07.85	85	45	0	6
Stoke C.	Tr	07.86	86-87	71	0	5
Arsenal	Tr	01.88	87-91	151	2	15

Lee Dixon (Burnley, Chester City, Bury, Stoke City, Arsenal & England)

League Club	Source	Date Signed	Seasons Played	Apps	Subs	Gls
DIXON, Michael						
Willesden, 14 March, 1937						(CF)
Luton T.	Hitchin T.	04.57	58-60	3	-	0
Coventry C.	Tr	05.61	61	18	-	12
DIXON, Michael G.						
Reading, 12 October, 1943 E Sch						(G)
Reading	Jnrs	08.61	62-67	113	0	0
Aldershot	Tr	07.69	69-70	38	0	0
DIXON, Milton						
Manchester, 30 March, 1925						(CF)
Huddersfield T.		02.48				
Stockport Co.	Tr	10.50	50	21	-	2
DIXON, Paul K.						
Derry (NI), 22 February, 1960						(CD)
Burnley	App	02.78	78-81	23	1	1
DIXON, Raymond						
Denaby, 31 December, 1930						(F)
Rotherham U.	Denaby U.	06.55	55-56	14	-	4
DIXON, Robert						
Felling, 11 January, 1936						(OL)
Arsenal	Crook T.	08.57				
Workington	Tr	11.58	58	28	-	5
West Bromwich A.	Tr	05.59	59	7	-	1

League Club	Source	Date Signed	Seasons Played	Apps	Subs	Gls
DIXON, Stanley						
Burnley, 28 August, 1920						(CH)
Plymouth Arg.	Hapton U.	12.38	46-50	60	-	1
DIXON, Thomas C.						
Newcastle, 8 June, 1929						(CF)
West Ham U.	Newcastle U. (Am)	02.51	52-54	39	-	21
Reading	Tr	03.55	54-58	123	-	64
Brighton & H.A.	Tr	10.58	58-59	35	-	12
Workington	Tr	07.60	60-61	53	-	17
Barrow	Tr	10.61	61-62	62	-	23
DIXON, Wilfred E. (Will)						
Wood Green, 2 February, 1950						(RB)
Arsenal	App	02.68				
Reading	Tr	07.69	69-72	150	3	0
Colchester U.	Tr	08.73				
Swindon T.	Tr	09.73	73-76	134	6	10
Aldershot	Tr	07.77	77-79	114	6	6
DOBBIE, Harold						
Bishop Auckland, 20 February, 1923 Died 1988						(IF)
Middlesbrough	South Bank	12.46	46-49	23	-	6
Plymouth Arg.	Tr	03.50	49-53	30	-	6
Torquay U.	Tr	10.53	53-56	110	-	47
DOBBIN, James						
Dunfermline, 17 September, 1963						(M)
Doncaster Rov.	Glasgow Celtic	03.84	83-86	56	8	13
Barnsley	Tr	09.86	86-90	116	13	12
Grimsby T.	Tr	07.91	91	32	0	6
DOBBING, Robert						
Sunderland, 27 June, 1949						(LB)
Coventry C.	App	06.67				
Hartlepool U.	Tr	07.69	69	34	0	1
DOBBINS, L. Wayne						
Bromsgrove, 30 August, 1968						(FB/M)
West Bromwich A.	App	08.86	86-90	30	15	0
Torquay U.	Tr	07.91	91	18	3	1
DOBBS, Eric						
Forehoe, 15 October, 1920						(FB)
Coventry C.		08.46	46-47	5	-	0
Bristol Rov.	Tr	07.48				
DOBBS, Gerald F.						
Lambeth, 24 January, 1971						(M)
Wimbledon	YT	07.89	91	2	2	0
DOBIE, Mark G.						
Carlisle, 8 November, 1963						(F)
Carlisle U.(N/C)	Workington	12.86	86	2	4	0
Cambridge U.	Gretna	12.90				
Torquay U.	Tr	08.91	91	18	2	2
DOBING, Brian G.						
Sheffield, 29 December, 1937						(G)
Crewe Alex.	Knutsford	04.59	58	1	-	0
DOBING, Peter A.						
Manchester, 1 December, 1938 Eu23-7/EF Lge						(IF)
Blackburn Rov.	Jnrs	12.55	55-60	179	-	88
Manchester C.	Tr	07.61	61-62	82	-	31
Stoke C.	Tr	08.63	63-72	303	0	80
DOBSON, Anthony J.						
Coventry, 5 February, 1969 Eu21-4						(D)
Coventry C.	App	07.86	86-90	51	3	1
Blackburn Rov.	Tr	01.91	90-91	21	1	0
DOBSON, Brian A.						
Colchester, 1 March, 1934						(WH)
Colchester U.		01.56	55-59	24	-	0
DOBSON, Colin						
Middlesbrough, 9 May, 1940 Eu23-2						(W)
Sheffield Wed.	Jnrs	11.57	61-65	177	0	49
Huddersfield T.	Tr	08.66	66-70	149	6	50
Brighton & H.A.	L	01.72	71	2	2	0
Bristol Rov.	Tr	07.72	72-75	62	0	4
DOBSON, George R.						
Chiswick, 24 August, 1949						(W)
Brentford	App	08.67	66-69	75	5	10

DOBSON, Ian
Hull, 3 October, 1957 (CD)

League Club	Source	Date Signed	Seasons Played	Apps	Subs	Gls
Hull C.	App	10.75	75-79	86	6	7
Hereford U.	Tr	06.80	80-81	41	0	5

DOBSON, J. Martin
Blackburn, 14 February, 1948 EF Lge/E-5 (M)

League Club	Source	Date Signed	Seasons Played	Apps	Subs	Gls
Bolton W.	Jnrs	07.66				
Burnley	Tr	08.67	67-74	220	4	43
Everton	Tr	08.74	74-78	190	0	29
Burnley	Tr	08.79	79-83	186	0	20
Bury	Tr	03.84	83-85	60	1	4

DOBSON, Paul
Hartlepool, 17 December, 1962 (F)

League Club	Source	Date Signed	Seasons Played	Apps	Subs	Gls
Hartlepool U.	Newcastle U. (Jnr)	11.81	81-82	23	8	8
Hartlepool U.	Horden Colly	12.83	83-85	60	20	24
Torquay U.	Tr	07.86	86-87	63	14	38
Doncaster Rov.	Tr	08.88	88	22	2	10
Scarborough	Tr	02.89	88-90	54	7	22
Halifax T.	L	10.90	90	1	0	1
Hereford U.	L	11.90	90	6	0	1
Lincoln C.	Tr	01.91	90-91	13	8	5

DOBSON, R. Peter
Frimley, 13 June, 1925 (F)

League Club	Source	Date Signed	Seasons Played	Apps	Subs	Gls
Ipswich T.	Wisbech T.	10.49	49-53	30	-	5

DOCHERTY, Bernard
Bellshill, 11 August, 1941 (IF)

League Club	Source	Date Signed	Seasons Played	Apps	Subs	Gls
Notts Co.	Cambuslang	08.64	64	25	-	2

DOCHERTY, James
Clydebank, 21 April, 1926 (F)

League Club	Source	Date Signed	Seasons Played	Apps	Subs	Gls
Northampton T.	Glasgow Celtic	07.50	50	1	-	0

DOCHERTY, James
Clydebank, 22 April, 1929 (WH)

League Club	Source	Date Signed	Seasons Played	Apps	Subs	Gls
Doncaster Rov.	Airdrieonians	05.51	51	11	-	4
Crewe Alex.	Limerick C.	02.57	56	2	-	0

DOCHERTY, James
Broxburn, 8 November, 1956 (F)

League Club	Source	Date Signed	Seasons Played	Apps	Subs	Gls
Chelsea	East Stirling	03.79	78	2	1	0

DOCHERTY, John
Glasgow, 28 February, 1935 (WH)

League Club	Source	Date Signed	Seasons Played	Apps	Subs	Gls
Colchester U.	Hearts	06.63	63-64	77	-	2

DOCHERTY, John
Glasgow, 29 April, 1940 (OR)

League Club	Source	Date Signed	Seasons Played	Apps	Subs	Gls
Brentford	St Rochs	07.59	60	17	-	2
Sheffield U.	Tr	03.61	60-65	41	0	9
Brentford	Tr	12.65	65-67	97	0	31
Reading	Tr	02.68	67-69	45	1	7
Brentford	Tr	03.70	70-73	137	4	34

DOCHERTY, Michael
Preston, 29 October, 1950 E Yth (FB)

League Club	Source	Date Signed	Seasons Played	Apps	Subs	Gls
Burnley	App	11.67	68-75	149	4	0
Manchester C.	Tr	04.76	75-76	8	0	0
Sunderland	Tr	12.76	76-78	72	1	6

DOCHERTY, Peter
Hebburn, 14 February, 1929 (OL)

League Club	Source	Date Signed	Seasons Played	Apps	Subs	Gls
Fulham		09.49				
Darlington	Tr	09.50	50	3	-	1

DOCHERTY, Thomas
Penshaw (Dm), 15 April, 1924 (OL)

League Club	Source	Date Signed	Seasons Played	Apps	Subs	Gls
Lincoln C.	Murton Colly	07.47	47-49	45	-	3
Norwich C.	Tr	06.50	50-52	85	-	4
Reading	Tr	07.53	53-54	53	-	2
Newport Co.	Tr	06.55	55-57	108	-	1

DOCHERTY, Thomas H.
Glasgow, 24 August, 1928 S'B'-1/S-25 (WH)

League Club	Source	Date Signed	Seasons Played	Apps	Subs	Gls
Preston N.E.	Glasgow Celtic	11.49	49-57	324	-	5
Arsenal	Tr	08.58	58-60	83	-	1
Chelsea	Tr	09.61	61	4	-	0

DOCKER, Ian
Norwich, 12 September, 1969 (M)

League Club	Source	Date Signed	Seasons Played	Apps	Subs	Gls
Gillingham	YT	09.87	87-90	73	14	3

DOCKER, John B.
Coventry, 25 September, 1947 (F)

League Club	Source	Date Signed	Seasons Played	Apps	Subs	Gls
Coventry C.	Jnrs	08.65				
Torquay U.	L	07.67	67	4	1	0

DODD, Alan
Stoke, 20 September, 1953 Eu23-6 (D)

League Club	Source	Date Signed	Seasons Played	Apps	Subs	Gls
Stoke C.	App	10.70	72-82	349	7	3
Wolverhampton W.	Tr	11.82	82-84	88	0	5
Stoke C.	Tr	01.85	84	16	0	0
Port Vale (N/C)	Sweden	11.86	86	2	0	0

DODD, James E.
Wallasey, 12 December, 1933 (F)

League Club	Source	Date Signed	Seasons Played	Apps	Subs	Gls
Tranmere Rov.	Upton	05.56	56-59	63	-	22

DODD, Jason R.
Bath, 2 November, 1970 Eu21-8 (RB)

League Club	Source	Date Signed	Seasons Played	Apps	Subs	Gls
Southampton	Bath C.	03.89	89-91	63	6	0

DODD, William
Bedlington, 30 September, 1936 (F)

League Club	Source	Date Signed	Seasons Played	Apps	Subs	Gls
Burnley	Whitley Bay	02.56				
Workington	Tr	09.58	58	1	-	1

DODD, William D.
Chester-le-Street, 25 August, 1933 Died 1982 (WH)

League Club	Source	Date Signed	Seasons Played	Apps	Subs	Gls
Shrewsbury T.	Derby Co. (Am)	08.50	50-54	28	-	1
Southport	Tr	06.57	57-58	70	-	2

DODDS, Ephraim (Jock)
Grangemouth, 7 September, 1915 (CF)

League Club	Source	Date Signed	Seasons Played	Apps	Subs	Gls
Huddersfield T.	Medomsley	02.33				
Lincoln C.	Tr	03.33				
Sheffield U.	Tr	05.34	34-38	178	-	114
Blackpool	Tr	03.39	38	12	-	10
Everton	Tr	11.46	46-48	55	-	36
Lincoln C.	Tr	10.48	48-49	60	-	38

DODDS, Gerald
Sheffield, 4 January, 1935 (OR)

League Club	Source	Date Signed	Seasons Played	Apps	Subs	Gls
Sheffield U.	Jnrs	02.52				
Chesterfield	Tr	06.55	55	4	-	0
Scunthorpe U.	South Shields	05.59				

DODDS, Leslie
Newcastle, 12 October, 1936 E Sch (G)

League Club	Source	Date Signed	Seasons Played	Apps	Subs	Gls
Sunderland	Jnrs	10.53	54-55	6	-	0

DODDS, Robert
Gateshead, 1 July, 1923 (WH)

League Club	Source	Date Signed	Seasons Played	Apps	Subs	Gls
Darlington		02.47	46-48	34	-	1

DODDS, Thomas B.
South Shields, 20 December, 1918 (IF)

League Club	Source	Date Signed	Seasons Played	Apps	Subs	Gls
Aston Villa	North Shields	01.39	46	1	-	0
Swansea C.	Tr	01.47	46-47	11	-	2

DODDS, William
New Cumnock, 5 February, 1969 (F)

League Club	Source	Date Signed	Seasons Played	Apps	Subs	Gls
Chelsea	App	05.86	86-88	0	3	0

DODGE, William C.
Hackney, 10 March, 1937 (WH)

League Club	Source	Date Signed	Seasons Played	Apps	Subs	Gls
Tottenham H.	Eton Manor	10.57	58-59	6	-	0
Crystal Palace	Tr	07.62	62	3	-	0

DODGIN, Norman
Gateshead, 1 November, 1921 (WH)

League Club	Source	Date Signed	Seasons Played	Apps	Subs	Gls
Newcastle U.	Whitehall B.C.	08.40	47-49	84	-	1
Reading	Tr	06.50	50	13	-	1
Northampton T.	Tr	09.51	51-52	19	-	1
Exeter C.	Tr	08.53	53-54	33	-	1

DODGIN, William
Felling, 4 November, 1931 Eu23-1 (CH)

League Club	Source	Date Signed	Seasons Played	Apps	Subs	Gls
Fulham	Southampton (Am)	09.49	51-52	35	-	0
Arsenal	Tr	12.52	52-59	191	-	0
Fulham	Tr	03.61	60-63	69	-	0

DODSON, David A.
Gravesend, 20 January, 1940 E Yth (OL)

League Club	Source	Date Signed	Seasons Played	Apps	Subs	Gls
Arsenal	Jnrs	11.57				
Swansea C.	Tr	07.59	59-61	30	-	12
Portsmouth	Tr	12.61	61-64	53	-	20
Aldershot	Tr	01.65	64-66	59	0	12

League Club	Source	Date Signed	Seasons Played	Career Record Apps	Subs	Gls

DOHERTY, James C.
Douglas, 31 January, 1957 (F)

League Club	Source	Date Signed	Seasons Played	Apps	Subs	Gls
Notts Co.	Cumnock Jnrs	07.79	79-80	6	2	0

DOHERTY, John
Manchester, 12 March, 1935 (IF)

League Club	Source	Date Signed	Seasons Played	Apps	Subs	Gls
Manchester U.	Jnrs	03.52	52-57	25	-	7
Leicester C.	Tr	10.57	57	12	-	5

DOHERTY, John M.
Ewell, 26 April, 1936 (CF)

League Club	Source	Date Signed	Seasons Played	Apps	Subs	Gls
Fulham	Chelsea (Am)	09.54	56-61	49	-	7
Aldershot	South Coast U. (Aus)	01.65	64-65	18	0	1

DOHERTY, Michael
Liverpool, 8 March, 1961 E Semi-Pro (F)

League Club	Source	Date Signed	Seasons Played	Apps	Subs	Gls
Reading	Basingstoke T.	10.82	82	23	2	5

DOHERTY, Peter D.
Magherafelt (NI), 5 June, 1913 Died 1990 NI-16 (IF)

League Club	Source	Date Signed	Seasons Played	Apps	Subs	Gls
Blackpool	Glentoran	11.33	33-35	83	-	28
Manchester C.	Tr	02.36	35-38	119	-	74
Derby Co.	Tr	12.45	46	15	-	7
Huddersfield T.	Tr	12.46	46-48	83	-	33
Doncaster Rov.	Tr	06.49	49-52	103	-	55

DOIG, Russell
Millport, 17 January, 1964 (W)

League Club	Source	Date Signed	Seasons Played	Apps	Subs	Gls
Leeds U.	East Stirling	07.86	86-87	3	3	0
Peterborough U.	L	10.86	86	7	0	0
Hartlepool U.	Tr	03.88	87-89	22	11	1

DOLAN, Andrew
Glasgow, 2 August, 1920 (IF)

League Club	Source	Date Signed	Seasons Played	Apps	Subs	Gls
Bury	Raith Rov.	08.48	48	10	-	2
Accrington St.	Tr	09.49	49	19	-	4

DOLAN, Eamonn J.
Dagenham, 20 September, 1967 IR Yth/IRu21-3 (F)

League Club	Source	Date Signed	Seasons Played	Apps	Subs	Gls
West Ham U.	App	03.85	86-89	9	6	3
Bristol C.	L	02.89	88	3	0	0
Birmingham C.	Tr	12.90	90-91	6	6	1
Exeter C.	Tr	09.91	91	5	2	0

DOLAN, Patrick D.
Dagenham, 20 September, 1967 IR Yth (D)

League Club	Source	Date Signed	Seasons Played	Apps	Subs	Gls
Arsenal	App	07.85				
Walsall	Tr	08.86	86	1	0	0

DOLAN, Terence P.
Bradford, 11 June, 1950 (M)

League Club	Source	Date Signed	Seasons Played	Apps	Subs	Gls
Bradford P.A.	Bradford C. (Am)	04.69	68-69	46	2	0
Huddersfield T.	Tr	10.70	71-75	157	5	14
Bradford C.	Tr	08.76	76-80	191	4	43
Rochdale	Tr	08.81	81	42	1	1

DOLBY, Peter
Derby, 18 May, 1940 (CH)

League Club	Source	Date Signed	Seasons Played	Apps	Subs	Gls
Shrewsbury T.	Heanor T.	02.60	60-75	304	22	21

DOLDING, D. Leonard
India, 13 December, 1922 Died 1954 (W)

League Club	Source	Date Signed	Seasons Played	Apps	Subs	Gls
Chelsea	Wealdstone	07.45	46-47	26	-	2
Norwich C.	Tr	07.48	48-49	12	-	1

DOLING, Stuart J.
Newport (IOW), 28 October, 1972 E Sch (M)

League Club	Source	Date Signed	Seasons Played	Apps	Subs	Gls
Portsmouth	YT	06.90	91	7	6	2

DOMINEY, Barry W.
Edmonton, 21 October, 1955 (CD)

League Club	Source	Date Signed	Seasons Played	Apps	Subs	Gls
Colchester U.	Enfield W.M.C.	01.74	73-76	56	15	3

DONACHIE, William
Glasgow, 5 October, 1951 Su23-2/S-35 (LB/M)

League Club	Source	Date Signed	Seasons Played	Apps	Subs	Gls
Manchester C.	Jnrs	12.68	69-79	347	4	2
Norwich C.	Portland (USA)	09.81	81	11	0	0
Burnley	Portland (USA)	11.82	82-84	60	0	3
Oldham Ath.	Tr	07.84	84-90	158	11	3

DONAGHY, Barry
Consett, 21 March, 1956 E Yth (M)

League Club	Source	Date Signed	Seasons Played	Apps	Subs	Gls
West Bromwich A.	App	05.73	73-74	4	2	1
Workington	Tr	12.75	75-76	40	4	3

DONAGHY, Malachy M. (Mal)
Belfast, 13 September, 1957 NIu21-1/NI-76 (CD)

League Club	Source	Date Signed	Seasons Played	Apps	Subs	Gls
Luton T.	Larne T.	06.78	78-88	410	0	16
Manchester U.	Tr	10.88	88-91	76	13	0
Luton T.	L	12.89	89	5	0	0

Mal Donaghy (Larne Town, Luton Town, Manchester United & Northern Ireland)

DONALD, Alexander
Edinburgh, 5 June, 1948 (W)

League Club	Source	Date Signed	Seasons Played	Apps	Subs	Gls
Port Vale	Jnrs	10.65	65-67	41	2	0

DONALD, Ian R.
Aberdeen, 28 November, 1951 S Sch (FB)

League Club	Source	Date Signed	Seasons Played	Apps	Subs	Gls
Manchester U.	Jnrs	07.69	72	4	0	0

DONALD, Warren R.
Hillingdon, 7 October, 1964 E Sch (M)

League Club	Source	Date Signed	Seasons Played	Apps	Subs	Gls
West Ham U.	App	10.82	83	1	1	0
Northampton T.	L	03.85	84	11	0	2
Northampton T.	Tr	10.85	85-89	169	8	11

DONALDSON, Andrew
Newcastle, 22 March, 1925 Died 1987 (CF)

League Club	Source	Date Signed	Seasons Played	Apps	Subs	Gls
Newcastle U.	Vickers Armstrong	09.43	46-48	19	-	6
Middlesbrough	Tr	01.49	48-50	21	-	7
Exeter C.	Peterborough U.	09.53	53-54	39	-	16

DONALDSON, Brian L.
Hove, 3 April, 1936 (OR)

League Club	Source	Date Signed	Seasons Played	Apps	Subs	Gls
Chelsea	Jnrs	07.53				
Swindon T.	Tr	10.57	57	1	-	0

DONALDSON, David
Hounslow, 28 December, 1941 (D)

League Club	Source	Date Signed	Seasons Played	Apps	Subs	Gls
Wimbledon	Walton & Hersham	08.74	77-78	61	0	0

DONALDSON, David J.
Islington, 12 November, 1954 E Sch (RB)

League Club	Source	Date Signed	Seasons Played	Apps	Subs	Gls
Arsenal	App	07.72				
Millwall	Tr	06.73	73-79	215	1	1
Cambridge U.	Tr	02.80	79-83	130	2	0

League Club	Source	Date Signed	Seasons Played	Apps	Subs	Gls

DONALDSON, L. Frederick
Stoke, 7 April, 1937 (FB)

League Club	Source	Date Signed	Seasons Played	Apps	Subs	Gls
Port Vale	Jnrs	07.54	54-59	47	-	4
Exeter C.	Tr	08.60	60	36	-	6
Chester C.	Tr	07.61	61	20	-	0

DONALDSON, James D.
South Shields, 11 June, 1927 (WH)

League Club	Source	Date Signed	Seasons Played	Apps	Subs	Gls
Chesterfield		11.48	49-50	17	-	4
Newport Co.	Tr	08.51	51-52	36	-	1

DONALDSON, Leslie
Glasgow, 30 July, 1922 (IF)

League Club	Source	Date Signed	Seasons Played	Apps	Subs	Gls
Wrexham	Rhyl	06.50	50-51	30	-	6

DONALDSON, O'Neill M.
Birmingham, 24 November, 1969 (F)

League Club	Source	Date Signed	Seasons Played	Apps	Subs	Gls
Shrewsbury T.	Hinckley T.	11.91	91	9	10	2

DONALDSON, Robert S.
South Shields, 26 February, 1921 (D)

League Club	Source	Date Signed	Seasons Played	Apps	Subs	Gls
Newcastle U.		01.43				
Hartlepool U.	Tr	07.47	47-51	131	-	4

DONALDSON, William
Edinburgh, 20 January, 1920 (OL)

League Club	Source	Date Signed	Seasons Played	Apps	Subs	Gls
Bradford P.A.	Leith Ath.	05.46	46-50	45	-	6
Mansfield T.	Tr	10.50	50-51	52	-	10

DONE, Cyril C.
Liverpool, 21 October, 1920 (CF)

League Club	Source	Date Signed	Seasons Played	Apps	Subs	Gls
Liverpool	Bootle B.B.	01.38	46-51	94	-	33
Tranmere Rov.	Tr	05.52	52-54	87	-	61
Port Vale	Tr	12.54	54-56	52	-	34

DONEGAL, Glen P.
Northampton, 20 June, 1969 (F)

League Club	Source	Date Signed	Seasons Played	Apps	Subs	Gls
Northampton T.	YT	08.87	87-89	7	13	3
Maidstone U.	Aylesbury U.	08.91	91	9	5	1

DONN, A. Nigel
Maidstone, 2 March, 1962 (M)

League Club	Source	Date Signed	Seasons Played	Apps	Subs	Gls
Gillingham	App	02.80	80-81	2	1	0
Leyton Orient	Karpalo (Fin)	08.82	82	22	1	2

DONNELLAN, Gary
Kensington, 3 July, 1962 (W)

League Club	Source	Date Signed	Seasons Played	Apps	Subs	Gls
Chelsea	App	07.80				
Watford	Tr	11.80				
Reading	Tr	11.81	81-82	33	8	5

DONNELLAN, Leo J.
Brent, 19 January, 1965 IRu21-1 (M)

League Club	Source	Date Signed	Seasons Played	Apps	Subs	Gls
Chelsea	App	08.82				
Leyton Orient	L	12.84	84	6	0	0
Fulham	Tr	08.85	85-89	54	25	4

DONNELLY, Andrew
Lanark, 1 May, 1943 (G)

League Club	Source	Date Signed	Seasons Played	Apps	Subs	Gls
Millwall	Clyde	05.63				
Torquay U.	Weymouth	08.67	67-71	160	0	0

DONNELLY, Darren C.
Liverpool, 28 December, 1971 (F)

League Club	Source	Date Signed	Seasons Played	Apps	Subs	Gls
Blackburn Rov.	YT	06.90	90	1	1	0

DONNELLY, James
Cork (Ire), 6 May, 1919 (IF)

League Club	Source	Date Signed	Seasons Played	Apps	Subs	Gls
Accrington St.	Sligo Rov.	08.51	51	4	-	1

DONNELLY, John
Glasgow, 8 March, 1961 (W)

League Club	Source	Date Signed	Seasons Played	Apps	Subs	Gls
Leeds U.	Dumbarton	03.83	82-84	36	4	4

DONNELLY, John
West Lothian, 17 December, 1936 (FB)

League Club	Source	Date Signed	Seasons Played	Apps	Subs	Gls
Preston N.E.	Glasgow Celtic	04.62	62-66	56	1	1

DONNELLY, Paul A.
Liverpool, 23 December, 1971 (W)

League Club	Source	Date Signed	Seasons Played	Apps	Subs	Gls
Halifax T.	YT	03.90	88-90	9	4	0

DONNELLY, Peter
Hull, 22 September, 1936 (CF)

League Club	Source	Date Signed	Seasons Played	Apps	Subs	Gls
Doncaster Rov.	Jnrs	03.54	53-56	6	-	1
Scunthorpe U.	Tr	07.58	58-59	39	-	19
Cardiff C.	Tr	06.60	60-61	30	-	8
Swansea C.	Tr	10.61	61	16	-	3
Brighton & H.A.	Tr	07.62	62-64	56	-	13
Bradford C.	Tr	03.65	64-65	13	0	5

DONNELLY, Peter J.
Chester, 11 May, 1965 (D)

League Club	Source	Date Signed	Seasons Played	Apps	Subs	Gls
Chester C. (N/C)	YT	08.83	83	1	0	0

DONOVAN, Donal C. (Don)
Cork (Ire), 23 December, 1929 IR-5 (FB)

League Club	Source	Date Signed	Seasons Played	Apps	Subs	Gls
Everton	Dalymount Rov.	05.49	51-57	179	-	2
Grimsby T.	Tr	08.58	58-63	238	-	1

DONOVAN, Frank J.
Pembroke, 21 February, 1919 W Amat (OR)

League Club	Source	Date Signed	Seasons Played	Apps	Subs	Gls
Swansea C.	Pembroke Bor.	05.50	50	15	-	2

DONOVAN, Kevin
Halifax, 17 December, 1971 (M)

League Club	Source	Date Signed	Seasons Played	Apps	Subs	Gls
Huddersfield T.	YT	10.89	89-91	9	8	1
Halifax T.	L	02.92	91	6	0	0

DONOVAN, Terence C.
Liverpool, 27 February, 1958 IRu21-1/IR-1 (F)

League Club	Source	Date Signed	Seasons Played	Apps	Subs	Gls
Grimsby T.	Louth U.	08.76	76-78	52	12	23
Aston Villa	Tr	09.79	79-81	17	0	6
Oxford U.	L	02.83	82	3	0	0
Burnley	Tr	02.83	82-83	13	2	6
Rotherham U.	Tr	09.83	83-84	9	4	0
Blackpool	L	10.84	84	2	0	0

DONOWA, B. Louie
Ipswich, 24 September, 1964 Eu21-3 (W)

League Club	Source	Date Signed	Seasons Played	Apps	Subs	Gls
Norwich C.	App	09.82	82-85	56	6	11
Stoke C.	L	12.85	85	4	0	1
Ipswich T.	Willem II Tilburg (Neth)	08.89	89	17	6	1
Bristol C.	Tr	08.90	90	11	13	3
Birmingham C.	Tr	08.91	91	20	6	2

DOOLAN, John
Liverpool, 10 November, 1968 (M)

League Club	Source	Date Signed	Seasons Played	Apps	Subs	Gls
Wigan Ath.	Knowsley U.	03.92	91	2	0	0

DOOLEY, Derek
Sheffield, 13 December, 1929 (CF)

League Club	Source	Date Signed	Seasons Played	Apps	Subs	Gls
Lincoln C. (Am)	Jnrs	09.46	46	2	-	2
Sheffield Wed.	Tr	06.47	49-52	61	-	62

DOOLEY, George W.
Chesterfield, 29 December, 1922 (IF)

League Club	Source	Date Signed	Seasons Played	Apps	Subs	Gls
Chesterfield	Parkhouse Colly	06.45				
Halifax T.	Tr	12.46	46	11	-	2

DOONAN, Thomas
West Calder, 5 October, 1922 (CF)

League Club	Source	Date Signed	Seasons Played	Apps	Subs	Gls
Bradford C.	Albion Rov.	06.49	49	13	-	7
Tranmere Rov.	Tr	07.50	50	4	-	2

DOONER, Gary J.
St Helens, 14 September, 1970 (W)

League Club	Source	Date Signed	Seasons Played	Apps	Subs	Gls
Stockport Co.(YT)	YT	09.87	88	1	0	0

DORAN, Robert R.
Carlisle, 26 December, 1933 (CH)

League Club	Source	Date Signed	Seasons Played	Apps	Subs	Gls
Carlisle U.		10.52	53-61	107	-	0

DORAN, Terence
Jarrow, 2 April, 1940

League Club	Source	Date Signed	Seasons Played	Apps	Subs	Gls
Gateshead (Am)	St. Mary's B.C.	09.59	59	1	-	0

DORE, Charles
Gosport, 30 September, 1928 (G)

League Club	Source	Date Signed	Seasons Played	Apps	Subs	Gls
Portsmouth	Fleetlands B.C.	05.50	51-53	18	-	0

DORIGO, Anthony R.
Melbourne (Aus), 31 December, 1965 Eu21-11/E'B'/E-10 (LB)

League Club	Source	Date Signed	Seasons Played	Apps	Subs	Gls
Aston Villa	App	07.83	83-86	106	5	1
Chelsea	Tr	05.87	87-90	146	0	11
Leeds U.	Tr	05.91	91	38	0	3

DORLING, George J.
Edmonton, 27 July, 1918 (FB)

League Club	Source	Date Signed	Seasons Played	Apps	Subs	Gls
Tottenham H.	Jnrs	03.46				
Gillingham	Tr	05.47	50	10	-	0

Derek Dooley (Lincoln City & Sheffield Wednesday)

DORMAN, Donald J.
Birmingham, 18 September, 1922 (IF)

League Club	Source	Date Signed	Seasons Played	Apps	Subs	Gls
Birmingham C.	Jnrs	05.46	46-51	59	-	4
Coventry C.	Tr	09.51	51-54	90	-	29
Walsall	Tr	10.54	54-56	115	-	33

DORNAN, Andrew
Aberdeen, 19 August, 1961 S Sch/S Yth (RB)

League Club	Source	Date Signed	Seasons Played	Apps	Subs	Gls
Walsall	Motherwell	08.86	86-89	117	1	1

DORNAN, Peter
Belfast, 30 June, 1953 (M)

League Club	Source	Date Signed	Seasons Played	Apps	Subs	Gls
Sheffield U.	Linfield	12.76	76	1	2	0
Swindon T.	Linfield	02.79	78	0	1	0

DORNEY, Alan J.
Bermondsey, 18 May, 1947 (CD)

League Club	Source	Date Signed	Seasons Played	Apps	Subs	Gls
Millwall	Jnrs	05.65	68-76	249	3	1

DORSETT, Richard (Dickie)
Brownhills, 3 December, 1919 (IF/WH)

League Club	Source	Date Signed	Seasons Played	Apps	Subs	Gls
Wolverhampton W.	Jnrs	12.36	37-46	46	-	32
Aston Villa	Tr	09.46	46-52	257	-	32

DOUGAL, James
Denny, 3 October, 1913 S-1 (IF)

League Club	Source	Date Signed	Seasons Played	Apps	Subs	Gls
Preston N.E.	Falkirk	01.34	33-46	171	-	51
Carlisle U.	Tr	10.46	46-48	70	-	15
Halifax T.	Tr	10.48	48	22	-	2

DOUGAL, John (Jack)
Falkirk, 7 August, 1934 E Amat (CH)

League Club	Source	Date Signed	Seasons Played	Apps	Subs	Gls
Halifax T. (Am)	Pegasus	05.56	56	2	-	0

DOUGAL, William
Falkirk, 30 October, 1923 (HB)

League Club	Source	Date Signed	Seasons Played	Apps	Subs	Gls
Preston N.E.	Glasgow Rangers	12.47	47-48	22	-	2
Barnsley	Tr	08.52	52	21	-	0

DOUGALL, Neil
Falkirk, 7 November, 1921 S-1 (IF)

League Club	Source	Date Signed	Seasons Played	Apps	Subs	Gls
Burnley	Jnrs	03.40				
Birmingham C.	Tr	10.45	46-48	93	-	15
Plymouth Arg.	Tr	03.49	48-58	274	-	26

DOUGALL, Thomas
Wishaw, 17 May, 1921 (OR)

League Club	Source	Date Signed	Seasons Played	Apps	Subs	Gls
Coventry C.		09.45				
Brentford	Tr	08.47	47	2	-	0
Sunderland	Tr	11.48	48	3	-	0

DOUGAN A. Derek
Belfast, 20 January, 1938 NI Sch/NI'B'-1/NI-43 (CF)

League Club	Source	Date Signed	Seasons Played	Apps	Subs	Gls
Portsmouth	Distillery	08.57	57-58	33	-	9
Blackburn Rov.	Tr	03.59	58-60	59	-	26
Aston Villa	Tr	08.61	61-62	51	-	19
Peterborough U.	Tr	06.63	63-64	77	-	38
Leicester C.	Tr	05.65	65-66	68	0	35
Wolverhampton W.	Tr	03.67	66-74	244	14	95

DOUGAN, George
Glasgow, 22 March, 1939 (WH)

League Club	Source	Date Signed	Seasons Played	Apps	Subs	Gls
Ipswich T.	Yiewsley	03.63	62-63	17	-	0

DOUGAN, John M.
Glasgow, 12 January, 1931 (IF)

League Club	Source	Date Signed	Seasons Played	Apps	Subs	Gls
Brighton & H.A.	Bellshill Ath.	12.51				
Torquay U.	Tr	02.54	53-54	20	-	3

DOUGAN, Maxwell S.
Stoneyburn, 23 May, 1938 S Amat (D)

League Club	Source	Date Signed	Seasons Played	Apps	Subs	Gls
Leicester C.	Queens Park	09.63	63-66	9	0	0
Luton T.	Tr	12.66	66-69	117	1	0

DOUGHERTY, Paul D.
Leamington, 12 May, 1966 (M)

League Club	Source	Date Signed	Seasons Played	Apps	Subs	Gls
Wolverhampton W.	App	05.84	83-86	24	17	3
Torquay U.	L	02.85	84	5	0	0

DOUGHERTY, Victor R.
Glasgow, 17 January, 1955 (FB)

League Club	Source	Date Signed	Seasons Played	Apps	Subs	Gls
Bury (App)	App	07.70	72	9	0	0

DOUGHTY, Eric
Radstock, 9 April, 1932 (LB)

League Club	Source	Date Signed	Seasons Played	Apps	Subs	Gls
Arsenal	Peasedown	05.51				
Plymouth Arg.	Tr	07.58	58	1	-	0

DOUGLAS, Bryan
Blackburn, 27 May, 1934 Eu23-5/E'B'-1/EF Lge/E-36 (OR)

League Club	Source	Date Signed	Seasons Played	Apps	Subs	Gls
Blackburn Rov.	Jnrs	04.52	54-68	438	0	100

DOUGLAS, Colin F.
Kilmarnock, 9 September, 1962 (D)

League Club	Source	Date Signed	Seasons Played	Apps	Subs	Gls
Doncaster Rov.	Glasgow Celtic	11.81	81-85	202	10	48
Rotherham U.	Tr	07.86	86-87	82	1	4
Doncaster Rov.	Tr	08.88	88-91	170	1	4

DOUGLAS, James S.
Sunderland, 16 September, 1941 (CF)

League Club	Source	Date Signed	Seasons Played	Apps	Subs	Gls
Hartlepool U (Am)	Evenwood T.	10.62	62	13	-	4

DOUGLAS, John S.
Stockton, 13 March, 1961 (F)

League Club	Source	Date Signed	Seasons Played	Apps	Subs	Gls
Darlington (N/C)	Stockton	01.86	85	3	0	0

DOUGLAS, John S.
Hartlepool, 1 December, 1917 (WH)

League Club	Source	Date Signed	Seasons Played	Apps	Subs	Gls
Hartlepool U.(Am)		09.38	38	5	-	0
Middlesbrough	Tr	09.45	46	2	-	0
Hartlepool U.	Tr	11.48	48-49	28	-	1

DOUGLAS, Patrick G.
Baschurch, 7 September, 1951 (IF)

League Club	Source	Date Signed	Seasons Played	Apps	Subs	Gls
Shrewsbury T.	App	07.69	68	12	1	1

DOUGLASS, Norman
Sunderland, 14 May, 1930 (FB)

League Club	Source	Date Signed	Seasons Played	Apps	Subs	Gls
Chelsea	Crook T.	03.52				
Exeter C.	Tr	06.53	53-54	63	-	0

DOVE, Henry W.
Stepney, 11 March, 1932 (CH)

League Club	Source	Date Signed	Seasons Played	Apps	Subs	Gls
Arsenal	Essex Co. Cadets	08.50				
Millwall	Tr	04.58	58	7	-	0

DOVEY, Alan R.
Stepney, 18 July, 1952 (G)

League Club	Source	Date Signed	Seasons Played	Apps	Subs	Gls
Chelsea	App	07.69				
Brighton & H.A.	Tr	03.71	70-72	6	0	0

DOW, David J.
Manchester, 10 June, 1947 (CH)

League Club	Source	Date Signed	Seasons Played	Apps	Subs	Gls
Rochdale (Am)	Avorton	02.66	66-67	8	0	0

DOWD, Harold W.
Manchester, 4 July, 1938 (G)

League Club	Source	Date Signed	Seasons Played	Apps	Subs	Gls
Manchester C.	Blackley I.C.I.	07.60	61-69	181	0	1
Stoke C.	L	10.69	69	3	0	0
Oldham Ath.	Tr	12.70	70-73	121	0	0

DOWD, Hugh O.
Lurgan (NI), 19 May, 1951 NI-3 (CD)

League Club	Source	Date Signed	Seasons Played	Apps	Subs	Gls
Sheffield Wed.	Glenavon	07.74	74-78	110	2	0
Doncaster Rov.	Tr	08.79	79-82	94	0	3

DOWEY, Walter L.
Lockton, 12 June, 1923 (RH)

League Club	Source	Date Signed	Seasons Played	Apps	Subs	Gls
Crewe Alex.		04.45	47-48	15	-	0

DOWIE, Iain
Hatfield, 9 January, 1965 NIu21-1/NI-12 (F)

League Club	Source	Date Signed	Seasons Played	Apps	Subs	Gls
Luton T.	Hendon	12.88	88-90	53	13	15
Fulham	L	09.89	89	5	0	1
West Ham U.	Tr	03.91	90	12	0	4
Southampton	Tr	08.91	91	25	5	9

DOWIE, John
Hamilton, 12 December, 1955 (M)

League Club	Source	Date Signed	Seasons Played	Apps	Subs	Gls
Fulham	App	05.73	73-76	32	5	2
Doncaster Rov.	Glasgow Celtic	07.79	79-80	21	0	0

DOWKER, Thomas
Liverpool, 7 November, 1922 (OL)

League Club	Source	Date Signed	Seasons Played	Apps	Subs	Gls
Oldham Ath.	South Liverpool	07.47	47	1	-	0

DOWLER, Michael J.
Caldicot, 12 October, 1957 W Sch (G)

League Club	Source	Date Signed	Seasons Played	Apps	Subs	Gls
Newport Co.	Hereford U.(App)	10.75	75-80	19	0	0

DOWLING, Michael L.
Bodmin, 3 October, 1952 (FB)

League Club	Source	Date Signed	Seasons Played	Apps	Subs	Gls
Plymouth Arg.	App	10.70	69-73	27	4	0

DOWMAN, Stephen J.
Ilford, 15 April, 1958 (CD)

League Club	Source	Date Signed	Seasons Played	Apps	Subs	Gls
Colchester U.	App	04.76	76-79	150	4	21
Wrexham	Tr	07.80	80-82	87	0	2
Charlton Ath.	Tr	08.83	83-84	60	1	5
Newport Co.	Tr	08.85	85	9	0	1
Cambridge U.	Tr	10.85	85-86	45	0	3

DOWN, David F.
Bristol, 7 July, 1948 (CF)

League Club	Source	Date Signed	Seasons Played	Apps	Subs	Gls
Bristol C.	App	09.65	66-67	6	1	3
Bradford P.A.	Tr	10.67	67-68	39	0	7
Oldham Ath.	Tr	09.68	68	8	0	1
Swindon T.	Tr	08.69	69-70	1	1	0

DOWN, William
Bristol, 8 November, 1963 (D)

League Club	Source	Date Signed	Seasons Played	Apps	Subs	Gls
Bristol C.	App	10.81	81	1	0	0

DOWNES, Christopher B.
Sheffield, 17 January, 1969 (FB/M)

League Club	Source	Date Signed	Seasons Played	Apps	Subs	Gls
Sheffield U.	YT	06.87	88	2	0	0
Scarborough	L	03.88	87	2	0	0
Stockport Co.	Tr	08.89	89	10	1	1
Crewe Alex. (N/C)	Tr	08.91	91	1	1	0

DOWNES, Eric R.
Wigan, 25 August, 1926 (CH)

League Club	Source	Date Signed	Seasons Played	Apps	Subs	Gls
Rochdale	Chester C. (Am)	05.49	50-53	54	-	0

DOWNES, Robert D.
Bloxwich, 18 August, 1949 (W)

League Club	Source	Date Signed	Seasons Played	Apps	Subs	Gls
West Bromwich A.	Jnrs	08.66				
Peterborough U.	Tr	09.67	67-68	23	3	3
Rochdale	Tr	08.69	69-73	164	10	10
Watford	Tr	05.74	74-79	192	7	19
Barnsley	Tr	03.80	79-80	43	0	1
Blackpool	Tr	07.82	82-83	27	1	3

DOWNES, Steven F.
Leeds, 2 December, 1949 (F)

League Club	Source	Date Signed	Seasons Played	Apps	Subs	Gls
Rotherham U.	Leeds M.D.B.C.	04.67	67-69	54	8	18
Sheffield Wed.	Tr	12.69	69-71	26	4	4
Chesterfield	Tr	08.72	72-73	37	4	11
Halifax T.	Tr	07.74	74-75	38	12	12
Blackburn Rov.	L	03.76	75	6	0	0

DOWNES, Walter J.
Hammersmith, 9 June, 1961 (M)

League Club	Source	Date Signed	Seasons Played	Apps	Subs	Gls
Wimbledon	App	01.79	78-86	194	14	14
Newport Co.	L	12.87	87	4	0	2
Sheffield U.	Tr	02.88	87	6	3	1

DOWNIE, John D.
Lanark, 19 July, 1925 (IF)

League Club	Source	Date Signed	Seasons Played	Apps	Subs	Gls
Bradford P.A.	Lanark A.T.C.	12.44	46-48	86	-	33
Manchester U.	Tr	03.49	48-52	110	-	35
Luton T.	Tr	08.53	53	26	-	12
Hull C.	Tr	07.54	54	27	-	5
Mansfield T.	Wisbech T.	10.58	58	18	-	4
Darlington	Tr	05.59	59	15	-	2

DOWNIE, Mitchell
Troon, 9 February, 1923 (G)

League Club	Source	Date Signed	Seasons Played	Apps	Subs	Gls
Bradford P.A.	Airdrieonians	08.50	50-53	156	-	0
Lincoln C.	Tr	05.54	54-58	157	-	0
Bradford C.	Goole T.	09.59	59-62	134	-	0
Doncaster Rov.	Tr	09.63	63	7	-	0

DOWNING, David W.
Bideford, 6 October, 1969 (W)

League Club	Source	Date Signed	Seasons Played	Apps	Subs	Gls
York C. (YT)	YT	07.86	87	1	0	0

DOWNING, Derrick G.
Doncaster, 3 November, 1945 (W)

League Club	Source	Date Signed	Seasons Played	Apps	Subs	Gls
Middlesbrough	Frickley Colly	02.65	65-71	172	10	39
Leyton Orient	Tr	05.72	72-74	100	4	12
York C.	Tr	07.75	75-76	44	3	2
Hartlepool U.	Tr	07.77	77	40	0	4

DOWNING, Keith G.
Oldbury, 23 July, 1965 (M)

League Club	Source	Date Signed	Seasons Played	Apps	Subs	Gls
Notts Co.	Mile Oak Rov.	05.84	84-86	23	0	1
Wolverhampton W.	Tr	07.87	87-91	139	21	6

DOWNS, David
Glasgow, 7 March, 1934 Died 1978 (HB)

League Club	Source	Date Signed	Seasons Played	Apps	Subs	Gls
Plymouth Arg.		11.57				
Torquay U.	Tr	07.59	59	3	-	0

DOWNS, Gregory
Nottingham, 13 December, 1958 (LB)

League Club	Source	Date Signed	Seasons Played	Apps	Subs	Gls
Norwich C.	App	12.76	77-84	162	7	7
Torquay U.	L	11.77	77	1	0	1
Coventry C.	Tr	07.85	85-89	142	4	4
Birmingham C.	Tr	07.90	90	16	1	0
Hereford U.	Tr	06.91	91	40	0	2

DOWNS, Ronald H.
Southwark, 27 August, 1932 (W)

League Club	Source	Date Signed	Seasons Played	Apps	Subs	Gls
Crystal Palace	Grove U.	12.52	52-53	23	-	2

DOWNSBOROUGH, Peter
Halifax, 13 September, 1943 (G)

League Club	Source	Date Signed	Seasons Played	Apps	Subs	Gls
Halifax T.	Jnrs	09.60	59-64	148	-	0
Swindon T.	Tr	08.65	65-72	274	0	0
Brighton & H.A.	L	08.73	73	3	0	0
Bradford C.	Tr	11.73	73-78	225	0	0

DOWSETT, Gilbert J. ("Dickie")
Chelmsford, 3 July, 1931 (CF)

League Club	Source	Date Signed	Seasons Played	Apps	Subs	Gls
Tottenham H.	Sudbury T.	05.52	54	1	-	1
Southend U.	Tr	05.55	55	20	-	4
Southampton	Tr	07.56	56	2	-	0
Bournemouth	Tr	06.57	57-62	169	-	79
Crystal Palace	Tr	11.62	62-64	54	-	22

DOWSON, Alan P.
Gateshead, 17 June, 1970 (LB)

League Club	Source	Date Signed	Seasons Played	Apps	Subs	Gls
Millwall	YT	05.88	90	1	0	0
Fulham	L	01.90	89	4	0	0
Bradford C.	Tr	07.91	91	16	2	0

DOWSON, John S.
Ashington, 18 September, 1926 (OR)

League Club	Source	Date Signed	Seasons Played	Apps	Subs	Gls
Manchester C.		03.50				
Darlington	Peterborough U.	06.52	52-53	65	-	11

DOYLE, Alistair
Limavady (NI), 25 October, 1949 (FB)

League Club	Source	Date Signed	Seasons Played	Apps	Subs	Gls
Oldham Ath.	Coleraine	10.66	67-68	31	2	0

DOYLE, J. Brian
Manchester, 15 July, 1930 (FB)

League Club	Source	Date Signed	Seasons Played	Apps	Subs	Gls
Stoke C.	Lostock Gralam	03.51	52	17	-	0
Exeter C.	Tr	04.54	54-56	100	-	0
Bristol Rov.	Tr	08.57	57-59	43	-	1

DOYLE, Ian P.
Torquay, 27 February, 1959 (W)

League Club	Source	Date Signed	Seasons Played	Apps	Subs	Gls
Bristol C.	Barnstaple	12.78	79-80	2	1	0

DOYLE, Jeffrey N.
Dublin, 25 February, 1967 (M)

League Club	Source	Date Signed	Seasons Played	Apps	Subs	Gls
Coventry C.	App	02.85				
Peterborough U.	Tr	08.86	86	13	1	0

DOYLE, John J.
Oxford, 8 February, 1960 (FB)

League Club	Source	Date Signed	Seasons Played	Apps	Subs	Gls
Oxford U.	App	02.78	77-81	66	0	0
Torquay U.	Tr	08.82	82	40	1	3

DOYLE, Maurice
Ellesmere Port, 17 October, 1969 (M)

League Club	Source	Date Signed	Seasons Played	Apps	Subs	Gls
Crewe Alex.	YT	07.88	87-88	6	2	2
Queens Park R.	Tr	04.89				
Crewe Alex.	L	01.91	90	6	1	2

DOYLE, Michael
Manchester, 25 November, 1946 Eu23-8/EF Lge/E-5 (CD)

League Club	Source	Date Signed	Seasons Played	Apps	Subs	Gls
Manchester C.	App	05.64	64-77	441	7	32
Stoke C.	Tr	06.78	78-81	115	0	5
Bolton W.	Tr	01.82	81-82	40	0	2
Rochdale	Tr	08.83	83	24	0	1

DOYLE, Robert
Dumbarton, 27 December, 1953 (M)

League Club	Source	Date Signed	Seasons Played	Apps	Subs	Gls
Barnsley	Jnrs	12.72	72-75	148	1	16
Peterborough U.	Tr	07.76	76-78	130	0	10
Blackpool	Tr	07.79	79-80	47	2	2
Portsmouth	Tr	12.80	80-85	169	8	16
Hull C.	Tr	08.85	85-86	43	0	2

DOYLE, Robert L.
Liverpool, 28 June, 1927 (D)

League Club	Source	Date Signed	Seasons Played	Apps	Subs	Gls
Everton	Jnrs	05.45				
Exeter C.	Tr	08.49	49-54	82	-	0

DOYLE, Stephen C.
Neath, 2 June, 1958 Wu21-2 (M)

League Club	Source	Date Signed	Seasons Played	Apps	Subs	Gls
Preston N.E.	App	06.75	74-81	178	19	8
Huddersfield T.	Tr	09.82	82-86	158	3	6
Sunderland	Tr	09.86	86-88	99	1	2
Hull C.	Tr	08.89	89-90	47	0	2
Rochdale	Tr	11.90	90-91	58	0	0

DOZZELL, Jason A. W.
Ipswich, 9 December, 1967 E Yth/Eu21-9 (M)

League Club	Source	Date Signed	Seasons Played	Apps	Subs	Gls
Ipswich T.	App	12.84	83-91	271	20	45

DRAKE, Kenneth L.
Skipton, 17 February, 1922 (CH)

League Club	Source	Date Signed	Seasons Played	Apps	Subs	Gls
Halifax T.		01.47	46-51	132	-	0

DRAKE, Leonard
Dorchester, 26 July, 1937 (CF)

League Club	Source	Date Signed	Seasons Played	Apps	Subs	Gls
Bristol Rov.	Dorchester T.	08.57	58-59	8	-	0

DRAKE, Raymond B.
Stockport, 24 October, 1934 (CF)

League Club	Source	Date Signed	Seasons Played	Apps	Subs	Gls
Stockport Co.		03.55	56-57	23	-	19

DRAKE, Robert J.
Southgate, 7 September, 1943 (FB)

League Club	Source	Date Signed	Seasons Played	Apps	Subs	Gls
Fulham	Chelsea (Am)	12.61	63-67	16	0	0

DRAKE, Stephen
Goole, 27 August, 1948 (G)

League Club	Source	Date Signed	Seasons Played	Apps	Subs	Gls
Huddersfield T.	Leeds U. (Am)	06.66				
Scunthorpe U.	Tr	07.67	67-69	23	0	0

DRAPER, Derek
Swansea, 11 May, 1943 Wu23-1 (M)

League Club	Source	Date Signed	Seasons Played	Apps	Subs	Gls
Swansea C.	Jnrs	05.62	62-65	61	0	10
Derby Co.	Tr	04.66	66	8	0	1
Bradford P.A.	Tr	09.67	67-68	60	3	9
Chester C.	Tr	01.69	68-76	316	6	55

DRAPER, Mark A.
Long Eaton, 11 November, 1970 Eu21-3 (W)

League Club	Source	Date Signed	Seasons Played	Apps	Subs	Gls
Notts Co.	YT	12.88	88-91	118	16	16

DRAPER, Richard W.
Leamington, 26 September, 1932 (CF)

League Club	Source	Date Signed	Seasons Played	Apps	Subs	Gls
Northampton T.	Lockheed Leamington	06.55	55-56	49	-	20

DREWERY, Michael S.
Snettisham, 16 January, 1949 (G)

League Club	Source	Date Signed	Seasons Played	Apps	Subs	Gls
Peterborough U.	Snettisham	07.67	68-73	209	0	0

DREYER, John B.
Alnwick, 11 June, 1963 (D)

League Club	Source	Date Signed	Seasons Played	Apps	Subs	Gls
Oxford U.	Wallingford T.	01.85	86-87	57	3	2
Torquay U.	L	12.85	85	5	0	0
Fulham	L	03.86	85	12	0	2
Luton T.	Tr	06.88	88-91	134	2	8

DRING, Raymond
Lincoln, 13 February, 1924 E Sch (G)

League Club	Source	Date Signed	Seasons Played	Apps	Subs	Gls
Huddersfield T.(Am)		06.47	47	4	-	0

DRINKELL, Kevin S.
Grimsby, 18 June, 1960 (F)

League Club	Source	Date Signed	Seasons Played	Apps	Subs	Gls
Grimsby T.	App	06.78	76-84	242	30	89
Norwich C.	Tr	08.85	85-87	121	0	50
Coventry C.	Glasgow Rangers	10.89	89-91	34	7	5
Birmingham C.	L	10.91	91	5	0	2

Peter Downsborough (Halifax Town, Swindon Town & Bradford City)

League Club | Source | Date Signed | Seasons Played | Career Record Apps | Subs | Gls

DRINKWATER, Charles J.
Willesden, 25 June, 1914 (OL)

League Club	Source	Date Signed	Seasons Played	Apps	Subs	Gls
Aston Villa	Walthamstow Ave.	11.35	35	2	-	1
Charlton Ath.	Tr	07.38	38	3	-	0
Watford	Tr	01.45	46	1	-	0

DRINKWATER, James A.
Northwich, 10 February, 1918 (FB)

League Club	Source	Date Signed	Seasons Played	Apps	Subs	Gls
Torquay U.	St Mirren	06.52	52-53	67	-	1

DRINKWATER, Raymond
Jarrow, 18 May, 1931 (G)

League Club	Source	Date Signed	Seasons Played	Apps	Subs	Gls
Portsmouth	Guildford C.	11.55	56	8	-	0
Queens Park R.	Tr	02.58	57-62	199	-	0

DRISCOLL, Andrew
Staines, 21 October, 1971 (RW)

League Club	Source	Date Signed	Seasons Played	Apps	Subs	Gls
Brentford	YT	03.90	88-91	10	4	2

DRIVER, Allenby
Blackwell (Dy), 29 September, 1918 (IF)

League Club	Source	Date Signed	Seasons Played	Apps	Subs	Gls
Sheffield Wed.	Mansfield Shoes	04.36	37-38	6	-	3
Luton T.	Tr	10.46	46-47	41	-	13
Norwich C.	Tr	01.48	47-49	49	-	19
Ipswich T.	Tr	01.50	49-51	86	-	25
Walsall	Tr	07.52	52	26	-	2

DRIVER, Philip A.
Huddersfield, 10 August, 1959 (W)

League Club	Source	Date Signed	Seasons Played	Apps	Subs	Gls
Wimbledon	Bedford T.	12.78	78-80	7	9	3
Chelsea	Tr	09.80	80-82	25	19	4
Wimbledon	Tr	07.83	83-84	2	2	0

DROY, Michael R.
Highbury, 7 May, 1951 (CD)

League Club	Source	Date Signed	Seasons Played	Apps	Subs	Gls
Chelsea	Slough T.	09.70	70-84	263	9	13
Luton T.	L	11.84	84	2	0	0
Crystal Palace	Tr	03.85	84-86	49	0	7
Brentford	Tr	11.86	86	19	0	3

DRUCE, Mark A.
Oxford, 3 March, 1974 (F)

League Club	Source	Date Signed	Seasons Played	Apps	Subs	Gls
Oxford U.	YT	12.91	91	0	2	0

DRUMMOND, Ian P.
Brechin, 27 August, 1923 (FB)

League Club	Source	Date Signed	Seasons Played	Apps	Subs	Gls
Portsmouth		05.45				
Bournemouth	Tr	06.49	49-55	265	-	1

DRUMMY, Dermot
Hackney, 16 January, 1961 (M)

League Club	Source	Date Signed	Seasons Played	Apps	Subs	Gls
Arsenal	App	01.79				
Blackpool	L	03.80	79	4	1	0

DRURY, Charles (Chuck)
Darlaston, 4 July, 1937 E Yth (WH)

League Club	Source	Date Signed	Seasons Played	Apps	Subs	Gls
West Bromwich A.	F.H. Lloyds	02.55	57-63	146	-	1
Bristol C.	Tr	08.64	64-66	51	0	2
Bradford P.A.	Tr	03.68	67-68	31	0	1

DRURY, George B.
Hucknall, 22 January, 1914 Died 1972 (IF)

League Club	Source	Date Signed	Seasons Played	Apps	Subs	Gls
Sheffield Wed.	Heanor T.	09.34	36-37	44	-	9
Arsenal	Tr	03.38	37-46	38	-	3
West Bromwich A.	Tr	10.46	46-47	29	-	8
Watford	Tr	07.48	48-49	35	-	3

DRURY, James
Cumnock, 29 May, 1924 (OL)

League Club	Source	Date Signed	Seasons Played	Apps	Subs	Gls
Rochdale	Stirling A.	05.51	51	4	-	1
Carlisle U.	Tr	08.52	52-53	35	-	5
Southport	Tr	07.54	54	24	-	2

DRYBURGH, Thomas J. D.
Kirkcaldy, 23 April, 1923 (OL)

League Club	Source	Date Signed	Seasons Played	Apps	Subs	Gls
Aldershot	Lochgelly Albert	06.47	47	19	-	2
Rochdale	Tr	07.48	48-49	77	-	17
Leicester C.	Tr	09.50	50-53	95	-	29
Hull C.	Tr	05.54	54	23	-	3
Oldham Ath.	Kings Lynn	08.57	57	1	-	0
Rochdale	Tr	11.57	57	5	-	0

DRYDEN, John G. (Jackie)
Sunderland, 16 September, 1919 (OR)

League Club	Source	Date Signed	Seasons Played	Apps	Subs	Gls
Charlton Ath.	Washington Chem.	03.46				
Swindon T.	Hylton Colly	05.47	47	21	-	3
Leyton Orient	Tr	06.48	48-49	40	-	10

DRYDEN, Richard A.
Stroud, 14 June, 1969 (LB/W)

League Club	Source	Date Signed	Seasons Played	Apps	Subs	Gls
Bristol Rov.	YT	07.87	86-88	12	1	0
Exeter C.	L	09.88	88	6	0	0
Exeter C.	Tr	03.89	88-90	86	0	13
Notts Co.	Tr	07.91	91	28	1	1

DRYHURST, Carl D.
Sutton Coldfield, 8 November, 1960 (F)

League Club	Source	Date Signed	Seasons Played	Apps	Subs	Gls
Halifax T.	Sutton Coldfield T.	11.79	79	4	4	0

DRYSDALE, Brian
Wingate (Dm), 24 February, 1943 (LB)

League Club	Source	Date Signed	Seasons Played	Apps	Subs	Gls
Lincoln C.	Jnrs	09.60	59-64	21	-	0
Hartlepool U.	Tr	07.65	65-68	169	1	2
Bristol C.	Tr	05.69	69-76	280	2	3
Reading	L	02.77	76	16	0	0
Oxford U.	Tr	07.77	77	15	0	0

DRYSDALE, Jason
Bristol, 17 November, 1970 E Yth (LB)

League Club	Source	Date Signed	Seasons Played	Apps	Subs	Gls
Watford	YT	09.88	89-91	79	8	5

DUBLIN, Dion
Leicester, 22 April, 1969 (F)

League Club	Source	Date Signed	Seasons Played	Apps	Subs	Gls
Norwich C.	Oakham U.	03.88				
Cambridge U.	Tr	08.88	88-91	133	23	53

DUBLIN, Keith B. L.
High Wycombe, 29 January, 1966 E Yth (D)

League Club	Source	Date Signed	Seasons Played	Apps	Subs	Gls
Chelsea	App	01.84	83-86	50	1	0
Brighton & H.A.	Tr	08.87	87-89	132	0	5
Watford	Tr	07.90	90-91	89	0	0

DUBOIS, Joseph M.
Monkstown (NI), 27 December, 1927 NI Amat (OR)

League Club	Source	Date Signed	Seasons Played	Apps	Subs	Gls
Doncaster Rov.	Brantwood	05.49	49-51	31	-	5
Grimsby T.	Bedford T.	07.53	53	6	-	1
Halifax T.	Tr	07.54	54-56	78	-	10

DUCHART, Alexander
Falkirk, 3 May, 1933 (W)

League Club	Source	Date Signed	Seasons Played	Apps	Subs	Gls
Southend U.	Hibernian	05.56	56	8	-	2

DUCK, George T.
Tottenham, 22 February, 1952 (F)

League Club	Source	Date Signed	Seasons Played	Apps	Subs	Gls
Millwall	App	02.70				
Southend U.	Tr	06.71	71	3	0	0

DUCKHOUSE, Edward
Walsall, 9 April, 1918 Died 1980 (CH)

League Club	Source	Date Signed	Seasons Played	Apps	Subs	Gls
Birmingham C.	Streetly Wks	08.38	38-49	119	-	4
Northampton T.	Tr	08.50	50-51	68	-	0

DUDDY, John M.
Manchester, 8 February, 1956 (M)

League Club	Source	Date Signed	Seasons Played	Apps	Subs	Gls
Oldham Ath.	App	02.74				
Stockport Co.	Tr	03.76	75	6	0	0

DUDLEY, Frank E.
Southend, 9 May, 1925 (IF)

League Club	Source	Date Signed	Seasons Played	Apps	Subs	Gls
Southend U.	Jnrs	10.45	46-48	88	-	32
Leeds U.	Tr	08.49	49-50	64	-	23
Southampton	Tr	02.51	50-53	67	-	32
Cardiff C.	Tr	09.53	53	4	-	1
Brentford	Tr	12.53	53-56	72	-	31

DUDLEY, James G.
Gartcosh, 24 August, 1928 S'B'-1 (WH)

League Club	Source	Date Signed	Seasons Played	Apps	Subs	Gls
West Bromwich A.	Jnrs	05.46	49-59	285	-	9
Walsall	Tr	12.59	59-63	167	-	3

DUDLEY, Philip W.
Basildon, 17 February, 1959 (FB)

League Club	Source	Date Signed	Seasons Played	Apps	Subs	Gls
Southend U.	App	02.77	77-82	107	3	3

DUDLEY, Reginald A.
Hemel Hempstead, 3 February, 1915 E Amat (FB)

League Club	Source	Date Signed	Seasons Played	Apps	Subs	Gls
Millwall	Apsley	03.35	35-46	42	-	0
Queens Park R.	Tr	12.46	46-49	57	-	0
Watford	Tr	07.50	50	1	-	0

DUERDEN, Harold
Barnsley, 5 March, 1948 (WH)

League Club	Source	Date Signed	Seasons Played	Apps	Subs	Gls
Barnsley	App	09.65	65-66	24	1	1

DUFF, William
Winchburgh, 6 February, 1935 Su23-1/SF Lge (G)

League Club	Source	Date Signed	Seasons Played	Apps	Subs	Gls
Charlton Ath.	Hearts	12.56	56-61	213	-	0
Peterborough U.	Tr	05.63	63-66	118	0	0

DUFF, William F. A.
Littleborough, 16 December, 1938 (OL)

League Club	Source	Date Signed	Seasons Played	Apps	Subs	Gls
Rochdale	Jnrs	05.56				
Scunthorpe U.	Tr	10.58				
Grimsby T.	Tr	10.59	59	3	-	1
Accrington St.	Toronto (Can)	10.60	60	14	-	3

DUFFETT, Edgar
Worcester, 29 August, 1926 (IF)

League Club	Source	Date Signed	Seasons Played	Apps	Subs	Gls
Norwich C.	West Bromwich A. (Am)	11.47				
Carlisle U.	Tr	08.50	50-52	47	-	8

DUFFEY, Christopher P.
Kirkby, 8 January, 1952 (W)

League Club	Source	Date Signed	Seasons Played	Apps	Subs	Gls
Bolton W.	App	09.69	69-71	8	0	0
Crewe Alex.	L	09.72	72	6	0	3
Crewe Alex.	Tr	07.73	73-74	54	3	12
Bury	Tr	10.74	74	17	4	8
Shrewsbury T.	Tr	05.75	75	4	4	1
Rochdale	L	11.75	75	2	0	0

DUFFIELD, Martin J.
Park Royal, 28 February, 1964 E Yth (M)

League Club	Source	Date Signed	Seasons Played	Apps	Subs	Gls
Queens Park R.	App	01.82	82	0	1	0
Bournemouth	L	09.83	83	6	0	1
Charlton Ath.	L	11.84	84	1	0	0

DUFFIELD, Peter
Middlesbrough, 4 February, 1969 (W)

League Club	Source	Date Signed	Seasons Played	Apps	Subs	Gls
Middlesbrough	App	11.86				
Sheffield U.	Tr	08.87	87-91	34	24	16
Halifax T.	L	03.88	87	12	0	6
Rotherham U.	L	03.91	90	17	0	5

DUFFIN, Lionel J.
Barrow, 8 August, 1945 (G)

League Club	Source	Date Signed	Seasons Played	Apps	Subs	Gls
Barrow	Jnrs	07.64	64-67	46	0	0

DUFFY, Alan
Stanley, 20 December, 1949 E Yth (M)

League Club	Source	Date Signed	Seasons Played	Apps	Subs	Gls
Newcastle U.	App	03.67	68-69	2	2	0
Brighton & H.A.	Tr	01.70	69-71	34	15	8
Tranmere Rov.	Tr	03.72	71-72	29	4	2
Darlington	Tr	08.73	73	19	5	0

DUFFY, Christopher
Methil, 21 October, 1918 Died 1978 (OL)

League Club	Source	Date Signed	Seasons Played	Apps	Subs	Gls
Charlton Ath.	Leith Ath.	09.45	46-52	162	-	33

DUFFY, Darrell G.
Birmingham, 18 January, 1971 E Yth (D)

League Club	Source	Date Signed	Seasons Played	Apps	Subs	Gls
Aston Villa	YT	07.89	88	1	0	0

DUFFY, Gerald
Middlewich, 12 September, 1934 (CF)

League Club	Source	Date Signed	Seasons Played	Apps	Subs	Gls
Oldham Ath.	Middlewich	05.56	56-58	58	-	21

DUFFY, John
Dunfermline, 6 September, 1943 (LH)

League Club	Source	Date Signed	Seasons Played	Apps	Subs	Gls
Darlington	Dunfermline Ath.	08.63	63	10	-	1

DUFFY, John
Glasgow, 24 April, 1922 (FB)

League Club	Source	Date Signed	Seasons Played	Apps	Subs	Gls
Norwich C.	Clyde	03.49	49-53	78	-	0

DUFFY, John G.
Dundee, 24 August, 1929 (WH)

League Club	Source	Date Signed	Seasons Played	Apps	Subs	Gls
Southend U.	Glasgow Celtic	05.54	54-59	113	-	4

DUFFY, Michael K.
Leicester, 12 June, 1961 (M)

League Club	Source	Date Signed	Seasons Played	Apps	Subs	Gls
Leicester C.	Jnrs	07.78	78-79	7	5	1

DUFFY, Vincent G.
Nottingham, 21 September, 1962 (M)

League Club	Source	Date Signed	Seasons Played	Apps	Subs	Gls
Scunthorpe U.	Nottingham F. (App)	12.80	80-81	3	5	0

DUGDALE, Alan
Liverpool, 11 September, 1952 E Yth (CD)

League Club	Source	Date Signed	Seasons Played	Apps	Subs	Gls
Coventry C.	App	11.69	72-77	139	3	0
Charlton Ath.	Tr	10.77	77-78	34	0	0
Barnsley	L	08.79	79	7	0	0

DUGDALE, Gordon
Liverpool, 21 February, 1924 (LB)

League Club	Source	Date Signed	Seasons Played	Apps	Subs	Gls
Everton	Jnrs	06.47	47-49	58	-	0

DUGDALE, James R.
Liverpool, 15 January, 1932 E'B'-3/EF Lge (CH)

League Club	Source	Date Signed	Seasons Played	Apps	Subs	Gls
West Bromwich A.	Harrowby	06.52	52-55	63	-	0
Aston Villa	Tr	01.56	55-61	215	-	3
Queens Park R.	Tr	10.62	62	10	-	0

DUGGAN, Andrew J.
Bradford, 19 September, 1967 (CD)

League Club	Source	Date Signed	Seasons Played	Apps	Subs	Gls
Barnsley	YT	07.85	86	1	1	0
Rochdale	L	11.87	87	3	0	0
Huddersfield T.	Tr	09.88	88-89	29	0	3
Hartlepool U.	L	08.90	90	2	0	0
Rochdale	Tr	03.91	90	1	0	0

DUGGAN, Edward J.
West Ham, 27 July, 1922 (IF)

League Club	Source	Date Signed	Seasons Played	Apps	Subs	Gls
Luton T.	Jnrs	08.39	46-48	47	-	20
Queens Park R.	Tr	02.49	48-50	47	-	5
Luton T.	Bedford T.	02.56				

DUGGAN, James
Droitwich, 17 November, 1920 Died 1981 (IF)

League Club	Source	Date Signed	Seasons Played	Apps	Subs	Gls
West Bromwich A.	Droitwich O.B.	12.39	46	25	-	8

DUGGINS, Eric E.
Tamworth, 24 November, 1928 (FB)

League Club	Source	Date Signed	Seasons Played	Apps	Subs	Gls
Portsmouth	Atherstone T.	08.48				
Southend U.	Tr	07.52	52-53	28	-	0

DUGGINS, Gordon
Tamworth, 8 December, 1932 (CF)

League Club	Source	Date Signed	Seasons Played	Apps	Subs	Gls
Barnsley	Gresley Rov.	11.55	55-57	17	-	6

DUGGINS, John
Tamworth, 4 August, 1931 (F)

League Club	Source	Date Signed	Seasons Played	Apps	Subs	Gls
Portsmouth	Atherstone T.	06.50				
Walsall	Tr	08.52	52	16	-	3

DUGNOLLE, John H.
India, 24 March, 1914 Died 1977 (HB)

League Club	Source	Date Signed	Seasons Played	Apps	Subs	Gls
Brighton & H.A.	Southwick	10.34	35-37	7	-	0
Plymouth Arg.	Tunbridge Wells	02.39	38	4	-	0
Brighton & H.A.	Tr	08.46	46-47	58	-	0

DUKE, George E.
Chichester, 6 September, 1920 (G)

League Club	Source	Date Signed	Seasons Played	Apps	Subs	Gls
Luton T.	Southwick	01.39	46-48	16	-	0
Bournemouth	Tr	05.49	49	10	-	0

DUKES, Harold P.
Portsmouth, 31 March, 1912 (G)

League Club	Source	Date Signed	Seasons Played	Apps	Subs	Gls
Norwich C.	Ipswich T.	08.34	34-38	105	-	0
Norwich C.	Bedford T.	09.46	46	13	-	0

DULIN, Michael C.
Stepney, 28 October, 1935 (OR)

League Club	Source	Date Signed	Seasons Played	Apps	Subs	Gls
Tottenham H.	Jnrs	11.52	55-57	10	-	2

DULSON, Gary
Nottingham, 21 December, 1953 (D)

League Club	Source	Date Signed	Seasons Played	Apps	Subs	Gls
Nottingham F.	App	10.71				
Port Vale	Tr	10.74	74-77	108	2	3
Crewe Alex.	Tr	11.78	78-79	33	5	0

DUMIGHAN, Joseph
Langley Park (Dm), 25 September, 1938 (F)

League Club	Source	Date Signed	Seasons Played	Apps	Subs	Gls
Sunderland	Jnrs	11.55				
Darlington	Tr	07.58	58	4	-	1

DUNBAR, Ian
Newcastle, 6 June, 1971 E Sch (F)

League Club	Source	Date Signed	Seasons Played	Apps	Subs	Gls
Hartlepool U. (N/C)	Jnrs	08.89	89-90	1	2	0

DUNCAN, Cameron
Shotts, 4 August, 1965 S Yth (G)

League Club	Source	Date Signed	Seasons Played	Apps	Subs	Gls
Sunderland	Jnrs	07.84	85	1	0	0

DUNCAN, Colin J.
Wantage, 5 August, 1957 (M)

League Club	Source	Date Signed	Seasons Played	Apps	Subs	Gls
Oxford U.	App	12.74	74-79	188	1	6
Gillingham	Tr	01.80	79-83	83	2	5
Reading	Tr	09.83	83-84	56	0	3
Aldershot	Tr	08.85	85	15	0	0

DUNCAN, David M.
East Fife, 21 November, 1921 Died 1991 SF Lge/S-3 (OL)

League Club	Source	Date Signed	Seasons Played	Apps	Subs	Gls
Crewe Alex.	Raith Rov.	08.55	55	22	-	0

DUNCAN, Douglas (Dally)
Aberdeen, 14 October, 1909 Died 1990 S-14 (W)

League Club	Source	Date Signed	Seasons Played	Apps	Subs	Gls
Hull C.	Aberdeen	08.28	28-31	111	-	47
Derby Co.	Tr	03.32	31-46	261	-	63
Luton T.	Tr	10.46	46-47	33	-	4

DUNCAN, George
Glasgow, 16 January, 1937 (OR)

League Club	Source	Date Signed	Seasons Played	Apps	Subs	Gls
Southend U.	Glasgow Rangers	06.60	60	6	-	2
Chesterfield	Tr	08.61	61-64	140	-	13

DUNCAN, James R.
Hull, 2 April, 1938 (F)

League Club	Source	Date Signed	Seasons Played	Apps	Subs	Gls
Hull C.	Jnrs	04.55	55-59	26	-	3
Bradford C.	Tr	06.60	60	18	-	5

DUNCAN, John G.
Glasgow, 10 December, 1926 (F)

League Club	Source	Date Signed	Seasons Played	Apps	Subs	Gls
Newcastle U.	Ayr U.	11.50	51-52	5	-	3

DUNCAN, John P.
Dundee, 22 February, 1949 SF Lge (F)

League Club	Source	Date Signed	Seasons Played	Apps	Subs	Gls
Tottenham H.	Dundee	10.74	74-78	101	2	53
Derby Co.	Tr	09.78	78-80	35	1	12
Scunthorpe U.	Tr	06.81	81-82	3	6	0

DUNCAN, Joseph J.
Liverpool, 24 February, 1950 (OR)

League Club	Source	Date Signed	Seasons Played	Apps	Subs	Gls
Wrexham (Am)	Jnrs	12.68	68	1	0	0

DUNCAN, Robert
Kirkcaldy, 2 November, 1943 (FB)

League Club	Source	Date Signed	Seasons Played	Apps	Subs	Gls
Southend U.	Jnrs	08.61	61	1	-	0

DUNCAN, Thomas M.
Banff, 15 July, 1936 (IF)

League Club	Source	Date Signed	Seasons Played	Apps	Subs	Gls
Newport Co. (L)	Airdrieonians	03.58	57	1	-	0

DUNCLIFFE, M. John
Brighton, 17 September, 1947 (FB)

League Club	Source	Date Signed	Seasons Played	Apps	Subs	Gls
Brighton & H.A.	App	09.65	66-67	22	0	0
Grimsby T.	Tr	06.68	68-69	71	1	0
Peterborough U.	Tr	07.70	70-72	120	0	0

DUNDERDALE, W. Leonard
Gainsborough, 6 February, 1915 Died 1989 (CF)

League Club	Source	Date Signed	Seasons Played	Apps	Subs	Gls
Walsall	Goole T.	03.36	35-37	33	-	18
Watford	Tr	05.38	38	30	-	18
Leeds U.	Tr	03.39	38	3	-	0
Watford	Tr	04.46	46-47	44	-	15

DUNGWORTH, John H.
Rotherham, 30 March, 1955 (F)

League Club	Source	Date Signed	Seasons Played	Apps	Subs	Gls
Huddersfield T.	App	04.72	72-74	18	5	1
Barnsley	L	10.74	74	2	1	1
Oldham Ath.	Tr	03.75	75	2	2	0
Rochdale	L	03.77	76	14	0	3
Aldershot	Tr	09.77	77-79	105	0	58
Shrewsbury T.	Tr	11.79	79-81	81	5	17
Hereford U.	L	10.81	81	7	0	3
Mansfield T.	Tr	08.82	82-83	50	6	16
Rotherham U.	Tr	02.84	83-87	177	11	16

DUNKLEY, Malcolm
Wolverhampton, 12 July, 1961 (F)

League Club	Source	Date Signed	Seasons Played	Apps	Subs	Gls
Lincoln C.	Bromsgrove Rov.	02.89	88	9	2	4

DUNKLEY, Maurice E. F.
Kettering, 19 February, 1914 Died 1989 (OR)

League Club	Source	Date Signed	Seasons Played	Apps	Subs	Gls
Northampton T.	Kettering T.	12.36	36-37	39	-	5
Manchester C.	Tr	03.38	37-46	51	-	5
Northampton T.	Kettering T.	07.49	49	4	-	0

DUNKLEY, Robert
Stoke, 6 April, 1922 (OL)

League Club	Source	Date Signed	Seasons Played	Apps	Subs	Gls
Stoke C.		01.41				
Barrow	Tr	08.46	46	11	-	0

DUNLEAVY, Christopher P.
Liverpool, 30 December, 1949 (CD)

League Club	Source	Date Signed	Seasons Played	Apps	Subs	Gls
Everton	Jnrs	03.68				
Southport	Tr	07.69	69-73	145	2	9
Chester C.	Tr	09.73	73-76	74	2	0
Halifax T.	Tr	10.76	76-80	181	0	13

DUNLOP, Albert
Liverpool, 21 April, 1932 Died 1990 (G)

League Club	Source	Date Signed	Seasons Played	Apps	Subs	Gls
Everton	Jnrs	08.49	56-62	211	-	0
Wrexham	Tr	11.63	63-64	15	-	0

DUNLOP, Rex W.
Glasgow, 21 September, 1927 (WH)

League Club	Source	Date Signed	Seasons Played	Apps	Subs	Gls
Workington	Glasgow Rangers	11.53	53-55	110	-	20

DUNLOP, William L.
Airdrie, 20 December, 1926 (IF)

League Club	Source	Date Signed	Seasons Played	Apps	Subs	Gls
Exeter C.	Dunfermline Ath.	07.50	50	4	-	0
Bristol Rov.	Ilfracombe	05.52				
Bradford P.A.	Tr	05.53	53	36	-	12
Darlington	Tr	10.54	54	18	-	2

DUNMORE, David G.I.
Whitehaven, 8 February, 1934 (CF)

League Club	Source	Date Signed	Seasons Played	Apps	Subs	Gls
York C.	Cliftonville	05.52	51-53	48	-	25
Tottenham H.	Tr	02.54	53-59	75	-	23
West Ham U.	Tr	03.60	59-60	36	-	16
Leyton Orient	Tr	03.61	60-64	147	-	54
York C.	Tr	06.65	65-66	61	2	13

DUNN, Barry
Harrogate, 17 December, 1939 (F)

League Club	Source	Date Signed	Seasons Played	Apps	Subs	Gls
Doncaster Rov.		02.58				
Halifax T.	Tr	09.59	59-60	7	-	1

DUNN, Barry
Sunderland, 15 February, 1952 (W)

League Club	Source	Date Signed	Seasons Played	Apps	Subs	Gls
Sunderland	Blue Star	09.79	79-80	16	7	2
Preston N.E.	Tr	10.81	81	8	0	1
Darlington	Tr	08.82	82	16	0	4

DUNN, Brian J.
Boston, 4 October, 1940 (OL)

League Club	Source	Date Signed	Seasons Played	Apps	Subs	Gls
Grimsby T.	Jnrs	10.57				
Hartlepool U.	Tr	06.58	58-60	27	-	1

DUNN, Iain G.W.
Howden, 1 April, 1970 E Yth (F)

League Club	Source	Date Signed	Seasons Played	Apps	Subs	Gls
York C.	Jnrs	07.88	88-90	46	31	11
Chesterfield	Tr	08.91	91	8	5	1

DUNN, James
Edinburgh, 25 November, 1923 (IF)

League Club	Source	Date Signed	Seasons Played	Apps	Subs	Gls
Wolverhampton W.	Maghull Ath.	11.42	46-52	123	-	33
Derby Co.	Tr	11.52	52-54	57	-	21

DUNN, James
Rutherglen, 23 October, 1922 (FB)

League Club	Source	Date Signed	Seasons Played	Apps	Subs	Gls
Leeds U.	Rutherglen Glencairn	06.47	47-58	422	-	1
Darlington	Tr	07.59	59	27	-	0

DUNN, John A.
Barking, 21 June, 1944 (G)

League Club	Source	Date Signed	Seasons Played	Apps	Subs	Gls
Chelsea	App	02.62	62-65	13	0	0
Torquay U.	Tr	10.66	66-67	44	0	0
Aston Villa	Tr	01.68	67-70	101	0	0
Charlton Ath.	Tr	07.71	71-74	104	0	0

DUNN, Joseph
Glasgow, 20 September, 1925 (CH)

League Club	Source	Date Signed	Seasons Played	Apps	Subs	Gls
Preston N.E.	Clyde	08.51	51-60	223	-	2

DUNN, Norman
South Shields, 20 October, 1928 (CH)

League Club	Source	Date Signed	Seasons Played	Apps	Subs	Gls
Aldershot	Murton Colly	08.51	52	1	-	0
Darlington	Tr	07.54				

DUNN, Richard
Easington, 23 December, 1919 Died 1986 (IF)

League Club	Source	Date Signed	Seasons Played	Apps	Subs	Gls
West Ham U.	Ferryhill Ath.	02.38	46-47	11	-	2
Hartlepool U.	Tr	08.49	49	13	-	2

DUNN, William C.
Hebburn, 25 March, 1920 (G)

League Club	Source	Date Signed	Seasons Played	Apps	Subs	Gls
Darlington		05.46	46-55	340	-	0

DUNNE, Anthony P.
Dublin, 24 July, 1941 IR-32 (LB)

League Club	Source	Date Signed	Seasons Played	Apps	Subs	Gls
Manchester U.	Shelbourne	04.60	60-72	414	0	2
Bolton W.	Tr	08.73	73-78	166	4	0

DUNNE, Austin
Limerick (Ire), 31 July, 1934

League Club	Source	Date Signed	Seasons Played	Apps	Subs	Gls
Colchester U.	Limerick	10.53	54	1	-	0

DUNNE, James C.
Dublin, 1 December, 1947 IR-1 (CD)

League Club	Source	Date Signed	Seasons Played	Apps	Subs	Gls
Millwall	Shelbourne	02.66				
Torquay U.	Tr	07.67	67-69	125	1	13
Fulham	Tr	07.70	70-73	142	1	2
Torquay U.	Tr	04.76	75-78	119	3	6

DUNNE, James P.
Dublin, 16 March, 1935 LOI/IR-3 (IF)

League Club	Source	Date Signed	Seasons Played	Apps	Subs	Gls
Leicester C.		09.53	54-55	4	-	0
Peterborough U.	St Patricks Ath.	07.60	60-61	4	-	1

DUNNE, Joseph J.
Dublin, 25 May, 1973 IR Yth/IRu21-1 (M/RB)

League Club	Source	Date Signed	Seasons Played	Apps	Subs	Gls
Gillingham	YT	08.90	90-91	32	5	0

DUNNE, Patrick A. J.
Dublin, 9 February, 1943 IR-5 (G)

League Club	Source	Date Signed	Seasons Played	Apps	Subs	Gls
Everton	Jnrs	05.60				
Manchester U.	Shamrock Rov.	05.64	64-65	45	0	0
Plymouth Arg.	Tr	02.67	66-70	152	0	0

DUNNE, Seamus
Wicklow (Ire), 13 April, 1930 IR-15 (FB)

League Club	Source	Date Signed	Seasons Played	Apps	Subs	Gls
Luton T.	Shelbourne	07.50	51-60	300	-	0

DUNNE, Thomas
Dublin, 19 March, 1927 Died 1988 LOI (WH)

League Club	Source	Date Signed	Seasons Played	Apps	Subs	Gls
Leicester C.	Shamrock Rov.	11.49	50-53	33	-	0
Exeter C.	Tr	07.54	54-55	37	-	1
Shrewsbury T.	Tr	08.56	56	3	-	0
Southport	Tr	07.57	57	21	-	0

DUNNE, Thomas J.
Glasgow, 22 June, 1946 (IF)

League Club	Source	Date Signed	Seasons Played	Apps	Subs	Gls
Leyton Orient	St Anthonys	05.64	64	1	-	0

DUNNIGAN, John Y.
Dalmuir, 30 November, 1920 (OR)

League Club	Source	Date Signed	Seasons Played	Apps	Subs	Gls
Barrow	Bridgeton Waverley	09.45	46	1	-	0

DUNNING, William S.
Bury, 15 November, 1952 (W)

League Club	Source	Date Signed	Seasons Played	Apps	Subs	Gls
Blackburn Rov.	App	11.70	70-71	10	3	2

DUNPHY, Eamonn M.
Dublin, 3 August, 1945 IR-23 (M)

League Club	Source	Date Signed	Seasons Played	Apps	Subs	Gls
Manchester U.	App	08.62				
York C.	Tr	08.65	65	22	0	3
Millwall	Tr	01.66	65-73	267	7	24
Charlton Ath.	Tr	11.73	73-74	39	3	3
Reading	Tr	07.75	75-76	74	3	3

DUNPHY, Sean
Maltby, 5 November, 1970 (CD)

League Club	Source	Date Signed	Seasons Played	Apps	Subs	Gls
Barnsley	YT	06.89	89	5	1	0
Lincoln C.	Tr	07.90	91	5	0	1

DUNS, Leonard
Newcastle, 28 September, 1916 (OR)

League Club	Source	Date Signed	Seasons Played	Apps	Subs	Gls
Sunderland	Newcastle W.E.	10.33	35-51	215	-	45

DUNWELL, Peter M.
Sheffield, 22 November, 1938 (OL)

League Club	Source	Date Signed	Seasons Played	Apps	Subs	Gls
Lincoln C.	Ecclesfield	09.58	59-60	14	-	1

DUNWELL, Richard K.
Islington, 17 June, 1971

League Club	Source	Date Signed	Seasons Played	Apps	Subs	Gls
Aldershot	Millwall (N/C)	11.90	90	0	1	0

DUQUEMIN, Leonard S.
Guernsey, 17 July, 1924 (CF)

League Club	Source	Date Signed	Seasons Played	Apps	Subs	Gls
Tottenham H.	Vauxbelets	09.46	47-56	274	-	114

DURANDT, Clifford M.
South Africa, 16 April, 1940 (OL)

League Club	Source	Date Signed	Seasons Played	Apps	Subs	Gls
Wolverhampton W.	Marist Bros (SA)	06.57	58-61	43	-	9
Charlton Ath.	Tr	03.63	62-64	36	-	4

DURBAN, W. Alan
Port Talbot, 7 July, 1941 Wu23-14/W-27 (M)

League Club	Source	Date Signed	Seasons Played	Apps	Subs	Gls
Cardiff C.	Jnrs	09.58	59-62	52	-	9
Derby Co.	Tr	07.63	63-72	336	10	93
Shrewsbury T.	Tr	09.73	73-77	150	6	33

DURHAM, Jonathan S.
Wombwell, 12 June, 1965 (F)

League Club	Source	Date Signed	Seasons Played	Apps	Subs	Gls
Rotherham U.	App	06.83	83	3	3	1
Torquay U.	Tr	03.85	84-85	20	4	2

DURHAM, R. Dennis
East Halton, 26 September, 1923 (LH)

League Club	Source	Date Signed	Seasons Played	Apps	Subs	Gls
Hull C.	East Halton	04.47	46-58	267	-	7

DURIE, David G.
Blackpool, 13 August, 1931 (IF)

League Club	Source	Date Signed	Seasons Played	Apps	Subs	Gls
Blackpool	Oxford Amats	05.52	52-63	301	-	84
Chester C.	Tr	09.64	64-66	87	2	4

DURIE, Gordon S.
Paisley, 6 December, 1965 Su21-4/S'B'/S-21 (F)

League Club	Source	Date Signed	Seasons Played	Apps	Subs	Gls
Chelsea	Hibernian	04.86	85-90	115	8	51
Tottenham H.	Tr	08.91	91	31	0	7

DURKAN, Kieron J.
Chester, 1 December, 1973 (M)

League Club	Source	Date Signed	Seasons Played	Apps	Subs	Gls
Wrexham (YT)	YT	07.90	91	0	1	0

DURKIN, John
Cowdenbeath, 18 April, 1930 (IF)

League Club	Source	Date Signed	Seasons Played	Apps	Subs	Gls
Gillingham	Hearts	08.53	53-54	30	-	5

DURKIN, William
Bradford, 29 September, 1921 (IF)

League Club	Source	Date Signed	Seasons Played	Apps	Subs	Gls
Bradford C.		01.47	46-47	28	-	1
Rotherham U.	Tr	08.48	48	2	-	0
Aldershot	Tr	08.49	49-53	127	-	15

DURNIN, John P.
Bootle, 18 August, 1965 (F)

League Club	Source	Date Signed	Seasons Played	Apps	Subs	Gls
Liverpool	Waterloo Dock	03.86				
West Bromwich A.	L	10.88	88	5	0	2
Oxford U.	Tr	02.89	88-91	106	18	33

DURRANT, Frederick H.
Dover, 19 June, 1921 (CF)

League Club	Source	Date Signed	Seasons Played	Apps	Subs	Gls
Brentford	Folkestone T.	05.39	46	4	-	3
Queens Park R.	Tr	09.46	46-48	51	-	27
Exeter C.	Tr	02.49	48-49	17	-	5

DURRANT, Paul
East Howdon, 21 February, 1943 (OL)

League Club	Source	Date Signed	Seasons Played	Apps	Subs	Gls
Wolverhampton W.	Sunderland (Am)	07.61				
Bury	Tr	07.62	63-64	21	-	6
Doncaster Rov.	Tr	07.65	65-66	13	2	1

DURRELL, Joseph T.
Stepney, 15 March, 1953 (OL)

League Club	Source	Date Signed	Seasons Played	Apps	Subs	Gls
West Ham U.	App	10.70	71	5	1	0
Bristol C.	Tr	07.73	73-74	5	3	0
Cardiff C.	L	08.75	75	2	0	0
Gillingham	Tr	11.75	75-76	43	6	9

DUTHIE, Ian M.
Forfar, 18 January, 1930 (F)

League Club	Source	Date Signed	Seasons Played	Apps	Subs	Gls
Huddersfield T.	Forfar Celtic	06.49	49-52	7	-	0
Bradford C.	Tr	06.54	54-55	28	-	4

DUTHIE, James
Letham (Angus), 23 September, 1923 (CH)

League Club	Source	Date Signed	Seasons Played	Apps	Subs	Gls
Grimsby T.		09.49	48-50	40	-	0
Hull C.	Tr	06.51	51-52	17	-	3
Southend U.	Tr	05.53	53-57	160	-	7

DUTHOIT, John
Leeds, 4 November, 1918 (LB)

League Club	Source	Date Signed	Seasons Played	Apps	Subs	Gls
Leeds U.	Carlton U.	04.45				
York C.	Tr	05.46	46-49	36	-	0

DUTTON, Charles A.
Rugeley, 10 April, 1934 (CF)

League Club	Source	Date Signed	Seasons Played	Apps	Subs	Gls
Coventry C.	Derby Co. (Am)	10.52	53-55	27	-	8
Northampton T.	Tr	03.56	55-56	10	-	2

DUTTON, Leonard L.
Cardiff, 17 January, 1922 W Sch (WH)

League Club	Source	Date Signed	Seasons Played	Apps	Subs	Gls
Arsenal	Jnrs	05.39				
Norwich C.	Tr	08.46	46-52	139	-	11

DUXBURY, Lee E.
Skipton, 7 October, 1969 (M)

League Club	Source	Date Signed	Seasons Played	Apps	Subs	Gls
Bradford C.	YT	07.88	88-91	100	4	11
Rochdale	L	01.90	89	9	1	0

DUXBURY, Michael
Accrington, 1 September, 1959 Eu21-7/E-10 (FB/M)

League Club	Source	Date Signed	Seasons Played	Apps	Subs	Gls
Manchester U.	App	10.76	80-89	274	25	6
Blackburn Rov.	Tr	08.90	90-91	25	2	0
Bradford C.	Tr	01.92	91	16	0	0

DWIGHT, Roy E.
Belvedere, 9 January, 1933 (OR)

League Club	Source	Date Signed	Seasons Played	Apps	Subs	Gls
Fulham	Jnrs	06.50	54-57	72	-	54
Nottingham F.	Tr	07.58	58-59	44	-	21
Coventry C.	Gravesend & Nft	01.62	61-62	31	-	8
Millwall	Tr	01.64	63-64	7	-	2

DWYER, Alan R.
Liverpool, 5 October, 1952 (FB)

League Club	Source	Date Signed	Seasons Played	Apps	Subs	Gls
Wrexham	Halewood Y.C.	10.73	74-80	169	11	2
Stockport Co.		10.81	81	4	0	0

DWYER, Noel M.
Dublin, 30 October, 1934 IR 'B'-1/IR-14 (G)

League Club	Source	Date Signed	Seasons Played	Apps	Subs	Gls
Wolverhampton W.	Ormeau	08.53	57	5	-	0
West Ham U.	Tr	12.58	58-59	36	-	0
Swansea C.	Tr	08.60	60-64	140	-	0
Plymouth Arg.	Tr	01.65	64-65	26	0	0
Charlton Ath.	Tr	12.65	65	6	0	0

DWYER, Philip J.
Cardiff, 28 October, 1953 W Sch/W Yth/Wu21-1/Wu23-5/W-10 (D)

League Club	Source	Date Signed	Seasons Played	Apps	Subs	Gls
Cardiff C.	Jnrs	10.71	72-84	466	5	41
Rochdale	L	03.85	84	15	0	1

DYAS, Gordon
Hednesford, 17 May, 1936 (HB)

League Club	Source	Date Signed	Seasons Played	Apps	Subs	Gls
Walsall	Hednesford T.	06.55	55	12	-	0

DYCHE, Sean M.
Kettering, 28 June, 1971 (RB/M)

League Club	Source	Date Signed	Seasons Played	Apps	Subs	Gls
Nottingham F.	YT	05.89				
Chesterfield	Tr	02.90	89-91	85	7	7

DYE, Dean C.
Lincoln, 5 March, 1969 (F)

League Club	Source	Date Signed	Seasons Played	Apps	Subs	Gls
Charlton Ath.	Lincoln U.	06.91				
Lincoln C. (N/C)	Tr	10.91	91	0	2	0

DYER, J. Alec
Crewe, 13 April, 1913 (OL/LB)

League Club	Source	Date Signed	Seasons Played	Apps	Subs	Gls
Crewe Alex.		10.33	33-36	51	-	9
Plymouth Arg.	Tr	02.37	36-46	53	-	3

DYER, Alexander C.
West Ham, 14 November, 1965 (W)

League Club	Source	Date Signed	Seasons Played	Apps	Subs	Gls
Blackpool	Watford (App)	10.83	83-86	101	7	19
Hull C.	Tr	02.87	86-88	59	1	14
Crystal Palace	Tr	11.88	88-89	16	1	2
Charlton Ath.	Tr	10.90	90-91	37	11	7

DYER, Paul D.
Leicester, 24 January, 1953 (M)

League Club	Source	Date Signed	Seasons Played	Apps	Subs	Gls
Notts Co.		09.72	72-73	1	6	0
Colchester U.	Tr	07.75	75-79	124	20	4

DYER, Peter R.F.
Devonport, 12 October, 1937 (G)

League Club	Source	Date Signed	Seasons Played	Apps	Subs	Gls
Plymouth Arg.	Oak Villa	06.55	55-56	8	-	0

DYER, Raymond
Stockport, 12 May, 1938 (F)

League Club	Source	Date Signed	Seasons Played	Apps	Subs	Gls
Stockport Co.	Bolton W. (Am)	09.56	56	1	-	0

DYER, Stephen P.
Chelmsford, 21 March, 1954 (D)

League Club	Source	Date Signed	Seasons Played	Apps	Subs	Gls
Southend U.	App	03.72	72-76	59	8	0

DYKE, Charles H.
Caerphilly, 23 September, 1926 (OR)

League Club	Source	Date Signed	Seasons Played	Apps	Subs	Gls
Chelsea	Troedyrhiw	11.47	47-50	24	-	2

DYKES, Donald W.
Ashby, 8 June, 1930 (WH)

League Club	Source	Date Signed	Seasons Played	Apps	Subs	Gls
Lincoln C.	M. & B.D.C.	06.49	49-58	95	-	4

DYMOND, William H.
Exeter, 13 February, 1920 (OR)

League Club	Source	Date Signed	Seasons Played	Apps	Subs	Gls
Bristol C.		09.45	46	8	-	1
Exeter C.	Tr	06.47	47-48	41	-	7

DYSON, J. Barry
Oldham, 6 September, 1942 (IF)

League Club	Source	Date Signed	Seasons Played	Apps	Subs	Gls
Bury	Jnrs	09.60				
Tranmere Rov.	Tr	07.62	62-66	174	0	99
Crystal Palace	Tr	09.66	66-67	33	1	9
Watford	Tr	01.68	67-68	38	0	19
Leyton Orient	Tr	12.68	68-72	154	6	28
Colchester U.	Tr	07.73	73-74	41	1	6

DYSON, Geoffrey
Huddersfield, 16 March, 1923 Died 1989 (IF)

League Club	Source	Date Signed	Seasons Played	Apps	Subs	Gls
Huddersfield T.	Jnrs	03.46				
Bradford C.	Tr	06.47	47	1	-	0
Accrington St.	Tr	01.48	47-48	20	-	1

DYSON, Jack
Oldham, 8 July, 1934 Eu23-1 (IF)

League Club	Source	Date Signed	Seasons Played	Apps	Subs	Gls
Manchester C.	Nelson	05.52	55-59	63	-	26

DYSON, James
Ryhope, 16 December, 1935 (G)

League Club	Source	Date Signed	Seasons Played	Apps	Subs	Gls
Hartlepool U.		04.55	54-58	63	-	0

DYSON, Keith
Consett, 10 February, 1950 Eu23-1 (IF)

League Club	Source	Date Signed	Seasons Played	Apps	Subs	Gls
Newcastle U.	Jnrs	08.68	68-71	74	2	22
Blackpool	Tr	10.71	71-75	91	3	30

DYSON, Paul I.
Birmingham, 27 December, 1959 Eu21-4 (CD)

League Club	Source	Date Signed	Seasons Played	Apps	Subs	Gls
Coventry C.	App	06.77	78-82	140	0	5
Stoke C.	Tr	07.83	83-85	106	0	5
West Bromwich A.	Tr	03.86	85-88	64	0	5
Darlington	Tr	03.89	88	12	0	3
Crewe Alex.	Tr	08.89	89	30	1	2

DYSON, Terence K.
Malton, 29 November, 1934 (OL)

League Club	Source	Date Signed	Seasons Played	Apps	Subs	Gls
Tottenham H.	Scarborough	04.55	54-64	184	-	41
Fulham	Tr	06.65	65	21	1	3
Colchester U.	Tr	08.68	68-69	53	3	4

DZIADULEWICZ, Mark
Wimbledon, 29 January, 1960 (M)

League Club	Source	Date Signed	Seasons Played	Apps	Subs	Gls
Southend U.	App	02.78				
Wimbledon	Chelmsford C.	02.79	78-79	22	6	1

DZIEKANOWSKI, Dariusz P. (Jackie)
Warsaw (Poland), 30 September, 1962 Polish Int (F)

League Club	Source	Date Signed	Seasons Played	Apps	Subs	Gls
Bristol C.	Glasgow Celtic	01.92	91	16	1	4

Dariusz Dziekanowski (Legia Warsaw, Glasgow Celtic, Bristol City & Poland)

Duncan Edwards (Manchester United & England)
The youngest player of modern times to appear for England before tragically losing his life in the Munich air disaster

League Club	Source	Date Signed	Seasons Played	Career Record Apps	Subs	Gls
EADES, Kevin M.						
Rotherham, 11 March, 1959						(OR)
Rotherham U.	App	03.77	75	1	0	0
EADES, Terence G.						
Banbridge (NI), 5 March, 1944						(CD)
Cambridge U.	Chelmsford C.	(N/L)	70-76	248	0	5
Watford	L	09.76	76	4	0	0
EADIE, Douglas						
Edinburgh, 22 September, 1946						(OL)
West Ham U.		09.66	66	2	0	0
Leyton Orient	L	09.67	67	2	0	0
EADIE, Gordon						
Glasgow, 17 November, 1950						(OL)
Bury (Am)	Glasgow U.	06.67	67	2	0	0
EADIE, James						
Kirkintilloch, 4 February, 1947						(G)
Cardiff C.	Kirkintilloch Rob Roy	09.66	69-71	43	0	0
Chester C.	L	08.72	72	6	0	0
Bristol Rov.	Tr	02.73	72-76	183	0	0
EAGLES, Alan J.						
Edgware, 6 September, 1933						(FB)
Leyton Orient	Carshalton Ath.	09.57	57-60	75	-	0
Colchester U.	Tr	01.61	60	16	-	1
Queens Park R.	Tr	08.61				
Aldershot	Tr	11.61	61-62	14	-	1
EALING, William H.						
Tamworth, 12 March, 1930						
Blackburn Rov.		02.50				
Walsall	Tr	07.52	52	1	-	0
EAMES, Terence						
Croydon, 13 October, 1957						(FB)
Wimbledon	Crystal Palace (Am)	(N/L)	77-79	46	1	1

League Club	Source	Date Signed	Seasons Played	Career Record Apps	Subs	Gls
EAMES, William						
Emsworth, 20 September, 1957						(F)
Portsmouth	App	09.75	75	9	3	1
Brentford	Tr	08.78	78	2	0	1
EARL, Albert T. (Sam)						
Gateshead, 10 February, 1915						(IF)
Bury	Dunston C.W.S.	03.32	33-36	35	-	7
York C.	Rhyl Ath.	07.37	37-38	58	-	9
Stockport Co.		08.46	46-47	42	-	12
Rochdale	Tr	11.47	47	4	-	1
New Brighton	Tr	03.48	47	9	-	1
EARL, Stanley W. J.						
Alton, 9 July, 1929						(FB)
Portsmouth	Alton T.	11.49	50-51	8	-	0
Leyton Orient	Tr	07.53	53-55	33	-	0
Swindon T.	Tr	11.56	56-57	23	-	0
EARL, Steven						
Scunthorpe, 31 August, 1956						(F)
Scunthorpe U.	Appleby Frodingham	09.74	74-79	37	2	10
EARLAM, Donald S.						
Altrincham, 25 June, 1931 Died 1988						(LH)
Southport (Am)	Stoke C. (Am)	08.54	54	2	-	0
EARLE, Robert G. (Robbie)						
Newcastle-u-Lyme, 27 January, 1965						(M)
Port Vale	Jnrs	07.82	82-90	284	10	77
Wimbledon	Tr	07.91	91	40	0	14
EARLE, Stephen J.						
Feltham, 1 November, 1945						(F)
Fulham	App	11.63	63-73	285	6	98
Leicester C.	Tr	11.73	73-77	91	8	20
Peterborough U.	L	11.77	77	1	0	0
EARLES, Patrick J.						
Titchfield (Hants), 22 March, 1955 E Sch						(F)
Southampton	App	11.72	74-76	4	8	1
Reading	Tr	01.77	76-82	240	7	68

Steve Earle (Fulham & Leicester City)

EARLS, Michael M.
Limerick (Ire), 25 March, 1954 (CD)

League Club	Source	Date Signed	Seasons Played	Apps	Subs	Gls
Southampton	App	03.72	73-74	8	0	0
Aldershot	Tr	06.75	75-78	68	5	0

EARLY, Michael
Dumbarton, 4 April, 1928 (OR)

League Club	Source	Date Signed	Seasons Played	Apps	Subs	Gls
Watford	Strathleven	06.46	46	5	-	1

EARNSHAW, Robert I.
Rotherham, 15 March, 1943 (OR)

League Club	Source	Date Signed	Seasons Played	Apps	Subs	Gls
Barnsley	Jnrs	06.62	62-72	220	6	34

EASDALE, John
Dumbarton, 16 January, 1919 (CH)

League Club	Source	Date Signed	Seasons Played	Apps	Subs	Gls
Liverpool		02.37	46	2	-	0
Stockport Co.	Tr	09.48	48	6	-	0

EAST, Keith M. G.
Southampton, 31 October, 1944 (CF)

League Club	Source	Date Signed	Seasons Played	Apps	Subs	Gls
Portsmouth	App	06.63				
Swindon T.	Tr	05.64	64-66	43	2	21
Stockport Co.	Tr	12.66	66-67	23	2	7
Bournemouth	Tr	11.67	67-69	93	1	34
Northampton T.	Tr	07.70	70	26	3	7
Crewe Alex.	Tr	07.71	71	32	2	8

EASTER, Graham P.
Epsom, 26 September, 1969 (W)

League Club	Source	Date Signed	Seasons Played	Apps	Subs	Gls
West Bromwich A.	YT	07.88				
Huddersfield T.	Tr	03.89				
Crewe Alex.	Tr	07.89	89	0	3	0
Preston N.E. (N/C)		10.90	90	1	0	0

EASTHAM, Brian
Bolton, 26 April, 1937 (FB)

League Club	Source	Date Signed	Seasons Played	Apps	Subs	Gls
Bury		09.58	58-66	188	1	3
Rochdale	Toronto (Can)	07.67	67	13	0	0

EASTHAM, George E.
Blackpool, 23 September, 1936 Eu23-6/EF Lge/E-19 (IF)

League Club	Source	Date Signed	Seasons Played	Apps	Subs	Gls
Newcastle U.	Ards	05.56	56-59	124	-	29
Arsenal	Tr	10.60	60-65	207	0	41
Stoke C.	Tr	08.66	66-73	184	10	4

EASTHAM, George R.
Blackpool, 13 September, 1914 E-1 (IF)

League Club	Source	Date Signed	Seasons Played	Apps	Subs	Gls
Bolton W.	Southshore Wed.	08.32	32-36	114	-	16
Brentford	Tr	05.37	37-38	49	-	1
Blackpool	Tr	11.38	38-46	45	-	9
Swansea C.	Tr	08.47	47	15	-	0
Rochdale	Tr	06.48	48	2	-	0
Lincoln C.	Tr	01.49	48-49	27	-	1

EASTHAM, Henry
Blackpool, 30 June, 1917 (IF)

League Club	Source	Date Signed	Seasons Played	Apps	Subs	Gls
Blackpool	Jnrs	06.34				
Liverpool	Tr	02.36	36-46	63	-	3
Tranmere Rov.	Tr	05.48	48-52	154	-	13
Accrington St.	Tr	07.53	53	42	-	3

EASTHAM, Stanley
Bolton, 26 November, 1913 E Amat (IF)

League Club	Source	Date Signed	Seasons Played	Apps	Subs	Gls
Liverpool		05.38				
Exeter C.	Tr	04.46				
Stockport Co.	Tr	06.46	46	14	-	1

EASTHOPE, Joseph D.
Liverpool, 26 September, 1929 (OL)

League Club	Source	Date Signed	Seasons Played	Apps	Subs	Gls
Everton		04.50	52	2	-	0
Stockport Co.	Tr	06.54	54	9	-	2

EASTMAN, Donald J.
Eastry, 9 August, 1923 (FB)

League Club	Source	Date Signed	Seasons Played	Apps	Subs	Gls
Crystal Palace (Am)	Jnrs	08.46	46	1	-	0

EASTOE, Peter R.
Tamworth, 2 August, 1953 E Yth (F)

League Club	Source	Date Signed	Seasons Played	Apps	Subs	Gls
Wolverhampton W.	App	06.71	71-73	4	2	0
Swindon T.	Tr	11.73	73-75	91	0	43
Queens Park R.	Tr	03.76	76-78	69	3	15
Everton	Tr	03.79	78-81	88	7	26
West Bromwich A.	Tr	08.82	82	30	1	8
Leicester C.	L	10.83	83	5	0	1
Huddersfield T.	L	03.84	83	8	2	0
Walsall	L	08.84	84	6	0	1
Leicester C.	L	10.84	84	6	0	1
Wolverhampton W.	L	02.85	84	8	0	0

EASTON, Harold M. B.
Shoreham, 12 September, 1938 (F)

League Club	Source	Date Signed	Seasons Played	Apps	Subs	Gls
Crystal Palace	Jnrs	11.56	59-61	8	-	1

EASTWAY, Raymond J.
Croydon, 12 April, 1929 (CH)

League Club	Source	Date Signed	Seasons Played	Apps	Subs	Gls
Watford		08.49	51	12	-	0

EASTWOOD, Eric
Heywood, 24 March, 1916 (CH)

League Club	Source	Date Signed	Seasons Played	Apps	Subs	Gls
Manchester C.	Heywood St James	04.35	38-46	16	-	0
Port Vale	Tr	03.47	46-48	28	-	1

EASTWOOD, Raymond
Manchester, 1 January, 1913 (FB)

League Club	Source	Date Signed	Seasons Played	Apps	Subs	Gls
Aldershot	Altrincham	06.38	38	9	-	0
Accrington St.	Tr	07.46	46	3	-	0

EATON, Jason C.
Bristol, 29 January, 1969 (F)

League Club	Source	Date Signed	Seasons Played	Apps	Subs	Gls
Bristol Rov.	Jnrs	06.87	87	0	3	0
Bristol C.	Clevedon	03.89	88-89	6	7	1

EATON, Joseph D.
Cuckney, 16 May, 1931 (IF)

League Club	Source	Date Signed	Seasons Played	Apps	Subs	Gls
Mansfield T.	Langwith B.C.	08.51	52-53	4	-	1

EATON, Stephen P.
Liverpool, 25 December, 1959 (FB)

League Club	Source	Date Signed	Seasons Played	Apps	Subs	Gls
Tranmere Rov.	Jnrs	06.77	78	1	0	0

EAVES, David M. C.
Blackpool, 13 February, 1973 (M)

League Club	Source	Date Signed	Seasons Played	Apps	Subs	Gls
Preston N.E.	YT	07.91	90	1	2	0

EAVES, Ernest
Bryn, 4 January, 1927 (CF)

League Club	Source	Date Signed	Seasons Played	Apps	Subs	Gls
New Brighton	Newton-le-Willows	10.48	48-50	14	-	3

EBANKS, M. Wayne A.
Birmingham, 2 October, 1964 (D)

League Club	Source	Date Signed	Seasons Played	Apps	Subs	Gls
West Bromwich A.	App	04.82	83	6	1	0
Stoke C.	L	08.84	84	10	0	0
Port Vale	Tr	03.85	84-86	36	3	0
Cambridge U. (N/C)	Tr	08.87	87	3	1	0

EBBRELL, John K.
Bromborough, 1 October, 1969 E Sch/E Yth/Eu21-14/E'B' (M)

League Club	Source	Date Signed	Seasons Played	Apps	Subs	Gls
Everton	YT	11.86	88-91	87	9	4

EBDON, Marc
Pontypool, 17 October, 1970 W Yth/Wu21-2 (M)

League Club	Source	Date Signed	Seasons Played	Apps	Subs	Gls
Everton	YT	07.89				
Peterborough U.	Tr	07.91	91	12	3	2

EBDON, Richard
Ottery St Mary, 3 May, 1913 Died 1987 (CF)

League Club	Source	Date Signed	Seasons Played	Apps	Subs	Gls
Exeter C.	Ottery St Mary	12.35	35-47	138	-	50
Torquay U.	Tr	07.48	48	5	-	1

ECCLES, Peter
Dublin, 24 August, 1962 IR-1 (CD)

League Club	Source	Date Signed	Seasons Played	Apps	Subs	Gls
Leicester C.	Dundalk	10.88	88	1	0	0

ECCLES, Terence S.
Leeds, 2 March, 1952 (CF)

League Club	Source	Date Signed	Seasons Played	Apps	Subs	Gls
Blackburn Rov.	App	08.69	69-72	33	13	6
Mansfield T.	Tr	07.73	73-76	115	3	47
Huddersfield T.	Tr	01.77	76-77	41	5	6
York C.	Ethnikos (Gre)	09.79	79-80	64	0	18

ECCLESHARE, Keith
Bolton, 14 December, 1950 E Yth (FB)

League Club	Source	Date Signed	Seasons Played	Apps	Subs	Gls
Bury	App	12.68	68-71	79	3	0

ECCLESTON, Stuart I.
Stoke, 4 October, 1961 (CD)

League Club	Source	Date Signed	Seasons Played	Apps	Subs	Gls
Stoke C.	App	10.79				
Hull C.	Tr	01.81	80-81	22	1	0
Port Vale	Tr	10.82				

ECKERSALL, Michael W.
Bury, 3 February, 1939 (WH)

League Club	Source	Date Signed	Seasons Played	Apps	Subs	Gls
Torquay U.	Mossley	10.59	60-62	28	-	2
Stockport Co.	Tr	07.63	63-65	39	1	2

ECKERSLEY, William
Southport, 16 July, 1926 Died 1982 EF Lge/E'B'-3/E-17 (FB)

League Club	Source	Date Signed	Seasons Played	Apps	Subs	Gls
Blackburn Rov.	High Park	03.48	47-60	406	-	20

ECKHARDT, Jeffrey E.
Sheffield, 7 October, 1965 (CD)

League Club	Source	Date Signed	Seasons Played	Apps	Subs	Gls
Sheffield U.	Jnrs	08.84	84-87	73	1	2
Fulham	Tr	11.87	87-91	182	2	14

ECONOMOU, Jon
Holloway, 25 October, 1961 (M)

League Club	Source	Date Signed	Seasons Played	Apps	Subs	Gls
Bristol C.	App	10.79	81-83	62	3	3

EDDOLLS, John D.
Bristol, 19 August, 1919 (G)

League Club	Source	Date Signed	Seasons Played	Apps	Subs	Gls
Bristol C.	Peasedown	09.45	46	6	-	0
Bristol Rov.	Tr	08.48				

EDDS, Ernest F.
Plymouth, 19 March, 1926 (F)

League Club	Source	Date Signed	Seasons Played	Apps	Subs	Gls
Plymouth Arg.	Portsmouth (Am)	10.46	46-49	59	-	18
Blackburn Rov.	Tr	12.49	49-50	18	-	3
Torquay U.	Tr	06.51	51-53	84	-	34
Plymouth Arg.	Tr	10.53	53-54	26	-	4
Swindon T.	Tr	07.55	55	3	-	0

EDDY, Keith
Barrow, 3 September, 1944 (M)

League Club	Source	Date Signed	Seasons Played	Apps	Subs	Gls
Barrow	Holker C.O.B.	06.62	62-65	127	1	5
Watford	Tr	07.66	66-71	239	1	26
Sheffield U.	Tr	08.72	72-75	113	1	16

EDELSTON, Maurice
Hull, 27 April, 1918 Died 1976 E Amat (CF)

League Club	Source	Date Signed	Seasons Played	Apps	Subs	Gls
Fulham (Am)	Jnrs	07.35	35-37	4	-	0
Brentford (Am)	Tr	12.37	37-38	21	-	6
Reading	Tr	05.39	46-51	202	-	70
Northampton T.	Tr	07.52	52-53	39	-	17

Maurice Edelston (Fulham, Brentford, Reading & Northampton Town)

EDEN, Alan
Sunderland, 8 October, 1958 (M)

League Club	Source	Date Signed	Seasons Played	Apps	Subs	Gls
Lincoln C.	Lambton Street B.C.	08.77	77-78	5	2	0

EDEN, Anthony F.
Birmingham, 15 March, 1941 (CH)

League Club	Source	Date Signed	Seasons Played	Apps	Subs	Gls
Aston Villa	Jnrs	04.58				
Walsall	Tr	07.60	60-62	14	-	0

EDGAR, Edward (Ted)
Bristol, 31 October, 1956 (G)

League Club	Source	Date Signed	Seasons Played	Apps	Subs	Gls
Newcastle U.	App	08.74				
Hartlepool U.	Tr	07.76	76-78	75	0	0

EDGAR, John
Barnsley, 9 April, 1936 (IF)

League Club	Source	Date Signed	Seasons Played	Apps	Subs	Gls
Barnsley	Jnrs	05.54	55-57	22	-	6
Gillingham	Tr	06.58	58	45	-	23
York C.	Tr	06.59	59-60	47	-	16
Hartlepool U.	Tr	06.61	61-62	72	-	31
Exeter C.	Tr	07.63	63	6	-	0

EDGAR, John D.
Aldershot, 1 December, 1930 (IF)

League Club	Source	Date Signed	Seasons Played	Apps	Subs	Gls
Darlington	Ferryhill Ath.	12.54	54-55	12	-	0

EDGE, Anthony
Wirral, 14 March, 1937 (CF)

League Club	Source	Date Signed	Seasons Played	Apps	Subs	Gls
Bristol Rov.	Devizes	08.59	59-60	13	-	4

EDGE, Declan J.
Malaysia, 18 September, 1965 NZ Int (F)

League Club	Source	Date Signed	Seasons Played	Apps	Subs	Gls
Notts Co.	Gisborne C. (NZ)	12.85	85	7	3	2

EDGE, Derek
Stoke, 14 February, 1942 (OR)

League Club	Source	Date Signed	Seasons Played	Apps	Subs	Gls
Port Vale	Stoke C. (Am)	09.60	61	2	-	0

EDGLEY, Brian K.
Shrewsbury, 26 August, 1937 (IF)

League Club	Source	Date Signed	Seasons Played	Apps	Subs	Gls
Shrewsbury T.	Jnrs	02.56	55-59	113	-	12
Cardiff C.	Tr	07.60	60	10	-	1
Brentford	Tr	06.61	61-62	31	-	9
Barnsley	Tr	11.62	62	4	-	0

EDINBURGH, Justin C.
Brentwood, 18 December, 1969 (LB)

League Club	Source	Date Signed	Seasons Played	Apps	Subs	Gls
Southend U.	YT	07.88	88-89	36	1	0
Tottenham H.	Tr	07.90	90-91	36	3	1

EDISBURY, William
Tyldesley, 12 November, 1937 (FB)

League Club	Source	Date Signed	Seasons Played	Apps	Subs	Gls
Bolton W.	Jnrs	10.56	56-57	2	-	0

EDMONDS, Darren
Watford, 12 April, 1971 (LW)

League Club	Source	Date Signed	Seasons Played	Apps	Subs	Gls
Leeds U.	YT	05.89				
Ipswich T.	Tr	09.91	91	0	2	0

EDMONDS, Derek J.
Luton, 9 October, 1950 E Yth (G)

League Club	Source	Date Signed	Seasons Played	Apps	Subs	Gls
Leeds U.	App	11.67				
Watford	Tr	05.70	70-71	15	0	0
Southport	South Africa	07.74	74	2	0	0

EDMONDS, Neil A.
Accrington, 18 October, 1968 (W)

League Club	Source	Date Signed	Seasons Played	Apps	Subs	Gls
Oldham Ath.	YT	06.86	86-87	3	2	0
Rochdale	Tr	09.88	88-89	36	7	8

EDMONDSON, D. Barry
Southport, 10 February, 1943 (WH)

League Club	Source	Date Signed	Seasons Played	Apps	Subs	Gls
Southport	Blackpool (Am)	12.61	61	1	-	0

EDMONDSON, Darren S.
Coniston, 4 November, 1971 (CD)

League Club	Source	Date Signed	Seasons Played	Apps	Subs	Gls
Carlisle U.	YT	07.90	90-91	56	2	2

EDMONDSON, Stanley G.
Bacup, 10 August, 1922 Died 1977 (OR)

League Club	Source	Date Signed	Seasons Played	Apps	Subs	Gls
Bradford C. (Am)	Bacup	05.46	46	3	-	0

EDMUNDS, Paul
Doncaster, 2 December, 1957 (W)

League Club	Source	Date Signed	Seasons Played	Apps	Subs	Gls
Leicester C.	Troston W.	04.79	79-80	8	0	2
Bournemouth	Tr	07.81	81	13	1	2

League Club	Source	Date Signed	Seasons Played	Career Record Apps	Subs	Gls

EDMUNDS, Redvern E.
Newport, 10 January, 1943 W Sch (OL)

Portsmouth	Jnrs	06.60	60	5	-	0
Newport Co.	Tr	07.61	61	4	-	0

EDWARDS, Alistair M.
Australia, 21 June, 1968 (F)

Brighton & H.A. (N/C)	Sydney Olympic (Aus)	11.89	89	1	0	0

EDWARDS, Andrew D.
Epping, 17 September, 1971 (D)

Southend U.	YT	12.89	88-91	17	3	1

EDWARDS, Andrew J.
Wrexham, 28 March, 1965 W Yth (W)

Wrexham	Jnrs	08.83	82-85	89	25	27

EDWARDS, Brian A.
Portsmouth, 6 October, 1930 (FB)

Portsmouth	Jnrs	10.48	51	1	-	0

EDWARDS, G. Bryan
Leeds, 27 October, 1930 (WH)

Bolton W.	Jnrs	10.47	50-64	482	-	8

EDWARDS, Clifford
Carmarthen, 4 December, 1928 (G)

Swansea C.		10.51	52	1	-	0

EDWARDS, Clifford L.
Cannock, 8 March, 1921 Died 1989 (WH)

West Bromwich A.	Cannock T.	10.38	46-47	40	-	1
Bristol C.	Tr	06.48	48-49	33	-	3

EDWARDS, David A.
(F)

Wrexham (Am)		11.49	49	1	-	1

EDWARDS, David J.
Treharris, 10 December, 1934 (WH)

Fulham	Treharris	05.52	56-63	38	-	0

EDWARDS, David J.
Bridgnorth, 13 January, 1974 (M)

Walsall	YT	01.92	91	13	9	1

EDWARDS, David S.
Bargoed, 11 September, 1916 (OL)

Newport Co.	Deri	09.37	37	1	-	0
Ipswich T.	Gloucester C.	06.39				
Swindon T.	Tr	06.46	46	3	-	1

EDWARDS, Dean S.
Wolverhampton, 25 February, 1962 (F)

Shrewsbury T.	App	02.80	79-81	7	6	1
Wolverhampton W.	Telford U.	10.85	85-86	28	3	9
Exeter C.	Tr	03.87	86-87	51	3	17
Torquay U.	Tr	08.88	88-91	98	18	26
Exeter C.	Tr	12.91	91	4	0	0
Northampton T. (N/C)	Tr	02.92	91	7	0	0

EDWARDS, Dennis
Slough, 19 January, 1937 E Amat (CF)

Charlton Ath.	Wycombe W.	02.59	58-64	171	-	61
Portsmouth	Tr	01.65	64-67	69	2	14
Brentford	L	09.67	67	11	0	2
Aldershot	Tr	12.67	67	11	3	1

EDWARDS, Donald
Wrexham, 2 August, 1930 (G)

Norwich C.	Wrexham Vic.	09.47	47	2	-	0

EDWARDS, Duncan
Dudley, 1 October, 1936 Died 1958 E Sch/E Yth/Eu23-6/E'B'-4/EF Lge/E-18 (WH)

Manchester U.	Jnrs	10.53	52-57	151	-	20

EDWARDS, Edward
Seaham, 13 February, 1936 (FB)

Hartlepool U.		02.57	57	1	-	0

EDWARDS, J. Elfyn
Aberystwyth, 4 May, 1960 (CD)

Wrexham	Jnrs	07.78				
Tranmere Rov.	Tr	07.79	79-80	62	0	1

EDWARDS, George
Treherbert, 2 December, 1920 W Amat/W-12 (OL)

Swansea C. (Am)	Jnrs	05.38	38	2	-	0
Birmingham C.	Tr	07.44	46-48	84	-	9
Cardiff C.	Tr	12.48	48-54	194	-	34

EDWARDS, George R.
Great Yarmouth, 1 April, 1918 (F)

Norwich C.	Yarmouth Caledonians	04.36	35-37	9	-	1
Aston Villa	Tr	06.38	38-50	138	-	34

EDWARDS, J. Gordon
Wrexham, 14 October, 1935 W Sch (CH)

Bolton W.	Jnrs	10.52	58	3	-	0

EDWARDS, Henry P.
Wigan, 13 February, 1932 (IF)

Blackpool		06.51				
Southport	Tr	08.53	54	1	-	0

EDWARDS, Howard
Tipton, 2 June, 1919 (HB)

Derby Co.	Stourbridge	01.47				
Crewe Alex.	Tr	06.52	52	5	-	0

EDWARDS, Ian R.
Wrexham, 30 January, 1955 Wu21-2/W-4

West Bromwich A.	Rhyl	02.73	74-76	13	3	3
Chester C.	Tr	11.76	76-79	104	0	36
Wrexham	Tr	11.79	79-81	71	4	20
Crystal Palace	Tr	07.82	82	16	2	4

EDWARDS, John (Jack)
Manchester, 23 February, 1924 Died 1978 (IF)

Nottingham F.	Long Eaton U.	05.44	46-48	77	-	20
Southampton	Tr	06.49	49-51	82	-	16
Notts Co.	Tr	11.52	52-53	25	-	3

EDWARDS, John
Wrexham, 23 May, 1940 (G)

Wrexham (Am)	Bradley Sports	10.65	65	1	0	0

EDWARDS, John F. (Jack)
Wath-on-Dearne, 27 December, 1921 (WH)

Rotherham U.	Manvers Main Colly	09.44	46-53	296	-	9

EDWARDS, John W. (Jack)
Risca, 6 July, 1929 (FB)

Crystal Palace	Lovells Ath.	09.49	49-58	223	-	0
Rochdale	Tr	06.59	59-60	68	-	1

EDWARDS, Keith
Stockton, 16 July, 1957 (F)

Sheffield U.	Jnrs	08.75	75-77	64	6	29
Hull C.	Tr	08.78	78-81	130	2	57
Sheffield U.	Tr	09.81	81-85	183	8	114
Leeds U.	Tr	08.86	86-87	28	10	6
Hull C.	Aberdeen	03.88	87-89	55	0	29
Stockport C.	Tr	09.89	89	26	1	10
Huddersfield T.	L	03.90	89	6	4	4
Huddersfield T.	Tr	08.90	90	10	8	4
Plymouth Arg.	L	12.90	90	3	0	1

EDWARDS, Keith B.
Chester, 10 June, 1944 (CF)

Chester C. (Am)		03.66	65-66	3	0	0

EDWARDS, M. Keith
Neath, 26 September, 1952 W Sch (CD)

Leeds U.	App	10.69	71	0	1	0

EDWARDS, Leonard O.
Wrexham, 30 May, 1930 (WH)

Sheffield Wed.	Wrexham (Am)	01.51	51	2	-	0
Brighton & H. A.	Tr	03.54	54	6	-	0
Crewe Alex.	Tr	12.55	55-56	40	-	0

EDWARDS, Leslie R.
Guildford, 12 April, 1924 (LB)

Bristol Rov.	Nailsea U.	05.48	50-56	47	-	0

EDWARDS, Levi W.
St Lucia (WI), 10 September, 1961 (M)

Crewe Alex.	Ashton U.	08.85	85	10	3	0
Stockport Co.	Altrincham	09.86	86-87	40	9	5

League Club	Source	Date Signed	Seasons Played	Apps	Subs	Gls

EDWARDS, Malcolm
Wrexham, 25 October, 1939 W Sch/Wu23-2 (LB)

League Club	Source	Date Signed	Seasons Played	Apps	Subs	Gls
Bolton W.	Jnrs	11.56	56-60	14	-	1
Chester C.	Tr	02.61	60-61	43	-	5
Tranmere Rov.	Tr	07.62	62-63	34	-	2
Barrow	Tr	07.64	64-68	177	0	9

EDWARDS, Matthew D.
Hammersmith, 15 June, 1971 (M)

League Club	Source	Date Signed	Seasons Played	Apps	Subs	Gls
Tottenham H.	YT	07.89				
Reading	L	03.91	90	6	2	0

EDWARDS, Neil A.
Rowley Regis, 14 March, 1966 (M)

League Club	Source	Date Signed	Seasons Played	Apps	Subs	Gls
Wolverhampton W.	Oldswinford	08.85	85-87	26	3	7

EDWARDS, Neil R.
Liverpool, 2 July, 1967 (F)

League Club	Source	Date Signed	Seasons Played	Apps	Subs	Gls
Burnley	Liverpool (App)	08.85	85	0	1	0

EDWARDS, Neil R.
Aberdare, 5 December, 1970 (G)

League Club	Source	Date Signed	Seasons Played	Apps	Subs	Gls
Leeds U.	YT	03.89				
Stockport Co.	Tr	09.91	91	39	0	0

EDWARDS, Nigel
Wrexham, 31 December, 1950 Wu23-3 (FB)

League Club	Source	Date Signed	Seasons Played	Apps	Subs	Gls
Chester C.	Blackburn Rov. (Am)	09.68	68-77	281	8	15
Aldershot	Tr	07.78	78-81	137	0	6
Chester C.	Tr	06.82	82	8	0	1

EDWARDS, Patrick K.
Wolverhampton, 9 December, 1939 (F)

League Club	Source	Date Signed	Seasons Played	Apps	Subs	Gls
Walsall	Jnrs	10.57	58	1	-	0
Chesterfield	Tr	07.59				

EDWARDS, Paul
Liverpool, 22 February, 1965 (G)

League Club	Source	Date Signed	Seasons Played	Apps	Subs	Gls
Crewe Alex.	Leek T.	02.89	88-91	29	0	0

EDWARDS, Paul F.
Crompton, 7 October, 1947 Eu23-3/EF Lge (CD)

League Club	Source	Date Signed	Seasons Played	Apps	Subs	Gls
Manchester U.	Jnrs	02.65	69-72	52	2	0
Oldham Ath.	Tr	09.72	72-77	108	4	7
Stockport Co.	L	01.77	76	2	0	0
Stockport Co.	Tr	08.78	78-79	64	3	2

EDWARDS, Paul R.
Birkenhead, 25 December, 1963 (LB)

League Club	Source	Date Signed	Seasons Played	Apps	Subs	Gls
Crewe Alex.	Altrincham	01.88	87-89	82	4	6
Coventry C.	Tr	03.90	89-91	32	4	0

EDWARDS, Reginald E.
Rugeley, 28 January, 1953 (G)

League Club	Source	Date Signed	Seasons Played	Apps	Subs	Gls
Port Vale	Nuneaton Bor.	08.72	72-74	8	0	0

EDWARDS, Reginald C.
Newton-le-Willows, 24 July, 1919 (OL)

League Club	Source	Date Signed	Seasons Played	Apps	Subs	Gls
Luton T.	Alloa Ath.	11.45				
Accrington St.	Tr	08.46	46-48	66	-	10

EDWARDS, Richard
Hartlepool, 9 November, 1964 (G)

League Club	Source	Date Signed	Seasons Played	Apps	Subs	Gls
Hartlepool U. (N/C)		08.86	86	1	0	0

EDWARDS, Richard L.
Kingsbury, 5 November, 1943 (FB)

League Club	Source	Date Signed	Seasons Played	Apps	Subs	Gls
Luton T.	Admult	06.64	64-65	15	2	1

EDWARDS, Richard T.
Kirkby-in-Ashfield, 20 November, 1942 (D)

League Club	Source	Date Signed	Seasons Played	Apps	Subs	Gls
Notts Co.	Jnrs	10.59	59-66	219	0	18
Mansfield T.	Tr	03.67	66-67	45	0	1
Aston Villa	Tr	03.68	67-69	68	0	2
Torquay U.	Tr	06.70	70-72	99	3	5
Mansfield T.	Tr	07.73	73	31	2	1

EDWARDS, Robert
Manchester, 23 February, 1970 (F)

League Club	Source	Date Signed	Seasons Played	Apps	Subs	Gls
Crewe Alex.	YT	07.88	87-91	48	23	18

EDWARDS, Robert H.
Guildford, 22 May, 1931 (IF)

League Club	Source	Date Signed	Seasons Played	Apps	Subs	Gls
Chelsea	Woking	11.51	52-54	13	-	2
Swindon T.	Tr	07.55	55-59	173	-	65
Norwich C.	Tr	12.59	59	1	-	0
Northampton T.	Tr	03.61	60-61	23	-	10

EDWARDS, Robert W.
Cockermouth, 1 July, 1972 W Yth/Wu21-2 (M)

League Club	Source	Date Signed	Seasons Played	Apps	Subs	Gls
Carlisle U.	YT	04.40	89-90	48	0	5
Bristol C.	Tr	03.91	91	12	8	1

EDWARDS, Ronald
Liverpool, 11 July, 1927 (IF)

League Club	Source	Date Signed	Seasons Played	Apps	Subs	Gls
Chesterfield	South Liverpool	07.53	53	13	-	2

EDWARDS, Roy
Sheffield, 26 November, 1920

League Club	Source	Date Signed	Seasons Played	Apps	Subs	Gls
Lincoln C.		06.47	47-48	6	-	0

EDWARDS, Stanley
West Bromwich, 11 December, 1942 (OL)

League Club	Source	Date Signed	Seasons Played	Apps	Subs	Gls
Everton	Jnrs	12.59				
Port Vale	Tr	05.61	61-62	49	-	9

EDWARDS, Stanley L.
Dawdon, 17 October, 1926 Died 1989 (CF)

League Club	Source	Date Signed	Seasons Played	Apps	Subs	Gls
Chelsea	Horden Colly	10.49				
Colchester U.	Tr	06.52	52	16	-	5
Leyton Orient	Tr	06.53	53	2	-	1

EDWARDS, Stephen G.
Birkenhead, 11 January, 1958 (D)

League Club	Source	Date Signed	Seasons Played	Apps	Subs	Gls
Oldham Ath.	App	01.76	77-82	77	3	0
Crewe Alex.	Tr	02.83	82-83	57	1	1
Rochdale	Tr	07.84	84	4	0	0
Tranmere Rov.	Tr	10.84	84-86	72	0	6

EDWARDS, W. Thomas
Llanelli, 13 March, 1923 (OL)

League Club	Source	Date Signed	Seasons Played	Apps	Subs	Gls
Fulham	Workington	08.46	47	2	-	0
Southend U.	Tr	03.48	47-48	11	-	1
Leicester C.	Tr	12.48	48	3	-	1
Walsall	Bath C.	05.52	52	12	-	0

EDWARDS, L. Trevor
Rhondda, 24 January, 1937 Wu23-2/W-2 (FB)

League Club	Source	Date Signed	Seasons Played	Apps	Subs	Gls
Charlton Ath.	Jnrs	05.55	56-59	64	-	0
Cardiff C.	Tr	06.60	60-63	73	-	3

EDWARDS, Walter
Mansfield, 26 June, 1924 (W)

League Club	Source	Date Signed	Seasons Played	Apps	Subs	Gls
Mansfield T.	Woodhouse	11.47	47-48	25	-	5
Leeds U.	Tr	03.49	48	2	-	0
Leicester C.	Tr	08.49				

EDWARDS, William
Paddington, 8 January, 1952 (D)

League Club	Source	Date Signed	Seasons Played	Apps	Subs	Gls
Wimbledon	Walton & Hersham	08.74	77	21	0	2

EDWARDS, William I.
Bowburn (Dm), 10 December, 1933 (CF)

League Club	Source	Date Signed	Seasons Played	Apps	Subs	Gls
Middlesbrough	Bowburn	03.52	52-54	16	-	4

EDWARDSON, Barry J.
Hindley, 4 November, 1972 (M)

League Club	Source	Date Signed	Seasons Played	Apps	Subs	Gls
Wigan Ath.	YT	07.91	91	0	1	0

EDWARDSON, John P.
Manchester, 9 March, 1944 (HB)

League Club	Source	Date Signed	Seasons Played	Apps	Subs	Gls
Crystal Palace	Bethesda	11.66				
Crewe Alex.	L	01.68	67	1	0	0

EDWORTHY, Marc
Barnstaple, 24 December, 1972 (M)

League Club	Source	Date Signed	Seasons Played	Apps	Subs	Gls
Plymouth Arg.	YT	03.91	91	7	8	0

EELES, Anthony G.
Chatham, 15 November, 1970 (M)

League Club	Source	Date Signed	Seasons Played	Apps	Subs	Gls
Gillingham	YT	07.89	88-91	42	17	3

EGAN, Christopher A.
Dublin, 6 August, 1953 (OL)

League Club	Source	Date Signed	Seasons Played	Apps	Subs	Gls
Derby Co.	Cork Celtic	10.73				
Newport Co.	Tr	08.76	76	5	2	0

EGAN, John
Kilsyth, 19 August, 1937 (W)

League Club	Source	Date Signed	Seasons Played	Apps	Subs	Gls
Halifax T.	Stenhousemuir	10.59	59	5	-	0
Accrington St.	Tr	08.60	60	1	-	0

EGDELL, Ernest
Newcastle, 29 May, 1922 (CH)

League Club	Source	Date Signed	Seasons Played	Apps	Subs	Gls
Darlington (Am)	Consett	08.46	46	1	-	0

EGERTON, Frank
Atherton, 5 April, 1926 (FB)

League Club	Source	Date Signed	Seasons Played	Apps	Subs	Gls
Blackburn Rov.	Atherton Colly	04.44				
Accrington St.	Tr	06.47	47-48	8	-	0

EGGLESTONE, Patrick
Penrith, 17 March, 1927 (G)

League Club	Source	Date Signed	Seasons Played	Apps	Subs	Gls
Bradford C. (Am)	Portsmouth (Am)	05.48	48	2	-	0
Halifax T.	Tr	09.49	49	20	-	0
Shrewsbury T.	Tr	08.50	50-52	109	-	0
Wrexham	Tr	02.53	52-55	84	-	0

EGGLESTON, Thomas
Mitcham, 21 February, 1920 (LH)

League Club	Source	Date Signed	Seasons Played	Apps	Subs	Gls
Derby Co.	Jnrs	02.37				
Leicester C.	Tr	08.46	46-47	34	-	2
Watford	Tr	02.48	47-52	177	-	6

EGLINGTON, Thomas J.
Dublin, 15 January, 1923 IR-24/NI-6 (OL)

League Club	Source	Date Signed	Seasons Played	Apps	Subs	Gls
Everton	Shamrock Rov.	07.46	46-56	394	-	76
Tranmere Rov.	Tr	06.57	57-60	172	-	36

EHIOGU, Ugochuku
Hackney, 3 November, 1972 Eu21-4 (CD)

League Club	Source	Date Signed	Seasons Played	Apps	Subs	Gls
West Bromwich A. (YT)	YT	07.89	90	0	2	0
Aston Villa	Tr	07.91	91	4	4	0

Ugo Ehiogu (West Bromwich Albion & Aston Villa)

EISENTRAGER, Alois (Alec)
Germany, 20 July, 1927 (IF)

League Club	Source	Date Signed	Seasons Played	Apps	Subs	Gls
Bristol C.	Trowbridge T.	01.50	49-57	229	-	47

EKNER, Daniel H.
Sweden, 5 February, 1927 Died 1975 (CF)

League Club	Source	Date Signed	Seasons Played	Apps	Subs	Gls
Portsmouth (Am)	Sweden	11.49	49	5	-	0

EKOKU, Efan
Manchester, 7 June, 1967 (F)

League Club	Source	Date Signed	Seasons Played	Apps	Subs	Gls
Bournemouth	Sutton U.	05.90	90-91	29	19	14

ELDER, Alexander
Perth, 11 September, 1923 (IF)

League Club	Source	Date Signed	Seasons Played	Apps	Subs	Gls
Hartlepool U.	Dundee U.	08.51	51-52	65	-	19

ELDER, Alexander R.
Lisburn (NI), 25 April, 1941 NI Sch/NIu23-1/NI-40 (LB)

League Club	Source	Date Signed	Seasons Played	Apps	Subs	Gls
Burnley	Glentoran	01.59	59-66	271	0	15
Stoke C.	Tr	08.67	67-72	80	3	1

ELDER, James
Perth, 5 March, 1928 (WH)

League Club	Source	Date Signed	Seasons Played	Apps	Subs	Gls
Portsmouth	Jeanfield Swifts	09.45	49	1	-	0
Colchester U.	Tr	07.50	50-54	199	-	15

ELEY, Kevin
Mexborough, 4 March, 1968 (W)

League Club	Source	Date Signed	Seasons Played	Apps	Subs	Gls
Rotherham U.	App	03.86	83-86	3	10	0
Chesterfield	Tr	08.87	87-89	72	9	2

ELGIN, Robert B.
Edinburgh, 23 June, 1949 (M)

League Club	Source	Date Signed	Seasons Played	Apps	Subs	Gls
Stockport Co.	Hearts	07.69	69-70	30	4	3

ELI, Roger
Bradford, 11 September, 1965 (W)

League Club	Source	Date Signed	Seasons Played	Apps	Subs	Gls
Leeds U.	App	09.83	84-85	1	1	0
Wolverhampton W.	Tr	01.86	85-86	16	2	0
Crewe Alex (N/C)	Cambridge U. (N/C)	09.87	87	20	7	1
York C. (N/C)	Pontefract Colly	11.88	88	3	1	1
Bury	Tr	12.88	88	0	2	0
Burnley	Tr	07.89	89-91	68	20	20

ELKINS, Gary
Wallingford, 4 May, 1966 E Yth (LB)

League Club	Source	Date Signed	Seasons Played	Apps	Subs	Gls
Fulham	App	12.83	84-89	100	4	2
Exeter C.	L	12.89	89	5	0	0
Wimbledon	Tr	08.90	90-91	25	3	1

ELLAM, Roy
Hemsworth, 13 January, 1943 (CH)

League Club	Source	Date Signed	Seasons Played	Apps	Subs	Gls
Bradford C.	Jnrs	05.61	61-65	149	0	12
Huddersfield T.	Tr	01.66	66-71	206	0	8
Leeds U.	Tr	08.72	72-73	9	2	0
Huddersfield T.	Tr	07.74	74	18	0	2

ELLAWAY, William
Crediton, 12 October, 1932 (IF)

League Club	Source	Date Signed	Seasons Played	Apps	Subs	Gls
Exeter C.	Barnstaple	11.54	53-55	31	-	9
Bournemouth	Tr	06.56	56-57	4	-	0

ELLERINGTON, William
Southampton, 30 June, 1923 E Sch/EF Lge/E'B'-1/E-2 (FB)

League Club	Source	Date Signed	Seasons Played	Apps	Subs	Gls
Southampton	Fatfield Colly	09.40	46-55	227	-	10

ELLIOTT, Andrew
Ashton-u-Lyne, 21 November, 1963 (M)

League Club	Source	Date Signed	Seasons Played	Apps	Subs	Gls
Manchester C.	App	11.81	81	1	0	0
Chester C.	Sligo Rov.	09.83	83	24	8	3

ELLIOTT, Anthony R.
Nuneaton, 30 November, 1969 E Yth (G)

League Club	Source	Date Signed	Seasons Played	Apps	Subs	Gls
Birmingham C.	YT	12.86				
Hereford U.	Tr	12.88	88-91	75	0	0

ELLIOTT, Bernard H.
Beeston, 3 May, 1925 (WH)

League Club	Source	Date Signed	Seasons Played	Apps	Subs	Gls
Nottingham F.	Beeston B.C.	10.42	47-48	10	-	0
Southampton	Tr	10.49	49-57	235	-	2

ELLIOTT, Charles S.
Bolsover, 24 April, 1912 (FB)

League Club	Source	Date Signed	Seasons Played	Apps	Subs	Gls
Chesterfield	Sheffield Wed. (Am)	11.30				
Coventry C.	Tr	08.31	31-47	95	-	2

ELLIOTT, David
Tantobie, 10 February, 1945 (M)

League Club	Source	Date Signed	Seasons Played	Apps	Subs	Gls
Sunderland	App	02.62	63-66	30	1	1
Newcastle U.	Tr	12.66	66-70	78	2	4
Southend U.	Tr	02.71	70-74	173	4	10
Newport Co.	Tr	07.75	75	21	0	0
Newport Co.	Bangor C.	10.78	78	0	2	0

ELLIOTT, Eamonn G.
Belfast, 27 August, 1971 (M)

League Club	Source	Date Signed	Seasons Played	Apps	Subs	Gls
Carlisle U.	YT	07.90	90	3	1	0

ELLIOTT, Edward
Carlisle, 24 May, 1919 (G)

League Club	Source	Date Signed	Seasons Played	Apps	Subs	Gls
Carlisle U.		12.37	37-38	11	-	0
Wolverhampton W.	Tr	02.39	46-47	7	-	0
Chester C.	Tr	10.48	48-50	59	-	0
Halifax T.	Tr	11.50	50-51	33	-	0

ELLIOTT, Frank F. G.
Merthyr Tydfil, 23 July, 1929 (G)

League Club	Source	Date Signed	Seasons Played	Apps	Subs	Gls
Swansea C.	Merthyr Tydfil	09.49				
Stoke C.	Tr	12.52	52-53	22	-	0
Fulham	Tr	03.54	53-55	25	-	0
Mansfield T.	Tr	07.56	56-57	63	-	0

ELLIOTT, Harvey
Middleton, 21 January, 1922 (IF)

League Club	Source	Date Signed	Seasons Played	Apps	Subs	Gls
Hull C.		12.46	46	4	-	0

ELLIOTT, Ian
Barrow, 16 December, 1953 (G)

League Club	Source	Date Signed	Seasons Played	Apps	Subs	Gls
Barrow (Am)	Jnrs	12.70	69	1	0	0

ELLIOTT, John
Eden Valley, 6 May, 1938 (IR)

League Club	Source	Date Signed	Seasons Played	Apps	Subs	Gls
Carlisle U.	Jnrs	08.58	55-57	2	-	1

ELLIOTT, John W.
Ashington, 23 December, 1946 (OL)

League Club	Source	Date Signed	Seasons Played	Apps	Subs	Gls
Notts Co.	Ashington	08.67	67-68	61	3	7

ELLIOTT, Kevin
Chilton, 5 September, 1958 (F)

League Club	Source	Date Signed	Seasons Played	Apps	Subs	Gls
Hartlepool U.	App	09.76	75-76	24	3	1

ELLIOTT, Lee
Ormskirk, 5 May, 1970 (F)

League Club	Source	Date Signed	Seasons Played	Apps	Subs	Gls
Crewe Alex.	Everton (YT)	06.88	88	1	0	0

ELLIOTT, Mark R.
Rhondda, 20 March, 1959 (M)

League Club	Source	Date Signed	Seasons Played	Apps	Subs	Gls
Brighton & H. A.	Merthyr Tydfil	02.77	76	3	0	0
Cardiff C.	Tr	09.79	79	6	1	0
Bournemouth	L	01.80	79	4	0	0
Wimbledon (N/C)		02.82	81	7	4	1

ELLIOTT, Matthew S.
Wandsworth, 1 November, 1968 (CD)

League Club	Source	Date Signed	Seasons Played	Apps	Subs	Gls
Charlton Ath.	Epsom & Ewell	05.88				
Torquay U.	Tr	03.89	88-91	123	1	15
Scunthorpe U.	L	03.92	91	8	0	1

ELLIOTT, Paul M.
Lewisham, 18 March, 1964 E Yth/Eu21-12 (CD)

League Club	Source	Date Signed	Seasons Played	Apps	Subs	Gls
Charlton Ath.	App	03.81	81-82	61	2	1
Luton T.	Tr	03.83	82-85	63	3	4
Aston Villa	Tr	12.85	85-86	56	1	7
Chelsea	Glasgow Celtic	07.91	91	35	0	3

ELLIOTT, Raymond C.
Southampton, 11 June, 1947 (F)

League Club	Source	Date Signed	Seasons Played	Apps	Subs	Gls
Charlton Ath.	App	06.65				
Exeter C.	Tr	03.66	65-66	28	0	3

ELLIOTT, Raymond J.
Rhondda, 23 March, 1929 (OR)

League Club	Source	Date Signed	Seasons Played	Apps	Subs	Gls
Millwall	Woking	11.46	47-48	2	-	0

ELLIOTT, Robert J.
Newcastle, 25 December, 1973 (LB)

League Club	Source	Date Signed	Seasons Played	Apps	Subs	Gls
Newcastle U.	YT	04.91	90-91	14	1	0

ELLIOTT, Shaun
Haydon Bridge, 26 January, 1957 E-'B' (CD)

League Club	Source	Date Signed	Seasons Played	Apps	Subs	Gls
Sunderland	App	01.75	76-85	316	5	11
Norwich C.	Tr	08.86	86-87	29	2	2
Blackpool	Tr	08.88	88-89	66	1	0

ELLIOTT, Stephen B.
Haltwhistle, 15 September, 1958 (F)

League Club	Source	Date Signed	Seasons Played	Apps	Subs	Gls
Nottingham F.	App	09.76	78	4	0	0
Preston N.E.	Tr	03.79	78-83	202	6	70
Luton T.	Tr	07.84	84	12	0	3

League Club	Source	Date Signed	Seasons Played	Apps	Subs	Gls
Walsall	Tr	12.84	84-85	68	1	21
Bolton W.	Tr	07.86	86-88	57	3	11
Bury	Tr	09.88	88	31	0	11
Rochdale	Tr	10.89	89-90	46	6	9

ELLIOTT, William
Poole, 23 October, 1961 (M)

League Club	Source	Date Signed	Seasons Played	Apps	Subs	Gls
Plymouth Arg.	App	03.79				
Bournemouth	Tr	05.80	80	6	5	1

ELLIOTT, William B.
Workington, 6 August, 1919 Died 1966 (OR)

League Club	Source	Date Signed	Seasons Played	Apps	Subs	Gls
Carlisle U.	Jnrs	11.36				
Wolverhampton W.	Dudley T.	07.37				
Bournemouth	Tr	05.38	38	10	-	1
West Bromwich A.	Tr	12.38	38-50	170	-	39

ELLIOTT, William H.
Bradford, 20 March, 1925 EF Lge/E-5 (OL)

League Club	Source	Date Signed	Seasons Played	Apps	Subs	Gls
Bradford P.A.	Jnrs	04.42	46-50	176	-	21
Burnley	Tr	09.51	51-52	74	-	14
Sunderland	Tr	06.53	53-58	193	-	23

ELLIS, Alan
Alfreton, 17 November, 1951 (M)

League Club	Source	Date Signed	Seasons Played	Apps	Subs	Gls
Charlton Ath.	App	11.69	70-72	9	5	0

ELLIS, Anthony J.
Salford, 20 October, 1964 (F)

League Club	Source	Date Signed	Seasons Played	Apps	Subs	Gls
Oldham Ath.	Horwich R.M.I.	08.86	86-87	5	3	0
Preston N.E.	Tr	10.87	87-89	80	6	28
Stoke C.	Tr	12.89	89-91	66	11	19

ELLIS, David
(W)

League Club	Source	Date Signed	Seasons Played	Apps	Subs	Gls
Bury	Pollok Jnrs	04.47				
Halifax T.	Tr	01.48	47	3	-	0
Barrow	Tr	10.48	48	1	-	0

ELLIS, Glenn D.
Dagenham, 31 October, 1957 E Sch (G)

League Club	Source	Date Signed	Seasons Played	Apps	Subs	Gls
Ipswich T.	App	10.75				
Colchester U.	L	12.76	76	2	0	0

ELLIS, Keith D.
Sheffield, 6 November, 1935 (CF)

League Club	Source	Date Signed	Seasons Played	Apps	Subs	Gls
Sheffield Wed.	Jnrs	04.55	54-63	102	-	52
Scunthorpe U.	Tr	03.64	63	10	-	5
Cardiff C.	Tr	09.64	64	22	-	10
Lincoln C.	Tr	06.65	65	7	0	0

ELLIS, Kenneth
Buckley, 22 January, 1928 (IF)

League Club	Source	Date Signed	Seasons Played	Apps	Subs	Gls
Chester C. (Am)	Jnrs	05.46	46	1	-	0
Wrexham (Am)		05.49	49	5	-	0

ELLIS, Kenneth
Sunderland, 29 May, 1948 (D/F)

League Club	Source	Date Signed	Seasons Played	Apps	Subs	Gls
Hartlepool U.	Scarborough	07.71	71	32	2	4
Darlington	Verna (Bel)	07.79	79	21	0	0

ELLIS, Mark E.
Bradford, 6 January, 1962 (W)

League Club	Source	Date Signed	Seasons Played	Apps	Subs	Gls
Bradford C.	Trinity Ath.	08.80	80-89	190	28	30
Halifax T.	Tr	10.90	90-91	33	4	4

ELLIS, Neil J.
Chester, 30 April, 1969 (LW)

League Club	Source	Date Signed	Seasons Played	Apps	Subs	Gls
Chester C.	Bangor C.	06.90	90	13	8	1
Maidstone U.	Tr	07.91	91	22	6	0

ELLIS, Peter J.
Portsmouth, 20 March, 1956 (C/D)

League Club	Source	Date Signed	Seasons Played	Apps	Subs	Gls
Portsmouth	App	03.74	73-83	226	21	1
Southend U.	Tr	09.84	84	12	0	1

ELLIS, Samuel
Ashton-u-Lyne, 12 September, 1946 Eu23-3 (CD)

League Club	Source	Date Signed	Seasons Played	Apps	Subs	Gls
Sheffield Wed.	Smiths (Manchester)	09.64	65-70	155	2	1
Mansfield T.	Tr	01.72	71-72	64	0	7
Lincoln C.	Tr	05.73	73-76	173	0	33
Watford	Tr	08.77	77-78	30	4	4

ELLIS, Sidney C.
Charlton, 16 August, 1931 Eu23-1 (FB)

League Club	Source	Date Signed	Seasons Played	Apps	Subs	Gls
Charlton Ath.	Crystal Palace (Am)	05.49	53-57	48	-	0
Brighton & H. A.	Tr	11.57	57-58	43	-	0

League Club	Source	Date Signed	Seasons Played	Apps	Subs	Gls

ELLISON, A. Lee
Bishop Auckland, 13 January, 1973 (F)

League Club	Source	Date Signed	Seasons Played	Apps	Subs	Gls
Darlington	YT	11.90	90-91	34	6	13

Lee Ellison (Darlington)

ELLISON, Norman
Bebington, 2 November, 1929 (F)

League Club	Source	Date Signed	Seasons Played	Apps	Subs	Gls
Tranmere Rov.		10.49	49-50	2	-	0

ELLISON, Raymond
Newcastle, 31 December, 1950 (FB)

League Club	Source	Date Signed	Seasons Played	Apps	Subs	Gls
Newcastle U.	App	10.68	71	5	0	0
Sunderland	Tr	03.73	72	2	0	0
Torquay U.	Tr	07.74	74	11	5	0
Workington	Tr	07.75	75-76	57	0	3

ELLISON, W. Roy
Newbiggin, 5 July, 1948 (M)

League Club	Source	Date Signed	Seasons Played	Apps	Subs	Gls
Newcastle U.	App	06.66				
Barrow	Tr	02.68	67-70	76	9	7
Hartlepool U.	L	10.70	70	5	0	0

ELLISON, Samuel W.
Leadgate, 27 August, 1923 (OR)

League Club	Source	Date Signed	Seasons Played	Apps	Subs	Gls
Sunderland	Mid. Crusaders	10.45	46	3	-	0
Reading	Consett	06.49	49	4	-	0

ELLSON, Peter E.
Audlem, 21 August, 1925 (G)

League Club	Source	Date Signed	Seasons Played	Apps	Subs	Gls
Crewe Alex.	Crewe R.P.	05.49	48-55	219	-	0

ELMES, Timothy
Croydon, 28 September, 1962 (M)

League Club	Source	Date Signed	Seasons Played	Apps	Subs	Gls
Chelsea	App	07.80	80	2	2	0

ELMS, James B.
Manchester, 16 September, 1940 E Yth (OL)

League Club	Source	Date Signed	Seasons Played	Apps	Subs	Gls
Manchester U.	Jnrs	04.58				
Crewe Alex.	Tr	10.60	60	1	-	0

ELSBY, Ian C.
Stoke, 13 September, 1960 (D)

League Club	Source	Date Signed	Seasons Played	Apps	Subs	Gls
Port Vale	Jnrs	06.78	78-80	32	11	1

ELSBY, James
Newcastle-u-Lyme, 1 August, 1928 (FB)

League Club	Source	Date Signed	Seasons Played	Apps	Subs	Gls
Port Vale		05.47	48-53	12	-	0

ELSE, Frederick
Golborne, 31 March, 1933 E'B'-1 (G)

League Club	Source	Date Signed	Seasons Played	Apps	Subs	Gls
Preston N.E.	Wigan Ath.	08.53	53-60	215	-	0
Blackburn Rov.	Tr	08.61	61-65	187	0	0
Barrow	Tr	07.66	66-69	148	0	0

ELSEY, W. John
Swansea, 23 December, 1938 W Sch (F)

League Club	Source	Date Signed	Seasons Played	Apps	Subs	Gls
Swansea C.	Jnrs	04.56	56	1	-	0
Wrexham	Tr	05.59				

ELSEY, Karl W.
Swansea, 20 November, 1958 (M)

League Club	Source	Date Signed	Seasons Played	Apps	Subs	Gls
Queens Park R.	Pembroke Bor.	01.79	78-79	6	1	0
Newport Co.	Tr	07.80	80-83	114	9	15
Cardiff C.	Tr	09.83	83-84	59	0	5
Gillingham	Tr	08.85	85-87	126	2	13
Reading	Tr	08.88	88	41	3	3
Maidstone U.	Tr	07.89	89-90	70	2	5
Gillingham	Tr	08.91	91	25	2	3

ELSTRUP, Lars
Denmark, 24 March, 1963 Danish Int (F)

League Club	Source	Date Signed	Seasons Played	Apps	Subs	Gls
Luton T.	B.K. Odense (Den)	08.89	89-90	50	10	19

ELSWORTHY, John T.
Pontypool, 26 July, 1931 (WH)

League Club	Source	Date Signed	Seasons Played	Apps	Subs	Gls
Ipswich T.	Newport Co. (Am)	05.49	49-64	396	-	44

ELVY, Reginald
Leeds, 25 November, 1920 Died 1991 (G)

League Club	Source	Date Signed	Seasons Played	Apps	Subs	Gls
Halifax T.		03.44	46	22	-	0
Bolton W.	Tr	03.47	47-49	31	-	0
Blackburn Rov.	Tr	11.51	51-55	192	-	0
Northampton T.	Tr	07.56	56-58	67	-	0

ELWELL, Terence T.
Newport, 13 April, 1926 (FB)

League Club	Source	Date Signed	Seasons Played	Apps	Subs	Gls
Swansea C.	Barry T.	08.48	48-50	48	-	0
Swindon T.	Tr	07.52	52-53	61	-	0

ELWISS, Michael P.
Doncaster, 2 May, 1954 (F)

League Club	Source	Date Signed	Seasons Played	Apps	Subs	Gls
Doncaster Rov.	Jnrs	07.71	71-73	96	1	30
Preston N.E.	Tr	02.74	73-77	191	1	60
Crystal Palace	Tr	07.78	78	19	1	7
Preston N.E.	L	03.80	79	8	2	3

ELWOOD, Joseph P.
Belfast, 26 October, 1939 NI Sch/NIu23-1/NI'B'-1 (OL)

League Club	Source	Date Signed	Seasons Played	Apps	Subs	Gls
Leyton Orient	Glenavon	04.58	58-65	101	2	25

EMANUEL, W. John (Ivor) M.
Swansea, 19 April, 1948 W Amat/W-2 (M)

League Club	Source	Date Signed	Seasons Played	Apps	Subs	Gls
Bristol C.	Ferndale	05.71	71-75	124	4	10
Swindon T.	L	01.75	75	6	0	0
Gillingham	L	02.76	75	4	0	0
Newport Co.	Tr	06.76	76-77	79	0	4

EMBERY, Benjamin J.
Barking, 10 October, 1944 (RB)

League Club	Source	Date Signed	Seasons Played	Apps	Subs	Gls
Tottenham H.	App	06.62				
Exeter C.	Tr	06.66	66-67	36	3	0

EMBLETON, David
Newcastle, 14 September, 1952 (D)

League Club	Source	Date Signed	Seasons Played	Apps	Subs	Gls
Newcastle U.	App	08.71				
Bury	Tr	07.72	72	6	1	0
Hartlepool U.	Tr	07.73	73-75	24	2	0

EMERSON, Dean
Salford, 27 December, 1962 (M)

League Club	Source	Date Signed	Seasons Played	Apps	Subs	Gls
Stockport Co.		02.82	81-84	156	0	7
Rotherham U.	Tr	07.85	85-86	55	0	8
Coventry C.	Tr	10.86	86-91	98	16	0

EMERY, Anthony J.
Lincoln, 4 November, 1927 (CH)

League Club	Source	Date Signed	Seasons Played	Apps	Subs	Gls
Lincoln C.	Jnrs	08.47	46-58	402	-	1
Mansfield T.	Tr	06.59	59-60	26	-	0

EMERY, Dennis
Sandy, 4 October, 1933 (IF)

League Club	Source	Date Signed	Seasons Played	Apps	Subs	Gls
Tottenham H.	Eynesbury Rov.	12.51				
Peterborough U.	Eynesbury Rov.	(N/L)	60-62	68	-	29

EMERY, Donald K. J.
Cardiff, 11 June, 1920 W Sch (LB)

League Club	Source	Date Signed	Seasons Played	Apps	Subs	Gls
Swindon T.	Cardiff C. (Am)	06.37	37-47	69	-	3

EMERY, James
Lisburn (NI), 2 March, 1940 (IR)

League Club	Source	Date Signed	Seasons Played	Apps	Subs	Gls
Exeter C.	Distillery	08.59				
Barrow	Tr	07.60	60	2	-	0

EMERY, Stephen R.
Ledbury, 7 February, 1956 (M)

League Club	Source	Date Signed	Seasons Played	Apps	Subs	Gls
Hereford U.	App	02.74	73-79	203	1	10
Derby Co.	Tr	09.79	79-81	73	2	4
Newport Co.	Tr	03.83				
Hereford U.	Tr	06.83	83-84	72	3	2
Wrexham	Tr	08.85	85	8	1	0

EMERY, Terence G.
Bristol, 8 September, 1936 (WH)

League Club	Source	Date Signed	Seasons Played	Apps	Subs	Gls
Bristol C.		02.57	56-57	11	-	0

EMMANUEL, J. Gary
Swansea, 1 February, 1954 Wu23-1 (M)

League Club	Source	Date Signed	Seasons Played	Apps	Subs	Gls
Birmingham C.	App	07.71	74-78	61	10	6
Bristol Rov.	Tr	12.78	78-80	59	6	2
Swindon T.	Tr	07.81	81-83	109	2	8
Newport Co.	Tr	07.84	84	12	0	0
Bristol C. (N/C)	Tr	08.85	85	2	0	0
Swansea C.	Tr	08.85	85-87	104	7	5

EMMANUEL, Leonard D.
Treboeth, 3 September, 1917 W Sch (FB)

League Club	Source	Date Signed	Seasons Played	Apps	Subs	Gls
Swansea C.		05.46	46	4	-	0
Newport Co.	Tr	05.47	46-47	33	-	7

EMMERSON, Mark
Cuddington, 7 August, 1965 (M)

League Club	Source	Date Signed	Seasons Played	Apps	Subs	Gls
Wrexham (N/C)	Jnrs	08.82	82	1	1	0

EMMERSON, Morris
Sunniside (Dm), 23 October, 1942 E Sch (G)

League Club	Source	Date Signed	Seasons Played	Apps	Subs	Gls
Middlesbrough	Jnrs	10.59	62	10	-	0
Peterborough U.	Tr	07.63	63	7	-	0

EMMERSON, Wayne E.
Canada, 2 November, 1947 (CF)

League Club	Source	Date Signed	Seasons Played	Apps	Subs	Gls
Manchester U.	Jnrs	09.65				
Crewe Alex.	Tr	07.68	68	6	1	1

EMPTAGE, Albert T.
Grimsby, 26 December, 1917 EF Lge (WH)

League Club	Source	Date Signed	Seasons Played	Apps	Subs	Gls
Manchester C.	Scunthorpe U.	02.37	37-50	136	-	1
Stockport Co.	Tr	01.51	50-52	36	-	1

EMSON, Paul D.
Lincoln, 22 October, 1958 (W)

League Club	Source	Date Signed	Seasons Played	Apps	Subs	Gls
Derby Co.	Brigg T.	09.78	78-82	112	15	13
Grimsby T.	Tr	08.83	83-85	90	7	15
Wrexham	Tr	07.86	86-87	42	7	5
Darlington	Tr	08.88	88-90	39	9	5

ENDEAN, Barry
Chester-le-Street, 22 March, 1946 (F)

League Club	Source	Date Signed	Seasons Played	Apps	Subs	Gls
Watford	Pelton Fell	09.68	68-70	72	5	28
Charlton Ath.	Tr	02.71	70-71	27	0	1
Blackburn Rov.	Tr	10.71	71-74	65	14	18
Huddersfield T.	Tr	03.75	74-75	8	4	1
Workington	L	10.75	75	8	0	2
Hartlepool U.	Tr	03.76	75-76	24	1	5

ENDERSBY, Scott A. G.
Lewisham, 20 February, 1962 E Yth (G)

League Club	Source	Date Signed	Seasons Played	Apps	Subs	Gls
Ipswich T.	App	03.79				
Tranmere Rov.	Tr	07.81	81-82	79	0	0
Swindon T.	Tr	08.83	83-85	85	0	0
Carlisle U.	Tr	11.85	85-86	52	0	0
York C.	Tr	07.87	87-88	35	0	0
Cardiff C.	L	12.87	87	4	0	0

ENGLAND, Frederick W.
Holmfirth, 11 July, 1923 (IF)

League Club	Source	Date Signed	Seasons Played	Apps	Subs	Gls
Halifax T. (Am)	Huddersfield T. (Am)	05.46	46-47	18	-	1

ENGLAND, Michael
Kingswood, 4 January, 1961 (CD)

League Club	Source	Date Signed	Seasons Played	Apps	Subs	Gls
Bristol Rov.	App	01.79	78	1	0	0
Bristol Rov.	Forest Green Rov.	09.85	85	17	0	0

ENGLAND, H. Michael
Holywell, 2 December, 1941 Wu23-11/W-44 (CH)

League Club	Source	Date Signed	Seasons Played	Apps	Subs	Gls
Blackburn Rov.	Jnrs	04.59	59-65	165	0	21
Tottenham H.	Tr	08.66	66-74	300	0	14
Cardiff C.	Tr	08.75	75	40	0	1

ENGLEFIELD, Graham W.
Eltham, 21 September, 1931 (WH)

League Club	Source	Date Signed	Seasons Played	Apps	Subs	Gls
Charlton Ath.	Jnrs	01.49				
Norwich C.	Tr	05.54	55-56	22	-	0

ENGLISH, Anthony K.
Luton, 19 October, 1966 E Yth (D)

League Club	Source	Date Signed	Seasons Played	Apps	Subs	Gls
Colchester U.	Coventry C. (App)	12.84	84-89	220	2	32

ENGLISH, John (Jack)
South Shields, 19 March, 1923 Died 1985 (OR)

League Club	Source	Date Signed	Seasons Played	Apps	Subs	Gls
Northampton T.		10.46	47-59	301	-	135

ENGLISH, Robert H.
Stockport, 19 April, 1939 (WH)

League Club	Source	Date Signed	Seasons Played	Apps	Subs	Gls
Manchester U.	Jnrs	03.57				
Southport	Tr	11.61	61-62	20	-	0

ENGLISH, Thomas S.
Cirencester, 18 October, 1961 E Yth (F)

League Club	Source	Date Signed	Seasons Played	Apps	Subs	Gls
Coventry C.	App	06.79	79-81	62	4	17
Leicester C.	Tr	09.82	82-83	29	15	3
Rochdale	Tr	09.84	84	3	0	1
Plymouth Arg.	Tr	09.84	84	0	4	1
Colchester U.	Canberra C. (Aus)	11.85	85-86	34	13	20
Colchester U.	Bishops Stortford	10.89	89	12	1	3

ENGWELL, Michael L.
Grays, 27 September, 1966 (F)

League Club	Source	Date Signed	Seasons Played	Apps	Subs	Gls
Southend U.	Jnrs	08.84	84-85	7	2	3
Crewe Alex. (N/C)	Tr	10.86	86	0	2	0

ENNIS, Mark E.
Bradford, 6 January, 1962 (D)

League Club	Source	Date Signed	Seasons Played	Apps	Subs	Gls
Rochdale (N/C)	Joiners Libs	11.83	83	1	0	0

ENTWISTLE, Robert P.
Bury, 6 October, 1938 (F)

League Club	Source	Date Signed	Seasons Played	Apps	Subs	Gls
Rochdale (Am)	Macclesfield T.	03.59	58	1	-	0
Accrington St.	Tr	09.60	60	2	-	0
Hartlepool U.	Llandudno	10.64	64	14	-	3

ENTWISTLE, Wayne P.
Bury, 6 August, 1958 E Yth (F)

League Club	Source	Date Signed	Seasons Played	Apps	Subs	Gls
Bury	App	08.76	76-77	25	6	7
Sunderland	Tr	11.77	77-79	43	2	13
Leeds U.	Tr	10.79	79	7	4	2
Blackpool	Tr	11.80	80-81	27	5	6
Crewe Alex.	Tr	03.82	81	11	0	0
Wimbledon	Tr	07.82	82	4	5	3
Bury	Grays Ath.	08.83	83-84	80	3	32
Carlisle U.	Tr	06.85	85	8	1	2
Bolton W.	Tr	10.85	85	5	3	0
Burnley	L	08.86	86	6	2	2
Stockport Co.	Tr	10.86	86-87	38	11	8
Bury (N/C)	Tr	08.88	88	0	2	0
Wigan Ath.	Tr	10.88	88	24	5	6
Hartlepool U.(N/C)	Altrincham	09.89	89	2	0	0

EPHGRAVE, George A.
Reading, 29 April, 1918 (G)

League Club	Source	Date Signed	Seasons Played	Apps	Subs	Gls
Aston Villa	Northfleet	10.36				
Swindon T.	Tr	03.39	38	1	-	0
Southampton	Tr	09.46	46-47	36	-	0
Norwich C.	Tr	07.48	48-50	5	-	0
Watford	Tr	08.51	51	4	-	0

ESHELBY, Paul
Sheffield, 29 May, 1970 (W)

League Club	Source	Date Signed	Seasons Played	Apps	Subs	Gls
Exeter C.	Endcliffe U.	12.89	89-90	10	9	1
Scarborough	Tr	03.91	90	2	1	0

ESSER, David
Altrincham, 20 June, 1957 (M)

League Club	Source	Date Signed	Seasons Played	Apps	Subs	Gls
Everton	App	05.75				
Rochdale	Tr	07.77	77-81	169	11	24

Mike England (Blackburn Rovers, Tottenham Hotspur, Cardiff City & Wales)

ESSERS, Pierre
Netherlands, 20 February, 1959 (F)

League Club	Source	Date Signed	Seasons Played	Apps	Subs	Gls
Walsall (N/C)	Charleroi (Bel)	09.91	91	1	0	0

ETHERIDGE, Brian G.
Northampton, 4 March, 1944 E Yth (IF)

League Club	Source	Date Signed	Seasons Played	Apps	Subs	Gls
Northampton T.	Jnrs	07.62	61-64	17	-	1
Brentford	Tr	02.66	65-66	22	0	2

ETHERIDGE, R. Keith
Ivybridge, 14 May, 1944 (F)

League Club	Source	Date Signed	Seasons Played	Apps	Subs	Gls
Plymouth Arg.	St Blazey	07.66	66-67	30	1	5

ETHERIDGE, Robert J.
Gloucester, 25 March, 1934 Died 1988 (WH)

League Club	Source	Date Signed	Seasons Played	Apps	Subs	Gls
Bristol C.	Gloucester C.	09.56	56-63	259	-	42

EUSTACE, Peter
Stocksbridge, 31 July, 1944 (M)

League Club	Source	Date Signed	Seasons Played	Apps	Subs	Gls
Sheffield Wed.	App	06.62	62-69	189	3	21
West Ham U.	Tr	01.70	69-71	41	2	6
Rotherham U.	L	03.72	71	6	0	1
Sheffield Wed.	Tr	08.72	72-74	48	8	4
Peterborough U.	Tr	07.75	75	42	1	5

EVANS, Allan J.
Dunfermline, 12 October, 1956 S-4 (CD)

League Club	Source	Date Signed	Seasons Played	Apps	Subs	Gls
Aston Villa	Dunfermline Ath.	05.77	77-88	374	6	51
Leicester C.	Tr	08.89	89	14	0	0
Darlington	Canada	03.91	90	0	1	0

EVANS, Alun J.
Penrycadery, 1 December, 1922 (IF)

League Club	Source	Date Signed	Seasons Played	Apps	Subs	Gls
West Bromwich A.	Wilden	01.43	47	18	-	0

EVANS, Alun W.
Bewdley, 30 April, 1949 E Sch/E Yth/Eu23-4 (F)

League Club	Source	Date Signed	Seasons Played	Apps	Subs	Gls
Wolverhampton W.	App	10.66	67-68	20	2	4
Liverpool	Tr	09.68	68-71	77	2	21
Aston Villa	Tr	06.72	72-73	53	7	11
Walsall	Tr	12.75	75-77	78	9	7

EVANS, Andrew D. S.
Rhondda, 3 October, 1957 W Sch/W Yth/Wu21-1 (W)

League Club	Source	Date Signed	Seasons Played	Apps	Subs	Gls
Bristol Rov.	App	09.75	75-77	34	8	2

EVANS, Anthony
Liverpool, 11 January, 1954 (F)

League Club	Source	Date Signed	Seasons Played	Apps	Subs	Gls
Blackpool	Formby	06.73	74	4	2	0
Cardiff C.	Tr	06.75	75-78	120	4	47
Birmingham C.	Tr	07.79	79-82	62	4	28
Crystal Palace	Tr	08.83	83	19	2	7
Wolverhampton W.	Tr	06.84	84	20	3	5
Bolton W.	L	02.85	84	4	0	0
Swindon T.	Tr	08.85	85	8	2	0

EVANS, Anthony W.
Colchester, 30 August, 1958 (M)

League Club	Source	Date Signed	Seasons Played	Apps	Subs	Gls
Colchester U.	App	03.78	77-80	21	9	2

EVANS, Arthur
Urmston, 13 May, 1933 E Yth (G)

League Club	Source	Date Signed	Seasons Played	Apps	Subs	Gls
Bury	Jnrs	06.50	50	2	-	0
Stockport Co.	Tr	08.52				
Gillingham	Tr	09.53	53-54	14	-	0

EVANS, Bernard
Chester, 4 January, 1937 (CF)

League Club	Source	Date Signed	Seasons Played	Apps	Subs	Gls
Wrexham	Jnrs	08.54	54-60	113	-	49
Queens Park R.	Tr	10.60	60-62	77	-	34
Oxford U.	Tr	12.62	62-63	13	-	3
Tranmere Rov.	Tr	10.63	63	12	-	5
Crewe Alex.	Tr	07.64				

EVANS, Bernard R.
Rotherhithe, 7 October, 1929

League Club	Source	Date Signed	Seasons Played	Apps	Subs	Gls
Millwall		03.50				
Watford	Tr	08.51	51	2	-	1

EVANS, Brian C.
Brynmawr, 2 December, 1942 Wu23-2/W-7 (W)

League Club	Source	Date Signed	Seasons Played	Apps	Subs	Gls
Swansea C.	Abergavenny Th.	07.63	63-72	351	4	58
Hereford U.	Tr	08.73	73-74	44	4	9

EVANS, Ceri L.
Christchurch (New Zealand), 2 October, 1963 (C/D)

League Club	Source	Date Signed	Seasons Played	Apps	Subs	Gls
Oxford U.	Oxford Univ.	02.89	88-91	72	3	3

EVANS, Charles J.
West Bromwich, 4 February, 1923 (IF)

League Club	Source	Date Signed	Seasons Played	Apps	Subs	Gls
West Bromwich A.	Cordley Vic.	08.41	1946	1	-	0

EVANS, Christopher B.
Rhondda, 13 October, 1962 (RB)

League Club	Source	Date Signed	Seasons Played	Apps	Subs	Gls
Arsenal	App	06.80				
Stoke C.	Tr	08.81				
York C.	Tr	08.82	82-85	93	3	1
Darlington	Tr	10.85	85-86	58	0	1

EVANS, A. Clive
Birkenhead, 1 May, 1957 (W/FB)

League Club	Source	Date Signed	Seasons Played	Apps	Subs	Gls
Tranmere Rov.	App	05.75	76-80	175	3	27
Wigan Ath.	Tr	07.81	81	29	3	2
Crewe Alex.	Tr	08.82	82	26	2	7
Stockport Co.	Tr	08.83	83-87	158	2	23
Lincoln C.	Tr	09.87	88	42	0	2

EVANS, David
Chester, 4 April, 1967 (D)

League Club	Source	Date Signed	Seasons Played	Apps	Subs	Gls
Chester C.	App	05.84	83-84	15	1	1

EVANS, David
Colwyn Bay, 19 June, 1934 (G)

League Club	Source	Date Signed	Seasons Played	Apps	Subs	Gls
Crewe Alex.	Llandudno	03.57	56-59	50	-	0

EVANS, David G.
West Bromwich, 20 May, 1958 (CD)

League Club	Source	Date Signed	Seasons Played	Apps	Subs	Gls
Aston Villa	App	02.76	78	2	0	0
Halifax T.	Tr	06.79	79-83	218	0	9
Bradford C.	Tr	06.84	84-89	222	1	3
Halifax T.	Tr	08.90	90-91	68	5	1

EVANS, David T.
Peterlee, 6 April, 1959 (F)

League Club	Source	Date Signed	Seasons Played	Apps	Subs	Gls
Hartlepool U.		07.78	78-79	2	2	0

EVANS, Dennis
Chester, 23 July, 1935 (FB)

League Club	Source	Date Signed	Seasons Played	Apps	Subs	Gls
Wrexham		03.55	55-57	11	-	0
Tranmere Rov.	Tr	06.58	58-59	3	-	0

EVANS, Dennis J.
Ellesmere Port, 18 May, 1930 (FB)

League Club	Source	Date Signed	Seasons Played	Apps	Subs	Gls
Arsenal	Ellesmere Port	01.51	53-59	189	-	10

EVANS, D. Douglas
Ystradygynlais, 27 September, 1956 (W)

League Club	Source	Date Signed	Seasons Played	Apps	Subs	Gls
Norwich C.	App	08.74	76-79	14	4	1
Cambridge U.	Tr	03.80	79-80	11	1	2

EVANS, Elfed E.
Ferndale, 28 August, 1926 Died 1988 (IF)

League Club	Source	Date Signed	Seasons Played	Apps	Subs	Gls
Cardiff C.	Treharris	05.49	49-51	46	-	18
Torquay U.	L	03.51	50	12	-	6
West Bromwich A.	Tr	06.52	52	17	-	3
Wrexham	Tr	06.55	55-56	34	-	13
Southport	Tr	12.56	56	13	-	0

EVANS, Emrys B.
Tonypandy, 16 September, 1930 (IF)

League Club	Source	Date Signed	Seasons Played	Apps	Subs	Gls
Newport Co.	Tottenham H. (Am)	08.52	52	18	-	4

EVANS, Frederick J.
Petersfield, 20 May, 1923 (IF)

League Club	Source	Date Signed	Seasons Played	Apps	Subs	Gls
Portsmouth		01.45	46	9	-	2
Notts Co.	Tr	07.47	47-50	40	-	14
Crystal Palace	Tr	03.51	50-52	52	-	11
Rochdale	Tr	06.53	53	12	-	0

EVANS, Gareth J.
Coventry, 14 January, 1967 (F)

League Club	Source	Date Signed	Seasons Played	Apps	Subs	Gls
Coventry C.	App	01.85	85-86	5	2	0
Rotherham U.	Tr	10.86	86-87	62	1	13
Stoke C. (L)	Hibernian	10.90	90	5	0	1
Northampton T. (L)	Hibernian	12.90	90	2	0	0

EVANS, Gary N.
Doncaster, 20 December, 1968 (F)

League Club	Source	Date Signed	Seasons Played	Apps	Subs	Gls
Chesterfield	Thorne Colly	08.91	91	1	4	0

EVANS, George A.
Wrexham, 26 July, 1935 (WH)

League Club	Source	Date Signed	Seasons Played	Apps	Subs	Gls
Wrexham	Oswestry T.	07.57	57-62	175	-	8
Chester C.	Tr	06.63	63-68	110	3	0

EVANS, Gwyn
Treorchy, 24 February, 1935 (CH)

League Club	Source	Date Signed	Seasons Played	Apps	Subs	Gls
Crystal Palace	Treorchy	03.55	58-62	80	-	0

EVANS, Harold A.
Lambeth, 17 April, 1919 Died 1952 (IF)

League Club	Source	Date Signed	Seasons Played	Apps	Subs	Gls
Southampton	Woking	10.43	46	1	-	0
Exeter C.	Tr	04.47	47-48	41	-	6
Aldershot	Tr	03.49	48-49	16	-	5

EVANS, Hubert W. R.
Swansea, 10 August, 1922 (WH)

League Club	Source	Date Signed	Seasons Played	Apps	Subs	Gls
Swansea C.		08.39				
Newport Co.	Lovells Ath.	04.51	50-51	14	-	1

EVANS, Hugh
Ynysybwl, 12 December, 1919 (IF)

League Club	Source	Date Signed	Seasons Played	Apps	Subs	Gls
Birmingham C.	Redditch U.	12.47	48-49	11	-	0
Bournemouth	Tr	06.50	50	22	-	8
Walsall	Tr	08.51	51	33	-	12
Watford	Tr	08.52	52	7	-	2

EVANS, Ian P.
Egham, 30 January, 1952 Wu23-2/W-13 (CD)

League Club	Source	Date Signed	Seasons Played	Apps	Subs	Gls
Queens Park R.	App	01.70	70-73	39	0	2
Crystal Palace	Tr	09.74	74-77	137	0	14
Barnsley	Tr	12.79	79-82	102	0	3
Exeter C.	L	08.83	83	4	0	0
Cambridge U.	L	10.83	83	1	0	0

EVANS, Ivor J.
Cardiff, 25 October, 1933 (IF)

League Club	Source	Date Signed	Seasons Played	Apps	Subs	Gls
Portsmouth	Guest Keen	09.56	56	1	-	0

EVANS, John
Hetton-le-Hole, 21 October, 1932 (IF)

League Club	Source	Date Signed	Seasons Played	Apps	Subs	Gls
Norwich C.	Jnrs	10.49				
Sunderland	Tr	08.54	54	1	-	0

EVANS, John A. (Taffy)
Aberystwyth, 22 October, 1922 Died 1956 (FB)

League Club	Source	Date Signed	Seasons Played	Apps	Subs	Gls
Millwall	Aberystwyth	09.43	46-49	73	-	2
Leyton Orient	Tr	06.50	50-53	149	-	0

EVANS, John C.
Torquay, 24 March, 1947 (OR)

League Club	Source	Date Signed	Seasons Played	Apps	Subs	Gls
Torquay U.	App	04.65	64-65	6	0	1

EVANS, John D.
Liverpool, 13 March, 1938 (IF)

League Club	Source	Date Signed	Seasons Played	Apps	Subs	Gls
Liverpool		05.58				
Bournemouth	Tr	05.59				
Stockport Co.	Army	10.62	62-63	52	-	21
Carlisle U.	Tr	02.64	63-65	78	0	37
Exeter C.	Tr	03.66	65-66	11	1	2
Barnsley	Tr	11.66	66-70	165	5	55

EVANS, John D.
Chester, 24 March, 1941 (FB)

League Club	Source	Date Signed	Seasons Played	Apps	Subs	Gls
Chester C.		08.61	61-64	40	-	0

EVANS, John J.
Coventry, 11 March, 1926 (CF)

League Club	Source	Date Signed	Seasons Played	Apps	Subs	Gls
Coventry C.	Mod Machines	06.47	48-50	8	-	1

EVANS, John L.
Newport, 4 October, 1937 (HB)

League Club	Source	Date Signed	Seasons Played	Apps	Subs	Gls
Gillingham	Lovells Ath.	04.56	57	7	-	0

EVANS, John R.
Rhondda, 28 July, 1932 (FB)

League Club	Source	Date Signed	Seasons Played	Apps	Subs	Gls
Swansea C.	Jnrs	08.50	51	14	-	0
Bristol Rov.	Tr	06.53				

EVANS, John W.
Tilbury, 28 August, 1929 EF Lge (IF)

League Club	Source	Date Signed	Seasons Played	Apps	Subs	Gls
Charlton Ath.	Tilbury Bata	05.50	50-53	90	-	38
Liverpool	Tr	12.53	53-57	96	-	49
Colchester U.	Tr	11.57	57-59	56	-	22

EVANS, Keith
Trealaw, 15 September, 1953 (CD)

League Club	Source	Date Signed	Seasons Played	Apps	Subs	Gls
Swansea C.	App	08.71	70-72	14	0	0

EVANS, Kenneth P.
Swansea, 17 July, 1931 (G)

League Club	Source	Date Signed	Seasons Played	Apps	Subs	Gls
Swansea C.	Carmarthen	06.50	54-56	13	-	0
Walsall	Tr	08.57	57	2	-	0

EVANS, Leslie N.
Kingswinford, 13 October, 1929 (OL)

League Club	Source	Date Signed	Seasons Played	Apps	Subs	Gls
Cardiff C.	Brierley Hill Alliance	10.50	50-51	3	-	0
Plymouth Arg.	Tr	06.52				

EVANS, Leslie T.
Rhondda, 26 December, 1924

League Club	Source	Date Signed	Seasons Played	Apps	Subs	Gls
Cardiff C.		09.45				
Torquay U.	Tr	07.47	47	24	-	0

EVANS, Mark
Leeds, 24 August, 1970 (G)

League Club	Source	Date Signed	Seasons Played	Apps	Subs	Gls
Bradford C.	YT	07.88	88-91	12	0	0

EVANS, Maurice G.
Didcot, 22 September, 1936 (WH)

League Club	Source	Date Signed	Seasons Played	Apps	Subs	Gls
Reading	Jnrs	09.53	55-66	407	0	13

EVANS, Medwyn J.
Brynteg, 8 November, 1964 W Sch (M)

League Club	Source	Date Signed	Seasons Played	Apps	Subs	Gls
Wrexham	Jnrs	08.83	82-83	13	4	0

EVANS, Michael
West Bromwich, 3 August, 1946 (LB)

League Club	Source	Date Signed	Seasons Played	Apps	Subs	Gls
Walsall	Vono	05.64	65-72	229	3	7
Swansea C.	Tr	12.72	72-74	92	0	7
Crewe Alex.	Tr	07.75	75-76	62	0	4

EVANS, Michael G.
Llanidloes, 4 June, 1947 W Sch/Wu23-2 (D)

League Club	Source	Date Signed	Seasons Played	Apps	Subs	Gls
Wolverhampton W.	App	07.64				
Wrexham	Tr	07.66	66-78	368	12	19

EVANS, Michael J.
Plymouth, 1 January, 1973 (F)

League Club	Source	Date Signed	Seasons Played	Apps	Subs	Gls
Plymouth Arg.	YT	03.91	90-91	12	5	0

EVANS, Nicholas
Trimdon, 23 November, 1925 (OR)

League Club	Source	Date Signed	Seasons Played	Apps	Subs	Gls
New Brighton (Am)	Heselden	03.47	46	1	-	0

EVANS, Nicholas J.
Bedford, 6 July, 1958 (F)

League Club	Source	Date Signed	Seasons Played	Apps	Subs	Gls
Queens Park R.	App	07.76				
Peterborough U.	Tr	08.77				
Barnet	Wycombe W.	01.91	91	7	2	1

EVANS, Oswald
Llanelli, 2 September, 1915 (G)

League Club	Source	Date Signed	Seasons Played	Apps	Subs	Gls
Fulham	Milford Haven	02.46	46	1	-	0

EVANS, Paul
Kiveton Park, 24 February, 1949 (G)

League Club	Source	Date Signed	Seasons Played	Apps	Subs	Gls
Sheffield Wed.	Jnrs	02.66				
Mansfield T.	Boston U.	10.75	75	6	0	0

EVANS, Paul A.
Brentwood, 14 September, 1964 (F)

League Club	Source	Date Signed	Seasons Played	Apps	Subs	Gls
Cardiff C.	Jnrs	09.82	83	0	2	0
Newport Co. (N/C)	Brecon Corries	07.87	87	9	1	2

EVANS, Paul S.
Oswestry, 1 September 1974 (M)

League Club	Source	Date Signed	Seasons Played	Apps	Subs	Gls
Shrewsbury T. (YT)	YT	07.91	91	1	1	0

EVANS, Philip A.
Swansea, 14 May, 1957 (CD)

League Club	Source	Date Signed	Seasons Played	Apps	Subs	Gls
Swansea C.	Jnrs	08.75	75	9	0	0

EVANS, D. Ralph
Hungerford, 9 October, 1915 (CF)

League Club	Source	Date Signed	Seasons Played	Apps	Subs	Gls
Bury		07.35				
Halifax T.	Yeovil T.	07.36	36	21	-	1
Watford	Tr	07.37	37-47	128	-	31

League Club	Source	Date Signed	Seasons Played	Career Record Apps	Subs	Gls

EVANS, Raymond
Mansfield, 27 November, 1927 (CF)

League Club	Source	Date Signed	Seasons Played	Apps	Subs	Gls
Coventry C.		05.48				
Mansfield T.	Stafford R.	11.49	49-52	39	-	12

EVANS, Raymond F.
Carlisle, 8 October, 1929 (G)

League Club	Source	Date Signed	Seasons Played	Apps	Subs	Gls
Crewe Alex.	Hightown Y.C.	10.48	48-50	21	-	0

EVANS, Raymond L.
Edmonton, 20 September, 1949 E Yth (RB)

League Club	Source	Date Signed	Seasons Played	Apps	Subs	Gls
Tottenham H.	App	06.67	68-74	130	4	2
Millwall	Tr	01.75	74-76	74	0	3
Fulham	Tr	03.77	76-78	86	0	6
Stoke C.	Tr	08.79	79-81	94	0	1

EVANS, Raymond P.
Preston, 21 June, 1933 (W)

League Club	Source	Date Signed	Seasons Played	Apps	Subs	Gls
Preston N.E.	Jnrs	05.51	53-56	33	-	2
Bournemouth	Tr	06.59	59-60	36	-	9

EVANS, Reginald
Consett, 18 March, 1939 (F)

League Club	Source	Date Signed	Seasons Played	Apps	Subs	Gls
Newcastle U.	Jnrs	03.56	58	4	-	0
Charlton Ath.	Tr	03.59	58-59	14	-	2

EVANS, Reuben
Dublin, 19 March, 1941 (IF)

League Club	Source	Date Signed	Seasons Played	Apps	Subs	Gls
Bradford P. A.	Glasgow Rangers	06.63	63	13	-	5

EVANS, Richard W.
Ebbw Vale, 12 April, 1968 (W)

League Club	Source	Date Signed	Seasons Played	Apps	Subs	Gls
Bristol Rov.	Weymouth	08.91	91	2	0	1

EVANS, Robert
Glasgow, 16 July, 1927 SF Lge/S-48 (CH)

League Club	Source	Date Signed	Seasons Played	Apps	Subs	Gls
Chelsea	Glasgow Celtic	05.60	60	32	-	0
Newport Co.	Tr	06.61	61	31	-	0

EVANS, Ronald
St Helens, 21 February, 1929 (HB)

League Club	Source	Date Signed	Seasons Played	Apps	Subs	Gls
Stockport Co.	Bolton W. (Am)	07.50	50-53	6	-	0

EVANS, Roy O.
Bootle, 4 October, 1948 E Sch (LB)

League Club	Source	Date Signed	Seasons Played	Apps	Subs	Gls
Liverpool	App	10.65	69-73	9	0	0

EVANS, Roy S.
Swansea, 5 June, 1943 Died 1969 Wu23-3/W-1 (FB)

League Club	Source	Date Signed	Seasons Played	Apps	Subs	Gls
Swansea C.	Jnrs	07.60	62-67	215	2	7

EVANS, J. Royson
Lampeter, 9 February, 1939 (W)

League Club	Source	Date Signed	Seasons Played	Apps	Subs	Gls
Wolverhampton W.	Bangor C.	08.56				
Wrexham	Tr	07.57				
Chester C.	Tr	10.57	57-59	23	-	4
Halifax T.	Tr	10.60	60	7	-	0

EVANS, Stewart J.
Maltby, 15 November, 1960 (F)

League Club	Source	Date Signed	Seasons Played	Apps	Subs	Gls
Rotherham U.	App	11.78				
Sheffield U.	Gainsborough Trin.	11.80				
Wimbledon	Tr	03.82	81-85	165	10	50
West Bromwich A.	Tr	08.86	86	13	1	1
Plymouth Arg.	Tr	03.87	86-88	36	9	10
Rotherham U.	Tr	11.88	88-90	45	20	14
Torquay U.	L	03.91	90	15	0	5
Crewe Alex.	Tr	09.91	91	13	4	3

EVANS, Terence W.
Hammersmith, 12 April, 1965 (CD)

League Club	Source	Date Signed	Seasons Played	Apps	Subs	Gls
Brentford	Hillingdon Bor.	07.85	85-91	217	1	23

EVANS, William E.
Birmingham, 5 September, 1921 Died 1960 (IF)

League Club	Source	Date Signed	Seasons Played	Apps	Subs	Gls
Aston Villa	Linread Wks	09.46	46-48	7	-	3
Notts Co.	Tr	06.49	49-52	94	-	14
Gillingham	Tr	07.53	53-54	89	-	12
Grimsby T.	Tr	06.55	55-57	102	-	28

EVANS, Wyndham E.
Llanelli, 19 March, 1951 (FB)

League Club	Source	Date Signed	Seasons Played	Apps	Subs	Gls
Swansea C.	Stoke C. (Am)	02.71	70-82	349	5	19
Swansea C. (N/C)	Llanelli	12.83	83-84	35	2	0

EVANSON, John M.
Newcastle-u-Lyme, 10 May, 1947 (M)

League Club	Source	Date Signed	Seasons Played	Apps	Subs	Gls
Oxford U.	Towcester	02.65	66-73	144	10	10
Blackpool	Tr	02.74	73-75	63	4	0
Fulham	Tr	08.76	76-78	84	11	5
Bournemouth	Tr	07.79	79-80	52	1	2

EVELEIGH, Gordon E.
Lymington, 26 July, 1922 (OL)

League Club	Source	Date Signed	Seasons Played	Apps	Subs	Gls
Bristol C.	Guildford C.	05.48	48	2	-	0

EVERALL, William F.
Nantwich, 18 July, 1928

League Club	Source	Date Signed	Seasons Played	Apps	Subs	Gls
Crewe Alex.		08.53	53	1	-	0

EVERETT, Harold
Worksop, 11 November, 1920 (LH)

League Club	Source	Date Signed	Seasons Played	Apps	Subs	Gls
Mansfield T.	Warsop Main	08.45	46	3	-	0

EVERETT, Harold P.
Worksop, 9 June, 1922 (LB)

League Club	Source	Date Signed	Seasons Played	Apps	Subs	Gls
Notts Co.		04.43				
Mansfield T.	Tr	09.46	46	15	-	0

EVERETT, Michael R.
Mile End, 21 March, 1958 (F)

League Club	Source	Date Signed	Seasons Played	Apps	Subs	Gls
Leyton Orient	Crystal Palace (App)	03.76	75	0	1	0

EVERITT, Michael D.
Clacton, 16 January, 1941 (LB)

League Club	Source	Date Signed	Seasons Played	Apps	Subs	Gls
Arsenal	Jnrs	02.58	59-60	9	-	1
Northampton T.	Tr	02.61	60-66	206	1	15
Plymouth Arg.	Tr	03.67	66-67	29	0	0
Brighton & H. A.	Tr	07.68	68-69	24	3	1

EVERITT, Richard E.
Carlisle, 3 May, 1922 (W)

League Club	Source	Date Signed	Seasons Played	Apps	Subs	Gls
Darlington	Sheffield W. (Am)	07.45	46	1	-	0

EVES, John R.
Sunderland, 28 February, 1922 (FB)

League Club	Source	Date Signed	Seasons Played	Apps	Subs	Gls
Sunderland		11.41				
Darlington	Tr	09.46	46-51	177	-	1

EVES, Melvyn J.
Wednesbury, 10 September, 1956 E'B' (F)

League Club	Source	Date Signed	Seasons Played	Apps	Subs	Gls
Wolverhampton W.	Jnrs	07.75	77-83	169	11	44
Huddersfield T.	L	03.84	83	7	0	4
Sheffield U.	Tr	12.84	84-85	25	1	10
Gillingham	Tr	08.86	86-87	19	8	9
Mansfield T.	L	10.87	87	3	0	0

EWING, David
Perth, 10 May, 1929 (CH)

League Club	Source	Date Signed	Seasons Played	Apps	Subs	Gls
Manchester C.	Luncarty Jnrs	06.49	52-61	279	-	1
Crewe Alex.	Tr	07.62	62-63	48	-	0

EWING, Thomas
Larkhall, 2 May, 1937 SF Lge/S-2 (OR)

League Club	Source	Date Signed	Seasons Played	Apps	Subs	Gls
Aston Villa	Partick Th.	02.62	61-63	39	-	4

EWING, Thomas M. H.
Musselburgh, 8 August, 1934 (HB)

League Club	Source	Date Signed	Seasons Played	Apps	Subs	Gls
Doncaster Rov.	Jnrs	08.51	51-57	39	-	6

EXLEY, William
Bradford, 2 May, 1924 (G)

League Club	Source	Date Signed	Seasons Played	Apps	Subs	Gls
Bradford C. (Am)		08.52	52	2	-	0

EYRE, S. Frederick
Manchester, 3 February, 1944 (WH)

League Club	Source	Date Signed	Seasons Played	Apps	Subs	Gls
Manchester C.	App	07.61				
Lincoln C.	Tr	07.63				
Bradford P.A.	Rossendale U.	12.69	69	1	0	0

EYRE, Leslie E.
Ilkeston, 7 January, 1922 (IF)

League Club	Source	Date Signed	Seasons Played	Apps	Subs	Gls
Norwich C.	Cardiff C. (Am)	07.46	46-51	185	-	58
Bournemouth	Tr	11.51	51-52	38	-	10

EYRES, David
Liverpool, 26 February, 1964 (LW)

League Club	Source	Date Signed	Seasons Played	Apps	Subs	Gls
Blackpool	Rhyl	08.89	89-91	101	11	22

Trevor Francis (Birmingham City, Nottingham Forest, Manchester City, Sampdoria, Atalanta, Glasgow Rangers, Queens Park Rangers, Sheffield Wednesday & England)
The former wonder-boy of English soccer who was still turning out as player-manager for Sheffield Wednesday last season

FACEY, Kenneth W.
Hackney, 12 October, 1927 (WH)

League Club	Source	Date Signed	Seasons Played	Apps	Subs	Gls
Leyton Orient	Leyton	06.52	52-60	301	-	74

FADIDA, Aharon
Israel, 20 September, 1961 (F)

League Club	Source	Date Signed	Seasons Played	Apps	Subs	Gls
Aldershot	Hapoel Haifa (Isr)	12.85	85-86	9	5	6

FAGAN, Bernard
Houghton-le-Spring, 29 January, 1949 (W)

League Club	Source	Date Signed	Seasons Played	Apps	Subs	Gls
Sunderland	App	02.66				
Northampton T.	Tr	07.69	69	6	0	0

FAGAN, Christopher J.
Manchester, 5 June, 1950 (FB)

League Club	Source	Date Signed	Seasons Played	Apps	Subs	Gls
Liverpool		07.70	70	1	0	0
Tranmere Rov.	Tr	07.71	71-74	77	7	2

FAGAN, Fionan (Paddy)
Dublin, 7 June, 1930 IR'B'/IR-8 (W)

League Club	Source	Date Signed	Seasons Played	Apps	Subs	Gls
Hull C.	Transport (Dublin)	03.51	51-53	26	-	2
Manchester C.	Tr	12.53	53-59	153	-	34
Derby Co.	Tr	03.60	59-60	24	-	6

FAGAN, George
Dundee, 27 September, 1934 (FB)

League Club	Source	Date Signed	Seasons Played	Apps	Subs	Gls
Leeds U.	Dundee St Joseph	11.53				
Halifax T.	Tr	06.58	58-61	67	-	3

FAGAN, Joseph F.
Liverpool, 12 March, 1921 (CH)

League Club	Source	Date Signed	Seasons Played	Apps	Subs	Gls
Manchester C.	Earlestown	10.38	46-50	148	-	2
Bradford P. A.	Nelson	08.53	53	3	-	0

FAGAN, Michael J.
Newcastle, 22 February, 1960 (D)

League Club	Source	Date Signed	Seasons Played	Apps	Subs	Gls
Hartlepool U.	Carlisle U. (N/C)	08.79	79-82	36	1	1

FAGAN, William
Musselburgh, 20 February, 1917 (IF)

League Club	Source	Date Signed	Seasons Played	Apps	Subs	Gls
Preston N.E.	Glasgow Celtic	10.36	36-37	35	-	6
Liverpool	Tr	10.37	37-51	158	-	47

FAHY, John J.
Paisley, 13 May, 1943 (CF)

League Club	Source	Date Signed	Seasons Played	Apps	Subs	Gls
Oxford U.	Bedford T.	01.64	63-65	23	0	14

FAIRBROTHER, Barrie E.
Hackney, 30 December, 1950 (F)

League Club	Source	Date Signed	Seasons Played	Apps	Subs	Gls
Leyton Orient	App	01.69	69-74	171	17	41
Millwall	Tr	06.74	75-76	12	3	1

FAIRBROTHER, Ian A.
Bootle, 2 October, 1966 (M)

League Club	Source	Date Signed	Seasons Played	Apps	Subs	Gls
Liverpool	App	07.84				
Bury	Tr	02.87	86-87	16	10	3
Wrexham	L	10.87	87	7	0	0

FAIRBROTHER, John (Jack)
Burton, 16 August, 1917 (G)

League Club	Source	Date Signed	Seasons Played	Apps	Subs	Gls
Preston N. E.	Burton T.	03.37	46	41	-	0
Newcastle U.	Tr	07.47	47-51	132	-	0

FAIRBROTHER, John
Cricklewood, 12 February, 1941 (CF)

League Club	Source	Date Signed	Seasons Played	Apps	Subs	Gls
Watford	Bennetts End	08.59	60-62	40	-	19
Peterborough U.	Worcester C.	05.65	65-67	69	3	37
Northampton T.	Tr	02.68	67-71	135	5	56
Mansfield T.	Tr	09.71	71-72	83	2	38
Torquay U.	Tr	06.73	73	15	0	3

FAIRCHILD, Michael P.
Northampton, 24 November, 1942 (OR)

League Club	Source	Date Signed	Seasons Played	Apps	Subs	Gls
Luton T.	Lowestoft T.	11.60	60-63	21	-	1
Reading	Tr	07.64	64-65	24	0	6

FAIRCLOUGH, Courtney H. (Chris)
Nottingham, 12 April, 1964 Eu21-7/E'B' (CD)

League Club	Source	Date Signed	Seasons Played	Apps	Subs	Gls
Nottingham F.	App	10.81	82-86	102	5	1
Tottenham H.	Tr	06.87	87-88	60	0	5
Leeds U.	Tr	03.89	88-91	117	1	15

FAIRCLOUGH, Cyril
Manchester, 21 April, 1923 (FB)

League Club	Source	Date Signed	Seasons Played	Apps	Subs	Gls
Bury	Urmston	09.45	46-57	191	-	2

FAIRCLOUGH, David
Liverpool, 5 January, 1957 Eu21-1 (F)

League Club	Source	Date Signed	Seasons Played	Apps	Subs	Gls
Liverpool	App	01.74	75-82	64	34	34
Norwich C.	Luzern (Switz)	03.85	84	1	1	0
Oldham Ath.	Tr	08.85	85	6	11	1
Tranmere Rov.	Beveren (Bel)	08.89	89	3	11	1
Wigan Ath.	Tr	08.90	90	4	3	1

FAIRCLOUGH, Michael J.
Drogheda (Ire), 21 October, 1952 IR-2 (M)

League Club	Source	Date Signed	Seasons Played	Apps	Subs	Gls
Huddersfield T.	Drogheda	08.71	71-74	25	11	2

FAIRCLOUGH, Wayne R.
Nottingham, 27 April, 1968 (D/M)

League Club	Source	Date Signed	Seasons Played	Apps	Subs	Gls
Notts Co.	App	04.86	85-89	39	32	0
Mansfield T.	Tr	03.90	89-91	72	7	9

FAIRFAX, Raymond J.
Smethwick, 13 January, 1941 (FB)

League Club	Source	Date Signed	Seasons Played	Apps	Subs	Gls
West Bromwich A.	Jnrs	08.59	62-67	79	2	0
Northampton T.	Tr	06.68	68-70	116	0	2

FAIRHURST, John
Bentley, 15 March, 1944 (WH)

League Club	Source	Date Signed	Seasons Played	Apps	Subs	Gls
Doncaster Rov.	App	07.61	61-65	21	0	0

FAIRLEY, Thomas P.
Houghton-le-Spring, 12 October, 1932 (G)

League Club	Source	Date Signed	Seasons Played	Apps	Subs	Gls
Sunderland	Bankhead Jnrs	10.51	52	2	-	0
Carlisle U.	Tr	05.56	56-58	56	-	0

FAIRWEATHER, Carlton
Camberwell, 22 September, 1961 (W)

League Club	Source	Date Signed	Seasons Played	Apps	Subs	Gls
Wimbledon	Tooting & Mitcham	12.84	84-91	118	20	26

FAIRWEATHER, John W.
Dornoch, 12 August, 1924 (RH)

League Club	Source	Date Signed	Seasons Played	Apps	Subs	Gls
Blackburn Rov.		04.44				
Carlisle U.		11.48	49	1	-	0

FALCO, Mark P.
Hackney, 22 October, 1960 E Yth (F)

League Club	Source	Date Signed	Seasons Played	Apps	Subs	Gls
Tottenham H.	App	07.78	78-86	162	12	68
Chelsea	L	11.82	82	3	0	0
Watford	Tr	10.86	86	33	0	14
Queens Park R.	Glasgow Rangers	12.87	87-90	65	22	27
Millwall	Tr	08.91	91	19	2	4

FALCONER, Andrew G.
South Africa, 27 June, 1925

League Club	Source	Date Signed	Seasons Played	Apps	Subs	Gls
Blackpool	South Africa	09.49	49	4	-	0

FALCONER, Henry
Newcastle, 22 December, 1954 (FB)

League Club	Source	Date Signed	Seasons Played	Apps	Subs	Gls
Bournemouth	Burnley (App)	07.72	74	4	3	0

FALCONER, William H.
Aberdeen, 5 April, 1966 S Sch/S Yth (LB/M)

League Club	Source	Date Signed	Seasons Played	Apps	Subs	Gls
Watford	Aberdeen	06.88	88-90	85	13	12
Middlesbrough	Tr	08.91	91	25	0	5

FALDER, David E. J.
Liverpool, 21 October, 1922 (CH)

League Club	Source	Date Signed	Seasons Played	Apps	Subs	Gls
Everton	Wigan Ath.	12.45	49-50	25	-	0

FALLON, Henry (Harry)
Paisley, 28 April, 1942 (G)

League Club	Source	Date Signed	Seasons Played	Apps	Subs	Gls
York C.	St Johnstone	09.65	65-67	67	0	0

FALLON, Kevin B.
Maltby, 3 December, 1948 (CH)

League Club	Source	Date Signed	Seasons Played	Apps	Subs	Gls
Rotherham U.	App	12.65				
Southend U.	Sligo Rov.	07.70	70	4	0	0

FALLON, Peter D.
Dublin, 19 October, 1922 (WH)

League Club	Source	Date Signed	Seasons Played	Apps	Subs	Gls
Exeter C.		06.47	47-52	110	-	8
Queens Park R.	Tr	08.53	53	1	-	0

FALLON, Shaun
Widnes, 10 September, 1970 (LB)

League Club	Source	Date Signed	Seasons Played	Apps	Subs	Gls
Wigan Ath.	YT	07.89	88-89	2	1	0

FALLON, Stephen P.
Whittlesey, 3 August, 1956 (CD)

League Club	Source	Date Signed	Seasons Played	Apps	Subs	Gls
Cambridge U.	Kettering T.	12.74	74-86	405	5	27

FALLON, William J.
Larne, 14 January, 1912 Died 1989 (OL)

League Club	Source	Date Signed	Seasons Played	Apps	Subs	Gls
Notts Co.	Dublin Dolphins	02.34	33-37	121	-	20
Sheffield Wed.	Tr	03.38	37-38	44	-	12
Notts Co.	Tr	06.46	46	16	-	3
Exeter C.	Tr	06.47	47	8	-	2

FANTHAM, John
Sheffield, 6 February, 1939 Eu23-1/EF Lge/E-1 (IF)

League Club	Source	Date Signed	Seasons Played	Apps	Subs	Gls
Sheffield Wed.	Jnrs	10.56	57-69	381	7	147
Rotherham U.	Tr	10.69	69-70	46	5	8

FAREY, John A.
Darlington, 22 July, 1922 Died 1962 (G)

League Club	Source	Date Signed	Seasons Played	Apps	Subs	Gls
Sunderland		02.44				
Carlisle U.		11.47	47	2	-	0

FARINA, Frank
Australia, 5 September, 1964 Australian Int (F)

League Club	Source	Date Signed	Seasons Played	Apps	Subs	Gls
Notts Co. (L)	Bari (Italy)	03.92	91	1	2	0

FARLEY, Alexander J.
Finchley, 11 May, 1925 (LB)

League Club	Source	Date Signed	Seasons Played	Apps	Subs	Gls
Leyton Orient	Finchley	11.45	46-47	15	-	0
Bournemouth	Tr	06.48				

FARLEY, Brian H.
Ross, 1 January, 1927 Died 1962 (CH)

League Club	Source	Date Signed	Seasons Played	Apps	Subs	Gls
Tottenham H.	Chelmsford C.	07.49	51	1	-	0

FARLEY, John D.
Middlesbrough, 21 September, 1951 (W)

League Club	Source	Date Signed	Seasons Played	Apps	Subs	Gls
Watford	Stockton	07.69	70-73	97	8	8
Halifax T.	L	09.71	71	6	0	3
Wolverhampton W.	Tr	05.74	74-77	35	5	0
Blackpool	L	10.76	76	1	0	0
Hull C.	Tr	05.78	78-79	59	1	5
Bury	Tr	08.80	80	17	1	2

George Farm (Hibernian, Blackpool & Scotland)

FARM, George N.
Slateford, 13 July, 1924 S-10 (G)

League Club	Source	Date Signed	Seasons Played	Apps	Subs	Gls
Blackpool	Hibernian	09.48	48-59	462	-	1

FARMER, F. Brian W.
Wordsley, 29 July, 1933 (FB)

League Club	Source	Date Signed	Seasons Played	Apps	Subs	Gls
Birmingham C.	Stourbridge	07.54	56-61	118	-	0
Bournemouth	Tr	01.62	61-64	132	-	0

FARMER, J. Edward (Ted)
Rowley Regis, 21 January, 1940 Eu23-2 (CF)

League Club	Source	Date Signed	Seasons Played	Apps	Subs	Gls
Wolverhampton W.	Jnrs	08.57	60-63	57	-	44

FARMER, John
Biddulph, 31 August, 1947 Eu23-1 (G)

League Club	Source	Date Signed	Seasons Played	Apps	Subs	Gls
Stoke C.	Jnrs	01.65	65-74	163	0	0
Leicester C.	L	12.74	74	2	0	0

FARMER, Kevin J.
Ramsgate, 24 January, 1960 (CD)

League Club	Source	Date Signed	Seasons Played	Apps	Subs	Gls
Leicester C.	App	11.77	77	1	0	0
Northampton T.	Tr	08.79	79-81	70	7	12

FARMER, Michael C.
Leicester, 22 November, 1944 (WH)

League Club	Source	Date Signed	Seasons Played	Apps	Subs	Gls
Birmingham C.	App	04.62	63	1	-	1
Lincoln C.	Tr	05.65	65	21	1	0

FARMER, Ronald J.
Guernsey, 6 March, 1936 (WH)

League Club	Source	Date Signed	Seasons Played	Apps	Subs	Gls
Nottingham F.	Jnrs	05.53	57	9	-	0
Coventry C.	Tr	11.58	58-67	281	4	48
Notts Co.	Tr	10.67	67-68	69	0	5

FARMER, Terence
Rotherham, 11 May, 1931 (CF)

League Club	Source	Date Signed	Seasons Played	Apps	Subs	Gls
Rotherham U.	Gainsborough Trin.	07.52	52-57	61	-	25
York C.	Tr	01.58	57-59	66	-	28

FARMER, William H.
Guernsey, 24 November, 1927 (G)

League Club	Source	Date Signed	Seasons Played	Apps	Subs	Gls
Nottingham F.	St Martins	05.51	53-56	52	-	0
Oldham Ath.	Tr	07.57	57	5	-	0

FARNABY, Craig
Hartlepool, 8 August, 1967 (M)

League Club	Source	Date Signed	Seasons Played	Apps	Subs	Gls
Hartlepool U. (N/C)	Jnrs	10.84	84	5	0	0
Middlesbrough	Tr	11.85				
Halifax T.	Tr	09.86	86	7	3	1
Stockport Co.	Shotton Comrades	09.87	87	17	5	1

FARNEN, Leslie
St Helens, 17 September, 1919 (CH)

League Club	Source	Date Signed	Seasons Played	Apps	Subs	Gls
Watford		05.46	46-48	77	-	0
Bradford C.	Tr	05.49	49	8	-	0

FARNSWORTH, Peter A.
Barnsley, 17 May, 1946 (WH)

League Club	Source	Date Signed	Seasons Played	Apps	Subs	Gls
Barnsley	App	09.63	64	1	-	0

FARNWORTH, Simon
Chorley, 28 October, 1963 (G)

League Club	Source	Date Signed	Seasons Played	Apps	Subs	Gls
Bolton W.	App	09.81	83-85	113	0	0
Stockport Co.	L	09.86	86	10	0	0
Tranmere Rov.	L	01.87	86	7	0	0
Bury	Tr	03.87	86-89	105	0	0
Preston N. E.	Tr	06.90	90-91	46	0	0

FARQUHAR, Douglas
Methil, 11 June, 1921 (WH)

League Club	Source	Date Signed	Seasons Played	Apps	Subs	Gls
Arsenal	St Andrews U.	05.44				
Reading	Tr	09.50	50-51	9	-	1

FARR, Brian S.
Swindon, 19 October, 1930 (WH)

League Club	Source	Date Signed	Seasons Played	Apps	Subs	Gls
Swindon T.		04.51	50-51	11	-	0

FARR, Ian S.
Swindon, 13 February, 1958 (F)

League Club	Source	Date Signed	Seasons Played	Apps	Subs	Gls
Swindon T. (App)	App	07.74	75	0	1	0

FARR, Thomas F. (Chick)
Bathgate, 19 February, 1914 Died 1980 (G)

League Club	Source	Date Signed	Seasons Played	Apps	Subs	Gls
Bradford P. A.	Broxburn Ath.	09.34	34-49	294	-	0

FARRALL, Alec
Hoylake, 3 March, 1936 E Sch (WH)

League Club	Source	Date Signed	Seasons Played	Apps	Subs	Gls
Everton	Jnrs	03.53	52-56	5	-	0
Preston N. E.	Tr	05.57	57-59	27	-	9
Gillingham	Tr	07.60	60-64	202	-	19
Lincoln C.	Tr	06.65	65	20	0	2
Watford	Tr	07.66	66-67	47	1	8

FARRAR, John N.
St Helens, 6 May, 1928

League Club	Source	Date Signed	Seasons Played	Apps	Subs	Gls
Manchester C.		03.48				
Crewe Alex.	Tr	01.51	50	2	-	0

FARRELL, Andrew J.
Colchester, 7 October, 1965 (W/D)

League Club	Source	Date Signed	Seasons Played	Apps	Subs	Gls
Colchester U.	App	09.83	83-86	98	7	5
Burnley	Tr	08.87	87-91	184	9	14

FARRELL, Arthur
Huddersfield, 1 October, 1920 (FB)

League Club	Source	Date Signed	Seasons Played	Apps	Subs	Gls
Bradford P. A.		05.40	46-50	156	-	4
Barnsley	Tr	05.51	51	18	-	0

FARRELL, Gerard W.
Liverpool, 19 March, 1952 (FB)

League Club	Source	Date Signed	Seasons Played	Apps	Subs	Gls
Wolverhampton W.	App	03.70				
Blackburn Rov.	Tr	10.71	71-72	21	1	1

FARRELL, Gregory J. P.
Motherwell, 19 March, 1944 (OR)

League Club	Source	Date Signed	Seasons Played	Apps	Subs	Gls
Birmingham C.	App	03.61	62-63	4	-	0
Cardiff C.	Tr	03.64	63-66	93	1	8
Bury	Tr	03.67	66-69	83	0	15

FARRELL, John
Perth, 22 June, 1933 (OL)

League Club	Source	Date Signed	Seasons Played	Apps	Subs	Gls
Accrington St.	Perth Celtic	08.54	54	2	-	0

FARRELL, K. Michael
Ilkley, 13 March, 1959 (M)

League Club	Source	Date Signed	Seasons Played	Apps	Subs	Gls
Scunthorpe U.	App	03.77	75-77	5	4	1

FARRELL, Paul A.
Liverpool, 1 November, 1958 (F)

League Club	Source	Date Signed	Seasons Played	Apps	Subs	Gls
Southport (App)	App	09.75	75	0	2	0

Peter Farrell (Shamrock Rovers, Everton, Tranmere Rovers & Republic of Ireland)

FARRELL, Peter D.
Dublin, 16 August, 1922 IR-28/NI-7 (WH)

League Club	Source	Date Signed	Seasons Played	Apps	Subs	Gls
Everton	Shamrock Rov.	08.46	46-56	422	-	13
Tranmere Rov.	Tr	10.57	57-59	114	-	1

FARRELL, Peter J.
Liverpool, 10 January, 1957 (M)

League Club	Source	Date Signed	Seasons Played	Apps	Subs	Gls
Bury	Ormskirk	09.75	75-78	49	5	9
Port Vale	Tr	11.78	78-81	85	4	10
Rochdale	Tr	08.82	82-84	71	2	17
Crewe Alex.	Tr	09.84	84	7	1	1
Crewe Alex.	Iceland	11.85	85	19	1	1

FARRELL, Raymond
Cardiff, 31 May, 1933 (CF)

League Club	Source	Date Signed	Seasons Played	Apps	Subs	Gls
Crystal Palace	Treharris	05.57	57-58	5	-	0

FARRELL, Sean P.
Watford, 28 February, 1969 (F)

League Club	Source	Date Signed	Seasons Played	Apps	Subs	Gls
Luton T.	App	02.87	89-91	14	11	1
Colchester U.	L	03.88	87	4	5	1
Northampton T.	L	09.91	91	4	0	1
Fulham	Tr	12.91	91	25	0	10

FARRELL, Stephen E.
Kilmarnock, 8 March, 1973 (M)

League Club	Source	Date Signed	Seasons Played	Apps	Subs	Gls
Stoke C.	YT	07.91	89	0	2	0

FARRELLY, Michael J.
Manchester, 1 January, 1962 E Sch/E Semi-Pro (M)

League Club	Source	Date Signed	Seasons Played	Apps	Subs	Gls
Preston N. E.		06.81	81-84	77	5	4

FARRIMOND, Sydney
Hindley, 17 July, 1940 E Yth (LB)

League Club	Source	Date Signed	Seasons Played	Apps	Subs	Gls
Bolton W.	Jnrs	01.58	58-70	364	1	1
Tranmere Rov.	Tr	02.71	70-73	132	2	0

FARRINGTON, John R.
Lynemouth, 19 June, 1947 (W)

League Club	Source	Date Signed	Seasons Played	Apps	Subs	Gls
Wolverhampton W.	App	06.65	66-69	31	3	2
Leicester C.	Tr	10.69	69-73	115	3	18
Cardiff C.	Tr	11.73	73-74	23	0	6
Northampton T.	Tr	10.74	74-79	224	8	29

FARRINGTON, Mark A.
Liverpool, 15 June, 1965 (F)

League Club	Source	Date Signed	Seasons Played	Apps	Subs	Gls
Norwich C.	Everton (App)	05.83	83-84	11	3	2
Cambridge U.	L	03.85	84	10	0	1
Cardiff C.	Tr	07.85	85	24	7	3
Brighton & H.A.	Feyenoord (Neth)	08.91	91	8	6	1

FARRINGTON, Roy A.
Tonbridge, 6 June, 1925 (IF)

League Club	Source	Date Signed	Seasons Played	Apps	Subs	Gls
Crystal Palace		11.47	47-48	3	-	0

FARROW, Desmond A.
Peterborough, 11 February, 1926 (IF)

League Club	Source	Date Signed	Seasons Played	Apps	Subs	Gls
Queens Park R.	Leicester C. (Am)	11.44	48-52	119	-	8
Stoke C.	Tr	10.52	52-53	8	-	0

FARROW, George H.
Whitburn, 4 October, 1913 (WH)

League Club	Source	Date Signed	Seasons Played	Apps	Subs	Gls
Stockport Co.	Jnrs	10.30	31	6	-	0
Wolverhampton W.	Tr	01.32	32	10	-	0
Bournemouth	Tr	07.33	33-35	106	-	12
Blackpool	Tr	06.36	36-47	144	-	16
Sheffield U.	Tr	01.48	47	1	-	0

FASCIONE, Joseph
Coatbridge, 5 February, 1945 (W)

League Club	Source	Date Signed	Seasons Played	Apps	Subs	Gls
Chelsea	Kirkintilloch Rob Roy	10.62	65-68	22	7	1

FASHANU, John
Kensington, 18 September, 1962 E-2 (F)

League Club	Source	Date Signed	Seasons Played	Apps	Subs	Gls
Norwich C.	Cambridge U. (Jnrs)	10.79	81-82	6	1	1
Crystal Palace	L	08.83	83	1	0	0
Lincoln C.	Tr	09.83	83-84	31	5	11
Millwall	Tr	11.84	84-85	50	0	12
Wimbledon	Tr	03.86	85-91	209	2	90

FASHANU, Justin S.
Hackney, 19 February, 1961 E Yth/Eu21-11 (F)

League Club	Source	Date Signed	Seasons Played	Apps	Subs	Gls
Norwich C.	App	12.78	78-80	84	6	35
Nottingham F.	Tr	08.81	81	31	1	3
Southampton	L	08.82	82	9	0	3
Notts Co.	Tr	12.82	82-84	63	1	20
Brighton & H.A.	Tr	06.85	85	16	0	2
Manchester C. (N/C)	(Retired)	10.89	89	0	2	0
West Ham U. (N/C)	Tr	11.89	89	2	0	0
Leyton Orient (N/C)	Tr	03.90	89	3	2	0
Torquay U.	Leatherhead	12.91	91	21	0	10

FAULKES, Brian K.
Abingdon, 10 April, 1945 (FB)

League Club	Source	Date Signed	Seasons Played	Apps	Subs	Gls
Reading	Jnrs	09.63	63-66	23	2	0
Northampton T.	Tr	07.67	67-68	51	1	2
Torquay U.	Tr	07.69	69	6	0	0

FAULKNER, John G.
Orpington, 10 March, 1948 (CD)

League Club	Source	Date Signed	Seasons Played	Apps	Subs	Gls
Leeds U.	Sutton U.	03.70	69	2	0	0
Luton T.	Tr	03.72	72-77	209	0	6

Justin Fashanu (Norwich City, Nottingham Forest, Notts County, Brighton & Hove Albion, Manchester City, West Ham United, Leyton Orient & Torquay United)

FAULKNER, Kenneth G.
Smethwick, 10 September, 1923 E Sch (OL)

League Club	Source	Date Signed	Seasons Played	Apps	Subs	Gls
Birmingham C.	Smethwick Highfield	09.44	46	2	-	0

FAULKNER, Michael
Conisborough, 3 January, 1950 (WH)

League Club	Source	Date Signed	Seasons Played	Apps	Subs	Gls
Sheffield U.	App	12.67				
Oldham Ath.	Tr	07.69	69	1	0	0

FAULKNER, Raymond A.
Horncastle, 26 May, 1934 (OR)

League Club	Source	Date Signed	Seasons Played	Apps	Subs	Gls
Grimsby T.	Jnrs	10.54	54	5	-	1

FAULKNER, Roy V.
Manchester, 28 June, 1935 (IF)

League Club	Source	Date Signed	Seasons Played	Apps	Subs	Gls
Manchester C.	Jnrs	12.52	55	7	-	4
Walsall	Tr	03.58	57-60	102	-	46

FAULKNER, Stephen A.
Sheffield, 18 December, 1954 (CD)

League Club	Source	Date Signed	Seasons Played	Apps	Subs	Gls
Sheffield U.	App	02.72	72-76	14	1	0
Stockport Co.	L	03.78	77	3	1	0
York C.	Tr	05.78	78-80	90	0	7

FAWCETT, Brian
Doncaster, 14 February, 1932 (OR)

League Club	Source	Date Signed	Seasons Played	Apps	Subs	Gls
Scunthorpe U.	Bentley Colly	02.55	54	1	-	0
Bradford P.A.	Tr	07.56				

FAWCETT, Roy
Leeds, 20 January, 1938 (F)

League Club	Source	Date Signed	Seasons Played	Apps	Subs	Gls
Blackpool	Jnrs	03.55	55-59	3	-	0

FAWELL, Derek S.
Hartlepool, 22 March 1944 (CF)

League Club	Source	Date Signed	Seasons Played	Apps	Subs	Gls
Notts Co.	Spennymoor U.	10.64	64	1	-	0
Lincoln C.	Tr	09.65	65	4	0	0

FAWLEY, Ronald
Ashton-u-Lyne, 22 April, 1927 (OL/LB)

League Club	Source	Date Signed	Seasons Played	Apps	Subs	Gls
Oldham Ath.	Ashton U.	08.50	50-57	94	-	9

FAZACKERLEY, Derek W.
Preston, 5 November, 1951 (CD)

League Club	Source	Date Signed	Seasons Played	Apps	Subs	Gls
Blackburn Rov.	App	10.69	70-86	593	3	23
Chester C.	Tr	01.87	86-87	66	0	0
York C.	Tr	07.88	88	16	0	0
Bury	Tr	12.88	88	7	7	0

FAZACKERLEY, Michael
Manchester, 8 April, 1932 (FB)

League Club	Source	Date Signed	Seasons Played	Apps	Subs	Gls
Bradford P. A.	Bradford C. (Am)	08.55	55	2	-	0

FEALEY, Nathan J.
Aldershot, 12 March, 1973 (CD)

League Club	Source	Date Signed	Seasons Played	Apps	Subs	Gls
Reading	YT	07.91	91	1	0	0

FEAR, Keith W.
Bristol, 8 May, 1952 (F)

League Club	Source	Date Signed	Seasons Played	Apps	Subs	Gls
Bristol C.	Jnrs	06.69	70-76	126	25	32
Hereford U.	L	09.77	77	6	0	0
Blackburn Rov.	L	12.77	77	5	0	2
Plymouth Arg.	Tr	02.78	77-79	40	5	9
Brentford	L	11.79	79	7	1	2
Chester C.	Tr	01.80	79-80	41	3	3

FEAR, Vivien J.
Bristol, 24 October, 1955 (F)

League Club	Source	Date Signed	Seasons Played	Apps	Subs	Gls
Hereford U.	Bristol C. (App)	07.74	74	2	1	0

FEARNLEY, Gordon
Bradford, 25 January, 1950 (F)

League Club	Source	Date Signed	Seasons Played	Apps	Subs	Gls
Sheffield Wed.	Jnrs	07.68				
Bristol Rov.	Tr	07.70	70-76	95	27	21

FEARNLEY, Harold
Penistone, 16 June, 1935 (G)

League Club	Source	Date Signed	Seasons Played	Apps	Subs	Gls
Huddersfield T.	Jnrs	12.52	55-62	90	-	0
Oxford U.	Tr	10.63	63-65	90	0	0
Doncaster Rov.	Tr	02.66	65-66	32	0	0

FEARNLEY, Harrison L. (Harry)
Morley, 27 May, 1923 (G)

League Club	Source	Date Signed	Seasons Played	Apps	Subs	Gls
Leeds U.	Bradford P.A. (Am)	11.45	46-48	28	-	0
Halifax T.	Tr	01.49	48	3	-	0
Newport Co.	Tr	07.49	49-52	103	-	0
Rochdale	Selby T.	07.55	55	1	-	0

FEARON, Ronald T.
Romford, 19 November, 1960 (G)

League Club	Source	Date Signed	Seasons Played	Apps	Subs	Gls
Reading	Dover T.	02.80	80-82	61	0	0
Ipswich T.	Sutton U.	08.87	87-88	28	0	0
Brighton & H. A.	L	09.88	88	7	0	0

FEASEY, Paul C.
Hull, 4 May, 1933 (CH)

League Club	Source	Date Signed	Seasons Played	Apps	Subs	Gls
Hull C.	Jnrs	05.50	52-64	271	-	0

FEATHERSTONE, Keith
Bradford, 30 August, 1935 (G)

League Club	Source	Date Signed	Seasons Played	Apps	Subs	Gls
Bradford P.A. (Am)	Wyke Celtic	12.55	55	1	-	0

FEE, Gregory P.
Halifax, 24 June, 1964 (CD)

League Club	Source	Date Signed	Seasons Played	Apps	Subs	Gls
Bradford C.	YT	05.83	82-83	6	1	0
Sheffield Wed.	Boston U.	08.87	87-89	16	10	0
Preston N.E.	L	09.90	90	10	0	0
Northampton T.	L	11.90	90	1	0	0
Preston N.E.	L	01.91	90	5	0	0
Leyton Orient	L	03.91	90	4	1	0
Mansfield T.	Tr	03.91	90-91	43	1	4

FEEHAN, Ignatius (Sonny)
Dublin, 17 September, 1926 (G)

League Club	Source	Date Signed	Seasons Played	Apps	Subs	Gls
Manchester U.	Waterford	11.48	49	12	-	0
Northampton T.	Tr	08.50	50-51	39	-	0
Brentford	Tr	08.54	54-58	30	-	0

FEELEY, Andrew J.
Hereford, 30 September, 1961 (FB/M)

League Club	Source	Date Signed	Seasons Played	Apps	Subs	Gls
Hereford U.	App	08.79	78-79	50	1	3
Leicester C.	Trowbridge T.	02.84	83-86	74	2	0
Brentford	Tr	08.87	87-88	57	10	0
Bury	Tr	07.89	89-90	46	11	3

FEELY, Peter J.
City of London, 3 January, 1950 E Yth/E Amat (F)

League Club	Source	Date Signed	Seasons Played	Apps	Subs	Gls
Chelsea	Enfield	05.70	70-72	4	1	2
Bournemouth	Tr	02.73	72-73	8	1	2
Fulham	Tr	07.74				
Gillingham	Tr	10.74	74-75	41	0	22
Sheffield Wed.	Tr	02.76	75-76	17	2	2
Stockport Co.	L	01.77	76	2	0	0

FEENEY, James M.
Belfast, 23 June, 1921 Died 1985 NI-2 (FB)

League Club	Source	Date Signed	Seasons Played	Apps	Subs	Gls
Swansea C.	Linfield	12.46	46-49	88	-	0
Ipswich T.	Tr	03.50	49-55	214	-	0

FEENEY, Joseph
Glasgow, 21 July, 1926 (IL)

League Club	Source	Date Signed	Seasons Played	Apps	Subs	Gls
Sunderland	St Theresa's	07.47				
Chester C.		09.51	51	5	-	0

FELGATE, David W.
Blaenau Ffestiniog, 4 March, 1960 W Sch/W-1 (G)

League Club	Source	Date Signed	Seasons Played	Apps	Subs	Gls
Bolton W.	Jnrs	08.78				
Rochdale	L	10.78	78	35	0	0
Crewe Alex.	L	09.79	79	14	0	0
Rochdale	L	03.80	79	12	0	0
Lincoln C.	Tr	09.80	80-84	198	0	0
Cardiff C.	L	11.84	84	4	0	0
Grimsby T.	Tr	02.85	84-86	36	0	0
Bolton W.	L	02.86	85	15	0	0
Bolton W.	Tr	02.87	86-91	223	0	0

FELIX, Gary M.
Manchester, 31 October, 1957 (M)

League Club	Source	Date Signed	Seasons Played	Apps	Subs	Gls
Leeds U.	App	11.75				
Chester C.	Manchester C. (N/C)	01.79	78	8	0	0

FELL, Geoffrey M.
Carlisle, 8 May, 1960 (F)

League Club	Source	Date Signed	Seasons Played	Apps	Subs	Gls
Carlisle U.	Jnrs	06.77	77-79	0	3	0

FELL, Gerald C.
Newark, 1 March, 1951 (F)

League Club	Source	Date Signed	Seasons Played	Apps	Subs	Gls
Brighton & H. A.	Long Eaton U.	11.74	74-77	65	14	19
Southend U.	Tr	11.77	77-79	43	2	10
Torquay U.	Tr	07.80	80-81	50	0	12
York C.	L	03.82	81	2	3	0

FELL, James I.
Grimsby, 4 January, 1936 (OL)

League Club	Source	Date Signed	Seasons Played	Apps	Subs	Gls
Grimsby T.	Waltham	04.54	56-60	166	-	35
Everton	Tr	03.61	60-61	27	-	4
Newcastle U.	Tr	03.62	61-62	49	-	16
Walsall	Tr	07.63	63	21	-	4
Lincoln C.	Tr	01.64	63-65	63	0	10

FELL, Leslie J.
West Ham, 16 December, 1920 (OR)

League Club	Source	Date Signed	Seasons Played	Apps	Subs	Gls
Charlton Ath.	Gravesend U.	12.45	46-51	13	-	2
Crystal Palace	Tr	10.52	52-53	65	-	6

FELLOWES, William J.
Bradford, 15 March, 1910 (WH)

League Club	Source	Date Signed	Seasons Played	Apps	Subs	Gls
Plymouth Arg.	Tavistock T.	07.27	29-32	5	-	0
Leyton Orient	Tr	07.33	33-34	78	-	1
Luton T.	Tr	05.35	35-37	110	-	3
Exeter C.	Tr	06.38	38-46	56	-	1

FELLOWS, Geoffrey A.
West Bromwich, 26 July, 1944 (LB)

League Club	Source	Date Signed	Seasons Played	Apps	Subs	Gls
Aston Villa	App	10.61				
Shrewsbury T.	Tr	06.65	65-72	277	4	2

FELLOWS, Gregory F. A.
Dudley, 10 October, 1953 (CF)

League Club	Source	Date Signed	Seasons Played	Apps	Subs	Gls
Aston Villa	App	09.71				
Crewe Alex.	L	02.73	72	3	0	1
Manchester U.	Tr	08.73				

FELLOWS, Stewart
Stockton, 9 October, 1948 (WH)

League Club	Source	Date Signed	Seasons Played	Apps	Subs	Gls
Newcastle U.	App	03.66				
York C.	Tr	06.67	67	0	2	0

FELTON, Graham M.
Cambridge, 1 March, 1949 E Yth (W)

League Club	Source	Date Signed	Seasons Played	Apps	Subs	Gls
Northampton T.	Cambridge U.	09.66	66-75	243	13	25
Barnsley	L	02.76	75	12	0	2
Barnsley	Tr	07.76	76	24	0	3

FELTON, Kenneth C.
Blackhall (Dm), 18 February, 1949 (LB)

League Club	Source	Date Signed	Seasons Played	Apps	Subs	Gls
Darlington	Jnrs	04.67	67-69	50	2	8

FELTON, Robert F. F.
Gateshead, 12 August, 1918 (FB)

League Club	Source	Date Signed	Seasons Played	Apps	Subs	Gls
Everton	Tr	08.37				
Port Vale	Tr	06.38	38	10	-	0
Crystal Palace	Tr	09.46	46	1	-	0

FELTON, Vivien E.
Southgate, 13 August, 1929 (CH)

League Club	Source	Date Signed	Seasons Played	Apps	Subs	Gls
Crystal Palace	Barnet	08.54	54-55	2	-	0

FENCOTT, Kenneth S.
Walsall, 27 December, 1943 (F)

League Club	Source	Date Signed	Seasons Played	Apps	Subs	Gls
Aston Villa	App	01.61	61-63	3	-	0
Lincoln C.	Tr	06.64	64-66	67	6	13

FENNEY, Stanley
Barry, 21 June, 1923 (LB)

League Club	Source	Date Signed	Seasons Played	Apps	Subs	Gls
Barrow	Stranraer	12.45	46	26	-	0

FENOUGHTY, Thomas
Rotherham, 7 June, 1941 (M)

League Club	Source	Date Signed	Seasons Played	Apps	Subs	Gls
Sheffield U.	Sheffield F.C.	11.63	63-68	47	2	4
Chesterfield	Tr	07.69	69-71	98	3	15

FENSOME, Andrew B.
Northampton, 18 February, 1969 (FB)

League Club	Source	Date Signed	Seasons Played	Apps	Subs	Gls
Norwich C.	App	02.87				
Cambridge U.	Bury T.	11.89	89-91	94	0	1

FENTON, Benjamin R. V.
West Ham, 28 October, 1918 Died 1992 (WH)

League Club	Source	Date Signed	Seasons Played	Apps	Subs	Gls
West Ham U.	Jnrs	10.35	37-38	21	-	9
Millwall	Tr	03.39	38-46	20	-	7
Charlton Ath.	Tr	01.47	46-54	264	-	22
Colchester U.	Tr	02.55	54-57	103	-	16

FENTON, Ewan A.
Dundee, 17 November, 1929 (WH)

League Club	Source	Date Signed	Seasons Played	Apps	Subs	Gls
Blackpool	Dundee N.E.	11.46	48-58	203	-	20
Wrexham	Tr	05.59	59	24	-	0

FENTON, Michael
Stockton, 30 October, 1913 E-1 (CF)

League Club	Source	Date Signed	Seasons Played	Apps	Subs	Gls
Middlesbrough	South Bank E.E.	03.33	32-49	240	-	147

FENTON, Ronald
South Shields, 2 September, 1940 (IF)

League Club	Source	Date Signed	Seasons Played	Apps	Subs	Gls
Burnley	Jnrs	09.57	60-61	11	-	1
West Bromwich A.	Tr	11.62	62-64	59	-	16
Birmingham C.	Tr	01.65	64-67	28	5	7
Brentford	Tr	01.68	67-69	87	4	19

FENTON, Stephen J.
Hartlepool, 25 February, 1951 E Yth (M)

League Club	Source	Date Signed	Seasons Played	Apps	Subs	Gls
Middlesbrough	Jnrs	08.69				
Bradford C.	Tr	06.72	72	9	1	1

FENTON, William H.
Hartlepool, 23 June, 1926 Died 1973 (OL)

League Club	Source	Date Signed	Seasons Played	Apps	Subs	Gls
Barnsley		11.44				
Blackburn Rov.	Horden Colly	12.48	48-50	33	-	7
York C.	Tr	05.51	51-57	258	-	118

FENWICK, Terence W.
Seaham, 17 November, 1959 E Yth/Eu21-11/E-20 (D)

League Club	Source	Date Signed	Seasons Played	Apps	Subs	Gls
Crystal Palace	App	12.76	77-80	62	8	0
Queens Park R.	Tr	12.80	80-87	256	0	33
Tottenham H.	Tr	12.87	87-91	87	1	8
Leicester C.	L	10.90	90	8	0	1

Les Ferdinand (Queens Park Rangers)

FERDINAND, Leslie
Acton, 18 December, 1966 (F)

League Club	Source	Date Signed	Seasons Played	Apps	Subs	Gls
Queens Park R.	Hayes	04.87	86-91	43	10	20
Brentford	L	03.88	87	3	0	0

FEREBEE, Stewart R.
Carshalton, 6 September, 1960 (F)

League Club	Source	Date Signed	Seasons Played	Apps	Subs	Gls
York C.	Harrogate T.	07.79	79-80	7	6	0
Darlington (N/C)	Whitley Bay	03.87	86	9	0	0
Halifax T.	Tr	07.87	87	6	6	0

FEREDAY, Wayne
Warley, 16 June, 1963 Eu21-5 (W)

League Club	Source	Date Signed	Seasons Played	Apps	Subs	Gls
Queens Park R.	App	09.80	80-88	167	30	21
Newcastle U.	Tr	06.89	89-90	27	6	0
Bournemouth	Tr	11.90	90-91	20	3	0
West Bromwich A.	Tr	12.91	91	19	3	2

FERGUSON, Alexander
Lochore, 4 August, 1904 (G)

League Club	Source	Date Signed	Seasons Played	Apps	Subs	Gls
Wigan Bor.	Vale of Clyde	11.24	24	1	-	0
Gillingham	Tr	06.25	25-26	67	-	0
Swansea C.	Tr	02.27	26-35	270	-	0
Bury	Tr	06.36	36-37	63	-	0
Newport Co.	Tr	06.38	38	41	-	0
Bristol C.	Tr	05.46	46	32	-	0
Swindon T.	Tr	09.47	47	7	-	0

FERGUSON, Archibald
Lochore (Fife), 9 December, 1918 (G)

League Club	Source	Date Signed	Seasons Played	Apps	Subs	Gls
Doncaster Rov.	Raith Rov.	12.41	46-47	61	-	0
Wrexham	Tr	07.48	48-52	126	-	0

FERGUSON, J. Brian
Irvine, 14 December, 1960 (M)

League Club	Source	Date Signed	Seasons Played	Apps	Subs	Gls
Newcastle U.	Mansfield T. (App)	01.79	79	4	1	1
Hull C.	Tr	12.80	80-81	24	4	2
Southend U.	Goole T.	08.83	83-84	31	3	6
Chesterfield	Tr	10.84	84	30	1	0

FERGUSON, Charles
Glasgow, 22 April, 1930 (FB)

League Club	Source	Date Signed	Seasons Played	Apps	Subs	Gls
Accrington St.	Hamilton Acad.	05.54	54	1	-	0
Rochdale	Tr	09.55	55-58	150	-	4
Oldham Ath.	Tr	07.59	59-60	57	-	0

FERGUSON, Darren
Glasgow, 9 February, 1972 S Yth/Su21-3 (M)

League Club	Source	Date Signed	Seasons Played	Apps	Subs	Gls
Manchester U.	YT	07.90	90-91	4	5	0

FERGUSON, David
Bonnybridge, 11 March, 1929 (OL)

League Club	Source	Date Signed	Seasons Played	Apps	Subs	Gls
Coventry C.	Alloa Ath.	10.56	56	4	-	0

FERGUSON, Donald S.
Ontario (Can), 2 January, 1963 Canada 'B' (G)

League Club	Source	Date Signed	Seasons Played	Apps	Subs	Gls
Wrexham (N/C)		01.86	85	20	0	0

FERGUSON, Edward B.
Dumbarton, 10 September, 1949 (M)

League Club	Source	Date Signed	Seasons Played	Apps	Subs	Gls
Rotherham U.	Dumbarton	02.71	70-73	64	3	5
Grimsby T.	L	11.71	71	1	1	0

FERGUSON, Hubert
Belfast, 23 May, 1926 (FB)

League Club	Source	Date Signed	Seasons Played	Apps	Subs	Gls
Bradford C.	Ballymena	07.48	48-52	132	-	0
Halifax T.	Tr	09.54	54-57	95	-	0

FERGUSON, Iain J. H.
Newarthill, 4 August, 1962 (F)

League Club	Source	Date Signed	Seasons Played	Apps	Subs	Gls
Charlton Ath. (L)	Hearts	11.89	89	1	0	0
Bristol C. (L)	Hearts	03.90	89	8	3	2

FERGUSON, James C. M.
Glasgow, 20 February, 1935 (G)

League Club	Source	Date Signed	Seasons Played	Apps	Subs	Gls
Oldham Ath.	Falkirk	05.59	59	36	-	0
Crewe Alex.	Tr	08.60	60-61	26	-	0
Darlington	Tr	07.62	62	32	-	0

FERGUSON, John
Maybole, 29 August, 1939 (OR)

League Club	Source	Date Signed	Seasons Played	Apps	Subs	Gls
Southend U.	Airdrieonians	06.67	67	13	1	2

FERGUSON, John T.
Edinburgh, 14 June, 1939 (OL)

League Club	Source	Date Signed	Seasons Played	Apps	Subs	Gls
Oldham Ath.	St Andrews U.	11.56	56	1	-	0

FERGUSON, Mark
Liverpool, 6 November, 1960 (W)

League Club	Source	Date Signed	Seasons Played	Apps	Subs	Gls
Tranmere Rov.		08.81	81-84	71	16	13

FERGUSON, Martin
Glasgow, 21 December, 1942 (IF)

League Club	Source	Date Signed	Seasons Played	Apps	Subs	Gls
Barnsley	Partick Th.	08.65	65	40	0	18
Doncaster Rov.	Tr	07.66	66	3	0	0

FERGUSON, Michael J.
Newcastle, 3 October, 1954 (F)

League Club	Source	Date Signed	Seasons Played	Apps	Subs	Gls
Coventry C.	App	12.71	74-80	121	6	51
Everton	Tr	08.81	81	7	1	4
Birmingham C.	Tr	11.82	82-84	22	0	9
Coventry C.	L	03.84	83	7	0	3
Brighton & H. A.	Tr	09.84	84-85	17	0	6
Colchester U.	Tr	03.86	85-86	25	1	11

FERGUSON, Michael K.
Burnley, 9 March, 1943 (M)

League Club	Source	Date Signed	Seasons Played	Apps	Subs	Gls
Accrington St.	Plymouth Arg. (Am)	07.60	60	23	-	1
Blackburn Rov.	Tr	03.62	62-67	220	0	29
Aston Villa	Tr	05.68	68-69	38	0	2
Queens Park R.	Tr	11.69	69-72	68	1	2
Cambridge U.	Tr	07.73	73	39	0	4
Rochdale	Tr	07.74	74-75	68	1	4
Halifax T.	I.A. Akranes (Ice)	12.76	76	2	0	0

FERGUSON, Robert
Ardrossan, 1 March, 1945 Su23-1/SF Lge/S-7 (G)

League Club	Source	Date Signed	Seasons Played	Apps	Subs	Gls
West Ham U.	Kilmarnock	06.67	67-79	240	0	0
Sheffield Wed.	L	02.74	73	5	0	0

FERGUSON, Robert
Grangetown, 27 July, 1917 (G)

League Club	Source	Date Signed	Seasons Played	Apps	Subs	Gls
Middlesbrough	Hurworth Jnrs	08.35	36-37	10	-	0
York C.	Tr	05.39	46	26	-	0

FERGUSON, Robert B.
Dudley (Nd), 8 January, 1938 (FB)

League Club	Source	Date Signed	Seasons Played	Apps	Subs	Gls
Newcastle U.	Jnrs	05.55	55-62	11	-	0
Derby Co.	Tr	10.62	62-65	121	0	0
Cardiff C.	Tr	12.65	65-68	87	1	0
Newport Co.	Barry T.	07.69	69-70	71	0	2

FERGUSON, Ronald C.
Accrington, 9 February, 1957 (F)

League Club	Source	Date Signed	Seasons Played	Apps	Subs	Gls
Sheffield Wed.	App	02.75	74	10	1	1
Scunthorpe U.	L	12.75	75	3	0	0
Darlington	Tr	02.76	75-79	101	13	18

FERN, Rodney A.
Measham, 13 December, 1948 (F)

League Club	Source	Date Signed	Seasons Played	Apps	Subs	Gls
Leicester C.	Measham Imps	12.66	67-71	133	19	32
Luton T.	Tr	06.72	72-74	34	5	5
Chesterfield	Tr	06.75	75-78	150	2	54
Rotherham U.	Tr	06.79	79-82	98	7	34

FERNEY, Martin J.
Lambeth, 8 November, 1971 (M)

League Club	Source	Date Signed	Seasons Played	Apps	Subs	Gls
Fulham	YT	07.90	90	12	2	0

FERNIE, James
Kirkcaldy, 31 October, 1936 (F)

League Club	Source	Date Signed	Seasons Played	Apps	Subs	Gls
Doncaster Rov.	Arbroath	10.58	58-60	89	-	30

FERNIE, D. William
East Fife, 22 November, 1928 SF Lge/S'B'-1/S-12 (IF)

League Club	Source	Date Signed	Seasons Played	Apps	Subs	Gls
Middlesbrough	Glasgow Celtic	12.58	58-60	65	-	3

FERNS, Philip
Liverpool, 14 November, 1937 (FB)

League Club	Source	Date Signed	Seasons Played	Apps	Subs	Gls
Liverpool		09.57	62-64	27	-	1
Bournemouth	Tr	08.65	65	46	0	0
Mansfield T.	Tr	08.66	66-67	55	1	1

FERNS, Philip D.
Liverpool, 12 September, 1961 (LB)

League Club	Source	Date Signed	Seasons Played	Apps	Subs	Gls
Bournemouth	App	02.79	78-80	94	1	6
Charlton Ath.	Tr	08.81	81-82	35	3	1
Wimbledon	L	12.82	82	7	0	0
Blackpool	Tr	08.83	83-84	44	3	0
Aldershot	Tr	07.85	85	24	0	2

FERRIDAY, Leslie
Manchester, 3 June, 1929 (WH)

League Club	Source	Date Signed	Seasons Played	Apps	Subs	Gls
Walsall	Buxton	05.54	54	32	-	1

FERRIER, Harold R.
Ratho, 20 May, 1920 (FB)

League Club	Source	Date Signed	Seasons Played	Apps	Subs	Gls
Barnsley		09.37				
Portsmouth	Tr	03.46	46-53	241	-	8

FERRIER, John
Edinburgh, 6 October, 1927 (LB)

League Club	Source	Date Signed	Seasons Played	Apps	Subs	Gls
Brighton & H. A.		10.46	46	1	-	1
Exeter C.	Clyde	05.56	56	31	-	0

FERRIER, Ronald J.
Cleethorpes, 26 April, 1914 Died 1991 (IF)

League Club	Source	Date Signed	Seasons Played	Apps	Subs	Gls
Grimsby T.		05.33				
Manchester U.	Tr	05.35	35-37	18	-	4
Oldham Ath.	Tr	03.38	37-46	45	-	25
Lincoln C.	Tr	08.47				

League Club	Source	Date Signed	Seasons Played	Career Record Apps	Subs	Gls
FERRIS, John O.						
Bristol, 4 September, 1939						(G)
Torquay U.		09.58	58	3	-	0
FERRIS, Paul J.						
Lisburn (NI), 10 July, 1965						(W)
Newcastle U.	App	03.83	81-84	1	10	0
FERRIS, Raymond O.						
Newry (NI), 22 September, 1920 NI-3						(WH)
Crewe Alex.		03.45	46-48	101	-	23
Birmingham C.	Tr	03.49	48-52	93	-	3
FERRIS, Samuel						
Motherwell, 14 March, 1951						(IF)
Chesterfield	Albion Rov.	03.72	71-73	25	6	3
Workington	L	02.74	73	2	1	0
FERRY, Gordon						
Sunderland, 22 December, 1943						(CH)
Arsenal	App	01.61	64	11	-	0
Leyton Orient	Tr	05.65	65	42	0	0
FERRY, William						
Sunderland, 21 November, 1966						(F)
Scunthorpe U.	YT	09.84	84-86	2	3	0
Barnsley	Tr	11.86	86	3	1	1
FETTIS, Alan						
Belfast, 1 February, 1971 NI-2						(G)
Hull C.	Ards	07.91	91	43	0	0
FEWINGS, Patrick J. H.						
Barnstaple, 21 January, 1931						(OR)
Torquay U.	Barnstaple	11.53	53-54	8	-	0
FIDLER, Dennis J.						
Stockport, 22 June, 1938						(OL)
Manchester C.	Manchester U. (Am)	01.57	57-58	5	-	1
Port Vale	Tr	06.60	60-61	38	-	12
Grimsby T.	Tr	10.61	61	9	-	3
Halifax T.	Tr	04.63	62-66	142	1	40
Darlington	Tr	10.66	66-67	32	2	3
FIDLER, Frank						
Middleton, 16 August, 1924						(CF)
Manchester U.	Jnrs	08.41				
Wrexham	Witton A.	05.50	50-51	36	-	15
Leeds U.	Tr	10.51	51-52	22	-	8
Bournemouth	Tr	12.52	52-54	61	-	32
FIDLER, Thomas G.						
Hounslow, 4 September, 1933						
Queens Park R.	Hounslow	05.54	54	12	-	2
FIELD, Anthony						
Halifax, 6 July, 1946						(F)
Halifax T.	Jnrs	07.63	63-65	21	0	3
Barrow	Tr	08.66	66-67	36	2	16
Southport	Tr	03.68	67-71	127	6	41
Blackburn Rov.	Tr	10.71	71-73	104	2	45
Sheffield U.	Tr	03.74	73-75	63	3	13
FIELD, Anthony F.						
Chester, 23 May, 1942						(F)
Chester C.		08.61	60	2	-	0
Southport	Tr	07.62				
FIELD, Norman						
Durham, 27 August, 1927						(WH)
Portsmouth		08.45				
Mansfield T.	Tr	06.50	51-52	20	-	0
FIELDER, Colin M. R.						
Winchester, 5 January, 1964						(M)
Aldershot	App	01.82	81-86	56	12	8
FIELDING, John A.						
Liverpool, 2 September, 1939						(IF)
Southport	Wigan Ath.	03.61	60-62	76	-	21
Brentford	Tr	03.63	62-65	82	0	18
Grimsby T.	Tr	12.65	65-66	29	1	8
FIELDING, Mark J.						
Bury, 10 November, 1956						(FB)
Preston N.E.	App	11.74	74	9	0	0

League Club	Source	Date Signed	Seasons Played	Career Record Apps	Subs	Gls
FIELDING, Michael A.						
Liverpool, 3 December, 1965						(FB)
Barnsley	Everton (YT)	08.84				
Rochdale	L	10.84	84	6	0	0
FIELDING, Paul A.						
Rochdale, 4 December, 1955						(M)
Rochdale	App	12.73	72-75	65	7	5
FIELDING, A. Walter						
Edmonton, 26 November, 1919						(IF)
Everton	Walthamstow Ave.	09.45	46-58	380	-	49
Southport	Tr	01.59	58-59	20	-	1
FIELDING, William J.						
Broadhurst, 17 June, 1915						(G)
Cardiff C.	Hurst	05.36	36-38	50	-	0
Bolton W.	Tr	06.44				
Manchester U.	Tr	01.47	46	6	-	0
FIELDS, Alfred G.						
West Ham, 15 November, 1918						(CH)
Arsenal	Margate	05.37	38-50	19	-	0
FIELDS, Maurice J. B.						
Chester, 12 August, 1935						(F)
Chester C.		08.55	55-57	20	-	1
FIFE, Adrian						
Peterborough, 13 September, 1969						(F)
Peterborough U. (N/C)	YT	07.88	86-87	1	1	0
FIFIELD, David						
Plymouth, 10 December, 1966						(M)
Torquay U. (YT)	YT	06.83	83	0	1	0
FIGGINS, Philip E.						
Portsmouth, 20 August, 1955						(G)
Portsmouth	Waterlooville	07.73	74-77	36	0	0
FILBY, Ian F.						
East Ham, 9 October, 1954						(W)
Leyton Orient	App	10.72				
Brentford	L	09.74	74	1	2	0
FILLERY, Michael C.						
Mitcham, 17 September, 1960 E Sch/E Yth						(M)
Chelsea	App	08.78	78-82	156	5	32
Queens Park R.	Tr	08.83	83-86	95	2	9
Portsmouth	Tr	07.87	87-90	62	5	6
Oldham Ath.	Tr	10.90	90	1	1	0
Millwall	L	03.91	90	1	0	0
Torquay U.	L	09.91	91	4	0	0
FILSON R. Martin						
St Helens, 25 June, 1968						(CD)
Wrexham (N/C)	Preston N.E. (N/C)	02.89	88-89	0	2	0
FINAN, Robert J.						
Old Kilpatrick, 13 January, 1912						(CF)
Blackpool	Yoker Ath.	08.33	33-38	173	-	82
Crewe Alex.	Tr	09.47	47-48	59	-	14
FINC, Robert						
Rochdale, 13 February, 1959						(M)
Rochdale (N/C)	Milton	10.77	77	0	1	0
FINCH, Derek						
Arley, 29 July, 1940						(FB)
West Bromwich A.	Jnrs	08.57				
Aldershot	Tr	06.60	60	3	-	0
FINCH, Desmond						
Worksop, 26 February, 1950						(G)
Mansfield T.		03.69	68-70	4	0	0
FINCH, John						
Lambeth, 5 July, 1966						(CD)
Fulham	Dorking	12.90	90-91	6	1	0
FINCH, Michael						
Stockton, 30 June, 1965						(G)
Hartlepool U. (N/C)		12.83	83-84	3	0	0

FINCH, Robert J.
Camberwell, 24 August, 1948 Died 1978 (FB)

League Club	Source	Date Signed	Seasons Played	Apps	Subs	Gls
Queens Park R.	App	08.66	67-68	5	1	0

FINCH, A. Roy
Barry, 7 April, 1922 (OL)

League Club	Source	Date Signed	Seasons Played	Apps	Subs	Gls
Swansea C.	Barians	08.39				
West Bromwich A.	Tr	06.44	46-48	15	-	1
Lincoln C.	Tr	02.49	48-58	275	-	57

FINCHAM, Gordon R.
Peterborough, 8 January, 1935 (CH)

League Club	Source	Date Signed	Seasons Played	Apps	Subs	Gls
Leicester C.	Fletton	11.52	52-57	50	-	0
Plymouth Arg.	Tr	07.58	58-62	136	-	4
Luton T.	Tr	07.63	63-64	64	-	0

FINDLAY, John W. (Jake)
Blairgowrie, 13 July, 1954 (G)

League Club	Source	Date Signed	Seasons Played	Apps	Subs	Gls
Aston Villa	App	06.72	73-76	14	0	0
Luton T.	Tr	11.78	78-84	167	0	0
Barnsley	L	09.83	83	6	0	0
Derby Co.	L	01.84	83	1	0	0
Swindon T.	Tr	07.85	85	4	0	0
Portsmouth	Tr	01.86				
Coventry C.	Tr	08.86				

FINDLAY, Kenneth
Pegswood, 24 March, 1926

League Club	Source	Date Signed	Seasons Played	Apps	Subs	Gls
Aldershot	Aberdeen	08.50	50	7	-	0

FINLAY, Allan J.
Edinburgh, 9 January, 1939 S Sch (IF)

League Club	Source	Date Signed	Seasons Played	Apps	Subs	Gls
Newport Co.	Hearts	07.61	61	20	-	1

FINLAY, John
Birtley, 16 February, 1919 (IF)

League Club	Source	Date Signed	Seasons Played	Apps	Subs	Gls
Sunderland	Ouston Jnrs	05.38	46	1	-	0

FINLAY, John
Glasgow, 1 July, 1925 (OR)

League Club	Source	Date Signed	Seasons Played	Apps	Subs	Gls
New Brighton	Clyde	03.51	50	15	-	2
Leeds U.	Tr	06.51	51	1	-	0
Walsall	Yeovil T.	08.53	53	11	-	0

FINLAY, Patrick
Birkenhead, 18 March, 1938 (OL)

League Club	Source	Date Signed	Seasons Played	Apps	Subs	Gls
Tranmere Rov.		08.59	61	3	-	0

FINLAYSON, Malcolm J.
Dumbarton, 14 June, 1930 (G)

League Club	Source	Date Signed	Seasons Played	Apps	Subs	Gls
Millwall	Renfrew Jnrs	02.48	47-55	230	-	0
Wolverhampton W.	Tr	08.56	56-63	179	-	0

FINLEY, Alan J.
Liverpool, 10 December, 1967 (CD)

League Club	Source	Date Signed	Seasons Played	Apps	Subs	Gls
Shrewsbury T.	Marine	06.88	88-89	60	3	2
Stockport Co.	Tr	08.90	90-91	34	3	4

FINLEY, Thomas
Frizington, 7 October, 1933 (FB)

League Club	Source	Date Signed	Seasons Played	Apps	Subs	Gls
Workington	Northside Jnrs	01.56	55-59	94	-	2
Southport	Tr	02.60	59	6	-	0

FINN, Michael G.
Liverpool, 1 May, 1954 (G)

League Club	Source	Date Signed	Seasons Played	Apps	Subs	Gls
Burnley	App	12.71	73-74	4	0	0

FINNEGAN, John
Glasgow, 3 July, 1943 (FB)

League Club	Source	Date Signed	Seasons Played	Apps	Subs	Gls
Millwall	Clyde	06.63	63	6	-	0

FINNEY, Alan
Langwith, 31 October, 1953 Eu23-3/E'B'-1 (OR)

League Club	Source	Date Signed	Seasons Played	Apps	Subs	Gls
Sheffield Wed.	Jnrs	11.50	50-65	455	0	83
Doncaster Rov.	Tr	01.66	65-66	30	0	3

FINNEY, R. Kenneth
St Helens, 10 March, 1929 (W)

League Club	Source	Date Signed	Seasons Played	Apps	Subs	Gls
Stockport Co.		12.47	47-57	192	-	32
Tranmere Rov.	Tr	03.58	57-62	180	-	26

FINNEY, Kevin
Newcastle-u-Lyme, 5 April, 1969 (M)

League Club	Source	Date Signed	Seasons Played	Apps	Subs	Gls
Port Vale	YT	06.87	87-89	20	17	1
Lincoln C.	Tr	07.91	91	21	2	2

FINNEY, Richard J.
Rotherham, 14 March, 1956 E Yth (W)

League Club	Source	Date Signed	Seasons Played	Apps	Subs	Gls
Rotherham U.	Jnrs	07.74	73-80	236	0	67

FINNEY, Shaun B.
Dinnington, 5 October, 1966 (F)

League Club	Source	Date Signed	Seasons Played	Apps	Subs	Gls
Scunthorpe U.	Nottingham F. (App)	10.84	84	1	1	0

FINNEY, Stephen K.
Hexham, 31 October, 1973 (W)

League Club	Source	Date Signed	Seasons Played	Apps	Subs	Gls
Preston N.E.	YT	05.92	91	0	2	1

FINNEY, Thomas
Belfast, 6 November, 1952 NI-14 (M)

League Club	Source	Date Signed	Seasons Played	Apps	Subs	Gls
Luton T.	Crusaders	08.73	73	13	1	5
Sunderland	Tr	07.74	74-75	8	7	1
Cambridge U.	Tr	08.76	76-83	259	9	56
Brentford	Tr	02.84	83-84	19	1	2
Cambridge U.	Tr	12.84	84-85	64	0	5

Tom Finney (Preston North End & England)

FINNEY, Thomas
Preston, 5 April, 1922 EF Lge/E-76 (F)

League Club	Source	Date Signed	Seasons Played	Apps	Subs	Gls
Preston N. E.	Jnrs	01.40	46-59	433	-	187

FINNEY, C. William
Stoke, 5 September, 1931 (IF)

League Club	Source	Date Signed	Seasons Played	Apps	Subs	Gls
Stoke C.	Crewe Alex. (Am)	05.49	52-54	57	-	14
Birmingham C.	Tr	11.55	55-56	14	-	0
Queens Park R.	Tr	05.57	57	10	-	1
Crewe Alex.	Tr	07.58	58	1	-	0
Rochdale	Tr	09.58	58	31	-	1

FINNIESTON, Stephen J.
Edinburgh, 30 November, 1954 S Yth (F)

League Club	Source	Date Signed	Seasons Played	Apps	Subs	Gls
Chelsea	App	12.71	74-77	78	2	34
Cardiff C.	L	10.74	74	9	0	2
Sheffield U.	Tr	06.78	78	23	0	4

FINNIGAN, Anthony
Wimbledon, 17 October, 1962 E Yth (M)

League Club	Source	Date Signed	Seasons Played	Apps	Subs	Gls
Fulham	App	10.80				
Crystal Palace	Corinthian Casuals	02.85	84-87	94	11	10
Blackburn Rov.	Tr	07.88	88-89	21	15	0
Hull C.	Tr	07.90	90	15	3	1
Swindon T.	Tr	03.91	90	2	1	0
Brentford (N/C)		01.92	91	3	0	0

FINNIGAN, Dennis V.
Sheffield, 23 March, 1940 (CH)

League Club	Source	Date Signed	Seasons Played	Apps	Subs	Gls
Sheffield U.		04.59	59-66	14	0	0
Chesterfield	Tr	09.68	68-69	27	0	0

FINNIGAN, Raymond W.
Wallsend, 22 January, 1947 (FB)

League Club	Source	Date Signed	Seasons Played	Apps	Subs	Gls
Newcastle U.	App	01.65				
Darlington	Tr	07.66	66-67	8	4	0

FINNIGAN, Trevor T.
Bedlington, 14 October, 1952 E Semi-Pro (F)

League Club	Source	Date Signed	Seasons Played	Apps	Subs	Gls
Everton		05.71				
Blackpool	Runcorn	03.77	76-77	13	4	3
Bournemouth	Tr	01.78	77-78	23	2	5

FINNIS, Harold A.
Liverpool, 21 October, 1920 (LB)

League Club	Source	Date Signed	Seasons Played	Apps	Subs	Gls
Everton		06.46	46	1	-	0

FIOCCA, Paul
Italy, 13 January, 1955 (M)

League Club	Source	Date Signed	Seasons Played	Apps	Subs	Gls
Swindon T.	App	01.73	73	1	0	0

FIORE, Mark J.
Southwark, 18 November, 1969 (LW)

League Club	Source	Date Signed	Seasons Played	Apps	Subs	Gls
Wimbledon	YT	07.88	88	1	0	0
Plymouth Arg.	Tr	03.90	89-91	74	8	8

FIRM, Neil J.
Bradford, 23 January, 1958 (CD)

League Club	Source	Date Signed	Seasons Played	Apps	Subs	Gls
Leeds U.	App	01.76	79-81	11	1	0
Oldham Ath.	L	03.82	81	9	0	0
Peterborough U.	Tr	08.82	82-84	71	1	3

FIRMAN, Kenneth
Felling, 5 February, 1941 (IL)

League Club	Source	Date Signed	Seasons Played	Apps	Subs	Gls
Gateshead (Am)	Jarrow Mercantile	02.59	58	1	-	0

FIRMANI, Edward R.
South Africa, 7 August, 1933 (IF)

League Club	Source	Date Signed	Seasons Played	Apps	Subs	Gls
Charlton Ath.	Clyde (SA)	02.50	51-54	100	-	50
Charlton Ath.	Sampdorla (It)	10.63	63-64	55	-	32
Southend U.	Tr	06.65	65-66	55	0	24
Charlton Ath.	Tr	03.67	66-67	10	0	6

FIRMANI, Peter W.
South Africa, 14 February, 1936 (FB)

League Club	Source	Date Signed	Seasons Played	Apps	Subs	Gls
Charlton Ath.	Marist Bros (SA)	09.53	55-58	31	-	2

FIRTH, Frank M.
Dewsbury, 27 May, 1956 (W)

League Club	Source	Date Signed	Seasons Played	Apps	Subs	Gls
Huddersfield T.	App	11.73	73-76	26	1	4
Halifax T.	Tr	02.78	77-81	157	11	19
Bury	Tr	08.82	82	33	0	4

FISHENDEN, Paul A.
Hillingdon, 2 August, 1963 (F)

League Club	Source	Date Signed	Seasons Played	Apps	Subs	Gls
Wimbledon	App	10.81	81-85	57	18	25
Fulham	L	12.85	85	3	0	0
Millwall	L	09.86	86	3	0	0
Leyton Orient	L	10.86	86	4	0	0
Crewe Alex.	Tr	02.88	87-89	79	2	25

FISHER, Alexander J.
Southampton, 30 January, 1973 (RB)

League Club	Source	Date Signed	Seasons Played	Apps	Subs	Gls
Aldershot	YT	07.91	90	2	0	0

FISHER, J Bernard
York, 23 February, 1934 (G)

League Club	Source	Date Signed	Seasons Played	Apps	Subs	Gls
Hull C.	Jnrs	11.55	55-62	126	-	0
Bradford C.	Tr	07.63	63-64	60	-	0

FISHER, Charles K.
Pontypridd, 4 January, 1915

League Club	Source	Date Signed	Seasons Played	Apps	Subs	Gls
Swansea	Lovells Ath.	08.39	46-47	65	-	0

FISHER, Frederick
Hetton-le-Hole, 28 November, 1924 (OR)

League Club	Source	Date Signed	Seasons Played	Apps	Subs	Gls
Reading	Slough T.	08.44	46-51	139	-	24
Shrewsbury T.	Tr	07.52	52-53	64	-	9
Leyton Orient	Tr	07.54	54	2	-	1

FISHER, Frederick T.
Wednesbury, 14 January, 1920 (FB)

League Club	Source	Date Signed	Seasons Played	Apps	Subs	Gls
Grimsby T.	Fallings Heath	05.37	38-50	166	-	0
Rochdale	Tr	06.51	51	1	-	0

FISHER, George S.
Bermondsey, 19 June, 1925 (LB)

League Club	Source	Date Signed	Seasons Played	Apps	Subs	Gls
Millwall		12.44	46-54	286	-	4
Fulham	Tr	11.54	54	8	-	0
Colchester U.	Tr	09.55	55-59	163	-	6

FISHER, Hugh D.
Glasgow, 9 January, 1944 (M)

League Club	Source	Date Signed	Seasons Played	Apps	Subs	Gls
Blackpool		08.62	63-66	51	3	1
Southampton	Tr	03.67	66-76	297	5	7
Southport	Tr	03.77	76-77	60	0	1

FISHER, James
Barrow, 12 June, 1934 (IF)

League Club	Source	Date Signed	Seasons Played	Apps	Subs	Gls
Barrow	Holker C.O.B.	10.55	52-57	10	-	1

FISHER, John A.
Bermondsey, 19 June, 1925 (FB)

League Club	Source	Date Signed	Seasons Played	Apps	Subs	Gls
Millwall		05.46	47-48	3	-	0
Bournemouth	Tr	06.49	49-52	52	-	0

FISHER, Kenneth D.
Westwood, 30 September, 1921 (FB)

League Club	Source	Date Signed	Seasons Played	Apps	Subs	Gls
Southampton		09.46				
Watford	Tr	08.47	47-50	106	-	2

FISHER, Leslie B.
Southampton, 8 January, 1948 (FB)

League Club	Source	Date Signed	Seasons Played	Apps	Subs	Gls
Blackpool		12.67	68	1	0	0

FISHER, Neil J.
St Helens, 7 November, 1970 (W)

League Club	Source	Date Signed	Seasons Played	Apps	Subs	Gls
Bolton W.	YT	07.89	91	4	3	1

FISHER, Paul B.
Mansfield, 19 January, 1951 (FB)

League Club	Source	Date Signed	Seasons Played	Apps	Subs	Gls
Huddersfield T.		02.69				
Darlington	Tr	06.70	70	2	1	0

FISHER, Peter M.
Edinburgh, 17 February, 1920 (FB)

League Club	Source	Date Signed	Seasons Played	Apps	Subs	Gls
Northampton T.		09.47	47	8	-	0
Shrewsbury T.	Tr	08.50	50-51	39	-	0
Wrexham	Tr	10.51	51-53	85	-	0

FISHER, Philip J.
Carmarthen, 10 January, 1958 (W)

League Club	Source	Date Signed	Seasons Played	Apps	Subs	Gls
Exeter C.	Bridgend T.	02.81	80-81	9	2	1
Swansea C. (N/C)	Merthyr Tydfil	03.85	84	2	0	0

FISHER, Robert P.
Wembley, 3 August, 1956 (FB)

League Club	Source	Date Signed	Seasons Played	Apps	Subs	Gls
Leyton Orient	App	08.73	73-82	308	6	4
Cambridge U.	Tr	11.82	82-83	42	0	0
Brentford	Tr	02.84	83-84	44	1	0

FISHER, Ronald
Sheffield, 9 March, 1923 (RB)

League Club	Source	Date Signed	Seasons Played	Apps	Subs	Gls
Halifax T.		08.50	50	6	-	0

FISHER, Stanley
Barnsley, 29 September, 1924 (CF)

League Club	Source	Date Signed	Seasons Played	Apps	Subs	Gls
Barnsley	Rockingham Colly	09.44	46	1	-	0
Halifax T.	Tr	01.47	46-47	26	-	7

FITCH, Barry E.
Brighton, 19 November, 1943 (FB)

League Club	Source	Date Signed	Seasons Played	Apps	Subs	Gls
Brighton & H.A.	Jnrs	11.61	63	1	-	0

FITTON, John
Oldham, 12 January, 1951 (G)

League Club	Source	Date Signed	Seasons Played	Apps	Subs	Gls
Oldham Ath.	Jnrs	10.68	69	3	0	0

FITZGERALD M. Alfred
Conisbrough, 25 January, 1911 Died 1981 (WH)

League Club	Source	Date Signed	Seasons Played	Apps	Subs	Gls
Reading	Denaby U.	08.34	34-35	6	-	1
Queens Park R.	Tr	05.36	36-38	94	-	1
Aldershot	Tr	11.45	46-47	59	-	1

FITZGERALD, Peter J.
Waterford, 17 June, 1937 LOI/IR-5 (F)

League Club	Source	Date Signed	Seasons Played	Apps	Subs	Gls
Leeds U.	Sparta Rotterdam (Neth)	08.60	60	8	-	0
Chester C.	Tr	07.61	61-63	80	-	12

FITZGERALD, Scott B.
Westminster, 13 August, 1969 IRu21-1/IR'B' (CD)

League Club	Source	Date Signed	Seasons Played	Apps	Subs	Gls
Wimbledon	YT	07.87	89-91	34	3	1

FITZPATRICK, Anthony C.
Glasgow, 3 March, 1956 Su21-5 (M)

League Club	Source	Date Signed	Seasons Played	Apps	Subs	Gls
Bristol C.	St Mirren	08.79	79-80	75	0	1

League Club	Source	Date Signed	Seasons Played	Career Record Apps	Subs	Gls
FITZPATRICK, Gary G.						
Birmingham, 5 August, 1971 IR Yth						(W)
Leicester C.	YT	01.90	89	0	1	0
FITZPATRICK, John H. N.						
Aberdeen, 18 August, 1946						(WH)
Manchester U.	Jnrs	09.63	64-72	111	6	8
FITZPATRICK, Paul J.						
Liverpool, 5 October, 1965						(D/M)
Bolton W.	Tranmere Rov. (Jnrs)	03.85	84-85	13	1	0
Bristol C.	Tr	08.86	86-88	40	4	7
Carlisle U.	Tr	10.88	88-90	106	3	4
Preston N. E.	L	12.88	88	2	0	0
Leicester C.	Tr	07.91	91	21	5	4
FITZPATRICK, Peter P.						
Bebington, 27 April, 1929						(IF)
New Brighton (Am)		01.50	49	1	-	0
FITZSIMONS, Arthur G.						
Dublin, 16 December, 1929 LOI/IR-26						(IF)
Middlesbrough	Shelbourne	05.49	49-58	223	-	49
Lincoln C.	Tr	03.59	58	7	-	0
Mansfield T.	Tr	08.59	59-60	62	-	23
FITZSIMONS, Eric J.						
Oldham, 23 October, 1948						(IR)
Bradford P.A. (Am)		02.70	69	1	0	0
FLACK, Douglas W.						
Staines, 24 October, 1920						(G)
Fulham	Jnrs	12.38	48-52	54	-	0
Walsall	Tr	08.53	53	11	-	0
FLACK, W. Leonard W.						
Cambridge, 1 June, 1916 E Sch						(FB)
Norwich C.	Cambridge T.	07.33	34-46	49	-	0
FLANAGAN, Daniel C.						
Dublin, 24 November, 1924						(CF)
Notts Co. (Am)	Dundalk	12.46	46	2	-	2
Manchester C.	Shelbourne	02.47				
Bradford C.	Tr	12.47	47	13	-	6
FLANAGAN, Michael A.						
Ilford, 9 November, 1952 E Yth						(F)
Charlton Ath.	Tottenham H. (Jnrs)	08.71	71-78	241	13	85
Crystal Palace	Tr	08.79	79-80	56	0	8
Queens Park R.	Tr	12.80	80-83	71	7	20
Charlton Ath.	Tr	01.84	83-85	89	4	24
Cambridge U. (N/C)	Tr	09.86	86	7	2	3
FLANAGAN, Shaun						
Doncaster, 25 December, 1960						(M)
Doncaster Rov.	App	01.79	78-80	41	9	3
FLANNIGAN, Raymond J.						
Margate, 15 March, 1949						(FB)
Reading	Margate	02.70	70-71	36	4	0
FLATLEY, Albert A.						
Bradford, 5 September, 1919 Died 1987						(IF)
York C.		02.39	38	4	-	0
Port Vale	Tr	06.39				
Bradford P.A.	Tr	07.44				
Bury		12.46				
Workington	Alessandria (It)	11.51	51	8	-	0
FLATT, Colin H.						
Blyth, 30 January, 1940						(CF)
Leyton Orient	Wisbech T.	05.65	65	32	1	8
Southend U.	Tr	06.66	66	20	2	8
FLAVELL, John A.						
Brierley Hill, 15 May, 1929						(FB)
West Bromwich A.	Lye T.	05.47				
Walsall	Tr	09.53	53	22	-	0
FLAVELL, Robert W.						
Berwick, 7 March, 1956						(FB)
Burnley	App	03.73				
Halifax T.	Tr	02.76	75-77	91	0	7
Chesterfield	Tr	08.78	78	27	2	2
Barnsley	Tr	07.79	79	25	0	0
Halifax T. (N/C)	Tr	12.80	80	1	0	0

League Club	Source	Date Signed	Seasons Played	Career Record Apps	Subs	Gls
FLAY, Stephen						
Poole, 2 October, 1954						(FB)
Oxford U.	App	10.72	73-74	3	0	0

Robert Fleck (Norwich City & Scotland)

League Club	Source	Date Signed	Seasons Played	Career Record Apps	Subs	Gls
FLECK, Robert						
Glasgow, 11 August, 1965 S Yth/Su21-7/S-4						(F)
Norwich C.	Glasgow Rangers	12.87	87-91	130	13	40
FLEET, Stephen						
Salford, 2 July, 1937						(G)
Manchester C.	Jnrs	02.55	57-60	5	-	0
Wrexham	Tr	06.63	63-65	79	0	0
Stockport Co.	Tr	01.66	65-67	36	0	0
FLEETING, James T.						
Glasgow, 8 April, 1955						(CD)
Norwich C.	Kilbirnie Ladeside	04.75	76	0	1	0
FLEETWOOD, Steven R.						
Sheffield, 27 February, 1962						
Rotherham U. (N/C)		02.87	86	0	1	0
FLEMING, Bernard J.						
Middlesbrough, 8 January, 1937						(FB)
Grimsby T.	R.A.F. Binbrook	04.57	57-60	22	-	0
Workington	Tr	07.61	61	19	-	0
Chester C.	Tr	05.62	62-63	64	-	0
FLEMING, Charles						
Dunfermline, 12 July, 1927 S-1						(CF)
Sunderland	East Fife	01.55	54-57	107	-	62
FLEMING, Craig						
Halifax, 6 October, 1971						(D)
Halifax T.	YT	03.90	88-90	56	1	0
Oldham Ath.	Tr	08.91	91	28	4	1
FLEMING, Curtis						
Manchester, 8 October, 1968 IRu21-1/IR'B'						(RB)
Middlesbrough	St Patricks Ath.	08.91	91	23	5	0
FLEMING, Frank						
South Shields, 21 December, 1945						(G)
Darlington		07.64	64	2	-	0
FLEMING, J. Gary						
Derry (NI), 17 February, 1967 NI-14						(FB)
Nottingham F.	App	11.84	84-87	71	3	0
Manchester C.	Tr	08.89	89	13	1	0
Notts Co.	L	03.90	89	3	0	0
Barnsley	Tr	03.90	89-91	96	2	0

FLEMING, George K.
Gourock, 25 February, 1935 (IF)

League Club	Source	Date Signed	Seasons Played	Apps	Subs	Gls
Watford	Morton	06.58	58-59	27	-	10
Carlisle U.	Tr	06.60	60	7	-	0
Barrow	Tr	09.60	60	17	-	3

FLEMING, James
Tannochside, 4 November, 1952 (M)

League Club	Source	Date Signed	Seasons Played	Apps	Subs	Gls
Carlisle U.	Manchester U. (App)	07.71				
Barrow	L	01.72	71	1	1	0

FLEMING, James F.
Glasgow, 7 January, 1929 (FB)

League Club	Source	Date Signed	Seasons Played	Apps	Subs	Gls
Workington	Stirling A.	05.54	54-57	89	-	1

FLEMING, James P.
Alloa, 7 January, 1942 (OL)

League Club	Source	Date Signed	Seasons Played	Apps	Subs	Gls
Luton T.	Partick Th.	11.60	60-62	66	-	9

FLEMING, John H. (Ian)
Maybole, 15 January, 1953 (W)

League Club	Source	Date Signed	Seasons Played	Apps	Subs	Gls
Sheffield Wed.	Aberdeen	02.79	78-79	13	0	1

FLEMING, John J.
Nottingham, 1 July, 1953 (M)

League Club	Source	Date Signed	Seasons Played	Apps	Subs	Gls
Oxford U.	Jnrs	09.70	71-74	67	8	2
Lincoln C.	Tr	07.75	75-78	109	12	17
Port Vale	Tr	03.80	79	3	0	0

FLEMING, Mark J.
Hammersmith, 11 August, 1969 (LB)

League Club	Source	Date Signed	Seasons Played	Apps	Subs	Gls
Queens Park R.	YT	01.88	87-88	1	2	0
Brentford	Tr	07.89	89-90	33	2	1

FLEMING, Michael A.
Rochdale, 23 February, 1928

League Club	Source	Date Signed	Seasons Played	Apps	Subs	Gls
Tranmere Rov.		09.53	53-57	115	-	8

FLEMING, Neil
Felixstowe, 9 January, 1950 (CH)

League Club	Source	Date Signed	Seasons Played	Apps	Subs	Gls
Lincoln C. (Am)	Swiss Cottage	07.73	73	1	0	0

FLEMING, Paul
Halifax, 6 September, 1967 (RB)

League Club	Source	Date Signed	Seasons Played	Apps	Subs	Gls
Halifax T.	YT	09.85	85-90	135	4	1
Mansfield T.	Tr	07.91	91	38	0	0

FLEMING, Terence M.
Marston Green, 5 January, 1973 (RW)

League Club	Source	Date Signed	Seasons Played	Apps	Subs	Gls
Coventry C.	YT	07.91	90	0	2	0

FLETCHER, Alan F.
Pendleton, 28 October, 1917 (IF)

League Club	Source	Date Signed	Seasons Played	Apps	Subs	Gls
Blackpool		01.37				
Bournemouth		06.38	38	12	-	0
Bristol Rov.	Tr	06.39				
Crewe Alex.		09.47	47	1	-	0

FLETCHER, Andrew M.
Saltburn, 12 August, 1971 (F)

League Club	Source	Date Signed	Seasons Played	Apps	Subs	Gls
Middlesbrough	YT	05.89				
Scarborough	Tr	02.91	90-91	15	12	6

FLETCHER, Christopher
Buncrana (Ire), 14 June, 1933 (F)

League Club	Source	Date Signed	Seasons Played	Apps	Subs	Gls
Brentford	Cheltenham T.	12.57	57	3	-	0

FLETCHER, Douglas
Sheffield, 17 September, 1930 (IF)

League Club	Source	Date Signed	Seasons Played	Apps	Subs	Gls
Sheffield Wed.	Hillsborough B.C.	01.48	48-49	4	-	0
Bury	Tr	05.51	51-55	67	-	17
Scunthorpe U.	Tr	07.56	56-57	64	-	26
Darlington	Tr	07.58	58	43	-	13
Halifax T.	Tr	06.59	59	20	-	4

FLETCHER, Gavin
Bellshill, 30 October, 1941 (IF)

League Club	Source	Date Signed	Seasons Played	Apps	Subs	Gls
Bradford C.	Third Lanark	07.63	63	8	-	1

FLETCHER, Hugh M.
Lochgilphead, 8 April, 1933 (FB)

League Club	Source	Date Signed	Seasons Played	Apps	Subs	Gls
Carlisle U.	Glasgow Celtic	05.56	56-60	124	-	18

FLETCHER, James
Houghton-le-Spring, 6 November, 1934 (CF)

League Club	Source	Date Signed	Seasons Played	Apps	Subs	Gls
Doncaster Rov.	Appleton Colly	01.58	57-59	45	-	15
Stockport Co.	Tr	01.60	59-60	61	-	19

FLETCHER, James A.
Wouldham, 10 November, 1931 E Amat (IF)

League Club	Source	Date Signed	Seasons Played	Apps	Subs	Gls
Gillingham	Maidstone U.	07.57	57	23	-	8
Southend U.	Tr	07.58				

FLETCHER, James R.
Brentwood, 23 December, 1926 (F)

League Club	Source	Date Signed	Seasons Played	Apps	Subs	Gls
Birmingham C.	Bilston U.	06.50				
Chester C.	Tr	07.51	51	23	-	9

FLETCHER, John
Sheffield, 22 February, 1943 (FB)

League Club	Source	Date Signed	Seasons Played	Apps	Subs	Gls
Doncaster Rov.		06.61	61	1	-	0

FLETCHER, Joseph M.
Manchester, 25 September, 1946 (CF)

League Club	Source	Date Signed	Seasons Played	Apps	Subs	Gls
Rochdale	Manchester C. (Am)	01.67	66-68	55	2	22
Grimsby T.	Tr	07.69	69	11	0	1
Barrow	Tr	10.69	69	7	1	1

FLETCHER, Kenneth
Liverpool, 31 December, 1931 (FB)

League Club	Source	Date Signed	Seasons Played	Apps	Subs	Gls
Everton	Jnrs	08.49				
Chester C.	Tr	07.53	53-55	34	-	0

FLETCHER, Leonard G. G.
Hammersmith, 28 April, 1929 (WH)

League Club	Source	Date Signed	Seasons Played	Apps	Subs	Gls
Ipswich T.	R.A.F. Didcot	11.49	49-54	20	-	0

FLETCHER, Mark R. J.
Barnsley, 1 April, 1965 (FB)

League Club	Source	Date Signed	Seasons Played	Apps	Subs	Gls
Barnsley	App	04.83	83	1	0	0
Bradford C.	Tr	06.84	84	4	2	0

FLETCHER, Paul J.
Bolton, 13 January, 1951 Eu23-4 (F)

League Club	Source	Date Signed	Seasons Played	Apps	Subs	Gls
Bolton W.	App	11.68	68-70	33	3	5
Burnley	Tr	03.71	70-79	291	2	71
Blackpool	Tr	02.80	79-81	19	1	8

FLETCHER, Peter
Manchester, 2 December, 1953 (F)

League Club	Source	Date Signed	Seasons Played	Apps	Subs	Gls
Manchester U.	App	12.70	72-73	2	5	0
Hull C.	Tr	05.74	74-75	26	10	5
Stockport Co.	Tr	05.76	76-77	43	8	13
Huddersfield T.	Tr	07.78	78-81	83	16	36

FLETCHER, J. Rodney
Preston, 23 September, 1945 (F)

League Club	Source	Date Signed	Seasons Played	Apps	Subs	Gls
Leeds U.		12.62				
Crewe Alex.		03.67	66	1	0	0
Lincoln C.	Tr	08.67	67-70	86	4	29
Scunthorpe U.	Tr	06.71	71-73	97	1	30
Grimsby T.	Tr	11.73	73-74	9	3	1

FLETCHER, Steven M.
Hartlepool, 26 July, 1972 (F)

League Club	Source	Date Signed	Seasons Played	Apps	Subs	Gls
Hartlepool U.	YT	08.90	90-91	19	13	4

FLEWIN, Reginald
Portsmouth, 28 November, 1920 (CH)

League Club	Source	Date Signed	Seasons Played	Apps	Subs	Gls
Portsmouth	Ryde Sports	11.37	38-52	150	-	0

FLEXNEY, Paul
Glasgow, 18 January, 1965 (CD)

League Club	Source	Date Signed	Seasons Played	Apps	Subs	Gls
Northampton T.	Clyde	08.88	88	12	0	0

FLINT, Kenneth
Kirkby, 12 November, 1923 (OL)

League Club	Source	Date Signed	Seasons Played	Apps	Subs	Gls
Tottenham H.	Bedford T.	07.47	47	5	-	1
Aldershot	Tr	07.50	50-57	324	-	70
Leyton Orient	Tr	06.58	58	4	-	0

FLITCROFT, Gary W.
Bolton, 6 November, 1972 E Sch/E Yth (M)

League Club	Source	Date Signed	Seasons Played	Apps	Subs	Gls
Manchester C.	YT	07.91				
Bury	L	03.92	91	12	0	0

FLOCKETT, Thomas W.
Ferryhill, 17 July, 1927 (FB)

League Club	Source	Date Signed	Seasons Played	Apps	Subs	Gls
Chesterfield	Spennymoor U.	04.49	49-56	200	-	1
Bradford C.	Tr	06.57	57-62	227	-	1

FLOOD, Edward D.
Liverpool, 19 November, 1952 (FB)

League Club	Source	Date Signed	Seasons Played	Apps	Subs	Gls
Liverpool	App	11.69				
Tranmere Rov.	Tr	07.72	72-80	313	2	6
York C.	Tr	08.81	81	13	2	0

FLOOD, John E.
Southampton, 21 October, 1932 E Sch (OR)

League Club	Source	Date Signed	Seasons Played	Apps	Subs	Gls
Southampton	Jnrs	11.49	52-57	122	-	28
Bournemouth	Tr	06.58	58	17	-	3

FLOOD, John G.
Glasgow, 25 December, 1960 (W)

League Club	Source	Date Signed	Seasons Played	Apps	Subs	Gls
Sheffield U.	App	10.78	78-80	16	3	1

FLOOD, Paul A.
Dublin, 29 June, 1948 (W)

League Club	Source	Date Signed	Seasons Played	Apps	Subs	Gls
Brighton & H.A.	Bohemians	06.67	67-70	32	3	7

FLOUNDERS, Andrew J.
Hull, 13 December, 1963 (F)

League Club	Source	Date Signed	Seasons Played	Apps	Subs	Gls
Hull C.	App	12.81	80-86	126	33	54
Scunthorpe U.	Tr	03.87	86-90	186	10	87
Rochdale	Tr	07.91	91	42	0	17

FLOWER, Anthony J.
Carlton, 2 February, 1945 (W)

League Club	Source	Date Signed	Seasons Played	Apps	Subs	Gls
Notts Co.	Jnrs	01.62	61-66	127	2	17
Halifax T.	Tr	07.67	67-69	78	1	6

FLOWER, John G.
Northampton, 9 December, 1964 (CD)

League Club	Source	Date Signed	Seasons Played	Apps	Subs	Gls
Sheffield U.	Corby T.	08.89				
Aldershot	Tr	10.90	90	30	2	2

FLOWERS, John E.
Doncaster, 26 August, 1944 (WH)

League Club	Source	Date Signed	Seasons Played	Apps	Subs	Gls
Stoke C.	App	09.61	63-65	8	0	0
Doncaster Rov.	Tr	08.66	66-70	162	2	4
Port Vale	Tr	08.71	71	34	0	0

FLOWERS, Malcolm
Mansfield, 9 August, 1938 (CH)

League Club	Source	Date Signed	Seasons Played	Apps	Subs	Gls
Mansfield T.	Jnrs	08.56	56	3	-	0

FLOWERS, Ronald
Doncaster, 28 July, 1934 Eu23-2/EF Lge/E-49 (WH)

League Club	Source	Date Signed	Seasons Played	Apps	Subs	Gls
Wolverhampton W.	Jnrs	08.51	52-66	467	0	33
Northampton T.	Tr	09.67	67-68	61	0	4

FLOWERS, Timothy D.
Kenilworth, 3 February, 1967 E Yth/Eu21-3 (G)

League Club	Source	Date Signed	Seasons Played	Apps	Subs	Gls
Wolverhampton W.	App	08.84	84-85	63	0	0
Southampton	Tr	06.86	86-91	138	0	0
Swindon T.	L	03.87	86	2	0	0
Swindon T.	L	11.87	87	5	0	0

FLOYD, Ronald C.
Coventry, 17 August, 1932 (G)

League Club	Source	Date Signed	Seasons Played	Apps	Subs	Gls
West Bromwich A.	Jnrs	11.49				
Crewe Alex.	Tr	07.53	53-54	39	-	0

FLYNN, Brian
Port Talbot, 12 October, 1955 W Sch/Wu23-2/W-66 (M)

League Club	Source	Date Signed	Seasons Played	Apps	Subs	Gls
Burnley	App	10.72	73-77	115	5	8
Leeds U.	Tr	11.77	77-82	152	2	11
Burnley	L	03.82	81	2	0	0
Burnley	Tr	11.82	82-84	76	4	11
Cardiff C.	Tr	11.84	84-85	32	0	0
Doncaster Rov.	Tr	11.85	85	27	0	0
Bury	Tr	07.86	86	19	0	0
Doncaster Rov. (N/C)	Limerick C.	08.87	87	18	6	1
Wrexham	Tr	02.88	87-91	90	8	5

FLYNN, John E.
Workington, 20 March, 1948 (CD)

League Club	Source	Date Signed	Seasons Played	Apps	Subs	Gls
Workington	Jnrs	09.67	66-68	35	3	0
Sheffield U.	Tr	07.69	69-77	185	5	8
Rotherham U.	Tr	07.78	78-79	30	1	1

FLYNN, Michael A.
Oldham, 23 February, 1969 (CD)

League Club	Source	Date Signed	Seasons Played	Apps	Subs	Gls
Oldham Ath.	App	02.87	87-88	37	3	1
Norwich C.	Tr	12.88				
Preston N. E.	Tr	12.89	89-91	99	2	5

FLYNN, Peter
Glasgow, 11 October, 1936 (WH)

League Club	Source	Date Signed	Seasons Played	Apps	Subs	Gls
Leeds U.	Jnrs	10.53	53	1	-	0
Bradford P. A.	Tr	06.57	58-65	130	1	9

FLYNN, Sean M.
Birmingham, 13 March, 1968 (M)

League Club	Source	Date Signed	Seasons Played	Apps	Subs	Gls
Coventry C.	Halesowen T.	12.91	91	21	1	2

FLYNN, William
Kirkmalden, 2 January, 1927

League Club	Source	Date Signed	Seasons Played	Apps	Subs	Gls
Rotherham U.	Maybold Jnrs	07.49	49	6	-	0

FOAN, Albert T.
Rotherhithe, 30 October, 1923 (IF)

League Club	Source	Date Signed	Seasons Played	Apps	Subs	Gls
Norwich C.		04.47	47-49	18	-	4
West Ham U.	Tr	07.50	50-56	53	-	6

FOGARTY, Ambrose G.
Dublin, 11 September, 1933 IR-11 (IF)

League Club	Source	Date Signed	Seasons Played	Apps	Subs	Gls
Sunderland	Glentoran	10.57	57-63	152	-	37
Hartlepool U.	Tr	11.63	63-66	127	1	22

FOGARTY, Kenneth A.
Manchester, 25 January, 1955 (CD)

League Club	Source	Date Signed	Seasons Played	Apps	Subs	Gls
Stockport Co.	App	11.72	71-79	265	4	6

FOGARTY, William F.
Dulwich, 27 June, 1957 (M)

League Club	Source	Date Signed	Seasons Played	Apps	Subs	Gls
Gillingham	App	07.75	75-76	25	4	0
Charlton Ath.	Tr	12.76				

FOGG, David
Liverpool, 28 May, 1951 (FB)

League Club	Source	Date Signed	Seasons Played	Apps	Subs	Gls
Wrexham		05.70	70-75	159	2	0
Oxford U.	Tr	07.76	76-84	289	4	16

FOGG, Ronald W. J.
Tilbury, 3 June, 1938 (CF)

League Club	Source	Date Signed	Seasons Played	Apps	Subs	Gls
Southend U. (Am)		08.59	59	2	-	0
Aldershot	Weymouth	07.63	63-64	64	-	29

FOGGO, Kenneth T.
Perth, 7 November, 1943 S Sch (OR)

League Club	Source	Date Signed	Seasons Played	Apps	Subs	Gls
West Bromwich A.	Peebles Y.M.C.A.	11.60	62-67	128	1	29
Norwich C.	Tr	10.67	67-72	181	4	54
Portsmouth	Tr	01.73	72-74	47	13	3
Southend U.	Tr	09.75	75	30	0	6

FOGGON, Alan
Chester-le-Street, 23 February, 1950 E Yth (W)

League Club	Source	Date Signed	Seasons Played	Apps	Subs	Gls
Newcastle U.	App	11.67	67-70	54	7	14
Cardiff C.	Tr	08.71	71-72	14	3	1
Middlesbrough	Tr	10.72	72-75	105	10	45
Manchester U.	Tr	07.76	76	0	3	0
Sunderland	Tr	09.76	76	7	1	0
Southend U.	Tr	06.77	77	22	0	0
Hartlepool U.	L	02.78	77	18	0	2

FOLDS, Robert J.
Bedford, 18 April, 1949 (LB)

League Club	Source	Date Signed	Seasons Played	Apps	Subs	Gls
Gillingham	App	04.67	68-70	38	5	1
Northampton T.	Tr	08.71	71	29	0	0

FOLEY, Charles
Salford, 7 January, 1952 (M)

League Club	Source	Date Signed	Seasons Played	Apps	Subs	Gls
Stockport Co.	App	01.70	69-70	6	1	0

FOLEY, Peter
Glasgow, 28 June, 1944 (W)

League Club	Source	Date Signed	Seasons Played	Apps	Subs	Gls
Workington	Preston Ath.	02.65	64-66	74	0	14
Scunthorpe U.	Tr	07.67	67-68	15	2	3
Chesterfield	Tr	08.69	69	2	0	0

FOLEY, Peter J.
Bicester, 10 September, 1956 IR Yth (F)

League Club	Source	Date Signed	Seasons Played	Apps	Subs	Gls
Oxford U.	App	09.74	74-82	262	15	71
Gillingham	L	02.83	82	5	0	0
Aldershot	Bulova (HK)	08.84	84	6	3	2
Exeter C. (N/C)		03.87	86	1	0	0

FOLEY, Stephen P.
Clacton, 21 June, 1953 (M)

League Club	Source	Date Signed	Seasons Played	Apps	Subs	Gls
Colchester U.	App	09.71	71-81	273	10	54

FOLEY, Steven
Liverpool, 4 October, 1962 (M)

League Club	Source	Date Signed	Seasons Played	Apps	Subs	Gls
Liverpool	App	09.80				
Fulham	L	12.83	83	2	1	0
Grimsby T.	Tr	08.84	84	31	0	2
Sheffield U.	Tr	08.85	85-86	56	10	14
Swindon T.	Tr	06.87	87-91	142	9	23
Stoke C.	Tr	01.92	91	20	0	1

FOLEY, Terence
Portsmouth, 8 February, 1938 (CF)

League Club	Source	Date Signed	Seasons Played	Apps	Subs	Gls
Portsmouth	Ryde	05.59	59	7	-	0
Chesterfield	Tr	07.60	60	28	-	11

FOLEY, Theodore C.
Dublin, 2 March, 1937 IR-9 (FB)

League Club	Source	Date Signed	Seasons Played	Apps	Subs	Gls
Exeter C.	Home Farm	03.55	55-60	155	-	1
Northampton T.	Tr	05.61	61-66	205	0	8
Charlton Ath.	Tr	08.67	67	6	0	0

FOLEY, William (Will)
Bellshill, 25 June, 1960 (F)

League Club	Source	Date Signed	Seasons Played	Apps	Subs	Gls
Swansea C. (N/C)	Frickley Ath.	01.86	85	4	1	2
Cardiff C. (N/C)	Tr	03.86	85	5	2	1

FOLLAN, Edward
Greenock, 3 October, 1929 (IF)

League Club	Source	Date Signed	Seasons Played	Apps	Subs	Gls
Aston Villa	Prescot Cables	06.52	54-55	34	-	7

FOLLAND, Robert
Hartlepool, 3 December, 1940 (CF)

League Club	Source	Date Signed	Seasons Played	Apps	Subs	Gls
Hartlepool U.		05.59	59-62	58	-	24

FOOTE, Christopher R. T.
Bournemouth, 19 November, 1950 (M)

League Club	Source	Date Signed	Seasons Played	Apps	Subs	Gls
Bournemouth	App	08.68	68-69	44	1	2
Cambridge U.	Tr	03.71	70-73	76	10	6

FOOTITT, Donald
Grantham, 24 May, 1929 (G)

League Club	Source	Date Signed	Seasons Played	Apps	Subs	Gls
Lincoln C.	St Johns	01.47	46	24	-	0
Crewe Alex.	Tr	07.49	49	1	-	0

FORBES, Alexander R.
Dundee, 21 January, 1925 S-14 (WH)

League Club	Source	Date Signed	Seasons Played	Apps	Subs	Gls
Sheffield U.	Dundee N.E.	12.44	46-47	61	-	6
Arsenal	Tr	02.48	47-55	217	-	20
Leyton Orient	Tr	08.56	56	8	-	0
Fulham	Tr	11.57	57	4	-	0

FORBES, Dudley D.
South Africa, 19 April, 1926 (WH)

League Club	Source	Date Signed	Seasons Played	Apps	Subs	Gls
Charlton Ath.	Marist Bros (SA)	12.47	48-50	57	-	1

FORBES, Duncan S.
Edinburgh, 19 June, 1941 (CD)

League Club	Source	Date Signed	Seasons Played	Apps	Subs	Gls
Colchester U.	Musselburgh	09.61	61-68	270	0	2
Norwich C.	Tr	09.68	68-80	289	6	10
Torquay U.	L	10.76	76	7	0	0

FORBES, George P.
Cheadle, 21 July, 1914 (CH)

League Club	Source	Date Signed	Seasons Played	Apps	Subs	Gls
Blackburn Rov.		01.37	36	2	-	1
Barrow	Tr	06.46	46-50	177	-	3

FORBES, Graeme S. A.
Forfar, 29 July, 1958 (CD)

League Club	Source	Date Signed	Seasons Played	Apps	Subs	Gls
Walsall	Motherwell	09.86	86-89	173	0	9

FORBES, Richard J.
Ashford (Sy), 12 March, 1955 (M)

League Club	Source	Date Signed	Seasons Played	Apps	Subs	Gls
Exeter C.	Woking	07.79	77-80	55	4	5
Plymouth Arg.	Bideford	08.83	83	3	0	0

FORBES, William
Glasgow, 25 May, 1922 (WH)

League Club	Source	Date Signed	Seasons Played	Apps	Subs	Gls
Wolverhampton W.	Dunfermline Ath.	09.46	46-49	71	-	23
Preston N.E.	Tr	12.49	49-55	192	-	7
Carlisle U.	Tr	07.56	56-57	25	-	0

FORD, Alan L.
Ferndale, 28 October, 1925 Died 1963 (G)

League Club	Source	Date Signed	Seasons Played	Apps	Subs	Gls
Workington (Am)		07.51	51-53	39	-	0

FORD, Andrew C.
Minehead, 4 May, 1954 (FB)

League Club	Source	Date Signed	Seasons Played	Apps	Subs	Gls
Bournemouth	Minehead	07.72				
Southend U.	Tr	05.73	73-76	135	3	3
Swindon T.	Tr	08.77	77-79	92	6	0
Gillingham	Tr	07.80	80-81	62	0	3

FORD, Anthony M.
Thornbury, 26 November, 1944 E Yth (FB)

League Club	Source	Date Signed	Seasons Played	Apps	Subs	Gls
Bristol C.	App	11.61	61-69	170	1	10
Bristol Rov.	Tr	12.69	69-70	28	0	1

FORD, Clive
West Bromwich, 10 April, 1945 (F)

League Club	Source	Date Signed	Seasons Played	Apps	Subs	Gls
Wolverhampton W.	App	10.62	64	2	-	0
Walsall	Tr	12.64	64-66	11	3	0
Lincoln C.	Tr	02.67	66-67	48	1	16

FORD, Colin
Lewisham, 18 September, 1960 (FB)

League Club	Source	Date Signed	Seasons Played	Apps	Subs	Gls
Gillingham	App	09.78	79	1	0	0

FORD, David
Sheffield, 2 March, 1945 Eu23-2 (IF)

League Club	Source	Date Signed	Seasons Played	Apps	Subs	Gls
Sheffield Wed.	App	01.63	65-69	117	5	31
Newcastle U.	Tr	12.69	69-70	24	2	3
Sheffield U.	Tr	01.71	70-72	21	6	2
Halifax T.	Tr	08.73	73-75	83	2	6

FORD, Francis M.
Bridgend, 3 February, 1967 (D)

League Club	Source	Date Signed	Seasons Played	Apps	Subs	Gls
Cardiff C.	YT	03.85	84	1	1	0

FORD, Frederick G. L.
Dartford, 10 February, 1916 Died 1981 (RH)

League Club	Source	Date Signed	Seasons Played	Apps	Subs	Gls
Charlton Ath.	Erith & Belvedere	03.36	36-37	22	-	0
Millwall	Tr	11.45	46	9	-	0
Carlisle U.	Tr	07.47	47	28	-	0

FORD, Gary
York, 8 February, 1961 (RW)

League Club	Source	Date Signed	Seasons Played	Apps	Subs	Gls
York C.	App	02.79	78-86	359	7	53
Leicester C.	Tr	06.87	87	15	1	2
Port Vale	Tr	12.87	87-90	66	9	12
Walsall	L	03.90	89	13	0	2
Mansfield T.	Tr	03.91	90-91	51	0	5

FORD, Jonathan S.
Birmingham, 12 April, 1968 (FB)

League Club	Source	Date Signed	Seasons Played	Apps	Subs	Gls
Swansea C.	Cradley T.	08.91	91	42	2	0

FORD, Kenneth S.
Sheffield, 1 December, 1940 (OR)

League Club	Source	Date Signed	Seasons Played	Apps	Subs	Gls
Sheffield Wed.	Jnrs	03.60				
Oldham Ath.	Tr	06.61	61	5	-	1

FORD, Michael P.
Bristol, 9 February, 1966 (D)

League Club	Source	Date Signed	Seasons Played	Apps	Subs	Gls
Leicester C.	App	02.84				
Cardiff C.	Devizes T.	09.84	84-87	144	1	13
Oxford U.	Tr	06.88	88-91	67	11	5

FORD, Peter L.
Stoke, 10 August, 1933 (LH)

League Club	Source	Date Signed	Seasons Played	Apps	Subs	Gls
Stoke C.	West Bromwich A. (Am)	05.53	56-58	14	-	0
Port Vale	Tr	09.59	59-62	104	-	5

FORD, Robert
Rutherglen, 13 August, 1934 (IF)

League Club	Source	Date Signed	Seasons Played	Apps	Subs	Gls
Aldershot	Vale of Clyde	07.57	57	2	-	0

FORD, Stephen D.
Shoreham, 17 February, 1959 (F)

League Club	Source	Date Signed	Seasons Played	Apps	Subs	Gls
Stoke C.	Lewes	07.81	81	1	1	0

FORD, Stuart T.
Sheffield, 20 July, 1971 (G)

League Club	Source	Date Signed	Seasons Played	Apps	Subs	Gls
Rotherham U.	YT	07.89	89-91	5	0	0
Scarborough	L	03.92	91	6	0	0

FORD, Tony
Grimsby, 14 May, 1959 E'B' (W)

League Club	Source	Date Signed	Seasons Played	Apps	Subs	Gls
Grimsby T.	App	05.77	75-85	321	34	55
Sunderland	L	03.86	85	8	1	1
Stoke C.	Tr	07.86	86-88	112	0	13
West Bromwich A.	Tr	03.89	88-91	114	0	15
Grimsby T.	Tr	11.91	91	17	5	1

FORD, Trevor
Swansea, 1 October, 1923 W-38 (CF)

League Club	Source	Date Signed	Seasons Played	Apps	Subs	Gls
Swansea C.	Jnrs	05.42	46	16	-	9
Aston Villa	Tr	01.47	46-50	120	-	60
Sunderland	Tr	10.50	50-53	108	-	67
Cardiff C.	Tr	12.53	53-56	96	-	39
Newport Co.	P.S.V. Eindhoven (Neth)	07.60	60	8	-	3

FORDE, Clevere
London, 14 November, 1958 (W)

League Club	Source	Date Signed	Seasons Played	Apps	Subs	Gls
Plymouth Arg.	Hounslow	12.78	78	4	1	0

League Club	Source	Date Signed	Seasons Played	Career Record Apps	Subs	Gls
FORDE, Steven						
South Kirkby, 29 August, 1914						(FB)
Sheffield Wed.	South Elmsall	01.33				
Rotherham U.	Tr	04.33	32-36	116	-	1
West Ham U.	Tr	01.37	37-51	170	-	1
FOREMAN, Darren						
Southampton, 12 February, 1968 E Sch						(F)
Barnsley	Fareham T.	08.86	86-89	33	14	8
Crewe Alex.	Tr	03.90	89-90	19	4	4
Scarborough	Tr	03.91	90-91	26	12	7
FOREMAN, Dennis J.						
South Africa, 1 February, 1933						(OL)
Brighton & H.A.	Hibs (SA)	03.52	52-60	212	-	62
FOREMAN, George A.						
West Ham, 1 March, 1914 Died 1969 E Amat						(CF)
West Ham U.	Walthamstow Ave.	03.38	38	6	-	1
Tottenham H.	Tr	02.46	46	36	-	14
FOREMAN, William E.						
Havant, 3 February, 1958						(M)
Bristol Rov.	Bournemouth (App)	05.76	76-77	0	2	0
FORGAN, Thomas C.						
Middlesbrough, 12 October, 1929						(G)
Hull C.	Sutton Est.	05.49	53	10	-	0
York C.	Tr	06.54	54-65	388	0	0
FORMAN, Matthew C.						
Evesham, 8 September, 1967						(M)
Aston Villa	App	09.85				
Wolverhampton W.	Tr	08.86	86	24	1	4
FORREST, Craig L.						
Canada, 30 September, 1967 Canadian Int						(G)
Ipswich T.	App	08.85	88-91	162	0	0
Colchester U.	L	03.88	87	11	0	0
FORREST, Ernest						
Sunderland, 19 February, 1919 Died 1987						(WH)
Bolton W.	Usworth Colly	01.38	38-47	69	-	1
Grimsby T.	Tr	05.48	48	33	-	1
Millwall	Tr	06.49	49	37	-	4
FORREST, Gerald						
Stockton, 21 January, 1957						(RB)
Rotherham U.	South Bank	02.77	77-85	357	0	7
Southampton	Tr	12.85	85-89	112	3	0
Rotherham U.	Tr	08.90	90	32	2	0
FORREST, James						
Glasgow, 22 September, 1944 S Sch/Su23-2/S-5						(CF)
Preston N.E.	Glasgow Rangers	03.67	66-67	24	2	3
FORREST, James						
Dalkeith, 14 November, 1929						(F)
Leeds U.	Musselburgh	12.50				
Accrington St.	Tr	11.51	51	5	-	2
FORREST, John A.						
Bury, 9 October, 1947						(G)
Bury	Jnrs	03.66	67-80	430	0	0
FORREST, Keith						
Hartlepool, 18 February, 1951						(IF)
Hartlepool U. (Am)		07.69	69-70	4	2	0
FORREST, J. Robert						
Rossington, 13 May, 1931						(IF)
Leeds U.	Retford T.	12.52	52-58	119	-	36
Notts Co.	Tr	02.59	58-61	117	-	37
FORREST, William						
Bo'ness, 19 January, 1945						(WH)
Carlisle U.	Hearts	07.62	62-63	10	-	0
Brighton & H. A.	Tr	07.64				
FORRESTER, Anthony C.						
Bournemouth, 14 January, 1940						(OR)
West Bromwich A.	Jnrs	03.57	58	6	-	3
Southend U.	Tr	04.59	59	10	-	1
FORRESTER, George H.						
Glasgow, 28 August, 1934						(FB)
Sunderland	Raith Rov.	03.53				
Accrington St.	Eyemouth U.	02.60	59-60	54	-	0

League Club	Source	Date Signed	Seasons Played	Career Record Apps	Subs	Gls
FORRESTER, George L.						
Cannock, 8 June, 1927 Died 1982						(WH)
Gillingham		08.47	50-54	100	-	3
Reading	Tr	07.55	55	6	-	2
FORSTER, Derek						
Newcastle, 19 February, 1949 E Sch						(G)
Sunderland	App	02.66	64-71	18	0	0
Charlton Ath.	Tr	07.73	73	9	0	0
Brighton & H. A.	Tr	07.74	74	3	0	0
FORSTER, Geoffrey P.						
Middlesbrough, 3 August, 1954						(F)
Rochdale (N/C)	Winnybanks	11.78	78	0	1	0
Hartlepool U.	Whitby T.	05.80	80	10	4	4
FORSTER, Leslie J.						
Newcastle, 22 July, 1915						(OR)
Blackpool	Walker Celtic	04.37	38	2	-	0
York C.	Tr	09.46	46	10	-	2
Gateshead	Tr	02.47	46-47	15	-	3
FORSTER, Mark E.						
Middlesbrough, 1 November, 1964						(F)
Leicester C.	Guisborough T.	06.83				
Darlington	Tr	03.84	83-85	31	7	13
FORSTER, Martyn G.						
Kettering, 1 February, 1963 E Sch						(FB)
Northampton T.	Kettering T.	10.83	83	41	1	0
FORSTER, Ronald						
Stockton, 19 August, 1935						(OR)
Darlington	Shotton Colly	05.56	56-59	57	-	4
FORSTER, Stanley G.						
Aylesham (Kt), 1 November, 1943						(OL)
Crystal Palace	Margate	11.61	62	2	-	1
FORSYTH, Alexander						
Swinton (Merse), 5 February, 1952 Su23-1/SF Lge/S-10						(LB)
Manchester U.	Partick Th.	12.72	72-77	99	2	4
FORSYTH, Alexander S.						
Falkirk, 29 September, 1928						(OL)
Darlington	Falkirk	08.52	52	26	-	7
FORSYTH, Campbell						
Stirling, 5 May, 1939 SF Lge/S-4						(G)
Southampton	Kilmarnock	12.65	65-67	48	0	0
FORSYTH, David						
Falkirk, 5 May, 1945						(FB)
Leyton Orient	Kirkintilloch Rob Roy	05.64	65-66	32	-	0
FORSYTH, John G.						
Dumbarton, 20 December, 1918						(OL)
Luton T.	Dumbarton	08.42				
New Brighton	Tr	07.46	46-47	64	-	4
Chester C.	Tr	07.48	48	32	-	1
FORSYTH, Michael E.						
Liverpool, 20 March, 1966 E Yth/Eu21-1/E'B'						(LB)
West Bromwich A.	App	11.83	83-85	28	1	0
Derby Co.	Tr	03.86	86-91	234	0	5
FORSYTH, E. Robert						
Belfast, 27 February, 1925						(OR)
Bradford C.	Ballymoney	07.48	48	1	-	0
FORSYTH, William A.						
Glasgow, 29 March, 1932						(FB)
Blackburn Rov.		08.49				
Southport	Tr	07.52	52-56	55	-	5
FORT, Samuel M.						
Bentley, 27 April, 1929 Died 1976						(FB)
Walsall	Retford T.	02.54	53-54	28	-	0
FOSS, Sidney R.						
Barking, 28 November, 1912						(LH)
Chelsea	Southall	05.36	36-47	41	-	3
FOSTER, Adrian M.						
Kidderminster, 19 March, 1971						(F)
West Bromwich A.	YT	07.89	89-91	13	14	2

Craig Forrest (Ipswich Town & Canada)

FOSTER, Alan
South Shields, 20 November, 1934 (CF)

League Club	Source	Date Signed	Seasons Played	Apps	Subs	Gls
Crewe Alex.	Northwich Vic.	08.59	59-60	19	-	7

FOSTER, Anthony J.
Dublin, 13 February, 1949 (IF)

League Club	Source	Date Signed	Seasons Played	Apps	Subs	Gls
Arsenal	Jnrs	02.66				
Oldham Ath.	Tr	09.66	66-67	8	1	0

FOSTER, Barry
Worksop, 21 September, 1951 E Yth (FB)

League Club	Source	Date Signed	Seasons Played	Apps	Subs	Gls
Mansfield T.	Jnrs	07.70	71-81	282	5	0

FOSTER, Clifford
Wigan, 14 January, 1931

League Club	Source	Date Signed	Seasons Played	Apps	Subs	Gls
Southport (Am)		08.51	51-52	10	-	2

FOSTER, Colin
Nottingham, 26 December, 1952 (CD)

League Club	Source	Date Signed	Seasons Played	Apps	Subs	Gls
Mansfield T.	App	12.70	71-78	195	10	17
Peterborough U.	Tr	06.79	79-80	71	0	5

FOSTER, Colin J.
Chiselhurst, 16 July, 1964 (CD)

League Club	Source	Date Signed	Seasons Played	Apps	Subs	Gls
Leyton Orient	App	02.82	81-86	173	1	10
Nottingham F.	Tr	02.87	86-89	68	4	5
West Ham U.	Tr	09.89	89-91	80	2	4

Colin Foster (Leyton Orient, Nottingham Forest & West Ham United)

FOSTER, Deane
Reading, 22 August, 1966 (D)

League Club	Source	Date Signed	Seasons Played	Apps	Subs	Gls
Reading	YT	03.85	84	0	2	0

FOSTER, Emanuel
Newcastle-u-Lyme, 4 December, 1921 (G)

League Club	Source	Date Signed	Seasons Played	Apps	Subs	Gls
Stoke C.		12.43	46	1	-	0

FOSTER, George W.
Plymouth, 26 September, 1956 (CD)

League Club	Source	Date Signed	Seasons Played	Apps	Subs	Gls
Plymouth Arg.	App	09.74	73-81	201	11	6
Torquay U.	L	10.76	76	6	0	3
Exeter C.	L	12.81	81	28	0	0
Derby Co.	Tr	06.82	82	30	0	0
Mansfield T.	Tr	08.83	83-91	363	0	0

FOSTER, Karl A.
Birmingham, 15 September, 1965 (F)

League Club	Source	Date Signed	Seasons Played	Apps	Subs	Gls
Shrewsbury T.	App	09.83	82	1	1	0

FOSTER, Michael S.
Leicester, 3 February, 1939 (W)

League Club	Source	Date Signed	Seasons Played	Apps	Subs	Gls
Leicester C.		08.59				
Colchester U.	Tr	05.61	61	36	-	8
Norwich C.	Tr	09.62				
Millwall	Tr	07.63	63	13	-	2

FOSTER, Nigel
Sutton-in-Ashfield, 23 March, 1968 (D)

League Club	Source	Date Signed	Seasons Played	Apps	Subs	Gls
Mansfield T.	YT	08.85	84	1	0	0

FOSTER, Robert J.
Sheffield, 19 July, 1929 E'B'-1 (IF)

League Club	Source	Date Signed	Seasons Played	Apps	Subs	Gls
Chesterfield	Jnrs	09.47	48-50	4	-	0
Preston N. E.	Tr	07.51	51-56	99	-	40
Rotherham U.	Tr	05.58	58	1	-	0

FOSTER, Ronald E.
Islington, 22 November, 1938 (IF)

League Club	Source	Date Signed	Seasons Played	Apps	Subs	Gls
Leyton Orient	Clapton	03.57	59-62	72	-	17
Grimsby T.	Tr	12.62	62-65	129	0	24
Reading	Tr	07.66	66-67	44	1	5
Brentford	Dallas (USA)	03.69	68	3	1	0

FOSTER, Stephen B.
Portsmouth, 24 September, 1957 Eu21-1/E-3 (CD)

League Club	Source	Date Signed	Seasons Played	Apps	Subs	Gls
Portsmouth	App	09.75	75-78	101	8	6
Brighton & H. A.	Tr	07.79	79-83	171	1	6
Aston Villa	Tr	03.84	83-84	15	0	3
Luton T.	Tr	11.84	84-88	163	0	11
Oxford U.	Tr	07.89	89-91	95	0	10

FOSTER, Trevor
Walsall, 11 January, 1941 (F)

League Club	Source	Date Signed	Seasons Played	Apps	Subs	Gls
Walsall	Jnrs	07.59	59-64	62	-	12

FOSTER, Wayne P.
Leigh, 11 September, 1963 E Yth (M)

League Club	Source	Date Signed	Seasons Played	Apps	Subs	Gls
Bolton W.	App	08.81	81-84	92	13	13
Preston N. E.	Tr	06.85	85	25	6	3

FOSTER, Winston A.
Birmingham, 1 November, 1941 (CH)

League Club	Source	Date Signed	Seasons Played	Apps	Subs	Gls
Birmingham C.	Jnrs	11.58	60-68	151	1	2
Crewe Alex.	L	03.69	68	13	0	0
Plymouth Arg.	Tr	06.69	69-70	33	0	0

FOTHERGILL, Ashley G.
Harrogate, 3 October, 1969 (M)

League Club	Source	Date Signed	Seasons Played	Apps	Subs	Gls
Rochdale	Middlesbrough (YT)	10.88	88	8	1	0

FOTHERINGHAM, James G.
Hamilton, 19 December, 1933 Died 1977 (CH)

League Club	Source	Date Signed	Seasons Played	Apps	Subs	Gls
Arsenal	Jnrs	03.51	54-58	72	-	0
Northampton T.	Hearts	08.59	59	11	-	0

FOULDS, Albert
Salford, 8 August, 1919 (IF)

League Club	Source	Date Signed	Seasons Played	Apps	Subs	Gls
Chester C.	Altrincham	08.48	49	31	-	15
Rochdale	Tr	09.50	50-52	62	-	24
Crystal Palace	Tr	07.53	53	17	-	4
Crewe Alex.	Tr	01.54	53	14	-	2

FOULKES, Reginald E.
Shrewsbury, 23 February, 1923 E Sch (CH)

League Club	Source	Date Signed	Seasons Played	Apps	Subs	Gls
Walsall	Birmingham C. (Am)	08.45	46-49	160	-	6
Norwich C.	Tr	05.50	50-55	216	-	8

FOULKES, William A.
St Helens, 5 January, 1932 Eu23-2/EF Lge/E-1 (D)

League Club	Source	Date Signed	Seasons Played	Apps	Subs	Gls
Manchester U.	Whiston B.C.	08.51	52-69	563	3	7

League Club	Source	Date Signed	Seasons Played	Career Record Apps	Subs	Gls

FOULKES, William I.
Merthyr Tydfil, 29 May, 1926 Died 1979 W-11 (IF)

League Club	Source	Date Signed	Seasons Played	Apps	Subs	Gls
Cardiff C.		02.45				
Chester C.	Winsford U.	05.48	48-51	117	-	14
Newcastle U.	Tr	10.51	51-53	58	-	8
Southampton	Tr	08.54	54	23	-	1
Chester C.	Tr	07.56	56-60	178	-	21

FOUNTAIN, John (Jack)
Leeds, 27 May, 1932 (WH)

League Club	Source	Date Signed	Seasons Played	Apps	Subs	Gls
Sheffield U.	Ashley Road	11.49	50-55	31	-	0
Swindon T.	Tr	01.57	56-59	81	-	2
York C.	Tr	08.60	60-63	130	-	3

FOWLER, Derek W.
Torquay, 28 November, 1961 (D)

League Club	Source	Date Signed	Seasons Played	Apps	Subs	Gls
Torquay U.	S.T.C. Paignton	03.84	83-85	65	8	4

FOWLER, John (Jack)
Rotherham, 13 April, 1935 (F)

League Club	Source	Date Signed	Seasons Played	Apps	Subs	Gls
Sheffield U.		07.54				
Halifax T.	Tr	06.56	56-58	19	-	3

FOWLER, John
Leith, 17 October, 1933 (LB)

League Club	Source	Date Signed	Seasons Played	Apps	Subs	Gls
Colchester U.	Bonnyrigg Rose	06.55	55-67	415	0	5

FOWLER, Lee E.
Eastwood, 26 January, 1969 (D)

League Club	Source	Date Signed	Seasons Played	Apps	Subs	Gls
Stoke C.	YT	07.88	87-91	42	7	0

FOWLER, Martin
York, 17 January, 1957 (M)

League Club	Source	Date Signed	Seasons Played	Apps	Subs	Gls
Huddersfield T.	App	01.74	73-77	62	11	2
Blackburn Rov.	Tr	07.78	78-79	36	2	0
Hartlepool U.	L	03.80	79	6	0	0
Stockport Co.	Tr	08.80	80-81	74	1	6
Scunthorpe U.	Tr	09.82	82	15	3	0

FOWLER, H. Norman
Stockton, 3 September, 1919 Died 1990 E Sch (FB)

League Club	Source	Date Signed	Seasons Played	Apps	Subs	Gls
Middlesbrough	South Bank	09.36	37-38	7	-	0
Hull C.	Tr	09.46	46-49	52	-	0
Gateshead	Tr	11.49	49-51	64	-	0

FOWLER, Thomas
Prescot, 16 December, 1924 (OL)

League Club	Source	Date Signed	Seasons Played	Apps	Subs	Gls
Northampton T.	Everton (Am)	03.45	46-61	521	-	82
Aldershot	Tr	12.61	61-62	14	-	0

FOWLER, Tony
Birmingham, 3 October, 1962 (G)

League Club	Source	Date Signed	Seasons Played	Apps	Subs	Gls
Torquay U.	Foxhole U.	03.85	84-85	9	0	0

FOX, Alan
Holywell, 10 July, 1936 Wu23-1 (CH)

League Club	Source	Date Signed	Seasons Played	Apps	Subs	Gls
Wrexham	Jnrs	04.54	53-63	350	-	3
Hartlepool U.	Tr	06.64	64-65	58	0	0
Bradford C.	Tr	10.65	65	33	0	0

FOX, Geoffrey R.
Bristol, 19 January, 1925 (FB)

League Club	Source	Date Signed	Seasons Played	Apps	Subs	Gls
Ipswich T.	M.C.W.	08.45	46	11	-	1
Bristol Rov.	Tr	06.47	47-54	276	-	2
Swindon T.	Tr	10.55	55-56	48	-	0

FOX, Kevin
Sheffield, 22 September, 1960 (G)

League Club	Source	Date Signed	Seasons Played	Apps	Subs	Gls
Lincoln C.	Jnrs	03.78	79	4	0	0

FOX, Matthew C.
Birmingham, 13 July, 1971 (CD)

League Club	Source	Date Signed	Seasons Played	Apps	Subs	Gls
Birmingham C.	YT	07.89	88-90	12	2	0

FOX, Oscar
Clowne, 1 January, 1921 Died 1990 (IF)

League Club	Source	Date Signed	Seasons Played	Apps	Subs	Gls
Sheffield Wed.		10.43	46-49	44	-	3
Mansfield T.	Tr	06.50	50-56	248	-	30

FOX, Peter D.
Scunthorpe, 5 July, 1957 (G)

League Club	Source	Date Signed	Seasons Played	Apps	Subs	Gls
Sheffield Wed.	App	06.75	72-76	49	0	0
Barnsley	L	12.77	77	1	0	0
Stoke C.	Tr	03.78	78-90	399	0	0

FOX, Raymond
Manchester, 13 December, 1934 (OL)

League Club	Source	Date Signed	Seasons Played	Apps	Subs	Gls
Oldham Ath. (Am)	Army	08.57	57	1	-	0

FOX, Raymond V.
Bristol, 28 January, 1921 (FB)

League Club	Source	Date Signed	Seasons Played	Apps	Subs	Gls
Bristol C.	St Aldheims	10.46	46-48	23	-	0

FOX, Reginald
Edmonton, 16 October, 1929 (FB)

League Club	Source	Date Signed	Seasons Played	Apps	Subs	Gls
Fulham		12.49				
Brighton & H. A.	Tr	10.52	52-55	20	-	0

FOX, Ruel A.
Ipswich, 14 January, 1968 (W)

League Club	Source	Date Signed	Seasons Played	Apps	Subs	Gls
Norwich C.	App	01.86	86-91	91	22	11

Ruel Fox (Norwich City)

FOX, Stephen D.
Tamworth, 17 February, 1958 (W)

League Club	Source	Date Signed	Seasons Played	Apps	Subs	Gls
Birmingham C.	App	02.76	76-78	26	3	1
Wrexham	Tr	12.78	78-82	136	6	10
Port Vale	Tr	10.82	82-83	71	3	6
Chester C.	Tr	07.84	84-85	29	4	4

FOX, Walter
Bolsover, 10 April, 1921 (FB)

League Club	Source	Date Signed	Seasons Played	Apps	Subs	Gls
Mansfield T.	Creswell Colly	05.46	46-49	62	-	0

FOXON, D. Neil
Nottingham, 10 July, 1948 (W)

League Club	Source	Date Signed	Seasons Played	Apps	Subs	Gls
Scunthorpe U.	Notts Co. (Am)	08.65	66-67	20	2	1

FOXTON, D. Graham
Harrogate, 2 October, 1949 (FB)

League Club	Source	Date Signed	Seasons Played	Apps	Subs	Gls
Scunthorpe U.	App	10.67	67-72	148	4	2

FOXTON, John D. (Jack)
Salford, 17 June, 1921 (LH)

League Club	Source	Date Signed	Seasons Played	Apps	Subs	Gls
Portsmouth	Bolton W. (Am)	05.45	46	1	-	0
Swindon T.	Tr	09.48	48-50	49	-	0

FOY, John
Liverpool, 28 May, 1950 (OL)

League Club	Source	Date Signed	Seasons Played	Apps	Subs	Gls
Southport (Am)	Ormskirk	08.74	74	1	0	0

FOYLE, Martin J.
Salisbury, 2 May, 1963 (F)

League Club	Source	Date Signed	Seasons Played	Apps	Subs	Gls
Southampton	App	08.80	82-83	6	6	1
Aldershot	Tr	07.84	84-86	98	0	35
Oxford U.	Tr	03.87	86-90	120	6	36
Port Vale	Tr	06.91	91	43	0	11

FRAIN, David

FRAIN, David
Sheffield, 11 October, 1962 (M)

League Club	Source	Date Signed	Seasons Played	Apps	Subs	Gls
Sheffield U.	Dronfield U.	09.85	85-87	35	9	6
Rochdale	Tr	07.88	88	42	0	12
Stockport Co.	Tr	07.89	89-91	105	6	9

FRAIN, John W.
Birmingham, 8 October, 1968 (M/LB)

League Club	Source	Date Signed	Seasons Played	Apps	Subs	Gls
Birmingham C.	App	10.86	85-91	165	7	15

FRAIN, Peter A.
Birmingham, 18 March, 1965 (F)

League Club	Source	Date Signed	Seasons Played	Apps	Subs	Gls
West Bromwich A.	App	03.82				
Mansfield T.	L	01.84	83	1	1	0

FRAME, William
Carluke, 7 May, 1912 (FB)

League Club	Source	Date Signed	Seasons Played	Apps	Subs	Gls
Leicester C.	Shawfield Jnrs	10.33	34-49	220	-	0

FRAME, William J.
Castleford, 1 August, 1939 (G)

League Club	Source	Date Signed	Seasons Played	Apps	Subs	Gls
Workington		11.58	58	9	-	0

FRANCE, Anthony
Huddersfield, 11 April, 1939 (IF)

League Club	Source	Date Signed	Seasons Played	Apps	Subs	Gls
Huddersfield T.	Jnrs	04.56	57-59	9	-	2
Darlington	Tr	12.61	61-62	47	-	9
Stockport Co.	Tr	07.63	63	30	-	8

FRANCE, Darren B.
Hull, 8 August, 1967 (F)

League Club	Source	Date Signed	Seasons Played	Apps	Subs	Gls
Hull C.	North Ferriby U.	11.91	91	10	7	4

FRANCE, Gary
Worksop, 18 June, 1955 (CF)

League Club	Source	Date Signed	Seasons Played	Apps	Subs	Gls
Sheffield U.	App	06.73	73-74	1	1	0

FRANCE, Gary L.
Stalybridge, 5 May, 1946 (IF)

League Club	Source	Date Signed	Seasons Played	Apps	Subs	Gls
Burnley	Stalybridge Celtic	04.66	66-67	1	2	0
Bury	Tr	07.68	68	0	1	0

FRANCE, John (Jack)
Stalybridge, 30 November, 1913 (WH)

League Club	Source	Date Signed	Seasons Played	Apps	Subs	Gls
Swindon T.	Bath C.	08.37	37	1	-	0
Halifax T.	Bath C.	06.39	46-47	50	-	1

FRANCE, M. Paul
Holmfirth, 10 September, 1968 (D)

League Club	Source	Date Signed	Seasons Played	Apps	Subs	Gls
Huddersfield T.	YT	06.87	87-88	7	4	0
Bristol C.	Tr	07.89				
Burnley	Tr	07.90	90-91	7	1	0

FRANCE, Peter
Huddersfield, 27 March, 1936 (G)

League Club	Source	Date Signed	Seasons Played	Apps	Subs	Gls
Huddersfield T.		09.56				
Bradford P.A.	Tr	05.57	57	16	-	0

FRANCIS, Carl E.
West Ham, 21 August, 1962 (F)

League Club	Source	Date Signed	Seasons Played	Apps	Subs	Gls
Birmingham C.	App	08.80	82	2	3	0
Hereford U.	L	12.83	83	5	0	0

FRANCIS, George E.
Acton, 4 February, 1934 (CF)

League Club	Source	Date Signed	Seasons Played	Apps	Subs	Gls
Brentford	Jnrs	01.53	54-60	228	-	109
Queens Park R.	Tr	05.61	61	2	-	1
Brentford	Tr	10.61	61	32	-	14
Gillingham	Tr	08.62	62-63	51	-	19

FRANCIS, Gerald
South Africa, 6 December, 1933 (OR)

League Club	Source	Date Signed	Seasons Played	Apps	Subs	Gls
Leeds U.	Johannesburg (SA)	07.57	57-61	46	-	9
York C.	Tr	10.61	61	16	-	4

FRANCIS, Gerald C. J.
Chiswick, 6 December, 1951 Eu23-6/E-12 (M)

League Club	Source	Date Signed	Seasons Played	Apps	Subs	Gls
Queens Park R.	App	06.69	69-78	289	4	53
Crystal Palace	Tr	07.79	79-80	59	0	7
Queens Park R.	Tr	02.81	80-81	17	0	4
Coventry C.	Tr	02.82	81-82	50	0	2
Exeter C.	Tr	08.83	83	28	0	3
Cardiff C. (N/C)	Tr	09.84	84	7	0	0
Swansea C. (N/C)	Tr	10.84	84	3	0	0
Portsmouth (N/C)	Tr	11.84	84	3	0	0
Bristol Rov. (N/C)	Tr	09.85	85-87	33	0	0

FRANCIS, John A.
Dewsbury, 21 November, 1963 (F)

League Club	Source	Date Signed	Seasons Played	Apps	Subs	Gls
Halifax T. (N/C)	Emley	02.85	84	1	3	0
Sheffield U.	Emley	09.88	88-89	14	28	6
Burnley	Tr	01.90	89-91	99	2	27

FRANCIS, Keith R.
Yeovil, 22 July, 1929 (WH)

League Club	Source	Date Signed	Seasons Played	Apps	Subs	Gls
Leyton Orient	Yeovil T.	06.50	50	3	-	0

FRANCIS, Kevin M. D.
Birmingham, 6 December, 1967 (F)

League Club	Source	Date Signed	Seasons Played	Apps	Subs	Gls
Derby Co.	Mile Oak Rov.	02.89	89-90	0	10	0
Stockport Co.	Tr	02.91	90-91	45	3	20

Kevin Francis (Derby County & Stockport County)

FRANCIS, Lee C.
Walthamstow, 24 October, 1969 (M/RB)

League Club	Source	Date Signed	Seasons Played	Apps	Subs	Gls
Arsenal	YT	11.87				
Chesterfield	L	03.90	89	2	0	0
Chesterfield	Tr	06.90	90-91	63	5	2

FRANCIS, Sean R.
Birmingham, 1 August, 1972 (F)

League Club	Source	Date Signed	Seasons Played	Apps	Subs	Gls
Birmingham C.	YT	07.90	90-91	0	6	0

FRANCIS, Stephen S.
Billericay, 29 May, 1964 E Yth (G)

League Club	Source	Date Signed	Seasons Played	Apps	Subs	Gls
Chelsea	App	04.82	81-85	71	0	0
Reading	Tr	02.87	86-91	182	0	0

FRANCIS, Terence
Hartlepool, 18 June, 1943 (IF)

League Club	Source	Date Signed	Seasons Played	Apps	Subs	Gls
Hartlepool U.		12.63	63-64	18	-	4

FRANCIS, Thomas G.
Bermondsey, 30 October, 1920 (G)

League Club	Source	Date Signed	Seasons Played	Apps	Subs	Gls
Millwall	Cheltenham T.	05.46	46	1	-	0

FRANCIS, Trevor J.
Plymouth, 19 April, 1954 E Yth/Eu23-5/E-52 (F)

League Club	Source	Date Signed	Seasons Played	Apps	Subs	Gls
Birmingham C.	App	05.71	70-78	278	2	118
Nottingham F.	Tr	02.79	78-81	69	1	28
Manchester C.	Tr	09.81	81	26	0	12
Queens Park R.	Glasgow Rangers	03.88	87-89	30	2	12
Sheffield Wed.	Tr	02.91	89-91	28	42	5

FRANCOMBE, Peter
Cardiff, 4 August, 1963 (D)

League Club	Source	Date Signed	Seasons Played	Apps	Subs	Gls
Cardiff C.	Crystal Palace (App)	09.81	81	2	1	0

FRANKLAND, Anthony
Greenwich, 11 October, 1972 (W/FB)

League Club	Source	Date Signed	Seasons Played	Apps	Subs	Gls
Exeter C.	YT	07.90	89-90	3	4	0

FRANKLIN, Graham N.
Bicester, 25 January, 1957 (F)

League Club	Source	Date Signed	Seasons Played	Apps	Subs	Gls
Southend U.	Lowestoft T.	12.77	77-78	1	5	1

FRANKLIN, Jeffrey T.
Darlington, 8 December, 1973 (W)

League Club	Source	Date Signed	Seasons Played	Apps	Subs	Gls
Torquay U. (YT)	Millwall (YT)	08.91	91	1	1	0

FRANKLIN, John L.
Stockton, 27 November, 1924 (OL)

League Club	Source	Date Signed	Seasons Played	Apps	Subs	Gls
Middlesrough		12.43				
Darlington	Bath C.	08.47	47	8	-	3

FRANKLIN, C. Neil
Stoke, 24 January, 1922 EF Lge/E-27 (CH)

League Club	Source	Date Signed	Seasons Played	Apps	Subs	Gls
Stoke C.	Jnrs	01.39	46-49	142	-	0
Hull C.	Santa Fe (Col)	02.51	50-55	95	-	0
Crewe Alex.	Tr	02.56	55-57	66	-	4
Stockport C.	Tr	10.57	57	20	-	0

FRANKLIN, Neil J.
Lincoln, 10 March, 1969 (FB)

League Club	Source	Date Signed	Seasons Played	Apps	Subs	Gls
Lincoln C. (YT)	YT	09.86	86	15	0	0
Lincoln C. (N/C)	Sweden	10.88	88	0	1	0

FRANKLIN, Paul L.
Hainault, 5 October, 1963 (CD)

League Club	Source	Date Signed	Seasons Played	Apps	Subs	Gls
Watford	App	08.81	82-86	32	0	0
Shrewsbury T.	L	10.86	86	6	0	0
Swindon T.	L	11.86	86	5	0	1
Reading	Tr	06.87	87-88	17	3	0

FRANKLIN, Stanley T.
Shrewsbury, 16 September, 1919 (FB)

League Club	Source	Date Signed	Seasons Played	Apps	Subs	Gls
Blackpool	Kenwood Jnrs	05.38				
Crewe Alex.	Tr	04.46	46-47	28	-	9

FRANKLIN, William M.
Tiverton, 3 March, 1955 (G)

League Club	Source	Date Signed	Seasons Played	Apps	Subs	Gls
Charlton Ath.	App	03.73	72-74	13	0	0

FRANKS, Albert J.
Bolton, 13 April, 1936 (WH)

League Club	Source	Date Signed	Seasons Played	Apps	Subs	Gls
Newcastle U.	Boldon Colly	12.53	56-59	72	-	4
Lincoln C.	Glasgow Rangers	11.61	61-62	58	-	5

FRANKS, Colin J.
Wembley, 16 April, 1951 (CD)

League Club	Source	Date Signed	Seasons Played	Apps	Subs	Gls
Watford	Wealdstone	07.69	69-72	99	13	8
Sheffield U.	Tr	07.73	73-78	139	11	7

FRANKS, Kenneth
Motherwell, 24 April, 1944 (OL)

League Club	Source	Date Signed	Seasons Played	Apps	Subs	Gls
Brighton & H. A.		06.62	62	1	-	0

FRASER, Andrew M.
Newtongrange, 29 August, 1940 (CH)

League Club	Source	Date Signed	Seasons Played	Apps	Subs	Gls
Hartlepool U.	Hearts	10.61	61-63	82	-	2

FRASER, J. Cameron (Cammie)
Blackford, 24 May, 1941 Su23-2 (FB)

League Club	Source	Date Signed	Seasons Played	Apps	Subs	Gls
Aston Villa	Dunfermline Ath.	10.62	62-63	33	-	1
Birmingham C.	Tr	02.65	64-65	38	1	0

FRASER, David M.
Newtongrange, 6 June, 1937 (OL)

League Club	Source	Date Signed	Seasons Played	Apps	Subs	Gls
Hull C.	Jnrs	07.54	55-57	11	-	7
Mansfield T.	Tr	07.58	58	6	-	1

FRASER, Douglas M.
Glasgow, 8 December, 1941 S-2 (D)

League Club	Source	Date Signed	Seasons Played	Apps	Subs	Gls
West Bromwich A.	Aberdeen	09.63	63-70	255	2	8
Nottingham F.	Tr	01.71	70-72	85	0	3
Walsall	Tr	07.73	73	26	1	0

FRASER, Gordon
Elgin, 27 November, 1943 (CF)

League Club	Source	Date Signed	Seasons Played	Apps	Subs	Gls
Cardiff C.	Forres Mechs	01.61	62	4	-	0
Millwall	Tr	09.63	63	5	-	0
Newport Co.	Barry T.	08.66	66	11	2	2

FRASER, James
Coatbridge, 17 November, 1932 (FB)

League Club	Source	Date Signed	Seasons Played	Apps	Subs	Gls
Barrow	Bellshill Ath.	03.58	57-58	32	-	0

FRASER, John
Hammersmith, 12 July, 1953 (RB)

League Club	Source	Date Signed	Seasons Played	Apps	Subs	Gls
Fulham	App	06.71	71-75	55	1	1
Brentford	Tr	07.76	76-79	121	2	6

FRASER, John W.
Belfast, 15 September, 1938 (OR)

League Club	Source	Date Signed	Seasons Played	Apps	Subs	Gls
Sunderland	Glentoran	03.59	58-59	22	-	1
Portsmouth	Tr	06.60	60	1	-	0
Watford	Margate	07.62	62-63	24	-	3

FRASER, Robert
Glasgow, 23 January, 1917 (CH)

League Club	Source	Date Signed	Seasons Played	Apps	Subs	Gls
Newcastle U.	Hibernian	01.47	46-48	26	-	0

FRASER, William A.
Australia, 24 February, 1929 S-2 (G)

League Club	Source	Date Signed	Seasons Played	Apps	Subs	Gls
Sunderland	Airdrieonians	03.54	53-58	127	-	0
Nottingham F.	Tr	12.58	58	2	-	0

FRASER, William T.
Edinburgh, 12 August, 1945 (OL)

League Club	Source	Date Signed	Seasons Played	Apps	Subs	Gls
Huddersfield T.	Jnrs	04.63	63-64	8	-	2

FREAR, Brian
Cleckheaton, 8 July, 1933 (IF)

League Club	Source	Date Signed	Seasons Played	Apps	Subs	Gls
Huddersfield T.	Jnrs	09.50	51-56	37	-	10
Chesterfield	Tr	02.57	56-63	281	-	84
Halifax T.	Tr	07.64	64	35	-	5

FREEBURN, William
Dunfermline, 7 April, 1930 (FB)

League Club	Source	Date Signed	Seasons Played	Apps	Subs	Gls
Grimsby T.	East Stirling	08.51	51-54	34	-	0

FREEMAN, Alfred G.
Bethnal Green, 2 January, 1920 (IF)

League Club	Source	Date Signed	Seasons Played	Apps	Subs	Gls
Southampton		11.43	46	7	-	2
Crystal Palace	Tr	04.48	48	2	-	0

FREEMAN, Anthony
Melton Mowbray, 29 August, 1928 (OR)

League Club	Source	Date Signed	Seasons Played	Apps	Subs	Gls
Notts Co.	Melton T.	01.46	46-49	43	-	2

FREEMAN, Clive R.
Leeds, 12 September, 1962 (M/D)

League Club	Source	Date Signed	Seasons Played	Apps	Subs	Gls
Swansea C.	Bridlington T.	08.90	90-91	10	4	0
Carlisle U.	L	01.92	91	4	0	0

FREEMAN, Donald R.
Dartford, 29 August, 1921 (WH)

League Club	Source	Date Signed	Seasons Played	Apps	Subs	Gls
Charlton Ath.	Dartford	03.46				
Bristol C.	Tr	05.49	49	8	-	0
Watford	Tr	11.50				
Gillingham	Tr	06.51				

FREEMAN, Henry G.
Woodstock, 4 November, 1918 (FB)

League Club	Source	Date Signed	Seasons Played	Apps	Subs	Gls
Fulham	Woodstock T.	10.37	38-51	179	-	6
Walsall	Tr	10.52	52	20	-	1

FREEMAN, Neil
Northampton, 16 February, 1955 (G)

League Club	Source	Date Signed	Seasons Played	Apps	Subs	Gls
Arsenal	Jnrs	06.72				
Grimsby T.	Tr	03.74	73-75	33	0	0
Southend U.	Tr	07.76	76-77	69	0	0
Birmingham C.	Tr	07.78	78-79	31	0	0
Walsall	L	08.80	80	8	0	0
Huddersfield T.	L	01.81	80	18	0	0
Peterborough U.	Tr	09.81	81	41	0	0
Northampton T. (N/C)	Tr	08.82	82	22	0	0

FREEMAN, Neville F.
Brixworth, 25 January, 1925 (G)

League Club	Source	Date Signed	Seasons Played	Apps	Subs	Gls
Northampton T.		10.49	50	1	-	0

FREEMAN, Percy R.
Newark, 4 July, 1945 (F)

League Club	Source	Date Signed	Seasons Played	Apps	Subs	Gls
West Bromwich A.	Stourbridge	04.68	69	2	1	0
Lincoln C.	Tr	06.70	70-72	76	4	30
Reading	Tr	01.73	72-74	53	7	13
Lincoln C.	Tr	01.75	74-76	62	10	34

League Club	Source	Date Signed	Seasons Played	Career Record Apps	Subs	Gls

FREESTONE, Roger
Caerleon, 19 August, 1968 (G)

League Club	Source	Date Signed	Seasons Played	Apps	Subs	Gls
Newport Co.	YT	04.86	86	13	0	0
Chelsea	Tr	04.87	86-88	42	0	0
Swansea C.	L	09.89	89	14	0	0
Hereford U.	L	03.90	89	8	0	0
Swansea C.	Tr	09.91	91	42	0	0

FREESTONE, Trevor
Market Bosworth, 16 February, 1954 (F)

League Club	Source	Date Signed	Seasons Played	Apps	Subs	Gls
Peterborough U.	Jnrs	01.73	72	2	1	1

FRENCH, George N.
Colchester, 10 November, 1926

League Club	Source	Date Signed	Seasons Played	Apps	Subs	Gls
Colchester U. (Am)		05.52	52-53	3	-	0

FRENCH, Graham E.
Wolverhampton, 6 April, 1945 E Yth (W)

League Club	Source	Date Signed	Seasons Played	Apps	Subs	Gls
Shrewsbury T.	App	11.62	61-62	27	-	1
Swindon T.	Tr	08.63	63	5	-	0
Watford	Tr	08.64	64	4	-	0
Luton T.	Wellington T.	10.65	65-72	179	2	22
Reading	L	11.73	73	3	0	0
Southport		03.76	75	2	0	0

Graham French (Shrewsbury Town, Swindon Town, Watford, Luton Town & Southport)

FRENCH, James R.
Stockton, 27 January, 1926 (IF)

League Club	Source	Date Signed	Seasons Played	Apps	Subs	Gls
Middlesbrough		08.45				
Northampton T.		08.51	51	1	-	0
Darlington	Tr	08.53	53-54	52	-	8

FRENCH, John W.
Stockton, 19 January, 1925 (WH)

League Club	Source	Date Signed	Seasons Played	Apps	Subs	Gls
Middlesbrough		10.43				
Southend U.	Tr	02.47	46-52	182	-	20
Nottingham F.	Tr	11.52	52-55	80	-	8
Southend U.	Tr	07.56	56	5	-	0

FRENCH, Michael J.
Eastbourne, 7 May, 1955 E Yth (F)

League Club	Source	Date Signed	Seasons Played	Apps	Subs	Gls
Queens Park R.	App	05.73				
Brentford	Tr	02.75	74-76	56	9	16
Swindon T.	Tr	02.77	76-77	5	5	1
Doncaster Rov.	Tr	07.78	78	36	0	5
Aldershot	Tr	05.79	79-81	70	4	16
Rochdale	Tr	08.82	82	35	1	11

League Club	Source	Date Signed	Seasons Played	Career Record Apps	Subs	Gls

FRENCH, Nigel P.
Swansea, 24 March, 1968 (W)

League Club	Source	Date Signed	Seasons Played	Apps	Subs	Gls
Swansea	App	03.86	85-86	13	13	3

FRENCH, Raymond
Wigton, 16 December, 1946 (CH)

League Club	Source	Date Signed	Seasons Played	Apps	Subs	Gls
Workington (Am)	Wigton	11.73	73	2	0	0

FRETWELL, David
Normanton, 18 February, 1952 (CD)

League Club	Source	Date Signed	Seasons Played	Apps	Subs	Gls
Bradford C.	Jnrs	07.70	70-77	247	6	5
Wigan Ath.	Chicago (USA)	10.78	78-80	111	1	0

FRIAR, J. Paul
Glasgow, 6 June, 1963 S Yth (LB)

League Club	Source	Date Signed	Seasons Played	Apps	Subs	Gls
Leicester C.	App	08.80	80-82	56	2	0
Rotherham U.	Tr	02.83	82-83	20	0	0
Charlton Ath	Tr	07.84	84-85	36	0	0
Northampton T.	L	03.86	85	14	0	0
Aldershot	Tr	08.86	86	29	0	1

FRIDAY, Robin
Hammersmith, 27 July, 1952 Died 1990 (F)

League Club	Source	Date Signed	Seasons Played	Apps	Subs	Gls
Reading	Hayes	02.74	73-76	121	0	46
Cardiff C.	Tr	12.76	76-77	20	1	6

FRIDAY, Terence J.
Sittingbourne, 1 May, 1936 (G)

League Club	Source	Date Signed	Seasons Played	Apps	Subs	Gls
Gillingham (Am)	Sheppey U.	03.61	60	2	-	0

FRIDGE, Leslie F.
Inverness, 27 August, 1968 S Yth/Su21-1 (G)

League Club	Source	Date Signed	Seasons Played	Apps	Subs	Gls
Chelsea	App	09.85	85	1	0	0

FRIEDMANIS, Edward
Latvia, 22 February, 1920 Latvian Int (CF)

League Club	Source	Date Signed	Seasons Played	Apps	Subs	Gls
Northampton T.	Peterborough U.	05.48	48-49	19	-	4

FRIEL, Bernard J.
Glasgow, 16 September, 1941 (IF)

League Club	Source	Date Signed	Seasons Played	Apps	Subs	Gls
Southend U.	Dumbarton	06.63	63-64	17	-	8

FRIEL, George P.
Reading, 11 October, 1970 (W)

League Club	Source	Date Signed	Seasons Played	Apps	Subs	Gls
Reading	YT	06.89	89-90	10	6	1

FRIEL, John P.
Glasgow, 1 September, 1923 (IF)

League Club	Source	Date Signed	Seasons Played	Apps	Subs	Gls
New Brighton	Third Lanark	06.50	50	3	-	0
Torquay U.	Queen of South	10.52				

FRIEL, Peter
Wishaw, 27 March, 1939 (W)

League Club	Source	Date Signed	Seasons Played	Apps	Subs	Gls
Workington	Cambuslang R.	08.61	61	4	-	0

FRIEND, Barry N.
Wandsworth, 13 October, 1951 E Amat (W)

League Club	Source	Date Signed	Seasons Played	Apps	Subs	Gls
Fulham	Leatherhead	10.73	73	2	1	0

FRITH, David W. M.
Liverpool, 17 March, 1929 (FB)

League Club	Source	Date Signed	Seasons Played	Apps	Subs	Gls
Blackpool	Jnrs	05.49	52-56	32	-	0
Tranmere Rov.	Tr	08.58	58-62	177	-	0

FRITH, William
Sheffield, 9 June, 1912 (WH)

League Club	Source	Date Signed	Seasons Played	Apps	Subs	Gls
Mansfield T.	Worksop	04.30				
Chesterfield	Tr	05.31	31	9	-	3
Coventry C.	Tr	05.32	32-46	169	-	4

FRIZZELL, James L.
Greenock, 16 February, 1937 (WH)

League Club	Source	Date Signed	Seasons Played	Apps	Subs	Gls
Oldham Ath.	Morton	05.60	60-69	308	9	56

FROGGATT, John (Jack)
Sheffield, 17 November, 1922 EF Lge/E-1 (OL/HB)

League Club	Source	Date Signed	Seasons Played	Apps	Subs	Gls
Portsmouth		09.45	46-53	280	-	66
Leicester C.	Tr	03.54	53-57	143	-	18

FROGGATT, John L.
Sutton-in-Ashfield, 13 December, 1945 (F)

League Club	Source	Date Signed	Seasons Played	Apps	Subs	Gls
Notts Co.	East Kirkby Colly	06.64	63-64	4	-	0
Colchester U.	Boston U.	07.74	74-77	155	0	29
Port Vale	Tr	02.78	77-78	12	2	3
Northampton T.	Tr	09.78	78	42	0	13

FROGGATT, Redfern
Sheffield, 23 August, 1924 EF Lge/E'B'/E-4 (IF)

League Club	Source	Date Signed	Seasons Played	Apps	Subs	Gls
Sheffield Wed.	Sheffield Y.M.C.A.	08.42	46-59	434	-	140

Redfern Froggatt (Sheffield Wednesday & England)

FROGGATT, Stephen J.
Lincoln, 9 March, 1973 (M)

League Club	Source	Date Signed	Seasons Played	Apps	Subs	Gls
Aston Villa	YT	01.91	91	6	3	0

FROST, Brian P.
Sheffield, 5 June, 1938 (F)

League Club	Source	Date Signed	Seasons Played	Apps	Subs	Gls
Chesterfield	Oswestry T.	05.59	59-64	103	-	20

FROST, Desmond
Congleton, 3 August, 1926 (CF)

League Club	Source	Date Signed	Seasons Played	Apps	Subs	Gls
Leeds U.	Congleton T.	04.49	49-50	10	-	2
Halifax T.	Tr	01.51	50-53	117	-	55
Rochdale	Tr	11.53	53-54	16	-	6
Crewe Alex.	Tr	09.54	54-55	42	-	12

FROST, John (Jack)
Wallsend, 13 February, 1920 Died 1988 (G)

League Club	Source	Date Signed	Seasons Played	Apps	Subs	Gls
Grimsby T.	North Shields	07.39				
York C.	Tr	07.48	48-51	45	-	0

FROST, Lee A.
Woking, 4 December, 1957 (W)

League Club	Source	Date Signed	Seasons Played	Apps	Subs	Gls
Chelsea	App	07.76	77-79	11	3	5
Brentford	L	10.78	78	5	1	0
Brentford	Tr	12.80	80	15	0	3

FROST, Ronald A.
Stockport, 16 January, 1947 (W)

League Club	Source	Date Signed	Seasons Played	Apps	Subs	Gls
Manchester C.	App	05.64	63	2	-	1

FROST, Stanley D.
Northampton, 19 October, 1922 (OR)

League Club	Source	Date Signed	Seasons Played	Apps	Subs	Gls
Leicester C.	Northampton T. (Am)	03.41				
Northampton T.	Tr	01.47	46	6	-	1

FROWEN, John
Trelewis, 11 October, 1931 (D)

League Club	Source	Date Signed	Seasons Played	Apps	Subs	Gls
Cardiff C.	Nelson	05.51	52-57	35	-	0
Bristol Rov.	Tr	08.58	58-62	84	-	0
Newport Co.	Tr	03.63	62-65	67	1	0

FRUDE, Roger G.
Plymouth, 19 November, 1946 (IF)

League Club	Source	Date Signed	Seasons Played	Apps	Subs	Gls
Bristol Rov.	App	12.64	63-67	38	3	8
Mansfield T.	Tr	09.67	67-68	14	1	0
Brentford	Tr	07.69	69	1	1	0

FRY, Barry F.
Bedford, 7 April, 1945 E Sch (IF)

League Club	Source	Date Signed	Seasons Played	Apps	Subs	Gls
Manchester U.	App	04.62				
Bolton W.	Tr	05.64	64	3	-	1
Luton T.	Tr	07.65	65	6	0	0
Leyton Orient	Gravesend & Nft	12.66	66	2	1	0
Leyton Orient	Bedford T.	06.67	67	5	5	0

FRY, Christopher D.
Cardiff, 23 October, 1969 W Sch (FB/W)

League Club	Source	Date Signed	Seasons Played	Apps	Subs	Gls
Cardiff C.	YT	07.88	88-90	22	33	1
Hereford U.	Tr	07.91	91	33	4	3

FRY, David P.
Bournemouth, 5 January, 1960 (G)

League Club	Source	Date Signed	Seasons Played	Apps	Subs	Gls
Crystal Palace	App	01.77	77-82	40	0	0
Gillingham	Tr	07.83	83-84	49	0	0
Torquay U.	Millwall (N/C)	10.85	85	30	0	0

FRY, Keith F.
Cardiff, 11 April, 1941 W Sch (OR)

League Club	Source	Date Signed	Seasons Played	Apps	Subs	Gls
Newport Co.	Jnrs	10.58	58-61	58	-	2
Notts Co.	Tr	02.62	61-63	73	-	9
Chesterfield	Merthyr Tydfil	01.66	65	2	0	1

FRY, Robert P.
Pontypridd, 29 June, 1935 (G)

League Club	Source	Date Signed	Seasons Played	Apps	Subs	Gls
Crystal Palace		04.56	55	6	-	0
Queens Park R.	Bath C.	08.57	57	1	-	0

FRY, Roger N.
Southampton, 18 August, 1948 (LB)

League Club	Source	Date Signed	Seasons Played	Apps	Subs	Gls
Southampton	Jnrs	10.67	70-71	23	0	0
Walsall	Tr	07.73	73-76	120	0	1

FRYATT, James E.
Southampton, 2 September, 1940 (CF)

League Club	Source	Date Signed	Seasons Played	Apps	Subs	Gls
Charlton Ath.	Jnrs	10.57	59	5	-	3
Southend U.	Tr	06.60	60-62	61	-	24
Bradford P.A.	Tr	06.63	63-65	101	0	38
Southport	Tr	03.66	65-66	39	0	15
Torquay U.	Tr	03.67	66-67	27	0	11
Stockport Co.	Tr	10.67	67-68	44	0	28
Blackburn Rov.	Tr	10.68	68-69	29	8	5
Oldham Ath.	Tr	02.70	69-71	76	0	40
Southport	Tr	11.71	71-73	102	2	24
Stockport Co.	Tr	09.74	74	1	0	1
Torquay U.	Tr	12.74	74	3	0	0

FRYE, John M.
Ardrossan, 27 July, 1933 (IF)

League Club	Source	Date Signed	Seasons Played	Apps	Subs	Gls
Sheffield Wed.	St Mirren	01.61				
Tranmere Rov.	Tr	10.61	61	21	-	6

FRYER, John H.
Manchester, 24 June, 1924 (CF)

League Club	Source	Date Signed	Seasons Played	Apps	Subs	Gls
Oldham Ath.	Goslings	04.47	47	9	-	3

FUCCILLO, Pasquale (Lil)
Bedford, 2 May, 1956 (M)

League Club	Source	Date Signed	Seasons Played	Apps	Subs	Gls
Luton T.	App	07.74	74-82	153	7	24
Southend U.	Tulsa (USA)	12.83	83-84	40	5	5
Peterborough U. (N/C)	Tr	08.85	85-86	82	0	3
Cambridge U. (N/C)	Malta	01.88	87	18	1	2

FUDGE, Michael H.
Bristol, 5 December, 1945 (IF)

League Club	Source	Date Signed	Seasons Played	Apps	Subs	Gls
West Bromwich A.	App	12.63	63-64	13	-	5
Exeter C.	Tr	06.67	67	32	2	6

FULBROOK, Gary
Bath, 4 May, 1966 (D)

League Club	Source	Date Signed	Seasons Played	Apps	Subs	Gls
Swindon T.	YT	09.84	84	0	1	0
Carlisle U.	Bath C.	09.87	87	6	0	0

FULLAM, John
Dublin, 22 March, 1940 IR'B'-1/IR-11 (WH)

League Club	Source	Date Signed	Seasons Played	Apps	Subs	Gls
Preston N. E.	Home Farm	10.58	59-60	49	-	6

FULLBROOK, John F.
Grays, 15 July, 1918 (FB)

League Club	Source	Date Signed	Seasons Played	Apps	Subs	Gls
Leyton Orient	Plymouth Arg. (Am)	04.46	46-47	36	-	1

FULLER, William J.
Brixton, 6 April, 1944 (FB)

League Club	Source	Date Signed	Seasons Played	Apps	Subs	Gls
Crystal Palace	Jnrs	01.63	62-64	3	-	0

FULLERTON, George
Ballymena (NI), 14 June, 1939 (G)

League Club	Source	Date Signed	Seasons Played	Apps	Subs	Gls
Leeds U.	Glentoran	05.58				
Barrow	Distillery	07.60	60	12	-	0

FULTON, Bryce
Prestwick, 7 August, 1935 (FB)

League Club	Source	Date Signed	Seasons Played	Apps	Subs	Gls
Manchester U.	Jnrs	03.53				
Plymouth Arg.	Tr	08.57	57-63	176	-	0
Exeter C.	Tr	07.64	64-65	37	0	0

FULTON, Raymond H.
Hendon, 24 September, 1953 (FB)

League Club	Source	Date Signed	Seasons Played	Apps	Subs	Gls
Leyton Orient	West Ham U. (App)	08.72	72	1	0	0

FUNNELL, Anthony
Eastbourne, 20 August, 1957 (F)

League Club	Source	Date Signed	Seasons Played	Apps	Subs	Gls
Southampton	Eastbourne	01.77	77-78	13	4	8
Gillingham	Tr	03.79	78-79	27	6	10
Brentford	Tr	03.80	79-80	29	3	8
Bournemouth	Tr	09.81	81-82	59	5	22

FUNNELL, Simon P.
Brighton, 8 August, 1974 (F)

League Club	Source	Date Signed	Seasons Played	Apps	Subs	Gls
Brighton & H.A.	YT	07.92	91	0	1	0

FURIE, John P. C.
Hammersmith, 13 May, 1948 (FB)

League Club	Source	Date Signed	Seasons Played	Apps	Subs	Gls
Watford	App	05.66	66	0	1	0
Gillingham	Tr	07.67	67	17	0	0

FURLONG, Paul A.
Wood Green, 1 October, 1968 E Semi-Pro (F)

League Club	Source	Date Signed	Seasons Played	Apps	Subs	Gls
Coventry C.	Enfield	07.91	91	27	10	4

FURNELL, James
Clitheroe, 23 November, 1937 (G)

League Club	Source	Date Signed	Seasons Played	Apps	Subs	Gls
Burnley	Jnrs	11.54	59-60	2	-	0
Liverpool	Tr	02.62	61-63	28	-	0
Arsenal	Tr	11.63	63-67	141	0	0
Rotherham U.	Tr	09.68	68-69	76	0	0
Plymouth Arg.	Tr	12.70	70-75	183	0	0

FURNESS, William I.
Washington, 8 June, 1909 Died 1980 E-1 (IF)

League Club	Source	Date Signed	Seasons Played	Apps	Subs	Gls
Leeds U.	Usworth Colly	08.28	29-36	243	-	62
Norwich C.	Tr	06.37	37-46	93	-	21

FURNISS, Frederick
Sheffield, 10 July, 1922 (FB)

League Club	Source	Date Signed	Seasons Played	Apps	Subs	Gls
Sheffield U.	Hallam	01.43	46-54	279	-	14
Chesterfield	Tr	08.55				

FURPHY, Keith
Stockton, 30 July, 1958 (LW)

League Club	Source	Date Signed	Seasons Played	Apps	Subs	Gls
Queens Park R.	Sheffield U. (App)	10.76				
Plymouth Arg.	Baltimore (USA)	08.87	87	6	0	1

FURPHY, Kenneth
Stockton, 28 May, 1931 (WH)

League Club	Source	Date Signed	Seasons Played	Apps	Subs	Gls
Everton		11.50				
Darlington	Runcorn	08.53	53-61	316	-	5
Workington	Tr	07.62	62-64	105	-	3
Watford	Tr	11.64	64-67	95	6	1

FURSDON, Alan H.
Grantham, 16 October, 1947 (FB)

League Club	Source	Date Signed	Seasons Played	Apps	Subs	Gls
Swindon T.		09.65				
Oxford U.		05.67	68	0	1	0

FURY, Paul
Swansea, 16 March, 1955 W Sch (FB)

League Club	Source	Date Signed	Seasons Played	Apps	Subs	Gls
Swansea C. (App)	App	09.70	71-72	11	0	0

FUSCHILLO, Paul M.
Islington, 20 October, 1948 E Amat (FB)

League Club	Source	Date Signed	Seasons Played	Apps	Subs	Gls
Blackpool	Wycombe W.	07.71	71-73	8	3	0
Brighton & H. A.	Tr	02.74	73-74	17	0	1

FUTCHER, Graham
Chester, 15 June, 1953 (CF)

League Club	Source	Date Signed	Seasons Played	Apps	Subs	Gls
Chester C.	Jnrs	08.71	71-72	5	5	0

FUTCHER, Paul
Chester, 25 September, 1956 Eu21-11 (CD)

League Club	Source	Date Signed	Seasons Played	Apps	Subs	Gls
Chester C.	App	01.74	72-73	20	0	0
Luton T.	Tr	06.74	74-77	131	0	1
Manchester C.	Tr	06.78	78-79	36	1	0
Oldham Ath.	Tr	08.80	80-82	98	0	1
Derby Co.	Tr	01.83	82-83	35	0	0
Barnsley	Tr	03.84	83-89	229	1	0
Halifax T.	Tr	07.90	90	15	0	0
Grimsby T.	Tr	01.91	90-91	51	0	0

FUTCHER, Ronald
Chester, 25 September, 1956 (F)

League Club	Source	Date Signed	Seasons Played	Apps	Subs	Gls
Chester C.	App	01.74	73	4	0	0
Luton T.	Tr	06.74	74-77	116	4	40
Manchester C.	Tr	08.78	78	10	7	7
Barnsley	N.A.C. Breda (Neth)	12.84	84	18	1	6
Oldham Ath.	Tr	07.85	85-86	65	0	30
Bradford C.	Tr	03.87	86-87	35	7	18
Port Vale	Tr	08.88	88-89	46	6	20
Burnley	Tr	11.89	89-90	52	5	25
Crewe Alex.	Tr	07.91	91	18	3	4

Ron Futcher (Chester City, Luton Town, Manchester City, NAC Breda, Barnsley, Oldham Athletic, Bradford City, Port Vale, Burnley & Crewe Alexandra)

FYFE, Anthony
Carlisle, 23 February, 1962 (F)

League Club	Source	Date Signed	Seasons Played	Apps	Subs	Gls
Carlisle U.	Penrith	09.87	87-89	28	20	12
Scarborough	L	12.89	89	6	0	1
Halifax T.	Tr	01.90	89-90	13	3	0
Carlisle U.	Tr	10.90	90-91	33	9	8

Paul Gascoigne (Newcastle United, Tottenham Hotspur, Lazio & England)
The most recent English soccer idol who equalled the British transfer fee record when signing for Lazio, following an horrendous injury in the 1991 FA Cup Final

League Club	Source	Date Signed	Seasons Played	Apps	Subs	Gls

GABBIADINI, Marco
Nottingham, 20 January, 1968 Eu21-2/E'B' (F)

League Club	Source	Date Signed	Seasons Played	Apps	Subs	Gls
York C.	App	09.85	84-87	42	18	14
Sunderland	Tr	09.87	87-91	155	2	75
Crystal Palace	Tr	09.91	91	15	0	5
Derby Co.	Tr	01.92	91	20	0	5

Marco Gabbiadini (York City, Sunderland, Crystal Palace & Derby County)

GABBIADINI, Riccardo
Newport, 11 March, 1970 (F)

League Club	Source	Date Signed	Seasons Played	Apps	Subs	Gls
York C. (YT)	YT	07.86	87	0	1	0
Sunderland	Tr	06.88	89	0	1	0
Blackpool	L	09.89	89	5	0	3
Grimsby T.	L	10.89	89	3	0	1
Brighton & H.A.	L	03.90	89	0	1	0
Crewe Alex.	L	10.90	90	1	1	0
Hartlepool U.	Tr	03.91	90-91	2	12	2
Scarborough	Tr	03.92	91	3	4	1

GABRIEL, James
Dundee, 16 October, 1940 S Sch/Su23-6/S-2 (WH)

League Club	Source	Date Signed	Seasons Played	Apps	Subs	Gls
Everton	Dundee	03.60	59-66	255	1	33
Southampton	Tr	07.67	67-71	190	1	25
Bournemouth	Tr	07.72	72-73	53	0	4
Swindon T.	L	10.73	73	6	0	0
Brentford	Tr	03.74	73	9	0	0

GADDES, Robert
Byfleet, 27 September, 1941 E Yth (G)

League Club	Source	Date Signed	Seasons Played	Apps	Subs	Gls
Portsmouth	Jnrs	06.60	59	1	-	0

GADSBY, Kenneth J.
Chesterfield, 3 July, 1916 (LB)

League Club	Source	Date Signed	Seasons Played	Apps	Subs	Gls
Leeds U.	Middlecliffe Rov.	10.34	36-47	78	-	0

GADSBY, Michael D.
Oswestry, 1 August, 1947 (G)

League Club	Source	Date Signed	Seasons Played	Apps	Subs	Gls
Notts Co.	Ashbourne	01.68	67	11	0	0
York C.	Tr	07.69	69	13	0	0
Grimsby T.	L	09.70	70	2	0	0
Bradford C.	L	12.70	70	6	0	0
Hartlepool U.	Tr	07.71	71	21	0	0

GADSTON, Joseph E.
Hanwell, 13 September, 1945 (CF)

League Club	Source	Date Signed	Seasons Played	Apps	Subs	Gls
Brentford	West Ham U. (Am)	08.64				
Bristol Rov.	Cheltenham T.	06.68	68	10	1	5
Exeter C.	Tr	11.69	69-71	85	0	31
Aldershot	Tr	07.72	72	2	2	0
Hartlepool U.	L	02.73	72	1	0	0

GAFFNEY, Terence
Hartlepool, 15 February, 1952 (M)

League Club	Source	Date Signed	Seasons Played	Apps	Subs	Gls
Hartlepool U.	Billingham Synth.	07.77	77	10	3	1

GAGE, Kevin W.
Chiswick, 21 April, 1964 E Yth (M/FB)

League Club	Source	Date Signed	Seasons Played	Apps	Subs	Gls
Wimbledon	App	01.82	80-86	135	33	15
Aston Villa	Tr	07.87	87-90	113	2	8
Sheffield U.	Tr	11.91	91	22	0	1

GAGE, Lawrence A. (Larry)
Walthamstow, 10 September, 1922 (G)

League Club	Source	Date Signed	Seasons Played	Apps	Subs	Gls
Leyton Orient	Walthamstow Ave.	08.43				
Fulham	Tr	08.44				
Aldershot	Tr	07.46	46-47	39	-	0
Fulham	Canada	08.48	48	3	-	0
Gillingham	Tr	06.50	50	40	-	0

GAGE, Wakely A. J.
Northampton, 5 May, 1958 (CD)

League Club	Source	Date Signed	Seasons Played	Apps	Subs	Gls
Northampton T.	Desborough T.	10.79	79-84	215	3	17
Chester C.	Tr	08.85	85	17	0	1
Peterborough U.	Tr	11.85	85-86	73	0	1
Crewe Alex.	Tr	06.87	87-88	45	9	1

GAGER, Horace E.
West Ham, 25 January, 1917 (CH)

League Club	Source	Date Signed	Seasons Played	Apps	Subs	Gls
Luton T.	Vauxhall Motors	11.37	46-47	59	-	2
Nottingham F.	Tr	02.48	47-54	258	-	11

GAILLARD, Marcel J.
Belgium, 15 January, 1927 (W)

League Club	Source	Date Signed	Seasons Played	Apps	Subs	Gls
Crystal Palace	Tonbridge	02.48	47-49	21	-	3
Portsmouth	Tr	02.51	50-52	58	-	7

GALBRAITH, Walter M.
Glasgow, 26 May, 1918 (LB)

League Club	Source	Date Signed	Seasons Played	Apps	Subs	Gls
New Brighton	Clyde	09.48	48-50	109	-	1
Grimsby T.	Tr	08.51	51-52	77	-	0
Accrington St.	Tr	06.53	53	21	-	0

GALE, Anthony P.
Westminster, 19 November, 1959 E Yth/Eu21-1 (CD)

League Club	Source	Date Signed	Seasons Played	Apps	Subs	Gls
Fulham	App	08.77	77-83	277	0	19
West Ham U.	Tr	07.84	84-91	241	4	4

GALE, Colin M.
Pontypridd, 31 August, 1932 (CH)

League Club	Source	Date Signed	Seasons Played	Apps	Subs	Gls
Cardiff C.	Jnrs	07.50	53-55	12	-	0
Northampton T.	Tr	03.56	55-60	212	-	1

GALE, Darren
Port Talbot, 25 October, 1963 Wu21-2 (F)

League Club	Source	Date Signed	Seasons Played	Apps	Subs	Gls
Swansea C.	App	10.80	81-84	26	11	6
Exeter C.	Tr	09.85	85-86	19	1	5

GALE, Ian J. C.
Slough, 3 March, 1961 (M)

League Club	Source	Date Signed	Seasons Played	Apps	Subs	Gls
Millwall	App	03.78	78	4	1	0

GALE, Shaun M.
Reading, 8 October, 1969 (FB)

League Club	Source	Date Signed	Seasons Played	Apps	Subs	Gls
Portsmouth	YT	07.88	90	2	1	0

GALE, Thomas
Durham, 4 January, 1920 (CH)

League Club	Source	Date Signed	Seasons Played	Apps	Subs	Gls
Sheffield Wed.	Gateshead (Am)	04.45	46	6	-	0
York C.	Tr	08.47	47-48	76	-	0

GALL, Mark I.
Brixton, 14 May, 1963 (F)

League Club	Source	Date Signed	Seasons Played	Apps	Subs	Gls
Maidstone U.	Greenwich Bor.	02.88	89-91	69	16	31
Brighton & H. A.	Tr	10.91	91	30	1	13

GALL, Norman A.
Wallsend, 30 September, 1942 (CH)

League Club	Source	Date Signed	Seasons Played	Apps	Subs	Gls
Brighton & H. A.	Gateshead	03.62	62-73	427	12	5

League Club	Source	Date Signed	Seasons Played	Apps	Subs	Gls
GALLACHER, Bernard						
Johnstone, 22 March, 1967						(LB)
Aston Villa	App	03.85	86-90	55	2	0
Blackburn Rov.	L	11.90	90	4	0	0
Doncaster Rov. (N/C)	Tr	09.91	91	2	0	0
Brighton & H.A.	Tr	10.91	91	31	0	1
GALLACHER, Connor						
Derry (NI), 24 April, 1922						(IF)
Middlesbrough	Lochee Harp.	01.47	46	1	-	0
Hull C.	Tr	05.47	47	18	-	3
Rochdale	Tr	03.48	47	6	-	1
GALLACHER, John						
Glasgow, 26 January, 1969						(W)
Newcastle U.	Falkirk	06.89	89-90	22	7	6
GALLACHER, Kevin W.						
Clydebank, 23 November, 1966 S Yth/Su21-7/S-12						(RW)
Coventry C.	Dundee U.	01.90	89-91	80	0	22
GALLACHER, Patrick						
Glasgow, 9 January, 1913 Died 1983						(IF)
Blackburn Rov.	Third Lanark	10.36	36-37	11	-	0
Bournemouth	Tr	06.38	38-47	35	-	3
GALLAGHER, Barry P.						
Bradford, 7 April, 1961						(M)
Bradford C.	App	04.79	77-82	66	5	22
Mansfield T.	L	01.83	82	2	1	0
Halifax T.	Tr	03.83	82-85	110	5	27
GALLAGHER, Brian						
Oldham, 22 July, 1938						(FB)
Bury	Ashton U.	10.56	57-64	130	-	1
Carlisle U.	Tr	05.65	65-66	42	2	1
Stockport Co.	Tr	07.67	67	13	0	0
GALLAGHER, James						
Bury, 2 September, 1911						(CH)
Bury	Tr	01.36				
Notts Co.	Tr	08.37	37-38	23	-	2
Exeter C.	Tr	06.39				
Exeter C.	Notts Co. (coach)	09.48	48	1	-	0
GALLAGHER, John C. (Jackie)						
Wisbech, 6 April, 1958						(F)
Lincoln C.	March T.	02.76	76	1	0	0
Peterborough U.	Kings Lynn	04.80	79-80	11	2	1
Torquay U. (N/C)	Hong Kong	08.82	82	38	4	7
Peterborough U.	Wisbech T.	08.85	85-86	78	4	19
Wolverhampton W.	Tr	06.87	87-88	10	17	4
GALLAGHER, Joseph A.						
Liverpool, 11 January, 1955 E'B'						(CD)
Birmingham C.	App	01.72	73-80	281	5	17
Wolverhampton W.	Tr	08.81	81-82	31	0	0
West Ham U.	Tr	12.82	82	8	1	0
Burnley	Tr	08.83	83-86	46	1	3
Halifax T.	L	10.83	83	4	0	0
GALLAGHER, Michael						
Cambuslang, 16 January, 1932 Died 1975						(OL)
Bolton W.	Benburb	01.52				
West Bromwich A.	Tr	12.52	52	1	-	0
GALLAGHER, Nicholas						
Boston, 28 January, 1971 E Sch						(W)
Doncaster Rov.	Jnrs	05.89	89	0	1	0
GALLANT, David						
Middlesbrough, 12 October, 1949						(F)
Leeds U.	Jnrs	12.66				
Darlington	L	01.68	67	1	0	0
GALLEGO, Antonio						
Spain, 2 June, 1924						(G)
Norwich C.	Cambridge T.	03.47	46	1	-	0
GALLEGO, Jose						
Spain, 8 April, 1923						(OL)
Brentford	Abbey U.	01.47	46-47	6	-	0
Southampton	Tr	05.48	48	1	-	0
Colchester U.	Tr	(N/L)	50	4	-	0

League Club	Source	Date Signed	Seasons Played	Apps	Subs	Gls
GALLEY, Gordon W.						
Worksop, 4 February, 1930						(OL)
Sheffield Wed.	Jnrs	06.47				
Darlington	Tr	10.48	48-51	60	-	12
GALLEY, John E.						
Clowne, 7 May, 1944						(CF)
Wolverhampton W.	Jnrs	05.61	62-64	5	-	2
Rotherham U.	Tr	12.64	64-67	112	0	48
Bristol C.	Tr	12.67	67-72	172	0	84
Nottingham F.	Tr	12.72	72-74	31	6	6
Peterborough U.	L	10.74	74	7	0	1
Hereford U.	Tr	12.74	74-76	77	3	10
GALLEY, Keith J.						
Worksop, 17 October, 1955						(F)
Southport	Morecambe	12.75	75-76	50	10	11
GALLEY, Maurice						
Clowne, 10 August, 1934						(WH)
Chesterfield	Jnrs	07.52	54-58	55	-	5
GALLEY, Thomas						
Hednesford, 4 August, 1915 EF Lge/E-2						(WH)
Wolverhampton W.	Notts Co. (Am)	04.34	34-47	183	-	41
Grimsby T.	Tr	11.47	47-48	32	-	2

Tom Galley (Wolverhampton Wanderers, Grimsby Town & England)

GALLIER, William H.
Cannock, 24 April, 1932 (LH)

League Club	Source	Date Signed	Seasons Played	Apps	Subs	Gls
West Bromwich A.	Beaudesert Sports	07.53				
Walsall	Tr	06.55	55	10	-	0

GALLIERS, Steven
Preston, 21 August, 1957 (M)

League Club	Source	Date Signed	Seasons Played	Apps	Subs	Gls
Wimbledon	Chorley	06.77	77-81	148	7	10
Crystal Palace	Tr	10.81	81	8	5	0
Wimbledon	Tr	08.82	82-87	145	1	5
Bristol C.	L	02.87	86	9	0	0
Bristol C.	Tr	09.87	87-88	65	3	6
Maidstone U.	Tr	07.89	89	7	1	0

GALLIMORE, Anthony M.
Crewe, 21 February, 1972 (LB)

League Club	Source	Date Signed	Seasons Played	Apps	Subs	Gls
Stoke C.	YT	07.90	89-91	6	5	0
Carlisle U.	L	10.91	91	8	0	0
Carlisle U.	L	02.92	91	8	0	0

GALLIMORE, Leonard
Northwich, 14 September, 1912 Died 1978 (FB)

League Club	Source	Date Signed	Seasons Played	Apps	Subs	Gls
Preston N. E.	Bainton Vic.	01.32	33-36	9	-	0
Watford	Tr	05.37	37-46	64	-	0

GALLOGLY, Charles
Banbridge (NI), 16 June, 1925 NI-2 (FB)

League Club	Source	Date Signed	Seasons Played	Apps	Subs	Gls
Huddersfield T.	Glenavon	12.49	49-51	76	-	0
Watford	Tr	08.52	52-53	47	-	0
Bournemouth	Tr	07.54				

GALLON, John W.
Burradon (Nd), 12 February, 1914 (IF)

League Club	Source	Date Signed	Seasons Played	Apps	Subs	Gls
Bradford C.	Bedlington U.	06.36	36-37	20	-	5
Bradford P. A.	Tr	02.38	37-38	31	-	1
Swansea C.	Tr	06.39				
Gateshead	Tr	03.46	46	20	-	2

GALLOWAY, John
Bo'ness, 29 October, 1918 (IF)

League Club	Source	Date Signed	Seasons Played	Apps	Subs	Gls
Chelsea	Glasgow Rangers	08.46	46-47	4	-	0

GALLOWAY, Michael
Oswestry, 30 May, 1965 S Yth (CD)

League Club	Source	Date Signed	Seasons Played	Apps	Subs	Gls
Mansfield T.		09.83	83-85	39	15	3
Halifax T.	Tr	02.86	85-87	79	0	5

GALLOWAY, Steven G.
West Germany, 13 February, 1963 (F)

League Club	Source	Date Signed	Seasons Played	Apps	Subs	Gls
Crystal Palace	Sutton U.	10.84	84-85	3	2	1
Cambridge U.	L	03.86	85	0	1	0

GALVIN, Anthony
Huddersfield, 12 July, 1956 IR-29 (LW)

League Club	Source	Date Signed	Seasons Played	Apps	Subs	Gls
Tottenham H.	Goole T.	01.78	78-86	194	7	20
Sheffield Wed.	Tr	08.87	87-88	21	15	1
Swindon T.	Tr	08.89	89	6	5	0

GALVIN, Christopher
Huddersfield, 24 November, 1951 E Yth (M)

League Club	Source	Date Signed	Seasons Played	Apps	Subs	Gls
Leeds U.	App	11.68	69-72	7	1	0
Hull C.	Tr	08.73	73-78	132	11	11
York C.	L	12.76	76	22	0	6
Stockport Co.	Tr	04.79	78-80	67	1	3

GALVIN, David
Denaby, 5 October, 1946 (CD)

League Club	Source	Date Signed	Seasons Played	Apps	Subs	Gls
Wolverhampton W.	Jnrs	05.65	68	5	0	0
Gillingham	Tr	10.69	69-76	239	6	17
Wimbledon	Tr	08.77	77-78	73	0	7

GAMBLE, Frank
Liverpool, 21 August, 1961 (W)

League Club	Source	Date Signed	Seasons Played	Apps	Subs	Gls
Derby Co.	Burscough	05.81	81-82	5	1	2
Rochdale (N/C)	Barrow	12.84	84-85	41	5	9

GAMBLE, S. William
Cottam (Nts), 5 March, 1968 (F)

League Club	Source	Date Signed	Seasons Played	Apps	Subs	Gls
Lincoln C.	App	01.86	85-88	44	20	14

GAMBLIN, Derek
Havant, 7 April, 1943 E Amat (FB)

League Club	Source	Date Signed	Seasons Played	Apps	Subs	Gls
Portsmouth (Am)	Sutton U.	07.65	65	1	0	0

GAMBRILL, Brian D.
Whitstable, 23 December, 1943 (G)

League Club	Source	Date Signed	Seasons Played	Apps	Subs	Gls
Millwall	Whitstable	12.65	65	1	0	0

GAME, Kirk M.
Southend, 22 October, 1966 (D)

League Club	Source	Date Signed	Seasons Played	Apps	Subs	Gls
Colchester U.	Southend U. (App)	08.85	85-86	28	1	0

GAMMON, Stephen G.
Swansea, 24 September, 1939 Wu23-2 (WH)

League Club	Source	Date Signed	Seasons Played	Apps	Subs	Gls
Cardiff C.	Jnrs	04.58	58-64	67	-	1

GANE, Alan
Chiswick, 11 June, 1950 (M)

League Club	Source	Date Signed	Seasons Played	Apps	Subs	Gls
Hereford U.	Slough T.	09.73	73	6	3	1

GANNON, Edward
Dublin, 3 January, 1921 Died 1989 IR-14 (WH)

League Club	Source	Date Signed	Seasons Played	Apps	Subs	Gls
Notts Co.	Shelbourne	08.46	46-48	106	-	2
Sheffield Wed.	Tr	03.49	48-54	204	-	4

GANNON, James P.
Southwark, 7 September, 1968 (M)

League Club	Source	Date Signed	Seasons Played	Apps	Subs	Gls
Sheffield U.	Dundalk	04.89				
Halifax T.	L	02.90	89	2	0	0
Stockport Co.	Tr	03.90	89-91	91	0	22

GANNON, John S.
Wimbledon, 18 December, 1966 (M)

League Club	Source	Date Signed	Seasons Played	Apps	Subs	Gls
Wimbledon	App	12.84	85-87	13	3	2
Crewe Alex.	L	12.86	86	14	1	0
Sheffield U.	L	02.89	88	8	8	1
Sheffield U.	Tr	06.89	89-91	90	3	4

GANNON, Michael J.
Liverpool, 2 February, 1943 (D)

League Club	Source	Date Signed	Seasons Played	Apps	Subs	Gls
Everton	Jnrs	02.60	61	3	-	0
Scunthorpe U.	Tr	05.62	62-63	15	-	0
Crewe Alex.	Tr	10.64	64-69	206	4	2

GARBETT, W. Edward
Dawley, 14 September, 1949 (W)

League Club	Source	Date Signed	Seasons Played	Apps	Subs	Gls
Shrewsbury T.	App	09.67	67-68	7	5	2
Barrow	Tr	07.69	69-71	119	0	27
Stockport Co.	Tr	07.72	72-73	63	7	11

GARBETT, Terence G.
Lanchester, 9 September, 1945 (M)

League Club	Source	Date Signed	Seasons Played	Apps	Subs	Gls
Middlesbrough	Stockton	08.63	65	7	0	1
Watford	Tr	08.66	66-71	196	4	46
Blackburn Rov.	Tr	09.71	71-73	90	0	6
Sheffield U.	Tr	02.74	73-75	26	5	0

GARBUTT, John E.
Scarborough, 27 March, 1920 (G)

League Club	Source	Date Signed	Seasons Played	Apps	Subs	Gls
Newcastle U.	Billingham Synth.	01.39	46-49	52	-	0

GARBUTT, Peter
Corbridge, 28 December, 1939 E Amat (HB)

League Club	Source	Date Signed	Seasons Played	Apps	Subs	Gls
Carlisle U.	Crook T.	08.64	64-70	134	2	12

GARBUTT, Raymond H.
Middlesbrough, 9 May, 1925 (CF)

League Club	Source	Date Signed	Seasons Played	Apps	Subs	Gls
Manchester C.	South Bank	09.47				
Watford	Spennymoor U.	05.50	50	22	-	8
Brighton & H.A.	Tr	03.51	50-51	32	-	18
Workington	Tr	10.52	52	8	-	2

GARDINER, Douglas
Douglas, 29 March, 1917 (WH)

League Club	Source	Date Signed	Seasons Played	Apps	Subs	Gls
Luton T.	Auchinleck Talbot	05.38	46-50	121	-	1

GARDINER, John
Chester-le-Street, 5 November, 1914 (IF)

League Club	Source	Date Signed	Seasons Played	Apps	Subs	Gls
Southend U. (Am)	Holfords	05.46	46	1	-	0

GARDINER, Mark C.
Cirencester, 25 December, 1966 (W)

League Club	Source	Date Signed	Seasons Played	Apps	Subs	Gls
Swindon T.	App	09.84	83-86	7	3	1
Torquay U.	Tr	02.87	86-87	37	12	4
Crewe Alex.	Tr	08.88	88-91	128	7	33

GARDINER, William S.
Glasgow, 15 August, 1929 S'B'-1 (CF)

League Club	Source	Date Signed	Seasons Played	Apps	Subs	Gls
Leicester C.	Glasgow Rangers	08.55	55-57	69	-	48
Reading	Tr	11.58	58-59	8	-	2

GARDNER, Charles C.
Dundee, 17 March, 1925

League Club	Source	Date Signed	Seasons Played	Apps	Subs	Gls
Aldershot	St Mirren	08.50	50	5	-	0

GARDNER, Donald C.
Jamaica (WI), 30 August, 1955 (M)

League Club	Source	Date Signed	Seasons Played	Apps	Subs	Gls
Wolverhampton W.	App	08.73	74	1	2	0

GARDNER, Frederick C.
Coventry, 4 June, 1922 (IF)

League Club	Source	Date Signed	Seasons Played	Apps	Subs	Gls
Birmingham C.		09.40				
Coventry C.	Tr	05.46	46-48	13	-	3
Newport Co.	Tr	05.49	49	4	-	2

GARDNER, Lee
Ayr, 11 July, 1970 (M)

League Club	Source	Date Signed	Seasons Played	Apps	Subs	Gls
Oxford U. (L)	Aberdeen	03.91	90	2	5	0

GARDNER, Paul A.
Southport, 22 September, 1957 (RB)

League Club	Source	Date Signed	Seasons Played	Apps	Subs	Gls
Blackpool	App	09.75	76-81	149	3	1
Bury	Tr	08.82	82-83	90	0	0
Swansea C. (N/C)	Tr	10.84	84	4	0	0
Wigan Ath. (N/C)	Preston N.E. (N/C)	01.85	84	5	0	0

GARDNER, Stephen D.
Hemsworth, 7 October, 1958 E Sch (M)

League Club	Source	Date Signed	Seasons Played	Apps	Subs	Gls
Ipswich T.	App	10.75				
Oldham Ath.	Tr	12.77	77-80	41	12	2

GARDNER, Stephen G.
Middlesbrough, 3 July, 1968 (CD)

League Club	Source	Date Signed	Seasons Played	Apps	Subs	Gls
Manchester U.	App	07.86				
Burnley	Tr	07.87	87-89	93	2	0
Bradford C.	Glossop	08.91	91	14	0	0

GARDNER, Thomas
Liverpool, 17 March, 1923 (OR)

League Club	Source	Date Signed	Seasons Played	Apps	Subs	Gls
Liverpool	South Liverpool	10.46				
Everton	Tr	06.47	47	1	-	0

GARDNER, Thomas
Huyton, 28 May, 1910 Died 1970 E-2 (WH)

League Club	Source	Date Signed	Seasons Played	Apps	Subs	Gls
Liverpool	Orrell	04.29	29	5	-	0
Grimsby T.	Tr	06.31	31	13	-	0
Hull C.	Tr	05.32	32-33	66	-	2
Aston Villa	Tr	02.34	33-37	77	-	1
Burnley	Tr	04.38	38	39	-	3
Wrexham	Tr	12.45	46	33	-	4

GARGAN, John
York, 6 June, 1928 (HB)

League Club	Source	Date Signed	Seasons Played	Apps	Subs	Gls
York C.	Cliftonville	08.45	46	1	-	0

GARIANI, Moshe
Israel, 18 June, 1957 Israel Int (M)

League Club	Source	Date Signed	Seasons Played	Apps	Subs	Gls
Brighton & H.A.	Macabbi Netanya (Isr)	06.80	80	0	1	0

GARLAND, Christopher S.
Bristol, 24 April, 1949 Eu23-1 (F)

League Club	Source	Date Signed	Seasons Played	Apps	Subs	Gls
Bristol C.	App	05.66	66-71	142	1	31
Chelsea	Tr	09.71	71-74	89	3	22
Leicester C.	Tr	02.75	74-76	52	3	15
Bristol C.	Tr	12.76	76-82	53	11	11

GARLAND, David
Grimsby, 18 June, 1948 (F)

League Club	Source	Date Signed	Seasons Played	Apps	Subs	Gls
Grimsby T.	Jnrs	07.65	65	2	0	0
Scunthorpe U.	Tr	07.67				

GARLAND, Peter J.
Croydon, 20 January, 1971 E Yth (RB)

League Club	Source	Date Signed	Seasons Played	Apps	Subs	Gls
Tottenham H.	YT	07.89	90	0	1	0
Newcastle U.	Tr	03.92	91	0	2	0

GARLAND, Ronald
Middlesbrough, 28 July, 1931 Died 1989 (CF)

League Club	Source	Date Signed	Seasons Played	Apps	Subs	Gls
Oldham Ath.	South Bank St Peter	12.51	54-55	9	-	3

GARNER, Alan H.
Lambeth, 2 February, 1951 (CD)

League Club	Source	Date Signed	Seasons Played	Apps	Subs	Gls
Millwall	App	02.69	70	2	0	0
Luton T.	Tr	07.71	71-74	88	0	3
Watford	Tr	02.75	74-79	200	0	15
Portsmouth	Tr	02.80	79-81	36	0	2

GARNER, Andrew
Stonebroom, 8 March, 1966 (F/M)

League Club	Source	Date Signed	Seasons Played	Apps	Subs	Gls
Derby Co.	App	12.83	83-87	48	23	17
Blackpool	Tr	08.88	88-91	147	7	37

GARNER, Darren J.
Plymouth, 10 December, 1971 (M)

League Club	Source	Date Signed	Seasons Played	Apps	Subs	Gls
Plymouth Arg.	YT	03.89	88-91	14	3	1

GARNER, Paul
Doncaster, 1 December, 1955 E Yth (LB)

League Club	Source	Date Signed	Seasons Played	Apps	Subs	Gls
Huddersfield T.	App	12.72	72-75	96	0	2
Sheffield U.	Tr	11.75	75-83	248	3	7
Gillingham	L	09.83	83	5	0	0
Mansfield T.	Tr	09.84	84-88	102	9	8

GARNER, Simon
Boston, 23 November, 1959 (F)

League Club	Source	Date Signed	Seasons Played	Apps	Subs	Gls
Blackburn Rov.	App	11.77	78-91	455	29	168

Simon Garner (Blackburn Rovers)

GARNER, Timothy J.
Hitchin, 30 March, 1961 (G)

League Club	Source	Date Signed	Seasons Played	Apps	Subs	Gls
Northampton T. (N/C)	Kidderminster H.	03.86	85	2	0	0

GARNER, William
Stirling, 24 July, 1955 (CD)

League Club	Source	Date Signed	Seasons Played	Apps	Subs	Gls
Rochdale (L)	Alloa Ath.	10.82	82	4	0	0

GARNER, William D.
Leicester, 14 December, 1947 (F)

League Club	Source	Date Signed	Seasons Played	Apps	Subs	Gls
Notts Co.	Jnrs	07.66	66	2	0	0
Southend U.	Bedford T.	11.69	69-72	101	1	41
Chelsea	Tr	09.72	72-78	94	11	30
Cambridge U.	Tr	11.78	78-79	17	7	3
Brentford (N/C)		08.83	83	2	1	1

GARNETT, Malcolm J.
Rotherham, 8 September, 1943 (CH)

League Club	Source	Date Signed	Seasons Played	Apps	Subs	Gls
Doncaster Rov.	Jnrs	07.61	61	1	-	0

GARNETT, Shaun M.
Wallasey, 22 November, 1969 (D)

League Club	Source	Date Signed	Seasons Played	Apps	Subs	Gls
Tranmere Rov.	YT	06.88	87-91	28	1	1

GARNEYS, Thomas T.
Leyton, 25 August, 1923 (CF)

League Club	Source	Date Signed	Seasons Played	Apps	Subs	Gls
Notts Co.	Leytonstone	08.48				
Brentford	Chingford T.	12.49	49-50	12	-	2
Ipswich T.	Tr	05.51	51-58	248	-	123

League Club	Source	Date Signed	Seasons Played	Career Record Apps	Subs	Gls

GARNHAM, Stuart E.
Selby, 30 November, 1955 (G)

League Club	Source	Date Signed	Seasons Played	Apps	Subs	Gls
Wolverhampton W.	App	12.73				
Northampton T.	L	09.74	74	1	0	0
Peterborough U.	Tr	03.77	76	2	0	0
Northampton T.	L	`08.77	77	11	0	0

GARRATT, Geoffrey
Whitehaven, 2 February, 1930 (OL)

League Club	Source	Date Signed	Seasons Played	Apps	Subs	Gls
Barrow	Barrow Social	09.51	52	2	-	0
Workington	Tr	08.53	53	2	-	0

GARRETT, Archibald C.
Lesmahagow, 17 June, 1919 (CF)

League Club	Source	Date Signed	Seasons Played	Apps	Subs	Gls
Preston N. E.	Hearts	12.38	38	2	-	2
Northampton T.	Hearts	09.46	46-47	51	-	35
Birmingham C.	Tr	12.47	47-48	18	-	5
Northampton T.	Tr	12.48	48-50	43	-	16

GARRETT, James E.
Dumfries, 15 March, 1939 (W)

League Club	Source	Date Signed	Seasons Played	Apps	Subs	Gls
Carlisle U.	Queen of South	08.63	63	1	-	0

GARRETT, Leonard G.
Hackney, 14 May, 1936 E Yth (FB)

League Club	Source	Date Signed	Seasons Played	Apps	Subs	Gls
Arsenal	Eton Manor	05.54				
Ipswich T.	Tr	05.58	58	1	-	0

GARRETT, Thomas H.
South Shields, 28 February, 1926 EF Lge/E-3 (FB)

League Club	Source	Date Signed	Seasons Played	Apps	Subs	Gls
Blackpool	Horden Colly	10.44	46-60	308	-	3
Millwall	Tr	05.61	61	12	-	0

GARRITY, Kenneth
Blackburn, 6 August, 1935 (F)

League Club	Source	Date Signed	Seasons Played	Apps	Subs	Gls
Accrington St.		02.56	58-59	37	-	5

GARROW, Herbert A.
Elgin, 24 January, 1942 (G)

League Club	Source	Date Signed	Seasons Played	Apps	Subs	Gls
Newcastle U.	Fochabers	02.60	60-62	4	-	0

GARTH, James
Bridgeton, 1 May, 1922 Died 1968 (F)

League Club	Source	Date Signed	Seasons Played	Apps	Subs	Gls
Preston N.E.	Morton	11.46	46-47	23	-	7

GARTLAND, Paul E.
Shipley, 8 February, 1959 (FB)

League Club	Source	Date Signed	Seasons Played	Apps	Subs	Gls
Huddersfield T.	App	02.77	76-78	8	0	0

GARTON, William F.
Salford, 15 March, 1965 (D)

League Club	Source	Date Signed	Seasons Played	Apps	Subs	Gls
Manchester U.	App	03.83	84-88	39	2	0
Birmingham C.	L	03.86	85	5	0	0

GARVEY, Brian
Hull, 3 July, 1937 (D)

League Club	Source	Date Signed	Seasons Played	Apps	Subs	Gls
Hull C.	Jnrs	01.58	57-64	232	-	3
Watford	Tr	07.65	65-69	179	1	2
Colchester U.	Tr	06.70	70-71	75	2	1

GARVEY, James
Paisley, 4 June, 1919 (WH)

League Club	Source	Date Signed	Seasons Played	Apps	Subs	Gls
Northampton T.		05.39				
Leicester C.	Tr	06.46	46-48	15	-	0

GARVEY, Stephen H.
Stalybridge, 22 November, 1973 (M)

League Club	Source	Date Signed	Seasons Played	Apps	Subs	Gls
Crewe Alex.	YT	10.91	90-91	8	4	0

GARVIE, John
Bellshill, 16 October, 1927 (CF)

League Club	Source	Date Signed	Seasons Played	Apps	Subs	Gls
Preston N. E.	Hibernian	08.49	49	5	-	0
Lincoln C.	Tr	08.50	50-55	183	-	73
Carlisle U.	Tr	05.56	56	25	-	6

GARWOOD, Colin A.
Heacham, 29 June, 1949 E Yth (F)

League Club	Source	Date Signed	Seasons Played	Apps	Subs	Gls
Peterborough U.	Jnrs	07.67	67-70	58	8	30
Oldham Ath.	Tr	07.71	71-74	84	9	35
Huddersfield T.	Tr	12.74	74-75	22	6	8
Colchester U.	Tr	02.76	75-77	83	4	25
Portsmouth	Tr	03.78	77-79	62	9	34
Aldershot	Tr	02.80	79-81	79	2	25

GARWOOD, Jason
Birmingham, 23 March, 1969 (W)

League Club	Source	Date Signed	Seasons Played	Apps	Subs	Gls
Leicester C.	App	03.87				
Northampton T.	L	09.88	88	5	1	0

GARWOOD, Leonard F.
India, 28 July, 1923 Died 1979 (WH)

League Club	Source	Date Signed	Seasons Played	Apps	Subs	Gls
Tottenham H.	Hitchin T.	05.46	48	2	-	0

GASCOIGNE, Paul J.
Gateshead, 27 May, 1967 Eu21-13/E'B'/E-20 (M)

League Club	Source	Date Signed	Seasons Played	Apps	Subs	Gls
Newcastle U.	App	05.85	84-87	83	9	21
Tottenham H.	Tr	07.88	88-90	91	1	19

GASKELL, Alec
Leigh, 30 July, 1932 (CF)

League Club	Source	Date Signed	Seasons Played	Apps	Subs	Gls
Southport	Manchester U. (Am)	11.52	51-53	44	-	18
Newcastle U.	Tr	10.53	53	1	-	0
Mansfield T.	Tr	06.54	54-55	42	-	17
Tranmere Rov.	Tr	06.57	57	6	-	6

GASKELL, David J.
Wigan, 5 October, 1940 E Sch/E Yth (G)

League Club	Source	Date Signed	Seasons Played	Apps	Subs	Gls
Manchester U.	Jnrs	10.57	57-66	96	0	0
Wrexham	Wigan Ath.	06.69	69-71	95	0	0

GASKELL, Edward
Bredbury, 19 December, 1916 (G)

League Club	Source	Date Signed	Seasons Played	Apps	Subs	Gls
Brentford		05.38	47-51	34	-	0

GASKELL, Ronald
Worsley, 1 March, 1926 (WH)

League Club	Source	Date Signed	Seasons Played	Apps	Subs	Gls
Southport	Walkden Hill	05.50	49-50	2	-	0

GASTON, Raymond
Belfast, 22 December, 1946 NIu23-1/NI-1 (CF)

League Club	Source	Date Signed	Seasons Played	Apps	Subs	Gls
Wolverhampton W.	Coleraine	05.65				
Oxford U.	Coleraine	09.68	68	12	0	2
Lincoln C.	L	02.70	69	4	0	1

GATE, B. Kenneth
Hartlepool, 26 October, 1948 (FB)

League Club	Source	Date Signed	Seasons Played	Apps	Subs	Gls
Hartlepool U. (Am)	St Josephs	08.68	68	1	0	0

GATER, Roy
Chesterton, 22 June, 1940 (CH)

League Club	Source	Date Signed	Seasons Played	Apps	Subs	Gls
Port Vale	Jnrs	04.60	60-61	5	-	0
Bournemouth	Tr	07.62	62-68	216	0	3
Crewe Alex.	Tr	01.69	68-72	156	0	5

GATES, Eric L.
Ferryhill, 28 June, 1955 E-2 (F)

League Club	Source	Date Signed	Seasons Played	Apps	Subs	Gls
Ipswich T.	App	10.72	73-84	267	29	73
Sunderland	Tr	08.85	85-89	163	18	43
Carlisle U.	Tr	06.90	90	33	5	8

GATES, William L.
Ferryhill, 8 May, 1944 E Yth (CH)

League Club	Source	Date Signed	Seasons Played	Apps	Subs	Gls
Middlesbrough	Jnrs	10.61	61-73	277	6	12

GATTING, Stephen P.
Willesden, 29 May, 1959 (CD)

League Club	Source	Date Signed	Seasons Played	Apps	Subs	Gls
Arsenal	App	03.77	78-80	50	8	5
Brighton & H. A.	Tr	09.81	81-90	313	3	19
Charlton Ath.	Tr	08.91	91	30	2	1

GAUDEN, Alan
Ashington, 20 November, 1944 (W)

League Club	Source	Date Signed	Seasons Played	Apps	Subs	Gls
Sunderland	Jnrs	03.62	65-67	40	4	6
Darlington	Tr	10.68	68-71	125	3	39
Grimsby T.	Tr	02.72	71-72	54	1	12
Hartlepool U.	Tr	08.73	73-74	63	0	15
Gillingham	Tr	12.74	74-75	41	0	3

GAUGHAN, Steven E.
Doncaster, 14 April, 1970 (W)

League Club	Source	Date Signed	Seasons Played	Apps	Subs	Gls
Doncaster Rov.	Hatfield Main	09.87	87-89	42	25	3
Sunderland	Tr	06.90				
Darlington	Tr	01.92	91	20	0	0

GAULD, James
Aberdeen, 9 May, 1931 (IF)

League Club	Source	Date Signed	Seasons Played	Apps	Subs	Gls
Charlton Ath.	Waterford	05.55	55-56	47	-	21
Everton	Tr	10.56	56	23	-	7
Plymouth Arg.	Tr	10.57	57-58	64	-	25
Swindon T.	Tr	08.59	59	40	-	14
Mansfield T.	St Johnstone	11.60	60	4	-	3

GAVAN, John T.
Walsall, 8 December, 1939 (G)

League Club	Source	Date Signed	Seasons Played	Apps	Subs	Gls
Aston Villa	Walsall Wood	11.62	62-65	9	0	0
Doncaster Rov.	Tr	07.67	67-68	21	0	0

GAVIN, John
Limerick (Ire), 20 April, 1928 IR-7 (OR)

League Club	Source	Date Signed	Seasons Played	Apps	Subs	Gls
Norwich C.	Limerick	08.48	48-54	203	-	76
Tottenham H.	Tr	10.54	54-55	32	-	15
Norwich C.	Tr	11.55	55-57	109	-	46
Watford	Tr	07.58	58	43	-	12
Crystal Palace	Tr	05.59	59-60	66	-	15

GAVIN, Mark W.
Baillieston, 10 December, 1963 (W)

League Club	Source	Date Signed	Seasons Played	Apps	Subs	Gls
Leeds U.	App	12.81	82-84	20	10	3
Hartlepool U.	L	03.85	84	7	0	0
Carlisle U.	Tr	07.85	85	12	1	1
Bolton W.	Tr	03.86	85-86	48	1	3
Rochdale	Tr	08.87	87	23	0	6
Bristol C.	Hearts	10.88	88-89	62	7	6
Watford	Tr	08.90	90	8	5	0
Bristol C.	Tr	12.91	91	12	2	1

GAVIN, Patrick J. O.
Drogheda (Ire), 6 June, 1929 IR'B'-1/LOI (FB)

League Club	Source	Date Signed	Seasons Played	Apps	Subs	Gls
Doncaster Rov.	Dundalk	06.53	53-59	145	-	6

GAVIN, Patrick J.
Hammersmith, 5 June, 1967 (F)

League Club	Source	Date Signed	Seasons Played	Apps	Subs	Gls
Gillingham	Hanwell T.	03.89	88	13	0	7
Leicester C.	Tr	06.89	90	1	2	0
Gillingham	L	09.89	89	18	16	1
Peterborough U.	Tr	03.91	90-91	18	4	5

GAWLER, Ronald N.
Canterbury, 10 July, 1924 (HB)

League Club	Source	Date Signed	Seasons Played	Apps	Subs	Gls
Southend U.	Canterbury C.	06.49	49-50	8	-	0

GAY, Geoffrey
Romford, 4 February, 1957 (M)

League Club	Source	Date Signed	Seasons Played	Apps	Subs	Gls
Bolton W.	App	01.75				
Exeter C.	L	03.77	76	5	1	0
Southport	Tr	08.77	77	40	0	5
Wigan Ath.	Tr	07.78	78	1	0	0

GAYLE, Andrew K.
Manchester, 17 September, 1970 (W)

League Club	Source	Date Signed	Seasons Played	Apps	Subs	Gls
Oldham Ath.	YT	07.89	88	0	1	0
Crewe Alex.	Tr	02.90	89	0	1	0
Bury	Tr	08.90				

GAYLE, Brian W.
Kingston, 6 March, 1965 (CD)

League Club	Source	Date Signed	Seasons Played	Apps	Subs	Gls
Wimbledon	Tooting & Mitcham	10.84	84-87	76	7	3
Manchester C.	Tr	07.88	88-89	55	0	3
Ipswich T.	Tr	01.90	89-91	58	0	4
Sheffield U.	Tr	09.91	91	33	0	4

GAYLE, Howard A.
Liverpool, 18 May, 1958 Eu21-3 (W)

League Club	Source	Date Signed	Seasons Played	Apps	Subs	Gls
Liverpool	Jnrs	11.77	80	3	1	1
Fulham	L	01.80	79	14	0	0
Newcastle U.	L	11.82	82	8	0	2
Birmingham C.	Tr	01.83	82-83	45	1	9
Sunderland	Tr	08.84	84-85	39	9	4
Stoke C.	Dallas (USA)	03.87	86	4	2	2
Blackburn Rov.	Tr	07.87	87-91	97	19	29

GAYLE, John
Bromsgrove, 30 July, 1964 (F)

League Club	Source	Date Signed	Seasons Played	Apps	Subs	Gls
Wimbledon	Burton A.	02.89	88-90	17	3	2
Birmingham C.	Tr	11.90	90-91	22	3	7

GAYLE, Marcus A.
Hammersmith, 27 September, 1970 E Yth (W)

League Club	Source	Date Signed	Seasons Played	Apps	Subs	Gls
Brentford	YT	07.89	88-91	52	31	12

GAYLE, Mark S. R.
Bromsgrove, 21 October, 1969 (G)

League Club	Source	Date Signed	Seasons Played	Apps	Subs	Gls
Leicester C.	YT	07.88				
Blackpool	Tr	07.89				
Walsall	Worcester C.	06.91	91	24	0	0

GAYNOR, James
Dublin, 22 August, 1928 LOI (OR)

League Club	Source	Date Signed	Seasons Played	Apps	Subs	Gls
Ipswich T.	Shamrock Rov.	03.52	51-52	47	-	3
Aldershot	Tr	09.53	53-57	165	-	37

GAYNOR, Leonard A.
Ollerton, 22 September, 1925 (IF)

League Club	Source	Date Signed	Seasons Played	Apps	Subs	Gls
Hull C.	Eastwood Colly	04.48	50	2	-	0
Bournemouth	Tr	06.51	51-53	51	-	12
Southampton	Tr	03.54	53	12	-	1
Aldershot	Tr	02.55	54-56	62	-	9
Oldham Ath.	Tr	07.57	57	5	-	0

GAYNOR, Thomas
Limerick, 29 January, 1963 (F)

League Club	Source	Date Signed	Seasons Played	Apps	Subs	Gls
Doncaster Rov.	Limerick C.	12.86	86-87	28	5	7
Nottingham F.	Tr	10.87	87-91	43	14	10
Newcastle U.	L	11.90	90	4	0	1

GAZZARD, Gerald
Cinderford, 15 March, 1925 (IF)

League Club	Source	Date Signed	Seasons Played	Apps	Subs	Gls
West Ham U.	Penzance	05.49	49-53	119	-	29
Brentford	Tr	01.54	53	13	-	6

GEARD, Leonard
Hammersmith, 12 February, 1934 (WH)

League Club	Source	Date Signed	Seasons Played	Apps	Subs	Gls
Fulham	Jnrs	05.51				
Brentford	Tr	03.53	54-55	4	-	0

GEBBIE, Robert B. R. (Bert)
Cambuslang, 18 November, 1934 (G)

League Club	Source	Date Signed	Seasons Played	Apps	Subs	Gls
Bradford P. A.	Queen of South	07.60	60-63	112	-	0

GEDDES, Andrew
Craigbank, 6 September, 1922 Died 1957 (WH)

League Club	Source	Date Signed	Seasons Played	Apps	Subs	Gls
Bradford C.	Kilmarnock	06.49	49-50	30	-	4
Mansfield T.	Tr	08.51	51	11	-	2
Halifax T.	Tr	07.52	52-54	50	-	4

GEDDES, James
Burntisland, 25 May, 1942 (WH)

League Club	Source	Date Signed	Seasons Played	Apps	Subs	Gls
Bradford P. A.	Third Lanark	08.65	65	1	0	0

GEDDES, Paul
Paisley, 19 April, 1961 (M)

League Club	Source	Date Signed	Seasons Played	Apps	Subs	Gls
Leicester C.	Kilbirnie Ladeside	04.79				
Wimbledon (N/C)	Hibernian	11.81	81	2	0	0

GEDDIS, David
Carlisle, 12 March, 1958 E Yth (F)

League Club	Source	Date Signed	Seasons Played	Apps	Subs	Gls
Ipswich T.	App	08.75	76-78	26	17	5
Luton T.	L	02.77	76	9	4	4
Aston Villa	Tr	09.79	79-82	43	4	12
Luton T.	L	12.82	82	4	0	0
Barnsley	Tr	09.83	83-84	45	0	24
Birmingham C.	Tr	12.84	84-86	45	1	18
Brentford	L	11.86	86	4	0	0
Shrewsbury T.	Tr	02.87	86-88	36	3	10
Swindon T.	Tr	10.88	88	8	2	3
Darlington	Tr	03.90	90	2	11	0

David Geddis (Ipswich Town, Aston Villa, Barnsley, Birmingham City, Shrewsbury Town, Swindon Town & Darlington)

GEDNEY, Christopher
Boston, 1 September, 1945 (IF)

League Club	Source	Date Signed	Seasons Played	Apps	Subs	Gls
Lincoln C. (Am)	Jnrs	05.62	62-65	9	0	1

GEE, Alan A.
Chesterfield, 16 March, 1932

League Club	Source	Date Signed	Seasons Played	Apps	Subs	Gls
Rotherham U. (Am)		08.52	52	2	-	0

GEE, James P.
Plymouth, 6 June, 1932 (G)

League Club	Source	Date Signed	Seasons Played	Apps	Subs	Gls
Plymouth Arg. (Am)	Launceston T.	08.56	56	1	-	0

GEE, Philip J.
Pelsall, 19 December, 1964 (F)

League Club	Source	Date Signed	Seasons Played	Apps	Subs	Gls
Derby Co.	Gresley Rov.	09.85	85-91	107	17	26
Leicester C.	Tr	03.92	91	14	0	2

GEIDMINTIS, Anthony J.
Stepney, 30 July, 1949 (D)

League Club	Source	Date Signed	Seasons Played	Apps	Subs	Gls
Workington	App	08.66	64-75	323	5	37
Watford	Tr	07.76	76-77	48	1	0
Northampton T.	Tr	02.78	77-78	63	0	1
Halifax T.	Tr	07.79	79	10	2	0

GELDARD, Albert
Bradford, 11 April, 1914 Died 1989 E Sch/EF Lge/E-4 (OR)

League Club	Source	Date Signed	Seasons Played	Apps	Subs	Gls
Bradford P. A.	Jnrs	09.29	29-32	34	-	1
Everton	Tr	11.32	32-37	167	-	31
Bolton W.	Tr	06.38	38-46	29	-	1

GELSON, Peter W. J.
Hammersmith, 18 October, 1941 (CH)

League Club	Source	Date Signed	Seasons Played	Apps	Subs	Gls
Brentford	Jnrs	03.60	61-74	468	3	17

GEMMELL, Andrew
Greenock, 27 July, 1945 (W)

League Club	Source	Date Signed	Seasons Played	Apps	Subs	Gls
Bradford C.	Morton	01.67	66	3	0	0

GEMMELL, Eric
Manchester, 7 April, 1921 (CF)

League Club	Source	Date Signed	Seasons Played	Apps	Subs	Gls
Manchester C.	Manchester U. (Am)	03.46				
Oldham Ath.	Tr	06.47	47-53	195	-	109
Crewe Alex.	Tr	02.54	53-54	15	-	5
Rochdale	Tr	09.54	54-55	65	-	32

GEMMELL, James
Sunderland, 17 November, 1911 (FB)

League Club	Source	Date Signed	Seasons Played	Apps	Subs	Gls
Bury	West Stanley	03.30	30-38	257	-	0
Southport	Tr	08.45	46	25	-	0

GEMMELL, Matthew
Glasgow, 10 March, 1931 (IF)

League Club	Source	Date Signed	Seasons Played	Apps	Subs	Gls
Portsmouth	Shawfield Jnrs	09.51	53-54	3	-	0
Swindon T.	Tr	10.54	54	8	-	2

GEMMELL, Thomas
Glasgow, 16 October, 1943 SF Lge/S-18 (FB)

League Club	Source	Date Signed	Seasons Played	Apps	Subs	Gls
Nottingham F.	Glasgow Celtic	12.71	71-72	39	0	6

GEMMILL, Archibald
Paisley, 24 March, 1947 Su23-1/S-43 (M)

League Club	Source	Date Signed	Seasons Played	Apps	Subs	Gls
Preston N. E.	St Mirren	06.67	67-70	93	6	13
Derby Co.	Tr	09.70	70-77	261	0	17
Nottingham F.	Tr	09.77	77-78	56	2	4
Birmingham C.	Tr	08.79	79-81	97	0	12
Wigan Ath. (N/C)	Jacksonville (USA)	09.82	82	11	0	0
Derby Co.	Tr	11.82	82-83	63	0	8

GEMMILL, Scot
Paisley, 2 January, 1971 Su21-4 (M)

League Club	Source	Date Signed	Seasons Played	Apps	Subs	Gls
Nottingham F.	YT	01.90	90-91	41	2	8

GENDALL, Richard M.
Wrexham, 25 September, 1960 (M)

League Club	Source	Date Signed	Seasons Played	Apps	Subs	Gls
Chester C.	App	09.78	80	4	1	0

GENNOE, Terence W.
Shrewsbury, 16 March, 1953 (G)

League Club	Source	Date Signed	Seasons Played	Apps	Subs	Gls
Bury	Bricklayer Sports	06.73	72-73	3	0	0
Halifax T.	Tr	05.75	75-77	78	0	0
Southampton	Tr	02.78	78-79	36	0	0
Crystal Palace	L	01.81	80	3	0	0
Blackburn Rov.	Tr	08.81	81-90	289	0	0

GENOVESE, Domenico
Peterborough, 2 February, 1961 (F)

League Club	Source	Date Signed	Seasons Played	Apps	Subs	Gls
Peterborough U.	Cambridge C.	03.88	87-88	8	8	1

GEORGE, F. Charles
Islington, 10 October, 1950 Eu23-5/E-1 (F)

League Club	Source	Date Signed	Seasons Played	Apps	Subs	Gls
Arsenal	App	03.68	69-74	113	20	31
Derby Co.	Tr	07.75	75-78	106	0	34
Southampton	Tr	12.78	78-80	44	0	11
Nottingham F.	L	01.80	79	2	0	0
Bournemouth	Bulova (HK)	03.82	81	2	0	0
Derby Co.	Tr	03.82	81	11	0	2

GEORGE, Frank R.
Stepney, 20 November, 1933 (G)

League Club	Source	Date Signed	Seasons Played	Apps	Subs	Gls
Leyton Orient	Carshalton Ath.	07.54	56-62	119	-	0
Watford	Tr	07.63	64	10	-	0

GEORGE, Richard S. (Ricki)
Barnet, 28 June, 1946 (W)

League Club	Source	Date Signed	Seasons Played	Apps	Subs	Gls
Tottenham H.	App	10.63				
Watford	Tr	08.64	64	4	-	0
Bournemouth	Tr	05.65	65	2	1	0
Oxford U.	Tr	07.66	66	6	0	0

GEORGE, Ronald A.
Bristol, 14 August, 1922 (FB)

League Club	Source	Date Signed	Seasons Played	Apps	Subs	Gls
Crystal Palace	Bristol Aero.	02.47	48-53	122	-	2
Colchester U.	Tr	07.54	54	5	-	0

GEORGESON, Roderick B. (Roddie)
Edinburgh, 31 July, 1948 (CF)

League Club	Source	Date Signed	Seasons Played	Apps	Subs	Gls
Port Vale		01.66	65-66	26	1	6

GEORGIOU, George J.
Camden, 19 August, 1972 (F)

League Club	Source	Date Signed	Seasons Played	Apps	Subs	Gls
Fulham	Wembley	08.91	91	1	3	0

GERHARDI, Hugh
South Africa, 5 May, 1933 (IF)

League Club	Source	Date Signed	Seasons Played	Apps	Subs	Gls
Liverpool	Thistle	08.52	52	6	-	0

GERMAN, David
Sheffield, 16 October, 1973 (M)

League Club	Source	Date Signed	Seasons Played	Apps	Subs	Gls
Halifax T. (YT)	YT	07.90	90-91	2	2	0

Scot Gemmill (Nottingham Forest)

GERNON, Frederick A. J. (Irvin)
Birmingham, 30 December, 1962 E Yth /Eu21-1 (D)

League Club	Source	Date Signed	Seasons Played	Apps	Subs	Gls
Ipswich T.	App	01.80	81-86	76	0	0
Northampton T.	L	11.86	86	9	0	0
Gillingham	Tr	03.87	86-87	33	2	1
Reading	Tr	09.88	88-89	21	4	0
Northampton T.	Tr	10.89	89-91	47	1	1

GERRIE, Sydney
Aberdeen, 14 June, 1927 (IF)

League Club	Source	Date Signed	Seasons Played	Apps	Subs	Gls
Hull C.	Dundee	11.50	50-56	146	-	59

GERULA, Stanislaus E. (Stan)
Poland, 21 February, 1914 Died 1979 Polish Amat Int (G)

League Club	Source	Date Signed	Seasons Played	Apps	Subs	Gls
Leyton Orient (Am)	Carpathians	05.48	48-49	30	-	0

GIAMATTEI, Aaron P.
Reading, 11 October, 1973

League Club	Source	Date Signed	Seasons Played	Apps	Subs	Gls
Reading (YT)	YT	07.90	91	0	2	0

GIBB, J. Barry
Workington, 21 May, 1940 (WH)

League Club	Source	Date Signed	Seasons Played	Apps	Subs	Gls
Workington	Jnrs	07.60	59-60	6	-	0

GIBB, Dean A.
Newcastle, 26 October, 1966 (M)

League Club	Source	Date Signed	Seasons Played	Apps	Subs	Gls
Hartlepool U.	Brandon U.	07.86	86-87	32	16	3

GIBB, Thomas
Bathgate, 13 December, 1944 Su23-1 (M)

League Club	Source	Date Signed	Seasons Played	Apps	Subs	Gls
Newcastle U.	Partick Th.	08.68	68-74	190	9	12
Sunderland	Tr	06.75	75-76	7	3	1
Hartlepool U.	Tr	07.77	77	40	0	4

GIBBINS, Edward
Shoreditch, 24 March, 1926 (CH)

League Club	Source	Date Signed	Seasons Played	Apps	Subs	Gls
Tottenham H.	Jnrs	09.46	52	1	-	0

GIBBINS, Roger G.
Enfield, 6 September, 1955 E Sch (M/CD)

League Club	Source	Date Signed	Seasons Played	Apps	Subs	Gls
Tottenham H.	App	12.72				
Oxford U.	Tr	08.75	75	16	3	2
Norwich C.	Tr	06.76	76-77	47	1	12
Cambridge U.	New England (USA)	09.79	79-81	97	3	12
Cardiff C.	Tr	08.82	82-85	135	4	17
Swansea C.	Tr	10.85	85	35	0	6
Newport Co.	Tr	08.86	86-87	79	0	8
Torquay U.	Tr	03.88	87-88	32	1	5
Cardiff C.	Newport Co.	03.89	88-91	131	3	7

GIBBON, Malcolm
Newcastle, 24 October, 1950 (WH)

League Club	Source	Date Signed	Seasons Played	Apps	Subs	Gls
Port Vale (App)	App	06.66	66-67	4	1	0

GIBBONS, Albert H. (Jack)
Fulham, 10 April, 1914 E Amat (CF)

League Club	Source	Date Signed	Seasons Played	Apps	Subs	Gls
Tottenham H. (Am)	Kingstonian	07.37	37	27	-	13
Brentford (Am)	Tr	08.38	38	12	-	1
Bradford P. A.	Tottenham H. (Am)	05.46	46	42	-	21
Brentford	Tr	08.47	47-48	56	-	16

GIBBONS, Arthur T.
Hartlepool, 24 May, 1937 (HB)

League Club	Source	Date Signed	Seasons Played	Apps	Subs	Gls
Hartlepool U.		09.58	58	13	-	0

GIBBONS, David
Belfast, 4 November, 1952 (FB)

League Club	Source	Date Signed	Seasons Played	Apps	Subs	Gls
Manchester C.	App	08.70				
Stockport Co.	L	02.72	71	1	0	0

GIBBONS, Ian K.
Stoke, 8 February, 1970

League Club	Source	Date Signed	Seasons Played	Apps	Subs	Gls
Stoke C. (YT)	YT	07.86	87	0	1	0

GIBBONS, John R.
Charlton, 8 April, 1925 (CF)

League Club	Source	Date Signed	Seasons Played	Apps	Subs	Gls
Queens Park R.	Dartford	12.47	48	8	-	2
Ipswich T.	Tr	05.49	49	11	-	3
Tottenham H.	Tr	03.50				

GIBBONS, Leonard
Wirral, 22 November, 1930 (FB)

League Club	Source	Date Signed	Seasons Played	Apps	Subs	Gls
Wolverhampton W.	Jnrs	02.48	51-53	25	-	0

GIBBS, Alan M.
Orpington, 7 February, 1934 (F)

League Club	Source	Date Signed	Seasons Played	Apps	Subs	Gls
Cardiff C.		10.54				
Swindon T.	Tr	05.56	56	16	-	5

GIBBS, Brian R.
Gillingham (Dst), 6 October, 1936 (IF)

League Club	Source	Date Signed	Seasons Played	Apps	Subs	Gls
Bournemouth	Gosport Bor.	10.57	57-62	58	-	15
Gillingham	Tr	10.62	62-68	259	0	101
Colchester U.	Tr	09.68	68-71	153	4	37

GIBBS, Derek W.
Fulham, 22 December, 1934 (IF)

League Club	Source	Date Signed	Seasons Played	Apps	Subs	Gls
Chelsea	Jnrs	04.55	56-60	23	-	5
Leyton Orient	Tr	11.60	60-62	33	-	4
Queens Park R.	Tr	08.63	63-64	27	-	0

GIBBS, Nigel J.
St Albans, 20 November, 1965 E Yth/Eu21-5 (RB)

League Club	Source	Date Signed	Seasons Played	Apps	Subs	Gls
Watford	App	11.83	83-91	261	3	3

GIBBS, Peter L.
Rhodesia, 24 August, 1956 (G)

League Club	Source	Date Signed	Seasons Played	Apps	Subs	Gls
Watford	Tring T.	07.75	75-76	4	0	0

GIBLIN, John
Stoke, 29 June, 1923 (HB)

League Club	Source	Date Signed	Seasons Played	Apps	Subs	Gls
Stoke C.		04.43	47	1	-	0

GIBSON, Aidan M.
Newcastle-u-Lyme, 17 May, 1963 (M)

League Club	Source	Date Signed	Seasons Played	Apps	Subs	Gls
Derby Co.	App	05.81	80-81	0	2	0
Exeter C.	Tr	07.82	82	17	1	1

GIBSON, Alexander
Glasgow, 25 January, 1925 (FB)

League Club	Source	Date Signed	Seasons Played	Apps	Subs	Gls
Hull C.	Clyde	03.50	49-50	21	-	0

GIBSON, Alexander P. S.
Kirkconnel, 28 November, 1939 (CH)

League Club	Source	Date Signed	Seasons Played	Apps	Subs	Gls
Notts Co.	Auchinleck Talbot	04.59	59-68	344	3	10

GIBSON, Alfred
Castleford, 9 September, 1919 (CH)

League Club	Source	Date Signed	Seasons Played	Apps	Subs	Gls
Rotherham U.	Army	10.45	46-53	152	-	0

GIBSON, Archibald
Girvan, 30 December, 1933 (WH)

League Club	Source	Date Signed	Seasons Played	Apps	Subs	Gls
Leeds U.	Colyston Jnrs	05.51	54-59	165	-	5
Scunthorpe U.	Tr	07.60	60-63	138	-	5

GIBSON, Brian
Huddersfield, 22 February, 1928 (FB)

League Club	Source	Date Signed	Seasons Played	Apps	Subs	Gls
Huddersfield T.	Paddock Ath.	05.51	51-60	157	-	1

GIBSON, Charles
Dumbarton, 12 June, 1961 (F)

League Club	Source	Date Signed	Seasons Played	Apps	Subs	Gls
Shrewsbury T.	St Anthony's	03.81	81	2	4	0

GIBSON, Colin H.
Middlesbrough, 16 September, 1923 Died 1992 E'B'-1/EF Lge (OR)

League Club	Source	Date Signed	Seasons Played	Apps	Subs	Gls
Cardiff C.	Penarth Pont.	04.44	46-47	71	-	16
Newcastle U.	Tr	07.48	48	23	-	5
Aston Villa	Tr	02.49	48-55	158	-	24
Lincoln C.	Tr	01.56	55-56	36	-	12

GIBSON, Colin J.
Bridport, 6 April, 1960 E Sch/Eu21-1 (LB/M)

League Club	Source	Date Signed	Seasons Played	Apps	Subs	Gls
Aston Villa	App	04.78	78-85	181	4	10
Manchester U.	Tr	11.85	85-89	74	5	9
Port Vale	L	09.90	90	5	1	2
Leicester C.	Tr	12.90	90-91	34	1	4

GIBSON, David
Seaham, 14 February, 1958 (M)

League Club	Source	Date Signed	Seasons Played	Apps	Subs	Gls
Hull C.	App	12.75	75-77	19	5	0
Scunthorpe U.	Tr	07.78	78-79	16	6	1

GIBSON, David J.
Runcorn, 18 March, 1931 (OR)

League Club	Source	Date Signed	Seasons Played	Apps	Subs	Gls
Everton	Jnrs	08.50	50-51	3	-	0
Swindon T.	Tr	11.54	54-56	70	-	6

GIBSON, David W.
Winchburgh, 23 September, 1938 S-7 (IF)

League Club	Source	Date Signed	Seasons Played	Apps	Subs	Gls
Leicester C.	Hibernian	01.62	61-69	274	6	41
Aston Villa	Tr	09.70	70-71	16	3	1
Exeter C.	Tr	01.72	71-72	69	2	3

GIBSON, T. R. Donald
Manchester, 12 May, 1929 (WH)

League Club	Source	Date Signed	Seasons Played	Apps	Subs	Gls
Manchester U.	Jnrs	08.47	50-54	108	-	0
Sheffield Wed.	Tr	06.55	55-59	80	-	2
Leyton Orient	Tr	06.60	60	8	-	0

GIBSON, Frank A.
Croxley Green, 7 June, 1914

League Club	Source	Date Signed	Seasons Played	Apps	Subs	Gls
Watford (Am)	Rickmansworth	05.46	46	1	-	0

GIBSON, Henry
Newcastle, 17 April, 1930 (HB)

League Club	Source	Date Signed	Seasons Played	Apps	Subs	Gls
Fulham	Spennymoor U.	11.52	54	1	-	0
Aldershot	Kings Lynn	08.56	56	3	-	0

GIBSON, Ian S.
Newton Stewart, 30 March, 1943 S Sch/Su23-2 (M)

League Club	Source	Date Signed	Seasons Played	Apps	Subs	Gls
Accrington St. (Am)	Jnrs	07.58	58	9	-	3
Bradford P. A.	Jnrs	04.60	59-61	88	-	18
Middlesbrough	Tr	03.62	61-65	168	-	44
Coventry C.	Tr	07.66	66-69	90	3	13
Cardiff C.	Tr	07.70	70-72	89	1	11
Bournemouth	Tr	10.72	72-73	17	3	0

GIBSON, James
Belfast, 4 September,1940 (WH)

League Club	Source	Date Signed	Seasons Played	Apps	Subs	Gls
Newcastle U.	Linfield	01.59	58-60	2	-	1
Luton T.	Cambridge U.	02.65	64-65	31	1	0

GIBSON, Joseph
Banknock, 20 March, 1926 (F)

League Club	Source	Date Signed	Seasons Played	Apps	Subs	Gls
Ipswich T.	Polkemmett Jnrs	09.47	48	1	-	0
West Ham U.	Tr	07.49				

GIBSON, Michael J.
Derby, 15 July, 1939 E Yth (G)

League Club	Source	Date Signed	Seasons Played	Apps	Subs	Gls
Shrewsbury T.	Nuneaton Bor.	03.60	60-62	76	-	0
Bristol C.	Tr	04.63	62-71	332	0	0
Gillingham	Tr	07.72	72-73	80	0	0

GIBSON, Reginald
Tideswell, 15 May, 1919 (CH)

League Club	Source	Date Signed	Seasons Played	Apps	Subs	Gls
Manchester U.		09.38				
Plymouth Arg.	Tr	02.46	46	6	-	0
Exeter C.	Tr	06.47	47-48	40	-	0

GIBSON, Robert
Washington, 29 December, 1916 (IF)

League Club	Source	Date Signed	Seasons Played	Apps	Subs	Gls
Southend U.		06.45	46	2	-	0

GIBSON, Robert H.
Ashington, 5 August, 1927 (CF)

League Club	Source	Date Signed	Seasons Played	Apps	Subs	Gls
Hull C.	Aberdeen	10.49	49	12	-	5
Lincoln C.	Ashington	05.51	51-54	41	-	20
Gateshead	Peterborough U.	03.57	56-58	49	-	27

GIBSON, Simon J.
Nottingham, 10 December, 1964 (CD)

League Club	Source	Date Signed	Seasons Played	Apps	Subs	Gls
Chelsea	App	12.82				
Swindon T.	Tr	11.83	83-84	29	2	3
Preston N. E.	Tr	12.84	84-85	42	0	5
Rochdale	Tr	08.86	86	3	2	0

GIBSON, J. Stephen
Huddersfield, 2 May, 1949 (D)

League Club	Source	Date Signed	Seasons Played	Apps	Subs	Gls
Bradford P.A.	Huddersfield T. (Am)	12.67	67-68	28	4	0

GIBSON, Terence B.
Walthamstow, 23 December, 1962 E Sch/E YthEu21-11 (F)

League Club	Source	Date Signed	Seasons Played	Apps	Subs	Gls
Tottenham H.	App	01.80	79-82	16	2	4
Coventry C.	Tr	08.83	83-85	97	1	43
Manchester U.	Tr	01.86	85-86	14	9	1
Wimbledon	Tr	08.87	87-91	74	4	20
Swindon T.	L	03.92	91	8	1	1

GIBSON, William
Lanark, 24 June, 1959 (FB)

League Club	Source	Date Signed	Seasons Played	Apps	Subs	Gls
Leicester C.	Easthouses B.C.	07.79	80-81	28	0	0

GIBSON, William
Glasgow, 17 September, 1926 (FB)

League Club	Source	Date Signed	Seasons Played	Apps	Subs	Gls
Brentford	Arsenal (Am)	01.47				
Tranmere Rov.	Tr	06.51	51-53	72	-	1

GIDMAN, John
Liverpool, 10 January, 1954 E Yth/Eu23-4/E-1 (RB)

League Club	Source	Date Signed	Seasons Played	Apps	Subs	Gls
Aston Villa	Liverpool (App)	08.71	72-79	196	1	9
Everton	Tr	10.79	79-80	64	0	2
Manchester U.	Tr	08.81	81-85	94	1	4
Manchester C.	Tr	10.86	86-87	52	1	1
Stoke C.	Tr	08.88	88	7	3	0
Darlington	Tr	02.89	88	13	0	1

GIGGS, Ryan J.
Cardiff, 29 November, 1973 W Yth/Wu21-1/W-3 (LW)

League Club	Source	Date Signed	Seasons Played	Apps	Subs	Gls
Manchester U.	YT	12.90	90-91	33	7	4

GILBERG, Harold
Tottenham, 27 June, 1923 (IF)

League Club	Source	Date Signed	Seasons Played	Apps	Subs	Gls
Tottenham H.	Jnrs	09.44	46-47	2	-	0
Queens Park R.	Tr	08.51	51-52	66	-	12
Brighton & H. A.	Tr	12.52	52-55	67	-	3

GILBERT, Carl G.
Folkestone, 20 March, 1948 (CF)

League Club	Source	Date Signed	Seasons Played	Apps	Subs	Gls
Gillingham	Jnrs	10.65	67-69	28	2	11
Bristol Rov.	Tr	12.69	69-70	38	7	15
Rotherham U.	Tr	03.71	70-73	78	16	37

GILBERT, David G.
Smethwick, 5 August, 1940 (OR)

League Club	Source	Date Signed	Seasons Played	Apps	Subs	Gls
Chesterfield	Redditch	05.60	60	22	-	2

GILBERT, David J.
Lincoln, 22 June, 1963 (M)

League Club	Source	Date Signed	Seasons Played	Apps	Subs	Gls
Lincoln C.	App	06.81	80-81	15	15	1
Scunthorpe U.	Tr	08.82	82	1	0	0
Northampton T.	Boston U.	06.86	86-88	120	0	21
Grimsby T.	Tr	03.89	88-91	141	0	27

GILBERT, Noel A.
North Walsham, 25 December, 1931 (OR)

League Club	Source	Date Signed	Seasons Played	Apps	Subs	Gls
Norwich C.	North Walsham	08.55	55	1	-	0

GILBERT, Phillip
Margate, 11 September, 1944 (IF)

League Club	Source	Date Signed	Seasons Played	Apps	Subs	Gls
Brighton & H. A.	Ramsgate	01.62	61-63	7	-	3

GILBERT, Timothy H.
South Shields, 28 August, 1958 (FB)

League Club	Source	Date Signed	Seasons Played	Apps	Subs	Gls
Sunderland	App	08.76	76-79	34	2	3
Cardiff C.	Tr	02.81	80-81	33	0	1
Darlington	Tr	08.82	82-83	62	3	3

Terry Gibson (Tottenham Hotspur, Coventry City, Manchester United & Wimbledon)

Ryan Giggs (Manchester United & Wales)

GILBERT William A.
Lewisham, 10 November, 1959 E Sch/E Yth/Eu21-11 (CD)

League Club	Source	Date Signed	Seasons Played	Apps	Subs	Gls
Crystal Palace	App	12.76	77-83	235	2	3
Portsmouth	Tr	06.84	84-88	133	7	0
Colchester U.		10.89	89	26	1	0
Maidstone U. (N/C)	Tr	10.90	90	2	1	0

GILBERT, William A.
Newcastle, 7 November, 1925 (G)

League Club	Source	Date Signed	Seasons Played	Apps	Subs	Gls
Coventry C.	Murton Colly	09.48	51-52	14	-	0
Stockport Co.	Snowdown Colly	07.54	54	33	-	0

GILCHRIST, Alexander
Holytown, 28 September, 1923 (OR)

League Club	Source	Date Signed	Seasons Played	Apps	Subs	Gls
Cardiff C.		05.48	48	1	-	0

GILCHRIST, John S.
Wishaw, 5 September, 1939 S Sch (FB)

League Club	Source	Date Signed	Seasons Played	Apps	Subs	Gls
Millwall	Airdrieonians	03.61	60-68	279	0	10
Fulham	Tr	07.69	69	20	3	1
Colchester U.	Tr	07.70	70-71	41	0	2

GILCHRIST, Paul A.
Dartford, 5 January, 1951 (F)

League Club	Source	Date Signed	Seasons Played	Apps	Subs	Gls
Charlton Ath.	App	03.68	69	5	2	0
Doncaster Rov.	Tr	07.71	71	22	0	8
Southampton	Tr	03.72	71-76	96	11	17
Portsmouth	Tr	03.77	76-77	38	2	3
Swindon T.	Tr	08.78	78-79	10	7	6
Hereford U.	Tr	03.80	79	11	0	1

GILCHRIST, Robert
Bellshill, 17 August, 1932 (FB)

League Club	Source	Date Signed	Seasons Played	Apps	Subs	Gls
Aldershot	Dumfermline Ath.	06.52	52-56	48	-	0

GILDER, Carlton E.
Newport, 25 July, 1957 (F)

League Club	Source	Date Signed	Seasons Played	Apps	Subs	Gls
Cambridge U.	Jnrs	01.75	74-75	0	2	0

GILES, Albert
Swansea, 4 May, 1924 (WH)

League Club	Source	Date Signed	Seasons Played	Apps	Subs	Gls
Bristol Rov.	Jnrs	05.41	46	1	-	0

GILES, Christopher
Dublin, 17 July, 1928 IR-1 (OR)

League Club	Source	Date Signed	Seasons Played	Apps	Subs	Gls
Doncaster Rov.	Drumcondra	06.50	50-51	27	-	4
Aldershot	Tr	08.53				

GILES, David C.
Cardiff, 21 September, 1956 W Sch/Wu21-4/W-12 (W)

League Club	Source	Date Signed	Seasons Played	Apps	Subs	Gls
Cardiff C.	App	09.74	74-78	51	8	3
Wrexham	Tr	12.78	78-79	38	0	2
Swansea C.	Tr	11.79	79-81	49	5	13
Leyton Orient	L	11.81	81	3	0	2
Crystal Palace	Tr	03.82	81-83	83	5	6
Birmingham C.	Tr	08.84				
Newport Co.	Tr	10.84	84	28	4	1
Cardiff C.	Tr	09.85	85-86	50	0	0

GILES, James A.
Kidlington, 21 April, 1946 (CD)

League Club	Source	Date Signed	Seasons Played	Apps	Subs	Gls
Swindon T.	Kidlington	03.65	65-67	12	1	0
Aldershot	Tr	10.68	68-70	80	1	3
Exeter C.	Tr	03.71	70-74	183	0	8
Charlton Ath.	Tr	06.75	75-77	`92	1	6
Exeter C.	Tr	12.77	77-80	130	0	5

GILES, John
Walsall, 4 June, 1933 (IF)

League Club	Source	Date Signed	Seasons Played	Apps	Subs	Gls
Walsall	Hednesford T.	12.50	52	1	-	0

GILES, John E.
Bristol, 7 November, 1947 (M)

League Club	Source	Date Signed	Seasons Played	Apps	Subs	Gls
Bristol C.	App	06.65	66	3	0	1
Bradford P. A.	L	03.68	67	9	0	0
Exeter C.	Tr	05.69	69-71	55	5	2

GILES, M. John
Dublin, 6 January, 1940 IR-60 (M)

League Club	Source	Date Signed	Seasons Played	Apps	Subs	Gls
Manchester U.	Home Farm	11.57	59-62	99	-	10
Leeds U.	Tr	08.63	63-74	380	3	88
West Bromwich A.	Tr	06.75	75-76	74	1	3

GILES, Paul A.
Cardiff, 21 February, 1961 Wu21-3 (W)

League Club	Source	Date Signed	Seasons Played	Apps	Subs	Gls
Cardiff C.	Jnrs	06.79	80-82	17	7	1
Exeter C.	L	03.82	81	9	0	1
Newport Co. (N/C)	Excelsior (Neth)	12.84	84	0	1	0
Newport Co.	Merthyr Tydfil	03.87	86-87	28	1	2

GILES, Philip R.
Walsall, 8 October, 1929 E Yth (OL)

League Club	Source	Date Signed	Seasons Played	Apps	Subs	Gls
Walsall	Jnrs	05.48	48-52	67	-	14

GILES, Terence
Halifax, 25 March, 1943 (F)

League Club	Source	Date Signed	Seasons Played	Apps	Subs	Gls
Halifax T. (Am)		09.61	61-62	2	-	1

GILFILLAN, Robert
Dunfermline, 14 March, 1926 (IF)

League Club	Source	Date Signed	Seasons Played	Apps	Subs	Gls
Blackpool	Jeanfield Swifts	07.47				
Rochdale	Cowdenbeath	06.51	51-53	62	-	11

GILFILLAN, Robert
Cowdenbeath, 29 June, 1938 (F)

League Club	Source	Date Signed	Seasons Played	Apps	Subs	Gls
Newcastle U.	Cowdenbeath	10.59	59-60	7	-	2
Southend U.	Raith Rov.	06.63	63-65	67	1	33
Doncaster Rov.	Tr	11.65	65-70	178	8	33

GILKES, Michael E.
Hackney, 20 July, 1965 (LW)

League Club	Source	Date Signed	Seasons Played	Apps	Subs	Gls
Reading	Leicester C. (Jnrs)	07.84	84-91	181	19	20
Chelsea	L	01.92	91	0	1	0
Southampton	L	03.92	91	4	2	0

GILL, Anthony G. D.
Bradford, 6 March, 1968 (FB)

League Club	Source	Date Signed	Seasons Played	Apps	Subs	Gls
Manchester U.	App	03.86	86-88	5	5	1

GILL, Colin J. P.
Swindon, 20 January, 1933 (G)

League Club	Source	Date Signed	Seasons Played	Apps	Subs	Gls
Swindon T.		10.55	55	1	-	0

GILL, Eric N.
Camden, 3 November, 1930 (G)

League Club	Source	Date Signed	Seasons Played	Apps	Subs	Gls
Charlton Ath.	Broomfields	04.48	51	1	-	0
Brighton & H. A.	Tr	06.52	52-59	280	-	0

GILL, Frank
Manchester, 5 December, 1948 (OL)

League Club	Source	Date Signed	Seasons Played	Apps	Subs	Gls
Manchester U.	App	12.65				
Tranmere Rov.	Tr	07.68	68-70	70	4	8

GILL, Gary
Middlesbrough, 28 November, 1964 (M)

League Club	Source	Date Signed	Seasons Played	Apps	Subs	Gls
Middlesbrough	App	11.82	83-89	69	8	2
Hull C.	L	12.83	83	0	1	0
Darlington	Tr	12.89	90-91	55	1	9
Cardiff C.	Tr	03.92	91	3	3	1

GILL, John B. A.
Wednesbury, 3 February, 1941 (CH)

League Club	Source	Date Signed	Seasons Played	Apps	Subs	Gls
Nottingham F.	Jnrs	03.58				
Mansfield T.	Tr	07.61	61-65	138	1	0
Hartlepool U.	Tr	02.66	65-70	202	3	1

GILL, Joseph
Sunderland, 10 November, 1945 (G)

League Club	Source	Date Signed	Seasons Played	Apps	Subs	Gls
Hartlepool U. (Am)	Ashington	01.69	68	4	0	0

GILL, Kenneth J.
Swindon, 5 November, 1955 (W)

League Club	Source	Date Signed	Seasons Played	Apps	Subs	Gls
Newport Co. (N/C)	Forest Green Rov.	09.85	85	13	6	1

GILL, Mervyn J.
Exeter, 13 April, 1931 (G)

League Club	Source	Date Signed	Seasons Played	Apps	Subs	Gls
Portsmouth (Am)		08.53	53	6	-	0
Southampton	Woking	04.56	55	1	-	0
Torquay U.	Tr	09.56	56-61	159	-	0

GILL, Raymond
Manchester, 8 December, 1924 (D)

League Club	Source	Date Signed	Seasons Played	Apps	Subs	Gls
Manchester C.		09.47	48-49	8	-	0
Chester C.	Tr	06.51	51-61	406	-	3

GILLARD, Ian T.
Hammersmith, 9 October, 1950 Eu23-5/E-3 (LB)

League Club	Source	Date Signed	Seasons Played	Apps	Subs	Gls
Queens Park R.	App	10.68	68-81	403	5	9
Aldershot	Tr	07.82	82-85	83	0	2

GILLESPIE, Gary T.
Bonnybridge, 5 July, 1960 Su21-8/S-13 (CD)

League Club	Source	Date Signed	Seasons Played	Apps	Subs	Gls
Coventry C.	Falkirk	03.78	78-82	171	1	6
Liverpool	Tr	07.83	83-90	152	4	14

League Club	Source	Date Signed	Seasons Played	Career Record Apps	Subs	Gls

GILLESPIE, Ian C.
Plymouth, 6 May, 1913 Died 1988 (F)

Crystal Palace	Harwich & Parkeston	02.37	36-38	21	-	4
Ipswich T.	Tr	04.66	46	6	-	1

GILLESPIE, Norman
Edinburgh, 20 April, 1940 (IF)

Wrexham	Falkirk	12.63	63	3	-	0

GILLESPIE, Patrick
Bellshill, 5 July, 1928 (WH)

Watford	Partick Th.	07.45	46	6	-	0
Northampton T.	Tr	08.47	47	1	-	0
Doncaster Rov.	Tr	11.47	47-48	8	-	1

GILLETT, David J.
Edinburgh, 2 April, 1951 (D)

Crewe Alex.	Hibernian	08.72	72-74	64	5	2

GILLIAM, Reginald
Farnham, 19 February, 1931 (G)

Aldershot	Farnham T.	02.56	56	1	-	0

GILLIBRAND, Ian V.
Blackburn, 24 November, 1948 (D)

Arsenal	App	12.65				
Wigan Ath.	Tr	(N/L)	78	7	0	0

GILLIES, Donald G.
Glencoe, 20 June, 1951 Su23-1 (FB)

Bristol C.	Morton	03.73	72-79	183	17	26
Bristol Rov.	Tr	06.80	80-81	56	3	0

GILLIES, John C.
Glasgow, 22 October, 1918 (OL)

Brentford	St Mirren	05.46	46	5	-	0

GILLIES, Matthew M.
Loganlea, 12 August, 1921 (CH)

Bolton W.	R.A.F. Weeton	10.42	46-51	145	-	1
Leicester C.	Tr	01.52	51-54	103	-	0

GILLIGAN, Augustus A. (Gus)
Abingdon, 19 August, 1959 (F)

Swindon T.	App	08.77	77	3	1	0
Doncaster Rov.	L	09.78	78	1	0	0

GILLIGAN, James M.
Hammersmith, 24 January, 1964 EYth (F)

Watford	App	08.81	81-84	18	9	6
Lincoln C.	L	10.82	82	0	3	0
Grimsby T.	Tr	08.85	85	19	5	4
Swindon T.	Tr	06.86	86	13	4	5
Newport Co.	L	02.87	86	4	1	1
Lincoln C.	Tr	03.87	86	11	0	1
Cardiff C.	Tr	07.87	87-89	99	0	35
Portsmouth	Tr	10.89	89	24	8	5
Swansea C.	Tr	08.90	90-91	60	2	23

GILLIGAN, John J.
Abingdon, 2 May, 1957 (M)

Swindon T.	App	10.75	75-76	2	4	0
Huddersfield T.	L	09.76	76	0	1	0
Northampton T.	L	01.77	76	5	0	1

GILLIGAN, Malcolm
Cardiff, 11 October, 1942 (OR)

Swansea C.		05.62	62	2	-	0

GILLIVER, Alan H.
Swallownest, 3 August, 1944 (CF)

Huddersfield T.	Jnrs	08.61	62-65	45	0	22
Blackburn Rov.	Tr	06.66	66-67	32	2	9
Rotherham U.	Tr	05.68	68	23	3	2
Brighton & H. A.	Tr	07.69	69-70	54	3	19
Lincoln C.	Tr	02.71	70-71	33	4	8
Bradford C.	Tr	06.72	72-73	68	2	30
Stockport Co.	Tr	06.74	74	22	3	5
Bradford C. (N/C)	Boston U.	08.78	78	1	1	0

GILLOTT, Peter
Barnsley, 20 July, 1935 EYth (FB)

Barnsley	Jnrs	05.53	55-58	5	-	0

GILMOUR, George R.
Barrhead, 7 May, 1919

Halifax T.		09.48	48-49	37	-	2

GILMOUR, Ronald
Workington, 28 February, 1935 (HB)

Workington	Jnrs	12.52	53	2	-	0

GILPIN, James
Edinburgh, 12 June, 1945 (OL)

Bradford P. A.	Raith Rov.	08.65	65	10	1	1

GILROY, Joseph
Glasgow, 19 October, 1941 (CF)

Fulham	Clyde	10.67	67-68	23	1	8

GILZEAN, Alan J.
Coupar Angus, 22 October, 1938 Su23-3/SF Lge/S-22 (CF)

Tottenham H.	Dundee	12.64	64-73	335	8	93

Alan Gilzean (Dundee, Tottenham Hotspur & Scotland)

GIPP, David T.
Stratford, 13 July, 1969 (F)

Brighton & H. A.	App	07.86	86-87	1	4	0

GIRLING, Howard M.
Birmingham, 24 May, 1922 Died 1992 (OL)

Crystal Palace		10.43	46	26	-	6
Brentford	Tr	02.47	46-49	86	-	8
Bournemouth	Tr	07.51	51	4	-	0

GISBOURNE, Charles J.
Bury, 7 October, 1952 (D)

Bury	App	10.70	72-74	13	3	1
Crewe Alex.	Tr	10.74	74	5	1	0

GISSING, John W.
Stapleford, 24 November, 1938 (OR)

Notts Co.	Stapleford B.C.	07.56	57-60	22	-	1
Chesterfield	Tr	07.61	61	2	-	0

GITSHAM, James W.
Hammersmith, 12 May, 1942 (FB)

Brentford	Jnrs	07.59	60-62	54	-	0

GITTENS, Jonathan
Birmingham, 22 January, 1964 (CD)

Southampton	Paget R.	10.85	85-86	18	0	0
Swindon T.	Tr	07.87	87-90	124	2	6
Southampton	Tr	03.91	90-91	16	3	0
Middlesbrough	L	02.92	91	9	3	0

GIVENS, Donald J.
Limerick (Ire), 9 August, 1949 IR-56 (F)

League Club	Source	Date Signed	Seasons Played	Apps	Subs	Gls
Manchester U.	App	12.66	69	4	4	1
Luton T.	Tr	04.70	70-71	80	3	19
Queens Park R.	Tr	07.72	72-77	242	0	76
Birmingham C.	Tr	08.78	78-80	49	10	10
Bournemouth	L	03.80	79	5	0	4
Sheffield U.	Tr	03.81	80	11	0	3

GLADWIN, Robin
Harlow, 12 August, 1940 (FB)

League Club	Source	Date Signed	Seasons Played	Apps	Subs	Gls
Norwich C.	Chelmsford C.	01.66	65-67	16	0	0
Oxford U.	Tr	07.68	68-69	44	0	0

GLAISTER, George
Newcastle, 18 May, 1918 (OL)

League Club	Source	Date Signed	Seasons Played	Apps	Subs	Gls
Blackburn Rov.	North Shields	05.37	46	8	-	1
Stockport Co.	Tr	04.47	46-49	92	-	21
Halifax T.	Tr	08.50	50	34	-	7
Accington St.	Tr	09.51	51	24	-	1

GLASBY, Herbert
Bradford, 21 September, 1919 (OR)

League Club	Source	Date Signed	Seasons Played	Apps	Subs	Gls
Bradford P. A.	Aldershot (Am)	05.46	46-48	11	-	1

GLAVIN, Ronald M.
Glasgow, 27 March, 1951 S-1 (M)

League Club	Source	Date Signed	Seasons Played	Apps	Subs	Gls
Barnsley	Glasgow Celtic	06.79	79-83	171	5	73
Barnsley (N/C)	Belenenses (Port)	08.85	85	5	1	0
Stockport Co. (N/C)	Tr	08.86	86	5	5	1

GLAZIER, William J.
Nottingham, 2 August, 1943 Eu23-3/EF Lge (G)

League Club	Source	Date Signed	Seasons Played	Apps	Subs	Gls
Crystal Palace	Jnrs	10.61	61-64	106	-	0
Coventry C.	Tr	10.64	64-74	346	0	0
Brentford	Tr	06.75	75	9	0	0

GLAZZARD, James
Normanton, 23 April, 1923 (CF)

League Club	Source	Date Signed	Seasons Played	Apps	Subs	Gls
Huddersfield T.	Altofts	10.43	46-55	299	-	141
Everton	Tr	09.56	56	3	-	0
Mansfield T.		12.56	56-57	21	-	10

GLAZZARD, Malcolm
Eastham, 1 July, 1931 (OL)

League Club	Source	Date Signed	Seasons Played	Apps	Subs	Gls
Liverpool	Jnrs	05.49				
Accrington St.	Tr	08.51	51	1	-	0

GLEADALL, Dennis
Sheffield, 15 February, 1934 (CH)

League Club	Source	Date Signed	Seasons Played	Apps	Subs	Gls
Bury		08.54				
Bradford P. A.	Tr	07.56	56-57	34	-	0

GLEADALL, Edward
Sheffield, 21 August, 1931 (OR)

League Club	Source	Date Signed	Seasons Played	Apps	Subs	Gls
Bury		01.52	51-56	74	-	17
Scunthorpe U.	Tr	03.57	56-57	6	-	2

GLEASURE, Peter F.
Luton, 8 October, 1960 (G)

League Club	Source	Date Signed	Seasons Played	Apps	Subs	Gls
Millwall	App	08.78	80-82	53	0	0
Northampton T.	Tr	03.83	82-90	344	0	0
Gillingham	L	03.91	90	3	0	0

GLEAVE, Colin
Stockport, 6 April, 1919 (D)

League Club	Source	Date Signed	Seasons Played	Apps	Subs	Gls
Stockport Co.		02.38	46-47	57	-	1

GLEDHILL, Samuel
Castleford, 7 July, 1913 (D)

League Club	Source	Date Signed	Seasons Played	Apps	Subs	Gls
York C.	Altofts	09.36	36-48	123	-	6

GLEDSTONE, Peter H.
Bournemouth, 4 April, 1934 (LB)

League Club	Source	Date Signed	Seasons Played	Apps	Subs	Gls
Bournemouth	Bournemouth G.W.	11.55	57-63	131	-	2

GLEESON, Percy
Acton, 18 July, 1921 (IF)

League Club	Source	Date Signed	Seasons Played	Apps	Subs	Gls
Brentford	Hounslow T.	03.47	47	9	-	1

GLEGHORN, Nigel W.
Seaham, 12 August, 1962 (W)

League Club	Source	Date Signed	Seasons Played	Apps	Subs	Gls
Ipswich T.	Seaham Red Star	08.85	85-87	54	12	11
Manchester C.	Tr	08.88	88-89	27	7	8
Birmingham C.	Tr	09.89	89-91	131	0	32

GLENDINNING, Brian
Newcastle, 26 December, 1934 (CF)

League Club	Source	Date Signed	Seasons Played	Apps	Subs	Gls
Darlington	Felham B.C.	05.55	55	12	-	2

GLENDINNING, Kevin
Corbridge, 23 January, 1962 (LB)

League Club	Source	Date Signed	Seasons Played	Apps	Subs	Gls
Darlington	Jnrs	08.80	80	4	0	0

GLENDON, Kevin W.
Manchester, 21 June, 1961 (M)

League Club	Source	Date Signed	Seasons Played	Apps	Subs	Gls
Manchester C.	App	06.79				
Crewe Alex.	Tr	08.80	80	3	1	0
Burnley	Hyde U.	12.83	83	4	0	0

GLENN, David A.
Wigan, 30 November, 1962 (RB)

League Club	Source	Date Signed	Seasons Played	Apps	Subs	Gls
Wigan Ath.	App	11.80	80-82	68	4	4
Blackburn Rov.	Tr	08.83	83-84	23	1	0
Chester C.	Tr	07.85	85-88	70	3	1

Bill Glazier (Crystal Palace, Coventry City & Brentford)

GLENNON, Christopher D.
Manchester, 29 October, 1949 (F)

League Club	Source	Date Signed	Seasons Played	Apps	Subs	Gls
Manchester C.	App	11.67	68-69	3	1	0
Tranmere Rov.	L	01.71	70	2	0	0

GLIDDEN, Gilbert S.
Sunderland, 15 December, 1915 E Sch (WH)

League Club	Source	Date Signed	Seasons Played	Apps	Subs	Gls
Sunderland	Jnrs	02.32				
Port Vale	Tr	05.35	35	5	-	1
Reading	Tr	05.36	36-49	111	-	25
Leyton Orient	Tr	11.50	50	1	-	0

GLOSSOP, Terence
Sheffield, 10 May, 1940 (OR)

League Club	Source	Date Signed	Seasons Played	Apps	Subs	Gls
Chesterfield		05.59	59	7	-	1

GLOVER, Alan R.
Staines, 21 October, 1950 (M)

League Club	Source	Date Signed	Seasons Played	Apps	Subs	Gls
Queens Park R.	App	03.68	68	5	1	0
West Bromwich A.	Tr	06.69	69-76	84	8	9
Southend U.	L	01.76	75	0	1	0
Brentford	L	10.76	76	6	0	0
Leyton Orient	Tr	03.77	76-77	37	0	5
Brentford	Tr	11.78	78-79	21	2	2

GLOVER, Alexander
Glasgow, 28 February, 1922 (OR)

League Club	Source	Date Signed	Seasons Played	Apps	Subs	Gls
Bradford P. A.	Partick Th.	03.48	47-49	48	-	5
Luton T.	Tr	09.49	49-50	56	-	6
Blackburn Rov.	Tr	09.51	51-53	65	-	4
Barrow	Tr	08.54	54-57	86	-	7

GLOVER, Arthur
Barnsley, 27 March, 1918 (CH)

League Club	Source	Date Signed	Seasons Played	Apps	Subs	Gls
Barnsley	Jnrs	03.35	37-52	187	-	6

GLOVER, Benjamin D.
Birmingham, 30 November, 1946 (HB)

League Club	Source	Date Signed	Seasons Played	Apps	Subs	Gls
Coventry C.		10.66	66	0	1	0

GLOVER, Bevil A.
Manchester, 25 March, 1926 (CH)

League Club	Source	Date Signed	Seasons Played	Apps	Subs	Gls
Stockport Co.	Cheadle	01.48	47-53	137	-	1
Rochdale	Tr	03.54	53-58	169	-	1

GLOVER, Dean V.
West Bromwich, 29 December, 1963 (CD)

League Club	Source	Date Signed	Seasons Played	Apps	Subs	Gls
Aston Villa	App	12.81	84-86	25	3	0
Sheffield U.	L	10.86	86	5	0	0
Middlesbrough	Tr	06.87	87-88	44	6	5
Port Vale	Tr	02.89	88-91	153	0	6

GLOVER, Gerald J.
Liverpool, 27 September, 1946 E Sch/E Yth (WH)

League Club	Source	Date Signed	Seasons Played	Apps	Subs	Gls
Everton	App	08.64	64-65	2	1	0
Mansfield T.	Tr	09.67	67	18	1	0

GLOVER, John J.
Workington, 6 February, 1935 (F)

League Club	Source	Date Signed	Seasons Played	Apps	Subs	Gls
Workington	Marsh B.C.	10.54	54	2	-	0

GLOVER, E. Lee
Kettering, 24 April, 1970 S Yth/Su21-3 (F)

League Club	Source	Date Signed	Seasons Played	Apps	Subs	Gls
Nottingham F.	YT	04.87	87-91	37	7	4
Leicester C.	L	09.89	89	3	2	1
Barnsley	L	01.90	89	8	0	0
Luton T.	L	09.91	91	1	0	0

GLOVER, Leonard
Kennington, 31 January, 1944 (OL)

League Club	Source	Date Signed	Seasons Played	Apps	Subs	Gls
Charlton Ath.	Jnrs	05.62	62-67	177	0	20
Leicester C.	Tr	11.67	67-75	245	7	38

GLOVER, Peter
Bradford, 16 October, 1936 (WH)

League Club	Source	Date Signed	Seasons Played	Apps	Subs	Gls
Bradford C.		11.57	57	1	-	0

GLOZIER, Robert
East Ham, 20 November, 1948 E Sch (FB)

League Club	Source	Date Signed	Seasons Played	Apps	Subs	Gls
West Ham U.	App	05.66				
Torquay U.	Tr	08.69	69-71	57	0	1

GLYNN, Terence R.
Hackney, 17 December, 1958 (F)

League Club	Source	Date Signed	Seasons Played	Apps	Subs	Gls
Leyton Orient	App	12.76	76	1	1	0

GOAD, Alan M.
Hilsham, 8 August, 1948 (D)

League Club	Source	Date Signed	Seasons Played	Apps	Subs	Gls
Exeter C.	Jnrs	12.65				
Hartlepool U.	Tr	07.67	67-77	366	9	11

GOALEN, H. Keith
Hindley, 24 May, 1933 (F)

League Club	Source	Date Signed	Seasons Played	Apps	Subs	Gls
Stockport Co.	Jnrs	04.53	50-55	18	-	2

GOATER, L. Shawn
Bermuda, 25 February, 1970 (F)

League Club	Source	Date Signed	Seasons Played	Apps	Subs	Gls
Manchester U.	Jnrs	05.89				
Rotherham U.	Tr	10.89	89-91	35	23	13

GOBLE, Stephen R.
Aylsham, 5 September, 1960 (LW)

League Club	Source	Date Signed	Seasons Played	Apps	Subs	Gls
Norwich C.	App	09.78	79-80	30	0	2
Norwich C.	Groningen (Neth)	08.84	84			
Cambridge C.(N/C)	Utrecht (Neth)	02.88	87	1	1	0

GODBOLD, Daryl M.
Ipswich, 5 September, 1964 (FB)

League Club	Source	Date Signed	Seasons Played	Apps	Subs	Gls
Norwich C.	App	09.82	83	0	2	0
Colchester U.	Tr	08.84	84	4	2	1

GODBOLD, Harold
Gateshead, 31 January, 1939 (W)

League Club	Source	Date Signed	Seasons Played	Apps	Subs	Gls
Sunderland	Usworth Colly	05.56	57-59	12	-	1
Hartlepool U.	Tr	01.61	60-62	66	-	8
Lincoln C.	Boston U.	03.66	65-66	22	0	3

GODDARD, Howard J.
Over Wallop, 10 May, 1957 (F)

League Club	Source	Date Signed	Seasons Played	Apps	Subs	Gls
Bournemouth	App	07.74	72-75	62	2	18
Swindon T.	Tr	06.76	76	10	3	0
Newport Co.	Tr	08.77	77-81	101	4	42
Blackpool	L	09.81	81	4	0	2
Bournemouth	Tr	12.81	81	6	3	2
Aldershot	Tr	08.82	82	26	2	9

GODDARD, Karl E.
Leeds, 29 December, 1967 E Sch (M/LB)

League Club	Source	Date Signed	Seasons Played	Apps	Subs	Gls
Manchester U.	App	12.85				
Bradford C.	Tr	06.86	86-89	67	6	0
Exeter C.	L	12.89	89	0	1	0
Colchester U.	L	01.90	89	16	0	1
Hereford U.	Tr	09.90	90-91	8	1	1

GODDARD, Paul
Harlington, 12 October, 1959 Eu21-8/E-1 (F)

League Club	Source	Date Signed	Seasons Played	Apps	Subs	Gls
Queens Park R.	App	07.77	77-79	63	7	23
West Ham U.	Tr	08.80	80-86	159	11	54
Newcastle U.	Tr	11.86	86-87	61	0	19
Derby Co.	Tr	08.88	88-89	49	0	15
Millwall	Tr	12.89	89-90	17	3	1
Ipswich T.	Tr	01.91	90-91	37	6	10

GODDARD, Raymond
Fulham, 13 February, 1949 (G)

League Club	Source	Date Signed	Seasons Played	Apps	Subs	Gls
Leyton Orient	Fulham (App)	02.67	66-73	278	0	0
Millwall	Tr	11.74	75-77	80	0	0
Wimbledon	Tr	02.78	77-80	119	0	1

GODDARD, Raymond
Birmingham, 17 October, 1920 Died 1974 (CH)

League Club	Source	Date Signed	Seasons Played	Apps	Subs	Gls
Wolverhampton W.	Red Rov.	09.38	38	4	-	0
Chelsea	Tr	09.46	46-47	14	-	1
Plymouth Arg.	Tr	07.48	48-49	43	-	1
Exeter C.	Tr	12.49	49-53	130	-	2

GODDEN, Anthony L.
Gillingham, 2 August, 1955 (G)

League Club	Source	Date Signed	Seasons Played	Apps	Subs	Gls
West Bromwich A.	Ashford T.	08.75	76-85	267	0	0
Luton T.	L	03.83	82	12	0	0
Walsall	L	10.83	83	19	0	0
Chlsea	Tr	03.86	85-86	34	0	0
Birmingham C.	Tr	07.87	87-88	29	0	0
Bury	L	12.88	88	1	0	0
Peterborough U.	Tr	07.89	89	24	0	0

GODDERIDGE, Alan E.
Tamworth, 23 May, 1928 (HB)

League Club	Source	Date Signed	Seasons Played	Apps	Subs	Gls
Swansea C.	Tamworth	10.50	51	1	-	0
Walsall	Tr	07.52	52	3	-	0

GODDING, Earl G.
Wrexham, 6 January, 1934 (G)

League Club	Source	Date Signed	Seasons Played	Apps	Subs	Gls
Wrexham	Jnrs	04.54	52-58	21	-	0
Workington	Tr	08.59	59	10	-	0

GODFREY, Anthony W.
Newbury, 30 April, 1939 (G)

League Club	Source	Date Signed	Seasons Played	Apps	Subs	Gls
Southampton	Basingstoke	04.58	58-65	141	0	0
Aldershot	Tr	12.65	65-69	172	0	0
Rochdale	Tr	07.70	70-71	71	0	0
Aldershot	Tr	07.72	72-75	68	0	0

GODFREY, Brian C.
Flint, 1 May, 1940 Wu23-1/W-3 (IF)

League Club	Source	Date Signed	Seasons Played	Apps	Subs	Gls
Everton	Flint Alex.	05.58	59	1	-	0
Scunthorpe U.	Tr	06.60	60-63	87	-	24
Preston N. E.	Tr	10.63	63-67	121	1	52
Aston Villa	Tr	09.67	67-70	139	4	22
Bristol Rov.	Tr	05.71	71-72	79	2	16
Newport Co.	Tr	06.73	73-75	117	1	14

GODFREY, Kevin A.
Kennington, 24 February, 1960 (W)

League Club	Source	Date Signed	Seasons Played	Apps	Subs	Gls
Leyton Orient	App	03.77	77-87	255	30	63
Plymouth Arg.	L	02.86	85	7	0	1
Brentford	Maidenhead U.	10.88	88-91	92	27	17

GODFREY, Paul
Derby, 27 September, 1972 (LM)

League Club	Source	Date Signed	Seasons Played	Apps	Subs	Gls
Chesterfield (YT)	YT	07.89	90	2	0	0

GODFREY, Peter R.
Woolwich, 15 March, 1938 (OR)

League Club	Source	Date Signed	Seasons Played	Apps	Subs	Gls
Charlton Ath.	Jnrs	11.55	60	1	-	0
Gillingham	Tr	07.61	61-64	66	-	9
Chesterfield	Tr	07.65	65	27	0	2
Exeter C.	Tr	06.66	66	42	0	4

GODSELL, John D.
Methil, 13 September, 1924 (LB)

League Club	Source	Date Signed	Seasons Played	Apps	Subs	Gls
Huddersfield T.		06.46				
Bradford C.	Tr	09.48	49	9	-	0
Southport	Tr	08.51	51	3	-	0

GODWIN, Donald
Bargoed, 5 July, 1932 (OL)

League Club	Source	Date Signed	Seasons Played	Apps	Subs	Gls
Cardiff C.	Bargoed	12.53	56	2	-	0

GODWIN, Robert G.
Wootton Bassett, 3 February, 1928 (IF)

League Club	Source	Date Signed	Seasons Played	Apps	Subs	Gls
Swindon T.		09.51	51	2	-	0

GODWIN, Thomas F.
Dublin, 20 August, 1927 LOI/IR-13 (G)

League Club	Source	Date Signed	Seasons Played	Apps	Subs	Gls
Leicester C.	Shamrock Rov.	10.49	49-51	45	-	0
Bournemouth	Tr	06.52	52-61	357	-	0

GODWIN, Verdi
Blackpool, 11 February, 1926 (F)

League Club	Source	Date Signed	Seasons Played	Apps	Subs	Gls
Blackburn Rov.		03.46	46-47	27	-	6
Manchester C.	Tr	06.48	48	8	-	3
Stoke C.	Tr	06.49	49	22	-	2
Mansfield T.	Tr	01.50	49-50	31	-	9
Middlesbrough	Tr	11.51				
Grimsby T.	Tr	01.52	51	1	-	0
Brentford	Tr	03.52	51-52	7	-	0
Southport	Tr	07.54	54	17	-	2
Barrow	Tr	08.55	55	16	-	3
Tranmere Rov.	Tr	08.56	56	14	-	2

GOFFIN, William C.
Tamworth, 12 December, 1920 Died 1987 (W)

League Club	Source	Date Signed	Seasons Played	Apps	Subs	Gls
Aston Villa	Jnrs	12.37	46-53	156	-	36
Walsall	Tr	08.54	54	8	-	1

GOLAC, Ivan
Yugoslavia, 15 June, 1950 Yugoslav Int (FB)

League Club	Source	Date Signed	Seasons Played	Apps	Subs	Gls
Southampton	Partizan Belgrade (Yug)	11.78	78-81	143	1	4
Bournemouth	L	11.82	82	9	0	0
Manchester C.	L	03.83	82	2	0	0
Southampton	Yugoslavia	03.84	83-85	24	0	0
Portsmouth	L	01.85	84	8	0	0

GOLDBERG, Leslie
Leeds, 3 January, 1918 E Sch (FB)

League Club	Source	Date Signed	Seasons Played	Apps	Subs	Gls
Leeds U.	Jnrs	05.35	37-46	31	-	0
Reading	Tr	03.47	46-49	71	-	1

GOLDER, James
Manchester, 28 March, 1955

League Club	Source	Date Signed	Seasons Played	Apps	Subs	Gls
Stockport Co. (App)	App	07.70	71	0	1	0

GOLDIE, James
Denny, 29 June, 1940 (F)

League Club	Source	Date Signed	Seasons Played	Apps	Subs	Gls
Luton T.	Kilsyth R.	04.62	62	7	-	2
York C.	Tr	06.63	63	22	-	7

GOLDIE, Peter
Dumbarton, 7 June, 1934 (FB)

League Club	Source	Date Signed	Seasons Played	Apps	Subs	Gls
Aldershot	Glasgow Celtic	06.58	58	5	-	0

GOLDING, Norman J.
Southwark, 23 January, 1937 (W)

League Club	Source	Date Signed	Seasons Played	Apps	Subs	Gls
Queens Park R.	Tonbridge	08.59	59-60	31	-	6

GOLDRING, Mark
Havant, 17 September, 1972 (G)

League Club	Source	Date Signed	Seasons Played	Apps	Subs	Gls
Chesterfield	YT	07.91	91	7	0	0

GOLDSMITH, Craig S. W.
Peterborough, 27 August, 1963 (LW)

League Club	Source	Date Signed	Seasons Played	Apps	Subs	Gls
Peterborough U.	Mirrlees Blackstone	08.88	88-89	39	7	6
Carlisle U.	Tr	12.89	89-90	21	9	1

GOLDSMITH, Martin
Walsall, 4 November, 1969 (F)

League Club	Source	Date Signed	Seasons Played	Apps	Subs	Gls
Walsall	YT	08.88	88-90	2	5	2

GOLDSMITH, Martin S.
Carmarthen, 25 May, 1962 (F)

League Club	Source	Date Signed	Seasons Played	Apps	Subs	Gls
Cambridge U.	Carmarthen	04.80	80-83	28	7	5
Cardiff C.	Tr	01.84	83	3	6	2

GOLDTHORPE, Robert J.
Osterley, 6 December, 1950 (CD)

League Club	Source	Date Signed	Seasons Played	Apps	Subs	Gls
Crystal Palace	Jnrs	07.68	71	1	0	0
Charlton Ath.	Tr	12.72	72-75	70	8	6
Aldershot	L	02.76	75	16	0	0
Brentford	Tr	07.76	76	19	0	2

GOLDTHORPE, Wayne
Staincross, 19 September, 1957 (F)

League Club	Source	Date Signed	Seasons Played	Apps	Subs	Gls
Huddersfield T.	App	09.75	75-77	19	7	7
Hartlepool U.	L	12.76	76	6	1	1
Hartlepool U.	Tr	08.78	78-79	43	4	8
Crewe Alex.	Tr	10.79	79	0	1	0

Ivan Golac (Partizan Belgrade, Southampton & Yugoslavia)

GOLLEY, Mark A.
Beckenham, 28 October, 1962 (CD)

League Club	Source	Date Signed	Seasons Played	Apps	Subs	Gls
Maidstone U.	Sutton U.	(N/L)	89-90	77	4	3

GOLLOGLY, John
Bridlington, 4 July, 1962 (M)

League Club	Source	Date Signed	Seasons Played	Apps	Subs	Gls
Hartlepool U. (N/C)	Whitby T.	03.85	84-86	29	2	5

GOMERSALL, Victor
Manchester, 17 June, 1942 (FB)

League Club	Source	Date Signed	Seasons Played	Apps	Subs	Gls
Manchester C.	Jnrs	07.60	61-65	39	0	0
Swansea C.	Tr	08.66	66-70	179	1	6

GOOCH, James A. G.
Ilford, 11 July, 1921 (G)

League Club	Source	Date Signed	Seasons Played	Apps	Subs	Gls
Preston N. E.	Becontree	05.42	46-51	135	-	0
Bradford C.	Tr	07.53	53	22	-	0
Watford	Tr	07.54	55-56	43	-	0

GOOD, John R.
Portsmouth, 29 January, 1933

League Club	Source	Date Signed	Seasons Played	Apps	Subs	Gls
Nottingham F.		06.53				
Bury	Tr	06.54				
Tranmere Rov.	Buxton	07.55	55	5	-	0

GOODALL, Bernard
Slough, 4 October, 1937 (FB)

League Club	Source	Date Signed	Seasons Played	Apps	Subs	Gls
Reading		07.59	59-61	98	-	0
Carlisle U.	Tr	07.63	63	1	-	0
Halifax T.	Tr	11.64	64	23	-	0

GOODALL, David G.
Madeley, 18 May, 1943 (CH)

League Club	Source	Date Signed	Seasons Played	Apps	Subs	Gls
Shrewsbury T.	Jnrs	05.61	61	1	-	0

GOODCHILD, Gary D.
Chelmsford, 27 January, 1958 E Sch (F)

League Club	Source	Date Signed	Seasons Played	Apps	Subs	Gls
Arsenal	App	01.75				
Hereford U.	Tr	06.76	76	1	3	0
Reading	Tr	09.77	77	0	1	0
Crystal Palace	Kramfors (Swe)	12.79	79-80	0	2	0

GOODCHILD, John
Gateshead, 2 January, 1939 (F)

League Club	Source	Date Signed	Seasons Played	Apps	Subs	Gls
Sunderland	Ludworth Jnrs	09.56	57-60	44	-	21
Brighton & H. A.	Tr	05.61	61-65	162	1	45
York C.	Tr	06.66	66	29	0	6
Darlington	Tr	07.67	67	2	0	0

GOODE, Terence J.
Islington, 29 October, 1961 (F)

League Club	Source	Date Signed	Seasons Played	Apps	Subs	Gls
Birmingham C.	App	09.79	80	0	2	0

GOODEVE, Kenneth G. A.
Manchester, 3 September, 1950 (CD)

League Club	Source	Date Signed	Seasons Played	Apps	Subs	Gls
Manchester U.	App	09.67				
Luton T.	Tr	04.70	70-72	9	6	0
Brighton & H. A.	Tr	12.73	73	5	1	0
Watford	Tr	06.74	74-75	67	0	4

GOODFELLOW, Derrick O.
Shilbottle, 26 June, 1914 (G)

League Club	Source	Date Signed	Seasons Played	Apps	Subs	Gls
Gateshead		03.35	34-35	30	-	0
Sheffield Wed.	Tr	05.36	36-46	69	-	0
Middlesbrough	Tr	06.47	47	36	-	0

GOODFELLOW, James
Bishop Auckland, 16 September, 1943 (M)

League Club	Source	Date Signed	Seasons Played	Apps	Subs	Gls
Port Vale	Bishop Auckland	06.66	66-68	77	8	11
Workington	Tr	07.69	69-73	199	0	15
Rotherham U.	Tr	01.74	73-77	192	0	8
Stockport Co.	Tr	08.78	78	2	1	0

GOODFELLOW, James B.
Edinburgh, 30 July, 1938 (F)

League Club	Source	Date Signed	Seasons Played	Apps	Subs	Gls
Leicester C.	Third Lanark	05.63	63-67	96	2	26
Mansfield T.	Tr	03.68	67-70	96	4	14

GOODFELLOW, Sidney
Newcastle-under-Lyme, 6 July, 1915 (WH)

League Club	Source	Date Signed	Seasons Played	Apps	Subs	Gls
Port Vale	Hanley	11.36	36	16	-	1
Rochdale	Glentoran	05.38	38	41	-	2
Chesterfield	Tr	04.39	46-47	80	-	0
Doncaster Rov.	Tr	05.48	48-49	65	-	2
Oldham Ath.	Tr	09.50	50-51	72	-	2
Accrington St.	Tr	06.52	52	28	-	3

GOODGAME, Anthony A.
Hammersmith, 19 February, 1946 (FB)

League Club	Source	Date Signed	Seasons Played	Apps	Subs	Gls
Fulham	App	02.64				
Leyton Orient	Tr	08.66	66	7	1	0

GOODING, Michael C.
Newcastle, 12 April, 1959 (M)

League Club	Source	Date Signed	Seasons Played	Apps	Subs	Gls
Rotherham U.	Bishop Auckland	07.79	79-82	90	12	10
Chesterfield	Tr	12.82	82	12	0	0
Rotherham U.	Tr	09.83	83-86	149	7	32
Peterborough U.	Tr	08.87	87-88	47	0	21
Wolverhampton W.	Tr	09.88	88-89	43	1	4
Reading	Tr	12.89	89-91	110	1	13

GOODING, Raymond
Hartlepool, 16 February, 1959 (M)

League Club	Source	Date Signed	Seasons Played	Apps	Subs	Gls
Coventry C.	App	06.76	76-81	46	3	5
Bristol C.	L	03.82	81	3	0	0
Plymouth Arg.	Tr	08.82	82	7	0	1

GOODISON, C. Wayne
Wakefield, 23 September, 1964 (FB)

League Club	Source	Date Signed	Seasons Played	Apps	Subs	Gls
Barnsley	App	09.82	82-85	31	5	0
Crewe Alex.	Tr	09.86	86-88	90	4	1
Rochdale	Tr	07.89	89-90	78	1	4

GOODLASS, Ronald
Liverpool, 6 September, 1953 E Sch (W)

League Club	Source	Date Signed	Seasons Played	Apps	Subs	Gls
Everton	App	07.71	75-77	31	4	2
Fulham	Den Haag (Neth)	09.80	80	21	1	2
Scunthorpe U.	Tr	03.82	81	9	0	0
Tranmere Rov.	Hong Kong	12.83	83-84	19	2	0

GOODMAN, Donald R.
Leeds, 9 May, 1966 (F)

League Club	Source	Date Signed	Seasons Played	Apps	Subs	Gls
Bradford C.	Collingham	10.83	83-86	65	5	14
West Bromwich A.	Tr	03.87	86-91	140	18	60
Sunderland	Tr	12.91	91	20	2	11

GOODMAN, John
Kings Lynn, 8 September, 1935 (G)

League Club	Source	Date Signed	Seasons Played	Apps	Subs	Gls
Crewe Alex.		10.58	58	1	-	0

GOODMAN, Jonathan
Walthamstow, 2 June, 1971 (F)

League Club	Source	Date Signed	Seasons Played	Apps	Subs	Gls
Millwall	Bromley	08.90	90-91	35	5	8

GOODMAN, Malcolm J.
Solihull, 6 May, 1961 (D)

League Club	Source	Date Signed	Seasons Played	Apps	Subs	Gls
Halifax T.	Bromsgrove Rov.	09.79	79-82	70	16	1

GOODWIN, David
Nantwich, 15 October, 1954 (F)

League Club	Source	Date Signed	Seasons Played	Apps	Subs	Gls
Stoke C.	App	06.72	73-77	22	4	3
Workington	L	10.76	76	7	0	0
Mansfield T.	Tr	11.77	77-79	42	4	5
Bury	Tr	09.80	80	2	2	0
Rochdale	Tr	08.81	81	34	5	6
Crewe Alex.	Tr	08.82	82	4	3	0

GOODWIN, Eric
Chesterfield, 6 March, 1929 (CH)

League Club	Source	Date Signed	Seasons Played	Apps	Subs	Gls
Mansfield T.		09.53	53-54	9	-	0

GOODWIN, Frederick
Heywood, 28 June, 1933 (WH)

League Club	Source	Date Signed	Seasons Played	Apps	Subs	Gls
Manchester U.		10.53	54-59	95	-	7
Leeds U.	Tr	03.60	59-63	107	-	2
Scunthorpe U.	Tr	12.64	65	5	1	1

GOODWIN, Frederick J.
Stockport, 4 January, 1944 (M)

League Club	Source	Date Signed	Seasons Played	Apps	Subs	Gls
Wolverhampton W.	Jnrs	01.61	61-65	44	1	0
Stockport Co.	Tr	01.66	65-69	171	5	20
Blackburn Rov.	Tr	03.70	69-71	63	1	4
Southport	Tr	10.71	71	10	2	0
Port Vale	Tr	08.72	72	27	0	2
Stockport Co.	Macclesfield T.	08.74	74	29	0	1

GOODWIN, Ian D.
Irlam, 14 November, 1950 (CD)

League Club	Source	Date Signed	Seasons Played	Apps	Subs	Gls
Coventry C.	Oldham Ath. (App)	12.68	70	4	0	0
Brighton & H.A.	Tr	10.70	70-73	52	4	0

GOODWIN, John W.
Worcester, 29 September, 1920 (OR)

League Club	Source	Date Signed	Seasons Played	Apps	Subs	Gls
Birmingham C.	Worcester C.	05.46	46-48	32	-	8
Brentford	Tr	04.49	49-53	131	-	23

GOODWIN, Leslie
Manchester, 30 April, 1924 (W)

League Club	Source	Date Signed	Seasons Played	Apps	Subs	Gls
Oldham Ath.	Blackpool (Am)	08.44	46	7	-	0
Southport	Tr	07.47	47-48	16	-	2

GOODWIN, Mark A.
Sheffield, 23 February, 1960 (M)

League Club	Source	Date Signed	Seasons Played	Apps	Subs	Gls
Leicester C.	App	11.77	77-80	69	22	8
Notts Co.	Tr	03.81	80-86	226	11	24
Walsall	Tr	07.87	87-89	81	11	2

GOODWIN, Samuel G.
Tarbolton, 14 March, 1943 (M)

League Club	Source	Date Signed	Seasons Played	Apps	Subs	Gls
Crystal Palace	Airdrieonians	09.71	71	18	7	0

GOODWIN, Shaun L.
Rotherham, 14 June, 1969 (M)

League Club	Source	Date Signed	Seasons Played	Apps	Subs	Gls
Rotherham U.	YT	06.87	87-91	142	13	18

GOODWIN, Stephen A.
Oldham, 23 February, 1954 (M)

League Club	Source	Date Signed	Seasons Played	Apps	Subs	Gls
Norwich C.	App	02.72	70-74	2	1	0
Scunthorpe U.	L	09.73	73	2	0	0
Southend U.	Tr	06.75	75-78	68	7	10

GOODYEAR, Clive
Lincoln, 15 January, 1961 (D)

League Club	Source	Date Signed	Seasons Played	Apps	Subs	Gls
Luton T.	Lincoln U.	10.78	79-83	85	5	4
Plymouth Arg.	Tr	08.84	84-86	99	7	5
Wimbledon	Tr	07.87	87-89	25	1	0
Brentford	Tr	03.91	90	10	0	0

GOODYEAR, George W.
Luton, 5 July, 1916 (WH)

League Club	Source	Date Signed	Seasons Played	Apps	Subs	Gls
Luton T.	Hitchin T.	10.38	46	10	-	0
Southend U.	Tr	07.47	47-48	59	-	1
Crystal Palace	Tr	06.49				

GORAM, Andrew L.
Bury, 13 April, 1964 Su21-1/S-23 (G)

League Club	Source	Date Signed	Seasons Played	Apps	Subs	Gls
Oldham Ath.	West Bromwich A.(App)	08.81	81-87	195	0	0

GORAM, Lewis A.
Edinburgh, 2 July, 1926 (G)

League Club	Source	Date Signed	Seasons Played	Apps	Subs	Gls
Bury	Third Lanark	06.50	50-56	111	-	0

GORDINE, Barry
Stepney, 1 September, 1948 (G)

League Club	Source	Date Signed	Seasons Played	Apps	Subs	Gls
Sheffield U.	Gravesend & Nft.	06.68				
Oldham Ath.	Tr	12.68	68-70	83	0	0

GORDON, Andrew
Bathgate, 6 July, 1944 (CF)

League Club	Source	Date Signed	Seasons Played	Apps	Subs	Gls
Darlington (Am)	West Auckland	08.69	69	1	2	0

GORDON, Colin K.
Stourbridge, 17 January, 1963 (F)

League Club	Source	Date Signed	Seasons Played	Apps	Subs	Gls
Swindon T.	Oldbury U.	10.84	84-85	70	2	34
Wimbledon	Tr	06.86	86	2	1	0
Gillingham	L	02.87	86	4	0	2
Reading	Tr	07.87	87-88	23	1	9
Bristol C.	L	03.88	87	8	0	4
Fulham	Tr	10.88	88	12	5	2
Birmingham C.	Tr	06.89	89-90	17	9	3
Hereford U.	L	09.90	90	6	0	0
Walsall	L	12.90	90	6	0	1
Bristol Rov.	L	01.91	90	1	3	0
Leicester C.	Tr	07.91	91	18	3	5

GORDON, Dale A.
Gt Yarmouth, 9 January, 1967 E Sch/E Yth/Eu21-4 (W)

League Club	Source	Date Signed	Seasons Played	Apps	Subs	Gls
Norwich C.	App	01.84	84-91	194	12	31

GORDON, Dean D. J.
Croydon, 10 February, 1973 (F)

League Club	Source	Date Signed	Seasons Played	Apps	Subs	Gls
Crystal Palace	YT	07.91	91	2	2	0

GORDON, Dennis W.
Wolverhampton, 7 June, 1924 (OR)

League Club	Source	Date Signed	Seasons Played	Apps	Subs	Gls
West Bromwich A.	Oxford C.	09.47	47-51	27	-	2
Brighton & H.A.	Tr	07.52	52-60	276	-	63

GORDON, Henry
Glasgow, 10 December, 1931 (HB)

League Club	Source	Date Signed	Seasons Played	Apps	Subs	Gls
Bury	Petershill	06.51	51-56	24	-	0

GORDON, Henry A.
Livingston, 25 July, 1940 (WH)

League Club	Source	Date Signed	Seasons Played	Apps	Subs	Gls
Bradford P.A.	Dundee U.	08.65	65-66	61	0	2

GORDON, James S.
Stretford, 3 October, 1955 E Sch (G)

League Club	Source	Date Signed	Seasons Played	Apps	Subs	Gls
Luton T.	Blackpool (App)	09.73				
Lincoln C.	Tr	07.74	76-77	4	0	0
Scunthorpe U.	Reading (N/C)	09.78	79-80	34	0	0

GORDON, James
Fauldhouse, 23 October, 1915 (WH)

League Club	Source	Date Signed	Seasons Played	Apps	Subs	Gls
Newcastle U.	Wishaw Jnrs	04.35	34-38	132	-	2
Middlesbrough	Tr	11.45	46-53	231	-	3

GORDON, John D. S.
Portsmouth, 11 September, 1931 (IF)

League Club	Source	Date Signed	Seasons Played	Apps	Subs	Gls
Portsmouth	Jnrs	01.49	51-58	209	-	69
Birmingham C.	Tr	09.58	58-60	96	-	32
Portsmouth	Tr	03.61	60-66	234	0	36

GORDON, Peter J.
Northampton, 21 May, 1932 (OR)

League Club	Source	Date Signed	Seasons Played	Apps	Subs	Gls
Norwich C.	L	12.49	53-57	160	-	34
Watford	Tr	07.58	58-59	43	-	13
Exeter C.	Tr	07.60	60-61	67	-	11
Newport Co.	Tr	07.62	62	8	-	1

GORDON, Robert B.
Ormiston, 5 September, 1923 (IF)

League Club	Source	Date Signed	Seasons Played	Apps	Subs	Gls
Millwall	Armadale Jnrs	01.45	46-47	5	-	0

GORDON, William J. W.
Carlisle, 22 November, 1926 (CF)

League Club	Source	Date Signed	Seasons Played	Apps	Subs	Gls
Carlisle U.		08.48	48	15	-	4
Barrow	Tr	07.50	49-57	301	-	145
Workington	Tr	03.58	57-58	33	-	7

GORE, Ian G.
Prescot, 10 January, 1968 (CD)

League Club	Source	Date Signed	Seasons Played	Apps	Subs	Gls
Birmingham C.	YT	05.86				
Blackpool	Southport	01.88	88-91	134	3	0

GORE, Shaun M.
West Ham, 21 September, 1968 (D)

League Club	Source	Date Signed	Seasons Played	Apps	Subs	Gls
Fulham	YT	06.86	85-88	25	1	0
Halifax T.	L	02.91	90	15	0	0

GORE, Thomas J.
Liverpool, 26 November, 1953 (M)

League Club	Source	Date Signed	Seasons Played	Apps	Subs	Gls
Wigan Ath.	Tranmere Rov. (N/C)	(N/L)	78-80	102	0	14
Bury	Tr	10.80	80-82	118	1	15
Port Vale	Tr	07.83	83	33	3	2

GORIN, Edward R.
Cardiff, 2 February, 1924 (CF)

League Club	Source	Date Signed	Seasons Played	Apps	Subs	Gls
Cardiff C.	Grange A.	10.48	48-49	6	-	2
Scunthorpe U.	Tr	07.50	50	26	-	12
Shrewsbury T.	Tr	01.51	50-51	18	-	3

GORING, Harry (Peter)
Bishops Cleeve, 2 January 1927 (CF/WH)

League Club	Source	Date Signed	Seasons Played	Apps	Subs	Gls
Arsenal	Cheltenham T.	01.48	49-58	220	-	51

GORMAN, Andrew D.
Cardiff, 13 September, 1974 (D)

League Club	Source	Date Signed	Seasons Played	Apps	Subs	Gls
Cardiff C. (YT)	YT	07.91	91	7	4	0

GORMAN, John.
Winchburgh, 16 August, 1949 (LB)

League Club	Source	Date Signed	Seasons Played	Apps	Subs	Gls
Carlisle U.	Glasgow Celtic	09.70	70-76	228	1	5
Tottenham H.	Tr	11.76	76-78	30	0	0

GORMAN, Keith
Bishop Auckland, 13 October, 1966 (W)

League Club	Source	Date Signed	Seasons Played	Apps	Subs	Gls
Ipswich T.	App	01.84				
Colchester U.	L	09.86	86	0	1	0
Darlington	Tr	01.87	86	4	3	2

GORMAN, Paul A.
Dublin, 6 August, 1963 IRu21-1 (M/FB)

League Club	Source	Date Signed	Seasons Played	Apps	Subs	Gls
Arsenal	App	10.80	81-83	5	1	0
Birmingham C.	Tr	06.84	84	6	0	0
Carlisle U.	Tr	03.85	84-89	137	11	7
Shrewsbury T.	Tr	11.89	89-91	58	6	1
Carlisle U.	Tr	12.91	91	5	0	0

League Club	Source	Date Signed	Seasons Played	Apps	Subs	Gls
GORMAN, Paul M.						
Macclesfield, 18 September, 1968						(F)
Doncaster Rov.	YT	07.87	87-88	1	15	2
Charlton Ath.	Fisher Ath.	03.91	90-91	7	9	5
GORMAN, William C.						
Sligo (Ire), 13 July, 1911 Died 1978 IR-13/NI-4						(FB)
Bury	Sheltleston Jnrs	09.34	36-38	52	-	0
Brentford	Tr	12.38	38-49	125	-	1
GORMLEY, Edward J.						
Dublin, 23 October, 1968						(M)
Tottenham H.	Bray W.	11.87				
Chesterfield	L	11.88	88	4	0	0
Doncaster Rov.	Tr	07.90	90-91	69	8	10
GORMLEY, Philip						
Greenock, 13 October, 1924						(CF)
Aldershot	Glasgow Celtic	08.50	50-52	65	-	9
GORNALL, John P.						
Preston, 28 March, 1941						(CH)
Preston N. E.	Jnrs	07.60	61-62	4	-	0
GORRIE, David A.						
Liverpool, 21 January, 1943						(WH)
Everton	Jnrs	05.60				
Stockport Co.	Tr	07.62	62	18	-	0
GORRY, Martin C.						
Derby, 29 December, 1954						(FB)
Barnsley	Jnrs	05.73	75-76	34	0	3
Newcastle U.	Tr	10.76	77	0	1	0
Hartlepool U.	Tr	07.78	78-79	59	0	0
GORTON, Andrew W.						
Salford, 23 September, 1966						(G)
Oldham Ath.	YT	07.84	85-87	26	0	0
Stockport Co.	L	12.86	86	14	0	0
Tranmere Rov.	L	05.88	87	1	0	0
Stockport Co.	Tr	08.88	88	34	0	0
Lincoln C.	Tr	08.89	89	20	0	0
Oldham Ath.	Glossop	02.91				
Crewe Alex. (N/C)	Tr	03.91	90	3	0	0

League Club	Source	Date Signed	Seasons Played	Apps	Subs	Gls
GOSLIN, Richard W.						
Bovey Tracey, 31 October, 1956						(F)
Torquay U.	Nottingham F. (App)	04.74	73-75	14	5	2
GOSNEY, Andrew R.						
Southampton, 8 November, 1963 E Yth						(G)
Portsmouth	App	11.81	81-91	48	0	0
York C.	L	10.91	91	5	0	0
GOSS, Jeremy						
Cyprus, 11 May, 1965 E Yth/W-3						(M)
Norwich C.	Jnrs	03.83	83-91	68	20	4
GOTSMANOV, Sergei						
USSR, 17 March, 1959						(F)
Brighton & H.A. (N/C)	Dinamo Minsk (USSR)	02.90	89	14	2	4
Southampton	Dinamo Minsk (USSR)	08.90	90	2	6	0
GOTTS, James						
Seaton Delaval, 17 January, 1917						
Brentford	Ashington	01.46				
Brighton & H. A.	Tr	07.46	46	2	-	0
GOUCK, Andrew S.						
Blackpool, 8 June, 1972						(M)
Blackpool	YT	07.90	89-91	26	11	3
GOUGH, Anthony M.						
Bath, 18 March, 1940						(M)
Bristol Rov.	Bath C.	05.58	58	1	-	0
Swindon T.	Bath C.	07.70	70	24	1	2
Torquay U.	Hereford U.	07.72	72	2	0	0
GOUGH, Charles S.						
Glasgow, 21 May, 1939						(WH)
Charlton Ath.	Alton T.	06.63	64	4	-	0
GOUGH, Keith						
Willenhall, 4 February, 1953 E Sch						(W)
Walsall	App	02.71	69-71	11	4	0
Oxford U.	Tr	07.72	72-74	32	7	5

Jeremy Goss (Norwich City & Wales)

League Club	Source	Date Signed	Seasons Played	Career Record Apps	Subs	Gls
GOUGH, Michael W.						
Nottingham, 29 December, 1935						(HB)
Aldershot		05.56	56-58	20	-	1
GOUGH, Raymond						
Belfast, 8 February, 1938						(WH)
Exeter C.	Linfield	10.63				
Millwall	Tr	10.64	64	13	-	0
GOUGH, Richard C.						
Stockholm (Swed), 5 April, 1962 Su21-5/S-59						(CD)
Tottenham H.	Dundee U.	08.86	86-87	49	0	2
GOUGH, Robert G.						
Birmingham, 20 July, 1949						(F)
Walsall	App	07.67	66	1	0	0
Port Vale	Tr	07.68	68-73	189	21	33
Stockport Co.	L	02.73	73	6	0	0
Southport	Tr	07.74	74-75	61	0	16
Colchester U.	Tr	01.76	75-80	195	1	65
GOULD, J. Barry						
Ammanford, 18 January, 1944						(WH)
Arsenal	App	11.61				
Chelsea	Tr	02.64				
Peterborough U.	Tr	07.65	65	18	0	3
GOULD, Geoffrey						
Blackburn, 7 January, 1945						(OL)
Bradford P. A.	App	01.62	62-68	129	2	18
Lincoln C.	L	02.68	67	1	0	0
Notts Co.	Tr	07.69	69	1	0	0
GOULD, Harold						
Birkenhead, 5 January, 1925						(IF)
Tranmere Rov.		09.46	46-48	5	-	2
Southport	Northwich Vic.	09.50	50	16	-	2
Tranmere Rov.	Tr	07.51				
GOULD, Jonathan A.						
Paddington, 18 July, 1968						(G)
Halifax T.	Clevedon T.	07.90	90-91	32	0	0
West Bromwich A.	Tr	01.92				
GOULD, Robert A.						
Coventry, 12 June, 1946						(F)
Coventry C.	App	06.64	63-67	78	4	40
Arsenal	Tr	02.68	67-69	57	8	16
Wolverhampton W.	Tr	06.70	70-71	39	1	18
West Bromwich A.	Tr	09.71	71-72	52	0	18
Bristol C.	Tr	12.72	72-73	35	0	15
West Ham U.	Tr	11.73	73-75	46	5	15
Wolverhampton W.	Tr	12.75	75-76	24	10	13
Bristol Rov.	Tr	10.77	77-78	35	1	12
Hereford U.	Tr	09.78	78-79	42	3	13
GOULD, Trevor R.						
Coventry, 5 March, 1950 E Sch						(M)
Coventry C.	Jnrs	07.67	69	9	0	0
Northampton T.	Tr	10.70	70-72	102	3	6
GOULD, Walter						
Rotherham, 25 September, 1938						(OR)
Sheffield U.	Rawmarsh Welfare	02.58	58	5	-	1
York C.	Tr	02.61	60-63	120	-	25
Brighton & H. A.	Tr	01.64	63-67	166	2	44
GOULDEN, Albert E.						
Salford, 5 February, 1945						(FB)
Bolton W.	Jnrs	02.62	62	1	-	0
GOULDEN, Leonard A.						
West Ham, 16 July, 1912 E Sch/EF Lge/E-14						(IF)
West Ham U.	Jnrs	04.33	32-38	239	-	54
Chelsea	Tr	08.45	46-49	99	-	17
GOULDEN, Roy L.						
Ilford, 22 September, 1937 E Sch						(IF)
Arsenal	Jnrs	09.54	58	1	-	0
Southend U.	Tr	05.61	61	9	-	2
Ipswich T.	Tr	07.62				
GOULDING, Eric						
Winsford, 22 November, 1924						(RB)
Everton	Over A.	10.45				
Crewe Alex.	Tr	10.46	46	1	-	0
GOULDING, Stephen						
Mexborough, 21 January, 1954						(FB)
Sheffield U.	App	05.71	71-75	28	0	0
GOULET, Brent						
USA, 19 June, 1964						(F)
Bournemouth	Seattle (USA)	11.87	87	2	4	0
Crewe Alex.	L	01.88	87	2	1	3
GOUNDRY, William						
Middlesbrough, 28 March, 1934						(WH)
Brentford	Huddersfield T. (Am)	05.55	55-60	141	-	12
GOURLAY, Archibald M.						
Greenock, 29 June, 1969						(M)
Newcastle U.	Morton	03.88	88-90	2	1	0
GOVAN, Alexander						
Glasgow, 16 June, 1929						(OL)
Plymouth Arg.	Jnrs	09.46	46-52	110	-	27
Birmingham C.	Tr	06.53	53-57	165	-	53
Portsmouth	Tr	03.58	57-58	11	-	2
Plymouth Arg.	Tr	09.58	58-59	32	-	8
GOVAN, Charles P.						
Belfast, 12 January, 1943 NI Sch						(IF)
Burnley	Jnrs	01.60				
Mansfield T.	Tr	06.63	63-64	11	-	0
GOVIER, Stephen						
Watford, 6 April, 1952						(CD)
Norwich C.	App	07.69	70-73	22	0	1
Brighton & H. A.	Tr	04.74	74	12	0	1
Grimsby T.	Tr	12.74	74-76	23	1	0
GOW, Gerald						
Glasgow, 29 May, 1952 Su23-1						(M)
Bristol C.	Jnrs	06.69	69-80	367	7	48
Manchester U.	Tr	10.80	80-81	26	0	5
Rotherham U.	Tr	01.82	81-82	58	0	4
Burnley	Tr	08.83	83	8	1	0
GOWANS, Peter T.						
Dundee, 25 May, 1944						(W)
Crewe Alex.	Glasgow Celtic	07.63	63-66	141	0	43
Aldershot	Tr	07.67	67-69	111	2	27
Rochdale	Tr	07.70	70-73	136	8	21
Southport	Tr	07.74	74	3	1	0
GOWLING, Alan E.						
Stockport, 16 March, 1949 E Amat/Eu23-1						(F)
Manchester U.	Manchester Univ.	04.67	67-71	64	7	18
Huddersfield T.	Tr	06.72	72-74	128	0	58
Newcastle U.	Tr	08.75	75-77	91	1	30
Bolton W.	Tr	03.78	77-81	147	2	28
Preston N. E.	Tr	09.82	82	37	3	5
GOY, Peter J.						
Beverley, 8 June, 1938						(G)
Arsenal	Jnrs	06.55	58	2	-	0
Southend U.	Tr	10.60	60-63	118	-	0
Watford	Tr	07.64	64	27	-	0
Huddersfield T.	Tr	07.65	66	4	0	0
GRACE, Derek G.						
Chiswick, 29 December, 1944						(IF)
Exeter C.	Queens Park R. (App)	05.62	62-64	40	-	4
Gillingham	Tr	07.65	65	4	0	0
GRACE, John M.						
Dublin, 16 February, 1964						(G)
Colchester U.	Tolka Rov.	07.89	89	19	0	0
GRAFTON, Stanley T.						
Heathton, 2 April, 1923 Died 1953						(HB)
Aldershot		08.47	47-48	2	-	0
GRAHAM, Alan W.						
Ryhope, 23 October, 1937						(FB)
Sunderland	Silksworth Jnrs	05.55	57	3	-	0
GRAHAM, Arthur						
Glasgow, 26 October, 1952 Su23-3/S-10						(W)
Leeds U.	Aberdeen	07.77	77-82	222	1	37
Manchester U.	Tr	08.83	83	33	4	5
Bradford C.	Tr	06.85	85-86	28	3	2

League Club	Source	Date Signed	Seasons Played	Apps	Subs	Gls
GRAHAM, Deiniol W. T.						
Cannock, 4 October, 1969 W Yth/Wu21-1						(F)
Manchester U.	YT	10.87	87-89	1	1	0
Barnsley	Tr	08.91	91	8	13	1
GRAHAM, Donald						
Oldham, 2 April, 1953						(FB)
Bury	Hyde U.	10.79	79-80	3	4	0
GRAHAM, Douglas						
Morpeth, 15 July, 1921						(FB)
Newcastle U.	Barrington U.	08.40	46-50	71	-	0
Preston N. E.	Tr	11.50				
Lincoln C.	Tr	12.51	51-56	182	-	0
GRAHAM, George						
Coatbridge, 30 November, 1944 S Sch/Su23-2/S-12						(F/M)
Aston Villa	App	12.61	62-63	8	-	2
Chelsea	Tr	07.64	64-66	72	0	35
Arsenal	Tr	09.66	66-72	219	8	59
Manchester U.	Tr	12.72	72-74	41	2	2
Portsmouth	Tr	11.74	74-76	61	0	5
Crystal Palace	Tr	11.76	76-77	43	1	2
GRAHAM, Gerald W.						
Aspatria, 31 January, 1941						(WH)
Blackpool	Jnrs	08.59				
Peterborough U.	Tr	07.60	60-63	17	-	1
Mansfield T.	Tr	06.64	64	18	-	3
Workington	Hereford U.	07.68	68	6	0	0

Arthur Graham (Aberdeen, Leeds United, Manchester United, Bradford City & Scotland)

League Club	Source	Date Signed	Seasons Played	Apps	Subs	Gls
GRAHAM, James						
Glasgow, 5 November, 1969						(LB)
Bradford C.	YT	09.88	88-89	6	1	0
Rochdale	L	11.89	89	11	0	0
Rochdale	Tr	07.90	90-91	55	4	1
GRAHAM, John J. (Jackie)						
Glasgow, 16 July, 1946						(M)
Brentford	Guildford C.	07.70	70-79	371	3	38
GRAHAM, John R.						
Leyland, 26 April, 1926						(IF)
Aston Villa	Leyland Wks	11.46	46-48	10	-	3
Wrexham	Tr	06.49	49-51	45	-	7
Rochdale	Tr	02.53	52	10	-	1
Bradford C.	Tr	07.53	53	18	-	1
GRAHAM, W. G. Leonard						
Belfast, 17 October, 1925 NI-14						(FB)
Doncaster Rov.	Brantwood	10.49	50-58	303	-	3
Torquay U.	Tr	11.58	58	20	-	0
GRAHAM, Leslie						
Manchester, 14 May, 1924						(IF)
Blackburn Rov.	Flixton	04.47	47-52	150	-	42
Newport Co.	Tr	02.53	52-54	97	-	40
Watford	Tr	07.55	56-57	90	-	26
Newport Co.	Tr	09.57	57-58	65	-	15
GRAHAM, Malcolm						
Wakefield, 26 January, 1934						(IF)
Barnsley	Hall Green	04.53	54-58	109	-	35
Bristol C.	Tr	05.59	59	14	-	8
Leyton Orient	Tr	06.60	60-62	75	-	29
Queens Park R.	Tr	07.63	63	21	-	7
Barnsley	Tr	07.64	64	20	-	5
GRAHAM, Michael A.						
Lancaster, 24 February, 1959						(D)
Bolton W.	App	02.77	77-80	43	3	0
Swindon T.	Tr	07.81	81-84	141	0	1
Mansfield T.	Tr	07.85	85-88	132	1	1
Carlisle U.	Tr	09.88	88-91	137	1	3
GRAHAM, Milton M.						
Tottenham, 2 November, 1962						(M)
Bournemouth	Jnrs	05.81	81-84	54	19	12
Chester C.	Tr	08.85	85-88	123	6	10
Peterborough U.	Tr	07.89	89	10	5	2
GRAHAM, Peter						
Barnsley, 19 April, 1947						(M)
Barnsley	Worsboro' Bridge	01.67	66-69	16	3	0
Halifax T.	L	03.70	69	6	0	0
Darlington	Tr	06.70	70-73	118	1	43
Lincoln C.	Tr	09.73	73-77	142	16	47
Cambridge U.	Tr	06.78	78-79	35	3	0
GRAHAM, Ralph C.						
Durham, 29 December, 1929						(W)
Doncaster Rov.	Broadway Ath.	05.47	48-49	15	-	0
Southport	Tr	07.50	50-51	29	-	9
GRAHAM, Richard D.						
Corby, 6 May, 1922						(G)
Leicester C.	Northampton T. (Am)	11.44				
Crystal Palace	Tr	12.45	46-50	155	-	0
GRAHAM, Robert						
Motherwell, 22 November, 1944						(F)
Liverpool	App	11.61	64-71	96	5	31
Coventry C.	Tr	03.72	71-72	19	-	3
Tranmere Rov.	L	01.73	72	10	0	3
GRAHAM, Thomas						
Glasgow, 31 March, 1958						(M)
Aston Villa	Arthurlie	04.78				
Barnsley	Tr	12.78	78-79	36	2	13
Halifax T.	Tr	10.80	80-81	68	3	17
Doncaster Rov. (N/C)	Tr	08.82	82	9	2	2
Scunthorpe U.	Tr	03.83	82-85	102	7	21
Scarborough	Tr	08.86	87-89	104	7	11
Halifax T.	Tr	01.90	89-91	56	2	4
GRAHAM, William R.						
Carlisle, 8 May, 1929						(IF)
Workington		07.51				
Carlisle U.	Consett	01.54	53-60	35	-	2

League Club	Source	Date Signed	Seasons Played	Apps	Subs	Gls

GRAHAM, William V.
Armagh (NI), 14 February, 1959 (M)

Brentford	Northampton T. (App)	08.77	77-80	42	6	3

GRAINGER, Colin
Wakefield, 10 June, 1933 EF Lge/E-7 (OL)

Wrexham	South Elmsall	10.50	50-52	5	-	0
Sheffield U.	Tr	07.53	53-56	88	-	26
Sunderland	Tr	02.57	56-59	120	-	14
Leeds U.	Tr	07.60	60	33	-	5
Port Vale	Tr	10.61	61-63	39	-	6
Doncaster Rov.	Tr	08.64	64-65	40	0	4

GRAINGER, Dennis
Royston, 5 March, 1920 (W)

Southport	South Kirkby	10.38				
Leeds U.	Tr	10.45	46-47	37	-	5
Wrexham	Tr	12.47	47-50	98	-	11
Oldham Ath.	Tr	06.51	51	3	-	0

GRAINGER, John (Jack)
South Elmsall, 17 July, 1912 Died 1976 (FB)

Barnsley	Royston Colly	08.32	32	1	-	0
Southport	Tr	08.33	33-46	222	-	0

GRAINGER, John (Jack)
Havercroft, 3 April, 1924 Died 1983 E'B'-1 (OR)

Rotherham U.	Frickley Colly	11.45	47-56	352	-	110
Lincoln C.	Tr	06.57	57-58	42	-	14

GRAINGER, Martin R.
Enfield, 23 August, 1972 (LW)

Colchester U. (YT)	YT	07.90	89	4	3	2

GRANGER, Keith W.
Southampton, 5 October, 1968 (G)

Southampton	App	10.86	85	2	0	0
Darlington	Tr	12.87	87	23	0	0

GRANGER, Michael
Leeds, 7 October, 1931 (G)

York C.	Cliftonville	12.51	54-61	71	-	0
Hull C.	Tr	07.62	62	2	-	0
Halifax T.	Tr	07.53	63-64	2	-	0

GRANT, Alan J.
Havant, 6 January, 1935 (HB)

Brighton & H. A.	Gosport Bor.	04.56	56	1	-	0
Exeter C.	Tr	06.60	60	4	-	0

GRANT, Alick F.
Camerton, 11 August, 1916 (G)

Bury	Sheffield U. (Am)	08.37				
Aldershot	Tr	05.38	38	5	-	0
Leicester C.	Tr	12.41	46	2	-	0
Derby Co.	Tr	11.46	46-47	12	-	0
Newport Co.	Tr	11.48	48	20	-	0
Leeds U.	Tr	08.49				
York C.	Tr	03.50	49	3	-	0

GRANT, Bernard
Airdrie, 23 May, 1920 (IF)

Exeter C.	Third Lanark	07.47	48	2	-	0

GRANT, Brian P.
Coatbridge, 10 May, 1943 (FB)

Nottingham F.	Jnrs	05.60	60-64	18	-	0
Hartlepool U.	Tr	01.66	65-66	35	0	0
Cambridge U.	Bradford C. (trial)	(N/L)	70	14	0	0

GRANT, Cyril
Wath, 10 July, 1920 (CF)

Lincoln C.	Mexborough	06.39				
Arsenal	Tr	07.46	46	2	-	0
Fulham	Tr	12.46	46-47	14	-	4
Southend U.	Tr	03.48	47-54	174	-	62

GRANT, David
Sheffield, 2 June, 1960 (LB)

Sheffield Wed.	App	02.78	77-81	132	1	4
Oxford U.	Tr	07.82	82-83	24	0	1
Chesterfield	L	09.83	83	7	0	0
Cardiff C.	Tr	03.84	83-84	25	0	0
Rochdale	Tr	03.85	84-86	97	0	2

GRANT, David B.
Edinburgh, 31 July, 1943 (F)

Reading	Third Lanark	05.63	63-64	17	-	3

League Club	Source	Date Signed	Seasons Played	Apps	Subs	Gls

GRANT, David J.
Liverpool, 18 December, 1947 E Sch (WH)

Everton	App	12.65				
Wrexham	Tr	09.66	66	6	5	0

GRANT, Edward A.
Greenock, 1 October, 1928 (IF)

Sheffield U.	Weymouth	05.50	50	4	-	0
Grimsby T.	Tr	07.52	52-53	15	-	5

GRANT, James
Chapelhall, 10 June, 1940

Scunthorpe U.	Larkhall Th.	11.58	58	1	-	0

GRANT, James

Brighton & H.A. (Am)		12.46	46	1	-	0

GRANT, John A.
High Spen, 8 September, 1924 (WH)

Everton	High Spen Ath.	12.42	46-54	121	-	10
Rochdale	Tr	05.56	56-58	102	-	3
Southport	Tr	01.59	58-59	40	-	0

GRANT, Kenneth
High Spen, 13 November, 1938 (CF)

Gateshead (Am)	Crook T.	12.58	58	5	-	0

GRANT, Kimberley T.
Ghana, 25 September, 1972 (F)

Charlton Ath.	YT	03.91	90-91	11	5	2

GRANT, Peter J.
Glasgow, 11 April, 1968 (D)

Stockport Co.	Ipswich T. (App)	07.86	86	1	0	0

GRANT, Robert
Edinburgh, 25 September, 1940 (CF)

Carlisle U.	St Johnstone	07.62	62	2	-	1

GRANT, Wilfred
Ashington, 3 August, 1920 Died 1990 E'B'-1 (CF)

Manchester C.		02.43				
Southampton	Tr	10.46	46-49	61	-	11
Cardiff C.	Tr	03.50	49-54	155	-	65
Ipswich T.	Tr	10.54	54-56	75	-	22

GRANT, William
Perth, 7 October, 1933 (HB)

Gillingham	Brechin C.	08.56	56	1	-	0

GRANVILLE, John H.
Tobago, 6 May, 1956 Trinidad Int (G)

Millwall (N/C)	Slough T.	10.85	85	6	0	0

GRANVILLE, Ralph
Glasgow, 23 April, 1931

Gateshead	Clyde	10.57	57	2	-	0

GRANVILLE, N. Trevor
Newport, 25 November, 1919 (OR)

Newport Co.	Cliftonville	01.46	46	1	-	0
Exeter C.	Tr	10.46	46-47	20	-	1

GRANYCOMBE, Neil
Middlesbrough, 23 October, 1958 (F)

Hartlepool U. (N/C)	South Bank	02.81	80	1	0	0

GRAPES, Stephen P.
Norwich, 25 February, 1953 (M)

Norwich C.	App	07.70	70-76	34	7	3
Bournemouth	L	03.76	75	7	0	1
Cardiff C.	Tr	10.76	76-81	138	9	6
Torquay U.	Tr	08.82	82	31	0	0

GRATRIX, Roy
Salford, 9 February, 1932 E'B'-1/EF Lge (CH)

Blackpool	Taylor Bros	03.53	53-64	400	-	0
Manchester C.	Tr	09.64	64	15	-	0

GRATTAN, James
Belfast, 30 November, 1958 (F)

Sunderland	App	10.76				
Mansfield T.	L	11.78	78	1	0	0

League Club	Source	Date Signed	Seasons Played	Career Record Apps	Subs	Gls
GRATTON, Dennis						
Rotherham, 21 April, 1934						(CH)
Sheffield U.	Worksop T.	10.52	55-58	6	-	0
Lincoln C.	Tr	09.59	59-60	45	-	0
GRAVER, Andrew M.						
Craghead (Dm), 12 September, 1927						(CF)
Newcastle U.	Annfield Plain	09.47	49	1	-	0
Lincoln C.	Tr	09.50	50-54	172	-	107
Leicester C.	Tr	12.54	54	11	-	3
Lincoln C.	Tr	07.55	55	15	-	4
Stoke C.	Tr	11.55	55-56	37	-	12
Lincoln C.	Boston U.	10.58	58-60	89	-	33
GRAVES, Mark T.						
Isleworth, 14 December, 1960						(F)
Plymouth Arg.	App	09.78	77-80	24	9	3
GRAVES, Robert E.						
Marylebone, 7 November, 1942						(G)
Lincoln C.	Kirton	04.60	59-64	77	-	0
GRAVETTE, Warren						
Thetford, 13 September, 1968						(M)
Tottenham H.	App	08.86				
Brentford	Tr	07.87	87	1	4	0
GRAY, Alexander D.						
Arbroath, 7 November, 1936						(FB)
Burnley	Dundee Violet	06.54				
Cardiff C.	Arbroath	03.57	58	1	-	0
GRAY, Andrew						
Southampton, 25 October, 1973						(W)
Reading (YT)	YT	09.90	91	0	1	0
GRAY, Andrew A.						
Lambeth, 22 February, 1964 Eu21-2/E-1						(M)
Crystal Palace	Dulwich Hamlet	11.84	84-87	91	7	27
Aston Villa	Tr	11.87	87-88	34	3	4
Queens Park R.	Tr	02.89	88	11	0	2
Crystal Palace	Tr	08.89	89-91	87	3	12
Tottenham H.	Tr	02.92	91	14	0	1
GRAY, Andrew M.						
Glasgow, 30 November, 1955 Su23-4/S-20						(F)
Aston Villa	Dundee U.	10.75	75-78	112	1	54
Wolverhampton W.	Tr	09.79	79-83	130	3	38
Everton	Tr	11.83	83-84	44	5	14
Aston Villa	Tr	07.85	85-86	53	1	5
Notts Co.	L	08.87	87	3	1	0
West Bromwich A.	Tr	09.87	87-88	32	3	10
GRAY, David						
Dundee, 8 February, 1922						(FB)
Preston N.E.	Glasgow Rangers	05.47	47	36	-	0
Blackburn Rov.	Tr	08.48	48-52	107	-	5
GRAY, David D.						
Clydebank, 13 April, 1923						(WH)
Bradford C.	Queensbury	09.48	48-55	242	-	13
GRAY, Edward						
Glasgow, 17 January, 1948 S Sch/Su23-2/S-12						(W)
Leeds U.	Jnrs	01.65	65-83	442	13	52
GRAY, Edward						
Bellshill, 19 October, 1934 S Sch						(IF)
Barrow	Yeovil T.	12.57	57-58	17	-	4
Accrington St.	Tr	07.59	59	6	-	0
GRAY, Frank T.						
Glasgow, 27 October, 1954 S Sch/Su23-2/S-32						(LB)
Leeds U.	App	11.71	72-78	188	5	17
Nottingham F.	Tr	08.79	79-80	81	0	5
Leeds U.	Tr	05.81	81-84	139	0	10
Sunderland	Tr	07.85	85-88	118	28	8
Darlington	Tr	07.89	90-91	49	0	7
GRAY, Gareth						
Longridge, 24 February, 1970						(G)
Bolton W.	Darwen	02.88				
Rochdale	Tr	07.90	91	6	0	0
GRAY, George						
Glasgow, 6 October, 1929						(F)
Scunthorpe U.	Sligo Rov.	08.51	51	9	-	3

League Club	Source	Date Signed	Seasons Played	Career Record Apps	Subs	Gls
GRAY, George						
						(OR)
Carlisle U.	Vale of Clyde	11.47	47	1	-	1
GRAY, George J. P.						
Sunderland, 7 July, 1925						(WH)
Grimsby T.	Derby Co. (Am)	01.47	50	3	-	0
Swindon T.	Tr	07.51	51-52	45	-	0
Darlington	Tr	07.53	53	6	-	0
GRAY, George W.						
Canning Town, 30 November, 1922						
Aldershot	West Ham U. (Am)	02.47	46-47	9	-	0
GRAY, Harold						
Hemsworth, 26 October, 1918						(IF)
Barnsley	Ardsley Rec.	02.38	46	9	-	1
Bournemouth	Tr	12.46	46-47	30	-	7
Southend U.	Tr	06.48	48-49	19	-	0
GRAY, Irvine W.						
Hoyland, 27 February, 1933						(W)
Barnsley		09.52				
Gillingham	Tr	08.56	56	9	-	0
GRAY, Kevin J.						
Sheffield, 7 January, 1972						(CD)
Mansfield T.	YT	07.90	88-91	56	10	1

Andy Gray (Dundee United, Aston Villa, Wolverhampton Wanderers, Everton, Aston Villa, West Bromwich Albion & Scotland)

League Club	Source	Date Signed	Seasons Played	Career Record Apps	Subs	Gls

GRAY, Mark S.
Pembroke, 24 November, 1959 (F)

League Club	Source	Date Signed	Seasons Played	Apps	Subs	Gls
Swansea C.	App	09.77	77	1	1	0
Fulham	Tr	01.78				
Leyton Orient	Tr	02.79	78	1	1	0

GRAY, Martin D.
Stockton, 17 August, 1971 (M)

League Club	Source	Date Signed	Seasons Played	Apps	Subs	Gls
Sunderland	YT	02.90	91	0	1	0
Aldershot	L	01.91	90	3	2	0

GRAY, Matthew
Renfrew, 11 July, 1936 (IF)

League Club	Source	Date Signed	Seasons Played	Apps	Subs	Gls
Manchester C.	Third Lanark	03.63	62-66	87	4	21

GRAY, Michael
(IF)

League Club	Source	Date Signed	Seasons Played	Apps	Subs	Gls
Aldershot	Glenavon	09.46	46	7	-	1
Watford	Tr	06.47	47	10	-	3

GRAY, Nigel R.
Fulham, 2 November, 1956 (CD)

League Club	Source	Date Signed	Seasons Played	Apps	Subs	Gls
Leyton Orient	App	07.74	74-82	233	0	3
Charlton Ath.	L	12.82	82	3	0	0
Swindon T.	Tr	07.83	83-84	33	0	1
Brentford	L	03.84	83	16	0	1
Aldershot	L	09.84	84	4	0	0

GRAY, R. Paul
Portsmouth, 28 January, 1970 (F)

League Club	Source	Date Signed	Seasons Played	Apps	Subs	Gls
Luton T.	YT	06.88	89	2	5	1
Wigan Ath.	Tr	05.91	91	2	3	0

GRAY, Philip
Belfast, 2 October, 1968 NI Sch/NI Yth/NIu23-1 (F)

League Club	Source	Date Signed	Seasons Played	Apps	Subs	Gls
Tottenham H.	App	08.86	86-90	4	5	0
Barnsley	L	01.90	89	3	0	0
Fulham	L	11.90	90	3	0	0
Luton T.	Tr	08.91	91	9	5	3

GRAY, Robert
Cambuslang, 18 June, 1927

League Club	Source	Date Signed	Seasons Played	Apps	Subs	Gls
Lincoln C.	Wishaw Jnrs	10.49	49	2	-	0

GRAY, Robert
Glasgow, 8 June, 1953 S Sch (M)

League Club	Source	Date Signed	Seasons Played	Apps	Subs	Gls
Workington	Nottingham F. (App)	08.72	72	0	1	0

GRAY, Robert
Newcastle, 14 December, 1923 (G)

League Club	Source	Date Signed	Seasons Played	Apps	Subs	Gls
Gateshead	Newcastle U. (Am)	03.44	47-58	432	-	0

GRAY, Robert H. W.
Aberdeen, 21 January, 1951 (G)

League Club	Source	Date Signed	Seasons Played	Apps	Subs	Gls
Torquay U. (Am)	Inverurie Loco.	11.69	69	2	0	0

GRAY, Roland (Ron)
North Shields, 25 June, 1920 (WH)

League Club	Source	Date Signed	Seasons Played	Apps	Subs	Gls
Sheffield U.		05.38				
Watford		08.45	46	16	-	0

GRAY, Stewart A.
Doncaster, 16 October, 1950 (D)

League Club	Source	Date Signed	Seasons Played	Apps	Subs	Gls
Doncaster Rov.	App	09.68	67-70	53	5	0
Grimsby T.	Tr	09.70	70-76	263	1	2
Doncaster Rov. (N/C)	Frickley Ath.	03.78	77	6	0	0

GRAY, Stuart
Withernsea, 19 April, 1960 (M/LB)

League Club	Source	Date Signed	Seasons Played	Apps	Subs	Gls
Nottingham F.	Withernsea Y.C.	03.78	80-82	48	1	3
Bolton W.	L	03.83	82	10	0	0
Barnsley	Tr	08.83	83-87	117	3	23
Aston Villa	Tr	11.87	87-90	102	4	9
Southampton	Tr	09.91	91	10	2	0

GRAY, Terence I.
Bradford, 3 June, 1954 E Yth (W)

League Club	Source	Date Signed	Seasons Played	Apps	Subs	Gls
Huddersfield T.	Ashley Road	08.72	73-78	146	17	36
Southend U.	Tr	07.79	79-81	106	4	28
Bradford C.	Tr	08.82	82-84	72	4	15
Preston N. E.	Tr	10.84	84-85	40	0	1

GRAY, William M.
Coventry, 3 December, 1931 (WH)

League Club	Source	Date Signed	Seasons Played	Apps	Subs	Gls
Coventry C.	Jnrs	12.48	51	2	-	0

GRAY, William P.
Ashington, 24 May, 1927 E'B'-1 (W)

League Club	Source	Date Signed	Seasons Played	Apps	Subs	Gls
Leyton Orient	Dinnington Colly	05.47	47-48	19	-	1
Chelsea	Tr	03.49	48-52	146	-	12
Burnley	Tr	08.53	53-56	120	-	30
Nottingham F.	Tr	06.57	57-62	201	-	29
Millwall	Tr	12.63	63-64	20	-	1

GRAYDON, Raymond J.
Bristol, 21 July, 1947 EYth (W)

League Club	Source	Date Signed	Seasons Played	Apps	Subs	Gls
Bristol Rov.	App	09.65	65-70	131	2	33
Aston Villa	Tr	06.71	71-76	188	4	68
Coventry C.	Tr	07.77	77	17	3	5
Oxford U.	Washington (USA)	11.78	78-80	36	6	10

GRAYSON, Barry J.
Manchester, 12 October, 1944 (F)

League Club	Source	Date Signed	Seasons Played	Apps	Subs	Gls
Manchester U.	App	11.61				
Bury	Tr	01.65	64	1	-	0

GRAYSON, Neil
York, 1 November, 1964 (W)

League Club	Source	Date Signed	Seasons Played	Apps	Subs	Gls
Doncaster Rov. (N/C)	Rowntree Mackintosh	03.90	89-90	21	8	6
York C.	Tr	03.91	90	0	1	0
Chesterfield	Tr	06.91	91	9	6	0

GRAYSON, Simon D.
Sheffield, 21 October, 1968 (F)

League Club	Source	Date Signed	Seasons Played	Apps	Subs	Gls
Sheffield U.	App	10.86				
Chesterfield	L	11.87	87	7	1	0
Hartlepool U.	Tr	04.88	87-89	39	5	12

GRAYSON, Simon N.
Ripon, 16 December, 1969 (M)

League Club	Source	Date Signed	Seasons Played	Apps	Subs	Gls
Leeds U.	YT	06.88	87	2	0	0
Leicester C.	Tr	03.92	91	13	0	0

GREALISH, Anthony P.
Paddington, 21 September, 1956 IR Yth/IR-44 (M)

League Club	Source	Date Signed	Seasons Played	Apps	Subs	Gls
Leyton Orient	App	07.74	74-78	169	2	10
Luton T.	Tr	08.79	79-80	78	0	2
Brighton & H. A.	Tr	07.81	81-83	95	5	6
West Bromwich A.	Tr	03.84	83-85	55	10	5
Manchester C.	Tr	10.86	86	11	0	0
Rotherham U.	Tr	08.87	87-89	105	5	7
Walsall	Tr	08.90	90-91	32	4	1

GREATREX, Edward
Nuneaton, 18 November, 1936 (G)

League Club	Source	Date Signed	Seasons Played	Apps	Subs	Gls
Norwich C.	Jnrs	06.54	57	1	-	0

GREAVES, Daniel T.
Upminster, 31 October, 1963 (F)

League Club	Source	Date Signed	Seasons Played	Apps	Subs	Gls
Southend U.	Tottenham H. (Jnr)	01.81	81-83	30	19	14
Cambridge U. (N/C)	Dagenham	09.84	84	2	2	1

GREAVES, Ian D.
Oldham, 26 May, 1932 (FB)

League Club	Source	Date Signed	Seasons Played	Apps	Subs	Gls
Manchester U.	Buxton	05.53	54-59	67	-	0
Lincoln C.	Tr	12.60	60	11	-	0
Oldham Ath.	Tr	05.61	61-62	22	-	0

GREAVES, James P.
East Ham, 20 February, 1940 E Yth/Eu23-12/EF Lge/E-57 (IF)

League Club	Source	Date Signed	Seasons Played	Apps	Subs	Gls
Chelsea	Jnrs	05.57	57-60	157	-	124
Tottenham H.	AC Milan (It)	12.61	61-69	321	0	220
West Ham U.	Tr	03.70	69-70	36	2	13

GREAVES, Philip G.
Chesterfield, 5 September, 1961 (W)

League Club	Source	Date Signed	Seasons Played	Apps	Subs	Gls
Chesterfield (N/C)	Alfreton T.	10.86	86	5	0	0

GREAVES, Roy
Farnworth, 4 April, 1947 (M)

League Club	Source	Date Signed	Seasons Played	Apps	Subs	Gls
Bolton W.	Jnrs	01.65	65-79	487	8	66
Rochdale	Seattle (USA)	11.82	82	19	2	0

GREAVES, Steven R.
Chelsea, 17 January, 1970 (D)

League Club	Source	Date Signed	Seasons Played	Apps	Subs	Gls
Fulham	YT	07.88	87	0	1	0
Preston N. E.	Tr	08.90	90	2	0	0
Ipswich T.	Tr	01.91				

GREEN, Adrian
Leicester, 22 October, 1957 (M)

League Club	Source	Date Signed	Seasons Played	Apps	Subs	Gls
Leicester C.	App	06.76				
Rochdale	L	12.77	77	7	0	0
Aldershot	Tr	07.78	78-79	7	14	0

League Club	Source	Date Signed	Seasons Played	Career Record Apps	Subs	Gls

GREEN, Alan
Darfield, 14 December, 1939 (FB)

League Club	Source	Date Signed	Seasons Played	Apps	Subs	Gls
Barnsley	Dodworth Colly	01.59	60-61	19	-	0
York C.	Tr	07.62				

GREEN, Alan P.
Worcester, 1 January, 1954 E Yth (F)

League Club	Source	Date Signed	Seasons Played	Apps	Subs	Gls
Coventry C.	App	01.71	71-78	98	19	30

GREEN, Alan P. C.
Fordingbridge, 19 April, 1951 (F)

League Club	Source	Date Signed	Seasons Played	Apps	Subs	Gls
Bournemouth	Jnrs	07.69				
Mansfield T.	Tr	07.72	72	1	0	0

GREEN, Anthony
Glasgow, 3 October, 1946 S-6 (M)

League Club	Source	Date Signed	Seasons Played	Apps	Subs	Gls
Blackpool	Albion Rov.	05.67	66-71	123	0	13
Newcastle U.	Tr	10.71	71-72	33	0	3

GREEN, Arthur
Liverpool, 28 April, 1928 (FB)

League Club	Source	Date Signed	Seasons Played	Apps	Subs	Gls
Huddersfield T.	Burscough	02.51	51	3	-	0

GREEN, Brian G.
Droylsden, 5 June, 1935 (CF)

League Club	Source	Date Signed	Seasons Played	Apps	Subs	Gls
Rochdale	Haggate Lads	08.55	54-58	46	-	8
Southport	Tr	03.59	58-59	20	-	7
Barrow	Colwyn Bay	09.60	60	3	-	0
Exeter C.	Altrincham	08.62	62	9	-	1
Chesterfield	Tr	02.63	62	2	-	0

GREEN, Clive P.
Portsmouth, 6 December, 1959 (F)

League Club	Source	Date Signed	Seasons Played	Apps	Subs	Gls
Portsmouth	Jnrs	07.76	76-77	34	6	4

GREEN, Colin R.
Wrexham, 10 February, 1942 Wu23-7/W-15 (FB)

League Club	Source	Date Signed	Seasons Played	Apps	Subs	Gls
Everton	Jnrs	02.59	60-61	15	-	1
Birmingham C.	Tr	12.62	62-70	183	0	1
Wrexham	L	01.71	70	3	0	0

GREEN, Donald
Needham Market, 30 November, 1924 (CH)

League Club	Source	Date Signed	Seasons Played	Apps	Subs	Gls
Ipswich T.	Bramford	03.47	46-51	52	-	0

GREEN, Donald
Blackburn, 13 May, 1932 (LB)

League Club	Source	Date Signed	Seasons Played	Apps	Subs	Gls
Accrington St. (Am)	Blackburn Rov. (Am)	05.52	52	12	-	0

Jimmy Greaves (Chelsea, AC Milan, Tottenham Hotspur, West Ham United & England)

GREEN, Frederick Z.
Sheffield, 9 September, 1916 (FB)

League Club	Source	Date Signed	Seasons Played	Apps	Subs	Gls
Torquay U.	Mosborough Trin.	06.35	35-37	86	-	0
Brighton & H.A.	Tr	06.38	38-47	26	-	0

GREEN, George F.
Northowram, 22 December, 1914 (WH)

League Club	Source	Date Signed	Seasons Played	Apps	Subs	Gls
Bradford P. A.		05.36	36	2	-	0
Huddersfield T.	Tr	10.44	46-47	9	-	1
Reading	Tr	10.47	47-48	44	-	6

GREEN, Horace
Barnsley, 23 April, 1918 (FB)

League Club	Source	Date Signed	Seasons Played	Apps	Subs	Gls
Halifax T.	Worsboro' Bridge	11.36	37-48	156	-	6
Lincoln C.	Tr	02.49	48-54	193	-	14

GREEN, Ivan D.
Bexhill, 29 July, 1933 (IF)

League Club	Source	Date Signed	Seasons Played	Apps	Subs	Gls
Millwall		09.53	54	1	-	0

GREEN, John
Warrington, 22 May, 1939 (WH)

League Club	Source	Date Signed	Seasons Played	Apps	Subs	Gls
Tranmere Rov.	Stockton Heath	02.58	58	17	-	5
Blackpool	Tr	03.59	59-66	135	0	9
Port Vale	Tr	09.67	67-70	92	2	7

GREEN, John R.
Rotherham, 7 August, 1958 (CD)

League Club	Source	Date Signed	Seasons Played	Apps	Subs	Gls
Rotherham U.	App	03.76	75-83	247	1	8
Scunthorpe U.	Tr	09.83	83-85	100	0	4
Darlington	Tr	10.85	85-86	45	0	2
Rotherham U.	Tr	12.86	86-88	84	1	3

GREEN, Kenneth
West Ham, 27 April, 1924 E'B'-2/EF Lge (FB)

League Club	Source	Date Signed	Seasons Played	Apps	Subs	Gls
Birmingham C.	Millwall (Am)	11.43	47-58	401	-	3

GREEN, Kenneth
Hull, 20 November, 1929 (CF)

League Club	Source	Date Signed	Seasons Played	Apps	Subs	Gls
Grimsby T.	Selby T.	04.51	51	1	-	0

GREEN, Leonard H.
Darlington, 2 October, 1936 (FB)

League Club	Source	Date Signed	Seasons Played	Apps	Subs	Gls
Darlington		10.55	55-60	48	-	0

GREEN, Leslie
Atherstone, 17 October, 1941 (G)

League Club	Source	Date Signed	Seasons Played	Apps	Subs	Gls
Hull C.	Atherstone T.	08.60	61	4	-	0
Hartlepool U.	Burton A.	07.65	65-66	34	0	0
Rochdale	Tr	04.67	67	44	0	0
Derby Co.	Tr	05.68	68-70	107	0	0

GREEN, Melvyn
Hull, 20 October, 1951 (CD)

League Club	Source	Date Signed	Seasons Played	Apps	Subs	Gls
Hull C.	App	10.69	71-72	10	0	0
Cambridge U.	Tr	07.74	74	3	0	0

GREEN, Michael C.
Carlisle, 8 September, 1946 (CD)

League Club	Source	Date Signed	Seasons Played	Apps	Subs	Gls
Carlisle U.	App	09.64	65	2	0	0
Gillingham	Tr	07.68	68-70	131	1	24
Bristol Rov.	Tr	07.71	71-73	74	3	2
Plymouth Arg.	Tr	07.74	74-76	108	0	8
Torquay U.	Tr	03.77	76-78	88	0	7

GREEN, Michael J.
Southend, 20 November, 1957 (D)

League Club	Source	Date Signed	Seasons Played	Apps	Subs	Gls
Exeter C.	App	11.75	76	0	1	0

GREEN, Philip
Cardiff, 30 October, 1957 (F)

League Club	Source	Date Signed	Seasons Played	Apps	Subs	Gls
Newport Co. (N/C)	Barry T.	03.84	83-84	11	5	2

GREEN, Richard (Rick)
Scunthorpe, 23 November, 1952 (F)

League Club	Source	Date Signed	Seasons Played	Apps	Subs	Gls
Scunthorpe U.	Appleby Frodingham	09.75	75-76	66	0	19
Chesterfield	Tr	02.77	76-77	45	3	13
Notts Co.	Tr	06.78	78	6	3	0
Scunthorpe U.	Tr	08.79	79-81	66	5	19

GREEN, Richard E.
Wolverhampton, 22 November, 1967 (D)

League Club	Source	Date Signed	Seasons Played	Apps	Subs	Gls
Shrewsbury T.	YT	07.86	86-89	120	5	5
Swindon T.	Tr	10.90				
Gillingham	Tr	03.92	91	12	0	4

GREEN, H. Rodney
Halifax, 24 June, 1939 (CF)

League Club	Source	Date Signed	Seasons Played	Apps	Subs	Gls
Halifax T.		08.60	60-61	9	-	2
Bradford P. A.	Tr	06.62	62	19	-	6
Bradford C.	Tr	01.63	62-63	66	-	39
Gillingham	Tr	07.64	64	33	-	17
Grimsby T.	Tr	08.65	65-66	65	0	20
Charlton Ath.	Tr	02.67	66	3	1	1
Luton T.	Tr	08.67	67	9	2	3
Watford	Tr	08.68	68-69	19	11	8

GREEN, Roger
Cardiff, 20 September, 1944 (D)

League Club	Source	Date Signed	Seasons Played	Apps	Subs	Gls
Newport Co.	Barry T.	01.72	71	1	0	0

GREEN, Ronald R.
Birmingham, 3 October, 1956 (G)

League Club	Source	Date Signed	Seasons Played	Apps	Subs	Gls
Walsall	Alvechurch	06.77	77-83	163	0	0
Shrewsbury T.	Tr	06.84	84	19	0	0
Bristol Rov.	Tr	02.85	84-85	56	0	0
Scunthorpe U.	Tr	08.86	86-87	78	0	0
Wimbledon	Tr	08.88	88	4	0	0
Shrewsbury T.	L	09.88	88	17	0	0
Walsall	Tr	03.89	88-90	67	0	0

GREEN, Roy
Loughborough, 8 June, 1931 (IF)

League Club	Source	Date Signed	Seasons Played	Apps	Subs	Gls
Reading	Bloxwich Strollers	12.52	55-56	14	-	3

GREEN, N. Russell
Donnington, 13 August, 1933 (WH)

League Club	Source	Date Signed	Seasons Played	Apps	Subs	Gls
Lincoln C.	Quadring	08.51	51-63	145	-	8

GREEN, Scott P.
Walsall, 15 January, 1970 (W)

League Club	Source	Date Signed	Seasons Played	Apps	Subs	Gls
Derby Co.	YT	07.88				
Bolton W.	Tr	03.90	89-91	63	20	10

GREEN, Stanley
West Bromwich, 6 September, 1928 (CH)

League Club	Source	Date Signed	Seasons Played	Apps	Subs	Gls
Bristol Rov.	Accles & Pollock	08.52	51	1	-	0

GREEN, Thomas
Birkenhead, 18 September, 1926 Died 1952 (RH)

League Club	Source	Date Signed	Seasons Played	Apps	Subs	Gls
Southport	West Lancs A.T.C.	05.46	46	4	-	0

GREEN, William
Newcastle, 22 December, 1950 (CD)

League Club	Source	Date Signed	Seasons Played	Apps	Subs	Gls
Hartlepool U.	Jnrs	06.69	69-72	128	3	9
Carlisle U.	Tr	07.73	73-75	119	0	4
West Ham U.	Tr	06.76	76-77	35	0	1
Peterborough U.	Tr	07.78	78	30	0	0
Chesterfield	Tr	06.79	79-82	160	0	5
Doncaster Rov.	Tr	06.83	83	10	1	1

GREEN, William C.
Hull, 9 October, 1927 (WH)

League Club	Source	Date Signed	Seasons Played	Apps	Subs	Gls
Wolverhampton W.	Jnrs	09.45				
Walsall	Tr	09.49	49-53	182	-	8
Wrexham	Tr	06.54	54-55	60	-	2

GREENALL, Colin A.
Billinge, 30 December, 1963 E Yth (CD)

League Club	Source	Date Signed	Seasons Played	Apps	Subs	Gls
Blackpool	App	01.81	80-86	179	4	9
Gillingham	Tr	09.86	86-87	62	0	5
Oxford U.	Tr	02.88	87-89	67	0	2
Bury	L	01.90	89	3	0	0
Bury	Tr	07.90	90-91	66	2	5
Preston N.E.	Tr	03.92	91	9	0	1

GREENALL, George E.
Liverpool, 5 November, 1937 (CH)

League Club	Source	Date Signed	Seasons Played	Apps	Subs	Gls
Manchester C.	Jnrs	11.58				
Oldham Ath.	Tr	09.60	60	25	-	0

GREENAWAY, Arthur R.
Swindon, 5 April, 1928 (IF)

League Club	Source	Date Signed	Seasons Played	Apps	Subs	Gls
Plymouth Arg.		08.47				
Exeter C.	Tr	05.50	50	1	-	0
Swansea C.	Tr	10.51				

GREENAWAY, Brian J.
Hammersmith, 26 September, 1957 (W)

League Club	Source	Date Signed	Seasons Played	Apps	Subs	Gls
Fulham	App	06.75	76-80	68	17	8

GREENER, Ronald
Easington, 31 January, 1934 (CH)

League Club	Source	Date Signed	Seasons Played	Apps	Subs	Gls
Newcastle U.	Easington Colly	05.51	53	3	-	0
Darlington	Tr	08.55	55-66	442	-	5

GREENHALGH, Brian A.
Chesterfield, 20 February, 1947 (F)

League Club	Source	Date Signed	Seasons Played	Apps	Subs	Gls
Preston N. E.	App	02.65	65-67	19	0	9
Aston Villa	Tr	09.67	67-68	37	3	12
Leicester C.	Tr	02.69	68	2	2	0
Huddersfield T.	Tr	06.69	69-70	15	0	0
Cambridge U.	Tr	07.71	71-73	116	0	47
Bournemouth	Tr	02.74	73-74	23	1	7
Torquay U.	L	06.74	74	9	0	1
Watford	Tr	03.75	74-75	17	1	1

GREENHALGH, James R.
Manchester, 25 August, 1923 (WH)

League Club	Source	Date Signed	Seasons Played	Apps	Subs	Gls
Hull C.	Newton Heath	08.46	46-50	148	-	5
Bury	Tr	12.50	50-54	122	-	1
Gillingham	Wigan Ath.	07.56	56	16	-	0

GREENHALGH, Norman H.
Bolton, 10 August, 1914 EF Lge (LB)

League Club	Source	Date Signed	Seasons Played	Apps	Subs	Gls
Bolton W.		09.33				
New Brighton	Tr	10.35	35-37	77	-	8
Everton	Tr	01.38	37-48	106	-	1

GREENHOFF, Brian
Barnsley, 28 April, 1953 Eu23-4/E'B'/E-18 (CD)

League Club	Source	Date Signed	Seasons Played	Apps	Subs	Gls
Manchester U.	App	06.70	73-78	218	3	13
Leeds U.	Tr	08.79	79-81	68	4	1
Rochdale	Hong Kong	03.83	82-83	15	1	0

GREENHOFF, Frank
Barnsley, 3 March, 1924 (OL)

League Club	Source	Date Signed	Seasons Played	Apps	Subs	Gls
Barnsley	Manchester C. (Am)	09.47				
Bradford C.	Tr	10.48	48-51	81	-	11

GREENHOFF, James
Barnsley, 19 June, 1946 Eu23-5/EF Lge (F)

League Club	Source	Date Signed	Seasons Played	Apps	Subs	Gls
Leeds U.	App	08.63	62-68	88	6	21
Birmingham C.	Tr	08.68	68	31	0	14
Stoke C.	Tr	08.69	69-76	274	0	76
Manchester U.	Tr	11.76	76-80	94	3	26
Crewe Alex.	Tr	12.80	80	11	0	4
Port Vale	Toronto (Can)	08.81	81-82	44	4	5
Rochdale	Tr	03.83	82-83	16	0	0

GREENMAN, Christopher
Bristol, 22 December, 1968 E Sch (CD)

League Club	Source	Date Signed	Seasons Played	Apps	Subs	Gls
Coventry C.	Jnrs	07.88	91	4	0	0

GREENOUGH, Richard A. (Ricky)
Mexborough, 30 May, 1961 (D)

League Club	Source	Date Signed	Seasons Played	Apps	Subs	Gls
Chester C.	Alfreton T.	01.85	84-87	123	9	15
Scarborough	Tr	07.88				
York C.	Tr	11.88	88-89	28	1	1

GREENSMITH, Ronald
Sheffield, 22 January, 1933 (OL)

League Club	Source	Date Signed	Seasons Played	Apps	Subs	Gls
Sheffield Wed.	Shiregreen W.M.C.	01.54	54-57	5	-	0
York C.	Tr	01.58	57-59	42	-	1

GREENWAY, Mark
Halifax, 10 April, 1966 (LB)

League Club	Source	Date Signed	Seasons Played	Apps	Subs	Gls
Halifax T.	App	04.84	83-84	15	1	1

GREENWELL, Donald
Chester-le-Street, 4 January, 1924 (HB)

League Club	Source	Date Signed	Seasons Played	Apps	Subs	Gls
York C.		12.46	46	1	-	0

GREENWOOD, Alexander J.
Fulham, 17 June, 1933 (FB)

League Club	Source	Date Signed	Seasons Played	Apps	Subs	Gls
Chelsea	Ferryhill Ath.	09.53				
Crystal Palace	Tr	05.54	54	2	-	0
Darlington	Scarborough	06.55	55	8	-	0

GREENWOOD, John E.
Manchester, 22 January, 1921 (WH)

League Club	Source	Date Signed	Seasons Played	Apps	Subs	Gls
Manchester C.		09.46	48	1	-	0
Exeter C.	Tr	06.49	49	31	-	2
Aldershot	Tr	03.51	50	12	-	0
Halifax T.	Tr	11.51				

GREENWOOD, Nigel P.
Preston, 27 November, 1966 (F)

League Club	Source	Date Signed	Seasons Played	Apps	Subs	Gls
Preston N.E.	App	09.84	84-85	36	9	14
Bury	Tr	08.86	86-89	78	32	24
Preston N.E.	Tr	02.90	89-91	24	6	4

GREENWOOD, Patrick G. (Paddy)
Hull, 17 October, 1946 (D)

League Club	Source	Date Signed	Seasons Played	Apps	Subs	Gls
Hull C.	Jnrs	11.64	65-71	137	12	3
Barnsley	Tr	11.71	71-73	110	1	6
Nottingham F.	Tr	10.74	74	15	0	0

GREENWOOD, Peter
Todmorden, 11 September, 1924 (W)

League Club	Source	Date Signed	Seasons Played	Apps	Subs	Gls
Burnley		10.46				
Chester C.	Tr	07.48	48-51	62	-	3

GREENWOOD, Peter
Rawtenstall, 3 April, 1938 (F)

League Club	Source	Date Signed	Seasons Played	Apps	Subs	Gls
Bury	Bolton W. (Am)	10.56	56	1	-	0

GREENWOOD, Ronald
Burnley, 11 November, 1921 E'B'-1 (CH)

League Club	Source	Date Signed	Seasons Played	Apps	Subs	Gls
Chelsea		10.43				
Bradford P. A.	Tr	12.45	46-47	59	-	0
Brentford	Tr	03.49	48-52	142	-	1
Chelsea	Tr	10.52	52-54	65	-	0
Fulham	Tr	02.55	54-55	42	-	0

GREENWOOD, Roy T.
Leeds, 26 September, 1952 (W)

League Club	Source	Date Signed	Seasons Played	Apps	Subs	Gls
Hull C.	App	10.70	71-75	118	8	24
Sunderland	Tr	01.76	75-78	45	11	9
Derby Co.	Tr	01.79	78-79	26	5	1
Swindon T.	Tr	02.80	79-81	49	4	7
Huddersfield T.	Tr	08.82	82-83	5	3	0
Tranmere Rov.	L	11.83	83	3	0	0

GREENWOOD, Roy T.
Croydon, 22 May, 1931 (FB)

League Club	Source	Date Signed	Seasons Played	Apps	Subs	Gls
Crystal Palace	Beckenham	11.54	54-58	111	-	0

GREER, Ross
Perth (Australia), 23 September, 1967 (F)

League Club	Source	Date Signed	Seasons Played	Apps	Subs	Gls
Chester C. (N/C)	Floreat Athena (Aus)	11.89	89	2	0	0

GREETHAM, Harold
Grimsby, 7 March, 1930 (FB)

League Club	Source	Date Signed	Seasons Played	Apps	Subs	Gls
Grimsby T.	Jnrs	06.50	50	4	-	0

GREGAN, Sean M.
Guisborough, 29 March, 1974 (CD)

League Club	Source	Date Signed	Seasons Played	Apps	Subs	Gls
Darlington	YT	12.91	91	17	0	0

GREGG, Frank
Stourbridge, 9 October, 1942 (FB)

League Club	Source	Date Signed	Seasons Played	Apps	Subs	Gls
Walsall	Jnrs	10.59	60-72	389	6	3

GREGG, Harold
Derry (NI), 25 October, 1932 NI Sch/NI Amat/Irish Lge/NI-24 (G)

League Club	Source	Date Signed	Seasons Played	Apps	Subs	Gls
Doncaster Rov.	Coleraine	10.52	52-57	93	-	0
Manchester U.	Tr	12.57	57-66	210	0	0
Stoke C.	Tr	12.66	66	2	0	0

GREGOIRE, Roland B.
Liverpool, 23 November, 1958 (F)

League Club	Source	Date Signed	Seasons Played	Apps	Subs	Gls
Halifax T.	Jnrs	08.76	77	5	0	0
Sunderland	Tr	11.77	77-78	6	3	1

GREGORY, Anthony C.
Luton, 16 May, 1937 E Yth (OL)

League Club	Source	Date Signed	Seasons Played	Apps	Subs	Gls
Luton T.	Vauxhall Motors	05.55	55-59	59	-	17
Watford	Tr	03.60	59-63	107	-	14

GREGORY, Anthony G.
Doncaster, 21 March, 1968 E Sch/E Yth (M)

League Club	Source	Date Signed	Seasons Played	Apps	Subs	Gls
Sheffield Wed.	App	01.86	85-88	14	4	1
Halifax T.	Tr	08.90	90-91	16	1	1

GREGORY, Anthony T.
Dawley, 10 March, 1947 (FB)

League Club	Source	Date Signed	Seasons Played	Apps	Subs	Gls
Shrewsbury T.	App	03.65	64-75	285	8	0

GREGORY, Brian C.
Gravesend, 11 January, 1955 (F)

League Club	Source	Date Signed	Seasons Played	Apps	Subs	Gls
Gillingham	Jnrs	08.74	74	1	1	0
Luton T.	Margate	06.76				

GREGORY, Charles F.
Doncaster, 24 October, 1911 (FB)

League Club	Source	Date Signed	Seasons Played	Apps	Subs	Gls
Doncaster Rov.	Brodsworth Colly	10.28	29	13	-	3
Manchester C.	Tr	03.30	31-33	21	-	2
Reading	Tr	03.34	33-37	128	-	6
Crystal Palace	Tr	12.37	37-38	43	-	9
Hartlepool U.	Tr	06.46	46	21	-	0
Rotherham U.	Tr	02.47	46	1	-	0

GREGORY, David H.
Peterborough, 6 October, 1951 (F)

League Club	Source	Date Signed	Seasons Played	Apps	Subs	Gls
Peterborough U.	Chatteris T.	08.73	73-76	125	17	32
Stoke C.	Tr	06.77	77	22	1	3
Blackburn Rov.	Tr	07.78	78	5	0	3
Bury	Tr	09.78	78-79	50	2	13
Portsmouth	Tr	12.79	79-81	64	10	18
Wrexham	Tr	08.82	82-85	145	8	31
Peterborough U.	Tr	08.86	86	16	15	8

GREGORY, David P.
Camden, 19 February, 1960 (FB)

League Club	Source	Date Signed	Seasons Played	Apps	Subs	Gls
Millwall	Crystal Palace (N/C)	08.78	78-80	52	0	2

GREGORY, David S.
Sudbury, 23 January, 1970 (M)

League Club	Source	Date Signed	Seasons Played	Apps	Subs	Gls
Ipswich T.	YT	03.87	88-91	15	13	1

GREGORY, Ernest
Stratford, 10 November, 1921 E'B'-1 (G)

League Club	Source	Date Signed	Seasons Played	Apps	Subs	Gls
West Ham U.	Leytonstone	05.39	46-59	382	-	0

GREGORY, Gordon (Harry)
Buckhurst Hill, 24 October, 1943 E Yth (M)

League Club	Source	Date Signed	Seasons Played	Apps	Subs	Gls
Leyton Orient	Jnrs	10.61	62-65	79	0	12
Charlton Ath.	Tr	08.66	66-70	146	3	24
Aston Villa	Tr	10.70	70-71	18	6	2
Hereford U.	Tr	08.72	72-74	71	2	6

GREGORY, John C.
Scunthorpe, 11 May, 1954 E-6 (M)

League Club	Source	Date Signed	Seasons Played	Apps	Subs	Gls
Northampton T.	App	05.72	72-76	187	0	8
Aston Villa	Tr	06.77	77-78	59	6	10
Brighton & H.A.	Tr	07.79	79-80	72	0	7
Queens Park R.	Tr	06.81	81-85	159	2	36
Derby Co.	Tr	11.85	85-87	103	0	22
Portsmouth	(Team Coach)	07.89				
Plymouth Arg. (N/C)	Tr	01.90	89	3	0	0
Bolton W. (N/C)	Tr	03.90	89	2	5	0

GREGORY, John E.
Shoreditch, 24 September, 1926 (IF)

League Club	Source	Date Signed	Seasons Played	Apps	Subs	Gls
West Ham U.	Bromley	06.51	51-52	24	-	6
Scunthorpe U.	Tr	06.53	53-56	147	-	64
Aldershot	Tr	06.57	57	6	-	2

GREGORY, John L. (Jack)
Southampton, 25 January, 1925 (FB)

League Club	Source	Date Signed	Seasons Played	Apps	Subs	Gls
Southampton	Jnrs	12.44	46-54	66	-	0
Leyton Orient	Tr	07.55	55-58	91	-	0
Bournemouth	Tr	07.59	59	17	-	0

GREGORY, Paul G.
Sheffield, 26 July, 1961 (G)

League Club	Source	Date Signed	Seasons Played	Apps	Subs	Gls
Chesterfield	App	07.79	80-83	23	0	0
Doncaster Rov.	Tr	03.84	84	1	0	0
Scunthorpe U.	Tr	10.84	84-86	69	0	0
Halifax T.	L	09.86	86	6	0	0

GREGSON, Colin
Newcastle, 19 January, 1958 (M)

League Club	Source	Date Signed	Seasons Played	Apps	Subs	Gls
West Bromwich A.	App	01.76				
Sheffield Wed.	Tr	07.77	77	1	1	0

GREGSON, John
Skelmersdale, 17 May, 1939 (W)

League Club	Source	Date Signed	Seasons Played	Apps	Subs	Gls
Blackpool	Skelmersdale U.	05.57	57-58	3	-	1
Chester C.	Tr	05.62	62	32	-	5
Shrewsbury T.	Tr	03.63	62-64	56	-	6
Mansfield T.	Tr	11.64	64-66	75	1	5
Lincoln C.	Tr	06.67	67	31	5	3
Cambridge U.	Tr	07.68	70	32	0	0

GREGSON, Peter G.
Blackpool, 12 May, 1953 (G)

League Club	Source	Date Signed	Seasons Played	Apps	Subs	Gls
Southport	Blackpool (App)	07.71	71-72	35	0	0

GREIG, Robert J.
Sunderland, 13 September, 1949 (W)

League Club	Source	Date Signed	Seasons Played	Apps	Subs	Gls
Leicester C.	App	01.67				
Workington	Tr	02.68	67	4	1	0

GRENFELL, Stephen J.
Enfield, 27 October, 1966 (M/LB)

League Club	Source	Date Signed	Seasons Played	Apps	Subs	Gls
Tottenham H.	App	08.84				
Colchester U.	Tr	10.86	86-88	67	3	1

GRESTY, Philip
Tarporley, 2 June, 1953 (OL)

League Club	Source	Date Signed	Seasons Played	Apps	Subs	Gls
Crewe Alex. (Am)	Jnrs	07.71	74	3	1	0

GREW, Mark S.
Bilston, 15 February, 1958 (G)

League Club	Source	Date Signed	Seasons Played	Apps	Subs	Gls
West Bromwich A.	Jnrs	06.76	81-82	33	0	0
Wigan Ath.	L	12.78	78	4	0	0
Leicester C.	Tr	07.83	83	5	0	0
Oldham Ath.	L	10.83	83	5	0	0
Ipswich T.	Tr	03.84	84	6	0	0
Fulham	L	09.85	85	4	0	0
West Bromwich A.	L	01.86	85	1	0	0
Port Vale	Tr	06.86	86-91	184	0	0
Blackburn Rov.	L	10.90	90	13	0	0

GREWCOCK, Neil
Leicester, 26 April, 1962 (W)

League Club	Source	Date Signed	Seasons Played	Apps	Subs	Gls
Leicester C.	App	07.79	79-80	7	1	1
Gillingham	Tr	03.82	81-82	30	4	4
Burnley	Shepshed Charthouse	06.84	84-90	180	22	27

GREY, W. Brian
Swansea, 7 September, 1948 (IF)

League Club	Source	Date Signed	Seasons Played	Apps	Subs	Gls
Swansea C.	App	09.66	67-69	28	3	9

GREYGOOSE, Dean
Thetford, 18 December, 1964 E Yth (G)

League Club	Source	Date Signed	Seasons Played	Apps	Subs	Gls
Cambridge U.	App	11.82	83-84	26	0	0
Lincoln C.	L	09.85	85	6	0	0
Leyton Orient	Tr	12.85	85	1	0	0
Crystal Palace	Tr	08.86				
Crewe Alex.	Tr	08.87	87-91	175	0	0

GRIBBIN, Brian T.
Newcastle, 2 June, 1954 (FB)

League Club	Source	Date Signed	Seasons Played	Apps	Subs	Gls
Hartlepool U.	Jnrs	07.73	72	1	0	0

GRICE, Michael J.
Woking, 3 November, 1931 (W)

League Club	Source	Date Signed	Seasons Played	Apps	Subs	Gls
Colchester U.	Lowestoft T.	06.52	52-55	107	-	16
West Ham U.	Tr	03.56	55-60	142	-	18
Coventry C.	Tr	08.61	61	37	-	6
Colchester U.	Tr	06.62	62-65	139	1	13

GRIDELET, Philip R.
Hendon, 30 April, 1967 (M)

League Club	Source	Date Signed	Seasons Played	Apps	Subs	Gls
Barnsley	Barnet	09.90	90	1	3	0

GRIERSON, Darrell P.
Blackpool, 30 October, 1968 (G)

League Club	Source	Date Signed	Seasons Played	Apps	Subs	Gls
Tranmere Rov.	App	10.86	86	4	0	0

GRIEVE, David
Selkirk, 15 February, 1929 (W)

League Club	Source	Date Signed	Seasons Played	Apps	Subs	Gls
Reading	Dalry Th.	02.52	51-53	19	-	1
Crystal Palace	Tr	04.54	54	22	-	3

GRIEVE, Richard M.
Aberdeen, 29 June, 1924

League Club	Source	Date Signed	Seasons Played	Apps	Subs	Gls
Rochdale	Montrose	05.50				
Wrexham	Tr	09.50	50	1	-	0

GRIEVES, Kenneth J.
Australia, 27 August, 1925 Died 1992 (G)

League Club	Source	Date Signed	Seasons Played	Apps	Subs	Gls
Bury	Wigan Ath.	04.47	47-49	59	-	0
Bolton W.	Tr	12.51	51-55	49	-	0
Stockport Co.	Tr	07.57	57	39	-	0

GRIEVSON, Henry
Easington, 10 April, 1941 (WH)

League Club	Source	Date Signed	Seasons Played	Apps	Subs	Gls
Sunderland	Jnrs	04.58				
Southend U.	Tr	07.61	61	24	-	1

GRIFFIN, Colin R.
Dudley, 8 January, 1956 (CD)

League Club	Source	Date Signed	Seasons Played	Apps	Subs	Gls
Derby Co.	App	01.74				
Shrewsbury T.	Tr	01.76	75-88	402	4	7

GRIFFIN, Frank A.
Pendlebury, 28 March, 1928 (OR)

League Club	Source	Date Signed	Seasons Played	Apps	Subs	Gls
Shrewsbury T.	St Augustines	03.51	50	37	-	5
West Bromwich A.	Tr	04.51	50-58	240	-	47
Northampton T.	Tr	07.59	59	18	-	0

GRIFFIN, Kevin R.
Plymouth, 5 October, 1953 (F)

League Club	Source	Date Signed	Seasons Played	Apps	Subs	Gls
Bristol C.	App	09.71	71-74	5	3	0
Mansfield T.	L	03.75	74	4	0	2
Cambridge U.	L	09.75	75	7	1	1

GRIFFIN, William
Bircotes, 24 September, 1940 (IF)

League Club	Source	Date Signed	Seasons Played	Apps	Subs	Gls
Sheffield Wed.	Jnrs	09.57	58-62	35	-	20
Bury	Tr	12.62	62-65	84	4	22
Workington	Tr	02.66	65-68	82	0	16
Rotherham U.	Tr	01.69	68-69	14	3	1

GRIFFITH, Cohen
Guyana, 26 December, 1962 Wu21-1 (W)

League Club	Source	Date Signed	Seasons Played	Apps	Subs	Gls
Cardiff C.	Kettering T.	10.89	89-91	107	13	19

GRIFFITHS, Arfon T.
Wrexham, 23 August, 1941 Wu23-3/W-17 (M)

League Club	Source	Date Signed	Seasons Played	Apps	Subs	Gls
Wrexham	Jnrs	05.59	59-60	42	-	8
Arsenal	Tr	01.61	60-61	15	-	2
Wrexham	Tr	09.62	62-78	544	6	115

GRIFFITHS, Ashley R.
Barry, 5 January, 1961 W Sch/W Yth (M)

League Club	Source	Date Signed	Seasons Played	Apps	Subs	Gls
Bristol Rov.	App	01.79	79-80	6	1	0
Torquay U.	Tr	08.81				

GRIFFITHS, Barry
Manchester, 21 November, 1940 (G)

League Club	Source	Date Signed	Seasons Played	Apps	Subs	Gls
Blackburn Rovers	Jnrs	07.62	59-62	2	-	0

GRIFFITHS, Brian
Penycae, 21 November, 1933 (F)

League Club	Source	Date Signed	Seasons Played	Apps	Subs	Gls
Wrexham		05.52	52-57	22	-	8
Chester C.	Tr	07.58	58	2	-	1

GRIFFITHS, Bryan
Liverpool, 21 November, 1938 (FB)

League Club	Source	Date Signed	Seasons Played	Apps	Subs	Gls
Everton	Jnrs	03.56	58	2	-	0
Southport	Tr	06.60	60-62	117	-	1

GRIFFITHS, Bryan K.
St Helens, 26 January, 1965 (LW)

League Club	Source	Date Signed	Seasons Played	Apps	Subs	Gls
Wigan Ath.	St Helens T.	11.88	88-91	133	12	31

GRIFFITHS, Carl B.
Welshpool, 16 July, 1971 W Yth/Wu21-1 (F)

League Club	Source	Date Signed	Seasons Played	Apps	Subs	Gls
Shrewsbury T.	YT	09.88	88-91	61	31	21

GRIFFITHS, Clive L.
Pontypridd, 22 January, 1955 W Sch/Wu23-2 (CD)

League Club	Source	Date Signed	Seasons Played	Apps	Subs	Gls
Manchester U.	App	01.72	73	7	0	0
Plymouth Arg.	L	07.74	74	10	1	0
Tranmere Rov.	Tr	11.75	75-76	59	0	0

GRIFFITHS, David
Woking, 13 December, 1937 (WH)

League Club	Source	Date Signed	Seasons Played	Apps	Subs	Gls
Portsmouth		03.56				
Aldershot	Tr	08.57	58-59	5	-	0

GRIFFITHS, David B.
Liverpool, 25 May, 1951 (FB)

League Club	Source	Date Signed	Seasons Played	Apps	Subs	Gls
Tranmere Rov.	Jnrs	02.70	69	6	0	0

GRIFFITHS, David J.
Newport, 20 May, 1962

League Club	Source	Date Signed	Seasons Played	Apps	Subs	Gls
Newport Co. (N/C)	Cwmbran T.	03.88	87	0	1	0

GRIFFITHS, Dennis
Ruabon, 12 August, 1935 (HB)

League Club	Source	Date Signed	Seasons Played	Apps	Subs	Gls
Wrexham	Jnrs	08.52	53-57	67	-	6

GRIFFITHS, Douglas J.
Birmingham, 23 October, 1948 (CH)

League Club	Source	Date Signed	Seasons Played	Apps	Subs	Gls
Wolverhampton W.	App	10.66				
Stockport Co.	Tr	07.68	68-69	20	1	0

GRIFFITHS, Estyn
Mold, 22 July, 1927 W Amat (CH)

League Club	Source	Date Signed	Seasons Played	Apps	Subs	Gls
Wrexham		04.50	50-51	11	-	0

GRIFFITHS, Evan G.
Aylesham, 19 April, 1943 (WH)

League Club	Source	Date Signed	Seasons Played	Apps	Subs	Gls
Gillingham	Jnrs	07.61	60	1	-	0

GRIFFITHS, George
Earlestown, 23 June, 1924 (FB)

League Club	Source	Date Signed	Seasons Played	Apps	Subs	Gls
Bury	Newton Park	03.42	46-53	241	-	7
Halifax T.	Tr	06.54	54-57	166	-	14

GRIFFITHS, Gerald
Swansea, 15 December, 1934 W Sch (HB)

League Club	Source	Date Signed	Seasons Played	Apps	Subs	Gls
Swansea C.	Jnrs	06.52				
Crewe Alex.	Tr	06.56	65	21	0	3

GRIFFITHS, J. Harold
Swansea, 4 January, 1931 Died 1978 W-1 (OR)

League Club	Source	Date Signed	Seasons Played	Apps	Subs	Gls
Swansea C.	Jnrs	06.49	49-63	424	-	68

GRIFFITHS, Harold S.
Liverpool, 17 November, 1912 Died 1981 (CH)

League Club	Source	Date Signed	Seasons Played	Apps	Subs	Gls
Everton		08.32				
Port Vale	Tr	05.35	36-46	76	-	3

GRIFFITHS, Ian J.
Birkenhead, 17 April, 1960 (LW)

League Club	Source	Date Signed	Seasons Played	Apps	Subs	Gls
Tranmere Rov.	Jnrs	02.79	78-82	110	6	5
Rochdale	Tr	08.83	83-84	40	2	5
Port Vale (N/C)	Tr	09.84	84	9	3	0
Wigan Ath.	Tr	07.85	85-87	73	9	7
Wigan Ath.	Mazda Hiroshima (Jap)	08.90	90	6	5	0
Wrexham	Tr	03.91	90-91	14	0	0

GRIFFITHS, Ivor
Port Talbot, 19 June, 1918 (IF)

League Club	Source	Date Signed	Seasons Played	Apps	Subs	Gls
Chester C.	Tottenham H. (Am)	09.46	46	1	-	0

GRIFFITHS, James T.
Gowerton, 5 October, 1941 (CF)

League Club	Source	Date Signed	Seasons Played	Apps	Subs	Gls
Stockport Co.		03.63	62	3	-	0

GRIFFITHS, Jeffrey K.
Swansea, 19 March, 1957 (F)

League Club	Source	Date Signed	Seasons Played	Apps	Subs	Gls
Swansea C. (N/C)		04.76	75-77	6	7	1

GRIFFITHS, John
Oldbury, 16 June, 1951 (M)

League Club	Source	Date Signed	Seasons Played	Apps	Subs	Gls
Aston Villa	App	11.68	68-69	1	2	0
Stockport Co.	Tr	05.70	70-74	167	16	31

GRIFFITHS, G. Keith
Chester, 30 December, 1927 (G)

League Club	Source	Date Signed	Seasons Played	Apps	Subs	Gls
Chester C.	Rhyl	07.55	55-58	54	-	0

GRIFFITHS, Kenneth G.
Cardiff, 11 November, 1925 Died 1985 (IF)

League Club	Source	Date Signed	Seasons Played	Apps	Subs	Gls
Cardiff C.	Jnrs	06.43				
Torquay U.	L	01.48	47-48	11	-	1
Newport Co.	Tr	09.49	49	14	-	6

GRIFFITHS, Kenneth J.
Stoke, 2 April, 1930 (IF)

League Club	Source	Date Signed	Seasons Played	Apps	Subs	Gls
Port Vale		03.50	49-57	179	-	52
Mansfield T.	Tr	01.58	57-58	42	-	7

GRIFFITHS, Malcolm W.
Merthyr Tydfil, 8 March, 1919 Died 1969 W-1 (OR)

League Club	Source	Date Signed	Seasons Played	Apps	Subs	Gls
Arsenal	Merthyr Tydfil	02.37	37	9	-	5
Leicester C.	Tr	09.38	38-55	373	-	66

GRIFFITHS, Neil
Stoke, 12 October, 1951 (FB)

League Club	Source	Date Signed	Seasons Played	Apps	Subs	Gls
Chester C.		11.70	70-73	89	1	4
Port Vale	Tr	12.73	73-80	214	4	13
Crewe Alex.	Tr	08.81	81	32	2	1

GRIFFITHS, Neil
Halifax, 4 September, 1972 (M)

League Club	Source	Date Signed	Seasons Played	Apps	Subs	Gls
Halifax T.	YT	07.91	90-91	1	2	0

GRIFFITHS, Peter J.
Barnstaple, 14 August, 1957 (W)

League Club	Source	Date Signed	Seasons Played	Apps	Subs	Gls
Stoke C.	Bideford	11.80	80-83	46	14	5
Bradford C.	L	03.84	83	2	0	0
Port Vale	Tr	07.84	84-85	32	4	4

GRIFFITHS, Raymond
Llanelli, 26 September, 1931 (HB)

League Club	Source	Date Signed	Seasons Played	Apps	Subs	Gls
Chester C.		09.55	55-59	18	-	0

GRIFFITHS, Richard D.
Earls Colne, 21 March, 1942 (FB)

League Club	Source	Date Signed	Seasons Played	Apps	Subs	Gls
Colchester U.	Jnrs	06.61	61-64	48	-	0

GRIFFITHS, Robert
Birmingham, 15 September, 1942 (WH)

League Club	Source	Date Signed	Seasons Played	Apps	Subs	Gls
Stoke C.	Rhyl	09.60				
Chester C.	Tr	07.62	62	2	-	0

GRIFFITHS, Roger D. N.
Hereford, 20 February, 1945 (FB)

League Club	Source	Date Signed	Seasons Played	Apps	Subs	Gls
Hereford U.	Worcester C.	(N/L)	72	7	2	0

GRIFFITHS J. Stephen
Barnsley, 23 February, 1914 (IF)

League Club	Source	Date Signed	Seasons Played	Apps	Subs	Gls
Chesterfield	Thurnscoe Vic.	10.34				
Halifax T.	Tr	07.37	37-38	76	-	14
Portsmouth	Tr	06.39				
Aldershot	Tr	06.46	46	42	-	9
Barnsley	Tr	07.47	47-50	65	-	27
York C.	Tr	06.51	51-52	74	-	12

GRIFFITHS, Stephen
Billingham, 28 November, 1957 (F)

League Club	Source	Date Signed	Seasons Played	Apps	Subs	Gls
Hartlepool U. (App)	App	09.74	74	0	1	0

GRIFFITHS, Vernon
Birmingham, 14 June, 1936 (WH)

League Club	Source	Date Signed	Seasons Played	Apps	Subs	Gls
Coventry C.	Sheldon T.	02.57	57-58	15	-	1

GRIFFITHS, William
Earlestown, 13 January, 1921 Died 1964 (CH)

League Club	Source	Date Signed	Seasons Played	Apps	Subs	Gls
Bury	Earlestown	05.39	46-51	191	-	11

GRIFFITHS, William E.
Warrington, 23 May, 1944 (W)

League Club	Source	Date Signed	Seasons Played	Apps	Subs	Gls
Torquay U.	App	05.62	62	1	-	0

GRIFFITHS, Wyn R.
Blaengwynfi, 17 October, 1919 (G)

League Club	Source	Date Signed	Seasons Played	Apps	Subs	Gls
Cardiff C. (Am)	Derby Co. (Am)	08.47	47	1	-	0
Newport Co. (Am)		01.52	51	3	-	0

GRIGGS, Robert J.
Petersfield, 12 December, 1952 (D)

League Club	Source	Date Signed	Seasons Played	Apps	Subs	Gls
Aldershot	App	07.70	68-69	3	1	0

GRIMES, A. Ashley
Dublin, 2 August, 1957 IRu21-2/IR-17 (LB)

League Club	Source	Date Signed	Seasons Played	Apps	Subs	Gls
Manchester U.	Bohemians	03.77	77-82	62	28	10
Coventry C.	Tr	08.83	83	29	3	1
Luton T.	Tr	08.84	84-88	85	2	3
Stoke C. (N/C)	Osasuna (Sp)	01.92	91	4	6	1

Ashley Grimes (Bohemians, Manchester United, Coventry City, Luton Town, Osasuna, Stoke City & Republic of Ireland)

GRIMES, Vincent
Scunthorpe, 13 May, 1954 (M)

League Club	Source	Date Signed	Seasons Played	Apps	Subs	Gls
Hull C.	App	05.72	73-77	84	5	9
Bradford C.	L	12.77	77	7	0	1
Scunthorpe U.	Tr	01.78	77-81	143	0	12

GRIMLEY, Thomas W.
Dinnington, 1 November, 1920 Died 1976 (G)

League Club	Source	Date Signed	Seasons Played	Apps	Subs	Gls
West Bromwich A.	Swallownest	04.39	46-47	30	-	0
New Brighton	Tr	08.48	48-50	94	-	0

GRIMSDITCH, S. Walter
Farnworth, 8 October, 1920 (G)

League Club	Source	Date Signed	Seasons Played	Apps	Subs	Gls
Southport	Rossendale U.	11.45	46	10	-	0

GRIMSHAW, Anthony
Manchester, 8 December, 1957 (M)

League Club	Source	Date Signed	Seasons Played	Apps	Subs	Gls
Manchester U.	App	12.74	75	0	1	0

GRIMSHAW, Christopher A.
Accrington, 1 October, 1965 (M)

League Club	Source	Date Signed	Seasons Played	Apps	Subs	Gls
Burnley	App	10.83				
Crewe Alex.	Tr	03.84	83	1	2	0
Bury	Tr	08.84	84-85	1	2	0

GRIMSHAW, Colin G.
Betchworth (Sy), 16 September, 1925 (WH)

League Club	Source	Date Signed	Seasons Played	Apps	Subs	Gls
Arsenal	Redhill	06.48				
Crystal Palace	Tr	10.52	52	32	-	3

GRINNEY, Ian
Crediton, 8 March, 1936 (OR)

League Club	Source	Date Signed	Seasons Played	Apps	Subs	Gls
Exeter C.	Crediton	09.54	55	2	-	0

GRIPTON, E. William
Tipton, 2 July, 1920 Died 1981 (CH)

League Club	Source	Date Signed	Seasons Played	Apps	Subs	Gls
West Bromwich A.	Jnrs	11.37	38-47	16	-	0
Luton T.	Tr	06.48	48	3	-	0
Bournemouth	Tr	07.50	50-51	79	-	0

GRITT, Stephen J.
Bournemouth, 31 October, 1957 (M)

League Club	Source	Date Signed	Seasons Played	Apps	Subs	Gls
Bournemouth	App	10.75	76	4	2	3
Charlton Ath.	Tr	07.77	77-88	320	27	24
Walsall	Tr	07.89	89	20	0	1
Charlton Ath.	Tr	02.90	89-91	11	15	1

GROBBELAAR, Bruce D.
Durban (SA), 6 October, 1957 Zimbabwe Int (G)

League Club	Source	Date Signed	Seasons Played	Apps	Subs	Gls
Crewe Alex. (N/C)	Vancouver W. (Can)	12.79	79	24	0	1
Liverpool	Vancouver W. (Can)	03.81	81-91	406	0	0

GROCOCK, Christopher R.
Grimsby, 30 October, 1968 (W)

League Club	Source	Date Signed	Seasons Played	Apps	Subs	Gls
Grimsby T.	Jnrs	06.87	85-88	18	25	1

GROGAN, John
Paisley, 30 October, 1915 (CH)

League Club	Source	Date Signed	Seasons Played	Apps	Subs	Gls
Leicester C.	Shawfield Jnrs	10.33	35-46	46	-	0
Mansfield T.	Tr	09.47	47-51	201	-	0

GROOMBRIDGE, David H.
Norbury, 13 April, 1930 (G)

League Club	Source	Date Signed	Seasons Played	Apps	Subs	Gls
Leyton Orient	Hayes	06.51	51-59	133	-	0

GROOME, Patrick B.
Nottingham, 16 March, 1934 (FB)

League Club	Source	Date Signed	Seasons Played	Apps	Subs	Gls
Notts Co.	Jnrs	11.51	52-54	29	-	0

GROTIER, Peter D.
Stratford, 18 October, 1950 (G)

League Club	Source	Date Signed	Seasons Played	Apps	Subs	Gls
West Ham U.	App	03.68	68-72	50	0	0
Cardiff C.	L	11.73	73	2	0	0
Lincoln C.	Tr	08.74	74-79	233	0	0
Cardiff C.	Tr	12.79	79-81	38	0	0
Grimsby T.	Tr	03.82	82-84	10	0	0

GROVES, Alan J.
Southport, 24 October, 1948 Died 1978 (W)

League Club	Source	Date Signed	Seasons Played	Apps	Subs	Gls
Southport	Blowick	12.68	68-69	10	4	2
Chester C.	Tr	07.70	70	21	0	3
Shrewsbury T.	Tr	02.71	70-72	76	0	11
Bournemouth	Tr	10.72	72-73	31	5	4
Oldham Ath.	Tr	02.74	73-77	136	4	12
Blackpool	Tr	11.77	77	11	4	1

GROVES, E. Gwyn
Merthyr Tydfil, 24 July, 1930 W Amat (G)

League Club	Source	Date Signed	Seasons Played	Apps	Subs	Gls
Swansea C.	Troedyrhiw	06.52	52-53	27	-	0

GROVES, John
Derby, 16 September, 1933 (WH)

League Club	Source	Date Signed	Seasons Played	Apps	Subs	Gls
Luton T.	Jnrs	10.50	53-62	218	-	16
Bournemouth	Tr	09.63	63-64	54	-	0

GROVES, Kenneth E. L.
Eton, 9 October, 1921 (G)

League Club	Source	Date Signed	Seasons Played	Apps	Subs	Gls
Preston N. E.	Windsor & Eton	03.39				
Reading	Tr	08.46	46	4	-	0

GROVES, Paul
Derby, 28 February, 1966 (M)

League Club	Source	Date Signed	Seasons Played	Apps	Subs	Gls
Leicester C.	Burton A.	04.88	87-88	7	9	1
Lincoln C.	L	08.89	89	8	0	1
Blackpool	Tr	01.90	89-91	106	1	21

GROVES, Perry
Bow, 19 April, 1965 (F)

League Club	Source	Date Signed	Seasons Played	Apps	Subs	Gls
Colchester U.	App	06.82	81-86	142	14	26
Arsenal	Tr	09.86	86-91	91	64	21

GROVES, Victor G.
Stepney, 5 November, 1932 E Yth/E Amat/Eu23-1/E'B'-1 (IF/WH)

League Club	Source	Date Signed	Seasons Played	Apps	Subs	Gls
Tottenham H. (Am)	Leytonstone	06.52	52-53	4	-	3
Leyton Orient	Walthamstow Ave.	10.54	54-55	42	-	24
Arsenal	Tr	11.55	55-63	185	-	31

GROZIER, William
Cumnock, 24 August, 1956 (FB)

League Club	Source	Date Signed	Seasons Played	Apps	Subs	Gls
Mansfield T.	App	08.74	73	1	0	0

GRUBB, Alan J.
Leven, 5 February, 1928 (W)

League Club	Source	Date Signed	Seasons Played	Apps	Subs	Gls
Tottenham H.	East Fife	03.52	52	2	-	0
Walsall	Tr	08.53	53	15	-	0

GRUMMETT, James
Hoyland, 31 July, 1921 (WH)

League Club	Source	Date Signed	Seasons Played	Apps	Subs	Gls
Lincoln C.	Ruston Sports	09.43	45-51	165	-	12
Accrington St.	Tr	09.52	52	40	-	1

Bruce Grobbelaar (Crewe Alexandra, Liverpool & Zimbabwe)

League Club	Source	Date Signed	Seasons Played	Career Record Apps	Subs	Gls

GRUMMETT, James
Barnsley, 11 July, 1945 EYth (WH)

Lincoln C.	Jnrs	06.63	63-70	246	4	19
Aldershot	Tr	07.71	71-72	81	0	6
Chester C.	Tr	06.73	73	15	1	0
Rochdale	Tr	12.73	73-74	32	1	2

GRUMMITT, Peter M.
Bourne, 19 August, 1942 Eu23-3/EF Lge (G)

Nottingham F.	Bourne T.	05.60	60-69	313	0	0
Sheffield Wed.	Tr	01.70	69-72	121	0	0
Brighton & H. A.	Tr	12.73	73-76	136	0	0

GRUNDY, Brian
Atherton, 9 May, 1945 (W)

Bury	Wigan Ath.	11.67	67-70	94	6	10

GRYBA, Raymond
Liverpool, 19 August, 1935 (IF)

Liverpool	Jnrs	08.52				
Southport	R.A.O.C. Feltham	10.55	55-57	72	-	14

GUARD, Anthony F.
Swansea, 19 April, 1964 (M)

Swansea C.	App	04.82	83	1	0	0

GUBBINS, Ralph G.
Ellesmere Port, 31 January, 1932 (IF)

Bolton W.	Shell Mex	10.52	52-59	97	-	15
Hull C.	Tr	10.59	59-60	45	-	10
Tranmere Rov.	Tr	03.61	60-63	107	-	37

GUDMUNDSSON, Albert S.
Iceland, 5 October, 1923 Iceland Int (IF)

Arsenal (Am)	Glasgow Rangers	09.46	46	2	-	0

GUEST, Brendan J.
Nottingham, 19 December, 1958 E Yth (RB)

Lincoln C.	App	12.76	76-79	99	5	2
Swindon T.	Tr	07.80				

GUEST, Gladstone
Rotherham, 26 June, 1917 (IF)

Rotherham U.	Rawmarsh Welfare	12.39	46-55	356	-	130

GUEST, William F.
Birmingham, 8 February, 1913 Died 1973 (OL)

Birmingham C.	Kingswinford Bromley	02.32	33-36	76	-	15
West Ham U.	Tr	03.36	36	3	-	1
Blackburn Rov.	Tr	01.37	36-46	88	-	30
Walsall	Tr	08.47	47	5	-	0

GUILD, Alan N.
Forfar, 27 March, 1947 S Amat (CD)

Luton T.	East Fife	07.69	70	1	0	0
Cambridge U.	Tr	05.71	71-73	117	10	1

GUILD, James
Glasgow, 10 December, 1928 (WH)

New Brighton	Dunoon Ath.	09.50	50	2	-	0

GULLAN, Stanley K.
Edinburgh, 26 January, 1926 (G)

Queens Park R.	Clyde	07.49	50-54	49	-	0

GULLIVER, Joffre
Merthyr Tydfil, 2 August, 1915 (FB)

Southend U.		08.34				
Leeds U.		03.38				
Reading	Tr	06.39	46-50	161	-	0
Swindon T.	Tr	08.51	51	11	-	0

GULLIVER, Terence R.
Salisbury, 30 September, 1944 (FB)

Bournemouth	Weymouth	08.66	66-71	162	1	2

GUMMER, Jason C.
Tredegar, 27 October, 1967 W Yth (M)

Cardiff C.	YT	07.85	85-89	28	6	5
Torquay U.	L	03.89	88	7	0	1

GUNBY, Peter
Leeds, 20 November, 1934 (WH)

Leeds U.		09.55				
Bradford C.	Tr	07.56	56	3	-	0

League Club	Source	Date Signed	Seasons Played	Career Record Apps	Subs	Gls

GUNN, Alfred H.
West Germany, 11 July, 1924 Died 1982 (CF)

Nottingham F.		02.47	46	2	-	0

GUNN, Alistair R.
Broughty Ferry, 2 November, 1924 (OR)

Huddersfield T.	Dundee	01.51	50-53	83	-	11
Bournemouth	Tr	06.54	54	27	-	2

GUNN, Andrew C.
Barking, 2 February, 1971 (LW)

Watford	YT	03.89				
Crewe Alex.	Tr	02.90	89-90	2	2	0

GUNN, Bryan
Thurso, 22 December, 1963 S Sch/S Yth/Su21-8/S'B'/S-1 (G)

Norwich C.	Aberdeen	10.86	86-91	200	0	0

Bryan Gunn (Aberdeen, Norwich City & Scotland)

GUNN, Bryn C.
Kettering, 21 August, 1958 (D)

Nottingham F.	App	08.75	75-84	129	2	1
Shrewsbury T.	L	11.85	85	9	0	0
Walsall	L	01.86	85	6	0	0
Mansfield T.	L	03.86	85	5	0	0
Peterborough U.	Tr	08.86	86-88	130	1	14
Chesterfield	Tr	07.89	89-91	89	2	10

GUNNING, Harold
Leigh-on-Sea, 8 February, 1932 (OL)

West Ham U.	Gravesend & Nft.	06.52	52	1	-	0
Crystal Palace	Tr	05.54	54-56	63	-	4
Reading	Tr	05.57	57	13	-	1

GUNNING, James M.
Helensburgh, 25 June, 1929 (OR)

Manchester C.	Hibernian	11.50	50-52	13	-	0
Barrow	Tr	07.54	54	10	-	1

GUNTER, David R.
Portsmouth, 4 March, 1933 (FB)

Southampton		05.55	55	7	-	0

League Club	Source	Date Signed	Seasons Played	Apps	Subs	Gls
GUNTER, Philip E.						
Portsmouth, 6 January, 1932 Eu23-1/E'B'-1						(D)
Portsmouth	Jnrs	08.49	51-63	321	-	2
Aldershot	Tr	07.64	64-65	78	0	8
GUNTHORPE, Kenneth						
Sheffield, 4 November, 1938						(HB)
Rotherham U.		05.58	58	2	-	0
GURINOVICH, Igor						
Minsk (USSR), 5 March, 1960 USSR Int						(F)
Brighton & H.A. (N/C)	Dinamo Minsk (USSR)	11.90	90	3	1	1
GURR, Gerald W.						
Brighton, 20 October, 1946						(G)
Southampton	Guildford C.	03.64	66-69	42	0	0
Aldershot	Tr	03.71	70-71	55	0	0
GUSCOTT, Lindon						
Lambeth, 29 March, 1972						(F)
Gillingham	YT	07.89	88	0	2	0
GUSCOTT, Raymond M.						
Newport, 18 November, 1957 W Sch						(M)
Bristol Rov.	App	11.75	76	1	0	0
Newport Co.	Minehead	10.77	77	12	5	1
GUTHRIE, Christopher W.						
Hexham, 7 September, 1953 E Sch						(F)
Newcastle U.	App	01.71	71	3	0	0
Southend U.	Tr	11.72	72-74	107	1	35
Sheffield U.	Tr	05.75	75-76	58	2	15
Swindon T.	Tr	07.77	77-78	44	1	12
Fulham	Tr	09.78	78-79	49	1	15
Millwall	Tr	03.80	79	7	0	1
GUTHRIE, James A. T.						
Perth, 6 June, 1912 Died 1981						(WH)
Portsmouth	Dundee	08.37	37-38	76	-	1
Crystal Palace	Guildford C.	10.46	46	5	-	0
GUTHRIE, Peter J.						
Newcastle, 10 October, 1961						(G)
Tottenham H.	Weymouth	01.88				
Swansea C.	L	02.88	87	14	0	0
Bournemouth	Barnet	08.90	90	10	0	0
GUTHRIE, Ralph						
Hartlepool, 13 September, 1932						(G)
Arsenal	Tow Law T.	05.53	54	2	-	0
Hartlepool U.	Tr	07.56	56-57	78	-	0
GUTHRIE, Ronald G.						
Burradon (Nd), 19 April, 1944						(LB)
Newcastle U.	Jnrs	07.63	66-72	52	3	2
Sunderland	Tr	01.73	72-74	66	0	1
GUTTRIDGE, Ronald						
Widnes, 28 April, 1916						(LB)
Aston Villa	Prescot Cables	03.37	46-47	15	-	0
Brighton & H. A.	Tr	06.48	48-49	17	-	0
GUTTRIDGE, William H.						
Darlaston, 4 March, 1931						(FB)
Wolverhampton W.	Metroshaft Wks	03.48	51-53	6	-	0
Walsall	Tr	11.54	54-61	197	-	0
GUY, Alan						
Jarrow, 8 September, 1957						(M)
Newcastle U.	App	09.75	76-78	3	1	0
Peterborough U.	Tr	03.79	78-80	42	11	4
GUY, Edward F.						
Hartlepool, 6 February, 1956						(G)
Hartlepool U.	App	02.74	74	1	0	0
GUY, Harold G.						
Wolverhampton, 1 January, 1932						(CH)
West Bromwich A.	Jnrs	03.50	50	1	-	0
GUY, Ivor						
Bristol, 27 February, 1926 Died 1986						(FB)
Bristol C.	Hambrook Villa	10.44	45-56	404	-	2
GUY, R. James						
Swansea, 29 January, 1921 Died 1990						(WH)
Norwich C.	R.A.F. St Athan	08.46	46-47	12	-	1

League Club	Source	Date Signed	Seasons Played	Apps	Subs	Gls
GUY, Keith						
Seaham, 19 May, 1959						(M)
Newcastle U.	App	06.77				
Hartlepool U.	Tr	06.78	78	7	3	0
GUY, Michael J.						
Limavady (NI), 4 February, 1953						(M)
Sheffield U.	Coleraine	03.78	77-78	12	6	2
Crewe Alex.	Tr	09.79	79-80	54	1	7
GUY, Richard						
Greenwich, 6 January, 1949						(G)
Wimbledon	Tooting & Mitcham	01.68	77	13	0	0
GUY, Ronald						
Salford, 25 April, 1936						(F)
Stockport Co.		09.58	58-59	9	-	2
GWATKIN, P. Arthur						
Harrow, 5 August, 1929						(OR)
Wrexham		10.52	53-55	56	-	8
Tranmere Rov.	Tr	06.56	56	21	-	6
GWINNETT, Melvyn L.						
Worcester, 14 May, 1963						(G)
Peterborough U.	Stourbridge	05.81				
Hereford U. (N/C)	Tr	09.82	82	1	0	0
Bradford C.	Gloucester C.	06.84				
Exeter C.	Tr	08.85	85-88	46	0	0
GWYTHER, David J. A.						
Birmingham, 6 December, 1948 Wu23-2						(F)
Swansea C.	South Gower	03.66	65-72	213	5	58
Halifax T.	Tr	08.73	73-75	104	0	26
Rotherham U.	Tr	02.76	75-79	162	0	45
Newport Co.	Tr	12.79	79-82	84	21	29
Crewe Alex.	L	01.82	81	7	0	1
Newport Co. (N/C)	Port Talbot Ath.	03.85	84	1	1	0
GYMER, John P.						
Romford, 11 November, 1966						(M)
Southend U.	App	08.84	83-86	30	25	12
Crewe Alex.	Tr	07.87	87	10	5	5
GYNN, Michael						
Peterborough, 19 August, 1961						(M)
Peterborough U.	App	04.79	78-82	152	4	33
Coventry C.	Tr	08.83	83-91	188	33	30

Micky Gynn (Peterborough United & Coventry City)

Glenn Hoddle (Tottenham Hotspur, AS Monaco, Swindon Town & England)
Still weaving his magic as the player-manager of Swindon Town

HAAG, Kelly J.
Enfield, 6 October, 1970 (F)

League Club	Source	Date Signed	Seasons Played	Apps	Subs	Gls
Brentford	YT	07.89	89	1	4	0
Fulham	Tr	08.90	90-91	30	27	9

HAASZ, John
Hungary, 7 July, 1937 (F)

League Club	Source	Date Signed	Seasons Played	Apps	Subs	Gls
Swansea C.		09.60	60	1	-	0
Workington	Tr	07.61	61-62	50	-	13

HABBIN, Richard L.
Cambridge, 6 January, 1949 (M)

League Club	Source	Date Signed	Seasons Played	Apps	Subs	Gls
Reading	Cambridge U.	03.69	69-74	204	14	42
Rotherham U.	Tr	01.75	74-77	79	5	19
Doncaster Rov.	Tr	09.77	77-78	57	3	12

HACKETT, Bernard
Ramsbottom, 7 September, 1933 (OR)

League Club	Source	Date Signed	Seasons Played	Apps	Subs	Gls
Aston Villa		11.53				
Chester C.	Tr	07.55	55-56	21	-	4

HACKETT, Gary S.
Stourbridge, 11 October, 1962 (W)

League Club	Source	Date Signed	Seasons Played	Apps	Subs	Gls
Shrewsbury T.	Bromsgrove Rov.	07.83	83-86	142	8	17
Stoke C.	Aberdeen	03.88	87-89	64	9	7
West Bromwich A.	Tr	03.90	89-91	22	12	2

HACKETT, Warren J.
Newham, 16 December, 1971 (D)

League Club	Source	Date Signed	Seasons Played	Apps	Subs	Gls
Leyton Orient	Tottenham H. (YT)	07.90	90-91	26	0	0

HACKING, John
Blackpool, 24 August, 1925 (G)

League Club	Source	Date Signed	Seasons Played	Apps	Subs	Gls
Accrington St.	Blackburn Rov. (Am)	09.45	46	8	-	0
Stockport Co.	Tr	11.46	46-49	4	-	0

HACKING, Robert
Blackburn, 30 March, 1918 (WH)

League Club	Source	Date Signed	Seasons Played	Apps	Subs	Gls
Luton T.		04.45	46	1	-	0
Brighton & H.A.	Tr	08.47	47	17	-	2
Southport	Tr	08.48	48-53	181	-	6

HADDINGTON, Harold
Scarborough, 7 August, 1931 (FB)

League Club	Source	Date Signed	Seasons Played	Apps	Subs	Gls
Bradford P.A.	Jnrs	02.49	52	2	-	0
West Bromwich A.	Tr	05.53				
Walsall	Tr	07.55	55-60	226	-	0

HADDINGTON, John (Jack)
Brierley Hill, 16 August, 1933 (OL)

League Club	Source	Date Signed	Seasons Played	Apps	Subs	Gls
Walsall	Cradley Heath	02.54	53	1	-	0

HADDINGTON, Raymond W.
Scarborough, 18 November, 1923 (IF)

League Club	Source	Date Signed	Seasons Played	Apps	Subs	Gls
Bradford C.	Bradford P.A. (Am)	09.46				
Oldham Ath.	Tr	08.47	47-50	117	-	63
Manchester C.	Tr	11.50	50	6	-	4
Stockport Co.	Tr	12.51	51	11	-	4
Bournemouth	Tr	07.52	52	2	-	0
Rochdale	Tr	10.52	52-53	38	-	12
Halifax T.	Tr	11.53	53	8	-	0

HADDOCK, Andrew
Edinburgh, 5 May, 1946 (W)

League Club	Source	Date Signed	Seasons Played	Apps	Subs	Gls
Chester C.	Jnrs	08.63	63	12	-	0
Crewe Alex.	Tr	08.64	64	4	-	0
Rotherham U.	Falkirk	12.66	66	4	0	0
Bradford P.A.	Tr	12.67	67	5	0	0
Chester C.	Tr	03.68	67	10	0	1

HADDOCK, Henry (Harry)
Glasgow, 26 July, 1925 (FB)

League Club	Source	Date Signed	Seasons Played	Apps	Subs	Gls
Exeter C.(Am)	Renfrew Jnrs	05.46	46	1	-	0

HADDOCK, Peter M.
Newcastle, 9 December, 1961 (D)

League Club	Source	Date Signed	Seasons Played	Apps	Subs	Gls
Newcastle U.	App	12.79	81-85	53	4	0
Burnley	L	03.86	85	7	0	0
Leeds U.	Tr	07.86	86-90	106	12	1

HADDON, Harold L.
Cardiff, 8 April, 1923 (IF)

League Club	Source	Date Signed	Seasons Played	Apps	Subs	Gls
Cardiff C.		04.46				
Newport Co.	Bangor C.	02.47	46-48	10	-	1
Bristol Rov.	Tr	11.48	48	2	-	0

HADDRICK, Robert
West Ham, 1 May, 1950 (CH)

League Club	Source	Date Signed	Seasons Played	Apps	Subs	Gls
Southend U. (App)	App	08.65	66	1	0	0

HADLEY, Anthony P. F.
Upminster, 5 July, 1955 (CD)

League Club	Source	Date Signed	Seasons Played	Apps	Subs	Gls
Southend U.	Basildon U.	07.74	74-82	243	22	16
Colchester U.	Tr	08.83	83	44	1	0
Southend U.	Tr	08.84	84	31	1	3

HADZIABDIC, Dzemal
Yugoslavia, 25 July, 1953 Yugoslav Int (LB)

League Club	Source	Date Signed	Seasons Played	Apps	Subs	Gls
Swansea C.	Velez Mostar (Yug)	08.80	80-82	87	2	2

HAFFEY, Frank
Glasgow, 28 November, 1938 S-2 (G)

League Club	Source	Date Signed	Seasons Played	Apps	Subs	Gls
Swindon T.	Glasgow Celtic	10.64	64	4	-	0

HAGAN, James
Monkstown (NI), 10 August, 1956 (CD)

League Club	Source	Date Signed	Seasons Played	Apps	Subs	Gls
Coventry C.	Larne T.	11.77	78	12	1	0
Torquay U.	L	09.79	79	7	0	0
Coventry C.	Hong Kong	07.81	81	3	0	0
Birmingham C.	Tr	05.82	82-86	124	13	0
Colchester U. (N/C)	Celta Vigo (Sp)	11.89	89	2	0	0

HAGAN, James
Washington, 21 November, 1918 E Sch/EF Lge/E-1 (IF)

League Club	Source	Date Signed	Seasons Played	Apps	Subs	Gls
Derby Co.	Washington Colly	01.35	35-38	30	-	7
Sheffield U.	Tr	11.38	38-57	361	-	116

HAGUE, Keith
Hull, 25 May, 1946 (WH)

League Club	Source	Date Signed	Seasons Played	Apps	Subs	Gls
York C.		10.65	65	0	1	0

HAGUE, Neil
Thurcroft, 1 December, 1949 E Yth (M)

League Club	Source	Date Signed	Seasons Played	Apps	Subs	Gls
Rotherham U.	App	12.66	67-71	135	11	23
Plymouth Arg.	Tr	11.71	71-73	98	0	15
Bournemouth	Tr	07.74	74-75	89	0	7
Huddersfield T.	Tr	06.76	76	25	0	2
Darlington	Tr	05.77	77-78	80	0	4

HAGUE, Paul
Consett, 16 September, 1972 (CD)

League Club	Source	Date Signed	Seasons Played	Apps	Subs	Gls
Gillingham	YTS	05.91	90	6	1	0

HAIG, Richard N.
Pontypridd, 29 December, 1970 (M)

League Club	Source	Date Signed	Seasons Played	Apps	Subs	Gls
Cardiff C.	YTS	07.89	88-89	1	4	0

HAIGH, Gordon
Barnsley, 18 August, 1921 (IF)

League Club	Source	Date Signed	Seasons Played	Apps	Subs	Gls
Burnley	Ransons	11.45	46-49	18	-	3
Bournemouth	Tr	04.50	49-50	17	-	3
Watford	Tr	08.51	51	29	-	5

HAIGH, Graham
Huddersfield, 16 September, 1946 (WH)

League Club	Source	Date Signed	Seasons Played	Apps	Subs	Gls
Halifax T. (App)	App	09.63	64	1	-	0

HAIGH, John (Jack)
Rotherham, 10 September, 1928 (IF)

League Club	Source	Date Signed	Seasons Played	Apps	Subs	Gls
Liverpool	Gainsborough Trin.	10.49	50-51	11	-	3
Scunthorpe U.	Tr	08.52	52-59	329	-	65
Doncaster Rov.	Tr	07.60	60-61	72	-	6

HAIGH, Paul
Scarborough, 4 May, 1958 Eu21-1 (D)

League Club	Source	Date Signed	Seasons Played	Apps	Subs	Gls
Hull C.	App	06.75	74-80	179	1	8
Carlisle U.	Tr	11.80	80-86	228	5	4
Hartlepool U.	Tr	07.87	87-88	49	1	0

HAILS, Julian
Lincoln, 20 November, 1967 (M)

League Club	Source	Date Signed	Seasons Played	Apps	Subs	Gls
Fulham	Hemel Hempstead	08.90	91	11	7	1

HAILS, William
Nettlesworth (Dm), 19 February, 1935 (OR)

League Club	Source	Date Signed	Seasons Played	Apps	Subs	Gls
Lincoln C.	Jnrs	03.53	53-54	9	-	0
Peterborough U.	Tr	(N/L)	60-62	94	-	28
Northampton T.	Tr	11.62	62-63	59	-	13
Luton T.	Tr	06.64	64	3	-	0

HAILWOOD, David J.
Nottingham, 17 October, 1954 (W)

League Club	Source	Date Signed	Seasons Played	Apps	Subs	Gls
Mansfield T.		07.73	74	1	0	0

HAINES, Donald N.
Ynysybwl, 23 September, 1925 (FB)

League Club	Source	Date Signed	Seasons Played	Apps	Subs	Gls
Bournemouth		10.48				
Newport Co.	Yeovil T.	12.50	50-53	77	-	1

HAINES, Ivan G.
Chatham, 14 September, 1968 (CD)

League Club	Source	Date Signed	Seasons Played	Apps	Subs	Gls
Gillingham	YT	06.87	87-90	45	6	0

HAINES, John T. W.
Evesham, 24 April, 1920 Died 1987 E-1 (IF)

League Club	Source	Date Signed	Seasons Played	Apps	Subs	Gls
Liverpool	Cheltenham T.	11.37				
Swansea C.	Tr	06.39	46	28	-	7
Leicester C.	Tr	06.47	47	12	-	3
West Bromwich A.	Tr	03.48	47-49	59	-	23
Bradford P.A.	Tr	12.49	49-53	136	-	34
Rochdale	Tr	10.53	53-54	60	-	16
Chester C.	Tr	07.55	55-56	47	-	8

HAINES, Keith H.
Wigston, 19 December, 1937 E Yth (CH)

League Club	Source	Date Signed	Seasons Played	Apps	Subs	Gls
Leeds U.	Matlock T.	05.59				
Lincoln C.	Tr	07.60	60-62	13	-	0

HAINES, Mervyn J.
Ynysybwl, 2 May, 1923 (W)

League Club	Source	Date Signed	Seasons Played	Apps	Subs	Gls
Bournemouth		10.48				
Newport Co.	Yeovil T.	05.50	50	15	-	1

HAINSWORTH, Leonard
Rotherham, 25 January, 1918 (FB)

League Club	Source	Date Signed	Seasons Played	Apps	Subs	Gls
Rotherham U.		03.39	38-47	32	-	8
Doncaster Rov.	Tr	07.48	48-50	65	-	0
Workington	Tr	07.51	51-52	75	-	0

HAIR, George
Ryton, 28 April, 1925 (OL)

League Club	Source	Date Signed	Seasons Played	Apps	Subs	Gls
Newcastle U.	Spen Jnrs	05.43	46-48	23	-	7
Grimsby T.	Tr	02.49	48-50	68	-	8

HAIR, K. Grenville A.
Burton, 16 November, 1931 Died 1968 (FB)

League Club	Source	Date Signed	Seasons Played	Apps	Subs	Gls
Leeds U.	Jnrs	11.48	50-63	443	-	1

HAIRE, Garry
Sedgefield, 24 July, 1963 (W)

League Club	Source	Date Signed	Seasons Played	Apps	Subs	Gls
Oxford U.	App	07.81				
Bradford C.	Whitley Bay	06.83	83-84	43	6	13
Darlington	Tr	02.85	84-85	16	9	2
Rochdale	L	10.85	85	3	0	0

HALBERT, Paul J.
St Albans, 28 October, 1973 (F)

League Club	Source	Date Signed	Seasons Played	Apps	Subs	Gls
Aldershot (YT)	YT	01.91	90	0	3	0

HALE, Alfred
Waterford (Ire), 28 August, 1939 IR Amat/IR-13 (IF)

League Club	Source	Date Signed	Seasons Played	Apps	Subs	Gls
Aston Villa	Waterford	06.60	60-61	5	-	1
Doncaster Rov.	Tr	07.62	62-64	119	-	42
Newport Co.	Tr	08.65	65	34	0	21

HALE, Denzil
Clevedon, 9 April, 1928 (CH)

League Club	Source	Date Signed	Seasons Played	Apps	Subs	Gls
Bristol Rov.	Clevedon	02.52	53-58	120	-	12

HALE, Kenneth O.
Blyth, 18 September, 1939 (IF)

League Club	Source	Date Signed	Seasons Played	Apps	Subs	Gls
Newcastle U.	Jnrs	10.56	57-62	30	-	15
Coventry C.	Tr	12.62	62-65	98	1	27
Oxford U.	Tr	03.66	65-67	64	2	13
Darlington	Tr	05.68	68-71	173	0	25
Halifax T.	Tr	07.72	72-73	52	0	4

HALE, Richard J. (Dixie)
Waterford (Ire), 29 May, 1935 (WH)

League Club	Source	Date Signed	Seasons Played	Apps	Subs	Gls
Swansea C.	Waterford	10.59	59-60	34	-	3
Barrow	Tr	07.61	61-63	118	-	16
Workington	Tr	08.64	64-66	131	0	10
Watford	Tr	07.67	67-69	95	3	7

HALES, Derek D.
Rainham (Kt), 15 December, 1951 (F)

League Club	Source	Date Signed	Seasons Played	Apps	Subs	Gls
Luton T.	Dartford	03.72	72	5	2	1
Charlton Ath.	Tr	10.73	73-76	126	3	72
Derby Co.	Tr	12.76	76-77	22	1	4
West Ham U.	Tr	09.77	77	23	1	10
Charlton Ath.	Tr	07.78	78-84	186	5	76
Gillingham	Tr	03.85	84-85	31	9	9

HALES, John
Glasgow, 15 May, 1940 (W)

League Club	Source	Date Signed	Seasons Played	Apps	Subs	Gls
Brentford	St Rochs	09.58	58-63	61	-	7

HALES, Kevin P.
Dartford, 13 January, 1961 (M)

League Club	Source	Date Signed	Seasons Played	Apps	Subs	Gls
Chelsea	App	01.79	79-82	18	2	2
Leyton Orient	Tr	08.83	83-91	256	15	22

HALES, Richard
Gillingham, 24 August, 1924 (RB)

League Club	Source	Date Signed	Seasons Played	Apps	Subs	Gls
Gillingham (Am)	Sittingbourne	08.51	51	5	-	0

HALES, William H.
Gillingham, 6 January, 1920 Died 1984 (CF)

League Club	Source	Date Signed	Seasons Played	Apps	Subs	Gls
Gillingham (Am)	Sittingbourne	07.50	50-51	15	-	9

HALEY, John
Sunderland, 24 April, 1932 Died 1956 (WH)

League Club	Source	Date Signed	Seasons Played	Apps	Subs	Gls
Gateshead		09.53	53-56	38	-	2

HALFORD, Carl
Oldham, 27 November, 1958 (M)

League Club	Source	Date Signed	Seasons Played	Apps	Subs	Gls
Manchester C.	App	08.76				
Stockport Co.	Tr	07.77	77-78	65	9	5
Bury	Tr	08.79	79-80	31	0	2

HALL, Alan S.
Manchester, 26 May, 1938 E Yth (WH)

League Club	Source	Date Signed	Seasons Played	Apps	Subs	Gls
Oldham Ath.	Manchester U. (Am)	11.57	57-60	74	-	5

HALL, Albert E. B.
Barry, 3 September, 1918 W Sch (OR)

League Club	Source	Date Signed	Seasons Played	Apps	Subs	Gls
Tottenham H.	Jnrs	10.35	35-46	40	-	10
Plymouth Arg.	Tr	07.47	47	9	-	0

HALL, Alec F.
Grimsby, 17 September, 1909 Died 1992 (WH)

League Club	Source	Date Signed	Seasons Played	Apps	Subs	Gls
Grimsby T.	Cleethorpes T.	05.29	29-47	358	-	4

HALL, Almer G.
Hove, 12 November, 1912 (IF)

League Club	Source	Date Signed	Seasons Played	Apps	Subs	Gls
Brighton & H.A.	Southwick	02.31				
Tottenham H.	Tr	09.33	34-35	16	-	3
Southend U.	Tr	05.37	37-38	37	-	10
Bradford C.	Tr	06.39				
West Ham U.	Tr	12.45	46-48	50	-	11

HALL, Anthony D.
Billingham, 17 January, 1969 (D)

League Club	Source	Date Signed	Seasons Played	Apps	Subs	Gls
Tranmere Rov.	Billingham T.	08.87	87	0	1	0
Hartlepool U.	Tr	10.87	87	0	1	0

HALL, Arthur
Sheffield, 23 November, 1925 (W)

League Club	Source	Date Signed	Seasons Played	Apps	Subs	Gls
Chesterfield	Gainsborough Trin.	07.47	47-48	23	-	4
Scunthorpe U.	Goole T.	08.51	51	15	-	3

HALL, Arthur B.
Witney, 24 March, 1937 (W)

League Club	Source	Date Signed	Seasons Played	Apps	Subs	Gls
Bristol Rov.	Witney T.	07.59	60-61	2	-	0

HALL, Bernard R. E.
Bath, 8 July, 1942 (G)

League Club	Source	Date Signed	Seasons Played	Apps	Subs	Gls
Bristol Rov.	Jnrs	09.59	61-66	163	0	0

HALL, Brian S.
Derby, 9 March, 1939 (OL/LB)

League Club	Source	Date Signed	Seasons Played	Apps	Subs	Gls
Mansfield T.	Belper T.	04.59	58-64	72	-	19
Colchester U.	Tr	03.65	64-72	324	4	29

HALL, Brian W.
Glasgow, 22 January, 1946 (M)

League Club	Source	Date Signed	Seasons Played	Apps	Subs	Gls
Liverpool	Manchester Univ.	07.68	68-75	140	13	15
Plymouth Arg.	Tr	07.76	76-77	49	2	16
Burnley	Tr	11.77	77-79	39	4	3

HALL, Colin T.
Wolverhampton, 2 February, 1948 E Yth (W)

League Club	Source	Date Signed	Seasons Played	Apps	Subs	Gls
Nottingham F.	Jnrs	03.66	67-69	27	9	2
Bradford C.	Tr	06.70	70-71	65	1	7
Bristol C.	Tr	07.72	72	0	1	0
Hereford U.	L	09.72	72	5	0	0

HALL, David A.
Doncaster, 26 September, 1960 (D)

League Club	Source	Date Signed	Seasons Played	Apps	Subs	Gls
Scunthorpe U.	App	09.78	78-79	16	1	0

HALL, David H.
Sheffield, 16 March, 1954 (M)

League Club	Source	Date Signed	Seasons Played	Apps	Subs	Gls
Sheffield Wed.	App	03.72				
Bradford C.	Tr	07.75	75-76	51	3	3

HALL, Dennis K.
Southwell, 24 December, 1930 (FB)

League Club	Source	Date Signed	Seasons Played	Apps	Subs	Gls
Portsmouth	Jnrs	09.48	52-53	10	-	0
Reading	Tr	08.54	54	13	-	0
Bournmouth	Tr	07.55				

HALL, Derek R.
Ashton-under-Lyme, 5 January, 1965 (M)

League Club	Source	Date Signed	Seasons Played	Apps	Subs	Gls
Coventry C.	App	10.82	82	1	0	0
Torquay U.	Tr	03.84	83-84	55	0	6
Swindon T.	Tr	07.85	85	9	1	0
Southend U.	Tr	08.86	86-88	120	3	15
Halifax T.	Tr	07.89	89-90	48	1	4
Hereford U.	Tr	07.91	91	15	5	0

HALL, Frederick
Norwich, 20 October, 1914 (G)

League Club	Source	Date Signed	Seasons Played	Apps	Subs	Gls
Norwich C.	Hellesden Hospital	09.34	35-46	90	-	0

HALL, Frederick
Worksop, 24 November, 1924 (CF)

League Club	Source	Date Signed	Seasons Played	Apps	Subs	Gls
Birmingham C.	Whitwell O.B.	03.47	46-48	5	-	2

HALL, Frederick W.
Chester-le-Street, 18 November, 1917 (CH)

League Club	Source	Date Signed	Seasons Played	Apps	Subs	Gls
Blackburn Rov.	Ouston Jnrs	11.35	36-38	29	-	0
Sunderland	Tr	08.46	46-54	215	-	1
Barrow	Tr	09.55	55	16	-	1

HALL, Gareth D.
Croydon, 20 March, 1969 E Sch/Wu21-1/W-9 (RB)

League Club	Source	Date Signed	Seasons Played	Apps	Subs	Gls
Chelsea	App	05.86	86-91	71	12	1

HALL, Ian
Whitehaven, 28 November, 1950 (D)

League Club	Source	Date Signed	Seasons Played	Apps	Subs	Gls
Workington	Jnrs	07.72	71-73	25	11	1
Southport	Tr	07.74	74	0	1	0

HALL, Ian W.
Chesterfield, 27 December, 1939 E Sch/E Yth (IF)

League Club	Source	Date Signed	Seasons Played	Apps	Subs	Gls
Derby Co.	Wolverhampton W. (Am)	09.59	59-61	44	-	13
Mansfield T.	Tr	09.62	62-67	145	0	10

HALL, James
Bootle, 5 October, 1959 (M)

League Club	Source	Date Signed	Seasons Played	Apps	Subs	Gls
Blackpool	App	10.77	78	1	0	0
Blackburn Rov.	Tr	07.80				

HALL, James F.
Manchester, 7 May, 1945 (FB)

League Club	Source	Date Signed	Seasons Played	Apps	Subs	Gls
Oldham Ath.	Mather & Platt	07.66	65	1	0	0

HALL, James L.
Northampton, 2 March, 1945 E Yth (F)

League Club	Source	Date Signed	Seasons Played	Apps	Subs	Gls
Northampton T.	Jnrs	07.63	63-67	54	2	7
Peterborough U.	Tr	12.67	67-74	298	4	122
Northampton T.	Tr	01.75	74-77	69	0	28
Cambridge U.	L	12.76	76	24	0	15

HALL, Jeffrey J.
Scunthorpe, 7 September, 1929 Died 1959 EF Lge/E'B'-1/E-17 (FB)

League Club	Source	Date Signed	Seasons Played	Apps	Subs	Gls
Birmingham C.	Bradford P.A. (Am)	05.50	50-58	227	-	1

HALL, John
Doncaster, 19 November, 1931 (F)

League Club	Source	Date Signed	Seasons Played	Apps	Subs	Gls
Doncaster Rov.		08.51	51	2	-	0

HALL, John F.
Bramley, 18 April, 1944 (OR)

League Club	Source	Date Signed	Seasons Played	Apps	Subs	Gls
Bradford C.	Jnrs	05.62	62-73	417	13	63

HALL, Joseph E.
Sherburn (Dm), 10 April, 1934 (IF)

League Club	Source	Date Signed	Seasons Played	Apps	Subs	Gls
Fulham	Jnrs	10.51	55	1	-	0

HALL, Lance
Darlington, 23 January, 1915 (CH)

League Club	Source	Date Signed	Seasons Played	Apps	Subs	Gls
Luton T.		01.37				
Barrow	Tr	07.38	38-48	108	-	1

HALL, Leslie F.
St Albans, 1 October, 1921 (CH)

League Club	Source	Date Signed	Seasons Played	Apps	Subs	Gls
Luton T.	St Albans C.	08.43	47-54	79	-	0

HALL, Mark
Doncaster, 11 May, 1970 (RB)

League Club	Source	Date Signed	Seasons Played	Apps	Subs	Gls
Doncaster Rov.	YT	06.88	87-88	1	1	0

HALL, Mark A.
Islington, 13 January, 1973 (W)

League Club	Source	Date Signed	Seasons Played	Apps	Subs	Gls
Southend U.	Tottenham H. (YT)	08.91	91	1	2	0

HALL, Paul A.
Manchester, 3 July, 1972 (W)

League Club	Source	Date Signed	Seasons Played	Apps	Subs	Gls
Torquay U.	YT	07.90	89-91	50	15	1

HALL, Peter
Stoke, 29 September, 1939 (W)

League Club	Source	Date Signed	Seasons Played	Apps	Subs	Gls
Port Vale	Stoke C. (Am)	05.58	58-60	16	-	4
Bournemouth	Tr	07.61				
Gillingham	Bedford T.	11.67	67	9	0	1

HALL, Richard A.
Ipswich, 14 March 1972 E Yth/Eu21-2 (CD)

League Club	Source	Date Signed	Seasons Played	Apps	Subs	Gls
Scunthorpe U.	YT	03.90	89-90	22	0	3
Southampton	Tr	02.91	90-91	21	6	3

HALL, Richard F.
Weymouth, 3 July, 1945 (WH)

League Club	Source	Date Signed	Seasons Played	Apps	Subs	Gls
Bournemouth	Weymouth	06.67	67	8	3	0

HALL, Ronald
Dudley, 8 February, 1933 (CF)

League Club	Source	Date Signed	Seasons Played	Apps	Subs	Gls
Walsall	Cradley Heath	06.54	54-55	2	-	0

HALL, Stanley A.
Southgate, 18 February, 1917 (G)

League Club	Source	Date Signed	Seasons Played	Apps	Subs	Gls
Leyton Orient	Finchley	03.38	38-46	26	-	0

HALL, Wayne
Rotherham, 25 October, 1968 (M/LB)

League Club	Source	Date Signed	Seasons Played	Apps	Subs	Gls
York C.	Hatfield Main Colly	03.89	88-91	104	8	7

HALL, Wilfred
Haydock, 14 October, 1934 (G)

League Club	Source	Date Signed	Seasons Played	Apps	Subs	Gls
Stoke C.	Earlestown	10.53	54-59	45	-	0
Ipswich T.	Tr	06.60	60-62	16	-	0

HALL, William
Gosport, 24 July, 1930 (CF)

League Club	Source	Date Signed	Seasons Played	Apps	Subs	Gls
Gillingham	Gosport Bor.	09.52	52	9	-	0

HALL, William F.
Walton-le-Dale, 6 February, 1926 Died 1986 (G)

League Club	Source	Date Signed	Seasons Played	Apps	Subs	Gls
Preston N.E.	Jnrs	02.48	47	7	-	0
Blackpool	Tr	07.49	52	3	-	0
Reading	Tr	07.53	53	16	-	0

HALL, William W.
Liverpool, 3 June, 1917

League Club	Source	Date Signed	Seasons Played	Apps	Subs	Gls
Liverpool		11.43				
Southport	Tr	06.46	46	16	-	1

HALLAM, Anthony K.
Chesterfield, 9 October, 1946 (FB)

League Club	Source	Date Signed	Seasons Played	Apps	Subs	Gls
Chesterfield	App	10.64	65-66	5	1	0

HALLAM, Norman
Stoke, 23 October, 1920

League Club	Source	Date Signed	Seasons Played	Apps	Subs	Gls
Port Vale		05.46	46-52	61	-	3
Halifax T.	Tr	10.53	53	3	-	0

HALLARD, William
St Helens, 28 August, 1913 Died 1979 (WH)

League Club	Source	Date Signed	Seasons Played	Apps	Subs	Gls
Bury	Runcorn	08.35	35	1	-	0
Bradford P.A.	Tr	06.37	37-38	69	-	5
Rochdale	Tr	06.46	46	17	-	2
Accrington St.	Tr	03.47	46	3	-	0

HALLAS, Geoffrey
Oldham, 8 December, 1930 (FB)

League Club	Source	Date Signed	Seasons Played	Apps	Subs	Gls
West Ham U.	Warminster	03.54	54	3	-	0

HALLE, Gunnar
Oslo (Norway), 11 August, 1965 Norwegian Int (RB)

League Club	Source	Date Signed	Seasons Played	Apps	Subs	Gls
Oldham Ath.	Lillestrom (Nor)	02.91	90-91	27	0	0

HALLETT, Thomas R.
Glyn-Neath, 10 April, 1939 W Sch (CH)

League Club	Source	Date Signed	Seasons Played	Apps	Subs	Gls
Leeds U.	Jnrs	04.56				
Swindon T.	Tr	07.63	63-65	26	0	0
Bradford C.	Tr	06.66	66-70	177	2	2

HALLIDAY, Brian
Farnworth, 19 January, 1938

League Club	Source	Date Signed	Seasons Played	Apps	Subs	Gls
Stockport Co.	Bolton W. (Am)	10.58	58	1	-	0

HALLIDAY, Brian J.
Liverpool, 30 December, 1944 (W)

League Club	Source	Date Signed	Seasons Played	Apps	Subs	Gls
Liverpool	Jnrs	05.63				
Tranmere Rov.	Tr	07.65				
Crewe Alex.	Tr	10.65	65	1	0	0

HALLIDAY, Bruce
Sunderland, 3 January, 1961 (CD)

League Club	Source	Date Signed	Seasons Played	Apps	Subs	Gls
Newcastle U.	App	01.79	80-81	32	0	1
Darlington	L	09.82	82	7	0	0
Bury	Tr	11.82	82	29	0	0
Bristol C.	Tr	08.83	83-84	52	1	0
Hereford U.	Tr	06.85	85-86	61	1	6

HALLIDAY, Gary
Bradford, 9 May, 1951 (F)

League Club	Source	Date Signed	Seasons Played	Apps	Subs	Gls
Bradford P.A.	Jnrs	08.68	68	0	1	0

HALLIDAY, Thomas
Ayr, 28 April, 1940 (CF)

League Club	Source	Date Signed	Seasons Played	Apps	Subs	Gls
Cardiff C.	Dumbarton	10.63	63-64	16	-	2

HALLOWS, Paul C. R.
Chester, 22 June, 1950 (FB)

League Club	Source	Date Signed	Seasons Played	Apps	Subs	Gls
Bolton W.	App	10.67	68-73	45	2	0
Rochdale	Tr	05.74	74-79	197	0	2

HALLWORTH, Jonathan G.
Stockport, 26 October, 1965 (G)

League Club	Source	Date Signed	Seasons Played	Apps	Subs	Gls
Ipswich T.	App	05.83	85-87	45	0	0
Bristol Rov.	L	01.85	84	2	0	0
Oldham Ath.	Tr	02.89	88-91	118	0	0

HALLYBONE, James M.
Leytonstone, 15 May, 1962 (M)

League Club	Source	Date Signed	Seasons Played	Apps	Subs	Gls
Leyton Orient	App	05.80	81	5	3	0
Halifax T.	Tr	07.82	82	11	5	0

HALOM, Victor L.
Swadlincote, 3 October, 1948 (F)

League Club	Source	Date Signed	Seasons Played	Apps	Subs	Gls
Charlton Ath.	App	01.66	65-67	9	3	0
Leyton Orient	Tr	08.67	67-68	53	0	12
Fulham	Tr	11.68	68-71	66	6	22
Luton T.	Tr	09.71	71-72	57	2	17
Sunderland	Tr	02.73	72-75	110	3	35
Oldham Ath.	Tr	07.76	76-79	121	2	43
Rotherham U.	Tr	02.80	79-80	19	1	2

HALPIN, John T.
Manchester, 5 June, 1927

League Club	Source	Date Signed	Seasons Played	Apps	Subs	Gls
Bury		11.48	48	2	-	0
Shrewsbury T.	Tr	08.51	51-52	42	-	0

HALPIN, John W.
Broxburn, 15 November, 1961 (LW)

League Club	Source	Date Signed	Seasons Played	Apps	Subs	Gls
Carlisle U.	Glasgow Celtic	10.84	84-90	148	5	17
Rochdale	Tr	07.91	91	22	9	1

HALSALL, Alan
Menai Bridge, 17 November, 1940 (G)

League Club	Source	Date Signed	Seasons Played	Apps	Subs	Gls
Blackpool	Skelmersdale U.	04.62	61	2	-	0
Oldham Ath.	Tr	07.63	63	2	-	0

HALSALL, Michael
Bootle, 21 July, 1961 (M)

League Club	Source	Date Signed	Seasons Played	Apps	Subs	Gls
Liverpool	App	05.79				
Birmingham C.	Tr	03.83	82-84	35	1	3
Carlisle U.	Tr	10.84	84-86	92	0	11
Grimsby T.	Tr	02.87	86	12	0	0
Peterborough U.	Tr	07.87	87-91	223	0	27

HALSEY, Mark A.
Romford, 1 December, 1959 (M)

League Club	Source	Date Signed	Seasons Played	Apps	Subs	Gls
Norwich C.	App	12.77	77-79	3	0	0

HALSTEAD, Roy
Whitworth, 26 July, 1931 (IR)

League Club	Source	Date Signed	Seasons Played	Apps	Subs	Gls
Burnley	Jnrs	06.53				
Chester C.	Tr	06.54	54	21	-	4

Gunnar Halle (Lillestrom, Oldham Athletic & Norway)

HALTON, Reginald L.
Leek, 11 July, 1916 Died 1988 (WH)

League Club	Source	Date Signed	Seasons Played	Apps	Subs	Gls
Manchester U.	Cheddington M.H.	10.36	36	4	-	1
Notts Co.	Tr	06.37	37	6	-	0
Bury	Tr	11.37	37-48	114	-	19
Chesterfield	Tr	12.48	48-50	61	-	10
Leicester C.	Tr	09.50	50-51	64	-	3

HAM, Michael T.
Plymouth, 6 December, 1963 (CD)

League Club	Source	Date Signed	Seasons Played	Apps	Subs	Gls
Plymouth Arg.	App	12.81	81-84	16	1	0

HAM, Robert S.
Bradford, 29 March, 1942 (F)

League Club	Source	Date Signed	Seasons Played	Apps	Subs	Gls
Bradford P.A.	Jnrs	10.61	61-62	25	-	6
Grimsby T.	Gainsborough Trin.	02.64	63	2	-	1
Bradford P.A.	Tr	08.64	64-67	134	0	47
Bradford C.	Tr	02.68	67-70	115	0	40
Preston N.E.	Tr	10.70	70-71	43	0	14
Rotherham U.	Tr	10.71	71-72	67	1	24
Bradford C.	Tr	07.73	73-74	72	1	24

HAMER, John A.
Bradford, 5 April, 1944 (LH)

League Club	Source	Date Signed	Seasons Played	Apps	Subs	Gls
Bradford C. (Am)		04.64	64	1	-	0

HAMER, Kevin J.
Merthyr Tydfil, 2 February, 1969 (D)

League Club	Source	Date Signed	Seasons Played	Apps	Subs	Gls
Newport Co.	YT	07.87	85-87	15	2	1

HAMILL, Stewart P.
Glasgow, 22 January, 1960 (W)

League Club	Source	Date Signed	Seasons Played	Apps	Subs	Gls
Leicester C.	Pollok Jnrs	09.80	80-81	10	0	2
Scunthorpe U.	L	03.82	81	4	0	0
Northampton T.	Nuneaton Bor.	03.86	85	3	0	1
Scarborough (N/C)	Altrincham	03.87	87	19	9	3

HAMILTON, Alexander M.
Kirkcolm, 21 November, 1937 (WH)

League Club	Source	Date Signed	Seasons Played	Apps	Subs	Gls
Accrington St.	Drumore Jnrs	08.57	58-60	82	-	0
York C.	Tr	03.62	61	11	-	0

HAMILTON, Bryan
Belfast, 21 December, 1946 NIu23-2/NI-50 (M)

League Club	Source	Date Signed	Seasons Played	Apps	Subs	Gls
Ipswich T.	Linfield	08.71	71-75	142	11	43
Everton	Tr	11.75	75-76	38	3	5
Millwall	Tr	07.77	77-78	48	1	6
Swindon T.	Tr	11.78	78-80	19	5	1
Tranmere Rov.	Tr	10.80	80-84	95	14	6

HAMILTON, Charles M.
Glasgow, 16 June, 1933 (F)

League Club	Source	Date Signed	Seasons Played	Apps	Subs	Gls
Plymouth Arg.	Jnrs	07.50				
Stockport Co.	Tr	11.55	55	27	-	1

HAMILTON, David
South Shields, 7 November, 1960 E Yth (M)

League Club	Source	Date Signed	Seasons Played	Apps	Subs	Gls
Sunderland	App	09.78				
Blackburn Rov.	Tr	01.81	80-85	104	10	7
Cardiff C.	L	03.85	84	10	0	0
Wigan Ath.	Tr	07.86	86-88	97	6	7
Chester C.	Tr	08.89	89	26	2	0
Burnley	Tr	08.90	90-91	11	4	0

HAMILTON, David S.
Carlisle, 8 February, 1919 (OR)

League Club	Source	Date Signed	Seasons Played	Apps	Subs	Gls
Newcastle U.	Shawfield Jnrs	05.39				
Southend U.	Tr	05.46	46	4	-	0

HAMILTON, Edward
Glasgow, 17 January, 1927 (IL)

League Club	Source	Date Signed	Seasons Played	Apps	Subs	Gls
Barnsley	Dundalk	04.49	49	1	-	0

HAMILTON, Gary J.
Glasgow, 27 December, 1965 S Yth (M)

League Club	Source	Date Signed	Seasons Played	Apps	Subs	Gls
Middlesbrough	App	06.83	82-88	217	12	25
Darlington	L	09.91	91	11	0	2

HAMILTON, Hugh
Glasgow, 16 June, 1942 (W)

League Club	Source	Date Signed	Seasons Played	Apps	Subs	Gls
Hartlepool U.	Falkirk	07.63	63-65	38	1	7

HAMILTON, Ian
Bristol, 12 September, 1940 (IF)

League Club	Source	Date Signed	Seasons Played	Apps	Subs	Gls
Bristol Rov.	Jnrs	01.58	58-67	149	0	60
Exeter C.	L	10.67	67	4	0	1
Newport Co.	Tr	07.68	68	13	2	2

HAMILTON, Ian M. ("Chico")
Streatham, 31 October, 1950 E Yth (M)

League Club	Source	Date Signed	Seasons Played	Apps	Subs	Gls
Chelsea	App	01.68	66	3	2	2
Southend U.	Tr	09.68	68	35	2	11
Aston Villa	Tr	06.69	69-75	189	19	40
Sheffield U.	Tr	07.76	76-77	55	5	13

HAMILTON, Ian R.
Stevenage, 14 December, 1967 (M)

League Club	Source	Date Signed	Seasons Played	Apps	Subs	Gls
Southampton	App	12.85				
Cambridge U.	Tr	03.88	87-88	23	1	1
Scunthorpe U.	Tr	12.88	88-91	139	6	18

HAMILTON, Ian W.
South Shields, 21 July, 1956 (M)

League Club	Source	Date Signed	Seasons Played	Apps	Subs	Gls
Darlington	Boldon Colly	11.79	79-81	99	4	19

HAMILTON, James
Uddingston, 14 June, 1955 (M)

League Club	Source	Date Signed	Seasons Played	Apps	Subs	Gls
Sunderland	App	06.72	71-73	8	8	2
Plymouth Arg.	Tr	11.75	76	6	2	0
Bristol Rov.	Tr	12.76	76-77	16	4	1
Carlisle U.	Tr	09.77	77-81	150	4	12
Hartlepool U.	Gretna	11.82	82	2	1	0

HAMILTON, John
Larkhall, 22 January, 1935 Su23-2/SF Lge (W)

League Club	Source	Date Signed	Seasons Played	Apps	Subs	Gls
Watford	Hearts	05.67	67	7	1	2

HAMILTON, John T.
Glasgow, 10 July, 1949 (F)

League Club	Source	Date Signed	Seasons Played	Apps	Subs	Gls
Millwall	Glasgow Rangers	06.78	78	1	1	0

HAMILTON, Neville R.
Leicester, 19 April, 1960 (M)

League Club	Source	Date Signed	Seasons Played	Apps	Subs	Gls
Leicester C.	App	11.77	77	4	0	0
Mansfield T.	Tr	01.79	78-80	84	5	4
Rochdale	Tr	08.81	81-83	72	2	5

HAMILTON, Robert M.
Edinburgh, 25 April, 1924 (W)

League Club	Source	Date Signed	Seasons Played	Apps	Subs	Gls
Chester C.	Hearts	11.45	46-47	69	-	10

HAMILTON, William
Hamilton, 1 September, 1918 (WH)

League Club	Source	Date Signed	Seasons Played	Apps	Subs	Gls
Preston N.E.	Blantyre Celtic	09.37	46	37	-	0

HAMILTON, William M.
Airdrie, 16 February, 1938 Died 1976 SF Lge/S-1 (IF)

League Club	Source	Date Signed	Seasons Played	Apps	Subs	Gls
Sheffield U.	Drumpelier	02.56	56-60	79	-	21
Middlesbrough	Tr	02.61	60-61	10	-	1
Aston Villa	Hibernian	08.65	65-66	49	0	9

HAMILTON, William R.
Belfast, 9 May, 1957 NIu21-1/NI-41 (F)

League Club	Source	Date Signed	Seasons Played	Apps	Subs	Gls
Queens Park R.	Linfield	04.78	78-79	9	3	2
Burnley	Tr	11.79	79-83	200	0	58
Oxford U.	Tr	08.84	84-86	32	0	12

HAMLETT, Thomas L.
Stoke, 24 January, 1917 (FB)

League Club	Source	Date Signed	Seasons Played	Apps	Subs	Gls
Bolton W.	Congleton T.	05.38	46-48	72	-	9
Port Vale	Tr	05.49	49-51	109	-	0

HAMMILL, John
Irvine, 8 January, 1924 (RH)

League Club	Source	Date Signed	Seasons Played	Apps	Subs	Gls
Newport Co.	Arbroath	04.47	46-47	12	-	0

HAMMOND, Albert W. A.
Hanwell, 5 February, 1924 (IF)

League Club	Source	Date Signed	Seasons Played	Apps	Subs	Gls
Brentford	Queens Park R. (Am)	01.46				
Exeter C.	Tr	06.46	46	2	-	0

HAMMOND, Cyril S.
Woolwich, 10 October, 1927 (WH)

League Club	Source	Date Signed	Seasons Played	Apps	Subs	Gls
Charlton Ath.	Erith & Belvedere	04.46	50-57	201	-	2
Colchester U.	Tr	07.58	58-60	95	-	5

HAMMOND, Geoffrey
Sudbury, 24 March, 1950 (FB)

League Club	Source	Date Signed	Seasons Played	Apps	Subs	Gls
Ipswich T.	Jnrs	07.68	70-73	52	3	2
Manchester C.	Tr	09.74	74-75	33	1	2
Charlton Ath.	Tr	07.76	76	15	1	0

HAMMOND, Nicholas D.
Hornchurch, 7 September, 1967 (G)

League Club	Source	Date Signed	Seasons Played	Apps	Subs	Gls
Arsenal	App	09.85				
Bristol Rov.	L	08.86	86	3	0	0
Swindon T.	Tr	06.87	87-91	34	0	0

HAMMOND, Paul A.
Nottingham, 26 July, 1953 (G)

League Club	Source	Date Signed	Seasons Played	Apps	Subs	Gls
Crystal Palace	App	07.71	72-76	117	0	0

HAMPSHIRE, Paul
Guildford, 10 October, 1961 (F)

League Club	Source	Date Signed	Seasons Played	Apps	Subs	Gls
Aldershot	Jnrs	06.79	80-81	4	1	2

HAMPSON, Alan
Prescot, 31 December, 1927 (IF)

League Club	Source	Date Signed	Seasons Played	Apps	Subs	Gls
Everton		08.49	50	1	-	0
Halifax T.	Tr	11.52	52-55	121	-	32
Bradford C.	Tr	07.56	56	6	-	4

HAMPSON, Eric
Norton, 11 November, 1921 (HB)

League Club	Source	Date Signed	Seasons Played	Apps	Subs	Gls
Stoke C.	Stafford R.	05.39	48-51	8	-	0

HAMPSON, Raymond G.
Manchester, 27 July, 1932 (F)

League Club	Source	Date Signed	Seasons Played	Apps	Subs	Gls
Manchester U.	Jnrs	04.51				
Reading	Tr	04.53				
Aldershot	Tr	07.55	55-56	20	-	2
Bournemouth	Tr	07.57	57-58	15	-	2

HAMPTON, Derek
Saltburn, 25 April, 1952 (W)

League Club	Source	Date Signed	Seasons Played	Apps	Subs	Gls
Hartlepool U.	Whitby T.	11.79	79-81	66	8	18

HAMPTON, Ivan K.
Kimberley, 15 October, 1942 (FB)

League Club	Source	Date Signed	Seasons Played	Apps	Subs	Gls
Notts Co.	Rotherham U. (Am)	03.61	60-66	139	2	1
Halifax T.	Tr	07.67	67-68	57	2	1
Peterborough U.	Tr	07.69	69	3	1	0

HAMPTON, Peter J.
Oldham, 12 September, 1954 E Yth (LB)

League Club	Source	Date Signed	Seasons Played	Apps	Subs	Gls
Leeds U.	App	09.71	72-79	63	5	2
Stoke C.	Tr	08.80	80-83	134	4	4
Burnley	Tr	08.84	84-86	116	2	2
Rochdale	Tr	08.87	87	19	0	1
Carlisle U.	Tr	12.87	87	12	0	0

HAMSON, Gary
Nottingham, 24 August, 1959 (LW)

League Club	Source	Date Signed	Seasons Played	Apps	Subs	Gls
Sheffield U.	App	11.76	76-78	107	1	8
Leeds U.	Tr	07.79	79-85	126	8	3
Bristol C.	Tr	07.86	86	12	0	2
Port Vale	Tr	12.86	86-87	36	2	3

HAMSTEAD, George W.
Rotherham, 24 January, 1946 (W)

League Club	Source	Date Signed	Seasons Played	Apps	Subs	Gls
York C.	Rotherham U. (Am)	09.64	64-65	32	3	1
Barnsley	Tr	07.66	66-70	147	2	23
Bury	Tr	07.71	71-78	189	7	29
Rochdale	L	01.77	76	3	1	0

HANCOCK, Anthony E.
Manchester, 31 January, 1967 (F)

League Club	Source	Date Signed	Seasons Played	Apps	Subs	Gls
Stockport Co.	Stockport Georgians	12.88	88	12	10	5
Burnley	Tr	06.89	89	9	8	0
Preston N.E.	Tr	01.90				

HANCOCK, Barry J.
Stoke, 30 December, 1938 (IF)

League Club	Source	Date Signed	Seasons Played	Apps	Subs	Gls
Port Vale		07.57	60-63	21	-	1
Crewe Alex.	Tr	08.64	64	3	-	0

HANCOCK, Charles
Stoke, 16 February, 1925 (G)

League Club	Source	Date Signed	Seasons Played	Apps	Subs	Gls
Port Vale		05.48	48-55	50	-	0

HANCOCK, David J.
Exeter, 24 July, 1938 (WH)

League Club	Source	Date Signed	Seasons Played	Apps	Subs	Gls
Plymouth Arg.	Jnrs	09.55	56	2	-	0
Torquay U.	Tr	01.59	58-63	177	-	12
Exeter C.	Tr	03.64	63-64	40	-	3

HANCOCK, Kenneth P.
Hanley, 25 November, 1937 (G)

League Club	Source	Date Signed	Seasons Played	Apps	Subs	Gls
Port Vale	Stoke C. (Am)	12.58	58-64	240	-	0
Ipswich T.	Tr	12.64	64-68	183	0	0
Tottenham H.	Tr	03.69	69-70	3	0	0
Bury	Tr	07.71	71-72	35	0	0

HANCOCK, Michael
Newport, 17 February, 1954 W Sch (CD)

League Club	Source	Date Signed	Seasons Played	Apps	Subs	Gls
Newport Co.	Jnrs	08.73	71-75	51	9	2

HANCOCKS, John
Oakengates, 30 April, 1919 EF Lge/E-3 (OR)

League Club	Source	Date Signed	Seasons Played	Apps	Subs	Gls
Walsall	Oakengates T.	08.38	38	30	-	8
Wolverhampton W.	Tr	05.46	46-55	343	-	158

HANCOX, David T.
Conisborough, 2 October, 1947 (CF)

League Club	Source	Date Signed	Seasons Played	Apps	Subs	Gls
Sheffield U.	App	09.65				
Chester C.	Tr	07.67	67	17	2	4

HANCOX, Paul A.
Manchester, 22 July, 1970

League Club	Source	Date Signed	Seasons Played	Apps	Subs	Gls
Rochdale (YT)	YT	12.87	87	0	2	0

HANCOX, Raymond
Mansfield, 1 May, 1929 (F)

League Club	Source	Date Signed	Seasons Played	Apps	Subs	Gls
Crystal Palace	Sutton U.	08.50	50-52	20	-	3
Southend U.	Tr	06.53				

HAND, Eoin K.
Dublin, 30 March, 1946 IR-19 (CD)

League Club	Source	Date Signed	Seasons Played	Apps	Subs	Gls
Swindon T.	Drumcondra	06.64				
Portsmouth	Drumcondra	10.68	68-75	259	1	12
Portsmouth	South Africa	12.77	77-78	15	2	2

HANDFORD, Philip M.
Sittingbourne, 18 July, 1964 (M)

League Club	Source	Date Signed	Seasons Played	Apps	Subs	Gls
Gillingham	App	07.82	82-83	29	3	1
Wimbledon	Tr	08.84	84	7	0	0
Crewe Alex.	L	01.86	85	9	0	0

HANDLEY, Brian
Wakefield, 21 June, 1936 Died 1982 (CF)

League Club	Source	Date Signed	Seasons Played	Apps	Subs	Gls
Aston Villa	Goole T.	09.57	59	3	-	0
Torquay U.	Tr	09.60	60-63	80	-	33
Rochdale	Bridgwater T.	02.66	65	3	0	0

HANDSCOMBE, Malcolm
Normanton, 29 June, 1934 (CH)

League Club	Source	Date Signed	Seasons Played	Apps	Subs	Gls
Chester C. (Am)		05.57	57	4	-	0

HANDYSIDES, Ian R.
Jarrow, 14 December, 1962 Died 1990 E Yth (W)

League Club	Source	Date Signed	Seasons Played	Apps	Subs	Gls
Birmingham C.	App	01.80	80-83	44	18	2
Walsall	Tr	01.84	83-85	58	8	11
Birmingham C.	Tr	03.86	85-87	53	3	4
Wolverhampton W.	L	09.86	86	11	0	2

HANFORD, Harold
Blaengwynfi, 9 October, 1907 W Sch/W-7 (CH)

League Club	Source	Date Signed	Seasons Played	Apps	Subs	Gls
Swansea C.	Ton Pentre	05.26	27-35	200	-	0
Sheffield Wed.	Tr	02.36	35-38	85	-	1
Exeter C.	Tr	05.46	46	36	-	0

HANKEY, Albert A.
Stoke, 24 May, 1914 (G)

League Club	Source	Date Signed	Seasons Played	Apps	Subs	Gls
Southend U.	Charlton Ath. (Am)	10.37	37-49	125	-	0

HANKIN, Raymond
Wallsend, 2 February, 1956 E Yth/Eu23-3 (F)

League Club	Source	Date Signed	Seasons Played	Apps	Subs	Gls
Burnley	App	02.73	72-76	110	2	37
Leeds U.	Tr	09.76	76-79	82	1	32
Middlesbrough	Vancouver (Can)	09.82	82	19	2	1
Peterborough U.	Tr	09.83	83-84	31	2	8
Wolverhampton W.	Tr	03.85	84	9	1	1

HANKINSON, James
Preston, 1 July, 1928 (F)

League Club	Source	Date Signed	Seasons Played	Apps	Subs	Gls
Preston N.E.		09.47				
Chester C.	Tr	06.50	50	15	-	1

HANLON, John J.
Manchester, 12 October, 1917 (CF)

League Club	Source	Date Signed	Seasons Played	Apps	Subs	Gls
Manchester U.	St Wilfreds	11.35	38-48	63	-	20
Bury	Tr	10.48	48-49	31	-	1

HANLON, Stephen H.
Chester, 18 July, 1963 (M)

League Club	Source	Date Signed	Seasons Played	Apps	Subs	Gls
Crewe Alex.	App	07.81	80-82	23	4	0

HANLON, Walter
Glasgow, 23 September, 1919 (OL)

League Club	Source	Date Signed	Seasons Played	Apps	Subs	Gls
Brighton & H.A.	Clyde	08.46	46-47	72	-	4
Bournemouth	Tr	05.48	48	19	-	3
Crystal Palace	Tr	07.49	49-54	126	-	8

HANN, Ralph
Whitburn, 4 July, 1911 (CH)

League Club	Source	Date Signed	Seasons Played	Apps	Subs	Gls
Derby Co.	Newcastle Swifts	03.32	32-38	115	-	0
Crystal Palace	Tr	04.47	46	1	-	0

HANNABY, Cyril
Doncaster, 11 October, 1923 (G)

League Club	Source	Date Signed	Seasons Played	Apps	Subs	Gls
Wolverhampton W.	Wath W.	03.44				
Hull C.	Tr	08.46	46-47	17	-	0
Halifax T.	Tr	02.48	47	2	-	0

HANNAH, George
Liverpool, 11 December, 1928 NI F Lge (IF)

League Club	Source	Date Signed	Seasons Played	Apps	Subs	Gls
Newcastle U.	Linfield	09.49	49-56	167	-	41
Lincoln C.	Tr	09.57	57-58	38	-	4
Manchester C.	Tr	09.58	58-63	114	-	15
Notts Co.	Tr	07.64	64-65	25	0	1
Bradford C.	Tr	10.65	65	29	1	2

HANNAH, John A.
Wakefield, 25 October, 1962 (F)

League Club	Source	Date Signed	Seasons Played	Apps	Subs	Gls
Darlington (N/C)	Fryston Colly	10.83	83-84	15	7	7

HANNAH, William K.
Shotts, 6 August, 1921 (IF)

League Club	Source	Date Signed	Seasons Played	Apps	Subs	Gls
Preston N.E.	Albion Rov.	12.47	47-49	15	-	4
Barrow	Tr	02.51	50-53	106	-	16

HANNAM, David V.
Islington, 10 May, 1944 (W)

League Club	Source	Date Signed	Seasons Played	Apps	Subs	Gls
Brighton & H.A.	Jnrs	06.61	62	5	-	2

HANNAWAY, John (Jack)
Bootle, 22 October, 1927 (WH)

League Club	Source	Date Signed	Seasons Played	Apps	Subs	Gls
Manchester C.	Seaforth Fellows	04.50	51-56	64	-	0
Gillingham	Tr	06.57	57-59	126	-	4
Southport	Tr	06.60	60-61	73	-	2

HANNIGAN, Brendan
Dublin, 3 September, 1943 (F)

League Club	Source	Date Signed	Seasons Played	Apps	Subs	Gls
Wrexham	Shelbourne	12.65	65	7	0	2

HANNIGAN, Ernest
Glasgow, 23 January, 1943 (W)

League Club	Source	Date Signed	Seasons Played	Apps	Subs	Gls
Preston N.E.	Queen of South	08.64	64-67	97	0	29
Coventry C.	Tr	11.67	67-69	43	4	6
Torquay U.	L	12.69	69	2	0	0

HANNIGAN, A. James
Islington, 26 January, 1971 (CD)

League Club	Source	Date Signed	Seasons Played	Apps	Subs	Gls
Arsenal	YT	03.89				
Torquay U.	L	03.90	89	5	2	0

HANNIGAN, John L.
Glasgow, 17 February, 1933 (W)

League Club	Source	Date Signed	Seasons Played	Apps	Subs	Gls
Sunderland	Morton	07.55	55-57	33	-	8
Derby Co.	Tr	05.58	58-60	72	-	19
Bradford P.A.	Tr	06.61	61-63	96	-	26

HANSBURY, Roger
Barnsley, 26 January, 1955 (G)

League Club	Source	Date Signed	Seasons Played	Apps	Subs	Gls
Norwich C.	App	01.73	74-80	78	0	0
Cambridge U.	L	11.77	77	11	0	0
Burnley	Hong Kong	08.83	83-84	83	0	0
Cambridge U.	Tr	07.85	85	37	0	0
Birmingham C.	Tr	03.86	86-89	57	0	0
Sheffield U.	L	10.87	87	5	0	0
Wolverhampton W.	L	03.89	88	3	0	0
Colchester U.	L	08.89	89	4	0	0
Cardiff C.	Tr	10.89	89-91	99	0	0

HANSELL, Ronald A.R.
Norwich, 3 October, 1930 (IF)

League Club	Source	Date Signed	Seasons Played	Apps	Subs	Gls
Norwich C.	Norwich St B.	06.50	53-55	29	-	7
Chester C.	Tr	06.56	56	38	-	9

HANSEN, Allan D.
Alloa, 13 June, 1955 Su23-3/S-26 (CD)

League Club	Source	Date Signed	Seasons Played	Apps	Subs	Gls
Liverpool	Partick Th.	04.77	77-89	434	0	8

Allan Hansen (Partick Thistle, Liverpool & Scotland)

HANSEN, Edwin
Denmark, 21 January, 1920 (IF)

League Club	Source	Date Signed	Seasons Played	Apps	Subs	Gls
Grimsby T. (Am)	Denmark	12.46	46	1	-	0

HANSEN, Karl A.
Denmark, 4 July, 1921 Died 1990 (IF)

League Club	Source	Date Signed	Seasons Played	Apps	Subs	Gls
Huddersfield T. (Am)	Denmark	01.49	48	15	-	2

HANSON, Frederick
Sheffield, 23 May, 1915 Died 1967 (OL)

League Club	Source	Date Signed	Seasons Played	Apps	Subs	Gls
Crystal Palace	Indus Sports	05.35	34	1	-	0
Rotherham U.	Tr	03.36	35-46	106	-	28

HANSON, John
Bradford, 3 December, 1962 (F)

League Club	Source	Date Signed	Seasons Played	Apps	Subs	Gls
Bradford C.	App	12.80	80	1	0	0

HANSON, Neil
Blackburn, 16 June, 1964 (F)

League Club	Source	Date Signed	Seasons Played	Apps	Subs	Gls
Preston N.E.	App	09.81				
Halifax T.	Tr	08.83	83	1	1	0

HANSON, Stanley
Bootle, 27 December, 1915 (G)

League Club	Source	Date Signed	Seasons Played	Apps	Subs	Gls
Bolton W.	Southport (Am)	10.35	36-55	384	-	0

HANVEY, Keith
Manchester, 18 January, 1952 (CD)

League Club	Source	Date Signed	Seasons Played	Apps	Subs	Gls
Manchester	Jnrs	08.71				
Swansea C.	Tr	07.72	72	11	0	0
Rochdale	Tr	07.73	73-76	121	0	10
Grimsby T.	Tr	02.77	76-77	54	0	2
Huddersfield T.	Tr	07.78	78-83	205	0	14
Rochdale	Tr	07.84	84	15	0	0

League Club	Source	Date Signed	Seasons Played	Apps	Subs	Gls
HAPGOOD, Anthony						
Kettering, 13 June, 1930						(F)
Burnley		03.48	51	7	-	2
Watford	Tr	07.53	53	1	-	0
HARBACH, Peter C.						
Carlisle, 30 April, 1967						(F)
Newcastle U.	App	04.85				
Carlisle U.	Tr	08.87	87	0	7	0
HARBER, William H.						
Hitchin, 3 December, 1944						(W)
Swindon T.	App	12.61	62	2	-	0
Luton T.	Tr	09.64	64-65	28	0	2
HARBERTSON, Ronald						
Redcar, 23 December, 1929						(IF)
Newcastle U.	North Shields	01.49				
Bradford C.	Tr	08.50	50	16	-	1
Brighton & H.A.	Tr	10.51				
Bradford C.	Tr	05.52	53	13	-	3
Grimsby T.	Tr	07.54	54	26	-	6
Darlington	Ashington	01.57	56-57	49	-	21
Lincoln C.	Tr	03.58	57-59	57	-	22
Wrexham	Tr	03.60	59-60	28	-	13
Darlington	Tr	01.61	60	14	-	2
Lincoln C.	Tr	07.61	61	29	-	3
HARBEY, Graham K.						
Chesterfield, 29 August, 1964						(LB)
Derby Co.	App	08.82	83-86	35	5	1
Ipswich T.	Tr	07.87	87-89	53	6	1
West Bromwich A.	Tr	11.89	89-91	97	0	2
HARBOTTLE, Mark S.						
Nottingham, 26 September, 1968 E Yth						(M)
Notts Co.	App	09.86	85	1	3	1
Doncaster Rov.	L	01.88	87	4	0	0
HARBURN, Peter A.						
Shoreditch, 18 June, 1931						(CF)
Brighton & H.A.	Portsmouth (Am)	02.56	54-57	126	-	64
Everton	Tr	08.58	58	4	-	1
Scunthorpe U.	Tr	01.59	58-59	20	-	8
Workington	Tr	10.59	59-60	67	-	23
HARBURN, Walter N.						
Stockton, 19 November, 1923						(CF)
Darlington (Am)		06.47	47	1	-	0

League Club	Source	Date Signed	Seasons Played	Apps	Subs	Gls
HARBY, Michael J.						
Nottingham, 7 November, 1948						(G)
Nottingham F.	Jnrs	07.66	67	3	0	0
HARDCASTLE, Cyril						
Halifax, 22 November, 1919						(CF)
Bradford C. (Am)		09.48	48	4	-	1
HARDCASTLE, Peter D.						
Leeds, 27 January, 1949 E Amat						(FB)
Blackpool	Skelmersdale U.	07.71	71-73	29	7	0
Plymouth Arg.	Tr	07.74	74-75	12	2	1
Bradford C.	Tr	07.76	76-77	62	0	1
HARDEN, Leslie J.						
Hartlepool, 7 May, 1923						(OL)
Hartlepool U.		05.46	46-55	170	-	47
HARDIE, John C.						
Edinburgh, 7 February, 1938						(G)
Oldham Ath.	Falkirk	07.60	60	17	-	0
Chester C.	Tr	07.61	61-62	82	-	0
Bradford P.A.	Tr	12.63	63-69	265	0	0
Crystal Palace	Tr	08.70				
HARDING, Alan						
Sunderland, 14 May, 1948						(W)
Darlington	Spennymoor U.	01.70	69-72	125	4	38
Lincoln C.	Tr	03.73	72-78	203	6	38
Hartlepool U.	Tr	03.79	78-82	79	5	8
HARDING, David						
Liverpool, 14 August, 1946						(W)
Wrexham		09.65	65	9	1	0
HARDING, Edward						
Croydon, 5 April, 1925						(FB)
Crystal Palace	Coalville	11.44	46-52	151	-	0
HARDING, Kevin R. C.						
Isleworth, 19 March, 1957						(FB)
Brentford (App)	App	07.72	73-74	8	0	0
HARDING, Paul J.						
Mitcham, 6 March, 1964						(M)
Notts Co.	Barnet	09.90	90-91	45	8	1

Paul Harding (Notts County)

HARDING, Stephen J.
Bristol, 23 July, 1956 (CD)

League Club	Source	Date Signed	Seasons Played	Apps	Subs	Gls
Bristol C.	App	07.74	75	2	0	0
Southend U.	L	01.76	75	2	0	0
Grimsby T.	L	09.76	76	8	0	0
Bristol Rov.	Tr	06.77	77-79	37	1	1
Brentford	L	01.80	79	3	1	0

HARDISTY, J. Robert E.
Chester-le-Street, 1 February, 1921 Died 1986 E Amat (WH)

League Club	Source	Date Signed	Seasons Played	Apps	Subs	Gls
Darlington (Am)	Bishop Auckland	12.46	46-48	6	-	0

HARDMAN, Colin A.
Altrincham, 13 November, 1955 (W)

League Club	Source	Date Signed	Seasons Played	Apps	Subs	Gls
Stockport Co.		03.76	75-76	6	3	1

HARDMAN, John A.
Bury, 17 December, 1940 (HB)

League Club	Source	Date Signed	Seasons Played	Apps	Subs	Gls
Rochdale	Bess's Boys	08.60	60-66	40	0	2

HARDS, Neil A.
Portsmouth, 28 January, 1962 (G)

League Club	Source	Date Signed	Seasons Played	Apps	Subs	Gls
Plymouth Arg.	App	01.80	79-82	6	0	0

HARDSTAFF, Cecil
Crewe, 14 November, 1931

League Club	Source	Date Signed	Seasons Played	Apps	Subs	Gls
Crewe Alex.	Wolverhampton W. (Am)	06.49	49	1	-	0

HARDWICK, George F. M.
Saltburn, 2 February, 1920 EF Lge/E-13 (FB)

League Club	Source	Date Signed	Seasons Played	Apps	Subs	Gls
Middlesbrough	South Bank	04.37	37-50	143	-	5
Oldham Ath.	Tr	11.50	50-55	190	-	14

HARDWICK, Kenneth
West Auckland, 6 January, 1924 (G)

League Club	Source	Date Signed	Seasons Played	Apps	Subs	Gls
Doncaster Rov.	Rossington Colly	04.45	47-56	308	-	0
Scunthorpe U.	Tr	04.57	56-59	96	-	0
Barrow	Tr	12.59	59	12	-	0

HARDWICK, Steven
Mansfield, 6 September, 1956 E Yth (G)

League Club	Source	Date Signed	Seasons Played	Apps	Subs	Gls
Chesterfield	Jnrs	07.74	74-76	38	0	0
Newcastle U.	Tr	12.76	77-82	92	0	0
Oxford U.	Tr	02.83	82-87	156	0	0
Crystal Palace	L	03.86	85	3	0	0
Sunderland	L	08.87	87	6	0	0
Huddersfield T.	Tr	07.88	88-90	109	0	0

HARDY, Edwin M.
Chesterfield, 16 October, 1953 (G)

League Club	Source	Date Signed	Seasons Played	Apps	Subs	Gls
Chesterfield	Jnrs	08.71	72	6	0	0

HARDY, Gordon D. (Bob)
Kingston, 23 May, 1923 (CH)

League Club	Source	Date Signed	Seasons Played	Apps	Subs	Gls
Millwall	Charlton Rov.	08.45	46	3	-	0
Southport	Tr	07.48	48-49	16	-	0
Bournemouth	Tr	06.50	51-53	76	-	0

HARDY, Herbert
Barrow, 6 December, 1929 (IF)

League Club	Source	Date Signed	Seasons Played	Apps	Subs	Gls
Barrow		05.52	51	2	-	1

HARDY, Jason P.
Manchester, 14 December, 1969 (FB)

League Club	Source	Date Signed	Seasons Played	Apps	Subs	Gls
Burnley	YT	07.88	86-91	38	5	1
Halifax T.	L	01.92	91	0	4	0

HARDY, John H.
Chesterfield, 15 June, 1910 Died 1978 (CH)

League Club	Source	Date Signed	Seasons Played	Apps	Subs	Gls
Chesterfield	Unstone	12.34	34-36	48	-	1
Hull C.	Tr	07.37	37-38	65	-	0
Lincoln C.	Tr	05.39	46	18	-	0

HARDY, Philip
Ellesmere Port, 9 April, 1973 (LB)

League Club	Source	Date Signed	Seasons Played	Apps	Subs	Gls
Wrexham	YT	11.90	89-91	75	0	0

HARDY, Robin
Worksop, 18 January, 1941 (WH)

League Club	Source	Date Signed	Seasons Played	Apps	Subs	Gls
Sheffield Wed.	Jnrs	02.58	61-63	30	-	1
Rotherham U.	Tr	02.65	64-65	41	0	2
Cambridge U.		(N/L)	70	15	1	0

HARDY, William
Whitehaven, 23 August, 1929 (HB)

League Club	Source	Date Signed	Seasons Played	Apps	Subs	Gls
Workington	Queen of South	10.51	51-53	55	-	2

HARDYMAN, Paul G.
Portsmouth, 11 March, 1964 Eu21-2 (LB)

League Club	Source	Date Signed	Seasons Played	Apps	Subs	Gls
Portsmouth	Waterlooville	07.83	83-88	113	4	3
Sunderland	Tr	07.89	89-91	101	5	9

HARE, Thomas
Motherwell, 1 April, 1944 (FB)

League Club	Source	Date Signed	Seasons Played	Apps	Subs	Gls
Southampton	Fauldhouse U.	04.63	65	13	0	0
Luton T.	Tr	07.67	67	12	0	0

HAREIDE, Age F.
Norway, 23 September, 1953 Norway Int (D)

League Club	Source	Date Signed	Seasons Played	Apps	Subs	Gls
Manchester C.	Molde F.K. (Nor)	10.81	81-82	17	7	0
Norwich C.	Tr	11.82	82-83	38	2	1

HARFIELD, Leslie P.
Southampton, 22 November, 1952 E Sch/E Yth (W)

League Club	Source	Date Signed	Seasons Played	Apps	Subs	Gls
Southampton	App	11.69	70	2	0	1
Luton T.	Tr	09.72	72	0	1	0

HARFORD, Michael G.
Sunderland, 12 February, 1959 E'B'/E-2 (F)

League Club	Source	Date Signed	Seasons Played	Apps	Subs	Gls
Lincoln C.	Lambton Street B.C.	07.77	77-80	109	6	41
Newcastle U.	Tr	12.80	80	18	1	4
Bristol C.	Tr	08.81	81	30	0	11
Birmingham C.	Tr	03.82	81-84	92	0	25
Luton T.	Tr	12.84	84-89	135	4	57
Derby Co.	Tr	01.90	89-91	58	0	15
Luton T.	Tr	09.91	91	29	0	12

Mick Harford (Lincoln City, Newcastle United, Bristol City, Birmingham City, Luton Town, Derby County, Luton Town & England)

HARFORD, Raymond T.
Halifax, 1 June, 1945 (CD)

League Club	Source	Date Signed	Seasons Played	Apps	Subs	Gls
Charlton Ath.	Jnrs	05.64	65	3	0	0
Exeter C.	Tr	01.66	65-66	55	0	1
Lincoln C.	Tr	07.67	67-70	161	0	10
Mansfield T.	Tr	06.71	71	7	0	0
Port Vale	Tr	12.71	71-72	20	0	1
Colchester U.	Tr	01.73	72-74	107	1	4

HARGREAVES, Alan
Dewsbury, 29 March, 1931 (CF)

League Club	Source	Date Signed	Seasons Played	Apps	Subs	Gls
Bradford C.		07.54	54-55	4	-	1

HARGREAVES, Christian
Cleethorpes, 12 May, 1972 (F)

League Club	Source	Date Signed	Seasons Played	Apps	Subs	Gls
Grimsby T.	YT	12.89	89-91	15	32	5

HARGREAVES, David
Accrington, 27 August, 1954 (F)

League Club	Source	Date Signed	Seasons Played	Apps	Subs	Gls
Blackburn Rov.	Accrington St.	12.77	77	2	0	0

HARGREAVES, John
Rotherham, 1 May, 1915 Died 1978 (OL)

League Club	Source	Date Signed	Seasons Played	Apps	Subs	Gls
Leeds U.		08.34	35-38	45	-	10
Bristol C.	Tr	08.45	46	26	-	9
Reading	Tr	04.47	46-47	15	-	1

HARGREAVES, Joseph
Accrington, 30 October, 1915 (CF)

League Club	Source	Date Signed	Seasons Played	Apps	Subs	Gls
Rochdale	Rossendale U.	10.45	46-47	35	-	24

HARGREAVES, Thomas
Blackburn, 29 October, 1917 (CF)

League Club	Source	Date Signed	Seasons Played	Apps	Subs	Gls
Blackburn Rov.		10.36	37	4	-	2
Rochdale	Tr	05.46	46	7	-	0

HARGREAVES, Wilfred O.
Rawmarsh, 15 December, 1921 (RH)

League Club	Source	Date Signed	Seasons Played	Apps	Subs	Gls
Rotherham U.	Rawmarsh Welfare	03.45	46-47	3	-	0

HARKER, Christopher J.
Shiremoor, 29 June, 1937 (G)

League Club	Source	Date Signed	Seasons Played	Apps	Subs	Gls
Newcastle U.	Jnrs	03.55	57	1	-	0
Bury	Aberdeen	12.61	61-66	178	0	0
Grimsby T.	Tr	06.67	67	10	0	0
Rochdale	Tr	07.68	68-69	92	0	0

John Harkes (Sheffield Wednesday & USA)

HARKES, John A.
New Jersey (USA), 8 March, 1967 USA Int (RB/M)

League Club	Source	Date Signed	Seasons Played	Apps	Subs	Gls
Sheffield Wed.	North Carolina (USA)	10.90	90-91	36	16	5

HARKIN, James
Brinsworth, 8 August, 1913 (IF)

League Club	Source	Date Signed	Seasons Played	Apps	Subs	Gls
Doncaster Rov.	Rossington Main Colly	08.34	34	1	-	0
Mansfield T.	Shrewsbury T.	02.39	38-46	23	-	5

HARKIN, Terence
Derry (NI), 14 September, 1941 NIu23-1/NI-5 (CF)

League Club	Source	Date Signed	Seasons Played	Apps	Subs	Gls
Port Vale	Coleraine	09.62	62-63	27	-	11
Crewe Alex.	Tr	06.64	64	42	-	34
Cardiff C.	Tr	08.65	65	19	2	10
Notts Co.	Tr	09.66	66	27	1	10
Southport	Tr	07.67	67-68	63	1	31
Shrewsbury T.	Tr	03.69	68-70	79	0	30

HARKNESS, James
Edinburgh, 19 May, 1940 (G)

League Club	Source	Date Signed	Seasons Played	Apps	Subs	Gls
Carlisle U.	Hamilton Acad.	08.61	61-62	17	-	0

HARKNESS, W. James
Glasgow, 21 July, 1918 (IF)

League Club	Source	Date Signed	Seasons Played	Apps	Subs	Gls
Carlisle U.		10.47				
Workington		(N/L)	51	7	-	1

HARKNESS, Steven
Carlisle, 27 August, 1971 E Yth (LB/W)

League Club	Source	Date Signed	Seasons Played	Apps	Subs	Gls
Carlisle U.	YT	03.89	88	12	1	0
Liverpool	Tr	07.89	91	7	4	0

HARKOUK, Rachid P.
Chelsea, 19 May, 1956 Algerian Int (F)

League Club	Source	Date Signed	Seasons Played	Apps	Subs	Gls
Crystal Palace	Feltham	06.76	76-77	51	3	21
Queens Park R.	Tr	06.78	78-79	15	5	3
Notts Co.	Tr	06.80	80-85	124	20	39

HARLAND, Stanley
Liverpool, 19 June, 1940 (WH)

League Club	Source	Date Signed	Seasons Played	Apps	Subs	Gls
Everton	New Brighton	12.59				
Bradford C.	Tr	07.61	61-63	120	-	20
Carlisle U.	Tr	06.64	64-65	77	0	7
Swindon T.	Tr	08.66	66-71	237	0	6
Birmingham C.	Tr	12.71	71-72	37	1	0

HARLE, David
Denaby, 15 August, 1963 E Yth (M)

League Club	Source	Date Signed	Seasons Played	Apps	Subs	Gls
Doncaster Rov.	App	11.80	79-81	48	13	3
Exeter C.	Tr	07.82	82-83	42	1	6
Doncaster Rov.	Tr	09.83	83-85	80	3	17
Leeds U.	Tr	12.85	85	3	0	0
Bristol C.	Tr	03.86	85-86	23	0	2
Scunthorpe U.	Tr	11.86	86-88	88	1	10
Peterborough U.	Tr	03.89	88-89	21	1	2
Doncaster Rov.	Tr	03.90	89-91	39	6	3

HARLE, Michael J. L.
Lewisham, 31 October, 1972 (LB/M)

League Club	Source	Date Signed	Seasons Played	Apps	Subs	Gls
Gillingham (YT)	YT	07.89	90	1	1	0

HARLEY, Albert G.
Chester, 17 April, 1940 (WH)

League Club	Source	Date Signed	Seasons Played	Apps	Subs	Gls
Shrewsbury T.	Jnrs	04.57	56-64	219	-	14
Swansea C.	Tr	09.64	64-65	25	1	0
Crewe Alex.	Guildford C.	07.66	66	22	0	4
Stockport Co.	Tr	02.67	66-68	78	3	11
Chester C.	Tr	06.69	69	3	0	1

HARLEY, Alexander
Glasgow, 20 April, 1936 Died 1969 (CF)

League Club	Source	Date Signed	Seasons Played	Apps	Subs	Gls
Manchester C.	Third Lanark	08.62	62	40	-	23
Birmingham C.	Tr	08.63	63-64	28	-	9

HARLEY, James
Methil, 21 February, 1917 (FB)

League Club	Source	Date Signed	Seasons Played	Apps	Subs	Gls
Liverpool	Hill of Beath	04.34	35-47	114	-	0

HARLEY, John R.
March, 22 April, 1949 (M)

League Club	Source	Date Signed	Seasons Played	Apps	Subs	Gls
Reading	Stevenage T.	09.69	69-72	64	10	6
Aldershot	Tr	07.73	73-74	16	12	0
Hartlepool U. (N/C)	Workingham T.	09.76	76	4	0	1

HARLEY, Lee
Crewe, 7 July, 1967 (F)

League Club	Source	Date Signed	Seasons Played	Apps	Subs	Gls
Chester C. (YT)	YT	12.84	85	0	1	0

HARLEY, Leslie A.
Chester, 26 September, 1946 (OR)

League Club	Source	Date Signed	Seasons Played	Apps	Subs	Gls
Chester C.	Jnrs	09.64	64-66	22	2	3
Blackpool	Tr	07.67				
Rochdale	L	02.68	67	5	0	0

HARLOCK, Desmond S.
Blaenau Ffestiniog, 20 December, 1922 Died 1981 (OR)

League Club	Source	Date Signed	Seasons Played	Apps	Subs	Gls
Tranmere Rov.		03.42	46-53	151	-	17

League Club	Source	Date Signed	Seasons Played	Career Record Apps	Subs	Gls

HARMAN, Peter R.
Guildford, 11 October, 1950 (CF)

League Club	Source	Date Signed	Seasons Played	Apps	Subs	Gls
Bournemouth	App	08.68	69	1	0	0
Reading	Tr	08.71	71-72	34	2	9

HARMER, Thomas C.
Hackney, 2 February, 1928 E'B'-1 (IF)

League Club	Source	Date Signed	Seasons Played	Apps	Subs	Gls
Tottenham H.	Finchley	08.48	51-59	205	-	47
Watford	Tr	10.60	60-61	63	-	6
Chelsea	Tr	09.62	62-63	8	-	1

HARMON, Darren J.
Northampton, 30 January, 1973 (M)

League Club	Source	Date Signed	Seasons Played	Apps	Subs	Gls
Notts Co.	YT	07.91				
Shrewsbury T.	Tr	02.92	91	1	4	2

HARMSTON, Michael J.
Sheffield, 7 April, 1950 (FB)

League Club	Source	Date Signed	Seasons Played	Apps	Subs	Gls
Sheffield U.	App	05.67	68	5	0	0
Southend U.	L	12.70	70	1	0	0

HARMSWORTH, Lee A.
Southwark, 27 October, 1967 (G)

League Club	Source	Date Signed	Seasons Played	Apps	Subs	Gls
Charlton Ath.	App	10.85	84	3	0	0

HARNBY, Donald R.
Darlington, 20 July, 1923 (FB)

League Club	Source	Date Signed	Seasons Played	Apps	Subs	Gls
Newcastle U.	Spennymoor U.	05.45				
York C.	Tr	08.47	47	1	-	0
Grimsby T.	Spennymoor U.	09.49	49-51	34	-	0

HARNEY, David
Jarrow, 2 March, 1947 (CF)

League Club	Source	Date Signed	Seasons Played	Apps	Subs	Gls
Grimsby T.	Jnrs	11.64				
Scunthorpe U.	Tr	07.67	67-68	20	5	1
Brentford	Tr	10.69	69	0	1	0

HARNEY, Stephen G.
Bradford, 18 February, 1951 (RB)

League Club	Source	Date Signed	Seasons Played	Apps	Subs	Gls
Bradford C. (Am)	Drum Rov.	07.68	68-70	13	1	0

HAROLD, Michael L.
Stockport, 22 September, 1943 (FB)

League Club	Source	Date Signed	Seasons Played	Apps	Subs	Gls
Stockport Co.	Manchester C. (Am)	08.64	64	4	-	0

HARPER, Alan
Liverpool, 1 November, 1960 E Yth (D/M)

League Club	Source	Date Signed	Seasons Played	Apps	Subs	Gls
Liverpool	App	04.78				
Everton	Tr	06.83	83-87	103	24	4
Sheffield Wed.	Tr	07.88	88-89	32	3	0
Manchester C.	Tr	12.89	89-90	46	4	1
Everton	Tr	08.91	91	29	4	0

HARPER, Anthony F.
Oxford, 26 May, 1925 Died 1982 (WH)

League Club	Source	Date Signed	Seasons Played	Apps	Subs	Gls
Brentford	Headington U.	04.48	48-54	173	-	6

HARPER, Colin G.
Ipswich, 25 July, 1946 (LB)

League Club	Source	Date Signed	Seasons Played	Apps	Subs	Gls
Ipswich T.	Jnrs	08.64	65-74	144	4	5
Grimsby T.	L	12.76	76	3	0	0
Cambridge U.	L	02.77	76	15	0	0
Port Vale	Tr	08.77	77	4	0	0

HARPER, David
Peckham, 29 September, 1938 E Yth (WH)

League Club	Source	Date Signed	Seasons Played	Apps	Subs	Gls
Millwall	Jnrs	05.57	57-64	165	-	4
Ipswich T.	Tr	03.65	64-66	70	2	2
Swindon T.	Tr	07.67	67	4	0	0
Leyton Orient	Tr	10.67	67-70	82	3	4

HARPER, Dennis
Wednesbury, 12 October, 1936 (IF)

League Club	Source	Date Signed	Seasons Played	Apps	Subs	Gls
Birmingham C.	Darlaston	08.56	56	1	-	0

HARPER, Donald
Blackwell, 26 October, 1921 (OR)

League Club	Source	Date Signed	Seasons Played	Apps	Subs	Gls
Chesterfield		12.43				
Mansfield T.	Tr	07.46	46	21	-	1

HARPER, Ian T.
Scunthorpe, 23 November, 1944 (FB)

League Club	Source	Date Signed	Seasons Played	Apps	Subs	Gls
Scunthorpe U.	Jnrs	07.62	63-64	21	-	0

HARPER, Ivor R.
Watford, 23 June, 1933 (IF)

League Club	Source	Date Signed	Seasons Played	Apps	Subs	Gls
Watford (Am)		10.51	51	3	-	0

HARPER, Joseph J.
Heathfield, 12 January, 1920 (FB)

League Club	Source	Date Signed	Seasons Played	Apps	Subs	Gls
Watford	Twechar U.	05.37	46-51	159	-	1

HARPER, Joseph M.
Greenock, 11 January, 1948 Su23-2/SF Lge/S-3 (CF)

League Club	Source	Date Signed	Seasons Played	Apps	Subs	Gls
Huddersfield T.	Morton	03.67	66-67	26	2	4
Everton	Aberdeen	12.72	72-73	40	3	12

HARPER, Kenneth
Worsborough, 15 April, 1917 (FB)

League Club	Source	Date Signed	Seasons Played	Apps	Subs	Gls
Walsall		03.35	37-38	22	-	1
Bradford C.	Tr	01.46	46-48	50	-	0

HARPER, Kenneth
Farnworth, 27 April, 1924 (CH)

League Club	Source	Date Signed	Seasons Played	Apps	Subs	Gls
Blackpool		12.45				
Rochdale		12.47				
Shrewsbury T.		08.50	50	1	-	0

HARPER, Robert
Glasgow, 6 June, 1920 Died 1980 (OL)

League Club	Source	Date Signed	Seasons Played	Apps	Subs	Gls
Huddersfield T.	Ayr U.	06.46				
Newport Co.	Tr	11.46	46-49	114	-	12
Southend U.	Tr	07.50	50	6	-	0

HARPER, Steven J.
Newcastle-u-Lyme, 3 February, 1969 (W)

League Club	Source	Date Signed	Seasons Played	Apps	Subs	Gls
Port Vale	YT	06.87	87-88	16	12	2
Preston N.E.	Tr	03.89	88-90	57	20	10
Burnley	Tr	07.91	91	31	4	3

HARRIGAN, Duncan
Paisley, 26 June, 1921 (CF)

League Club	Source	Date Signed	Seasons Played	Apps	Subs	Gls
Crewe Alex.	St Mirren (Am)	08.46	46-47	55	-	24
Aston Villa	Tr	04.48				
Chester C.	Tr	10.48	48	20	-	4

HARRINGTON, Alan C.
Cardiff, 17 November, 1933 W-11 (FB)

League Club	Source	Date Signed	Seasons Played	Apps	Subs	Gls
Cardiff C.	Cardiff Nomads	10.51	52-65	349	0	6

HARRINGTON, Colin A.
Bicester, 3 April, 1943 (OL)

League Club	Source	Date Signed	Seasons Played	Apps	Subs	Gls
Oxford U.	Wolverhampton W. (Am)	10.62	62-70	230	4	29
Mansfield T.	Tr	06.71	71	7	6	0

HARRINGTON, Paul
Hartlepool, 26 September, 1964 (M)

League Club	Source	Date Signed	Seasons Played	Apps	Subs	Gls
Hartlepool U.		04.83	83	0	2	0

HARRINGTON, Philip
Bangor, 20 November, 1963 W Yth (G)

League Club	Source	Date Signed	Seasons Played	Apps	Subs	Gls
Chester C.	App	11.81	81-84	76	0	0
Blackpool	Tr	03.85				
Burnley	L	11.85	85	2	0	0
Preston N.E.	L	02.86	85	2	0	0

HARRIS, Alan J.
Hackney, 28 December, 1942 E Sch/E Yth (LB)

League Club	Source	Date Signed	Seasons Played	Apps	Subs	Gls
Chelsea	Jnrs	06.60	60-64	70	-	0
Coventry C.	Tr	11.64	64-65	60	0	0
Chelsea	Tr	05.66	66	12	2	0
Queens Park R.	Tr	07.67	67-70	90	3	0
Plymouth Arg.	Tr	03.71	70-72	64	0	0
Cambridge U.	Tr	07.73	73	6	0	0

HARRIS, Albert E.
Bootle, 21 November, 1931 (G)

League Club	Source	Date Signed	Seasons Played	Apps	Subs	Gls
Everton		01.55	55	5	-	0
Tranmere Rov.	Tr	05.57	57-59	33	-	0
Southport	Tr	07.60	60-64	159	-	0

HARRIS, Alexander
Hong Kong, 22 October, 1934 (F)

League Club	Source	Date Signed	Seasons Played	Apps	Subs	Gls
Blackpool	Jnrs	11.51	52-57	21	-	4

HARRIS, Andrew
Birmingham, 17 November, 1970 (M)

League Club	Source	Date Signed	Seasons Played	Apps	Subs	Gls
Birmingham C.	YT	07.89	89	0	1	0
Oxford U.	L	10.91	91	1	0	0
Exeter C.	Tr	11.91	91	5	1	0

HARRIS, Anthony T.
Berrington, 20 December, 1945 (HB)

League Club	Source	Date Signed	Seasons Played	Apps	Subs	Gls
Shrewsbury T.	App	07.63	63-66	54	1	4
Bradford P.A.	Tr	07.68	68	10	0	0

League Club	Source	Date Signed	Seasons Played	Apps	Subs	Gls

HARRIS, Arthur
Coventry, 28 July, 1914 Died 1973 (RH)

Southend U.	Nuneaton T.	07.36	36-46	113	-	1

HARRIS, Brian
Bebington, 16 May, 1935 E Yth (WH)

Everton	Port Sunlight	01.54	55-66	310	0	23
Cardiff C.	Tr	10.66	66-70	147	2	0
Newport Co.	Tr	07.71	71-73	85	0	0

HARRIS, Carl S.
Neath, 3 November, 1956 W Sch/Wu23-1/W-24 (W)

Leeds U.	App	11.73	74-81	123	30	26
Charlton Ath.	Tr	07.82	82-84	73	3	7
Bury	Leeds U. (N/C)	12.85	85-86	33	5	4
Rochdale (N/C)	Cardiff C. (N/C)	01.88	87-88	24	1	3
Exeter C.	Tr	12.88	88	11	5	1

HARRIS, Christopher R.
Hastings, 23 January, 1957 (F)

Millwall	Bexhill U.	10.76	76	3	0	0

HARRIS, David
Stoke, 19 November, 1953 (CD)

Port Vale		08.73	73-78	175	1	8
Halifax T.	Tr	07.79	79-80	69	2	3

HARRIS, Frederick
Birmingham, 2 July, 1912 EF Lge (IF/WH)

Birmingham C.	Osborne Ath.	04.33	34-49	280	-	61

HARRIS, Gary W.
Birmingham, 31 May, 1959 (W)

Cardiff C.	App	05.77	78-79	4	0	0

HARRIS, Geoffrey R.
Manchester, 1 February, 1956 (F)

Oldham Ath.	App	02.74				
Halifax T.	Tr	07.75	75-76	10	5	1

League Club	Source	Date Signed	Seasons Played	Apps	Subs	Gls

HARRIS, George
Lanchester, 24 August, 1936 (F)

Preston N.E.		08.57				
Southport	Tr	07.59	59	1	-	0

HARRIS, George A.
Lambeth, 10 June, 1940 (OL)

Newport Co.	Woking	07.61	61	31	-	8
Watford	Tr	04.62	61-65	162	1	55
Reading	Tr	07.66	66-69	134	2	56
Cambridge U.	Tr	07.70	70-71	33	2	11

HARRIS, Gerald W.
Bridgnorth, 8 October, 1935 Eu23-4 (FB)

Wolverhampton W.	Bebington	01.54	56-65	235	0	2
Walsall	Tr	04.66	65-67	13	2	1

HARRIS, Gordon
Worksop, 2 June, 1940 Eu23-2/EF Lge/E-1 (OL)

Burnley	Firbeck Colly	01.58	58-67	258	0	69
Sunderland	Tr	01.68	67-71	124	1	16

HARRIS, Gordon W.
Perth, 19 February, 1943 (FB)

Cardiff C.	Forfar Ath.	03.65	64	5	-	0

HARRIS, D. Harold
Undy, 2 November, 1933 (IF)

Newport Co.	Undy U.	09.54	54-57	156	-	56
Portsmouth	Tr	07.58	58-70	378	2	48
Newport Co.	L	10.70	70	17	0	2

HARRIS, James
Birkenhead, 18 August, 1933 Eu23-1/EF Lge (CF)

Everton	Jnrs	09.51	55-60	191	-	65
Birmingham C.	Tr	12.60	60-63	93	-	37
Oldham Ath.	Tr	07.64	64-65	28	1	9

HARRIS, Jamie
Exeter, 4 June, 1969 (F)

Exeter C.	YT	08.86	87-88	6	8	1

Carl Harris (Leeds United, Charlton Athletic, Bury, Rochdale, Exeter City & Wales)

League Club	Source	Date Signed	Seasons Played	Apps	Subs	Gls
HARRIS, Jason M.						
Rochdale, 26 December, 1969						(M)
Burnley	YT	07.88	86	4	0	0
HARRIS, Jeffrey B.						
Stepney, 11 June, 1942 E Amat						(WH)
Leyton Orient	Enfield	05.64	64	14	-	0
HARRIS, John						
Glasgow, 30 June, 1917						(D)
Swansea C.	Swindon T. (Am)	08.34	36-38	28	-	4
Tottenham H.	Tr	02.39				
Wolverhampton W.	Tr	05.39				
Chelsea	Tr	08.45	46-55	326	-	14
Chester C.	Tr	07.56	56	27	-	1
HARRIS, John D.						
Gornal, 3 April, 1939						(FB)
Wolverhampton W.	Jnrs	05.58	61-62	3	-	0
Walsall	Tr	01.65	64-68	73	5	2
HARRIS, John P.						
Bermondsey, 20 December, 1931						(IF)
Millwall (Am)		06.56	56	1	-	0
HARRIS, T. John						
Swansea, 18 May, 1934						(CH)
Leeds U.		11.51				
Halifax T.	Tr	10.55	55-56	9	-	0
HARRIS, Joseph						
Belfast, 8 April, 1929						(CF)
Blackburn Rov.	Distillery	01.51	50-51	35	-	15
Oldham Ath.	Tr	03.53	52-53	27	-	4
HARRIS, Joseph A.						
Liverpool, 20 September, 1926						(OR)
Everton		07.50	50-52	14	-	4
HARRIS, Kevin						
Dublin, 20 February, 1918						(WH)
Notts Co.		09.45				
Brentford		08.48	48	4	-	0
HARRIS, Leonard J.						
Nuneaton, 29 May, 1949						(FB)
Nottingham F.	Jnrs	06.66	68-69	2	0	0
Doncaster Rov.	L	09.70	70	4	0	0
HARRIS, Leslie						
Llanfair, 1 November, 1941						(FB)
Swansea C.	Aberystwyth Univ.	08.63	63-64	4	-	0
HARRIS, Leslie H.						
Stocksbridge, 29 May, 1955						(F)
Barnsley	Jnrs	05.74	75-76	11	15	2
HARRIS, Mark A.						
Reading, 15 July, 1963						(CD)
Crystal Palace	Wokingham T.	02.88	88	0	2	0
Burnley	L	08.89	89	4	0	0
Swansea C.	Tr	09.89	89-91	126	0	6
HARRIS, Martin						
Doncaster, 22 December, 1955						(W)
Workington	Grimsby T. (App)	07.74	74-76	97	9	13
Hartlepool U.	Tr	12.77	77	0	1	0
HARRIS, Neil						
Glasgow, 9 February, 1920						(CF)
Queens Park R.		09.46	46	1	-	1
HARRIS, Neil J.						
Manchester, 7 November, 1969						(W)
Crewe Alex.	YT	07.88	87	3	0	0
HARRIS, Paul E.						
Hackney, 19 May, 1953						(CD)
Leyton Orient	App	07.70	70-74	96	0	4
Swansea C.	Tr	07.75	75-76	47	2	2
HARRIS, Peter						
Neath, 9 August, 1953						(W)
Newport Co.	App	08.71	70-72	20	11	1
HARRIS, Peter P.						
Portsmouth, 19 December, 1925 EF Lge/E-2						(OR)
Portsmouth	Gosport Bor.	11.44	46-59	480	-	194
HARRIS, Philip J.						
Swindon, 18 December, 1958						(M)
Swindon T. (App)	App	07.75	76	0	1	0
HARRIS, Ronald E.						
Hackney, 13 November, 1944 E Sch/E Yth/Eu23-4						(D)
Chelsea	App	11.61	61-79	646	9	13
Brentford	Tr	05.80	80-83	60	1	0
HARRIS, Thomas A.						
Chelsea, 8 November, 1924						(IF)
Fulham		09.47				
Leyton Orient	Tr	09.51	51-52	31	-	11
Colchester U.	Tr	06.53	53	3	-	0
HARRIS, Thomas J. G.						
Ogmore, 15 February, 1916						(G)
Charlton Ath.		08.39				
Plymouth Arg.	Aberaman	05.48	48	3	-	0
HARRIS, W. Thomas						
Aberbargoed, 30 June, 1913						(FB)
Watford	New Tredegar	04.33	35-48	94	-	6
HARRIS, Trevor J.						
Colchester, 6 February, 1936						(WH)
Colchester U.	Jnrs	07.54	54-62	100	-	6
HARRIS, William						
Dudley, 1 December, 1918						(G)
West Bromwich A.	Whiteheath	02.37	37	2	-	0
Oldham Ath.	Tr	06.46	46	32	-	0
Accrington St.	Tr	08.47	47-49	99	-	0
HARRIS, William C.						
Swansea, 31 October, 1928 Died 1989 W-6						(IF/WH)
Hull C.	Llanelli	03.50	49-53	131	-	6
Middlesbrough	Tr	03.54	53-64	360	-	69
Bradford C.	Tr	03.65	64-65	9	0	1
HARRISON, Andrew F.						
Long Eaton, 13 September, 1957						(FB)
Scarborough	Kettering T.	(N/L)	87	3	1	0
HARRISON, Anthony L.						
Gateshead, 9 January, 1954						(G)
Southport	Whitley Bay	02.77	76-77	48	0	0
Carlisle U.	Tr	06.78	80	8	0	0
HARRISON, Bernard R. S.						
Worcester, 28 September, 1934						(W)
Crystal Palace	Portsmouth (Am)	10.55	55-58	92	-	12
Southampton	Tr	08.59	59	3	-	0
Exeter C.	Tr	07.60	60	18	-	4
HARRISON, Christopher C.						
Launceston, 17 October, 1956						(D)
Plymouth Arg.	App	10.74	75-84	315	9	7
Swansea C.	Tr	09.85	85-87	114	3	14
HARRISON, Colin G.						
Pelsall, 18 March, 1946						(D)
Walsall	Jnrs	11.63	64-81	452	15	33
HARRISON, Derek						
Leicester, 9 February, 1950						(CD)
Leicester C.	App	02.67				
Torquay U.	Tr	01.71	70-74	124	3	4
Colchester U.	Tr	06.75	75	5	2	0
HARRISON, Eric G.						
Hebden Bridge, 5 February, 1938						(WH)
Halifax T.	Mytholmroyd	07.57	57-63	199	-	10
Hartlepool U.	Tr	08.64	64-65	81	0	4
Barrow	Tr	07.66	66-68	127	3	1
Southport	Tr	06.69	69-70	75	0	0
Barrow	Tr	07.71	71	31	1	1
HARRISON, Francis N.						
Eston, 19 September, 1963						(LB)
Middlesbrough	Guisborough T.	09.82				
Lincoln C. (N/C)	Carnegie Col.	11.85	85	0	1	0
Halifax T.	Guiseley	03.87	86-89	48	6	1

League Club	Source	Date Signed	Seasons Played	Apps	Subs	Gls

HARRISON, Frank J.
Gateshead, 12 November, 1931 Died 1981 E Yth (FB)

Hull C.	Jnrs	05.49	52-59	199	-	0

HARRISON, Gerald R.
Lambeth, 15 April, 1972 (M)

Watford	YT	12.89	89-90	6	3	0
Bristol C.	Tr	06.91	91	0	4	0
Cardiff C.	L	01.92	91	10	0	1

HARRISON, Harold
Sunderland, 26 June, 1917 (FB)

Chesterfield		06.37				
Southport		07.39	46-50	135	-	1

HARRISON, Herbert K. G.
Burnley, 23 January, 1916 (OR)

Accrington St. (Am)	Morecambe	10.47	47	3	-	0

HARRISON, James C.
Leicester, 12 February, 1921 (FB)

Leicester C.	Jnrs	12.41	46-48	81	-	1
Aston Villa	Tr	07.49	49	8	-	1
Coventry C.	Tr	07.51	51-52	20	-	2

HARRISON, James H.
Hammersmith, 31 July, 1928 (F)

Queens Park R.		02.52	52	5	-	1

HARRISON, John
Swansea, 30 September, 1932 (G)

Crewe Alex.		08.56	56	2	-	0

HARRISON, John G.
Worksop, 18 May, 1946 (W)

Sheffield U.	Worksop T.	01.67				
Lincoln C.	Tr	07.68	68	4	0	0

HARRISON, John J.
York, 7 June, 1961 (FB)

York C.	App	06.79	79	8	0	0

HARRISON, John M.
Stepney, 16 January, 1958 (W)

Charlton Ath.	App	01.76	75	5	0	2

HARRISON, John W.
Leicester, 27 September, 1927 (FB)

Aston Villa		08.48				
Colchester U.	Tr	07.50	50-56	237	-	1

HARRISON, Kenneth
Stockton, 20 January, 1926 (OR)

Hull C.	Billingham Synth.	04.47	46-54	238	-	47
Derby Co.	Tr	07.54	54-55	15	-	3

HARRISON, Lee D.
Billericay, 12 September, 1971 G)

Charlton Ath.	YT	07.90				
Gillingham	L	03.92	91	2	0	0

HARRISON, Mark S.
Derby, 11 December, 1960 (G)

Southampton	App	12.78				
Port Vale	Tr	02.80	80-81	70	0	0
Stoke C.	Tr	08.82	82	7	0	0

HARRISON, Michael
Leicester, 21 February, 1952 (CD)

Birmingham C.	App	02.70	70-71	3	0	0
Southend U.	Tr	07.72	72	16	0	0

HARRISON, Michael J.
Ilford, 18 April, 1940 E Sch/Eu23-3 (OL)

Chelsea	Jnrs	04.57	56-62	61	-	8
Blackburn Rov.	Tr	09.62	62-67	160	0	40
Plymouth Arg.	Tr	09.67	67	15	0	3
Luton T.	Tr	06.68	68-69	29	3	6

HARRISON, Peter
Sleaford, 25 October, 1927 (W)

Leeds U.	Peterborough U.	01.49	49-51	65	-	9
Bournemouth	Tr	08.52	52-56	172	-	34
Reading	Tr	06.57	57-58	39	-	5
Southport	Tr	07.59	59-61	126	-	22

HARRISON, Ralph
Clayton-le-Moors, 18 December, 1926 (OL)

Leeds U.	Great Harwood	01.49	49	2	-	0

HARRISON, Raymond W.
Boston, 21 June, 1921 (CF)

Burnley	Boston U.	04.46	46-49	60	-	19
Doncaster Rov.	Tr	01.50	49-53	126	-	47
Grimsby T.	Tr	07.54	54	38	-	7

HARRISON, Reginald F.
Derby, 22 June, 1923 (OR)

Derby Co.	Jnrs	03.44	46-54	254	-	52

HARRISON, Robert A.
Chatham, 25 December, 1947 (IF)

Gillingham	Jnrs	06.67	66	1	0	0

HARRISON, Robert J.
Manchester, 23 December, 1930 (OR)

Carlisle U.	Army	02.53	52-54	66	-	16
Stockport Co.	Tr	07.56				

HARRISON, Ronald
Hebburn, 15 May, 1923 (F)

Darlington	Gateshead (Am)	08.45	46	8	-	3
Gateshead	Tr	07.47	47	6	-	1

HARRISON, Stephen J.
Blackpool, 26 December, 1952 (LB)

Blackpool	App	12.70	71-77	141	7	0
Watford	Vancouver (Can)	09.78	78-80	82	1	0
Charlton Ath.	Tr	07.81	81	3	0	0

HARRISON, Terence J.
Thornaby, 12 September, 1950 (CF)

Newcastle U.	Stockton	11.67				
Barrow	Tr	07.70	70	4	0	0

HARRISON, Walter E.
Coalville, 16 January, 1923 E'B'-2 (WH)

Leicester C.	Jnrs	08.45	46-50	125	-	3
Chesterfield	Tr	12.50	50-52	74	-	13

HARRISON, Wayne
Stockport, 15 November, 1967 (F)

Oldham Ath.	App	12.84	84	5	1	1
Liverpool	Tr	03.85				
Crewe Alex.	L	12.88	88	3	0	0

HARRISON, Wayne M.
Whitehaven, 16 October, 1957 (M)

Workington (N/C)	Everton (Jnr)	08.75	75	1	3	0
Blackpool	Sheffield Wed. (N/C)	09.79	79-81	81	5	6
Carlisle U. (N/C)	Workington	08.87	87	1	1	0

HARRITY, Michael D.
Sheffield, 5 October, 1946 (FB)

Rotherham U.		10.65	65-68	36	3	0
Doncaster Rov.	Tr	09.68	68	2	1	0

HARROLD, Mark A.
Halifax, 29 January, 1957 (M)

Halifax T.	Jnrs	08.74	74-75	8	5	1

HARROP, John (Jack)
Manchester, 25 June, 1929 (FB)

Swansea C.		08.52	52-53	10	-	0
Watford	Tr	07.56	56-59	111	-	0

HARROP, Robert W.
Manchester, 25 August, 1936 (CH)

Manchester U.	Benchill Y.C.	05.54	57-58	10	-	0
Tranmere Rov.	Tr	11.59	59-60	41	-	2

HARROW, Andrew
Kirkcaldy, 6 November, 1956 (F)

Luton T.	Raith Rov.	09.80	80	3	1	0

HARROWER, James
Alva, 18 August, 1935 Su23-1 (IF)

Liverpool	Hibernian	01.58	57-60	96	-	21
Newcastle U.	Tr	03.61	60-61	5	-	0

HARROWER, James S.
Dunfermline, 19 June, 1924 (FB)

League Club	Source	Date Signed	Seasons Played	Apps	Subs	Gls
Accrington St.	Third Lanark	12.54	54-60	246	-	2

HARROWER, Steven G.
Exeter, 9 October, 1961 (RB)

League Club	Source	Date Signed	Seasons Played	Apps	Subs	Gls
Exeter C.	Dawlish	01.84	83-89	165	22	10

HARROWER, William
Dunfermline, 13 April, 1922 (IF)

League Club	Source	Date Signed	Seasons Played	Apps	Subs	Gls
Torquay U.	Third Lanark	05.46	46-47	16	-	3
Exeter C.	Tr	07.48	48-51	85	-	11

HARSTON, John C.
Barnsley, 7 October, 1920 (FB)

League Club	Source	Date Signed	Seasons Played	Apps	Subs	Gls
Wolverhampton W.		10.37				
Barnsley	Tr	09.38	46-48	19	-	1
Bradford C.	Tr	06.49	49	24	-	1

HART, Alan M.
Woolwich, 21 February, 1956 (M)

League Club	Source	Date Signed	Seasons Played	Apps	Subs	Gls
Charlton Ath.	App	02.74	74	3	0	2
Millwall	Tr	06.75	75	13	3	0

HART, Andrew
Yarmouth, 14 January, 1963 (D)

League Club	Source	Date Signed	Seasons Played	Apps	Subs	Gls
Norwich C.	App	01.81	81	0	1	0

HART, Brian P.
Farnworth, 14 July, 1959 (CD)

League Club	Source	Date Signed	Seasons Played	Apps	Subs	Gls
Rochdale	Bolton W. (App)	07.77	77-79	73	5	0

HART, Harold
Sheffield, 29 September, 1926 (IF)

League Club	Source	Date Signed	Seasons Played	Apps	Subs	Gls
Rotherham U.		12.45	49	10	-	3
Coventry C.	Tr	06.50	50-51	10	-	1
Grimsby T.	Tr	12.52	52	13	-	3

HART, John P.
Golborne, 8 June, 1928 (IF)

League Club	Source	Date Signed	Seasons Played	Apps	Subs	Gls
Manchester C.	Jnrs	06.45	47-60	169	-	67

HART, J. Leslie
Ashton, 28 February, 1917 (CH)

League Club	Source	Date Signed	Seasons Played	Apps	Subs	Gls
Bury	Ashton National	12.36	38-53	280	-	1

HART, Nigel
Golborne, 1 October, 1958 (CD)

League Club	Source	Date Signed	Seasons Played	Apps	Subs	Gls
Wigan Ath.		08.78	79	1	0	0
Leicester C.	Tr	10.79				
Blackpool	Tr	08.81	81-82	36	1	0
Crewe Alex.	Tr	11.82	82-86	139	3	10
Bury	Tr	02.87	86-87	33	12	2
Stockport Co.	Tr	07.88	88-89	38	1	2
Chesterfield	Tr	08.89	89-90	45	1	2
York C. (N/C)	Tr	02.91	90	1	0	0

HART, Paul A.
Golborne, 4 May, 1953 (CD)

League Club	Source	Date Signed	Seasons Played	Apps	Subs	Gls
Stockport Co.	Jnrs	09.70	70-72	88	0	5
Blackpool	Tr	06.73	73-77	143	0	17
Leeds U.	Tr	03.78	77-82	191	0	16
Nottingham F.	Tr	05.83	83-84	70	0	1
Sheffield Wed.	Tr	08.85	85-86	52	0	2
Birmingham C.	Tr	12.86	86	1	0	0
Notts Co.	Tr	06.87	87	23	0	0

HART, Peter A.
Wickersley, 6 September, 1949 (FB)

League Club	Source	Date Signed	Seasons Played	Apps	Subs	Gls
Bradford P.A. (Am)	Rotherham U. (App)	03.68	67	3	0	0

HART, Peter O.
Mexborough, 14 August, 1957 (CD)

League Club	Source	Date Signed	Seasons Played	Apps	Subs	Gls
Huddersfield T.	App	08.74	73-79	208	2	7
Walsall	Tr	08.80	80-89	389	1	12

HART, Roy E.
Acton, 30 May, 1933 E Sch (CH)

League Club	Source	Date Signed	Seasons Played	Apps	Subs	Gls
Brentford	Jnrs	06.50	54	2	-	0

HART, Stuart M.
Derby, 15 January, 1941 (OR)

League Club	Source	Date Signed	Seasons Played	Apps	Subs	Gls
Exeter C.	Long Eaton U.	08.67	67	20	2	1

HART, William R.
North Shields, 1 April, 1923 (RH)

League Club	Source	Date Signed	Seasons Played	Apps	Subs	Gls
Newcastle U.		09.40				
Chesterfield	Tr	03.45	46	1	-	0
Bradford C.	Tr	05.47	46-48	25	-	0

HARTBURN, John
Houghton-le-Spring, 20 December, 1920 (OL)

League Club	Source	Date Signed	Seasons Played	Apps	Subs	Gls
Queens Park R.	Yeovil T.	03.47	47-48	58	-	10
Watford	Tr	09.49	49-50	66	-	19
Millwall	Tr	03.51	50-53	104	-	29
Leyton Orient	Tr	06.54	54-57	112	-	36

HARTERY, John
Waterford (Ire), 25 November, 1920 LOI (RB)

League Club	Source	Date Signed	Seasons Played	Apps	Subs	Gls
Plymouth Arg.	Limerick	06.48	49	1	-	0

HARTFIELD, Charles J.
Lambeth, 4 September, 1971 E Yth (M/FB)

League Club	Source	Date Signed	Seasons Played	Apps	Subs	Gls
Arsenal	YT	09.89				
Sheffield U.	Tr	08.91	91	6	1	0

HARTFORD, R. Asa
Clydebank, 24 October, 1950 Su21-1/Su23-5/S-50 (M)

League Club	Source	Date Signed	Seasons Played	Apps	Subs	Gls
West Bromwich A.	Jnrs	11.67	67-73	206	8	18
Manchester C.	Tr	08.74	74-78	184	1	22
Nottingham F.	Tr	07.79	79	3	0	0
Everton	Tr	08.79	79-81	81	0	6
Manchester C.	Tr	10.81	81-83	75	0	7
Norwich C.	Fort Lauderdale (USA)	10.84	84	28	0	2
Bolton W.	Tr	07.85	85-86	81	0	8
Stockport Co.	Tr	06.87	87-88	42	3	0
Oldham Ath.	Tr	03.89	88	3	4	0
Shrewsbury T.	Tr	08.89	89-90	22	3	0

Asa Hartford (West Bromwich Albion, Manchester City, Nottingham Forest, Everton, Manchester City, Norwich City, Bolton Wanderers, Stockport County, Oldham Athletic, Shrewsbury Town & Scotland)

HARTLAND, Michael L.
Birmingham, 7 January, 1944 (M)

League Club	Source	Date Signed	Seasons Played	Apps	Subs	Gls
Oxford U.	Nuneaton Bor.	06.63	63-64	19	-	6
Barrow	Tr	07.65	65-70	169	7	20
Crewe Alex.	Tr	12.70	70	3	0	2
Southport	Tr	07.71	71-72	32	5	4

HARTLE, Barry
Salford, 8 August, 1939 (OL)

League Club	Source	Date Signed	Seasons Played	Apps	Subs	Gls
Watford	Jnrs	08.56	58-59	39	-	7
Sheffield U.	Tr	06.60	60-65	101	0	16
Carlisle U.	Tr	07.66	66-67	28	1	1
Stockport Co.	Tr	09.67	67-69	87	0	1
Oldham Ath.	Tr	06.70	70	8	1	2
Southport	Tr	07.71	71	37	4	6

HARTLE, L. Roy
Bromsgrove, 4 October, 1931 EF Lge (FB)

League Club	Source	Date Signed	Seasons Played	Apps	Subs	Gls
Bolton W.	Bromsgrove Rov.	02.51	52-65	446	1	11

HARTLEY, Edmund
Burnley, 5 May, 1932 (OR)

League Club	Source	Date Signed	Seasons Played	Apps	Subs	Gls
Burnley	Jnrs	11.50				
Oldham Ath.	Rossendale U.	07.56	56	1	-	0

HARTLEY, Thomas W.
Gateshead, 7 May, 1917 (IF)

League Club	Source	Date Signed	Seasons Played	Apps	Subs	Gls
Gateshead	Birtley B.C.	02.36	35-36	5	-	1
Bury	Tr	05.38				
Chesterfield	Tr	05.39				
Leicester C.	North Shields	01.48				
Watford	Tr	02.48	47	6	-	1

HARTLEY, Trevor J.
Doncaster, 16 March, 1947 (W)

League Club	Source	Date Signed	Seasons Played	Apps	Subs	Gls
West Ham U.	Jnrs	07.64	66-68	4	1	0
Bournemouth	Tr	07.69	69-70	35	7	2

HARTNETT, James B.
Dublin, 21 March, 1927 LOI/IR-2 (OL)

League Club	Source	Date Signed	Seasons Played	Apps	Subs	Gls
Middlesbrough	Dundalk	06.48	48-54	48	-	8
Hartlepool U.	Barry T.	09.57	57	7	-	1
York C.	Tr	08.58	58	2	-	1

HARVEY, Alexander
Ayr, 28 September, 1928 (IF)

League Club	Source	Date Signed	Seasons Played	Apps	Subs	Gls
Chesterfield	Saltcoats Vic.	11.50	50-52	27	-	9

HARVEY, Alexander
Kirkconnel, 28 August, 1925 (LH)

League Club	Source	Date Signed	Seasons Played	Apps	Subs	Gls
Carlisle U.	Queen of South	08.46	46	1	-	0

HARVEY, Brian
Liverpool, 12 January, 1947 (WH)

League Club	Source	Date Signed	Seasons Played	Apps	Subs	Gls
Chester C.	Sheffield Wed. (App)	09.64	64	1	-	0

HARVEY, Bryan R.
Stepney, 26 August, 1938 (G)

League Club	Source	Date Signed	Seasons Played	Apps	Subs	Gls
Newcastle U.	Wisbech T.	09.58	58-60	86	-	0
Blackpool	Cambridge C.	02.62	61-63	11	-	0
Northampton T.	Tr	10.63	63-67	165	0	0

HARVEY, J. Colin
Liverpool, 16 November, 1944 Eu23-5/EF Lge/E-1 (M)

League Club	Source	Date Signed	Seasons Played	Apps	Subs	Gls
Everton	App	10.62	63-74	317	3	18
Sheffield Wed.	Tr	09.74	74-75	45	0	2

HARVEY, David
Hetton-le-Hole, 15 February, 1954 (OR)

League Club	Source	Date Signed	Seasons Played	Apps	Subs	Gls
Hartlepool U. (App)	App	10.69	70	3	2	0

HARVEY, David
Leeds, 7 February, 1948 S-16

League Club	Source	Date Signed	Seasons Played	Apps	Subs	Gls
Leeds U.	Jnrs	02.65	65-79	276	0	0
Leeds U.	Vancouver (Can)	09.82	82-84	73	0	0
Bradford C. (N/C)	Tr	02.85	84	6	0	0

HARVEY, Gary
Colchester, 19 November, 1961 (F)

League Club	Source	Date Signed	Seasons Played	Apps	Subs	Gls
Colchester U.	App	11.79	79-80	6	0	2

HARVEY, James
Lurgan (NI), 2 May, 1958 NIu23-1 (M)

League Club	Source	Date Signed	Seasons Played	Apps	Subs	Gls
Arsenal	Glenavon	08.77	77-78	2	1	0
Hereford U.	Tr	03.80	79-86	276	2	39
Bristol C.	Tr	03.87	86-87	2	1	0
Wrexham	L	09.87	87	6	0	0
Tranmere Rov.	Tr	10.87	87-91	174	10	18

HARVEY, Joseph
Doncaster, 11 June, 1918 Died 1989 (WH)

League Club	Source	Date Signed	Seasons Played	Apps	Subs	Gls
Bradford P.A.	Edlington R.	05.36	36	3	-	0
Wolverhampton W.	Tr	11.36				
Bournemouth	Tr	05.37	37-38	3	-	0
Newcastle U.	Tr	10.45	46-52	224	-	12

HARVEY Keith W.
Crediton, 25 December, 1934 (CH)

League Club	Source	Date Signed	Seasons Played	Apps	Subs	Gls
Exeter C.	Crediton	08.52	52-68	483	0	28

HARVEY, Laurence (Lol)
Heanor, 25 July, 1934 (FB)

League Club	Source	Date Signed	Seasons Played	Apps	Subs	Gls
Coventry C.	Jnrs	07.51	51-60	140	-	1

HARVEY, Lee D.
Harlow, 21 December, 1966 E Yth (W/F)

League Club	Source	Date Signed	Seasons Played	Apps	Subs	Gls
Leyton Orient	App	12.84	83-91	116	47	19

HARVEY, Leighton
Neath, 27 August, 1959 (W)

League Club	Source	Date Signed	Seasons Played	Apps	Subs	Gls
Swansea C. (App)	App	08.75	75-76	1	1	0

HARVEY, Martin
Belfast, 19 September, 1941 NI Sch/NIu23-3/NI'B'-1/NI-33 (WH)

League Club	Source	Date Signed	Seasons Played	Apps	Subs	Gls
Sunderland	Jnrs	09.58	59-71	310	4	5

HARVEY, Richard G.
Letchworth, 19 April, 1969 E Sch/E Yth (LB)

League Club	Source	Date Signed	Seasons Played	Apps	Subs	Gls
Luton T.	App	01.87	86-91	90	14	2

HARVEY, William D.
Doncaster, 30 September, 1934 (FB)

League Club	Source	Date Signed	Seasons Played	Apps	Subs	Gls
Doncaster Rov.	Jnrs	11.51	52	2	-	0

HARVEY, William J.
Clydebank, 23 November, 1929 (IF)

League Club	Source	Date Signed	Seasons Played	Apps	Subs	Gls
Bradford P.A.	Dunfermline Ath.	01.59	58-59	26	-	1

HARWOOD, Lee
Southall, 4 October, 1960 (CD)

League Club	Source	Date Signed	Seasons Played	Apps	Subs	Gls
Southampton	App	10.78				
Wimbledon	Tr	01.79	78	1	0	0
Port Vale	Leatherhead	02.80	79-80	19	0	1

HARWOOD, Richard A.
Sheffield, 13 September, 1960 (M)

League Club	Source	Date Signed	Seasons Played	Apps	Subs	Gls
Sheffield U.	App	07.78	78	2	1	0

HASELDEN, John J.
Doncaster, 3 August, 1943 (CD)

League Club	Source	Date Signed	Seasons Played	Apps	Subs	Gls
Rotherham U.	Denaby U.	02.62	61-68	100	2	0
Doncaster Rov.	Tr	09.68	68-73	168	4	20
Mansfield T.	L	02.72	71	4	0	0

HASFORD, Jason M.
Manchester, 1 April, 1971 (F)

League Club	Source	Date Signed	Seasons Played	Apps	Subs	Gls
Rochdale	Manchester C. (YT)	07.89	89	0	1	0

HASKINS, Anthony J.
Northampton, 26 July, 1935 (FB)

League Club	Source	Date Signed	Seasons Played	Apps	Subs	Gls
Northampton T.		01.59	59-61	8	-	0

HASLAM, Graham
Doncaster, 29 April, 1956 (G)

League Club	Source	Date Signed	Seasons Played	Apps	Subs	Gls
Rotherham U.	App	04.74	75	2	0	0

HASLAM, Harold
Manchester, 30 July, 1921 Died 1986 (FB)

League Club	Source	Date Signed	Seasons Played	Apps	Subs	Gls
Oldham Ath.	Rochdale (Am)	05.46	46	2	-	0
Brighton & H.A.	Tr	09.47				
Leyton Orient	Tr	07.48	48	7	-	0

HASLEGRAVE, Sean M.
Stoke, 7 June, 1951 (M)

League Club	Source	Date Signed	Seasons Played	Apps	Subs	Gls
Stoke C.	Jnrs	11.68	70-75	106	7	5
Nottingham F.	Tr	07.76	76	5	2	1
Preston N.E.	Tr	09.77	77-80	111	2	2
Crewe Alex.	Tr	08.81	81-82	78	4	1
York C.	Tr	07.83	83-86	137	5	0
Torquay U.	Tr	08.87	87-88	32	4	1

HASPELL, Alan
Northwich, 23 January, 1943 (IF)

League Club	Source	Date Signed	Seasons Played	Apps	Subs	Gls
Burnley	Jnrs	01.60				
Doncaster Rov.	Tr	07.63	63	1	-	0

HASSALL, Harold W.
Tyldesley, 4 March, 1929 EF Lge/E-5 (IF)

League Club	Source	Date Signed	Seasons Played	Apps	Subs	Gls
Huddersfield T.	Astley	09.46	48-51	74	-	26
Bolton W.	Tr	01.52	51-54	102	-	34

HASSALL, Wilfred
Manchester, 23 September, 1923 (FB)

League Club	Source	Date Signed	Seasons Played	Apps	Subs	Gls
Hull C.	R.M. Alsager	09.46	46-52	141	-	3

HASSELL, Richard (Rick)
Coatbridge, 12 January, 1951 (WH)

League Club	Source	Date Signed	Seasons Played	Apps	Subs	Gls
Carlisle U.	Jnrs	01.69	68-69	3	3	0

HASSELL, Thomas W.
Stonham, 5 April, 1919 Died 1984 (F)

League Club	Source	Date Signed	Seasons Played	Apps	Subs	Gls
Southampton		02.40				
Aldershot	Tr	05.46	46-49	113	-	16
Brighton & H.A.	Tr	08.50	50	11	-	3

HASTIE, John K. G.
South Africa, 6 September, 1928 (IF)

League Club	Source	Date Signed	Seasons Played	Apps	Subs	Gls
Leeds U.	Clyde Ath. (SA)	08.52	52	4	-	2

HASTY, Patrick J. (Paddy)
Belfast, 17 March, 1932 NI Amat (CF)

League Club	Source	Date Signed	Seasons Played	Apps	Subs	Gls
Leyton Orient(Am)	Tooting & Mitcham	07.58	58	2	-	2
Queens Park R. (Am)	Tr	10.59	59	1	-	0
Aldershot	Tooting & Mitcham	03.61	60-62	35	-	14

HATCH, Peter D.
Wargrave, 22 October, 1949 (LB/M)

League Club	Source	Date Signed	Seasons Played	Apps	Subs	Gls
Oxford U.	App	10.66	67-72	15	4	2
Exeter C.	Tr	12.73	73-81	343	3	18

HATCHER, Clifford H.
Currie Dando, 27 June, 1925 (G)

League Club	Source	Date Signed	Seasons Played	Apps	Subs	Gls
Reading		06.46	47-48	2	-	0

HATCHER, Douglas T.
Carshalton, 6 March, 1962 (G)

League Club	Source	Date Signed	Seasons Played	Apps	Subs	Gls
Fulham	App	03.80				
Aldershot (N/C)	Wokingham T.	08.83	83	1	0	0

HATELEY, Anthony
Derby, 13 June, 1941 (CF)

League Club	Source	Date Signed	Seasons Played	Apps	Subs	Gls
Notts Co.	Jnrs	06.58	58-62	131	-	77
Aston Villa	Tr	08.63	63-66	127	0	68
Chelsea	Tr	10.66	66	26	1	6
Liverpool	Tr	07.67	67-68	42	0	17
Coventry C.	Tr	09.68	68	17	0	4
Birmingham C.	Tr	08.69	69-70	28	0	6
Notts Co.	Tr	11.70	70-71	57	0	32
Oldham Ath.	Tr	07.72	73	1	4	1

HATELEY, Mark W.
Liverpool, 7 November, 1961 E Yth/Eu21-10/E-32 (F)

League Club	Source	Date Signed	Seasons Played	Apps	Subs	Gls
Coventry C.	App	12.78	78-82	86	6	25
Portsmouth	Tr	06.83	83	38	0	22

HATHAWAY, Ian A.
Wordsley, 22 August, 1968 (W)

League Club	Source	Date Signed	Seasons Played	Apps	Subs	Gls
Mansfield T.	Bedworth U.	03.89	88-90	21	23	2
Rotherham U.	Tr	03.91	90-91	5	8	1

Mark Hateley (Coventry City, Portsmouth, Glasgow Rangers & England)

HATSELL, Dennis
Preston, 9 June, 1930 (CF)

League Club	Source	Date Signed	Seasons Played	Apps	Subs	Gls
Preston N.E.	Jnrs	06.48	53-59	115	-	54

HATTER, Stephen J.
East Ham, 21 October, 1958 (CD)

League Club	Source	Date Signed	Seasons Played	Apps	Subs	Gls
Fulham	App	05.76	77-80	25	1	1
Exeter C.	L	09.82	82	11	0	1
Wimbledon	Tr	11.82	82-84	83	1	4
Southend U.	Tr	03.85	84-85	62	0	2

HATTON, Cyril
Nottingham, 14 September, 1918 Died 1987 (IF)

League Club	Source	Date Signed	Seasons Played	Apps	Subs	Gls
Notts Co.	Grantham Co-op.	07.36	36-38	62	-	15
Queens Park R.	Tr	04.46	46-52	164	-	63
Chesterfield	Tr	06.53	53	36	-	10

HATTON, David H.
Farnworth, 30 October, 1943 (CD)

League Club	Source	Date Signed	Seasons Played	Apps	Subs	Gls
Bolton W.	Jnrs	11.60	61-69	231	0	8
Blackpool	Tr	09.69	69-75	249	1	6
Bury	Tr	08.76	76-78	96	1	2

HATTON, Robert J.
Hull, 10 April, 1947 (F)

League Club	Source	Date Signed	Seasons Played	Apps	Subs	Gls
Wolverhampton W.	Jnrs	11.64	66	10	0	7
Bolton W.	Tr	03.67	66-67	23	1	2
Northampton T.	Tr	10.68	68	29	4	8
Carlisle U.	Tr	07.69	69-71	93	0	37
Birmingham C.	Tr	10.71	71-75	170	5	58
Blackpool	Tr	07.76	76-77	75	0	32
Luton T.	Tr	07.78	78-79	81	1	29
Sheffield U.	Tr	07.80	80-82	92	3	34
Cardiff C.	Tr	12.82	82	29	1	9

HAUGHEY, Frederick
Conisborough, 12 May, 1921 (LB)

League Club	Source	Date Signed	Seasons Played	Apps	Subs	Gls
Bradford C. (Am)	Halifax T. (Am)	08.46	46	3	-	0

HAUGHEY, William
Glasgow, 20 December, 1932 (IF)

League Club	Source	Date Signed	Seasons Played	Apps	Subs	Gls
Everton	Larkhall Th.	06.56	56-57	4	-	1

HAUSER, Peter B.
South Africa, 20 April, 1934 (WH)

League Club	Source	Date Signed	Seasons Played	Apps	Subs	Gls
Blackpool	South Africa	11.55	57-61	83	-	10
Chester C.	Cheltenham T.	08.63	63-66	117	3	3

HAUSER, Thomas
West Germany, 10 April, 1965 (F)

League Club	Source	Date Signed	Seasons Played	Apps	Subs	Gls
Sunderland	F.C. Basel (Swi)	02.89	88-91	22	31	9

HAVENGA, William S.
South Africa, 6 November, 1924 (IF)

League Club	Source	Date Signed	Seasons Played	Apps	Subs	Gls
Birmingham C.	Bremner O.B.	07.48	49	1	-	0
Luton T.	Tr	05.50	50-51	18	-	6
Ipswich T.	Tr	01.52	51-52	19	-	3

HAVENHAND, Keith
Dronfield, 11 September, 1937 E Yth (IF)

League Club	Source	Date Signed	Seasons Played	Apps	Subs	Gls
Chesterfield	Jnrs	09.54	53-61	176	-	58
Derby Co.	Tr	10.61	61	26	-	14
Oxford U.	Tr	12.63	63-64	12	-	3

HAVERSON, Paul T.
Chigwell, 19 February, 1959 E Sch (D)

League Club	Source	Date Signed	Seasons Played	Apps	Subs	Gls
Queens Park R.	App	08.76				
Wimbledon	Tr	10.78	78-79	27	1	2

HAVERTY, Joseph
Dublin, 17 February, 1936 IR-32 (OL)

League Club	Source	Date Signed	Seasons Played	Apps	Subs	Gls
Arsenal	St Patricks Ath.	07.54	54-60	114	-	25
Blackburn Rov.	Tr	08.61	61-62	27	-	1
Millwall	Tr	09.62	62-63	68	-	8
Bristol Rov.	Glasgow Celtic	12.64	64	13	-	1

HAWDEN, Kenneth
Huddersfield, 16 September, 1931 (F)

League Club	Source	Date Signed	Seasons Played	Apps	Subs	Gls
Derby Co.	Ashenhurst S.C.	04.53	53	2	-	0

HAWKE, Warren R.
Durham, 20 September, 1970 (F)

League Club	Source	Date Signed	Seasons Played	Apps	Subs	Gls
Sunderland	YT	11.88	88-91	7	16	1
Chesterfield	L	09.91	91	7	0	1

HAWKER, David
Hull, 29 November, 1958 (M)

League Club	Source	Date Signed	Seasons Played	Apps	Subs	Gls
Hull C.	App	08.76	77-79	33	2	2
Darlington	Tr	03.80	79-82	84	4	2

HAWKER, Philip N.
Solihull, 7 December, 1962 E Yth (D/M)

League Club	Source	Date Signed	Seasons Played	Apps	Subs	Gls
Birmingham C.	App	06.80	80-82	34	1	1
Walsall	Tr	12.82	82-89	159	18	10
West Bromwich A.	Tr	09.90	90	1	0	0

HAWKES, Barry
Easington (Dm), 21 March, 1938 (IF)

League Club	Source	Date Signed	Seasons Played	Apps	Subs	Gls
Luton T.	Shotton Colly	11.55	58-59	8	-	0
Darlington	Tr	06.60	60	13	-	3
Hartlepool U.	Tr	07.61	61	9	-	0

HAWKES, Kenneth
Easington (Dm), 6 May, 1933 (FB)

League Club	Source	Date Signed	Seasons Played	Apps	Subs	Gls
Luton T.	Shotton Colly	10.51	57-60	90	-	1
Peterborough U.	Tr	06.61	61	1	-	0

HAWKINGS, Barry
Birmingham, 7 November, 1931 (IF)

League Club	Source	Date Signed	Seasons Played	Apps	Subs	Gls
Coventry C.	Jnrs	01.49	53-55	34	-	12
Lincoln C.	Tr	03.56	55-56	15	-	6
Northampton T.	Tr	06.57	57-58	64	-	25

HAWKINS, Bertram W.
Bristol, 29 September, 1923 (CF0)

League Club	Source	Date Signed	Seasons Played	Apps	Subs	Gls
Bristol Rov.	De Veys	08.47				
Bristol C.	Tr	05.49	49	8	-	4
West Ham U.	Bath C.	09.51	51-52	34	-	16
Queens Park R.	Tr	06.53	53	8	-	3

HAWKINS, David J.
Kingston, 11 August, 1931 (CF)

League Club	Source	Date Signed	Seasons Played	Apps	Subs	Gls
Gillingham (Am)	Sheppey U.	01.56	55	14	-	8

HAWKINS, Dennis R.
Swansea, 22 October, 1947 W Sch/Wu23-6 (F)

League Club	Source	Date Signed	Seasons Played	Apps	Subs	Gls
Leeds U.	App	10.64	66-67	2	0	0
Shrewsbury T.	Tr	10.68	68-69	51	7	9
Chester C.	L	09.70	70	6	2	1
Workington	L	03.72	71	6	0	1
Newport Co.	Tr	05.72	72	9	0	1

HAWKINS, Graham N.
Darlaston, 5 March, 1946 (CD)

League Club	Source	Date Signed	Seasons Played	Apps	Subs	Gls
Wolverhampton W.	App	06.63	64-67	28	6	0
Preston N.E.	Tr	01.68	67-73	241	4	3
Blackburn Rov.	Tr	06.74	74-77	108	1	4
Port Vale	Tr	01.78	77-79	61	1	3

HAWKINS, Harold
Middlesbrough, 24 November, 1915 (CF)

League Club	Source	Date Signed	Seasons Played	Apps	Subs	Gls
Middlesbrough	South Bank E.E.	02.35	35	1	-	0
Watford	Tr	06.37	37	5	-	0
Southport	Tr	07.38	38-46	79	-	31
Gateshead	Tr	06.47	47	27	-	12
Hartlepool U.	Tr	03.48	47-48	30	-	4

HAWKINS, Herbert H.
Lambeth, 15 July, 1923 (CF)

League Club	Source	Date Signed	Seasons Played	Apps	Subs	Gls
Leyton Orient	Gravesend & Nft	06.51	51-52	5	-	0

HAWKINS, Nigel S.
Bristol, 7 September, 1968 (F)

League Club	Source	Date Signed	Seasons Played	Apps	Subs	Gls
Bristol C.	YT	02.87	87-88	8	10	2
Blackpool	Tr	10.89	89	4	3	0

HAWKINS, Peter M.
Swansea, 18 December, 1951 W Sch (F)

League Club	Source	Date Signed	Seasons Played	Apps	Subs	Gls
Northampton T.	App	12.68	68-73	49	10	10

HAWKSBY, John F.
York, 12 June, 1942 E Yth (IF)

League Club	Source	Date Signed	Seasons Played	Apps	Subs	Gls
Leeds U.	Jnrs	06.59	60-62	37	-	2
Lincoln C.	Tr	08.64	64-65	64	1	4
York C.	Tr	03.66	65-67	72	2	7

HAWKSFORD, Edward
Liverpool, 7 November, 1931 (OR)

League Club	Source	Date Signed	Seasons Played	Apps	Subs	Gls
Mansfield T.	Army	03.52	52	1	-	0

HAWKSWORTH, Anthony
Sheffield, 15 January, 1938 E Sch/E Yth (G)

League Club	Source	Date Signed	Seasons Played	Apps	Subs	Gls
Manchester U.	Jnrs	04.55	56	1	-	0

HAWKSWORTH, Derek M.
Bradford, 16 July, 1927 E'B'-1 (OL)

League Club	Source	Date Signed	Seasons Played	Apps	Subs	Gls
Bradford C.	Huddersfield T. (Am)	10.48	48-50	75	-	20
Sheffield U.	Tr	12.50	50-57	255	-	88
Huddersfield T.	Tr	05.58	58-59	55	-	14
Lincoln C.	Tr	02.60	59-60	36	-	14
Bradford C.	Tr	01.61	60-61	44	-	8

HAWLEY, Alan J.
Woking, 7 June, 1946 (FB)

League Club	Source	Date Signed	Seasons Played	Apps	Subs	Gls
Brentford	App	06.63	62-73	316	2	5

HAWLEY, John E.
Withernsea, 8 May, 1954 (F)

League Club	Source	Date Signed	Seasons Played	Apps	Subs	Gls
Hull C.	Jnrs	04.72	72-77	101	13	22
Leeds U.	Tr	04.78	78-79	30	3	16
Sunderland	Tr	10.79	79-80	25	0	11
Arsenal	Tr	09.81	81-82	14	6	3
Leyton Orient	L	10.82	82	4	0	1
Hull C.	L	12.82	82	3	0	1
Bradford C.	Happy Valley(HK)	09.83	83-84	61	6	28
Scunthorpe U.	Tr	07.85	85	18	3	7

HAWORTH, Gary
Bury, 25 April, 1959 (F)

League Club	Source	Date Signed	Seasons Played	Apps	Subs	Gls
Rochdale (N/C)	Radcliffe Bor.	08.84	84	1	0	0

HAWORTH, Herbert
Accrington, 5 May, 1920 (IF)

League Club	Source	Date Signed	Seasons Played	Apps	Subs	Gls
Accrington St. (Am)	Woodcock Amats	10.46	46	2	-	0

HAWSON, Alexander
Auchincaim, 23 October, 1923 (RH)

League Club	Source	Date Signed	Seasons Played	Apps	Subs	Gls
Rochdale	Aberdeen	12.48	48	1	-	0

HAWTIN, Craig S.
Buxton, 29 March, 1970 (FB)

League Club	Source	Date Signed	Seasons Played	Apps	Subs	Gls
Chester C.	Port Vale (YT)	09.88	87-88	6	1	1
Burnley (N/C)	Tr	08.89				

HAY, Alan B.
Dunfermline, 28 November, 1958 (LB)

League Club	Source	Date Signed	Seasons Played	Apps	Subs	Gls
Bolton W.	Dundee	03.77				
Bristol C.	Tr	07.78	79-81	72	2	1
York C.	Tr	08.82	82-85	147	3	2
Tranmere Rov.	Tr	08.86	86	27	1	0
York C. (N/C)	Hill of Beath	12.88	88	1	0	0
Sunderland	Tr	02.89	88	1	0	0
Torquay U.	Tr	09.89	89-90	10	0	0

HAY, David
Paisley, 29 January, 1948 Su23-3/SF Lge/S-27 (D)

League Club	Source	Date Signed	Seasons Played	Apps	Subs	Gls
Chelsea	Glasgow Celtic	08.74	74-78	107	1	2

HAYCOCK, Frederick J.
Liverpool, 19 April, 1912 Died 1989 (IL)

League Club	Source	Date Signed	Seasons Played	Apps	Subs	Gls
Aston Villa	Prescot Cables	02.34	36-38	99	-	28
Wrexham	Tr	12.45	46	6	-	1

HAYCOCK, T. Paul
Sheffield, 8 July, 1962 (F)

League Club	Source	Date Signed	Seasons Played	Apps	Subs	Gls
Rotherham U.	Burton A.	08.86	86-89	77	20	22

HAYDE, Michael P.
St Helens, 20 June, 1971 (FB)

League Club	Source	Date Signed	Seasons Played	Apps	Subs	Gls
Chester C.	Liverpool (YT)	08.89	89	0	1	0

HAYDOCK, Frank
Eccles, 29 November, 1940 (CH)

League Club	Source	Date Signed	Seasons Played	Apps	Subs	Gls
Manchester U.	Jnrs	12.58	60-62	6	-	0
Charlton Ath.	Tr	08.63	63-65	84	0	4
Portsmouth	Tr	12.65	65-68	71	0	1
Southend U.	Tr	01.69	68-69	29	4	4

HAYDOCK, William E.
Salford, 19 January, 1937 (FB)

League Club	Source	Date Signed	Seasons Played	Apps	Subs	Gls
Manchester C.	Buxton	03.59	59-60	3	-	1
Crewe Alex.	Tr	03.61	60-64	142	-	30
Grimsby T.	Tr	11.64	64	21	-	4
Stockport Co.	Tr	08.65	65-70	257	4	4
Southport	Port Elizabeth (SA)	11.71	71	7	0	0

HAYES, Austin W. P.
Hammersmith, 15 July, 1958 Died 1986 IRu21-1/IR-1 (W)

League Club	Source	Date Signed	Seasons Played	Apps	Subs	Gls
Southampton	App	07.76	76-79	22	9	5
Millwall	Tr	02.81	80-82	40	7	5
Northampton T.	Tr	08.83	83-84	60	3	13

HAYES, Hugh
Bangor, 23 June, 1925 (WH)

League Club	Source	Date Signed	Seasons Played	Apps	Subs	Gls
Ipswich T.	Bangor	06.46	48-49	9	-	0

HAYES, Joseph
Kearsley, 20 January, 1936 Eu23-2 (IF)

League Club	Source	Date Signed	Seasons Played	Apps	Subs	Gls
Manchester C.	Jnrs	08.53	53-64	331	-	142
Barnsley	Tr	07.65	65	26	0	2

HAYES, Martin
Walthamstow, 21 March, 1966 Eu21-3 (W)

League Club	Source	Date Signed	Seasons Played	Apps	Subs	Gls
Arsenal	App	11.83	85-89	70	32	26
Wimbledon (L)	Glasgow Celtic	09.92	91	1	1	0

HAYES, Michael
Newport, 11 September, 1954 (D)

League Club	Source	Date Signed	Seasons Played	Apps	Subs	Gls
Newport Co. (N/C)		01.76	75	4	0	0

HAYES, Michael C.
Aberdare, 24 April, 1944 W Sch (WH)

League Club	Source	Date Signed	Seasons Played	Apps	Subs	Gls
Swansea C.	Jnrs	06.61	62	3	-	0

HAYES, Philip H.
Chiswick, 23 December, 1935 (F)

League Club	Source	Date Signed	Seasons Played	Apps	Subs	Gls
Millwall	Slough T.	12.56	56-58	16	-	1

HAYES, Samuel
Accrington, 21 June, 1920 Died 1959 (G)

League Club	Source	Date Signed	Seasons Played	Apps	Subs	Gls
Accrington St. (Am)	Blackburn Rov. (Am)	10.46	46	13	-	0

HAYES, Stephen C.
Smethwick, 28 January, 1952 (CD)

League Club	Source	Date Signed	Seasons Played	Apps	Subs	Gls
Shrewsbury T.	Warley Bor.	02.74	74-79	69	3	0
Torquay U.	L	09.75	75	1	0	0
Torquay U.	Tr	07.80	80	25	0	0

HAYES, William
Runcorn, 8 June, 1919 (HB)

League Club	Source	Date Signed	Seasons Played	Apps	Subs	Gls
Oldham Ath.	Halton Jnrs	01.37	38-50	126	-	3

HAYES, William
Newcastle-u-Lyme, 2 March, 1918 (CH)

League Club	Source	Date Signed	Seasons Played	Apps	Subs	Gls
Crewe Alex.	R.O.F. Radway Green	09.46	46	29	-	0

HAYES, William E.
Cork (Ire), 7 November, 1915 IR-2/NI-4 (FB)

League Club	Source	Date Signed	Seasons Played	Apps	Subs	Gls
Huddersfield T.	Jnrs	04.33	34-49	181	-	5
Burnley	Tr	02.50	49-50	12	-	0

HAYES, William J.
Limerick (Ire), 30 March, 1928 LOI/IR Amat/IR-1 (G)

League Club	Source	Date Signed	Seasons Played	Apps	Subs	Gls
Wrexham	Limerick	07.50	50	14	-	0
Torquay U.	Ellesmere Port	08.52	52-55	54	-	0

HAYHURST, Stanley
Leyland, 13 May, 1925 (G)

League Club	Source	Date Signed	Seasons Played	Apps	Subs	Gls
Blackburn Rov.	Leyland Motors	01.43	46-48	27	-	0
Tottenham H.	Tr	10.48				
Barrow	Tr	06.50	50	26	-	0
Grimsby T.	Tr	01.51	50-52	62	-	0

HAYLOCK, Garry A.
Bradford, 31 December, 1970 (F)

League Club	Source	Date Signed	Seasons Played	Apps	Subs	Gls
Huddersfield T.	YT	07.89	90-91	10	3	4

HAYLOCK, Paul
Lowestoft, 24 March, 1963 (RB)

League Club	Source	Date Signed	Seasons Played	Apps	Subs	Gls
Norwich C.	App	01.81	81-85	154	1	3
Gillingham	Tr	08.86	86-89	149	3	0
Maidstone U.	Tr	03.91	90-91	47	1	1

HAYMAN, James
Ramsbottom, 19 February, 1928 (FB)

League Club	Source	Date Signed	Seasons Played	Apps	Subs	Gls
Bury	Radcliffe Bor.	11.50	50	5	-	0

HAYNES, Arthur E. T.
Birmingham, 23 May, 1924 (OR)

League Club	Source	Date Signed	Seasons Played	Apps	Subs	Gls
Aston Villa		01.46	46	4	-	0
Walsall	Tr	05.48	48	2	-	0

HAYNES, Eric
Sheffield, 18 June, 1936 (F)

League Club	Source	Date Signed	Seasons Played	Apps	Subs	Gls
Rotherham U.	Thorncliffe	04.56	55	1	-	0

HAYNES, John, N.
Edmonton, 17 October, 1934 E Sch/E Yth/Eu23-8/E'B'-5/EF Lge/E-56 (IF)

League Club	Source	Date Signed	Seasons Played	Apps	Subs	Gls
Fulham	Jnrs	05.52	52-69	594	0	146

HAYRETTIN, Hakan
Enfield, 4 February, 1970 (M)

League Club	Source	Date Signed	Seasons Played	Apps	Subs	Gls
Leyton Orient	YT	07.88				
Barnet	Tr	08.89	91	0	4	0

HAYS, C. John (Jack)
Ashington, 12 December, 1918 Died 1938 (OR)

League Club	Source	Date Signed	Seasons Played	Apps	Subs	Gls
Bradford P.A.	Ipswich T.	08.38	38	17	-	0
Burnley	Tr	05.39	46-50	146	-	12
Bury	Tr	09.51	51-52	27	-	2

HAYTON, Eric
Carlisle, 14 January, 1922 (OR)

League Club	Source	Date Signed	Seasons Played	Apps	Subs	Gls
Carlisle U.		08.45	46-50	49	-	5
Rochdale	Tr	05.51	51	12	-	0
Workington	Tr	10.52	52	19	-	0

HAYWARD, C. Basil
Leek, 7 April, 1928 Died 1989 (CH)

League Club	Source	Date Signed	Seasons Played	Apps	Subs	Gls
Port Vale	Northwood Heath	05.46	46-57	349	-	32
Portsmouth	Tr	07.58	58-59	44	-	4

HAYWARD, Douglas S.
Wellington, 23 August, 1920 (FB)

League Club	Source	Date Signed	Seasons Played	Apps	Subs	Gls
Huddersfield T.		05.39				
Bristol Rov.		09.46	46	1	-	0
Newport Co.	Tr	11.46	46-55	259	-	11

HAYWARD, L. Eric
Newcastle-u-Lyme, 2 August, 1917 Died 1976 (CH)

League Club	Source	Date Signed	Seasons Played	Apps	Subs	Gls
Port Vale	Wardles	08.34	34-36	34	-	0
Blackpool	Tr	07.37	37-51	269	-	0

HAYWARD, Keith W.
Hove, 21 November, 1951 (G)

League Club	Source	Date Signed	Seasons Played	Apps	Subs	Gls
Charlton Ath. (App)	App	10.67	68	1	0	0

HAYWARD, Steven L.
Pelsall, 8 September, 1971 E Yth (M)

League Club	Source	Date Signed	Seasons Played	Apps	Subs	Gls
Derby Co.	Jnrs	09.88	89-91	4	7	0

HAYWOOD, Clive
Ramsgate, 1 November, 1960 (F)

League Club	Source	Date Signed	Seasons Played	Apps	Subs	Gls
Coventry C.	App	08.78	80	1	0	0

HAYWOOD, Raymond J.
Dudley, 12 January, 1949 (F)

League Club	Source	Date Signed	Seasons Played	Apps	Subs	Gls
Shrewsbury T.	Stourbridge	05.74	74-76	75	12	27
Northampton T.	Tr	03.77	76-77	14	2	2

HAZARD, Michael
Sunderland, 5 February, 1960 (M)

League Club	Source	Date Signed	Seasons Played	Apps	Subs	Gls
Tottenham H.	App	02.78	79-85	73	18	13
Chelsea	Tr	09.85	85-89	78	3	9
Portsmouth	Tr	01.90	89	8	0	1
Swindon T.	Tr	09.90	90-91	75	3	14

HAZEL, Clifford
Woolwich, 14 September, 1937 (IF)

League Club	Source	Date Signed	Seasons Played	Apps	Subs	Gls
Gillingham	Hastings U.	07.55	57	2	-	0
Millwall	Tr	07.58				

Johnny Haynes (Fulham & England)

HAZEL, Desmond L.
Bradford, 15 July, 1967 (W)

League Club	Source	Date Signed	Seasons Played	Apps	Subs	Gls
Sheffield Wed.	App	07.85	87	5	1	0
Grimsby T.	L	10.86	86	9	0	2
Rotherham U.	Tr	07.88	88-91	131	21	19

HAZEL, Ian
Merton, 1 December, 1967 (M)

League Club	Source	Date Signed	Seasons Played	Apps	Subs	Gls
Wimbledon	App	12.85	87-88	4	3	0
Bristol Rov.	L	02.89	88	3	0	0
Bristol Rov.	Tr	07.89	89-90	4	10	0
Maidstone U. (N/C)	Tr	03.92	91	6	2	0

HAZELDEN, Walter
Ashton-in-Makerfield, 13 February, 1941 E Yth (IF)

League Club	Source	Date Signed	Seasons Played	Apps	Subs	Gls
Aston Villa	Jnrs	02.58	57-58	17	-	5

HAZELL, Anthony P.
High Wycombe, 19 September, 1947 E Yth (D)

League Club	Source	Date Signed	Seasons Played	Apps	Subs	Gls
Queens Park R.	Jnrs	10.64	64-74	362	7	4
Millwall	Tr	12.74	74-78	153	0	6
Crystal Palace	Tr	11.78	78	5	0	0
Charlton Ath.	Tr	09.79	79-80	37	0	0

HAZELL, Robert
Jamaica, 14 June, 1959 E Yth/Eu21-1/E'B' (CD)

League Club	Source	Date Signed	Seasons Played	Apps	Subs	Gls
Wolverhampton W.	App	05.77	77-78	32	1	1
Queens Park R.	Tr	09.79	79-83	100	6	8
Leicester C.	Tr	09.83	83-84	41	0	2
Wolverhampton W.	L	09.85	85	1	0	0
Reading	Luton T. (trial)	11.86	86	4	0	0
Port Vale	Tr	12.86	86-88	81	0	1

HAZLEDINE, Albert V.
Royton, 28 July, 1918 (LH)

League Club	Source	Date Signed	Seasons Played	Apps	Subs	Gls
Halifax T.	West Ham U. (Am)	11.45	46	10	-	2

HAZLEDINE, Donald
Derby, 10 July, 1929 (IF)

League Club	Source	Date Signed	Seasons Played	Apps	Subs	Gls
Derby Co.	Notts Regent	08.51	52-53	26	-	6
Northampton T.	Tr	06.54	54	22	-	4

HAZLEDINE, Geoffrey
Derby, 27 February, 1932 (F)

League Club	Source	Date Signed	Seasons Played	Apps	Subs	Gls
Derby Co.	Notts Regent	07.52	53	1	-	0
Southport	Boston U.	07.57	57	29	-	5

HAZLETT, George
Glasgow, 10 March, 1923 (OR)

League Club	Source	Date Signed	Seasons Played	Apps	Subs	Gls
Bury	Belfast Celtic	08.49	49-51	101	-	9
Cardiff C.	Tr	08.52	52	7	-	1
Millwall	Tr	05.53	53-57	131	-	10

HAZZLETON, James
Bolton, 29 September, 1930 (IF)

League Club	Source	Date Signed	Seasons Played	Apps	Subs	Gls
Bury	Atherton Colly	05.50				
Rochdale	Tr	08.51	51	11	-	1
Accrington St.	Tr	07.52	52	4	-	0

HEAD, Bertram J.
Midsomer Norton, 8 June, 1916 (CH)

League Club	Source	Date Signed	Seasons Played	Apps	Subs	Gls
Torquay U.	Midsomer Norton	10.36	36-50	223	-	4
Bury	Tr	02.52	51-52	22	-	0

HEAD, David G.
Midsomer Norton, 11 August, 1940 (IF)

League Club	Source	Date Signed	Seasons Played	Apps	Subs	Gls
Swindon T.	Jnrs	08.58				
Arsenal	Tr	03.59				
Reading	Tr	07.60	60	12	-	0
Bristol Rov.	Tr	07.61				

HEAD, Michael
Hull, 13 April, 1933 (OR)

League Club	Source	Date Signed	Seasons Played	Apps	Subs	Gls
Hull C.	Bridlington C.U.	12.53	54	3	-	0

HEALD, Paul A.
Wath, 20 September, 1968 (G)

League Club	Source	Date Signed	Seasons Played	Apps	Subs	Gls
Sheffield U.	YT	06.87				
Leyton Orient	Tr	11.88	88-91	105	0	0
Coventry C.	L	03.92	91	2	0	0

HEALE, Gary J.
Canvey Island, 15 July, 1958 (F)

League Club	Source	Date Signed	Seasons Played	Apps	Subs	Gls
Luton T.	Canvey	12.76	77	7	0	1
Exeter C.	L	12.77	77	3	1	0
Reading	Tr	08.79	79-81	68	8	20

HEALER, Ernest
Birtley, 13 November, 1941 (IF)

League Club	Source	Date Signed	Seasons Played	Apps	Subs	Gls
Darlington		08.61				
Brighton & H.A.	Berwick R.	10.63	63	3	-	1

HEALEY, Daniel K.
Manchester, 2 December, 1953 (W)

League Club	Source	Date Signed	Seasons Played	Apps	Subs	Gls
Manchester U.	App	01.71				
Bolton W.	Tr	05.73				
Workington	Tr	07.74	74	13	4	2

HEALEY, Jonathan P.
Morecambe, 30 December, 1966 (M)

League Club	Source	Date Signed	Seasons Played	Apps	Subs	Gls
Oldham Ath.	YT	06.85				
Crewe Alex.	Alsager College	12.87	87	7	3	2

HEALEY, Ronald
Manchester, 30 August, 1952 IR-2 (G)

League Club	Source	Date Signed	Seasons Played	Apps	Subs	Gls
Manchester C.	App	10.69	70-73	30	0	0
Coventry C.	L	12.71	71	3	0	0
Preston N.E.	L	12.73	73	6	0	0
Cardiff C.	Tr	03.74	73-81	216	0	0

HEALEY, William R.
Liverpool, 22 May, 1926 (FB)

League Club	Source	Date Signed	Seasons Played	Apps	Subs	Gls
Arsenal	Chorley	05.49				
Fulham	Tr	12.52	52	1	-	0
Hartlepool U.	Tr	08.55	55	6	-	0

HEALY, Patrick J. (Felix)
Derry (NI), 27 September, 1955 (M)

League Club	Source	Date Signed	Seasons Played	Apps	Subs	Gls
Port Vale	Finn Harps	10.78	78-79	40	1	2

HEANEY, Anthony
Plymouth, 9 May, 1940 E Yth (FB)

League Club	Source	Date Signed	Seasons Played	Apps	Subs	Gls
Southampton	Jnrs	06.58	60	1	-	0

HEANEY, Neil A.
Middlesbrough, 3 November, 1971 E Yth/Eu21-4 (W)

League Club	Source	Date Signed	Seasons Played	Apps	Subs	Gls
Arsenal	YT	11.89	91	0	1	0
Hartlepool U.	L	01.91	90	2	1	0
Cambridge U.	L	01.92	91	9	4	2

HEAP, Stuart
Nelson, 7 February, 1965 (M)

League Club	Source	Date Signed	Seasons Played	Apps	Subs	Gls
Tranmere Rov. (N/C)	Clitheroe	03.85	84	0	3	0

HEARD, T. Patrick
Hull, 17 March, 1960 E Yth (LB/W)

League Club	Source	Date Signed	Seasons Played	Apps	Subs	Gls
Everton	App	03.78	78-79	10	1	0
Aston Villa	Tr	10.79	79-82	20	4	2
Sheffield Wed.	Tr	01.83	82-84	22	3	3
Newcastle U.	Tr	09.84	84	34	0	2
Middlesbrough	Tr	08.85	85	25	0	2
Hull C.	Tr	03.86	85-87	79	1	5
Rotherham U.	Tr	07.88	88-89	41	3	7
Cardiff C.	Tr	08.90	90-91	45	1	4

HEARN, Frank G.
Camden, 5 November, 1929 (IF)

League Club	Source	Date Signed	Seasons Played	Apps	Subs	Gls
Torquay U.		08.50				
Northampton T.	Tr	10.51				
Crystal Palace	Tr	06.54	54	8	-	1

HEASLEGRAVE, Samuel E.
Smethwick, 1 October, 1916 Died 1975 (IR)

League Club	Source	Date Signed	Seasons Played	Apps	Subs	Gls
West Bromwich A.	Brierley Hill Alliance	10.34	36-38	49	-	16
Northampton T.	Tr	10.45	46-47	42	-	4

HEATH, Adrian P.
Stoke, 11 January, 1961 Eu21-8 (F)

League Club	Source	Date Signed	Seasons Played	Apps	Subs	Gls
Stoke C.	App	01.79	78-81	94	1	16
Everton	Tr	01.82	81-88	206	20	71
Aston Villa	Espanol (Sp)	08.89	89	8	1	0
Manchester C.	Tr	02.90	89-91	58	17	3
Stoke C.	Tr	03.92	91	5	1	0

HEATH, Dennis J.
Chiswick, 28 September, 1934 (OR)

League Club	Source	Date Signed	Seasons Played	Apps	Subs	Gls
Brentford	Jnrs	09.52	54-60	125	-	20

HEATH, Donald
Stockton, 26 December, 1944 (W)

League Club	Source	Date Signed	Seasons Played	Apps	Subs	Gls
Middlesbrough	App	12.62				
Norwich C.	Tr	07.64	64-67	79	3	15
Swindon T.	Tr	09.67	67-69	82	6	2
Oldham Ath.	Tr	07.70	70-71	43	2	1
Peterborough U.	Tr	07.72	72	43	1	4
Hartlepool U.	Tr	07.73	73-74	36	1	2

Adrian Heath (Stoke City, Everton, Espanol, Aston Villa, Manchester City & Stoke City)

League Club	Source	Date Signed	Seasons Played	Career Record Apps	Subs	Gls

HEATH, Duncan N.
Stoke, 23 October, 1961 (D)

Aston Villa	App	07.79				
Crewe Alex.	Tr	11.80	81	17	6	0

HEATH, Herbert G.
Wolverhampton, 29 March, 1970 (CD)

Exeter C.	Walsall Wood	02.89	88	3	2	0

HEATH, John
Heywood, 5 June, 1936 (G)

Bury	Blackburn Rov. (Am)	09.56	56-61	8	-	0
Tranmere Rov.	Tr	01.62	61-63	58	-	0
Rochdale	Wigan Ath.	02.66	65	6	0	0

HEATH, Michael F.
Hillingdon, 9 January, 1953 (IF)

Brentford (Am)	Walton & Hersham	04.71	70	1	0	0

HEATH, Norman H.
Wolverhampton, 31 January, 1924 Died 1983 (G)

West Bromwich A.	Meadows B.C.	10.43	47-53	121	-	0

HEATH, Philip A.
Stoke, 24 November, 1964 (LW)

Stoke C.	App	10.82	82-87	144	12	17
Oxford U.	Tr	06.88	88-89	24	13	1
Cardiff C.	Tr	03.91	90	11	0	1
Aldershot	Tr	08.91				

HEATH, Seamus M. J. P.
Belfast, 6 December, 1961 (D)

Luton T.	Jnrs	04.79				
Lincoln C.	L	08.82	82	6	1	0
Wrexham	Tr	08.83	83	32	0	1
Tranmere Rov.	Tr	08.84	84	6	11	0

HEATH, R. Terence
Leicester, 17 November, 1943 (M)

Leicester C.	App	11.61	62-63	8	-	2
Hull C.	Tr	05.64	64-67	27	6	1
Scunthorpe U.	Tr	03.68	67-72	174	3	50
Lincoln C.	Tr	02.73	72-73	17	0	1

HEATH, William H. M.
Bournemouth, 15 April, 1934 (G)

Bournemouth	Jnrs	12.51	56-57	34	-	0
Lincoln C.	Tr	11.58	58-61	84	-	0

HEATH, William J.
Stepney, 26 June, 1920 (FB)

Queens Park R.		09.45	46-52	93	-	3

HEATHCOTE, Michael
Kelloe (Dm), 10 September, 1965 (CD)

Sunderland	Spennymoor U.	08.87	87-89	6	3	0
Halifax T.	L	12.87	87	7	0	1
York C.	L	01.90	89	3	0	0
Shrewsbury T.	Tr	07.90	90-91	43	1	6
Cambridge U.	Tr	09.91	91	17	5	5

HEATHCOTE, Peter G. S.
Leicester, 13 November, 1932 (G)

Southend U.	Jnrs	11.51	51	2	-	0

HEATHCOTE, Wilfred
Hemsworth, 29 June, 1911 (CF)

Queens Park R.		10.43	46	5	-	1
Millwall	Tr	12.46	46	8	-	2

HEATHER, John L.
Winchcomb, 25 April, 1933 (IF)

Mansfield T.	Belper T.	08.52	53	1	-	0

HEATON, J. Michael
Sheffield, 15 January, 1947 (FB)

Sheffield U.	App	11.64	66-70	31	2	0
Blackburn Rov.	Tr	10.71	71-75	168	2	1

HEATON, Paul J.
Hyde, 24 January, 1961 (M)

Oldham Ath.	App	01.79	77-83	124	12	28
Rochdale	Tr	03.84	83-85	85	4	9

HEATON, William H.
Leeds, 26 August, 1918 (OL)

Leeds U.	Whitkirk	12.37	46-48	59	-	6
Southampton	Tr	02.49	48	15	-	0
Rochdale	Tr	11.50	50	5	-	0

League Club	Source	Date Signed	Seasons Played	Career Record Apps	Subs	Gls

HEAVISIDE, John
Ferryhill, 7 October, 1943 Died 1990 (LB)

Darlington (Am)	Bishops Middleham	08.63	63	2	-	0

HEBBERD, Trevor N.
Alresford, 19 June, 1958 (M)

Southampton	App	06.76	76-81	69	28	7
Bolton W.	L	09.81	81	6	0	0
Leicester C.	L	11.81	81	4	0	1
Oxford U.	Tr	03.82	81-87	260	0	37
Derby Co.	Tr	08.88	88-90	70	11	10
Portsmouth (N/C)	Tr	10.91	91	1	3	0
Chesterfield	Tr	11.91	91	22	2	0

HEBDITCH, Alan F.
Wigan, 11 October, 1961 (D)

Bradford C.	Leeds U. (Jnr)	08.80	80	2	0	0

HECKMAN, Ronald E.
Peckham, 23 November, 1929 Died 1990 E Amat (OL)

Leyton Orient	Bromley	07.55	55-57	87	-	38
Millwall	Tr	11.57	57-59	92	-	21
Crystal Palace	Tr	07.60	60-62	84	-	25

HECTOR, Kevin J.
Leeds, 2 November, 1944 EF Lge/E-2 (F)

Bradford P.A.	Jnrs	07.62	62-66	176	0	113
Derby Co.	Tr	09.66	66-77	426	4	147
Derby Co.	Vancouver (Can)	10.80	80-81	52	4	8

HEDLEY, Graeme
Easington (Dm), 1 March, 1957 (M)

Middlesbrough	App	03.75	76-81	36	14	6
Sheffield Wed.	L	02.78	77	6	0	1
Darlington	L	03.79	78	14	0	1
York C.	L	10.81	81	5	0	1

HEDLEY, John R. (Jack)
Willington Quay, 11 December, 1923 (FB)

Everton	North Shields	04.45	47-49	54	-	0
Sunderland	Tr	08.50	50-58	269	-	0
Gateshead	Tr	07.59	59	11	-	0

HEDMAN, Rudi G.
Lambeth, 16 November, 1964 (D)

Colchester U.		02.84	83-88	166	10	10
Crystal Palace	Tr	12.88	88-91	10	11	0
Leyton Orient	L	12.89	89	5	0	0

HEDWORTH, Christopher
Wallsend, 5 January, 1964 (D)

Newcastle U.	App	01.82	82-85	8	1	0
Barnsley	Tr	08.86	86-87	19	6	0
Halifax T.	Tr	08.88	88-89	38	0	0
Blackpool	Tr	09.90	90-91	24	0	0

HEELEY, D. Mark
Peterborough, 8 September, 1959 (W)

Peterborough U.	App	11.76	75-76	12	5	3
Arsenal	Tr	09.77	77-78	9	6	1
Northampton T.	Tr	03.80	79-82	84	8	3

HEENAN, Thomas
Glasgow, 16 June, 1932 (IF)

Bradford P.A.	Stirling A.	05.58	58	5	-	1

HEEPS, James A.
Luton, 16 May, 1971 (G)

Swansea C.	YT	07.89	89	1	0	0

HEESOM, Darren L.
Warrington, 8 May, 1968 (LB)

Burnley	App	12.85	85-86	36	2	1

HEFFER, Paul V.
West Ham, 21 December, 1947 (CH)

West Ham U.	Jnrs	08.65	66-71	11	4	0

HEFFER, Robert W.
Mildenhall, 9 November, 1935 (W)

Norwich C.	R.A.F. St Faiths	04.56	56	2	-	1

HEFFERNAN, Thomas P.
Dublin, 30 April, 1955 (RB)

Tottenham H.	Dunleary Celtic	10.77				
Bournemouth	Tr	05.79	79-82	152	2	21
Sheffield U.	Tr	08.83	83-84	82	0	5
Bournemouth	Tr	06.85	85-87	58	5	6

HEFFRON, Charles
Belfast, 13 August, 1927 (G)

League Club	Source	Date Signed	Seasons Played	Apps	Subs	Gls
Bradford P.A.	Belfast Celtic	06.49	51-52	25	-	0

HEGAN, Daniel
Coatbridge, 14 June, 1943 NI-7 (M)

League Club	Source	Date Signed	Seasons Played	Apps	Subs	Gls
Sunderland	Albion Rov.	09.61				
Ipswich T.	Tr	07.63	63-68	207	0	34
West Bromwich A.	Tr	05.69	69	13	1	2
Wolverhampton W.	Tr	05.70	70-73	49	4	6
Sunderland	Tr	11.73	73	3	3	0

HEGARTY, Kevin M.
Edinburgh, 30 July, 1950 (F)

League Club	Source	Date Signed	Seasons Played	Apps	Subs	Gls
Carlisle U.	Hearts	09.71	71	1	6	0

HEGGARTY, James P.
Lame (NI), 4 August, 1965 (CD)

League Club	Source	Date Signed	Seasons Played	Apps	Subs	Gls
Brighton & H.A.	Larne T.	09.84				
Burnley	Tr	08.85	85	33	3	1

HEGGIE, William C.
Perth, 7 June, 1927 (CF)

League Club	Source	Date Signed	Seasons Played	Apps	Subs	Gls
New Brighton	Jeanfield Swifts	02.51	50	10	-	5
Leeds U.	Tr	06.51				
Wrexham	Tr	08.52	52-54	33	-	13
Accrington St.	Winsford U.	02.55	54	1	-	0

HEGGS, Carl S.
Leicester, 11 October, 1970 (LW)

League Club	Source	Date Signed	Seasons Played	Apps	Subs	Gls
West Bromwich A.	Leicester U.	08.91	91	3	0	0

HEGINBOTHAM, Brian
Hyde, 3 October, 1937 (HB)

League Club	Source	Date Signed	Seasons Played	Apps	Subs	Gls
Stockport Co.	Jnrs	10.54	58-59	11	-	0

HEIGHWAY, Stephen D.
Dublin, 25 November, 1947 IR-33 (W)

League Club	Source	Date Signed	Seasons Played	Apps	Subs	Gls
Liverpool	Skelmersdale U.	05.70	70-80	312	17	50

Steve Heighway (Liverpool & Republic of Ireland)

HELLAWELL, John R.
Keighley, 20 December, 1943 (IF)

League Club	Source	Date Signed	Seasons Played	Apps	Subs	Gls
Bradford C.	Salts	06.63	62-64	48	-	13
Rotherham U.	Tr	01.65	64-65	5	1	2
Darlington	Tr	07.66	66	6	3	1
Bradford P.A.		10.68	68	1	0	0

HELLAWELL, Michael S.
Keighley, 30 June, 1938 E-2 (OR)

League Club	Source	Date Signed	Seasons Played	Apps	Subs	Gls
Queens Park R.	Salts	08.55	55-56	45	-	7
Birmingham C.	Tr	05.57	57-64	178	-	30
Sunderland	Tr	01.65	64-66	43	1	2
Huddersfield T.	Tr	09.66	66-67	45	1	1
Peterborough U.	Tr	12.68	68	9	0	0

HELLEWELL, Keith
Barnsley, 1 April, 1944 (G)

League Club	Source	Date Signed	Seasons Played	Apps	Subs	Gls
Doncaster Rov.	Jnrs	05.61	62-63	12	-	0

HELLIN, Anthony
Merthyr Tydfill, 26 September, 1944 W Sch (LB)

League Club	Source	Date Signed	Seasons Played	Apps	Subs	Gls
Swindon T.	App	06.62				
Torquay U.	Tr	07.64	64-65	29	0	1

HELLIN, Matthew K.
Merthyr Tydfil, 12 September, 1966 (D)

League Club	Source	Date Signed	Seasons Played	Apps	Subs	Gls
Aston Villa	App	09.84				
Wolverhampton W.	Tr	08.86	86	1	0	0

HELLINGS, Dennis
Lincoln, 9 December, 1923

League Club	Source	Date Signed	Seasons Played	Apps	Subs	Gls
Lincoln C.		12.45	46	3	-	0

HELLIWELL, David
Blackburn, 28 March, 1948 (W)

League Club	Source	Date Signed	Seasons Played	Apps	Subs	Gls
Blackburn Rov.	App	05.66	66-68	15	0	1
Lincoln C.	Tr	05.69	69	11	2	1
Workington	Tr	07.70	70-75	184	13	20
Rochdale	Tr	07.76	76	20	11	3

HELLIWELL, Ian
Rotherham, 7 November, 1962 (F)

League Club	Source	Date Signed	Seasons Played	Apps	Subs	Gls
York C.	Matlock T.	10.87	87-90	158	2	40
Scunthorpe U.	Tr	08.91	91	38	1	9

HEMMERMAN, Jeffrey L.
Hull, 25 February, 1955 (F)

League Club	Source	Date Signed	Seasons Played	Apps	Subs	Gls
Hull C.	App	03.73	73-76	45	14	10
Scunthorpe U.	L	09.75	75	4	1	1
Port Vale	Tr	06.77	77	13	2	5
Portsmouth	Tr	07.78	78-81	114	9	38
Cardiff C.	Tr	07.82	82-83	54	1	22

HEMMING, Christopher A. J.
Newcastle-u-Lyme, 13 April, 1966 (CD)

League Club	Source	Date Signed	Seasons Played	Apps	Subs	Gls
Stoke C.	Jnrs	04.84	83-88	85	8	2
Wigan Ath.	L	01.89	88	4	0	0
Hereford U.	Tr	08.89	89-90	39	2	3

HEMSLEY, Edward J. O. (Ted)
Stoke, 1 September, 1943 (D)

League Club	Source	Date Signed	Seasons Played	Apps	Subs	Gls
Shrewsbury T.	Jnrs	07.61	60-68	234	1	21
Sheffield U.	Tr	08.68	68-76	247	0	8
Doncaster Rov.	Tr	07.77	77-78	32	0	1

HEMSTEAD, Derek W.
Scunthorpe, 22 May, 1943 (FB)

League Club	Source	Date Signed	Seasons Played	Apps	Subs	Gls
Scunthorpe U.	Jnrs	05.60	60-68	249	0	2
Carlisle U.	Tr	07.69	69-72	96	1	1

HEMSTOCK, Brian
Goldthorpe, 9 February, 1949 (F)

League Club	Source	Date Signed	Seasons Played	Apps	Subs	Gls
Barnsley	Jnrs	12.66	66	1	0	0
Bradford P.A.	Tr	07.68	68	4	0	0

HENCHER, Kenneth E. E.
Romford, 2 February, 1928 (CH)

League Club	Source	Date Signed	Seasons Played	Apps	Subs	Gls
Millwall		12.49	49-55	48	-	0

HENCHER, Nicholas H.
Wrexham, 24 August, 1961 (W)

League Club	Source	Date Signed	Seasons Played	Apps	Subs	Gls
Wrexham (N/C)	Lex	08.85	85-87	26	6	5

HENDERSON, Anthony J.
Newcastle, 14 January, 1954 (CH)

League Club	Source	Date Signed	Seasons Played	Apps	Subs	Gls
Rotherham U.	App	01.72	73	5	1	0

HENDERSON, Brian C.
Allendale, 12 June, 1930 (FB)

League Club	Source	Date Signed	Seasons Played	Apps	Subs	Gls
Carlisle U.		05.50				
Darlington	Tr	07.52	52-63	422	-	3

HENDERSON, George
Hartlepool, 7 March, 1946 (CF)

League Club	Source	Date Signed	Seasons Played	Apps	Subs	Gls
Hartlepool U. (Am)	Bishop Auckland	11.70	70	1	0	0

HENDERSON, John
Montrose, 22 September, 1941 (IF)

League Club	Source	Date Signed	Seasons Played	Apps	Subs	Gls
Charlton Ath.	Montrose Vic.	06.59	62	4	-	1
Exeter C.	Tr	11.62	62-63	46	-	14
Doncaster Rov.	Tr	07.64	64	10	-	0
Chesterfield	Tr	07.65	65	28	0	3

HENDERSON, John G. (Jackie)
Glasgow, 17 January, 1932 S'B'-2/S-7 (CF)

League Club	Source	Date Signed	Seasons Played	Apps	Subs	Gls
Portsmouth	Jnrs	01.49	51-57	217	-	70
Wolverhampton W.	Tr	03.58	57-58	9	-	3
Arsenal	Tr	10.58	58-61	103	-	29
Fulham	Tr	01.62	61-63	45	-	7

HENDERSON, John S. P.
Glasgow, 13 October, 1923 (IF)

League Club	Source	Date Signed	Seasons Played	Apps	Subs	Gls
Rotherham U.	Third Lanark	11.53	53-54	47	-	7
Leeds U.	Tr	03.55	54-55	15	-	4

HENDERSON, Joseph
Cleland, 21 December, 1924 (G)

League Club	Source	Date Signed	Seasons Played	Apps	Subs	Gls
Northampton T.	Albion Rov.	05.49				
Accrington St.	Stenhousemuir	07.53	53	14	-	0

HENDERSON, W. Martin
Kirkcaldy, 3 May, 1956 (F)

League Club	Source	Date Signed	Seasons Played	Apps	Subs	Gls
Leicester C.	Philadelphia (USA)	10.78	78-80	79	12	12
Chesterfield	Tr	09.81	81-83	87	0	23
Port Vale	Tr	10.83	83	27	0	7

HENDERSON, Michael R.
Newcastle, 31 March, 1956 (M)

League Club	Source	Date Signed	Seasons Played	Apps	Subs	Gls
Sunderland	App	03.74	75-78	81	3	2
Watford	Tr	11.79	79-81	50	1	0
Cardiff C.	Tr	03.82	81	11	0	0
Sheffield U.	Tr	08.82	82-84	65	2	0
Chesterfield	Tr	01.85	84-88	135	1	10

HENDERSON, Peter
Berwick, 29 September, 1952 (W)

League Club	Source	Date Signed	Seasons Played	Apps	Subs	Gls
Chester C.	Witton A.	12.78	78-79	59	5	10
Gillingham	Tr	07.80	80	6	1	3
Crewe Alex.	L	09.81	81	6	1	0
Chester C.	Tr	12.81	81	28	0	5

HENDERSON, Raymond
Wallsend, 31 March, 1937 (OR)

League Club	Source	Date Signed	Seasons Played	Apps	Subs	Gls
Middlesbrough	Ashington	05.57	57-60	9	-	5
Hull C.	Tr	06.61	61-67	226	3	54
Reading	Tr	10.68	68	5	0	0

HENDERSON, Stanley
Barrow, 15 October, 1925 Died 1980 (OR)

League Club	Source	Date Signed	Seasons Played	Apps	Subs	Gls
Barrow	Holker C.O.B.	06.46	46-47	25	-	3

HENDERSON, Stewart J.
Bridge of Allan, 5 June, 1947 S Sch (FB)

League Club	Source	Date Signed	Seasons Played	Apps	Subs	Gls
Chelsea	Jnrs	07.64				
Brighton & H.A.	Tr	07.65	65-72	198	0	1
Reading	Tr	06.73	73-82	159	7	6

HENDERSON, Thomas
Consett, 6 April, 1949 (W)

League Club	Source	Date Signed	Seasons Played	Apps	Subs	Gls
Bradford P.A.	Tow Law T.	02.69	68-69	22	0	3
York C.	Tr	10.70	70-71	63	1	7

HENDERSON, Thomas
Burnley, 1 October, 1927 (OR)

League Club	Source	Date Signed	Seasons Played	Apps	Subs	Gls
Burnley	Jnrs	08.45	48	2	-	0

HENDERSON, Thomas W.
Larkhall, 25 July, 1943 (W)

League Club	Source	Date Signed	Seasons Played	Apps	Subs	Gls
Leeds U.	St Mirren	11.62	62-64	24	-	2
Bury	Tr	06.65	65	7	0	1
Swindon T.	Tr	01.66	65	11	0	3
Stockport Co.	Tr	07.66	66	17	2	4

HENDERSON, William
Baillieston, 24 January, 1944 S Sch/Su23-2/SF Lge/S-29 (W)

League Club	Source	Date Signed	Seasons Played	Apps	Subs	Gls
Sheffield Wed.	Glasgow Rangers	07.72	72-73	42	6	5

HENDERSON, William J.
Dumfries, 13 November, 1918 (G)

League Club	Source	Date Signed	Seasons Played	Apps	Subs	Gls
Rochdale	Queen of South	07.46	46	17	-	0
Southport	Tr	06.47	47	20	-	0

HENDON, Ian M.
Ilford, 5 December, 1971 E Yth/Eu21-4 (CD)

League Club	Source	Date Signed	Seasons Played	Apps	Subs	Gls
Tottenham H.	YT	12.89	90-91	0	4	0
Portsmouth	L	01.92	91	1	3	0
Leyton Orient	L	03.92	91	5	1	0

HENDRIE, John G.
Lennoxtown, 24 October, 1963 S Sch (RW)

League Club	Source	Date Signed	Seasons Played	Apps	Subs	Gls
Coventry C.	App	05.81	81-83	15	6	2
Hereford U.	L	01.84	83	6	0	0
Bradford C.	Tr	06.84	84-87	173	0	46
Newcastle U.	Tr	06.88	88	34	0	4
Leeds U.	Tr	06.89	89	22	5	5
Middlesbrough	Tr	06.90	90-91	78	1	6

John Hendrie (Coventry City, Bradford City, Newcastle United, Leeds United & Middlesbrough)

HENDRIE, Paul F.
Glasgow, 27 March, 1954 (W)

League Club	Source	Date Signed	Seasons Played	Apps	Subs	Gls
Birmingham C.	Kirkintilloch Rob Roy	03.72	72-75	19	3	1
Bristol Rov.	Portland (USA)	09.77	77-78	17	13	1
Halifax T.	Tr	07.79	79-83	187	0	11
Stockport Co.	Tr	08.84	84-88	114	7	6

HENDRY, E. Colin J.
Keith, 7 December, 1965 (CD)

League Club	Source	Date Signed	Seasons Played	Apps	Subs	Gls
Blackburn Rov.	Dundee	03.87	86-89	99	3	22
Manchester C.	Tr	11.89	89-91	57	6	5
Blackburn Rov.	Tr	11.91	91	26	4	4

HENDRY, Ian
Glasgow, 19 October, 1959 (M)

League Club	Source	Date Signed	Seasons Played	Apps	Subs	Gls
Aston Villa	App	09.77				
Hereford U.	Tr	02.79	78-79	21	0	0

HENDRY, John
Glasgow, 6 January, 1970 Su21-1 (F)

League Club	Source	Date Signed	Seasons Played	Apps	Subs	Gls
Tottenham H.	Dundee	07.90	90-91	3	6	3
Charlton Ath.	L	02.92	91	1	4	1

HENLEY, Leslie
Lambeth, 26 September, 1922 E Sch (IF)

League Club	Source	Date Signed	Seasons Played	Apps	Subs	Gls
Arsenal	Jnrs	09.40				
Reading	Tr	12.46	46-52	181	-	28

HENNESSEY, W. Terence
Llay, 1 September, 1942 W Sch/Wu23-6/W-39 (HB)

League Club	Source	Date Signed	Seasons Played	Apps	Subs	Gls
Birmingham C.	Jnrs	09.59	60-65	178	0	3
Nottingham F.	Tr	11.65	65-69	159	0	5
Derby Co.	Tr	02.70	69-72	62	1	4

HENNIGAN, Michael
Rotherham, 20 December, 1942 (CH)

League Club	Source	Date Signed	Seasons Played	Apps	Subs	Gls
Sheffield Wed.	Rotherham U. (Am)	03.61				
Southampton	Tr	06.62	63	3	-	0
Brighton & H.A.	Tr	07.64	64	4	-	0

HENNIN, Derek
Prescot, 28 December, 1931 Died 1987 E Yth (WH)

League Club	Source	Date Signed	Seasons Played	Apps	Subs	Gls
Bolton W.	Prescot Cables	06.49	53-60	164	-	8
Chester C.	Tr	02.61	60-61	54	-	4

HENNINGS, Roberts I.
Glyncorrwg, 30 December, 1931 (F)

League Club	Source	Date Signed	Seasons Played	Apps	Subs	Gls
Swansea C.		10.49	55-56	10	-	1

HENRY, Anthony
Houghton-le-Spring, 26 November, 1957 (M)

League Club	Source	Date Signed	Seasons Played	Apps	Subs	Gls
Manchester C.	App	12.74	76-81	68	11	6
Bolton W.	Tr	09.81	81-82	70	0	22
Oldham Ath.	Tr	03.83	82-87	185	5	25
Stoke C.	Tr	11.87	87-88	59	3	11
Shrewsbury T.	Mazda (Jap)	08.91	91	39	1	7

HENRY, Charles A.
Acton, 13 February, 1962 (M)

League Club	Source	Date Signed	Seasons Played	Apps	Subs	Gls
Swindon T.	App	02.80	80-88	200	23	26
Torquay U.	L	02.87	86	6	0	1
Northampton T.	L	03.87	86	4	0	1
Aldershot	Tr	08.89	89-90	81	0	18

HENRY, Gerald R.
Hemsworth, 5 October, 1920 (IF)

League Club	Source	Date Signed	Seasons Played	Apps	Subs	Gls
Leeds U.	Outwood Stormcocks	10.37	38-47	44	-	4
Bradford P.A.	Tr	11.47	47-49	79	-	31
Sheffield Wed.	Tr	02.50	49-51	40	-	7
Halifax T.	Tr	12.51	51-52	24	-	3

HENRY, Gordon
Troon, 9 October, 1930 (CH)

League Club	Source	Date Signed	Seasons Played	Apps	Subs	Gls
Aldershot	St Mirren	06.56	56-63	176	-	15

HENRY, Liburd A.
Dominica (WI), 29 August, 1967 (FB)

League Club	Source	Date Signed	Seasons Played	Apps	Subs	Gls
Watford	Leytonstone & Ilford	11.87	88-89	8	2	1
Halifax T.	L	09.88	88	1	4	0
Maidstone U.	Tr	06.90	90-91	61	6	9

HENRY, Nicholas I.
Liverpool, 21 February, 1969 (M)

League Club	Source	Date Signed	Seasons Played	Apps	Subs	Gls
Oldham Ath.	YT	06.87	87-91	142	7	10

HENRY, Ronald P.
Shoreditch, 17 August, 1934 E-1 (LB)

League Club	Source	Date Signed	Seasons Played	Apps	Subs	Gls
Tottenham H.	Redbourne	03.52	54-65	247	0	1

HENSHAW, Gary
Leeds, 18 February, 1965 (W)

League Club	Source	Date Signed	Seasons Played	Apps	Subs	Gls
Grimsby T.	App	02.83	83-86	46	4	9
Bolton W.	Tr	06.87	87-90	49	21	4
Rochdale	L	03.90	89	8	1	1

HENSON, Anthony, H.
Dronfield, 15 October, 1960 (M)

League Club	Source	Date Signed	Seasons Played	Apps	Subs	Gls
Chesterfield	Alfreton T.	11.81	81-82	26	2	0

HENSON, Leonard
Hull, 6 August, 1921 (WH)

League Club	Source	Date Signed	Seasons Played	Apps	Subs	Gls
Gillingham		05.50	50	8	-	0

HENSON, Philip M.
Manchester, 30 March, 1953 (M)

League Club	Source	Date Signed	Seasons Played	Apps	Subs	Gls
Manchester C.	App	07.70	71-74	12	4	0
Swansea C.	L	07.72	72	1	0	0
Sheffield Wed.	Tr	02.75	74-76	65	8	9
Stockport Co.	Sparta Rotterdam (Neth)	09.78	78-79	65	2	13
Rotherham U.	Tr	02.80	79-83	87	5	7

HENWOOD, Rodney C.
Portsmouth, 27 November, 1931 (OL)

League Club	Source	Date Signed	Seasons Played	Apps	Subs	Gls
Portsmouth	Kingston B.C.	05.50	53	2	-	0

HEPBURN, John
Paisley, 10 March, 1921 (OR)

League Club	Source	Date Signed	Seasons Played	Apps	Subs	Gls
Workington	Morton	08.51	51	1	-	0

HEPPELL, George B.
Hartlepool, 2 September, 1916 (G)

League Club	Source	Date Signed	Seasons Played	Apps	Subs	Gls
Wolverhampton W.		09.36				
Port Vale	Tr	05.37	37-51	193	-	0

HEPPLE, Gordon
Sunderland, 16 September, 1925 Died 1980 (FB)

League Club	Source	Date Signed	Seasons Played	Apps	Subs	Gls
Middlesbrough	North Sands	07.45	46-53	41	-	0
Norwich C.	Tr	06.54	54	5	-	0

HEPPLE, John A.
Middlesbrough, 12 March, 1970 (F)

League Club	Source	Date Signed	Seasons Played	Apps	Subs	Gls
Sunderland	YT	07.87				
Hartlepool U.	L	03.89	88	1	1	0

HEPPLEWHITE, George
Edmondsley (Dm), 5 September, 1919 (CH)

League Club	Source	Date Signed	Seasons Played	Apps	Subs	Gls
Huddersfield T.	Horden Colly	05.39	46-50	156	-	3
Preston N.E.	Tr	03.51				
Bradford C.	Tr	07.53	53-54	57	-	2

HEPPLEWHITE, Wilson
Washington, 11 June, 1946 (OL)

League Club	Source	Date Signed	Seasons Played	Apps	Subs	Gls
Carlisle U.	Crook T.	03.65	65	3	0	0
Hartlepool U.	Tr	07.67	67-68	50	2	2

HEPPOLETTE, Richard A. W. (Ricky)
India, 8 April, 1949 (M)

League Club	Source	Date Signed	Seasons Played	Apps	Subs	Gls
Preston N.E.	App	09.64	67-72	149	5	13
Leyton Orient	Tr	12.72	72-76	113	0	10
Crystal Palace	Tr	10.76	76	13	2	0
Chesterfield	Tr	02.77	76-78	46	1	3
Peterborough U.	Tr	08.79	79	5	0	0

HEPTON, Stanley
Leeds, 3 December, 1932 (IF)

League Club	Source	Date Signed	Seasons Played	Apps	Subs	Gls
Blackpool	Ashley Road	03.50	52-56	7	-	3
Huddersfield T.	Tr	08.57	57-58	6	-	1
Bury	Tr	06.59	59	14	-	3
Rochdale	Tr	07.60	60-63	149	-	21
Southport	Tr	07.64	64	22	-	2

HEPWORTH, Maurice
Hexham, 6 September, 1953 (FB)

League Club	Source	Date Signed	Seasons Played	Apps	Subs	Gls
Sunderland	App	09.70	70	2	0	0
Darlington	L	01.75	74	4	0	0

HEPWORTH, Ronald
Barnsley, 25 January, 1919 (FB)

League Club	Source	Date Signed	Seasons Played	Apps	Subs	Gls
Chesterfield		05.36				
Bradford P.A.	Tr	05.39	46-50	101	-	0

League Club	Source	Date Signed	Seasons Played	Career Record Apps	Subs	Gls
HERBERT, David R.						
Sheffield, 23 January, 1956						(F)
Sheffield Wed.	App	01.74	74-75	12	5	5
HERBERT, Frank						
Stocksbridge, 29 June, 1916 Died 1972						(RH)
Sheffield Wed.		05.38				
Bury	Tr	10.45				
Oldham Ath.	Tr	06.46	46	4	-	0
HERBERT, Richard L. (Rikki)						
New Zealand, 10 April, 1961 NZ Int						(CD)
Wolverhampton W.	Sydney Olympic (Aus)	10.84	84-85	44	1	0
HERBERT, Robert						
Glasgow, 21 November, 1925						(WH)
Doncaster Rov.	Blantyre Vic.	06.50	50-55	108	-	15
HERBERT, Stanley						
Whitehaven, 29 August, 1946						(IF)
Workington (Am)	Jnrs	09.66	66	1	0	0
HERBERT, Trevor E.						
Reading, 3 June, 1929						(CF)
Leyton Orient		08.49				
Crystal Palace	Tr	07.50	50	8	-	2
HERD, Alexander						
Bowhill, 8 November, 1911 Died 1982 SF Lge						(IF)
Manchester C.	Hamilton Acad.	02.33	32-47	257	-	107
Stockport Co.	Tr	03.48	47-51	110	-	35
HERD, David G.						
Hamilton, 15 April, 1934 S-5						(CF)
Stockport Co.	Jnrs	04.51	50-53	16	-	6
Arsenal	Tr	08.54	54-60	166	-	97
Manchester U.	Tr	07.61	61-67	201	1	114
Stoke C.	Tr	07.68	68-69	39	5	11

Dave Herd (Stockport County, Arsenal, Manchester United, Stoke City & Scotland)

League Club	Source	Date Signed	Seasons Played	Career Record Apps	Subs	Gls
HERD, George						
Gartcosh, 6 May, 1936 Su23-2/SF Lge/S-5						(IF)
Sunderland	Clyde	04.61	60-68	275	3	47
Hartlepool U.	Tr	06.70	70	9	4	0
HERITAGE, Peter M.						
Bexhill, 8 November, 1960						(F)
Gillingham	Hythe T.	08.89	89-90	42	15	11
Hereford U.	Tr	02.91	90-91	55	2	9

Peter Heritage (Gillingham & Hereford United)

League Club	Source	Date Signed	Seasons Played	Career Record Apps	Subs	Gls
HERNON, James						
Cleland, 6 December, 1924						(IF)
Leicester C.	Mossvale Y.M.C.A.	04.42	46-47	31	-	7
Bolton W.	Tr	09.48	48-50	43	-	2
Grimsby T.	Tr	08.51	51-53	91	-	23
Watford	Tr	07.54	54-55	43	-	10
HEROD, Dennis J.						
Stoke, 27 October, 1923						(G)
Stoke C.	Jnrs	01.41	46-52	191	-	1
Stockport Co.	Tr	07.53	53	33	-	0
HERON, Brian						
Dumbarton, 19 June, 1948						(W)
Oxford U.	Dumbarton	07.74	74-76	40	3	8
Scunthorpe U.	Tr	07.77	77	20	5	1

League Club	Source	Date Signed	Seasons Played	Career Record Apps	Subs	Gls

HERON, Thomas R. F.
Irvine, 31 March, 1936 (LB)

Manchester U.	Portadown	03.58	57-60	3	-	0
York C.	Tr	05.61	61-65	192	0	6

HERON, William B.
Washington, 29 March, 1932 (IF)

Gateshead		02.55	54-56	21	-	1

HERRERA, Roberto
Torquay, 12 June, 1970 (FB)

Queens Park R.	YT	02.88	88-90	4	2	0
Torquay U.	L	03.92	91	11	0	0

HERRING, Harold
Hartlepool, 4 January, 1939 (F)

Hartlepool U.		08.58	58	2	-	0

HERRING, Paul J.
Hyde, 1 July, 1973 (M)

Rochdale	YT	07.91	90	0	1	0

HERRINGTON, Eric
Rotherham, 30 October, 1943 (CH)

Doncaster Rov.	Jnrs	01.61	61	1	-	0

HERRIOT, James
Airdrie, 20 December, 1939 SF Lge/S-8 (G)

Birmingham C.	Dunfermline Ath.	05.65	65-69	181	0	0
Mansfield T.	L	11.70	70	5	0	0

HERRITTY, Alan M.
Newport, 24 October, 1941 W Sch (FB)

Newport Co.	Jnrs	12.58	59-61	28	-	0

HERRITTY, William R.
Newport, 2 September, 1938 (IR)

Newport Co.	Jnrs	05.57	56-62	62	-	12

HERRON, Alan
Washington, 6 October, 1932 (CH)

Blackburn Rov.	Newcastle U. (Am)	08.50	55-56	4	-	0

HERRON, John
Widdrington (Nd), 2 March, 1938 (F)

Leeds U.		10.56				
Gateshead	Tr	06.57	57-58	8	-	0

HESELTINE, George V.
Wolverhampton, 25 March, 1926 (IF)

Walsall	Hednesford T.	02.49	48-49	8	-	0

HESELTINE, Wayne A.
Bradford, 3 December, 1969 (D)

Manchester U.	YT	12.87				
Oldham Ath.	Tr	12.89	89	1	0	0

HESFORD, Iain
Kenya, 4 March, 1960 E Yth/Eu21-7 (G)

Blackpool	App	08.77	77-82	202	0	0
Sheffield Wed.	Tr	08.83				
Fulham	L	01.85	84	3	0	0
Notts Co.	L	11.85	85	10	0	0
Sunderland	Tr	08.86	86-88	97	0	0
Hull C.	Tr	12.88	88-90	91	0	0
Maidstone U.	Tr	08.91	91	42	0	1

HESFORD, Robert T.
Bolton, 13 April, 1916 Died 1982 (G)

Huddersfield T.	South Shore	09.33	34-49	203	-	0

HESLOP, Brian
Carlisle, 4 August, 1947 (D)

Carlisle U.	App	08.65	65-66	5	0	0
Sunderland	Tr	05.67	67-70	57	1	0
Northampton T.	Tr	03.71	70-71	49	1	0
Workington	Tr	09.72	72-75	139	1	5

HESLOP, George W.
Wallsend, 1 July, 1940 (CH)

Newcastle U.	Dudley Welfare	02.59	59-61	27	-	0
Everton	Tr	03.62	62-65	10	0	0
Manchester C.	Tr	09.65	65-71	159	3	1
Bury	Tr	08.72	72	37	0	0

HESLOP, Norman
Bolton, 1 August, 1920 (IF)

Southport	Bolton W. (Am)	10.46	46-47	30	-	4

HESSENTHALER, Andrew
Dartford, 17 August, 1965 (W)

Watford	Redbridge F.	09.91	91	35	0	2

HETHERINGTON, R. Brent
Carlisle, 6 December, 1961 (F)

Carlisle U.	Workington	08.87	87-89	61	27	23

HETHERINGTON, Harold
Chester-le-Street, 7 November, 1928 (OR)

Sunderland	Shiney Row	05.46	47	2	-	0
Gateshead	Tr	01.49	48	2	-	1

HETHERINGTON, Thomas B.
Newcastle, 22 January, 1911 (G)

Burnley	Walker Celtic	12.33	33-38	67	-	0
Barnsley	Jarrow	02.39				
Gateshead	Tr	10.46	46	1	-	0

HETHERSTON, Peter
Bellshill, 6 November, 1964 (W)

Watford	Falkirk	07.87	87	2	3	0
Sheffield U.	Tr	02.88	87	11	0	0

HETZKE, Stephen E. R.
Marlborough, 3 June, 1955 (CD)

Reading	App	06.73	71-81	254	7	23
Blackpool	Tr	07.82	82-85	140	0	18
Sunderland	Tr	03.86	85-86	31	0	0
Chester C.	Tr	06.87	87	14	0	0
Colchester U.	Tr	03.88	87-88	27	2	2

HEWARD, Brian
Lincoln, 17 July, 1935 (CH)

Scunthorpe U.	Jnrs	03.54	53-60	135	-	0
Lincoln C.	Tr	07.61	61-65	97	0	1

HEWARD, Graham K.
Newcastle, 13 October, 1965 (F)

Cambridge U.	App	10.83	83	1	0	0

HEWIE, John D.
South Africa, 13 December, 1927 Su23-1/S'B'/S-19 (FB)

Charlton Ath.	Arcadia Shep. (SA)	10.49	51-65	495	0	37

HEWITT, Daren P.
Chichester, 1 September, 1969 (M)

Aldershot	YT	08.88	88	0	2	0

HEWITT, Gerald
Sheffield, 28 January, 1935 (WH)

Sheffield U.	Jnrs	07.54	55-56	3	-	0
Workington	Tr	06.58				

HEWITT, Harold
Chesterfield, 24 June, 1919 (OR)

Mansfield T.		11.45	46	1	-	0

HEWITT, Jamie R.
Chesterfield, 17 May, 1968 (D/M)

Chesterfield	YT	04.86	85-91	240	9	14

HEWITT, John
Aberdeen, 9 February, 1963 S Sch/S Yth/Su21-6 (M)

Middlesbrough (L)	Glasgow Celtic	09.91	91	0	2	0

HEWITT, Leonard
Wrexham, 20 March, 1920 Died 1979 (CF)

Wrexham		05.46	46	5	-	2

HEWITT, Martin D.
Hartlepool, 24 July, 1965 (F)

Hartlepool U. (N/C)		08.84	85-86	11	3	2

HEWITT, Richard
South Elmsall, 25 May, 1943 (M)

Huddersfield T.	Moorthorpe B.C.	05.61				
Bradford C.	Tr	07.64	64	20	-	7
Barnsley	Tr	07.65	65-68	95	2	20
York C.	Tr	03.69	68-71	87	4	7

HEWITT, Ronald
Chesterfield, 25 January, 1924 (G)

League Club	Source	Date Signed	Seasons Played	Apps	Subs	Gls
Sheffield U.		11.44				
Lincoln C.		08.46	48	3	-	0

HEWITT, Ronald
Flint, 21 June, 1928 W-5 (IF)

League Club	Source	Date Signed	Seasons Played	Apps	Subs	Gls
Wolverhampton W.		07.48				
Walsall	Tr	10.49	49	8	-	2
Darlington	Tr	06.50	50	36	-	3
Wrexham	Tr	07.51	51-56	204	-	84
Cardiff C.	Tr	06.57	57-58	64	-	27
Wrexham	Tr	07.59	59	27	-	11
Coventry C.	Tr	03.60	59-61	59	-	23
Chester C.	Tr	03.62	61-62	29	-	6

HEWITT, Stephen
Hull, 17 April, 1973 (G)

League Club	Source	Date Signed	Seasons Played	Apps	Subs	Gls
Scarborough	YT	01.92	91	2	0	0

HEWKINS, Kenneth J. R.
South Africa, 30 October, 1929 (G)

League Club	Source	Date Signed	Seasons Played	Apps	Subs	Gls
Fulham	Clyde	11.55	55-61	38	-	0

HEWSON, Patrick G.
Gateshead, 2 June, 1926 (FB)

League Club	Source	Date Signed	Seasons Played	Apps	Subs	Gls
West Bromwich A.	Crook T.	11.50				
Gateshead	Tr	07.53	53-57	130	-	0

HEYDON, Cecil
Birkenhead, 24 May, 1919 (WH)

League Club	Source	Date Signed	Seasons Played	Apps	Subs	Gls
New Brighton	Victory Social	02.39	38	1	-	0
Derby Co.	Tr	06.39				
Doncaster Rov.	Tr	10.45	46-47	6	-	0
Rochdale	Tr	07.48	48	1	-	0

HEYDON, John (Jack)
Birkenhead, 19 October, 1928 (WH)

League Club	Source	Date Signed	Seasons Played	Apps	Subs	Gls
Liverpool	Everton (Am)	01.49	50-52	63	-	0
Millwall	Tr	05.53	53-55	75	-	1
Tranmere Rov.	Tr	07.56	56-60	76	-	1

HEYES, Darren L.
Swansea, 11 January, 1967 E Sch/E Yth (G)

League Club	Source	Date Signed	Seasons Played	Apps	Subs	Gls
Nottingham F.	App	01.84				
Wrexham	L	01.87	86	2	0	0
Scunthorpe U. (N/C)	Tr	07.87	87	3	0	0

HEYES, George
Bolton, 16 November, 1937 (G)

League Club	Source	Date Signed	Seasons Played	Apps	Subs	Gls
Rochdale	Jnrs	04.56	58-59	24	-	0
Leicester C.	Tr	07.60	60-65	25	0	0
Swansea C.	Tr	09.65	65-68	99	0	0
Barrow	Tr	07.69	69	26	0	0

HEYES, Kenneth
Haydock, 4 January, 1936 E Sch/E Yth (FB)

League Club	Source	Date Signed	Seasons Played	Apps	Subs	Gls
Everton	Jnrs	02.53				
Preston N.E.	Tr	05.57	59	3	-	0

HEYS, Michael
Preston, 23 June, 1938 (G)

League Club	Source	Date Signed	Seasons Played	Apps	Subs	Gls
Preston N.E.	Jnrs	05.57				
Barrow	Tr	03.59	58-61	70	-	0
Workington	Tr	08.62				
Halifax T.		11.63	63	1	-	0

HEYWOOD, Albert E.
Hartlepool, 12 May, 1913 (G)

League Club	Source	Date Signed	Seasons Played	Apps	Subs	Gls
Sunderland	Spennymoor U.	03.37	38	4	-	0
Hartlepool U.	Tr	05.46	46	39	-	0

HEYWOOD, David I.
Wolverhampton, 25 July, 1967 (LB)

League Club	Source	Date Signed	Seasons Played	Apps	Subs	Gls
Wolverhampton W.	YT	11.84	84	7	0	0

HIBBERD, Stuart
Sheffield, 11 October, 1961 (W)

League Club	Source	Date Signed	Seasons Played	Apps	Subs	Gls
Lincoln C.	App	10.79	80-82	36	6	3

HIBBITT, Kenneth
Bradford, 3 January, 1951 Eu23-1 (M)

League Club	Source	Date Signed	Seasons Played	Apps	Subs	Gls
Bradford P.A.	App	11.68	67-68	13	2	0
Wolverhampton W.	Tr	11.68	68-83	447	19	89
Coventry C.	Tr	08.84	84-85	42	5	4
Bristol Rov.	Tr	08.86	86-88	51	2	5

HIBBITT, Terence A.
Bradford, 1 December, 1947 (M)

League Club	Source	Date Signed	Seasons Played	Apps	Subs	Gls
Leeds U.	Jnrs	12.64	65-70	32	15	9
Newcastle U.	Tr	08.71	71-75	138	0	7
Birmingham C.	Tr	08.75	75-77	110	0	11
Newcastle U.	Tr	05.78	78-80	89	1	5

HIBBS, Garry T.
Hammersmith, 26 January, 1957 (M)

League Club	Source	Date Signed	Seasons Played	Apps	Subs	Gls
Leyton Orient	App	07.74	75	1	0	0
Aldershot	Tr	02.77	76	4	2	0

HICK, Leslie D.
York, 23 April, 1927 (OR)

League Club	Source	Date Signed	Seasons Played	Apps	Subs	Gls
Bradford C.		07.48	48	1	-	0

HICKIE, George M.
Larkhall, 29 September, 1920 (FB)

League Club	Source	Date Signed	Seasons Played	Apps	Subs	Gls
Barnsley		05.46				
Carlisle U.	Tr	09.46	46	1	-	0

HICKLIN, A. William
Dudley, 20 September, 1924 (HB)

League Club	Source	Date Signed	Seasons Played	Apps	Subs	Gls
Birmingham C.	West Bromwich A. (Am)	03.45				
Watford	Tr	06.47	47	21	-	5
West Bromwich A.	Tr	05.48				

HICKMAN, Geoffrey B.
West Bromwich, 7 January, 1950 (G)

League Club	Source	Date Signed	Seasons Played	Apps	Subs	Gls
West Bromwich A.	App	01.68				
Bradford P.A.	Tr	06.69	69	9	0	0

HICKMAN, Michael F. T.
Elstead (Sy), 2 October, 1946 (M)

League Club	Source	Date Signed	Seasons Played	Apps	Subs	Gls
Brighton & H.A.	Jnrs	06.65	65-67	12	3	0
Grimsby T.	Tr	06.68	68-74	247	7	48
Blackburn Rov.	Tr	02.75	74-75	23	3	8
Torquay U.	Tr	10.75	75-76	17	0	1

HICKS, Anthony J.
Swindon, 20 August, 1945 (G)

League Club	Source	Date Signed	Seasons Played	Apps	Subs	Gls
Swindon T.	App	10.62	64-66	51	0	0

HICKS, James M.
Ipswich, 16 September, 1960 (CD)

League Club	Source	Date Signed	Seasons Played	Apps	Subs	Gls
Exeter C. (N/C)	St Lukes College	09.83	83	3	0	0
Oxford U.	Tr	08.84				
Fulham	Tr	08.85	85-87	39	1	1

HICKS, Keith
Oldham, 9 August, 1954 E Yth (CD)

League Club	Source	Date Signed	Seasons Played	Apps	Subs	Gls
Oldham Ath.	App	08.72	71-79	240	2	11
Hereford U.	Tr	09.80	80-84	201	0	2
Rochdale	Tr	07.85	85-86	32	0	1

HICKS, Martin
Stratford-on-Avon, 27 February, 1957 (CD)

League Club	Source	Date Signed	Seasons Played	Apps	Subs	Gls
Charlton Ath.	Stratford T.	02.77				
Reading	Tr	02.78	77-90	499	1	23
Birmingham C.	Tr	08.91	91	41	1	1

HICKS, Stuart J.
Peterborough, 30 May, 1967 (CD)

League Club	Source	Date Signed	Seasons Played	Apps	Subs	Gls
Peterborough U.	YT	07.84				
Colchester U.	Wisbech T.	03.88	87-89	57	7	0
Scunthorpe U.	Tr	08.90	90-91	67	0	1

HICKSON, David
Ellesmere Port, 30 October, 1929 (CF)

League Club	Source	Date Signed	Seasons Played	Apps	Subs	Gls
Everton	Ellesmere Port	05.48	51-55	139	-	63
Aston Villa	Tr	09.55	55	12	-	1
Huddersfield T.	Tr	11.55	55-56	54	-	28
Everton	Tr	08.57	57-59	86	-	32
Liverpool	Tr	11.59	59-60	60	-	37
Bury	Cambridge C.	01.62	61	8	-	0
Tranmere Rov.	Tr	08.62	62-63	45	-	21

HICKSON, Geoffrey G.
Crewe, 26 September, 1939 (G)

League Club	Source	Date Signed	Seasons Played	Apps	Subs	Gls
Stoke C.	Blackburn Rov. (Am)	08.57	59-60	11	-	0
Crewe Alex.	Tr	07.62	62-66	105	0	0
Port Vale	L	08.68	68	17	0	0
Southport	Tr	12.68	68	3	0	0

HICKTON, John
Chesterfield, 24 September, 1944 (F)

League Club	Source	Date Signed	Seasons Played	Apps	Subs	Gls
Sheffield Wed.	Jnrs	01.62	63-65	52	1	21
Middlesbrough	Tr	09.66	66-77	395	20	159
Hull C.	L	01.77	76	6	0	1

League Club	Source	Date Signed	Seasons Played	Apps	Subs	Gls

HICKTON, Roy
Chesterfield, 19 September, 1948 (FB)

League Club	Source	Date Signed	Seasons Played	Apps	Subs	Gls
Chesterfield	App	11.65	68-70	48	2	1

HIGGINBOTTOM, Andrew J.
Chesterfield, 22 October, 1964 (M)

League Club	Source	Date Signed	Seasons Played	Apps	Subs	Gls
Chesterfield	App	10.82	82	1	2	0
Everton	Tr	07.83				
Cambridge U.	Tr	08.84	84	1	0	0
Crystal Palace		09.85	85-86	16	7	2

HIGGINBOTTOM, Michael
Sheffield, 13 October, 1962 (M)

League Club	Source	Date Signed	Seasons Played	Apps	Subs	Gls
Chesterfield (N/C)		08.83	83	4	1	0

HIGGINS, Andrew M.
Bolsover, 12 February, 1960 (CD)

League Club	Source	Date Signed	Seasons Played	Apps	Subs	Gls
Chesterfield	App	02.78	78	1	0	0
Port Vale	Tr	02.81	80-81	11	3	0
Hartlepool U.	Tr	09.82	82	3	1	1
Rochdale	Kings Lynn	03.83	82-83	31	2	6
Chester C.	Tr	07.84	84	16	3	1

HIGGINS, Augustine
Dublin, 19 January, 1931 (CF)

League Club	Source	Date Signed	Seasons Played	Apps	Subs	Gls
Aston Villa	Shamrock Rov.	11.49				
Ipswich T.	Tr	07.52	52	2	-	0

HIGGINS, Charles
Bellshill, 12 May, 1921 (LB)

League Club	Source	Date Signed	Seasons Played	Apps	Subs	Gls
Chester C.	Arbroath	08.46	46	11	-	0

HIGGINS, David A.
Liverpool, 19 August, 1961 (RB)

League Club	Source	Date Signed	Seasons Played	Apps	Subs	Gls
Tranmere Rov.	Eagle	08.83	83-84	27	1	0
Tranmere Rov.	Caernarfon T.	07.87	87-91	185	2	6

HIGGINS, Frederick T.
Hackney, 21 January, 1930 (CH)

League Club	Source	Date Signed	Seasons Played	Apps	Subs	Gls
Crystal Palace	Wood Green	03.52	52-53	11	-	0

HIGGINS, George
Batley, 12 September, 1932 (HB)

League Club	Source	Date Signed	Seasons Played	Apps	Subs	Gls
Huddersfield T.	Jnrs	12.49				
Halifax T.	Tr	07.57	57	5	-	0

HIGGINS, George
Dundee, 16 June, 1925 (FB)

League Club	Source	Date Signed	Seasons Played	Apps	Subs	Gls
Blackburn Rov.	Lochee Harp	10.46	46-50	53	-	0
Bolton W.	Tr	07.51	51-53	69	-	0
Grimsby T.	Tr	05.54	54-56	47	-	0

HIGGINS, James T.
Dublin, 3 February, 1926 IR-1 (F)

League Club	Source	Date Signed	Seasons Played	Apps	Subs	Gls
Birmingham C.	Dundalk	11.49	49-52	50	-	12

HIGGINS, John O.
Bakewell, 15 November, 1932 (CH)

League Club	Source	Date Signed	Seasons Played	Apps	Subs	Gls
Bolton W.	Buxton	10.50	52-60	183	-	0

HIGGINS, John W.
Kilmarnock, 27 January, 1933 (FB)

League Club	Source	Date Signed	Seasons Played	Apps	Subs	Gls
Swindon T.	St Mirren	05.59	59-60	28	-	0

HIGGINS, Mark N.
Buxton, 29 September, 1958 E Schl/E Yth (CD)

League Club	Source	Date Signed	Seasons Played	Apps	Subs	Gls
Everton	App	08.76	76-83	150	2	6
Manchester U.	(Retired)	12.85	85	6	0	0
Bury	Tr	01.87	86-88	67	1	0
Stoke C.	Tr	09.88	88-89	37	2	1

HIGGINS, Michael
Rossendale, 5 September, 1956 (W)

League Club	Source	Date Signed	Seasons Played	Apps	Subs	Gls
Blackburn Rov.	App	12.73				
Workington	Tr	07.76	76	11	4	1

HIGGINS, Peter
Mansfield, 1 August, 1944 (CH)

League Club	Source	Date Signed	Seasons Played	Apps	Subs	Gls
Oxford U.	Blidworth Y.C.	07.62	62-68	35	5	0
Crewe Alex.	Tr	06.69	69-71	56	3	0

HIGGINS, Peter C.
Cardiff, 12 November, 1950 (W)

League Club	Source	Date Signed	Seasons Played	Apps	Subs	Gls
Bristol Rov.	App	02.69	68-72	36	1	5
Doncaster Rov.	Tr	07.73	73-75	63	5	10
Torquay U.	L	03.76	75	3	1	1

HIGGINS, Robert J.
Bolsover, 23 December, 1958 (D)

League Club	Source	Date Signed	Seasons Played	Apps	Subs	Gls
Burnley	App	07.76	77	3	0	0
Hartlepool U.	L	11.79	79	2	0	0
Rochdale	Tr	10.80	80	4	1	0

HIGGINS, Ronald V.
Silvertown, 14 February, 1923 (CF)

League Club	Source	Date Signed	Seasons Played	Apps	Subs	Gls
Leyton Orient(Am)	Green & Siley Wks	12.49	49	2	-	0
Brighton & H.A.	Tonbridge	01.52	51-52	9	-	0
Queens Park R.	Tr	01.53	52	3	-	1

HIGGINS, William C.
Birkenhead, 26 February, 1924 (F)

League Club	Source	Date Signed	Seasons Played	Apps	Subs	Gls
Everton	Tranmere Rov. (Am)	03.46	46-49	48	-	8

HIGGINSON, Thomas
Newtongrange, 6 January, 1937 (WH)

League Club	Source	Date Signed	Seasons Played	Apps	Subs	Gls
Brentford	Kilmarnock	06.59	59-69	383	3	15

HIGH, David H.
Reading, 22 February, 1941 E Yth (FB)

League Club	Source	Date Signed	Seasons Played	Apps	Subs	Gls
Reading	Jnrs	02.58	59-63	72	-	2

HIGH, Sidney W.
Waterbeach, 30 September, 1922 (OR)

League Club	Source	Date Signed	Seasons Played	Apps	Subs	Gls
Luton T.	Cambridge U.	10.46				
Watford	Tr	08.48	48	7	-	3

HIGHAM, John P.
Liverpool, 22 November, 1956 (CD)

League Club	Source	Date Signed	Seasons Played	Apps	Subs	Gls
Liverpool	App	05.74				
Southport	Tr	01.76	75-77	96	0	1

HIGHAM, Peter
Wigan, 8 November, 1930 (CF)

League Club	Source	Date Signed	Seasons Played	Apps	Subs	Gls
Portsmouth (Am)		11.49	49	1	-	0
Bolton W.	Tr	11.50				
Preston N.E.	Tr	05.52	53-54	15	-	10
Nottingham F.	Tr	08.55	55-57	61	-	20
Doncaster Rov.	Tr	03.58	57-58	22	-	6

HIGNETT, Alan J.
Liverpool, 1 November, 1946 E Sch (FB)

League Club	Source	Date Signed	Seasons Played	Apps	Subs	Gls
Liverpool	App	11.63	64	1	-	0
Chester C.	Tr	08.66	66	6	0	0

HIGNETT, Craig J.
Prescot, 12 January, 1970 (W)

League Club	Source	Date Signed	Seasons Played	Apps	Subs	Gls
Crewe Alex.	Liverpool (YT)	05.88	88-91	94	13	34

HILAIRE, Vincent M.
Forest Hill, 10 October, 1959 E Yth/Eu21-9/E'B' (LW)

League Club	Source	Date Signed	Seasons Played	Apps	Subs	Gls
Crystal Palace	App	10.76	76-83	239	16	29
Luton T.	Tr	07.84	84	5	1	0
Portsmouth	Tr	11.84	84-87	144	2	25
Leeds U.	Tr	07.88	88-89	42	2	6
Stoke C.	L	11.89	89	5	0	1
Stoke C.	Tr	11.90	90	10	0	2
Exeter C.	Tr	09.91	91	24	9	4

HILDERSLEY, Ronald
Kirkcaldy, 6 April, 1965 (M)

League Club	Source	Date Signed	Seasons Played	Apps	Subs	Gls
Manchester C.	App	04.83	82	1	0	0
Chester C.	L	01.84	83	9	0	0
Chester C.	Tr	07.84	84	5	4	0
Rochdale (N/C)	Tr	08.85	85	12	4	0
Preston N.E.	Tr	06.86	86-87	54	4	3
Cambridge U.	L	02.88	87	9	0	3
Blackburn Rov.	Tr	07.88	88-89	25	5	4
Wigan Ath.	Tr	08.90	90	4	0	0
Halifax T.		11.91	91	14	4	0

HILDITCH, Mark W.
Royton, 20 August, 1960 (F)

League Club	Source	Date Signed	Seasons Played	Apps	Subs	Gls
Rochdale	Jnrs	11.78	77-82	184	13	40
Tranmere Rov.	Tr	08.83	83-85	47	2	12
Wigan Ath.	Altrincham	09.86	86-89	89	14	26
Rochdale	Tr	08.90	90-91	12	4	2

HILEY, Scott P.
Plymouth, 27 September, 1968 (RB)

League Club	Source	Date Signed	Seasons Played	Apps	Subs	Gls
Exeter C.	YT	08.86	87-91	172	5	9

HILL, E. Alan
Bromborough, 1 July, 1933 (OL)

League Club	Source	Date Signed	Seasons Played	Apps	Subs	Gls
Tranmere Rov. (Am)	Bebington	11.56	56	6	-	1

HILL, Alan
Barnsley, 3 November, 1943 (G)

League Club	Source	Date Signed	Seasons Played	Apps	Subs	Gls
Barnsley	Jnrs	04.61	60-65	131	0	0
Rotherham U.	Tr	06.66	66-68	82	0	0
Nottingham F.	Tr	03.69	68-69	41	0	0

HILL, Alan G.
Chester, 22 June, 1955 (FB)

League Club	Source	Date Signed	Seasons Played	Apps	Subs	Gls
Wrexham	Jnrs	07.73	74-82	173	26	7

HILL, Alistair G.
Glasgow, 25 April, 1934 (OR)

League Club	Source	Date Signed	Seasons Played	Apps	Subs	Gls
Bristol C.	Dundee	11.59	59	3	-	0

HILL, Andrew R.
Maltby, 20 January, 1965 E Yth (RB)

League Club	Source	Date Signed	Seasons Played	Apps	Subs	Gls
Manchester U.	App	01.83				
Bury	Tr	07.84	84-90	264	0	10
Manchester C.	Tr	12.90	90-91	43	1	5

HILL, Andrew R.
Ilkeston, 10 November, 1960 (F)

League Club	Source	Date Signed	Seasons Played	Apps	Subs	Gls
Derby Co.	Kimberley T.	06.81	81-83	19	3	2
Carlisle U.	Tr	09.83	83-85	73	12	15

HILL, Arthur
Chesterfield, 12 November, 1921 (OR)

League Club	Source	Date Signed	Seasons Played	Apps	Subs	Gls
Chesterfield		09.46	47	1	-	0

HILL, Bert
West Ham, 8 March, 1930 (WH)

League Club	Source	Date Signed	Seasons Played	Apps	Subs	Gls
Chelsea	Jnrs	05.50				
Colchester U.	Tr	10.52	52-57	104	-	3

HILL, Brian
Sheffield, 6 October, 1937 Died 1968 (FB)

League Club	Source	Date Signed	Seasons Played	Apps	Subs	Gls
Sheffield Wed.	Jnrs	04.55	56-65	116	1	1

HILL, Brian
Mansfield, 15 December, 1942 (OL)

League Club	Source	Date Signed	Seasons Played	Apps	Subs	Gls
Grimsby T.	Ollerton Colly	08.60	60-66	180	0	26
Huddersfield T.	Tr	11.66	66-68	85	3	6
Blackburn Rov.	Tr	09.69	69-70	34	3	4
Torquay U.	Tr	07.71	71	6	1	1

HILL, Brian W.
Bedworth, 31 July, 1941 (D)

League Club	Source	Date Signed	Seasons Played	Apps	Subs	Gls
Coventry C.	Jnrs	08.58	57-70	240	4	7
Bristol C.	L	03.71	70	7	0	0
Torquay U.	Tr	10.71	71-72	49	0	1

HILL, Charles J. (Midge)
Cardiff, 6 September, 1918 (IF)

League Club	Source	Date Signed	Seasons Played	Apps	Subs	Gls
Cardiff C.		06.38	38-46	19	-	4
Torquay U.	Tr	07.47	47-48	63	-	15
Queens Park R.	Tr	03.49	48-49	20	-	1
Swindon T.	Tr	09.50	50	4	-	0

HILL, Colin F.
Uxbridge, 12 November, 1963 NI-6 (D)

League Club	Source	Date Signed	Seasons Played	Apps	Subs	Gls
Arsenal	App	08.81	82-84	46	0	1
Colchester U.	Maritima (Port)	10.87	87-88	64	5	0
Sheffield U.	Tr	07.89	89-91	77	5	1
Leicester C.	L	03.92	91	10	0	0

HILL, David
Bradford, 25 May, 1965 (F)

League Club	Source	Date Signed	Seasons Played	Apps	Subs	Gls
Bradford C. (N/C)	YT	08.82	82-83	2	3	1

HILL, David M.
Nottingham, 6 June, 1966 (LW)

League Club	Source	Date Signed	Seasons Played	Apps	Subs	Gls
Scunthorpe U.	YT	02.85	83-87	139	1	10
Ipswich T.	Tr	07.88	88-90	54	7	0
Scunthorpe U.	L	03.91	90	8	1	1
Scunthorpe U.	Tr	09.91	91	36	1	5

HILL, David R.
Kettering, 28 September, 1953 (G)

League Club	Source	Date Signed	Seasons Played	Apps	Subs	Gls
Northampton T.	App	07.70	70	1	0	0

HILL, Dennis
Willenhall, 16 August, 1929 (OL)

League Club	Source	Date Signed	Seasons Played	Apps	Subs	Gls
Birmingham C.	Darlaston	06.51	53-55	4	-	0

HILL, Dilwyn
Porth, 1 April, 1937 Died 1963 (IF)

League Club	Source	Date Signed	Seasons Played	Apps	Subs	Gls
Exeter C.	Pontypridd	06.55	57-59	14	-	3

HILL, Frank R.
Forfar, 21 May, 1906 S-3 (WH)

League Club	Source	Date Signed	Seasons Played	Apps	Subs	Gls
Arsenal	Aberdeen	05.32	32-35	76	-	4
Blackpool	Tr	06.36	36-37	45	-	8
Southampton	Tr	09.37	37-38	51	-	4
Crewe Alex.	Preston N.E.	07.44	46-47	20	-	0

HILL, Frederick
Sheffield, 17 January, 1940 Eu23-10/EF Lge/E-2 (IF)

League Club	Source	Date Signed	Seasons Played	Apps	Subs	Gls
Bolton W.	Jnrs	03.57	57-68	373	2	74
Halifax T.	Tr	07.69	69	25	0	3
Manchester C.	Tr	05.70	70-72	28	7	3
Peterborough U.	Tr	08.73	73-74	73	2	7

HILL, Geoffrey R.
Carlisle, 31 August, 1929 (FB)

League Club	Source	Date Signed	Seasons Played	Apps	Subs	Gls
Carlisle U.		10.49	49-57	188	-	0

HILL, Gordon A.
Sunbury, 1 April, 1954 Eu23-1/E-6 (W)

League Club	Source	Date Signed	Seasons Played	Apps	Subs	Gls
Millwall	Southall	01.73	72-75	79	7	20
Manchester U.	Tr	11.75	75-77	100	1	39
Derby Co.	Tr	04.78	77-79	22	2	5
Queens Park R.	Tr	11.79	79-80	10	4	1

Gordon Hill (Millwall, Manchester United, Derby County, Queens Park Rangers & England)

HILL, Henry A.
Lambeth, 19 September, 1947 (M)

League Club	Source	Date Signed	Seasons Played	Apps	Subs	Gls
Ipswich T.	Canada	03.69				
Gillingham	South Africa	07.71	71	0	1	0
Hereford U. (N/C)	South Africa	11.78	78	0	1	0

HILL, James
Wilshaw, 19 August, 1931 (OL)

League Club	Source	Date Signed	Seasons Played	Apps	Subs	Gls
Coventry C.	Jnrs	08.48	49-55	66	-	8
Millwall	Tr	07.56	56	1	-	0
Shrewsbury T.	Tr	07.57	57	8	-	0

League Club	Source	Date Signed	Seasons Played	Apps	Subs	Gls
HILL, James M.						
Carrickfergus (NI), 31 October, 1935 NI Amat/NI'B'-2/NI-7						(IF)
Newcastle U.	Linfield	07.57	57	11	-	2
Norwich C.	Tr	07.58	58-62	161	-	55
Everton	Tr	08.63	63	7	-	1
Port Vale	Tr	10.65	65-67	63	0	8
HILL, James W. T.						
Balham, 22 July, 1928						(IF)
Brentford	Reading (Am)	05.49	49-51	83	-	10
Fulham	Tr	03.52	51-60	276	-	41

Jimmy Hill (Brentford & Fulham)

League Club	Source	Date Signed	Seasons Played	Apps	Subs	Gls
HILL, John E.						
Yeovil, 29 November, 1948						(FB)
Bournemouth	App	08.66	67	3	1	0
HILL, Jonathan W.						
Wigan, 26 August, 1970						(LM)
Rochdale	Crewe Alex. (YT)	07.89	89-90	25	11	1
HILL, Keith J.						
Bolton, 17 May, 1969						(CD)
Blackburn Rov.	Jnrs	05.87	87-91	89	6	4
HILL, Kenneth						
Walsall, 28 April, 1938						(WH)
Walsall	Bescot U.	11.56	58-62	115	-	1
Norwich C.	Tr	07.63	63-65	44	0	0
Walsall	Tr	10.66	66	15	0	0
HILL, Kenneth G.						
Canterbury, 7 March, 1953 E Semi-Pro						(CD)
Gillingham	App	03.71	71-76	120	5	7
Lincoln C.	L	12.74	74	1	0	0
HILL, Leonard W.						
Caerleon, 14 April, 1942 W Yth						(M)
Newport Co.	Lovells Ath.	11.62	62-69	265	2	49
Swansea C.	Tr	07.70	70	12	0	1
Newport Co.	Tr	01.72	71-73	93	4	13
HILL, Mark S.						
Perivale, 21 January, 1961						(FB)
Queens Park R.	App	07.79				
Brentford	Tr	07.80	80-81	54	2	3

League Club	Source	Date Signed	Seasons Played	Apps	Subs	Gls
HILL, Maurice						
Halifax, 2 May, 1920 Died 1966						(CH)
Everton	Park Side	05.39				
New Brighton	Tr	07.46	46-47	73	-	0
HILL, Michael R.						
Hereford, 3 December, 1947 W-2						(CF)
Sheffield U.	Bethesda Ath.	09.65	66-69	35	2	9
Ipswich T.	Tr	10.69	69-72	63	3	18
Crystal Palace	Tr	12.73	73-75	43	2	6
HILL, Paul J.						
Nottingham, 28 January, 1973						(D)
Peterborough U.	YT	07.89	90	1	0	0
HILL, Peter						
Heanor, 8 August, 1931						(IF)
Coventry C.	Jnrs	08.48	48-61	285	-	73
HILL, Raymond W.						
Stourbridge, 15 February, 1936						(F)
Coventry C.	Redditch U.	11.57	57-58	14	-	5
HILL, Richard W.						
Hinckley, 20 September, 1963						(LW)
Leicester C.	Jnrs	11.81				
Northampton T.	Nuneaton Bor.	06.85	85-86	86	0	46
Watford	Tr	05.87	87	2	2	0
Oxford U.	Tr	09.87	87-88	48	15	13
HILL, Ricky A.						
Hammersmith, 5 March, 1959 E Yth/E-3						(M)
Luton T.	App	05.76	75-88	429	7	54
Leicester C.	Le Havre (Fr)	08.90	90	19	7	0
HILL, Robert						
Edinburgh, 9 June, 1938						(IF)
Colchester U.	Jnrs	06.55	55-64	238	-	20
HILL, Stephen T. (Mandy)						
Blackpool, 15 February, 1940 Eu23-4						(W)
Blackpool	Jnrs	05.59	59-63	71	-	1
Tranmere Rov.	Tr	09.64	64-67	130	0	10
HILL, William						
Sheffield, 6 January, 1936						(F)
York C.	Rawmarsh Welfare	02.54	56-59	29	-	3
HILL, William H.						
Skegby, 15 March, 1920						(IF)
Mansfield T.	Skegby M.W.	11.47	47	2	-	0
HILL, William L.						
Uxbridge, 9 June, 1930						(F)
Queens Park R.	Uxbridge T.	04.51	51	10	-	1
HILLARD, Douglas A.						
Bristol, 10 August, 1935						(FB)
Bristol Rov.	Bristol M.H.	05.57	58-67	313	5	12
HILLARD, John G.						
Aberdeen, 3 September, 1916						
Torquay U.		09.46	46	6	-	0
HILLEY, David						
Glasgow, 20 December, 1938 Su23-1/SF Lge						(IF)
Newcastle U.	Third Lanark	08.62	62-67	194	0	31
Nottingham F.	Tr	12.67	67-70	72	16	14
HILLIER, Barry G.						
Redcar, 8 April, 1936						(FB)
Southampton	Jnrs	04.53	57-58	9	-	0
HILLIER, David						
Blackheath, 19 December, 1969 Eu21-1						(M)
Arsenal	YT	02.88	90-91	36	7	1
HILLIER, John						
Halsall, 10 September, 1933						(G)
Chester C. (Am)	Llanrwst	11.54	54	6	-	0
HILLMAN, Dennis V.						
Southend, 27 November, 1918						(OR)
Brighton & H.A.		11.44				
Colchester U.	Tr	(N/L)	50	4	-	0
Gillingham	Tr	08.51	51	21	-	0

HILLS, John R.
Northfleet, 24 February, 1934 (FB)

League Club	Source	Date Signed	Seasons Played	Apps	Subs	Gls
Tottenham H.	Gravesend & Nft	08.53	57-59	29	-	0
Bristol Rov.	Tr	07.61	61	7	-	0

HILLYARD, Ronald W.
Rotherham, 31 March, 1952 (G)

League Club	Source	Date Signed	Seasons Played	Apps	Subs	Gls
York C.	Jnrs	12.69	69-73	61	0	0
Hartlepool U.	L	01.72	71	23	0	0
Gillingham	Tr	07.74	74-90	563	0	0

HILTON, Gary
Manchester, 4 March, 1961 (G)

League Club	Source	Date Signed	Seasons Played	Apps	Subs	Gls
Bury (N/C)		08.83	83	1	0	0

HILTON, John (Jack)
Rochdale, 20 February, 1925 (CF)

League Club	Source	Date Signed	Seasons Played	Apps	Subs	Gls
Wrexham	Hyde U.	07.50	50	3	-	0

HILTON, Joseph
Bromborough, 20 July, 1931 (F)

League Club	Source	Date Signed	Seasons Played	Apps	Subs	Gls
Leeds U.	Jnrs	09.48	49	1	-	0
Chester C.	Tr	08.50	50-53	62	-	9

HILTON, Mark G.J.
Middleton, 15 January, 1960 (M)

League Club	Source	Date Signed	Seasons Played	Apps	Subs	Gls
Oldham Ath.	App	01.78	77-80	48	2	2
Bury	Tr	08.81	81-82	29	3	3

HILTON, Patrick J.
Aylesham (Kt), 1 May, 1954 (W)

League Club	Source	Date Signed	Seasons Played	Apps	Subs	Gls
Brighton & H.A.	Canterbury C.	02.73	72-73	18	2	1
Blackburn Rov.	Tr	05.74	74	16	0	2
Gillingham	Tr	09.75	75-76	16	10	1
Aldershot	L	03.77	76	12	1	0
Southport	Tr	07.77	77	22	5	5

HILTON, Paul
Oldham, 8 October, 1959 (CD)

League Club	Source	Date Signed	Seasons Played	Apps	Subs	Gls
Bury	Chadderton	07.78	78-83	136	12	39
West Ham U.	Tr	02.84	83-88	47	13	7

HILTON, Peter B.
Tamworth, 20 March, 1929 Died 1965 (FB)

League Club	Source	Date Signed	Seasons Played	Apps	Subs	Gls
West Bromwich A.	Tamworth	07.49				
Swindon T.	Tr	07.53	53-55	50	-	0

HIMSWORTH, Gary P.
Pickering, 19 December, 1969 (W)

League Club	Source	Date Signed	Seasons Played	Apps	Subs	Gls
York C.	YT	01.88	87-90	74	14	8
Scarborough	Tr	12.90	90-91	56	3	5

HINCE, Paul F.
Manchester, 2 March, 1945 (W)

League Club	Source	Date Signed	Seasons Played	Apps	Subs	Gls
Manchester C.		10.66	66-67	7	0	4
Charlton Ath.	Tr	02.68	67-68	23	0	2
Bury	Tr	12.68	68-69	38	0	3
Crewe Alex.	Tr	07.70	70	23	3	2

HINCH, James A.
Sheffield, 8 November, 1947 (F)

League Club	Source	Date Signed	Seasons Played	Apps	Subs	Gls
Tranmere Rov.	Portmadoc	03.70	69-70	36	3	10
Plymouth Arg.	Tr	02.71	70-73	102	5	28
Hereford U.	Tr	10.73	73	22	5	7
York C.	Tr	07.74	74-76	56	12	12
Southport	L	03.75	74	7	0	2
Sheffield Wed.	Tr	10.77	77	0	1	0
Barnsley	Tr	12.77	77	9	3	4

HINCHCLIFFE, Andrew G.
Manchester, 5 February, 1969 E Yth/Eu21-1 (LB)

League Club	Source	Date Signed	Seasons Played	Apps	Subs	Gls
Manchester C.	App	06.86	87-89	107	5	8
Everton	Tr	07.90	90-91	36	3	1

HINCHCLIFFE, Thomas
Denaby, 6 December, 1913 Died 1978 (IF)

League Club	Source	Date Signed	Seasons Played	Apps	Subs	Gls
Grimsby T.	Denaby U.	10.33	36-37	27	-	5
Huddersfield T.	Tr	02.38	37-38	13	-	4
Derby Co.	Tr	11.38	38	6	-	1
Nottingham F.	Tr	05.46	46	1	-	0

HINCHLEY, Gary
Guisborough, 14 November, 1968 (RB)

League Club	Source	Date Signed	Seasons Played	Apps	Subs	Gls
Darlington	Jnrs	08.86	86-87	13	1	0
Darlington	Guisborough T.	02.92	91	6	0	0

HINCHLIFFE, Alan A.
Chesterfield, 8 December, 1936 (G)

League Club	Source	Date Signed	Seasons Played	Apps	Subs	Gls
Sheffield Wed.	Jnrs	12.53	56	2	-	0
Chesterfield	Tr	07.59				

HINCHLIFFE, John
Tillicoultry, 4 June, 1938 S Sch (WH)

League Club	Source	Date Signed	Seasons Played	Apps	Subs	Gls
Aston Villa	Jnrs	09.56	57	2	-	0
Workington	Tr	06.58	58-61	116	-	4
Hartlepool U.	Tr	10.61	61-63	88	-	8

HINDLE, Frank J.
Blackburn, 22 June, 1925 (FB)

League Club	Source	Date Signed	Seasons Played	Apps	Subs	Gls
Blackburn Rov.		01.43				
Chester C.	Tr	06.49	49-50	81	-	0
Bradford P.A.	Tr	04.51	50-56	204	-	0

HINDLE, John R. (Jack)
Preston, 10 November, 1921 Died 1987 (G)

League Club	Source	Date Signed	Seasons Played	Apps	Subs	Gls
Preston N.E.		11.46	47	1	-	0
Barrow	Tr	05.48	48-49	84	-	0
Aston Villa	Tr	06.50	50	15	-	0
Barrow	Tr	08.51	51-55	182	-	0

HINDLE, Thomas
Keighley, 22 February, 1921 (IF)

League Club	Source	Date Signed	Seasons Played	Apps	Subs	Gls
Leeds U.	Keighley T.	09.43	46-48	43	-	2
York C.	Tr	02.49	48-49	19	-	3
Halifax T.	Tr	09.49	49-51	85	-	17
Rochdale	Tr	03.52	51	6	-	1

HINDLEY, Frank C.
Worksop, 2 November, 1914 (F)

League Club	Source	Date Signed	Seasons Played	Apps	Subs	Gls
Nottingham F.	Netherton U.	12.37	38	6	-	3
Brighton & H.A.	Tr	05.39	46	10	-	4

HINDLEY, Peter
Worksop, 19 May, 1944 Eu23-1 (RB)

League Club	Source	Date Signed	Seasons Played	Apps	Subs	Gls
Nottingham F.	Jnrs	06.61	62-73	366	0	10
Coventry C.	Tr	01.74	73-75	33	0	0
Peterborough U.	Tr	07.76	76-78	112	0	1

HINDMARCH, Robert
Morpeth, 27 April, 1961 E Yth (CD)

League Club	Source	Date Signed	Seasons Played	Apps	Subs	Gls
Sunderland	App	04.78	77-83	114	1	2
Portsmouth	L	12.83	83	2	0	0
Derby Co.	Tr	07.84	84-89	164	0	9
Wolverhampton W.	Tr	06.90	90	40	0	2

HINDMARSH, Edward
Sunderland, 7 September, 1921 (HB)

League Club	Source	Date Signed	Seasons Played	Apps	Subs	Gls
Sunderland		10.43				
Carlisle U.	Tr	07.45	46	15	-	0

HINDMARSH, J. Walter
Crook, 26 December, 1919 (FB)

League Club	Source	Date Signed	Seasons Played	Apps	Subs	Gls
Portsmouth	Willington	04.39	46-50	55	-	0
Swindon T.	Tr	07.51	51	11	-	0

HINDSON, Gordon
Stanley, 8 January, 1950 (W)

League Club	Source	Date Signed	Seasons Played	Apps	Subs	Gls
Newcastle U.	Jnrs	08.68	68-71	7	0	1
Luton T.	Tr	10.71	71-74	62	6	3
Carlisle U.	L	09.75	75	1	2	0
Blackburn Rov.	Tr	10.75	75	10	0	0

HINE, Mark
Middlesbrough, 18 May, 1964 (M)

League Club	Source	Date Signed	Seasons Played	Apps	Subs	Gls
Grimsby T.	Whitby T.	10.83	84-85	20	2	1
Darlington	Tr	06.86	86-88	126	2	8
Peterborough U.	Tr	01.90	89-90	55	0	8
Scunthorpe U.	Tr	03.91	90-91	19	3	2

HINES, Derek J.
Moira, 8 February, 1931 E Yth (CF)

League Club	Source	Date Signed	Seasons Played	Apps	Subs	Gls
Leicester C.	Jnrs	03.48	47-60	299	-	116
Shrewsbury T.	Tr	11.61	61-62	16	-	5

HINNIGAN, Joseph P.
Liverpool, 3 December, 1955 (FB)

League Club	Source	Date Signed	Seasons Played	Apps	Subs	Gls
Wigan Ath.	South Liverpool	(N/L)	78-79	66	0	10
Sunderland	Tr	02.80	79-82	63	0	4
Preston N.E.	Tr	12.82	82-83	51	1	8
Gillingham	Tr	08.84	84-86	99	4	7
Wrexham	Tr	07.87	87	28	1	1
Chester C.	Tr	08.88	88-89	52	2	2

HINSHELWOOD, Martin
Reading, 16 June, 1953 (M)

League Club	Source	Date Signed	Seasons Played	Apps	Subs	Gls
Crystal Palace	App	08.70	72-77	66	3	4

HINSHELWOOD, Paul A.
Bristol, 14 August, 1956 Eu21-2 (RB)

League Club	Source	Date Signed	Seasons Played	Apps	Subs	Gls
Crystal Palace	App	08.73	73-82	271	5	22
Oxford U.	Tr	08.83	83-84	45	0	7
Millwall	Tr	01.85	84-86	59	2	2
Colchester U.	Tr	09.86	86-87	81	0	6

HINSHELWOOD, Walter A.
Lambeth, 27 October, 1929 (OR)

League Club	Source	Date Signed	Seasons Played	Apps	Subs	Gls
Fulham	Jnrs	10.46	46-50	19	-	1
Chelsea	Tr	01.51	50	12	-	1
Fulham	Tr	05.51	51	2	-	0
Reading	Tr	12.52	52-55	135	-	31
Bristol C.	Tr	02.56	55-59	148	-	16
Millwall	Tr	06.60	60	19	-	1
Newport Co.	Canada	11.61	61	3	-	0

HINSHELWOOD, William
Airdrie, 11 May, 1935 (WH)

League Club	Source	Date Signed	Seasons Played	Apps	Subs	Gls
Hartlepool U.	Airdrieonians	07.63	63	17	-	3

HINSLEY, George
Sheffield, 19 July, 1914 (HB)

League Club	Source	Date Signed	Seasons Played	Apps	Subs	Gls
Barnsley	Denaby U.	09.35	35-38	9	-	0
Bradford C.	Tr	10.38	38-48	114	-	17
Halifax T.	Tr	07.49	49	32	-	0

HINTON, Alan T.
Wednesbury, 6 October, 1942 E Yth/Eu23-7/E-3 (OL)

League Club	Source	Date Signed	Seasons Played	Apps	Subs	Gls
Wolverhampton W.	Jnrs	10.59	61-63	75	-	29
Nottingham F.	Tr	01.64	63-67	108	4	24
Derby Co.	Tr	09.67	67-75	240	13	64

HINTON, Edward
Belfast, 20 May, 1922 NI-7 (G)

League Club	Source	Date Signed	Seasons Played	Apps	Subs	Gls
Fulham	Distillery	08.46	46-48	82	-	0
Millwall	Tr	07.49	49-51	91	-	0

HINTON, Marvin
Norwood, 2 February, 1940 Eu23-3 (CH)

League Club	Source	Date Signed	Seasons Played	Apps	Subs	Gls
Charlton Ath.	Jnrs	04.57	57-63	131	-	2
Chelsea	Tr	08.63	63-74	257	8	3

HINTON, Ronald
Keighley, 27 November, 1943 (CH)

League Club	Source	Date Signed	Seasons Played	Apps	Subs	Gls
Doncaster Rov.	App	07.61				
Chesterfield	Tr	07.63	63	1	-	0

HIPKIN, Reginald W.
Syderstone (Nk), 31 December, 1921 (RH)

League Club	Source	Date Signed	Seasons Played	Apps	Subs	Gls
Wolverhampton W.		07.39				
Charlton Ath.	Tr	09.46	47	2	-	0
Brighton & H.A.	Tr	02.48	47-48	15	-	1

HIRD, R. Keith B.
Annfield Plain, 25 November, 1939 (G)

League Club	Source	Date Signed	Seasons Played	Apps	Subs	Gls
Sunderland	Annfield Plain	09.57	60	1	-	0
Darlington	Tr	07.63	63	17	-	0

HIRD, Kevin
Colne, 11 February, 1955 (M)

League Club	Source	Date Signed	Seasons Played	Apps	Subs	Gls
Blackburn Rov.	App	02.73	73-78	129	3	20
Leeds U.	Tr	03.79	78-83	165	16	19
Burnley	Tr	08.84	84-85	83	0	23

HIRON, Raymond M. C.
Gosport, 22 July, 1943 (F)

League Club	Source	Date Signed	Seasons Played	Apps	Subs	Gls
Portsmouth	Fareham T.	05.64	64-74	324	7	110
Reading	Tr	07.75	75-77	88	4	14

HIRONS, Paul T.
Bath, 6 March, 1971 (F)

League Club	Source	Date Signed	Seasons Played	Apps	Subs	Gls
Torquay U.	Bristol C. (YT)	01.89	88-89	10	11	0

HIRST, David E.
Cudworth, 7 December, 1967 E Yth/Eu21-7/E'B'/E-3 (F)

League Club	Source	Date Signed	Seasons Played	Apps	Subs	Gls
Barnsley	App	11.85	85	26	2	9
Sheffield Wed.	Tr	08.86	86-91	168	21	72

HIRST, Keith R. H.
Bradford, 15 October, 1932 (OR)

League Club	Source	Date Signed	Seasons Played	Apps	Subs	Gls
Bradford P.A.	Lowmoor Celtic	01.54	53	1	-	0

HIRST, Lee W.
Sheffield, 26 January, 1969 (CD)

League Club	Source	Date Signed	Seasons Played	Apps	Subs	Gls
Scarborough	Sheffield Parks	02.90	89-91	72	0	4

HIRST, Malcolm W.
Cudworth, 28 December, 1937 (CF)

League Club	Source	Date Signed	Seasons Played	Apps	Subs	Gls
Barnsley	Darfield Colly	05.56	56	1	-	0

HIRST, Martyn P.
Batley, 26 October, 1961 E Sch (M)

League Club	Source	Date Signed	Seasons Played	Apps	Subs	Gls
Bristol C.	Bath Univ.	10.83	83-85	36	5	1
Torquay U.	L	09.85	85	4	0	0

HITCH, George A.
Hammersmith, 15 March, 1930 (FB)

League Club	Source	Date Signed	Seasons Played	Apps	Subs	Gls
Queens Park R.		12.50	51	1	-	0

HITCHCOCK, Alan P.
Bracknell, 5 October, 1949 (FB)

League Club	Source	Date Signed	Seasons Played	Apps	Subs	Gls
Reading	App	10.67	68-69	4	0	0

HITCHCOCK, Kevin J.
Canning Town, 5 October, 1962 (G)

League Club	Source	Date Signed	Seasons Played	Apps	Subs	Gls
Nottingham F.	Barking	08.83				
Mansfield T.	L	02.84	83	14	0	0
Mansfield T.	Tr	06.84	84-87	168	0	0
Chelsea	Tr	03.88	87-91	35	0	0
Northampton T.	L	12.90	90	17	0	0

Kevin Hitchcock (Nottingham Forest, Mansfield Town & Chelsea)

HITCHEN, Harold
Liverpool, 22 October, 1922 (WH)

League Club	Source	Date Signed	Seasons Played	Apps	Subs	Gls
New Brighton	Formby	09.46	46-47	70	-	2
Sheffield U.	Tr	05.48	48-52	154	-	15
Bury	Tr	05.53	53	2	-	0

HITCHEN, Trevor
Sowerby Bridge, 25 September, 1926 (WH)

League Club	Source	Date Signed	Seasons Played	Apps	Subs	Gls
Notts Co.	Halifax T. (Am)	05.45				
Southport	Wellington T.	01.49	48-55	242	-	34
Oldham Ath.	Tr	08.56	56	3	-	0
Southport	Wigan Ath.	08.58	58	5	-	0

HITCHENS, Gerald A.
Kidderminster, 8 October, 1934 Died 1983 Eu23-1/EF Lge/E-7 (CF)

League Club	Source	Date Signed	Seasons Played	Apps	Subs	Gls
Cardiff C.	Kidderminster Hrs	01.55	54-57	95	-	40
Aston Villa	Tr	12.57	57-60	132	-	78

HITCHON, John
Carlisle, 30 August, 1919 (G)

League Club	Source	Date Signed	Seasons Played	Apps	Subs	Gls
Carlisle U.		04.47	46-49	5	-	0

HOADLEY, Philip F. W.
Battersea, 6 January, 1952 E Yth (CD)

League Club	Source	Date Signed	Seasons Played	Apps	Subs	Gls
Crystal Palace	App	01.69	67-71	62	11	1
Leyton Orient	Tr	10.71	71-77	255	0	9
Norwich C.	Tr	08.78	78-81	74	3	0

HOBBINS, Sidney G.
Plumstead, 6 May, 1916 Died 1984 (G)

League Club	Source	Date Signed	Seasons Played	Apps	Subs	Gls
Charlton Ath.	Bromley	05.34	37-46	2	-	0
Millwall	Tr	05.48	48	15	-	0
Leyton Orient	Tr	12.49	49	11	-	0

HOBBIS, Harold H. F.
Dartford, 9 March, 1913 Died 1991 E-2 (OL)

League Club	Source	Date Signed	Seasons Played	Apps	Subs	Gls
Charlton Ath.	Bromley	03.31	31-47	248	-	76

HOBBS, John E.
Swanage, 17 April, 1930 (CF)

League Club	Source	Date Signed	Seasons Played	Apps	Subs	Gls
Bournemouth	Swanage	10.52	53-54	6	-	1

HOBBS, Ronald G.
Aldershot, 23 August, 1921 (W)

League Club	Source	Date Signed	Seasons Played	Apps	Subs	Gls
Aldershot	Woking	11.44	46-53	170	-	15

HOBSON, Albert
Glossop, 7 April, 1925 (OR)

League Club	Source	Date Signed	Seasons Played	Apps	Subs	Gls
Blackpool	Glossop	08.45	47-53	62	-	3
Huddersfield T.	Tr	07.54	54-55	9	-	0
York C.	Tr	03.56	55-56	22	-	1

HOBSON, Gary
North Ferriby, 12 November, 1972 (D)

League Club	Source	Date Signed	Seasons Played	Apps	Subs	Gls
Hull C.	YT	07.91	90-91	19	1	0

HOBSON, Gordon
Sheffield, 27 November, 1957 (F)

League Club	Source	Date Signed	Seasons Played	Apps	Subs	Gls
Lincoln C.	Sheffield R.	12.77	77-84	260	12	73
Grimsby T.	Tr	06.85	85-86	50	2	18
Southampton	Tr	11.86	86-87	32	1	8
Lincoln C.	Tr	09.88	88-89	61	0	23
Exeter C.	Tr	08.90	90-91	37	1	7
Walsall (N/C)	Tr	09.91	91	3	0	0

HOBSON, John
Barnsley, 1 June, 1946 (W)

League Club	Source	Date Signed	Seasons Played	Apps	Subs	Gls
Blackpool	Jnrs	09.63				
Barnsley	Tr	07.65	65-68	30	8	7
Notts Co.	Tr	05.69	69-70	46	3	6

HOBSON, Norman
Shrewsbury, 22 August, 1933 (FB)

League Club	Source	Date Signed	Seasons Played	Apps	Subs	Gls
Shrewsbury T.	Oswestry T.	10.54	55-60	212	-	5

HOBSON, Wilfred
Consett, 26 January, 1932 (WH)

League Club	Source	Date Signed	Seasons Played	Apps	Subs	Gls
Oldham Ath.	West Stanley	01.53	54-58	170	-	1
Gateshead	Tr	06.59	59	31	-	1

HOCKADAY, David
Billingham, 9 November, 1957 (FB)

League Club	Source	Date Signed	Seasons Played	Apps	Subs	Gls
Blackpool	Billingham Synth.	06.75	76-82	131	16	24
Swindon T.	Tr	08.83	83-90	227	18	7
Hull C.	Tr	09.90	90-91	47	0	1

HOCKEY, Trevor J.
Keighley, 1 May, 1943 Died 1987 W-9 (M)

League Club	Source	Date Signed	Seasons Played	Apps	Subs	Gls
Bradford C.	Jnrs	05.60	59-61	53	-	5
Nottingham F.	Tr	11.61	61-63	73	-	6
Newcastle U.	Tr	11.63	63-65	52	0	3
Birmingham C.	Tr	11.65	65-70	195	1	8
Sheffield U.	Tr	01.71	70-72	68	0	4
Norwich C.	Tr	02.73	72	13	0	0
Aston Villa	Tr	06.73	73	24	0	1
Bradford C.	Tr	06.74	74-75	43	1	1

HODDER, Kenneth
Stockport, 20 August, 1930 (CH)

League Club	Source	Date Signed	Seasons Played	Apps	Subs	Gls
Stockport Co.	Jnrs	03.49	51-63	238	-	0

HODDLE, Carl
Harlow, 8 March, 1967 (M)

League Club	Source	Date Signed	Seasons Played	Apps	Subs	Gls
Tottenham H.	App	07.84				
Leyton Orient	Bishops Stortford	07.89	89-90	19	9	2
Barnet	Tr	07.91	91	10	3	0

HODDLE, Glenn
Hayes, 27 October, 1957 E Yth/Eu21-12/E'B'/E-53 (M)

League Club	Source	Date Signed	Seasons Played	Apps	Subs	Gls
Tottenham H.	App	04.75	75-86	371	7	88
Swindon T.	A.S. Monaco (Fr)	04.91	91	22	0	0

HODDY, Kevin R.
Romford, 6 January, 1968 (M)

League Club	Source	Date Signed	Seasons Played	Apps	Subs	Gls
Fulham	App	01.86	86-88	13	9	1

HODGE, Eric
Edmonton, 1 June, 1928 Died 1963 (G)

League Club	Source	Date Signed	Seasons Played	Apps	Subs	Gls
Tottenham H.		08.48				
Newport Co.	Tr	08.49	49	7	-	0

HODGE, Eric R. C.
South Africa, 3 April, 1933 (HB)

League Club	Source	Date Signed	Seasons Played	Apps	Subs	Gls
Brighton & H.A.	South Africa	10.56	57	3	-	0
Aldershot	Tr	07.59	59	17	-	0

HODGE, James O.
Perth, 23 October, 1926 (LB)

League Club	Source	Date Signed	Seasons Played	Apps	Subs	Gls
Newport Co.	York C. (Am)	08.46	46	1	-	0

HODGE, John
Skelmersdale, 1 April, 1969 (W)

League Club	Source	Date Signed	Seasons Played	Apps	Subs	Gls
Exeter C.	Falmouth	09.91	91	16	7	1

HODGE, Martin J.
Southport, 4 February, 1959 (G)

League Club	Source	Date Signed	Seasons Played	Apps	Subs	Gls
Plymouth Arg.	App	02.77	77-78	43	0	0
Everton	Tr	07.79	79-80	25	0	0
Preston N.E.	L	12.81	81	28	0	0
Oldham Ath.	L	07.82	82	4	0	0
Gillingham	L	01.83	82	4	0	0
Preston N.E.	L	02.83	82	16	0	0
Sheffield Wed.	Tr	08.83	83-87	197	0	0
Leicester C.	Tr	08.88	88-90	75	0	0
Hartlepool U.	Tr	08.91	91	40	0	0

HODGE, Robert W.
Exeter, 30 April, 1954 (W)

League Club	Source	Date Signed	Seasons Played	Apps	Subs	Gls
Exeter C.		07.74	74-78	120	8	18
Colchester U.	Tr	09.78	78-80	87	5	14
Torquay U.	Tr	08.81	81	3	1	1

HODGE, Stephen B.
Nottingham, 25 October, 1962 Eu21-8/E'B'/E-24 (M)

League Club	Source	Date Signed	Seasons Played	Apps	Subs	Gls
Nottingham F.	App	10.80	81-85	122	1	30
Aston Villa	Tr	08.85	85-86	53	0	12
Tottenham H.	Tr	12.86	86-87	44	1	7
Nottingham F.	Tr	08.88	88-90	79	3	20
Leeds U.	Tr	07.91	91	12	11	7

HODGES, Cyril L.
Hackney, 18 September, 1919 Died 1980 (W)

League Club	Source	Date Signed	Seasons Played	Apps	Subs	Gls
Arsenal		04.45	46	2	-	0
Brighton & H.A.	Tr	10.46	46	9	-	3

HODGES, David
Ross-on-Wye, 17 January, 1970 (M)

League Club	Source	Date Signed	Seasons Played	Apps	Subs	Gls
Mansfield T.	Jnrs	08.87	86-90	67	18	7
Torquay U.	Tr	01.91	90-91	8	8	0

HODGES, Glyn P.
Streatham, 30 April, 1963 W Yth/Wu21-5/W-16 (LW)

League Club	Source	Date Signed	Seasons Played	Apps	Subs	Gls
Wimbledon	App	02.81	80-86	200	32	49
Newcastle U.	Tr	07.87	87	7	0	0
Watford	Tr	10.87	87-89	82	4	15
Crystal Palace	Tr	07.90	90	5	2	0
Sheffield U.	Tr	01.91	90-91	34	4	6

HODGES, Kevin
Bridport, 12 June, 1960 (M)

League Club	Source	Date Signed	Seasons Played	Apps	Subs	Gls
Plymouth Arg.	App	03.78	78-91	500	26	81
Torquay U.	L	01.92	91	3	0	0

HODGES, Leonard H.
Bristol, 17 February, 1920 (IR)

League Club	Source	Date Signed	Seasons Played	Apps	Subs	Gls
Bristol Rov.	Soundwell	08.46	46-49	118	-	20
Swansea C.	Tr	08.50	50	2	-	0
Reading	Tr	08.51	51-52	6	-	2

Glyn Hodges (Wimbledon, Newcastle United, Watford, Crystal Palace, Sheffield United & Wales)

HODGES, Mark
Sheffield, 24 October, 1971 (CD)

League Club	Source	Date Signed	Seasons Played	Apps	Subs	Gls
Rotherham U.	YT	07.90	90	3	1	0

HODGETTS, Frank
Dudley, 30 September, 1924 (OL)

League Club	Source	Date Signed	Seasons Played	Apps	Subs	Gls
West Bromwich A.	Jnrs	10.42	46-48	67	-	11
Millwall	Tr	08.49	49-52	34	-	6

HODGKINS, Jeffrey
Portsmouth, 8 October, 1942 (CF)

League Club	Source	Date Signed	Seasons Played	Apps	Subs	Gls
Portsmouth	Jnrs	06.60	60	3	-	0

HODGKINSON, Alan
Sheffield, 16 August, 1936 *Eu23-7/EF Lge/E-5* (G)

League Club	Source	Date Signed	Seasons Played	Apps	Subs	Gls
Sheffield U.	Worksop T.	08.53	54-70	576	0	0

HODGKINSON, Derek
Margate, 30 April, 1944 (IF)

League Club	Source	Date Signed	Seasons Played	Apps	Subs	Gls
Manchester C.	Margate	08.61	63	1	-	1
Stockport Co.	Tr	06.64	64-65	46	0	9

HODGKINSON, Edwin
Ilkeston, 27 November, 1920 (WH)

League Club	Source	Date Signed	Seasons Played	Apps	Subs	Gls
Leeds U.		12.46	46-47	2	-	0
Halifax T.	Tr	07.48	48-49	12	-	2

HODGKISS, Robert
Farnworth, 22 March, 1918 (FB)

League Club	Source	Date Signed	Seasons Played	Apps	Subs	Gls
Southport	Walkden Meths	11.38	38	10	-	0
Everton	Tr	08.46				
Southport	Tr	07.47	47-48	20	-	0

HODGKISSON, W. Kenneth
West Bromwich, 12 March, 1933 (IF)

League Club	Source	Date Signed	Seasons Played	Apps	Subs	Gls
West Bromwich A.	Jnrs	04.50	52-55	21	-	4
Walsall	Tr	01.56	55-65	333	1	54

HODGSON, Brian G.
Cleethorpes, 29 January, 1936 (F)

League Club	Source	Date Signed	Seasons Played	Apps	Subs	Gls
Grimsby T.	Askern W.M.C.	09.56	56	7	-	1
Workington	Tr	10.59	59	1	-	0

HODGSON, David J.
Gateshead, 1 November, 1960 *Eu21-6* (F)

League Club	Source	Date Signed	Seasons Played	Apps	Subs	Gls
Middlesbrough	Jnrs	08.78	78-81	116	9	16
Liverpool	Tr	08.82	82-83	21	7	4
Sunderland	Tr	08.84	84-85	32	8	5
Norwich C.	Tr	07.86	86	3	3	1
Middlesbrough	L	02.87	86	2	0	0
Sheffield Wed.	Jerez (Ap.)	08.88	88	6	5	1
Swansea C. (N/C)	Metz (Fr)	03.92	91	1	2	0

HODGSON, Donald
Liversedge, 22 December, 1922 (IF)

League Club	Source	Date Signed	Seasons Played	Apps	Subs	Gls
Bradford P.A.	Bradford U.	04.48	48-51	41	-	7
York C.	Tr	08.52				

HODGSON, Gordon H.
Newcastle, 13 October, 1952 *E Yth* (M)

League Club	Source	Date Signed	Seasons Played	Apps	Subs	Gls
Newcastle U.	Jnrs	06.71	71-73	8	1	0
Mansfield T.	Tr	05.74	74-78	184	0	23
Oxford U.	Tr	09.78	78-79	66	1	3
Peterborough U.	Tr	08.80	80-81	82	1	5

HODGSON, John P.
Dawdon, 10 May, 1922 (G)

League Club	Source	Date Signed	Seasons Played	Apps	Subs	Gls
Leeds U.	Murton Colly	11.43	46-47	20	-	0
Middlesbrough	Tr	03.48	47-54	13	-	0

HODGSON, John V. (Jack)
Seaham, 30 September, 1913 *Died 1970* (FB)

League Club	Source	Date Signed	Seasons Played	Apps	Subs	Gls
Grimsby T.	Seaham Colly	01.32	32-47	212	-	2
Doncaster Rov.	Tr	01.48	47-51	96	-	2

HODGSON, Kenneth
Newcastle, 19 January, 1942 (F)

League Club	Source	Date Signed	Seasons Played	Apps	Subs	Gls
Newcastle U.	Jnrs	05.59	60	6	-	0
Scunthorpe U.	Tr	12.61	61-63	88	-	30
Bournemouth	Tr	06.64	64-65	77	1	24
Colchester U.	Tr	07.66	66-68	56	1	19

HODGSON, Lawrence
Birkenhead, 19 January, 1917 (FB)

League Club	Source	Date Signed	Seasons Played	Apps	Subs	Gls
Tranmere Rov.	Silver Green	01.39	46-50	78	-	0

HODGSON, Michael
Newcastle, 6 July, 1945 (OR)

League Club	Source	Date Signed	Seasons Played	Apps	Subs	Gls
Hartlepool U. (Am)	Billingham Synth.	08.64	64	1	-	0

HODGSON, Noel
Workington, 25 December, 1938 (W)

League Club	Source	Date Signed	Seasons Played	Apps	Subs	Gls
Workington	Jnrs	08.57	57-62	51	-	12

HODGSON, Ronald
Birkenhead, 21 November, 1922 (CH)

League Club	Source	Date Signed	Seasons Played	Apps	Subs	Gls
Tranmere Rov.		02.41				
Manchester C.	Tr	10.44	46	1	-	0
Southport	Tr	06.47	47-48	42	-	1
Crewe Alex.	Tr	02.49	48-49	31	-	0

HODGSON, Samuel
Seaham, 21 January, 1919 (WH)

League Club	Source	Date Signed	Seasons Played	Apps	Subs	Gls
Grimsby T.	Seaham Colly	01.36	46-47	21	-	0
Mansfield T.	Tr	07.48	48	2	-	0

HODGSON, William
Glasgow, 9 July, 1935 (IF)

League Club	Source	Date Signed	Seasons Played	Apps	Subs	Gls
Sheffield U.	St Johnstone	05.57	57-63	152	-	32
Leicester C.	Tr	09.63	63-64	46	-	10
Derby Co.	Tr	06.65	65-67	78	0	17
Rotherham U.	Tr	09.67	67	9	0	0
York C.	Tr	12.67	67-69	98	0	3

HODKINSON, Andrew J.
Ashton-u-Lyne, 4 November, 1965 *E Sch* (W)

League Club	Source	Date Signed	Seasons Played	Apps	Subs	Gls
Oldham Ath.	Bolton W. (App)	08.83	83-84	4	1	1
Stockport Co.	Tr	08.85	85-87	114	4	18
Scunthorpe U.	Tr	08.88	88-89	59	3	8

HODKINSON, David
Lancaster, 18 January, 1945 (OL)

League Club	Source	Date Signed	Seasons Played	Apps	Subs	Gls
Oldham Ath.	App	02.63	61	2	-	0

HODSON, Simeon P.
Lincoln, 5 March, 1966 (RB)

League Club	Source	Date Signed	Seasons Played	Apps	Subs	Gls
Notts Co.	App	03.84	83-84	27	0	0
Charlton Ath.	Tr	03.85	84	5	0	0
Lincoln C.	Tr	01.86	85-86	54	2	0
Newport Co.	Tr	08.87	87	34	0	1
West Bromwich A.	Tr	03.88	87-91	77	4	0

HODSON, Stuart W.
Peterborough, 5 November, 1950 (D)

League Club	Source	Date Signed	Seasons Played	Apps	Subs	Gls
Peterborough U.	Chatteris T.	11.74	74-76	24	10	0

HOEKMAN, Daniel
Nijmegen (Neth.), 21 September, 1964 (M)

League Club	Source	Date Signed	Seasons Played	Apps	Subs	Gls
Manchester C. (N/C)	Den Haag (Neth)	10.91	91	0	1	0

HOGAN, Charles
Bury, 23 April, 1926 (OR)

League Club	Source	Date Signed	Seasons Played	Apps	Subs	Gls
Bury	Spartan Ath.	06.48	47	1	-	0
Accrington St.	Tr	08.49	49-50	56	-	4
Southport	Tr	08.51	51	9	-	1
Rochdale	Tr	08.52	52	3	-	0

HOGAN, T. Eric
Cork, 17 December, 1971 (M)

League Club	Source	Date Signed	Seasons Played	Apps	Subs	Gls
Birmingham C.	Cobh Ramblers	08.91	91	0	1	0

HOGAN, Roy D.
Hartlepool, 24 September, 1960 (M)

League Club	Source	Date Signed	Seasons Played	Apps	Subs	Gls
Hartlepool U.	App	09.78	77-82	133	10	15
Hartlepool U.	Consett	12.83	83-86	138	3	17

HOGAN, Terence
Hartlepool, 3 June, 1933

League Club	Source	Date Signed	Seasons Played	Apps	Subs	Gls
Hartlepool U.		08.57	57	9	-	1

HOGAN, William J.
Salford, 9 January, 1924 (IF)

League Club	Source	Date Signed	Seasons Played	Apps	Subs	Gls
Manchester C.		05.42	48	3	-	0
Carlisle U.	Tr	09.49	49-55	191	-	27

HOGARTH, Gordon
Sunderland, 18 November, 1936 (G)

League Club	Source	Date Signed	Seasons Played	Apps	Subs	Gls
Gateshead	Throckley Welfare	06.57	57-58	12	-	0

HOGG, Adam
Airdrie, 26 April, 1934 (FB)

League Club	Source	Date Signed	Seasons Played	Apps	Subs	Gls
Swindon T.	Airdrieonians	06.56	56	1	-	0

League Club	Source	Date Signed	Seasons Played	Apps	Subs	Gls
HOGG, Derek						
Stockton, 4 November, 1930 EF Lge						(OL)
Leicester C.	Chorley	10.52	52-57	161	-	26
West Bromwich A.	Tr	04.58	58-60	81	-	11
Cardiff C.	Tr	10.60	60-61	41	-	7
HOGG, Frederick						
Bishop Auckland, 24 April, 1918						(WH)
Luton T.		12.36	37	4	-	0
Mansfield T.	Tr	11.45	46-47	45	-	8
Halifax T.	Tr	10.47	47-49	49	-	3
HOGG, Graeme J.						
Aberdeen, 17 June, 1964 Su21-4						(CD)
Manchester U.	App	06.82	83-87	82	1	1
West Bromwich A.	L	11.87	87	7	0	0
Portsmouth	Tr	08.88	88-90	97	3	2
HOGG, Graham S.						
Neath, 15 January, 1922 W Amat						(F)
Cardiff C.	Cardiff Corries	06.48	48	1	-	0
HOGG, John						
Blyth, 7 October, 1931						(F)
Sunderland		12.49				
Portsmouth	Blyth Spartans	12.54				
Gateshead	Peterborough U.	07.57	57-59	80	-	21
HOGG, Matthew						
Wideopen (Nd), 14 April, 1941						(HB)
Newcastle U.	Jnrs	05.59				
Darlington	Tr	07.61	61	1	-	0
HOGG, A. Raymond						
Lowick (Nd), 11 December, 1929						(FB)
Aston Villa	Berwick R.	03.55	54-56	21	-	0
Mansfield T.	Tr	07.58	58-59	11	-	0
Peterborough U.	Tr	08.60	60	2	-	0
HOGGAN, David M.						
Falkirk, 10 August, 1961						(M)
Bolton W.	App	08.79	79-82	83	10	11
HOGGART, Dennis J.						
Glasgow, 2 January, 1939						(IF)
Leeds U.	Ferndale Ath.	02.57				
York C.	Tr	08.60	60-63	45	-	11
Stockport Co.	Tr	08.64	64-65	30	0	6
HOLAH, Eric T.						
Hull, 3 August, 1937						(CF)
Hull C. (Am)	Malet Lambert O.B.	06.60	60	1	-	1
Bradford C.	Tr	08.61	61	4	-	2
HOLBROOK, Ian C.						
Warrington, 24 November, 1955						(G)
Bolton W.	Jnrs	07.74				
Stockport Co.	Tr	07.76	76	37	0	0
HOLBROOK, Stephen						
Richmond (NYorks), 16 September, 1952 E Sch						(W)
Hull C.	App	09.70	70-71	2	1	0
Darlington	Tr	06.72	72-76	104	12	12
HOLBUTT, Barry L.						
Birmingham, 11 February, 1943						(CF)
Aston Villa	Jnrs	10.60				
Walsall	Nuneaton Bor.	03.65	65	0	1	0
HOLD, John D.						
Southampton, 28 March, 1948						(F)
Bournemouth	App	11.64	65-70	80	5	25
Crewe Alex.	L	01.69	68	0	2	0
Northampton T.	Tr	08.71	71-72	42	2	11
HOLD, Oscar						
Barnsley, 19 October, 1918						(IF)
Barnsley		08.37				
Aldershot	Tr	04.39	46	14	-	4
Norwich C.	Tr	03.47	46-48	44	-	18
Notts Co.	Tr	10.48	48	19	-	9
Everton	Chelmsford C.	02.50	49-50	22	-	5
Queens Park R.	Tr	02.52	51-52	4	-	1
HOLDEN, Alan						
Haslingden, 12 October, 1941						(WH)
Blackburn Rov.		01.62	63	1	-	0
Stockport Co.	Tr	07.66	66	1	0	0
HOLDEN, Andrew I.						
Flint, 14 September, 1962 Wu21-1/W-1						(CD)
Chester C.	Rhyl	08.83	83-86	100	0	17
Wigan Ath.	Tr	10.86	86-88	48	1	4
Oldham Ath.	Tr	01.89	88-90	21	0	4
HOLDEN, A. Douglas						
Manchester, 28 September, 1930 E Yth/EFLge/E-5						(OR)
Bolton W.	Jnrs	01.50	51-62	419	-	40
Preston N.E.	Tr	11.62	62-64	89	-	13
HOLDEN, Melvyn G.						
Dundee, 25 August, 1954 Died 1981						(F)
Preston N.E.	App	09.72	72-74	69	3	22
Sunderland	Tr	05.75	75-77	66	7	23
Blackpool	Tr	07.78	78	2	1	0
HOLDEN, Richard W. (Rick)						
Skipton, 9 September, 1964						(LW)
Burnley (N/C)	Carnegie Coll.	03.86	85	0	1	0
Halifax T.	Tr	09.86	86-87	66	1	12
Watford	Tr	03.88	87-88	42	0	8
Oldham Ath.	Tr	08.89	89-91	125	4	19

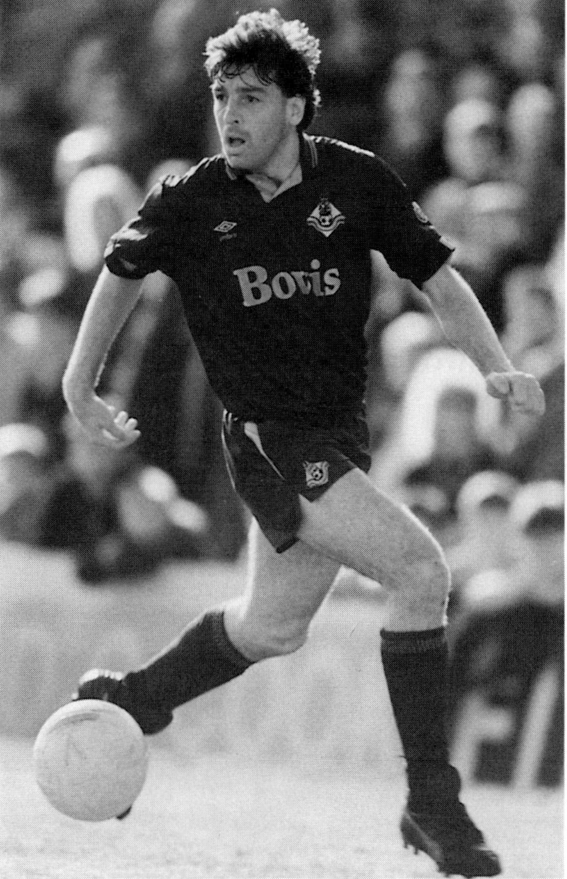

Rick Holden (Burnley, Halifax Town, Watford & Oldham Athletic)

League Club	Source	Date Signed	Seasons Played	Apps	Subs	Gls
HOLDEN, Robert						
Sunderland, 28 October, 1965						(F)
Scunthorpe U.	Sunderland (App)	09.83	83	6	1	1
HOLDEN, Simon J.						
Littleborough, 9 March, 1968						(M)
Rochdale	Jnrs	07.85				
Rochdale		01.87	86-87	35	14	4
HOLDEN, Stephen A. D.						
Luton, 4 September, 1972						(CD)
Leicester C.	YT	03.91	91	1	0	0
HOLDEN, J. Stuart						
Grange Moor, 21 April, 1942						(D)
Huddersfield T.	Jnrs	04.59	60-64	28	-	2
Oldham Ath.	Tr	07.65	65-66	39	3	5
Rochdale	Tr	01.67	66	21	0	0

League Club	Source	Date Signed	Seasons Played	Apps	Subs	Gls

HOLDEN, William
Bolton, 1 April, 1928 Died E'B'-1 (CF)

League Club	Source	Date Signed	Seasons Played	Apps	Subs	Gls
Burnley	Everton (Am)	11.49	50-55	187	-	75
Sunderland	Tr	12.55	55	19	-	5
Stockport Co.	Tr	10.56	56-58	87	-	38
Bury	Tr	03.59	58-61	101	-	33
Halifax T.	Tr	06.62	62	37	-	11

HOLDER, Alan M.
Oxford, 10 December, 1931 (F)

League Club	Source	Date Signed	Seasons Played	Apps	Subs	Gls
Nottingham F.		04.52	54	3	-	0
Lincoln C.	Tr	07.55	55	1	-	0
Tranmere Rov.	Tr	12.56	56	13	-	1

HOLDER, Colin W.
Cheltenham, 6 January, 1944 (CF)

League Club	Source	Date Signed	Seasons Played	Apps	Subs	Gls
Coventry C.	App	05.61	60-61	9	-	4

HOLDER, David J.
Cheltenham, 15 December, 1943 (CH)

League Club	Source	Date Signed	Seasons Played	Apps	Subs	Gls
Notts Co.	Cardiff C. (Am)	10.62	63	8	-	0
Barrow	Tr	07.64	64	29	-	0

HOLDER, Philip
Kilburn, 19 January, 1952 E Yth (M)

League Club	Source	Date Signed	Seasons Played	Apps	Subs	Gls
Tottenham H.	App	02.69	71-73	9	4	1
Crystal Palace	Tr	02.75	74-77	93	2	5
Bournemouth	Tr	03.79	78-79	58	0	4

HOLDER, Stephen W.
Nottingham, 21 April, 1952 (OR)

League Club	Source	Date Signed	Seasons Played	Apps	Subs	Gls
Notts Co.	App	04.70	69	0	1	0

HOLDING, Edwin J.
Wolverhampton, 15 October, 1930 (F)

League Club	Source	Date Signed	Seasons Played	Apps	Subs	Gls
Walsall		01.49	50-53	39	-	6
Barrow		07.54	54	5	-	5

HOLDSWORTH, David G.
Walthamstow, 8 November, 1968 Eu21-1 (CD)

League Club	Source	Date Signed	Seasons Played	Apps	Subs	Gls
Watford	App	11.86	88-91	119	6	8

HOLDSWORTH, Dean C.
Walthamstow, 8 November, 1968 (F)

League Club	Source	Date Signed	Seasons Played	Apps	Subs	Gls
Watford	App	11.86	87-89	2	14	3
Carlisle U.	L	02.88	87	4	0	1
Port Vale	L	03.88	87	6	0	2
Swansea C.	L	08.88	88	4	1	1
Brentford	L	10.88	88	2	5	1
Brentford	Tr	09.89	89-91	106	4	53

Dean Holdsworth (Watford & Brentford)

HOLE, Alan V.
Swansea, 26 December, 1930 (CH)

League Club	Source	Date Signed	Seasons Played	Apps	Subs	Gls
Swansea C.		07.53	53	20	-	0

HOLE, Barry G.
Swansea, 16 September, 1942 W Sch/Wu23-5/W-30 (WH)

League Club	Source	Date Signed	Seasons Played	Apps	Subs	Gls
Cardiff C.	Jnrs	09.59	59-65	211	0	16
Blackburn Rov.	Tr	07.66	66-68	79	0	13
Aston Villa	Tr	09.68	68-69	47	0	6
Swansea C.	Tr	07.70	70-71	78	0	3

HOLE, Colin D.
Swansea, 1 September, 1932 W Sch

League Club	Source	Date Signed	Seasons Played	Apps	Subs	Gls
Swansea C.	Jnrs	03.50	53	1	-	0

HOLLAND, David W.
Chorley, 6 March, 1935 (WH)

League Club	Source	Date Signed	Seasons Played	Apps	Subs	Gls
Stockport Co.	Horwich R.M.I.	06.59	59-60	25	-	4

HOLLAND, Eric R.
Sutton-in-Ashfield, 23 January, 1940 E Sch/E Yth (FB)

League Club	Source	Date Signed	Seasons Played	Apps	Subs	Gls
Manchester U.	Jnrs	05.57				
Wrexham	Tr	03.60	59-65	118	0	0
Chester C.	Tr	03.66	65-66	5	1	0

HOLLAND, Kenneth A.
Doncaster, 18 April, 1922 (IF)

League Club	Source	Date Signed	Seasons Played	Apps	Subs	Gls
Bury	Wolverhampton W. (Am)	09.44				
Bournemouth	Tr	09.48	48	3	-	0

HOLLAND, Patrick G.
Poplar, 13 September, 1950 (W)

League Club	Source	Date Signed	Seasons Played	Apps	Subs	Gls
West Ham U.	App	04.69	68-80	227	18	23
Bournemouth	L	03.71	70	10	0	0

HOLLAND, Paul
Lincoln, 8 July, 1973 (M)

League Club	Source	Date Signed	Seasons Played	Apps	Subs	Gls
Mansfield T.	Jnrs	07.91	90-91	39	0	6

HOLLAND, Robert J.
Willesden, 18 August, 1965 (LB)

League Club	Source	Date Signed	Seasons Played	Apps	Subs	Gls
Crewe Alex. (N/C)	Harrow Bor.	09.85	85	7	0	0

HOLLAND, Simon L. D.
Sunderland, 26 March, 1973 (F)

League Club	Source	Date Signed	Seasons Played	Apps	Subs	Gls
Doncaster Rov.	YT	01.91	90	1	0	0

HOLLETT, Ivan R.
Pinxton, 22 April, 1940 (F)

League Club	Source	Date Signed	Seasons Played	Apps	Subs	Gls
Mansfield T.	Sutton T.	08.58	58-64	98	-	40
Chesterfield	Tr	12.64	64-68	157	0	62
Crewe Alex.	Tr	11.68	68-70	55	4	19
Cambridge U.	Tr	11.70	70-71	37	1	13
Hereford U.	Tr	01.72	72	11	0	2

HOLLEY, Thomas
Sunderland, 15 November, 1913 (CH)

League Club	Source	Date Signed	Seasons Played	Apps	Subs	Gls
Barnsley		09.32	33-35	75	-	4
Leeds U.	Tr	07.36	36-48	162	-	1

HOLLIDAY, Edwin
Barnsley, 7 June, 1939 Eu23-5/EF Lge/E-3 (OL)

League Club	Source	Date Signed	Seasons Played	Apps	Subs	Gls
Middlesbrough	Jnrs	08.56	57-61	134	-	17
Sheffield Wed.	Tr	03.62	61-63	55	-	12
Middlesbrough	Tr	06.65	65	23	0	4
Workington	Hereford U.	02.68	67-68	56	0	4
Peterborough U.	Tr	07.69	69	12	4	1

HOLLIDAY, John R.
Penrith, 13 March, 1970 (CD)

League Club	Source	Date Signed	Seasons Played	Apps	Subs	Gls
Carlisle U.		09.89	90-91	17	0	0

HOLLIDAY, Kenneth J.
Darwen, 19 August, 1925 (D)

League Club	Source	Date Signed	Seasons Played	Apps	Subs	Gls
Blackburn Rov.	Darwen	10.46	47-51	29	-	0
Accrington St.	Tr	07.52	52-54	96	-	5
Barrow	Tr	09.55	55	5	-	0

HOLLIFIELD, Michael
Middlesbrough, 2 May, 1961 (LB)

League Club	Source	Date Signed	Seasons Played	Apps	Subs	Gls
Wolverhampton W.	App	04.79	80-81	21	0	0
Hull C.	Tr	08.83	83-84	45	0	1
Tranmere Rov.	Tr	07.85	85	0	1	0

HOLLINS, David M.
Bangor, 4 February, 1938 Wu23-2/W-11 (G)

League Club	Source	Date Signed	Seasons Played	Apps	Subs	Gls
Brighton & H.A.	Merrow	11.55	57-60	66	-	0
Newcastle U.	Tr	03.61	60-66	112	0	0
Mansfield T.	Tr	02.67	66-69	111	0	0
Nottingham F.	L	03.70	69	9	0	0
Aldershot	Tr	07.70	70	16	0	0

HOLLINS, John W.
Guildford, 16 July, 1946 E Yth/Eu23-12/E'B'/EF Lge/E-1 (M)

League Club	Source	Date Signed	Seasons Played	Apps	Subs	Gls
Chelsea	App	07.63	63-74	436	0	47
Queens Park R.	Tr	06.75	75-78	148	3	5
Arsenal	Tr	07.79	79-82	123	4	9
Chelsea	Tr	06.83	83	29	0	1

HOLLINSHEAD, Shaun R.
Sandbach, 21 February, 1961 (M)

League Club	Source	Date Signed	Seasons Played	Apps	Subs	Gls
Crewe Alex. (App)	App	06.77	77	2	3	0

HOLLIS, Andrew
Huntingdon, 16 September, 1963 (F)

League Club	Source	Date Signed	Seasons Played	Apps	Subs	Gls
Cambridge U.	Ramsey T.	04.87	86-87	3	1	0

HOLLIS, Harold
Shotton, 12 December, 1913 (FB)

League Club	Source	Date Signed	Seasons Played	Apps	Subs	Gls
Chester C.		09.40				
Wrexham	Connahs Quay	08.46	46	1	-	0

HOLLIS, K. Michael
Loughborough, 14 November, 1949 (W)

League Club	Source	Date Signed	Seasons Played	Apps	Subs	Gls
Leicester C.	App	11.66				
Barrow	Tr	07.69	69-71	88	3	13
Chester C.	Tr	07.72	72	34	3	8
Stockport Co.	Tr	07.73	73-75	106	6	33
Reading	Tr	03.76	75-76	18	7	6

HOLLIS, Roy W.
Yarmouth, 24 December, 1925 (CF)

League Club	Source	Date Signed	Seasons Played	Apps	Subs	Gls
Norwich C.	Great Yarmouth	05.47	47-51	96	-	52
Tottenham H.	Tr	12.52	52	3	-	1
Southend U.	Tr	02.54	53-59	240	-	122

HOLLOW, Michael J.
Nazeing (Ex), 5 September, 1943 (FB)

League Club	Source	Date Signed	Seasons Played	Apps	Subs	Gls
Leyton Orient	Bishops Stortford	08.62	63-64	34	-	0
Peterborough U.	Tr	07.65	65	14	0	1

HOLLOWAY, Ian S.
Kingswood, 12 March, 1963 (RW)

League Club	Source	Date Signed	Seasons Played	Apps	Subs	Gls
Bristol Rov.	App	03.81	80-84	104	7	14
Wimbledon	Tr	07.85	85	19	0	2
Brentford	Tr	03.86	85-87	27	3	2
Torquay U.	L	01.87	86	5	0	0
Bristol Rov.	Tr	08.87	87-90	179	0	26
Queens Park R.	Tr	08.91	91	34	6	0

HOLLOWBREAD, John F.
Enfield, 2 January, 1934 (G)

League Club	Source	Date Signed	Seasons Played	Apps	Subs	Gls
Tottenham H.	Enfield	01.52	58-63	67	-	0
Southampton	Tr	05.64	64-65	36	0	0

HOLLYMAN, Kenneth C.
Cardiff, 18 November, 1922 (WH)

League Club	Source	Date Signed	Seasons Played	Apps	Subs	Gls
Cardiff C.	Cardiff Nomads	04.42	46-53	188	-	8
Newport Co.	Tr	11.53	53-59	231	-	3

HOLLYWOOD, Dennis
Govan, 3 November, 1944 Su23-1 (LB)

League Club	Source	Date Signed	Seasons Played	Apps	Subs	Gls
Southampton	App	12.61	62-71	234	0	4

HOLMAN, Harold
Exeter, 16 November, 1957 E Sch (F)

League Club	Source	Date Signed	Seasons Played	Apps	Subs	Gls
Exeter C.	Chelsea (App)	07.76	76-78	47	5	9
Peterborough U.	Tr	12.78	78	9	0	1

HOLMAN, Harold W.
Exeter, 25 September, 1920 Died 1977 (CF)

League Club	Source	Date Signed	Seasons Played	Apps	Subs	Gls
Exeter C.	Budleigh Salterton	12.46	46	4	-	2

HOLME, Philip C.
Briton Ferry, 21 June, 1947 (IF)

League Club	Source	Date Signed	Seasons Played	Apps	Subs	Gls
Swansea C.	Bridgend T.	03.71	70-71	19	4	5
Hull C.	Tr	07.72	72-73	29	9	11

HOLMES, Albert V.
Ecclesfield, 14 February, 1942 (FB)

League Club	Source	Date Signed	Seasons Played	Apps	Subs	Gls
Chesterfield	E.M.Gas Board	06.61	61-75	457	3	10

HOLMES, Andrew J.
Stoke, 7 January, 1969 (CD)

League Club	Source	Date Signed	Seasons Played	Apps	Subs	Gls
Stoke C.	App	01.87	87-89	6	1	0
Doncaster Rov.	Tr	07.90	90	10	1	0

HOLMES, Barry
Bradford, 4 October, 1942 (W)

League Club	Source	Date Signed	Seasons Played	Apps	Subs	Gls
Halifax T.	Ossett A.	09.66	66-72	82	8	8

HOLMES, Colin A.
Winchester, 28 March, 1939 E Yth (HB)

League Club	Source	Date Signed	Seasons Played	Apps	Subs	Gls
Southampton	Jnrs	02.57	59	1	-	0

HOLMES, David J.
Derby, 22 November, 1972 (F)

League Club	Source	Date Signed	Seasons Played	Apps	Subs	Gls
Scarborough	YT	05.90	89-91	4	7	1

HOLMES, Herbert F. (Bert)
Norwich, 27 September, 1924 (CH)

League Club	Source	Date Signed	Seasons Played	Apps	Subs	Gls
Norwich C.	Gothic	08.47	48-54	58	-	1

HOLMES, Ian M.
Wombwell, 8 December, 1950 (M)

League Club	Source	Date Signed	Seasons Played	Apps	Subs	Gls
Sheffield U.	Jnrs	01.68	71-72	4	2	0
York C.	Tr	07.73	73-77	152	7	30
Huddersfield T.	Tr	10.77	77-79	65	8	21

HOLMES, James P.
Dublin, 11 November, 1953 IR-30 (LB)

League Club	Source	Date Signed	Seasons Played	Apps	Subs	Gls
Coventry C.	App	11.70	71-76	122	6	6
Tottenham H.	Tr	03.77	76-78	81	0	2
Leicester C. (N/C)	Vancouver (Can)	10.82	82	2	0	0
Brentford (N /C)	Tr	02.83	82	4	0	0
Torquay U. (N/C)	Tr	03.83	82-83	25	0	3
Peterborough U.	Tr	11.83	83-85	48	1	7

HOLMES, Joseph
Clay Cross, 10 February, 1926 (WH)

League Club	Source	Date Signed	Seasons Played	Apps	Subs	Gls
Chesterfield	Parkhouse Colly	09.46	47-51	29	-	3

HOLMES, Kyle J.
Abergavenny, 25 September, 1959 (M)

League Club	Source	Date Signed	Seasons Played	Apps	Subs	Gls
Hereford U.	App	10.77	77-79	25	3	3

HOLMES, Lee J.
Aveley, 28 September, 1955 (F)

League Club	Source	Date Signed	Seasons Played	Apps	Subs	Gls
Brentford	Haringey Bor.	06.79	79	26	2	6

HOLMES, Matthew J. E.
Luton, 1 August, 1969 (M)

League Club	Source	Date Signed	Seasons Played	Apps	Subs	Gls
Bournemouth	YT	08.88	88-91	105	9	8
Cardiff C.	L	03.89	88	0	1	0

HOLMES, Michael A.
Blackpool, 9 September, 1965 (M)

League Club	Source	Date Signed	Seasons Played	Apps	Subs	Gls
Bradford C. (N/C)	Yeadon Celtic	07.83	84	0	5	0
Wolverhampton W.	Burnley (N/C)	11.85	85-87	74	9	13
Huddersfield T.	Tr	07.88	88	3	4	0
Cambridge U.	Tr	02.89	88	7	4	0
Rochdale	Tr	07.89	89-90	47	7	7
Torquay U.	Tr	12.90	90-91	34	6	3
Carlisle U.	Tr	02.92	91	15	0	4

HOLMES, Nicholas C.
Southampton, 11 November, 1954 (M)

League Club	Source	Date Signed	Seasons Played	Apps	Subs	Gls
Southampton	App	11.72	73-86	437	7	56

HOLMES, Paul
Stocksbridge, 18 February, 1968 (RB)

League Club	Source	Date Signed	Seasons Played	Apps	Subs	Gls
Doncaster Rov.	App	02.86	85-87	42	5	1
Torquay U.	Tr	08.88	88-91	127	11	4

HOLMES, Roger W.
Scunthorpe, 9 September, 1942 (M)

League Club	Source	Date Signed	Seasons Played	Apps	Subs	Gls
Lincoln C.	Jnrs	09.59	59-71	276	2	37

HOLMES, Stanley
Easington, 27 November, 1920

League Club	Source	Date Signed	Seasons Played	Apps	Subs	Gls
Hartlepool U.		07.47	49	1	-	0

HOLMES, Thomas
Hemsworth, 14 December, 1934 (IF)

League Club	Source	Date Signed	Seasons Played	Apps	Subs	Gls
Barnsley	Hemsworth Y.C.	03.53	54-58	35	-	7
Halifax T.	Tr	07.59	59-60	50	-	15
Chesterfield	Tr	07.61	61	20	-	3

League Club	Source	Date Signed	Seasons Played	Career Record Apps	Subs	Gls

HOLMES, William
Leeds, 29 October, 1926 E Amat (CF)

League Club	Source	Date Signed	Seasons Played	Apps	Subs	Gls
Doncaster Rov.	Morecambe	10.50	50	2	-	0
Blackburn Rov.	Morecambe	01.52	51-52	21	-	16
Bradford C.	Morecambe	09.53	53	22	-	5
Southport	Tr	07.54	54-55	56	-	21

HOLMES, William G.
Balham, 4 February, 1951 Died 1987 (F)

League Club	Source	Date Signed	Seasons Played	Apps	Subs	Gls
Millwall	Woking	07.70	70	0	1	0
Luton T.	Tr	07.73	73	0	1	0
Wimbledon	Barnet	07.75	77	15	0	5
Hereford U.	Tr	11.77	77-78	21	10	5
Brentford	Tr	08.79	79	8	7	2

HOLSGROVE, John W.
Southwark, 27 September, 1945 E Yth (CD)

League Club	Source	Date Signed	Seasons Played	Apps	Subs	Gls
Crystal Palace	Tottenham H. (Am)	02.64	64	18	-	2
Wolverhampton W.	Tr	05.65	65-70	178	2	7
Sheffield Wed.	Tr	06.71	71-74	103	1	5
Stockport Co.	Tr	08.75	75	9	0	0

HOLSGROVE, Paul
Telford, 26 August, 1969 (F)

League Club	Source	Date Signed	Seasons Played	Apps	Subs	Gls
Aldershot	YT	02.87	87-88	0	3	0
Luton T.	Wokingham T.	01.91	90-91	0	1	0

HOLT, David
Padiham, 26 February, 1952 (D)

League Club	Source	Date Signed	Seasons Played	Apps	Subs	Gls
Bury	App	10.69	69-74	174	4	9
Oldham Ath.	Tr	12.74	74-79	141	1	1
Burnley	Tr	07.80	80-82	84	0	1

HOLT, David E.
Sunniside (Dm), 7 January, 1945 (CH)

League Club	Source	Date Signed	Seasons Played	Apps	Subs	Gls
Blackburn Rov.	Jnrs	04.63	65-66	10	0	0

HOLT, George
Halifax, 28 February, 1927 (IF)

League Club	Source	Date Signed	Seasons Played	Apps	Subs	Gls
Halifax T.		07.47	47-53	57	-	11

HOLT, Raymond
Thorne, 29 October, 1939 (CH)

League Club	Source	Date Signed	Seasons Played	Apps	Subs	Gls
Huddersfield T.	Moor End	08.58	61-63	16	-	0
Oldham Ath.	Tr	07.65	65	14	1	0
Halifax T.	Tr	07.66	66-67	86	0	0
Scunthorpe U.	Tr	07.68	68-69	50	0	0

HOLT, William K.
Boldon, 31 March, 1926 (CH)

League Club	Source	Date Signed	Seasons Played	Apps	Subs	Gls
Blackburn Rov.	Boldon Colly	01.49	48-52	78	-	0
Barrow	Weymouth	06.54	54-56	72	-	0

HOLTHAM, Dean M.
Pontypridd, 30 September, 1963 (D)

League Club	Source	Date Signed	Seasons Played	Apps	Subs	Gls
Cardiff C.	App	09.81				
Swansea C.	Tr	08.82	82	6	0	0
Newport Co. (N/C)	Ebbw Vale	09.87	87	4	2	0

HOLTON, Clifford C.
Oxford, 29 April, 1929 (CF)

League Club	Source	Date Signed	Seasons Played	Apps	Subs	Gls
Arsenal	Oxford C.	11.47	50-58	198	-	83
Watford	Tr	10.58	58-61	120	-	84
Northampton T.	Tr	09.61	61-62	62	-	50
Crystal Palace	Tr	12.62	62-64	101	-	40
Watford	Tr	05.65	65	24	0	12
Charlton Ath.	Tr	02.66	65	18	0	7
Leyton Orient	Tr	07.66	66-67	47	0	17

HOLTON, James A.
Lesmahagow, 11 April, 1951 Su23-1/S-15 (CD)

League Club	Source	Date Signed	Seasons Played	Apps	Subs	Gls
West Bromwich A.	Jnrs	04.68				
Shrewsbury T.	Tr	06.71	71-72	67	0	4
Manchester U.	Tr	01.73	72-74	63	0	5
Sunderland	Tr	09.76	76	15	0	0
Coventry C.	Tr	03.77	76-79	91	0	0
Sheffield Wed.	Tr	08.81				

HOLTON, Patrick
Hamilton, 23 December, 1935 (FB)

League Club	Source	Date Signed	Seasons Played	Apps	Subs	Gls
Chelsea	Motherwell	03.59	58	1	-	0
Southend U.	Tr	08.60	60	11	-	0

HOLYOAK, Philip
Sunderland, 22 May, 1959 (CD)

League Club	Source	Date Signed	Seasons Played	Apps	Subs	Gls
Tottenham H.	App	05.77				
Scunthorpe U.	L	02.78	77	1	0	0

HOLZMAN, Mark R.
Bracknell, 21 February, 1973 (FB)

League Club	Source	Date Signed	Seasons Played	Apps	Subs	Gls
Reading	YT	07.91	91	11	5	1

HONE, Mark J.
Croydon, 31 March, 1968 (D)

League Club	Source	Date Signed	Seasons Played	Apps	Subs	Gls
Crystal Palace	Jnrs	07.85	87-88	4	0	0

HONEYWOOD, Brian R.
Chelmsford, 8 May, 1949 (WH)

League Club	Source	Date Signed	Seasons Played	Apps	Subs	Gls
Ipswich T.	App	05.67				
Colchester U.	Tr	06.68	68	12	5	0

HONOR, Christian R.
Bristol, 5 June, 1968 (D)

League Club	Source	Date Signed	Seasons Played	Apps	Subs	Gls
Bristol C.	App	06.86	85-89	44	16	1
Torquay U.	L	11.86	86	3	0	0
Hereford U.	L	12.89	89	2	1	0
Swansea C.	L	01.91	90	2	0	0

HONOUR, Brian
Horden, 16 February, 1964 (RW)

League Club	Source	Date Signed	Seasons Played	Apps	Subs	Gls
Darlington	App	02.82	81-83	59	15	4
Hartlepool U.	Peterlee Newtown	02.85	84-91	247	17	18

Jim Holton (West Bromwich Albion, Shrewsbury Town, Manchester United, Sunderland, Coventry City, Sheffield Wednesday & Scotland)

League Club	Source	Date Signed	Seasons Played	Apps	Subs	Gls

HONOUR, John
Horden, 1 November, 1953 (M)

West Bromwich A.	App	05.71				
Hartlepool U.	Tr	07.72	72-75	107	5	6
Workington	Tr	03.76	75-76	38	1	1

HOOD, Derek
Washington, 17 December, 1958 (M)

West Bromwich A.	App	12.76				
Hull C.	Tr	08.77	77-79	20	4	0
York C.	Tr	02.80	79-87	287	13	32

HOOD, George W.
Houghton-le-Spring, 27 November, 1920

Gateshead		10.47	47-48	30	-	0

HOOD, Glyn O.
Pentwyn (Gwent), 12 March, 1925 (WH)

West Bromwich A.	Nuffield Wks	09.45	46-49	69	-	0

HOOD, Harold A.
Glasgow, 3 October, 1944 Su23-1 (CF)

Sunderland	Clyde	11.64	64-66	31	0	9

HOOD, John O. (Jack)
Glasgow, 8 January, 1938 (CF)

Everton	Shettleston	10.56				
Tranmere Rov.	Tr	12.59	59	3	-	2

HOOD, Melvyn
Reading, 5 October, 1939 (F)

Reading	Jnrs	10.56	56-57	10	-	0

HOOD, Ronald G.
Cowdenbeath, 18 November, 1922 (IF)

Aldershot	Hamilton Acad.	08.47	47	14	-	6
Rochdale	Tr	11.48	48	9	-	1

HOOKER, Alan T.
Exeter, 23 June, 1956 (FB)

Exeter C.	Jnrs	07.74	74-76	46	4	0

HOOKER, Keith W.
Fleet, 31 January, 1950 (WH)

Brentford	App	02.68	66-68	24	8	2

HOOKS, Paul
Wallsend, 30 May, 1959 (M)

Notts Co.	App	06.77	76-82	144	29	30
Derby Co.	Tr	03.83	82-84	46	2	4

HOOKS, Victor R.
Belfast, 4 July, 1955 (F)

Grimsby T.	Manchester U. (App)	10.72	72	0	1	0

HOOLE, David
Chesterfield, 16 October, 1970 (M/RB)

Chesterfield	YT	07.89	88-89	6	8	0

HOOLEY, Joseph W.
Barnsley, 26 December, 1938 (W)

Barnsley	Jnrs	04.56	56	1	-	0
Sheffield U.	Tr	12.57				
Workington	Tr	06.58	58	6	-	2
Bradford P.A.	Holbeach U.	11.59	59-60	13	-	4
Accrington St.	Bedford T.	10.61				

HOOLICKIN, Gary J.
Middleton, 29 October, 1957 (D)

Oldham Ath.	App	07.75	76-86	209	2	2

HOOLICKIN, Stephen J.
Manchester, 13 December, 1951 (RB)

Oldham Ath.	App	12.69	69-72	8	0	0
Bury	Tr	08.73	73-76	140	0	5
Carlisle U.	Tr	10.76	76-80	143	0	2
Hull C.	Tr	12.80	80-81	31	0	0

HOOPER, Harold
Burnley, 16 December, 1910 Died 1970 (FB)

Nelson	Nelson Trades	11.28	29	8	-	0
Sheffield U.	Tr	02.30	30-38	269	-	12
Hartlepool U.	Tr	07.47	47-49	67	-	4

HOOPER, Harold
Pittington (Dm), 14 June, 1933 Eu23-2/EF Lge/E'B'-6 (OR)

West Ham U.	Hylton Colly	11.50	50-55	119	-	39
Wolverhampton W.	Tr	03.56	56	39	-	19
Birmingham C.	Tr	12.57	57-60	105	-	34
Sunderland	Tr	09.60	60-62	65	-	16

HOOPER, Michael D.
Bristol, 10 February, 1964 (G)

Bristol C.	Mangotsfield	01.84	84	1	0	0
Wrexham	Tr	02.85	84-85	34	0	0
Liverpool	Tr	10.85	86-91	42	0	0
Leicester C.	L	09.90	90	14	0	0

HOOPER, Percy W. G.
Lambeth, 17 December, 1914 (G)

Tottenham H.	Islington Corries	01.35	34-38	97	-	0
Swansea C.	Tr	03.47	46-47	13	-	0

HOOPER, Peter J.
Teignmouth, 2 February, 1933 EF Lge (OL)

Bristol Rov.	Dawlish	05.53	53-61	297	-	101
Cardiff C.	Tr	07.62	62	40	-	22
Bristol C.	Tr	07.63	63-65	54	0	14

HOOPER, Stuart R. J.
Lytham St Annes, 16 June, 1970 (F)

Burnley	Jnrs	07.88	88	0	1	0

HOOPER, Wynne
Seven Sisters, 5 June, 1952 W Yth (W)

Newport Co.	App	06.70	68-76	166	14	21
Swindon T.	Tr	12.76	76	4	2	0
Aldershot	Tr	07.77	77-78	21	19	1

HOPE, Alexander J. H.
Musselburgh, 22 June, 1924 (OL)

Swindon T.	Morton	06.54	54	11	-	1

HOPE, Darren
Stoke, 3 April, 1971 (W)

Stoke C.	YT	07.89				
Stockport Co.	Tr	03.90	89	4	0	0

HOPE, Eric
Oakengates, 2 December, 1927 (IF)

Manchester C.		01.46				
Shrewsbury T.	Tr	08.50	50-51	27	-	3
Wrexham	Tr	10.51	51-53	36	-	9

HOPE, George
Haltwhistle, 4 April, 1954 (F)

Newcastle U.	App	04.72	73	6	0	1
Charlton Ath.	Tr	06.75	75-76	13	0	2
York C.	Tr	11.76	76-77	34	8	8

HOPE, James
(OL)

Manchester C.	Ardeer Rec.	02.39	46	7	-	0

HOPE, James G.
East Wemyss (Fife), 4 October, 1919 (HB)

New Brighton	East Fife	08.47	47-49	43	-	0

HOPE, John W. M.
Shildon, 30 March, 1949 (G)

Darlington	App	05.67	64-68	14	0	0
Newcastle U.	Tr	03.69	68	1	0	0
Sheffield U.	Tr	01.71	70-73	63	0	0
Hartlepool U.	Tr	07.75	75	23	0	0

HOPE, Robert
Bridge of Allan, 28 September, 1943 S Sch/Su23-1/S-2 (M)

West Bromwich A.	Jnrs	09.60	59-71	331	5	33
Birmingham C.	Tr	06.72	72-75	33	1	5
Sheffield Wed.	Tr	09.76	76-77	39	3	7

HOPGOOD, Ronald F.
Battersea, 24 November, 1934 (G)

Crystal Palace	Spicers Ath.	05.57	57-59	14	-	0

HOPKIN, Gareth G.
Swansea, 12 April, 1923 (W)

Swansea C.		11.46	47	2	-	0

League Club	Source	Date Signed	Seasons Played	Career Record Apps	Subs	Gls

HOPKINS, Anthony
Pontypool, 17 February, 1971 (LB/W)

Newport Co. (YT)	YT	08.87	87	2	4	0
Bristol C.	Chelsea (YT)	10.89				
Aldershot	I.F.K. Uddev'la (Swe)	02.91	90	9	1	0

HOPKINS, Brian
Derby, 15 March, 1933 (OR)

Port Vale (Am)	Keele Univ.	08.57	57	2	-	0

HOPKINS, Idris J.
Merthyr Tydfil, 11 October, 1907 W-12 (OR)

Crystal Palace	Ramsgate Ath.	05.32	32	4	-	0
Brentford	Tr	11.32	32-46	290	-	75
Bristol C.	Tr	05.47	47	24	-	0

HOPKINS, Jeffrey
Swansea, 14 April, 1964 W Yth/Wu21-2/W-14 (CD)

Fulham	App	09.81	80-87	213	6	4
Crystal Palace	Tr	08.88	88-89	70	0	2
Plymouth Arg.	L	10.91	91	8	0	0
Bristol Rov.	Tr	03.92	91	4	2	0

HOPKINS, Kelvin R.
Perivale, 26 July, 1953 (G)

Aldershot	App	07.71	70-71	2	0	0

HOPKINS, Melvyn
Rhondda, 7 November, 1934 Wu23-1/W-34 (FB)

Tottenham H.	Jnrs	05.52	52-63	219	-	0
Brighton & H.A.	Tr	10.64	64-66	57	1	2
Bradford P.A.	Ballymena U.	01.69	68-69	29	1	0

HOPKINS, Oliver T.
South Kirkby, 15 November, 1935 (CH)

Barnsley	Burntwood	03.54	57-60	50	-	10
Peterborough U.	Tr	07.61	61-64	104	-	0

HOPKINS, Robert A.
Birmingham, 25 October, 1961 (W)

Aston Villa	App	07.79	79-82	1	2	1
Birmingham C.	Tr	03.83	82-86	123	0	20
Manchester C.	Tr	08.86	86	7	0	1
West Bromwich A.	Tr	10.86	86-88	81	2	11
Birmingham C.	Tr	03.89	88-90	43	7	9
Shrewsbury T.	Tr	06.91	91	18	9	3

HOPKINSON, Alan
Chapeltown, 15 April, 1953 (F)

Barnsley	App	04.71	70-73	24	3	5

HOPKINSON, Edward
Royton, 29 October, 1935 Eu23-6/EF Lge/E-14 (G)

Oldham Ath. (Am)	Jnrs	06.51	51	3	-	0
Bolton W.	Tr	11.52	56-69	519	0	0

HOPKINSON, Gordon
Sheffield, 19 June, 1933 (FB)

Doncaster Rov.	Beighton M.W.	06.57	57	10	-	0
Bristol C.	Tr	07.58	58-60	67	-	1

HOPKINSON, Ian J.
Newcastle, 19 October, 1950 (F)

Barrow	Newcastle U. (App)	01.69	68-70	17	5	1
Workington	Tr	07.71	71	13	6	7
Darlington	Berwick R.	12.72	72	7	2	1

HOPKINSON, Michael E.
Ambergate, 24 February, 1942 (D)

Derby Co.	Jnrs	07.59	60-67	112	3	4
Mansfield T.	Tr	07.68	68-69	46	0	1
Port Vale	Tr	07.70	70	12	1	0

HOPKINSON, Paul E.
Royton, 17 January, 1958 (G)

Stockport Co.	Manchester C. (App)	10.75	75-76	39	0	0

HOPKINSON, Stanley
Kiveton Park, 15 March, 1922 (G)

Watford (Am)	Hemel Hempstead	05.47	46	1	-	0

HOPPER, Alan
Newcastle, 17 July, 1937 (RB)

Newcastle U.		10.59				
Barnsley	South Shields	03.61	61-64	135	-	4
Bradford C.	Tr	07.65	65	8	0	0

League Club	Source	Date Signed	Seasons Played	Career Record Apps	Subs	Gls

HOPPER, William
Bishop Auckland, 20 February, 1938 (CF)

Halifax T.	West Auckland	12.61	61-62	35	-	9
Workington	Tr	07.63	63-64	46	-	14
Darlington	Tr	07.65	65	6	0	0

HORE, K. John
St Austell, 10 February, 1947 (D)

Plymouth Arg.	App	12.64	64-75	393	7	17
Exeter C.	Tr	03.76	75-79	193	0	0

HORMANTSCHUK, Peter
Coventry, 11 September, 1962 (FB)

Coventry C.	App	09.80	81-83	18	6	1

HORN, Graham R.
Westminster, 23 August, 1954 (G)

Arsenal	App	04.72				
Portsmouth	L	06.72	72	22	0	0
Luton T.	Tr	02.73	72-74	58	0	0
Brentford	L	11.75	75	3	0	0
Charlton Ath.	Los Angeles (USA)	12.76				
Southend U.	Kettering T.	12.77	77-78	9	0	0
Aldershot	Tr	01.80	79-81	9	0	0
Torquay U.	Tr	08.82	82-83	47	0	0

HORN, Robert I.
Westminster, 15 December, 1961 E Yth (G)

Crystal Palace	App	04.79				
Barnsley	Tr	11.80	81-83	67	0	0
Cambridge U.	L	11.83	83	8	0	0
Crystal Palace	Tr	07.84				

HORN, William
Glasgow, 13 May, 1938 (OL)

Brentford	Kilmarnock	10.58	58	1	-	0

HORNBY, Eric V.
Birkenhead, 31 March, 1923 (FB)

Tranmere Rov.	Jnrs	11.44	47-48	32	-	0
Crewe Alex.	Tr	08.49	49-50	4	-	0

HORNBY, Ronald
Rochdale, 13 April, 1914 (OL)

Rochdale (Am)	Rochdale St Clements	02.32	31	2	-	0
Oldham Ath.	Tr	07.33				
Burnley	Stalybridge Celtic	05.34	34-47	123	-	16

HORNE, Alfred T.
Brixworth, 6 September, 1926 (WH)

Northampton T.		09.44	48	1	-	0

HORNE, Barry
St Asaph, 18 May, 1962 W-31 (M)

Wrexham	Rhyl	06.84	84-86	136	0	17
Portsmouth	Tr	07.87	87-88	66	4	7
Southampton	Tr	03.89	88-91	111	1	6

HORNE, Brian S.
Billericay, 5 October, 1967 E Yth/Eu21-5 (G)

Millwall	App	10.85	86-90	163	0	0

HORNE, Desmond T.
South Africa, 12 December, 1939 (OL)

Wolverhampton W.	Jnrs	12.56	58-60	40	-	16
Blackpool	Tr	03.61	60-65	117	1	17

HORNE, George
Glasgow, 23 November, 1933 (OL)

Carlisle U.	Maryhill Jnrs	08.57	57	4	-	2

HORNE, John R.
Dudley, 4 November, 1961 (FB)

Walsall	App	11.79	79-81	10	6	1

HORNE, Kenneth W.
Burton, 25 June, 1926 (FB)

Blackpool	Wolverhampton W. (Am)	06.49				
Brentford	Tr	05.50	50-59	223	-	1

HORNE, Leslie H.
Dudley, 2 May, 1923 Died 1986 (CH)

West Bromwich A.	Netherton W.	04.48	49-51	13	-	0
Plymouth Arg.	Tr	07.52				
Walsall	Tr	11.52	52-53	52	-	1

HORNE, Stanley F.
Clanfield, 17 December, 1944 (M)

League Club	Source	Date Signed	Seasons Played	Apps	Subs	Gls
Aston Villa	App	12.61	63	6	-	0
Manchester C.	Tr	09.65	65-67	48	2	0
Fulham	Tr	02.69	68-72	73	6	0
Chester C.	Tr	08.73	73	17	1	0
Rochdale	Tr	12.73	73-74	48	0	5

HORNER, Philip M.
Leeds, 10 November, 1966 E Yth (CD/M)

League Club	Source	Date Signed	Seasons Played	Apps	Subs	Gls
Leicester C.	App	11.84	86-87	7	3	0
Rotherham U.	L	03.86	85	3	1	0
Halifax T.	Tr	08.88	88-89	70	2	4
Blackpool	Tr	09.90	90-91	64	2	11

HORNER, William
Cassop (Dm), 7 September, 1942 (D)

League Club	Source	Date Signed	Seasons Played	Apps	Subs	Gls
Middlesbrough	Jnrs	09.59	60-68	184	3	11
Darlington	Tr	06.69	69-74	211	7	5

HORNSBY, Brian G.
Great Shelford, 10 September, 1954 E Sch/E Yth (M)

League Club	Source	Date Signed	Seasons Played	Apps	Subs	Gls
Arsenal	App	07.72	72-75	23	3	6
Shrewsbury T.	Tr	06.76	76-77	75	0	16
Sheffield Wed.	Tr	03.78	77-81	102	4	25
Chester C.	L	11.81	81	4	0	0
Carlisle U.	Edmonton (Can)	08.82	82-83	9	1	1
Chesterfield	L	12.83	83	1	0	0

HORNSBY, John
Ferryhill, 3 August, 1945 (OL)

League Club	Source	Date Signed	Seasons Played	Apps	Subs	Gls
Colchester U.	Evenwood T.	10.64	65	11	0	1

HOROBIN, Roy
Brownhills, 10 March, 1935 (IF)

League Club	Source	Date Signed	Seasons Played	Apps	Subs	Gls
West Bromwich A.	Jnrs	10.52	55-57	54	-	6
Notts Co.	Tr	11.58	58-61	123	-	37
Peterborough U.	Tr	06.62	62-63	80	-	20
Crystal Palace	Tr	07.64	64	4	-	0

HORREY, Rowland G.
Bishop Auckland, 9 March, 1943 (W)

League Club	Source	Date Signed	Seasons Played	Apps	Subs	Gls
Blackburn Rov.	Ferryhill Ath.	12.63	64-65	3	0	0
York C.	Tr	07.66	66-67	74	0	9
Cambridge U.	Tr	(N/L)	70-71	37	1	4

HORRIDGE, Peter
Manchester, 31 May, 1934 (FB)

League Club	Source	Date Signed	Seasons Played	Apps	Subs	Gls
Manchester C.	Newton Heath P.	11.52	58	3	-	0
Crewe Alex.	Tr	06.59				

HORRIGAN, Kenneth P.
Gravesend, 7 December, 1919 (WH)

League Club	Source	Date Signed	Seasons Played	Apps	Subs	Gls
Carlisle U.	Imp.Paper Mill	08.46	46	16	-	1

HORRIX, Dean V.
Maidenhead, 21 November, 1961 Died 1990 (F)

League Club	Source	Date Signed	Seasons Played	Apps	Subs	Gls
Millwall	App	04.79	80-82	65	7	19
Gillingham	Tr	03.83	82	7	7	0
Reading	Tr	08.83	83-87	135	23	35
Cardiff C.	L	02.87	86	9	0	3
Millwall	Tr	03.88	87-89	5	6	1
Bristol C.	Tr	03.90	89	3	0	0

HORROBIN, Thomas
Doncaster, 8 August, 1943 (FB)

League Club	Source	Date Signed	Seasons Played	Apps	Subs	Gls
Sheffield Wed.	Jnrs	08.60	62	3	-	0

HORSBURGH, John J.
Edinburgh, 17 November, 1936 (G)

League Club	Source	Date Signed	Seasons Played	Apps	Subs	Gls
Oldham Ath.	Dundee	08.61	61	1	-	0

HORSCROFT, Grant
Fletching (E Sx), 30 July, 1961 (CD)

League Club	Source	Date Signed	Seasons Played	Apps	Subs	Gls
Brighton & H.A.	Lewes	03.87	87	2	0	0

HORSFALL, George F.
Australia, 19 September, 1924 (WH)

League Club	Source	Date Signed	Seasons Played	Apps	Subs	Gls
Southampton		05.47	46	2	-	0
Southend U.	Tr	07.49	49	1	-	0

HORSFALL, Thomas W.
Hamilton, 7 January, 1951 (W)

League Club	Source	Date Signed	Seasons Played	Apps	Subs	Gls
Southend U.	Dover T.	11.72	72-73	11	5	1
Bury	L	11.73	73	0	1	0
Scunthorpe U.	L	11.73	73	5	0	2
Cambridge U.	Tr	12.74	74-76	79	4	28
Halifax T.	Tr	07.77	77	15	1	3

HORSFIELD, Alec
Selby, 4 August, 1921 (IF)

League Club	Source	Date Signed	Seasons Played	Apps	Subs	Gls
Arsenal	Selby T.	11.46				
Bradford P.A.	Tr	12.50	50	4	-	2

HORSFIELD, Arthur
Newcastle, 5 July, 1946 E Yth (F)

League Club	Source	Date Signed	Seasons Played	Apps	Subs	Gls
Middlesbrough	App	07.63	63-68	107	4	51
Newcastle U.	Tr	01.69	68	7	2	3
Swindon T.	Tr	06.69	69-71	107	1	42
Charlton Ath.	Tr	06.72	72-75	139	0	54
Watford	Tr	09.75	75-76	78	0	16

HORSMAN, Leslie
Burley-in-Wharfedale, 26 May, 1920 (CH)

League Club	Source	Date Signed	Seasons Played	Apps	Subs	Gls
Bradford P.A.	Guiseley	06.45	46-52	239	-	18
Halifax T.	Tr	08.53	53-56	120	-	8

HORSTEAD, J. Barry
Brigg, 8 May, 1935 (D)

League Club	Source	Date Signed	Seasons Played	Apps	Subs	Gls
Scunthorpe U.	Jnrs	05.56	56-67	319	2	3

HORSWILL, Michael F.
Annfield Plain, 6 March, 1953 (M)

League Club	Source	Date Signed	Seasons Played	Apps	Subs	Gls
Sunderland	App	03.70	71-73	68	1	3
Manchester C.	Tr	03.74	73-74	11	3	0
Plymouth Arg.	Tr	06.75	75-77	98	4	3
Hull C.	Tr	07.78	78-81	82	2	6
Carlisle U. (N/C)	Happy Valley (HK)	08.83	83	1	0	0

HORTON, Brian
Hednesford, 4 February, 1949 (M)

League Club	Source	Date Signed	Seasons Played	Apps	Subs	Gls
Port Vale	Hednesford T.	07.70	70-75	232	4	33
Brighton & H.A.	Tr	02.76	75-80	217	1	33
Luton T.	Tr	08.81	81-83	118	0	8
Hull C.	Tr	07.84	84-86	38	0	0

HORTON, Duncan
Maidstone, 18 February, 1967 (M)

League Club	Source	Date Signed	Seasons Played	Apps	Subs	Gls
Charlton Ath. (N/C)	App	02.85	84	1	0	0
Barnet	Welling U.	03.91	91	24	5	3

HORTON, Henry
Malvern, 18 April, 1923 (WH)

League Club	Source	Date Signed	Seasons Played	Apps	Subs	Gls
Blackburn Rov.	Worcester C.	01.47	46-50	92	-	5
Southampton	Tr	06.51	51-53	75	-	12
Bradford P.A.	Tr	05.54	54	26	-	0

HORTON, Kenneth J.
Preston, 26 August, 1922 (IF)

League Club	Source	Date Signed	Seasons Played	Apps	Subs	Gls
Preston N.E.	Jnrs	10.45	46-52	166	-	36
Hull C.	Tr	10.52	52-54	76	-	16
Barrow	Tr	08.55	55	22	-	4

HORTON, Leonard

League Club	Source	Date Signed	Seasons Played	Apps	Subs	Gls
Walsall		06.47	46	1	-	0

HORTON, Leslie
Salford, 12 July, 1921 (D)

League Club	Source	Date Signed	Seasons Played	Apps	Subs	Gls
Rochdale	Tyldesley U.	04.41				
Oldham Ath.	Tr	01.43	46-47	79	-	2
Carlisle U.	Tr	08.48	48-49	66	-	0
Rochdale	Tr	04.50				
York C.	Tr	07.50	50	21	-	0
Halifax T.	Tr	03.51	50-51	34	-	1

HORTON, William G.
Aldershot, 27 August, 1942 (IF)

League Club	Source	Date Signed	Seasons Played	Apps	Subs	Gls
Aldershot	Jnrs	11.61	62-64	9	-	2

HORWOOD, Neil K.
Peterhead, 4 August, 1964 (F)

League Club	Source	Date Signed	Seasons Played	Apps	Subs	Gls
Grimsby T.	Kings Lynn	08.86	86	0	1	0
Halifax T.	L	12.86	86	3	0	0
Tranmere Rov.	L	03.87	86	4	0	1
Cambridge U. (N/C)	Tr	08.87	87	4	10	2

HOSIE, James
Aberdeen, 3 April, 1940 (OR)

League Club	Source	Date Signed	Seasons Played	Apps	Subs	Gls
Barnsley	Aberdeen	07.62	62	37	-	0

HOSKER, Robert C.
Harrogate, 27 February, 1955 (W)

League Club	Source	Date Signed	Seasons Played	Apps	Subs	Gls
Middlesbrough	App	03.72				
York C.	Tr	08.73	75-76	16	9	1

League Club	Source	Date Signed	Seasons Played	Career Record Apps	Subs	Gls
HOSKIN, J. Ashley						
Accrington, 27 March, 1968						(LW)
Burnley	App	12.85	85-88	72	16	11
HOSKIN, Michael A.						
Chesterfield, 3 November, 1966						(D)
Chesterfield (N/C)	YT	08.84	83-84	1	1	0
HOSKINS, John F.						
Southampton, 10 May, 1931						(OL)
Southampton	Winchester C.	07.52	52-58	220	-	64
Swindon T.	Tr	07.59	59	10	-	3
HOTTE, Timothy A.						
Bradford, 4 October, 1963						(F)
Huddersfield T.	Arsenal (App)	09.81	81-82	14	2	4
Halifax T.	Harrogate T.	08.85	85	2	2	0
Hull C.	North Ferriby U.	10.87	87-88	1	4	0
York C.	L	09.88	88	1	1	0
HOUCHEN, Keith M.						
Middlesbrough, 25 July, 1960						(F)
Hartlepool U.	Chesterfield (Jnrs)	02.78	77-81	160	10	65
Leyton Orient	Tr	03.82	81-83	74	2	20
York C.	Tr	03.84	83-85	56	11	19
Scunthorpe U.	Tr	03.86	85	9	0	2
Coventry C.	Tr	06.86	86-88	43	11	7
Port Vale	Hibernian	08.91	91	18	3	4
HOUGH, David J.						
Crewe, 20 February, 1966 W Yth						(RB)
Swansea C.	App	02.84	83-91	202	25	9
HOUGH, Frederick						
Stoke, 23 December, 1935						(F)
Port Vale		06.55	57	4	-	0
HOUGH, Harold						
Chapeltown, 26 September, 1924						(G)
Barnsley	Thorncliffe W.	09.47	47-58	345	-	0
Bradford P.A.	Tr	06.59	59-60	57	-	0
HOUGH, John						
Halifax, 9 June, 1954						(G)
Halifax T.	Irish Dems	09.79	79	1	0	0
HOUGH, Thomas						
Preston, 17 January, 1922						(IF)
Preston N.E.	Jnrs	05.39				
Barrow	Tr	10.46	46	3	-	0
HOUGHTON, H. Brian (Bud)						
India, 1 September, 1936						(CF)
Bradford P.A.	St Wrefords Y.C.	10.55	55-57	28	-	7
Birmingham C.	Tr	10.57	57-58	4	-	1
Southend U.	Tr	10.58	58-60	67	-	32
Oxford U.	Tr	03.61	62-63	53	-	17
Lincoln C.	Tr	10.63	63-64	54	-	22
HOUGHTON, W. Eric						
Billingborough, 29 June, 1910 EF Lge/E-7						(OL)
Aston Villa	Billingborough	08.27	29-46	361	-	160
Notts Co.	Tr	12.46	46-48	51	-	7
HOUGHTON, Frank C.						
Preston, 15 February, 1926						(WH)
Newcastle U.	Ballymena	12.47	47-50	55	-	10
Exeter C.	Tr	08.54	54-56	27	-	10
HOUGHTON, Keith						
Backworth, 10 March, 1954 E Semi-Pro						(CD)
Carlisle U.	Blyth Spartans	01.80	79-82	82	5	2
Lincoln C.	Tr	08.83	83	26	0	0
HOUGHTON, Kenneth						
Rotherham, 18 October, 1939						(IF)
Rotherham U.	Silverwood Colly	05.60	60-64	148	-	56
Hull C.	Tr	01.65	64-72	253	11	79
Scunthorpe U.	Tr	06.73	73	33	0	5
HOUGHTON, Peter						
Liverpool, 30 November, 1954						(F)
Wigan Ath.	South Liverpool	(N/L)	78-83	169	16	62
Preston N.E.	Tr	10.83	83-84	52	4	16
Wrexham	L	11.84	84	5	0	2
Chester C.	Tr	08.85	85-87	78	7	13

League Club	Source	Date Signed	Seasons Played	Career Record Apps	Subs	Gls
HOUGHTON, Raymond J.						
Glasgow, 9 January, 1962 IR-46						(M)
West Ham U.	Jnrs	07.79	81	0	1	0
Fulham	Tr	07.82	82-85	129	0	16
Oxford U.	Tr	09.85	85-87	83	0	10
Liverpool	Tr	10.87	87-91	147	6	28

Ray Houghton (West Ham United, Fulham, Oxford United, Liverpool & Republic of Ireland)

League Club	Source	Date Signed	Seasons Played	Career Record Apps	Subs	Gls
HOUGHTON, Scott A.						
Hitchin, 22 October, 1971 E Sch/E Yth						(F)
Tottenham H.	YT	07.90	91	0	10	2
Ipswich T.	L	03.91	90	7	1	1
HOUGHTON, William G.						
Hemsworth, 20 February, 1939 E Yth						(D)
Barnsley	Jnrs	08.57	57-63	206	-	10
Watford	Tr	07.64	64-65	48	0	2
Ipswich T.	Tr	06.66	66-68	107	0	3
Leicester C.	Tr	07.69	69	6	1	0
Rotherham U.	Tr	01.70	69-73	139	0	1
HOULAHAN, Harold						
Coundon (Dm), 14 February, 1930						(IL)
Newcastle U.	Durham C.	02.51				
Oldham Ath.	Tr	05.52	52-53	6	-	3
Darlington	Tr	01.54	53-54	23	-	8
HOULT, Alan J.						
Hinckley, 7 October, 1957 E Sch						(F)
Leicester C.	Jnrs	09.75				
Hull C.	L	01.78	77	3	0	1
Lincoln C.	L	03.78	77	2	2	1
Bristol Rov.	Tr	07.78				
HOULT, Russell						
Leicester, 22 November, 1972						(G)
Leicester C.	YT	03.91				
Lincoln C.	L	08.91	91	2	0	0

League Club	Source	Date Signed	Seasons Played	Apps	Subs	Gls
HOUNSLEA, William H.						
Liverpool, 15 August, 1926						(RB)
New Brighton	Unity B.C.	12.47	47	16	-	0
Chester C.	Tr	08.48	48	1	-	0
HOUSAM, Arthur						
Sunderland, 10 October, 1917 Died 1975						(WH)
Sunderland	Hylton Colly	05.37	37-47	55	-	2
HOUSDEN, Dennis						
City of London, 15 March, 1953						(F)
Gillingham	App	08.71	71-72	12	4	1
HOUSEMAN, Peter M.						
Battersea, 24 December, 1945 Died 1977						(W)
Chelsea	App	12.62	63-74	252	17	20
Oxford U.	Tr	05.75	75-76	65	0	2
HOUSLEY, Stuart						
Doncaster, 15 September, 1948						(W)
Grimsby T.	App	07.66	66-68	34	0	3
HOUSTON, David						
Glasgow, 7 July, 1948						(WH)
Cardiff C.	Jnrs	07.65	65-66	17	1	0
Crystal Palace	Tr	01.67				
HOUSTON, Graham R.						
Gibraltar, 24 February, 1960						(W)
Preston N.E.	Jnrs	03.78	79-84	90	38	11
Burnley (N/C)	Tr	09.85				
Wigan Ath.	Tr	06.86	86	16	1	4
Carlisle U. (N/C)	Northwich Vic.	10.87	87	8	8	1
HOUSTON, Joseph						
Wishaw, 27 December, 1926						(G)
Aldershot	Dunfermline Ath.	07.51	51-52	46	-	0
HOUSTON, Stewart M.						
Dunoon, 20 August, 1949 Su23-2/S-1						(D)
Chelsea	Port Glasgow	08.67	67-69	6	3	0
Brentford	Tr	03.72	71-73	77	0	9
Manchester U.	Tr	12.73	73-79	204	1	13
Sheffield U.	Tr	07.80	80-82	93	1	1
Colchester U.	Tr	08.83	83-85	106	1	5
HOW, Trevor A.						
Amersham, 8 August, 1957						(FB)
Watford	App	03.75	74-79	90	1	2
HOWARD, Andrew P.						
Southport, 7 October, 1971						(F)
Blackpool	Liverpool (YT)	09.91	91	0	1	0
HOWARD, Barry P.						
Ashton-u-Lyne, 19 February, 1950 E Semi-Pro						(F)
Stockport Co.	Runcorn	02.78	77	12	1	1
HOWARD, David F.						
Hartlepool, 3 June, 1962						(F)
Newcastle U.	Jnrs	07.79				
Hartlepool U.	Tr	03.81	80-81	6	3	4
HOWARD, Frank H.						
South Africa, 30 January, 1931						(OL)
Brighton & H.A.	Guildford C.	05.50	50-58	198	-	26
HOWARD, Jonathan						
Sheffield, 7 October, 1971						(F)
Rotherham U.	YT	07.90	90-91	9	2	3
HOWARD, Lee						
Worksop, 6 February, 1967						(W)
Mansfield T. (YT)	YT	08.84	84	0	1	0
HOWARD, Mark E.						
Kings Lynn, 25 October, 1964						(W)
Stockport Co.	Kings Lynn	04.88	87-89	13	6	2
Cambridge U.	L	03.89	88	0	2	0
HOWARD, Matthew J.						
Watford, 5 December, 1970						(D)
Brentford (YT)	YT	07.87	87	0	1	0

League Club	Source	Date Signed	Seasons Played	Apps	Subs	Gls
HOWARD, Patrick						
Dodworth, 7 October, 1947						(CD)
Barnsley	Jnrs	10.65	65-71	176	1	6
Newcastle U.	Tr	09.71	71-76	182	2	7
Arsenal	Tr	09.76	76	15	1	0
Birmingham C.	Tr	08.77	77-78	40	0	0
Bury	Tr	07.79	79-81	117	1	5
HOWARD, Richard						
Birkenhead, 10 June, 1943						(G)
Chester C.		09.65	65	1	0	0
HOWARD, Stanley						
Chorley, 1 July, 1934						(W)
Huddersfield T.	Chorley	07.52	57-59	62	-	13
Bradford C.	Tr	06.60	60	18	-	6
Barrow	Tr	01.61	60-63	86	-	22
Halifax T.	Tr	07.64	64	21	-	1
HOWARD, Terence						
Stepney, 26 February, 1966 E Yth						(D)
Chelsea	App	02.84	84-86	6	0	0
Crystal Palace	L	01.86	85	4	0	0
Chester C.	L	01.87	86	2	0	0
Leyton Orient	Tr	03.87	86-91	235	0	23
HOWARD, Trevor E.						
Kings Lynn, 2 June, 1949						(M)
Norwich C.	App	07.67	67-73	81	42	13
Bournemouth	Tr	08.74	74-75	86	0	11
Cambridge U.	Tr	07.76	76-78	105	0	5

Stewart Houston (Chelsea, Brentford, Manchester United, Sheffield United, Colchester United & Scotland)

League Club	Source	Date Signed	Seasons Played	Apps	Subs	Gls
HOWARTH, Frank						
Budleigh Salterton, 19 November, 1964						(D)
Exeter C.	App	11.82	81-84	21	16	1
HOWARTH, John (Jack)						
Crook, 27 February, 1945						(CF)
Chelsea	Stanley U.	10.63				
Swindon T.	Tr	10.64	64	2	-	0
Aldershot	Tr	07.65	65-71	258	1	113
Rochdale	Tr	01.72	71-72	40	0	12
Aldershot	Tr	11.72	72-76	163	0	58
Bournemouth	Tr	01.77	76-77	39	3	6
Southport (N/C)	Dorchester T.	03.78	77	9	0	1
HOWARTH, Lee						
Bolton, 3 January, 1968						(CD)
Peterborough U.	Chorley	08.91	91	6	1	0
HOWARTH, Neil						
Farnworth, 15 November, 1971						(CD)
Burnley	YT	07.90	89	0	1	0
HOWARTH, Sydney						
Newport, 28 June, 1923						(CF)
Aston Villa	Merthyr Tydfil	06.48	48-49	8	-	2
Swansea C.	Tr	09.50	50-51	39	-	7
Walsall	Tr	09.52	52	6	-	0
HOWAT, Ian S.						
Wrexham, 29 July, 1958						(F)
Chester C.	App	07.76	76-81	48	9	10
Crewe Alex.	Tr	02.82	81	16	1	1
HOWCROFT, Brian						
Farnworth, 20 June, 1938						(FB)
Bury	Jnrs	09.56	57-58	20	-	0
HOWDON, Stephen						
Prudhoe, 1 February, 1922						(F)
Newcastle U.	Hexham Hearts	08.41				
Gateshead	Tr	11.44	46	2	-	1
HOWE, Albert R. H. (Bert)						
Charlton, 16 November, 1938						(FB)
Crystal Palace	Faversham	12.58	58-66	192	1	0
Leyton Orient	Tr	01.67	66-68	91	0	0
Colchester U.	Tr	07.69	69	29	0	1
HOWE, Anthony V.						
Colchester, 14 February, 1939						(OL)
Colchester U.	Colchester Casuals	03.63	60	10	-	2
Southend U.	Haverhill Rov.	07.64	64	2	-	0
HOWE, Denis C.						
West Ham, 14 September, 1928						(CH)
West Ham U.		05.49				
Darlington	Tr	08.51	51-53	89	-	1
Southend U.	Tr	08.54	54-57	101	-	0
Aldershot	Tr	07.58	58	33	-	0
HOWE, Donald						
Wakefield, 26 November, 1917						(WH)
Bolton W.	Jnrs	11.34	36-51	266	-	35
HOWE, Donald						
Wolverhampton, 12 October, 1935 Eu23-6/E'B"-1/EF Lge/E-23						(FB)
West Bromwich A.	Jnrs	11.52	55-63	342	-	17
Arsenal	Tr	04.64	64-66	70	0	1
HOWE, Ernest J.						
Chiswick, 15 February, 1953						(CD)
Fulham	Hounslow	10.73	73-77	68	2	10
Queens Park R.	Tr	12.77	77-81	89	0	3
Portsmouth	Tr	08.82	82-83	35	0	4
HOWE, Frederick						
Bredbury, 24 September, 1912						(CF)
Stockport Co.	Wilmslow	09.31	31-32	2	-	0
Liverpool	Hyde U.	03.35	34-37	89	-	36
Manchester C.	Tr	06.38	38	6	-	5
Grimsby T.	Tr	10.38	38	29	-	15
Oldham Ath.	Tr	07.46	46	30	-	20
HOWE, George						
Wakefield, 10 January, 1924 Died 1991						(FB)
Huddersfield T.	Carlton U.	05.42	46-53	40	-	0
York C.	Tr	06.54	54-60	307	-	0

League Club	Source	Date Signed	Seasons Played	Apps	Subs	Gls
HOWE, Herbert A.						
Rugby, 1 April, 1916						(LB)
Leicester C.	Leicester Nomads	02.37	38-46	28	-	0
Notts Co.	Tr	07.47	47-48	52	-	0
HOWE, Jeremy R.						
Dewsbury, 5 September, 1973 E Yth						(M)
Bradford C.	YT	07.92	91	3	0	0
HOWE, John R. (Jack)						
Hartlepool, 7 October, 1915 Died 1987 E-13						(FB)
Hartlepool U.		06.34	34-35	24	-	0
Derby Co.	Tr	03.36	35-49	223	-	2
Huddersfield T.	Tr	10.49	49-50	29	-	1
HOWE, Robert J.						
Chadwell St Mary, 22 December, 1945						(CD)
West Ham U.	App	01.63	66-71	68	7	4
Bournemouth	Tr	01.72	71-73	100	0	6
HOWELL, David C.						
Hammersmith, 10 October, 1958 E Semi-Pro						(CD)
Barnet	Enfield	(N/L)	91	34	0	3
HOWELL, Graham F.						
Manchester, 18 February, 1951						(FB)
Manchester C.	App	10.68				
Bradford C.	Tr	06.71	71-72	45	0	0
Brighton & H.A.	Tr	08.72	72-73	40	4	0
Cambridge U.	Tr	07.74	74-75	68	3	3
HOWELL, Reginald W.						
Wolverhampton, 12 August, 1938						(G)
Plymouth Arg.		11.56	56	1	-	0
Aston Villa	Tr	02.58				
HOWELL, Ronald R.						
Tottenham, 22 May, 1949						(M)
Millwall	App	03.67	66-69	7	7	0
Cambridge U.	Tr	09.70	70	10	2	1
Swindon T.	Kettering T.	07.72	72	22	3	1
Brighton & H.A.	Tr	07.73	73	26	1	9
HOWELLS, David G.						
Guildford, 15 December, 1967 E Yth						(M)
Tottenham H.	YT	01.85	85-91	106	28	14

David Howells (Tottenham Hotspur)

HOWELLS, Gareth J.
Guildford, 13 June, 1970 (G)

League Club	Source	Date Signed	Seasons Played	Apps	Subs	Gls
Tottenham H.	YT	07.88				
Torquay U.	Tr	08.90	90-91	83	0	0

HOWELLS, Jeffrey D.
Shoreham, 26 September, 1940 (WH)

League Club	Source	Date Signed	Seasons Played	Apps	Subs	Gls
Millwall	Fulham (Am)	10.57	58-60	55	-	3

HOWELLS, Peter
Middlesbrough, 23 September, 1932 (W)

League Club	Source	Date Signed	Seasons Played	Apps	Subs	Gls
Sheffield Wed.		10.53	54-55	3	-	1
Hartlepool U.	Tr	11.56	56	1	-	0

HOWELLS, Raymond G.
Rhondda, 27 June, 1926 (OL)

League Club	Source	Date Signed	Seasons Played	Apps	Subs	Gls
Crystal Palace		06.47	46-49	25	-	5
Exeter C.	Tr	07.51	51-52	15	-	3

HOWELLS, Roger W.
Swansea, 18 September, 1931 (FB)

League Club	Source	Date Signed	Seasons Played	Apps	Subs	Gls
Swansea C.	Llanelli	03.50				
Darlington	Tr	02.53	52-53	2	-	0
Swansea C.	Tr	07.54				

HOWELLS, Ronald
Rhondda, 3 August, 1935 (WH)

League Club	Source	Date Signed	Seasons Played	Apps	Subs	Gls
Wolverhampton W.	Nuneaton Bor.	11.52	55-57	9	-	0
Portsmouth	Tr	03.59	58-60	65	-	2
Scunthorpe U.	Tr	06.61	61-62	69	-	4
Walsall	Tr	07.63	63	13	-	0

HOWELLS, Ronald G.
Swansea, 12 January, 1927 W-2 (G)

League Club	Source	Date Signed	Seasons Played	Apps	Subs	Gls
Swansea C.		04.48	47	8	-	0
Cardiff C.	Barry T.	07.50	51-56	154	-	0
Chester C.	Worcester C.	09.58	58-59	80	-	0

HOWELLS, William M.
Grimsby, 20 March, 1943 (CH)

League Club	Source	Date Signed	Seasons Played	Apps	Subs	Gls
Grimsby T.	Jnrs	10.61	63	6	-	0

HOWEY, Peter
Kinsley, 23 January, 1958 (W)

League Club	Source	Date Signed	Seasons Played	Apps	Subs	Gls
Huddersfield T.	App	01.76	76-78	20	2	3
Leeds U.	Tr	07.79				
Newport Co.	Tr	11.79				

HOWEY, Stephen N.
Sunderland, 26 October, 1971 (F)

League Club	Source	Date Signed	Seasons Played	Apps	Subs	Gls
Newcastle U.	YT	12.89	88-91	16	17	1

HOWFIELD, Robert M.
Manchester, 3 December, 1936 (F)

League Club	Source	Date Signed	Seasons Played	Apps	Subs	Gls
Watford	Bushey U.	09.57	57-58	47	-	9
Crewe Alex.	Tr	07.59	59	5	-	0
Aldershot	Tr	10.59	59-61	76	-	44
Watford	Tr	07.62	62-63	45	-	13
Fulham	Tr	11.63	63-64	26	-	9
Aldershot	Tr	08.65	65-66	33	1	10

HOWITT, David J.
Birmingham, 4 August, 1952 (FB)

League Club	Source	Date Signed	Seasons Played	Apps	Subs	Gls
Birmingham C.	App	08.69	72	2	0	0
Bury	Tr	08.73	73	11	9	4
Workington	Tr	07.74	74	30	5	1
Aldershot	Tr	06.75	75-79	126	11	2

HOWITT, Robert G.
Glasgow, 15 July, 1929 SF Lge (IF/WH)

League Club	Source	Date Signed	Seasons Played	Apps	Subs	Gls
Sheffield U.	Partick Th.	07.55	55-57	88	-	30
Stoke C.	Tr	04.58	58-62	133	-	14

HOWLETT, Gary P.
Dublin, 2 April, 1963 IR Yth/IR-1 (M)

League Club	Source	Date Signed	Seasons Played	Apps	Subs	Gls
Coventry C.	Home Farm	11.80				
Brighton & H.A.	Tr	08.82	82-84	30	2	2
Bournemouth	Tr	12.84	84-86	56	4	7
Aldershot	L	08.87	87	1	0	0
Chester C.	L	12.87	87	6	0	1
York C.	Tr	01.88	87-90	94	7	13

HOWLETT, Robert V.
Basildon, 12 December, 1948 (D)

League Club	Source	Date Signed	Seasons Played	Apps	Subs	Gls
Chelsea	App	12.65				
Southend U.	Tr	09.67	67-68	4	2	0
Colchester U.	Tr	07.69	69	10	6	0

HOWSAM, A. Dennis
Sheffield, 21 October, 1922 (CF)

League Club	Source	Date Signed	Seasons Played	Apps	Subs	Gls
Sheffield Wed.		11.45				
Chesterfield	Tr	03.47	46-47	12	-	4
Halifax T.	Tr	06.48	48	19	-	4

HOWSHALL, Gerald T.
Stoke, 27 October, 1944 (WH)

League Club	Source	Date Signed	Seasons Played	Apps	Subs	Gls
West Bromwich A.	App	05.62	63-67	43	2	3
Norwich C.	Tr	11.67	67-70	36	4	0

HOY, Robert
Halifax, 10 January, 1950 E Yth (W)

League Club	Source	Date Signed	Seasons Played	Apps	Subs	Gls
Huddersfield T.	App	11.67	66-74	140	4	18
Blackburn Rov.	Tr	03.75	74-75	13	6	0
Halifax T.	Tr	06.76	76	30	0	7
York C.	Tr	08.77	77	10	4	1
Rochdale	Tr	12.77	77-80	61	5	12

HOY, Roger E.
Bow, 6 December, 1946 (M)

League Club	Source	Date Signed	Seasons Played	Apps	Subs	Gls
Tottenham H.	Jnrs	05.64	65-67	10	0	0
Crystal Palace	Tr	09.68	68-69	54	0	7
Luton T.	Tr	06.70	70	32	0	0
Cardiff C.	Tr	08.71	71-72	14	2	0

HOYLAND, Jamie W.
Sheffield, 23 January, 1966 E Yth (M)

League Club	Source	Date Signed	Seasons Played	Apps	Subs	Gls
Manchester C.	App	11.83	83-84	2	0	0
Bury	Tr	07.86	86-89	169	3	35
Sheffield U.	Tr	07.90	90-91	40	7	4

HOYLAND, Thomas
Sheffield, 14 June, 1932 (WH)

League Club	Source	Date Signed	Seasons Played	Apps	Subs	Gls
Sheffield U.	Jnrs	10.49	49-60	181	-	18
Bradford C.	Tr	10.61	61-62	27	-	6

HOYLE, Colin R.
Wirksworth, 15 January, 1972 (CD)

League Club	Source	Date Signed	Seasons Played	Apps	Subs	Gls
Arsenal	YT	01.90				
Chesterfield	L	02.90	89	3	0	0
Barnsley	Tr	06.90				

HOYLE, Herbert
Baildon, 22 April, 1920 (G)

League Club	Source	Date Signed	Seasons Played	Apps	Subs	Gls
Wolverhampton W.		05.46				
Exeter C.	Tr	08.46	46-49	82	-	0
Bristol Rov.	Tr	05.50	50-52	105	-	0

HUBBARD, John
Wath, 24 March, 1925 (WH)

League Club	Source	Date Signed	Seasons Played	Apps	Subs	Gls
Notts Co.		02.45	46	18	-	2
Scunthorpe U.	Scarborough	08.50	50-59	359	-	12

HUBBARD, John G.
South Africa, 16 December, 1930 SF Lge (OL)

League Club	Source	Date Signed	Seasons Played	Apps	Subs	Gls
Bury	Glasgow Rangers	04.59	59-61	109	-	29

HUBBARD, Philip J.
Lincoln, 25 January, 1949 (M)

League Club	Source	Date Signed	Seasons Played	Apps	Subs	Gls
Lincoln C.	App	07.66	65-71	150	1	41
Norwich C.	Tr	12.71	71-72	6	4	1
Grimsby T.	Tr	10.72	72-75	144	2	37
Lincoln C.	Tr	08.76	76-79	100	9	11

HUBBARD, Terence J.
Pontypool, 6 November, 1950 W Sch/Wu23-2 (M)

League Club	Source	Date Signed	Seasons Played	Apps	Subs	Gls
Swindon T.	App	11.68	70-75	83	1	2

HUBBICK, David
South Shields, 16 March, 1960 (F)

League Club	Source	Date Signed	Seasons Played	Apps	Subs	Gls
Ipswich T.	App	01.78				
Wimbledon	Tr	09.80	80-81	22	4	6
Colchester U. (N/C)	Dagenham	10.83	83-84	4	11	1

HUBBICK, Henry (Harry)
Jarrow, 12 November, 1914 Died 1992 (FB)

League Club	Source	Date Signed	Seasons Played	Apps	Subs	Gls
Burnley	Blyth Spartans	03.35	35-36	58	-	1
Bolton W.	Tr	02.37	36-46	128	-	0
Port Vale	Tr	10.47	47-48	50	-	1
Rochdale	Tr	01.49	48-50	90	-	0

HUCKER, Peter I.
Hampstead, 28 October, 1959 Eu21-2 (G)

League Club	Source	Date Signed	Seasons Played	Apps	Subs	Gls
Queens Park R.	App	07.77	80-85	160	0	0
Oxford U.	Tr	02.87	86-89	66	0	0
West Bromwich A.	L	01.88	87	7	0	0
Millwall	Tr	11.89				
Aldershot	Tr	11.90	90	27	0	0

League Club	Source	Date Signed	Seasons Played	Apps	Subs	Gls
HUDD, David C.						
Bristol, 9 July, 1944						(IF)
Bristol Rov.	Jnrs	07.63	64	5	-	1
HUDDART, David J.						
Maryport, 18 November, 1937						(G)
Aldershot	Army	06.61				
Gillingham	Tr	07.62	62-64	10	-	0
HUDDLESTONE, Edward						
Nottingham, 29 September, 1935						(CF)
Nottingham F.	Blackpool (Am)	12.56	56	1	-	0
HUDGELL, Arthur J.						
Hackney, 28 December, 1920						(FB)
Crystal Palace	Eton Manor	12.37	46	25	-	1
Sunderland	Tr	01.47	46-56	260	-	0
HUDSON, Alan A.						
Chelsea, 21 June, 1951 Eu23-10/E-2						(M)
Chelsea	App	06.68	68-73	144	1	10
Stoke C.	Tr	01.74	73-76	105	0	9
Arsenal	Tr	12.76	76-77	36	0	0
Chelsea	Seattle (USA)	08.83				
Stoke C.	Tr	01.84	83-85	38	1	0
HUDSON, Albert G.						
Swansea, 17 June, 1920 W Sch						(IL)
Fulham	Caerau	08.37	46	1	-	0
HUDSON, Carl B.						
Bradford, 10 October, 1966						(CD)
Rochdale	Bradford C. (YT)	08.86	86	13	2	0
HUDSON, Charles A.						
Stamford, 3 April, 1920						(CF)
Accrington St. (Am)	Guiseley	06.46	46	11	-	3
HUDSON, Christopher B.						
Rotherham, 13 March, 1951						(FB)
Rotherham U.	App	03.86	68-71	53	9	1
HUDSON, Colin A.R.						
Undy, 5 October, 1935						(OR)
Newport Co.	Undy U.	04.54	53-56	82	-	20
Cardiff C.	Tr	07.57	57-60	61	-	9
Brighton & H.A.	Tr	06.61	61	1	-	0
Newport Co.	Tr	02.62	62	30	-	2
HUDSON, Gary						
West Auckland, 1 November, 1955						(G)
Preston N.E. (Am)		08.73	73	1	-	0
HUDSON, Gary P.						
Bradford, 25 February, 1951						(FB)
Bradford P.A.	Jnrs	07.68	67-69	38	1	0
HUDSON, Geoffrey A.						
Leeds, 14 October, 1931						(FB)
Bradford P.A.	Jnrs	12.49	50-56	95	-	0
Bradford C.	Tr	02.57	56-58	34	-	0
Halifax T.	Tr	08.59	59-60	52	-	0
Exeter C.	Tr	07.61	61	41	-	0
Crewe Alex.	Tr	07.62	62	1	-	0
Gillingham	Tr	07.63	63-64	81	-	1
Lincoln C.	Tr	05.65	65	33	0	0
Rotherham U.	Tr	06.66				
HUDSON, George A.						
Manchester, 14 March, 1937						(CF)
Blackburn Rov.		01.58	58	4	-	1
Accrington St.	Tr	07.60	60	44	-	35
Peterborough U.	Tr	10.61	61-62	65	-	39
Coventry C.	Tr	04.63	62-65	113	0	62
Northampton T.	Tr	03.66	65-66	18	0	6
Tranmere Rov.	Tr	01.67	66-68	53	1	20
HUDSON, George W. (Garth)						
Havant, 26 October, 1923						(CH)
Portsmouth		08.45	47	1	-	0
Swindon T.	Tr	09.48	48-59	401	-	11
HUDSON, C. John						
Middleton, 25 November, 1964						(LW)
Oldham Ath.	Manchester C. (Jnrs)	09.82	82-83	16	4	0
Rochdale (N/C)	Sweden	02.87	86	18	1	1
HUDSON, John (Jackie)						
Blaydon, 5 October, 1921						(OR)
Chesterfield	West Stanley	10.46	46-51	169	-	33
Shrewsbury T.	Bangor C.	09.53	53-54	48	-	20
HUDSON, Maurice						
Barnsley, 12 September, 1930						(FB)
Barnsley	Jnrs	01.49	50-53	35	-	0
Bradford C.	Tr	07.55	55	4	-	0
HUDSON, Raymond J.						
Slough, 21 November, 1937						(FB)
Reading	Jnrs	11.54	55-58	11	-	0
HUDSON, Raymond W.						
Gateshead, 24 March, 1955						(M)
Newcastle U.	App	03.73	73-77	16	4	1
HUDSON, Stanley R.						
Fulham, 10 February, 1923 Died 1951						(F)
Queens Park R.		09.48	48-49	23	-	8
HUDSON, William A.						
Swansea, 10 March, 1928 W Amat						(OR)
Leeds U.	Pembroke Bor.	05.51	51	4	-	0
Sheffield U.	Tr	05.52	53	1	-	0
Mansfield T.	Tr	05.54	54	8	-	1
HUFFER, Philip						
Bedworth, 23 January, 1932						
Derby Co.	Bedworth T.	10.53				
Northampton T.	Tr	05.54	54	1	-	0
HUGGINS, Joseph E.						
India, 24 February, 1930						(IF)
Aldershot	Alton T.	12.55	55	6	-	5
HUGHES, Adrian F. S.						
Billinge, 19 December, 1970						(CD)
Preston N.E.	YT	03.89	87-91	91	9	3
HUGHES, Alan						
Wallasey, 5 October, 1948						(CF)
Liverpool	Jnrs	09.66				
Chester C.	L	11.67	67	9	0	2
HUGHES, Alan L						
Swansea, 11 March, 1951						(FB)
Swansea C.	App	03.69	68	2	0	0
HUGHES, Arthur						
Linlithgow, 23 November, 1927						(IF)
Notts Co.	Jeanfield Swifts	07.49				
Nottingham F.	Tr	05.51				
Grimsby T.	Canterbury C.	06.54	54	25	-	11
Gillingham	Tr	05.55	55	5	-	1
HUGHES, Brian						
Swansea, 22 November, 1937 W Sch/Wu23-2						(WH)
Swansea C.	Jnrs	07.56	58-68	231	0	6
HUGHES, Brian D.						
Ludgershall, 20 August, 1962						(M)
Swindon T.	App	07.80	80-82	67	3	5
Torquay U.	Tr	08.83	83	33	5	6
HUGHES, Ceri M.						
Pontypridd, 26 February, 1971 W Yth/Wu21-2/W-1						(M)
Luton T.	YT	07.89	89-91	24	12	1
HUGHES, Charles						
Manchester, 17 September, 1927						(W)
Manchester U.	Jnrs	09.46				
Leeds U.	Tr	09.50	50-51	21	-	2
HUGHES, Charles J.						
Blackpool, 7 September, 1939						(G)
Wrexham		10.58	59-60	35	-	0
HUGHES, Darren J.						
Prescot, 6 October, 1965						(LB/M)
Everton	App	10.83	83-84	3	0	0
Shrewsbury T.	Tr	06.85	85-86	34	3	1
Brighton & H.A.	Tr	09.86	86	26	0	2
Port Vale	Tr	09.87	87-91	183	1	4

League Club	Source	Date Signed	Seasons Played	Career Record Apps	Subs	Gls

HUGHES, David J.
Liverpool, 23 September, 1951 (OR)

Wrexham (Am)		05.70	70	1	0	0

HUGHES, David J.
Connah's Quay, 27 April, 1943 (OR)

Wrtexham	Jnrs	05.61	61	1	-	0
Tranmere Rov.	Tr	07.62	62	2	-	0

HUGHES, David R.
Blackburn, 7 September, 1948 (W)

Preston N.E.	Jnrs	09.65	66-71	22	9	0
Southport	Tr	07.72	72	40	0	1
Bury	Tr	08.73	73	12	0	3
Southport	Tr	11.73	73-76	109	4	4
Crewe Alex. (N/C)		08.78	78	12	1	0

HUGHES, David T.
Birmingham, 19 March, 1958 (M)

Aston Villa	App	02.76	76	3	1	1
Lincoln C.	Tr	04.77	77-80	61	1	1
Scunthorpe U.	Tr	06.81	81	17	4	0
Lincoln C.	Tr	03.82				

HUGHES, Dennis
Stoke, 9 April, 1931 (F)

Stoke C.	Jnrs	09.48	50	1	-	0

League Club	Source	Date Signed	Seasons Played	Career Record Apps	Subs	Gls

HUGHES, Emlyn W.
Barrow, 28 August, 1947 Eu23-8/EF Lge/E-62 (D/M)

Blackpool	Jnrs	09.64	65-66	27	1	0
Liverpool	Tr	03.67	66-78	474	0	35
Wolverhampton W.	Tr	08.79	79-80	56	2	2
Rotherham U.	Tr	09.81	81-82	55	1	6
Hull C.	Tr	03.83	82	9	0	0
Swansea C.	Mansfield T. (N/C)	09.83	83	7	0	0

HUGHES, Glyn
Wrexham, 29 November, 1931 (OR)

Sheffield Wed.		01.51				
Wrexham	Tr	08.52	52-54	92	-	20
Newport Co.	Tr	07.55	55	4	-	0

HUGHES, Gordon
Washington, 19 June, 1936 (OR)

Newcastle U.	Tow Law T.	08.56	56-62	133	-	18
Derby Co.	Tr	08.63	63-67	184	0	22
Lincoln C.	Tr	03.68	67-70	117	0	8

HUGHES, T. Gwyn
Blaenau Ffestiniog, 7 May, 1922 (WH)

Northampton T.	Blaenau Ffestiniog	12.45	46-55	224	-	15

HUGHES, Harold A.
Thurcroft, 12 August, 1937 (FB)

Rotherham U.		06.59	59	1	-	0

Emlyn Hughes (Blackpool, Liverpool, Wolverhampton Wanderers, Rotherham United, Hull City, Swansea City & England)

HUGHES, Harold J.
Nuneaton, 8 October, 1929 (CH)

League Club	Source	Date Signed	Seasons Played	Apps	Subs	Gls
Southport	Symingtons	08.50				
Chelsea	Tr	02.51	51	1	-	0
Bournemouth	Tr	06.52	52-57	77	-	2
Gillingham	Tr	07.58	58-62	204	-	15

HUGHES, Ian
Bangor, 2 August, 1974 Wu21-1 (FB)

League Club	Source	Date Signed	Seasons Played	Apps	Subs	Gls
Bury	YT	11.91	91	13	4	0

HUGHES, Ian J.
Sunderland, 24 August, 1961 (D)

League Club	Source	Date Signed	Seasons Played	Apps	Subs	Gls
Sunderland	App	08.79	79	1	0	0
Barnsley	Tr	07.81				

HUGHES, R. Ian
Cefn Mawr, 17 March, 1946 (OR)

League Club	Source	Date Signed	Seasons Played	Apps	Subs	Gls
Wrexham	Oswestry T.	02.66	65	9	0	3
Bradford P.A.	Tr	07.67	67	13	0	0

HUGHES, Iorwerth
Abergele, 26 May, 1925 W Amat/W-4 (G)

League Club	Source	Date Signed	Seasons Played	Apps	Subs	Gls
Luton T.	Llandudno	04.49	49-50	36	-	0
Cardiff C.	Tr	08.51	51	26	-	0
Newport Co.	Worcester C.	08.53	53-57	106	-	0

HUGHES, James A.
Leeds, 28 August, 1918 (D)

League Club	Source	Date Signed	Seasons Played	Apps	Subs	Gls
Fulham		09.46	46	1	-	0

HUGHES, John
Edinburgh, 19 September, 1964 (F)

League Club	Source	Date Signed	Seasons Played	Apps	Subs	Gls
Swansea C.	Berwick R.	11.89	89	16	8	4

HUGHES, John
Coatbridge, 3 April, 1943 Su23-4/SF Lge/S-8 (CF)

League Club	Source	Date Signed	Seasons Played	Apps	Subs	Gls
Crystal Palace	Glasgow Celtic	10.71	71-72	20	0	4
Sunderland	Tr	01.73	72	1	0	0

HUGHES, John
West Bromwich, 13 September, 1929 (IF)

League Club	Source	Date Signed	Seasons Played	Apps	Subs	Gls
Walsall	Golden Lion	05.50	50-52	44	-	10

HUGHES, John G.
Prestatyn, 18 February, 1942 (CF)

League Club	Source	Date Signed	Seasons Played	Apps	Subs	Gls
Chester C.	Rhyl	07.62	62	2	-	0

HUGHES, John I.
Bangor, 4 May, 1951 (W)

League Club	Source	Date Signed	Seasons Played	Apps	Subs	Gls
Blackpool	Jnrs	07.69	69-70	5	3	0
Southport	L	03.71	70	7	1	1
Stockport Co.	Altrincham	01.76	75	11	1	3

HUGHES, John M.
Manchester, 29 November, 1962 (M)

League Club	Source	Date Signed	Seasons Played	Apps	Subs	Gls
Bury		11.80	81-82	1	1	0

HUGHES, John N.
Tamworth, 10 July, 1921 (W)

League Club	Source	Date Signed	Seasons Played	Apps	Subs	Gls
Birmingham C.	Tamworth Castle	06.47	47-48	6	-	0

HUGHES, Kenneth D.
Barmouth, 9 January, 1966 (G)

League Club	Source	Date Signed	Seasons Played	Apps	Subs	Gls
Crystal Palace	Jnrs	08.85				
Shrewsbury T.	Tr	07.86	86-91	74	0	0

HUGHES, Laurence
Liverpool, 2 March, 1924 E'B'-1/E-3 (CH)

League Club	Source	Date Signed	Seasons Played	Apps	Subs	Gls
Liverpool	Tranmere Rov. (Am)	02.43	46-57	303	-	1

HUGHES, Lyndon J.
Smethwick, 16 September, 1950 E Sch/E Yth (FB/M)

League Club	Source	Date Signed	Seasons Played	Apps	Subs	Gls
West Bromwich A.	App	01.68	68-74	89	9	3
Peterborough U.	Tr	07.75	75-77	75	2	5

HUGHES, L. Mark
Wrexham, 1 November, 1963 W Sch/W Yth/Wu21-5/W-43 (F)

League Club	Source	Date Signed	Seasons Played	Apps	Subs	Gls
Manchester U.	App	11.80	83-85	85	4	37
Manchester U.	Barcelona (Sp)	07.88	88-91	141	4	47

HUGHES, Mark
Port Talbot, 3 February, 1962 W Yth (CD)

League Club	Source	Date Signed	Seasons Played	Apps	Subs	Gls
Bristol Rov.	App	02.80	79-83	73	1	3
Torquay U.	L	12.82	82	9	0	1
Swansea C.	Tr	07.84	84	12	0	0
Bristol C.	Tr	02.85	84-85	21	1	0
Tranmere Rov.	Tr	09.85	85-91	244	3	9

HUGHES, Mark C.
Swindon, 17 July, 1967 W Yth (M)

League Club	Source	Date Signed	Seasons Played	Apps	Subs	Gls
Swindon T. (App)	App	07.83	83	0	1	0

HUGHES, Michael E.
Larne (NI), 2 August, 1971 NI Sch/NI Yth/NIu21-1/NI-4 (W)

League Club	Source	Date Signed	Seasons Played	Apps	Subs	Gls
Manchester C.	Carrick R.	08.88	88-91	25	1	1

HUGHES, E. Michael
Llanidloes, 3 September, 1940 (WH)

League Club	Source	Date Signed	Seasons Played	Apps	Subs	Gls
Cardiff C.	Jnrs	12.58	58	1	-	0
Exeter C.	Tr	07.61	61-62	36	-	0
Chesterfield	Tr	07.63	63-68	208	2	9

HUGHES, Michael R.
Bridgend, 19 August, 1964 W Yth (G)

League Club	Source	Date Signed	Seasons Played	Apps	Subs	Gls
Swnasea C.	App	08.82	83-87	139	0	0

HUGHES, Paul
Denton, 19 December, 1968 (FB)

League Club	Source	Date Signed	Seasons Played	Apps	Subs	Gls
Bolton W.	YT	07.87	87-89	12	1	0

HUGHES, Patrick J.
Coatbridge, 28 February, 1945 (OL)

League Club	Source	Date Signed	Seasons Played	Apps	Subs	Gls
Darlington	St Mirren	08.65	65	3	0	0

HUGHES, Philip A.
Manchester, 19 November, 1964 NI Yth/NI-3 (G)

League Club	Source	Date Signed	Seasons Played	Apps	Subs	Gls
Leeds U.	Manchester U. (App)	01.83	83-84	6	0	0
Bury	Tr	07.85	85-87	80	0	0
Wigan Ath.	Tr	11.87	87-90	99	0	0
Scarborough	Rochdale (N/C)	10.91	91	17	0	0

HUGHES, Richard M.
Barrow, 27 December, 1950 (F)

League Club	Source	Date Signed	Seasons Played	Apps	Subs	Gls
Barrow (Am)	Jnrs	08.70	71	0	2	0

HUGHES, Ronald
Mold, 1 July, 1930 (WH)

League Club	Source	Date Signed	Seasons Played	Apps	Subs	Gls
Chester C.	Mold U.	09.50	51-61	400	-	21

HUGHES, Ronald H.
Workington, 17 August, 1955 (G)

League Club	Source	Date Signed	Seasons Played	Apps	Subs	Gls
Workington	R.N.A.D.	12.75	75	15	0	0

Mark Hughes (Manchester United, Barcelona, Bayern Munich, Manchester United & Wales)

HUGHES, Roy
Manchester, 13 August, 1949 (WH)

League Club	Source	Date Signed	Seasons Played	Apps	Subs	Gls
Bury	App	09.66	67-71	45	3	1

HUGHES, Stephen J.
Warrington, 4 January, 1958 (F)

League Club	Source	Date Signed	Seasons Played	Apps	Subs	Gls
Crewe Alex. (N/C)	Manchester C. (App)	03.76	75	0	2	0

HUGHES, Stephen J. (Billy)
Folkestone, 29 July, 1960 (M)

League Club	Source	Date Signed	Seasons Played	Apps	Subs	Gls
Gillingham	Jnrs	07.77	75-80	110	16	8
Crystal Palace	Tr	07.81	81	3	4	0
Wimbledon (N/C)	Tr	03.82	81	2	0	0

HUGHES, Terence P.
Llanidloes, 10 March, 1953 (F)

League Club	Source	Date Signed	Seasons Played	Apps	Subs	Gls
Shrewsbury T.	App	03.71	69-73	66	5	22

HUGHES, Thomas A.
Dalmuir, 11 July, 1947 Su23-2 (G)

League Club	Source	Date Signed	Seasons Played	Apps	Subs	Gls
Chelsea	Clydebank	07.65	66-69	11	0	0
Aston Villa	Tr	06.71	71	16	0	0
Brighton & H.A.	L	02.73	72	3	0	0
Hereford U.	Tr	08.73	73-81	240	0	0

HUGHES, Walter C. J.
Liverpool, 15 March, 1934 (OR)

League Club	Source	Date Signed	Seasons Played	Apps	Subs	Gls
Liverpool	Winsford U.	10.54				
Sheffield U.	Winsford U.	01.56	55	2	-	0
Bradford P.A.	Wisbech T.	04.57	56-57	20	-	0
Southport	Tr	02.58	57	11	-	0

HUGHES, B. Wayne
Port Talbot, 8 March, 1958 W Sch/Wu21-3 (M)

League Club	Source	Date Signed	Seasons Played	Apps	Subs	Gls
West Bromwich A.	App	03.76	76-77	3	3	2
Cardiff C.	Tulsa (USA)	10.79	79-81	42	4	1

HUGHES, William
Glasgow, 3 March, 1929 (OR)

League Club	Source	Date Signed	Seasons Played	Apps	Subs	Gls
York C.	Newcastle U. (Am)	05.51	51-61	349	-	55

HUGHES, William
Ballymena (NI), 9 May, 1929 NI-1 (OR)

League Club	Source	Date Signed	Seasons Played	Apps	Subs	Gls
Bolton W.	Larne T.	08.48	48-52	47	-	2
Bournemouth	Tr	06.53	53	16	-	1

HUGHES, William
Coatbridge, 30 December, 1948 S-1 (F)

League Club	Source	Date Signed	Seasons Played	Apps	Subs	Gls
Sunderland	Jnrs	02.66	66-76	264	23	74
Derby Co.	Tr	08.77	77	17	2	8
Leicester C.	Tr	12.77	77-78	36	1	5
Carlisle U.	L	09.79	79	5	0	0

HUGHES, William A.
Colwyn Bay, 2 February, 1919 Died 1992 W-5 (G)

League Club	Source	Date Signed	Seasons Played	Apps	Subs	Gls
Huddersfield T.	Newry T.	05.39				
Tottenham H.	Tr	12.45	46-47	2	-	0
Blackburn Rov.	Tr	10.48	48-49	27	-	0
Rochdale	Tr	09.50	50	9	-	0
Crystal Palace	Tr	02.51	50-51	18	-	0

HUGHES, William H.
Cardiff, 2 October, 1920 W Sch (CH)

League Club	Source	Date Signed	Seasons Played	Apps	Subs	Gls
Hartlepool U.		05.46	46-49	123	-	2

HUGHES, William M.
Llanelli, 6 March, 1918 Died 1981 W-10 (FB)

League Club	Source	Date Signed	Seasons Played	Apps	Subs	Gls
Birmingham C.	Watchers Celtic	05.35	35-46	104	-	0
Luton T.	Tr	07.47	47	31	-	0
Chelsea	Tr	03.48	47-50	93	-	0

HUGHES, Zacari D.
Australia, 6 June, 1971 (CD)

League Club	Source	Date Signed	Seasons Played	Apps	Subs	Gls
Rochdale	YT	08.89	87	2	0	0

HUGHTON, Christopher W. G.
Stratford, 11 December, 1958 IRu21-1/IR-53 (FB)

League Club	Source	Date Signed	Seasons Played	Apps	Subs	Gls
Tottenham H.	Jnrs	06.77	79-89	293	4	12
West Ham U.	Tr	11.90	90-91	32	1	0
Brentford	Tr	03.92	91	12	0	0

HUGHTON, Henry T.
Stratford, 18 November, 1959 (D)

League Club	Source	Date Signed	Seasons Played	Apps	Subs	Gls
Leyton Orient	App	12.76	78-81	104	7	2
Crystal Palace	Tr	07.82	82-85	113	5	1
Brentford	Tr	09.86	86	5	3	0
Leyton Orient	Tr	12.86	86-87	16	2	0

HUGO, Roger V.
Woking, 6 September, 1942 (IF)

League Club	Source	Date Signed	Seasons Played	Apps	Subs	Gls
West Ham U.	Jnrs	10.60	63	3	-	2
Watford	Tr	05.65	65	24	1	6

HUKIN, Arthur
Sheffield, 22 October, 1937 Died 1983 (F)

League Club	Source	Date Signed	Seasons Played	Apps	Subs	Gls
Sheffield Wed.	Jnrs	10.54	54	6	-	3

HULL, Alan E.
Southend, 4 September, 1962 (F)

League Club	Source	Date Signed	Seasons Played	Apps	Subs	Gls
Leyton Orient	Barking	05.87	87-89	54	25	16

HULL, Gary
Sheffield, 21 June, 1956 (FB)

League Club	Source	Date Signed	Seasons Played	Apps	Subs	Gls
Sheffield Wed.	App	06.74	75	6	2	0

HULL, Jeffrey
Southend, 25 August, 1960 (W)

League Club	Source	Date Signed	Seasons Played	Apps	Subs	Gls
Southend U.	App	08.78	78-80	10	5	1
Colchester U.	Basildon U.	12.82	82-85	82	1	10

HULLETT, William A.
Liverpool, 19 November, 1915 Died 1982 (CF)

League Club	Source	Date Signed	Seasons Played	Apps	Subs	Gls
Everton		12.35				
New Brighton	Tr	01.37	36	13	-	8
Plymouth Arg.	Tr	10.37	37-38	29	-	20
Manchester U.	Tr	03.39				
Cardiff C.	Merthyr Tydfil	02.48	47-48	27	-	15
Nottingham F.	Tr	11.48	48	13	-	2

HULLIGAN, Michael J.
Liverpool, 28 February, 1923 (OR)

League Club	Source	Date Signed	Seasons Played	Apps	Subs	Gls
Liverpool		12.42				
Port Vale	Tr	07.48	48-54	197	-	22

HULME, Eric M.
Houghton-le-Spring, 14 January, 1949 (G)

League Club	Source	Date Signed	Seasons Played	Apps	Subs	Gls
Nottingham F.	Spennymoor U.	03.70	71	5	0	0
Lincoln C.	Tr	09.72	72-73	23	0	0

HULME, John
Mobberley, 6 February, 1945 (CD)

League Club	Source	Date Signed	Seasons Played	Apps	Subs	Gls
Bolton W.	Jnrs	02.62	62-71	186	2	7
Notts Co.	L	03.72	71	8	0	0
Reading	Tr	07.72	72-73	86	1	0
Bury	Tr	07.74	74-75	86	0	5

HULME, Kevin
Farnworth, 2 December, 1967 (F)

League Club	Source	Date Signed	Seasons Played	Apps	Subs	Gls
Bury	Radcliffe Bor.	03.89	88-91	50	28	12
Chester C.	L	10.89	89	4	0	0

HULMES, Gary
Manchester, 28 February, 1957 (F)

League Club	Source	Date Signed	Seasons Played	Apps	Subs	Gls
Rochdale	Manchester C. (Jnr)	12.74	74-75	4	6	1

HULSE, Robert A.
Crewe, 5 November, 1948 E Yth (CF)

League Club	Source	Date Signed	Seasons Played	Apps	Subs	Gls
Stoke C.	Nantwich T.	04.67	67	2	0	0

HULSE, Robert J.
Gateshead, 5 January, 1957 (M)

League Club	Source	Date Signed	Seasons Played	Apps	Subs	Gls
Darlington (N/C)	Stade Quimper (Fr)	09.83	83	3	1	0

HUMBLE, Douglas
Weardale, 16 February, 1920 Died 1989 (CF)

League Club	Source	Date Signed	Seasons Played	Apps	Subs	Gls
Sunderland	Bishop Auckland	05.45				
Southport	Tr	06.47	47	11	-	4

HUMBLE, J. Wilfred
Ashington, 10 May, 1936 Died 1988 (FB)

League Club	Source	Date Signed	Seasons Played	Apps	Subs	Gls
Mansfield T.	Ashington	05.59	59-65	198	0	1

HUME, Robert M.
Kirkintilloch, 18 March, 1941 (OL)

League Club	Source	Date Signed	Seasons Played	Apps	Subs	Gls
Middlesbrough	Glasgow Rangers	09.62	62	19	-	5

HUME, William S.
Armadale, 18 December, 1935 (F)

League Club	Source	Date Signed	Seasons Played	Apps	Subs	Gls
Birmingham C.	Dunfermline Ath.	02.58	58-59	10	-	1

HUMES, Anthony
Blyth, 19 March, 1966 (CD)

League Club	Source	Date Signed	Seasons Played	Apps	Subs	Gls
Ipswich T.	App	05.83	86-91	107	13	10
Wrexham	Tr	03.92	91	8	0	0

HUMES, James
Carlisle, 6 August, 1942 (W)

League Club	Source	Date Signed	Seasons Played	Apps	Subs	Gls
Preston N.E.	Jnrs	09.59	59-61	18	-	1
Bristol Rov.	Tr	06.62	62	2	-	0
Chester C.	Tr	07.63	63-66	127	0	31
Barnsley	Tr	07.67	67	7	0	1

HUMPHREY, John
Paddington, 31 January, 1961 (RB)

League Club	Source	Date Signed	Seasons Played	Apps	Subs	Gls
Wolverhampton W.	App	01.79	79-84	149	0	3
Charlton Ath.	Tr	07.85	85-89	194	0	3
Crystal Palace	Tr	06.90	90-91	74	1	1

John Humphrey (Wolverhampton Wanderers, Charlton Athletic & Crystal Palace)

HUMPHREY, John M.
Guildford, 2 July, 1969 (F)

League Club	Source	Date Signed	Seasons Played	Apps	Subs	Gls
Millwall	Leatherhead	02.91				
Exeter C.	L	12.91	91	2	0	0

HUMPHREY, Thomas R.
Houghton-le-Spring, 27 October, 1937 (F)

League Club	Source	Date Signed	Seasons Played	Apps	Subs	Gls
Aldershot	Army	03.59	58-60	22	-	3

HUMPHREYS, Alan
Chester, 18 October, 1939 (G)

League Club	Source	Date Signed	Seasons Played	Apps	Subs	Gls
Shrewsbury T.	Jnrs	10.56	56-59	32	-	0
Leeds U.	Tr	02.60	59-61	40	-	0
Mansfield T.	Gravesend & Nft.	01.64	64-67	58	0	0
Chesterfield	Tr	07.68	68-69	51	0	0

HUMPHREYS, Derek J. B.
Belfast, 5 October, 1949 (G)

League Club	Source	Date Signed	Seasons Played	Apps	Subs	Gls
Arsenal	Jnrs	10.66				
Sunderland	Crusaders	11.67				
Hartlepool U.	L	10.69	69	4	0	0

HUMPHREYS, Gerald
Llandudno, 14 January, 1946 W Sch/Wu23-5 (W)

League Club	Source	Date Signed	Seasons Played	Apps	Subs	Gls
Everton	App	09.63	65-69	12	0	2
Crystal Palace	Tr	06.70	70	4	7	0
Crewe Alex.	Tr	01.72	71-76	184	9	30

HUMPHREYS, John S.
Farnworth, 18 July, 1964 (F)

League Club	Source	Date Signed	Seasons Played	Apps	Subs	Gls
Oldham Ath.	App	07.82	82-83	7	6	0
Rochdale	L	03.84	83	6	0	0

HUMPHREYS, John V.
Llandudno, 13 January, 1920 Died 1954 W-1 (CH)

League Club	Source	Date Signed	Seasons Played	Apps	Subs	Gls
Everton	Llandudno	04.43	46-50	53	-	0

HUMPHREYS, Percy R.
Bradford, 28 October, 1924 (OR)

League Club	Source	Date Signed	Seasons Played	Apps	Subs	Gls
Halifax T.	Boothtown	11.43	46	3	-	1

HUMPHREYS, Ronald H.
Tonypandy, 4 April, 1925 (FB)

League Club	Source	Date Signed	Seasons Played	Apps	Subs	Gls
Southend U.	Snowdown Colly	05.45	46	3	-	0

HUMPHRIES, Charles
Birmingham, 19 March, 1922 (FB)

League Club	Source	Date Signed	Seasons Played	Apps	Subs	Gls
Walsall	Paget R.	09.46	47	6	-	0

HUMPHRIES, David W.
Wolverhampton, 10 August, 1939 (CH)

League Club	Source	Date Signed	Seasons Played	Apps	Subs	Gls
Shrewsbury T.		03.60	60	3	-	0

HUMPHRIES, Glenn
Hull, 11 August, 1964 E Yth (CD)

League Club	Source	Date Signed	Seasons Played	Apps	Subs	Gls
Doncaster Rov.	App	08.82	80-87	174	6	8
Lincoln C.	L	03.87	86	9	0	0
Bristol C.	Tr	10.87	87-90	81	4	0
Scunthorpe U.	Tr	03.91	90-91	42	0	4

HUMPHRIES, Robert
Hindhead, 4 July, 1933 (WH)

League Club	Source	Date Signed	Seasons Played	Apps	Subs	Gls
Sheffield U.		12.55				
Brighton & H.A.	Tr	11.56	56	10	-	2
Millwall	Tr	08.57	57-59	47	-	4

HUMPHRIES, Stephen R.
Hull, 29 May, 1961 E Semi-Pro (G)

League Club	Source	Date Signed	Seasons Played	Apps	Subs	Gls
Leicester C.	App	09.78				
Doncaster Rov.	Tr	06.81	81	13	0	0
Cardiff C.	Tr	08.82	82	1	0	0
Wrexham	Tr	09.82	82	2	0	0
Oldham Ath.	Tr	10.82				
Leicester C.	Tr	01.83				

HUMPHRIES, William M.
Belfast, 8 July, 1936 NI-4 (OR)

League Club	Source	Date Signed	Seasons Played	Apps	Subs	Gls
Leeds U.	Ards	09.58	58-59	25	-	2
Coventry C.	Ards	04.62	61-64	109	-	23
Swansea C.	Tr	03.65	64-67	143	0	22

HUMPSTON, Ronald
Derby, 14 December, 1923 (G)

League Club	Source	Date Signed	Seasons Played	Apps	Subs	Gls
Portsmouth		01.46	47-50	9	-	0
Huddersfield T.	Tr	11.51	51	5	-	0

HUNT, Andrew
Grays, 9 June, 1970 (W)

League Club	Source	Date Signed	Seasons Played	Apps	Subs	Gls
Newcastle U.	Kettering T.	01.91	90-91	34	9	11

HUNT, David
Leicester, 17 April, 1959 (M)

League Club	Source	Date Signed	Seasons Played	Apps	Subs	Gls
Derby Co.	App	04.77	77	5	0	0
Notts Co.	Tr	03.78	77-86	331	5	28
Aston Villa	Tr	06.87	87-88	12	1	0
Mansfield T.	Tr	06.89	89	21	1	0

HUNT, Dennis P.
Portsmouth, 8 September, 1937 (FB)

League Club	Source	Date Signed	Seasons Played	Apps	Subs	Gls
Gillingham		09.58	58-67	319	2	6
Brentford	Tr	06.68	68	12	0	0

HUNT, Douglas A.
Shipton, 19 May, 1914 (CF)

League Club	Source	Date Signed	Seasons Played	Apps	Subs	Gls
Tottenham H.	Gravesend & Nft	03.34	34-36	17	-	6
Barnsley	Tr	03.37	36-37	36	-	17
Sheffield Wed.	Tr	03.38	37-38	42	-	30
Leyton Orient	Tr	04.46	46-47	61	-	16

HUNT, George H.
Bethnal Green, 5 March, 1917

League Club	Source	Date Signed	Seasons Played	Apps	Subs	Gls
Barnsley	Regent Street Congs	05.38				
Watford	Tr	06.46	47-49	35	-	0

HUNT, George R. A.
Swindon, 27 February, 1922 (RB)

League Club	Source	Date Signed	Seasons Played	Apps	Subs	Gls
Swindon T.		01.47	48-57	306	-	0

HUNT, George S.
Barnsley, 22 February, 1910 E-3 (CF)

League Club	Source	Date Signed	Seasons Played	Apps	Subs	Gls
Chesterfield	Regent Street Congs	09.29	29	14	-	9
Tottenham H.	Tr	06.30	30-36	185	-	125
Arsenal	Tr	10.37	37	18	-	3
Bolton W.	Tr	02.38	37-46	45	-	24
Sheffield Wed.	Tr	11.46	46-47	32	-	8

HUNT, Jonathan R.
Camden, 2 November, 1971 (M)

League Club	Source	Date Signed	Seasons Played	Apps	Subs	Gls
Barnet (N/C)	Jnrs	(N/L)	91	2	12	0

HUNT, Mark G.
Farnworth, 5 October, 1969 (F)

League Club	Source	Date Signed	Seasons Played	Apps	Subs	Gls
Rochdale (YT)	YT	08.86	86-87	1	1	1

HUNT, Morgan W.
Bridgend, 5 March, 1931 (HB)

League Club	Source	Date Signed	Seasons Played	Apps	Subs	Gls
Doncaster Rov.	Askern Welfare	02.52	53-57	50	-	2
Norwich C.	Tr	07.58	58	7	-	0
Port Vale	Tr	08.59	59	2	-	0

HUNT, Paul C.
Swindon, 8 October, 1970 (F)

League Club	Source	Date Signed	Seasons Played	Apps	Subs	Gls
Swindon T.	YT	07.89	89-90	2	4	0

HUNT, Paul L.
Hereford, 7 March, 1959 (D)

League Club	Source	Date Signed	Seasons Played	Apps	Subs	Gls
Hereford U.	Coventry C. (App)	06.77	78-80	41	10	4

HUNT, Peter J.
Stepney, 2 July, 1952 E Yth (M)

League Club	Source	Date Signed	Seasons Played	Apps	Subs	Gls
Southend U.	App	09.69	68-71	49	8	1
Charlton Ath.	Tr	12.72	72-76	138	20	6
Gillingham	Tr	08.77	77	23	0	0

HUNT, Ralph A.R.
Portsmouth, 14 August, 1933 Died 1964

League Club	Source	Date Signed	Seasons Played	Apps	Subs	Gls
Portsmouth	Jnrs	08.50	52-53	5	-	0
Bournemouth	Tr	02.54	53-54	33	-	7
Norwich C.	Tr	07.55	55-57	124	-	67
Derby Co.	Tr	08.58	58	24	-	10
Grimsby T.	Tr	08.59	59-60	53	-	39
Swindon T.	Tr	07.61	61	21	-	13
Port Vale	Tr	12.61	61	14	-	6
Newport Co.	Tr	07.62	62-63	83	-	37
Chesterfield	Tr	07.64	64	17	-	5

HUNT, Richard A.
Reading, 5 January, 1971 (CD)

League Club	Source	Date Signed	Seasons Played	Apps	Subs	Gls
Aldershot	Queens Park R. (YT)	07.89	89	1	1	0

HUNT, Robert
Liverpool, 4 September, 1934 (WH)

League Club	Source	Date Signed	Seasons Played	Apps	Subs	Gls
Wrexham		07.56				
Chester C.	Tr	05.58	58-60	84	-	2

HUNT, Robert R.
Colchester, 1 October, 1942 (F)

League Club	Source	Date Signed	Seasons Played	Apps	Subs	Gls
Colchester U.	Jnrs	11.59	59-63	148	-	80
Northampton T.	Tr	03.64	63-65	40	0	10
Millwall	Tr	09.66	66-67	43	0	13
Ipswich T.	Tr	11.67	67-70	16	10	4
Charlton Ath.	Tr	09.70	70-72	34	2	11
Northampton T.	L	11.72	72	5	0	3
Reading	Tr	01.73	72-73	15	1	3

HUNT, Robert S.
Newcastle, 20 September, 1966 (G)

League Club	Source	Date Signed	Seasons Played	Apps	Subs	Gls
Halifax T. (N/C)	Barnsley (YT)	01.85	84	3	0	0

HUNT, Roger
Golborne, 20 July, 1938 EF Lge/E-34 (IF)

League Club	Source	Date Signed	Seasons Played	Apps	Subs	Gls
Liverpool	Stockton Heath	05.59	59-69	401	3	245
Bolton W.	Tr	12.69	69-71	72	4	24

HUNT, Roger P. (Ernie)
Swindon, 17 March, 1943 Eu23-3 (F)

League Club	Source	Date Signed	Seasons Played	Apps	Subs	Gls
Swindon T.	Jnrs	03.60	59-65	214	0	82
Wolverhampton W.	Tr	09.65	65-67	74	0	32
Everton	Tr	09.67	67	12	2	3
Coventry C.	Tr	03.68	67-73	140	6	45
Doncaster Rov.	L	01.73	72	9	0	1
Bristol C.	Tr	12.73	73-74	9	3	2

HUNT, Ronald G.
Paddington, 19 December, 1945 (CH)

League Club	Source	Date Signed	Seasons Played	Apps	Subs	Gls
Queens Park R.	App	03.63	64-72	214	5	1

HUNT, Ronald M.
Colchester, 26 September, 1933 (WH)

League Club	Source	Date Signed	Seasons Played	Apps	Subs	Gls
Colchester U.	Jnrs	10.51	51-63	177	-	3

HUNT, Simon
Chester, 17 November, 1962 (M)

League Club	Source	Date Signed	Seasons Played	Apps	Subs	Gls
Wrexham	Jnrs	08.81	81-83	102	6	18

HUNT, Stephen K.
Birmingham, 4 August, 1956 E-2 (M)

League Club	Source	Date Signed	Seasons Played	Apps	Subs	Gls
Aston Villa	App	01.74	74-76	4	3	1
Coventry C.	New York (USA)	08.78	78-83	178	7	27
West Bromwich A.	Tr	03.84	83-85	68	0	15
Aston Villa	Tr	03.86	85-87	61	1	6

Steve Hunt (Aston Villa, Coventry City, West Bromwich Albion, Aston Villa & England)

HUNT, William E.
Colchester, 25 November, 1934 (WH)

League Club	Source	Date Signed	Seasons Played	Apps	Subs	Gls
Colchester U.	Jnrs	08.53	53	1	-	0

HUNT, William S.
Halesowen, 19 November, 1934 (FB)

League Club	Source	Date Signed	Seasons Played	Apps	Subs	Gls
Aston Villa	Jnrs	01.52	52	1	-	0

HUNT-BROWN, Peter
Halifax, 19 February, 1937 (CF)

League Club	Source	Date Signed	Seasons Played	Apps	Subs	Gls
Halifax T. (Am)	Elland U.	12.58	58	1	-	0

League Club	Source	Date Signed	Seasons Played	Apps	Subs	Gls

HUNTER, Alan
Strabane (NI), 30 June, 1946 NI Amat/NIu23-1/NI-53 (CD)

League Club	Source	Date Signed	Seasons Played	Apps	Subs	Gls
Oldham Ath.	Coleraine	01.67	66-68	83	0	1
Blackburn Rov.	Tr	06.69	69-71	84	0	1
Ipswich T.	Tr	09.71	71-80	280	0	8
Colchester U.	Tr	05.82	81-82	18	1	0

HUNTER, Christopher P.
Hong Kong, 18 January, 1964 (F)

League Club	Source	Date Signed	Seasons Played	Apps	Subs	Gls
Preston N.E.	App	09.81	82	0	1	0
Preston N.E.	Chorley	09.84	84	3	3	0

HUNTER, Donald
Thorne, 10 March, 1927 (WH)

League Club	Source	Date Signed	Seasons Played	Apps	Subs	Gls
Huddersfield T.	Jnrs	03.44	48-50	26	-	1
Halifax T.	Tr	08.51	51	11	-	0
Southport	Tr	08.52	52-56	174	-	1

HUNTER, Edward
Tillicoultry, 7 March, 1928 (WH)

League Club	Source	Date Signed	Seasons Played	Apps	Subs	Gls
Accrington St.	Falkirk	08.54	54-58	169	-	4

HUNTER, Geoffrey
Hull, 27 October, 1959 (M)

League Club	Source	Date Signed	Seasons Played	Apps	Subs	Gls
Manchester U.	App	11.76				
Crewe Alex.	Tr	08.79	79-80	86	1	8
Port Vale	Tr	08.81	81-86	218	3	15
Wrexham	Tr	08.87	87-90	116	6	14

HUNTER, George I.
Troon, 29 August, 1930 Died 1990 (G)

League Club	Source	Date Signed	Seasons Played	Apps	Subs	Gls
Derby Co.	Glasgow Celtic	06.54	54	19	-	0
Exeter C.	Tr	08.55	55-58	147	-	0
Darlington	Yiewsley	06.61	61	20	-	0
Lincoln C.	Burton A.	09.65	65	1	0	0

HUNTER, Gordon G.
Lyneham, 8 November, 1954 (D)

League Club	Source	Date Signed	Seasons Played	Apps	Subs	Gls
York C.	Shrewsbury T. (Am)	07.73	73-77	70	7	1

HUNTER, John D.
Backworth, 20 September, 1934 (G)

League Club	Source	Date Signed	Seasons Played	Apps	Subs	Gls
Gateshead		08.54	55	4	-	0

HUNTER, John S.
Coalburn, 26 May, 1934 (OL)

League Club	Source	Date Signed	Seasons Played	Apps	Subs	Gls
Rotherham U.	Coltness U.	06.56	56	5	-	1
Carlisle U.	Tr	07.57	57	1	-	0
Barrow	Kings Lynn	07.59	59-60	24	-	0

HUNTER, Lee
Oldham, 5 October, 1969 (M)

League Club	Source	Date Signed	Seasons Played	Apps	Subs	Gls
Colchester U.	YT	06.88	87-88	5	4	0

HUNTER, Leslie
Middlesbrough, 15 January, 1958 (CD)

League Club	Source	Date Signed	Seasons Played	Apps	Subs	Gls
Chesterfield	App	08.75	75-81	156	9	8
Scunthorpe U.	Tr	07.82	82-83	61	0	8
Chesterfield	Tr	01.84	83-85	99	0	9
Scunthorpe U.	Tr	03.86	85-86	49	0	5
Chesterfield	Lincoln C.	12.87	87-88	31	0	3

HUNTER, Michael
Hexham, 27 May, 1948 (F)

League Club	Source	Date Signed	Seasons Played	Apps	Subs	Gls
Blackpool		01.66				
Darlington	Tr	07.67	67	2	1	0

HUNTER, Norman
Gateshead, 29 October, 1943 Eu23-3/E-28 (CD)

League Club	Source	Date Signed	Seasons Played	Apps	Subs	Gls
Leeds U.	Jnrs	04.61	62-76	540	0	18
Bristol C.	Tr	10.76	76-78	108	0	4
Barnsley	Tr	06.79	79-82	28	3	0

HUNTER, Paul
Kirkcaldy, 30 August, 1968 Su21-3 (F)

League Club	Source	Date Signed	Seasons Played	Apps	Subs	Gls
Hull C.	East Fife	03.90	89-91	18	24	5

HUNTER, Philip
Hartlepool, 28 September, 1950 (OR)

League Club	Source	Date Signed	Seasons Played	Apps	Subs	Gls
Hartlepool U. (Am)	Jnrs	08.69	69	1	0	0

HUNTER, J. Reginald
Colwyn Bay, 25 October, 1938 (W)

League Club	Source	Date Signed	Seasons Played	Apps	Subs	Gls
Manchester U.	Colwyn Bay	11.56	58	1	-	0
Wrexham	Tr	02.60	59-61	34	-	3

HUNTER, Robert
Gateshead, 25 March, 1951 (W)

League Club	Source	Date Signed	Seasons Played	Apps	Subs	Gls
Hartlepool U.		02.71	70	1	0	0

HUNTER, Robert R.
Lanark, 12 March, 1931 (OR)

League Club	Source	Date Signed	Seasons Played	Apps	Subs	Gls
Swindon T.	Motherwell	08.54	54	16	-	3

HUNTER, Roy I.
Middlesbrough, 29 October, 1973 (M)

League Club	Source	Date Signed	Seasons Played	Apps	Subs	Gls
West Bromwich A.	YT	03.92	91	2	4	1

HUNTER, William N.
Cambuslang, 7 April, 1942 (IF)

League Club	Source	Date Signed	Seasons Played	Apps	Subs	Gls
Bradford P.A.	Glasgow Rangers	07.64	64	14	-	0

HUNTLEY, John
Lumley, 5 November, 1967 (D)

League Club	Source	Date Signed	Seasons Played	Apps	Subs	Gls
Darlington (N/C)	Chester-le-Street	10.85	85	5	1	0

HUNTLEY, Keith S. M.
Swansea, 12 February, 1931 W Amat (OL)

League Club	Source	Date Signed	Seasons Played	Apps	Subs	Gls
Swansea C.		08.50	50	2	-	0

HUNTLEY, Richard B.
Sunderland, 5 January, 1949 (CH)

League Club	Source	Date Signed	Seasons Played	Apps	Subs	Gls
Sunderland	Jnrs	08.67	68	1	0	0

HUNTON, Keith
Wellington, 18 July, 1961 (G)

League Club	Source	Date Signed	Seasons Played	Apps	Subs	Gls
Carlisle U. (N/C)	Workington	02.87	86	3	0	0

HURFORD, David G.
Bristol, 17 January, 1945 (OR)

League Club	Source	Date Signed	Seasons Played	Apps	Subs	Gls
Bristol Rov.	App	01.63	62-64	6	-	0

HURLEY, Charles J.
Cork, 4 October, 1936 IR-40 (CH)

League Club	Source	Date Signed	Seasons Played	Apps	Subs	Gls
Millwall	Jnrs	10.53	53-57	105	-	2
Sunderland	Tr	09.57	57-68	357	1	23
Bolton W.	Tr	06.69	69-70	41	1	3

Charlie Hurley (Millwall, Sunderland, Bolton Wanderers & Republic of Ireland)

HURLEY, Christopher J.
Cork, 20 November, 1943 (CF)

League Club	Source	Date Signed	Seasons Played	Apps	Subs	Gls
Millwall	Rainham T.	03.64	63-64	4	-	2

HURLEY, William H.
Leytonstone, 11 December, 1959 E Sch (F)

League Club	Source	Date Signed	Seasons Played	Apps	Subs	Gls
Leyton Orient	App	01.77	76	1	1	0

HURLOCK, Terence A.
Hackney, 22 September, 1958 E 'B' (M)

League Club	Source	Date Signed	Seasons Played	Apps	Subs	Gls
Brentford	Leytonstone & Ilford	08.80	80-85	220	0	18
Reading	Tr	02.86	85-86	29	0	0
Millwall	Tr	02.87	86-89	103	1	8
Southampton	Glasgow Rangers	09.91	91	27	2	0

Terry Hurlock (Brentford, Reading, Millwall, Glasgow Rangers & Southampton)

HURLSTONE, Gary
Mexborough, 25 April, 1963 (F)

League Club	Source	Date Signed	Seasons Played	Apps	Subs	Gls
York C. (N/C)	Hatfield Main Colly	03.89	88	1	1	0

HURRELL, William P.
Dundee, 28 January, 1920 (IF)

League Club	Source	Date Signed	Seasons Played	Apps	Subs	Gls
Millwall	Raith Rov.	01.46	46-52	121	-	32
Queens Park R.	Tr	07.53	53	6	-	1

HURRELL, William T.
Newcastle, 15 September, 1955 (CH)

League Club	Source	Date Signed	Seasons Played	Apps	Subs	Gls
Northampton T.	App	08.72	72	5	0	0

HURST, Charles
Denton, 25 January, 1919 (IF)

League Club	Source	Date Signed	Seasons Played	Apps	Subs	Gls
Bristol Rov.		09.38				
Oldham Ath.		01.43				
Rochdale	Tr	06.46	46	4	-	1

HURST, Geoffrey C.
Ashton-u-Lyne, 8 December, 1941 E Yth/Eu23-4/EF Lge/E-49 (F)

League Club	Source	Date Signed	Seasons Played	Apps	Subs	Gls
West Ham U.	Jnrs	04.59	59-71	410	1	180
Stoke C.	Tr	08.72	72-74	103	5	30
West Bromwich A.	Tr	08.75	75	10	0	2

HURST, Gordon
Oldham, 9 October, 1924 Died 1980 EF Lge (W)

League Club	Source	Date Signed	Seasons Played	Apps	Subs	Gls
Charlton Ath.	Ramsgate	05.46	46-57	369	-	75

HURST, Graham J.
Oldham, 23 November, 1967 (M)

League Club	Source	Date Signed	Seasons Played	Apps	Subs	Gls
Rochdale	YT	07.85	84	0	1	0

HURST, G. John (Jack)
Bolton, 27 October, 1914 (CH)

League Club	Source	Date Signed	Seasons Played	Apps	Subs	Gls
Bolton W.	Lever Bridge	05.33	34-46	60	-	2
Oldham Ath.	Tr	02.47	46-50	98	-	2

HURST, John W.
Blackpool, 6 February, 1947 E Sch/Eu23-9 (CD)

League Club	Source	Date Signed	Seasons Played	Apps	Subs	Gls
Everton	App	10.64	65-75	336	11	29
Oldham Ath.	Tr	06.76	76-80	169	1	2

HURST, Lee J.
Nuneaton, 21 September, 1970 (LB)

League Club	Source	Date Signed	Seasons Played	Apps	Subs	Gls
Coventry C.	YT	05.89	90-91	11	3	0

HURST, William R.
Brierfield, 4 March, 1921 (W)

League Club	Source	Date Signed	Seasons Played	Apps	Subs	Gls
Burnley	Jnrs	03.38				
Plymouth Arg.	Tr	06.39	46	4	-	0
Bury	Nelson	09.47	47	1	-	0
Accrington St.	Northwich Vic.	10.48	48	1	-	0

HUSBAND, James
Newcastle, 15 October, 1947 E Sch/E Yth/Eu23-5 (F)

League Club	Source	Date Signed	Seasons Played	Apps	Subs	Gls
Everton	App	10.64	64-73	158	6	44
Luton T.	Tr	11.73	73-77	138	5	44

HUSSEY, Malcolm F.
Darfield, 11 September, 1933 (CH)

League Club	Source	Date Signed	Seasons Played	Apps	Subs	Gls
Rotherham U.	Jnrs	04.52	52-55	24	-	0
Scunthorpe U.	Tr	08.56	56-57	23	-	0
Rochdale	Tr	03.59	58	1	-	0

HUTCHINGS, Christopher
Winchester, 5 July, 1957 (FB)

League Club	Source	Date Signed	Seasons Played	Apps	Subs	Gls
Chelsea	Harrow Bor.	07.80	80-83	83	4	3
Brighton & H.A.	Tr	11.83	83-87	153	0	4
Huddersfield T.	Tr	12.87	87-89	110	0	10
Walsall	Tr	08.90	90	40	0	0
Rotherham U.	Tr	07.91	91	41	0	4

HUTCHINGS, Dennis
Axminster, 1 December, 1924 (OR)

League Club	Source	Date Signed	Seasons Played	Apps	Subs	Gls
Exeter C.	Axminster	04.47	46-51	82	-	13

HUTCHINS, Donald
Middlesbrough, 8 May, 1948 (W)

League Club	Source	Date Signed	Seasons Played	Apps	Subs	Gls
Leicester C.	Stockton	02.66	67-68	4	0	0
Plymouth Arg.	Tr	07.69	69-71	94	1	23
Blackburn Rov.	Tr	07.72	72-73	37	3	6
Bradford C.	Tr	06.74	74-80	252	4	44

Geoff Hurst (West Ham United, Stoke City, West Bromwich Albion & England)

HUTCHINSON, J. Barry
Sheffield, 27 January, 1936 (IF)

League Club	Source	Date Signed	Seasons Played	Apps	Subs	Gls
Chesterfield	Bolton W. (Am)	04.53	54-59	154	-	16
Derby Co.	Tr	07.60	60-63	107	-	51
Lincoln C.	Weymouth	07.65	65	24	0	18
Darlington	Tr	02.66	65-66	28	2	14
Halifax T.	Tr	11.66	66	25	0	14
Rochdale	Tr	07.67	67	27	0	3

HUTCHINSON, Colin
Lanchester, 20 October, 1936 (IF)

League Club	Source	Date Signed	Seasons Played	Apps	Subs	Gls
Stoke C.	Jnrs	11.53	54-57	9	-	0

HUTCHINSON, David N.
Grimsby, 25 September, 1941 (CF)

League Club	Source	Date Signed	Seasons Played	Apps	Subs	Gls
Scunthorpe U.	Brigg T.	07.71	71	5	4	0

HUTCHINSON, Douglas
Gateshead, 3 May, 1922 (CF)

League Club	Source	Date Signed	Seasons Played	Apps	Subs	Gls
Gateshead	Stirling A.	08.46	46	3	-	0

HUTCHINSON, George H.
Castleford, 31 October, 1929 (W)

League Club	Source	Date Signed	Seasons Played	Apps	Subs	Gls
Huddersfield T.	Jnrs	01.47	47	1	-	0
Sheffield U.	Tr	03.48	48-52	73	-	10
Tottenham H.	Tr	06.53	53	5	-	1
Leeds U.	Tr	08.55	55	11	-	5
Halifax T.	Tr	07.56	56-57	44	-	12

HUTCHINSON, Ian
Derby, 4 August, 1948 Eu23-2 (CF)

League Club	Source	Date Signed	Seasons Played	Apps	Subs	Gls
Chelsea	Cambridge U.	07.68	68-75	112	7	43

HUTCHINSON, Ian N.
Stockton, 7 November, 1972 (LB)

League Club	Source	Date Signed	Seasons Played	Apps	Subs	Gls
Halifax T.	YT	07.91	90-91	7	1	1

HUTCHINSON, James A.
Sheffield, 28 December, 1915 (IF)

League Club	Source	Date Signed	Seasons Played	Apps	Subs	Gls
Sheffield U.		11.37				
Bournemouth	Tr	06.46	46	8	-	3
Lincoln C.	Tr	11.46	46-48	85	-	54
Oldham Ath.	Tr	02.49	48-49	14	-	3

HUTCHINSON, John A. (Jack)
Codnor, 1 June, 1921 (FB)

League Club	Source	Date Signed	Seasons Played	Apps	Subs	Gls
Nottingham F.		08.43	46-58	241	-	0

HUTCHINSON, Keith G.
South Shields, 7 September, 1920 (FB)

League Club	Source	Date Signed	Seasons Played	Apps	Subs	Gls
Darlington		05.46	46-48	31	-	0

HUTCHINSON, C. Mark
Stoke, 2 November, 1963 (M)

League Club	Source	Date Signed	Seasons Played	Apps	Subs	Gls
Aston Villa	App	11.81				
Leicester C.	Tr	08.83				
Carlisle U.	L	08.84	84	6	0	0
Northampton T.	Tr	02.85	84	1	1	0

HUTCHINSON, Paul
Eaglescliffe, 20 February, 1953 (FB)

League Club	Source	Date Signed	Seasons Played	Apps	Subs	Gls
Darlington	Jnrs	09.71	71-72	8	2	0

HUTCHINSON, Robert
Glasgow, 19 June, 1953 (M)

League Club	Source	Date Signed	Seasons Played	Apps	Subs	Gls
Wigan Ath.	Hibernian	07.80	80	34	1	3
Tranmere Rov.	Tr	08.81	81-82	32	3	6
Mansfield T.	Tr	10.82	82-83	35	0	3
Tranmere Rov.	Tr	01.84	83	21	0	4
Bristol C.	Tr	07.84	84-86	89	3	10
Walsall	Tr	02.87	86-87	8	8	0
Blackpool	L	09.87	87	3	3	0
Carlisle U.	L	01.88	87	12	1	2

HUTCHINSON, Robert
Bolton, 9 May, 1955 (F)

League Club	Source	Date Signed	Seasons Played	Apps	Subs	Gls
Rochdale	Radcliffe Bor.	12.74	74	2	0	1

HUTCHISON, Donald
Gateshead, 9 May, 1971 (M)

League Club	Source	Date Signed	Seasons Played	Apps	Subs	Gls
Hartlepool U.	YT	03.90	89-90	19	5	3
Liverpool	Tr	11.90	91	0	3	0

HUTCHISON, Thomas
Cardenden, 22 September, 1947 Su23-1/S-17 (LW)

League Club	Source	Date Signed	Seasons Played	Apps	Subs	Gls
Blackpool	Alloa Ath.	02.68	67-72	163	2	10
Coventry C.	Tr	10.72	72-80	312	2	24
Manchester C.	Tr	10.80	80-81	44	2	4
Burnley	Hong Kong	08.83	83-84	92	0	4
Swansea C.	Tr	07.85	85-90	163	15	9

HUTT, Geoffrey
Hazelwood, 28 September, 1949 (FB)

League Club	Source	Date Signed	Seasons Played	Apps	Subs	Gls
Huddersfield T.	App	09.67	68-75	245	0	4
Blackburn Rov.	L	09.75	75	10	0	1
York C.	Haarlem (Neth)	02.77	76-77	63	0	1
Halifax T.	Tr	04.78	78-79	75	1	0

HUTTON, Alexander S.
Edinburgh, 10 October, 1941 (FB)

League Club	Source	Date Signed	Seasons Played	Apps	Subs	Gls
Southend U.		08.63	64	1	-	0

HUTTON, John (Jack)
Bellshill, 23 April, 1944 (W)

League Club	Source	Date Signed	Seasons Played	Apps	Subs	Gls
Scunthorpe U.	Hamilton Acad.	06.63	63-65	53	1	7

HUTTON, Joseph
Dundee, 18 November, 1927 (IF)

League Club	Source	Date Signed	Seasons Played	Apps	Subs	Gls
Reading	Albion Rov.	10.50	49-50	8	-	0
Stoke C.	Ayr U.	12.53	53-56	34	-	7
Gillingham	Tr	08.57	57	36	-	6
Millwall	Tr	08.58	58-59	24	-	9

HUTTON, Thomas O.
Gateshead, 10 September, 1922 (FB)

League Club	Source	Date Signed	Seasons Played	Apps	Subs	Gls
Accrington St.	Red Rose	05.45	46	18	-	0
Carlisle U.	Tr	08.47	47-48	44	-	0
Rochdale	Tr	08.49				
Tranmere Rov.	Nelson	08.50				

HUXFORD, Clifford G.
Stroud, 8 June, 1937 (WH)

League Club	Source	Date Signed	Seasons Played	Apps	Subs	Gls
Chelsea	Jnrs	02.55	58	6	-	0
Southampton	Tr	05.59	59-66	276	2	4
Exeter C.	Tr	06.67	67	40	1	1

HUXFORD, Colin J.
Stroud, 26 May, 1944 E Yth (FB)

League Club	Source	Date Signed	Seasons Played	Apps	Subs	Gls
Chelsea	App	10.61				
Swindon T.	Tr	11.62	62	1	-	0

HYDE, Frank L.
Wath, 11 January, 1927 (G)

League Club	Source	Date Signed	Seasons Played	Apps	Subs	Gls
Bradford C.	Wath W.	12.48	48-51	34	-	0

HYDE, Gary S.
Wolverhampton, 28 December, 1969 (W)

League Club	Source	Date Signed	Seasons Played	Apps	Subs	Gls
Darlington	YT	07.88	87-88	31	7	3
Leicester C.	Tr	04.90				
Scunthorpe U.	Tr	08.91	91	1	7	0

HYDE, Graham
Doncaster, 10 November, 1970 (M)

League Club	Source	Date Signed	Seasons Played	Apps	Subs	Gls
Sheffield Wed.	YT	05.88	91	9	4	0

HYDE, Stephen L.
High Wycombe, 18 December, 1943 (W)

League Club	Source	Date Signed	Seasons Played	Apps	Subs	Gls
Oxford U.	Wycombe W.	01.65	64-65	9	0	0

HYDES, Arthur J. E.
Barnsley, 24 November, 1910 (IF)

League Club	Source	Date Signed	Seasons Played	Apps	Subs	Gls
Leeds U.	Ardsley Rec.	05.30	30-36	127	-	74
Newport Co.	Tr	05.38	38	27	-	13
Exeter C.	Tr	02.46	46	4	-	0

HYMERS, Thomas
Thorne, 29 April, 1935 (FB)

League Club	Source	Date Signed	Seasons Played	Apps	Subs	Gls
Doncaster Rov.	Frickley Colly	11.58	59-60	23	-	0

HYND, J. Roger S.
Falkirk, 2 February, 1942 (CD)

League Club	Source	Date Signed	Seasons Played	Apps	Subs	Gls
Crystal Palace	Glasgow Rangers	07.69	69	29	1	0
Birmingham C.	Tr	07.70	70-75	162	8	4
Oxford U.	L	10.75	75	5	0	0
Walsall	Tr	12.75	75-77	89	0	1

HYNON, John C.
Bath, 19 January, 1934 (CF)

League Club	Source	Date Signed	Seasons Played	Apps	Subs	Gls
Crystal Palace		08.54	54	1	-	0

HYSEN, Glenn I.
Goteborg (Swe), 30 October, 1959 Swedish Int (CD)

League Club	Source	Date Signed	Seasons Played	Apps	Subs	Gls
Liverpool	Fiorentina (It)	07.89	89-90	70	2	1

HYSLOP, Christian T.
Watford, 14 June, 1972 (D)

League Club	Source	Date Signed	Seasons Played	Apps	Subs	Gls
Southend U.	YT	04.90	90-91	12	1	0

Paul Ince (West Ham United, Manchester United & England)
Exciting midfield player who is finally beginning to make his mark on the game.

I'ANSON, Paul
Shipley, 3 May, 1946 (WH)

League Club	Source	Date Signed	Seasons Played	Apps	Subs	Gls
Bradford P.A.	App	06.64	63-67	49	1	2

IBBOTSON, Daniel
Morecambe, 5 October, 1968 (W)

League Club	Source	Date Signed	Seasons Played	Apps	Subs	Gls
Preston N.E.(YT)	YT	08.85	85	1	0	0

IBBOTSON, Dennis
Rotherham, 4 December, 1920 E Sch (FB)

League Club	Source	Date Signed	Seasons Played	Apps	Subs	Gls
Rotherham U.(Am)	Rotherham Y.M.C.A.	11.46	46	4	-	0

IBBOTSON, Wilfred
Sheffield, 1 October, 1926 (IF)

League Club	Source	Date Signed	Seasons Played	Apps	Subs	Gls
Sheffield Wed.	Jnrs	04.44	47	1	-	0
Mansfield T.	Tr	08.48	48	2	-	0

ICETON, O. Lloyd
Workington, 30 March, 1920 (OL)

League Club	Source	Date Signed	Seasons Played	Apps	Subs	Gls
Preston N.E.		05.38				
Carlisle U.	Tr	10.46	46-49	77	-	18
Tranmere Rov.	Tr	06.50	50-54	140	-	18

ICKE, David V.
Leicester, 29 May, 1952 (G)

League Club	Source	Date Signed	Seasons Played	Apps	Subs	Gls
Coventry C.	App	09.69				
Hereford U.	Tr	08.71	72	37	0	0

IDDON, Harold
Preston, 20 February, 1921

League Club	Source	Date Signed	Seasons Played	Apps	Subs	Gls
Preston N.E.	Jnrs	02.43				
Barrow	Tr	10.46	46	25	-	6
Southport	Tr	06.47	47-48	42	-	3

IGGLEDEN, Horatio (Ray)
Hull, 17 March, 1925 (IF)

League Club	Source	Date Signed	Seasons Played	Apps	Subs	Gls
Leicester C.	Jnrs	03.42	46-47	11	-	2
Leeds U.	Tr	01.49	48-54	169	-	47
Exeter C.	Tr	07.55	55	27	-	8

IKIN, David
Stoke, 18 February, 1946 (G)

League Club	Source	Date Signed	Seasons Played	Apps	Subs	Gls
Port Vale		08.65	65	2	0	0

ILES, Richard
Bristol, 21 May, 1967 (D)

League Club	Source	Date Signed	Seasons Played	Apps	Subs	Gls
Bristol Rov. (N/C)	Longwell Green	03.86	85	1	0	0

ILES, Robert J.
Leicester, 2 September, 1955 (G)

League Club	Source	Date Signed	Seasons Played	Apps	Subs	Gls
Chelsea	Weymouth	06.78	78-82	14	0	0

ILEY, James
South Kirkby, 15 December, 1935 Eu23-1/EF Lge (WH)

League Club	Source	Date Signed	Seasons Played	Apps	Subs	Gls
Sheffield U.	Jnrs	06.53	54-57	99	-	7
Tottenham H.	Tr	08.57	57-58	53	-	1
Nottingham F.	Tr	07.59	59-62	93	-	4
Newcastle U.	Tr	09.62	62-68	227	5	15
Peterborough U.	Tr	01.69	68-72	64	4	4

IMLACH, Michael T.
Croydon, 19 September, 1962 (FB)

League Club	Source	Date Signed	Seasons Played	Apps	Subs	Gls
Preston N.E.	Everton (App)	08.80				
Leeds U.	Tr	11.81				
Peterborough U.	Tr	08.82	82-83	37	5	1
Tranmere Rov.	Tr	08.84	84	4	0	0

IMLACH, J. J. Stuart
Lossiemouth, 6 January, 1932 S-4 (OL)

League Club	Source	Date Signed	Seasons Played	Apps	Subs	Gls
Bury	Lossiemouth	10.52	52-53	71	-	14
Derby Co.	Tr	05.54	54	36	-	2
Nottingham F.	Tr	07.55	55-59	184	-	43
Luton T.	Tr	06.60	60	8	-	0
Coventry C.	Tr	10.60	60-61	73	-	11
Crystal Palace	Tr	07.62	62-64	35	-	2
Crystal Palace	Chelmsford C.	02.66	65-66	16	0	1

IMPEY, Andrew R.
Hammersmith, 30 September, 1971 (W)

League Club	Source	Date Signed	Seasons Played	Apps	Subs	Gls
Queens Park R.	Yeading	06.90	91	13	0	0

IMPEY, John E.
Minehead, 11 August, 1954 E Sch/E Yth (CD)

League Club	Source	Date Signed	Seasons Played	Apps	Subs	Gls
Cardiff C.	App	08.72	72-74	13	8	0
Bournemouth	Tr	07.75	75-82	280	4	7
Torquay U.	Tr	08.83	83-84	72	0	0
Exeter C.	Tr	08.85	85	26	0	0
Torquay U.	Tr	07.86	86-87	58	0	2

IMRIE, Adam
Dumfries, 1 October, 1933 (OR)

League Club	Source	Date Signed	Seasons Played	Apps	Subs	Gls
Carlisle U.	Kilmarnock	05.57	57	10	-	5

INCE, Paul E. C.
Ilford, 21 October, 1967 E Yth/Eu21-2/E'B' (M)

League Club	Source	Date Signed	Seasons Played	Apps	Subs	Gls
West Ham U.	YT	07.85	86-89	66	6	7
Manchester U.	Tr	09.89	89-91	87	3	6

INGER, James
Nottingham, 10 August, 1953 (G)

League Club	Source	Date Signed	Seasons Played	Apps	Subs	Gls
Walsall (Am)	Long Eaton U.	03.73	72	2	0	0

INGHAM, Anthony
Harrogate, 18 February, 1925 (FB)

League Club	Source	Date Signed	Seasons Played	Apps	Subs	Gls
Leeds U.	Harrogate T.	04.47	47-49	3	-	0
Queens Park R.	Tr	06.50	50-62	514	-	3

INGHAM, Frederick R.
Manchester, 3 April, 1954 (F)

League Club	Source	Date Signed	Seasons Played	Apps	Subs	Gls
Stockport Co.	App	04.72	71-72	12	5	0
Blackburn Rov.	Tr	08.73				
Exeter C.	Falmouth	03.78	77-78	4	4	1

INGHAM, R. John
Hebburn, 18 October, 1924 (OR)

League Club	Source	Date Signed	Seasons Played	Apps	Subs	Gls
Gateshead	Newburn	08.47	47-57	431	-	109

INGHAM, William C.
Stakeford (Nd), 22 October, 1952 (M)

League Club	Source	Date Signed	Seasons Played	Apps	Subs	Gls
Burnley	App	11.69	71-79	181	30	22
Bradford C.	Tr	08.80	80-81	78	0	4

INGLE, Stephen P.
Bradford, 22 October, 1946 (FB)

League Club	Source	Date Signed	Seasons Played	Apps	Subs	Gls
Bradford C.	App	08.64	64-66	89	1	15
Southend U.	Tr	01.67	66	14	1	3
Wrexham	Tr	07.67	67-71	145	4	5
Stockport Co.	Tr	07.72	72	29	0	0
Southport	Tr	07.73	73	2	0	0
Darlington	Tr	10.73	73	8	0	0

Andy Impey (Queens Park Rangers)

League Club	Source	Date Signed	Seasons Played	Apps	Subs	Gls

INGLETHORPE, Alexander M.
Epsom, 14 November, 1971 (F)

League Club	Source	Date Signed	Seasons Played	Apps	Subs	Gls
Watford	Jnrs	07.90	90-91	1	2	0

INGLIS, James M.
Glasgow, 14 February, 1924

League Club	Source	Date Signed	Seasons Played	Apps	Subs	Gls
Bury	Falkirk	05.50	50	2	-	0

INGLIS, John
Gateshead, 5 August, 1933 (G)

League Club	Source	Date Signed	Seasons Played	Apps	Subs	Gls
Gateshead (Am)	Blyth Spartans	06.57	57	2	-	0

INGLIS, John F.
Leven, 19 May, 1947 (CF)

League Club	Source	Date Signed	Seasons Played	Apps	Subs	Gls
Aston Villa	Glenrothes	09.65	67	1	1	0
Crewe Alex.	Tr	07.68	68-69	46	1	10

INGRAM, Alexander
Edinburgh, 2 January, 1945 S Amat/SF Lge (CF)

League Club	Source	Date Signed	Seasons Played	Apps	Subs	Gls
Nottingham F.	Ayr U.	12.69	69-70	28	0	3

INGRAM, Gerald
Merthyr Tydfil, 28 January, 1951 W Sch (M)

League Club	Source	Date Signed	Seasons Played	Apps	Subs	Gls
Swansea C.		08.70	70-72	35	2	1

INGRAM, Gerald
Hull, 19 August, 1947 (F)

League Club	Source	Date Signed	Seasons Played	Apps	Subs	Gls
Blackpool	Hull Brunswick	03.67	66-67	33	1	18
Preston N.E.	Tr	09.68	68-71	107	3	40
Bradford C.	Tr	03.72	71-76	171	3	60

INGRAM, Godfrey P.
Luton, 25 October, 1959 E Sch/E Yth (F)

League Club	Source	Date Signed	Seasons Played	Apps	Subs	Gls
Luton T.	App	10.77	77-81	22	5	6
Northampton T.	L	03.80	79	10	0	4
Cardiff C.	San Jose (USA)	09.82	82	7	4	2

INSKIP, Frederick C.
Cheadle, 20 October, 1924

League Club	Source	Date Signed	Seasons Played	Apps	Subs	Gls
Nottingham F.		12.44				
Crewe Alex.	Tr	04.48	47-48	26	-	4

INWOOD, Gordon F.
Kislingbury, 18 June, 1928 (OL)

League Club	Source	Date Signed	Seasons Played	Apps	Subs	Gls
West Bromwich A.	Rushden T.	01.49	49	10	-	0
Hull C.	Tr	05.50	50	3	-	0

IORFA, Dominic
Lagos (Nigeria), 1 October, 1968 (F)

League Club	Source	Date Signed	Seasons Played	Apps	Subs	Gls
Queens Park R.	Royal Antwerp (Bel)	03.90	89-91	1	7	0

IOVAN, Stefan
Romania, 23 August, 1960 (D)

League Club	Source	Date Signed	Seasons Played	Apps	Subs	Gls
Brighton & H.A.	Stoava Bucarest (Rom)	03.91	90-91	4	2	0

IPPOLITO, Mario
Peterborough, 16 April, 1964 (F)

League Club	Source	Date Signed	Seasons Played	Apps	Subs	Gls
Peterborough U.	Jnrs	04.83	82	8	0	3

IRELAND, Geoffrey J. C.
Paddington, 1 December, 1935 (OR)

League Club	Source	Date Signed	Seasons Played	Apps	Subs	Gls
Tottenham H.	Finchley	11.57	57-58	3	-	0
Shrewsbury T.	Tr	06.59	59	38	-	4

IRELAND, Jeremy
Chester, 14 September, 1938 (WH)

League Club	Source	Date Signed	Seasons Played	Apps	Subs	Gls
Chester C.		09.57	57-61	40	-	8

IRELAND, Roy P.
Exeter, 3 February, 1961 (M)

League Club	Source	Date Signed	Seasons Played	Apps	Subs	Gls
Exeter C.	App	02.79	78-80	17	3	0

IRELAND, Simon P.
Barnstaple, 23 November, 1971 (W)

League Club	Source	Date Signed	Seasons Played	Apps	Subs	Gls
Huddersfield T.	Jnrs	07.90	90-91	6	9	0
Wrexham	L	03.92	91	2	3	0

IRONS, Kenneth
Liverpool, 4 November, 1970 (M)

League Club	Source	Date Signed	Seasons Played	Apps	Subs	Gls
Tranmere Rov.	YT	11.89	89-91	69	9	13

IRONSIDE, Ian
Sheffield, 8 March, 1964 (G)

League Club	Source	Date Signed	Seasons Played	Apps	Subs	Gls
Barnsley	Jnrs	09.82				
Scarborough	North Ferriby U.	03.88	87-90	88	0	0
Middlesbrough	Tr	08.91	91	1	0	0
Scarborough	L	03.92	91	7	0	0

IRONSIDE, Roy
Sheffield, 28 May, 1935 (G)

League Club	Source	Date Signed	Seasons Played	Apps	Subs	Gls
Rotherham U.	Jnrs	07.54	56-64	220	-	0
Barnsley	Tr	07.65	65-68	113	0	0

IRVIN, Derek V.
Stockton, 23 August, 1943 (W)

League Club	Source	Date Signed	Seasons Played	Apps	Subs	Gls
Middlesbrough		09.61				
Watford	Brechin C.	06.67	67	0	2	1

IRVINE, J. Alan
Glasgow, 12 July, 1958 (RW)

League Club	Source	Date Signed	Seasons Played	Apps	Subs	Gls
Everton	Queens Park	05.81	81-83	51	9	4
Crystal Palace	Tr	08.84	84-86	108	1	12
Blackburn Rov.	Dundee U.	10.89	89-91	40	18	3

IRVINE, Alan J.
Broxburn, 29 November, 1962 (F)

League Club	Source	Date Signed	Seasons Played	Apps	Subs	Gls
Liverpool	Falkirk	11.86	86	0	2	0
Shrewsbury T.	Dundee U.	02.88	87-88	32	5	6

Stefan Iovan (Stoava Bucarest & Brighton & Hove Albion)

IRVINE, Archibald
Coatbridge, 25 June, 1946 (M)

League Club	Source	Date Signed	Seasons Played	Apps	Subs	Gls
Sheffield Wed.	Airdrieonians	09.68	68-69	25	4	1
Doncaster Rov.	Tr	12.69	69-74	220	8	16
Scunthorpe U.	Tr	07.75	75	22	1	1

IRVINE, James D.
Whitburn, 17 August, 1940 S Sch (CF)

League Club	Source	Date Signed	Seasons Played	Apps	Subs	Gls
Middlesbrough	Dundee U.	05.64	64-66	90	1	37
Barrow	Hearts	07.70	70-71	67	0	17

IRVINE, Robert J.
Carrickfergus (NI), 17 January, 1942 NI Sch/NIu23-1/NI-8 (G)

League Club	Source	Date Signed	Seasons Played	Apps	Subs	Gls
Stoke C.	Linfield	06.63	63-65	25	0	0

IRVINE, Samuel
Glasgow, 7 January, 1956 (M)

League Club	Source	Date Signed	Seasons Played	Apps	Subs	Gls
Shrewsbury T.	App	01.74	72-77	198	9	18
Stoke C.	Tr	06.78	78-79	67	0	11

IRVINE, William J.
Carrickfergus (NI), 18 June, 1943 NI Sch/NIu23-3/NI-23 (CF)

League Club	Source	Date Signed	Seasons Played	Apps	Subs	Gls
Burnley	Jnrs	06.60	62-67	124	2	78
Preston N.E.	Tr	03.68	67-70	77	4	27
Brighton & H.A.	Tr	03.71	70-72	66	3	27
Halifax T.	Tr	12.72	72	9	1	1

IRVING, David
Workington, 10 September, 1951 E Yth (F)

League Club	Source	Date Signed	Seasons Played	Apps	Subs	Gls
Workington	Jnrs	05.70	70-72	57	8	16
Everton	Tr	01.73	73-75	4	2	0
Sheffield U.	Tr	09.75	75	0	2	0
Oldham Ath.	Tr	06.76	76-77	18	3	7

IRVING, Gerald
Maryport, 19 September, 1937 (W)

League Club	Source	Date Signed	Seasons Played	Apps	Subs	Gls
Workington		08.56	56	1	-	0

IRVING, Russell
Wallsend, 4 January, 1964 (F)

League Club	Source	Date Signed	Seasons Played	Apps	Subs	Gls
Ipswich T.	App	05.81				
Colchester U.	Tr	08.84	84-85	36	14	9

IRWIN, Cecil
Ellington (Nd), 8 April, 1942 E Yth (RB)

League Club	Source	Date Signed	Seasons Played	Apps	Subs	Gls
Sunderland	Jnrs	04.59	58-71	312	3	1

IRWIN, Colin T.
Liverpool, 9 February, 1957 (CD)

League Club	Source	Date Signed	Seasons Played	Apps	Subs	Gls
Liverpool	Jnrs	12.74	79-80	26	3	3
Swansea C.	Tr	08.81	81-83	48	0	0

IRWIN, Dennis J.
Cork, 31 October, 1965 IRSch/IRYth/IRu21-3/IR-13 (RB)

League Club	Source	Date Signed	Seasons Played	Apps	Subs	Gls
Leeds U.	App	10.83	83-85	72	0	1
Oldham Ath.	Tr	05.86	86-89	166	1	4
Manchester U.	Tr	06.90	90-91	70	2	4

IRWIN, William J. N.
Newtonards (NI), 23 July, 1951 NI Amat (G)

League Club	Source	Date Signed	Seasons Played	Apps	Subs	Gls
Cardiff C.	Bangor C.	10.71	71-77	180	0	0

ISAAC, James
Cramlington, 23 October, 1916 (IF)

League Club	Source	Date Signed	Seasons Played	Apps	Subs	Gls
Huddersfield T.	Cramlington	11.34	36-38	33	-	8
Bradford C.	Tr	04.45	46	24	-	3
Hartlepool U.	Tr	07.47	47-48	56	-	9

ISAAC, Robert C.
Hackney, 30 November, 1965 E Yth (CD)

League Club	Source	Date Signed	Seasons Played	Apps	Subs	Gls
Chelsea	App	11.83	84-86	9	0	0
Brighton & H.A.	Tr	02.87	86-88	30	0	0

ISAAC, William H.
Pontypridd, 16 May, 1935 (G)

League Club	Source	Date Signed	Seasons Played	Apps	Subs	Gls
Stoke C.		03.53				
Northampton T.	Barry T.	07.58	59	8	-	0

ISAACS, Anthony B.
Middlesbrough, 8 April, 1973 (M)

League Club	Source	Date Signed	Seasons Played	Apps	Subs	Gls
Darlington	YT	07.91	91	4	5	0

ISHERWOOD, Dennis
Brierley Hill, 20 January, 1947 (FB)

League Club	Source	Date Signed	Seasons Played	Apps	Subs	Gls
Birmingham C.	App	01.64	66	5	0	1

ISHERWOOD, Dennis
Northwich, 9 January, 1924 Died 1974 (F)

League Club	Source	Date Signed	Seasons Played	Apps	Subs	Gls
Wrexham		08.44				
Chester C.	Tr	04.46	46	3	-	0

ISHERWOOD, Roy E.
Blackburn, 24 January, 1934 (OR)

League Club	Source	Date Signed	Seasons Played	Apps	Subs	Gls
Blackburn Rov.	Nelson	10.57	57-61	49	-	9

ITHELL, W. James
Hawarden, 7 February, 1916 (CH)

League Club	Source	Date Signed	Seasons Played	Apps	Subs	Gls
Bolton W.		11.36				
Swindon T.	Tr	05.46	46-49	107	-	1

IVERSON, Robert J.
Folkestone, 17 October, 1910 Died 1953 (WH)

League Club	Source	Date Signed	Seasons Played	Apps	Subs	Gls
Lincoln C.	Ramsgate P.W.	09.33	33	40	-	13
Wolverhampton W.	Tr	02.35	34-36	37	-	7
Aston Villa	Tr	12.36	36-47	135	-	9

IVEY, George H.
West Stanley, 29 October, 1923 Died 1979 (W)

League Club	Source	Date Signed	Seasons Played	Apps	Subs	Gls
York C.	Stanley U.	06.48	48-50	79	-	13

IVEY, Paul H.W.
Westminster, 1 April, 1961 (F)

League Club	Source	Date Signed	Seasons Played	Apps	Subs	Gls
Birmingham C.	App	01.79	78-80	4	3	0
Chesterfield (N/C)	Kettering T.	12.82	82	0	6	0

Dennis Irwin (Leeds United, Oldham Athletic, Manchester United & Republic of Ireland)

Rob Jones (Crewe Alexandra, Liverpool & England)
Made an impressive international debut last season after just 17 League games for Liverpool

League Club	Source	Date Signed	Seasons Played	Career Record Apps	Subs	Gls
JACK, Andrew M.						
Glasgow, 30 June, 1923						(F)
Tranmere Rov.	Wishaw Jnrs	06.48	48	3	-	3
JACK, J. Ross						
Inverness, 21 March, 1959						(F)
Everton	App	02.77	78	1	0	1
Norwich C.	Tr	12.79	80-82	31	25	10
Lincoln C.	Tr	08.83	83-84	52	8	16
JACK, Vincent						
Fortrose, 6 August, 1933						(CH)
Bury	Inverness Jnrs	04.54	55-56	10	-	0
Swindon T.	Tr	10.56	56-58	26	-	0
Accrington St.	Tr	07.59	59	22	-	0
JACKETT, Frank						
Pontardawe, 5 July, 1927						(WH)
Watford		11.49	49-52	14	-	0
Leyton Orient	Tr	07.53	53	4	-	0
JACKETT, Kenneth F.						
Watford, 5 January, 1962 W Yth/Wu21-2/W-31						(M/LB)
Watford	App	01.80	79-89	328	7	26
JACKMAN, Clive E. J.						
Farnborough, 2 December, 1936						(G)
Aldershot	Jnrs	05.53	52-56	38	-	0
West Bromwich A.	Tr	06.57	57-58	21	-	0
JACKMAN, Derek C.						
Colchester, 20 August, 1927						(WH)
Crystal Palace	Chelmsford C.	03.45				
West Ham U.	Tr	08.48	48-50	8	-	0
JACKS, George C.						
Stepney, 14 March, 1946						(M)
Queens Park R.	App	01.64	64	1	-	0
Millwall	Tr	07.65	65-70	144	7	5
Gillingham	Tr	07.72	72-75	159	0	20
JACKSON, Alan						
Swadlincote, 22 August, 1938						(IF)
Wolverhampton W.	Jnrs	08.55	57-58	4	-	1
Bury	Tr	06.59	59-62	124	-	43
Brighton & H.A.	Tr	11.62	62-63	21	-	5
JACKSON, Alan E.						
Scunthorpe, 14 February, 1938						(W)
Lincoln C.	Brigg T.	11.58	58-60	5	-	0
JACKSON, Albert						
Manchester, 12 September, 1943						(CH)
Oldham Ath.	Manchester U. (Jnr)	12.62	63-65	22	0	4
JACKSON, Alec						
Tipton, 29 May, 1937 EF Lge						(F)
West Bromwich A.	Jnrs	09.54	54-63	192	-	50
Birmingham C.	Tr	06.64	64-66	78	0	11
Walsall	Tr	02.67	66-67	35	2	7
JACKSON, Alexander J.						
Glasgow, 28 November, 1935						(CF)
Birmingham C.	Shettleston	04.58	58	6	-	6
Plymouth Arg.	Tr	03.60	59-63	67	-	23
JACKSON, Alexander W.						
Lesmahagow, 2 October, 1921						(WH)
York C.		09.46	46-49	50	-	5
JACKSON, Anthony T.						
Tarleton (Lancs), 16 August, 1942						(FB)
Southport	Preston N.E. (Am)	08.62	62-64	12	-	0
JACKSON, Arnold						
Manchester, 10 November, 1925						(IF)
Shrewsbury T.		(N/L)	50-53	144	-	40
Stockport Co.	Tr	06.54	54-58	153	-	46
JACKSON, C. Barry						
York, 2 February, 1938						(CH)
York C.	Cliftonville	12.56	58-69	481	1	9
JACKSON, Brian						
Maltby, 2 February, 1936						(WH)
Rotherham U.	Maltby Main Colly	09.54	55-64	131	-	6
Barnsley	Tr	07.65	65	29	0	0
JACKSON, Brian H.						
Walton-on-Thames, 1 April, 1933 E Sch						(OR)
Leyton Orient	Arsenal (Am)	10.50	50-51	38	-	2
Liverpool	Tr	11.51	51-57	124	-	12
Port Vale	Tr	07.58	58-61	159	-	29
Peterborough U.	Tr	07.62	62-63	47	-	4
Lincoln C.	Tr	05.64	64	10	-	1
JACKSON, Clifford						
Swindon, 3 September, 1941 E Sch						(F)
Swindon T.	Jnrs	09.58	58-62	91	-	30
Plymouth Arg.	Tr	06.63	63-66	72	0	19
Crystal Palace	Tr	09.66	66-69	100	6	26
Torquay U.	Tr	08.70	70-73	114	13	13
JACKSON, Craig						
Newark, 15 September, 1968						(CD)
Notts Co.	YT	08.86	85-86	3	2	0
JACKSON, Darren						
Edinburgh, 25 July, 1966						(W)
Newcastle U.	Meadowbank Th.	10.86	86-88	53	16	7
JACKSON, Darren W.						
Keynsham, 24 September, 1971						(CD)
Oxford U.	YT	05.90	89-91	9	2	0
JACKSON, David						
Stoke, 23 January, 1937						(IF)
Wrexham (Am)	Jnrs	07.54	54	7	-	1
Bradford C.	Marine	03.55	54-60	250	-	61
Tranmere Rov.	Tr	07.61	61-62	38	-	5
Halifax T.	Tr	07.63	63-64	66	-	2
JACKSON, David P.						
Bradford, 16 September, 1958						(F)
Manchester U.	App	09.75				
Bradford C.	Tr	09.78	78	9	3	3
JACKSON, Dennis L.						
Birmingham, 8 March, 1932						(FB)
Aston Villa	Hednesford T.	10.54	56-58	8	-	0
Millwall	Tr	05.59	59-60	80	-	0
JACKSON, Ernest						
Sheffield, 11 June, 1914						(WH)
Sheffield U.	Atlas & Norfolk	09.32	32-48	229	-	8
JACKSON, Gary A.						
Swinton, 30 September, 1964						(M)
Manchester C.	Jnrs	10.81	81	6	2	0
Exeter C.	Tr	09.85	85-86	34	1	2
JACKSON, George						
Liverpool, 14 January, 1911						(FB)
Everton	Walton Parish	05.32	34-47	75	-	0
JACKSON, George						
Stretford, 10 February, 1952						(M)
Stoke C.	App	07.69	71	8	0	0
JACKSON, Harold						
Halifax, 20 July, 1917						(FB)
Halifax T.	Sutherley W.E.	08.36	36-46	49	-	3
Stockport Co.	Tr	08.47	47	2	-	0
JACKSON, Harold						
Blackburn, 30 December, 1918						(CF)
Burnley	Darwen	01.42				
Manchester C.	Tr	06.46	46-47	8	-	2
Preston N.E.	Tr	12.47	47-48	18	-	5
Blackburn Rov.	Tr	12.48	48	1	-	0
Chester C.	Tr	07.49	49	21	-	10
JACKSON, Harold						
Shaw, 12 May, 1934						(F)
Oldham Ath.	Jnrs	06.51	51-55	10	-	1
Rochdale	Tr	10.55	55	1	-	1
JACKSON, James						
Glasgow, 26 March, 1931						(CF)
Notts Co.	Mapperley Celtic	03.49	48-57	113	-	47
JACKSON, James						
Glasgow, 1 January, 1921						(IF)
Bolton W.		06.39	47-49	11	-	1
Carlisle U.	Tr	07.50	50-54	100	-	22

JACKSON, James P.
Glasgow, 4 August, 1924

League Club	Source	Date Signed	Seasons Played	Apps	Subs	Gls
Bury	Third Lanark	05.50	50	1	-	0

JACKSON, James W.
Ashington, 30 December, 1933 E Sch (FB)

League Club	Source	Date Signed	Seasons Played	Apps	Subs	Gls
Newcastle U.	Jnrs	01.51				
Aldershot	Tr	07.55	55-60	195	-	19

JACKSON, John
Newcastle, 7 January, 1923 (F)

League Club	Source	Date Signed	Seasons Played	Apps	Subs	Gls
Stoke C.		05.41	46-47	4	-	3

JACKSON, John K.
Hammersmith, 5 September, 1942 E Yth/EF Lge (G)

League Club	Source	Date Signed	Seasons Played	Apps	Subs	Gls
Crystal Palace	Jnrs	03.62	64-73	346	0	0
Leyton Orient	Tr	10.73	73-78	226	0	0
Millwall	Tr	08.79	79-80	79	0	0
Ipswich T.	Tr	08.81	81	1	0	0
Hereford U.	Tr	08.82	82	4	0	0

JACKSON, Joseph G.
Wolverhampton, 22 April, 1966 (M)

League Club	Source	Date Signed	Seasons Played	Apps	Subs	Gls
Wolverhampton W.	Jnrs	08.83	83	1	0	0

JACKSON, Leonard
Stockport, 10 May, 1923

League Club	Source	Date Signed	Seasons Played	Apps	Subs	Gls
Manchester C.		01.45				
Rochdale	Tr	09.45	46-47	61	-	0

JACKSON, Leonard W.
Birmingham, 6 September, 1922

League Club	Source	Date Signed	Seasons Played	Apps	Subs	Gls
Birmingham C.		09.46				
Northampton T.	Tr	07.48	48	2	-	0

JACKSON, Matthew A.
Leeds, 19 October, 1971 E Sch/Eu21-4 (D)

League Club	Source	Date Signed	Seasons Played	Apps	Subs	Gls
Luton T.	Jnrs	07.90	91	7	2	0
Preston N.E.	L	03.91	90	3	1	0
Everton	Tr	10.91	91	30	0	1

Matthew Jackson (Luton Town & Everton)

JACKSON, Maurice
Barnsley, 6 November, 1928 (FB)

League Club	Source	Date Signed	Seasons Played	Apps	Subs	Gls
Barnsley	Carlton U.	09.49	49-55	34	-	0
Barrow	Tr	08.56	56-58	74	-	0

JACKSON, Michael J.
Chester, 4 December, 1973 E Yth (CD)

League Club	Source	Date Signed	Seasons Played	Apps	Subs	Gls
Crewe Alex.	YT	06.92	91	1	0	0

JACKSON, Nigel A.
Pudsey, 27 June, 1950 (FB)

League Club	Source	Date Signed	Seasons Played	Apps	Subs	Gls
Scunthorpe U.	App	07.68	68-72	112	3	5

JACKSON, Norman E.
Bradford, 6 July, 1925 (FB)

League Club	Source	Date Signed	Seasons Played	Apps	Subs	Gls
Sheffield Wed.	Manningham Mills	10.48	49-52	31	-	0
Bristol C.	Tr	06.54	54-55	8	-	0
Oldham Ath.	Tr	07.56	56	2	-	0

JACKSON, Peter
Stoke, 23 January, 1937 Died 1991 (WH)

League Club	Source	Date Signed	Seasons Played	Apps	Subs	Gls
Wrexham (Am)	Jnrs	07.54	54	7	-	0
Bradford C.	Marine	03.55	54-60	199	-	15
Tranmere Rov.	Tr	07.61	61-64	81	-	3

JACKSON, Peter A.
Bradford, 6 April, 1961 (CD)

League Club	Source	Date Signed	Seasons Played	Apps	Subs	Gls
Bradford C.	App	04.79	78-86	267	11	24
Newcastle U.	Tr	10.86	86-88	60	0	3
Bradford C.	Tr	09.88	88-89	55	3	5
Huddersfield T.	Tr	09.90	90-91	83	0	2

JACKSON, Philip J.
Manchester, 8 September, 1958 (M)

League Club	Source	Date Signed	Seasons Played	Apps	Subs	Gls
Stockport Co.	Manchester C. (App)	08.76	76-77	15	3	1

JACKSON, Richard G.
Rotherham, 13 December, 1932 (G)

League Club	Source	Date Signed	Seasons Played	Apps	Subs	Gls
Rotherham U.	Jnrs	07.51				
York C.	Tr	08.54				
Rotherham U.		07.56	56	1	-	0

JACKSON, Robert
Middleton, 5 June, 1934 (D)

League Club	Source	Date Signed	Seasons Played	Apps	Subs	Gls
Oldham Ath.	Jnrs	08.51	51-54	29	-	1
Lincoln C.	Tr	03.55	55-63	233	-	0

JACKSON, Robert G.
Altrincham, 9 February, 1973 (F)

League Club	Source	Date Signed	Seasons Played	Apps	Subs	Gls
Walsall	Manchester C. (YT)	03.91	90-91	8	2	2

JACKSON, Robert G.
Cornsay (Dm), 12 May, 1915 (WH)

League Club	Source	Date Signed	Seasons Played	Apps	Subs	Gls
Southend U.	Stanley U.	07.34	35-47	149	-	0

JACKSON, Ronald
Crook, 15 October, 1919 Died 1980 (FB)

League Club	Source	Date Signed	Seasons Played	Apps	Subs	Gls
Wrexham		09.45	46-49	108	-	0
Leicester C.	Tr	12.49	49-54	161	-	0

JACKSON, Roy L.
Swindon, 22 October, 1931 (WH)

League Club	Source	Date Signed	Seasons Played	Apps	Subs	Gls
Swindon T.		11.53	54	2	-	0

JACKSON, Thomas A.
Belfast, 3 November, 1946 NIu23-1/NI-35 (M)

League Club	Source	Date Signed	Seasons Played	Apps	Subs	Gls
Everton	Glentoran	02.68	67-70	30	2	0
Nottingham F.	Tr	10.70	70-74	73	8	6
Manchester U.	Tr	07.75	75-76	18	1	0

JACKSON, William P.
Liverpool, 8 December, 1924 (IF)

League Club	Source	Date Signed	Seasons Played	Apps	Subs	Gls
Swindon T.		10.47	48-49	4	-	1
Tranmere Rov.	Tr	04.51	51-53	14	-	1

JACOBS, Frank A.
Bristol, 22 April, 1940 (WH)

League Club	Source	Date Signed	Seasons Played	Apps	Subs	Gls
Bristol C.	Jnrs	05.58	59-60	5	-	0

JACOBS, Stephen D.
West Ham, 5 July, 1961 (D)

League Club	Source	Date Signed	Seasons Played	Apps	Subs	Gls
Coventry C.	App	11.78	79-83	94	7	0
Brighton & H.A.	Tr	06.84	84-85	47	1	3
Charlton Ath.	Tr	08.86				
Gillingham	Tr	12.86	86	6	1	0

JACOBS, Trevor F.
Bristol, 28 November, 1946 (FB)

League Club	Source	Date Signed	Seasons Played	Apps	Subs	Gls
Bristol C.	Jnrs	07.65	66-72	130	1	3
Plymouth Arg.	L	09.72	72	4	0	0
Bristol Rov.	Tr	05.73	73-75	82	0	3

JACOBS, Wayne G.
Sheffield, 3 February, 1969 (LB)

League Club	Source	Date Signed	Seasons Played	Apps	Subs	Gls
Sheffield Wed.	App	01.87	87	5	1	0
Hull C.	Tr	03.88	87-91	127	2	4

JACOBSEN, Viggo L.
Denmark, 11 August, 1953 (M)

League Club	Source	Date Signed	Seasons Played	Apps	Subs	Gls
Charlton Ath.	Kastrup (Den)	11.79	79	9	0	0

JACQUES, Anthony
Oddington (Oxon), 10 October, 1942 (WH)

League Club	Source	Date Signed	Seasons Played	Apps	Subs	Gls
Oxford U.	Jnrs	(N/L)	62	7	-	0

JACQUES, Joseph
Consett, 12 September, 1944 Died 1981 (WH)

League Club	Source	Date Signed	Seasons Played	Apps	Subs	Gls
Preston N.E.	Jnrs	09.61				
Lincoln C.	Tr	05.64	64	22	-	0
Darlington	Tr	07.65	65-69	150	3	5
Southend U.	Tr	10.69	69-72	85	2	0
Gillingham	Tr	11.72	72-74	73	0	1
Hartlepool U.	Dartford	01.76	75	5	0	0

JAGGER, George N.
Great Houghton, 30 September, 1941 (W)

League Club	Source	Date Signed	Seasons Played	Apps	Subs	Gls
Barnsley	Houghton Main Colly	06.60	60-62	46	-	2

JAGO, Gordon H.
Poplar, 22 October, 1932 E Sch/E Yth (CH)

League Club	Source	Date Signed	Seasons Played	Apps	Subs	Gls
Charlton Ath.	Dulwich Hamlet	05.51	54-61	137	-	1

JAKEMAN, Leslie
Nuneaton, 14 March, 1930 (WH)

League Club	Source	Date Signed	Seasons Played	Apps	Subs	Gls
Derby Co.	Atherstone T.	06.47				
Leicester C.	Hinckley Ath.	05.51	54	1	-	0

JAKUB, Yanek (Joe)
Falkirk, 7 December, 1956 (M)

League Club	Source	Date Signed	Seasons Played	Apps	Subs	Gls
Burnley	App	12.73	75-79	42	0	0
Bury	Tr	10.80	80-86	262	3	27
Chester C.	A.Z.67 Alkmaar (Neth)	08.88	88	42	0	1
Burnley	Tr	07.89	89-91	130	1	8

JALES, Richard A.
Chiswick, 3 April, 1922 (FB)

League Club	Source	Date Signed	Seasons Played	Apps	Subs	Gls
Bradford C.		06.45				
Aldershot	Tr	05.46	46-50	77	-	1

JALINK, Nico
Rotterdam (Neth.), 22 June, 1964 (M)

League Club	Source	Date Signed	Seasons Played	Apps	Subs	Gls
Port Vale	Waalwijk (Neth)	07.91	91	20	8	1

JAMES, T. Anthony G.
Ynysybwl, 16 September, 1919 (IF)

League Club	Source	Date Signed	Seasons Played	Apps	Subs	Gls
Brighton & H.A.	Folkestone T.	06.39	46-48	70	-	19
Bristol Rov.	Tr	06.49	49-50	21	-	5

JAMES, Anthony C.
Sheffield, 27 June, 1967 (CD)

League Club	Source	Date Signed	Seasons Played	Apps	Subs	Gls
Lincoln C.	Gainsborough Trin.	08.88	88-89	24	5	0
Leicester C.	Tr	08.89	89-91	73	9	10

JAMES, Anthony R.
Swansea, 24 February, 1960 (M)

League Club	Source	Date Signed	Seasons Played	Apps	Subs	Gls
Swansea C.	App	12.77	77-79	6	5	1

JAMES, Christopher
Sheffield, 16 January, 1969 (RB)

League Club	Source	Date Signed	Seasons Played	Apps	Subs	Gls
Scarborough	Worksop T.	08.91	91	12	1	0

JAMES, David
Swansea, 29 September, 1917 Died 1981 (CF)

League Club	Source	Date Signed	Seasons Played	Apps	Subs	Gls
Chelsea	Mossley	04.38				
Swansea C.	Tr	06.47	47	12	-	7

JAMES, David
Welwyn GC, 1 August, 1970 Eu21-10 (G)

League Club	Source	Date Signed	Seasons Played	Apps	Subs	Gls
Watford	YT	07.88	90-91	89	0	0

JAMES, David
Cambuslang, 12 December, 1942 (OR)

League Club	Source	Date Signed	Seasons Played	Apps	Subs	Gls
Brighton & H.A.	Blantyre Vic.	05.62	62	5	-	0

JAMES, David J.
Southend, 11 March, 1948 (D)

League Club	Source	Date Signed	Seasons Played	Apps	Subs	Gls
West Ham U.	App	03.65				
Torquay U.	Tr	05.67	67	8	0	0

JAMES, W. George
Swansea, 15 June, 1924 (CF)

League Club	Source	Date Signed	Seasons Played	Apps	Subs	Gls
Swansea C.	Tawe U.	08.42	49	4	-	0
Newport Co.	Tr	07.50	50-51	13	-	5

JAMES, Glyn
Llangollen, 17 December, 1941 Wu23-2/W-9 (CH)

League Club	Source	Date Signed	Seasons Played	Apps	Subs	Gls
Blackpool	Jnrs	05.59	60-74	393	6	22

JAMES, John B.
Stoke, 24 October, 1948 (F)

League Club	Source	Date Signed	Seasons Played	Apps	Subs	Gls
Port Vale	Jnrs	04.66	65-72	202	7	40
Chester C.	Tr	02.73	72-75	97	1	40
Tranmere Rov.	Tr	09.75	75-77	59	14	22

JAMES, John E.
Birmingham, 19 February, 1934 (WH)

League Club	Source	Date Signed	Seasons Played	Apps	Subs	Gls
Birmingham C.	Jnrs	03.51	52-53	5	-	2
Torquay U.	Tr	06.55	55-60	123	-	11

JAMES, John S.
South Shields, 12 September, 1923 (FB)

League Club	Source	Date Signed	Seasons Played	Apps	Subs	Gls
Bradford P.A.	South Shields	08.44	49-50	13	-	1

JAMES, Joseph
Bootle, 9 September, 1954 (CD)

League Club	Source	Date Signed	Seasons Played	Apps	Subs	Gls
Liverpool	Jnrs	01.74				
Southport	Tr	07.75	75	11	2	0

JAMES, Julian C.
Tring, 22 March, 1970 Eu21-2 (RB)

League Club	Source	Date Signed	Seasons Played	Apps	Subs	Gls
Luton T.	YT	06.88	87-91	58	11	4
Preston N.E.	L	09.91	91	6	0	0

JAMES, Keith A.
Hillingdon, 18 August, 1961 E Yth (FB)

League Club	Source	Date Signed	Seasons Played	Apps	Subs	Gls
Portsmouth	App	07.79	78-79	5	1	0

JAMES, Leighton
Loughor, 16 February, 1953 W Sch/Wu23-7/W-54 (LW)

League Club	Source	Date Signed	Seasons Played	Apps	Subs	Gls
Burnley	App	02.70	70-75	180	1	44
Derby Co.	Tr	10.75	75-77	67	1	15
Queens Park R.	Tr	10.77	77-78	27	1	4
Burnley	Tr	09.78	78-79	76	0	9
Swansea C.	Tr	04.80	79-82	88	10	27
Sunderland	Tr	01.83	82-83	50	2	4
Bury	Tr	08.84	84	46	0	5
Newport Co.	Tr	08.85	85	21	7	2
Burnley	Tr	08.86	86-88	75	4	13

Leighton James (Burnley, Derby County, Queens Park Rangers, Burnley, Swansea City Sunderland, Bury, Newport County, Burnley & Wales)

League Club	Source	Date Signed	Seasons Played	Apps	Subs	Gls
JAMES, Leslie						
						(OL)
Darlington (Am)		05.53	53	4	-	0
JAMES, Martin C.						
Slough, 18 February, 1953						(CD)
Reading	Jnrs	08.71	71	21	0	0
JAMES, Martin J.						
Crosby, 18 May, 1971						(LW/B)
Preston N.E.	YT	07.89	90-91	70	3	6
JAMES, Paul J.						
Cardiff, 11 November, 1963 Canadian Int						(M)
Doncaster Rov.	Hamilton (Can)	11.87	87	7	1	0
JAMES, Percy G. B.						
Rhondda, 9 March, 1917 W Amat						
Luton T.	Oxford C.	08.49	49	2	-	1
JAMES, Robert M. (Robbie)						
Swansea, 23 March, 1957 Wu21-3/W-47						(M)
Swansea C.	App	04.74	72-82	386	8	99
Stoke C.	Tr	07.83	83-84	48	0	6
Queens Park R.	Tr	10.84	84-86	78	9	5
Leicester C.	Tr	06.87	87	21	2	0
Swansea C.	Tr	01.88	87-89	82	8	16
Bradford C.	Tr	08.90	90-91	89	0	6

Robbie James (Swansea City, Stoke City, Queens Park Rangers, Leicester City, Swansea City, Bradford City & Wales)

League Club	Source	Date Signed	Seasons Played	Apps	Subs	Gls
JAMES, Ronald						
Birmingham, 16 March, 1922						(WH)
Birmingham C.		10.47				
Northampton T.	L	07.48	48	4	-	1
JAMES, Roy W.						
Bristol, 19 February, 1941						(CF)
Bristol Rov.		07.60	60	1	-	0
JAMES, Steven R.						
Coseley, 29 November, 1949 E Yth						(CD)
Manchester U.	App	12.66	68-74	129	0	4
York C.	Tr	01.76	75-79	105	0	1

League Club	Source	Date Signed	Seasons Played	Apps	Subs	Gls
JAMES, Tyrone S.						
Paddington, 19 September, 1956						(D)
Fulham	Jnrs	09.74	75-77	18	2	0
Plymouth Arg.	Tr	03.78	77-81	77	4	0
Torquay U.	L	03.83	82	13	0	1
JAMES, William J.						
Cardiff, 18 October, 1921 Died 1980						(CF)
Cardiff C.	Cardiff Corries	08.39	46	6	-	2
JAMESON, John C.						
Belfast, 11 March, 1958						(W)
Huddersfield T.	Bangor (NI)	03.77	77	1	0	0
JAMIESON, Ian						
Edinburgh, 22 October, 1934						(F)
Crewe Alex.	Third Lanark	08.56	56	4	-	2
Birmingham C.	Tr	07.57				
JAMIESON, Ian W.						
Dumbarton, 14 October, 1928						(WH)
Coventry C.	Aberdeen	01.49	48-57	181	-	6
JANKOVIC, Bozo						
Yugoslavia, 22 May, 1951 Yugoslav Int						(F)
Middlesbrough	Zeljeznicar (Yug)	02.79	79-80	42	8	16
JANTUNEN, Pertti K.						
Finland, 25 June, 1952 Finland Int						(M)
Bristol C.	Eskilstuna (Swe)	03.79	78-79	7	1	1
JARDINE, Alexander						
Motherwell, 12 April, 1926 Died 1978						(RB)
Millwall	Dundee U.	08.50	50-57	299	-	25
JARDINE, Frederick						
Edinburgh, 27 September, 1941						(LB)
Luton T.	Dundee U.	05.61	61-69	218	2	9
Torquay U.	Tr	02.71	70-71	11	0	0
JARMAN, Harold J.						
Bristol, 4 May, 1939						(OR)
Bristol Rov.	Clifton St Vincent	08.59	59-72	440	12	127
Newport Co.	Tr	05.73	73	34	6	8
JARMAN, John E.						
Rhymney, 4 February, 1931						(WH)
Wolverhampton W.	Lowhill Y.C.	07.49				
Barnsley	Tr	10.50	51-55	45	-	1
Walsall	Tr	06.56	56-57	37	-	2
JARMAN, William B.						
Pontypridd, 18 July, 1920						(CF)
Bury	Llanbradach	10.46	46	10	-	1
JARRIE, Frederick						
Hartlepool, 2 August, 1922						(G)
Hartlepool U. (Am)		08.47	47	1	-	0
JARVIS, Alan L.						
Wrexham, 4 August, 1943 W-3						(M)
Everton	Jnrs	07.61				
Hull C.	Tr	06.64	65-70	148	11	12
Mansfield T.	Tr	03.71	70-72	76	6	0
JARVIS, Anthony						
Radcliffe, 18 March, 1964						(F)
Oldham Ath.	Irlam T.	03.86				
Crewe Alex.	Tr	10.86	86	6	3	1
JARVIS, J. Brian						
Bangor-on-Dee, 26 August, 1933						(WH)
Wrexham		07.52	53-58	64	-	3
Oldham Ath.	Tr	07.59	59-62	88	-	2
JARVIS, Harold						
Maltby, 8 October, 1928						(WH)
Notts Co.	Worksop T.	05.51	52-54	29	-	0
JARVIS, Joseph						
Farnworth, 27 June, 1929						(FB)
Stockport Co.		09.53	54-56	43	-	0
JARVIS, Mervin J.						
Bristol, 20 October, 1924						(OL)
Bristol C.		05.48	48	4	-	0

JARVIS, Nicholas C.
Mansfield, 19 September, 1955 (LB)

League Club	Source	Date Signed	Seasons Played	Apps	Subs	Gls
Scunthorpe U.	Grantham	07.80	80	21	0	0

JARVIS, Nigel B.
Totnes, 6 November, 1963 (FB)

League Club	Source	Date Signed	Seasons Played	Apps	Subs	Gls
Plymouth Arg.	App	11.81				
Torquay U. (N/C)	Yeovil T.	02.85	84	8	3	0

JASPER, Brian
Plymouth, 25 November, 1933 (FB)

League Club	Source	Date Signed	Seasons Played	Apps	Subs	Gls
Plymouth Arg.	Astor Inst.	07.54	56	2	-	0

JASPER, Dale W.
Croydon, 14 January, 1964 (M/D)

League Club	Source	Date Signed	Seasons Played	Apps	Subs	Gls
Chelsea	App	01.82	83-84	10	0	0
Brighton & H.A.	Tr	05.86	86-87	44	5	6
Crewe Alex.	Tr	07.88	88-91	103	8	2

JAYES, Brian
Leicester, 13 December, 1932 (WH)

League Club	Source	Date Signed	Seasons Played	Apps	Subs	Gls
Leicester C.	Jnrs	07.54	55	3	-	0
Mansfield T.	Tr	07.56	56-59	115	-	1

JAYES, Carl G.
Leicester, 15 March, 1954 E Sch (G)

League Club	Source	Date Signed	Seasons Played	Apps	Subs	Gls
Leicester C.	Jnrs	06.71	74	5	0	0
Northampton T.	Tr	11.77	77-79	68	0	0

JAYES, A. Gordon
Leicester, 26 September, 1923 E Sch (IF)

League Club	Source	Date Signed	Seasons Played	Apps	Subs	Gls
Notts Co.	Leicester C. (Am)	11.46	46-47	27	-	7

JEAVONS, Patrick
Deptford, 5 July, 1946 (G)

League Club	Source	Date Signed	Seasons Played	Apps	Subs	Gls
Lincoln C.	Gravesend & Nft	02.66	65	1	0	0

JEFFELS, Simon
Barnsley, 18 January, 1966 E Yth (CD)

League Club	Source	Date Signed	Seasons Played	Apps	Subs	Gls
Barnsley	App	01.84	83-87	39	3	0
Preston N.E.	L	10.87	87	1	0	0
Carlisle U.	Tr	07.88	88-91	75	2	5

JEFFERIES, Alfred J.
Oxford, 9 February, 1922 (G)

League Club	Source	Date Signed	Seasons Played	Apps	Subs	Gls
Brentford	Oxford C.	09.47	49-53	116	-	0
Torquay U.	Tr	06.54	54	45	-	0

JEFFERS, John J.
Liverpool, 5 October, 1968 (LW/LB)

League Club	Source	Date Signed	Seasons Played	Apps	Subs	Gls
Liverpool	App	10.86				
Port Vale	Tr	12.88	88-91	105	14	6

JEFFERSON, Arthur
Goldthorpe, 14 December, 1916 (FB)

League Club	Source	Date Signed	Seasons Played	Apps	Subs	Gls
Queens Park R.	Peterborough U.	02.36	36-49	213	-	1
Aldershot	Tr	03.50	49-54	170	-	0

JEFFERSON, Derek
Morpeth, 5 September, 1948 (CD)

League Club	Source	Date Signed	Seasons Played	Apps	Subs	Gls
Ipswich T.	App	02.66	67-72	163	3	1
Wolverhampton W.	Tr	10.72	72-75	41	1	0
Sheffield Wed.	L	10.76	76	5	0	0
Hereford U.	Tr	11.76	76-77	39	0	0

JEFFERSON, Stanley
Doncaster, 26 June, 1931 Died 1973 (FB)

League Club	Source	Date Signed	Seasons Played	Apps	Subs	Gls
Aldershot	Dearne Ath.	08.52	52-57	82	-	0
Southend U.	Tr	07.58				

JEFFREY, Alick J.
Rawmarsh, 29 January, 1939 E Sch/E Yth/E Amat/Eu23-2 (IF)

League Club	Source	Date Signed	Seasons Played	Apps	Subs	Gls
Doncaster Rov.	Jnrs	02.56	54-56	71	-	34
Doncaster Rov.	Skegness	12.63	63-68	190	1	95
Lincoln C.	Tr	01.69	68-69	14	3	3

JEFFREY, Michael R.
Liverpool, 11 August, 1971 (F)

League Club	Source	Date Signed	Seasons Played	Apps	Subs	Gls
Bolton W.	YT	02.89	88-91	9	6	0
Doncaster Rov.	L	03.92	91	11	0	6

JEFFREY, Robert
Aberdeen, 14 May, 1920 (WH)

League Club	Source	Date Signed	Seasons Played	Apps	Subs	Gls
Derby Co.		12.43				
Exeter C.	Aberdeen	10.47	47	7	-	0

JEFFREY, William G.
Clydebank, 25 October, 1956 (M)

League Club	Source	Date Signed	Seasons Played	Apps	Subs	Gls
Oxford U.	App	10.73	73-81	311	3	24
Blackpool	Tr	06.82	82	12	2	1
Northampton T.	Tr	03.83	82-83	53	1	6

JEFFRIES, Derek
Manchester, 22 March, 1951 (CD)

League Club	Source	Date Signed	Seasons Played	Apps	Subs	Gls
Manchester C.	App	08.68	69-72	64	9	0
Crystal Palace	Tr	09.73	73-75	107	0	1
Peterborough U.	L	10.76	76	7	0	0
Millwall	L	03.77	76	10	1	0
Chester C.	Tr	07.77	77-80	116	5	2

JEFFRIES, Ronald J.
Birmingham, 24 March, 1930 (CF)

League Club	Source	Date Signed	Seasons Played	Apps	Subs	Gls
Aston Villa	Moor Green	12.50	50	2	-	0
Walsall	Tr	11.53	53	3	-	0

JEFFRIES, William A.
Acton, 11 March, 1921 Died 1981 (IF)

League Club	Source	Date Signed	Seasons Played	Apps	Subs	Gls
Mansfield T.		03.46	46	2	-	0
Hull C.	Tr	01.47				

JELLY, H. Edward (Ted)
Leicester, 28 August, 1921 (FB)

League Club	Source	Date Signed	Seasons Played	Apps	Subs	Gls
Leicester C.		05.46	46-50	56	-	1
Plymouth Arg.	Tr	08.51	52-53	11	-	0

JEMSON, Nigel B.
Preston, 10 August, 1969 Eu21-1 (F)

League Club	Source	Date Signed	Seasons Played	Apps	Subs	Gls
Preston N.E.	YT	06.87	85-87	28	4	8
Nottingham F.	Tr	03.88	89-91	45	2	13
Bolton W.	L	12.88	88	4	1	0
Preston N.E.	L	03.89	88	6	3	2
Sheffield Wed.	Tr	09.91	91	11	9	4

JENKIN, Kenneth
Grimsby, 27 November, 1931 (OR)

League Club	Source	Date Signed	Seasons Played	Apps	Subs	Gls
Grimsby T.	Jnrs	07.50	50-53	23	-	6

JENKINS, Brian
Treherbert, 1 August, 1935 (W)

League Club	Source	Date Signed	Seasons Played	Apps	Subs	Gls
Cardiff C.	Cwmparc	04.57	56-60	30	-	7
Exeter C.	Tr	06.61	61-62	73	-	12
Bristol Rov.	Tr	07.63	63	7	-	0

JENKINS, David J.
Bristol, 2 September, 1946 (F)

League Club	Source	Date Signed	Seasons Played	Apps	Subs	Gls
Arsenal	App	10.63	67-68	16	1	3
Tottenham H.	Tr	10.68	68-69	11	3	2
Brentford	Tr	07.72	72	13	5	1
Hereford U.	Tr	03.73	72-73	18	4	3
Newport Co.	L	03.74	73	6	0	1
Shrewsbury T.	Tr	08.74	74	2	0	1
Workington	South Africa	10.75	75	6	0	0

JENKINS, Iain
Prescot, 24 November, 1972 (D)

League Club	Source	Date Signed	Seasons Played	Apps	Subs	Gls
Everton	YT	06.91	90-91	2	2	0

JENKINS, Iori C.
Neath, 11 December, 1959 W Sch (D)

League Club	Source	Date Signed	Seasons Played	Apps	Subs	Gls
Chelsea	App	08.78				
Brentford	Tr	11.79	79-80	12	3	1

JENKINS, Lee R.
West Bromwich, 17 March, 1961 E Yth (M)

League Club	Source	Date Signed	Seasons Played	Apps	Subs	Gls
Aston Villa	App	01.79	78-79	0	3	0
Port Vale	Tr	11.80	80	1	0	0
Birmingham C.	Rovaniemi (Fin)	10.85	85	1	0	0

JENKINS, J. Lindley
West Bromwich, 6 April, 1954 (M)

League Club	Source	Date Signed	Seasons Played	Apps	Subs	Gls
Birmingham C.	App	07.71	73	2	0	0
Walsall	Tr	07.74	74	3	0	0

JENKINS, Peter L.
Bow, 7 February, 1947 (FB)

League Club	Source	Date Signed	Seasons Played	Apps	Subs	Gls
Charlton Ath.	Chelsea (App)	03.65	65	2	0	0

JENKINS, Randolph J.
Sligo (Ire), 5 September, 1923 (IF)

League Club	Source	Date Signed	Seasons Played	Apps	Subs	Gls
Walsall		01.45				
Northampton T.	Tr	06.46	46-47	18	-	6
Fulham	Tr	05.48				
Gillingham	Tr	06.50	50	2	-	0

League Club	Source	Date Signed	Seasons Played	Career Record Apps	Subs	Gls
JENKINS, Reginald						
Millbrook, 7 October, 1938						(IF)
Plymouth Arg.	Truro C.	10.57	58-59	16	-	3
Exeter C.	Tr	12.60	60	20	-	6
Torquay U.	Tr	07.61	61-63	88	-	23
Rochdale	Tr	06.64	64-72	294	11	119
JENKINS, Ross A.						
Kensington, 4 November, 1951						(F)
Crystal Palace	App	11.69	71-72	15	0	2
Watford	Tr	11.72	72-82	312	27	118
JENKINS, Stephen R.						
Merthyr Tydfil, 16 July, 1972 W Yth						(RB)
Swansea C.	YT	07.90	90-91	31	4	0
JENKINS, Thomas E.						
Bethnal Green, 2 December, 1947						(OL)
Leyton Orient		01.66	65	1	0	0
Reading	Margate	07.69	69	21	0	5
Southampton	Tr	12.69	69-72	84	0	4
Swindon T.	Tr	11.72	72-75	89	11	4
JENKINS, Thomas F.						
Stockton, 5 December, 1925						(IF)
Chelsea	Queen of South	07.49	49	5	-	0
Leicester C.	Kettering T.	07.54				
JENKINSON, Leigh						
Thorne, 9 July, 1969						(LW)
Hull C.	YT	06.87	87-91	70	34	9
Rotherham U.	L	09.90	90	5	2	0
JENNINGS, Dennis B.						
Kidderminster, 20 July, 1910						(LB)
Huddersfield T.	Kidderminster Hrs	10.30	30-32	33	-	5
Grimsby T.	Tr	09.32	32-35	99	-	29
Birmingham C.	Tr	01.36	35-49	192	-	12
JENNINGS, Kentoine (Jed)						
Bermuda, 15 October, 1971 Bermuda Int						(D)
Hereford U.	Pembroke (Ber)	08.91	91	9	2	0
JENNINGS, Nicholas						
Wellington (Som), 18 January, 1946						(OL)
Plymouth Arg.	Wellington	08.63	63-66	98	0	11
Portsmouth	Tr	01.67	66-73	198	8	45
Aldershot	L	11.73	73	4	0	1
Exeter C.	Tr	05.74	74-77	119	5	15
JENNINGS, Patrick A.						
Newry (NI), 12 June, 1945 NI Yth/NIu23-1/NI-119						(G)
Watford	Newry T.	05.63	62-63	48	-	0
Tottenham H.	Tr	06.64	64-76	472	0	0
Arsenal	Tr	08.77	77-84	237	0	0
JENNINGS, Roy T. E.						
Swindon, 31 December, 1931 E Yth						(CH)
Brighton & H.A.	Southampton (Am)	05.52	52-63	277	-	22
JENNINGS, H. William						
Norwich, 7 January, 1920 Died 1969						(CF)
Northampton T.		10.38	38-46	11	-	2
Ipswich T.	Tr	05.47	47-50	102	-	41
Rochdale	Tr	06.51	51	3	-	1
Crystal Palace	Tr	09.51				
JENNINGS, William J.						
Hackney, 20 February, 1952 E Yth						(F)
Watford	Jnrs	04.70	70-74	80	12	33
West Ham U.	Tr	09.74	74-78	89	10	34
Leyton Orient	Tr	08.79	79-81	64	3	21
Luton T.	Tr	03.82	81	0	2	1

Pat Jennings (Watford, Tottenham Hotspur, Arsenal & Northern Ireland)

JENSEN, H. Viggo
Denmark, 29 March, 1921 Danish Int (LB/IF)

League Club	Source	Date Signed	Seasons Played	Apps	Subs	Gls
Hull C.	Esbjerg (Den)	10.48	48-56	308	-	51

JEPPSON, Hans O.
Sweden, 10 May, 1925 Swedish Int (CF)

League Club	Source	Date Signed	Seasons Played	Apps	Subs	Gls
Charlton Ath. (Am)	Djurgardens (Swe)	01.51	50	11	-	9

JEPSON, Arthur E.
Nottingham, 12 July, 1915 (G)

League Club	Source	Date Signed	Seasons Played	Apps	Subs	Gls
Mansfield T. (Am)		11.34	34	2	-	0
Port Vale	Grantham	06.38	38	39	-	0
Stoke C.	Tr	09.46	46-47	28	-	0
Lincoln C.	Tr	12.48	48-49	58	-	0

JEPSON, C. Barry
Alfreton, 29 December, 1929 (CF)

League Club	Source	Date Signed	Seasons Played	Apps	Subs	Gls
Chesterfield	Jnrs	11.48				
Mansfield T.	Ilkeston T.	03.54	53-56	55	-	36
Chester C.	Tr	01.57	56-59	89	-	41
Southport	Tr	11.59	59	24	-	7

JEPSON, Ronald F.
Stoke, 12 May, 1963 (F)

League Club	Source	Date Signed	Seasons Played	Apps	Subs	Gls
Port Vale	Nantwich T.	03.89	88-90	12	10	0
Peterborough U.	L	01.90	89	18	0	5
Preston N.E.	Tr	02.91	90-91	36	2	8

JERVIS, William J.
Liverpool, 22 January, 1942 (OR)

League Club	Source	Date Signed	Seasons Played	Apps	Subs	Gls
Blackburn Rov.	Jnrs	01.59				
Gillingham	Tr	07.61	61	1	-	0

JESSOP, Stanley T.
Liverpool, 5 August, 1932 (F)

League Club	Source	Date Signed	Seasons Played	Apps	Subs	Gls
Southport	Kidderminster Hrs	08.53	53	11	-	1

JESSOP, William
Preston, 2 April, 1922 (OL)

League Club	Source	Date Signed	Seasons Played	Apps	Subs	Gls
Preston N.E.	Jnrs	09.40	46	4	-	0
Stockport Co.	Tr	04.47	46-47	17	-	4
Oldham Ath.	Tr	02.48	47-50	94	-	16
Wrexham	Tr	06.51	51	14	-	2

JEST, Sydney T.
Ramsgate, 4 June, 1943 (FB)

League Club	Source	Date Signed	Seasons Played	Apps	Subs	Gls
Brighton & H.A.	Ramsgate	12.61	61-62	12	-	0

JEWELL, Paul
Liverpool, 28 September, 1964 (F/M)

League Club	Source	Date Signed	Seasons Played	Apps	Subs	Gls
Liverpool	App	09.82				
Wigan Ath	Tr	12.84	84-87	117	20	35
Bradford C.	Tr	07.88	88-91	105	32	19

JEWELL, Ronald P.
Plymouth, 6 December, 1920 (OL)

League Club	Source	Date Signed	Seasons Played	Apps	Subs	Gls
Torquay U.	Plymouth Arg. (Am)	09.46	46	1	-	0

JEZZARD, Bedford
Clerkenwell, 19 October, 1927 EF Lge/E'B'-3/E-2 (CF)

League Club	Source	Date Signed	Seasons Played	Apps	Subs	Gls
Fulham	Croxley B.C.	10.48	48-55	292	-	154

JINKS, James T.
Camberwell, 19 August, 1916 Died 1981 (CF)

League Club	Source	Date Signed	Seasons Played	Apps	Subs	Gls
Millwall	Downham Com.	11.38	38-47	45	-	16
Fulham	Tr	08.48	48-49	11	-	3
Luton T.	Tr	03.50	49-50	9	-	2
Aldershot	Tr	09.51	51	5	-	1

JOBLING, Keith A.
Grimsby, 26 March, 1934 (CH)

League Club	Source	Date Signed	Seasons Played	Apps	Subs	Gls
Grimsby T.	Jnrs	07.53	53-68	450	0	5

JOBLING, Kevin A.
Sunderland, 1 January, 1968 (M/LB)

League Club	Source	Date Signed	Seasons Played	Apps	Subs	Gls
Leicester C.	App	01.86	86-87	4	5	0
Grimsby T.	Tr	02.88	87-91	155	6	8

JOBSON, Richard I.
Holderness, 9 May, 1963 E'B' (CD)

League Club	Source	Date Signed	Seasons Played	Apps	Subs	Gls
Watford	Burton A.	11.82	82-84	26	2	4
Hull C.	Tr	02.85	84-90	219	2	17
Oldham Ath.	Tr	09.90	90-91	79	1	3

JOEL, Stephen P.
Liverpool, 13 October, 1954 (M)

League Club	Source	Date Signed	Seasons Played	Apps	Subs	Gls
Southport (N/C)	Portmadoc	11.77	77	0	1	0

JOHANNESON, Albert
South Africa, 12 March, 1940 (OL)

League Club	Source	Date Signed	Seasons Played	Apps	Subs	Gls
Leeds U.	Germiston Callies (SA)	04.61	60-69	170	2	48
York C.	Tr	07.70	70-71	26	0	3

JOHN, Dennis C.J.
Swansea, 27 January, 1935 (FB)

League Club	Source	Date Signed	Seasons Played	Apps	Subs	Gls
Plymouth Arg.	Jnrs	02.52	55-56	3	-	0
Swansea C.	Tr	08.58	58	4	-	0
Scunthorpe U.	Tr	08.59	59-61	88	-	0
Millwall	Tr	06.62	62-65	101	5	6

JOHN, Dilwyn J.
Tonypandy, 3 June, 1944 Wu23-1 (G)

League Club	Source	Date Signed	Seasons Played	Apps	Subs	Gls
Cardiff C.	Jnrs	06.61	61-66	88	0	0
Swansea C.	Tr	03.67	66-69	80	0	0

JOHN, Malcolm
Bridgend, 9 December, 1950 (F)

League Club	Source	Date Signed	Seasons Played	Apps	Subs	Gls
Bristol Rov.	Swansea C. (Am)	09.71	71-73	4	1	2
Northampton T.	Tr	03.74	73-74	34	7	9

JOHN, Raymond C.
Swansea, 22 November, 1932 (F)

League Club	Source	Date Signed	Seasons Played	Apps	Subs	Gls
Barnsley	Tottenham H. (Am)	05.53				
Exeter C.	Tr	07.54	54-58	144	-	18
Oldham Ath.	Tr	12.58	58-59	32	-	5

JOHN, Stephen P.
Brentwood, 22 December, 1966 (FB)

League Club	Source	Date Signed	Seasons Played	Apps	Subs	Gls
Leyton Orient	App	12.84	85-86	23	0	0

JOHNROSE, Leonard
Preston, 29 November, 1969 (F)

League Club	Source	Date Signed	Seasons Played	Apps	Subs	Gls
Blackburn Rov.	YT	06.88	87-91	20	22	11
Preston N.E.	L	01.92	91	1	2	1
Hartlepool U.	Tr	02.92	91	15	0	2

JOHNS, Mark S.
Bristol, 17 May, 1959 (F)

League Club	Source	Date Signed	Seasons Played	Apps	Subs	Gls
Bristol Rov. (N/C)	Bristol Manor Farm	09.86	86	2	0	1

JOHNS, Nicholas P.
Bristol, 8 June, 1957 (G)

League Club	Source	Date Signed	Seasons Played	Apps	Subs	Gls
Millwall	Minehead	02.76	76-77	50	0	0
Sheffield U. (L)	Tampa Bay (USA)	09.78	78	1	0	0
Charlton Ath.	Tr	12.78	78-87	288	0	0
Queens Park R.	Tr	12.87	87-88	10	0	0
Maidstone U.	L	10.89	89	2	0	0
Maidstone U.	Tr	03.90	89-90	40	0	0

JOHNS, F. Stanley
Liverpool, 28 June, 1924 (IF)

League Club	Source	Date Signed	Seasons Played	Apps	Subs	Gls
West Ham U.	South Liverpool	08.50	50	6	-	2

JOHNSEN, Erland
Norway, 5 April, 1967 Norwegian Int (CD)

League Club	Source	Date Signed	Seasons Played	Apps	Subs	Gls
Chelsea	Bayern Munchen (Ger)	11.89	89-91	30	1	0

JOHNSON, Alan
Stoke, 13 March, 1947 (OR)

League Club	Source	Date Signed	Seasons Played	Apps	Subs	Gls
Port Vale	Jnrs	09.64	65	2	0	1

JOHNSON, Alan K.
Wigan, 19 February, 1971 (CD)

League Club	Source	Date Signed	Seasons Played	Apps	Subs	Gls
Wigan Ath.	YT	03.89	88-91	111	17	11

JOHNSON, Albert
Morpeth, 7 September, 1923 (FB)

League Club	Source	Date Signed	Seasons Played	Apps	Subs	Gls
Bradford C.	Ashington	05.47	46-49	35	-	0

JOHNSON, Albert
Weaverham, 15 July, 1920 (OR)

League Club	Source	Date Signed	Seasons Played	Apps	Subs	Gls
Everton		03.46	46-47	9	-	0
Chesterfield	Tr	09.48	48	20	-	1

JOHNSON, Andrew J.
Bath, 2 May, 1974 (M)

League Club	Source	Date Signed	Seasons Played	Apps	Subs	Gls
Norwich C.	YT	03.92	91	2	0	0

JOHNSON, Arthur
Liverpool, 23 January, 1933 (G)

League Club	Source	Date Signed	Seasons Played	Apps	Subs	Gls
Blackburn Rov.	Jnrs	01.50	51	1	-	0
Halifax T.	Tr	03.55	54-59	216	-	0
Wrexham	Tr	06.60	60-61	52	-	0
Chester C.	L	08.62	62	3	-	0

League Club	Source	Date Signed	Seasons Played	Career Record Apps	Subs	Gls

JOHNSON, Brian
Gateshead, 20 March, 1936 (CF)

Millwall		10.57	57	7	-	2

JOHNSON, Brian
Newcastle, 12 November, 1948 (W)

Sunderland	App	11.65				
Luton T.	Tr	07.66	66-67	9	1	0

JOHNSON, Brian A.
Nantwich, 28 May, 1930 (F)

Wrexham		04.50	50-51	14	-	2

JOHNSON, Brian F.
Isleworth, 21 October, 1955 (W)

Plymouth Arg.	App	08.73	73-80	186	11	40
Torquay U.	L	01.79	78	5	0	2
Torquay U.	L	09.81	81	2	0	0

JOHNSON, Brian J.
Liverpool, 29 October, 1948 (M)

Tranmere Rov.	Jnrs	05.67	68	0	1	0

JOHNSON, David
Blackburn, 17 April, 1951 (G)

Tranmere Rov.	Atherstone T.	07.74	74-75	3	0	0
Southport	L	01.76	75	6	0	0

JOHNSON, David
South Shields, 19 November, 1955 E Yth (F)

Bristol C.	Doncaster Rov. (Am)	05.74				
Hartlepool U.	Tr	02.75	74	1	0	0

JOHNSON, David A.
Dinnington, 29 October, 1970 (F)

Sheffield Wed.	YT	07.89	91	5	1	0
Hartlepool U.	L	10.91	91	7	0	2

JOHNSON, David D.
Northampton, 10 March, 1967 (LB)

Northampton T.	Irthlingboro Diamonds	07.89	89-91	23	24	0

JOHNSON, David E.
Liverpool, 23 October, 1951 E-8 (F)

Everton	App	04.69	70-72	47	3	11
Ipswich T.	Tr	11.72	72-75	134	3	35
Liverpool	Tr	08.76	76-81	128	20	55
Everton	Tr	08.82	82-83	32	8	4
Barnsley	L	02.84	83	4	0	1
Manchester C.	Tr	03.84	83	4	2	1
Preston N.E.	Tulsa (USA)	10.84	84	20	4	3

JOHNSON, David N.
Gloucester, 26 December, 1963 (F)

Watford	Redhill	03.82	81-83	4	3	0
Peterborough U.	Tr	08.84	84-85	28	7	4

JOHNSON, Dennis
Seaham, 20 May, 1934 (F)

Hartlepool U.		02.54	57	2	-	0

JOHNSON, Eric
Moulton (Ches), 25 May, 1927 (W)

Coventry C.	Winsford U.	09.52	52-56	91	-	7
Torquay U.	Tr	07.57	57-58	48	-	1

JOHNSON, Eric
Birkenhead, 16 December, 1944 (WH)

Wrexham	Everton (Am)	06.63	63-65	28	0	0

JOHNSON, Gary J.
Peckham, 14 September, 1959 (F)

Chelsea	App	09.77	78-80	16	3	9
Brentford	Tr	12.80	80-82	55	5	13
Aldershot	South Africa	08.85	85-87	73	2	20

JOHNSON, Gavin
Eye, 10 October, 1970 (M)

Ipswich T.	YT	02.89	88-91	45	14	5

JOHNSON, George
Manchester, 27 April, 1936 (IF)

Rochdale		12.54	54	1	-	0
Southport	Ashton U.	01.63	62	6	-	0

JOHNSON, George J.
Esh (Dm), 6 October, 1932 (OL)

Lincoln C.		09.51	51	3	-	1

JOHNSON, L. Glenn
Canada, 22 April, 1951 (F)

West Bromwich A.	Vancouver (Can)	10.69	71	2	1	0

JOHNSON, Glenn W.
Barrow, 7 March, 1952 E Yth (G)

Arsenal	App	07.69				
Doncaster Rov.	Tr	06.70	70-72	95	0	0
Walsall	L	12.72	72	3	0	0
Aldershot	Tr	07.73	73-82	424	0	0

JOHNSON, W. Herbert
Stockton, 4 June, 1916 (WH)

Charlton Ath.	Spennymoor U.	03.39	46-52	142	-	1

JOHNSON, Howard
Sheffield, 17 July, 1925 (CH)

Sheffield U.	Norton Woodseats	03.51	50-56	92	-	0
York C.	Tr	08.57	57	28	-	0

JOHNSON, Ian
Oldham, 11 November, 1960 (D)

Rochdale	Chadderton	09.84	84-86	74	7	1

JOHNSON, Ian
Newcastle, 14 February, 1969 (CD)

Northampton T.	Gateshead	11.87	88	2	1	0

JOHNSON, James
Stockton, 26 February, 1923 Died 1987 (CF)

Grimsby T.	York C. (Am)	03.45	46-49	6	-	1
Carlisle U.	Tr	03.51	50	8	-	1

JOHNSON, Jeffrey
Manchester, 29 October, 1950 E Semi-Pro (M)

Stockport Co.	Hyde U.	09.76	76	6	2	0

JOHNSON, Jeffrey D.
Cardiff, 26 November, 1953 W Sch (M)

Manchester C.	App	12.70	70-71	4	2	0
Swansea C.	L	07.72	72	37	2	4
Crystal Palace	Tr	12.73	73-75	82	5	4
Sheffield Wed.	Tr	07.76	76-80	175	5	6
Newport Co.	Tr	08.81	81	34	0	2
Gillingham	Tr	09.82	82-84	85	3	4
Port Vale	Tr	07.85	85	10	0	1

JOHNSON, John
Hazel Grove, 11 December, 1921 (OR)

Stockport Co.	Tr	01.41				
Millwall	Tr	12.45	46-56	309	-	46

JOHNSON, John E.
South Shields, 4 February, 1929 (F)

Manchester C.		05.49				
Gateshead	North Shields	01.51	50-54	73	-	13

JOHNSON, John W.
Newcastle, 12 February, 1919 Died 1975 (OR)

Huddersfield T.	Leicester Nomads	06.36	36-38	18	-	2
Grimsby T.	Tr	04.39	46-47	44	-	2

JOHNSON, Joseph
South Kirkby, 16 May, 1916 (RH)

Doncaster Rov.		12.38				
Southport	Folkestone T.	12.46	46	5	-	0

JOHNSON, Joseph R.
Greenock, 13 September, 1920

Lincoln C.	Glasgow Rangers	11.52	52	11	-	2
Workington	Tr	07.53	53	38	-	5

JOHNSON, Kenneth
Hartlepool, 15 February, 1931 (IF)

Hartlepool U.	Seaton H.T.	05.49	49-63	384	-	98

JOHNSON, Kevin P.
Doncaster, 29 August, 1952 (M)

Sheffield Wed.	App	07.70	70	0	1	0
Southend U.	Tr	09.72	72-73	13	4	1
Gillingham	L	02.74	73	1	0	0
Workington	Tr	07.74	74	15	0	1
Hartlepool U.	Tr	02.75	74-76	60	1	9
Huddersfield T.	Tr	09.76	76-77	80	1	23
Halifax T.	Tr	08.78	78-80	51	6	10
Hartlepool U.	Tr	01.81	80-83	74	13	3

JOHNSON, Marvin A.
Wembley, 29 October, 1968 (CD)

League Club	Source	Date Signed	Seasons Played	Apps	Subs	Gls
Luton T.	App	10.86	87-90	54	9	0

JOHNSON, Michael
York, 4 October, 1933 (W)

League Club	Source	Date Signed	Seasons Played	Apps	Subs	Gls
Newcastle U.	Jnrs	04.51				
Brighton & H.A.		12.55	56	2	-	0
Fulham	Gloucester C.	08.58	58-61	23	-	6
Doncaster Rov.	Tr	07.62	62	15	-	2
Barrow	Tr	03.63	62	12	-	1

JOHNSON, Michael G.
Swansea, 13 October, 1941 Wu23-2/W-1 (CH)

League Club	Source	Date Signed	Seasons Played	Apps	Subs	Gls
Swansea C.	Jnrs	10.58	59-65	167	0	1

JOHNSON, Michael J.
Oxford, 24 February, 1928 (IF)

League Club	Source	Date Signed	Seasons Played	Apps	Subs	Gls
Preston N.E.	Lytham St Annes	09.50				
Accrington St.	Tr	06.51	51	3	-	0

JOHNSON, Michael O.
Nottingham, 4 July, 1973 (CD)

League Club	Source	Date Signed	Seasons Played	Apps	Subs	Gls
Notts Co.	YT	07.91	91	5	0	0

JOHNSON, Neil J.
Grimsby, 3 December, 1946 (W)

League Club	Source	Date Signed	Seasons Played	Apps	Subs	Gls
Tottenham H.	App	06.64	65-70	27	7	5
Charlton Ath.	L	02.71	70	1	0	0
Torquay U.	Tr	07.71	71	5	1	1

JOHNSON, Nigel M.
Rotherham, 23 June, 1964 (CD)

League Club	Source	Date Signed	Seasons Played	Apps	Subs	Gls
Rotherham U.	App	06.82	82-84	89	0	1
Manchester C.	Tr	06.85	85	4	0	0
Rotherham U.	Tr	07.87	87-91	141	3	7

JOHNSON, Owen E.
Grimsby, 13 November, 1919 (OL)

League Club	Source	Date Signed	Seasons Played	Apps	Subs	Gls
Derby Co.		11.37				
Bradford C.	Tr	10.46	46	10	-	1

JOHNSON, Paul
Stoke, 25 May, 1959 (LB)

League Club	Source	Date Signed	Seasons Played	Apps	Subs	Gls
Stoke C.	App	05.77	78-80	33	1	0
Shrewsbury T.	Tr	05.81	81-86	178	2	3
York C.	Tr	07.87	87-88	83	0	1

JOHNSON, Paul
Scunthorpe, 10 May, 1963 (G)

League Club	Source	Date Signed	Seasons Played	Apps	Subs	Gls
Scunthorpe U.	App	05.81	81	2	0	0
Scunthorpe U. (N/C)		01.85	85	12	0	0

JOHNSON, Paul A.
Stoke, 19 September, 1955 (M)

League Club	Source	Date Signed	Seasons Played	Apps	Subs	Gls
Stoke C.	App	06.73	76-81	51	5	0
Chester C.	Tr	08.82	82	18	1	0

JOHNSON, Peter
Rotherham, 31 July, 1931 (RB)

League Club	Source	Date Signed	Seasons Played	Apps	Subs	Gls
Rotherham U.	Rawmarsh Welfare	03.53	53-57	153	-	23
Sheffield Wed.	Tr	12.57	57-64	181	-	6
Peterborough U.	Tr	07.65	65-66	42	0	1

JOHNSON, Peter E.
Harrogate, 5 October, 1958 (LB)

League Club	Source	Date Signed	Seasons Played	Apps	Subs	Gls
Middlesbrough	App	10.76	77-79	42	1	0
Newcastle U.	Tr	10.80	80	16	0	0
Bristol C.	L	09.82	82	20	0	0
Doncaster Rov.	Tr	03.83	82	12	0	0
Darlington	Tr	08.83	83-84	89	0	2
Crewe Alex. (N/C)	Whitby T.	10.85	85	8	0	0
Exeter C. (N/C)	Whitby T.	03.86	85	5	0	0
Southend U.	Tr	08.86	86-88	126	0	3
Gillingham	Tr	08.89	89-90	67	2	2
Peterborough U. (N/C)		10.91	91	11	0	0

JOHNSON, Peter J.
Hackney, 18 February, 1954 (W)

League Club	Source	Date Signed	Seasons Played	Apps	Subs	Gls
Leyton Orient	Tottenham H. (Am)	04.72	71-72	1	2	0
Crystal Palace	Greece	10.74	74-75	5	2	0
Bournemouth	Tr	06.76	76-78	99	8	11

JOHNSON, V. Ralph
Hethersett (Nk), 15 April, 1922 (CF)

League Club	Source	Date Signed	Seasons Played	Apps	Subs	Gls
Norwich C.	Chesterfield (Am)	05.46	46	18	-	8
Leyton Orient	Tr	04.47	47-48	7	-	2

JOHNSON, Richard M.
Australia, 27 April, 1974 (M)

League Club	Source	Date Signed	Seasons Played	Apps	Subs	Gls
Watford	YT	05.92	91	1	1	0

JOHNSON, Richard R.
Liverpool, 20 February, 1953 (G)

League Club	Source	Date Signed	Seasons Played	Apps	Subs	Gls
Tranmere Rov.	Jnrs	08.72	71-81	355	0	0

JOHNSON, Robert E.
Fencehouses (Dm), 25 October, 1911 Died 1982 (CH)

League Club	Source	Date Signed	Seasons Played	Apps	Subs	Gls
Burnley	Bishop Auckland	09.34	34-48	78	-	0

JOHNSON, Robert N.
Kensington, 30 March, 1962 (D)

League Club	Source	Date Signed	Seasons Played	Apps	Subs	Gls
Arsenal	App	02.80				
Brentford	Tr	03.81	80-81	2	0	0

JOHNSON, Robert S. (Rob)
Bedford, 22 February, 1962 (FB)

League Club	Source	Date Signed	Seasons Played	Apps	Subs	Gls
Luton T.	App	08.79	83-88	91	6	0
Lincoln C.	L	08.83	83	4	0	0
Leicester C.	Tr	08.89	89-90	19	6	0
Barnet (N/C)	Tr	08.91	91	2	0	0

JOHNSON, Rodney
Leeds, 8 January, 1945 E Yth (M)

League Club	Source	Date Signed	Seasons Played	Apps	Subs	Gls
Leeds U.	Jnrs	03.62	62-67	18	4	4
Doncaster Rov.	Tr	03.68	67-70	106	1	23
Rotherham U.	Tr	12.70	70-73	108	2	8
Bradford C.	Tr	12.73	73-78	190	2	16

JOHNSON, Roy
Swindon, 18 May, 1933 (CF)

League Club	Source	Date Signed	Seasons Played	Apps	Subs	Gls
Swindon T.		04.52	52-55	31	-	4

JOHNSON, Samuel
Barnton, 10 February, 1919 (RB)

League Club	Source	Date Signed	Seasons Played	Apps	Subs	Gls
Hull C.	Northwich Vic.	04.47	46-47	10	-	0

JOHNSON, Stephen A.
Liverpool, 23 June, 1957 (F)

League Club	Source	Date Signed	Seasons Played	Apps	Subs	Gls
Bury	Altrincham	11.77	77-82	139	15	52
Rochdale	Tr	08.83	83	17	2	7
Wigan Ath.	Tr	02.84	83-84	50	1	18
Bristol C.	Tr	03.85	84-85	14	7	3
Rochdale	L	12.85	85	3	3	1
Chester C.	L	03.86	85	10	0	6
Scunthorpe U.	Tr	07.86	86-87	59	13	20
Chester C.	Tr	08.88	88	35	3	10
Rochdale	Huskvarna (Swe)	10.89	89	20	4	4

JOHNSON, Steven
Nottingham, 23 March, 1961 (LB)

League Club	Source	Date Signed	Seasons Played	Apps	Subs	Gls
Mansfield T.	App	03.79	80	1	0	0

JOHNSON, Terence
Newcastle, 30 August, 1949 (W)

League Club	Source	Date Signed	Seasons Played	Apps	Subs	Gls
Newcastle U.	Longbenton Jnrs	05.67				
Darlington	L	11.69	69	4	0	1
Southend U.	Tr	01.71	70-74	155	2	34
Brentford	Tr	11.74	74-76	98	3	27

JOHNSON, Thomas
Gateshead, 21 September, 1921 (IF)

League Club	Source	Date Signed	Seasons Played	Apps	Subs	Gls
Gateshead		09.41	46-47	52	-	19
Nottingham F.	Tr	08.48	48-51	68	-	27

JOHNSON, Thomas
Stockton, 5 March, 1926 (LH)

League Club	Source	Date Signed	Seasons Played	Apps	Subs	Gls
Middlesbrough		01.45				
Darlington	Tr	08.47	47	6	-	1
Bradford P.A.		08.52	52	1	-	0

JOHNSON, Thomas
Ecclesfield, 4 May, 1911 (CH)

League Club	Source	Date Signed	Seasons Played	Apps	Subs	Gls
Sheffield U.	Ecclesfield	09.28	29-38	182	-	0
Lincoln C.	Tr	03.46	46-48	75	-	0

JOHNSON, Thomas
Newcastle, 15 January, 1971 Eu21-7 (F)

League Club	Source	Date Signed	Seasons Played	Apps	Subs	Gls
Notts Co.	YT	01.89	88-91	100	18	47
Derby Co.	Tr	03.92	91	12	0	2

JOHNSTON, Alan K.
Workington, 23 September, 1944 (FB)

League Club	Source	Date Signed	Seasons Played	Apps	Subs	Gls
Blackpool	Jnrs	10.61				
Workington	Tr	07.62	62-64	65	-	0

League Club	Source	Date Signed	Seasons Played	Career Record Apps	Subs	Gls

JOHNSTON, Clement
Lothian, 3 September, 1933

Walsall	Haddington	08.56	56	7	-	2

JOHNSTON, Craig P.
South Africa, 8 December, 1960 Eu21-2 (W)

Middlesbrough	App	02.78	77-80	61	3	16
Liverpool	Tr	04.81	81-87	165	25	30

JOHNSTON, David
Scothern (Lincs), 17 September, 1941 (FB)

Leicester C.	Bishop Auckland	02.60				
Exeter C.	Tr	05.62	62	10	-	0
Stockport Co.	Tr	07.63	63	26	-	0

JOHNSTON, George
Glasgow, 21 March, 1947 (F)

Cardiff C.	Jnrs	05.64	64-66	57	3	21
Arsenal	Tr	03.67	67-68	17	4	3
Birmingham C.	Tr	05.69	69	6	3	1
Walsall	L	09.70	70	5	0	1
Fulham	Tr	10.70	70-71	33	6	12
Hereford U.	Tr	08.72	72	15	3	5
Newport Co.	Tr	09.73	73	2	1	0

JOHNSTON, Henry (Harry)
Manchester, 26 September, 1919 Died 1973 EF Lge/E-10 (CH)

Blackpool	Droylsden Ath.	10.36	37-54	386	-	11

JOHNSTON, Ian
Workington, 19 September, 1957 (CD)

Workington	Jnrs	08.75	74-76	46	2	0

JOHNSTON, James C.
Aberdeen, 12 April, 1923 (WH)

Leicester C.	Aberdeen	04.47	48-49	35	-	0
Reading	Tr	05.50	50-52	120	-	0
Swindon T.	Tr	03.53	52-54	75	-	0

JOHNSTON, John
Belfast, 2 May, 1947 NIu23-1 (M)

Blackpool	Glentoran	11.68	68-71	19	5	2
Halifax T.	L	10.71	71	3	1	1

Tommy Johnson (Notts County & Derby County)

League Club	Source	Date Signed	Seasons Played	Career Record Apps	Subs	Gls
Bradford C.	Tr	07.72	72-73	55	4	4
Southport	Tr	07.74	74-75	82	0	6
Halifax T.	Tr	07.76	76-78	67	6	7

JOHNSTON, Leslie H.
Glasgow, 16 August, 1920 S-2 (IF)

Stoke C.	Glasgow Celtic	10.49	49-52	88	-	21
Shrewsbury T.	Tr	07.53	53	16	-	6

JOHNSTON, Maurice T. (Mo)
Glasgow, 30 April, 1963 Su21-3/S-38 (F)

Watford	Partick Th.	11.83	83-84	37	1	23
Everton	Glasgow Rangers	11.91	91	21	0	7

JOHNSTON, C. Patrick (Paddy)
Dublin, 16 July, 1924 Died 1971 LOI (WH)

Middlesbrough	Shelbourne	12.47	47-48	3	-	0
Grimsby T.	Tr	02.49	48-56	250	-	16

JOHNSTON, Robert
Carlisle, 28 January, 1933 (WH)

Carlisle U.		11.51	51-59	122	-	1

JOHNSTON, Ronald
Glasgow, 3 April, 1921 (CF)

Rochdale	Glasgow Perthshire	11.47	47	17	-	7
Exeter C.	Tr	06.48	48	10	-	2
Brighton & H.A.	Headington U.	11.50	50	1	-	0

Harry Johnston (Blackpool & England)

League Club	Source	Date Signed	Seasons Played	Career Record Apps	Subs	Gls

JOHNSTON, Stanley
Wallsend, 23 February, 1934 (F)

Fulham	Jnrs	08.51				
Gateshead	Durham C.	09.54	54	10	-	1

JOHNSTON, Thomas B.
Loanhead, 18 August, 1927 (CF)

Darlington	Kilmarnock	04.51	51	27	-	9
Oldham Ath.	Tr	03.52	51	5	-	3
Norwich C.	Tr	06.52	52-54	60	-	28
Newport Co.	Tr	10.54	54-55	63	-	45
Leyton Orient	Tr	02.56	55-57	87	-	70
Blackburn Rov.	Tr	03.58	57-58	36	-	21
Leyton Orient	Tr	02.59	58-60	93	-	51
Gillingham	Tr	09.61	61	35	-	10

JOHNSTON, Thomas D.
Berwick, 30 December, 1918 (OL)

Nottingham F.	Peterborough U.	05.44	46-47	64	-	26
Notts Co.	Tr	08.48	48-56	268	-	86

JOHNSTON, William
(G)

Barrow	Morton	04.47	46	1	-	0

JOHNSTON, William C.
Dungannon, 21 May, 1942 NI-2 (IF)

Oldham Ath.	Glenavon	06.66	66-68	28	1	6

JOHNSTON, William J.
Sunderland, 3 September, 1948 (F)

Northampton T.		07.67	67	0	1	0

JOHNSTON, William M.
Glasgow, 19 December, 1946 Su23-2/SF Lge/S-22 (W)

West Bromwich A.	Glasgow Rangers	12.72	72-78	203	4	18
Birmingham C.	Vancouver (Can)	10.79	79	15	0	0

JOHNSTONE, Cyril
Hamilton, 21 December, 1920 (FB)

Exeter C.	Hamilton Acad.	07.47	47-50	134	-	0

JOHNSTONE, Derek J.
Dundee, 4 November, 1953 Su23-6/S-14 (F)

Chelsea	Glasgow Rangers	09.83	83-84	1	3	0

JOHNSTONE, Eric
Newcastle, 22 March, 1943 (OL)

Carlisle U.	Tow Law T.	06.63	63-64	15	-	3
Darlington	Tr	07.65	65-66	27	1	10

JOHNSTONE, R. Gordon
Edinburgh, 19 November, 1934 (WH)

West Ham U.	Ormiston Primrose	04.53	56	2	-	0
Ipswich T.	Tr	07.57	57-58	35	-	4

JOHNSTONE, Ian D.
Galashiels, 2 March, 1939 (F)

Colchester U.	Ormiston Primrose	06.58	58-59	2	-	0

JOHNSTONE, James C.
Glasgow, 30 September, 1944 Su23-2/SF Lge/S-23 (W)

Sheffield U.	Glasgow Celtic	11.75	75-76	11	0	2

JOHNSTONE, Robert
Cleland, 13 September, 1918 (WH)

Tranmere Rov.	Raith Rov.	09.46	46-47	40	-	0

JOHNSTONE, Robert
Selkirk, 7 September, 1929 SF Lge/S-17 (IF)

Manchester C.	Hibernian	03.55	54-59	124	-	42
Oldham Ath.	Hibernian	10.60	60-64	143	-	36

JOHNSTONE, Stanley
Shiremoor, 28 October, 1940

Gateshead	Durham C.	12.58	58	5	-	1

JOICEY, Brian
Winlaton, 19 December, 1945 (F)

Coventry C.	North Shields	06.69	69-71	31	8	9
Sheffield Wed.	Tr	08.71	71-75	144	1	48
Barnsley	Tr	07.76	76-78	77	16	43

JOL, Martin C.
Netherlands, 16 January, 1956 (M)

West Bromwich A.	Twente Enschede (Neth)	10.81	81-83	63	1	4
Coventry C.	Tr	07.84	84	15	0	0

League Club	Source	Date Signed	Seasons Played	Career Record Apps	Subs	Gls

JOLLEY, Charles
Liverpool, 3 March, 1936 E Yth (CF)

Tranmere Rov.	Liverpool (Am)	07.53	53-54	6	-	2
Chester C.	Tr	05.55	55	7	-	3

JOLLEY, Terence A.
Greenhithe, 13 April, 1959 (F)

Gillingham	Jnrs	11.76	76-79	14	7	5

JONES, J. Alan
Wrexham, 12 September, 1939 (G)

Cardiff C.	Druids	06.57	57	1	-	0
Exeter C.	Tr	07.59	59-61	90	-	0
Norwich C.	Tr	07.62	62	9	-	0
Wrexham	Tr	08.63	63	18	-	0

JONES, Alan
Abermodda, 13 January, 1944 (OR)

Wrexham		07.64	64	2	-	0

JONES, Alan
Grimethorpe, 21 January, 1951 (W)

Huddersfield T.	App	12.68	70-72	30	2	0
Halifax T.	Tr	08.73	73-76	109	0	6
Chesterfield	Tr	09.76	76-77	39	0	5
Lincoln C.	Tr	11.77	77-78	24	2	4
Bradford C.	Tr	09.79	79	16	3	1
Rochdale	Tr	08.80	80	40	4	5

JONES, Alan H.
Wrexham, 22 September, 1949 W Sch (CH)

Shrewsbury T.	App	05.67	68	3	0	0

JONES, Alan M.
Swansea, 6 October, 1945 (CD)

Swansea C.	App	10.63	64-67	59	0	5
Hereford U.	Tr	07.68	72-73	52	1	2
Southport	Tr	08.74	74-75	49	0	2

JONES, Alan P.
Flint, 6 January, 1940 W Sch (FB)

Liverpool	Jnrs	05.57	59-62	5	-	0
Brentford	Tr	08.63	63-69	244	5	2

JONES, Alan R.
Burton, 3 November, 1941 (W)

Aston Villa	Jnrs	11.58	61	1	-	0

JONES, Alan W. E.
Paddington, 19 September, 1940 (CF)

Fulham	Jnrs	04.58	59	7	-	3

JONES, Alexander
Blackburn, 27 November, 1964 (CD)

Oldham Ath.	App	12.82	82-84	8	1	0
Stockport Co.	L	10.84	84	3	0	0
Preston N.E.	Tr	06.86	86-89	100	1	3
Carlisle U.	Tr	09.89	89-90	62	0	4
Rochdale	Tr	06.91	91	12	1	0

JONES, Alfred
Liverpool, 2 March, 1937 (FB)

Leeds U.	Marine	04.60	60-61	25	-	0
Lincoln C.	Tr	06.62	62-66	177	1	3

JONES, Andrew M.
Wrexham, 9 January, 1963 W-6 (F)

Port Vale	Rhyl	06.85	85-87	87	3	47
Charlton Ath.	Tr	09.87	87-90	51	15	15
Port Vale	L	02.89	88	8	9	3
Bristol C.	L	11.89	89	2	2	1
Bournemouth	Tr	10.90	90-91	36	4	8
Leyton Orient	Tr	10.91	91	20	10	5

JONES, Anthony P.
Birmingham, 12 November, 1937 (IF/WH)

Oxford U.	Birmingham C. (Am)	09.59	62-67	226	0	41
Newport Co.	Tr	11.67	67-68	53	1	9

JONES, Arthur
(OR)

Rochdale	Goslings	06.45	46	1	-	0

JONES, Barrie
Barnsley, 31 October, 1938 (CF)

Notts Co.		09.61	61-63	42	-	15

JONES, Barrie S.
Swansea, 10 October, 1941 Wu23-8/W-15 (OR)

League Club	Source	Date Signed	Seasons Played	Apps	Subs	Gls
Swansea C.	Jnrs	04.59	59-64	166	-	23
Plymouth Arg.	Tr	09.64	64-66	98	1	9
Cardiff C.	Tr	03.67	66-69	107	0	18

JONES, T. Benjamin
Frodsham, 23 March, 1920 Died 1973 (W)

League Club	Source	Date Signed	Seasons Played	Apps	Subs	Gls
Tranmere Rov.	Ellesmere Port	09.41	46-47	54	-	19
Chelsea	Tr	11.47	47-51	55	-	11
Accrington St.	Tr	07.53	53	14	-	0

JONES, Bernard
Coventry, 10 April, 1934 (IF)

League Club	Source	Date Signed	Seasons Played	Apps	Subs	Gls
Northampton T.		10.52	53-55	43	-	16
Cardiff C.	Tr	03.56	55-56	9	-	0
Shrewsbury T.	Tr	07.57	57-58	43	-	4

JONES, Bernard
Stoke, 27 September, 1924

League Club	Source	Date Signed	Seasons Played	Apps	Subs	Gls
Port Vale		10.48	48	6	-	0

JONES, Brian
Barnsley, 15 September, 1938 (FB)

League Club	Source	Date Signed	Seasons Played	Apps	Subs	Gls
Barnsley	Jnrs	05.57	57-58	15	-	0
York C.	Tr	05.59	59	1	-	0

JONES, Brian
Doncaster, 5 September, 1933

League Club	Source	Date Signed	Seasons Played	Apps	Subs	Gls
Walsall		11.53	53	2	-	0

JONES, Bryn
Merthyr Tydfil, 14 February, 1912 Died 1985 W-17 (IF)

League Club	Source	Date Signed	Seasons Played	Apps	Subs	Gls
Wolverhampton W.	Aberaman	10.33	33-37	163	-	52
Arsenal	Tr	08.38	38-48	71	-	7
Norwich C.	Tr	06.49	49	23	-	1

Andy Jones (Port Vale, Charlton Athletic, Bournemouth & Leyton Orient)

JONES, Bryn E.
Bagillt, 26 May, 1939 (FB)

League Club	Source	Date Signed	Seasons Played	Apps	Subs	Gls
Watford	Holywell	01.63	62	2	-	0
Chester C.	Tr	08.64	64-66	30	0	0

JONES, Bryn H.
Llandrindod Wells, 8 February, 1948 W Sch/Wu23-1 (M)

League Club	Source	Date Signed	Seasons Played	Apps	Subs	Gls
Cardiff C.	App	02.66	66-67	1	2	0
Newport Co.	L	02.69	68	13	0	0
Bristol Rov.	Tr	06.69	69-74	84	6	6

JONES, Bryn R.
Swansea, 20 May, 1931 Died 1990 (FB)

League Club	Source	Date Signed	Seasons Played	Apps	Subs	Gls
Swansea C.		09.51	52-57	121	-	4
Newport Co.	Tr	06.58	58-59	71	-	11
Bournemouth	Tr	02.60	59-63	118	-	5
Northampton T.	Tr	10.63	63	7	-	0
Watford	Tr	11.63	63-66	90	1	1

JONES, Brynley
St Asaph, 16 May, 1959 (M)

League Club	Source	Date Signed	Seasons Played	Apps	Subs	Gls
Chester C.	App	05.77	76-81	149	13	17

JONES, Christopher H.
Jersey, 18 April, 1956 Eu21-1

League Club	Source	Date Signed	Seasons Played	Apps	Subs	Gls
Tottenham H.	App	05.73	74-81	149	15	37
Manchester C.	Tr	09.82	82	3	0	0
Crystal Palace	Tr	11.82	82	18	0	3
Charlton Ath.	Tr	09.83	83	17	6	2
Leyton Orient	Tr	09.84	84-86	106	1	19

JONES, Christopher M. N.
Altrincham, 19 November, 1945 (F)

League Club	Source	Date Signed	Seasons Played	Apps	Subs	Gls
Manchester C.	Jnrs	05.64	66-67	6	1	2
Swindon T.	Tr	07.68	68-71	49	19	18
Oldham Ath.	L	01.72	71	3	0	1
Walsall	Tr	02.72	71-72	54	5	14
York C.	Tr	06.73	73-75	94	1	34
Huddersfield T.	Tr	08.76	76	9	5	2
Doncaster Rov.	Tr	07.77	77-78	14	6	4
Darlington	L	01.78	77	14	2	3
Rochdale	Tr	12.78	78-79	51	5	19

JONES, Clifford W.
Swansea, 7 February, 1935 Wu23-1/EF Lge/W-59 (W)

League Club	Source	Date Signed	Seasons Played	Apps	Subs	Gls
Swansea C.	Jnrs	05.52	52-57	168	-	47
Tottenham H.	Tr	02.58	57-68	314	4	135
Fulham	Tr	10.68	68-69	23	2	2

JONES, G. Colin
Chester, 8 September, 1940 (HB)

League Club	Source	Date Signed	Seasons Played	Apps	Subs	Gls
Chester C.	Jnrs	06.60	59	2	-	0

JONES, Colin M.
Birmingham, 30 October, 1963 (W)

League Club	Source	Date Signed	Seasons Played	Apps	Subs	Gls
West Bromwich A.	App	10.81				
Mansfield T. (N/C)		01.85	84	5	0	0

JONES, Cyril
Rhos, 17 July, 1920 (RB)

League Club	Source	Date Signed	Seasons Played	Apps	Subs	Gls
Wrexham	Johnstown	02.42	46	29	-	0

JONES, David
Blaenau Ffestiniog, 8 September, 1914 (G)

League Club	Source	Date Signed	Seasons Played	Apps	Subs	Gls
Stoke C.	Colwyn Bay U.	03.37	38	1	-	0
Carlisle U.	Tr	05.39	46-47	66	-	0

JONES, David
Wrexham, 6 May, 1971 (W)

League Club	Source	Date Signed	Seasons Played	Apps	Subs	Gls
Aston Villa	YT	06.89				
Wrexham	Tr	01.92	91	0	1	0

JONES, David
Whitwell, 9 April, 1914 (WH)

League Club	Source	Date Signed	Seasons Played	Apps	Subs	Gls
Bury	Worksop T.	08.34	34-49	257	-	12

JONES, David
Swansea, 3 March, 1935 (G)

League Club	Source	Date Signed	Seasons Played	Apps	Subs	Gls
Swansea C.		12.55	56-57	3	-	0

League Club	Source	Date Signed	Seasons Played	Career Record Apps	Subs	Gls

JONES, David
Aberdare, 7 January, 1932 (G)

Brentford	Dover T.	12.51				
Reading	Tr	07.53	53-60	215	-	0
Aldershot	Tr	07.61	61-65	187	0	0

JONES, David A. B. (Dai)
Neath, 31 March, 1941 W Yth (F)

Millwall	Ton Pentre	03.64	63-64	12	-	3
Newport Co.	Tr	07.65	65-67	81	0	25
Mansfield T.	Tr	11.67	67-71	116	14	32
Newport Co.	Tr	11.71	71-73	43	4	12

JONES, David B.
Harrow, 3 July, 1964 (F)

Chelsea	New Zealand	11.87				
Bury (N/C)	Barnet	09.88	88	0	1	0
Leyton Orient (N/C)	Barnet	12.88	88	0	2	0
Burnley (N/C)	Barnet	02.89	88	4	0	0
Ipswich T. (N/C)	U.S.A.	10.89				
Doncaster Rov.	Tr	11.89	89-90	34	6	14
Bury	Tr	09.91	91	0	9	0

JONES, David E.
Chester, 5 March, 1936 (W)

Wrexham		04.55	56-58	70	-	11
Crewe Alex.	Tr	07.59	59	1	-	1

JONES, David E.
Gosport, 11 February,1952 Wu23-4/W-8 (CD)

Bournemouth	App	01.70	70-74	128	6	5
Nottingham F.	Tr	08.74	74	36	0	1
Norwich C.	Tr	09.75	75-79	120	3	4

JONES, David F.
Brixham, 18 May, 1950 (M)

Arsenal	App	02.68				
Oxford U.	Middlesbrough	10.68	68-70	17	4	0
Torquay U.	Tr	07.72	72	0	1	0

JONES, David H.
Tetbury, 4 August, 1937 (HB)

Leeds U.	Gloucester C.	12.54				
Crewe Alex.	Tr	05.60	60-61	15	-	0

JONES, David H.
Bradford, 29 December, 1950 (W)

Wolverhampton W.		08.68				
York C.	Tr	08.70	70	3	0	0

JONES, David J.
Ruabon, 16 September, 1952 (F)

Hereford U.	Telford U.	05.78	78-79	44	3	11

JONES, David O.
Cardiff, 28 October, 1910 Died 1971 W-7 (FB)

Leyton Orient	Ebbw Vale	08.31	31-32	55	-	0
Leicester C.	Tr	05.33	32-46	227	-	4
Mansfield T.	Tr	10.47	47-48	74	-	0

JONES, David R.
Onllwyn, 18 January, 1946 (G)

Derby Co.		07.65				
Newport Co.	Burton A.	05.68	67-68	3	0	0

JONES, David R.
Liverpool, 17 August, 1956 E Yth/Eu21-1 (CD)

Everton	App	05.74	75-78	79	7	1
Coventry C.	Tr	06.79	79-80	8	3	0
Preston N.E.	Seiko (HK)	08.83	83-84	50	0	1

JONES, David W. L.
Kingsley (Ches), 9 April, 1940 E Yth (IF)

Crewe Alex. (Am)	Jnrs	05.56	56	10	-	1
Birmingham C.	Tr	04.57	57-58	9	-	0
Millwall	Tr	12.59	59-63	165	-	71

JONES, Dennis J.
Aberdare, 19 October, 1930 (OR)

Norwich C.	Yarmouth T.	04.51	51-52	5	-	2

JONES, F. W. Derek
Ellesmere Port, 24 April, 1929 (FB)

Tranmere Rov.	Ellesmere Port	07.53	53-60	155	-	19

League Club	Source	Date Signed	Seasons Played	Career Record Apps	Subs	Gls

JONES, Desmond
Rhondda, 15 March, 1930 (W)

Swansea C.	Jnrs	01.48				
Bristol Rov.	Tr	06.52	52	6	-	0
Workington	Tr	07.54	54-59	210	-	23

JONES, Dilwyn B.
Swansea, 2 January, 1937 (HB)

Leeds U.	Jnrs	01.54				
Crewe Alex.	Tr	02.58	57	15	-	1

JONES, Edward M.
Abercynon, 20 March, 1914 W Sch (OR)

Bolton W. (Am)	Abercynon	04.33	33	1	-	1
Swindon T.	Tr	05.36	36-46	124	-	18

JONES, Edward W.G.
Finchley, 17 September, 1952 W Sch (FB)

Tottenham H.	Jnrs	10.70				
Millwall	Tr	07.73	73-75	58	1	0

JONES, Eric
Ulverston, 23 June, 1931 (W)

Preston N.E.	Notts Co. (Am)	01.52	53-54	13	-	0
Nottingham F.	Tr	09.55	55-57	18	-	3
Doncaster Rov.	Tr	03.58	57-58	15	-	2
Accrington St.	Tr	07.59	59	18	-	0
Southport	Tr	07.60	60-61	76	-	18

JONES, Eric J.
Dover, 5 March, 1938 (HB)

Coventry C.	Snowdown Colly	05.55	55-60	14	-	0

JONES, Eric N.
Birmingham, 5 February, 1915 (W)

Wolverhampton W.	Kidderminster Hrs	10.36	36	3	-	0
Portsmouth	Tr	11.37	37	1	-	0
Stoke C.	Tr	09.38				
West Bromwich A.	Tr	05.39				
Brentford	Tr	12.45				
Crewe Alex.	Tr	07.46	46-47	53	-	14

JONES, W. Ernest A.
Swansea, 12 November, 1920 W-4 (W)

Swansea C.	Bolton W. (Am)	10.43	46	37	-	3
Tottenham H.	Tr	06.47	46-48	56	-	14
Southampton	Tr	05.49	49-51	44	-	4
Bristol C.	Tr	11.51	51-53	50	-	7

JONES, Ernest
Ruabon, 9 December, 1919 (F)

Chester C.		08.49	49-50	6	-	1

JONES, Ernest J.
Bristol, 12 May, 1919 (LH)

Bristol C.	Jnrs	08.39	46-47	27	-	1

JONES, Frank
Llandudno, 3 October, 1960 Wu21-1 (D)

Wrexham	Jnrs	07.79	78-80	8	0	0
Wrexham		09.84	84-86	30	1	0

JONES, Frederick A.
Stoke, 21 October, 1922

Port Vale	South Liverpool	06.46	46	12	-	1

JONES, Frederick G.
Gelligaer, 11 January, 1938 Wu23-2 (OL)

Arsenal	Hereford U.	01.58				
Brighton & H.A.	Tr	09.58	58-60	69	-	14
Swindon T.	Tr	12.60	60	18	-	1
Grimsby T.	Tr	07.61	61-62	58	-	9
Reading	Tr	07.63	63	30	-	5

JONES, Gary
Huddersfield, 6 April, 1969 (F)

Doncaster Rov.	Rossington Main Colly	01.89	88-89	10	10	2

JONES, Gary A.
Cardiff, 18 June, 1952 (W)

Torquay U.		10.72	72-73	11	5	0
Bournemouth	Tr	03.74	73-74	1	3	0

JONES, Gary E.
Wythenshawe, 11 December, 1950 (F)

Bolton W.	App	01.68	68-78	195	8	41
Sheffield U.	L	02.75	74	3	0	1
Blackpool	Tr	11.78	78-79	18	9	5
Hereford U.	Tr	08.80	80	21	4	4

League Club	Source	Date Signed	Seasons Played	Career Record Apps	Subs	Gls
JONES, Gary K.						
Whiston, 5 January, 1951						(W)
Everton	Jnrs	10.68	70-75	76	6	12
Birmingham C.	Tr	07.76	76-77	33	2	1
JONES, George						
Wrexham, 19 July, 1930						(WH)
Wrexham		08.50	50-53	113	-	5
JONES, George A.						
Radcliffe, 21 April, 1945 E Yth						(F)
Bury	App	06.62	61-63	63	-	14
Blackburn Rov.	Tr	03.64	63-66	36	3	14
Bury	Tr	11.66	66-72	249	7	100
Oldham Ath.	Tr	03.73	72-75	63	8	19
Halifax T.	Tr	02.76	75-76	18	1	4
Southport	Tr	01.77	76-77	54	1	11
JONES, George H.						
Sheffield, 27 November, 1918						(OL)
Sheffield U.	Woodburn Alliance	08.36	36-50	141	-	35
Barnsley	Tr	02.51	50-51	22	-	6
JONES, Gerald						
Burslem, 30 December, 1945						(W)
Stoke C.	App	06.63	64-66	7	0	0
JONES, Gerald K.						
Newport, 21 April, 1950						(W)
Luton T.	Barry T.	07.72				
Crewe Alex.	L	02.73	72	6	1	1
JONES, Glanville						
Merthyr Tydfil, 27 February, 1921						(OL)
Hull C.	Merthyr Tydfil	06.46	46	7	-	0
Bournemouth	Tr	05.47	48	9	-	3
Crewe Alex.	Tr	03.49				
JONES, Glyn						
Rotherham, 8 April, 1936 E Yth						(F)
Sheffield U.	Rotherham U. (Am)	06.54	55-57	29	-	4
Rotherham U.	Tr	12.57	57-58	22	-	6
Mansfield T.	Tr	07.59	59-60	45	-	18
JONES, Glyn A.						
Newport, 29 March, 1959						(G)
Bristol Rov.	App	03.77	77-79	9	0	0
Shrewsbury T.	Tr	07.80				
Newport Co. (N/C)	Newport Y.M.C.A.	09.83	83	3	0	0
JONES, Gordon E.						
Sedgefield, 6 March, 1943 E Yth/Eu23-9						(FB)
Middlesbrough	Jnrs	03.60	60-72	457	5	4
Darlington	Tr	02.73	72-74	80	5	5
JONES, Graham						
Worsley, 2 June, 1959						(CD)
Luton T.	App	06.76	75-79	31	8	0
Torquay U.	Tr	01.80	79-82	114	0	6
Stockport Co.	Tr	07.83	83	32	3	2
JONES, Graham						
Bradford, 5 October, 1957						(D)
Bradford C. (N/C)	Jnrs	06.76	75-77	1	3	0
JONES, Graham O.						
Wrexham, 16 September, 1949						(CH)
Wrexham	Jnrs	10.67	67	3	0	0
JONES, Grenville A.						
Nuneaton, 23 November, 1932 E Sch/E Yth						(OR)
West Bromwich A.	Jnrs	12.49	53	2	-	0
Wrexham	Tr	06.55	55-60	241	-	36
JONES, J. Gwllym						
Cardigan, 3 April, 1925						(CF)
Torquay U.	Abergwynfi	09.47	47	6	-	1
JONES, Gwyn						
Llandwrog, 20 March, 1935						(FB)
Wolverhampton W.	Caernarfon T.	09.55	55-61	21	-	0
Bristol Rov.	Tr	08.62	62-65	153	0	0
JONES, Gwyn						
Newport, 20 November, 1932						(F)
Leeds U.	Llanelli	08.50				
York C.	Tr	09.53				
Walsall	Tr	11.53	53	11	-	0

League Club	Source	Date Signed	Seasons Played	Career Record Apps	Subs	Gls
JONES, Harold						
Liverpool, 22 May, 1933						(HB)
Liverpool	Jnrs	02.52	53	1	-	0
JONES, Harvey C.						
Rhos, 16 August, 1936						(HB)
Wrexham (Am)	Liverpool (Am)	11.59	59	13	-	0
Chester C.	Tr	08.60	60	19	-	0
JONES, Haydn						
Caernarfon, 8 May, 1946						(FB)
Wrexham	Caernarfon T.	06.64	64-65	15	1	0
JONES, Henry						
Hartlepool, 28 September, 1918						(WH)
Hartlepool U.		09.46	46-48	75	-	1
JONES, Herbert N.						
Mold, 20 January, 1929						(IF)
Wrexham	Colwyn Bay	07.51	51	1	-	0
JONES, Idwal G.						
Ton Pentre, 3 August, 1924						(OR)
Swansea C.	Ton Pentre	10.46	46	4	-	0
JONES, Islwyn						
Merthyr Tydfil, 8 April, 1935						(CH)
Cardiff C.	Jnrs	11.52	54-55	26	-	0
JONES, Ivor J.						
Rhondda, 1 April, 1925						(OR)
Crystal Palace		06.46	46	1	-	1
JONES, B. James						
Rhondda, 16 November, 1919 Died 1976 W Amat						(FB)
Watford	Slough T.	09.47	47-53	158	-	0
JONES, James A.						
Birkenhead, 3 August, 1927						(G)
Everton		12.45				
New Brighton	Tr	08.50	50	32	-	0
Lincoln C.	Tr	08.51	51-53	76	-	0
Accrington St.	Tr	02.54	53-54	46	-	0
Rochdale	Tr	09.55	55-60	177	-	0
JONES, James M.						
Manchester						(IF)
Hull C. (Am)		05.47	46	1	-	0
JONES, John						
Gourock						(IL)
Bradford C.	Third Lanark	09.46	46	2	-	1
JONES, John						
Wrexham, 9 April, 1921						(IF)
Wrexham		09.46	46-47	20	-	1
Doncaster Rov.	Tr	07.48	48	6	-	0
New Brighton	Tr	08.49	49-50	77	-	11
JONES, John E.						
Bromborough, 3 July, 1913						(FB)
Everton	Ellesmere Port	03.32	33-37	98	-	10
Sunderland	Tr	12.45	46	24	-	0
JONES, John M.						
Llanelli, 31 October, 1924						(OL)
Fulham	Larne	01.47	47	1	-	0
Millwall	Tr	03.50	49-50	27	-	7
JONES, John T.						
Holywell, 25 November, 1916 W Sch						(G)
Port Vale		12.36	36	3	-	0
Northampton T.	Tr	05.37	38-47	71	-	0
Oldham Ath.	Tr	08.48	48	22	-	0
JONES, Joseph P.						
Llandudno, 4 March, 1955 Wu23-4/W-72						(D)
Wrexham	Jnrs	01.73	72-74	98	0	2
Liverpool	Tr	07.75	75-77	72	0	3
Wrexham	Tr	10.78	78-82	145	1	6
Chelsea	Tr	10.82	82-84	76	2	2
Huddersfield T.	Tr	08.85	85-86	67	1	3
Wrexham	Tr	08.87	87-91	131	1	11
JONES, Keith						
Nantyglo, 23 October, 1928 W-1						(G)
Aston Villa	Kidderminster Hrs	05.46	47-56	185	-	0
Port Vale	Tr	07.57	57-58	66	-	0
Crewe Alex.	Tr	04.59	58-59	46	-	0
Southport	Tr	07.60				

JONES, Keith A.
Dulwich, 14 October, 1965 E Sch/E Yth (M)

League Club	Source	Date Signed	Seasons Played	Apps	Subs	Gls
Chelsea	App	08.83	82-86	43	9	7
Brentford	Tr	09.87	87-91	167	2	13
Southend U.	Tr	10.91	91	33	1	5

JONES, Kenneth
Easington, 1 October, 1936 E Sch (FB)

League Club	Source	Date Signed	Seasons Played	Apps	Subs	Gls
Sunderland	Jnrs	10.53	59	10	-	0
Hartlepool U.	Tr	01.61	60-61	33	-	0

JONES, Kenneth
Aberdare, 2 January, 1936 Wu23-1 (G)

League Club	Source	Date Signed	Seasons Played	Apps	Subs	Gls
Cardiff C.	Jnrs	05.53	57-58	24	-	0
Scunthorpe U.	Tr	12.58	58-63	168	-	0
Charlton Ath.	Tr	09.64	64-65	25	0	0
Exeter C.	Tr	06.66	66	17	0	0

JONES, Kenneth
Havercroft, 26 June, 1944 (FB)

League Club	Source	Date Signed	Seasons Played	Apps	Subs	Gls
Bradford P.A.	Monkton Colly	09.61	62-64	100	-	3
Southampton	Tr	06.65	65-69	79	0	0
Cardiff C.	Tr	07.71	71	6	0	0

JONES, Kenneth B.
Rhos, 11 May, 1937 (FB)

League Club	Source	Date Signed	Seasons Played	Apps	Subs	Gls
Wrexham	Jnrs	05.54	57-59	31	-	0
Crystal Palace	Tr	06.60	60	4	-	0
Swindon T.	Tr	03.61	60-61	35	-	0

JONES, Kenneth B.
Keighley, 9 February, 1941 (M)

League Club	Source	Date Signed	Seasons Played	Apps	Subs	Gls
Southend U.		10.60	60-63	86	-	35
Millwall	Tr	09.64	64-69	175	3	11
Colchester U.	Tr	11.69	69-71	72	5	23

JONES, Kevin R.
Wrexham, 16 February, 1974 (F)

League Club	Source	Date Signed	Seasons Played	Apps	Subs	Gls
Wrexham (YT)	YT	07.90	91	0	1	0

JONES, P. Lee
Wrexham, 29 May, 1973 W Yth/Wu21-1 (F)

League Club	Source	Date Signed	Seasons Played	Apps	Subs	Gls
Wrexham	YT	07.91	90-91	24	15	9
Liverpool	Tr	03.92				

JONES, Leonard
Barnsley, 9 June, 1913 (OR)

League Club	Source	Date Signed	Seasons Played	Apps	Subs	Gls
Barnsley	Huddersfield T. (Am)	08.33	34-37	57	-	0
Plymouth Arg.	Chelmsford C.	05.39	46-48	39	-	2
Southend U.	Tr	08.49	49	29	-	0
Colchester U.	Tr	07.50	50-52	71	-	3

JONES, Leslie
Ynysybwl, 8 December, 1922 (IF)

League Club	Source	Date Signed	Seasons Played	Apps	Subs	Gls
Millwall		12.47	48-51	7	-	1

JONES, Leslie A.
Wrexham, 9 November, 1940 W Sch (IF)

League Club	Source	Date Signed	Seasons Played	Apps	Subs	Gls
Bolton W.	Jnrs	11.57				
Tranmere Rov.	Tr	07.62	62-64	68	-	29
Chester C.	Tr	04.65	65-68	132	3	35

JONES, Leslie C.
Mountain Ash, 1 January, 1930 (FB)

League Club	Source	Date Signed	Seasons Played	Apps	Subs	Gls
Luton T.	Craig Ath.	10.50	50-57	99	-	1
Aston Villa	Tr	01.58	57	5	-	0

JONES, Leslie J.
Aberdare, 1 July, 1911 Died 1981 W-11 (IF)

League Club	Source	Date Signed	Seasons Played	Apps	Subs	Gls
Cardiff C.	Aberdare Ath.	08.29	29-33	139	-	31
Coventry C.	Tr	01.34	33-37	138	-	70
Arsenal	Tr	11.37	37-38	46	-	3
Swansea C.	Tr	06.46	46	2	-	0
Brighton & H.A.	Barry T.	08.48	48	3	-	0

JONES, Linden
Tredegar, 5 March, 1961 Wu21-3 (RB/M)

League Club	Source	Date Signed	Seasons Played	Apps	Subs	Gls
Cardiff C.	App	03.79	78-83	142	3	2
Newport Co.	Tr	09.83	83-86	141	0	5
Reading	Tr	07.87	87-91	147	5	8

JONES, Mark
Barnsley, 15 June, 1933 Died 1958 E Sch (CH)

League Club	Source	Date Signed	Seasons Played	Apps	Subs	Gls
Manchester U.	Jnrs	07.50	50-57	103	-	1

JONES, Mark
Brownhills, 4 January, 1968 (RW/B)

League Club	Source	Date Signed	Seasons Played	Apps	Subs	Gls
Walsall	App	01.86	87	6	2	0
Exeter C.	L	11.88	88	5	0	0
Hereford U.	Tr	08.89	89	40	2	7

JONES, Mark
Berinsfield, 26 September, 1961 (M)

League Club	Source	Date Signed	Seasons Played	Apps	Subs	Gls
Oxford U.	App	09.79	79-85	101	28	7
Swindon T.	Tr	09.86	86	39	1	9
Cardiff C.	Tr	08.90	90-91	33	3	2

JONES, Mark A. W.
Warley, 22 October, 1961 (RB)

League Club	Source	Date Signed	Seasons Played	Apps	Subs	Gls
Aston Villa	App	07.79	81-83	24	0	0
Brighton & H.A.	Tr	03.84	83-84	9	0	0
Birmingham C.	Tr	10.84	84-86	33	1	0
Shrewsbury T.	Tr	03.87				
Hereford U.	Tr	06.87	87-90	155	1	2

JONES, Mark D.
Doncaster, 2 October, 1958 (M)

League Club	Source	Date Signed	Seasons Played	Apps	Subs	Gls
Doncaster Rov.	App	11.75	75-77	10	3	0

JONES, Mark G.
Bristol, 2 December, 1965

League Club	Source	Date Signed	Seasons Played	Apps	Subs	Gls
Bristol C. (App)	App	06.82	82	0	1	0

JONES, Mark R.
Mansfield, 21 December, 1965 (M)

League Club	Source	Date Signed	Seasons Played	Apps	Subs	Gls
Notts Co.	App	12.83	83-84	4	2	0

JONES, Mark T.
Liverpool, 16 September, 1960 (FB)

League Club	Source	Date Signed	Seasons Played	Apps	Subs	Gls
Preston N.E.	Runcorn	02.84	83-85	76	0	3

JONES Matthew L.
Chiswick, 9 October, 1970 (W)

League Club	Source	Date Signed	Seasons Played	Apps	Subs	Gls
Southend U.	YT	05.89	88-89	2	3	0

JONES, J. Mervyn
Bangor, 30 April, 1931 (W)

League Club	Source	Date Signed	Seasons Played	Apps	Subs	Gls
Liverpool	Bangor C.	12.51	51-52	4	-	0
Scunthorpe U.	Tr	08.53	53-58	240	-	29
Crewe Alex.	Tr	06.59	59-60	84	-	14
Chester C.	Tr	08.61	61-62	61	-	10
Lincoln C.		10.63	63	1	-	0

JONES, Michael
Sunderland, 24 March, 1947 (CD)

League Club	Source	Date Signed	Seasons Played	Apps	Subs	Gls
Derby Co.	Jnrs	11.64				
Notts Co.	Tr	07.69	69-72	82	20	1
Peterborough U.	Tr	08.73	73-75	82	6	4

JONES, Michael A.
Sutton-in-Ashfield, 4 December, 1942 (FB)

League Club	Source	Date Signed	Seasons Played	Apps	Subs	Gls
Mansfield T.	Mansfield Co-op.	10.60	62-65	91	0	0

JONES, Michael D.
Worksop, 24 April, 1945 Eu23-9/E-3 (CF)

League Club	Source	Date Signed	Seasons Played	Apps	Subs	Gls
Sheffield U.	App	11.62	62-67	149	0	63
Leeds U.	Tr	09.67	67-73	215	4	77

JONES, Michael H.
Llangurig, 25 August, 1938 (W)

League Club	Source	Date Signed	Seasons Played	Apps	Subs	Gls
Shrewsbury T.		07.59	58-61	22	-	1

JONES, Michael K.
Berkhamsted, 8 January, 1945 (FB)

League Club	Source	Date Signed	Seasons Played	Apps	Subs	Gls
Fulham	App	01.63				
Chelsea	Tr	12.64				
Leyton Orient	Tr	02.66	65-71	223	5	16
Charlton Ath.	Tr	12.71	71-73	58	1	0

JONES, W. Morris
Liverpool, 30 November, 1919 (IF)

League Club	Source	Date Signed	Seasons Played	Apps	Subs	Gls
Port Vale	South Liverpool	06.46	46-47	53	-	26
Swindon T.	Tr	11.47	47-49	94	-	48
Crystal Palace	Tr	05.50	50	17	-	3
Watford	Tr	03.51	50-51	27	-	7

JONES, Murray L.
Bexley, 7 October, 1964 (F)

League Club	Source	Date Signed	Seasons Played	Apps	Subs	Gls
Southend U.	App	08.82				
Crystal Palace	Carshalton Ath.	10.89				
Bristol C.	Tr	08.90				
Doncaster Rov.	L	10.90	90	5	0	0
Exeter C.	Tr	01.91	90	16	4	3
Grimsby T.	Tr	07.91	91	14	14	3

JONES, Norman G.
Rhostyllen, 15 November, 1923 W Sch (G)

League Club	Source	Date Signed	Seasons Played	Apps	Subs	Gls
Wrexham	Jnrs	09.41	46	1	-	0

JONES, Patrick J.
Plymouth, 7 September, 1920 Died 1990 (FB)

League Club	Source	Date Signed	Seasons Played	Apps	Subs	Gls
Plymouth Arg.	Astor Inst.	03.47	46-57	425	-	2

JONES, Paul A.
Walsall, 6 September, 1965 (M)

League Club	Source	Date Signed	Seasons Played	Apps	Subs	Gls
Walsall	App	09.83	82-89	125	18	15
Wrexham	L	03.89	88	5	0	0
Wolverhampton W.	Tr	11.89	89-90	7	7	0

JONES, Paul B.
Ellesmere Port, 13 May, 1953 (CD)

League Club	Source	Date Signed	Seasons Played	Apps	Subs	Gls
Bolton W.	App	06.70	70-82	441	4	38
Huddersfield T.	Tr	07.83	83-85	73	0	8
Oldham Ath.	Tr	12.85	85-86	32	0	1
Blackpool	Tr	03.87	86-87	31	6	0
Rochdale	Stalybridge Celtic	03.89	88	14	0	2
Stockport Co.	Tr	06.89	89	25	0	0

JONES, Paul S.
Stockport, 10 September, 1953 (M)

League Club	Source	Date Signed	Seasons Played	Apps	Subs	Gls
Manchester U.	App	12.70				
Mansfield T.	Tr	06.73	73	15	5	1

JONES, Paul T.
Solihull, 6 February, 1974 (W)

League Club	Source	Date Signed	Seasons Played	Apps	Subs	Gls
Birmingham C.	YT	02.92	91	0	1	0

JONES, E. Peter
Manchester, 30 November, 1937 E Yth (D)

League Club	Source	Date Signed	Seasons Played	Apps	Subs	Gls
Manchester U.	Jnrs	04.55	57	1	-	0
Wrexham	Tr	03.60	59-65	225	1	7
Stockport Co.	Tr	07.66	66-67	51	3	1

JONES, Peter
Caerphilly, 22 September, 1957 (LB)

League Club	Source	Date Signed	Seasons Played	Apps	Subs	Gls
Newport Co.	Merthyr Tydfil	08.85	85-86	54	1	1

JONES, Peter A.
Ellesmere Port, 25 November, 1949 E Sch/E Yth (FB)

League Club	Source	Date Signed	Seasons Played	Apps	Subs	Gls
Burnley	App	05.67	68-69	2	0	0
Swansea C.	Tr	07.71	71-73	80	0	1

JONES, Philip A.
Liverpool, 1 December, 1969 (RB)

League Club	Source	Date Signed	Seasons Played	Apps	Subs	Gls
Everton	YT	06.88	87	0	1	0
Blackpool	L	03.90	89	6	0	0
Wigan Ath.	Tr	01.91	90-91	59	2	2

JONES, Philip E.
Ellesmere Port, 30 March, 1948 (IF)

League Club	Source	Date Signed	Seasons Played	Apps	Subs	Gls
Blackpool	Jnrs	01.66				
Wrexham	Blackburn Rov. (trial)	05.67	66	1	0	0

JONES, Philip H.
Mansfield, 12 September, 1961 (M)

League Club	Source	Date Signed	Seasons Played	Apps	Subs	Gls
Sheffield U.	App	06.79	78-80	25	3	1

JONES, Ralph
Maesteg, 19 May, 1921 (FB)

League Club	Source	Date Signed	Seasons Played	Apps	Subs	Gls
Leicester C.		10.44				
Newport Co.	Tr	05.46	46-47	19	-	0
Bristol Rov.	Tr	12.47	47-49	13	-	1

JONES, Raymond M.
Chester, 4 June, 1944 (FB)

League Club	Source	Date Signed	Seasons Played	Apps	Subs	Gls
Chester C.	Jnrs	10.62	62-68	169	1	0

JONES, G. Richard
Llanrwst, 25 June, 1932 (HB)

League Club	Source	Date Signed	Seasons Played	Apps	Subs	Gls
Crewe Alex.	Holyhead	01.57	56-59	75	-	2

JONES, Richard J.
Usk, 26 April, 1969 (M)

League Club	Source	Date Signed	Seasons Played	Apps	Subs	Gls
Newport Co.	YT	07.87	86-87	31	10	1
Hereford U.	Tr	08.88	88-91	108	5	6

JONES, Richard K.
Llanelli, 16 April, 1926 (FB)

League Club	Source	Date Signed	Seasons Played	Apps	Subs	Gls
Coventry C.	Llanelli	11.49	51-55	83	-	0

JONES, Robert
Coventry, 17 November, 1964 (F)

League Club	Source	Date Signed	Seasons Played	Apps	Subs	Gls
Leicester C.	Manchester C. (App)	09.82	82-85	12	3	3
Walsall	Tr	08.86	86	1	4	0

JONES, Robert M.
Wrexham, 5 November, 1971 W Sch/E Yth/E-1 (RB)

League Club	Source	Date Signed	Seasons Played	Apps	Subs	Gls
Crewe Alex.	YT	12.88	87-91	59	16	2
Liverpool	Tr	10.91	91	28	0	0

JONES, Robert S.
Bristol, 28 October, 1938 (F)

League Club	Source	Date Signed	Seasons Played	Apps	Subs	Gls
Bristol Rov.	Soundwell	05.56	57-66	250	0	64
Northampton T.	Tr	09.66	66	18	0	1
Swindon T.	Tr	02.67	66	11	0	0
Bristol Rov.	Tr	08.67	67-72	160	11	37

JONES, Robert S.
Liverpool, 12 November, 1971 (M)

League Club	Source	Date Signed	Seasons Played	Apps	Subs	Gls
Wrexham	YT	07.90	89-90	5	2	1

JONES, Robert W.
Liverpool, 28 March, 1933 (G)

League Club	Source	Date Signed	Seasons Played	Apps	Subs	Gls
Southport	Jnrs	07.51	51-52	22	-	0
Chester C.	Tr	08.53	53-57	167	-	0
Blackburn Rov.	Tr	03.58	58-65	49	0	0

JONES, Roderick
Rhiwderyn, 14 June, 1946 (F)

League Club	Source	Date Signed	Seasons Played	Apps	Subs	Gls
Newport Co.	Lovells Ath.	10.69	69-78	271	17	66

JONES, Rodney E.
Ashton-u-Lyne, 23 September, 1945 (G)

League Club	Source	Date Signed	Seasons Played	Apps	Subs	Gls
Rotherham U.	Ashton U.	06.65	65-66	35	0	0
Burnley	Tr	03.67	67-68	9	0	0
Rochdale	Tr	06.71	71-73	19	0	0

JONES, Roger
Upton-on-Severn, 8 November, 1946 Eu23-1 (G)

League Club	Source	Date Signed	Seasons Played	Apps	Subs	Gls
Portsmouth	App	11.64				
Bournemouth	Tr	05.65	65-69	160	0	0
Blackburn Rov.	Tr	01.70	69-75	242	0	0
Newcastle U.	Tr	03.76	75	5	0	0
Stoke C.	Tr	02.77	76-79	101	0	0
Derby Co	Tr	07.80	80-81	59	0	0
Birmingham C.	L	02.82	81	4	0	0
York C.	Tr	08.82	82-84	122	0	0

JONES, Ronald
Crewe, 9 April, 1918 (OL)

League Club	Source	Date Signed	Seasons Played	Apps	Subs	Gls
Crewe Alex.	Heslington Vic.	05.37	37-46	3	-	2

JONES, Ronald J.
Rhondda, 27 February, 1926

League Club	Source	Date Signed	Seasons Played	Apps	Subs	Gls
Swansea C.		07.49				
Scunthorpe U.	Tr	08.50	50	3	-	0

JONES, Roy
Stoke, 20 February, 1924 (CH)

League Club	Source	Date Signed	Seasons Played	Apps	Subs	Gls
Stoke C.		10.43	47-49	7	-	0

JONES, Roy J.
Clacton, 26 July, 1942 (G)

League Club	Source	Date Signed	Seasons Played	Apps	Subs	Gls
Swindon T.	R.A.F.	10.67	67-71	34	0	0

JONES, Samuel
Lurgan (NI), 14 September, 1911 NI-2 (WH)

League Club	Source	Date Signed	Seasons Played	Apps	Subs	Gls
Blackpool	Distillery	10.33	33-46	168	-	7

JONES, Selwyn T.
Rhos, 3 April, 1929 (OR)

League Club	Source	Date Signed	Seasons Played	Apps	Subs	Gls
Everton		07.49				
Sheffield Wed.		08.51				
Leyton Orient	Tr	07.52	52	6	-	0

JONES, Shane G.
Tredegar, 8 November, 1972 (M)

League Club	Source	Date Signed	Seasons Played	Apps	Subs	Gls
Hereford U.	YT	08.91	89-91	12	26	1

JONES, E. Sidney
Wrexham, 10 October, 1921 Died 1981 (OL)

League Club	Source	Date Signed	Seasons Played	Apps	Subs	Gls
Bolton W.		05.39				
Norwich C.	Tr	12.45	46-47	40	-	9

JONES, Sidney
Rothwell, 15 February, 1921 (FB)

League Club	Source	Date Signed	Seasons Played	Apps	Subs	Gls
Arsenal	Kippax Jnrs	05.39				
Walsall	Tr	07.48	48-51	146	-	1

JONES, Simon C.
Nettleham (Lincs), 16 May, 1945 (G)

League Club	Source	Date Signed	Seasons Played	Apps	Subs	Gls
Rochdale	Gainsborough Trin.	06.63	63-66	47	0	0
Chester C.	Bangor C.	10.67	67	3	0	0

League Club	Source	Date Signed	Seasons Played	Career Record Apps	Subs	Gls

JONES, Stanley G.
Highley, 16 November, 1938 (CH)

League Club	Source	Date Signed	Seasons Played	Apps	Subs	Gls
Walsall	Kidderminster Hrs	05.56	57-59	30	-	0
West Bromwich A.	Tr	05.60	60-66	239	0	2
Walsall	Tr	03.68	67-72	204	1	7

JONES, Stanley J.

League Club	Source	Date Signed	Seasons Played	Apps	Subs	Gls
Crewe Alex.		08.47	47-48	14	-	1

JONES, Stephen A.
Wrexham, 28 November, 1962 (F)

League Club	Source	Date Signed	Seasons Played	Apps	Subs	Gls
Wrexham	Jnrs	08.81	80-81	3	2	0
Crewe Alex.	Tr	08.82	82	6	4	1

JONES, Stephen A.
Plymouth, 11 March, 1974

League Club	Source	Date Signed	Seasons Played	Apps	Subs	Gls
Plymouth Arg. (YT)	YT	07.90	91	0	1	0

JONES, Stephen R.
Eastbourne, 12 November, 1958 (FB)

League Club	Source	Date Signed	Seasons Played	Apps	Subs	Gls
Queens Park R.	App	10.74				
Walsall	Tr	01.79	78	15	0	0
Wimbledon	Tr	07.79	79-82	77	2	0

JONES, Stephen T.
Harrogate, 6 September, 1955 (G)

League Club	Source	Date Signed	Seasons Played	Apps	Subs	Gls
Bradford C.	App	09.73	72	2	0	0

JONES, Steven
Stockton, 31 January, 1974 (G)

League Club	Source	Date Signed	Seasons Played	Apps	Subs	Gls
Hartlepool U.	YT	05.92	91	6	0	0

JONES, Steven F.
Liverpool, 18 October, 1960 (M)

League Club	Source	Date Signed	Seasons Played	Apps	Subs	Gls
Manchester U.	App.	10.77				
Port Vale	Tr	05.79	79-80	24	1	3

JONES, Steven W.
Wrexham, 23 October, 1964 (D)

League Club	Source	Date Signed	Seasons Played	Apps	Subs	Gls
Wrexham	Jnrs	08.83	82-83	9	1	1

Tom Jones (Aberdeen & Swindon Town)

JONES, Tecwyn
Holywell, 3 January, 1930 (FB)

League Club	Source	Date Signed	Seasons Played	Apps	Subs	Gls
Brentford		03.50	51-52	5	-	0
Wrexham	Tr	07.53	53	4	-	0

JONES, Tecwyn L.
Ruabon, 27 January, 1941 Wu23-1 (WH)

League Club	Source	Date Signed	Seasons Played	Apps	Subs	Gls
Wrexham	Jnrs	05.59	61-64	57	-	2
Colchester U.	Tr	10.64	64-65	28	0	0
Crewe Alex.	Tr	10.65	65	8	0	0

JONES, Thomas
Aldershot, 7 October, 1964 (M)

League Club	Source	Date Signed	Seasons Played	Apps	Subs	Gls
Swindon T.	Aberdeen	09.88	88-91	162	6	13

JONES, Thomas E.
Liverpool, 11 April, 1930 E Yth (CH)

League Club	Source	Date Signed	Seasons Played	Apps	Subs	Gls
Everton	Jnrs	01.48	50-61	383	-	14

JONES, Thomas G.
Connahs Quay, 12 October, 1917 W Sch/W-17 (CH)

League Club	Source	Date Signed	Seasons Played	Apps	Subs	Gls
Wrexham	Llanerch Celtic	11.34	35	6	-	0
Everton	Tr	03.36	36-49	165	-	4

JONES, Thomas W.
Oakengates, 23 March, 1907 Died 1980 (IF)

League Club	Source	Date Signed	Seasons Played	Apps	Subs	Gls
West Bromwich A.	Oakengates T.	07.29				
Burnley	Tr	11.30	30-33	94	-	24
Blackpool	Tr	09.33	33-37	155	-	40
Grimsby T.	Tr	07.38	38-46	48	-	8

JONES, Trevor
Aberdare, 27 January, 1923

League Club	Source	Date Signed	Seasons Played	Apps	Subs	Gls
Plymouth Arg.		05.48				
Watford	Tr	08.49	49	15	-	2

JONES, Vaughan
Tonyrefail, 2 September, 1959 W Yth/Wu21-2 (LB)

League Club	Source	Date Signed	Seasons Played	Apps	Subs	Gls
Bristol Rov.	App	09.77	76-81	93	8	3
Newport Co.	Tr	08.82	82-83	67	1	4
Cardiff C.	Tr	07.84	84	11	0	0
Bristol Rov.	Tr	12.84	84-91	265	3	9

JONES, Vincent P. (Vinny)
Watford, 5 January, 1965 (M)

League Club	Source	Date Signed	Seasons Played	Apps	Subs	Gls
Wimbledon	Wealdstone	11.86	86-88	77	0	9
Leeds U.	Tr	06.89	89-90	44	2	5
Sheffield U.	Tr	09.90	90-91	35	0	2
Chelsea	Tr	08.91	91	35	0	3

JONES, Walter
Lurgan (NI), 4 April, 1925 (WH)

League Club	Source	Date Signed	Seasons Played	Apps	Subs	Gls
Blackpool	Linfield	12.47				
Doncaster Rov.	Tr	06.50	50-52	69	-	2
York C.	Grimsby T. (trial)	11.54	54	1	-	0

JONES, Walter S.
Rochdale, 9 January, 1925 (CF)

League Club	Source	Date Signed	Seasons Played	Apps	Subs	Gls
Rochdale	St Chads	11.46	46	2	-	2

JONES, P. Wayne
Treorchy, 20 October, 1948 Wu23-6/W-1 (M)

League Club	Source	Date Signed	Seasons Played	Apps	Subs	Gls
Bristol Rov.	Jnrs	10.66	66-72	218	6	28

JONES, William H.
Whalley, 13 May, 1921 EF Lge/E'B'-1/E-2 (WH)

League Club	Source	Date Signed	Seasons Played	Apps	Subs	Gls
Liverpool	Hayfield St Mathews	09.38	46-53	257	-	17

JONES, William J.
Aberbargoed, 5 May, 1925 (HB)

League Club	Source	Date Signed	Seasons Played	Apps	Subs	Gls
Ipswich T.	Bargoed	04.49	49-50	33	-	1

JONES, William J. B.
Liverpool, 6 June, 1924 (F)

League Club	Source	Date Signed	Seasons Played	Apps	Subs	Gls
Manchester C.		05.48	48-49	3	-	0
Chester C.	Tr	06.51	51	29	-	5

JONES, C. Wilson
Wrexham, 29 April, 1914 Died 1985 W-2 (CF)

League Club	Source	Date Signed	Seasons Played	Apps	Subs	Gls
Wrexham	Brymbo Green	08.32	32-33	6	-	3
Birmingham C.	Tr	09.34	34-46	135	-	63
Nottingham F.	Tr	09.47	47	7	-	5

JONSSON, Siggi
Iceland, 27 September, 1966 Iceland Int (M)

League Club	Source	Date Signed	Seasons Played	Apps	Subs	Gls
Sheffield Wed.	Akranes (Ice)	02.85	84-88	59	8	4
Barnsley	L	01.86	85	5	0	0
Arsenal	Tr	07.89	89-90	2	6	1

JOPLING, Joseph
South Shields, 21 April, 1951 (FB)

League Club	Source	Date Signed	Seasons Played	Apps	Subs	Gls
Aldershot	Horton Westhoe	08.69	69-70	35	0	2
Leicester C.	Tr	09.70	70-73	2	1	0
Torquay U.	L	01.74	73	6	0	0
Aldershot	Tr	03.74	73-83	321	11	11

JORDAN, Brian A.
Doncaster, 31 January, 1932 (CH)

League Club	Source	Date Signed	Seasons Played	Apps	Subs	Gls
Derby Co.		10.51				
Rotherham U.	Denaby U.	07.53	53-58	38	-	0
Middlesbrough	Tr	11.58	58	5	-	0
York C.	Tr	07.60	60	8	-	0

JORDAN, Clarence (Clarrie)
South Kirkby, 20 June, 1922 Died 1992 (CF)

League Club	Source	Date Signed	Seasons Played	Apps	Subs	Gls
Doncaster Rov.	Upton Colly	04.40	46-47	60	-	47
Sheffield Wed.	Tr	02.48	47-54	92	-	36

JORDAN, Colin
Hemsworth, 2 June, 1934 (FB)

League Club	Source	Date Signed	Seasons Played	Apps	Subs	Gls
Bradford P.A.	Fitzwilliam Y.C.	04.52	53-56	27	-	0

JORDAN, David C.
Gillingham, 26 October, 1971 (F)

League Club	Source	Date Signed	Seasons Played	Apps	Subs	Gls
Gillingham	YT	06.90	90	0	2	0

JORDAN, Gerald
Seaham, 4 April, 1949 (FB)

League Club	Source	Date Signed	Seasons Played	Apps	Subs	Gls
Northampton T.	Jnrs	06.66	66	1	0	0

JORDAN, James
Glasgow, 25 February, 1944 (OR)

League Club	Source	Date Signed	Seasons Played	Apps	Subs	Gls
Reading	Glasgow Celtic	10.48	48	3	-	0
Brentford	Tr	10.49				

JORDAN, John W.
Bromley, 8 November, 1921 (IF)

League Club	Source	Date Signed	Seasons Played	Apps	Subs	Gls
Tottenham H.	Grays Ath.	08.47	47	24	-	10
Birmingham C.	Juventus (It)	03.49	48-49	24	-	2
Sheffield Wed.	Tr	09.50	50	10	-	2

JORDAN, Joseph
Carluke, 15 December, 1951 Su23-1/S-52 (F)

League Club	Source	Date Signed	Seasons Played	Apps	Subs	Gls
Leeds U.	Morton	10.70	71-77	139	30	35
Manchester U.	Tr	01.78	77-80	109	0	37
Southampton	Verona (It)	08.84	84-86	48	0	12
Bristol C.	Tr	02.87	86-89	38	19	8

Vinny Jones (Wimbledon, Leeds United, Sheffield United & Chelsea)

JORDAN, Michael
Exeter, 8 January, 1956 (W)

League Club	Source	Date Signed	Seasons Played	Apps	Subs	Gls
Exeter C.		07.75	75-76	15	3	3

JORDAN, Timothy E.
Littleborough, 12 April, 1960 (F)

League Club	Source	Date Signed	Seasons Played	Apps	Subs	Gls
Oldham Ath.	Jnrs	06.78	78-79	2	3	0

JOSEPH, Francis
Kilburn, 6 March, 1960 (F)

League Club	Source	Date Signed	Seasons Played	Apps	Subs	Gls
Wimbledon	Hillingdon Bor.	11.80	80-81	42	9	14
Brentford	Tr	07.82	82-86	103	7	44
Wimbledon	L	03.87	86	2	3	1
Reading	Tr	07.87	87	5	6	2
Bristol Rov.	L	01.88	87	3	0	0
Aldershot	L	03.88	87	9	1	2
Sheffield U.	Tr	07.88	88	5	8	3
Gillingham	Tr	03.89	88-89	12	6	1
Crewe Alex.	Tr	12.89	89	9	7	2
Fulham	Tr	08.90	90	2	2	0
Barnet (N/C)	Belgium	10.91	91	1	0	0

JOSEPH, Leon
Stepney, 26 February, 1920 Died 1983 E Amat (OL)

League Club	Source	Date Signed	Seasons Played	Apps	Subs	Gls
Tottenham H. (Am)	Leytonstone	02.47	46	1	-	0

JOSEPH, Roger A.
Paddington, 24 December, 1965 E'B' (RB)

League Club	Source	Date Signed	Seasons Played	Apps	Subs	Gls
Brentford	Southall	10.84	84-87	103	1	2
Wimbledon	Tr	08.88	88-91	108	6	0

JOSLIN, Philip J.
Kingsteignton, 1 September, 1916 Died 1981 (G)

League Club	Source	Date Signed	Seasons Played	Apps	Subs	Gls
Torquay U.	Plymouth Arg. (Am)	01.36	35-47	135	-	0
Cardiff C.	Tr	05.48	48-50	108	-	0

JOSLYN, Roger D. W.
Colchester, 7 May, 1950 (M)

League Club	Source	Date Signed	Seasons Played	Apps	Subs	Gls
Colchester U.	Jnrs	05.68	67-70	91	7	4
Aldershot	Tr	10.70	70-74	186	0	17
Watford	Tr	11.74	74-79	178	4	17
Reading	Tr	11.79	79-81	67	1	1

JOVANOVIC, Nikola
Yugoslavia, 18 September, 1952 Yugoslavia Int (CD)

League Club	Source	Date Signed	Seasons Played	Apps	Subs	Gls
Manchester U.	Red Star Belgrade (Yug)	01.80	79-80	20	1	4

JOWETT, Albert W.

League Club	Source	Date Signed	Seasons Played	Apps	Subs	Gls
Halifax T. (Am)		11.46	46	7	-	0

JOWETT, Harold O.
Halifax, 15 November, 1923

League Club	Source	Date Signed	Seasons Played	Apps	Subs	Gls
Halifax T.		09.50	50	9	-	1

JOWETT, Kenneth S.
Bradford, 9 March, 1927 (W)

League Club	Source	Date Signed	Seasons Played	Apps	Subs	Gls
Halifax T.	Fryston Colly	02.47	46-48	22	-	2

JOWETT, S. James
Sheffield, 27 January, 1926 (OL)

League Club	Source	Date Signed	Seasons Played	Apps	Subs	Gls
York C. (Am)	Sheffield U. (Am)	09.46	46	1	-	0

JOY, Bernard
Fulham, 29 October, 1911 Died 1984 E Amat (CH)

League Club	Source	Date Signed	Seasons Played	Apps	Subs	Gls
Fulham (Am)	Corinthian Casuals	02.31	33	1	-	0
Arsenal (Am)	Corinthian Casuals	05.35	35-46	86	-	0

JOY, Brian W.
Reading, 26 February, 1951 (FB)

League Club	Source	Date Signed	Seasons Played	Apps	Subs	Gls
Blackburn Rov.	Coventry C. (Am)	08.68				
Torquay U.	Tr	08.69	69	26	1	0
Tranmere Rov.	Tr	06.70	70	21	0	1
Doncaster Rov.	Tr	07.72	72	28	6	1
Exeter C.	Tr	07.73	73-75	89	1	2
York C.	Tr	09.76	76	18	0	0

JOY, David F.
Barnard Castle, 23 September, 1943 E Yth (FB)

League Club	Source	Date Signed	Seasons Played	Apps	Subs	Gls
Huddersfield T.	Evenwood T.	07.62	65	1	0	0
York C.	Tr	06.67	67	13	2	0

JOY, Harold C.
Ebbw Vale, 8 January, 1921 (CF)

League Club	Source	Date Signed	Seasons Played	Apps	Subs	Gls
Norwich C.	Lovells Ath.	02.47	46	8	-	4
Newport Co.	Tr	01.48	47	2	-	0

JOYCE Anthony J.
Wembley, 24 September, 1971 (LB)

League Club	Source	Date Signed	Seasons Played	Apps	Subs	Gls
Queens Park R.	YT	03.90				
Aldershot (N/C)	Tr	05.91	90	3	0	0

JOYCE, Christopher
Dumbarton, 19 April, 1933 (F)

League Club	Source	Date Signed	Seasons Played	Apps	Subs	Gls
Nottingham F.	Vale of Leven	09.56	57	10	-	0
Notts Co.	Tr	07.59	59-61	62	-	19

JOYCE, Eric
Durham, 3 July, 1924 Died 1977 (RH)

League Club	Source	Date Signed	Seasons Played	Apps	Subs	Gls
Bradford C.	Eppleton Colly	11.45	46	5	-	0

JOYCE, John
Easington, 6 January, 1949 (OR)

League Club	Source	Date Signed	Seasons Played	Apps	Subs	Gls
Hartlepool U. (Am)	Peterlee Jnrs	03.67	66-68	4	0	0

JOYCE, Joseph P.
Consett, 18 March, 1961 (RB)

League Club	Source	Date Signed	Seasons Played	Apps	Subs	Gls
Barnsley	Jnrs	11.79	79-90	332	2	4
Scunthorpe U.	Tr	02.91	90-91	61	0	2

JOYCE, Nicholas J.
Leeds, 27 July, 1947 (W)

League Club	Source	Date Signed	Seasons Played	Apps	Subs	Gls
Bradford C. (Am)	Ashley Road	11.71	71	5	0	1

JOYCE, Sean W.
Doncaster, 15 February, 1967 (M)

League Club	Source	Date Signed	Seasons Played	Apps	Subs	Gls
Doncaster Rov.	YT	09.86	85-87	39	2	2
Exeter C.	L	11.86	86	1	0	0
Torquay U.	Tr	08.88	88-91	117	14	12

JOYCE, Walter
Oldham, 10 September, 1937 (WH)

League Club	Source	Date Signed	Seasons Played	Apps	Subs	Gls
Burnley	Jnrs	10.54	60-63	70	-	3
Blackburn Rov.	Tr	02.64	63-67	119	1	4
Oldham Ath.	Tr	09.67	67-69	68	3	2

JOYCE, Warren G.
Oldham, 20 January, 1965 (M)

League Club	Source	Date Signed	Seasons Played	Apps	Subs	Gls
Bolton W.	Jnrs	06.82	82-87	180	4	17
Preston N.E.	Tr	10.87	87-91	170	7	34

JUDD, Jeremy L.
Bristol, 18 June, 1965 (G)

League Club	Source	Date Signed	Seasons Played	Apps	Subs	Gls
Bournemouth	Jnrs	07.82				
Torquay U. (N/C)	Dorchester T.	08.84	84	2	0	0

JUDD, Michael D.
Southampton, 18 June, 1948 (F)

League Club	Source	Date Signed	Seasons Played	Apps	Subs	Gls
Southampton	App	08.65	67-69	14	1	3

JUDD, Walter J.
Salisbury, 25 October, 1926 Died 1964 (F)

League Club	Source	Date Signed	Seasons Played	Apps	Subs	Gls
Southampton	Nomansland	08.49	50-52	34	-	13

JUDGE, Alan G.
Kingsbury, 14 May, 1960 (G)

League Club	Source	Date Signed	Seasons Played	Apps	Subs	Gls
Luton T.	Jnrs	01.78	79-82	11	0	0
Reading	Tr	09.82	82-84	77	0	0
Oxford U.	Tr	12.84	85-90	80	0	0
Lincoln C.	L	11.85	85	2	0	0
Cardiff C.	L	10.87	87	8	0	0
Hereford U.	Tr	07.91	91	24	0	0

JUDGES, Barry J.
Rainham, 23 September, 1940 (CH)

League Club	Source	Date Signed	Seasons Played	Apps	Subs	Gls
Gillingham	Jnrs	12.57	57-58	3	-	0

JUKES, Norman G.
Leeds, 14 October, 1932 (RB)

League Club	Source	Date Signed	Seasons Played	Apps	Subs	Gls
Huddersfield T.		07.51				
York C.	Tr	10.53	53	1	-	0

JULES, Mark A.
Bradford, 5 September, 1971 (W)

League Club	Source	Date Signed	Seasons Played	Apps	Subs	Gls
Bradford C.	YT	07.90				
Scarborough	Tr	08.91	91	30	11	8

JULIANS, Leonard B.
Tottenham, 19 June, 1933 (CF)

League Club	Source	Date Signed	Seasons Played	Apps	Subs	Gls
Leyton Orient	Walthamstow Ave.	06.55	55-58	66	-	35
Arsenal	Tr	12.58	58-59	18	-	7
Nottingham F.	Tr	06.60	60-63	58	-	24
Millwall	Tr	01.64	63-66	125	0	58

JULIUSSEN, Albert L.
Blyth, 20 February, 1920 (CF)

League Club	Source	Date Signed	Seasons Played	Apps	Subs	Gls
Portsmouth	Dundee	03.48	47	7	-	4
Everton	Tr	09.48	48	10	-	1

JUMP, Stewart P.
Manchester, 27 January, 1952 (D)

League Club	Source	Date Signed	Seasons Played	Apps	Subs	Gls
Stoke C.	App	07.69	70-73	36	8	1
Crystal Palace	Tr	12.73	73-77	79	1	2
Fullham	L	01.77	76	3	0	0

JURYEFF, Ian M.
Gosport, 24 November, 1962 (F)

League Club	Source	Date Signed	Seasons Played	Apps	Subs	Gls
Southampton	App	11.80	83	0	2	0
Mansfield T.	L	03.84	83	12	0	5
Reading	L	11.84	84	7	0	1
Leyton Orient	Tr	02.85	84-88	106	5	45
Ipswich T.	L	02.89	88	0	2	0
Halifax T.	Tr	08.89	89	15	2	7
Hereford U.	Tr	12.89	89-90	25	3	4
Halifax T.	Tr	09.90	90-91	71	0	13

Ian Juryeff (Southampton, Leyton Orient, Halifax Town, Hereford United & Halifax Town)

Kevin Keegan (Scunthorpe United, Liverpool, SV Hamburg, Southampton, Newcastle United & England)
Now managing his former club, Newcastle United, after a career that scaled the peaks

League Club	Source	Date Signed	Seasons Played	Apps	Subs	Gls
KABIA, James P.						
Mansfield, 11 November, 1954						(F)
Chesterfield	App	11.72	72-73	10	1	1
KABIA, Jason T.						
Sutton-in-Ashfield, 28 May, 1969						(F)
Lincoln C.	Oakham U.	01.92	91	10	5	3
KAILE, Gordon W.						
Blandford Camp, 7 December, 1924 Died 1988						(OL)
Nottingham F.		05.45	47-49	65	-	8
Preston N.E.	Tr	07.51	51-53	7	-	1
Exeter C.	Tr	08.54	54	6	-	1
KAISER, Rudi						
Netherlands, 26 December, 1960						(W)
Coventry C.	Antwerp (Bel)	08.81	81	11	5	3
KAMARA, Alan						
Sheffield, 15 July, 1958						(FB)
York C.	Kiveton Park	07.79	79	10	0	0
Darlington	Tr	06.80	80-82	134	0	1
Scarborough	Burton A.	11.87	87-90	158	1	2
Halifax T.	Tr	08.91	91	34	1	0
KAMARA, Christopher						
Middlesbrough, 25 December, 1957						(M)
Portsmouth	App	12.75	75-76	56	7	7
Swindon T.	Tr	08.77	77-80	133	14	21
Portsmouth	Tr	08.81	81	11	0	0
Brentford	Tr	10.81	81-84	150	2	28
Swindon T.	Tr	08.85	85-87	86	1	6
Stoke C.	Tr	07.88	88-89	60	0	5
Leeds U.	Tr	01.90	89-91	15	5	1
Luton T.	Tr	11.91	91	28	0	0
KAMINSKY, Jason M. G.						
Leicester, 3 December, 1973						(F)
Nottingham F.	YT	07.91	91	0	1	0
KANE, Alan						
Falkirk, 20 January, 1957						(M)
Portsmouth	Hibernian	03.75	74-75	6	1	0
KANE, John P.						
Hackney, 15 December, 1960						(D)
Leyton Orient	App	12.78	78	0	1	0
KANE, Leonard R.						
Belfast, 27 January, 1926						
Preston N.E.	Glentoran	05.47	48-49	5	-	0
Plymouth Arg.	Tr	01.50				
KANE, Paul J.						
Edinburgh, 20 June, 1965						(M/RB)
Oldham Ath.	Hibernian	01.91	90-91	13	8	0
KANE, Peter						
Petershill, 4 April, 1939						(IF)
Northampton T.	Queens Park	10.59	59	28	-	16
Arsenal	Tr	07.60	60	4	-	1
Northampton T.	Tr	09.63	63	18	-	8
Crewe Alex.	Tr	03.64	63-66	82	1	31
KANE, Robert						
Cambuslang, 11 May, 1911 Died 1985						(CH)
Leeds U.	St Rochs	08.35	35-46	57	-	0
KANTCHELSKIS, Andrei						
Kirowograd (USSR), 23 January, 1969 USSR Int						(RW)
Manchester U.	Shakytor Donetsk (USSR)	03.91	90-91	29	6	5
KAPENGWE, Emment						
Zambia, 27 March, 1943						(OR)
Aston Villa	Atlanta (USA)	09.69	69	3	0	0
KAPLER, Konrad						
Poland, 25 February, 1925 Died 1991						(OL)
Rochdale	Glasgow Celtic	05.49	49	4	-	0
KARAA, Roch D.						
Tunisia, 3 April, 1964						(G)
Darlington		03.85	84	1	0	0
KASULE, Victor P. A.						
Glasgow, 28 May, 1965						(W)
Shrewsbury T.	Meadowbank Th.	01.88	87-89	28	12	4

League Club	Source	Date Signed	Seasons Played	Apps	Subs	Gls
KATALINIC, Ivan						
Yugoslavia, 17, May, 1951 Yugoslav Int						(G)
Southampton	Red Star Belgrade (Yug)	02.80	79-81	48	0	
KAVANAGH, Eamonn A.						
Manchester, 5 January, 1954						(M)
Manchester C.	Jnrs	06.71				
Rochdale	Tr	10.73	73	2	2	0
Workington	Bury (N/C)	03.74	73-76	123	6	11
Scunthorpe U.	Tr	08.77	77-79	68	8	3
KAVANAGH, Edward						
Glasgow, 20 July, 1941						(OR)
Notts Co.	Cambuslang	05.64	64	25	-	4
KAVANAGH, Jason C.						
Meriden, 23 November, 1971 E Yth						(RB)
Derby Co.	YT	12.88	90-91	27	9	0
KAVANAGH, Michael						
Dublin, 27 December, 1927						
Brighton & H.A.		02.48	48-49	26	-	7
KAVANAGH, Peter J.						
Romford, 3 November, 1938						(OL)
Fulham	Dagenham	10.56				
Everton	Romford	02.61	60	6	-	0
KAY, Anthony H.						
Sheffield, 13 May, 1937 Eu23-7/EF Lge/E-1						(LH)
Sheffield Wed.	Jnrs	05.54	54-62	179	-	10
Everton	Tr	12.62	62-63	50	-	4
KAY, James						
Preston, 3 May, 1932						(F)
Stockport Co.	Leyland Motors	05.53	54-55	9	-	3
Crewe Alex.	Tr	12.56	56	4	-	0
KAY, John						
Great Lumley (Dm), 29 January, 1964						(RB)
Arsenal	App	08.81	82-83	13	1	0
Wimbledon	Tr	07.84	84-86	63	0	2

Andrei Kantchelskis (Shakytor Donetsk, Manchester United & Russia)

League Club	Source	Date Signed	Seasons Played	Apps	Subs	Gls
Middlesborough	L	01.85	84	8	0	0
Sunderland	Tr	07.87	87-91	157	3	0

KAY, Kenneth
Newark, 9 March, 1920 (OL)

League Club	Source	Date Signed	Seasons Played	Apps	Subs	Gls
Mansfield T.	Ransome & Marles	06.47	47	1	-	0

KAY, Robert
Edinburgh, 24 October, 1949 (FB)

League Club	Source	Date Signed	Seasons Played	Apps	Subs	Gls
York C.	Hearts	07.78	78-81	160	0	8

KAYE, Arthur
Barnsley, 9 May, 1933 E Sch/Eu23-1/EF Lge (OR)

League Club	Source	Date Signed	Seasons Played	Apps	Subs	Gls
Barnsley	Jnrs	05.50	50-58	265	-	54
Blackpool	Tr	05.59	59-60	38	-	9
Middlesbrough	Tr	11.60	60-64	164	-	38
Colchester U.	Tr	06.65	65-66	48	1	3

KAYE, David N.
Huddersfield, 14 November, 1959 (G)

League Club	Source	Date Signed	Seasons Played	Apps	Subs	Gls
Rotherham U.	App	11.77				
Chester C. (N/C)	Mexborough T.	03.85	84-85	10	0	0

KAYE, G. Harold
Liverpool, 19 April, 1919 (W/H)

League Club	Source	Date Signed	Seasons Played	Apps	Subs	Gls
Liverpool		04.41	46	1	-	0
Swindon T.	Tr	05.47	47-52	170	-	5

KAYE, John
Goole, 3 March, 1940 EF Lge (D/CF)

League Club	Source	Date Signed	Seasons Played	Apps	Subs	Gls
Scunthorpe U.	Goole T.	09.60	60-62	77	-	25
West Bromwich A.	Tr	06.63	63-71	281	3	45
Hull C.	Tr	11.71	71-73	71	1	9

KEAN, Stephen
Glasgow, 30 September, 1967 (W)

League Club	Source	Date Signed	Seasons Played	Apps	Subs	Gls
Swansea C. (L)	Glasgow Celtic	02.87	86	3	1	0

KEANE, Roy M.
Cork, 10 August, 1971 IRu21/IR-7 (M)

League Club	Source	Date Signed	Seasons Played	Apps	Subs	Gls
Nottingham F	Cobh Ramblers	05.90	90-91	74	0	16

KEANE, Thomas J.
Galway (Ire), 16 September, 1968 IRYth (F)

League Club	Source	Date Signed	Seasons Played	Apps	Subs	Gls
Bournemouth	App	09.86	85-87	1	2	0
Colchester U.	Tr	12.87	87	9	7	0

KEANE, Thomas R.
Limerick (Ire), 31 August, 1922 IR-4/NI-1 (FB)

League Club	Source	Date Signed	Seasons Played	Apps	Subs	Gls
Swansea C.	Limerick	06.47	47-54	164	-	0

KEAR, Michael P.
Coleford, 27 June, 1943 (OR)

League Club	Source	Date Signed	Seasons Played	Apps	Subs	Gls
Newport Co.	Cinderford T.	08.63	63	6	-	0
Nottingham F.	Tr	12.63	63-66	26	1	5
Middlesbrough	Tr	09.67	67-69	56	2	7
Barnsley	L	08.70	70	6	0	1

KEARNEY, Mark J.
Ormskirk, 12 June, 1962 (M/LB)

League Club	Source	Date Signed	Seasons Played	Apps	Subs	Gls
Everton	Marine	10.81				
Mansfield T.	Tr	03.83	82-90	248	2	29
Bury	Tr	01.91	90-91	65	0	2

KEARNEY, Michael J.
Glasgow, 18 February, 1953 (F)

League Club	Source	Date Signed	Seasons Played	Apps	Subs	Gls
Shrewsbury T.	Petershill	12.72	72-76	143	6	41
Chester C.	Tr	03.77	76-77	37	1	5
Reading	Tr	01.78	77-79	78	9	24
Chester C.	Tr	07.80	80	9	0	0
Reading	Tr	10.80	80-82	57	1	12

KEARNEY, Noel M.
Ipswich, 7 October, 1942 (F)

League Club	Source	Date Signed	Seasons Played	Apps	Subs	Gls
Ipswich T.	Jnrs	10.60				
Colchester U.	Tr	09.64	64	3	-	0

KEARNEY, Sidney F.
Liverpool, 28 March, 1917 Died 1982 (L/H)

League Club	Source	Date Signed	Seasons Played	Apps	Subs	Gls
Leicester C.	Crowndale	08.36				
Tranmere Rov.	Tr	05.37	37-38	31	-	3
Accrington St.	Tr	11.38	38-46	30	-	7
Bristol C.	Tr	01.47	46-49	65	-	5

KEARNS, Frederick T.
Cork (Ire), 8 November, 1927 IR-1 (CF)

League Club	Source	Date Signed	Seasons Played	Apps	Subs	Gls
West Ham U.	Shamrock Rov.	05.48	49-53	43	-	14
Norwich C.	Tr	06.54	54-55	28	-	11

KEARNS, Jamie A.
Hammersmith, 28 October, 1971 (FB)

League Club	Source	Date Signed	Seasons Played	Apps	Subs	Gls
Cambridge U. (N/C)	YT	07.90	90	1	0	0

KEARNS, Michael
Banbury, 26 November, 1950 IR-18 (G)

League Club	Source	Date Signed	Seasons Played	Apps	Subs	Gls
Oxford U.	App	07.68	69-71	67	0	0
Plymouth Arg.	L	10.72	72	1	0	0
Charlton Ath.	L	02.73	72	4	0	0
Walsall	Tr	07.73	73-78	249	0	0
Wolverhampton W.	Tr	07.79	79-80	9	0	0
Walsall	Tr	08.82	82-84	26	0	0

KEARNS, Michael D.
Nuneaton, 10 March, 1938 (D)

League Club	Source	Date Signed	Seasons Played	Apps	Subs	Gls
Coventry C.	Stockingford	09.55	57-67	344	0	14

KEARNS, Oliver A.
Banbury, 12 June, 1956 (F)

League Club	Source	Date Signed	Seasons Played	Apps	Subs	Gls
Reading	Banbury U.	03.77	76-79	75	11	40
Oxford U.	Tr	08.81	81	9	9	4
Walsall	Tr	08.82	82	31	7	11
Hereford U.	Tr	06.83	83-87	166	4	58
Wrexham	Tr	12.87	87-89	36	10	14

KEARNS, Peter V.
Wellingborough, 26 March, 1937 (IF)

League Club	Source	Date Signed	Seasons Played	Apps	Subs	Gls
Plymouth Arg.	Wellingborough T.	04.56	56-59	65	-	8
Aldershot	Corby T.	12.62	62-67	184	1	64
Lincoln C.	Tr	03.68	67-68	45	1	11

KEARTON, Jason B.
Australia, 9 July, 1969 (G)

League Club	Source	Date Signed	Seasons Played	Apps	Subs	Gls
Everton	Brisbane Lions (Aus)	10.88				
Stoke C.	L	08.91	91	16	0	0
Blackpool	L	01.92	91	14	0	0

KEATING, Brian A.
Lewisham, 19 March, 1935 (F)

League Club	Source	Date Signed	Seasons Played	Apps	Subs	Gls
Crewe Alex. (Am)	Barry T.	07.56	56-57	7	-	1

KEATING, Dennis
Cork (Ire), 18 October, 1940 (OL)

League Club	Source	Date Signed	Seasons Played	Apps	Subs	Gls
Chester C.		06.62	62	1	-	0

Jason Kearton (Everton)

KEATING, Patrick J.
Cork (Ire), 17 September, 1930 (OL)

League Club	Source	Date Signed	Seasons Played	Apps	Subs	Gls
Sheffield U.	Cork	02.50	50	3	-	0
Bradford P.A.	Wisbech T.	09.53	53	2	-	0
Chesterfield	Tr	10.53	53-56	95	-	21

KEATING, Robert
Oldham, 24 June, 1917 Died 1985 (W)

League Club	Source	Date Signed	Seasons Played	Apps	Subs	Gls
Oldham Ath.		08.41				
Accrington St.	Hereford U.	12.46	46	5	-	0

KEAY, John P. (Jack)
Glasgow, 14 June, 1960 (CD)

League Club	Source	Date Signed	Seasons Played	Apps	Subs	Gls
Shrewsbury T.	Glasgow Celtic (Jnr)	07.77	77-81	152	3	20
Wrexham	Tr	09.82	82-85	156	0	9

KEE, Paul J.
Derry (NI), 21 February, 1967 NI Yth (D)

League Club	Source	Date Signed	Seasons Played	Apps	Subs	Gls
Mansfield T.	App	01.84	83	0	1	0
Nottingham F.	Tr	01.85				

KEE, Paul V.
Belfast, 8 November, 1969 NI Yth/NI-7 (G)

League Club	Source	Date Signed	Seasons Played	Apps	Subs	Gls
Oxford U.	Ards	05.88	89-91	42	0	0

KEEBLE, Brian B.
Holbeach, 11 July, 1938 (LB)

League Club	Source	Date Signed	Seasons Played	Apps	Subs	Gls
Grimsby T.	Holbeach U.	05.59	59-64	172	-	1
Darlington	Tr	07.65	65-68	154	0	2

KEEBLE, Frederick W.
Coventry, 30 August, 1919 (IF)

League Club	Source	Date Signed	Seasons Played	Apps	Subs	Gls
Grimsby T.	Albion Rov.	09.46	46	7	-	1
Notts Co.	Tr	07.47	47	4	-	1

KEEBLE, Victor A. W.
Colchester, 25 June, 1930 (CF)

League Club	Source	Date Signed	Seasons Played	Apps	Subs	Gls
Colchester U.	King George Y.C.	(N/L)	50-51	46	-	23
Newcastle U.	Tr	02.52	51-57	104	-	56
West Ham U.	Tr	10.57	57-59	76	-	45

KEEFE, David E.
Dagenham, 23 June, 1957 (W)

League Club	Source	Date Signed	Seasons Played	Apps	Subs	Gls
Southend U.	App	07.75	74-75	4	2	1
Torquay U.	Tr	08.77	77	2	0	0

KEEGAN, Gerard A. (Ged)
Walkden, 3 October, 1955 Eu21-1 (M)

League Club	Source	Date Signed	Seasons Played	Apps	Subs	Gls
Manchester C.	App	03.73	74-78	32	5	2
Oldham Ath.	Tr	02.79	78-82	139	5	5
Mansfield T.		10.83	83	18	0	1
Rochdale	Tr	07.84	84	2	0	0

KEEGAN, J. Kevin
Doncaster, 14 February, 1951 Eu23-5/E-63 (F)

League Club	Source	Date Signed	Seasons Played	Apps	Subs	Gls
Scunthorpe U.	App	12.68	68-70	120	4	18
Liverpool	Tr	05.71	71-76	230	0	68
Southampton	S.V. Hamburg (Ger)	07.80	80-81	68	0	37
Newcastle U.	Tr	08.82	82-83	78	0	48

KEELAN, Kevin D.
India, 5 January, 1941 (G)

League Club	Source	Date Signed	Seasons Played	Apps	Subs	Gls
Aston Villa	Jnrs	07.58	59-60	5	-	0
Stockport Co.	Tr	04.61	60	3	-	0
Wrexham	Kidderminster Hrs	11.61	61-62	68	-	0
Norwich C.	Tr	07.63	63-79	571	0	0

KEELEY, Andrew J.
Basildon, 16 September, 1956 E Yth (D)

League Club	Source	Date Signed	Seasons Played	Apps	Subs	Gls
Tottenham U.	App	01.74	76	5	1	0
Sheffield U.	Tr	12.77	77-80	28	0	0
Scunthorpe U.	Tr	07.81	81-82	75	2	1

KEELEY, Damian
Salford, 14 February, 1963 (F)

League Club	Source	Date Signed	Seasons Played	Apps	Subs	Gls
Torquay U. (N/C)		09.81	81	1	2	0

KEELEY, Glenn M.
Barking, 1 September, 1954 E Yth (CD)

League Club	Source	Date Signed	Seasons Played	Apps	Subs	Gls
Ipswich T.	App	08.72	72-73	4	0	0
Newcastle U.	Tr	07.74	74-75	43	1	2
Blackburn Rov.	Tr	08.76	76-86	365	5	23
Everton	L	10.82	82	1	0	0
Oldham Ath.	Tr	08.87	87	10	1	0
Colchester U.	L	02.88	87	4	0	0
Bolton W.	Tr	09.88	88	20	0	0

KEELEY, John H.
Plaistow, 27 July, 1961 (G)

League Club	Source	Date Signed	Seasons Played	Apps	Subs	Gls
Southend U.	App	07.79	79-84	63	0	0
Brighton & H.A.	Chelmsford C.	08.86	86-89	138	0	0
Oldham Ath.	Tr.	08.90	91	1	0	0
Oxford U.	L	11.91	91	6	0	0
Reading	L	02.92	91	6	0	0

KEELEY, John J. (Jack)
Liverpool, 18 October, 1936 E Sch/E Yth (IF)

League Club	Source	Date Signed	Seasons Played	Apps	Subs	Gls
Everton	Jnrs	05.54	57	4	-	1
Accrington St.	Tr	07.59	59	10	-	1
Southport	Tr	12.59	59	4	-	0

KEELEY, Nolan B.
Fakenham, 24 May, 1951 (M)

League Club	Source	Date Signed	Seasons Played	Apps	Subs	Gls
Scunthorpe U.	Yarmouth T.	07.73	72-79	255	4	37
Lincoln C.	Tr	01.80	79-80	52	0	3

KEELEY, Raymond B.
Battersea, 25 December, 1946 (IF)

League Club	Source	Date Signed	Seasons Played	Apps	Subs	Gls
Charlton Ath.	App	12.64	64	1	-	0
Exeter C.	Tr	03.66	65-66	45	1	10
Mansfield T.	Crawley T.	06.68	68-69	48	4	5

KEELEY, Walter
Manchester, 1 April, 1921 (IF)

League Club	Source	Date Signed	Seasons Played	Apps	Subs	Gls
Accrington St.		12.44	46-47	48	-	21
Bury	Tr	10.47	47	7	-	0
Port Vale	Tr	01.48	47-48	18	-	3
Accrington St.	Tr	09.48	48-51	101	-	35
Rochdale	Tr	10.51	51	4	-	0

KEEN, Alan
Barrow, 29 May, 1930 (IF)

League Club	Source	Date Signed	Seasons Played	Apps	Subs	Gls
Barrow	Barrow Social	05.49	49-53	95	-	14
Chesterfield	Tr	07.54	54-55	54	-	12
Bradford P.A.	Cheltenham T.	02.57	56	11	-	1
Carlisle U.	Cheltenham T.	09.58	58-59	8	-	0

KEEN, Herbert
Barrow, 9 September, 1926 (OL)

League Club	Source	Date Signed	Seasons Played	Apps	Subs	Gls
Barrow	Netherfield	07.53	53	8	-	0

KEEN, John
Barrow, 26 January, 1929 (WH)

League Club	Source	Date Signed	Seasons Played	Apps	Subs	Gls
Barrow	West Bromwich A. (Am)	01.48	47-58	273	-	19
Workington	Tr	07.59	59	19	-	0

KEEN, Kevin I.
Amersham, 25 February, 1967 E Sch/E Yth (M)

League Club	Source	Date Signed	Seasons Played	Apps	Subs	Gls
West Ham U.	App	03.84	86-91	141	32	14

KEEN, Michael A. C.
Wrexham, 12 February, 1963 W Sch (G)

League Club	Source	Date Signed	Seasons Played	Apps	Subs	Gls
Chester C.	Jnrs	09.81				
Wrexham (N/C)		06.85	85	5	0	0

KEEN, Michael T.
High Wycombe, 19 March, 1940 (WH)

League Club	Source	Date Signed	Seasons Played	Apps	Subs	Gls
Queens Park R.	Jnrs	06.58	59-68	393	0	41
Luton T.	Tr	01.69	68-71	144	1	11
Watford	Tr	07.72	72-74	124	2	5

KEEN, Nigel J.
Barrow, 23 October, 1961 (M)

League Club	Source	Date Signed	Seasons Played	Apps	Subs	Gls
Manchester U.	App	02.79				
Preston N.E.	Barrow	05.85	85	24	0	0

KEENAN, Gerald P.
Liverpool, 25 July, 1954 (FB)

League Club	Source	Date Signed	Seasons Played	Apps	Subs	Gls
Bury		04.75	74-78	69	2	3
Port Vale	Tr	09.78	78-81	105	1	7
Rochdale		11.82	82-83	35	0	1

KEENAN, William G.
Llanelli, 29 December, 1918 (OL)

League Club	Source	Date Signed	Seasons Played	Apps	Subs	Gls
Everton	Hereford U.	01.39				
Newport Co.	Tr	06.46	46	4	-	1

KEENE, Douglas C.
Hendon, 30 August, 1928 (OL)

League Club	Source	Date Signed	Seasons Played	Apps	Subs	Gls
Brentford	Jnrs	09.47	48-49	13	-	1
Brighton & H.A.	Tr	06.50	50-52	61	-	10
Colchester U.	Tr	07.53	53	22	-	1

KEEP, Vernon J.
Chester, 23 May, 1963

League Club	Source	Date Signed	Seasons Played	Apps	Subs	Gls
Wrexham (N/C)		10.84	84	0	1	0

KEERS, James
Stanley, 10 December, 1931 (OR)

League Club	Source	Date Signed	Seasons Played	Apps	Subs	Gls
Darlington	Evenwood T.	03.52	51-55	73	-	15

KEERY, Stanley
Derby, 9 September, 1931 (WH)

League Club	Source	Date Signed	Seasons Played	Apps	Subs	Gls
Shrewsbury T.	Blackburn Rov. (Am)	08.52	52	15	-	2
Newcastle U.	Tr	11.52	52-56	19	-	1
Mansfield T.	Tr	05.57	57-58	53	-	17
Crewe Alex.	Tr	10.58	58-64	254	-	23

KEETCH, Robert D.
Tottenham, 25 October, 1941 (CH)

League Club	Source	Date Signed	Seasons Played	Apps	Subs	Gls
Fulham	West Ham U. (Am)	04.59	62-65	106	0	2
Queens Park R.	Tr	11.66	66-68	48	3	0

KEETLEY, Albert E.
Nottingham, 22 February, 1930 (FB)

League Club	Source	Date Signed	Seasons Played	Apps	Subs	Gls
Bury		03.50	50	4	-	0
Bournemouth	Tr	07.52	53-57	86	-	0

KEETON, Albert
Chesterfield, 15 January, 1918 (RB)

League Club	Source	Date Signed	Seasons Played	Apps	Subs	Gls
Torquay U.	Mosborough Trin.	06.37	37-47	77	-	0

KEIGHLEY, J. Paul
Ribchester (Lancs), 15 February, 1961 (M)

League Club	Source	Date Signed	Seasons Played	Apps	Subs	Gls
Bolton W.	App	02.79				
Crewe Alex.	Tr	08.81	81	25	4	0

KEIR, Colin W.
Bournemouth, 14 January, 1938 (W)

League Club	Source	Date Signed	Seasons Played	Apps	Subs	Gls
Portsmouth	Jnrs	05.55				
Workington	Tr	06.59	59	4	-	0

KEIRS, John
Irvine, 14 August, 1947 (CH)

League Club	Source	Date Signed	Seasons Played	Apps	Subs	Gls
Charlton Ath.	Annbank U	06.65	65-70	73	5	1

KEITH, Adrian J.
Colchester, 16 December, 1962 (D)

League Club	Source	Date Signed	Seasons Played	Apps	Subs	Gls
West Ham U.	App	12.80				
Colchester U. (N/C)		12.82	82	4	0	0

KEITH, Richard M.
Belfast, 15 May, 1933 Died 1967 NI'B'-1/NI-3 (RB)

League Club	Source	Date Signed	Seasons Played	Apps	Subs	Gls
Newcastle U.	Linfield	09.56	56-63	208	-	2
Bournemouth	Tr	02.64	63-65	47	0	0

KELL, G. Allan
Spennymoor, 9 April, 1949

League Club	Source	Date Signed	Seasons Played	Apps	Subs	Gls
Darlington (Am)		08.66	67	0	2	0

KELL, Leonard W.
Billingham, 27 May, 1932 (IF)

League Club	Source	Date Signed	Seasons Played	Apps	Subs	Gls
Chelsea	Jnrs	02.52	53	3	-	0
Norwich C.	Tr	06.54	54	2	-	0

KELLARD, Robert S. W.
Edmonton, 1 March, 1943 E Yth (M)

League Club	Source	Date Signed	Seasons Played	Apps	Subs	Gls
Southend U.	Jnrs	05.60	59-62	106	-	15
Crystal Palace	Tr	09.63	63-65	77	0	6
Ipswich T.	Tr	11.65	65	13	0	3
Portsmouth	Tr	03.66	65-67	91	0	8
Bristol C.	Tr	07.68	68-69	77	0	6
Leicester C.	Tr	08.70	70-71	48	0	8
Crystal Palace	Tr	09.71	71-72	44	2	4
Portsmouth	Tr	12.72	72-74	62	1	6
Hereford U.	L	01.75	74	3	0	1
Torquay U.	South Africa	09.75	75	2	0	0

KELLER, Kasey
Washington (USA), 27 November, 1969 (G)

League Club	Source	Date Signed	Seasons Played	Apps	Subs	Gls
Millwall	Portland Univ. (USA)	02.92	91	1	0	0

KELLEY, Alan W.
Liverpool, 24 December, 1952 (FB)

League Club	Source	Date Signed	Seasons Played	Apps	Subs	Gls
Southport	App	12.70	70-71	17	6	2
Crewe Alex.	Tr	08.72	72-75	105	2	0

KELLEY, Stanley R.
Foleshill, 14 June, 1920 (FB)

League Club	Source	Date Signed	Seasons Played	Apps	Subs	Gls
Coventry C.	Herberts Ath.	08.39	46	4	-	0

KELLOCK, William
Glasgow, 7 February, 1954 S Sch (M)

League Club	Source	Date Signed	Seasons Played	Apps	Subs	Gls
Cardiff C.	Aston Villa (App)	02.72	71-72	33	2	2
Norwich C.	Tr	06.73	73	1	2	0
Millwall	Tr	07.74				
Peterborough U.	Kettering T.	08.79	79-81	134	0	43
Luton T.	Tr	07.82	82	2	5	0
Wolverhampton W.	Tr	03.83	82-83	12	0	3
Southend U.	Tr	09.83	83-84	53	0	9
Port Vale	Tr	12.84	84	10	1	4
Halifax T.	Tr	07.85	85	41	2	17

KELLOW, Anthony
Falmouth, 1 May, 1952 (F)

League Club	Source	Date Signed	Seasons Played	Apps	Subs	Gls
Exeter C.	Falmouth	07.76	76-78	107	0	40
Blackpool	Tr	11.78	78-79	57	0	23
Exeter C.	Tr	03.80	79-83	140	3	61
Plymouth Arg.	Tr	11.83	83	8	2	2
Swansea C. (N/C)	Tr	10.84	84	0	1	0
Newport Co. (N/C)	Tr	11.84	84	17	3	8
Exeter C.	Tr	07.85	85-87	51	31	28

KELLY, J. Alan
Dublin, 5 July 1936, IR-47 (G)

League Club	Source	Date Signed	Seasons Played	Apps	Subs	Gls
Preston N.E.	Drumcondra	04.58	60-73	447	0	0

KELLY Alan T.
Preston, 11 August, 1968 IR Yth/IRu21-3 (G)

League Club	Source	Date Signed	Seasons Played	Apps	Subs	Gls
Preston N.E.	YT	09.85	85-91	142	0	0

KELLY, N. Anthony
Meriden, 14 February, 1966 (W)

League Club	Source	Date Signed	Seasons Played	Apps	Subs	Gls
Bristol C. (N/C)	Jnrs	09.82	82	2	4	1
Stoke C.	St Albans C.	01.90	89-91	31	20	5
Hull C.	L	01.92	91	6	0	1

KELLY, Anthony G.
Prescot, 1 January, 1964 (M)

League Club	Source	Date Signed	Seasons Played	Apps	Subs	Gls
Liverpool	App	09.82				
Wigan Ath.	Prescot Cables	01.84	83-85	98	3	15
Stoke C.	Tr	04.86	85-86	33	3	4
West Bromwich A.	Tr	07.87	87	26	0	1
Chester C.	L	09.88	88	5	0	0
Colchester U.	L	10.88	88	13	0	2
Shrewsbury T.	Tr	01.89	88-90	100	1	15
Bolton W.	Tr	08.91	91	31	0	2

KELLY, Arthur
Belfast, 12 March, 1914 Died 1973 (CF)

League Club	Source	Date Signed	Seasons Played	Apps	Subs	Gls
Barrow	Belfast Celtic	09.46	46	8	-	2

KELLY, Bernard
Motherwell, 21 October, 1932 S'B'-1/SF Lge (IF)

League Club	Source	Date Signed	Seasons Played	Apps	Subs	Gls
Leicester C.	Raith Rov.	07.58	58	24	-	13
Nottingham F.	Tr	04.59	58	2	-	0

KELLY, Bernard A.
Kensington, 21 August, 1928 OR)

League Club	Source	Date Signed	Seasons Played	Apps	Subs	Gls
Brentford	Bath C.	08.50	50	1	-	1

KELLY, Brian L.
Bradford, 22 May, 1943 (FB)

League Club	Source	Date Signed	Seasons Played	Apps	Subs	Gls
Bradford C.	Jnrs	05.60	61-64	83	-	2
Doncaster Rov.	Tr	01.65	64-67	130	1	3
York C.	Tr	07.68	68-69	32	1	0

KELLY, Christopher M.
Epsom, 14 October, 1948 E Amat (F)

League Club	Source	Date Signed	Seasons Played	Apps	Subs	Gls
Millwall	Leatherhead	01.75	74	9	2	0

KELLY, David T.
Birmingham, 25 November, 1965 IRu21-1/IR'B'/IR-13 (F)

League Club	Source	Date Signed	Seasons Played	Apps	Subs	Gls
Walsall	Alvechurch	12.83	83-87	115	32	63
West Ham U.	Tr	08.88	88-89	29	12	7
Leicester C.	Tr	03.90	89-91	63	3	22
Newcastle U.	Tr	12.91	91	25	0	11

KELLY, Desmond C.
Limerick (Ire), 1 November, 1950 (G)

League Club	Source	Date Signed	Seasons Played	Apps	Subs	Gls
Norwich C.	Limerick	07.70				
Colchester U.	Tr	06.72	72	1	0	0

KELLY, Donald J.
Market Harborough, 2 July, 1922 (CF)

League Club	Source	Date Signed	Seasons Played	Apps	Subs	Gls
Torquay U.	Coventry C. (Am)	07.47	46-47	5	-	3

KELLY, Douglas C.
Barnsley, 30 May, 1934 (CF)

League Club	Source	Date Signed	Seasons Played	Apps	Subs	Gls
Barnsley	Jnrs	08.51	52-54	18	-	7
Bradford C.	Tr	06.55	55-56	43	-	14
Chesterfield	Tr	06.57	57	1	-	1

KELLY, Edward P.
Glasgow, 7 February, 1951 (M)

League Club	Source	Date Signed	Seasons Played	Apps	Subs	Gls
Arsenal	Jnrs	02.68	69-75	168	7	13
Queens Park R.	Tr	09.76	76	28	0	1
Leicester C.	Tr	07.77	77-79	85	0	3
Notts Co.	Tr	07.80	80	26	1	1
Bournemouth	Tr	08.81	81	13	0	0
Leicester C.	Tr	12.81	81-82	34	0	0
Torquay U. (N/C)	Melton T.	10.84	84-85	35	0	1

KELLY, Errington E.
St Vincent (WI), 8 April, 1958 (W)

League Club	Source	Date Signed	Seasons Played	Apps	Subs	Gls
Bristol Rov.	Ledbury T.	09.81	81-82	12	6	3
Lincoln C. (N/C)	Tr	01.83	82	0	2	0
Bristol C.	Tr	02.83	82	4	1	1
Coventry C.	Tr	08.83				
Peterborough U.	Tr	03.84	83-85	59	13	22
Peterborough U.		12.86	86-87	36	10	6

KELLY, Frederick C.
Wednesbury, 11 February, 1921

League Club	Source	Date Signed	Seasons Played	Apps	Subs	Gls
Walsall		12.45	46-47	16	-	6

KELLY, Garry
Drogheda (IR), 9 July, 1974 IR Yth /IRu21 (F)

League Club	Source	Date Signed	Seasons Played	Apps	Subs	Gls
Leeds U.	Home Farm	09.91	91	0	2	0

KELLY, Gary A.
Preston, 3 August, 1966 (G)

League Club	Source	Date Signed	Seasons Played	Apps	Subs	Gls
Newcastle U.	App	06.84	86-89	53	0	0
Blackpool	L	10.88	88	5	0	0
Bury	Tr	10.89	89-91	130	0	0

KELLY, Gavin J.
Beverley, 29 September, 1968 (G)

League Club	Source	Date Signed	Seasons Played	Apps	Subs	Gls
Hull C.	YT	05.87	88-89	11	0	0
Bristol Rov.	Tr	06.90	90-91	10	0	0

KELLY, George L.
Aberdeen, 29 June, 1933 (IF)

League Club	Source	Date Signed	Seasons Played	Apps	Subs	Gls
Stoke C	Aberdeen	02.56	55-57	67	-	35
Cardiff C.	Tr	05.58	58	8	-	4
Stockport Co.	Tr	07.59	59	34	-	4

KELLY, Hugh R.
Belfast, 17 August, 1919 Died 1977 Irish Lge/NI-4 (G)

League Club	Source	Date Signed	Seasons Played	Apps	Subs	Gls
Fulham	Belfast Celtic	03.49	49	25	-	0
Southampton	Tr	08.50	50	28	-	0
Exeter C.	Tr	06.52	52-55	99	-	0

KELLY, Hugh T.
Valleyfield (Fife), 23 July 1923 S'B'-1/S-1 (WH)

League Club	Source	Date Signed	Seasons Played	Apps	Subs	Gls
Blackpool	Jeanfield Swifts	08.44	46-59	429	-	5

KELLY, James
Bellshill, 4 June, 1933 (CF)

League Club	Source	Date Signed	Seasons Played	Apps	Subs	Gls
Preston N.E.	Peterborough U.	05.55				
Swindon T.	Tr	02.58	57-58	30	-	14
Walsall	Tr	02.59	58	8	-	1

KELLY, James
Liverpool, 14 February, 1973 (M)

League Club	Source	Date Signed	Seasons Played	Apps	Subs	Gls
Wrexham	YT	07.91	90-91	11	10	0
Wolverhampton W.	Tr	02.92	91	0	3	0

KELLY, James
Bradford, 1 July, 1938 (WH)

League Club	Source	Date Signed	Seasons Played	Apps	Subs	Gls
Halifax T.	Queensbury U.	10.62	63	3	-	0

KELLY, James
Morpeth, 11 August, 1931 (WH)

League Club	Source	Date Signed	Seasons Played	Apps	Subs	Gls
Watford	Blyth Spartans	03.49	50-54	119	-	4
Blackpool	Tr	10.54	54-60	198	-	9

KELLY, James
Aldergrove (NI), 6 February, 1954 (W)

League Club	Source	Date Signed	Seasons Played	Apps	Subs	Gls
Wolverhampton W.	Cliftonville	12.71	73-77	20	2	0
Wrexham	L	09.75	75	4	0	0
Walsall	Tr	08.76	78-79	19	7	3

KELLY, James
Drogheda (Ire), 16 February, 1925 (OL)

League Club	Source	Date Signed	Seasons Played	Apps	Subs	Gls
Tottenham H.	Glenavon	07.49				
Carlisle U.	Tr	02.50	49-51	43	-	6

KELLY, James E.
Seaham, 29 December, 1907 Died 1984 (FB)

League Club	Source	Date Signed	Seasons Played	Apps	Subs	Gls
Southport	Murton Colly	11.28	28-30	7	-	0
Barrow	Tr	08.31	31-32	63	-	0
Grimsby T.	Tr	03.33	32-37	160	-	3
Bradford P.A.	Tr	05.38	38	2	-	0
York C.	Tr	12.38	38	24	-	0
Barrow	Norway	06.46	46	1	-	0

KELLY, James J.
(CF)

League Club	Source	Date Signed	Seasons Played	Apps	Subs	Gls
Barrow		02.46	46	1	-	0

KELLY, James L.
Holborn, 14 July, 1926 (IF)

League Club	Source	Date Signed	Seasons Played	Apps	Subs	Gls
Gillingham	Dartford	05.51	51	3	-	0

KELLY, James P.
Seaham, 22 November, 1951 (FB)

League Club	Source	Date Signed	Seasons Played	Apps	Subs	Gls
Hartlepool U.		08.70	71	5	0	0

KELLY, James W.
Carlisle, 2 May, 1957 (M)

League Club	Source	Date Signed	Seasons Played	Apps	Subs	Gls
Manchester U.	App	05.74	75	0	1	0

KELLY, John
Bebington, 20 October, 1960 IRu21-1 (W/M)

League Club	Source	Date Signed	Seasons Played	Apps	Subs	Gls
Tranmere Rov.	Cammell Laird	09.79	79-81	55	9	9
Preston N.E.	Tr	10.81	81-84	120	10	27
Chester C.	Tr	08.85	85-86	85	0	17
Swindon T.	Tr	06.87	87	3	4	1
Oldham Ath.	Tr	11.87	87-88	51	1	6
Walsall	Tr	08.89	89-90	36	3	1
Huddersfield T.	L	03.90	89	9	1	1
Huddersfield T.	Tr	02.91	90-91	16	2	0

KELLY, John C.
Paisley, 21 February, 1921 S-2 (W)

League Club	Source	Date Signed	Seasons Played	Apps	Subs	Gls
Barnsley	Morton	12.45	46-52	217	-	24
Halifax T.	Morton	07.56	56-57	38	-	2

KELLY, John G.
Glasgow, 14 December, 1935 S Sch (WH)

League Club	Source	Date Signed	Seasons Played	Apps	Subs	Gls
Crewe Alex.	Third Lanark	08.59	59	20	-	1

KELLY Laurence
Wolverhampton, 28 April, 1925 (LB)

League Club	Source	Date Signed	Seasons Played	Apps	Subs	Gls
Wolverhampton W.	Jnrs	03.43	47-49	60	-	0
Huddersfield T.	Tr	10.50	50-56	225	-	2

KELLY, Mark D.
Blackpool, 7 October, 1966 (M)

League Club	Source	Date Signed	Seasons Played	Apps	Subs	Gls
Shrewsbury T.		12.85				
Cardiff C.	Tr	06.87	87-89	93	12	2
Fulham	Tr	06.90	90-91	36	3	1

KELLY, Mark J.
Sutton, 27 November, 1969 E Yth/IRu21-2/IR-4 (W)

League Club	Source	Date Signed	Seasons Played	Apps	Subs	Gls
Portsmouth	YT	11.86	87-90	24	25	2

KELLY, Michael J.
Northampton, 18 October, 1942 E Amat (G)

League Club	Source	Date Signed	Seasons Played	Apps	Subs	Gls
Queens Park R.	Wimbledon	03.66	67-69	54	0	0
Birmingham C.	Tr	08.70	70-74	62	0	0

KELLY, Michael J.
(OL)

League Club	Source	Date Signed	Seasons Played	Apps	Subs	Gls
Wolverhampton W.		06.39				
Crewe Alex.	Tr	11.45	46	15	-	2

KELLY, Michael L.
Belvedere, 22 October, 1954 (M)

League Club	Source	Date Signed	Seasons Played	Apps	Subs	Gls
Millwall	App	10.72	72-74	16	2	2
Charlton Ath.	Tr	12.74	74	10	0	3

KELLY, Noel
Dublin, 28 December, 1921 LOI/IR-1 (IF)

League Club	Source	Date Signed	Seasons Played	Apps	Subs	Gls
Arsenal	Glentoran	10.47	49	1	-	0
Crystal Palace	Tr	03.50	49-50	42	-	5
Nottingham F.	Tr	08.51	51-54	48	-	11
Tranmere Rov.	Tr	07.55	55-56	52	-	6

League Club	Source	Date Signed	Seasons Played	Career Record Apps	Subs	Gls

KELLY, Norman
Belfast, 10 October, 1970 NI Yth (M)

League Club	Source	Date Signed	Seasons Played	Apps	Subs	Gls
Oldham Ath.	YT	07.89	87-88	0	2	0
Wigan Ath.	L	10.89	89	0	4	0

KELLY, Paul A.
Eccles, 6 March, 1971 (M)

League Club	Source	Date Signed	Seasons Played	Apps	Subs	Gls
Manchester C.	YT	02.90				
Crewe Alex.	Tr	02.92	91	0	1	0

KELLY, Paul L. M.
Hillingdon, 24 February, 1974 (M)

League Club	Source	Date Signed	Seasons Played	Apps	Subs	Gls
Fulham	YT	07.92	91	3	0	0

KELLY, Paul M.
Bexley, 12 October, 1969 E Yth (M)

League Club	Source	Date Signed	Seasons Played	Apps	Subs	Gls
West Ham U.	YT	06.88	89	0	1	0

KELLY, Patrick
South Africa, 9 April, 1918 NI-1 (G)

League Club	Source	Date Signed	Seasons Played	Apps	Subs	Gls
Barnsley	Aberdeen	10.46	46-50	145	-	0
Crewe Alex.	Tr	02.52	51-52	38	-	0

KELLY, Peter A.
East Kilbride, 6 December, 1956 (FB)

League Club	Source	Date Signed	Seasons Played	Apps	Subs	Gls
Newcastle U.	App	07.74	75-80	31	2	0

KELLY, Philip J. V.
Dublin, 10 July, 1939 IR-5 (FB)

League Club	Source	Date Signed	Seasons Played	Apps	Subs	Gls
Wolverhampton W.	Sheldon T.	09.57	58-61	16	-	0
Norwich C.	Tr	08.62	62-66	114	1	2

KELLY, Robert
Kirkcaldy, 16 November, 1919 (WH)

League Club	Source	Date Signed	Seasons Played	Apps	Subs	Gls
Millwall	Raith Rov.	06.46	46-47	52	-	1
Bury	Tr	05.48	48	9	-	0

KELLY, Robert A.
Birmingham, 21 December, 1964 (M)

League Club	Source	Date Signed	Seasons Played	Apps	Subs	Gls
Leicester C.	App	12.82	83-86	17	7	1
Tranmere Rov.	L	12.84	84	5	0	2
Wolverhampton W.	Tr	03.87	86-88	13	3	2

KELLY, Terence J.
Gateshead, 14 May, 1942 (CF)

League Club	Source	Date Signed	Seasons Played	Apps	Subs	Gls
Newcastle U.	Jnrs	05.60				
Lincoln C.	Tr	07.62	62	8	-	3

KELLY, Terence W. J.
Luton, 16 January, 1932 (CHO

League Club	Source	Date Signed	Seasons Played	Apps	Subs	Gls
Luton T.	Vauxhall Motors	04.50	54-62	136	-	1

KELLY, Thomas J.
Bellshill, 28 March, 1964 (M/LB)

League Club	Source	Date Signed	Seasons Played	Apps	Subs	Gls
Hartlepool U.	Queen of South	08.85	85	14	1	0
Torquay U.	Tr	07.86	86-88	116	4	0
York C.	Tr	06.89	89	35	0	2
Exeter C.	Tr	03.90	89-91	56	10	8

KELLY, Thomas W.
Darlington, 22 November, 1919 (FB)

League Club	Source	Date Signed	Seasons Played	Apps	Subs	Gls
Darlington		11.37	37-50	157	-	3
York C.	Tr	08.51				

KELLY, Walter M.
Cowdenbeath, 15 April, 1929 (CF)

League Club	Source	Date Signed	Seasons Played	Apps	Subs	Gls
Bury	Raith Rov.	08.52	52-56	160	-	76
Doncaster Rov.	Tr	06.57	57	29	-	6
Stockport Co.	Tr	03.58	57-59	48	-	12
Chester C.	Tr	08.59	59-60	56	-	24

KELLY, William B.
Isleworth, 25 September, 1937

League Club	Source	Date Signed	Seasons Played	Apps	Subs	Gls
Queens Park R.		11.58	58	6	-	0

KELLY, William M.
Cowdenbeath, 14 August, 1922 (CH)

League Club	Source	Date Signed	Seasons Played	Apps	Subs	Gls
Blackburn Rov.	Airdrieonians	09.51	51-56	186	-	1
Accrington St.	Mossley	09.57	57	24	-	0

KELSALL, Charles
Hawarden, 15 April, 1921 (HB)

League Club	Source	Date Signed	Seasons Played	Apps	Subs	Gls
Wrexham		08.39	46-51	39	-	0

KELSEY, A. John (Jack)
Llansamlet, 19 November, 1929 Died 1992 EF Lge/W-41 (G)

League Club	Source	Date Signed	Seasons Played	Apps	Subs	Gls
Arsenal	Winch Wen	08.49	50-61	327	-	0

KEMBER, Stephen D.
Croydon, 8 December, 1948 Eu23-3 (M)

League Club	Source	Date Signed	Seasons Played	Apps	Subs	Gls
Crystal Palace	App	12.65	65-71	216	2	35
Chelsea	Tr	09.71	71-74	125	5	13
Leicester C.	Tr	07.75	75-78	115	2	6
Crystal Palace	Tr	10.78	78-79	39	3	1

KEMP, David M.
Harrow, 20 February, 1953 (F)

League Club	Source	Date Signed	Seasons Played	Apps	Subs	Gls
Crystal Palace	Slough T.	04.75	74-76	32	3	10
Portsmouth	Tr	11.76	76-77	63	1	32
Carlisle U.	Tr	03.78	77-79	60	1	22
Plymouth Arg.	Tr	09.79	79-81	82	2	39
Gillingham	L	12.81	81	9	0	2
Brentford	L	03.82	81	3	0	1

KEMP, Frederick G.
Italy, 27 February, 1946 (M)

League Club	Source	Date Signed	Seasons Played	Apps	Subs	Gls
Wolverhampton W.	App	06.63	64	3	-	0
Southampton	Tr	06.65	65-69	58	3	10
Blackpool	Tr	11.70	70-71	20	2	1
Halifax T.	Tr	12.71	71-73	106	5	10
Hereford U.	Tr	07.74	74	12	1	2

KEMP, John J.
Clydebank, 11 April, 1934 (OL)

League Club	Source	Date Signed	Seasons Played	Apps	Subs	Gls
Leeds U.	Clyde	12.57	58	1	-	0
Barrow	Tr	03.59	58-63	170	-	46
Crewe Alex.	Tr	12.63	63-65	47	0	7

KEMP, Raymond W.
Bristol, 18 January, 1922 (G)

League Club	Source	Date Signed	Seasons Played	Apps	Subs	Gls
Reading (Am)	Grays Ath.	09.49	49	3	-	0

KEMP, Robert
Falkirk, 15 August, 1941 (OL)

League Club	Source	Date Signed	Seasons Played	Apps	Subs	Gls
Carlisle U.	Falkirk	11.60	60	1	-	0

KEMP, Samuel P.
Stockton, 29 August, 1932 (OR)

League Club	Source	Date Signed	Seasons Played	Apps	Subs	Gls
Sunderland	Whitby T.	03.52	52-56	17	-	2
Sheffield U.	Tr	02.57	56-57	16	-	1
Mansfield T.	Tr	05.58	58	3	-	1
Gateshead	Tr	10.58	58	7	-	1

KEMP, Stephen D.
Shrewsbury, 2 May, 1955 (CD)

League Club	Source	Date Signed	Seasons Played	Apps	Subs	Gls
Shrewsbury T.	App	07.73	72-73	7	1	0

KENDAL, Stephen J.
Birtley, 4 August, 1961 (W)

League Club	Source	Date Signed	Seasons Played	Apps	Subs	Gls
Nottingham F.	App	08.79	81	1	0	0
Chesterfield	Tr	12.82	82-86	122	3	14
Torquay U. (N/C)	Tr	10.86	86	4	0	0

KENDALL, Arnold
Halifax, 6 April, 1925 (W)

League Club	Source	Date Signed	Seasons Played	Apps	Subs	Gls
Bradford C.	Ossett T.	02.49	48-52	113	-	13
Rochdale	Tr	09.53	53-56	111	-	25
Bradford P.A.	Tr	09.56	56-58	90	-	12

KENDALL, Howard
Ryton-on-Tyne, 22 May, 1946 E Sch/E Yth/Eu23-6/EF Lge (M)

League Club	Source	Date Signed	Seasons Played	Apps	Subs	Gls
Preston N.E.	App	05.63	62-66	104	0	13
Everton	Tr	03.67	66-73	227	2	21
Birmingham C.	Tr	02.74	73-76	115	0	16
Stoke C.	Tr	08.77	77-78	82	0	9
Blackburn Rovers	Tr	07.79	79-80	79	0	6
Everton (N/C)	Tr	08.81	81	4	0	0

KENDALL, Ian
Blackburn, 11 December, 1947 (OL)

League Club	Source	Date Signed	Seasons Played	Apps	Subs	Gls
Blackburn Rov.	App	12.65				
Southport	Tr	08.67	67	1	1	0

KENDALL, James B.
Birtley, 4 October, 1922 (IF)

League Club	Source	Date Signed	Seasons Played	Apps	Subs	Gls
Barrow	Gateshead U.	05.47	46-48	44	-	16
Gateshead	Tr	11.48	48-51	57	-	21
Barrow	Tr	10.51	51-52	22	-	6
Accrington St.	Tr	09.52	52	26	-	8

KENDALL, Mark
Blackwood, 20 September, 1958 W SchW Yth/Wu21-1 G)

League Club	Source	Date Signed	Seasons Played	Apps	Subs	Gls
Tottenham H.	App	07.76	78-80	29	0	0
Chesterfield	L	11.79	79	9	0	0
Newport Co.	Tr	09.80	80-86	272	0	0
Wolverhampton W.	Tr	12.86	86-89	147	0	0
Swansea C.	Tr	07.90	90-91	12	0	0
Burnley	L	12.91	91	2	0	0

League Club	Source	Date Signed	Seasons Played	Apps	Subs	Gls
KENDALL, Mark I.						
Nuneaton, 10 December, 1961 E Yth						(G)
Aston Villa	App	11.79				
Northampton T.	Tr	06.82	82	11	0	0
Birmingham C.	Tr	02.84	83	1	0	0
KENDALL, Paul S.						
Halifax, 19 October, 1964						(CD)
Halifax T.	App	10.82	81-85	91	15	4
Scarborough	Tr	07.86	87	22	5	1
Halifax T.	Tr	03.88	87	9	1	0
KENNA, Jeffrey J.						
Dublin, 27 August, 1970 IRu21-3						(LB)
Southampton	YT	04.89	90-91	15	1	0
KENNEDY, Alan P.						
Sunderland, 31 August, 1954 Eu23-6/E-2						(LB)
Newcastle U.	App	08.72	72-77	155	3	9
Liverpool	Tr	08.78	78-85	249	2	15
Sunderland	Tr	09.85	85-86	54	0	2
Hartlepool U. (N/C)	Sweden	10.87	87	4	1	0
Wigan Ath.	Grantham	12.87	87	22	0	0
Wrexham (N/C)	Colne Dynamoes	03.90	89-90	15	1	0

Alan Kennedy (Newcastle United, Liverpool, Sunderland, Hartlepool United, Wigan Athletic, Wrexham & England)

League Club	Source	Date Signed	Seasons Played	Apps	Subs	Gls
KENNEDY, Andrew J.						
Stirling, 8 October, 1964						(F)
Birmingham C.	Hong Kong	03.85	84-87	51	25	19
Sheffield U.	L	03.87	86	8	1	1
Blackburn Rov.	Tr	06.88	88-89	49	10	23
Watford	Tr	08.90	90-91	17	8	4
Bolton W.	L	10.91	91	1	0	0
KENNEDY, David						
Birkenhead, 14 February, 1949						(W)
Tranmere Rov.	Jnrs	05.67	67-69	16	1	0
Chester C.	Tr	05.70	70-73	79	7	9
Torquay U.	Tr	09.73	73-76	144	7	7

League Club	Source	Date Signed	Seasons Played	Apps	Subs	Gls
KENNEDY, David						
Sunderland, 30 November, 1950						(CD)
Leeds U.	App	05.68	69	2	0	1
Lincoln C.	Tr	07.71	71	6	2	1
KENNEDY, Gordon M.						
Dundee, 15 April, 1924						(FB)
Blackpool		10.43	46-49	8	-	0
Bolton W.	Tr	09.50	50	17	-	0
Stockport Co.	Tr	08.53	53	20	-	1
KENNEDY, John						
Newtonards (NI), 4 September, 1930						(G)
Lincoln C.	Glasgow Celtic	07.67	67-73	251	0	0
KENNEDY, John						
Kilwinning, 26 February, 1941						(IF)
Charlton Ath.	Saltcoats Vic.	03.62	61-64	46	-	8
Exeter C.	Tr	11.65	65-66	40	1	6
KENNEDY, Joseph P.						
Cleator Moor, 15 November, 1925 Died 1986 E'B'-3						(CH)
West Bromwich A.	Altrincham	12.48	48-60	364	-	3
Chester C.	Tr	06.61	61	33	-	0
KENNEDY, Keith V.						
Sunderland, 5 March, 1952						(LB)
Newcastle U.	App	07.70	71	1	0	0
Bury	Tr	10.72	72-81	405	0	4
Mansfield T.	Tr	08.82	82	32	2	0
KENNEDY, Malcolm S. J.						
Swansea, 13 October, 1939						(HB)
Swansea C.	Jnrs	05.57	57-60	19	-	0
KENNEDY, Michael F.						
Salford, 9 April, 1961 IRu-21-1/IR-2						(M)
Halifax T.	App	01.79	78-79	74	2	4
Huddersfield T.	Tr	08.80	80-81	80	1	9
Middlesbrough	Tr	08.82	82-83	68	0	5
Portsmouth	Tr	06.84	84-87	129	0	4
Bradford C.	Tr	01.88	87-88	45	0	2
Leicester C.	Tr	03.89	88	9	0	0
Luton T.	Tr	08.89	89	30	2	0
Stoke C.	Tr	08.90	90-91	51	1	3
KENNEDY, Patrick A.						
Dublin, 9 October, 1934						(FB)
Manchester U.	Jnrs	02.53	54	1	-	0
Blackburn Rov.	Tr	08.56	57	3	-	0
Southampton	Tr	07.59	59	2	-	0
KENNEDY, Raymond						
Seaton Delaval, 28 July, 1951 Eu23-6/E-17						(M)
Arsenal	App	11.68	69-73	156	2	53
Liverpool	Tr	07.74	74-81	272	3	51
Swansea C.	Tr	01.82	81-83	42	0	2
Hartlepool U.	Tr	11.83	83	18	5	3
KENNEDY, Robert						
Motherwell, 23 June, 1937 Su23-1						(FB)
Manchester C.	Kilmarnock	07.61	61-68	216	3	9
Grimsby T.	Tr	03.69	68-70	84	0	1
KENNEDY, Stephen						
Manchester, 22 July, 1965						(FB)
Burnley	App	07.83	83-86	18	0	0
KENNERLEY, Kevin R.						
Chester, 26 April, 1954						(M)
Burnley	Arsenal (App)	05.72	75	6	0	1
Port Vale	Tr	05.76	76-77	16	8	1
Swansea C.	L	02.78	77	2	0	0
KENNING, Michael J.						
Birmingham, 18 August, 1940						(W)
Aston Villa	Jnrs	10.59	60	3	-	0
Shrewsbury T.	Tr	05.61	61-62	62	-	17
Charlton Ath.	Tr	11.62	62-66	152	2	43
Norwich C.	Tr	12.66	66-67	44	0	9
Wolverhampton W.	Tr	01.68	67-68	35	6	5
Charlton Ath.	Tr	03.69	68-71	60	7	12
Watford	Tr	12.71	71-72	35	6	2
KENNON, Neil S. (Sandy)						
South Africa, 28 November, 1933						(G)
Huddersfield T.	Bulawayo (Rhod)	08.56	56-58	78	-	0
Norwich C.	Tr	02.59	58-64	213	-	0
Colchester U.	Tr	03.65	64-66	77	0	0

KENNY, Frederick
Manchester, 14 January, 1923 Died 1985 (FB)

League Club	Source	Date Signed	Seasons Played	Apps	Subs	Gls
Stockport Co.		12.47	48-56	204	-	0

KENNY, Vincent
Sheffield, 29 December, 1924 (FB)

League Club	Source	Date Signed	Seasons Played	Apps	Subs	Gls
Sheffield Wed.	Atlas Wks	11.45	46-54	144	-	0
Carlisle U.	Tr	07.55	55-57	103	-	3

KENNY, William A.
Liverpool, 23 October, 1951 (M)

League Club	Source	Date Signed	Seasons Played	Apps	Subs	Gls
Everton	App	07.69	70-74	10	2	0
Tranmere Rov.	Tr	03.75	74-76	36	18	6

KENT, Kevin J.
Stoke, 19 March, 1965 (W)

League Club	Source	Date Signed	Seasons Played	Apps	Subs	Gls
West Bromwich A.	App	12.82	83	1	1	0
Newport Co.	Tr	07.84	84	23	10	1
Mansfield T.	Tr	08.85	85-90	223	6	36
Port Vale	Tr	03.91	90-91	24	10	0

KENT, Michael J.
Dinnington, 12 January, 1951 (M)

League Club	Source	Date Signed	Seasons Played	Apps	Subs	Gls
Wolverhampton W.	Wath W.	08.68	69-71	0	2	0
Gillingham	L	03.71	70	11	0	0
Sheffield Wed.	Tr	09.73	73	4	0	0

KENT, Paul
Rotherham, 23 February, 1954 (FB)

League Club	Source	Date Signed	Seasons Played	Apps	Subs	Gls
Norwich C.	App	02.72	73	1	2	0
Halifax T.	Tr	08.76	76	12	0	0

KENT, Terence
Battersea, 21 October, 1939 (HB)

League Club	Source	Date Signed	Seasons Played	Apps	Subs	Gls
Southend U.		05.58	58	1	-	0
Millwall	Tr	08.60				

KENWORTHY, Anthony D.
Leeds, 30 October, 1958 E Yth (CD)

League Club	Source	Date Signed	Seasons Played	Apps	Subs	Gls
Sheffield U.	App	07.76	75-85	281	5	34
Mansfield T.	Tr	03.86	85-89	98	2	0

KENWORTHY, Stephen
Wrexham, 6 November, 1959 (LB)

League Club	Source	Date Signed	Seasons Played	Apps	Subs	Gls
Wrexham	Jnrs	11.77	77-80	19	1	0
Bury	Tr	08.81	82	14	0	0

KENYON, Frederick
Carlisle, 14 January, 1922 (CH)

League Club	Source	Date Signed	Seasons Played	Apps	Subs	Gls
Carlisle U.		09.43	47-48	4	-	0

KENYON, John F.
Blackburn, 2 December, 1953 (F)

League Club	Source	Date Signed	Seasons Played	Apps	Subs	Gls
Blackburn Rov.	Great Harwood	12.72	72-75	32	14	7

KENYON, Roger N.
Blackpool, 4 January, 1949 (CD)

League Club	Source	Date Signed	Seasons Played	Apps	Subs	Gls
Everton	App	09.66	67-78	254	12	6
Bristol C.	Vancouver (Can)	10.79	79	4	0	0

KENYON, Roy
Manchester, 10 March, 1933 (F)

League Club	Source	Date Signed	Seasons Played	Apps	Subs	Gls
Leeds U.	Bolton W. (Am)	12.50				
Southport	Tr	09.54	54	1	-	0

KEOUGH, Daniel P.
Bacup, 31 January, 1963 (M)

League Club	Source	Date Signed	Seasons Played	Apps	Subs	Gls
Manchester U.	App	02.80				
Exeter C.	Bury (N/C)	10.85	85-86	71	1	0

KEOWN, Martin R.
Oxford, 24 July, 1966 E Yth/Eu21-8/E-9 (CD)

League Club	Source	Date Signed	Seasons Played	Apps	Subs	Gls
Arsenal	App	01.84	85	22	0	0
Brighton & H.A.	L	02.85	84-85	21	2	1
Aston Villa	Tr	06.86	86-88	109	3	3
Everton	Tr	06.89	89-91	79	4	0

KERFOOT, Eric
Ashton-u-Lyne, 31 July, 1924 (WH)

League Club	Source	Date Signed	Seasons Played	Apps	Subs	Gls
Leeds U.	Stalybridge Celtic	12.49	49-58	336	-	9
Chesterfield	Tr	07.59	59	9	-	0

KERFOOT, Jason J. T.
Preston, 17 April, 1973 (F)

League Club	Source	Date Signed	Seasons Played	Apps	Subs	Gls
Preston N.E.	YT	07.91	90-91	0	4	0

KERNAGHAN, Alan N.
Otley, 25 April, 1967 NI Sch (CD)

League Club	Source	Date Signed	Seasons Played	Apps	Subs	Gls
Middlesbrough	App	03.85	84-91	144	40	13
Charlton Ath.	L	01.91	90	13	0	0

KERNAN, Anthony P.
Letterkenny (Ire), 31 August, 1963 IR Yth (M)

League Club	Source	Date Signed	Seasons Played	Apps	Subs	Gls
Wolverhampton W.	App	01.81	81	1	0	0

KERNICK, Dudley
Camelford, 29 August, 1921 (F)

League Club	Source	Date Signed	Seasons Played	Apps	Subs	Gls
Torquay U.	Tintagel	01.39	46-47	38	-	7
Northampton T.	Tr	08.48				
Birmingham C.	Tr	12.48				

KERR, Albert W.
Lanchester, 11 August, 1917 Died 1979 (OR)

League Club	Source	Date Signed	Seasons Played	Apps	Subs	Gls
Aston Villa	Medomsley Jnrs	07.36	36-46	29	-	4

KERR, Andrew
Cumnock, 29 June, 1932 S'B'-1/SF Lge/S-2 (CF)

League Club	Source	Date Signed	Seasons Played	Apps	Subs	Gls
Manchester C	Partick Th.	06.59	59	10	-	0
Sunderland	Kilmarnock	04.63	62-63	18	-	5

KERR, Andrew A.
West Bromwich, 7 April, 1966 (RB)

League Club	Source	Date Signed	Seasons Played	Apps	Subs	Gls
Shrewsbury T.	YT	04.84	84-85	9	1	0
Cardiff C.	Tr	08.86	86	31	0	1

KERR, Archibald
Motherwell, 30 August, 1935 (F)

League Club	Source	Date Signed	Seasons Played	Apps	Subs	Gls
Shrewsbury T.	Motherwell	01.57	56	13	-	0

KERR, Charles C.
Glasgow, 10 December, 1933 (OR)

League Club	Source	Date Signed	Seasons Played	Apps	Subs	Gls
Carlisle U.	Morton	08.56	56-57	9	-	3
Barrow		07.59	59	20	-	3

KERR, David
Glasgow, 4 December, 1936 (F)

League Club	Source	Date Signed	Seasons Played	Apps	Subs	Gls
Liverpool		04.56				
Southport	Tr	07.58	58	32	-	4

Martin Keown (Arsenal, Aston Villa, Everton & England)

KERR, Dylan
Malta, 14 January, 1967 (FB)

League Club	Source	Date Signed	Seasons Played	Apps	Subs	Gls
Sheffield Wed.	YT	09.84				
Leeds U.	Arcadia Shep (SA)	01.89	88-89	3	5	0
Doncaster Rov.	L	08.91	91	7	0	1
Blackpool	L	12.91	91	12	0	1

KERR, George A. M.
Dumbarton, 9 January, 1943 (IF)

League Club	Source	Date Signed	Seasons Played	Apps	Subs	Gls
Barnsley	Vale of Leven	05.60	61-65	166	0	40
Bury	Tr	03.66	65-66	15	0	2
Oxford U.	Tr	09.66	66-67	40	1	5
Scunthorpe U.	Tr	02.68	67-72	151	6	32

KERR, James
Newburn, 3 March, 1932 (OL)

League Club	Source	Date Signed	Seasons Played	Apps	Subs	Gls
Lincoln C.	Blyth Spartans	11.52	52-53	15	-	1
Oldham Ath.	Tr	06.54	54-55	34	-	4

KERR, James P.
Glasgow, 2 September, 1949 S Sch (M)

League Club	Source	Date Signed	Seasons Played	Apps	Subs	Gls
Bury	Jnrs	09.66	65-69	150	2	37
Blackburn Rov.	Tr	05.70	70	11	0	0

KERR, John
Birkenhead, 23 November, 1959 (F)

League Club	Source	Date Signed	Seasons Played	Apps	Subs	Gls
Tranmere Rov.	App	11.77	78-82	145	9	38
Bristol C.	Tr	08.83	83	13	1	4
Stockport Co.	Tr	01.84	83-84	47	0	16
Bury	Tr	03.85	84-85	21	10	4

KERR, John J.
Scarborough, 6 March, 1965 USA Int (F)

League Club	Source	Date Signed	Seasons Played	Apps	Subs	Gls
Portsmouth	Harrow Bor.	08.87	87	2	2	0
Peterborough U.	L	12.87	87	10	0	1

KERR, Paul A.
Portsmouth, 9 June, 1964 (M)

League Club	Source	Date Signed	Seasons Played	Apps	Subs	Gls
Aston Villa	App	05.82	83-86	16	8	3
Middlesbrough	Tr	01.87	86-90	114	11	13
Millwall	Tr	03.91	90-91	42	2	14

KERR, Peter
Paisley, 25 September, 1943 (F)

League Club	Source	Date Signed	Seasons Played	Apps	Subs	Gls
Reading	Third Lanark	05.63	63-64	41	-	7

KERR, Peter
Glasgow, 3 January, 1928 (IR)

League Club	Source	Date Signed	Seasons Played	Apps	Subs	Gls
Hartlepool U.	Maryhill Hearts	09.49	49	2	-	0

KERR, Robert
Dumbarton, 16 November, 1947 (M)

League Club	Source	Date Signed	Seasons Played	Apps	Subs	Gls
Sunderland	Jnrs	11.64	66-78	355	13	56
Blackpool	Tr	03.79	78-79	18	4	2
Hartlepool U.	Tr	07.80	80-81	48	1	2

KERR, Robert
West Lothian, 10 July, 1942 (CF)

League Club	Source	Date Signed	Seasons Played	Apps	Subs	Gls
Millwall	Arbroath	08.62	62	1	-	0

KERR, Robert J.
Coatbridge, 29 November, 1929 (IF)

League Club	Source	Date Signed	Seasons Played	Apps	Subs	Gls
Darlington	Third Lanark	10.52	52	10	-	2

KERRAY, James R.
Stirling, 2 December, 1935 (IF)

League Club	Source	Date Signed	Seasons Played	Apps	Subs	Gls
Huddersfield T.	Dunfermline Ath.	08.60	60-61	54	-	12
Newcastle U.	Tr	02.62	61-62	38	-	10

KERRIGAN, Donald M.
Seamill, 7 May, 1942 Died 1990 (OR)

League Club	Source	Date Signed	Seasons Played	Apps	Subs	Gls
Fulham	Dunfermline Ath.	02.68	67-68	4	2	1
Lincoln C.	L	03.69	68	12	0	0

KERRINS, Patrick M.
Fulham, 13 September, 1936 (OL)

League Club	Source	Date Signed	Seasons Played	Apps	Subs	Gls
Queens Park R.	Jnrs	12.53	53-59	145	-	30
Crystal Palace	Tr	06.60	60	5	-	0
Southend U.	Tr	07.61	61	11	-	0

KERRINS, Wayne M.
Brentwood, 5 August, 1965 (M/LB)

League Club	Source	Date Signed	Seasons Played	Apps	Subs	Gls
Fulham	App	08.83	84-88	51	15	1
Port Vale	L	03.85	84	6	2	0
Leyton Orient	L	03.89	88	3	0	0

KERRY, Brian P.
Maltby, 18 December, 1948 (F)

League Club	Source	Date Signed	Seasons Played	Apps	Subs	Gls
Grimsby T.	App	01.66	65	0	1	0
Huddersfield T.	Tr	04.67				

KERRY, David T.
Derby, 6 February, 1937 E Yth (CF)

League Club	Source	Date Signed	Seasons Played	Apps	Subs	Gls
Preston N.E.	Derby Co. (Am)	05.55				
Chesterfield	Tr	07.61	61-62	55	-	23
Rochdale	Tr	07.63	63	12	-	4

KERSHAW, Alan D.
Southport, 23 April, 1954 (FB)

League Club	Source	Date Signed	Seasons Played	Apps	Subs	Gls
Preston N.E.	App	09.72				
Southport	Tr	07.74	74	19	5	0

KERSLAKE, David
Stepney, 19 June, 1966 E Sch/E Yth/Eu21-1 (FB)

League Club	Source	Date Signed	Seasons Played	Apps	Subs	Gls
Queens Park R.	App	06.83	84-89	38	20	6
Swindon T.	Tr	11.89	89-91	103	1	1

KERSLAKE, Michael L.
Bethnal Green, 27 February, 1958 E Yth (FB)

League Club	Source	Date Signed	Seasons Played	Apps	Subs	Gls
Fulham	App	10.75	75-77	1	2	0
Brighton & H.A.	Tr	06.78				

KETTERIDGE, Stephen J.
Stevenage, 7 November, 1959 (M)

League Club	Source	Date Signed	Seasons Played	Apps	Subs	Gls
Wimbledon	Derby Co. (App)	04.78	78-84	229	8	32
Crystal Palace	Tr	08.85	85-86	58	1	6
Leyton Orient	Tr	07.87	87-88	26	5	3
Cardiff C.	L	10.88	88	6	0	2

KETTLE, Albert H.
Colchester, 3 June, 1922 (RB)

League Club	Source	Date Signed	Seasons Played	Apps	Subs	Gls
Colchester U.	Arkwright Sports	(N/L)	50-54	23	-	0

KETTLE, Brian
Prescot, 22 April, 1956 E Yth (FB)

League Club	Source	Date Signed	Seasons Played	Apps	Subs	Gls
Liverpool	App	05.73	75-76	3	0	0
Wigan Ath.	Houston (USA)	08.80	80	14	0	1

KETTLEBOROUGH, Keith F.
Rotherham, 29 June, 1935 (IF)

League Club	Source	Date Signed	Seasons Played	Apps	Subs	Gls
Rotherham U.	Rotherham Y.M.C.A.	12.55	55-60	119	-	20
Sheffield U.	Tr	12.60	60-65	154	0	17
Newcastle U.	Tr	12.65	65-66	30	0	0
Doncastle Rov.	Tr	12.66	66-67	35	1	0
Chesterfield	Tr	11.67	67-68	66	0	3

KETTLEY, Spencer C.
Rhondda, 22 May, 1921 (WH)

League Club	Source	Date Signed	Seasons Played	Apps	Subs	Gls
Luton T.	Newbury T.	08.44	46	1	-	0

KEVAN, David J.
Wigtown, 31 August, 1968 (M)

League Club	Source	Date Signed	Seasons Played	Apps	Subs	Gls
Notts Co.	App	08.86	85-89	82	7	3
Cardiff C.	L	09.89	89	6	1	0
Stoke C.	Tr	01.90	89-91	64	1	1
Maidstone U.	L	02.91	90	3	0	0

KEVAN, Derek T.
Ripon, 6 March, 1935 Eu23-4/EF Lge/E-14 (IF)

League Club	Source	Date Signed	Seasons Played	Apps	Subs	Gls
Bradford P.A.	Ripon Y.M.C.A.	10.52	52	15	-	8
West Bromwich A.	Tr	07.53	55-62	262	-	157
Chelsea	Tr	03.63	62	7	-	1
Manchester C.	Tr	08.63	63-64	67	-	48
Crystal Palace	Tr	07.65	65	21	0	5
Peterborough U.	Tr	03.66	65-66	16	1	2
Luton T.	Tr	12.66	66	11	0	4
Stockport Co.	Tr	03.67	66-67	38	2	10

KEWLEY, Kevin J.
Liverpool, 2 March, 1955 (M)

League Club	Source	Date Signed	Seasons Played	Apps	Subs	Gls
Liverpool	App	03.72	77	0	1	0

KEY, John P.
Chelsea, 5 November, 1937 (OR)

League Club	Source	Date Signed	Seasons Played	Apps	Subs	Gls
Fulham	Jnrs	05.56	58-65	163	0	29
Coventry C.	Tr	05.66	66-67	27	1	7
Leyton Orient	Tr	03.68	67-68	9	1	0

KEY, Richard M.
Cambridge, 13 April, 1956 (G)

League Club	Source	Date Signed	Seasons Played	Apps	Subs	Gls
Exeter C.	Coventry C. (Jnr)	07.75	75-77	109	0	0
Cambridge U.	Tr	08.78	78-82	52	0	0
Northampton T.	L	11.82	82	2	0	0

League Club	Source	Date Signed	Seasons Played	Apps	Subs	Gls
Leyton Orient	Tr	08.83	83	42	0	0
Brentford	Tr	08.84	84	1	0	0
Sunderland	Tr	10.84				
Cambridge U.	L	03.85	84	13	0	0
Brentford (N/C)	Tr	08.85	85	3	0	0

KEYES, Anthony J.
Salford, 29 October, 1953 (M)

League Club	Source	Date Signed	Seasons Played	Apps	Subs	Gls
Stockport Co.	Witton A.	10.71	71-73	7	1	0

KEYS, Paul
Ipswich, 4 September, 1962 (F)

League Club	Source	Date Signed	Seasons Played	Apps	Subs	Gls
Luton T.		07.81				
Halifax T.	L.	03.82	81	1	1	0

KEYWORTH, Kenneth
Rotherham, 24 February, 1934 (CF/WH)

League Club	Source	Date Signed	Seasons Played	Apps	Subs	Gls
Rotherham U.	Wolverhampton W. (Am)	01.52	55-57	85	-	7
Leicester C.	Tr	05.58	58-64	177	-	63
Coventry C.	Tr	12.64	64	7	-	3
Swindon T.	Tr	08.65	65	6	0	0

KICHENBRAND, Donald B.
South Africa, 13 August, 1933 (CF)

League Club	Source	Date Signed	Seasons Played	Apps	Subs	Gls
Sunderland	Glasgow Rangers	03.58	57-59	53	-	28

KIDD, Brian
Manchester, 29 May, 1949 E Yth/Eu23-10/EF Lge/E-2 (F)

League Club	Source	Date Signed	Seasons Played	Apps	Subs	Gls
Manchester U.	App	06.66	67-73	195	8	52
Arsenal	Tr	08.74	74-75	77	0	30
Manchester C.	Tr	07.76	76-78	97	1	44
Everton	Tr	03.79	78-79	40	0	12
Bolton W.	Tr	05.80	80-81	40	3	14

KIDD, John O.
Birkenhead, 15 January, 1936 (F)

League Club	Source	Date Signed	Seasons Played	Apps	Subs	Gls
Tranmere Rov.	Everton (Am)	08.55	55-58	34	-	4

KIDD, Ryan A.
Radcliffe, 6 October, 1971 (FB)

League Club	Source	Date Signed	Seasons Played	Apps	Subs	Gls
Port Vale	YT	07.90	91	1	0	0

KIDD, William E.
Morpeth, 31 January, 1907 Died 1978 (FB)

League Club	Source	Date Signed	Seasons Played	Apps	Subs	Gls
Chesterfield	Pegswood U.	03.32	31-47	316	-	1

KIELY, Dean L.
Salford, 10 October, 1970 E Yth (G)

League Club	Source	Date Signed	Seasons Played	Apps	Subs	Gls
Coventry C.	YT	10.87				
York C.	Tr	05.90	90-91	38	0	0

KIERAN, Leonard V.
Birkenhead, 25 July, 1926 Died 1981 (WH)

League Club	Source	Date Signed	Seasons Played	Apps	Subs	Gls
Tranmere Rov.	Jnrs	09.43	47-56	346	-	6

KIERNAN, Daniel J.
Northampton, 16 December, 1973 (M)

League Club	Source	Date Signed	Seasons Played	Apps	Subs	Gls
Northampton T. (YT)	YT	07.90	91	6	3	0

KIERNAN, Frederick W.
Dublin, 7 July 1919 Died 1981 IR-5 (G)

League Club	Source	Date Signed	Seasons Played	Apps	Subs	Gls
Southampton	Shamrock Rov.	10.51	51-55	132	-	0

KIERNAN, Joseph
Coatbridge, 22 October, 1942 (WH)

League Club	Source	Date Signed	Seasons Played	Apps	Subs	Gls
Sunderland	Jnrs	11.59	62	1	-	0
Northampton T.	Tr	07.63	63-71	303	3	13

KIERNAN, Thomas
Coatbridge, 20 October, 1918 SF Lge (IF)

League Club	Source	Date Signed	Seasons Played	Apps	Subs	Gls
Stoke C.	Glasgow Celtic	09.47	47-48	28	-	6
Luton T.	Tr	11.48	48-50	55	-	10

Brian Kidd (Manchester United, Arsenal, Manchester City, Everton, Bolton Wanderers & England)

League Club	Source	Date Signed	Seasons Played	Career Record Apps	Subs	Gls

KIERNAN, William E.
Croydon, 22 May, 1925 E'B'-1 (OL)

League Club	Source	Date Signed	Seasons Played	Apps	Subs	Gls
Charlton Ath.	Hong Kong	07.49	49-60	378	-	89

KILCLINE, Brian
Nottingham, 7 May, 1962 Eu21-2 (CD)

League Club	Source	Date Signed	Seasons Played	Apps	Subs	Gls
Notts Co.	App	05.80	79-83	156	2	9
Coventry C.	Tr	06.84	84-90	173	0	28
Oldham Ath.	Tr	08.91	91	8	0	0
Newcastle U.	Tr	02.92	91	12	0	0

Brian Kilcline (Notts County, Coventry City, Oldham Athletic & Newcastle United)

KILEY, Thomas J.
Swansea, 15 June, 1924 (CH)

League Club	Source	Date Signed	Seasons Played	Apps	Subs	Gls
Swansea C.		06.47	49-56	130	-	2

KILFORD, John D.
Derby, 8 November, 1938 (FB)

League Club	Source	Date Signed	Seasons Played	Apps	Subs	Gls
Notts Co.	Derby Corries	07.57	58	26	-	0
Leeds U.	Tr	02.59	58-61	21	-	0

KILGALLON, Mark C.
Glasgow, 20 December, 1962 (D)

League Club	Source	Date Signed	Seasons Played	Apps	Subs	Gls
Hull C.	Ipswich T. (App)	08.80	80	0	1	0

KILGANNON, John
Stenhousemuir, 26 June, 1936 Died 1967 (F)

League Club	Source	Date Signed	Seasons Played	Apps	Subs	Gls
Luton T.	Stenhousemuir	04.59	58-59	13	-	1

KILKELLY, Thomas F.
Galway (Ire), 22 August, 1955 IR Yth (D)

League Club	Source	Date Signed	Seasons Played	Apps	Subs	Gls
Leicester C.	App	07.73				
Northampton T.	L	09.74	74	2	2	0

KILKENNY, James
Stanley, 21 November, 1934 (WH)

League Club	Source	Date Signed	Seasons Played	Apps	Subs	Gls
Doncaster Rov.	Annfield Plain	05.52	55-60	131	-	1

KILLARNEY, Arthur
Huddersfield, 26 February, 1921 (IR)

League Club	Source	Date Signed	Seasons Played	Apps	Subs	Gls
Halifax T.		05.46	46	2	-	0

KILLIN, Harold R.
Canada, 18 July, 1929 (FB)

League Club	Source	Date Signed	Seasons Played	Apps	Subs	Gls
Manchester U		04.49				
Lincoln C.	Tr	08.52	53	7	-	0

KILMORE, Kevin
Scunthorpe, 11 November, 1959 E Yth (M)

League Club	Source	Date Signed	Seasons Played	Apps	Subs	Gls
Scunthorpe U.	Jnrs	01.77	76-79	93	9	28
Grimsby T.	Tr	09.79	79-82	70	32	27
Rotherham U.	Tr	08.83	83-84	82	2	20
Lincoln C.	Belgium	01.86	85-86	40	6	6

KILNER, Andrew W.
Bolton, 11 October, 1966 E Yth (LW)

League Club	Source	Date Signed	Seasons Played	Apps	Subs	Gls
Burnley	App	07.84	85	2	3	0
Stockport Co.	Jonsereds (Swe)	12.90	90-91	34	8	14
Rochdale	L	01.92	91	3	0	0

KILNER, John I.
Bolton, 3 October, 1959 (G)

League Club	Source	Date Signed	Seasons Played	Apps	Subs	Gls
Preston N.E.	App	10.77				
Halifax T.	Tr	02.79	78-81	114	0	0
Wigan Ath. (N/C)	South Africa	07.83	83	4	0	0

KILSHAW, Edward
Prescot, 25 December, 1919 (OR)

League Club	Source	Date Signed	Seasons Played	Apps	Subs	Gls
Bury	Prescot Cables	10.37	37-48	111	-	13
Sheffield Wed.	Tr	12.48	48	17	-	1

KILSHAW, Frederick
Wrexham, 24 August, 1916 (IR)

League Club	Source	Date Signed	Seasons Played	Apps	Subs	Gls
Leicester C.		01.45				
New Brighton	Tr	07.46	46	8	-	1

KIMBERLEY, S. Kenneth
Walsall, 7 August, 1920 (G)

League Club	Source	Date Signed	Seasons Played	Apps	Subs	Gls
Walsall	Cannock Colly	05.46	46	1	-	0

KIMBLE, Alan F.
Dagenham, 6 August, 1966 (LB)

League Club	Source	Date Signed	Seasons Played	Apps	Subs	Gls
Charlton Ath.	Jnrs	08.84	84	6	0	0
Exeter C.	L	08.85	85	1	0	0
Cambridge U.	Tr	08.86	86-91	249	4	20

KIMBLE, Gary L.
Dagenham, 6 August, 1966 (LW)

League Club	Source	Date Signed	Seasons Played	Apps	Subs	Gls
Charlton Ath.	Jnrs	08.84	84	7	2	1
Exeter C.	L	08.85	85	1	0	0
Cambridge U.	Tr	08.86	86-87	39	2	2
Doncaster Rov.	Tr	10.87	87-88	60	5	1
Fulham	Tr	08.89	89	1	2	0
Maidstone U.	Tr	10.89				
Gillingham	St Albans C.	02.90	89-90	35	13	1
Peterborough U.	Tr	07.91	91	30	0	4

KINDON, Stephen M.
Warrington, 17 December, 1950 E Yth (F)

League Club	Source	Date Signed	Seasons Played	Apps	Subs	Gls
Burnley	App	12.67	68-71	102	7	28
Wolverhampton W.	Tr	07.72	72-77	111	27	28
Burnley	Tr	11.77	77-79	73	3	18
Huddersfield T.	Tr	12.79	79-81	69	4	35

KING, Adam
Hillingdon, 4 October, 1969 E Yth (M)

League Club	Source	Date Signed	Seasons Played	Apps	Subs	Gls
West Ham U.	YT	06.88				
Plymouth Arg.	Tr	03.90	89-90	9	7	0

KING, Alan
Birkenhead, 18 January, 1945 (WH)

League Club	Source	Date Signed	Seasons Played	Apps	Subs	Gls
Tranmere Rov.	Jnrs	07.62	62-71	342	0	33

KING, Alan
Gateshead, 25 November, 1947 (OL)

League Club	Source	Date Signed	Seasons Played	Apps	Subs	Gls
Hartlepool U. (Am)	Horden Colly	08.67	67	0	1	0

KING, Andrew E.
Luton, 14 August, 1956 Eu21-2 (M)

League Club	Source	Date Signed	Seasons Played	Apps	Subs	Gls
Luton T	App	07.74	74-75	30	3	9
Everton	Tr	04.76	75-79	150	1	38
Queens Park R.	Tr	09.80	80-81	28	2	9
West Bromwich A.	Tr	09.81	81	21	4	4
Everton	Tr	07.82	82-83	43	1	11
Wolverhampton W.	Cambuur (Neth)	01.85	84-85	28	0	10
Luton T.	Tr	12.85	85	3	0	0
Aldershot	Tr	08.86	86	36	0	11

KING, Andrew J.
Thatcham, 30 March, 1970 (F)

League Club	Source	Date Signed	Seasons Played	Apps	Subs	Gls
Reading	Tr	06.88	88	0	1	0

KING, Barry
Chesterfield, 30 March, 1935 (OR)

League Club	Source	Date Signed	Seasons Played	Apps	Subs	Gls
Chelsea	Norton Woodseats	02.58				
Reading	Tr	03.58	57	3	-	0

KING, M. Brian
Bishops Stortford, 18 May, 1947 (G)

League Club	Source	Date Signed	Seasons Played	Apps	Subs	Gls
Millwall	Chelmsford C.	06.67	67-74	302	0	0
Coventry C.	Tr	08.75	75	23	0	0

KING, David J.
Hull, 24 October, 1940 (IF)

League Club	Source	Date Signed	Seasons Played	Apps	Subs	Gls
Hull C.	Jnrs	10.58	59-62	65	-	24

KING, David M.
Colchester, 18 September, 1962 (M)

League Club	Source	Date Signed	Seasons Played	Apps	Subs	Gls
Derby Co.	App	09.80				
York C. (N/C)	Gresley Rov.	03.83	82	0	1	0

KING, Dennis
Bearpark (Dm), 16 September, 1932 (W)

League Club	Source	Date Signed	Seasons Played	Apps	Subs	Gls
Bradford P.A.		09.50				
Oldham Ath.	Spennymoor U.	05.54	54-55	22	-	7

KING, Derek A.
Hackney, 15 August, 1929 (CH)

League Club	Source	Date Signed	Seasons Played	Apps	Subs	Gls
Tottenham H.	Jnrs	08.50	51-54	19	-	0
Swansea C.	Tr	08.56	56	5	-	0

KING, Frederick A. R.
Northampton, 19 September, 1919 (OR)

League Club	Source	Date Signed	Seasons Played	Apps	Subs	Gls
Northampton T.		10.37	37-38	42	-	6
Wolverhampton W.	Tr	11.39	46	6	-	3
Northampton T.	Tr	12.47	47-49	56	-	17

KING, George
Warkworth (Nd), 5 January, 1923 (CF)

League Club	Source	Date Signed	Seasons Played	Apps	Subs	Gls
Newcastle U.	R.A.F.	08.46	46	2	-	0
Hull C.	Tr	03.48	47-48	3	-	0
Port Vale	Tr	04.49	48-49	10	-	5
Barrow	Tr	02.50	49-51	86	-	35
Bradford C.	Tr	01.52	51-52	23	-	9
Gillingham	Tr	10.52	52	19	-	5

KING, Gerald H.
Radnor, 9 April, 1947 W Sch (W)

League Club	Source	Date Signed	Seasons Played	Apps	Subs	Gls
Cardiff C.	Jnrs	06.64	64	6	-	0
Torquay U.	Tr	06.65	65	17	0	2
Luton T.	Tr	06.66	66	21	1	4
Newport Co.	Tr	07.67	67-68	49	3	9

KING, Jeffrey
Fauldhouse, 9 November, 1953 (M)

League Club	Source	Date Signed	Seasons Played	Apps	Subs	Gls
Derby Co.	Albion Rov.	04.74	75-77	12	2	0
Notts Co.	L	01.76	75	3	0	0
Portsmouth	L	03.76	75	4	0	0
Walsall	Tr	11.77	77-78	50	1	4
Sheffield Wed.	Tr	08.79	79-81	54	3	5
Sheffield U.	Tr	01.82	81-82	35	2	5
Chesterfield (N/C)		10.83	83	1	0	0

KING, John
Ferndale, 29 November, 1933 Died 1982 W Sch/W-1 (G)

League Club	Source	Date Signed	Seasons Played	Apps	Subs	Gls
Swansea C.	Jnrs	02.51	50-63	368	-	0

KING, John (Jake)
Glasgow, 29 January, 1955 (RB)

League Club	Source	Date Signed	Seasons Played	Apps	Subs	Gls
Shrewsbury T.	App	01.73	71-81	304	2	20
Wrexham	Tr	08.82	82-84	91	1	5
Cardiff C.	Tr	11.84	84-85	30	0	0

KING, John A. (Ian)
Loanhead, 27 May, 1937 S Sch (CH)

League Club	Source	Date Signed	Seasons Played	Apps	Subs	Gls
Leicester C.	Arniston Rov.	06.57	57-65	244	0	6
Charlton Ath.	Tr	03.66	65-67	63	0	0

KING, John A.
Liverpool, 15 April, 1938 (WH)

League Club	Source	Date Signed	Seasons Played	Apps	Subs	Gls
Everton	Jnrs	03.56	57-59	48	-	1
Bournemouth	Tr	07.60	60	21	-	1
Tranmere R.	Tr	02.61	60-67	239	2	4
Port Vale	Tr	07.68	68-70	99	2	0

KING, John C.
Great Gidding, 5 November, 1926 (WH)

League Club	Source	Date Signed	Seasons Played	Apps	Subs	Gls
Leicester C.	Peterborough U.	09.44	46-54	197	-	5

KING, John W.
Wrenbury (Ches), 9 August, 1932 (CF)

League Club	Source	Date Signed	Seasons Played	Apps	Subs	Gls
Crewe Alex.	Jnrs	10.49	50-53	48	-	17
Stoke C.	Tr	09.53	53-60	284	-	105
Cardiff C.	Tr	08.61	61	33	-	6
Crewe Alex.	Tr	06.62	62-66	178	0	43

KING, Martyn N. G.
Birmingham, 23 August, 1937 (CF)

League Club	Source	Date Signed	Seasons Played	Apps	Subs	Gls
Colchester U.	Pegasus	05.57	56-64	212	-	131
Wrexham	Tr	10.64	64-65	45	0	15

KING, Peter
Liverpool, 5 July, 1964 (M)

League Club	Source	Date Signed	Seasons Played	Apps	Subs	Gls
Liverpool	App	07.82				
Crewe Alex.	Tr	08.83	83-84	55	9	5

KING, Peter C.
Worcester, 3 April, 1943 (F)

League Club	Source	Date Signed	Seasons Played	Apps	Subs	Gls
Cardiff C.	Worcester C.	09.60	61-73	352	2	66

KING, Philip G.
Bristol, 28 December, 1967 E'B' (LB)

League Club	Source	Date Signed	Seasons Played	Apps	Subs	Gls
Exeter C.	App	01.85	84-85	24	3	0
Torquay U.	Tr	07.86	86	24	0	3
Swindon T.	Tr	02.87	86-89	112	4	4
Sheffield Wed.	Tr	11.89	89-91	106	1	1

KING, Raymond
Warkworth, 15 August, 1924 E'B'-1 (G)

League Club	Source	Date Signed	Seasons Played	Apps	Subs	Gls
Newcastle U.		04.42				
Leyton Orient	Tr	10.46	46	1	-	0
Port Vale	Ashington	05.49	49-56	252	-	0

KING, Robert E.
Edinburgh, 7 September, 1941 (FB)

League Club	Source	Date Signed	Seasons Played	Apps	Subs	Gls
Southend U.	Glasgow Rangers	08.63	63-65	77	2	2

KING, Simon A.
Ebbw Vale, 19 July, 1964 (D)

League Club	Source	Date Signed	Seasons Played	Apps	Subs	Gls
Newport Co. (N/C)	Cwmbran T.	10.84	84	1	0	0

KING, Thomas
Edinburgh, 18 July, 1933 (G)

League Club	Source	Date Signed	Seasons Played	Apps	Subs	Gls
Watford	Ormiston Primrose	03.54	55	20	-	0

KING, Thomas F.
Barrow, 2 April, 1934 (WH)

League Club	Source	Date Signed	Seasons Played	Apps	Subs	Gls
Barrow	Holker C.O.B.	03.53	52-59	73	-	1

KINGSHOTT, Frederick J.
Camden, 20 June, 1929 (G)

League Club	Source	Date Signed	Seasons Played	Apps	Subs	Gls
Doncaster Rov.		02.53	52	2	-	0
Gillingham	Tr	11.55	55-56	45	-	0

KINGSNORTH, Thomas H.
Sittingbourne, 16 April, 1917 (CH)

League Club	Source	Date Signed	Seasons Played	Apps	Subs	Gls
Gillingham	Lloyds Paper Mill	09.46	50	29	-	0

KINGSTON, Andrew K.
Oxford, 21 February, 1959 E Sch/E Yth (RB)

League Club	Source	Date Signed	Seasons Played	Apps	Subs	Gls
Oxford U.	App	10.76	76-81	44	6	0

KINLOCH, Thomas S.
Glasgow, 22 February, 1927 (WH)

League Club	Source	Date Signed	Seasons Played	Apps	Subs	Gls
Carlisle U.	Falkirk	05.50	50-55	182	-	15
Workington	Tr	07.56	56-57	70	-	12
Southampton	Tr	02.58	57-58	53	-	0

KINNEAR, Joseph P.
Dublin, 27 December, 1946 IR-25 (RB)

League Club	Source	Date Signed	Seasons Played	Apps	Subs	Gls
Tottenham H.	St Albans C.	02.65	65-74	189	7	2
Brighton & H.A.	Tr	08.75	75	15	1	1

KINNELL, George
Cowdenbeath, 22 December, 1937 (CH)

League Club	Source	Date Signed	Seasons Played	Apps	Subs	Gls
Stoke C.	Aberdeen	11.63	63-65	89	2	6
Oldham Ath.	Tr	08.66	66	12	0	8
Sunderland	Tr	10.66	66-68	67	2	3
Middlesbrough	Tr	10.68	68	12	1	1

KINSELL, T. Harold
Cannock, 3 May, 1921 (FB)

League Club	Source	Date Signed	Seasons Played	Apps	Subs	Gls
West Bromwich A.	Jnrs	06.38	46-48	83	-	0
Bolton W.	Tr	06.49	49	17	-	0
Reading	Tr	05.50	50	12	-	0
West Ham U.	Tr	01.51	50-54	101	-	2

KINSELLA, Anthony S.
Grays, 30 October, 1961 IRu21-2 (LW)

League Club	Source	Date Signed	Seasons Played	Apps	Subs	Gls
Millwall	App	11.78	78-80	55	6	1
Ipswich T.	Tampa Bay (USA)	04.82	82-83	7	2	0
Millwall	Tr	06.84	84-85	20	2	1
Doncaster Rov.	Enfield	02.87	86-87	29	1	4

KINSELLA, Leonard
Dumbarton, 14 May, 1946 (M)

League Club	Source	Date Signed	Seasons Played	Apps	Subs	Gls
Burnley	App	05.63	65-69	7	6	0
Carlisle U.	Tr	09.70	70-71	10	4	0
Rochdale	Tr	09.71	71-73	82	3	4

KINSELLA, Mark A.
Dublin, 12 August, 1972 IRu21-1 (M)

League Club	Source	Date Signed	Seasons Played	Apps	Subs	Gls
Colchester U.	YT	08.89	89	1	5	0

KINSELLA, Patrick G.
Liverpool, 8 November, 1943 (M)

League Club	Source	Date Signed	Seasons Played	Apps	Subs	Gls
Liverpool	Jnrs	11.60				
Tranmere Rov.	Bangor C.	08.66	66	1	0	0
Stockport Co.	Rhyl	10.68	68	12	1	0

KINSEY, Albert J.
Liverpool, 19 September, 1945 E Sch (F)

League Club	Source	Date Signed	Seasons Played	Apps	Subs	Gls
Manchester U.	App	10.62				
Wrexham	Tr	03.66	65-72	245	8	80
Crewe Alex.	Tr	03.73	72-74	30	2	1

KINSEY, Brian R.
Charlton, 4 March, 1938 (LB)

League Club	Source	Date Signed	Seasons Played	Apps	Subs	Gls
Charlton Ath.	Bromley	09.56	56-70	371	6	19

KINSEY, Noel
Treorchy, 24 December, 1925 W-7 (IF)

League Club	Source	Date Signed	Seasons Played	Apps	Subs	Gls
Cardiff C.	Jnrs	06.44				
Norwich C.	Tr	05.47	47-52	223	-	57
Birmingham C.	Tr	05.53	53-57	149	-	48
Port Vale	Tr	02.58	57-60	72	-	6

Noel Kinsey (Cardiff City, Norwich City, Birmingham City, Port Vale & Wales)

KINSEY, Stephen
Manchester, 2 January, 1963 E Yth (W)

League Club	Source	Date Signed	Seasons Played	Apps	Subs	Gls
Manchester C.	App	01.80	80-85	87	14	15
Chester C.	L	09.82	82	3	0	1
Chesterfield	L	11.82	82	3	0	0
Rochdale (N/C)	Tacoma (USA)	10.91	91	3	3	1

KIPPAX, Dennis H.
Sheffield, 7 August, 1926 Died 1970 (OR)

League Club	Source	Date Signed	Seasons Played	Apps	Subs	Gls
Sheffield Wed.	Stocksbridge Wks	03.46	46	1	-	0

KIPPAX, F. Peter
Burnley, 17 July, 1922 E Amat/EF Lge (OL)

League Club	Source	Date Signed	Seasons Played	Apps	Subs	Gls
Burnley (Am)	Jnrs	07.46	46-47	32	-	6
Liverpool (Am)	Tr	01.49	48	1	-	0

KIRBY, Alan
Barrow, 19 December, 1926 (G)

League Club	Source	Date Signed	Seasons Played	Apps	Subs	Gls
Notts Co.		05.45				
Barrow		09.47	50-51	21	-	0

KIRBY, Dennis
Leeds, 8 November, 1924 (WH)

League Club	Source	Date Signed	Seasons Played	Apps	Subs	Gls
Leeds U.		09.42	47	8	-	0

KIRBY, Eric
Sheffield, 12 October, 1926 (WH)

League Club	Source	Date Signed	Seasons Played	Apps	Subs	Gls
Sheffield Wed.		12.49	50	1	-	0
York Co.	Tr	08.52	52	1	-	0

KIRBY, George A.
Liverpool, 20 December, 1933 (CF)

League Club	Source	Date Signed	Seasons Played	Apps	Subs	Gls
Everton	Jnrs	06.52	55-57	26	-	9
Sheffield Wed.	Tr	03.59	59	3	-	0
Plymouth Arg.	Tr	01.60	59-62	93	-	38
Southampton	Tr	09.62	62-63	63	-	28
Coventry C.	Tr	03.64	63-64	18	-	10
Swansea C.	Tr	10.64	64	26	-	8
Walsall	Tr	05.65	65-66	74	1	25
Brentford	New York (USA)	10.68	68	5	0	1

KIRK, Harold J.
Saltcoats, 25 August, 1944 (W)

League Club	Source	Date Signed	Seasons Played	Apps	Subs	Gls
Middlesbrough	Ardeer Rec.	05.63	63	1	-	0
Darlington	Dumbarton	06.67	67-69	59	3	7
Hartlepool U.	Tr	10.69	69-70	42	3	5
Scunthorpe U.	Tr	11.70	70-72	112	0	16
Stockport Co.	Tr	09.73	73-74	60	8	7

KIRK, James
Tarbolton (Ayrs), 12 November, 1925 (G)

League Club	Source	Date Signed	Seasons Played	Apps	Subs	Gls
Bury	St Mirren	08.51	51-53	79	-	0
Colchester U.	Tr	06.54	54	32	-	0
Torquay U.	Tr	08.55	55	39	-	0
Aldershot	Tr	07.56	56	5	-	0

KIRK, John F.
Leicester, 7 February, 1922 (OL)

League Club	Source	Date Signed	Seasons Played	Apps	Subs	Gls
Nottingham F.		08.48				
Darlington	Tr	08.51	51	31	-	4

KIRK, John M.
Canada, 13 March, 1930 (IF)

League Club	Source	Date Signed	Seasons Played	Apps	Subs	Gls
Portsmouth	Montrose	01.51				
Accrington St.	Tr	03.53	52-53	14	-	1

KIRK, Roy
Bolsover, 11 June, 1929 Died 1983 (D)

League Club	Source	Date Signed	Seasons Played	Apps	Subs	Gls
Leeds U.	Bolsover Colly	10.48	50-51	34	-	1
Coventry C.	Tr	03.52	51-59	330	-	6

KIRK, Stephen D.
Kirkcaldy, 3 January, 1963 (FB)

League Club	Source	Date Signed	Seasons Played	Apps	Subs	Gls
Stoke C.	East Fife	05.80	81	12	0	0

KIRKALDIE, John (Jack)
Coventry, 2 August, 1917 Died 1985 (OR)

League Club	Source	Date Signed	Seasons Played	Apps	Subs	Gls
Southend U.		02.36				
West Ham U.	Tr	02.37	36-38	11	-	1
Doncaster Rov.	Tr	04.39	38-47	53	-	17

KIRKBY, John
USA, 29 November, 1929 Died 1953 (FB)

League Club	Source	Date Signed	Seasons Played	Apps	Subs	Gls
Stoke C.	Jnrs	12.46	48	1	-	0
Wrexham	Tr	08.51	51-52	5	-	0

KIRKHAM, John
Ellesmere Port, 16 June, 1918 (F)

League Club	Source	Date Signed	Seasons Played	Apps	Subs	Gls
Wolverhampton W.	Ellesmere Port	03.36	37-38	13	-	5
Bournemouth	Tr	10.38	38-46	47	-	26

KIRKHAM, John K.
Wednesbury, 13 May, 1941 E Yth/Eu23-2 (WH)

League Club	Source	Date Signed	Seasons Played	Apps	Subs	Gls
Wolverhampton W.	Jnrs	05.58	59-64	100	-	12
Peterborough U.	Tr	11.65	65-67	46	0	2
Exeter C.	Tr	07.68	68	31	1	6

KIRKHAM, Paul
Manchester, 5 July, 1969 (F)

League Club	Source	Date Signed	Seasons Played	Apps	Subs	Gls
Huddersfield T.	Manchester U. (YT)	09.87	87	0	1	0

KIRKHAM, Raymond
Thorne, 16 December, 1934 (G)

League Club	Source	Date Signed	Seasons Played	Apps	Subs	Gls
Mansfield T.	Thorne T.	12.57	57-59	42	-	0

KIRKHAM, Reginald
Ormskirk, 8 May, 1919 (FB)

League Club	Source	Date Signed	Seasons Played	Apps	Subs	Gls
Wolverhampton W.	Ormskirk	03.46				
Burnley	Tr	03.47	48-50	13	-	1

KIRKHAM, Royce
Ollerton, 17 October, 1937 (FB)

League Club	Source	Date Signed	Seasons Played	Apps	Subs	Gls
Notts Co.	Ollerton Colly	05.55	56	1	-	0

KIRKLAND, James W.
Bedford, 30 October, 1946 (FB)

League Club	Source	Date Signed	Seasons Played	Apps	Subs	Gls
Grimsby T.	Aberdeen	07.70	70	12	0	0

KIRKMAN, Alan J.
Bolton, 21 June, 1936 (IF)

League Club	Source	Date Signed	Seasons Played	Apps	Subs	Gls
Manchester C.	Bacup Bor.	02.56	56-58	7	-	6
Rotherham U.	Tr	03.59	58-63	143	-	58
Newcastle U.	Tr	09.63	63	5	-	1
Scunthorpe U.	Tr	12.63	63-64	32	-	5
Torquay U.	Tr	07.65	65-66	58	1	8
Workington	Tr	01.67	66-67	56	0	3

KIRKMAN, Kenneth R.
Bolton, 20 March, 1931

League Club	Source	Date Signed	Seasons Played	Apps	Subs	Gls
Bournemouth		07.51				
Southport	Tr	08.53	53	1	-	0

KIRKMAN, Norman
Bolton, 6 March, 1920 (FB)

League Club	Source	Date Signed	Seasons Played	Apps	Subs	Gls
Burnley		09.39				
Rochdale	Tr	09.46	46-47	53	-	0
Chesterfield	Tr	12.47	47-48	41	-	0
Leicester C.	Tr	08.49	49	12	-	0
Southampton	Tr	07.50	50-51	20	-	0
Exeter C.	Tr	03.52	51-52	11	-	1

KIRKPATRICK, John
Annan, 3 March, 1919 (IF)

League Club	Source	Date Signed	Seasons Played	Apps	Subs	Gls
Carlisle U.	Jnrs	11.37	46	35	-	2

KIRKPATRICK, Roger W.
Chester, 29 May, 1923 (WH)

League Club	Source	Date Signed	Seasons Played	Apps	Subs	Gls
Chester C.		08.47	47-52	110	-	26

KIRKUP, Brian A.
Slough, 16 April, 1932 (CF)

League Club	Source	Date Signed	Seasons Played	Apps	Subs	Gls
Reading	Bedford T.	08.55	55-57	55	-	19
Northampton T.	Tr	07.58	58-59	26	-	7
Aldershot	Tr	11.59	59-61	59	-	14

KIRKUP, Frank W.
Spennymoor, 12 January, 1939 (OL)

League Club	Source	Date Signed	Seasons Played	Apps	Subs	Gls
Blackburn Rov.	Spennymoor U.	02.57				
Workington	Tr	06.59	59-62	140	-	31
Carlisle U.	Tr	12.62	62-64	76	-	15
Notts Co.	Tr	06.65	65	29	0	0
Workington		11.66	66	8	0	0

KIRKUP, Graeme S.
Cramlington, 31 May, 1965 (RB)

League Club	Source	Date Signed	Seasons Played	Apps	Subs	Gls
Exeter C.	App	05.83	81-85	102	5	1

KIRKUP, Joseph R.
Hexham, 17 December, 1939 E Yth/Eu23-3 (FB)

League Club	Source	Date Signed	Seasons Played	Apps	Subs	Gls
West Ham U.	Jnrs	05.57	58-65	165	0	6
Chelsea	Tr	03.66	65-67	48	5	2
Southampton	Tr	02.68	67-73	169	0	3

KIRKWOOD, Ian
Edinburgh, 29 November, 1932 (IR)

League Club	Source	Date Signed	Seasons Played	Apps	Subs	Gls
Reading	Wokingham T.	02.53	52-54	5	-	1

KIRKWOOD, John F.
Falkirk, 27 February, 1932 (G)

League Club	Source	Date Signed	Seasons Played	Apps	Subs	Gls
Reading	Blairhall Colly	12.49	52-53	31	-	0

KIRMAN, Harold
Hull, 3 December, 1930 (FB)

League Club	Source	Date Signed	Seasons Played	Apps	Subs	Gls
Hull C.	Fred Askew Y.C.	12.50				
Gillingham	Tr	07.52	53	8	-	0
Hull C.		01.55	55	2	-	0

KIRSTEN, Kenneth
South Africa, 28 October, 1922 (W)

League Club	Source	Date Signed	Seasons Played	Apps	Subs	Gls
Charlton Ath.	Park Villa	03.48				
Aldershot	Tr	08.51	51	5	-	0

KIRTLEY, J. Harold
Washington, 23 May, 1930 (IF)

League Club	Source	Date Signed	Seasons Played	Apps	Subs	Gls
Sunderland	Fatfield Jnrs	05.48	48-54	95	-	18
Cardiff C.	Tr	05.55	55	38	-	4
Gateshead	Tr	03.57	56-59	96	-	14

KIRTON, John
Aberdeen, 4 March, 1916 (WH)

League Club	Source	Date Signed	Seasons Played	Apps	Subs	Gls
Stoke C.	Banks o'Dee	11.35	46-52	162	-	2
Bradford C.	Tr	07.53	53	8	-	0

KISBY, Christopher N.
Pudsey, 7 November, 1952 (D)

League Club	Source	Date Signed	Seasons Played	Apps	Subs	Gls
Scunthorpe U.	App	10.70	70-72	30	9	2
Workington	Tr	08.73	73-76	162	2	2
Southport	Tr	08.77	77	42	0	1

KITCHEN, John (Jack)
Whitehaven, 28 February, 1925 Died 1992 (CH)

League Club	Source	Date Signed	Seasons Played	Apps	Subs	Gls
Barnsley	Ketts. Ath.	10.44	46-51	54	-	0

KITCHEN, Peter M.
Mexborough, 16 February, 1952 (F)

League Club	Source	Date Signed	Seasons Played	Apps	Subs	Gls
Doncaster Rov.	Jnrs	07.70	70-76	221	7	89
Leyton Orient	Tr	07.77	77-78	64	1	28
Fulham	Tr	02.79	78-79	21	3	6
Cardiff C.	Tr	08.80	80-81	64	3	21
Leyton Orient	Happy Valley (HK)	12.82	82-83	46	3	21
Chester C. (N/C)	Dagenham	03.85	84	3	2	1

KITCHENER, Barry R.
Dagenham, 11 December, 1947 (CD)

League Club	Source	Date Signed	Seasons Played	Apps	Subs	Gls
Millwall	App	08.65	66-81	518	5	25

KITCHENER, Raymond A.
Letchworth, 31 October, 1930 (OL)

League Club	Source	Date Signed	Seasons Played	Apps	Subs	Gls
Chelsea	Hitchin T.	07.54	55	1	-	0
Norwich C.	Tr	09.56	56	18	-	0

KITCHENER, William H.
Arlesey, 3 November, 1946 (FB)

League Club	Source	Date Signed	Seasons Played	Apps	Subs	Gls
West Ham U.	App	11.63	66-67	11	0	0
Torquay U.	L	09.66	66	25	0	3
Torquay U.	Tr	12.67	67-70	142	0	5
Bournemouth	Tr	07.71	71	36	0	2

KITCHING, Phillip J.
Lewisham, 30 September, 1967 (M)

League Club	Source	Date Signed	Seasons Played	Apps	Subs	Gls
York C. (N/C)	Bradford C. (N/C)	08.87	87	7	6	0

KITE, Philip D.
Bristol, 26 October, 1962 E Sch/E Yth (G)

League Club	Source	Date Signed	Seasons Played	Apps	Subs	Gls
Bristol Rov.	App	10.80	80-83	96	0	0
Southampton	Tr	08.84	84-85	4	0	0
Middlesbrough	L	03.86	85	2	0	0
Gillingham		02.87	86-88	70	0	0
Bournemouth	Tr	06.89	89	7	0	0
Sheffield U.	Tr	08.90	90-91	11	0	0
Mansfield T.	L	11.91	91	11	0	0

KITSON, Paul
Peterlee, 9 January, 1971 Eu21-7 (W)

League Club	Source	Date Signed	Seasons Played	Apps	Subs	Gls
Leicester C.	YT	12.88	89-91	39	11	6
Derby Co.	Tr	03.92	91	12	0	4

League Club	Source	Date Signed	Seasons Played	Apps	Subs	Gls
KIWOMYA, Andrew D.						
Huddersfield, 1 October, 1967 E Yth						(W)
Barnsley	YT	07.85	85	1	0	0
Sheffield Wed.	Tr	10.86				
KIWOMYA, Christopher M.						
Huddersfield, 2 December, 1969						(F)
Ipswich T.	YT	03.87	88-91	112	23	32

Chris Kiwomya (Ipswich Town)

League Club	Source	Date Signed	Seasons Played	Apps	Subs	Gls
KLETZENBAUER, C. Frank						
Coventry, 21 July, 1936						(FB)
Coventry C.	Coventry M.S.C.	03.56	56-63	122	-	3
Walsall	Tr	03.64	63-64	12	-	0
KLONER, Hymie R.						
Poland, 23 May, 1929						(WH)
Birmingham C.	Marist Bros (SA)	11.50	50	1	-	0
KLUG, Bryan P.						
Coventry, 8 October, 1960 E Yth						(M)
Ipswich T.	App	11.77				
Wimbledon	L	03.80	79	10	1	0
Chesterfield	Tr	08.83	83	27	7	2
Peterborough U.	Tr	08.84	84	39	0	2
KNAPP, Anthony						
Newstead (Nts), 13 October, 1936 EF Lge						(CH)
Leicester C.	Jnrs	12.53	55-60	86	-	0
Southampton	Tr	08.61	61-66	233	0	2
Coventry C.	Tr	08.67	67	11	0	0
Tranmere Rov.	Los Angeles (USA)	10.69	69-70	36	0	1
KNIGHT, Alan E.						
Balham, 3 July, 1961 E Yth/Eu21-2						(G)
Portsmouth	App	03.79	77-91	446	0	0
KNIGHT, Anthony						
Romford, 6 March, 1959						(G)
Luton T.	App	05.76	76-77	6	0	0
Brighton & H.A.	Dover T.	08.79				

League Club	Source	Date Signed	Seasons Played	Apps	Subs	Gls
KNIGHT, Arnold W.						
Guisborough, 30 May, 1919						(IF)
Leeds U.		10.37				
Plymouth Arg.	Tr	07.47	47	7	-	0
Bradford C.	Tr	02.48	47-48	7	-	0
KNIGHT, Brian M.						
Dundee, 28 March, 1949						(FB)
Huddersfield T.	Dundee	07.69				
Northampton T.	Tr	10.69	69	9	3	0
KNIGHT, Brian T.						
High Wycombe, 14 November, 1946						(OL)
Reading	App	11.64	64-65	4	0	1
KNIGHT, Craig						
Wrexham, 24 October, 1973						(D)
Wrexham (YT)	YT	07.90	91	1	0	0
KNIGHT, Frank						
Hucknall, 26 October, 1921						(LH)
Nottingham F.		05.43	46-49	48	-	1
KNIGHT, George R.						
Bolton, 12 May, 1921						(IR)
Burnley	Jnrs	05.38	38-46	9	-	2
KNIGHT, Graham J.						
Rochester, 5 January, 1952						(FB/M)
Gillingham	App	01.70	70-78	229	16	10
KNIGHT, Ian J.						
Hartlepool, 26 October, 1966 Eu21-2						(CD)
Barnsley	App	10.84				
Sheffield Wed.	Tr	08.85	85-88	21	0	0
Scunthorpe U.	L	08.89	89	2	0	0
Grimsby T.	Tr	01.90	89-91	16	5	2
KNIGHT, Jeffrey W.						
Sudbury, 10 December, 1926						(F)
Derby Co.		05.46				
Walsall	Tr	08.52	52	4	-	0
KNIGHT, John						
Bolton, 12 September, 1922						(IL)
Burnley	Jnrs	08.45	46-48	26	-	5
Preson N.E.	Tr	12.48	48-49	39	-	7
Chesterfield	Tr	07.51	51	35	-	6
KNIGHT, Keith						
Cheltenham, 16 February, 1969 E Sch						(W)
Reading	Cheltenham T.	09.88	88-90	39	4	8
KNIGHT, Lyndon A.						
Lydbrook, 3 February, 1961						(G)
Hereford U.	App	02.79	78	2	0	0
KNIGHT, Peter R.						
Brighton, 12 November, 1939						(W)
Brighton & H.A.	Lewes	01.64	63-65	9	1	1
KNIGHT, Peter R.						
Ilford, 26 December, 1937						(OR)
Southend U.		06.58				
Nottingham F.	Tr	08.59	59	4	-	0
Oxford U.	Tr	07.60	62-64	94	-	12
Reading	Tr	11.64	64-65	26	0	3
KNIGHT, Terence G.						
Camden, 1 February, 1932						(G)
Aldershot (Am)	Alton T.	10.58	58	4	-	0
KNIGHTON, Kenneth						
Barnsley, 20 February, 1944						(M)
Wolverhampton W.	App	02.61	64-66	13	3	0
Oldham Ath.	Tr	11.66	66-67	45	0	4
Preston N.E.	Tr	11.67	67-68	62	0	3
Blackburn Rov.	Tr	06.69	69-70	70	0	11
Hull C.	Tr	03.71	70-72	79	1	9
Sheffield Wed.	Tr	08.73	73-75	71	5	2
KNIGHTS, Anthony F.						
Grimsby, 13 March, 1940						(LH)
Grimsby T.	Jnrs	06.58	59-63	75	-	1
Luton T.	Tr	08.64	64	2	-	0
Aldershot	Tr	07.65	65	20	0	0

League Club	Source	Date Signed	Seasons Played	Career Record Apps	Subs	Gls
KNILL, Alan R.						
Slough, 8 October, 1964 W Yth/W-1						(CD)
Southampton	App	10.82				
Halifax T.	Tr	07.84	84-86	118	0	6
Swansea C.	Tr	08.87	87-88	89	0	3
Bury	Tr	08.89	89-91	95	3	3
KNOTT, Herbert						
Goole, 5 December, 1914						(CF)
Walsall	Brierley Hill Alliance	08.37	39	9	-	2
Hull Co.	Brierley Hill Alliance	10.40	46	6	-	1
KNOTT, William F.						
Leeds, 16 March, 1934 E Yth						
Leeds U.	Jnrs	05.51				
Walsall	Tr	02.55	54	1	-	0
KNOWLES, J. Barry						
Wigan, 25 April, 1959						(LB)
Wigan Ath.	Barrow	10.84	84-87	124	3	3
KNOWLES, Cyril B.						
Fitzwilliam, 13 July, 1944 Died 1991 Eu23-6/EF Lge/E-4						(LB)
Middlesbrough	Monkton Colly	10.62	62-63	37	-	0
Tottenham H.	Tr	05.64	64-75	402	1	15
KNOWLES, Darren T.						
Sheffield, 8 October, 1970						(RB/M)
Sheffield U.	YT	07.89				
Stockport Co.	Tr	09.89	89-91	41	11	0
KNOWLES, J. David						
Halifax, 11 April, 1941						(G)
Halifax T.	Jnrs	12.58	58-62	72	-	0
Bury	Tr	07.63	64	1	-	0
Bradford C.	Tr	08.66	66	21	0	0
KNOWLES, Harold F.						
Hednesford, 6 September, 1932						(OL)
Walsall	Excelsior	09.50	50	10	-	0
Cardiff C.	Worcester C.	02.59	58-59	8	-	0
KNOWLES, James						
Preston, 31 July, 1934						(G)
Preston N.E.	Jnrs	10.57	57	2	-	0
Barrow	Tr	08.58	58-59	11	-	0
KNOWLES, Peter R.						
Fitzwilliam, 30 September, 1945 Eu21-4/E Yth						(IF)
Wolverhampton W.	App	10.62	63-69	171	3	61
KNOWLES, Raymond						
Willesden, 30 September, 1952						(F)
Wimbledon	Southall	07.78	78-79	31	8	6
KNOX, James						
Brechin, 26 November, 1935						(F)
Coventry C.	Raith Rov.	05.57	57	2	-	0
KNOX, Robert P.						
Ulverston, 26 February, 1946						(F)
Barrow	Jnrs	07.65	64-71	94	12	19
KNOX, Thomas						
Glasgow, 5 September, 1939						(OL)
Chelsea	East Stirling	06.62	62-64	20	-	0
Newcastle U.	Tr	02.65	64-66	24	1	1
Mansfield T.	Tr	03.67	66-67	34	0	5
Northampton T.	Tr	11.67	67-68	27	2	0
KNOX, William J.						
Kilmarnock, 9 September, 1937 S Sch						
Barrow	Third Lanark	07.59	59	1	-	0
KOENEN, Frans L. A.						
Netherlands, 4 November, 1958 Dutch u21 Int						(M)
Newcastle U.	Nijmegen (Neth)	08.80	80	11	1	1
KOFFMAN, S. John (Jack)						
Prestwich, 3 August, 1920 Died 1977						(OL)
Manchester U.	Northwich Vic.	08.45				
Hull C.	Tr	06.46	46	4	-	0
Oldham Ath.	Congleton T.	06.47	47	3	-	0
KOPEL, Frank						
Falkirk, 28 March, 1949 S Sch						(FB)

League Club	Source	Date Signed	Seasons Played	Career Record Apps	Subs	Gls
Manchester U.	Jnrs	04.66	67-68	8	2	0
Blackburn Rov.	Tr	03.69	68-71	23	2	0
KOSMINA, A. John						
Australia, 17 August, 1956						(F)
Arsenal	Polonia (Aus)	03.78	78	0	1	0
KOWALSKI, Andrew M.						
Warsop, 26 February, 1953						(M)
Chesterfield	Alfreton T.	02.73	72-82	354	11	30
Doncaster Rov.	Tr	07.83	83-84	45	7	1
Peterborough U.	Tr	08.85	85	35	0	4
Chesterfield	Tr	08.86	86	19	9	1

Peter Knowles (Wolverhampton Wanderers)

League Club	Source	Date Signed	Seasons Played	Career Record Apps	Subs	Gls

KOWENICKI, Ryszard
Poland, 22 December, 1948 (M)

Oldham Ath.	Widzew Lodz (Pol)	12.79	79-80	40	2	5

KOZMA, Istvan
Hungary, 3 December, 1964 Hungary Int (M)

Liverpool	Dunfermline Ath.	02.92	91	3	2	0

KRAAY, Hans
Netherlands, 22 December, 1959 (M)

Brighton & H.A.	N.A.C. Breda (Neth)	02.84	83-84	19	4	3

KRISTENSEN, Bjorn
Denmark, 10 October, 1963 Danish Int (CD)

Newcastle U.	Aahus G.F. (Den)	03.89	88-91	69	11	4

KRUSE, Patrick K.
Biggleswade, 30 November, 1953 (CD)

Leicester C.	App	02.72	73	2	0	0
Mansfield T.	L	09.74	74	6	0	1
Torquay U.	Tr	03.75	74-76	79	0	4
Brentford	Tr	03.77	76-81	186	0	12
Northampton T.	L	02.82	81	18	0	0

KRUSZYNSKI Zbigniew (Detzi)
Germany, 14 October, 1961 (M)

Wimbledon	F.C. 08 Homburg (Ger)	12.88	88-91	65	6	4
Brentford	L	03.92	91	8	0	0

KRZYWICKI, Richard L.
Penley, 2 February, 1947 W-8/Wu23-3 (W)

West Bromwich A.	App	02.65	64-69	51	6	9
Huddersfield T.	Tr	03.70	69-73	39	8	7
Scunthorpe U.	L	02.73	72	2	0	0
Northampton T.	L	11.73	73	8	0	3
Lincoln C.	Tr	07.74	74-75	55	13	11

KUBICKI, Dariusz
Warsaw (Poland), 6 June, 1963 Poland Int (RB)

Aston Villa	Legia Warsaw (Pol)	08.91	91	23	0	0

KUBICKI, Eryk
Poland (OL)

York C. (Am)	Polish Army	10.46	46	5	-	0

KUHL, Martin
Frimley, 10 January, 1965 (M)

Birmingham C.	App	01.83	82-86	103	8	5
Sheffield U.	Tr	03.87	86-87	38	0	4
Watford	Tr	02.88	87	4	0	0
Portsmouth	Tr	09.88	88-91	143	11	26

KURILA, John
Glasgow, 10 April, 1941 (WH)

Northampton T.	Glasgow Celtic	08.62	62	40	-	1
Bristol C.	Tr	08.63	63	6	-	0
Northampton T.	Tr	11.63	63-67	105	2	3
Southend U.	Tr	07.68	68-69	87	1	1
Colchester U.	Tr	05.70	70-71	53	0	4
Lincoln C.	Tr	12.71	71	23	1	0

KURZ, Frederick J.
Grimsby, 3 September, 1918 Died 1978 (CF)

Grimsby T.	Grimsby Y.M.C.A.	05.36	38	3	-	0
Crystal Palace	Tr	12.45	46-50	148	-	48

KWIATKOWSKI, Richard A.
Peterborough, 7 April, 1948 (FB/M)

Peterborough U.	Jnrs	07.67	67-71	49	11	0

KYDD, David R.
Penge, 22 December, 1945 (WH)

Brighton & H.A.	App	09.63	65	2	-	0

KYLE, Maurice
Darlington, 8 November, 1937 (CH)

Wolverhampton W.	Jnrs	09.55				
Oxford U.	Tr	02.59	62-69	275	-	2
Southend U.	L	03.70	69	8	-	0

KYNMAN, David J.
Hull, 20 May, 1962 (M)

Hull C.	App	05.80	80-81	11	-	0

Dariusz Kubicki (Legia Warsaw, Aston Villa & Poland)

L

Gary Lineker (Leicester City, Everton, Barcelona, Tottenham Hotspur & England)
Now retired from the international scene, he fell just one goal short of Bobby Charlton's England record tally of 49

LA RONDE, Everald
West Ham, 24 January, 1963 (FB)

League Club	Source	Date Signed	Seasons Played	Apps	Subs	Gls
West Ham U.	App	01.81	81	6	1	0
Bournemouth	Tr	09.83	83-84	24	0	0
Peterborough U.	L	01.85	84	6	0	0

LABONE, Brian L.
Liverpool, 23 January, 1940 E-26/Eu23-7/EF Lge (CH)

League Club	Source	Date Signed	Seasons Played	Apps	Subs	Gls
Everton	Jnrs	07.57	57-71	451	0	2

LACEY, Anthony J.
Leek, 18 March, 1944 (FB)

League Club	Source	Date Signed	Seasons Played	Apps	Subs	Gls
Stoke C.		10.65	67-68	2	2	0
Port Vale	Tr	02.70	69-74	193	7	9
Rochdale	Tr	07.75	75-76	83	0	0

LACEY, Desmond P.
Dublin, 3 August, 1925 Died 1974 (OR)

League Club	Source	Date Signed	Seasons Played	Apps	Subs	Gls
Chester C. (Am)		07.46	46	1	-	0

LACEY, William
Tynemouth, 17 November, 1931 Died 1988 (CF)

League Club	Source	Date Signed	Seasons Played	Apps	Subs	Gls
Middlesbrough		05.52				
Aldershot	Tr	02.53	52-58	211	-	59
Reading	Tr	07.59	59-62	90	-	40

LACK, Harold
Bolsover, 29 November, 1930 (OL)

League Club	Source	Date Signed	Seasons Played	Apps	Subs	Gls
Leeds U.		07.51				
Blackburn Rov.	Tr	08.52				
Chesterfield	Tr	08.53	53	1	-	0

LACKENBY, George
Newcastle, 22 May, 1931 (D)

League Club	Source	Date Signed	Seasons Played	Apps	Subs	Gls
Newcastle U.	Jnrs	10.50	51-56	19	-	0
Exeter C.	Tr	12.56	56	24	-	4
Carlisle U.	Tr	07.57	57-58	46	-	0
Gateshead	Tr	07.59	59	43	-	2
Hartlepool U.	Tr	08.60	60-62	86	-	1

LACY, John
Liverpool, 14 August, 1951 (CD)

League Club	Source	Date Signed	Seasons Played	Apps	Subs	Gls
Fulham	Kingstonian	06.71	72-77	164	4	7
Tottenham H.	Tr	07.78	78-82	99	5	2
Crystal Palace	Tr	08.83	83	24	3	0

LADD, Ian M.
Peterborough, 22 November, 1958 (CD)

League Club	Source	Date Signed	Seasons Played	Apps	Subs	Gls
Notts Co.		09.77	77	1	0	0

LAHTINEN, Aki A.
Finland, 31 October, 1958 Finland Int (CD)

League Club	Source	Date Signed	Seasons Played	Apps	Subs	Gls
Notts Co.	O.P.S. Oulu (Fin)	09.81	81-84	37	8	2

LAIDLAW, John
Aldershot, 5 July, 1936 (RB)

League Club	Source	Date Signed	Seasons Played	Apps	Subs	Gls
Colchester U.	Easthouses	06.57	59-60	41	-	1

LAIDLAW, Joseph D.
Whickham, 12 July, 1950 (M)

League Club	Source	Date Signed	Seasons Played	Apps	Subs	Gls
Middlesbrough	App	08.67	67-71	104	5	20
Carlisle U.	Tr	07.72	72-75	146	5	44
Doncaster Rov.	Tr	06.76	76-78	127	1	27
Portsmouth	Tr	06.79	79-80	60	0	19
Hereford U.	Tr	12.80	80-81	61	1	8
Mansfield T.	Tr	07.82	82	4	0	0

LAIDLER, John R. (Jackie)
Windermere, 5 January, 1919 (OL)

League Club	Source	Date Signed	Seasons Played	Apps	Subs	Gls
Barrow		09.36	36-38	40	-	6
Carlisle U.	Netherfield	06.46	46	27	-	3

LAIDMAN, Frederick
Durham, 20 June, 1913 (IF)

League Club	Source	Date Signed	Seasons Played	Apps	Subs	Gls
Everton		12.36				
Bristol C.	Tr	06.38	38	10	-	1
Darlington	Stockton	07.48	49	2	-	0

LAING, David
Strathmiglo (Fife), 20 February, 1925 SF Lge (WH)

League Club	Source	Date Signed	Seasons Played	Apps	Subs	Gls
Gillingham	Hibernian	08.57	57-58	82	-	5

LAING, Frederick J.
Glasgow, 25 February, 1920 (IF)

League Club	Source	Date Signed	Seasons Played	Apps	Subs	Gls
Luton T.	Ashfield Jnrs	06.38				
Middlesbrough	Tr	07.47				
Bristol Rov.	Tr	07.48	48	2	-	0

LAING, Robert S.
Glasgow, 1 February, 1925 Died 1985 (OL)

League Club	Source	Date Signed	Seasons Played	Apps	Subs	Gls
Birmingham C.	Falkirk	03.46	47-49	19	-	2
Watford	Tr	06.50	50-51	60	-	8

LAIRD, Alexander
Newmains, 2 June, 1926 (OR)

League Club	Source	Date Signed	Seasons Played	Apps	Subs	Gls
Chelsea	Stirling A.	11.51				
Notts Co.	Tr	07.53	53	1	-	0

LAIRD, Alexander W.
Edinburgh, 23 October, 1928 (FB)

League Club	Source	Date Signed	Seasons Played	Apps	Subs	Gls
Barrow	Dunfermline Ath.	11.57	57	22	-	0
Scunthorpe U.	Tr	08.58				

LAIRD, David S.
Rutherglen, 11 February, 1936 (IF)

League Club	Source	Date Signed	Seasons Played	Apps	Subs	Gls
Aldershot	St Mirren	07.57				
Northampton T.	St Mirren	06.60	60	12	-	1

LAIRD, David W.
Clackmannan, 9 May, 1926 (WH)

League Club	Source	Date Signed	Seasons Played	Apps	Subs	Gls
Aldershot	Alloa Ath.	05.48	48-53	126	-	22

LAISBY, John
Ulverston, 27 March, 1957 (G)

League Club	Source	Date Signed	Seasons Played	Apps	Subs	Gls
Liverpool	App	04.75				
Workington (N/C)	Barrow	03.77	76	2	0	0

LAITT, David
Colchester, 1 November, 1946 (FB)

League Club	Source	Date Signed	Seasons Played	Apps	Subs	Gls
Colchester U.	Colchester Casuals	08.65	65	0	1	0

LAKE, Huw G. T.
Swansea, 20 August, 1963 W Sch (M)

League Club	Source	Date Signed	Seasons Played	Apps	Subs	Gls
Swansea C.	App	08.81	82-83	14	5	2

LAKE, Leslie E.
Luton, 29 January, 1923 Died 1976 (FB)

League Club	Source	Date Signed	Seasons Played	Apps	Subs	Gls
Luton T.	Holly R.	09.41	46-50	59	-	0

LAKE, Michael C.
Denton, 15 November, 1966 (M)

League Club	Source	Date Signed	Seasons Played	Apps	Subs	Gls
Sheffield U.	Macclesfield T.	10.89	89-91	13	16	4

Michael Lake (Sheffield United)

League Club	Source	Date Signed	Seasons Played	Career Record Apps	Subs	Gls

LAKE, Paul A.
Denton, 28 October, 1968 Eu21-5/E'B' (M)

Manchester C.	YT	05.87	86-90	104	4	7

Paul Lake (Manchester City)

LAKING, George E.
Harthill, 17 March, 1913 (FB)

Wolverhampton W.	Dinnington	05.34	35-36	27	-	0
Middlesbrough	Tr	10.36	36-46	94	-	1

LALLY, Patrick A. M.
Paddington, 11 January, 1952 (CD)

Millwall	App	01.70	69	1	0	0
York C.	Tr	07.71	71-72	64	7	5
Swansea C.	Tr	08.73	73-78	152	8	10
Aldershot	L	10.75	75	3	0	0
Doncaster Rov.	Tr	09.78	78-81	118	4	0

LAMB, Alan
Gateshead, 30 January, 1970 (F)

Nottingham F.	YT	02.88				
Hereford U.	L	03.89	88	9	1	2
Hartlepool U.	Tr	09.89	89-90	4	10	0
Newcastle U.	Brandon U.	10.91				

LAMB, Alan D.
Falkirk, 3 July, 1952 Su23-1 (M)

Preston N.E.	App	05.70	72-76	76	4	2
Port Vale	Tr	03.77	76-77	54	0	3

LAMB, Harold E.
Bebington, 3 June, 1925 Died 1982 (IF)

Tranmere Rov.	Jnrs	08.42	47-52	88	-	12

LAMB Harold T.
Stourbridge, 20 April, 1928 (FB)

Aston Villa	Wordsley	10.49				
Scunthorpe U.	Tr	06.54	54-55	36	-	0

LAMB, Stephen P.
Southend, 2 October, 1955 (F)

Southend U.	App	10.73	74-75	6	1	0

LAMBDEN, Victor D.
Bristol, 24 October, 1925 (CF)

Bristol Rov.	Oldland	10.45	46-54	269	-	117

LAMBERT, Anton J.
Nottingham, 29 November, 1959 (M)

Scunthorpe U.	Long Eaton U.	07.80	80-81	35	4	3

LAMBERT, Brian
Sutton-in-Ashfield, 10 July, 1936 (FB)

Mansfield T.	Sutton T.	10.54	54-59	24	-	0

LAMBERT, David
Ruabon, 7 July, 1939 (FB)

Cardiff C.		03.59				
Wrexham	Tr	07.63	63	5	-	0

LAMBERT, Eric V.
Derby, 4 August, 1920 (CH)

Derby Co.	Nottingham F. (Am)	10.44				
Hartlepool U.	Tr	06.46	46	16	-	0

LAMBERT, Gilbert J.
Preston, 16 March, 1937 Died 1986 (OL)

Preston N.E.	Jnrs	03.55	58-60	22	-	6

LAMBERT, Kenneth
Sheffield, 7 June, 1928 (IF)

Barnsley	Ecclesfield	01.50	50-51	11	-	2
Gillingham	Tr	07.52	52	37	-	10
Swindon T.	Tr	07.53	53-54	30	-	5
Bradford C.	Tr	11.54	54	19	-	4

LAMBERT, Martin C.
Southampton, 24 September, 1965 E Sch/E Yth (F)

Brighton & H.A.	App	08.83	83	2	1	0
Torquay U.	Tr	07.85	85	4	2	2
Brighton & H.A.	Sedan (Fr)	07.89	89	0	1	0

LAMBERT, Matthew R.
Morecambe, 28 September, 1971 (D)

Preston N.E.	YT	07.90	90-91	11	5	2

LAMBERT, Michael A.
Balsham (Cam), 20 May, 1950 (W)

Ipswich T.	Newmarket	11.67	68-78	180	30	39
Peterborough U.	Tr	07.79	79-80	15	6	2

LAMBERT, Raymond
Bagillt, 18 July, 1922 W Sch/W-5 (FB)

Liverpool	Jnrs	07.39	46-55	308	-	2

LAMBERT, Roy
Chapeltown, 16 July, 1933 (WH)

Rotherham U.	Thorncliffe Colly	07.54	56-64	306	-	6
Barnsley	Tr	11.65	65	3	0	0

LAMBLE, John
Reading, 10 November, 1948 (W)

Reading	App	11.66	67	3	2	0

LAMBOURNE, Dennis J.
Swansea, 7 October, 1945 (CF)

Wrexham	Llanelli	07.64	64-65	15	0	4

LAMBTON, Colin G.
Newcastle, 21 February, 1942 (WH)

Newcastle U.	Chester Moor	02.60				
Doncaster Rov.	Tr	07.63	63	6	-	0

LAMBTON, William E.
Nottingham, 2 December, 1914 Died 1976 (G)

Nottingham F.	Basford N.E.	05.35				
Exeter C.		04.46				
Doncaster Rov.	Tr	10.46	46	3	-	0

LAMIE, Robert
Newarthill, 28 December, 1928 (IF)

Cardiff C.	Stonehouse Violet	10.49	49-50	6	-	1
Swansea C.	Tr	03.51	51	2	-	0

LAMONT, David
Glasgow, 2 April, 1949 (HB)

Colchester U.	App	04.67	67	0	1	0

LAMONT, William T.
Glasgow, 25 December, 1926 (FB)

New Brighton	Kilmarnock	07.50	50	27	-	0
Tranmere Rov.	Tr	09.51	51-55	143	-	3

League Club	Source	Date Signed	Seasons Played	Career Record Apps	Subs	Gls

LAMPARD, Frank R. G.
West Ham, 20 September, 1948 E Yth/Eu23-4/E-2 (FB)

League Club	Source	Date Signed	Seasons Played	Apps	Subs	Gls
West Ham U.	App	09.65	67-84	546	5	18
Southend U.	Tr	08.85	85	34	0	1

LAMPE, Derek
Edmonton, 20 May, 1937 E Yth (CH)

League Club	Source	Date Signed	Seasons Played	Apps	Subs	Gls
Fulham	Jnrs	05.54	56-62	88	-	0

LAMPKIN, Stephen C. A.
Silsden, 15 October, 1964 (W)

League Club	Source	Date Signed	Seasons Played	Apps	Subs	Gls
Bradford C.		03.83	82-83	5	2	1

LANCASHIRE, Carl P.
Blackpool, 17 January, 1969 (M)

League Club	Source	Date Signed	Seasons Played	Apps	Subs	Gls
Blackpool	YT	06.87	87	2	5	0

LANCASHIRE, Graham
Blackpool, 19 October, 1972 (F)

League Club	Source	Date Signed	Seasons Played	Apps	Subs	Gls
Burnley	YT	06.91	90-91	9	17	8

LANCASTER, Brian
Bradford, 8 May, 1939 (CH)

League Club	Source	Date Signed	Seasons Played	Apps	Subs	Gls
Torquay U.		07.60	61	18	-	0

LANCASTER, David
Preston, 8 September, 1961 (F)

League Club	Source	Date Signed	Seasons Played	Apps	Subs	Gls
Blackpool	Colne Dynamoes	08.90	90	7	1	1
Chesterfield	L	02.91	90	12	0	4
Chesterfield	Tr	08.91	91	27	2	7

LANCASTER, Desmond C.
Burnley, 16 July, 1937 (F)

League Club	Source	Date Signed	Seasons Played	Apps	Subs	Gls
Burnley	Jnrs	08.54	56	1	-	0
Darlington	Tr	03.58	57-58	31	-	18
Tranmere Rov.	Tr	06.59	59	1	-	0

LANCASTER, Joseph G.
Stockport, 28 April, 1926 (G)

League Club	Source	Date Signed	Seasons Played	Apps	Subs	Gls
Manchester U.	Heaton Mersey O.B.	02.50	49	2	-	0
Accrington St.	Tr	11.50	50	1	-	0

LANCASTER, Raymond
Rotherham, 17 August, 1941 (WH)

League Club	Source	Date Signed	Seasons Played	Apps	Subs	Gls
Rotherham U.	Jnrs	11.58	60-64	66	-	2
Grimsby T.	Tr	12.64	64-66	16	2	0
Lincoln C.	Tr	01.67	66-67	24	0	0

LANCELOTTE, Eric C.
India, 26 February, 1917 (IF)

League Club	Source	Date Signed	Seasons Played	Apps	Subs	Gls
Charlton Ath.	Jnrs	05.35	37-47	40	-	6
Brighton & H.A.	Tr	02.48	47-49	60	-	15

LANDSBOROUGH, Murray
Thornhill, 30 December, 1915 (FB)

League Club	Source	Date Signed	Seasons Played	Apps	Subs	Gls
Carlisle U.	Kilmarnock	08.47	47	1	-	0

LANE, Frank
Wallasey, 20 July, 1948 (G)

League Club	Source	Date Signed	Seasons Played	Apps	Subs	Gls
Tranmere Rovs.		08.68	69-71	76	0	0
Liverpool	Tr	09.71	72	1	0	0
Notts Co.	Tr	07.75	75	2	0	0

LANE, Henry
Hednesford, 21 March, 1909 (F)

League Club	Source	Date Signed	Seasons Played	Apps	Subs	Gls
Birmingham C.	Bloxwich Strollers	12.29	30	2	-	0
Southend U.	Tr	05.33	33-37	155	-	51
Plymouth Arg.	Tr	03.38	37-38	47	-	8
Southend U.		05.46	46-48	65	-	13

LANE, John G.
Birmingham, 10 November, 1931 (CF)

League Club	Source	Date Signed	Seasons Played	Apps	Subs	Gls
Birmingham C.	Boldmere St Michael	09.49	52-55	46	-	14
Notts Co.	Tr	07.56	56-58	57	-	19

LANE, Kevin J.
Wolverhampton, 11 May, 1957 (F)

League Club	Source	Date Signed	Seasons Played	Apps	Subs	Gls
Torquay U.	Walsall (App)	08.75	75-76	17	13	5

LANE, Martin J.
Altrincham, 12 April, 1961 (D)

League Club	Source	Date Signed	Seasons Played	Apps	Subs	Gls
Manchester U.	Jnrs	05.79				
Chester C.	Tr	08.82	82-86	175	0	3
Coventry C.	Tr	01.87	86-87	0	3	0
Wrexham	L	10.88	88	6	0	0
Chester C.	Tr	01.89	88-90	97	2	0
Walsall	Tr	08.91	91	6	4	0

LANE, Michael E.
Wellington (Som), 6 December, 1966 (FB)

League Club	Source	Date Signed	Seasons Played	Apps	Subs	Gls
Exeter C.	App	12.84	83	1	0	0

LANE, Sean B.
Bristol, 16 January, 1964 E Sch (M)

League Club	Source	Date Signed	Seasons Played	Apps	Subs	Gls
Hereford U.	App	03.81	80-82	39	11	3
Derby Co.	Tr	05.83	83	1	0	0

LANG, Gavan
Lanark, 21 March, 1926 (OL)

League Club	Source	Date Signed	Seasons Played	Apps	Subs	Gls
Chester C.	Hereford U.	08.56	56	3	-	0

LANG, Gavin T.
Hereford, 10 November, 1951 (W)

League Club	Source	Date Signed	Seasons Played	Apps	Subs	Gls
Chester C.	Newcastle U. (App)	11.69				
Crewe Alex.	Tr	09.70	70	3	0	1

LANG, Malcolm C.
Barnsley, 14 January, 1941 (OL)

League Club	Source	Date Signed	Seasons Played	Apps	Subs	Gls
York C.	Bridlington T.	08.63	63	12	-	2

LANG, Thomas
Larkhall, 3 April, 1906 (OL)

League Club	Source	Date Signed	Seasons Played	Apps	Subs	Gls
Newcastle U.	Larkhall Th.	10.26	27-34	215	-	53
Huddersfield T.	Tr	12.34	34-35	24	-	5
Manchester U.	Tr	12.35	35-36	12	-	1
Swansea C.	Tr	04.37	37	33	-	1
Ipswich T.	Queen of South	10.46	46	5	-	1

LANGAN, David F.
Dublin, 15 February, 1957 IR-25 (RB)

League Club	Source	Date Signed	Seasons Played	Apps	Subs	Gls
Derby Co.	App	02.75	76-79	143	0	1
Birmingham C.	Tr	07.80	80-82	92	0	3
Oxford U.	Tr	08.84	84-87	112	2	2
Leicester C.	L	10.87	87	5	0	0
Bournemouth	Tr	12.87	87	19	1	0
Peterborough U.	Tr	08.88	88	18	1	0

LANGE, Anthony S.
West Ham, 10 December, 1964 (G)

League Club	Source	Date Signed	Seasons Played	Apps	Subs	Gls
Charlton Ath.	App	12.82	83-85	12	0	0
Aldershot	L	08.85	85	7	0	0
Aldershot	Tr	07.86	86-88	125	0	0
Wolverhampton W.	Tr	07.89	89-90	8	0	0
Aldershot	L	11.90	90	2	0	0
Torquay U.	L	09.91	91	1	0	0

LANGFORD, John W.
Kirkby-in-Ashfield, 4 August, 1937 (OL)

League Club	Source	Date Signed	Seasons Played	Apps	Subs	Gls
Nottingham F.	Leicester C. (Am)	08.55	55	4	-	0
Notts Co.	Tr	08.58	58	16	-	0

LANGLAND, John R.
Easington, 9 November, 1929 (F)

League Club	Source	Date Signed	Seasons Played	Apps	Subs	Gls
Sunderland		06.48				
Chesterfield	Consett	01.51	52-53	7	-	0
Hartlepool U.	Blyth Spartans	07.58	58-59	38	-	11

LANGLEY, Geoffrey R.
Gateshead, 31 March, 1962 (F)

League Club	Source	Date Signed	Seasons Played	Apps	Subs	Gls
Bolton W.	App	03.80	81	3	3	0

LANGLEY, E. James
Kilburn, 7 February, 1929 EF Lge/E'B'-3/E-3 (LB)

League Club	Source	Date Signed	Seasons Played	Apps	Subs	Gls
Leeds U.	Guildford C.	06.52	52	9	-	3
Brighton & H.A.	Tr	07.53	53-56	166	-	14
Fulham	Tr	02.57	56-64	323	-	31
Queens Park R.	Tr	07.65	65-66	86	1	9

LANGLEY, Kevin J.
St Helens, 24 May, 1964 (M)

League Club	Source	Date Signed	Seasons Played	Apps	Subs	Gls
Wigan Ath.	App	05.82	81-85	156	4	6
Everton	Tr	07.86	86	16	0	2
Manchester C.	Tr	03.87	86	9	0	0
Chester C.	L	01.88	87	9	0	0
Birmingham C.	Tr	03.88	87-89	74	2	2
Wigan Ath.	Tr	09.90	90-91	83	1	4

LANGLEY, Richard J.
Lambeth, 20 March, 1965 (FB)

League Club	Source	Date Signed	Seasons Played	Apps	Subs	Gls
Fulham	Corinthian Casuals	11.86	86-90	43	7	0

LANGLEY, Thomas W.
Lambeth, 8 February, 1958 E Sch/E Yth/Eu21-1 (F)

League Club	Source	Date Signed	Seasons Played	Apps	Subs	Gls
Chelsea	App	04.75	74-79	129	13	40
Queens Park R.	Tr	08.80	80	24	1	8
Crystal Palace	Tr	03.81	80-82	54	5	8
Coventry C.	A.E.K. Athens (Gr)	03.84	83	2	0	0
Wolverhampton W.	Tr	07.84	84	22	1	4
Aldershot	L	03.85	84	16	0	4
Aldershot	Hong Kong	08.86	86-87	80	1	21
Exeter C.	Tr	07.88	88	14	7	2

LANGMAN, H. Neil
Bere Alston, 21 February, 1932 (F)

League Club	Source	Date Signed	Seasons Played	Apps	Subs	Gls
Plymouth Arg.	Tavistock	09.53	53-57	97	-	49
Colchester U.	Tr	11.57	57-60	128	-	50

LANGMAN, Peter J. H.
Bere Alston, 1 April, 1928 (CH)

League Club	Source	Date Signed	Seasons Played	Apps	Subs	Gls
Plymouth Arg.	Tavistock	06.51	54-57	90	-	0

LANGRIDGE, John
Newcastle, 14 November, 1957 (F)

League Club	Source	Date Signed	Seasons Played	Apps	Subs	Gls
Hartlepool U. (N/C)	Easington Colly	10.82	82	5	1	0

LANGSTRETH, H. Lawrence
Blackburn, 19 July, 1931 (FB)

League Club	Source	Date Signed	Seasons Played	Apps	Subs	Gls
Accrington St.	Blackburn Rov. (Am)	07.53	53	3	-	0
Torquay U.	Netherfield	08.56	56	1	-	0

LANGTON, Robert
Burscough, 8 September, 1918 E'B'-3/EF Lge/E-11 (OL)

League Club	Source	Date Signed	Seasons Played	Apps	Subs	Gls
Blackburn Rov.	Burscough Vic.	09.38	38-47	107	-	24
Preston N.E.	Tr	08.48	48-49	55	-	14
Bolton W.	Tr	11.49	49-52	118	-	16
Blackburn Rov.	Tr	09.53	53-55	105	-	33

LANSDOWNE, William
Epping, 28 April, 1959 (F)

League Club	Source	Date Signed	Seasons Played	Apps	Subs	Gls
West Ham U.	Jnrs	06.78	78-79	5	4	1
Charlton Ath.	Tr	07.81	81-82	28	4	4
Gillingham	L	01.83	82	6	0	2

LANSDOWNE, William T. M.
Shoreditch, 9 November, 1935 (WH)

League Club	Source	Date Signed	Seasons Played	Apps	Subs	Gls
West Ham U.	Woodford T.	02.56	55-62	57	-	5

LAPOT, Stanley
Edinburgh, 20 January, 1944 (WH)

League Club	Source	Date Signed	Seasons Played	Apps	Subs	Gls
Preston N.E.	Smeaton B.C.	06.62	62-66	16	3	2

LARAMAN, Peter K.
Rochester, 24 October, 1940 E Yth (IF)

League Club	Source	Date Signed	Seasons Played	Apps	Subs	Gls
Charlton Ath.	Jnrs	02.58	58-59	2	-	1
Torquay U.	Tr	07.61	61	9	-	5

LARGE, Frank
Leeds, 26 January, 1940 (CF)

League Club	Source	Date Signed	Seasons Played	Apps	Subs	Gls
Halifax T.	Halifax B.R.	06.59	58-61	133	-	50
Queens Park R.	Tr	06.62	62	18	-	5
Northampton T.	Tr	03.63	62-63	47	-	30
Swindon T.	Tr	03.64	63-64	17	-	4
Carlisle U.	Tr	09.64	64-65	51	0	18
Oldham Ath.	Tr	12.65	65-66	34	0	18
Northampton T.	Tr	12.66	66-67	37	0	15
Leicester C.	Tr	11.67	67	26	0	8
Fulham	Tr	06.68	68-69	20	4	3
Northampton T.	Tr	08.69	69-72	133	2	42
Chesterfield	Tr	11.72	72-73	46	0	15

LARKIN, Anthony G.
Wrexham, 12 January, 1956 (D)

League Club	Source	Date Signed	Seasons Played	Apps	Subs	Gls
Wrexham	Jnrs	07.75				
Shrewsbury T.	Tr	07.78	78-80	54	1	0
Carlisle U.	Tr	07.81	81-82	47	2	2
Hereford U.	Tr	03.83	82-84	28	7	2

LARKIN, Bernard P. (Bunny)
Birmingham, 11 January, 1936 (IF)

League Club	Source	Date Signed	Seasons Played	Apps	Subs	Gls
Birmingham C.	Jnrs	07.54	56-59	79	-	23
Norwich C.	Tr	03.60	59-61	41	-	12
Doncaster Rov.	Tr	09.61	61	25	-	12
Watford	Tr	06.62	62-64	49	-	3
Lincoln C.	Tr	11.64	64-65	25	2	3

LARKIN, Gordon T.
Hartlepool, 12 October, 1958 (W)

League Club	Source	Date Signed	Seasons Played	Apps	Subs	Gls
Hartlepool U.		07.77	77-79	5	9	1

LARMOUR, Albert A. J.
Belfast, 27 May, 1951 (CD)

League Club	Source	Date Signed	Seasons Played	Apps	Subs	Gls
Cardiff C.	Linfield	07.72	72-78	152	2	0
Torquay U.	Tr	06.79	79-81	46	4	4

LARNACH, Ian J.
Ferryhill, 10 July, 1951 (F)

League Club	Source	Date Signed	Seasons Played	Apps	Subs	Gls
Darlington	App	07.69	69	1	1	1

LARNACH, Michael
Lybster, 9 November, 1952 (F)

League Club	Source	Date Signed	Seasons Played	Apps	Subs	Gls
Newcastle U.	Clydebank	12.77	77	12	1	0

LARYEA, Benjamin M.
Ghana, 20 March, 1962 (F)

League Club	Source	Date Signed	Seasons Played	Apps	Subs	Gls
Torquay U. (N/C)	Maidenhead U.	03.84	83-84	10	2	3

LASKEY, Russell G.
Norwich, 17 March, 1937 (F)

League Club	Source	Date Signed	Seasons Played	Apps	Subs	Gls
Norwich C.	Gothic	01.56	56	4	-	2

LATCHAM, Leslie A.
Stanley, 22 December, 1942 (LM)

League Club	Source	Date Signed	Seasons Played	Apps	Subs	Gls
Burnley	Jnrs	01.60	64-70	149	4	10
Plymouth Arg.	Tr	07.71	71-72	83	0	13
Bradford C.	Tr	07.73	73	15	0	2

LATCHFORD, David B.
Birmingham, 9 April, 1949 (G)

League Club	Source	Date Signed	Seasons Played	Apps	Subs	Gls
Birmingham C.	App	07.66	68-77	206	0	0
Bury	Motherwell	03.79	78	2	0	0

LATCHFORD, Peter W.
Birmingham, 27 September, 1952 Eu23-2 (G)

League Club	Source	Date Signed	Seasons Played	Apps	Subs	Gls
West Bromwich A.	App	10.69	72-74	81	0	0

LATCHFORD, Robert D.
Birmingham, 18 January, 1951 E Yth/Eu23-6/EF Lge/E-12 (F)

League Club	Source	Date Signed	Seasons Played	Apps	Subs	Gls
Birmingham C.	App	08.68	68-73	158	2	68
Everton	Tr	02.74	73-80	235	1	106
Swansea C.	Tr	07.81	81-83	87	0	35
Coventry C.	N.A.C. Breda (Neth)	07.84	84	11	1	2
Lincoln C.	Tr	08.85	85	14	1	2
Newport Co.	Tr	01.86	85	20	0	5

Bob Latchford (Birmingham City, Everton, Swansea City, NEC Breda, Coventry City, Lincoln City, Newport County & England)

LATHAM, David C.
Manchester, 17 October, 1943 (W)

League Club	Source	Date Signed	Seasons Played	Apps	Subs	Gls
Manchester U.	App	10.61				
Southport	Tr	07.63	63	22	-	0

League Club	Source	Date Signed	Seasons Played	Career Record Apps	Subs	Gls

LATHAM, Harold
Sheffield, 9 January, 1921 Died 1983 (CH)

League Club	Source	Date Signed	Seasons Played	Apps	Subs	Gls
Sheffield U.	Jnrs	10.38	46-52	190	-	1

LATHAM, Leslie
Coventry, 31 December, 1917 E Sch (CH)

League Club	Source	Date Signed	Seasons Played	Apps	Subs	Gls
Aston Villa		10.36				
Coventry C.	Tr	10.46	46	1	-	0

LATHAN, John G.
Sunderland, 12 April, 1952 (M)

League Club	Source	Date Signed	Seasons Played	Apps	Subs	Gls
Sunderland	App	04.69	69-73	41	12	14
Mansfield T.	Tr	02.74	73-75	72	2	14
Carlisle U.	Tr	02.76	75-77	55	6	8
Barnsley	L	02.77	76	6	1	0
Portsmouth	Tr	03.78	77-79	56	2	4
Mansfield T.	Tr	08.79	79	29	0	1

LATIMER, Frank J.
Durham, 3 October, 1923 (WH)

League Club	Source	Date Signed	Seasons Played	Apps	Subs	Gls
Brentford	Snowdown Colly	11.45	46-55	171	-	3

LAUGHTON, Dennis
Dingwall, 22 January, 1948 (D)

League Club	Source	Date Signed	Seasons Played	Apps	Subs	Gls
Newcastle U.	Morton	10.73	73-74	7	0	0

LAUREL, John A.
Dartford, 11 June, 1935 E Yth (CH)

League Club	Source	Date Signed	Seasons Played	Apps	Subs	Gls
Tottenham H.	Jnrs	07.52				
Ipswich T.	Tr	06.59	60-62	4	-	0

LAVERICK, Michael G.
Trimdon, 13 March, 1954 (M)

League Club	Source	Date Signed	Seasons Played	Apps	Subs	Gls
Mansfield T.	Jnrs	01.72	72-75	73	16	13
Southend U.	Tr	10.76	76-78	108	2	18
Huddersfield T.	Tr	07.79	79-81	74	0	9
York C.	Tr	01.82	81-82	38	3	6
Huddersfield T.	L	01.83	82	2	0	0

LAVERICK, Peter H.
Grimsby, 29 January, 1939 (IF)

League Club	Source	Date Signed	Seasons Played	Apps	Subs	Gls
Grimsby T.	Jnrs	03.56	57-60	4	-	0

LAVERICK, Robert M.
Trimdon, 11 June, 1938 E Yth (OL)

League Club	Source	Date Signed	Seasons Played	Apps	Subs	Gls
Chelsea	Jnrs	06.55	56-57	7	-	0
Everton	Tr	02.59	58-59	22	-	6
Brighton & H.A.	Tr	06.60	60-61	63	-	20
Coventry C.	Tr	07.62	62	4	-	0

LAVERTY, Patrick J.
Gorseinon, 24 May, 1934 (IF)

League Club	Source	Date Signed	Seasons Played	Apps	Subs	Gls
Sheffield U.	Wellington T.	05.56	56-59	7	-	0
Southend U.	Tr	07.60	60	21	-	6

LAVERY, James
Glasgow, 13 December, 1948 (G)

League Club	Source	Date Signed	Seasons Played	Apps	Subs	Gls
Scunthorpe U.		08.66	67	15	0	0
Scunthorpe U.	Brigg T.	08.74	74	11	0	0

LAVERY, John
Belfast, 24 November, 1919 NI Sch (OL)

League Club	Source	Date Signed	Seasons Played	Apps	Subs	Gls
Bradford C.	Dundalk	08.48	48	5	-	0
Halifax T.	Tr	09.48	48	3	-	1

LAVIN, Gerard
Corby, 5 February, 1974 (W)

League Club	Source	Date Signed	Seasons Played	Apps	Subs	Gls
Watford	YT	05.92	91	0	1	0

LAW, Brian J.
Merthyr Tydfil, 1 January, 1970 W Yth/Wu21-1/W-1 (CD)

League Club	Source	Date Signed	Seasons Played	Apps	Subs	Gls
Queens Park R.	YT	08.87	87-90	19	1	0

LAW, Cecil R
Rhodesia, 10 March, 1930 (OL)

League Club	Source	Date Signed	Seasons Played	Apps	Subs	Gls
Derby Co.	Alexandra (SA)	08.51	52-53	33	-	2
Bury	Tr	05.54	54-55	44	-	5

LAW, Denis
Aberdeen, 24 February, 1940 Su23-3/EF Lge/S-55 (IF)

League Club	Source	Date Signed	Seasons Played	Apps	Subs	Gls
Huddersfield T.	Jnrs	02.57	56-59	81	-	16
Manchester C.	Tr	03.60	59-60	44	-	21
Manchester U.	Torino (It)	08.62	62-72	305	4	171
Manchester C.	Tr	07.73	73	22	2	9

Denis Law (Huddersfield Town, Manchester City, Torino, Manchester United, Manchester City & Scotland)

LAW, Nicholas
Greenwich, 8 September, 1961 E Sch (CD)

League Club	Source	Date Signed	Seasons Played	Apps	Subs	Gls
Arsenal	App	07.79				
Barnsley	Tr	08.81	81-85	113	1	1
Blackpool	Tr	08.85	85-86	64	2	1
Plymouth Arg.	Tr	03.87	86-87	37	1	5
Notts Co.	Tr	06.88	88-89	44	3	4
Scarborough	L	11.89	89	12	0	0
Rotherham U.	Tr	07.90	90-91	72	2	2

LAWFORD, Craig B.
Dewsbury, 25 November, 1972 (FB)

League Club	Source	Date Signed	Seasons Played	Apps	Subs	Gls
Bradford C.	YT	07.91	89	0	1	0

LAWLER, Christopher
Liverpool, 20 October, 1943 E Yth/Eu23-4/EF Lge/E-4 (RB)

League Club	Source	Date Signed	Seasons Played	Apps	Subs	Gls
Liverpool	Jnrs	10.60	62-74	406	0	41
Portsmouth	Tr	10.75	75-76	35	1	0
Stockport Co.	Tr	08.77	77	33	3	3

LAWLER, James H.
Dublin, 20 November, 1923 (WH)

League Club	Source	Date Signed	Seasons Played	Apps	Subs	Gls
Portsmouth	Glentoran	10.47				
Southend U.	Tr	01.49	48-56	269	-	18

LAWLER, Joseph F. (Robin)
Dublin, 28 August, 1925 LOI/IR-8 (D)

League Club	Source	Date Signed	Seasons Played	Apps	Subs	Gls
Fulham	Belfast Celtic	03.49	49-61	281	-	0

LAWLESS, A. Trevor
Retford, 23 March, 1932 (CH)

League Club	Source	Date Signed	Seasons Played	Apps	Subs	Gls
Plymouth Arg.	Worcester C.	07.55	55	8	-	0
Oldham Ath.	Tr	07.56	56	9	-	0
Aldershot	Tr	07.57	57	2	-	0
Southport	Tr	07.58	58	15	-	0

LAWLOR, James J.
Dublin, 10 May, 1933 (CH)

League Club	Source	Date Signed	Seasons Played	Apps	Subs	Gls
Doncaster Rov.	Drumcondra	08.52	54	9	-	0
Bradford C.	Coleraine	03.57	56-61	153	-	5

LAWLOR, John B.
Glasgow, 30 January, 1937 S Sch (OL)

League Club	Source	Date Signed	Seasons Played	Apps	Subs	Gls
Aldershot	Kilmarnock	05.59	59-60	57	-	17

LAWLOR, John C.
Dublin, 3 December, 1922 IR-3 (F)

League Club	Source	Date Signed	Seasons Played	Apps	Subs	Gls
Doncaster Rov.	Drumcondra	06.50	50-54	128	-	46

LAWRENCE, Cyril
Salford, 12 June, 1920 (OR)

League Club	Source	Date Signed	Seasons Played	Apps	Subs	Gls
Blackpool	Jnrs	02.46				
Rochdale	Tr	04.47	46-49	44	-	5
Wrexham	Tr	09.50	50-51	50	-	9

LAWRENCE, David W.
Swansea, 18 January, 1947 W Amat (FB)

League Club	Source	Date Signed	Seasons Played	Apps	Subs	Gls
Swansea C.	Merthyr Tydfil	05.67	67-70	94	3	2

LAWRENCE, David
Poole, 12 May, 1933 (FB)

League Club	Source	Date Signed	Seasons Played	Apps	Subs	Gls
Bristol Rov.	Poole T.	06.55	56	5	-	0
Reading	Tr	06.57	57-58	23	-	0

LAWRENCE, George R.
Kensington, 14 September, 1962 (W)

League Club	Source	Date Signed	Seasons Played	Apps	Subs	Gls
Southampton	App	09.80	81-82	7	3	1
Oxford U.	L	03.82	81	15	0	4
Oxford U.	Tr	11.82	82-84	63	0	21
Southampton	Tr	01.85	84-86	58	12	11
Millwall	Tr	07.87	87-88	26	2	4
Bournemouth	Tr	08.89	89-91	47	28	5

LAWRENCE, Keith D
Orpington, 25 March, 1954 (CD)

League Club	Source	Date Signed	Seasons Played	Apps	Subs	Gls
Chelsea	App	03.72				
Brentford	Tr	05.74	74-75	78	0	1

LAWRENCE, Leslie O.
Wolverhampton, 18 May, 1957 (F)

League Club	Source	Date Signed	Seasons Played	Apps	Subs	Gls
Shrewsbury T.	Stourbridge	02.75	75-76	10	4	2
Torquay U.	Telford U.	07.77	77-81	170	19	45
Port Vale	Tr	08.82	82	5	3	0
Aldershot	Tr	07.83	83	39	0	22
Rochdale	Tr	08.84	84	15	0	4
Burnley	Tr	11.84	84-85	22	9	8
Peterborough U.	Tr	07.86	86-87	28	5	8
Cambridge U.	Tr	02.88	87	11	2	0

LAWRENCE, Mark
Middlesbrough, 4 December, 1958 (M)

League Club	Source	Date Signed	Seasons Played	Apps	Subs	Gls
Hartlepool U.		08.77	77-83	155	13	24
Port Vale	L	03.83	82	10	1	0

LAWRENCE, Thomas
Dailly (Ayrs), 14 May, 1940 Su23-1/S-3 (G)

League Club	Source	Date Signed	Seasons Played	Apps	Subs	Gls
Liverpool	Jnrs	10.57	62-70	306	0	0
Tranmere Rov.	Tr	09.71	71-73	80	0	0

LAWRENSON, Mark T.
Preston, 2 June, 1957 IR-38 (D)

League Club	Source	Date Signed	Seasons Played	Apps	Subs	Gls
Preston N.E.	Jnrs	08.74	74-76	73	0	2
Brighton & H.A.	Tr	07.77	77-80	152	0	5
Liverpool	Tr	08.81	81-87	233	8	11

LAWRENSON, Thomas
Preston, 24 May, 1929

League Club	Source	Date Signed	Seasons Played	Apps	Subs	Gls
Preston N.E.		04.49	54	1	-	0
Southport	Tr	07.55	55-56	37	-	0

LAWRIE, Samuel
Glasgow, 15 December, 1934 Died 1979 (OR)

League Club	Source	Date Signed	Seasons Played	Apps	Subs	Gls
Middlesbrough	Jnrs	02.52	51-56	36	-	5
Charlton Ath.	Tr	11.56	56-62	193	-	70
Bradford P.A.	Tr	10.62	62-65	72	1	16

LAWS, Brian
Wallsend, 14 October, 1961 E'B'/EF Lge (M/RB)

League Club	Source	Date Signed	Seasons Played	Apps	Subs	Gls
Burnley	App	10.79	79-82	125	0	12
Huddersfield T.	Tr	08.83	83-84	56	0	1
Middlesbrough	Tr	03.85	84-87	103	5	12
Nottingham F.	Tr	07.88	88-91	98	9	4

Brian Laws (Burnley, Huddersfield Town, Middlesbrough & Nottingham Forest)

LAWS, Jonathan
Peterborough, 1 September, 1964 (M)

League Club	Source	Date Signed	Seasons Played	Apps	Subs	Gls
Wolverhampton W.	App	09.82				
Mansfield T.	Tr	03.83	82	0	1	0

LAWSON, Alan
Lennoxtown, 13 September, 1941 (CD)

League Club	Source	Date Signed	Seasons Played	Apps	Subs	Gls
Oldham Ath.	Glasgow Celtic	06.64	64-69	128	10	1

LAWSON, David
Wallsend, 22 December, 1947 (G)

League Club	Source	Date Signed	Seasons Played	Apps	Subs	Gls
Newcastle U.	Jnrs	04.66				
Bradford P.A.	Shrewsbury T.	10.67	67-68	13	0	0
Huddersfield T.	Tr	05.69	70-71	51	0	0
Everton	Tr	06.72	72-76	124	0	0
Luton T.	Tr	10.78	78	5	0	0
Stockport Co.	Tr	03.79	78-80	106	0	0

LAWSON, F. Ian
Ouston (Dm), 24 March, 1939 E Yth (CF)

League Club	Source	Date Signed	Seasons Played	Apps	Subs	Gls
Burnley	Jnrs	03.56	56-60	23	-	7
Leeds U.	Tr	03.62	61-64	44	-	17
Crystal Palace	Tr	06.65	65	15	2	6
Port Vale	Tr	08.66	66	7	1	0

LAWSON, James J.
Middlesbrough, 11 December, 1947 (W)

League Club	Source	Date Signed	Seasons Played	Apps	Subs	Gls
Middlesbrough	Jnrs	12.64	65-67	25	6	3
Huddersfield T.	Tr	08.68	68-75	234	11	42
Halifax T.	Tr	06.76	76-78	93	0	9

LAWSON, John R.
York, 3 February, 1925 (OR)

League Club	Source	Date Signed	Seasons Played	Apps	Subs	Gls
York C.	Dringhouses	08.44	46	1	-	0

LAWSON, Norman
Houghton-le-Spring, 6 April, 1935 (OL)

League Club	Source	Date Signed	Seasons Played	Apps	Subs	Gls
Bury	Hednesford T.	09.55	55-57	56	-	8
Swansea C.	Tr	07.58	58-59	24	-	3
Watford	Tr	07.60				

LAWSON, William
Dundee, 28 November, 1947 (W)

League Club	Source	Date Signed	Seasons Played	Apps	Subs	Gls
Sheffield Wed.	Brechin C.	10.69	69-70	9	1	0

LAWTHER, W. Ian
Belfast, 20 October, 1939 NI'B'-1/NI-4 (CF)

League Club	Source	Date Signed	Seasons Played	Apps	Subs	Gls
Sunderland	Crusaders	03.58	59-60	75	-	41
Blackburn Rov.	Tr	07.61	61-62	59	-	21
Scunthorpe U.	Tr	07.63	63-64	60	-	21
Brentford	Tr	11.64	64-67	138	1	43
Halifax T.	Tr	08.68	68-70	87	14	23
Stockport Co.	Tr	07.71	71-75	158	6	29

LAWTON, James M.
Middlesbrough, 6 July, 1942 (CF)

League Club	Source	Date Signed	Seasons Played	Apps	Subs	Gls
Darlington	Middlesbrough (Am)	10.61	61-65	120	0	60
Swindon T.	Tr	09.65	65-66	11	0	3
Watford	Tr	03.67	66-67	10	3	1
Darlington	Tr	03.68	67-68	22	0	3

LAWTON, John K.
Woore, 6 July, 1936 (F)

League Club	Source	Date Signed	Seasons Played	Apps	Subs	Gls
Stoke C.	Jnrs	06.54	55	9	-	3

LAWTON, H. Malcolm
Leeds, 7 November, 1935 (FB)

League Club	Source	Date Signed	Seasons Played	Apps	Subs	Gls
Leeds U.	Jnrs	11.52				
Bradford P.A.	Tr	06.57	57-62	113	-	0

LAWTON, Norbert (Nobby)
Manchester, 25 March, 1940 (M)

League Club	Source	Date Signed	Seasons Played	Apps	Subs	Gls
Manchester U.	Jnrs	04.58	59-62	36	-	6
Preston N.E.	Tr	03.63	62-67	143	0	22
Brighton & H.A.	Tr	09.67	67-70	112	0	14
Lincoln C.	Tr	02.71	70-71	20	0	0

LAWTON, Peter
Barnsley, 25 February, 1944 (FB)

League Club	Source	Date Signed	Seasons Played	Apps	Subs	Gls
Barnsley	Jnrs	05.62	62-63	2	-	0

LAWTON, Thomas
Bolton, 6 October, 1919 EF Lge/E-23 (CF)

League Club	Source	Date Signed	Seasons Played	Apps	Subs	Gls
Burnley	Jnrs	03.36	35-36	25	-	16
Everton	Tr	01.37	36-38	87	-	65
Chelsea	Tr	11.45	46-47	42	-	30
Notts Co.	Tr	11.47	47-51	151	-	90
Brentford	Tr	03.52	51-53	50	-	17
Arsenal	Tr	09.53	53-55	35	-	13

LAWTON, William
Ashton-u-Lyme, 4 June, 1920 (WH)

League Club	Source	Date Signed	Seasons Played	Apps	Subs	Gls
Oldham Ath.	Ferranti	02.45	46-48	10	-	0
Chester C.	Tr	10.49				

LAY, Peter J
Stratford, 4 December, 1931 (FB)

League Club	Source	Date Signed	Seasons Played	Apps	Subs	Gls
Nottingham F.		04.53	54	1	-	0
Queens Park R.	Tr	07.56	56	1	-	0

LAYBOURNE, Keith E.
Sunderland, 27 January, 1959 (LB)

League Club	Source	Date Signed	Seasons Played	Apps	Subs	Gls
Lincoln C.	Lambton Street B.C.	07.77	77-78	18	0	1

LAYNE, David R.
Sheffield, 29 July, 1939 (CF)

League Club	Source	Date Signed	Seasons Played	Apps	Subs	Gls
Rotherham U.	Jnrs	07.57	57-58	11	-	4
Swindon T.	Tr	06.59	59-60	41	-	28
Bradford C.	Tr	12.60	60-61	65	-	44
Sheffield Wed.	Tr	02.62	62-63	74	-	52
Sheffield Wed.	(Retired)	06.72				
Hereford U.	L	12.72	72	4	0	0

LAYTON, Alan
Bury, 27 November, 1928 (OR)

League Club	Source	Date Signed	Seasons Played	Apps	Subs	Gls
Bolton W.		04.49				
Barrow	Tr	10.50	50-55	142	-	19

LAYTON, John H.
Hereford, 29 June, 1951 (CD)

League Club	Source	Date Signed	Seasons Played	Apps	Subs	Gls
Hereford U.	Gloucester C.	09.74	74-79	198	2	13
Newport Co. (N/C)	Trowbridge T.	01.84	83	1	0	0

LAYTON, William H.
Birmingham, 13 January, 1915 Died 1984 (WH)

League Club	Source	Date Signed	Seasons Played	Apps	Subs	Gls
Reading	Shirley T.	03.37	37-46	51	-	17
Bradford P.A.	Tr	01.47	46-48	47	-	5
Colchester U.	Tr	08.50	50	7	-	0

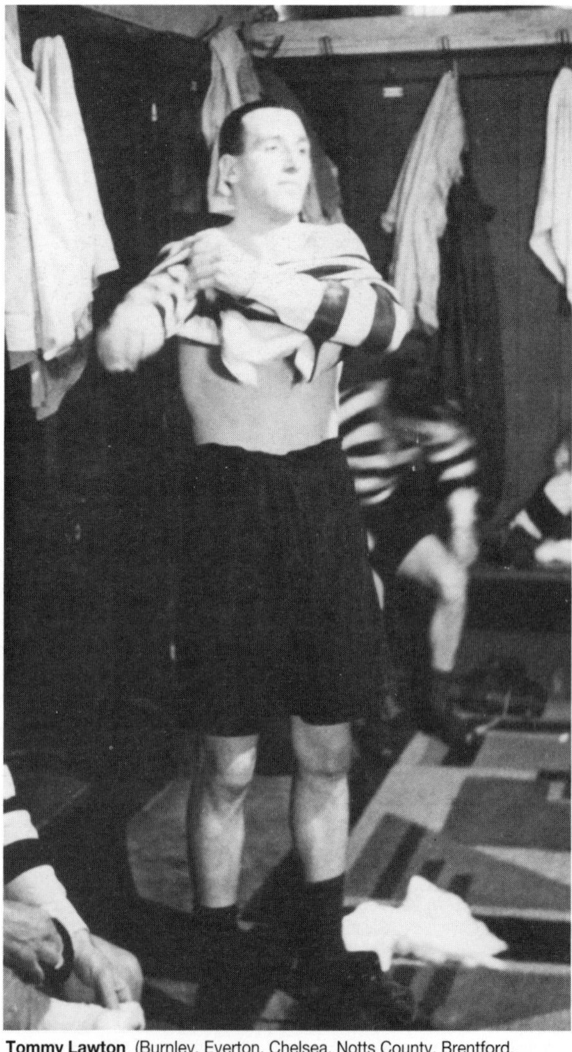

Tommy Lawton (Burnley, Everton, Chelsea, Notts County, Brentford, Arsenal & England)

League Club	Source	Date Signed	Seasons Played	Career Record Apps	Subs	Gls

LAZARUS, Mark
Stepney, 5 December, 1938 (W)

League Club	Source	Date Signed	Seasons Played	Apps	Subs	Gls
Leyton Orient	Barking	11.57	58-60	20	-	4
Queens Park R.	Tr	09.60	60-61	37	-	19
Wolverhampton W.	Tr	09.61	61	9	-	3
Queens Park R.	Tr	02.62	61-63	81	-	29
Brentford	Tr	01.64	63-65	62	0	21
Queens Park R.	Tr	11.65	65-67	86	2	29
Crystal Palace	Tr	11.67	67-69	63	0	17
Leyton Orient	Tr	10.69	69-71	81	1	14

LAZARUS, Paul
Stepney, 4 September, 1962 (F)

League Club	Source	Date Signed	Seasons Played	Apps	Subs	Gls
Charlton Ath.	Jnrs	08.80	80	2	0	1
Wimbledon	T.P.S. Turun (Fin)	10.81	81	17	1	6

LE CORNU, Craig D.
Birkenhead, 17 September, 1960 (M)

League Club	Source	Date Signed	Seasons Played	Apps	Subs	Gls
Liverpool	App	09.78				
Tranmere Rov.	Tr	12.80	80	3	3	0

LE FLEM, Richard P. ("Flip")
Bradford-on-Avon, 12 July, 1942 Eu23-1 (OL)

League Club	Source	Date Signed	Seasons Played	Apps	Subs	Gls
Nottingham F.	Guernsey	05.60	60-63	132	-	18
Wolverhampton W.	Tr	01.64	63-64	19	-	5
Middlesbrough	Tr	02.65	64-65	9	0	1
Leyton Orient	Tr	03.66	65-66	11	0	2

LE ROUX, Daniel L.
South Africa, 25 November, 1933 SA Am Int (OR)

League Club	Source	Date Signed	Seasons Played	Apps	Subs	Gls
Arsenal	Queens Park (SA)	02.57	57	5	-	0

LE SAUX, Graham P.
Jersey, 17 October, 1968 Eu21-4/E'B' (LB/W)

League Club	Source	Date Signed	Seasons Played	Apps	Subs	Gls
Chelsea	St Pauls (Jersey)	12.87	88-91	67	9	8

LE TISSIER, Matthew P.
Guernsey, 14 October, 1968 E'B'/E YTh (W/F)

League Club	Source	Date Signed	Seasons Played	Apps	Subs	Gls
Southampton	App	10.86	86-91	143	30	60

Matthew Le Tissier (Southampton)

LEA, Cyril
Wrexham, 5 August, 1934 W Amat/W-2 (WH)

League Club	Source	Date Signed	Seasons Played	Apps	Subs	Gls
Leyton Orient	Bradley R.	07.57	57-64	205	-	0
Ipswich T.	Tr	11.64	64-68	103	4	2

LEA, Harold
Wigan, 14 September, 1931 (G)

League Club	Source	Date Signed	Seasons Played	Apps	Subs	Gls
Stockport Co.	Horwich R.M.I.	05.58	58-63	117	-	1

LEA, Leslie
Manchester, 5 October, 1942 (W)

League Club	Source	Date Signed	Seasons Played	Apps	Subs	Gls
Blackpool	Jnrs	10.59	60-67	159	1	13
Cardiff C.	Tr	11.67	67-69	75	1	7
Barnsley	Tr	08.70	70-75	198	7	32

LEABURN, Carl W.
Lewisham, 30 March, 1969 (F)

League Club	Source	Date Signed	Seasons Played	Apps	Subs	Gls
Charlton Ath.	App	03.87	86-91	96	23	14
Northampton T.	L	03.90	89	9	0	0

LEACH, Albert
Bolton, 10 July, 1931 (G)

League Club	Source	Date Signed	Seasons Played	Apps	Subs	Gls
Shrewsbury T.		11.51	51	2	-	0

LEACH, Brian E.
Reading, 20 July, 1932 (WH)

League Club	Source	Date Signed	Seasons Played	Apps	Subs	Gls
Reading		11.50	52-56	108	-	1

LEACH, John N.
Whitehaven, 17 January, 1919 (OL)

League Club	Source	Date Signed	Seasons Played	Apps	Subs	Gls
Barrow	Barrow Celtic	09.47	47-49	74	-	10

LEACH, Michael J. C.
Hackney, 16 January, 1947 Died 1992 E Yth (M)

League Club	Source	Date Signed	Seasons Played	Apps	Subs	Gls
Queens Park R.	App	02.64	64-77	291	22	61
Cambridge U.	Detroit (USA)	09.78	78	18	1	1

LEADBETTER, Albert
Newton-le-Willows, 17 August, 1921 (OL)

League Club	Source	Date Signed	Seasons Played	Apps	Subs	Gls
Accrington St. (Am)	Earlestown	12.46	46	4	-	0

LEADBETTER, James H.
Edinburgh, 15 July, 1928 (OL)

League Club	Source	Date Signed	Seasons Played	Apps	Subs	Gls
Chelsea	Edinburgh Th.	07.49	51	3	-	0
Brighton & H.A.	Tr	08.52	52-54	107	-	29
Ipswich T.	Tr	06.55	55-64	344	-	43

LEADBITTER, Christopher J.
Middlesbrough, 17 October, 1967 (W)

League Club	Source	Date Signed	Seasons Played	Apps	Subs	Gls
Grimsby T.	App	09.85				
Hereford U.	Tr	08.86	86-87	32	4	1
Cambridge U.	Tr	08.88	88-91	110	28	12

LEADBITTER, John
Sunderland, 7 May, 1953 (CD)

League Club	Source	Date Signed	Seasons Played	Apps	Subs	Gls
Sunderland	App	05.70				
Darlington	Tr	08.72	72	15	4	0

LEAF, Andrew K.
York, 18 January, 1962 (FB)

League Club	Source	Date Signed	Seasons Played	Apps	Subs	Gls
York C.	App	01.80	79	1	0	0

LEAHY, Stephen D.
Battersea, 23 September, 1959 E Sch (F)

League Club	Source	Date Signed	Seasons Played	Apps	Subs	Gls
Crystal Palace	App	10.76	80-81	3	1	0

LEAKE, Albert G.
Stoke, 7 April, 1930 E Yth (WH)

League Club	Source	Date Signed	Seasons Played	Apps	Subs	Gls
Port Vale	Stoke C. (Am)	02.50	50-59	269	-	34

LEAMON, Frederick W.
Jersey, 11 May, 1919 Died 1981 (CF)

League Club	Source	Date Signed	Seasons Played	Apps	Subs	Gls
Newport Co.	Bath C.	02.46	46	4	-	3
Bristol Rov.	Tr	10.46	46-47	43	-	21
Brighton & H.A.	Tr	07.49	49	11	-	4

LEAN, David R.
Plymouth, 28 August, 1945 (CD)

League Club	Source	Date Signed	Seasons Played	Apps	Subs	Gls
Plymouth Arg.	Embankment	08.69	69-70	44	1	0

LEANING, Andrew J.
Howden, 18 May, 1963 (G)

League Club	Source	Date Signed	Seasons Played	Apps	Subs	Gls
York C.	Rowntree-Mackintosh	06.85	85-86	69	0	0
Sheffield U.	Tr	05.87	87	21	0	0
Bristol C.	Tr	09.88	88-91	74	0	0

LEAR, Graham J.
Exeter, 18 December, 1930 (G)

League Club	Source	Date Signed	Seasons Played	Apps	Subs	Gls
Exeter C. (Am)	Exeter T.	06.50	50-51	20	-	0

LEARY, Stuart E.
South Africa, 30 April, 1933 Died 1988 Eu23-1 (CF)

League Club	Source	Date Signed	Seasons Played	Apps	Subs	Gls
Charlton Ath.	Clyde (SA)	02.50	51-61	376	-	153
Queens Park R.	Tr	12.62	62-65	94	0	28

LEATH, Terence
Liverpool, 6 November, 1934 (FB)

League Club	Source	Date Signed	Seasons Played	Apps	Subs	Gls
Southport		07.59	58-59	17	-	0

LEATHER, Maurice P.
Eastleigh, 9 November, 1929 E Yth (G)

League Club	Source	Date Signed	Seasons Played	Apps	Subs	Gls
Portsmouth	Southampton (Am)	01.50	50-52	18	-	0

LEAVER, Derek
Blackburn, 13 November, 1930 (F)

League Club	Source	Date Signed	Seasons Played	Apps	Subs	Gls
Blackburn Rov.		05.49	50-54	14	-	5
Bournemouth	Tr	07.55	55	29	-	5
Crewe Alex.	Tr	03.56	55-56	28	-	6

LEAVY, Stephen
Longford (Ire), 18 June, 1925 LOI (FB)

League Club	Source	Date Signed	Seasons Played	Apps	Subs	Gls
Swansea C.	Sligo Rov.	07.50	50-57	36	-	1

LECK, Derek A.
Deal, 8 February, 1937 (WH)

League Club	Source	Date Signed	Seasons Played	Apps	Subs	Gls
Millwall		05.55	55-57	7	-	2
Northampton T.	Tr	06.58	58-65	247	0	46
Brighton & H.A.	Tr	11.65	65-66	29	1	0

LEDGARD, Ian
Stockport, 9 February, 1948 (FB)

League Club	Source	Date Signed	Seasons Played	Apps	Subs	Gls
Blackburn Rov.	Leeds U. (Am)	07.67				
Stockport Co.	Tr	10.67	67-68	4	4	0

LEDGER, Robert H.
Stanley, 5 October, 1937 (OR)

League Club	Source	Date Signed	Seasons Played	Apps	Subs	Gls
Huddersfield T.	Jnrs	10.54	55-61	58	-	7
Oldham Ath.	Tr	05.62	62-67	229	1	37
Mansfield T.	Tr	11.67	67-69	51	6	14
Barrow	Tr	10.69	69	21	1	2

LEDGER, Roy
Barnsley, 9 December, 1930 (IF)

League Club	Source	Date Signed	Seasons Played	Apps	Subs	Gls
Barnsley	Jnrs	04.48	50	1	-	0

LEDGERTON, Terence
Liverpool, 7 October, 1930 (OL)

League Club	Source	Date Signed	Seasons Played	Apps	Subs	Gls
Brentford		05.50	51-53	40	-	8
Millwall	Tr	05.54	54	6	-	2

LEE, Alan R.
West Germany, 19 June, 1960 (W)

League Club	Source	Date Signed	Seasons Played	Apps	Subs	Gls
Leicester C.	Philadelphia (USA)	02.79	78-79	6	0	0

LEE, Alfred
Farnworth, 11 June, 1927 (WH)

League Club	Source	Date Signed	Seasons Played	Apps	Subs	Gls
Bolton W.		10.48				
Oldham Ath.	Tr	07.50	50	3	-	1

LEE, Andrew G.
Liverpool, 14 September, 1962 (D)

League Club	Source	Date Signed	Seasons Played	Apps	Subs	Gls
Tranmere Rov.	Stafford R.	07.84	84	14	4	0
Cambridge U. (N/C)	Tr	09.85	85	8	1	0

LEE, Anthony
Manchester, 4 June, 1937 (OL)

League Club	Source	Date Signed	Seasons Played	Apps	Subs	Gls
Southport (Am)	Cheadle Rov.	02.58	57-58	10	-	1

LEE, J. Anthony
Middlesbrough, 26 November, 1947 (F)

League Club	Source	Date Signed	Seasons Played	Apps	Subs	Gls
Leicester C.		10.65				
Bradford C.	Tr	07.67	67	6	2	3
Darlington	Stockton	05.68	68	10	4	0

LEE, Christopher
Batley, 18 June, 1971 (M)

League Club	Source	Date Signed	Seasons Played	Apps	Subs	Gls
Bradford C.	YT	07.89				
Rochdale	Tr	06.90	90	24	2	2
Scarborough	Tr	03.91	90-91	49	1	2

LEE, Colin
Torquay, 12 June, 1956 (F/CD)

League Club	Source	Date Signed	Seasons Played	Apps	Subs	Gls
Bristol C.	App	06.74				
Hereford U.	L	11.74	74	7	2	0
Torquay U.	Tr	01.77	76-77	35	0	14
Tottenham H.	Tr	10.77	77-79	57	5	18
Chelsea	Tr	01.80	79-86	167	18	36
Brentford	Tr	07.87	87-88	20	4	1

LEE, David J.
Kingswood, 26 November, 1959 E Yth/Eu21-10 (M/CD)

League Club	Source	Date Signed	Seasons Played	Apps	Subs	Gls
Chelsea	YT	06.88	88-91	53	19	6
Reading	L	01.92	91	5	0	5
Plymouth Arg.	L	03.92	91	9	0	1

LEE, David M.
Blackburn, 5 November, 1967 (W)

League Club	Source	Date Signed	Seasons Played	Apps	Subs	Gls
Bury	YT	08.86	85-91	203	5	35
Southampton	Tr	08.91	91	11	8	0

David Lee (Bury & Southampton)

LEE, Eric G.
Chester, 18 October, 1922 E Amat (CH)

League Club	Source	Date Signed	Seasons Played	Apps	Subs	Gls
Chester C.		05.46	46-56	360	-	8

LEE, Francis H.
Westhoughton, 29 April, 1944 E Yth/EF Lge/E-27 (F)

League Club	Source	Date Signed	Seasons Played	Apps	Subs	Gls
Bolton W.	Jnrs	05.61	60-67	189	0	92
Manchester C.	Tr	10.67	67-73	248	1	112
Derby Co.	Tr	08.74	74-75	62	0	24

LEE, Frank
Chorley, 17 February, 1944 (W)

League Club	Source	Date Signed	Seasons Played	Apps	Subs	Gls
Preston N.E.	Jnrs	11.61	62-70	144	9	22
Southport	Tr	11.70	70-73	115	0	20
Stockport Co.	Tr	07.74	74	13	0	1

LEE, Garth
Sheffield, 39 September, 1943 E Yth (OL)

League Club	Source	Date Signed	Seasons Played	Apps	Subs	Gls
Sheffield U.	Jnrs	05.61				
Chester C.	Tr	09.63	63-64	29	-	7

LEE, Gary
Doncaster, 30 April, 1966 (D)

League Club	Source	Date Signed	Seasons Played	Apps	Subs	Gls
Doncaster Rov. (N/C)	YT	07.84	84	1	0	0

LEE, George
York, 4 June, 1919 Died 1991 (OL)

League Club	Source	Date Signed	Seasons Played	Apps	Subs	Gls
York C.	Jnrs	06.36	36-46	37	-	11
Nottingham F.	Tr	08.47	47-48	76	-	20
West Bromwich A.	Tr	07.49	49-57	271	-	59

Francis Lee (Bolton Wanderers, Manchester City, Derby County & England)

LEE, Gordon F.
Hednesford, 13 July, 1934 (FB)

League Club	Source	Date Signed	Seasons Played	Apps	Subs	Gls
Aston Villa	Hednesford T.	10.55	58-64	118	-	2
Shrewsbury T.	Tr	07.66	66	2	0	0

LEE, Harold
Mexborough, 13 January, 1933 (F)

League Club	Source	Date Signed	Seasons Played	Apps	Subs	Gls
Derby Co.	Thomas Hill Y.C.	10.50				
Mansfield T.		08.55	55	3	-	2

LEE, James
Rotherham, 26 January, 1926 (FB)

League Club	Source	Date Signed	Seasons Played	Apps	Subs	Gls
Wolverhampton W.	Wath W.	02.45				
Hull C.	Tr	10.48	49	3	-	1
Halifax T.	Tr	02.51	50-51	26	-	0
Chelsea	Tr	10.51				
Leyton Orient	Tr	07.54	54-55	67	-	1
Swindon T.	Tr	11.56	56-58	35	-	0

LEE, Jason B.
Forest Gate, 9 May, 1971 (F)

League Club	Source	Date Signed	Seasons Played	Apps	Subs	Gls
Charlton Ath.	YT	05.89	89	0	1	0
Stockport Co.	L	02.91	90	2	0	0
Lincoln C.	Tr	03.91	90-91	50	2	9

LEE, Jeffrey W.
Countesthorpe (Lei), 3 October, 1945 (LB)

League Club	Source	Date Signed	Seasons Played	Apps	Subs	Gls
Halifax T.	Huddersfield T. (Am)	01.65	64-72	231	9	2
Peterborough U.	Tr	08.73	73-77	170	2	12

LEE, John (Jack)
Sileby (Leics), 4 November, 1920 E-1 (CF)

League Club	Source	Date Signed	Seasons Played	Apps	Subs	Gls
Leicester C.	Quorn	02.41	46-49	123	-	74
Derby Co.	Tr	07.50	50-53	93	-	54
Coventry C.	Tr	11.54	54	15	-	8

LEE, Michael J.
Chester, 27 June, 1938 W Sch (OL)

League Club	Source	Date Signed	Seasons Played	Apps	Subs	Gls
West Bromwich A.	Saltney Jnrs	08.56	56	1	-	0
Crewe Alex.	Tr	06.58	58	1	-	0

LEE, Norman T.
Rhondda, 29 May, 1939 (WH)

League Club	Source	Date Signed	Seasons Played	Apps	Subs	Gls
Tottenham H.	Jnrs	11.57				
Bournemouth	Tr	09.61				
Southend U.	Tr	02.62	61-62	22	-	1

LEE, Paul A.
Oxford, 30 May, 1952 (F)

League Club	Source	Date Signed	Seasons Played	Apps	Subs	Gls
Hereford U.	Oxford C.	09.72	73-74	21	7	5

LEE, Raymond M.
Bristol, 19 September, 1970 (W)

League Club	Source	Date Signed	Seasons Played	Apps	Subs	Gls
Arsenal	YT	10.88				
Scarborough (N/C)		02.91	90	2	8	0

LEE, Richard
Sheffield, 11 September, 1944 (WH)

League Club	Source	Date Signed	Seasons Played	Apps	Subs	Gls
Rotherham U.	Jnrs	05.63				
Notts Co.	Tr	06.64				
Mansfield T.	Tr	08.65	65	3	1	0
Halifax T.	Tr	07.66	66-67	16	0	0

LEE, Robert
Newcastle, 23 December, 1957 (M)

League Club	Source	Date Signed	Seasons Played	Apps	Subs	Gls
Doncaster Rov.	App	05.74	74	1	0	0
Scunthorpe U.	Tr	07.76	76-77	17	2	0

LEE, Robert G.
Melton Mowbray, 2 February, 1953 (F)

League Club	Source	Date Signed	Seasons Played	Apps	Subs	Gls
Leicester C.	Blaby B.C.	02.72	71-76	55	8	17
Doncaster Rov.	L	08.74	74	14	0	4
Sunderland	Tr	09.76	76-79	101	8	32
Bristol Rov.	Tr	08.80	80	19	4	2
Carlisle U.	Tr	08.81	81-82	47	8	12
Darlington	Hong Kong	08.83	83	5	0	0

LEE, Robert M.
West Ham, 1 February, 1966 Eu21-2 (RW)

League Club	Source	Date Signed	Seasons Played	Apps	Subs	Gls
Charlton Ath.	Hornchurch	07.83	83-91	267	24	58

LEE, Samuel
Liverpool, 7 February, 1959 E Yth/Eu21-6/E-14 (M)

League Club	Source	Date Signed	Seasons Played	Apps	Subs	Gls
Liverpool	App	04.76	77-85	190	7	13
Queens Park R.	Tr	08.86	86	29	1	0
Southampton	Osasuna (Sp)	01.90	89	0	2	0
Bolton W.	Tr	10.90	90	4	0	0

LEE, F. Stuart
Manchester, 11 February, 1953 (F)

League Club	Source	Date Signed	Seasons Played	Apps	Subs	Gls
Bolton W.	App	02.71	71-74	77	8	20
Wrexham	Tr	11.75	75-77	46	8	12
Stockport Co.	Tr	08.78	78-79	49	0	21
Manchester C.	Tr	09.79	79	6	1	2

LEE, Terence W. G.
Stepney, 20 September, 1952 (G)

League Club	Source	Date Signed	Seasons Played	Apps	Subs	Gls
Tottenham H.	Jnrs	05.70	73	1	0	0
Torquay U.	Tr	07.75	75-77	106	0	0
Newport Co.	Tr	11.78	78	1	0	0

LEE, Thomas J.
Horden, 19 December, 1949 (F)

League Club	Source	Date Signed	Seasons Played	Apps	Subs	Gls
Hartlepool U.		11.68	69	6	0	0

LEE, Trevor C.
Lewisham, 3 July, 1954 (F)

League Club	Source	Date Signed	Seasons Played	Apps	Subs	Gls
Millwall	Epsom & Ewell	10.75	75-78	99	9	22
Colchester U.	Tr	11.78	78-80	95	1	35
Gillingham	Tr	01.81	80-82	43	4	14
Leyton Orient	L	10.82	82	5	0	0
Bournemouth	Tr	11.82	82-83	28	6	9
Cardiff C.	Tr	12.83	83	21	0	5
Northampton T.	Tr	07.84	84	24	0	0
Fulham (N/C)	Tr	03.85	84	1	0	0

LEE, William R.
Darwen, 24 October, 1919 (WH)

League Club	Source	Date Signed	Seasons Played	Apps	Subs	Gls
Blackburn Rov.		08.38	38	1	-	0
Barrow	Tr	05.47	46-52	158	-	1

LEEBROOK, Peter D.
Saltburn, 18 September, 1969 (RB)

League Club	Source	Date Signed	Seasons Played	Apps	Subs	Gls
Burnley	YT	05.87	86-87	52	0	0

LEECH, Frederick
Stalybridge, 5 December, 1923 (CF)

League Club	Source	Date Signed	Seasons Played	Apps	Subs	Gls
Bradford C.	Hurst	12.45	46	7	-	2

LEECH, Vincent G.
Rochdale, 6 February, 1940 (D)

League Club	Source	Date Signed	Seasons Played	Apps	Subs	Gls
Blackburn Rov.	Burnley (Am)	04.59				
Bury	Tr	07.61	61-67	108	3	0
Rochdale	Tr	07.68	68-70	59	1	1

LEEDER, Frederick
Seaton Delaval, 15 September, 1936 (FB)

League Club	Source	Date Signed	Seasons Played	Apps	Subs	Gls
Everton		03.55	57	1	-	0
Darlington	Tr	07.58	58-59	21	-	0
Southport	Tr	07.60	60-61	63	-	0

LEEDHAM, John R.
Morden, 8 November, 1942 (WH)

League Club	Source	Date Signed	Seasons Played	Apps	Subs	Gls
Millwall	Epsom & Ewell	10.62	62-63	9	-	0
Walsall	Tr	05.64	64	13	-	0
Leyton Orient	Tr	08.65				

LEEK, Kenneth
Ynysybwl, 26 July, 1935 Wu23-1/W-13 (CF)

League Club	Source	Date Signed	Seasons Played	Apps	Subs	Gls
Northampton T.	Pontypridd	08.52	55-57	71	-	26
Leicester C.	Tr	05.58	58-60	93	-	34
Newcastle U.	Tr	06.61	61	13	-	6
Birmingham C.	Tr	11.61	61-64	104	-	49
Northampton T.	Tr	12.64	64-65	15	0	4
Bradford C.	Tr	11.65	65-67	99	0	25

LEEMING, Clifford
Turton, 2 February, 1920 (IF)

League Club	Source	Date Signed	Seasons Played	Apps	Subs	Gls
Bury	Bolton W. (Am)	10.46	46	1	-	0
Tranmere Rov.	Tr	07.47	47	13	-	2

LEES, Alfred
Worsley, 28 July, 1923 (CH)

League Club	Source	Date Signed	Seasons Played	Apps	Subs	Gls
Bolton W.		05.47	47	2	-	0
New Brighton	Tr	08.49	49-50	72	-	0
Crewe Alex.	Tr	09.51	51-55	185	-	5

LEES, Geoffrey
Rotherham, 1 October, 1933 (HB)

League Club	Source	Date Signed	Seasons Played	Apps	Subs	Gls
Barnsley	Jnrs	03.51				
Bradford C.	Tr	07.55	55	3	-	0

LEES, Norman
Newcastle, 18 November, 1948 (D)

League Club	Source	Date Signed	Seasons Played	Apps	Subs	Gls
Hull C.	App	11.66	66-70	4	1	0
Hartlepool U.	L	12.70	70	20	0	1
Darlington	Tr	07.71	71-76	108	12	5

LEES, Terence
Stoke, 30 June, 1952 (FB)

League Club	Source	Date Signed	Seasons Played	Apps	Subs	Gls
Stoke C.	App	07.69	70-73	17	7	0
Crewe Alex.	L	03.75	74	6	0	0
Port Vale	Tr	08.75	75	40	1	2
Birmingham C.	Roda (Neth)	07.79	79-80	11	1	0
Newport Co.	Tr	08.81	81	25	0	0
Scunthorpe U.	Stafford R.	09.84	84	30	1	0

LEES, Walter J.
Glasgow, 2 February, 1947 (CD)

League Club	Source	Date Signed	Seasons Played	Apps	Subs	Gls
Watford	Kilsyth R.	06.68	68-75	220	6	10

LEESE, William
Stoke, 10 March, 1961 (CD)

League Club	Source	Date Signed	Seasons Played	Apps	Subs	Gls
Port Vale	App	03.79	79	1	0	0

LEESON, Donald
Askern, 25 August, 1935 (G)

League Club	Source	Date Signed	Seasons Played	Apps	Subs	Gls
Barnsley	Askern B.C.	05.54	56-60	98	-	0

LEET, Norman D.
Leicester, 13 March, 1962 (FB)

League Club	Source	Date Signed	Seasons Played	Apps	Subs	Gls
Leicester C.	Jnrs	06.80	80-82	19	0	0

LEGATE, Roland A.
Arlesey, 4 May, 1939 (OL)

League Club	Source	Date Signed	Seasons Played	Apps	Subs	Gls
Luton T.	Jnrs	05.56	56-61	15	-	8

LEGG, Andrew
Neath, 28 July, 1966 (LW)

League Club	Source	Date Signed	Seasons Played	Apps	Subs	Gls
Swansea C.	Briton Ferry	08.88	88-91	109	8	17

LEGG, Richard D.
Chippenham, 23 April, 1952 (F)

League Club	Source	Date Signed	Seasons Played	Apps	Subs	Gls
Swindon T.	Chippenham T.	08.71	71-73	13	7	3

LEGG, William C.
Bradford, 17 April, 1948 (LB)

League Club	Source	Date Signed	Seasons Played	Apps	Subs	Gls
Huddersfield T.	App	05.65	64-68	54	2	4

LEGGAT, Graham
Aberdeen, 20 June, 1934 Su23-1/SF Lge/S-18 (W)

League Club	Source	Date Signed	Seasons Played	Apps	Subs	Gls
Fulham	Aberdeen	08.58	58-66	251	3	127
Birmingham C.	Tr	01.67	66-67	13	3	3
Rotherham U.	Tr	07.68	68	13	3	7

LEGGETT, Peter R.
Newton-le-Willows, 16 December, 1943 (W)

League Club	Source	Date Signed	Seasons Played	Apps	Subs	Gls
Swindon T.	Weymouth	05.62	63-64	15	-	1
Brighton & H.A.	Tr	07.65	65	2	1	0
Cambridge U.	Chelmsford C.	(N/L)	70	21	0	0

LEIGH, Dennis
Barnsley, 26 February, 1949 (LB)

League Club	Source	Date Signed	Seasons Played	Apps	Subs	Gls
Doncaster Rov.	App	03.67	66-67	34	2	1
Rotherham U.	Tr	02.68	67-72	154	5	10
Lincoln C.	Tr	02.73	72-78	201	5	3

LEIGH, Ian R.
Ilfracombe, 11 June, 1962 (G)

League Club	Source	Date Signed	Seasons Played	Apps	Subs	Gls
Bournemouth	Swaythling	10.79	81-85	123	0	0
Bristol C.	L	01.85	84	1	0	0
Torquay U.	L	09.85	85	4	0	0

LEIGH, Mark B.
Manchester, 4 October, 1961 (F)

League Club	Source	Date Signed	Seasons Played	Apps	Subs	Gls
Stockport Co. (N/C)	Manchester C. (App)	11.79	80-83	6	5	1

LEIGH, Peter
Wythenshawe, 4 March, 1939 (LB)

League Club	Source	Date Signed	Seasons Played	Apps	Subs	Gls
Manchester C.	Stamford Lads	08.57	59	2	-	0
Crewe Alex.	Tr	06.61	61-71	430	0	3

LEIGHTON, Anthony
Leeds, 27 November, 1939 Died 1978 (CF)

League Club	Source	Date Signed	Seasons Played	Apps	Subs	Gls
Leeds U.	Ashley Road	12.56				
Doncaster Rov.	Tr	06.59	59-61	83	-	45
Barnsley	Tr	05.62	62-64	106	-	59
Huddersfield T.	Tr	01.65	64-67	89	1	40
Bradford C.	Tr	03.68	67-69	84	4	23

LEIGHTON, James
Johnstone, 24 July, 1958 Su21-1/S-58 (G)

League Club	Source	Date Signed	Seasons Played	Apps	Subs	Gls
Manchester U.	Aberdeen	05.88	88-89	73	0	0
Reading	L	11.91	91	8	0	0

LEIPER, John
Aberdeen, 26 June, 1938 (G)

League Club	Source	Date Signed	Seasons Played	Apps	Subs	Gls
Plymouth Arg.	Aberdeen E.E.	04.58	60-66	75	0	0

LEISHMAN, Graham
Salford, 6 April, 1968 (F)

League Club	Source	Date Signed	Seasons Played	Apps	Subs	Gls
Mansfield T.	Irlam T.	12.88	88-90	8	19	3

LEISHMAN, Thomas
Stenhousemuir, 3 September, 1937 (WH)

League Club	Source	Date Signed	Seasons Played	Apps	Subs	Gls
Liverpool	St Mirren	11.59	59-62	107	-	6

LEITCH, Andrew B.
Bristol, 27 March, 1950 (F)

League Club	Source	Date Signed	Seasons Played	Apps	Subs	Gls
Swansea C.		07.75	75	15	2	6

LEITCH, Grant
South Africa, 31 October, 1972 (F)

League Club	Source	Date Signed	Seasons Played	Apps	Subs	Gls
Blackpool	Jnrs	08.91	91	1	5	0

LEIVERS, William E
Bolsover, 29 January, 1932 (FB)

League Club	Source	Date Signed	Seasons Played	Apps	Subs	Gls
Chesterfield	Jnrs	02.50	51-52	27	-	0
Manchester C.	Tr	11.53	54-63	250	-	4
Doncaster Rov.	Tr	07.64	64-65	24	0	1

LELLO, Cyril F.
Ludlow, 24 February, 1920 (WH)

League Club	Source	Date Signed	Seasons Played	Apps	Subs	Gls
Lincoln C.		02.44				
Everton	Shrewsbury T.	09.47	47-56	237	-	9
Rochdale	Tr	11.56	56	11	-	0

LEMAN, Dennis
Newcastle, 1 December, 1954 E Sch (M)

League Club	Source	Date Signed	Seasons Played	Apps	Subs	Gls
Manchester C.	App	12.71	73-75	10	7	1
Sheffield Wed.	Tr	12.76	76-81	89	15	9
Wrexham	L	02.82	81	17	0	1
Scunthorpe U.	Tr	08.82	82-83	38	0	3

LEMON, Arthur
Neath, 25 January, 1932 (F)

League Club	Source	Date Signed	Seasons Played	Apps	Subs	Gls
Nottingham F.		02.51	52-54	24	-	1

Jim Leighton (Aberdeen, Manchester United & Scotland)

League Club	Source	Date Signed	Seasons Played	Apps	Subs	Gls

LEMON, Paul A.
Middlesbrough, 3 June, 1966 (M)

League Club	Source	Date Signed	Seasons Played	Apps	Subs	Gls
Sunderland	App	05.84	84-88	91	16	15
Carlisle U.	L	12.84	84	2	0	0
Walsall	L	11.89	89	2	0	0
Reading	L	12.89	89	3	0	0
Chesterfield	Tr	09.90	90-91	52	2	4

LENARDUZZI, Robert I.
Canada, 1 May, 1955 Canadian Int (D)

League Club	Source	Date Signed	Seasons Played	Apps	Subs	Gls
Reading	App	05.73	71-75	63	4	2

LENG, Michael
Rotherham, 14 June, 1952 (D)

League Club	Source	Date Signed	Seasons Played	Apps	Subs	Gls
Rotherham U.	App	07.71	71-75	94	7	2
Workington	Tr	07.76	76	43	0	2

LENIHAN, Michael M.
Swansea, 15 October, 1946 (F)

League Club	Source	Date Signed	Seasons Played	Apps	Subs	Gls
Swansea C.	Swansea G.P.O.	08.72	72-73	9	4	0

LENNARD, David H.
Manchester, 31 December, 1944 (M)

League Club	Source	Date Signed	Seasons Played	Apps	Subs	Gls
Bolton W.	Jnrs	12.61	62-68	114	5	3
Halifax T.	Tr	07.69	69-71	97	0	16
Blackpool	Tr	10.71	71-72	42	3	9
Cambridge U.	Tr	08.73	73-74	39	1	6
Chester C.	Tr	09.74	74-75	73	2	11
Stockport Co.	Tr	07.76	76	39	0	4
Bournemouth	Tr	09.77	77-78	56	3	4

LENNON, Alexander V.
Glasgow, 23 October, 1925 (IL)

League Club	Source	Date Signed	Seasons Played	Apps	Subs	Gls
Rotherham U.		11.44				
Queens Park R.		01.47	48	1	-	0
Mansfield T.	Tr	02.49	48	3	-	0

LENNON, Neil F.
Lurgan (NI), 25 June, 1971 NI Yth (M)

League Club	Source	Date Signed	Seasons Played	Apps	Subs	Gls
Manchester C.	YT	08.89	87	1	0	0
Crewe Alex.	Tr	08.90	90	32	2	3

LENNOX, Stephen J. M.
Aberdeen, 14 November, 1964 (M)

League Club	Source	Date Signed	Seasons Played	Apps	Subs	Gls
Stoke C.	App	12.81	82	1	1	0
Torquay U.	L	12.83	83	11	0	0

LEONARD, Carleton C.
Oswestry, 3 February, 1958 (FB)

League Club	Source	Date Signed	Seasons Played	Apps	Subs	Gls
Shrewsbury T.	Jnrs	09.75	75-82	224	3	1
Hereford U.	Tr	06.83	83-84	29	1	0
Cardiff C. (N/C)	Tr	07.85	85	4	0	0

LEONARD, Christopher
Jarrow, 11 July, 1927 (CH)

League Club	Source	Date Signed	Seasons Played	Apps	Subs	Gls
Darlington	South Shields	03.52	51-53	26	-	0

LEONARD, Gary A.
Newcastle, 28 November, 1965 (M)

League Club	Source	Date Signed	Seasons Played	Apps	Subs	Gls
West Bromwich A.	App	11.83				
Shrewsbury T.	Tr	07.85	85-87	48	19	1
Hereford U.	L	03.88	87	11	0	1
Bury	Tr	07.88	88	4	5	1
Stockport Co.	Tr	03.89	88-89	15	2	1

LEONARD, Gary E.
Northampton, 23 March, 1962 (M)

League Club	Source	Date Signed	Seasons Played	Apps	Subs	Gls
Northampton T.	App	03.80	79-80	2	0	0

LEONARD, Henry (Harry)
Jarrow, 19 May, 1924 (FB)

League Club	Source	Date Signed	Seasons Played	Apps	Subs	Gls
Bradford P.A.	Darlington (Am)	05.45	47	1	-	0
Hartlepool U.	Tr	11.48	48	2	-	0

LEONARD, Keith A.
Birmingham, 10 November, 1950 (F)

League Club	Source	Date Signed	Seasons Played	Apps	Subs	Gls
Aston Villa	Highgate U.	04.72	72-75	36	2	11

LEONARD, Mark A.
St Helens, 27 September, 1962 (F)

League Club	Source	Date Signed	Seasons Played	Apps	Subs	Gls
Everton	Witton A.	02.82				
Tranmere Rov.	L	03.83	82	6	1	0
Crewe Alex.	Tr	06.83	83-84	51	3	15
Stockport Co.	Tr	02.85	84-86	73	0	23
Bradford C.	Tr	09.86	86-91	120	37	29
Rochdale	Tr	03.92	91	9	0	1

LEONARD, Michael C.
Carshalton, 9 May, 1959 (G)

League Club	Source	Date Signed	Seasons Played	Apps	Subs	Gls
Halifax T.	Epsom & Ewell	07.76	76-79	69	0	0
Notts Co.	Tr	09.79	79-88	204	0	0
Chesterfield	Tr	03.89	88-91	127	0	0
Halifax T.	L	11.90	90	3	0	0

LEONARD, Patrick D.
Dublin, 25 July, 1929 (IF)

League Club	Source	Date Signed	Seasons Played	Apps	Subs	Gls
Bristol Rov.	Bath C.	07.52	52-53	14	-	2
Colchester U.	Tr	07.54	54	34	-	5

LEONARD, Stanley
Hawarden, 8 October, 1925 (OR)

League Club	Source	Date Signed	Seasons Played	Apps	Subs	Gls
Chester C. (Am)		01.47	46	1	-	0

LESLIE, John A.
Plumstead, 25 October, 1955 (F)

League Club	Source	Date Signed	Seasons Played	Apps	Subs	Gls
Wimbledon	Dulwich Hamlet	12.75	77-82	242	11	85
Gillingham	Tr	08.83	83-84	60	5	12
Millwall	Tr	08.85	85-86	12	7	2

LESLIE, Lawrence G.
Edinburgh, 17 March, 1935 SF Lge/S-5 (G)

League Club	Source	Date Signed	Seasons Played	Apps	Subs	Gls
West Ham U.	Airdrieonians	06.61	61-62	57	-	0
Stoke C.	Tr	10.63	63-65	78	0	0
Millwall	Tr	07.66	66-67	67	0	0
Southend U.	Tr	07.68	68	13	0	0

LESLIE, Maurice H.
India, 19 August, 1923 (FB)

League Club	Source	Date Signed	Seasons Played	Apps	Subs	Gls
Swindon T.		06.47	46	1	-	0

LESLIE, Steven R. W.
Brentwood, 4 September, 1952 E Yth (M)

League Club	Source	Date Signed	Seasons Played	Apps	Subs	Gls
Colchester U.	Jnrs	05.71	70-83	411	21	40

LESSLIE, Kenneth G.
West Ham, 4 January, 1923 (OR)

League Club	Source	Date Signed	Seasons Played	Apps	Subs	Gls
Ipswich T.		08.47				
Watford		07.48	48	7	-	1

LESTER, A. Benjamin
Sheffield, 10 February, 1920 (CF)

League Club	Source	Date Signed	Seasons Played	Apps	Subs	Gls
Hull C.	Selby T.	09.46	46-47	27	-	17
Lincoln C.	Tr	01.48	47-48	37	-	10
Stockport Co.	Tr	08.49	49	8	-	2

LESTER, Leslie J.
Cardiff, 17 November, 1923 Died 1991 (RH)

League Club	Source	Date Signed	Seasons Played	Apps	Subs	Gls
Cardiff C.	Cardiff Corries	04.44				
Torquay U.	Tr	08.48	48-49	31	-	1
Newport Co.	Tr	09.50	50	2	-	0

LESTER, Michael J.
Manchester, 4 August, 1954 (M)

League Club	Source	Date Signed	Seasons Played	Apps	Subs	Gls
Oldham Ath.	App	08.72	72-73	26	1	2
Manchester C.	Tr	11.73	73-76	1	1	0
Stockport Co.	L	08.75	75	8	1	1
Grimsby T.	Washington (USA)	11.77	77-79	45	3	10
Barnsley	Tr	10.79	79-80	64	0	11
Exeter C.	Tr	08.81	81	18	1	6
Bradford C.	Tr	02.82	81-82	46	3	2
Scunthorpe U.	Tr	03.83	82-85	106	0	9
Hartlepool U.	L	01.86	85	11	0	1
Stockport Co.	Tr	09.86	86	11	0	0
Blackpool	Sweden	12.87	87	11	0	1

LETHERAN, Glan
Llanelli, 1 May, 1956 Wu21-2/Wu23-1 (G)

League Club	Source	Date Signed	Seasons Played	Apps	Subs	Gls
Leeds U.	App	05.73	74	1	0	0
Scunthorpe U.	L	08.76	76	27	0	0
Chesterfield	Tr	12.77	77-79	63	0	0
Swansea C.	Tr	09.79	79	21	0	0

LEUTY, Leon H.
Shrewsbury, 23 October, 1920 Died 1955 EF Lge/E'B'-3 (CH)

League Club	Source	Date Signed	Seasons Played	Apps	Subs	Gls
Derby Co.	Notts Co. (Am)	05.44	46-49	131	-	1
Bradford P.A.	Tr	03.50	49-50	19	-	0
Notts Co.	Tr	09.50	50-55	187	-	3

LEVER, Arthur R.
Cardiff, 25 March, 1920 W-1 (FB)

League Club	Source	Date Signed	Seasons Played	Apps	Subs	Gls
Cardiff C.	Jnrs	08.43	46-50	156	-	9
Leicester C.	Tr	09.50	50-53	119	-	0
Newport Co.	Tr	07.54	54-56	72	-	0

League Club	Source	Date Signed	Seasons Played	Career Record Apps	Subs	Gls

LEVER, Mark
Beverley, 29 March, 1970 (CD)

League Club	Source	Date Signed	Seasons Played	Apps	Subs	Gls
Grimsby T.	YT	07.88	87-91	147	5	6

LEVERTON, Roland ("Tot")
Whitwell, 8 May, 1926 (IF)

League Club	Source	Date Signed	Seasons Played	Apps	Subs	Gls
Nottingham F.	Jnrs	10.43	46-53	103	-	36
Notts Co.	Tr	10.53	53-55	45	-	6
Walsall	Tr	07.56	56	17	-	3

LEVY, Anthony S.
Edmonton, 20 October, 1959 (F)

League Club	Source	Date Signed	Seasons Played	Apps	Subs	Gls
Plymouth Arg.	App	10.77	78	0	1	0
Torquay U.	Tr	07.79	79	8	5	1

LEVY, Leonard
Stepney, 24 December, 1926 (G)

League Club	Source	Date Signed	Seasons Played	Apps	Subs	Gls
Aldershot		10.50	50	2	-	0

LEWIN, Derek J.
Manchester, 18 May, 1930 E Amat (IF)

League Club	Source	Date Signed	Seasons Played	Apps	Subs	Gls
Oldham Ath. (Am)	St Annes Ath.	08.53	53-54	10	-	1
Accrington St. (Am)	Bishop Auckland	10.57	57	1	-	0

LEWIN, D. Ronald
Edmonton, 21 June, 1920 (FB)

League Club	Source	Date Signed	Seasons Played	Apps	Subs	Gls
Bradford C.		09.43				
Fulham	Tr	06.46	46-48	41	-	0
Gillingham	Tr	06.50	50-54	191	-	1

LEWINGTON, Raymond
Lambeth, 7 September, 1956 (M)

League Club	Source	Date Signed	Seasons Played	Apps	Subs	Gls
Chelsea	App	02.74	75-78	80	5	4
Wimbledon (L)	Vancouver (Can)	09.79	79	23	0	0
Fulham	Tr	03.80	79-84	172	2	20
Sheffield U.	Tr	07.85	85	36	0	0
Fulham	Tr	07.86	86-89	58	2	1

LEWIS, Alan T.
Oxford, 19 August, 1954 E Yth (LB)

League Club	Source	Date Signed	Seasons Played	Apps	Subs	Gls
Derby Co.	App	05.72	72	2	0	0
Peterborough U.	Tr	03.74	73	10	0	1
Brighton & H.A.	Tr	01.75	74	3	0	0
Reading	Tr	07.77	77-81	147	4	5

LEWIS, Allan
Pontypridd, 31 May, 1971 (D)

League Club	Source	Date Signed	Seasons Played	Apps	Subs	Gls
Cardiff C.	YT	07.89	89-91	27	23	0

LEWIS, Bernard
Aberfan, 12 March, 1945 Wu23-5 (OL)

League Club	Source	Date Signed	Seasons Played	Apps	Subs	Gls
Cardiff C.	Jnrs	04.64	63-67	87	1	7
Watford	Tr	12.67	67-69	41	10	9
Southend U.	Tr	09.70	70-71	55	3	5

LEWIS, Brian
Woking, 26 January, 1943 (M)

League Club	Source	Date Signed	Seasons Played	Apps	Subs	Gls
Crystal Palace	Jnrs	04.60	60-62	32	-	4
Portsmouth	Tr	07.63	63-66	134	0	24
Coventry C.	Tr	01.67	66-67	33	2	2
Luton T.	Tr	07.68	68-69	45	4	22
Oxford U.	Tr	01.70	69-70	12	2	4
Colchester U.	Tr	12.70	70-71	46	0	17
Portsmouth	Tr	04.72	71-74	44	14	8

LEWIS, Charles R.
Liverpool, 11 May, 1921

League Club	Source	Date Signed	Seasons Played	Apps	Subs	Gls
Halifax T.	South Liverpool	10.47	47-48	24	-	4

LEWIS, David S.
Swansea, 12 February, 1936 (W)

League Club	Source	Date Signed	Seasons Played	Apps	Subs	Gls
Swansea C.		12.57	57-58	19	-	1
Torquay U.	Tr	07.60	60	16	-	2

LEWIS, Dennis G.
Treherbert, 21 April, 1925 (WH)

League Club	Source	Date Signed	Seasons Played	Apps	Subs	Gls
Swansea C.		08.46				
Torquay U.	Tr	08.47	47-58	443	-	30

LEWIS, Derek I. E.
Edmonton, 10 June, 1929 Died 1953 (IF)

League Club	Source	Date Signed	Seasons Played	Apps	Subs	Gls
Gillingham	Fulham (Am)	05.50	50-51	48	-	31
Preston N.E.	Tr	02.52	51-52	37	-	14

LEWIS, Dudley K.
Swansea, 17 November, 1962 W Sch/Wu21-9/W-1 (CD)

League Club	Source	Date Signed	Seasons Played	Apps	Subs	Gls
Swansea C.	App	11.79	80-88	228	2	2
Huddersfield T.	Tr	07.89	89-90	32	2	0
Halifax T.	L	10.91	91	11	0	0
Wrexham	Tr	03.92	91	8	1	0

LEWIS, Edward
Manchester, 3 January, 1935 (FB)

League Club	Source	Date Signed	Seasons Played	Apps	Subs	Gls
Manchester U.	Jnrs	01.52	52-55	20	-	9
Preston N.E.	Tr	12.55	55-56	12	-	2
West Ham U.	Tr	11.56	56-57	31	-	12
Leyton Orient	Tr	06.58	58-63	143	-	5

LEWIS, Edward
Birmingham (G)

League Club	Source	Date Signed	Seasons Played	Apps	Subs	Gls
West Bromwich A.		11.44				
Leyton Orient	Tr	03.46	46	5	-	0

LEWIS, Frederick A.
Broughton, 27 July, 1923 (FB)

League Club	Source	Date Signed	Seasons Played	Apps	Subs	Gls
Chelsea	Aylesbury T.	03.46	46-52	23	-	0
Colchester U.	Tr	07.53	53-54	85	-	0

LEWIS, T. George
Troedyrhiw, 20 October, 1913 (CF)

League Club	Source	Date Signed	Seasons Played	Apps	Subs	Gls
Watford	New Tredegar	05.34	36-38	25	-	11
Southampton	Tr	07.46	46-47	43	-	12
Brighton & H.A.	Tr	06.48	48	24	-	8

LEWIS, Glyn
Abertillery, 3 July, 1921 (W)

League Club	Source	Date Signed	Seasons Played	Apps	Subs	Gls
Crystal Palace		05.42	46-47	60	-	4
Bristol C.	Tr	07.48	48	18	-	0

LEWIS, Gwyn
Bangor, 22 April, 1931 W Yth (CF)

League Club	Source	Date Signed	Seasons Played	Apps	Subs	Gls
Everton	Jnrs	05.48	51-55	10	-	6
Rochdale	Tr	06.56	56	27	-	10
Chesterfield	Tr	02.57	56-60	123	-	58

LEWIS, Idris
Tonypandy, 26 August, 1915 (OR)

League Club	Source	Date Signed	Seasons Played	Apps	Subs	Gls
Swansea C.		05.35	35-37	66	-	2
Sheffield Wed.	Tr	08.38	38	18	-	7
Swansea C.	Tr	03.39	38	12	-	2
Bristol Rov.	Tr	07.46	46	13	-	2
Newport Co.	Tr	10.46	46-47	27	-	4

LEWIS, James L.
Hackney, 26 June, 1927 E Amat (CF)

League Club	Source	Date Signed	Seasons Played	Apps	Subs	Gls
Leyton Orient (Am)	Walthamstow Ave.	11.50	50	4	-	0
Chelsea (Am)	Walthamstow Ave.	09.52	52-57	90	-	38

LEWIS, F. John (Jack)
Long Eaton, 22 March, 1948 Wu23-1 (F)

League Club	Source	Date Signed	Seasons Played	Apps	Subs	Gls
Lincoln C.	Long Eaton U.	03.67	66-69	47	15	9
Grimsby T.	Tr	01.70	69-76	231	27	74
Blackburn Rov.	Tr	08.77	77	24	4	6
Doncaster Rov.	Tr	08.78	78-79	48	16	10

LEWIS, John
Tredegar, 15 October, 1955 Wu21-1 (M)

League Club	Source	Date Signed	Seasons Played	Apps	Subs	Gls
Cardiff C.	Pontllanfraith	08.78	78-83	135	5	9
Newport Co.	Tr	09.83	83-87	153	0	8
Swansea C.	Tr	10.87	87	25	0	0

LEWIS, John
Tamworth, 1 May, 1920 (G)

League Club	Source	Date Signed	Seasons Played	Apps	Subs	Gls
Walsall	Boldmere St Michael	12.45	46-52	271	-	0

LEWIS, John (Jack)
Walsall, 26 August, 1919 (WH)

League Club	Source	Date Signed	Seasons Played	Apps	Subs	Gls
Crystal Palace	West Bromwich A. (Am)	07.38	38-49	124	-	6
Bournemouth	Tr	11.49	49-50	25	-	1
Reading	Tr	07.51	51-52	74	-	17

LEWIS, John
Birmingham, 6 October, 1923 (WH)

League Club	Source	Date Signed	Seasons Played	Apps	Subs	Gls
West Bromwich A.	Jnrs	10.45				
Mansfield T.	Tr	08.48	48-52	163	-	11

LEWIS, John G.
Hackney, 9 May, 1954 E Yth (M)

League Club	Source	Date Signed	Seasons Played	Apps	Subs	Gls
Leyton Orient	Tottenham H. (Am)	07.72	72	0	2	0

LEWIS, Kenneth
Cardiff, 7 November, 1924 (FB)

League Club	Source	Date Signed	Seasons Played	Apps	Subs	Gls
Torquay U.		01.50	50-52	27	-	0

LEWIS, Kenneth
Bangor, 12 October, 1929 (IF)

League Club	Source	Date Signed	Seasons Played	Apps	Subs	Gls
Walsall	Bangor C.	03.54	53-54	18	-	1
Scunthorpe U.	Bangor C.	08.56	56	1	-	0

LEWIS, Kevin
Ellesmere Port, 19 September, 1940 E Yth (W)

League Club	Source	Date Signed	Seasons Played	Apps	Subs	Gls
Sheffield U.	Jnrs	10.57	57-59	62	-	23
Liverpool	Tr	06.60	60-62	71	-	39
Huddersfield T.	Tr	08.63	63-64	45	-	13

LEWIS, Kevin
Hull, 17 October, 1970 (D)

League Club	Source	Date Signed	Seasons Played	Apps	Subs	Gls
Stoke C. (YT)	YT	07.87	87	0	1	0

LEWIS, Kevin W.
Hull, 25 September, 1952 E Sch (FB)

League Club	Source	Date Signed	Seasons Played	Apps	Subs	Gls
Manchester U.	App	09.69				
Stoke C.	Tr	07.72	72-75	15	0	0
Crewe Alex.	Tr	06.79	79-81	117	5	2

LEWIS, Michael
Birmingham, 15 February, 1965 E Yth (M)

League Club	Source	Date Signed	Seasons Played	Apps	Subs	Gls
West Bromwich A.	App	02.82	81-84	22	2	0
Derby Co.	Tr	11.84	84-87	37	6	1
Oxford U.	Tr	08.88	88-91	155	0	6

LEWIS, Michael
Ollerton, 26 August, 1950 (OL)

League Club	Source	Date Signed	Seasons Played	Apps	Subs	Gls
Rotherham U.	App	12.67	67	0	1	0

LEWIS, Morgan R.
Bournemouth, 8 September, 1965 (M)

League Club	Source	Date Signed	Seasons Played	Apps	Subs	Gls
Bournemouth	Jnrs	07.84	83-86	11	1	0

LEWIS, Norman
Shifnal, 28 May, 1927 (LB)

League Club	Source	Date Signed	Seasons Played	Apps	Subs	Gls
Shrewsbury T.	Oakengates T.	08.50	50-52	62	-	0
Newport Co.	Gravesend & Nft.	06.54	54	15	-	0

LEWIS, Paul S.
Rhondda, 27 September, 1956 W Yth (G)

League Club	Source	Date Signed	Seasons Played	Apps	Subs	Gls
Bristol Rov.	App	10.74	75	1	0	0

LEWIS, Reginald J.
Bilston, 7 March, 1920 E'B'-2 (CF)

League Club	Source	Date Signed	Seasons Played	Apps	Subs	Gls
Arsenal	Jnrs	03.37	37-51	154	-	103

LEWIS, Roland
Sandbach, 21 September, 1925 (F)

League Club	Source	Date Signed	Seasons Played	Apps	Subs	Gls
Port Vale		03.50	50-53	7	-	0

LEWIS, Ronald
Belfast, 10 February, 1932 (IF)

League Club	Source	Date Signed	Seasons Played	Apps	Subs	Gls
Burnley	Glentoran	06.49				
Barrow	Tr	05.54	54	5	-	1

LEWIS, Russell
Blaengwynfi, 15 September, 1956 (CD)

League Club	Source	Date Signed	Seasons Played	Apps	Subs	Gls
Swindon T.	Bridgend T.	10.76	76-82	175	6	7
Northampton T.	Tr	08.83	83-85	131	1	6

LEWIS, Terence J.
Newport, 22 October, 1950 W Sch (WH)

League Club	Source	Date Signed	Seasons Played	Apps	Subs	Gls
Cardiff C.	App	10.68	68-69	2	0	0

LEWIS, Trevor
Aberbargoed, 6 January, 1921 (W)

League Club	Source	Date Signed	Seasons Played	Apps	Subs	Gls
Coventry C.	Redditch	02.48	47-52	11	-	0
Gillingham	Tr	02.53	52-54	26	-	4

LEWIS, Wilfred
Cardiff, 4 July, 1923 (OR)

League Club	Source	Date Signed	Seasons Played	Apps	Subs	Gls
Cardiff C.		07.41	46-47	9	-	0
Newport Co.	Tr	10.47	47-49	49	-	11

LEWIS, William A.
West Ham, 23 November, 1921 E Sch (FB)

League Club	Source	Date Signed	Seasons Played	Apps	Subs	Gls
Blackpool	West Ham U. (Am)	07.45	46-49	30	-	0
Norwich C.	Tr	11.49	49-55	232	-	1

LEWORTHY, David J.
Portsmouth, 22 October, 1962 (F)

League Club	Source	Date Signed	Seasons Played	Apps	Subs	Gls
Portsmouth	App	09.80	81	0	1	0
Tottenham H.	Fareham T.	08.84	84-85	8	3	3
Oxford U.	Tr	12.85	85-88	25	12	8
Shrewsbury T.	L	10.87	87	6	0	3
Reading	Tr	07.89	89-91	23	21	7

LEY, George O. A.
Exminster, 7 April, 1946 (LB)

League Club	Source	Date Signed	Seasons Played	Apps	Subs	Gls
Exeter C.	Hitchin T.	09.63	63-66	93	0	7
Portsmouth	Tr	05.67	66-72	183	1	10
Brighton & H.A.	Tr	09.72	72-73	47	0	1
Gillingham	Tr	08.74	74-75	87	0	2

LEYDEN, Darren S.
Warley, 20 February, 1970 (CD)

League Club	Source	Date Signed	Seasons Played	Apps	Subs	Gls
Torquay U.	YT	07.88	88	7	2	0

LEYFIELD, John G.
Chester, 5 August, 1923 (WH)

League Club	Source	Date Signed	Seasons Played	Apps	Subs	Gls
Wrexham		07.46	46-49	34	-	1
Southport	Tr	08.50	50	26	-	0

LEYLAND, Harold K.
Liverpool, 12 May, 1930 (G)

League Club	Source	Date Signed	Seasons Played	Apps	Subs	Gls
Everton	Jnrs	08.50	51-55	35	-	0
Blackburn Rov.	Tr	08.56	56-60	166	-	0
Tranmere Rov.	Tr	03.61	60-65	180	0	0

LIDDELL, Andrew M.
Leeds, 28 June, 1973 (F)

League Club	Source	Date Signed	Seasons Played	Apps	Subs	Gls
Barnsley	YT	06.91	91	0	1	0

LIDDELL, Gary
Bannockburn, 27 August, 1954 (F)

League Club	Source	Date Signed	Seasons Played	Apps	Subs	Gls
Leeds U.	App	09.71	72-74	2	1	0
Grimsby T.	Tr	03.77	76-80	90	15	22
Doncaster Rov.	Hearts	03.82	81-82	25	12	4

LIDDELL, John

League Club	Source	Date Signed	Seasons Played	Apps	Subs	Gls
Leyton Orient		03.44				
Brighton & H.A.		03.47	46	4	-	1

LIDDELL, John C.
Stirling, 13 December, 1933 (CF)

League Club	Source	Date Signed	Seasons Played	Apps	Subs	Gls
Oldham Ath.	St Johnstone	09.60	60-61	23	-	10

LIDDELL, William B.
Dumfermline, 10 January, 1922 S-28 (F)

League Club	Source	Date Signed	Seasons Played	Apps	Subs	Gls
Liverpool	Lochgelly Viollet	04.39	46-60	495	-	216

LIDDLE, Bryan
Durham, 23 June, 1961 (LB)

League Club	Source	Date Signed	Seasons Played	Apps	Subs	Gls
Hartlepool U.	Brandon U.	08.84	84	12	1	0

LIDDLE, Daniel H. S.
Bo'ness, 19 February, 1912 Died 1982 S-3 (IF)

League Club	Source	Date Signed	Seasons Played	Apps	Subs	Gls
Leicester C.	East Fife	05.32	32-38	255	-	63
Mansfield T.	Tr	07.46	46	1	-	0

LIDDLE, David N.
Bedford, 21 May, 1957 (CD)

League Club	Source	Date Signed	Seasons Played	Apps	Subs	Gls
Northampton T.	App	05.75	77-78	28	3	3

LIDDLE, Gavin
Houghton-le-Spring, 9 May, 1963 (FB)

League Club	Source	Date Signed	Seasons Played	Apps	Subs	Gls
Darlington	Hartlepool U. (App)	08.81	81-82	33	0	4

LIDDLE, Kenneth
Gateshead, 6 October, 1928 (F)

League Club	Source	Date Signed	Seasons Played	Apps	Subs	Gls
Sunderland		12.49				
Darlington	Tr	06.50	50	1	-	0

LIDDLE, Thomas B.
Middleton, 22 April, 1921 (D)

League Club	Source	Date Signed	Seasons Played	Apps	Subs	Gls
Bournemouth		02.47	47	1	-	0

LIEVESLEY, Dennis
Chesterfield, 19 September, 1919 (CH)

League Club	Source	Date Signed	Seasons Played	Apps	Subs	Gls
Aldershot		08.46	46-48	8	-	0

LIGGITT, Norman
Thornaby, 21 July, 1941 (CH)

League Club	Source	Date Signed	Seasons Played	Apps	Subs	Gls
Middlesbrough	Jnrs	08.59				
Southend U.	Tr	07.62	62	1	-	0

LIGHT, Daniel
Chiswick, 10 July, 1948 (W)

League Club	Source	Date Signed	Seasons Played	Apps	Subs	Gls
Crystal Palace	App	12.65	66-67	18	1	5
Colchester U.	Tr	08.68	68-69	65	2	17

LIGHT, James P.
Oxford, 13 January, 1954 (FB)

League Club	Source	Date Signed	Seasons Played	Apps	Subs	Gls
Oxford U.	App	01.72	72-75	64	0	1

LIGHTBOWN, Trevor J.
Blackburn, 21 November, 1939 (CF)

League Club	Source	Date Signed	Seasons Played	Apps	Subs	Gls
Accrington St. (Am)	Burnley (Am)	08.59	59	8	-	0
Bradford P.A. (Am)	Tr	08.60	60	2	-	0

LIGHTENING, Arthur D.
South Africa, 1 August, 1936 (G)

League Club	Source	Date Signed	Seasons Played	Apps	Subs	Gls
Nottingham F.	South Africa	12.56	57-58	6	-	0
Coventry C.	Tr	11.58	58-62	150	-	0
Middlesbrough	Tr	08.62	62	15	-	0

LIGHTFOOT, Christopher I.
Warrington, 1 April, 1970 (CD)

League Club	Source	Date Signed	Seasons Played	Apps	Subs	Gls
Chester C.	YT	07.88	87-91	161	12	15

LIGHTLY, Brian
Portsmouth, 12 May, 1936 (WH)

League Club	Source	Date Signed	Seasons Played	Apps	Subs	Gls
Exeter C.	Portsmouth (Am)	06.57	57	4	-	0

LIGHTOWLER, Gerard A.
Bradford, 5 September, 1940 (FB)

League Club	Source	Date Signed	Seasons Played	Apps	Subs	Gls
Bradford P.A.	St. Bede's	12.58	58-67	206	2	1
Bradford C.	Los Angeles (USA)	10.68	68	11	1	0

LILEY, Henry J. G.
Bristol, 19 August, 1918 (G)

League Club	Source	Date Signed	Seasons Played	Apps	Subs	Gls
Bristol Rov.	Dockland Settlement	10.46	46-49	27	-	0

LILL, David A.
Aldbrough, 17 February, 1947 (M)

League Club	Source	Date Signed	Seasons Played	Apps	Subs	Gls
Hull C.	Jnrs	03.65	66-69	16	2	2
Rotherham U.	Tr	10.69	67-70	33	7	5
Cambridge U.	Tr	07.71	71-75	166	6	22

LILL, James A.
Wentworth, 4 June, 1933 (OL)

League Club	Source	Date Signed	Seasons Played	Apps	Subs	Gls
Mansfield T.	Wentworth	03.54	53-55	3	-	0

LILL, Michael J.
Romford, 3 August, 1936 E Yth (OL)

League Club	Source	Date Signed	Seasons Played	Apps	Subs	Gls
Wolverhampton W.	Storey Ath.	06.54	57-59	30	-	15
Everton	Tr	02.60	59-61	31	-	11
Plymouth Arg.	Tr	06.62	62	21	-	7
Portsmouth	Tr	03.63	62-64	39	-	5

LILLIS, Jason W.
Chatham, 1 October, 1969 (F)

League Club	Source	Date Signed	Seasons Played	Apps	Subs	Gls
Gillingham	YT	10.87	87-88	15	14	3
Maidstone U.	Queens Park R. (N/C)	07.89	89-91	57	18	18
Carlisle U.	L	02.91	90	4	0	1

LILLIS, Mark A.
Manchester, 17 January, 1960 (F/M)

League Club	Source	Date Signed	Seasons Played	Apps	Subs	Gls
Huddersfield T.	Manchester C. (Jnr)	07.78	78-84	199	7	56
Manchester C.	Tr	06.85	85	39	0	11
Derby Co.	Tr	08.86	86-87	6	9	1
Aston Villa	Tr	09.87	87-88	30	1	4
Scunthorpe U.	Tr	09.89	89-90	62	6	23
Stockport Co.	Tr	09.91	91	9	2	2

LILYGREEN, Christopher L.
Newport, 9 June, 1965 (F)

League Club	Source	Date Signed	Seasons Played	Apps	Subs	Gls
Newport Co.	Jnrs	08.83	83-84	18	13	4

LIM, Harvey C.
Halesworth, 30 August, 1967 (G)

League Club	Source	Date Signed	Seasons Played	Apps	Subs	Gls
Norwich C.	YT	07.85				
Gillingham	Ornskoldsvik (Swe)	11.89	89-91	82	0	0

LIMBER, Nicholas
Doncaster, 23 January, 1974 (LB)

League Club	Source	Date Signed	Seasons Played	Apps	Subs	Gls
Doncaster Rov.	YT	12.91	90-91	13	0	1
Manchester C.	Tr	01.92				

LIMPAR, Anders
Sweden, 24 August, 1965 Swedish Int (LW)

League Club	Source	Date Signed	Seasons Played	Apps	Subs	Gls
Arsenal	Cremonese (It)	07.90	90-91	55	8	16

LINACRE, John
Middlesbrough, 13 December, 1955 (M)

League Club	Source	Date Signed	Seasons Played	Apps	Subs	Gls
Hartlepool U.	Whitby T.	07.77	77-83	207	4	12

LINACRE, Philip
Middlesbrough, 17 May, 1962 (F)

League Club	Source	Date Signed	Seasons Played	Apps	Subs	Gls
Hartlepool U.	Coventry C. (App)	08.80	80-83	78	4	17
Darlington	Newcastle Blue Star	03.90	90	6	2	3

LINACRE, William
Chesterfield, 10 August, 1924 (F)

League Club	Source	Date Signed	Seasons Played	Apps	Subs	Gls
Chesterfield	Jnrs	02.44	46-47	22	-	3
Manchester C.	Tr	10.47	47-49	75	-	6
Middlesbrough	Tr	09.49	49-51	31	-	2
Hartlepool U.	Goole T.	08.53	53-55	89	-	10
Mansfield T.	Tr	10.55	55	13	-	0

LINAKER, John E.
Southport, 14 January, 1927 (OR)

League Club	Source	Date Signed	Seasons Played	Apps	Subs	Gls
Manchester C.	Everton (Am)	08.45				
Southport	Tr	11.46	46	15	-	1
Nottingham F.	Tr	09.47	48-49	15	-	2
York C.	Tr	06.50	50-51	59	-	16
Hull C.	Tr	10.51	51-52	26	-	3
York C.	Tr	05.53	53-55	39	-	4
Crewe Alex.	Scarborough	07.57	57	34	-	3

LINDLEY, Edwin
Epworth, 22 April, 1931 Died 1951 (IF)

League Club	Source	Date Signed	Seasons Played	Apps	Subs	Gls
Nottingham F.	Scunthorpe U.	10.49	49	1	-	0
Scunthorpe U.	Tr	08.51				

LINDLEY, W. Maurice
Keighley, 5 December, 1915 (CH)

League Club	Source	Date Signed	Seasons Played	Apps	Subs	Gls
Everton	Keighley T.	03.36	47-51	51	-	0

LINDORES, William R.H.
Newcastleton, 3 May, 1933 S Sch (FB)

League Club	Source	Date Signed	Seasons Played	Apps	Subs	Gls
Barrow	Hearts Liddleston	07.59	59	5	-	0

LINDSAY, Alec
Bury, 27 February, 1948 E Yth/E-4 (LB)

League Club	Source	Date Signed	Seasons Played	Apps	Subs	Gls
Bury	App	03.65	64-68	126	0	14
Liverpool	Tr	03.69	69-76	168	2	12
Stoke C.	Tr	08.77	77	20	0	3

LINDSAY, David
Dumbarton, 23 September, 1919 (CH)

League Club	Source	Date Signed	Seasons Played	Apps	Subs	Gls
Luton T.	St Mirren	05.48	48	7	-	0
Barnsley	Tr	11.48	48-51	78	-	3

Anders Limpar (Cremonese, Arsenal & Sweden)

League Club	Source	Date Signed	Seasons Played	Apps	Subs	Gls
LINDSAY, David						
Cambuslang, 29 June, 1926						(FB)
Sunderland	Blantyre Vic.	08.46	46	1	-	0
Southend U.	Tr	05.48	48-50	52	-	1
LINDSAY, David J.						
Romford, 17 May, 1966						(LB)
Crystal Palace	App	05.84	83-85	18	3	0
LINDSAY, Hugh M.						
Ickenham, 23 August, 1938 E Amat						(IF)
Southampton (Am)	Kingstonian	07.60	60	2	-	0
LINDSAY, Ian						
Canonble, 10 February, 1944						(G)
Workington	Hearts Liddleston	11.64	64-65	10	0	0
LINDSAY, James Y.						
Hamilton, 12 July, 1949						(M)
West Ham U.	Jnrs	08.66	68-70	36	3	2
Watford	Tr	08.71	71-73	64	1	12
Colchester U.	Tr	07.74	74	45	0	6
Hereford U.	Tr	08.75	75-76	79	0	6
Shrewsbury T.	Tr	08.77	77-80	80	6	0
LINDSAY, John M.						
Cambuslang, 11 December, 1921						(CF)
Sheffield Wed.	Morton	03.45	46	1	-	1
Bury	Tr	10.46	46	11	-	7
Carlisle U.	Tr	08.47	47-50	103	-	46
Southport	Tr	03.51	50-51	50	-	20
Carlisle U.	Wigan Ath.	01.55	54	13	-	2
LINDSAY, John S.						
Auchinleck, 8 August, 1924						(FB)
Everton	Glasgow Rangers	03.51	50-53	105	-	2
Bury	Tr	05.56	56	7	-	0
LINDSAY, Laurence						
Dumbarton, 7 October, 1921						(CH)
Crewe Alex.	Hibernian	01.48	47-48	40	-	0
LINDSAY, Malcolm						
Ashington, 26 September, 1940						(CF)
Cambridge U.	Kings Lynn	(N/L)	70	6	0	0
LINDSAY, Mark E.						
Lambeth, 6 March, 1955						(M)
Crystal Palace	App	03.73	73-74	27	3	0
LINDSEY, Barry						
Scunthorpe, 17 April, 1944						(WH)
Scunthorpe U.	App	05.61	61-70	209	6	14
LINDSEY, Keith						
Scunthorpe, 25 November, 1946						(RB)
Scunthorpe U.	App	12.64	65	16	0	0
Doncaster Rov.	Tr	07.66	66	16	2	0
Southend U.	Cambridge U.	01.69	68-71	88	3	4
Port Vale	Tr	12.71	71-72	24	0	0
Gillingham	Tr	12.72	72-74	73	0	5
LINEKER, Gary W.						
Leicester, 30 November, 1960 E'B'/E-80						(F)
Leicester C.	App	11.89	78-84	187	7	95
Everton	Tr	07.85	85	41	0	30
Tottenham H.	Barcelona (Sp)	07.89	89-91	105	0	67
LINES, Barry						
Bletchley, 16 May, 1942						(OL)
Northampton T.	Bletchley T.	09.60	60-69	259	7	49
LINEY, Patrick						
Paisley, 14 July, 1936						(G)
Bradford P.A.	St Mirren	06.66	66	11	0	0
Bradford C.	Tr	09.67	67-71	147	0	0
LINFORD, John R.						
Norwich, 6 February, 1957						(F)
Ipswich T.	Gorleston	08.81				
Colchester U.	L	01.83	82	7	0	0
Southend U.	L	03.83	82	6	0	3
Birmingham C.	L	11.84	84	1	1	0
LING, Martin						
West Ham, 15 July, 1966						(W)
Exeter C.	App	01.84	82-85	109	8	14
Swindon T.	Tr	07.86	86	2	0	0
Southend U.	Tr	10.86	86-90	126	12	30
Mansfield T.	L	01.91	90	3	0	0
Swindon T.	Tr	03.91	90-91	17	5	3

League Club	Source	Date Signed	Seasons Played	Apps	Subs	Gls
LINIGHAN, Andrew						
Hartlepool, 18 June, 1962 E'B'						(CD)
Hartlepool U.		09.80	80-83	110	0	4
Leeds U.	Tr	05.84	84-85	66	0	3
Oldham Ath.	Tr	01.86	85-87	87	0	6
Norwich C.	Tr	03.88	87-89	86	0	8
Arsenal	Tr	06.90	90-91	22	5	0

Andy Linighan (Hartlepool United, Leeds United, Oldham Athletic, Norwich City & Arsenal)

League Club	Source	Date Signed	Seasons Played	Apps	Subs	Gls
LINIGHAN, Brian						
Hartlepool, 17 March, 1936						(HB)
Lincoln C.		12.53				
Darlington	L	10.58	58	1	-	1
LINIGHAN, David						
Hartlepool, 9 January, 1965						(CD)
Hartlepool U.	Jnrs	03.82	81-85	84	7	5
Derby Co.	Tr	08.86				
Shrewsbury T.	Tr	12.86	86-87	65	0	1
Ipswich T.	Tr	06.88	88-91	162	1	8
LINK, Thomas H.						
Halifax, 15 December, 1918						(OR)
Bradford C.		05.48	47-48	6	-	0
LINNECOR, Albert R. (Bert)						
Birmingham, 30 November, 1933						(IF/WH)
Birmingham C.	Jnrs	05.52	55-56	17	-	0
Lincoln C.	Tr	04.57	56-63	264	-	52
LINNELL, John L.						
Northampton, 2 January, 1944						(WH)
Northampton T.	Jnrs	09.63				
Peterborough U.	Tr	07.67	67	24	2	1
LINNEY, David W.						
Birmingham, 5 September, 1961						(RB)
Birmingham C.	App	09.79	81	0	1	0
Oxford U.	Tr	08.82	82	26	0	0

LINSTREM, Kenneth R.
Salford, 12 October, 1928 (HB)

League Club	Source	Date Signed	Seasons Played	Apps	Subs	Gls
Crewe Alex.		06.50	50-51	13	-	1
Bournemouth	Tr	08.52				

LINTERN, Melvyn
Newcastle, 17 May, 1950 (CH)

League Club	Source	Date Signed	Seasons Played	Apps	Subs	Gls
Port Vale	Jnrs	03.68	66	0	1	0

LINTON, Desmond M.
Birmingham, 5 September, 1971 (CD)

League Club	Source	Date Signed	Seasons Played	Apps	Subs	Gls
Leicester C.	YT	01.90	89-91	6	5	0
Luton T.	Tr	10.91	91	2	1	0

LINTON, Ivor
West Bromwich, 20 November, 1959 (M)

League Club	Source	Date Signed	Seasons Played	Apps	Subs	Gls
Aston Villa	App	09.77	76-81	16	11	0
Peterborough U.	Tr	08.82	82-83	24	3	3
Birmingham C.	Tr	12.83	83	3	1	0

LINTON, James A.
Glasgow, 2 December, 1930 (G)

League Club	Source	Date Signed	Seasons Played	Apps	Subs	Gls
Notts Co.	Kirkintilloch Rob Roy	11.52	52-58	112	-	0
Watford	Tr	07.59	59-62	71	-	0

LINTON, Malcolm W.
Southend, 13 February, 1952 (CD)

League Club	Source	Date Signed	Seasons Played	Apps	Subs	Gls
Leyton Orient	Southend U. (Am)	08.72	72-74	14	5	0

LINTON, Thomas G. N.
Falkirk, 15 October, 1920

League Club	Source	Date Signed	Seasons Played	Apps	Subs	Gls
Southend U.		05.45	46-48	68	-	0

LINWOOD, Alexander B.
Glasgow, 13 March, 1920 SF Lge/S-1 (IF)

League Club	Source	Date Signed	Seasons Played	Apps	Subs	Gls
Middlesbrough	St Mirren	06.46	46	14	-	3

LIPTROTT, David A.
Stockport, 26 February, 1965 (F)

League Club	Source	Date Signed	Seasons Played	Apps	Subs	Gls
Stockport Co. (N/C)	Jnrs	09.82	82	0	1	0

LISHMAN, Douglas J.
Birmingham, 14 September, 1923 E'B'-1/EF Lge (IF)

League Club	Source	Date Signed	Seasons Played	Apps	Subs	Gls
Walsall	Paget R.	08.46	46-47	59	-	26
Arsenal	Tr	07.48	48-55	226	-	125
Nottingham F.	Tr	03.56	55-56	38	-	22

LISTER, Alexander O.
Glasgow, 20 January, 1924 (IF)

League Club	Source	Date Signed	Seasons Played	Apps	Subs	Gls
Rochdale	Alloa Ath.	05.52	52	2	-	0

LISTER, Eric
Willenhall, 13 August, 1933 (OL)

League Club	Source	Date Signed	Seasons Played	Apps	Subs	Gls
Notts Co.	Wolverhampton W. (Am)	09.51	54-56	8	-	0

LISTER, Herbert F.
Manchester, 4 October, 1939 (CF)

League Club	Source	Date Signed	Seasons Played	Apps	Subs	Gls
Manchester C.	Jnrs	11.57	58	2	-	0
Oldham Ath.	Tr	10.60	60-64	135	-	81
Rochdale	Tr	01.65	64-66	56	0	16
Stockport Co.	Tr	01.67	66	16	0	11

LISTER, Stephen H.
Doncaster, 18 November, 1961 (CD)

League Club	Source	Date Signed	Seasons Played	Apps	Subs	Gls
Doncaster Rov.	App	05.79	78-84	229	8	30
Scunthorpe U.	Tr	07.85	85-91	176	6	30
York C.	L	03.91	90	4	0	1

LITCHFIELD, Peter
Manchester, 27 July, 1956 (G)

League Club	Source	Date Signed	Seasons Played	Apps	Subs	Gls
Preston N.E.	Droylsden	01.79	80-84	107	0	0
Bradford C.	Tr	07.85	85-88	88	0	0
Oldham Ath.	L	10.88	88	3	0	0
Scunthorpe U.	Tr	07.89	89-90	25	0	0

LITHGO, Gordon
Hartlepool, 14 August, 1942 (OL)

League Club	Source	Date Signed	Seasons Played	Apps	Subs	Gls
Hartlepool U.	Jnrs	08.59	60-63	37	-	8

LITT, Stephen E.
Carlisle, 21 May, 1954 (CD)

League Club	Source	Date Signed	Seasons Played	Apps	Subs	Gls
Luton T.	Blackpool (App)	06.72	73-75	15	0	0
Northampton T.	Minnesota (USA)	09.77	77	19	1	0

LITTLE, Alan
Horden, 5 February, 1955 (M)

League Club	Source	Date Signed	Seasons Played	Apps	Subs	Gls
Aston Villa	App	01.73	74	2	1	0
Southend U.	Tr	12.74	74-76	102	1	12
Barnsley	Tr	08.77	77-79	91	0	14
Doncaster Rov.	Tr	12.79	79-82	84	1	11
Torquay U.	Tr	10.82	82-83	51	0	4
Halifax T.	Tr	11.83	83-84	68	0	6
Hartlepool U.	Tr	07.85	85	12	0	1

LITTLE, Barry B.
Greenwich, 25 August, 1964 E Yth (M)

League Club	Source	Date Signed	Seasons Played	Apps	Subs	Gls
Charlton Ath.	App	07.82	82	2	0	1

LITTLE, Brian
Horden, 25 November, 1953 E-1 (F)

League Club	Source	Date Signed	Seasons Played	Apps	Subs	Gls
Aston Villa	App	03.71	71-79	242	5	60

LITTLE, George
Newcastle, 30 June, 1915 (W)

League Club	Source	Date Signed	Seasons Played	Apps	Subs	Gls
Doncaster Rov.	Throckley Welfare	08.36	36-47	50	-	11
York C.	Tr	12.47	47	15	-	2

LITTLE, John A.
Gateshead, 17 May, 1912 (W)

League Club	Source	Date Signed	Seasons Played	Apps	Subs	Gls
Ipswich T.	Needham Market	11.37	38-49	150	-	18

LITTLE, Ronald
Carlisle, 24 January, 1934 (OR)

League Club	Source	Date Signed	Seasons Played	Apps	Subs	Gls
Carlisle U. (Am)	Sowerby Hearts	05.55	55	5	-	0

LITTLE, Roy
Manchester, 1 June, 1931 (FB)

League Club	Source	Date Signed	Seasons Played	Apps	Subs	Gls
Manchester C.	Greenwood Vic.	08.49	52-58	168	-	2
Brighton & H.A.	Tr	10.58	58-60	83	-	0
Crystal Palace	Tr	05.61	61-62	38	-	1

LITTLEJOHN, Adrian S.
Wolverhampton, 26 September, 1970 E Yth (W)

League Club	Source	Date Signed	Seasons Played	Apps	Subs	Gls
Walsall	West Bromwich A. (YT)	05.89	89-90	26	18	1
Sheffield U.	Tr	08.91	91	5	2	0

LITTLEJOHN, Roy D.
Bournemouth, 2 June, 1933 E Amat (CF)

League Club	Source	Date Signed	Seasons Played	Apps	Subs	Gls
Bournemouth (Am)	Jnrs	05.52	52-55	22	-	2

LITTLEJOHNS, Colin
Liverpool, 8 September, 1968 (M)

League Club	Source	Date Signed	Seasons Played	Apps	Subs	Gls
Cambridge U. (N/C)	YT	10.85	85-86	10	2	0

LITTLER, J. Eric
St Helens, 14 April, 1929 (CF)

League Club	Source	Date Signed	Seasons Played	Apps	Subs	Gls
Leicester C.	Stubshaw Cross	05.51	51-54	5	-	2
Lincoln C.	Tr	12.54	54	6	-	2
Wrexham	Tr	06.55	55	12	-	1
Crewe Alex.	Tr	12.55	55	10	-	2

LITTLER, Thomas
Stockport, 6 March, 1936 (F)

League Club	Source	Date Signed	Seasons Played	Apps	Subs	Gls
Stockport Co.		04.55	55	1	-	0

LIVERMORE, Douglas E.
Liverpool, 27 December, 1947 (M)

League Club	Source	Date Signed	Seasons Played	Apps	Subs	Gls
Liverpool	Jnrs	11.65	67-70	13	3	0
Norwich C.	Tr	11.70	70-74	113	1	4
Bournemouth	L	03.75	74	10	0	0
Cardiff C.	Tr	08.75	75-77	84	4	5
Chester C.	Tr	10.77	77-78	71	0	6

LIVERSIDGE, Ronald
Huddersfield, 12 September, 1934 (CF)

League Club	Source	Date Signed	Seasons Played	Apps	Subs	Gls
Bradford C.	Ossett T.	10.56	56-58	48	-	27

LIVESEY, Charles E.
West Ham, 6 February, 1938 (CF)

League Club	Source	Date Signed	Seasons Played	Apps	Subs	Gls
Southampton	Wolverhampton W. (Am)	03.56	58	25	-	14
Chelsea	Tr	05.59	59-60	39	-	17
Gillingham	Tr	08.61	61-62	47	-	17
Watford	Tr	10.62	62-63	64	-	26
Northampton T.	Tr	08.64	64-65	28	0	4
Brighton & H.A.	Tr	09.65	65-68	124	1	30

LIVESEY, John
Preston, 8 March, 1924 (IF)

League Club	Source	Date Signed	Seasons Played	Apps	Subs	Gls
Preston N.E.		04.44				
Bury	Tr	05.46	46	7	-	1
Doncaster Rov.	Tr	01.47	47	3	-	0
Rochdale	Tr	04.48	47-50	113	-	36
Southport	Tr	07.51	51	31	-	9

LIVETT, Simon R.
East Ham, 8 January, 1969 (M)

League Club	Source	Date Signed	Seasons Played	Apps	Subs	Gls
West Ham U.	App	01.87	90	1	0	0

LIVIE, Gordon
Billingham, 10 June, 1932 (D)

League Club	Source	Date Signed	Seasons Played	Apps	Subs	Gls
Leicester C.	Jnrs	12.49				
Mansfield T.	Tr	07.52	52-53	21	-	0

LIVINGSTONE, Archibald
Pencaitland, 15 November, 1915 Died 1961 (IF)

League Club	Source	Date Signed	Seasons Played	Apps	Subs	Gls
Newcastle U.	Ormiston Primrose	05.35	35-37	33	-	5
Bury	Tr	06.38	38	23	-	8
Everton	Tr	05.46	46	4	-	2
Southport	Tr	06.47	47	23	-	2

LIVINGSTONE, Joseph
Middlesbrough, 18 June, 1942 (CF)

League Club	Source	Date Signed	Seasons Played	Apps	Subs	Gls
Middlesbrough	Jnrs	01.60	60-62	20	-	7
Carlisle U.	Tr	11.62	62-65	79	1	41
Hartlepool U.	Tr	05.66	65-66	15	0	5

LIVINGSTONE, Stephen
Middlesbrough, 8 September, 1968 (F)

League Club	Source	Date Signed	Seasons Played	Apps	Subs	Gls
Coventry C.	YT	07.86	86-90	17	14	5
Blackburn Rov.	Tr	01.91	90-91	24	4	10

LIVINGSTONE, Wilfred
Barrow, 22 October, 1919 (CF)

League Club	Source	Date Signed	Seasons Played	Apps	Subs	Gls
Barrow	Holker C.O.B.	09.47	47-48	4	-	0

LIVINGSTONE, William
Coventry, 13 August, 1964 S Yth (F)

League Club	Source	Date Signed	Seasons Played	Apps	Subs	Gls
Wolverhampton W.	App	08.82	82-83	21	3	4
Derby Co.	Tr	07.84				

LIVINGSTONE, William R.
Greenock, 8 February, 1929 (CH)

League Club	Source	Date Signed	Seasons Played	Apps	Subs	Gls
Reading	Ardeer Rec.	04.49	49-54	49	-	2
Chelsea	Tr	06.55	56-57	20	-	0
Brentford	Tr	07.59	59	19	-	0

LIVSEY, Gordon W.
Keighley, 24 January, 1947 (G)

League Club	Source	Date Signed	Seasons Played	Apps	Subs	Gls
Wrexham	Kettering T.	01.67	67-70	79	0	0
Chester C.	Tr	08.71	71	44	0	0
Hartlepool U.	Kettering T.	12.77	77	6	0	0

LLEWELLYN, Andrew D.
Bristol, 26 February, 1966 E Yth (FB)

League Club	Source	Date Signed	Seasons Played	Apps	Subs	Gls
Bristol C.	App	02.84	82-91	269	12	3

LLEWELLYN, David J.
Cardiff, 9 August, 1949 Wu23-1 (W)

League Club	Source	Date Signed	Seasons Played	Apps	Subs	Gls
West Ham U.	Jnrs	08.66	69-71	2	4	0
Peterborough U.	Tr	08.73	73-74	11	2	3
Mansfield T.	L	08.74	74	6	2	0

LLEWELLYN, Herbert A.
Golborne, 5 February, 1939 E Yth (CF)

League Club	Source	Date Signed	Seasons Played	Apps	Subs	Gls
Everton	Jnrs	05.56	56-57	11	-	2
Crewe Alex.	Tr	07.58	58-60	96	-	51
Port Vale	Tr	11.60	60-62	88	-	42
Northampton T.	Tr	02.63	62	1	-	0
Walsall	Tr	02.64	62-64	17	-	6

LLOYD, Barry, D.
Hillingdon, 19 February, 1949 E Yth (M)

League Club	Source	Date Signed	Seasons Played	Apps	Subs	Gls
Chelsea	App	02.66	66-68	8	2	0
Fulham	Tr	12.68	68-75	249	8	29
Hereford U.	Tr	10.76	76	12	2	0
Brentford	Tr	06.77	77	26	5	4

LLOYD, Brian W.
St Asaph, 18 March, 1948 Wu23-2/W-3 (G)

League Club	Source	Date Signed	Seasons Played	Apps	Subs	Gls
Stockport Co.	Rhyl	03.67	67-68	32	0	0
Southend U.	Tr	09.69	69-70	46	0	0
Wrexham	Tr	08.71	71-77	266	0	0
Chester C.	Tr	09.77	77-79	94	0	0
Port Vale	L	02.81	80	16	0	0
Stockport Co.	Tr	08.81	81-82	91	0	1

LLOYD, Clifford
Ellesmere Port, 14 November, 1916 (LB)

League Club	Source	Date Signed	Seasons Played	Apps	Subs	Gls
Wrexham	Brymbo Steel Wks	07.37	37-38	13	-	2
Fulham		12.43	46	2	-	0
Bristol Rov.	Tr	05.50				

LLOYD, R. Clive
Merthyr Tydfil, 4 September, 1945 (IF)

League Club	Source	Date Signed	Seasons Played	Apps	Subs	Gls
Norwich C.	App	09.62				
Cardiff C.	Tr	08.64	64	2	-	0

LLOYD, David
Gateshead, 1 June, 1928 (CF)

League Club	Source	Date Signed	Seasons Played	Apps	Subs	Gls
Sheffield U.		09.49				
York C.	Tr	03.51	50	1	-	0

LLOYD, Frank
Barnsley, 16 January, 1928 (LH)

League Club	Source	Date Signed	Seasons Played	Apps	Subs	Gls
Bradford C.		07.51	51-53	24	-	0

LLOYD, Geoffrey R.
Wrexham, 18 August, 1942 (CF)

League Club	Source	Date Signed	Seasons Played	Apps	Subs	Gls
Wrexham		10.66	66	13	1	5
Bradford P.A.	Tr	07.67	67	32	0	10

LLOYD, Graham
Liverpool, 10 January, 1951 (G)

League Club	Source	Date Signed	Seasons Played	Apps	Subs	Gls
Liverpool	App	01.68				
Portsmouth	Motherwell	07.75	75-76	73	0	0

LLOYD, Harold
Flint, 12 March, 1920 (G)

League Club	Source	Date Signed	Seasons Played	Apps	Subs	Gls
Tranmere Rov.	Flint T.	10.45	45-56	189	-	0

LLOYD John D.
Hitchin, 10 December, 1944 (LB)

League Club	Source	Date Signed	Seasons Played	Apps	Subs	Gls
Swindon T.	App	01.62				
Oxford U.	Tr	10.64	65-68	68	4	0
Aldershot	Tr	02.69	68-69	11	2	0

LLOYD, John W.
Rossett, 15 February, 1948 (OR)

League Club	Source	Date Signed	Seasons Played	Apps	Subs	Gls
Wrexham (Am)	Jnrs	08.65	65-66	2	0	0

LLOYD, Joseph M.
Shotton, 30 September, 1910 (WH)

League Club	Source	Date Signed	Seasons Played	Apps	Subs	Gls
Everton	Connah's Quay	02.31				
Swansea C.		08.32	32-38	212	-	0
Wrexham	Tr	07.46	46	20	-	0

LLOYD, Kevin J.J.
Wolverhampton, 12 June, 1958 (F)

League Club	Source	Date Signed	Seasons Played	Apps	Subs	Gls
Cardiff C.	Darlaston	05.79	79	0	1	0
Gillingham	Tr	07.80	80	0	1	0

Cliff Lloyd (Wrexham, Fulham & Bristol Rovers)

LLOYD, Laurence V. (Larry)
Bristol, 6 October, 1948 E Yth/Eu23-8/E-4 (CD)

League Club	Source	Date Signed	Seasons Played	Apps	Subs	Gls
Bristol Rov.	Jnrs	07.67	68	43	0	1
Liverpool	Tr	04.69	69-73	150	0	4
Coventry C.	Tr	08.74	74-76	50	0	5
Nottingham F.	Tr	10.76	76-80	148	0	6
Wigan Ath.	Tr	03.81	80-82	52	0	2

LLOYD, Norman P.
Neath, 8 March, 1930 (WH)

League Club	Source	Date Signed	Seasons Played	Apps	Subs	Gls
Cardiff C.		03.48				
Torquay U.	Tr	08.49	52-56	29	-	1

LLOYD, Norman W.
Glasgow, 6 September, 1949 (M)

League Club	Source	Date Signed	Seasons Played	Apps	Subs	Gls
Preston N.E.	Jnrs	09.66	68-70	18	2	6
Stockport Co.	L	01.71	70	10	0	0
Southport	Tr	07.71	71-73	93	9	13
Stockport Co.	Tr	07.74	74	36	2	2

LLOYD, Peter J.
Pattingham, 26 April, 1933 (OL)

League Club	Source	Date Signed	Seasons Played	Apps	Subs	Gls
Walsall	Pattingham	03.51	53	5	-	0

LLOYD, Philip R.
Hemsworth 26 December, 1964 (CD)

League Club	Source	Date Signed	Seasons Played	Apps	Subs	Gls
Middlesbrough	App	12.82				
Barnsley (N/C)	Tr	09.83				
Darlington	Tr	03.84	83-86	127	0	3
Torquay U.	Tr	08.87	87-91	169	1	7

LLOYD, Raymond
Seaham, 6 December, 1930

League Club	Source	Date Signed	Seasons Played	Apps	Subs	Gls
Lincoln C.	Seaham Colly	01.50	50	1	-	0

LLOYD, W. Stanley
West Auckland, 1 October, 1924 E Sch (W)

League Club	Source	Date Signed	Seasons Played	Apps	Subs	Gls
Sunderland	Jnrs	12.41	46-47	24	-	5
Grimsby T.	Tr	08.48	48-52	148	-	23
Scunthorpe U.	Worksop T.	07.54	54	1	-	0

LLOYD, William F.
Poplar, 10 July, 1934 (G)

League Club	Source	Date Signed	Seasons Played	Apps	Subs	Gls
Millwall	Bromley	08.56	56-57	74	-	0

LLOYD, William L.
Rhondda, 22 May, 1915 (D)

League Club	Source	Date Signed	Seasons Played	Apps	Subs	Gls
Swindon T.	Milford Haven	08.39	46-50	107	-	2

LOADWICK, Derek
Middlesbrough, 4 October, 1956 (M)

League Club	Source	Date Signed	Seasons Played	Apps	Subs	Gls
Leeds U.	App	10.73				
Stockport Co.	Tr	07.76	76-78	84	0	0
Hartlepool U.	Tr	10.78	78-79	49	2	1

LOASBY, Alan A.
Wellingborough, 19 March, 1937 (IF)

League Club	Source	Date Signed	Seasons Played	Apps	Subs	Gls
Luton T.	Jnrs	04.54				
Northampton T.	Tr	07.58	58	2	-	0

LOBBETT, John
Exeter, 8 January, 1938 (G)

League Club	Source	Date Signed	Seasons Played	Apps	Subs	Gls
Exeter C.	Barnstaple	03.56	58-60	42	-	0

LOCHERTY, Joseph
Dundee, 5 September, 1925 (WH)

League Club	Source	Date Signed	Seasons Played	Apps	Subs	Gls
Sheffield Wed.	Dundee	09.47	48-49	10	-	0
Colchester U.	Tr	07.50	50	10	-	1

LOCHHEAD, Andrew L.
Milngavie, 9 March, 1941 Su23-1 (CF)

League Club	Source	Date Signed	Seasons Played	Apps	Subs	Gls
Burnley	Renfrew Jnrs	12.58	60-68	225	1	101
Leicester C.	Tr	10.68	68-69	40	4	12
Aston Villa	Tr	02.70	69-72	127	4	34
Oldham Ath.	Tr	08.73	73-74	44	1	10

LOCK, Frank W.
Whitechapel, 12 March, 1922 Died 1985 (LB)

League Club	Source	Date Signed	Seasons Played	Apps	Subs	Gls
Charlton Ath.	Finchley	12.45	46-53	222	-	8
Liverpool	Tr	12.53	53-54	41	-	0
Watford	Tr	06.55	55-56	42	-	1

LOCK, Kevin J.
Plaistow, 27 December, 1953 E Yth/Eu23-4 (D)

League Club	Source	Date Signed	Seasons Played	Apps	Subs	Gls
West Ham U.	App	12.71	71-77	122	10	2
Fulham	Tr	05.78	78-84	210	1	27
Southend U.	Tr	08.85	85	10	0	0

LOCKE, Adam S.
Croydon, 20 August, 1970 (W)

League Club	Source	Date Signed	Seasons Played	Apps	Subs	Gls
Crystal Palace	YT	06.88				
Southend U.	Tr	08.90	90-91	23	15	3

LOCKE, Gary R.
Kingsbury, 12 July, 1954 E Yth (RB)

League Club	Source	Date Signed	Seasons Played	Apps	Subs	Gls
Chelsea	App	07.71	72-82	270	2	3
Crystal Palace	Tr	01.83	82-85	84	0	1

LOCKE, Leslie C.
Perth, 24 January, 1934 S Amat (IF)

League Club	Source	Date Signed	Seasons Played	Apps	Subs	Gls
Queens Park R.	Bromley	05.58	56-59	77	-	22

LOCKER, Stephen
Ashington, 5 November, 1970

League Club	Source	Date Signed	Seasons Played	Apps	Subs	Gls
Hartlepool U.	Nottingham F. (YT)	09.88	88	0	1	0

LOCKETT, Philip B.
Stockport, 6 September, 1972 (M)

League Club	Source	Date Signed	Seasons Played	Apps	Subs	Gls
Rochdale	YT	07.91	89-90	1	2	0

LOCKHART, Crichton (Jock)
Perth, 6 March, 1930 (F)

League Club	Source	Date Signed	Seasons Played	Apps	Subs	Gls
Southend U.	Chertsey	08.50	50-56	45	-	11
Rochdale	Tr	06.57	57	40	-	11

LOCKHART, Keith S.
Wallsend, 19 July 1964 (W)

League Club	Source	Date Signed	Seasons Played	Apps	Subs	Gls
Cambridge U.	App	07.82	81-85	55	3	8
Wolverhampton W.	Tr	03.86	85-86	24	1	4
Hartlepool U. (N/C)	Tr	12.86	86	2	0	0

LOCKHART, Norman H.
Belfast, 4 March, 1924 NI-8 (OL)

League Club	Source	Date Signed	Seasons Played	Apps	Subs	Gls
Swansea C.	Linfield	10.46	46-47	47	-	13
Coventry C.	Tr	10.47	47-52	182	-	41
Aston Villa	Tr	09.52	52-55	74	-	10
Bury	Tr	11.56	56-57	41	-	6

LOCKIE, Alexander J.
South Shields, 11 April, 1915 (CH)

League Club	Source	Date Signed	Seasons Played	Apps	Subs	Gls
Sunderland	South Shields	09.35	36-38	40	-	1
Notts Co.	Tr	09.46	46	23	-	0

LOCKIER, Maurice R.
Bristol, 27 November, 1924 (OL)

League Club	Source	Date Signed	Seasons Played	Apps	Subs	Gls
Bristol Rov.		07.47	49	2	-	0

LOCKWOOD, Edward
Barnburgh, 4 August, 1925 (FB)

League Club	Source	Date Signed	Seasons Played	Apps	Subs	Gls
Scunthorpe U.	Denaby U.	06.51	51-53	11	-	0

LOCKWOOD, Roy
Barnsley, 20 June, 1933 E Yth (FB)

League Club	Source	Date Signed	Seasons Played	Apps	Subs	Gls
Sheffield Wed.	Jnrs	04.51				
Norwich C.	Tr	09.55	55-57	36	-	0

LODGE, Frank
Oldham, 28 November, 1919 Died 1973 (CF)

League Club	Source	Date Signed	Seasons Played	Apps	Subs	Gls
Stockport Co. (Am)	Ward Street O.B.	03.47	46	1	-	0

LODGE, George
Wallsend, 27 January, 1943 (OL)

League Club	Source	Date Signed	Seasons Played	Apps	Subs	Gls
Workington		12.61				
Newcastle U.	Tr	07.62				
Barrow	Tr	07.63	63	6	-	0

LODGE, T. Joseph
Huddersfield, 16 April, 1921 (LH)

League Club	Source	Date Signed	Seasons Played	Apps	Subs	Gls
Huddersfield T.	Jnrs	08.39	46-47	2	-	0

LODGE, Paul
Liverpool, 13 February, 1961 E Sch (M)

League Club	Source	Date Signed	Seasons Played	Apps	Subs	Gls
Everton	App	02.79	80-81	20	4	0
Wigan Ath.	L	08.82	82	5	0	1
Rotherham U.	L	01.83	82	4	0	0
Preston N.E.	Tr	02.83	82-83	36	2	0
Bolton W.	Tr	07.84	84	4	0	0
Port Vale	L	11.84	84	3	0	0
Stockport Co.	Tr	03.85	84-85	10	3	2

LODGE, Robert W.
Retford, 1 July, 1941 (OR)

League Club	Source	Date Signed	Seasons Played	Apps	Subs	Gls
Sheffield Wed.		05.59	60	3	-	2
Doncaster Rov.	Tr	05.61	61	23	-	4

League Club	Source	Date Signed	Seasons Played	Apps	Subs	Gls
LOFTHOUSE, Nathaniel (Nat)						
Bolton, 27 August, 1925 E'B'-1/EF Lge/E-33						(CF)
Bolton W.	Jnrs	08.42	46-60	452	-	255
LOFTUS, Robert						
Liverpool, 15 December, 1931						(IF)
Bradford P.A.	Llanelli	12.55	55	3	-	0
LOFTY, James K.						
Farnham, 5 December, 1945						(W)
Reading	Jnrs	05.63	63	2	-	0
Birmingham C.	Tr	07.64				
LOGAN, David						
Middlesbrough, 5 December, 1963						(LB)
Mansfield T.	Whitby T.	06.84	84-86	67	0	1
Northampton T.	Tr	02.87	86-87	39	2	1
Halifax T.	Tr	08.88	88	3	0	0
Stockport Co.	Tr	10.88	88-89	60	0	4
Scarborough	Tr	08.90	90-91	54	1	1
LOGAN, Douglas						
Aberdeen, 30 August, 1933 Died 1984						(WH)
Southampton		01.54	55-57	21	-	0
LOGAN, Gordon T.						
Edinburgh, 3 October, 1949						(FB)
Port Vale		03.67	66-69	34	2	1
LOGAN, John W.						
Horden, 16 August, 1912						(WH)
Charlton Ath.		07.34				
Darlington	Tr	05.35	35-36	65	-	5
Barnsley	Tr	03.37	36-46	99	-	5
Sheffield Wed.	Tr	01.47	46	4	-	0
LOGGIE, David M.						
Newbiggin, 31 May, 1957						(F)
Burnley	App	06.74	75-77	6	1	0
York C.	Tr	06.78	78-79	47	3	11
LOGIE, James T.						
Edinburgh, 23 November, 1919 Died 1984 S-1						(IF)
Arsenal	Lochore Welfare	06.39	46-54	296	-	68
LOGUE, Samuel W.						
Glasgow, 9 April, 1934						(IF)
Accrington St.	Clyde	06.60	60	2	-	0
LOHMAN, Jan H. P.						
Netherlands, 18 February, 1959 Netherlands u21 Int						(W)
Watford	Lokeren (Bel)	10.81	81-85	51	12	6
LOMAS, Albert						
Tyldesley, 14 October, 1924						(G)
Leeds U.	Bolton W. (Am)	09.48	48	1	-	0
Rochdale	Mossley	05.50	50	9	-	0
Chesterfield	Tr	07.51	51	29	-	0
LOMAS, Clive I.						
Ealing, 18 January, 1947						(WH)
Watford	App	01.65	65	6	1	0
LOMAS, Peter						
Manchester, 9 May, 1933						(FB)
Southport		04.52	51-56	18	-	0
LOMAX, Geoffrey W.						
Droylsden, 6 July, 1964						(D)
Manchester C.	Jnrs	07.81	82-84	23	2	1
Wolverhampton W.	L	10.85	85	5	0	0
Carlisle U.	Tr	12.85	85-86	37	0	0
Rochdale	Tr	07.87	87-88	70	1	0
LONG, Christopher						
Hatfield, 7 February, 1948						(OL)
Luton T.	Hatfield T.	02.66	65	1	0	0
LONG, John W.						
Southampton, 8 May, 1921						(FB)
Exeter C.	Chester C. (Am)	04.46	46	1	-	0
LONG, Nigel S.						
Doncaster, 31 March, 1955						(WH)
Doncaster Rov. (N/C)		05.74	74	1	0	0

League Club	Source	Date Signed	Seasons Played	Apps	Subs	Gls
LONG, Raymond						
Stickney, 4 October, 1936						(CH)
Lincoln C.	Louth U.	12.58	59	1	-	0
LONG, Terence A.						
Beaconsfield, 17 November, 1934						(D)
Crystal Palace	Wycombe W.	05.55	55-68	432	10	15
LONG, Trevor G.						
Smethwick, 1 July, 1931						(W)
Wolverhampton W.	Mitchell & Butlers	12.50				
Gillingham	Tr	07.52	52-54	67	-	15
Reading	Tr	07.55	55	12	-	5
LONG, Wilfred R.						
Wallasey, 28 December, 1922						(OL)
New Brighton (Am)	Everton (Am)	07.46	46	2	-	0
LONGBOTTOM, Arthur						
Leeds, 30 January, 1933						(IF)
Queens Park R.	Methley U.	03.54	54-60	201	-	62
Port Vale	Tr	05.61	61-62	62	-	15
Millwall	Tr	01.63	62	10	-	1
Oxford U.	Tr	08.63	63-64	34	-	14
Colchester U.	Tr	10.64	64	33	-	12
LONGDEN, Colin						
Rotherham, 21 July, 1933 E Sch						(OR)
Rotherham U.	Jnrs	08.50	52	3	-	0
York C.		08.55	57	2	-	0
LONGDEN, D. Paul						
Wakefield, 28 September, 1962						(LB)
Barnsley	App	09.80	81-82	5	0	0
Scunthorpe U.	Tr	08.83	83-91	344	4	0
LONGDON, Charles W.						
Mansfield, 6 May, 1917						(WH)
Brighton & H.A.		05.39				
Bournemouth	Tr	05.46	46	9	-	1
Rochdale	Tr	07.47	47	2	-	0
LONGHORN, Dennis						
Southampton, 12 September, 1950						(M)
Bournemouth	App	08.68	67-71	23	7	1
Mansfield T.	Tr	12.71	71-73	93	3	5
Sunderland	Tr	02.74	73-76	35	5	3
Sheffield U.	Tr	10.76	76-77	34	2	1
Aldershot	Tr	02.78	77-79	46	7	3
Colchester U.	Tr	05.80	80-82	62	9	0
LONGHURST, David J.						
Northampton, 15 January, 1965 Died 1990						(F)
Nottingham F.	App	01.83				
Halifax T.	Tr	07.85	85-86	85	0	24
Northampton T.	Tr	06.87	87-88	34	3	7
Peterborough U.	Tr	10.88	88-89	51	7	7
York C.	Tr	01.90	89-90	6	0	2
LONGLAND, John						
Southampton, 24 September, 1932						(HB)
Brighton & H.A.		04.54	54	3	-	0
LONGLEY, Nicholas						
Mexborough, 21 May, 1961						(G)
Crewe Alex.		05.81	81-85	23	0	0
LONGLEY, Scott E.						
Wakefield, 16 July, 1973						(M)
Halifax T. (YT)	YT	05.91	91	1	0	0
LONGRIDGE, George						
Glasgow, 23 August, 1931						(G)
Leyton Orient	Dennistoun	07.50				
Darlington	Tr	09.51	51	2	-	0
LONSDALE, J. Stanley						
Washington, 13 April, 1931						(WH)
Huddersfield T.	Seaham Jnrs	12.48				
Halifax T.	Tr	03.55	54-59	202	-	21
Hartlepool U.	Tr	11.60	60	9	-	0
LORAM, Mark J.						
Paignton, 13 August, 1967						(M)
Torquay U.	Brixham Villa	01.85	84-85	50	2	8
Queens Park R.	Tr	05.86				
Torquay U.	Tr	03.87	86-91	188	21	41
Stockport Co.	L	03.92	91	1	3	0

League Club	Source	Date Signed	Seasons Played	Career Record Apps	Subs	Gls

LORD, Albert E.
Farnworth, 10 September, 1944 (G)

Bolton W.	Jnrs	01.63				
Southport	Tr	03.66	65	16	0	0

LORD, Barry
Goole, 17 November, 1937 (G)

Hull C.	Goole Buchanan	04.56	58-60	5	-	0

LORD, Frank
Chadderton, 13 March, 1936 (CF)

Rochdale	Jnrs	10.53	53-60	122	-	54
Crewe Alex.	Tr	07.61	61-63	108	-	68
Plymouth Arg.	Tr	11.63	63-65	69	1	23
Stockport Co.	Tr	02.66	65-66	27	0	18
Blackburn Rov.	Tr	12.66	66	10	0	1
Chesterfield	Tr	06.67	67	12	0	6
Plymouth Arg.	Tr	10.67	68	6	0	2

LORD, W. Graham
Rawtenstall, 9 July, 1936 (FB)

Accrington St.	Rossendale U.	07.57	58-60	67	-	0

LORD, Malcolm
Driffield, 25 October, 1946 (M)

Hull C.	Jnrs	08.65	66-78	271	27	24

LORD, Walter
Grimsby, 1 November, 1933 (IF)

Grimsby T.	Jnrs	08.51	52-53	7	-	1
Lincoln C.	Tr	05.56	56	1	-	0

LORENSON, Roy V.
Liverpool, 8 April, 1932 (CH)

Halifax T.	St Elizabeths	02.52	51-60	216	-	7
Tranmere Rov.	Tr	10.60	60-61	14	-	0

LORENZO, Nestor G.
Argentina, 28 February, 1966 Argentina Int (CD)

Swindon T	F.C. Bari (It)	10.90	90-91	20	4	2

LORIMER, Peter P.
Dundee, 14 December, 1946 S Sch/S Yth/Su23-2/S-21 (F)

Leeds U.	Jnrs	12.63	62-78	430	20	151
York C.	Toronto (Can)	09.79	79	29	0	8
Leeds U.	Vancouver (Can)	03.84	83-85	74	2	17

LORMOR, Anthony
Ashington, 29 October, 1970 (F)

Newcastle U.	YT	02.88	87-88	6	2	3
Lincoln C.	Tr	01.90	89-91	85	5	29

LORNIE, John
Aberdeen, 2 March, 1939 S Sch (IF)

Leicester C.	Banks o'Dee	03.58	58-60	8	-	3
Luton T.	Tr	06.61	61-62	19	-	6
Carlisle U.	Tr	06.63	63	4	-	0
Tranmere Rov.	Tr	06.64	64-65	33	2	7

LOSKA, Anthony S. P.
Chesterton, 11 February, 1950 (LB)

Shrewsbury T.	App	03.68	68-70	12	0	0
Port Vale	Tr	07.71	71-73	74	6	5
Chester C.	Tr	12.73	73-76	103	7	5
Halifax T.	Tr	10.76	76-78	101	1	0

LOUGH, John D.
Gateshead, 31 October, 1922

Gateshead (Am)		09.46	46	1	-	0

LOUGHLAN, Anthony J.
Croydon, 19 January, 1970 (W)

Nottingham F.	Leicester U.	08.89	90	2	0	1

LOUGHLAN, John
Coatbridge, 12 June, 1943 (FB)

Leicester C.		08.61				
Crystal Palace	Morton	09.68	68-71	58	2	0
Wrexham	L	03.72	71	5	0	0

LOUGHNANE, J. Brian
Manchester, 16 June, 1930 (F)

Leeds U.		08.52				
Shrewsbury T.	Tr	07.53	53-55	42	-	7
Bournemouth	Tr	07.56	56-58	43	-	6

League Club	Source	Date Signed	Seasons Played	Career Record Apps	Subs	Gls

LOUGHNANE, Peter B.
Bournemouth, 18 March, 1958 (F)

Manchester U.	App	03.75				
Shrewsbury T.	Tr	02.77	76-78	24	7	4

LOUGHRAN, Joseph L.
Consett, 12 August, 1915 (FB)

Birmingham C.	Dudley Colly	08.33	35-36	31	-	2
Luton T.	Tr	05.37	37-38	25	-	0
Burnley	TR	07.39	46-49	65	-	0
Southend U.	Tr	09.49	49-52	147	-	1

LOUGHTON, Michael G.
Colchester, 8 December, 1942 (CH)

Colchester U.	Jnrs	08.61	64-67	121	1	6

LOUKES, Gordon
Sheffield, 15 June, 1928

Sheffield U.		04.49	50	1	-	0
Southend U.	Tr	07.51	51	2	-	0

LOVATT, John (Jack)
Burton, 23 August, 1941 (CF)

West Bromwich A.	Jnrs	12.58	60-62	18	-	5

LOVATT, John
Middlesbrough, 21 January, 1962 (FB)

Derby Co.	App	01.80	81	2	2	0

LOVE, Alistair J.
Edinburgh, 9 May, 1955 (M)

West Bromwich A.	Melbourne Th.	03.73				
Southend U.	Tr	05.74	74	6	5	0
Newport Co.	Tr	07.75	75	41	1	2

LOVE, Ian J.
Cardiff, 1 March, 1958 (F)

Swansea C.	Barry T.	08.86	86-88	33	8	9
Torquay U.	Tr	03.89	88	8	1	0
Cardiff C. (N/C)	Tr	09.89	89	1	1	0

LOVE, John
Eynsham, 11 March, 1937 (OL)

Oxford U.	Wolverhampton W. (Am)	03.55	62-63	25	-	5

LOVE, John E.
Hillingdon, 22 April, 1951 (CD)

Crystal Palace	Staines T.	01.75	74	1	0	0

LOVE, John T.
Edinburgh, 18 March, 1924 (IF)

Nottingham F.	Albion Rov.	02.49	48-51	59	-	21
Walsall	Llanelli	03.55	54-55	39	-	11

LOVELL, Alan J.
Swansea, 17 May, 1940 (F)

Swansea C.	Jnrs	06.57				
Stockport Co.	Tr	07.60	60	1	-	0

LOVELL, Frederick W.
Crewe, 18 June, 1929 (IF)

Notts Co. (Am)	Loughborough Col.	04.53	52-53	7	-	2

LOVELL, Mark A.
Kensington, 20 January, 1961 (M)

Fulham	App	08.78	77-78	4	2	0

LOVELL, Michael G.
Doncaster, 28 October, 1946 (FB)

Doncaster Rov.	App	10.64	65	2	0	0

LOVELL, Stephen J.
Swansea, 16 July, 1960 W Sch/W-6 (F)

Crystal Palace	App	08.77	80-82	68	6	3
Stockport Co.	L	10.79	79	12	0	0
Millwall	Tr	03.83	82-85	143	3	43
Swansea C.	L	02.87	86	2	0	1
Gillingham	Tr	02.87	86-91	211	9	91

LOVELL, Stuart A.
Sydney (Aus), 9 January, 1972 (W)

Reading	YT	07.90	90-91	38	16	6

LOVELL, Trevor
Halifax, 19 January, 1940 (W)

Halifax T. (Am)	Jnrs	08.60	60-62	9	-	0

LOVEMAN, Robert K.
Greenock, 30 September, 1921 (G)

League Club	Source	Date Signed	Seasons Played	Apps	Subs	Gls
Newport Co.	Ballieston Jnrs	03.48	47-48	20	-	0

LOVERIDGE, James C.
Swansea, 19 October, 1962 W Sch/Wu21-3 (M)

League Club	Source	Date Signed	Seasons Played	Apps	Subs	Gls
Swansea C.	App	11.79	79-84	40	7	4
Charlton Ath.	Tr	06.85	85	5	1	0

LOVERIDGE, John
Wolverhampton, 28 February, 1959 (M)

League Club	Source	Date Signed	Seasons Played	Apps	Subs	Gls
West Bromwich A.	App	03.77				
Walsall	Tr	08.81	81	23	3	2

LOVERING, John
Nuneaton, 10 December, 1922 (LH)

League Club	Source	Date Signed	Seasons Played	Apps	Subs	Gls
Coventry C.	Holbrooks O.B.	06.46	46-47	6	-	0

LOVESEY, William S
Marylebone, 8 December, 1922 (WH)

League Club	Source	Date Signed	Seasons Played	Apps	Subs	Gls
Swindon T.	Wolverhampton W. (Am)	05.45	46	4	-	0

LOVETT, Eric
Radcliffe, 20 August, 1925 (CH)

League Club	Source	Date Signed	Seasons Played	Apps	Subs	Gls
Accrington St.		11.49	49-50	41	-	1

LOVETT, Graham J.
Birmingham, 5 August, 1947 (M)

League Club	Source	Date Signed	Seasons Played	Apps	Subs	Gls
West Bromwich A.	App	11.64	64-70	106	8	8
Southampton	L	11.71	71	3	0	0

LOVETT, John E.
Portsmouth, 31 October, 1940 (OR)

League Club	Source	Date Signed	Seasons Played	Apps	Subs	Gls
Portsmouth		09.58				
Millwall	Tr	03.60	59	6	-	2

LOVETT, Percy R.
Bayston, 1 August, 1921 (G)

League Club	Source	Date Signed	Seasons Played	Apps	Subs	Gls
Everton	Kenwood Jnrs	08.38				
Wrexham	Tr	02.47	46	13	-	0

LOVIE, James T. H.
Peterhead, 19 September, 1932 (WH)

League Club	Source	Date Signed	Seasons Played	Apps	Subs	Gls
Bury	Peterhead	01.57	57-59	51	-	10
Bournemouth	Tr	07.60	60	9	-	0
Chesterfield	Tr	07.61	61-63	94	-	7

LOW, Gordon A.
Aberdeen, 11 July, 1940 (WH)

League Club	Source	Date Signed	Seasons Played	Apps	Subs	Gls
Huddersfield T.	Jnrs	07.57	57-60	67	-	6
Bristol C.	Tr	03.61	60-67	203	2	12
Stockport Co.	Tr	07.68	68-69	63	1	8
Crewe Alex.	Tr	08.70	70	5	0	0

LOW, Norman H.
Aberdeen, 23 March, 1941 (CH)

League Club	Source	Date Signed	Seasons Played	Apps	Subs	Gls
Liverpool	Rosehill	10.33	34-36	13	-	0
Newport Co.	Tr	11.36	36-46	112	-	0
Norwich C.	Tr	10.46	46-49	150	-	0

LOW, Roy A.
Watford, 8 July, 1944 E Sch (IF)

League Club	Source	Date Signed	Seasons Played	Apps	Subs	Gls
Tottenham H.	Jnrs	07.61	64-66	6	2	1
Watford	Tr	02.67	66-68	25	1	4

LOWDEN, George
Isleworth, 2 March, 1933 (FB)

League Club	Source	Date Signed	Seasons Played	Apps	Subs	Gls
Brentford	Jnrs	05.51	53-56	29	-	0

LOWDER, Thomas W.
Worksop, 17 October, 1924 (OL)

League Club	Source	Date Signed	Seasons Played	Apps	Subs	Gls
Rotherham U.	Crystal Palace (Am)	08.47	48	8	-	5
Southampton	Boston U.	10.49	49-52	39	-	2
Southend U.	Tr	05.53	53	21	-	3

LOWE, David A.
Liverpool, 30 August, 1965 E Yth/Eu21-2 (RW)

League Club	Source	Date Signed	Seasons Played	Apps	Subs	Gls
Wigan Ath.	App	06.83	82-86	179	9	40
Ipswich T.	Tr	06.87	87-91	121	13	37
Port Vale	L	03.92	91	8	1	2

LOWE, Edward
Halesowen, 11 July, 1925 E-3 (WH)

League Club	Source	Date Signed	Seasons Played	Apps	Subs	Gls
Aston Villa	Kynoch Wks	05.45	46-49	104	-	3
Fulham	Tr	05.50	50-62	473	-	8
Notts Co.	Tr	09.63	63-64	9	-	0

LOWE, Garry
Prescot, 21 February, 1967 (FB)

League Club	Source	Date Signed	Seasons Played	Apps	Subs	Gls
Bury	YT	06.86	85	3	1	0

LOWE, Gary W.
Manchester, 25 September, 1959 (M)

League Club	Source	Date Signed	Seasons Played	Apps	Subs	Gls
Crystal Palace	App	10.76				
Manchester C.	Tr	12.79				
Hereford U.	Tr	06.80	80	9	0	0

LOWE, Kenneth
Sedgefield, 6 November, 1961 (M)

League Club	Source	Date Signed	Seasons Played	Apps	Subs	Gls
Hartlepool U.	App	11.78	81-83	50	4	3
Scarborough	Barrow	01.88	87	4	0	0
Barnet	Barrow	03.91	91	26	10	3

LOWE, Matthew I.
Birmingham, 25 February, 1974 (G)

League Club	Source	Date Signed	Seasons Played	Apps	Subs	Gls
Torquay U.	YT	07.92	91	7	0	0

LOWE, Nicholas P.
Oxford, 28 October, 1952 (CD)

League Club	Source	Date Signed	Seasons Played	Apps	Subs	Gls
Oxford U.	App	07.70	72-76	71	0	3
Halifax T.	L	08.74	74	9	0	0

LOWE, Reginald
Halesowen, 15 December, 1926 (LB)

League Club	Source	Date Signed	Seasons Played	Apps	Subs	Gls
Aston Villa	Finchley	08.44				
Fulham	Tr	05.50	50-52	66	-	0

LOWE, Simon J.
Westminster, 26 December, 1962 (F)

League Club	Source	Date Signed	Seasons Played	Apps	Subs	Gls
Barnsley	Ossett T.	12.83	83	2	0	0
Halifax T.	Tr	07.84	84-85	74	3	19
Hartlepool U.	Tr	08.86	86	12	2	1
Colchester U.	Tr	12.86	86-87	32	4	8
Scarborough	Tr	11.87	87	14	2	3

LOWE, Terence J.
Cheadle, 27 May, 1943 (FB)

League Club	Source	Date Signed	Seasons Played	Apps	Subs	Gls
Port Vale	Stoke C. (Am)	06.60	61-65	55	0	0

LOWELL, Eric J.
Cheadle, 8 March, 1935 (IF)

League Club	Source	Date Signed	Seasons Played	Apps	Subs	Gls
Derby Co.	Jnrs	03.52	53	1	-	1
Stoke C.	Tr	05.55	55	7	-	3

LOWERY, Anthony W.
Wallsend, 6 July, 1961 (M)

League Club	Source	Date Signed	Seasons Played	Apps	Subs	Gls
West Bromwich A.	Ashington	03.81	81	1	0	0
Walsall	L	02.82	81	4	2	1
Mansfield T.	Tr	04.83	82-90	249	3	19
Walsall	L	10.90	90	6	0	0
Carlisle U.		10.91	91	6	1	0

LOWERY, Harold
Whitehaven, 26 February, 1918 (WH)

League Club	Source	Date Signed	Seasons Played	Apps	Subs	Gls
West Bromwich A.	Moor Celtic	05.35	37	17	-	0
Northampton T.	Tr	11.45	46-48	76	-	2

LOWERY, Jeremiah
Newcastle, 19 October, 1924 (G)

League Club	Source	Date Signed	Seasons Played	Apps	Subs	Gls
Newcastle U.	C.A. Parsons	06.47	49-51	6	-	0
Lincoln C.	Tr	03.52	52-53	51	-	0
Barrow	Peterborough U.	06.56	56-57	86	-	0
Crewe Alex.	Tr	07.58	58	4	-	0

LOWERY, Stewart
Thornaby, 21 February, 1951 (IF)

League Club	Source	Date Signed	Seasons Played	Apps	Subs	Gls
Watford	Bishop Auckland	01.70				
Walsall	L	11.70	70	0	1	0

LOWES, Arnold R.
Sunderland, 27 February, 1919 (WH)

League Club	Source	Date Signed	Seasons Played	Apps	Subs	Gls
Sheffield Wed.	Washington Chemicals	10.37	38-47	42	-	8
Doncaster Rov.	Tr	02.48	47-50	72	-	3

LOWES, Barry T.
Barrow, 16 March, 1939 (OR)

League Club	Source	Date Signed	Seasons Played	Apps	Subs	Gls
Barrow	Holker C.O.B.	01.60	59-61	55	-	15
Blackpool	Tr	11.61				
Workington	Tr	08.62	62-65	121	0	34
Bury	Tr	02.66	65-66	33	0	6
Coventry C.	Tr	03.67	66	3	0	0
Swindon T.	Tr	08.67	67	2	0	0

LOWEY, John A.
Manchester, 7 March, 1958 (M)

League Club	Source	Date Signed	Seasons Played	Apps	Subs	Gls
Manchester U.	App	03.75				
Blackburn Rov.	Chicago (USA)	07.77				
Port Vale	Tr	12.77				
Sheffield Wed.	California (USA)	10.78	78-79	35	7	4
Blackburn Rov.	Tr	11.80	80-85	136	5	14
Wigan Ath.	Tr	07.86	86	1	2	0
Chesterfield	L	11.86	86	2	0	0
York C.	L	03.87	86	3	3	0
Preston N.E.	Tr	08.87	87	4	0	1
Chester C.	Tr	03.88	87	9	0	0

LOWIS, Paul N.
Shap, 17 October, 1937 (WH)

League Club	Source	Date Signed	Seasons Played	Apps	Subs	Gls
Blackpool	B.A.B.C.	05.57				
Stockport Co.	Tr	06.59	59	9	-	0

LOWNDES, Stephen R.
Cwmbran, 17 June, 1960 Wu21-4/W-10 (W)

League Club	Source	Date Signed	Seasons Played	Apps	Subs	Gls
Newport Co.	Jnrs	10.77	77-82	200	8	39
Millwall	Tr	08.83	83-85	95	1	16
Barnsley	Tr	08.86	86-89	108	8	20
Hereford U.	Tr	10.90	90-91	45	4	4

LOWNDS, Mark U.
Sunderland, 28 November, 1940 (WH)

League Club	Source	Date Signed	Seasons Played	Apps	Subs	Gls
Luton T.	Ryhope Colly	01.60	61-64	59	-	3

LOWREY, Patrick
Newcastle, 11 October, 1950 E Sch (W)

League Club	Source	Date Signed	Seasons Played	Apps	Subs	Gls
Sunderland	Newcastle U. (App)	11.67	68-71	13	2	3
Darlington	R.U. Bruges (Bel)	08.75	75	14	6	2
Workington	Tr	07.76	76	15	0	3

LOWRIE, George
Rhondda, 19 December, 1919 Died 1989 W-4 (CF)

League Club	Source	Date Signed	Seasons Played	Apps	Subs	Gls
Swansea C.	Tonypandy	01.37				
Preston N.E.	Tr	12.37	37	5	-	0
Coventry C.	Tr	06.39	46-47	56	-	44
Newcastle U.	Tr	03.48	47-49	12	-	5
Bristol C.	Tr	09.49	49-51	48	-	21
Coventry C.	Tr	02.52	51-52	27	-	12

LOWRIE, Thomas
Glasgow, 14 January, 1928 (WH)

League Club	Source	Date Signed	Seasons Played	Apps	Subs	Gls
Manchester U.	Troon Ath.	08.47	48-49	13	-	0
Oldham Ath.	Aberdeen	08.52	52-54	79	-	5

LOWRY, Brian T.
Manchester, 12 December, 1936 (OR)

League Club	Source	Date Signed	Seasons Played	Apps	Subs	Gls
Grimsby T.	Manchester U. (Am)	08.54	54-55	12	-	1
Aldershot	Tr	07.56				

LOWRY, Thomas
Liverpool, 26 August, 1946 (RB)

League Club	Source	Date Signed	Seasons Played	Apps	Subs	Gls
Liverpool	App	04.63	64	1	-	0
Crewe Alex.	Tr	07.66	66-77	435	1	2

LOWTHER, Shaun
North Shields, 24 January, 1962 (D)

League Club	Source	Date Signed	Seasons Played	Apps	Subs	Gls
Peterborough U.	Middlesbrough (N/C)	01.85	84	1	0	0

LOXLEY, Anthony D.
Nottingham, 14 December, 1959 (D)

League Club	Source	Date Signed	Seasons Played	Apps	Subs	Gls
Lincoln C.	App	12.77	78	1	0	0

LOXLEY, Herbert
Matlock, 3 February, 1934 (WH)

League Club	Source	Date Signed	Seasons Played	Apps	Subs	Gls
Notts Co.	Jnrs	03.52	54-63	245	-	9
Mansfield T.	Tr	07.64				
Lincoln C.	Lockheed Leamington	10.66	66	7	0	0

LOYDEN, Edward
Liverpool, 22 December, 1945 (CF)

League Club	Source	Date Signed	Seasons Played	Apps	Subs	Gls
Blackpool	Jnrs	12.63	64	2	-	0
Carlisle U.	Tr	06.66				
Chester C.	Tr	07.67	67	37	0	22
Shrewsbury T.	Tr	05.68	68	11	1	2
Barnsley	Tr	12.68	68-70	64	1	22
Chester C.	Tr	11.70	70-71	62	0	26
Tranmere Rov.	Tr	06.72	72-73	61	0	22

LUCAS, Alec L.
Bradley, 1 December, 1945 Wu23-1 (FB)

League Club	Source	Date Signed	Seasons Played	Apps	Subs	Gls
Wrexham	Queens Park R. (App)	08.65	65-66	51	4	0

LUCAS, Brian A.
Farnborough, 31 January, 1961 (M)

League Club	Source	Date Signed	Seasons Played	Apps	Subs	Gls
Aldershot	Jnrs	07.78	79-83	112	13	19

LUCAS, Frederick C.
Slade Green, 29 September, 1933 (WH)

League Club	Source	Date Signed	Seasons Played	Apps	Subs	Gls
Charlton Ath.	Jnrs	01.52	55-63	185	-	29
Crystal Palace	Tr	10.63	63-64	16	-	0

LUCAS, P. Malcolm
Wrexham, 7 October, 1938 Wu23-1/W-4 (WH)

League Club	Source	Date Signed	Seasons Played	Apps	Subs	Gls
Leyton Orient	Bradley R.	09.58	58-64	157	-	6
Norwich C.	Tr	09.64	64-69	180	3	8
Torquay U.	Tr	03.70	69-73	118	4	3

LUCAS, Oliver
Paisley, 14 January, 1923 (FB)

League Club	Source	Date Signed	Seasons Played	Apps	Subs	Gls
Leyton Orient	St Mirren	07.48	48-49	2	-	0

LUCAS, Paul
Coseley, 27 April, 1936 (IF)

League Club	Source	Date Signed	Seasons Played	Apps	Subs	Gls
Aston Villa	Jnrs	04.54				
Gillingham	Tr	08.56	56-57	44	-	7

LUCAS, Richard
Chapeltown, 22 September, 1970 (FB)

League Club	Source	Date Signed	Seasons Played	Apps	Subs	Gls
Sheffield U.	YT	07.89	90-91	8	2	0

LUCAS, Richard J.
Witney, 22 January, 1948 (FB)

League Club	Source	Date Signed	Seasons Played	Apps	Subs	Gls
Oxford U.	Jnrs	07.65	67-74	190	1	2

LUCAS, Robert W.
Bethnal Green, 6 January, 1925 (G)

League Club	Source	Date Signed	Seasons Played	Apps	Subs	Gls
Crystal Palace	Hendon	06.46	46	4	-	0

LUCAS, William H.
Newport, 15 January, 1918 W-7 (IF)

League Club	Source	Date Signed	Seasons Played	Apps	Subs	Gls
Wolverhampton W.		05.36				
Swindon T.	Tr	05.37	37-47	141	-	32
Swansea C.	Tr	03.48	47-53	203	-	35
Newport Co.	Tr	12.53	53-57	94	-	6

LUCKETT, Paul
Coventry, 12 January, 1957 (FB)

League Club	Source	Date Signed	Seasons Played	Apps	Subs	Gls
Halifax T.	Coventry C. (App)	08.74	74-75	26	1	0
Hartlepool U.	Tr	03.76	75-76	19	0	0

LUCKETTI, Christopher J.
Littleborough, 28 September, 1971 (CD)

League Club	Source	Date Signed	Seasons Played	Apps	Subs	Gls
Rochdale (YT)	YT	07.88	88	1	0	0
Stockport Co.	Tr	08.90				
Halifax T.	Tr	07.91	91	31	5	0

LUDFORD, George A.
Barnet, 22 March, 1915 (WH)

League Club	Source	Date Signed	Seasons Played	Apps	Subs	Gls
Tottenham H.	Jnrs	05.36	36-49	75	-	7

LUDLAM, Steven J.
Chesterfield, 18 October, 1955 (M)

League Club	Source	Date Signed	Seasons Played	Apps	Subs	Gls
Sheffield U.	App	01.73	75-76	26	1	1
Carlisle U.	Tr	05.77	77-79	90	6	11
Chester C.	Tr	07.80	80-82	100	2	12

LUFF, Neil J.
Bletchley, 9 April, 1969 (M)

League Club	Source	Date Signed	Seasons Played	Apps	Subs	Gls
Gillingham	Jnrs	06.87	87	0	1	0

LUGG, Raymond J.
Jarrow, 18 July, 1948 (M)

League Club	Source	Date Signed	Seasons Played	Apps	Subs	Gls
Middlesbrough	Jnrs	07.65	66-68	34	3	3
Watford	Tr	11.69	69-71	51	8	3
Plymouth Arg.	Tr	07.72	72	22	2	1
Crewe Alex.	Tr	07.73	73-77	183	2	10
Bury	Tr	07.78	78-79	68	3	2

LUKE, George
Hetton-le-Hole, 8 November, 1948 Died 1968 E Sch (WH)

League Club	Source	Date Signed	Seasons Played	Apps	Subs	Gls
Newcastle U.	App	03.66				
Chelsea	Tr	03.67	66	1	0	0

LUKE, George B.
Lanchester, 20 October, 1932 (F)

League Club	Source	Date Signed	Seasons Played	Apps	Subs	Gls
Sheffield U.		01.52	53-54	7	-	0
Scunthorpe U.	Tr	05.56	56	18	-	6

LUKE, George T.
Newcastle, 17 December, 1933 (OL)

League Club	Source	Date Signed	Seasons Played	Apps	Subs	Gls
Newcastle U.	Jnrs	12.50				
Hartlepool U.	Tr	10.53	53-59	186	-	61
Newcastle U.	Tr	10.59	59-60	27	-	4
Darlington	Tr	01.61	60-62	68	-	10

LUKE, Noel E.
Birmingham, 28 December, 1964 (W/RB)

League Club	Source	Date Signed	Seasons Played	Apps	Subs	Gls
West Bromwich A.	App	04.82	82-83	8	1	1
Mansfield T.	Tr	07.84	84-85	41	9	9
Peterborough U.	Tr	08.86	86-91	248	1	27

LUKE, William
Aberdeen, 19 April, 1932 (IL)

League Club	Source	Date Signed	Seasons Played	Apps	Subs	Gls
Crewe Alex.	East Fife	10.55	55	1	-	0

LUKIC, John
Chesterfield, 11 December, 1960 E Yth/Eu21-7/E'B' (G)

League Club	Source	Date Signed	Seasons Played	Apps	Subs	Gls
Leeds U.	App	12.78	79-82	146	0	0
Arsenal	Tr	07.83	83-89	223	0	0
Leeds U.	Tr	06.90	90-91	80	0	0

LUMBY, James A.
Grimsby, 2 October, 1954 (F)

League Club	Source	Date Signed	Seasons Played	Apps	Subs	Gls
Grimsby T.	Jnrs	10.72	73-74	28	3	12
Scunthorpe U.	Brigg T.	03.77	76-77	55	0	28
Carlisle U.	Tr	04.78	77-78	24	3	7
Tranmere Rov.	Tr	07.79	79-80	43	3	21
Mansfield T.	Tr	01.81	80-81	49	2	18

LUMLEY, Robert
Leadgate, 6 January, 1933 (IF)

League Club	Source	Date Signed	Seasons Played	Apps	Subs	Gls
Charlton Ath.	Jnrs	01.50	53-54	6	-	0
Hartlepool U.	Tr	02.55	54-57	106	-	20
Chesterfield	Tr	12.57	57-58	25	-	2
Gateshead	Tr	06.59	59	40	-	5
Hartlepool U.	Tr	07.60	60	38	-	6

LUMLEY, I. Thomas
Leadgate, 9 December, 1924 (IF)

League Club	Source	Date Signed	Seasons Played	Apps	Subs	Gls
Charlton Ath.	Consett	12.48	48-51	37	-	10
Barnsley	Tr	03.52	51-55	145	-	36
Darlington	Tr	08.56	56	15	-	3

LUMSDEN, Alexander
Fife, 24 May, 1946 (F)

League Club	Source	Date Signed	Seasons Played	Apps	Subs	Gls
Southend U.	Camelon Jnrs	02.66	65-66	2	0	0

LUMSDEN, James
Glasgow, 7 November, 1947 (M)

League Club	Source	Date Signed	Seasons Played	Apps	Subs	Gls
Leeds U.	Jnrs	11.66	66-69	3	1	0
Southend U.	Tr	09.70	70	12	1	0

LUMSDEN, John D.
Stoke, 30 July, 1956 (RB)

League Club	Source	Date Signed	Seasons Played	Apps	Subs	Gls
Stoke C.	App	08.73	75-77	26	2	0
Port Vale	L	03.78	77	5	0	0

LUMSDEN, John I.
Heanor, 1 July, 1942 (LB)

League Club	Source	Date Signed	Seasons Played	Apps	Subs	Gls
Aston Villa	Jnrs	07.59				
Workington	Tr	02.52	61-67	249	2	7
Chesterfield	Tr	03.68	67-70	94	0	0

LUMSDEN, John W.
Edinburgh, 15 December, 1960 (M)

League Club	Source	Date Signed	Seasons Played	Apps	Subs	Gls
Stoke C.	East Fife	02.80	79-81	2	4	0

LUND, Gary J.
Grimsby, 13 September, 1964 E Yth/Eu21-3 (F)

League Club	Source	Date Signed	Seasons Played	Apps	Subs	Gls
Grimsby T.	Jnrs	07.83	83-85	47	13	24
Lincoln C.	Tr	08.86	86	41	3	13
Notts Co.	Tr	06.87	87-91	135	16	42

LUNDON, Sean
Liverpool, 7 March, 1969 (D)

League Club	Source	Date Signed	Seasons Played	Apps	Subs	Gls
Chester C.	YT	12.86	86-90	48	8	4

LUNDSTRUM, Colin F.
Colchester, 9 October, 1938 (W)

League Club	Source	Date Signed	Seasons Played	Apps	Subs	Gls
Ipswich T.	West Ham U. (Am)	11.56	57-59	13	-	1
Colchester U.	Tr	08.61	61	1	-	0

LUNN, Dennis
Barnsley, 20 November, 1938 (CH)

League Club	Source	Date Signed	Seasons Played	Apps	Subs	Gls
Doncaster Rov.	Wombwell	10.58	59-61	85	-	0

LUNN, George
Bolton-on-Dearne, 28 June, 1915 (CH)

League Club	Source	Date Signed	Seasons Played	Apps	Subs	Gls
Aston Villa	Frickley Colly	05.38				
Birmingham C.	Tr	09.46				
Watford	Tr	10.47	47	5	-	0

LUNN, Grant H.
Guildford, 26 August, 1967 (G)

League Club	Source	Date Signed	Seasons Played	Apps	Subs	Gls
Aldershot (N/C)	Chelsea (App)	08.85	85	9	0	0

LUNN, Henry (Harry)
Lurgan (NI), 20 March, 1925 (OR)

League Club	Source	Date Signed	Seasons Played	Apps	Subs	Gls
Notts Co.	Lurgan	07.46	46	24	-	5
Portsmouth	Tr	07.47	47	1	-	0
Swindon T.	Tr	05.48	48-53	195	-	30

LUNN, John (Jack)
Barnsley, 14 October, 1937 Died 1989 (OL)

League Club	Source	Date Signed	Seasons Played	Apps	Subs	Gls
Barnsley	Jnrs	05.56	56-60	56	-	19
Chesterfield	Tr	07.61	61	40	-	13

LUNN, William J.
Lurgan (NI), 8 May, 1923 NI Sch (IF)

League Club	Source	Date Signed	Seasons Played	Apps	Subs	Gls
West Bromwich A.	Glenavon	02.46	46-47	10	-	5
Bournemouth	Tr	02.48	47-49	47	-	19
Newport Co.	Tr	07.50	50-51	6	-	1

LUNNISS, Roy E.
Islington, 4 November, 1939 (FB)

League Club	Source	Date Signed	Seasons Played	Apps	Subs	Gls
Crystal Palace	Carshalton Ath.	04.60	59-62	25	-	1
Portsmouth	Tr	06.63	63-65	69	0	1
Luton T.	South Africa	12.66	66	1	0	0

LUNT, Robert J.
Widnes, 11 December, 1973 (LW)

League Club	Source	Date Signed	Seasons Played	Apps	Subs	Gls
Wrexham (YT)	YT	07.90	90-91	1	8	0

LUSCOMBE, Lee J.
Guernsey, 16 July, 1971 (W)

League Club	Source	Date Signed	Seasons Played	Apps	Subs	Gls
Southampton	YT	04.89				
Brentford	Tr	10.91	91	10	3	3

LUSTED, Leslie R.
Reading, 20 September, 1931 (IF)

League Club	Source	Date Signed	Seasons Played	Apps	Subs	Gls
Leyton Orient	Harwich & Parkeston	12.52	52-53	23	-	6
Aldershot	Tr	07.54	54-55	9	-	1

LUTTON, Robert J.
Banbridge (NI), 13 July, 1950 NI-6 (W)

League Club	Source	Date Signed	Seasons Played	Apps	Subs	Gls
Wolverhampton W.	Jnrs	09.67	68-70	16	5	1
Brighton & H.A.	Tr	09.71	71-72	18	11	4
West Ham U.	Tr	01.73	72-73	8	4	1

LYALL, George
Wick, 4 May, 1947 (M)

League Club	Source	Date Signed	Seasons Played	Apps	Subs	Gls
Preston N.E.	Raith Rov.	03.66	65-71	90	15	16
Nottingham F.	Tr	05.72	72-75	108	8	24
Hull C.	Tr	12.75	75-76	42	0	5

LYALL, John A.
Ilford, 24 February, 1940 E Yth (LB)

League Club	Source	Date Signed	Seasons Played	Apps	Subs	Gls
West Ham U.	Jnrs	05.57	59-62	31	-	0

LYDERSEN, Pal
Norway, 10 September, 1965 Norway Int (FB)

League Club	Source	Date Signed	Seasons Played	Apps	Subs	Gls
Arsenal	F.K. Stort (Nor)	09.91	91	5	2	0

LYDIATE, Jason L.
Manchester, 29 October, 1971 (CD)

League Club	Source	Date Signed	Seasons Played	Apps	Subs	Gls
Manchester U.	YT	07.90				
Bolton W.	Tr	03.92	91	1	0	0

LYDON, George W.
Sunderland, 25 November, 1933 E Sch (OL)

League Club	Source	Date Signed	Seasons Played	Apps	Subs	Gls
Sunderland	Jnrs	12.50				
Leeds U.	Tr	06.54	54	4	-	1
Gateshead	Tr	11.55	55-58	106	-	24

LYMAN, Colin C.
Northampton, 9 March, 1914 Died 1986 (F)

League Club	Source	Date Signed	Seasons Played	Apps	Subs	Gls
Southend U.		03.34	33	1	-	0
Northampton T.	Tr	11.34	34-37	85	-	31
Tottenham H.	Tr	10.37	37-38	46	-	10
Port Vale	Tr	05.46	46	11	-	1
Nottingham F.	Tr	10.46	46	23	-	9
Notts Co.	Tr	08.47	47	21	-	5

John Lukic (Leeds United, Arsenal & Leeds United)

LYNAM, Christopher A.
Manchester, 22 January, 1962 (W)

League Club	Source	Date Signed	Seasons Played	Apps	Subs	Gls
Manchester U.	App	01.80				
Carlisle U.	Ryoden (HK)	08.86	86	1	1	0

LYNCH, Anthony J.
Paddington, 20 January, 1966 (W)

League Club	Source	Date Signed	Seasons Played	Apps	Subs	Gls
Brentford	Jnrs	01.84	83-85	35	10	6
Barnet	Wealdstone	10.90	91	1	5	0

LYNCH, Barrie J.
Birmingham, 8 June, 1951 (FB)

League Club	Source	Date Signed	Seasons Played	Apps	Subs	Gls
Aston Villa	App	01.69	68-69	2	0	0
Grimsby T.	Atlanta (USA)	09.72	72	10	4	0
Scunthorpe U.	Tr	07.73	73-74	62	2	0
Torquay U.	Portland T. (USA)	09.75	75-76	67	3	2

LYNCH, John
Uddingston, 22 September, 1917 (G)

League Club	Source	Date Signed	Seasons Played	Apps	Subs	Gls
Workington	St Mirren	10.52	52	2	-	0

LYNCH, Patrick
Belfast, 22 January, 1950 (D)

League Club	Source	Date Signed	Seasons Played	Apps	Subs	Gls
Middlesbrough	Cliftonville	06.70	71	0	1	0

LYNCH, Terence J.
Newport, 17 May, 1952 (G)

League Club	Source	Date Signed	Seasons Played	Apps	Subs	Gls
Newport Co.	Jnrs	11.69	69-71	56	0	0

LYNCH, Thomas M.
Limerick, 10 October, 1964 (M/LB)

League Club	Source	Date Signed	Seasons Played	Apps	Subs	Gls
Sunderland	Limerick	08.88	88	4	0	0
Shrewsbury T.	Tr	01.90	89-91	93	8	4

LYNE, Neil G.F.
Leicester, 4 April, 1970 (F)

League Club	Source	Date Signed	Seasons Played	Apps	Subs	Gls
Nottingham F.	Leicester U.	08.89				
Walsall	L	03.90	89	6	1	0
Shrewsbury T.	L	03.91	90	16	0	6
Shrewsbury T.	Tr	07.91	91	43	1	8

LYNEX, Steven C.
West Bromwich, 23 January, 1958 (W)

League Club	Source	Date Signed	Seasons Played	Apps	Subs	Gls
West Bromwich A.	App	01.76				
Birmingham C.	Shamrock Rov.	04.79	78-80	28	18	10
Leicester C.	Tr	02.81	80-86	200	13	57
Birmingham C.	L	10.86	86	10	0	2
West Bromwich A.	Tr	03.87	86-87	26	3	3
Cardiff C.	Tr	07.88	88-89	56	6	2

LYNN, Frank
Consett, 29 May, 1929 (OL)

League Club	Source	Date Signed	Seasons Played	Apps	Subs	Gls
Grimsby T	Blackhall Colly	12.47	48	2	-	0

LYNN, Joseph
Seaton Sluice (Nd), 31 January, 1925 (IF)

League Club	Source	Date Signed	Seasons Played	Apps	Subs	Gls
Huddersfield T.	Cramlington	05.47	49	5	-	0
Exeter C.	Tr	06.50	50	29	-	2
Rochdale	Tr	07.51	51-55	193	-	23

LYNN, Samuel
St Helens, 25 December, 1920 (WH)

League Club	Source	Date Signed	Seasons Played	Apps	Subs	Gls
Manchester U.	Jnrs	01.38	47-49	13	-	0
Bradford P.A.	Tr	02.51	50-52	73	-	0

LYNN, Stanley
Bolton, 18 June, 1928 (FB)

League Club	Source	Date Signed	Seasons Played	Apps	Subs	Gls
Accrington St.	Whitworths	07.47	46-49	35	-	2
Aston Villa	Tr	03.50	50-61	281	-	36
Birmingham C.	Tr	10.61	61-65	131	0	26

LYNN, William
Newcastle, 20 January, 1947 (OL)

League Club	Source	Date Signed	Seasons Played	Apps	Subs	Gls
Huddersfield T.		07.65	65-66	4	0	0
Rotherham U.	Tr	04.67				

LYNNE, Michael G. A.
Kettering, 20 March, 1938 (G)

League Club	Source	Date Signed	Seasons Played	Apps	Subs	Gls
Preston N.E.	Jnrs	03.56	58	2	-	0
Bournemouth	Tr	06.59	59-60	17	-	0

LYON, David E.
Oldham, 21 November, 1948 (M)

League Club	Source	Date Signed	Seasons Played	Apps	Subs	Gls
Bolton W.	App	11.66				
Southport	Wigan Ath.	09.76	76	11	2	1

LYON, David G.
Northwich, 18 January, 1951 (CD)

League Club	Source	Date Signed	Seasons Played	Apps	Subs	Gls
Bury	App	01.69	68-71	65	6	0
Huddersfield T.	Tr	09.71	71-73	24	1	0
Mansfield T.	L	11.73	73	2	0	0
Cambridge U.	TR	07.74	74-76	84	1	11
Northampton T.	Tr	10.77	77	6	0	0

LYON, Thomas K.
Clydebank, 17 March, 1915 (CF)

League Club	Source	Date Signed	Seasons Played	Apps	Subs	Gls
Blackpool	Albion Rov.	03.37	36-37	7	-	0
Chesterfield	Tr	09.38	38-47	41	-	22
New Brighton	Tr	07.48	48	36	-	7

LYONS, A. Edward
Rochdale, 20 May, 1920 (FB)

League Club	Source	Date Signed	Seasons Played	Apps	Subs	Gls
Bury		04.45	47-48	2	-	0
Millwall	Tr	03.50	49-51	6	-	0
Crewe Alex.	Tr	07.52	52-53	23	-	0
Rochdale	Tr	12.53	53-54	19	-	1

LYONS, Barry
Shirebrook, 14 March, 1945 (W)

League Club	Source	Date Signed	Seasons Played	Apps	Subs	Gls
Rotherham U.	Jnrs	09.62	63-66	125	0	24
Nottingham F.	Tr	11.66	66-72	201	2	28
York C.	Tr	09.73	73-75	80	5	10
Darlington	Tr	07.76	76-78	97	0	10

LYONS, Brian
Darfield, 3 December, 1948 (CH)

League Club	Source	Date Signed	Seasons Played	Apps	Subs	Gls
Bradford P.A. (Am)	Houghton Colly	03.68	67	3	0	0

LYONS, Darren P.
Manchester, 9 November, 1966 (W)

League Club	Source	Date Signed	Seasons Played	Apps	Subs	Gls
Bury	Ashton U.	03.92	91	9	1	4

LYONS, George W.
Rochdale, 1 May, 1935 (OR)

League Club	Source	Date Signed	Seasons Played	Apps	Subs	Gls
Rochdale		12.53	53-56	29	-	4

LYONS, John P.
Buckley, 8 November, 1956 Died 1982 (F)

League Club	Source	Date Signed	Seasons Played	Apps	Subs	Gls
Wrexham	Jnrs	06.75	74-78	63	23	23
Millwall	Tr	07.79	79-80	55	0	20
Cambridge U.	Tr	10.80	80-81	20	1	6
Colchester U.	Tr	02.82	81-82	31	2	9

LYONS, Michael
Liverpool, 8 December, 1951 Eu23-5/E'B' (CD)

League Club	Source	Date Signed	Seasons Played	Apps	Subs	Gls
Everton	App	07.69	70-81	364	26	48
Sheffield Wed.	Tr	08.82	82-85	129	0	12
Grimsby T.	Tr	11.85	85-86	50	0	4

LYONS, Michael C.
Bristol, 31 January, 1932 (FB)

League Club	Source	Date Signed	Seasons Played	Apps	Subs	Gls
Bristol C.	Jnrs	06.50	50-51	2	-	0
Bristol Rov.	Tr	07.53	53	2	-	0
Bournemouth	Tr	07.56	56-58	105	-	0
Swindon T.	Tr	11.59	59	2	-	0

LYONS, Terence
Bradford, 14 April, 1929 (OL)

League Club	Source	Date Signed	Seasons Played	Apps	Subs	Gls
Burnley		10.49	50	12	-	3
Bradford P.A.	Tr	09.51	51-52	38	-	6

LYSKE, James H. A.
Lurgan (NI), 7 October, 1932 (FB)

League Club	Source	Date Signed	Seasons Played	Apps	Subs	Gls
Sunderland	Glenavon	11.57				
Darlington	Tr	02.58	57-58	16	-	0

LYTHGOE, Arnold P.
Bolton, 7 March, 1922 (LH)

League Club	Source	Date Signed	Seasons Played	Apps	Subs	Gls
Accrington St.	Ashton National	09.45	46	10	-	0

LYTHGOE, Derek
Bolton, 5 May, 1933 (W)

League Club	Source	Date Signed	Seasons Played	Apps	Subs	Gls
Blackpool	Jnrs	05.50	55-57	4	-	1
Norwich C.	Tr	03.58	57-61	62	-	22
Bristol C.	Tr	08.62	62-63	13	-	2

LYTHGOE, Philip
Norwich, 18 December, 1959 (W)

League Club	Source	Date Signed	Seasons Played	Apps	Subs	Gls
Norwich C.	App	12.77	77-79	9	3	1
Bristol Rov.	L	09.78	78	6	0	0
Oxford U.	Tr	08.80	80-81	23	5	3

Stanley Matthews (Stoke City, Blackpool, Stoke City & England)
The one and only "wizard of the dribble" and a legend in his own lifetime

League Club	Source	Date Signed	Seasons Played	Career Record Apps	Subs	Gls
McADAM, David						
Hereford, 3 April, 1923						(FB)
Leeds U.	Stapenhill W.	05.48	48-49	24	-	0
Wrexham	Tr	05.50	50	10	-	0
McADAM, Neil B.						
East Kilbride, 30 July, 1957						(G)
Port Vale	Northwich Vic.	08.82	82	2	0	0
McADAM, Steven						
Portadown (NI), 2 April, 1960						(FB)
Burnley	Portadown	05.78	79	5	0	0
Wigan Ath	Barnsley (N/C)	11.80	80-81	26	0	0
McADAM, Thomas						
Glasgow, 9 April, 1954						(CD)
Stockport Co.	Glasgow Celtic	08.86	86	5	0	1
McADAMS, William J.						
Belfast, 20 January, 1934 NI-15						(CF)
Manchester C.	Distillery	12.53	53-59	127	-	62
Bolton W.	Tr	09.60	60-61	44	-	26
Leeds U.	Tr	12.61	61	11	-	3
Brentford	Tr	07.62	62-64	75	-	36
Queens Park R.	Tr	09.64	64-65	33	0	13
Barrow	Tr	07.66	66-67	53	0	9
McALEA, Robert J.						
Belfast, 13 September, 1920						(IF)
Bradford C.	Ballymoney	07.48	48	4	-	0
McALEER, Frank						
Glasgow, 16 October, 1945						(M)
Barrow	Morton	08.70	70	9	1	0
McALINDEN, James						
Belfast, 31 December, 1917 IR Lge/IR-2/NI-4						(WH)
Portsmouth	Belfast Celtic	12.38	38-47	53	-	9
Stoke C.	Tr	09.47	47-48	33	-	2
Southend U.	Tr	10.48	48-53	218	-	12
McALINDEN, John						
Carlisle, 25 December, 1930						(F)
Shrewsbury T.	Glasgow Celtic	05.57	57	12	-	3
McALINDEN, Robert J.						
Salford, 22 May, 1946						(W)
Manchester C.	Aston Villa (App)	05.64	63	1	-	0
Port Vale	Tr	09.65				
Bournemouth	Los Angeles (USA)	09.76	76	1	0	0
McALISTER, Thomas G.						
Clydebank, 10 December, 1952						(G)
Sheffield U.	App	05.70	71-75	63	0	0
Rotherham U.	Tr	01.76	75-78	159	0	0
Blackpool	Tr	07.79	79	16	0	0
Swindon T.	Tr	05.80	80	1	0	0
Bristol Rov.	L	02.81	80	13	0	0
West Ham U.	Tr	05.81	81-88	85	0	0
Colchester U.	L	02.89	88	20	0	0
McALLE, John E.						
Liverpool, 31 January, 1950						(CD)
Wolverhampton W.	App	02.67	67-80	394	12	0
Sheffield U.	Tr	08.81	81	18	0	0
Derby Co.	Tr	04.82	81-83	51	7	1
McALLISTER, Brian						
Glasgow, 30 November, 1970						(D)
Wimbledon	YT	02.89	89-91	10	3	0
Plymouth Arg.	L	12.90	90	7	1	0
McALLISTER, Donald						
Radcliffe, 26 May, 1953						(D)
Bolton W.	App	06.70	69-74	155	1	2
Tottenham H.	Tr	02.75	74-80	168	4	9
Charlton Ath.	Tr	08.81	81-82	55	0	6
Rochdale (N/C)	Tampa Bay (USA)	11.84	84	3	0	0
McALLISTER, Gary						
Motherwell, 25 December, 1964 Su21-1/S'B'/S-18						(M)
Leicester C.	Motherwell	08.85	85-89	199	2	46
Leeds U.	Tr	06.90	90-91	79	1	7

Gary McAllister (Motherwell, Leicester City, Leeds United & Scotland)

League Club	Source	Date Signed	Seasons Played	Career Record Apps	Subs	Gls
McALLISTER, James						
Barrhead, 30 October, 1931						(IF)
Millwall	Neilston Jnrs	06.54	54-55	20	-	6
Bradford P.A.	Morton	05.59	59-60	43	-	14
McALLISTER, Kevin						
Falkirk, 8 November, 1962						(W)
Chelsea	Falkirk	05.85	85-90	78	28	7
McALONE, Robert						
Whitehaven, 16 February, 1928						*(CH)*
Workington		(N/L)	51-53	68	-	3
McALOON, Gerald						
Glasgow, 13 September, 1916						*(IF)*
Brentford	St Francis	06.34	37-38	21	-	9
Wolverhampton W.	Tr	03.39	38	2	-	1
Brentford	Tr	12.45	46	7	-	3
McANDREW, Anthony						
Glasgow, 11 April, 1956						(CD)
Middlesbrough	App	08.73	73-81	245	2	13
Chelsea	Tr	09.82	82-83	20	0	4
Middlesbrough	Tr	09.84	84-85	66	0	2
Darlington	(Retired)	11.88	88	11	0	0
Hartlepool U.	Tr	03.89	88	4	0	0
MacANDREW, Robert						
Derby, 6 April, 1943						(HB)
Derby Co.	Jnrs	06.61	63	1	-	0
McANEARNEY, James						
Dundee, 20 March, 1935						(IF)
Sheffield Wed.	Jnrs	03.52	53-59	38	-	10
Plymouth Arg.	Tr	01.60	59-63	135	-	34
Watford	Tr	11.63	63-66	84	2	19
Bradford C.	Tr	09.66	66-67	41	4	5
McANEARNEY, Thomas						
Dundee, 6 January, 1933						(WH)
Sheffield Wed.	Dundee St Stephens	10.51	52-64	352	-	19
Peterborough U.	Tr	11.65	65	12	0	0
Aldershot	Tr	03.66	65-68	106	0	5
McARTHUR, Barry						
Nottingham, 6 May, 1947						(CF)
Nottingham F.	Jnrs	05.65	65	7	1	4
Barrow	Tr	07.69	69	5	2	0
York C.	Tr	12.69	69	1	0	0
McARTHUR, Thomas						
Neilston, 23 April, 1925						(CH)
Leicester C.	Neilston Vic.	01.47	46-53	97	-	0
Plymouth Arg.	Tr	01.54	53	2	-	0
McARTHUR, Walter J.						
Denaby, 21 March, 1912 Died 1980						(WH)
Bristol Rov.	Goldthorpe Colly	01.33	32-49	261	-	14
McATEER, Andrew W.						
Preston, 24 April, 1961						(LB)
Preston N.E.	App	04.79	79-86	236	2	8
Blackpool	Tr	12.86	86-87	37	4	0
Preston N.E.	Tr	05.88	88	11	2	1
McAUGHTRIE, David						
Cumnock, 30 January, 1963						(CD)
Stoke C.	App	01.81	80-83	48	3	1
Carlisle U.	Tr	07.84	84	28	0	1
York C.	Tr	06.85	85-86	64	0	1
Darlington	Tr	07.87	87-88	36	3	0
MACAULAY, Archibald R.						
Falkirk, 30 July, 1915 S-7						(WH)
West Ham U.	Glasgow Rangers	06.37	37-46	83	-	29
Brentford	Tr	10.46	46	26	-	2
Arsenal	Tr	07.47	47-49	103	-	1
Fulham	Tr	06.50	50-52	48	-	4
McAULEY, Hugh A.						
Bootle, 8 January, 1953						(W)
Liverpool	App	01.70				
Tranmere Rov.	L	08.73	73	13	0	1
Plymouth Arg.	Tr	10.74	74-76	76	1	7
Charlton Ath.	Tr	12.76	76-77	55	0	9
Tranmere Rov.	Tr	08.78	78	41	2	0
Carlisle U.	Tr	07.79	79-80	14	3	1

League Club	Source	Date Signed	Seasons Played	Career Record Apps	Subs	Gls
MACAULEY, James A. R.						
Edinburgh, 19 October, 1922						(WH)
Chelsea	Edinburgh Th.	10.46	46-49	86	-	5
Aldershot	Tr	08.51	51	31	-	3
McAULEY, Patrick J.						
Barrhead, 31 July, 1921 SF Lge						(WH)
Luton T.	Glasgow Celtic	12.50	50	8	-	1
McAULEY, Stephen R.						
Lytham, 4 March, 1969						(CD)
Manchester C.	YT	11.87				
Crewe Alex.	Fleetwood T.	03.92	91	9	0	1
McAVENNIE, Frank						
Glasgow, 22 November, 1959 Su21-5/S-5						(F)
West Ham U.	St Mirren	06.85	85-87	85	0	33
West Ham U.	Glasgow Celtic	03.89	88-91	49	19	16

Frank McAvennie (St Mirren, West Ham United, Glasgow Celtic, West Ham United & Scotland)

League Club	Source	Date Signed	Seasons Played	Career Record Apps	Subs	Gls
McAVOY, Alan J.						
Wigton, 4 October, 1963						(M)
Blackpool		02.81	81	6	0	0
McAVOY, Douglas H.						
Kilmarnock, 29 November, 1918						(IF)
Liverpool	Kilmarnock	12.47	47-48	2	-	0
McBAIN, Alan						
Aberdeen, 10 February, 1940						(FB)
Swansea C.	Aberdeen E.E.	01.59				
Carlisle U.	Tr	06.60	60-62	70	-	0
Luton T.	Tr	06.63	63-64	60	-	0
McBAIN, Gordon A.						
Glasgow, 4 September, 1934						(F)
Rochdale	Kilmarnock	05.58	58	10	-	1
McBAIN, Neil						
Campbeltown, 15 November, 1895 Died 1974 S-3						(WH)
Manchester U.	Ayr U.	11.21	21-22	42	-	2
Everton	Tr	01.23	22-25	97	-	1
Liverpool	St Johnstone	03.28	27-28	12	-	0
Watford	Tr	11.28	28-31	84	-	4
New Brighton	(Team Manager)	03.47	46	1	-	0
MacBENNETT, Seamus						
Newcastle (NI), 16 November, 1925						(OR)
Cardiff C.		09.47	47	4	-	2
Tranmere Rov.	Tr	11.48	48-49	12	-	1

League Club	Source	Date Signed	Seasons Played	Apps	Subs	Gls
McBETH, George						
Belfast, 4 September, 1954						(W)
Manchester C.	App	10.71				
Stockport Co.	Tr	07.76	76-77	51	5	3
McBLAIN, Andrew						
Bo'ness, 11 August, 1926						(LH)
Newport Co.	Forth W.	02.47	46-48	36	-	1
McBRIDE, Andrew D.						
Kenya, 15 March, 1954						(CD)
Crystal Palace	App	10.71	73	1	0	0
McBRIDE, John						
Kilsyth, 31 December, 1923						(G)
Reading	Third Lanark	03.48	47-52	100	-	0
Shrewsbury T.	Tr	12.52	52-55	78	-	0
McBRIDE, Joseph						
Glasgow, 17 August, 1960 S Sch/Su21-1						(W)
Everton	App	08.78	79-81	51	6	9
Rotherham U.	Tr	08.82	82-83	45	0	12
Oldham Ath.	Tr	09.83	83-84	28	8	5
McBRIDE, Joseph						
Kilmarnock, 10 June, 1938 SF Lge/S-2						(CF)
Wolverhampton W.	Kilmarnock	12.59				
Luton T.	Tr	02.60	59-60	25	-	9
McBRIDE, Peter P						
Motherwell, 22 December, 1946						(WH)
Manchester U.	Jnrs	12.63				
Southport	Tr	07.66	66	1	2	0
Bradford P.A.	Tr	07.67	67	5	2	0
McBRIDE, Vincent						
Manchester, 21 January, 1934						(G)
Walsall	Ashton U.	05.54	54	11	-	0
Aston Villa	Tr	03.56				
Mansfield T.	Tr	07.58	58	10	-	0
McBRIDE, William						
Newtown, 8 November, 1913						(LB)
Carlisle U.		02.46	46	15	-	1
McBURNEY, Michael L.						
Wrexham, 12 September, 1953 W Sch						(F)
Wrexham	Jnrs	07.71	70-72	20	4	4
Bolton W.	Tr	05.73	73	1	0	0
Hartlepool U.	L	11.74	74	5	1	1
Tranmere Rov.	L	03.75	74	4	1	0
MacCABE, Andrew B.						
Glasgow, 22 February, 1935 Died 1964						(W)
Chesterfield	Corby T.	11.55	55-58	53	-	7
McCABE, James J.						
Derry (NI), 17 September, 1918 Died 1991 NI-6						(WH)
Middlesbrough	South Bank	05.37	46-47	34	-	0
McCAFFERTY, James						
Motherwell, 10 July, 1957						(W)
Hereford U.	Bristol C. (App)	04.75	75	0	3	0
McCAFFREY, Aiden						
Newcastle, 30 August, 1957 E Yth						(CD)
Newcastle U.	App	01.74	74-77	57	2	4
Derby Co.	Tr	08.78	78-79	31	6	4
Bristol Rov.	Tr	08.80	80-84	183	1	11
Bristol C.	L	02.82	81	6	0	1
Torquay U.	L	03.85	84	6	0	0
Exeter C.	Tr	07.85	85-86	55	3	0
Hartlepool U.	Tr	02 87	86	6	0	1
Carlisle U.	Whitley Bay	01.88	87	14	0	0
McCAFFREY, James						
Luton, 12 October, 1951 E Yth						(W)
Nottingham F.	App	03.69	69	2	6	1
Mansfield T.	Tr	07.72	72-76	170	8	21
Huddersfield T.	Tr	01.77	76-77	23	4	0
Portsmouth	Tr	02.78	77-78	11	1	1
Northampton T.	Tr	12.78	78-79	56	1	6
McCAIG, Robert A. M.						
Dumfries, 15 August, 1923						(OR)
Carlisle U.		08.48	48	5	-	0
Blackburn Rov.	Tr	12.48	48-50	30	-	2
Stockport Co.	Tr	08.51	51	15	-	2
Halifax T.	Tr	01.52	51	17	-	2
Crewe Alex.	Tr	08.52	52-53	19	-	1

League Club	Source	Date Signed	Seasons Played	Apps	Subs	Gls
McCALL, Alexander H.						
Annan, 26 March, 1939						(WH)
Carlisle U.		09.58	59	1	-	0
McCALL, Andrew						
Hamilton, 15 March, 1925						(W)
Blackpool	Blantyre Vic.	07.47	47-50	84	-	15
West Bromwich A.	Tr	01.51	50-51	31	-	3
Leeds U.	Tr	08.52	52-54	62	-	8
Halifax T.	Tr	07.56	56-59	139	-	15
McCALL, Anthony E.						
Thatcham, 15 January, 1936						(F)
Reading	Jnrs	05.53	55-56	8	-	1
McCALL, David						
Carlisle, 24 January, 1948						(OR)
Workington	Jnrs	01.66	66	1	0	0
McCALL, Ian H.						
Dumfries, 30 September, 1964						(M)
Bradford C.	Glasgow Rangers	01.90	89	11	1	1
McCALL, John						
Glasgow, 29 September, 1918						(WH)
Bradford P.A.	Workington	09.37	37-47	41	-	5
McCALL, Peter						
West Ham, 11 September, 1936						(WH)
Bristol C.	Kings Lynn	04.55	57-61	78	-	1
Oldham Ath.	Tr	05.62	62-64	108	-	5
McCALL, Robert H.						
Worksop, 29 December, 1915						(FB)
Nottingham F.	Worksop T.	02.35	35-51	162	-	1
McCALL, Stephen H.						
Carlisle, 15 October, 1960 E Yth/Eu21-6						(LB)
Ipswich T.	App	10.78	79-86	249	8	7
Sheffield Wed.	Tr	06.87	87-90	21	8	2
Carlisle U.	L	02.90	89	6	0	0
Plymouth Arg.	Tr	03.92	91	9	0	1
McCALL, Stuart M.						
Leeds, 10 June, 1964 Su21-2/S-20						(M)
Bradford C.	App	06.82	82-87	235	3	37
Everton	Tr	06.88	88-90	99	4	5

Stuart McCall (Bradford City, Everton, Glasgow Rangers & Scotland)

League Club	Source	Date Signed	Seasons Played	Apps	Subs	Gls
McCALL, William						
Glasgow, 14 November, 1920						(OL)
Newcastle U.	Aberdeen	01.48	47-48	16	-	4
McCALLIOG, James						
Glasgow, 23 September, 1946 S Sch/Su23-2/S-5						(M)
Chelsea	Leeds U. (Am)	09.63	64-65	7	0	2
Sheffield Wed.	Tr	10.65	65-68	150	0	19
Wolverhampton W.	Tr	08.69	69-73	158	5	34
Manchester U.	Tr	03.74	73-74	31	0	7
Southampton	Tr	02.75	74-76	70	2	8
Lincoln C.	Chicago (USA)	09.78	78	9	0	0
MacCALLUM, Stewart						
Dumbarton, 9 May, 1927						(HB)
Wrexham	Rhyl	06.50	50-52	67	-	0
Workington	Kettering T.	06.54	54-55	10	-	1
Coventry C.	Tr	02.56				
Hartlepool U.	Tr	07.56	56	2	-	0
Southport	Tr	08.57	57	9	-	0
McCALMAN, Donald S.						
Greenock, 18 October, 1935						(CH)
Bradford P.A.	Hibernian	06.59	59-65	297	0	5
Barrow	Tr	07.66	66	13	0	0
McCAMBRIDGE, David T.						
Larne (NI), 26 July, 1921						(WH)
Barrow	Larne T.	09.46	46-49	15	-	1
McCANN, Albert						
Maidenhead, 1 November, 1941						(IF)
Luton T.	Jnrs	04.59	59-60	6	-	0
Coventry C.	Tr	08.61	61	22	-	3
Portsmouth	Tr	08.62	62-73	331	7	84
McCANN, James						
Dundee, 20 May, 1954						(F)
Nottingham F.	App	05.72	74-75	2	4	1
Stockport Co.	L	10.75	75	4	1	0
Halifax T.	L	10.76	76	2	0	1
McCANN, John						
Glasgow, 23 July, 1934 S'B'-1						(OL)
Barnsley	Bridgeton B.C.	12.55	55-58	118	-	17
Bristol C.	Tr	05.59	59-60	30	-	0
Huddersfield T.	Tr	10.60	60-62	20	-	1
Derby Co.	Tr	09.62	62-63	55	-	2
Darlington	Tr	08.64	64	4	-	0
Chesterfield	Tr	10.64	64-65	41	0	9
McCARRICK, Mark B.						
Liverpool, 4 February, 1962						(FB)
Birmingham C.	Witton A.	05.83	83	12	3	0
Lincoln C.	Tr	07.84	84-85	42	2	0
Crewe Alex. (N/C)	Tr	02.86	85	10	1	0
Tranmere Rov.	Runcorn	08.87	87-90	125	0	14
McCARRISON, Dugald						
Lanarkshire, 22 December, 1969						(F)
Darlington (L)	Glasgow Celtic	10.91	91	5	0	2
McCARRON, Frank P.						
Glasgow, 1 October, 1943						(WH)
Carlisle U.	Glasgow Celtic	07.67	67	7	2	1
McCARTER, James J.						
Glasgow, 19 March, 1923						(OL)
Sheffield Wed.	Vale of Clyde	01.46	46	6	-	0
Mansfield T.	Tr	08.48	48-49	67	-	10
McCARTHY, Alan J.						
Wandsworth, 11 January, 1972 E Yth						(CD)
Queens Park R.	YT	12.89	90-91	4	1	0
McCARTHY, Daniel J.						
Abergavenny, 26 September, 1942						(W)
Cardiff C.	Abergavenny Th.	07.60	61	7	-	0
McCARTHY, Gerard						
Limerick (Ire), 30 March, 1934						(CH)
Charlton Ath.	Limerick	07.56	56	4	-	0
McCARTHY, Ian						
Porth, 4 September, 1960						(F)
Swansea C.	Coventry C. (App)	03.78	77	0	1	0

League Club	Source	Date Signed	Seasons Played	Apps	Subs	Gls
McCARTHY, John F.						
Cork (Ire), 22 January, 1922						(CF)
Bristol C.	Cork	07.49	49	3	-	0
McCARTHY, Jonathan D.						
Middlesbrough, 18 August, 1970						(M)
Hartlepool U. (N/C)	Jnrs	11.87	87	0	1	0
York C.	Shepshed Charterhouse	03.90	90-91	68	1	8
McCARTHY, Kevin J.						
Bethnal Green, 24 December, 1957						(M)
Watford	App	01.76	75-77	35	1	1
McCARTHY, Michael J.						
Barnsley, 7 February, 1959 IR-57						(CD)
Barnsley	App	07.77	77-83	272	0	7
Manchester C.	Tr	12.83	83-86	140	0	2
Millwall	Olimpique Lyon (Fr)	03.90	89-91	31	4	2
McCARTHY, Paul J.						
Cork, 4 August, 1971 IR Yth/IRu21-4						(CD)
Brighton & H.A.	YT	04.89	89-91	43	1	0
McCARTHY, Philip						
Liverpool, 19 February, 1944						(OL)
Oldham Ath.	Skelmersdale U.	07.65	65	2	1	0
Halifax T.	Tr	01.66	65-70	180	1	14
McCARTHY, Robert Z.						
Overton, 2 November, 1948						(RB)
Southampton	App	11.65	67-74	112	0	2
McCARTHY, Roy S.						
Barnsley, 17 January, 1945						(OR)
Barnsley	Jnrs	05.62	61-62	3	-	0
Barrow	Tr	07.64	64-68	188	0	41
Southport	Tr	06.69	69	33	1	4
McCARTHY, Sean C.						
Bridgend, 12 September, 1965						(F)
Swansea C.	Bridgend T.	10.85	85-87	76	15	25
Plymouth Arg.	Tr	08.88	88-89	67	3	19
Bradford C.	Tr	07.90	90-91	69	2	29
McCARTHY, William E.						
Bootle, 25 November, 1941 E Sch						(CH)
Liverpool	Jnrs	12.58				
Southport	Tr	10.60	60-62	27	-	1
McCARTNEY, Michael						
Edinburgh, 28 September, 1954 S Sch						(LB)
West Bromwich A.	App	12.71				
Carlisle U.	Tr	05.73	73-79	148	8	17
Southampton	Tr	07.80	80	22	0	1
Plymouth Arg.	Tr	08.81	81-82	49	0	5
Carlisle U.	Tr	03.83	82-86	130	1	7
McCARTNEY, William R.						
Musselburgh, 1 August, 1947						(F)
Port Vale		06.66	66	14	1	1
McCAVANA, William T.						
Belfast, 24 January, 1921 NI Amat/IR Lge/NI-2						(CH)
Notts Co. (Am)	Coleraine	08.48	48	3	-	0
McCLAIR, Brian J.						
Bellshill, 8 December, 1963 Su21-8/S'B'/S-26						(F)
Manchester U.	Glasgow Celtic	07.87	87-91	190	3	70
McCLAREN, Christopher						
Bristol, 14 March, 1963						(D)
Darlington (N/C)		03.87	86	1	2	0
McCLAREN, Stephen						
York, 3 May, 1961						(M)
Hull C.	App	04.79	79-84	171	7	16
Derby Co.	Tr	08.85	85-87	23	2	0
Lincoln C.	L	02.87	86	8	0	0
Bristol C.	Tr	02.88	87-88	60	1	2
Oxford U.	Tr	08.89	89-91	27	6	0
McCLATCHEY, Derek H.						
Whiston, 29 April, 1956						(F)
Liverpool	App	05.73				
Southport	L	02.76	75	2	1	0

McCLEAN, Christian A.
Colchester, 17 October, 1963 (F)

League Club	Source	Date Signed	Seasons Played	Apps	Subs	Gls
Bristol Rov.	Clacton T.	03.88	87-90	28	23	6
Swansea C.	Tr	07.91	91	4	0	0
Northampton T.	Tr	11.91	91	19	0	3

MacCLELLAN, Sidney B.
Dagenham, 11 June, 1925 (IF)

League Club	Source	Date Signed	Seasons Played	Apps	Subs	Gls
Tottenham H.	Chelmsford C.	08.49	50-55	68	-	29
Portsmouth	Tr	11.56	56-57	37	-	9
Leyton Orient	Tr	07.58	58	12	-	4

McCLELLAND, Charles
Manchester, 8 January, 1924 (IF)

League Club	Source	Date Signed	Seasons Played	Apps	Subs	Gls
Blackburn Rov.	Hyde U.	12.46	46-48	13	-	2
Exeter C.	Tr	07.49	49-54	183	-	60

McCLELLAND, David
Newcastle, 25 December, 1941 (W)

League Club	Source	Date Signed	Seasons Played	Apps	Subs	Gls
Port Vale	Bishop Auckland	08.67	67	2	2	0

McCLELLAND, John
Belfast, 7 December, 1955 NI-53 (CD)

League Club	Source	Date Signed	Seasons Played	Apps	Subs	Gls
Cardiff C.	Portadown	02.74	74	1	3	1
Mansfield T.	Bangor C.	05.78	78-80	122	3	8
Watford	Glasgow Rangers	11.84	84-88	184	0	3
Leeds U.	Tr	06.89	89-91	22	2	0
Watford	L	01.90	89	1	0	0
Notts Co.	L	03.92	91	6	0	0

John McClelland (Portadown, Cardiff City, Bangor City, Mansfield Town, Glasgow Rangers, Watford, Leeds United & Northern Ireland)

McCLELLAND, John B.
Bradford, 5 March, 1935 (OR)

League Club	Source	Date Signed	Seasons Played	Apps	Subs	Gls
Manchester C.	Manchester Y.M.C.A.	03.53	56-58	8	-	2
Lincoln C.	Tr	09.58	58-61	121	-	32
Queens Park R.	Tr	09.61	61-62	71	-	23
Portsmouth	Tr	05.63	62-67	135	1	36
Newport Co.	Tr	07.68	68	36	0	10

McCLELLAND, John T.
Lurgan (NI), 19 May, 1940 Died 1976 NI-6 (G)

League Club	Source	Date Signed	Seasons Played	Apps	Subs	Gls
Arsenal	Glenavon	10.60	60-63	46	-	0
Fulham	Tr	12.64	65-68	51	0	0
Lincoln C.	L	12.68	68	12	0	0

McCLELLAND, John W.
Colchester, 11 August, 1930 (IF)

League Club	Source	Date Signed	Seasons Played	Apps	Subs	Gls
Colchester U.		09.51				
Stoke C.	Tr	06.52	52	4	-	0
Swindon T.	Tr	06.54	54	14	-	1
Rochdale	Tr	06.55	55	24	-	5

McCLELLAND, Joseph
Edinburgh, 12 October, 1935 (FB)

League Club	Source	Date Signed	Seasons Played	Apps	Subs	Gls
Wrexham	Hibernian	06.64	64	32	-	0

McCLENAGHAN, Albert
Hamilton, 7 July, 1954 (D)

League Club	Source	Date Signed	Seasons Played	Apps	Subs	Gls
Watford	Larne T.	12.77	77	2	0	0

McCLURE, Douglas H.
Islington, 6 September, 1964 E Yth (FB)

League Club	Source	Date Signed	Seasons Played	Apps	Subs	Gls
Queens Park R.	App	08.82				
Exeter C. (N/C)	Tr	11.84	84	0	1	0
Torquay U. (N/C)	Tr	12.84	84	3	1	0
Wimbledon	Tr	01.85	84	2	0	0
Peterborough U.	Finland	10.85	85	4	0	0
Crewe Alex. (N/C)	Tr	01.86	85	3	0	0

McCLURE, William
Shotts, 16 May, 1921 (OL)

League Club	Source	Date Signed	Seasons Played	Apps	Subs	Gls
Preston N.E.	Albion Rov.	12.47	47	12	-	2
New Brighton	Tr	07.48	48-49	45	-	7
Carlisle U.	Tr	10.49	49	8	-	1
Hartlepool U.	Tr	08.50	50-52	119	-	24

McCLUSKEY, Andrew
Manchester, 29 March, 1951 (WH)

League Club	Source	Date Signed	Seasons Played	Apps	Subs	Gls
Hartlepool U.		09.69	69	4	2	0

McCLUSKEY, George Mc.
Hamilton, 19 September, 1957 Su21-6 (F)

League Club	Source	Date Signed	Seasons Played	Apps	Subs	Gls
Leeds U.	Glasgow Celtic	08.83	83-85	57	16	16

McCLUSKEY, Ronald
Johnstone, 3 November, 1938 (G)

League Club	Source	Date Signed	Seasons Played	Apps	Subs	Gls
Accrington St.	East Fife	11.60	60	4	-	0

McCLUSKIE, James A.
Rossendale, 29 September, 1966 (M)

League Club	Source	Date Signed	Seasons Played	Apps	Subs	Gls
Rochdale	Jnrs	07.84	83-85	14	5	0

McCOIST, Alistair M.
Glasgow, 24 September, 1962 S Yth/Su21-1/S-41 (F)

League Club	Source	Date Signed	Seasons Played	Apps	Subs	Gls
Sunderland	St Johnstone	08.81	81-82	38	18	8

McCOLE, John
Glasgow, 18 September, 1936 (CF)

League Club	Source	Date Signed	Seasons Played	Apps	Subs	Gls
Bradford C.	Falkirk	09.58	58-59	42	-	32
Leeds U.	Tr	09.59	59-61	78	-	45
Bradford C.	Tr	10.61	61-62	46	-	15
Rotherham U.	Tr	12.62	62	14	-	5
Newport Co.	Shelbourne	10.64	64	6	-	2

McCOLL, Duncan
Glasgow, 28 December, 1945 (IF)

League Club	Source	Date Signed	Seasons Played	Apps	Subs	Gls
Barnsley	Partick Th.	01.66	65	5	0	0

McCOLL, Thomas G.
Glasgow, 19 September, 1945 (IF)

League Club	Source	Date Signed	Seasons Played	Apps	Subs	Gls
Colchester U.	Dennistoun	06.63	63-64	11	-	2
Chelsea	Tr	12.64				

McCONNELL, Peter
Stockport, 3 March, 1937 (WH)

League Club	Source	Date Signed	Seasons Played	Apps	Subs	Gls
Leeds U.	Jnrs	03.54	58-61	49	-	4
Carlisle U.	Tr	08.62	62-68	272	1	27
Bradford C.	Tr	07.69	69-70	76	3	0

McCONVILLE, Ian J.
Doncaster, 1 May, 1959 (W)

League Club	Source	Date Signed	Seasons Played	Apps	Subs	Gls
Doncaster Rov.	App	04.77	75-77	9	2	1

McCORD, Brian J.
Derby, 24 August, 1968 (RB/W)

League Club	Source	Date Signed	Seasons Played	Apps	Subs	Gls
Derby Co.	App	06.87	87-89	3	2	0
Barnsley	L	11.89	89	5	0	0
Barnsley	Tr	03.90	89-91	35	3	2

McCORKINDALE, John
Campbeltown, 10 August, 1934 (W)

League Club	Source	Date Signed	Seasons Played	Apps	Subs	Gls
Gillingham	Tonbridge	10.57	57	8	-	0

McCORMACK, J. Cecil
Newcastle, 15 February, 1922 (CF)

League Club	Source	Date Signed	Seasons Played	Apps	Subs	Gls
Gateshead		09.41	46	27	-	19
Middlesbrough	Tr	04.47	46-48	37	-	15
Barnsley	Chelmsford C.	07.50	50-51	50	-	43
Notts Co.	Tr	11.51	51-55	82	-	35

McCORMACK, Frank A.
Glasgow, 25 September, 1924 (HB)

League Club	Source	Date Signed	Seasons Played	Apps	Subs	Gls
Oldham Ath.	Clyde	11.49	49	14	-	0

McCORMACK, Murdoch
Glasgow, 7 October, 1920 Died 1951 (OL)

League Club	Source	Date Signed	Seasons Played	Apps	Subs	Gls
Manchester C.	Glasgow Rangers	04.47	46	1	-	0
Blackpool	Tr	07.47	47	12	-	3
Crewe Alex.	Tr	07.48	48	31	-	3

McCORMICK, David
Halifax, 3 November, 1920 (G)

League Club	Source	Date Signed	Seasons Played	Apps	Subs	Gls
Halifax T.		10.47	47-54	117	-	0

McCORMICK, David J.
Southwark, 29 December, 1951 (F)

League Club	Source	Date Signed	Seasons Played	Apps	Subs	Gls
Peterborough U.	Biggleswade	08.75	75	1	0	0

McCORMICK, Henry (Harry)
Coleraine (NI), 10 January, 1924 IR Lge (OL)

League Club	Source	Date Signed	Seasons Played	Apps	Subs	Gls
Derby Co.	Coleraine	10.46	46-47	7	-	0
Everton	Tr	07.48	48	4	-	0

McCORMICK, James
Rotherham, 26 September, 1912 Died 1968 (IF)

League Club	Source	Date Signed	Seasons Played	Apps	Subs	Gls
Rotherham U.		03.31	30-31	19	-	2
Chesterfield	Tr	08.32	32	14	-	2
Tottenham H.	Tr	03.33	32-38	137	-	26
Fulham	Tr	04.46	46	9	-	2
Lincoln C.	Tr	08.47	47-48	64	-	6
Crystal Palace	Tr	02.49	48	13	-	2

McCORMICK, James
Rotherham, 1 April, 1937

League Club	Source	Date Signed	Seasons Played	Apps	Subs	Gls
Sheffield U.		10.56	56	1	-	0
Rotherham U.	Tr	07.57				

McCORMICK, John
Glasgow, 18 July, 1936 (CH)

League Club	Source	Date Signed	Seasons Played	Apps	Subs	Gls
Crystal Palace	Aberdeen	05.66	66-72	194	0	6

McCORMICK, Joseph M.
Holywell, 15 July, 1916 (RH)

League Club	Source	Date Signed	Seasons Played	Apps	Subs	Gls
Bolton W.		10.37				
Rochdale		05.46	46-47	66	-	0
Scunthorpe U.	Boston U.	(N/L)	50	7	-	0

McCOURT, Frank J.
Portadown (NI), 9 December, 1925 NI-6 (WH)

League Club	Source	Date Signed	Seasons Played	Apps	Subs	Gls
Bristol Rov.	Shamrock Rov.	11.45				
Bristol Rov.	Shamrock Rov.	03.49	49	32	-	1
Manchester C.	Tr	12.50	50-53	61	-	4
Colchester U.	Tr	06.54	54	12	-	0

McCOY, Michael
Sunderland, 29 January, 1934 (F)

League Club	Source	Date Signed	Seasons Played	Apps	Subs	Gls
Burnley		10.53				
Southport	Tr	07.57	57	5	-	1

McCOY, Peter J.
Wingate (Dm), 31 July, 1923 (FB)

League Club	Source	Date Signed	Seasons Played	Apps	Subs	Gls
Newcastle U.	Shotton Jnrs	09.46				
Norwich C.	Tr	02.49	48	6	-	0

McCOY, Wilfred
Birmingham, 4 March, 1921 (CH)

League Club	Source	Date Signed	Seasons Played	Apps	Subs	Gls
Portsmouth		08.46	46-47	18	-	0
Northampton T.	Tr	12.48	48-49	61	-	0
Brighton & H.A.	Tr	01.51	50-53	112	-	0

McCRAE, Alexander
Stoneyburn, 2 January, 1920 (IF)

League Club	Source	Date Signed	Seasons Played	Apps	Subs	Gls
Charlton Ath.	Hearts	05.47	47-48	43	-	8
Middlesbrough	Tr	11.48	48-52	122	-	47

McCRAE, Ian
West Ham, 1 October, 1935 (D)

League Club	Source	Date Signed	Seasons Played	Apps	Subs	Gls
Accrington St.		07.57	59-60	14	-	0

McCREADIE, Edward

League Club	Source	Date Signed	Seasons Played	Apps	Subs	Gls
Walsall		09.53	53	4	-	0

McCREADIE, Edward G.
Glasgow, 15 April, 1940 S-23 (FB)

League Club	Source	Date Signed	Seasons Played	Apps	Subs	Gls
Chelsea	East Stirling	04.62	62-73	327	4	4

McCREADIE, W. Harvey
Stranraer, 1 October, 1942 (CF)

League Club	Source	Date Signed	Seasons Played	Apps	Subs	Gls
Accrington St.	Jnrs	10.59	58-59	28	-	10
Luton T.	Tr	01.60	59	1	-	0
Wrexham	Tr	11.60	60	10	-	2

McCREADIE, Thomas S.
Port Glasgow, 28 September, 1923

League Club	Source	Date Signed	Seasons Played	Apps	Subs	Gls
Hartlepool U.		08.49	49	34	-	3
Lincoln C.	Tr	08.50	50	11	-	1

McCREADY, Bernard T.
Dumbarton, 23 April, 1937 (G)

League Club	Source	Date Signed	Seasons Played	Apps	Subs	Gls
Rochdale	Glasgow Celtic	05.57	57-58	29	-	0
Oldham Ath.	Tr	03.59	58	7	-	0

McCREADY, Thomas
Johnstone, 19 October, 1943 S Sch (FB)

League Club	Source	Date Signed	Seasons Played	Apps	Subs	Gls
Watford	Hibernian	07.63	63	1	-	0

McCREDIE, Norman J.
Glasgow, 17 May, 1928 (FB)

League Club	Source	Date Signed	Seasons Played	Apps	Subs	Gls
Accrington St.	Partick Th.	05.55	55-56	51	-	3
Southport	Tr	08.57	57	33	-	2
Barrow	Tr	08.58	58	23	-	0

McCREERY, David
Belfast, 16 September, 1957 NI Sch/NIu21-1/NI-67 (M)

League Club	Source	Date Signed	Seasons Played	Apps	Subs	Gls
Manchester U.	App	10.74	74-78	48	39	7
Queens Park R.	Tr	08.79	79-80	56	1	4
Newcastle U.	Tulsa (USA)	10.82	82-88	237	6	2
Hartlepool U.	Hearts	08.91	91	27	3	0

McCREESH, Andrew
Billingham, 8 September, 1962 (FB)

League Club	Source	Date Signed	Seasons Played	Apps	Subs	Gls
Middlesbrough	App	09.80	81	2	0	0

McCRINDLE, William
Kilmarnock, 28 July, 1923 Died 1982 (IF)

League Club	Source	Date Signed	Seasons Played	Apps	Subs	Gls
Newport Co.	Pollok Jnrs	12.48	48	2	-	0

McCROHAN, Roy
Reading, 22 September, 1930 (WH)

League Club	Source	Date Signed	Seasons Played	Apps	Subs	Gls
Reading	Jnrs	01.49	49-50	4	-	1
Norwich C.	Tr	08.51	51-61	385	-	20
Colchester U.	Tr	09.62	62-63	62	-	5
Bristol Rov.	Tr	08.64	64	10	-	1

McCRORY, Samuel
Belfast, 11 October, 1924 NI'B'-1/NI-1 (CF)

League Club	Source	Date Signed	Seasons Played	Apps	Subs	Gls
Swansea C.	Linfield	10.46	46-49	103	-	46
Ipswich T.	Tr	03.50	49-51	97	-	39
Plymouth Arg.	Tr	08.52	52-54	50	-	11
Southend U.	Tr	06.55	55-59	205	-	90

McCRYSTAL, Dennis
Welwyn Garden City, 13 January, 1932 (G)

League Club	Source	Date Signed	Seasons Played	Apps	Subs	Gls
Watford	Kingsway Y.C.	03.50	50	1	-	0

McCUBBIN, Robert
Kilmarnock, 13 February, 1943 (OR)

League Club	Source	Date Signed	Seasons Played	Apps	Subs	Gls
Hartlepool U.	Ayr U.	06.63	63	2	-	0

McCUE, Alexander B.
Greenock, 25 November, 1927 (W)

League Club	Source	Date Signed	Seasons Played	Apps	Subs	Gls
Carlisle U.	Falkirk	10.50	50	32	-	11
Grimsby T.	Tr	07.51	51-52	37	-	15
Shrewsbury T.	Tr	05.53	53-55	91	-	28

McCUE, John W.
Stoke, 22 August, 1922 (FB)

League Club	Source	Date Signed	Seasons Played	Apps	Subs	Gls
Stoke C.	Jnrs	04.40	46-59	502	-	2
Oldham Ath.	Tr	09.60	60-61	56	-	0

McCULLOCH, Adam B.
Crossford, 4 June, 1920 (CF)

League Club	Source	Date Signed	Seasons Played	Apps	Subs	Gls
Northampton T.	Third Lanark	06.49	49-51	89	-	38
Shrewsbury T.	Tr	01.52	51-52	46	-	17
Aldershot	Tr	02.53	52-54	78	-	33

McCULLOCH, Andrew
Northampton, 3 January, 1950 (F)

League Club	Source	Date Signed	Seasons Played	Apps	Subs	Gls
Queens Park R.	Walton & Hersham	10.70	70-72	30	12	10
Cardiff C.	Tr	10.72	72-73	58	0	24
Oxford U.	Tr	07.74	74-75	41	0	9
Brentford	Tr	03.76	75-78	115	2	48
Sheffield Wed.	Tr	06.79	79-82	122	3	44
Crystal Palace	Tr	08.83	83	25	0	3
Aldershot	Tr	11.84	84	16	0	2

McCULLOCH, David
Hamilton, 5 October, 1911 Died 1979 SF Lge/S-7 (CF)

League Club	Source	Date Signed	Seasons Played	Apps	Subs	Gls
Brentford	Hearts	11.35	35-38	116	-	85
Derby Co.	Tr	10.38	38	31	-	16
Leicester C.	Tr	08.46	46	4	-	2

McCULLOCH, Iain
Kilmarnock, 28 December, 1954 Su21-2 (W)

League Club	Source	Date Signed	Seasons Played	Apps	Subs	Gls
Notts Co.	Kilmarnock	04.78	78-83	212	3	51

McCULLOCH, Thomas
Dumfries, 25 December, 1921 (OR)

League Club	Source	Date Signed	Seasons Played	Apps	Subs	Gls
Northampton T.	Queen of South	12.49	49	2	-	0
Bradford C.	Tr	01.51	50-53	109	-	9
Crewe Alex.	Tr	07.54	54	28	-	5

McCULLOCH, William D.
Edinburgh, 25 June, 1922 Died 1961 (FB)

League Club	Source	Date Signed	Seasons Played	Apps	Subs	Gls
Stockport Co.		03.44	46-53	309	-	4
Rochdale	Tr	07.54	54-57	140	-	2

McCULLOUGH, Paul J.
Birmingham, 26 October, 1959 (G)

League Club	Source	Date Signed	Seasons Played	Apps	Subs	Gls
Reading	Brixham	09.78				
Brentford	Dawlish	07.80	80	7	0	0

McCULLOUGH, William J.
Carrickfergus (NI), 27 July, 1935 NI-10 (LB)

League Club	Source	Date Signed	Seasons Played	Apps	Subs	Gls
Arsenal	Portadown	09.58	58-65	253	0	4
Millwall	Tr	08.66	66	17	2	0

McCUNNELL, Barry
Hull, 20 September, 1948 (OL)

League Club	Source	Date Signed	Seasons Played	Apps	Subs	Gls
Hull C.	Endike Jnrs	10.66	69	0	1	0

McCURDY, Colin C.
Belfast, 18 July, 1954 NI-1 (F)

League Club	Source	Date Signed	Seasons Played	Apps	Subs	Gls
Fulham	Larne T.	11.77	77	1	0	0

McCURLEY, Kevin
Consett, 2 April, 1926 (CF)

League Club	Source	Date Signed	Seasons Played	Apps	Subs	Gls
Brighton & H.A.		09.48	48-50	21	-	9
Liverpool	Tr	06.51				
Colchester U.	Tr	03.52	51-59	224	-	91
Oldham Ath.	Tr	06.60	60	1	-	0

McCUSKER, James
Maghera (NI), 27 December, 1939 (G)

League Club	Source	Date Signed	Seasons Played	Apps	Subs	Gls
Bradford C.	Jnrs	02.57	58	7	-	0
Stockport Co.	Tr	08.59	59	2	-	0

McDERMENT, William S.
Paisley, 5 January, 1943 (WH)

League Club	Source	Date Signed	Seasons Played	Apps	Subs	Gls
Leicester C.	Johnstone Burgh	05.61	62-66	20	3	1
Luton T.	Tr	07.67	67-68	28	12	1
Notts Co.	Tr	05.69	69	2	1	0

McDERMOTT, Brian J.
Slough, 8 April, 1961 E Yth (W)

League Club	Source	Date Signed	Seasons Played	Apps	Subs	Gls
Arsenal	App	02.79	78-83	38	23	12
Fulham	L	03.83	82	0	3	0
Oxford U.	Tr	12.84	84-86	16	8	2
Huddersfield T.	L	10.86	86	4	0	1
Cardiff C.	Tr	08.87	87-88	49	2	8
Exeter C.	Tr	02.89	88-90	65	3	4

McDERMOTT, James
Earlestown, 25 May, 1932 (F)

League Club	Source	Date Signed	Seasons Played	Apps	Subs	Gls
Southport	Crompton Rec.	07.55	55-58	157	-	30

McDERMOTT, John
Middlesbrough, 3 February, 1969 (RB)

League Club	Source	Date Signed	Seasons Played	Apps	Subs	Gls
Grimsby T.	YT	06.87	86-91	191	9	2

McDERMOTT, John C.
Manchester, 14 October, 1959 (M)

League Club	Source	Date Signed	Seasons Played	Apps	Subs	Gls
Manchester U.	App	10.76				
Rochdale	Wigan Ath.	09.79	79	5	3	1

McDERMOTT, Maurice P.
Pelton Fell, 21 February, 1923 (LB)

League Club	Source	Date Signed	Seasons Played	Apps	Subs	Gls
Sunderland	Consett	11.45				
York C.	Consett	07.47	47	7	-	0

McDERMOTT, Steven
Gateshead, 30 December, 1964 (F)

League Club	Source	Date Signed	Seasons Played	Apps	Subs	Gls
Darlington	Sunderland (App)	02.83	82	0	2	0

McDERMOTT, Terence
Kirkby, 8 December, 1951 Eu23-1/E'B'/E-25 (M)

League Club	Source	Date Signed	Seasons Played	Apps	Subs	Gls
Bury	App	10.69	69-72	83	7	8
Newcastle U.	Tr	02.73	72-74	55	1	6
Liverpool	Tr	11.74	74-82	221	11	54
Newcastle U.	Tr	09.82	82-83	74	0	12

McDEVITT, Kenneth R.
Liverpool, 4 March, 1929 (IF)

League Club	Source	Date Signed	Seasons Played	Apps	Subs	Gls
Tranmere Rov.		01.50	51-59	237	-	39

McDONAGH, James M. (Seamus)
Rotherham, 6 October, 1952 E Yth/IR-24 (G)

League Club	Source	Date Signed	Seasons Played	Apps	Subs	Gls
Rotherham U.	App	10.70	70-75	121	0	0
Bolton W.	Tr	08.76	76-79	161	0	0
Everton	Tr	07.80	80	40	0	0
Bolton W.	Tr	08.81	81-82	81	0	1
Notts Co.	Tr	07.83	83-84	35	0	0
Birmingham C.	L	09.84	84	1	0	0
Gillingham	L	03.85	84	10	0	0
Sunderland	L	08.85	85	7	0	0
Scarborough	Wichita (USA)	11.87	87	9	0	0
Huddersfield T.	L	01.88	87	6	0	0
Charlton Ath.	Tr	03.88				

McDONALD, Alan
Belfast, 12 October, 1963 NI Sch/NI Yth/NI-33 (CD)

League Club	Source	Date Signed	Seasons Played	Apps	Subs	Gls
Queens Park R.	App	09.81	83-91	242	5	8
Charlton Ath.	L	03.83	82	9	0	0

McDONALD, Colin A.
Tottington, 15 October, 1930 EF Lge/E-8 (G)

League Club	Source	Date Signed	Seasons Played	Apps	Subs	Gls
Burnley	Hankshaw St Marys	10.48	53-58	186	-	0

McDONALD, Colin B.
Norwich, 15 May, 1950 (W)

League Club	Source	Date Signed	Seasons Played	Apps	Subs	Gls
Norwich C.	App	07.67	67	4	0	0
Scunthorpe U.	Tr	07.70	70-72	78	8	11

MacDONALD, David A.
Dundee, 9 May, 1931 (G)

League Club	Source	Date Signed	Seasons Played	Apps	Subs	Gls
Crystal Palace	Dundee Violet	03.51	52-54	30	-	0

McDONALD, David H.
Dublin, 2 January, 1971 IR Yth/IRu21-3 (RB)

League Club	Source	Date Signed	Seasons Played	Apps	Subs	Gls
Tottenham H.	YT	07.88				
Gillingham	L	09.90	90	10	0	0

MacDONALD, Garry
Middlesbrough, 26 March, 1962 (F)

League Club	Source	Date Signed	Seasons Played	Apps	Subs	Gls
Middlesbrough	App	03.80	80-83	40	13	5
Carlisle U.	Tr	07.84	84	7	2	0
Darlington	Tr	10.84	84-88	153	9	35
Stockport Co.	Tr	07.89	89	1	0	0
Hartlepool U.	Tr	12.89	89-90	10	8	1

McDONALD, Gary
Sunderland, 20 November, 1969 (F)

League Club	Source	Date Signed	Seasons Played	Apps	Subs	Gls
Mansfield T.	Ipswich T. (YT)	08.89	89	1	1	0

McDONALD, Gavin J.
Salford, 6 October, 1970 (F)

League Club	Source	Date Signed	Seasons Played	Apps	Subs	Gls
Chesterfield (YT)	YT	08.87	88	5	7	1

McDONALD, Gerard
Milnthorpe, 3 December, 1952 (M)

League Club	Source	Date Signed	Seasons Played	Apps	Subs	Gls
Blackburn Rov.	App	12.70	71	19	2	2
Halifax T.	Tr	08.73	73	10	3	0

McDONALD, Gordon
Hampstead, 7 February, 1932 (LB)

League Club	Source	Date Signed	Seasons Played	Apps	Subs	Gls
Crystal Palace	Eastbourne	12.54	54-56	13	-	0
Swindon T.	Tr	07.57	57	10	-	0

McDONALD, Harold
Salford, 11 September, 1926 (FB)

League Club	Source	Date Signed	Seasons Played	Apps	Subs	Gls
Crystal Palace	Ashton U.	09.50	50-54	140	-	1

McDONALD, Ian
Inverness, 5 February, 1951 (M)

League Club	Source	Date Signed	Seasons Played	Apps	Subs	Gls
Wolverhampton W.	Jnrs	08.68				
Darlington	Tr	09.70	70	21	4	3

McDONALD, Ian C.
Barrow, 10 May, 1953 (M)

League Club	Source	Date Signed	Seasons Played	Apps	Subs	Gls
Barrow	App	05.71	70-71	30	5	2
Workington	Tr	02.73	72-73	42	0	4
Liverpool	Tr	01.74				
Colchester U.	L	02.75	74	5	0	2
Mansfield T.	Tr	07.75	75-76	47	9	4
York C.	Tr	11.77	77-81	175	0	29
Aldershot	Tr	11.81	81-88	340	0	49

McDONALD, Ian C. A.
West Germany, 30 August, 1953 (CD)

League Club	Source	Date Signed	Seasons Played	Apps	Subs	Gls
Carlisle U.	St Johnstone	05.76	76-80	186	1	7

McDONALD, James
Greenock, 18 April, 1932 (W)

League Club	Source	Date Signed	Seasons Played	Apps	Subs	Gls
Gillingham	Dumbarton	08.56	56	1	-	0

MacDONALD, John
Liverpool, 1 September, 1921 (FB)

League Club	Source	Date Signed	Seasons Played	Apps	Subs	Gls
Liverpool		08.44				
Tranmere Rov.	Tr	06.49	49-51	89	-	0

MacDONALD, John
Glasgow, 15 April, 1961 S Sch/S Yth/Su21-8 (F)

League Club	Source	Date Signed	Seasons Played	Apps	Subs	Gls
Charlton Ath.	Hong Kong	09.86	86	2	0	0
Barnsley	Tr	11.86	86-89	87	7	20
Scarborough	Tr	11.89	89-90	39	1	6

McDONALD, John C.
Maltby, 27 August, 1921 (OL)

League Club	Source	Date Signed	Seasons Played	Apps	Subs	Gls
Wolverhampton W.	Jnrs	09.38	38	2	-	0
Bournemouth	Tr	05.39	46-47	80	-	35
Fulham	Tr	06.48	48-51	75	-	19
Southampton	Tr	08.52	52	16	-	4
Southend U.	Tr	05.53	53-54	28	-	6

MacDONALD, John S.
Edinburgh, 23 September, 1922

League Club	Source	Date Signed	Seasons Played	Apps	Subs	Gls
Notts Co.	Carshalton Ath.	08.48	48	1	-	0
Queens Park R.	Tr	03.49				

McDONALD, Joseph
Hamilton, 10 February, 1929 S-2 (LB)

League Club	Source	Date Signed	Seasons Played	Apps	Subs	Gls
Sunderland	Falkirk	03.54	53-57	137	-	1
Nottingham F.	Tr	07.58	58-60	109	-	0

MacDONALD, Kevin D.
Inverness, 22 November, 1960 (M)

League Club	Source	Date Signed	Seasons Played	Apps	Subs	Gls
Leicester C.	Inverness Caledonians	05.80	80-84	133	5	8
Liverpool	Tr	11.84	84-88	29	11	1
Leicester C.	L	12.87	87	3	0	0
Coventry C.	Tr	07.89	89-90	26	5	0
Cardiff C.	L	03.91	90	8	0	0
Walsall	Tr	07.91	91	20	0	3

MacDONALD, Leslie
Newcastle, 2 April, 1934 (LB)

League Club	Source	Date Signed	Seasons Played	Apps	Subs	Gls
Portsmouth		05.55				
Exeter C.	Tr	06.57	57-65	294	0	0

McDONALD, Malcolm
Glasgow, 26 October, 1913 (RB)

League Club	Source	Date Signed	Seasons Played	Apps	Subs	Gls
Brentford	Kilmarnock	10.46	46-48	86	-	1

MacDONALD, Malcolm I.
Fulham, 7 January, 1950 Eu23-4/EF Lge/E-14 (F)

League Club	Source	Date Signed	Seasons Played	Apps	Subs	Gls
Fulham	Tonbridge	08.68	68	10	3	5
Luton T.	Tr	07.69	69-70	88	0	49
Newcastle U.	Tr	05.71	71-75	187	0	95
Arsenal	Tr	08.76	76-78	84	0	42

MacDONALD, Martin
Ballymena (NI), 5 September, 1931 (FB)

League Club	Source	Date Signed	Seasons Played	Apps	Subs	Gls
Portsmouth	Jnrs	11.48				
Bournemouth	Tr	11.51	52-55	51	-	1

McDONALD, Michael F.
Glasgow, 8 November, 1950 (G)

League Club	Source	Date Signed	Seasons Played	Apps	Subs	Gls
Stoke C.	Clydebank	10.72	72-73	5	0	0

McDONALD, Neil J.
Barrow, 27 May, 1954 (W)

League Club	Source	Date Signed	Seasons Played	Apps	Subs	Gls
Workington (N/C)		03.77	76	5	1	0

McDONALD, Neil R.
Wallsend, 2 November, 1965 E Sch/E Yth/Eu21-5 (RB/M)

League Club	Source	Date Signed	Seasons Played	Apps	Subs	Gls
Newcastle U.	App	02.83	82-87	163	17	24
Everton	Tr	08.88	88-91	76	14	4
Oldham Ath.	Tr	10.91	91	14	3	1

McDONALD, Richard
Paisley, 18 December, 1933 (CF)

League Club	Source	Date Signed	Seasons Played	Apps	Subs	Gls
Barnsley	Saltcoats Vic.	12.57	58	1	-	0

MacDONALD, Robert
Kilpatrick, 26 October, 1935 (FB)

League Club	Source	Date Signed	Seasons Played	Apps	Subs	Gls
Manchester C.	Vale of Leven	09.56	61	5	-	0
Bournemouth	Tr	09.63	63	1	-	0

McDONALD, Robert R.
Hull, 22 January, 1959 (F)

League Club	Source	Date Signed	Seasons Played	Apps	Subs	Gls
Hull C.	App	01.77	76-79	17	8	2
Newcastle U.	P.S.V. Eindhoven (Neth)	11.88	88	6	4	1

McDONALD, Robert W.
Aberdeen, 13 April, 1955 (LB)

League Club	Source	Date Signed	Seasons Played	Apps	Subs	Gls
Aston Villa	App	09.72	72-75	33	6	3
Coventry C.	Tr	08.76	76-80	161	0	14
Manchester C.	Tr	10.80	80-82	96	0	11
Oxford U.	Tr	09.83	83-86	93	1	14
Leeds U.	Tr	02.87	86-87	18	0	1
Wolverhampton W.	L	02.88	87	6	0	0

McDONALD, Rodney
Westminster, 20 March, 1967 (F)

League Club	Source	Date Signed	Seasons Played	Apps	Subs	Gls
Walsall	Colne Dynamoes	08.90	90-91	69	6	23

McDONALD, Roger
Glasgow, 2 February, 1933 (FB)

League Club	Source	Date Signed	Seasons Played	Apps	Subs	Gls
Mansfield T.	St Mirren	03.55	54-55	14	-	0

McDONALD, Terence
Belfast, 5 February, 1947 (FB)

League Club	Source	Date Signed	Seasons Played	Apps	Subs	Gls
Middlesbrough	Jnrs	02.64				
Southport	Tr	07.65	65-66	33	0	1
Barrow	Tr	07.67	67-68	35	1	0

Malcolm MacDonald (Fulham, Luton Town, Newcastle United, Arsenal & England)

McDONALD, Terence J.
Plaistow, 12 November, 1938 E Yth (OL)

League Club	Source	Date Signed	Seasons Played	Apps	Subs	Gls
West Ham U.	Jnrs	04.56				
Leyton Orient	Tr	07.59	59-64	152	-	23
Reading	Tr	05.65	65	13	0	2

McDONALD, Thomas
Glasgow, 24 May, 1930 S'B'-1 (OR)

League Club	Source	Date Signed	Seasons Played	Apps	Subs	Gls
Wolverhampton W.	Hibernian	04.54	54-55	5	-	1
Leicester C.	Tr	07.56	56-59	113	-	27

McDONALD, William L.
Longriggend, 30 August, 1918 (WH)

League Club	Source	Date Signed	Seasons Played	Apps	Subs	Gls
Carlisle U.	Airdrieonians	08.46	46	3	-	0

McDONNELL, Charles
Birkenhead, 15 July, 1936 (IF)

League Club	Source	Date Signed	Seasons Played	Apps	Subs	Gls
Tranmere Rov.		09.57	57-60	67	-	25
Stockport Co.	Tr	06.61	61-63	85	-	32
Tranmere Rov.	Tr	10.63	63-64	45	-	25
Southport	Tr	07.65	65	10	0	1

McDONNELL, Martin
Newton-le-Willows, 27 April, 1924 Died 1988 (CH)

League Club	Source	Date Signed	Seasons Played	Apps	Subs	Gls
Everton		08.42				
Southport	Tr	08.46	46	38	-	0
Birmingham C.	Tr	05.47	47-49	32	-	0
Coventry C.	Tr	10.49	49-54	232	-	0
Derby Co.	Tr	07.55	55-57	93	-	0
Crewe Alex.	Tr	07.58	58	17	-	0

McDONNELL, Peter A.
Kendal, 11 June, 1953 (G)

League Club	Source	Date Signed	Seasons Played	Apps	Subs	Gls
Bury	Netherfield	10.73	73	1	0	0
Liverpool	Tr	08.74				
Oldham Ath.	Tr	08.78	78-81	137	0	0

McDONOUGH, Darren K.
Antwerp (Bel), 7 November, 1962 (M/CD)

League Club	Source	Date Signed	Seasons Played	Apps	Subs	Gls
Oldham Ath.	App	01.80	80-86	178	5	14
Luton T.	Tr	09.86	86-91	88	17	5
Newcastle U.	Tr	03.92	91	2	1	0

McDONOUGH, Roy
Solihull, 16 October, 1958 (F)

League Club	Source	Date Signed	Seasons Played	Apps	Subs	Gls
Birmingham C.	App	10.76	76	2	0	1
Walsall	Tr	09.78	78-80	76	6	15
Chelsea	Tr	10.80				
Colchester U.	Tr	02.81	80-82	84	4	24
Southend U.	Tr	08.83	83	22	0	4
Exeter C.	Tr	01.84	83-84	19	1	1
Cambridge U.	Tr	10.84	84	30	2	5
Southend U.	Tr	08.85	85-89	163	23	30

McDOUGALL, Edward J. (Ted)
Inverness, 8 January, 1947 S-7 (F)

League Club	Source	Date Signed	Seasons Played	Apps	Subs	Gls
Liverpool	I.C.I. Recs (Widnes)	01.66				
York C.	Tr	07.67	67-68	84	0	34
Bournemouth	Tr	07.69	69-72	146	0	103
Manchester U.	Tr	09.72	72	18	0	5
West Ham U.	Tr	03.73	72-73	24	0	5
Norwich C.	Tr	12.73	73-76	112	0	51
Southampton	Tr	09.76	76-78	86	0	42
Bournemouth	Tr	11.78	78-79	51	1	16
Blackpool	Tr	03.80	79-80	11	2	0

McDOUGALL, Laybourne
Tynemouth, 12 May, 1917 (LB)

League Club	Source	Date Signed	Seasons Played	Apps	Subs	Gls
Carlisle U.		06.37	37	3	-	0
Preston N.E.	Tr	03.38				
Blackpool	Tr	05.39				
Gateshead	Tr	10.46	46-48	60	-	0

McDOWALL, Daniel
Kirkintilloch, 22 May, 1929 (IF)

League Club	Source	Date Signed	Seasons Played	Apps	Subs	Gls
Middlesbrough		02.47				
Workington	Kilmarnock	08.51	51-52	82	-	23
Lincoln C.	Tr	07.53	53	17	-	4
Millwall	Tr	06.54	54-55	10	-	1

McDOWALL, Duncan J.
Paddington, 18 December, 1963 (F)

League Club	Source	Date Signed	Seasons Played	Apps	Subs	Gls
Birmingham C	App	08.81	81	2	0	0

McDOWALL, James C.
Glasgow, 25 October, 1940 (G)

League Club	Source	Date Signed	Seasons Played	Apps	Subs	Gls
Notts Co.	Baillieston	09.59				
Scunthorpe U.	Boston U.	12.61	61	1	-	0

McDOWALL, Kenneth F.
Manchester, 6 May, 1938 (OL)

League Club	Source	Date Signed	Seasons Played	Apps	Subs	Gls
Manchester U.	Rhyl	09.59				
Rochdale	Tr	10.60	60	6	-	0

McDOWALL, Leslie J.
India, 25 October, 1912 Died 1991 (CH)

League Club	Source	Date Signed	Seasons Played	Apps	Subs	Gls
Sunderland	Glentyre Th.	12.32	34-37	13	-	0
Manchester C.	Tr	03.38	37-48	120	-	8
Wrexham	Tr	11.49	49	3	-	0

McDOWELL, John A.
East Ham, 7 September, 1951 E Yth/Eu23-13 (RB)

League Club	Source	Date Signed	Seasons Played	Apps	Subs	Gls
West Ham U.	App	08.69	70-78	243	6	7
Norwich C.	Tr	08.79	79-80	40	1	1

McELHINNEY, Gerard M. A.
Derry (NI), 19 September, 1956 NI-6 (CD)

League Club	Source	Date Signed	Seasons Played	Apps	Subs	Gls
Bolton W.	Distillery	09.80	80-84	107	2	2
Rochdale	L	11.82	82	20	0	1
Plymouth Arg.	Tr	01.85	84-87	90	1	2
Peterborough U.	Tr	08.88	88-90	87	0	1

McELVANEY, David A.
Chesterfield, 3 November, 1954 (M)

League Club	Source	Date Signed	Seasons Played	Apps	Subs	Gls
Chesterfield		10.75	75	4	0	1

McEVOY, M. Andrew
Dublin, 15 July, 1938 IR-17 (IF)

League Club	Source	Date Signed	Seasons Played	Apps	Subs	Gls
Blackburn Rov.	Bray W.	10.56	58-66	183	0	89

McEVOY, Donald W.
Golcar, 3 December, 1928 (CH)

League Club	Source	Date Signed	Seasons Played	Apps	Subs	Gls
Huddersfield T.	Bradley R.	09.47	49-54	148	-	3
Sheffield Wed.	Tr	12.54	54-57	105	-	1
Lincoln C.	Tr	01.59	58-59	23	-	0
Barrow	Tr	07.60	60-61	74	-	1

McEVOY, Richard P.
Gibraltar, 6 August, 1967 IR Yth (M)

League Club	Source	Date Signed	Seasons Played	Apps	Subs	Gls
Luton T.	App	08.85	86	0	1	0
Cambridge U.	L	02.87	86	10	1	1

Ted McDougall (Liverpool, York City, Bournemouth, Manchester United, West Ham United, Norwich City, Southampton, Bournemouth, Blackpool & Scotland)

League Club	Source	Date Signed	Seasons Played	Career Record Apps	Subs	Gls
MacEWAN, James						
Dundee, 22 March, 1929						(OR)
Aston Villa	Raith Rov.	07.59	59-65	143	0	28
Walsall	Tr	08.66	66	10	0	1
McEWAN, Peter M.						
South Africa, 23 May, 1933						(CF)
Luton T.	Pretoria (SA)	02.54	53-55	27	-	15
McEWAN, Stanley						
Wishaw, 8 June, 1957						(CD)
Blackpool	App	07.74	74-81	204	10	24
Exeter C.	Tr	07.82	82-83	65	0	15
Hull C.	Tr	03.84	83-87	113	0	25
Wigan Ath.	Tr	12.87	87-88	26	3	4
Hartlepool U.	Tr	08.89	89	14	0	2
McEWAN, Stephen						
Selkirk, 28 March, 1930						(IF)
Liverpool		07.50				
Accrington St.	Tr	08.51	51	2	-	1
McEWAN, William						
Glasgow, 29 August, 1914						(OR)
Queens Park R.	Petershill	06.38	38-49	96	-	17
Leyton Orient	Tr	02.50	49-50	21	-	3
McEWAN, William J. M.						
Wishaw, 20 June, 1951						(M)
Blackpool	Hibernian	05.73	73	4	0	0
Brighton & H. A.	Tr	02.74	73-74	27	0	3
Chesterfield	Tr	11.74	74-76	79	1	7
Mansfield T.	Tr	01.77	76-77	32	0	3
Peterborough U.	Tr	11.77	77-78	62	1	3
Rotherham U.	Tr	07.79	79-83	86	9	10
McEWEN, Francis K.						
Dublin, 15 February, 1948						(M)
Manchester U.	App	05.65				
Rochdale	Tr	11.66	66-67	17	0	2
McFADDEN, Anthony						
Hexham, 18 May, 1957						(F)
Darlington	Reyrolles	08.81	81-82	44	3	10
McFADZEAN, Clive S.						
Kilmarnock, 11 March, 1958						(F)
Bradford C.	App	03.76	75-76	3	1	2
McFADZEAN, John P.						
Sheffield, 2 April, 1966						(F)
Rotherham U. (App)	App	06.82	83	0	1	0
McFALL, David P.						
Ballymena (NI), 14 March, 1935						(IF)
Aldershot	Sittingbourne	10.58	58	3	-	0
McFARLAND, Roy L.						
Liverpool, 5 April, 1948 Eu23-5/EF Lge/E-28						(CD)
Tranmere Rov.	Jnrs	07.66	66-67	35	0	0
Derby Co.	Tr	08.67	67-80	434	0	44
Bradford C.	Tr	06.81	81-82	40	0	1
Derby Co. (N/C)	Tr	08.83	83	3	5	0
McFARLANE, Andrew A.						
Wolverhampton, 30 November, 1966						(F)
Portsmouth	Cradley T.	11.90	91	0	2	0
McFARLANE, Ian						
Lanarkshire, 26 January, 1933						(FB)
Chelsea	Aberdeen	08.56	56-57	40	-	0
Leicester C.	Tr	05.58	58	1	-	0
McFARLANE, Noel W.						
Bray (Ire), 20 December, 1934						(F)
Manchester U.	Jnrs	04.52	53	1	-	0
McFARLANE, Robert R.						
Bo'ness, 12 October, 1913 Died 1971						(WH)
Arsenal		03.36				
Doncaster Rov.	Tr	05.37	46-47	131	-	4
McFAUL, William S.						
Coleraine (NI), 1 October, 1943 NI Amat/NI-6						(G)
Newcastle U.	Linfield	11.66	66-74	290	0	0
McFEAT, Archibald						
Kincardine, 23 January, 1924						(G)
Torquay U.	Morton	05.48	48	9	-	0
McGAIRY, Thomas						
Glasgow, 25 November, 1927						
Walsall	Dumbarton	08.54	54	7	-	1
McGANN, William T. A.						
Wilmslow, 12 July, 1923						(FB)
Stockport Co.		05.48	49-50	14	-	0
Bournemouth	Tr	07.51				
McGARRIGLE, Dennis						
Luton, 4 November, 1936						(G)
Bristol C.	Gourock Jnrs	02.60				
Crewe Alex.	Tr	06.60	60-61	12	-	0
MacGARRITY, Thomas W.						
Scotstoun, 24 November, 1922						(IF)
Southampton	Morton	11.52	52	5	-	1
McGARRY, Ronald						
Cockermouth, 25 October, 1938						(WH)
Workington		07.60	60	2	-	0
McGARRY, Ronald J.						
Whitehaven, 5 December, 1937						(IF)
Workington	Whitehaven	10.58	58-61	92	-	25
Bolton W.	Tr	02.62	61-62	27	-	7
Newcastle U.	Tr	12.62	62-66	118	3	41
Barrow	Tr	03.67	66-67	30	0	4
Barrow	Australia	09.70	70	14	3	4
McGARRY, William H.						
Stoke, 10 June, 1927 EF Lge/E'B'-1/E-4						(WH)
Port Vale	Northwood Mission	06.45	46-50	146	-	5
Huddersfield T.	Tr	03.51	50-60	363	-	25
Bournemouth	Tr	03.61	60-62	78	-	2
McGARVEY, Scott T.						
Glasgow, 22 April, 1963 Su21-4						(F)
Manchester U.	App	04.80	80-82	13	12	3
Wolverhampton W.	L	03.84	83	13	0	2
Portsmouth	Tr	07.84	84-85	17	6	6
Carlisle U.	L	01.86	85	10	0	3
Carlisle U.	Tr	07.86	86	25	0	8
Grimsby T.	Tr	03.87	86-87	49	1	7
Bristol C.	Tr	09.88	88	20	6	9
Oldham Ath.	Tr	05.89	89	2	2	1
Wigan Ath	L	09.89	89	3	0	0
McGEACHIE, George						
Falkirk, 9 September, 1939						(OL)
Darlington	Dundee	01.64	63-66	119	0	9
McGEACHIE, George						
Calder, 26 October, 1916						(WH)
New Brighton	St Johnstone	07.46	46-47	63	-	4
Leyton Orient	Tr	07.48				
Rochdale	Tr	12.48	48-50	90	-	6
Crystal Palace	Tr	06.51	51	46	-	5
McGEACHY, Joseph						
Glasgow, 21 April, 1920						(OL)
Leyton Orient	Third Lanark	05.48	48-50	74	-	5
Hereford U.	Workington	09.52	52	2	-	1
McGEADY, John T.						
Glasgow, 17 April, 1950						(W)
Sheffield U.	Third Lanark	01.76	75-76	13	3	0
Newport Co.	California (USA)	10.78	78	2	0	0
McGEE, Owen E.						
Middlesbrough, 29 April, 1970						(FB)
Middlesbrough	YT	07.88	89-90	18	3	1
Scarborough	Leicester C. (N/C)	03.92	91	8	0	0
McGEE, Paul						
Dublin, 17 May, 1968 IRu21-3						(W)
Colchester U.	Bohemians	02.89	88	3	0	0
Wimbledon	Tr	03.89	88-91	53	4	9
McGEE, Paul G.						
Dublin, 19 June, 1954 IRu21-2/IR-16						(F)
Queens Park R.	Sligo Rov.	11.77	77-78	31	8	7
Preston N.E.	Tr	10.79	79-81	62	4	13
Burnley	Tr	11.81	81-82	33	1	9

League Club	Source	Date Signed	Seasons Played	Career Record Apps	Subs	Gls

McGEENEY, Patrick M. (Paddy)
Sheffield, 31 October, 1966 (M)

League Club	Source	Date Signed	Seasons Played	Apps	Subs	Gls
Sheffield U.	App	10.84	84-85	15	1	0
Rochdale	L	11.86	86	3	0	0
Chesterfield	Tr	08.87	87-88	45	4	1

McGEORGE, James L.
Sunderland, 8 June, 1945 (W)

League Club	Source	Date Signed	Seasons Played	Apps	Subs	Gls
Leyton Orient	Spennymoor U.	03.64	64-65	16	0	0
Mansfield T.	Tr	07.66	66	5	4	0

McGEOUGH, James
Waterford (Ire.), 14 July, 1946 (M)

League Club	Source	Date Signed	Seasons Played	Apps	Subs	Gls
Lincoln C.	Waterford	06.72	72-74	61	4	0
Hartlepool U.	L	03.73	72	1	1	0

McGETTIGAN, John A.
Motherwell, 28 November, 1945 (OL)

League Club	Source	Date Signed	Seasons Played	Apps	Subs	Gls
Workington		03.68	67-68	13	1	0

McGETTIGAN, Lawrence
Hackney, 25 December, 1952 (W)

League Club	Source	Date Signed	Seasons Played	Apps	Subs	Gls
Watford	App	11.70	71-74	40	10	3

McGHEE, James W.
Motherwell, 21 August, 1930 (CF)

League Club	Source	Date Signed	Seasons Played	Apps	Subs	Gls
Darlington	Kilmarnock	07.52	52	15	-	4
Newport Co.	Barry T.	05.54	54	10	-	1

McGHEE, Mark E.
Glasgow, 25 May, 1957 Su21-1/S-4 (F)

League Club	Source	Date Signed	Seasons Played	Apps	Subs	Gls
Newcastle U.	Morton	12.77	77-78	21	7	5
Newcastle U.	Glasgow Celtic	08.89	89-90	63	4	24
Reading	Tr	05.91	91	23	9	5

McGHEE, Thomas E.
Manchester, 10 May, 1929 E Amat/E'B'-1 (FB)

League Club	Source	Date Signed	Seasons Played	Apps	Subs	Gls
Portsmouth	Wealdstone	05.54	54-58	136	-	0
Reading	Tr	07.59	59	8	-	0

McGHIE, William L.
Lanarkshire, 19 January, 1958 (M)

League Club	Source	Date Signed	Seasons Played	Apps	Subs	Gls
Leeds U.	App	01.76	76	2	0	1
York C.	Tr	12.79	79-81	39	4	1

McGIBBON, Douglas
Southampton, 24 February, 1919 (CF)

League Club	Source	Date Signed	Seasons Played	Apps	Subs	Gls
Southampton		12.38	38-46	13	-	9
Fulham	Tr	01.47	46-47	42	-	18
Bournemouth	Tr	09.48	48-50	103	-	65

McGIFFORD, Graham L.
Carshalton, 1 May, 1955 (FB)

League Club	Source	Date Signed	Seasons Played	Apps	Subs	Gls
Huddersfield T.	App	07.72	72-75	41	1	0
Hull C.	Tr	05.76	76	1	0	0
Port Vale	Tr	06.77	77	20	0	0

McGILL, Andrew
Glasgow, 11 July, 1924 (WH)

League Club	Source	Date Signed	Seasons Played	Apps	Subs	Gls
Bradford C.	Clyde	11.47	47-51	164	-	24
Scunthorpe U.	Tr	07.52	52-56	182	-	15

McGILL, Austin M.
Dumfries, 29 January, 1935 (F)

League Club	Source	Date Signed	Seasons Played	Apps	Subs	Gls
Carlisle U.	Queen of South	08.59	59	30	-	12

McGILL, James
Kilsyth, 10 March, 1926 (IF)

League Club	Source	Date Signed	Seasons Played	Apps	Subs	Gls
Bury		12.45	46	1	-	0
Derby Co.	Tr	03.47	46-47	8	-	0

McGILL, James H.
Bellshill, 2 October, 1939 (FB)

League Club	Source	Date Signed	Seasons Played	Apps	Subs	Gls
Oldham Ath	Partick Th.	05.59	59	38	-	2
Crewe Alex.	Tr	08.60	60-62	81	-	2
Chester C.	Tr	10.62	62-63	32	-	0
Wrexham	Tr	10.63	63	17	-	1

McGILL, James M.
Glasgow, 27 November, 1946 (M)

League Club	Source	Date Signed	Seasons Played	Apps	Subs	Gls
Arsenal	Possilpark Jnrs	07.65	65-66	6	4	0
Huddersfield T.	Tr	09.67	67-71	161	3	8
Hull C.	Tr	10.71	71-75	141	6	2
Halifax T.	Tr	02.76	75-76	31	1	0

McGILLIVRAY, Findlay
Newtongrange, 19 March, 1940 (FB)

League Club	Source	Date Signed	Seasons Played	Apps	Subs	Gls
Bradford P.A.	Glasgow Rangers	05.66	66	38	1	0

McGINLAY, John
Inverness, 8 April, 1964 (F)

League Club	Source	Date Signed	Seasons Played	Apps	Subs	Gls
Shrewsbury T.	Elgin C.	02.89	88-89	58	2	27
Bury	Tr	07.90	90	16	9	9
Millwall	Tr	03.91	90-91	21	6	8

McGINLAY, Patrick D.
Glasgow, 30 May, 1967 (M)

League Club	Source	Date Signed	Seasons Played	Apps	Subs	Gls
Blackpool		05.85	86	2	10	0

McGINLEY, John
Rowlands Gill, 11 June, 1959 (LW)

League Club	Source	Date Signed	Seasons Played	Apps	Subs	Gls
Sunderland	Gateshead	01.82	81	3	0	0
Lincoln C.	Charleroi (Bel)	09.84	84-86	69	2	11
Rotherham U.	Tr	09.86	86	1	2	0
Hartlepool U.	L	01.87	86	2	0	0
Lincoln C.	Tr	01.87	86-88	36	5	7
Doncaster Rov.	Tr	06.89	89	4	6	0

McGINLEY, William D.
Dumfries, 12 November, 1954 S Sch (W)

League Club	Source	Date Signed	Seasons Played	Apps	Subs	Gls
Leeds U.	App	01.72	72	0	1	0
Huddersfield T.	Tr	09.74	74	11	4	1
Bradford C.	Tr	06.75	75-76	52	8	11
Crewe Alex.	Tr	08.77	77	36	2	2

McGINN, Francis
Cambuslang, 2 March, 1919 (OL)

League Club	Source	Date Signed	Seasons Played	Apps	Subs	Gls
Wrexham		04.47	46	2	-	0
Ipswich T.	Tr	08.48	48	8	-	2

McGINN, William B.
Ardrossan, 2 February, 1943 (FB)

League Club	Source	Date Signed	Seasons Played	Apps	Subs	Gls
Oldham Ath.	Ardrossan Winton	11.63	63-65	37	1	0

McGIVEN, Michael
Newcastle, 7 February, 1951 (CD)

League Club	Source	Date Signed	Seasons Played	Apps	Subs	Gls
Sunderland	Jnrs	07.68	69-73	107	6	9
West Ham U.	Tr	11.73	73-77	46	2	0

McGLASHAN, John
Dundee, 3 June, 1967 (M)

League Club	Source	Date Signed	Seasons Played	Apps	Subs	Gls
Millwall	Montrose	08.90	90-91	9	7	0

McGLEISH, John J.
Airdrie, 9 November, 1951 (W)

League Club	Source	Date Signed	Seasons Played	Apps	Subs	Gls
Northampton T.	Jnrs	11.68	70-72	7	1	0

McGLEN, William
Bedlington, 27 April, 1921 (WH)

League Club	Source	Date Signed	Seasons Played	Apps	Subs	Gls
Manchester U.	Blyth Spartans	05.46	46-51	110	-	2
Lincoln C.	Tr	07.52	52	13	-	0
Oldham Ath.	Tr	02.53	52-55	68	-	3

McGLENNON, Thomas
Whitehaven, 20 October, 1933 (WH)

League Club	Source	Date Signed	Seasons Played	Apps	Subs	Gls
Blackpool	Jnrs	11.50				
Rochdale	Tr	05.57	57-58	61	-	2
Barrow	Burton A.	11.59	59-60	60	-	6

McGOLDRICK, Edward J. P.
Corby, 30 April, 1965 IR-4 (RW)

League Club	Source	Date Signed	Seasons Played	Apps	Subs	Gls
Northampton T.	Nuneaton Bor.	08.86	86-88	97	10	9
Crystal Palace	Tr	01.89	88-91	97	8	3

McGOLDRICK, John
Coatbridge, 23 September, 1963 (RB)

League Club	Source	Date Signed	Seasons Played	Apps	Subs	Gls
Leeds U.	Glasgow Celtic	06.83	83	7	0	0

McGOLDRICK, Thomas J.
Doncaster, 20 September, 1929 (IF)

League Club	Source	Date Signed	Seasons Played	Apps	Subs	Gls
Rotherham U.	Maltby	11.49	51	5	-	2
Chesterfield	Tr	05.53	53-54	36	-	16

McGONIGAL, Robert E.
Cookstown (NI), 2 May, 1942 NI Sch (G)

League Club	Source	Date Signed	Seasons Played	Apps	Subs	Gls
Brighton & H.A.	Glentoran	02.62	62-65	57	0	0

McGORRIGHAN, Frank C.
Easington, 20 November, 1921 (IF)

League Club	Source	Date Signed	Seasons Played	Apps	Subs	Gls
Middlesbrough	Eppleton Colly	04.44				
Carlisle U.	Tr	10.45				
Hull C.	Tr	08.46	46	20	-	1
Blackburn Rov.	Tr	02.47	46-47	5	-	0
Hull C.	Tr	09.47	47	6	-	0
Southport	Tr	08.48	48	4	-	0

McGORRY, Brian P.
Liverpool, 16 April, 1970 (M)

League Club	Source	Date Signed	Seasons Played	Apps	Subs	Gls
Bournemouth	Weymouth	08.91	91	4	4	0

McGOVERN, John P.
Montrose, 28 October, 1949 Su23-2 (M)

League Club	Source	Date Signed	Seasons Played	Apps	Subs	Gls
Hartlepool U.	App	05.67	65-68	69	3	5
Derby Co.	Tr	09.68	68-73	186	4	16
Leeds U.	Tr	08.74	74	4	0	0
Nottingham F.	Tr	02.75	74-81	249	4	6
Bolton W.	Tr	06.82	82-83	16	0	0

McGOVERN, Michael J.
Hayes, 15 February, 1951 (M)

League Club	Source	Date Signed	Seasons Played	Apps	Subs	Gls
Queens Park R.	App	11.68	67-71	10	2	0
Watford	L	08.72	72	4	0	0
Swindon T.	Tr	02.73	72-74	26	4	2
Aldershot	L	03.75	74	6	0	1

McGOVERN, Patrick M.
Edinburgh, 14 May, 1948 (IF)

League Club	Source	Date Signed	Seasons Played	Apps	Subs	Gls
Notts Co.	Royston B.C.	07.67	67	1	2	0

McGOVERN, Simon
Bradford, 25 February, 1965 (M)

League Club	Source	Date Signed	Seasons Played	Apps	Subs	Gls
Bradford C. (N/C)	Jnrs	08.82	82	1	0	0

McGOWAN, Aloysius (Ally)
Whitburn, 22 January, 1930 (FB)

League Club	Source	Date Signed	Seasons Played	Apps	Subs	Gls
Wrexham	St Johnstone	05.53	53-64	408	-	2

McGOWAN, Andrew
Corby, 17 May, 1956 E Yth (M)

League Club	Source	Date Signed	Seasons Played	Apps	Subs	Gls
Northampton T.	Corby T.	06.75	75-77	93	12	15

McGOWAN, Daniel
Dublin, 8 November, 1924 LOI/IR-3 (WH)

League Club	Source	Date Signed	Seasons Played	Apps	Subs	Gls
West Ham U.	Shelbourne	05.48	48-53	81	-	8

McGOWAN, George
Carluke, 30 November, 1943 (CF)

League Club	Source	Date Signed	Seasons Played	Apps	Subs	Gls
Preston N.E.	Wishaw Jnrs	08.62				
Chester C.	Tr	03.63	62-63	18	-	3
Stockport Co.	Tr	09.64	64	5	-	0

McGOWAN, Gerard A.
Kilwinning, 4 August, 1944 (OL)

League Club	Source	Date Signed	Seasons Played	Apps	Subs	Gls
Oldham Ath.	Ardeer Rec.	11.63	65	5	0	1

McGOWAN, James
Cambuslang, 12 January, 1924 Died 1984 (WH)

League Club	Source	Date Signed	Seasons Played	Apps	Subs	Gls
Grimsby T.	Dumbarton	07.46	46-48	34	-	4
Southampton	Tr	03.50	49-57	78	-	9

McGOWAN, James
Glasgow, 31 July, 1939 (OR)

League Club	Source	Date Signed	Seasons Played	Apps	Subs	Gls
Mansfield T.	St Johnstone	06.61	61	3	-	0

McGOWAN, Kenneth J.
Wolverhampton, 13 May, 1920

League Club	Source	Date Signed	Seasons Played	Apps	Subs	Gls
Walsall		10.47	47-48	11	-	4

McGRATH, R. Christopher
Belfast, 29 November, 1954 NI-21 (W)

League Club	Source	Date Signed	Seasons Played	Apps	Subs	Gls
Tottenham H.	App	01.72	73-75	30	8	5
Millwall	L	02.76	75	15	0	3
Manchester U.	Tr	10.76	76-80	12	16	1

McGRATH, Derek B. J.
Dublin, 21 January, 1972 (M)

League Club	Source	Date Signed	Seasons Played	Apps	Subs	Gls
Brighton & H.A.	YT	12.89	89-90	2	4	0

McGRATH, James A.
Belfast, 15 November, 1921 (WH)

League Club	Source	Date Signed	Seasons Played	Apps	Subs	Gls
Barrow		08.45	46	3	-	0

McGRATH, John
Tidworth, 21 May, 1932 (F)

League Club	Source	Date Signed	Seasons Played	Apps	Subs	Gls
Notts Co.		08.53	55-57	54	-	5
Darlington	Tr	05.58	58	25	-	6

McGRATH, John T.
Manchester, 23 August, 1938 Eu23-1/EF Lge (CH)

League Club	Source	Date Signed	Seasons Played	Apps	Subs	Gls
Bury	Bolton W. (Am)	10.55	56-60	148	-	2
Newcastle U.	Tr	02.61	60-67	169	1	2
Southampton	Tr	02.68	67-73	167	1	1
Brighton & H. A.	L	12.72	72	3	0	0

McGRATH, Lloyd A.
Birmingham, 24 February, 1965 E Yth/Eu21-1 (M)

League Club	Source	Date Signed	Seasons Played	Apps	Subs	Gls
Coventry C.	App	12.82	83-91	170	8	4

McGRATH, Martin L.
Hendon, 15 October, 1960 E Sch (M)

League Club	Source	Date Signed	Seasons Played	Apps	Subs	Gls
Southampton	App	10.78	79	0	1	0
Bournemouth	Tr	06.80	80	17	5	0

McGRATH, Michael
Dublin, 7 April, 1936 IR'B'-1/IR-22 (WH)

League Club	Source	Date Signed	Seasons Played	Apps	Subs	Gls
Blackburn Rov.	Home Farm	08.54	55-65	268	0	8
Bradford P.A.	Tr	03.66	65-66	50	0	2

McGRATH, Paul
Ealing, 4 December, 1959 IR-55 (CD/M)

League Club	Source	Date Signed	Seasons Played	Apps	Subs	Gls
Manchester U.	St Patricks Ath.	04.82	82-88	159	4	12
Aston Villa	Tr	07.89	89-91	111	0	2

Paul McGrath (St Patricks, Manchester United, Aston Villa & Republic of Ireland)

McGRAW, Ian
Glasgow, 30 August, 1926 (G)

League Club	Source	Date Signed	Seasons Played	Apps	Subs	Gls
Leicester C.	Arbroath	12.48	48-50	13	-	0

McGREAL, John
Liverpool, 2 June, 1972 (CD)

League Club	Source	Date Signed	Seasons Played	Apps	Subs	Gls
Tranmere Rov.	YT	07.90	91	3	0	0

McGREEVEY, Brian E
Prestwich, 29 September, 1935 (F)

League Club	Source	Date Signed	Seasons Played	Apps	Subs	Gls
Arsenal	Preston N.E. (Am)	03.54				
Stockport Co.	Tr	03.57	56	1	-	0

McGREGOR, Alexander G. P.
Glasgow, 12 November, 1950 (W)

League Club	Source	Date Signed	Seasons Played	Apps	Subs	Gls
Shrewsbury T.	Hibernian	01.75	74-75	46	3	7
Aldershot	Tr	09.76	76-81	168	9	17

MacGREGOR, Colin
Bradford, 13 November, 1940 (OR)

League Club	Source	Date Signed	Seasons Played	Apps	Subs	Gls
Bradford P. A.	Bradford C. (Am)	03.58	58-59	3	-	0

McGREGOR, James P.
Hartlepool, 22 December, 1931 (HB)

League Club	Source	Date Signed	Seasons Played	Apps	Subs	Gls
Hartlepool U.		02.50	52-56	5	-	0

McGREGOR, John R.
Airdrie, 5 January, 1963 (D)

League Club	Source	Date Signed	Seasons Played	Apps	Subs	Gls
Liverpool	Queens Park	06.82				
Leeds U.	L	10.85	85	5	0	0

MacGREGOR, Terence J.
Hartlepool, 24 May, 1938 (WH)

League Club	Source	Date Signed	Seasons Played	Apps	Subs	Gls
Hartlepool U.		12.56	56-62	47	-	2

McGREGOR, William
Paisley, 1 December, 1923 (FB)

League Club	Source	Date Signed	Seasons Played	Apps	Subs	Gls
Leicester C.	Mossdale Y.M.C.A.	04.47	47-51	9	-	0
Mansfield T.	Tr	09.53	53-55	119	-	0

McGRELLIS, Frank
Falkirk, 5 October, 1958 (F)

League Club	Source	Date Signed	Seasons Played	Apps	Subs	Gls
Coventry C.	App	10.76				
Huddersfield T.	L	08.78	78	4	1	0
Hereford U.	Tr	03.79	78-81	80	5	24

McGROARTY, James M.
Derry (NI), 30 August, 1957 (W)

League Club	Source	Date Signed	Seasons Played	Apps	Subs	Gls
Stoke C.	Finn Harps	09.77	77-78	6	1	2

McGROGAN, Hugh
Dumbarton, 1 March, 1957 (W)

League Club	Source	Date Signed	Seasons Played	Apps	Subs	Gls
Oxford U.	App	03.75	74-79	101	25	13
Carlisle U.	Tr	05.80	80	1	1	0

McGRORY, Shaun P.
Coventry, 29 February, 1968 (FB)

League Club	Source	Date Signed	Seasons Played	Apps	Subs	Gls
Coventry C.	YT	07.86				
Burnley	Tr	07.87	87-89	34	12	2

McGROTTY, William
Glasgow, 12 August, 1952 (W)

League Club	Source	Date Signed	Seasons Played	Apps	Subs	Gls
Blackpool	Yoker Ath.	06.70	70-72	2	2	1

McGUCKIN, George K.
Dundee, 11 August, 1938 (HB)

League Club	Source	Date Signed	Seasons Played	Apps	Subs	Gls
Cardiff C.	Dundee Shamrock	12.55	57	4	-	0

McGUCKIN, T. Ian
Middlesbrough, 24 April, 1973 (CD)

League Club	Source	Date Signed	Seasons Played	Apps	Subs	Gls
Hartlepool U.	YT	05.91	91	7	0	0

McGUFFIE, Alwyn S.
Stranraer, 13 April, 1937 (WH)

League Club	Source	Date Signed	Seasons Played	Apps	Subs	Gls
Luton T.	Queen of South	09.54	55-63	79	-	10

McGUGAN, John H.
Airdrie, 12 June, 1939 (CH)

League Club	Source	Date Signed	Seasons Played	Apps	Subs	Gls
Leeds U.	St Mirren	08.60	60	1	-	0
Tranmere Rov.	Tr	02.61	60-61	35	-	0

McGUGAN, Paul J.
Glasgow, 17 July, 1964 (CD)

League Club	Source	Date Signed	Seasons Played	Apps	Subs	Gls
Barnsley	Glasgow Celtic	10.87	87-88	47	2	2
Chesterfield	Tr	01.91	90-91	59	0	4

McGUIGAN, James
Addlewell, 1 March, 1924 Died 1988 (WH)

League Club	Source	Date Signed	Seasons Played	Apps	Subs	Gls
Sunderland	Hamilton Acad.	06.47	47-48	3	-	1
Stockport Co.	Tr	06.49	49-50	43	-	9
Crewe Alex.	Tr	08.50	50-55	207	-	32
Rochdale	Tr	08.56	56-58	70	-	2

McGUIGAN, John J.
Motherwell, 29 October, 1932 (IF)

League Club	Source	Date Signed	Seasons Played	Apps	Subs	Gls
Southend U.	St Mirren	05.55	55-57	126	-	35
Newcastle U.	Tr	07.58	58-61	50	-	15
Scunthorpe U.	Tr	01.62	61-62	57	-	17
Southampton	Tr	08.63	63-64	33	-	8
Swansea C.	Tr	03.65	64-65	27	0	5

McGUIGAN, Thomas
Whitburn, 22 November, 1922 (IF)

League Club	Source	Date Signed	Seasons Played	Apps	Subs	Gls
Hartlepool U.	Ayr U.	08.50	50-57	324	-	76

McGUINNESS, Henry
Saltcoats, 17 February, 1928 (CH)

League Club	Source	Date Signed	Seasons Played	Apps	Subs	Gls
Torquay U.		03.48	49-54	81	-	0

McGUINNESS, Paul E.
Manchester, 2 March, 1966 (M)

League Club	Source	Date Signed	Seasons Played	Apps	Subs	Gls
Manchester U.	Jnrs	07.84				
Crewe Alex.	Tr	08.86	86	11	2	0
Manchester U.		07.89				
Chester C.	Bury (N/C)	07.91	91	3	4	0

McGUINNESS, Robert F.
Motherwell, 29 January, 1954 (F)

League Club	Source	Date Signed	Seasons Played	Apps	Subs	Gls
Portsmouth	Motherwell	07.75	75-76	27	4	3

McGUINNESS, Wilfred
Manchester, 25 October, 1937 E Sch/E Yth/Eu23-4/EF Lge/E-2 (WH)

League Club	Source	Date Signed	Seasons Played	Apps	Subs	Gls
Manchester U.	Jnrs	11.54	55-59	81	-	2

McGUIRE, Bernard P.
Liverpool, 23 November, 1932

League Club	Source	Date Signed	Seasons Played	Apps	Subs	Gls
Shrewsbury T.		07.53	53	2	-	0

McGUIRE, Douglas J.
Bathgate, 6 September, 1967 S Yth (W)

League Club	Source	Date Signed	Seasons Played	Apps	Subs	Gls
Sunderland (L)	Glasgow Celtic	03.88	87	1	0	0
Coventry C.	Tr	08.88	89	1	3	0

McGUIRE, Gary J.
Askern, 30 September, 1938 (G)

League Club	Source	Date Signed	Seasons Played	Apps	Subs	Gls
Torquay U.	Hakoah (Aus)	02.66	65-66	32	0	0

McGUIRE, Michael J.
Blackpool, 4 September, 1952 E Yth (M)

League Club	Source	Date Signed	Seasons Played	Apps	Subs	Gls
Coventry C.	Jnrs	11.69	71-74	60	12	1
Norwich C.	Tr	01.75	74-82	172	10	11
Barnsley	Tr	03.83	82-84	44	3	6
Oldham Ath.	Tr	01.85	84-86	65	4	3

McGUIRE, Reginald A.
Birkenhead, 24 August, 1959 (F)

League Club	Source	Date Signed	Seasons Played	Apps	Subs	Gls
Tranmere Rov. (N/C)		08.82	82	0	4	0

McHALE, John
Oldham, 7 May, 1954 (CH)

League Club	Source	Date Signed	Seasons Played	Apps	Subs	Gls
Reading (Am)	Alton T.	01.75	74	1	0	0

McHALE, J. Kevin
Darfield, 1 October, 1939 E Sch/E Yth (OR)

League Club	Source	Date Signed	Seasons Played	Apps	Subs	Gls
Huddersfield T.	Jnrs	10.56	56-67	345	0	60
Crewe Alex.	Tr	01.68	67-70	116	0	22
Chester C.	Tr	10.70	70-71	61	3	5

McHALE, Raymond
Sheffield, 12 August, 1950 (M)

League Club	Source	Date Signed	Seasons Played	Apps	Subs	Gls
Chesterfield		08.70	71-74	123	1	27
Halifax T	Tr	10.74	74-76	86	0	21
Swindon T.	Tr	09.76	76-79	171	2	32
Brighton & H. A.	Tr	05.80	80	9	2	0
Barnsley	Tr	03.81	80-81	52	1	1
Sheffield U.	Tr	08.82	82-84	66	1	2
Bury	L	02.83	82	6	0	0
Swansea	Tr	01.85	84-85	45	2	1
Rochdale (N/C)	Tr	08.86	86	6	1	0
Scarborough (N/C)	Tr	12.86	87	25	0	3

McHALE, Thomas A.
Liverpool, 3 September, 1951 (FB)

League Club	Source	Date Signed	Seasons Played	Apps	Subs	Gls
Bradford C.	Prescot Cables	09.71	71-72	34	2	0

McHALE, William
East Fife, 9 August, 1929 (IL)

League Club	Source	Date Signed	Seasons Played	Apps	Subs	Gls
Carlisle U.		08.53	53	1	-	0
Halifax T.		03.55	54	3	-	0

McHARD, Archibald
Dumbarton, 10 June, 1934 (W)

League Club	Source	Date Signed	Seasons Played	Apps	Subs	Gls
Bradford P.A.	Clyde	05.59	59-60	27	-	3

McHUGH, Michael B.
Donegal, 3 April, 1971 (M)

League Club	Source	Date Signed	Seasons Played	Apps	Subs	Gls
Bradford C.	Jnrs	12.89	90-91	5	5	0

McILHARGEY, Stephen
Glasgow, 23 August, 1964 (G)

League Club	Source	Date Signed	Seasons Played	Apps	Subs	Gls
Walsall	Blantyre Celtic	07.87				
Blackpool	Tr	08.89	89-91	94	0	0

McILHATTON, John
Ardrossan, 3 January, 1921 Died 1954 (OR)

League Club	Source	Date Signed	Seasons Played	Apps	Subs	Gls
Everton	Albion Rov.	04.46	46-48	55	-	1

McILMOYLE, Hugh
Cambuslang, 29 January, 1940 (CF)

League Club	Source	Date Signed	Seasons Played	Apps	Subs	Gls
Leicester C.	Port Glasgow	08.59	60-61	20	-	5
Rotherham U.	Tr	07.62	62	12	-	4
Carlisle U.	Tr	03.63	62-64	77	-	44
Wolverhampton W.	Tr	10.64	64-66	90	0	35
Bristol C.	Tr	03.67	66-67	20	0	4
Carlisle U.	Tr	09.67	67-69	79	0	30
Middlesbrough	Tr	09.69	69-70	69	1	19
Preston N.E.	Tr	07.71	71-72	59	1	10
Carlisle U.	Morton	07.74	74	15	3	2

McILROY, James
Lisburn (NI), 25 October, 1931 EF Lge/ NI-55 (IF)

League Club	Source	Date Signed	Seasons Played	Apps	Subs	Gls
Burnley	Glentoran	03.50	50-62	439	-	116
Stoke C.	Tr	03.63	62-65	96	2	16
Oldham Ath.	Tr	03.66	65-67	35	4	1

McILROY, Samuel B.
Belfast, 2 August, 1954 NI-88 (M)

League Club	Source	Date Signed	Seasons Played	Apps	Subs	Gls
Manchester U.	App	08.71	71-81	320	22	57
Stoke C.	Tr	02.82	81-84	132	1	14
Manchester C.	Tr	08.85	85	12	0	1
Manchester C.	Orgryte (Swe)	11.86	86	1	0	0
Bury	Tr	03.87	86-87	43	0	6
Bury	V.F.B. Mödling (Aus)	08.88	88-89	52	5	2
Preston N.E.	Tr	02.90	89	20	0	0

McILVENNY, Edward
Glasgow, 21 October, 1924 USA Int (WH)

League Club	Source	Date Signed	Seasons Played	Apps	Subs	Gls
Wrexham		03.47	46-47	7	-	1
Manchester U.	Philadelphia (USA)	08.50	50	2	-	0

McILVENNY, Harold J.
Bradford, 5 October, 1922 E Amat (CF)

League Club	Source	Date Signed	Seasons Played	Apps	Subs	Gls
Bradford P. A. (Am)	Yorkshire Amats	08.46	46-49	43	-	17

McILVENNY, John A.
Hinckley, 2 March, 1930 (OR)

League Club	Source	Date Signed	Seasons Played	Apps	Subs	Gls
West Bromwich A.	Hinckley U.	10.49				
Bristol Rov.	Cheltenham T.	07.52	52-58	80	-	11
Reading	Tr	06.59	59-60	77	-	4

McILVENNY, Patrick D.
Belfast, 11 September, 1924 (OR)

League Club	Source	Date Signed	Seasons Played	Apps	Subs	Gls
Cardiff C.	Merthr Tydfil	05.50				
Brighton & H. A.	Tr	07.51	51-54	61	-	5
Aldershot	Tr	12.55	55-56	17	-	0

McILVENNY, Robert
Belfast, 7 July, 1926 (IF)

League Club	Source	Date Signed	Seasons Played	Apps	Subs	Gls
Oldham Ath.	Merthyr Tydfil	03.50	49-53	139	-	36
Bury	Tr	08.54	54	12	-	1
Southport	Tr	08.55	55-56	77	-	16
Barrow	Tr	07.57	57-58	43	-	11

McILWAINE, Matthew
Glasgow, 20 September, 1920 (WH)

League Club	Source	Date Signed	Seasons Played	Apps	Subs	Gls
Bolton W.	Ayr U.	08.51	52	2	-	0

McILWRAITH, James M.
Troon, 17 April, 1954 (M)

League Club	Source	Date Signed	Seasons Played	Apps	Subs	Gls
Bury	Motherwell	09.75	75-77	80	9	21
Portsmouth	Tr	07.78	78	16	3	2
Bury	Tr	07.79	79	28	1	3
Halifax T.	Tr	10.80	80-81	33	3	6

McINALLY, Alan B.
Ayr, 10 February, 1963 S-8 (F)

League Club	Source	Date Signed	Seasons Played	Apps	Subs	Gls
Aston Villa	Glasgow Celtic	07.87	87-88	50	8	18

McINALLY, Charles
Glasgow, 1 February, 1939 (HB)

League Club	Source	Date Signed	Seasons Played	Apps	Subs	Gls
Brentford	St Rochs	09.58	59	1	-	0

McINALLY, James E.
Glasgow, 19 February, 1964 S Yth (FB)

League Club	Source	Date Signed	Seasons Played	Apps	Subs	Gls
Nottingham F.	Glasgow Celtic	06.84	84-85	36	0	0
Coventry C.	Tr	01.86	85	5	0	0

McINALLY, John S.
Gatehouse of Fleet, 26 September, 1951 S Sch (G)

League Club	Source	Date Signed	Seasons Played	Apps	Subs	Gls
Manchester U.	Jnrs	03.69				
Lincoln C.	Tr	08.70	70-71	22	0	0
Colchester U.	Tr	11.72	72	27	0	0

McINCH, James
Glasgow, 27 June, 1953 (F)

League Club	Source	Date Signed	Seasons Played	Apps	Subs	Gls
Cardiff C.	Jnrs	08.70	72-74	11	2	0

McINDEWAR, Archibald
Glasgow, 26 August, 1921 (G)

League Club	Source	Date Signed	Seasons Played	Apps	Subs	Gls
Workington	Glasgow Rangers	08.51	51	20	-	0

McINERNEY, Ian
Limerick, 1 September, 1972 (F)

League Club	Source	Date Signed	Seasons Played	Apps	Subs	Gls
Peterborough U.	YT	07.91	91	3	7	1

McINERNEY, Ian D.
Liverpool, 26 January, 1964 (W)

League Club	Source	Date Signed	Seasons Played	Apps	Subs	Gls
Huddersfield T.	Newcastle Blue Star	08.88	88	5	5	1
Stockport Co.	Tr	07.89	89-90	37	5	8
Rochdale	L	02.91	90	4	0	1

McINNES, Graham J.
Aberdeen, 7 April, 1938 (F)

League Club	Source	Date Signed	Seasons Played	Apps	Subs	Gls
Bury	Aberdeen	06.59	60	1	-	0

McINNES, Ian
Hamilton, 22 March, 1967 (W)

League Club	Source	Date Signed	Seasons Played	Apps	Subs	Gls
Rotherham U.	App	09.84	83-84	6	3	0
Lincoln C.	Tr	01.86	85-86	38	5	4

McINNES, John
Ayr, 29 March, 1923 (IF)

League Club	Source	Date Signed	Seasons Played	Apps	Subs	Gls
Bradford C.	Partick Th.	05.49	49-50	21	-	6

McINNES, John S.
Glasgow, 11 August, 1927 Died 1973 (IF)

League Club	Source	Date Signed	Seasons Played	Apps	Subs	Gls
Chelsea	Morton	05.47	46-49	37	-	5

McINNES, Joseph C.
Glasgow, 9 December, 1932 (OL)

League Club	Source	Date Signed	Seasons Played	Apps	Subs	Gls
Accrington St.	Partick Th.	03.56	55	14	-	2

McINNES, William
Lesmahagow, 20 May, 1931 (G)

League Club	Source	Date Signed	Seasons Played	Apps	Subs	Gls
Accrington St.	Alloa Ath.	10.55	55-60	153	-	0
Southport	Tr	07.61	61-62	26	-	0

McINTOSH, Alan
Llandudno, 29 July, 1939 W Amat (W)

League Club	Source	Date Signed	Seasons Played	Apps	Subs	Gls
Cardiff C.	Llandudno	02.62	61-63	64	-	11

McINTOSH, Albert
Dundee, 6 April, 1930 (CF)

League Club	Source	Date Signed	Seasons Played	Apps	Subs	Gls
Swansea C.		03.54	53-56	14	-	3

McINTOSH, Alexander
Derry, 14 April, 1916 (IF)

League Club	Source	Date Signed	Seasons Played	Apps	Subs	Gls
Wolverhampton W.	Folkestone T.	10.37	37-46	44	-	7
Birmingham C.	Tr	01.47	46-47	23	-	4
Coventry C.	Tr	02.48	47-48	20	-	3

McINTOSH, Alexander J.
Aberdeen, 19 October, 1923 (FB)

League Club	Source	Date Signed	Seasons Played	Apps	Subs	Gls
Barrow	Dundee	04.47	46-49	89	-	1
Carlisle U.	Tr	10.49	49-54	228	-	4

McINTOSH, David
Girvan, 4 May, 1925 (G)

League Club	Source	Date Signed	Seasons Played	Apps	Subs	Gls
Sheffield Wed.	Girvan Ath.	10.47	47-57	293	-	0
Doncaster Rov.	Tr	01.58	57-58	15	-	0

McINTOSH, James M.
Dumfries, 5 April, 1918 (CF)

League Club	Source	Date Signed	Seasons Played	Apps	Subs	Gls
Blackpool	Droylsden	09.35	35-37	5	-	0
Preston N.E.	Tr	11.37	37-38	27	-	3
Blackpool	Tr	05.46	46-48	69	-	25
Everton	Tr	03.49	48-50	58	-	19

McINTOSH, James W.
Forfar, 19 August, 1950 (W)

League Club	Source	Date Signed	Seasons Played	Apps	Subs	Gls
Nottingham F.	Montrose	10.70	70-75	45	7	2
Chesterfield	L	01.76	75	3	0	0
Hull C.	Tr	03.76	75-76	20	0	1

McINTOSH, Malcolm P.
Oxford, 6 July, 1959 (D)

League Club	Source	Date Signed	Seasons Played	Apps	Subs	Gls
Oxford U.	App	07.77	78-80	53	3	0
Oxford U. (N/C)	Kettering T.	08.82	82	2	0	0

League Club	Source	Date Signed	Seasons Played	Apps	Subs	Gls
McINTOSH, McGregor J.						
Glasgow, 14 September, 1933						(F)
Bury	Partick Th.	12.57	57-58	29	-	13
McINTOSH, William D.						
Glasgow, 7 December, 1919						(CF)
Preston N.E.	St Johnstone	05.46	46-48	91	-	46
Blackpool	Tr	01.49	48-51	51	-	12
Stoke C.	Tr	09.51	51-52	26	-	6
Walsall	Tr	11.52	52	22	-	9
McINTYRE, James						
Motherwell, 22 March, 1933						(G)
Accrington St.	Motherwell	03.57	56	4	-	0
McINTYRE, James						
Glasgow, 24 May, 1972						(W)
Bristol C.	Duntocher B.C.	10.91	91	1	0	0
McINTYRE, Joseph G.						
Manchester, 19 June, 1971						(LB)
Rochdale (YT)	Port Vale (YT)	10.88	88	2	2	0
McINTYRE, Patrick F.						
Aylesham (Kent), 14 March, 1943						(FB)
Gillingham	Jnrs	07.61	60-62	10	-	0
McINTYRE, Stephen						
Ayr, 15 May, 1966						(RB)
Hereford U.	Ayr U.	07.91	91	12	0	0
McIVER, Frederick						
Birtley, 14 February, 1952						(M)
Sunderland	App	04.69	71	1	0	0
Sheffield Wed.	Racing Jet (Bel)	07.74	74-75	34	3	0

League Club	Source	Date Signed	Seasons Played	Apps	Subs	Gls
McIVOR, Ronald W.						
Edinburgh, 23 March, 1951						(FB)
Wigan Ath.	East Fife	10.79	79	3	0	1
McJANNET, W. Leslie						
Cumnock, 2 August, 1961						(RB)
Mansfield T.	Jnrs	08.79	79-81	73	1	0
Scarborough	Matlock T.	08.87	87-88	29	5	0
Darlington	Tr	12.88	88-91	83	2	5
McJARROW, Hugh						
Motherwell, 29 January, 1928						(CF)
Chesterfield	Maryhill Jnrs	03.46	46-49	33	-	11
Sheffield Wed.	Tr	03.50	49-51	46	-	21
Luton T.	Tr	02.52	51-53	15	-	10
Plymouth Arg.	Tr	12.53	53-55	30	-	3
MACKAY, Angus M.						
Glasgow, 24 April, 1925						(IF)
Ipswich T.	Hamilton Acad.	05.46	46	5	-	0
Exeter C.	Tr	09.47	47-54	257	-	78
Millwall	Tr	06.55	55	17	-	4
MACKAY, David C.						
Edinburgh, 14 November, 1934	*S Sch/Su23-4/SF Lge/S-22*					(LH)
Tottenham H.	Hearts	03.59	58-67	268	0	42
Derby Co.	Tr	07.68	68-70	122	0	5
Swindon T.	Tr	05.71	71	25	1	1
McKAY, Derek						
Banff, 13 December, 1949						(W)
Barrow	Aberdeen	09.71	71	18	0	0
MACKAY, Donald S.						
Glasgow, 19 March, 1940						(G)
Southend U.	Dundee U.	07.72	72-73	13	0	0

Dave Mackay (Hearts, Tottenham Hotspur, Derby County, Swindon Town & Scotland)

League Club	Source	Date Signed	Seasons Played	Apps	Subs	Gls
McKAY, James						
Stirling, 11 June, 1918						
Tranmere Rov.		08.49	49	12	-	1
McKAY, Joffre						
Conan Bridge, 21 January, 1937						(G)
Bury	Ross Co.	12.58				
Rochdale	Tr	07.60	60	9	-	0
McKAY, John						
Port Glasgow, 27 June, 1927						(OL)
Queens Park R.	Irvine	03.49	49-51	16	-	1
McKAY, Mark B.						
Edinburgh, 12 November, 1967						(W)
Doncaster Rov.	Dalkeith Jnrs	01.90	89	0	1	0
McKAY, Paul W.						
Banbury, 28 January, 1971						(RB)
Burnley	YT	11.89	89	8	4	0
McKAY, Peter W.						
Newburgh, 23 February, 1925						(CF)
Burnley	Dundee U.	05.54	54-56	60	-	36
MACKAY, Robert						
Harthill, 6 June, 1948						(M)
Leicester C.	Harthill Jnrs	05.65	68	6	1	1
McKAY, William						
Rothesay, 10 March, 1927						
Queens Park R.	Deal T.	07.55	55	6	-	0
McKEARNEY, David J.						
Crosby, 20 June, 1968						(LB)
Bolton W.	Prescot Cables	11.87				
Crewe Alex.	Northwich Vic.	10.89	89-91	67	12	6
McKECHNIE, Ian H.						
Bellshill, 4 October, 1941						(G)
Arsenal	Jnrs	05.59	61-63	23	-	0
Southend U.	Tr	05.64	64-65	62	0	0
Hull C.	Tr	08.66	66-73	255	0	0
McKECHNIE, Thomas S.						
Milngavie, 9 February, 1940						(IF)
Luton T.	Kirkintiloch Rob Roy	05.61	61-65	129	2	31
Bournemouth	Tr	07.66	66	14	0	2
Colchester U.	Tr	09.67	67	23	1	5
McKEE, Frank						
Cowdenbeath, 25 January, 1923						(WH)
Birmingham C.	Dundee U.	02.48	48-50	22	-	0
Gillingham	Tr	07.52	52-54	53	-	0
McKEE, Raymond T.						
Plaistow, 16 June, 1926						(G)
Northampton T.	Finchley	03.47	46	5	-	0
McKEE Stephen						
Belfast, 15 April, 1956						(W)
Sheffield U.	Linfield	12.76	76	4	3	0
McKEE, William A.						
Warrington, 6 June, 1928						(WH)
Blackburn Rov.		11.49	50	1	-	0
McKEENAN, A. Peter						
Port Glasgow, 26 February, 1924						(IF)
Leyton Orient	Port Glasgow	06.46	46	1	-	0
McKELLAR, David N.						
Irvine, 22 May, 1956						(G)
Ipswich T.	App	03.74				
Derby Co.	Ardrossan Winton	04.78	78-79	41	0	0
Brentford	Tr	09.80	80-81	84	0	0
Carlisle U.	Tr	08.83	83-84	82	0	0
Newcastle U. (L)	Hibernian	02.86	85	10	0	0
Hartlepool U. (L)	Dumfermline Ath.	08.88	88	5	0	0
Carlisle U.	Tr	10.88	88-89	69	0	0
McKENNA, Alan M.						
Edinburgh, 4 August, 1961						(F)
Millwall	App	10.78	78-81	23	7	4
McKENNA, Brian F. J.						
Dublin, 30 January, 1972 IRu21-2						(G)
Brighton & H.A.	Home Farm	07.89	90	1	0	0
McKENNA, Frank						
Blaydon, 8 January, 1933 E Amat						(W)
Leeds U.	Bishop Auckland	07.56	56	6	-	4
Carlisle U.	Tr	02.58	57-58	45	-	11
Hartlepool U.	Tr	07.59	59	32	-	5
McKENNA, John						
Belfast, 6 June, 1926 Died 1980 NI-7						(OR)
Huddersfield T.	Linfield	09.48	48-52	134	-	8
Blackpool	Tr	07.54	54-56	25	-	2
Southport	Tr	07.57	57	15	-	1
McKENNA, Kenneth M.						
Birkenhead, 2 July, 1960						(F)
Tranmere Rov. (N/C)	Poulton Vic.	08.82	82	2	2	0
Tranmere Rov.	Telford U.	08.87	87-88	13	2	3
McKENNA, Michael J.						
Darkley, 3 November, 1916 Died 1974						
Northampton T.	Bromsgrove Rov.	07.46	46	4	-	0
McKENNA, Patrick						
Glasgow, 26 April, 1920						(FB)
Plymouth Arg.	Aberdeen	08.52	52	1	-	0
McKENNA, Thomas						
Paisley, 11 November, 1919						(WH)
Reading	St Mirren	06.46	46-47	28	-	1
Grimsby T.	Tr	06.48	48-49	50	-	2
McKENNAN, Peter S.						
Airdrie, 16 July, 1918 Died 1991 SF Lge						(IF)
West Bromwich A.	Partick Th.	10.47	47	11	-	4
Leicester C.	Tr	03.48	47-48	18	-	7
Brentford	Tr	09.48	48	24	-	6
Middlesbrough	Tr	05.49	49-50	40	-	18
Oldham Ath.	Tr	07.51	51-53	78	-	28
MacKENZIE, Aiden						
Athlone, 15 July, 1959						(W)
Lincoln C.	Galway Rov.	12.78	79	4	2	0
MacKENZIE, Donald A.						
Liverpool, 30 January, 1942						(W)
Everton		01.63				
Rochdale	Tr	10.63	63-64	41	-	7
McKENZIE, Donald C.						
Glasgow, 9 June, 1927						(IF)
Grimsby T.	Glasgow Rangers	08.51	51	4	-	0
McKENZIE, Duncan						
Grimsby, 10 June, 1950						(F)
Nottingham F.	Jnrs	07.68	69-73	105	6	41
Mansfield T.	L	03.70	69	7	3	3
Mansfield T.	L	02.73	72	6	0	7
Leeds U.	Tr	08.74	74-75	64	2	27
Everton	Anderlecht (Bel)	12.76	76-77	48	0	14
Chelsea	Tr	09.78	78	15	0	4
Blackburn Rov.	Tr	03.79	78-80	74	0	16
MacKENZIE, Hamish J. T.						
Denny, 11 March, 1945						(FB)
Liverpool	App	03.62				
Brentford	Dunfermline Ath.	08.64	65-66	19	0	0
McKENZIE, Ian E.						
Wallsend, 22 August, 1966						(LB)
Barnsley (N/C)	Newcastle U. App	08.85	85	1	0	0
Stockport Co.	Tr	09.86	86-88	51	8	0
MacKENZIE, Ian S.						
Rotherham, 27 September, 1950						(CD)
Sheffield U.	Jnrs	06.68	69-73	43	2	1
Southend U.	L	03.75	74	5	1	0
Mansfield T.	Tr	07.75	75-77	69	1	1
McKENZIE, John A.						
Glasgow, 4 September, 1925 SF Lge/S-9						(W)
Bournemouth	Partick Th.	08.47	47	38	-	9
MaCKENZIE, M. Laurence						
Kilpatrick, 7 July, 1924						(IF)
Sheffield Wed.	Clydebank Ath.	12.45	46-47	6	-	0
Grimsby T.	Tr	07.49	49-50	58	-	11

League Club	Source	Date Signed	Seasons Played	Career Record Apps	Subs	Gls
McKENZIE, Malcolm J.						
Edinburgh, 1 May, 1950 (OL)						
Port Vale	Jnrs	05.67	65-67	7	1	0
McKENZIE, Paul A.						
Aberdeen, 4 October, 1969 (M)						
Sunderland	YT	07.87				
Burnley	Peterhead	02.92	91	1	3	0
McKENZIE, Roger M.						
Sheffield, 27 January, 1973 (F)						
Doncaster Rov.	YT	07.91	91	7	10	1
MacKENZIE, Stephen						
Romford, 23 November, 1961 E Yth/Eu21-3/E'B' (M)						
Crystal Palace	App	07.79				
Manchester C.	Tr	07.79	79-80	56	2	8
West Bromwich A.	Tr	08.81	81-86	153	3	23
Charlton Ath.	Tr	06.87	87-90	92	8	7
Sheffield Wed.	Tr	02.91	90-91	5	10	2
Shrewsbury T.	Tr	12.91	91	13	0	1
McKENZIE, Stuart R.						
Hull, 19 September, 1967 (FB)						
York C.	YT	12.85	85-87	30	2	0
McKEOWN, Gary J.						
Oxford, 19 October, 1970 E Yth (M)						
Arsenal	YT	11.88				
Shrewsbury T.	L	03.92	91	8	0	1
McKEOWN, Joseph						
Bannockburn, 9 April, 1924 (IF)						
Hartlepool U.	Stirling A.	08.50	50	46	-	7
McKEOWN, Lindsay I.						
Belfast, 11 July, 1957 (M)						
Manchester U.	App	07.74				
Sheffield Wed.	Tr	07.76	76-77	6	5	0
McKEOWN, Thomas						
Cleland, 2 October, 1930 (OR)						
Accrington St.	Queen of South	05.54	54	12	-	2
McKERNON, Craig A.						
Gloucester, 23 February, 1968 (RB)						
Mansfield T.	App	02.86	84-89	79	15	0
Arsenal	Tr	12.89				
MACKIE, Thomas F.						
Burntisland, 30 March, 1918 (LB)						
New Brighton	St Johnstone	05.47	47	2	-	0
Chester C.	Tr	08.48	48	5	-	0
McKIM, John						
Greenock, 22 January, 1926 (IF)						
Chelsea	Port Glasgow	06.47				
Colchester U.	Tr	08.50	50-54	129	-	42
McKINLAY, Ian J.						
Liverpool, 21 June, 1949 (OR)						
Southport	Wrexham (Am)	09.66	66-67	11	1	1
McKINLAY, Robert						
Lochgelly, 10 October, 1932 (CH)						
Nottingham F.	Bowhill Rov.	10.49	51-69	611	3	9
McKINNEY, William E.						
Newcastle, 20 July, 1936 (RB)						
Newcastle U.	Wallsend St Luke	05.56	57-64	85	-	6
Bournemouth	Tr	08.65	65	17	0	0
Mansfield T.	Tr	07.66	66-67	51	1	2
McKINNON, Paul J.						
Frimley, 1 August, 1958 (F)						
Blackburn Rov.	Sutton U.	12.86	86	5	0	0
McKINNON, Robert						
Glasgow, 31 July, 1966 (LB)						
Newcastle U.	Rutherglen Glencairn	11.84	85	1	0	0
Hartlepool U.	Tr	07.86	86-91	246	1	7
McKINVEN, John J.						
Campbeltown, 1 May, 1941 (OL)						
Southend U.	Raith Rov.	05.60	60-69	284	2	62
Cambridge U.	Tr	12.69	70	18	0	2
McKNIGHT, Allen D.						
Antrim (NI), 27 January, 1964 NIu21/NI-10 (G)						
West Ham U.	Albion Rov.	07.88	88	23	0	0
Rotherham U. (N/C)	Stockport Co. (N/C)	10.91	91	3	0	0
Walsall	Tr	11.91	91	8	0	0

League Club	Source	Date Signed	Seasons Played	Career Record Apps	Subs	Gls
McKNIGHT, George						
Belfast, 17 November, 1923 (CF)						
Blackpool	Linfield	06.46	46-53	41	-	9
Chesterfield	Tr	07.55	55	5	-	1
Southport		09.57	57	1	-	0
McKNIGHT, Philip						
Glasgow, 15 June, 1924 (WH)						
Chelsea	Alloa Ath.	01.47	47-53	33	-	1
Leyton Orient	Tr	07.54	54-58	161	-	2
McLACHLAN, Dugald						
Falkirk, 10 September, 1953 (F)						
Preston N.E.	App	11.71				
Halifax T.	L	10.72	72	1	1	0
Peterborough U.	Tr	07.73	73	1	0	0
McLACHLAN, Stephen						
Kirkcudbright, 19 September, 1918 (WH)						
Derby Co.	Dalbeattie	03.38	38-52	58	-	1
McLAFFERTY, Maurice						
Lanark, 7 August, 1922						
Sheffield U.		08.51	51	18	-	0
Brighton & H.A.	Tr	07.52	52	21	-	0
McLAIN, Thomas						
Linton, 19 January, 1922 (WH)						
Sunderland	Ashington	08.46	46-51	67	-	1
Northampton T.	Tr	07.52	52-55	96	-	10
McLAREN, Andrew						
Larkhall, 24 January, 1922 S-4 (IF)						
Preston N.E.	Larkhall Th.	02.39	46-48	69	-	29
Burnley	Tr	12.48	48	3	-	1
Sheffield U.	Tr	03.49	48-50	31	-	4
Barrow	Tr	02.51	50-54	155	-	52
Bradford P.A.	Tr	10.54	54	18	-	7
Southport	Tr	06.55	55	4	-	1
Rochdale	Tr	11.55	55-56	44	-	12
MacLAREN, David						
Auchterarder, 12 June, 1934 (G)						
Leicester C.	Dundee	01.57	56-59	85	-	0
Plymouth Arg.	Tr	06.60	60-64	131	-	0
Wolverhampton W.	Tr	01.65	64-66	44	0	0
Southampton	Tr	09.66	66	22	0	0
McLAREN, Edward						
Dundee, 8 September, 1929 (WH)						
Blackpool	Dunkeld Jnrs	06.48				
Reading	Tr	10.52	53-58	184	-	2
McLAREN, Hugh						
Hamilton, 24 June, 1926 Died 1988 (OL)						
Derby Co.	Kilmarnock	10.49	49-53	119	-	53
Nottingham F.	Tr	01.54	53-54	33	-	15
Walsall	Tr	07.55	55	31	-	8
McLAREN, James D.						
Birkenhead, 29 July, 1936 (OR)						
Chesterfield	Wigan Ath.	06.58	59	11	-	1
McLAREN, Robert						
Glasgow, 5 August, 1929 (IF)						
Cardiff C.	Barry T.	02.50	49	1	-	0
Scunthorpe U.	Tr	08.51	51	6	-	0
McLAREN, Ross						
Edinburgh, 14 April, 1962 (CD/M)						
Shrewsbury T.	Glasgow Rangers (Jnrs)	08.80	80-84	158	3	18
Derby Co.	Tr	07.85	85-87	113	9	4
Swindon T.	Tr	08.88	88-91	160	0	9
McLAREN, J. J. Roy						
Auchterarder, 12 February, 1930 (G)						
Bury	St Johnstone	12.55	55-58	86	-	0
Sheffield Wed.	Tr	10.58	58-63	31	-	0
MacLAREN, Scott J.						
Crieff, 26 November, 1921 (G)						
Chester C.	Berwick R.	01.47	46-48	30	-	0
Carlisle U.	Tr	12.48	48-54	261	-	0
McLAREN, Thomas						
Livingston, 1 June, 1949 Died 1978 (M)						
Port Vale		11.67	67-76	301	32	28
McLARTY, Jesse J.						
Ayr, 3 March, 1920 (IF)						
Wrexham	Chester C. (Am)	09.45	46-47	24	-	9

League Club	Source	Date Signed	Seasons Played	Apps	Subs	Gls
McLAUGHLAN, Alexander D.						
Kilwinning, 17 July, 1936 SF Lge						(G)
Sunderland	Kilmarnock	09.64	64-65	43	0	0
McLAUGHLIN, Hugh						
Glasgow, 2 September, 1943						(WH)
Brentford	St Rochs	09.61	63-65	4	1	0
McLAUGHLIN, James						
Paisley, 11 February, 1926						(CH)
Walsall	Glasgow Celtic	06.48	48-49	15	-	0
McLAUGHLIN, James						
Stirling, 10 December, 1926						
Hartlepool U.		07.53	53	13	-	2
McLAUGHLIN, James C.						
Derry (NI), 22 December, 1940 NIu23-2/NI-12						(W)
Birmingham C.	Derry C.	06.58				
Shrewsbury T.	Tr	07.60	60-62	124	-	56
Swansea C.	Tr	05.63	63-66	120	3	45
Peterborough U.	Tr	03.67	66	8	0	2
Shrewsbury T.	Tr	09.67	67-72	159	14	21
Swansea C.	Tr	11.72	72-73	20	8	2
McLAUGHLIN, John						
Lennoxtown, 13 November, 1936						(F)
Millwall	Morton	07.63	63	21	-	5
McLAUGHLIN, John						
Edmonton, 29 October, 1954 E Yth						(LB)
Colchester U.	App	05.72	71-73	66	0	2
Swindon T.	Tr	12.73	73-78	199	3	9
Portsmouth	Tr	07.79	79-83	172	0	1
McLAUGHLIN, John I.						
Stirling, 3 January, 1948						(FB)
Everton	Falkirk	10.71	71-75	59	2	1
McLAUGHLIN, John M. L.						
Clarkston, 12 April, 1936						(G)
Shrewsbury T.	Third Lanark	09.63	63	5	-	0
McLAUGHLIN, John T.						
Liverpool, 25 February, 1952						(M)
Liverpool	App	02.69	69-73	38	2	2
Portsmouth	L	10.75	75	5	0	0
McLAUGHLIN, Joseph						
Greenock, 2 June, 1960 Su21-10						(CD)
Chelsea	Morton	06.83	83-88	220	0	5
Charlton Ath.	Tr	08.89	89	31	0	0
Watford	Tr	08.90	90-91	46	0	2
McLAUGHLIN, Michael A.						
Newport, 5 January, 1943						(CD)
Newport Co.		11.61				
Newport Co.	Lovells Ath.	08.68	68-69	90	0	3
Hereford U.	Tr	08.70	72-74	84	0	1
Newport Co. (N/C)	Cheltenham T.	03.78	77	7	0	0
McLAUGHLIN, Robert						
Belfast, 6 December, 1925 IR Lge						(WH)
Wrexham	Distillery	01.50	49	17	-	0
Cardiff C.	Tr	04.50	50-53	48	-	3
Southampton	Tr	10.53	53-58	169	-	5
McLAUGHLIN, William J.						
USA, 31 January, 1918 Died 1972						
Crewe Alex.		10.46	46	1	-	0
McLEAN, Angus						
Queensferry, 20 September, 1925 Died 1979						(FB)
Wolverhampton W.	Aberystwyth	11.42	46-50	144	-	1
Bury	Bromsgrove Rov.	05.53	53	12	-	0
Crewe Alex.	Tr	06.54	54	39	-	11
McLEAN, Colin						
Stirling, 16 May, 1928						(IF)
Southport	Forfar Ath.	06.52	52-53	59	-	18
Crewe Alex.	Tr	07.54	54	14	-	0
McLEAN, David J.						
Newcastle, 24 November, 1957 E Sch						(M)
Newcastle U.	App	11.75	75-77	7	2	0
Carlisle U.	Tr	03.78	77-78	9	6	0
Darlington	Tr	08.79	79-85	289	5	46
Scunthorpe U.	Tr	07.86	86-87	23	1	3
Hartlepool U.	L	03.87	86	6	0	0

League Club	Source	Date Signed	Seasons Played	Apps	Subs	Gls
McLEAN, Derek J.						
Brotton, 21 December, 1932						(IF)
Middlesbrough		10.52	55-61	119	-	30
Hartlepool U.	Tr	10.61	61-63	89	-	17
McLEAN, George R.						
Paisley, 16 September, 1937						(CF)
Norwich C.	Glasgow Rangers	03.62				
Grimsby T.	Tr	09.62	62-64	91	-	41
Exeter C.	Tr	06.65	65-66	47	0	12
Workington	Tr	01.67	66-67	53	0	16
Barrow	Tr	06.68	68	26	1	9
MacLEAN, Hugh						
Stornoway, 20 January, 1952						(W)
West Bromwich A.	Jnrs	02.69	71-72	4	2	0
Swindon T.	Tr	07.74	74	17	2	1
McLEAN, James						
Alloa, 3 April, 1934						(F)
Port Vale	Alva R.	03.58	57	3	-	0
McLEAN, Peter Y.						
East Fife, 27 November, 1923						(WH)
Reading	Bo'ness U.	01.49	49-52	70	-	6
Exeter C.	Tr	08.53	53	15	-	0
McLEAN, Stewart D.						
Barrhead, 30 August, 1923						(IL)
Rotherham U.	Partick Th.	05.46	46-47	35	-	18
McLEAN, William						
Liverpool, 14 August, 1931						(OR)
Blackburn Rov.	Burscough	02.53	53	12	-	0
McLEAN, William						
						(OR)
New Brighton	Queen of South	06.47	47	12	-	2
McLEAN, William G.						
Dumbarton, 14 October, 1933						
Walsall		02.54	53	2	-	0
McLEARY, Alan T.						
Lambeth, 6 October, 1964 E Yth/Eu21-1/E'B'						(CD)
Millwall	App	10.81	82-91	285	16	5

Alan McLeary (Millwall)

League Club	Source	Date Signed	Seasons Played	Apps	Subs	Gls
McLEISH, Hugh						
Shotts, 10 June, 1948						(CF)
Sunderland	Dundee U.	08.67				
Luton T.	Tr	11.67	67	1	0	0
McLELLAN, Alistair A.						
Glasgow, 16 April, 1922						(IF)
New Brighton	Albion Rov.	08.46	46-47	34	-	7
Tranmere Rov.	Tr	05.48	48	2	-	0

McLEOD, Alexander H. M.
Glasgow, 1 January, 1951 (F)

League Club	Source	Date Signed	Seasons Played	Apps	Subs	Gls
Southampton	St Mirren	05.73	73	2	1	0
Huddersfield T.	L	10.74	74	3	1	1

MacLEOD, Alistair R.
Glasgow, 26 February, 1931 (W)

League Club	Source	Date Signed	Seasons Played	Apps	Subs	Gls
Blackburn Rov.	St Mirren	06.56	56-60	193	-	47

McLEOD, George J.
Inverness, 30 November, 1932 (OL)

League Club	Source	Date Signed	Seasons Played	Apps	Subs	Gls
Luton T.	Inverness Clach.	01.55	55-58	51	-	6
Brentford	Tr	10.58	58-63	207	-	20
Queens Park R.	Tr	01.64	63-64	41	-	4

McLEOD, John M.
Edinburgh, 23 November, 1938 Su23-1/SF Lge/S-4 (OR)

League Club	Source	Date Signed	Seasons Played	Apps	Subs	Gls
Arsenal	Hibernian	07.61	61-64	101	-	23
Aston Villa	Tr	09.64	64-67	123	2	16

McLEOD, Norman A.
Manchester, 29 July, 1930

League Club	Source	Date Signed	Seasons Played	Apps	Subs	Gls
Crewe Alex.	Hyde U.	08.57	57-58	25	-	1

McLEOD, Robert A.
Inverness, 24 February, 1947 (CH)

League Club	Source	Date Signed	Seasons Played	Apps	Subs	Gls
Hartlepool U.		11.65	65-68	23	5	0

McLEOD, Robert B.
Govan Hill, 22 January, 1919

League Club	Source	Date Signed	Seasons Played	Apps	Subs	Gls
Brighton & H.A.		11.47	47	1	-	0

McLEOD, Samuel M.
Glasgow, 4 January, 1934 (IF)

League Club	Source	Date Signed	Seasons Played	Apps	Subs	Gls
Colchester U.	Easthouses	06.55	55-62	156	-	23

McLEOD, Thomas
Musselburgh, 26 December, 1920 (IF)

League Club	Source	Date Signed	Seasons Played	Apps	Subs	Gls
Liverpool		10.45	46-48	7	-	0
Chesterfield	Tr	07.51	51	25	-	3

McLINTOCK, Frank
Glasgow, 28 December, 1939 Su23-1/S-9 (CD)

League Club	Source	Date Signed	Seasons Played	Apps	Subs	Gls
Leicester C.	Shawfield Jnrs	01.57	59-64	168	-	25
Arsenal	Tr	10.64	64-72	312	2	26
Queens Park R.	Tr	06.73	73-76	126	1	5

McLOUGHLIN, Alan F.
Manchester, 20 April, 1967 IR'B'/IR-12 (M)

League Club	Source	Date Signed	Seasons Played	Apps	Subs	Gls
Manchester U.	App	04.85				
Swindon T.	Tr	08.86	86-90	101	5	18
Torquay U.	L	03.87	86	16	0	1
Torquay U.	L	08.87	87	5	3	3
Southampton	Tr	12.90	90-91	22	2	1
Portsmouth	Tr	02.92	91	14	0	2

Alan McLoughlin (Manchester United, Swindon Town, Southampton, Portsmouth & Republic of Ireland)

McLOUGHLIN, Anthony
Liverpool, 24 September, 1946 (OL)

League Club	Source	Date Signed	Seasons Played	Apps	Subs	Gls
Everton	Jnrs	02.64				
Wrexham	Tr	07.66	66-67	27	2	9
Chester C.	Tr	10.67	67	2	2	0

McLOUGHLIN, Paul B.
Bristol, 23 December, 1963 (F)

League Club	Source	Date Signed	Seasons Played	Apps	Subs	Gls
Cardiff C.	Gisborne (NZ)	12.84	84-85	40	9	4
Bristol C. (N/C)	Sweden	01.87				
Hereford U.	Tr	06.87	87-88	72	2	14
Wolverhampton W.	Tr	07.89	89-91	12	16	4
Walsall	L	09.91	91	9	0	4
York C.	L	01.92	91	1	0	0
Mansfield T.	Tr	01.92	91	10	2	3

MacLUCKIE, George R.
Falkirk, 19 September, 1931 (OL)

League Club	Source	Date Signed	Seasons Played	Apps	Subs	Gls
Blackburn Rov.	Lochore Welfare	08.52	52	20	-	2
Ipswich T.	Tr	05.53	53-57	141	-	24
Reading	Tr	06.58	58-60	85	-	8

McLUCKIE, Robert J.
Doncaster, 5 October, 1955 (M)

League Club	Source	Date Signed	Seasons Played	Apps	Subs	Gls
Doncaster Rov.	App	10.73	72-73	2	2	0

McMAHON, Desmond
Reading, 22 March, 1956 (F)

League Club	Source	Date Signed	Seasons Played	Apps	Subs	Gls
Reading (N/C)	Hungerford T.	08.82	82	0	2	0

McMAHON, Frank G.
Belfast, 4 January, 1950 (M)

League Club	Source	Date Signed	Seasons Played	Apps	Subs	Gls
Coventry C.	Distillery	10.69				
Lincoln C.	Waterford	07.71	71-72	54	1	2
Darlington	Tr	03.73	72-73	19	4	1
Hartlepool U.	L	10.73	73	7	0	0

McMAHON, Hugh
Grangetown, 24 September, 1909 (OL)

League Club	Source	Date Signed	Seasons Played	Apps	Subs	Gls
Reading		09.32	32	1	-	0
Southend U.	Mexborough	05.33	33	10	-	3
Reading	Tr	06.34	34-35	10	-	2
Queens Park R.	Tr	05.36	36-37	41	-	3
Sunderland	Tr	11.37	37-38	8	-	1
Hartlepool U.	Tr	06.45	46-47	28	-	7
Rotherham U.	Tr	09.47	47-48	59	-	8

McMAHON, Ian D.
Wells, 7 October, 1964 (M)

League Club	Source	Date Signed	Seasons Played	Apps	Subs	Gls
Oldham Ath.	App	10.82	82	2	0	0
Rochdale	Tr	01.84	83-85	89	2	8

McMAHON, John A.
Middlesbrough, 25 October, 1965 (F)

League Club	Source	Date Signed	Seasons Played	Apps	Subs	Gls
Middlesbrough	App	10.83				
Darlington (N/C)	Tr	03.85	84	0	4	0

McMAHON, John J.
Manchester, 7 December, 1949 (RB)

League Club	Source	Date Signed	Seasons Played	Apps	Subs	Gls
Preston N.E.	App	12.67	70-78	256	1	7
Southend U.	L	09.70	70	3	0	0
Chesterfield	L	09.79	79	1	0	0
Crewe Alex.	Tr	10.79	79-80	67	0	2
Wigan Ath.	Tr	08.81	81-82	71	0	5
Tranmere Rov.	Tr	08.83	83	39	1	0

McMAHON, Kevin
Tantobie, 1 March, 1946 (F)

League Club	Source	Date Signed	Seasons Played	Apps	Subs	Gls
Newcastle U.	Consett	08.67				
York C.	Tr	05.69	69-71	85	8	31
Bolton W.	L	03.72	71	4	2	1
Barnsley	Tr	07.72	72	4	1	0
Hartlepool U.	Tr	07.73	73-75	104	3	28

McMAHON, Patrick
Kilsyth, 19 September, 1945 (M)

League Club	Source	Date Signed	Seasons Played	Apps	Subs	Gls
Aston Villa	Glasgow Celtic	06.69	69-74	121	9	25

McMAHON, Peter J.
Marylebone, 30 April, 1934 (WH)

League Club	Source	Date Signed	Seasons Played	Apps	Subs	Gls
Leyton Orient	Chertsey	05.51	51-57	66	-	1
Aldershot	Tr	10.58	58-59	39	-	0

McMAHON, Stephen
Liverpool, 20 August, 1961 Eu21-6/E'B'/EF Lge/E-17 (M)

League Club	Source	Date Signed	Seasons Played	Apps	Subs	Gls
Everton	App	08.79	80-82	99	1	11
Aston Villa	Tr	05.83	83-85	74	1	7
Liverpool	Tr	09.85	85-91	202	2	29
Manchester C.	Tr	12.91	91	18	0	0

Steve McMahon (Everton, Aston Villa, Liverpool, Manchester City & England)

McMANAMAN, Steven
Bootle, 11 February, 1972 E Yth/Eu21-2 (F)

League Club	Source	Date Signed	Seasons Played	Apps	Subs	Gls
Liverpool	YT	02.90	90-91	26	6	5

Steve McManaman (Liverpool)

McMANUS, Brendan
Kilkeel (NI), 2 December, 1923 (G)

League Club	Source	Date Signed	Seasons Played	Apps	Subs	Gls
Huddersfield T.	Newry T.	10.45	46	1	-	0
Oldham Ath.	Tr	07.47	47	35	-	0
Bradford C.	Tr	10.48	48-52	125	-	0

McMANUS, C. Eric
Limavady (NI), 14 November, 1950 NI Amat (G)

League Club	Source	Date Signed	Seasons Played	Apps	Subs	Gls
Coventry C.	Coleraine	08.68	69-71	6	0	0
Notts Co.	Tr	05.72	72-78	229	0	0
Stoke C.	Tr	10.79	81	4	0	0
Lincoln C.	L	12.79	79	21	0	0
Bradford C.	Tr	08.82	82-84	113	0	0
Middlesbrough	L	01.86	85	2	0	0
Peterborough U.	L	03.86	85	18	0	0
Tranmere Rov.	Tr	08.86	86	3	0	0

McMANUS, Edward J.
Ramsgate, 8 August, 1937 (CF)

League Club	Source	Date Signed	Seasons Played	Apps	Subs	Gls
Bournemouth	Dover T.	08.54	58-59	4	-	0
Gillingham	Tr	08.60	60	3	-	0

McMANUS, Stanley
Carlisle, 31 October, 1932

League Club	Source	Date Signed	Seasons Played	Apps	Subs	Gls
Bury		01.56				
Southport	Tr	07.57	57	5	-	0

McMANUS, Stuart J.
Falkirk, 19 March, 1965 (F)

League Club	Source	Date Signed	Seasons Played	Apps	Subs	Gls
Southampton	Jnrs	07.84	85	2	0	1
Newport Co.	L	08.85	85	4	1	0

McMASTER, Christopher
Darlington, 16 June, 1959 (F)

League Club	Source	Date Signed	Seasons Played	Apps	Subs	Gls
Hartlepool U.	App	07.77	76-77	3	1	0

McMENEMY, Paul C.
Farnborough, 5 November, 1966 (F)

League Club	Source	Date Signed	Seasons Played	Apps	Subs	Gls
West Ham U.	App	11.84				
Aldershot	L	03.86	85	10	0	5
Northampton T.	L	01.87	86	4	0	2

McMICHAEL, Alfred
Belfast, 1 October, 1927 IR Lge/NI-40 (FB)

League Club	Source	Date Signed	Seasons Played	Apps	Subs	Gls
Newcastle U.	Linfield	09.49	49-62	402	-	1

McMILLAN, L. Andrew
South Africa, 22 June, 1968 (FB)

League Club	Source	Date Signed	Seasons Played	Apps	Subs	Gls
York C.	Hull C. (trial)	10.87	87-91	127	8	2

MacMILLAN, Duncan
Glasgow, 18 January, 1922 Died 1992 (CH)

League Club	Source	Date Signed	Seasons Played	Apps	Subs	Gls
Grimsby T.	Glasgow Celtic	03.49	48-54	188	-	2

McMILLAN, Eric
Beverley, 2 November, 1936 (WH)

League Club	Source	Date Signed	Seasons Played	Apps	Subs	Gls
Chelsea		04.58	59	5	-	0
Hull C.	Tr	07.60	60-63	150	-	3
Halifax T.	Tr	07.65	65-66	49	1	8

McMILLAN, George S.
Motherwell, 15 March, 1930 (F)

League Club	Source	Date Signed	Seasons Played	Apps	Subs	Gls
Wrexham	Aberdeen	05.52	52	1	-	0

McMILLAN, George S.
Stonehouse, 10 August, 1929 (G)

League Club	Source	Date Signed	Seasons Played	Apps	Subs	Gls
Ipswich T.	Newarthill Jnrs	02.53	54-57	53	-	0

McMILLAN, John S.
Dumbarton, 14 April, 1937 (OR)

League Club	Source	Date Signed	Seasons Played	Apps	Subs	Gls
Cardiff C.	Dumbarton	02.58	60	2	-	0
Exeter C.	Tr	10.61	61-62	20	-	1

McMILLAN, Paul A.
Lennoxtown, 13 July,1950 (WH)

League Club	Source	Date Signed	Seasons Played	Apps	Subs	Gls
Chelsea	Jnrs	08.67	67	1	0	0

McMILLAN, Samuel
Belfast, 29 September, 1941 NIu23-1/NI-2 (IF)

League Club	Source	Date Signed	Seasons Played	Apps	Subs	Gls
Manchester U.	Boyland Y.C.	11.59	61-62	15	-	6
Wrexham	Tr	12.63	63-67	149	0	52
Southend U.	Tr	09.67	67-69	76	1	5
Chester C.	Tr	12.69	69	16	2	0
Stockport Co.	Tr	07.70	70-71	74	0	29

McMILLAN, Thomas
Glasgow, 12 February, 1931 (OL)

League Club	Source	Date Signed	Seasons Played	Apps	Subs	Gls
Norwich C.	Glasgow Celtic	07.54	54	19	-	2
Workington	Tr	09.55	55	2	-	0

McMILLAN, Thomas P.
Auchinleck, 16 January, 1936 (WH)

League Club	Source	Date Signed	Seasons Played	Apps	Subs	Gls
Watford	Maybole Jnrs	09.56	56-57	33	-	13
Carlisle U.	Tr	07.58	58-60	89	-	7

McMILLEN, Walter S.
Belfast, 24 November, 1913 (HB)

League Club	Source	Date Signed	Seasons Played	Apps	Subs	Gls
Manchester U.	Cliftonville	08.33	33-34	27	-	2
Chesterfield	Tr	12.36	36-38	85	-	16
Millwall	Tr	05.39	46-49	91	-	0

McMINN, Kevin C. (Ted)
Castle Douglas, 28 September, 1962 (W)

League Club	Source	Date Signed	Seasons Played	Apps	Subs	Gls
Derby Co.	Seville (Sp)	02.88	87-91	102	2	7

McMINN, Robert W.
Doncaster, 9 October, 1946 (FB)

League Club	Source	Date Signed	Seasons Played	Apps	Subs	Gls
Doncaster Rov.	App	10.64	63-65	4	1	0

McMORDIE, Alexander A. (Eric)
Belfast, 12 August, 1946 NIu23-1/NI-21 (M)

League Club	Source	Date Signed	Seasons Played	Apps	Subs	Gls
Middlesbrough	Dundela	09.64	65-73	231	10	22
Sheffield Wed.	L	10.74	74	9	0	6
York C.	Tr	05.75	75-76	42	0	2
Hartlepool U.	Tr	12.76	76-77	46	1	2

McMORRAN, Edward J.
Larne (NI), 2 September, 1923 Died 1984 NI Sch/IR Lge/NI-15 (IF)

League Club	Source	Date Signed	Seasons Played	Apps	Subs	Gls
Manchester C.	Belfast Celtic	08.47	47-48	33	-	12
Leeds U.	Tr	01.49	48-49	38	-	6
Barnsley	Tr	07.50	50-52	104	-	30
Doncaster Rov.	Tr	02.53	52-57	126	-	32
Crewe Alex.	Tr	11.57	57	24	-	6

McMORRAN, James W.
Muirkirk, 29 October, 1942 S Sch (IF)

League Club	Source	Date Signed	Seasons Played	Apps	Subs	Gls
Aston Villa	Jnrs	10.59	60-61	11	-	1
Walsall	Third Lanark	11.64	64-67	95	2	10
Swansea C.	Tr	06.68	68	14	0	2
Walsall	Tr	11.68	68	9	0	1
Notts Co.	Tr	07.69	69	6	0	0

Ted McMinn (Queen of South, Glasgow Rangers, Seville & Derby County)

League Club	Source	Date Signed	Seasons Played	Apps	Subs	Gls
McMORRAN, John						
Forth, 11 May, 1934						(IF)
Bradford C.	Forth W.	12.54	54	1	-	0
McMORRAN, Robert						
Forth, 12 March, 1926						
Manchester U.	Glasgow Rangers	02.47				
Walsall	Tr	02.50	49-50	10	-	1
McMULLEN, David						
Denny, 13 June, 1960						(M)
Wigan Ath.	Cumbernauld U.	02.80	79-80	20	7	1
McMULLEN, David						
Harrington, 6 January, 1936						(WH)
Workington		08.59	59	1	-	0
McMULLEN, Ian						
Hoylake, 17 November, 1965						(M)
Tranmere Rov. (N/C)		08.84	84	2	0	0
McMURRAY, John						
Billingham, 5 October, 1931						(WH)
Middlesbrough	Billingham Synth.	05.49	53-54	3	-	0
McNAB, Alexander						
Birmingham, 6 April, 1932 S Sch						(WH)
Shrewsbury T.		12.54	54-55	4	-	0
McNAB, Alexander						
Glasgow, 27 December, 1911 Died 1962 S-2						(WH)
Sunderland	Pollock Jnrs	05.32	32-37	97	-	6
West Bromwich A.	Tr	03.38	37-38	49	-	2
Newport Co.	Tr	04.46	46	3	-	0
McNAB, James						
Denny, 13 April, 1940 S Sch						(WH)
Sunderland	Jnrs	06.57	58-66	284	1	13
Preston N.E.	Tr	03.67	66-73	222	2	6
Stockport Co.	Tr	07.74	74-75	30	0	1
McNAB, Neil						
Greenock, 4 June, 1957 S Sch/Su21-1						(M)
Tottenham H.	Morton	02.74	73-78	63	9	3
Bolton W.	Tr	11.78	78-79	33	2	4
Brighton & H.A.	Tr	02.80	79-82	100	3	4
Leeds U.	L	12.82	82	5	0	0
Manchester C.	Tr	07.83	83-89	216	5	16
Tranmere Rov.	Tr	01.90	89-91	64	10	4
Huddersfield T.	L	01.92	91	11	0	0
McNAB, Robert						
Huddersfield, 20 July, 1943 EF Lge/E-4						(LB)
Huddersfield T.	Moldgreen Y.C.	04.62	63-66	68	0	0
Arsenal	Tr	10.66	66-74	277	1	4
Wolverhampton W.	Tr	07.75	75	13	0	0
McNAB, Samuel						
Glasgow, 20 October, 1926						(IF)
Sheffield U.	Dalry Th.	01.52	52-53	11	-	4
York C.	Tr	05.54	54	19	-	3
McNAB, Thomas C.						
Glasgow, 15 July, 1933						(WH)
Nottingham F.	Partick Th.	03.54				
Wrexham	Partick Th.	03.57	56-58	43	-	5
Barrow	Tr	03.59	58-60	44	-	4
McNALLY, Bernard A.						
Shrewsbury, 17 February, 1963 NI-5						(M)
Shrewsbury T.	App	02.81	80-88	278	4	23
West Bromwich A.	Tr	07.89	89-91	78	9	7
McNALLY, J. Brendan						
Dublin, 22 January, 1935 IR'B'-1/IR-3						(FB)
Luton T.	Shelbourne	05.56	56-62	134	-	2
McNALLY, Errol A.						
Lurgan (NI), 27 August, 1943						(G)
Chelsea	Portadown	12.61	61-63	9	-	0
McNALLY, Paul A.						
Consett, 19 December, 1949						(IF)
Bradford C.	Consett Jnrs	07.67	68	1	2	0

League Club	Source	Date Signed	Seasons Played	Apps	Subs	Gls
McNAMARA, Anthony						
Liverpool, 3 October, 1929						(OR)
Everton		05.50	51-57	111	-	22
Liverpool	Tr	12.57	57	10	-	3
Crewe Alex.	Tr	07.58	58	9	-	2
Bury	Tr	09.58	58	14	-	0
McNAMARA, Dennis A.						
Liverpool, 8 March, 1935						
Tranmere Rov.		11.54	54	1	-	0
McNAMEE, Gerard						
Consett, 16 August, 1960						(W)
Hartlepool U.		11.79	79-82	2	2	1
McNAMEE, John						
Coatbridge, 11 June, 1941						(CD)
Newcastle U.	Hibernian	12.66	66-71	115	2	8
Blackburn Rov.	Tr	11.71	71-72	56	0	9
Hartlepool U.	Morton	12.73	73	2	0	0
Workington (N/C)	Lancaster C.	08.75	75	2	0	0
McNAMEE, John J.						
Edinburgh, 31 July, 1942						(OL)
Reading	Montrose	12.64				
Tranmere Rov.	Raith Rov.	08.67	67-69	67	5	11
McNAMEE, Peter						
Glasgow, 20 March, 1935						(OL)
Peterborough U.	Lanark A.	(N/L)	60-65	192	0	60
Notts Co.	Kings Lynn	01.66	65	3	0	0
McNAUGHT, John						
Glasgow, 19 June, 1964						(M)
Chelsea	Hamilton Acad.	04.86	85-87	9	1	2
McNAUGHT, Kenneth						
Kirkcaldy, 11 January, 1955						(CD)
Everton	App	05.72	74-76	64	2	3
Aston Villa	Tr	08.77	77-82	207	0	8
West Bromwich A.	Tr	08.83	83	42	0	1
Manchester C.	L	12.84	84	7	0	0
Sheffield U.	Tr	07.85	85	34	0	5
McNEE, Terence A.						
Birkenhead, 5 June, 1925						(G)
Wrexham	Park Villa	12.46	46	11	-	0
McNEICE, Vincent						
Cricklewood, 25 October, 1938						(CH)
Watford	Jnrs	03.57	57-63	231	-	0
McNEIL, David						
Chester, 14 May, 1921						(LB)
Chester C.	Chester Rov.	05.42	46-50	114	-	1
McNEIL, Hamish						
Alva, 16 November, 1934						(F)
Colchester U.	Bonnyrigg Rose	08.57	57	2	-	1
McNEIL, Mark J.						
Forest Gate, 3 December, 1962						(F)
Leyton Orient	App	12.79	81-84	76	13	12
Aldershot	Tr	12.84	84-85	20	5	2
McNEIL, Matthew A.						
Glasgow, 28 July, 1927						(CH)
Newcastle U.	Hibernian	12.49	50	9	-	0
Barnsley	Tr	08.51	51-52	69	-	1
Brighton & H.A.	Tr	07.53	53-55	53	-	0
Norwich C.	Tr	03.56	55-56	44	-	2
McNEIL, Michael						
Middlesbrough, 7 February, 1940 Eu23-9/EF Lge/E-9						(FB)
Middlesbrough	Jnrs	06.57	58-63	178	-	3
Ipswich T.	Tr	07.64	64-71	141	5	4
McNEIL, Richard (Dixie)						
Melton Mowbray, 16 January, 1947						(F)
Leicester C.	Holwell Wks	11.64				
Exeter C.	Tr	06.66	66	31	0	11
Northampton T.	Corby T.	05.69	69-71	85	1	33
Lincoln C.	Tr	01.72	71-73	96	1	53
Hereford U.	Tr	08.74	74-77	128	1	85
Wrexham	Tr	09.77	77-82	166	1	54
Hereford U.	Tr	10.82	82	12	0	3

League Club	Source	Date Signed	Seasons Played	Career Record Apps	Subs	Gls

McNEIL, Robert M.
Hamilton, 1 November, 1962 (RB)

League Club	Source	Date Signed	Seasons Played	Apps	Subs	Gls
Hull C.	App	11.80	80-84	135	3	3
Lincoln C. (N/C)	Blackpool (N/C)	10.85	85	4	0	0
Preston N.E.	Tr	12.85	85-86	43	0	0
Carlisle U.	Tr	08.87	87	18	1	0

McNEILL, Alan A.
Belfast, 16 August, 1945 NI Amat (M)

League Club	Source	Date Signed	Seasons Played	Apps	Subs	Gls
Middlesbrough	Crusaders	08.67	67-68	3	0	0
Huddersfield T.	Tr	11.68	68	1	1	0
Oldham Ath.	Tr	10.69	69-74	154	16	19
Stockport Co.	Tr	07.75	75-76	69	2	1

McNEILL, Brian
Newcastle, 1 April, 1956 (FB)

League Club	Source	Date Signed	Seasons Played	Apps	Subs	Gls
Bristol C.	App	04.74	75-76	0	3	0
Plymouth Arg.	Tr	12.78	78-80	47	0	0

McNEILL, Edward V.
Warrenpoint (NI), 26 March, 1929 (G)

League Club	Source	Date Signed	Seasons Played	Apps	Subs	Gls
Sunderland	Portadown	12.51	53	7	-	0

McNEILL, Ian M.
Glasgow, 24 February, 1932 (IF)

League Club	Source	Date Signed	Seasons Played	Apps	Subs	Gls
Leicester C.	Aberdeen	03.56	55-58	72	-	26
Brighton & H.A.	Tr	03.59	58-61	116	-	12
Southend U.	Tr	07.62	62-63	41	-	3

McNEISH, Samuel
Bo'ness, 4 August, 1930 (F)

League Club	Source	Date Signed	Seasons Played	Apps	Subs	Gls
Leeds U.	Linlithgow Rose	02.51	50	1	-	0

McNICHOL, Alexander
Baillieston, 10 October, 1919 (IF)

League Club	Source	Date Signed	Seasons Played	Apps	Subs	Gls
Aldershot	Dunfermline Ath.	08.47	47-50	109	-	20
Rochdale	Tr	01.51	50	17	-	3

McNICHOL, James A.
Glasgow, 9 June, 1958 Su21-7 (CD)

League Club	Source	Date Signed	Seasons Played	Apps	Subs	Gls
Luton T.	Ipswich T. (App)	07.76	76-78	13	2	0
Brentford	Tr	10.78	78-83	151	4	22
Exeter C.	Tr	07.84	84-85	87	0	10
Torquay U.	Tr	07.86	86-88	124	0	13
Exeter C.	Tr	08.89	89-90	42	0	8
Torquay U.	Tr	07.91	91	2	0	0

McNICHOL, John
Kilmarnock, 20 August, 1925 (IF)

League Club	Source	Date Signed	Seasons Played	Apps	Subs	Gls
Newcastle U.	Hurlford Jnrs	08.46				
Brighton & H.A.	Tr	08.48	48-51	158	-	36
Chelsea	Tr	08.52	52-57	181	-	60
Crystal Palace	Tr	03.58	57-62	189	-	15

McNICHOL, Robert H.
Dumbarton, 13 February, 1933 (FB)

League Club	Source	Date Signed	Seasons Played	Apps	Subs	Gls
Accrington St.	Stirling A.	05.56	56-58	134	-	5
Brighton & H.A.	Tr	06.59	59-61	93	-	0
Carlisle U.	Gravesend & Nft.	10.63	63	1	-	0

McNIVEN, David S.
Larkhall, 9 September, 1955 Su21-3 (F)

League Club	Source	Date Signed	Seasons Played	Apps	Subs	Gls
Leeds U.	App	09.72	75-77	15	7	6
Bradford C.	Tr	02.78	77-82	202	10	64
Blackpool	Tr	02.83	82-83	45	4	11
Halifax T. (N/C)	Pittsburgh (USA)	03.85	84	12	0	4

McNULTY, Joseph
Dundalk (Ire), 17 July, 1923 Died 1986 (G)

League Club	Source	Date Signed	Seasons Played	Apps	Subs	Gls
Burnley	Ards.	05.49	50-51	8	-	0
Sheffield U.	Tr	06.52				

McNULTY, Thomas
Salford, 30 December, 1929 (FB)

League Club	Source	Date Signed	Seasons Played	Apps	Subs	Gls
Manchester U.	Jnrs	06.47	49-53	57	-	0
Liverpool	Tr	02.54	53-57	36	-	0

McNULTY, William G.
Edinburgh, 9 February, 1949 (G)

League Club	Source	Date Signed	Seasons Played	Apps	Subs	Gls
Port Vale	Jnrs	04.66	66	1	0	0
Chesterfield	Tr	07.68	68	6	0	0

McPARLAND, Ian J.
Edinburgh, 4 October, 1961 (F)

League Club	Source	Date Signed	Seasons Played	Apps	Subs	Gls
Notts Co.	Ormiston Primrose	12.80	80-88	190	31	69
Hull C.	Tr	03.89	88-90	31	16	8
Walsall	L	03.91	90	11	0	6

McPARLAND, Peter J.
Newry (NI), 25 April, 1934 EF Lge/NI-34 (OL)

League Club	Source	Date Signed	Seasons Played	Apps	Subs	Gls
Aston Villa	Dundalk	09.52	52-61	293	-	98
Wolverhampton W.	Tr	01.62	61-62	21	-	10
Plymouth Arg.	Tr	01.63	62-63	38	-	14

McPARTLAND, Desmond
Middlesbrough, 5 October, 1947 E Yth (G)

League Club	Source	Date Signed	Seasons Played	Apps	Subs	Gls
Middlesbrough	App	10.64	65-67	35	0	0
Carlisle U.	Tr	12.67	67	5	0	0
Northampton T.	Tr	07.69	69	6	0	0
Hartlepool U.	Tr	03.70	69-70	56	0	0

McPEAKE, Matthew
Ballymena (NI), 19 June, 1919 (LH)

League Club	Source	Date Signed	Seasons Played	Apps	Subs	Gls
Everton	Ballymena U.	07.46				
Grimsby T.	Tr	06.47				
New Brighton	Tr	07.48	48-49	50	-	2

MacPHAIL, John
Dundee, 7 December, 1955 (CD)

League Club	Source	Date Signed	Seasons Played	Apps	Subs	Gls
Sheffield U.	Dundee	01.79	78-82	135	0	7
York C.	Tr	02.83	82-85	141	1	24
Bristol C.	Tr	07.86	86	26	0	1
Sunderland	Tr	07.87	87-90	130	0	22
Hartlepool U.	Tr	09.90	90-91	82	1	2

McPHEAT, William
Caldercruix, 4 September, 1942 (IF)

League Club	Source	Date Signed	Seasons Played	Apps	Subs	Gls
Sunderland	Jnrs	09.59	60-62	58	-	19
Hartlepool U.	Tr	09.65	65	13	2	2

McPHEE, John
Motherwell, 21 November, 1937 (WH)

League Club	Source	Date Signed	Seasons Played	Apps	Subs	Gls
Blackpool	Motherwell	07.62	62-69	249	10	15
Barnsley	Tr	06.70	70	26	0	3
Southport	Tr	07.71	71-72	85	0	1

McPHEE, Magnus G.
Edinburgh, 30 April, 1914 Died 1960 (CF)

League Club	Source	Date Signed	Seasons Played	Apps	Subs	Gls
Bradford P.A.	Workington	10.36	36	30	-	17
Coventry C.	Tr	06.37	37	12	-	6
Reading	Tr	05.38	38-48	132	-	85

McPHEE, Stewart D.
Middlesbrough, 15 January, 1965 (M)

League Club	Source	Date Signed	Seasons Played	Apps	Subs	Gls
Middlesbrough		08.83				
Darlington	Whitby T.	09.86	86	7	2	1

McPHERSON, Albert
Salford, 8 July, 1927 (CH)

League Club	Source	Date Signed	Seasons Played	Apps	Subs	Gls
Bury		06.49				
Walsall	Stalybridge Celtic	05.54	54-63	351	-	8

McPHERSON, Angus
Glasgow, 11 October, 1968 (D)

League Club	Source	Date Signed	Seasons Played	Apps	Subs	Gls
Exeter C. (L)	Glasgow Rangers	03.90	89	11	0	1

McPHERSON, Ian B.
Glasgow, 26 July, 1920 Died 1983 (W)

League Club	Source	Date Signed	Seasons Played	Apps	Subs	Gls
Notts Co.	Glasgow Rangers	08.45				
Arsenal	Tr	08.46	46-50	152	-	19
Notts Co.	Tr	08.51	51-52	52	-	6
Brentford	Tr	07.53	53	4	-	0

McPHERSON, Keith A.
Greenwich, 11 September, 1963 (CD)

League Club	Source	Date Signed	Seasons Played	Apps	Subs	Gls
West Ham U.	App	09.81	84	1	0	0
Cambridge U.	L	09.85	85	11	0	1
Northampton T.	Tr	01.86	85-89	182	0	8
Reading	Tr	08.90	90-91	90	0	4

McPHERSON, Kenneth
Hartlepool, 25 March, 1927 (CF/CH)

League Club	Source	Date Signed	Seasons Played	Apps	Subs	Gls
Notts Co.		08.50	50-52	24	-	11
Middlesbrough	Tr	08.53	53-55	33	-	15
Coventry C.	Tr	11.55	55-57	89	-	38
Newport Co.	Tr	06.58	58-60	128	-	51
Swindon T.	Tr	08.61	61-64	107	-	3

McPHILLIPS, Terence
Manchester, 1 October, 1968 (F)

League Club	Source	Date Signed	Seasons Played	Apps	Subs	Gls
Halifax T.	Liverpool (YT)	09.87	87-90	61	32	29
Northampton T.	L	11.89	89	0	1	0
Crewe Alex. (N/C)	Tr	08.91	91	5	1	1

McQUADE, James
Renfrew, 14 October, 1933 (F)

League Club	Source	Date Signed	Seasons Played	Apps	Subs	Gls
Halifax T.	Dumbarton	08.57	57	9	-	2

League Club	Source	Date Signed	Seasons Played	Career Record Apps	Subs	Gls

McQUADE, Terence J.
Hackney, 24 February, 1941 (W)

League Club	Source	Date Signed	Seasons Played	Apps	Subs	Gls
Millwall	Enfield	10.61	61-62	34	-	7
Queens Park R.	Tr	07.63	63	20	-	2
Millwall	Leyton Orient	11.65	65	3	0	1

McQUAID, Thomas J.
Dublin, 1 February, 1936 (WH)

League Club	Source	Date Signed	Seasons Played	Apps	Subs	Gls
Bradford C.	Thackley	11.57	58-59	23	-	2

McQUARRIE, Andrew
Glasgow, 2 October, 1939 (IF)

League Club	Source	Date Signed	Seasons Played	Apps	Subs	Gls
Chesterfield	Albion Rov.	11.62	62-63	38	-	12
Brighton & H.A.	Tr	07.64	64	2	-	1

McQUEEN, Gordon
Kilbirnie, 26 June, 1952 S-30 (CD)

League Club	Source	Date Signed	Seasons Played	Apps	Subs	Gls
Leeds U.	St Mirren	09.72	72-77	140	0	15
Manchester U.	Tr	02.78	77-84	184	0	20

McQUEEN, Ian D.
Manchester, 4 February, 1946 (CF)

League Club	Source	Date Signed	Seasons Played	Apps	Subs	Gls
Rochdale		01.66	65-66	14	2	4

McQUEEN, Thomas
West Calder, 21 February, 1929 (G)

League Club	Source	Date Signed	Seasons Played	Apps	Subs	Gls
Accrington St.	Queen of South	06.54	54-56	80	-	0

McQUEEN, Thomas F.
Bellshill, 1 April, 1963 (LB)

League Club	Source	Date Signed	Seasons Played	Apps	Subs	Gls
West Ham U.	Aberdeen	03.87	86-89	24	6	0

McQUILLAN, Dennis
Derby, 16 March, 1934 (OR)

League Club	Source	Date Signed	Seasons Played	Apps	Subs	Gls
Derby Co.	Jnrs	03.51	52-55	18	-	1
Aldershot	Tr	07.56				
Luton T.	Tr	03.57				

McQUILLAN, Patrick G.
Belfast, 27 June, 1961 (RB)

League Club	Source	Date Signed	Seasons Played	Apps	Subs	Gls
Swansea C.		08.79				
Swansea C.	Pembroke Bor.	12.83	83-84	25	1	0

MacRAE, Keith
Glasgow, 5 February, 1951 Su23-2/SF Lge (G)

League Club	Source	Date Signed	Seasons Played	Apps	Subs	Gls
Manchester C.	Motherwell	10.73	73-80	56	0	0
Leeds U.	Portland (USA)	03.82				

MacREADY, Brian L.
Leicester, 25 March, 1942 (IF)

League Club	Source	Date Signed	Seasons Played	Apps	Subs	Gls
West Bromwich A.	Willerby B.C.	02.60	60-63	14	-	1
Mansfield T.	Tr	07.64	64-65	49	1	11

McSEVENEY, John H.
Shotts, 8 February, 1931 (OL)

League Club	Source	Date Signed	Seasons Played	Apps	Subs	Gls
Sunderland	Hamilton Acad.	10.51	51-54	35	-	3
Cardiff C.	Tr	05.55	55-56	75	-	18
Newport Co.	Tr	07.57	57-60	171	-	53
Hull C.	Tr	07.61	61-64	161	-	60

McSHANE, Anthony
Belfast, 28 February, 1927 (WH)

League Club	Source	Date Signed	Seasons Played	Apps	Subs	Gls
Plymouth Arg.	Brantwood	12.48	49-54	85	-	2
Swindon T.	Tr	06.55	55-56	41	-	0

McSHANE, Harold
Holytown, 8 April, 1920 (W)

League Club	Source	Date Signed	Seasons Played	Apps	Subs	Gls
Blackburn Rov.	Bellshill Ath.	04.37	37	2	-	0
Huddersfield T.	Tr	09.46	46	15	-	1
Bolton W.	Tr	07.47	47-50	93	-	6
Manchester U.	Tr	09.50	50-53	56	-	8
Oldham Ath.	Tr	02.54	53-54	41	-	5

McSTAY, James G.
Newry (NI), 4 August, 1922 LOI (W)

League Club	Source	Date Signed	Seasons Played	Apps	Subs	Gls
Grimsby T.	Dundalk	08.48	48-50	61	-	2

McSTAY, William J.
Hamilton, 26 November, 1961 (D)

League Club	Source	Date Signed	Seasons Played	Apps	Subs	Gls
Huddersfield T.	Glasgow Celtic	03.87	86-87	4	5	0
Notts Co.	Tr	02.88	87-89	33	12	1
Hartlepool U.	L	11.89	89	3	0	0

McTAFF, Stephen
Tanfield (Dm), 11 March, 1922 (WH)

League Club	Source	Date Signed	Seasons Played	Apps	Subs	Gls
Bradford P.A.	East Tanfield	05.45	46-47	29	-	2
New Brighton	Tr	07.48	48-50	100	-	3

McTAVISH, John R.
Glasgow, 2 February, 1932 (CH)

League Club	Source	Date Signed	Seasons Played	Apps	Subs	Gls
Manchester C.	Dalry Th.	06.52	53-59	93	-	0

McTURK, John
Cumnock, 11 July, 1936 (FB)

League Club	Source	Date Signed	Seasons Played	Apps	Subs	Gls
Wrexham	St Mirren	07.57	57	2	-	0

McVAY, David R.
Workington, 5 March, 1955 (D)

League Club	Source	Date Signed	Seasons Played	Apps	Subs	Gls
Notts Co.	Jnrs	07.73	73-78	101	12	2
Torquay U.	L	09.77	77	8	0	0
Peterborough U.	Tr	07.79	79-80	47	2	1
Lincoln C.	Tr	08.81	81	13	0	0

McVEIGH, James
Bamford (Dy), 2 July, 1949 (FB)

League Club	Source	Date Signed	Seasons Played	Apps	Subs	Gls
Wolverhampton W.		05.68	68	2	0	0
Gillingham	Tr	10.70	70-71	48	0	1

McVICAR, Donald
Perth, 6 November, 1962 (M)

League Club	Source	Date Signed	Seasons Played	Apps	Subs	Gls
Tranmere Rov. (N/C)	St Johnstone	08.85	85	7	0	0

MacVINISH, Thomas
Inverness, 1 January, 1921 (OL)

League Club	Source	Date Signed	Seasons Played	Apps	Subs	Gls
Preston N.E.	Hamilton Acad.	08.48				
Darlington	Tr	08.50	50	1	-	0

McVITIE, George J.
Carlisle, 7 September, 1948 E Sch (W)

League Club	Source	Date Signed	Seasons Played	Apps	Subs	Gls
Carlisle U.	App	12.65	65-70	124	4	21
West Bromwich A.	Tr	08.70	70-71	42	0	5
Oldham Ath.	Tr	08.72	72-75	108	5	19
Carlisle U.	Tr	12.75	75-80	191	7	20

McWHINNIE, Archibald
Glasgow, 17 July, 1926 (WH)

League Club	Source	Date Signed	Seasons Played	Apps	Subs	Gls
Wrexham	Rutherglen Glencairn	05.51	51	2	-	0

MABBUTT, Gary V.
Bristol, 23 August, 1961 E Yth/Eu21-7/E'B'/E-16 (CD)

League Club	Source	Date Signed	Seasons Played	Apps	Subs	Gls
Bristol Rov.	App	01.79	78-81	122	9	10
Tottenham H.	Tr	08.82	82-91	326	13	25

Gary Mabbutt (Bristol Rovers, Tottenham Hotspur & England)

MABBUTT, Kevin R.
Bristol, 5 December, 1958 (F)

League Club	Source	Date Signed	Seasons Played	Apps	Subs	Gls
Bristol C.	App	01.76	77-81	112	17	29
Crystal Palace	Tr	10.81	81-84	67	8	22

MABBUTT, Raymond W.
Aylesbury, 13 March, 1936 (WH)

League Club	Source	Date Signed	Seasons Played	Apps	Subs	Gls
Bristol Rov.	Oxford C.	08.56	57-68	392	3	27
Newport Co.	Tr	09.69	69-70	38	6	14

MABEE, Gary L.
Oxford, 1 February, 1955 (F)

League Club	Source	Date Signed	Seasons Played	Apps	Subs	Gls
Tottenham H.	App	02.72				
Northampton T.	Tr	08.74	74-75	29	4	13

MACARI, Luigi (Lou)
Aberdeen, 4 June, 1949 Su23-2/S-24 (F)

League Club	Source	Date Signed	Seasons Played	Apps	Subs	Gls
Manchester U.	Glasgow Celtic	01.73	72-83	311	18	78
Swindon T.	Tr	07.84	84-85	33	3	3

Lou Macari (Glasgow Celtic, Manchester United, Swindon Town & Scotland)

MACEDO, Anthony
Gibraltar, 22 February, 1938 Eu23-10 (G)

League Club	Source	Date Signed	Seasons Played	Apps	Subs	Gls
Fulham	Jnrs	10.55	57-67	346	0	0
Colchester U.	Tr	09.68	68	38	0	0

MACEY, John R. T.
Bristol, 13 November, 1947 E Sch (G)

League Club	Source	Date Signed	Seasons Played	Apps	Subs	Gls
Bristol C.	App	05.65				
Grimsby T.	Tr	07.68	68-69	36	1	0
Newport Co.	Tr	07.70	70-75	194	0	0

MACHENT, Stanley C.
Chesterfield, 23 March, 1921 (IF)

League Club	Source	Date Signed	Seasons Played	Apps	Subs	Gls
Sheffield U.		10.38	46-47	22	-	2
Chesterfield	Tr	11.47	47-48	21	-	7

MACHIN, Alec H.
Hampstead, 6 July, 1920 (WH)

League Club	Source	Date Signed	Seasons Played	Apps	Subs	Gls
Chelsea	Royal Hants Regt	10.44	46-47	53	-	8
Plymouth Arg.	Tr	06.48	48-50	26	-	1

MACHIN, Ernest T.
Walkden, 26 April, 1944 (M)

League Club	Source	Date Signed	Seasons Played	Apps	Subs	Gls
Coventry C.	Nelson	03.62	62-72	255	2	33
Plymouth Arg.	Tr	12.72	72-73	57	0	6
Brighton & H.A.	Tr	08.74	74-75	64	0	2

MACHIN, Melvyn
Newcastle-u-Lyme, 16 April, 1945 (M)

League Club	Source	Date Signed	Seasons Played	Apps	Subs	Gls
Port Vale	Jnrs	07.62	62-65	29	1	6
Gillingham	Tr	07.66	66-70	155	1	11
Bournemouth	Tr	12.70	70-73	110	0	7
Norwich C.	Tr	12.73	73-77	93	3	4

MACKEN, Anthony
Dublin, 30 July, 1950 IR-1 (RB)

League Club	Source	Date Signed	Seasons Played	Apps	Subs	Gls
Derby Co.	Waterford	08.74	75-77	20	3	1
Portsmouth	L	11.75	75	10	0	1
Walsall	Tr	10.77	77-81	190	0	1

MACKIN, John
Glasgow, 18 November, 1943 (RB)

League Club	Source	Date Signed	Seasons Played	Apps	Subs	Gls
Northampton T.		11.63	65-68	95	9	11
Lincoln C.	Tr	07.69	69	3	0	0
York C.	Tr	09.69	69-72	157	3	7
Darlington	L	03.73	72	2	0	0

MACKLEWORTH, Colin
Bow, 24 March, 1947 (G)

League Club	Source	Date Signed	Seasons Played	Apps	Subs	Gls
West Ham U.	App	04.64	66	3	0	0
Leicester C.	Tr	11.67	67-70	6	0	0

MACKRETH, Stephen F.
Wrexham, 1 July, 1950 (FB)

League Club	Source	Date Signed	Seasons Played	Apps	Subs	Gls
Wrexham	Jnrs	10.67	68	1	1	0

MACOWAT, Ian S.
Liverpool, 19 November, 1965 E Sch/E Yth (LB)

League Club	Source	Date Signed	Seasons Played	Apps	Subs	Gls
Everton	App	11.83				
Gillingham	Tr	01.85	84-85	4	1	0
Crewe Alex.	Tr	07.86	86-88	64	8	1

MACROW, Geoffrey C.
East Harling (Nk), 26 September, 1932 (OR)

League Club	Source	Date Signed	Seasons Played	Apps	Subs	Gls
Ipswich T.	Thetford T.	08.55	55-56	2	-	0

MADDEN, Craig A.
Manchester, 25 September, 1958 (F)

League Club	Source	Date Signed	Seasons Played	Apps	Subs	Gls
Bury	Northern Nomads	03.78	77-85	278	19	129
West Bromwich A.	Tr	03.86	85-86	10	2	3
Blackpool	Tr	02.87	86-89	73	18	24
Wrexham	L	01.90	89	6	2	0
York C.	Tr	03.90	89	3	1	0

MADDEN, David J.
Stepney, 6 January, 1963 (M)

League Club	Source	Date Signed	Seasons Played	Apps	Subs	Gls
Southampton	App	01.81				
Bournemouth	L	01.83	82	5	0	0
Arsenal	Tr	08.83	83	2	0	0
Charlton Ath.	Tr	06.84	84	19	1	1
Reading	Los Angeles (USA)	11.87	87	7	2	1
Crystal Palace	Tr	08.88	88-89	19	8	5
Birmingham C.	L	01.90	89	5	0	1
Maidstone U.	Tr	06.90	90	10	0	0

MADDEN, Lawrence D.
Hackney, 28 September, 1955 (CD)

League Club	Source	Date Signed	Seasons Played	Apps	Subs	Gls
Mansfield T. (N/C)	Arsenal (N/C)	03.75	74-75	9	1	0
Charlton Ath.	Manchester Univ.	03.78	77-81	109	4	7
Millwall	Tr	03.82	81-82	44	3	1
Sheffield Wed.	Tr	08.83	83-90	200	12	2
Leicester C.	L	01.91	90	3	0	0
Wolverhampton W.	Tr	08.91	91	43	0	1

MADDEN, Neil
Luton, 6 February, 1962 (M)

League Club	Source	Date Signed	Seasons Played	Apps	Subs	Gls
Luton T.	App	12.79	79	1	0	0

MADDEN, Peter
Bradford, 31 October, 1934 (CH)

League Club	Source	Date Signed	Seasons Played	Apps	Subs	Gls
Rotherham U.	Thornton	10.55	55-65	308	2	7
Bradford P.A.	Tr	07.66	66	25	3	1
Aldershot	Tr	07.67	67	26	1	1

MADDISON, Donald
Washington, 13 February, 1927 (G)

League Club	Source	Date Signed	Seasons Played	Apps	Subs	Gls
Bradford P.A.	Sunderland (Am)	06.46				
Blackpool	Tr	02.48				
Darlington	Tr	08.50	50	1	-	0

MADDISON, Frank
Worksop, 6 May, 1934 (FB)

League Club	Source	Date Signed	Seasons Played	Apps	Subs	Gls
Notts Co.		08.53	56-57	15	-	0

League Club	Source	Date Signed	Seasons Played	Apps	Subs	Gls
MADDISON, George *Hull, 6 October, 1930*						(G)
Aldershot		08.48	48	2	-	0
York C.	Tr	09.52	53	11	-	0
MADDISON, W. Hartley *Sunderland, 6 April, 1954*						(OR)
Hartlepool U. (Am)		08.73	73-74	3	1	0
MADDISON, James P. *South Shields, 9 November, 1924 Died 1992*						(OL)
Middlesbrough	Jnrs	12.45	46	1	-	0
Darlington	Tr	08.49	49	41	-	7
Grimsby T.	Tr	06.50	50-58	272	-	40
Chesterfield	Tr	03.59	58-60	98	-	15
MADDISON, John A. (Jack) *Barrow, 1 October, 1940*						(W)
Barrow	Holker C.O.B.	07.60	61-64	88	-	18
MADDISON, Lee R. *Bristol, 5 October, 1972*						(LB)
Bristol Rov.	YT	05.91	91	8	2	0
MADDISON, Neil S. *Darlington, 2 October, 1969*						(M)
Southampton	YT	04.88	88-91	8	9	2
MADDISON, Ralph *Doncaster, 28 August, 1918*						(W)
Doncaster Rov.	Bentley Colly	01.46	46-47	61	-	19
Stockport Co.	Tr	05.48	48	5	-	0
Southport	Tr	02.49	48-49	34	-	4
MADDIX, Daniel S. *Ashford, 11 October, 1967*						(CD)
Tottenham H.	App	07.85				
Southend U.	L	10.86	86	2	0	0
Queens Park R.	Tr	07.87	87-91	113	12	6
MADDOCK, Cyril *Sandbach, 14 June, 1933*						
Crewe Alex.	Jnrs	05.51	51	1	-	0
MADDREN, William D. *Billingham, 11 January, 1951 Eu23-5*						(CD)
Middlesbrough	App	06.68	68-77	293	3	19
MADDY, Paul M. *Cwmcarn, 17 August, 1962 Wu21-1*						(LM)
Cardiff C.	App	08.80	80-82	35	8	3
Hereford U.	L	03.83	82	9	0	1
Swansea C.	Tr	08.83	83	18	2	3
Hereford U.	Tr	03.84	83-85	75	2	16
Brentford	Tr	07.86	86	29	2	5
Chester C.	Tr	07.87	87	17	1	1
Hereford U.	Tr	03.88	87-88	27	8	1
MADELEY, Paul E. *Leeds, 20 September, 1944 E Yth/EF Lge/E-24*						(D)
Leeds U.	Farsley Celtic	05.62	63-80	528	8	25
MADRICK, Carl J. *Bolton, 20 September, 1968*						(F)
Huddersfield T.	YT	06.87	87	3	5	1
Peterborough U.	Tr	09.88	88	3	5	0
MAFFEY, Dennis *Sunderland, 22 February, 1922*						(CF)
Ipswich T.	Walton U.	07.47	47	5	-	1
MAGEE, Eric *Lurgan (NI), 24 August, 1947 NI Amat*						(F)
Oldham Ath.	Glenavon	06.67	67-68	41	4	9
Port Vale	Tr	07.69	69	11	7	1
MAGGIORE, Anthony *Sunderland, 28 October, 1957*						(CD)
Hartlepool U.	Sunderland (App)	11.75	75-76	24	4	0
MAGILL, Edward J. *Lurgan (NI), 17 May, 1939 NIu23-1/NI-26*						(FB)
Arsenal	Portadown	05.59	59-64	116	-	0
Brighton & H.A.	Tr	10.65	65-67	50	0	1
MAGILTON, James *Belfast, 6 May, 1969 NIu23-1/NI-9*						(M)
Liverpool	App	05.86				
Oxford U.	Tr	10.90	90-91	81	0	18
MAGUIRE, Gavin T. *Hammersmith, 24 November, 1967 W'B'/W-7*						(CD)
Queens Park R.	App	10.85	86-88	33	7	0
Portsmouth	Tr	01.89	88-90	69	1	0
Newcastle U.	L	10.91	91	3	0	0
MAGUIRE, James E. *Brandon, 23 July, 1917*						(OR)
Wolverhampton W.	Willington	11.35	36-38	79	-	7
Swindon T.	Tr	05.47	47	28	-	4
Halifax T.	Tr	10.48	48-49	55	-	8
MAGUIRE, James S. *Eaglesham, 3 February, 1932*						(OL)
Rochdale	Queen of South	08.58	58	15	-	0
MAGUIRE, Leslie G. R. *Bethnal Green, 31 January, 1929*						(IF)
Gillingham		(N/L)	50-51	6	-	2
MAGUIRE, Paul B. *Glasgow, 21 August, 1956*						(W)
Shrewsbury T.	Kilbirnie Ladeside	08.76	76-79	143	8	35
Stoke C.	Tr	09.80	80-83	93	14	24
Port Vale	Tacoma (USA)	07.85	85-87	101	14	22
MAGUIRE, Peter J. *Holmfirth, 11 September, 1969*						(F)
Leeds U.	YT	06.88	87	2	0	0
Huddersfield T.	Tr	09.89	89-90	1	6	1
Stockport Co.	L	09.90	90	0	2	0
MAGUIRE, Thomas *Dublin, 22 July, 1955*						(M)
Liverpool	App	11.72				
Crewe Alex.	Tr	02.74	73-75	23	4	1
MAHER, Aiden *Liverpool, 1 December, 1946 E Sch*						(OL)
Everton	App	12.64	67	1	0	0
Plymouth Arg.	Tr	10.68	68-70	64	0	3
Tranmere Rov.	Tr	06.71	71	2	5	1
MAHER, John *Manchester, 6 November, 1933*						(F)
Walsall	Manchester C. (Am)	05.54	54	1	-	0
Gillingham	Tr	07.55	55	2	-	1
MAHON, Michael J. *Manchester, 17 September, 1944 E Amat*						(W)
Port Vale	North Shields	04.67	66-68	91	1	22
York C.	Tr	07.69	69	27	2	10
Colchester U.	Tr	05.70	70-73	131	5	26
MAHONEY, Anthony J. *Barking, 29 September, 1959 E Yth*						(F)
Fulham	App	08.77	76-80	53	6	10
Northampton T.	L	10.81	81	6	0	0
Brentford	Tr	07.82	82-83	33	8	12
Crystal Palace	Tr	06.84	84	17	1	4
MAHONEY, Brian *Huddersfield, 12 May, 1952*						(F)
Huddersfield T.	App	11.69	70-71	18	2	2
Barnsley	Tr	03.72	71-74	82	8	15
MAHONEY, John F. *Cardiff, 20 September, 1946 Wu23-3/W-51*						(M)
Crewe Alex.	Ashton U.	03.66	65-66	16	2	5
Stoke C.	Tr	03.67	66-76	272	12	25
Middlesbrough	Tr	08.77	77-78	77	0	1
Swansea C.	Tr	07.79	79-82	106	4	1
MAHONEY, Michael J. *Bristol, 25 October, 1950*						(G)
Bristol C.	App	08.68	67-69	4	0	0
Torquay U.	Tr	08.70	70-74	157	0	0
Newcastle U.	Tr	03.75	74-78	108	0	0
MAHY, Barry *Doncaster, 21 January, 1942*						(IF)
Scunthorpe U.	Jersey	05.63	63-66	21	1	2

MAIDMENT, Ian M.
Newbury, 9 August, 1947 (OL)

League Club	Source	Date Signed	Seasons Played	Apps	Subs	Gls
Reading	App	08.65	65	7	0	0

MAIL, David
Bristol, 12 September, 1962 (CD)

League Club	Source	Date Signed	Seasons Played	Apps	Subs	Gls
Aston Villa	App	07.80				
Blackburn Rov.	Tr	01.82	82-89	200	6	4
Hull C.	Tr	07.90	90-91	71	2	2

MAILER, Ronald G.
Auchterarder, 18 May, 1932 (F)

League Club	Source	Date Signed	Seasons Played	Apps	Subs	Gls
Darlington	Dunfermline Ath.	03.54	54	11	-	2

MAILEY, William
Duntocher, 13 June, 1943 S Sch (G)

League Club	Source	Date Signed	Seasons Played	Apps	Subs	Gls
Everton	Jnrs	06.60				
Crewe Alex.	Tr	03.63	63-69	215	0	0

MAIN, Ian
Swindon, 31 October, 1959 (G)

League Club	Source	Date Signed	Seasons Played	Apps	Subs	Gls
Exeter C.	Gloucester C.	09.78	78-81	78	0	0

MAIORANA, Giuliano
Cambridge, 18 April, 1969 (LW)

League Club	Source	Date Signed	Seasons Played	Apps	Subs	Gls
Manchester U.	Histon	11.88	88-89	2	5	0

MAIR, Gordon
Coatbridge, 18 December, 1958 S Sch (W)

League Club	Source	Date Signed	Seasons Played	Apps	Subs	Gls
Notts Co.	App	12.76	76-83	123	8	19
Lincoln C.	Tr	08.84	84-85	57	0	3

MAITLAND, Lloyd C.
Coleshill, 21 March, 1957 (W)

League Club	Source	Date Signed	Seasons Played	Apps	Subs	Gls
Huddersfield T.	App	03.74	74-76	31	8	2
Darlington	Tr	03.77	76-78	58	13	6

MAJOR, John L. (Jack)
Islington, 12 March, 1929 E Amat (W)

League Club	Source	Date Signed	Seasons Played	Apps	Subs	Gls
Hull C. (Am)	Hull Amats	04.47	46	3	-	0
Hull C.	Bishop Auckland	06.55	55-56	10	-	0

MAJOR, Leslie D.
Yeovil, 25 January, 1926 (G)

League Club	Source	Date Signed	Seasons Played	Apps	Subs	Gls
Leicester C.	Loughborough Corries	06.43	47-48	26	-	0
Plymouth Arg.	Tr	05.49	49-55	75	-	0

MAKEL, Lee R.
Sunderland, 11 January, 1973 (M)

League Club	Source	Date Signed	Seasons Played	Apps	Subs	Gls
Newcastle U.	YT	02.91	90-91	6	6	1

MAKEPEACE, Brian
Rossington, 6 October, 1931 (FB)

League Club	Source	Date Signed	Seasons Played	Apps	Subs	Gls
Doncaster Rov.	Rossington Colly	03.49	50-60	353	-	0

MAKIN, Joseph
Manchester, 21 September, 1950 (FB)

League Club	Source	Date Signed	Seasons Played	Apps	Subs	Gls
Oldham Ath.	App	10.67	66-67	6	0	0

MAKIN, Samuel H.
Radcliffe, 14 November, 1925 Died 1981 (W)

League Club	Source	Date Signed	Seasons Played	Apps	Subs	Gls
Rochdale	Moss Rov.	05.44	46	5	-	1

MALAM, Albert
Liverpool, 20 January, 1913 Died 1992 (IF)

League Club	Source	Date Signed	Seasons Played	Apps	Subs	Gls
Chesterfield	Colwyn Bay	11.32	32-34	58	-	26
Huddersfield T.	Tr	09.34	34-35	21	-	11
Doncaster Rov.	Tr	09.36	36-38	96	-	22
Wrexham	Tr	02.46	46	6	-	1

MALAN, Norman F.
South Africa, 23 November, 1923 (G)

League Club	Source	Date Signed	Seasons Played	Apps	Subs	Gls
Middlesbrough	Defos (SA)	10.45	46	2	-	0
Darlington	Tr	08.48				
Scunthorpe U.	Tr	06.50	50-55	136	-	0
Bradford P.A.	Tr	07.56	56	24	-	0

MALCOLM, Alexander A.
Hamilton, 13 February, 1956 (LB)

League Club	Source	Date Signed	Seasons Played	Apps	Subs	Gls
Luton T.	App	07.73				
Northampton T.	Tr	08.76	76	2	0	0

MALCOLM, Alexander M.
Alloa, 15 December, 1921 (W)

League Club	Source	Date Signed	Seasons Played	Apps	Subs	Gls
Barnsley	Alloa Ath.	06.46	46-47	5	-	0

MALCOLM, Andrew
West Ham, 4 May, 1933 E Sch/E Yth/EF Lge (WH)

League Club	Source	Date Signed	Seasons Played	Apps	Subs	Gls
West Ham U.	Jnrs	07.50	53-61	283	-	4
Chelsea	Tr	11.61	61	27	-	1
Queens Park R.	Tr	10.62	62-64	84	-	4

MALCOLM, Grant W.L.
Musselburgh, 25 October, 1940 S Sch (F)

League Club	Source	Date Signed	Seasons Played	Apps	Subs	Gls
Newcastle U.	Dalkeith Th.	11.57	59	1	-	0

MALCOLM, John M.
Clackmannan, 20 May, 1917 (WH)

League Club	Source	Date Signed	Seasons Played	Apps	Subs	Gls
Accrington St.		10.44	46	25	-	0
Tranmere Rov.	Tr	07.47	47	22	-	0

MALCOLM, Kenneth C.
Aberdeen, 25 July, 1926 (FB)

League Club	Source	Date Signed	Seasons Played	Apps	Subs	Gls
Ipswich T.	Arbroath	05.54	54-62	274	-	2

MALCOLM, Paul A.
Felling, 11 December, 1964 (G)

League Club	Source	Date Signed	Seasons Played	Apps	Subs	Gls
Newcastle U.	App	12.82				
Rochdale	Durham C.	09.84	84	24	0	0
Shrewsbury T.	Tr	07.85				
Barnsley	Tr	08.86	86	3	0	0
Doncaster Rov.	Tr	07.88	88	34	0	0

MALE, C. George
West Ham, 8 May, 1910 EF Lge/E-19 (FB)

League Club	Source	Date Signed	Seasons Played	Apps	Subs	Gls
Arsenal	Clapton	05.30	30-47	285	-	0

MALE, Norman A.
West Bromwich, 27 May, 1917 (FB)

League Club	Source	Date Signed	Seasons Played	Apps	Subs	Gls
West Bromwich A.	Bush Rov.	10.34	37	3	-	1
Walsall	Tr	06.38	38-48	70	-	2

MALKIN, Christopher G.
Hoylake, 4 June, 1967 (F)

League Club	Source	Date Signed	Seasons Played	Apps	Subs	Gls
Tranmere Rov.	Stork	07.87	87-91	80	45	28

MALKIN, John
Stoke, 9 November, 1925 (IF)

League Club	Source	Date Signed	Seasons Played	Apps	Subs	Gls
Stoke C.		07.47	47-55	175	-	23

MALLALIEU, Anthony M.
Prestatyn, 3 October, 1946 (F)

League Club	Source	Date Signed	Seasons Played	Apps	Subs	Gls
Manchester U.	Rhyl	06.64				
Stockport Co.		03.70	69	0	1	0

MALLENDER, Gary
Barnsley, 12 March, 1959 (M)

League Club	Source	Date Signed	Seasons Played	Apps	Subs	Gls
Barnsley	App	03.77	76-78	0	2	0

MALLENDER, Kenneth
Thrybergh, 10 December, 1943 (D)

League Club	Source	Date Signed	Seasons Played	Apps	Subs	Gls
Sheffield U.	App	02.61	61-68	141	2	2
Norwich C.	Tr	10.68	68-70	46	0	1
Hereford U.	Tr	07.71	72-73	71	1	1

MALLENDER, Paul R.
Norwich, 30 November, 1969 (D)

League Club	Source	Date Signed	Seasons Played	Apps	Subs	Gls
Hereford U. (YT)	YT	09.86	87	0	1	0

MALLETT, Joseph
Gateshead, 8 January, 1916 (WH)

League Club	Source	Date Signed	Seasons Played	Apps	Subs	Gls
Charlton Ath.	Dunston Colly	11.35	38	2	-	0
Queens Park R.	Tr	02.39	38-46	42	-	9
Southampton	Tr	02.47	46-52	215	-	3
Leyton Orient	Tr	07.53	53-54	27	-	1

MALLEY, Philip
Felling, 1 November, 1965 (M)

League Club	Source	Date Signed	Seasons Played	Apps	Subs	Gls
Hartlepool U.	Sunderland (App)	11.83	83	0	1	0
Burnley	Berwick R. (trial)	02.84	83-87	91	4	5
Stockport Co.	L	11.84	84	3	0	0

MALLINSON, David J.
Sheffield, 7 July, 1946 (WH)

League Club	Source	Date Signed	Seasons Played	Apps	Subs	Gls
Mansfield T.	Jnrs	03.65	65	10	1	1

MALLINSON, Trevor
Huddersfield, 25 April, 1945 (FB)

League Club	Source	Date Signed	Seasons Played	Apps	Subs	Gls
Halifax T. (Am)	Huddersfield T.	12.64	64	3	-	0

MALLON, James G.
Glasgow, 28 August, 1938 (FB)

League Club	Source	Date Signed	Seasons Played	Apps	Subs	Gls
Oldham Ath.	Partick Th.	03.59	58-59	31	-	8
Barrow	Morton	10.65	65-68	149	1	3

MALLORY, Richard J. L.
Bermuda, 10 August, 1942 (OL)

League Club	Source	Date Signed	Seasons Played	Apps	Subs	Gls
Cardiff C.	Bermuda	05.63	63	3	-	0

MALLOY, Daniel
Dennyloan, 6 November, 1930 S'B'-2/SF Lge (CH)

League Club	Source	Date Signed	Seasons Played	Apps	Subs	Gls
Cardiff C.	Dundee	10.53	55-60	225	-	1
Doncaster Rov.	Tr	08.61	61	42	-	0

MALONE, Richard P.
Motherwell, 22 August, 1947 Su23-1 (RB)

League Club	Source	Date Signed	Seasons Played	Apps	Subs	Gls
Sunderland	Ayr U.	10.70	70-76	235	1	2
Hartlepool U.	Tr	07.77	77-78	36	0	1
Blackpool	Tr	11.78	78-79	48	0	1

MALONEY, Derek T.
Newton, 27 March, 1936

League Club	Source	Date Signed	Seasons Played	Apps	Subs	Gls
Crewe Alex.		02.58	57	15	-	0

MALONEY, Joseph J.
Liverpool, 26 January, 1934 (CH)

League Club	Source	Date Signed	Seasons Played	Apps	Subs	Gls
Liverpool	Jnrs	01.51	52-53	12	-	0
Shrewsbury T.	Tr	07.54	54-59	237	-	0
Port Vale	Tr	07.61	61	1	-	0
Crewe Alex.	Tr	08.61	61-62	26	-	0

MALONEY, Paul J.
Doncaster, 13 January, 1952 (M)

League Club	Source	Date Signed	Seasons Played	Apps	Subs	Gls
Huddersfield T.	App	11.69				
York C.	Tr	02.70	69-71	3	5	0

MALONEY, Sean
Hyde, 4 October, 1962 (F)

League Club	Source	Date Signed	Seasons Played	Apps	Subs	Gls
Stockport Co. (N/C)	Jnrs	08.79	79	0	1	0

MALOY, Kenneth F.
Edmonton, 16 September, 1940 (OL)

League Club	Source	Date Signed	Seasons Played	Apps	Subs	Gls
Plymouth Arg.	Ilford	09.59	60-63	62	-	11
Peterborough U.	Tr	07.64	64	6	-	1
Aldershot	Tr	07.65	65-66	51	1	12

MALOY, Kevin W.
Aldershot, 12 November, 1966 (G)

League Club	Source	Date Signed	Seasons Played	Apps	Subs	Gls
Exeter C.	Taunton T.	07.91	91	4	0	0

MALPASS, Frank L.
Consett, 16 October, 1932 (G)

League Club	Source	Date Signed	Seasons Played	Apps	Subs	Gls
Gateshead	Jnrs	10.49	49	3	-	0

MALPASS, Samuel T.
Consett, 12 September, 1918 Died 1983 (FB)

League Club	Source	Date Signed	Seasons Played	Apps	Subs	Gls
Huddersfield T.		10.36				
Fulham	Tr	05.39	46	2	-	0
Watford	Tr	01.47	46-48	41	-	0

MALT, Robert
Ryhope, 4 November, 1951 (CF)

League Club	Source	Date Signed	Seasons Played	Apps	Subs	Gls
Leeds U.	App	11.68				
Darlington	Tr	06.70	70	2	2	0

MALTBY, John
Leadgate, 31 July, 1939 (IF)

League Club	Source	Date Signed	Seasons Played	Apps	Subs	Gls
Sunderland	Jnrs	08.57	56-60	22	-	4
Darlington	Tr	06.61	61-64	115	-	32
Bury	Tr	07.65	65-66	56	1	8

MANCINI, Michael L.
London, 8 June, 1956 (F)

League Club	Source	Date Signed	Seasons Played	Apps	Subs	Gls
Leyton Orient (N/C)		03.84	83	2	0	0

MANCINI, Terence J.
Camden Town, 4 October, 1942 IR-5 (CD)

League Club	Source	Date Signed	Seasons Played	Apps	Subs	Gls
Watford	Jnrs	07.61	61-65	66	1	0
Leyton Orient	Port Elizabeth (SA)	11.67	67-71	167	0	16
Queens Park R.	Tr	10.71	71-74	94	0	3
Arsenal	Tr	10.74	74-75	52	0	1
Aldershot	Tr	09.76	76	21	0	0

MANDERS, Ronald E.
Shrewsbury, 13 November, 1931 (HB)

League Club	Source	Date Signed	Seasons Played	Apps	Subs	Gls
Shrewsbury T.	Jnrs	12.54	54-55	6	-	0

MANDERSON, David A.
Glasgow, 18 October, 1973

League Club	Source	Date Signed	Seasons Played	Apps	Subs	Gls
Scarborough (YT)	YT	08.90	91	0	1	0

MANKELOW, Jamie A.
Clapton, 4 September, 1964 (F)

League Club	Source	Date Signed	Seasons Played	Apps	Subs	Gls
Leyton Orient	App	09.82	82	1	1	0

MANKTELOW, Brian
Farnham, 29 March, 1951 (CF)

League Club	Source	Date Signed	Seasons Played	Apps	Subs	Gls
Aldershot (App)	App	09.66	68	1	0	0

MANLEY, Malcolm R.
Johnstone, 1 December, 1949 S Sch (CD)

League Club	Source	Date Signed	Seasons Played	Apps	Subs	Gls
Leicester C.	Johnstone Burgh	01.67	67-72	109	11	5
Portsmouth	Tr	12.73	73-74	11	0	0

MANLEY, Thomas
Northwich, 7 October, 1912 (OL)

League Club	Source	Date Signed	Seasons Played	Apps	Subs	Gls
Manchester U.	Northwich Vic.	05.31	31-38	188	-	40
Brentford	Tr	07.39	46-50	116	-	6

MANN, Adrian G.
Northampton, 12 July, 1967 (M)

League Club	Source	Date Signed	Seasons Played	Apps	Subs	Gls
Northampton T.	YT	05.85	83-87	71	11	5
Torquay U.	L	03.87	86	6	2	0
Newport Co.	Tr	11.87	87	17	0	1

MANN, Arthur F.
Burntisland, 23 January, 1948 (M)

League Club	Source	Date Signed	Seasons Played	Apps	Subs	Gls
Manchester C.	Hearts	11.68	68-70	32	3	0
Blackpool	L	11.71	71	3	0	0
Notts Co.	Tr	07.72	72-78	243	10	21
Shrewsbury T.	Tr	06.79	79	8	0	1
Mansfield T.	Tr	10.79	79-81	114	2	3

MANN, James A.
Goole, 15 December, 1952 (M)

League Club	Source	Date Signed	Seasons Played	Apps	Subs	Gls
Leeds U.	App	12.69	71-72	2	0	0
Bristol C.	Tr	05.74	74-81	205	26	31
Barnsley	Tr	02.82	81-82	14	1	0
Scunthorpe U. (N/C)	Tr	01.83	82	2	0	0
Doncaster Rov.	Tr	02.83	82	13	0	0

MANN, Ronald H.
Doncaster, 8 October, 1932 (FB)

League Club	Source	Date Signed	Seasons Played	Apps	Subs	Gls
Notts Co.		12.50	50	1	-	0
Aldershot	Tr	07.56	56-57	26	-	4

MANNERS, Peter J.
Sunderland, 31 July, 1959 (M)

League Club	Source	Date Signed	Seasons Played	Apps	Subs	Gls
Newcastle U.	App	07.77	78	2	0	0

MANNERS, Wingrove
West Indies, 7 March, 1955 (F)

League Club	Source	Date Signed	Seasons Played	Apps	Subs	Gls
Bradford C. (App)	App	01.72	71	1	0	0

MANNING, John J.
Liverpool, 11 December, 1940 (CF)

League Club	Source	Date Signed	Seasons Played	Apps	Subs	Gls
Tranmere Rov.	Liverpool (Am)	05.62	62-66	130	0	70
Shrewsbury T.	Tr	10.66	66-67	39	0	18
Norwich C.	Tr	09.67	67-68	60	0	21
Bolton W.	Tr	03.69	68-70	27	2	7
Walsall	Tr	07.71	71	13	1	6
Tranmere Rov.	Tr	03.72	71	5	0	1
Crewe Alex.	Tr	08.72	72	37	1	6
Barnsley	Tr	09.73	73-74	41	4	7
Crewe Alex.		11.75	75	7	0	5

MANNION, Gerard P.
Warrington, 21 December, 1939 E Yth/Eu23-2 (OR)

League Club	Source	Date Signed	Seasons Played	Apps	Subs	Gls
Wolverhampton W.	Jnrs	11.57	59-60	17	-	7
Norwich C.	Tr	09.61	61-67	100	0	17
Chester C.	Tr	01.68	67	6	0	0

MANNION, Wilfred J.
South Bank, 16 May, 1918 E'B'-2/EF Lge/E-26 (IF)

League Club	Source	Date Signed	Seasons Played	Apps	Subs	Gls
Middlesbrough	South Bank St Peters	09.36	36-53	341	-	99
Hull C.	Tr	12.54	54	16	-	1

MANNS, Paul H.
Stafford, 15 April, 1961 (F)

League Club	Source	Date Signed	Seasons Played	Apps	Subs	Gls
Notts Co.	Cardiff C. (N/C)	08.79	79-80	5	2	1
Chester C.	Tr	03.83	82-83	28	0	3

League Club	Source	Date Signed	Seasons Played	Career Record Apps	Subs	Gls

MANSELL, Barry R.
Petersfield, 8 March, 1932 (FB)

League Club	Source	Date Signed	Seasons Played	Apps	Subs	Gls
Portsmouth	Jnrs	08.49	51-53	16	-	0
Reading	Tr	02.54	53-55	84	-	1
Bournemouth	Tr	06.57				

MANSELL, George W.
Doncaster, 19 January, 1943 (CF)

League Club	Source	Date Signed	Seasons Played	Apps	Subs	Gls
Doncaster Rov.		09.62	62	1	-	0

MANSELL, John (Jack)
Manchester, 22 August, 1927 E'B'-2/EF Lge (FB)

League Club	Source	Date Signed	Seasons Played	Apps	Subs	Gls
Brighton & H.A.	Manchester U. (Am)	03.49	48-52	116	-	11
Cardiff C.	Tr	10.52	52-53	24	-	0
Portsmouth	Tr	11.53	53-57	134	-	7

MANSFIELD, Frederick C. A.
Cambridge, 9 March, 1915 (RB)

League Club	Source	Date Signed	Seasons Played	Apps	Subs	Gls
Brentford	Cambridge C.	04.39				
Norwich C.	Tr	02.47	46-47	34	-	0

MANSFIELD, John V.
Colchester, 13 September, 1946 (IF)

League Club	Source	Date Signed	Seasons Played	Apps	Subs	Gls
Colchester U.	Jnrs	08.64	64-68	28	6	3

MANSFIELD, Ronald W.
Romford, 31 December, 1923 (OL)

League Club	Source	Date Signed	Seasons Played	Apps	Subs	Gls
Millwall	Ilford	04.41	46-52	97	-	25
Southend U.	Tr	11.52	52	7	-	3

MANSLEY, Alan
Liverpool, 31 August, 1946 (W)

League Club	Source	Date Signed	Seasons Played	Apps	Subs	Gls
Blackpool	Skelmersdale U.	06.67				
Brentford	Tr	01.68	67-70	94	1	24
Fulham	Tr	12.70	70	1	0	0
Notts Co.	L	03.71	71	11	0	2
Lincoln C.	L	12.71	71	3	0	0

MANSLEY, V. Clifford
Skipton, 5 April, 1921 (WH)

League Club	Source	Date Signed	Seasons Played	Apps	Subs	Gls
Preston N.E.		09.40				
Barnsley	Tr	11.45	46-47	31	-	0
Chester C.	Tr	06.48	48	22	-	0
Leyton Orient	Yeovil T.	07.52	52	10	-	0

MANUEL, William A. J.
Hackney, 28 June, 1969 (M/LB)

League Club	Source	Date Signed	Seasons Played	Apps	Subs	Gls
Tottenham H.	App	06.87				
Gillingham	Tr	02.89	88-90	74	13	5
Brentford	Tr	06.91	91	27	8	0

MAPSON, John D.
Birkenhead, 2 May, 1917 (G)

League Club	Source	Date Signed	Seasons Played	Apps	Subs	Gls
Reading	Guildford C.	04.35	35	2	-	0
Sunderland	Tr	03.36	35-52	345	-	0

MARANGONI, Claudio O.
Argentina, 17 November, 1954 Argentine Int (M)

League Club	Source	Date Signed	Seasons Played	Apps	Subs	Gls
Sunderland	San Lorenzo (Arg)	12.79	79-80	19	1	3

MARCH, John E.
Norwich, 12 May, 1940 (LB)

League Club	Source	Date Signed	Seasons Played	Apps	Subs	Gls
Norwich C.	Jnrs	05.57				
Bradford P.A.	Tr	06.61	61-62	62	-	1

MARCH, Stanley A.
Manchester, 26 December, 1938 (F)

League Club	Source	Date Signed	Seasons Played	Apps	Subs	Gls
Port Vale	Altrincham	08.59	59	1	-	0

MARCH, William
Chester-le-Street, 28 February, 1925 (FB)

League Club	Source	Date Signed	Seasons Played	Apps	Subs	Gls
Barnsley	Ferryhill Ath.	11.47	51	2	-	0
Gateshead	Tr	07.52	52-56	134	-	0

MARCHANT, Marwood
Milford Haven, 19 June, 1922 (F)

League Club	Source	Date Signed	Seasons Played	Apps	Subs	Gls
Cardiff C.	Milford U.	01.51	50	12	-	3
Torquay U.	Tr	11.51	51-52	40	-	19

MARCHI, Anthony V.
Edmonton, 21 January, 1933 E Sch/E Yth/E'B'-1 (WH)

League Club	Source	Date Signed	Seasons Played	Apps	Subs	Gls
Tottenham H.	Jnrs	06.50	49-56	131	-	2
Tottenham H.	Juventus (It)	07.59	59-64	101	-	5

MARDEN, Reuben J.
Fulham, 10 February, 1927 (OL)

League Club	Source	Date Signed	Seasons Played	Apps	Subs	Gls
Arsenal	Chelmsford C.	02.50	50-54	42	-	11
Watford	Tr	06.55	55-56	41	-	11

MARDENBOROUGH, Stephen A.
Birmingham, 11 September, 1964 (F)

League Club	Source	Date Signed	Seasons Played	Apps	Subs	Gls
Coventry C.	App	08.82				
Wolverhampton W.	Tr	09.83	83	9	0	1
Cambridge U.	L	02.84	83	6	0	0
Swansea C.	Tr	07.84	84	32	4	7
Newport Co.	Tr	07.85	85-86	50	14	11
Cardiff C.	Tr	03.87	86-87	18	14	1
Hereford U.	Tr	07.88	88	20	7	0
Darlington	Cheltenham T.	02.90	90-91	38	26	7

MARDON, Paul J.
Bristol, 14 September, 1969 (CD)

League Club	Source	Date Signed	Seasons Played	Apps	Subs	Gls
Bristol C.	YT	01.88	87-90	29	13	0
Doncaster Rov.	L	09.90	90	3	0	0
Birmingham C.	Tr	08.91	91	31	4	0

MARGERRISON, John W.
Bushey, 20 October, 1955 (M)

League Club	Source	Date Signed	Seasons Played	Apps	Subs	Gls
Tottenham H.	App	12.72				
Fulham	Tr	07.75	75-78	63	8	9
Leyton Orient	Tr	07.79	79-81	77	3	6

MARGETSON, Martyn W.
Neath, 8 September, 1971 W Sch/W Yth/Wu21-1 (G)

League Club	Source	Date Signed	Seasons Played	Apps	Subs	Gls
Manchester C.	YT	07.90	90-91	5	0	0

MARINELLO, Peter
Edinburgh, 20 February, 1950 Su23-2 (W)

League Club	Source	Date Signed	Seasons Played	Apps	Subs	Gls
Arsenal	Hibernian	01.70	69-72	32	6	3
Portsmouth	Tr	07.73	73-75	92	3	7
Fulham	Motherwell	12.78	78-79	25	2	1

Peter Marinello (Hibernian, Arsenal, Portsmouth, Motherwell & Fulham)

MARINER, Paul
Bolton, 22 May, 1953 E-35 (F)

League Club	Source	Date Signed	Seasons Played	Apps	Subs	Gls
Plymouth Arg.	Chorley	07.73	73-76	134	1	56
Ipswich T.	Tr	09.76	76-83	260	0	96
Arsenal	Tr	02.84	83-85	52	8	14
Portsmouth	Tr	07.86	86-87	49	7	9

MARKER, Nicholas R. T.
Budleigh Salterton, 3 May, 1965 (CD)

League Club	Source	Date Signed	Seasons Played	Apps	Subs	Gls
Exeter C.	App	05.83	81-87	196	6	3
Plymouth Arg.	Tr	10.87	87-91	194	1	10

League Club	Source	Date Signed	Seasons Played	Career Record Apps	Subs	Gls
MARKHAM, Colin						
Clowne, 2 March, 1916 Died 1967						(FB)
Torquay U.		07.37	37-46	25	-	1
MARKHAM, Leo S.						
Aylesbury, 22 March, 1953						(CD)
Watford	Marlow	08.72	72-74	22	11	3
MARKHAM, Peter						
Scunthorpe, 18 March, 1954						(RB)
Scunthorpe U.	App	03.72	71-76	121	1	1
MARKIE, John						
Bo'ness, 16 December, 1944 S Sch						(CH)
Newcastle U.	App	04.62	63	2	-	0
MARKLEW, Roger K.						
Sheffield, 30 January, 1940						(W)
Sheffield Wed.	Sheffield U. (Am)	05.58				
Accrington St.	Tr	05.59				
Grimsby T.	Tr	08.60	60	6	-	1
MARKS, Charles W.						
Eccles (Kt), 21 December, 1919						(FB)
Gillingham	Tooting & Mitcham	(N/L)	50-56	265	-	8
MARKS, George W.						
Amesbury, 9 April, 1915						(G)
Arsenal	Salisbury Corries	03.36	38	2	-	0
Blackburn Rov.	Tr	08.46	46-47	67	-	0
Bristol C.	Tr	08.48	48	9	-	0
Reading	Tr	10.48	48-52	118	-	0
MARKS, Michael D.						
Lambeth, 23 March, 1968						(F)
Millwall	App	07.86	86	36	0	10
Mansfield T.	L	01.88	87	0	1	0
Leyton Orient	Tr	02.88	87	3	0	0
MARLEY, Alan						
Durham, 29 February, 1956						(FB)
Grimsby T.	App	11.73	74-75	39	1	2
MARLEY, George						
Gateshead, 22 April, 1921						
Gateshead		09.47	47-49	22	-	2
MARLOW, Frederick						
Sheffield, 9 November, 1928						(WH)
Arsenal	Hillsboro B.C.	09.47				
Sheffield Wed.	Tr	09.50				
Grimsby T.	Buxton	08.51	51	12	-	6
York C.	Boston U.	10.53	53-54	24	-	0
MARLOW, Geoffrey A.						
Worksop, 13 December, 1914 Died 1978						(OL)
Lincoln C.	Dinnington	05.37	37-48	80	-	25
MARLOWE, Richard R.						
Edinburgh, 10 August, 1950						(CF)
Derby Co.		06.69				
Shrewsbury T.	Tr	12.73	73	31	0	4
Brighton & H.A.	Tr	07.74	74	24	1	5
Aldershot	L	01.76	75	2	0	0
MARMON, Neale G.						
Bournemouth, 21 April, 1961						(CD)
Torquay U. (N/C)		03.80	79	4	0	0
Colchester U.	Hanover 96 (Ger)	01.90	89	22	0	4
MARPLES, Christopher						
Chesterfield, 3 August, 1964						(G)
Chesterfield	Goole T.	03.84	84-86	84	0	0
Stockport Co.	Tr	03.87	86-87	57	0	0
York C.	Tr	07.88	88-91	136	0	0
Scunthorpe U.	L	02.92	91	1	0	0
MARRIOTT, Andrew						
Sutton-in-Ashfield, 11 October, 1970 E Sch/E Yth/Eu21-1						(G)
Arsenal	YT	10.88				
Nottingham F.	Tr	06.89	91	6	0	0
West Bromwich A.	L	09.89	89	3	0	0
Blackburn Rov.	L	12.89	89	2	0	0
Colchester U.	L	03.90	89	10	0	0
Burnley	L	08.91	91	15	0	0

League Club	Source	Date Signed	Seasons Played	Career Record Apps	Subs	Gls
MARRIOTT, Ernest						
Sutton-in-Ashfield, 25 January, 1913 Died 1989						(FB)
Brighton & H.A.	Sutton T.	01.34	34-47	163	-	1
MARRIOTT, John						
Sheffield, 16 July, 1915 Died 1989						(CF)
Doncaster Rov.	Normanton Sports	02.45	46-47	6	-	0
Southport	Tr	12.47	47-48	23	-	5
MARRIOTT, John L. (Jack)						
Scunthorpe, 1 April, 1928						(OR)
Sheffield Wed.	Scunthorpe U.	02.47	46-54	153	-	19
Huddersfield T.	Tr	07.55	55-56	38	-	4
Scunthorpe U.	Tr	06.57	57-63	212	-	26
MARRIOTT, Paul W.						
Liverpool, 26 September, 1973						(F)
Cardiff C. (YT)	YT	07.90	91	0	1	0
MARRIOTT, Stanley						
Rochdale, 21 July, 1929						(CF)
Rochdale (Am)	Rochdale Y.M.C.A.	12.52	52	6	-	2
MARRON, Christopher						
Jarrow, 7 February, 1925 Died 1986						(CF)
Chesterfield	South Shields	10.47	47-51	108	-	44
Mansfield T.	Tr	07.52	52-53	53	-	25
Bradford P.A.	Tr	07.54	54	2	-	1
MARSDEN, Anthony J.						
Bolton, 11 September, 1948						(CF)
Blackpool	App	07.66	67-68	4	1	0
Doncaster Rov.	Tr	07.69	69-70	14	3	2
Grimsby T.	L	11.69	69	2	0	0
MARSDEN, Christopher						
Sheffield, 3 January, 1969						(M)
Sheffield U.	App	01.87	87	13	3	1
Huddersfield T.	Tr	07.88	88-91	105	7	9
MARSDEN, Eric						
Bolsover, 3 January, 1930						(CF)
Crystal Palace	Winchester C.	04.50	50-52	34	-	11
Southend U.	Tr	10.52	52	14	-	6
Shrewsbury T.	Tr	03.53	52-53	11	-	0
MARSDEN, Frederick						
Blackburn, 6 September, 1911						(FB)
Accrington St.		10.34	34	5	-	0
Wolverhampton W.	Tr	01.35	35	1	-	0
Bournemouth	Tr	05.36	36-48	194	-	1
MARSDEN, James						
Rotherham, 10 April, 1928						(F)
Rotherham U.	Parkgate W.	08.52	52-54	12	-	2
MARSDEN, John						
Leeds, 17 December, 1931						(CH)
Leeds U.	Osmondthorpe	08.50	52-58	71	-	0
Barrow	Tr	03.59	58-59	47	-	0
Carlisle U.	Tr	09.60	60-63	88	-	0
Doncaster Rov.	Tr	07.64	64	2	-	0
MARSDEN, Keith						
Matlock, 10 April, 1934 Died 1986						(CF)
Chesterfield	Youlgreave B.C.	06.52	53-54	22	-	15
Manchester C.	Tr	07.55	55-57	14	-	1
Accrington St.	Tr	08.59				
MARSDEN, Liddell						
Fatfield, 13 May, 1936						(HB)
Workington	South Shields	11.56	56	2	-	0
MARSH, Arthur						
Dudley, 4 May, 1947						(CD)
Bolton W.	App	05.65	66-70	71	2	0
Rochdale	Tr	12.71	71-73	89	1	0
Darlington	Tr	07.74	74	23	0	1
MARSH, Christopher J.						
Sedgley, 14 January, 1970						(M)
Walsall	YT	07.88	87-91	61	24	3
MARSH, Clifford						
Atherton, 29 December, 1920						(IF)
Leeds U.	Winsford U.	09.48	48	4	-	1
Bournemouth	Tr	05.49	49-51	39	-	2

MARSH, W. Edmund (Eddie)
Croydon, 14 December, 1927 (G)

League Club	Source	Date Signed	Seasons Played	Apps	Subs	Gls
Charlton Ath.	Erith & Belvedere	12.45	50-56	26	-	0
Luton T.	Tr	06.57	57-58	2	-	0
Torquay U.	Tr	07.59	59-61	61	-	0

MARSH, Frank K.
Bolton, 7 June, 1916 (WH)

League Club	Source	Date Signed	Seasons Played	Apps	Subs	Gls
Bolton W.		05.38	38	3	-	0
Chester C.	Tr	05.39	46-47	70	-	2

MARSH, Ian J.
Swansea, 27 October, 1969 (LB)

League Club	Source	Date Signed	Seasons Played	Apps	Subs	Gls
Swansea C.	YT	07.88	87	1	0	0
Bradford C.	Tr	07.89				

MARSH, John H.
Stoke, 31 May, 1948 (RB)

League Club	Source	Date Signed	Seasons Played	Apps	Subs	Gls
Stoke C.	App	06.65	67-78	344	8	2

MARSH, John K.
Mansfield, 8 October, 1922 (IF)

League Club	Source	Date Signed	Seasons Played	Apps	Subs	Gls
Notts Co.		08.42	46-48	42	-	18
Coventry C.	Tr	09.48	48-49	20	-	7
Leicester C.	Tr	03.50	49-50	14	-	4
Chesterfield	Tr	09.50	50	26	-	4

MARSH, John S.
Bolton, 31 August, 1940 (IF)

League Club	Source	Date Signed	Seasons Played	Apps	Subs	Gls
Oldham Ath.	Jnrs	10.57	59	2	-	0

MARSH, John W.
Leeds, 17 December, 1947 (G)

League Club	Source	Date Signed	Seasons Played	Apps	Subs	Gls
Bradford C.	New Farnley Jnrs	05.66	66-67	12	0	0

MARSH, Kevin W.
Liverpool, 27 March, 1949 (F)

League Club	Source	Date Signed	Seasons Played	Apps	Subs	Gls
Liverpool	App	03.66				
Southport	Tr	05.70	70	35	2	8

MARSH, Michael A.
Liverpool, 21 July, 1969 (M)

League Club	Source	Date Signed	Seasons Played	Apps	Subs	Gls
Liverpool	Kirkby T.	08.87	88-91	20	19	0

MARSH, Rodney W.
Hatfield, 11 October, 1944 Eu23-2/E-9 (F)

League Club	Source	Date Signed	Seasons Played	Apps	Subs	Gls
Fulham	App	10.62	62-65	63	0	22
Queens Park R.	Tr	03.66	65-71	211	0	106
Manchester C.	Tr	03.72	71-75	116	2	36
Fulham	Tampa Bay (USA)	08.76	76	16	0	5

MARSHALL, Alexander S.
Alloa, 27 November, 1935 (IF)

League Club	Source	Date Signed	Seasons Played	Apps	Subs	Gls
Accrington St.	Stirling A.	10.60	60	8	-	2

MARSHALL, Alfred G.
Dagenham, 21 May, 1933 (FB)

League Club	Source	Date Signed	Seasons Played	Apps	Subs	Gls
Colchester U.	Dagenham	10.57	58-60	29	-	0

MARSHALL, Brian
Bolton-on-Dearne, 20 September, 1954 (CD)

League Club	Source	Date Signed	Seasons Played	Apps	Subs	Gls
Huddersfield T.	App	12.71	72-74	30	2	0
Scunthorpe U.	L	10.74	74	3	0	0

MARSHALL, Clifford
Liverpool, 4 November, 1955 E Sch (W)

League Club	Source	Date Signed	Seasons Played	Apps	Subs	Gls
Everton	App	11.73	74-75	6	1	0
Southport	Tr	09.76	76	11	2	0

MARSHALL, Colin
Glasgow, 1 November, 1969 (F)

League Club	Source	Date Signed	Seasons Played	Apps	Subs	Gls
Barnsley	YT	04.88	88-90	0	4	0
Wrexham	L	09.91	91	3	0	0
Scarborough	Tr	03.92	91	4	0	1

MARSHALL, David H.
Manchester, 12 November, 1955 (M)

League Club	Source	Date Signed	Seasons Played	Apps	Subs	Gls
Workington (N/C)	Headley Colly	11.76	76	2	0	0

MARSHALL, Dwight W.
Jamaica, 3 October, 1965 (F)

League Club	Source	Date Signed	Seasons Played	Apps	Subs	Gls
Plymouth Arg.	Grays Ath.	08.91	91	44	0	14

MARSHALL, Ernest
Dinnington, 23 May, 1918 Died 1983 (WH)

League Club	Source	Date Signed	Seasons Played	Apps	Subs	Gls
Sheffield U.		05.35	36-37	13	-	0
Cardiff C.		05.39	46	1	-	0

MARSHALL, Frank
Sheffield, 26 January, 1929 (WH)

League Club	Source	Date Signed	Seasons Played	Apps	Subs	Gls
Rotherham U.	Scarborough	05.51	51-56	118	-	5
Scunthorpe U.	Tr	07.57	57-58	80	-	0
Doncaster Rov.	Tr	10.59	59-61	35	-	0

MARSHALL, Gary
Bristol, 20 April, 1964 (W)

League Club	Source	Date Signed	Seasons Played	Apps	Subs	Gls
Bristol C.	Shepton Mallet	07.83	83-87	48	20	7
Torquay U.	L	12.84	84	7	0	1
Carlisle U.	Tr	07.88	88	18	3	2
Scunthorpe U.	Tr	07.89	89-90	38	3	3
Exeter C.	Tr	10.90	90-91	48	12	6

MARSHALL, Gordon
Farnham, 2 July, 1939 Eu23-1 (G)

League Club	Source	Date Signed	Seasons Played	Apps	Subs	Gls
Newcastle U.	Hearts	06.63	63-67	177	0	0
Nottingham F.	Tr	10.68	68	7	0	0

MARSHALL, Ian P.
Liverpool, 20 March, 1966 (CD/F)

League Club	Source	Date Signed	Seasons Played	Apps	Subs	Gls
Everton	App	03.84	85-87	9	6	1
Oldham Ath.	Tr	03.88	87-91	139	4	34

MARSHALL, John
Rawtenstall, 1 November, 1938 (G)

League Club	Source	Date Signed	Seasons Played	Apps	Subs	Gls
Accrington St.		05.57	57-58	7	-	0

MARSHALL, John G.
Bolton, 29 May, 1917 (FB)

League Club	Source	Date Signed	Seasons Played	Apps	Subs	Gls
Burnley	Jnrs	11.36	38-46	26	-	0

MARSHALL, John J.
Glasgow, 12 February, 1949 (W)

League Club	Source	Date Signed	Seasons Played	Apps	Subs	Gls
Preston N.E.		02.67				
Rotherham U.	Ross Co.	09.68	68	4	0	0

MARSHALL, John P.
Balham, 18 August, 1964 (RB/M)

League Club	Source	Date Signed	Seasons Played	Apps	Subs	Gls
Fulham	App	08.82	83-91	293	13	23

Rodney Marsh (Fulham, Queens Park Rangers, Manchester City, Fulham & England)

MARSHALL, Julian P.
Swansea, 6 July, 1957 (CD)

League Club	Source	Date Signed	Seasons Played	Apps	Subs	Gls
Hereford U.	Merthyr Tydfil	08.75	76-79	91	1	4
Bristol C.	Tr	08.80	80-81	29	0	0
Walsall	Tr	08.82	82	10	0	0

MARSHALL, Peter
Barrow, 2 October, 1947 (OR)

League Club	Source	Date Signed	Seasons Played	Apps	Subs	Gls
Barrow	Holker C.O.B.	01.66	65-66	4	0	1

MARSHALL, Peter W.
Worksop, 5 December, 1934 (G)

League Club	Source	Date Signed	Seasons Played	Apps	Subs	Gls
Scunthorpe U.	Worksop T.	09.54	54-56	64	-	0

MARSHALL, Ralph
Airdrie, 30 January, 1944 (FB)

League Club	Source	Date Signed	Seasons Played	Apps	Subs	Gls
Crewe Alex.	Glasgow Rangers	09.64	64-66	72	1	0

MARSHALL, Richard
Leicester, 23 November, 1945 (W)

League Club	Source	Date Signed	Seasons Played	Apps	Subs	Gls
Leicester C.	App	08.63				
Southport	Tr	07.65	65-66	29	2	7

MARSHALL, Roy C.
Fulham, 22 May, 1932 (G)

League Club	Source	Date Signed	Seasons Played	Apps	Subs	Gls
Brighton & H.A.	Jnrs	06.50				
Aldershot	Tr	08.57	57-60	34	-	0

MARSHALL, Stanley K.
Goole, 20 April, 1946 (IF)

League Club	Source	Date Signed	Seasons Played	Apps	Subs	Gls
Middlesbrough	Goole T.	08.63	65	2	0	0
Notts Co.	Tr	06.66	66-67	43	6	17

MARSHALL, Terence W. J.
Wisbech, 26 December, 1935 (OR)

League Club	Source	Date Signed	Seasons Played	Apps	Subs	Gls
Newcastle U.	Wisbech T.	12.58	58-60	5	-	1

MARSHALL, William
Belfast, 11 July, 1936 NI'B'-2 (FB)

League Club	Source	Date Signed	Seasons Played	Apps	Subs	Gls
Burnley	Distillery	10.53	59-60	6	-	0
Oldham Ath.	Tr	08.62	62-63	57	-	0
Hartlepool U.	Tr	08.64	64-65	57	0	0

MARSHALL, William F.
Rutherglen, 9 May, 1933 (CF)

League Club	Source	Date Signed	Seasons Played	Apps	Subs	Gls
Bradford C.	Rutherglen Glencairn	01.57	56-58	33	-	16
Swindon T.	Tr	02.59	58-59	30	-	12

MARSLAND, Gordon
Blackpool, 20 March, 1945 (WH)

League Club	Source	Date Signed	Seasons Played	Apps	Subs	Gls
Blackpool	App	05.62				
Carlisle U.	Tr	06.65	65-68	62	1	4
Bristol Rov.	Tr	06.69	69	16	0	1
Crewe Alex.	L	09.70	70	5	0	0
Oldham Ath.	L	03.71	70	1	3	0

MARSTON, Joseph
Australia, 7 January, 1926 EF Lge (CH)

League Club	Source	Date Signed	Seasons Played	Apps	Subs	Gls
Preston N.E.	Leichardt (Aus)	02.50	50-54	185	-	0

MARSTON, Maurice
Trimdon (Dm), 24 March, 1929 (FB)

League Club	Source	Date Signed	Seasons Played	Apps	Subs	Gls
Sunderland	Jnrs	06.49	51-52	9	-	0
Northampton T.	Tr	07.53	53-56	149	-	2

MARTIN, Alan J.
Stoke, 23 November, 1923 (WH)

League Club	Source	Date Signed	Seasons Played	Apps	Subs	Gls
Port Vale		12.42	46-51	169	-	28
Stoke C.	Tr	09.51	51-54	104	-	6
Port Vale	Bangor C.	07.57	57-58	19	-	0

MARTIN, Alvin E.
Bootle, 29 July, 1958 E Yth/E'B'/E-17 (CD)

League Club	Source	Date Signed	Seasons Played	Apps	Subs	Gls
West Ham U.	App	07.76	77-91	399	2	24

MARTIN, Barrie
Birmingham, 29 September, 1935 (FB)

League Club	Source	Date Signed	Seasons Played	Apps	Subs	Gls
Blackpool	Jnrs	12.53	57-63	189	-	1
Oldham Ath.	Tr	08.64	64	42	-	4
Tranmere Rov.	Tr	06.65	65-67	99	3	0

MARTIN, Cornelius J. (Con)
Dublin, 20 March, 1923 IR-30/NI-6 (CH)

League Club	Source	Date Signed	Seasons Played	Apps	Subs	Gls
Leeds U.	Glentoran	01.47	46-48	47	-	1
Aston Villa	Tr	10.48	48-55	194	-	1

MARTIN, David
East Ham, 25 April, 1963 E Yth (M/D)

League Club	Source	Date Signed	Seasons Played	Apps	Subs	Gls
Millwall	App	05.80	79-84	131	9	6
Wimbledon	Tr	09.84	84-85	30	5	3
Southend U.	Tr	08.86	86-91	186	9	18

MARTIN, Dean E.
Islington, 31 August, 1972 (M)

League Club	Source	Date Signed	Seasons Played	Apps	Subs	Gls
West Ham U.	Fisher Ath.	06.91	91	1	1	0

MARTIN, Dean S.
Halifax, 9 September, 1967 (M)

League Club	Source	Date Signed	Seasons Played	Apps	Subs	Gls
Halifax T.	App	09.85	86-90	149	4	7
Scunthorpe U.	Tr	07.91	91	36	1	2

MARTIN, Dennis V.
Southampton, 8 November, 1928 (HB)

League Club	Source	Date Signed	Seasons Played	Apps	Subs	Gls
Bournemouth	Jnrs	08.47	48-53	23	-	0

MARTIN, Dennis W.
Edinburgh, 27 October, 1947 (W)

League Club	Source	Date Signed	Seasons Played	Apps	Subs	Gls
West Bromwich A.	Kettering T.	07.67	67-69	14	2	1
Carlisle U.	Tr	07.70	70-77	271	4	48
Newcastle U.	Tr	10.77	77	9	2	2
Mansfield T.	Tr	03.78	77-78	46	0	3

MARTIN, Donald
Corby, 15 February, 1944 E Yth (F)

League Club	Source	Date Signed	Seasons Played	Apps	Subs	Gls
Northampton T.	Jnrs	07.62	62-67	135	0	52
Blackburn Rov.	Tr	02.68	67-75	218	6	58
Northampton T.	Tr	11.75	75-77	77	15	17

MARTIN, Edward
Baillieston, 31 March, 1921 (IF)

League Club	Source	Date Signed	Seasons Played	Apps	Subs	Gls
Accrington St.	Alloa Ath.	08.50	50	2	-	0

MARTIN, Eliot J.
Plumstead, 27 September, 1972 (LB)

League Club	Source	Date Signed	Seasons Played	Apps	Subs	Gls
Gillingham	YT	05.91	91	22	0	0

MARTIN, Eric
Perth, 31 March, 1946 (G)

League Club	Source	Date Signed	Seasons Played	Apps	Subs	Gls
Southampton	Dunfermline Ath.	03.67	66-74	248	0	0

MARTIN, Frederick A.
Nottingham, 13 December, 1925 (F)

League Club	Source	Date Signed	Seasons Played	Apps	Subs	Gls
Nottingham F.		10.44	47-48	5	-	0

MARTIN, Frederick J.
Nottingham, 14 April, 1925 (WH)

League Club	Source	Date Signed	Seasons Played	Apps	Subs	Gls
Blackburn Rov.	Sutton T.	12.49				
Accrington St.	Tr	07.50	50-51	64	-	0

MARTIN, Geoffrey
Clay Cross, 9 March, 1940 (OL)

League Club	Source	Date Signed	Seasons Played	Apps	Subs	Gls
Chesterfield	Parkhouse Colly	10.58	58	2	-	0
Leeds U.	Tr	05.60				
Darlington	Tr	07.61	61	20	-	6
Carlisle U.	Tr	05.62	61-62	15	-	2
Workington	Tr	12.62	62-66	144	0	24
Grimsby T.	Tr	11.66	66-67	71	0	5
Chesterfield	Tr	07.68	68-69	43	0	4

MARTIN, Harold J.
Blackburn, 15 March, 1955 (CD)

League Club	Source	Date Signed	Seasons Played	Apps	Subs	Gls
Bolton W.		11.73				
Rochdale	Tr	07.74	74	11	2	0

MARTIN, James C.
Dundee, 27 May, 1938 (CF)

League Club	Source	Date Signed	Seasons Played	Apps	Subs	Gls
Blackpool	Evenwood T.	12.61				
Reading	Tr	06.62	62-63	22	-	6

MARTIN, James P.
Glasgow, 3 March, 1937 (OL)

League Club	Source	Date Signed	Seasons Played	Apps	Subs	Gls
Nottingham F.	Baillieston	06.58	58	1	-	0

MARTIN, John G.
Dundee, 20 August, 1935 (FB)

League Club	Source	Date Signed	Seasons Played	Apps	Subs	Gls
Sheffield Wed.	Dundee N.E.	02.54	54-60	63	-	0
Rochdale	Tr	06.62	62-63	24	-	1

MARTIN, John J.
Ashington, 4 December, 1946 (W)

League Club	Source	Date Signed	Seasons Played	Apps	Subs	Gls
Aston Villa	App	07.64	64	1	-	0
Colchester U.	Tr	05.66	66-68	76	1	11
Workington	Tr	07.69	69-73	206	1	32
Southport	Tr	08.74	74-75	54	9	7

League Club	Source	Date Signed	Seasons Played	Career Record Apps	Subs	Gls

MARTIN, John R.
Birmingham, 5 August, 1914 (IF)

League Club	Source	Date Signed	Seasons Played	Apps	Subs	Gls
Aston Villa	Hednesford T.	01.35	36-48	81	-	22

MARTIN, Lee A.
Hyde, 5 February, 1968 Eu21-2 (LB)

League Club	Source	Date Signed	Seasons Played	Apps	Subs	Gls
Manchester U.	YT	05.86	87-91	55	17	1

Lee Martin (Manchester United)

MARTIN, Lee B.
Huddersfield, 9 September, 1968 (G)

League Club	Source	Date Signed	Seasons Played	Apps	Subs	Gls
Huddersfield T.	YT	06.87	87-91	54	0	0

MARTIN, Lionel J.
Ludlow, 15 May, 1947 (M)

League Club	Source	Date Signed	Seasons Played	Apps	Subs	Gls
Aston Villa	App	07.64	66-70	36	12	4
Doncaster Rov.	L	03.71	70	2	0	0

MARTIN, Michael P.
Dublin, 9 July, 1951 IR Amat/IR-51 (M)

League Club	Source	Date Signed	Seasons Played	Apps	Subs	Gls
Manchester U.	Bohemians	01.73	72-74	33	7	2
West Bromwich A.	Tr	10.75	75-78	85	4	11
Newcastle U.	Tr	12.78	78-82	139	8	5
Cardiff C.	Vancouver (Can)	11.84	84	7	0	0
Peterborough U.	Tr	01.85	84	12	0	0
Rotherham U.	Tr	08.85	85	5	0	0
Preston N.E.	Tr	09.85	85	35	0	0

MARTIN, Neil
Tranent, 20 October, 1940 Su23-1/SF Lge/S-3 (CF)

League Club	Source	Date Signed	Seasons Played	Apps	Subs	Gls
Sunderland	Hibernian	10.65	65-67	86	0	38
Coventry C.	Tr	02.68	67-70	106	0	40
Nottingham F.	Tr	02.71	70-74	116	3	28
Brighton & H.A.	Tr	07.75	75	13	4	8
Crystal Palace	Tr	03.76	75	8	1	1

MARTIN, Peter
South Shields, 29 December, 1950 (W)

League Club	Source	Date Signed	Seasons Played	Apps	Subs	Gls
Middlesbrough	Chilton B.C.	06.69				
Darlington	Tr	07.71	71	3	0	0
Barnsley	Tr	10.71	71-72	18	7	6

MARTIN, Raymond B.
Wolverhampton, 23 January, 1945 (FB)

League Club	Source	Date Signed	Seasons Played	Apps	Subs	Gls
Birmingham C.	Aston Villa (Am)	05.62	63-75	325	8	1

MARTIN, Roy
Kilbirnie, 16 May, 1929 (FB)

League Club	Source	Date Signed	Seasons Played	Apps	Subs	Gls
Birmingham C.	Kilwinning R.	03.50	50-55	69	-	0
Derby Co.	Tr	03.56	55-59	81	-	0
Chesterfield	Tr	07.60				

MARTIN, Thomas
Glasgow, 21 December, 1924 (WH)

League Club	Source	Date Signed	Seasons Played	Apps	Subs	Gls
Doncaster Rov.	Stirling A.	07.50	50-52	71	-	9
Nottingham F.	Tr	11.52	52-54	47	-	4
Hull C.	Tr	06.55	55-56	32	-	2

MARTIN, Wayne L.
Basildon, 16 December, 1965 (D)

League Club	Source	Date Signed	Seasons Played	Apps	Subs	Gls
Crystal Palace	App	07.82	83	1	0	0

MARTINDALE, David
Liverpool, 9 April, 1964 (M)

League Club	Source	Date Signed	Seasons Played	Apps	Subs	Gls
Tranmere Rov.	Caernarfon T.	07.87	87-91	98	29	7

MARTINDALE, Leonard
Bolton, 30 June, 1920 (WH)

League Club	Source	Date Signed	Seasons Played	Apps	Subs	Gls
Burnley	Jnrs	07.37	37-50	69	-	2
Accrington St.	Tr	12.51	51	16	-	0

MARTINEZ, Eugene
Chelmsford, 6 July, 1957 (M)

League Club	Source	Date Signed	Seasons Played	Apps	Subs	Gls
Bradford C.	Harrogate R.I.	07.77	77-79	38	14	5
Rochdale	Tr	07.80	80-82	110	6	16
Newport Co.	Tr	08.83	83	18	2	1
Northampton T.	L	02.84	83	12	0	2

MARTYN, A. Nigel
St Austell, 11 August, 1966 Eu21-11/E'B'/E-2 (G)

League Club	Source	Date Signed	Seasons Played	Apps	Subs	Gls
Bristol Rov.	St Blazey	08.87	87-89	101	0	0
Crystal Palace	Tr	11.89	89-91	101	0	0

Nigel Martyn (Bristol Rovers, Crystal Palace & England)

MARUSTIK, Christopher
Swansea, 10 August, 1961 W Sch/Wu21-7/W-6 (M)

League Club	Source	Date Signed	Seasons Played	Apps	Subs	Gls
Swansea C.	App	08.78	78-85	144	8	11
Cardiff C.	Tr	10.85	85-86	43	0	1

MARVIN, Walter
Derby, 6 July, 1920 (CF)

League Club	Source	Date Signed	Seasons Played	Apps	Subs	Gls
Accrington St.	Newport Co. (Am)	12.46	46-47	9	-	3

MARWOOD, Brian
Seaham, 5 February, 1960 E-1 (W)

League Club	Source	Date Signed	Seasons Played	Apps	Subs	Gls
Hull C.	App	02.78	79-83	154	4	51
Sheffield Wed.	Tr	08.84	84-87	125	3	27
Arsenal	Tr	03.88	87-89	52	0	16
Sheffield U.	Tr	09.90	90-91	14	8	3
Middlesbrough	L	10.91	91	3	0	0

MASEFIELD, Keith L.
Birmingham, 26 February, 1957 (FB)

League Club	Source	Date Signed	Seasons Played	Apps	Subs	Gls
Aston Villa	App	10.74	74-76	1	3	0

MASEFIELD, Paul D.
Lichfield, 21 October, 1970 (RB)

League Club	Source	Date Signed	Seasons Played	Apps	Subs	Gls
Birmingham C.	YT	07.89				
Exeter C. (N/C)	Cheltenham T.	02.92	91	1	0	0

MASIELLO, Luciano
Italy, 2 January, 1951 (W)

League Club	Source	Date Signed	Seasons Played	Apps	Subs	Gls
Charlton Ath.	App	01.69	69-70	6	0	0

MASKELL, Craig D.
Aldershot, 10 April, 1968 (F)

League Club	Source	Date Signed	Seasons Played	Apps	Subs	Gls
Southampton	App	04.86	85-86	2	4	1
Huddersfield T.	Tr	05.88	88-89	86	1	43
Reading	Tr	08.90	90-91	60	12	26

MASKELL, Dennis
Mountain Ash, 16 April, 1931 (OL)

League Club	Source	Date Signed	Seasons Played	Apps	Subs	Gls
Watford		09.51	51	5	-	0

MASKELL, Michael R.
Eynsham (Oxon), 25 January, 1952 (FB)

League Club	Source	Date Signed	Seasons Played	Apps	Subs	Gls
Chelsea	App	02.69				
Brentford	Tr	07.70	70	1	0	0

MASKERY, Christopher P.
Stoke, 25 September, 1964 (M)

League Club	Source	Date Signed	Seasons Played	Apps	Subs	Gls
Stoke C.	App	09.82	82-86	82	10	3

MASON, Andrew J. P.
Stretford, 26 October, 1966 (M)

League Club	Source	Date Signed	Seasons Played	Apps	Subs	Gls
Crewe Alex. (N/C)	YT	08.84	84	1	1	0

MASON, Clifford E.
York, 27 November, 1929 (FB)

League Club	Source	Date Signed	Seasons Played	Apps	Subs	Gls
Sunderland		01.50				
Darlington	Tr	07.52	52-54	107	-	0
Sheffield U.	Tr	08.55	55-61	97	-	2
Leeds U.	Tr	03.62	61-62	31	-	0
Scunthorpe U.	Tr	02.64	63	12	-	1
Chesterfield	Tr	07.64	64	5	-	0

MASON, George W.
Birmingham, 5 September, 1913 E Sch (CH)

League Club	Source	Date Signed	Seasons Played	Apps	Subs	Gls
Coventry C.	Redhill Amats	11.31	31-51	330	-	6

MASON, James
Glasgow, 17 April, 1933 (OL)

League Club	Source	Date Signed	Seasons Played	Apps	Subs	Gls
Accrington St.	Dundee	06.55	55-56	14	-	1
Chester C.	Tr	06.57	57-58	65	-	6
Crystal Palace	Chelmsford C.	05.60				

MASON, John F.
Coventry, 23 January, 1943 E Amat (CF)

League Club	Source	Date Signed	Seasons Played	Apps	Subs	Gls
Peterborough U.	Alvechurch	05.66	66-67	37	0	18

MASON, Keith M.
Leicester, 19 July, 1958 (G)

League Club	Source	Date Signed	Seasons Played	Apps	Subs	Gls
Huddersfield T.	Leicester C. (N/C)	07.82	82-85	30	0	0

MASON, Maurice
Sedgefield, 25 June, 1927 (IF)

League Club	Source	Date Signed	Seasons Played	Apps	Subs	Gls
Huddersfield T.		01.48				
Darlington	Blackhall Colly	07.52	52	3	-	0

MASON, Michael B.
Bloxwich, 20 October, 1944 (IF)

League Club	Source	Date Signed	Seasons Played	Apps	Subs	Gls
Walsall	App	09.62	63	4	-	0
West Bromwich A.	Tr	07.64				

MASON, Richard J.
Arley, 2 April, 1918 (FB)

League Club	Source	Date Signed	Seasons Played	Apps	Subs	Gls
Coventry C.	Nuneaton Bor.	05.46	46-53	253	-	2

MASON, Robert H.
Tipton, 22 March, 1936 (IF)

League Club	Source	Date Signed	Seasons Played	Apps	Subs	Gls
Wolverhampton W.	Jnrs	05.53	55-61	146	-	44
Leyton Orient	Chelmsford C.	03.63	62-63	23	-	0

MASON, Stuart J.
Whitchurch, 2 June, 1948 E Yth (FB)

League Club	Source	Date Signed	Seasons Played	Apps	Subs	Gls
Wrexham	Jnrs	07.66	65-66	28	0	0
Liverpool	Tr	10.66				
Doncaster Rov.	L	11.67	67	1	0	0
Wrexham	Tr	06.68	68-72	144	13	3
Chester C.	Tr	06.73	73-77	132	5	7
Rochdale	L	12.76	76	2	0	0
Crewe Alex.	L	10.77	77	4	0	1

MASON, Thomas H. A.
Buxton, 20 February, 1953 (M)

League Club	Source	Date Signed	Seasons Played	Apps	Subs	Gls
Derby Co.	App	07.72				
Brighton & H.A.	Tr	09.74	74	23	2	2

MASON, Thomas J. R.
Fulham, 19 June, 1960 (FB)

League Club	Source	Date Signed	Seasons Played	Apps	Subs	Gls
Fulham	App	01.78	77-79	6	0	0
Brighton & H.A.	Tr	06.81				

MASON, Thomas W. M.
Hartlepool, 21 April, 1925 (CH)

League Club	Source	Date Signed	Seasons Played	Apps	Subs	Gls
Hartlepool U.	Railway Ath.	05.46	46	4	-	0

MASSART, David L.
Birmingham, 2 November, 1919 (CF)

League Club	Source	Date Signed	Seasons Played	Apps	Subs	Gls
Birmingham C.	Bells Ath.	02.39	46	3	-	0
Walsall	Tr	06.47	47	27	-	23
Bury	Tr	03.48	47-50	85	-	45
Chesterfield	Tr	02.51	50	11	-	5

MASSEY, Andrew T.
New Cross, 20 October, 1961 IR Yth (M)

League Club	Source	Date Signed	Seasons Played	Apps	Subs	Gls
Millwall	Jnrs	03.79	80-83	74	15	8
Port Vale	L	03.84	83	4	0	1
Aldershot	Tr	05.84	84-85	65	6	3

MASSEY, Bernard W.
Ripley, 5 November, 1920 (WH)

League Club	Source	Date Signed	Seasons Played	Apps	Subs	Gls
Halifax T.	Peterborough U.	09.38	38-50	84	-	6

MASSEY, Eric
Derby, 11 September, 1923 (WH)

League Club	Source	Date Signed	Seasons Played	Apps	Subs	Gls
Bury	Arsenal (Am)	09.46	46-56	202	-	6

MASSEY, Kevin J.
Gainsborough, 30 November, 1965 (M)

League Club	Source	Date Signed	Seasons Played	Apps	Subs	Gls
Cambridge U.	App	12.83	83-85	8	8	1

MASSEY, Richard
Wolverhampton, 11 October, 1968 (CD)

League Club	Source	Date Signed	Seasons Played	Apps	Subs	Gls
Exeter C.	YT	07.86	85-87	22	6	1

MASSEY, Robert W.
Bournemouth, 6 April, 1940 (FB)

League Club	Source	Date Signed	Seasons Played	Apps	Subs	Gls
Bournemouth	Jnrs	05.58	59-60	5	-	0

MASSEY, Roy
Mexborough, 10 September, 1943 E Yth (CF)

League Club	Source	Date Signed	Seasons Played	Apps	Subs	Gls
Rotherham U.		07.64	64-66	15	1	6
Leyton Orient	Tr	09.67	67-68	58	5	13
Colchester U.	Tr	07.69	69-70	30	4	11

MASSEY, Stephen
Denton, 28 March, 1958 (F)

League Club	Source	Date Signed	Seasons Played	Apps	Subs	Gls
Stockport Co.	App	07.75	74-77	87	14	20
Bournemouth	Tr	07.78	78-80	85	12	19
Peterborough U.	Tr	08.81	81	13	5	2
Northampton T.	Tr	02.82	81-82	60	0	26
Hull C.	Tr	07.83	83-84	34	8	9
Cambridge U.	Tr	08.85	85	28	3	11
Wrexham	Tr	07.86	86-87	38	5	10

MASSIE, Leslie
Aberdeen, 20 July, 1935 (IF)

League Club	Source	Date Signed	Seasons Played	Apps	Subs	Gls
Huddersfield T.	Banks O'Dee	08.53	56-66	334	1	100
Darlington	Tr	10.66	66	20	0	2
Halifax T.	Tr	06.67	67-68	89	0	41
Bradford P.A.	Tr	08.69	69	14	0	2
Workington	Tr	12.69	69-70	62	0	15

MASSIMO, Franco
Horsham, 23 September, 1968 (F)

League Club	Source	Date Signed	Seasons Played	Apps	Subs	Gls
Brighton & H.A.	App	09.86	85	0	1	0

MASSON, Donald S.
Banchory, 26 August, 1946 S-17 (M)

League Club	Source	Date Signed	Seasons Played	Apps	Subs	Gls
Middlesbrough	Jnrs	09.63	64-67	50	3	6
Notts Co.	Tr	09.68	68-74	273	0	81
Queens Park R.	Tr	12.74	74-77	116	0	18
Derby Co.	Tr	10.77	77	23	0	1
Notts Co.	Tr	08.78	78-81	129	0	11

MASTERS, Graham J.
Bristol, 13 August, 1931 (W)

League Club	Source	Date Signed	Seasons Played	Apps	Subs	Gls
Bristol C.	Jnrs	08.48	51	9	-	1

MATHER, Harold
Bolton, 24 January, 1921 (FB)

League Club	Source	Date Signed	Seasons Played	Apps	Subs	Gls
Burnley	Jnrs	05.38	46-54	301	-	0

MATHER, Shaun L.
Hereford, 9 September, 1965 (M)

League Club	Source	Date Signed	Seasons Played	Apps	Subs	Gls
Newport Co. (N/C)	Presteigne	08.83	83	0	1	0

MATHIAS, Raymond
Liverpool, 13 December, 1946 (FB)

League Club	Source	Date Signed	Seasons Played	Apps	Subs	Gls
Tranmere Rov.	App	12.64	67-84	557	10	6

MATHIE, David
Motherwell, 15 August, 1919 Died 1954 (CF)

League Club	Source	Date Signed	Seasons Played	Apps	Subs	Gls
Workington	Kilmarnock	10.53	53	2	-	0

MATIER, Gerald
Lisburn (NI), 1 December, 1912 (G)

League Club	Source	Date Signed	Seasons Played	Apps	Subs	Gls
Blackburn Rov.	Coleraine	07.37	37-38	20	-	0
Bradford C.	Tr	08.39				
Plymouth Arg.	Tr	09.46				
Torquay U.	Tr	11.46	46	17	-	0

MATTHEW, Damian
Islington, 23 September, 1970 Eu21-9 (M)

League Club	Source	Date Signed	Seasons Played	Apps	Subs	Gls
Chelsea	YT	06.89	89-91	10	7	0

MATTHEWS, Barry J.
Sheffield, 18 January, 1926

League Club	Source	Date Signed	Seasons Played	Apps	Subs	Gls
Lincoln C. (Am)	Sheffield U. (Am)	10.49	49	2	-	0

MATTHEWS, David
Hackney, 20 November, 1965 (F)

League Club	Source	Date Signed	Seasons Played	Apps	Subs	Gls
West Ham U.	App	11.82				
Walsall	Basildon U.	11.87				
Southend U.	Tr	03.88	88	1	5	0

MATTHEWS, David I.
Rhondda, 24 September, 1921 (G)

League Club	Source	Date Signed	Seasons Played	Apps	Subs	Gls
Cardiff C.		09.47				
Newport Co.	Tr	04.48	48-49	9	-	0

MATTHEWS, Francis J.
London, 7 January, 1948 (FB)

League Club	Source	Date Signed	Seasons Played	Apps	Subs	Gls
Southend U.	App	01.66	65-67	21	6	0
Torquay U.	Tr	06.68	68	6	1	0

MATTHEWS, Graham
Stoke, 2 November, 1942 (F)

League Club	Source	Date Signed	Seasons Played	Apps	Subs	Gls
Stoke C.	Jnrs	11.59	60-62	16	-	3
Walsall	Tr	08.63	63-64	67	-	21
Crewe Alex.	Tr	08.65	65-66	55	1	19

MATTHEWS, John M.
Camden, 1 November, 1955 (M)

League Club	Source	Date Signed	Seasons Played	Apps	Subs	Gls
Arsenal	App	08.73	74-77	38	7	2
Sheffield U.	Tr	08.78	78-81	98	5	14
Mansfield T.	Tr	08.82	82-83	70	2	6
Chesterfield	Tr	08.84	84	38	0	1
Plymouth Arg.	Tr	08.85	85-88	131	4	4
Torquay U.	Tr	07.89	89	22	3	0

MATTHEWS, Keith J.
Wrexham, 7 March, 1934 (F)

League Club	Source	Date Signed	Seasons Played	Apps	Subs	Gls
Wrexham		12.52	52-54	9	-	0

MATTHEWS, Mark
Reading, 17 September, 1961 (M)

League Club	Source	Date Signed	Seasons Played	Apps	Subs	Gls
Reading (N/C)		07.81	81-83	5	3	1

MATTHEWS, Michael
Hull, 25 September, 1960 (M)

League Club	Source	Date Signed	Seasons Played	Apps	Subs	Gls
Wolverhampton W.	App	10.78	80-83	72	4	7
Scunthorpe U.	Tr	02.84	83-85	56	2	5
Halifax T.	North Ferriby U.	09.86	86-88	98	1	8
Scarborough	Tr	12.88	88	7	0	1
Stockport Co.	Tr	02.89	88-89	35	0	3
Scarborough	Tr	12.89	89-90	64	2	4
Hull C.	Tr	08.91	91	10	6	2

MATTHEWS, Neil
Grimsby, 19 September, 1966 (F)

League Club	Source	Date Signed	Seasons Played	Apps	Subs	Gls
Grimsby T.	App	09.84	84-86	9	2	1
Scunthorpe U.	L	11.85	85	1	0	0
Halifax T.	L	10.86	86	9	0	2
Bolton W.	L	03.87	86	1	0	0
Halifax T.	Tr	08.87	87-89	99	6	29
Stockport Co.	Tr	06.90	90-91	26	12	14
Halifax T.	L	09.91	91	3	0	0

MATTHEWS, Neil P.
Manchester, 3 December, 1967 NIu21-1 (RB)

League Club	Source	Date Signed	Seasons Played	Apps	Subs	Gls
Blackpool	App	12.85	85-89	67	9	1
Cardiff C.	Tr	08.90	90-91	48	4	1

MATTHEWS, Paul W.
Leicester, 30 September, 1946 (M)

League Club	Source	Date Signed	Seasons Played	Apps	Subs	Gls
Leicester C.	App	08.64	64-70	56	5	5
Southend U.	L	09.72	72	1	0	0
Mansfield T.	Tr	12.72	72-77	121	3	6
Rotherham U.	Tr	10.77	77	8	0	0
Northampton T.	L	03.79	78	13	0	0

MATTHEWS, Reginald D.
Coventry, 20 December, 1933 Eu23-4/E'B'-3/EF Lge/E-5 (G)

League Club	Source	Date Signed	Seasons Played	Apps	Subs	Gls
Coventry C.	Jnrs	05.50	52-56	111	-	0
Chelsea	Tr	11.56	56-60	135	-	0
Derby Co.	Tr	10.61	61-67	225	0	0

MATTHEWS, Robert
Slough, 14 October, 1970 (M)

League Club	Source	Date Signed	Seasons Played	Apps	Subs	Gls
Notts Co.	Shepshed A.	03.92	91	1	4	3

MATTHEWS, Roy H.
Slough, 29 March, 1940 (IF)

League Club	Source	Date Signed	Seasons Played	Apps	Subs	Gls
Charlton Ath.	Arbroath Vic.	04.57	59-66	160	0	46

MATTHEWS, Stanley (Sir)
Hanley, 1 February, 1915 E Sch/EF Lge/E-54 (OR)

League Club	Source	Date Signed	Seasons Played	Apps	Subs	Gls
Stoke C.	Jnrs	02.32	31-46	259	-	51
Blackpool	Tr	05.47	47-61	379	-	17
Stoke C.	Tr	10.61	61-64	59	-	3

MATTHEWS, Terence G.
Leyton, 25 February, 1936 (IF)

League Club	Source	Date Signed	Seasons Played	Apps	Subs	Gls
West Ham U.	Jnrs	02.53	55	9	-	1
Aldershot	Tr	07.57	57-61	62	-	22
Gillingham	Tr	08.62	62	11	-	1

MATTHEWS, Wayne J.
Cardiff, 11 September, 1964 (M)

League Club	Source	Date Signed	Seasons Played	Apps	Subs	Gls
Cardiff C.	Jnrs	01.83	83	4	10	0

MATTHEWSON, Reginald
Sheffield, 6 August, 1939 (CH)

League Club	Source	Date Signed	Seasons Played	Apps	Subs	Gls
Sheffield U.	Jnrs	06.58	61-67	146	3	3
Fulham	Tr	02.68	67-72	156	2	1
Chester C.	Tr	01.73	72-75	86	1	1

MATTHEWSON, Robert
Newcastle, 13 April, 1930 (CH)

League Club	Source	Date Signed	Seasons Played	Apps	Subs	Gls
Bolton W.	Byker Y.C.	03.48	50-52	3	-	0
Lincoln C.	Tr	06.53				

MATTHEWSON, Trevor
Sheffield, 12 February, 1963 (CD)

League Club	Source	Date Signed	Seasons Played	Apps	Subs	Gls
Sheffield Wed.	App	02.81	80-82	3	0	0
Newport Co.	Tr	10.83	83-84	73	2	0
Stockport Co.	Tr	09.85	85-86	79	1	0
Lincoln C.	Tr	08.87	88	43	0	2
Birmingham C.	Tr	07.89	89-91	127	1	10

MATTHIAS, Terence
Wrexham, 10 November, 1949 W Sch (D)

League Club	Source	Date Signed	Seasons Played	Apps	Subs	Gls
Shrewsbury T.	App	05.67	65-73	96	3	0

MATTINSON, Harold
Ireby, 20 July, 1925 (CH)

League Club	Source	Date Signed	Seasons Played	Apps	Subs	Gls
Middlesbrough		11.45	46	3	-	0
Preston N.E.	Tr	03.49	48-58	124	-	0

MAUCHLEN, Alistair H.
West Kilbride, 29 June, 1960 (M/RB)

League Club	Source	Date Signed	Seasons Played	Apps	Subs	Gls
Leicester C.	Motherwell	08.85	85-91	228	11	11

MAUGE, Ronald C.
Islington, 10 March, 1969 (M)

League Club	Source	Date Signed	Seasons Played	Apps	Subs	Gls
Charlton Ath.	YT	07.87				
Fulham	Tr	09.88	88-89	47	3	2
Bury	Tr	07.90	90-91	41	10	6

MAUGHAN, Wesley J.
Southampton, 17 February, 1939 (CF)

League Club	Source	Date Signed	Seasons Played	Apps	Subs	Gls
Southampton	Cowes (IOW)	05.57	58-61	6	-	1
Reading	Tr	03.62	61-62	16	-	3

MAUND, John H.
Hednesford, 5 January, 1916 (OR)

League Club	Source	Date Signed	Seasons Played	Apps	Subs	Gls
Aston Villa	Hednesford T.	10.34	35-37	47	-	8
Nottingham F.	Tr	05.39				
Walsall	Tr	10.46	46-47	30	-	7

MAW, John
Scunthorpe, 22 December, 1934 (HB)

League Club	Source	Date Signed	Seasons Played	Apps	Subs	Gls
Scunthorpe U.		06.57	57	1	-	0

MAWER, Shaun K.
Ulceby, 6 August, 1959 (FB)

League Club	Source	Date Signed	Seasons Played	Apps	Subs	Gls
Grimsby T.	App	08.77	77-79	57	3	0

MAWSON, Joseph
Workington, 7 January, 1934

League Club	Source	Date Signed	Seasons Played	Apps	Subs	Gls
Workington (Am)		06.55	55	1	-	0

MAWSON, Ronald
Bishop Auckland, 16 September, 1914 (G)

League Club	Source	Date Signed	Seasons Played	Apps	Subs	Gls
Crewe Alex.	R.A.F. Tern Hill	06.45	46-47	23	-	0
Wrexham	Tr	09.48	48	6	-	0

MAXFIELD, John
Carlisle, 17 June, 1919 (CF)

League Club	Source	Date Signed	Seasons Played	Apps	Subs	Gls
Carlisle U.		01.47	46-50	25	-	4
Workington	Tr	07.51	51	13	-	4

MAXWELL, Alistair
Hamilton, 29 June, 1960 (G)

League Club	Source	Date Signed	Seasons Played	Apps	Subs	Gls
Bolton W. (L)	Motherwell	03.92	91	3	0	0

MAXWELL, Hugh
Rigghead, 14 May, 1938 (IF)

League Club	Source	Date Signed	Seasons Played	Apps	Subs	Gls
Bradford P.A.	Stirling A.	04.62	61-62	12	-	5

MAXWELL, Kenneth
Glasgow, 11 February, 1928 (FB)

League Club	Source	Date Signed	Seasons Played	Apps	Subs	Gls
Northampton T.	Kilmarnock	06.49	50	2	-	0
Bradford P.A.	Canada	11.57	57	2	-	0

MAXWELL, Patrick
Ayr, 10 January, 1929 (IF)

League Club	Source	Date Signed	Seasons Played	Apps	Subs	Gls
Chesterfield	Saltcoats Vic.	08.51	51-52	18	-	3

MAY, Andrew M. P.
Bury, 26 January, 1964 Eu21-1 (M)

League Club	Source	Date Signed	Seasons Played	Apps	Subs	Gls
Manchester C.	App	01.82	80-86	141	9	8
Huddersfield T.	Tr	07.87	87-89	112	2	5
Bolton W.	L	03.88	87	9	1	2
Bristol C.	Tr	08.90	90-91	88	2	4

MAY, David
Oldham, 24 June, 1970 (CD)

League Club	Source	Date Signed	Seasons Played	Apps	Subs	Gls
Blackburn Rov.	YT	06.88	88-91	49	0	1

MAY, Donald T.
Broseley, 31 May, 1931 (WH)

League Club	Source	Date Signed	Seasons Played	Apps	Subs	Gls
Bury		03.51	51-61	133	-	11

MAY, Edward
Edinburgh, 30 August, 1967 S Yth/Su21-2 (M)

League Club	Source	Date Signed	Seasons Played	Apps	Subs	Gls
Brentford	Hibernian	07.89	89-90	46	1	10

MAY, Edward C.
Epping, 19 May, 1943 (CD)

League Club	Source	Date Signed	Seasons Played	Apps	Subs	Gls
Southend U.	Dagenham	01.65	64-67	107	4	3
Wrexham	Tr	06.68	68-75	330	4	34
Swansea C.	Tr	08.76	76-77	90	0	8

MAY, Gary C.
Darlington, 7 May, 1967 (M)

League Club	Source	Date Signed	Seasons Played	Apps	Subs	Gls
Darlington (N/C)		11.86	86	1	1	0

MAY, Harold
Glasgow, 15 October, 1928 (FB)

League Club	Source	Date Signed	Seasons Played	Apps	Subs	Gls
Cardiff C.	Thorniewood U.	08.48	49	1	-	0
Swindon T.	Tr	06.50	50-51	78	-	1
Barnsley	Tr	05.52	52-54	106	-	0
Southend U.	Tr	09.55	55	19	-	1

MAY, John
Crosby, 28 January, 1960 E Sch (CD)

League Club	Source	Date Signed	Seasons Played	Apps	Subs	Gls
Blackpool	App	11.78	78	4	0	0
Exeter C.	Tr	08.80				

MAY, Lawrence C. (Larry)
Sutton Coldfield, 26 December, 1958 (CD)

League Club	Source	Date Signed	Seasons Played	Apps	Subs	Gls
Leicester C.	App	12.76	76-82	180	7	12
Barnsley	Tr	09.83	83-86	122	0	3
Sheffield Wed.	Tr	02.87	86-87	30	1	1
Brighton & H.A.	Tr	09.88	88	24	0	3

MAY, Leroy A.
Wolverhampton, 12 August, 1969 (F)

League Club	Source	Date Signed	Seasons Played	Apps	Subs	Gls
Walsall	Tividale	01.92	91	1	3	0

MAY, Warren D.
Southend, 31 December, 1964 (D)

League Club	Source	Date Signed	Seasons Played	Apps	Subs	Gls
Southend U.	App	01.83	82-85	78	12	4

MAYBANK, Edward G. (Teddy)
Lambeth, 11 October, 1956 (F)

League Club	Source	Date Signed	Seasons Played	Apps	Subs	Gls
Chelsea	App	02.74	74-76	28	0	6
Fulham	Tr	11.76	76-77	27	0	14
Brighton & H.A.	Tr	11.77	77-79	62	2	16
Fulham	Tr	12.79	79	19	0	3

MAYERS, Alan
Chester, 20 April, 1937 (OR)

League Club	Source	Date Signed	Seasons Played	Apps	Subs	Gls
Chester C.	Jnrs	05.55	55	1	-	0

MAYERS, Derek
Liverpool, 24 January, 1935 (OR)

League Club	Source	Date Signed	Seasons Played	Apps	Subs	Gls
Everton	Jnrs	08.52	52-56	18	-	7
Preston N.E.	Tr	05.57	57-60	118	-	25
Leeds U.	Tr	06.61	61	20	-	5
Bury	Tr	07.62	62-63	32	-	6
Wrexham	Tr	10.63	63	21	-	2

MAYES, Alan K.
Edmonton, 11 December, 1953 (F)

League Club	Source	Date Signed	Seasons Played	Apps	Subs	Gls
Queens Park R.	App	07.71				
Watford	Tr	11.74	74-78	110	23	31
Northampton T.	L	01.76	75	10	0	4
Swindon T.	Tr	02.79	78-80	89	0	38
Chelsea	Tr	12.80	80-82	61	5	18
Swindon T.	Tr	07.83	83-84	52	10	27
Carlisle U.	Tr	07.85	85	8	2	2
Newport Co.	L	02.86	85	3	0	1
Blackpool	Tr	09.86	86	12	1	6

MAYFIELD, Leslie
Mansfield, 19 January, 1926 (FB)

League Club	Source	Date Signed	Seasons Played	Apps	Subs	Gls
Mansfield T.		09.48	49-52	34	-	0

MAYLE, Robert J.
Llandysul, 18 December, 1938 (F)

League Club	Source	Date Signed	Seasons Played	Apps	Subs	Gls
Shrewsbury T.	Sentinel Jnrs	05.57	57	8	-	0

MAYMAN, Paul F.
Crewe, 29 May, 1958 E Semi-Pro (M)

League Club	Source	Date Signed	Seasons Played	Apps	Subs	Gls
Crewe Alex.	Jnrs	07.76	75-76	42	1	3

MAYNARD, Michael C.
Guyana, 7 January, 1947 (FB)

League Club	Source	Date Signed	Seasons Played	Apps	Subs	Gls
Crystal Palace	Hounslow T.	03.66				
Peterborough U.	Tr	07.67	67	2	1	0

MAYO, Joseph
Tipton, 25 May, 1951 (F)

League Club	Source	Date Signed	Seasons Played	Apps	Subs	Gls
Walsall	Dudley T.	09.72	72	2	5	1
West Bromwich A.	Tr	02.73	73-76	67	5	16
Leyton Orient	Tr	03.77	76-81	150	5	36
Cambridge U.	Tr	09.81	81-82	35	1	14
Blackpool	L	10.82	82	5	0	1

MAYS, Albert E.
Rhondda, 18 April, 1929 Died 1973 (WH)

League Club	Source	Date Signed	Seasons Played	Apps	Subs	Gls
Derby Co.	Jnrs	05.46	49-59	272	-	21
Chesterfield	Tr	07.60	60	37	-	5

MAZZON, Giorgio
Cheshunt, 4 September, 1960 (D/M)

League Club	Source	Date Signed	Seasons Played	Apps	Subs	Gls
Tottenham H.	Hertford T.	04.79	80-82	3	1	0
Aldershot	Tr	08.83	83-88	184	11	6

MEACHAM, Jeffrey
Bristol, 6 February, 1962 (F)

League Club	Source	Date Signed	Seasons Played	Apps	Subs	Gls
Bristol Rov.	Trowbridge T.	03.87	86-87	19	7	9

MEACHIN, Paul
Bebington, 17 July, 1956 (F)

League Club	Source	Date Signed	Seasons Played	Apps	Subs	Gls
Southport (Am)	Ashville	10.74	74	3	0	0

MEACOCK, Kevin M.
Bristol, 16 September, 1963 (F)

League Club	Source	Date Signed	Seasons Played	Apps	Subs	Gls
Cardiff C.	Devizes T.	12.84	84-85	20	5	3

MEAD, Peter S.
Luton, 9 September, 1956 (FB)

League Club	Source	Date Signed	Seasons Played	Apps	Subs	Gls
Luton T.	App	07.74				
Northampton T.	Tr	08.77	77-78	75	2	4

MEADE, Raphael J.
Islington, 22 November, 1962 (F)

League Club	Source	Date Signed	Seasons Played	Apps	Subs	Gls
Arsenal	App	06.90	81-84	25	16	14
Luton T.	Dundee U.	03.89	88	2	2	0
Ipswich T. (N/C)	B.K. Odense (Den)	01.90	89	0	1	0
Plymouth Arg.	B.K. Odense (Den)	01.91	90	2	3	0
Brighton & H.A.	Tr	08.91	91	35	5	9

MEADOWS, Frank
Maltby, 27 June, 1933 (WH)

League Club	Source	Date Signed	Seasons Played	Apps	Subs	Gls
Rotherham U.		04.52	53-55	8	-	0
Coventry C.	Tr	06.56	56	8	-	0

MEADOWS, James
Bolton, 21 July, 1931 EF Lge/E-1 (OR)

League Club	Source	Date Signed	Seasons Played	Apps	Subs	Gls
Southport	Bolton Y.M.C.A.	03.49	48-50	60	-	6
Manchester C.	Tr	03.51	50-54	130	-	30

MEADOWS, John A.
Hoxton, 13 November, 1930 (WH)

League Club	Source	Date Signed	Seasons Played	Apps	Subs	Gls
Watford	St Albans C.	06.51	51-59	222	-	42

MEADOWS, Robert
Melton Mowbray, 25 April, 1938 (FB)

League Club	Source	Date Signed	Seasons Played	Apps	Subs	Gls
Stoke C.	Jnrs	05.55				
Doncaster Rov.	Northwich Vic.	12.62	62-63	43	-	0

MEADOWS, J. Ronald
Lancaster, 4 December, 1920 (G)

League Club	Source	Date Signed	Seasons Played	Apps	Subs	Gls
Burnley	Glasson Dock	09.46				
Bournemouth	Tr	04.50	50-51	16	-	0
Accrington St.	Tr	07.52	52	18	-	0

MEAGAN, Michael K.
Dublin, 29 May, 1934 IR Sch/IR'B'-1/IR-17 (FB)

League Club	Source	Date Signed	Seasons Played	Apps	Subs	Gls
Everton	Johnville Jnrs	09.52	57-63	165	-	1
Huddersfield T.	Tr	07.64	64-67	118	1	1
Halifax T.	Tr	07.68	68	23	0	0

MEAGAN, Thomas P.
Liverpool, 14 November, 1959 (M)

League Club	Source	Date Signed	Seasons Played	Apps	Subs	Gls
Doncaster Rov.	App	11.77	77-78	32	5	1
Doncaster Rov. (N/C)		09.82	82	2	0	0

MEAGON, John G.
Shap, 11 November, 1935 (FB)

League Club	Source	Date Signed	Seasons Played	Apps	Subs	Gls
Workington	Jnrs	12.52	52-54	3	-	0

MEAKER, Michael J.
Greenford, 18 August, 1971 (W)

League Club	Source	Date Signed	Seasons Played	Apps	Subs	Gls
Queens Park R.	YT	12.89	90-91	0	9	0
Plymouth Arg.	L	11.91	91	4	0	0

MEAKIN, Harold
Stoke, 8 September, 1919 (FB)

League Club	Source	Date Signed	Seasons Played	Apps	Subs	Gls
Stoke C.		11.45	46-49	35	-	0

MEALAND, K. Barry
Carshalton, 24 January, 1943 (FB)

League Club	Source	Date Signed	Seasons Played	Apps	Subs	Gls
Fulham	Jnrs	10.61	61-67	28	1	0
Rotherham U.	Tr	08.68	68-69	44	1	0

MEANEY, John F.
Stoke, 19 November, 1919 (IF)

League Club	Source	Date Signed	Seasons Played	Apps	Subs	Gls
Crewe Alex.	Ravensdale	03.47	46-53	288	-	31

MEANEY, Terence
Stoke, 25 May, 1922 (F)

League Club	Source	Date Signed	Seasons Played	Apps	Subs	Gls
Bury	Ravensdale	05.44	46	4	-	2
Crewe Alex.	Tr	07.47	47	3	-	2

MEASHAM, Ian
Barnsley, 14 December, 1964 (RB)

League Club	Source	Date Signed	Seasons Played	Apps	Subs	Gls
Huddersfield T.	App	12.82	84	17	0	0
Lincoln C.	L	10.85	85	6	0	0
Rochdale	L	03.86	85	12	0	0
Cambridge U.	Tr	07.86	86	46	0	0
Burnley	Tr	11.88	88-91	136	1	2

MEASURES, George A.
Walthamstow, 17 December, 1958 (F)

League Club	Source	Date Signed	Seasons Played	Apps	Subs	Gls
Cambridge U. (N/C)	Bowers U.	11.83	83	4	0	0

MEATH, Trevor J.
Wednesbury, 20 March, 1944 (M)

League Club	Source	Date Signed	Seasons Played	Apps	Subs	Gls
Walsall	Darlaston	05.64	64-69	59	8	11
Lincoln C.	Tr	10.69	69-71	42	1	5

MEDD, Gordon E.
Birmingham, 17 August, 1925 (OL)

League Club	Source	Date Signed	Seasons Played	Apps	Subs	Gls
Birmingham C.	Worcester C.	10.46				
Walsall	Worcester C.	06.49	49	22	-	2
Rochdale	Tr	07.50	50	5	-	1
York C.	Tr	01.51	50	1	-	0

MEDHURST, Harold E.
Byfleet, 5 February, 1916 Died 1984 (G)

League Club	Source	Date Signed	Seasons Played	Apps	Subs	Gls
West Ham U.	Woking	11.36	38-46	24	-	0
Chelsea	Tr	01.47	46-51	143	-	0
Brighton & H.A.	Tr	11.52	52	12	-	0

MEDLEY, Leslie D.
Edmonton, 3 September, 1920 E Sch/EF Lge/E-6 (OL)

League Club	Source	Date Signed	Seasons Played	Apps	Subs	Gls
Tottenham H.	Jnrs	02.39	46-52	150	-	45

MEDLOCK, Owen W.
Peterborough, 8 March, 1938 (G)

League Club	Source	Date Signed	Seasons Played	Apps	Subs	Gls
Chelsea	Jnrs	05.55				
Swindon T.	Tr	02.59	59	3	-	0
Oxford U.	Tr	12.59	62	19	-	0

MEDWIN, Terence C.
Swansea, 25 September, 1932 W Sch/W-30 (W)

League Club	Source	Date Signed	Seasons Played	Apps	Subs	Gls
Swansea C.	Jnrs	11.49	51-55	148	-	60
Tottenham H.	Tr	04.56	56-62	197	-	65

MEE, George E.
Blackpool, 20 May, 1923 Died 1974 (IF)

League Club	Source	Date Signed	Seasons Played	Apps	Subs	Gls
Nottingham F.	Jnrs	05.40	46	9	-	1

MEECHAM, David A.
Loganlea, 10 November, 1943 (CF)

League Club	Source	Date Signed	Seasons Played	Apps	Subs	Gls
Sheffield Wed.	Burnley (Am)	12.60				
Scunthorpe U.	Tr	06.61				
York C.	Tr	06.63	63	6	-	0

MEEK, George
Glasgow, 15 February, 1934 (W)

League Club	Source	Date Signed	Seasons Played	Apps	Subs	Gls
Leeds U.	Hamilton Acad.	08.52	52-59	196	-	19
Walsall	L	01.54	53-54	44	-	6
Leicester C.	Tr	08.60	60	13	-	0
Walsall	Tr	07.61	61-64	129	-	22

MEENS, Harold
Doncaster, 5 October, 1919 (CH)

League Club	Source	Date Signed	Seasons Played	Apps	Subs	Gls
Hull C.	Jnrs	10.38	38-51	146	-	0

MEESON, David J.
Oxford, 6 July, 1934 (G)

League Club	Source	Date Signed	Seasons Played	Apps	Subs	Gls
Wolverhampton W.	Oxford C.	02.52				
Reading	Tr	08.54	54-62	156	-	0
Coventry C.	Tr	09.62	62-64	24	-	0

MEGSON, Donald H.
Sale, 12 June, 1936 EF Lge (LB)

League Club	Source	Date Signed	Seasons Played	Apps	Subs	Gls
Sheffield Wed.	Jnrs	05.53	59-69	386	0	6
Bristol Rov.	Tr	03.70	69-70	31	0	1

MEGSON, Gary J.
Manchester, 2 May, 1959 (M)

League Club	Source	Date Signed	Seasons Played	Apps	Subs	Gls
Plymouth Arg.	App	05.77	77-79	78	0	10
Everton	Tr	12.79	79-80	20	2	2
Sheffield Wed.	Tr	08.81	81-83	123	0	13
Nottingham F.	Tr	08.84				
Newcastle U.	Tr	11.84	84-85	21	3	1
Sheffield Wed.	Tr	12.85	85-88	107	3	12
Manchester C.	Tr	01.89	88-91	78	4	2

Gary Megson (Plymouth Argyle, Everton, Sheffield Wednesday, Nottingham Forest, Newcastle United, Sheffield Wednesday & Manchester City)

MEGSON, Kevin C.
Halifax, 1 July, 1971 (W)

League Club	Source	Date Signed	Seasons Played	Apps	Subs	Gls
Bradford C.	YT	07.89	89-90	24	3	0
Halifax T.	Tr	03.91	90-91	13	2	0

MEHEW, David S.
Camberley, 29 October, 1967 (M)

League Club	Source	Date Signed	Seasons Played	Apps	Subs	Gls
Bristol Rov.	Leeds U. (YT)	07.85	85-91	181	17	60

MEHMET, David N.
Camberwell, 2 December, 1960 (M)

League Club	Source	Date Signed	Seasons Played	Apps	Subs	Gls
Millwall	App	12.77	76-80	97	17	15
Charlton Ath.	Tampa Bay (USA)	01.82	81-82	29	0	2
Gillingham	Tr	03.83	82-85	128	4	39
Millwall	Tr	07.86	86-87	17	2	1

MEIJER, Geert
Netherlands, 15 March, 1951 Dutch Int (W)

League Club	Source	Date Signed	Seasons Played	Apps	Subs	Gls
Bristol C.	Ajax (Neth)	03.79	78-79	12	3	2

MELDRUM, Colin
Glasgow, 26 November, 1941 (LB)

League Club	Source	Date Signed	Seasons Played	Apps	Subs	Gls
Arsenal	Jnrs	12.58				
Watford	Tr	12.60	60-62	32	-	0
Reading	Tr	04.63	62-69	265	1	8
Cambridge U.	Tr	10.69	70	37	1	0
Workington		12.74	74	0	2	0

MELIA, James J.
Liverpool, 1 November, 1937 E Sch/E Yth/EF Lge/E-2 (M)

League Club	Source	Date Signed	Seasons Played	Apps	Subs	Gls
Liverpool	Jnrs	11.54	55-63	269	-	76
Wolverhampton W.	Tr	03.64	63-64	24	-	4
Southampton	Tr	11.64	64-68	139	0	11
Aldershot	Tr	11.68	68-71	135	0	14
Crewe Alex.	Tr	02.72	71	2	2	0

MELL, Stewart A.
Doncaster, 15 October, 1957 E Semi-Pro (F)

League Club	Source	Date Signed	Seasons Played	Apps	Subs	Gls
Doncaster Rov.	Appleby Frodingham	02.80	79-82	62	14	14
Halifax T.	Tr	07.83	83	22	8	8
Scarborough	Burton A.	07.86	87-88	30	9	8

MELLEDEW, Stephen T.
Rochdale, 28 November, 1945 (M)

League Club	Source	Date Signed	Seasons Played	Apps	Subs	Gls
Rochdale	Whipp & Bourne	12.66	66-69	88	9	23
Everton	Tr	09.69				
Aldershot	Tr	07.71	71-73	90	2	27
Bury	Tr	11.73	73-74	14	6	2
Crewe Alex.	Tr	10.74	74-75	49	7	2
Rochdale	Tr	07.76	76-77	76	2	12

MELLING, Terence
Billingham, 24 January, 1940 (IF)

League Club	Source	Date Signed	Seasons Played	Apps	Subs	Gls
Newcastle U.	Tow Law T.	12.65				
Watford	Tr	05.66	65-66	23	1	5
Newport Co.	Tr	02.67	66-67	34	0	14
Mansfield T.	Tr	11.67	67-68	33	0	7
Rochdale	Tr	09.68	68	20	0	8
Darlington	Tr	03.67	68-69	21	0	6

MELLISH, Stuart M.
Hyde, 19 November, 1969 (M)

League Club	Source	Date Signed	Seasons Played	Apps	Subs	Gls
Rochdale	YT	07.88	87-88	24	3	1

MELLON, Michael J.
Paisley, 18 March, 1972 (W)

League Club	Source	Date Signed	Seasons Played	Apps	Subs	Gls
Bristol C.	YT	12.89	89-91	19	6	0

MELLOR, J. Allan
Droylsden, 16 October, 1921 (WH)

League Club	Source	Date Signed	Seasons Played	Apps	Subs	Gls
Hull C.	Ashton U.	05.47	47-51	104	-	4

MELLOR, R. Brett
Huddersfield, 4 February, 1960 (CD)

League Club	Source	Date Signed	Seasons Played	Apps	Subs	Gls
Huddersfield T.	App	02.78	77	1	0	0
Barnsley	Tr	08.80				

MELLOR, Ian
Sale, 19 February, 1950 (W)

League Club	Source	Date Signed	Seasons Played	Apps	Subs	Gls
Manchester C.	Wythenshawe Amats	12.69	70-72	36	4	7
Norwich C.	Tr	03.73	72-73	28	1	2
Brighton & H.A.	Tr	04.74	74-77	116	6	31
Chester C.	Tr	02.78	77-78	38	2	11
Sheffield Wed.	Tr	06.79	79-81	54	16	11
Bradford C.	Tr	06.82	82-83	27	9	4

MELLOR, Kenneth E.
Leicester, 22 August, 1934 (CH)

League Club	Source	Date Signed	Seasons Played	Apps	Subs	Gls
Leicester C.		07.55				
Mansfield T.	Tr	07.57	57-58	66	-	0
Swindon T.	Tr	07.59	59-60	32	-	4

MELLOR, Peter J.
Prestbury, 20 November, 1947 E Yth (G)

League Club	Source	Date Signed	Seasons Played	Apps	Subs	Gls
Burnley	Witton A.	04.69	69-71	69	0	0
Chesterfield	L	01.72	71	4	0	0
Fulham	Tr	02.72	71-76	190	0	0
Hereford U.	Tr	09.77	77	32	0	0
Portsmouth	Tr	07.78	78-80	129	0	0

MELLOR, William
Manchester, 29 June, 1925 (FB)

League Club	Source	Date Signed	Seasons Played	Apps	Subs	Gls
Accrington St.	Droylsden	06.50	50-53	138	-	2

MELLOWS, Michael A.
Epsom, 14 November, 1947 E Amat/E Yth (M)

League Club	Source	Date Signed	Seasons Played	Apps	Subs	Gls
Reading (Am)	Sutton U.	09.70	70	14	2	2
Portsmouth	Winchester C.	09.73	73-77	174	7	16

League Club	Source	Date Signed	Seasons Played	Apps	Subs	Gls

MELROSE, James M.
Glasgow, 7 October, 1958 S Sch/Su21-8/SF Lge (F)

League Club	Source	Date Signed	Seasons Played	Apps	Subs	Gls
Leicester C.	Partick Th.	07.80	80-82	57	15	21
Coventry C.	Tr	09.82	82	21	3	8
Wolverhampton W.	Glasgow Celtic (L)	09.84	84	6	1	2
Manchester C.	Glasgow Celtic	11.84	84-85	27	7	8
Charlton Ath.	Tr	03.86	85-87	44	4	19
Leeds U.	Tr	09.87	87	3	1	0
Shrewsbury T.	Tr	02.88	87-89	27	22	3

MELVILLE, Alan A.
Hartlepool, 13 March, 1941 (CH)

League Club	Source	Date Signed	Seasons Played	Apps	Subs	Gls
Hartlepool U.	Jnrs	09.60	60-61	5	-	0

MELVILLE, Andrew R.
Swansea, 29 November, 1968 Wu21-1/W-13 (CD)

League Club	Source	Date Signed	Seasons Played	Apps	Subs	Gls
Swansea C.	YT	07.86	85-89	165	10	22
Oxford U.	Tr	07.90	90-91	91	0	7

MELVILLE, Leslie
Ormskirk, 29 November, 1930 E Yth (HB)

League Club	Source	Date Signed	Seasons Played	Apps	Subs	Gls
Everton	Jnrs	04.50				
Bournemouth	Tr	07.56	56-57	25	-	0
Oldham Ath.	Tr	03.58	57	2	-	0

MENDHAM, Peter S.
Kings Lynn, 9 April, 1960 (M)

League Club	Source	Date Signed	Seasons Played	Apps	Subs	Gls
Norwich C.	App	04.78	78-86	200	11	23

MENDONCA, Clive P.
Islington, 9 September, 1968 (F)

League Club	Source	Date Signed	Seasons Played	Apps	Subs	Gls
Sheffield U.	App	09.86	86-87	8	5	4
Doncaster Rov.	L	02.88	87	2	0	0
Rotherham U.	Tr	03.88	87-90	71	13	27
Sheffield U.	Tr	07.91	91	4	6	1
Grimsby T.	L	01.92	91	3	0	1
Grimsby T.	L	03.92	91	7	0	2

MENMUIR, William F.
Glasgow, 3 February, 1952 (M)

League Club	Source	Date Signed	Seasons Played	Apps	Subs	Gls
Bristol C.		06.69	69-70	1	1	0

MENZIES, Norman
Washington, 20 June, 1926 (IF)

League Club	Source	Date Signed	Seasons Played	Apps	Subs	Gls
Barnsley	Hexham Hearts	10.49				
Aldershot	Tr	05.50	50-57	221	-	95

MENZIES, Ross
Glasgow, 31 October, 1934 S Sch (HB)

League Club	Source	Date Signed	Seasons Played	Apps	Subs	Gls
Cardiff C.	Glasgow Rangers	08.57	57	1	-	0

MEOLA, Anthony M.
USA, 21 February, 1969 USA Int (G)

League Club	Source	Date Signed	Seasons Played	Apps	Subs	Gls
Brighton & H.A. (N/C)		08.90	90	1	0	0

MERCER, Arthur D.
Hull, 14 February, 1918

League Club	Source	Date Signed	Seasons Played	Apps	Subs	Gls
Torquay U.		02.46	46-48	66	-	8

MERCER, James R.
Dunfermline, 17 March, 1935 (F)

League Club	Source	Date Signed	Seasons Played	Apps	Subs	Gls
Bury	Rosyth R.	06.57	57-58	18	-	1
Crewe Alex.	Tr	06.59	59	3	-	0

MERCER, Joseph
Ellesmere Port, 9 August, 1914 Died 1990 EF Lge/E-5 (WH)

League Club	Source	Date Signed	Seasons Played	Apps	Subs	Gls
Everton	Ellesmere Port	09.32	32-46	170	-	1
Arsenal	Tr	12.46	46-53	247	-	2

MERCER, Keith A.
Lewisham, 10 October, 1956 (F)

League Club	Source	Date Signed	Seasons Played	Apps	Subs	Gls
Watford	App	09.74	72-79	109	25	46
Southend U.	Tr	02.80	79-82	132	0	35
Blackpool	Tr	08.83	83	31	0	9

MERCER, Stanley
Birkenhead, 11 September, 1919 (CF)

League Club	Source	Date Signed	Seasons Played	Apps	Subs	Gls
Blackpool		01.44				
Leicester C.	Tr	11.44	46	1	-	0
Accrington St.	Tr	01.47	46-48	68	-	36
Mansfield T.	Tr	10.48	48	12	-	6

MERCER, Stephen J.
Barking, 1 May, 1965 (D)

League Club	Source	Date Signed	Seasons Played	Apps	Subs	Gls
Peterborough U.	Cambridge U. (N/C)	09.82	82	3	0	0

MERCER, William
Liverpool, 22 May, 1969 (G)

League Club	Source	Date Signed	Seasons Played	Apps	Subs	Gls
Liverpool	YT	08.87				
Rotherham U.	Tr	02.89	89-91	50	0	0

MEREDITH, John F
Doncaster, 23 September, 1940 (W)

League Club	Source	Date Signed	Seasons Played	Apps	Subs	Gls
Doncaster Rov.	Jnrs.	01.58	58-60	58	-	8
Sheffield Wed.	Tr	02.61	60	1	-	0
Chesterfield	Tr	07.62	62-63	81	-	6
Gillingham	Tr	03.64	63-68	227	1	7
Bournemouth	Tr	08.69	69-70	51	0	1

MEREDITH, Robert G.
Swansea, 3 September, 1917 W Sch (OR)

League Club	Source	Date Signed	Seasons Played	Apps	Subs	Gls
Carlisle U.		01.47	46	1	-	0

MEREDITH, Trevor G.
Bridgnorth, 25 December, 1936 (OR)

League Club	Source	Date Signed	Seasons Played	Apps	Subs	Gls
Burnley	Kidderminster Hrs	11.57	59-63	37	-	8
Shrewsbury T.	Tr	04.64	64-71	229	6	42

MERRICK, Alan R.
Birmingham, 20 June, 1950 E Yth (FB)

League Club	Source	Date Signed	Seasons Played	Apps	Subs	Gls
West Bromwich A.	App	08.67	68-75	131	8	5
Peterborough U.	L	09.75	75	5	0	0

MERRICK, Geoffrey
Bristol, 29 April, 1951 E Sch (CD)

League Club	Source	Date Signed	Seasons Played	Apps	Subs	Gls
Bristol C.	App	08.68	67-81	361	6	10

MERRICK, Gilbert H. (Gil)
Birmingham 26 January, 1922 EF Lge/E-23 (G)

League Club	Source	Date Signed	Seasons Played	Apps	Subs	Gls
Birmingham C.	Solihull T.	08.39	46-59	486	-	0

Gil Merrick (Birmingham City & England)

MERRICK, Neil G.
Birmingham, 6 April, 1952 E Semi-Pro (CD)

League Club	Source	Date Signed	Seasons Played	Apps	Subs	Gls
Bournemouth	Worcester C.	09.74	74	13	2	0

MERRIFIELD, Roy G.
Mile End, 11 October, 1931 (W)

League Club	Source	Date Signed	Seasons Played	Apps	Subs	Gls
Chelsea	Rainham T.	02.54				
Millwall	Tr	06.56	56	2	-	0

MERRINGTON, David R.
Newcastle, 26 January, 1945 (CH)

League Club	Source	Date Signed	Seasons Played	Apps	Subs	Gls
Burnley	App	02.62	64-70	96	2	1
Bristol C.	Tr	07.71				

MERRITT, Harold G.
Ormskirk, 22 September, 1920 (IF)

League Club	Source	Date Signed	Seasons Played	Apps	Subs	Gls
Everton	Jnrs	12.37				
Leyton Orient	Tr	09.46	46	1	-	0

MERSON, Paul C.
Harlesden, 20 March, 1968 E Yth/Eu21-4/E'B'/E-7 (F)

League Club	Source	Date Signed	Seasons Played	Apps	Subs	Gls
Arsenal	App	11.85	86-91	139	28	49
Brentford	L	01.87	86	6	1	0

METCALF, Colin C. A.
Norwich, 3 March, 1939 (CH)

League Club	Source	Date Signed	Seasons Played	Apps	Subs	Gls
Norwich C.	Norman O.B.	07.60	62-63	12	-	1
Southend U.	Tr	09.64	64	3	-	0

League Club	Source	Date Signed	Seasons Played	Career Record Apps	Subs	Gls
METCALF, Mark P.						
Norwich, 25 September, 1965						(M)
Norwich C.	App	09.83	82	0	1	0
METCALF, Michael						
Liverpool, 24 May, 1939						(IF)
Wrexham	Everton (Am)	05.57	57-63	120	-	58
Chester C.	Tr	12.63	63-68	221	0	68
METCALFE, John						
Birmingham, 2 June, 1935						(W)
Birmingham C.	Jnrs	10.52	52	2	-	0
York C.	Tr	06.57	57	3	-	2
Walsall	Tr	07.58	58	2	-	0
METCALFE, Ronald						
South Shields, 8 December, 1947						(W)
Derby Co.	Jnrs	01.65	66	1	0	0
METCALFE, Stuart M.						
Blackburn, 6 October, 1950 E Yth						(M)
Blackburn Rov.	App	01.68	67-69	375	11	21
Carlisle U.	Tr	07.80	80	23	2	3
Blackburn Rov. (N/C)	Carolina (USA)	10.82	82	1	0	0
Crewe Alex. (N/C)	Tr	01.83	82	3	0	0
METCALFE, Victor						
Barrow, 3 February, 1922 EF Lge/E-2						(OL)
Huddersfield T.	Ravensthorpe	01.40	46-57	434	-	87
Hull C.	Tr	06.58	58-59	6	-	3
METCHICK, David J.						
Bakewell, 14 August, 1943 E Yth						(IF)
Fulham	Jnrs	08.61	61-64	47	-	9
Leyton Orient	Tr	12.64	64-66	75	0	15
Peterborough U.	Tr	03.67	66-67	38	0	6
Queens Park R.	Tr	08.68	68-69	0	3	1
Arsenal	Tr	09.70				
Brentford	Atlanta (USA)	09.73	73-74	57	4	4
METGOD, John A. B.						
Netherlands, 27 February, 1958 Neth Int						(M)
Nottingham F.	Real Madrid (Sp)	08.84	84-86	113	3	15
Tottenham H.	Tr	07.87	87	5	7	0
METHLEY, Irvin						
Barnsley, 22 September, 1925						(FB)
Wolverhampton W.		10.42				
Walsall	Tr	03.46	46-50	112	-	0

Johnny Metgod (DWS, Real Madrid, Nottingham Forest, Tottenham Hotspur & Holland)

League Club	Source	Date Signed	Seasons Played	Career Record Apps	Subs	Gls
METHVEN, Colin J.						
India, 10 December, 1955						(CD)
Wigan Ath.	East Fife	10.79	79-85	295	1	21
Blackpool	Tr	07.86	86-89	166	7	11
Carlisle U.	L	09.90	90	12	0	0
Walsall	Tr	11.90	90-91	74	0	3
MEYER, Adrian M.						
Yate, 22 September, 1970						(CD)
Scarborough	YT	06.89	89-91	65	0	8
MEYER, Barry J.						
Bournemouth, 21 August, 1932						(IF)
Bristol Rov.	Jnrs	11.49	50-57	139	-	60
Plymouth Arg.	Tr	08.58	58	8	-	5
Newport Co.	Tr	02.59	58-60	70	-	27
Bristol C.	Tr	09.61	61-62	11	-	8
MICALLEF, Constantinous (Tarki)						
Cardiff, 24 January, 1961 W Sch/Wu21-3						(M)
Cardiff C.	App	01.79	78-82	67	14	11
Newport Co.	Tr	09.83	83	22	2	2
Gillingham	Tr	08.84	84	2	0	0
Cardiff C. (N/C)	Tr	09.84	84-85	26	14	1
Bristol Rov.	Tr	08.86	86	15	3	1
MICKLEWHITE, Gary						
Southwark, 21 March, 1961						(RW)
Manchester U.	App	03.78				
Queens Park R.	Tr	07.79	80-84	97	9	11
Derby Co.	Tr	02.85	84-91	219	15	31
MICKLEWRIGHT, Andrew A. J.						
Birmingham, 31 January, 1931						(IF)
Bristol Rov.	Smethwick	01.52	51-52	8	-	1
Bristol C.	Tr	05.53	53-54	39	-	17
Swindon T.	Tr	09.55	55-58	114	-	31
Exeter C.	Tr	07.59	59	38	-	11
MICKLEWRIGHT, Leslie J.						
Stoke, 13 October, 1915						(WH)
Crewe Alex.	Stafford R.	09.46	46-49	71	-	0
MIDDLEBROUGH, Alan						
Rochdale, 4 December, 1925						(CF)
Bolton W.		07.46	46-47	5	-	1
Bradford C.	Tr	08.48	48	4	-	0
Rochdale	Tr	10.48	48-51	47	-	25
MIDDLEMASS, Clive						
Leeds, 25 August, 1944						(D)
Leeds U.	Jnrs	08.62				
Workington	Tr	11.63	63-69	168	1	6
MIDDLEMISS, Ernest						
Newcastle, 30 August, 1920						(CF)
Lincoln C.	South Shields	06.48	48	2	-	0
MIDDLETON, Craig D.						
Nuneaton, 10 September, 1970						(M)
Coventry C.	YT	05.89	89-91	1	1	0
MIDDLETON, Derek						
Ashby-de-la-Zouch, 30 May, 1934						(WH)
York C.	Burton A.	11.58	58	1	-	0
MIDDLETON, Frederick T.						
Hartlepool, 2 August, 1930						(WH)
Newcastle U.	Jnrs	04.48				
Lincoln C.	Tr	05.54	54-62	300	-	16
MIDDLETON, Harold						
Birmingham, 18 March, 1937 E Yth						(CF)
Wolverhampton W.	Jnrs	08.54	55	1	-	0
Scunthorpe U.	Tr	09.59	59-60	29	-	11
Portsmouth	Tr	06.61	61	17	-	5
Shrewsbury T.	Tr	02.62	61-64	85	-	37
Mansfield T.	Tr	11.64	64-65	45	1	24
Walsall	Tr	03.66	65-67	56	2	26
MIDDLETON, James						
Armadale, 25 April, 1922						(WH)
Bradford C.	Third Lanark	05.49	49	8	-	0
MIDDLETON, John						
Rawmarsh, 11 July, 1955						(CD)
Bradford C.	App	07.73	72-78	188	4	5

MIDDLETON, John
Lincoln, 24 December, 1956 E Yth/Eu21-3 (G)

League Club	Source	Date Signed	Seasons Played	Apps	Subs	Gls
Nottingham F.	App	11.74	74-77	90	0	0
Derby Co.	Tr	09.77	77-79	73	0	0

MIDDLETON, Lee J.
Nuneaton, 10 September, 1970 (CD)

League Club	Source	Date Signed	Seasons Played	Apps	Subs	Gls
Coventry C.	YT	05.89	89	0	2	0

MIDDLETON, Matthew Y.
Jarrow, 24 October, 1907 Died 1979 (G)

League Club	Source	Date Signed	Seasons Played	Apps	Subs	Gls
Southport	Boldon Colly	02.31	31-32	63	-	0
Sunderland	Tr	08.33	33-38	57	-	0
Plymouth Arg.	Tr	05.39				
Bradford C.	Hordon Colly	08.46	46-48	94	-	0
York C.	Tr	02.49	48-49	55	-	0

MIDDLETON, Peter W.
Rawmarsh, 13 September, 1948 Died 1977 (M)

League Club	Source	Date Signed	Seasons Played	Apps	Subs	Gls
Sheffield Wed.	App	09.65				
Bradford C.	Tr	06.68	68-72	127	4	25
Plymouth Arg.	Tr	09.72	72	1	0	1

MIDDLETON, Raymond
Boldon, 6 September, 1919 Died 1977 E'B'-4 (G)

League Club	Source	Date Signed	Seasons Played	Apps	Subs	Gls
Chesterfield	Washington	10.37	38-50	250	-	0
Derby Co.	Tr	06.51	51-53	116	-	0

MIDDLETON, Robert R.
Retford, 8 December, 1933 (F)

League Club	Source	Date Signed	Seasons Played	Apps	Subs	Gls
Southend U.	Bulford U.	11.57	57	5	-	1
Workington	Luton T. (trial)	10.58	58	2	-	2
Swindon T.	Tr	12.58	58	5	-	0
Aldershot	Tr	07.59	59	5	-	0

MIDDLETON, Stephen R.
Portsmouth, 28 March, 1953 (G)

League Club	Source	Date Signed	Seasons Played	Apps	Subs	Gls
Southampton	App	07.70	73-76	24	0	0
Torquay U.	L	03.75	74	10	0	0
Portsmouth	Tr	07.77	77	26	0	0

MIELCZAREK, Raymond
Caernarfon, 10 February, 1946 Wu23-2/W-1 (CD)

League Club	Source	Date Signed	Seasons Played	Apps	Subs	Gls
Wrexham	Jnrs	05.64	64-67	76	0	0
Huddersfield T.	Tr	09.67	67-70	25	1	1
Rotherham U.	Tr	01.71	70-73	114	1	7

MIHALY, Ronald R.
Chesterfield, 14 October, 1952 (CD)

League Club	Source	Date Signed	Seasons Played	Apps	Subs	Gls
Chesterfield	Jnrs	08.71	71	4	0	0

MIKE, Adrian R.
Manchester, 16 November, 1973 E Sch (F)

League Club	Source	Date Signed	Seasons Played	Apps	Subs	Gls
Manchester C.	YT	07.92	91	2	0	1

MIKLOSKO, Ludek
Czechoslovakia, 9 December, 1961 Czech Int (G)

League Club	Source	Date Signed	Seasons Played	Apps	Subs	Gls
West Ham U.	Banik Ostrava (Cz)	02.90	89-91	100	0	0

MILBURN, George W.
Ashington, 24 June, 1910 Died 1980 (FB)

League Club	Source	Date Signed	Seasons Played	Apps	Subs	Gls
Leeds U.	Ashington	03.28	28-36	157	-	1
Chesterfield	Tr	05.37	37-47	105	-	16

MILBURN, James
Ashington, 21 September, 1919 (FB)

League Club	Source	Date Signed	Seasons Played	Apps	Subs	Gls
Leeds U.	Ashington	10.36	46-51	207	-	15
Bradford P.A.	Tr	06.52	52-54	90	-	10

MILBURN, John (Jack)
Ashington, 18 March, 1908 Died 1979 (FB)

League Club	Source	Date Signed	Seasons Played	Apps	Subs	Gls
Leeds U.	Spen Black	11.27	29-38	386	-	28
Norwich C.	Tr	02.39	38	15	-	0
Bradford C.	Tr	10.46	46	14	-	3

MILBURN, John E. T. (Jackie)
Ashington, 11 May, 1924 Died 1988 EF Lge/E-13 (CF)

League Club	Source	Date Signed	Seasons Played	Apps	Subs	Gls
Newcastle U.	Ashington	08.43	46-56	353	-	177

Jackie Milburn (Newcastle United & England)

MILBURN, Stanley
Ashington, 22 October, 1926 E'B'-1/EF Lge (FB)

League Club	Source	Date Signed	Seasons Played	Apps	Subs	Gls
Chesterfield	Ashington	01.47	46-51	179	-	0
Leicester C.	Tr	03.52	51-57	173	-	1
Rochdale	Tr	01.59	58-64	238	-	26

MILBURN, William R.
Sunniside, 25 January, 1932 (HB)

League Club	Source	Date Signed	Seasons Played	Apps	Subs	Gls
Gateshead		04.55	56	2	-	0

MILES, Andrew
Tredegar, 25 May, 1961 (W)

League Club	Source	Date Signed	Seasons Played	Apps	Subs	Gls
Newport Co. (N/C)	Ebbw Vale	08.85	85	3	1	2

MILES, Dennis
Normanton, 6 August, 1936 (OR)

League Club	Source	Date Signed	Seasons Played	Apps	Subs	Gls
Bradford P.A.	Jnrs	09.53	53-54	24	-	1
Southport	Tr	06.55	55-56	51	-	12

MILES, Jeffrey M.
Caldicot, 17 January, 1949 (G)

League Club	Source	Date Signed	Seasons Played	Apps	Subs	Gls
Newport Co. (Am)	Jnrs	04.68	67-68	4	0	0

MILES, Sidney G.
Bournemouth, 16 May, 1934 (HB)

League Club	Source	Date Signed	Seasons Played	Apps	Subs	Gls
Bournemouth		12.56	57	1	-	0

MILES, Terence
Stoke, 7 May, 1937 (WH)

League Club	Source	Date Signed	Seasons Played	Apps	Subs	Gls
Port Vale	Milton Y.C.	06.55	56-67	358	7	17

MILKINS, A. John
Dagenham, 3 January, 1944 E Yth (G)

League Club	Source	Date Signed	Seasons Played	Apps	Subs	Gls
Portsmouth	Jnrs	05.61	60-73	344	0	0
Oxford U.	Tr	08.74	74-78	53	0	0

MILLAR, Alistair
Glasgow, 15 January, 1952 (M)

League Club	Source	Date Signed	Seasons Played	Apps	Subs	Gls
Barnsley	Benburb	02.71	70-79	273	16	17
York C.	Tr	07.80	80	11	1	0

MILLAR, James
Dunfermline, 21 December, 1927 (FB)

League Club	Source	Date Signed	Seasons Played	Apps	Subs	Gls
Crewe Alex.	Deal	08.58	58-59	56	-	1

MILLAR John
Coatbridge, 8 December, 1966 (M/FB)

League Club	Source	Date Signed	Seasons Played	Apps	Subs	Gls
Chelsea	Jnrs	08.84	85-86	11	0	0
Northampton T.	L	01.87	86	1	0	0
Blackburn Rov.	Tr	07.87	87-90	122	4	2

MILLAR, John R.
Armadale, 25 October, 1923 (CF)

League Club	Source	Date Signed	Seasons Played	Apps	Subs	Gls
Bradford C.	Albion Rov.	06.49	49	3	-	1

MILLAR, John W.
Auchterderran, 31 December, 1927 (IF)

League Club	Source	Date Signed	Seasons Played	Apps	Subs	Gls
Bradford C.	Queen of South	10.48	49-51	44	-	7
Grimsby T.	Tr	05.52	52	5	-	2

MILLAR, Paul W.
Belfast, 16 November, 1966 NIu23-1 (F)

League Club	Source	Date Signed	Seasons Played	Apps	Subs	Gls
Port Vale	Portadown	12.88	89-90	19	21	6
Hereford U.	L	10.90	90	5	0	2
Cardiff C.	Tr	08.91	91	8	7	0

MILLAR, Thomas T.
Edinburgh, 3 December, 1938 (FB)

League Club	Source	Date Signed	Seasons Played	Apps	Subs	Gls
Colchester U.	Bo'ness U.	06.59	59-61	46	-	4

MILLAR, William
Mansfield, 7 February, 1952 (G)

League Club	Source	Date Signed	Seasons Played	Apps	Subs	Gls
Doncaster Rov. (Am)	Folkhouse O.B.	02.75	74	1	0	0

MILLAR, William
Irvine, 24 July, 1924 (W)

League Club	Source	Date Signed	Seasons Played	Apps	Subs	Gls
Swindon T.	Stirling A.	08.50	50-52	75	-	18
Gillingham	Tr	07.53	53-55	91	-	35
Accrington St.	Tr	07.56	56	26	-	11

MILLARD, Lance J.
Bristol, 24 June, 1938 (G)

League Club	Source	Date Signed	Seasons Played	Apps	Subs	Gls
Aldershot	Army	03.61	60	12	-	0
Barrow	Tr	07.64	64-65	52	0	0

MILLARD, Leonard
Coseley, 7 March, 1919 (FB)

League Club	Source	Date Signed	Seasons Played	Apps	Subs	Gls
West Bromwich A.	Sunbeam	05.37	46-57	436	-	7

MILLARD, Robert
South Shields, 2 June, 1927 (IF)

League Club	Source	Date Signed	Seasons Played	Apps	Subs	Gls
Middlesbrough		12.45				
Reading	Blyth Spartans	06.49	49	2	-	0
Walsall	Tr	06.50	50	7	-	1

MILLBANK, Joseph H.
Edmonton, 30 September, 1919 (CH)

League Club	Source	Date Signed	Seasons Played	Apps	Subs	Gls
Wolverhampton W.		07.38				
Crystal Palace		08.39	46-47	38	-	1
Queens Park R.	Tr	07.48	48	1	-	0

MILLEN Keith
Croydon, 26 September, 1966 (CD)

League Club	Source	Date Signed	Seasons Played	Apps	Subs	Gls
Brentford	Jnrs	08.84	84-91	258	4	13

MILLER, Alfred G. A.
Portsmouth, 25 March, 1917 (WH)

League Club	Source	Date Signed	Seasons Played	Apps	Subs	Gls
Portsmouth		11.35				
Southport	Tr	10.37	37-38	32	-	2
Plymouth Arg.	Tr	07.39	46-47	9	-	0

MILLER, Alistair W.
Glasgow, 24 January, 1936 (OL)

League Club	Source	Date Signed	Seasons Played	Apps	Subs	Gls
Brighton & H. A.	St Mirren	04.62	61	1	-	0
Norwich C.	Tr	05.62	62-63	23	-	2

MILLER, Alan J.
Epping, 29 March, 1970 E Yth/Eu21-4 (G)

League Club	Source	Date Signed	Seasons Played	Apps	Subs	Gls
Arsenal	YT	05.88				
Plymouth Arg.	L	11.88	88	13	0	0
West Bromwich A.	L	08.91	91	3	0	0
Birmingham C.	L	12.91	91	15	0	0

MILLER, Alan J.
Preston, 13 September, 1970 (W)

League Club	Source	Date Signed	Seasons Played	Apps	Subs	Gls
Torquay U. (N/C)	Bury (YT)	08.89	89	3	1	0

MILLER, Anthony W.
Colchester, 26 October, 1937 (W)

League Club	Source	Date Signed	Seasons Played	Apps	Subs	Gls
Colchester U.	Jnrs	05.58	59-63	6	-	0

MILLER, Archibald
Larkhall, 5 September, 1913 S-1 (WH)

League Club	Source	Date Signed	Seasons Played	Apps	Subs	Gls
Blackburn Rov.	Hearts	11.47	47	6	-	0
Carlisle U.	Kilmarnock	09.50	50	1	-	0
Workington	Hearts	02.52				

MILLER, Brian G.
Burnley, 19 January, 1937 Eu23-3/EF Lge/E-1 (WH)

League Club	Source	Date Signed	Seasons Played	Apps	Subs	Gls
Burnley	Jnrs	02.54	55-66	379	0	29

MILLER, Colin F.
Lanarkshire, 4 October, 1964 Canadian Int (M)

League Club	Source	Date Signed	Seasons Played	Apps	Subs	Gls
Doncaster Rov.	Glasgow Rangers	12.86	86-87	61	0	3

MILLER, David
Middlesbrough, 21 January, 1921 (WH)

League Club	Source	Date Signed	Seasons Played	Apps	Subs	Gls
Middlesbrough		09.38				
Wolverhampton W.	Tr	08.45	46	2	-	0
Derby Co.	Tr	04.47	47	1	-	0
Doncaster Rov.	Tr	01.48	47-52	140	-	3
Aldershot	Tr	03.54	53	11	-	0

MILLER, David B.
Burnley, 8 January, 1964 (RB/W)

League Club	Source	Date Signed	Seasons Played	Apps	Subs	Gls
Burnley	App	01.82	82-84	27	5	3
Crewe Alex.	L	03.83	82	3	0	0
Tranmere Rov.	Tr	07.85	85	25	4	1
Preston N. E.	Colne Dynamoes	12.86	86-89	50	8	2
Burnley	L	02.89	88	4	0	0
Carlisle U.	Tr	09.89	89-91	108	1	7
Stockport Co.	Tr	03.92	91	0	3	0

MILLER, Edward
Ulverston, 21 June, 1920 (IF)

League Club	Source	Date Signed	Seasons Played	Apps	Subs	Gls
Barrow	Ulverston	05.46	46-50	124	-	32

MILLER, E. George
South Africa, 17 October, 1927 (IF)

League Club	Source	Date Signed	Seasons Played	Apps	Subs	Gls
Leeds U.	Arcadia (SA)	11.50	50-51	13	-	1
Workington	Tr	03.52	51	11	-	0

MILLER, George
Larkhall, 20 May, 1939 SF Lge (WH)

League Club	Source	Date Signed	Seasons Played	Apps	Subs	Gls
Wolverhampton W.	Dunfermline Ath.	10.64	64-65	37	0	3

MILLER, Graham J. P.
South Africa, 25 August, 1927

League Club	Source	Date Signed	Seasons Played	Apps	Subs	Gls
Workington		12.52	52	8	-	1

MILLER, Ian
Perth, 13 May, 1955 (RW)

League Club	Source	Date Signed	Seasons Played	Apps	Subs	Gls
Bury	Jnrs	08.73	73	9	6	0
Nottingham F.	Tr	08.74				
Doncaster Rov.	Tr	08.75	75-77	124	0	14
Swindon T.	Tr	07.78	78-80	123	4	9
Blackburn Rov.	Tr	08.81	81-88	252	16	16
Port Vale	Tr	07.89	89	14	7	0
Scunthorpe U.	Tr	08.90	90	8	4	0

MILLER, John T.
Ipswich, 21 September, 1950 (W)

League Club	Source	Date Signed	Seasons Played	Apps	Subs	Gls
Ipswich T.	Jnrs	07.68	68-73	38	13	2
Norwich C.	Tr	10.74	74-75	22	1	3
Mansfield T.	Tr	07.76	76-79	109	4	14
Port Vale (N/C)	Tr	09.80	80	22	4	4

MILLER, Joseph Mc.
Glasgow, 2 October, 1934 (OL)

League Club	Source	Date Signed	Seasons Played	Apps	Subs	Gls
Swindon T.	Hamilton Acad.	06.56	56	12	-	0

MILLER, Keith R.
Lewisham, 26 January, 1948 (M)

League Club	Source	Date Signed	Seasons Played	Apps	Subs	Gls
West Ham U.	Walthamstow Ave.	09.65	68-69	1	2	0
Bournemouth	Tr	07.70	70-79	381	2	19

MILLER, Kevin
Falmouth, 15 March, 1969 (G)

League Club	Source	Date Signed	Seasons Played	Apps	Subs	Gls
Exeter C.	Newquay	03.89	88-91	119	0	0

MILLER, Lumley R.
Blaydon, 3 August, 1938 (W)

League Club	Source	Date Signed	Seasons Played	Apps	Subs	Gls
Sheffield U.		07.62				
Hartlepool U.	Tr	11.62	62	9	-	2

MILLER, Mark J.
Newcastle, 22 September, 1962 (W)

League Club	Source	Date Signed	Seasons Played	Apps	Subs	Gls
Gillingham	Whitley Bay	10.81	81-82	5	4	1
Doncaster Rov.	Whitley Bay	08.83	83	21	9	4
Darlington	Tr	08.84	84	4	3	1

MILLER, J. Paul
Wolverhampton, 9 December, 1940 Died 1963 (G)

League Club	Source	Date Signed	Seasons Played	Apps	Subs	Gls
Shrewsbury T.	St Nicks B.C.	07.59	59-62	77	-	0

MILLER, Paul A.
Woking, 31 January, 1968 (F)

League Club	Source	Date Signed	Seasons Played	Apps	Subs	Gls
Wimbledon	Yeovil T.	08.87	87-91	54	7	9
Newport Co.	L	10.87	87	6	0	2
Bristol C.	L	01.90	89	0	3	0

MILLER, Paul R.
Stepney, 11 October, 1959 (CD)

League Club	Source	Date Signed	Seasons Played	Apps	Subs	Gls
Tottenham H.	App	05.77	78-86	206	2	7
Charlton Ath.	Tr	02.87	86-88	40	2	2
Watford	Tr	10.88	88	20	0	1
Bournemouth	Tr	08.89	89-90	43	4	1
Brentford	L	11.89	89	3	0	0
Swansea C.	Tr	01.91	90	8	4	0

MILLER, Peter D.
Hoyland, 4 December, 1929 (HB)

League Club	Source	Date Signed	Seasons Played	Apps	Subs	Gls
Bradford C.		08.52	52-55	18	-	2

MILLER, Ralph E.
Slough, 22 June, 1941 (D)

League Club	Source	Date Signed	Seasons Played	Apps	Subs	Gls
Charlton Ath.	Slough T.	09.63	64	8	-	0
Gillingham	Tr	05.65	65-67	103	0	4
Bournemouth	Tr	07.68	68-70	71	1	1

MILLER, Roger, L.
Northampton, 18 August, 1938 (F)

League Club	Source	Date Signed	Seasons Played	Apps	Subs	Gls
Northampton T.	Jnrs	11.56	56-58	4	-	1

MILLER, Walter
Cornforth (Dm), 11 August, 1930 (WH)

League Club	Source	Date Signed	Seasons Played	Apps	Subs	Gls
Hartlepool U.		09.48	49	1	-	0
Luton T.	Spennymoor U.	02.52				

MILLETT, Glynne
Crickhowell, 13 October, 1968 (W)

League Club	Source	Date Signed	Seasons Played	Apps	Subs	Gls
Newport Co.	YT	07.87	86-87	23	14	2

MILLIGAN, Charles
Ardrossan, 26 July, 1930 (CH)

League Club	Source	Date Signed	Seasons Played	Apps	Subs	Gls
Colchester U.	Ardrossan Winton	05.56	56-60	186	-	3

MILLIGAN, Dudley
South Africa, 7 November, 1916 NI-1 (CF)

League Club	Source	Date Signed	Seasons Played	Apps	Subs	Gls
Chesterfield	Clyde	11.38	38-46	47	-	18
Bournemouth	Tr	08.47	47-48	45	-	26
Walsall	Tr	10.48	48	5	-	1

MILLIGAN, Laurence C.
Liverpool, 20 April, 1958 (FB)

League Club	Source	Date Signed	Seasons Played	Apps	Subs	Gls
Blackpool	App	04.76	76-78	19	0	0
Portsmouth	L	03.79	78	7	0	0
Rochdale	Aldershot (N/C)	10.79	79	8	1	0

MILLIGAN, Michael J.
Manchester, 20 February, 1967 IRu-21-1/IR'B'/IR-1 (M)

League Club	Source	Date Signed	Seasons Played	Apps	Subs	Gls
Oldham Ath.	YT	02.85	85-89	161	1	17
Everton	Tr	08.90	90	16	1	1
Oldham Ath.	Tr	07.91	91	36	0	3

Mike Milligan (Oldham Athletic, Everton, Oldham Athletic & Republic of Ireland)

MILLIGAN, Stephen J. F.
Hyde, 13 June, 1973 (D)

League Club	Source	Date Signed	Seasons Played	Apps	Subs	Gls
Rochdale (YT)	YT	07.89	89	5	0	1

MILLIGAN, Terence J.
Manchester, 10 January, 1966 (M)

League Club	Source	Date Signed	Seasons Played	Apps	Subs	Gls
Manchester C.	App	11.83				
Oldham Ath.	New Zealand	02.86				
Crewe Alex.	Tr	07.86	86-87	71	6	5

MILLIN, Alfred
Rotherham, 18 December, 1933 (FB)

League Club	Source	Date Signed	Seasons Played	Apps	Subs	Gls
Derby Co.	Jnrs	08.51	55	1	-	0

MILLINGTON, Anthony H.
Hawarden, 5 June, 1943 Wu23-4/W-21 (G)

League Club	Source	Date Signed	Seasons Played	Apps	Subs	Gls
West Bromwich A.	Jnrs	07.60	61-62	40	-	0
Crystal Palace	Tr	10.64	64-65	16	0	0
Peterborough U.	Tr	03.66	66-68	118	0	0
Swansea C .	Tr	07.69	69-73	178	0	0

League Club	Source	Date Signed	Seasons Played	Career Record Apps	Subs	Gls
MILLINGTON, Grenville						
Queensferry, 10 December, 1951 W Amat						(G)
Chester C. (Am)	Rhyl	07.68	68	1	0	0
Chester C.	Witton A.	09.73	73-82	289	0	0
Wrexham (N/C)	Oswestry T.	12.83	83	13	0	0
MILLINGTON, John H.						
Coseley, 21 February, 1930						(HB)
Aston Villa	Jnrs	09.48				
Walsall	Tr	07.51	51-52	23	-	0
MILLINGTON, Ralph V.						
Neston, 18 June, 1930						(CH)
Tranmere Rov.	Neston	01.50	50-60	357	-	3
MILLION, Esmond						
Ashington, 15 March, 1938						(G)
Middlesbrough	Amble Jnrs	05.56	56-61	52	-	0
Bristol Rov.	Tr	06.62	62	38	-	0
MILLS, Brian						
Stafford, 26 December, 1971 E Yth						(F)
Port Vale	YT	04.90	90-91	14	9	4
MILLS, David J.						
Whitby, 6 December, 1951 Eu23-8/E-'B'						(F)
Middlesbrough	App	12.68	68-78	275	18	76
West Bromwich A.	Tr	01.79	78-82	44	15	6
Newcastle U.	L	01.82	81	23	0	4
Sheffield Wed.	Tr	01.83	82	15	0	3
Newcastle U.	Tr	08.83	83	10	6	5
Middlesbrough	Tr	06.84	84	31	1	14
Darlington (N/C)	Tr	08.86	86	12	5	2
MILLS, Donald						
Rotherham, 17 August, 1926						(IF)
Queens Park R.		08.46	46-48	43	-	6
Torquay U.	Tr	03.49	48-49	34	-	13
Queens Park R.	Tr	01.50	49-50	30	-	3
Cardiff C.	Tr	02.51	50	1	-	0
Leeds U.	Tr	09.51	51-52	34	-	9
Torquay U.	Tr	12.52	52-61	310	-	68
MILLS, Gary R.						
Northampton, 11 November, 1961 E Sch/E Yth/Eu21-2						(W/M)
Nottingham F.	App	11.78	78-81	50	8	8
Derby Co.	Seatle (USA)	10.82	82	18	0	2
Nottingham F.	Seatle (USA)	12.83	83-86	63	15	4
Notts Co.	Tr	08.87	87-88	75	0	8
Leicester C.	Tr	03.89	88-91	131	2	15
MILLS, Henry						
Bishop Auckland, 23 July, 1922						(F)
Sheffield U.		06.46	46	3	-	2
Rotherham U.	Tr	03.48	47	7	-	5
Rochdale	Tunbridge Wells	04.51	50	1	-	0
Halifax T.	Tr	08.52				
MILLS, Henry O.						
Blyth, 23 August, 1922						(G)
Huddersfield T.	Blyth Spartans	03.48	47-55	157	-	0
Halifax T	Tr	12.55	55-56	26	-	0
MILLS, James						
Rotherham, 30 September, 1915						(WH)
Rotherham U.	Dinnington Colly	08.37	37-38	53	-	4
Hull C.	Tr	10.46	46-47	42	-	1
Halifax T.	Tr	12.47	47	19	-	0
MILLS, John						
Bagillt, 19 December, 1920						(RH)
Chester C.		05.46	46	3	-	0
MILLS, Keith						
Newcastle, 30 December, 1963						(M)
Carlisle U. (N/C)	North Shields	02.88	87	0	1	0
MILLS, Keith D.						
Egham, 29 December, 1942						(WH)
Grimsby T.	Jnrs	01.60	60	2	-	0
MILLS, Michael D.						
Godalming, 4 January, 1949 E Yth/Eu23-5/EF Lge/E-42						(FB)
Ipswich T.	Portsmouth (App)	02.66	65-82	588	3	22
Southampton	Tr	11.82	82-84	103	0	3
Stoke C.	Tr	07.85	85-87	38	0	0

League Club	Source	Date Signed	Seasons Played	Career Record Apps	Subs	Gls
MILLS, Neil						
Littleborough, 27 October, 1963						(F)
Rochdale	Tin Bobbins	08.86	86	4	6	0
Stockport Co. (N/C)	Tr	08.87	87	5	2	0
MILLS, Robert B.						
Edmonton, 16 March, 1955						(M)
Colchester U.	App	12.72	71-73	20	6	0
MILLS, Ronald W.G. (Roly)						
Daventry, 22 June, 1933 E Yth						(OR/WH)
Northampton T.	Jnrs	05.51	54-63	305	-	30
MILLS, Sean D.						
Ebbw Vale, 1 June, 1968						(M)
Newport Co.	Sunderland (App)	08.86	86	5	2	0
MILLS, Simon A.						
Sheffield, 16 August, 1964 E Yth						(RB/M)
Sheffield Wed.	App	08.82	82-84	1	4	0
York C.	Tr	06.85	85-87	97	2	4
Port Vale	Tr	12.87	87-91	177	4	8
MILLS, Stephen J.						
Portsmouth, 9 December, 1953 Died 1988 Eu23-1						(FB)
Southampton	App	07.71	72-76	57	4	0
MILLWARD, H. Douglas						
Sheffield, 10 July, 1931						(IF)
Southampton	Doncaster Rov. (Am)	02.52				
Ipswich T.	Tr	07.55	55-62	143	-	35
MILNE, Alexander S.						
Dundee, 4 June, 1937 Su23-1						(FB)
Cardiff C.	Arbroath	03.57	57-64	172	-	1
MILNE, Gordon						
Preston, 29 March, 1937 EF Lge/E-14						(WH)
Preston N. E.	Morecambe	01.56	56-60	81	-	3
Liverpool	Tr	09.60	60-66	234	2	18
Blackpool	Tr	05.67	67-69	60	4	4

Mick Mills (Ipswich Town, Southampton, Stoke City & England)

MILNE, John B.
Rosehearty, 27 April, 1911 (FB)

League Club	Source	Date Signed	Seasons Played	Apps	Subs	Gls
Plymouth Arg.	Fraserburgh	05.33	34-36	3	-	0
Southend U.	Tr	06.37	37-38	67	-	1
Barrow	Tr	08.46	46	33	-	0
Oldham Ath.	Tr	08.47	47	13	-	0

MILNE, Maurice
Dundee, 21 October, 1932 (OL)

League Club	Source	Date Signed	Seasons Played	Apps	Subs	Gls
Norwich C.	Dundee U.	05.57	57	5	-	0

MILNE, Michael
Aberdeen, 17 August, 1959 (D)

League Club	Source	Date Signed	Seasons Played	Apps	Subs	Gls
Sunderland	App	05.77				
Rochdale		02.79	78	1	1	0

MILNE, Ralph
Dundee, 13 May, 1961 S Yth/Su21-3 (W)

League Club	Source	Date Signed	Seasons Played	Apps	Subs	Gls
Charlton Ath.	Dundee U.	01.87	86-87	19	3	0
Bristol C.	Tr	01.88	87-88	29	1	6
Manchester U.	Tr	11.88	88-89	19	4	3

MILNER, Alfred J. G.
Harrogate, 6 February, 1919 (OR)

League Club	Source	Date Signed	Seasons Played	Apps	Subs	Gls
Aldershot		08.46	46	7	-	1
Darlington		03.48	47-48	28	-	4

MILNER, Andrew J.
Kendal, 10 February, 1967 (F)

League Club	Source	Date Signed	Seasons Played	Apps	Subs	Gls
Manchester C.	Netherfield	01.89				
Rochdale	Tr	01.90	89-91	72	12	19

MILNER, James E.
Newcastle, 3 February, 1933 (IF)

League Club	Source	Date Signed	Seasons Played	Apps	Subs	Gls
Burnley	Blyth Spartans	12.52	53	1	-	0
Darlington	Tr	12.57	57-60	148	-	27
Accrington St	Tr	09.61				
Tranmere Rov.	Tr	06.62	62	16	-	3

MILNER, John
Huddersfield, 14 May, 1942 (WH)

League Club	Source	Date Signed	Seasons Played	Apps	Subs	Gls
Huddersfield T.	Jnrs	05.59	60-62	17	-	0
Lincoln C.	Tr	10.63	63-66	109	0	6
Bradford P.A.	Tr	02.67	66	6	2	0

MILNER, Michael
Hull, 21 September, 1939 (CH)

League Club	Source	Date Signed	Seasons Played	Apps	Subs	Gls
Hull C.	Jnrs	07.57	58-67	160	0	0
Stockport Co.	Tr	07.68	68	41	0	0
Barrow	Tr	09.69	69	11	0	0
Bradford C.	Tr	12.69	69	0	1	0

MILTON, C. Arthur
Bristol, 10 March, 1928 E-1 (OR)

League Club	Source	Date Signed	Seasons Played	Apps	Subs	Gls
Arsenal	Jnrs	07.46	50-54	75	-	18
Bristol C.	Tr	02.55	54	14	-	3

MILTON, Roy
Brixham, 27 November, 1934 (G)

League Club	Source	Date Signed	Seasons Played	Apps	Subs	Gls
Bury	Jnrs	10.52				
Torquay U.	Tr	08.56	56	1	-	0

MILTON, Simon C.
Fulham, 23 August, 1963 (M)

League Club	Source	Date Signed	Seasons Played	Apps	Subs	Gls
Ipswich T.	Bury T.	07.87	87-91	131	18	35
Exeter C.	L	11.87	87	2	0	3
Torquay U.	L	03.88	87	4	0	1

MILTON, Stephen
Fulham, 13 April, 1963 (F)

League Club	Source	Date Signed	Seasons Played	Apps	Subs	Gls
West Ham U.	App	04.81				
Fulham	Whyteleafe	10.89	89-91	39	19	9

MIMMS Robert A.
York, 12 October, 1963 Eu21-3 (G)

League Club	Source	Date Signed	Seasons Played	Apps	Subs	Gls
Halifax T.	App	08.81				
Rotherham U.	Tr	11.81	81-84	83	0	0
Everton	Tr	06.85	85-87	29	0	0
Notts Co.	L	03.86	85	2	0	0
Sunderland	L	12.86	86	4	0	0
Blackburn Rov.	L	01.87	86	6	0	0
Manchester C.	L	09.87	87	3	0	0
Tottenham H.	Tr	02.88	87-89	37	0	0
Blackburn Rov.	Tr	12.90	90-91	67	0	0

MINETT, Jason K.
Peterborough, 12 August, 1971 (LB)

League Club	Source	Date Signed	Seasons Played	Apps	Subs	Gls
Norwich C.	YT	07.89	90	0	2	0

MINNOCK, John J.
Tullamore (Ire), 12 November, 1949 (W)

League Club	Source	Date Signed	Seasons Played	Apps	Subs	Gls
Charlton Ath.	St Patricks Ath.	02.69	69	0	1	0

MINSHULL, Raymond
Bolton, 15 July, 1920 (G)

League Club	Source	Date Signed	Seasons Played	Apps	Subs	Gls
Liverpool	High Park	09.46	46-49	28	-	0
Southport	Tr	07.51	51-57	217	-	0
Bradford P. A.	Tr	12.57	57-58	28	-	0

MINTO, Scott C.
Heswall, 6 August, 1971 E Yth/Eu21-4 (W/LB)

League Club	Source	Date Signed	Seasons Played	Apps	Subs	Gls
Charlton Ath.	YT	01.89	88-91	95	7	4

MINTON, Albert E.
Walsall, 22 September, 1937 E Yth (CF)

League Club	Source	Date Signed	Seasons Played	Apps	Subs	Gls
Blackpool	Derby Co. (Am)	10.54				
Scunthorpe U.	Tr	07.57	57-58	5	-	0
Doncaster Rov.	Tr	12.58	58	11	-	2

MINTON, Jeffrey S. T.
Hackney, 28 December, 1973 (M)

League Club	Source	Date Signed	Seasons Played	Apps	Subs	Gls
Tottenham H.	YT	01.92	91	2	0	1

MINTON, Roger C.
Birmingham, 4 June, 1951 (FB)

League Club	Source	Date Signed	Seasons Played	Apps	Subs	Gls
West Bromwich A.	App	06.69	70-74	24	2	1

MIRANDINHA, Da Silva Francisco
Brazil, 2 July, 1959 Brazilian Int (F)

League Club	Source	Date Signed	Seasons Played	Apps	Subs	Gls
Newcastle U.	Palmeiras (Br)	08.87	87-88	47	7	20

MIROCEVIC, Anton
Yugoslavia, 6 August, 1952 Yugoslav Int (M)

League Club	Source	Date Signed	Seasons Played	Apps	Subs	Gls
Sheffield Wed.	F.C.Budocnost (Yug)	10.80	80-82	58	3	6

MITCHELL, Albert J.
Stoke, 22 January, 1922 E'B'-1 (OL)

League Club	Source	Date Signed	Seasons Played	Apps	Subs	Gls
Stoke C.	Jnrs	05.41	46-47	10	-	2
Blackburn Rov.	Tr	02.48	47	3	-	0
Northampton T.	Tr	05.49	49-50	81	-	19
Luton T.	Tr	07.51	51-54	106	-	41
Middlesbrough	Tr	09.54	54-55	50	-	6
Southport	Tr	08.56	56	16	-	3

Bobby Mimms (Halifax Town, Rotherham United, Everton, Tottenham Hotspur & Blackburn Rovers)

MITCHELL, Alexander R.
Greenock, 24 May, 1918 (FB)

League Club	Source	Date Signed	Seasons Played	Apps	Subs	Gls
Ipswich T.	Bute	08.46	47-49	42	-	2

MITCHELL, Anthony J.
Guildford, 7 September, 1959 (FB)

League Club	Source	Date Signed	Seasons Played	Apps	Subs	Gls
Exeter C.	Leatherhead	07.77	78-81	60	0	0

MITCHELL, Arnold
Rotherham, 1 December, 1929 (WH)

League Club	Source	Date Signed	Seasons Played	Apps	Subs	Gls
Derby Co.	Sheffield Wed. (Am)	02.48				
Nottingham F.	Tr	03.50				
Notts Co.	Tr	05.51	51	1	-	0
Exeter C.	Tr	07.52	52-65	495	0	44

MITCHELL, Barrie
Aberdeen, 15 March, 1947 (F)

League Club	Source	Date Signed	Seasons Played	Apps	Subs	Gls
Tranmere Rov.	Aberdeen	02.74	73-75	77	6	10
Preston N.E.	Tr	07.76	76	7	4	2
York C.	Tr	09.77	77	1	2	0

MITCHELL, C. Brian
Stonehaven, 16 July, 1963 (RB)

League Club	Source	Date Signed	Seasons Played	Apps	Subs	Gls
Bradford C.	Aberdeen	02.87	86-91	170	8	9

MITCHELL, David J.
Stoke, 24 August, 1945 (CF)

League Club	Source	Date Signed	Seasons Played	Apps	Subs	Gls
Port Vale	Jnrs	03.64	64-65	21	0	4
Ipswich T.	Tr	08.66	66	0	2	0

MITCHELL, David S.
Glasgow, 13 June, 1962 Australian Int (F)

League Club	Source	Date Signed	Seasons Played	Apps	Subs	Gls
Chelsea	Feyenoord (Neth)	12.88	88-90	6	1	0
Newcastle U.	L	01.91	90	2	0	1
Swindon T.	Tr	07.91	91	24	3	5

MITCHELL, Frank R.
Australia, 3 June, 1922 Died 1984 (WH)

League Club	Source	Date Signed	Seasons Played	Apps	Subs	Gls
Birmingham C.	Coventry C. (Am)	09.43	46-48	93	-	6
Chelsea	Tr	01.49	48-51	75	-	1
Watford	Tr	08.52	52-56	193	-	0

MITCHELL, Graham L.
Shipley, 16 February, 1968 (CD)

League Club	Source	Date Signed	Seasons Played	Apps	Subs	Gls
Huddersfield T.	YT	06.86	86-91	201	5	2

MITCHELL, Ian D.
Tredegar, 1 October, 1971 (F)

League Club	Source	Date Signed	Seasons Played	Apps	Subs	Gls
Hereford U.	Merthyr Tydfil	10.90	90	0	3	0

MITCHELL, Ian J.
Falkirk, 9 May, 1946 S Sch/Su23-2 (OL)

League Club	Source	Date Signed	Seasons Played	Apps	Subs	Gls
Newcastle U.	Dundee U.	07.70	70	2	1	0

MITCHELL, James D.
Ilkeston, 1 July, 1937 (G)

League Club	Source	Date Signed	Seasons Played	Apps	Subs	Gls
Derby Co.	Ilkeston T.	10.58	58-59	6	-	0

MITCHELL, James R.
Liverpool, 13 June, 1967 (FB)

League Club	Source	Date Signed	Seasons Played	Apps	Subs	Gls
Wigan Ath.	App	06.85	84	2	0	0

MITCHELL, John
St Albans, 12 March, 1952 (F)

League Club	Source	Date Signed	Seasons Played	Apps	Subs	Gls
Fulham	St Albans C.	02.72	72-77	158	11	57
Millwall	Tr	06.78	78-80	78	3	18

MITCHELL, John D.
Titchfield, 19 January, 1928 (OL)

League Club	Source	Date Signed	Seasons Played	Apps	Subs	Gls
Southampton		03.49	50	7	-	0

MITCHELL, John G.
Gateshead, 1 August, 1919 Died 1977 (CF)

League Club	Source	Date Signed	Seasons Played	Apps	Subs	Gls
Hartlepool U.	Billingham Synth.	11.46	46	3	-	2

MITCHELL, Kenneth
Sunderland, 26 May, 1957 (CD)

League Club	Source	Date Signed	Seasons Played	Apps	Subs	Gls
Newcastle U.	App	04.75	76-80	61	5	2
Darlington	Tr	08.81	81	12	1	1

MITCHELL, Kenneth S.
Wearhead, 26 December, 1933 (F)

League Club	Source	Date Signed	Seasons Played	Apps	Subs	Gls
Plymouth Arg.	Whitby Rov.	03.56	55-56	8	-	4

MITCHELL, Neil N.
Lytham, 7 November, 1974 (F)

League Club	Source	Date Signed	Seasons Played	Apps	Subs	Gls
Blackpool (YT)	YT	07.91	91	0	1	0

MITCHELL, Norman
Sunderland, 7 November, 1931 (OR)

League Club	Source	Date Signed	Seasons Played	Apps	Subs	Gls
Chesterfield	West Stanley	10.51	51-52	66	-	7
Workington	West Stanley	11.53	53-57	138	-	23
Hartlepool U.	Tr	03.58	57-58	23	-	6

MITCHELL, Paul R.
Bournemouth, 20 October, 1971 E Yth (M)

League Club	Source	Date Signed	Seasons Played	Apps	Subs	Gls
Bournemouth	YT	08.89	90-91	3	4	0

MITCHELL, Peter
Oldham, 5 August, 1946 (FB)

League Club	Source	Date Signed	Seasons Played	Apps	Subs	Gls
Oldham Ath.	Jnrs	07.66	65	0	1	0

MITCHELL, Robert
South Shields, 4 January, 1955 (M)

League Club	Source	Date Signed	Seasons Played	Apps	Subs	Gls
Sunderland	App	01.72	73-75	1	2	0
Blackburn Rov.	Tr	07.76	76-77	17	12	6
Grimsby T.	Tr	06.78	78-81	142	0	6
Carlisle U.	Tr	08.82	82	2	0	0
Rotherham U.	Tr	03.83	82-84	86	9	2
Lincoln C.	Malta	01.86	85-86	41	3	2

MITCHELL, Robert
Campbeltown, 17 January, 1927 (CF)

League Club	Source	Date Signed	Seasons Played	Apps	Subs	Gls
Exeter C.	Third Lanark	07.51	51	3	-	0

MITCHELL, Robert
Glasgow, 16 August, 1924 SF Lge/S-2 (OL)

League Club	Source	Date Signed	Seasons Played	Apps	Subs	Gls
Newcastle U.	Third Lanark	02.49	48-60	367	-	95

MITCHELL, Robert
Petersfield, 17 December, 1948 (F)

League Club	Source	Date Signed	Seasons Played	Apps	Subs	Gls
Aldershot	Alton T.	09.69	69-70	5	7	1

MITCHELL, Ronald G.
Morcambe, 13 February, 1935 (FB)

League Club	Source	Date Signed	Seasons Played	Apps	Subs	Gls
Leeds U.	Morecambe	11.58	58	4	-	0

MITCHELL, Ronald J.
Barrhead, 27 May, 1925 (OR)

League Club	Source	Date Signed	Seasons Played	Apps	Subs	Gls
Exeter C.	Glasgow Celtic	08.49	49	2	-	0

MITCHELL, Roy
Liverpool, 10 March, 1964 (M)

League Club	Source	Date Signed	Seasons Played	Apps	Subs	Gls
Stockport Co. (N/C)		10.86	86	2	1	0

MITCHELL, Stewart A.
Glasgow, 3 March, 1933 (G)

League Club	Source	Date Signed	Seasons Played	Apps	Subs	Gls
Newcastle U.	Benburb	09.53	54-62	45	-	0

MITCHELSON, Kenneth G.
Edmonton, 16 May, 1928 (FB)

League Club	Source	Date Signed	Seasons Played	Apps	Subs	Gls
Charlton Ath.	Tottenham H. (Am)	09.47				
Bristol C.	Tr	05.49	49-52	28	-	0

MITCHESON, Francis J.
Stalybridge, 10 March, 1924 (IF)

League Club	Source	Date Signed	Seasons Played	Apps	Subs	Gls
Doncaster Rov.	Droylsden	05.44	46-48	22	-	5
Crewe Alex.	Tr	11.48	48-53	181	-	34
Rochdale	Tr	06.54	54-55	50	-	8

MITCHINSON, Thomas W.
Sunderland, 24 February, 1943 (M)

League Club	Source	Date Signed	Seasons Played	Apps	Subs	Gls
Sunderland	Jnrs	12.60	62-65	16	1	2
Mansfield T.	Tr	01.66	65-67	76	0	15
Aston Villa	Tr	08.67	67-68	49	0	9
Torquay U.	Tr	05.69	68-71	108	0	9
Bournemouth	Tr	12.71	71-72	13	1	1

MITTEN, Charles
Burma, 17 January, 1921 (OL)

League Club	Source	Date Signed	Seasons Played	Apps	Subs	Gls
Manchester U.	Jnrs	01.38	46-49	142	-	50
Fulham	Tr	01.52	51-55	154	-	32
Mansfield T.	Tr	02.56	55-57	100	-	25

MITTEN, Charles E.
Altrincham, 14 December, 1943 (F)

League Club	Source	Date Signed	Seasons Played	Apps	Subs	Gls
Mansfield T.	Newcastle U. (App)	11.61				
Halifax T.	Altrincham	10.65	65	1	0	0

MITTEN, John
Manchester, 30 March, 1941 E Sch/E Yth (W)

League Club	Source	Date Signed	Seasons Played	Apps	Subs	Gls
Mansfield T. (Am)	Jnrs	01.58	57	3	-	0
Newcastle U.	Tr	09.58	58-60	9	-	3
Leicester C.	Tr	09.61	61	12	-	0
Coventry C.	Manchester U. (trial)	08.63	63-66	34	2	5
Plymouth Arg.	Tr	01.67	66-67	43	0	8
Exeter C .	Tr	07.68	68-70	96	4	17

MITTON, G. Keith
Leyland, 30 December, 1928 (G)

League Club	Source	Date Signed	Seasons Played	Apps	Subs	Gls
Preston N.E.	Leyland Motors	05.50	53	2	-	0
Carlisle U.	Tr	06.54	54-56	48	-	0

MOBLEY, David L.
Oxford, 24 August, 1948 (FB)

League Club	Source	Date Signed	Seasons Played	Apps	Subs	Gls
Sheffield Wed.	Jnrs	09.65				
Grimsby T.	Tr	07.69	69	26	1	0

MOBLEY, Victor J.
Oxford, 11 October, 1943 Eu23-13/EF Lge (CH)

League Club	Source	Date Signed	Seasons Played	Apps	Subs	Gls
Sheffield Wed.	Oxford C.	09.61	63-69	187	0	8
Queens Park R.	Tr	10.69	69-70	24	1	0

MOCHAN, Dennis
Falkirk, 12 December, 1935 (FB)

League Club	Source	Date Signed	Seasons Played	Apps	Subs	Gls
Nottingham F.	Raith Rov.	06.62	62-65	108	0	1
Colchester U.	Tr	09.66	66-69	114	3	2

MOCHAN, Neil
Larbert, 6 April, 1927 S'B'-1/S-3 (CF)

League Club	Source	Date Signed	Seasons Played	Apps	Subs	Gls
Middlesbrough	Morton	05.51	51-52	38	-	14

MOCKLER, Andrew J.
Stockton, 18 November, 1970 (M)

League Club	Source	Date Signed	Seasons Played	Apps	Subs	Gls
Arsenal	YT	11.88				
Scarborough	Tr	07.90	90-91	52	6	9

MOFFAT, Adam
Dunfermline, 1 April, 1941 (IF)

League Club	Source	Date Signed	Seasons Played	Apps	Subs	Gls
Newport Co.	East Fife	10.61	61	17	-	5

MOFFATT, Gregory T.
Liverpool, 8 January, 1964 (D)

League Club	Source	Date Signed	Seasons Played	Apps	Subs	Gls
Chester C.	App	01.82	82	6	1	0

MOFFATT, John B.
Greenock, 22 December, 1929

League Club	Source	Date Signed	Seasons Played	Apps	Subs	Gls
Brighton & H. A.	Bellshill Ath.	12.51	52	2	-	0

MOFFATT, Norman
Bootle, 18 November, 1920 (IF)

League Club	Source	Date Signed	Seasons Played	Apps	Subs	Gls
Workington		08.51	51	1	-	0

MOFFATT, Robert W.
Portsmouth, 7 October, 1945 (WH)

League Club	Source	Date Signed	Seasons Played	Apps	Subs	Gls
Portsmouth	App	10.63				
Gillingham	Tr	05.65	65-67	23	1	1

MOFFITT, Kenneth
Newcastle, 2 February, 1933 (FB)

League Club	Source	Date Signed	Seasons Played	Apps	Subs	Gls
Brentford	Berwick R.	08.53				
Gateshead	Berwick R.	09.57	57-59	76	-	2

MOGFORD, Reginald W. G.
Newport, 12 June, 1919 (CF)

League Club	Source	Date Signed	Seasons Played	Apps	Subs	Gls
Newport Co.	Jnrs	06.38	38-47	20	-	9

MOHAN, Nicholas
Middlesbrough, 6 October, 1970 (D)

League Club	Source	Date Signed	Seasons Played	Apps	Subs	Gls
Middlesbrough	Charlton Ath. (Jnr)	11.87	88-91	53	2	2

MOIR, Ian
Aberdeen, 30 June, 1943 (W)

League Club	Source	Date Signed	Seasons Played	Apps	Subs	Gls
Manchester U.	Jnrs	07.60	60-64	45	-	5
Blackpool	Tr	02.65	64-66	61	0	12
Chester C.	Tr	05.67	67	25	0	3
Wrexham	Tr	01.68	67-71	144	6	20
Shrewsbury T.	Tr	03.72	71-72	22	3	2
Wrexham	Tr	07.73	73-74	11	4	0

MOIR, James M. M.
Newcastle, 23 March, 1918 (CF)

League Club	Source	Date Signed	Seasons Played	Apps	Subs	Gls
Accrington St.	Newcastle W.E.	10.37	37-38	20	-	9
Carlisle U.	Tr	08.46	46-47	42	-	18

MOIR, Richard J.
Glasgow, 22 October, 1945 (M)

League Club	Source	Date Signed	Seasons Played	Apps	Subs	Gls
Shrewsbury T.	Cumnock Jnrs	03.69	69-73	159	7	30
Halifax T.	Tr	07.74	74	16	3	5

MOIR, William
Aberdeen, 19 April, 1922 Died 1988 S'B'-1/S-1 (IF)

League Club	Source	Date Signed	Seasons Played	Apps	Subs	Gls
Bolton W.	R.A.F. Kirkham	04.43	46-55	325	-	118
Stockport Co.	Tr	09.55	55-57	69	-	26

MOKONE, Stephen V.
South Africa, 23 March, 1932 (OR)

League Club	Source	Date Signed	Seasons Played	Apps	Subs	Gls
Coventry C.	Pretoria (SA)	10.56	56	4	-	1
Cardiff C.	Netherlands	06.59	59	3	-	1

MOLBY, Jan
Denmark, 4 July, 1963 Danish Int (M)

League Club	Source	Date Signed	Seasons Played	Apps	Subs	Gls
Liverpool	Ajax (Neth)	08.84	84-91	164	19	37

Jan Molby (Kolding, Ajax, Liverpool & Denmark)

MOLLATT, Ronald V.
Edwinstowe, 24 February, 1932 (WH)

League Club	Source	Date Signed	Seasons Played	Apps	Subs	Gls
Leeds U.	Jnrs	02.50	51-54	17	-	0
York C.	Tr	07.55	55-59	124	-	1
Bradford C.	Tr	07.60	60-62	88	-	0

MOLLER, Jan B.
Sweden, 17 September, 1953 Swedish Int (G)

League Club	Source	Date Signed	Seasons Played	Apps	Subs	Gls
Bristol C.	Malmo (Swe)	12.80	80-81	48	0	0

MOLLOY, Gerard
Rochdale, 13 March, 1936 (OL)

League Club	Source	Date Signed	Seasons Played	Apps	Subs	Gls
Rochdale	Jnrs	11.55	55-56	6	-	0

MOLLOY, Peter (Paddy)
Rossendale, April, 1911 NIF Lge (WH)

League Club	Source	Date Signed	Seasons Played	Apps	Subs	Gls
Fulham		12.31	31	4	-	0
Bristol Rov.	Tr	05.33	33	6	-	0
Cardiff C.	Tr	02.34	33-34	23	-	0
Queens Park R.	Tr	07.35	35	3	-	0
Stockport Co.	Tr	07.36	36	10	-	0
Carlisle U.	Tr	05.37	37	33	-	0
Bradford C.	Tr	05.38	38	25	-	0
Notts Co.	Distillery	04.48	47	1	-	0

MOLLOY, G. William
Coventry, 28 August, 1929 (RH)

League Club	Source	Date Signed	Seasons Played	Apps	Subs	Gls
Southampton	Army	10.49	49	1	-	0
Newport Co.	Lockheed Leamington	11.50	50	3	-	0

MOLYNEUX, Bernard
Prescot, 17 September, 1933

League Club	Source	Date Signed	Seasons Played	Apps	Subs	Gls
Everton	Jnrs	12.51				
Tranmere Rov.	Tr	05.56	56	12	-	3

MOLYNEUX, Frederick G.
Wallasey, 25 July, 1944 (CD)

League Club	Source	Date Signed	Seasons Played	Apps	Subs	Gls
Liverpool	Jnrs	06.62				
Southport	Tr	08.65	65-68	123	0	1
Plymouth Arg.	Tr	08.68	68-70	79	0	5
Exeter C.	L	02.71	70	2	0	0
Tranmere Rov.	Tr	02.71	70-72	71	1	0
Southport	Tr	07.73	73	32	1	1

MOLYNEUX, Geoffrey B.
Warrington, 23 January, 1943 (OR)

League Club	Source	Date Signed	Seasons Played	Apps	Subs	Gls
Chester C. (Am)	Rylands Y.C.	05.62	62	1	-	0

MOLYNEUX, John A.
Warrington, 3 February, 1931 E Yth (RB)

League Club	Source	Date Signed	Seasons Played	Apps	Subs	Gls
Chester C.	Jnrs	02.49	49-54	178	-	1
Liverpool	Tr	06.55	55-61	229	-	2
Chester C.	Tr	08.62	62-64	67	-	0

MOLYNEUX, Raymond
Kearsley, 13 June, 1930 E Yth (RB)

League Club	Source	Date Signed	Seasons Played	Apps	Subs	Gls
Bradford C.		12.48	48	2	-	1

MOLYNEUX, William S.
Liverpool, 10 January, 1944 (G)

League Club	Source	Date Signed	Seasons Played	Apps	Subs	Gls
Liverpool	Earle	11.63	64	1	-	0
Oldham Ath.	Tr	06.67	68	8	0	0

MONAGHAN, Derek J.
Bromsgrove, 20 January, 1959 E Yth (F)

League Club	Source	Date Signed	Seasons Played	Apps	Subs	Gls
West Bromwich A.	App	01.77	79-83	14	5	2
Port Vale	Tr	07.84	84	4	3	0

MONCRIEFF, James C.
Todmorden, 14 June, 1922 Died 1975 (CF)

League Club	Source	Date Signed	Seasons Played	Apps	Subs	Gls
Halifax T. (Am)	Pegasus	06.46	46-54	42	-	13

MONCUR, John F.
Stepney, 22 September, 1966 (M)

League Club	Source	Date Signed	Seasons Played	Apps	Subs	Gls
Tottenham H.	App	08.84	86-90	10	11	1
Doncaster Rov.	L	09.86	86	4	0	0
Cambridge U.	L	03.87	86	3	1	0
Portsmouth	L	03.89	88	7	0	0
Brentford	L	10.89	89	5	0	1
Ipswich T.	L	10.91	91	5	1	0
Swindon T.	Tr	03.92	91	1	2	0

MONCUR, Robert
Perth, 19 January, 1945 S Sch/Su23-1/S-16 (CD)

League Club	Source	Date Signed	Seasons Played	Apps	Subs	Gls
Newcastle U.	App	04.62	62-73	293	3	3
Sunderland	Tr	06.74	74-76	86	0	2
Carlisle U.	Tr	11.76	76	11	0	0

MONEY, Richard
Lowestoft, 13 October, 1955 E'B' (CD)

League Club	Source	Date Signed	Seasons Played	Apps	Subs	Gls
Scunthorpe U.	Lowestoft T.	07.73	73-77	165	8	4
Fulham	Tr	12.77	77-79	106	0	3
Liverpool	Tr	04.80	80	12	2	0
Derby Co.	L	12.81	81	5	0	0
Luton T.	Tr	03.82	81-82	44	0	1
Portsmouth	Tr	08.83	83-85	17	0	0
Scunthorpe U.	Tr	10.85	85-89	105	1	0

MONINGTON, Mark D.
Bilsthorpe (Nts), 21 October, 1970 (CD)

League Club	Source	Date Signed	Seasons Played	Apps	Subs	Gls
Burnley	Jnrs	03.89	88-91	27	6	2

MONK, Brian
Leeds, 15 May, 1937 (F)

League Club	Source	Date Signed	Seasons Played	Apps	Subs	Gls
Leeds U.	Jnrs	02.55				
Crewe Alex.	Tr	05.58	58	5	-	0

MONK, Frederick J.
Brighton, 9 October, 1920 Died 1987 E Sch (RB/CF)

League Club	Source	Date Signed	Seasons Played	Apps	Subs	Gls
Brentford	Guildford C.	03.48	47-53	205	-	48
Aldershot	Tr	07.54	54-55	48	-	0

MONKHOUSE, Alan W.
Stockton, 23 October, 1930 (F)

League Club	Source	Date Signed	Seasons Played	Apps	Subs	Gls
Millwall	Thornaby	08.50	49-53	65	-	20
Newcastle U.	Tr	10.53	53-55	21	-	9
York C.	Tr	06.56	56	12	-	1

MONKHOUSE, Graham
Carlisle, 26 April, 1954 (G)

League Club	Source	Date Signed	Seasons Played	Apps	Subs	Gls
Workington	Penrith	08.76	76	4	0	0

MONKOU, Kenneth J.
Surinam, 29 November, 1964 Neth u21 Int (CD)

League Club	Source	Date Signed	Seasons Played	Apps	Subs	Gls
Chelsea	Feyenoord (Neth)	03.89	88-91	92	2	2

MONKS, John
Stockport, 3 June, 1921 (WH)

League Club	Source	Date Signed	Seasons Played	Apps	Subs	Gls
Stockport Co.		04.47	46-52	91	-	1

MONOGHAN, William
Glasgow, 2 September, 1919 (RB)

League Club	Source	Date Signed	Seasons Played	Apps	Subs	Gls
Bury	Alloa Ath.	08.46				
Carlisle U.	Tr	08.47	47-49	19	-	0

MONTGOMERY, Alec W.
Tamworth, 16 September, 1926

League Club	Source	Date Signed	Seasons Played	Apps	Subs	Gls
Walsall	Baddesley	08.49	51-52	29	-	0

MONTGOMERY, Derek
Houghton-le-Spring, 5 May, 1950 (M)

League Club	Source	Date Signed	Seasons Played	Apps	Subs	Gls
Leeds U.	App	12.67				
Bradford C.	Tr	08.68	68	4	0	0

MONTGOMERY, James
Sunderland, 9 October, 1943 E Yth/Eu23-6 (G)

League Club	Source	Date Signed	Seasons Played	Apps	Subs	Gls
Sunderland	Jnrs	10.60	61-76	537	0	0
Southampton	L	10.76	76	5	0	0
Birmingham C.	Tr	02.77	76-78	66	0	0
Nottingham F.	Tr	08.79				
Sunderland	Tr	08.80				

MONTGOMERY, Stanley W. J.
West Ham, 7 July, 1920 (CH)

League Club	Source	Date Signed	Seasons Played	Apps	Subs	Gls
Hull C.	Romford	09.44	46	5	-	0
Southend U.	Tr	09.46	46-48	96	-	6
Cardiff C.	Tr	12.48	48-54	231	-	4
Newport Co.	Worcester C.	11.55	55	9	-	0

MOODY, Alan
Middlesbrough, 18 January, 1951 E Sch (D)

League Club	Source	Date Signed	Seasons Played	Apps	Subs	Gls
Middlesbrough	App	01.68	68-72	44	2	0
Southend U.	Tr	10.72	72-83	444	2	41

MOODY, Kenneth G.
Grimsby, 12 November, 1924 Died 1990 (FB)

League Club	Source	Date Signed	Seasons Played	Apps	Subs	Gls
Grimsby T.	Humber U.	10.42	47-50	114	-	0

Bobby Moncur (Newcastle United, Sunderland, Carlisle United & Scotland)

Jim Montgomery (Sunderland, Birmingham City, Nottingham Forest & Sunderland)

League Club	Source	Date Signed	Seasons Played	Apps	Subs	Gls
MOODY, Paul						
Portsmouth, 13 June, 1967						(F)
Southampton	Waterlooville	07.91	91	2	2	0
MOODY, V. Roy						
Worksop, 12 March, 1923						(OR)
Lincoln C.		11.46	46	1	-	0
MOONEY, Brian J.						
Dublin, 2 February, 1966 IR Yth						(W)
Liverpool	Home Farm	08.83				
Wrexham	L	12.85	85	9	0	2
Preston N.E.	Tr	10.87	87-90	125	3	20
Sunderland	Tr	02.91	90-91	11	4	0
MOONEY, Dean F.						
Paddington, 24 July, 1956						(F)
Leyton Orient	App	07.74	74-75	16	6	3
Bournemouth	Sweden	12.80	80-81	27	0	10
Torquay U. (N/C)	R.S. Southampton	08.84	84	15	0	2
MOONEY, Frank						
Fauldhouse, 1 January, 1932						(OR)
Manchester U.	Bathgate St M.	05.49				
Blackburn Rov.	Tr	02.54	53-55	58	-	19
Carlisle U.	Tr	05.56	56-59	124	-	23
MOONEY, John						
Fauldhouse, 21 February, 1926						(OR)
Doncaster Rov.	Hamilton Acad.	05.53	53-58	171	-	32
MOONEY, Kevin W.						
Liverpool, 23 August, 1959						(D)
Bury	Bangor C.	03.80	80	1	0	0
Tranmere Rov.	Telford U.	08.82	82	21	1	0
MOONEY, Thomas J.						
Middlesbrough, 11 August, 1971						(F)
Aston Villa	YT	11.89				
Scarborough	Tr	07.90	90-91	57	10	20
MOOR, Anthony J.						
York, 18 January, 1940						(G)
York C.	Scarborough	05.62	62-64	57	-	0
Darlington	Tr	07.65	65-71	239	0	0
MOORCROFT, David S.						
Liverpool, 16 March, 1947						(D)
Tranmere Rov.	Skelmersdale U.	12.68	68-71	107	1	1
MOORCROFT, Maurice						
Chesterfield, 4 November, 1929 E Yth						(G)
Sheffield U.	Jnrs	07.48				
Gillingham	Tr	07.52	52	8	-	0
MOORE, Alan						
Hebburn, 7 March, 1927						(OR)
Sunderland		05.46				
Chesterfield	Spennymoor U.	12.48	48-50	67	-	2
Hull C.	Tr	07.51	51	13	-	4
Nottingham F.	Tr	01.52	51-54	102	-	38
Coventry C.	Tr	12.54	54-56	57	-	13
Swindon T.	Tr	07.57	57-58	19	-	3
Rochdale	Tr	11.58	58	11	-	2
MOORE, Andrew D.						
Wantage, 2 October, 1964						(M)
Reading (App)	App	09.81	81	0	1	0
MOORE, Andrew R.						
Cleethorpes, 14 November, 1965						(CD)
Grimsby T.	App	11.83	83-86	62	3	1
MOORE, Anthony P.						
Wolverhampton, 19 September, 1957						(FB)
Sheffield U.	Burton A.	07.79	79-81	29	0	0
Crewe Alex.	Tr	08.82	82	17	0	2
Rochdale (N/C)	Worksop T.	10.84	84	1	2	0
MOORE, Anthony P.						
Scarborough, 4 September, 1947						(W)
Chesterfield	App	01.65	64-70	148	7	13
Grimsby T.	L	03.71	70	2	1	0
Chester C.	Tr	08.71	71	9	4	3
MOORE, Anthony P.						
York, 7 February, 1943						(CF)
York C. (Am)	Heworth	05.62	62	2	-	0
MOORE, J. F. Beriah						
Cardiff, 25 December, 1919						(OL)
Cardiff C.	Bangor C.	09.41	47-48	6	-	4
Newport Co.	Bangor C.	07.50	50-52	121	-	45
MOORE, Bernard J.						
Brighton, 18 December, 1923						(CF)
Brighton & H.A.	Jnrs	09.45	47	8	-	2
Luton T.	Hastings U.	01.51	50-53	73	-	31
Brighton & H.A.	Tr	03.54	53-54	29	-	10
MOORE, Brian						
Hemsworth, 24 December, 1938						(OR)
Mansfield T. (Am)	Loughborough Col.	09.60	60	4	-	0
Notts Co.	Tr	12.61	61-62	27	-	3
Doncaster Rov.	Tr	07.63	63	1	-	0
MOORE, Brian M.						
Belfast, 29 December, 1933						(IF)
West Ham U.	Glentoran	02.55	54-55	9	-	1
MOORE, Christian						
Derby, 4 November, 1972						(F)
Stockport Co.	Leicester C. (YT)	08.91	91	0	1	0
MOORE, Darren M.						
Birmingham, 22 April, 1974						(CD)
Torquay U. (YT)	YT	11.90	91	5	0	1
MOORE, David						
Grimsby, 17 December, 1959						(RB)
Grimsby T.	App	12.77	78-82	136	0	2
Carlisle U.	Tr	08.83	83	13	0	1
Blackpool	Tr	12.83	83-86	114	1	1
Grimsby T.	Tr	12.86	86-87	3	1	0
Darlington	Tr	08.88	88	25	5	1
MOORE, Eric						
St Helens, 16 July, 1926						(FB)
Everton		02.49	49-56	171	-	0
Chesterfield	Tr	01.57	56	6	-	0
Tranmere Rov.	Tr	07.57	57	36	-	0
MOORE, Gary						
Sunderland, 4 November, 1945						(F)
Sunderland	Jnrs	11.62	64-66	13	0	2
Grimsby T.	Tr	02.67	66-68	52	1	15
Southend U.	Tr	11.68	68-73	156	6	46
Colchester U.	L	03.74	73	11	0	7
Chester C.	Tr	08.74	74-75	29	14	4
Swansea C.	Tr	07.76	76-77	30	4	8
MOORE, Gary S.						
Greenwich, 29 December, 1968						(F)
Maidstone U. (N/C)	Alma Swanley	03.91	90	0	5	1
MOORE, Gordon A.						
Greenock, 27 June, 1968						(W)
Bristol C.	Jnrs	06.86	85	0	1	0
MOORE, Graham						
Hengoed, 7 March, 1941 Wu23-9/EF Lge/W-21						(M)
Cardiff C.	Jnrs	05.58	58-61	85	-	23
Chelsea	Tr	12.61	61-63	68	-	13
Manchester U.	Tr	11.63	63	18	-	4
Northampton T.	Tr	12.65	65-66	53	0	10
Charlton Ath.	Tr	06.67	67-70	110	0	8
Doncaster Rov.	Tr	09.71	71-73	67	2	3
MOORE, Howard						
Canterbury, 5 March, 1947						(W)
Coventry C.	Ashford T.	03.66				
Gillingham	Tr	07.67	67	17	0	0
Southend U.	Tr	01.68	67-68	6	2	0
MOORE, John						
Consett, 1 October, 1966						(F)
Sunderland	App	10.84	84-87	4	12	1
Newport Co.	L	12.85	85	2	0	0
Darlington	L	11.86	86	2	0	1
Mansfield T.	L	03.87	86	5	0	1
Rochdale	L	01.88	87	10	0	2
Hull C.	Tr	06.88	88	11	3	1
Sheffield U.	L	03.89	88	4	1	0
Shrewsbury T.	F.C. Utrecht (Neth)	07.90	90	7	1	1
Crewe Alex. (N/C)	Tr	01.91	90	0	1	0
Scarborough	F.C. Utrecht (Neth)	08.91	91	3	4	1

League Club	Source	Date Signed	Seasons Played	Apps	Subs	Gls

MOORE, John
Liverpool, 9 September, 1945 (CD)

League Club	Source	Date Signed	Seasons Played	Apps	Subs	Gls
Stoke C.	Everton (App)	07.63	67	12	1	0
Shrewsbury T.	Tr	08.68	68-72	144	0	3
Swansea C.	Tr	01.73	72-73	31	0	0

MOORE, John
Harthill, 21 December, 1943 (CD)

League Club	Source	Date Signed	Seasons Played	Apps	Subs	Gls
Luton T.	Motherwell	05.65	65-72	263	9	13
Brighton & H.A.	L	10.72	72	5	0	0
Northampton T.	Tr	08.74	74	14	0	0

MOORE, John M.
Carlton, 1 February, 1943 (OR)

League Club	Source	Date Signed	Seasons Played	Apps	Subs	Gls
Lincoln C.	Arnold St Marys	11.61	61-64	30	-	5

MOORE, John W.
Chiswick, 25 September, 1923 (WH)

League Club	Source	Date Signed	Seasons Played	Apps	Subs	Gls
Brentford		09.46	46-47	4	-	0
Colchester U.	Tr	07.50	51	2	-	0

MOORE, Jonathan
Cardiff, 17 November, 1955 W Sch/W Yth (FB)

League Club	Source	Date Signed	Seasons Played	Apps	Subs	Gls
Bristol Rov.	App	11.73				
Millwall	Tr	12.74	74-78	119	0	5
Bournemouth	Tr	05.79	79-80	36	0	2

MOORE, Kenneth
Bradford, 13 September, 1921

League Club	Source	Date Signed	Seasons Played	Apps	Subs	Gls
Halifax T.		11.47	47-49	31	-	2

MOORE, Kevin
Loughborough, 20 October, 1957 (M)

League Club	Source	Date Signed	Seasons Played	Apps	Subs	Gls
Shrewsbury T.	App	10.75	74-77	15	3	1

MOORE, Kevin J.
Blackpool, 30 January, 1956 (W)

League Club	Source	Date Signed	Seasons Played	Apps	Subs	Gls
Blackpool	App	10.73	74-76	33	5	3
Bury	L	12.76	76	4	0	0
Swansea C.	Tr	07.77	77-78	51	4	6
Newport Co.	Tr	02.79	78-82	140	8	13
Swindon T.	L	03.83	82	1	0	0

MOORE, Kevin T.
Grimsby, 29 April, 1958 E Sch (CD)

League Club	Source	Date Signed	Seasons Played	Apps	Subs	Gls
Grimsby T.	Jnrs	07.76	76-86	397	3	28
Oldham Ath.	Tr	02.87	86	13	0	1
Southampton	Tr	07.87	87-91	112	4	8
Bristol Rov.	L	01.92	91	7	0	0

MOORE, J. Leslie
Sheffield, 7 July, 1933 (CH)

League Club	Source	Date Signed	Seasons Played	Apps	Subs	Gls
Derby Co.	Worksop T.	11.57	57-63	144	-	3
Lincoln C.	Boston U.	10.65	65-66	59	0	0

MOORE, Malcolm
Silksworth, 18 December, 1948 (F)

League Club	Source	Date Signed	Seasons Played	Apps	Subs	Gls
Sunderland	App	12.65	67-68	10	2	3
Crewe Alex.	L	03.70	69	8	0	0
Tranmere Rov.	Tr	07.70	70-72	83	8	21
Hartlepool U.	Tr	08.73	73-75	127	2	34
Workington	Tr	08.76	76	22	0	2

MOORE, Martin T.
Middlesbrough, 10 January, 1966 (LW)

League Club	Source	Date Signed	Seasons Played	Apps	Subs	Gls
Peterborough U.	Stockton	01.90	89	6	1	0

MOORE, Michael
Chorley, 20 July, 1952 (F)

League Club	Source	Date Signed	Seasons Played	Apps	Subs	Gls
Preston N.E.		06.70				
Southport	Tr	07.71	71-73	62	21	10
Port Vale	Wigan Ath.	03.78	77	13	0	0
Wigan Ath.	Tr	08.78	78-79	57	7	12

MOORE, Norman W.
Grimsby, 15 October, 1919 (CF)

League Club	Source	Date Signed	Seasons Played	Apps	Subs	Gls
Grimsby T.	Jnrs	03.39	46	7	-	1
Hull C.	Tr	04.47	46-49	81	-	46
Blackburn Rov.	Tr	03.50	49-50	7	-	1
Bury	Tr	08.51	51	2	-	0

MOORE, Raymond
Workington, 2 November, 1956 (W)

League Club	Source	Date Signed	Seasons Played	Apps	Subs	Gls
Workington (N/C)	Sekers	11.75	75	3	0	0

MOORE, Robert
Askern, 14 December, 1932 (F)

League Club	Source	Date Signed	Seasons Played	Apps	Subs	Gls
Rotherham U.	Worksop T.	05.55	55-56	19	-	2
Chesterfield	Tr	10.56	56-58	19	-	3

MOORE, Robert F.
Barking, 12 April, 1941 E Yth/Eu23-8/EF Lge/E-108 (CD)

League Club	Source	Date Signed	Seasons Played	Apps	Subs	Gls
West Ham U.	Jnrs	06.58	58-73	543	1	22
Fulham	Tr	03.74	73-76	124	0	1

Bobby Moore (West Ham United, Fulham & England)

MOORE, Ronald D.
Liverpool, 29 January, 1953 (F/CD)

League Club	Source	Date Signed	Seasons Played	Apps	Subs	Gls
Tranmere Rov.	Jnrs	05.71	71-78	248	1	72
Cardiff C.	Tr	02.79	78-79	54	2	6
Rotherham U.	Tr	08.80	80-83	124	1	51
Charlton Ath.	Tr	09.83	83-84	60	2	13
Rochdale	Tr	07.85	85	43	0	9
Tranmere Rov.	Tr	07.86	86-88	75	0	6

MOORE, T. Roy
Grimsby, 18 December, 1923 Died 1991 (CH)

League Club	Source	Date Signed	Seasons Played	Apps	Subs	Gls
Grimsby T.		06.47	48-49	3	-	0

MOORE, Samuel C.
Birmingham, 6 September, 1934 (IF)

League Club	Source	Date Signed	Seasons Played	Apps	Subs	Gls
Wolverhampton W.	Aldershot (Am)	11.54				
Walsall	Tr	05.55	55-57	64	-	12
Gillingham	Tr	06.58	58-59	33	-	9

MOORE, Stephen J.
Chester, 17 December, 1969

League Club	Source	Date Signed	Seasons Played	Apps	Subs	Gls
Chester C. (YT)	YT	08.86	87	0	1	0

MOORE, Thomas L.
Trimdon (Dm), 25 July, 1936 (G)

League Club	Source	Date Signed	Seasons Played	Apps	Subs	Gls
Darlington (Am)	Trimdon	08.56	56	1	-	0

MOORE, Watson (Watty)
Hartlepool, 30 August, 1925 (CH)

League Club	Source	Date Signed	Seasons Played	Apps	Subs	Gls
Hartlepool U.		05.48	48-59	448	-	1

MOORES, J. Craig
Macclesfield, 1 February, 1961 (F)

League Club	Source	Date Signed	Seasons Played	Apps	Subs	Gls
Bolton W.	App	02.79	80	0	1	0
Swindon T.	Tr	07.81	81	1	1	0

League Club	Source	Date Signed	Seasons Played	Apps	Subs	Gls

MOORES, Ian R.
Chesterton, 5 October, 1954 Eu23-2 (F)

League Club	Source	Date Signed	Seasons Played	Apps	Subs	Gls
Stoke C.	App	06.72	73-75	40	10	14
Tottenham H.	Tr	08.76	76-78	25	4	6
Leyton Orient	Tr	10.78	78-81	110	7	26
Bolton W.	Tr	07.82	82	23	3	3
Barnsley	L	02.83	82	3	0	0

MOORHOUSE, Alan
Wardle, 12 October, 1925

League Club	Source	Date Signed	Seasons Played	Apps	Subs	Gls
Rochdale	Blackburn Rov. (Am)	03.47	46-47	17	-	3

MORAH, Olisa H.
Islington, 30 September, 1972 E Sch/E Yth (F)

League Club	Source	Date Signed	Seasons Played	Apps	Subs	Gls
Tottenham H.	YT	07.91				
Hereford U.	L	11.91	91	0	2	0

MORALEE, Jamie D.
Wandsworth, 2 December, 1971 (F)

League Club	Source	Date Signed	Seasons Played	Apps	Subs	Gls
Crystal Palace	YT	07.90	91	2	4	0

MORAN, Brian J.
Hemsworth, 3 June, 1947 (OR)

League Club	Source	Date Signed	Seasons Played	Apps	Subs	Gls
Barnsley	Jnrs	01.67	66	1	0	0

MORAN, Douglas W.
Musselburgh, 29 July, 1934 (IF)

League Club	Source	Date Signed	Seasons Played	Apps	Subs	Gls
Ipswich T.	Falkirk	07.61	61-63	104	-	31

MORAN, Edward
Cleland, 20 July, 1930 (IF)

League Club	Source	Date Signed	Seasons Played	Apps	Subs	Gls
Leicester C.	Cleland B.C.	09.47	48-50	8	-	1
Stockport Co.	Tr	10.51	51-56	110	-	42
Rochdale	Tr	02.57	56-58	43	-	13
Crewe Alex.	Tr	09.58	58	22	-	8

MORAN, James
Wishaw, 6 March, 1935 (IF)

League Club	Source	Date Signed	Seasons Played	Apps	Subs	Gls
Leicester C.	Wishaw Jnrs.	12.55	56	3	-	1
Norwich C.	Tr	11.57	57-59	36	-	17
Northampton T.	Tr	01.61	60-61	24	-	5
Darlington	Tr	08.62	62	27	-	6
Workington	Tr	07.63	63-65	100	0	22

MORAN, John
Cleland, 9 March, 1933 (IF)

League Club	Source	Date Signed	Seasons Played	Apps	Subs	Gls
Derby Co.	Coltness U.	11.54	54	2	-	0

MORAN, Kevin B.
Dublin, 29 April, 1956 IR-62 (CD)

League Club	Source	Date Signed	Seasons Played	Apps	Subs	Gls
Manchester U.	Pegasus (Gaelic)	02.78	78-87	228	3	21
Blackburn Rov.	Sporting Gijon (Sp)	01.90	89-91	88	4	5

MORAN, Lister F.
Ryton-on-Tyne, 24 June, 1930 (WH)

League Club	Source	Date Signed	Seasons Played	Apps	Subs	Gls
Gateshead	Wearmouth Colly	10.50	51-56	22	-	0

MORAN, Michael E.
Leek, 26 December, 1935

League Club	Source	Date Signed	Seasons Played	Apps	Subs	Gls
Port Vale		07.54				
Crewe Alex.	Tr	07.57	57	14	-	3

MORAN, Paul
Enfield, 22 May, 1968 (W)

League Club	Source	Date Signed	Seasons Played	Apps	Subs	Gls
Tottenham H.	YT	07.85	86-90	14	14	2
Portsmouth	L	01.89	88	3	0	0
Leicester C.	L	11.89	89	10	0	2
Newcastle U.	L	02.91	90	1	0	0
Southend U.	L	03.91	90	1	0	0

MORAN, Richard
Hammersmith, 9 September, 1963 (F)

League Club	Source	Date Signed	Seasons Played	Apps	Subs	Gls
Birmingham C.	Fujita Tokyo (Jap)	08.90	90	2	6	1

MORAN, Ronald
Liverpool, 28 February, 1934 EF Lge (LB)

League Club	Source	Date Signed	Seasons Played	Apps	Subs	Gls
Liverpool	Jnrs	01.52	52-64	343	-	14

MORAN, Stephen J.
Croydon, 10 January, 1961 Eu21-2 (F)

League Club	Source	Date Signed	Seasons Played	Apps	Subs	Gls
Southampton	Jnrs	08.79	79-85	173	7	78
Leicester C.	Tr	09.86	86-87	35	8	14
Reading	Tr	11.87	87-90	91	25	30
Exeter C.	Tr	08.91	91	31	3	19

MORAN, Thomas
Glasgow, 31 May, 1924 (WH)

League Club	Source	Date Signed	Seasons Played	Apps	Subs	Gls
Accrington St.	Alloa Ath.	08.53	53	7	-	0

MORAN, Thomas
Edinburgh, 5 February, 1930 (OL)

League Club	Source	Date Signed	Seasons Played	Apps	Subs	Gls
Carlisle U.	Cowdenbeath	05.54	54-55	36	-	5
Darlington	Tr	05.56	56-57	66	-	13

MORDUE, James
Seaton Delaval, 18 February, 1924 (WH)

League Club	Source	Date Signed	Seasons Played	Apps	Subs	Gls
Bradford P.A.	North Shields	09.46	48	2	-	0

MORDUE, William
Durham, 23 February, 1937 (D)

League Club	Source	Date Signed	Seasons Played	Apps	Subs	Gls
Doncaster Rov.	Bentley Colly	03.58	57-60	78	-	0

MOREFIELD, John W.
Gloucester, 26 October, 1922 (FB)

League Club	Source	Date Signed	Seasons Played	Apps	Subs	Gls
Halifax T.		05.46	46-48	66	-	0

MORELAND, Victor
Belfast, 15 June, 1957 NIu21-1/NI-6 (M)

League Club	Source	Date Signed	Seasons Played	Apps	Subs	Gls
Derby Co.	Glentoran	09.78	78-79	38	4	1

MORELINE, David J.
Stepney, 2 December, 1950 (FB)

League Club	Source	Date Signed	Seasons Played	Apps	Subs	Gls
Fulham	App	01.68	68-73	63	7	0
Reading	Tr	06.74	74-80	166	0	0

MOREMONT, Ralph
Sheffield, 24 September, 1924 (WH)

League Club	Source	Date Signed	Seasons Played	Apps	Subs	Gls
Sheffield U.		09.46	49	2	-	0
Chester C.	Tr	05.50	50-52	121	-	19
Rochdale		08.55	55	1	-	0

MORGAN, Alan
Swansea, 2 January, 1936

League Club	Source	Date Signed	Seasons Played	Apps	Subs	Gls
Leeds U.		01.54				
Crewe Alex.	Tr	09.56	56-57	6	-	0

MORGAN, Arthur R.
Ogmore Vale, 13 September, 1930 (FB/IF)

League Club	Source	Date Signed	Seasons Played	Apps	Subs	Gls
Swansea C.		12.48	50-52	13	-	0
Plymouth Arg.	Tr	11.53	53-56	36	-	4

Kevin Moran (Manchester United, Sporting Gijon, Blackburn Rovers & Republic of Ireland)

Steve Moran (Southampton, Leicester City, Reading & Exeter City)

MORGAN, Clifford I.
Bristol, 26 September, 1913 (WH)

League Club	Source	Date Signed	Seasons Played	Apps	Subs	Gls
Bristol C.	Bristol B.B.	06.33	33-48	235	-	8

MORGAN, Darren J.
Camberwell, 5 November, 1967 W Yth (M)

League Club	Source	Date Signed	Seasons Played	Apps	Subs	Gls
Millwall	App	11.85	86-90	35	9	2
Bradford C.	L	03.90	89	2	0	0
Peterborough U.	L	03.91	90	5	0	0
Bradford C.	Tr	08.91	91	9	2	0

MORGAN, Denley J.
Llanelli, 13 February, 1951 (FB)

League Club	Source	Date Signed	Seasons Played	Apps	Subs	Gls
Swansea C.	Jnrs	02.71	68-71	14	1	0

MORGAN, R. Dennis
Neath, 22 September, 1925 Died 1980 (FB)

League Club	Source	Date Signed	Seasons Played	Apps	Subs	Gls
Cardiff C.	Briton Ferry	04.44				
Norwich C.	Tr	10.46	46-55	225	-	3

MORGAN, Donald
Huddersfield, 8 June, 1925 Died 1976 (WH)

League Club	Source	Date Signed	Seasons Played	Apps	Subs	Gls
Accrington St.	Huddersfield T. (Am)	06.47	46-47	8	-	1
Tranmere Rov.	Tr	05.48				

MORGAN, Ernest
Barnsley, 13 January, 1927 (CF)

League Club	Source	Date Signed	Seasons Played	Apps	Subs	Gls
Lincoln C.	Royston Y.C.	09.49	52	3	-	0
Gillingham	Tr	08.53	53-56	155	-	73

MORGAN, Gary
Consett, 1 April, 1961 (LB)

League Club	Source	Date Signed	Seasons Played	Apps	Subs	Gls
Darlington	Berwick R.	07.85	85-88	146	0	3

MORGAN, George W.
Cardiff, 28 March, 1923 (W)

League Club	Source	Date Signed	Seasons Played	Apps	Subs	Gls
Norwich C.	Cardiff C. (Am)	01.47	46-49	65	-	15
Newport Co.	Tr	06.50				

MORGAN, Gerald
Llanidloes, 23 February, 1950 (G)

League Club	Source	Date Signed	Seasons Played	Apps	Subs	Gls
Walsall (Am)		03.74	73	1	0	0

MORGAN, Huw
Neath, 20 August, 1964 (M)

League Club	Source	Date Signed	Seasons Played	Apps	Subs	Gls
Swansea C.	App	08.82	83	5	2	0

MORGAN, Ian A.
Walthamstow, 14 November, 1946 (W)

League Club	Source	Date Signed	Seasons Played	Apps	Subs	Gls
Queens Park R.	App	09.64	64-72	161	11	26
Watford	Tr	10.73	73	15	1	1

MORGAN, W. James
Bristol, 19 June, 1922 (IF)

League Club	Source	Date Signed	Seasons Played	Apps	Subs	Gls
Bristol Rov.		04.46	46-51	104	-	24

MORGAN, Jonathan P.
Cardiff, 10 July, 1970 W Yth (M)

League Club	Source	Date Signed	Seasons Played	Apps	Subs	Gls
Cardiff C.	YT	07.88	88-90	43	12	3

MORGAN, Keith
Trowbridge, 19 February, 1940 (WH)

League Club	Source	Date Signed	Seasons Played	Apps	Subs	Gls
Swindon T.	Westbury U.	08.58	58-66	325	0	6

MORGAN, Kenneth S.
Swansea, 28 July, 1932 (OR)

League Club	Source	Date Signed	Seasons Played	Apps	Subs	Gls
Fulham	Rickmansworth	09.50				
Watford	Tr	09.52				
Northampton T.		09.54				
Crystal Palace	Brentford (trial)	10.55	55	1	-	0

MORGAN, Laurie (Lol)
Rotherham, 5 May, 1931 (FB)

League Club	Source	Date Signed	Seasons Played	Apps	Subs	Gls
Huddersfield T.	Sheffield U. (Am)	03.49	49-50	7	-	0
Rotherham U.	Tr	08.54	54-63	290	-	0
Darlington	Tr	07.64	64-65	29	1	0

MORGAN, Lewis
Cowdenbeath, 30 April, 1911 (FB)

League Club	Source	Date Signed	Seasons Played	Apps	Subs	Gls
Portsmouth	Dundee	08.35	35-38	122	-	0
Watford	Tr	07.46	46-47	50	-	0

MORGAN, Nicholas
East Ham, 30 October, 1959 (F)

League Club	Source	Date Signed	Seasons Played	Apps	Subs	Gls
West Ham U.	App	11.77	78-82	14	7	2
Portsmouth	Tr	03.83	82-86	79	16	32
Stoke C.	Tr	11.86	86-89	73	15	20
Bristol C.	Tr	03.90	89-91	65	5	20

MORGAN, Peter W.
Cardiff, 28 October, 1951 (D)

League Club	Source	Date Signed	Seasons Played	Apps	Subs	Gls
Cardiff C.	Jnrs	11.69	72	16	0	0
Hereford U.	Tr	08.74	74	16	0	0
Newport Co.	Tr	03.76	75-76	22	2	1

MORGAN, Richard L. (Richie)
Cardiff, 3 October, 1946 W Sch/Wu23-1 (CD)

League Club	Source	Date Signed	Seasons Played	Apps	Subs	Gls
Cardiff C.	Cardiff Corries	02.66	67-76	69	0	0

MORGAN, Roger E.
Walthamstow, 14 November, 1946 E Yth/Eu23-1 (W)

League Club	Source	Date Signed	Seasons Played	Apps	Subs	Gls
Queens Park R.	App	09.64	64-68	180	0	39
Tottenham H.	Tr	02.69	68-71	66	2	8

MORGAN, Ronald
Twynrodyn, 6 September, 1915 (CF)

League Club	Source	Date Signed	Seasons Played	Apps	Subs	Gls
Bournemouth	Wolverhampton W. (Am)	06.35	35	2	-	1
Doncaster Rov.	Tr	05.37	37-38	5	-	1
Accrington St.	Tr	06.39	46	4	-	0

MORGAN, Samuel J.
Belfast, 3 December, 1946 NI-18 (F)

League Club	Source	Date Signed	Seasons Played	Apps	Subs	Gls
Port Vale	Gorleston	07.70	69-72	109	4	24
Aston Villa	Tr	08.73	73-75	35	5	9
Brighton & H.A.	Tr	12.75	75-76	19	16	8
Cambridge U.	Tr	08.77	77	34	3	4

MORGAN, Simon C.
Birmingham, 5 September, 1966 Eu21-2 (FB)

League Club	Source	Date Signed	Seasons Played	Apps	Subs	Gls
Leicester C.	YT	11.84	85-89	147	13	3
Fulham	Tr	10.90	90-91	66	2	3

MORGAN, Simon D.
Merthyr Tydfil, 3 September, 1970

League Club	Source	Date Signed	Seasons Played	Apps	Subs	Gls
Newport Co. (YT)	YT	08.87	87	0	2	0

MORGAN, Stanley A.
Abergwynfl, 10 October, 1920 (IF)

League Club	Source	Date Signed	Seasons Played	Apps	Subs	Gls
Arsenal	Gwynfil Welfare	12.41	46	2	-	0
Walsall	Tr	06.48	48	10	-	1
Millwall	Tr	12.48	48-52	156	-	41
Leyton Orient	Tr	05.53	53-55	96	-	24

MORGAN, Stephen A.
Oldham, 19 September, 1968 (LB)

League Club	Source	Date Signed	Seasons Played	Apps	Subs	Gls
Blackpool	App	08.86	85-89	135	9	10
Plymouth Arg.	Tr	07.90	90-91	85	0	5

MORGAN, Stephen J.
Wrexham, 28 December, 1970 W Yth (W)

League Club	Source	Date Signed	Seasons Played	Apps	Subs	Gls
Oldham Ath.	YT	07.89	87-88	1	1	0
Wrexham	L	03.90	89	7	0	1
Rochdale	Tr	03.91	90-91	12	11	3

MORGAN, Stuart E.
Swansea, 23 September, 1949 (CD)

League Club	Source	Date Signed	Seasons Played	Apps	Subs	Gls
West Ham U.	Jnrs	03.67				
Torquay U.	L	02.69	68	14	0	0
Reading	Tr	11.69	69-71	42	4	1
Colchester U.	Tr	08.72	72-74	79	2	10
Bournemouth	Tr	03.75	74-76	80	1	5

MORGAN, Sidney S.
Bristol, 1 August, 1926 (G)

League Club	Source	Date Signed	Seasons Played	Apps	Subs	Gls
Bristol C.	A.G. Farmers	12.47	48-53	71	-	0
Millwall	Tr	03.58	57-58	16	-	0

MORGAN, Trevor J.
Forest Gate, 30 September, 1956 (F)

League Club	Source	Date Signed	Seasons Played	Apps	Subs	Gls
Bournemouth	Leytonstone	09.80	80-81	53	0	13
Mansfield T.	Tr	11.81	81	12	0	6
Bournemouth	Tr	03.82	81-83	88	0	33
Bristol C.	Tr	03.84	83-84	32	0	8
Exeter C.	Tr	11.84	84-85	30	0	9
Bristol Rov.	Tr	09.85	85-86	54	1	24
Bristol C.	Tr	01.87	86	19	0	7
Bolton W.	Tr	06.87	87-88	65	12	17
Colchester U.	Tr	10.89	89	31	1	12
Exeter C.	Happy Valley (HK)	11.90	90	14	3	3

MORGAN, Wendell
Gorseinon, 22 April, 1935 (W)

League Club	Source	Date Signed	Seasons Played	Apps	Subs	Gls
Cardiff C.	Jnrs	05.52				
Brentford	Tr	06.54	55-57	47	-	6
Gillingham	Tr	09.57	57	34	-	3
Swansea C.	Tr	07.58	58	7	-	0
Newport Co.	Tr	06.59	59	26	-	3
Carlisle U.	Tr	06.60	60	35	-	2

League Club	Source	Date Signed	Seasons Played	Career Record Apps	Subs	Gls

MORGAN, William
Glasgow, 2 October, 1944 Su23-1/S-21 (W)

League Club	Source	Date Signed	Seasons Played	Apps	Subs	Gls
Burnley	Jnrs	10.61	62-67	183	0	19
Manchester U.	Tr	08.68	68-74	236	2	25
Burnley	Tr	06.75	75	12	1	0
Bolton W.	Tr	03.76	75-79	154	1	10
Blackpool	Minnesota (USA)	09.80	80-81	41	1	4

Willie Morgan (Burnley, Manchester United, Burnley, Bolton Wanderers, Blackpool & Scotland)

MORGAN, William A.
Rotherham, 26 September, 1926 (WH)

League Club	Source	Date Signed	Seasons Played	Apps	Subs	Gls
Wolverhampton W.	Jnrs	11.43				
Sheffield U.	Tr	09.46				
Halifax T.	Tr	08.48	48-52	109	-	3
Rochdale	Tr	07.53	53-54	29	-	0

MORGAN, Wynffrwd
Abergwynfl, 7 August, 1925 (OR)

League Club	Source	Date Signed	Seasons Played	Apps	Subs	Gls
Bristol Rov. (Am)		12.46	46	2	-	0

MORGANS, Jeffrey
Farnborough, 12 August, 1942 (OR)

League Club	Source	Date Signed	Seasons Played	Apps	Subs	Gls
Crewe Alex.	Jnrs	09.59	60-61	9	-	2

MORGANS, Kenneth G.
Swansea, 16 March, 1939 Wu23-2 (IF)

League Club	Source	Date Signed	Seasons Played	Apps	Subs	Gls
Manchester U.	Jnrs	04.56	57-60	17	-	0
Swansea C.	Tr	03.61	60-63	55	-	8
Newport Co.	Tr	06.64	64-66	125	0	46

MORGANS, Morgan G.
Blaenau Ffestiniog, 20 April, 1932 (HB)

League Club	Source	Date Signed	Seasons Played	Apps	Subs	Gls
Northampton T.		08.55				
Wrexham	Tr	07.56	56-57	29	-	2
Southport	Tr	07.58	58	14	-	0

MORLEY, Anthony W.
Ormskirk, 26 August, 1954 E Yth/Eu23-1/E'B'/E-6 (LW)

League Club	Source	Date Signed	Seasons Played	Apps	Subs	Gls
Preston N.E.	App	08.72	72-75	78	6	15
Burnley	Tr	02.76	75-78	78	13	5
Aston Villa	Tr	06.79	79-83	128	9	25
West Bromwich A.	Tr	12.83	83-84	33	0	4
Birmingham C.	L	11.84	84	4	0	3
West Bromwich A.	Den Haag (Neth)	08.87	87	27	1	7
Burnley	L	10.88	88	5	0	0

Tony Morley (Preston North End, Burnley, Aston Villa, West Bromwich Albion, Den Haag, West Bromwich Albion & England)

MORLEY, Brian J.
Fleetwood, 4 October, 1960 (LB)

League Club	Source	Date Signed	Seasons Played	Apps	Subs	Gls
Blackburn Rov.	App	10.78	78-79	20	0	0
Tranmere Rov.	Tr	08.81	81	10	6	2

MORLEY, Trevor W.
Nottingham, 20 March, 1961 E Semi-Pro (F)

League Club	Source	Date Signed	Seasons Played	Apps	Subs	Gls
Northampton T.	Nuneaton Bor.	06.85	85-87	107	0	39
Manchester C.	Tr	01.88	87-89	69	3	18
West Ham U.	Tr	12.89	89-91	69	12	24

MORLEY, William
Nottingham, 30 July, 1925 Died 1981 (WH)

League Club	Source	Date Signed	Seasons Played	Apps	Subs	Gls
Nottingham F.	Mapperley Celtic	08.45	46-58	282	-	10

MORONEY, Thomas
Cork (Ire), 10 November, 1923 Died 1981 LOI/IR-12 (WH)

League Club	Source	Date Signed	Seasons Played	Apps	Subs	Gls
West Ham U.	Cork U.	08.47	47-52	148	-	8

MORRAD, Frank G.
Brentford, 28 February, 1920 (CF)

League Club	Source	Date Signed	Seasons Played	Apps	Subs	Gls
Notts Co.		08.44	46	1	-	0
Leyton Orient	Tr	11.46	46	25	-	11
Fulham	Tr	08.47				
Brighton & H.A.	Tr	02.48	47-50	43	-	3
Brentford	Tr	08.51	51-52	7	-	2

MORRALL, Alfred D.
Birmingham, 1 July, 1916 (WH)

League Club	Source	Date Signed	Seasons Played	Apps	Subs	Gls
Northampton T.		10.44	46-47	34	-	1
Newport Co.	Tr	07.48	48	28	-	0

League Club	Source	Date Signed	Seasons Played	Apps	Subs	Gls

MORRALL, Stephen A.
Torquay, 25 September, 1952 (W)

League Club	Source	Date Signed	Seasons Played	Apps	Subs	Gls
Torquay U.	Jnrs	08.72	72-76	133	31	12

MORRALL, Terence S.
Smethwick, 24 November, 1938 (CH)

League Club	Source	Date Signed	Seasons Played	Apps	Subs	Gls
Aston Villa	Jnrs	11.55	59-60	8	-	0
Shrewsbury T.	Tr	05.61	60-62	31	-	0
Wrexham	Tr	07.63	63-64	42	-	0
Southport	Tr	07.65	65	1	0	0

MORRELL, Paul D. P.
Poole, 23 March, 1961 (LB)

League Club	Source	Date Signed	Seasons Played	Apps	Subs	Gls
Bournemouth	Weymouth	06.83	83-91	317	5	8

MORRELL, Robert I.
Heselden (Dm), 4 June, 1944 (WH)

League Club	Source	Date Signed	Seasons Played	Apps	Subs	Gls
Hartlepool U.		03.64	63-64	34	-	0

MORREY, Bernard J.
Liverpool, 8 April, 1927 (OR)

League Club	Source	Date Signed	Seasons Played	Apps	Subs	Gls
Tranmere Rov.		08.44				
Newport Co.	Llandudno	10.52	52-53	24	-	2
Chester C.	Tr	12.53	53-54	29	-	6

MORRIN, Anthony J.
Swinton, 31 July, 1946 (M)

League Club	Source	Date Signed	Seasons Played	Apps	Subs	Gls
Bury	App	10.63	63-64	3	-	0
Burnley	Tr	07.65				
Stockport Co.		10.66	66-68	27	5	2
Barrow	Tr	03.69	68-70	97	3	6
Exeter C.	Tr	07.71	71-76	180	2	15
Stockport Co.	Tr	03.77	76	13	0	1
Rochdale	Tr	08.77	77-78	29	1	0

MORRIS, Alan
Swansea, 6 April, 1941 (W)

League Club	Source	Date Signed	Seasons Played	Apps	Subs	Gls
Swansea C.	Jnrs	06.58	57-62	12	-	1
Reading	Tr	08.63	63	12	-	0

MORRIS, Alan G.
Chester, 15 July, 1954 (D)

League Club	Source	Date Signed	Seasons Played	Apps	Subs	Gls
Chester C.	Bangor C.	06.84	84	0	1	0

MORRIS, Alfred
Cadishead (WH)

League Club	Source	Date Signed	Seasons Played	Apps	Subs	Gls
Accrington St.		10.45	46-47	15	-	0

MORRIS, Andrew D.
Sheffield, 17 November, 1967 (F)

League Club	Source	Date Signed	Seasons Played	Apps	Subs	Gls
Rotherham U.	Jnrs	07.85	84-86	0	7	0
Chesterfield	Tr	01.88	87-91	105	13	19
Exeter C.	L	03.92	91	4	3	2

MORRIS, Christopher B.
Newquay, 24 December, 1963 E Sch/IR-34 (FB)

League Club	Source	Date Signed	Seasons Played	Apps	Subs	Gls
Sheffield Wed.		10.82	83-86	61	13	1

MORRIS, Christopher J.
Spilsby (Lincs), 12 October, 1939 (OR)

League Club	Source	Date Signed	Seasons Played	Apps	Subs	Gls
Hull C.	Jnrs	10.57	58-60	17	-	4
York C.	Tr	06.61				

MORRIS, Colin
Blyth, 22 August, 1953 (RW)

League Club	Source	Date Signed	Seasons Played	Apps	Subs	Gls
Burnley	App	08.71	74-75	9	1	0
Southend U.	Tr	01.77	76-79	133	0	25
Blackpool	Tr	12.79	79-81	87	0	26
Sheffield U.	Tr	02.82	81-87	235	5	68
Scarborough	Tr	07.88	88-89	20	4	3

MORRIS, David K.
Greenwich, 19 November, 1971 (CD)

League Club	Source	Date Signed	Seasons Played	Apps	Subs	Gls
Bournemouth	YT	07.90	90	0	1	0

MORRIS, David M.
Swansea, 20 September, 1957 (F)

League Club	Source	Date Signed	Seasons Played	Apps	Subs	Gls
Manchester U.	App	10.74				
York C.	L	03.77	76	1	6	0

MORRIS, Douglas
Durham, 29 July, 1925

League Club	Source	Date Signed	Seasons Played	Apps	Subs	Gls
Hartlepool U.		01.46	46-50	19	-	3

MORRIS, Edwin C.
Pontypool, 6 May, 1921 (G)

League Club	Source	Date Signed	Seasons Played	Apps	Subs	Gls
Cardiff C.	Bewdley	05.48	48-50	8	-	0

MORRIS, Elfed
Colwyn Bay, 9 June, 1942 (OL)

League Club	Source	Date Signed	Seasons Played	Apps	Subs	Gls
Wrexham		05.60	60-61	11	-	6
Chester C.	Tr	06.62	62-67	164	3	69
Halifax T.	Tr	03.68	67-68	9	0	2

MORRIS, E. Eric
Mold, 15 April, 1940 (FB)

League Club	Source	Date Signed	Seasons Played	Apps	Subs	Gls
Chester C.		06.60	60	1	-	0

MORRIS, Ernest
Stocksbridge, 11 May, 1921 (CF)

League Club	Source	Date Signed	Seasons Played	Apps	Subs	Gls
Nottingham F.		08.47	47	4	-	1
York C.	Tr	06.48				
Halifax T.	Grantham	11.50	50	1	-	0

MORRIS, Frank
Penge, 28 March, 1932 (OL)

League Club	Source	Date Signed	Seasons Played	Apps	Subs	Gls
Crystal Palace		03.56	56	8	-	0

MORRIS, Frederick A.
Sheffield, 11 March, 1920 Died 1973 (W)

League Club	Source	Date Signed	Seasons Played	Apps	Subs	Gls
Barnsley		09.46	46-48	23	-	9
Southend U.	Tr	01.49	48-49	34	-	16

MORRIS, Frederick W.
Oswestry, 15 June, 1929 (OR)

League Club	Source	Date Signed	Seasons Played	Apps	Subs	Gls
Walsall	Oswestry T.	05.50	50-56	210	-	43
Mansfield T.	Tr	03.57	56-57	56	-	17
Liverpool	Tr	05.58	58-59	47	-	14
Crewe Alex.	Tr	06.60	60	8	-	1
Gillingham	Tr	01.61	60	11	-	1
Chester C.	Tr	07.61	61	27	-	3

MORRIS, Geoffrey
Birmingham, 8 February, 1949 (OL)

League Club	Source	Date Signed	Seasons Played	Apps	Subs	Gls
Walsall	App	02.66	65-72	172	5	35
Shrewsbury T.	Tr	01.73	72-74	71	4	9
Port Vale	Tr	08.75	75	10	5	1

MORRIS, George E.
Birkenhead, 22 November, 1929 (FB)

League Club	Source	Date Signed	Seasons Played	Apps	Subs	Gls
Crewe Alex.	Crewe Cadets	08.48	48-54	30	-	0

MORRIS, Gordon J.
Wrottesley, 27 June, 1926 (OL)

League Club	Source	Date Signed	Seasons Played	Apps	Subs	Gls
West Bromwich A.	East Park	11.44				
Walsall	Tr	07.49	49-50	9	-	2

MORRIS, Ian G.
Manchester, 10 June, 1948 (W)

League Club	Source	Date Signed	Seasons Played	Apps	Subs	Gls
Stockport Co.	Bolton W. (Am)	03.68	67	1	1	0

MORRIS, James
St Helens, 16 November, 1915 (CH)

League Club	Source	Date Signed	Seasons Played	Apps	Subs	Gls
Stockport Co.	St Helens T.	08.39	46-48	61	-	3

MORRIS, John
Radcliffe, 27 September, 1924 E'B'-1/EF Lge/E-3 (IF)

League Club	Source	Date Signed	Seasons Played	Apps	Subs	Gls
Manchester U.	Jnrs	03.41	46-48	83	-	32
Derby Co.	Tr	03.49	48-52	130	-	44
Leicester C.	Tr	10.52	52-57	206	-	33

MORRIS, John E.
Crewe, 27 November, 1937

League Club	Source	Date Signed	Seasons Played	Apps	Subs	Gls
Crewe Alex.	Jnrs	12.54	54	3	-	0

MORRIS, John R.
Canning Town, 13 April, 1934

League Club	Source	Date Signed	Seasons Played	Apps	Subs	Gls
Crewe Alex.		08.54	54	1	-	0

MORRIS, Kevin G.
Much Wenlock, 22 September, 1953 (RB)

League Club	Source	Date Signed	Seasons Played	Apps	Subs	Gls
Shrewsbury T.	App	07.71	70-71	9	0	0

MORRIS, Maldwyn J. G.
Swansea, 3 August, 1932 (F)

League Club	Source	Date Signed	Seasons Played	Apps	Subs	Gls
Swansea C.	Pembroke Bor.	10.56	56-57	15	-	5

MORRIS, Mark
Chester, 1 August, 1968 (G)

League Club	Source	Date Signed	Seasons Played	Apps	Subs	Gls
Wrexham	YT	08.87	85-91	63	0	0

MORRIS, Mark J.
Morden, 26 September, 1962 (CD)

League Club	Source	Date Signed	Seasons Played	Apps	Subs	Gls
Wimbledon	App	09.80	81-86	167	1	9
Aldershot	L	09.85	85	14	0	0
Watford	Tr	07.87	87-88	41	0	1
Sheffield U.	Tr	07.89	89-90	53	3	3
Bournemouth	Tr	07.91	91	43	0	3

MORRIS, Michael J.
Plaistow, 20 January, 1943 (W)

League Club	Source	Date Signed	Seasons Played	Apps	Subs	Gls
Oxford U.	Faversham	07.64	64-66	89	1	15
Port Vale	Tr	08.67	67-71	176	7	25

MORRIS, Neil A.
Sheffield, 3 May, 1970 (F)

League Club	Source	Date Signed	Seasons Played	Apps	Subs	Gls
York C.	Doncaster Rov. (YT)	09.88	88	3	1	0
Doncaster R. (N/C)		02.92	91	0	1	0

MORRIS, Paul W.
Glasfryn, 8 January, 1957 (F)

League Club	Source	Date Signed	Seasons Played	Apps	Subs	Gls
Hereford U.	Llanelli	02.80	79-80	2	2	1

MORRIS, Peter A.
Farnworth, 23 November, 1958 (W)

League Club	Source	Date Signed	Seasons Played	Apps	Subs	Gls
Preston N.E.	App	10.76				
Blackburn Rov.	Tr	07.78	78	2	2	0

MORRIS, Peter J.
New Houghton, 8 November, 1943 (M)

League Club	Source	Date Signed	Seasons Played	Apps	Subs	Gls
Mansfield T.	Jnrs	11.60	60-67	286	1	50
Ipswich T.	Tr	03.68	67-73	213	7	13
Norwich C.	Tr	06.74	74-75	66	0	1
Mansfield T.	Tr	07.76	76-77	41	0	3
Peterborough U.	Newcastle U. (Coach)	08.79	79	1	0	0

MORRIS, Ronald
Birmingham, 25 September, 1970 (W)

League Club	Source	Date Signed	Seasons Played	Apps	Subs	Gls
Birmingham C.	YT	09.88	87-88	3	8	0

MORRIS, Samuel
Warrington, 12 February, 1930 (WH)

League Club	Source	Date Signed	Seasons Played	Apps	Subs	Gls
Chester C.	Stockton Heath	12.51	51-56	92	-	0

MORRIS, Stephen A.
Bristol, 6 July, 1949 (M/LB)

League Club	Source	Date Signed	Seasons Played	Apps	Subs	Gls
Bristol C.	App	06.67				
Exeter C.	Tr	06.69	69-71	61	11	2

MORRIS, Steven G.
Swansea, 8 October, 1958 (LB)

League Club	Source	Date Signed	Seasons Played	Apps	Subs	Gls
Swansea C.	App	06.76	75-78	33	6	1
Plymouth Arg.	Tr	01.80				

MORRIS, William
Radcliffe, 1 April, 1931

League Club	Source	Date Signed	Seasons Played	Apps	Subs	Gls
Bury	Jnrs	05.48				
Derby Co.	Tr	10.51				
Rochdale	Tr	11.52	52	4	-	1

MORRIS, William
Colwyn Bay, 30 July, 1918 W-5 (IF)

League Club	Source	Date Signed	Seasons Played	Apps	Subs	Gls
Burnley	Llandudno	01.39	38-52	211	-	47

MORRIS, William H.
Swansea, 28 September, 1920

League Club	Source	Date Signed	Seasons Played	Apps	Subs	Gls
Swansea C.		05.46	47-48	16	-	1
Brighton & H.A.	Tr	09.49	49-50	27	-	4

MORRIS, William W.
Birmingham, 26 March, 1913 E-3 (FB)

League Club	Source	Date Signed	Seasons Played	Apps	Subs	Gls
Wolverhampton W.	Halesowen T.	05.33	33-46	175	-	2

MORRISON, Andrew C.
Inverness, 30 July, 1970 (D/M)

League Club	Source	Date Signed	Seasons Played	Apps	Subs	Gls
Plymouth Arg.	YT	07.88	87-91	76	8	7

MORRISON, Angus C.
Dingwall, 26 April, 1924 S'B'-1 (OL)

League Club	Source	Date Signed	Seasons Played	Apps	Subs	Gls
Derby Co.	Ross Co.	10.44	46-47	52	-	21
Preston N.E.	Tr	11.48	48-56	262	-	70
Millwall	Tr	10.57	57	15	-	4

MORRISON, Charles
Newton Aycliffe, 12 January, 1953 (D)

League Club	Source	Date Signed	Seasons Played	Apps	Subs	Gls
Chelsea	App	08.70				
Doncaster Rov.	Tr	07.72	72	5	1	0

MORRISON, George C.
Ayr, 27 November, 1924

League Club	Source	Date Signed	Seasons Played	Apps	Subs	Gls
Hartlepool U.	St Johnstone	08.51	51	2	-	0

MORRISON, John
Greenock, 4 August, 1929

League Club	Source	Date Signed	Seasons Played	Apps	Subs	Gls
Torquay U.	Morton	07.51	51	2	-	0

MORRISON, John
Kettering, 27 July, 1970 (M)

League Club	Source	Date Signed	Seasons Played	Apps	Subs	Gls
Torquay U.	YT	07.88	88-89	24	8	0

MORRISON, Murdoch
Glasgow, 9 October, 1924 Died 1975 (G)

League Club	Source	Date Signed	Seasons Played	Apps	Subs	Gls
Luton T.	Bell Haven Star	09.45	46	1	-	0
Leyton Orient	Tr	08.47	47	10	-	0

MORRISON, Robert
Glasgow, 16 February, 1933 (IF)

League Club	Source	Date Signed	Seasons Played	Apps	Subs	Gls
Nottingham F.	Glasgow Rangers	07.58	58	1	-	0
Workington	Tr	07.59	59-60	53	-	20

MORRISON, Thomas
Croy, 6 March, 1943 (IF)

League Club	Source	Date Signed	Seasons Played	Apps	Subs	Gls
Port Vale	Aberdeen	08.65	65	5	1	0

MORRISON, William
Edinburgh, 31 March, 1934 (WH)

League Club	Source	Date Signed	Seasons Played	Apps	Subs	Gls
Sunderland	Merchiston Th.	05.51	54-56	19	-	0
Southend U.	Tr	01.58	57-59	60	-	4

MORRISON, William
Croy, 10 October, 1939 (FB)

League Club	Source	Date Signed	Seasons Played	Apps	Subs	Gls
Portsmouth	Croy Guilds	05.58	58	3	-	0

MORRISSEY, John J.
Liverpool, 18 April, 1940 E Sch/EF Lge (OL)

League Club	Source	Date Signed	Seasons Played	Apps	Subs	Gls
Liverpool	Jnrs	05.57	57-60	36	-	6
Everton	Tr	09.62	62-71	257	2	43
Oldham Ath.	Tr	05.72	72	6	0	1

MORRISSEY, John J.
Liverpool, 8 March, 1965 E Yth (RW)

League Club	Source	Date Signed	Seasons Played	Apps	Subs	Gls
Everton	App	03.83	84	1	0	0
Wolverhampton W.	Tr	08.85	85	5	5	1
Tranmere Rov.	Tr	10.85	85-91	237	21	38

MORRISSEY, Patrick J.
Enniscorthy (Ire), 23 February, 1948 (M)

League Club	Source	Date Signed	Seasons Played	Apps	Subs	Gls
Coventry C.	App	07.65	66-67	6	4	0
Torquay U.	Tr	07.68	68	19	2	0
Crewe Alex.	Tr	07.69	69-71	95	1	28
Chester C.	Tr	10.71	71	9	0	1
Watford	Tr	12.71	71-74	101	6	27
Aldershot	Tr	11.74	74-76	109	0	27
Swansea C.	L	10.77	77	3	1	0

MORRITT, Gordon R.
Rotherham, 8 February, 1942 (G)

League Club	Source	Date Signed	Seasons Played	Apps	Subs	Gls
Rotherham U.	Steel Peach & Tozer	06.61	61-65	77	0	0
Doncaster Rov.	Durban C. (SA)	09.67	67-68	40	0	0
Northampton T.	Tr	08.68	68-69	42	0	0
York C.	Tr	10.69	69-71	41	0	0
Rochdale	Tr	08.72	72	31	0	0
Darlington	Tr	08.73	73	34	0	0

MORROW, Grant R.
Glasgow, 4 October, 1970 (F)

League Club	Source	Date Signed	Seasons Played	Apps	Subs	Gls
Doncaster Rov.	Rowntree-Mackintosh	07.89	89-91	29	12	3

MORROW, Hugh J. E.
Larne (NI), 9 July, 1930 (OR)

League Club	Source	Date Signed	Seasons Played	Apps	Subs	Gls
West Bromwich A.	Jnrs	08.47	48	5	-	2
Northampton T.	Lockheed Leamington	06.56	56	30	-	3

MORROW, Stephen J.
Bangor (NI), 2 July, 1970 NI Sch/NI Yth/NIu21-1/NI-7 (D)

League Club	Source	Date Signed	Seasons Played	Apps	Subs	Gls
Arsenal	YT	05.88	91	0	2	0
Reading	L	01.91	90	10	0	0
Watford	L	08.91	91	7	1	0
Reading	L	10.91	91	3	0	0
Barnet	L	03.92	91	1	0	0

MORSE, Richard A.
Newport, 17 December, 1966 (D)

League Club	Source	Date Signed	Seasons Played	Apps	Subs	Gls
Newport Co. (N/C)	Jnrs	08.83	83	0	1	0

MORTENSEN, Henrik
Denmark, 12 February, 1968 (F)

League Club	Source	Date Signed	Seasons Played	Apps	Subs	Gls
Norwich C.	Aarhus G.F. (Den)	10.89	89-90	12	6	0

MORTENSEN, Stanley H.
South Shields, 26 May, 1921 Died 1991 EF Lge/E-25 (CF)

League Club	Source	Date Signed	Seasons Played	Apps	Subs	Gls
Blackpool	Jnrs	05.38	46-55	317	-	197
Hull C.	Tr	11.55	55-56	42	-	18
Southport	Tr	02.57	56-57	36	-	10

Stan Mortensen (Blackpool, Hull City, Southport & England)

MORTIMER, Dennis G.
Liverpool, 5 April, 1952 E Yth/Eu23-6/E'B' (M)

League Club	Source	Date Signed	Seasons Played	Apps	Subs	Gls
Coventry C.	App	09.69	69-75	179	14	10
Aston Villa	Tr	12.75	75-84	316	1	31
Sheffield U.	L	12.84	84	7	0	0
Brighton & H.A.	Tr	08.85	85	40	0	2
Birmingham C.	Tr	08.86	86	33	0	4

MORTIMER, John M.
Birkenhead, 5 December, 1923 (FB)

League Club	Source	Date Signed	Seasons Played	Apps	Subs	Gls
Wrexham		01.47	46-48	23	-	0
New Brighton	Tr	10.49	49-50	5	-	0

MORTIMER, Paul H.
Kensington, 8 May, 1968 Eu21-2 (M)

League Club	Source	Date Signed	Seasons Played	Apps	Subs	Gls
Charlton Ath.	Farnborough T.	09.87	87-90	108	5	17
Aston Villa	Tr	07.91	91	10	2	1
Crystal Palace	Tr	10.91	91	17	4	2

MORTIMORE, Charles T.
Gosport, 12 April, 1928 E Amat (CF)

League Club	Source	Date Signed	Seasons Played	Apps	Subs	Gls
Aldershot (Am)	Woking	08.49	49-52	67	-	27
Portsmouth (Am)	Woking	10.53	53	1	-	0
Aldershot (Am)	Woking	12.55	55	2	-	0

MORTIMORE, John H.
Farnborough, 23 September, 1934 E Amat/E Yth (CH)

League Club	Source	Date Signed	Seasons Played	Apps	Subs	Gls
Chelsea	Woking	04.56	55-64	249	-	8
Queens Park R.	Tr	09.65	65	10	0	0

MORTON, Alan
Erith, 13 April, 1950 (CF)

League Club	Source	Date Signed	Seasons Played	Apps	Subs	Gls
Crystal Palace	Woking	11.67				
Stockport Co.	L	08.69	69	10	2	1
Fulham	Nuneaton Bor.	08.70	70	1	0	1

MORTON, Alan
Peterborough, 6 March, 1942 (IF)

League Club	Source	Date Signed	Seasons Played	Apps	Subs	Gls
Arsenal	Peterborough U.	04.59				
Peterborough U.	Tr	10.61	61-62	7	-	2
Lincoln C.	Wisbech T.	07.63	63-64	58	-	20
Chesterfield	Tr	07.65	65	28	1	6

MORTON, Albert
Newcastle, 27 July, 1919 (G)

League Club	Source	Date Signed	Seasons Played	Apps	Subs	Gls
Sheffield Wed.	St Peters A.	03.38	47-50	41	-	0
Rochdale	Tr	07.53	53-56	89	-	0

MORTON, Geoffrey D.
Acton, 27 July, 1922 (G)

League Club	Source	Date Signed	Seasons Played	Apps	Subs	Gls
Watford	Chelmsford C.	10.48	48-51	107	-	0
Southend U.	Tr	02.52	51-52	25	-	0
Exeter C.		09.54	54	6	-	0

MORTON, George E.
Liverpool, 30 September, 1943 (IF)

League Club	Source	Date Signed	Seasons Played	Apps	Subs	Gls
Everton	Jnrs	10.60				
Rochdale	Tr	07.62	62-65	146	1	51

MORTON, Gerald W.
Newcastle, 17 March, 1944 (CH)

League Club	Source	Date Signed	Seasons Played	Apps	Subs	Gls
Newcastle U.	North Shields	08.62				
Workington	Tr	04.63	62-63	3	-	0

MORTON, Keith
Ferryhill, 11 August, 1934 (CF)

League Club	Source	Date Signed	Seasons Played	Apps	Subs	Gls
Crystal Palace (Am)		08.53	53	5	-	3
Sunderland	Tr	07.54				
Darlington	Tr	05.55	55-60	175	-	50

MORTON, Kenneth
Chorley, 19 May, 1947 E Sch (OL)

League Club	Source	Date Signed	Seasons Played	Apps	Subs	Gls
Manchester U.	App	05.64				
York C.	Tr	05.65	65	9	1	2
Blackpool	Tr	08.66				
Darlington	Fleetwood	07.68	68	3	1	0

Dennis Mortimer (Coventry City, Aston Villa, Brighton & Hove Albion & Birmingham City)

League Club	Source	Date Signed	Seasons Played	Career Record Apps	Subs	Gls

MORTON, Neil
Congleton, 21 December, 1968 (W)

League Club	Source	Date Signed	Seasons Played	Apps	Subs	Gls
Crewe Alex.	YT	09.87	86-88	18	13	1
Chester C.	Northwich Vic.	10.90	90-91	43	25	9

MORTON, Norman
Barnsley, 22 May, 1925 Died 1977 (CF)

League Club	Source	Date Signed	Seasons Played	Apps	Subs	Gls
Leeds U.	Woolley Colly	12.47	47	1	-	0

MORTON, Robert H.
Aston Clinton, 25 September, 1927 E'B'-1 (WH)

League Club	Source	Date Signed	Seasons Played	Apps	Subs	Gls
Luton T.	Eaton Bray	02.46	48-63	494	-	49

MORTON, Roy S.
Birmingham, 29 October, 1955 E Yth (M)

League Club	Source	Date Signed	Seasons Played	Apps	Subs	Gls
Manchester U.	App	11.72				
Birmingham C.	Tr	09.73	74	3	0	0

MORTON, William
Grangemouth, 2 April, 1928 (CH)

League Club	Source	Date Signed	Seasons Played	Apps	Subs	Gls
Millwall		10.45	46-50	11	-	0

MOSBY, Harold
Kippax, 25 June, 1926 (F)

League Club	Source	Date Signed	Seasons Played	Apps	Subs	Gls
Rotherham U.	Huddersfield T. (Am)	01.47	47-49	25	-	9
Scunthorpe U.	Tr	07.50	50-54	147	-	22
Crewe Alex.	Worksop T.	08.56	56	38	-	4

MOSELEY, Graham
Manchester, 16 November, 1953 E Yth (G)

League Club	Source	Date Signed	Seasons Played	Apps	Subs	Gls
Blackburn Rov.	App	09.71				
Derby Co.	Tr	09.71	72-76	32	0	0
Aston Villa	L	08.74	74	3	0	0
Walsall	L	10.77	77	3	0	0
Brighton & H.A.	Tr	11.77	77-85	189	0	0
Cardiff C.	Tr	08.86	86-87	38	0	0

MOSES, George
High Spen, 11 September, 1920 (IR)

League Club	Source	Date Signed	Seasons Played	Apps	Subs	Gls
Newcastle U.		10.39				
Hartlepool U.	Tr	08.46	46	19	-	4

MOSES, Remi M.
Manchester, 14 November, 1960 Eu21-8 (M)

League Club	Source	Date Signed	Seasons Played	Apps	Subs	Gls
West Bromwich A.	App	11.78	79-81	63	0	5
Manchester U.	Tr	09.81	81-87	143	7	7

MOSS, Amos
Birmingham, 28 August, 1921 (WH)

League Club	Source	Date Signed	Seasons Played	Apps	Subs	Gls
Aston Villa	Jnrs	05.39	46-55	103	-	5

MOSS, Craig A.
Birmingham, 11 March, 1961 (W)

League Club	Source	Date Signed	Seasons Played	Apps	Subs	Gls
Wolverhampton W.	App	03.79	78-81	4	0	0

MOSS, David J.
Witney, 18 March, 1952 (W)

League Club	Source	Date Signed	Seasons Played	Apps	Subs	Gls
Swindon T.	Witney T.	07.69	71-77	217	13	60
Luton T.	Tr	05.78	78-84	218	3	88
Swindon T.	Tr	07.85	85	4	0	0

MOSS, Donald R.
Tamworth, 27 June, 1925 (WH)

League Club	Source	Date Signed	Seasons Played	Apps	Subs	Gls
Cardiff C.	Boldmere St Michael	05.51				
Crystal Palace	Tr	05.53	53-56	56	-	2

MOSS, Edward
Skelmersdale, 27 October, 1939 (IF)

League Club	Source	Date Signed	Seasons Played	Apps	Subs	Gls
Liverpool	Skelmersdale U.	10.58				
Southport	Tr	07.59	59-60	51	-	15

MOSS, Ernest
Chesterfield, 19 October, 1949 (F)

League Club	Source	Date Signed	Seasons Played	Apps	Subs	Gls
Chesterfield	Chesterfield Tube	10.68	68-75	271	0	95
Peterborough U.	Tr	01.76	75-76	34	1	9
Mansfield T.	Tr	12.76	76-78	56	1	21
Chesterfield	Tr	01.79	78-80	105	2	33
Port Vale	Tr	06.81	81-82	74	0	23
Lincoln C.	Tr	03.83	82	10	1	2
Doncaster Rov.	Tr	06.83	83	41	3	15
Chesterfield	Tr	07.84	84-86	90	1	33
Stockport Co.	Tr	12.86	86	26	0	7
Scarborough	Tr	08.87	87	22	1	4
Rochdale	L	03.88	87	10	0	2

MOSS, Frank
Birmingham, 16 September, 1917 (CH)

League Club	Source	Date Signed	Seasons Played	Apps	Subs	Gls
Sheffield Wed.	Worcester Nondescripts	11.35	36-37	22	-	0
Aston Villa	Tr	05.38	38-54	296	-	3

MOSS, John (Jack)
Blackrod, 1 September, 1923 (IF)

League Club	Source	Date Signed	Seasons Played	Apps	Subs	Gls
Bury		12.43	46	7	-	2
Rochdale	Tr	01.47	46-48	58	-	17
Leeds U.	Tr	01.49	48-50	23	-	2
Halifax T.	Tr	01.51	50-53	124	-	10

MOSS, Paul M.
Birmingham, 2 August, 1957 (M)

League Club	Source	Date Signed	Seasons Played	Apps	Subs	Gls
Wolverhampton W.	Northfield Jnrs	07.76				
Hull C.	Tr	09.79	79-80	53	1	7
Scunthorpe U.	Tr	09.81	81	42	0	7

MOSS, Robert
Chigwell, 13 February, 1952 (F)

League Club	Source	Date Signed	Seasons Played	Apps	Subs	Gls
Leyton Orient	App	02.70	70	2	3	1
Colchester U.	Tr	05.72	72	16	1	3

MOSS, Robert S.
Harrow, 15 February, 1949 (W)

League Club	Source	Date Signed	Seasons Played	Apps	Subs	Gls
Fulham	App	02.66	67	8	1	3
Peterborough U.	Tr	07.69	69-72	86	18	17

Remi Moses (West Bromwich Albion & Manchester United)

MOSS, Roy G.
Maldon (Ex), 5 September, 1941 E Sch (IF)

League Club	Source	Date Signed	Seasons Played	Apps	Subs	Gls
Tottenham H.	Jnrs	01.60				
Gillingham	Tr	09.62	62-63	14	-	3

MOSS, Terence J.
Bristol, 2 January, 1932 (OL)

League Club	Source	Date Signed	Seasons Played	Apps	Subs	Gls
Swindon T. (Am)		03.56	55	7	-	0

MOSSMAN, David J.
Sheffield, 27 July, 1964 (W)

League Club	Source	Date Signed	Seasons Played	Apps	Subs	Gls
Sheffield Wed.	Jnrs	08.82				
Bradford C.	L	03.85	84	0	3	1
Stockport Co.	L	10.85	85	9	0	4
Rochdale	Tr	01.86	85	8	0	0
Stockport Co.	Tr	03.86	85-86	28	2	1

MOSSOP, Graham
Wellington, 11 January, 1958 (M)

League Club	Source	Date Signed	Seasons Played	Apps	Subs	Gls
Workington	Liverpool (App)	11.75	75	1	0	0
Carlisle U.		07.79	80	2	0	0

MOSTYN, Roger
Wrexham, 31 August, 1953 (F)

League Club	Source	Date Signed	Seasons Played	Apps	Subs	Gls
Wrexham	Jnrs	11.71	71-73	16	3	4

MOTTERSHEAD, Brian L.
Rochdale, 13 July, 1935

League Club	Source	Date Signed	Seasons Played	Apps	Subs	Gls
Notts Co.	Jnrs	09.52				
Rochdale	Tr	08.53	53	1	-	0

MOTTERSHEAD, Keith A.
Stafford, 12 December, 1944 (OR)

League Club	Source	Date Signed	Seasons Played	Apps	Subs	Gls
Doncaster Rov.	Stafford R.	10.66	66-67	34	5	0

MOUGHTON, Colin E.
Harrow, 30 December, 1947 (WH)

League Club	Source	Date Signed	Seasons Played	Apps	Subs	Gls
Queens Park R.	App	12.65	65-66	6	0	0
Colchester U.	Tr	07.68	68	4	0	0

MOULD, William
Stoke, 6 October, 1919 (FB)

League Club	Source	Date Signed	Seasons Played	Apps	Subs	Gls
Stoke C.	Summerbank	07.36	37-51	176	-	1
Crewe Alex.	Tr	07.52	52-53	66	-	1

MOULDEN, Anthony
Farnworth, 28 August, 1942 (IF)

League Club	Source	Date Signed	Seasons Played	Apps	Subs	Gls
Bury	Blackburn Rov. (Am)	05.60	60-61	4	-	0
Rochdale	Tr	06.62	62	5	-	1
Peterborough U.	Tr	11.62	62-64	62	-	9
Notts Co.	Tr	05.65	65	23	0	1
Rochdale	Tr	09.66	66	1	1	0

MOULDEN, Paul A.
Farnworth, 6 September, 1967 E Yth (F)

League Club	Source	Date Signed	Seasons Played	Apps	Subs	Gls
Manchester C.	App	09.84	85-88	48	16	18
Bournemouth	Tr	07.89	89	32	0	13
Oldham Ath.	Tr	03.90	89-91	16	18	4

MOULSON, George B.
Clogheen, 6 August, 1914 IR-3 (G)

League Club	Source	Date Signed	Seasons Played	Apps	Subs	Gls
Grimsby T.	Jnrs	07.36	46	1	-	0
Lincoln C.	Tr	06.47	47-48	60	-	0

MOUNCER, Frank E.
Grimsby, 22 November, 1920 E Sch (RB)

League Club	Source	Date Signed	Seasons Played	Apps	Subs	Gls
Grimsby T.	Humber U.	09.38	46-48	22	-	0

MOUNTAIN, Robert B.
Wombwell, 11 September, 1956 (F)

League Club	Source	Date Signed	Seasons Played	Apps	Subs	Gls
Huddersfield T.	App	11.73	73	1	0	0

MOUNTFIELD, Derek N.
Liverpool, 2 November, 1962 Eu21-1 (CD)

League Club	Source	Date Signed	Seasons Played	Apps	Subs	Gls
Tranmere Rov.	App	11.80	80-81	26	0	1
Everton	Tr	06.82	82-87	100	6	19
Aston Villa	Tr	06.88	88-91	88	2	9
Wolverhampton W.	Tr	11.91	91	28	0	1

MOUNTFORD, David
Hanley, 9 January, 1931 (W)

League Club	Source	Date Signed	Seasons Played	Apps	Subs	Gls
Crewe Alex.	Jnrs	11.48	48-51	33	-	5
West Bromwich A.	Tr	12.51	52	4	-	0
Crewe Alex.	Tr	10.53	53-56	27	-	7

MOUNTFORD, Derek
Stoke, 24 March, 1934 (HB)

League Club	Source	Date Signed	Seasons Played	Apps	Subs	Gls
Port Vale	Jnrs	05.51	54-56	26	-	0
Crewe Alex.	Tr	07.57	57	13	-	0

MOUNTFORD, Frank
Stoke, 30 March, 1923 (CH)

League Club	Source	Date Signed	Seasons Played	Apps	Subs	Gls
Stoke C.	Jnrs	04.40	46-57	392	-	21

MOUNTFORD, George F.
Stoke, 30 March, 1921 (IF)

League Club	Source	Date Signed	Seasons Played	Apps	Subs	Gls
Stoke C.	Jnrs	09.38	46-52	147	-	27
Queens Park R.	Tr	10.52	52-53	34	-	2

MOUNTFORD, Peter
Stoke, 13 September, 1960 (M)

League Club	Source	Date Signed	Seasons Played	Apps	Subs	Gls
Norwich C.	App	09.78	81-82	1	3	0
Charlton Ath.	Tr	09.83	83	10	1	1
Leyton Orient	Tr	01.85	84-86	27	6	2

MOUNTFORD, Raymond
Mexborough, 28 April, 1958 (G)

League Club	Source	Date Signed	Seasons Played	Apps	Subs	Gls
Manchester U.	App	04.75				
Rotherham U.	Tr	07.78	78-82	123	0	0
Bury	L	11.83	83	4	0	0

MOUNTFORD, Robert W.
Stoke, 23 February, 1952 (F)

League Club	Source	Date Signed	Seasons Played	Apps	Subs	Gls
Port Vale	App	02.70	68-74	64	13	9
Scunthorpe U.	L	10.74	74	1	2	0
Crewe Alex.	L	12.74	74	5	0	0
Rochdale	Tr	01.75	74-77	97	1	37
Huddersfield T.	Tr	10.77	77	12	2	4
Halifax T.	Tr	03.78	77-79	56	6	11
Crewe Alex.	Tr	08.80	80	3	0	0
Stockport Co.	Tr	11.80	80	6	1	3

MOVERLEY, Robert
Batley, 18 January, 1969 (G)

League Club	Source	Date Signed	Seasons Played	Apps	Subs	Gls
Bradford C.	YT	06.87				
Hartlepool U.	Tr	12.88	88-89	29	0	0

MOWBRAY, Anthony M.
Saltburn, 22 November, 1963 E'B' (CD)

League Club	Source	Date Signed	Seasons Played	Apps	Subs	Gls
Middlesbrough	App	11.81	82-91	345	3	25

Derek Mountfield (Tranmere Rovers, Everton, Aston Villa & Wolverhampton Wanderers)

League Club	Source	Date Signed	Seasons Played	Apps	Subs	Gls

MOWBRAY, Henry
Hamilton, 1 May, 1947 (FB)

League Club	Source	Date Signed	Seasons Played	Apps	Subs	Gls
Blackpool	Cowdenbeath	05.67	67-70	88	3	0
Bolton W.	Tr	06.71	71-72	31	0	0

MOWER, Kenneth M.
Walsall, 1 December, 1960 (LB)

League Club	Source	Date Signed	Seasons Played	Apps	Subs	Gls
Walsall	App	11.78	78-90	410	5	8

MOWL, William J.
Bulwell, 23 June, 1922 (G)

League Club	Source	Date Signed	Seasons Played	Apps	Subs	Gls
Notts Co.		10.44	48	3	-	0
Mansfield T.	Tr	07.49				

MOXHAM, Graham
Exeter, 3 January, 1949 (W)

League Club	Source	Date Signed	Seasons Played	Apps	Subs	Gls
Bournemouth	Preston N.E. (App)	07.66				
Exeter C.	Bideford	07.75	75	4	2	0

MOXHAM, Robert
Barrow, 5 July, 1922 (CF)

League Club	Source	Date Signed	Seasons Played	Apps	Subs	Gls
Barrow	Holker C.O.B.	09.48	48	5	-	1

MOYES, David W.
Glasgow, 25 April, 1963 (CD)

League Club	Source	Date Signed	Seasons Played	Apps	Subs	Gls
Cambridge U.	Glasgow Celtic	10.83	83-85	79	0	1
Bristol C.	Tr	10.85	85-87	83	0	6
Shrewsbury T.	Tr	10.87	87-89	91	5	11

MOYES, John K.
Belper, 17 July, 1951 (CD)

League Club	Source	Date Signed	Seasons Played	Apps	Subs	Gls
Chesterfield	App	07.69	68-71	13	0	0

MOYSE, Alec R.
Mitcham, 5 August, 1935 (CF)

League Club	Source	Date Signed	Seasons Played	Apps	Subs	Gls
Crystal Palace	Chatham	02.56	55-56	4	-	1
Swindon T.	Tr	08.58	58	4	-	0
Millwall	Tr	09.58	58-59	22	-	3

MOYSE, Ronald
Portsmouth, 2 April, 1920 (FB)

League Club	Source	Date Signed	Seasons Played	Apps	Subs	Gls
Reading		10.46	46-52	189	-	0

MOYSES, Christopher R.
Lincoln, 1 November, 1965 (D)

League Club	Source	Date Signed	Seasons Played	Apps	Subs	Gls
Lincoln C. (N/C)	App	11.83	83	2	2	0
Halifax T.	Tr	07.84	84	21	4	0

MOZLEY, Bertram
Derby, 23 September, 1923 EF Lge/E-3 (FB)

League Club	Source	Date Signed	Seasons Played	Apps	Subs	Gls
Derby Co.	Shelton U.	06.46	46-54	297	-	2

MUDD, Paul A.
Hull, 13 November, 1970 (FB)

League Club	Source	Date Signed	Seasons Played	Apps	Subs	Gls
Hull C.	YT	07.89	88	1	0	0
Scarborough	Tr	07.90	90-91	57	3	1

MUDIE, John K. (Jackie)
Dundee, 10 April, 1930 Died 1992 S-17 (IF)

League Club	Source	Date Signed	Seasons Played	Apps	Subs	Gls
Blackpool	Stobswell Jnrs	05.47	49-60	320	-	143
Stoke C.	Tr	03.61	60-63	89	-	32
Port Vale	Tr	11.63	63-66	54	0	9

MUGGLETON, Carl D.
Leicester, 13 September, 1968 Eu21-1 (G)

League Club	Source	Date Signed	Seasons Played	Apps	Subs	Gls
Leicester C.	App	09.86	88-91	29	0	0
Chesterfield	L	09.87	87	17	0	0
Blackpool	L	02.88	87	2	0	0
Hartlepool U.	L	10.88	88	8	0	0
Stockport Co.	L	03.90	89	4	0	0

MUHREN, Arnold J. H.
Netherlands, 2 June, 1951 (M)

League Club	Source	Date Signed	Seasons Played	Apps	Subs	Gls
Ipswich T.	Twente Enschede (Neth)	08.78	78-81	161	0	21
Manchester U.	Tr	08.82	82-84	65	5	13

Arnold Muhren (Twente Enschede, Ipswich Town & Manchester United)

League Club	Source	Date Signed	Seasons Played	Apps	Subs	Gls
MUIR, Alexander J.						
Inverkeithing, 10 December, 1923						(OR)
Liverpool	Lochgelly Violet	07.47	47	4	-	0
MUIR, Ian B.						
Motherwell, 16 February, 1929						(CH)
Bristol Rov.	Motherwell	05.53	53-56	26	-	0
Oldham Ath.	Tr	06.57	57	35	-	0
MUIR, Ian J.						
Coventry, 5 May, 1963 E Sch/E Yth						(F)
Queens Park R.	App	09.80	80	2	0	2
Burnley	L	11.82	82	1	1	1
Birmingham C.	Tr	08.83	83	1	0	0
Brighton & H.A.	Tr	02.84	83-84	3	1	0
Swindon T.	L	01.85	84	2	0	0
Tranmere Rov.	Tr	07.85	85-91	254	14	122

Ian Muir (Queens Park Rangers, Birmingham City, Brighton & Hove Albion & Tranmere Rovers)

League Club	Source	Date Signed	Seasons Played	Apps	Subs	Gls
MUIR, John G.						
Sedgley, 26 April, 1963						(F)
Doncaster Rov.	Dudley T.	02.90	89-91	64	11	18
Stockport Co.	Tr	02.92	91	3	1	0
MUIR, Maurice						
Wimbledon, 19 March, 1963 E Sch						(M)
Northampton T.	App	02.82	79-83	15	13	0
MUIR, William M.						
Ayr, 27 August, 1925						(F)
Queens Park R.	Irvine	02.49	48-52	18	-	4
Torquay U.	Tr	10.52	52	9	-	0
MUIR, William N.						
Port Glasgow, 14 August, 1934						(F)
Aldershot	St Mirren	05.56	56	7	-	4
MULDOON, John P.						
Bebington, 21 November, 1964						(W)
Wrexham	Jnrs	12.82	82-85	64	19	11

League Club	Source	Date Signed	Seasons Played	Apps	Subs	Gls
MULDOON, Terence						
Ashington, 10 August, 1951 Died 1971						(W)
Scunthorpe U. (Am)		05.70	70	1	0	0
MULGREW, Thomas						
Motherwell, 13 April, 1929						(IF)
Northampton T.	Morton	07.49	50-52	8	-	1
Newcastle U.	Tr	10.52	52-53	14	-	1
Southampton	Tr	07.54	54-61	293	-	90
Aldershot	Tr	08.62	62-64	112	-	2
MULGROVE, Keith A.						
Haltwhistle, 21 August, 1959						(FB)
Newcastle U.	App	07.77	78	0	1	0
MULHALL, George						
Falkirk, 8 May, 1936 SF Lge/S-3						(OL)
Sunderland	Aberdeen	09.62	62-68	249	4	55
MULHEARN, Kenneth J.						
Liverpool, 16 October, 1945						(G)
Everton	App	07.63				
Stockport Co.	Tr	08.64	64-67	100	0	0
Manchester C.	Tr	09.67	67-69	50	0	0
Shrewsbury T.	Tr	03.71	70-79	370	0	0
Crewe Alex.	Tr	08.80	80-81	88	0	0
MULHERON, Peter						
Glasgow, 21 June, 1921						(IF)
Crystal Palace	Tonbridge	10.48	48-49	38	-	2
MULHOLLAND, Frank G.						
Belfast, 28 October, 1927 NI Lge						(WH)
Middlesbrough	Glentoran	10.51	51-57	46	-	0
MULHOLLAND, George R.						
Ayr, 4 August, 1928						(FB)
Stoke C.		07.50	50	3	-	0
Bradford C.	Tr	07.53	53-59	277	-	0
Darlington	Tr	07.60	60-62	106	-	0
MULHOLLAND, James						
Glasgow, 10 April, 1938						(IF)
Chelsea	East Stirling	10.62	62-63	11	-	2
Barrow	Morton	08.65	65-68	132	2	47
Stockport Co.	Tr	10.68	68-69	29	4	5
Crewe Alex.	Tr	08.70	70	0	10	0
MULHOLLAND, John A.						
Dumbarton, 20 January, 1932						(F)
Southampton	Condorat Th.	12.51				
Chester C.	Tr	07.56	56	8	-	1
Halifax T.	Tr	06.57	57	8	-	1
MULHOLLAND, John R.						
Dumbarton, 7 December, 1928						(OR)
Plymouth Arg.	Renton Boys Guild	10.46				
Grimsby T.	Tr	08.49	49-50	2	-	0
Scunthorpe U.	Tr	10.50	50	6	-	1
MULKERRIN, James						
Dumbarton, 25 December, 1931 S'B'-1						(IF)
Accrington St.	Hibernian	03.57	56-58	70	-	36
Tranmere Rov.	Tr	08.59	59-60	38	-	8
MULLAN, Brendan G. J.						
Coleraine (NI), 2 January, 1950 NIu23-1						(CF)
Fulham	Coleraine	02.68	67-68	2	2	0
Millwall	Tr	07.69				
MULLARD, Albert T.						
Walsall, 22 November, 1920 Died 1985						(IF)
Walsall	Hinckley U.	11.45	46-48	63	-	12
Crewe Alex.	Tr	06.49	49-50	44	-	14
Stoke C.	Tr	08.50	50-51	21	-	3
Port Vale	Tr	09.51	51-55	164	-	22
MULLEN, Andrew						
Newcastle, 28 July, 1928						(OL)
Aston Villa		07.48				
Workington	Annfield Plain	08.51	51-52	66	-	5
Scunthorpe U.	South Shields	08.55	55-56	10	-	1
MULLEN, James						
Newcastle, 6 January, 1923 Died 1987 E Sch/E'B'-3/EF Lge/E-12						(OL)
Wolverhampton W.	Jnrs	01.40	38-58	445	-	98

League Club	Source	Date Signed	Seasons Played	Apps	Subs	Gls

MULLEN, James
Oxford, 16 March, 1947 (W)

League Club	Source	Date Signed	Seasons Played	Apps	Subs	Gls
Reading	Oxford C.	11.66	66-67	8	0	1
Charlton Ath.	Tr	11.67	67-68	7	0	0
Rotherham U.	Tr	02.69	68-73	173	3	24
Blackburn Rov.	Tr	08.74	74-75	6	4	0
Bury	Tr	06.76	76	2	2	0
Rochdale	L	03.77	76	6	2	1

MULLEN, James W.
Larne (NI), 10 January, 1921 (OL)

League Club	Source	Date Signed	Seasons Played	Apps	Subs	Gls
Barrow	Larne T.	02.46	46-47	55	-	8
Crystal Palace	Tr	07.48	48	11	-	0
Bristol C.	Tr	02.49	48-49	17	-	2
Barrow	Tr	09.50	50	9	-	0

MULLEN, James
Jarrow, 8 November, 1952 (CD)

League Club	Source	Date Signed	Seasons Played	Apps	Subs	Gls
Sheffield Wed.	App	10.70	70-79	222	8	10
Rotherham U.	Tr	08.80	80-81	49	0	1
Preston N.E.	L	11.81	81	1	0	0
Cardiff C.	Tr	03.82	81-85	128	5	12
Newport Co.	Tr	06.86	86	19	0	0

MULLEN, Roger C.
Cowbridge, 2 March, 1966 W Yth (D)

League Club	Source	Date Signed	Seasons Played	Apps	Subs	Gls
Swansea C.	App	03.84	83-84	2	1	0

MULLEN, Stephen A.
Glasgow, 8 September, 1959 (W)

League Club	Source	Date Signed	Seasons Played	Apps	Subs	Gls
Bury	Darwen	02.79	78-81	76	17	5

MULLERY, Alan P.
Notting Hill, 23 November, 1941 Eu23-3/EF Lge/E-35 (WH)

League Club	Source	Date Signed	Seasons Played	Apps	Subs	Gls
Fulham	Jnrs	12.58	58-63	199	-	13
Tottenham H.	Tr	03.64	63-71	312	0	25
Fulham	Tr	03.72	71-75	164	1	24

MULLETT, Joseph
Blackheath, 2 October, 1936 (FB)

League Club	Source	Date Signed	Seasons Played	Apps	Subs	Gls
Birmingham C.	Malt Hill U.	02.55	57	3	-	0
Norwich C.	Tr	02.59	58-67	211	2	2

MULLIGAN, Patrick G. (Paddy)
Dublin, 17 March, 1945 IR-51 (RB)

League Club	Source	Date Signed	Seasons Played	Apps	Subs	Gls
Chelsea	Shamrock Rov.	10.69	69-72	55	3	2
Crystal Palace	Tr	09.72	72-74	57	0	2
West Bromwich A.	Tr	09.75	75-77	109	0	1

MULLIGAN, Peter G.
Barnsley, 17 July, 1942 (IF)

League Club	Source	Date Signed	Seasons Played	Apps	Subs	Gls
Barnsley	Jnrs	07.63	59-63	9	-	0

MULLINEUX, Ian J.
Salford, 10 November, 1968 (W)

League Club	Source	Date Signed	Seasons Played	Apps	Subs	Gls
Bolton W. (YT)	YT	07.86	86	1	1	0

MULLINGTON, Philip T.
Oldham, 25 September, 1956 (M)

League Club	Source	Date Signed	Seasons Played	Apps	Subs	Gls
Oldham Ath.	App	07.75				
Rochdale	Tr	01.76	75-76	59	7	6
Crewe Alex. (N/C)	Northwich Vic.	01.78	77	1	0	0
Rochdale	Winsford U.	08.78	78	8	1	0

MULRANEY, Ambrose
Wishaw, 18 May, 1916 (OR)

League Club	Source	Date Signed	Seasons Played	Apps	Subs	Gls
Ipswich T.	Dartford	11.36	38	28	-	8
Birmingham C.	Tr	10.45	46	28	-	9
Aston Villa	Shrewsbury T.	09.48	48	12	-	2

MULVANEY, James
Sunderland, 13 May, 1941 Died 1982 (IF)

League Club	Source	Date Signed	Seasons Played	Apps	Subs	Gls
Hartlepool U.	Whitby T.	08.65	65-67	67	2	32
Barrow	Tr	11.67	67-69	71	8	34
Stockport Co.	Tr	07.70	70-71	38	2	8

MULVANEY, James
Airdrie, 27 April, 1921 (D)

League Club	Source	Date Signed	Seasons Played	Apps	Subs	Gls
Luton T.	Dumbarton	06.48	48-49	8	-	2
Brighton & H.A.	Tr	08.50	50	8	-	0
Bradford C.	Tr	10.51	51	19	-	0
Halifax T.	Bath C.	11.52	52	1	-	0

MULVANEY, Richard
Sunderland, 5 August, 1942 (CD)

League Club	Source	Date Signed	Seasons Played	Apps	Subs	Gls
Blackburn Rov.	Billingham Synth.	02.64	64-70	135	6	4
Oldham Ath.	Tr	08.71	71-74	88	4	2
Rochdale	Tr	10.74	74-76	72	1	4

MULVEY, Edward P. N.
Dublin, 29 December, 1934 (F)

League Club	Source	Date Signed	Seasons Played	Apps	Subs	Gls
Stockport Co.	Glentoran	11.57	57-59	26	-	5

MULVOY, Terence
Manchester, 2 December, 1938 (F)

League Club	Source	Date Signed	Seasons Played	Apps	Subs	Gls
Rochdale		02.56	56	2	-	0

MUMBY, Peter
Bradford, 22 February, 1969 (W)

League Club	Source	Date Signed	Seasons Played	Apps	Subs	Gls
Leeds U.	App	07.87	87-88	3	3	0
Burnley	Tr	07.89	89-91	36	10	9

MUMFORD, Wayne E.
Rhymney, 3 November, 1964 (FB)

League Club	Source	Date Signed	Seasons Played	Apps	Subs	Gls
Birmingham C.	Manchester C. (App)	09.82	82-83	5	2	0

MUNCIE, William
Carluke, 28 August, 1911 (W)

League Club	Source	Date Signed	Seasons Played	Apps	Subs	Gls
Leicester C.	Shettleston Jnrs	08.34	34-37	42	-	11
Southend U.	Tr	05.38	38	14	-	2
Crewe Alex.		10.46	46	2	-	0

MUNDAY, Stuart C.
Newham, 28 September, 1972 (RB)

League Club	Source	Date Signed	Seasons Played	Apps	Subs	Gls
Brighton & H.A.	YT	07.90	91	14	0	1

MUNDEE, Brian G.
Hammersmith, 12 January, 1964 (LB)

League Club	Source	Date Signed	Seasons Played	Apps	Subs	Gls
Bournemouth	Hungerford T.	01.82	82	3	1	0
Northampton T.	Tr	10.83	83-85	96	4	3
Cambridge U.	Tr	03.86	85-86	16	0	1

MUNDEE, Dennis W. J.
Swindon, 10 October, 1968 (FB)

League Club	Source	Date Signed	Seasons Played	Apps	Subs	Gls
Swindon T.	Queens Park R. (App)	08.86				
Bournemouth	Salisbury	05.88	88-91	53	21	4
Torquay U.	L	09.89	89	9	0	0

MUNDY, Albert E.
Gosport, 12 May, 1926 (IF)

League Club	Source	Date Signed	Seasons Played	Apps	Subs	Gls
Portsmouth	Gosport Bor.	01.51	50-53	51	-	12
Brighton & H.A.	Tr	11.53	53-57	166	-	86
Aldershot	Tr	02.58	57-60	130	-	11

MUNDY, H. James
Wythenshawe, 2 September, 1948 (M)

League Club	Source	Date Signed	Seasons Played	Apps	Subs	Gls
Manchester C.	Ashland Rov.	08.66	68-69	2	1	0
Oldham Ath.	L	09.70	70	3	5	2

MUNGALL, Steven H.
Bellshill, 22 May, 1958 (D/M)

League Club	Source	Date Signed	Seasons Played	Apps	Subs	Gls
Tranmere Rov.	Motherwell	07.79	79-91	420	13	10

MUNKS, David
Sheffield, 29 April, 1947 E Yth (D)

League Club	Source	Date Signed	Seasons Played	Apps	Subs	Gls
Sheffield U.	App	08.64	65-68	108	4	1
Portsmouth	Tr	05.69	69-73	132	5	2
Swindon T.	Tr	12.73	73-74	21	0	0
Exeter C.	Tr	12.74	74-75	20	0	0

MUNRO, A. Iain F.
Uddingston, 24 August, 1951 S-7 (LB)

League Club	Source	Date Signed	Seasons Played	Apps	Subs	Gls
Stoke C.	St Mirren	10.80	80	32	0	1
Sunderland	Tr	08.81	81-83	80	0	0

MUNRO, Alexander
Glasgow, 3 October, 1944 (D)

League Club	Source	Date Signed	Seasons Played	Apps	Subs	Gls
Bristol Rov.	Drumchapel Jnrs	10.62	62-70	157	10	11

MUNRO, Alexander D.
Corridon, 6 April, 1912 Died 1986 S-3 (OR)

League Club	Source	Date Signed	Seasons Played	Apps	Subs	Gls
Blackpool	Hearts	03.37	36-48	141	-	17

MUNRO, Francis M.
Broughty Ferry, 25 October, 1947 Su23-4/S-9 (CD)

League Club	Source	Date Signed	Seasons Played	Apps	Subs	Gls
Wolverhampton W.	Aberdeen	01.68	67-76	290	6	14

MUNRO, James F.
Garmouth (Sc), 25 March, 1926 (OR)

League Club	Source	Date Signed	Seasons Played	Apps	Subs	Gls
Manchester C.	Waterford	11.47	47-49	25	-	4
Oldham Ath.	Tr	03.50	49-52	119	-	20
Lincoln C.	Tr	02.53	52-57	161	-	24
Bury	Tr	01.58	57-58	41	-	8

League Club	Source	Date Signed	Seasons Played	Apps	Subs	Gls
MUNRO, Malcolm G.						
Melton Mowbray, 21 May, 1953 E Sch/E Yth						(CD)
Leicester C.	App	05.70	71-74	69	1	1
MUNRO, Rodney A.						
Inverness, 27 July, 1920						(FB)
Brentford		05.46	46-52	199	-	0
MUNRO, Stuart						
Falkirk, 15 September, 1962 S'B'						(LB)
Blackburn Rov.	Glasgow Rangers	07.91	91	1	0	0
MUNRO, William D.						
Glasgow, 21 June, 1934						(IF)
Barrow	Kilmarnock	06.59	59-60	15	-	2
MUNROE, William J.						
Dublin, 28 November, 1933						(IF)
Bristol C.	Ards.	12.57	57	1	-	0
Scunthorpe U.	Tr	07.58				
MURCHISON, Ronald A.						
Kilmarnock, 12 February, 1927						(HB)
Ipswich T.	Auchterader Primrose	06.50	50-54	42	-	2
MURCOTT, Stephen						
Streetly, 17 January, 1961						(G)
Coventry C.	App	11.78	79	1	0	0
MURDOCH, Robert W.						
Bothwell, 17 August, 1944 Su23-1/SF Lge/S-12						(M)
Middlesbrough	Glasgow Celtic	09.73	73-75	93	2	6
MURDOCH, W. Robert						
Liverpool, 25 January, 1936						(IF)
Liverpool		05.57	57-58	17	-	5
Barrow	Tr	05.59	59	42	-	17
Stockport Co.	Tr	08.60	60-61	58	-	18
Carlisle U.	Tr	01.62	61	10	-	1
Southport	Tr	07.62	62	33	-	10
MURPHY, Aidan J.						
Manchester, 17 September, 1967 E Sch/E Yth						(M)
Manchester U.	App	09.84				
Lincoln C.	L	10.86	86	2	0	0
Crewe Alex.	Tr	05.87	87-91	94	19	13
MURPHY, Andrew C.						
Preston, 18 October, 1966						(M)
Preston N.E.	YT	07.84	83-84	9	1	0
MURPHY, Barry L.						
Consett, 10 February, 1940						(RB)
Barnsley	South Shields	07.62	62-77	509	4	3
MURPHY, Bernard A. P.						
Dublin, 19 November, 1947						(WH)
Torquay U.	App	11.65	64-66	6	0	0
MURPHY, Daniel						
Burtonwood, 10 May, 1922						(WH)
Bolton W.	Burtonwood Ath.	02.43	46-50	66	-	1
Crewe Alex.	Tr	01.52	51-53	106	-	1
Rochdale	Tr	07.54	54-56	109	-	0
MURPHY, Donal P.						
Dublin, 23 February, 1955						(OL)
Coventry C.	App	08.72	75-77	33	10	10
Millwall	L	10.77	77	3	0	0
Torquay U.	Tr	05.78	78-79	81	4	20
Plymouth Arg.	Tr	06.80	80-81	44	4	9
Torquay U.	L	12.81	81	2	1	0
Blackburn Rov.	Tr	02.82	81	1	2	0
MURPHY T. Edward						
Middlesbrough, 25 March, 1921						(IF)
Middlesbrough	South Bank	05.39	46-47	9	-	1
Blackburn Rov.	Tr	12.47	47-48	31	-	6
Halifax T.	Tr	03.49	48-53	217	-	30
MURPHY, Edward						
Hamilton, 13 May, 1924						(IF)
Northampton T.	Morton	06.49	49-50	71	-	14
Barnsley	Tr	03.51	50-51	18	-	2
Exeter C.	Tr	06.52	52-55	94	-	13
MURPHY, Edward C.						
Glasgow, 1 June, 1934						(CH)
Oldham Ath.	Clyde	05.56	56-58	72	-	0
MURPHY, Francis J.						
Edinburgh, 16 August, 1949						(WH)
Notts Co.	Edina Jnrs	08.67	67-68	17	2	2
MURPHY, Frank						
Glasgow, 1 June, 1959						(F)
Barnet	Kettering T.	08.88	91	3	12	5
MURPHY, George						
Crosskeys, 22 July, 1915 Died 1983						(CF)
Bradford C.	Cwmfelinfach Jnr	11.34	34-47	180	-	43
Hull C.	Tr	12.47	47	15	-	9
MURPHY, James						
Islington, 17 November, 1971						(M)
Aldershot	Leyton Orient (YT)	07.90	90	1	2	0
MURPHY, James B.						
Glasgow, 29 November, 1942						(IF)
Notts Co.	Raith Rov.	02.68	67-68	33	0	7
MURPHY, Jeremy M.						
Stepney, 23 September, 1959 E Sch/IR-3						(LM)
Crystal Palace	App	10.76	76-84	214	15	20
Chelsea	Tr	08.85	85-87	34	0	3
MURPHY, Joseph P.						
Waterford (Ire), 30 March, 1924						(FB)
Brighton & H.A.		02.48				
Crystal Palace	Shelbourne	02.49	48-50	37	-	0
MURPHY, Marcus M.						
Tavistock, 16 November, 1914						(IF)
Plymouth Arg.	Plymouth U.	08.46	46-47	15	-	1
MURPHY, Michael						
Reading, 15 April, 1939						(G)
Reading (Am)	Thorneycroft A.	04.58	57	1	-	0
MURPHY, Nicholas M.						
West Bromwich, 25 December, 1946						(M)
Manchester U.	Jnrs	02.66				
Reading	Tr	07.70	70	3	1	0
MURPHY, Patrick						
Merthyr Tydfil, 19 December, 1947						(HB)
Cardiff C.	App	12.65	65	0	1	0
MURPHY, Paul						
Ashington, 16 March, 1954						(F)
Rotherham U.	Ashington	02.72	73	1	0	0
Workington	L	08.73	73	10	2	1
MURPHY, Peter						
Hartlepool, 7 March, 1922 Died 1975						(IF)
Coventry C.	Birmingham C. (Am)	05.46	46-49	114	-	37
Tottenham H.	Tr	06.50	50-51	38	-	14
Birmingham C.	Tr	01.52	51-59	245	-	107
MURPHY, Philip						
Liverpool, 21 November, 1960						(F)
Blackpool	Nacional (Port)	09.84	84	5	0	0
Burnley (N/C)		11.86	86	12	3	5
MURPHY, Terence						
Liverpool, 14 January, 1940						(WH)
Crewe Alex.		09.61	61	1	-	0
MURPHY, J. William						
Birstall, 21 November, 1921						(WH)
Bradford C.	Liverpool (Am)	09.46	46-51	146	-	9
MURPHY, William R.						
Barrhead, 22 March, 1928						(W)
Exeter C.	Stirling A.	11.49	49	2	-	0
Bristol Rov.	Tr	07.50	50	3	-	0

League Club	Source	Date Signed	Seasons Played	Apps	Subs	Gls

MURRAY, Alan
Newcastle, 5 November, 1949 (M)

Middlesbrough	Jnrs	09.67	69-70	6	4	1
York C.	L	01.72	71	4	0	0
Brentford	Tr	06.72	72	42	3	7
Doncaster Rov.	Tr	07.73	73-76	133	13	21

MURRAY, Albert G. (Bert)
Hoxton, 22 September, 1942 E Sch/E Yth/Eu23-6 (OR)

Chelsea	Jnrs	05.61	61-65	156	4	39
Birmingham C.	Tr	08.66	66-70	126	6	22
Brighton & H.A.	Tr	02.71	70-73	99	3	25
Peterborough U.	Tr	09.73	73-75	123	0	10

MURRAY, Alistair
Longtown, 22 December, 1943 (IF)

Sunderland	Jnrs	01.61				
Barnsley	Tr	07.63	63	21	-	1
Carlisle U.	Tr	07.64				

MURRAY, David I.
Otterburn, 11 July, 1949 (F)

Workington		03.74	73-75	79	3	22

MURRAY, David R.
Chorley, 30 September, 1967 (F)

Chester C.	Wigan Ath. (Jnr)	09.85	85	3	3	1

MURRAY, Dennis P.
Stoke, 11 June, 1932 (G)

Crewe Alex.	Jnrs	10.50	51	2	-	0

MURRAY, Donald J.
Elgin, 18 January, 1946 Su23-1 (CD)

Cardiff C.	Jnrs	01.63	62-74	406	0	6
Swansea C.	L	10.74	74	5	0	0
Newport Co.	Hearts	10.76	76	16	2	0

MURRAY, Edwin J.
Ilford, 31 August, 1973 (FB)

Swindon T.	YT	07.91	90	0	1	0

MURRAY, Edward J.
Crosby, 10 July, 1962 (W)

Tranmere Rov.	Stork	08.87	87-88	11	16	1

MURRAY, Hugh
Drybridge, 3 August, 1936 (F)

Manchester C.	Dalry Th.	04.55	55	1	-	0

MURRAY, Ivan H.
Ballymoney, 29 May, 1944 (WH)

Fulham	Coleraine	02.68	67-68	4	1	0

MURRAY, A. James
Thornton, 4 February, 1945 (W)

Southport	Jnrs	07.65	64	3	-	0

MURRAY, James
Motherwell, 13 July, 1922 (FB)

Exeter C.	Shawfield Jnrs	08.45	46	1	-	0

MURRAY, James
Edinburgh, 4 February, 1933 (F)

Reading	Hearts	02.54	53-54	7	-	3

MURRAY, James R.
Dover, 11 October, 1935 Eu23-2/EF Lge (CF)

Wolverhampton W.	Jnrs	11.53	55-63	273	-	155
Manchester C.	Tr	11.63	63-66	70	0	43
Walsall	Tr	05.67	66-68	54	4	13

MURRAY, James W.
Lambeth, 16 March, 1935 (IF)

Crystal Palace	Jnrs	07.55	55-57	37	-	13
Walsall	Tr	01.58	57-58	14	-	2

MURRAY, Jamie G.
Glasgow, 27 December, 1958 (LB)

Cambridge U.	Rivet Sports	09.76	76-83	213	16	3
Sunderland	L	03.84	83	0	1	0
Brentford	Tr	07.84	84-87	130	0	3
Cambridge U.	Tr	09.87	87	13	0	0

League Club	Source	Date Signed	Seasons Played	Apps	Subs	Gls

MURRAY, John
Newcastle, 2 March, 1948 (W)

Burnley	Jnrs	03.65	66-69	20	2	6
Blackpool	Tr	03.70	69-70	5	3	1
Bury	Tr	02.71	70-73	117	9	37
Reading	Tr	08.74	74-77	123	8	44
Brentford	Tr	02.78	77	2	3	1

MURRAY, John
Glasgow, 9 March, 1945 (LB)

Lincoln C.	Stirling A.	11.66	66	4	0	0

MURRAY, John A.
Saltcoats, 5 February, 1949 (FB)

Cambridge U.	Morton	07.71	71	3	0	0

MURRAY, John G.
Lambeth, 15 July, 1927 (FB)

Leyton Orient	Chelmsford C.	08.49				
Gillingham	Sittingbourne	06.51	51	4	-	0

MURRAY, Joseph E.
Liverpool, 5 November, 1971 (M)

Wrexham (N/C)	Marine	03.91	90	11	0	0

MURRAY, Kenneth
Darlington, 2 April, 1928 (F)

Darlington	Bishop Auckland	07.50	50-52	70	-	19
Mansfield T.	Tr	07.53	53-56	140	-	60
Oldham Ath.	Tr	03.57	56-57	35	-	14
Wrexham	Tr	02.58	57-58	32	-	12
Gateshead	Tr	08.59	59	18	-	7

MURRAY, Leslie
East Fife, 29 September, 1928

Rochdale	Arbroath	05.52	52	16	-	3

MURRAY, Malcolm
Buckie, 26 July, 1964 (FB)

Hull C.	Hearts	03.89	88-89	9	2	0
Mansfield T.	Tr	12.89	89-90	56	3	0

MURRAY, Mark
Manchester, 13 June, 1973 (LB)

Blackpool	Jnrs	10.90	91	2	0	0

MURRAY, Matthew
Paisley, 25 December, 1929 (OL)

Barrow	St Mirren	08.58	58	33	-	2
Carlisle U.	Tr	07.59	59	28	-	4

MURRAY, Maxwell
Falkirk, 7 November, 1935 S Amat/Su23-2 (CF)

West Bromwich A.	Glasgow Rangers	11.62	62	3	-	0

MURRAY, Robert L.
Kemnay, 24 April, 1932 (FB)

Stockport Co.	Inverurie Loco	11.51	52-62	465	-	31

MURRAY, Shaun
Newcastle, 7 December, 1970 E Yth (M)

Tottenham H.	YT	12.87				
Portsmouth	Tr	06.89	90-91	19	8	1

MURRAY, Steven
Kilmarnock, 1 December, 1967 S Yth (M)

Nottingham F.	App	04.85				
York C.	L	09.86	86	2	1	0

MURRAY, Terence
Dublin, 22 May, 1958 IRF Lge/IR-1 (IF)

Hull C.	Dundalk	10.51	51-53	32	-	6
Bournemouth	Tr	03.54	53-54	13	-	1

MURRAY, Thomas
Airdrie, 5 February, 1933 (IF)

Darlington	Headington U.	06.56	56	3	-	0

MURRAY, Thomas
Bellshill, 14 January, 1933 (OR)

Leeds U.	Queen of South	08.60	60	7	-	2
Tranmere Rov.	Tr	03.61	60-61	10	-	1

League Club	Source	Date Signed	Seasons Played	Career Record Apps	Subs	Gls
MURRAY, Thomas						
Caldercruix, 1 June, 1943						(F)
Carlisle U.	Airdrieonians	03.67	66-70	123	10	37
MURRAY, Thomas A.						
Barrow, 16 October, 1944						(FB)
Barrow	Jnrs	07.64	63-64	8	-	0
MURRAY, William						
Burnley, 26 January, 1922						(WH)
Manchester C.	Arbroath	01.47	46-49	20	-	1
MURTY, Joseph						
Glasgow, 6 November, 1957						(M)
Rochdale	App	11.75	74-75	15	5	2
Bury	Tr	08.76	77	0	1	0
MUSGRAVE, David						
South Shields, 20 April, 1928						(OL)
Manchester U.	Johannesburg (SA)	12.47				
New Brighton	Fleetwood	08.50	50	35	-	2
Preston N.E.	Tr	08.51				
Southport	Tr	10.51	51-52	52	-	7
Accrington St.	Tr	09.53	53	30	-	7
MUSGROVE, Malcolm						
Lynemouth, 8 July, 1933						(OL)
West Ham U.	Lynemouth Colly	12.53	53-62	283	-	84
Leyton Orient	Tr	12.62	62-65	83	0	14
MUSGROVE, Martin						
Wanstead, 21 November, 1961						(M)
Torquay U. (N/C)	Heavitree U.	03.82	81	1	1	0
MUSIAL, Adam						
Poland, 18 December, 1948 Polish Int						(D)
Hereford U.	Arkagdynia (Pol)	08.80	80-82	44	2	0
MUSKER, Russell						
Teignmouth, 10 July, 1962						(W)
Bristol C.	App	08.79	80-83	44	2	1
Exeter C.	L	10.83	83	6	0	0
Gillingham	Tr	11.83	83-85	54	10	7
Torquay U.	Tr	08.86	86-87	36	9	0
Torquay U.	(Retired)	07.90	90	20	1	1
Walsall	Tr	08.91	91	3	0	0
MUSSELWHITE, Paul S.						
Portsmouth, 22 December, 1968						(G)
Portsmouth (N/C)	App	12.86				
Scunthorpe U.	Tr	03.88	88-91	132	0	0
MUSSON, Ian S.						
Lincoln, 13 December, 1953						(W)
Sheffield Wed.	App	02.71				
Lincoln C.	Tr	07.73	73	11	0	0
MUSSON, Walter U. (Chick)						
Belper, 8 October, 1920 Died 1955 EF Lge						(WH)
Derby Co.	Jnrs	10.37	46-53	246	-	0
MUSTARD, William						
South Shields, 28 November, 1920 Died 1976						(OR)
Exeter C.	Bath C.	05.46	46	14	-	0
MUSTOE, Robert						
Witney, 28 August, 1968						(M)
Oxford U.	Jnrs	07.86	86-89	78	13	10
Middlesbrough	Tr	07.90	90-91	67	4	6
MUTCH, Andrew T.						
Liverpool, 28 December, 1963 Eu21-1/E'B'						(F)
Wolverhampton W.	Southport	02.86	85-91	243	7	87
MUTCH, George						
Aberdeen, 21 September, 1912 S Sch/S-1						(IF)
Manchester U.	Arbroath	05.34	34-37	112	-	46
Preston N.E.	Tr	09.37	37-46	80	-	25
Bury	Tr	10.46	46	21	-	8
Southport	Tr	10.47	47	14	-	2
MUTRIE, Leslie A.						
Newcastle, 1 April, 1952 E Semi-Pro						(F)
Carlisle U.	Gateshead	06.77	77	4	1	0
Hull C.	Blyth Spartans	12.80	80-83	114	1	49
Doncaster Rov.	L	12.83	83	6	0	1
Colchester U.	Tr	01.84	83	10	4	2
Hartlepool U.	Tr	08.84	84	18	0	4

League Club	Source	Date Signed	Seasons Played	Career Record Apps	Subs	Gls
MUTTOCK, Jonathan L.						
Oxford, 23 December, 1961						(D)
Oxford U.	YT	05.90	89	1	0	0
MUXWORTHY, Graham J.						
Bristol, 11 October, 1938						(OL)
Crystal Palace	Exeter U.	09.57	57	2	-	0
Bristol Rov.	Chippenham T.	06.60	62	8	-	0
MUZINIC, Drazen						
Yugoslavia, 25 January, 1953 Yugoslav Int						(D)
Norwich C.	Hadjuk Split (Yug)	09.80	80-81	15	4	0
MWILA, Frederick						
Zambia, 6 July, 1946						(IF)
Aston Villa	Atlanta (USA)	06.69	69	1	0	0
MYCOCK, Albert						
Manchester, 31 January, 1923						(F)
Manchester U.		05.44				
Crystal Palace	Tr	06.46	46-47	59	-	9
Barrow	Tr	07.48	48-49	42	-	4
MYCOCK, David						
Sunderland, 30 August, 1921						(WH)
Halifax T.	Sunderland (Am)	05.46	46-51	170	-	17
MYCOCK, David C.						
Todmorden, 18 September, 1969						(FB)
Rochdale	YT	07.88	87-88	19	3	0
MYCOCK, John (Jack)						
Manchester, 11 February, 1936						(OR)
Shrewsbury T. (Am)	Congleton T.	12.58	58	6	-	1
MYCOCK, Thomas						
Ryhope, 22 August, 1923 Died 1988 IR F Lge						(HB)
Southport	Swansea C. (Am)	10.46	46	19	-	3
Aldershot	Tr	04.47	46-47	16	-	4
Brentford	Distillery	12.50				
Tranmere Rov.	Tr	05.52	52-53	46	-	2
Bradford C.	Tr	02.54	53-54	21	-	3
MYERS, Andrew J.						
Hounslow, 3 November, 1973 E Yth						(LB)
Chelsea	YT	06.91	90-91	9	5	1
MYERS, Christopher						
Yeovil, 1 April, 1969						(M)
Torquay U.	YT	06.87	86	8	1	0
Torquay U.	Barnstaple T.	08.90	90-91	60	8	6
MYERS, Clifford W.						
Southwark, 23 September, 1946						(M)
Charlton Ath.	App	09.64	65-66	16	2	2
Brentford	Tr	06.67	67	7	3	0
Torquay U.	Yeovil T.	07.73	73-75	80	6	11
MYERS, J. Rodney						
Sheffield, 16 February, 1939						(FB)
Doncaster Rov.	Scarborough	01.63	63	19	-	0
MYERSCOUGH, H. William						
Bolton, 22 June, 1930 Died 1977						(IF)
Walsall	Ashfield	06.54	54	26	-	6
Aston Villa	Tr	07.55	56-58	64	-	15
Rotherham U.	Tr	07.59	59	39	-	11
Coventry C.	Tr	07.60	60-61	58	-	16
Chester C.	Tr	03.62	61-62	36	-	11
Wrexham	Tr	07.63	63	35	-	5
MYLES, Neil T.						
Falkirk, 17 June, 1927						(WH)
Ipswich T.	Third Lanark	08.49	49-59	223	-	15
MYNARD, Leslie D.						
Bewdley, 19 December, 1925						(OL)
Wolverhampton W.	Bewdley	05.45	47	3	-	0
Derby Co.	Tr	07.49	49-50	14	-	2
Scunthorpe U.	Tr	08.52	52	18	-	3
MYTON, Brian						
York, 26 September, 1950						(LB)
Middlesbrough	App	09.67	68-70	10	0	0
Southend U.	L	11.71	71	0	1	0

Charlie Nicholas (Glasgow Celtic, Arsenal, Aberdeen, Glasgow Celtic & Scotland)
Fully expected to be a sensation in English football, he failed to scale the peaks and was transferred to Aberdeen after four seasons with the "Gunners"

League Club	Source	Date Signed	Seasons Played	Career Record Apps	Subs	Gls

NAGY, Niklos
Hungary, 1 May, 1929 (IF)

Scunthorpe U.		01.51				
Swindon T.	Tr	08.51	51	2	-	0

NAIL, Desmond R.
St Columb, 28 December, 1924 (CF)

Plymouth Arg.	St Blazey	10.47	47	1	-	0

NAINBY, L. John
Seaton Delaval, 2 January, 1940 (F)

Sheffield Wed.		02.58				
Darlington	Tr	07.59	59	3	-	1

NAPIER, Alexander S.
Kirkcaldy, 8 August, 1935 (IF)

Darlington	Raith Rov.	05.55	55	1	-	0

NAPIER, Christopher R. A. (Kit)
Dunblane, 26 September, 1943 (CF)

Blackpool	Jnrs	11.60	62	2	-	0
Preston N.E.	Tr	06.63	63	1	-	0
Workington	Tr	07.64	64-65	58	0	25
Newcastle U.	Tr	11.65	65	8	0	0
Brighton & H.A.	Tr	09.66	66-72	249	7	84
Blackburn Rov.	Tr	08.72	72-73	53	1	10

NAPIER, R. John
Lurgan (NI), 23 September, 1946 NIu23-2/NI-1 (CD)

Bolton W.	Jnrs	09.63	64-66	69	0	2
Brighton & H.A.	Tr	08.67	67-72	218	1	5
Bradford C.	Tr	10.72	72-76	106	1	3

NARBETT, Jonathan V.
Birmingham, 21 November, 1968 (M)

Shrewsbury T.	App	09.86	86-87	20	6	3
Hereford U.	Tr	10.88	88-91	148	1	31

NARDIELLO, Donato
Cardigan, 9 January, 1957 Wu21-1/W-2 (W)

Coventry C.	App	04.74	77-79	32	1	1

NARDIELLO, Gerardo
Warley, 5 May, 1966 E Yth (F)

Shrewsbury T.	App	05.84	82-85	32	6	11
Cardiff C.	L	03.86	85	7	0	4
Torquay U.	Tr	07.86	86-87	28	9	11

NASH, Frank C.
Middlesbrough, 30 June, 1919 (G)

Middlesbrough	South Bank	09.37	37-47	19	-	0
Southend U.	Tr	12.47	47-50	57	-	0

NASH, Robert G.
Hammersmith, 8 February, 1946 (FB)

Queens Park R.	Jnrs	02.64	64	17	-	0
Exeter C.	Tr	06.66	66	1	0	0

NASSARI, Derek J.
Salford, 20 October, 1971

Chester C. (YT)	YT	07.88	89	0	1	0

NASTRI, Carlo L. F.
Finchley, 22 October, 1935 (W)

Crystal Palace	Kingstonian	07.58	58	2	-	0

NATTRASS, Irving
Fishburn (Dm), 12 December, 1952 Eu23-1 (RB)

Newcastle U.	App	07.70	70-78	226	12	16
Middlesbrough	Tr	08.79	79-85	186	5	2

NATTRESS, Clive
Durham, 24 May, 1951 (D)

Blackpool	Consett	08.70				
Darlington	Tr	08.72	72-79	297	5	15
Halifax T.	Tr	06.80	80	37	0	5
Darlington (N/C)	Bishop Auckland	08.85	85	1	0	0

NAUGHTON, William B.S.
Catrine (Ayrs), 20 March, 1962 (LW)

Preston N.E.	App	03.80	79-84	148	14	10
Walsall	Tr	03.85	84-88	139	12	16
Shrewsbury T.	Tr	08.89	89-90	43	6	4
Walsall	Tr	01.91	90	15	1	1

NAYIM, Mohamed A. A.
Morocco, 5 November, 1966 Moroccan Int (M)

Tottenham H.	Barcelona (Sp)	11.88	88-91	80	14	8

Mohamed Nayim (Barcelona, Tottenham Hotspur & Morocco)

NAYLOR, Anthony J.
Manchester, 29 March, 1967 (F)

Crewe Alex.	Droylsden	03.90	89-91	39	11	16

NAYLOR, Dominic J.
Watford, 12 August, 1970 (LB)

Watford	YT	09.88				
Halifax T.	Tr	12.89	89	5	1	1
Barnet	Hong Kong	08.91	91	26	0	0

NAYLOR, Edward A.
Bradford, 24 December, 1921

Bradford P.A.		05.45				
Halifax T.	Tr	09.48	48	7	-	0

NAYLOR, Geoffrey
Goole, 28 September, 1949 (WH)

Scunthorpe U.	App	09.67	67	9	1	0

NAYLOR, Glenn
Howden, 11 August, 1972 (F)

York C.	YT	03.90	89-91	31	11	13

NAYLOR, Harold F.
Leeds, 6 June, 1928 (CF)

Oldham Ath. (Am)		04.51	50	1	-	0

NAYLOR, Stuart W.
Wetherby, 6 December, 1962 E Yth/E'B' (G)

Lincoln C.	Yorkshire Amats	06.80	81-85	49	0	0
Peterborough U.	L	02.83	82	8	0	0
Crewe Alex.	L	10.83	83-84	55	0	0
West Bromwich A.	Tr	02.86	85-91	234	0	0

NAYLOR, Terence M. P.
Islington, 5 December, 1948 (CD)

Tottenham H.	Smithfield Market	07.69	69-79	237	6	0
Charlton Ath.	Tr	11.80	80-83	69	4	0

NAYLOR, Thomas V.
Blackburn, 1 April, 1946 (D)

League Club	Source	Date Signed	Seasons Played	Apps	Subs	Gls
Bournemouth	App	10.63	64-70	139	3	3
Hereford U.	Tr	08.72	72-74	73	2	4

NAYLOR, T. William
Leeds, 7 December, 1924 (FB)

League Club	Source	Date Signed	Seasons Played	Apps	Subs	Gls
Huddersfield T.	Outwood Stormcocks	02.43				
Oldham Ath.	Tr	03.48	47-58	224	-	0

NAYLOR, William H.
Sheffield, 23 November, 1919 (IF)

League Club	Source	Date Signed	Seasons Played	Apps	Subs	Gls
Crystal Palace	Hampton Sports	01.39	46	18	-	9
Brentford	Tr	02.47	46	11	-	2
Leyton Orient	Tr	06.47	47-49	64	-	14

NDLOVU, Peter
Bulawayo (Zimbabwe), 25 February, 1973 Zimbabwe Int (F)

League Club	Source	Date Signed	Seasons Played	Apps	Subs	Gls
Coventry C.	Highlanders (Zim)	07.91	91	9	14	2

NEAL, Christopher
Kirkby-in-Ashfield, 27 June, 1947 (W)

League Club	Source	Date Signed	Seasons Played	Apps	Subs	Gls
Darlington (Am)	Crook T.	06.67	67	5	0	0

NEAL, Dean J.
Edmonton, 5 January, 1961 (F)

League Club	Source	Date Signed	Seasons Played	Apps	Subs	Gls
Queens Park R.	App	01.79	79-80	20	3	8
Millwall	Tulsa (USA)	10.81	81-84	101	19	42
Southend U.	Tr	01.86	85-87	35	5	6
Cambridge U.	L	12.87	87	4	0	0

NEAL, George
Wellingborough, 29 December, 1919 (RH)

League Club	Source	Date Signed	Seasons Played	Apps	Subs	Gls
Northampton T.	Kettering T.	01.45	46	3	-	0

NEAL, John
Silksworth, 3 April, 1932 (FB)

League Club	Source	Date Signed	Seasons Played	Apps	Subs	Gls
Hull C.	Silksworth Jnrs	08.49	49-55	60	-	1
Swindon T.	Kings Lynn	07.57	57-58	91	-	2
Aston Villa	Tr	07.59	59-62	96	-	0
Southend U.	Tr	11.62	62-65	101	0	1

NEAL, John J.
Hornsey, 11 March, 1966 E Sch (F)

League Club	Source	Date Signed	Seasons Played	Apps	Subs	Gls
Millwall	App	03.83	83	3	3	1

NEAL, Philip G.
Irchester, 29 February, 1951 E-50 (RB)

League Club	Source	Date Signed	Seasons Played	Apps	Subs	Gls
Northampton T.	App	12.68	68-74	182	4	29
Liverpool	Tr	10.74	74-85	453	2	41
Bolton W.	Tr	12.85	85-88	56	8	3

NEAL, Richard M.
Dinnington, 1 October, 1933 Eu23-4 (WH)

League Club	Source	Date Signed	Seasons Played	Apps	Subs	Gls
Wolverhampton W.	Jnrs	03.51				
Lincoln C.	Tr	07.54	54-56	115	-	11
Birmingham C.	Tr	04.57	56-61	165	-	15
Middlesbrough	Tr	10.61	61-62	33	-	4
Lincoln C.	Tr	08.63	63-64	41	-	4

NEALE, Duncan F.
Hove, 1 October, 1939 (WH)

League Club	Source	Date Signed	Seasons Played	Apps	Subs	Gls
Newcastle U.	Ilford	06.59	60-62	88	-	8
Plymouth Arg.	Tr	08.63	63-69	141	5	8

NEALE, John W.
Barnstaple, 15 January, 1949 (W)

League Club	Source	Date Signed	Seasons Played	Apps	Subs	Gls
Exeter C.	Barnstaple	03.72	71-74	51	14	5

NEALE, Keith I.
Birmingham, 19 January, 1935 (IF)

League Club	Source	Date Signed	Seasons Played	Apps	Subs	Gls
Birmingham C.	Jnrs	02.54	56-57	5	-	1
Lincoln C.	Tr	11.57	57-58	8	-	1

NEALE, Peter
Chesterfield, 9 April, 1934 (CH)

League Club	Source	Date Signed	Seasons Played	Apps	Subs	Gls
Oldham Ath.	Chesterfield (Jnrs)	01.53	55-58	117	-	28
Scunthorpe U.	Tr	10.58	58-66	221	5	7
Chesterfield	Tr	10.66	66-67	69	0	4

NEALE, Philip A.
Scunthorpe, 5 June, 1954 (LB)

League Club	Source	Date Signed	Seasons Played	Apps	Subs	Gls
Lincoln C.	Scunthorpe U. (Am)	10.74	74-84	327	8	22

NEALE, William
Wallsend, 20 May, 1933 (HB)

League Club	Source	Date Signed	Seasons Played	Apps	Subs	Gls
Sunderland	Jnrs	06.50				
Darlington	North Shields	05.57	57	15	-	0

NEARY, H. Frank
Aldershot, 6 March, 1921 (CF)

League Club	Source	Date Signed	Seasons Played	Apps	Subs	Gls
Queens Park R.	Finchley	07.45	46	9	-	4
West Ham U.	Tr	01.47	46-47	17	-	15
Leyton Orient	Tr	11.47	47-49	78	-	44
Queens Park R.	Tr	10.49	49	18	-	5
Millwall	Tr	08.50	50-53	123	-	50

NEATE, Derek G. S.
Uxbridge, 1 October, 1927 (OL)

League Club	Source	Date Signed	Seasons Played	Apps	Subs	Gls
Brighton & H.A.	Hayes	04.56	55-56	24	-	6

NEATE, Gordon
Reading, 14 March, 1941 (FB)

League Club	Source	Date Signed	Seasons Played	Apps	Subs	Gls
Reading	Jnrs	03.58	58-65	99	0	2

NEAVE, I.J. Gordon
Glasgow, 10 October, 1924 (HB)

League Club	Source	Date Signed	Seasons Played	Apps	Subs	Gls
Portsmouth	Pollok Jnrs	03.47				
Bournemouth	Tr	06.49	50-53	85	-	0
Aldershot	Tr	07.55	55-57	79	-	1

NEBBELING, Gavin M.
South Africa, 15 May, 1963 (CD)

League Club	Source	Date Signed	Seasons Played	Apps	Subs	Gls
Crystal Palace	Arcadia Shep. (SA)	08.81	81-88	145	6	8
Northampton T.	L	10.85	85	11	0	0
Fulham	Tr	07.89	89-91	57	1	0
Hereford U.	L	12.91	91	3	0	0

NEEDHAM, Andrew P.
Harlow, 13 September, 1955 (F)

League Club	Source	Date Signed	Seasons Played	Apps	Subs	Gls
Birmingham C.	App	08.73	75	2	1	1
Blackburn Rov.	Tr	07.76	76	4	1	0
Aldershot	Tr	03.77	76-79	92	3	29

NEEDHAM, Anthony
Scunthorpe, 4 January, 1941 (FB)

League Club	Source	Date Signed	Seasons Played	Apps	Subs	Gls
Scunthorpe U.	Jnrs	07.59	59-64	33	-	0

NEEDHAM, David W.
Leicester, 21 May, 1949 (CD)

League Club	Source	Date Signed	Seasons Played	Apps	Subs	Gls
Notts Co.	App	07.66	65-76	428	1	32
Queens Park R.	Tr	06.77	77	18	0	3
Nottingham F.	Tr	12.77	77-81	81	5	9

NEEDHAM, Paul A.
Buxton, 15 June, 1961 (FB)

League Club	Source	Date Signed	Seasons Played	Apps	Subs	Gls
Chester C.	App	06.79	80-82	55	2	1

NEENAN, Joseph P.
Manchester, 17 March, 1959 (G)

League Club	Source	Date Signed	Seasons Played	Apps	Subs	Gls
York C.	App	03.77	76-79	56	0	0
Scunthorpe U.	Tr	01.80	79-84	191	0	0
Burnley	L	01.85	84	9	0	0
Burnley	Tr	07.85	85-86	81	0	0
Peterborough U.	Tr	07.87	87-88	55	0	0
Scarborough	L	01.88	87	6	0	0

NEIGHBOUR, James E.
Chingford, 15 November, 1950 (W)

League Club	Source	Date Signed	Seasons Played	Apps	Subs	Gls
Tottenham H.	App	11.68	70-76	104	15	8
Norwich C.	Tr	09.76	76-79	104	2	5
West Ham U.	Tr	09.79	79-82	66	7	5
Bournemouth	L	01.83	82	6	0	0

NEIL, Hugh M.
Cumnock, 2 October, 1936 S Sch (FB)

League Club	Source	Date Signed	Seasons Played	Apps	Subs	Gls
Carlisle U.	St Johnstone	06.61	61-68	246	1	2

NEIL, Patrick
Portsmouth, 24 October, 1937 E Amat (OL)

League Club	Source	Date Signed	Seasons Played	Apps	Subs	Gls
Portsmouth (Am)	Jnrs	06.55	55	9	-	3
Wolverhampton W. (Am)	Tr	08.56	56	4	-	1
Portsmouth	Pegasus	05.62	62	1	-	0

NEIL, William M.
Lanark, 20 April, 1924 (IF)

League Club	Source	Date Signed	Seasons Played	Apps	Subs	Gls
Bradford P.A.	Morton	12.47	47	3	-	0

League Club	Source	Date Signed	Seasons Played	Career Record Apps	Subs	Gls

NEIL, William W.
Roslin, 10 November, 1944 (LW)

League Club	Source	Date Signed	Seasons Played	Apps	Subs	Gls
Millwall	Bonnyrigg Rose	04.64	64-71	178	8	26

NEILL, Terence W. J.
Belfast, 8 May, 1942 NI Sch/NIu23-4/NI-59 (CH)

League Club	Source	Date Signed	Seasons Played	Apps	Subs	Gls
Arsenal	Bangor	12.59	60-69	240	1	8
Hull C.	Tr	07.70	70-72	103	0	4

NEILL, Thomas K.
Methil, 3 October, 1930 (WH)

League Club	Source	Date Signed	Seasons Played	Apps	Subs	Gls
Bolton W.	R.A.F. Wharton	09.50	52-56	40	-	2
Bury	Tr	12.56	56-59	90	-	9
Tranmere Rov.	Tr	10.60	60-62	79	-	2

NEILL, Warren A.
Acton, 21 November, 1962 E Sch (RB)

League Club	Source	Date Signed	Seasons Played	Apps	Subs	Gls
Queens Park R.	App	09.80	80-87	177	4	3
Portsmouth	Tr	07.88	88-91	146	2	1

NEILSON, Alan B.
Wegburg, (WG), 26 September, 1972 W-1 (FB)

League Club	Source	Date Signed	Seasons Played	Apps	Subs	Gls
Newcastle U.	YT	02.91	90-91	18	1	1

NEILSON, Gordon
Glasgow, 28 May, 1947 (W)

League Club	Source	Date Signed	Seasons Played	Apps	Subs	Gls
Arsenal	Glasgow U.	06.64	65-66	14	0	2
Brentford	Tr	10.68	68-71	80	11	15

NEILSON, John C.
Hamilton, 2 August, 1921 (CF)

League Club	Source	Date Signed	Seasons Played	Apps	Subs	Gls
Bradford C.	Clyde	10.47	47-48	29	-	11
Wrexham	Tr	10.48				

NEILSON, Stephen B.
Newtongrange, 25 April, 1931

League Club	Source	Date Signed	Seasons Played	Apps	Subs	Gls
Rotherham U.		07.55	56	9	-	0

NEILSON, Thomas
Armadale, 28 July, 1922 (HB)

League Club	Source	Date Signed	Seasons Played	Apps	Subs	Gls
Ipswich T.	Hearts	05.48	48	1	-	0

NEKREWS, Thomas J.
Chatham, 20 March, 1933 (CH)

League Club	Source	Date Signed	Seasons Played	Apps	Subs	Gls
Gillingham	Chelsea (Am)	09.53	53-57	42	-	0
Watford	Tr	07.58				

NELMES, Alan V.
Hackney, 20 October, 1948 (D)

League Club	Source	Date Signed	Seasons Played	Apps	Subs	Gls
Chelsea	Jnrs	10.65				
Brentford	Tr	07.67	67-75	311	5	2

NELSON, Andrew N.
Canning Town, 5 July, 1935 (CH)

League Club	Source	Date Signed	Seasons Played	Apps	Subs	Gls
West Ham U.	Jnrs	12.53	57-58	15	-	1
Ipswich T.	Tr	06.59	59-64	193	-	0
Leyton Orient	Tr	09.64	64-65	43	0	0
Plymouth Arg.	Tr	10.65	65-67	94	0	1

NELSON, J. Anthony
Newport, 12 April, 1930 W Amat (CH)

League Club	Source	Date Signed	Seasons Played	Apps	Subs	Gls
Newport Co.		06.52	51-53	19	-	6
Bristol C.	Tr	05.54				
Bournemouth	Tr	06.56	56-64	195	-	1

NELSON, Colin A.
Boldon, 13 March, 1938 (FB)

League Club	Source	Date Signed	Seasons Played	Apps	Subs	Gls
Sunderland	Usworth Colly	03.58	58-64	146	-	2
Mansfield T.	Tr	03.65	64-65	38	0	0

NELSON, David
Douglas Water, 3 February, 1918 Died 1988 (WH)

League Club	Source	Date Signed	Seasons Played	Apps	Subs	Gls
Arsenal	St Bernards	05.36	36-46	27	-	4
Fulham	Tr	12.46	46	23	-	2
Brentford	Tr	08.47	47-49	106	-	5
Queens Park R.	Tr	02.50	49-50	31	-	0
Crystal Palace	Tr	03.52	51-52	12	-	0

NELSON, Dennis N.
Edinburgh, 25 February, 1950 (M)

League Club	Source	Date Signed	Seasons Played	Apps	Subs	Gls
Crewe Alex.	Dunfermline Ath.	07.74	74-75	65	6	18
Reading	Tr	03.76	75-77	53	6	6
Crewe Alex.	Tr	07.78	78-80	97	10	15

NELSON, Garry P.
Braintree, 16 January, 1961 (W)

League Club	Source	Date Signed	Seasons Played	Apps	Subs	Gls
Southend U.	Jnrs	07.79	79-82	106	23	17
Swindon T.	Tr	08.83	83-84	78	1	7
Plymouth Arg.	Tr	07.85	85-86	71	3	20
Brighton & H.A.	Tr	07.87	87-90	132	12	45
Notts Co.	L	11.90	90	0	2	0
Charlton Ath.	Tr	08.91	91	41	0	6

NELSON, George
Mexborough, 5 February, 1925 (IF)

League Club	Source	Date Signed	Seasons Played	Apps	Subs	Gls
Sheffield U.		08.43				
Lincoln C.	Tr	09.46	46	1	-	0

NELSON, James F.
Newcastle, 4 November, 1943 (FB)

League Club	Source	Date Signed	Seasons Played	Apps	Subs	Gls
Sunderland		08.62				
Ipswich T.	Tr	07.63				
Barrow	Tr	01.65	64-65	15	0	0

NELSON, Samuel
Belfast, 1 April, 1949 NIu23-1/NI-51 (LB)

League Club	Source	Date Signed	Seasons Played	Apps	Subs	Gls
Arsenal	Jnrs	04.66	69-80	245	10	10
Brighton & H.A.	Tr	09.81	81-82	40	0	0

NELSON, Samuel E.
Belfast, 26 May, 1924 NI Sch (OR)

League Club	Source	Date Signed	Seasons Played	Apps	Subs	Gls
Blackpool	Linfield Swifts	10.46	46-47	14	-	0
Luton T.	Tr	01.48	47-48	4	-	1

NELSON, William E.
Silvertown, 20 September, 1929 (WH)

League Club	Source	Date Signed	Seasons Played	Apps	Subs	Gls
West Ham U.		10.50	54	2	-	0
Queens Park R.	Tr	07.55	55	9	-	0

NESBIT, Anthony
Sunderland, 26 January, 1968 E Sch (M)

League Club	Source	Date Signed	Seasons Played	Apps	Subs	Gls
Newcastle U.	App	01.86	86	1	2	0

NESBITT, Edward
Boldon, 12 October, 1951 (G)

League Club	Source	Date Signed	Seasons Played	Apps	Subs	Gls
Hartlepool U. (Am)	Longbenton Jnrs	08.71	71	1	0	0

NESBITT, John
Washington, 24 September, 1933 (CH)

League Club	Source	Date Signed	Seasons Played	Apps	Subs	Gls
Newcastle U.	Ashington	12.55	57	3	-	0

NESBITT, Mark T.
Doncaster, 11 January, 1972 (FB)

League Club	Source	Date Signed	Seasons Played	Apps	Subs	Gls
Middlesbrough	YT	01.90				
Hartlepool U.	Tr	03.91	90-91	2	0	0

NESBITT, Michael D.
Doncaster, 8 January, 1969 E Yth (F)

League Club	Source	Date Signed	Seasons Played	Apps	Subs	Gls
Doncaster Rov.	App	01.86	85-87	6	5	1

NESS, Hugh P.
Dunfermline, 30 April, 1940 (FB)

League Club	Source	Date Signed	Seasons Played	Apps	Subs	Gls
Accrington St.	Cowdenbeath	07.59	59	14	-	1
Halifax T.	Tr	06.60				

NETHERCOTT, Kenneth W. S.
Bristol, 22 July , 1925 E'B'-1 (G)

League Club	Source	Date Signed	Seasons Played	Apps	Subs	Gls
Norwich C.	Cardiff C. (Am)	04.47	47-58	378	-	0

NETHERCOTT, Stuart D.
Ilford, 21 March, 1973 (CD)

League Club	Source	Date Signed	Seasons Played	Apps	Subs	Gls
Tottenham H.	YT	07.91				
Maidstone U.	L	09.91	91	13	0	1
Barnet	L	02.92	91	3	0	0

NETTLESHIP, Reginald
Worksop, 23 February, 1925 (F)

League Club	Source	Date Signed	Seasons Played	Apps	Subs	Gls
Sheffield U.		06.43				
Mansfield T.	Tr	07.46	46	1	-	0

NETTLETON, Ernest
Sheffield, 7 January, 1918 (OL)

League Club	Source	Date Signed	Seasons Played	Apps	Subs	Gls
York C.		07.46	46	7	-	2

NEVILLE, Christopher W.
Downham Market, 22 October, 1970 (G)

League Club	Source	Date Signed	Seasons Played	Apps	Subs	Gls
Ipswich T.	YT	05.89	89	1	0	0

NEVILLE, David R.
Birmingham, 8 January, 1929 (D)

League Club	Source	Date Signed	Seasons Played	Apps	Subs	Gls
Bournemouth	Paget R.	04.49				
Chelsea	Tr	07.50				
Rochdale	Burton A.	08.55	55	1	-	0

NEVILLE, Steven F.
Walthamstow, 18 September, 1957 (W)

League Club	Source	Date Signed	Seasons Played	Apps	Subs	Gls
Southampton	App	09.75	77	5	1	1
Exeter C.	Tr	09.78	78-80	90	3	22
Sheffield U.	Tr	10.80	80-81	40	9	6
Exeter C.	Tr	10.82	82-84	89	3	27
Bristol C.	Tr	11.84	84-87	128	6	40
Exeter C.	Tr	07.88	88-90	115	5	40

NEVILLE, William
Cork (Ire), 15 May, 1935 IR'B'-1 (F)

League Club	Source	Date Signed	Seasons Played	Apps	Subs	Gls
West Ham U.	Wembley T.	11.56	57	3	-	0

NEVIN, Patrick K. F.
Glasgow, 6 September, 1963 S Yth/Su21-5/S'B'/S-14 (RW)

League Club	Source	Date Signed	Seasons Played	Apps	Subs	Gls
Chelsea	Clyde	07.83	83-87	190	3	36
Everton	Tr	07.88	88-91	81	28	16
Tranmere Rov.	L	03.92	91	8	0	0

Pat Nevin (Clyde, Chelsea, Everton & Scotland)

NEVIN, Paul R.
London, 23 June, 1969 (F)

League Club	Source	Date Signed	Seasons Played	Apps	Subs	Gls
Carlisle U.	U.S.A.	09.91	91	2	6	0

NEVIN, Ridley W.
Liverpool, 28 July, 1956 (M)

League Club	Source	Date Signed	Seasons Played	Apps	Subs	Gls
Everton	App	05.74				
Workington	Tr	08.75	75	3	1	0

NEVINS, Laurence
Gateshead, 2 July, 1920

League Club	Source	Date Signed	Seasons Played	Apps	Subs	Gls
Newcastle U.		09.40				
Brighton & H.A.	Tr	05.47	47	5	-	0
Hartlepool U.	Tr	03.48	47-48	18	-	8

NEW, Martin P.
Swindon, 11 May, 1959 E Sch (G)

League Club	Source	Date Signed	Seasons Played	Apps	Subs	Gls
Arsenal	App	03.77				
Mansfield T.	Tr	06.78	78-79	21	0	0
Barnsley	Tr	06.80	80	24	0	0

NEWALL, Daniel J.
Newport, 5 June, 1921 (WH)

League Club	Source	Date Signed	Seasons Played	Apps	Subs	Gls
Newport Co.	Jnrs	06.38	38-54	231	-	4

NEWBERRY, Peter J.
Derby, 4 March, 1938 (CF)

League Club	Source	Date Signed	Seasons Played	Apps	Subs	Gls
Derby Co.	Jnrs	03.55	58-60	5	-	2

NEWBOLD, Alfred
Hartlepool, 7 August, 1921 (RB)

League Club	Source	Date Signed	Seasons Played	Apps	Subs	Gls
Huddersfield T.	Ouston W.	12.45	46	2	-	0
Newport Co.	Tr	10.46	46	22	-	0

NEWBY, T. Geoffrey
Barrow, 9 October, 1949 (WH)

League Club	Source	Date Signed	Seasons Played	Apps	Subs	Gls
Barrow (Am)	Jnrs	11.68	68	1	0	0

NEWCOMBE, Bernard J. (Len)
Swansea, 28 February, 1931 (OL)

League Club	Source	Date Signed	Seasons Played	Apps	Subs	Gls
Fulham	Jnrs	05.48	51-54	23	-	3
Brentford	Tr	04.56	55-58	84	-	10

NEWCOMBE, Giles A.
Doncaster, 9 July, 1968 (G)

League Club	Source	Date Signed	Seasons Played	Apps	Subs	Gls
Rotherham U.	YT	06.87	86	6	0	0

NEWELL, Edgar
Swansea, 17 April, 1920 (CH)

League Club	Source	Date Signed	Seasons Played	Apps	Subs	Gls
Swansea C.		08.46	47-50	24	-	0

NEWELL, George
Rochdale, 7 March, 1936

League Club	Source	Date Signed	Seasons Played	Apps	Subs	Gls
Rochdale		04.57	57	1	-	0

NEWELL, Michael C.
Liverpool, 27 January, 1965 Eu21-4/E'B' (F)

League Club	Source	Date Signed	Seasons Played	Apps	Subs	Gls
Crewe Alex.	Liverpool (Jnr)	09.83	83	3	0	0
Wigan Ath.	Tr	10.83	83-85	64	8	25
Luton T.	Tr	01.86	85-87	62	1	18
Leicester C.	Tr	09.87	87-88	81	0	21
Everton	Tr	06.89	89-91	48	20	15
Blackburn Rov.	Tr	11.91	91	18	2	6

NEWELL, Paul C.
Woolwich, 23 February, 1969 (G)

League Club	Source	Date Signed	Seasons Played	Apps	Subs	Gls
Southend U.	YT	06.87	87-88	15	0	0
Leyton Orient	Tr	08.90	90-91	18	0	0

NEWHOUSE, Aiden R.
Wallasey, 23 May, 1972 E Sch/E Yth (F)

League Club	Source	Date Signed	Seasons Played	Apps	Subs	Gls
Chester C.	YT	07.89	87-89	29	15	6
Wimbledon	Tr	02.90	89-91	7	15	2

NEWLANDS, Douglas H.
Edinburgh, 29 October, 1931 (OR)

League Club	Source	Date Signed	Seasons Played	Apps	Subs	Gls
Burnley	Aberdeen	03.55	54-58	98	-	21
Stoke C.	Tr	07.59	59	32	-	8

NEWLANDS, Malcolm
Glasgow, 28 March, 1925 (G)

League Club	Source	Date Signed	Seasons Played	Apps	Subs	Gls
Preston N.E.	St Mirren	07.48	48-52	80	-	0
Workington	Tr	11.52	52-59	251	-	0

NEWLOVE, Peter
Bradford, 27 December, 1947 (HB)

League Club	Source	Date Signed	Seasons Played	Apps	Subs	Gls
Bradford C.	App	01.66	64-66	2	1	0

NEWMAN, Albert
Lichfield, 1 March, 1915 Died 1982 (WH)

League Club	Source	Date Signed	Seasons Played	Apps	Subs	Gls
Walsall	Brierley Hill Alliance	11.39	46-49	136	-	2

NEWMAN, Darren L.
Brighton, 14 August, 1968 (D)

League Club	Source	Date Signed	Seasons Played	Apps	Subs	Gls
Brighton & H.A.	App	08.86	85	1	0	0

NEWMAN, Eric I. A.
Romford, 24 November, 1924 Died1971 (G)

League Club	Source	Date Signed	Seasons Played	Apps	Subs	Gls
Arsenal	Romford	10.46				
Ipswich T.	Tr	09.50	52	18	-	0

League Club	Source	Date Signed	Seasons Played	Career Record Apps	Subs	Gls
NEWMAN, John H. G.						
Hereford, 13 December, 1933						(WH)
Birmingham C.	Jnrs	03.51	51-57	60	-	0
Leicester C.	Tr	11.57	57-59	61	-	2
Plymouth Arg.	Tr	01.60	59-67	298	0	9
Exeter C.	Tr	11.67	67-71	91	1	1
NEWMAN, Keith						
Farnham, 20 November, 1949 E Sch						(WH)
Aldershot	App	11.66	66-69	19	4	0
York C.	Tr	07.70	70	3	1	0
NEWMAN, H. Michael						
Canada, 2 April, 1932						(IF)
West Ham U.	Dagenham	02.57	56-57	7	-	2
NEWMAN, Richard A.						
Guildford, 5 August, 1970						(M)
Crystal Palace	Jnrs	01.88				
Maidstone U.	L	02.92	91	9	1	1
NEWMAN, Robert N.						
Bradford-on-Avon, 13 December, 1963						(D/M)
Bristol C.	App	10.81	81-90	382	12	52
Norwich C.	Tr	07.91	91	41	0	7
NEWMAN, Ronald						
Pontypridd, 1 May, 1933						(IF)
Northampton T.	Ynysybwl	10.53	54-55	18	-	5
Coventry C.	Tr	03.56	55-56	13	-	2
Torquay U.	Tr	07.57	57	5	-	0
NEWMAN, Ronald V.						
Fareham, 19 January, 1934						(W)
Portsmouth	Woking	01.55	54-60	109	-	21
Leyton Orient	Tr	01.61	60-61	14	-	1
Crystal Palace	Tr	10.62	62	6	-	0
Gillingham	Tr	09.63	63-65	90	3	20
NEWSHAM, Stanley						
Farnworth, 24 May, 1931						(IF)
Bournemouth		06.52	52-56	142	-	74
Notts Co.	Tr	08.57	57-61	99	-	45
NEWSOME, Jonathan						
Sheffield, 6 September, 1970						(FB)
Sheffield Wed.	YT	07.89	89-90	6	1	0
Leeds U.	Tr	06.91	91	7	3	2

League Club	Source	Date Signed	Seasons Played	Career Record Apps	Subs	Gls
NEWSOME, Robin						
Hebden Bridge, 25 September, 1919						(IF)
West Bromwich A.	Congleton T.	03.39				
Coventry C.	Tr	06.47	47	7	-	2
NEWSON, Mark J.						
Stepney, 7 December, 1960 E Semi-Pro						(FB)
Charlton Ath.	App	12.78				
Bournemouth	Maidstone U.	05.85	85-89	172	5	23
Fulham	Tr	02.90	89-91	72	1	4
NEWTON, Benjamin						
Grimsby, 10 October, 1934						(IF)
Grimsby T.	Jnrs	07.53	53	3	-	0
NEWTON, S. Douglas						
Newcastle, 16 January, 1959						(M)
Scarborough (N/C)	Boston U.	03.88	87	4	1	0
NEWTON, Edward J. I.						
Hammersmith, 13 December, 1971 E Yth						(M)
Chelsea	YT	05.90	91	0	1	1
Cardiff C.	L	01.92	91	18	0	4
NEWTON, Eric						
Sheffield, 21 June, 1932						(IF)
Halifax T.	Norton Woodseats	12.54	54	10	-	3
NEWTON, Graham W.						
Bilston, 22 December, 1942						(IF)
Blackpool	Wolverhampton W. (Am)	08.61				
Walsall	Tr	02.62	62-63	30	-	10
Coventry C.	Tr	01.64	63	8	-	3
Bournemouth	Tr	12.64	64-66	27	1	3
Port Vale	Atlanta (USA)	11.68	68	4	0	0
NEWTON, Henry A.						
Nottingham, 18 February, 1944 Eu23-4/EF Lge						(M/LB)
Nottingham F.	Jnrs	06.61	63-70	282	0	17
Everton	Tr	10.70	70-73	76	1	5
Derby Co.	Tr	09.73	73-76	111	6	5
Walsall	Tr	07.77	77	16	0	0
NEWTON, John						
Edinburgh, 19 January, 1940						(WH)
Notts Co.	Craiglea Th.	10.57	58-60	5	-	0

Henry Newton (Nottingham Forest, Everton, Derby County & Walsall)

NEWTON, John L.
Bishop Auckland, 25 May, 1925 (WH)

League Club	Source	Date Signed	Seasons Played	Apps	Subs	Gls
Newcastle U.		05.44				
Hartlepool U.	Tr	05.46	46-57	332	-	15

NEWTON, Keith R.
Manchester, 23 June, 1941 Eu23-4/EF Lge/E-27 (FB)

League Club	Source	Date Signed	Seasons Played	Apps	Subs	Gls
Blackburn Rov.	Jnrs	10.58	60-69	306	0	9
Everton	Tr	12.69	69-71	48	1	1
Burnley	Tr	06.72	72-77	209	0	5

NEWTON, Reginald W.
Bow, 30 June, 1926 (G)

League Club	Source	Date Signed	Seasons Played	Apps	Subs	Gls
Leyton Orient	Dagenham Wks	04.48	48	23	-	0
Brentford	Tr	07.49	49-56	87	-	0

Reg Newton (Leyton Orient & Brentford)

NEWTON, Robert
Chesterfield, 23 November, 1956 (F)

League Club	Source	Date Signed	Seasons Played	Apps	Subs	Gls
Huddersfield T.	App	11.73	73-76	37	5	7
Hartlepool U.	Tr	08.77	77-82	150	0	48
Port Vale	Tr	09.82	82-83	48	0	22
Chesterfield	Tr	10.83	83-84	78	0	29
Hartlepool U.	Tr	07.85	85	8	3	2
Stockport Co.	L	03.86	85	6	0	1
Bristol Rov. (N/C)		02.87	86	7	1	0

NEWTON, Robert A.
Earl Shilton, 19 January, 1946 (OL)

League Club	Source	Date Signed	Seasons Played	Apps	Subs	Gls
Leicester C.	App	08.63	64	2	-	0
Bradford C.	Tr	05.65	65	19	1	4

NGATA, Heremaia (Herry)
New Zealand, 24 August, 1971 (F)

League Club	Source	Date Signed	Seasons Played	Apps	Subs	Gls
Hull C. (N/C)	Jnrs	07.89	89-91	8	17	0

NIBLETT, Victor
Aldershot, 9 December, 1924 (CH)

League Club	Source	Date Signed	Seasons Played	Apps	Subs	Gls
Reading	Jnrs	08.44	46-49	6	-	0
West Ham U.	Tr	06.50				
Gillingham	Tr	08.51	51-55	154	-	0

NIBLOE, John A.
Sheffield, 1 June, 1939 Died 1964 (CF)

League Club	Source	Date Signed	Seasons Played	Apps	Subs	Gls
Sheffield U.		08.58	58-60	25	-	4
Stoke C.	Tr	10.61	61-62	19	-	4
Doncaster Rov.	Tr	10.62	62-63	36	-	7
Stockport Co.	Tr	07.64	64	19	-	1

NIBLOE, Joseph
Glasgow, 10 December, 1926 (FB)

League Club	Source	Date Signed	Seasons Played	Apps	Subs	Gls
Cardiff C.	Clydebank Jnrs	03.48	48	1	-	0

NICHOL, George W.
Bannockburn, 20 July, 1923 (G)

League Club	Source	Date Signed	Seasons Played	Apps	Subs	Gls
Aldershot	Falkirk	08.51	51	19	-	0

NICHOL, Robert W.
Carlisle, 19 January, 1941 (OL)

League Club	Source	Date Signed	Seasons Played	Apps	Subs	Gls
Carlisle U. (Am)	Jnrs	06.58	58-59	3	-	1

NICHOLAS, Anthony W. L.
West Ham, 16 April, 1938 E Yth (IF)

League Club	Source	Date Signed	Seasons Played	Apps	Subs	Gls
Chelsea	Jnrs	05.55	56-59	46	-	13
Brighton & H.A.	Tr	11.60	60-61	65	-	22
Leyton Orient	Chelmsford C.	06.65	65	8	1	2

NICHOLAS, C. Brian
Aberdare, 20 April, 1933 E Sch (WH)

League Club	Source	Date Signed	Seasons Played	Apps	Subs	Gls
Queens Park R.	Jnrs	05.50	48-54	115	-	2
Chelsea	Tr	07.55	55-57	39	-	6
Coventry C.	Tr	02.58	57-61	113	-	0

NICHOLAS, Charles
Glasgow, 30 December, 1961 S Yth/Su21-6/S-20 (F)

League Club	Source	Date Signed	Seasons Played	Apps	Subs	Gls
Arsenal	Glasgow Celtic	07.83	83-87	145	6	34

NICHOLAS, Glyn
Dartmouth, 2 December, 1946 (CF)

League Club	Source	Date Signed	Seasons Played	Apps	Subs	Gls
Plymouth Arg.	App	09.64	64-65	2	0	0
Crewe Alex.	L	03.66	65	2	0	1

NICHOLAS, John T.
Derby, 26 November, 1910 Died 1977 W Sch (WH)

League Club	Source	Date Signed	Seasons Played	Apps	Subs	Gls
Derby Co.	Jnrs	12.27	28-46	347	-	14

NICHOLAS, Kenneth W.
Northampton, 3 February, 1938 E Sch/E Yth (FB)

League Club	Source	Date Signed	Seasons Played	Apps	Subs	Gls
Arsenal	Jnrs	05.55				
Watford	Tr	05.59	59-64	198	-	4

NICHOLAS, Peter
Newport, 10 November, 1959 W Sch/Wu21-3/W-73 (M)

League Club	Source	Date Signed	Seasons Played	Apps	Subs	Gls
Crystal Palace	App	12.76	77-80	127	0	7
Arsenal	Tr	03.81	80-82	57	3	1
Crystal Palace	Tr	10.83	83-84	47	0	7
Luton T.	Tr	01.85	84-86	102	0	1
Chelsea	Aberdeen	08.88	88-90	79	1	3
Watford	Tr	03.91	90-91	40	0	1

NICHOLL, Christopher J.
Wilmslow, 12 October, 1946 NI-51 (CD)

League Club	Source	Date Signed	Seasons Played	Apps	Subs	Gls
Burnley	Jnrs	04.65				
Halifax T.	Witton A.	06.68	68-69	42	0	3
Luton T.	Tr	08.69	69-71	98	0	6
Aston Villa	Tr	03.72	71-76	210	0	11
Southampton	Tr	06.77	77-82	228	0	8
Grimsby T.	Tr	08.83	83-84	70	0	0

NICHOLL, James M.
Canada, 28 February, 1956 NI Sch/NIu21-1/NI-73 (RB)

League Club	Source	Date Signed	Seasons Played	Apps	Subs	Gls
Manchester U.	App	02.74	74-81	188	9	3
Sunderland	L	12.81	81	3	0	0
Sunderland	Toronto (Can)	09.82	82	29	0	0
West Bromwich A.	Toronto (Can)	11.84	84-85	56	0	0

NICHOLL, Terence J.
Wilmslow, 16 September, 1952 (M)

League Club	Source	Date Signed	Seasons Played	Apps	Subs	Gls
Crewe Alex.		02.72	71-72	46	0	7
Sheffield U.	Tr	03.73	73-74	12	10	1
Southend U.	Tr	05.75	75-76	50	0	3
Gillingham	Tr	10.76	76-80	184	0	11

NICHOLLS, Alan
Plymouth, 10 February, 1963 (CD)

League Club	Source	Date Signed	Seasons Played	Apps	Subs	Gls
Bristol C.	App	02.80	80-82	70	0	5

NICHOLLS, David
Bradford, 3 November, 1956 E Sch (M)

League Club	Source	Date Signed	Seasons Played	Apps	Subs	Gls
Huddersfield T.	App	11.73				
Bradford C. (N/C)	Tr	08.75	75	0	4	0

NICHOLLS, James H.
Coseley, 27 November, 1919 (G)

League Club	Source	Date Signed	Seasons Played	Apps	Subs	Gls
Bradford P.A.		05.46	46-49	36	-	0
Rochdale	Tr	08.51	51-52	50	-	0

NICHOLLS, John
Wolverhampton, 3 April, 1931 Eu23-1/E-2 (IF)

League Club	Source	Date Signed	Seasons Played	Apps	Subs	Gls
West Bromwich A.	Heath T.	08.51	51-56	131	-	58
Cardiff C.	Tr	05.57	57	8	-	2
Exeter C.	Tr	11.57	57-58	55	-	23

NICHOLLS, Phillip R.
Bilston, 22 June, 1952 (CD)

League Club	Source	Date Signed	Seasons Played	Apps	Subs	Gls
Wolverhampton W.	App	07.70				
Crewe Alex.	Tr	09.72	72-76	155	8	8
Bradford C.	Tr	03.77	76-77	19	2	2
Crewe Alex.	Tr	08.78	78	10	3	0

NICHOLLS, Raymond I.
Peterborough, 7 April, 1965 (M)

League Club	Source	Date Signed	Seasons Played	Apps	Subs	Gls
Cambridge U.	App	08.82	81-83	18	5	1

NICHOLLS, Ronald B.
Sharpness, 4 December, 1933 (G)

League Club	Source	Date Signed	Seasons Played	Apps	Subs	Gls
Bristol Rov.	Fulham (Am)	11.54	55-57	71	-	0
Cardiff C.	Tr	08.58	58-60	51	-	0
Bristol C.	Tr	07.61	61-63	39	-	0

NICHOLLS, Ronald H.
Cannock, 18 October, 1935

League Club	Source	Date Signed	Seasons Played	Apps	Subs	Gls
West Bromwich A.	Jnrs	11.52				
Walsall	Tr	08.53	53	2	-	0

NICHOLLS, Wayne K.
Leicester, 21 October, 1952 (F)

League Club	Source	Date Signed	Seasons Played	Apps	Subs	Gls
Leicester C.	Wolverhampton W. (App)	11.70				
Workington	Tr	08.71	71-72	21	12	1

NICHOLS, Adam A.
Ilford, 14 September, 1962 (D)

League Club	Source	Date Signed	Seasons Played	Apps	Subs	Gls
Ipswich T.	App	10.79				
Colchester U. (N/C)	South Africa	09.83	83	4	2	1

NICHOLS, Brian A.
Dagenham, 30 May, 1945 (FB)

League Club	Source	Date Signed	Seasons Played	Apps	Subs	Gls
Fulham	App	07.63	65-67	50	1	1
Millwall	Tr	07.68	68-69	9	1	0

NICHOLSON, Derek
Chertsey, 8 April, 1936 (OR)

League Club	Source	Date Signed	Seasons Played	Apps	Subs	Gls
Leyton Orient	Chertsey	11.53	57	6	-	0

NICHOLSON, Gary A.
Newcastle, 4 November, 1960 (LW)

League Club	Source	Date Signed	Seasons Played	Apps	Subs	Gls
Newcastle U.	App	11.78	78-80	7	5	0
Mansfield T.	Tr	08.81	81-83	112	6	21
York C.	Tr	07.84	84	23	1	4
Halifax T.	Tr	07.85	85-86	54	6	4

NICHOLSON, G. Harold
Carlisle, 25 January, 1932 (G)

League Club	Source	Date Signed	Seasons Played	Apps	Subs	Gls
Grimsby T.	Carlisle U. (Am)	08.52	53	17	-	0
Nottingham F.	Tr	07.55	55-56	72	-	0
Accrington St.	Tr	03.58	58	1	-	0
Leyton Orient	Tr	03.59	59	4	-	0
Bristol C.	Tr	07.60	60	1	-	0

NICHOLSON, James J.
Belfast, 27 February, 1943 NI Sch/NIu23-4/NI'B'-1/NI-4 (M)

League Club	Source	Date Signed	Seasons Played	Apps	Subs	Gls
Manchester U.	Jnrs	02.60	60-62	58	-	5
Huddersfield T.	Tr	12.64	64-73	280	1	25
Bury	Tr	12.73	73-75	79	4	0

NICHOLSON, John P.
Liverpool, 2 September, 1936 Died 1966 (CH)

League Club	Source	Date Signed	Seasons Played	Apps	Subs	Gls
Liverpool		01.57	59	1	-	0
Port Vale	Tr	08.61	61-65	184	0	1
Doncaster Rov.	Tr	09.65	65-66	41	0	0

NICHOLSON, John R.
Harrington, 23 June, 1928 (OL)

League Club	Source	Date Signed	Seasons Played	Apps	Subs	Gls
Barrow	Frizington	05.49	49	4	-	1

NICHOLSON, Maxwell
Leeds, 3 October, 1971 (F)

League Club	Source	Date Signed	Seasons Played	Apps	Subs	Gls
Doncaster Rov.	YT	07.90	89-91	23	4	2

NICHOLSON, Peter
Cleator Moor, 12 January, 1951 (FB)

League Club	Source	Date Signed	Seasons Played	Apps	Subs	Gls
Blackpool	Carlisle U. (App)	08.69	70	3	3	0
Bolton W.	Tr	06.71	71-81	303	15	12
Rochdale (N/C)	Lytham	11.82	82	7	0	0
Carlisle U. (N/C)	Lytham	03.83	82-83	1	2	0

NICHOLSON, Peter W.
Hull, 11 December, 1936 (CF)

League Club	Source	Date Signed	Seasons Played	Apps	Subs	Gls
Hull C. (Am)	Kingburn Ath.	06.60	60	1	-	0

NICHOLSON, Reece
Bircotes, 4 April, 1936 (IF)

League Club	Source	Date Signed	Seasons Played	Apps	Subs	Gls
Doncaster Rov.	Jnrs	09.53	54-57	28	-	8

NICHOLSON, Shane M.
Newark, 3 June, 1970 (M/LB)

League Club	Source	Date Signed	Seasons Played	Apps	Subs	Gls
Lincoln C.	YT	07.88	86-91	122	11	7

NICHOLSON, Stanley
Middlesbrough, 20 August, 1931 (IF)

League Club	Source	Date Signed	Seasons Played	Apps	Subs	Gls
Middlesbrough	South Bank	05.49				
Leeds U.	Tr	08.51				
Hartlepool U.	Horden Colly	07.58	58	7	-	1

NICHOLSON, William E.
Scarborough, 26 January, 1919 E'B'-3/EF Lge/E-1 (WH)

League Club	Source	Date Signed	Seasons Played	Apps	Subs	Gls
Tottenham H.	Jnrs	08.38	38-54	315	-	6

NICKALLS, James
Amble, 29 May, 1934 (CH)

League Club	Source	Date Signed	Seasons Played	Apps	Subs	Gls
Sunderland		04.53				
Darlington	Tr	05.54	54	18	-	0

NICKEAS, Mark
Southport, 20 October, 1956 (CD)

League Club	Source	Date Signed	Seasons Played	Apps	Subs	Gls
Plymouth Arg.	App	07.74				
Chester C.	Tr	08.75	75-78	58	2	1

NICKLAS, Charles
Sunderland, 26 April, 1930 (CF)

League Club	Source	Date Signed	Seasons Played	Apps	Subs	Gls
Hull C.	Silksworth Jnrs	12.50	51	6	-	1
Darlington	Tr	05.53	53	17	-	6

NICOL, Bennett
Glasgow, 10 March, 1921

League Club	Source	Date Signed	Seasons Played	Apps	Subs	Gls
Bolton W.		11.46				
Rochdale	Winsford U.	07.49	49	5	-	1

NICOL, Paul J.
Scunthorpe, 31 October, 1967 (CD)

League Club	Source	Date Signed	Seasons Played	Apps	Subs	Gls
Scunthorpe U.	YT	07.86	86-89	68	7	2

NICOL, Robert B. M.
Edinburgh, 11 May, 1936 S Sch (WH)

League Club	Source	Date Signed	Seasons Played	Apps	Subs	Gls
Barnsley	Hibernian	08.62	62-63	37	-	1

NICOL, Stephen
Irvine, 11 December, 1961 Su21-14/S-27 (FB/M)

League Club	Source	Date Signed	Seasons Played	Apps	Subs	Gls
Liverpool	Ayr U.	10.81	82-91	265	11	35

NICOLL, Paul
Chester, 10 November, 1966

League Club	Source	Date Signed	Seasons Played	Apps	Subs	Gls
Wrexham (N/C)	Jnrs	07.84	84	0	1	0

NIEDZWIECKI, A. Edward
Bangor, 3 May, 1959 W Sch/W-2 (G)

League Club	Source	Date Signed	Seasons Played	Apps	Subs	Gls
Wrexham	Jnrs	07.76	77-82	111	0	0
Chelsea	Tr	06.83	83-87	136	0	0

NIELSEN, Kent
Denmark, 28 December, 1961 Danish Int (CD)

League Club	Source	Date Signed	Seasons Played	Apps	Subs	Gls
Aston Villa	Brondby (Den)	06.89	89-91	74	5	4

NIELSON, Norman F.
South Africa, 6 November, 1928 (CH)

League Club	Source	Date Signed	Seasons Played	Apps	Subs	Gls
Charlton Ath.	Arcadia (SA)	07.49	49	1	-	0
Derby Co.	Tr	09.51	51-53	57	-	8
Bury	Tr	05.54	54-56	100	-	5
Hull C.	Tr	04.57	56-57	25	-	0

NIEUWENHUYS, Berry
South Africa, 5 November, 1911 (OR)

League Club	Source	Date Signed	Seasons Played	Apps	Subs	Gls
Liverpool	Germiston Callies (SA)	09.33	33-46	239	-	74

NIGHTINGALE, Albert J.
Thrybergh, 10 November, 1923 (IF)

League Club	Source	Date Signed	Seasons Played	Apps	Subs	Gls
Sheffield U.	Thurcroft	06.41	46-47	62	-	14
Huddersfield T.	Tr	03.48	47-51	119	-	20
Blackburn Rov.	Tr	10.51	51-52	35	-	5
Leeds U.	Tr	10.52	52-56	130	-	48

Steve Nicol (Ayr United, Liverpool & Scotland)

NIGHTINGALE, David R.
Liverpool, 15 August, 1927 (RB)

League Club	Source	Date Signed	Seasons Played	Apps	Subs	Gls
Tranmere Rov.		09.46	46	3	-	0

NIGHTINGALE, Mark B. D.
Salisbury, 1 February, 1957 E Yth (D/M)

League Club	Source	Date Signed	Seasons Played	Apps	Subs	Gls
Bournemouth	App	07.74	74-75	44	5	4
Crystal Palace	Tr	06.76				
Norwich C.	Tr	07.77	77-81	28	7	0
Bournemouth	Bulova (HK)	11.82	82-85	144	6	4
Peterborough U.	Tr	07.86	86-87	71	7	2

NIGHTINGALE, Ronald
Darwen, 27 January, 1937 (WH)

League Club	Source	Date Signed	Seasons Played	Apps	Subs	Gls
Accrington St.		07.57	58-60	14	-	0

NIKOLIC, Dusan
Yugoslavia, 23 January, 1953 Yugoslav Int (W)

League Club	Source	Date Signed	Seasons Played	Apps	Subs	Gls
Bolton W.	Red Star Belgrade (Yug)	10.80	80-81	22	0	2

NILSSON, N. L. Roland
Sweden, 27 November, 1963 Swedish Int (RB)

League Club	Source	Date Signed	Seasons Played	Apps	Subs	Gls
Sheffield Wed.	I.F.K. Göteborg (Swe)	11.89	89-91	81	0	1

Roland Nilsson (IFK Goteborg, Sheffield Wednesday & Sweden)

NIMMO, Ian W.
Boston, 23 January, 1958 (F)

League Club	Source	Date Signed	Seasons Played	Apps	Subs	Gls
Sheffield Wed.	App	01.76	75-78	26	19	10
Peterborough U.	L	01.77	76	4	0	1
Doncaster Rov.	Tr	06.79	79-81	77	9	29

NIMMO, William B.
Forth (LK), 11 January, 1934 (G)

League Club	Source	Date Signed	Seasons Played	Apps	Subs	Gls
Leeds U.	Alloa Ath.	02.56	57	1	-	0
Doncaster Rov.	Tr	03.58	57-61	182	-	0
Mansfield T.	Tr	07.62				

NISBET, Gordon J. M.
Wallsend, 18 September, 1951 Eu23-1 (RB)

League Club	Source	Date Signed	Seasons Played	Apps	Subs	Gls
West Bromwich A.	Jnrs	09.68	69-75	136	0	0
Hull C.	Tr	09.76	76-80	190	3	1
Plymouth Arg.	Tr	12.80	80-86	281	0	14
Exeter C.	Tr	06.87	87	12	0	0

NISH, David J.
Burton, 26 September, 1947 E Yth/Eu23-10/EF Lge/E-5 (LB)

League Club	Source	Date Signed	Seasons Played	Apps	Subs	Gls
Leicester C.	Measham Imp.	07.66	66-72	228	0	25
Derby Co.	Tr	08.72	72-78	184	4	10

NIX, Peter
Rotherham, 25 January, 1958 (W)

League Club	Source	Date Signed	Seasons Played	Apps	Subs	Gls
Rotherham U.	Jnrs	08.76	77-79	22	0	2

NIXON, Eric W.
Manchester, 4 October, 1962 (G)

League Club	Source	Date Signed	Seasons Played	Apps	Subs	Gls
Manchester C.	Curzon Ashton	12.83	85-87	58	0	0
Wolverhampton W.	L	08.86	86	16	0	0
Bradford C.	L	11.86	86	3	0	0
Southampton	L	12.86	86	4	0	0
Carlisle U.	L	01.87	86	16	0	0
Tranmere Rov.	L	03.88	87	8	0	0
Tranmere Rov.	Tr	07.88	88-91	180	0	0

NIXON, Jonathan C.
Ilkeston, 20 January, 1948 (W)

League Club	Source	Date Signed	Seasons Played	Apps	Subs	Gls
Derby Co.	Jnrs	09.65				
Notts Co.	Ilkeston T.	01.70	69-74	167	12	32
Peterborough U.	Tr	09.74	74-76	104	6	16
Shrewsbury T.	Tr	08.77	77	21	2	3
Barnsley	Tr	03.78	77	5	4	0
Halifax T.	Tr	06.78	78	12	7	1

NIXON, Paul
Seaham, 23 September, 1963 NZ Int (F)

League Club	Source	Date Signed	Seasons Played	Apps	Subs	Gls
Bristol Rov.	Seaham Red Star	01.89	88-90	31	13	6

NIXON, Thomas J.
Backworth, 25 May, 1931 (LH)

League Club	Source	Date Signed	Seasons Played	Apps	Subs	Gls
Darlington (Am)	Newcastle U. (Am)	05.51	51	1	-	0

NIXON, William J.
Ballynahinch (NI), 28 September, 1941 NI Sch (IF)

League Club	Source	Date Signed	Seasons Played	Apps	Subs	Gls
Norwich C.	Distillery	03.61	61	1	-	0
Shrewsbury T.	Tr	03.62	61-64	17	-	1

NOAKE, David J.
Dorchester, 9 June, 1940 (W)

League Club	Source	Date Signed	Seasons Played	Apps	Subs	Gls
Luton T.	Dorchester T.	11.59	59-60	17	-	0
Bristol C.	Tr	06.61	61	11	-	3

NOAKES, Alfred G.
Stratford, 14 August, 1933 (FB)

League Club	Source	Date Signed	Seasons Played	Apps	Subs	Gls
West Ham U.	Jnrs	08.50				
Crystal Palace	Sittingbourne	06.55	55-61	195	-	14
Portsmouth	Tr	07.62	62-63	13	-	0

NOBBS, A. Keith
Bishop Auckland, 19 September, 1961 (RB)

League Club	Source	Date Signed	Seasons Played	Apps	Subs	Gls
Middlesbrough	App	09.79	80	1	0	0
Halifax T.	Tr	08.82	82-83	87	0	1
Hartlepool U.	Bishop Auckland	08.85	85-91	247	6	1

NOBLE, Alfred W. T.
Hackney, 18 September, 1924 E Amat (IF)

League Club	Source	Date Signed	Seasons Played	Apps	Subs	Gls
Colchester U. (Am)	Briggs Sports	09.55	55	1	-	0

NOBLE, Barry
Stockton, 5 June, 1951 (G)

League Club	Source	Date Signed	Seasons Played	Apps	Subs	Gls
Hartlepool U. (Am)	Jnrs	08.70	71	1	0	0

NOBLE, Daniel W.T.
Hull, 2 September, 1970 (G)

League Club	Source	Date Signed	Seasons Played	Apps	Subs	Gls
Stoke C.	YT	07.89	89-90	3	0	0
Crewe Alex.	Tr	06.91	91	7	0	0

NOBLE, Frank
Sheffield, 26 October, 1945 (FB)

League Club	Source	Date Signed	Seasons Played	Apps	Subs	Gls
Sheffield Wed.	Jnrs	05.63	63-65	2	0	0
Peterborough U.	Tr	07.67	67-71	205	2	1

NOBLE, John
Manchester, 20 May, 1919 (WH)

League Club	Source	Date Signed	Seasons Played	Apps	Subs	Gls
Stockport Co.	Warte Villa	03.39	46	1	-	0

NOBLE, Norman
Barnsley, 8 August, 1923 Died 1973 (FB)

League Club	Source	Date Signed	Seasons Played	Apps	Subs	Gls
Huddersfield T.		06.43				
Bradford C.	Tr	10.45				
Rotherham U.	Ransome & Marles	05.48	48-57	326	-	21

League Club	Source	Date Signed	Seasons Played	Career Record Apps	Subs	Gls

NOBLE, Peter
Newcastle, 19 August, 1944 (M)

League Club	Source	Date Signed	Seasons Played	Apps	Subs	Gls
Newcastle U.	Consett	11.64	65-67	22	3	7
Swindon T.,	Tr	01.68	67-72	212	4	62
Burnley	Tr	06.73	73-79	241	2	63
Blackpool	Tr	01.80	79-82	95	2	14

NOBLE, Robert
Newcastle, 25 May, 1949 (CD)

League Club	Source	Date Signed	Seasons Played	Apps	Subs	Gls
Newcastle U.	App	04.67				
Barrow	L	08.69	69	19	0	3
Bury	Tr	08.70	70	6	0	0
Barrow	Tr	10.70	70-71	72	1	5
Colchester U.	Tr	08.72	72	25	2	0
Southport	Tr	03.73	72-74	61	2	6
Darlington	Tr	08.75	75-76	54	0	3

NOBLE, Robert
Manchester, 18 December, 1945 E Yth (FB)

League Club	Source	Date Signed	Seasons Played	Apps	Subs	Gls
Manchester U.	App	12.62	65-66	31	0	0

NOBLE, Wayne I.
Bristol, 11 June, 1967 (M)

League Club	Source	Date Signed	Seasons Played	Apps	Subs	Gls
Bristol Rov.	App	03.85	85-86	16	6	1

NOGAN, Kurt
Cardiff, 9 September, 1970 Wu21-2 (F)

League Club	Source	Date Signed	Seasons Played	Apps	Subs	Gls
Luton T.	YT	07.89	89-91	17	16	3

NOGAN, Lee M.
Cardiff, 21 May, 1969 Wu21-1/W'B'/W-1 (F)

League Club	Source	Date Signed	Seasons Played	Apps	Subs	Gls
Oxford U.	YT	03.87	87-91	57	7	10
Brentford	L	03.87	86	10	1	2
Southend U.	L	09.87	87	6	0	1
Watford	Tr	12.91	91	23	0	5

NOLAN, David J.
Liverpool, 24 February, 1968 (M)

League Club	Source	Date Signed	Seasons Played	Apps	Subs	Gls
Chester C. (N/C)	Bromborough	01.92	91	1	0	0

NOLAN, George
Liverpool, 9 December, 1925 (LH)

League Club	Source	Date Signed	Seasons Played	Apps	Subs	Gls
Southport	A.I. Control	06.46	46	3	-	0

NOLAN, Ian R.
Liverpool, 9 July, 1970 (LB)

League Club	Source	Date Signed	Seasons Played	Apps	Subs	Gls
Tranmere Rov.	Marine	08.91	91	34	0	1

NOLAN, Michael W.
Dublin, 8 July, 1950 (FB)

League Club	Source	Date Signed	Seasons Played	Apps	Subs	Gls
Oldham Ath.	App	08.67	66-67	2	0	0

NOLAN, Philip
Edmonton, 29 December, 1923 (CH)

League Club	Source	Date Signed	Seasons Played	Apps	Subs	Gls
Watford	Hayes	10.47	47-54	91	-	8

NOLAN, Terence S.
Whiston, 16 March, 1956 (F)

League Club	Source	Date Signed	Seasons Played	Apps	Subs	Gls
Southport (N/C)	Prescot Cables	02.78	77	0	1	0

NOON, Harold
Sutton-in-Ashfield, 6 October, 1937 (FB)

League Club	Source	Date Signed	Seasons Played	Apps	Subs	Gls
Notts Co.	Bentinck Methodists	05.55	57-61	122	-	0
Bradford C.	Tr	07.62	62	1	-	0

NORBURY, Michael S.
Hemsworth, 22 January, 1969 (F)

League Club	Source	Date Signed	Seasons Played	Apps	Subs	Gls
Scarborough	Ossett T.	12.89				
Cambridge U.	Bridlington T.	02.92	91	4	10	2

NORCROSS, William
Preston, 29 December, 1937 (CF)

League Club	Source	Date Signed	Seasons Played	Apps	Subs	Gls
Southport (Am)	Chorley	07.59	59	1	-	0

NORMAN, Anthony J.
Deeside, 24 February, 1958 W'B'/W-5 (G)

League Club	Source	Date Signed	Seasons Played	Apps	Subs	Gls
Burnley	Jnrs	08.76				
Hull C.	Tr	02.80	79-88	372	0	0
Sunderland	Tr	12.88	88-91	133	0	0

NORMAN, Derek A.
Birmingham, 11 February, 1946 E Yth (WH)

League Club	Source	Date Signed	Seasons Played	Apps	Subs	Gls
Southampton	Alvechurch	01.64				
Aldershot	Tr	05.65	65	22	1	0

NORMAN, Griffith A.
Cardiff, 20 February, 1926 (WH)

League Club	Source	Date Signed	Seasons Played	Apps	Subs	Gls
Cardiff C.		04.50	51	1	-	0
Torquay U.	Tr	10.52	52-57	216	-	6

NORMAN, Malcolm A.
Cardiff, 24 October, 1934 (G)

League Club	Source	Date Signed	Seasons Played	Apps	Subs	Gls
Bristol Rov.	Cardiff Corries	05.58	58-61	69	-	0

NORMAN, Maurice
Mulbarton (Nk), 8 May, 1934 Eu23-3/EF Lge/E-23 (CH)

League Club	Source	Date Signed	Seasons Played	Apps	Subs	Gls
Norwich C.	Wymondham O.B.	09.52	54-55	35	-	0
Tottenham H.	Tr	11.55	55-65	357	0	15

NORMAN, Richard
Newcastle, 5 September, 1935 (LB)

League Club	Source	Date Signed	Seasons Played	Apps	Subs	Gls
Leicester C.	Horden Colly	11.58	59-67	303	0	2
Peterborough U.	Tr	07.68	68	9	1	0

NORMAN, Sean
Lowestoft, 27 November, 1966 (LB/LM)

League Club	Source	Date Signed	Seasons Played	Apps	Subs	Gls
Colchester U.	Lowestoft T.	07.85	86-87	18	4	1

NORMANTON, Graham S.
Hartlepool, 13 November, 1959 (FB)

League Club	Source	Date Signed	Seasons Played	Apps	Subs	Gls
Hartlepool U.	Middlesbrough (App)	07.78	79-80	17	1	0

NORMANTON, Sidney (Skinner)
Barnsley, 20 August, 1926 (WH)

League Club	Source	Date Signed	Seasons Played	Apps	Subs	Gls
Barnsley	Barnsley M.C.W.	09.45	47-53	123	-	2
Halifax T.	Tr	07.54	54	14	-	0

NORRIE, Craig T.
Hull, 22 July, 1960 (F)

League Club	Source	Date Signed	Seasons Played	Apps	Subs	Gls
Hull C.	App	08.78	78-81	22	9	4

NORRIS, Derek
Beighton, 19 June, 1935 (WH)

League Club	Source	Date Signed	Seasons Played	Apps	Subs	Gls
Peterborough U.	Gainsborough Trin.	(N/L)	60	5	-	0

NORRIS, George A.
Aldershot, 19 September, 1935 (CF)

League Club	Source	Date Signed	Seasons Played	Apps	Subs	Gls
Aldershot	Farnborough T.	12.58	58-63	106	-	58

NORRIS, Graham J.
Hampton, 8 February, 1954 (W)

League Club	Source	Date Signed	Seasons Played	Apps	Subs	Gls
Crystal Palace	App	02.72				
Southend U.	L	03.73	72	1	0	0

NORRIS, Michael
Retford, 27 February, 1957 (G)

League Club	Source	Date Signed	Seasons Played	Apps	Subs	Gls
Scunthorpe U.	App	02.75	73-75	25	0	0

NORRIS, Oliver P.
Derry (NI), 1 April, 1929 (CF)

League Club	Source	Date Signed	Seasons Played	Apps	Subs	Gls
Middlesbrough	Jnrs	07.48	51-53	12	-	3
Bournemouth	Worcester C.	07.55	55-58	96	-	34
Northampton T.	Tr	09.58	58	14	-	1
Rochdale	Ashford T.	01.61	60	2	-	1

NORRIS, Raymond G.
Bristol, 15 July, 1922 (CH)

League Club	Source	Date Signed	Seasons Played	Apps	Subs	Gls
Bristol C.	Bedminster	05.47	47	3	-	0

NORRIS, Russell
Hoo, 1 February, 1971 (RB)

League Club	Source	Date Signed	Seasons Played	Apps	Subs	Gls
Gillingham	YT	07.89	89	2	3	0

NORRIS, Stephen M.
Coventry, 22 September, 1961 (F)

League Club	Source	Date Signed	Seasons Played	Apps	Subs	Gls
Scarborough	Telford U.	07.88	88-89	35	10	13
Notts Co.	L	11.89	89	0	1	0
Carlisle U.	Tr	12.89	89-90	21	8	5
Halifax T.	Tr	10.90	90-91	56	0	35
Chesterfield	Tr	01.92	91	21	0	10

NORTH, Eric
Halifax, 6 October, 1923 (OL)

League Club	Source	Date Signed	Seasons Played	Apps	Subs	Gls
Halifax T. (Am)	Lee Mount	08.48	48	1	-	0

League Club	Source	Date Signed	Seasons Played	Career Record Apps	Subs	Gls
NORTH, Marcus V.						
Ware, 29 May, 1966						(F)
Luton T.	App	03.84	85-86	11	7	3
Lincoln C.	L	03.85	84	4	0	0
Scunthorpe U.	L	01.87	86	4	1	2
Birmingham C.	L	03.87	86	4	1	1
Grimsby T.	Tr	08.87	87-88	64	3	17
Leicester C.	Tr	03.89	88-90	51	20	9
Grimsby T.	Luton T. (N/C)	08.91	91	0	1	0
NORTH, Stacey S.						
Luton, 25 November, 1964 E Yth						(CD)
Luton T.	App	08.82	83-87	24	1	0
Wolverhampton W.	L	11.85	85	3	0	0
West Bromwich A.	Tr	12.87	87-89	96	2	0
Fulham	Tr	10.90	90	38	0	0
NORTH, Thomas W.						
Barrow-on-Soar, 31 October, 1919						(IF)
Nottingham F.	Banbury Spencer	01.45	46	1	-	0
NORTHCOTT, George E.						
Torquay, 7 May, 1935						(CH)
Torquay U.	Jnrs	10.52	54-61	164	-	2
Exeter C.	Cheltenham T.	08.63	63	1	-	0
NORTHCOTT, Thomas T.						
Torquay, 5 December, 1931 E Yth						(IF)
Torquay U.	Jnrs	12.48	48-52	60	-	10
Cardiff C.	Tr	10.52	52-54	71	-	13
Lincoln C.	Tr	07.55	55-57	94	-	34
Torquay U.	Tr	11.57	57-65	347	2	125
NORTHOVER, Stanley O.						
Weymouth, 3 July, 1926						(IF)
Luton T. (Am)	Weymouth	02.50	49	1	-	0
NORTON, David J.						
Gateshead, 24 January, 1957						(FB)
Hartlepool U.	Whickham	12.78	78-79	14	3	1
NORTON, David W.						
Cannock, 3 March, 1965 E Yth						(M/RB)
Aston Villa	App	03.83	84-87	42	2	2
Notts Co.	Tr	08.88	88-90	22	5	1
Rochdale	L	10.90	90	9	0	0
Hull C.	L	01.91	90	15	0	0
Hull C.	Tr	08.91	91	45	0	2
NORTON, Paul						
Mexborough, 17 September, 1969						(G)
Hartlepool U.	Sheffield U. (YT)	08.88	88	5	0	0
NORTON, Peter						
Manchester, 11 November, 1947						(FB)
Bournemouth	Jnrs	11.66	66-67	18	0	1
Crewe Alex.	Tr	07.68				
NORTON, Ralph						
Aylesham, 11 October, 1942						(IF)
Reading	Jnrs	10.59	60-65	99	1	9
Bournemouth	Tr	07.66	66-67	44	4	4
NOTEMAN, Kevin S.						
Preston, 15 October, 1969						(LW/B)
Leeds U.	YT	06.88	87	0	1	0
Doncaster Rov.	Tr	11.89	89-91	105	1	20
Mansfield T.	Tr	03.92	91	6	0	0
NOVACKI, Jan						
Manchester, 4 December, 1958 E Yth						(W)
Bolton W.	App	12.76				
York C.	L	12.77	77	24	1	3
NOWAK, Tadeusz						
Poland, 28 November, 1948 Polish Int						(W)
Bolton W.	Legia Warsaw (Pol)	03.79	78-80	22	2	1
NTAMARK, Charles B.						
Paddington, 22 July, 1964 Cameroon Int						(M)
Walsall	Boreham Wood	08.90	90-91	81	2	6
NUGENT, Arthur						
Glasgow, 30 May, 1926						(RB)
Darlington	Canterbury C.	06.56	56	5	-	0
NUGENT, W. Clifford						
Bicester, 3 March, 1929						(OL)
Cardiff C.	Headington U.	01.51	51-58	117	-	19
Mansfield T.	Tr	11.58	58-59	52	-	7
NUGENT, Kevin P.						
Edmonton, 10 April, 1969						(F)
Leyton Orient	YT	07.87	87-91	86	8	19
Plymouth Arg.	Tr	03.92	91	2	2	0
NUGENT, Richard J.						
Birmingham, 20 March, 1964						(CD)
Barnet	St Albans C.	10.88	91	2	0	0
NUGENT, Stephen						
Orrell, 7 May, 1973						(W)
Wigan Ath.	YT	08.91	89-91	2	2	0
NULTY, Geoffrey O.						
Prescot, 13 February, 1949						(M)
Stoke C.	Jnrs	07.67				
Burnley	Tr	07.68	69-74	123	7	20
Newcastle U.	Tr	12.74	74-77	101	0	11
Everton	Tr	07.78	78-79	22	6	2
NUNDY, Jeffrey W.						
Hull, 29 November, 1935						(CH)
Huddersfield T.		12.53				
Bradford C.	Tr	07.57	57-59	32	-	0
NUNN, Walter						
Deptford, 16 January, 1920 Died 1965						(HB)
Charlton Ath.	Bexleyheath & Welling	05.39				
Swindon T.	Tr	06.47	47	4	-	0
NURSE, Melvyn T. G.						
Swansea, 11 October, 1937 W Sch/Wu23-2/W-12						(CH)
Swansea C.	Jnrs	06.55	55-62	158	-	9
Middlesbrough	Tr	10.62	62-65	113	0	8
Swindon T.	Tr	09.65	65-67	122	1	10
Swansea C.	Tr	06.68	68-70	97	1	3
NUTE, Stephen L. R.						
Plymouth, 18 April, 1962						(G)
Exeter C.	App	04.80	80	5	0	0
NUTLEY, Robert						
Paisley, 10 September, 1916						(W)
Portsmouth	Hibernian	08.46	46	9	-	1
NUTT, Gordon E.						
Birmingham, 8 November, 1932						(W)
Coventry C.	Jnrs	11.49	51-54	76	-	12
Cardiff C.	Tr	12.54	54-55	17	-	4
Arsenal	Tr	09.55	55-59	49	-	10
Southend U.	Tr	10.60	60	16	-	2
NUTT, Philip J.						
Westminster, 18 May, 1958						(F)
Queens Park R.	App	07.75	75-76	0	4	1
NUTTALL, James						
Liverpool, 14 October, 1929						(CF)
Southport	Skelmersdale U.	05.50	50-52	67	-	29
NUTTALL, Martin						
Oldham, 12 September, 1961						(F)
Oldham Ath.	App	09.79	80-81	8	5	1
Halifax T.	Tr	08.82	82-83	39	11	10
NUTTALL, William						
Preston, 7 December, 1920						(FB)
Preston N.E.		07.46	46	2	-	0
Barrow	Tr	08.48	48-50	65	-	0
NUTTELL, Michael J.						
Boston, 22 November, 1968						(F)
Peterborough U.	YT	08.87	85-87	12	9	0
Crewe Alex.	L	12.87	87	2	1	1
Carlisle U.	L	11.88	88	1	2	0
NUTTON, Michael W.						
St Johns Wood, 3 October, 1959						(CD)
Chelsea	App	10.77	78-82	77	2	0
Reading	L	02.83	82	6	0	0
Millwall	Tr	03.83	82-85	81	1	4
NWAJIOBI, Chukwuemeka (Emeka)						
Nigeria, 25 May, 1959						(F)
Luton T.	Dulwich Hamlet	12.83	83-87	59	13	17

Peter Osgood (Chelsea, Southampton, Chelsea & England)
But for suffering a broken leg early in his career, he would surely have been one of England's greatest ever players

O'BERG, Paul J.
Hull, 8 May, 1958 (M)

League Club	Source	Date Signed	Seasons Played	Apps	Subs	Gls
Scunthorpe U.	Bridlington T.	07.79	79-83	117	13	24
Wimbledon	Tr	08.84	84	2	1	0
Stockport Co.	L	11.84	84	2	0	0
Chester C.	L	12.84	84	5	0	1

O'BRIEN, Anthony
Liverpool, 4 September, 1956 (FB)

League Club	Source	Date Signed	Seasons Played	Apps	Subs	Gls
Southport (N/C)		08.74	74-76	17	3	1

O'BRIEN, Colin
Dunfermline, 19 April, 1956 (W)

League Club	Source	Date Signed	Seasons Played	Apps	Subs	Gls
Bristol C.	Swaythling	11.77				
Hereford U.	L	12.78	78	1	1	0

O'BRIEN, George
Dunfermline, 22 November, 1935 (IF)

League Club	Source	Date Signed	Seasons Played	Apps	Subs	Gls
Leeds U.	Dunfermline Ath.	03.57	56-58	43	-	6
Southampton	Tr	07.59	59-65	244	0	154
Leyton Orient	Tr	03.66	65-66	17	0	3
Aldershot	Tr	12.66	66-67	38	3	8

O'BRIEN, George
Liverpool, 21 October, 1939 (IF)

League Club	Source	Date Signed	Seasons Played	Apps	Subs	Gls
Everton	Jnrs	02.59				
Southport	Tr	07.60	60	3	-	1

O'BRIEN, Gerald
Glasgow, 10 November, 1949 (W)

League Club	Source	Date Signed	Seasons Played	Apps	Subs	Gls
Southampton	Clydebank	03.70	69-75	66	12	2
Bristol Rov.	L	03.74	73	3	0	0
Swindon T.	Tr	03.76	75-76	24	3	0

O'BRIEN, Jonathan M.
Southend, 2 November, 1961 (G)

League Club	Source	Date Signed	Seasons Played	Apps	Subs	Gls
Southend U.	Maldon T.	01.85	84	11	0	0

O'BRIEN, Joseph
Dundalk (Ire), 9 May, 1924 (OL)

League Club	Source	Date Signed	Seasons Played	Apps	Subs	Gls
Luton T.	Dundalk	11.47	47-48	11	-	3
Ipswich T.	Tr	06.49	49-50	50	-	12

O'BRIEN, Noel W.
Islington, 18 December, 1956 (M)

League Club	Source	Date Signed	Seasons Played	Apps	Subs	Gls
Arsenal	App	01.74				
Mansfield T.	Tr	06.75	75	7	0	0

O'BRIEN, Raymond C.
Dublin, 21 May, 1951 IR-4 (FB)

League Club	Source	Date Signed	Seasons Played	Apps	Subs	Gls
Manchester U.	Shelbourne	05.73				
Notts Co.	Tr	03.74	73-82	323	0	30
Derby Co.	L	09.83	83	4	0	0

O'BRIEN, William
Middlesbrough, 26 January, 1929 (HB)

League Club	Source	Date Signed	Seasons Played	Apps	Subs	Gls
Darlington		02.50	50	2	-	0

O'BRIEN, William F. (Liam)
Dublin, 5 September, 1964 IR-9 (M)

League Club	Source	Date Signed	Seasons Played	Apps	Subs	Gls
Manchester U.	Shamrock Rov.	10.86	86-88	16	15	2
Newcastle U.	Tr	11.88	88-91	94	18	13

O'CALLAGHAN, Brendan
Bradford, 23 July, 1955 IRu21-1/IR-7 (F/CD)

League Club	Source	Date Signed	Seasons Played	Apps	Subs	Gls
Doncaster Rov.	Jnrs	07.73	73-77	184	3	65
Stoke C.	Tr	03.78	77-84	255	10	45
Oldham Ath.	Tr	02.85	84-85	10	0	0

O'CALLAGHAN, Kevin
Dagenham, 19 October, 1961 IR Yth/IRu21-1/IR-20 (LW)

League Club	Source	Date Signed	Seasons Played	Apps	Subs	Gls
Millwall	App	11.78	78-79	15	5	3
Ipswich T.	Tr	01.80	79-84	72	43	3
Portsmouth	Tr	01.85	84-86	84	3	16
Millwall	Tr	06.87	87-90	65	11	14
Southend U.	Tr	07.91	91	2	6	0

O'CONNELL, Brendan J.
Lambeth, 12 November, 1966 (F/W)

League Club	Source	Date Signed	Seasons Played	Apps	Subs	Gls
Portsmouth	YT	07.85				
Exeter C.	Tr	07.86	86-87	73	8	19
Burnley	Tr	06.88	88-89	62	2	17
Huddersfield T.	L	11.89	89	11	0	1
Barnsley	Tr	03.90	89-91	75	17	15

O'CONNELL, Brian E. (Pat)
Kensington, 13 September, 1937 (OL)

League Club	Source	Date Signed	Seasons Played	Apps	Subs	Gls
Fulham	Jnrs	03.56	58-65	152	0	26
Crystal Palace	Tr	07.66	66	20	1	2

O'CONNELL, Iain A.
Southend, 9 October, 1970 (W)

League Club	Source	Date Signed	Seasons Played	Apps	Subs	Gls
Southend U.	YT	07.89	89	0	4	0

O'CONNELL, Seamus
Carlisle, 1 January, 1930 E Amat (IF)

League Club	Source	Date Signed	Seasons Played	Apps	Subs	Gls
Middlesbrough (Am)	Queens Park	05.53	53	3	-	2
Chelsea (Am)	Bishop Auckland	08.54	54-55	16	-	11
Carlisle U. (Am)	Crook T.	02.58	57	4	-	2

O'CONNOR, Douglas
Barnsley, 29 April, 1954 (F)

League Club	Source	Date Signed	Seasons Played	Apps	Subs	Gls
Barnsley	App	04.72	70-73	27	9	7
Mansfield T.	Tr	07.74	74	11	6	2
Scunthorpe U.	Tr	07.75	75-76	28	3	9

O'CONNOR, James K.
Lanark, 27 June, 1951 (W)

League Club	Source	Date Signed	Seasons Played	Apps	Subs	Gls
Bury		07.70	70	7	0	2

O'CONNOR, Malcolm J.
Ashton-u-Lyne, 25 April, 1965 (F)

League Club	Source	Date Signed	Seasons Played	Apps	Subs	Gls
Rochdale (N/C)	Curzon Ashton	03.83	82-83	12	4	3

O'CONNOR, Mark A.
Southend, 10 March, 1963 (M)

League Club	Source	Date Signed	Seasons Played	Apps	Subs	Gls
Queens Park R.	App	06.80	81-82	2	1	0
Exeter C.	L	10.83	83	38	0	1
Bristol Rov.	Tr	08.84	84-85	79	1	10
Bournemouth	Tr	03.86	85-89	115	13	12
Gillingham	Tr	12.89	89-91	91	4	7

O'CONNOR, Michael
Romford, 11 January, 1952 (W)

League Club	Source	Date Signed	Seasons Played	Apps	Subs	Gls
Southend U. (App)	App	06.68	69	1	0	0

O'CONNOR, Patrick
Wishaw, 1 May, 1934 (IF)

League Club	Source	Date Signed	Seasons Played	Apps	Subs	Gls
Barrow	Bellshill	06.58	58-59	20	-	4

O'CONNOR, Philip K.
Romford, 10 October, 1953 Died 1985 (W)

League Club	Source	Date Signed	Seasons Played	Apps	Subs	Gls
Luton T.	Bexley U.	12.72	72	1	1	0
Lincoln C.	L	01.75	74	4	0	1

Liam O'Brien (Shamrock Rovers, Manchester United, Newcastle United & Republic of Ireland)

League Club	Source	Date Signed	Seasons Played	Career Record Apps	Subs	Gls

O'CONNOR, Robert T.
Gateshead, 9 August, 1940 (OL)

Gateshead (Am)	Jnrs	05.58	58	2	-	0

O'CONNOR, Timothy D.
Neath, 3 October, 1967 W Yth (M)

Cardiff C.	Afan Lido	01.85	85	1	1	0

O'CONNOR, Turlough
Athlone (Ire), 22 July, 1946 IR Amat/IR-7 (OL)

Fulham	Bohemians	05.66	67	1	0	0

O'CONNOR, Vincent J.
Durham, 12 March, 1929

Hartlepool U.	Middlesbrough (Am)	12.47	48	2	-	0

O'DELL, Andrew
Hull, 2 January, 1963 (M)

Grimsby T.	App	01.81	81-82	18	2	0
Rotherham U.	Tr	08.83	83-84	16	2	0
Torquay U.	Tr	03.85	84	12	2	1
Darlington	North Ferriby U.	09.87	87	1	2	0

O'DELL, Robert
Isle of Wight, 10 December, 1934 (CH)

Reading	Jnrs	07.52	53	2	-	0

O'DOHERTY, Kenneth B.
Dublin, 30 March, 1963 (CD)

Crystal Palace	U.C. Dublin	02.85	85-87	41	1	0
Huddersfield T.	Tr	06.88	88-91	63	2	1
Exeter C.	L	08.91	91	2	0	0

O'DONNELL, Brian F.
Glasgow, 8 August, 1957 (M)

Bristol Rov.	Bournemouth (App)	05.76				
Bournemouth	Blacktown C. (Aus)	01.82	81-82	9	5	0
Torquay U. (N/C)	Tr	10.82	82	19	0	0

O'DONNELL, Christopher
Newcastle, 26 May, 1968 (D)

Ipswich T.	App	06.85	86-88	10	4	0
Northampton T.	L	01.88	87	1	0	0
Leeds U.	Tr	07.89	89	0	1	0
Exeter C.	Tr	08.91	91	2	0	0

O'DONNELL, Daniel
Dunbar, 27 February, 1939 (IF)

Brentford	Kirkintilloch Rob Roy	02.60	60-61	11	-	0

O'DONNELL, Edward
Barrow, 5 February, 1921 (FB)

Barrow		09.46	46-52	33	-	0

O'DONNELL, Frank
Buckhaven, 31 August, 1911 Died 1952 S-6 (CF)

Preston N.E.	Glasgow Celtic	05.35	35-37	92	-	36
Blackpool	Tr	11.37	37-38	29	-	17
Aston Villa	Tr	11.38	38	29	-	14
Nottingham F.	Tr	01.46	46	11	-	5

O'DONNELL, Hugh
Buckhaven, 15 February, 1913 Died 1964 (OL)

Preston N.E.	Glasgow Celtic	05.35	35-38	132	-	29
Blackpool	Tr	03.39	38-46	10	-	2
Rochdale	Tr	03.47	46-47	40	-	14
Halifax T.	Tr	03.48	47-48	13	-	1

O'DONNELL, James
Methil, 18 April, 1934 (IF)

Blackburn Rov.	Wellesley Jnrs	05.52				
Oldham Ath.	Tr	10.53	54-55	15	-	3
Leeds U.	Stalybridge Celtic	01.57				

O'DONNELL, John D.
Leeds, 21 March, 1954 (FB)

Leeds U.	App	03.71				
Cambridge U.	Tr	07.73	73-75	79	0	8
Colchester U.	L	08.75	75	1	0	0
Hartlepool U.	Tr	07.76	76	30	1	1
Scunthorpe U.	Tr	07.77	77-79	60	0	0

O'DONNELL, Neil
Glasgow, 21 December, 1949 (M)

Norwich C.	Jnrs	12.66	67-73	31	19	2
Gillingham	Tr	08.74	74-75	18	6	0
Sheffield Wed.	Tr	10.75	75-76	40	0	1

O'DONNELL, Ralph
Cudworth, 17 October, 1931 (CH)

Sheffield Wed.	Upton Colly	05.49	51-61	170	-	3

O'DONNELL, William
Clydebank, 9 August, 1924 (CF)

Northampton T.	Partick Th.	06.51	51-53	104	-	43
Shrewsbury T.	Tr	07.54	54-57	130	-	46

O'DONOGHUE, Michael G.
Redhill, 13 September, 1956 (F)

Southampton	Wembley T.	01.79				
Northampton T.	L	11.79	79	4	0	1

O'DOWD, Adrian G.
Solihull, 16 September, 1959 (F)

Aston Villa	App	08.77				
Oxford U.	Tr	02.80	79-80	8	2	1

O'DOWD, Gregory H.
Dublin, 16 March, 1973 (CD)

Brighton & H.A.	YT	11.90	91	0	1	0

O'DRISCOLL, John F.
Cork (Ire), 20 September, 1921 IR-3/NI-3 (W)

Swansea C.	Cork	05.47	47-51	117	-	26

O'DRISCOLL, Sean M.
Wolverhampton, 1 July, 1957 IR-3 (RW)

Fulham	Alvechurch	11.79	79-83	141	7	13
Bournemouth	Tr	02.84	83-91	354	9	19

O'FARRELL, Frank
Cork (Ire), 9 October, 1927 IR-9 (WH)

West Ham U.	Cork	01.48	50-56	197	-	6
Preston N.E.	Tr	11.56	56-60	118	-	3

O'FLANAGAN, Kevin P.
Dublin, 10 June, 1919 NI Amat/IR-10 (W)

Arsenal (Am)	Bohemians	10.45	46	14	-	3
Brentford (Am)	Barnet	11.49	49	6	-	0

Kevin O'Flanagan (Bohemians, Arsenal, Brentford & Republic of Ireland)

O'GORMAN, David J.
Chester, 20 June, 1972 (F)

Wrexham	YT	07.90	90	8	9	0

O'GRADY, Michael
Leeds, 11 October, 1942 Eu23-3/EF Lge/E-2 (OL)

Huddersfield T.	Jnrs	10.59	59-65	160	0	26
Leeds U.	Tr	10.65	65-69	90	1	12
Wolverhampton W.	Tr	09.69	69-72	28	5	5
Birmingham C.	L	02.72	71	2	1	0
Rotherham U.	Tr	11.72	72-73	24	0	2

League Club	Source	Date Signed	Seasons Played	Apps	Subs	Gls
O'HAGAN, Patrick J.						
Caerphilly, 15 March, 1971						(G)
Newport Co. (YT)	YT	08.87	87	3	0	0
Cardiff C.	YT	07.89				
O'HALLORAN, Neil						
Cardiff, 21 June, 1933						(F)
Cardiff C.		08.54	55-56	10	-	4
Newport Co.	Tr	07.57	57	14	-	2
O'HANLON Kelham G.						
Saltburn, 16 May, 1962 IR-1						(G)
Middlesbrough	App	05.80	82-84	87	0	0
Rotherham U.	Tr	08.85	85-90	248	0	0
Carlisle U.	Tr	08.91	91	42	0	0
O'HARA, Daniel						
Airdrie, 28 September, 1937						(F)
Mansfield T.	Cork Celtic	06.61	61	3	-	1
O'HARA, Edward A.						
Glasgow, 28 October, 1935 S Sch/Su23-3						(OL)
Everton	Falkirk	06.58	58-59	29	-	2
Rotherham U.	Tr	02.60	59-60	20	-	3
Barnsley	Morton	07.62	62-64	127	-	37
O'HARA, Edward P.						
Dublin, 22 February, 1927 Died 1987						(OL)
Birmingham C.	Dundalk	11.49	49-50	6	-	0
O'HARA, Gerald J.						
Wolverhampton, 3 December, 1956						(M)
Wolverhampton W.	App	12.74	75-76	7	2	0
Hereford U. (N/C)	Tr	08.78	78	1	0	0
O'HARA, Michael J.						
Belfast, 30 August, 1944						(G)
Luton T.	App	11.61	60	2	-	0
Swindon T.	Tr	11.61	61-62	30	-	0
O'HARA, Stephen						
Lanarkshire, 21 February, 1971						(D)
Walsall	YT	07.89	89-91	67	8	3
O'HARE, John						
Renton, 24 September, 1946 Su23-3/S-13						(F)
Sunderland	Jnrs	10.63	64-66	51	0	14
Derby Co.	Tr	08.67	67-73	247	1	65
Leeds U.	Tr	08.74	74	6	0	1
Nottingham F.	Tr	02.75	74-79	94	7	14
O'KAMBACK, Joseph						
Tottenham, 13 March, 1915 Died 1981						(WH)
Millwall		04.46	46	1	-	0
O'KANE, Vincent						
Stepney, 20 November, 1952						(M)
Charlton Ath.	App	12.70	70-72	29	3	1
O'KANE, William J. (Liam)						
Derry (NI), 17 June, 1948 NI-20						(CD)
Nottingham F.	Derry C.	12.68	68-75	186	3	0
O'KEEFE, Eamonn						
Manchester, 13 March, 1953 E Semi-Pro/IR-5						(F)
Plymouth Arg.	Stalybridge Celtic	02.74				
Everton	Mossley	07.79	79-81	26	14	6
Wigan Ath.	Tr	01.82	81-82	56	2	25
Port Vale	Tr	07.83	83-84	50	9	17
Blackpool	Tr	03.85	84-86	33	3	23
Chester C.	Cork C.	03.89	88-89	12	5	4

John O'Hare (Sunderland, Derby County, Leeds United, Nottingham Forest & Scotland)

League Club	Source	Date Signed	Seasons Played	Career Record Apps	Subs	Gls

O'KEEFE, Patrick J.
Peterborough, 17 July, 1967 (M)

League Club	Source	Date Signed	Seasons Played	Apps	Subs	Gls
Peterborough U.	YT	07.85	84	0	1	0

O'KEEFE, J. Vincent
Birmingham, 2 April, 1957 (G)

League Club	Source	Date Signed	Seasons Played	Apps	Subs	Gls
Birmingham C.	Jnrs	07.75				
Walsall	Tr	07.76				
Exeter C.	A.P.Leamington	06.78	78-79	53	0	0
Torquay U.	Tr	02.80	79-81	108	0	0
Blackburn Rov.	Tr	08.82	82-88	68	0	0
Bury	L	10.83	83	2	0	0
Blackpool	L	12.86	86	1	0	0
Blackpool	L	02.89	88	6	0	0
Wrexham	Tr	07.89	89-91	83	0	0

O'KELLY, Richard F.
West Bromwich, 8 January, 1957 (F)

League Club	Source	Date Signed	Seasons Played	Apps	Subs	Gls
Walsall	Alvechurch	10.79	80-85	189	15	55
Port Vale	Tr	07.86	86-87	26	2	4
Walsall	Tr	01.88	87	7	5	1
Grimsby T.	Tr	07.88	88	38	1	10

O'LEARY, Daniel
Cork (Ire), 11 January, 1951 (IF)

League Club	Source	Date Signed	Seasons Played	Apps	Subs	Gls
Millwall	App	05.68				
Fulham	Tr	07.69	69	0	1	0

O'LEARY, David A.
Stoke Newington, 2 May, 1958 IR-66 (CD)

League Club	Source	Date Signed	Seasons Played	Apps	Subs	Gls
Arsenal	App	07.75	75-91	517	30	11

O'LEARY, Donal
Limehouse, 24 June, 1936 (OL)

League Club	Source	Date Signed	Seasons Played	Apps	Subs	Gls
Blackburn Rov.		10.54	55	6	-	1

O'LINN, Sydney
South Africa, 5 May, 1927 (IF)

League Club	Source	Date Signed	Seasons Played	Apps	Subs	Gls
Charlton Ath.	Green Point (SA)	12.47	47-56	187	-	32

O'LOUGHLIN, Nigel
Denbigh, 19 January, 1954 (M)

League Club	Source	Date Signed	Seasons Played	Apps	Subs	Gls
Shrewsbury T.	Rhyl	08.72	72-75	23	10	7
Rochdale	Tr	08.76	76-81	242	3	17

O'LOUGHLIN, William
Bolton, 18 January, 1937 (W)

League Club	Source	Date Signed	Seasons Played	Apps	Subs	Gls
Oldham Ath.	Rossendale U.	02.60	59-60	27	-	0

O'MAHONEY, Francis K.
Aldershot, 5 April, 1935 (CF)

League Club	Source	Date Signed	Seasons Played	Apps	Subs	Gls
Swindon T.		04.57	56-57	8	-	5

O'MAHONY, Matthew T.
Waterford (Ire), 9 January, 1913 IR-6/NI-1 (CH)

League Club	Source	Date Signed	Seasons Played	Apps	Subs	Gls
Southport		04.35				
Wolverhampton W.		05.35				
Newport Co.	Tr	03.36	35-36	8	-	0
Bristol Rov.	Tr	05.36	36-38	101	-	6
Ipswich T.	Tr	07.39	46-48	58	-	4

O'MARA, John
Farnworth, 19 March, 1947 (CF)

League Club	Source	Date Signed	Seasons Played	Apps	Subs	Gls
Gillingham	Margate	10.65				
Brentford	Wimbledon	03.71	70-72	53	0	28
Blackburn Rov.	Tr	09.72	72-73	30	5	10
Bradford C.	Chelmsford C.	12.74	74	3	0	1

O'MEARA, Alan M.
Grantham, 15 December, 1958 (G)

League Club	Source	Date Signed	Seasons Played	Apps	Subs	Gls
Scunthorpe U.	App	07.76	75-76	41	0	0

O'NEIL, Brian
Bedlington, 4 January, 1944 Eu23-1/EF Lge (M)

League Club	Source	Date Signed	Seasons Played	Apps	Subs	Gls
Burnley	Jnrs	01.61	62-69	231	4	22
Southampton	Tr	05.71	70-74	148	1	16
Huddersfield T.	Tr	10.74	74-75	60	1	3

O'NEIL, Joseph
Glasgow, 15 August, 1931 (IF)

League Club	Source	Date Signed	Seasons Played	Apps	Subs	Gls
Southend U. (L)	Aberdeen	11.52	52-53	24	-	11
Leicester C.	Aberdeen	03.56	57	5	-	2
Northampton T.	Tr	10.57	57-58	28	-	4

O'NEIL, Thomas P.
St Helens, 25 October, 1952 E Sch (M)

League Club	Source	Date Signed	Seasons Played	Apps	Subs	Gls
Manchester U.	App	11.69	70-72	54	0	0
Blackpool	L	01.73	72	7	0	0
Southport	Tr	08.73	73-77	192	6	17
Tranmere Rov.	Tr	06.78	78-79	74	0	10
Halifax T.	Tr	08.80	80-81	39	1	2

O'NEILL, Alan
Leadgate, 13 November, 1937 (IF)

League Club	Source	Date Signed	Seasons Played	Apps	Subs	Gls
Sunderland	Jnrs	02.55	56-60	74	-	27
Aston Villa	Tr	10.60	60-62	23	-	6
Plymouth Arg.	Tr	11.62	62-63	40	-	14
Bournemouth	Tr	02.64	63-65	37	0	8

O'NEILL, Alan
Cork (IR), 27 August, 1973 (M)

League Club	Source	Date Signed	Seasons Played	Apps	Subs	Gls
Birmingham C.	Cobh Ramblers	02.92	91	2	2	0

O'NEILL, Frank S.
Dublin, 13 April, 1940 IR-20 (OR)

League Club	Source	Date Signed	Seasons Played	Apps	Subs	Gls
Arsenal	Home Farm	04.59	60	2	-	0

O'NEILL, George
Port Glasgow, 26 July, 1942 (WH)

League Club	Source	Date Signed	Seasons Played	Apps	Subs	Gls
Barrow	Glasgow Celtic	10.64	64	7	-	0

O'NEILL, George P.
Liverpool, 21 July, 1923 (OL)

League Club	Source	Date Signed	Seasons Played	Apps	Subs	Gls
Port Vale (Am)	Ellesmere Port	11.48	48	5	-	0

O'NEILL, James
Lurgan (NI), 24 November, 1941 NI Sch/NIu23-1/NI-1 (CF)

League Club	Source	Date Signed	Seasons Played	Apps	Subs	Gls
Sunderland	Jnrs	11.58	61	7	-	6
Walsall	Tr	12.62	62-64	38	-	13
Darlington	Hakoah (Aus)	10.67	67	20	3	4

O'NEILL, James A.
Dublin, 13 October, 1931 IR-17 (G)

League Club	Source	Date Signed	Seasons Played	Apps	Subs	Gls
Everton	Bulfin U.	05.49	50-59	201	-	0
Stoke C.	Tr	07.60	60-63	130	-	0
Darlington	Tr	03.64	63-64	32	-	0
Port Vale	Tr	02.65	64-65	42	0	0

O'NEILL, James J. (Shaun)
Belfast, 24 February, 1952 (D)

League Club	Source	Date Signed	Seasons Played	Apps	Subs	Gls
Leeds U.	App	05.69				
Chesterfield	Tr	07.74	74-85	437	5	6

O'NEILL, John
Dublin, 8 September, 1935 IR-1 (D)

League Club	Source	Date Signed	Seasons Played	Apps	Subs	Gls
Preston N.E.	Drumcondra	04.58	58-62	50	-	0
Barrow	Tr	07.63	63	35	-	3

O'NEILL, John P.
Derry (NI), 11 March, 1958 NI-39 (CD)

League Club	Source	Date Signed	Seasons Played	Apps	Subs	Gls
Leicester C.	Derry B.C.	03.76	78-86	313	0	10
Queens Park R.	Tr	07.87	87	2	0	0
Norwich C.	Tr	12.87	87	1	0	0

O'NEILL, Leslie A.
Blyth, 4 December, 1943 (M)

League Club	Source	Date Signed	Seasons Played	Apps	Subs	Gls
Newcastle U.	Blyth Spartans	11.61	63	1	-	0
Darlington	Tr	01.65	64-69	178	1	35
Bradford C.	Tr	03.70	69-71	95	2	17
Carlisle U.	Tr	05.72	72-76	148	7	20

O'NEILL, Martin H. M.
Kilrea (NI), 1 March, 1952 NI-64 (M)

League Club	Source	Date Signed	Seasons Played	Apps	Subs	Gls
Nottingham F.	Derry C.	10.71	71-80	264	21	48
Norwich C.	Tr	02.81	80	11	0	1
Manchester C.	Tr	06.81	81	12	1	0
Norwich C.	Tr	01.82	81-82	54	1	11
Notts Co.	Tr	08.83	83-84	63	1	5

O'NEILL, Michael A.
Portadown (NI), 5 July, 1969 NI-10 (F)

League Club	Source	Date Signed	Seasons Played	Apps	Subs	Gls
Newcastle U.	Coleraine	10.87	87-88	36	12	15

O'NEILL, Thomas
Glasgow, 2 February, 1958 (M)

League Club	Source	Date Signed	Seasons Played	Apps	Subs	Gls
Cambridge U.	Ipswich T. (App)	07.76	76-82	96	20	8
Northampton T.	Tr	06.83	83	43	0	6

O'NEILL, Thomas H.
Spennymoor, 5 January, 1925 Died 1978 (RB)

League Club	Source	Date Signed	Seasons Played	Apps	Subs	Gls
Newcastle U.	Spennymoor U.	09.42				
Newport Co.	Tr	04.48	48	9	-	0

O'NEILL, William
Glasgow, 30 December, 1940 (FB)

League Club	Source	Date Signed	Seasons Played	Apps	Subs	Gls
Carlisle U.	Glasgow Celtic	05.69	69	15	0	0

O'NEILL, William A.
Cork (Ire), 29 December, 1919 (IF)

League Club	Source	Date Signed	Seasons Played	Apps	Subs	Gls
Burnley	Chelmsford C.	06.49	50	1	-	1
Walsall	Tr	01.51	50-51	55	-	16

O'REGAN, Kieran
Cork (Ire.), 9 November, 1963 IR-4 (D/M)

League Club	Source	Date Signed	Seasons Played	Apps	Subs	Gls
Brighton & H.A.	Tramore Ath.	04.83	82-86	69	17	2
Swindon T.	Tr	08.87	87	23	3	1
Huddersfield T.	Tr	08.88	88-91	150	8	20

O'REILLY, Gary M.
Isleworth, 21 March, 1961 IR Yth (CD)

League Club	Source	Date Signed	Seasons Played	Apps	Subs	Gls
Tottenham H.	Jnrs	09.79	80-83	39	6	0
Brighton & H.A.	Tr	08.84	84-86	78	1	3
Crystal Palace	Tr	01.87	86-89	65	5	2
Birmingham C.	L	03.91	90	1	0	0
Brighton & H.A.	Tr	07.91	91	28	0	3

O'RILEY, Paul J.
Liverpool, 17 October, 1950 (F)

League Club	Source	Date Signed	Seasons Played	Apps	Subs	Gls
Hull C.	App	10.68	68-73	19	11	2
Scunthorpe U.	L	03.71	70	11	0	4
Barnsley	Tr	07.74	74	11	3	2
Southport	Goole T.	03.75	74-76	19	11	4

O'RIORDAN, Donal J.
Dublin, 14 May, 1957 IRu21-1 (CD/M)

League Club	Source	Date Signed	Seasons Played	Apps	Subs	Gls
Derby Co	App	05.75	76-77	2	4	1
Doncaster Rov.	L	01.78	77	2	0	0
Preston N.E.	Tulsa (USA)	10.78	78-82	153	5	8
Carlisle U.	Tr	08.83	83-84	84	0	18
Middlesbrough	Tr	08.85	85	41	0	2
Grimsby T.	Tr	08.86	86-87	86	0	14
Notts Co.	Tr	07.88	88-91	87	5	4
Mansfield T.	L	09.89	89	6	0	0

O'ROURKE, James
Glasgow, 17 October, 1948 (FB)

League Club	Source	Date Signed	Seasons Played	Apps	Subs	Gls
Arsenal	Possilpark Jnrs	10.65				
Carlisle U.	Tr	10.67	67	0	1	0

O'ROURKE, John
Northampton, 11 February, 1945 E Yth/Eu23-1 (CF)

League Club	Source	Date Signed	Seasons Played	Apps	Subs	Gls
Chelsea	Arsenal (Am)	04.62				
Luton T.	Tr	12.63	63-65	84	0	64
Middlesbrough	Tr	07.66	66-67	63	1	38
Ipswich T.	Tr	02.68	67-69	69	0	30
Coventry C.	Tr	11.69	69-71	52	2	17
Queens Park R.	Tr	10.71	71-72	33	1	12
Bournemouth	Tr	01.74	73-74	21	1	4

O'ROURKE, Kenneth
Lambeth, 8 December, 1949 (IF)

League Club	Source	Date Signed	Seasons Played	Apps	Subs	Gls
Arsenal	Leyton Orient (App)	02.67				
Colchester U.	Ipswich T. (Trial)	10.68	68	1	0	0

O'ROURKE, William J.
Nottingham, 2 April, 1960 (G)

League Club	Source	Date Signed	Seasons Played	Apps	Subs	Gls
Burnley	App	02.78	79-82	14	0	0
Blackpool	L	08.83	83	6	0	0
Chester C.	Tr	03.84	83	5	0	0
Blackpool	Tr	07.84	84-85	92	0	0
Tranmere Rov.	L	09.86	86	15	0	0
Tranmere Rov.	Tr	02.87	86-87	38	0	0

O'SHAUGHNESSY, Brian
Wednesbury, 8 September, 1932 (IF)

League Club	Source	Date Signed	Seasons Played	Apps	Subs	Gls
Walsall		03.54	53	1	-	0

O'SHAUGHNESSY, Michael
Poplar, 15 April, 1955 (G)

League Club	Source	Date Signed	Seasons Played	Apps	Subs	Gls
Leyton Orient	App	08.73	73	1	0	0

O'SHAUGHNESSY, Stephen
Wrexham, 13 October, 1967 W Yth (M)

League Club	Source	Date Signed	Seasons Played	Apps	Subs	Gls
Leeds U.	YT	10.85				
Bradford C.	Tr	11.85	87	0	1	0
Rochdale	Tr	08.88	88-90	101	8	16
Exeter C.	Tr	07.91	91	1	2	0
Darlington	Tr	01.92	91	15	0	1

O'SHEA, Daniel E.
Kensington, 26 March, 1963 (D/M)

League Club	Source	Date Signed	Seasons Played	Apps	Subs	Gls
Arsenal	App	12.80	82	6	0	0
Charlton Ath.	L	02.84	83	9	0	0
Exeter C.	Tr	08.84	84	45	0	2
Southend U.	Tr	08.85	85-88	116	2	12
Cambridge U.	Tr	08.89	89-91	83	14	1

O'SHEA, Timothy J.
Pimlico, 12 November, 1966 IR Yth (M)

League Club	Source	Date Signed	Seasons Played	Apps	Subs	Gls
Tottenham H.	App	08.84	86-87	1	2	0
Newport Co.	L	10.86	86	10	0	0
Leyton Orient	Tr	07.88	88	7	2	1
Gillingham	Tr	02.89	88-91	102	10	2

O'SULLIVAN, Cyril J.
Lewisham, 22 February, 1920 (G)

League Club	Source	Date Signed	Seasons Played	Apps	Subs	Gls
Reading	Crown Villa	09.46	46-47	36	-	0

O'SULLIVAN, John
Cork (Ire), 30 May, 1922 (W)

League Club	Source	Date Signed	Seasons Played	Apps	Subs	Gls
Swansea C.	Waterford	01.48	47	2	-	0
Aldershot	Lovells Ath.	11.51				

O'SULLIVAN, Peter A.
Colwyn Bay, 4 March, 1951 W Sch/Wu23-6/W-3 (M)

League Club	Source	Date Signed	Seasons Played	Apps	Subs	Gls
Manchester U.	App	03.68				
Brighton & H.A.	Tr	04.70	70-80	432	3	38
Fulham	Tr	06.81	81-82	45	1	1
Charlton Ath.	L	10.82	82	5	0	0
Reading	L	11.82	82	9	0	0
Aldershot	Hong Kong	07.83	83	13	1	0

O'SULLIVAN, William F.
Lambeth, 5 October, 1959 IR Yth (W)

League Club	Source	Date Signed	Seasons Played	Apps	Subs	Gls
Charlton Ath.	App	10.77	76-77	1	1	0

O'TOOLE, C. Patrick
Dublin, 2 January, 1965 (M)

League Club	Source	Date Signed	Seasons Played	Apps	Subs	Gls
Leicester C.	Shelbourne	02.90				
Exeter C.	L	12.90	90	6	0	0
Shrewsbury T.	Tr	03.91	90-91	24	14	0

OAKES, Alan A.
Winsford, 1 September, 1942 EF Lge (M)

League Club	Source	Date Signed	Seasons Played	Apps	Subs	Gls
Manchester C.	Jnrs	09.59	59-75	561	3	26
Chester C.	Tr	07.76	76-81	211	0	15
Port Vale (N/C)	(Team Coach)	10.83	83	1	0	0

OAKES, Dennis R.
Bedworth, 10 April, 1946 (M)

League Club	Source	Date Signed	Seasons Played	Apps	Subs	Gls
Coventry C.	App	08.64				
Notts Co.	Tr	06.67	67-70	108	12	0
Peterborough U.	Tr	05.71	71-72	84	1	5

OAKES, Donald J.
Rhyl, 8 October, 1928 Died 1977 (WH)

League Club	Source	Date Signed	Seasons Played	Apps	Subs	Gls
Arsenal	Downend	07.46	52-54	11	-	1

OAKES, George
Orrell, 18 October, 1918 (CF)

League Club	Source	Date Signed	Seasons Played	Apps	Subs	Gls
Southport	Red Triangle Y.M.C.A.	08.45	46	7	-	0

OAKES, John
Hamilton, 16 January, 1921 (CF)

League Club	Source	Date Signed	Seasons Played	Apps	Subs	Gls
Rochdale	Queen of South	02.47	46	1	-	0

OAKES, John
Hamilton, 6 December, 1919 (W)

League Club	Source	Date Signed	Seasons Played	Apps	Subs	Gls
Huddersfield T.	Queen of South	11.43				
Blackburn Rov.	Queen of South	02.47	46-47	35	-	9
Manchester C.	Tr	06.48	48-50	77	-	9

OAKES, John
Northwich, 13 September, 1905 Died 1992 (CH)

League Club	Source	Date Signed	Seasons Played	Apps	Subs	Gls
Nottingham F.	Chilton Colly	08.28	29-30	2	-	0
Southend U.	Newark T.	05.31	31	2	-	0
Aldershot	Spennymoor U.	08.34	34-35	61	-	3
Charlton Ath	Tr	03.36	35-46	130	-	3
Plymouth Arg.	Tr	07.47	47	36	-	0

OAKES, Keith B.
Bedworth, 3 July, 1956 (CD)

League Club	Source	Date Signed	Seasons Played	Apps	Subs	Gls
Peterborough U.	App	07.73	72-77	48	14	2
Newport Co.	Tr	09.78	78-83	232	0	27
Gillingham	Tr	08.84	84-86	84	2	7
Fulham	Tr	09.86	86-87	76	0	3
Peterborough U.	Tr	08.88	88-90	95	2	9

OAKES, Scott J.
Leicester, 5 August, 1972 (W)

League Club	Source	Date Signed	Seasons Played	Apps	Subs	Gls
Leicester C.	YT	05.90	89-91	1	2	0
Luton T.	Tr	10.91	91	15	6	2

OAKES, Thomas
Manchester, 6 February, 1922 (OR)

League Club	Source	Date Signed	Seasons Played	Apps	Subs	Gls
Manchester C.	Manchester U. (Am)	04.47	46	1	-	0

OAKEY, Graham
Worcester, 5 October, 1954 (RB)

League Club	Source	Date Signed	Seasons Played	Apps	Subs	Gls
Coventry C.	App	10.72	74-77	87	1	0

OAKLEY, Kenneth
Rhymney, 9 May, 1929 (CF)

League Club	Source	Date Signed	Seasons Played	Apps	Subs	Gls
Cardiff C.	Ebbw Vale	03.50	50-53	7	-	0
Northampton T.	Tr	07.54	54	13	-	6

League Club	Source	Date Signed	Seasons Played	Career Record Apps	Subs	Gls

OAKLEY, Norman
Stockton, 4 June, 1939 (G)

Doncaster Rov.	Jnrs	04.57				
Hartlepool U.	Scunthorpe U. (trial)	09.58	58-63	182	-	0
Swindon T.	Tr	03.64	63-64	21	-	0
Grimsby T.	Tr	09.66	66	15	0	0

OAKLEY, Royston
Tipton, 5 January, 1928 (FB)

Southampton	Guernsey	11.50	53-55	6	-	0

OATES, Graham
Scunthorpe, 4 December, 1943 (W)

Blackpool	App	05.61	61-68	118	3	26
Grimsby T.	Tr	10.68	68-70	80	1	9

OATES, Graham
Bradford, 14 March, 1949 (M)

Bradford C.	Manningham Mills	02.70	69-73	158	3	19
Blackburn Rov.	Tr	06.74	74-75	76	0	10
Newcastle U.	Tr	03.76	75-77	26	9	3

OATES, Robert A.
Leeds, 26 July, 1956 E Yth (CD)

Scunthorpe U.	Ashley Road	08.74	74-82	306	9	17
Rochdale	Tr	08.83	83	42	0	1

OBENEY, Henry R. (Harry)
Bethnal Green, 9 March, 1938 (WH/CF)

West Ham U.	Brigg Sports	05.56	56-60	25	-	12
Millwall	Tr	06.61	61-63	76	-	10

OBI, Anthony L.
Birmingham, 15 September, 1965 E Yth (W)

Aston Villa	App	09.83				
Walsall	L	12.84	84	1	1	0
Plymouth Arg.	L	02.85	84	5	0	0
Bristol Rov. (N/C)	Tr	08.85	85	1	0	0
Oxford U.	Tr	10.85	86	0	1	0
Brentford	L	08.86	86	10	0	0

OELOFSE, Ralph J.
South Africa, 12 November, 1926 (WH)

Chelsea	Berea Park (SA)	10.51	51-52	8	-	0
Watford	Tr	07.53	53	15	-	0

OGBURN, Michael G.
Portsmouth, 19 February, 1948 (FB)

Brentford	Portsmouth (App)	05.65	66	12	0	0

OGDEN, Alan
Thrybergh, 15 April, 1954 (FB)

Sheffield U.	App	05.71	71-73	6	6	0
York C.	Tr	09.74	74	7	0	0

OGDEN, Christopher J.
Oldham, 3 February, 1953 (G)

Oldham Ath.	Jnrs	07.71	71-77	128	0	0
Swindon T.	Tr	08.78	78-79	24	0	0
Rotherham U.	Tr	11.79	79	3	0	0

OGDEN, Frederick
Oldham, 3 April, 1925 (G)

Oldham Ath.	Edge Lane B.C.	12.47	47-54	151	-	0
Chesterfield	Tr	06.55				
Oldham Ath.	Tr	03.56	55	5	-	0

OGDEN, Paul
Leek, 18 December, 1946 (W)

Port Vale (Am)	Leek Castle	11.65	65	2	0	0

OGDEN, Paul
Salford, 16 October, 1969 (M)

Hartlepool U.	Oldham Ath. (YT)	08.88	88-89	9	3	0

OGDEN, Trevor
Culcheth, 12 June, 1945 (CF)

Manchester C.		09.64	64	9	-	3
Doncaster Rov.	Tr	06.65	65-66	39	0	14

OGHANI, George W.
Manchester, 2 September, 1960 (F)

Bury	Sheffield U. (Jnrs)	02.78				
Bolton W.	Hyde U.	10.83	83-86	86	13	27
Wrexham	L	03.87	86	6	1	0
Burnley	Tr	06.87	87-88	73	1	21
Stockport Co.	Tr	06.89	89	5	3	2
Hereford U.	Tr	10.89	89	7	1	2
Scarborough	Hyde U.	02.90	89-90	43	7	18

League Club	Source	Date Signed	Seasons Played	Career Record Apps	Subs	Gls

OGILVIE, Gary F.
Dundee, 16 November, 1967 (LB)

Sunderland	Dundee	03.88	88	0	1	0

OGILVIE, John F.
Motherwell, 28 October, 1928 (FB)

Leicester C.	Hibernian	09.55	55-58	82	-	2
Mansfield T.	Tr	01.60	59-60	24	-	1

OGILVIE, John L.
Workington, 20 December, 1943 (FB)

Workington	Blackpool (Am)	04.63	62-74	386	4	14

OGLEY, Alan
Barnsley, 4 February, 1946 E Sch (G)

Barnsley	App	03.63	62	9	-	0
Manchester C.	Tr	07.63	63-67	51	0	0
Stockport Co.	Tr	09.67	67-74	240	0	0
Darlington	Tr	08.75	75-76	80	0	0

OGLEY, Mark A.
Barnsley, 10 March, 1967 (CD)

Barnsley	App	03.85	85-86	19	0	0
Aldershot	L	12.87	87	6	2	0
Carlisle U.	Tr	03.88	87-89	33	0	1
Aldershot	Tr	11.89	89-90	58	4	0
York C.	Tr	04.92				

OGRIZOVIC, Steven
Mansfield, 12 September, 1957 (G)

Chesterfield	Mansfield Y.C.	07.77	77	16	0	0
Liverpool	Tr	11.77	77-80	4	0	0
Shrewsbury T.	Tr	08.82	82-83	84	0	0
Coventry C.	Tr	06.84	84-91	316	0	1

OGSTON, John K.
Aberdeen, 15 January, 1939 Su23-3 (G)

Liverpool	Aberdeen	08.65	66	1	0	0
Doncaster Rov.	Tr	08.68	68-70	70	0	0

OKAI, Stephen P.
Ghana, 3 December, 1973 (W)

Leyton Orient	Jnrs	07.92	91	1	0	1

OKENLA, Floronso
Nigeria, 9 October, 1967 (W)

Birmingham C.	Burnley (N/C)	08.91	91	2	5	1

OLAH, Bela
Hungary, 8 June, 1938 (W)

Northampton T.	Bedford T.	12.58	58-60	41	-	8

OLDFIELD, Craig
Wortley, 24 November, 1963 (F)

Colchester U.		03.83	83	0	3	0

OLDFIELD, David C.
Australia, 30 May, 1968 Eu21-1 (F)

Luton T.	App	05.86	87-88	21	8	4
Manchester C.	Tr	03.89	88-89	18	8	6
Leicester C.	Tr	01.90	89-91	87	16	16

OLDFIELD, John E.
Helsby, 13 July, 1918 (RH)

Port Vale	Helsby	03.46	46	1	-	0

OLDFIELD, John S.
Lindrick (Nts), 19 August, 1943 (G)

Huddersfield T.	Jnrs	08.61	63-68	152	0	0
Wolverhampton W.	Tr	12.69	69-70	19	0	0
Crewe Alex.	L	11.71	71	5	0	0
Bradford C.	Tr	12.71	71-72	31	0	0

OLDFIELD, Terence J.
Bristol, 1 April, 1939 (WH)

Bristol Rov.	Clifton St Vincent	02.58	60-65	131	1	11
Wrexham	Tr	07.66	66	40	1	6

OLDHAM, Eric
Newcastle, 27 June, 1933 (FB)

Bolton W.	Seaton Delaval	10.53				
Gateshead	Tr	07.56	56-57	53	-	0
Hartlepool U.	Kidderminster Hrs	06.59	59	12	-	0

League Club	Source	Date Signed	Seasons Played	Career Record Apps	Subs	Gls
OLDHAM, George						
Glossop, 20 April, 1920						(LB)
Stoke C.		10.37	38	2	-	0
Newport Co.	Tr	09.46	46-47	63	-	0
OLDHAM, John						
Oswaldtwistle, 30 January, 1926						(CH)
Accrington St.	Oswaldtwistle Imps	08.50	50-52	10	-	0
OLDHAM, John						
Nottingham, 24 October, 1949						(CF)
Mansfield T.		02.67	66	0	1	0
OLDRIDGE, A. Robert						
Barton-on-Humber, 17 November, 1957						(F)
Grimsby T.		01.76	75-76	9	6	1
OLDROYD, Darren R.						
Ormskirk, 1 November, 1966						(RB)
Everton	App	11.84	84	0	1	0
Wolverhampton W.	Tr	08.86	86	10	0	0
OLINYK, Peter						
Bolton, 4 October, 1953						(M)
Bolton W.	App	06.71	73-74	7	3	0
Stockport Co.	Tr	11.74	74	4	0	0
OLIPHANT, David						
Carlisle, 29 January, 1942						(WH)
Wolverhampton W.	Jnrs	06.59				
Carlisle U.	Tr	12.60	60-64	109	-	11
OLIVE, R. Leslie						
Salford, 27 April, 1928						(G)
Manchester U. (Am)		01.53	52	2	-	0
OLIVER J. Alan						
Blyth, 8 September, 1924						(OL)
Derby Co.	Crofton Colly	10.46	47-49	16	-	2
Stockport Co.	Tr	08.50	50-53	139	-	28
Gateshead	Tr	07.54	54-57	146	-	36
OLIVER, Anthony J.						
Portsmouth, 22 September, 1967						(G)
Brentford (N/C)	Portsmouth (N/C)	08.87	87	11	0	0
OLIVER, Brian C.						
Liverpool, 6 March, 1957						(G)
Rochdale	Bury (App)	03.75	75	3	0	0
Southport	L	12.75	75	2	0	0
OLIVER, Edmund A.						
Manchester, 17 March, 1961						(FB)
Rochdale	App	03.79	77-79	19	3	1
OLIVER, Eric						
Spennymoor, 8 July, 1940						(G)
Darlington (Am)	West Auckland	12.63	63	2	-	0
OLIVER, Gavin R.						
Felling, 6 September, 1962						(CD)
Sheffield Wed.	App	08.80	80-84	14	6	0
Tranmere Rov.	L	01.83	82	17	0	1
Brighton & H.A.	L	08.85	85	15	1	0
Bradford C.	Tr	11.85	85-91	223	4	7
OLIVER, George						
Houghton-le-Spring, 22 January, 1919 Died 1981						(OL)
Halifax T.		10.45				
Gateshead	Tr	10.46	46	13	-	1
OLIVER, Harold S.						
Sunderland, 16 February, 1921 E Sch						(CH)
Hartlepool U.		03.38	37	9	-	0
Brentford	Tr	05.38	46-47	18	-	0
Watford	Tr	05.48	48-51	122	-	2
OLIVER, Howard D.						
Sunderland, 16 April, 1950						(W)
Sheffield Wed.	Jnrs	04.67				
Hartlepool U.	Tr	08.68	68	0	1	0
OLIVER, James						
Fern, 13 January, 1958						(M)
Wigan Ath.	Montrose	08.80	80	1	1	0
OLIVER, James						
Uxbridge, 28 August, 1949						(FB)
Crystal Palace	App	03.67	67-69	3	0	0
OLIVER, James R.						
Falkirk, 3 December, 1941 S Sch						(M)
Norwich C.	Falkirk	08.62	62-64	40	-	14
Brighton & H.A.	Tr	03.65	64-67	37	6	5
Colchester U.	Tr	02.68	67-69	65	10	10
OLIVER, John						
Bradford, 21 September, 1946						(FB)
Bradford P.A.	Jnrs	09.66	65	1	0	0
OLIVER, John						
Red Row (Nd), 6 October, 1920						(IL)
Chesterfield	Amble	10.46	46-47	24	-	5
OLIVER, J. H. Kenneth						
Loughborough, 10 August, 1924						(CH)
Sunderland	Brush Sports	08.46	47-48	8	-	1
Derby Co.	Tr	09.49	49-57	184	-	1
Exeter C.	Tr	01.58	57-59	92	-	0
OLIVER, Kenneth						
Pelton (Dm), 26 November, 1938						(IF)
Sunderland	Birtley R.O.F.	05.58				
Barnsley	South Shields	02.60	59-62	94	-	38
Watford	Tr	07.63	63-64	58	-	26
Workington	Tr	02.65	65-66	84	0	20
Bournemouth	Tr	01.67	66	14	0	4
OLIVER, Neil						
Berwick, 11 April, 1967						(FB)
Blackburn Rov.	Berwick R.	08.89	89-90	5	1	0
OLIVER, Peter F. R.						
Cowdenbeath, 18 August, 1948						(FB)
York C.	Hearts	07.74	74-75	41	0	0
Huddersfield T.	Tr	05.76	76	41	0	1
OLIVER, Ralph						
Tredegar, 30 March, 1934						(HB)
Shrewsbury T.	Hereford U.	08.55	55-57	8	-	0
OLLERENSHAW, John						
Stockport, 3 April, 1925						(FB)
Arsenal	Manchester C. (Am)	09.46				
Hartlepool U.	Tr	06.50	50	2	-	0
Oldham Ath.	Tr	03.51				
OLNEY, Ian D.						
Luton, 17 December, 1969 E Yth/Eu21-10						(F)
Aston Villa	YT	07.88	88-91	62	26	16
OLNEY, Kevin						
Doncaster, 12 February, 1959						(FB)
Doncaster Rov.	Jnrs	08.76	76-78	65	1	1
OLSEN, Jesper						
Denmark, 20 March, 1961 Danish Int						(LW)
Manchester U.	Ajax (Neth)	07.84	84-88	119	20	21
OLSSON, Paul						
Hull, 24 December, 1965						(M)
Hull C.	App	12.83				
Exeter C.	Tr	03.87	86-87	38	5	2
Scarborough	Tr	08.88	88-89	34	14	5
Hartlepool U.	Tr	12.89	89-91	94	6	9
OMAN, Alan J.						
Northampton, 6 October, 1952						(FB)
Northampton T.	App	10.70	70-74	83	5	3
ONSLOW, Leslie G.						
Swindon, 29 August, 1926						(HB)
Swindon T.		10.45	46-48	4	-	0
ONSLOW, Roy E.						
Swindon, 12 September, 1928						(IF)
Swindon T.		11.47	47-55	140	-	23
ONUORA, Ifem						
Glasgow, 28 July, 1967						(W)
Huddersfield T.	Bradford Univ.	07.89	89-91	73	31	18

ONWERE, Udo A.
Hammersmith, 9 November, 1971 (M)

League Club	Source	Date Signed	Seasons Played	Apps	Subs	Gls
Fulham	YT	07.90	90-91	24	10	4

ONYEALI, Elkanah
Nigeria, 7 June, 1939 (CF)

League Club	Source	Date Signed	Seasons Played	Apps	Subs	Gls
Tranmere Rov.	Nigeria	08.60	60	13	-	8

OOSTHUIZEN, Ronald
South Africa, 16 March, 1936 (OL)

League Club	Source	Date Signed	Seasons Played	Apps	Subs	Gls
Charlton Ath.	Marist Bros (SA)	09.53	55	1	-	0
Carlisle U.	Poole T.	09.59	59	1	-	0

ORAM, Dennis G.
Bristol, 14 January, 1920 (CH)

League Club	Source	Date Signed	Seasons Played	Apps	Subs	Gls
Bristol C. (Am)	St Pancras B.C.	08.46	46	3	-	0

ORD, Brian R.
Gateshead, 21 June, 1939 (FB)

League Club	Source	Date Signed	Seasons Played	Apps	Subs	Gls
Charlton Ath.	Bleach Green	11.57	61-62	13	-	1

ORD, Kenneth
South Shields, 21 September, 1939 (WH)

League Club	Source	Date Signed	Seasons Played	Apps	Subs	Gls
Sunderland	Cleadon Colly	11.57				
Chesterfield	Tr	06.61	61	3	-	0

ORD, Richard J.
Murton, 3 March, 1970 Eu21-3 (CD)

League Club	Source	Date Signed	Seasons Played	Apps	Subs	Gls
Sunderland	YT	07.87	87-91	58	11	2
York C.	L	02.90	89	3	0	0

ORD, Thomas
Woolwich, 15 October, 1952 (F)

League Club	Source	Date Signed	Seasons Played	Apps	Subs	Gls
Chelsea	Erith & Belvedere	12.72	72	3	0	1

ORGILL, Harold
Hucknall, 1 October, 1920 Died1980 (G)

League Club	Source	Date Signed	Seasons Played	Apps	Subs	Gls
Nottingham F.		04.47	46	7	-	0
Notts Co.	Tr	06.47	47	2	-	0

ORHAN, Yilmaz
Cyprus, 13 March, 1955 (F)

League Club	Source	Date Signed	Seasons Played	Apps	Subs	Gls
West Ham U.	Aveley	10.72	75-76	6	2	0

ORLYGSSON, Thorvaldur (Toddy)
Odense (Den), 2 August, 1966 Iceland Int (W)

League Club	Source	Date Signed	Seasons Played	Apps	Subs	Gls
Nottingham F.	K.A. Akureyri (Ice)	11.89	89-91	16	1	1

ORMANDY, John (Jack)
Liverpool, 25 January, 1912 (OL)

League Club	Source	Date Signed	Seasons Played	Apps	Subs	Gls
Bradford C.	Prescot Cables	06.32	32-35	63	-	9
Bury	Tr	06.36	36-38	87	-	18
Southend U.	Tr	06.39				
Oldham U.	Tr	07.46	46	30	-	5
Halifax T.	Tr	07.47	47	7	-	0

ORMOND, John L.
Larkhall, 10 August, 1947 (W)

League Club	Source	Date Signed	Seasons Played	Apps	Subs	Gls
Barnsley	New Zealand	12.67	68	1	0	1

ORMOND, William
Greenock, 26 August, 1926 (OL)

League Club	Source	Date Signed	Seasons Played	Apps	Subs	Gls
Blackpool	Partick Th.	10.47				
Oldham Ath.	Tr	12.49	49-53	122	-	25
Barrow	Tr	02.54	53-57	139	-	31
Scunthorpe U.	Tr	08.58	58	3	-	0

ORMONDROYD, Ian
Bradford, 22 September, 1964 (F)

League Club	Source	Date Signed	Seasons Played	Apps	Subs	Gls
Bradford C.	Thackley	09.85	85-88	72	15	20
Oldham Ath.	L	03.87	86	8	2	1
Aston Villa	Tr	02.89	88-91	41	15	6
Derby Co.	Tr	09.91	91	25	0	8
Leicester C.	Tr	03.92	91	14	0	1

ORMROD, Leslie
Stockport, 8 October, 1952 E Sch (FB)

League Club	Source	Date Signed	Seasons Played	Apps	Subs	Gls
Stockport Co.	Everton (App)	03.70	69-73	103	5	0

ORMSBY, Brendan T. C.
Birmingham, 1 October, 1960 E Sch/E Yth (CD)

League Club	Source	Date Signed	Seasons Played	Apps	Subs	Gls
Aston Villa	App	10.78	78-85	115	2	4
Leeds U.	Tr	02.86	85-88	46	0	5
Shrewsbury T.	L	01.90	89	1	0	0
Doncaster Rov.	Tr	07.90	90-91	78	0	7

ORMSTON, Alexander
Stoke, 10 February, 1919 Died 1975 EF Lge (W)

League Club	Source	Date Signed	Seasons Played	Apps	Subs	Gls
Stoke C.	Jnrs	07.36	37-51	173	-	27

ORPHAN, Leslie
Newport, 17 April, 1923 W Amat (IL)

League Club	Source	Date Signed	Seasons Played	Apps	Subs	Gls
Newport Co.	Girlings	02.49	48	1	-	0

ORR, Anderson (Alan)
Glasgow, 19 December, 1923 (WH)

League Club	Source	Date Signed	Seasons Played	Apps	Subs	Gls
Nottingham F.	Third Lanark	08.51	51-54	46	-	0

ORR, Douglas M.
Glasgow, 8 November, 1937 S Amat (W)

League Club	Source	Date Signed	Seasons Played	Apps	Subs	Gls
Queens Park R. (Am)	Hendon	06.57	57	5	-	0

ORR, Henry
Lisburn (NI), 31 June, 1936 (WH)

League Club	Source	Date Signed	Seasons Played	Apps	Subs	Gls
Sheffield U.	Distillery	11.58	58-62	10	-	1
Peterborough U.	Tr	07.64	64-66	47	1	0

ORR, Neil I.
Greenock, 13 May, 1959 Su21-7 (D)

League Club	Source	Date Signed	Seasons Played	Apps	Subs	Gls
West Ham U.	Morton	01.82	81-87	133	13	4

ORRITT, Bryan
Caernarfon, 22 February, 1937 Wu23-3 (IF)

League Club	Source	Date Signed	Seasons Played	Apps	Subs	Gls
Birmingham C.	Bangor C.	01.56	56-61	99	-	23
Middlesbrough	Tr	03.62	61-65	115	3	22

OSBORN, Kenneth G.
Hampstead, 23 November, 1948 (OR)

League Club	Source	Date Signed	Seasons Played	Apps	Subs	Gls
Gillingham	Queens Park R. (App)	06.66	68-69	2	0	0

OSBORN, Simon E.
Croydon, 19 January, 1972 (M)

League Club	Source	Date Signed	Seasons Played	Apps	Subs	Gls
Crystal Palace	YT	01.90	90-91	15	3	2

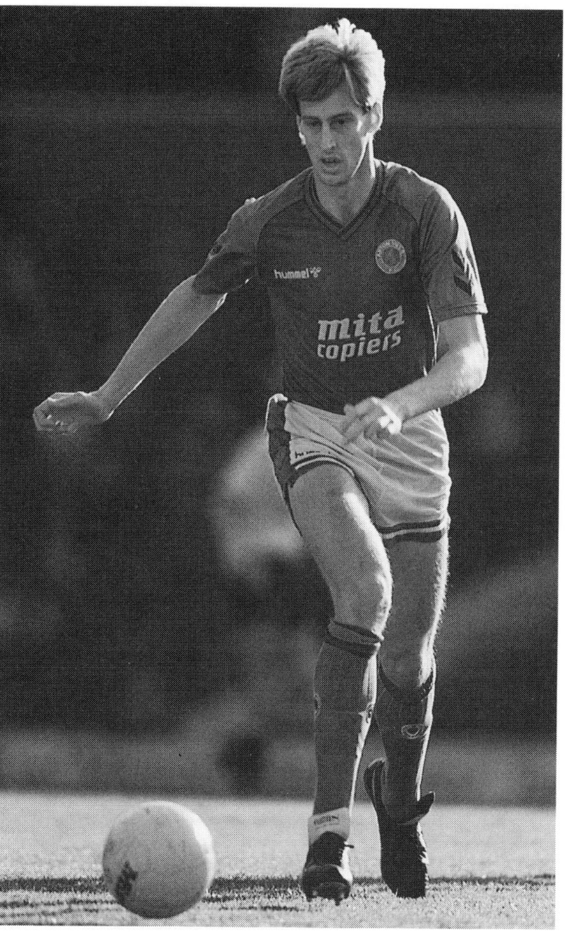

Ian Ormondroyd (Bradford City, Aston Villa, Derby County & Leicester City)

OSBORNE, Glyn
Crewe, 23 August, 1954 (CF)

League Club	Source	Date Signed	Seasons Played	Apps	Subs	Gls
Crewe Alex. (App)	App	09.69	70-71	2	5	0

OSBORNE, Ian L.
Leicester, 28 October, 1952 (FB)

League Club	Source	Date Signed	Seasons Played	Apps	Subs	Gls
Birmingham C.	App	10.70	75	10	0	0
Port Vale	Tr	06.76	76	14	1	0

OSBORNE, John
Barlborough, 1 December, 1940 E Sch (G)

League Club	Source	Date Signed	Seasons Played	Apps	Subs	Gls
Chesterfield	Jnrs	09.60	60-66	110	0	0
West Bromwich A.	Tr	01.67	66-76	250	0	0
Walsall	L	02.73	72	3	0	0

OSBORNE, John
Renfrew, 14 October, 1919 (IF)

League Club	Source	Date Signed	Seasons Played	Apps	Subs	Gls
Leicester C.		09.38				
Watford	Tr	02.48	47-48	34	-	13

OSBORNE, Lawrence W.
West Ham, 20 October, 1967 (M)

League Club	Source	Date Signed	Seasons Played	Apps	Subs	Gls
Arsenal	App	07.85				
Newport Co.	Huddersfield T. (N/C)	11.87	87	15	0	0
Maidstone U.	Redbridge Forest	07.90	90-91	49	4	8
Gillingham	Tr	12.91	91	4	1	0

OSBORNE, Roger C.
Otley (Sfk), 9 March, 1950 (M)

League Club	Source	Date Signed	Seasons Played	Apps	Subs	Gls
Ipswich T.	Grundisburgh	03.71	73-80	109	15	9
Colchester U.	Tr	02.81	80-85	196	10	11

OSBORNE, Steven C.
Middlesbrough, 3 March, 1969 (F)

League Club	Source	Date Signed	Seasons Played	Apps	Subs	Gls
Peterborough U.	South Bank	03.89	88-90	18	42	7
York C.	Tr	08.91	91	6	3	0

OSBOURNE, C. Gary J.
Wolverhampton, 22 October, 1969 (FB)

League Club	Source	Date Signed	Seasons Played	Apps	Subs	Gls
Shrewsbury T.	YT	07.88	88	3	4	0

OSCROFT, Harold
Mansfield, 10 March, 1926 (OL)

League Club	Source	Date Signed	Seasons Played	Apps	Subs	Gls
Mansfield T.	Mansfield Colly	04.47	46-49	113	-	41
Stoke C.	Tr	01.50	49-58	326	-	100
Port Vale	Tr	09.59	59-60	47	-	12

OSGOOD, Keith
Isleworth, 8 May, 1955 E Sch/E Yth (CD)

League Club	Source	Date Signed	Seasons Played	Apps	Subs	Gls
Tottenham H.	App	05.72	73-77	112	1	13
Coventry C.	Tr	01.78	77-78	24	1	1
Derby Co.	Tr	10.79	79-81	61	8	10
Leyton Orient	Tr	12.81	81-83	36	0	0
Cambridge U.	Tr	11.84	84-85	34	1	1

OSGOOD, Peter L.
Windsor, 20 February, 1947 E Yth/Eu23-6/EF Lge/E-4 (F)

League Club	Source	Date Signed	Seasons Played	Apps	Subs	Gls
Chelsea	Jnrs	09.64	65-73	276	3	103
Southampton	Tr	03.74	73-77	122	4	28
Norwich C.	L	11.76	76	3	0	0
Chelsea	Philadelphia (USA)	12.78	78-79	10	0	2

OSGOOD, Stephen
Bracknell, 20 January, 1962 (G)

League Club	Source	Date Signed	Seasons Played	Apps	Subs	Gls
Aldershot (N/C)	Newbury T.	02.89	88	1	0	0

OSMAN, Harold J.
Alton, 29 January, 1911 (OL)

League Club	Source	Date Signed	Seasons Played	Apps	Subs	Gls
Plymouth Arg.	Poole T.	12.35	35-36	5	-	0
Southampton	Tr	06.37	37-38	70	-	31
Millwall	Tr	03.39	38-47	34	-	3
Bristol C.	Tr	10.47	47	18	-	1

OSMAN, Rex C.
Derby, 4 April, 1932 E Yth (FB)

League Club	Source	Date Signed	Seasons Played	Apps	Subs	Gls
Derby Co.	Jnrs	07.49	53-54	2	-	0

OSMAN, Russell C.
Repton (Dy), 14 February, 1959 E Yth/Eu21-7/E-11 (CD)

League Club	Source	Date Signed	Seasons Played	Apps	Subs	Gls
Ipswich T.	App	03.76	77-84	294	0	17
Leicester C.	Tr	07.85	85-87	108	0	8
Southampton	Tr	06.88	88-91	92	4	6
Bristol C.	Tr	10.91	91	30	1	2

OSMOND, Avery N.
Huddersfield, 25 December, 1924

League Club	Source	Date Signed	Seasons Played	Apps	Subs	Gls
Southend U.	Peterborough U.	05.48	48	2	-	0

OSMOND, Colin A. E.
Whitchurch, 15 May, 1937 E Yth (FB)

League Club	Source	Date Signed	Seasons Played	Apps	Subs	Gls
Portsmouth	Jnrs	05.54	57	1	-	0

OSTERGAARD, John B.
Denmark, 6 February, 1955 (F)

League Club	Source	Date Signed	Seasons Played	Apps	Subs	Gls
Charlton Ath.	Ikast (Den)	11.79	79-80	8	4	1

OSVOLD, Kjetll
Norway, 5 June, 1961 Norwegian Int (W)

League Club	Source	Date Signed	Seasons Played	Apps	Subs	Gls
Nottingham F.	Lillestrom (Nor)	03.87	86-87	5	2	0
Leicester C.	L	12.87	87	3	1	0

OTTEWELL, Sydney
Horsley (Dy), 23 October, 1919 (IF)

League Club	Source	Date Signed	Seasons Played	Apps	Subs	Gls
Chesterfield	Holbrook Colly	11.36	36-46	42	-	12
Birmingham C.	Tr	06.47	47	5	-	2
Luton T.	Tr	12.47	47	15	-	4
Nottingham F.	Tr	07.48	48-49	32	-	3
Mansfield T.	Tr	01.50	49-51	67	-	21
Scunthorpe U.	Tr	03.52	51-52	30	-	10

OTTO, Heine M.
Netherlands, 24 August, 1954 Netherland Int (M)

League Club	Source	Date Signed	Seasons Played	Apps	Subs	Gls
Middlesbrough	Twente Enschede (Neth)	08.81	81-84	163	3	24

OTTO, Ricky
London, 9 November, 1967 (W)

League Club	Source	Date Signed	Seasons Played	Apps	Subs	Gls
Leyton Orient	Haringey Bor.	11.90	90-91	23	10	5

OTULAKOWSKI, Anton
Dewsbury, 29 January, 1956 (M)

League Club	Source	Date Signed	Seasons Played	Apps	Subs	Gls
Barnsley	Ossett T.	03.75	75-76	42	0	2
West Ham U.	Tr	10.76	76-77	10	7	0
Southend U.	Tr	03.79	78-82	161	2	8
Millwall	Tr	03.83	82-85	114	0	14
Crystal Palace	Tr	08.86	86	12	0	1

OUTHART, Anthony J.
Scarborough, 17 September, 1963 (F)

League Club	Source	Date Signed	Seasons Played	Apps	Subs	Gls
Scarborough	Bridlington T.	11.87	87-88	3	3	1

OUTHWAITE, George
Ferryhill, 19 May, 1928 (G)

League Club	Source	Date Signed	Seasons Played	Apps	Subs	Gls
Oldham Ath. (Am)	Chilton Colly	03.56	55	4	-	0

OUTTERSIDE, Mark J.
Hexham, 13 January, 1967 (RB)

League Club	Source	Date Signed	Seasons Played	Apps	Subs	Gls
Sunderland	App	01.85	86	1	0	0
Darlington	Tr	07.87	87	37	1	0

OVARD, Frank C.
Evesham, 16 December, 1955 E Semi-Pro (F)

League Club	Source	Date Signed	Seasons Played	Apps	Subs	Gls
Gillingham	Maidstone U.	12.81	81	4	2	0

OVER, Eric
Sheffield, 5 July, 1933 (OL)

League Club	Source	Date Signed	Seasons Played	Apps	Subs	Gls
Sheffield U.		11.54	54	2	-	0
Barrow	Tr	01.56	55-57	19	-	1
Oldham Ath.	Tr	12.57	57	21	-	2

OVERFIELD, John (Jack)
Leeds, 14 May, 1932 (OL)

League Club	Source	Date Signed	Seasons Played	Apps	Subs	Gls
Leeds U.	Yorkshire Amats	05.53	55-59	159	-	20
Sunderland	Tr	08.60	60-62	65	-	5
Peterborough U.	Tr	02.63	62	1	-	0
Bradford C.	Tr	07.64	64	11	-	0

OVERSON, Richard J.
Kettering, 3 June, 1959 (D)

League Club	Source	Date Signed	Seasons Played	Apps	Subs	Gls
Burnley	App	06.77	77-79	5	1	0
Hereford U.	Tr	05.80	80-81	6	5	1

OVERSON, Vincent D.
Kettering, 15 May, 1962 E Yth (CD)

League Club	Source	Date Signed	Seasons Played	Apps	Subs	Gls
Burnley	App	11.79	79-85	207	4	6
Birmingham C.	Tr	06.86	86-90	179	3	3
Stoke C.	Tr	08.91	91	34	1	3

Russell Osman (Ipswich Town, Leicester City, Southampton, Bristol City & England)

OVERTON, John
Rotherham, 2 May, 1956 (CD)

League Club	Source	Date Signed	Seasons Played	Apps	Subs	Gls
Aston Villa	App	01.74	75	2	1	0
Halifax T.	L	03.76	75	14	0	2
Gillingham	Tr	06.76	76-80	177	1	10

OVERTON, Paul H.
Soham, 18 April, 1961 (G)

League Club	Source	Date Signed	Seasons Played	Apps	Subs	Gls
Ipswich T.	App	07.78	77	1	0	0
Peterborough U.	Tr	05.79				
Northampton T.	Tr	06.80				

OWEN, Aled W.
Anglesey, 7 January, 1934 (W)

League Club	Source	Date Signed	Seasons Played	Apps	Subs	Gls
Tottenham H.	Bangor C.	09.53	53	1	-	0
Ipswich T.	Tr	07.58	58-61	30	-	3
Wrexham	Tr	07.63	63	3	-	0

OWEN, Brian E.
Harefield, 2 November, 1944 (W)

League Club	Source	Date Signed	Seasons Played	Apps	Subs	Gls
Watford	App	07.62	62-69	148	5	17
Colchester U.	Tr	05.70	70-71	11	2	2
Wolverhampton W.	Tr	01.72	72	4	0	0

OWEN, Brian G.
Bath, 7 July, 1942 (F)

League Club	Source	Date Signed	Seasons Played	Apps	Subs	Gls
Hereford U.	Bath C.	(N/L)	72-73	46	8	13

OWEN, Bryn
Rochdale, 25 April, 1939 (FB)

League Club	Source	Date Signed	Seasons Played	Apps	Subs	Gls
Rochdale		08.60	60-61	6	-	0

OWEN R. Derek
Ellesmere Port, 25 September, 1938 (G)

League Club	Source	Date Signed	Seasons Played	Apps	Subs	Gls
Chester C. (Am)	Ellesmere Port	05.58	58-60	7	-	0

OWEN, Derek W.
Shrewsbury, 11 March, 1938 (F)

League Club	Source	Date Signed	Seasons Played	Apps	Subs	Gls
Shrewsbury T.	Coton Rov.	01.57	56-57	12	-	3

OWEN, Gareth
Chester, 21 October, 1971 Wu21-3 (M)

League Club	Source	Date Signed	Seasons Played	Apps	Subs	Gls
Wrexham	YT	07.90	89-91	65	11	9

OWEN, Gary A.
St Helens, 7 July, 1958 E Yth/Eu21-22/E'B' (M)

League Club	Source	Date Signed	Seasons Played	Apps	Subs	Gls
Manchester C.	App	08.75	75-78	101	2	19
West Bromwich A.	Tr	06.79	79-85	185	2	21
Sheffield Wed.	Panionios (Gre)	08.87	87	12	2	0

OWEN, Gordon
Barnsley, 14 June, 1959 (RW)

League Club	Source	Date Signed	Seasons Played	Apps	Subs	Gls
Sheffield Wed.	Jnrs	11.76	77-82	32	15	5
Rotherham U.	L	03.80	79	9	0	0
Doncaster Rov.	L	11.82	82	9	0	0
Chesterfield	L	03.83	82	6	0	2
Cardiff C.	Tr	08.83	83	38	1	14
Barnsley	Tr	08.84	84-85	68	0	25
Bristol C.	Tr	08.86	86-87	51	2	11
Hull C.	L	12.87	87	3	0	0
Mansfield T.	Tr	01.88	87-88	54	4	8
Blackpool	Tr	07.89	89-90	21	8	2
Carlisle U.	L	10.90	90	4	1	0
Exeter C.	L	12.90	90	4	0	0

OWEN, J. Leslie
Hawarden, 11 April, 1933 (FB)

League Club	Source	Date Signed	Seasons Played	Apps	Subs	Gls
Chester C.		07.54	56	1	-	0

OWEN, Maurice
Abingdon, 4 July, 1924 (CF/CH)

League Club	Source	Date Signed	Seasons Played	Apps	Subs	Gls
Swindon T.	Abingdon	12.46	46-62	555	-	150

OWEN, Neil
Bury, 14 October, 1959 (M)

League Club	Source	Date Signed	Seasons Played	Apps	Subs	Gls
Sheffield Wed. (App)	App	08.76	76	1	0	0

OWEN, Robert
Farnworth, 17 October, 1947 (F)

League Club	Source	Date Signed	Seasons Played	Apps	Subs	Gls
Bury	App	08.65	64-67	81	2	38
Manchester C.	Tr	07.68	68-69	18	4	3
Swansea C.	L	03.70	69	5	1	1
Carlisle U.	Tr	06.70	70-76	185	19	51
Northampton T.	L	10.76	76	5	0	0
Workington	L	12.76	76	8	0	2
Bury	L	02.77	76	4	0	1
Doncaster Rov.	Tr	07.77	77-78	74	3	22

OWEN, Robert G.
Sunderland, 5 May, 1924 (WH)

League Club	Source	Date Signed	Seasons Played	Apps	Subs	Gls
Huddersfield T.		04.45				
Lincoln C.	Murton Colly	01.47	46-54	246	-	4

OWEN Sidney W.
Birmingham, 29 February, 1922 EF Lge/E-3 (CH)

League Club	Source	Date Signed	Seasons Played	Apps	Subs	Gls
Birmingham C.		10.45	46	5	-	0
Luton T.	Tr	06.47	47-58	388	-	3

OWEN, L. Terence
Liverpool, 11 September, 1949 (W)

League Club	Source	Date Signed	Seasons Played	Apps	Subs	Gls
Everton	App	12.66	67	2	0	0
Bradford C.	Tr	06.70	70-71	41	11	6
Chester C.	Tr	06.72	72-76	161	15	40
Cambridge U.	Tr	08.77	77	1	0	0
Rochdale	Tr	09.77	77-78	80	3	21
Port Vale	Tr	07.79	79	14	4	3

OWEN Trefor
Flint, 20 February, 1933 W Amat (CH)

League Club	Source	Date Signed	Seasons Played	Apps	Subs	Gls
Leyton Orient	Tooting & Mitcham	01.58	58-60	15	-	0

OWEN, William M.
Llanfairfechan, 30 June, 1914 Died 1976 (WH/F)

League Club	Source	Date Signed	Seasons Played	Apps	Subs	Gls
Manchester C.	Northwich Vic.	06.34	35	9	-	3
Tranmere Rov.	Tr	03.36	35	6	-	4
Newport Co.	Tr	06.36	36-46	72	-	5
Exeter C.	Tr	10.46	46	20	-	9

OWENS, John G.
Ynysybwl, 25 March, 1932 (WH)

League Club	Source	Date Signed	Seasons Played	Apps	Subs	Gls
Exeter C.	Pontypridd	10.53	53-54	14	-	0
Bournemouth	Tr	09.56				

OWENS, T. Leslie
Sunderland, 17 October, 1919 Died 1974 (CF)

League Club	Source	Date Signed	Seasons Played	Apps	Subs	Gls
Charlton Ath.	Washington C.W.	09.37	37-38	12	-	5
Doncaster Rov.	Tr	02.39	38-47	21	-	11
Southport	Tr	12.47	47-48	53	-	11
Hartlepool U.	Tr	07.49	49	28	-	12
Norwich C.	Tr	03.50	49-50	20	-	8
Reading	Tr	07.51	51	8	-	4
Brighton & H.A.	Tr	06.52	52	15	-	4

OWER, John C.T. (Ian)
Glasgow, 2 January, 1939 (G)

League Club	Source	Date Signed	Seasons Played	Apps	Subs	Gls
Workington	St Johnstone	02.63	62-67	199	0	0

OWERS, Adrian R.
Danbury (Ex), 26 February, 1965 (M)

League Club	Source	Date Signed	Seasons Played	Apps	Subs	Gls
Southend U.	App	02.83	82-84	18	9	0
Brighton & H.A.	Chelmsford C.	12.87	87-90	32	8	4
Gillingham	L	03.91	90	9	1	0
Maidstone U. (N/C)		10.91	91	1	0	0

OWERS, Gary
Newcastle, 3 October, 1968 (M)

League Club	Source	Date Signed	Seasons Played	Apps	Subs	Gls
Sunderland	App	10.86	87-91	178	8	20

OWERS, Philip
Bishop Auckland, 28 April, 1955 (G)

League Club	Source	Date Signed	Seasons Played	Apps	Subs	Gls
Darlington	Jnrs	06.73	72-74	45	0	0
Gillingham	Tr	07.75	75	2	0	0
Darlington	Tr	07.76	76-79	69	0	0
Hartlepool U. (N/C)	Brandon U.	08.87	87	2	0	0

OXBROW, Darren W.
Ipswich, 1 September, 1969 (CD)

League Club	Source	Date Signed	Seasons Played	Apps	Subs	Gls
Ipswich T.	YT	06.88				
Maidstone U.	Tr	08.89	89-91	84	1	2

OXFORD, Kenneth
Oldham, 14 November, 1929 E Yth (G)

League Club	Source	Date Signed	Seasons Played	Apps	Subs	Gls
Manchester C.	Jnrs	10.47	47	1	-	0
Chesterfield		06.50				
Norwich C.	Tr	07.51	53-57	128	-	0
Derby Co.	Tr	12.57	57-62	151	-	0
Doncaster Rov.	Tr	07.64	64	16	-	0
Port Vale	Tr	03.65				

OXLEY, Albert
Gateshead, 21 October, 1915 (IF)

League Club	Source	Date Signed	Seasons Played	Apps	Subs	Gls
Gateshead	Windy Nook	01.35	34-46	120	-	25

OXTOBY, Richard J.
Chesterfield, 5 September, 1939 (CH)

League Club	Source	Date Signed	Seasons Played	Apps	Subs	Gls
Bolton W.	Jnrs	01.57	59	3	-	0
Tranmere Rov.	Tr	07.63	63	5	-	0

David Platt (Manchester United, Crewe Alexandra, Aston Villa, Bari, Juventus & England)
Once a Manchester United reject, he now stars in the Italian League with Juventus

PACE, Derek J. (Doc)
Bloxwich, 11 March, 1932 Died 1989 (CF)

League Club	Source	Date Signed	Seasons Played	Apps	Subs	Gls
Aston Villa	Bloxwich Strollers	09.49	50-57	98	-	40
Sheffield U.	Tr	12.57	57-64	253	-	140
Notts Co.	Tr	12.64	64-65	29	0	15
Walsall	Tr	07.66	66	4	1	1

PACEY, David
Luton, 2 October, 1936 Eu23-1 (WH)

League Club	Source	Date Signed	Seasons Played	Apps	Subs	Gls
Luton T.	Hitchin T.	08.56	57-64	246	-	16

PACEY, Dennis F.
Feltham, 27 September, 1928 (CF)

League Club	Source	Date Signed	Seasons Played	Apps	Subs	Gls
Leyton Orient	Walton & Hersham	12.51	51-54	120	-	46
Millwall	Tr	10.54	54-58	133	-	37
Aldershot	Tr	09.58	58-59	32	-	13

PACK, Roy J.
Islington, 20 September, 1946 (FB)

League Club	Source	Date Signed	Seasons Played	Apps	Subs	Gls
Arsenal	App	11.63	65	1	0	0
Portsmouth	Tr	07.66	66-68	92	0	0

PACKARD, J. Edgar
Mansfield, 7 March, 1919 (CH)

League Club	Source	Date Signed	Seasons Played	Apps	Subs	Gls
Sheffield Wed.	Clipstone Colly	12.36	46-51	124	-	1
Halifax T.	Tr	08.52	52-53	85	-	0

PACKER, Leslie J.
Sunderland, 8 April, 1959 (F)

League Club	Source	Date Signed	Seasons Played	Apps	Subs	Gls
Doncaster Rov.		09.78	78-79	5	2	2

PACKER, Michael D.
Willesden, 20 April, 1950 (D)

League Club	Source	Date Signed	Seasons Played	Apps	Subs	Gls
Watford	App	04.68	68-72	57	11	2
Crewe Alex.	L	03.72	71	12	0	0
Colchester U.	Tr	07.73	73-82	237	7	20

PACKER, Norman J.
Ynysybwl, 14 June, 1931 (HB)

League Club	Source	Date Signed	Seasons Played	Apps	Subs	Gls
Exeter C.	Pontypridd	07.55	55-60	18	-	0

PADDON, Graham C.
Manchester, 24 August, 1950 Eu23-1 (M)

League Club	Source	Date Signed	Seasons Played	Apps	Subs	Gls
Coventry C.	App	05.68	68-69	3	2	1
Norwich C.	Tr	10.69	69-73	162	0	19
West Ham U.	Tr	12.73	73-76	115	0	11
Norwich C.	Tr	11.76	76-81	126	2	6
Millwall	L	12.81	81	5	0	1

PAGE, Donald R.
Manchester, 18 January, 1964 (F)

League Club	Source	Date Signed	Seasons Played	Apps	Subs	Gls
Wigan Ath.	Runcorn	03.89	88-90	62	12	15
Rotherham U.	Tr	08.91	91	29	2	11

PAGE, John
Frimley, 21 October, 1934 (D)

League Club	Source	Date Signed	Seasons Played	Apps	Subs	Gls
Southampton	Jnrs	10.51	52-60	190	-	24

PAGE, Malcolm E.
Knucklas, 5 February, 1947 W Sch/Wu23-6/W-28 (D)

League Club	Source	Date Signed	Seasons Played	Apps	Subs	Gls
Birmingham C.	App	09.64	64-80	328	8	8
Oxford U.	Tr	02.81	80-81	14	0	1

PAGE, Raymond M.
Swindon, 26 September, 1930 (FB)

League Club	Source	Date Signed	Seasons Played	Apps	Subs	Gls
Swindon T.		04.51	50-54	32	-	0

PAINE, Terence L.
Winchester, 23 March, 1939 Eu23-4/EF Lge /E-19 (W)

League Club	Source	Date Signed	Seasons Played	Apps	Subs	Gls
Southampton	Winchester C.	02.57	56-73	709	4	160
Hereford U.	Tr	08.74	74-76	106	5	8

PAINTER, Edward G.
Swindon, 23 June, 1921 (WH)

League Club	Source	Date Signed	Seasons Played	Apps	Subs	Gls
Swindon T.		10.38	46-50	77	-	0

PAINTER, Ian J.
Wombourne, 28 December, 1964 E Yth/Eu21-1 (F)

League Club	Source	Date Signed	Seasons Played	Apps	Subs	Gls
Stoke C.	App	12.82	82-83	105	8	20
Coventry C.	Tr	07.68	86	0	3	0

PAINTER, P. Robert
Wigan, 26 January, 1971 (M)

League Club	Source	Date Signed	Seasons Played	Apps	Subs	Gls
Chester C.	YT	07.89	87-90	58	26	8
Maidstone U.	Tr	07.91	91	27	3	5
Burnley	Tr	03.92	91	9	0	2

PAINTER, Trevor A.
Norwich, 2 July, 1949 (CH)

League Club	Source	Date Signed	Seasons Played	Apps	Subs	Gls
Norwich C.	App	07.67	67	2	0	0
Colchester U.	Tr	05.70	70	1	0	0

PAISLEY, Robert
Hetton-le-Hole, 23 January, 1919 (WH)

League Club	Source	Date Signed	Seasons Played	Apps	Subs	Gls
Liverpool	Bishop Auckland	05.39	46-53	253	-	10

PALADINO, Giuseppe (Joe)
Prescot, 21 August, 1965 (G)

League Club	Source	Date Signed	Seasons Played	Apps	Subs	Gls
Wigan Ath.	St Helens T.	12.90	90	7	0	0

PALETHORPE, Christopher G.
Maidenhead, 6 November, 1942 (OR)

League Club	Source	Date Signed	Seasons Played	Apps	Subs	Gls
Reading	Jnrs	11.59	60-62	55	-	10
Aldershot	Tr	06.63	63-64	56	-	5

PALFREYMAN, George
Sheffield, 13 March, 1933 (G)

League Club	Source	Date Signed	Seasons Played	Apps	Subs	Gls
Halifax T. (Am)	Sheffield F.C.	01.54	53	1	-	0

PALGRAVE, Brian U.
Birmingham, 12 July, 1966 (F)

League Club	Source	Date Signed	Seasons Played	Apps	Subs	Gls
Walsall	Alvechurch	07.84	84-87	5	3	1

PALIN, Grenville
Doncaster, 13 February, 1940 (FB)

League Club	Source	Date Signed	Seasons Played	Apps	Subs	Gls
Wolverhampton W.	Jnrs	03.57				
Walsall	Tr	07.60	60-63	129	-	10

PALIN, Leigh G.
Worcester, 12 September, 1965 E Yth (M)

League Club	Source	Date Signed	Seasons Played	Apps	Subs	Gls
Aston Villa	App	09.83				
Shrewsbury T.	L	12.84	84	2	0	0
Nottingham F.	Tr	11.85				
Bradford C.	Tr	10.86	86-88	65	6	10
Stoke C.	Tr	09.89	89	17	2	3
Hull C.	Tr	03.90	89-91	57	0	7
Rochdale	L	10.91	91	3	0	0

PALIOS, Mark
Birkenhead, 9 November, 1952 (M)

League Club	Source	Date Signed	Seasons Played	Apps	Subs	Gls
Tranmere Rov.		07.73	73-79	177	13	25
Crewe Alex.	Tr	01.80	79-82	114	4	23
Tranmere Rov.	Tr	03.83	82-84	55	4	7

Malcolm Page (Birmingham City, Oxford United & Wales)

League Club	Source	Date Signed	Seasons Played	Apps	Subs	Gls

PALLISTER, Gary A.
Ramsgate, 30 June, 1965 E-'B'/EF Lge/E-5 (CD)

Middlesbrough	Billingham T.	11.84	85-89	156	0	5
Darlington	L	10.85	85	7	0	0
Manchester U.	Tr	08.89	89-91	108	3	4

Gary Pallister (Middlesbrough, Manchester United & England)

PALLISTER, Gordon
Crook, 2 April, 1917 EF Lge (FB)

Bradford C.	Willington	05.34	37-38	28	-	0
Barnsley	Tr	10.38	38-51	220	-	3

PALMER, Calvin I.
Skegness, 21 October, 1940 (WH)

Nottingham F.	Skegness T.	03.58	58-63	91	-	14
Stoke C.	Tr	09.63	63-67	165	0	24
Sunderland	Tr	02.68	67-69	35	5	5
Crewe Alex.	Cape Town C. (SA)	10.71	71	2	0	0

PALMER, Carlton L.
Rowley Regis, 5 December, 1965 Eu21-4/E-7 (CD/M)

West Bromwich A.	YT	12.84	85-88	114	7	4
Sheffield Wed.	Tr	02.89	88-91	134	0	8

PALMER, Charles A.
Aylesbury, 10 July, 1963 (RB)

Watford	App	07.81	83	10	0	1
Derby Co.	Tr	07.84	84-85	51	0	2
Hull C.	Tr	02.87	86-88	69	1	1
Notts Co.	Tr	02.89	88-91	126	3	6

PALMER, David J.
Bristol, 10 April, 1961 (FB)

Bristol Rov.	App	01.79	78	1	0	0

PALMER, Desmond F.
Swansea, 23 September, 1931 W-3 (IF)

Swansea C.	Jnrs	04.50	52-58	83	-	37
Liverpool	Tr	03.59				
Derby Co.	Durban C. (SA)	06.61	61	18	-	6

League Club	Source	Date Signed	Seasons Played	Apps	Subs	Gls

PALMER, Frank
Sunderland, 29 October, 1923 (OL)

Gateshead (Am)	Bishop Auckland	02.51	50	1	-	1

PALMER, Frederick W.
Barrow, 23 October, 1922 (WH)

Crewe Alex.		12.45	46	1	-	0

PALMER, Geoffrey
Barnsley, 12 November, 1940 (FB)

Bristol C.	Doncaster Rov. (Am)	08.58	61	1	-	0

PALMER, Geoffrey
Cannock, 11 July, 1954 Eu23-12 (RB)

Wolverhampton W.	App	07.72	73-84	389	5	13
Burnley	Tr	11.84	84-85	34	0	0
Wolverhampton W.	Tr	12.85	85-86	21	1	0

PALMER, John N.
Bristol, 1 July, 1958 (M)

Bristol C.	Weston-super-Mare	03.83	82	2	6	0

PALMER, Lee J.
Croydon, 19 September, 1970 (LB)

Gillingham	YT	07.89	87-91	62	10	4

PALMER, Leslie
Barrow, 16 December, 1923 (WH)

Barrow	Holker C.O.B.	10.49	49	1	-	0

PALMER, Leslie J.
Birmingham, 5 September, 1971 (F)

West Bromwich A.	YT	07.90	90-91	5	3	1

PALMER, Roger N.
Manchester, 30 January, 1959 (F)

Manchester C.	App	01.77	77-80	22	9	9
Oldham Ath.	Tr	11.80	80-91	413	28	141

Carlton Palmer (West Bromwich Albion, Sheffield Wednesday & England)

League Club	Source	Date Signed	Seasons Played	Career Record Apps	Subs	Gls
PALMER, Stephen L.						
Brighton, 31 March, 1968						(M)
Ipswich T.	Cambridge Univ.	08.89	89-91	37	14	1
PAMMENT, Michael I.						
Huddersfield, 12 May, 1945 E Yth						(CF)
Bradford C. (Am)	Jnrs	07.64	64	1	-	0
PAMPHLETT, Antony J.						
Westminster, 13 April, 1960						(CD)
Maidstone U.	Dartford	07.86	89	7	0	0
PANES, Simon M.						
Almondsbury, 22 February, 1960						(F)
Bristol C.	Melksham T.	08.82	82	2	2	0
PANTER, Derek						
Blackpool, 22 November, 1943						(F)
Manchester C.	West Bromwich A. (Am)	08.62	63	1	-	0
Torquay U.	Tr	05.64	64	5	-	1
Southport	Tr	07.65				
PAPE, Andrew M.						
Hammersmith, 22 March, 1962 E Semi-Pro						(G)
Queens Park R.	Jnrs	07.80	79	1	0	0
Barnet	Enfield	08.91	91	36	0	0
PARDEW, Alan S.						
Wimbledon, 18 July, 1961						(M)
Crystal Palace	Yeovil T.	03.87	87-91	111	17	8
Charlton Ath.	Tr	11.91	91	23	1	2

Alan Pardew (Crystal Palace & Charlton Athletic)

League Club	Source	Date Signed	Seasons Played	Apps	Subs	Gls
PARDOE, Glyn						
Winsford, 1 June, 1946 E Sch/Eu23-4						(LB)
Manchester C.	App	06.63	61-74	303	2	17
PARFITT, Henry E.						
Cardiff, 26 September, 1929						(FB)
Cardiff C.		05.49	53	1	-	0
Torquay U.	L	10.52	52-53	58	-	0

League Club	Source	Date Signed	Seasons Played	Career Record Apps	Subs	Gls
PARIS, Alan D.						
Slough, 15 August, 1964						(LB)
Watford	Slough T.	11.82				
Peterborough U.	Tr	08.85	85-87	135	2	2
Leicester C.	Tr	07.88	88-90	80	8	3
Notts Co.	Tr	01.91	90-91	39	3	1
PARK, Colin S. J.						
Swansea, 8 February, 1945						(G)
Swansea C.	Jnrs	09.63	63	1	-	0
PARK, Robert						
Douglas, 7 April, 1930						(G)
Crewe Alex.	Airdrieonians	08.55	55-56	61	-	0
PARK, Robert						
Coatbridge, 5 January, 1952						(M)
Sunderland	Jnrs	01.69	69-71	50	15	4
PARK, Robert C.						
Edinburgh, 3 July, 1946						(M)
Aston Villa	App	07.63	64-68	60	14	7
Wrexham	Tr	05.69	69-71	98	4	8
Peterborough U.	Tr	06.72	72	15	3	1
Northampton T.	Tr	02.73	72-73	21	3	0
Hartlepool U.	Tr	07.74	74	14	3	0
PARK, Terence						
Liverpool, 7 February, 1957						(M)
Wolverhampton W.	Jnrs	03.74				
Stockport Co.	Blackpool (N/C)	07.76	76-79	87	3	8
Stockport Co.	Minnesota K. (USA)	03.81	80-82	72	0	7
Manchester C.	L	01.83	82	0	2	0
Bury	Tr	07.83	83	18	3	1
PARK, William						
Gateshead, 23 February, 1919						(CH)
Blackpool	Felling Red Star	05.38	38	3	-	0
York C.	Tr	09.46	46	22	-	1
PARKE, John						
Belfast, 6 August, 1937 NI-14						(FB)
Sunderland	Hibernian	11.64	64-67	83	2	0
PARKER, Albert E.						
Liverpool, 13 September, 1927						(FB)
Crewe Alex.	South Liverpool	12.48	48-51	111	-	0
Wrexham	Tr	11.51	51-58	216	-	1
PARKER, Alexander H.						
Irvine, 2 August, 1935 Su23-6/SF Lge/S-15						(RB)
Everton	Falkirk	06.58	58-64	198	-	5
Southport	Tr	09.65	65-67	76	0	0
PARKER, Brian T.						
Chorley, 4 August, 1955 E Semi-Pro						(G)
Crewe Alex.	Jnrs	08.72	73	26	0	0
Arsenal	Tr	08.75				
PARKER, Carl						
Burnley, 25 March, 1971						(M)
Rochdale	Rosendale U.	02.92	91	5	1	1
PARKER, Clifford H.						
Denaby, 6 November, 1913 Died 1983						(OL)
Doncaster Rov.	Denaby U.	08.31	31-33	52	-	11
Portsmouth	Tr	12.33	33-50	241	-	58
PARKER, Derek						
Colchester, 23 June, 1926						(WH)
West Ham U.	Grays Ath.	10.44	46-55	199	-	9
Colchester U.	Tr	03.57	56-60	130	-	1
PARKER, Derrick						
Wallsend, 7 February, 1957						(F)
Burnley	App	02.74	74-75	5	1	2
Southend U.	Tr	02.77	76-79	129	0	43
Barnsley	Tr	02.80	79-82	104	3	32
Oldham Ath.	Tr	08.83	83-84	54	3	11
Doncaster Rov.	L	12.84	84	5	0	1
Burnley	Tr	10.85	85-86	43	0	10
Rochdale (N/C)	Finland	10.87	87	6	1	1

League Club	Source	Date Signed	Seasons Played	Career Record Apps	Subs	Gls

PARKER, Garry S.
Oxford, 7 September, 1965 E Yth/Eu21-6/E'B' (M)

League Club	Source	Date Signed	Seasons Played	Apps	Subs	Gls
Luton T.	App	05.83	82-85	31	11	3
Hull C.	Tr	02.86	85-87	82	2	8
Nottingham F.	Tr	03.88	87-91	99	4	17
Aston Villa	Tr	11.91	91	25	0	1

Garry Parker (Luton Town, Hull City, Nottingham Forest & Aston Villa)

PARKER, Graham S.
Coventry, 23 May, 1946 (M)

League Club	Source	Date Signed	Seasons Played	Apps	Subs	Gls
Aston Villa	App	05.63	63-67	16	1	1
Rotherham U.	Tr	12.67	67	3	1	0
Lincoln C.	Tr	07.68	68	4	1	0
Exeter C.	Tr	03.69	68-73	180	1	12
Torquay U.	Tr	05.74	74-75	41	2	3

PARKER, Harold
Blackburn, 8 February, 1933 (OR)

League Club	Source	Date Signed	Seasons Played	Apps	Subs	Gls
Blackburn Rov.		08.51	51	3	-	0

PARKER, Jeffrey S.
Liverpool, 23 January, 1969 (F)

League Club	Source	Date Signed	Seasons Played	Apps	Subs	Gls
Crewe Alex.	YT	07.87	87	7	3	0

PARKER, John W.
Birkenhead, 5 July, 1925 Died 1988 (IF)

League Club	Source	Date Signed	Seasons Played	Apps	Subs	Gls
Everton	St Lawrence C.Y.M.S.	12.48	50-55	167	-	82
Bury	Tr	05.56	56-58	81	-	43

PARKER, Martin T.
Exeter, 18 October, 1970 (M)

League Club	Source	Date Signed	Seasons Played	Apps	Subs	Gls
Exeter C. (YT)	YT	07.87	88	0	1	0

PARKER, Neil
Blackburn, 19 October, 1957 (FB)

League Club	Source	Date Signed	Seasons Played	Apps	Subs	Gls
Leeds U.	App	10.75	77	0	1	0

PARKER, Patrick J.
Bow (Devon), 15 July, 1929 (CH)

League Club	Source	Date Signed	Seasons Played	Apps	Subs	Gls
Southampton	Newton Abbot	08.51	51-58	132	-	0

PARKER, Paul A.
West Ham, 4 April, 1964 E Yth/Eu21-8/E'B'/E-17 (D)

League Club	Source	Date Signed	Seasons Played	Apps	Subs	Gls
Fulham	App	04.82	80-86	140	13	2
Queens Park R.	Tr	06.87	87-90	121	4	1
Manchester U.	Tr	08.91	91	24	2	0

Paul Parker (Fulham, Queens Park Rangers, Manchester United & England)

PARKER, Raymond D.
Doncaster, 27 January, 1925 (CH)

League Club	Source	Date Signed	Seasons Played	Apps	Subs	Gls
Chesterfield	Thurcroft	02.45	47	14	-	0
Sheffield Wed.	Tr	04.48	48	1	-	0
Bradford C.	Buxton	06.51	51-52	41	-	1

PARKER, Reginald E.
Pontyclun, 10 June, 1921 (CF)

League Club	Source	Date Signed	Seasons Played	Apps	Subs	Gls
Cardiff C.		11.46	47	2	-	0
Newport Co.	Tr	08.48	48-53	201	-	99

PARKER, Robert
Coventry, 11 November, 1952 E Yth (D)

League Club	Source	Date Signed	Seasons Played	Apps	Subs	Gls
Coventry C.	App	05.70	69-73	77	3	0
Carlisle U.	Tr	06.74	74-83	373	2	6

PARKER, Robert W.
Seaham, 26 November, 1935 (FB)

League Club	Source	Date Signed	Seasons Played	Apps	Subs	Gls
Huddersfield T.	Murton Colly	06.54	59-64	65	-	0
Barnsley	Tr	07.65	65-68	108	0	0

PARKER, Samuel
Liverpool, 5 April, 1924 (CF/FB)

League Club	Source	Date Signed	Seasons Played	Apps	Subs	Gls
Accrington St.	Marine	07.48	48	13	-	6
Barnsley	Tr	12.48				
Accrington St.	Tr	09.49	49-50	36	-	6
Crewe Alex.	Tr	11.50	50-51	43	-	5

PARKER, Sean
Newcastle, 23 August, 1973 (D)

League Club	Source	Date Signed	Seasons Played	Apps	Subs	Gls
Northampton T.	YT	07.91	91	5	1	0

PARKER, Stanley F.
Worksop, 31 July, 1920 (IF)

League Club	Source	Date Signed	Seasons Played	Apps	Subs	Gls
Ipswich T.	Worksop L.B.O.B.	05.46	46-50	126	-	43
Norwich C.	Tr	08.51				

League Club	Source	Date Signed	Seasons Played	Apps	Subs	Gls
PARKER, Stuart J.						
Preston, 16 February, 1954						(F)
Blackpool	App	04.72	72-74	10	6	2
Southend U.	Tr	07.75	75-76	62	2	23
Chesterfield	Tr	02.77	76-77	30	4	8
Blackburn Rov.	Sparta Rotterdam (Neth)	07.79	79	5	4	1
Bury	Frecheville C.A.	09.82	82	26	8	9
Chester C. (N/C)	R.C. Mechelen (Bel)	09.83	83	9	0	5
Stockport Co. (N/C)	Blackpool (N/C)	02.84	83	0	1	0
PARKER, Stuart K.						
Nantwich, 13 April, 1963						(G)
Wrexham	Jnrs	08.81	82-84	31	0	0
PARKER, Thomas R.						
Hartlepool, 13 February, 1924						(IF)
Ipswich T.		08.46	46-56	428	-	86
PARKER, Walter						
Doncaster, 28 June, 1929						(FB)
Hull C.	Jnrs	08.47				
Crewe Alex.	Tr	08.51	51-55	56	-	0
PARKER, William						
Liverpool, 15 August, 1925						(OL)
Reading	Runcorn	06.50	50-52	32	-	6
Swindon T.	Tr	02.53	52	10	-	0
Exeter C.	Tr	07.53	53	18	-	2
PARKER, William F.						
Liverpool, 29 March, 1932						(HB)
Liverpool	Burscough	04.53				
Southport	Shelbourne	07.59	59	9	-	0
PARKER, William T.						
Bolsover, 6 October, 1920 Died 1953						(G)
Crewe Alex.		07.47	47-48	17	-	0
PARKES, Alan						
Hartlepool, 12 January, 1929						(CF)
Charlton Ath.	Murton Colly	10.49				
Darlington		03.55	54	1	-	0
PARKES, Anthony						
Sheffield, 5 May, 1949						(M)
Blackburn Rov.	Buxton	05.70	70-80	345	5	38
PARKES, Barry J.						
Hartlepool, 21 January, 1940						(IF)
Hartlepool U.		11.60	60-62	27	-	9
PARKES, Harold A.						
Birmingham, 4 January, 1920						(FB)
Aston Villa	Boldmere St Michael	04.39	46-54	320	-	3
PARKES, Philip						
West Bromwich, 14 July, 1947						(G)
Wolverhampton W.	Jnrs	09.64	66-77	303	0	0
PARKES, Phillip B. F.						
Sedgley, 8 August, 1950 Eu21-1/Eu23-6/E-'B'/E-1						(G)
Walsall	Jnrs	01.68	68-69	52	0	0
Queens Park R.	Tr	06.70	70-78	344	0	0
West Ham U.	Tr	02.79	78-89	344	0	0
Ipswich T.	Tr	08.90	90	3	0	0
PARKES, Sidney						
Hartlepool, 20 September, 1919						(G)
Hartlepool U.	Hetton U.	08.46	46-47	6	-	0
PARKHILL, James						
Belfast, 27 July, 1934						(G)
Exeter C.	Cliftonville	09.63	63	1	-	0
PARKHOUSE, R. Robert						
Calne, 13 August, 1914						(FB)
Swindon T.	Calne T.	10.35	35-46	26	-	0
PARKIN, Albert G.						
Mansfield, 11 April, 1928						(F)
Derby Co.	Jnrs	05.46	49	9	-	0
PARKIN, Brian						
Birkenhead, 12 October, 1965						(G)
Oldham Ath.	Jnrs	03.83	83-84	6	0	0
Crewe Alex.	Tr	11.84	84-87	98	0	0
Crystal Palace	Tr	06.88	88-89	20	0	0
Bristol Rov.	Tr	11.89	89-91	112	0	0

League Club	Source	Date Signed	Seasons Played	Apps	Subs	Gls
PARKIN, Derek						
Newcastle, 2 January, 1948 Eu23-5/EF Lge						(RB)
Huddersfield T.	Jnrs	05.65	64-67	60	1	1
Wolverhampton W.	Tr	02.68	67-81	500	1	6
Stoke C.	Tr	03.82	81-82	40	0	0
PARKIN, Herbert B.						
Sheffield, 10 April, 1920						(FB)
Sheffield U.		04.42	47-50	35	-	0
Chesterfield	Tr	08.51	51-52	55	-	0
PARKIN, Maurice						
Sheffield, 8 September, 1949						(FB)
Leeds U.	App	10.67				
Shrewsbury T.	Tr	07.68	68	4	2	0
PARKIN, Stephen J.						
Mansfield, 7 November, 1965 E Sch/E Yth/Eu21-5						(M/LB)
Stoke C.	App	11.83	82-88	104	9	5
West Bromwich A.	Tr	06.89	89-91	44	4	2
PARKIN, Thomas A.						
Gateshead, 1 February, 1956						(M)
Ipswich T.	App	12.73	77-86	52	18	0
Grimsby T.	L	03.76	75	6	0	0
Peterborough U.	L	07.76	76	3	0	0
PARKIN, Timothy J.						
Penrith, 31 December, 1957						(CD)
Blackburn Rov.	App	03.76	76-78	13	0	0
Bristol Rov.	F.K. Malmö (Swe)	08.81	81-85	205	1	12
Swindon T.	Tr	07.86	86-89	109	1	6
Port Vale	Tr	12.89	89-91	41	7	1
Shrewsbury T.	L	09.91	91	5	0	0
PARKINSON, Alfred A.						
Camden Town, 30 April, 1922						(WH)
Queens Park R.		09.43	46-50	77	-	2
PARKINSON, Alan						
Normanton, 5 May, 1932						(CF)
Bradford P. A.	Jnrs	10.50	51-54	13	-	4
PARKINSON, Alan						
Dagenham, 12 April, 1945						(G)
Leyton Orient (Am)	Aveley	03.67	66	1	0	0
PARKINSON, Alan A.						
Longton, 19 July, 1933						(FB)
Southport	Leyland Motors	08.53	53-58	106	-	0
PARKINSON, Andrew J.						
South Africa, 5 May, 1959						(F)
Newcastle U.	Highlands Park (SA)	03.78	77-78	0	3	0
Peterborough U.	Tr	08.79	79	12	1	5
PARKINSON, Eric						
Longridge, 14 December, 1930						(HB)
Preston N. E.	Jnrs	02.51				
Southport	Tr	06.56	57	4	-	0
PARKINSON, Gary A.						
Thornaby, 10 January, 1968						(RB)
Middlesbrough	Everton (Jnrs)	01.86	86-91	190	8	5
PARKINSON, John						
Trimdon, 2 June, 1953						(WH)
Hartlepool U. (Am)	Trimdon Jnrs	09.71	71	1	0	0
PARKINSON, Joseph S.						
Eccles, 11 June, 1971						(M/RB)
Wigan Ath.	YT	03.89	88-91	102	4	6
PARKINSON, Keith J.						
Preston, 28 January, 1956						(CD)
Leeds U.	App	02.73	75-80	25	6	0
Hull C.	L	11.81	81	0	1	0
Doncaster Rov. (N/C)	Tr	01.82	81	5	0	0
PARKINSON, Noel D.						
Hull, 16 November, 1959 E Yth						(W)
Ipswich T.	App	12.76				
Bristol Rov.	L	11.79	79	5	0	1
Brentford	L	02.80	79	9	1	0
Mansfield T.	Tr	07.80	80-81	66	4	13
Scunthorpe U.	Tr	08.82	82-83	39	2	7
Colchester U.	Tr	08.84	84-85	79	0	13

League Club	Source	Date Signed	Seasons Played	Career Record Apps	Subs	Gls

PARKINSON, Philip J.
Chorley, 1 December, 1967 (M)

Southampton	App	12.85				
Bury	Tr	03.88	87-91	133	12	5

PARKS, Albert
Lurgan (NI), 9 February, 1926 (IF)

Notts Co.	Glenavon	11.45	46-47	28	-	4

PARKS, Anthony
Hackney, 28 January, 1963 (G)

Tottenham H.	App	09.80	81-87	37	0	0
Oxford U.	L	10.86	86	5	0	0
Gillingham	L	09.87	87	2	0	0
Brentford	Tr	08.88	88-90	71	0	0
Fulham	Tr	02.91	90	2	0	0
West Ham U.	Tr	08.91	91	6	0	0

PARKS, John A.
Wath, 14 September, 1943 (CF)

Sheffield U.	App	11.60	63	1	-	0
Halifax T.	Tr	09.66	66-67	40	0	14

PARLANE, Derek J.
Helensburgh, 5 May, 1953 Su21-1/Su23-5/S-12 (F)

Leeds U.	Glasgow Rangers	03.80	79-82	45	5	10
Manchester C.	Hong Kong	08.83	83-84	47	1	20
Swansea C.	Tr	01.85	84	21	0	3
Rochdale	Hong Kong	12.86	86-87	42	0	10

Derek Parlane (Glasgow Rangers, Leeds United, Manchester City, Swansea City, Rochdale & Scotland)

PARLOUR, Raymond
Romford, 7 March, 1973 Eu21-4 (M)

Arsenal	YT	03.91	91	2	4	1

PARMENTER, Terence L.
Romford, 21 October, 1947 (W)

Fulham	App	11.64	64-68	18	1	1
Leyton Orient	Tr	02.69	68-70	34	3	3
Gillingham	Tr	08.71	71-72	48	1	0

League Club	Source	Date Signed	Seasons Played	Career Record Apps	Subs	Gls

PARNABY, Thomas W.
South Shields, 6 January, 1922 (OL)

Plymouth Arg.		07.39				
Oldham Ath.	Tr	02.47	47	7	-	1

PARNELL, Dennis R.
Farnborough, 17 January, 1940 E Yth (W)

Aldershot	West Bromwich A. (Am)	08.58	58-60	66	-	11
Norwich C.	Tr	07.61	61	2	-	0

PARNELL, Frank W.
Birkenhead, 4 November, 1935 (F)

Tranmere Rov.		01.56	55-56	4	-	3

PARNELL, Roy
Birkenhead, 8 October, 1943 (FB)

Everton	Jnrs	10.60	60-63	3	-	0
Tranmere Rov.	Tr	08.64	64-66	105	0	2
Bury	Tr	02.67	66-69	97	0	2

PARODI, Leslie V.
Lambeth, 1 April, 1954 (FB)

Bournemouth	Slough T.	09.72	73-74	45	4	2

PARR, Gordon J.
Bristol, 6 December, 1938 (WH)

Bristol C.	Jnrs	02.57	57-71	281	6	4

PARR, Henry
Newark, 23 October, 1915 E Amat (WH)

Lincoln C. (Am)	Leyton Orient (Am)	08.46	46-49	112	-	14

PARR, John (Jack)
Derby, 21 November, 1920 Died 1985 (FB)

Derby Co.	Long Eaton St Peters	03.38	46-52	112	-	0
Shrewsbury T.	Tr	07.53	53-55	112	-	0

PARR, John B.
Weston-super-Mare, 23 November, 1942 (G)

Nottingham F.	Ransome & Marles	11.62	63	1	-	0

PARR, Stephen V.
Preston, 22 December, 1926 (FB)

Liverpool	Farrington Vic.	05.48	51-52	20	-	0
Exeter C.	Tr	05.55	55-56	8	-	0
Rochdale	Tr	12.56	56-57	16	-	1

Ray Parlour (Arsenal)

League Club	Source	Date Signed	Seasons Played	Career Record Apps	Subs	Gls
PARR, Trevor W.						
Bradford, 21 December, 1961						(F)
Birmingham C.	App	12.79				
Bradford C.	Tr	07.80				
Huddersfield T.	Tr	11.80				
Peterborough U. (N/C)	Thackley	11.84	84	0	1	0
PARRIS, George M. R.						
Ilford, 11 September, 1964 E Sch						(M/FB)
West Ham U.	App	09.82	84-91	201	22	12

George Parris (West Ham United)

League Club	Source	Date Signed	Seasons Played	Career Record Apps	Subs	Gls
PARRISH, Donald A.						
Bilston, 22 November, 1944						(F)
Wrexham	Jnrs	06.63	62-65	4	0	0
PARRISH, Sean						
Wrexham, 14 March, 1972						(M)
Shrewsbury T.	YT	07.90	89-90	1	2	0
PARROTT, John F.						
Scunthorpe, 5 June, 1934						(F)
Scunthorpe U.		12.55	55	1	-	0
PARRY, Anthony J.						
Burton, 8 September, 1945						(CD)
Hartlepool U.	Burton A.	11.65	65-71	181	6	5
Derby Co.	Tr	01.72	72	4	2	0
Mansfield T.	L	01.74	73	0	1	0
PARRY, Bryn J.						
Swansea, 11 January, 1924 W-1						(G)
Swansea C.	Clydach	09.46	46-50	99	-	0
Ipswich T.	Tr	08.51	51-54	138	-	0
PARRY, Colin						
Stockport, 16 February, 1941						(CH)
Stockport Co.	Vernon Park	07.62	62-67	132	1	0
Bradford C.	L	09.65	65	5	0	0
Rochdale	Tr	07.68	68-71	154	2	1
PARRY, Cyril						
Derby, 13 December, 1937 E Sch						(F)
Notts Co.	Derby Co. (Am)	05.55	57-58	12	-	2

League Club	Source	Date Signed	Seasons Played	Career Record Apps	Subs	Gls
PARRY, David E.						
Southport, 11February, 1948						(W)
Blackpool	App	12.65				
Tranmere Rov.	Tr	07.67	67	3	0	0
Halifax T.	Tr	09.68	68	2	0	0
PARRY, John (Jack)						
Derby, 29 July, 1931						(IF)
Derby Co.	Jnrs	07.48	48-65	482	1	105
PARRY, John E.						
Flint, 4 September, 1939						(FB)
Liverpool	Jnrs	09.56				
Doncaster Rov.	Tr	09.61	61	14	-	0
PARRY, Leslie I.						
Wallasey, 13 November, 1953						(D)
Tranmere Rov.	Jnrs	09.72	72-83	254	4	4
PARRY, Mark						
Wrexham, 21 May, 1970						(W)
Chester C. (YT)	YT	08.86	87	4	1	1
PARRY, Oswald						
Merthyr Tydfil, 16 August, 1908						(FB)
Crystal Palace	Wimbledon	05.31	31-35	141	-	0
Ipswich T.	Tr	06.36	38-48	104	-	0
PARRY, Raymond A.						
Derby, 19 January, 1936 E Sch/E Yth/Eu23-4/EF Lge/E-2						(IF)
Bolton W.	Jnrs	01.53	51-60	270	-	68
Blackpool	Tr	10.60	60-64	128	-	27
Bury	Tr	10.64	64-71	136	10	17
PARRY, Stephen						
Upton, 11 December, 1956						(G)
Barnsley	App	12.74	73-74	5	0	0
PARRY, William						
Blaenau Ffestiniog, 18 February, 1933						(FB)
Tottenham H.	Portmadoc	09.53				
Gillingham	Tr	07.55	55-60	200	-	4
PARSELLE, Norman J.						
Newport, 8 January, 1970						(M)
Newport Co. (YT)	YT	08.86	87	4	6	0
PARSLEY, Neil R.						
Liverpool, 25 April, 1966						(FB)
Leeds U.	Witton A.	11.88				
Chester C.	L	12.89	89	6	0	0
Huddersfield T.	Tr	07.90	90-91	11	2	0
Doncaster Rov.	L	02.91	90	2	1	0
PARSLEY, Norman N.						
Shildon, 28 November, 1923						(WH)
Darlington	Shildon Wks	10.45	46-52	161	-	14
PARSONS, Dennis R.						
Birmingham, 29 May, 1925 Died 1980						(G)
Wolverhampton W.	B.S.A. Cycles	11.44	48-51	23	-	0
Aston Villa	Hereford U.	09.52	52-54	36	-	0
PARSONS, Derek J.						
Hammersmith, 24 October, 1929						(IF)
Queens Park R.		02.50	52	2	-	1
PARSONS, Edward J.						
Bristol, 22 March, 1928						(CF)
Bristol Rov.	Frome T.	08.49	49	5	-	2
PARSONS, Eric G.						
Worthing, 9 November, 1923 E'B'-2						(OR)
West Ham U.	Jnrs	10.43	46-50	146	-	34
Chelsea	Tr	12.50	50-56	158	-	37
Brentford	Tr	11.56	56-60	119	-	18
PARSONS, Frank R.						
Amersham, 29 October, 1947						(G)
Crystal Palace	Jnrs	07.65	66	4	0	0
Cardiff C.	Tr	08.70	70-72	17	0	0
Reading	Tr	09.74	74	1	0	0
PARSONS, Geoffrey						
Belper, 2 August, 1931						(OL)
Mansfield T.	Jnrs	05.51				
Chesterfield	Tr	07.52	52	1	-	0

League Club	Source	Date Signed	Seasons Played	Career Record Apps	Subs	Gls

PARSONS, John S.
Cardiff, 10 December, 1950 W Sch (F)

League Club	Source	Date Signed	Seasons Played	Apps	Subs	Gls
Cardiff C.	App	12.68	70-72	7	8	6
Bournemouth	Tr	02.73	72-74	7	1	1
Newport Co.	Tr	03.75	74-76	57	3	22

PARSONS, Lindsay W.
Bristol, 20 March, 1946 (LB)

League Club	Source	Date Signed	Seasons Played	Apps	Subs	Gls
Bristol Rov.	App	04.64	63-76	354	5	0
Torquay U.	Tr	08.77	77-78	56	0	0

PARSONS, Mark C.
Luton, 24 February, 1975 (RB)

League Club	Source	Date Signed	Seasons Played	Apps	Subs	Gls
Northampton T. (YT)	YT	07.91	91	13	0	0

PARSONS, Stephen P. J.
Hammersmith, 7 October, 1957 (M)

League Club	Source	Date Signed	Seasons Played	Apps	Subs	Gls
Wimbledon	Walton & Hersham	12.77	77-79	91	3	19
Leyton Orient	Tr	03.80	79-80	36	0	6

PARSONS, Stuart
Staveley, 24 May, 1948 (WH)

League Club	Source	Date Signed	Seasons Played	Apps	Subs	Gls
Chesterfield	Jnrs	08.67	66	1	0	0

PARTON, Jeffrey J.
Swansea, 24 February, 1953 W Sch/Wu23-3 (G)

League Club	Source	Date Signed	Seasons Played	Apps	Subs	Gls
Burnley	App	03.70	71-73	3	0	0
Northampton T.	Tr	07.75	75-77	25	0	0

PARTRIDGE, Brendan
Manchester, 17 September, 1941 (OL)

League Club	Source	Date Signed	Seasons Played	Apps	Subs	Gls
Stockport Co.		11.60	60-61	31	-	6
Darlington	Tr	07.62	62	3	-	0

PARTRIDGE, Cyril
York, 12 October, 1931 (OL)

League Club	Source	Date Signed	Seasons Played	Apps	Subs	Gls
Queens Park R.		08.54				
Rotherham U.		08.57	57	7	-	2

PARTRIDGE, Donald
Bolton, 22 October, 1925 (HB)

League Club	Source	Date Signed	Seasons Played	Apps	Subs	Gls
Rochdale	Farnworth	10.45	46-55	103	-	2

PARTRIDGE, John T.
Chesterfield, 14 September, 1962 (LB)

League Club	Source	Date Signed	Seasons Played	Apps	Subs	Gls
Chesterfield	App	09.80	81-82	34	4	0
Mansfield T.	L	09.83	83	1	0	0

PARTRIDGE, Malcolm
Chesterfield, 28 August, 1950 (F)

League Club	Source	Date Signed	Seasons Played	Apps	Subs	Gls
Mansfield T.	App	09.68	67-70	65	2	20
Leicester C.	Tr	09.70	70-73	25	11	4
Charlton Ath.	L	01.72	71	1	1	0
Grimsby T.	Tr	03.75	74-78	134	4	25
Scunthorpe U.	Tr	07.79	79-81	91	6	21

PARTRIDGE, Maurice E.
Birmingham, 20 February, 1941 (FB)

League Club	Source	Date Signed	Seasons Played	Apps	Subs	Gls
Birmingham C.	Jnrs	03.58				
Walsall	Tr	07.61	61-62	3	-	0

PASCOE, Colin J.
Port Talbot, 9 April, 1965 W Yth/Wu21-3/W-10 (LW)

League Club	Source	Date Signed	Seasons Played	Apps	Subs	Gls
Swansea C.	App	04.83	82-87	167	7	39
Sunderland	Tr	03.88	87-91	116	10	22

PASHLEY, Robert
Sheffield, 9 September, 1937 (IF)

League Club	Source	Date Signed	Seasons Played	Apps	Subs	Gls
Sheffield U.	Sheffield Wed. (Am)	01.56				
Scunthorpe U.	Gainsborough Trin.	05.59	59	3	-	1
Barrow	Tr	06.60	60	26	-	2

PASHLEY, Terence
Chesterfield, 11 October, 1956 E Sch (LB)

League Club	Source	Date Signed	Seasons Played	Apps	Subs	Gls
Burnley	App	10.73	75-77	16	2	0
Blackpool	Tr	08.78	78-82	201	0	7
Bury	Tr	08.83	83-88	205	12	5

PASKIN, W. John
Cape Town (SA), 1 February, 1962 (F)

League Club	Source	Date Signed	Seasons Played	Apps	Subs	Gls
West Bromwich A.	Seiko (HK)	08.88	88	14	11	5
Wolverhampton W.	Tr	06.89	89-91	21	13	2
Stockport Co.	L	09.91	91	3	2	1
Birmingham C.	L	11.91	91	8	2	3
Shrewsbury T.	L	02.92	91	1	0	0
Wrexham	Tr	02.92	91	14	3	3

PASSEY, Peter T. J.
Birmingham, 13 July, 1952 E Yth (D)

League Club	Source	Date Signed	Seasons Played	Apps	Subs	Gls
Birmingham C.	App	07.69				
Newport Co.	Tr	01.72	71-75	136	0	2

PASSMOOR, Thomas
Chester-le-Street, 12 February, 1937 (CH)

League Club	Source	Date Signed	Seasons Played	Apps	Subs	Gls
Sunderland	Jnrs	05.54				
Scunthorpe U.	South Shields	05.59	59-63	27	-	0
Carlisle U.	Tr	12.63	63-69	242	2	0

PASSMORE, Ernest
Moorsley, 28 April, 1922 (CF)

League Club	Source	Date Signed	Seasons Played	Apps	Subs	Gls
Swansea C.	Portsmouth (Am)	02.44	46	6	-	2
Gateshead	Tr	04.47	46-49	41	-	26

PATCHING, Martin
Rotherham, 1 November, 1958 E Sch/E Yth (M)

League Club	Source	Date Signed	Seasons Played	Apps	Subs	Gls
Wolverhampton W.	App	03.76	75-79	78	12	10
Watford	Tr	12.79	79-83	24	1	3
Northampton T.	L	01.83	82	6	0	1

PATE, Alexander M. (Sandy)
Lennoxtown, 15 August, 1943 (RB)

League Club	Source	Date Signed	Seasons Played	Apps	Subs	Gls
Watford	Renfrew Jnrs	03.65	64-66	14	1	0
Mansfield T.	Tr	10.67	67-77	412	1	2

PATERSON, Alexander
Peterculter, 18 March, 1922 (WH)

League Club	Source	Date Signed	Seasons Played	Apps	Subs	Gls
New Brighton	Alloa Ath.	07.46	46-47	67	-	10
Stockport Co.	Tr	03.48	47-52	160	-	7

PATERSON, George D.
Denny, 26 September, 1914 SF Lge/S-1 (WH)

League Club	Source	Date Signed	Seasons Played	Apps	Subs	Gls
Brentford	Glasgow Celtic	10.46	46-49	62	-	0

PATERSON, George L.
Aberdeen, 19 December, 1916 (IF)

League Club	Source	Date Signed	Seasons Played	Apps	Subs	Gls
Liverpool		05.37	38	2	-	0
Swindon T.	Tr	10.46	46-49	53	-	7

PATERSON, Jamie R.
Dumfries, 26 April, 1973 (W)

League Club	Source	Date Signed	Seasons Played	Apps	Subs	Gls
Halifax T.	YT	07.91	90-91	16	5	3

PATERSON, Steven W.
Elgin, 8 April, 1958 (F)

League Club	Source	Date Signed	Seasons Played	Apps	Subs	Gls
Manchester U.	Nairn Co.	07.75	76-79	3	3	0

PATERSON, Toby L.
Cresswell, 15 May, 1971

League Club	Source	Date Signed	Seasons Played	Apps	Subs	Gls
Halifax T. (YT)	YT	07.87	88	0	1	0

PATERSON, Thomas
Newcastle, 30 March, 1954 (F)

League Club	Source	Date Signed	Seasons Played	Apps	Subs	Gls
Middlesbrough	Leicester C. (Am)	09.74	74	1	0	0
Bournemouth	Tr	04.76	76-77	45	12	10
Darlington	Tr	06.78	78	6	1	2

PATERSON, Thomas A.
Lochore, 3 April, 1927 (W)

League Club	Source	Date Signed	Seasons Played	Apps	Subs	Gls
Leicester C.	Lochgelly Albert	03.48	48-49	17	-	4
Newcastle U.	Tr	06.50	50-51	2	-	0
Watford	Tr	07.52	52-54	45	-	7

PATTERSON, William
Bellshill, 6 October, 1927 (CF)

League Club	Source	Date Signed	Seasons Played	Apps	Subs	Gls
Accrington St.	Morton	08.49	49	1	-	0

PATERSON, William A. K.
Kinlochleven, 25 February, 1930 S 'B'-1 (CH)

League Club	Source	Date Signed	Seasons Played	Apps	Subs	Gls
Doncaster Rov.	Ransome & Marles	03.50	50-54	113	-	0
Newcastle U.	Tr	10.54	54-57	22	-	1

PATES, Colin G.
Carshalton, 10 August, 1961 E Yth (CD)

League Club	Source	Date Signed	Seasons Played	Apps	Subs	Gls
Chelsea	App	07.79	79-88	280	1	10
Charlton Ath.	Tr	10.88	88-89	37	1	0
Arsenal	Tr	01.90	89-91	10	4	0
Brighton & H.A.	L	03.91	90	17	0	0

PATON, David S. C.
Saltcoats, 13 December, 1943 (CH)

League Club	Source	Date Signed	Seasons Played	Apps	Subs	Gls
Southampton	St Mirren	07.63	63-67	13	0	0
Aldershot	Tr	11.69	69-70	31	0	0

League Club	Source	Date Signed	Seasons Played	Apps	Subs	Gls

PATON, John A.
Glasgow, 2 April, 1923 (OL)

League Club	Source	Date Signed	Seasons Played	Apps	Subs	Gls
Chelsea	Glasgow Celtic	11.46	46	18	-	3
Brentford	Glasgow Celtic	09.49	49-51	90	-	14
Watford	Tr	07.52	52-54	84	-	17

PATON, Robert (Danny)
West Calder, 27 January, 1936 (IF)

League Club	Source	Date Signed	Seasons Played	Apps	Subs	Gls
Oxford U.	Hearts	07.64	64	2	-	1

PATON, Thomas G.
Saltcoats, 22 December, 1918 (D)

League Club	Source	Date Signed	Seasons Played	Apps	Subs	Gls
Wolverhampton W.		06.37				
Swansea C.	Tr	10.38	38	6	-	0
Bournemouth	Tr	02.39	38-47	46	-	8
Watford	Tr	01.48	47-51	141	-	1

PATRICK, Alfred
York, 25 September, 1921 (CF)

League Club	Source	Date Signed	Seasons Played	Apps	Subs	Gls
York C.	Cooks	09.46	46-52	228	-	109

PATRICK, Bert
Kilsyth, 26 April, 1946 (FB)

League Club	Source	Date Signed	Seasons Played	Apps	Subs	Gls
Preston N. E.	Jnrs	08.63	64-69	50	0	1
Barrow	Tr	07.71	71	34	0	1

PATRICK, Matthew
Slamannan, 13 June, 1919 (F/FB)

League Club	Source	Date Signed	Seasons Played	Apps	Subs	Gls
York C.	Cowdenbeath	09.40	46-53	249	-	47

PATRICK, Roy
Overseal, 4 December, 1935 (FB)

League Club	Source	Date Signed	Seasons Played	Apps	Subs	Gls
Derby Co.	Jnrs	02.52	52-55	49	-	0
Nottingham F.	Tr	05.59	59-60	57	-	0
Southampton	Tr	06.61	61-62	31	-	0
Exeter C.	Tr	03.63	62-64	50	-	0

PATRICK, William C. G.
Lochgelly, 12 March, 1932 (IF)

League Club	Source	Date Signed	Seasons Played	Apps	Subs	Gls
Coventry C.	Snowdon Colly	11.54	55-57	44	-	6
Gillingham	Tr	06.58	58-59	47	-	13

PATTERSON, Darren J.
Belfast, 15 October, 1969 (CD)

League Club	Source	Date Signed	Seasons Played	Apps	Subs	Gls
West Bromwich A.	YT	07.88				
Wigan Ath.	Tr	04.89	89-91	69	28	6

PATTERSON, George T.
Sunderland, 15 September, 1934 (WH)

League Club	Source	Date Signed	Seasons Played	Apps	Subs	Gls
Hull C.	Silksworth Jnrs	10.52	54-55	7	-	1
York C.	South Shields	05.57	57-59	57	-	4
Hartlepool U.	Tr	06.60	60	18	-	1

PATTERSON, John G.
Cramlington, 6 July, 1922 (G)

League Club	Source	Date Signed	Seasons Played	Apps	Subs	Gls
Blackburn Rov.	North Shields	04.45	48-56	107	-	0

PATTERSON, Mark
Leeds, 13 September, 1968 (RB)

League Club	Source	Date Signed	Seasons Played	Apps	Subs	Gls
Carlisle U.	YT	08.87	86-87	19	3	0
Derby Co.	Tr	11.87	88-91	24	9	3

PATTERSON, Mark A.
Darwen, 24 May, 1965 (LW)

League Club	Source	Date Signed	Seasons Played	Apps	Subs	Gls
Blackburn Rov.	App	05.83	83-87	89	12	20
Preston N. E.	Tr	06.88	88-89	54	1	19
Bury	Tr	02.90	89-90	42	0	10
Bolton W.	Tr	01.90	90-91	54	1	4

PATTERSON, Robert A.
Newcastle, 12 March, 1935 (G)

League Club	Source	Date Signed	Seasons Played	Apps	Subs	Gls
Gateshead	Stanley U.	03.59	58-59	26	-	0

PATTERSON, Ronald L.
Gateshead, 30 October, 1929 (FB)

League Club	Source	Date Signed	Seasons Played	Apps	Subs	Gls
Middlesbrough	Whitehall Jnrs	06.49	51	1	-	0
Northampton T.	Tr	06.52	52-61	301	-	5

PATTISON, Frank M.
Barrhead, 23 December, 1930 (W)

League Club	Source	Date Signed	Seasons Played	Apps	Subs	Gls
Barnsley	Alloa Ath.	12.51	51-54	31	-	5

PATTISON, John M.
Glasgow, 19 December, 1918 (OL)

League Club	Source	Date Signed	Seasons Played	Apps	Subs	Gls
Queens Park R.	Motherwell	05.37	37-49	90	-	17
Leyton Orient	Tr	02.50	49-50	43	-	10

PATTISON, John W. P.
Portsmouth, 23 February, 1925 (RH)

League Club	Source	Date Signed	Seasons Played	Apps	Subs	Gls
Reading	Portsmouth C.S.	07.45	46	2	-	0

PAUL, Anthony G.
Isleworth, 6 April, 1961 (M)

League Club	Source	Date Signed	Seasons Played	Apps	Subs	Gls
Crystal Palace	App	04.78	80	0	1	0

PAUL, David D.
Kirkcaldy, 19 February, 1936 S Sch (G)

League Club	Source	Date Signed	Seasons Played	Apps	Subs	Gls
Derby Co.	Jnrs	02.53	53-55	2	-	0

PAUL, Ian K.
Wolverhampton, 23 January, 1961 (M)

League Club	Source	Date Signed	Seasons Played	Apps	Subs	Gls
Walsall	App	08.78	77-80	68	2	9

PAUL, Roy
Ton Pentre, 18 April, 1920 W-33 (WH)

League Club	Source	Date Signed	Seasons Played	Apps	Subs	Gls
Swansea C.	Ton Pentre	10.38	46-49	160	-	14
Manchester C.	Tr	07.50	50-56	270	-	9

Roy Paul (Swansea City, Manchester City & Wales)

PAUL, Thomas
Grimsby, 14 May, 1933 (OR)

League Club	Source	Date Signed	Seasons Played	Apps	Subs	Gls
Grimsby T.		05.55	58	1	-	0

PAVITT, William E.
West Ham, 30 June, 1920 (D)

League Club	Source	Date Signed	Seasons Played	Apps	Subs	Gls
Fulham	R.A.F. Debden	08.46	49-52	50	-	1
Southend U.	Tr	05.53	53-54	80	-	0

PAWSON, Anthony H.
Chertsey, 22 August, 1921 E Amat (W)

League Club	Source	Date Signed	Seasons Played	Apps	Subs	Gls
Charlton Ath. (Am)	Pegasus	12.51	51-52	2	-	1

PAXTON, John W.
Wolverhampton, 24 March, 1928 (FB)

League Club	Source	Date Signed	Seasons Played	Apps	Subs	Gls
Wolverhampton W.	Jnrs	04.45				
Notts Co.	Tr	05.50	50	2	-	0

PAYE, Michael C.
Orpington, 30 July, 1966 (D)

League Club	Source	Date Signed	Seasons Played	Apps	Subs	Gls
Charlton Ath. (App)	App	04.83	83	2	0	0

PAYNE, Albert C.
Liverpool, 11 November, 1923

League Club	Source	Date Signed	Seasons Played	Apps	Subs	Gls
Tranmere Rov.		08.46	46-48	13	-	0

PAYNE, Brian
Altrincham, 4 November, 1937 (W)

League Club	Source	Date Signed	Seasons Played	Apps	Subs	Gls
Huddersfield T.	Jnrs	10.55				
Gillingham	Tr	07.57	57-59	36	-	3

PAYNE, Clive E.
Aylsham (Nk), 2 March, 1950 (FB)

League Club	Source	Date Signed	Seasons Played	Apps	Subs	Gls
Norwich C.	App	03.68	68-73	122	3	0
Bournemouth	Tr	12.73	73-75	101	0	3

PAYNE, David R.
Croydon, 25 April, 1947 Eu23-1 (D)

League Club	Source	Date Signed	Seasons Played	Apps	Subs	Gls
Crystal Palace	App	11.64	64-72	281	3	9
Leyton Orient	Tr	08.73	73-77	88	5	0

PAYNE, Derek R.
Edgware, 26 April, 1967 (M)

League Club	Source	Date Signed	Seasons Played	Apps	Subs	Gls
Barnet	Hayes	12.88	91	13	1	1

PAYNE, Donald
Swansea, 18 November, 1950 (G)

League Club	Source	Date Signed	Seasons Played	Apps	Subs	Gls
Swansea C.	Jnrs	12.70	71	11	0	0
Torquay U.	Tr	06.72				
Newport Co.	Tr	08.73	73-74	32	0	0

PAYNE, Frank E.
Ipswich, 18 March, 1926

League Club	Source	Date Signed	Seasons Played	Apps	Subs	Gls
Derby Co.	Ollerton Colly	10.47				
Hull C.	Tr	08.48				
Lincoln C.	Tr	08.49	49	5	-	0

PAYNE, George H.
Liverpool, 22 August, 1921 (G)

League Club	Source	Date Signed	Seasons Played	Apps	Subs	Gls
Tranmere Rov.		04.47	46-60	435	-	0

PAYNE, Irving E. H. (Joe)
Briton Ferry, 29 June, 1921 (IF)

League Club	Source	Date Signed	Seasons Played	Apps	Subs	Gls
Swansea C.	Jnrs	07.38	46-48	53	-	10
Newport Co.	Tr	10.49	49	12	-	1
Scunthorpe U.	Tr	07.50	50	18	-	1
Northampton T.	Tr	08.51	51	32	-	5

PAYNE, James
West Bromwich, 25 May, 1936

League Club	Source	Date Signed	Seasons Played	Apps	Subs	Gls
Walsall		08.55	55	1	-	0

PAYNE, James B.
Liverpool, 10 March, 1926 E 'B'-3 (OR)

League Club	Source	Date Signed	Seasons Played	Apps	Subs	Gls
Liverpool	Bootle A.T.C.	11.44	48-55	224	-	37
Everton	Tr	04.56	55-56	5	-	2

PAYNE, Jeremy (Jess)
Dartford, 7 March, 1958 (CD)

League Club	Source	Date Signed	Seasons Played	Apps	Subs	Gls
Leicester C.	Jnrs	07.76				
Torquay U.	Tr	12.77	77-78	25	0	1

PAYNE, Joseph
Bolsover, 17 January, 1914, Died 1975 E-1 (CF)

League Club	Source	Date Signed	Seasons Played	Apps	Subs	Gls
Luton T.	Biggleswade T.	06.34	34-37	72	-	83
Chelsea	Tr	03.38	37-38	36	-	21
West Ham U.	Tr	12.46	46	10	-	6

PAYNE, Lee J.
Luton, 12 December, 1966 (LW)

League Club	Source	Date Signed	Seasons Played	Apps	Subs	Gls
Newcastle U.	Barnet	09.88	88	6	1	0
Reading	Tr	03.89	88-89	25	2	3

PAYNE, Mark I.
India, 2 September, 1966 (W)

League Club	Source	Date Signed	Seasons Played	Apps	Subs	Gls
Swindon T.	App	09.84	84	0	3	0

PAYNE, Mark R. C.
Cheltenham, 3 August, 1960 (M)

League Club	Source	Date Signed	Seasons Played	Apps	Subs	Gls
Stockport Co.	S.C. Cambuur (Neth)	08.88	88-90	77	10	16
Rochdale	Tr	05.91	91	32	2	2

PAYNE, Russell J.
Wigan, 8 July, 1970 (W)

League Club	Source	Date Signed	Seasons Played	Apps	Subs	Gls
Liverpool	Skelmersdale U.	03.90				
Crewe Alex.	L	10.91	91	3	3	0

PAYTON, Andrew P.
Whalley, 3 October, 1967 (F)

League Club	Source	Date Signed	Seasons Played	Apps	Subs	Gls
Hull C.	YT	05.86	86-91	116	28	53
Middlesbrough	Tr	11.91	91	8	11	3

PAYTON, Clifford C.
Brighton, 16 October, 1935 (IF)

League Club	Source	Date Signed	Seasons Played	Apps	Subs	Gls
Accrington St.	Wisbech T.	07.56				
Gillingham	Tonbridge	03.59	58-59	24	-	5

PEACH, David S.
Bedford, 21 January, 1951 Eu21-3/Eu23-8 (LB)

League Club	Source	Date Signed	Seasons Played	Apps	Subs	Gls
Gillingham	App	01.69	69-73	186	1	30
Southampton	Tr	01.74	73-79	221	3	34
Swindon T.	Tr	03.80	79-81	52	1	2
Leyton Orient	Tr	03.82	81-82	47	0	6

PEACH, Geoffrey L.
Plymouth, 11 October, 1932 (F)

League Club	Source	Date Signed	Seasons Played	Apps	Subs	Gls
Plymouth Arg.	Millwall (Am)	07.56	56	1	-	0

PEACH, John (Jack)
Barnsley, 4 April, 1923 (IF)

League Club	Source	Date Signed	Seasons Played	Apps	Subs	Gls
Barnsley	York C. (Am)	11.45				
Hull C.	Tr	10.46	46-47	19	-	2

PEACHEY, John M.
Cambridge, 21 July, 1952 (F)

League Club	Source	Date Signed	Seasons Played	Apps	Subs	Gls
York C.	Hillingdon Bor.	08.73	73-74	6	2	3
Barnsley	Tr	11.74	74-78	116	10	32
Darlington	L	12.75	75	5	1	3
Darlington	Tr	03.79	78-79	16	4	6
Plymouth Arg.	Tr	07.80	80	1	2	0

PEACOCK, Alan
Middlesbrough, 29 October, 1937 E Yth/E-6 (CF)

League Club	Source	Date Signed	Seasons Played	Apps	Subs	Gls
Middlesbrough	Jnrs	11.54	55-63	218	-	125
Leeds U.	Tr	02.64	63-66	54	0	27
Plymouth Arg.	Tr	10.67	67	11	0	1

PEACOCK, Darren
Bristol, 3 February, 1968 (CD)

League Club	Source	Date Signed	Seasons Played	Apps	Subs	Gls
Newport Co.	YT	02.86	85-87	24	4	0
Hereford U.	Tr	03.89	88-90	56	3	5
Queens Park R.	Tr	12.90	90-91	58	0	1

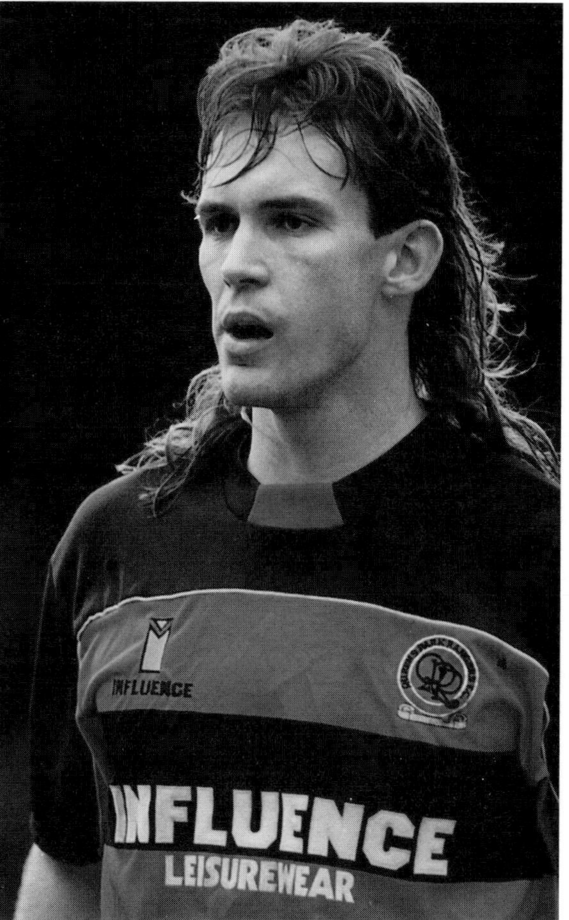

Darren Peacock (Newport County, Hereford United & Queens Park Rangers)

League Club	Source	Date Signed	Seasons Played	Career Record Apps	Subs	Gls
PEACOCK, Dennis						
Lincoln, 19 April, 1953						(G)
Nottingham F.	App	04.71	72-74	22	0	0
Walsall	L	03.73	72	10	0	0
Doncaster Rov.	Tr	07.75	75-79	199	0	0
Bolton W.	Tr	03.80	80-81	16	0	0
Doncaster Rov.	Tr	08.82	82-85	130	0	0
Burnley	L	09.85	85	8	0	0
PEACOCK, Ernest						
Bristol, 11 December, 1924 Died 1966						(WH)
Notts Co.	Syston	03.45				
Bristol C.	Tr	10.46	46-58	343	-	7
PEACOCK, Ernest A.						
Renfrew, 10 August, 1942						(WH)
Workington	Falkirk	01.64	63	1	-	0
PEACOCK, Frank E.						
Bolton, 17 May, 1945						(WH)
Stockport Co.	Blackburn Rov. (Am)	11.64	64	4	-	0
PEACOCK, Gavin K.						
Eltham, 18 November, 1967 E Sch/E Yth						(M)
Queens Park R.	App	11.84	86-87	7	10	1
Gillingham	L	10.87	87	6	0	0
Gillingham	Tr	12.87	87-88	63	1	11
Bournemouth	Tr	07.89	89-90	56	0	8
Newcastle U.	Tr	11.90	90-91	73	0	23
PEACOCK, George						
Pontypool, 10 February, 1924						(FB)
Bristol Rov.	Newport Co. (Am)	05.46	46	7	-	0
PEACOCK, John C.						
Leeds, 27 March, 1956						(LB)
Scunthorpe U.		08.74	74-79	185	5	1
PEACOCK, Keith						
Bexleyheath, 2 May, 1945						(M)
Charlton Ath.	Jnrs	07.62	62-78	512	21	92
PEACOCK, Michael R.						
Fishburn (Dm), 28 September, 1940						(G)
Darlington	Shildon	08.60	60-62	46	-	0
PEACOCK, Robert J.						
Rushden, 18 December, 1937						(HB)
Northampton T.	Rushden T.	02.57	57	2	-	0
PEACOCK, Terence						
Hull, 18 April, 1935						(CF)
Hull C.	Jnrs	12.52	55	2	-	0
Queens Park R.	Tr	08.56	56-57	17	-	4
PEAKE, Andrew M.						
Market Harborough, 1 November, 1961 E Yth/Eu21-1						(M)
Leicester C.	App	01.79	78-84	141	6	13
Grimsby T.	Tr	08.85	85-86	39	0	4
Charlton Ath.	Tr	09.86	86-91	174	3	5
Middlesbrough	Tr	11.91	91	20	3	0
PEAKE, Dudley J.						
Swansea, 26 October, 1934						(CH)
Swansea C.	Tower U.	04.56	55-57	57	-	2
Newport Co.	Tr	06.58	58-62	128	-	0
PEAKE, Jason W.						
Leicester, 29 September, 1971						(M)
Leicester C.	YT	01.90	90	4	4	1
Hartlepool U.	L	02.92	91	5	1	1
PEAKE, Trevor						
Nuneaton, 10 February, 1957 E Semi Pro						(CD)
Lincoln C.	Nuneaton Bor.	06.79	79-82	171	0	7
Coventry C.	Tr	07.83	83-91	277	1	6
Luton T.	Tr	08.91	91	38	0	0
PEAPELL, F. Dennis						
Swindon, 16 November, 1945						(FB/WH)
Swindon T.	App	11.63	64	2	-	0
Exeter C.	Tr	07.65	65	23	1	1
PEARCE, Alan J.						
Middlesbrough, 25 October, 1965						(LW)
York C.	Jnrs	10.83	83-86	76	2	9
Torquay U.	Tr	08.87	87	20	7	2

League Club	Source	Date Signed	Seasons Played	Career Record Apps	Subs	Gls
PEARCE, Andrew J.						
Bradford-on-Avon, 20 April, 1966						(CD)
Coventry C.	Halesowen T.	05.90	90-91	47	0	3
PEARCE, Christopher L.						
Newport, 7 August, 1961 W Sch						(G)
Blackburn Rov.	Wolverhampton W. (App)	10.79				
Rochdale	L	08.80	80	5	0	0
Rochdale	Tr	08.82	82	36	0	0
Port Vale	Tr	06.83	83-85	48	0	0
Wrexham	Tr	07.86	86	25	0	0
Burnley	Tr	07.87	87-91	181	0	0
PEARCE, David G.						
Scunthorpe, 19 December, 1934						(HB)
Scunthorpe U.		07.56	58	2	-	0
PEARCE, David H.						
Northolt, 7 December, 1959 E Semi-Pro						(F)
Millwall		02.78	77	1	0	0
PEARCE, Graham						
Hammersmith, 8 July, 1959						(LB)
Brighton & H. A.	Barnet	01.82	82-85	87	1	2
Gillingham	Tr	07.86	86-87	65	0	0
Brentford	Tr	09.88	88	11	7	0
Maidstone U.	Tr	07.89	89	24	3	0
PEARCE, Ian A.						
Bury St Edmunds, 7 May, 1974						(D)
Chelsea	Jnrs	08.91	90-91	0	3	0
PEARCE, James J.						
Tottenham, 27 November, 1947 E Sch						(W)
Tottenham H.	App	05.65	68-72	108	33	21
PEARCE, John						
Watford, 12 December, 1950						(FB)
Watford	Jnrs	07.69	70	0	1	0
PEARCE, John A.						
Grimsby, 29 February, 1940						(WH)
Grimsby T.	Jnrs	12.58	58-61	48	-	0
PEARCE, Reginald S.						
Liverpool, 12 January, 1930 EF Lge						(WH)
Luton T.	Winsford U.	11.54	54-57	75	-	6
Sunderland	Tr	02.58	57-60	61	-	4
Peterborough U.	Cambridge C.	08.63	63	28	-	2
PEARCE, Stuart						
Hammersmith, 24 April, 1962 Eu21-1/E-50						(LB)
Coventry C.	Wealdstone	10.83	83-84	52	0	4
Nottingham F.	Tr	06.85	85-91	236	0	39
PEARCE, Trevor G.						
Canterbury, 30 May, 1949						(W)
Arsenal	Folkestone T.	02.70				
Aldershot	Tr	05.71	71-72	19	6	2
PEARCEY, Jason						
Leamington, 23 July, 1971						(G)
Mansfield T.	YT	07.89	88-91	32	0	0
PEARS, Jeffrey						
York, 14 June, 1920						(G)
York C.		09.47	47-48	3	-	0
PEARS, Stephen						
Brandon, 22 January, 1962						(G)
Manchester U.	App	01.79	84	4	0	0
Middlesbrough	L	11.83	83	12	0	0
Middlesbrough	Tr	07.85	85-91	250	0	0
PEARSON, Andrew J.						
Newmarket, 19 November, 1960						(F)
Luton T.	App	11.78	79	1	1	0
PEARSON, David A. J.						
Connahs Quay, 13 October, 1947 W Sch/Wu23-1						(FB)
Everton	App	10.65				
Southport	Tr	08.67	67-69	91	2	0
Rochdale	Tr	09.70	70	3	0	0

Stuart Pearce (Coventry City, Nottingham Forest & England)

League Club	Source	Date Signed	Seasons Played	Career Record Apps	Subs	Gls
PEARSON, David T.						
Dunfermline, 9 November, 1932						(CF)
Blackburn Rov.	Jnrs	11.49				
Ipswich T.	Tr	05.54				
Oldham Ath.	Darwen	08.56	56	25	-	12
Rochdale	Tr	03.57	56-57	32	-	17
Crewe Alex.	Tr	05.58	58	9	-	2
PEARSON, Donald J.						
Swansea, 14 March, 1930						(WH)
Swansea C.		06.50	52-57	50	-	1
Aldershot	Tr	07.58	58	31	-	2
PEARSON, Ian T.						
Leeds, 18 September, 1950						(F)
Plymouth Arg.	Goole T.	07.74	74-75	6	6	0
Millwall	Wycombe W.	08.77	77-78	41	3	9
Exeter C.	Tr	11.78	78-80	67	2	10
Plymouth Arg.	Bideford	08.83	83	5	3	1
PEARSON, James F.						
Falkirk, 24 March, 1953 Su23-6						(F)
Everton	St Johnstone	07.74	74-77	76	17	15
Newcastle U.	Tr	08.78	78-79	11	0	3
PEARSON, John						
Wigan, 18 October, 1946 E Sch						(OR)
Manchester U.	App	11.63				
York C.	Tr	07.65	65	14	1	4
PEARSON, John						
Ferryhill, 8 May, 1951						(IF)
Hartlepool U. (Am)	Ferryhill Ath.	01.69	68	1	0	0
PEARSON, John A.						
Isleworth, 23 April, 1935						(F)
Brentford	Jnrs	11.52	55-56	5	-	0
Queens Park R.	Tr	06.58	58-59	21	-	9
PEARSON, John G.						
Gateshead, 10 April, 1931						
Hartlepool U.		04.53	52	1	-	0
PEARSON, John S.						
Sheffield, 1 September, 1963 E Yth						(F)
Sheffield Wed.	App	05.81	80-84	64	41	24
Charlton Ath.	Tr	05.85	85-86	52	9	15
Leeds U.	Tr	01.87	86-90	51	48	12
Rotherham U.	L	03.91	90	11	0	5
Barnsley	Tr	07.91	91	8	2	1
Hull C.	L	01.92	91	15	0	0
PEARSON, Lawrence						
Wallsend, 2 July, 1965						(LB)
Hull C.	Gateshead	06.84	84-86	58	1	0
Bristol C.	Tr	06.87				
Port Vale	Tr	08.87	87	3	0	0
PEARSON, Mark						
Sheffield, 28 October, 1939 E Sch/E Yth						(IF)
Manchester U.	Jnrs	05.57	57-62	68	-	12
Sheffield Wed.	Tr	10.63	63-64	39	-	9
Fulham	Tr	05.65	65-67	53	5	7
Halifax T.	Tr	03.68	68	2	3	0
PEARSON, Michael						
Bilston, 5 December, 1942						(IF)
Manchester C.	Jnrs	12.59				
Walsall	Tr	05.62	62	3	-	1
PEARSON, Nigel G.						
Nottingham, 21 August, 1963						(CD)
Shrewsbury T.	Heanor T.	11.81	82-87	153	0	5
Sheffield Wed.	Tr	10.87	87-91	159	0	13
PEARSON, Richard						
Ulcombe, 18 October, 1970						(CD)
Gillingham	YT	07.89	88-89	7	2	0
PEARSON, Richard J.						
Portsmouth, 14 June, 1931						(IF)
Portsmouth	Gosport Bor.	05.49	53	4	-	1
PEARSON, Stanley C.						
Salford, 11 January, 1919 EF Lge/E-8						(IF)
Manchester U.	Adelphi B.C.	05.36	37-53	312	-	127
Bury	Tr	02.54	53-57	122	-	56
Chester C.	Tr	10.57	57-58	57	-	16

League Club	Source	Date Signed	Seasons Played	Career Record Apps	Subs	Gls
PEARSON, Stuart J.						
Hull, 21 June, 1949 Eu23-1/E-15						(F)
Hull C.	Jnrs	07.68	69-73	126	3	44
Manchester U.	Tr	05.74	74-77	138	1	55
West Ham U.	Tr	08.79	79-81	29	5	6
PEARSON, Thomas U.						
Edinburgh, 6 March, 1913 SF Lge/S-2						(OL)
Newcastle U.	Murrayfield Ath.	03.33	33-47	212	-	46
PEARSON, Trevor						
Sheffield, 4 April, 1952						(G)
Sheffield W. (Am)	Woodseats W.M.C.	03.72	71	4	0	0
PEARSON, Walter						
Ottershaw, 13 November, 1928						(G)
Aldershot (Am)	Tooting & Mitcham	03.61	60	1	-	0
PEARSON, William G. A.						
Clonmel (Ire), 23 October, 1921						(W)
Grimsby T.		09.43	46-48	35	-	8
Chester C.	Tr	06.49	49	12	-	3
PEART, Robert C.						
Swindon, 17 December, 1926						(CF)
Swindon T.	Burnley (Am)	04.48	49-51	13	-	5
PEART, Ronald						
Brandon, 8 March, 1920						(WH)
Hartlepool U.		09.38	38	8	-	0
Derby Co.	Tr	05.39	46	1	-	0
York C.	Tr	06.48	48	5	-	0
PEAT, W. Arthur						
Liverpool, 1 September, 1940						(WH)
Everton	Jnrs	04.59				
Southport	Tr	07.61	61-71	401	0	27
Crewe Alex.	Tr	07.72	72-73	82	0	5
PEAT, James L.						
Birmingham, 29 May, 1951						(OL)
Workington	Cadburys	08.73	73	0	1	0

Nigel Pearson (Shrewsbury Town & Sheffield Wednesday)

League Club	Source	Date Signed	Seasons Played	Career Record Apps	Subs	Gls
PEAT, John						
Workington		10.53	53	1	-	0
PEATTIE, Donald S.						
York, 5 April, 1963						(F)
Sheffield U.	Gretna	08.84	84	3	2	0
Doncaster Rov.	L	01.86	85	3	1	0
PECK, Trevor D.						
Llanelli, 25 May, 1938						(FB)
Cardiff C.	Llanelli	02.58	59-64	42	-	0
PECKETT, Andrew R.						
Sheffield, 19 September, 1969						(M)
Doncaster Rov.	YT	06.88	87-88	2	7	0
PEDDELTY, John						
Bishop Auckland, 2 April, 1955 E Yth						(CD)
Ipswich T.	App	01.73	72-76	44	0	5
Plymouth Arg.	Tr	10.76	76-77	30	3	1
PEDDELTY, Maurice J.						
Carlisle, 23 May, 1950						(M)
Carlisle U.	App	12.67	68-70	9	5	1
Darlington	Tr	07.70	70-71	51	5	1
PEDEN, George W.						
Rosewell, 12 April, 1943						(FB)
Lincoln C.	Hearts	04.67	66-73	223	2	15
PEEBLES, Richard						
Glasgow, 30 August, 1923						(IF)
Swindon T.	St Johnstone	05.50	50	12	-	1
PEEK, James						
Hartlepool, 7 July, 1933						(RB)
Hartlepool U. (Am)	Fosten W.	12.59	59	7	-	0
PEEL, Kenneth						
Manchester, 8 January, 1922						(IR)
Crewe Alex.	Rusholme	09.46	46	1	-	0
PEEL, Nathan J.						
Blackburn, 17 May, 1972						(F)
Preston N. E.	YT	07.90	90	1	9	1
Sheffield U.	Tr	07.91	91	0	1	0
PEEL, Trevor						
Huddersfield, 25 October, 1945						(FB)
Bradford P. A.	Huddersfield T. (Am)	04.67	66-67	11	0	0
PEER, Dean						
Stourbridge, 8 August, 1969						(M)
Birmingham C.	YT	07.87	86-91	93	14	7
PEGG, David						
Doncaster, 20 September, 1935 Died 1958 E Sch/Eu23-3/E'B'-1/E-1						(OL)
Manchester U.	Jnrs	09.52	52-57	127	-	24
PEGG, James K.						
Salford, 4 January, 1926						(G)
Manchester U.	Jnrs	11.47	47	2	-	0
Torquay U.	Tr	08.49	49	2	-	0
York C.	Tr	08.50	50	1	-	0
PEJIC, Melvyn						
Newcastle-u-Lyme, 27 April, 1959						(CD)
Stoke C.	Jnrs	07.77	79	1	0	0
Hereford U.	Tr	06.80	80-91	404	8	14
Wrexham	Tr	01.92	91	6	1	1
PEJIC, Michael						
Chesterton, 25 January, 1950 Eu23-8/E-4						(LB)
Stoke C.	App	01.68	68-76	274	0	6
Everton	Tr	02.77	76-78	76	0	2
Aston Villa	Tr	09.79	79	10	0	0
PELL, Dennis						
Normanton, 19 April, 1929						(IF)
Rotherham U.	Methley	05.52	52-55	12	-	3
Grimsby T.	Tr	10.55	55-56	3	-	1
PEMBERTON, James H. A.						
Wolverhampton, 30 April, 1916						(FB)
West Bromwich A.	Brownhills A.	08.38	46-50	162	-	0

League Club	Source	Date Signed	Seasons Played	Career Record Apps	Subs	Gls
PEMBERTON, James T.						
Birmingham, 14 November, 1925						(OL)
West Bromwich A.	Round Oak	05.45				
Luton T.	Stourbridge	11.47	50-56	92	-	8
PEMBERTON, John M.						
Oldham, 18 November, 1964						(RB)
Rochdale (N/C)	Chadderton	09.84	84	1	0	0
Crewe Alex.	Chadderton	03.85	84-87	116	5	1
Crystal Palace	Tr	03.88	87-89	76	2	2
Sheffield U.	Tr	07.90	90-91	40	1	0
PEMBERTON, Selwyn R.						
Cardiff, 13 October, 1928						(RB)
Newport Co.		03.52	52	1	-	0
PEMBERY, Gordon D.						
Cardiff, 10 October, 1926						(WH)
Norwich C.	Cardiff Nomads	01.47	46	1	-	0
Cardiff C.	Tr	08.48	49	1	-	0
Torquay U.	Tr	06.50	50-51	51	-	7
Charlton Ath.	Tr	01.52	51-55	18	-	1
Swindon T.	Tr	06.56	56	37	-	2
PEMBRIDGE, Mark A.						
Merthyr Tydfil, 29 November, 1970 Wu21-1/W'B'/W-5						(M)
Luton T.	YT	07.89	90-91	60	0	6
PENDER, John P.						
Luton, 19 November, 1963 IR Yth/IRu21-1						(CD)
Wolverhampton W.	App	11.81	81-84	115	2	3
Charlton Ath.	Tr	07.85	85-87	41	0	0
Bristol C.	Tr	10.87	87-89	83	0	3
Burnley	Tr	09.90	90-91	79	0	3
PENDERGAST, William J.						
Pen-y-groes, 13 April, 1915						(CF)
Manchester U.	Wrexham (Am)	12.35				
Wolverhampton W.	Tr	01.36				
Bristol Rov.	Tr	05.36	36-37	7	-	3
Chester C.	Tr	07.38	38	34	-	26
New Brighton	Tr	08.46	46-47	69	-	26
PENDLEBURY, Keith D.						
Stockport, 22 January, 1934						(HB)
Stockport Co.	Jnrs	03.51	53	2	-	0
PENDREY, Gary J. S.						
Birmingham, 9 February, 1949						(D)
Birmingham C.	App	10.66	66-78	287	19	4
West Bromwich A.	Tr	08.79	79	18	0	0
Torquay U.	Tr	08.81	81	12	0	0
Bristol Rov.	Tr	12.81	81	1	0	0
Walsall	Tr	08.82	82	8	0	1
PENFOLD, Mark						
Woolwich, 10 December, 1956						(RB)
Charlton Ath.	App	04.74	73-78	65	5	0
Leyton Orient	Tr	07.79	79	3	0	1
PENFORD, Dennis H.						
Reading, 31 August, 1931						(RB)
Reading		05.52	53-58	101	-	6
Torquay U.	Tr	06.59	59-61	77	-	0
PENGELLY, Richard N.						
Looe, 6 October, 1919						(HB)
Plymouth Arg.	Looe	05.47	47-49	9	-	0
PENHALIGON, Gary						
St Austell, 13 May, 1970						(G)
Plymouth Arg.	YT	07.88	88	1	0	0
PENK, Harold						
Wigan, 19 July, 1934						(W)
Portsmouth	Wigan Ath.	09.55	55-56	9	-	2
Plymouth Arg.	Tr	06.57	57-59	104	-	14
Southampton	Tr	07.60	60-63	52	0	6
PENMAN, Christopher						
Durham, 12 September, 1945						(G)
Darlington	Preston N.E. (App)	12.62	62-63	30	-	0
PENMAN, William S. T.						
Wemyss (Fife), 7 August, 1939						(M)
Newcastle U.	Glasgow Rangers	04.63	62-65	62	1	18
Swindon T.	Tr	09.66	66-69	87	11	18
Walsall	Tr	08.70	70-72	118	5	6

League Club	Source	Date Signed	Seasons Played	Apps	Subs	Gls
PENN, Donald J.						
Smethwick, 15 March, 1960						(F)
Walsall	Warley Bor.	01.78	77-82	132	9	54
PENN, Frank R.						
Edmonton, 15 April, 1927						(OL)
Crystal Palace (Am)	Fulham (Am)	09.49	49	1	-	0
PENNEY, David M.						
Wakefield, 17 August, 1964						(W)
Derby Co.	Pontefract Colly	09.85	86-88	6	13	0
Oxford U.	Tr	06.89	89-91	40	21	7
Swansea C.	L	03.91	90	12	0	3
PENNEY, Stephen A.						
Ballymena (NI), 16 January, 1964 NI-17						(W)
Brighton & H.A.	Ballymena U.	11.83	83-88	125	13	15
PENNICK, Raymond						
Ferryhill, 30 November, 1946						(IF)
York C. (Am)	Willington	03.69	68	0	1	0
PENNINGTON, James						
Golborne, 26 April, 1939						(OR)
Manchester C.	Jnrs	08.56	58	1	-	0
Crewe Alex.	Tr	03.61	60-62	34	-	2
Grimsby T.	Tr	04.63	62-64	89	-	8
Oldham Ath.	Tr	07.65	65	23	0	0
Rochdale	Tr	07.66	66	14	0	0
PENNINGTON, James						
Warrington, 13 November, 1928 Died 1976						(IL)
Huddersfield T.		08.49				
Southport	Tr	07.51	51-53	55	-	11
PENNINGTON, John						
Marsden, 12 September, 1928						(CF)
Halifax T.	Marsden	11.53	53-54	7	-	2
PENNOCK, Adrian B.						
Ipswich, 27 March, 1971						(CD)
Norwich C.	YT	07.89	89	1	0	0
PENNOCK, Anthony						
Swansea, 10 April, 1971						(G)
Stockport Co.	Clydach U.	08.90				
Wigan Ath.	L	12.90	90	2	0	0
Wigan Ath.	Tr	06.91				
PENNY, Christian V.						
Southend, 16 February, 1973						(FB)
Doncaster Rov. (N/C)	Brigg T.	02.92	91	1	0	0
PENNY, John						
Plymouth, 19 August, 1938						(OR)
Plymouth Arg.	Jnrs	11.55	57-59	7	-	0
PENNY, Shaun						
Bristol, 24 September, 1957 E Sch						(F)
Bristol C.	App	09.74				
Bristol Rov.	Tr	08.79	79-81	57	3	13
PENNYFATHER, Glenn J.						
Billericay, 11 February, 1963						(M)
Southend U.	App	02.81	80-87	231	7	36
Crystal Palace	Tr	11.87	87-88	31	3	1
Ipswich T.	Tr	10.89	89-91	9	2	1
PENRICE, Gary K.						
Bristol, 23 March, 1964						(F)
Bristol Rov.	Mangotsfield	11.84	84-89	186	2	53
Watford	Tr	11.89	89-90	41	2	17
Aston Villa	Tr	03.91	90-91	14	6	1
Queens Park R.	Tr	10.91	91	13	6	3
PENROSE, Colin R.						
Bradford, 1 November, 1949						(IF)
Bradford P. A. (Am)	Sedbergh Y.C.	09.68	68	6	0	1
PENROSE, Norman						
Consett, 10 March, 1922 E Sch						(WH)
Grimsby T.	Jnrs	05.39	46-47	9	-	0
PENTECOST, Michael E.						
Hounslow, 13 April, 1948						(FB)
Fulham	Sutton U.	08.66	66-72	81	6	0

League Club	Source	Date Signed	Seasons Played	Apps	Subs	Gls
PEPLOW, Ronald R.						
Willesden, 4 May, 1935						(WH)
Brentford	Southall	08.55	55-60	61	-	5
PEPLOW, Stephen T.						
Liverpool, 8 January, 1949						(W)
Liverpool	App	01.66	69	2	0	0
Swindon T.	Tr	05.70	70-72	37	3	11
Nottingham F.	Tr	07.73	73	3	0	0
Mansfield T.	L	12.73	73	4	0	3
Tranmere Rov.	Tr	01.74	73-80	232	16	44
PEPPER, Nigel C.						
Rotherham, 25 April, 1968						(M)
Rotherham U.	App	04.86	85-89	35	10	1
York C.	Tr	07.90	90-91	71	3	7
PEPPITT, Sydney						
Stoke, 8 September, 1919 E Sch						(OR)
Stoke C.	Jnrs	09.36	36-49	93	-	28
Port Vale	Tr	05.50	50	11	-	3
PERCIVAL, John						
Partington, 16 May, 1913						(WH)
Manchester C.	Durham C.	10.32	33-46	161	-	8
Bournemouth	Tr	05.47	47-48	52	-	1
PERCIVAL, Ronald F. J.						
Lambeth, 19 April, 1924						(WH)
Huddersfield T.	Tunbridge Wells	02.48	47-49	8	-	0
Chesterfield	Tr	05.50	50	6	-	0
PERDOMO, Jose T.						
Uruguay, 6 January, 1965 Uruguay Int						(M)
Coventry C. (N/C)	Genoa (It)	08.90	90	4	0	0
PERKINS, Eric						
West Bromwich, 19 August, 1934						(FB)
West Bromwich A.	Jnrs	06.52	55	2	-	0
Walsall	Tr	06.56	56-58	67	-	1
PERKINS, Glen S.						
Little Billing, 12 October, 1960						(M)
Northampton T.	App	10.78	78	0	1	0
PERKINS, Stephen A.						
Stepney, 3 October, 1954						(FB)
Chelsea	App	11.71				
Queens Park R.	Tr	06.77	77	2	0	0
Wimbledon	Tr	10.78	78-80	52	0	0
PERKS, Stephen J.						
Bridgnorth, 19 April, 1963						(G)
Shrewsbury T.	App	04.81	84-91	243	0	0
PERRETT, George R.						
Kenilworth, 2 May, 1915 Died 1952						(WH)
Ipswich T.	Fulham (Am)	06.36	38-49	131	-	4
PERRIN, Stephen C.						
Paddington, 13 February, 1952						(F)
Crystal Palace	Wycombe W.	03.76	76-77	45	3	13
Plymouth Arg.	Tr	03.78	77-79	34	1	6
Portsmouth	Tr	11.79	79-80	18	10	3
Northampton T. (N/C)	Hillingdon Bor.	12.81	81-82	22	0	5
PERRY, Andrew						
Dulwich, 28 December, 1962						(F)
Portsmouth	Dulwich Hamlet	11.86	87	1	3	0
Gillingham	Tr	08.88	88	8	5	0
PERRY, Arthur						
Doncaster, 15 October, 1932						(FB)
Hull C.		12.50				
Bradford P. A.	Tr	07.56	56-57	60	-	0
Rotherham U.	Tr	07.58	58	2	-	0
PERRY, David						
Sheffield, 17 May, 1967						(D)
Chesterfield	Jnrs	07.87	85-87	12	5	0
PERRY, Frederick N.						
Cheltenham, 30 October, 1933						(FB)
Liverpool	Worthing	07.54	55	1	-	0

PERRY, Jason
Newport, 2 April, 1970 W Yth/W'B'/Wu21-3 (CD)

League Club	Source	Date Signed	Seasons Played	Apps	Subs	Gls
Cardiff C.	Jnrs	08.87	86-91	118	1	0

PERRY, Leonard
Walsall, 14 May, 1930 (FB)

League Club	Source	Date Signed	Seasons Played	Apps	Subs	Gls
Walsall	Jnrs	10.50	53	3	-	0

PERRY, Michael A.
Wimbledon, 4 April, 1964 (F)

League Club	Source	Date Signed	Seasons Played	Apps	Subs	Gls
West Bromwich A.	App	02.82	82-83	14	6	5
Torquay U.	L	10.84	84	5	0	1
Northampton T.	L	12.84	84	4	0	0
Torquay U.	Tr	03.85	84-85	18	0	2

PERRY, Peter
Rotherham, 11 April, 1936 (FB)

League Club	Source	Date Signed	Seasons Played	Apps	Subs	Gls
Rotherham U.	Treeton R.R.	07.56	57-61	97	-	12
York C.	Tr	07.62	62	23	-	0

PERRY, William
South Africa, 10 September, 1930 E'B'-2/EF Lge/E-3 (OL)

League Club	Source	Date Signed	Seasons Played	Apps	Subs	Gls
Blackpool	Johannesburg (SA)	11.49	49-61	394	-	120
Southport	Tr	06.62	62	26	-	0

PERRYMAN, Gerald
West Haddon, 3 October, 1947 (FB)

League Club	Source	Date Signed	Seasons Played	Apps	Subs	Gls
Northampton T.	Jnrs	09.66	66	1	0	0
Colchester U.	Tr	07.68	68	1	1	0

PERRYMAN, Stephen J.
Ealing, 21 December, 1951 E Sch/E Yth/Eu23-17/E-1 (M)

League Club	Source	Date Signed	Seasons Played	Apps	Subs	Gls
Tottenham H.	App	01.69	69-85	653	2	31
Oxford U.	Tr	03.86	85-86	17	0	0
Brentford	Tr	11.86	86-89	44	9	0

PETCHEY, George W.
Stepney, 24 June, 1931 (WH)

League Club	Source	Date Signed	Seasons Played	Apps	Subs	Gls
West Ham U.	Jnrs	08.48	52	2	-	0
Queens Park R.	Tr	07.53	53-59	255	-	22
Crystal Palace	Tr	06.60	60-63	143	-	12

PETERS, Alan G.
Newport, 14 October, 1958 (M)

League Club	Source	Date Signed	Seasons Played	Apps	Subs	Gls
Hereford U.	Aston Villa (App)	06.76	76	1	0	0

PETERS, Gary D.
Carshalton, 3 August, 1954 (D)

League Club	Source	Date Signed	Seasons Played	Apps	Subs	Gls
Reading	Guildford C.	05.75	75-78	150	6	7
Fulham	Tr	08.79	79-81	57	7	2
Wimbledon	Tr	07.82	82-83	83	0	7
Aldershot	Tr	07.84	84	17	0	1
Reading	Tr	02.85	84-87	93	7	3
Fulham (N/C)	Tr	08.88	88-89	7	4	2

PETERS, Jeffrey
Wideopen (Nd), 7 March, 1961 (LB)

League Club	Source	Date Signed	Seasons Played	Apps	Subs	Gls
Middlesbrough	App	03.79	79	6	0	0

PETERS, Martin S.
Plaistow, 8 November, 1943 E Sch/E Yth/Eu23-5/EF Lge/E-67 (M)

League Club	Source	Date Signed	Seasons Played	Apps	Subs	Gls
West Ham U.	App	11.60	61-69	302	0	81
Tottenham H.	Tr	03.70	69-74	189	0	46
Norwich C.	Tr	03.75	74-79	206	1	44
Sheffield U.	Tr	08.80	80	23	1	4

PETERS, Robert A. G.
Kensington, 18 May, 1971 (M)

League Club	Source	Date Signed	Seasons Played	Apps	Subs	Gls
Brentford	YT	07.89	89-91	8	9	1

PETERS, Roger D. (Lou)
Cheltenham, 5 March, 1944 E Yth (W)

League Club	Source	Date Signed	Seasons Played	Apps	Subs	Gls
Bristol C.	App	03.61	60-67	158	0	25
Bournemouth	Tr	06.68	68-69	35	2	3

PETERS, Thomas J.
Droylsden, 22 October, 1920 (IF)

League Club	Source	Date Signed	Seasons Played	Apps	Subs	Gls
Doncaster Rov.		05.44				
Bury	Tr	12.46	47	10	-	1
Leeds U.	Tr	08.48				
Mansfield T.	Tr	03.49	48	6	-	2
Accrington St.	Tr	10.49	49	4	-	2

PETERSON, Brian
South Africa, 20 October, 1936 (IF)

League Club	Source	Date Signed	Seasons Played	Apps	Subs	Gls
Blackpool	Berea Park (SA)	10.56	56-61	103	-	16

PETERSON, Frank
London, 3 April, 1951 (F)

League Club	Source	Date Signed	Seasons Played	Apps	Subs	Gls
Millwall	App	02.69	68-69	3	1	0

PETERSON, Paul W.
Luton, 22 December, 1949 (FB)

League Club	Source	Date Signed	Seasons Played	Apps	Subs	Gls
Leeds U.	App	12.66	69	3	1	0
Swindon T.	Tr	06.71	71	1	0	0

PETHARD, Frederick J.
Glasgow, 7 October, 1950 S Sch (LB)

League Club	Source	Date Signed	Seasons Played	Apps	Subs	Gls
Cardiff C.	Glasgow Celtic	08.69	71-78	161	10	0
Torquay U.	Tr	08.79	79-81	104	1	0

PETHERBRIDGE, George E.
Plymouth, 19 May, 1927 (W)

League Club	Source	Date Signed	Seasons Played	Apps	Subs	Gls
Bristol Rov.	Jnrs	01.45	46-61	452	-	85

PETROVIC, Vladimir
Yugoslavia, 1 July, 1955 (M)

League Club	Source	Date Signed	Seasons Played	Apps	Subs	Gls
Arsenal	Red Star Belgrade (Yug)	12.82	82	10	3	2

PETTIT, Raymond J.
Hull, 11 December, 1946 (CD)

League Club	Source	Date Signed	Seasons Played	Apps	Subs	Gls
Hull C.	App	12.64	66-71	78	1	0
Barnsley	Tr	09.72	72-73	49	2	1

PETTS, John W. F. J.
Edmonton, 2 October, 1938 E Yth (WH)

League Club	Source	Date Signed	Seasons Played	Apps	Subs	Gls
Arsenal	Jnrs	05.56	57-61	32	-	0
Reading	Tr	10.62	62-64	34	-	0
Bristol Rov.	Tr	07.65	65-69	88	4	3

PETTS, Paul A.
Hackney, 27 September, 1961 E Yth (W)

League Club	Source	Date Signed	Seasons Played	Apps	Subs	Gls
Bristol Rov.	App	06.79	78-79	12	1	0
Shrewsbury T.	Tr	08.80	80-84	138	11	16

PEVERELL, John R.
Richmond (N Yorks), 17 September, 1941 (RB)

League Club	Source	Date Signed	Seasons Played	Apps	Subs	Gls
Darlington	Ferryhill Ath.	09.59	61-71	418	1	13

PEYTON, Gerald J.
Birmingham, 20 May, 1956 IR-33 (G)

League Club	Source	Date Signed	Seasons Played	Apps	Subs	Gls
Burnley	Atherstone T.	05.75	75-76	30	0	0
Fulham	Tr	12.76	76-85	345	0	0
Southend U.	L	09.83	83	10	0	0
Bournemouth	Tr	07.86	86-90	202	0	0
Everton	Tr	07.91				
Bolton W.	L	02.92	91	1	0	0

PEYTON, Noel
Dublin, 4 December, 1935 IR'B'-1/IR-6 (IF)

League Club	Source	Date Signed	Seasons Played	Apps	Subs	Gls
Leeds U.	Shamrock Rov.	01.58	57-62	104	-	17
York C.	Tr	07.63	63-64	37	-	4

PEYTON, Robert A.
Birmingham, 1 May, 1954 (M)

League Club	Source	Date Signed	Seasons Played	Apps	Subs	Gls
Port Vale	Chelmsley T.	01.72	71	1	0	0

PHELAN, Albert
Sheffield, 27 April, 1945 (CD)

League Club	Source	Date Signed	Seasons Played	Apps	Subs	Gls
Chesterfield	Jnrs	07.64	64-74	385	5	14
Halifax T.	Tr	10.74	74-76	118	0	4

PHELAN, Michael C.
Nelson, 24 September, 1962 E Yth/E-1 (M)

League Club	Source	Date Signed	Seasons Played	Apps	Subs	Gls
Burnley	App	07.80	80-84	166	2	9
Norwich C.	Tr	07.85	85-88	155	1	9
Manchester U.	Tr	06.89	89-91	82	7	2

PHELAN, Terence M.
Manchester, 16 March, 1967 IR Yth/IRu21-1/IR'B'/IR-8 (LB)

League Club	Source	Date Signed	Seasons Played	Apps	Subs	Gls
Leeds U.	YT	08.84	85	12	2	0
Swansea C.	Tr	07.86	86	45	0	0
Wimbledon	Tr	07.87	87-91	155	4	1

PHILIP, Ian F.
Dundee, 14 February, 1951 S Sch/Su23-1/SF Lge (M)

League Club	Source	Date Signed	Seasons Played	Apps	Subs	Gls
Crystal Palace	Dundee	09.72	72-73	35	0	1

PHILLIBEN, John
Stirling, 14 March, 1964 S Yth (D)

League Club	Source	Date Signed	Seasons Played	Apps	Subs	Gls
Doncaster Rov.	Stirling A.	03.84	83-86	66	5	1
Cambridge U.	L	12.85	85	6	0	0

PHILLIPS, Benjamin
Hazel Grove, 9 June, 1960 (FB)

League Club	Source	Date Signed	Seasons Played	Apps	Subs	Gls
Bury	Macclesfield T.	09.80	80	14	0	0

PHILLIPS, Brendan U.
West Indies, 16 July, 1954 E Semi-Pro (M)

League Club	Source	Date Signed	Seasons Played	Apps	Subs	Gls
Leicester C.	App	07.72				
Peterborough U.	Tr	08.73	73	1	0	0
Mansfield T.	Boston U.	08.80	80	17	0	0

PHILLIPS, Brian J.
Manchester, 9 November, 1931 (CH)

League Club	Source	Date Signed	Seasons Played	Apps	Subs	Gls
Middlesbrough	Altrincham	06.54	54-59	121	-	2
Mansfield T.	Tr	06.60	60-62	103	-	3

PHILLIPS, Cornelius
Liverpool, 10 May, 1938 (F)

League Club	Source	Date Signed	Seasons Played	Apps	Subs	Gls
Liverpool	Jnrs	06.55				
Southport	Tr	07.57	57	19	-	6

PHILLIPS, David O.
West Germany, 29 July, 1963 W Yth/Wu21-3/W-39 (M)

League Club	Source	Date Signed	Seasons Played	Apps	Subs	Gls
Plymouth Arg.	App	08.81	81-83	65	8	15
Manchester C.	Tr	08.84	84-85	81	0	13
Coventry C.	Tr	06.86	86-88	93	7	8
Norwich C.	Tr	06.89	89-91	110	0	9

PHILLIPS, Donald
Llanelli, 3 March, 1933 (F)

League Club	Source	Date Signed	Seasons Played	Apps	Subs	Gls
Swansea C.	Llanelli	12.56	56-57	3	-	0

PHILLIPS, Edward J. (Ted)
Leiston, 21 August, 1933 (IF)

League Club	Source	Date Signed	Seasons Played	Apps	Subs	Gls
Ipswich T.	Leiston	12.53	53-63	269	-	161
Leyton Orient	Tr	03.64	63-64	36	-	17
Luton T.	Tr	02.65	64	12	-	8
Colchester U.	Tr	09.65	65	32	0	13

PHILLIPS, Ernest
North Shields, 29 November, 1923 (FB)

League Club	Source	Date Signed	Seasons Played	Apps	Subs	Gls
Manchester C.	Ashington	01.47	48-51	80	-	0
Hull C.	Tr	11.51	51-53	42	-	0
York C.	Tr	06.54	54-57	164	-	2

PHILLIPS, Gary C.
St Albans, 20 September, 1961 E Semi-Pro (G)

League Club	Source	Date Signed	Seasons Played	Apps	Subs	Gls
West Bromwich A.	Brighton & H. A. (App)	06.79				
Brentford	Barnet	12.84	84-87	143	0	0
Reading	Tr	08.88	88	24	0	0
Hereford U.	L	09.89	89	6	0	0
Barnet	Tr	12.89	91	6	0	0

PHILLIPS, Gordon D.
Hayes, 17 January, 1946 (G)

League Club	Source	Date Signed	Seasons Played	Apps	Subs	Gls
Brentford	Hayes	11.63	64-72	206	0	0

PHILLIPS, Ian A.
Edinburgh, 23 April, 1959 (LB)

League Club	Source	Date Signed	Seasons Played	Apps	Subs	Gls
Mansfield T.	Ipswich T. (App)	08.77	77-78	18	5	0
Peterborough U.	Tr	08.79	79-81	97	0	3
Northampton T.	Tr	08.82	82	42	0	1
Colchester U.	Tr	09.83	83-86	150	0	10
Aldershot	Tr	08.87	87-89	106	0	2

PHILLIPS, James N.
Bolton, 8 February, 1966 (LB)

League Club	Source	Date Signed	Seasons Played	Apps	Subs	Gls
Bolton W.	App	08.83	83-86	103	5	2
Oxford U.	Glasgow Rangers	08.88	88-89	79	0	6
Middlesbrough	Tr	03.90	89-91	99	0	4

PHILLIPS, John E.
Portsmouth, 4 March, 1937 (WH)

League Club	Source	Date Signed	Seasons Played	Apps	Subs	Gls
Portsmouth	Jnrs	05.55	55-59	77	-	0

PHILLIPS, John T. S.
Shrewsbury, 7 July, 1951 Wu23-4/W-4 (G)

League Club	Source	Date Signed	Seasons Played	Apps	Subs	Gls
Shrewsbury T.	App	11.68	68-69	51	0	0
Aston Villa	Tr	10.69	69	15	0	0
Chelsea	Tr	08.70	70-78	125	0	0
Crewe Alex.	L	08.79	79	6	0	0
Brighton & H. A.	Tr	03.80	80	1	0	0
Charlton Ath.	Tr	07.81	81	2	0	0
Crystal Palace	Tr	01.83				

PHILLIPS, Joseph R. W.
Cardiff, 8 July, 1923 (FB)

League Club	Source	Date Signed	Seasons Played	Apps	Subs	Gls
Cardiff C.	Cardiff Corries	04.42	46	2	-	0

PHILLIPS, Justin L.
Derby, 17 December, 1971 E Yth (CD)

League Club	Source	Date Signed	Seasons Played	Apps	Subs	Gls
Derby Co.	YT	07.90	90	3	0	1

PHILLIPS, Leighton
Briton Ferry, 25 September, 1949 W Sch/Wu21-1/Wu23-4/W-58 (CD)

League Club	Source	Date Signed	Seasons Played	Apps	Subs	Gls
Cardiff C.	App	04.67	67-74	169	11	11
Aston Villa	Tr	09.74	74-78	134	6	4
Swansea C.	Tr	11.78	78-80	97	0	0
Charlton Ath.	Tr	08.81	81-82	45	0	1
Exeter C. (N/C)	Tr	03.83	82	10	0	0

PHILLIPS, Leonard H.
Hackney, 11 September, 1922 EF Lge/E-3 (IF)

League Club	Source	Date Signed	Seasons Played	Apps	Subs	Gls
Portsmouth	Hillside Y.C.	01.46	46-54	244	-	47

PHILLIPS, Leslie M.
Lambeth, 7 January, 1963 (M)

League Club	Source	Date Signed	Seasons Played	Apps	Subs	Gls
Birmingham C.	App	08.80	81-83	36	8	3
Oxford U.	Tr	03.84	83-91	156	12	11

PHILLIPS, Lionel R.
Hereford, 13 December, 1929 (F)

League Club	Source	Date Signed	Seasons Played	Apps	Subs	Gls
Portsmouth	Yeovil T.	02.53	53	4	-	1

PHILLIPS, Michael S.
Cumnock, 18 January, 1933 (CF)

League Club	Source	Date Signed	Seasons Played	Apps	Subs	Gls
Grimsby T.	Cumnock Jnrs.	01.55	54	6	-	1

PHILLIPS, Nicholas
West Ham, 19 November, 1960 (M)

League Club	Source	Date Signed	Seasons Played	Apps	Subs	Gls
Coventry C.	App	08.78	79	4	1	0

PHILLIPS, Peter S.
Wellingborough, 29 June, 1946 E Amat (F)

League Club	Source	Date Signed	Seasons Played	Apps	Subs	Gls
Luton T.	Bishops Stortford	06.69	69	2	3	0
Torquay U.	L	01.71	70	2	0	1
Cambridge U.	Tr	03.71	70-72	40	13	13

PHILLIPS, Ralph
Houghton-le-Spring, 9 August, 1933 (FB)

League Club	Source	Date Signed	Seasons Played	Apps	Subs	Gls
Middlesbrough		05.54				
Northampton T.	Tr	08.58	58-60	83	-	1
Darlington	Tr	06.61	61-62	29	-	2

PHILLIPS, Reginald R.
Llanelli, 9 March, 1921 (CF)

League Club	Source	Date Signed	Seasons Played	Apps	Subs	Gls
Crewe Alex.	Shrewsbury T.	05.49	49-51	64	-	35

PHILLIPS, Ronald D.
Worsley, 30 March, 1947 (W)

League Club	Source	Date Signed	Seasons Played	Apps	Subs	Gls
Bolton W.	Jnrs	10.65	66-74	135	10	17
Chesterfield	L	01.75	74	5	0	0
Bury	Tr	06.75	75-76	68	4	5
Chester C.	Tr	09.77	77-80	128	2	21

PHILLIPS, Russell G. T.
Exeter, 22 June, 1916

League Club	Source	Date Signed	Seasons Played	Apps	Subs	Gls
Millwall		01.45				
Torquay U.	Tr	01.46	46	30	-	3

PHILLIPS, Stephen E.
Edmonton, 4 August, 1954 E Yth (F)

League Club	Source	Date Signed	Seasons Played	Apps	Subs	Gls
Birmingham C.	App	08.71	71-75	15	5	1
Torquay U.	L	12.74	74	6	0	0
Northampton T.	Tr	10.75	75-76	50	1	8
Brentford	Tr	02.77	76-79	156	1	65
Northampton T.	Tr	08.80	80-81	75	0	29
Southend U.	Tr	03.82	81-85	157	1	66
Torquay U.	Tr	01.86	85-86	32	0	11
Peterborough U.	Tr	11.86	86-87	46	2	16
Exeter C.	L	09.87	87	5	1	1
Chesterfield	L	01.88	87	9	0	2

PHILLIPS, Stewart G.
Halifax, 30 December, 1961 (F)

League Club	Source	Date Signed	Seasons Played	Apps	Subs	Gls
Hereford U.	App	11.79	77-87	285	8	83
West Bromwich A.	Tr	03.88	87-88	15	0	4
Swansea C.	Tr	01.89	88-89	10	10	1
Hereford U.	Tr	08.90	90	31	6	10
Wrexham (N/C)	Tr	08.91	91	1	1	1

League Club	Source	Date Signed	Seasons Played	Apps	Subs	Gls

PHILLIPS, Trevor
Rotherham, 18 September, 1952 E Yth (F)

Rotherham U.	App	03.70	69-78	289	33	81
Hull C.	Tr	06.79	79	22	0	3
Chester C.	Tr	03.80	79-81	57	7	11
Stockport Co.	Tr	03.82	81-82	49	2	13
Chester C. (N/C)	Tr	08.83	83	9	1	2

PHILLIPS, Wayne
Bangor, 15 December, 1970 (M)

Wrexham	YT	08.89	89-91	54	9	3

PHILLIPSON, William E.
Barrow, 4 April, 1917 Died 1974 (G)

Barrow	Holker C.O.B.	10.38	46-47	14	-	0

PHILLIPSON-MASTERS, Forbes E.
Bournemouth, 14 November, 1955 (CD)

Southampton	App	11.73	76-77	9	0	0
Exeter C.	L	09.76	76	6	0	0
Bournemouth	L	09.77	77	7	0	2
Luton Town	L	03.79	78	10	0	0
Plymouth Arg.	Tr	08.79	79-82	119	0	0
Bristol C.	Tr	11.82	82-84	94	0	4
Exeter C.	L	03.85	84	5	2	1

PHILLISKIRK, Anthony
Sunderland, 10 February, 1965 E Sch (F)

Sheffield U.	Jnrs	08.83	83-87	62	18	20
Rotherham U.	L	10.86	86	6	0	1
Oldham Ath.	Tr	07.88	88	3	7	1
Preston N. E.	Tr	02.89	88	13	1	6
Bolton W.	Tr	06.89	89-91	130	1	50

PHILP, David
Fowey, 8 July, 1960 (G)

Plymouth Arg.	Newquay	07.84	84	7	0	0

PHILPOTT, Alan
Stoke, 8 November, 1942 (M)

Stoke C.	Jnrs	11.59	60-67	41	4	1
Oldham Ath.	Tr	11.67	67-68	28	3	1

PHILPOTT, Lee
Barnet, 21 February, 1970 (W)

Peterborough U.	YT	07.88	87-88	1	3	0
Cambridge U.	Tr	05.89	89-91	102	16	15

PHILPOTTS, David R.
Bromborough, 31 March, 1954 (CD)

Coventry C.	App	10.71	73	3	0	0
Southport	L	01.74	73	8	0	0
Tranmere Rov.	Tr	09.74	74-77	174	1	5
Tranmere Rov.	Carolina (USA)	10.83	83-84	36	0	6

PHIPPS, Harold J.
Dartford, 15 January, 1916 (CH)

Charlton Ath.	Middlesex Regt	10.43	46-50	185	-	2
Watford	Tr	06.52	52-53	47	-	0

PHOENIX, W. Brian
Tyldesley, 10 December, 1937 (F)

Southport	Boothstown	12.57	57-58	15	-	3

PHOENIX, Eric W.
Manchester, 20 January, 1932 (IF)

Gillingham	Hastings U.	07.54	54-55	17	-	2
Exeter C.	Tr	07.56	56	5	-	0

PHOENIX, Peter P.
Manchester, 31 December, 1936 (OL)

Oldham Ath.	Lastock Gralam	02.58	57-62	161	-	27
Rochdale	Tr	10.62	62-63	36	-	4
Exeter C.	Tr	10.63	63	15	-	1
Southport	Tr	01.64	63	10	-	0
Stockport Co.	Tr	07.64	64	20	-	1

PHOENIX, Ronald J.
Stretford, 30 June, 1929 (WH)

Manchester C.	Humphrey Park	03.50	51-58	53	-	2
Rochdale	Tr	02.60	60-61	64	-	0

PHYTHIAN, Ernest R.
Farnworth, 16 July, 1942 E Yth (CF)

Bolton W.	Jnrs	07.59	59-61	10	-	3
Wrexham	Tr	03.62	61-64	134	-	44
Hartlepool U.	Tr	06.65	65-67	124	0	50

League Club	Source	Date Signed	Seasons Played	Apps	Subs	Gls

PICKARD, Leonard J.
Barnstaple, 29 November, 1924 (CF)

Bristol Rov.	Barnstaple	01.51	51	4	-	1
Bristol C.	Tr	05.53				
Bradford P. A.	Tr	10.53	53-55	76	-	31

Len Pickard (Bristol Rovers, Bristol City & Bradford Park Avenue)

PICKARD, Owen A.
Barnstaple, 18 November, 1969 (F)

Plymouth Arg.	YT	07.88	88-91	6	10	1

PICKERING, Alistair G.
Manchester, 22 June, 1967 (FB)

Rotherham U.	Buxton	02.90	89-91	37	1	0

PICKERING, Frederick
Blackburn, 19 January, 1941 Eu23-3/EF Lge/E-3 (CF)

Blackburn Rov.	Jnrs	01.58	59-63	123	-	59
Everton	Tr	03.64	63-66	97	0	56
Birmingham C.	Tr	08.67	67-68	74	0	27
Blackpool	Tr	06.69	69-70	48	1	24
Blackburn Rov.	Tr	03.71	70	11	0	2

PICKERING, John
Chapeltown, 18 December, 1908 EF Lge/E-1 (IF)

Sheffield U.	Jnrs	12.25	26-47	343	-	104

PICKERING, John
Stockton, 7 November, 1944 (CD)

Newcastle U.	Stockton	07.63				
Halifax T.	Tr	09.65	65-73	364	3	5
Barnsley	Tr	07.74	74	42	1	2

PICKERING, Michael J.
Heckmondwike, 29 September, 1956 (CD)

Barnsley	Jnrs	10.74	74-76	100	0	1
Southampton	Tr	06.77	77-78	44	0	0
Sheffield Wed.	Tr	10.78	78-82	106	4	1
Norwich C.	L	09.83	83	0	1	0
Bradford C.	L	11.83	83	4	0	0
Barnsley	L	12.83	83	3	0	0
Rotherham U.	Tr	01.84	83-85	102	0	1
York C.	Tr	07.86	86	31	1	1
Stockport Co.	Tr	07.87	87-88	15	1	0

PICKERING, Nicholas

League Club	Source	Date Signed	Seasons Played	Career Record Apps	Subs	Gls

PICKERING, Nicholas
Newcastle, 4 August, 1963 E Yth/Eu21-15/E-1 (LM)

League Club	Source	Date Signed	Seasons Played	Apps	Subs	Gls
Sunderland	App	08.81	81-85	177	2	18
Coventry C.	Tr	01.86	85-87	76	2	9
Derby Co.	Tr	08.88	88-91	35	10	3
Darlington	Tr	10.91	91	29	0	5

Nick Pickering (Sunderland, Coventry City, Derby County, Darlington & England)

PICKERING, Peter B.
York, 24 March, 1926 (G)

League Club	Source	Date Signed	Seasons Played	Apps	Subs	Gls
York C.	Earswick	04.44	46-47	49	-	0
Chelsea	Tr	05.48	48-50	27	-	0
Northampton T.	Kettering T.	07.55	55-57	86	-	0

PICKERING, William H.
Sheffield, 10 February, 1919 Died 1983 E Amat (FB)

League Club	Source	Date Signed	Seasons Played	Apps	Subs	Gls
Sheffield Wed.	Jnrs	10.37	38	3	-	0
Oldham Ath.	Tr	07.48	48-49	78	-	0

PICKETT, Reginald A.
India, 6 January, 1927 (WH)

League Club	Source	Date Signed	Seasons Played	Apps	Subs	Gls
Portsmouth	Weymouth	03.49	49-56	123	-	2
Ipswich T.	Tr	07.57	57-62	140	-	3

PICKRELL, Anthony D.
Neath, 3 November, 1942 (OL)

League Club	Source	Date Signed	Seasons Played	Apps	Subs	Gls
Cardiff C.	Jnrs	09.60	60-61	18	-	4

PICKUP, John A.
Wakefield, 3 December, 1931 (IL)

League Club	Source	Date Signed	Seasons Played	Apps	Subs	Gls
Bradford P. A.	Frickley Colly	09.55	55	2	-	0

PICKUP, Reginald J.
Stoke, 6 September, 1929 (WH)

League Club	Source	Date Signed	Seasons Played	Apps	Subs	Gls
Stoke C.	Jnrs	08.49	49	1	-	0

PICKWICK, Donald H. J.
Rhondda, 7 February, 1925 (WH)

League Club	Source	Date Signed	Seasons Played	Apps	Subs	Gls
Norwich C.	Cardiff C. (Am)	08.47	47-55	224	-	9

PIDCOCK, Frederick C.
Canada, 29 June, 1933 (G)

League Club	Source	Date Signed	Seasons Played	Apps	Subs	Gls
Walsall (Am)	Moor Green	09.53	53	1	-	0

PIEKALNIETIS, John
Penrith, 23 September, 1951 E Yth (CD)

League Club	Source	Date Signed	Seasons Played	Apps	Subs	Gls
Nottingham F.	Jnrs	03.69				
Southend U.	Tr	04.71	70	1	0	0

PIERCE, J. Barry
Liverpool, 13 August, 1934 (IF)

League Club	Source	Date Signed	Seasons Played	Apps	Subs	Gls
Crystal Palace	Truro C.	08.55	55-58	85	-	23
Millwall	Tr	05.59	59-60	46	-	17
York C.	Tr	07.61	61	12	-	5
Exeter C.	Tr	07.62	62	28	-	4

PIERCE, Gary
Bury, 2 March, 1951 (G)

League Club	Source	Date Signed	Seasons Played	Apps	Subs	Gls
Huddersfield T.	Mossley	02.71	71-72	23	0	0
Wolverhampton W.	Tr	08.73	73-78	98	0	0
Barnsley	Tr	07.79	79-82	81	0	0
Blackpool	Tr	08.83	83	27	0	0

PIGGOTT, Gary D.
Warley, 1 April, 1969 (F)

League Club	Source	Date Signed	Seasons Played	Apps	Subs	Gls
West Bromwich A.	Dudley T.	03.91	91	3	2	0

PIKE, Christopher
Cardiff, 19 October, 1961 (F)

League Club	Source	Date Signed	Seasons Played	Apps	Subs	Gls
Fulham	Barry T.	03.85	85-87	32	10	4
Cardiff C.	L	12.86	86	6	0	2
Cardiff C.	Tr	07.89	89-91	114	6	53

PIKE, Geoffrey A.
Clapton, 28 September, 1956 (M)

League Club	Source	Date Signed	Seasons Played	Apps	Subs	Gls
West Ham U.	App	09.74	75-86	275	16	32
Notts Co.	Tr	07.87	87-88	80	2	17
Leyton Orient	Tr	09.89	89-90	36	8	1

PIKE, Martin R.
South Shields, 21 October, 1964 (LB)

League Club	Source	Date Signed	Seasons Played	Apps	Subs	Gls
West Bromwich A.	App	10.82				
Peterborough U.	Tr	08.83	83-85	119	7	8
Sheffield U.	Tr	08.86	86-89	127	2	5
Tranmere Rov.	L	11.89	89	2	0	0
Bolton W.	L	12.89	89	5	0	1
Fulham	Tr	02.90	89-91	110	1	7

PILGRIM, Alan J.
Billingborough, 20 July, 1947 (D)

League Club	Source	Date Signed	Seasons Played	Apps	Subs	Gls
Lincoln C.	Billingborough	05.65	65-71	20	3	1

PILKINGTON, Brian
Leyland, 12 February, 1933 E'B'-2/EF Lge/E-1 (OL)

League Club	Source	Date Signed	Seasons Played	Apps	Subs	Gls
Burnley	Leyland Motors	04.51	52-60	300	-	67
Bolton W.	Tr	03.61	60-63	82	-	11
Bury	Tr	02.64	63-64	19	-	0
Barrow	Tr	02.65	64-66	86	1	9

PILKINGTON, George
Hemsworth, 3 June, 1926 (RB)

League Club	Source	Date Signed	Seasons Played	Apps	Subs	Gls
Rotherham U.	Great Houghton	11.48	49	1	-	0
Chester C.	Tr	07.52	52	16	-	0
Stockport Co.	Tr	05.53	53-55	77	-	4

PILKINGTON, Leslie
Darwen, 23 June, 1925 (IF)

League Club	Source	Date Signed	Seasons Played	Apps	Subs	Gls
Arsenal	Darwen Corries	03.48				
Watford	Tr	03.50	49-50	5	-	0

PILLING, Andrew J.
Wigan, 30 June, 1969 (M)

League Club	Source	Date Signed	Seasons Played	Apps	Subs	Gls
Preston N.E. (YT)	YT	07.85	85	1	0	0
Wigan Ath.	Tr	07.87	87-91	104	21	16

PILLING, John J.
St Helens, 4 June, 1913 (LH)

League Club	Source	Date Signed	Seasons Played	Apps	Subs	Gls
Liverpool	South Liverpool	09.42				
Southport	Tr	02.46	46	9	-	0

PILLING, Stuart
Sheffield, 26 March, 1951 (W)

League Club	Source	Date Signed	Seasons Played	Apps	Subs	Gls
Preston N. E.	Jnrs	07.69				
Hull C.	Tr	07.70				
Scunthorpe U.	Tr	05.73	73-81	246	16	26

PILLING, Vincent J.
Bolton, 8 January, 1932 (W)

League Club	Source	Date Signed	Seasons Played	Apps	Subs	Gls
Bolton W.	Lomax's	10.52	52-54	7	-	0
Bradford P. A.	Tr	08.55	55	9	-	1

PIMBLETT, Frank R.
Liverpool, 12 March, 1957 E Sch (M)

League Club	Source	Date Signed	Seasons Played	Apps	Subs	Gls
Aston Villa	App	10.74	74-75	9	0	0
Newport Co.	L	03.76	75	7	0	0
Stockport Co.	Tr	07.76	76	0	1	0
Hartlepool U.	Brisbane C. (Aus.)	03.80	79	3	0	0

PIMBLEY, Douglas W.
Birmingham, 19 June, 1917 (OL)

League Club	Source	Date Signed	Seasons Played	Apps	Subs	Gls
Birmingham C.	Stourbridge	07.46	46	2	-	0
Notts Co.	Tr	03.48	47-49	23	-	2

PIMLOTT, John G.
Radcliffe, 21 January, 1939 (IF)

League Club	Source	Date Signed	Seasons Played	Apps	Subs	Gls
Bury		12.57				
Chester C.	Tr	08.59	59-60	41	-	11

PINCHBECK, Clifford B.
Cleethorpes, 20 January, 1925 (CF)

League Club	Source	Date Signed	Seasons Played	Apps	Subs	Gls
Everton	Scunthorpe U.	12.47	47	3	-	0
Brighton & H. A.	Tr	08.49	49	14	-	5
Port Vale	Tr	11.49	49-51	69	-	34
Northampton T.	Tr	12.51	51	3	-	3

PINCOTT, Frederick
Bristol, 19 March, 1913 (CH)

League Club	Source	Date Signed	Seasons Played	Apps	Subs	Gls
Wolverhampton W.		11.31	32	2	-	0
Bournemouth	Tr	05.34	34-38	196	-	0
Newport Co.	Gravesend & Nft.	07.47	47	14	-	0

PINDER, John J. (Jack)
York, 1 December, 1912 E Sch (RB)

League Club	Source	Date Signed	Seasons Played	Apps	Subs	Gls
York C.	Jnrs	02.30	32-47	199	-	4

PINGEL, Frank
Denmark, 9 May, 1964 Danish Int (F)

League Club	Source	Date Signed	Seasons Played	Apps	Subs	Gls
Newcastle U.	Aarhus G.F. (Den)	01.89	88	13	1	1

PINKNEY, Alan J.
Battersea, 1 January, 1947 (M)

League Club	Source	Date Signed	Seasons Played	Apps	Subs	Gls
Exeter C. (Am)	St Lukes College	02.68	67-68	7	0	1
Crystal Palace	Tr	07.69	69-73	19	5	0
Fulham	L	01.73	72	11	1	0

PINNER, Michael J.
Boston, 16 February, 1934 E Amat (G)

League Club	Source	Date Signed	Seasons Played	Apps	Subs	Gls
Aston Villa (Am)	Pegasus	05.54	54-56	4	-	0
Sheffield W. (Am)	Corinthian Casuals	12.57	57-58	7	-	0
Queens Park R. (Am)	Tr	07.59	59	19	-	0
Manchester U. (Am)	Tr	02.61	60	4	-	0
Chelsea (Am)	Tr	10.61	61	1	-	0
Swansea C. (Am)	Tr	05.62	61	1	-	0
Leyton Orient	Hendon	10.62	62-64	77	-	0

PIPER, Gilbert H.
Northfleet, 21 June, 1921 (HB)

League Club	Source	Date Signed	Seasons Played	Apps	Subs	Gls
Tottenham H.		01.40				
Gillingham	Tr	08.46	50	4	-	0

PIPER, Norman J.
North Tawton, 8 January, 1948 E Yth/Eu23-4 (M)

League Club	Source	Date Signed	Seasons Played	Apps	Subs	Gls
Plymouth Arg.	App	02.65	64-69	215	0	35
Portsmouth	Tr	05.70	70-77	310	4	51

PIPER, Ronald D.
Lowestoft, 16 March, 1943 (IF)

League Club	Source	Date Signed	Seasons Played	Apps	Subs	Gls
Tottenham H.	Arsenal (Am)	10.60	62	1	-	0

PIPER, Stephen P. H.
Brighton, 2 November, 1953 (CD)

League Club	Source	Date Signed	Seasons Played	Apps	Subs	Gls
Brighton & H. A.	Jnrs	09.72	72-77	160	2	9
Portsmouth	Tr	02.78	77-78	27	2	2

PIRIE, Frederick W.
Coupar Angus, 19 January, 1934 (FB)

League Club	Source	Date Signed	Seasons Played	Apps	Subs	Gls
Accrington St.	Coupar Angus	01.54	54-59	17	-	0

PISANTI, David
Israel, 27 May, 1962 (M)

League Club	Source	Date Signed	Seasons Played	Apps	Subs	Gls
Queens Park R.	F.C. Köln (Ger)	09.87	87-88	16	6	0

PITCHER, Darren E. J.
Stepney, 12 October, 1969 E Sch (RB)

League Club	Source	Date Signed	Seasons Played	Apps	Subs	Gls
Charlton Ath.	YT	01.88	90-91	88	2	5

PITT, John H. (Jack)
Willenhall, 20 May, 1920 (RH)

League Club	Source	Date Signed	Seasons Played	Apps	Subs	Gls
Bristol Rov.	Bath C.	05.46	46-57	467	-	16

PITT, Richard E.
Ryhope, 22 October, 1951 E Sch (CD)

League Club	Source	Date Signed	Seasons Played	Apps	Subs	Gls
Sunderland	Jnrs	11.68	68-73	126	0	7

PITT, Stephen W.
Willesden, 1 August, 1948 (W)

League Club	Source	Date Signed	Seasons Played	Apps	Subs	Gls
Tottenham H.	App	08.65	65	1	0	0
Colchester U.	Tr	06.69	69	4	2	0

PITTMAN, Stephen
North Carolina (USA), 18 July, 1967 (LB)

League Club	Source	Date Signed	Seasons Played	Apps	Subs	Gls
Shrewsbury T.	East Fife	03.89	88-89	31	1	2

PLACE, Brendan A.
Dublin, 13 December, 1965 (CD)

League Club	Source	Date Signed	Seasons Played	Apps	Subs	Gls
Gillingham	Athlone T.	10.89	89	3	1	0

PLACE, Charles A.
Ilkeston, 26 November, 1937 (OL)

League Club	Source	Date Signed	Seasons Played	Apps	Subs	Gls
Derby Co.	Jnrs	11.54	55	2	-	0

PLACE, Mark G.
Mansfield, 16 November, 1969 (CD)

League Club	Source	Date Signed	Seasons Played	Apps	Subs	Gls
Mansfield T.	YT	07.88	88-89	12	3	0
Doncaster Rov.	Tr	08.90	90	1	0	0

PLANT, Kenneth G.
Coventry, 15 August, 1925 (CF)

League Club	Source	Date Signed	Seasons Played	Apps	Subs	Gls
Bury	Nuneaton Bor.	02.50	49-53	119	-	55
Colchester U.	Tr	01.54	53-58	190	-	82

PLASKETT, Stephen C.
Newcastle, 24 April, 1971 (RB)

League Club	Source	Date Signed	Seasons Played	Apps	Subs	Gls
Hartlepool U.	YT	07.89	88-89	19	1	0

PLATNAUER, Nicholas R.
Leicester, 10 June, 1961 (LB)

League Club	Source	Date Signed	Seasons Played	Apps	Subs	Gls
Bristol Rov.	Bedford T.	08.82	82	21	3	7
Coventry C.	Tr	08.83	83-84	38	6	6
Birmingham C.	Tr	12.84	84-85	23	5	2
Reading	L	01.86	85	7	0	0
Cardiff C.	Tr	09.86	86-88	110	5	6
Notts Co.	Tr	07.89	89-90	57	0	1
Port Vale	L	01.91	90	14	0	0
Leicester C.	Tr	07.91	91	26	3	0

PLATT, David A.
Oldham, 10 June, 1966 Eu21-3/E'B'/E-32 (F)

League Club	Source	Date Signed	Seasons Played	Apps	Subs	Gls
Manchester U.	Chadderton	07.84				
Crewe Alex.	Tr	01.85	84-87	134	0	55
Aston Villa	Tr	02.88	87-90	121	0	50

PLATT, Edward H.
Newcastle-under-Lyme, 26 March, 1921 (G)

League Club	Source	Date Signed	Seasons Played	Apps	Subs	Gls
Arsenal	Colchester U.	01.39	46-52	53	-	0
Portsmouth	Tr	09.53	53-54	31	-	0
Aldershot	Tr	08.55	55	16	-	0

PLATT, James A.
Ballymoney (NI), 26 January, 1952 NI Amat/NI-22 (G)

League Club	Source	Date Signed	Seasons Played	Apps	Subs	Gls
Middlesbrough	Ballymena	05.70	71-82	401	0	0
Hartlepool U.	L	08.78	78	13	0	0
Cardiff C.	L	11.78	78	4	0	0

PLATT, John R.
Ashton-u-Lyne, 22 August, 1954 (G)

League Club	Source	Date Signed	Seasons Played	Apps	Subs	Gls
Oldham Ath.	Ashton U.	06.72	75-80	109	0	0
Bury	Tr	08.81	81-82	20	0	0
Bolton W.	Tr	07.83	83	10	0	0
Tranmere Rov.	L	11.84	84	8	0	0
Preston N. E.	Tr	02.85	84-85	38	0	0

PLATT, John S.
Bermondsey, 29 June, 1942 (OR)

League Club	Source	Date Signed	Seasons Played	Apps	Subs	Gls
Charlton Ath.	Brookhill B.C.	06.61	61	2	-	0

PLATTS, Lawrence
Worksop, 31 October, 1921 (G)

League Club	Source	Date Signed	Seasons Played	Apps	Subs	Gls
Nottingham F.	Jnrs	10.43	46-49	6	-	0
Chesterfield	Tr	07.51	51	11	-	0
Stockport Co.	Burton A.	02.53	52-53	28	-	0

PLATTS, Peter
Dinnington, 14 January, 1928 (CF)

League Club	Source	Date Signed	Seasons Played	Apps	Subs	Gls
Scunthorpe U. (Am)		07.51	51	2	-	2

League Club	Source	Date Signed	Seasons Played	Apps	Subs	Gls

PLAYER, P. Roy I.
Portsmouth, 10 May, 1928 Died 1992 (CH)

Grimsby T.	Portsmouth (Am)	08.52	52-58	57	-	0
Oldham Ath.	Tr	05.59	59	2	-	0

PLEAT, David J.
Nottingham, 15 January, 1945 E Sch/E Yth (W)

Nottingham F.	Jnrs	03.62	61-63	6	-	1
Luton T.	Tr	08.64	64-66	67	3	9
Shrewsbury T.	Tr	07.67	67	10	2	1
Exeter C.	Tr	07.68	68-69	66	2	13
Peterborough U.	Tr	07.70	70	28	0	2

PLENDERLEITH, John B. (Jackie)
Bellshill, 6 October, 1937 S Sch/Su23-5/S-1 (CH)

Manchester C.	Hibernian	07.60	60-62	41	-	0

PLLU, Charles
Saltcoats, 28 February, 1934 (G)

Sheffield Wed.	Scarborough	12.56	56-57	19	-	0

PLUCKROSE, Alan
Southwater (Sx), 3 July, 1963 (LB)

Torquay U. (N/C)	Falmouth	03.83	82	3	0	0

PLUMB, Richard K.
Swindon, 24 September, 1946 (CF)

Swindon T.	App	12.63				
Bristol Rov.	Tr	04.65	65-68	39	0	9
Charlton Ath.	Yeovil T.	09.70	70-71	32	11	10
Exeter C.	Tr	08.72	72-73	59	0	17

PLUME, Richard W.
Tottenham, 10 June, 1949 (M)

Millwall	App	03.67	66-68	12	4	0
Leyton Orient	Tr	05.69	69-70	12	6	1

PLUMLEY, Gary E.
Birmingham, 24 March, 1956 (G)

Leicester C.	App	03.74				
Newport Co.	Tr	06.76	76-80	182	0	0
Hereford U. (N/C)	Hong Kong	09.82	82	13	0	0
Newport Co.	Tr	12.82	82	2	0	0
Cardiff C.	Happy Valley (HK)	08.83	83-84	25	0	0
Newport Co.	L	08.84	84	2	0	0
Newport Co. (N/C)	Ebbw Vale	03.87	86	1	0	0

PLUMMER, Calvin A.
Nottingham, 14 February, 1963 (W)

Nottingham F.	App	02.81	81-82	10	2	2
Chesterfield	Tr	12.82	82	28	0	7
Derby Co.	Tr	08.83	83	23	4	3
Barnsley	Tr	03.84	83-86	41	13	6
Nottingham F.	Tr	12.86				
Nottingham F.	Lahden Reipas (Fin)	10.87	87	8	0	2
Plymouth Arg.	Tr	09.88	88	17	6	1
Chesterfield	Tr	07.89	89-90	67	4	12

PLUMMER, Norman L.
Leicester, 12 January, 1924 (CH)

Leicester C.	Leicester A.T.C.	11.42	47-51	66	-	1
Mansfield T.	Tr	07.52	52-55	166	-	5

PLUNKETT, Sidney E.
Norwich, 2 October, 1920 Died 1986 (W)

Norwich C.	Norwich Y.M.C.A.	04.38	38	3	-	1
Wolverhampton W.	Tr	04.39				
Norwich C.	Tr	02.46	46	28	-	7

PODD, Cyril M. (Ces)
St Kitts (WI), 7 August, 1952 (FB)

Bradford C.	Jnrs	08.70	70-83	494	8	3
Halifax T.	Tr	08.84	84-85	52	5	0
Scarborough (N/C)	Tr	07.86	87	3	0	0

PODMORE, Edgar V.
Fenton, 21 April, 1918 (G)

Stoke C.		08.43				
Crewe Alex.		08.47	47	1	-	0

POINTER, Keith C.
Norwich, 16 February, 1951 (M)

West Ham U.	Norwich C. (Am)	06.68				
Cambridge U.	Tr	03.72	71-72	6	2	2

League Club	Source	Date Signed	Seasons Played	Apps	Subs	Gls

POINTER, Raymond
Cramlington, 10 October, 1936 Eu23-5/EF Lge/E-3 (CF)

Burnley	Dudley Welfare	08.57	57-64	223	-	118
Bury	Tr	08.65	65	19	0	17
Coventry C.	Tr	12.65	65-66	26	0	13
Portsmouth	Tr	01.67	66-72	149	4	31

POINTER, Reginald E.
Norwich, 28 January, 1935 (CH)

Norwich C. (Am)	C.N.S.O.B.U.	06.56	56	11	-	0

POINTON, Neil G.
Warsop, 28 November, 1964 (LB)

Scunthorpe U.	App	08.82	81-85	159	0	2
Everton	Tr	11.85	85-89	95	7	5
Manchester C.	Tr	07.90	90-91	74	0	2

Neil Pointon (Scunthorpe United, Everton & Manchester City)

POINTON, Raymond E.
Birkenhead, 6 November, 1947 (D)

Tranmere Rov.	App	11.65	67-70	41	5	0

POINTON, William J.
Hanley, 25 November, 1920 (F)

Port Vale		07.40	46-48	74	-	26
Queens Park R.	Tr	01.49	48-49	26	-	6
Brentford	Tr	02.50	49-50	16	-	2

POLAND, George
Penarth, 21 September, 1913 Died 1988 W-2 (G)

Cardiff C.		11.35	35-36	24	-	0
Wrexham		07.38	38	39	-	0
Liverpool	Tr	07.39				
Cardiff C.	Tr	08.46	46	2	-	0

POLE, H. Edward W. (Ted)
Kessingland (Sk), 25 March, 1922 (F)

Ipswich T.		10.46	46-50	39	-	13
Leyton Orient	Tr	07.51	51-52	12	-	0

POLK, Stanley
Liverpool, 28 October, 1921 (WH)

Liverpool	South Liverpool	03.40	46-47	13	-	0
Port Vale	Tr	07.48	48-51	159	-	14

POLLARD, Brian E.
York, 22 May, 1954 E Yth (W)

League Club	Source	Date Signed	Seasons Played	Apps	Subs	Gls
York C.	Jnrs	03.72	71-77	151	11	34
Watford	Tr	11.77	77-79	68	3	8
Mansfield T.	Tr	01.80	79-80	45	9	5
Blackpool	Tr	08.81	81	0	1	0
York C.	Tr	09.81	81-83	98	4	26
Chesterfield (N/C)	Tr	09.84	84	0	1	0
Hartlepool U. (N/C)	Scarborough	01.85	84	2	0	0

POLLARD, Gary
Staveley, 30 December, 1959 (CD)

League Club	Source	Date Signed	Seasons Played	Apps	Subs	Gls
Chesterfield	Jnrs	07.77	77-82	83	4	1
Port Vale	Tr	06.83	83	18	0	0
Mansfield T.	Tr	07.84	84-86	66	1	1
Peterborough U.	Tr	08.87	87-88	20	0	0

POLLARD, James R.
Liverpool, 4 June, 1920 (OL)

League Club	Source	Date Signed	Seasons Played	Apps	Subs	Gls
Newport Co.	Tredomen	05.46				
Tranmere Rov.		11.47	47-48	24	-	1

POLLARD, K. John
Chelmsford, 17 November, 1971 (CD)

League Club	Source	Date Signed	Seasons Played	Apps	Subs	Gls
Colchester U. (YT)	YT	07.88	88-89	1	8	1

POLLITT, John (Jack)
Famworth, 29 March, 1937 (CF)

League Club	Source	Date Signed	Seasons Played	Apps	Subs	Gls
Bolton W.	Jnrs	12.54				
Bury	Tr	08.58	58	4	-	0
Accrington St.	Tr	03.60	59	3	-	1
Rochdale	Tr	08.60	60	6	-	1

POLLOCK, Jamie
Stockton, 16 February, 1974 (M)

League Club	Source	Date Signed	Seasons Played	Apps	Subs	Gls
Middlesbrough	YT	12.91	90-91	21	6	1

POLLOCK, Maitland A. I.
Dumfries, 31 October, 1952 S Sch (W)

League Club	Source	Date Signed	Seasons Played	Apps	Subs	Gls
Nottingham F.	App	10.70				
Walsall	Tr	07.73	73	1	1	0
Luton T.	Burton A.	03.74	75	3	3	0
Portsmouth	Tr	07.76	76-77	50	4	10

POLLOCK, Stewart
Bellshill, 25 September, 1933 (IF)

League Club	Source	Date Signed	Seasons Played	Apps	Subs	Gls
Gillingham	Motherwell	07.56	56	10	-	0

POLLOCK, William
Barrhead, 7 June, 1920 (RH)

League Club	Source	Date Signed	Seasons Played	Apps	Subs	Gls
Oldham Ath.	Manchester U. (Am)	07.47	47	4	-	0

POLSTON, Andrew A.
Walthamstow, 26 July, 1970 (CD)

League Club	Source	Date Signed	Seasons Played	Apps	Subs	Gls
Tottenham H.	YT	07.88	89	0	1	0
Cambridge U.	L	10.89	89	3	0	0
Gillingham	L	11.91	91	1	1	0

POLSTON, Jonathan D.
Walthamstow, 10 June, 1968 E Yth (CD)

League Club	Source	Date Signed	Seasons Played	Apps	Subs	Gls
Tottenham H.	App	07.85	86-89	17	7	1
Norwich C.	Tr	07.90	90-91	43	3	5

POLYCARPOU, Andrew
Islington, 15 August, 1958 (M)

League Club	Source	Date Signed	Seasons Played	Apps	Subs	Gls
Southend U.		09.76	76-80	43	20	10
Cambridge U.	Tr	08.81	81	1	4	0
Cardiff C.	Tr	04.82	81	7	0	0

POMPHREY, Edric A. (Syd)
Stretford, 31 May, 1916 (FB)

League Club	Source	Date Signed	Seasons Played	Apps	Subs	Gls
Notts Co.	Hyde U.	09.44				
Rochdale	Tr	10.45	46	9	-	0

PONTE, Raimondo
Switzerland, 4 April, 1954 Swiss Int (M)

League Club	Source	Date Signed	Seasons Played	Apps	Subs	Gls
Nottingham F.	Grasshoppers (Swi)	08.80	80	17	4	3

PONTIN, Keith
Pontyclun, 14 June, 1956 Wu21-1/W-2 (CD)

League Club	Source	Date Signed	Seasons Played	Apps	Subs	Gls
Cardiff C.	App	05.74	76-82	193	0	5

POOK, David C.
Plymouth, 16 January, 1955 (W)

League Club	Source	Date Signed	Seasons Played	Apps	Subs	Gls
Torquay U.	App	01.73	71-72	13	3	1

POOLE, Andrew J.
Chesterfield, 6 July, 1960 (G)

League Club	Source	Date Signed	Seasons Played	Apps	Subs	Gls
Northampton T.	Mansfield T. (App)	07.78	78-81	141	0	0
Wolverhampton W.	Tr	08.82				
Port Vale	Tr	03.83	82	2	0	0

POOLE, Cyril J.
Mansfield, 13 March, 1921 (FB)

League Club	Source	Date Signed	Seasons Played	Apps	Subs	Gls
Mansfield T.	Gillingham	02.44	49-50	16	-	1

POOLE, Gary J.
Stratford, 11 September, 1967 (FB)

League Club	Source	Date Signed	Seasons Played	Apps	Subs	Gls
Tottenham H.	Jnrs	07.85				
Cambridge U.	Tr	08.87	87-88	42	1	0
Barnet	Tr	03.89	91	39	1	2

POOLE, Harold
Stoke, 31 January, 1935 (IF)

League Club	Source	Date Signed	Seasons Played	Apps	Subs	Gls
Port Vale	Oxford C.	04.56	55-67	449	1	73

POOLE, John A. F.
Stoke, 12 December, 1932 (G)

League Club	Source	Date Signed	Seasons Played	Apps	Subs	Gls
Port Vale		09.53	55-60	32	-	0

POOLE, Joseph
Huddersfield, 25 May, 1923 (W)

League Club	Source	Date Signed	Seasons Played	Apps	Subs	Gls
Huddersfield T.	David Brown Wks	06.41	46	2	-	0
Bradford C.	Tr	02.47	46-48	56	-	5

POOLE, Kenneth J.
Blaencwm, 2 July, 1933 (FB)

League Club	Source	Date Signed	Seasons Played	Apps	Subs	Gls
Swansea C.	Jnrs	11.53				
Northampton T.	Tr	06.56	56	4	-	0

POOLE, Kevin
Bromsgrove, 21 July, 1963 (G)

League Club	Source	Date Signed	Seasons Played	Apps	Subs	Gls
Aston Villa	App	06.81	84-86	28	0	0
Northampton T.	L	11.84	84	3	0	0
Middlesbrough	Tr	08.87	87-89	34	0	0
Hartlepool U.	L	03.91	90	12	0	0
Leicester C.	Tr	07.91	91	42	0	0

POOLE, Michael D.
Morley, 23 April, 1955 (G)

League Club	Source	Date Signed	Seasons Played	Apps	Subs	Gls
Rochdale	Coventry C. (App)	09.73	73-77	192	0	0
Rochdale	Portland (USA)	08.81	81	27	0	0

POOLE, Richard J.
Heston, 3 July, 1957 (F)

League Club	Source	Date Signed	Seasons Played	Apps	Subs	Gls
Brentford	App	07.75	73-75	12	9	1
Watford	Tr	07.76	76	3	4	1

POOLE, Roy
Sheffield, 2 December, 1939 (FB/CF)

League Club	Source	Date Signed	Seasons Played	Apps	Subs	Gls
Wolverhampton W.	Jnrs	01.57				
Rotherham U.	Tr	07.58				
Chesterfield	Tr	07.61	61-63	50	-	14

POOLE, Terence
Sheffield, 8 December, 1937 (WH)

League Club	Source	Date Signed	Seasons Played	Apps	Subs	Gls
Sheffield Wed.	Jnrs	04.55				
Darlington	Tr	07.59	59-60	41	-	3

POOLE, Terence
Chesterfield, 16 December, 1949 (G)

League Club	Source	Date Signed	Seasons Played	Apps	Subs	Gls
Manchester U.	Jnrs	02.67				
Huddersfield T.	Tr	08.68	68-76	207	0	0
Bolton W.	Tr	01.77	80	29	0	0
Sheffield U.	L	03.80	79	7	0	0

POPE, David W.
London, 8 January, 1936 (FB)

League Club	Source	Date Signed	Seasons Played	Apps	Subs	Gls
Crystal Palace	Jnrs	09.53				
Swansea C.		09.56	57	4	-	0

POPE, Neil L.
Ashton-u-Lyne, 9 October, 1972 (M)

League Club	Source	Date Signed	Seasons Played	Apps	Subs	Gls
Peterborough U. (N/C)	Cambridge U. (YT)	03.91	90	1	1	0

POPE, Terence J.
Newport, 27 January, 1926 (G)

League Club	Source	Date Signed	Seasons Played	Apps	Subs	Gls
Newport Co.	Bargoed	07.50	50-54	83	-	0

POPELY, Peter C. F.
York, 7 April, 1943 (FB)

League Club	Source	Date Signed	Seasons Played	Apps	Subs	Gls
York C.	Cliftonville	08.62	62-66	24	1	0

League Club	Source	Date Signed	Seasons Played	Career Record Apps	Subs	Gls
POPPITT, John						
Bedlington, 20 January, 1923						(FB)
Derby Co.	West Sleekburn	05.45	46-49	16	-	0
Queens Park R.	Tr	09.50	50-53	106	-	0
POPPY, Arthur P. C.						
Yeovil, 6 January, 1961						(D)
Northampton T. (App)	App	09.77	77	1	0	0
PORRITT, Walter M.						
Heckmondwike, 19 July, 1914						(OR)
Huddersfield T.		05.35				
York C.	Tr	08.36	36-46	40	-	5
PORT, Bernard H.						
Burton, 14 December, 1925						(G)
Hull C.	Newhall	09.50				
Chester C.	Tr	08.51	51-52	9	-	0
PORTEOUS, John R.						
India, 12 January, 1933						(IF)
Aldershot	Alton T.	02.56	55	1	-	0
PORTEOUS, John R.						
Motherwell, 5 December, 1921						(WH)
Plymouth Arg.	Alloa Ath.	07.49	49-55	215	-	13
Exeter C.	Tr	03.56	55-56	40	-	0
PORTEOUS, Joseph						
Shildon, 20 April, 1925						(LH)
York C.	Chesterfield (Am)	08.46	46	23	-	0
PORTEOUS, Trevor						
Hull, 9 October, 1933						(WH)
Hull C.	Jnrs	10.50	51-55	61	-	1
Stockport Co.	Tr	06.56	56-64	336	-	9
PORTER, Andrew M.						
Macclesfield, 17 September, 1968						(M)
Port Vale	YT	06.87	86-91	114	15	3
PORTER, Andrew						
Stewarton, 21 January, 1937						(WH)
Watford	Darvel Jnrs	06.59	59-62	72	-	4
PORTER, Christopher J.						
North Petherton, 30 April, 1949						(W)
Swindon T.	Bridgwater T.	11.69	70-73	33	3	4
PORTER, Derek						
Ulverston, 22 June, 1936						(OL)
Barrow	Dalton T.	05.57	57-58	15	-	1
PORTER, Gary M.						
Sunderland, 6 March, 1966 E Yth/Eu21-12						(M)
Watford	App	03.84	83-91	219	29	34
PORTER, George						
Chirk, 5 February, 1935						(OL)
Wrexham (Am)	Chirk A.A.A.	05.59	59	1	-	0
PORTER, Leslie						
Gateshead, 5 May, 1923						(WH)
Newcastle U.	Redheugh Wks	09.44				
York C.	Tr	03.49	48-53	39	-	1
PORTER, Michael R.						
Stoke, 19 May, 1945						(IF)
Port Vale	Jnrs	07.62	63-64	13	-	2
PORTER, Trevor J.						
Guildford, 16 October, 1956						(G)
Fulham	App	05.74				
Brentford	Slough T.	08.78	78-79	15	0	0
PORTER, William						
Durham, 23 November, 1923 Died 1975						(OL)
Hartlepool U.	Horden Colly	09.43	46	2	-	0
PORTERFIELD, Ian						
Dunfermline, 11 February, 1946						(M)
Sunderland	Raith Rov.	12.67	67-75	218	12	17
Reading	L	11.76	76	5	0	0
Sheffield Wed.	Tr	07.77	77-79	103	3	3

League Club	Source	Date Signed	Seasons Played	Career Record Apps	Subs	Gls
PORTWOOD, Clifford E.						
Salford, 17 October, 1937						(IF)
Preston N. E.	Manchester Ath.	02.55				
Port Vale	Tr	08.59	59-60	61	-	32
Grimsby T.	Tr	07.61	61-63	92	-	35
Portsmouth	Tr	05.64	64-68	95	3	28
POSKETT, Malcolm						
Middlesbrough, 19 July, 1953						(F)
Middlesbrough	South Bank	04.73	73	0	1	0
Hartlepool U.	Whitby T.	11.76	76-77	50	1	20
Brighton & H. A.	Tr	02.78	77-79	33	12	16
Watford	Tr	01.80	79-81	57	6	17
Carlisle U.	Tr	08.82	82-84	108	2	40
Darlington	Tr	07.85	85	18	3	4
Stockport Co.	Tr	01.86	85	8	0	1
Hartlepool U.	L	03.86	85	4	1	0
Carlisle U.	Tr	08.86	86-87	67	9	20
POSKETT, Thomas W.						
Esh Winning, 26 December, 1909 Died 1972						(G)
Grimsby T.	Crook T.	12.28	28-30	2	-	0
Lincoln C.	Tr	05.32	33	10	-	0
Notts Co.	Tr	05.34	34	10	-	0
Tranmere Rov.	Tr	08.35	35-36	22	-	0
Crewe Alex.	Tr	07.37	37-46	99	-	0
POSSEE, Derek J.						
Southwark, 14 February, 1946						(W)
Tottenham H.	App	03.63	63-65	19	0	4
Millwall	Tr	08.67	67-72	222	1	79
Crystal Palace	Tr	01.73	72-73	51	2	13
Leyton Orient	Tr	07.74	74-76	77	2	11
POSTLEWHITE, Dennis J.						
Birkenhead, 13 October, 1957						(CD)
Tranmere Rov.	App	07.76	76-78	31	2	1
POTRAC, Anthony J.						
Victoria, 21 January, 1953						(F)
Chelsea	App	08.70	71	1	0	0
POTTER, Frederick						
Cradley Heath, 29 November, 1940						(G)
Aston Villa	Jnrs	07.59	60	3	-	0
Doncaster Rov.	Tr	07.62	62-65	123	0	0
Hereford U.	Burton A.	07.70	72-73	10	0	0

Ian Porterfield (Raith Rovers, Sunderland & Sheffield Wednesday)

POTTER, Gary C.
Chester, 6 August, 1952 (CD)

League Club	Source	Date Signed	Seasons Played	Apps	Subs	Gls
Chester C.		07.73	73-74	11	0	0

POTTER, George R.
Arbroath, 7 October, 1946 (FB)

League Club	Source	Date Signed	Seasons Played	Apps	Subs	Gls
Luton T.	Forfar Ath.	03.68	67-68	3	4	0
Torquay U.	Tr	07.69	69-70	32	6	0
Hartlepool U.	Tr	07.71	71-76	211	2	4

POTTER, Harold
Tyldesley, 20 May, 1923 (FB)

League Club	Source	Date Signed	Seasons Played	Apps	Subs	Gls
Shrewsbury T.	Winsford U.	(N/L)	50-51	67	-	0
Rochdale	Tr	06.52	52-53	52	-	0

POTTER, James
Belfast, 20 November, 1941 (WH)

League Club	Source	Date Signed	Seasons Played	Apps	Subs	Gls
Sunderland	Jnrs	11.58				
Darlington	Tr	09.63	63	19	-	1

POTTER, Raymond J.
Beckenham, 7 May, 1936 (G)

League Club	Source	Date Signed	Seasons Played	Apps	Subs	Gls
Crystal Palace	Jnrs	05.53	53-57	44	-	0
West Bromwich A.	Tr	06.58	58-66	217	0	0
Portsmouth	Tr	05.67	67-69	3	0	0

POTTER, Ronald C.
Wolverhampton, 5 December, 1948 (CD)

League Club	Source	Date Signed	Seasons Played	Apps	Subs	Gls
West Bromwich A.	App	12.66	68-69	8	1	0
Swindon T.	Tr	11.70	70-74	84	2	0

POTTER, Stephen D.
Belper, 1 October, 1955 (G)

League Club	Source	Date Signed	Seasons Played	Apps	Subs	Gls
Manchester C.	App	10.73				
Swansea C.	Tr	08.74	74-77	118	0	0

POTTS, Brian
Sunderland, 3 September, 1948 (FB)

League Club	Source	Date Signed	Seasons Played	Apps	Subs	Gls
Leicester C.	App	09.65	67-68	9	1	0
Peterborough U.	Tr	07.69	69-70	49	1	0

POTTS, Craig
Carlisle, 25 February, 1974 (W)

League Club	Source	Date Signed	Seasons Played	Apps	Subs	Gls
Carlisle U. (YT)	YT	07.90	91	3	3	0

POTTS, Eric T.
Liverpool, 16 March, 1950 (W)

League Club	Source	Date Signed	Seasons Played	Apps	Subs	Gls
Sheffield Wed.	Oswestry T.	12.69	70-76	142	17	21
Brighton & H. A.	Tr	06.77	77	19	14	5
Preston N. E.	Tr	08.78	78-80	50	7	5
Burnley	Tr	09.80	80-81	48	8	5
Bury	Tr	10.82	82-83	46	5	7

POTTS, Harold
Hetton-le-Hole, 22 October, 1920 (IF)

League Club	Source	Date Signed	Seasons Played	Apps	Subs	Gls
Burnley	Jnrs	11.37	46-50	165	-	47
Everton	Tr	10.50	50-55	59	-	15

POTTS, Henry J.
Carlisle, 23 January, 1925 E Amat (OL)

League Club	Source	Date Signed	Seasons Played	Apps	Subs	Gls
Northampton T. (Am)	Pegasus	08.50	50	9	-	0

POTTS, Reginald
Stoke, 31 July, 1927 (FB)

League Club	Source	Date Signed	Seasons Played	Apps	Subs	Gls
Port Vale	Northwood Mission	08.45	48-56	277	-	3

POTTS, Steven J.
USA, 7 May, 1967 E Yth (RB)

League Club	Source	Date Signed	Seasons Played	Apps	Subs	Gls
West Ham U.	App	05.84	84-91	139	10	1

POTTS, Victor E.
Birmingham, 20 August, 1915 (RB)

League Club	Source	Date Signed	Seasons Played	Apps	Subs	Gls
Tottenham H.	Metro Welfare	08.34				
Doncaster Rov.	Tr	08.38	38	23	-	0
Aston Villa	Tr	08.45	46-47	62	-	0

POULTON, George H.
Holborn, 23 April, 1929 (OL)

League Club	Source	Date Signed	Seasons Played	Apps	Subs	Gls
Gillingham		08.49	51	5	-	1
Leyton Orient	Tr	07.52	52-54	61	-	24

POUND, J. H. Kenneth
Portsmouth, 24 August, 1944 (W)

League Club	Source	Date Signed	Seasons Played	Apps	Subs	Gls
Swansea C.	Yeovil T.	07.64	64-65	27	2	4
Bournemouth	Tr	08.66	66-68	102	0	24
Gillingham	Tr	07.69	69-70	62	10	11

POUNDER, John A.
Sheffield, 16 March, 1935 (OR)

League Club	Source	Date Signed	Seasons Played	Apps	Subs	Gls
Luton T.	Atlas Sports	12.55	55-56	3	-	0
Coventry C.	Tr	06.57	57	6	-	1
Crewe Alex.	Tr	12.57	57-58	29	-	6

POUNDER, Albert W.
Charlton, 27 July, 1931 (OR)

League Club	Source	Date Signed	Seasons Played	Apps	Subs	Gls
Charlton Ath.	Harvey Sports	02.50	52	1	-	0
Queens Park R.	Tr	02.54	53-55	52	-	6

POUNDER, Antony M.
Yeovil, 11 March, 1966 (LW)

League Club	Source	Date Signed	Seasons Played	Apps	Subs	Gls
Bristol Rov.	Weymouth	07.90	90-91	77	8	7

POUNTNEY, David H.
Baschurch, 12 October, 1939 (WH)

League Club	Source	Date Signed	Seasons Played	Apps	Subs	Gls
Shrewsbury T.	Myddle	09.57	57-63	176	-	11
Aston Villa	Tr	10.63	63-67	109	4	7
Shrewsbury T.	Tr	02.68	67-69	54	4	1
Chester C.	Tr	06.70	70-72	135	0	1

POUNTNEY, Ronald A.
Bilston, 19 March, 1955 (M)

League Club	Source	Date Signed	Seasons Played	Apps	Subs	Gls
Walsall	Jnrs	07.73	72	1	0	0
Port Vale	Tr	10.73				
Southend U.	Bilston	01.75	74-84	326	22	26

POUTCH, Neil A.
Dublin, 27 November, 1969 IRu21-5 (FB)

League Club	Source	Date Signed	Seasons Played	Apps	Subs	Gls
Luton T.	YT	11.87	89	0	1	0

POVEY, Victor R.
Wolverhampton, 15 March, 1944 (W)

League Club	Source	Date Signed	Seasons Played	Apps	Subs	Gls
Wolverhampton W.	Jnrs	07.61				
Notts Co.	Tr	08.63	63-64	35	-	3

POVEY, William
Billingham, 11 January, 1943 (W)

League Club	Source	Date Signed	Seasons Played	Apps	Subs	Gls
Middlesbrough	Jnrs	05.60	62	6	-	0
York C.	Tr	03.64	64	3	-	0

POWELL, Andrew
Plymouth, 27 June, 1955 (G)

League Club	Source	Date Signed	Seasons Played	Apps	Subs	Gls
Hereford U. (N/C)	Jnrs	10.82	82	4	0	0

POWELL, Anthony
Severn Beach, 11 February, 1947 (CD)

League Club	Source	Date Signed	Seasons Played	Apps	Subs	Gls
Bournemouth	Bath C.	04.68	68-73	214	5	10
Norwich C.	Tr	08.74	74-80	235	2	3

Harry Potts (Burnley & Everton)

POWELL, Aubrey
Swansea, 19 April, 1918 W-8 (IF)

League Club	Source	Date Signed	Seasons Played	Apps	Subs	Gls
Leeds U.	Swansea C. (Am)	11.35	36-47	112	-	25
Everton	Tr	07.48	48-49	35	-	5
Birmingham C.	Tr	08.50	50	15	-	1

POWELL, Baden
Hebburn, 17 June, 1931 (OR)

League Club	Source	Date Signed	Seasons Played	Apps	Subs	Gls
Darlington	South Shields	10.50	50-53	9	-	0

POWELL, Barry I.
Kenilworth, 29 January, 1954 Eu23-4 (M)

League Club	Source	Date Signed	Seasons Played	Apps	Subs	Gls
Wolverhampton W.	App	01.72	72-74	58	6	7
Coventry C.	Tr	09.75	75-79	162	2	27
Derby Co.	Tr	10.79	79-81	86	0	7
Burnley	Hong Kong	07.84	84	9	2	0
Swansea C.	Tr	02.85	84	8	0	0
Wolverhampton W.	Hong Kong	11.86	86-87	10	4	0

POWELL, Christopher G. R.
Lambeth, 8 September, 1969 (LB)

League Club	Source	Date Signed	Seasons Played	Apps	Subs	Gls
Crystal Palace	YT	12.87	88	2	1	0
Aldershot	L	01.90	89	11	0	0
Southend U.	Tr	08.90	90-91	87	2	1

POWELL, Clifford G.
Watford, 21 February, 1968 (D)

League Club	Source	Date Signed	Seasons Played	Apps	Subs	Gls
Watford	App	02.86				
Hereford U.	L	12.87	87	7	0	0
Sheffield U.	Tr	03.88	87-88	7	3	0
Doncaster Rov.	L	03.89	88	4	0	0
Cardiff C.	L	11.89	89	0	1	0

POWELL, Colin D.
Hendon, 7 July, 1948 (W)

League Club	Source	Date Signed	Seasons Played	Apps	Subs	Gls
Charlton Ath.	Barnet	01.73	72-78	230	14	23
Charlton Ath.	New England (USA)	08.79	79-80	71	6	8
Gillingham	Tr	08.81	81-82	54	1	1

POWELL, Darryl A.
Lambeth, 15 November, 1971 (M)

League Club	Source	Date Signed	Seasons Played	Apps	Subs	Gls
Portsmouth	YT	12.88	88-91	28	19	6

POWELL, David
Conwy, 15 October, 1944 Wu23-4/W-11 (CD)

League Club	Source	Date Signed	Seasons Played	Apps	Subs	Gls
Wrexham	Gwydyn Rov.	05.63	62-68	132	2	4
Sheffield U.	Tr	09.68	68-70	89	0	2
Cardiff C.	Tr	09.72	72-74	36	0	1

POWELL, David M. (Dai)
Swansea, 19 January, 1935 (FB)

League Club	Source	Date Signed	Seasons Played	Apps	Subs	Gls
Blackpool		12.52				
Rochdale	Tr	07.58	58-60	76	-	1

POWELL, David R.
Hednesford, 24 September, 1967 (G)

League Club	Source	Date Signed	Seasons Played	Apps	Subs	Gls
West Bromwich A.	Cherry Valley	04.86	87	2	0	0
Wrexham	L	02.87	86	2	0	0

POWELL, Gary
Hoylake, 2 April, 1969 (F)

League Club	Source	Date Signed	Seasons Played	Apps	Subs	Gls
Everton	YT	07.87				
Lincoln C.	L	09.90	90	11	0	0
Scunthorpe U.	L	11.90	90	3	1	1
Wigan Ath.	L	03.91	90	13	1	4
Wigan Ath.	Tr	08.91	91	22	12	7

POWELL, George R.
Fulham, 11 October, 1924 (FB)

League Club	Source	Date Signed	Seasons Played	Apps	Subs	Gls
Queens Park R.	Fulham (Am)	12.46	47-52	125	-	0

POWELL, Ivor V.
Bargoed, 5 July, 1916 W-8 (WH)

League Club	Source	Date Signed	Seasons Played	Apps	Subs	Gls
Queens Park R.	Bargoed	09.37	38-48	112	-	2
Aston Villa	Tr	12.48	48-50	79	-	5
Port Vale	Tr	08.51	51	6	-	0
Bradford C.	Barry T.	06.52	52-54	83	-	9

POWELL, B. John E.
York, 10 March, 1936 (OL)

League Club	Source	Date Signed	Seasons Played	Apps	Subs	Gls
York C.	Cliftonville	09.56	56-59	27	-	5

POWELL, Kenneth
Mansfield, 2 March, 1920 Died 1976 (OL)

League Club	Source	Date Signed	Seasons Played	Apps	Subs	Gls
Derby Co.	Mansfield C.W.S.	05.39	46	13	-	0
Southport	Tr	06.47	47-50	90	-	18

POWELL, Kenneth L.
Chester, 25 September, 1924 (WH)

League Club	Source	Date Signed	Seasons Played	Apps	Subs	Gls
Cardiff C.		09.47				
Exeter C.	Tr	06.48	48-49	22	-	1
Bristol Rov.	Tr	07.51	51	4	-	0

POWELL, Lee
Caerleon, 2 June, 1973 Wu21-2 (W)

League Club	Source	Date Signed	Seasons Played	Apps	Subs	Gls
Southampton	YT	05.91	91	1	3	0

POWELL, Michael J.
Newport, 26 April, 1951 (D)

League Club	Source	Date Signed	Seasons Played	Apps	Subs	Gls
Newport Co. (N/C)	Newport Y.M.C.A.	01.76	75-77	7	2	0

POWELL, Michael P.
Slough, 18 April, 1933 (CH)

League Club	Source	Date Signed	Seasons Played	Apps	Subs	Gls
Queens Park R.	Jnrs	01.51	51-58	123	-	0

POWELL, Neville D.
Flint, 2 September, 1963 (W)

League Club	Source	Date Signed	Seasons Played	Apps	Subs	Gls
Tranmere Rov.	App	08.81	80-84	76	10	4

POWELL, Raymond
Swansea, 5 August, 1924 (CF)

League Club	Source	Date Signed	Seasons Played	Apps	Subs	Gls
Swansea C.	Haverfordwest	05.47	47-50	17	-	5
Scunthorpe U.	Tr	08.51	51	31	-	14

POWELL, Richard
Chesterfield, 3 September, 1969 (G)

League Club	Source	Date Signed	Seasons Played	Apps	Subs	Gls
Blackpool	YT	06.88	86-87	14	0	0

POWELL, Ronald W. H.
Knighton, 2 December, 1929 (G)

League Club	Source	Date Signed	Seasons Played	Apps	Subs	Gls
Manchester C.	Knighton T.	11.48	49	12	-	0
Chesterfield	Tr	06.52	52-64	471	-	0

POWELL, Stephen
Derby, 20 September, 1955 E Sch/E Yth/Eu23-1 (M/D)

League Club	Source	Date Signed	Seasons Played	Apps	Subs	Gls
Derby Co.	App	11.72	71-84	342	10	20

POWELL, Thomas
Derby, 12 April, 1925 (OR)

League Club	Source	Date Signed	Seasons Played	Apps	Subs	Gls
Derby Co.	Jnrs	04.42	48-61	380	-	57

POWELL, Wayne
Caerphilly, 25 October, 1956 W Yth (F)

League Club	Source	Date Signed	Seasons Played	Apps	Subs	Gls
Bristol Rov.	App	10.74	75-77	25	7	10
Halifax T.	L	10.77	77	4	0	1
Hereford U.	Tr	06.78	78	6	0	2

POWER, John
Chelsea, 10 December, 1959 (G)

League Club	Source	Date Signed	Seasons Played	Apps	Subs	Gls
Brentford (N/C)	Kingstonian	03.87	86	2	0	0

POWER, Lee M.
Lewisham, 30 June, 1972 IRu21-5 (F)

League Club	Source	Date Signed	Seasons Played	Apps	Subs	Gls
Norwich C.	YT	07.90	89-91	15	6	4

POWER, Michael D.
Stockport, 3 October, 1961 (F)

League Club	Source	Date Signed	Seasons Played	Apps	Subs	Gls
Stockport Co.	Jnrs	08.80	80-85	67	4	16

POWER, Paul C.
Manchester, 30 October, 1953 E-'B (LM)

League Club	Source	Date Signed	Seasons Played	Apps	Subs	Gls
Manchester C.	Leeds Polytechnic	09.73	75-85	358	7	26
Everton	Tr	06.86	86-87	52	2	6

POWER, Philip D.
Salford, 25 July, 1966 (W)

League Club	Source	Date Signed	Seasons Played	Apps	Subs	Gls
Crewe Alex.	Witton A.	08.85	85-86	18	9	3

POWLING, Richard F.
Barking, 21 May, 1956 E Yth (D)

League Club	Source	Date Signed	Seasons Played	Apps	Subs	Gls
Arsenal	App	07.73	73-77	50	5	3

POWNER, Robert J.
Newcastle-u-Lyme, 2 July, 1967 (G)

League Club	Source	Date Signed	Seasons Played	Apps	Subs	Gls
Crewe Alex.	Jnrs	06.86	85-86	6	0	0

POWNEY, Bryan W.
Seaford, 7 October, 1944 (G)

League Club	Source	Date Signed	Seasons Played	Apps	Subs	Gls
Brighton & H. A.	App	11.61	61-73	351	0	0

POWTON, Brian
Newcastle, 29 August, 1929 (G)

League Club	Source	Date Signed	Seasons Played	Apps	Subs	Gls
Newcastle U.		10.50				
Preston N. E.	Tr	08.51				
Hartlepool U.	Tr	07.52	52	4	-	0

League Club	Source	Date Signed	Seasons Played	Apps	Subs	Gls

POYNER, Robert C.
Newport, 25 December, 1932 Died 1977 W Sch/W Yth (HB)

Newport Co.	Jnrs	01.51	50-51	2	-	0

POYNTON, William
Shiremoor, 30 June, 1944 (FB)

Burnley	Jnrs	07.61				
Mansfield T.	Tr	07.64	64-65	20	0	0
Lincoln C.	Lockheed Leamington	10.66	66	0	1	0

POYSER, George H.
Stanton Hill, 6 February, 1910 (FB)

Wolverhampton W.		05.28				
Port Vale	Mansfield T.	05.31	31-33	73	-	0
Brentford	Tr	06.34	34-38	150	-	0
Plymouth Arg.	Tr	04.46	46	3	-	0

PRAGG, Michael K.
Shrewsbury, 8 October, 1941 E Amat (IF)

Shrewsbury T. (Am)	Jnrs	05.59	60-62	5	-	1

PRANGLEY, Samuel
Newport, 30 September, 1924 (CH)

Newport Co.	Lovells Ath.	11.46	46	7	-	0

PRASKI, Josef
France, 22 January, 1926 (OR)

Notts Co.	Jeanfield Swifts	03.49	48	3	-	0

PRATLEY, Richard G.
Banbury, 12 January, 1963 (CD)

Derby Co.	Banbury U.	07.83	83-86	29	2	1
Scunthorpe U.	L	03.84	83	10	0	0
Shrewsbury T.	Tr	02.88	87-89	44	2	1

PRATT, John A.
Hackney, 26 June, 1948 (M)

Tottenham H.	Jnrs	11.65	68-79	307	24	39

PRATT, John L.
Atherstone, 1 March, 1943 (G)

Reading	Wycombe W.	07.69	69-71	29	0	0

PRATT, Lee S.
Cleethorpes, 31 March, 1970 (G)

Grimsby T.	YT	06.88	86	1	0	0

PRATT, Michael W.
Newport, 15 January, 1966 W Yth (F)

Newport Co.		08.83	83-84	4	5	2

PRATT, Raymond E.
Burry Port, 11 November, 1955 W Yth (F)

Exeter C.	Merthyr Tydfil	03.80	79-85	127	46	62

PRATT, Wayne
Southampton, 1 March, 1960 (M)

Southampton	App	03.78	80	1	0	0

PRECIOUS, Derek
Crewe, 2 June, 1931 (F)

Crewe Alex.		09.55	55-56	18	-	3

PREECE, Andrew P.
Evesham, 27 March, 1967 (F)

Northampton T. (N/C)	Evesham U.	08.88	88	0	1	0
Wrexham	Worcester C.	03.90	89-91	44	7	7
Stockport Co.	Tr	12.91	91	23	2	13

PREECE, Brian J.
Hereford, 16 February, 1958 Died 1992 (W)

Hereford U.	App	02.76	74-76	5	1	0
Newport Co.	Tr	03.77	76-77	38	6	12

PREECE, David W.
Bridgnorth, 28 May, 1963 E-'B' (LM)

Walsall	App	07.80	80-84	107	4	5
Luton T.	Tr	12.84	84-91	215	7	9

PREECE, John C. (Jack)
Wolverhampton, 30 April, 1914 (FB)

Wolverhampton W.		05.31	33	2	-	0
Bristol Rov.	Tr	05.35	35-37	79	-	0
Bradford C.	Tr	07.38	38	3	-	0
Southport	Tr	05.39	46	36	-	0
Swindon T.	Tr	06.47	47	7	-	0

PREECE, Paul W.
Penarth, 16 May, 1957 (W)

Newport Co.	App	06.75	74-75	17	6	0

PREECE, Roger
Much Wenlock, 9 June, 1969 (RB/W)

Wrexham	Coventry C. (YT)	08.86	86-89	89	21	12
Chester C.	Tr	08.90	90-91	61	3	0

PREECE, Ryan
Neath, 10 January, 1969 (M)

Newport Co. (N/C)	YT	10.87	87	7	3	2

PRENDERGAST, Michael J.
Denaby, 24 November, 1950 (F)

Sheffield Wed.	App	11.67	68-77	170	13	53
Barnsley	Tr	05.78	77-78	12	7	2
Halifax T.	L	10.78	78	4	0	1

PRENTIS, John
Liverpool, 22 March, 1939 (FB)

Blackpool		10.62	64-65	6	0	0
Stockport Co.	Tr	10.66	66-67	16	3	0

PRESCOTT, Francis S.
Birkenhead, 12 August, 1922 Died 1969 (CF)

Tranmere Rov.	St Annes	10.46	46	2	-	0

PRESCOTT, James L.
Warrington, 2 November, 1930 (IF)

Southport		03.54	53-54	53	-	9
York C.	Tr	06.55	55	18	-	5
Southport	Tr	10.56	56	17	-	1

PRESLAND, Edward R.
Loughton, 27 March, 1943 (FB)

West Ham U.	Jnrs	10.60	64-65	6	0	1
Crystal Palace	Tr	01.67	66-68	61	0	0
Colchester U.	L	10.69	69	5	0	0

PRESLEY, Derek C.
Warminster, 8 March, 1930 (WH)

Bristol C.	Warminster T.	03.50	50-51	9	-	0
Bristol Rov.	Tr	05.52				

PRESSDEE, James S.
Swansea, 19 June, 1933 W Sch (FB)

Swansea C.	Jnrs	08.51	53-55	8	-	0

PRESSMAN, Kevin P.
Fareham, 6 November, 1967 E Sch/E Yth/E u21-1 (G)

Sheffield Wed.	App	11.85	87-91	59	0	0
Stoke C.	L	03.92	91	4	0	0

PRESTON, Richard F.
Nottingham, 10 June, 1967 (F)

Scarborough	Stanton	03.88	87	1	3	0

PRICE, Albert E.
Langwith, 4 April, 1926 (G)

Crewe Alex.	Creswell Colly	12.46	46	5	-	0

PRICE, Allen D.
Gelligaer, 24 March, 1968 W Yth (D)

Cardiff C. (N/C)	Newport Co. (Jnr)	08.85	85	2	0	0

PRICE, Arthur
Rowlands Gill, 12 January, 1921 (WH)

Leeds U.	Consett	05.46	46	6	-	0

PRICE, Brynley
Treorchy, 15 November, 1936 (WH)

Barnsley	Treorchy B.C.	05.55	56-57	2	-	0

PRICE, Cecil A.
Cardiff, 2 December, 1919 (OL)

Cardiff C.		09.48	48	1	-	0
Bradford C.	Tr	06.49	49	7	-	0

PRICE, Christopher J.
Hereford, 30 March, 1960 E Yth (RB)

Hereford U.	App	01.78	76-85	327	3	27
Blackburn Rov.	Tr	07.86	86-87	83	0	11
Aston Villa	Tr	05.88	88-91	109	2	2
Blackburn Rov.	Tr	02.92	91	11	2	3

PRICE, David J.
Caterham, 23 June, 1955 E Sch/E Yth (M)

League Club	Source	Date Signed	Seasons Played	Apps	Subs	Gls
Arsenal	App	08.72	72-80	116	10	16
Peterborough U.	L	01.75	74	6	0	1
Crystal Palace	Tr	03.81	80-81	25	2	2
Leyton Orient (N/C)		03.83	82	10	0	0

PRICE Derek E.
Wellington, 14 February, 1932 (OR)

League Club	Source	Date Signed	Seasons Played	Apps	Subs	Gls
Shrewsbury T.	Donnington	02.53	53-57	125	-	28
Aldershot	Tr	07.58	58-59	4	-	1

PRICE, T. Dudley
Swansea, 17 November, 1931 (IF)

League Club	Source	Date Signed	Seasons Played	Apps	Subs	Gls
Swansea C.	Jnrs	04.50	53-57	33	-	9
Southend U.	Tr	01.58	57-60	91	-	41
Hull C.	Tr	09.60	60-62	76	-	26
Bradford C.	Tr	07.63	63-64	62	-	21

PRICE, Ernest
Horden, 12 May, 1926 (WH)

League Club	Source	Date Signed	Seasons Played	Apps	Subs	Gls
Sunderland		01.45				
Darlington		12.48	48-50	68	-	0
Crystal Palace	Tr	07.51	51-52	34	-	5

PRICE, Gareth
Swindon, 21 February, 1970 (M/FB)

League Club	Source	Date Signed	Seasons Played	Apps	Subs	Gls
Mansfield T.	YT	07.88				
Bury	Tr	07.89	89-90	1	3	0

PRICE, George
Crewe, 2 December, 1929

League Club	Source	Date Signed	Seasons Played	Apps	Subs	Gls
Crewe Alex.		02.54	53	4	-	0

PRICE, John
Middlewich, 28 April, 1960 (M)

League Club	Source	Date Signed	Seasons Played	Apps	Subs	Gls
Rochdale	Nantwich T.	01.78	77-78	10	2	0

PRICE, John
Easington, 25 October, 1943 (W)

League Club	Source	Date Signed	Seasons Played	Apps	Subs	Gls
Burnley	Horden Colly	11.60	63-64	21	-	2
Stockport Co.	Tr	05.65	65-71	241	6	23
Blackburn Rov.	Tr	09.71	71-73	63	14	12
Stockport Co.	Tr	03.74	73-75	51	15	1

PRICE, John
Shotton (Dm), 29 August, 1918 (IF)

League Club	Source	Date Signed	Seasons Played	Apps	Subs	Gls
Hartlepool U.		06.38	38-48	89	-	12
York C.	Tr	12.48	48	2	-	2

PRICE, John
Consett, 14 April, 1947 (W)

League Club	Source	Date Signed	Seasons Played	Apps	Subs	Gls
Leeds U.	App	05.65				
Southport	Tr	07.66	66	16	2	2

PRICE, John D.
Camden, 31 December, 1932 (FB)

League Club	Source	Date Signed	Seasons Played	Apps	Subs	Gls
Tottenham H.	Eastbourne U.	09.54				
Aldershot	Tr	01.57	56-58	85	-	1
Watford	Tr	06.59	59	22	-	0

PRICE, John G.
Aberystwyth, 22 November, 1936 (FB)

League Club	Source	Date Signed	Seasons Played	Apps	Subs	Gls
Liverpool		10.54	55	1	-	0
Aston Villa	Tr	03.57				
Walsall	Tr	07.57				
Shrewsbury T.	Tr	07.58	58-59	9	-	0

PRICE, Kenneth E.
Ellesmere Port, 25 March, 1939 (F)

League Club	Source	Date Signed	Seasons Played	Apps	Subs	Gls
Aston Villa	West Bromborough	08.59				
Tranmere Rov.	Tr	12.60	60	3	-	2
Hartlepool U.	Tr	07.61	61	8	-	3

PRICE, Kenneth G.
Dudley, 26 February, 1955 (F)

League Club	Source	Date Signed	Seasons Played	Apps	Subs	Gls
Southend U.	Dudley T.	05.76	76	1	0	0
Gillingham	Tr	12.76	76-82	247	8	78
Reading	Tr	01.83	82-84	40	3	6

PRICE, Leslie E.
Consett, 26 August, 1930 (OL)

League Club	Source	Date Signed	Seasons Played	Apps	Subs	Gls
Sunderland		08.50				
Gateshead	Tr	07.52	52-53	39	-	12

PRICE, Mark A. R.
Keighley, 15 October, 1973 (M)

League Club	Source	Date Signed	Seasons Played	Apps	Subs	Gls
Scarborough (YT)	YT	07.90	91	2	1	1

PRICE, Neil
Hemel Hempstead, 15 February, 1964 (LB)

League Club	Source	Date Signed	Seasons Played	Apps	Subs	Gls
Watford	App	02.82	83	7	1	0
Plymouth Arg.	L	02.84	83	1	0	0
Blackpool	L	03.85	84	13	0	0
Swansea C.	Tr	07.85	85	1	2	0

PRICE, Paul T.
St Albans, 23 March, 1954 Wu21-1/W-25 (CD)

League Club	Source	Date Signed	Seasons Played	Apps	Subs	Gls
Luton T.	Jnrs	07.71	72-80	206	1	8
Tottenham H.	Tr	06.81	81-83	35	4	0
Swansea C.	Minnesota (USA)	01.85	84-85	61	0	1
Peterborough U.	Tr	08.86	86-87	86	0	0

PRICE, Peter
Yarbolton, 26 February, 1932 (IF)

League Club	Source	Date Signed	Seasons Played	Apps	Subs	Gls
Darlington		01.54	53-54	3	-	0

PRICE, Peter W.
Wrexham, 17 August, 1949 Wu23-4 (F)

League Club	Source	Date Signed	Seasons Played	Apps	Subs	Gls
Liverpool	App	08.66				
Peterborough U.	Tr	07.68	68-71	114	5	62
Portsmouth	Tr	06.72	72-73	13	1	2
Peterborough U.	L	07.74	74	2	0	0
Barnsley	Tr	11.74	74-77	72	7	28

PRICE, Raymond
Durham, 18 May, 1944 (FB)

League Club	Source	Date Signed	Seasons Played	Apps	Subs	Gls
Norwich C.	Jnrs	07.63	63	1	-	0
Colchester U.	Tr	07.64	64-66	15	2	0

PRICE, Raymond J.
Northampton, 30 November, 1948 (CF)

League Club	Source	Date Signed	Seasons Played	Apps	Subs	Gls
Northampton T.	App	12.66	66-67	7	0	0

PRICE, Terence E.
Colchester, 11 October, 1945 (W)

League Club	Source	Date Signed	Seasons Played	Apps	Subs	Gls
Leyton Orient	App	08.63	64-67	86	1	18
Colchester U.	Tr	09.67	67-68	54	2	5

PRICE, Trevor H. R.
Ellesmere Port, 27 December, 1944 (W)

League Club	Source	Date Signed	Seasons Played	Apps	Subs	Gls
Workington		06.64	64	2	-	1

PRICE, Walter B.
Neston, 14 February, 1921

League Club	Source	Date Signed	Seasons Played	Apps	Subs	Gls
Tranmere Rov.		03.41	46	3	-	0
Rochdale	Tr	08.48	48	1	-	0

PRICE, A. J. William
Wellington, 10 April, 1917 (CF)

League Club	Source	Date Signed	Seasons Played	Apps	Subs	Gls
Huddersfield T.	Wrockwardine Wood	10.37	37-47	51	-	23
Reading	Tr	10.47	47-48	15	-	2
Hull C.	Tr	01.49	48	8	-	5
Bradford C.	Tr	11.49	49-51	54	-	28

PRIDAY, Marcus A.
Knighton, 16 October, 1971 W Yth (G)

League Club	Source	Date Signed	Seasons Played	Apps	Subs	Gls
Hereford U.	YT	08.90	89	3	0	0

PRIDAY, Robert H.
South Africa, 29 March, 1925 (W)

League Club	Source	Date Signed	Seasons Played	Apps	Subs	Gls
Liverpool	Cape Town (SA)	12.45	46-48	33	-	6
Blackburn Rov.	Tr	03.49	48-50	44	-	11
Accrington St.	Northwich Vic.	12.52	52	5	-	0
Rochdale	Tr	08.53	53	5	-	1

PRIDDLE, Sean P.
Hammersmith, 14 December, 1965 (M)

League Club	Source	Date Signed	Seasons Played	Apps	Subs	Gls
Wimbledon	App	12.83				
Crewe Alex.	Tr	02.85	84	6	5	0
Exeter C.	Wimbledon (N/C)	07.86	86	18	0	1
Brentford		07.87	87	5	1	0

PRIDDY, Paul J.
Isleworth, 11 July, 1953 (G)

League Club	Source	Date Signed	Seasons Played	Apps	Subs	Gls
Brentford	Walton & Hersham	10.72	72-76	121	0	0
Wimbledon (N/C)	Tooting & Mitcham	10.78	78	1	0	0
Brentford	Hayes	08.81	81	1	0	0

PRIEST, Harold
Clay Cross, 26 October, 1935 (F)

League Club	Source	Date Signed	Seasons Played	Apps	Subs	Gls
Sheffield U.	Clay Cross Wks	02.54	56	2	-	1
Halifax T.	Tr	01.58	57-58	30	-	12

PRIEST, Philip
Warley, 9 September, 1966 E Sch/E Yth (M)

League Club	Source	Date Signed	Seasons Played	Apps	Subs	Gls
Chelsea	App	09.83				
Blackpool	L	12.86	86	1	0	0
Brentford	L	03.87	86	3	2	1
Shrewsbury T.	Tr	07.87	87-89	54	6	3

League Club	Source	Date Signed	Seasons Played	Career Record Apps	Subs	Gls
PRIESTLEY, Derek						
Queensbury, 22 December, 1926						(OL)
Halifax T.		10.50	51-55	145	-	19
Bradford P. A.	Tr	07.56				
PRIESTLEY, Gordon (Gerry)						
Halifax, 2 March, 1931						(W)
Nottingham F.		12.50				
Exeter C.	Tr	06.53	53-54	42	-	6
Grimsby T.	Tr	06.55	55-58	110	-	11
Crystal Palace	Tr	11.58	58-59	28	-	2
Halifax T.	Tr	07.60	60-62	105	-	23
PRIESTLEY, Jason A.						
Leeds, 25 October, 1970						(G)
Carlisle U.	YT	07.89	90	22	0	0
Hartlepool U.	L	12.89	89	16	0	0
Scarborough	L	08.91	91	9	0	0
PRIESTLEY, Maurice						
Bradford, 27 October, 1922						(F)
Bradford P. A.		09.46				
Halifax T.	Tr	01.48	47-48	24	-	8
PRIESTLEY, Royston M.						
Barnsley, 26 November, 1948						(CF)
Barnsley (Am)	Jnrs	08.67	67	1	0	0
PRINCE, Eric						
Ipstones, 11 December, 1924						(IF)
Port Vale		09.44	46	14	-	2
PRINCE, Francis A.						
Penarth, 1 December, 1949 Wu23-4						(M)
Bristol Rov.	App	12.67	67-79	360	2	22
Exeter C.	Tr	07.80	80-81	27	4	2
PRINCE, Harold						
Stoke, 4 December, 1921						(G)
Port Vale		08.44	46-48	5	-	0
PRINDIVILLE, Steven A.						
Harlow, 26 December, 1968						(LB)
Leicester C.	App	12.86	87	0	1	0
Chesterfield	Tr	06.88	88	43	0	1
Mansfield T.	Tr	06.89	89-90	26	2	0
Doncaster Rov. (N/C)	India	02.92	91	16	0	0
PRING, Dennis F.						
Newport, 1 November, 1940						(IF)
Southampton	Newport Y.M.C.A.	02.59	58	4	-	0
PRING, Keith D.						
Newport, 11 March, 1943 W-3						(W)
Newport Co.	Jnrs	11.61	61-64	61	-	3
Rotherham U.	Tr	10.64	64-67	80	2	6
Notts Co.	Tr	12.67	67-68	41	3	2
Southport	Tr	07.69	69-70	48	0	4
PRINGLE, Brian						
Chathill (Nd), 12 March, 1949						(IF)
Hartlepool U. (Am)	Alnwick T.	04.73	72	1	0	0
PRINGLE, William A.						
Liverpool, 24 February, 1932						(IF)
Liverpool	Jnrs	08.49				
Grimsby T.	Tr	05.54	54	2	-	0
PRINS, Jason						
Wisbech, 1 November, 1974						(F)
Carlisle U. (YT)	YT	07.91	91	3	1	0
PRIOR, Kenneth G.						
Ashington, 13 October, 1932						(OL)
Newcastle U.	Sunderland (Am)	03.52	51-52	8	-	3
Millwall	Tr	05.54	54-55	61	-	16
Newcastle U.	Tr	07.56	56	2	-	0
PRIOR, Spencer J.						
Southend, 22 April, 1971						(CD)
Southend U.	YT	05.89	88-91	90	0	3
PRISCOTT, Anthony J.						
Burlesdon, 19 March, 1941						(W)
Portsmouth	Jnrs	07.59	59-61	35	-	6
Aldershot	Tr	08.62	62-65	141	0	43
Bournemouth	Tr	01.66	65-66	60	1	6
Aldershot	Tr	08.67	67-70	126	12	26

League Club	Source	Date Signed	Seasons Played	Career Record Apps	Subs	Gls
PRITCHARD, Alan S.						
Chester, 24 August, 1943						(IF)
Chester C.	Jnrs	10.60	60-63	19	-	6
PRITCHARD, Alfred V.						
Chester, 31 August, 1920						(IF)
Wrexham	Dumbarton	08.46	46-49	36	-	8
PRITCHARD, David M.						
Wolverhampton, 27 May, 1972						(W)
West Bromwich A.	YT	07.90	91	1	4	0
PRITCHARD, Harvey J.						
Meriden, 30 January, 1918						(W)
Coventry C.	Exhall Colly	10.35	36	5	-	2
Crystal Palace	Tr	06.37	37	30	-	6
Manchester C.	Tr	03.38	37-38	22	-	5
Southend U.	Tr	02.47	46-51	72	-	8
PRITCHARD, Howard K.						
Cardiff, 18 October, 1958 W Yth/W-1						(W)
Bristol C.	App	08.76	78-80	31	7	2
Swindon T.	Tr	08.81	81-82	59	6	11
Bristol C.	Tr	08.83	83-85	117	2	22
Gillingham	Tr	08.86	86-87	84	4	20
Walsall	Tr	07.88	88-89	40	5	7
Maidstone U.	Tr	10.89	89-90	29	4	6
PRITCHARD, Joseph H.						
Birkenhead, 4 September, 1943						(M)
Tranmere Rov.	Liverpool (Am)	09.62	62-69	177	3	29
PRITCHARD, Keith						
Wallasey, 20 October, 1919						(F)
New Brighton (Am)	Northern Nomads	07.46	46-47	25	-	8
PRITCHARD, Philip J.						
Stourbridge, 9 January, 1965						(G)
Stoke C.	App	01.82				
Southend U.	L	03.84	83	9	0	0
PRITCHARD, Raymond						
Liverpool, 23 June, 1954						(FB)
Tranmere Rov.	Everton (App)	02.73	72-73	13	1	0
Southport	L	01.74	73	3	0	0
PRITCHARD, Roy T.						
Dawley, 9 May, 1925						(FB)
Wolverhampton W.	Jnrs	05.42	46-54	202	-	0
Aston Villa	Tr	02.55	55-57	3	-	0
Notts Co.	Tr	11.57	57	18	-	0
Port Vale	Tr	08.58	58-59	23	-	0
PRITCHETT, Darrol W.						
Bentley, 22 May, 1933						(FB)
Hull C.	Jnrs	01.51				
Walsall	Tr	05.54	54	1	-	0
PRITCHETT, Keith B.						
Glasgow, 8 November, 1953						(LB)
Wolverhampton W.		04.72				
Doncaster Rov.	Tr	07.73	73	6	0	0
Queens Park R.		03.74	74	4	0	0
Brentford	Tr	07.76	76	11	0	1
Watford	Tr	11.76	76-81	133	7	9
Blackpool	Tr	11.82	82-83	36	1	1
PRITTY, George						
Birmingham, 4 March, 1915						(WH)
Aston Villa	H.B. Metro	05.33	36-37	3	-	0
Nottingham F.	Tr	12.38	38-47	49	-	1
PROBERT, Eric W.						
South Kirkby, 17 February, 1952 E Yth						(M)
Burnley	App	02.69	68-72	62	5	11
Notts Co.	Tr	07.73	73-76	122	0	14
Darlington	Tr	07.78	78-79	20	1	0
PROCTOR, David						
Belfast, 10 October, 1929						(FB)
Blackpool	Portadown	08.49				
Norwich C.	Tr	01.53	52-53	17	-	0
Barrow	Northwich Vic.	10.54	54-58	160	-	2
Wrexham	Tr	08.59	59	2	-	0
PROCTOR, Harold M.						
Ushaw Moor, 10 July, 1912 Died 1984						(WH)
Hartlepool U.	Portsmouth (Am)	07.32	32-33	61	-	14
Norwich C.	Tr	05.34	34-46	108	-	3

League Club	Source	Date Signed	Seasons Played	Apps	Subs	Gls
PROCTOR, Mark G.						
Middlesbrough, 30 January, 1961 E Yth/Eu21-4						(M)
Middlesbrough	App	09.78	78-80	107	2	12
Nottingham F.	Tr	08.81	81-82	60	4	5
Sunderland	Tr	03.83	82-87	115	2	19
Sheffield Wed.	Tr	09.87	87-88	59	0	4
Middlesbrough	Tr	03.89	88-91	95	14	6
PROLZE, Brian J.						
Altrincham, 11 April, 1932						(CF)
Crewe Alex. (Am)	Altrincham	02.54	53	1	-	0
PROPHETT, Colin G.						
Crewe, 8 March, 1947						(CD)
Sheffield Wed.	Crewe Y.C.	06.68	69-72	111	6	7
Norwich C.	Tr	06.73	73	34	1	0
Swindon T.	Tr	09.74	74-77	158	2	10
Chesterfield	Tr	09.78	78-79	35	2	1
Crewe Alex.	Tr	10.79	79-80	79	0	1
PROSSER, Neil A.						
Edmonton, 8 March, 1957						(F)
Bournemouth	Harlow T.	07.80	80	1	1	0
Tranmere Rov. (N/C)		09.82	82	1	1	0
PROUDLER, Arthur						
Kingswinford, 3 October, 1929						(HB)
Aston Villa	Halesowen T.	12.47	54	1	-	0
Crystal Palace	Tr	06.56	56-58	26	-	2
PROUDLOCK, George T.						
Morpeth, 19 September, 1919						(IF)
West Ham U.	Amble Jnrs	11.37	38-47	18	-	5
PROUDLOCK, Paul						
Hartlepool, 25 October, 1965						(W)
Hartlepool U.		09.84	84-85	8	7	0
Middlesbrough		11.86	86-88	2	3	1
Carlisle U.	Tr	03.89	88-91	113	16	18
PROUDLOVE, Andrew G.						
Buxton, 15 January, 1955						(W)
Reading (App)	App	09.70	71	4	1	0
Sheffield Wed.	Buxton	09.75	75	10	5	0
Norwich C.	Tr	02.76	76	0	1	0
Hereford U.	Tr	05.77	77	6	5	0
Port Vale	Tr	11.78	78	5	0	0
PROUTON, Ralph O.						
Southampton, 1 March, 1926						(LH)
Arsenal	Romsey T.	08.49				
Swindon T.	Tr	08.52	52	13	-	0
PROVAN, Andrew M. H. (Drew)						
Greenock, 1 January, 1944						(W)
Barnsley	St Mirren	05.63	63	3	-	0
York C.	Tr	08.64	64-68	159	1	49
Chester C.	Tr	08.68	68-69	77	3	19
Wrexham	Tr	04.70	70-71	49	2	10
Southport	Tr	07.72	72-73	82	1	28
Torquay U.	Tr	08.74	74-76	83	8	14
PROVAN, David						
Glasgow, 11 March, 1941 Su23-1/SF Lge/S-3						(FB)
Crystal Palace	Glasgow Rangers	06.70	70	1	0	0
Plymouth Arg.	Tr	03.71	70-74	128	1	10
PROVERBS, Roy J.						
Wednesbury, 8 July, 1932						(D)
Coventry C.	Stratford T.	05.56	56	10	-	0
Bournemouth	Tr	07.57				
Gillingham	Tr	02.58	57-61	143	-	2
PRUDHAM, C. Edward						
Gateshead, 12 April, 1952						(F)
Sheffield Wed.	Jnrs	07.69	70-74	14	5	2
Carlisle U.	Tr	11.74	74-76	15	2	2
Hartlepool U.	L	09.76	76	3	0	0
Workington	L	02.77	76	15	0	6
Stockport Co.	Tr	07.77	77-79	80	7	22
Bournemouth	Tr	05.80	80	2	2	0
PRUDHOE, Mark						
Washington, 11 November, 1963						(G)
Sunderland	App	09.81	82	7	0	0
Hartlepool U.	L	11.83	83	3	0	0
Birmingham C.	Tr	09.84	84	1	0	0
Walsall	Tr	02.86	85-86	26	0	0

League Club	Source	Date Signed	Seasons Played	Apps	Subs	Gls
Doncaster Rov.	L	12.86	86	5	0	0
Grimsby T.	L	03.87	86	8	0	0
Hartlepool U.	L	08.87	87	13	0	0
Bristol C.	L	11.87	87	3	0	0
Carlisle U.	Tr	12.87	87-88	34	0	0
Darlington	Tr	03.89	88-91	104	0	0
PRYCE, Idris						
Wrexham, 24 February, 1941						(W)
Wrexham	Jnrs	09.59	59	3	-	0
PRYDE, David						
Edinburgh, 10 November, 1913						(WH)
Arsenal	Margate	05.35	38	4	-	0
Torquay U.	Tr	10.46	46-49	64	-	0
PRYDE, Robert I.						
Methil, 25 April, 1913 EF Lge						(CH)
Blackburn Rov.	St Johnstone	05.33	33-48	320	-	11
PRYDE, William						
Falkirk, 20 May, 1919						
Southend U.	Bo'ness	07.47	47-48	17	-	1
PRYER, Terence						
London, 4 December, 1967						(D)
Southend U. (N/C)	YT	10.85	85	2	0	0
PUCKETT, David C.						
Southampton, 29 October, 1960						(F)
Southampton	App	10.78	80-85	51	43	14
Bournemouth	Tr	07.86	86-88	29	6	14
Stoke C.	L	03.88	87	7	0	0
Swansea C.	L	11.88	88	7	1	3
Aldershot	Tr	01.89	88-90	113	0	50
Bournemouth	Tr	03.92	91	1	3	0
PUGH, Daral J.						
Neath, 5 June, 1961 Wu21-2						(W)
Doncaster Rov.	App	12.78	78-82	136	18	15
Huddersfield T.	Tr	09.82	82-84	52	33	7
Rotherham U.	Tr	07.85	85-87	106	6	6
Cambridge U.	L	12.87	87	6	0	1
Torquay U.	Tr	08.88	88-89	29	3	0
PUGH, David						
Blackwood, 22 January, 1947 W Sch/Wu23-2						(M)
Newport Co.	Jnrs	04.64	64-67	73	5	9
Chesterfield	Tr	12.67	67-72	212	1	12
Halifax T.	Tr	08.73	73-75	91	5	3
Rotherham U.	Tr	07.76	76-78	57	1	0
York C.	Tr	11.78	78-80	73	4	2
PUGH, David						
Liverpool, 19 September, 1964						(M)
Chester C.	Runcorn	07.89	89-91	97	10	6
PUGH, Gary						
Wrexham, 10 January, 1967						(W)
Wrexham (N/C)	Jnrs	07.84	84	1	0	0
PUGH, Gary K.						
Ramsgate, 11 February, 1961						(M)
West Ham U.	Jnrs	02.78				
Bournemouth (N/C)	Dover T.	01.81	80	0	3	1
Torquay U. (N/C)	Canterbury C.	11.84	84	4	0	0
PUGH, J. Graham						
Chester, 12 February, 1961 Eu23-1						(M)
Sheffield Wed.	App	02.65	65-71	136	6	7
Huddersfield T.	Tr	05.72	72-74	80	0	1
Chester C.	Tr	02.75	74-76	67	2	3
Barnsley	Tr	10.76	76-79	128	1	8
Scunthorpe U.	Tr	01.80	79-80	54	1	0
PUGH, Kevin J.						
Corbridge, 11 October, 1960						(M)
Newcastle U.	App	10.78	81	0	1	0
Darlington	Gateshead	09.83	83	0	2	0
PUGH, Stephen J.						
Wolverhampton, 1 February, 1965						(FB)
Wolverhampton W.	App	12.82				
Torquay U.	Tr	10.83	83-85	115	5	4
Exeter C.	Tr	08.86	86	23	1	1
PUGSLEY, David G.						
Merthyr Tydfil, 15 August, 1931						(G)
Newport Co. (Am)	Gloucester C.	03.53	52	1	-	0

Dave Puckett (Southampton, Bournemouth, Aldershot & Bournemouth)

League Club	Source	Date Signed	Seasons Played	Apps	Subs	Gls
PULIS, Anthony R.						
Newport, 16 January, 1958						(D/M)
Bristol Rov.	App	09.75	75-80	78	7	3
Bristol Rov.	Hong Kong	06.82	82-83	44	1	2
Newport Co.	Tr	07.84	84-85	75	2	0
Bournemouth	Tr	08.86	86-88	68	6	3
Gillingham	Tr	06.89	89	16	0	0
Bournemouth	Tr	08.90	90-91	12	4	1
PULIS, Raymond J.						
Newport, 21 November, 1964						(F)
Newport Co.	App	11.82	82	0	1	0
PULLAN, Christopher J.						
Durham, 14 December, 1967						(M)
Watford	Jnrs	07.86	86-90	5	7	0
Halifax T.	L	02.89	88	5	0	1
Maidstone U.	Tr	03.91	90	0	1	0
PULLAR, David H.						
Durham, 13 February, 1959						(W/FB)
Portsmouth	App	02.77	75-78	84	9	4
Exeter C.	Tr	07.79	79-82	124	6	22
Crewe Alex.	Tr	07.83	83-86	120	12	7
PULLEN, Walter E.						
Ripley (Sy), 2 August, 1919						(IF)
Leyton Orient	Fulham (Am)	01.46	46-50	117	-	37
PULLEY, Gordon A.						
Stourbridge, 18 September, 1936						(OL)
Millwall	Oswestry T.	09.56	56-57	60	-	9
Gillingham	Tr	05.58	58-65	203	0	46
Peterborough U.	Tr	11.65	65-66	16	1	4
PUNTER, Brian						
Bromsgrove, 16 August, 1935 E Yth						(CF)
Wolverhampton W.	Jnrs	09.53				
Leicester C.	Bromsgrove Rov.	05.58				
Lincoln C.	Tr	11.59	59-63	75	-	21
PUNTON, William						
Morpeth, 18 December, 1957						(G)
Bradford C. (N/C)	Gainsborough Trin.	08.75	75-76	7	0	0
PUNTON, William H.						
Glenkindrie, 4 May, 1934						(OL)
Newcastle U.	Portadown	02.54	53-57	23	-	1
Southend U.	Tr	07.58	58	38	-	6
Norwich C.	Tr	07.59	59-66	219	0	24
Sheffield U.	Tr	11.66	66-67	16	0	1
Scunthorpe U.	Tr	01.68	67-68	45	1	2
PURCELL, Brian P. J.						
Swansea, 23 November, 1938 Died 1969						(FB)
Swansea C.	Tower U.	01.58	59-67	160	2	1
PURCELL, Daniel						
Chesterfield, 15 September, 1948						(F)
Chesterfield (Am)	Jnrs	05.65	65	0	1	0
PURDIE, Bernard C.						
Wrexham, 20 April, 1949						(F)
Wrexham	Jnrs	10.67	68-69	7	3	3
Chester C.	Tr	07.71	71-72	54	9	14
Crewe Alex.	Tr	07.73	73-79	203	10	44
Huddersfield T.	Tr	10.79	79-81	37	9	1
Crewe Alex.	Tr	08.82	82	14	2	0
PURDIE, Ian						
Motherwell, 7 March, 1953 Su23-1						(W)
Wigan Ath.	Motherwell	07.78	78-79	54	1	12
Portsmouth	Tr	11.79	79	4	1	1
PURDIE, James J.						
Berwick, 24 May, 1918						(G)
Millwall	Airdrieonians	02.46	46-47	50	-	0
Southport	Kilmarnock	02.49	48	6	-	0
Aldershot	Tunbridge Wells	10.50	50	16	-	0
PURDIE, Jonathan						
Corby, 22 February, 1967 E Sch						(W)
Arsenal	App	01.85				
Wolverhampton W.	Tr	07.85	85-87	82	7	12
Cambridge U.	L	10.87	87	7	0	2
Oxford U.	Tr	07.88	88	5	6	0
Brentford	Tr	03.89	88	5	1	0
Shrewsbury T.	Tr	06.89	89	9	3	1
PURDON, Edward J. (Ted)						
South Africa, 1 March, 1930						(CF)
Birmingham C.	Marist Bros (SA)	08.50	51-53	64	-	27
Sunderland	Tr	01.54	53-56	90	-	39

League Club	Source	Date Signed	Seasons Played	Apps	Subs	Gls
Workington	Tr	03.57	56-57	33	-	9
Barrow	Tr	03.58	57-58	37	-	11
Bristol Rov.	Bath C.	08.60	60	4	-	1
PURNELL, Philip						
Bristol, 16 September, 1964						(LW)
Bristol Rov.	Mangotsfield	09.85	85-91	130	23	22
Swansea C.	L	12.91	91	5	0	1
PURSELL, Robert W.						
Glasgow, 28 September, 1919						
Port Vale		12.39	46-47	39	-	0
PURVES, Charles R.						
High Spen, 17 February, 1921						(IF)
Charlton Ath.	Spennymoor U.	10.46	46-49	46	-	4
Southampton	Tr	06.51	51-53	30	-	2
PURVIS, Bartholomew						
Gateshead, 15 October, 1921						(LB)
Everton	North Shields	01.46				
Gateshead	Tr	10.46	46	1	-	0
Plymouth Arg.	Tr	06.47				
Notts Co.	Tr	05.48	48-50	25	-	0
Carlisle U.	Tr	08.51	51	4	-	0
PURVIS, William Y. R.						
Berwick, 14 December, 1938						(CF)
Grimsby T.	Berwick R.	08.61	61-62	7	-	2
Doncaster Rov.	Tr	12.62	62	2	-	0
PUTNEY, Trevor A.						
Harold Hill, 9 April, 1960						(M)
Ipswich T.	Brentwood & Warley	09.80	82-85	94	9	8
Norwich C.	Tr	06.86	86-88	76	6	9
Middlesbrough	Tr	07.89	89-90	45	3	1
Watford	Tr	08.91	91	26	2	2
PUTTNAM, David P.						
Leicester, 3 February, 1967						(W)
Leicester C.	Leicester U.	02.89	88-89	4	3	0
Lincoln C.	Tr	01.90	89-91	98	7	13
PYATT, John H.						
Barnet, 26 September, 1948						(IF)
Liverpool	Chesham U.	07.67				
Peterborough U.	Tr	07.68	68	15	1	1
PYE, Frederick						
Stockport, 11 March, 1928						(IF)
Accrington St.	Stalybridge Celtic	04.48	47-48	4	-	0
PYE, Jesse						
Rotherham, 22 December, 1919, Died 1984 E'B'-3/EF Lge/E-1						(CF)
Sheffield U.	Treeton	12.38				
Notts Co.		08.45				
Wolverhampton W.	Tr	05.46	46-51	188	-	90
Luton T.	Tr	07.52	52-54	60	-	32
Derby Co.	Tr	10.54	54-56	61	-	24
PYE, William						
St Helens, 8 November, 1930						(IF)
Stockport Co.		08.49				
Chester C.	Tr	07.52	53-55	28	-	11
PYGALL, David A.						
Watford, 23 January, 1939						(IF)
Watford	Jnrs	01.56	55-60	20	-	2
PYKE, Malcolm						
Eltham, 6 March, 1938						(WH)
West Ham U.	Jnrs	03.55	56-57	17	-	0
Crystal Palace	Tr	06.59	59	2	-	0
PYLE, W. David						
Trowbridge, 12 December, 1936						(CH)
Bristol Rov.	Trowbridge T.	07.55	56-61	139	-	0
Bristol C.	Tr	07.62	62	8	-	0
PYLE, Elijah S.						
Chester-le-Street, 22 September, 1918						(IF)
York C.		11.47	47-48	10	-	3
PYLE, Stephen						
North Shields, 28 September, 1963						(M)
Cambridge U.	App	07.81	80-85	56	13	8
Torquay U.	Tr	12.85	85-86	27	6	5
PYM, Ernest F.						
Torquay, 23 March, 1935						(W)
Torquay U.	St Marychurch	09.57	57-64	283	-	81

Albert Quixall (Sheffield Wednesday, Manchester United, Oldham Athletic, Stockport County & England)
The original "golden boy" of English soccer

League Club	Source	Date Signed	Seasons Played	Apps	Subs	Gls
QUAIRNEY, John						
Girvan, 7 January, 1927						(G)
Rotherham U.	Girvan Jnrs	07.48	48-59	260	-	0
QUAMINA, Mark E.						
Guyana, 25 November, 1969						(M/RB)
Wimbledon	YT	07.88	88	1	0	0
Plymouth Arg.	Tr	07.91	91	4	1	0
QUARTERMAIN, Patrick						
Oxford, 16 April, 1937						(LB)
Oxford U.	Jnrs	09.55	62-66	184	1	0
QUEEN, Gerald						
Glasgow, 15 January, 1945						(F)
Crystal Palace	Kilmarnock	07.69	69-72	101	7	24
Leyton Orient	Tr	09.72	72-76	149	7	34
QUESTED, Leonard W.						
Folkestone, 9 January, 1925 E'B'-1						(WH)
Fulham	Folkestone T.	08.46	46-51	175	-	6
Huddersfield T.	Tr	11.51	51-56	220	-	8
QUIGLEY, Edward						
Bury, 13 July, 1921 E'B'-2						(IF)
Bury	Jnrs	09.41	46-47	42	-	18
Sheffield Wed.	Tr	10.47	47-49	74	-	49
Preston N.E.	Tr	12.49	49-51	52	-	17
Blackburn Rov.	Tr	11.51	51-55	159	-	92
Bury	Tr	08.56	56	10	-	3
QUIGLEY, Gilbert						
Ulverston, 17 February, 1921						(LB)
Barrow	Vickers Sports	12.45	46-48	27	-	0
QUIGLEY, John						
Glasgow, 28 June, 1935						(IF)
Nottingham F.	Ashfield Jnrs	07.57	57-64	236	-	51
Huddersfield T.	Tr	02.65	64-66	66	1	4
Bristol C.	Tr	10.66	66-67	66	0	7
Mansfield T.	Tr	07.68	68-70	105	0	2
QUIGLEY, Michael A.						
Manchester, 2 October, 1970						(M)
Manchester C.	YT	07.89	91	0	5	0
QUIGLEY, Thomas						
Mid Calder, 26 March, 1932						(F)
Portsmouth	Barry T.	12.55				
Queens Park R.	Tr	06.56	56	16	-	7
QUINLAN, Edward M.						
Finsbury Park, 15 August, 1931						(F)
Tottenham H.	Great Yarmouth T.	03.52				
Reading	Tr	06.53	53-55	51	-	12
QUINLAN, Michael						
Barnsley, 4 December, 1941						(CH)
Bristol C.	Doncaster Rov. (Am)	03.59	60	2	-	0
QUINLAN, Philip E.						
Southport, 17 April, 1971 E Yth						(F)
Everton	YT	07.89				
Huddersfield T.	L	03.91	90	7	1	2
QUINN, Albert						
Lanchester, 18 April, 1920						(F)
Sunderland	Esh Winning Jnrs	11.46	47	6	-	2
Darlington	Tr	05.48	48-50	86	-	43
QUINN, Anthony M.						
Liverpool, 24 July, 1959						(F)
Wigan Ath.	Everton (N/C)	01.79	79-80	36	7	14
QUINN, Desmond						
Co Down (NI), 21 March, 1926						(FB)
Blackburn Rov.		08.47	47	1	-	0
Millwall	Tr	06.49	49-54	43	-	0
QUINN, Gordon P.						
Hammersmith, 11 May, 1932						(IF)
Queens Park R.	Eastcote B.C.	08.52	52-56	21	-	1
Plymouth Arg.	Tr	09.56	56-57	14	-	2
QUINN, James						
Kilsyth, 23 November, 1947						(LB)
Sheffield Wed.	Glasgow Celtic	01.75	74-75	46	0	1
QUINN, James M.						
Belfast, 18 November, 1959 NI-29						(F)
Swindon T.	Oswestry T.	12.81	81-83	34	15	10
Blackburn Rov.	Tr	08.84	84-86	58	13	17
Swindon T.	Tr	12.86	86-87	61	3	30
Leicester C.	Tr	06.88	88	13	18	6
Bradford C.	Tr	03.89	88-89	35	0	13
West Ham U.	Tr	12.89	89-90	34	13	19
Bournemouth	Tr	08.91	91	43	0	19
QUINN, John D.						
St Helens, 30 May, 1938						(M)
Sheffield Wed.	Prescot Cables	05.59	59-67	166	7	20
Rotherham U.	Tr	11.67	67-71	114	0	7
Halifax T.	Tr	07.72	72-74	88	4	1
QUINN, Michael						
Liverpool, 2 May, 1962						(F)
Wigan Ath.	Derby Co. (App)	09.79	79-81	56	13	19
Stockport Co.	Tr	07.82	82-83	62	1	39
Oldham Ath.	Tr	01.84	83-85	78	2	34
Portsmouth	Tr	03.86	85-88	115	6	54
Newcastle U.	Tr	07.89	89-91	106	4	57

Mick Quinn (Wigan Athletic, Stockport County, Oldham Athletic, Portsmouth & Newcastle United)

League Club	Source	Date Signed	Seasons Played	Apps	Subs	Gls
QUINN, Niall J.						
Dublin, 6 October, 1966 IR Yth/IRu21-1/IR-31						(F)
Arsenal	Jnrs	11.83	85-89	59	8	14
Manchester C.	Tr	03.90	89-91	82	0	36
QUINN, Noel						
Dublin, 2 November, 1949						(OR)
Oldham Ath.	Manchester U. (Am)	01.67	67	4	0	0
QUINN, Patrick						
Glasgow, 26 April, 1936 SF Lge/S-4						(IF)
Blackpool	Motherwell	11.62	62-63	34	-	9
QUINN, Patrick						
Croy, 18 June, 1918 Died 1979						(IF)
Halifax T.	Ashfield Jnrs	07.46	46	25	-	6
QUINNEY, Henry J.						
Rugby, 15 October, 1922						(FB)
Northampton T.	Wolverhampton W. (Am)	01.43	46	3	-	0
QUINNEY, John						
Rugby, 2 October, 1932						(FB)
Coventry C.	Jnrs	11.49	52	3	-	0
QUINTON, Walter						
Anston, 13 December, 1917						(LB)
Rotherham U.		07.38	38	32	-	0
Birmingham C.	Tr	07.39	47	8	-	0
Brentford	Tr	04.49	48-50	42	-	0
Southend U.	Tr	08.52				
Shrewsbury T.	Tr	10.52	52	3	-	0
QUIRKE, David J.						
Ballina (Ire), 11 January, 1947						(CD)
Gillingham	Bedford T.	07.66	67-73	221	9	0
QUIXALL, Albert						
Sheffield, 9 August, 1933 E Sch/Eu23-1/E'B'-3/EF Lge/E-5						(IF)
Sheffield Wed.	Jnrs	08.50	50-58	241	-	63
Manchester U.	Tr	09.58	58-63	165	-	50
Oldham Ath.	Tr	09.64	64-65	36	0	11
Stockport Co.	Tr	07.66	66	13	0	0
QUOW, Trevor S.						
Peterborough, 28 September, 1960						(M)
Peterborough U.	App	09.78	78-85	191	12	17
Gillingham	Tr	08.86	86-88	64	15	3
Northampton T.	Tr	01.89	88-91	78	10	2

Alf Ramsey (Southampton, Tottenham Hotspur & England)
Knighted for services to football as the manager who steered England to victory in the 1966 World Cup

RABJOHN, Christopher S.
Sheffield, 10 March, 1945 (M)

League Club	Source	Date Signed	Seasons Played	Apps	Subs	Gls
Rotherham U.	Jnrs	07.63	65-67	76	2	4
Doncaster Rov.	Tr	02.68	67-72	137	16	8

RACKHAM, Derek R.
Norwich, 14 June, 1928 (OL)

League Club	Source	Date Signed	Seasons Played	Apps	Subs	Gls
Norwich C.	Norman Y.C.	11.49	51	8	-	2

RACKLEY, Robert W.
Teignmouth, 15 March, 1940 (OL)

League Club	Source	Date Signed	Seasons Played	Apps	Subs	Gls
Exeter C.	Newton Abbot Sports	03.58				
Bristol Rov.	Tr	07.60				
Oldham Ath.	Tr	10.60	60	19	-	7

RACKSTRAW, Charles
Sheffield, 23 April, 1938 (IF)

League Club	Source	Date Signed	Seasons Played	Apps	Subs	Gls
Chesterfield		03.58	58-63	172	-	48
Gillingham	Tr	05.64	64-66	93	1	25
Bradford C.	Tr	01.67	66-69	94	10	27

RADCLIFFE, Mark
Hyde, 26 October, 1919 (G)

League Club	Source	Date Signed	Seasons Played	Apps	Subs	Gls
Oldham Ath.		12.42				
Fulham	Tr	08.46	46-47	11	-	0
Rochdale	Witton A.	11.52	52	1	-	0

RADCLIFFE, Vincent
Manchester, 9 June, 1945 (CH)

League Club	Source	Date Signed	Seasons Played	Apps	Subs	Gls
Portsmouth	App	06.63	64-66	10	0	0
Peterborough U.	Tr	07.67	67	2	0	0
Rochdale	Tr	07.68	68	26	0	1

RADFORD, Arthur (Alf)
Rotherham, 7 October, 1925 (FB)

League Club	Source	Date Signed	Seasons Played	Apps	Subs	Gls
Huddersfield T.		10.44				
Rotherham U.		05.47	47-49	44	-	0
Rochdale	Tr	06.51	51	27	-	0
Swindon T.	Tr	08.52	52	16	-	0

RADFORD, W. Howard
Abercynon, 8 September, 1930 (G)

League Club	Source	Date Signed	Seasons Played	Apps	Subs	Gls
Bristol Rov.	Penrhiwceiber	08.51	51-61	244	-	0

RADFORD, John
Hemsworth, 22 February, 1947 Eu23-4/EF Lge/E-2 (F)

League Club	Source	Date Signed	Seasons Played	Apps	Subs	Gls
Arsenal	App	03.64	63-76	375	4	111
West Ham U.	Tr	12.76	76-77	28	0	0
Blackburn Rov.	Tr	02.78	77-78	36	0	10

RADFORD, Mark
Leicester, 20 December, 1968 (LB/M)

League Club	Source	Date Signed	Seasons Played	Apps	Subs	Gls
Colchester U.	Jnrs	05.87	87-89	47	17	5

RADFORD, Ronald
South Elmsall, 12 July, 1943 (M)

League Club	Source	Date Signed	Seasons Played	Apps	Subs	Gls
Leeds U.	Sheffield Wed. (Am)	10.61				
Newport Co.	Cheltenham T.	07.69	69-70	63	3	7
Hereford U.	Tr	07.71	72-73	61	0	6

RAE, Alexander M.
Glasgow, 23 August, 1946 (M)

League Club	Source	Date Signed	Seasons Played	Apps	Subs	Gls
Bury	East Fife	05.69	69	10	1	0

RAE, Alexander S.
Glasgow, 30 September, 1969 Su21-8 (M)

League Club	Source	Date Signed	Seasons Played	Apps	Subs	Gls
Millwall	Falkirk	08.90	90-91	73	4	21

RAE, Ian J.
Grangemouth, 19 January, 1933 Su23-1/S'B'-1 (FB)

League Club	Source	Date Signed	Seasons Played	Apps	Subs	Gls
Bristol C.	Falkirk	10.57	57	12	-	0

RAE, Joseph
Glasgow, 6 March, 1925

League Club	Source	Date Signed	Seasons Played	Apps	Subs	Gls
Torquay U.	Glasgow Celtic	07.48	48	20	-	4

RAFFELL, Stephen C.
Blyth, 27 April, 1970 (CD)

League Club	Source	Date Signed	Seasons Played	Apps	Subs	Gls
Doncaster Rov.	YT	06.88	87-89	45	9	0

RAFFERTY, Bernard
Manchester, 9 July, 1948 (F)

League Club	Source	Date Signed	Seasons Played	Apps	Subs	Gls
Bradford P.A.		10.69	69	8	5	1

RAFFERTY, James
Manchester, 7 November, 1930 (LH)

League Club	Source	Date Signed	Seasons Played	Apps	Subs	Gls
Manchester C.		12.48				
Bradford P.A.	Tr	06.52	52	2	-	0

RAFFERTY, Kevin B.
Kenya, 9 November, 1960 (G)

League Club	Source	Date Signed	Seasons Played	Apps	Subs	Gls
Crewe Alex.	App	11.78	78-79	22	0	0

RAFFERTY, Patrick T.
Stoke, 28 November, 1925

League Club	Source	Date Signed	Seasons Played	Apps	Subs	Gls
Port Vale		01.49	48-49	5	-	0

RAFFERTY, Ronald
South Shields, 6 May, 1934 (IF)

League Club	Source	Date Signed	Seasons Played	Apps	Subs	Gls
Portsmouth	Wycombe W.	07.54	54-56	23	-	5
Grimsby T.	Tr	12.56	56-62	264	-	145
Hull C.	Tr	07.63	63-64	16	-	6
Aldershot	Tr	07.66	66-68	79	2	10

RAFFERTY, William H.
Glasgow, 30 December, 1950 (F)

League Club	Source	Date Signed	Seasons Played	Apps	Subs	Gls
Coventry C.	Port Glasgow	07.68	69-72	27	0	3
Blackpool	Tr	10.72	72-73	35	1	9
Plymouth Arg.	Tr	03.74	73-75	89	1	35
Carlisle U.	Tr	05.76	76-77	72	0	27
Wolverhampton W.	Tr	03.78	77-79	41	3	6
Newcastle U.	Tr	10.79	79-80	34	5	6
Portsmouth	Tr	12.80	80-82	98	4	40
Bournemouth	Tr	02.84	83-84	58	0	19

RAFTER, Sean
Southend, 20 May, 1957 (G)

League Club	Source	Date Signed	Seasons Played	Apps	Subs	Gls
Southend U.	App	06.75	75-77	23	0	0
Leicester C.	Tr	01.78				
Leyton Orient	Tr	07.79	80	2	0	0

RAGGETT, Brian C.
Barnsley, 11 January, 1949 (D)

League Club	Source	Date Signed	Seasons Played	Apps	Subs	Gls
Barnsley	App	01.67	66-71	56	5	0

RAINE, David
Stone, 28 March, 1937 (D)

League Club	Source	Date Signed	Seasons Played	Apps	Subs	Gls
Port Vale		05.57	56-61	144	-	0
Doncaster Rov.	Tr	07.62	62-64	107	-	2
Colchester U.	Tr	06.65	65-66	44	4	0

RAINE, Robert R.
Chesterfield, 17 November, 1927 (CF)

League Club	Source	Date Signed	Seasons Played	Apps	Subs	Gls
Chesterfield	Newbold Colly	02.49	49	1	-	0
Aldershot	Kidderminster Hrs	02.51	50-53	48	-	20

RAINEY, Hugh
Dumbarton, 7 January, 1935 (HB)

League Club	Source	Date Signed	Seasons Played	Apps	Subs	Gls
Portsmouth	Renton Guild	06.53				
Queens Park R.	Tr	06.55				
Aldershot	Tr	07.57	57	8	-	0

RAINFORD, John W.
Camden, 11 December, 1930 (IF)

League Club	Source	Date Signed	Seasons Played	Apps	Subs	Gls
Crystal Palace	Jnrs	03.49	48-52	64	-	8
Cardiff C.	Tr	05.53	53	3	-	1
Brentford	Tr	10.53	53-61	299	-	42

RAINFORD, Kenneth S.
Saughall Massie, 4 November, 1926 (CF)

League Club	Source	Date Signed	Seasons Played	Apps	Subs	Gls
New Brighton (Am)	New Brighton Baptists	02.48	47	3	-	1

RAJKOVIC, Ante
Yugoslavia, 17 August, 1952 Yugoslav Int (CD)

League Club	Source	Date Signed	Seasons Played	Apps	Subs	Gls
Swansea C.	Sarajevo (Yug)	03.81	80-84	79	1	2

RALSTON, Peter
Fauldhouse, 31 January, 1929 (CH)

League Club	Source	Date Signed	Seasons Played	Apps	Subs	Gls
Accrington St.	Falkirk	08.57	57-58	6	-	0

RALSTON, Walter
Glasgow, 3 October, 1935 (HB)

League Club	Source	Date Signed	Seasons Played	Apps	Subs	Gls
Aldershot (L)	Partick Th.	06.58	58	3	-	0

RAMAGE, Alan
Guisborough, 29 November, 1957 (CD)

League Club	Source	Date Signed	Seasons Played	Apps	Subs	Gls
Middlesbrough	App	12.75	75-79	65	4	2
Derby Co.	Tr	07.80	80-81	32	1	2

RAMAGE, Craig D.
Derby, 30 March, 1970 Eu21-3 (F/M)

League Club	Source	Date Signed	Seasons Played	Apps	Subs	Gls
Derby Co.	YT	07.88	89-91	30	6	4
Wigan Ath.	L	02.89	88	10	0	2

RAMAGE, George M.
Dalkeith, 29 January, 1937 (G)

League Club	Source	Date Signed	Seasons Played	Apps	Subs	Gls
Colchester U.	Third Lanark	08.61	62-63	38	-	0
Leyton Orient	Tr	07.64	64	4	-	0
Luton T.	Tr	11.65	65	7	0	0

RAMMELL, Andrew V.
Nuneaton, 10 February, 1967 (F)

League Club	Source	Date Signed	Seasons Played	Apps	Subs	Gls
Manchester U.	Atherstone U.	09.89				
Barnsley	Tr	09.90	90-91	63	14	20

Andy Rammell (Manchester United & Barnsley)

RAMPLING, Dennis W.
Gainsborough, 25 November, 1923 (OR)

League Club	Source	Date Signed	Seasons Played	Apps	Subs	Gls
Fulham		11.42	47	2	-	0
Bournemouth	Tr	07.48	48	24	-	4
Brentford	Tr	05.49	49	1	-	0

RAMPLING, Edward
Wigan, 17 February, 1948 (OL)

League Club	Source	Date Signed	Seasons Played	Apps	Subs	Gls
Chester C.		03.67	67	2	1	0

RAMSAY, George A.
Sunderland, 24 April, 1923 (OR)

League Club	Source	Date Signed	Seasons Played	Apps	Subs	Gls
Gateshead	Raith Rov.	11.46	46	7	-	1

RAMSBOTTOM, Neil
Blackburn, 25 February, 1946 (G)

League Club	Source	Date Signed	Seasons Played	Apps	Subs	Gls
Bury	Jnrs	07.64	65-70	174	0	0
Blackpool	Tr	02.71	70-71	13	0	0
Crewe Alex.	L	01.72	71	3	0	0
Coventry C.	Tr	03.72	72-74	51	0	0
Sheffield Wed.	Tr	08.75	75	18	0	0
Plymouth Arg.	Tr	07.76	76	39	0	0
Blackburn Rov.	Tr	01.78	78	10	0	0
Sheffield U.	Miami (USA)	10.79	79	2	0	0
Bradford C.	Tr	08.80	80-82	73	0	0
Bournemouth (N/C)	Tr	08.83	83	4	0	0

RAMSCAR, Frederick T.
Salford, 24 January, 1919 (IF)

League Club	Source	Date Signed	Seasons Played	Apps	Subs	Gls
Wolverhampton W.	Stockport Co. (Am)	09.45	46	16	-	1
Queens Park R.	Tr	10.47	47-49	51	-	4
Preston N.E.	Tr	11.49	49-50	19	-	4
Northampton T.	Tr	07.51	51-54	139	-	56
Millwall	Tr	09.54	54	30	-	5

RAMSDEN, Bernard
Sheffield, 8 November, 1917 (FB)

League Club	Source	Date Signed	Seasons Played	Apps	Subs	Gls
Liverpool		03.35	37-47	57	-	0
Sunderland	Tr	03.48	47-48	12	-	0
Hartlepool U.	Tr	01.50	49	13	-	0

RAMSEY, Alfred E. (Sir)
Dagenham, 22 January, 1920 EF Lge/E-32 (FB)

League Club	Source	Date Signed	Seasons Played	Apps	Subs	Gls
Southampton	Portsmouth (Am)	04.44	46-48	90	-	8
Tottenham H.	Tr	05.49	49-54	226	-	24

RAMSEY, Christopher L.
Birmingham, 28 April, 1962 (RB)

League Club	Source	Date Signed	Seasons Played	Apps	Subs	Gls
Brighton & H.A.	Bristol C. (App)	08.80	80-83	30	0	0
Swindon T.	Tr	08.84	84-86	99	1	5
Southend U.	Tr	08.87	87	8	5	0

RAMSEY, Craig J.
Dunfermline, 19 September, 1962 (F)

League Club	Source	Date Signed	Seasons Played	Apps	Subs	Gls
Lincoln C.	App	09.80	79-80	3	2	2

RAMSEY, Donald
Manchester, 27 September, 1928 (OR)

League Club	Source	Date Signed	Seasons Played	Apps	Subs	Gls
Oldham Ath.		11.46	49	2	-	0

RAMSEY, Paul C.
Derry (NI), 3 September, 1962 NI-14 (M/RB)

League Club	Source	Date Signed	Seasons Played	Apps	Subs	Gls
Leicester C.	App	04.80	80-90	278	12	13
Cardiff C.	Tr	08.91	91	39	0	3

RAMSEY, Robert
Sunderland, 24 February, 1935 (FB)

League Club	Source	Date Signed	Seasons Played	Apps	Subs	Gls
Huddersfield T.	Jnrs	01.53				
York C.	Tr	05.58	58-60	75	-	0

RANDALL, Adrian J.
Amesbury, 10 November, 1968 E Yth (M)

League Club	Source	Date Signed	Seasons Played	Apps	Subs	Gls
Bournemouth	App	08.86	85-87	3	0	0
Aldershot	Tr	09.88	88-90	102	5	12
Burnley	Tr	12.91	91	11	7	2

RANDALL, Ernest A. W.
Bognor Regis, 13 January, 1926 (IF)

League Club	Source	Date Signed	Seasons Played	Apps	Subs	Gls
Chelsea	Bognor Regis T.	12.50	51	3	-	1
Crystal Palace	Tr	06.53	53-54	22	-	11

RANDALL, Kevin
Ashton-u-Lyne, 20 August, 1945 (F)

League Club	Source	Date Signed	Seasons Played	Apps	Subs	Gls
Bury	Droylsden	10.65	65	4	0	0
Chesterfield	Tr	07.66	66-71	258	0	96
Notts Co.	Tr	08.72	72-75	119	2	38
Mansfield T.	Tr	11.75	75-77	62	4	20
York C.	Tr	10.77	77-80	96	11	27

RANDALL, Maurice
Manchester, 4 August, 1919 Died 1976 (LB)

League Club	Source	Date Signed	Seasons Played	Apps	Subs	Gls
Crewe Alex.	Droylsden	02.47	46-48	41	-	0

RANDALL, Paul
Liverpool, 16 February, 1958 (F)

League Club	Source	Date Signed	Seasons Played	Apps	Subs	Gls
Bristol Rov.	Frome T.	08.77	77-78	49	3	33
Stoke C.	Tr	12.78	78-80	38	8	7
Bristol Rov.	Tr	01.81	80-85	169	15	61

RANDELL, Colin W.
Neath, 12 December, 1952 W Sch/Wu23-1 (M)

League Club	Source	Date Signed	Seasons Played	Apps	Subs	Gls
Coventry C.	App	05.70				
Plymouth Arg.	Tr	09.73	73-76	137	2	9
Exeter C.	Tr	09.77	77-78	78	0	4
Plymouth Arg.	Tr	07.79	79-81	110	0	8
Blackburn Rov.	Tr	08.82	82-84	72	1	7
Newport Co.	L	03.84	83	15	0	0
Swansea C.	Tr	07.85	85-86	20	2	1

RANDLES, Thomas
Blackpool, 13 October, 1940 (IF)

League Club	Source	Date Signed	Seasons Played	Apps	Subs	Gls
Stoke C.	Ellesmere Port	02.60	61	2	-	0

RANKIN, Andrew G.
Bootle, 11 May, 1944 Eu23-1 (G)

League Club	Source	Date Signed	Seasons Played	Apps	Subs	Gls
Everton	Jnrs	10.61	63-70	85	0	0
Watford	Tr	11.71	71-79	299	0	0
Huddersfield T.	Tr	12.79	79-81	71	0	0

RANKIN, George
Liverpool, 29 January, 1930 E Yth (FB)

League Club	Source	Date Signed	Seasons Played	Apps	Subs	Gls
Everton	Jnrs	08.48	50-55	36	-	0
Southport	Tr	07.56	56-59	144	-	0

RANKIN, James
Gateshead, 8 September, 1927 (OR)

League Club	Source	Date Signed	Seasons Played	Apps	Subs	Gls
Newcastle U.	Jnrs	09.44				
Brighton & H.A.		08.49				
Grimsby T.	Tr	01.50	49-50	5	-	1

RANKINE, S. Mark
Doncaster, 30 September, 1969 (M)

League Club	Source	Date Signed	Seasons Played	Apps	Subs	Gls
Doncaster Rov.	YT	06.88	87-91	160	4	20
Wolverhampton W.	Tr	01.92	91	10	5	1

RANKMORE, Frank E. J.
Cardiff, 21 July, 1939 Wu23-2/W-1 (CH)

League Club	Source	Date Signed	Seasons Played	Apps	Subs	Gls
Cardiff C.	Cardiff Corries	12.57	61-62	67	-	0
Peterborough U.	Tr	08.63	63-67	201	0	7
Northampton T.	Tr	08.68	68-70	103	0	14

RANSHAW, John W.
Lincoln, 19 December, 1916 (OL)

League Club	Source	Date Signed	Seasons Played	Apps	Subs	Gls
Lincoln C.	Grantham	03.46	46	3	-	0

RANSHAW, Richard W. G.
Sleaford, 17 April, 1970 (F)

League Club	Source	Date Signed	Seasons Played	Apps	Subs	Gls
Lincoln C. (N/C)	YT	08.88	88	0	1	0

RANSON, Raymond
St Helens, 12 June, 1960 E Yth/Eu21-10 (RB)

League Club	Source	Date Signed	Seasons Played	Apps	Subs	Gls
Manchester C.	App	06.77	78-83	181	2	1
Birmingham C.	Tr	11.84	84-88	136	1	0
Newcastle U.	Tr	12.88	88-91	75	5	1

RANTANEN, Jari J.
Finland, 31 December, 1961 Finnish Int (F)

League Club	Source	Date Signed	Seasons Played	Apps	Subs	Gls
Leicester C.	Gothenburg (Swe)	09.87	87	10	3	3

RAPER, Kenneth
Consett, 15 May, 1956 (M)

League Club	Source	Date Signed	Seasons Played	Apps	Subs	Gls
Stoke C.	App	06.73				
Torquay U.	Tr	07.77	77-78	51	1	8

RAPLEY, Peter D.
Portsmouth, 24 October, 1936 (OR)

League Club	Source	Date Signed	Seasons Played	Apps	Subs	Gls
Exeter C.	Portsmouth (Am)	06.57	57-59	10	-	4

RATCLIFFE, J. Barrie
Blackburn, 21 September, 1941 (OL)

League Club	Source	Date Signed	Seasons Played	Apps	Subs	Gls
Blackburn Rov.	Jnrs	09.58	59-63	36	-	4
Scunthorpe U.	Tr	05.64	64	26	-	7
Rochdale	Tr	07.65	65	12	0	1

RATCLIFFE, Beaumont
Bolton-on-Dearne, 24 April, 1909 (CH)

League Club	Source	Date Signed	Seasons Played	Apps	Subs	Gls
New Brighton	Bolton A.	10.31	31-34	131	-	4
Oldham Ath.	Le Havre (Fr)	06.35	35-38	156	-	1
Reading	Tr	05.46	46-47	32	-	0
Watford	Tr	05.48	48	24	-	0

RATCLIFFE, David
Dewsbury, 9 March, 1957 (CD)

League Club	Source	Date Signed	Seasons Played	Apps	Subs	Gls
Bradford C.	App	03.75	74-77	17	11	1

RATCLIFFE, Donald
Newcastle-u-Lyme, 13 November, 1934 (W)

League Club	Source	Date Signed	Seasons Played	Apps	Subs	Gls
Stoke C.		05.53	54-63	237	-	15
Middlesbrough	Tr	09.63	63-65	65	0	3
Darlington	Tr	02.66	65-67	84	1	12
Crewe Alex.	Tr	01.68	67-68	45	3	2

RATCLIFFE, Kevin
Deeside, 12 November, 1960 W Sch/Wu21-2/W-58 (CD)

League Club	Source	Date Signed	Seasons Played	Apps	Subs	Gls
Everton	App	11.78	79-91	356	3	2

RATCLIFFE, Patrick C. (Paddy)
Dublin, 31 December, 1919 (RB)

League Club	Source	Date Signed	Seasons Played	Apps	Subs	Gls
Notts Co.	Bohemians	11.45				
Wolverhampton W.	Tr	06.46	46	2	-	0
Plymouth Arg.	Tr	06.47	47-55	236	-	10

RATCLIFFE, Raymond
St Helens, 3 November, 1929

League Club	Source	Date Signed	Seasons Played	Apps	Subs	Gls
Stockport Co.		03.49	48	1	-	0

RATCLIFFE, Simon
Urmston, 8 February, 1967 E Sch/E Yth (M/RB)

League Club	Source	Date Signed	Seasons Played	Apps	Subs	Gls
Manchester U.	App	02.85				
Norwich C.	Tr	06.87	87	6	3	0
Brentford	Tr	01.89	88-91	107	9	7

Kevin Ratcliffe (Everton & Wales)

RATHBONE, Graham C.
Newport, 22 August, 1942 (CD)

League Club	Source	Date Signed	Seasons Played	Apps	Subs	Gls
Newport Co.	Merthyr Tydfil	03.61	60-66	191	0	6
Grimsby T.	Tr	11.66	66-72	232	1	11
Cambridge U.	Tr	02.73	72-73	35	1	0

RATHBONE, Michael J.
Birmingham, 6 November, 1958 E Yth (LB)

League Club	Source	Date Signed	Seasons Played	Apps	Subs	Gls
Birmingham C.	App	11.76	76-78	17	3	0
Blackburn Rov.	Tr	03.79	78-86	270	3	2
Preston N.E.	Tr	07.87	87-90	82	9	4

RATTRAY, Peter K.
Bannockburn, 7 November, 1925 (IF)

League Club	Source	Date Signed	Seasons Played	Apps	Subs	Gls
Plymouth Arg.	Dundee	09.50	50-51	54	-	22
Norwich C.	Tr	06.52	52-53	24	-	5

RAVEN, Paul D.
Salisbury, 28 July, 1970 E Sch (CD)

League Club	Source	Date Signed	Seasons Played	Apps	Subs	Gls
Doncaster Rov.	Jnrs	06.88	87-88	52	0	4
West Bromwich A.	Tr	03.89	88-91	27	3	1
Doncaster Rov.	L	11.91	91	7	0	0

RAWCLIFFE, Frank
Blackburn, 10 December, 1921 (CF)

League Club	Source	Date Signed	Seasons Played	Apps	Subs	Gls
Notts Co.		02.43				
Newport Co.	Tr	06.46	46	37	-	14
Swansea C.	Tr	05.47	47	25	-	17
Aldershot	Tr	07.48	48	35	-	14

RAWCLIFFE, Peter
Cleethorpes, 8 December, 1963 (F)

League Club	Source	Date Signed	Seasons Played	Apps	Subs	Gls
Grimsby T.	Louth U.	09.86	86-87	9	13	2
Lincoln C. (N/C)	Holbeach U.	08.90	90	0	1	0

RAWES, Herbert
Frizington, 23 November, 1932 (OR)

League Club	Source	Date Signed	Seasons Played	Apps	Subs	Gls
Carlisle U.		09.53	53-54	11	-	1

RAWLINGS, Charles J.
Coleshill, 4 November, 1932 (WH)

League Club	Source	Date Signed	Seasons Played	Apps	Subs	Gls
West Bromwich A.	Erdington A.	03.50				
Walsall	Tr	06.56	56-62	201	-	5
Port Vale	Tr	07.63	63-64	31	-	2

RAWLINGS, David
Wrexham, 12 December, 1943 (OL)

League Club	Source	Date Signed	Seasons Played	Apps	Subs	Gls
Wrexham (Am)		11.65	65	1	0	0

RAWLINGS, James S.D.
Wombwell, 5 May, 1913 Died 1956 (OR)

League Club	Source	Date Signed	Seasons Played	Apps	Subs	Gls
Preston N.E.		03.32	33	12	-	1
Huddersfield T.	Tr	03.34	33-34	11	-	2
West Bromwich A.	Tr	03.35	34-35	10	-	1
Northampton T.	Tr	06.36	36-37	51	-	19
Millwall	Tr	12.37	37-38	53	-	27
Everton	Tr	11.45				
Plymouth Arg.	Tr	05.46	46-47	56	-	20

RAWLINGSON, John
Wallsend, 7 April, 1944 (CH)

League Club	Source	Date Signed	Seasons Played	Apps	Subs	Gls
Bury	Corinthian Jnrs	07.62	64	2	-	0
Barrow	Tr	07.65	65	19	0	2

RAWSON, Colin
Shirebrook, 12 November, 1926 (WH)

League Club	Source	Date Signed	Seasons Played	Apps	Subs	Gls
Nottingham F.	Welbeck Colly	09.44	46	1	-	0
Rotherham U.	Peterborough U.	07.48	49-52	113	-	12
Sheffield U.	Tr	03.53	53-55	70	-	1
Millwall	Tr	10.55	55-58	159	-	5
Torquay U.	Tr	07.59	59-61	86	-	2

RAWSON, J. Kenneth
Nottingham, 31 March, 1921 (CH)

League Club	Source	Date Signed	Seasons Played	Apps	Subs	Gls
Nottingham F.		12.46	47-49	6	-	0

RAWSON, Kenneth
Ripley, 18 September, 1931 (CH)

League Club	Source	Date Signed	Seasons Played	Apps	Subs	Gls
Notts Co.		05.53	54-60	34	-	0

RAY, Cecil H.
West Grinstead, 25 October, 1911 (F)

League Club	Source	Date Signed	Seasons Played	Apps	Subs	Gls
Aldershot	Lewes U.	01.36	35-46	89	-	38

RAY, John D.
Wolverhampton, 7 November, 1946 (WH)

League Club	Source	Date Signed	Seasons Played	Apps	Subs	Gls
Shrewsbury T.		01.65	65	7	0	0

RAY, John W.
Newmarket, 21 November, 1968 (CD)

League Club	Source	Date Signed	Seasons Played	Apps	Subs	Gls
Colchester U.	YT	10.87	87	0	1	0

RAY, Philip
Wallsend, 21 November, 1964 (FB)

League Club	Source	Date Signed	Seasons Played	Apps	Subs	Gls
Burnley	App	11.82	82	1	0	0
Hartlepool U.	L	10.83	83	5	0	1

RAYBOULD, Eric
Manchester, 8 December, 1940 (WH)

League Club	Source	Date Signed	Seasons Played	Apps	Subs	Gls
Chester C.		07.60	60-61	10	-	0

RAYBOULD, Philip E.
Caerphilly, 26 May, 1948 W Sch/W Amat (M)

League Club	Source	Date Signed	Seasons Played	Apps	Subs	Gls
Swansea C.	Bridgend T.	07.67	67-68	10	2	4
Newport Co.	Tr	09.69	69	5	1	1

RAYMENT, Joseph W.
Hartlepool, 25 September, 1934 (OR)

League Club	Source	Date Signed	Seasons Played	Apps	Subs	Gls
Middlesbrough	Jnrs	10.51	52-54	24	-	4
Hartlepool U.	Tr	07.55	55-57	63	-	17
Darlington	Tr	07.58	58-64	173	-	28

RAYMENT, Patrick J.
Peterborough, 11 April, 1965 (W/FB)

League Club	Source	Date Signed	Seasons Played	Apps	Subs	Gls
Peterborough U.	App	04.83	81-84	24	6	3
Cambridge U.	Tr	10.84	84-86	42	6	2

RAYNER, A. Edward
Salford, 18 August, 1932 (WH)

League Club	Source	Date Signed	Seasons Played	Apps	Subs	Gls
Stoke C.	Northwich Vic.	05.55	56-59	4	-	0

RAYNER, Edward
Hemsworth, 28 September, 1916 Died 1988 (G)

League Club	Source	Date Signed	Seasons Played	Apps	Subs	Gls
Halifax T.	Scarborough	10.40	46-50	137	-	0

RAYNER, James P.
Cornsay (Dm), 31 March, 1935 (WH)

League Club	Source	Date Signed	Seasons Played	Apps	Subs	Gls
Grimsby T.	Jnrs	05.52	52-53	12	-	3
Bury	Tr	05.54				
Hartlepool U.	Tr	11.54				
Bury	Tr	06.55				
Barrow	Tr	09.55	55	11	-	1
Peterborough U.	Grantham	07.58	60-62	119	-	12
Notts Co.	Grantham	09.64	64	32	-	13

RAYNER, Warren A.
Bradford, 24 April, 1957 (W)

League Club	Source	Date Signed	Seasons Played	Apps	Subs	Gls
Bradford C.	App	04.75	74-76	13	4	0

RAYNES, John
Sheffield, 4 November, 1928 (OL)

League Club	Source	Date Signed	Seasons Played	Apps	Subs	Gls
Sheffield U.	Jnrs	11.45				
Rotherham U.		03.49	49	5	-	1
Northampton T.	Worksop T.	07.51				

RAYNES, William
Sheffield, 30 October, 1964 (LW)

League Club	Source	Date Signed	Seasons Played	Apps	Subs	Gls
Rotherham U.	Heanor T.	09.83	83-84	17	3	2
Stockport Co.	L	01.85	84	2	0	0
Wolverhampton W.	Tr	12.85	85	6	1	0

RAYNOR, Paul E.
Chester, 3 September, 1957 (FB)

League Club	Source	Date Signed	Seasons Played	Apps	Subs	Gls
Chester C.	App	09.75	76-81	196	1	9
Chester C. (N/C)	Oswestry T.	08.83	83	3	0	0

RAYNOR, Paul J.
Nottingham, 29 April, 1966 (F/W)

League Club	Source	Date Signed	Seasons Played	Apps	Subs	Gls
Nottingham F.	App	04.84	84	3	0	0
Bristol Rov.	L	03.85	84	7	1	0
Huddersfield T.	Tr	08.85	85-86	38	12	9
Swansea C.	Tr	03.87	86-91	170	21	27
Wrexham	L	10.88	88	6	0	0
Cambridge U.	Tr	03.92	91	5	3	0

RAYNOR, Robert
Nottingham, 30 August, 1940 (G)

League Club	Source	Date Signed	Seasons Played	Apps	Subs	Gls
Nottingham F.		05.64				
Halifax T.	Tr	08.65	65-66	17	0	0

REA, Kenneth W.
Liverpool, 17 February, 1935 (WH)

League Club	Source	Date Signed	Seasons Played	Apps	Subs	Gls
Everton	Jnrs	06.52	56-58	46	-	0

REA, Wallace
Uddingston, 21 August, 1935 (W)

League Club	Source	Date Signed	Seasons Played	Apps	Subs	Gls
Bradford C.	Motherwell	07.59	59	11	-	2

READ, J. Anthony
Haydock, 5 July, 1942 (G/F)

League Club	Source	Date Signed	Seasons Played	Apps	Subs	Gls
Sheffield Wed.	Wolverhampton W. (Am)	01.60				
Peterborough U.	Tr	05.64	64	2	-	0
Luton T.	Tr	03.65	65-71	195	3	12

READ, David P.
West Bromwich, 15 January, 1941 (W)

League Club	Source	Date Signed	Seasons Played	Apps	Subs	Gls
Wolverhampton W.	Jnrs	10.58				
Chester C.	Tr	10.62	62-66	68	4	6

READER, Peter
East Ham, 8 March, 1941 E Yth (G)

League Club	Source	Date Signed	Seasons Played	Apps	Subs	Gls
West Ham U.	Jnrs	06.59				
Millwall	Tr	06.61	61	1	-	0

READFERN, T. Edward
Crook, 9 July, 1944 (CF)

League Club	Source	Date Signed	Seasons Played	Apps	Subs	Gls
West Bromwich A.	Jnrs	08.61	63	4	-	0

READY, Karl
Neath, 14 August, 1972 W Sch/Wu21-1 (FB)

League Club	Source	Date Signed	Seasons Played	Apps	Subs	Gls
Queens Park R.	YT	08.90	91	1	0	0

REAGAN, C. Martin
York, 12 May, 1924 (W)

League Club	Source	Date Signed	Seasons Played	Apps	Subs	Gls
York C.		09.46	46	1	-	0
Hull C.	Tr	04.47	46-47	18	-	1
Middlesbrough	Tr	02.48	47-50	24	-	4
Shrewsbury T.	Tr	08.51	51-52	58	-	9
Portsmouth	Tr	01.53	52	5	-	0
Norwich C.	Tr	06.54	54-55	34	-	4

REANEY, Paul
Fulham, 22 October, 1944 Eu23-5/EF Lge/E-3 (RB)

League Club	Source	Date Signed	Seasons Played	Apps	Subs	Gls
Leeds U.	Jnrs	10.61	62-77	550	8	6
Bradford C.	Tr	06.78	78-79	37	1	0

REAY, Edwin P.
Tynemouth, 5 August, 1914

League Club	Source	Date Signed	Seasons Played	Apps	Subs	Gls
Queens Park R.		11.37	37-49	34	-	0

RECK, Sean M.
Oxford, 5 May, 1967 (M)

League Club	Source	Date Signed	Seasons Played	Apps	Subs	Gls
Oxford U.	App	04.85	86-88	11	3	0
Newport Co.	L	08.85	85	15	0	0
Reading	L	03.86	85	1	0	0
Wrexham	Tr	07.89	89-90	41	4	2

REDDIE, Thomas M.
Stirling, 5 October, 1926 (HB)

League Club	Source	Date Signed	Seasons Played	Apps	Subs	Gls
Aldershot	Falkirk	07.51	51-56	97	-	1

REDDING, Thomas R.
Grimsby, 17 March, 1932 (D)

League Club	Source	Date Signed	Seasons Played	Apps	Subs	Gls
Grimsby T.	Brigg T.	07.54	54-56	4	-	0

REDDISH, Shane
Bolsover, 5 May, 1971 (FB)

League Club	Source	Date Signed	Seasons Played	Apps	Subs	Gls
Mansfield T.	YT	07.89				
Doncaster Rov.	Tr	02.90	89-91	24	5	2

REDFEARN, Brian
Bradford, 20 February, 1935 (OL)

League Club	Source	Date Signed	Seasons Played	Apps	Subs	Gls
Bradford P.A.	Jnrs	08.52	52-57	130	-	32
Blackburn Rov.	Tr	12.57				
Darlington	Tr	06.59	59-60	49	-	15
Halifax T.	Tr	06.61	61-62	67	-	10
Bradford C.	Tr	07.63	63	7	-	2

REDFEARN, Neil D.
Dewsbury, 20 June, 1965 (W)

League Club	Source	Date Signed	Seasons Played	Apps	Subs	Gls
Bolton W.	Nottingham F. (App)	06.82	82-83	35	0	1
Lincoln C.	Tr	03.84	83-85	96	4	13
Doncaster Rov.	Tr	08.86	86	46	0	14
Crystal Palace	Tr	07.87	87-88	57	0	10
Watford	Tr	11.88	88-89	22	2	3
Oldham Ath.	Tr	01.90	89-90	56	6	16
Barnsley	Tr	09.91	91	35	1	4

REDFERN, David
Sheffield, 8 November, 1962 (G)

League Club	Source	Date Signed	Seasons Played	Apps	Subs	Gls
Sheffield Wed.	Jnrs	06.81				
Rochdale	Tr	03.85	84-86	87	0	0
Wigan Ath.	L	10.87	87	3	0	0
Stockport Co.	Gainsborough Trin.	07.89	89-91	42	0	0

REDFERN, Edward
Liverpool, 24 June, 1920 (WH)

League Club	Source	Date Signed	Seasons Played	Apps	Subs	Gls
New Brighton	Unity B.C.	01.48	47-49	22	-	0

REDFERN, Frederick
Hyde, 28 September, 1914 (RB)

League Club	Source	Date Signed	Seasons Played	Apps	Subs	Gls
Stockport Co.	Hyde U.	08.45	46-47	36	-	0

REDFERN, James
Kirkby, 1 August, 1952 (W)

League Club	Source	Date Signed	Seasons Played	Apps	Subs	Gls
Bolton W.	App	08.69	69-72	19	5	2
Chester C.	Tr	08.73	73-76	98	8	15

REDFERN, Robert
Crook, 3 March, 1918 (OR)

League Club	Source	Date Signed	Seasons Played	Apps	Subs	Gls
Wolverhampton W.		05.36				
Bournemouth	Cradley Heath	02.37	36-46	89	-	5
Brighton & H.A.	Tr	08.47	47	5	-	1

REDFORD, Ian P.
Perth, 5 April, 1960 S Yth/Su21-6 (W)

League Club	Source	Date Signed	Seasons Played	Apps	Subs	Gls
Ipswich T.	Dundee U.	11.88	88-90	59	9	8

REDHEAD, William S.
Newcastle, 10 October, 1935 (HB)

League Club	Source	Date Signed	Seasons Played	Apps	Subs	Gls
Newcastle U.	Fatfield Jnrs	08.54	56	1	-	0
Gateshead	Tr	08.59	59	19	-	0

REDKNAPP, Harold J.
Poplar, 2 March, 1947 E Yth (W)

League Club	Source	Date Signed	Seasons Played	Apps	Subs	Gls
West Ham U.	App	03.64	65-71	146	3	7
Bournemouth	Tr	08.72	72-75	96	5	5
Brentford	Tr	09.76	76	1	0	0
Bournemouth (N/C)	(Team Coach)	09.82	82	1	0	0

REDKNAPP, Jamie F.
Barton-on-Sea, 25 June, 1973 E Sch/E Yth (M)

League Club	Source	Date Signed	Seasons Played	Apps	Subs	Gls
Bournemouth	YT	06.90	89-90	6	7	0
Liverpool	Tr	01.91	91	5	1	1

REDMAN, William
Manchester, 29 January, 1928 (FB)

League Club	Source	Date Signed	Seasons Played	Apps	Subs	Gls
Manchester U.	Jnrs	11.46	50-53	36	-	0
Bury	Tr	06.54	54-55	37	-	1

REDMOND, Harold
Manchester, 24 March, 1933 (FB)

League Club	Source	Date Signed	Seasons Played	Apps	Subs	Gls
Crystal Palace	Tavistock	04.57	57	2	-	0
Millwall	Tr	05.58	58-60	54	-	0

REDMOND, Stephen
Liverpool, 2 November, 1967 E Yth/Eu21-14 (CD)

League Club	Source	Date Signed	Seasons Played	Apps	Subs	Gls
Manchester C.	App	12.84	85-91	231	4	7

REDROBE, W. Eric
Wigan, 23 August, 1944 E Yth (F)

League Club	Source	Date Signed	Seasons Played	Apps	Subs	Gls
Bolton W.	Jnrs	02.62	63-65	4	0	1
Southport	Tr	08.66	66-72	186	6	55
Hereford U.	Tr	10.72	72-77	75	12	17

REDSHAW, Raymond
Salford, 23 December, 1958 (F)

League Club	Source	Date Signed	Seasons Played	Apps	Subs	Gls
Wigan Ath.	Horwich R.M.I.	07.84	84	2	2	0

REDWOOD, Barry K.
Torquay, 11 September, 1946 (CF)

League Club	Source	Date Signed	Seasons Played	Apps	Subs	Gls
Exeter C.	App	09.64	64	1	-	0

REDWOOD, Toby R. B.
Newton Abbot, 7 October, 1973 (FB)

League Club	Source	Date Signed	Seasons Played	Apps	Subs	Gls
Exeter C.	YT	06.92	91	1	0	0

REECE, Andrew J.
Shrewsbury, 5 September, 1962 (M)

League Club	Source	Date Signed	Seasons Played	Apps	Subs	Gls
Bristol Rov.	Dudley T.	08.87	87-91	208	5	15

REECE, Gilbert I.
Cardiff, 2 July, 1942 W Sch/W-29 (W)

League Club	Source	Date Signed	Seasons Played	Apps	Subs	Gls
Cardiff C.	Jnrs	05.61				
Newport Co.	Pembroke Bor.	06.63	63-64	32	-	9
Sheffield U.	Tr	04.65	65-72	197	13	58
Cardiff C.	Tr	09.72	72-75	94	6	23
Swansea C.	Tr	07.76	76	0	2	0

League Club	Source	Date Signed	Seasons Played	Apps	Subs	Gls
REECE, Paul J.						
Nottingham, 16 July, 1968						(G)
Stoke C.	App	07.86	86	2	0	0
Grimsby T.	Kettering T.	07.88	88-91	54	0	0
REECE, Thomas S.						
Wolverhampton, 17 May, 1919						(LH)
Wolverhampton W.		07.37				
Crystal Palace	Tr	09.38	38-47	76	-	5
REED, Adam M.						
Bishop Auckland, 18 February, 1975						(M)
Darlington (YT)	YT	07.91	91	0	1	0
REED, Barry R. F.						
Huntingdon, 24 November, 1937						(FB)
Leicester C.	St Neots	03.55				
Luton T.	Tr	05.61	61	1	-	0
REED, Frank N.						
Seaham, 12 October, 1933 Died 1975						(G)
Charlton Ath.	Murton Colly	08.54	55-62	29	-	0
REED, George						
Normanton, 16 July, 1938						(CH)
Halifax T.		08.61	62	2	-	0
REED, Graham						
Kings Lynn, 6 February, 1938						(WH)
Sunderland	Kings Lynn	02.55	57	5	-	0
REED, Graham						
Doncaster, 24 June, 1961						(RB)
Barnsley	App	06.79	78-79	3	0	0
Northampton T.	Frickley Colly	06.85	85-88	105	7	2
REED, Hugh D.						
Dumbarton, 23 August, 1950						(W)
West Bromwich A.	Jnrs	08.67	68-70	5	3	2
Plymouth Arg.	Tr	11.71	71-73	44	12	9
Brentford	L	10.73	73	3	1	0

Steve Redmond (Manchester City)

League Club	Source	Date Signed	Seasons Played	Apps	Subs	Gls
Crewe Alex.	Tr	07.74	74-75	38	9	9
Hartlepool U.	Huddersfield T. (N/C)	10.76	76	6	0	1
REED, John P.						
Rotherham, 27 August, 1972						(W)
Sheffield U.	YT	07.90	91	0	1	0
Scarborough	L	01.91	90	14	0	5
Scarborough	L	09.91	91	5	1	0
REED, Kevin D.						
Leicester, 22 September, 1960						(W)
Leicester C.	App	05.78	78	0	1	0
REED, Stephen E.						
Doncaster, 6 January, 1956						(D)
Doncaster Rov.	App	01.74	72-78	137	3	2
REED, Thomas R.						
Haltwhistle, 4 October, 1934						(WH)
Newport Co.	Army	01.54	53-54	2	-	0
REED, William G.						
Rhondda, 25 January, 1928 W Sch/W Amat/W-2						(OR)
Cardiff C.	Rhondda T.	07.47				
Brighton & H.A.	Tr	08.48	48-52	129	-	39
Ipswich T.	Tr	07.53	53-57	155	-	43
Swansea C.	Tr	02.58	57	8	-	0
REES, Anthony A.						
Merthyr Tydfil, 1 August, 1964 W Sch/W Yth/Wu21-1/W-1						(F)
Aston Villa	App	08.82				
Birmingham C.	Tr	07.83	83-87	75	20	12
Peterborough U.	L	10.85	85	5	0	2
Shrewsbury T.	L	03.86	85	1	1	0
Barnsley	Tr	03.88	87-88	27	4	3
Grimsby T.	Tr	08.89	89-91	93	1	28
REES, Barry G.						
Rhyl, 4 February, 1944 Died 1965						(WH)
Everton	Jnrs	09.61	63-64	4	-	2
Brighton & H.A.	Tr	01.65	64	12	-	1
REES, R. Clive						
Nantymoel, 7 September, 1937						(G)
Newport Co. (Am)	Caerau	03.63	62	4	-	0
REES, Derek W.						
Swansea, 18 February, 1934						(OL)
Portsmouth		05.54	54-56	46	-	15
Ipswich T.	Tr	05.57	57-60	90	-	29
REES, Douglas C.						
Neath, 12 February, 1923 W Amat						(CH)
Ipswich T.	Troedyrhiw	02.49	48-58	356	-	1
REES, Graham J.						
Pontypridd, 28 August, 1937						(W)
Exeter C.	Pontypridd Y.C.	09.54	54-65	345	0	85
REES, Ian D.						
Crosshands, 21 September, 1943						(IF)
Swansea C.	Ammanford	12.61	64	1	0	0
Swansea C.		08.68	68	1	2	0
REES, Jason M.						
Aberdare, 22 December, 1969 W Yth/Wu21-3/W'B'/W-1						(W)
Luton T.	YT	06.88	89-91	22	18	0
REES, John F.						
Bedlinog, 3 February, 1933 W Amat						(CF)
Newport Co. (Am)	Troedyrhiw	08.52	52	2	-	0
REES, Maldwyn J. F.						
Neath, 21 April, 1924						
Norwich C.		05.47				
Brighton & H.A.		09.49	49	2	-	0
Scunthorpe U.	Tr	07.50	50	18	-	1
REES, Mark						
Smethwick, 13 October, 1961 E Sch						(W)
Walsall	App	08.79	78-89	188	49	36
Rochdale	L	10.86	86	2	1	0

REES, Melvyn J.
Cardiff, 25 January, 1967 W Yth (G)

League Club	Source	Date Signed	Seasons Played	Apps	Subs	Gls
Cardiff C.	YT	09.84	84-86	31	0	0
Watford	Tr	07.87	87	3	0	0
Crewe Alex.	L	08.89	89	6	0	0
Leyton Orient	L	01.90	89	9	0	0
West Bromwich A.	Tr	09.90	90	18	0	0
Sheffield U.	Tr	03.92	91	8	0	0

REES, Nigel R.
Bridgend, 11 July, 1953 (W)

League Club	Source	Date Signed	Seasons Played	Apps	Subs	Gls
Cardiff C.	Jnrs	08.70	70-72	21	6	1

REES, Peter N.
Machynlleth, 5 May, 1932 (IF)

League Club	Source	Date Signed	Seasons Played	Apps	Subs	Gls
Tranmere Rov. (Am)	Llanidloes	10.56	56	9	-	4

REES, Ronald R.
Ystradgynlais, 4 April, 1944 Wu23-7/W-39 (W)

League Club	Source	Date Signed	Seasons Played	Apps	Subs	Gls
Coventry C.	App	05.62	62-67	230	0	42
West Bromwich A.	Tr	03.68	67-68	34	1	9
Nottingham F.	Tr	02.69	68-71	76	9	12
Swansea C.	Tr	01.72	71-74	88	1	5

REES, William
Blaengarw, 10 March, 1924 W-4 (IF)

League Club	Source	Date Signed	Seasons Played	Apps	Subs	Gls
Cardiff C.	Carn Rov.	02.44	46-48	101	-	33
Tottenham H.	Tr	06.49	49	11	-	3
Leyton Orient	Tr	07.50	50-55	184	-	58

REES, William
Swansea, 31 September, 1937 (OL)

League Club	Source	Date Signed	Seasons Played	Apps	Subs	Gls
Swansea C.	Jnrs	10.54	54-57	6	-	0
Crystal Palace	Peterborough U.	05.59	59	17	-	1

REESON, M. Anthony
Rotherham, 24 September, 1933 Died 1991 (IF)

League Club	Source	Date Signed	Seasons Played	Apps	Subs	Gls
Rotherham U.	Jnrs	11.53	54	4	-	1
Grimsby T.	Tr	06.55	55-57	76	-	20
Doncaster Rov.	Tr	02.58	57-58	21	-	6
Southport	Tr	06.59	59	42	-	9

REEVE, Edward G.
Hounslow, 3 December, 1947 (WH)

League Club	Source	Date Signed	Seasons Played	Apps	Subs	Gls
Brentford	App	12.65	65-67	20	4	0

REEVE, Frederick W.
Clapton, 1 May, 1918 (WH)

League Club	Source	Date Signed	Seasons Played	Apps	Subs	Gls
Crystal Palace	Ashford T.	05.35	36	1	-	0
Tottenham H.	Tr	05.37				
Rochdale	Tr	07.38	38	27	-	3
Grimsby T.	Tr	07.39	46-47	46	-	0
Reading	Tr	06.48	48-49	34	-	1

REEVE, Kenneth E.
Grimsby, 13 January, 1921 (IF)

League Club	Source	Date Signed	Seasons Played	Apps	Subs	Gls
Grimsby T.	Humber U.	02.38	46-47	24	-	5
Doncaster Rov.	Tr	07.48	48	30	-	12
Mansfield T.	Tr	07.49	49-53	139	-	62

REEVES, Alan
Birkenhead, 19 November, 1967 (D)

League Club	Source	Date Signed	Seasons Played	Apps	Subs	Gls
Norwich C.	Heswall	09.88				
Gillingham	L	02.89	88	18	0	0
Chester C.	Tr	08.89	89-90	31	9	2
Rochdale	Tr	07.91	91	33	1	3

REEVES, T. Brian
Skelmersdale, 18 February, 1939 (G)

League Club	Source	Date Signed	Seasons Played	Apps	Subs	Gls
Blackburn Rov.	Burscough	08.60	60-61	12	-	0
Scunthorpe U.	Tr	04.62	62-64	38	-	0
Southport	Tr	07.65	65-68	143	0	0

REEVES, David
Birkenhead, 19 November, 1967 (F)

League Club	Source	Date Signed	Seasons Played	Apps	Subs	Gls
Sheffield Wed.	Heswall	08.86	88	8	9	2
Scunthorpe U.	L	12.86	86	3	1	2
Scunthorpe U.	L	10.87	87	6	0	4
Burnley	L	11.87	87	16	0	8
Bolton W.	Tr	08.89	89-91	101	19	29

REEVES, Dennis J.
Lochmaben, 1 December, 1944 (G)

League Club	Source	Date Signed	Seasons Played	Apps	Subs	Gls
Chester C.		09.63	63-66	139	0	0
Wrexham	Tr	10.67	67-68	15	0	0

REEVES, Derek B.
Poole, 27 August, 1934 (CF)

League Club	Source	Date Signed	Seasons Played	Apps	Subs	Gls
Southampton	Bournemouth G.W.	12.54	54-62	273	-	145
Bournemouth	Tr	11.62	62-64	35	-	8

REEVES, Frank
Peckham, 11 July, 1921 (HB)

League Club	Source	Date Signed	Seasons Played	Apps	Subs	Gls
Millwall	Sidcup	02.47	47-54	179	-	1

REEVES, John C.
Hackney, 8 July, 1963 (LM)

League Club	Source	Date Signed	Seasons Played	Apps	Subs	Gls
Fulham	App	06.81	81-84	9	5	0
Colchester U.	Tr	08.85	85-87	58	3	7

REEVES, Kevin P.
Burley (Hants), 20 October, 1957 E Yth/Eu23-10/E'B'/E-2 (F)

League Club	Source	Date Signed	Seasons Played	Apps	Subs	Gls
Bournemouth	App	07.75	74-76	60	3	20
Norwich C.	Tr	01.77	76-79	118	1	37
Manchester C.	Tr	03.80	79-82	129	1	34
Burnley	Tr	07.83	83	20	1	12

REEVES, Michael R.
Saltash, 13 January, 1943 (FB)

League Club	Source	Date Signed	Seasons Played	Apps	Subs	Gls
Plymouth Arg.	Saltash U.	06.61	62-69	107	3	0

REEVES, Peter J.
Eltham, 7 February, 1949 E Yth (CD)

League Club	Source	Date Signed	Seasons Played	Apps	Subs	Gls
Charlton Ath.	App	02.66	65-73	263	5	2

REEVES, Peter P.
Swansea, 20 January, 1959 (M)

League Club	Source	Date Signed	Seasons Played	Apps	Subs	Gls
Coventry C.	App	12.76				
Swansea C.	Tr	07.78	78	2	2	0

REEVES, Raymond H. E.
Reading, 12 August, 1931 E Yth (FB)

League Club	Source	Date Signed	Seasons Played	Apps	Subs	Gls
Reading		05.49	52-60	284	-	29
Brentford	Tr	07.61	61	5	-	0

REEVES-JONES, Adrian
Stoke, 18 October, 1966 (W)

League Club	Source	Date Signed	Seasons Played	Apps	Subs	Gls
Port Vale (N/C)	App	10.84	84	2	1	0

REGAN, Douglas J. T.
Yeovil, 3 June, 1922 (W)

League Club	Source	Date Signed	Seasons Played	Apps	Subs	Gls
Exeter C.		03.45	46-52	206	-	63
Bristol C.	Tr	12.52	52-55	36	-	11

REGAN, James
Hemsworth, 7 December, 1927 (WH)

League Club	Source	Date Signed	Seasons Played	Apps	Subs	Gls
Rotherham U.	Moorthorpe Colly	08.49	51-52	12	-	0
Bristol C.	Tr	06.53	53-55	51	-	0
Coventry C.	Tr	03.56	55-56	26	-	0

REGAN, John H.
Dalton-in-Furness, 8 June, 1925 (OL)

League Club	Source	Date Signed	Seasons Played	Apps	Subs	Gls
Barrow	Swarthmoor	01.48	48-50	9	-	1

REGAN, M. John
Worcester, 18 June, 1944 (CF)

League Club	Source	Date Signed	Seasons Played	Apps	Subs	Gls
Birmingham C.	Jnrs	09.61	62-63	5	-	2
Shrewsbury T.	Tr	10.64	64-65	21	0	6
Brentford	Tr	03.66	65-66	14	0	5
Crewe Alex.	Tr	11.66	66-68	48	3	17
Doncaster Rov.	Tr	09.68	68-70	91	4	25

REGAN Terence
Bradford, 26 June, 1926 (OR)

League Club	Source	Date Signed	Seasons Played	Apps	Subs	Gls
Bradford C. (Am)	Salts	10.48	48	1	-	0

REGIS, Cyrille
French Guyana, 9 February, 1958 Eu21-6/E'B'/E-5 (F)

League Club	Source	Date Signed	Seasons Played	Apps	Subs	Gls
West Bromwich A.	Hayes	05.77	77-84	233	4	82
Coventry C.	Tr	10.84	84-90	231	7	47
Aston Villa	Tr	07.91	91	39	0	11

REGIS, David R.
Paddington, 3 March, 1964 (F)

League Club	Source	Date Signed	Seasons Played	Apps	Subs	Gls
Notts Co.	Barnet	09.90	90-91	31	15	16
Oxford U.	Tr	11.91	91	21	3	2

REGIS, Robert A.
Huddersfield, 24 January, 1967 (F)

League Club	Source	Date Signed	Seasons Played	Apps	Subs	Gls
Burnley (N/C)		08.86	86	3	1	1

League Club	Source	Date Signed	Seasons Played	Apps	Subs	Gls
REHN, J. Stefan						
Sweden, 22 September, 1966 Swedish Int						(W)
Everton	Djurgarden (Swe)	06.89	89	1	3	0
REID, Anthony J.						
Nottingham, 9 May, 1963						(M)
Derby Co.	App	05.80	80-82	27	3	1
Scunthorpe U.	L	02.83	82	6	0	0
Newport Co.	Tr	03.83	82-84	74	2	12
Chesterfield	Tr	07.85	85-87	63	4	6
REID, Alexander D.						
Glasgow, 2 March, 1947						(M)
Newcastle U.	Dundee	10.71	71-72	15	8	0
REID, David A.						
Glasgow, 3 January, 1923						(WH)
Rochdale	Glasgow Perthshire	01.48	47-50	36	-	2
Bradford P.A.	Tr	09.50	50-51	13	-	0
Workington		07.53	53	8	-	1
Crewe Alex.	Tr	08.54	54	3	-	0
REID, Douglas J.						
Mauchline, 3 October, 1917						(IF)
Stockport Co.		08.35	36-38	84	-	22
Portsmouth	Tr	03.46	46-55	309	-	129
REID, Ernest J.						
Merthyr Tydfil, 25 March, 1914						(RB)
Swansea C.	Troedyrhiw	07.32				
Chelsea	Tr	09.37	38	1	-	0
Norwich C.	Tr	06.45	46	5	-	0
REID, Frank J.						
Mauchline, 16 June, 1920						(IF)
Huddersfield T.	Cumnock Jnrs	08.46	46-48	7	-	0
Stockport Co.	Tr	06.49	49-50	23	-	0
REID, James						
Dundee, 14 December, 1935						(F)
Bury	Dundee U.	01.57	56-58	21	-	9
Stockport Co.	Tr	03.59	58	11	-	2

Cyrille Regis (West Bromwich Albion, Coventry City, Aston Villa & England)

League Club	Source	Date Signed	Seasons Played	Apps	Subs	Gls
REID, John						
Newmains (Lk), 20 August, 1932						(IF)
Bradford C.	Hamilton Acad.	12.57	57-61	147	-	32
Northampton T.	Tr	11.61	61-63	85	-	14
Luton T.	Tr	11.63	63-65	110	0	7
Torquay U.	Tr	06.66	66	21	2	1
Rochdale	Tr	07.67	67	37	2	3
REID, John						
Edinburgh, 23 July, 1935						(F)
Watford	Airdrieonians	12.56	56	1	-	1
Norwich C.	Airdrieonians	06.58				
Barrow	Tr	07.59	59	20	-	4
REID, John H.						
Edinburgh, 4 May, 1925						
Torquay U.	Hibernian	05.49	49-51	51	-	10
REID, Mark						
Kilwinning, 15 September, 1961 S Yth/Su21-2						(LB)
Charlton Ath.	Glasgow Celtic	05.85	85-90	209	2	15
REID, Michael J.						
Wolverhampton, 7 August, 1927						(CF)
Wolverhampton W.		02.48				
Bournemouth	Tr	02.49	48	5	-	2
Portsmouth	Tr	07.50	50	5	-	1
Watford	Tr	12.52	52	19	-	8
REID, Nicholas S.						
Urmston, 30 October, 1960 Eu21-6						(D/M)
Manchester C.	App	10.78	78-86	211	5	2
Blackburn Rov.	Tr	07.87	87-91	160	14	9
REID, Paul R.						
Oldbury, 19 January, 1968						(W)
Leicester C.	App	01.86	86-91	140	22	21
Bradford C.	L	03.92	91	7	0	0
REID, Peter						
Huyton, 20 June, 1956 Eu21-6/E-13						(M)
Bolton W.	App	05.74	74-82	222	3	23
Everton	Tr	12.82	82-88	155	4	8
Queens Park R.	Tr	02.89	88-89	29	0	1
Manchester C.	Tr	12.89	89-91	75	4	1

Peter Reid (Bolton Wanderers, Everton, Queens Park Rangers, Manchester City & England)

League Club	Source	Date Signed	Seasons Played	Apps	Subs	Gls

REID, Robert
Hamilton, 19 February, 1911 Died 1987 SF Lge/S-2 (OL)

Brentford	Hamilton Acad.	01.36	35-38	103	-	34
Sheffield U.	Tr	02.39	38-46	14	-	4
Bury	Tr	11.46	46	17	-	1

REID, Robert B. A.
Dundee, 18 November, 1936 (G)

Swansea C.	Downfield Jnrs	09.57	57-59	17	-	0

REID, Ronald E.
Liversedge, 9 November, 1944 (CF)

Chesterfield	Retford T.	07.67	67	6	1	1

REID, Shaun
Huyton, 13 October, 1965 (M)

Rochdale	YT	09.83	83-88	126	7	4
Preston N.E.	L	12.85	85	3	0	0
York C.	Tr	12.88	88-91	104	2	7

REID, Wesley A.
Lewisham, 10 September, 1968 (M)

Arsenal	YT	07.86				
Millwall	Tr	06.87	88-89	5	1	0
Bradford C.	Tr	01.91	90-91	31	4	3

REID, William D.
Ayr, 13 January, 1920 (RH)

Newport Co.	Cumnock Jnrs	05.48	49	9	-	0

REILLY, Daniel
Peterborough, 17 November, 1966

Peterborough U.	YT	08.84	84	0	1	0

REILLY, David J.
Chester, 24 November, 1966

Wrexham (N/C)	Jnrs	07.84	84	0	1	0

REILLY, Felix
Musselburgh, 12 September, 1933 (CF)

Bradford P.A.	East Fife	03.60	59-61	31	-	12
Crewe Alex.	Tr	12.61	61	6	-	0

REILLY, George G.
Bellshill, 14 September, 1957 (F)

Northampton T.	Corby T.	06.76	76-79	124	3	46
Cambridge U.	Tr	11.79	79-82	136	2	36
Watford	Tr	08.83	83-84	46	2	14
Newcastle U.	Tr	02.85	84-85	31	0	10
West Bromwich A.	Tr	12.85	85-87	42	1	9
Cambridge U.	Tr	07.88	88	20	0	7

REILLY, Leonard H.
Rotherhithe, 31 January, 1917 (CH)

Norwich C.	Diss T.	02.36	37-46	30	-	0

REILLY, Terence
Culross (Fife), 1 July, 1924 (FB)

Chesterfield	Bo'ness U.	03.49				
Southport	Tr	08.50	50-54	191	-	2
Bradford P.A.	Tr	06.55	55	14	-	0

REINELT, Robert S.
Loughton, 11 March, 1974 (M)

Aldershot (YT)	YT	07.90	90	3	2	0

RELISH, John D.
Liverpool, 5 October, 1953 (LB)

Chester C.	App	10.71	72-73	10	1	1
Newport Co.	Tr	06.74	74-86	319	19	9

RENNIE, David
Edinburgh, 29 August, 1964 S Yth (M/CD)

Leicester C.	App	05.82	83-85	21	0	1
Leeds U.	Tr	01.86	85-88	95	6	5
Bristol C.	Tr	07.89	89-91	101	3	8
Birmingham C.	Tr	02.92	91	17	0	2

RENNIE, Paul A.
Nantwich, 26 October, 1971 (CD)

Crewe Alex. (YT)	YT	08.88	89	1	1	0
Stoke C.	Tr	05.90	90-91	4	0	0

RENSHAW, Derek
Gateshead, 18 September, 1924 (FB)

Sunderland		12.47				
Barrow	Tr	06.50	50-54	150	-	0

League Club	Source	Date Signed	Seasons Played	Apps	Subs	Gls

RENTON, William
Cardenden, 4 February, 1942 (M)

Barrow	Dunfermline Ath.	01.71	70-71	23	1	2

RENWICK, Craig
Motherwell, 22 September, 1958 (CD)

Sheffield U.	East Stirling	04.78	78-79	8	1	0

RENWICK, Richard
Gilsland (Nd), 27 November, 1942 (FB)

Grimsby T.	Jnrs	12.59				
Aldershot	Tr	07.63	63-68	203	2	5
Brentford	Tr	02.69	68-70	96	0	5
Stockport Co.	Tr	10.71	71	30	0	1
Rochdale	Tr	07.72	72-73	48	1	0
Darlington	L	01.74	73	19	0	0

RESTARICK, Stephen L. J.
Barking, 28 November, 1971 (F)

Colchester U. (YT)	YT	09.88	89	0	1	0

REVEL, Gordon H.
Mansfield, 19 September, 1927 (CH)

Mansfield T.		08.50	52	1	-	0

REVELL, Charles H.
Belvedere, 5 June, 1919 (WH)

Charlton Ath.	Gravesend & Nflt	05.39	46-50	104	-	15
Derby Co.	Tr	03.51	50-51	22	-	2

REVIE, Donald G.
Middlesbrough, 10 July, 1927 Died 1989 EF Lge/E'B'-1/E-6 (IF)

Leicester C.	Jnrs	08.44	46-49	96	-	25
Hull C.	Tr	11.49	49-51	76	-	12
Manchester C.	Tr	10.51	51-56	162	-	37
Sunderland	Tr	11.56	56-58	64	-	15
Leeds U.	Tr	12.58	58-61	77	-	11

Don Revie (Leicester City, Hull City, Manchester City, Sunderland, Leeds United & England)

REW, Royston E.
Belfast, 26 May, 1924 (CF)

Exeter C.	Sea Mills	02.49	48-49	4	-	1

REYNOLDS, A. Brayley
Blackwood, 30 May, 1935 (CF)

Cardiff C.	Lovells Ath.	05.56	56-58	54	-	15
Swansea C.	Tr	05.59	59-64	151	-	57

REYNOLDS, Graham E. A.
Newport, 23 January, 1937 W Amat (CF)

League Club	Source	Date Signed	Seasons Played	Apps	Subs	Gls
Newport Co. (Am)	Caerleon	10.56	56	4	-	1
Newport Co.	Brecon Corries	07.63	63-66	42	1	11

REYNOLDS, Hugh
Wishaw, 19 September, 1926

League Club	Source	Date Signed	Seasons Played	Apps	Subs	Gls
Torquay U.	Morton	05.48	48	3	-	0

REYNOLDS, Jamie A.
Swindon, 27 October, 1967 E Yth (M)

League Club	Source	Date Signed	Seasons Played	Apps	Subs	Gls
Swindon T.	App	09.85	84-86	0	2	0

REYNOLDS, Joseph
Cleland, 13 February, 1939 (CH)

League Club	Source	Date Signed	Seasons Played	Apps	Subs	Gls
Crewe Alex.		08.60	60	7	-	0

REYNOLDS, Mark D.
Glapwell, 1 January, 1966 (FB)

League Club	Source	Date Signed	Seasons Played	Apps	Subs	Gls
Mansfield T. (App)	App	07.82	82	4	0	0

REYNOLDS, Richard J.
Looe, 15 February, 1948 E Yth (M)

League Club	Source	Date Signed	Seasons Played	Apps	Subs	Gls
Plymouth Arg.	App	02.65	64-70	123	8	24
Portsmouth	Tr	07.71	71-75	134	6	24

REYNOLDS, Ronald S. M.
Haslemere, 2 June, 1928 (G)

League Club	Source	Date Signed	Seasons Played	Apps	Subs	Gls
Aldershot	Jnrs	12.45	46-49	115	-	0
Tottenham H.	Tr	07.50	53-57	86	-	0
Southampton	Tr	03.60	59-63	90	-	0

REYNOLDS, Thomas
Felling, 2 October, 1922 (OR)

League Club	Source	Date Signed	Seasons Played	Apps	Subs	Gls
Sunderland	Felling Jnrs	07.46	46-52	167	-	18
Darlington	Kings Lynn	12.54	54-55	42	-	6

RHOADES-BROWN, Peter
Hampton, 2 January, 1962 (LW)

League Club	Source	Date Signed	Seasons Played	Apps	Subs	Gls
Chelsea	App	07.79	79-83	86	10	4
Oxford U.	Tr	01.84	83-88	87	25	13

RHODES, Alan
Bradford, 5 January, 1946 (WH)

League Club	Source	Date Signed	Seasons Played	Apps	Subs	Gls
Bradford C. (Am)	Salts	07.64	64-65	7	0	0

RHODES, Albert
Dinnington, 29 April, 1936 (FB)

League Club	Source	Date Signed	Seasons Played	Apps	Subs	Gls
Queens Park R.	Worksop T.	12.54	55-56	5	-	0

RHODES, Andrew C.
Askern, 23 August, 1964 (G)

League Club	Source	Date Signed	Seasons Played	Apps	Subs	Gls
Barnsley	App	08.82	83-84	36	0	0
Doncaster Rov.	Tr	10.85	85-87	106	0	0
Oldham Ath.	Tr	03.88	87-89	69	0	0

RHODES, J. Anthony
Dover, 17 September, 1946 (CD)

League Club	Source	Date Signed	Seasons Played	Apps	Subs	Gls
Derby Co.	Jnrs	10.63	64-70	5	0	0
Halifax T.	Tr	11.70	70-75	233	0	9
Southport	Tr	08.76	76	7	2	0

RHODES, Brian W.
Marylebone, 23 October, 1937 (G)

League Club	Source	Date Signed	Seasons Played	Apps	Subs	Gls
West Ham U.	Jnrs	01.55	57-62	61	-	0
Southend U.	Tr	09.63	63	11	-	0

RHODES, Mark N.
Sheffield, 26 August, 1957 (M)

League Club	Source	Date Signed	Seasons Played	Apps	Subs	Gls
Rotherham U.	App	08.75	75-84	235	23	13
Darlington	L	10.82	82	14	0	0
Mansfield T.	L	03.83	82	4	0	0
Burnley	Tr	03.85	84-85	12	1	0

RHODES, Stanley
Sheffield, 19 April, 1929 (F)

League Club	Source	Date Signed	Seasons Played	Apps	Subs	Gls
Leeds U.		05.48				
Sheffield U.	Worksop T.	11.51	51	1	-	0

RHODES, Trevor C.
Southend, 9 August, 1948 (WH)

League Club	Source	Date Signed	Seasons Played	Apps	Subs	Gls
Arsenal	App	09.65				
Millwall	Tr	09.66	66	4	0	0
Bristol Rov.	Tr	07.68	68	2	0	0

RICE, Brian
Bellshill, 11 October, 1963 S Yth/Su21-1 (LW)

League Club	Source	Date Signed	Seasons Played	Apps	Subs	Gls
Nottingham F.	Hibernian	08.85	85-90	86	5	9
Grimsby T.	L	10.86	86	4	0	0
West Bromwich A.	L	01.89	88	2	1	0
Stoke C.	L	02.91	90	18	0	0

RICE, Patrick J.
Belfast, 17 March, 1949 NIu23-2/NI-49 (RB)

League Club	Source	Date Signed	Seasons Played	Apps	Subs	Gls
Arsenal	Jnrs	03.66	67-80	391	6	12
Watford	Tr	11.80	80-83	112	0	1

RICE, Ronald H.
Birkenhead, 13 April, 1923 (IL)

League Club	Source	Date Signed	Seasons Played	Apps	Subs	Gls
Bradford C.	Huddersfield T. (Am)	09.46	46	1	-	0
Tranmere Rov.	Tr	10.46	46	4	-	1

RICHARDS, Anthony W.
Birmingham, 6 March, 1934 (CF)

League Club	Source	Date Signed	Seasons Played	Apps	Subs	Gls
Birmingham C.	Jnrs	12.51				
Walsall	Tr	09.54	54-62	334	-	184
Port Vale	Tr	03.63	62-65	59	4	30

RICHARDS, Anthony
New Houghton, 9 June, 1944 (HB)

League Club	Source	Date Signed	Seasons Played	Apps	Subs	Gls
Mansfield T.	App	06.62	61-63	3	-	0

RICHARDS, Carroll L. (Carl)
Jamaica, 1 December, 1960 E Semi-Pro (F)

League Club	Source	Date Signed	Seasons Played	Apps	Subs	Gls
Bournemouth	Enfield	07.86	86-88	57	14	16
Birmingham C.	Tr	10.88	88	18	1	2
Peterborough U.	Tr	07.89	89	16	4	5
Blackpool	Tr	01.90	89-91	32	9	8
Maidstone U.	L	10.91	91	4	0	2

RICHARDS, Craig A.
Neath, 10 October, 1959 (M)

League Club	Source	Date Signed	Seasons Played	Apps	Subs	Gls
Queens Park R.	App	07.77				
Wimbledon	Tr	06.79	79	2	0	0

RICHARDS, Dean I.
Bradford, 9 June, 1974 (CD)

League Club	Source	Date Signed	Seasons Played	Apps	Subs	Gls
Bradford C.	YT	07.92	91	5	2	1

RICHARDS, Gary V.
Swansea, 2 August, 1963 (D)

League Club	Source	Date Signed	Seasons Played	Apps	Subs	Gls
Swansea C.	App	08.81	81-84	63	3	1
Lincoln C. (N/C)		11.85	85	2	5	0
Cambridge U. (N/C)	Tr	03.86	85	8	0	0
Torquay U.	Tr	07.86	86	24	1	1

RICHARDS, Geoffrey M.
Bilston, 24 April, 1929 (OR)

League Club	Source	Date Signed	Seasons Played	Apps	Subs	Gls
West Bromwich A.	Albion Wks	08.46	46-47	3	-	1

RICHARDS, Gordon
Rhos, 23 October, 1933 (OL)

League Club	Source	Date Signed	Seasons Played	Apps	Subs	Gls
Wrexham	Jnrs	05.52	52-57	96	-	24
Chester C.	Tr	01.58	57-60	75	-	18

RICHARDS, John B.
West Bromwich, 14 June, 1931 (F)

League Club	Source	Date Signed	Seasons Played	Apps	Subs	Gls
Swindon T.		11.55	55-59	105	-	36
Norwich C.	Tr	12.59	59	5	-	2
Aldershot	Tr	10.60	60	19	-	8

RICHARDS, John P.
Warrington, 9 November, 1950 Eu21-2/Eu23-6/EF Lge/E-1 (F)

League Club	Source	Date Signed	Seasons Played	Apps	Subs	Gls
Wolverhampton W.	Jnrs	07.69	69-82	365	20	144
Derby Co.	L	11.82	82	10	0	2

RICHARDS, Lloyd G.
Jamaica (WI), 11 February, 1958 (M)

League Club	Source	Date Signed	Seasons Played	Apps	Subs	Gls
Notts Co.	App	02.76	75-77	7	2	0
York C.	Tr	06.80	80	17	1	1

RICHARDS, Michael J.
Wolverhampton, 26 May, 1939 (G)

League Club	Source	Date Signed	Seasons Played	Apps	Subs	Gls
Oxford U.	Wellington T.	07.62	62-63	30	-	0
Shrewsbury T.	Tr	11.63				

RICHARDS, Pedro
Edmonton, 1 November, 1956 (RB)

League Club	Source	Date Signed	Seasons Played	Apps	Subs	Gls
Notts Co.	App	11.74	74-85	397	2	5

RICHARDS, Stanley V.
Cardiff, 21 January, 1917 Died 1987 W-1 (CF)

League Club	Source	Date Signed	Seasons Played	Apps	Subs	Gls
Cardiff C.	Tufnell Park	01.46	46-47	57	-	40
Swansea C.	Tr	06.48	48-50	65	-	35

League Club	Source	Date Signed	Seasons Played	Career Record Apps	Subs	Gls

RICHARDS, Stephen C.
Dundee, 24 October, 1961 (CD)

League Club	Source	Date Signed	Seasons Played	Apps	Subs	Gls
Hull C.	App	10.79	79-82	55	3	2
York C. (N/C)	Gainsborough Trin.	12.84	84	6	1	0
Lincoln C.	Tr	08.85	85	21	0	0
Cambridge U. (N/C)	Tr	03.86	85	4	0	2
Scarborough	Tr	08.86	87-90	164	0	13
Halifax T.	Tr	08.91	91	24	1	0

RICHARDS, Wayne
Scunthorpe, 10 May, 1961 (FB)

League Club	Source	Date Signed	Seasons Played	Apps	Subs	Gls
Derby Co.	App	05.79	79-81	16	3	0

RICHARDSON, Anthony F.
Alford (Lincs), 5 November, 1943 (CF)

League Club	Source	Date Signed	Seasons Played	Apps	Subs	Gls
Nottingham F.	Jnrs	11.60				
Bradford C. (Am)	Cheltenham T.	05.62	62	2	-	1

RICHARDSON, Anthony J.
Southwark, 7 January, 1932 (FB)

League Club	Source	Date Signed	Seasons Played	Apps	Subs	Gls
Queens Park R.	Slough S.C.	04.51	51	2	-	0

RICHARDSON, Barry
Wallsend, 5 August, 1969 (G)

League Club	Source	Date Signed	Seasons Played	Apps	Subs	Gls
Sunderland	YT	05.88				
Scunthorpe U.	Tr	03.89				
Scarborough	Seaham Red Star	12.89	89-90	30	0	0
Stockport Co.	Tr	08.91				
Northampton T.	Tr	09.91	91	27	0	0

RICHARDSON, Brian
Sheffield, 5 October, 1934 (WH)

League Club	Source	Date Signed	Seasons Played	Apps	Subs	Gls
Sheffield U.		12.54	55-64	291	-	9
Swindon T.	Tr	01.66	65	11	0	0
Rochdale	Tr	07.66	66	19	0	1

RICHARDSON, Damien J.
Dublin, 2 August, 1947 IR-3 (F)

League Club	Source	Date Signed	Seasons Played	Apps	Subs	Gls
Gillingham	Shamrock Rov.	10.72	72-80	314	9	94

RICHARDSON, David
Billingham, 11 March, 1932 (FB)

League Club	Source	Date Signed	Seasons Played	Apps	Subs	Gls
Leicester C.	Jnrs	11.49	54	2	-	0
Grimsby T.	Tr	06.55	55-59	175	-	1
Swindon T.	Tr	06.60				
Barrow	Tr	07.61	61-62	31	-	0

RICHARDSON, Derek W.
Hackney, 13 July, 1956 E Yth/E Semi-Pro (G)

League Club	Source	Date Signed	Seasons Played	Apps	Subs	Gls
Chelsea	App	02.74				
Queens Park R.	Tr	04.76	76-78	31	0	0
Sheffield U.	Tr	12.79	79-80	42	0	0
Coventry C.	Tr	03.82				

RICHARDSON, Frederick
Spennymoor, 18 August, 1925 (CF)

League Club	Source	Date Signed	Seasons Played	Apps	Subs	Gls
Chelsea	Bishop Auckland	09.46	46	2	-	0
Hartlepool U.	Tr	10.47	47-48	43	-	16
Barnsley	Tr	10.48	48-49	41	-	12
West Bromwich A.	Tr	06.50	50-51	29	-	8
Chester C.	Tr	02.52	51-52	23	-	6
Hartlepool U.	Tr	11.52	52-55	106	-	24

RICHARDSON, Garbutt
Newcastle, 24 October, 1938 (CH)

League Club	Source	Date Signed	Seasons Played	Apps	Subs	Gls
Huddersfield T.	Jnrs	10.55				
Preston N.E.	Tr	07.57	59-60	15	-	1
Accrington St.	Tr	07.61				
Halifax T.	Carlisle U. (Trial)	11.62	62-63	20	-	1
Barrow	Tr	07.64	64	30	-	5

RICHARDSON, George
Worksop, 12 December, 1912 Died 1968 (F)

League Club	Source	Date Signed	Seasons Played	Apps	Subs	Gls
Huddersfield T.	Manton Colly	04.33	33	1	-	0
Sheffield U.	Tr	05.34	36-38	30	-	9
Hull C.	Tr	11.38	38-47	36	-	15

RICHARDSON, Graham C.
Sedgefield, 20 March, 1958 (G)

League Club	Source	Date Signed	Seasons Played	Apps	Subs	Gls
Hartlepool U.	Darlington (Am)	08.75	75-80	89	0	0

RICHARDSON, Ian P.
Ely, 9 May, 1964 (F)

League Club	Source	Date Signed	Seasons Played	Apps	Subs	Gls
Watford	App	05.82	83-84	5	3	2
Blackpool	L	12.82	82	4	1	2
Rotherham U.	L	02.85	84	5	0	2
Chester C.	Tr	11.85	85-86	31	4	10
Scunthorpe U.	Tr	10.86	86-88	11	7	4

RICHARDSON, James R.
Ashington, 8 February, 1911 Died 1964 E Sch/EF Lge/E-2 (IF)

League Club	Source	Date Signed	Seasons Played	Apps	Subs	Gls
Newcastle U.	Blyth Spartans	04.28	29-34	136	-	42
Huddersfield T.	Tr	10.34	34-37	120	-	32
Newcastle U.	Tr	10.37	37	14	-	4
Millwall	Tr	03.38	37-38	52	-	16
Leyton Orient	Tr	01.48	47	15	-	0

RICHARDSON, John
Birkenhead, 24 May, 1933 (G)

League Club	Source	Date Signed	Seasons Played	Apps	Subs	Gls
Southport	Canterbury C.	07.56	56-59	103	-	0

RICHARDSON, John
Worksop, 20 April, 1945 (FB)

League Club	Source	Date Signed	Seasons Played	Apps	Subs	Gls
Derby Co.	App	04.62	62-70	118	0	4
Notts Co.	Tr	07.71	71	0	2	0

RICHARDSON, John P.
Ashington, 5 February, 1949 (CD)

League Club	Source	Date Signed	Seasons Played	Apps	Subs	Gls
Millwall (App)	App	12.64	65	1	0	0
Brentford	Tr	08.66	66-69	83	2	7
Fulham	Tr	08.69	69-72	61	10	6
Aldershot	Tr	07.73	73-76	120	1	6

RICHARDSON, Joseph A. S.
Sheffield, 17 March, 1942 Died 1966 (IF)

League Club	Source	Date Signed	Seasons Played	Apps	Subs	Gls
Birmingham C.	Winsford U.	09.59				
Sheffield U.	Tr	01.60				
Rochdale	Tr	10.60	60-64	115	-	31
Tranmere Rov.	Tr	07.65				

RICHARDSON, Kevin
Newcastle, 4 December, 1962 (LM)

League Club	Source	Date Signed	Seasons Played	Apps	Subs	Gls
Everton	App	12.80	81-86	95	14	16
Watford	Tr	09.86	86	39	0	2
Arsenal	Tr	08.87	87-89	88	8	5
Aston Villa	Real Sociedad (Sp)	08.91	91	42	0	6

RICHARDSON, Lee J.
Halifax, 12 March, 1969 (M)

League Club	Source	Date Signed	Seasons Played	Apps	Subs	Gls
Halifax T.	YT	07.87	86-88	43	13	2
Watford	Tr	02.89	88-89	40	1	1
Blackburn Rov.	Tr	08.90	90-91	50	12	3

RICHARDSON, Neil T.
Sunderland, 3 March, 1968 (M)

League Club	Source	Date Signed	Seasons Played	Apps	Subs	Gls
Rotherham U.	Brandon U.	07.89	89-91	36	0	4

RICHARDSON, Nicholas
Halifax, 11 April, 1967 (F)

League Club	Source	Date Signed	Seasons Played	Apps	Subs	Gls
Halifax T.	Emley	11.88	88-91	89	12	17

RICHARDSON, Norman
Consett, 15 April, 1915 (FB)

League Club	Source	Date Signed	Seasons Played	Apps	Subs	Gls
Bolton W.	Medomsley Jnrs	05.33				
New Brighton	Tr	02.36	35-50	213	-	0

RICHARDSON, Paul
Shirebrook, 25 October, 1949 E Yth (M)

League Club	Source	Date Signed	Seasons Played	Apps	Subs	Gls
Nottingham F.	App	08.67	67-76	199	24	18
Chester C.	Tr	10.76	76	28	0	2
Stoke C.	Tr	06.77	77-80	124	3	10
Sheffield U.	Tr	08.81	81-82	35	1	2
Blackpool	L	01.83	82	4	0	0
Swindon T.	Tr	07.83	83	7	0	0
Swansea C. (N/C)	Tr	09.84	84	12	0	0

RICHARDSON, Paul A.
Hucknall, 7 November, 1962 (M)

League Club	Source	Date Signed	Seasons Played	Apps	Subs	Gls
Derby Co.	Nuneaton Bor.	08.84	84	7	7	0

RICHARDSON, Roderick K.
Hunstanton, 1 October, 1942 (IF)

League Club	Source	Date Signed	Seasons Played	Apps	Subs	Gls
Torquay U.	Norwich C. (Am)	07.62	62-63	7	-	1

RICHARDSON, Russell
Sheffield, 21 October, 1964 (FB)

League Club	Source	Date Signed	Seasons Played	Apps	Subs	Gls
Scunthorpe U. (N/C)	YT	08.83	83	2	0	0

RICHARDSON, Stanley
Harrington, 28 April, 1924 (W)

League Club	Source	Date Signed	Seasons Played	Apps	Subs	Gls
Workington		08.51	51	8	-	1

RICHARDSON, Steven E.
Slough, 11 February, 1962 (LB)

League Club	Source	Date Signed	Seasons Played	Apps	Subs	Gls
Southampton	App	02.80				
Reading	Tr	07.82	82-91	362	3	3

League Club	Source	Date Signed	Seasons Played	Apps	Subs	Gls

RICHARDSON, Stuart
Leeds, 12 June, 1938 (WH)

League Club	Source	Date Signed	Seasons Played	Apps	Subs	Gls
Queens Park R.	Methley U.	11.56	58	1	-	0
Oldham Ath.	Tr	07.59	59	22	-	0

RICHARDSON, Thomas
Reading, 1 February, 1931 (WH)

League Club	Source	Date Signed	Seasons Played	Apps	Subs	Gls
Middlesbrough		09.52				
Southport	Tr	05.54				
Aldershot	Tr	07.55	55-57	41	-	9

RICHARDSON, William
Bedlington, 25 October, 1943 (FB)

League Club	Source	Date Signed	Seasons Played	Apps	Subs	Gls
Sunderland	Jnrs	10.60				
Mansfield T.	Tr	10.65	65-67	61	2	0
York C.	Tr	06.68	68	24	0	0

RICHLEY, Lionel
Gateshead, 2 July, 1924 (HB)

League Club	Source	Date Signed	Seasons Played	Apps	Subs	Gls
Hartlepool U.	Tonbridge	06.51	51-53	72	-	0

RICHMOND, John F.
Derby, 17 September, 1938 (FB)

League Club	Source	Date Signed	Seasons Played	Apps	Subs	Gls
Derby Co.	Derby Corries	01.56	57-62	6	-	0

RICKABY, Stanley
Stockton, 12 March, 1924 EF Lge/E-1 (FB)

League Club	Source	Date Signed	Seasons Played	Apps	Subs	Gls
Middlesbrough	South Bank	07.46	47-49	10	-	0
West Bromwich A.	Tr	02.50	49-54	189	-	2

RICKARD, Derek B. P.
Plymouth, 1 October, 1947 (F)

League Club	Source	Date Signed	Seasons Played	Apps	Subs	Gls
Plymouth Arg.	St Austell	12.69	69-73	101	9	41
Bournemouth	Tr	07.74	74-75	22	10	6

RICKARDS, Kenneth
Middlesbrough, 22 March, 1929 (IR)

League Club	Source	Date Signed	Seasons Played	Apps	Subs	Gls
Hull C.	Middlesbrough A.	05.47				
Darlington	Tr	01.50	49	8	-	0

RICKETT, Horace F. J.
Orsett, 3 January, 1912 (G)

League Club	Source	Date Signed	Seasons Played	Apps	Subs	Gls
Leyton Orient	Chelmsford C.	02.43				
Reading		06.46	46-47	22	-	0

RICKETT, Walter
Sheffield, 20 March, 1917 E'B'-1 (OR)

League Club	Source	Date Signed	Seasons Played	Apps	Subs	Gls
Sheffield U.		05.39	46-47	57	-	16
Blackpool	Tr	01.48	47-49	45	-	8
Sheffield Wed.	Tr	10.49	49-52	95	-	13
Rotherham U.	Tr	09.52	52	28	-	4
Halifax T.	Tr	08.53	53	31	-	2

RICKETTS, Alan
Crawley, 30 October, 1962 (F)

League Club	Source	Date Signed	Seasons Played	Apps	Subs	Gls
Crewe Alex.	Wrexham (N/C)	08.81	81	14	3	2

RICKETTS, Graham A.
Oxford, 30 July, 1939 E Yth (WH)

League Club	Source	Date Signed	Seasons Played	Apps	Subs	Gls
Bristol Rov.	Jnrs	08.56	56-60	32	-	0
Stockport Co.	Tr	07.61	61-63	119	-	6
Doncaster Rov.	Tr	07.64	64-67	143	8	15
Peterborough U.	Tr	03.68	67-68	46	3	1

RICKIS, Victor
Edinburgh, 26 November, 1940 (OL)

League Club	Source	Date Signed	Seasons Played	Apps	Subs	Gls
Millwall	Dalkeith Th.	12.59	60	3	-	1

RIDDICK, Gordon G.
Watford, 6 November, 1943 (M)

League Club	Source	Date Signed	Seasons Played	Apps	Subs	Gls
Luton T.	Jnrs	04.61	62-66	101	1	16
Gillingham	Tr	03.67	66-69	114	0	24
Charlton Ath.	Tr	11.69	69-70	26	3	5
Leyton Orient	Tr	10.70	70-72	13	8	3
Northampton T.	Tr	12.72	72-73	28	0	3
Brentford	Tr	10.73	73-76	104	4	5

RIDEOUT, Brian J.
Bristol, 15 September, 1940 (FB)

League Club	Source	Date Signed	Seasons Played	Apps	Subs	Gls
Bristol Rov.		02.59	60	1	-	0

RIDEOUT, Paul D.
Bournemouth, 14 August, 1964 E Sch/E Yth/Eu21-5 (F)

League Club	Source	Date Signed	Seasons Played	Apps	Subs	Gls
Swindon T.	App	08.81	80-82	90	5	38
Aston Villa	Tr	06.83	83-84	50	4	19
Southampton	Bari (It)	07.88	88-91	68	7	19
Swindon T.	L	03.91	90	9	0	1
Notts Co.	Tr	09.91	91	9	2	3

Paul Rideout (Swindon Town, Aston Villa, Bari, Southampton & Notts County)

RIDGE, Roy
Sheffield, 21 October, 1934 (FB)

League Club	Source	Date Signed	Seasons Played	Apps	Subs	Gls
Sheffield U.	Ecclesfield	11.51	53-60	11	-	0
Rochdale	Tr	08.64	64-65	85	0	0

RIDING, Alan
Preston, 14 March, 1945 (CF)

League Club	Source	Date Signed	Seasons Played	Apps	Subs	Gls
Exeter C.	Colchester U. (Am)	07.64	65	1	0	0

RIDLEY, David G. H.
Pontypridd, 16 December, 1916

League Club	Source	Date Signed	Seasons Played	Apps	Subs	Gls
Millwall	Bedford T.	01.45				
Brighton & H.A.	Tr	07.46	46	5	-	0

RIDLEY, John
Consett, 27 April, 1952 (CD)

League Club	Source	Date Signed	Seasons Played	Apps	Subs	Gls
Port Vale	Sheffield Univ.	08.73	73-78	149	7	3
Leicester C.	Tr	10.78	78	17	7	0
Chesterfield	Tr	08.79	79-81	121	3	8
Port Vale	Tr	08.82	82-84	105	9	5

RIDLEY, Robert M.
Reading, 30 May, 1942 (W)

League Club	Source	Date Signed	Seasons Played	Apps	Subs	Gls
Portsmouth	Jnrs	06.60				
Gillingham	Tr	07.61	61-66	71	2	8

RIDYARD, Alfred
Cudworth, 5 May, 1908 (CH)

League Club	Source	Date Signed	Seasons Played	Apps	Subs	Gls
Barnsley		08.28	30-31	21	-	3
West Bromwich A.	Tr	06.32	32-36	31	-	0
Queens Park R.	Tr	03.38	37-47	28	-	0

RIGBY, Edward
Atherton, 20 April, 1925

League Club	Source	Date Signed	Seasons Played	Apps	Subs	Gls
Manchester C.		02.48				
Barrow	Tr	07.49	49	19	-	0

RIGBY, Ernest
Kirkham, 8 April, 1928 (FB)

League Club	Source	Date Signed	Seasons Played	Apps	Subs	Gls
Accrington St.	Blackpool (Am)	02.51	50-51	10	-	0

RIGBY, John (Jack)
Golborne, 29 July, 1924 (CH)

League Club	Source	Date Signed	Seasons Played	Apps	Subs	Gls
Manchester C.	Bryn Boys Brigade	12.46	46-52	100	-	0

RIGBY, Jonathan K.
Bury St Edmunds, 31 January, 1965 (F)

League Club	Source	Date Signed	Seasons Played	Apps	Subs	Gls
Norwich C.	App	08.82	83-84	7	3	0
Aldershot	Tr	03.86	85	1	0	0
Cambridge U.	Tr	10.86	86-87	28	3	6

RIGBY, Norman
Newark, 23 May, 1923 (CH)

League Club	Source	Date Signed	Seasons Played	Apps	Subs	Gls
Notts Co.		09.44	47-50	46	-	0
Peterborough U.	Tr	(N/L)	60-61	55	-	0

RIGBY, William A.
Chester, 9 June, 1921 (G)

League Club	Source	Date Signed	Seasons Played	Apps	Subs	Gls
Chester C.	Jnrs	08.46	46	1	-	0

RIGG, Thomas
Bedlington, 20 February, 1920 (G)

League Club	Source	Date Signed	Seasons Played	Apps	Subs	Gls
Middlesbrough		02.39				
Watford		06.46	46-48	80	-	0
Gillingham	Consett	08.51	51-55	192	-	0

RIGGS, Leslie J.
Portsmouth, 30 May, 1935 (WH)

League Club	Source	Date Signed	Seasons Played	Apps	Subs	Gls
Gillingham	Jnrs	06.52	53-57	152	-	3
Newport Co.	Tr	06.58	58-60	110	-	3
Bury	Tr	06.61	61	6	-	0
Crewe Alex.	Tr	02.63	62-63	67	-	6
Gillingham	Tr	09.64	64-65	17	1	1

RILEY, Brian F.
Bolton, 14 September, 1937 (OL)

League Club	Source	Date Signed	Seasons Played	Apps	Subs	Gls
Bolton W.	Jnrs	12.54	56-58	8	-	1

RILEY, Christopher J.
Rhyl, 19 January, 1939 (IF)

League Club	Source	Date Signed	Seasons Played	Apps	Subs	Gls
Crewe Alex.	Rhyl	03.58	57-63	136	-	47
Tranmere Rov.	Tr	07.64				

RILEY, David S.
Northampton, 8 December, 1960 (F)

League Club	Source	Date Signed	Seasons Played	Apps	Subs	Gls
Nottingham F.	Keyworth U.	01.84	83-86	7	5	2
Darlington	L	02.87	86	6	0	2
Peterborough U.	L	07.87	87	12	0	2
Port Vale	Tr	10.87	87-89	75	1	11
Peterborough U.	Tr	03.90	89-91	73	11	21

RILEY, Glyn
Barnsley, 24 July, 1958 (F)

League Club	Source	Date Signed	Seasons Played	Apps	Subs	Gls
Barnsley	App	07.76	74-81	102	28	16
Doncaster Rov.	L	12.79	79	7	1	2
Bristol C.	Tr	08.82	82-86	184	15	61
Torquay U.	L	09.87	87	6	0	1
Aldershot	Tr	10.87	87-88	48	10	5

RILEY, Howard
Leicester, 18 August, 1938 E Yth/Eu23-2 (OR)

League Club	Source	Date Signed	Seasons Played	Apps	Subs	Gls
Leicester C.	Jnrs	08.55	55-64	193	-	38
Walsall	Tr	01.66	65	24	0	3
Barrow	Atlanta (USA)	07.68	68	21	3	6

RILEY, Hughen W.
Accrington, 12 June, 1947 (M)

League Club	Source	Date Signed	Seasons Played	Apps	Subs	Gls
Rochdale		12.66	67-71	81	12	12
Crewe Alex.	Tr	12.71	71-74	116	5	9
Bury	Tr	12.74	74-75	47	4	4
Bournemouth	Tr	04.76	76-77	69	3	7

RILEY, Ian M.
Tollesbury, 8 February, 1947 (FB)

League Club	Source	Date Signed	Seasons Played	Apps	Subs	Gls
Southend U.	Maldon T.	11.67	67-68	3	1	0

RILEY, Joseph
Stockton (F)

League Club	Source	Date Signed	Seasons Played	Apps	Subs	Gls
Darlington (Am)	Stockton	08.49	49	8	-	2

RIMMER, Gilbert H.
Southport, 14 July, 1932 E Amat

League Club	Source	Date Signed	Seasons Played	Apps	Subs	Gls
Southport (Am)	Leyland Road	07.55	55	2	-	0

RIMMER, J. James
Southport, 10 February, 1948 E-1 (G)

League Club	Source	Date Signed	Seasons Played	Apps	Subs	Gls
Manchester U.	App	05.65	67-72	34	0	0
Swansea C.	L	10.73	73	17	0	0
Arsenal	Tr	02.74	73-76	124	0	0
Aston Villa	Tr	08.77	77-82	229	0	0
Swansea C.	Tr	08.83	83-85	66	0	0

RIMMER, Neill
Liverpool, 13 November, 1967 E Sch/E Yth (M)

League Club	Source	Date Signed	Seasons Played	Apps	Subs	Gls
Everton (App)	App	04.84	84	0	1	0
Ipswich T.	Tr	08.85	85-87	19	3	3
Wigan Ath.	Tr	07.88	88-91	105	1	6

RIMMER, Raymond
Marshside, 6 August, 1938 (OL)

League Club	Source	Date Signed	Seasons Played	Apps	Subs	Gls
Southport (Am)	Formby Dons	08.55	55-57	8	-	0

RIMMER, Stuart A.
Southport, 12 October, 1964 E Yth (F)

League Club	Source	Date Signed	Seasons Played	Apps	Subs	Gls
Everton	App	10.82	81-83	3	0	0
Chester C.	Tr	01.85	84-87	110	4	68
Watford	Tr	03.88	87-88	10	0	1
Notts Co.	Tr	11.88	88	3	1	2
Walsall	Tr	02.89	88-90	85	3	31
Barnsley	Tr	03.91	90	10	5	1
Chester C.	Tr	08.91	91	44	0	13

RIMMER, Warwick R.
Birkenhead, 1 March, 1941 E Sch (D)

League Club	Source	Date Signed	Seasons Played	Apps	Subs	Gls
Bolton W.	Jnrs	03.58	60-74	462	7	17
Crewe Alex.	Tr	03.75	74-78	114	14	0

RIMMINGTON, Norman
Barnsley, 29 November, 1923 (G)

League Club	Source	Date Signed	Seasons Played	Apps	Subs	Gls
Barnsley	Mapplewell	02.45	46	27	-	0
Hartlepool U.	Tr	12.47	47-51	124	-	0

RING, Michael P.
Brighton, 13 February, 1961 (W)

League Club	Source	Date Signed	Seasons Played	Apps	Subs	Gls
Brighton & H.A.	App	02.79	81-83	1	4	0
Hull C.	Ballymena U.	07.84	84-85	17	7	2
Bolton W.	L	03.86	85	1	2	0
Aldershot	Tr	07.86	86-88	53	26	16

RING, Thomas
Glasgow, 8 August, 1930 S-12/SF Lge (OL)

League Club	Source	Date Signed	Seasons Played	Apps	Subs	Gls
Everton	Clyde	01.60	59-60	27	-	6
Barnsley	Tr	11.61	61-62	21	-	1

RINGER, Walter A.
Wakefield, 7 October, 1941 (OL)

League Club	Source	Date Signed	Seasons Played	Apps	Subs	Gls
Halifax T.		12.59	59-60	6	-	0

RINGSTEAD, Alfred
Dublin, 14 October, 1927 IR-20 (OL)

League Club	Source	Date Signed	Seasons Played	Apps	Subs	Gls
Sheffield U.	Northwich Vic.	11.50	50-58	247	-	101
Mansfield T.	Tr	07.59	59	27	-	3

RINTANEN, Mauno O.
Finland, 28 April, 1925 (G)

League Club	Source	Date Signed	Seasons Played	Apps	Subs	Gls
Hull C. (Am)	H.J.K. Helsinki (Fin)	09.56	56	4	-	0

RIOCH, Bruce D.
Aldershot, 6 September, 1947 S-24 (M)

League Club	Source	Date Signed	Seasons Played	Apps	Subs	Gls
Luton T.	App	09.64	64-68	148	1	47
Aston Villa	Tr	07.69	69-73	149	5	34
Derby Co.	Tr	02.74	73-76	106	0	34
Everton	Tr	12.76	76-77	30	0	3
Derby Co.	Tr	11.77	77-79	40	1	4
Birmingham C.	L	12.78	78	3	0	0
Sheffield U.	L	03.79	78	8	0	1
Torquay U.	Seattle (USA)	10.80	80-83	64	7	6

RIOCH, Neil G.
Paddington, 13 April, 1951 E Yth (CD)

League Club	Source	Date Signed	Seasons Played	Apps	Subs	Gls
Luton T.	App	07.68				
Aston Villa	Tr	09.69	69-74	17	5	3
York C.	L	02.72	71	0	1	0
Northampton T.	L	03.72	71	14	0	4
Plymouth Arg.	Tr	05.75	75	3	2	0

RIPLEY, Keith A.
Normanton, 10 October, 1954 (FB)

League Club	Source	Date Signed	Seasons Played	Apps	Subs	Gls
Huddersfield T.	Gainsborough Trin.	08.78	78	2	3	0
Doncaster Rov.	Tr	08.79	79	5	0	0

RIPLEY, S. Keith
Normanton, 29 March, 1935 (WH)

League Club	Source	Date Signed	Seasons Played	Apps	Subs	Gls
Leeds U.	Jnrs	04.52	54-57	68	-	15
Norwich C.	Tr	08.58	58	12	-	6
Mansfield T.	Tr	11.58	58-59	31	-	5
Peterborough U.	Tr	07.60	60-61	82	-	12
Doncaster Rov.	Tr	08.62	62-65	123	5	7

League Club	Source	Date Signed	Seasons Played	Career Record Apps	Subs	Gls

RIPLEY, Stuart E.
Middlesbrough, 20 November, 1967 E Yth/Eu21-8 (LW)

Middlesbrough	App	11.85	84-91	210	39	26
Bolton W.	L	02.86	85	5	0	1

RISDON, Stanley W.
Exeter, 13 August, 1913 Died 1979 (WH)

Exeter C.	St Marys Majors	10.33	33-35	35	-	1
Brighton & H.A.	Tr	08.36	36-46	23	-	0

RISEBOROUGH, Cyril
Doncaster, 22 February, 1933 (OR)

Swindon T.		02.55	54-56	26	-	1

RIST, Frank H.
Hackney, 30 March, 1914 (CH)

Leyton Orient	Grays Ath.	08.32				
Charlton Ath.	Tr	06.33	34-46	47	-	1

RITCHIE, Andrew T.
Manchester, 28 November, 1960 E Sch/E Yth/Eu21-1 (F)

Manchester U.	App	12.77	77-80	26	7	13
Brighton & H.A.	Tr	10.80	80-82	82	7	23
Leeds U.	Tr	03.83	82-86	127	9	40
Oldham Ath.	Tr	08.87	87-91	139	11	67

Andy Ritchie (Manchester United, Brighton & Hove Albion, Leeds United & Oldham Athletic)

RITCHIE, David M.
Stoke, 20 January, 1971 (F)

Stoke C.	YT	07.89				
Stockport Co.	Tr	03.90	89	0	1	0

RITCHIE, John
Paddington, 28 February, 1951 E Amat (CF)

Arsenal	Slough T.	04.72				
Hereford U.	Tr	03.74	73-74	19	3	4

RITCHIE, John
Ashington, 10 April, 1944 E Amat (FB)

Port Vale	Whitley Bay	12.65	65-66	50	0	3
Preston N.E.	Tr	04.67	66-71	93	0	5
Bradford C.	Tr	03.72	71-72	20	0	0

RITCHIE, John
Blairhall, 31 March, 1927 (WH)

Accrington St.	Crossgates Primrose	06.49	49	13	-	0

RITCHIE, John B.
Auchterderran (Fife), 12 June, 1947 (G)

Bradford C.	Brechin C.	07.71	71-73	64	0	0

RITCHIE, John H.
Kettering, 12 July, 1941 (CF)

Stoke C.	Kettering T.	06.62	62-66	110	0	64
Sheffield Wed.	Tr	11.66	66-68	88	1	34
Stoke C.	Tr	07.69	69-74	151	9	71

RITCHIE, Robert
Glasgow, 1 February, 1920

Watford	Rickmansworth	02.48	48	1	-	0

RITCHIE, Stephen K.
Glasgow, 17 February, 1954 S Sch (LB)

Bristol C.	App	09.71	72	1	0	0
Hereford U.	Morton	06.75	75-77	102	0	3
Torquay U.	Aberdeen	03.79	78-79	58	0	2

RITCHIE, Stuart A.
Southampton, 20 May, 1968 (M)

Aston Villa	App	05.86	86	0	1	0
Crewe Alex.	Tr	06.87	87	13	5	0

RITCHIE, Thomas
Bangor, 10 July, 1930 (OL)

Manchester U.	Bangor C.	12.50				
Reading	Tr	02.53	52-54	18	-	5
Grimsby T.	Dartford	08.58	58	1	-	0
Barrow	Tr	12.58	58	16	-	6

RITCHIE, Thomas G.
Edinburgh, 2 January, 1952 (F)

Bristol C.	Bridgend Th.	07.69	72-80	308	13	77
Sunderland	Tr	01.81	80-81	32	3	8
Carlisle U.	L	03.82	81	14	1	0
Bristol C.	Tr	06.82	82-84	92	1	25

RITCHIE, William S.
Dundee, 13 November, 1932 (F)

Bury	Dundee	06.57	57-58	13	-	7
Stockport Co.	Tr	03.59	58-60	52	-	12

RITSON, John A.
Liverpool, 6 September, 1949 (RB)

Bolton W.	App	09.66	67-77	321	3	9
Bury	Tr	09.78	78-79	41	0	2

RITSON, Ledger
Gateshead, 28 April, 1921 Died 1977 (LB)

Leyton Orient		03.46	46-48	84	-	0

RIVERS, Alan D.
Portsmouth, 27 January, 1946 (CH)

Luton T.	App	01.64	65-66	25	5	1
Watford	Tr	09.67	67	0	2	0

RIX, Graham
Askern, 23 October, 1957 Eu21-7/E-17 (M)

Arsenal	App	01.75	76-87	338	13	41
Brentford	L	12.87	87	6	0	0

ROAST, Jesse
Barking, 16 March, 1964 (FB)

Maidstone U.	Walthamstow Ave.	01.87	89-90	31	1	0

ROBB, David T.
Broughty Ferry, 15 December, 1947 Su23-3/S-5 (F)

Norwich C.	Tampa Bay (USA)	09.78	78	4	1	1

ROBB, George
Finsbury Park, 1 June, 1926 E Amat/EF Lge/E'B'-3/E-1 (OL)

Tottenham H.	Finchley	12.51	51-58	182	-	53

ROBB, Ian A.
Doncaster, 1 June, 1955 (CD)

York C.	Jnrs	02.73	73-74	4	0	0

ROBB, William L.
Cambuslang, 23 December, 1927 (WH)

Leyton Orient	Aberdeen	05.50	50	5	-	0
Bradford C.	Albion Rov.	10.54	54-57	127	-	4

League Club	Source	Date Signed	Seasons Played	Apps	Subs	Gls
ROBBINS, Gordon						
Barnsley, 7 February, 1936						(HB)
Rotherham U.	Wombwell	05.53				
Crewe Alex.	Goole T.	12.58	58	4	-	0
ROBBINS, Robert						
Newton Abbot, 20 September, 1953						(G)
Torquay U. (N/C)		08.76	76	19	0	0
ROBER, H. Jurgen						
West Germany, 25 December, 1933						(M)
Nottingham F.	Chicago (USA)	12.81	81	21	1	3
ROBERTS, Alan						
Newcastle, 8 December, 1964						(RW)
Middlesbrough	App	12.82	82-85	28	10	2
Darlington	Tr	09.85	85-87	116	3	19
Sheffield U.	Tr	07.88	88-89	31	5	2
Lincoln C.	Tr	10.89	89	10	0	0
ROBERTS, Alan						
Bury, 23 April, 1946						(FB)
Bradford P.A.	Mossley	11.69	69	15	0	0
ROBERTS, Andrew J.						
Dartford, 20 March, 1974						(M)
Millwall	YT	10.91	91	5	2	0
ROBERTS, Anthony M.						
Holyhead, 4 August, 1969 W Yth/Wu21-2						(G)
Queens Park R.	YT	07.87	87-91	19	0	0
ROBERTS, A. Arthur						
Barnsley, 27 January, 1907 Died 1957						(CH)
Southampton	Ardsley	08.29	30-37	156	-	0
Swansea C.	Tr	08.38	38	14	-	0
York C.	Tr	07.46	46	1	-	0
ROBERTS, Brian J.						
Windsor, 3 February, 1967						(F)
Reading	YT	07.85	84-85	0	5	0
ROBERTS, Brian L. F.						
Manchester, 6 November, 1955						(FB)
Coventry C.	App	11.73	75-83	209	6	1
Hereford U.	L	02.75	74	5	0	0
Birmingham C.	Tr	03.84	83-89	182	5	0
Wolverhampton W.	Tr	06.90	90	17	4	0
ROBERTS, Cledwyn						
Colwyn Bay, 12 August, 1947						(WH)
Wrexham	Glan Conwy	08.65	65	1	0	0
ROBERTS, Colin						
Castleford, 16 September, 1933						(WH)
Bradford P.A.	Altofts Colly	10.51	53-55	75	-	0
Bradford C.	Frickley Colly	06.59	59-60	57	-	0
ROBERTS, J. Dale						
Newcastle, 8 October, 1956 E Yth						(CD)
Ipswich T.	App	09.74	74-77	17	1	0
Hull C.	Tr	02.80	79-84	149	4	6
ROBERTS, David A.						
Birmingham, 21 December, 1946						(W)
Aston Villa	Jnrs	12.63	65-67	15	1	1
Shrewsbury T.	Tr	03.68	67-73	224	6	21
Swansea C.	Tr	05.74	74	32	5	1
ROBERTS, David F.						
Southampton, 26 January, 1949 Wu23-4/W-18						(CD)
Fulham	App	09.67	68-70	21	1	0
Oxford U.	Tr	02.71	70-74	160	1	7
Hull C.	Tr	02.75	74-77	86	0	4
Cardiff C.	Tr	08.78	78-80	40	1	2
ROBERTS, David G.						
Plymouth, 8 May, 1944						(FB)
Plymouth Arg.	App	12.61	61-63	11	-	0
ROBERTS, Dean						
Mexborough, 12 January, 1967						(F)
Bolton W.	App	01.85				
Exeter C.	Tr	07.86	86	23	2	7
ROBERTS, Dennis						
Bretton, 5 February, 1918						(CH)
Notts Co.		08.37				
Bristol C.	Tr	05.38	38-53	303	-	2
ROBERTS, Donald C.						
Arlecdon, 3 February, 1933						(IF)
Workington	Whitehaven	07.52	52-53	21	-	0
Barrow		10.57	57-58	22	-	2
ROBERTS, Dudley E.						
Derby, 16 October, 1945						(F)
Coventry C.	Jnrs	11.63	65-67	11	1	6
Mansfield T.	Tr	03.68	67-73	194	6	66
Doncaster Rov.	L	02.73	72	7	0	0
Scunthorpe U.	Tr	02.74	73-75	56	3	17
ROBERTS, Edward						
Chesterfield, 2 November, 1916						(CF)
Derby Co.	Glapwell Colly	04.34	35	4	-	0
Coventry C.	Tr	03.37	36-51	212	-	85
ROBERTS, Edward J.						
Liverpool, 16 November, 1947						(G)
Tranmere Rov.	Harrowby Jnrs	05.67	68-69	7	0	0
ROBERTS, Eric						
						(OL)
Halifax T.	Altofts Colly	08.47	47	5	-	1
ROBERTS, Frederick						
Rhyl, 7 May, 1916 Died 1985						(OR)
Bury	Rhyl	04.38	38-46	12	-	5
Leyton Orient	Tr	11.46	46	18	-	2
ROBERTS, Garreth W.						
Hull, 15 November, 1960 Wu21-1						(W)
Hull C.	App	11.78	78-90	409	5	47
ROBERTS, Gary P. M.						
Rhyl, 5 April, 1960						(F)
Brentford	Wembley	10.80	80-85	180	7	45
ROBERTS, Geoffrey M.						
Liverpool, 29 December, 1949						(FB)
Bolton W.	App	01.67	67-69	5	0	0
ROBERTS, D. Gordon						
Coventry, 30 May, 1925						(W)
Wolverhampton W.	Jnrs	09.42				
Northampton T.	Tr	09.45	46-48	57	-	7
Brighton & H.A.	Tr	03.49	48-49	17	-	3
Accrington St.	Tr	07.51	51	39	-	11
ROBERTS, Gordon R.						
Cardiff, 30 December, 1946 W Sch						(W)
Wolverhampton W.	App	01.64				
Bury	Tr	09.65	65	2	0	0
ROBERTS, Graham P.						
Southampton, 3 July, 1959 E-6						(CD)
Portsmouth (N/C)	Sholing	03.77				
Tottenham H.	Weymouth	05.80	80-86	200	9	23
Chelsea	Glasgow Rangers	08.88	88-89	70	0	18
West Bromwich A.	Tr	11.90	90-91	39	0	6
ROBERTS, Griffith O.						
Blaenau Ffestiniog, 2 October, 1920						(G)
Nottingham F.	Blaenau Ffestiniog	05.46	46	9	-	0
ROBERTS, Harold						
Liverpool, 12 January, 1920						(OL)
Chesterfield	Harrowby Jnrs	08.39	46-48	92	-	9
Birmingham C.	Tr	11.48	48-50	34	-	2
Shrewsbury T.	Tr	06.51	51-52	70	-	16
Scunthorpe U.	Tr	07.53	53-54	17	-	1
ROBERTS, Ian M.						
Colwyn Bay, 28 February, 1961						(M)
Wrexham	Jnrs	07.79	78-79	2	4	0
ROBERTS, Ian P.						
Glasgow, 28 September, 1955						(LB)
Shrewsbury T.	App	09.72	71-75	93	3	0
Crewe Alex.	Tr	07.76	76-78	89	4	0

League Club	Source	Date Signed	Seasons Played	Career Record Apps	Subs	Gls

ROBERTS, Iwan W.
Bangor, 26 June, 1968 W Yth/W-3 (F)

League Club	Source	Date Signed	Seasons Played	Apps	Subs	Gls
Watford	YT	06.86	85-89	40	23	9
Huddersfield T.	Tr	07.90	90-91	90	0	37

ROBERTS, James N.
Stirling, 12 June, 1923 (OL)

League Club	Source	Date Signed	Seasons Played	Apps	Subs	Gls
Ipswich T.	Dundee	09.49	49-51	73	-	15
Barrow	Tr	07.52	52	11	-	2

ROBERTS, Jeremy
Middlesbrough, 24 November, 1966 E Yth (G)

League Club	Source	Date Signed	Seasons Played	Apps	Subs	Gls
Hartlepool U. (N/C)	Jnrs	12.83	83	1	0	0
Leicester C.	Tr	07.84	85	3	0	0
Darlington	Luton T. (Trial)	03.87	86-87	29	0	0
Brentford (N/C)	Tr	09.88	88	5	0	0

ROBERTS, John D.
Wrexham, 22 July, 1928 (F)

League Club	Source	Date Signed	Seasons Played	Apps	Subs	Gls
Wrexham (Am)	Brymbo Steel Wks	04.51	50	1	-	0

ROBERTS, John G.
Abercynon, 11 September, 1946 Wu21-1/Wu23-5/W-22 (CD)

League Club	Source	Date Signed	Seasons Played	Apps	Subs	Gls
Swansea C.	Abercynon A.	07.64	65-67	36	1	16
Northampton T.	Tr	11.67	67-68	62	0	11
Arsenal	Tr	05.69	69-72	56	3	4
Birmingham C.	Tr	10.72	72-75	61	5	1
Wrexham	Tr	08.76	76-79	145	0	5
Hull C.	Tr	08.80	80	26	0	1

ROBERTS, John H.
Swansea, 30 June, 1918 W-1 (FB)

League Club	Source	Date Signed	Seasons Played	Apps	Subs	Gls
Bolton W.	Cwmburia	04.36	37-50	162	-	19
Swansea C.	Tr	09.50	50	16	-	1

ROBERTS, John T.
Australia, 24 March, 1944 (G)

League Club	Source	Date Signed	Seasons Played	Apps	Subs	Gls
Chelsea	Leichardt (Aus)	01.66				
Blackburn Rov.	Tr	04.66	65	3	0	0
Chesterfield	L	08.67	67	46	0	0
Bradford C.	Tr	08.68	68-70	44	0	0
Southend U.	Tr	01.71	70-71	47	0	0
Northampton T.	Tr	07.72	72	13	0	0

Graham Roberts (Portsmouth, Tottenham Hotspur, Glasgow Rangers, Chelsea, West Bromwich Albion & England)

ROBERTS, Jonathan W.
Ferndale, 30 December, 1968 W Yth (G)

League Club	Source	Date Signed	Seasons Played	Apps	Subs	Gls
Cardiff C.	YT	11.87	87-88	9	0	0

ROBERTS, Kenneth
Crewe, 10 March, 1931 (IF)

League Club	Source	Date Signed	Seasons Played	Apps	Subs	Gls
Aston Villa	Crewe Villa	08.51	51-53	42	-	7

ROBERTS, Kenneth O.
Cefn-mawr, 27 March, 1936 (OR)

League Club	Source	Date Signed	Seasons Played	Apps	Subs	Gls
Wrexham (Am)	Jnrs	05.51	51	1	-	0
Aston Villa	Tr	05.53	53-57	38	-	3

ROBERTS, Kevin J.
Bristol, 25 July, 1955 (G)

League Club	Source	Date Signed	Seasons Played	Apps	Subs	Gls
Swindon T.	Welton Rov.	03.77	77	1	0	0

ROBERTS, Lee J.
Market Drayton, 23 March, 1957 (CD)

League Club	Source	Date Signed	Seasons Played	Apps	Subs	Gls
Shrewsbury T.	App	01.75	73-77	9	6	1
Exeter C.	L	03.77	76	5	2	0
Exeter C.	Tr	09.77	77-82	135	9	12

ROBERTS, Maurice E. S.
Bristol, 5 July, 1922 (OL)

League Club	Source	Date Signed	Seasons Played	Apps	Subs	Gls
Brentford		08.46	46	10	-	0
Bristol C.	Tr	05.47				

ROBERTS, Michael J.
Birmingham, 21 May, 1960 (M)

League Club	Source	Date Signed	Seasons Played	Apps	Subs	Gls
Shrewsbury T.		07.78	78	0	1	0

ROBERTS, Owen J.
Maerdy, 16 February, 1919 (G)

League Club	Source	Date Signed	Seasons Played	Apps	Subs	Gls
Plymouth Arg.		02.38				
Swansea C.	Aberaman	10.45	46-47	24	-	0
Newport Co.	Tr	08.48	48	7	-	0

ROBERTS, Paul
West Ham, 27 April, 1962 (FB)

League Club	Source	Date Signed	Seasons Played	Apps	Subs	Gls
Millwall	App	04.79	78-82	142	4	0
Brentford	Tr	09.83	83-84	61	1	0
Swindon T. (N/C)	Finland	09.85	85	25	2	0
Southend U.	Tr	07.86	86	38	0	0
Aldershot	Tr	08.87	87	36	3	0
Exeter C. (N/C)	Leytonstone & Ilford	12.88	88	3	0	0
Southend U.	Tr	01.89	88-89	53	1	0

ROBERTS, Peter
Chesterfield, 21 July, 1955 (W)

League Club	Source	Date Signed	Seasons Played	Apps	Subs	Gls
Chesterfield (N/C)	Jnrs	09.73	74-75	2	0	0

ROBERTS, Peter L.
Sherburn, 16 July, 1925 (IF)

League Club	Source	Date Signed	Seasons Played	Apps	Subs	Gls
Leeds U.	Newcastle U. (Am)	09.46				
New Brighton	Tr	07.48	48	3	-	0

ROBERTS, Philip S.
Cardiff, 24 February, 1950 Wu23-6/W-4 (RB)

League Club	Source	Date Signed	Seasons Played	Apps	Subs	Gls
Bristol Rov.	App	11.68	69-72	174	1	6
Portsmouth	Tr	05.73	73-77	152	1	1
Hereford U.	Tr	07.78	78	3	0	0
Exeter C.	Tr	02.79	78-81	103	2	0

ROBERTS, Robert
Edinburgh, 2 September, 1940 Su23-1/SF Lge (M)

League Club	Source	Date Signed	Seasons Played	Apps	Subs	Gls
Leicester C.	Motherwell	09.63	63-69	224	5	26
Mansfield T.	Tr	09.70	70-71	76	4	4
Colchester U.	Coventry C. (Coach)	07.73	73	0	2	0

ROBERTS, Ronald
Wrexham, 14 September, 1942 Wu23-2 (OL)

League Club	Source	Date Signed	Seasons Played	Apps	Subs	Gls
Wrexham	Jnrs	04.60	59-62	68	-	4
Tranmere Rov.	Tr	03.63	62-63	56	-	2

ROBERTS, Stanley
Wrexham, 10 April, 1921 (OR)

League Club	Source	Date Signed	Seasons Played	Apps	Subs	Gls
Wrexham	Cross Street	09.46	46-47	27	-	9
New Brighton	Tr	07.48	48-50	103	-	25

ROBERTS, Stuart W.
Chirk, 25 March, 1967 W Yth (G)

League Club	Source	Date Signed	Seasons Played	Apps	Subs	Gls
Stoke C.	App	03.85	84	3	0	0

League Club	Source	Date Signed	Seasons Played	Apps	Subs	Gls
ROBERTS, Thomas						
Liverpool, 28 July, 1927						(FB)
Blackburn Rov.	Skelmersdale U.	12.51	51-53	6	-	0
Watford	Tr	12.54	54	1	-	0
Chester C.	Tr	02.56	55	5	-	0
ROBERTS, Thomas						
Liverpool, 27 December, 1945						(OL)
Everton	App	11.63				
Stockport Co.	Tr	03.65	64-65	20	0	0
Southport	Tr	07.66	66	4	0	1
ROBERTS, Thomas W. G.						
Reading, 11 June, 1932						(F)
Birmingham C.		05.53				
Barrow	Tr	10.55	55-56	40	-	14
ROBERTS, Trevor E.						
Caernarfon, 25 February, 1942 Died 1972 W Amat						(G)
Liverpool	Liverpool Univ.	06.63				
Southend U.	Tr	01.66	65-69	171	0	0
Cambridge U.	Tr	08.70	70-71	36	0	0
ROBERTS, Trevor L.						
Southampton, 9 May, 1961						(D)
Portsmouth	Southampton (App)	02.79	78-79	1	2	0
ROBERTS, Walter						
Wrexham, 23 November, 1917						(D)
Wrexham		08.38	38-47	60	-	1
Bournemouth	Tr	07.48	48-49	14	-	0
ROBERTS, William E.						
Flint, 22 October, 1918						(G)
Rochdale		04.46	46-48	43	-	0
ROBERTS, William J.						
Bradford, 9 April, 1963						(F)
Rochdale (N/C)	Farsley Celtic	11.88	88	1	0	0
ROBERTS, Winston						
Hartlepool, 5 July, 1939						(F)
Hartlepool U.		09.58	58	3	-	0
ROBERTSON, Alistair						
Linlithgow, 9 September, 1952 S Sch						(CD)
West Bromwich A.	App	09.69	69-85	504	2	8
Wolverhampton W.	Tr	09.86	86-89	107	0	0
ROBERTSON, David						
Baillieston, 12 January, 1945						(OR)
Crewe Alex.	Motherwell	07.63	63	10	-	2
ROBERTSON, Edward H. Y.						
Edinburgh, 19 December, 1935 Died 1981						(FB)
Bury	Linithgow Rose	07.54	56-62	196	-	5
Wrexham	Tr	10.63	63	24	-	0
Tranmere Rov.	Tr	07.64	64-68	143	4	1
ROBERTSON, George J.						
Bainsford, 20 April, 1930						(FB)
Plymouth Arg.	Gairdoch Jnrs	01.50	50-63	359	-	2
ROBERTSON, James						
Leith, 7 July, 1940						(IR)
Newport Co.	Aberdeen	07.61	61	29	-	5
ROBERTSON, James						
Gateshead, 24 November, 1969						(RB)
Carlisle U.	YT	07.88	87-89	10	3	0
ROBERTSON, James G.						
Glasgow, 17 December, 1944 Su23-4/S-1						(W)
Tottenham H.	St Mirren	03.64	63-68	153	4	25
Arsenal	Tr	10.68	68-69	45	1	7
Ipswich T.	Tr	03.70	69-71	87	0	10
Stoke C.	Tr	06.72	72-76	99	15	12
Walsall	Tr	09.77	77	16	0	0
Crewe Alex.	Tr	09.78	78	32	1	0
ROBERTSON, James W.						
Falkirk, 20 February, 1929						(W)
Arsenal	Dunipace Th.	06.48	51	1	-	0
Brentford	Tr	09.53	53-55	85	-	11
ROBERTSON, John C.						
Aberdeen, 15 July, 1928						(CF)
Portsmouth	Ayr U.	08.55	55	12	-	4
York C.	Tr	06.57	57	17	-	5
Barrow	Tr	08.58	58-61	156	-	48
ROBERTSON, John G.						
Edinburgh, 2 October, 1964 Su21-1/S-4						(F)
Newcastle U.	Hearts	04.88	88	7	5	0
ROBERTSON, John N.						
Uddingston, 20 January, 1953 S Sch/S Yth/S-28						(LW)
Nottingham F.	App	05.70	70-82	374	13	61
Derby Co.	Tr	06.83	83-84	72	0	3
Nottingham F.	Tr	08.85	85	10	1	0
ROBERTSON, A. Lamond (Lammie)						
Paisley, 27 September, 1947						(M)
Burnley	Jnrs	09.66				
Bury	Tr	06.68	68	3	2	0
Halifax T.	Tr	02.69	68-72	142	7	20
Brighton & H.A.	Tr	12.72	72-73	42	4	9
Exeter C.	Tr	05.74	74-77	132	1	25
Leicester C.	Tr	09.77	77	6	1	0
Peterborough U.	Tr	08.78	78	12	3	1
Bradford C.	Tr	01.79	78-80	41	2	3
ROBERTSON, Leonard V.						
Middlesbrough, 1 March, 1916						(IF)
Watford	Stockton	06.46	46	6	-	2
Hull C.	Tr	04.47	46-47	9	-	2
Accrington St.	Tr	07.48	48	3	-	0
ROBERTSON, Paul						
Manchester, 5 February, 1972						(LB)
Stockport Co.	York C. (YT)	08.89	89-90	7	3	0
Bury	Tr	07.91	91	5	0	0
ROBERTSON, Stuart						
Glasgow, 29 September, 1959						(W)
Burnley	App	07.77	78-81	30	2	0
Exeter C.	Tr	03.82	81	5	1	0
Doncaster Rov. (N/C)	Tr	10.82	82	25	0	0
ROBERTSON, Stuart J.						
Nottingham, 16 December, 1946						(CD)
Nottingham F.	Jnrs	08.64				
Doncaster Rov.	Tr	07.66	66-71	224	3	8
Northampton T.	Tr	05.72	72-78	254	0	24
ROBERTSON, Thomas						
Coventry, 28 September, 1944						(W)
Crystal Palace	St Mirren	10.66	66	5	0	0
ROBERTSON, William G.						
Glasgow, 13 November, 1928 Died 1973						(G)
Chelsea	Arthurlie	07.46	50-59	199	-	0
Leyton Orient	Tr	09.60	60-62	47	-	0
ROBERTSON, William G.						
Glasgow, 4 November, 1936						(W)
Middlesbrough	Jnrs	11.53	54	5	-	2
ROBERTSON, William H.						
Crowthorne, 25 March, 1923						(G)
Chelsea	R.A.F. Lossiemouth	10.45	46-47	37	-	0
Birmingham C.	Tr	12.48	48-51	2	-	0
Stoke C.	Tr	06.52	52-59	238	-	0
ROBERTSON, William J.						
Montrose, 9 November, 1923						(HB)
Preston N.E.	Montrose Roselea	03.42	46-52	52	-	0
Southport	Tr	07.55	55	28	-	0
ROBINS, Ian						
Bury, 22 February, 1952						(F)
Oldham Ath.	App	02.70	69-76	202	18	40
Bury	Tr	07.77	77-78	49	0	5
Huddersfield T.	Tr	09.78	78-81	145	11	59
ROBINS, Mark G.						
Ashton-u-Lyne, 22 December, 1969 Eu21-6						(F)
Manchester U.	YT	12.86	88-91	19	29	11
ROBINSON, Alan						
Grantham, 2 December, 1955						(IF)
Sheffield Wed.	App	12.73				
Scunthorpe U.	Tr	08.75	75	1	0	0

ROBINSON, Albert
Chester, 1 June, 1948 (WH)

League Club	Source	Date Signed	Seasons Played	Apps	Subs	Gls
Chester C.	Jnrs	07.68	67-68	5	1	0

ROBINSON, Andrew C.
Oldham, 10 March, 1966 (M)

League Club	Source	Date Signed	Seasons Played	Apps	Subs	Gls
Manchester U.	App	03.84				
Burnley	L	10.85	85	5	0	1
Bury	Tr	01.86	85-86	12	7	0
Carlisle U.	Tr	03.87	86-87	43	3	3

ROBINSON, Anthony
Hebburn, 5 November, 1958 (W)

League Club	Source	Date Signed	Seasons Played	Apps	Subs	Gls
Hartlepool U. (N/C)	Blue Star	09.86	86	1	1	0

ROBINSON, Bernard C.
Cambridge, 5 December, 1911 (WH)

League Club	Source	Date Signed	Seasons Played	Apps	Subs	Gls
Norwich C.	Kings Lynn	12.31	31-48	360	-	13

ROBINSON, Brian T. A.
Paddington, 2 April, 1946 (G)

League Club	Source	Date Signed	Seasons Played	Apps	Subs	Gls
Peterborough U.	App	04.64	64-65	8	0	0

ROBINSON, Colin R.
Birmingham, 15 May, 1960 (F)

League Club	Source	Date Signed	Seasons Played	Apps	Subs	Gls
Shrewsbury T.	Mile Oak Rov.	11.82	82-87	176	18	41
Birmingham C.	Tr	01.88	87-88	34	3	6
Hereford U.	Tr	08.89	89-90	41	23	6

ROBINSON, Cyril
Nottingham, 4 March, 1929 (WH)

League Club	Source	Date Signed	Seasons Played	Apps	Subs	Gls
Blackpool	Mansfield T. (Am)	09.49	51-54	22	-	2
Bradford P.A.	Northwich Vic.	06.56	56-58	89	-	3
Southport	Tr	07.59	59	37	-	0

ROBINSON, David
Birmingham, 14 July, 1948 (CD)

League Club	Source	Date Signed	Seasons Played	Apps	Subs	Gls
Birmingham C.	App	07.66	68-71	110	2	2
Walsall	Tr	02.73	72-76	164	1	3

ROBINSON, David A.
Middlesbrough, 14 January, 1965 (CD)

League Club	Source	Date Signed	Seasons Played	Apps	Subs	Gls
Hartlepool U.	Jnrs	08.83	83-85	64	2	1
Halifax T.	Tr	08.86	86-88	72	0	1
Peterborough U.	Tr	07.89	89-91	94	0	9

ROBINSON, David J.
Newcastle, 27 November, 1969 (F)

League Club	Source	Date Signed	Seasons Played	Apps	Subs	Gls
Newcastle U.	YT	06.88	88-91	0	8	0
Peterborough U.	L	02.91	90	7	0	3
Reading (N/C)	Tr	03.92	91	8	0	0

ROBINSON, David S.
Exeter, 6 January, 1937 (W)

League Club	Source	Date Signed	Seasons Played	Apps	Subs	Gls
Exeter C.	Whipton	12.54	57-58	16	-	4
Oldham Ath.	Tr	07.59				

ROBINSON, David W.
Manchester, 25 November, 1921

League Club	Source	Date Signed	Seasons Played	Apps	Subs	Gls
Shrewsbury T.		08.50	50	10	-	0

ROBINSON, Edward
Bywell, 15 January, 1922 (FB)

League Club	Source	Date Signed	Seasons Played	Apps	Subs	Gls
Gateshead		11.45	46-52	90	-	7

ROBINSON, Eric M.
Manchester, 1 July, 1935 (F)

League Club	Source	Date Signed	Seasons Played	Apps	Subs	Gls
West Bromwich A.	Altrincham	03.57	57	1	-	0
Rotherham U.	Tr	01.59	58-59	14	-	1

ROBINSON, Frederick J.
Rotherham, 29 December, 1954 (LB)

League Club	Source	Date Signed	Seasons Played	Apps	Subs	Gls
Rotherham U.	App	01.73	73	4	0	0
Doncaster Rov.	Tr	10.75	75-78	111	8	3
Huddersfield T.	Tr	08.79	79-80	72	0	2

ROBINSON, George D.
Liverpool, 28 May, 1937

League Club	Source	Date Signed	Seasons Played	Apps	Subs	Gls
Southport		02.59	58	2	-	0

ROBINSON, George F.
Melton Mowbray, 17 June, 1925 (FB)

League Club	Source	Date Signed	Seasons Played	Apps	Subs	Gls
Notts Co.	Holwell Wks	08.44	46	29	-	0

ROBINSON, George H.
Heanor, 11 January, 1908 Died 1963 (IF)

League Club	Source	Date Signed	Seasons Played	Apps	Subs	Gls
Sunderland	Ilkeston U.	04.27	27-30	31	-	8
Charlton Ath.	Tr	06.31	31-46	238	-	42

ROBINSON Henry
Southport, 14 September, 1947 (OR)

League Club	Source	Date Signed	Seasons Played	Apps	Subs	Gls
Blackpool	App	01.65				
Southport	Tr	02.66				
Newport Co.		11.67	67-68	39	1	3

ROBINSON, Herbert
Padiham, 30 April, 1922 (CF)

League Club	Source	Date Signed	Seasons Played	Apps	Subs	Gls
Accrington St.	Barnoldswick T.	12.46	46	5	-	4

ROBINSON, John
Chorley, 18 April, 1936 (OR)

League Club	Source	Date Signed	Seasons Played	Apps	Subs	Gls
Bury	Leyland Motors	09.54	54-59	120	-	21
Oldham Ath.	Tr	07.61	61	3	-	0

ROBINSON, John
Middlesbrough, 10 February, 1934 (IF)

League Club	Source	Date Signed	Seasons Played	Apps	Subs	Gls
Middlesbrough	Jnrs	10.51	53-54	3	-	0
Hartlepool U.	Tr	06.59	59	9	-	0

ROBINSON, John
Lurgan (NI), 2 April, 1920 Died 1981

League Club	Source	Date Signed	Seasons Played	Apps	Subs	Gls
Wolverhampton W.	Glenavon	01.42				
Walsall	Tr	03.47	46	4	-	0

ROBINSON, John (Jackie)
Shiremoor, 10 August, 1917 EF Lge/E-4 (IF)

League Club	Source	Date Signed	Seasons Played	Apps	Subs	Gls
Sheffield Wed.	Shiremoor	10.34	34-36	108	-	34
Sunderland	Tr	10.46	46-48	82	-	32
Lincoln C.	Tr	10.49	49	8	-	5

ROBINSON, John J.
Blackburn, 23 April, 1918 (G)

League Club	Source	Date Signed	Seasons Played	Apps	Subs	Gls
Accrington St.	Sacred Heart	05.35	35-36	16	-	0
Manchester C.	Tr	04.37	38-46	2	-	0
Bury	Tr	11.46	46	12	-	0
Southend U.	Tr	08.47	47	6	-	0

ROBINSON, John R. C.
Bulawayo (Zimbabwe), 29 August, 1971 Wu21-1 (W)

League Club	Source	Date Signed	Seasons Played	Apps	Subs	Gls
Brighton & H.A.	YT	04.89	89-91	51	5	6

ROBINSON, Joseph
Lanchester, 14 November, 1918 (WH)

League Club	Source	Date Signed	Seasons Played	Apps	Subs	Gls
Norwich C.	Ouston U.	11.37	46	2	-	0

ROBINSON, Joseph
Morpeth, 4 March, 1919 Died 1991 (G)

League Club	Source	Date Signed	Seasons Played	Apps	Subs	Gls
Hartlepool U.	Hexham Hearts	05.38	38	11	-	0
Blackpool	Tr	07.46	47-48	25	-	0
Hull C.	Tr	02.49	48-52	70	-	0

ROBINSON Joseph W.
Chester-le-Street, 13 April, 1932 (F)

League Club	Source	Date Signed	Seasons Played	Apps	Subs	Gls
Newcastle U.	Jnrs	09.51				
Hartlepool U.	West Stanley	07.54	55-57	43	-	6
Gateshead	Tr	08.58	58	22	-	4

ROBINSON, Keith
Bolton, 30 December, 1937 (IF)

League Club	Source	Date Signed	Seasons Played	Apps	Subs	Gls
Oldham Ath.		09.58	58-60	40	-	4

ROBINSON, Leonard J.
Nottingham, 1 October, 1946 (FB)

League Club	Source	Date Signed	Seasons Played	Apps	Subs	Gls
Notts Co.	Nottingham F. (Am)	03.64	63-64	4	-	0

ROBINSON, Leslie
Shirebrook, 1 March, 1967 (RB)

League Club	Source	Date Signed	Seasons Played	Apps	Subs	Gls
Mansfield T.	Chesterfield (Jnrs)	10.84	84-86	11	4	0
Stockport Co.	Tr	11.86	86-87	67	0	3
Doncaster Rov.	Tr	03.88	87-89	82	0	12
Oxford U.	Tr	03.90	89-91	71	0	0

ROBINSON, S. Liam
Bradford, 29 December, 1965 (F)

League Club	Source	Date Signed	Seasons Played	Apps	Subs	Gls
Huddersfield T.	Nottingham F. (App)	01.84	83-85	17	4	2
Tranmere Rov.	L	12.85	85	4	0	3
Bury	Tr	07.86	86-91	234	14	82

ROBINSON, Mark J.
Nottingham, 26 November, 1960 (F)

League Club	Source	Date Signed	Seasons Played	Apps	Subs	Gls
Notts Co.	Ilkeston T.	01.85	84-85	12	14	1

League Club	Source	Date Signed	Seasons Played	Career Record Apps	Subs	Gls

ROBINSON, Mark J.
Rochdale, 21 November, 1968 (RB/W)

League Club	Source	Date Signed	Seasons Played	Apps	Subs	Gls
West Bromwich A. (App)	App	07.85	85-86	2	0	0
Barnsley	Tr	06.87	87-91	89	19	5

ROBINSON, Mark W.
Middlesbrough, 22 October, 1961 (M)

League Club	Source	Date Signed	Seasons Played	Apps	Subs	Gls
Middlesbrough	App	10.79				
Hartlepool U.	Hull C. (N/C)	01.83	82-83	34	1	4

ROBINSON, Martin J.
Ilford, 17 July, 1957 (W)

League Club	Source	Date Signed	Seasons Played	Apps	Subs	Gls
Tottenham H.	App	05.75	75-77	5	1	2
Charlton Ath.	Tr	02.78	77-84	218	10	58
Reading	L	09.82	82	6	0	2
Gillingham	Tr	10.84	84-86	91	5	24
Southend U.	Tr	07.87	87-88	43	13	14
Cambridge U.	Tr	08.89	89	7	9	1

ROBINSON, Maurice
Newark, 9 November, 1929 (OL)

League Club	Source	Date Signed	Seasons Played	Apps	Subs	Gls
Leeds U.		04.49				
Doncaster Rov.	Gainsborough Trin.	12.52	53	18	-	7
Northampton T.	Kettering T.	06.57	57	11	-	2

ROBINSON, Michael A.
Sunderland, 30 October, 1968 (FB)

League Club	Source	Date Signed	Seasons Played	Apps	Subs	Gls
Newcastle U.	YT	08.87				
Darlington	Tr	07.88	88	0	1	0

ROBINSON, Michael J.
Leicester, 12 July, 1958 IR-23 (F)

League Club	Source	Date Signed	Seasons Played	Apps	Subs	Gls
Preston N.E.	App	07.76	75-78	45	3	15
Manchester C.	Tr	07.79	79	29	1	8
Brighton & H.A.	Tr	07.80	80-82	111	2	37
Liverpool	Tr	08.83	83-84	26	4	6
Queens Park R.	Tr	12.84	84-86	41	7	6

ROBINSON, Neil
Liverpool, 20 April, 1957 (RB/M)

League Club	Source	Date Signed	Seasons Played	Apps	Subs	Gls
Everton	App	05.74	75-78	13	3	1
Swansea C.	Tr	10.79	79-84	114	9	7
Grimsby T.	Tr	09.84	84-87	109	0	6
Darlington	Tr	07.88	88	36	2	1

ROBINSON, J. Norman
Middlesbrough, 15 January, 1921 (CH)

League Club	Source	Date Signed	Seasons Played	Apps	Subs	Gls
Middlesbrough	South Bank St Peter	01.46	46-47	16	-	0
Grimsby T.	Tr	06.48	48	5	-	0

ROBINSON, Paul
Hampstead, 5 January, 1963 E Sch/E Yth (LB)

League Club	Source	Date Signed	Seasons Played	Apps	Subs	Gls
Millwall	App	01.80	79-83	56	3	2

ROBINSON, Paul J.
Nottingham, 21 February, 1971 (F)

League Club	Source	Date Signed	Seasons Played	Apps	Subs	Gls
Scarborough	Bury (YT)	05.89	89	13	7	3
Plymouth Arg.	Tr	05.90	90	7	4	3
Hereford U.	Tr	06.91	91	7	4	0

ROBINSON, Peter
Ashington, 4 September, 1957 E Semi-Pro (CD)

League Club	Source	Date Signed	Seasons Played	Apps	Subs	Gls
Burnley	Jnrs	06.76	76-79	48	7	3
Rochdale (N/C)	Blyth Spartans	03.85	84	9	3	0
Darlington	Tr	08.85	85-87	110	2	5
Halifax T.	L	12.85	85	3	2	0

ROBINSON, Peter
Manchester, 29 January, 1922 (WH)

League Club	Source	Date Signed	Seasons Played	Apps	Subs	Gls
Manchester C.	Jnrs	05.40	46	1	-	0
Chesterfield	Tr	10.47	47-48	60	-	0
Notts Co.	Buxton	02.50	49-52	82	-	1

ROBINSON, Peter J.
St Ives, 11 April, 1944 (D)

League Club	Source	Date Signed	Seasons Played	Apps	Subs	Gls
Southend U.	Cambridge U.	03.69	68-69	1	4	0

ROBINSON, Philip B.
Doncaster, 21 November, 1942 (W)

League Club	Source	Date Signed	Seasons Played	Apps	Subs	Gls
Huddersfield T.	Montrose Vic.	04.60				
Doncaster Rov.	Tr	08.61	61-65	157	0	19
Bradford P.A.	Tr	07.66	66-68	108	8	8
Darlington	Tr	07.69	69	26	1	4

ROBINSON, Philip J.
Stafford, 6 January, 1967 (M)

League Club	Source	Date Signed	Seasons Played	Apps	Subs	Gls
Aston Villa	App	01.85	86	2	1	1
Wolverhampton W.	Tr	06.87	87-88	63	8	8
Notts Co.	Tr	08.89	89-91	65	1	5
Birmingham C.	L	03.91	90	9	0	0

ROBINSON, Raymond M.
Durham, 2 December, 1950 (IF)

League Club	Source	Date Signed	Seasons Played	Apps	Subs	Gls
Preston N.E.	App	12.68	68	2	0	0

ROBINSON, Richard
Whitburn, 19 January, 1927 EF Lge (FB)

League Club	Source	Date Signed	Seasons Played	Apps	Subs	Gls
Middlesbrough	Jnrs	04.45	46-58	390	-	1
Barrow	Tr	06.59	59-62	139	-	0

ROBINSON, Robert
Ashington, 23 June, 1921 (G)

League Club	Source	Date Signed	Seasons Played	Apps	Subs	Gls
Sunderland	Newbiggin	02.47	47-51	31	-	0
Newcastle U.	Tr	08.52	52	5	-	0

ROBINSON, Ronald
Sunderland, 22 October, 1966 (D)

League Club	Source	Date Signed	Seasons Played	Apps	Subs	Gls
Ipswich T.	S.C. Vaux	10.84				
Leeds U.	S.C. Vaux	11.85	85-86	27	0	0
Doncaster Rov.	Tr	02.87	86-88	76	2	5
West Bromwich A.	Tr	03.89	88	1	0	0
Rotherham U.	Tr	08.89	89-91	86	0	2
Peterborough U.	Tr	12.91	91	24	3	0

ROBINSON, Simon W.
West Bromwich, 6 April, 1965 (M)

League Club	Source	Date Signed	Seasons Played	Apps	Subs	Gls
Blackpool	Alvechurch	12.90				
Walsall (N/C)	Alvechurch	12.91	91	0	1	0

ROBINSON, Steven M.
Sheffield, 14 June, 1964 (M)

League Club	Source	Date Signed	Seasons Played	Apps	Subs	Gls
Chesterfield	App	06.82	81-82	8	1	0

ROBINSON, Stuart A.
Middlesbrough, 16 January, 1959 (W)

League Club	Source	Date Signed	Seasons Played	Apps	Subs	Gls
Newcastle U.	App	07.77	77-78	11	1	2
Aldershot	Tr	07.80	80-82	71	6	10

ROBINSON, Terence A. C.
Stewkley, 24 March, 1954 (F)

League Club	Source	Date Signed	Seasons Played	Apps	Subs	Gls
Luton T.	App	03.72				
Cambridge U.	L	09.72	72	6	0	1
Crewe Alex.	Tr	12.72	72-73	7	4	1

ROBINSON, Terence H.
Woodhams, 8 November, 1929 E Amat (FB)

League Club	Source	Date Signed	Seasons Played	Apps	Subs	Gls
Brentford (Am)	Loughborough Col.	09.54	54-56	34	-	3
Northampton T. (Am)	Tr	07.57	57	13	-	0

ROBINSON, William
Manchester, 17 November, 1925 Died 1953 (D)

League Club	Source	Date Signed	Seasons Played	Apps	Subs	Gls
Stockport Co.		08.49	49	9	-	2
Accrington St.	Tr	12.50	50-52	96	-	2

ROBINSON, William
Whitburn, 4 April, 1919 (CF)

League Club	Source	Date Signed	Seasons Played	Apps	Subs	Gls
Sunderland	Jnrs	04.36	37-38	24	-	14
Charlton Ath.	Tr	05.46	46-48	52	-	16
West Ham U.	Tr	01.49	48-51	101	-	60

ROBLEDO, Edward O. (Ted)
Chile, 26 July, 1928 Died 1970 (WH)

League Club	Source	Date Signed	Seasons Played	Apps	Subs	Gls
Barnsley	Jnrs	03.46	47-48	5	-	0
Newcastle U.	Tr	02.49	49-52	37	-	0
Notts Co.	Cola Cola (Chile)	09.57	57	2	-	0

ROBLEDO, George O.
Chile, 14 April, 1926 Died 1989 Chilean Int (IF)

League Club	Source	Date Signed	Seasons Played	Apps	Subs	Gls
Barnsley	Huddersfield T. (Am)	04.43	46-48	105	-	47
Newcastle U.	Tr	01.49	48-52	146	-	82

ROBLEY, Keith
Cockermouth, 3 June, 1944 (W)

League Club	Source	Date Signed	Seasons Played	Apps	Subs	Gls
Workington (Am)	Corinthian Jnrs	08.65	65	2	0	0

ROBSHAW, Harold W.
Edmonton, 10 May, 1927 (WH)

League Club	Source	Date Signed	Seasons Played	Apps	Subs	Gls
Tottenham H.	Jnrs	11.48	51	1	-	0
Reading	Tr	02.53	52-53	20	-	1

ROBSON, Albert P.
Crook, 14 November, 1916 (F)

League Club	Source	Date Signed	Seasons Played	Apps	Subs	Gls
Crystal Palace	Godalming	12.34	36-47	85	-	22

ROBSON, Benjamin T.
Gateshead, 31 January, 1922 (WH)

League Club	Source	Date Signed	Seasons Played	Apps	Subs	Gls
Southport	Aberdeen	08.49	49	2	-	0

ROBSON, Bryan
Witton Gilbert (Dm), 11 January, 1957 E Yth/Eu21-7/E'B'/EF Lge/E-90 (M)

League Club	Source	Date Signed	Seasons Played	Apps	Subs	Gls
West Bromwich A.	App	08.74	74-81	194	4	39
Manchester U.	Tr	10.81	81-91	311	5	72

Bryan Robson (West Bromwich Albion, Manchester United & England)

ROBSON, Bryan S. (Pop)
Sunderland, 11 November, 1945 Eu23-2/EF Lge (F)

League Club	Source	Date Signed	Seasons Played	Apps	Subs	Gls
Newcastle U.	Jnrs	11.62	64-70	205	1	82
West Ham U.	Tr	02.71	70-73	120	0	47
Sunderland	Tr	07.74	74-76	90	0	34
West Ham U.	Tr	10.76	76-78	107	0	47
Sunderland	Tr	06.79	79-80	49	3	23
Carlisle U.	Tr	03.81	80-81	48	0	21
Chelsea	Tr	08.82	82	11	4	3
Carlisle U.	L	03.83	82	11	0	4
Sunderland	Tr	08.83	83	7	5	3
Carlisle U.	Tr	07.84	84-85	10	3	1

ROBSON, David M.
Hesleden (Dm), 5 October, 1966 (M)

League Club	Source	Date Signed	Seasons Played	Apps	Subs	Gls
Hartlepool U. (N/C)		11.86	86	1	0	0

ROBSON, Donald J.
Winlaton, 5 February, 1934 (F)

League Club	Source	Date Signed	Seasons Played	Apps	Subs	Gls
Doncaster Rov.		07.51				
Gateshead	Tr	09.53	53-56	34	-	11

ROBSON, Gary
Chester-le-Street, 6 July, 1965 (M)

League Club	Source	Date Signed	Seasons Played	Apps	Subs	Gls
West Bromwich A.	App	05.83	82-91	168	28	26

ROBSON, James
Chester-le-Street, 23 January, 1939 Eu23-1 (IF)

League Club	Source	Date Signed	Seasons Played	Apps	Subs	Gls
Burnley	Jnrs	01.56	56-64	202	-	79
Blackpool	Tr	03.65	64-67	60	3	13
Barnsley	Tr	01.68	67-69	87	0	15
Bury	Tr	08.70	70-72	100	3	3

ROBSON, John D.
Consett, 15 July, 1950 Eu23-7/EF Lge (FB)

League Club	Source	Date Signed	Seasons Played	Apps	Subs	Gls
Derby Co.	Birtley Y.C.	10.67	67-72	170	1	3
Aston Villa	Tr	10.72	72-77	141	3	1

ROBSON, John D.
Washington, 20 July, 1942 (CH)

League Club	Source	Date Signed	Seasons Played	Apps	Subs	Gls
Darlington		10.62	62-64	33	-	0

ROBSON, Keith
Hetton-le-Hole, 15 November, 1953 (W)

League Club	Source	Date Signed	Seasons Played	Apps	Subs	Gls
Newcastle U.	Jnrs	05.71	72-73	14	0	3
West Ham U.	Tr	09.74	74-76	65	3	13
Cardiff C.	Tr	08.77	77	21	0	5
Norwich C.	Tr	02.78	77-80	61	4	13
Leicester C.	Tr	09.81	81	8	1	0
Carlisle U.	L	03.83	82	10	1	4

ROBSON, Lance
Newcastle, 27 December, 1939 (CF)

League Club	Source	Date Signed	Seasons Played	Apps	Subs	Gls
Newcastle U.	Stannington	10.58				
Darlington	Tr	07.60	60-63	144	-	49
Darlington	(Retired)	07.68	68-69	69	0	17
Hartlepool U.	Tr	02.70	69	8	0	2

ROBSON, C. Leslie
South Shields, 1 November, 1931 (OR)

League Club	Source	Date Signed	Seasons Played	Apps	Subs	Gls
Hull C.	North Hull Jnrs	05.50	51	3	-	1
Darlington	Tr	05.53	53-54	68	-	19
Liverpool	Tr	07.55				
Crewe Alex.	Tr	01.56	55	14	-	2

ROBSON, Mark A.
Newham, 22 May, 1969 (LW)

League Club	Source	Date Signed	Seasons Played	Apps	Subs	Gls
Exeter C.	App	12.86	86	26	0	7
Tottenham H.	Tr	07.87	88-89	3	5	0
Reading	L	03.88	87	5	2	0
Watford	L	10.89	89	1	0	0
Plymouth Arg.	L	12.89	89	7	0	0
Exeter C.	L	01.92	91	7	1	1

ROBSON, Matthew
Easington, 29 December, 1954 (F)

League Club	Source	Date Signed	Seasons Played	Apps	Subs	Gls
Sunderland	App	01.72				
Darlington	L	03.75	74	1	0	0

ROBSON, T. Raymond
Newcastle, 11 August, 1928 (FB)

League Club	Source	Date Signed	Seasons Played	Apps	Subs	Gls
Cardiff C.		02.49				
Bradford C.	Tr	07.50	50-51	10	-	0
Grimsby T.	Tr	06.52	52-54	58	-	2

ROBSON, Robert W.
Sacriston (Dm), 18 February, 1933 Eu23-1/EF Lge/E-20 (IF)

League Club	Source	Date Signed	Seasons Played	Apps	Subs	Gls
Fulham	Langley Park Jnrs	05.50	50-55	152	-	68
West Bromwich A.	Tr	03.56	55-61	239	-	56
Fulham	Tr	08.62	62-66	192	0	9

ROBSON, Ronald
Sunderland, 12 September, 1932 (HB)

League Club	Source	Date Signed	Seasons Played	Apps	Subs	Gls
Gateshead	Albion S.C.	06.57	57-58	7	-	0

ROBSON, Stewart I.
Billericay, 6 November, 1964 E Yth/Eu21-8 (M)

League Club	Source	Date Signed	Seasons Played	Apps	Subs	Gls
Arsenal	App	11.81	81-86	150	1	16
West Ham U.	Tr	01.87	86-90	68	1	4
Coventry C.	Tr	03.91	90-91	40	1	3

ROBSON, Thomas
Sunderland, 1 February, 1936 (CH)

League Club	Source	Date Signed	Seasons Played	Apps	Subs	Gls
Sunderland	Jnrs	09.57	58-59	5	-	0
Darlington	Tr	08.60	60	1	-	0

ROBSON, Thomas H.
Gateshead, 31 July, 1944 E Yth (W)

League Club	Source	Date Signed	Seasons Played	Apps	Subs	Gls
Northampton T.	App	08.61	61-65	73	1	20
Chelsea	Tr	12.65	65	6	1	0
Newcastle U.	Tr	12.66	66-68	46	2	11
Peterborough U.	Tr	11.68	68-80	440	42	113

ROBSON, Trevor
Stoke, 4 January, 1959 (F)

League Club	Source	Date Signed	Seasons Played	Apps	Subs	Gls
Port Vale	App	01.77	75	0	1	0

ROBSON, William H.
Whitehaven, 13 October, 1931 (IF)

League Club	Source	Date Signed	Seasons Played	Apps	Subs	Gls
Workington	Kells	08.51	51-59	130	-	55
Carlisle U.	Tr	11.59	59	10	-	1

ROBY, Donald
Wigan, 15 November, 1933 (OR)

League Club	Source	Date Signed	Seasons Played	Apps	Subs	Gls
Notts Co.	Jnrs	02.51	50-60	226	-	37
Derby Co.	Tr	08.61	61-64	70	-	6

ROCASTLE, David
Lewisham, 2 May, 1967 Eu21-14/E'B'/E-14 (RW)

League Club	Source	Date Signed	Seasons Played	Apps	Subs	Gls
Arsenal	App	12.84	85-91	204	14	24

David Rocastle (Arsenal & England)

ROCCA, Jonathan C.
Sheffield, 4 November, 1972 (D)

League Club	Source	Date Signed	Seasons Played	Apps	Subs	Gls
Scarborough	YT	06.91	91	3	0	0

ROCHE, David
Newcastle, 13 December, 1970 (M)

League Club	Source	Date Signed	Seasons Played	Apps	Subs	Gls
Newcastle U.	YT	08.88	88-91	23	13	0

ROCHE, John A.
Poplar, 18 May, 1932 (F)

League Club	Source	Date Signed	Seasons Played	Apps	Subs	Gls
Millwall	Margate	06.57	57-58	25	-	14
Crystal Palace	Tr	05.59	59	36	-	11

ROCHE, Patrick J.
Dublin, 4 January, 1951 IR-7 (G)

League Club	Source	Date Signed	Seasons Played	Apps	Subs	Gls
Manchester U.	Shelbourne	10.73	74-81	46	0	0
Brentford	Tr	08.82	82-83	71	0	0
Halifax T.	Tr	07.84	84-88	184	0	0

ROCHFORD, William
Airdrie, 23 May, 1913 Died 1984 EF Lge (FB)

League Club	Source	Date Signed	Seasons Played	Apps	Subs	Gls
Portsmouth	Cuckfield	08.31	32-38	128	-	1
Southampton	Tr	07.46	46-49	128	-	0
Colchester U.	Tr	07.50	50	2	-	0

ROCKETT, Trevor D.
Finchampstead, 8 October, 1951 (G)

League Club	Source	Date Signed	Seasons Played	Apps	Subs	Gls
Aldershot	Fleet	07.76	76-77	5	0	0

RODAWAY, William V.
Liverpool, 26 September, 1954 E Sch (CD)

League Club	Source	Date Signed	Seasons Played	Apps	Subs	Gls
Burnley	App	09.71	71-80	201	2	1
Peterborough U.	Tr	07.81	81-82	80	1	0
Blackpool	Tr	08.83	83	41	0	0
Tranmere Rov.	Tr	07.84	84-85	55	3	5
Burnley	Tr	08.86	86	44	0	2

RODDOM, Joseph
Spennymoor, 16 May, 1924 (WH)

League Club	Source	Date Signed	Seasons Played	Apps	Subs	Gls
Chesterfield	Blyth Spartans	01.48				
Darlington	Tr	06.50	50	6	-	0

RODGER, Graham
Glasgow, 1 April, 1967 Eu21-4 (CD)

League Club	Source	Date Signed	Seasons Played	Apps	Subs	Gls
Wolverhampton W. (App)	App	08.83	83	1	0	0
Coventry C.	Tr	02.85	85-88	31	5	2
Luton T.	Tr	07.89	89-91	27	1	2
Grimsby T.	Tr	01.92	91	16	0	0

RODGER, James M.
Cleland, 15 September, 1933 (F)

League Club	Source	Date Signed	Seasons Played	Apps	Subs	Gls
Newport Co.	St Mirren	02.57	56-57	5	-	1

RODGER, Richard J.
Hemsworth, 1 July, 1936 (W)

League Club	Source	Date Signed	Seasons Played	Apps	Subs	Gls
Halifax T.	Jnrs	09.54	54-56	15	-	3

RODGER, Simon L.
Shoreham, 3 October, 1971 (M)

League Club	Source	Date Signed	Seasons Played	Apps	Subs	Gls
Crystal Palace	YT	07.90	91	20	2	0

RODGER, William
Dalkeith, 24 June, 1947 (IF)

League Club	Source	Date Signed	Seasons Played	Apps	Subs	Gls
Bradford P.A.	Newtongrange Star	04.65	65-66	6	2	0

RODGERS, Alwyn
Chesterfield, 29 May, 1938 (FB)

League Club	Source	Date Signed	Seasons Played	Apps	Subs	Gls
Doncaster Rov.		11.56	58	1	-	0

RODGERS, Arnold W.
Rotherham, 5 December, 1923 (CF)

League Club	Source	Date Signed	Seasons Played	Apps	Subs	Gls
Huddersfield T.	Wickersley	03.42	46-49	28	-	17
Bristol C.	Tr	10.49	49-55	195	-	106
Shrewsbury T.	Tr	06.56	56	13	-	3

RODGERS, Clifford F.
Rotherham, 3 October, 1921 Died 1990 (LB)

League Club	Source	Date Signed	Seasons Played	Apps	Subs	Gls
York C.	R.A.F. Pocklington	11.45	46	26	-	0

RODGERS, David M.
Bristol, 28 February, 1952 E Sch (CD)

League Club	Source	Date Signed	Seasons Played	Apps	Subs	Gls
Bristol C.	Jnrs	07.69	70-81	190	2	15
Torquay U. (N/C)	Tr	02.82	81	5	0	1
Lincoln C. (N/C)	Tr	03.82	81	3	0	0

RODGERS, Mark
Broxburn, 20 September, 1967 (M)

League Club	Source	Date Signed	Seasons Played	Apps	Subs	Gls
Preston N.E. (N/C)	YT	09.85	85	1	0	0

RODGERSON, Alan R.
Easington, 19 March, 1939 E Sch (IF)

League Club	Source	Date Signed	Seasons Played	Apps	Subs	Gls
Middlesbrough	Jnrs	05.56	58-60	13	-	3

RODGERSON, Ian
Hereford, 9 April, 1966 (W/RB)

League Club	Source	Date Signed	Seasons Played	Apps	Subs	Gls
Hereford U.	Jnrs	06.85	85-87	95	5	6
Cardiff C.	Tr	08.88	88-90	98	1	4
Birmingham C.	Tr	12.90	90-91	63	1	11

RODI, Joseph
Glasgow, 23 July, 1913 Died 1965 (F)

League Club	Source	Date Signed	Seasons Played	Apps	Subs	Gls
Grimsby T.		04.45				
Rochdale	Tr	04.46	46	9	-	3

RODON, Christopher P.
Swansea, 9 June, 1963 (F)

League Club	Source	Date Signed	Seasons Played	Apps	Subs	Gls
Brighton & H.A.	Pontardawe	01.83	82	0	1	0
Cardiff C.	L	08.83	83	4	0	0

RODON, Peter C.
Swansea, 5 February, 1945 (CF)

League Club	Source	Date Signed	Seasons Played	Apps	Subs	Gls
Swansea C.	Jnrs	11.62				
Bradford C.	Tr	07.64	64-66	60	4	15

RODRIGUES, Peter J.
Cardiff, 21 April, 1944 W Sch/Wu23-5/W-40 (RB)

League Club	Source	Date Signed	Seasons Played	Apps	Subs	Gls
Cardiff C.	Jnrs	05.61	63-65	85	0	2
Leicester C.	Tr	01.66	65-70	139	1	6
Sheffield Wed.	Tr	10.70	70-74	162	0	2
Southampton	Tr	07.75	75-76	59	0	3

RODWELL, Anthony
Southport, 26 August, 1962 (RW)

League Club	Source	Date Signed	Seasons Played	Apps	Subs	Gls
Blackpool	Colne Dynamoes	08.90	90-91	83	2	14

RODWELL, James R.
Lincoln, 20 November, 1970 (D)

League Club	Source	Date Signed	Seasons Played	Apps	Subs	Gls
Darlington (YT)	YT	07.87	88	1	0	0

RODWELL, Joseph
Southport, 13 October, 1928 (W)

League Club	Source	Date Signed	Seasons Played	Apps	Subs	Gls
Accrington St. (Am)	Birkdale Ath.	09.48	48	2	-	0

ROE, John
Broxburn, 7 January, 1938 (FB)

League Club	Source	Date Signed	Seasons Played	Apps	Subs	Gls
Colchester U.	West Calder	07.58	59	2	-	0

ROE, Leonard M.
Hayes, 11 January, 1932 (WH)

League Club	Source	Date Signed	Seasons Played	Apps	Subs	Gls
Brentford	Ruislip Manor	05.51	54-56	7	-	0

ROEDER, Glenn V.
Woodford, 13 December, 1955 E-'B' (CD)

League Club	Source	Date Signed	Seasons Played	Apps	Subs	Gls
Leyton Orient	App	12.73	74-77	107	8	4
Queens Park R.	Tr	08.78	78-83	157	0	17
Notts Co.	L	11.83	83	4	0	0
Newcastle U.	Tr	12.83	83-88	193	0	8
Watford	Tr	07.89	89-90	74	4	2
Leyton Orient (N/C)	Tr	01.91	91	6	2	0

ROFE, Dennis
Epping, 1 June, 1950 Eu23-1 (LB)

League Club	Source	Date Signed	Seasons Played	Apps	Subs	Gls
Leyton Orient	App	02.68	67-72	170	1	6
Leicester C.	Tr	08.72	72-79	290	0	6
Chelsea	Tr	02.80	79-81	58	1	0
Southampton	Tr	07.82	82-83	18	2	0

ROFFEY, William R.
Stepney, 6 February, 1954 (FB)

League Club	Source	Date Signed	Seasons Played	Apps	Subs	Gls
Crystal Palace	App	05.71	72-73	24	0	0
Leyton Orient	Tr	10.73	73-83	324	4	8
Brentford	L	03.84	83	13	0	1
Millwall	Tr	08.84	84-85	36	1	2

ROFFI, Guido (George)
Ynsybwl, 6 March, 1924 Died 1973 (CF)

League Club	Source	Date Signed	Seasons Played	Apps	Subs	Gls
Newport Co.	Arsenal (Am)	02.47	46-50	112	-	27

ROGAN, Anton G. P.
Belfast, 25 March, 1966 NI-17 (LB)

League Club	Source	Date Signed	Seasons Played	Apps	Subs	Gls
Sunderland	Glasgow Celtic	10.91	91	33	0	1

ROGAN, L. Michael
Fleetwood, 29 May, 1948 (G)

League Club	Source	Date Signed	Seasons Played	Apps	Subs	Gls
Workington	App	08.66	66-76	390	0	0
Stockport Co.	Tr	06.77	77-80	73	0	0
Crewe Alex.	L	03.79	78	3	0	0

ROGERS, Alan J.
Plymouth, 6 July, 1954 (LW)

League Club	Source	Date Signed	Seasons Played	Apps	Subs	Gls
Plymouth Arg.	App	07.72	73-78	107	10	5
Portsmouth	Tr	07.79	79-83	154	7	14
Southend U.	Tr	03.84	83-85	84	3	4
Cardiff C.	Tr	08.86	86	25	2	1

ROGERS, Alfred
Eccleshall, 10 April, 1921 (IF)

League Club	Source	Date Signed	Seasons Played	Apps	Subs	Gls
Sheffield Wed.	Birley Carr	06.42	46-49	30	-	8

ROGERS, Alfred H.
Willenhall, 17 January, 1920 (FB)

League Club	Source	Date Signed	Seasons Played	Apps	Subs	Gls
Aldershot	West Bromwich A. (Am)	05.46	46-53	317	-	5

ROGERS, Andrew
Chatteris, 1 December, 1956 (LW)

League Club	Source	Date Signed	Seasons Played	Apps	Subs	Gls
Peterborough U.	Chatteris T.	07.76	75-77	25	4	1
Southampton	Hampton	02.80	79-81	0	5	0
Plymouth Arg.	Tr	09.81	81-84	159	4	15
Reading	Tr	07.85	85-86	44	0	5
Southend U.	Tr	10.86	86-87	40	5	2

ROGERS, Darren J.
Birmingham, 9 April, 1970 (CD)

League Club	Source	Date Signed	Seasons Played	Apps	Subs	Gls
West Bromwich A. (YT)		07.88	90-91	7	7	1

ROGERS, Dennis
Chorley, 28 March, 1936 (G)

League Club	Source	Date Signed	Seasons Played	Apps	Subs	Gls
Accrington St.	Netherfield	03.59	58	3	-	0

ROGERS, Donald E.
Paulton, 25 October, 1945 E Yth/Eu23-2/EF Lge (W)

League Club	Source	Date Signed	Seasons Played	Apps	Subs	Gls
Swindon T.	App	10.62	62-72	400	0	146
Crystal Palace	Tr	11.72	72-74	69	1	28
Queens Park R.	Tr	09.74	74	13	5	5
Swindon T.	Tr	03.76	75-76	11	1	2

Don Rogers (Swindon Town, Crystal Palace, Queens Park Rangers & Swindon Town)

ROGERS, Eamonn
Dublin, 16 April, 1947 IR-19 (W)

League Club	Source	Date Signed	Seasons Played	Apps	Subs	Gls
Blackburn Rov.	App	05.65	65-71	159	6	30
Charlton Ath.	Tr	10.71	71-72	37	2	3
Northampton T.	L	11.72	72	4	0	1

ROGERS, Ehud (Tim)
Chirk, 15 October, 1909 W Amat (OR)

League Club	Source	Date Signed	Seasons Played	Apps	Subs	Gls
Wrexham	Oswestry T.	05.34	34	11	-	2
Arsenal	Tr	01.35	34-35	16	-	5
Newcastle U.	Tr	06.36	36-38	56	-	10
Swansea C.	Tr	05.39				
Wrexham	Tr	12.45	46	1	-	0

ROGERS, Graham R.
Newport, 5 September, 1955 (D)

League Club	Source	Date Signed	Seasons Played	Apps	Subs	Gls
Newport Co.	App	09.73	74	0	4	0
Newport Co. (N/C)	Forest Green Rov.	08.85	85	6	1	0

ROGERS, James R.
Wednesbury, 31 December, 1929 (F)

League Club	Source	Date Signed	Seasons Played	Apps	Subs	Gls
Wolverhampton W.	Rubery Owen	05.48				
Bristol C.	Tr	05.50	50-56	155	-	74
Coventry C.	Tr	12.56	56-58	77	-	27
Bristol C.	Tr	12.58	58-61	115	-	28

ROGERS, John C.
Liverpool, 16 September, 1950 E Semi-Pro (F)

League Club	Source	Date Signed	Seasons Played	Apps	Subs	Gls
Port Vale	Wigan Ath.	10.76	76	25	1	6
Wigan Ath.	Altrincham	08.82	82	4	2	2

ROGERS, Kenneth J.
Chatham, 21 November, 1954 (OL)

League Club	Source	Date Signed	Seasons Played	Apps	Subs	Gls
Gillingham	App	11.72	72-73	11	2	1

ROGERS, Kevin P.
Merthyr Tydfil, 23 September, 1963 W Sch/W Yth (M)

League Club	Source	Date Signed	Seasons Played	Apps	Subs	Gls
Aston Villa	App	09.81				
Birmingham C.	Tr	04.83	83	8	1	1
Wrexham	Tr	07.84	84	30	5	3

ROGERS, Lee J.
Doncaster, 28 October, 1966 (D)

League Club	Source	Date Signed	Seasons Played	Apps	Subs	Gls
Doncaster Rov. (N/C)	YT	07.84				
Chesterfield	Tr	08.86	86-91	174	13	0

ROGERS, Lee M.
Bristol, 8 April, 1967 (CD)

League Club	Source	Date Signed	Seasons Played	Apps	Subs	Gls
Bristol C.	App	12.84	84-86	30	0	0
Hereford U.	L	03.87	86	13	0	0
York C.	L	12.87	87	5	2	0
Exeter C.	Tr	06.88	88-90	74	4	0

ROGERS, Martyn
Bristol, 7 March, 1955 Died 1992 E Yth (RB)

League Club	Source	Date Signed	Seasons Played	Apps	Subs	Gls
Bristol C.	App	03.73				
Exeter C.	Bath C.	07.79	79-84	129	3	5

ROGERS, Martyn
Nottingham, 26 January, 1960 E Sch (FB)

League Club	Source	Date Signed	Seasons Played	Apps	Subs	Gls
Manchester U.	App	01.77	77	1	0	0
Queens Park R.	Tr	07.79	79	2	0	0

ROGERS, Paul A.
Portsmouth, 21 March, 1965 E Semi-Pro (M)

League Club	Source	Date Signed	Seasons Played	Apps	Subs	Gls
Sheffield U.	Sutton U.	01.92	91	13	0	0

ROGERS, Peter P.
Bristol, 22 April, 1953 (F)

League Club	Source	Date Signed	Seasons Played	Apps	Subs	Gls
Exeter C.	Bath C.	02.79	78-83	194	11	39

ROGERS, William
Ulverston, 3 July, 1919 (W)

League Club	Source	Date Signed	Seasons Played	Apps	Subs	Gls
Preston N.E.		08.37				
Blackburn Rov.	Tr	06.38	38-47	73	-	24
Barrow	Tr	10.47	47-52	197	-	14

ROGERSON, Lee A.
Darwen, 21 March, 1967 (F)

League Club	Source	Date Signed	Seasons Played	Apps	Subs	Gls
Wigan Ath.	Clitheroe	01.90	89-90	1	3	0

ROLES, Albert G.
Southampton, 29 September, 1921 (FB)

League Club	Source	Date Signed	Seasons Played	Apps	Subs	Gls
Southampton		08.42	48	1	-	0

ROLFE, James
Liverpool, 8 February, 1932 (OR)

League Club	Source	Date Signed	Seasons Played	Apps	Subs	Gls
Liverpool	Jnrs	07.52				
Chester C.	Tr	07.53	53-54	52	-	4
Crewe Alex.	Tr	08.55	55-57	101	-	13
Barrow	Tr	07.58	58	12	-	4

ROLLINGS, Andrew N.
Portishead, 14 December, 1954 (CD)

League Club	Source	Date Signed	Seasons Played	Apps	Subs	Gls
Norwich C.	App	12.72	73	4	0	0
Brighton & H.A.	Tr	04.74	74-79	168	0	10
Swindon T.	Tr	05.80	80	11	1	1
Portsmouth	Tr	05.81	81-82	29	0	1
Torquay U. (N/C)	Tr	08.83	83	2	0	0
Brentford (N/C)	Tr	11.83	83	1	0	0

ROLLINS, Kevin
Halifax, 2 January, 1947 (FB)

League Club	Source	Date Signed	Seasons Played	Apps	Subs	Gls
Halifax T. (App)	App	07.63	64	1	-	0

ROLLO, Alexander
Dumbarton, 18 September, 1926 (FB)

League Club	Source	Date Signed	Seasons Played	Apps	Subs	Gls
Workington	Dumbarton	06.57	57-59	127	-	3

ROLLO, James S.
Perth, 16 November, 1937 (G)

League Club	Source	Date Signed	Seasons Played	Apps	Subs	Gls
Oldham Ath.	Poole T.	05.60	60-62	59	-	0
Southport	Tr	07.63	63	38	-	0
Bradford C.	Tr	07.64	64-65	37	0	0

ROLPH, Andrew J. P.
Meriden, 28 October, 1969 (W)

League Club	Source	Date Signed	Seasons Played	Apps	Subs	Gls
Chesterfield	Mile Oak Rov.	01.89	88-90	14	22	1

ROLPH, Darren G.
Romford, 19 November, 1968 (FB)

League Club	Source	Date Signed	Seasons Played	Apps	Subs	Gls
Barnsley	Kings Lynn	08.87	87	1	1	0

ROLPH, Gary L.
Stepney, 24 February, 1960 (F)

League Club	Source	Date Signed	Seasons Played	Apps	Subs	Gls
Brentford	App	02.78	76-78	8	4	1

RONALDSON, Kenneth
Edinburgh, 27 September, 1945 (IF)

League Club	Source	Date Signed	Seasons Played	Apps	Subs	Gls
Bristol Rov.	Aberdeen	07.65	65-68	72	4	15
Gillingham	Tr	11.69	69-70	6	0	0

RONSON, Brian
Durham, 7 August, 1935 (G)

League Club	Source	Date Signed	Seasons Played	Apps	Subs	Gls
Fulham	Willington	03.53	53	2	-	0
Southend U.	Tr	08.56	56-58	30	-	0
Norwich C.	Tr	08.59	59	1	-	0
Peterborough U.	Tr	07.61	61-62	50	-	0

RONSON, William
Fleetwood, 22 January, 1957 (M)

League Club	Source	Date Signed	Seasons Played	Apps	Subs	Gls
Blackpool	App	02.74	74-78	124	4	12
Cardiff C.	Tr	07.79	79-81	90	0	4
Wrexham	Tr	10.81	81	31	1	1
Barnsley	Tr	08.82	82-85	111	2	3
Birmingham C.	L	11.85	85	2	0	0
Blackpool (N/C)	Tr	01.86	85	3	0	0

ROOKE, Rodney
Grays, 7 April, 1970 (FB)

League Club	Source	Date Signed	Seasons Played	Apps	Subs	Gls
Colchester U.	YT	06.88	89	4	0	0

ROOKE, Ronald
Carlisle, 12 December, 1926 (OR)

League Club	Source	Date Signed	Seasons Played	Apps	Subs	Gls
Carlisle U. (Am)	Carlisle Young Libs	09.49	49	1	-	0

ROOKE, Ronald L.
Guildford, 7 December, 1911 Died 1985 (CF)

League Club	Source	Date Signed	Seasons Played	Apps	Subs	Gls
Crystal Palace	Guildford C.	03.33	33-36	18	-	6
Fulham	Tr	10.36	36-46	105	-	69
Arsenal	Tr	12.46	46-48	88	-	68
Crystal Palace	Tr	06.49	49-50	45	-	26

ROOKES, Philip W.
Dulverton, 23 April, 1919 (FB)

League Club	Source	Date Signed	Seasons Played	Apps	Subs	Gls
Bradford C.	Worksop T.	10.36	37	11	-	0
Portsmouth	Tr	01.38	38-50	114	-	0
Colchester U.	Tr	07.51	51-52	68	-	0

ROOKS, Richard
Sunderland, 29 May, 1940 (CH)

League Club	Source	Date Signed	Seasons Played	Apps	Subs	Gls
Sunderland	Jnrs	06.57	60-64	34	-	2
Middlesbrough	Tr	08.65	65-68	136	0	14
Bristol C.	Tr	06.69	69-71	96	0	4

ROONEY, James
Dundee, 10 December, 1945 (OL)

League Club	Source	Date Signed	Seasons Played	Apps	Subs	Gls
Peterborough U.	Lochee Harp	07.65	65-66	7	0	2

ROONEY, Robert
Glasgow, 26 October, 1920 S Sch (CH)

League Club	Source	Date Signed	Seasons Played	Apps	Subs	Gls
Leyton Orient	Falkirk	05.48	48-50	66	-	2
Workington	Tr	06.51	51	27	-	0

ROONEY, Robert M.
Cowie, 8 July, 1938 (W)

League Club	Source	Date Signed	Seasons Played	Apps	Subs	Gls
Sheffield U.	Clydebank	06.58	58-59	14	-	3
Doncaster Rov.	Tr	10.62	62	5	-	1
Lincoln C.	Tr	01.63	62-63	28	-	3

ROONEY, Simon A.
Manchester, 10 July, 1970 (F)

League Club	Source	Date Signed	Seasons Played	Apps	Subs	Gls
Blackpool	YT	07.88	87-88	4	5	0

ROOST, William C.
Bristol, 22 March, 1924 (IF)

League Club	Source	Date Signed	Seasons Played	Apps	Subs	Gls
Bristol Rov.	Stonehouse	09.48	48-56	177	-	49
Swindon T.	Tr	05.57	57-58	18	-	3

ROPER, Alan J.
Tipton, 21 May, 1939 (FB)

League Club	Source	Date Signed	Seasons Played	Apps	Subs	Gls
Walsall		05.59	62-64	53	-	2

ROPER, David
Ilkley, 26 September, 1944 E Yth (G)

League Club	Source	Date Signed	Seasons Played	Apps	Subs	Gls
Bradford C. (Am)	Salts	09.62	62	13	-	0

ROPER, Donald G. B.
Botley, 14 December, 1922 E'B'-1/EF Lge (W)

League Club	Source	Date Signed	Seasons Played	Apps	Subs	Gls
Southampton	Bitterne Nomads	06.40	46	40	-	8
Arsenal	Tr	08.47	47-56	297	-	88
Southampton	Tr	01.57	56-58	80	-	32

ROSARIO, Robert M.
Hammersmith, 4 March, 1966 Eu21-4 (F)

League Club	Source	Date Signed	Seasons Played	Apps	Subs	Gls
Norwich C.	Hillingdon Bor.	12.83	83-90	115	11	18
Wolverhampton W.	L	12.85	85	2	0	1
Coventry C.	Tr	03.91	90-91	26	5	4

Robert Rosario (Norwich City & Coventry City)

ROSCOE, Philip
Barnsley, 3 March, 1934 (FB)

League Club	Source	Date Signed	Seasons Played	Apps	Subs	Gls
Barnsley	Jnrs	08.51				
Halifax T.	Tr	07.56	56-63	257	-	5

ROSE, Colin J.
Winsford, 22 January, 1972 (M)

League Club	Source	Date Signed	Seasons Played	Apps	Subs	Gls
Crewe Alex.	YT	04.90	90-91	17	5	1

ROSE, Frederick
Stannington, 27 March, 1955 (W)

League Club	Source	Date Signed	Seasons Played	Apps	Subs	Gls
Huddersfield T.	App	04.72				
Workington	Tr	07.74	74	0	2	0

ROSE, Gordon
Sheffield, 22 March, 1935 (F)

League Club	Source	Date Signed	Seasons Played	Apps	Subs	Gls
Sheffield U.		10.56				
Halifax T.	Tr	07.58	58	8	-	1

ROSE, James
Clayton-le-Moors, 4 March, 1918 (G)

League Club	Source	Date Signed	Seasons Played	Apps	Subs	Gls
Accrington St.	Clayton Villa	02.39	38-46	20	-	0

ROSE, John
Sheffield, 26 October, 1921

League Club	Source	Date Signed	Seasons Played	Apps	Subs	Gls
Queens Park R.		03.45	46-47	18	-	0

ROSE, John W.
Woolwich, 12 August, 1920 (IF)

League Club	Source	Date Signed	Seasons Played	Apps	Subs	Gls
Bournemouth	Salisbury	02.46	46	1	-	0

ROSE, Kenneth
Eckington, 18 August, 1930 (CF)

League Club	Source	Date Signed	Seasons Played	Apps	Subs	Gls
Chesterfield		11.50				
Exeter C.	Tr	06.52	52	11	-	3
Rochdale	Tr	07.53	53	11	-	0
Workington	Tr	06.54	54	6	-	2

ROSE, Kevin P.
Evesham, 23 November, 1960 (G)

League Club	Source	Date Signed	Seasons Played	Apps	Subs	Gls
Lincoln C.	Ledbury T.	08.79				
Hereford U.	Ledbury T.	03.83	82-88	268	0	0
Bolton W.	Tr	07.89	89-91	10	0	0
Carlisle U.	L	03.90	89	11	0	0
Rochdale	L	02.91	90	3	0	0
Rochdale	Tr	11.91	91	28	0	0

ROSE, Michael J.
New Barnet, 22 July, 1943 (G)

League Club	Source	Date Signed	Seasons Played	Apps	Subs	Gls
Charlton Ath.	St Albans C.	07.63	63-66	75	0	0
Notts Co.	Tr	03.67	66-69	109	0	0
Mansfield T.	L	08.70	70	3	0	0

ROSENIOR, Leroy D.G.
Clapton, 24 March, 1964 E Sch/E Yth (F)

League Club	Source	Date Signed	Seasons Played	Apps	Subs	Gls
Fulham	Jnrs	08.82	82-84	53	1	15
Queens Park R.	Tr	08.85	85-86	27	11	7
Fulham	Tr	06.87	87	34	0	20
West Ham U.	Tr	03.88	87-91	44	9	15
Fulham	L	09.90	90	11	0	3
Charlton Ath.	L	11.91	91	3	0	0
Bristol C.	Tr	03.92	91	5	3	5

ROSENTHAL, Abraham W.
Liverpool, 12 October, 1921 Died 1986 (IF)

League Club	Source	Date Signed	Seasons Played	Apps	Subs	Gls
Tranmere Rov.	Liverpool (Am)	01.39	38-46	27	-	8
Bradford C.	Tr	04.47	46-48	44	-	11
Tranmere Rov.	Oldham Ath. (Trial)	08.49	49-51	69	-	24
Bradford C.	Tr	01.52	52-53	63	-	32
Tranmere Rov.	Tr	07.54	54	21	-	3
Bradford C.	Tr	07.55	55	1	-	0

ROSENTHAL, Ronny
Haifa (Israel), 4 October, 1963 Israeli Int (F)

League Club	Source	Date Signed	Seasons Played	Apps	Subs	Gls
Liverpool	Standard Liege (Bel)	03.90	89-91	16	28	15

Ronny Rosenthal (Maccabi Haifa, Bruges, Standard Liege, Liverpool & Israel)

ROSS, Alan
Ellesmere Port, 7 February, 1933 (G)

League Club	Source	Date Signed	Seasons Played	Apps	Subs	Gls
Oldham Ath. (Am)	Bishop Auckland	09.56	56	3	-	0
Accrington St. (Am)	Blackburn Rov. (Am)	03.59	58	1	-	0

ROSS, J. Alan
Glasgow, 26 May, 1942 (G)

League Club	Source	Date Signed	Seasons Played	Apps	Subs	Gls
Luton T.	Petershill Jnrs	04.62				
Carlisle U.	Tr	06.63	63-78	465	1	0

ROSS, Alexander M. C.
Glasgow, 17 December, 1923 (WH)

League Club	Source	Date Signed	Seasons Played	Apps	Subs	Gls
West Bromwich A.	Shawfield Jnrs	10.47				
Crystal Palace	Tr	08.48	48-50	34	-	0

ROSS, Bryce T.
Edinburgh, 4 December, 1927 Died 1969 (CF)

League Club	Source	Date Signed	Seasons Played	Apps	Subs	Gls
Newcastle U.	Jnrs	12.43				
Carlisle U.		11.46	46-47	3	-	0

ROSS, Colin
Dailly (Ayrs), 29 August, 1962 (M)

League Club	Source	Date Signed	Seasons Played	Apps	Subs	Gls
Middlesbrough	App	09.80	80-82	37	1	0
Chesterfield	L	03.83	82	6	0	0
Darlington	Tr	08.83	83-84	14	0	0

ROSS, W. Eric
Belfast, 19 September, 1944 NIu23-1/NI-1 (M)

League Club	Source	Date Signed	Seasons Played	Apps	Subs	Gls
Newcastle U.	Glentoran	08.67	67-68	2	0	0
Northampton T.	Tr	08.69	69-71	51	7	5
Hartlepool U.	L	11.71	71	2	0	0

ROSS, George
Inverness, 15 April, 1943 (FB)

League Club	Source	Date Signed	Seasons Played	Apps	Subs	Gls
Preston N.E.	Jnrs	04.60	60-72	384	2	3
Southport	Tr	11.72	72-73	31	0	0

ROSS, George A.
Deptford, 1 November, 1920 (FB)

League Club	Source	Date Signed	Seasons Played	Apps	Subs	Gls
Millwall	Metro Gas	01.46				
Carlisle U.	Tr	05.47	47	9	-	0

ROSS, Ian
Glasgow, 26 November, 1947 (CD)

League Club	Source	Date Signed	Seasons Played	Apps	Subs	Gls
Liverpool	Jnrs	08.65	66-71	42	6	2
Aston Villa	Tr	02.72	71-75	175	0	3
Notts Co.	L	10.76	76	4	0	1
Northampton T.	L	11.76	76	2	0	0
Peterborough U.	Tr	12.76	76-78	112	0	1
Wolverhampton W.	Tr	08.79				
Hereford U. (N/C)	(Team Coach)	10.82	82	15	0	0

ROSS, Louis A.
Dublin, 19 September, 1920 (FB)

League Club	Source	Date Signed	Seasons Played	Apps	Subs	Gls
Walsall	Queen of South	08.48	48	8	-	0

ROSS, Michael P.
Southampton, 2 September, 1971 (F)

League Club	Source	Date Signed	Seasons Played	Apps	Subs	Gls
Portsmouth	YT	12.88	88-91	0	4	0

ROSS, Robert
Glasgow, 2 February, 1917

League Club	Source	Date Signed	Seasons Played	Apps	Subs	Gls
Watford	Dumbarton	07.46	46	33	-	6

ROSS, Robert A.
Wishaw, 25 May, 1927 (FB)

League Club	Source	Date Signed	Seasons Played	Apps	Subs	Gls
Leeds U.	Workington	08.50	51	5	-	0
Stockport Co.	Tr	06.54	54	9	-	0

ROSS, Robert C.
Edinburgh, 9 September, 1941 (M)

League Club	Source	Date Signed	Seasons Played	Apps	Subs	Gls
Grimsby T.	St Mirren	06.65	65-70	208	4	18

ROSS, Robert H.
Edinburgh, 18 May, 1942 (M)

League Club	Source	Date Signed	Seasons Played	Apps	Subs	Gls
Shrewsbury T.	Hearts	06.63	63-65	99	0	29
Brentford	Tr	03.66	65-72	288	2	59
Cambridge U.	Tr	10.72	72-73	57	8	14

ROSS, Robert R.
Cowdenbeath, 13 December, 1925 (CH)

League Club	Source	Date Signed	Seasons Played	Apps	Subs	Gls
Millwall	Dundee	08.52	52	1	-	0

ROSS, Stewart
Woking, 1 September, 1945 (FB)

League Club	Source	Date Signed	Seasons Played	Apps	Subs	Gls
Wolverhampton W.		11.65	67-68	1	2	0

ROSS, Thomas
Tain, 27 February, 1947 (F)

League Club	Source	Date Signed	Seasons Played	Apps	Subs	Gls
Peterborough U.	Lochee Harp	07.65	65-66	5	2	2
York C.	Tr	06.67	67-68	56	5	20

ROSS, Trevor W.
Ashton-u-Lyne, 16 January, 1957 E Sch/Su21-1 (M)

League Club	Source	Date Signed	Seasons Played	Apps	Subs	Gls
Arsenal	App	06.74	74-77	57	1	5
Everton	Tr	11.77	77-82	120	6	16
Portsmouth	L	10.82	82	5	0	0
Sheffield U.	L	12.82	82	4	0	0
Sheffield U.	A.E.K. Athens (Gr)	01.84	83	4	0	0
Bury	Tr	08.84	84-86	96	2	11

ROSS, William
Glasgow, 2 May, 1919 (CF)

League Club	Source	Date Signed	Seasons Played	Apps	Subs	Gls
Bradford C.	Arbroath	07.50	50	4	-	2

ROSS, William B.
Swansea, 8 November, 1924 (OR)

League Club	Source	Date Signed	Seasons Played	Apps	Subs	Gls
Cardiff C.		03.43	46-47	8	-	0
Sheffield U.	Tr	05.48	48	3	-	1
Southport	Tr	08.49	49-50	47	-	13

ROSSER, Douglas R.
Swansea, 8 September, 1948 (CH)

League Club	Source	Date Signed	Seasons Played	Apps	Subs	Gls
Swansea C.	Jnrs	05.67	68-70	28	2	1
Crewe Alex.	Tr	08.71	71	28	1	0

ROSSITER, Donald P.
Strood, 8 June, 1935 E Yth (IF)

League Club	Source	Date Signed	Seasons Played	Apps	Subs	Gls
Arsenal	Jnrs	06.52				
Leyton Orient	Tr	03.56	56	1	-	0
Gillingham	Dartford	07.57	57	1	-	0

ROSSITER, John D.
Kingsbridge, 28 October, 1942 (FB)

League Club	Source	Date Signed	Seasons Played	Apps	Subs	Gls
Torquay U.		07.61	62-63	24	-	0

ROSTRON, J. Wilfred
Sunderland, 29 September, 1956 E Sch (LB)

League Club	Source	Date Signed	Seasons Played	Apps	Subs	Gls
Arsenal	App	10.73	74-76	12	5	2
Sunderland	Tr	07.77	77-79	75	1	17
Watford	Tr	10.79	79-88	306	11	22
Sheffield Wed.	Tr	01.89	88	7	0	0
Sheffield U.	Tr	09.89	89-90	33	3	3
Brentford	Tr	01.91	90-91	33	7	2

Wilf Rostron (Arsenal, Sunderland, Watford, Sheffield Wednesday, Sheffield United & Brentford)

ROTHWELL, Edward
Atherton, 3 September, 1917 (W)

League Club	Source	Date Signed	Seasons Played	Apps	Subs	Gls
Bolton W.		02.36	37-48	48	-	2
Southport	Tr	08.49	49-50	40	-	5

League Club	Source	Date Signed	Seasons Played	Apps	Subs	Gls
ROTHWELL, George						
Bolton, 22 November, 1923						(WH)
Accrington St.	Chorley	08.44	46-51	202	-	10
ROTHWELL, John						
Farnworth, 29 March, 1920						(CF)
Southport	Walkden Heath	11.38	38-46	18	-	9
Birmingham C.	Tr	03.47				
Crewe Alex.	Tr	10.49	49	3	-	1
ROTHWELL, Ronald						
Bury, 10 July, 1920						(FB)
Rochdale	Dunfermline Ath.	10.46	46-51	48	-	0
ROUGVIE, Douglas						
Ballingry, (Fife), 24 May, 1956 S-1						(D)
Chelsea	Aberdeen	08.84	84-86	74	0	3
Brighton & H.A.	Tr	06.87	87	35	0	2
Shrewsbury T.	Tr	08.88	88	20	1	3
Fulham	Tr	02.89	88	18	0	1
ROUND, Leonard F.						
Kingswinford, 21 May, 1928						(G)
Hull C.	Ayr U.	06.57	57	17	-	0
ROUND, Paul G.						
Blackburn, 22 June, 1959						(CD)
Blackburn Rov.	App	08.77	76-80	41	10	5
ROUND, Stephen C.						
Dudley, 28 February, 1963						(F)
Walsall	App	03.80	81-82	5	19	3
ROUND, Stephen J.						
Burton, 9 November, 1970						(FB)
Derby Co.	YT	07.89	91	2	1	0
ROUNSEVELL, Anthony E.						
Liskeard, 1 April, 1945						(FB)
Plymouth Arg.	App	12.62	63-67	34	1	0

Darren Rowbotham (Plymouth Argyle, Exeter City, Torquay United & Birmingham City)

League Club	Source	Date Signed	Seasons Played	Apps	Subs	Gls
ROUSE, Herbert						
Doncaster, 29 November, 1920						(FB)
Doncaster Rov.		06.48	48-54	35	-	0
ROUSE, R. Victor						
Swansea, 16 March, 1936 Wu23-1/W-1						(G)
Millwall	Jnrs	03.53				
Crystal Palace	Tr	08.56	56-62	238	-	0
Oxford U.	Tr	08.63	63-64	22	-	0
Leyton Orient	Tr	07.65	65-66	40	0	0
ROUTLEDGE, T. Alan						
Wallsend, 6 May, 1960						(FB)
Bristol Rov.	Bath Univ.	10.80	80	0	1	0
ROUTLEDGE, Ronald W.						
Ashington, 14 October, 1937						(G)
Sunderland	Jnrs	10.54	56-57	2	-	0
Bradford P.A.	Tr	05.58	58-61	39	-	0
ROWAN, Barry						
Willesden, 24 April, 1942						(OR)
Brentford	Watford (Am)	10.60				
Millwall	Dover T.	07.64	64-66	72	0	13
Colchester U.	Detroit (USA)	11.68	68	2	0	0
Reading	Tr	08.69	69	1	0	0
Plymouth Arg.	Tr	09.69	69	10	0	1
Exeter C.	Tr	07.70	70-72	76	5	14
ROWAN, Brian						
Glasgow, 28 June, 1948						(FB)
Aston Villa	Baillieston Jnrs	04.69	69	1	0	0
Watford	Tr	10.71	71	8	4	0
ROWBOTHAM, Darren						
Cardiff, 22 October, 1966						(F)
Plymouth Arg.	Jnrs	11.84	84-87	22	24	2
Exeter C.	Tr	10.87	87-91	110	8	46
Torquay U.	Tr	09.91	91	14	0	3
Birmingham C	Tr	01.92	91	21	1	4
ROWBOTHAM, Jason						
Cardiff, 3 January, 1969						(FB)
Plymouth Arg.	YT	07.87	87-90	8	1	0
ROWBOTHAM, Michael G.						
Sheffield, 2 September, 1965						(M)
Manchester U.	App	09.83				
Grimsby T.	Tr	08.84	84	3	1	0
ROWDEN, Leonard A.						
Swansea, 31 May, 1927						(CF)
Swansea C.	Clydach	10.53	53	1	-	0
ROWE, Benjamin P.						
Hull, 1 October, 1970						(F)
Exeter C.	Bristol C. (Jnrs)	09.89	89-90	5	7	2
ROWE, Brian						
Sunderland, 24 October, 1971						(M)
Doncaster Rov.	YT	10.90	90-91	21	8	0
ROWE, Colwyn K.						
Ipswich, 22 March, 1956						(W)
Colchester U.	App	01.74	73-74	4	8	2
ROWE, Graham E.						
Southport, 28 August, 1945						(WH)
Blackpool	App	07.63	63-70	100	5	12
Tranmere Rov.	L	11.70	70	6	1	0
Bolton W.	Tr	05.71	71	4	2	0
ROWE, Mark T.						
Bodmin, 9 June, 1964						(M)
Plymouth Arg.	App	09.81	81-84	46	9	1
Torquay U. (N/C)	Saltash U.	09.86	86	7	0	0
ROWE, Norman						
Halesowen, 20 March, 1940						(W)
Walsall	Aston Villa (Am)	03.59	59-60	6	-	0
ROWE, V. Norman						
Shouldham (Nk), 14 February, 1926						(FB)
Derby Co.	Kings Lynn	12.49	51	2	-	0
Walsall	Tr	08.52	52	26	-	0

ROWE, E. Stanley
Exeter, 20 August, 1921 (LB)

League Club	Source	Date Signed	Seasons Played	Apps	Subs	Gls
Exeter C.		10.47	47-53	139	-	0

ROWE, N. Terence S.
Fulham, 8 June, 1964 (FB)

League Club	Source	Date Signed	Seasons Played	Apps	Subs	Gls
Brentford	App	06.82	81-84	63	3	1

ROWELL, Gary
Seaham, 6 June, 1957 Eu21-1 (W)

League Club	Source	Date Signed	Seasons Played	Apps	Subs	Gls
Sunderland	App	07.74	75-83	229	25	88
Norwich C.	Tr	08.84	84	2	4	1
Middlesbrough	Tr	08.85	85	27	0	10
Brighton & H.A.	Tr	08.86	86-87	9	3	0
Carlisle U.	Tr	03.88	87	7	0	0
Burnley	Tr	08.88	88-89	8	11	1

ROWELL, John F.
Dawdon (Dm), 31 December, 1918 (F)

League Club	Source	Date Signed	Seasons Played	Apps	Subs	Gls
Bournemouth		09.41	46-47	31	-	11
Wrexham	Tr	07.48	48-49	41	-	4
Aldershot	Tr	08.50	50	5	-	0

ROWETT, Gary
Bromsgrove, 6 March, 1974 (W)

League Club	Source	Date Signed	Seasons Played	Apps	Subs	Gls
Cambridge U.	YT	08.91	91	10	3	2

ROWLAND, Alfred
Stokesley, 2 September, 1920 (CH)

League Club	Source	Date Signed	Seasons Played	Apps	Subs	Gls
Aldershot	Stockton	08.46	46-48	93	-	0
Cardiff C.	Tr	02.49	48-49	3	-	0

ROWLAND, Andrew A.
Derby, 8 September, 1954 E Yth (F)

League Club	Source	Date Signed	Seasons Played	Apps	Subs	Gls
Derby Co.	Jnrs	09.72				
Bury	Tr	08.74	74-78	169	5	58
Swindon T.	Tr	09.78	78-85	280	7	80

ROWLAND, Andrew J.
Taunton, 1 October, 1965 (F)

League Club	Source	Date Signed	Seasons Played	Apps	Subs	Gls
Southampton	Exmouth T.	11.89				
Torquay U.	Tr	03.91	90-91	9	7	1

ROWLAND, David C.
Arlesey, 12 September, 1940 E Sch (F)

League Club	Source	Date Signed	Seasons Played	Apps	Subs	Gls
Luton T.	Arlesey	01.58	57	1	-	0

ROWLAND, John D.
Riddings, 7 April, 1941 E Yth (W)

League Club	Source	Date Signed	Seasons Played	Apps	Subs	Gls
Nottingham F.	Ironville Amats	04.61	60-61	26	-	3
Port Vale	Tr	08.62	62-66	147	2	40
Mansfield T.	Tr	09.66	66-67	49	0	16
Tranmere Rov.	Tr	07.68	68	25	1	3

ROWLAND, John O.
Newport, 16 March, 1936 Wu23-1 (WH)

League Club	Source	Date Signed	Seasons Played	Apps	Subs	Gls
Newport Co.	Lovells Ath.	06.58	58-68	461	1	9

ROWLAND, Keith
Portadown (NI), 1 September, 1971 NI Yth (LB)

League Club	Source	Date Signed	Seasons Played	Apps	Subs	Gls
Bournemouth	YT	10.89	91	34	3	0

ROWLAND, Leonard C.
Manchester, 23 June, 1925 E Amat (HB)

League Club	Source	Date Signed	Seasons Played	Apps	Subs	Gls
Wrexham (Am)	Mansfield T. (Am)	05.49	49-50	18	-	0
Stockport Co.	Ashton U.	12.52	52-56	61	-	0

ROWLANDS, John H.
Liverpool, 7 February, 1945 (F)

League Club	Source	Date Signed	Seasons Played	Apps	Subs	Gls
Mansfield T.		10.67	67	12	1	3
Torquay U.	Tr	06.68	68	18	0	4
Exeter C.	L	01.69	68	1	0	0
Stockport Co.	Tr	08.69	69-70	45	1	13
Barrow	Tr	01.71	70-71	52	2	6
Workington	Tr	07.72	72-73	50	1	11
Crewe Alex.	Tr	11.73	73-74	31	4	1
Hartlepool U.	Seattle (USA)	09.75	75-76	47	2	10

ROWLANDS, Trevor I.
Rhondda, 2 February, 1922 Died 1973 W Sch (FB)

League Club	Source	Date Signed	Seasons Played	Apps	Subs	Gls
Norwich C.	Cardiff Nomads	08.46	47-49	10	-	2
Colchester U.	Tr	07.50	50-52	46	-	5

ROWLES, A. Edward J.
Gosport, 10 March, 1951 (F)

League Club	Source	Date Signed	Seasons Played	Apps	Subs	Gls
Bournemouth	App	03.68	67-70	58	8	12
York C.	Tr	07.71	71-72	61	6	14
Torquay U.	Tr	06.73	73-74	54	5	13
Darlington	Tr	08.75	75-77	96	7	21
Colchester U.	Tr	12.77	77-81	79	12	17

ROWLEY, Antonio C. (Tony)
Porthcawl, 19 September, 1929 W-1 (IF)

League Club	Source	Date Signed	Seasons Played	Apps	Subs	Gls
Birmingham C.	Wellington T.	01.49				
Liverpool	Stourbridge	10.53	53-57	60	-	38
Tranmere Rov.	Tr	03.58	57-60	100	-	47

ROWLEY, Arthur
Liverpool, 9 May, 1933 (IF)

League Club	Source	Date Signed	Seasons Played	Apps	Subs	Gls
Liverpool	F. Melly B.C.	05.51	52	11	-	0
Wrexham	Tr	11.54	54-56	54	-	8
Crewe Alex.	Tr	02.57	56-57	34	-	7

Arthur Rowley (West Bromwich Albion, Fulham, Leicester City & Shrewsbury Town)

ROWLEY, G. Arthur
Wolverhampton, 21 April, 1926 E'B'-1/EF Lge (IF)

League Club	Source	Date Signed	Seasons Played	Apps	Subs	Gls
West Bromwich A.	Wolverhampton W. (Am)	05.44	46-48	24	-	4
Fulham	Tr	12.48	48-49	56	-	26
Leicester C.	Tr	07.50	50-57	303	-	251
Shrewsbury T.	Tr	06.58	58-64	236	-	152

ROWLEY, John
Wolverhampton, 23 June, 1944 (FB)

League Club	Source	Date Signed	Seasons Played	Apps	Subs	Gls
Bradford P.A.	Wellington T.	10.67	67	35	0	0

ROWLEY, John F. (Jack)
Wolverhampton, 7 October, 1920 EF Lge/E'B'-1/E-6 (CF)

League Club	Source	Date Signed	Seasons Played	Apps	Subs	Gls
Wolverhampton W.		11.35				
Bournemouth	Cradley Heath	02.37	36-37	22	-	12
Manchester U.	Tr	10.37	37-54	380	-	182
Plymouth Arg.	Tr	02.55	54-56	56	-	14

ROWLEY, Kenneth F.
Pelsall, 29 August, 1926 (IF)

League Club	Source	Date Signed	Seasons Played	Apps	Subs	Gls
Wolverhampton W.	Elkingtons	10.47	49	1	-	0
Birmingham C.	Tr	01.51	50-54	40	-	19
Coventry C.	Tr	11.54	54	3	-	0

ROXBURGH, Alexander W.
Manchester, 19 September, 1910 (G)

League Club	Source	Date Signed	Seasons Played	Apps	Subs	Gls
Blackpool	Manchester C. (Am)	01.31	32-38	62	-	0
Barrow	Tr	08.46	46-47	69	-	0

ROY, Andrew
Tillicoultry, 4 July, 1928 (IF)

League Club	Source	Date Signed	Seasons Played	Apps	Subs	Gls
Exeter C.	Dunfermline Ath.	08.49	49	2	-	0

ROY, John R.
Southampton, 23 March, 1914 Died 1980 (OR)

League Club	Source	Date Signed	Seasons Played	Apps	Subs	Gls
Norwich C.	Sholing	08.33	34-35	6	-	0
Mansfield T.	Tr	04.36	36	25	-	2
Sheffield Wed.	Tr	02.37	36-37	15	-	1
Notts Co.	Tr	03.38	37-38	14	-	0
Tranmere Rov.	Tr	12.38	38	19	-	2
Ipswich T.	Aberaman	02.46	46	15	-	2

ROYCE, Simon E.
Forest Gate, 9 September, 1971 (G)

League Club	Source	Date Signed	Seasons Played	Apps	Subs	Gls
Southend U.	Heybridge Swifts	10.91	91	1	0	0

ROYLE, Joseph
Liverpool, 8 April, 1949 Eu23-10/EF Lge/E-6 (F)

League Club	Source	Date Signed	Seasons Played	Apps	Subs	Gls
Everton	App	08.66	65-74	229	3	102
Manchester C.	Tr	12.74	74-77	98	1	23
Bristol C.	Tr	11.77	77-79	100	1	18
Norwich C.	Tr	08.80	80-81	40	2	9

Joe Royle (Everton, Manchester City, Bristol City, Norwich City & England)

ROYSTON, Robert
Newcastle, 1 December, 1915 (RB)

League Club	Source	Date Signed	Seasons Played	Apps	Subs	Gls
Sunderland		01.35				
Southport	Tr	10.36	37-38	70	-	2
Plymouth Arg.	Tr	03.39	38-46	39	-	0

RUARK, Anthony
West Ham, 23 March, 1933 (HB)

League Club	Source	Date Signed	Seasons Played	Apps	Subs	Gls
Southend U.		05.56	56	9	-	0

RUDD, Edward
Wigan, 7 January, 1929 (WH)

League Club	Source	Date Signed	Seasons Played	Apps	Subs	Gls
Bolton W.		08.50				
Accrington St.	Tr	08.51	51	2	-	0

RUDD, J. James
Dublin, 25 October, 1919 Died 1985 (OL)

League Club	Source	Date Signed	Seasons Played	Apps	Subs	Gls
Manchester C.	Teremure Ath.	01.38	46	2	-	0
York C.	Tr	03.47	46-48	83	-	23
Leeds U.	Tr	02.49	48-49	18	-	1
Rotherham U.	Tr	10.49	49-51	75	-	10
Scunthorpe U.	Tr	10.51	51	32	-	5
Workington	Tr	09.52	52	17	-	1

RUDD, William T.
Manchester, 13 December, 1941 (M)

League Club	Source	Date Signed	Seasons Played	Apps	Subs	Gls
Birmingham C.	Stalybridge Celtic	10.59	59-61	24	-	3
York C.	Tr	11.61	61-65	193	0	30
Grimsby T.	Tr	07.66	66-67	59	1	9
Rochdale	Tr	02.68	67-69	108	0	8
Bury	Tr	06.70	70-76	174	15	18

RUDDOCK, Neil
Wandsworth, 9 May, 1968 E Yth/Eu21-4 (CD)

League Club	Source	Date Signed	Seasons Played	Apps	Subs	Gls
Millwall	App	03.86				
Tottenham H.	Tr	04.86	86-87	7	2	0
Millwall	Tr	06.88	88	0	2	1
Southampton	Tr	02.89	88-91	100	7	9

Neil Ruddock (Millwall, Tottenham Hotspur, Millwall & Southampton)

RUDGE, Dale A.
Wolverhampton, 9 September, 1963 (M)

League Club	Source	Date Signed	Seasons Played	Apps	Subs	Gls
Wolverhampton W.	App	08.81	82-83	23	4	0
Preston N.E.	Tr	07.84	84-85	46	1	2

RUDGE, David H.
Wolverhampton, 21 January, 1948 (W)

League Club	Source	Date Signed	Seasons Played	Apps	Subs	Gls
Aston Villa	App	05.65	66-69	49	6	10
Hereford U.	Tr	08.72	72-75	75	7	8
Torquay U.	Tr	12.75	75-77	60	4	4

RUDGE, John R.
Wolverhampton, 21 October, 1944 (F)

League Club	Source	Date Signed	Seasons Played	Apps	Subs	Gls
Huddersfield T.	Jnrs	11.61	62-66	5	0	0
Carlisle U.	Tr	12.66	66-68	45	5	16
Torquay U.	Tr	01.69	68-71	93	2	35
Bristol Rov.	Tr	02.72	71-74	50	20	17
Bournemouth	Tr	03.75	74-76	18	3	2

RUDGE, Simon J.
Warrington, 30 December, 1964 (M)

League Club	Source	Date Signed	Seasons Played	Apps	Subs	Gls
Bolton W.	App	12.82	82-85	77	13	14

RUDHAM, Keith R. (Doug)
South Africa, 3 May, 1926 Died 1991 S African Amat Int (G)

League Club	Source	Date Signed	Seasons Played	Apps	Subs	Gls
Liverpool	Johannesburg (SA)	11.54	54-59	63	-	0

RUDKIN, Thomas W.
Peterborough, 17 June, 1919 (OL)

League Club	Source	Date Signed	Seasons Played	Apps	Subs	Gls
Lincoln C.		05.38	38	2	-	1
Arsenal	Peterborough U.	01.47	46	5	-	2
Southampton	Tr	08.47	47-48	9	-	0
Bristol C.	Tr	05.49	49-50	34	-	4

RUDMAN, Harold
Whitworth, 4 November, 1924 (FB)

League Club	Source	Date Signed	Seasons Played	Apps	Subs	Gls
Burnley		12.42	46-56	71	-	0
Rochdale	Tr	07.57	57	21	-	1

RUECROFT, Jacob
Lanchester, 1 May, 1915 (FB)

League Club	Source	Date Signed	Seasons Played	Apps	Subs	Gls
Halifax T.	Goole T.	05.38	38-46	60	-	2
Bradford C.	Scarborough	01.48	47-48	43	-	0

RUFFETT, Raymond D.
Luton, 20 July, 1924 (WH)

League Club	Source	Date Signed	Seasons Played	Apps	Subs	Gls
Luton T.	Jnrs	10.41	48	1	-	0

RUGGIERO, John S.
Stoke, 26 November, 1954 (M)

League Club	Source	Date Signed	Seasons Played	Apps	Subs	Gls
Stoke C.	App	05.72	76	9	0	2
Workington	L	01.76	75	3	0	0
Brighton & H.A.	Tr	06.77	77	4	4	2
Portsmouth	L	12.77	77	6	0	1
Chester C.	Tr	04.79	79	9	3	1

RULE, Alan H.
Southampton, 10 January, 1930 (WH)

League Club	Source	Date Signed	Seasons Played	Apps	Subs	Gls
Chelsea	Winchester C.	11.52				
Norwich C.	Tr	09.56	56	8	-	0
Bournemouth	Tr	06.57	57	25	-	0

RUMBLE, Paul
Hemel Hempstead, 14 March, 1969 (LB)

League Club	Source	Date Signed	Seasons Played	Apps	Subs	Gls
Watford	App	03.87				
Scunthorpe U.	L	08.88	88	8	0	1
Maidstone U.	Tr	08.89	89-91	48	7	3

RUMBOLD, George A.
Alton, 10 July, 1911 (FB)

League Club	Source	Date Signed	Seasons Played	Apps	Subs	Gls
Crystal Palace	Faringdon	10.34	35	5	-	0
Leyton Orient	Tr	06.37	37-38	52	-	0
Ipswich T.	Tr	05.46	46-49	121	-	11

RUMNEY, J. Edgar
Abberton (Ex), 15 September, 1936 (FB)

League Club	Source	Date Signed	Seasons Played	Apps	Subs	Gls
Colchester U.	Jnrs	05.57	57-64	50	-	0

RUNDLE, Charles R.
Fowey, 17 January, 1923 (IF)

League Club	Source	Date Signed	Seasons Played	Apps	Subs	Gls
Tottenham H.	St Blazey	02.46	46-48	28	-	12
Crystal Palace	Tr	06.50	50-51	38	-	2

RUNDLE, Sidney S.K.
Fowey, 19 October, 1921 Died 1987 (WH)

League Club	Source	Date Signed	Seasons Played	Apps	Subs	Gls
Plymouth Arg.	St Blazey	06.45	46-52	53	-	1

RUSH, David
Sunderland, 15 May, 1971 (F)

League Club	Source	Date Signed	Seasons Played	Apps	Subs	Gls
Sunderland	Notts Co. (YT)	07.89	90-91	28	8	6
Hartlepool U.	L	08.91	91	8	0	2

RUSH, Ian J.
St Asaph, 20 October, 1961 W Sch/Wu21-2/W-54 (F)

League Club	Source	Date Signed	Seasons Played	Apps	Subs	Gls
Chester C.	App	09.79	78-79	33	1	14
Liverpool	Tr	04.80	80-86	224	0	139
Liverpool	Juventus (It)	08.88	88-91	105	10	45

RUSH, Jonathan
New Zealand, 13 October, 1961 (G)

League Club	Source	Date Signed	Seasons Played	Apps	Subs	Gls
Blackpool	New Zealand	11.79	80	11	-	0
Carlisle U.	Tr	08.82				

RUSH, Matthew J.
Hackney, 6 August, 1971 (M)

League Club	Source	Date Signed	Seasons Played	Apps	Subs	Gls
West Ham U.	YT	03.90	90-91	5	10	2

RUSHBURY, David G.
Wolverhampton, 20 February, 1956 (D)

League Club	Source	Date Signed	Seasons Played	Apps	Subs	Gls
West Bromwich A.	App	02.74	74-75	28	0	0
Sheffield Wed.	Tr	11.76	76-78	111	1	7
Swansea C.	Tr	07.79	79-80	51	1	0
Carlisle U.	Tr	08.81	81-84	120	9	1
Gillingham	Tr	03.85	84	12	0	0
Doncaster Rov.	Tr	07.85	85-86	66	0	2
Cambridge U.	L	02.87	86	1	0	0
Bristol Rov.	Tr	02.87	86	14	2	0

RUSHBY, Alan
Doncaster, 27 December, 1933 (CH)

League Club	Source	Date Signed	Seasons Played	Apps	Subs	Gls
Doncaster Rov.		01.52	52-53	2	-	0
Mansfield T.	Tr	03.57	56-57	20	-	0
Bradford P.A.	Tr	11.57	57-58	12	-	0

RUSHFORTH, Peter
Carlisle, 6 December, 1945 (FB)

League Club	Source	Date Signed	Seasons Played	Apps	Subs	Gls
Workington (Am)		09.66	66	5	0	0

RUSHTON, Brian W. E.
Sedgley, 21 October, 1943 (RB)

League Club	Source	Date Signed	Seasons Played	Apps	Subs	Gls
Birmingham C.	App	10.60	62-63	12	-	0
Notts Co.	Tr	06.67	67	2	2	0

RUSHWORTH, Peter T.
Bristol, 12 April, 1927 (WH)

League Club	Source	Date Signed	Seasons Played	Apps	Subs	Gls
Leicester C.	Cheltenham T.	11.51				
Bournemouth	Tr	06.53	53-56	88	-	1

RUSLING, Graham
Keadby, 4 April, 1948 (F)

League Club	Source	Date Signed	Seasons Played	Apps	Subs	Gls
Scunthorpe U.		01.67	66-70	71	10	17

RUSSELL, Allan
Aberdeen, 16 November, 1953 (M)

League Club	Source	Date Signed	Seasons Played	Apps	Subs	Gls
Peterborough U.	Leicester C. (App)	08.71	71-72	7	8	1

RUSSELL, Alec C.
Bristol, 17 April, 1925 (IF)

League Club	Source	Date Signed	Seasons Played	Apps	Subs	Gls
Bristol C.		11.47	47-48	3	-	0

RUSSELL, Alexander
Seaham, 21 February, 1944 (M)

League Club	Source	Date Signed	Seasons Played	Apps	Subs	Gls
Everton	Jnrs	12.61				
Southport	Tr	11.63	63-69	262	1	63
Blackburn Rov.	Tr	08.70	70	22	2	4
Tranmere Rov.	Tr	07.71	71-72	54	1	7
Crewe Alex.	L	10.72	72	4	0	0
Southport	Tr	11.72	72-74	84	1	12

RUSSELL, Colin
Liverpool, 21 January, 1961 (F)

League Club	Source	Date Signed	Seasons Played	Apps	Subs	Gls
Liverpool	App	04.78	80	0	1	0
Huddersfield T.	Tr	09.82	82-83	64	2	23
Stoke C.	L	03.84	83	11	0	2
Bournemouth	Tr	08.84	84-85	65	3	14
Doncaster Rov.	Tr	07.86	86-87	43	0	5
Scarborough	Tr	10.87	87	12	1	2
Wigan Ath.	Tr	07.88	88	8	0	3

RUSSELL, Craig S.
South Shields, 4 February, 1974 (F)

League Club	Source	Date Signed	Seasons Played	Apps	Subs	Gls
Sunderland	YT	07.92	91	1	3	0

RUSSELL, Edward T.
Cranwell, 15 July, 1928 (WH)

League Club	Source	Date Signed	Seasons Played	Apps	Subs	Gls
Wolverhampton W.	St Chads Coll.	04.46	48-50	30	-	0
Middlesbrough	Tr	12.51	51-52	29	-	1
Leicester C.	Tr	10.53	53-57	90	-	5
Notts Co.	Tr	08.58	58	9	-	0

RUSSELL, Guy R.
Birmingham, 28 September, 1967 (F)

League Club	Source	Date Signed	Seasons Played	Apps	Subs	Gls
Birmingham C.	YT	05.86	84-87	7	4	0
Carlisle U.	L	03.87	86	9	3	2

RUSSELL, Hugh W.
Redcar, 10 March, 1921 (IF)

League Club	Source	Date Signed	Seasons Played	Apps	Subs	Gls
Gillingham	Bishop Auckland	08.46	50-51	61	-	8

RUSSELL, James W.
Edinburgh, 14 September, 1916 (IF)

League Club	Source	Date Signed	Seasons Played	Apps	Subs	Gls
Sunderland	Hearts	06.34	35-37	5	-	0
Norwich C.	Tr	05.38	38-46	12	-	2
Crystal Palace	Tr	12.46	46-47	43	-	6
New Brighton	Tr	07.48	48	24	-	1

RUSSELL, John M.
Plymouth, 22 April, 1938 (F)

League Club	Source	Date Signed	Seasons Played	Apps	Subs	Gls
Plymouth Arg.		01.59				
Southport	Tr	07.60	60	1	-	0

Ian Rush (Chester City, Liverpool, Juventus, Liverpool & Wales)

RUSSELL, Kevin J.

League Club	Source	Date Signed	Seasons Played	Career Record Apps	Subs	Gls

RUSSELL, Kevin J.
Brighton, 6 December, 1966 E Yth (F)

League Club	Source	Date Signed	Seasons Played	Apps	Subs	Gls
Portsmouth	Brighton & H.A.	10.84	85-86	3	1	0
Wrexham	Tr	07.87	87-88	84	0	43
Leicester C.	Tr	06.89	89-91	24	19	10
Peterborough U.	L	09.90	90	7	0	3
Cardiff C.	L	01.91	90	3	0	0
Hereford U.	L	11.91	91	3	0	1
Stoke C.	L	01.92	91	5	0	1

Kevin Russell (Portsmouth, Wrexham & Leicester City)

RUSSELL, Lee E.
Southampton, 3 September, 1969 (FB)

League Club	Source	Date Signed	Seasons Played	Apps	Subs	Gls
Portsmouth	YT	07.88	88-91	25	8	1

RUSSELL, Malcolm
Halifax, 9 November, 1945 (FB)

League Club	Source	Date Signed	Seasons Played	Apps	Subs	Gls
Halifax T.	App	03.63	62-68	184	1	0
Southport	Tr	09.68	68-70	92	0	2
Barrow	Tr	12.70	70-71	64	0	2
Stockport Co.	Tr	07.72	72	11	0	0

RUSSELL, Martin C.
Dublin, 27 April, 1967 IR Yth/IRu21-1 (M)

League Club	Source	Date Signed	Seasons Played	Apps	Subs	Gls
Manchester U.	App	04.84				
Birmingham C.	L	10.86	86	3	2	0
Leicester C.	Tr	03.87	86-88	13	7	0
Scarborough	Tr	02.89	88-89	51	0	9
Middlesbrough	Tr	03.90	90	10	1	2

RUSSELL, Peter W.
Gornal, 16 January, 1935 (HB)

League Club	Source	Date Signed	Seasons Played	Apps	Subs	Gls
Wolverhampton W.	Jnrs	10.52	54-55	3	-	0
Notts Co.	Tr	03.56	55-58	106	-	6

RUSSELL, Raymond J.
Walsall, 9 March, 1930 (IF)

League Club	Source	Date Signed	Seasons Played	Apps	Subs	Gls
West Bromwich A.	Jnrs	05.48				
Shrewsbury T.	Burton A.	05.54	54-59	168	-	56
Crewe Alex.	Tr	03.60	59	13	-	4

RUSSELL, Robert I.
Aberdour, 27 December, 1919 (WH)

League Club	Source	Date Signed	Seasons Played	Apps	Subs	Gls
Chelsea	Airdrieonians	12.44	46	2	-	0
Notts Co.	Tr	08.48	48	2	-	0
Leyton Orient	Tr	10.48				

RUSSELL, Roger
Corby, 20 November, 1957 (F)

League Club	Source	Date Signed	Seasons Played	Apps	Subs	Gls
Northampton T. (N/C)		09.81	81	0	1	0

RUSSELL, Sidney E. J.
Feltham, 4 October, 1937 (FB)

League Club	Source	Date Signed	Seasons Played	Apps	Subs	Gls
Brentford	Jnrs	08.56	56-59	54	-	0

RUSSELL, William
Hounslow, 7 July, 1935 E Amat (IF)

League Club	Source	Date Signed	Seasons Played	Apps	Subs	Gls
Sheffield U.	Rhyl	11.57	57-62	145	-	55
Bolton W.	Tr	03.63	62-64	22	-	2
Rochdale	Tr	07.66	66-67	61	1	8

RUSSELL, William H.
Coatbridge, 19 October, 1919 (IF)

League Club	Source	Date Signed	Seasons Played	Apps	Subs	Gls
Hartlepool U.		05.46	46-47	13	-	1

RUSSELL, William M.
Glasgow, 14 September, 1959 S Yth (RB)

League Club	Source	Date Signed	Seasons Played	Apps	Subs	Gls
Everton	App	07.77				
Doncaster Rov.	Glasgow Celtic	07.79	79-84	241	3	15
Scunthorpe U.	Tr	08.85	85-87	113	4	7
Rotherham U.	Tr	08.88	88-91	103	2	2

RUSSO, Gary
Hemsby (Nk), 2 August, 1956 (FB)

League Club	Source	Date Signed	Seasons Played	Apps	Subs	Gls
Ipswich T.	App	08.74				
Bournemouth	Tr	07.75	75	1	0	0

RUSSON, Ronald
Wednesbury, 10 December, 1928 Died 1981 (CH)

League Club	Source	Date Signed	Seasons Played	Apps	Subs	Gls
Wolverhampton W.	Jnrs	04.46				
Walsall	Hednesford T.	05.48	48-54	141	-	1

RUTHERFORD, Colin
Rowlands Gill, 11 July, 1944 (HB)

League Club	Source	Date Signed	Seasons Played	Apps	Subs	Gls
Sunderland	Jnrs	07.61				
Barnsley	Tr	06.63	63	1	-	0

RUTHERFORD, Ian S.
Hitchin, 24 December, 1972 (F)

League Club	Source	Date Signed	Seasons Played	Apps	Subs	Gls
Crewe Alex.	Luton T. (YT)	06.91	91	0	1	0

RUTHERFORD, Joseph H.
Chester-le-Street, 20 September, 1914 (G)

League Club	Source	Date Signed	Seasons Played	Apps	Subs	Gls
Southport		10.36	36-38	88	-	0
Aston Villa	Tr	02.39	38-51	148	-	0

RUTHERFORD, Mark R.
Birmingham, 25 March, 1972 (M)

League Club	Source	Date Signed	Seasons Played	Apps	Subs	Gls
Birmingham C.	YT	07.90	89-90	1	4	0

RUTHERFORD, Michael A.
Greenwich, 6 June, 1972 (M)

League Club	Source	Date Signed	Seasons Played	Apps	Subs	Gls
Queens Park R.	YT	12.89	89	1	1	0

RUTHERFORD, Robert
South Shields, 20 April, 1922 (HB)

League Club	Source	Date Signed	Seasons Played	Apps	Subs	Gls
Newcastle U.		03.44				
Gateshead	Tr	11.45	46-52	10	-	2

RUTHERFORD, Robert A.
Carlisle, 28 July, 1953 E Sch (M)

League Club	Source	Date Signed	Seasons Played	Apps	Subs	Gls
Leeds U.	App	08.70				
Workington	Tr	11.72	72	1	1	0

RUTHERFORD, William J.
Bellshill, 23 January, 1930 Died 1980 (WH)

League Club	Source	Date Signed	Seasons Played	Apps	Subs	Gls
Darlington	Stirling A.	07.52	52-58	253	-	3
Southport	Tr	07.59	59-63	176	-	7

RUTLEY, Peter
Exeter, 19 May, 1946 (WH)

League Club	Source	Date Signed	Seasons Played	Apps	Subs	Gls
Exeter C.	App	07.63	62-64	16	-	0

RUTTER, D. Brian
Poplar, 11 May, 1933 (IF)

League Club	Source	Date Signed	Seasons Played	Apps	Subs	Gls
Crystal Palace (Am)	Cardiff C. (Am)	11.54	54	3	-	1

RUTTER, Charles F.
Poplar, 22 December, 1927 E'B'-1 (FB)

League Club	Source	Date Signed	Seasons Played	Apps	Subs	Gls
Cardiff C.	Taunton T.	09.49	50-57	118	-	0
Exeter C.	Tr	08.58				

Vaughan Ryan (Wimbledon)

RUTTER, Cyril H.
Leeds, 21 February, 1933 (CH)

League Club	Source	Date Signed	Seasons Played	Apps	Subs	Gls
Portsmouth	Jnrs	07.51	53-62	171	-	0

RUTTER, John T.
Warrington, 13 September, 1952 (FB)

League Club	Source	Date Signed	Seasons Played	Apps	Subs	Gls
Wolverhampton W.	App	09.70				
Bournemouth	Tr	08.73	73	2	2	0
Exeter C.	Tr	07.74	74-75	31	1	1
Stockport Co.	Tr	08.76	76-85	400	4	10

RUTTER, Keith G.
Leeds, 10 September, 1931 (CH)

League Club	Source	Date Signed	Seasons Played	Apps	Subs	Gls
Queens Park R.	Methley U.	07.54	54-62	340	-	1
Colchester U.	Tr	02.63	62-63	63	-	0

RUTTER, Stephen J.
London, 24 July, 1968 (F)

League Club	Source	Date Signed	Seasons Played	Apps	Subs	Gls
Maidstone U. (N/C)	Iceland	02.92	91	0	1	0

RYALLS, Brian
Grimethorpe, 7 July, 1932 (G)

League Club	Source	Date Signed	Seasons Played	Apps	Subs	Gls
Sheffield Wed.	Grimethorpe Colly	01.53	53-57	41	-	0

RYAN, Darren T.
Oswestry, 3 July, 1972 (F)

League Club	Source	Date Signed	Seasons Played	Apps	Subs	Gls
Shrewsbury T.	YT	10.90	90-91	3	1	0

RYAN, David P.
Manchester, 5 January, 1957 (G)

League Club	Source	Date Signed	Seasons Played	Apps	Subs	Gls
Manchester U.	App	07.74				
Port Vale	L	01.76	75	1	0	0
Southport	Tr	03.76	75-76	23	0	0

RYAN, Derek A.
Dublin, 2 January, 1967 (M)

League Club	Source	Date Signed	Seasons Played	Apps	Subs	Gls
Wolverhampton W.	App	10.84	84-86	23	10	5

RYAN, Eric W.
Oswestry, 6 January, 1933 (FB)

League Club	Source	Date Signed	Seasons Played	Apps	Subs	Gls
Mansfield T.	Oswestry T.	05.51	54-56	20	-	0

RYAN, George
Glasgow, 29 December, 1931 (CF)

League Club	Source	Date Signed	Seasons Played	Apps	Subs	Gls
Sheffield U.	Hull C. (Am)	05.52				
Chesterfield	Third Lanark	07.54	54	3	-	0

RYAN, Gerard J.
Dublin, 4 October, 1955 IR-16 (W)

League Club	Source	Date Signed	Seasons Played	Apps	Subs	Gls
Derby Co.	Bohemians	09.77	77-78	30	0	4
Brighton & H.A.	Tr	09.78	78-84	131	41	32

RYAN, James
Stirling, 12 May, 1945 (W)

League Club	Source	Date Signed	Seasons Played	Apps	Subs	Gls
Manchester U.	Corrie Hearts	01.63	65-69	21	3	4
Luton T.	Tr	04.70	70-76	172	12	21

RYAN, James P.
Rhyl, 6 September, 1942 Wu23-1 (CF)

League Club	Source	Date Signed	Seasons Played	Apps	Subs	Gls
Charlton Ath.	Dulwich Hamlet	02.63	62-64	16	-	8
Millwall	Tr	02.65	64-65	12	0	2
Exeter C.	Hastings U.	01.67	66	20	0	5

RYAN, John B.
Ashton-u-Lyne, 18 February, 1962 Eu21-1 (LB/M)

League Club	Source	Date Signed	Seasons Played	Apps	Subs	Gls
Oldham Ath.	App	02.80	81-82	77	0	8
Newcastle U.	Tr	08.83	83-84	28	0	1
Sheffield Wed.	Tr	09.84	84	5	3	1
Oldham Ath.	Tr	08.85	85-86	20	3	0
Mansfield T.	Tr	10.87	87-88	53	9	1
Chesterfield	Tr	06.89	89-90	81	1	6
Rochdale	Tr	06.91	91	29	3	2

RYAN, John G.
Lewisham, 20 July, 1947 (M/RB)

League Club	Source	Date Signed	Seasons Played	Apps	Subs	Gls
Arsenal	Maidstone U.	10.64				
Fulham	Tr	07.65	65-68	42	5	1
Luton T.	Tr	07.69	69-75	264	2	10
Norwich C.	Tr	08.76	76-79	113	3	26
Sheffield U.	Seattle (USA)	09.80	80-81	56	0	2
Manchester C.	Tr	01.82	81	19	0	0
Stockport Co. (N/C)	Tr	08.83	83	1	1	0
Chester C. (N/C)	Tr	09.83	83	4	0	0
Cambridge U. (N/C)		10.84	84	5	0	0

RYAN, John J. ("Buck")
Alloa, 16 October, 1930 (CF)

League Club	Source	Date Signed	Seasons Played	Apps	Subs	Gls
Charlton Ath.	Chippenham T.	02.54	54-58	61	-	32
Newcastle U.	Tr	03.59				
Bristol C.	Tr	07.60	60	3	-	0

RYAN, John O.
Liverpool, 28 October, 1944 (W)

League Club	Source	Date Signed	Seasons Played	Apps	Subs	Gls
Tranmere Rov.		08.64				
Luton T.	Wigan Ath.	10.67	67-68	17	1	1
Notts Co.	Tr	05.69	69	22	2	1

RYAN, Kenneth
Accrington, 20 September, 1936 (G)

League Club	Source	Date Signed	Seasons Played	Apps	Subs	Gls
Accrington St. (Am)	Accrington Colly	04.59	58	1	-	0

RYAN, Laurence J.
Watford, 15 October, 1963 (F)

League Club	Source	Date Signed	Seasons Played	Apps	Subs	Gls
Cambridge U.	Dunstable T.	04.88	87-89	39	12	13

RYAN, Michael J.
Welwyn, 14 October, 1930 (OR)

League Club	Source	Date Signed	Seasons Played	Apps	Subs	Gls
Arsenal	Chertsey	07.48				
Lincoln C.	Tr	06.52	52	7	-	0
York C.	Tr	01.53	52	4	-	0

RYAN, Reginald A.
Dublin, 30 October, 1925 IR-16/NI-1 (IF)

League Club	Source	Date Signed	Seasons Played	Apps	Subs	Gls
West Bromwich A.	Nuneaton Bor.	04.45	46-54	234	-	28
Derby Co.	Tr	07.55	55-58	133	-	30
Coventry C.	Tr	09.58	58-60	65	-	9

RYAN, Thomas S.
Windlesham, 9 July, 1952 (D)

League Club	Source	Date Signed	Seasons Played	Apps	Subs	Gls
Reading	App	05.70	70	1	0	0

RYAN, Vaughan W.
Westminster, 2 September, 1968 (M)

League Club	Source	Date Signed	Seasons Played	Apps	Subs	Gls
Wimbledon	App	08.86	86-91	67	15	3
Sheffield U.	L	01.89	88	2	1	0

RYDEN, Hugh J.
Dumbarton, 7 April, 1943 (M)

League Club	Source	Date Signed	Seasons Played	Apps	Subs	Gls
Leeds U.	Yoker Ath.	10.60				
Bristol Rov.	Tr	06.62	62	8	-	4
Stockport Co.	Tr	07.63	63	38	-	9
Chester C.	Tr	06.64	64-67	140	1	44
Halifax T.	Tr	11.67	67-69	54	1	6
Stockport Co.	Tr	12.69	69-72	112	12	15

RYDEN, John J.
Alexandria, 18 February, 1931 (CH)

League Club	Source	Date Signed	Seasons Played	Apps	Subs	Gls
Accrington St.	Alloa Ath.	02.54	53-55	80	-	1
Tottenham H.	Tr	11.55	55-58	63	-	2
Watford	Tr	06.61	61	24	-	1

RYDER, Derek F.
Leeds, 18 February, 1947 (FB)

League Club	Source	Date Signed	Seasons Played	Apps	Subs	Gls
Leeds U.	Jnrs	02.64				
Cardiff C.	Tr	06.66	66	4	0	0
Rochdale	Tr	07.68	68-71	168	0	1
Southport	Tr	07.72	72-73	80	2	2

RYDER, Robert
Bolton, 11 July, 1943 (FB)

League Club	Source	Date Signed	Seasons Played	Apps	Subs	Gls
Gillingham	Nantwich T.	01.65	64-67	6	0	0

RYDER, Terence R.
Norwich, 3 June, 1928 (F)

League Club	Source	Date Signed	Seasons Played	Apps	Subs	Gls
Norwich C.	City W.	09.46	46-49	46	-	12
Portsmouth	Tr	10.50	50-51	14	-	4
Swindon T.	Tr	07.52	52	34	-	13

RYECRAFT, Frederick
Southall, 29 August, 1939 (G)

League Club	Source	Date Signed	Seasons Played	Apps	Subs	Gls
Brentford	Southall	09.59	62-63	33	-	0

RYLANDS, David R.
Liverpool, 7 March, 1953 (CD)

League Club	Source	Date Signed	Seasons Played	Apps	Subs	Gls
Liverpool	App	03.70				
Hereford U.	Tr	09.74	74-75	22	0	0
Newport Co.	L	03.75	74	3	0	1
Hartlepool U.	L	03.76	75	11	0	0
Halifax T.	Tr	06.76	76	5	0	0

RYMER, George H.
Barnsley, 6 October, 1923 (G)

League Club	Source	Date Signed	Seasons Played	Apps	Subs	Gls
Barnsley	Ardsley Vic.	12.43	46	3	-	0
Accrington St.	Tr	02.47	46	8	-	0

Peter Shilton (Leicester City, Stoke City, Nottingham Forest, Southampton, Derby County, Plymouth Argyle & England)
Currently the player-manager with Plymouth Argyle, he is the most capped Englishman, with 125 appearances to his credit

League Club	Source	Date Signed	Seasons Played	Career Record Apps	Subs	Gls
SABELLA, Alejandro (Alex)						
Argentina, 5 November, 1954						(M)
Sheffield U.	River Plate (Arg)	08.78	78-79	76	0	8
Leeds U.	Tr	06.80	80	22	1	2
SABIN, Arthur H.						
Birmingham, 25 January, 1939 Died 1958						(G)
Aston Villa	Jnrs	01.57	56-57	2	-	0
SADDINGTON, Nigel J.						
Sunderland, 9 December, 1965						(CD)
Doncaster Rov.	S.C. Vaux	09.84	84	5	0	0
Sunderland	Roker	01.86	86	3	0	0
Carlisle U.	Tr	02.88	87-89	97	0	15
SADLER, David						
Yalding (Kt), 5 February, 1946 E Yth/E Amat/Eu23-3/EF Lge/E-4						(CD)
Manchester U.	Maidstone U.	02.63	63-73	266	6	22
Preston N. E.	Tr	11.73	73-76	104	1	3
SADLER, George H.						
Whitwell, 7 May, 1915						(FB)
West Ham U.	Gainsborough Trin.	12.38	46	1	-	0
SAGAR, Edward (Ted)						
Thorne, 7 February, 1910 Died 1986 EF Lge/E-4						(G)
Everton	Thorne Colly	03.29	29-52	463	-	0
SAGE, Frank R.						
Chipping Sodbury, 31 May, 1924						(WH)
Cardiff C.		02.45				
Newport Co.	Tr	04.48	47-48	3	-	0
SAGE, Melvyn						
Gillingham, 24 March, 1964						(RB)
Gillingham	App	03.82	81-85	126	6	5
Derby Co.	Tr	08.86	86-91	137	3	4
SAILE, Michael A.						
Heywood, 31 December, 1950 E Yth						(FB)
Bury	App	01.69	68-72	92	1	0
SAINSBURY, Kim C.						
Reading, 21 September, 1957						(F)
Reading (App)	App	08.74	74	0	1	0

League Club	Source	Date Signed	Seasons Played	Career Record Apps	Subs	Gls
ST. JOHN, Ian						
Motherwell, 7 June, 1938 Su23-2/SF Lge/S-21						(M)
Liverpool	Motherwell	04.61	61-70	334	2	95
Coventry C.	Hellenic (SA)	09.71	71	18	0	3
Tranmere Rov.	Tr	10.72	72	9	0	1
SAINTY, John A.						
Poplar, 24 March, 1946 E Sch						(M)
Tottenham H.	App	07.63				
Reading	Tr	08.67	67-69	63	8	19
Bournemouth	Tr	02.70	69-73	111	7	21
Mansfield T.	L	11.72	72	3	0	0
Aldershot	Tr	08.74	74-75	26	3	0
SALAKO, Andrew O.						
Nigeria, 8 November, 1972						(FB)
Charlton Ath.	YT	04.91	90	1	0	0
SALAKO, John A.						
Nigeria, 11 February, 1969 E-5						(LW)
Crystal Palace	App	11.86	86-91	87	38	11
Swansea C.	L	08.89	89	13	0	3
SALATHIEL, D. Neil						
Wrexham, 19 November, 1962 W Sch						(RB)
Wrexham (N/C)	Sheffield Wed. (Jnr)	05.80	80	4	0	0
Crewe Alex.	Tr	06.81	81-82	64	1	0
Wrexham	Arcadia Shep. (S.A.)	12.83	83-89	239	1	3
SALE, Mark D.						
Burton, 27 February, 1972						(F)
Stoke C.	YT	07.90	89	0	2	0
Cambridge U.	Tr	05.91				
Birmingham C.	Rocester	03.92	91	2	4	0
SALES, Ronald D.						
South Shields, 19 September, 1920						(CH)
Newcastle U.	Reyrolles	07.42				
Leyton Orient	Tr	05.47	47-48	46	-	3
Hartlepool U.	Tr	08.50	50	3	-	0
SALISBURY, Gareth						
Caernarfon, 11 March, 1941						(IF)
Wrexham	Jnrs	05.59	59-61	11	-	0
Norwich C.	Tr	07.62				
Luton T.	Tr	07.63	63	12	-	2
Colchester U.	Tr	07.64	64	15	-	2
Chesterfield	Tr	07.65	65	34	0	9

John Salako (Crystal Palace & England)

SALMAN, Danis M. M.
Cyprus, 12 March, 1960 E Yth (D)

League Club	Source	Date Signed	Seasons Played	Apps	Subs	Gls
Brentford	App	08.77	75-85	316	9	8
Millwall	Tr	08.86	86-89	85	8	4
Plymouth Arg.	Tr	03.90	89-91	71	3	4
Peterborough U.	L	03.92	91	1	0	0

SALMON, Leonard A.
West Kirby, 24 June, 1912 (WH)

League Club	Source	Date Signed	Seasons Played	Apps	Subs	Gls
New Brighton	Hoylake	10.34	34-35	30	-	2
Burnley	South Liverpool	09.41				
Tranmere Rov.	Tr	09.46	46-47	30	-	1

SALMON, Michael B.
Leyland, 14 July, 1964 (G)

League Club	Source	Date Signed	Seasons Played	Apps	Subs	Gls
Blackburn Rov.	Jnrs	10.81	81	1	0	0
Chester C.	L	10.82	82	16	0	0
Stockport Co.	Tr	08.83	83-85	118	0	0
Bolton W.	Tr	07.86	86	26	0	0
Wrexham	Tr	03.87	86-88	100	0	0
Charlton Ath.	Tr	07.89	90	7	0	0

SALMONS, Geoffrey
Mexborough, 14 January, 1948 (M)

League Club	Source	Date Signed	Seasons Played	Apps	Subs	Gls
Sheffield U.	Jnrs	02.66	67-73	170	10	8
Stoke C.	Tr	07.74	74-77	115	3	14
Sheffield U.	L	09.77	77	5	0	0
Leicester C.	Tr	10.77	77	25	1	4
Chesterfield	Tr	08.78	78-81	119	1	15

SALT, Samuel J.
Southport, 30 December, 1938 (WH)

League Club	Source	Date Signed	Seasons Played	Apps	Subs	Gls
Blackpool	Jnrs	01.56	60	18	-	0

SALTER, Kenneth
Cullompton, 16 November, 1933 (G)

League Club	Source	Date Signed	Seasons Played	Apps	Subs	Gls
Exeter C.	Jnrs	11.50	50	1	-	0

SALTON, Darren B.
Edinburgh, 16 March, 1972 S Sch/S Yth/Su21-4 (D)

League Club	Source	Date Signed	Seasons Played	Apps	Subs	Gls
Luton T.	YT	03.89	91	2	1	0

SALVAGE, Barry J.
Bristol, 21 December, 1947 Died 1986 (W)

League Club	Source	Date Signed	Seasons Played	Apps	Subs	Gls
Fulham	Eastbourne	09.67	67-68	7	0	0
Millwall	Tr	03.69	68	1	1	0
Queens Park R.	Tr	03.71	70-72	16	5	1
Brentford	Tr	02.73	72-74	87	0	8
Millwall	Tr	08.75	75-76	43	12	9

SAMBROOK, Raymond
Wolverhampton, 31 May, 1933 (W)

League Club	Source	Date Signed	Seasons Played	Apps	Subs	Gls
Coventry C.	Wednesfield	09.53	54-57	96	-	25
Manchester C.	Tr	01.58	57-61	62	-	13
Doncaster Rov.	Tr	06.62	62	8	-	0
Crewe Alex.	Tr	01.63				

SAMMELS, Jonathan C.
Ipswich, 23 July, 1945 E Yth/Eu23-9/EF Lge (M)

League Club	Source	Date Signed	Seasons Played	Apps	Subs	Gls
Arsenal	App	08.62	62-70	212	3	39
Leicester C.	Tr	07.71	71-77	236	5	21

SAMPLE, James
Morpeth, 5 November, 1921 (IF)

League Club	Source	Date Signed	Seasons Played	Apps	Subs	Gls
Bradford C.	Ashington	08.47	47-48	8	-	2

SAMPSON, Ian
Wakefield, 14 November, 1968 (CD)

League Club	Source	Date Signed	Seasons Played	Apps	Subs	Gls
Sunderland	Goole T.	11.90	91	7	1	0

SAMPSON, Peter S.
Pitsea (Ex), 9 July, 1927 (WH)

League Club	Source	Date Signed	Seasons Played	Apps	Subs	Gls
Bristol Rov.	Devizes	06.48	48-60	339	-	4

SAMPSON, Raymond V.
Swindon, 6 February, 1935 (IF)

League Club	Source	Date Signed	Seasons Played	Apps	Subs	Gls
Swindon T.	Jnrs	05.52	53-58	64	-	10

SAMPSON, Thomas W.
Southwark, 18 August, 1954 (D)

League Club	Source	Date Signed	Seasons Played	Apps	Subs	Gls
Millwall	App	06.72	72	0	1	0

SAMUELS, Leslie
Oldham, 8 December, 1928 (IF)

League Club	Source	Date Signed	Seasons Played	Apps	Subs	Gls
Burnley		12.49	50	2	-	0
Exeter C.	Tr	07.53	53	12	-	1
Wrexham	Tr	03.54	53-54	26	-	11
Crewe Alex.	Tr	11.54	54-55	42	-	13
Bradford C.	Tr	12.55	55-57	84	-	38
Stockport Co.	Tr	03.58	57-58	25	-	5

SAMUELS, Robert W.
Aberdeen, 18 May, 1946 (IF)

League Club	Source	Date Signed	Seasons Played	Apps	Subs	Gls
Lincoln C.	Aberdeen	07.67	67	3	1	0

SAMWAYS, Mark
Doncaster, 11 November, 1968 (G)

League Club	Source	Date Signed	Seasons Played	Apps	Subs	Gls
Doncaster Rov.	YT	08.87	87-91	121	0	0
Scunthorpe U.	L	03.92	91	8	0	0

SAMWAYS, Vincent (Vinny)
Bethnal Green, 27 October, 1968 E Yth/Eu21-5 (M)

League Club	Source	Date Signed	Seasons Played	Apps	Subs	Gls
Tottenham H.	App	10.85	86-91	92	28	8

SANAGHAN, Joseph
Motherwell, 12 December, 1914 (FB)

League Club	Source	Date Signed	Seasons Played	Apps	Subs	Gls
Bradford P.A.		08.35	35	5	-	0
Bournemouth	Tr	06.37	37-48	170	-	0
Stockport Co.	Tr	08.49	49-50	52	-	0

SANCHEZ, John
Paddington, 21 October, 1940 E Sch/E Yth (WH)

League Club	Source	Date Signed	Seasons Played	Apps	Subs	Gls
Arsenal	Jnrs	10.57				
Watford	Tr	06.59	59-60	19	-	0

SANCHEZ, Lawrence P.
Lambeth, 22 October, 1959 E Sch/NI-3 (M)

League Club	Source	Date Signed	Seasons Played	Apps	Subs	Gls
Reading	Thatcham T.	09.77	77-84	249	13	28
Wimbledon	Tr	12.84	84-91	216	12	27

SANDEMAN, Bradley R.
Northampton, 24 February, 1970 (M)

League Club	Source	Date Signed	Seasons Played	Apps	Subs	Gls
Northampton T.	YT	07.88	87-90	28	30	2
Maidstone U.	Tr	02.91	90-91	55	2	7

SANDER, Christopher A.
Swansea, 11 November, 1962 (G)

League Club	Source	Date Signed	Seasons Played	Apps	Subs	Gls
Swansea C.	App	11.79	81-83	20	0	0
Wrexham	L	09.84	84	5	0	0
Cardiff C. (N/C)	Tr	08.85	85	8	0	0
Cardiff C. (N/C)	Haverfordwest	03.86	85	5	0	0

SANDERCOCK, Kenneth L.
Plymouth, 31 January, 1951 (M)

League Club	Source	Date Signed	Seasons Played	Apps	Subs	Gls
Torquay U.	App	01.69	68-69	42	4	1
Leicester C.	Tr	11.69	69	5	5	0
Torquay U.	Tr	11.71	71-74	113	6	5

SANDERCOCK, Philip J.
Plymouth, 21 June, 1953 (LB)

League Club	Source	Date Signed	Seasons Played	Apps	Subs	Gls
Torquay U.	App	09.71	69-76	199	6	13
Huddersfield T.	Tr	06.77	77-78	81	0	1
Northampton T.	Tr	09.79	79-80	69	0	3

SANDERS, Alan
Salford, 31 January, 1934 (FB)

League Club	Source	Date Signed	Seasons Played	Apps	Subs	Gls
Manchester C.		08.55				
Everton	Tr	07.56	57-59	56	-	0
Swansea C.	Tr	11.59	59-62	92	-	0
Brighton & H. A.	Tr	01.63	62-65	80	0	0

SANDERS, Alan J.
Newport, 29 October, 1963 W Sch (M)

League Club	Source	Date Signed	Seasons Played	Apps	Subs	Gls
Cardiff C.	Jnrs	11.81	81	1	1	0

SANDERS, James A.
Hackney, 5 July, 1920 (G)

League Club	Source	Date Signed	Seasons Played	Apps	Subs	Gls
Charlton Ath.	Longlands	02.44				
West Bromwich A.	Tr	11.45	48-57	327	-	0
Coventry C.	Tr	07.58	58	10	-	0

SANDERS, James C. F.
Marlborough, 15 October, 1932 (WH)

League Club	Source	Date Signed	Seasons Played	Apps	Subs	Gls
Bristol C.		11.51				
Crystal Palace	Tr	03.55	55-58	46	-	0
Exeter C.	Cheltenham T.	08.62	62	20	-	1

SANDERS, Peter C. W.
Newport, 7 September, 1942 W Yth (CF)

League Club	Source	Date Signed	Seasons Played	Apps	Subs	Gls
Newport Co.	Jnrs	10.59	60	3	-	0
Gillingham	Tr	07.61	61	2	-	0

SANDERS, Roy J.
Stepney, 22 September, 1940 (OR)

League Club	Source	Date Signed	Seasons Played	Apps	Subs	Gls
Northampton T.	Romford	05.62	62	15	-	2

League Club	Source	Date Signed	Seasons Played	Career Record Apps	Subs	Gls
SANDERSON, Eric						
Chapeltown, 10 November, 1921						(FB)
Rotherham U.	Paramore	09.47	47	2	-	1
SANDERSON, Ian						
Torquay, 26 August, 1956						(F)
Torquay U. (N/C)		08.77	77	0	1	0
SANDERSON, John R.						
Carlisle, 5 February, 1918						(LB)
Carlisle U.		05.38	38	15	-	0
Wolverhampton W.	Tr	02.39				
Luton T.	Tr	05.46	46	6	-	0
SANDERSON, Keith						
Hull, 9 October, 1940						(IF)
Plymouth Arg.	Bath C.	08.64	64	29	-	2
Queens Park R.	Tr	06.65	65-68	98	6	11
SANDERSON, Michael						
West Germany, 26 October, 1966						(M)
Darlington (N/C)	Hartlepool U. (YT)	03.86	85	1	0	0
SANDERSON, Paul D.						
Blackpool, 16 December, 1966						(W)
Manchester C.	Fleetwood T.	11.83				
Chester C.	Tr	02.84	83	24	0	3
Halifax T.	Tr	08.84	84-86	88	16	5
Cardiff C.	Tr	07.87	87	8	13	1
Walsall	Tr	03.88	87	0	3	0
SANDERSON, Philip						
Barnsley, 1 November, 1953						(OL)
Barnsley (N/C)	Worsboro' Bridge	10.74	74	2	0	1
SANDFORD, Lee R.						
Basingstoke, 22 April, 1968 E Yth						(D)
Portsmouth	App	12.85	85-89	66	6	1
Stoke C.	Tr	12.89	89-91	92	1	4
SANDIFORD, Ian R .						
Chorley, 26 February, 1946						(CF)
Blackburn Rov.	App	02.64				
Stockport Co.	Tr	06.64	64-65	47	0	9
Crewe Alex.	Tr	01.66	65-66	48	4	18
SANDLANDS, Herbert						
Nantwich, 9 August, 1931						
Crewe Alex. (Am)	Nantwich T.	08.54	54	1	-	0
SANDY, Adam V. C.						
Peterborough, 22 September, 1958						(M)
Northampton T.	Wolverton T.	02.80	79-82	88	16	7
SANDYS, Harold A.						
Fulham, 8 October, 1932						(F)
Torquay U.	Yeovil T.	08.54	54	2	-	0
SANFORD, Mark A.						
London, 10 September, 1960						(IF)
Aldershot	Jnrs	06.79	79-82	72	12	23
SANG, Neil						
Liverpool, 23 May, 1972						(M)
Everton	YT	05.90				
Torquay U.	Tr	06.91	91	8	6	0
SANKEY, John						
Winsford, 19 March, 1912 Died 1985						(WH)
West Bromwich A.	Winsford U.	11.30	33-38	144	-	5
Northampton T.	Tr	10.45	46-47	42	-	0
SANKEY, Martin A.						
Wellington, 4 May, 1964						(F)
Shrewsbury T.	App	02.82	82	0	5	0
SANSBY, Clifford P.						
Peterborough, 24 November, 1934						(FB)
Peterborough U.	March T.	(N/L)	60	1	-	0
SANSOM, Kenneth G.						
Camberwell, 26 September, 1958 E Sch/E Yth/Eu21-8/E-86						(LB)
Crystal Palace	App	12.75	74-79	172	0	3
Arsenal	Tr	08.80	80-87	314	0	6
Newcastle U.	Tr	12.88	88	20	0	0
Queens Park R.	Tr	06.89	89-90	64	0	0
Coventry C.	Tr	03.91	90-91	30	0	0

League Club	Source	Date Signed	Seasons Played	Career Record Apps	Subs	Gls
SANSOME, Paul E.						
New Addington, 6 October, 1961						(G)
Millwall	Crystal Palace (App)	04.80	81-87	156	0	0
Southend U.	Tr	03.88	87-91	187	0	0
SAPHIN, Reginald F. E.						
Kilburn, 8 August, 1916						(G)
Queens Park R.	Walthamstow Ave.	06.46	46-50	34	-	0
Watford	Tr	07.51	51-53	57	-	0
SARGENT, Gary S.						
Bedford, 11 September, 1952						(F)
Norwich C.	App	09.70	71	0	1	0
Scunthorpe U.	Tr	07.72	72	14	1	1
Peterborough U.	Bedford T.	07.77	77-78	27	7	5
Northampton T.	Tr	06.79	79-80	41	2	4
SARSON, Albert						
Rossington, 31 December, 1930						(F)
Doncaster Rov.	Mansfield T. (Am)	08.49	49-50	2	-	0
SARTORI, Carlo						
Italy, 10 February, 1948						(M)
Manchester U.	Jnrs	02.65	68-71	26	13	4
SATCHWELL, Kenneth R.						
Birmingham, 17 January, 1940						(F)
Coventry C.	Jnrs	09.58	58-61	68	-	21
Walsall	Nuneaton Bor.	01.65	64-66	54	3	7
SAUL, Frank L.						
Canvey Island, 23 August, 1943 E Yth						(W)
Tottenham H.	Jnrs	08.60	60-67	112	4	37
Southampton	Tr	01.68	67-69	47	3	2
Queens Park R.	Tr	05.70	70-71	40	3	4
Millwall	Tr	03.72	71-75	85	11	4
SAUNDERS, Carl S.						
Marston Green, 26 November, 1964						(F)
Stoke C.		03.83	82-89	130	34	23
Bristol Rov.	Tr	02.90	89-91	86	8	31

Kenny Sansom (Crystal Palace, Arsenal, Newcastle United, Queens Park Rangers, Coventry City & England)

League Club	Source	Date Signed	Seasons Played	Career Record Apps	Subs	Gls

SAUNDERS, Dean N.
Swansea, 21 June, 1964 W-34 (F)

League Club	Source	Date Signed	Seasons Played	Apps	Subs	Gls
Swansea C.	App	06.82	83-84	42	7	12
Cardiff C.	L	03.85	84	3	1	0
Brighton & H. A.	Tr	08.85	85-86	66	6	20
Oxford U.	Tr	03.87	86-88	57	2	22
Derby Co.	Tr	10.88	88-90	106	0	42
Liverpool	Tr	07.91	91	36	0	10

Dean Saunders (Swansea City, Brighton & Hove Albion, Oxford United, Derby County, Liverpool & Wales)

SAUNDERS, Dennis F.
Scarborough, 19 December, 1924 E Amat (CH)

League Club	Source	Date Signed	Seasons Played	Apps	Subs	Gls
Newport Co. (Am)	Huddersfield T. (Am)	11.46	46	7	-	0

SAUNDERS, Derek W.
Ware, 6 January, 1928 E Amat (WH)

League Club	Source	Date Signed	Seasons Played	Apps	Subs	Gls
Chelsea	Walthamstow Ave.	07.53	53-58	203	-	9

SAUNDERS, George E.
Birkenhead, 1 March, 1918 Died 1982 (RB)

League Club	Source	Date Signed	Seasons Played	Apps	Subs	Gls
Everton		02.39	46-51	133	-	0

SAUNDERS, Glyn
Nottingham, 16 June, 1956 (FB)

League Club	Source	Date Signed	Seasons Played	Apps	Subs	Gls
Nottingham F.	App	06.74	76	4	0	0

SAUNDERS, F. John
Middlesbrough, 24 August, 1924 (CH)

League Club	Source	Date Signed	Seasons Played	Apps	Subs	Gls
Darlington		09.46	46-47	67	-	0
Chelsea	Tr	05.48	49-53	52	-	0
Crystal Palace	Tr	08.54	54-55	59	-	0
Chester C.	Tr	05.57	57-58	67	-	3

SAUNDERS, John G.
Worksop, 1 December, 1950 (CD)

League Club	Source	Date Signed	Seasons Played	Apps	Subs	Gls
Mansfield T.	App	12.68	69-72	89	0	2
Huddersfield T.	Tr	10.72	72-75	121	0	1

League Club	Source	Date Signed	Seasons Played	Apps	Subs	Gls
Barnsley	Tr	12.75	75-78	149	0	7
Lincoln C.	Tr	06.79	79	25	1	1
Doncaster Rov.	Tr	08.80	80	27	1	2

SAUNDERS, John H.
Maidenhead, 18 December, 1943 (OR)

League Club	Source	Date Signed	Seasons Played	Apps	Subs	Gls
Charlton Ath.	Jnrs	08.62	62	1	-	0

SAUNDERS, John T.
Newport, 2 October, 1950 W Sch (D)

League Club	Source	Date Signed	Seasons Played	Apps	Subs	Gls
Newport Co.	Birmingham C. (App)	08.69	69-70	26	1	0
Leeds U.	Tr	07.71				
Walsall	Tr	10.72	72-75	94	5	2

SAUNDERS, Leonard J.
Liverpool, 7 January, 1928 (CF)

League Club	Source	Date Signed	Seasons Played	Apps	Subs	Gls
New Brighton (Am)	Stoneycroft	01.51	50	4	-	2

SAUNDERS, Paul B.
Watford, 17 December, 1959 (D)

League Club	Source	Date Signed	Seasons Played	Apps	Subs	Gls
Watford	App	12.77				
Northampton T.	Tr	07.78	78-82	114	12	5

SAUNDERS, Robert C.
Poole, 26 August, 1945 (IF)

League Club	Source	Date Signed	Seasons Played	Apps	Subs	Gls
Bournemouth	App	06.63	65	2	1	0

SAUNDERS, Ronald
Birkenhead, 6 November, 1932 E Yth (CF)

League Club	Source	Date Signed	Seasons Played	Apps	Subs	Gls
Everton	Jnrs	02.51	54	3	-	0
Gillingham	Tonbridge	05.57	57-58	49	-	20
Portsmouth	Tr	09.58	58-64	234	-	140
Watford	Tr	09.64	64-65	39	0	18
Charlton Ath.	Tr	08.65	65-66	64	1	24

SAUNDERS, Ronald A.
Malmesbury, 14 January, 1923 (CH)

League Club	Source	Date Signed	Seasons Played	Apps	Subs	Gls
Swindon T. (Am)		04.48	47	1	-	0

SAUNDERS, Roy
Salford, 4 September, 1930 E Yth (WH)

League Club	Source	Date Signed	Seasons Played	Apps	Subs	Gls
Liverpool	Hull C. (Am)	05.48	52-58	132	-	1
Swansea C.	Tr	03.59	58-62	95	-	3

SAUNDERS, Steven J. P.
Warrington, 21 September, 1964 (F)

League Club	Source	Date Signed	Seasons Played	Apps	Subs	Gls
Bolton W.	App	09.82	83	3	0	0
Crewe Alex.	Tr	07.85	85	15	7	1
Preston N. E. (N/C)	Tr	08.86				
Grimsby T.	Tr	08.87	87-88	70	6	13
Scarborough	Tr	08.89	89	23	9	1

SAUNDERS, Wesley
Sunderland, 23 February, 1963 (CD)

League Club	Source	Date Signed	Seasons Played	Apps	Subs	Gls
Newcastle U.	Jnrs	06.81	81-84	79	0	0
Bradford C.	L	03.85	84	1	3	0
Carlisle U.	Tr	08.85	85-87	97	0	11
Torquay U.	Dundee	07.90	90-91	54	1	6

SAVAGE, John A.
Bromley, 14 December, 1929 (G)

League Club	Source	Date Signed	Seasons Played	Apps	Subs	Gls
Hull C.	R.A.F.	09.50	50	4	-	0
Halifax T.	Tr	03.52	51-53	57	-	1
Manchester C.	Tr	11.53	54-57	30	-	0
Walsall	Tr	01.58	57-58	51	-	0

SAVAGE, Reginald
Eccles, 5 July, 1912 (G)

League Club	Source	Date Signed	Seasons Played	Apps	Subs	Gls
Leeds U.	Stalybridge Celtic	02.31	34-38	79	-	0
Nottingham F.	Queen of South	05.46	46	20	-	0
Accrington St.	Tr	08.47				

SAVAGE, Robert J.
Liverpool, 8 January, 1960 (M)

League Club	Source	Date Signed	Seasons Played	Apps	Subs	Gls
Liverpool	App	01.78				
Wrexham	L	10.82	82	27	0	10
Stoke C.	Tr	07.83	83	5	2	0
Bournemouth	Tr	12.83	83-86	80	2	18
Bradford C.	Tr	12.86	86-87	11	0	0
Bolton W.	Tr	09.87	87-89	83	4	11

SAVILLE, Andrew V.
Hull, 12 December, 1964 (F)

League Club	Source	Date Signed	Seasons Played	Apps	Subs	Gls
Hull C.		09.83	83-88	74	27	18
Walsall	Tr	03.89	88-89	28	10	5
Barnsley	Tr	03.90	89-91	71	11	20
Hartlepool U.	Tr	03.92	91	1	0	0

SAVILLE, Peter W.
Dalbeattie, 29 August, 1948 (W)

League Club	Source	Date Signed	Seasons Played	Apps	Subs	Gls
Carlisle U.		07.66	67	1	0	0
Bradford P. A.	Hawick Royal Albert	03.69	68-69	31	0	1

SAVIN, Keith A.
Oxford, 5 June, 1929 (FB)

League Club	Source	Date Signed	Seasons Played	Apps	Subs	Gls
Derby Co.	Oxford C.	05.50	50-55	65	-	0
Mansfield T.	Tr	05.57	57-58	68	-	0

SAVINO, Raymond J.
Norwich, 16 November, 1938 (OR)

League Club	Source	Date Signed	Seasons Played	Apps	Subs	Gls
Norwich C.	Thorpe Village	02.57	56-61	22	-	3
Bristol C.	Tr	07.62	62-67	75	0	2

SAWARD, Leonard R.
Aldershot, 6 July, 1927 (IF)

League Club	Source	Date Signed	Seasons Played	Apps	Subs	Gls
Crystal Palace	Beddington	03.49	48-50	9	-	1
Newport Co.	Cambridge U.	01.54	53-54	25	-	4

SAWARD, Patrick
Cork (Ire), 17 August, 1928 IR-18 (WH)

League Club	Source	Date Signed	Seasons Played	Apps	Subs	Gls
Millwall	Crystal Palace (Am)	07.51	51-54	118	-	14
Aston Villa	Tr	08.55	55-60	152	-	2
Huddersfield T.	Tr	03.61	60-62	59	-	1

SAWBRIDGE, John
Wigan, 20 September, 1920 Died 1984 (G)

League Club	Source	Date Signed	Seasons Played	Apps	Subs	Gls
Oldham Ath.	Crossens	12.45	46-47	8	-	0

SAWYER, Brian
Rotherham, 28 January, 1938 (CF)

League Club	Source	Date Signed	Seasons Played	Apps	Subs	Gls
Rotherham U.	Rawmarsh Welfare	01.58	57-62	92	-	31
Bradford C.	Tr	12.62	62-63	15	-	2

SAWYER, Roy
Barnsley, 29 March, 1940 (CH)

League Club	Source	Date Signed	Seasons Played	Apps	Subs	Gls
Barnsley	Worsboro' Bridge	05.58	60-61	2	-	0

SAWYERS, Keith W.
Banbury, 14 June, 1960 (M)

League Club	Source	Date Signed	Seasons Played	Apps	Subs	Gls
Carlisle U.	Carlisle Spartans	01.78	77-79	5	4	0

SAXBY, Gary P.
Mansfield, 11 December, 1959 (M)

League Club	Source	Date Signed	Seasons Played	Apps	Subs	Gls
Mansfield T.	App	12.77	78	14	2	1
Northampton T.	Tr	08.80	80-82	86	10	11

SAXBY, Michael W.
Mansfield, 12 August, 1957 (CD)

League Club	Source	Date Signed	Seasons Played	Apps	Subs	Gls
Mansfield T.	App	01.75	75-78	76	3	5
Luton T.	Tr	07.79	79-81	82	0	6
Grimsby T.	L	03.83	82	10	0	0
Lincoln C.	L	11.83	83	10	0	1
Newport Co.	Tr	07.84	84	6	0	0
Middlesbrough	Tr	09.84	84	15	0	0

SAXTON, Robert
Doncaster, 6 September, 1943 (CD)

League Club	Source	Date Signed	Seasons Played	Apps	Subs	Gls
Derby Co.	Denaby U.	02.62	64-67	94	2	1
Plymouth Arg.	Tr	02.68	67-75	224	7	7
Exeter C.	Tr	09.75	75-77	92	0	3

SAYER, Andrew C.
Brent, 6 June, 1966 (F)

League Club	Source	Date Signed	Seasons Played	Apps	Subs	Gls
Wimbledon	App	06.84	83-87	46	12	15
Cambridge U.	L	02.88	87	2	3	0
Fulham	Tr	08.88	88-89	44	9	15
Leyton Orient	Tr	02.90	89-91	23	7	6
Sheffield U.	L	03.91	90	0	3	0

SAYER, Peter A.
Cardiff, 2 May, 1955 Wu21-2/W-7 (W)

League Club	Source	Date Signed	Seasons Played	Apps	Subs	Gls
Cardiff C.	Jnrs	07.73	73-77	70	12	14
Brighton & H. A.	Tr	02.78	77-79	46	9	6
Preston N. E.	Tr	08.80	80-83	42	3	6
Cardiff C.	L	09.81	81	4	0	1
Chester C.	Tr	07.84	84	36	0	6

SBRAGIA, Richard
Lennoxtown, 26 May, 1956 (CD)

League Club	Source	Date Signed	Seasons Played	Apps	Subs	Gls
Birmingham C.	App	05.74	74-77	14	1	1
Walsall	Tr	10.78	78-79	77	0	4
Blackpool	Tr	07.80	80-81	24	2	1
York C.	Tr	08.82	82-86	149	0	7
Darlington	L	08.85	85	6	0	0

SCAIFE, Robert H.
Northallerton, 12 October, 1955 (M)

League Club	Source	Date Signed	Seasons Played	Apps	Subs	Gls
Middlesbrough	App	10.72				
Halifax T.	L	01.75	74	5	1	1
Hartlepool U.	Tr	09.75	75-77	77	3	10
Rochdale	Tr	10.77	77-79	95	3	9

SCALES, George
Northwich, 14 March, 1923 (G)

League Club	Source	Date Signed	Seasons Played	Apps	Subs	Gls
Chester C.	Manchester C. (Am)	08.44	46-48	81	-	0

SCALES, John R.
Harrogate, 4 July, 1966 (D)

League Club	Source	Date Signed	Seasons Played	Apps	Subs	Gls
Bristol Rov.	Leeds U. (YT)	07.85	85-86	68	4	2
Wimbledon	Tr	07.87	87-91	163	5	10

SCALES, Terence A.
West Ham, 18 November, 1951 (CD)

League Club	Source	Date Signed	Seasons Played	Apps	Subs	Gls
West Ham U.	App	08.69				
Brentford	Tr	07.71	71-76	212	0	5

SCANLON, Albert J.
Manchester, 10 October, 1935 Eu23-5/EF Lge (OL)

League Club	Source	Date Signed	Seasons Played	Apps	Subs	Gls
Manchester U.	Jnrs	12.52	54-60	115	-	34
Newcastle U.	Tr	11.60	60-61	22	-	5
Lincoln C.	Tr	02.62	61-62	47	-	11
Mansfield T.	Tr	04.63	62-65	108	0	21

SCANLON, Ian
Stirling, 13 July, 1952 (W)

League Club	Source	Date Signed	Seasons Played	Apps	Subs	Gls
Notts Co.	East Stirling	07.72	72-77	99	12	31

SCANNELL, Thomas
Youghal (Ire), 3 June, 1925 IR-1 (G)

League Club	Source	Date Signed	Seasons Played	Apps	Subs	Gls
Southend U.	Tilbury	12.49	50-54	98	-	0

SCARBOROUGH, Brian
Ironville, 11 December, 1941 (OL)

League Club	Source	Date Signed	Seasons Played	Apps	Subs	Gls
Derby Co.	Jnrs	01.59	58-60	4	-	0

SCARBOROUGH, James A.
Nottingham, 10 June, 1931 (CF)

League Club	Source	Date Signed	Seasons Played	Apps	Subs	Gls
Darlington		09.51	51-53	49	-	15

SCARLETT, John E.
Wolverhampton, 1 August, 1934 Died 1960 (IF)

League Club	Source	Date Signed	Seasons Played	Apps	Subs	Gls
Walsall		03.52	52-53	10	-	2

SCARROTT, Alan R.
Malmesbury, 22 November, 1944 (W)

League Club	Source	Date Signed	Seasons Played	Apps	Subs	Gls
West Bromwich A.	Chippenham T.	12.61				
Bristol Rov.	Tr	06.64				
Reading	Tr	04.65	65-67	90	0	7

SCARTH, James W.
North Shields, 26 August, 1926 (IF)

League Club	Source	Date Signed	Seasons Played	Apps	Subs	Gls
Tottenham H.	Percy Main Colly	08.48	49-51	7	-	3
Gillingham	Tr	02.52	51-54	139	-	25

SCATTERGOOD, Eric
Barnsley, 9 September, 1929 (WH)

League Club	Source	Date Signed	Seasons Played	Apps	Subs	Gls
Barnsley	Jnrs	02.47	49-51	11	-	0

SCHIAVI, Mark A.
City of London, 1 May, 1964 E Yth (LW)

League Club	Source	Date Signed	Seasons Played	Apps	Subs	Gls
West Ham U.	App	11.81				
Bournemouth	L	09.83	83	10	0	0
Bournemouth	Tr	07.84	84	14	5	0
Northampton T.	Tr	07.85	85-86	31	4	5
Cambridge U.	Tr	09.86	86	24	6	2

SCHMEICHEL, Peter B.
Denmark, 18 November, 1968 Denmark Int (G)

League Club	Source	Date Signed	Seasons Played	Apps	Subs	Gls
Manchester U.	Brondby (Den)	07.91	91	40	0	0

SCHOFIELD, Ernest
Sheffield, 29 March, 1921 (IL)

League Club	Source	Date Signed	Seasons Played	Apps	Subs	Gls
Bradford C.		06.45	46	1	-	0

SCHOFIELD, Gary P.
Eccles, 27 March, 1957 (D)

League Club	Source	Date Signed	Seasons Played	Apps	Subs	Gls
Stockport Co. (N/C)		03.78	77	0	1	0

SCHOFIELD, Graham
Manchester, 18 December, 1950 (CD)

League Club	Source	Date Signed	Seasons Played	Apps	Subs	Gls
Oldham Ath.	Jnrs	08.69	69	1	0	0

SCHOFIELD, John D.
Barnsley, 16 May, 1965 (M)

League Club	Source	Date Signed	Seasons Played	Apps	Subs	Gls
Lincoln C.	Gainsborough Trin.	11.88	88-91	137	2	8

SCHOFIELD, John R.
Atherstone, 8 February, 1931 (G)

League Club	Source	Date Signed	Seasons Played	Apps	Subs	Gls
Birmingham C.	Nuneaton Bor.	02.50	52-65	212	0	0
Wrexham	Tr	07.66	66-67	52	0	0

SCHOFIELD, Malcolm
Failsworth, 8 October, 1918 (G)

League Club	Source	Date Signed	Seasons Played	Apps	Subs	Gls
Oldham Ath.		11.37	46	7	-	0

SCHOFIELD, Mark A.
Wigan, 10 October, 1966 (D)

League Club	Source	Date Signed	Seasons Played	Apps	Subs	Gls
Wigan Ath.	App	07.85	83-84	1	1	0

SCHOFIELD, A. Stewart
Blackburn, 24 July, 1933 (IF)

League Club	Source	Date Signed	Seasons Played	Apps	Subs	Gls
Southport	Blackburn Rov. (Am)	07.57	57-58	36	-	9

SCHOFIELD, Thomas
Halifax, 22 June, 1926 (G)

League Club	Source	Date Signed	Seasons Played	Apps	Subs	Gls
Halifax T. (Am)	Boothtown	10.52	52	1	-	0

SCHOLES, Martin
Barrow, 28 January, 1954 (CD)

League Club	Source	Date Signed	Seasons Played	Apps	Subs	Gls
Workington (N/C)		11.76	76	3	1	0

SCHROEDER, Nico
Netherlands, 19 November, 1947 (G)

League Club	Source	Date Signed	Seasons Played	Apps	Subs	Gls
Swansea C.		07.76	76	1	0	0

SCONCE, Mark A.
Wrexham, 18 February, 1968 (FB)

League Club	Source	Date Signed	Seasons Played	Apps	Subs	Gls
Chester C.	YT	07.86	85	1	1	0

SCOPE, David F.
Newcastle, 10 May, 1967 (W)

League Club	Source	Date Signed	Seasons Played	Apps	Subs	Gls
Northampton T.	Blyth Spartans	09.89	89-91	6	13	1

SCOTHORN, Gary
Hoyland, 6 June, 1950 (G)

League Club	Source	Date Signed	Seasons Played	Apps	Subs	Gls
Sheffield Wed.	App	06.67	67	1	0	0
Mansfield T.	Sligo Rov.	08.74				

SCOTSON, Reginald
Stockton, 22 September, 1919 (WH)

League Club	Source	Date Signed	Seasons Played	Apps	Subs	Gls
Sunderland	Ouston Jnrs	04.39	46-50	61	-	1
Grimsby T.	Tr	12.50	50-54	164	-	4

SCOTT, Alexander M.
St Andrews, 17 November, 1922 (FB)

League Club	Source	Date Signed	Seasons Played	Apps	Subs	Gls
Leicester C.	Lochgelly Albert	03.47	47-49	31	-	1
Carlisle U.	Tr	01.50	49-55	203	-	3

SCOTT, Alexander S.
Falkirk, 22 November, 1936 Su23-1/S'B'-2/SF Lge/S-16 (OR)

League Club	Source	Date Signed	Seasons Played	Apps	Subs	Gls
Everton	Glasgow Rangers	02.63	62-66	149	0	23

SCOTT, Anthony J. E.
Edmonton, 1 April, 1941 E Yth (W)

League Club	Source	Date Signed	Seasons Played	Apps	Subs	Gls
West Ham U.	Jnrs	05.58	59-65	83	0	16
Aston Villa	Tr	10.65	65-67	47	3	3
Torquay U.	Tr	09.67	67-69	82	5	4
Bournemouth	Tr	07.70	70-71	59	2	6
Exeter C.	Tr	06.72	72-73	51	0	2

SCOTT, Augustus F.
Sunderland, 19 February, 1921 (IF)

League Club	Source	Date Signed	Seasons Played	Apps	Subs	Gls
Luton T.	Hylton Colly	03.39				
Southampton	Tr	07.47	47-49	45	-	9
Colchester U.	Tr	08.51	51-53	120	-	11

SCOTT, Christopher
Wallsend, 11 September, 1963 (CD)

League Club	Source	Date Signed	Seasons Played	Apps	Subs	Gls
Northampton T.	Blyth Spartans	07.87				
Lincoln C.	Tr	03.88	88	4	0	0

SCOTT, Colin
Glasgow, 19 May, 1970 (G)

League Club	Source	Date Signed	Seasons Played	Apps	Subs	Gls
Brentford (L)	Glasgow Rangers	03.90	89	6	0	0

SCOTT, David P.
Belfast, 6 June, 1918 Died 1977 (G)

League Club	Source	Date Signed	Seasons Played	Apps	Subs	Gls
Northampton T.	Linfield	05.45	46-47	11	-	0

SCOTT, Derek E.
Gateshead, 8 February, 1958 E Sch (RB)

League Club	Source	Date Signed	Seasons Played	Apps	Subs	Gls
Burnley	App	02.75	74-84	277	8	24
Bolton W.	Tr	07.85	85-87	119	0	0

SCOTT, Donald
Elland, 20 October, 1922

League Club	Source	Date Signed	Seasons Played	Apps	Subs	Gls
Halifax T.		09.48	48-49	20	-	5

SCOTT, Frederick H.
Fatfield, 6 October, 1916 E Sch (OR)

League Club	Source	Date Signed	Seasons Played	Apps	Subs	Gls
Bolton W.		01.35				
Bradford P. A.	Tr	05.36				
York C.	Tr	02.37	36-46	74	-	16
Nottingham F.	Tr	09.46	46-56	301	-	40

SCOTT, Geoffrey S.
Birmingham, 31 October, 1956 (D)

League Club	Source	Date Signed	Seasons Played	Apps	Subs	Gls
Stoke C.	Highgate U.	04.77	77-79	76	2	3
Leicester C.	Tr	02.80	79-81	39	0	0
Birmingham C.	Tr	02.82	81-82	18	1	0
Charlton Ath.	Tr	10.82	82	2	0	0
Middlesbrough	Tr	06.84	84	2	0	0
Northampton T.	Tr	09.84	84	16	1	0
Cambridge U.	Tr	07.85	85	19	0	0

SCOTT, George W.
Aberdeen, 25 October, 1944 (M)

League Club	Source	Date Signed	Seasons Played	Apps	Subs	Gls
Liverpool	App	10.61				
Tranmere Rov.	South Africa	11.68	68-69	35	1	0

SCOTT, Ian
Radcliffe, 20 September, 1967 E Sch (M)

League Club	Source	Date Signed	Seasons Played	Apps	Subs	Gls
Manchester C.	App	09.85	87-88	20	4	3
Stoke C.	Tr	07.89	89-91	21	9	2
Crewe Alex.	L	03.91	90	12	0	1

SCOTT, Ian R.
Otley, 4 March, 1969 (D)

League Club	Source	Date Signed	Seasons Played	Apps	Subs	Gls
Manchester U.	App	03.87				
Stockport Co.	Tr	09.87	87-88	23	2	0

SCOTT, James
Falkirk, 21 August, 1940 S-1 (W)

League Club	Source	Date Signed	Seasons Played	Apps	Subs	Gls
Newcastle U.	Hibernian	08.67	67-69	70	4	6
Crystal Palace	Tr	02.70	69-71	36	7	5

SCOTT, James A.
Newcastle, 28 February, 1960 (M)

League Club	Source	Date Signed	Seasons Played	Apps	Subs	Gls
Newcastle U.	App	03.78	77-78	9	1	0

SCOTT, James D.
Dagenham, 5 September, 1945 (IF)

League Club	Source	Date Signed	Seasons Played	Apps	Subs	Gls
Leyton Orient	Chelsea (Am)	11.62	63-65	22	1	6

SCOTT, James J.
Glasgow, 26 December, 1927 (IF)

League Club	Source	Date Signed	Seasons Played	Apps	Subs	Gls
Workington	Alloa Ath.	06.54	54	6	-	1

SCOTT, James J.
Hetton-le-Hole, 7 September, 1934 E Sch (WH)

League Club	Source	Date Signed	Seasons Played	Apps	Subs	Gls
Burnley	Jnrs	09.51	54-60	3	-	0
Oldham Ath.	Tr	06.61	61-63	76	-	0

SCOTT, John
Normanton, 2 January, 1942 (IF)

League Club	Source	Date Signed	Seasons Played	Apps	Subs	Gls
Bradford C.	Jnrs	08.60	61-62	11	-	2
Chesterfield	Tr	07.63	63	5	-	1

SCOTT, John
Belfast, 22 December, 1933 Died 1978 NI'B'-1/NI-2 (OR)

League Club	Source	Date Signed	Seasons Played	Apps	Subs	Gls
Manchester U.	Ormond Star	10.51	52-55	3	-	0
Grimsby T.	Tr	06.56	56-62	240	-	51
York C.	Tr	06.63	63	21	-	3

SCOTT, John A.
Workington, 18 July, 1928 (G)

League Club	Source	Date Signed	Seasons Played	Apps	Subs	Gls
Leeds U.	Workington	05.50	50-54	111	-	0

SCOTT, John M.
Edinburgh, 21 August, 1953 (D)

League Club	Source	Date Signed	Seasons Played	Apps	Subs	Gls
Workington	Brechin C.	08.75	75	1	1	0

SCOTT, Joseph
Plymouth, 11 January, 1953 (F)

League Club	Source	Date Signed	Seasons Played	Apps	Subs	Gls
Bournemouth	Falmouth	06.78	78	18	3	4

SCOTT, Joseph C.
Fatfield (Dm), 9 January, 1930 (IF)

League Club	Source	Date Signed	Seasons Played	Apps	Subs	Gls
Newcastle U.		04.49				
Luton T.	Spennymoor U.	02.52	52-53	13	-	2
Middlesbrough	Tr	09.54	54-58	93	-	26
Hartlepool U.	Tr	01.59	58-59	62	-	10
York C.	Tr	06.60	60	17	-	2

SCOTT, Keith
Westminster, 9 June, 1967 (F)

League Club	Source	Date Signed	Seasons Played	Apps	Subs	Gls
Lincoln C.	Leicester U.	03.90	89-90	7	9	2

SCOTT, Kenneth
Maltby, 13 August, 1931 (OR)

League Club	Source	Date Signed	Seasons Played	Apps	Subs	Gls
Derby Co.	Denaby U.	08.50	50	2	-	0
Mansfield T.	Denaby U.	08.52	52	5	-	2

SCOTT, Kevin A.
Lincoln, 12 November, 1954 (D)

League Club	Source	Date Signed	Seasons Played	Apps	Subs	Gls
Lincoln C. (N/C)	Sheffield Univ.	02.74	73	1	0	0

SCOTT, Kevin W.
Easington, 17 December, 1966 (CD)

League Club	Source	Date Signed	Seasons Played	Apps	Subs	Gls
Newcastle U.	App	12.84	86-91	164	0	6

SCOTT, Laurence
Sheffield, 23 April, 1917 EF Lge/E'B'-4/E-17 (FB)

League Club	Source	Date Signed	Seasons Played	Apps	Subs	Gls
Bradford C.	Jnrs	05.35	35-36	39	-	0
Arsenal	Tr	02.37	46-51	115	-	0
Crystal Palace	Tr	10.51	51-52	28	-	0

SCOTT, Lloyd E.
Stepney, 13 October, 1961 (G)

League Club	Source	Date Signed	Seasons Played	Apps	Subs	Gls
Leyton Orient	App	10.79				
Blackpool	Tr	07.82	82	2	0	0

SCOTT, Malcolm E.
South Shields, 8 May, 1936 (WH)

League Club	Source	Date Signed	Seasons Played	Apps	Subs	Gls
Newcastle U.	Cleadon Jnrs	09.55	56-60	25	-	2
Darlington	Tr	10.61	61-62	47	-	2
York C.	Tr	10.63	63	19	-	0

SCOTT, Martin
Sheffield, 7 January, 1968 (LB)

League Club	Source	Date Signed	Seasons Played	Apps	Subs	Gls
Rotherham U.	App	01.86	84-90	93	1	3
Bristol C.	Tr	12.90	90-91	73	0	4

SCOTT, Melvyn D.
Claygate, 26 September, 1939 E Yth/Eu23-3 (CH)

League Club	Source	Date Signed	Seasons Played	Apps	Subs	Gls
Chelsea	Jnrs	11.56	57-61	97	-	0
Brentford	Tr	03.63	62-66	156	0	2

SCOTT, Michael R.
Newcastle, 4 December, 1945 (OL)

League Club	Source	Date Signed	Seasons Played	Apps	Subs	Gls
Burnley	App	12.62				
Hartlepool U.	Tr	07.64	64	2	-	0

SCOTT, Morrys J.
Swansea, 17 December, 1970 (F)

League Club	Source	Date Signed	Seasons Played	Apps	Subs	Gls
Cardiff C.	YT	07.89	89	1	8	0
Southend U.	Colchester U.	10.90				
Plymouth Arg.	Tr	06.91	91	3	3	0

SCOTT, Peter R.
Notting Hill, 1 October, 1963 (M)

League Club	Source	Date Signed	Seasons Played	Apps	Subs	Gls
Fulham	App	09.81	81-91	268	9	27

SCOTT, Peter W.
Liverpool, 19 September, 1952 E Yth/NI-6 (FB)

League Club	Source	Date Signed	Seasons Played	Apps	Subs	Gls
Everton	App	07.70	71-74	42	2	1
Southport	L	01.74	73	4	0	0
York C.	Tr	12.75	75-78	99	1	3
Aldershot	Tr	03.79	78-82	114	7	2

SCOTT, Richard S. A.
Thetford, 26 October, 1941 (WH)

League Club	Source	Date Signed	Seasons Played	Apps	Subs	Gls
Norwich C.	Jnrs	11.58	60-62	28	-	1
Cardiff C.	Tr	07.63	63-64	37	-	5
Scunthorpe U.	Tr	09.64	64-65	47	0	8
Lincoln C.	Tr	07.66	66	9	1	1

SCOTT, Robert
Bathgate, 13 January, 1964 (F)

League Club	Source	Date Signed	Seasons Played	Apps	Subs	Gls
Colchester U.	Whitburn Jnrs	03.89	88-89	26	11	8

SCOTT, Robert
Bellshill, 20 May, 1930 (W)

League Club	Source	Date Signed	Seasons Played	Apps	Subs	Gls
Accrington St.	Alloa Ath.	09.54	54-58	149	-	32
Wrexham	Tr	07.59	59	2	-	0
Oldham Ath.	Tr	10.59	59	9	-	1

SCOTT, Robert A.
Liverpool, 29 October, 1913 Died 1962 E Sch (G)

League Club	Source	Date Signed	Seasons Played	Apps	Subs	Gls
Liverpool		05.31				
Burnley	Tr	05.33	33-35	57	-	0
Wolverhampton W.	Tr	02.36	35-38	119	-	0
Crewe Alex.	Tr	08.47	47-48	44	-	0

SCOTT, Robert J.
Dundee, 16 March, 1937 (WH)

League Club	Source	Date Signed	Seasons Played	Apps	Subs	Gls
Cardiff C.	Dundee Violet	02.57	57	3	-	0
Swindon T.	Tr	06.61				
Newport Co.	Tr	11.61	61-62	18	-	0
Southport	Sankeys	07.63	63	3	-	0

SCOTT, Robert W.
Liverpool, 22 February, 1953 (CD)

League Club	Source	Date Signed	Seasons Played	Apps	Subs	Gls
Wrexham	Jnrs	07.71	70-75	15	4	0
Reading	L	01.75	74	5	0	0
Hartlepool U.	Tr	07.76	76	37	0	0
Rochdale	Tr	07.77	77-78	71	0	3
Crewe Alex.	Tr	08.79	79-85	238	1	15
Wrexham (N/C)	Northwich Vic.	01.86	85	2	1	0

SCOTT, Samuel
Ashington, 14 June, 1922 (CF)

League Club	Source	Date Signed	Seasons Played	Apps	Subs	Gls
Hartlepool U.	Ashington	02.46	46-47	49	-	17

SCOTT, Stephen R.
Wrexham, 5 November, 1966 (D)

League Club	Source	Date Signed	Seasons Played	Apps	Subs	Gls
Wrexham (N/C)	Oswestry T.	03.86	87	0	2	0

SCOTT, Stuart R.
Shrewsbury, 31 March, 1946 (W)

League Club	Source	Date Signed	Seasons Played	Apps	Subs	Gls
Shrewsbury T.	Jnrs	04.64	63-65	18	0	2

SCOTT, Walter
Douglas, 23 June, 1932 (G)

League Club	Source	Date Signed	Seasons Played	Apps	Subs	Gls
Halifax T.	Dumbarton	08.54	54	13	-	0

SCOTT, William J.
Preston, 14 June, 1921 (FB)

League Club	Source	Date Signed	Seasons Played	Apps	Subs	Gls
Preston N. E.	Jnrs	05.39	46-53	207	-	0

SCOTT, William R.
Willington, 6 December, 1907 Died 1969 E-1 (IF)

League Club	Source	Date Signed	Seasons Played	Apps	Subs	Gls
Middlesbrough	Howden B.L.	05.27	30-31	26	-	5
Brentford	Tr	05.32	32-46	269	-	83
Aldershot	Tr	07.47	47	21	-	0

SCOTTING, Allen
Dartford, 22 April, 1966 (FB)

League Club	Source	Date Signed	Seasons Played	Apps	Subs	Gls
Gillingham (N/C)	Charlton Ath. (Jnrs)	02.84	83	2	0	0

SCOULAR, James
Livingston, 11 January, 1925 S-9 (WH)

League Club	Source	Date Signed	Seasons Played	Apps	Subs	Gls
Portsmouth	Gosport Bor.	12.45	46-52	249	-	8
Newcastle U.	Tr	06.53	53-60	247	-	6
Bradford P. A.	Tr	01.61	60-63	108	-	5

SCREEN, Anthony L.
Swansea, 9 May, 1952 Wu23-1 (FB)

League Club	Source	Date Signed	Seasons Played	Apps	Subs	Gls
Swansea C.	App	05.70	68-74	125	3	9

SCREEN, William R.
Swansea, 8 November, 1948 Wu23-2 (M)

League Club	Source	Date Signed	Seasons Played	Apps	Subs	Gls
Swansea C.	Jnrs	03.67	67-71	131	10	14
Newport Co.	Tr	06.72	72-75	137	5	7

SCRIMGEOUR, Brian
Dundee, 11 August, 1959 (D/M)

League Club	Source	Date Signed	Seasons Played	Apps	Subs	Gls
Chesterfield	Dundee	07.83	83-86	117	4	16

SCRIMSHAW, Stanley
Hartlepool, 7 August, 1915 (WH)

League Club	Source	Date Signed	Seasons Played	Apps	Subs	Gls
Hartlepool U.		01.36	35-36	18	-	1
Bradford C.	Tr	06.37	37-46	20	-	0
Halifax T.	Frickley Colly	10.47	47-49	52	-	0

SCRINE, Frank H.
Swansea, 9 January, 1925 W-2 (IF)

League Club	Source	Date Signed	Seasons Played	Apps	Subs	Gls
Swansea C.		03.44	47-53	142	-	45
Oldham Ath.	Tr	10.53	53-55	78	-	21

League Club	Source	Date Signed	Seasons Played	Career Record Apps	Subs	Gls

SCRINE, William H.
Swansea, 3 December, 1934

League Club	Source	Date Signed	Seasons Played	Apps	Subs	Gls
Swansea C.	Jnrs	12.51	52	1	-	0

SCRIVENS, Stephen J.
Ewell, 11 March, 1957 (W)

League Club	Source	Date Signed	Seasons Played	Apps	Subs	Gls
Fulham	App	03.75	74-75	3	1	1
Brentford	L	12.76	76	5	0	0

SCRIVENS, William
Rotherham, 26 May, 1936 (G)

League Club	Source	Date Signed	Seasons Played	Apps	Subs	Gls
Rotherham U.		08.56	56	3	-	0

SCRUGHAM, Robert
Cleator Moor, 15 May, 1932 (G)

League Club	Source	Date Signed	Seasons Played	Apps	Subs	Gls
Workington	Cleator Moor	08.53	53	3	-	0

SCULLION, Stewart M. A.
Bo'ness, 18 April, 1946 (W)

League Club	Source	Date Signed	Seasons Played	Apps	Subs	Gls
Charlton Ath.	Chesham U.	03.65				
Watford	Tr	02.66	65-70	217	8	30
Sheffield U.	Tr	05.71	71-73	53	4	7
Watford	Tr	12.73	73-75	87	0	19

SCULLY, Patrick J.
Dublin, 23 June, 1970 IRu21-3/IR-1 (CD)

League Club	Source	Date Signed	Seasons Played	Apps	Subs	Gls
Arsenal	YT	09.87				
Preston N. E.	L	09.89	89	13	0	1
Northampton T.	L	08.90	90	15	0	0
Southend U.	Tr	01.91	90-91	65	0	3

SCURR, David W.
Netley, 25 September, 1939 Died 1991 (FB)

League Club	Source	Date Signed	Seasons Played	Apps	Subs	Gls
Southampton		04.58	59-60	2	-	0

SCURR, John T.
North Shields, 30 September, 1940 (IF)

League Club	Source	Date Signed	Seasons Played	Apps	Subs	Gls
Arsenal	North Shields B.C.	09.59				
Carlisle U.	Tr	01.61	60-61	15	-	1

SEACOLE, Jason P.
Oxford, 11 April, 1960 E Sch/E Yth (F)

League Club	Source	Date Signed	Seasons Played	Apps	Subs	Gls
Oxford U.	App	04.77	76-81	104	16	22

SEADEN, John C.
Southend, 4 June, 1967 (M)

League Club	Source	Date Signed	Seasons Played	Apps	Subs	Gls
Southend U.	App	03.85	84-85	19	1	0

SEAGRAVES, Christopher A.
Liverpool, 7 October, 1964 (RB)

League Club	Source	Date Signed	Seasons Played	Apps	Subs	Gls
Liverpool	App	09.82				
Grimsby T.	Tr	08.84	84	22	1	0

SEAGRAVES, Mark
Bootle, 22 October, 1966 E Sch/E Yth (CD)

League Club	Source	Date Signed	Seasons Played	Apps	Subs	Gls
Liverpool	App	11.83				
Norwich C.	L	11.86	86	3	0	0
Manchester C.	Tr	09.87	87-89	36	6	0
Bolton W.	Tr	09.90	90-91	71	1	1

SEAL, James
Pontefract, 9 December, 1950 (F)

League Club	Source	Date Signed	Seasons Played	Apps	Subs	Gls
Wolverhampton W.	Jnrs	03.68	68	1	0	0
Walsall	L	01.70	69-70	40	0	14
Barnsley	Tr	05.71	71	43	0	12
York C.	Tr	07.72	72-76	152	9	43
Darlington	Tr	11.76	76-79	115	7	19
Rochdale	Tr	11.79	79-80	44	9	4

SEALEY, Alan W.
Canning Town, 22 April, 1942 (OR)

League Club	Source	Date Signed	Seasons Played	Apps	Subs	Gls
Leyton Orient	Memorial Sports	08.59	60	4	-	1
West Ham U.	Tr	03.61	60-66	107	0	22
Plymouth Arg.	Tr	09.67	67	4	0	0

SEALEY, John A.
Wallasey, 27 December, 1945 (F)

League Club	Source	Date Signed	Seasons Played	Apps	Subs	Gls
Liverpool	Warrington	12.63	64	1	-	1
Chester C.	Tr	06.66	66-67	3	1	0

SEALEY, Leslie J.
Bethnal Green, 29 September, 1957 (G)

League Club	Source	Date Signed	Seasons Played	Apps	Subs	Gls
Coventry C.	App	03.76	76-82	158	0	0
Luton T.	Tr	08.83	83-88	207	0	0
Plymouth Arg.	L	10.84	84	6	0	0
Manchester U.	L	03.90	89	2	0	0
Manchester U.	Tr	06.90	90	31	0	0
Aston Villa	Tr	07.91	91	18	0	0
Coventry C.	L	03.92	91	2	0	0

SEALY, Anthony J.
Hackney, 7 May, 1959 (F)

League Club	Source	Date Signed	Seasons Played	Apps	Subs	Gls
Southampton	App	05.77	77-78	2	5	0
Crystal Palace	Tr	03.79	78-80	16	8	5
Port Vale	L	02.80	79	17	0	6
Queens Park R.	Tr	03.81	80-83	57	6	18
Port Vale	L	02.82	81	6	0	4
Fulham	L	12.83	83	5	0	1
Fulham	L	08.84	84	3	1	1
Fulham	Tr	01.85	84-85	14	2	9
Leicester C.	Tr	09.85	85-86	28	11	7
Bournemouth	L	03.87	86	8	5	2
Brentford (N/C)	Sporting Lisbon (Port)	03.89	88	11	1	4
Bristol Rov.	Tr	09.89	89-90	21	16	7
Brentford	Finland	10.91	91	9	9	0

SEAMAN, David A.
Rotherham, 19 September, 1963 Eu21-10/E'B'/E-9 (G)

League Club	Source	Date Signed	Seasons Played	Apps	Subs	Gls
Leeds U.	App	09.81				
Peterborough U.	Tr	08.82	82-84	91	0	0
Birmingham C.	Tr	10.84	84-85	75	0	0
Queens Park R.	Tr	08.86	86-89	141	0	0
Arsenal	Tr	05.90	90-91	80	0	0

David Seaman (Leeds United, Peterborough United, Birmingham City, Queens Park Rangers, Arsenal & England)

SEAR, Clifford R.
Rhostyllen, 22 September, 1936 Wu23-2/W-1 (LB)

League Club	Source	Date Signed	Seasons Played	Apps	Subs	Gls
Manchester C.	Oswestry T.	01.57	56-65	248	0	1
Chester C.	Tr	04.68	68-69	49	2	1

SEARGEANT, Stephen G.
Liverpool, 2 January, 1951 E Sch (D)

League Club	Source	Date Signed	Seasons Played	Apps	Subs	Gls
Everton	App	07.68	71-77	77	3	1

SEARLE, Damon P.
Cardiff, 26 October, 1971 W Yth/Wu21-2 (LB)

League Club	Source	Date Signed	Seasons Played	Apps	Subs	Gls
Cardiff C.	YT	08.90	90-91	76	1	1

SEARLE, Eric F.
Guildford, 20 July, 1925 (G)

League Club	Source	Date Signed	Seasons Played	Apps	Subs	Gls
Aldershot		10.47	47-49	12	-	0

SEARS, Douglas R.
Eton, 5 January, 1919 (IF)

League Club	Source	Date Signed	Seasons Played	Apps	Subs	Gls
Grimsby T.		10.43				
Reading	Tr	05.46	46	5	-	0
Aldershot	Tr	06.47	47-49	47	-	14

SEARS, Gerald
Chesterfield, 13 January, 1935 (LB)

League Club	Source	Date Signed	Seasons Played	Apps	Subs	Gls
Chesterfield	Jnrs	01.52	52-67	412	0	4

SEARSON, Harold V.
Mansfield, 3 June, 1924 (G)

League Club	Source	Date Signed	Seasons Played	Apps	Subs	Gls
Sheffield Wed.	Bilsthorpe Colly	08.46				
Mansfield T.	Tr	06.47	47-48	42	-	0
Leeds U.	Tr	01.49	48-51	104	-	0
York C.	Tr	11.52	52-53	62	-	0

SEARY, Raymond M.
Slough, 18 September, 1952 (LB)

League Club	Source	Date Signed	Seasons Played	Apps	Subs	Gls
Queens Park R.	App	09.70	71	0	1	0
Cambridge U.	Tr	03.74	73-75	55	2	0

SEASMAN, John
Liverpool, 21 February, 1955 (M)

League Club	Source	Date Signed	Seasons Played	Apps	Subs	Gls
Tranmere Rov.	App	02.73	72-74	15	2	0
Luton T.	Tr	01.75	74-75	7	1	2
Millwall	Tr	02.76	75-79	157	1	35
Rotherham U.	Tr	08.80	80-83	93	7	25
Cardiff C.	Tr	08.84	84	10	2	2
Rochdale	L	11.84	84	8	0	0
Chesterfield	Tr	01.85	84	8	2	1
Rochdale	Tr	07.85	85-87	86	1	4

SEATHERTON, Raymond
Tiverton, 20 May, 1932 (CF)

League Club	Source	Date Signed	Seasons Played	Apps	Subs	Gls
Bristol Rov.	Minehead	02.55	55	2	-	2

SEATON, Gordon
Wick, 1 September, 1945 (WH)

League Club	Source	Date Signed	Seasons Played	Apps	Subs	Gls
Chester C.	Rhyl	12.66	66-67	45	3	2

SEDDON, Andrew J.
Worsley, 23 November, 1959 (D)

League Club	Source	Date Signed	Seasons Played	Apps	Subs	Gls
Stockport Co. (N/C)		08.77	78-82	4	3	0

SEDDON, Benjamin P.
Liverpool, 5 February, 1952 (CD)

League Club	Source	Date Signed	Seasons Played	Apps	Subs	Gls
Tranmere Rov.	Formby	04.73	73	1	0	0

SEDDON, David A.
Rochdale, 13 April, 1951 (FB)

League Club	Source	Date Signed	Seasons Played	Apps	Subs	Gls
Rochdale	Stafford R.	01.74	73-74	18	2	0

SEDDON, Frank O.
Stockton, 1 May, 1928 (CH)

League Club	Source	Date Signed	Seasons Played	Apps	Subs	Gls
Notts Co.		05.46				
Hull C.	Tr	05.47	49	3	-	0
Halifax T.	Tr	01.51	50-51	4	-	0

SEDDON, Ian W.
Prestbury, 14 October, 1950 (M)

League Club	Source	Date Signed	Seasons Played	Apps	Subs	Gls
Bolton W.	App	06.69	69-72	51	13	4
Chester C.	Tr	09.73	73-75	62	11	7
Stockport Co.	L	11.75	75	4	0	0
Chesterfield	L	01.76	75	2	0	0
Cambridge U.	Tr	02.76	75-76	34	3	3
Rochdale	Tr	07.77	77	30	1	3
Wigan Ath.	Tr	07.78	78	1	0	0

SEDDON, Thomas
Rotherham, 25 October, 1935 (HB)

League Club	Source	Date Signed	Seasons Played	Apps	Subs	Gls
Rotherham U.		03.54	58	1	-	0

SEDGLEY, Stephen P.
Enfield, 26 May, 1968 Eu21-11 (CD)

League Club	Source	Date Signed	Seasons Played	Apps	Subs	Gls
Coventry C.	App	05.86	86-88	81	3	3
Tottenham H.	Tr	07.89	89-91	85	15	0

SEED, Trevance F.
Preston, 3 September, 1923 (CH)

League Club	Source	Date Signed	Seasons Played	Apps	Subs	Gls
Preston N.E.	Jnrs	07.46				
Carlisle U.	Tr	12.46	46-49	81	-	0
Accrington St.	Tr	09.50	50	1	-	0

SEEMLEY, Ivor J.
Sheffield, 30 June, 1929 (RB)

League Club	Source	Date Signed	Seasons Played	Apps	Subs	Gls
Sheffield Wed.	Jnrs	07.46	53-54	15	-	0
Stockport Co.	Tr	06.55	55-56	81	-	0
Chesterfield	Tr	06.57	57-58	78	-	0

SEGERS, Johannes C. A. (Hans)
Netherlands, 30 October, 1961 (G)

League Club	Source	Date Signed	Seasons Played	Apps	Subs	Gls
Nottingham F.	P.S.V. Eindhoven (Neth)	08.84	84-87	58	0	0
Stoke C.	L	02.87	86	1	0	0
Sheffield U.	L	11.87	87	10	0	0
Wimbledon	Tr	09.88	88-91	149	0	0

Hans Segers (PSV Eindhoven, Nottingham Forest & Wimbledon)

SEIGEL, Arnold W.
Islington, 21 March, 1919 (WH)

League Club	Source	Date Signed	Seasons Played	Apps	Subs	Gls
Leyton Orient	Hendon	06.46	46	9	-	0

SEITH, Robert
Coatbridge, 9 March, 1932 (WH)

League Club	Source	Date Signed	Seasons Played	Apps	Subs	Gls
Burnley	Jnrs	03.49	53-59	211	-	6

SELBY, Dennis
Broughton, 15 October, 1920 Died 1969 (W)

League Club	Source	Date Signed	Seasons Played	Apps	Subs	Gls
Chester C. (Am)		07.46	46	5	-	1

SELF, Glen W.
Norwich, 4 December, 1953 (F)

League Club	Source	Date Signed	Seasons Played	Apps	Subs	Gls
Norwich C.	App	09.70	70-72	4	1	2
Torquay U.	L	03.73	72	3	0	0

SELKIRK, John (Jack)
Doncaster, 20 January, 1923 (RB)

League Club	Source	Date Signed	Seasons Played	Apps	Subs	Gls
Rotherham U.	Edlington Colly	10.44	46-56	427	-	12

SELLARS, Geoffrey
Stockport, 20 May, 1930 (OR)

League Club	Source	Date Signed	Seasons Played	Apps	Subs	Gls
Leeds U.	Altrincham	04.50				
Aston Villa	Tr	08.50	50	2	-	0

SELLARS, John
Stoke, 28 April, 1924 (WH)

League Club	Source	Date Signed	Seasons Played	Apps	Subs	Gls
Stoke C.	Jnrs	10.41	46-57	384	-	14

SELLARS, Peter
Market Rasen, 15 March, 1958 (F)

League Club	Source	Date Signed	Seasons Played	Apps	Subs	Gls
Lincoln C. (App)	App	08.74	75	0	1	0

SELLARS, Scott
Sheffield, 27 November, 1965 *Eu21-3* (W)

League Club	Source	Date Signed	Seasons Played	Apps	Subs	Gls
Leeds U.	App	07.83	82-85	72	4	12
Blackburn Rov.	Tr	07.86	86-91	194	8	35

SELLS, Charles E.
Paddington, 24 September, 1939 (IF)

League Club	Source	Date Signed	Seasons Played	Apps	Subs	Gls
Exeter C.	Wealdstone	08.62	62	14	-	3

SEMARK, Robin H.
Portsmouth, 5 September, 1972 (M)

League Club	Source	Date Signed	Seasons Played	Apps	Subs	Gls
Cardiff C.	YT	07.91	91	4	2	0

SEMLEY, Alan
Barnsley, 21 February, 1966 (F)

League Club	Source	Date Signed	Seasons Played	Apps	Subs	Gls
Barnsley	App	02.84	83	1	3	0

SENDALL, Richard A.
Stamford, 10 July, 1967 (F)

League Club	Source	Date Signed	Seasons Played	Apps	Subs	Gls
Blackpool	Watford (App)	07.85	85-86	6	5	0
Carlisle U.	Tr	07.88	88-91	48	26	13
Cardiff C.	L	09.89	89	3	1	0

SENIOR, Alan G.
Dewsbury, 29 September, 1930

League Club	Source	Date Signed	Seasons Played	Apps	Subs	Gls
Halifax T.		08.52	52	1	-	0

SENIOR, Colin
Dewsbury, 3 June, 1927 (HB)

League Club	Source	Date Signed	Seasons Played	Apps	Subs	Gls
Huddersfield T.	Stocksbridge	06.45	50	5	-	1
Accrington St.	Tr	06.51	51	27	-	1

SENIOR, Karl R.
Northwich, 3 September, 1972 (M)

League Club	Source	Date Signed	Seasons Played	Apps	Subs	Gls
Chester C. (YT)	YT	07.89	89	0	1	0

SENIOR, Philip M.
Darton, 29 May, 1943 (FB)

League Club	Source	Date Signed	Seasons Played	Apps	Subs	Gls
Barnsley	Jnrs	06.61				
Southport	Tr	07.63	63	2	-	0

SENIOR, Roy V.
Barnsley, 21 June, 1940 (W)

League Club	Source	Date Signed	Seasons Played	Apps	Subs	Gls
Doncaster Rov.		08.60	60	13	-	5
Peterborough U.	Tr	07.61	61-63	38	-	11
Millwall	Tr	03.64	63-64	15	-	3
Barnsley	Tr	11.64	64	20	-	4

SENIOR, Stephen
Sheffield, 15 May, 1963 (RB)

League Club	Source	Date Signed	Seasons Played	Apps	Subs	Gls
York C.	App	05.81	80-86	158	10	6
Darlington	L	10.84	84	5	0	0
Northampton T.	Tr	06.87	87	1	3	0
Wigan Ath.	Tr	10.87	87-89	107	2	3
Preston N. E.	Tr	07.90	90-91	73	0	3

SENIOR, Stuart
Barnsley, 26 October, 1953 (W)

League Club	Source	Date Signed	Seasons Played	Apps	Subs	Gls
Barnsley	App	11.71	72	1	1	0

SENIOR, Trevor J.
Dorchester, 28 November, 1961 (F)

League Club	Source	Date Signed	Seasons Played	Apps	Subs	Gls
Portsmouth	Dorchester T.	12.81	81-82	11	0	2
Aldershot	L	03.83	82	10	0	7
Reading	Tr	08.83	83-86	164	0	102
Watford	Tr	07.87	87	22	2	1
Middlesbrough	Tr	03.88	87-88	9	1	2
Reading	Tr	10.88	88-91	127	10	51

SERELLA, David E.
Kings Lynn, 24 September, 1952 (CD)

League Club	Source	Date Signed	Seasons Played	Apps	Subs	Gls
Nottingham F.	App	08.70	71-74	65	3	0
Walsall	Tr	11.74	74-81	265	2	12
Blackpool	Tr	08.82	82-83	34	1	3

SERMANNI, Thomas D.
Glasgow, 1 July, 1954 *S Sch* (M)

League Club	Source	Date Signed	Seasons Played	Apps	Subs	Gls
Blackpool	Albion Rov.	03.78	78	6	4	0
Torquay U.	Tr	08.79	79-82	83	6	12

SERTORI, Mark A.
Manchester, 1 September, 1967 (CD)

League Club	Source	Date Signed	Seasons Played	Apps	Subs	Gls
Stockport Co.		02.87	86-87	3	1	0
Lincoln C.	Tr	08.87	88-89	43	7	9
Wrexham	Tr	02.90	89-91	81	2	2

SETTERS, Maurice E.
Honiton, 16 December, 1936 *E Sch/E Yth/Eu23-16* (WH)

League Club	Source	Date Signed	Seasons Played	Apps	Subs	Gls
Exeter C.	Jnrs	01.54	53-54	10	-	0
West Bromwich A.	Tr	01.55	55-59	120	-	10
Manchester U.	Tr	01.60	59-64	159	-	12
Stoke C.	Tr	11.64	64-67	87	0	5
Coventry C.	Tr	11.67	67-69	50	1	3
Charlton Ath.	Tr	01.70	69	8	0	1

Maurice Setters (Exeter City, West Bromwich Albion, Manchester United, Stoke City, Coventry City & Charlton Athletic)

SEWARD, Bruce W.
Uxbridge, 10 February, 1939 (F)

League Club	Source	Date Signed	Seasons Played	Apps	Subs	Gls
Brighton & H. A.	Yiewsley	05.57				
Aldershot	Tr	07.59	59	1	-	0

SEWARD, Gary
Paddington, 1 October, 1961 (F)

League Club	Source	Date Signed	Seasons Played	Apps	Subs	Gls
Blackpool	App	11.79	79	0	1	0

SEWELL, Arthur
Comforth (Dm), 15 July, 1934 (IL)

League Club	Source	Date Signed	Seasons Played	Apps	Subs	Gls
Bradford C. (Am)	Bishop Auckland	06.54	54	1	-	0

SEWELL, John (Jackie)
Whitehaven, 24 January, 1927 *EF Lge/E-6* (IF)

League Club	Source	Date Signed	Seasons Played	Apps	Subs	Gls
Notts Co.	Whitehaven	10.44	46-50	179	-	97
Sheffield Wed.	Tr	03.51	50-55	164	-	87
Aston Villa	Tr	12.55	55-59	123	-	36
Hull C.	Tr	10.59	59-60	44	-	8

SEWELL, John D.
Brockley, 7 July, 1936 (FB)

League Club	Source	Date Signed	Seasons Played	Apps	Subs	Gls
Charlton Ath.	Bexleyheath & Welling	01.55	56-63	185	-	5
Crystal Palace	Tr	10.63	63-70	228	3	6
Leyton Orient	Tr	08.71	71	5	2	0

SEXTON, David J.
Islington, 6 April, 1930 (IF)

League Club	Source	Date Signed	Seasons Played	Apps	Subs	Gls
Luton T.	Chelmsford C.	06.51	51-52	9	-	1
West Ham U.	Tr	04.52	52-55	74	-	27
Leyton Orient	Tr	06.56	56-57	24	-	4
Brighton & H. A.	Tr	10.57	57-58	47	-	26
Crystal Palace	Tr	05.59	59	27	-	11

SEYMOUR, Christopher D.
Reading, 14 September, 1971 (M)

League Club	Source	Date Signed	Seasons Played	Apps	Subs	Gls
Reading	YT	07.90	90-91	10	3	0

SEYMOUR, Ian P.
Edenbridge, 17 March, 1948 (G)

League Club	Source	Date Signed	Seasons Played	Apps	Subs	Gls
Fulham	Tonbridge	08.66	66-70	64	0	0
Brighton & H. A.	L	02.71	70	3	0	0

SHACKLETON, Alan
Padiham, 3 February, 1934 (CF)

League Club	Source	Date Signed	Seasons Played	Apps	Subs	Gls
Burnley	Jnrs	05.54	56-58	31	-	18
Leeds U.	Tr	10.58	58-59	30	-	16
Everton	Tr	09.59	59	26	-	10
Oldham Ath.	Nelson	08.61	61	10	-	7

SHACKLETON, Leonard F.
Bradford, 3 May, 1922 E Sch/EF Lge/E 'B'-1/E-5 (IF)

League Club	Source	Date Signed	Seasons Played	Apps	Subs	Gls
Bradford P. A.	Arsenal (Am)	12.40	46	7	-	4
Newcastle U.	Tr	10.46	46-47	57	-	26
Sunderland	Tr	02.48	47-57	320	-	98

Len Shackleton (Bradford Park Avenue, Newcastle United, Sunderland & England)

SHADBOLT, William H.
Shrewsbury, 4 August, 1932 (OL)

League Club	Source	Date Signed	Seasons Played	Apps	Subs	Gls
Sheffield Wed.	Oswestry T.	01.53	52	7	-	0
Halifax T.	Tr	03.54	53	3	-	1

SHAKESPEARE, Craig R.
Birmingham, 26 October, 1963 (M)

League Club	Source	Date Signed	Seasons Played	Apps	Subs	Gls
Walsall	App	10.81	82-88	276	8	45
Sheffield Wed.	Tr	06.89	89	15	2	0
West Bromwich A.	Tr	02.90	89-91	92	6	10

SHANAHAN, Terence C.
Paddington, 5 December, 1951 (F)

League Club	Source	Date Signed	Seasons Played	Apps	Subs	Gls
Ipswich T.	Tottenham H. (App)	07.69	70	3	1	0
Blackburn Rov.	L	09.71	71	6	0	2
Halifax T.	Tr	11.71	71-74	88	8	23
Chesterfield	Tr	10.74	74-75	56	4	28
Millwall	Tr	04.76	76	13	7	5
Bournemouth	Tr	07.77	77	14	4	1
Aldershot	Tr	07.78	78-79	16	0	4

SHANKLAND, Andrew J.
Stoke, 8 April, 1964 (M)

League Club	Source	Date Signed	Seasons Played	Apps	Subs	Gls
Port Vale	App	03.82	81-85	15	10	2

SHANKLY, William
Glenbuck, 2 September, 1913 Died 1981 S-5 (WH)

League Club	Source	Date Signed	Seasons Played	Apps	Subs	Gls
Carlisle U.		07.32	32	16	-	0
Preston N. E.	Tr	07.33	33-48	296	-	13

SHANKS, Donald
Hammersmith, 2 October, 1952 E Yth (FB)

League Club	Source	Date Signed	Seasons Played	Apps	Subs	Gls
Luton T.	Fulham (App)	07.70	71-74	89	1	2
Queens Park R.	Tr	11.74	74-80	176	4	10
Brighton & H. A.	Tr	08.81	81-82	45	1	0
Wimbledon (N/C)	Eastern (HK)	01.84	83	1	0	0

SHANKS, James
Barrow, 31 October, 1918 (OL)

League Club	Source	Date Signed	Seasons Played	Apps	Subs	Gls
Barrow	Vickers Sports	10.45	46	23	-	5

SHANKS, Robert
Sunnyside (Dm), 14 December, 1912 (WH)

League Club	Source	Date Signed	Seasons Played	Apps	Subs	Gls
Swindon T.		05.35	35-36	25	-	1
Crystal Palace	Tr	05.37	37-38	18	-	0
Swindon T.	Tr	10.46	46	1	-	0

SHANKS, Walter G.
Malta, 1 May, 1923 (WH)

League Club	Source	Date Signed	Seasons Played	Apps	Subs	Gls
Chelsea		10.46				
Luton T.	Tr	12.46	46-56	266	-	6

SHANNON, David L.
Liverpool, 4 May, 1953 (FB)

League Club	Source	Date Signed	Seasons Played	Apps	Subs	Gls
Sunderland	App	05.70				
Stockport Co.	Tr	07.73	73	3	1	1

SHANNON, Leslie
Liverpool, 12 March, 1926 E'B'-3 (WH)

League Club	Source	Date Signed	Seasons Played	Apps	Subs	Gls
Liverpool	Jnrs	11.44	47-48	11	-	1
Burnley	Tr	11.49	49-58	262	-	39

SHANNON, Robert
Bellshill, 20 April, 1966 Su21-7 (LB)

League Club	Source	Date Signed	Seasons Played	Apps	Subs	Gls
Middlesbrough (L)	Dundee	09.91	91	0	1	0

SHARDLOW, Paul
Stone, 29 April, 1943 Died 1968 (G)

League Club	Source	Date Signed	Seasons Played	Apps	Subs	Gls
Stoke C.	Northwich Vic.	05.66	66-67	3	0	0

SHARKEY, Dominic (Nick)
Helensburgh, 4 May, 1943 S Sch/Su23-2 (CF)

League Club	Source	Date Signed	Seasons Played	Apps	Subs	Gls
Sunderland	Jnrs	05.60	59-66	99	0	51
Leicester C.	Tr	10.66	66-67	6	0	5
Mansfield T.	Tr	03.68	67-69	67	2	17
Hartlepool U.	Tr	07.70	70-71	55	5	12

SHARKEY, Patrick G.
Omagh (NI), 26 August, 1953 NI-1 (M)

League Club	Source	Date Signed	Seasons Played	Apps	Subs	Gls
Ipswich T.	Portadown	09.73	75-76	17	1	1
Millwall	L	11.76	76	7	0	0
Mansfield T.	Tr	08.77	77	31	1	5
Colchester U.	Tr	06.78	78	5	1	0
Peterborough U.	Tr	03.79	78-79	15	0	0

SHARMAN, Donald W.
Rothwell, 2 February, 1932 (G)

League Club	Source	Date Signed	Seasons Played	Apps	Subs	Gls
Derby Co.	Jnrs	02.49	50	2	-	0

SHARP, Duncan
Barnsley, 16 March, 1933 (CH)

League Club	Source	Date Signed	Seasons Played	Apps	Subs	Gls
Barnsley	Jnrs	05.50	53-61	213	-	0

SHARP, Frank
Edinburgh, 28 May, 1947 (W)

League Club	Source	Date Signed	Seasons Played	Apps	Subs	Gls
Carlisle U.	Hearts	03.67	66-68	31	0	0
Cardiff C.	Tr	02.69	68-69	13	1	1
Barnsley	Tr	08.70	70-72	125	0	7
Grimsby T.	Tr	07.73	73	26	3	2
Port Vale	Tr	05.74	74	17	7	2

League Club	Source	Date Signed	Seasons Played	Apps	Subs	Gls

SHARP, George H.
Bedlington, 20 July, 1935 (OL)

Darlington (Am)		05.57	57	3	-	0
Oldham Ath. (Am)	Tr	11.57	57	1	-	0

SHARP, Graeme M.
Glasgow, 16 October, 1960 Su21-1/S-12 (F)

Everton	Dumbarton	04.80	79-90	306	16	111
Oldham Ath.	Tr	07.91	91	42	0	12

Graeme Sharp (Dumbarton, Everton, Oldham Athletic & Scotland)

SHARP, John
Castleford, 25 April, 1937 (OL)

Halifax T.	Fryston Colly	01.55	54-58	92	-	16

SHARP, Norman W.
Liverpool, 26 November, 1919 (IF)

Everton		11.38				
Wrexham	Tr	09.46	46-49	122	-	17

SHARP, Ronald
Canada, 22 November, 1932 (W)

Doncaster Rov.	Arbroath	10.58	58-59	58	-	11

SHARP, Thomas A.
Newmains, 30 July, 1957 (CD)

Everton	App	08.75				
Brentford	Tr	01.76	75-76	4	12	1

SHARPE, Frederick A.
Norwich, 26 January, 1924

Wrexham (Am)		05.48	48	1	-	0

SHARPE, Frederick C.
Brockley, 11 November, 1937 (CH)

Tottenham H.	Jnrs	05.56	58	2	-	1
Norwich C.	Tr	07.63	63-68	107	4	0
Reading	Tr	07.69	69-70	64	0	1

SHARPE, Gerald R.
Gloucester, 17 March, 1946 (F)

Bristol C.	App	03.64	64-70	149	4	48

League Club	Source	Date Signed	Seasons Played	Apps	Subs	Gls

SHARPE, John W. H.
Portsmouth, 9 October, 1957 (RB)

Southampton	App	10.75	76-77	21	0	0
Gillingham	Tr	09.78	78-84	192	2	2
Swansea (N/C)	Southampton (N/C)	09.85	85	5	0	0

SHARPE, Lee S.
Halesowen, 27 May, 1971 Eu21-8/E'B'/E-1 (LW/LB)

Torquay U.	YT	05.88	87	9	5	3
Manchester U.	Tr	05.88	88-91	60	17	4

SHARPE, Leonard T.
Scunthorpe, 29 November, 1932 (WH)

Scunthorpe U.	Jnrs	05.50	51-61	186	-	3
Hull C.	Tr	06.62	62-65	58	0	4

SHARPE, Philip
Leeds, 26 January, 1968 (F)

Halifax T.	Doncaster Rov. (YT)	08.86	86	0	1	0

SHARPE, Robert
Kirkcaldy, 20 December, 1925 (RB)

Darlington	Raith Rov.	08.52	52	14	-	0

SHARPLES, Brian
Bradford, 6 September, 1944 (CH)

Birmingham C.	App	12.61	62-68	60	1	2
Exeter C.	Tr	12.68	68-70	68	0	4

SHARPLES, George F. V.
Ellesmere Port, 20 September, 1943 E Sch/E Yth (WH)

Everton	Jnrs	09.60	60-63	10	-	0
Blackburn Rov.	Tr	03.65	64-68	99	4	5
Southport	Tr	07.71	71	23	2	0

SHARPLES, John
Wolverhampton, 8 August, 1934 (FB)

Aston Villa	Heath Town	10.55	58	13	-	0
Walsall	Tr	08.59	59-63	124	-	1

SHARRATT, Christopher M.
West Kirby, 13 August, 1970 (W)

Wigan Ath.	Stalybridge Celtic	12.91	91	0	4	0

SHARRATT, Harold
Wigan, 16 December, 1929 E Amat (G)

Blackpool (Am)	Wigan Ath.	05.52	52	1	-	0
Oldham Ath. (Am)	Bishop Auckland	03.56	55	1	-	0
Nottingham F. (Am)	Bishop Auckland	01.58	57	1	-	0

SHARRATT, Stuart E.
Stoke, 26 February, 1942 (G)

Port Vale	Oswestry T.	03.66	65-71	144	0	0

SHARROCK, Anthony
Warrington, 8 September, 1955 (G)

Southport (N/C)	Marine	11.73	73	1	0	0

SHAW, Adrian
Murton (Dm), 13 April, 1966 (D/M)

Nottingham F.	App	12.83				
Halifax T.	Tr	12.84	84-87	95	5	1
York C. (N/C)	Bridlington T.	10.88	88	5	0	0
Chesterfield	Tr	12.88	88-90	40	10	3

SHAW, Alan
Preston, 9 October, 1943 (OL)

Preston N. E.	Jnrs	10.60				
Hull C.	Tr	08.61	61-63	15	-	1

SHAW, Alexander

Crewe Alex.		12.44	46	13	-	4

SHAW, Arthur
Limehouse, 9 April, 1924 (WH)

Brentford	Southall	05.46	46	4	-	0
Arsenal	Tr	04.48	49-54	57	-	0
Watford	Tr	06.55	55	3	-	0

SHAW, Barry
Chilton (Dm), 31 October, 1948 (OL)

Darlington (Am)	Crowboro Ath.	03.68	67	2	0	0

SHAW, Bernard
Sheffield, 14 March, 1945 E Yth/Eu23-2 (FB)

Sheffield U.	App	10.62	62-68	135	1	2
Wolverhampton W.	Tr	07.69	69-72	113	3	2
Sheffield Wed.	Tr	06.73	73-75	100	4	3

SHAW, Bernard
Selby, 4 September, 1929 (OR)

League Club	Source	Date Signed	Seasons Played	Apps	Subs	Gls
Hull C.	Buckley Jnrs	05.48				
Lincoln C.	Goole T.	10.53	53-54	9	-	1

SHAW, Cecil E.
Mansfield, 22 June, 1911 Died 1977 (FB)

League Club	Source	Date Signed	Seasons Played	Apps	Subs	Gls
Wolverhampton W.	Rufford Colly	02.30	30-36	174	-	8
West Bromwich A.	Tr	12.36	36-46	110	-	10

SHAW, Christopher J.
Bournemouth, 23 August, 1965 (M)

League Club	Source	Date Signed	Seasons Played	Apps	Subs	Gls
Bournemouth	Jnrs	06.83	82-85	13	12	2

SHAW, Colin M.
St Albans, 19 June, 1943 E Yth (IF)

League Club	Source	Date Signed	Seasons Played	Apps	Subs	Gls
Chelsea	Jnrs	05.60	61	1	-	0
Norwich C.	Tr	08.63	63-64	3	-	0
Leyton Orient	Tr	03.65	65	7	0	0

SHAW, David G.
Huddersfield, 11 October, 1948 (F)

League Club	Source	Date Signed	Seasons Played	Apps	Subs	Gls
Huddersfield T.	Jnrs	01.67	66-68	23	3	2
Oldham Ath.	Tr	09.69	69-72	155	0	70
West Bromwich A.	Tr	03.73	72-74	65	17	17
Oldham Ath.	Tr	10.75	75-77	55	4	21

SHAW, Eric L.
Barnsley, 12 February, 1947 (FB)

League Club	Source	Date Signed	Seasons Played	Apps	Subs	Gls
Barnsley	App	02.65	64-65	2	0	0

SHAW, Gary R.
Birmingham, 21 January, 1961 E Yth/Eu21-7 (F)

League Club	Source	Date Signed	Seasons Played	Apps	Subs	Gls
Aston Villa	App	01.79	78-87	158	7	59
Blackpool	L	02.88	87	4	2	0
Walsall	Klagenfurt (Aut)	02.90	89	4	5	3
Shrewsbury T.	Kilmarnock	09.90	90	20	2	5

SHAW, Gordon
Wigan, 5 May, 1927 (RB)

League Club	Source	Date Signed	Seasons Played	Apps	Subs	Gls
Southport (Am)	Crompton Rec.	07.46	46	2	-	0

SHAW, Graham L.
Sheffield, 9 July, 1934 Eu23-5/EF Lge/E-5 (LB)

League Club	Source	Date Signed	Seasons Played	Apps	Subs	Gls
Sheffield U.	Jnrs	07.51	51-66	442	0	12
Doncaster Rov.	Tr	09.67	67	22	0	0

SHAW, Graham P.
Stoke, 7 June, 1967 (F)

League Club	Source	Date Signed	Seasons Played	Apps	Subs	Gls
Stoke C.	App	06.85	85-88	83	16	18
Preston N.E.	Tr	07.89	89-91	113	8	29

SHAW, Hugh
Clydebank, 29 April, 1929

League Club	Source	Date Signed	Seasons Played	Apps	Subs	Gls
Tranmere Rov.	Rhyl	06.55	55	3	-	0

SHAW, John
Stirling, 4 February, 1954 (G)

League Club	Source	Date Signed	Seasons Played	Apps	Subs	Gls
Leeds U.	App	02.71				
Bristol C.	Tr	05.74	76-84	295	0	0
Exeter C.	Tr	07.85	85-87	109	0	0

SHAW, John S. (Jack)
Doncaster, 10 April, 1924 (CF)

League Club	Source	Date Signed	Seasons Played	Apps	Subs	Gls
Rotherham U.	Yorkshire Main Colly	04.45	46-52	262	-	124
Sheffield Wed.	Tr	06.53	53-57	56	-	21

SHAW, Joseph
Murton (Dm), 23 June, 1928 EF Lge (CH)

League Club	Source	Date Signed	Seasons Played	Apps	Subs	Gls
Sheffield U.	Upton Colly	07.45	48-65	629	0	9

SHAW, Kenneth
Dukinfield, 15 December, 1920 (W)

League Club	Source	Date Signed	Seasons Played	Apps	Subs	Gls
Stockport Co.		10.42	46-47	41	-	18

SHAW, Mark W.
St Helens, 15 October, 1964 (M)

League Club	Source	Date Signed	Seasons Played	Apps	Subs	Gls
Wigan Ath. (N/C)	Jnrs	11.82	82	3	0	0

SHAW, Martin J.
Bristol, 14 September, 1960 (M)

League Club	Source	Date Signed	Seasons Played	Apps	Subs	Gls
Bristol Rov.	App	09.78	78	1	1	0

SHAW, Peter K.
Northolt, 9 January, 1956 (CD)

League Club	Source	Date Signed	Seasons Played	Apps	Subs	Gls
Charlton Ath.	Staines T.	12.77	77-80	100	5	5
Exeter C.	L	11.81	81	3	0	0
Gillingham	Tr	02.82	81-85	140	3	2

Gary Shaw (Aston Villa, Klagenfurt, Walsall, Kilmarnock & Shrewsbury Town)

SHAW, Raymond
Walsall, 18 May, 1913 Died 1980 (WH)

League Club	Source	Date Signed	Seasons Played	Apps	Subs	Gls
Birmingham C.	Darlaston	04.37	37-46	12	-	0

SHAW, Richard E.
Brentford, 11 September, 1968 (FB)

League Club	Source	Date Signed	Seasons Played	Apps	Subs	Gls
Crystal Palace	App	09.86	87-91	75	9	1
Hull C.	L	12.89	89	4	0	0

SHAW, Ronald
Bolton-on-Dearne, 1 January, 1924 (IF)

League Club	Source	Date Signed	Seasons Played	Apps	Subs	Gls
Torquay U.	Harrow T.	02.47	46-57	384	-	99

SHAW, Samuel
Caverswell, 14 September, 1934

League Club	Source	Date Signed	Seasons Played	Apps	Subs	Gls
Crewe Alex.	Foley	08.56	56	19	-	3

SHAW, Simon R.
Middlesbrough, 21 September, 1973 (M)

League Club	Source	Date Signed	Seasons Played	Apps	Subs	Gls
Darlington (YT)	YT	07.90	91	0	1	0

SHAW, Steven
Manchester, 10 August, 1960 (M)

League Club	Source	Date Signed	Seasons Played	Apps	Subs	Gls
Rochdale (App)	App	07.77	77	6	0	0

SHAW, Stuart
Liverpool, 9 October, 1944 (OR)

League Club	Source	Date Signed	Seasons Played	Apps	Subs	Gls
Everton	Jnrs	12.61	64-65	3	0	0
Crystal Palace	Tr	12.66				
Southport	Tr	03.67	66-68	66	1	6
Port Vale	Tr	07.69	69	1	2	0

SHAWCROSS, F. David
Stretford, 3 July, 1941 E Yth/Eu23-1 (WH)

League Club	Source	Date Signed	Seasons Played	Apps	Subs	Gls
Manchester C.	Jnrs	06.58	58-64	47	-	2
Stockport Co.	Tr	06.65	65-66	59	1	14
Halifax T.	Tr	03.67	66-69	126	6	17

SHEARD, Frank
Spilsby, 29 January, 1922 Died 1990 (CH)

League Club	Source	Date Signed	Seasons Played	Apps	Subs	Gls
Leicester C.	Skegness	08.41				
Southend U.	Tr	05.46	46-52	180	-	1

SHEARER, Alan
Newcastle, 13 August, 1970 E Yth/Eu21-11/E'B'/E-3 (F)

League Club	Source	Date Signed	Seasons Played	Apps	Subs	Gls
Southampton	YT	04.88	87-91	105	13	23

Alan Shearer (Southampton & England)

SHEARER, David J.
Inverness, 16 October, 1958 (F)

League Club	Source	Date Signed	Seasons Played	Apps	Subs	Gls
Middlesbrough	Inverness Clach.	01.78	77-82	88	9	23
Wigan Ath.	L	03.80	79	11	0	9
Grimsby T.	Tr	08.83	83	1	3	0
Gillingham	Tr	08.84	84-87	82	11	42
Bournemouth	Tr	10.87	87	8	3	3
Scunthorpe U.	Tr	02.88	87-88	16	0	7
Darlington	Tr	12.88	88	6	1	0

SHEARER, Duncan N.
Fort William, 28 August, 1962 (F)

League Club	Source	Date Signed	Seasons Played	Apps	Subs	Gls
Chelsea	Inverness Clach.	11.83	85	2	0	1
Huddersfield T.	Tr	03.86	85-87	80	3	38
Swindon T.	Tr	06.88	88-91	156	3	78
Blackburn Rov.	Tr	03.92	91	5	1	1

SHEARER, John M.
Dunfermline, 8 July, 1917 (IF)

League Club	Source	Date Signed	Seasons Played	Apps	Subs	Gls
Derby Co.		03.46				
Bradford C.	Tr	10.46	46-48	75	-	17
Grimsby T.	Tr	02.49	48-50	34	-	9

SHEARER, Peter A.
Coventry, 4 February, 1967 (M)

League Club	Source	Date Signed	Seasons Played	Apps	Subs	Gls
Birmingham C.	App	02.85	84	2	2	0
Rochdale	Tr	07.86	86	1	0	0
Bournemouth	Cheltenham T.	03.89	88-91	42	9	6

SHEARING, Peter F.
Uxbridge, 26 August, 1938 (G)

League Club	Source	Date Signed	Seasons Played	Apps	Subs	Gls
West Ham U.	Hendon	06.60	60	6	-	0
Portsmouth	Tr	07.61	61-63	17	-	0
Exeter C.	Tr	06.64	64-65	80	0	0
Plymouth Arg.	Tr	06.66	66-67	24	0	0
Exeter C.	Tr	07.68	68-70	79	0	0
Bristol Rov.	Tr	02.71				
Gillingham	Tr	08.71	71-72	39	0	0

SHEAVILLS, James E.
Ayesham (Kt), 28 July, 1940 (W)

League Club	Source	Date Signed	Seasons Played	Apps	Subs	Gls
Leeds U.	Jnrs	09.57				
Peterborough U.	Holbeach U.	(N/L)	60-62	30	-	8
Barnsley	Tr	06.63	63-64	65	-	6

SHEEDY, Kevin M.
Builth Wells, 21 October, 1959 IR Yth/IRu21-1/IR-43 (LM)

League Club	Source	Date Signed	Seasons Played	Apps	Subs	Gls
Hereford U.	App	10.76	75-77	47	4	4
Liverpool	Tr	07.78	80-81	1	2	0
Everton	Tr	08.82	82-91	263	11	67
Newcastle U.	Tr	03.92	91	13	0	1

SHEEN, John
Airdrie, 30 August, 1920 (IF)

League Club	Source	Date Signed	Seasons Played	Apps	Subs	Gls
Sheffield U.		09.37				
Hull C.	Tr	07.46	46	5	-	1

SHEFFIELD, Jonathan
Bedworth, 1 February, 1969 (G)

League Club	Source	Date Signed	Seasons Played	Apps	Subs	Gls
Norwich C.	App	02.87	88	1	0	0
Aldershot	L	09.89	89	11	0	0
Aldershot	L	08.90	90	15	0	0
Cambridge U.	Tr	03.91	90-91	15	0	0

SHEFFIELD, Laurence J.
Swansea, 27 April, 1939 W Sch (CF)

League Club	Source	Date Signed	Seasons Played	Apps	Subs	Gls
Bristol Rov.	Jnrs	07.56				
Newport Co.	Barry T.	04.62	61-64	91	-	46
Doncaster Rov.	Tr	08.65	65-66	58	0	34
Norwich C.	Tr	11.66	66-67	27	0	16
Rotherham U.	Tr	08.67	67	19	0	7
Oldham Ath.	Tr	12.67	67	18	0	6
Luton T.	Tr	07.68	68-69	31	3	12
Doncaster Rov.	Tr	10.69	69	13	2	6
Peterborough U.	Tr	08.70	70	17	1	6

SHELDON, Kevin J.
Stoke, 14 June, 1956 (W)

League Club	Source	Date Signed	Seasons Played	Apps	Subs	Gls
Stoke C.	App	06.73	75-80	12	3	0
Wigan Ath.	Tr	08.81	81-82	29	0	1
Port Vale	L	08.82	82	5	0	0
Crewe Alex (N/C)	Tr	08.83	83	2	0	0

SHELL, Frank H.
Hackney, 2 January, 1912 Died 1988 (F)

League Club	Source	Date Signed	Seasons Played	Apps	Subs	Gls
Aston Villa	Ford Sports	05.37	37-38	23	-	8
Birmingham C.	Tr	09.46				
Mansfield T.	Hereford U.	06.47	47	22	-	1

League Club	Source	Date Signed	Seasons Played	Apps	Subs	Gls
SHELLITO, Kenneth J.						
East Ham, 18 April, 1940 Eu23-1/E-1						(RB)
Chelsea	Jnrs	04.57	58-65	114	0	2
SHELTON, Gary						
Nottingham, 21 March, 1958 Eu21-1						(M)
Walsall	App	03.76	75-77	12	12	0
Aston Villa	Tr	01.78	78-81	24	0	7
Notts Co.	L	03.80	79	8	0	0
Sheffield Wed.	Tr	03.82	81-86	195	3	18
Oxford U.	Tr	07.87	87-88	60	5	1
Bristol C.	Tr	08.89	89-91	104	1	19
SHELTON, John B. T.						
Wollaston, 9 November, 1912						
Walsall	Worcester C.	08.34	34-46	103	-	5
SHEPHERD, Anthony						
Glasgow, 16 November, 1966 S Sch/S Yth						(M)
Bristol C. (L)	Glasgow Celtic	12.88	88	2	1	0
Carlisle U.	Glasgow Celtic	07.89	89-90	73	2	8
SHEPHERD, Arthur L.						
Liverpool, 11 May, 1922						(W)
Liverpool		04.46				
New Brighton	Tr	08.49	49-50	30	-	10
SHEPHERD, Brian A.						
Leicester, 29 January, 1935						(FB)
Coventry C.	Hinckley Ath.	10.56	57-59	29	-	0
SHEPHERD, Ernest						
Wombwell, 14 August, 1919						(OL)
Fulham	Bradford Rov.	04.38	46-48	72	-	13
West Bromwich A.	Tr	12.48	48	4	-	0
Hull C.	Tr	03.49	48-49	15	-	3
Queens Park R.	Tr	08.50	50-55	219	-	51
SHEPHERD, J. Greig						
Edinburgh, 29 September, 1960						(F)
Norwich C.	Musselburgh Windsor	03.79	79-81	13	3	2
Southend U.	Hong Kong	08.83	83-84	47	6	11
Peterborough U.	Tr	12.84	84-86	53	2	14
SHEPHERD, James						
Wigan, 25 June, 1938						(WH)
Blackburn Rov.		11.55				
Everton	Tr	07.59				
Crewe Alex.	Tr	06.60	60-63	50	-	4
Southport	Tr	02.64	63	13	-	6
SHEPHERD, John A.						
Rotherham, 20 September, 1945						(IF)
Rotherham U.		04.66	65-67	21	2	2
York C.	Tr	09.68	68	5	0	0
Oxford U.	Tr	10.69	69	9	2	1
SHEPHERD, John H. W.						
Kensington, 29 May, 1932						(CF)
Millwall		10.52	52-57	149	-	63
Brighton & H. A.	Tr	06.58	58-59	45	-	19
Gillingham	Tr	02.60	59-60	53	-	23
SHEPHERD, Peter D.						
Edrington, 27 August, 1965						(G)
Exeter C. (N/C)	Plymouth Arg. (Jnrs)	06.82	82	1	0	0
SHEPHERD, Trevor						
Sutton-in-Ashfield, 25 December, 1946						(F)
Nottingham F.	Jnrs	12.63				
Coventry C.	Tr	10.66	67-68	12	2	1
Torquay U.	L	03.68	67	14	0	6
Plymouth Arg.	Tr	06.69	69-70	36	3	4
SHEPHERD, J. William						
Liverpool, 25 September, 1920						(FB)
Liverpool	Elm Bank	12.45	48-51	53	-	0
SHEPHERDSON, Harold						
Middlesbrough, 28 October, 1918						(CH)
Middlesbrough	Jnrs	05.36	36-46	17	-	0
Southend U.	Tr	05.47				
SHEPPARD, Hedley H.						
East Ham, 26 November, 1909						(FB)
West Ham U.	Ilford	11.32				
Aldershot	Tr	07.34	34-48	249	-	1

League Club	Source	Date Signed	Seasons Played	Apps	Subs	Gls
SHEPPARD, Richard J.						
Bristol, 14 February, 1945						(G)
West Bromwich A.	App	02.63	65-68	39	0	0
Bristol Rov.	Tr	06.69	69-74	151	0	0
Torquay U.	L	12.73	73	2	0	0
SHEPPEARD, Howard T.						
Ynysybwl, 31 January, 1933						(IF)
Sunderland	Gnasyshard Y.C.	12.51	53	1	-	0
Cardiff C.	Tr	05.55				
Newport Co.	Tr	06.56	56-57	31	-	6
SHEPSTONE, Paul T. A.						
Coventry, 8 November, 1970 E Yth						(M)
Coventry C.	YT	11.87				
Birmingham C.	Tr	07.89				
Blackburn Rov.	Atherstone U.	05.90	90-91	16	10	1
York C.	L	03.92	91	2	0	0
SHERGOLD, Wilfred F.						
Swindon, 18 September, 1943						(WH)
Swindon T.	Jnrs	10.60	63-65	37	0	0
Bradford C.	Tr	06.66	66-67	22	6	2
SHERGOLD, William R.						
Newport, 22 January, 1923 Died 1968 W Amat						(W)
Newport Co.	Bishop Auckland	07.47	47-55	277	-	49
SHERIDAN, Alexander						
Motherwell, 19 July, 1948						(FB)
Brighton & H. A.	Queens Park	08.70	70	12	4	2
SHERIDAN, Frank M.						
Stepney, 9 December, 1961						(M)
Derby Co.	App	07.78	80-81	41	2	5
Torquay U.	Tr	08.82	82-83	24	3	3
SHERIDAN, George F.						
Wigan, 30 October, 1929						(OR)
Bolton W.		09.50				
Bradford C.	Colwyn Bay	01.52	51-52	12	-	1
SHERIDAN, John						
Ramsgate, 25 May, 1938						(WH)
Notts Co.	Linby Colly	07.55	56-65	287	0	9
Hartlepool U.	Tr	07.66	66-69	117	3	1
SHERIDAN, John J.						
Manchester, 1 October, 1964 IR Yth/IRu21-1/IR-14						(M)
Leeds U.	Manchester C. (Jnrs)	03.82	82-88	225	5	47
Nottingham F.	Tr	07.89	89			
Sheffield Wed.	Tr	11.89	89-91	96	1	18

John Sheridan (Leeds United, Nottingham Forest, Sheffield Wednesday & Republic of Ireland)

SHERINGHAM, Edward P. (Teddy)
Walthamstow, 2 April, 1966 E Yth/Eu21-1/E'B' (F)

League Club	Source	Date Signed	Seasons Played	Apps	Subs	Gls
Millwall	App	01.84	83-90	205	15	93
Aldershot	L	02.85	84	4	1	0
Nottingham F.	Tr	07.91	91	39	0	13

Teddy Sheringham (Millwall & Nottingham Forest)

SHERLOCK, Stephen E.
Birmingham, 10 May, 1959 (LB)

League Club	Source	Date Signed	Seasons Played	Apps	Subs	Gls
Manchester C.	App	05.77				
Luton T.	Tr	06.78	78	2	0	0
Stockport Co.	Tr	08.79	79-85	236	9	7
Cardiff C.	Tr	07.86	86	14	1	0
Newport Co.	L	12.86	86	5	0	0
Newport Co.	Tr	03.87	86-87	42	2	2

SHERON, Michael N.
Liverpool, 11 January, 1972 Eu21-2 (F)

League Club	Source	Date Signed	Seasons Played	Apps	Subs	Gls
Manchester C.	YT	07.90	91	20	9	6
Bury	L	03.91	90	1	4	1

SHERRATT, Brian
Stoke, 29 March, 1944 (G)

League Club	Source	Date Signed	Seasons Played	Apps	Subs	Gls
Stoke C.	App	04.61	61	1	-	0
Oxford U.	Tr	08.65	65-67	44	0	0
Nottingham F.	L	10.68	68	1	0	0
Barnsley	Tr	06.69	69	15	0	0
Colchester U.	Tr	08.70	70	9	0	0

SHERRATT, James A.
Warrington, 24 December, 1921 (FB)

League Club	Source	Date Signed	Seasons Played	Apps	Subs	Gls
Arsenal		12.46				
Hartlepool U.	Tr	12.48	48	20	-	4
Leyton Orient	Tr	08.49	49-51	39	-	8
Workington	Tr	08.52	52-53	48	-	3

SHERRATT, John H.
Stoke, 9 March, 1923

League Club	Source	Date Signed	Seasons Played	Apps	Subs	Gls
Port Vale (Am)		03.49	48	2	-	0

SHERWOOD, Alfred T.
Aberdare, 13 November, 1923 Died 1989 W Sch/W-41 (FB)

League Club	Source	Date Signed	Seasons Played	Apps	Subs	Gls
Cardiff C.	Aberaman	07.42	46-55	353	-	15
Newport Co.	Tr	07.56	56-60	205	-	21

SHERWOOD, Henry W.
Reading, 3 September 1913 Died 1985 (WH)

League Club	Source	Date Signed	Seasons Played	Apps	Subs	Gls
Reading	Jnrs	06.38	38	9	-	1
Aldershot	Tr	09.47	47-48	47	-	5
Crystal Palace	Tr	07.49	49	2	-	0

SHERWOOD, Jeffrey
Bristol, 5 October, 1959 (FB)

League Club	Source	Date Signed	Seasons Played	Apps	Subs	Gls
Bristol Rov.	Bath C.	06.82	82	16	2	0

SHERWOOD, Stephen
Selby, 10 December, 1953 (G)

League Club	Source	Date Signed	Seasons Played	Apps	Subs	Gls
Chelsea	App	07.71	71-75	16	0	0
Millwall	L	10.73	73	1	0	0
Brentford	L	01.74	73-74	62	0	0
Watford	Tr	11.76	76-86	211	0	1
Grimsby T.	Tr	07.87	87-91	176	0	0

SHERWOOD, Timothy A.
St Albans, 6 February, 1969 Eu21-4 (M/D)

League Club	Source	Date Signed	Seasons Played	Apps	Subs	Gls
Watford	App	02.87	87-88	23	9	2
Norwich C.	Tr	07.89	89-91	66	5	10
Blackburn Rov.	Tr	02.92	91	7	4	0

SHIELDS, Duncan
Dumbarton, 6 November, 1949 (CH)

League Club	Source	Date Signed	Seasons Played	Apps	Subs	Gls
Workington		08.69	69	7	1	0

SHIELDS, James
Glasgow, 28 November, 1931 (F)

League Club	Source	Date Signed	Seasons Played	Apps	Subs	Gls
Shrewsbury T.	Hibernian	05.56	56	25	-	5

SHIELDS, R. James
Derry (NI), 26 September, 1931 NI Amat/LOI/NI-1 (CF)

League Club	Source	Date Signed	Seasons Played	Apps	Subs	Gls
Sunderland	Crusaders	03.54				
Southampton	Tr	07.56	56-58	38	-	20

SHIELDS, Samuel M.
Denny, 21 March, 1928 (F)

League Club	Source	Date Signed	Seasons Played	Apps	Subs	Gls
Liverpool	Cowdenbeath	05.49	49	1	-	0
Darlington	Airdrieonians	06.52	52	21	-	2

SHIELS, Dennis P.
Belfast, 24 August, 1938 NI'B'-1 (CF)

League Club	Source	Date Signed	Seasons Played	Apps	Subs	Gls
Sheffield U.	Distillery	12.58	58-63	32	-	8
Peterborough U.	Tr	07.64	64	12	-	4
Notts Co.	Tr	07.65	65	28	1	7

SHIELS, James M.
Derry (NI), 24 February, 1938 NI'B'-1 (FB)

League Club	Source	Date Signed	Seasons Played	Apps	Subs	Gls
Manchester U.	Waterside B.C.	09.56				
Southend U.	Tr	06.61	61	25	-	0

SHILTON, Peter L.
Leicester, 18 September, 1949 E Sch/E Yth/Eu23-13/EF Lge/E-125 (G)

League Club	Source	Date Signed	Seasons Played	Apps	Subs	Gls
Leicester C.	App	09.66	65-74	286	0	1
Stoke C.	Tr	11.74	74-77	110	0	0
Nottingham F.	Tr	09.77	77-81	202	0	0
Southampton	Tr	08.82	82-86	188	0	0
Derby Co.	Tr	07.87	87-91	175	0	0
Plymouth Arg. (N/C)	Tr	03.92	91	7	0	0

SHIMWELL, Edward
Matlock, 27 February, 1920 E-1 (FB)

League Club	Source	Date Signed	Seasons Played	Apps	Subs	Gls
Sheffield U.	Wirksworth	01.39	46	14	-	0
Blackpool	Tr	12.46	46-56	283	-	5
Oldham Ath.	Tr	05.57	57	7	-	0

SHINER, Roy A. J.
Ryde (IOW), 15 November, 1924 Died 1988 (CF)

League Club	Source	Date Signed	Seasons Played	Apps	Subs	Gls
Huddersfield T.	Cheltenham T.	12.51	51-54	21	-	6
Sheffield Wed.	Tr	07.55	55-59	153	-	93
Hull C.	Tr	11.59	59	22	-	8

SHINNERS, Paul
Westminster, 8 January, 1959 (F)

League Club	Source	Date Signed	Seasons Played	Apps	Subs	Gls
Gillingham	Fisher Ath.	10.84	84	1	3	0
Colchester U.	L	03.85	84	6	0	1
Leyton Orient	Tr	07.85	85-88	73	4	32

SHINTON, Robert T.
West Bromwich, 6 January, 1952 (F)

League Club	Source	Date Signed	Seasons Played	Apps	Subs	Gls
Walsall	Lye T.	03.72	71-73	78	1	20
Cambridge U.	Tr	03.74	73-75	99	0	25
Wrexham	Tr	07.76	76-78	128	0	37
Manchester C.	Tr	07.79	79	5	0	0
Millwall	L	02.80	79	5	0	3
Newcastle U.	Tr	03.80	79-81	41	1	10
Millwall	Tr	03.82	81-82	29	5	4

League Club	Source	Date Signed	Seasons Played	Apps	Subs	Gls
SHIPLEY, George M.						
Newcastle, 7 March, 1959						(M)
Southampton	App	03.77	79	2	1	0
Reading	L	03.79	78	11	1	1
Lincoln C.	Tr	01.80	79-84	229	1	42
Charlton Ath.	Tr	07.85	85-86	61	0	6
Gillingham	Tr	08.87	87-88	27	2	3
SHIPLEY, Mark E.						
Hemsworth, 11 February, 1959						(G)
Blackburn Rov.	App	08.77				
Doncaster Rov.	Tr	08.79	79-80	6	0	0
SHIPPERLEY, David J.						
Uxbridge, 12 April, 1952						(CD)
Charlton Ath.	App	04.70	70-73	92	8	8
Plymouth Arg.	L	02.74	73	1	0	0
Gillingham	Tr	05.74	74-77	144	0	11
Charlton Ath.	Tr	02.78	77-79	53	0	6
Reading	Tr	09.79	79-80	18	1	0
SHIPWRIGHT, William K.						
Camden, 22 December, 1932						(CH)
Watford	Chesham U.	04.53	53-58	146	-	0
Aldershot	Tr	06.59	59-62	123	-	0
SHIRES, Alan J.						
Leigh-on-Sea, 29 June, 1948						(OR)
Southend U. (App)	App	07.64	65	0	1	0
Colchester U.	Tr	07.66	66-67	23	0	3
SHIRLEY, Alexander G.						
Milngavie, 31 October, 1921						(OR)
New Brighton	Dundee U.	10.46	46	18	-	3
Bradford C.	Tr	08.47	47	1	-	0
SHIRTLIFF, Paul R.						
Hoyland, 3 November, 1962 E Semi Pro						(FB)
Sheffield Wed.	App	11.80	80-82	7	2	0
Northampton T.	Tr	07.84	84	27	2	0
SHIRTLIFF, Peter A.						
Hoyland, 6 April, 1961						(CD)
Sheffield Wed.	App	10.78	78-85	188	0	4
Charlton Ath.	Tr	07.86	86-88	102	1	7
Sheffield Wed.	Tr	07.89	89-91	84	0	4
SHOEMAKE, Kevin P.						
Wickford, 28 January, 1965						(G)
Leyton Orient	App	01.83	83	4	0	0
Peterborough U.	Welling U.	09.86	86-87	40	0	0
SHONE, George F.						
Runcorn, 15 February, 1922						
Tranmere Rov.		12.46	46	4	-	0
SHORE, Andrew W.						
Kirkby-in-Ashfield, 29 December, 1955						(D)
Mansfield T.	Jnrs	07.74	74	1	0	0
SHORE, Brian						
Huddersfield, 1 February, 1935						
Halifax T.		10.56	56-57	9	-	3
SHORE, Edward G.						
Nuneaton, 18 October, 1927						(OL)
Port Vale		10.45	47	3	-	0
Coventry C.	Tr	07.48	48-49	2	-	0
SHORT, Alan J. M.						
Plymouth, 5 July, 1928						(OR)
Exeter C.	Tamerton	08.50	50	5	-	1
SHORT, Christian M.						
West Germany, 9 May, 1970						(CD)
Scarborough	Jnrs	07.88	88-89	42	1	1
Notts Co.	Tr	09.90	90-91	31	11	1
SHORT, J. Craig						
Bridlington, 25 June, 1968						(CD)
Scarborough	Pickering T.	10.87	87-88	61	2	7
Notts Co.	Tr	07.89	89-91	125	0	5
SHORT, David						
St Neots, 14 April, 1941						(F)
Lincoln C.	St Neots	11.58	58-59	4	-	0

League Club	Source	Date Signed	Seasons Played	Apps	Subs	Gls
SHORT, John						
Barnsley, 18 February, 1928 Died 1976						(FB)
Wolverhampton W.	Wath W.	05.48	50-53	98	-	0
Stoke C.	Tr	08.54	54-55	55	-	2
Barnsley	Tr	10.56	56-59	109	-	0
SHORT, John D.						
Gateshead, 25 January, 1921						(WH)
Leeds U.	Jnrs	01.38	46-48	60	-	18
Millwall	Tr	11.48	48-55	245	-	19
SHORT, Maurice						
Middlesbrough, 29 December, 1949						(G)
Middlesbrough	App	02.67	67-69	16	0	0
Oldham Ath.	Tr	06.70	70	5	0	0
Grimsby T.	L	01.71	70	10	0	0
SHORT, Russell D. V.						
Ilford, 4 September, 1968						(D)
Southend U.	YT	06.87	86	0	1	0
SHORTHOUSE, William H.						
Bilston, 27 May, 1922						(FB)
Wolverhampton W.	St Mirren O.B.	04.46	47-56	344	-	1
SHORTT, William W.						
Wrexham, 13 October, 1920 W-12						(G)
Chester C.		05.39				
Plymouth Arg.	Tr	02.46	46-55	342	-	0
SHOTTON, John M.						
Hartlepool, 17 August, 1971						(M)
Manchester U.	YT	05.89				
Hartlepool U.	Tr	09.90	90	0	1	0
SHOTTON, Malcolm						
Newcastle, 16 February, 1957						(CD)
Leicester C.	App	02.75				
Oxford U.	Nuneaton Bor.	05.80	80-87	262	1	12
Portsmouth	Tr	08.87	87	10	0	0
Huddersfield T.	Tr	02.88	87-88	16	0	1
Barnsley	Tr	09.88	88-89	64	2	6
Hull C.	Tr	02.90	89-91	58	1	2

Craig Short (Scarborough & Notts County)

SHOULDER, Alan
Bishop Auckland, 4 February, 1953 (F)

League Club	Source	Date Signed	Seasons Played	Apps	Subs	Gls
Newcastle U.	Blyth Spartans	12.78	78-81	99	8	35
Carlisle U.	Tr	08.82	82-84	110	2	32
Hartlepool U.	Tr	06.85	85-87	66	0	24

SHOULDER, James
Esh Winning, 11 September, 1946 (FB)

League Club	Source	Date Signed	Seasons Played	Apps	Subs	Gls
Sunderland	Jnrs	02.64	66	3	0	0
Hartlepool U.	Scarborough	08.73	73-74	62	1	3

SHOWELL, George W.
Bilston, 9 February, 1934 (D)

League Club	Source	Date Signed	Seasons Played	Apps	Subs	Gls
Wolverhampton W.	Jnrs	08.51	54-64	200	-	3
Bristol C.	Tr	05.65	65	9	2	0
Wrexham	Tr	11.66	66-67	48	0	1

SHOWERS, Derek
Merthyr Tydfil, 28 January, 1953 W Sch/Wu23-6/W-2 (F)

League Club	Source	Date Signed	Seasons Played	Apps	Subs	Gls
Cardiff C.	Jnrs	08.70	70-76	76	7	10
Bournemouth	Tr	07.77	77-78	58	2	19
Portsmouth	Tr	02.79	78-80	36	3	8
Hereford U.	Tr	12.80	80-82	87	2	13

SHOWLER, Kenneth
Doncaster, 3 February, 1933 (OR)

League Club	Source	Date Signed	Seasons Played	Apps	Subs	Gls
Chesterfield	Bentley Colly	11.52	53	7	-	0

SHOWLER, Paul
Doncaster, 10 October, 1966 (W)

League Club	Source	Date Signed	Seasons Played	Apps	Subs	Gls
Barnet	Altrincham	08.91	91	39	0	7

SHREEVE, John T. T.
Boldon, 18 August, 1917 Died 1966 (FB)

League Club	Source	Date Signed	Seasons Played	Apps	Subs	Gls
Charlton Ath.	Boldon Colly	01.35	36-50	145	-	0

SHREEVE, Peter
Neath, 30 November, 1940 (IF)

League Club	Source	Date Signed	Seasons Played	Apps	Subs	Gls
Reading	Finchley	01.59	58-65	112	1	17

SHREWSBURY, Philip
Durham, 25 March, 1947 E Yth (WH)

League Club	Source	Date Signed	Seasons Played	Apps	Subs	Gls
Notts Co.	Jnrs	09.65	66	1	1	0

SHRUBB, Paul J.
Guildford, 1 August, 1955 (D/M)

League Club	Source	Date Signed	Seasons Played	Apps	Subs	Gls
Fulham	App	08.72	72	1	0	0
Brentford	Hellenic (SA)	03.77	76-81	170	12	8
Aldershot	Tr	08.82	82-86	165	9	5

SHUFFLEBOTTOM, Frank C.
Chesterfield, 9 October, 1917 (FB)

League Club	Source	Date Signed	Seasons Played	Apps	Subs	Gls
Ipswich T.		06.38	38	2	-	0
Nottingham F.	Tr	09.42	46	2	-	0
Bradford C.	Tr	10.46	46-47	56	-	0

SHUKER, John
Manchester, 8 May, 1942 (LB)

League Club	Source	Date Signed	Seasons Played	Apps	Subs	Gls
Oxford U.		12.61	62-76	473	5	46

SHUTE, Philip
Darlington, 15 December, 1953 (F)

League Club	Source	Date Signed	Seasons Played	Apps	Subs	Gls
Darlington (N/C)	Shildon	03.84	85	2	0	0

SHUTT, Carl S.
Sheffield, 10 October, 1961 (F)

League Club	Source	Date Signed	Seasons Played	Apps	Subs	Gls
Sheffield Wed.	Spalding U.	05.85	85-87	36	4	16
Bristol C.	Tr	10.87	87-88	39	7	10
Leeds U.	Tr	03.89	88-91	40	25	17

SHUTT, Stephen J.
Barnsley, 29 November, 1964 (F)

League Club	Source	Date Signed	Seasons Played	Apps	Subs	Gls
Barnsley	App	11.82	82	1	0	0
Scunthorpe U. (N/C)	Goole T.	02.85	84	2	0	1

SHYNE, Christopher
Rochdale, 10 December, 1950 (G)

League Club	Source	Date Signed	Seasons Played	Apps	Subs	Gls
Rochdale	Dyers Arms	01.77	76-78	20	0	0
Wigan Ath.	Tr	08.79	79	10	0	0

SIBBALD, Robert L.
Hebburn, 25 January, 1948 (FB)

League Club	Source	Date Signed	Seasons Played	Apps	Subs	Gls
Leeds U.	Jnrs	01.65	66-67	1	1	0
York C.	Tr	02.69	68-70	74	5	7
Southport	Tr	07.71	71-76	240	0	13

SIBLEY, Albert
Southend, 6 October, 1919 (OR)

League Club	Source	Date Signed	Seasons Played	Apps	Subs	Gls
Southend U.	Jnrs	05.39	46	21	-	3
Newcastle U.	Tr	02.47	46-49	31	-	6
Southend U.	Tr	07.50	50-55	193	-	37

SIBLEY, Eric S.
Christchurch, 17 November, 1915 (FB)

League Club	Source	Date Signed	Seasons Played	Apps	Subs	Gls
Bournemouth		08.37	37	7	-	0
Blackpool	Tr	10.37	37-46	80	-	0
Grimsby T.	Tr	12.47	47-48	23	-	0
Chester C.	Tr	07.49	49	7	-	0

SIBLEY, Frank P.
Uxbridge, 4 December, 1947 E Yth (WH)

League Club	Source	Date Signed	Seasons Played	Apps	Subs	Gls
Queens Park R.	App	02.65	63-70	147	3	3

SIBLEY, Thomas I.
Porth, 27 October, 1920 (OL)

League Club	Source	Date Signed	Seasons Played	Apps	Subs	Gls
Birmingham C.	Ton Pentre	09.43				
Rochdale	Tr	03.47	46-47	23	-	3

SIDDALL, A. Barry
Northwich, 2 May, 1930 (IF)

League Club	Source	Date Signed	Seasons Played	Apps	Subs	Gls
Stoke C.	Northwich Vic.	02.51	50-53	59	-	10
Bournemouth	Tr	01.54	53-56	86	-	14
Ipswich T.	Tr	05.57	57-60	58	-	6

SIDDALL, Barry
Ellesmere Port, 12 September, 1954 E Yth (G)

League Club	Source	Date Signed	Seasons Played	Apps	Subs	Gls
Bolton W.	App	01.72	72-76	137	0	0
Sunderland	Tr	09.76	76-81	167	0	0
Darlington	L	10.80	80	8	0	0
Port Vale	Tr	08.82	82-84	81	0	0
Blackpool	L	10.83	83	7	0	0
Stoke C.	Tr	01.85	84-85	20	0	0
Tranmere Rov.	L	10.85	85	12	0	0
Manchester C.	L	03.86	85	6	0	0
Blackpool	Tr	08.86	86-88	110	0	0
Stockport Co.	Tr	06.89	89	21	0	0
Hartlepool U.	Tr	03.90	89	11	0	0
West Bromwich A. (N/C)	Tr	08.90				
Carlisle U.	Mossley	11.90	90	24	0	0
Chester C.	Tr	07.91	91	9	0	0

SIDEBOTTOM, Arnold
Barnsley, 1 April, 1954 (CD)

League Club	Source	Date Signed	Seasons Played	Apps	Subs	Gls
Manchester U.	Jnrs	02.72	72-74	16	0	0
Huddersfield T.	Tr	01.76	75-77	56	5	5
Halifax T.	Tr	10.78	78	21	0	2

SIDEBOTTOM, Geoffrey
Mapplewell, 29 December, 1936 (G)

League Club	Source	Date Signed	Seasons Played	Apps	Subs	Gls
Wolverhampton W.	Jnrs	09.54	58-60	28	-	0
Aston Villa	Tr	02.61	60-64	70	-	0
Scunthorpe U.	Tr	01.65	64-66	59	0	0
Brighton & H. A.	New York (USA)	01.69	68-70	40	0	0

SIDLOW, Cyril
Colwyn Bay, 26 November, 1915 W Amat/W-7 (G)

League Club	Source	Date Signed	Seasons Played	Apps	Subs	Gls
Wolverhampton W.	Llandudno	05.37	37-38	4	-	0
Liverpool	Tr	02.46	46-50	149	-	0

SIEVWRIGHT, George E.
Broughty Ferry, 10 September, 1937 (WH)

League Club	Source	Date Signed	Seasons Played	Apps	Subs	Gls
Oldham Ath.	Dundee U.	06.63	63	37	-	4
Tranmere Rov.	Tr	06.64				
Rochdale	Tr	07.65	65	31	1	1

SILK, George H.
Bootle, 18 October, 1916 Died 1969 (FB)

League Club	Source	Date Signed	Seasons Played	Apps	Subs	Gls
Southport		09.35	35-36	14	-	0
Plymouth Arg.	Tr	08.37	37-50	86	-	1

SILKMAN, Barry
Stepney, 29 June, 1952 (M)

League Club	Source	Date Signed	Seasons Played	Apps	Subs	Gls
Hereford U.	Barnet	08.74	74-75	18	19	2
Crystal Palace	Tr	08.76	76-78	40	8	6
Plymouth Arg.	Tr	10.78	78	14	0	2
Luton T.	L	02.79	78	3	0	0
Manchester C.	Tr	03.79	78-79	19	0	3
Brentford	Tr	08.80	80	14	0	1
Queens Park R.	Tr	10.80	80	22	1	2
Leyton Orient	Tr	09.81	81-84	133	7	14
Southend U.	Tr	07.85	85	38	2	1
Crewe Alex. (N/C)	Tr	09.86	86	1	1	0

SILLE, Leslie T.
Liverpool, 12 April, 1928 (OL)

League Club	Source	Date Signed	Seasons Played	Apps	Subs	Gls
Bournemouth (Am)	Tranmere Rov. (Am)	03.47	46	1	-	0
Crystal Palace (Am)	Ipswich T. (Am)	09.48	47	3	-	0
Tranmere Rov. (Am)	Tr	02.49	48	1	-	0

SILLETT, John C.
Southampton, 20 July, 1936 EF Lge (FB)

League Club	Source	Date Signed	Seasons Played	Apps	Subs	Gls
Chelsea	Southampton (Am)	04.54	56-61	93	-	0
Coventry C.	Tr	04.62	61-65	108	1	1
Plymouth Arg.	Tr	07.66	66-67	37	1	1

SILLETT, R. Peter
Southampton, 1 February, 1933 E Yth/Eu23-3/EF Lge/E'B'-1/E-3 (FB)

League Club	Source	Date Signed	Seasons Played	Apps	Subs	Gls
Southampton	Jnrs	06.50	51-52	59	-	4
Chelsea	Tr	06.53	53-61	260	-	29

SILMAN, David A.
Hampstead, 28 October, 1959 (D)

League Club	Source	Date Signed	Seasons Played	Apps	Subs	Gls
Brentford	Wolverhampton W. (App)	02.78	78	1	0	0

SILMAN, Roy
Rotherham, 12 May, 1934 (FB)

League Club	Source	Date Signed	Seasons Played	Apps	Subs	Gls
Rotherham U.	Edlington Colly	04.52	52-59	105	-	1
Barnsley	Tr	07.60				

SILVESTER, Peter D.
Wokingham, 19 February, 1948 (F)

League Club	Source	Date Signed	Seasons Played	Apps	Subs	Gls
Reading	App	02.66	65-69	76	3	26
Norwich C.	Tr	09.69	69-73	99	1	37
Colchester U.	L	10.73	73	4	0	0
Southend U.	Tr	02.74	73-76	79	2	32
Reading	L	03.75	74	2	0	0
Blackburn Rov.	L	10.76	76	5	0	1
Cambridge U.	Washington (USA)	08.77	77	2	2	1

SIM, John
Glasgow, 4 December, 1922

League Club	Source	Date Signed	Seasons Played	Apps	Subs	Gls
Brighton & H. A.	Kirkintilloch Rob Roy	10.46	46-49	32	-	5

SIMCOE, Kenneth E.
Nottingham, 14 February, 1937 (CF)

League Club	Source	Date Signed	Seasons Played	Apps	Subs	Gls
Nottingham F.	Jnrs	12.56	57	2	-	1
Coventry C.	Tr	05.59	59	8	-	1
Notts Co.	Tr	07.60	60	2	-	0

SIMM, John
Ashton-in-Makerfield, 24 November, 1929 (W)

League Club	Source	Date Signed	Seasons Played	Apps	Subs	Gls
Bolton W.		10.47	47	1	-	0
Bury	Tr	05.51	51-54	47	-	8
Bradford C.	Tr	03.55	54-58	95	-	22

SIMMONDS, Christopher K.
Plymouth, 5 August, 1920 (F)

League Club	Source	Date Signed	Seasons Played	Apps	Subs	Gls
Millwall	Barry T.	05.47	46-49	67	-	14
Leyton Orient	Tr	06.50	50	15	-	1
Workington	Tr	06.51	51-53	119	-	34

SIMMONDS, R. Lyndon
Pontypool, 11 November, 1966 W Yth (F)

League Club	Source	Date Signed	Seasons Played	Apps	Subs	Gls
Leeds U.	App	11.84	84-85	6	3	3
Swansea C.	L	10.86	86	7	1	1
Rochdale	Tr	02.87	86-87	65	0	22

SIMMONDS, Melvyn R.
Reading, 20 December, 1951 E Sch (M)

League Club	Source	Date Signed	Seasons Played	Apps	Subs	Gls
Reading	Manchester U. (App)	01.69				
Bournemouth	Tr	07.69	69	4	2	0

SIMMONITE, Gordon
Sheffield, 25 April, 1957 E Semi-Pro (FB)

League Club	Source	Date Signed	Seasons Played	Apps	Subs	Gls
Sheffield Wed.	Rotherham U. (App)	08.75	76	1	0	0
Blackpool	Boston U.	09.80	80-82	63	0	1
Lincoln C.	Tr	11.82	82-84	71	1	0

SIMMONS, Anthony J.
Stocksbridge, 9 February, 1965 E Yth (F)

League Club	Source	Date Signed	Seasons Played	Apps	Subs	Gls
Sheffield Wed.	App	02.83	81-82	1	3	0
Queens Park R.	Tr	11.83				
Rotherham U.	Tr	03.84	83-86	85	11	27
Lincoln C.	Tr	09.86	86	14	5	5
Cardiff C.	L	02.87	86	4	1	1

SIMMONS, David J.
Gosport, 24 October, 1948 (F)

League Club	Source	Date Signed	Seasons Played	Apps	Subs	Gls
Arsenal	App	11.65				
Bournemouth	L	11.68	68	7	0	3
Aston Villa	Tr	02.69	68-70	13	4	7
Walsall	L	10.70	70	5	0	2
Colchester U.	Tr	12.70	70-72	57	5	11
Cambridge U.	Tr	03.73	72-73	19	5	3
Brentford	Tr	03.74	73-75	47	5	17
Cambridge U.	Tr	11.75	75	16	1	5

SIMMS, Gordon H.
Leamington, 20 December, 1936 (W)

League Club	Source	Date Signed	Seasons Played	Apps	Subs	Gls
Coventry C. (Am)	Flavells	10.57	57	1	-	0

SIMNER, Joseph
Sedgley, 13 March, 1923 (F)

League Club	Source	Date Signed	Seasons Played	Apps	Subs	Gls
Chelsea	Folkestone T.	10.47	47	1	-	0
Swindon T.	Tr	07.49	49-50	30	-	12

SIMONS, Alan G.
Wrexham, 2 September, 1968 (G)

League Club	Source	Date Signed	Seasons Played	Apps	Subs	Gls
Port Vale (N/C)	YT	09.87	87	1	0	0

SIMONSEN, Allan
Denmark, 15 December, 1952 Danish Int (F)

League Club	Source	Date Signed	Seasons Played	Apps	Subs	Gls
Charlton Ath.	Barcelona (Sp)	11.82	82	16	0	9

SIMPKIN, Christopher J.
Hull, 24 April, 1944 (M)

League Club	Source	Date Signed	Seasons Played	Apps	Subs	Gls
Hull C.	App	04.62	62-71	284	1	19
Blackpool	Tr	10.71	71-72	31	3	1
Scunthorpe U.	Tr	10.73	73-74	61	0	2
Huddersfield T.	Tr	08.75	75	25	0	0
Hartlepool U.	Tr	12.76	76-77	47	0	0

SIMPKIN, Joseph
Skelmersdale, 26 September, 1921 Died 1969 (CH)

League Club	Source	Date Signed	Seasons Played	Apps	Subs	Gls
Southport		04.44	46-47	10	-	2

SIMPKINS, Kenneth
Wrexham, 21 December, 1943 Wu23-1 (G)

League Club	Source	Date Signed	Seasons Played	Apps	Subs	Gls
Wrexham	Jnrs	05.62	62-63	4	-	0
Hartlepool U.	Tr	03.64	63-67	121	0	1

SIMPSON, Alexander
Glasgow, 24 November, 1924 (WH)

League Club	Source	Date Signed	Seasons Played	Apps	Subs	Gls
Wolverhampton W.	Benburb	01.47	47-48	2	-	0
Notts Co.	Tr	10.49	49-52	74	-	6
Southampton	Tr	11.52	52-54	68	-	1
Shrewsbury T.	Tr	07.55	55-57	99	-	4

SIMPSON, Archibald
Dundee, 8 June, 1933 S Sch (FB)

League Club	Source	Date Signed	Seasons Played	Apps	Subs	Gls
Newcastle U.	Dundee	07.55				
Barrow	Tr	07.56	56-58	76	-	1

SIMPSON, Charles W. P.
Rochdale, 11 July, 1954 (M)

League Club	Source	Date Signed	Seasons Played	Apps	Subs	Gls
Rochdale	App	07.72	72	1	0	1

SIMPSON, Cyril
Aylesham, 18 August, 1942 (WH)

League Club	Source	Date Signed	Seasons Played	Apps	Subs	Gls
Gillingham	Jnrs	06.60	59-61	18	-	0

SIMPSON, David
Glasgow, 5 January, 1931 (WH)

League Club	Source	Date Signed	Seasons Played	Apps	Subs	Gls
Coventry C.	Third Lanark	05.55	55	4	-	1

SIMPSON, Dennis E.
Coventry, 1 November, 1919 (OR)

League Club	Source	Date Signed	Seasons Played	Apps	Subs	Gls
Coventry C.	Jnrs	05.39	46-49	67	-	5
Reading	Tr	05.50	50-54	172	-	31
Exeter C.	Tr	05.55	55-56	30	-	4

SIMPSON, Fitzroy
Bradford-on-Avon, 26 February, 1970 (LW)

League Club	Source	Date Signed	Seasons Played	Apps	Subs	Gls
Swindon T.	YT	07.88	88-91	78	27	9
Manchester C.	Tr	03.92	91	9	2	1

SIMPSON, Gary
Chesterfield, 10 June, 1959 (F)

League Club	Source	Date Signed	Seasons Played	Apps	Subs	Gls
Chesterfield	App	07.77	76-80	36	7	8
Chester C.	Tr	08.81	81-82	57	6	18

Fitzroy Simpson (Swindon Town & Manchester City)

League Club	Source	Date Signed	Seasons Played	Career Record Apps	Subs	Gls
SIMPSON, George L.						
Shirebrook, 3 December, 1933						(IF)
Mansfield T.	Jnrs	08.51	52-53	8	-	0
Gillingham	Hereford U.	08.56	56	8	-	1
SIMPSON, Harold						
Ashton-u-Lyne, 2 August, 1927						(OL)
Accrington St. (Am)	Lytham	04.49	48	1	-	0
SIMPSON, James						
Clay Cross, 8 December, 1923						(IF)
Chesterfield	Parkhouse Colly	05.45	46	3	-	0
SIMPSON, John						
Hull, 27 October, 1918						(LB)
Huddersfield T.	Bridlington T.	03.39	46	5	-	0
York C.	Tr	03.48	47-53	207	-	0
SIMPSON, John L.						
Appleby, 5 October, 1933						(G)
Lincoln C.	Netherfield	03.57	56	5	-	0
Gillingham	Tr	06.57	57-71	571	0	0
SIMPSON, Kenneth						
Sheffield, 12 June, 1931						(F)
Rotherham U.	Ransome & Marles	09.55	55-57	7	-	0
SIMPSON, Neil						
Hackney, 15 November, 1961 E Yth/Su21-11/S-4						(M)
Newcastle U.	Aberdeen	07.90	90	1	3	0
SIMPSON, Noel H.						
Mansfield, 23 December, 1922 Died 1987						(WH)
Nottingham F.		05.45	46-47	47	-	3
Coventry C.	Tr	08.48	48-56	258	-	7
Exeter C.	Tr	02.57	56-57	33	-	0
SIMPSON, Owen						
Stocksfield (Nd), 18 September, 1943						(FB)
Rotherham U.		10.62	64-66	6	0	0
Leyton Orient	Tr	09.67	67	36	0	4
Colchester U.	Tr	08.68	68	41	1	4
Southend U.	Tr	08.69	69-70	64	0	1
Darlington	Tr	03.71	70	11	0	0
Grimsby T.	Tr	08.71	71	6	1	0
SIMPSON, Paul D.						
Carlisle, 26 July, 1966 E Yth/Eu21-5						(LW)
Manchester C.	App	08.83	82-88	99	22	18
Oxford U.	Tr	10.88	88-91	138	6	43
Derby Co.	Tr	02.92	91	16	0	7
SIMPSON, Peter F.						
Great Yarmouth, 13 January, 1945						(CD)
Arsenal	App	04.62	63-77	353	17	10
SIMPSON, Peter W.						
Sunderland, 21 September, 1940 E Sch						(F)
Burnley	Jnrs	11.57	61-62	3	-	0
Bury	Tr	08.63	63	4	-	0
SIMPSON, Reginald						
Blackburn, 14 June, 1923						(CH)
Preston N. E.		11.43	46	4	-	0
Carlisle U.	Tr	08.48	48	36	-	0
SIMPSON, Robert						
Bishop Auckland, 15 September, 1915						(OL)
Darlington	West Auckland	08.36	36-46	97	-	0
Hartlepool U.	Tr	07.47	47	13	-	1
SIMPSON, Ronald						
Carlisle, 25 February, 1934						(OL)
Huddersfield T.	Holme Head Wks	02.51	51-57	110	-	24
Sheffield U.	Tr	05.58	58-64	203	-	45
Carlisle U.	Tr	12.64	64-65	45	0	6
SIMPSON, Ronald C.						
Glasgow, 11 October, 1930 S Amat/S'B'-2/SF Lge/S-5						(G)
Newcastle U.	Third Lanark	02.51	51-59	262	-	0
SIMPSON, Terence J. N.						
Southampton, 8 October, 1938						(WH)
Southampton		06.57	58-61	22	-	1
Peterborough U.	Tr	06.62	62	45	-	4
West Bromwich A.	Tr	06.63	63-66	71	1	3
Walsall	Tr	03.67	66-67	50	1	4
Gillingham	Tr	07.68	68	35	1	4
SIMPSON, Thomas						
Airdrie, 31 July, 1931						(FB)
Darlington	Dundee U.	08.56	56-57	4	-	0
SIMPSON, William						
Carlisle, 2 October, 1919						(IL)
Carlisle U.	Tottenham H. (Am)	08.46	46	12	-	2
SIMPSON, William G.						
Glasgow, 22 May, 1928						(F/WH)
Aston Villa	Trentside Jnrs	05.50				
Crystal Palace	Tr	08.52	52-54	38	-	13
SIMS, Christopher H.						
Liverpool, 6 December, 1939						(FB)
Blackburn Rov.	Clitheroe	04.59	63-64	13	-	0
SIMS, Frank						
Lincoln, 12 September, 1931						(CH)
Lincoln C.	Ruston Sports	08.51	51-55	3	-	0
SIMS, John						
Belper, 14 August, 1952						(F)
Derby Co.	App	08.70	72	2	1	0
Luton T.	L	11.73	73	3	0	1
Oxford U.	L	09.74	74	6	1	1
Colchester U.	L	01.75	74	2	0	0
Notts Co.	Tr	12.75	75-77	48	13	13
Exeter C.	Tr	12.78	78-79	33	1	11
Plymouth Arg.	Tr	10.79	79-82	161	2	43
Torquay U.	Tr	08.83	83	30	0	8
Exeter C.	Tr	02.84	83-84	23	2	6
Torquay U.	Tr	11.84	84	15	2	3

Peter Simpson (Arsenal)

SIMS, Nigel D.
Coton-in-Elms, 9 August, 1931 EF Lge (G)

League Club	Source	Date Signed	Seasons Played	Apps	Subs	Gls
Wolverhampton W.	Jnrs	09.48	48-55	38	-	0
Aston Villa	Tr	03.56	55-63	264	-	0
Peterborough U.	Tr	09.64	64	16	-	0

SIMS, Steven F.
Lincoln, 2 July, 1957 Eu21-10/E-'B' (CD)

League Club	Source	Date Signed	Seasons Played	Apps	Subs	Gls
Leicester C.	App	08.74	75-78	78	1	3
Watford	Tr	12.78	78-83	150	2	4
Notts Co.	Tr	09.84	84-86	85	0	5
Watford	Tr	10.86	86	19	0	1
Aston Villa	Tr	06.87	87-88	41	0	0
Lincoln C. (N/C)	Burton A.	10.90	90	5	0	0

SINCLAIR, Brian W.
Liverpool, 2 August, 1958 (W)

League Club	Source	Date Signed	Seasons Played	Apps	Subs	Gls
Blackpool	Bury (N/C)	08.77	77	0	2	0
Port Vale	Tr	08.78	78	14	4	2

SINCLAIR, Colin M.
Edinburgh, 1 December, 1947 (F)

League Club	Source	Date Signed	Seasons Played	Apps	Subs	Gls
Darlington	Raith Rov.	06.71	71-76	201	2	59
Hereford U.	Tr	10.76	76-77	20	2	2
Newport Co.	Tr	01.78	77-78	29	1	5

SINCLAIR, Dennis
Middlesbrough, 20 November, 1931 (OR)

League Club	Source	Date Signed	Seasons Played	Apps	Subs	Gls
Derby Co.		05.52				
Mansfield T.	Tr	07.53	53	1	-	0

SINCLAIR, Frank M.
Lambeth, 3 December, 1971 (FB)

League Club	Source	Date Signed	Seasons Played	Apps	Subs	Gls
Chelsea	YT	05.90	90-91	12	0	1
West Bromwich A.	L	12.91	91	6	0	1

SINCLAIR, Graeme
Paisley, 1 July, 1957 (D)

League Club	Source	Date Signed	Seasons Played	Apps	Subs	Gls
Manchester C. (L)	Glasgow Celtic	11.84	84	1	0	0

SINCLAIR, Harvey P.
Bournemouth, 30 November, 1933 (G)

League Club	Source	Date Signed	Seasons Played	Apps	Subs	Gls
Fulham	Bournemouth (Am)	12.50				
Leicester C.	Cambridge U.	08.56	56	1	-	0
Bristol Rov.	Yeovil T.	09.58	58	1	-	0

SINCLAIR, Jade
Saltburn, 6 November, 1971 (M)

League Club	Source	Date Signed	Seasons Played	Apps	Subs	Gls
Hartlepool U. (YT)	Middlesbrough (YT)	06.89	89	4	0	0

SINCLAIR, John E. W. (Jackie)
Culross (Fife), 21 July, 1943 S-1 (W)

League Club	Source	Date Signed	Seasons Played	Apps	Subs	Gls
Leicester C.	Dunfermline Ath.	05.65	65-67	103	0	50
Newcastle U.	Tr	01.68	67-69	42	1	6
Sheffield Wed.	Tr	12.69	69-72	97	4	14
Chesterfield	L	03.73	72	10	0	3

SINCLAIR, Michael J.
Grimsby, 13 October, 1938 (CF)

League Club	Source	Date Signed	Seasons Played	Apps	Subs	Gls
Grimsby T.	Jnrs	09.57	57-60	6	-	1

SINCLAIR, Nicholas J. T.
Manchester, 3 January, 1960 (RB)

League Club	Source	Date Signed	Seasons Played	Apps	Subs	Gls
Oldham Ath.	Jnrs	06.78	78-84	73	2	1
Wolverhampton W.	L	09.84	84	1	0	0
Tranmere Rov.	Tr	10.84	84-85	22	0	1

SINCLAIR, Robert A.
Greenwich, 9 April, 1974 (F)

League Club	Source	Date Signed	Seasons Played	Apps	Subs	Gls
Maidstone U. (YT)	YT	06.90	91	1	0	0

SINCLAIR, Robert D.
Winchburgh, 29 June, 1915 (OR)

League Club	Source	Date Signed	Seasons Played	Apps	Subs	Gls
Chesterfield		05.39				
Darlington	Tr	06.46	46-47	69	-	11

SINCLAIR, Ronald M.
Stirling, 19 November, 1964 S Sch/S Yth (G)

League Club	Source	Date Signed	Seasons Played	Apps	Subs	Gls
Nottingham F.	App	10.82				
Wrexham	L	03.84	83	11	0	0
Leeds U.	Tr	06.86	86	8	0	0
Halifax T.	L	03.87	86	4	0	0
Halifax T.	L	12.88	88	10	0	0
Bristol C.	Tr	09.89	89-90	44	0	0
Walsall	L	09.91	91	10	0	0
Stoke C.	Tr	11.91	91	26	0	0

SINCLAIR, Roy
Liverpool, 10 December, 1944 (M)

League Club	Source	Date Signed	Seasons Played	Apps	Subs	Gls
Tranmere Rov.	Liverpool (Am)	10.63	63-68	130	5	17
Watford	Tr	03.69	68-71	32	11	3
Chester C.	L	12.71	71	5	0	2
Tranmere Rov.	Tr	07.72	72	12	0	0

SINCLAIR, Thomas
Wigan, 13 October, 1921 (OL)

League Club	Source	Date Signed	Seasons Played	Apps	Subs	Gls
Aldershot	Gainsborough Trin.	08.44	46-50	70	-	9
Brentford	Tr	08.50	50	16	-	5
Bradford C.	Tr	08.51	51	9	-	0

SINCLAIR, Trevor L.
Dulwich, 2 March, 1973 E Yth (F)

League Club	Source	Date Signed	Seasons Played	Apps	Subs	Gls
Blackpool	YT	08.90	89-91	39	28	4

SINCLAIR, William
Southport, 11 September, 1920 Died 1978 (WH)

League Club	Source	Date Signed	Seasons Played	Apps	Subs	Gls
Southport	High Park	09.45	46	15	-	1

SINCLAIR, William I.
Glasgow, 21 March, 1947 (WH)

League Club	Source	Date Signed	Seasons Played	Apps	Subs	Gls
Chelsea	Morton	09.64	64	1	-	0

SINCLAIR, William M.
Blairhall, 14 October, 1934 (IF)

League Club	Source	Date Signed	Seasons Played	Apps	Subs	Gls
Huddersfield T.	Falkirk	12.58	58-59	15	-	5
Tranmere Rov.	Tr	06.60	60	4	-	0
Halifax T.	Tr	10.60	60	21	-	3

SINDALL, Mark
Shirebrook, 3 September, 1964 (M)

League Club	Source	Date Signed	Seasons Played	Apps	Subs	Gls
Mansfield T.	Notts Co. (App)	08.82	82-83	18	3	0

SINGER, D. James
Gilfach Goch, 30 August, 1937 (IF)

League Club	Source	Date Signed	Seasons Played	Apps	Subs	Gls
Newport Co.	Hengoed F.D.L.	05.56	57-60	52	-	28
Birmingham C.	Tr	09.60	60-61	20	-	8
Bournemouth	Tr	09.62	62-63	59	-	22
Newport Co.	Tr	07.64	64	8	-	5

SINGLETON, Anthony J.
Preston, 30 March, 1936 (CH)

League Club	Source	Date Signed	Seasons Played	Apps	Subs	Gls
Preston N. E.	Jnrs	05.55	60-67	286	1	0

SINGLETON, Bernard (Barney)
Conisbrough, 14 April, 1924 Died 1981 (G)

League Club	Source	Date Signed	Seasons Played	Apps	Subs	Gls
Wolverhampton W.	Lincoln C. (Am)	05.41				
Exeter C.	Tr	01.46	46-53	177	-	1

SINGLETON, Martin D.
Banbury, 2 August, 1963 E Yth (M)

League Club	Source	Date Signed	Seasons Played	Apps	Subs	Gls
Coventry C.	App	01.81	81-84	20	3	1
Bradford C.	Tr	12.84	84-86	69	2	3
West Bromwich A.	Tr	12.86	86-87	15	4	1
Northampton T.	Tr	11.87	87-89	45	5	4
Walsall	Tr	09.90	90	20	8	1

SINGLETON, Thomas W.
Blackpool, 8 September, 1940 (FB)

League Club	Source	Date Signed	Seasons Played	Apps	Subs	Gls
Blackpool	Jnrs	11.58				
Peterborough U.	Tr	06.62	62-64	85	-	1
Chester C.	Tr	06.65	65-67	87	1	1
Bradford P. A.	Tr	07.68	68	32	0	1

SINNOTT, Lee
Pelsall, 12 July, 1965 E Yth/Eu21-1 (CD)

League Club	Source	Date Signed	Seasons Played	Apps	Subs	Gls
Walsall	App	11.82	81-83	40	0	2
Watford	Tr	09.83	83-86	71	7	2
Bradford C.	Tr	07.87	87-90	173	0	6
Crystal Palace	Tr	08.91	91	35	1	0

SINTON, Andrew
Newcastle, 19 March, 1966 E Sch/E'B'/E-5 (LW)

League Club	Source	Date Signed	Seasons Played	Apps	Subs	Gls
Cambridge U.	App	04.83	82-85	90	3	13
Brentford	Tr	12.85	85-88	149	0	28
Queens Park R.	Tr	03.89	88-91	124	0	15

SIRREL, James
Glasgow, 2 February, 1922 (IF)

League Club	Source	Date Signed	Seasons Played	Apps	Subs	Gls
Bradford P. A.	Glasgow Celtic	05.49	49-50	12	-	2
Brighton & H. A.	Tr	08.51	51-53	55	-	15
Aldershot	Tr	08.54	54-56	33	-	2

SISSONS, J. Graham
Chester-le-Street, 20 May, 1934 (D)

League Club	Source	Date Signed	Seasons Played	Apps	Subs	Gls
Birmingham C.	Country Girl	07.54	56-62	91	-	0
Peterborough U.	Tr	12.61	62-64	68	-	0
Walsall	Tr	11.64	64-67	95	5	1

SISSONS, John L.
Hayes, 30 September, 1945 E Sch/E Yth/Eu23-10 (OL)

League Club	Source	Date Signed	Seasons Played	Apps	Subs	Gls
West Ham U.	App	10.62	62-69	210	3	37
Sheffield Wed.	Tr	08.70	70-73	114	1	14
Norwich C.	Tr	12.73	73	17	0	2
Chelsea	Tr	08.74	74	10	1	0

SITFORD, J. Anthony
Crowborough, 28 January, 1940 (FB)

League Club	Source	Date Signed	Seasons Played	Apps	Subs	Gls
Brighton & H. A.		03.59	60-61	22	-	2

SITTON, John E.
Hackney, 21 October, 1959 (D)

League Club	Source	Date Signed	Seasons Played	Apps	Subs	Gls
Chelsea	App	10.77	78-79	11	2	0
Millwall	Tr	02.80	79-80	43	2	1
Gillingham	Tr	09.81	81-84	102	5	5
Leyton Orient	Tr	07.85	85-90	166	4	7

SIVEBAEK, John
Denmark, 25 October, 1961 Danish Int (RB)

League Club	Source	Date Signed	Seasons Played	Apps	Subs	Gls
Manchester U.	Vejle B.K. (Den)	02.86	85-86	29	2	1

SIVELL, Laurence
Lowestoft, 8 February, 1951 (G)

League Club	Source	Date Signed	Seasons Played	Apps	Subs	Gls
Ipswich T.	App	02.69	69-83	141	0	0
Lincoln C.	L	01.79	78	2	0	0

SIX, Didier
France, 21 August, 1954 French Int (W)

League Club	Source	Date Signed	Seasons Played	Apps	Subs	Gls
Aston Villa	Mulhouse (Fr)	10.84	84	13	3	2

SJOBERG, John
Aberdeen, 12 June, 1941 S Sch (D)

League Club	Source	Date Signed	Seasons Played	Apps	Subs	Gls
Leicester C.	Banks O'Dee	08.58	60-72	334	1	15
Rotherham U.	Tr	06.73	73	6	0	0

SKEECH, H. Gordon
Warrington, 15 May, 1934 (FB)

League Club	Source	Date Signed	Seasons Played	Apps	Subs	Gls
Shrewsbury T.	Runcorn	11.54	54-62	223	-	4

SKEELS, Eric T.
Eccles, 27 October, 1939 (D)

League Club	Source	Date Signed	Seasons Played	Apps	Subs	Gls
Stoke C.	Stockport Co. (Am)	12.58	59-75	494	12	7
Port Vale	Seattle (USA)	09.76	76	5	0	1

SKEEN, George
Gateshead, 4 August, 1920 (WH)

League Club	Source	Date Signed	Seasons Played	Apps	Subs	Gls
Gateshead		10.46	46-49	86	-	3

SKEEN, Kenneth A.
Cheltenham, 20 March, 1942 (M)

League Club	Source	Date Signed	Seasons Played	Apps	Subs	Gls
Swindon T.	Trowbridge T.	09.64	64-66	14	0	4
Oxford U.	Tr	07.67	67-73	214	20	27

SKEET, Stuart C.
Cheshunt, 6 July, 1948 (G)

League Club	Source	Date Signed	Seasons Played	Apps	Subs	Gls
Tottenham H.	App	12.65				
Northampton T.	L	03.69	68	1	0	0

SKEETE, Leo S.
Liverpool, 3 August, 1949 (F)

League Club	Source	Date Signed	Seasons Played	Apps	Subs	Gls
Rochdale	Ellesmere Port	04.73	72-74	39	1	14

SKELTON, George A.
Thurcroft, 27 November, 1919 (IF)

League Club	Source	Date Signed	Seasons Played	Apps	Subs	Gls
Huddersfield T.	Thurcroft Welfare	12.45	46	1	-	0
Leyton Orient	Tr	07.47	47	3	-	0

SKIDMORE, William
Barnsley, 15 March, 1925

League Club	Source	Date Signed	Seasons Played	Apps	Subs	Gls
Wolverhampton W.		05.42				
Walsall	Tr	05.46	46-50	98	-	10

SKILLEN, Keith
Cockermouth, 26 May, 1948 (F)

League Club	Source	Date Signed	Seasons Played	Apps	Subs	Gls
Workington	Netherfield	12.73	73-74	56	8	9
Hartlepool U.	Tr	07.75	75	4	2	1

SKINGLEY, Brian G.
Romford, 28 August, 1937 (FB)

League Club	Source	Date Signed	Seasons Played	Apps	Subs	Gls
Bristol Rov.	Ilfracombe	01.55				
Crystal Palace	Tr	09.58	58	11	-	0
Queens Park R.	Tr	07.59				

SKINNER, Craig R.
Heywood, 21 October, 1970 (W)

League Club	Source	Date Signed	Seasons Played	Apps	Subs	Gls
Blackburn Rov.	YT	06.89	90-91	11	5	0

SKINNER, George E. H.
Erith, 26 June, 1917 (IF)

League Club	Source	Date Signed	Seasons Played	Apps	Subs	Gls
Tottenham H.	Callenders	09.38	46	1	-	0
Brighton & H. A.	Gillingham	02.48				

SKINNER, Justin
Hounslow, 30 January, 1969 (M)

League Club	Source	Date Signed	Seasons Played	Apps	Subs	Gls
Fulham	App	11.86	86-90	111	24	23
Bristol Rov.	Tr	08.91	91	41	1	2

SKIPPER, Peter D.
Hull, 11 April, 1958 (CD)

League Club	Source	Date Signed	Seasons Played	Apps	Subs	Gls
Hull C.	Schultz Y. C.	02.79	78-79	22	1	2
Scunthorpe U.	L	02.80	79	0	1	0
Darlington	Tr	05.80	80-81	91	0	4
Hull C.	Tr	08.82	82-88	264	1	17
Oldham Ath.	Tr	10.88	88	27	0	1
Walsall	Tr	07.89	89-90	81	0	2
Wrexham (N/C)	Tr	09.91	91	2	0	0
Wigan Ath. (N/C)	Tr	10.91	91	15	3	0

SKIRTON, Alan F. G.
Bath, 23 January, 1939 (W)

League Club	Source	Date Signed	Seasons Played	Apps	Subs	Gls
Arsenal	Bath C.	01.59	60-66	144	1	53
Blackpool	Tr	09.66	66-68	76	1	25
Bristol C.	Tr	11.68	68-70	75	3	14
Torquay U.	Tr	07.71	71	36	2	7

SKIVINGTON, Glenn
Barrow, 19 January, 1962 (M)

League Club	Source	Date Signed	Seasons Played	Apps	Subs	Gls
Derby Co.	Barrow	07.80	80-82	39	7	2
Halifax T.	L	03.83	82	4	0	0
Southend U.	Tr	08.83	83	2	2	0

SKIVINGTON, Michael N.
Glasgow, 24 December, 1921 LOI (CH)

League Club	Source	Date Signed	Seasons Played	Apps	Subs	Gls
Bury		06.47				
Rochdale	Tr	01.48	47	1	-	0
Leyton Orient	Dundalk	10.49	49	5	-	0
Gillingham	Tr	07.50	50	8	-	0
Brentford	Tr	09.51				

SKULL, John
Swindon, 25 August, 1932 E Yth (OR)

League Club	Source	Date Signed	Seasons Played	Apps	Subs	Gls
Wolverhampton W.	Swindon T. (Am)	06.50				
Swindon T.	Banbury Spencer	09.57	57-58	33	-	11

SLACK, Andrew
Heywood, 9 June, 1959 (G)

League Club	Source	Date Signed	Seasons Played	Apps	Subs	Gls
Rochdale	Bolton W. (App)	01.78	77-78	15	0	0

SLACK, R. Geoffrey
Peterborough, 11 April, 1940 (G)

League Club	Source	Date Signed	Seasons Played	Apps	Subs	Gls
Leicester C.		09.58				
Queens Park R.	Tr	03.61	61	1	-	0

SLACK, Melvyn
Bishop Auckland, 7 March, 1944 (WH)

League Club	Source	Date Signed	Seasons Played	Apps	Subs	Gls
Sunderland	Jnrs	03.61	64	2	-	1
Southend U.	Tr	08.65	65-68	107	4	5
Cambridge U.	Tr	01.69	70	33	2	0

SLACK, Robert G.
Morecambe, 13 July, 1934 (F)

League Club	Source	Date Signed	Seasons Played	Apps	Subs	Gls
Stockport Co.	Morecambe	11.58	58	8	-	1

SLACK, Trevor C.
Peterborough, 26 September, 1962 E Yth (CD)

League Club	Source	Date Signed	Seasons Played	Apps	Subs	Gls
Peterborough U.	App	08.80	80-85	201	1	18
Rotherham U.	Tr	08.86	86	14	1	1
Grimsby T.	Tr	08.87	87	21	0	0
Northampton T.	Tr	02.88	87	13	0	1
Chesterfield	Tr	09.88	88-89	23	0	0

SLADE, Robert F.
Hounslow, 15 July, 1927 (G)

League Club	Source	Date Signed	Seasons Played	Apps	Subs	Gls
Millwall (Am)	Acton T.	10.48	48	1	-	0

SLATER, J. Brian
Sheffield, 20 October, 1932 (IF)

League Club	Source	Date Signed	Seasons Played	Apps	Subs	Gls
Sheffield Wed.		05.51	52	3	-	0
Grimsby T.	Tr	07.54	54	4	-	0
Rotherham U.	Tr	09.55	56	17	-	5
Chesterfield	Tr	06.57	57	15	-	3

SLATER, Frederick
Burton, 25 September, 1925 (CF)

League Club	Source	Date Signed	Seasons Played	Apps	Subs	Gls
Birmingham C.	Burton A.	11.47	48-49	5	-	1
York C.	Tr	06.51	51	13	-	3

SLATER, James J.
Wrexham, 27 October, 1968 (F)

League Club	Source	Date Signed	Seasons Played	Apps	Subs	Gls
Wrexham	Jnrs	07.87	87	0	3	0

SLATER, John
Heywood, 8 May, 1917 (RH)

League Club	Source	Date Signed	Seasons Played	Apps	Subs	Gls
Rochdale		04.40				
Crewe Alex.	Tr	08.46	46	3	-	0

SLATER, Malcolm B.
Buckie, 22 October, 1939 (W)

League Club	Source	Date Signed	Seasons Played	Apps	Subs	Gls
Southend U.	Montrose	11.63	63-66	83	0	6
Leyton Orient	Tr	01.67	66-69	111	0	4
Colchester U.	L	10.69	69	4	0	0

SLATER, Raymond
Seaton Delaval, 22 August, 1931 (CF)

League Club	Source	Date Signed	Seasons Played	Apps	Subs	Gls
Chesterfield	South Shields	06.56	56	2	-	1
Gateshead	Tr	10.56	56	6	-	2

SLATER, Robert
Musselburgh, 5 May, 1936 Su23-1 (G)

League Club	Source	Date Signed	Seasons Played	Apps	Subs	Gls
Liverpool	Falkirk	05.59	59-61	99	-	0
Watford	Dundee	05.65	65-68	134	0	0

SLATER, Stuart I.
Sudbury, 27 March, 1969 Eu21-3 (LW)

League Club	Source	Date Signed	Seasons Played	Apps	Subs	Gls
West Ham U.	App	03.87	87-91	134	7	11

SLATER, William J.
Clitheroe, 29 April, 1927 E Amat/E-12 (WH)

League Club	Source	Date Signed	Seasons Played	Apps	Subs	Gls
Blackpool (Am)	Jnrs	05.49	49-51	30	-	9
Brentford (Am)	Tr	12.51	51	7	-	1
Wolverhampton W.	Tr	08.52	52-62	310	-	24
Brentford	Tr	07.63	63	5	-	2

SLATTER, Leslie A. H.
Reading, 22 November, 1931 (OR)

League Club	Source	Date Signed	Seasons Played	Apps	Subs	Gls
Luton T.	Mount Pleasant Y.C.	03.49	49	1	-	0
Aston Villa	Crusaders	08.53				
York C.	Tr	07.54	54	13	-	0

SLATTER, Neil J.
Cardiff, 30 May, 1964, W Yth/Wu21-6/W-22 (D)

League Club	Source	Date Signed	Seasons Played	Apps	Subs	Gls
Bristol Rov.	App	05.82	80-84	147	1	4
Oxford U.	Tr	07.85	85-89	88	3	6
Bournemouth	L	03.90	89	5	1	0

SLATTERY, J. Clive
Swansea, 21 July, 1946 (W)

League Club	Source	Date Signed	Seasons Played	Apps	Subs	Gls
Swansea C.	North End	10.68	68-71	65	6	10
Hereford U.	Tr	07.72	72	3	5	0

SLATTERY, Joseph W.
Newcastle, 3 June, 1926 (CF)

League Club	Source	Date Signed	Seasons Played	Apps	Subs	Gls
Accrington St.	Hexham Hearts	06.50	50	13	-	2

SLAVEN, Bernard J.
Paisley, 13 November, 1960 IR-6 (F)

League Club	Source	Date Signed	Seasons Played	Apps	Subs	Gls
Middlesbrough	Albion Rov.	09.85	85-91	273	16	115

SLAWSON, Stephen M.
Nottingham, 13 November, 1972 (F)

League Club	Source	Date Signed	Seasons Played	Apps	Subs	Gls
Notts Co.	YT	07.91	91	3	10	1

SLEE, Carl D.
Swansea, 30 November, 1947 W Sch (D)

League Club	Source	Date Signed	Seasons Played	Apps	Subs	Gls
Swansea C.	Jnrs	01.66	67-70	111	4	0

SLEEUWENHOEK, John C.
Wednesfield, 26 February, 1944 Died 1989 E Sch/E Yth/Eu23-2/EF Lge (CH)

League Club	Source	Date Signed	Seasons Played	Apps	Subs	Gls
Aston Villa	App	03.61	60-67	226	0	1
Birmingham C.	Tr	11.67	67-70	29	1	0
Torquay U.	L	03.71	70	11	0	0
Oldham Ath.	Tr	07.71	71	2	0	0

SLEIGHT, Geoffrey
Royston, 20 June, 1943 (OL)

League Club	Source	Date Signed	Seasons Played	Apps	Subs	Gls
Bolton W.	Jnrs	08.61	61	2	-	0

SLINGSBY, Lee
Rossington, 27 November, 1970 (M)

League Club	Source	Date Signed	Seasons Played	Apps	Subs	Gls
Scarborough	Doncaster Rov. (YT)	07.89	89	0	1	0

SLOAN, David
Lisburn (NI), 28 October, 1941 NI Amat/NIu23-1/NI-2 (W)

League Club	Source	Date Signed	Seasons Played	Apps	Subs	Gls
Scunthorpe U.	Bangor	11.63	63-67	133	3	42
Oxford U.	Tr	02.68	67-72	166	8	29
Walsall	Tr	07.73	73-74	44	5	3

SLOAN, James
Newcastle, 22 February, 1924 (CF)

League Club	Source	Date Signed	Seasons Played	Apps	Subs	Gls
Newcastle U.	C.A. Parsons	01.45				
Hartlepool U.	Tr	10.46	46-51	83	-	28

SLOAN, Josiah W. (Paddy)
Lurgan (NI), 30 April, 1921 IR-2/NI-1 (WH)

League Club	Source	Date Signed	Seasons Played	Apps	Subs	Gls
Manchester U.	Glenavon	09.37				
Tranmere Rov.	Tr	05.39				
Arsenal	Tr	05.46	46-47	33	-	1
Sheffield U.	Tr	02.48	47	12	-	2
Norwich C.	Brescla (It)	12.51	51	6	-	0

SLOAN, Scott
Wallsend, 14 December, 1967 (F)

League Club	Source	Date Signed	Seasons Played	Apps	Subs	Gls
Newcastle U.	Berwick R.	07.90	90	11	5	1

SLOAN, Thomas
Ballymena (NI), 10 July, 1959 NIu21-1/NI-3 (M)

League Club	Source	Date Signed	Seasons Played	Apps	Subs	Gls
Manchester U.	Ballymena	08.78	78-80	4	7	0
Chester C.	Tr	08.82	82	44	0	3

SLOCOMBE, Michael
Bristol, 3 May, 1941 (WH)

League Club	Source	Date Signed	Seasons Played	Apps	Subs	Gls
Bristol Rov.	Jnrs	06.61	61-62	32	-	0

SLOUGH, Alan P.
Luton, 24 September, 1947 (D)

League Club	Source	Date Signed	Seasons Played	Apps	Subs	Gls
Luton T.	App	05.65	65-72	265	10	28
Fulham	Tr	08.73	73-76	154	0	13
Peterborough U.	Tr	07.77	77-80	104	1	10
Millwall	Tr	06.81	81	14	0	0

SLYNN, Frank
Birmingham, 10 February, 1924 (WH)

League Club	Source	Date Signed	Seasons Played	Apps	Subs	Gls
Sheffield Wed.	Batchelor Sports	09.46	46-50	44	-	5
Bury	Tr	12.50	50-52	41	-	0
Walsall	Tr	09.53	53	10	-	0

SMALE, Thomas H.
Swansea, 16 July, 1928 (FB)

League Club	Source	Date Signed	Seasons Played	Apps	Subs	Gls
Shrewsbury T.	Derby Co. (Am)	(N/L)	50-51	14	-	1
Aldershot	Tr	08.52	52	1	-	0

SMALES, Kenneth
Hull, 3 May, 1932 (FB)

League Club	Source	Date Signed	Seasons Played	Apps	Subs	Gls
Hull C.	Brunswick Inst.	05.53	56	1	-	0

SMALL, Bryan
Birmingham, 15 November, 1971 E Yth (LB)

League Club	Source	Date Signed	Seasons Played	Apps	Subs	Gls
Aston Villa	YT	07.90	91	8	0	0

SMALL, Colin
Stockport, 9 November, 1970 (M)

League Club	Source	Date Signed	Seasons Played	Apps	Subs	Gls
Rochdale	Manchester C. (YT)	07.89	89	5	2	1

SMALL, David
Dundee, 17 July, 1930 (W)

League Club	Source	Date Signed	Seasons Played	Apps	Subs	Gls
Watford	Dundee N.E.	06.50	50-51	5	-	0

SMALL, John H.
Billingham, 14 January, 1945 (G)

League Club	Source	Date Signed	Seasons Played	Apps	Subs	Gls
Hartlepool U. (Am)		06.65	65	2	0	0

SMALL, Martin L.
Gateshead, 2 February, 1920 (IF)

League Club	Source	Date Signed	Seasons Played	Apps	Subs	Gls
Gateshead		08.46	46-51	96	-	29

SMALL, Michael A.
Birmingham, 2 January, 1962 E Yth (F)

League Club	Source	Date Signed	Seasons Played	Apps	Subs	Gls
Luton T.		10.79	81-82	0	4	0
Peterborough U.	L	10.82	82	2	2	1
Brighton & H. A.	P.A.O.K. Salonika (Gre)	08.90	90	39	0	15
West Ham U.	Tr	08.91	91	37	3	13

League Club	Source	Date Signed	Seasons Played	Apps	Subs	Gls
SMALL, Peter V.						
Horsham, 23 October, 1924						(W)
Luton T.	Horsham	08.47	47-49	27	-	5
Leicester C.	Tr	02.50	49-54	65	-	16
Nottingham F.	Tr	09.54	54-56	87	-	20
Brighton & H. A.	Tr	07.57	57	8	-	3
SMALL, Samuel J.						
Birmingham, 15 May, 1912						(WH)
Birmingham C.	Bromsgrove Rov.	05.34	34-36	6	-	0
West Ham U.	Tr	01.37	36-47	108	-	39
Brighton & H. A.	Tr	03.48	47-49	38	-	0
SMALLER, Paul A.						
Scunthorpe, 18 September, 1970						(M)
Grimsby T.	YT	07.89	88-89	1	1	0
SMALLEY, Mark A.						
Newark, 2 January, 1965 E Yth						(CD)
Nottingham F.	App	01.83	82-84	1	2	0
Birmingham C.	L	03.86	85	7	0	0
Bristol Rov.	L	08.86	86	10	0	0
Leyton Orient	Tr	02.87	86-89	59	5	4
Mansfield T.	Tr	11.89	89-90	49	0	2
Maidstone U.	Tr	05.91	91	33	1	2
SMALLEY, Paul T.						
Nottingham, 17 November, 1966 E Yth						(RB)
Notts Co.	App	11.84	85-87	112	6	0
Scunthorpe U.	Tr	09.88	88-90	84	2	1
Blackpool	L	10.90	90	6	0	0
Leeds U. (N/C)	Tr	12.90				
Doncaster R. (N/C)	Tr	03.91	90	14	0	0
SMALLEY, Thomas						
Kinsley, 13 January, 1912 Died 1984 E-1						(FB)
Wolverhampton W.	South Kirkby Colly	05.31	31-37	179	-	11
Norwich C.	Tr	08.38	38	42	-	1
Northampton T.	Tr	10.45	46-50	200	-	2
SMALLMAN, David P.						
Connahs Quay, 22 March, 1953 Wu23-5/W-7						(F)
Wrexham	Jnrs	11.71	72-74	100	1	38
Everton	Tr	03.75	74-76	19	2	6
SMALLWOOD, James W.						
Bearpark (Dm), 1 September, 1925						(WH)
Chesterfield	Spennymoor U.	12.49	49-60	345	-	14
SMALLWOOD, Neil						
York, 3 December, 1966						(G)
York C.	Jnrs	06.85	86-87	13	0	0
Darlington	Tr	08.88	88	4	0	0
SMART, Gary J.						
Totnes, 29 April, 1964						(FB)
Oxford U.	Wokingham T.	07.88	88-91	107	4	0
SMART, Gary M.						
Bristol, 8 December, 1963						(M)
Bristol Rov.	Mangotsfield	09.85	85-86	11	8	4
SMART, James						
Dundee, 9 January, 1947						(W)
Chelsea	Morton	02.65	64	1	-	0
SMART, Jason						
Rochdale, 15 February, 1969						(CD)
Rochdale	YT	08.86	85-88	116	1	4
Crewe Alex.	Tr	07.89	89-91	87	2	2
SMART, Kevin G.						
Newcastle, 17 October, 1958						(RB)
Plymouth Arg.	App	10.76	76-77	32	0	0
Wigan Ath.	Tr	07.78	78-79	48	1	1
SMART, Richard						
Bishop Auckland, 19 June, 1921						(IF)
Exeter C.	Stanley U.	08.46	46-51	103	-	33
SMART, Roger W.						
Swindon, 25 March, 1943						(M)
Swindon T.	Jnrs	05.60	61-72	341	6	43
Charlton Ath.	Tr	05.73	73	30	1	1
SMEDLEY, Lawrence						
Sheffield, 7 May, 1922						(IF)
Lincoln C.		05.45	46-48	11	-	6
SMEE, Roger G.						
Reading, 14 August, 1948						(CF)
Chelsea	Jnrs	03.66				
Reading	Tr	01.67	66-69	49	1	16
Reading	(Retired)	07.73	73	6	3	1
SMELT, Lee A.						
Edmonton, 13 March, 1958						(G)
Colchester U.	Jnrs	07.75				
Nottingham F.	Gravesend & Nft.	06.80	80	1	0	0
Peterborough U.	L	08.81	81	5	0	0
Halifax T.	Tr	10.81	81-83	119	0	0
Cardiff C.	Tr	08.84	84-85	37	0	0
Exeter C.	L	03.85	84	13	0	0
SMETHURST, Derek						
South Africa, 24 October, 1947						(F)
Chelsea	Durban U. (SA)	12.68	70-71	14	0	4
Millwall	Tr	09.71	71-74	66	5	9
SMETHURST, Edward						
Doncaster, 5 March, 1938						(G)
Chesterfield	Denaby U.	08.59	59	19	-	0
SMETHURST, Peter J.						
South Africa, 8 August, 1940						(F)
Blackpool	Durban U. (SA)	02.60	59	1	-	0
SMEULDERS, John						
Hackney, 28 March, 1957 E Yth						(G)
Leyton Orient	App	07.74				
Bournemouth	Tr	07.79	79-80	14	0	0
Bournemouth	Weymouth	01.84	83-85	75	0	0
Torquay U.	Tr	07.86	86	18	0	0
Peterborough U.	L	12.86	86	1	0	0
Bournemouth (N/C)	Poole T.	08.87	87-88	9	0	0
Brentford (N/C)	L	10.88	88	8	0	0
SMILLIE, Andrew T.						
Ilford, 15 March, 1941 E Yth						(IF)
West Ham U.	Jnrs	06.58	58-60	20	-	3
Crystal Palace	Tr	06.61	61-62	53	-	23
Scunthorpe U.	Tr	07.63	63-64	13	-	2
Southend U.	Tr	09.64	64-68	163	0	29
Gillingham	Tr	10.68	68-70	88	6	7
SMILLIE, Neil						
Barnsley, 19 July, 1958						(LW)
Crystal Palace	App	10.75	76-81	71	12	7
Brentford	L	01.77	76	3	0	0
Brighton & H. A.	Tr	08.82	82-84	62	13	2
Watford	Tr	06.85	85	10	6	3
Reading	L	12.86	86	6	0	0
Reading	Tr	03.87	86-87	32	1	0
Brentford	Tr	08.88	88-91	145	6	17
SMILLIE, Ronald D.						
Grimethorpe, 27 September, 1933						(OR)
Barnsley	Jnrs	12.50	51-55	28	-	1
Lincoln C.	Tr	06.56	56-59	91	-	15
Barnsley	Tr	07.60	60-61	85	-	16
SMIRKE, Alfred H.						
Pershore, 14 March, 1917 E Sch						(OL)
Southend U.		05.38	38-47	100	-	25
Gateshead	Tr	03.48	47	11	-	4
SMITH, Alan						
						(OL)
Hull C. (Am)		09.46	46	1	-	0
SMITH, Alan						
Newcastle, 15 October, 1921						(OL)
Arsenal		05.46	46	3	-	0
Brentford	Tr	12.46	46-48	13	-	4
Leyton Orient	Tr	07.49	49	6	-	1
SMITH, C. Alan						
Salford, 7 June, 1940						(G)
Stockport Co. (Am)	Manchester C. (Am)	06.60	60	6	-	0
SMITH, Alan D.						
Sheffield, 7 December, 1966						(D)
Sheffield Wed.	App	12.84				
Darlington	Tr	09.86	86-88	26	5	1

SMITH, Alan F.
Newport, 3 September, 1949 W Sch (M)

League Club	Source	Date Signed	Seasons Played	Apps	Subs	Gls
Newport Co.	Jnrs	09.66	66-71	88	14	7

SMITH, Alan G.
Bromsgrove, 7 April, 1936 (HB)

League Club	Source	Date Signed	Seasons Played	Apps	Subs	Gls
Aston Villa	Bromsgrove Rov.	06.54	55	1	-	0

SMITH, Alan M.
Harrogate, 1 September, 1950 (OL)

League Club	Source	Date Signed	Seasons Played	Apps	Subs	Gls
York C. (Am)	Harrogate R.I.	12.70	70	1	1	0

SMITH, Alan M.
Bromsgrove, 21 November, 1962 E Semi-Pro/EF Lge/E 'B'/E-13 (F)

League Club	Source	Date Signed	Seasons Played	Apps	Subs	Gls
Leicester C.	Alvechurch	06.82	82-86	190	10	76
Arsenal	Tr	05.87	87-91	177	12	78

Alan Smith (Leicester City, Arsenal & England)

SMITH, J. Alan
Birkenhead, 8 June, 1939 (CH)

League Club	Source	Date Signed	Seasons Played	Apps	Subs	Gls
Torquay U.	Port Sunlight	08.56	57-68	277	1	3

SMITH, Albert O. S.
Bargoed, 18 October, 1923 (G)

League Club	Source	Date Signed	Seasons Played	Apps	Subs	Gls
Cardiff C.		04.44				
Newport Co.	Tr	05.47	46-47	27	-	0

SMITH, Albert W.
Stoke, 27 August, 1918 Died 1992

League Club	Source	Date Signed	Seasons Played	Apps	Subs	Gls
Queens Park R.		05.39	46-48	63	-	3

SMITH, Alexander
Dundee, 4 September, 1927 (FB)

League Club	Source	Date Signed	Seasons Played	Apps	Subs	Gls
Blackpool		08.46				
Bradford P. A.	Tr	06.49	49-50	5	-	0

SMITH, Alexander
Dewsbury, 11 May, 1947 (FB)

League Club	Source	Date Signed	Seasons Played	Apps	Subs	Gls
Bradford C.	Ossett T.	12.64	65-67	91	2	2
Huddersfield T.	Tr	03.68	67-68	29	0	0
Southend U.	Tr	04.70	70-73	130	1	1
Colchester U.	Tr	01.73	73-74	51	1	1
Halifax T.	Tr	02.75	74-75	46	1	1

SMITH, Alexander
Lancaster, 29 October, 1938 (G)

League Club	Source	Date Signed	Seasons Played	Apps	Subs	Gls
Accrington St.	Weymouth	08.61				
Bolton W.	Tr	03.62	62-67	19	0	0
Halifax T.	Tr	01.68	67-75	341	0	0
Preston N. E.	Tr	05.76	76	8	0	0

SMITH, R. Alexander
Billingham, 6 February, 1944 (D)

League Club	Source	Date Signed	Seasons Played	Apps	Subs	Gls
Middlesbrough	Jnrs	12.61	65-71	119	2	1
Darlington	Bangor C.	07.74	74-75	43	0	0

SMITH, Alfred

League Club	Source	Date Signed	Seasons Played	Apps	Subs	Gls
Walsall		10.53	53	1	-	0

SMITH, Anthony
Sunderland, 31 December, 1943 (CF)

League Club	Source	Date Signed	Seasons Played	Apps	Subs	Gls
West Ham U.	Consett	11.63				
Watford	Tr	06.66	66	3	0	0
Hartlepool U.		10.67	67	2	0	1

SMITH, Anthony
Sunderland, 20 February, 1957 (CD)

League Club	Source	Date Signed	Seasons Played	Apps	Subs	Gls
Newcastle U.	Jnrs	07.75	77	1	1	0
Peterborough U.	Tr	03.79	78-81	68	0	5
Halifax T.	Tr	08.82	82-83	81	2	3
Hartlepool U.	Tr	08.84	84-88	200	0	8

SMITH, Anthony
Sunderland, 21 September, 1971 E Yth (LB)

League Club	Source	Date Signed	Seasons Played	Apps	Subs	Gls
Sunderland	YT	07.90	90-91	11	0	0
Hartlepool U.	L	01.92	91	4	1	0

SMITH, Archibald N.
Larkhall, 23 October, 1924 (CF)

League Club	Source	Date Signed	Seasons Played	Apps	Subs	Gls
Exeter C.	Hamilton Acad.	05.48	48-51	115	-	43
Carlisle U.	Tr	08.52	52-53	31	-	8

SMITH, Arthur E.
Bourne, 13 February, 1922 (FB)

League Club	Source	Date Signed	Seasons Played	Apps	Subs	Gls
Luton T.		05.45				
Aldershot	Tr	08.47	47-48	2	-	0

SMITH, Arthur E.
Whetstone (Leics), 5 September, 1921 (IF)

League Club	Source	Date Signed	Seasons Played	Apps	Subs	Gls
Leicester C.	Jnrs	02.41	46-47	17	-	3
West Bromwich A.	Tr	06.48	48-51	49	-	12
Plymouth Arg.	Tr	08.52	52-53	28	-	9
Crewe Alex.	Tr	06.54	54	4	-	0

SMITH, Barrie A.
Colchester, 3 March, 1953 (G)

League Club	Source	Date Signed	Seasons Played	Apps	Subs	Gls
Colchester U.	Jnrs	07.71	71-72	49	0	0

SMITH, Barry J.
Wigan, 21 September, 1969

League Club	Source	Date Signed	Seasons Played	Apps	Subs	Gls
Wigan Ath. (YT)	YT	07.86	87	0	1	0

SMITH, J. Barry
South Kirkby, 15 March, 1934 (F)

League Club	Source	Date Signed	Seasons Played	Apps	Subs	Gls
Leeds U.	Farsley Celtic	10.51	52	2	-	1
Bradford P. A.	Tr	05.55	55-56	64	-	38
Wrexham	Tr	06.57	57	18	-	10
Stockport Co.	Tr	07.58	58	17	-	5
Oldham Ath.	Headington U.	08.60	60	1	-	0

SMITH, Brian
Bolton, 12 September, 1955 E Yth (M)

League Club	Source	Date Signed	Seasons Played	Apps	Subs	Gls
Bolton W.	App	09.73	74-78	43	6	3
Bradford C.	L	10.77	77	8	0	0
Blackpool	Tr	08.79	79	18	1	1
Bournemouth	Tr	12.80	80-81	40	0	2
Bury	Tr	03.82	81	6	0	0

SMITH, Brian
Sheffield, 27 October, 1966 (D)

League Club	Source	Date Signed	Seasons Played	Apps	Subs	Gls
Sheffield U.	App	10.84	84-88	81	3	0
Scunthorpe U.	L	03.87	86	6	0	1

SMITH, Charles
Oswaldwistle, 27 June, 1930 (CF)

League Club	Source	Date Signed	Seasons Played	Apps	Subs	Gls
Accrington St. (Am)	Oswaldwistle Imms	06.50	50	1	-	0

SMITH, Charles J.
Cardiff, 26 August, 1915 (OR)

League Club	Source	Date Signed	Seasons Played	Apps	Subs	Gls
Torquay U.	Aberdeen	04.46	46	23	-	0

League Club	Source	Date Signed	Seasons Played	Apps	Subs	Gls
SMITH, Christopher J.						
Christchurch, 28 March, 1966						(RB)
Bristol Rov. (N/C)	Cheltenham T.	05.85	84	1	0	0
SMITH, Colin						
Bishop Auckland, 30 November, 1951						(D)
Leeds U.	App	11.69				
Darlington (N/C)		09.84	84	2	0	0
SMITH, Colin R.						
Ruddington, 3 November, 1958						(CD)
Nottingham F.	Jnrs	06.77				
Norwich C.	Tr	08.82	82	2	2	0
Cardiff C.	Hong Kong	10.83	83-84	50	0	3
Aldershot	Tr	12.84	84-89	185	5	4
SMITH, E. Colin						
Doncaster, 3 March, 1936						(CF)
Hull C.		01.57	56-59	65	-	39
Rotherham U.	Tr	06.60	60	9	-	3
SMITH, W. Conway						
Huddersfield, 13 July, 1926						(IF)
Huddersfield T.	Jnrs	05.45	47-50	37	-	5
Queens Park R.	Tr	03.51	50-55	175	-	82
Halifax T.	Tr	06.56	56-61	183	-	73
SMITH, Daniel						
Armadale, 7 September, 1921						(W)
West Bromwich A.	Coltness U.	05.45	47	7	-	1
Chesterfield	Tr	06.48	48	15	-	4
Crewe Alex.	Tr	08.49	49-51	110	-	15
SMITH, F. David						
Chesterfield, 27 July, 1936						(W)
Chesterfield	Jnrs	09.53	53	7	-	0
Mansfield T.	Boston U.	08.55	55-56	31	-	4
Derby Co.	Tr	07.57				
Coventry C.	Tr	11.57	57-58	28	-	2
SMITH, David						
Durham, 12 October, 1915						(OR)
Newcastle U.		10.35	35	1	-	0
Northampton T.	South Shields	09.43	46-50	128	-	30
SMITH, David						
Thornaby, 8 December, 1947 E Sch						(M)
Middlesbrough	App	12.64	67	1	1	0
Lincoln C.	Tr	07.68	68-77	358	13	52
Rotherham U.	Tr	07.78	78-79	32	1	3
SMITH, David						
Stonehouse (Glos), 29 March, 1968 Eu21-10						(LW)
Coventry C.	YT	07.86	87-91	138	10	18
SMITH, David A.						
Sidcup, 25 June, 1961						(LW)
Gillingham	Welling U.	08.86	86-88	90	14	10
Bristol C.	Tr	08.89	89-91	94	3	10
Plymouth Arg.	Tr	12.91	91	14	4	2
SMITH, David B.						
Sheffield, 11 December, 1950						(F)
Huddersfield T.	Jnrs	04.69	71-73	27	7	7
Stockport Co.	L	12.73	73	7	1	0
Halifax T.	L	03.74	73	12	1	4
Cambridge U.	Tr	07.74	74	15	2	3
Hartlepool U.	Tr	02.75	74-75	42	0	13
SMITH, David B.						
Dundee, 22 September, 1933						(FB)
Burnley	Jnrs	09.50	54-60	99	-	1
Brighton & H. A.	Tr	07.61	61	15	-	0
Bristol C.	Tr	07.62	62	3	-	0
SMITH, David C.						
Liverpool, 26 December, 1970						(M)
Norwich C.	YT	07.89	89-91	3	2	0
SMITH, David F.						
Nottingham, 11 March, 1956						(M)
Notts Co.	App	03.74	75-77	45	5	0
Torquay U.	Tr	06.79	79	20	3	1
SMITH, David J.						
Frome, 13 October, 1964						(D)
Bristol Rov. (App)	Jnrs	07.81	81	0	1	0
SMITH, David R.						
Bristol, 5 October, 1934 E Yth						(OL)
Bristol C.	Jnrs	04.53	55-58	21	-	1
Millwall	Tr	09.59	59	13	-	1
SMITH, Dean						
Leicester, 28 November, 1958						(F)
Leicester C.	App	12.76	77	8	2	1
Brentford	Tr	10.78	78-80	48	6	16
SMITH, Dean						
West Bromwich, 19 March, 1971						(CD)
Walsall	YT	07.89	88-91	63	1	0
SMITH, Denis N.						
Grimsby, 23 December, 1932						(FB)
Grimsby T.	Jnrs	07.50	52-53	4	-	0
SMITH, Dennis						
Stoke, 19 November, 1947						(CD)
Stoke C.	Jnrs	09.66	68-81	406	1	30
York C.	L	03.82	81	7	0	1
York C. (N/C)	Tr	08.82	82	30	0	4
SMITH, Dennis						
Nelson, 22 August, 1925						(WH)
Hull C.	Frickley Colly	07.46	46	15	-	0
Accrington St.	Tr	10.47	47-53	155	-	15
SMITH, Derek L.						
Liverpool, 5 July, 1946						(CF)
Everton	App	11.63	65-66	3	1	0
Tranmere Rov.	Tr	03.68	67-68	78	5	21
SMITH, Edward F.						
Stoke, 19 October, 1920						(CF)
Arsenal	Margate	05.38				
Aldershot	Tr	06.47	47	7	-	2
SMITH, Edward W. A.						
London, 23 March, 1929						(CF)
Chelsea	Wealdstone	05.50				
Bournemouth	Tr	08.52				
Watford	Tr	07.53	53-54	38	-	12
Northampton T.	Tr	01.55	54-55	53	-	8
Colchester U.	Tr	06.56	56	35	-	13
Queens Park R.	Tr	07.57	57	18	-	0
SMITH, Edward W. J.						
Grays, 3 September, 1914						(FB)
Millwall	Barking	05.35	35-47	143	-	1
SMITH, J. Eric						
Glasgow, 29 July, 1934 S-2						(WH)
Leeds U.	Glasgow Celtic	06.60	60-62	65	-	3
SMITH, Eric T. H.						
Tamworth, 3 November, 1921						(CH)
Leicester C.	Castle Bromwich	04.43	46	5	-	0
SMITH, Eric V.						
Reading, 20 March, 1928 Died 1992						(HB)
Reading		04.49	52-55	61	-	1
SMITH, Frank A.						
Colchester, 30 April, 1936						(G)
Tottenham H.	Colchester Casuals	02.54				
Queens Park R.	Tr	05.62	62-65	64	0	0
SMITH, Frederick A.						
Aberdeen, 14 February, 1926						(IF)
Hull C.	Aberdeen	10.49	49-50	17	-	1
Sheffield U.	Tr	04.51	50-52	40	-	12
Millwall	Tr	01.53	52-55	92	-	20
Chesterfield	Tr	07.56	56	7	-	1
SMITH, Frederick E.						
Draycott, 7 May, 1926						(CF)
Derby Co.	Draycott	06.47	47	1	-	0
Sheffield U.	Tr	03.48	47-51	53	-	17
Manchester C.	Tr	05.52	52	2	-	1
Grimsby T.	Tr	09.52	52-53	50	-	24
Bradford C.	Tr	07.54	54	9	-	3
SMITH, Frederick G. S.						
West Sleekburn, 25 December, 1942						(FB)
Burnley	Jnrs	12.59	63-69	84	0	1
Portsmouth	Tr	07.70	70-72	82	0	1
Halifax T.	Tr	09.74	74	3	0	0

SMITH, Gary A.
Trowbridge, 12 November, 1962 (W)

League Club	Source	Date Signed	Seasons Played	Apps	Subs	Gls
Bristol C.	App	11.79	80	7	7	0

SMITH, Gary E.
Chasetown, 30 December, 1968 (M)

League Club	Source	Date Signed	Seasons Played	Apps	Subs	Gls
Walsall	App	01.87				
Gillingham (N/C)	Chasetown	07.89	89	0	1	0

SMITH, Gary M.
Greenford, 4 November, 1955 (CD)

League Club	Source	Date Signed	Seasons Played	Apps	Subs	Gls
Brentford		01.74	74	3	0	0

SMITH, Gary N.
Harlow, 3 December, 1968 (D)

League Club	Source	Date Signed	Seasons Played	Apps	Subs	Gls
Fulham	App	08.86	85	0	1	0
Colchester U. (N/C)	Tr	09.87	87	11	0	0

SMITH, Gavin
Cambuslang, 25 September, 1917 (OR)

League Club	Source	Date Signed	Seasons Played	Apps	Subs	Gls
Barnsley	Dumbarton	02.39	46-53	257	-	36

SMITH, Geoffrey
Bingley, 14 March, 1928 (G)

League Club	Source	Date Signed	Seasons Played	Apps	Subs	Gls
Bradford C.	Rossendale U.	12.52	52-58	253	-	0

SMITH, George
Newcastle, 7 October, 1945 (M)

League Club	Source	Date Signed	Seasons Played	Apps	Subs	Gls
Newcastle U.	App	09.63				
Barrow	Tr	03.65	64-66	91	1	11
Portsmouth	Tr	05.67	67-68	64	0	3
Middlesbrough	Tr	01.69	68-70	74	0	0
Birmingham C.	Tr	03.71	70-72	36	3	0
Cardiff C.	Tr	06.73	73-74	43	2	1
Swansea C.	Tr	05.75	75-77	86	2	8
Hartlepool U.	Tr	10.77	77-79	81	4	2

SMITH, George B.
Fleetwood, 7 February, 1921 (IF)

League Club	Source	Date Signed	Seasons Played	Apps	Subs	Gls
Manchester C.	Salford Adelphi	05.38	46-51	166	-	75
Chesterfield	Tr	10.51	51-57	250	-	97

SMITH, George C.
Bromley, 23 April, 1915 Died 1983 (CH)

League Club	Source	Date Signed	Seasons Played	Apps	Subs	Gls
Charlton Ath.	Bexleyheath	08.38	38	1	-	0
Brentford	Tr	11.45	46	41	-	1
Queens Park R.	Tr	06.47	47-48	75	-	1
Ipswich T.	Tr	09.49	49	8	-	0

SMITH, George C. R.
Portsmouth, 24 March, 1919 (WH)

League Club	Source	Date Signed	Seasons Played	Apps	Subs	Gls
Southampton	Guernsey R.	07.38	38-48	95	-	1
Crystal Palace	Tr	05.50	50	7	-	0

SMITH, George H.
Nottingham, 13 April, 1936 (G)

League Club	Source	Date Signed	Seasons Played	Apps	Subs	Gls
Notts Co.	Dale R.	07.53	55-66	323	0	0
Hartlepool U.	Tr	07.67	67-69	112	0	0

SMITH, George T.

League Club	Source	Date Signed	Seasons Played	Apps	Subs	Gls
Walsall (Am)		09.53	53	1	-	0

SMITH, Gerald
Huddersfield, 18 November, 1939 (OL)

League Club	Source	Date Signed	Seasons Played	Apps	Subs	Gls
Huddersfield T.	Jnrs	05.58				
Bradford C.	Tr	07.60	60	7	-	0

SMITH, Gordon D.
Kilwinning, 29 December, 1954 Su21-1 (W)

League Club	Source	Date Signed	Seasons Played	Apps	Subs	Gls
Brighton & H. A.	Glasgow Rangers	06.80	80-83	97	12	22
Manchester C.	Tr	03.84	83-85	40	2	13
Oldham Ath.	Tr	01.86	85	14	1	0

SMITH, Gordon M.
Glasgow, 3 July, 1954 (FB)

League Club	Source	Date Signed	Seasons Played	Apps	Subs	Gls
Aston Villa	St Johnstone	08.76	76-78	76	3	0
Tottenham H.	Tr	02.79	78-81	34	4	1
Wolverhampton W.	Tr	08.82	82-83	35	3	3

SMITH, Graham
Wimbledon, 7 August, 1951 (CD)

League Club	Source	Date Signed	Seasons Played	Apps	Subs	Gls
Brentford	Wimbledon	08.74	74	7	0	0

SMITH, Graham L.
Pudsey, 20 June, 1946 (RB)

League Club	Source	Date Signed	Seasons Played	Apps	Subs	Gls
Leeds U.	Jnrs	02.64				
Rochdale	Tr	06.66	66-73	316	1	3
Stockport Co.	Tr	07.74	74-78	147	4	2

SMITH, Graham W. C.
Liverpool, 2 November, 1947 (G)

League Club	Source	Date Signed	Seasons Played	Apps	Subs	Gls
Notts Co.	Loughborough Col.	08.68	68	10	0	0
Colchester U.	Tr	06.69	69-71	95	0	0
West Bromwich A.	Tr	12.71	71-72	10	0	0
Cambridge U.	Tr	01.73	72-75	85	0	0

SMITH, Granville
Mountain Ash, 4 February, 1937 (W)

League Club	Source	Date Signed	Seasons Played	Apps	Subs	Gls
Bristol Rov.		05.57	58-59	21	-	2
Newport Co.	Tr	06.60	60-67	241	0	36

SMITH, Harold A.
Wolverhampton, 10 October, 1932 (FB)

League Club	Source	Date Signed	Seasons Played	Apps	Subs	Gls
Torquay U.	West Bromwich A. (Am)	01.54	53-60	188	-	0
Bristol C.	Tr	07.61	61	1	-	0

SMITH, Henry S. (Harry)
Chester, 27 August, 1930 (WH)

League Club	Source	Date Signed	Seasons Played	Apps	Subs	Gls
Chester C.		01.53	52-57	74	-	7

SMITH, Henry S.
Newburn, 11 October, 1908 (FB)

League Club	Source	Date Signed	Seasons Played	Apps	Subs	Gls
Darlington		08.37	37-38	65	-	1
Bristol Rov.	Tr	08.39	46	3	-	0

SMITH, Herbert H.
Birmingham, 17 December, 1922 (OR)

League Club	Source	Date Signed	Seasons Played	Apps	Subs	Gls
Aston Villa	Moor Green	05.47	49-53	51	-	8
Southend U.	Tr	06.54	54	5	-	0

SMITH, Ian L. T.
Edinburgh, 2 April, 1952 (F)

League Club	Source	Date Signed	Seasons Played	Apps	Subs	Gls
Birmingham C.	Queens Park	03.75	74	0	2	0

SMITH, Ian R.
Rotherham, 15 February, 1957 E Yth (FB)

League Club	Source	Date Signed	Seasons Played	Apps	Subs	Gls
Tottenham H.	App	04.74	75	2	0	0
Rotherham U.	Tr	06.76	77	3	1	0

SMITH, James
(OR)

League Club	Source	Date Signed	Seasons Played	Apps	Subs	Gls
Burnley		03.43				
Leyton Orient	Tr	04.46	46-47	22	-	3

SMITH, James
Johnstone, 22 November, 1969 (F)

League Club	Source	Date Signed	Seasons Played	Apps	Subs	Gls
Torquay U.	YT	07.88	87-89	28	17	5

SMITH, James
Glasgow, 20 January, 1947 Su23-1/SF Lge/S-4 (M)

League Club	Source	Date Signed	Seasons Played	Apps	Subs	Gls
Newcastle U.	Aberdeen	08.69	69-74	124	5	13

SMITH, James A.
Coatbridge, 9 September, 1925 (OL)

League Club	Source	Date Signed	Seasons Played	Apps	Subs	Gls
Walsall	Coatdyke Jnrs	06.48	48	2	-	0

SMITH, James A. G.
Arbroath, 16 October, 1937 S Sch (D)

League Club	Source	Date Signed	Seasons Played	Apps	Subs	Gls
Preston N. E.	Arbroath Lads	10.55	58-68	314	0	13
Stockport Co.	Tr	10.69	69-70	78	0	2

SMITH, James H.
Sheffield, 6 December, 1930 (W)

League Club	Source	Date Signed	Seasons Played	Apps	Subs	Gls
Chelsea	Shildon	04.51	51-53	19	-	3
Leyton Orient	Tr	07.55	55-57	37	-	3

SMITH, James M.
Sheffield, 17 October, 1940 (WH)

League Club	Source	Date Signed	Seasons Played	Apps	Subs	Gls
Sheffield U.		01.59				
Aldershot	Tr	07.61	61-64	74	-	1
Halifax T.	Tr	07.65	65-67	112	1	7
Lincoln C.	Tr	03.68	67-68	54	0	0
Colchester U.	Boston U.	11.72	72	7	1	0

SMITH, Jeffrey E.
Macclesfield, 8 December, 1935 (LB)

League Club	Source	Date Signed	Seasons Played	Apps	Subs	Gls
Sheffield U.	Jnrs	06.53	56	1	-	0
Lincoln C.	Tr	02.58	57-66	318	0	2

SMITH, Jeremy
Leeds, 20 July, 1971 (F)

League Club	Source	Date Signed	Seasons Played	Apps	Subs	Gls
Wigan Ath.	Goole T.	08.91	91	0	6	0

SMITH, John
Coatbridge, 27 November, 1956 (F)

League Club	Source	Date Signed	Seasons Played	Apps	Subs	Gls
Preston N. E.	App	11.74	73-78	80	11	14
Halifax T. (N/C)		11.79	79	26	2	6

League Club	Source	Date Signed	Seasons Played	Career Record Apps	Subs	Gls

SMITH, John
Liverpool, 14 March, 1953 E Sch (M)

League Club	Source	Date Signed	Seasons Played	Apps	Subs	Gls
Everton	App	09.70	73	2	0	0
Carlisle U.	Tr	06.76	76	4	1	0
Southport	L	02.77	76	17	1	2

SMITH, John (Jack)
Hartlepool, 24 April, 1936 (CF)

League Club	Source	Date Signed	Seasons Played	Apps	Subs	Gls
Hartlepool U.	Jnrs	05.53	53-59	119	-	49
Watford	Tr	07.60	60	20	-	8
Swindon T.	Tr	06.61	61-63	97	-	37
Brighton & H. A.	Tr	01.64	63-66	88	0	33
Notts Co.	Tr	09.66	66-68	74	4	12

SMITH, John
Shoreditch, 4 January, 1939 Died 1988 E Yth/Eu23-1 (IF)

League Club	Source	Date Signed	Seasons Played	Apps	Subs	Gls
West Ham U.	Jnrs	01.56	56-59	127	-	20
Tottenham H.	Tr	03.60	59-63	21	-	1
Coventry C.	Tr	03.64	63-65	34	1	1
Leyton Orient	Tr	10.65	65-66	38	1	3
Torquay U.	Tr	10.66	66-67	68	0	8
Swindon T.	Tr	06.68	68-70	79	5	9
Walsall	Tr	06.71	71	13	0	1

SMITH, John
Stocksbridge, 15 September, 1910 Died 1986 (G)

League Club	Source	Date Signed	Seasons Played	Apps	Subs	Gls
Sheffield U.	Worksop T.	10.30	30-49	348	-	0

SMITH, John
Wrexham, 13 September, 1944 (FB)

League Club	Source	Date Signed	Seasons Played	Apps	Subs	Gls
Wrexham	Jnrs	05.63	64-65	23	0	0

SMITH, John
Batley, 17 February, 1915 (CF)

League Club	Source	Date Signed	Seasons Played	Apps	Subs	Gls
Huddersfield T.	Whitehall Print	06.32	32-34	45	-	24
Newcastle U.	Tr	09.34	34-37	104	-	69
Manchester U.	Tr	02.38	37-38	36	-	14
Blackburn Rov.	Tr	03.46	46	30	-	12
Port Vale	Tr	05.47	46-47	29	-	11

SMITH, John
Liverpool (IF)

League Club	Source	Date Signed	Seasons Played	Apps	Subs	Gls
Ipswich T.		12.45	46	2	-	0

SMITH, John
Liverpool, 23 July, 1970 (M)

League Club	Source	Date Signed	Seasons Played	Apps	Subs	Gls
Tranmere Rov.	Jnrs	11.87	88	1	1	0

SMITH, John E.
Romford, 9 November, 1930 Died 1991 E Yth (LB)

League Club	Source	Date Signed	Seasons Played	Apps	Subs	Gls
Millwall	Barking	04.56	55-57	64	-	1

SMITH, John O.
Leicester, 4 September, 1928 (WH)

League Club	Source	Date Signed	Seasons Played	Apps	Subs	Gls
Northampton T.		09.49	50-59	189	-	12

SMITH, John T.
Birkenhead, 21 December, 1927 (CF)

League Club	Source	Date Signed	Seasons Played	Apps	Subs	Gls
Liverpool	Bromborough	03.51	51-53	57	-	14
Torquay U.	Tr	05.54	54-57	65	-	16

SMITH, John V.
Plymouth, 12 November, 1927 (FB)

League Club	Source	Date Signed	Seasons Played	Apps	Subs	Gls
Plymouth Arg.	Plymouth U.	07.50	50-52	3	-	0
Torquay U.	Tr	07.54	54-59	164	-	0

SMITH, John W. (Jackie)
Camden, 27 May, 1920 (OR)

League Club	Source	Date Signed	Seasons Played	Apps	Subs	Gls
Bradford P. A.		10.43	46-52	204	-	26

SMITH, Keith
Sheffield, 17 October, 1963 (F)

League Club	Source	Date Signed	Seasons Played	Apps	Subs	Gls
Exeter C.	Alfreton T.	01.89	88	2	13	2

SMITH, Keith W.
Swadlincote, 15 September, 1940 (CF)

League Club	Source	Date Signed	Seasons Played	Apps	Subs	Gls
West Bromwich A.	Jnrs	01.58	59-62	63	-	30
Peterborough U.	Tr	06.63	63-64	55	-	28
Crystal Palace	Tr	11.64	64-65	47	3	14
Darlington	Tr	11.66	66	17	0	2
Leyton Orient	Tr	05.67	66	3	0	0
Notts Co.	Tr	07.67	67-69	85	4	7

SMITH, Kenneth
South Shields, 21 May, 1932 (CF)

League Club	Source	Date Signed	Seasons Played	Apps	Subs	Gls
Sunderland	Jnrs	08.49	50-52	5	-	2
Blackpool	Headington U.	12.54	54-57	6	-	4
Shrewsbury T.	Tr	10.57	57-58	44	-	20
Gateshead	Tr	11.58	58-59	41	-	16
Darlington	Tr	12.59	59	24	-	7
Carlisle U.	Tr	07.60	60	13	-	12
Halifax T.	Canada	10.61	61	23	-	8

SMITH, Kenneth
Consett, 7 December, 1927 (F)

League Club	Source	Date Signed	Seasons Played	Apps	Subs	Gls
Blackpool	Annfield Plain	04.49				
Gateshead	Tr	08.52	52-58	259	-	74

SMITH, Kenneth G.
Norwich, 22 April, 1936 (FB)

League Club	Source	Date Signed	Seasons Played	Apps	Subs	Gls
Norwich C.	Gothic	09.55	55-56	10	-	0

SMITH, Kevan
Eaglescliffe, 13 December, 1959 (CD)

League Club	Source	Date Signed	Seasons Played	Apps	Subs	Gls
Darlington	Stockton	09.79	79-84	242	3	11
Rotherham U.	Tr	07.85	85-86	59	0	4
Coventry C.	Tr	12.86	87	5	1	0
York C.	Tr	05.88	88	30	1	5
Darlington	Tr	06.89	90-91	85	0	5

SMITH, Kevin J.
Wallsend, 20 April, 1965 (M)

League Club	Source	Date Signed	Seasons Played	Apps	Subs	Gls
Cambridge U.	App	11.82	82-84	30	8	4
Exeter C.	Tr	10.84	84	21	4	2
Torquay U.	Tr	07.85	85	20	3	1

SMITH, Kevin P.
St Pauls Cray, 5 December, 1962 (M)

League Club	Source	Date Signed	Seasons Played	Apps	Subs	Gls
Charlton Ath.	App	08.80	79-83	79	25	14

SMITH, Leslie
Manchester, 2 October, 1920 (RH)

League Club	Source	Date Signed	Seasons Played	Apps	Subs	Gls
Huddersfield T.	Stockport Co. (Am)	03.46	46-47	37	-	0
Oldham Ath.	Tr	07.49	49-55	178	-	3

SMITH, Leslie ("Snowy")
Tamworth, 16 November, 1921 (RH)

League Club	Source	Date Signed	Seasons Played	Apps	Subs	Gls
Mansfield T.	Nottingham F. (Am)	08.45	46-47	38	-	0

SMITH, Leslie G. F.
Ealing, 13 March, 1918 E-1 (OL)

League Club	Source	Date Signed	Seasons Played	Apps	Subs	Gls
Brentford	Hayes	03.36	36-38	62	-	7
Aston Villa	Tr	10.45	46-51	181	-	31
Brentford	Tr	06.52	52	14	-	1

SMITH, Leslie J.
Halesowen, 24 December, 1927 (OR)

League Club	Source	Date Signed	Seasons Played	Apps	Subs	Gls
Wolverhampton W.	Jnrs	04.46	47-55	88	-	22
Aston Villa	Tr	02.56	55-58	115	-	24

SMITH, Lindsay J.
Enfield, 18 September, 1954 (CD)

League Club	Source	Date Signed	Seasons Played	Apps	Subs	Gls
Colchester U.	App	03.72	70-76	185	27	16
Charlton Ath.	L	08.77	77	1	0	0
Millwall	L	09.77	77	4	1	0
Cambridge U.	Tr	10.77	77-82	173	1	7
Lincoln C.	L	09.81	81	5	0	0
Plymouth Arg.	Tr	10.82	82-83	76	0	5
Millwall	Tr	07.84	84-85	54	1	5
Cambridge U.	Tr	07.86	86-88	102	0	16

SMITH, Lionel
Mexborough, 23 August, 1920 Died 1980 EF Lge/E-6 (FB)

League Club	Source	Date Signed	Seasons Played	Apps	Subs	Gls
Arsenal	Denaby U.	08.39	47-53	162	-	0
Watford	Tr	06.54	54	7	-	0

SMITH, Malcolm
Stockton, 21 September, 1953 (F)

League Club	Source	Date Signed	Seasons Played	Apps	Subs	Gls
Middlesbrough	App	10.70	71-75	32	24	11
Bury	L	10.75	75	5	0	1
Blackpool	L	01.76	75	8	0	5
Burnley	Tr	09.76	76-79	82	3	17
York C.	Tr	08.80	80-81	28	7	6

SMITH, Malcolm A.
Maidstone, 3 August, 1970 (M)

League Club	Source	Date Signed	Seasons Played	Apps	Subs	Gls
Gillingham	YT	06.88	87	1	1	0

SMITH, Mark
Redruth, 21 September, 1963 (LB)

League Club	Source	Date Signed	Seasons Played	Apps	Subs	Gls
Bristol C.	App	09.81	81	1	4	0
Plymouth Arg. (N/C)	Exmouth T.	03.84	83	3	0	0

SMITH, Mark A.
Torquay, 9 October, 1961 (FB)

League Club	Source	Date Signed	Seasons Played	Apps	Subs	Gls
Torquay U. (N/C)		09.81	81-83	28	2	0

SMITH, Mark A.
Bellshill, 16 December, 1964 (W)

League Club	Source	Date Signed	Seasons Played	Apps	Subs	Gls
Stoke C. (L)	Dunfermline Ath.	02.90	89	2	0	0
Nottingham F.	Tr	03.90				
Reading	L	12.90	90	3	0	0
Mansfield T.	L	03.91	90	6	1	0
Shrewsbury T.	Tr	08.91	91	19	3	1

SMITH, Mark C.
Sheffield, 21 March, 1960 Eu21-5 (CD)

League Club	Source	Date Signed	Seasons Played	Apps	Subs	Gls
Sheffield Wed.	App	03.78	77-86	281	1	16
Plymouth Arg.	Tr	07.87	87-89	82	0	6
Barnsley	Tr	11.89	89-91	98	2	10

SMITH, Mark C.
Sheffield, 19 December, 1961 (LW)

League Club	Source	Date Signed	Seasons Played	Apps	Subs	Gls
Sheffield U.	Jnrs	08.80				
Scunthorpe U. (N/C)	Gainsborough Trin.	09.85	85	0	1	0
Rochdale	Kettering T.	07.88	88	26	1	7
Huddersfield T.	Tr	02.89	88-90	85	11	11
Grimsby T.	Tr	03.91	90-91	29	22	4

SMITH, Mark L.
Canning Town, 10 October, 1961 (LB)

League Club	Source	Date Signed	Seasons Played	Apps	Subs	Gls
West Ham U.	App	10.79	79	1	0	0

SMITH, Mark S.
Carlisle, 4 April, 1962 E Yth (FB)

League Club	Source	Date Signed	Seasons Played	Apps	Subs	Gls
Leyton Orient	App	12.79	78-79	3	0	0

SMITH, Martyn C.
Stoke, 16 September, 1961 (W)

League Club	Source	Date Signed	Seasons Played	Apps	Subs	Gls
Port Vale	Leek T.	07.84	84	12	1	1

SMITH, Michael
Sunderland, 28 October, 1958 (CD)

League Club	Source	Date Signed	Seasons Played	Apps	Subs	Gls
Lincoln C.	Lambton Street B.C.	07.77	77-78	20	5	0
Wimbledon	Tr	12.79	79-86	203	2	14
Aldershot	L	10.84	84	7	0	0
Hartlepool U.	Seaham Red Star	10.89	89-91	53	2	5

SMITH, Michael
Haddington, 15 October, 1923 (CF)

League Club	Source	Date Signed	Seasons Played	Apps	Subs	Gls
Plymouth Arg.	Preston A.	02.48	47	1	-	0
Chelsea	Tr	06.48				

SMITH, Michael J.
Derby, 22 September, 1935 E Sch (CH)

League Club	Source	Date Signed	Seasons Played	Apps	Subs	Gls
Derby Co.	Jnrs	10.52	57-60	22	-	0
Bradford C.	Tr	06.61	61-65	134	0	0

SMITH, Michael K.
Hull, 19 December, 1968 (W)

League Club	Source	Date Signed	Seasons Played	Apps	Subs	Gls
Hull C.	YT	05.87	88-90	14	5	1

SMITH, Neil
Warley, 10 February, 1970 (M)

League Club	Source	Date Signed	Seasons Played	Apps	Subs	Gls
Shrewsbury T.	YT	07.88	87	0	1	0
Lincoln C.	Redditch U.	03.90	89-91	13	4	0

SMITH, Neil J.
Lambeth, 30 September, 1971 (M)

League Club	Source	Date Signed	Seasons Played	Apps	Subs	Gls
Tottenham H.	YT	07.90				
Gillingham	Tr	10.91	91	26	0	2

SMITH, Nicholas L.
Berkeley, 28 January, 1969 (LW)

League Club	Source	Date Signed	Seasons Played	Apps	Subs	Gls
Southend U.	YT	07.87	86-89	49	11	6

SMITH, Nigel G.
Manchester, 22 April, 1959 (CD)

League Club	Source	Date Signed	Seasons Played	Apps	Subs	Gls
Stockport Co.	Blackburn Rov. (Am)	08.79	80-85	118	5	1

SMITH, Nigel K.
Bath, 12 January, 1966 (M)

League Club	Source	Date Signed	Seasons Played	Apps	Subs	Gls
Bristol C.	App	01.84	82	2	0	0
Exeter C.	L	11.84	84	1	0	0

SMITH, Nigel P.
Banstead, 3 January, 1958 (CD)

League Club	Source	Date Signed	Seasons Played	Apps	Subs	Gls
Brentford	Banstead	03.75	74-78	81	4	0
Cambridge U.	Tr	11.78	78	0	1	0

SMITH, Nigel P.
Leeds, 21 December, 1969 (W)

League Club	Source	Date Signed	Seasons Played	Apps	Subs	Gls
Leeds U. (N/C)	YT	07.88				
Burnley	Tr	07.89	89-90	6	7	0
Bury	Tr	08.91	91	30	4	3

SMITH, Norman
Darwen, 2 January, 1925 (WH)

League Club	Source	Date Signed	Seasons Played	Apps	Subs	Gls
Arsenal	Darwen	07.47				
Barnsley	Tr	10.52	52-58	156	-	14

SMITH, Norman H.
Burton, 27 January, 1924 (IF)

League Club	Source	Date Signed	Seasons Played	Apps	Subs	Gls
Accrington St.		02.46	46-47	39	-	6
Oldham Ath.	Tr	06.48	48	1	-	0

SMITH, Norman L.
Boldon, 23 November, 1919 (CF)

League Club	Source	Date Signed	Seasons Played	Apps	Subs	Gls
Coventry C.	Standard Apps	05.38	38-47	13	-	0
Millwall	Tr	12.47	47	10	-	0

SMITH, Norman L.
Carshalton, 2 July, 1928 E Amat (WH)

League Club	Source	Date Signed	Seasons Played	Apps	Subs	Gls
Fulham	Bishop Auckland	07.48	52-56	60	-	0

SMITH, Paul A.
Bath, 12 September, 1953 (M)

League Club	Source	Date Signed	Seasons Played	Apps	Subs	Gls
Manchester C.	Jnrs	09.70				
Portsmouth	Tr	06.73	73	0	1	0

SMITH, Paul M.
Rotherham, 9 November, 1964 (F/RB)

League Club	Source	Date Signed	Seasons Played	Apps	Subs	Gls
Sheffield U.	App	11.82	82-85	29	7	1
Stockport Co.	L	08.85	85	7	0	5
Port Vale	Tr	07.86	86-87	42	2	7
Lincoln C.	Tr	08.87	88-91	143	3	24

SMITH, Paul S.
Wembley, 5 October, 1967 (RW)

League Club	Source	Date Signed	Seasons Played	Apps	Subs	Gls
Arsenal	App	10.85				
Brentford	Tr	08.87	87	10	7	1
Bristol Rov.	Tr	07.88	88	14	2	1
Torquay U.	Tr	03.89	88-91	65	9	12

SMITH, Paul W.
Doncaster, 15 October, 1954 (M)

League Club	Source	Date Signed	Seasons Played	Apps	Subs	Gls
Huddersfield T.	App	12.71	72-73	1	1	0
Cambridge U.	Tr	09.74	74-75	35	3	3

SMITH, Paul W.
Lenham (Kt), 18 September, 1971 (M)

League Club	Source	Date Signed	Seasons Played	Apps	Subs	Gls
Southend U.	YT	03.90	89-90	10	2	1

SMITH, Peter
Gosport, 6 May, 1932 (CF)

League Club	Source	Date Signed	Seasons Played	Apps	Subs	Gls
Gillingham	Gosport Bor.	11.54	54-56	6	-	0

SMITH, Peter A.
Islington, 20 November, 1964 (CD)

League Club	Source	Date Signed	Seasons Played	Apps	Subs	Gls
Leyton Orient	App	11.82	82	8	6	0

SMITH, Peter J.
Balham, 27 May, 1935 (WH)

League Club	Source	Date Signed	Seasons Played	Apps	Subs	Gls
Gillingham	Tunbridge Wells	06.58	58-59	39	-	2

SMITH, Philip N.
Fleetwood, 20 November, 1961 (F)

League Club	Source	Date Signed	Seasons Played	Apps	Subs	Gls
Blackpool	App	11.79	79	1	0	0

SMITH, Raymond
Portadown (NI), 20 November, 1950 (F)

League Club	Source	Date Signed	Seasons Played	Apps	Subs	Gls
Oldham Ath.	Glenavon	01.68	67	0	2	0

SMITH, H. Raymond
Hull, 13 September, 1934 (IF)

League Club	Source	Date Signed	Seasons Played	Apps	Subs	Gls
Hull C.	Jnrs	08.52	54-55	23	-	2
Peterborough U.	Tr	07.56	60-62	92	-	33
Northampton T.	Tr	10.62	62-63	23	-	7
Luton T.	Tr	10.63	63	10	-	1

SMITH, Raymond J.
Islington, 18 April, 1943 (CF)

League Club	Source	Date Signed	Seasons Played	Apps	Subs	Gls
Southend U.	Basildon U.	12.61	61-66	150	0	55
Wrexham	Tr	07.67	67-71	161	11	62
Peterborough U.	Tr	07.72	72	22	0	8

SMITH, Raymond S.
Evenwood, 14 April, 1929 (WH)

League Club	Source	Date Signed	Seasons Played	Apps	Subs	Gls
Luton T.	Evenwood T.	02.50	51-56	12	-	0
Southend U.	Tr	08.57	57-59	46	-	1

SMITH, Richard F.
Reading, 22 October, 1967 (W)

League Club	Source	Date Signed	Seasons Played	Apps	Subs	Gls
Wolverhampton W.	YT	07.85	85	0	1	0
Mansfield T. (N/C)	Moor Green	03.87	86	1	1	0

SMITH, Richard G.
Lutterworth, 3 October, 1970 (CD)

League Club	Source	Date Signed	Seasons Played	Apps	Subs	Gls
Leicester C.	YT	12.88	89-91	25	8	1
Cambridge U.	L	09.89	89	4	0	0

SMITH, Robert
Barnsley, 20 June, 1941 (WH)

League Club	Source	Date Signed	Seasons Played	Apps	Subs	Gls
Barnsley	Jnrs	06.60	62	3	-	0

SMITH, Robert A.
Skelton, 22 February, 1933 E-15 (CF)

League Club	Source	Date Signed	Seasons Played	Apps	Subs	Gls
Chelsea	Jnrs	05.50	50-55	74	-	23
Tottenham H.	Tr	12.55	55-63	271	-	176
Brighton & H. A.	Tr	05.64	64	31	-	18

SMITH, Robert G. J.
Bournemouth, 15 December, 1941 (WH)

League Club	Source	Date Signed	Seasons Played	Apps	Subs	Gls
Portsmouth	Jnrs	05.59				
Gillingham	Tr	07.62	62	7	-	0

SMITH, Robert M. S.
Hull, 25 April, 1950 (FB)

League Club	Source	Date Signed	Seasons Played	Apps	Subs	Gls
Hull C.	App	11.67				
Grimsby T.	Tr	09.71	71	10	1	0
Hartlepool U.	Tr	07.72	72-75	141	11	4

SMITH, Robert N.
Dalkeith, 21 December, 1953 (LB)

League Club	Source	Date Signed	Seasons Played	Apps	Subs	Gls
Leicester C.	Hibernian	12.78	78-85	175	6	21
Peterborough U.	L	02.82	81	5	0	0

SMITH, Robert W.
Prestbury, 14 March, 1944 E Yth (M)

League Club	Source	Date Signed	Seasons Played	Apps	Subs	Gls
Manchester U.	App	04.61				
Scunthorpe U.	Tr	03.65	64-66	82	0	12
Grimsby T.	Tr	01.67	66-67	48	4	1
Brighton & H. A.	Tr	06.68	68-70	72	3	2
Chester C.	Tr	06.71	71	2	0	0
Hartlepool U.	Tr	10.71	71-72	67	2	7

SMITH, Roger A.
Welwyn, 3 November, 1944 (OL)

League Club	Source	Date Signed	Seasons Played	Apps	Subs	Gls
Tottenham H.	App	06.62				
Exeter C.	Tr	06.66	66	6	0	3

SMITH, Roger W.
Tamworth, 19 February, 1945 (W)

League Club	Source	Date Signed	Seasons Played	Apps	Subs	Gls
Walsall	App	09.62	62-64	44	0	2
Port Vale	Tr	08.65	65	29	1	5
Walsall	Tr	05.66	66	8	1	0

SMITH, Ronald
Aberystwyth, 9 April, 1934 Died 1987 (RB)

League Club	Source	Date Signed	Seasons Played	Apps	Subs	Gls
Arsenal	Maidenhead U.	07.54				
Watford	Tr	08.55	55	2	-	0

SMITH, Ronald
Liverpool, 7 June, 1936 (OL)

League Club	Source	Date Signed	Seasons Played	Apps	Subs	Gls
Liverpool		12.57				
Bournemouth	Tr	05.59	59-60	36	-	6
Crewe Alex.	Tr	07.61	61-63	89	-	11
Port Vale	Tr	10.63	63-64	59	-	6
Southport	Tr	07.65	65-66	77	2	14

SMITH, Ronald H.
York, 25 November, 1929 (CH)

League Club	Source	Date Signed	Seasons Played	Apps	Subs	Gls
York C.	Harrogate R.I.	05.54	54	1	-	0

SMITH, Roy H.
India, 19 March, 1936 (F)

League Club	Source	Date Signed	Seasons Played	Apps	Subs	Gls
West Ham U.	Woodford Y.C.	06.55	55-56	6	-	1
Portsmouth	Hereford U.	01.62	61-62	10	-	3

SMITH, Roy L.
Shirebrook, 22 September, 1916 (G)

League Club	Source	Date Signed	Seasons Played	Apps	Subs	Gls
Sheffield Wed.	Selby T.	02.36	36-47	84	-	0
Notts Co.	Tr	12.48	48-52	110	-	0

SMITH, Roy P.
Haydock, 18 June, 1936 Died 1959 (CF)

League Club	Source	Date Signed	Seasons Played	Apps	Subs	Gls
Southport	Wigan Ath.	09.58	58	23	-	4

SMITH, Septimus C.
Whitburn, 15 March, 1912 E Sch/EF Lge/E-1 (WH)

League Club	Source	Date Signed	Seasons Played	Apps	Subs	Gls
Leicester C.	Whitburn	03.29	29-48	351	-	33

SMITH, G. Shaun
Leeds, 9 April, 1971 (LB)

League Club	Source	Date Signed	Seasons Played	Apps	Subs	Gls
Halifax T.	YT	07.89	88-89	6	1	0
Crewe Alex.	Emley	12.91	91	8	2	0

SMITH, Stanley J.
Kidsgrove, 24 February, 1931 (F)

League Club	Source	Date Signed	Seasons Played	Apps	Subs	Gls
Port Vale	Stoke C. (Am)	05.50	54-56	59	-	14
Crewe Alex.	Tr	07.57	57	28	-	6
Oldham Ath.	Tr	03.58	57	4	-	0

SMITH, Stanley W.
Coventry, 24 February, 1925 (WH)

League Club	Source	Date Signed	Seasons Played	Apps	Subs	Gls
Coventry C.	Nuffield Mechs	08.46	47-48	29	-	0

SMITH, C. Stephen
Birmingham, 13 January, 1961 (F)

League Club	Source	Date Signed	Seasons Played	Apps	Subs	Gls
Walsall	Bromsgrove Rov.	08.80	80-81	17	2	3

SMITH, Stephen
Huddersfield, 28 April, 1946 (M)

League Club	Source	Date Signed	Seasons Played	Apps	Subs	Gls
Huddersfield T.	Jnrs	10.63	64-76	330	12	30
Bolton W.	L	12.74	74	3	0	0
Halifax T.	Tr	08.77	77-78	78	3	4

SMITH, Stephen J.
Lydney, 12 June, 1957 (G)

League Club	Source	Date Signed	Seasons Played	Apps	Subs	Gls
Birmingham C.	App	07.75	75	2	0	0
Bradford C.	Tr	03.78	78-81	105	0	0
Crewe Alex.	Tr	08.82	82-83	54	0	0

SMITH, Terence P.
Cheltenham, 10 June, 1951 (F)

League Club	Source	Date Signed	Seasons Played	Apps	Subs	Gls
Stoke C.	App	12.68	70-71	4	1	0
Shrewsbury T.	L	02.73	72	2	0	0

SMITH, Terence V.
Rainworth, 10 July, 1942 (WH)

League Club	Source	Date Signed	Seasons Played	Apps	Subs	Gls
Mansfield T.	Jnrs	04.60	60	8	-	0

SMITH, Thomas
Liverpool, 5 April, 1945 E Yth/Eu23-10/EF Lge/E-1 (D)

League Club	Source	Date Signed	Seasons Played	Apps	Subs	Gls
Liverpool	App	04.62	62-77	467	0	36
Swansea C.	Tr	08.78	78	34	2	2

SMITH, Thomas
Easington, 2 February, 1923 (CH)

League Club	Source	Date Signed	Seasons Played	Apps	Subs	Gls
Newcastle U.	Horden Colly	03.41	46-49	8	-	0

SMITH, Thomas E.
Wolverhampton, 30 July, 1959 (F)

League Club	Source	Date Signed	Seasons Played	Apps	Subs	Gls
Sheffield U.	Bromsgrove Rov.	04.78	78	2	1	1
Huddersfield T.	Tr	03.79	78	0	1	0

SMITH, Timothy C.
Gloucester, 19 April, 1959 (M)

League Club	Source	Date Signed	Seasons Played	Apps	Subs	Gls
Luton T.	App	05.76	76-77	1	1	0

SMITH, J. Trevor
West Stanley, 8 September, 1910 (IF)

League Club	Source	Date Signed	Seasons Played	Apps	Subs	Gls
Charlton Ath.	Annfield Plain	05.33	33-34	23	-	6
Fulham	Tr	03.35	34-37	93	-	19
Crystal Palace	Tr	02.38	37-38	57	-	14
Watford	Colchester U.	06.47	47	10	-	0

SMITH, Trevor
Brierley Hill, 13 April, 1936 Eu23-15/E'B'-2/EF Lge/E-2 (CH)

League Club	Source	Date Signed	Seasons Played	Apps	Subs	Gls
Birmingham C.	Jnrs	05.53	53-64	365	-	3
Walsall	Tr	10.64	64-65	11	0	0

SMITH, Trevor J.
Birmingham, 7 May, 1954 E Sch (W)

League Club	Source	Date Signed	Seasons Played	Apps	Subs	Gls
Coventry C.	App	05.71				
Walsall	Tr	08.72	72	2	1	0

SMITH, Trevor M.
Middlesbrough, 4 April, 1949 (D)

League Club	Source	Date Signed	Seasons Played	Apps	Subs	Gls
Hartlepool U.	Whitby T.	07.77	76-78	27	6	1
Hartlepool U.	Whitby T.	08.82	82	30	2	2

SMITH, Trevor R.
Lowestoft, 12 August, 1946 (FB)

League Club	Source	Date Signed	Seasons Played	Apps	Subs	Gls
Ipswich T.	App	08.64	64-65	22	1	0

SMITH, Wilfred
Manchester, 20 January, 1935 (F)

League Club	Source	Date Signed	Seasons Played	Apps	Subs	Gls
Stockport Co.		02.57	57-59	6	-	1

SMITH, Wilfred S.
West Germany, 3 September, 1946 E Yth/Eu23-6/EF Lge (FB)

League Club	Source	Date Signed	Seasons Played	Apps	Subs	Gls
Sheffield Wed.	App	09.63	64-70	206	0	4
Coventry C.	Tr	08.70	70-74	132	3	1
Brighton & H. A.	L	10.74	74	5	0	0
Millwall	L	01.75	74	5	0	0
Bristol Rov.	Tr	03.75	74-76	54	0	2
Chesterfield	Tr	11.76	76	26	1	2

SMITH, Wilfred V.
Pucklechurch, 7 April, 1918 Died 1968 (FB)

League Club	Source	Date Signed	Seasons Played	Apps	Subs	Gls
Bristol Rov.		05.36	37-46	26	-	0
Newport Co.	Tr	12.46	46-47	9	-	0

SMITH, William
Stoke, 18 April, 1917

League Club	Source	Date Signed	Seasons Played	Apps	Subs	Gls
Port Vale		10.36	36-48	86	-	0

SMITH, William
Cumnock, 12 October, 1942 (IF)

League Club	Source	Date Signed	Seasons Played	Apps	Subs	Gls
Sheffield U.		07.65	66	2	0	1

SMITH, William
Glasgow, 6 December, 1943 (WH)

League Club	Source	Date Signed	Seasons Played	Apps	Subs	Gls
Brentford	Glasgow Celtic	06.63	63-65	25	0	0

SMITH, William
London, 29 September, 1948 E Amat (D)

League Club	Source	Date Signed	Seasons Played	Apps	Subs	Gls
Wimbledon	Leatherhead	08.77	77	2	0	0

SMITH, William
Aberdeen, 23 December, 1938 (IL)

League Club	Source	Date Signed	Seasons Played	Apps	Subs	Gls
Darlington	Raith Rov.	07.63	63	26	-	7

SMITH, William
Lambeth, 2 November, 1938 (G)

League Club	Source	Date Signed	Seasons Played	Apps	Subs	Gls
Crystal Palace	Jnrs	12.56				
Watford	Tr	08.57	58	10	-	0

SMITH, William H.
Plymouth, 7 September, 1926 (WH/IF)

League Club	Source	Date Signed	Seasons Played	Apps	Subs	Gls
Plymouth Arg.	Plymouth U.	08.45				
Reading	Tr	08.47	47	3	-	0
Northampton T.	Tr	07.48	48	26	-	8
Birmingham C.	Tr	02.50	50-52	55	-	21
Blackburn Rov.	Tr	12.52	52-59	119	-	10
Accrington St.	Tr	07.60	60	34	-	3

SMITH, William R.
Stafford, 20 December, 1930

League Club	Source	Date Signed	Seasons Played	Apps	Subs	Gls
Crewe Alex.		12.55	55-56	43	-	0

SMITHERS, Timothy
Ramsgate, 22 January, 1956 E Semi-Pro (LB)

League Club	Source	Date Signed	Seasons Played	Apps	Subs	Gls
Oxford U.	Nuneaton Bor.	05.80	80-82	95	4	6

SMITHIES, Michael H.
Hartlepool, 18 September, 1962 (D)

League Club	Source	Date Signed	Seasons Played	Apps	Subs	Gls
Hartlepool U.		08.83	82-83	27	2	0
Hartlepool U. (N/C)		08.86	86	5	1	0

SMITHSON, Rodney G.
Leicester, 9 October, 1943 E Sch/E Yth (CD)

League Club	Source	Date Signed	Seasons Played	Apps	Subs	Gls
Arsenal	App	10.60	62	2	-	0
Oxford U.	Tr	07.64	65-74	150	6	6

SMOUT, John R.
Newtown, 30 October, 1941 (G)

League Club	Source	Date Signed	Seasons Played	Apps	Subs	Gls
Crystal Palace		08.65	65	1	0	0
Exeter C.	Tr	06.66	66-67	75	0	0

SMYTH, Cecil
Belfast, 4 May, 1941 (FB)

League Club	Source	Date Signed	Seasons Played	Apps	Subs	Gls
Exeter C.	Distillery	08.62	62-68	270	3	1
Torquay U.	Tr	08.69	69-70	22	2	0

SMYTH, John M.
Dublin, 28 April, 1970 (RB)

League Club	Source	Date Signed	Seasons Played	Apps	Subs	Gls
Liverpool	Dundalk	05.87				
Burnley	Tr	08.90				
Wigan Ath.	Tr	09.91	91	2	6	0

SMYTH, Michael
Dublin, 13 May, 1940 IR-1 (G)

League Club	Source	Date Signed	Seasons Played	Apps	Subs	Gls
Barrow	Drumcondra	08.62	62-63	8	-	0

SMYTH, Peter
Derry (NI), 3 December, 1924 (IF)

League Club	Source	Date Signed	Seasons Played	Apps	Subs	Gls
Exeter C.	Albion Rov.	06.50	50	5	-	0
Southport	Tr	07.51	51	5	-	0

SMYTH, H. Robert
Manchester, 28 February, 1921 (WH)

League Club	Source	Date Signed	Seasons Played	Apps	Subs	Gls
Ipswich T.		12.45	46-47	2	-	0
Halifax T.	Tr	08.50	50	2	-	0
Rochdale	Tr	09.50	50	3	-	1
Accrington St.	Tr	01.51	50	7	-	0

SMYTH, Samuel
Belfast, 25 February, 1925 LOI/NI-9 (IF)

League Club	Source	Date Signed	Seasons Played	Apps	Subs	Gls
Wolverhampton W.	Linfield	07.47	47-51	102	-	34
Stoke C.	Tr	09.51	51-52	40	-	19
Liverpool	Tr	01.53	52-53	45	-	20

SNAPE, John
Birmingham, 2 July, 1917 (RH)

League Club	Source	Date Signed	Seasons Played	Apps	Subs	Gls
Coventry C.	Solihull T.	05.36	37-49	106	-	2

SNEDDEN, John D.
Bonnybridge, 3 February, 1942 S Sch (CH)

League Club	Source	Date Signed	Seasons Played	Apps	Subs	Gls
Arsenal	Jnrs	02.59	59-64	83	-	0
Charlton Ath.	Tr	03.65	64-65	18	2	0
Leyton Orient	Tr	07.66	66-67	26	1	3
Halifax T.	L	11.67	67	5	0	0

SNEDDON, Charles
Bo'ness, 10 June, 1930 (CH)

League Club	Source	Date Signed	Seasons Played	Apps	Subs	Gls
Accrington St.	Stenhousemuir	10.53	53-60	213	-	3

SNEDDON, David
Kilwinning, 24 April, 1936 Su23-1 (IF)

League Club	Source	Date Signed	Seasons Played	Apps	Subs	Gls
Preston N. E.	Dundee	04.59	58-61	91	-	17

SNEDDON, Thomas
Livingston, 26 August, 1912 (FB)

League Club	Source	Date Signed	Seasons Played	Apps	Subs	Gls
Rochdale	Queen of South	07.37	37-46	67	-	0

SNEDDON, William C.
Wishaw, 1 April, 1914 (WH)

League Club	Source	Date Signed	Seasons Played	Apps	Subs	Gls
Brentford	Falkirk	06.37	37-38	66	-	2
Swansea C.	Tr	02.46	46	2	-	0
Newport Co.	Tr	10.46	46	18	-	0

SNELL, Albert E.
Dunscroft, 7 February, 1931 (WH)

League Club	Source	Date Signed	Seasons Played	Apps	Subs	Gls
Sunderland		08.49	52-54	9	-	1
Halifax T.	Tr	11.55	55-56	25	-	0

SNELL, Victor D. R.
Ipswich, 29 October, 1927 (FB)

League Club	Source	Date Signed	Seasons Played	Apps	Subs	Gls
Ipswich T.		11.45	49-58	64	-	2

SNODIN, Glynn
Rotherham, 14 February, 1960 (LB/W)

League Club	Source	Date Signed	Seasons Played	Apps	Subs	Gls
Doncaster Rov.	App	10.77	76-84	288	21	61
Sheffield Wed.	Tr	06.85	85-86	51	8	1
Leeds U.	Tr	07.87	87-90	83	11	10
Oldham Ath.	L	08.91	91	8	0	1
Rotherham U.	L	02.92	91	3	0	0

SNODIN, Ian
Rotherham, 15 August, 1963 E Yth/Eu21-4/E 'B' (M/RB)

League Club	Source	Date Signed	Seasons Played	Apps	Subs	Gls
Doncaster Rov.	App	08.80	79-84	181	7	25
Leeds U.	Tr	05.85	85-86	51	0	6
Everton	Tr	01.87	86-90	93	3	2

SNOOKES, Eric
Birmingham, 6 March, 1955 (LB)

League Club	Source	Date Signed	Seasons Played	Apps	Subs	Gls
Preston N. E.	App	03.73	72-73	20	0	0
Crewe Alex.	Tr	07.74	74	33	1	0
Southport	Tr	07.75	75-77	106	4	2
Rochdale	Tr	07.78	78-82	183	0	1
Bolton W.	Tr	07.83	83	6	0	0

SNOW, Simon G.
Sheffield, 3 April, 1966 (F)

League Club	Source	Date Signed	Seasons Played	Apps	Subs	Gls
Scunthorpe U. (N/C)	App	08.83	82-83	1	1	0
Preston N. E.	Sutton T.	08.89	89	1	0	0

SNOWBALL, Raymond
Sunderland, 10 March, 1932 (G)

League Club	Source	Date Signed	Seasons Played	Apps	Subs	Gls
Darlington (Am)	Crook T.	10.64	64-66	13	0	0

League Club	Source	Date Signed	Seasons Played	Career Record Apps	Subs	Gls
SNOWDON, Brian V. S.						
Bishop Auckland, 1 January, 1935						(CH)
Blackpool		09.52	55-59	18	-	1
Portsmouth	Tr	10.59	59-63	114	-	0
Millwall	Tr	10.63	63-66	128	0	0
Crystal Palace	Detroit (USA)	02.69	68	1	4	0
SODEN, Walter J.						
Birmingham, 22 January, 1921						(CF)
Coventry C.	Boldmere St Michael	03.48	47-48	2	-	0
SOLAN, Kenneth						
Middlesbrough, 13 October, 1948 Died 1972						(IF)
Middlesbrough		11.66				
Hartlepool U.	L	10.68	68	5	0	1
Darlington	L	03.69	68	8	0	1
SOLOMAN, Jason R.						
Welwyn Garden City, 6 October, 1970 E Yth						(CD)
Watford	YT	12.88	90-91	24	13	0
SOMERFIELD, Alfred G.						
South Kirkby, 22 March, 1918						(F)
Mansfield T.	Frickley Colly	05.38	38	15	-	6
Wolverhampton W.	Tr	03.39				
Wrexham	Tr	06.47	46	2	-	1
Crystal Palace	Tr	09.47	47	10	-	3
SOMERS, Michael R.						
Nottingham, 27 February, 1945						(OL)
Chelsea	Nottingham F. (Am)	11.62				
Torquay U.	Tr	05.64	64-65	40	1	3
Hartlepool U.	Tr	07.66	66-68	64	3	3
SOMMER, Jurgen P.						
New York (USA), 27 February, 1969						(G)
Luton T.		08.91				
Brighton & H.A.	L	11.91	91	1	0	0
SONNER, Daniel J.						
Wigan, 9 January, 1972						(F)
Burnley	Wigan Ath. (YT)	07.90	90-91	1	4	0

League Club	Source	Date Signed	Seasons Played	Career Record Apps	Subs	Gls
SOO, Frank C.						
Buxton, 8 March, 1914 Died 1991						(WH)
Stoke C.	Prescot Cables	01.33	33-38	173	-	5
Leicester C.	Tr	09.45				
Luton T.	Tr	07.46	46-47	71	-	4
SORRELL, Anthony C.						
Hornchurch, 17 October, 1966						(M)
Maidstone U.	Barking	08.88	89-90	46	9	8
SORRELL, Dennis J.						
Lambeth, 7 October, 1940						(WH)
Leyton Orient	Jnrs	10.57	58-60	37	-	1
Chelsea	Tr	02.62	61-63	3	-	0
Leyton Orient	Tr	09.64	64-66	74	0	3
SORVEL, Neil S.						
Prescot, 2 March, 1973						(M)
Crewe Alex.	YT	07.91	91	5	4	0
SOUNESS, Graeme J.						
Edinburgh, 6 May, 1953 S Sch/Su23-2/S-40						(M)
Tottenham H.	App	05.70				
Middlesbrough	Tr	01.73	72-77	174	2	22
Liverpool	Tr	01.78	77-83	246	1	38
SOUTAR, Timothy J.						
Oxford, 25 February, 1946						(IF)
Brentford	Jnrs	07.63	63	1	-	0
SOUTAR, William						
Dundee, 3 May, 1931						(FB)
Burnley	Broughty Ath.	12.53				
Chester C.	Tr	06.57	57-59	51	-	1
SOUTER, Donald D.						
Hammersmith, 1 December, 1961						(CD)
Ipswich T.	App	01.79				
Barnsley	Tr	08.82	82	19	2	0
Aldershot	Tr	08.83	83-84	45	0	0
SOUTH, Alexander						
Brighton, 7 July, 1931						(CH)
Brighton & H. A.	Jnrs	03.49	49-54	79	-	4
Liverpool	Tr	12.54	54	6	-	1
Halifax T.	Tr	10.56	56-64	302	-	12

Graeme Souness (Tottenham Hotspur, Middlesbrough, Liverpool, Sampdoria, Glasgow Rangers & Scotland)

SOUTH, John A.
Bow, 30 November, 1952 (CH)

League Club	Source	Date Signed	Seasons Played	Apps	Subs	Gls
Colchester U.	Leyton Orient (Am)	07.72	72	4	0	0

SOUTH, John E.
Lambeth, 8 April, 1948 (CF)

League Club	Source	Date Signed	Seasons Played	Apps	Subs	Gls
Brentford	Fulham (App)	11.66	66	1	0	0

SOUTH, William A.
Brighton, 24 February, 1928 (HB)

League Club	Source	Date Signed	Seasons Played	Apps	Subs	Gls
Brighton & H. A.	Jnrs	08.51	51	2	-	0

SOUTHALL, Neville
Llandudno, 16 September, 1958 W-61 (G)

League Club	Source	Date Signed	Seasons Played	Apps	Subs	Gls
Bury	Winsford U.	06.80	80	39	0	0
Everton	Tr	07.81	81-91	371	0	0
Port Vale	L	01.83	82	9	0	0

Neville Southall (Bury, Everton & Wales)

SOUTHALL, L. Nicholas
Stockton, 28 January, 1972 (F)

League Club	Source	Date Signed	Seasons Played	Apps	Subs	Gls
Hartlepool U.	Darlington (YT)	11.90	91	13	9	3

SOUTHALL, Robert
Rotherham, 10 May, 1922 (WH)

League Club	Source	Date Signed	Seasons Played	Apps	Subs	Gls
Chesterfield	Jnrs	12.43	47-52	127	-	11

SOUTHAM, James H.
Willenhall, 19 August, 1917 Died 1982 (FB)

League Club	Source	Date Signed	Seasons Played	Apps	Subs	Gls
West Bromwich A.	Shornhill Rec.	12.42				
Newport Co.	Tr	05.46	46	8	-	0
Birmingham C.	Tr	11.46	47	1	-	0
Northampton T.	Tr	06.49	49-54	144	-	1

SOUTHEY, Peter C.
Putney, 4 January, 1962 Died 1983 (FB)

League Club	Source	Date Signed	Seasons Played	Apps	Subs	Gls
Tottenham H.	App	10.79	79	1	0	0

SOUTHGATE, Gareth
Watford, 3 September, 1970 (CD)

League Club	Source	Date Signed	Seasons Played	Apps	Subs	Gls
Crystal Palace	YT	01.89	90-91	27	4	0

SOUTHREN, Thomas
Sunderland, 1 August, 1927 (W)

League Club	Source	Date Signed	Seasons Played	Apps	Subs	Gls
West Ham U.	Peartree O.B.	12.49	50-53	64	-	2
Aston Villa	Tr	12.54	54-58	63	-	6
Bournemouth	Tr	10.58	58-59	64	-	11

SOUTHWELL, Aubrey A.
Grantham, 21 August, 1921 (FB)

League Club	Source	Date Signed	Seasons Played	Apps	Subs	Gls
Notts Co.	Nottingham F. (Am)	12.44	46-56	327	-	2

SOWDEN, Maurice
Doncaster, 21 October, 1954 (M)

League Club	Source	Date Signed	Seasons Played	Apps	Subs	Gls
Scunthorpe U.	App	10.72	72	3	0	0

SOWDEN, Peter T.
Bradford, 1 May, 1929 (F)

League Club	Source	Date Signed	Seasons Played	Apps	Subs	Gls
Blackpool	Jnrs	06.47				
Hull C.	Bacup Bor.	09.48				
Aldershot	Elgin C.	10.50	50	4	-	0
Hull C.	Tr	08.51				
Gillingham	Tr	08.52	52-55	134	-	27
Accrington St.	Tr	09.56	56-57	54	-	13
Wrexham	Tr	06.58	58-59	38	-	4

SOWDEN, William
Manchester, 8 December, 1930 (CF)

League Club	Source	Date Signed	Seasons Played	Apps	Subs	Gls
Manchester C.	Jnrs	04.49	52-53	11	-	2
Chesterfield	Tr	11.54	54-56	97	-	59
Stockport Co.	Tr	06.57	57	15	-	7

SOWERBY, William H. R.
Hull, 31 August, 1932 (IF)

League Club	Source	Date Signed	Seasons Played	Apps	Subs	Gls
Wolverhampton W.	Pilkington Rec.	05.50				
Grimsby T.		01.54	53-54	12	-	1

SPACKMAN, Nigel J.
Romsey, 2 December, 1960 (M)

League Club	Source	Date Signed	Seasons Played	Apps	Subs	Gls
Bournemouth	Andover	05.80	80-82	118	1	10
Chelsea	Tr	06.83	83-86	139	2	12
Liverpool	Tr	02.87	86-88	39	12	0
Queens Park R.	Tr	02.89	88-89	27	2	1

SPALDING, William
Glasgow, 24 November, 1926 (OR)

League Club	Source	Date Signed	Seasons Played	Apps	Subs	Gls
Bristol C.	Ballymena	01.50	49-50	10	-	0

SPARHAM, Sean R.
Bexley, 4 December, 1968 (LB)

League Club	Source	Date Signed	Seasons Played	Apps	Subs	Gls
Millwall	Jnrs	05.87	87-89	22	6	0
Brentford	L	03.90	89	5	0	1

SPARK, Alexander M.
Stenhousemuir, 16 October, 1949 (CD)

League Club	Source	Date Signed	Seasons Played	Apps	Subs	Gls
Preston N. E.	Jnrs	11.66	67-75	207	18	6
Bradford C.	Motherwell	12.76	76-77	32	2	0

SPARKS, Christopher J.
Islington, 22 May, 1960 (FB)

League Club	Source	Date Signed	Seasons Played	Apps	Subs	Gls
Crystal Palace	App	11.77				
Reading	L	08.79	79	3	0	0

SPARROW, Brian E.
Bethnal Green, 24 June, 1962 (LB)

League Club	Source	Date Signed	Seasons Played	Apps	Subs	Gls
Arsenal	App	02.80	83	2	0	0
Wimbledon	L	01.83	82	17	0	1
Millwall	L	12.83	83	5	0	2
Gillingham	L	01.84	83	5	0	1
Crystal Palace	Tr	07.84	84-86	62	1	2

SPARROW, John P.
Bethnal Green, 3 June, 1957 E Sch/E Yth (LB)

League Club	Source	Date Signed	Seasons Played	Apps	Subs	Gls
Chelsea	App	08.74	73-79	63	6	2
Millwall	L	03.79	78	7	0	0
Exeter C.	Tr	01.81	80-82	62	1	3

SPAVIN, Alan
Lancaster, 20 February, 1942 (M)

League Club	Source	Date Signed	Seasons Played	Apps	Subs	Gls
Preston N. E.	Jnrs	08.59	60-73	411	6	26
Preston N. E.	Washington (USA)	11.77	77-78	3	4	0

SPEAKMAN, Samuel
Huyton, 27 January, 1934 (OL)

League Club	Source	Date Signed	Seasons Played	Apps	Subs	Gls
Bolton W.		09.51				
Middlesbrough	Tr	07.53				
Tranmere Rov.	Tr	09.54	54-55	68	-	9

SPEARING, Anthony
Romford, 7 October, 1964 *E Yth* (LB)

League Club	Source	Date Signed	Seasons Played	Apps	Subs	Gls
Norwich C.	App	10.82	83-87	67	2	0
Stoke C.	L	11.84	84	9	0	0
Oxford U.	L	02.85	84	5	0	0
Leicester C.	Tr	07.88	88-90	71	2	1
Plymouth Arg.	Tr	06.91	91	30	0	0

SPEARRITT, Edward A.
Lowestoft, 31 January, 1947 (W)

League Club	Source	Date Signed	Seasons Played	Apps	Subs	Gls
Ipswich T.	App	02.65	65-68	62	10	13
Brighton & H. A.	Tr	01.69	68-73	203	7	22
Carlisle U.	Tr	06.74	74-75	29	2	1
Gillingham	Tr	08.76	76	19	0	1

SPEARS, Alan F.
Amble, 27 December, 1938 *E Sch* (W)

League Club	Source	Date Signed	Seasons Played	Apps	Subs	Gls
Newcastle U.	Jnrs	02.56				
Millwall	Tr	06.60	60-62	31	-	6
Lincoln C.	Tr	07.63	63	2	-	0

SPECTOR, Miles D.
Hendon, 4 August, 1934 *E Yth/E Amat* (OL)

League Club	Source	Date Signed	Seasons Played	Apps	Subs	Gls
Chelsea (Am)	Jnrs	05.52	52-53	3	-	0
Millwall (Am)	Hendon	05.56	56	1	-	0

SPEDDING, Thomas W.
Tynemouth, 8 December, 1925

League Club	Source	Date Signed	Seasons Played	Apps	Subs	Gls
Doncaster Rov.		03.49	48	1	-	0

SPEED, Gary A.
Hawarden, 8 September, 1969 *W Yth/Wu21-3/W-14* (LW)

League Club	Source	Date Signed	Seasons Played	Apps	Subs	Gls
Leeds U.	YT	06.88	88-91	89	16	17

SPEED, Leslie
Wrexham, 3 October, 1923 (FB)

League Club	Source	Date Signed	Seasons Played	Apps	Subs	Gls
Wrexham	Llandudno	04.45	46-54	211	-	0

SPEEDIE, David R.
Glenrothes, 20 February, 1960 *Su21-1/S-10* (F/M)

League Club	Source	Date Signed	Seasons Played	Apps	Subs	Gls
Barnsley	Jnrs	10.78	78-79	10	13	0
Darlington	Tr	06.80	80-81	88	0	21
Chelsea	Tr	06.82	82-86	155	7	47
Coventry C.	Tr	07.87	87-90	121	1	31
Liverpool	Tr	02.91	90	8	4	6
Blackburn Rov.	Tr	08.91	91	34	2	23

SPEIGHT, Michael
Upton, 1 November, 1951 *E-'B'* (M)

League Club	Source	Date Signed	Seasons Played	Apps	Subs	Gls
Sheffield U.	App	05.69	71-79	184	15	14
Blackburn Rov.	Tr	07.80	80-81	50	1	4
Grimsby T.	Tr	08.82	82-83	35	3	2
Chester C.	Tr	08.84	84-85	40	0	1

SPEIRS, Gardner
Airdrie, 14 April, 1963 *S Yth* (M)

League Club	Source	Date Signed	Seasons Played	Apps	Subs	Gls
Hartlepool U. (N/C)	St Mirren	08.89	89	0	1	0

SPELMAN, Isaac
Newcastle, 9 March, 1914 (WH)

League Club	Source	Date Signed	Seasons Played	Apps	Subs	Gls
Southend U.		05.35	35-36	43	-	2
Tottenham H.	Tr	05.37	37-38	28	-	2
Hartlepool U.	Tr	05.46	46	26	-	0

SPELMAN, Michael T.
Newcastle, 8 December, 1950 (M)

League Club	Source	Date Signed	Seasons Played	Apps	Subs	Gls
Wolverhampton W.	Whitley Bay	11.69				
Watford	Tr	08.71				
Hartlepool U.	Tr	10.71	71-76	115	6	4
Darlington	L	12.72	72	4	0	0

SPELMAN, Ronald E.
Blofield, 22 May, 1938 (OR)

League Club	Source	Date Signed	Seasons Played	Apps	Subs	Gls
Norwich C.	C.N.S.O.B.U.	08.56	57-60	2	-	0
Northampton T.	Tr	11.60	60-61	33	-	3
Bournemouth	Tr	03.62	61-63	28	-	4
Watford	Tr	09.63	63-64	40	-	3
Oxford U.	Tr	05.65	65	15	1	1

SPENCE, Alan N.
Seaham, 7 February, 1940 *E Yth* (IF)

League Club	Source	Date Signed	Seasons Played	Apps	Subs	Gls
Sunderland	Murton Jnrs	05.57	57	5	-	1
Darlington	Tr	06.60	60-61	24	-	10
Southport	Tr	07.62	62-68	225	5	98
Oldham Ath.	Tr	12.68	68-69	26	1	12
Chester C.	Tr	12.69	69	5	2	2

SPENCE, Colin
Glasgow, 7 January, 1960 (F)

League Club	Source	Date Signed	Seasons Played	Apps	Subs	Gls
Crewe Alex. (N/C)	App	02.78	76-78	10	8	1

SPENCE, Derek W.
Belfast, 18 January, 1952 *NI-29* (F)

League Club	Source	Date Signed	Seasons Played	Apps	Subs	Gls
Oldham Ath.	Crusaders	09.70	71-72	5	1	0
Bury	Tr	02.73	72-76	140	0	44
Blackpool	Tr	10.76	76	24	3	2
Blackpool	Olympiakos (Gre)	08.78	78-79	58	0	18
Southend U.	Tr	12.79	79-81	100	4	32
Bury	See Bee (HK)	08.83	83	9	4	1

SPENCE, Joseph L.
Salford, 13 October, 1925 (D)

League Club	Source	Date Signed	Seasons Played	Apps	Subs	Gls
Chesterfield	Buxton	01.48				
York C.	Tr	07.50	50-53	110	-	0

SPENCE, Richard
Barnsley, 18 July, 1908 *E-2* (OR)

League Club	Source	Date Signed	Seasons Played	Apps	Subs	Gls
Barnsley	Thorpe Colly	02.33	32-34	64	-	25
Chelsea	Tr	10.34	34-47	221	-	62

SPENCE, Ronald
Spennymoor, 7 January, 1927 (WH)

League Club	Source	Date Signed	Seasons Played	Apps	Subs	Gls
York C.	Rossington Colly	03.48	47-58	280	-	25

SPENCE, William J.
Hartlepool, 10 January, 1926 (CH)

League Club	Source	Date Signed	Seasons Played	Apps	Subs	Gls
Portsmouth		03.47	49-50	19	-	0
Queens Park R.	Tr	12.51	51-53	56	-	0

SPENCER, Anthony R.
Chiswick, 23 April, 1965 (FB)

League Club	Source	Date Signed	Seasons Played	Apps	Subs	Gls
Brentford	App	04.83	81-83	17	1	0
Aldershot	L	12.84	84	10	0	0

SPENCER, Derek
Coventry, 10 January, 1931 (G)

League Club	Source	Date Signed	Seasons Played	Apps	Subs	Gls
Coventry C.	Lockheed Leamington	12.51	51-52	20	-	0

David Speedie (Barnsley, Darlington, Chelsea, Coventry City, Liverpool, Blackburn Rovers & Scotland)

League Club	Source	Date Signed	Seasons Played	Career Record Apps	Subs	Gls

SPENCER, Harold
Burnley, 30 April, 1919 (HB)

League Club	Source	Date Signed	Seasons Played	Apps	Subs	Gls
Burnley	Jnrs	09.37	46	4	-	1
Wrexham	Tr	07.50	50	11	-	0

SPENCER, John R.
Bradfield, 20 November, 1934 E Yth (F)

League Club	Source	Date Signed	Seasons Played	Apps	Subs	Gls
Sheffield U.	Jnrs	06.54	54-56	24	-	10

SPENCER, John S.
Bacup, 24 August, 1920 (IF)

League Club	Source	Date Signed	Seasons Played	Apps	Subs	Gls
Burnley		06.48	48-50	37	-	8
Accrington St.	Tr	06.51	51	29	-	7

SPENCER, Leslie
Manchester, 16 September, 1936 (W)

League Club	Source	Date Signed	Seasons Played	Apps	Subs	Gls
Rochdale		01.58	57-59	74	-	17
Luton T.	Tr	07.60	60	7	-	1

SPENCER, Raymond
Birmingham, 25 May, 1933 E Sch (WH)

League Club	Source	Date Signed	Seasons Played	Apps	Subs	Gls
Aston Villa	Jnrs	06.50				
Darlington	Tr	03.58	57-60	98	-	5
Torquay U.	Tr	06.61	61-63	59	-	1

SPENCER, Thomas H.
Glasgow, 28 November, 1945 (CD)

League Club	Source	Date Signed	Seasons Played	Apps	Subs	Gls
Southampton	Glasgow Celtic	07.65	65	3	0	0
York C.	Tr	06.66	66-67	54	3	21
Workington	Tr	03.68	67-71	167	0	10
Lincoln C.	Tr	01.72	71-73	67	7	10
Rotherham U.	Tr	07.74	74-77	137	1	10

SPERRIN, Martyn R.
Edmonton, 6 December, 1956 (F)

League Club	Source	Date Signed	Seasons Played	Apps	Subs	Gls
Luton T.	Edgware T.	10.77	77	0	1	0

SPERRIN, William T.
Wood Green, 9 April, 1922 (IF)

League Club	Source	Date Signed	Seasons Played	Apps	Subs	Gls
Brentford	Finchley	09.49	49-55	90	-	28

SPERRING, George B.
Epsom, 30 April, 1935 (CF)

League Club	Source	Date Signed	Seasons Played	Apps	Subs	Gls
Gillingham (Am)		07.55	55	1	-	0

SPERTI, Franco
Italy, 28 January, 1955 (FB)

League Club	Source	Date Signed	Seasons Played	Apps	Subs	Gls
Swindon T.	App	01.73	73	1	0	0

SPICER, Edward W.
Liverpool, 20 September, 1922 E Sch (FB)

League Club	Source	Date Signed	Seasons Played	Apps	Subs	Gls
Liverpool	Jnrs	10.39	46-53	158	-	2

SPIERS, George
Belfast, 3 September, 1941 (OL)

League Club	Source	Date Signed	Seasons Played	Apps	Subs	Gls
Exeter C.	Crusaders	08.63	63	5	-	0

SPIERS, Richard A.
Benson (Oxon), 27 November, 1937 (CH)

League Club	Source	Date Signed	Seasons Played	Apps	Subs	Gls
Reading	Chertsey	10.55	55-69	451	2	3

SPINK, Anthony A.
Doncaster, 16 November, 1929 (F)

League Club	Source	Date Signed	Seasons Played	Apps	Subs	Gls
Sheffield Wed.		12.49				
Chester C.	Tr	06.50	51-52	13	-	3
Workington	Tr	07.55				
Sunderland	Tr	12.55				
Tranmere Rov.	Tr	06.56	56	7	-	3

SPINK, Dean P.
Birmingham, 22 January, 1967 (CD/F)

League Club	Source	Date Signed	Seasons Played	Apps	Subs	Gls
Aston Villa	Halesowen T.	06.89				
Scarborough	L	11.89	89	3	0	2
Bury	L	02.90	89	6	0	1
Shrewsbury T.	Tr	03.90	89-91	77	19	13

SPINK, Nigel P.
Chelmsford, 8 August, 1958 E'B'/EF Lge/E-1 (G)

League Club	Source	Date Signed	Seasons Played	Apps	Subs	Gls
Aston Villa	Chelmsford C.	01.77	79-91	306	0	0

SPINKS, Henry
Great Yarmouth, 1 February, 1920 (CF)

League Club	Source	Date Signed	Seasons Played	Apps	Subs	Gls
Norwich C. (Am)	C.E.Y.M.S.	12.46	46	2	-	1

SPINNER, Terence J.
Woking, 6 November, 1953 (F)

League Club	Source	Date Signed	Seasons Played	Apps	Subs	Gls
Southampton	App	07.71	72-73	1	1	0
Walsall	Tr	07.74	74-75	10	6	5

SPIRING, Peter J.
Glastonbury, 13 December, 1950 E Yth (M)

League Club	Source	Date Signed	Seasons Played	Apps	Subs	Gls
Bristol C.	Jnrs	06.68	69-72	58	5	16
Liverpool	Tr	03.73				
Luton T.	Tr	11.74	74-75	12	3	2
Hereford U.	Tr	02.76	75-82	205	22	20

SPITTLE, Paul D.
Wolverhampton, 16 December, 1964 (M)

League Club	Source	Date Signed	Seasons Played	Apps	Subs	Gls
Oxford U.	App	10.82				
Crewe Alex.	Tr	08.83	83	4	2	1

SPOFFORTH, David J.
York, 21 March, 1969 (D)

League Club	Source	Date Signed	Seasons Played	Apps	Subs	Gls
York C.	Jnrs	07.87	87	3	0	0

SPOONER, Nicholas M.
Manchester, 5 June, 1971 (RB)

League Club	Source	Date Signed	Seasons Played	Apps	Subs	Gls
Bolton W.	YT	07.89	91	14	1	1

SPOONER, Stephen A.
Sutton, 25 January, 1961 (M)

League Club	Source	Date Signed	Seasons Played	Apps	Subs	Gls
Derby Co.	App	12.78	78-81	7	1	0
Halifax T.	Tr	12.81	81-82	71	1	13
Chesterfield	Tr	07.83	83-85	89	4	14
Hereford U.	Tr	07.86	86-87	84	0	19
York C.	Tr	07.88	88-89	72	0	11
Rotherham U.	Tr	07.90	90	15	4	1
Mansfield T.	Tr	03.91	90-91	43	0	2

SPRAGGON, Frank
Whickham, 27 October, 1945 (D)

League Club	Source	Date Signed	Seasons Played	Apps	Subs	Gls
Middlesbrough	App	11.62	63-75	277	3	3
Hartlepool U. (N/C)	Minnesota (USA)	11.76	76	1	0	0

SPRAGUE, Martyn L.
Risca, 10 April, 1949 (FB)

League Club	Source	Date Signed	Seasons Played	Apps	Subs	Gls
Newport Co.	Lovells Ath.	08.68	69-73	155	1	1

SPRAKE, Gary
Swansea, 3 April, 1945 Wu23-5/W-37 (G)

League Club	Source	Date Signed	Seasons Played	Apps	Subs	Gls
Leeds U.	App	05.62	61-72	381	0	0
Birmingham C.	Tr	10.73	73-74	16	0	0

SPRATLEY, Alan S.
Maidenhead, 5 June, 1949 (G)

League Club	Source	Date Signed	Seasons Played	Apps	Subs	Gls
Queens Park R.	App	05.67	68-72	29	0	0
Swindon T.	Tr	07.73	73	7	0	0

SPRATT, Graham W.
Leicester, 17 July, 1939 (G)

League Club	Source	Date Signed	Seasons Played	Apps	Subs	Gls
Coventry C.	Oadby T.	12.56	57-58	28	-	0

SPRATT, Thomas
Cambois (Nd), 20 December, 1941 E Sch/E Yth (M)

League Club	Source	Date Signed	Seasons Played	Apps	Subs	Gls
Manchester U.	Jnrs	12.59				
Bradford P. A.	Tr	02.61	60-63	118	-	45
Torquay U.	Weymouth	07.65	65-66	60	1	19
Workington	Tr	01.67	66-67	51	0	14
York C.	Tr	03.68	67-68	26	3	1
Workington	Tr	03.69	68-71	142	2	27
Stockport Co.	Tr	06.72	72-73	65	1	6

SPRIDGEON, Frederick
Swansea, 13 July, 1935 (FB)

League Club	Source	Date Signed	Seasons Played	Apps	Subs	Gls
Leeds U.	Jnrs	08.52				
Crewe Alex.	Tr	07.56	56	7	-	0

Nigel Spink (Aston Villa & England)

SPRIGGS, Stephen
Doncaster, 16 February, 1956 (M)

League Club	Source	Date Signed	Seasons Played	Apps	Subs	Gls
Huddersfield T.	App	02.73	74	2	2	0
Cambridge U.	Tr	07.75	75-86	411	5	58
Middlesbrough	L	03.87	86	3	0	0

SPRING, Andrew J.
Gateshead, 17 November, 1965 (FB)

League Club	Source	Date Signed	Seasons Played	Apps	Subs	Gls
Coventry C.	App	11.83	83-84	3	2	0
Bristol Rov.	Tr	07.85	85	18	1	0
Cardiff C.	L	10.85	85	1	0	0

SPRINGETT, Peter J.
Fulham, 8 May, 1946 E Yth/Eu23-6 (G)

League Club	Source	Date Signed	Seasons Played	Apps	Subs	Gls
Queens Park R.	App	05.63	62-66	139	0	0
Sheffield Wed.	Tr	05.67	67-74	180	0	0
Barnsley	Tr	07.75	75-79	191	0	0

SPRINGETT, Ronald D.
Fulham, 22 July, 1935 EF Lge/E-33 (G)

League Club	Source	Date Signed	Seasons Played	Apps	Subs	Gls
Queens Park R.	Victoria U.	02.53	55-57	89	-	0
Sheffield Wed.	Tr	03.58	57-66	345	0	0
Queens Park R.	Tr	06.67	67-68	45	0	0

SPRINGTHORPE, Terence A.
Draycott, 4 December, 1923 (FB)

League Club	Source	Date Signed	Seasons Played	Apps	Subs	Gls
Wolverhampton W.	Jnrs	12.40	47-49	35	-	0
Coventry C.	Tr	12.50	50	12	-	0

SPROATES, Alan
Hetton-le-Hole, 30 June, 1944 (M)

League Club	Source	Date Signed	Seasons Played	Apps	Subs	Gls
Sunderland	Jnrs	07.61				
Swindon T.	Tr	08.63	63-64	3	-	0
Darlington	Tr	09.65	65-73	305	11	17
Scunthorpe U.	Tr	08.74	74	19	5	0

SPROATES, John
Houghton-le-Spring, 11 April, 1943 (WH)

League Club	Source	Date Signed	Seasons Played	Apps	Subs	Gls
Barnsley	West Auckland	12.63	63	2	-	0

SPROSON, Philip J.
Stoke, 13 October, 1959 (CD)

League Club	Source	Date Signed	Seasons Played	Apps	Subs	Gls
Port Vale	Jnrs	12.77	77-88	422	4	33
Birmingham C.	Tr	07.89	89	12	0	0

SPROSON, Roy
Stoke, 23 September, 1930 (D)

League Club	Source	Date Signed	Seasons Played	Apps	Subs	Gls
Port Vale	Stoke C. (Am)	07.49	50-71	756	5	29

SPROSTON, Bert
Sandbach, 22 June, 1915 EF Lge/E-11 (FB)

League Club	Source	Date Signed	Seasons Played	Apps	Subs	Gls
Leeds U.	Sandbach Ramblers	06.33	33-37	130	-	1
Tottenham H.	Tr	06.38	38	9	-	0
Manchester C.	Tr	11.38	38-49	125	-	5

SPROSTON, Neil R.
Dudley, 20 November, 1970 (CD)

League Club	Source	Date Signed	Seasons Played	Apps	Subs	Gls
Birmingham C.	YT	07.89	87	0	1	0

SPRUCE, George D.
Chester, 3 April, 1923 (CH)

League Club	Source	Date Signed	Seasons Played	Apps	Subs	Gls
Wrexham		10.48	48-51	135	-	3
Barnsley	Tr	05.52	52-56	149	-	0
Chester C.	Tr	07.58	58-60	64	-	0

SPRUCE, Philip T.
Chester, 16 November, 1929 (FB)

League Club	Source	Date Signed	Seasons Played	Apps	Subs	Gls
Wrexham		11.50	51-55	23	-	0

SPUHLER, John O.
Sunderland, 18 September, 1917 E Sch (CF)

League Club	Source	Date Signed	Seasons Played	Apps	Subs	Gls
Sunderland		09.34	36-38	35	-	4
Middlesbrough	Tr	10.45	46-53	216	-	69
Darlington	Tr	06.54	54-55	67	-	19

SPURDLE, William
Guernsey, 28 January, 1926 (WH)

League Club	Source	Date Signed	Seasons Played	Apps	Subs	Gls
Oldham Ath.	Jnrs	03.48	47-49	56	-	5
Manchester C.	Tr	01.50	49-56	160	-	32
Port Vale	Tr	11.56	56	21	-	7
Oldham Ath.	Tr	06.57	57-62	144	-	19

SQUIRE, Michael R.
Poole, 18 October, 1963 E Sch (F)

League Club	Source	Date Signed	Seasons Played	Apps	Subs	Gls
Fulham		07.82				
Torquay U.	Dorchester T.	03.84	83	12	1	3

SQUIRES, Alan
Fleetwood, 26 February, 1923 (LB)

League Club	Source	Date Signed	Seasons Played	Apps	Subs	Gls
Preston N. E.		12.44				
Carlisle U.	Tr	12.46	46-47	25	-	0

SQUIRES, Barry
Birmingham, 29 July, 1931 (OL)

League Club	Source	Date Signed	Seasons Played	Apps	Subs	Gls
Birmingham C.	Lye T.	05.53	53	1	-	0
Bradford C.	Tr	06.54	54	7	-	0

SQUIRES, Frank
Swansea, 8 March, 1921 Died 1988 (IF)

League Club	Source	Date Signed	Seasons Played	Apps	Subs	Gls
Swansea C.	Jnrs	05.38	46-47	36	-	5
Plymouth Arg.	Tr	10.47	47-49	86	-	13
Grimsby T.	Tr	07.50	50	36	-	2

SQUIRES, Robert
Selby, 6 April, 1919 (WH)

League Club	Source	Date Signed	Seasons Played	Apps	Subs	Gls
Doncaster Rov.	Selby T.	09.37	47	21	-	0
Exeter C.	Tr	07.49	49	1	-	0

SRNICEK, Pavel
Czechoslavakia, 10 March, 1968 (G)

League Club	Source	Date Signed	Seasons Played	Apps	Subs	Gls
Newcastle U.	Banik Ostrava (Cz)	02.91	90-91	20	0	0

STABB, George H.
Paignton, 26 September, 1912 (CF)

League Club	Source	Date Signed	Seasons Played	Apps	Subs	Gls
Torquay U.		09.31	31-34	95	-	43
Port Vale	Tr	07.35	35-36	32	-	9
Bradford P. A.	Tr	09.36	36-46	94	-	4

STACEY, Stephen D.
Bristol, 27 August, 1944 (FB)

League Club	Source	Date Signed	Seasons Played	Apps	Subs	Gls
Bristol C.	App	11.61				
Wrexham	Tr	02.66	65-68	101	3	6
Ipswich T.	Tr	09.68	68	3	0	0
Chester C.	L	12.69	69	1	0	0
Charlton Ath.	L	01.70	69	1	0	1
Bristol C.	Tr	09.70	70	9	0	0
Exeter C.	Tr	09.71	71-72	57	2	0

STACEY, Terence J.
Mitcham, 28 September, 1936 E Amat (FB)

League Club	Source	Date Signed	Seasons Played	Apps	Subs	Gls
Plymouth Arg.	Carshalton Ath.	05.59	59-61	22	-	0
Watford	Tr	07.62				
Gillingham	Tr	08.63	63-64	16	-	0

STACK, William J.
Liverpool, 17 January, 1948 (OL)

League Club	Source	Date Signed	Seasons Played	Apps	Subs	Gls
Crystal Palace	Jnrs	01.65	65	2	0	0

STAFF, Paul
Hartlepool, 30 August, 1962 (W)

League Club	Source	Date Signed	Seasons Played	Apps	Subs	Gls
Hartlepool U.	App	08.80	79-83	88	10	14
Aldershot	Tr	08.84	84-85	25	12	11

STAFFORD, Andrew G.
Littleborough, 28 October, 1960 (W)

League Club	Source	Date Signed	Seasons Played	Apps	Subs	Gls
Halifax T.	Blackburn Rov. (N/C)	01.79	78-80	33	8	1
Stockport Co.	Tr	08.81	81	21	4	1
Rochdale	Tr	08.82	82	1	0	1

STAFFORD, Clive A.
Ipswich, 4 April, 1963 (LB)

League Club	Source	Date Signed	Seasons Played	Apps	Subs	Gls
Colchester U.	Diss T.	02.89	88-89	31	2	0
Exeter C.	L	02.90	89	2	0	0

STAFFORD, Ellis
Sheffield, 17 August, 1929 (FB)

League Club	Source	Date Signed	Seasons Played	Apps	Subs	Gls
Peterborough U.	Scarborough	(N/L)	60-62	17	-	0

STAGG, William
Ealing, 17 October, 1957 (M)

League Club	Source	Date Signed	Seasons Played	Apps	Subs	Gls
Brentford (App)	App	04.74	74	4	0	0

STAINROD, Simon A.
Sheffield, 1 February, 1959 E Yth (F)

League Club	Source	Date Signed	Seasons Played	Apps	Subs	Gls
Sheffield U.	App	07.76	75-78	59	8	14
Oldham Ath.	Tr	03.79	78-80	69	0	21
Queens Park R.	Tr	11.80	80-84	143	2	48
Sheffield Wed.	Tr	02.85	84-85	8	7	2
Aston Villa	Tr	09.85	85-87	58	5	16
Stoke C.	Tr	12.87	87-88	27	1	6

STAINSBY, John
Barnsley, 25 September, 1937 (CF)

League Club	Source	Date Signed	Seasons Played	Apps	Subs	Gls
Barnsley	Wolverhampton W. (Am)	12.55	59-60	34	-	12
York C.	Tr	07.61	61-62	69	-	21
Stockport Co.	Tr	07.63	63	5	-	0

STAINTON, Bryan E.
Scampton (Lincs), 8 January, 1942 (FB)

League Club	Source	Date Signed	Seasons Played	Apps	Subs	Gls
Lincoln C.	Ingham	03.62	61-64	25	-	0

STAINTON, James K.
Sheffield, 14 December, 1931 (FB)

League Club	Source	Date Signed	Seasons Played	Apps	Subs	Gls
Bradford P. A.		04.53				
Mansfield T.	Tr	08.54	55-56	9	-	0

STAINWRIGHT, David P.
Nottingham, 13 June, 1948 (CF)

League Club	Source	Date Signed	Seasons Played	Apps	Subs	Gls
Nottingham F.	App	08.65	65-66	4	3	1
Doncaster Rov.	Tr	07.68	68	1	0	0
York C.	Tr	07.69	69	6	2	1

STALKER, Alan
Ponteland, 18 March, 1939 (G)

League Club	Source	Date Signed	Seasons Played	Apps	Subs	Gls
Gateshead (Am)	Bishop Auckland	05.58	58	4	-	0

STALKER, John A. H.
Musselburgh, 12 March, 1959 (F)

League Club	Source	Date Signed	Seasons Played	Apps	Subs	Gls
Leicester C.		07.79				
Darlington	Tr	10.79	79-82	107	9	36
Hartlepool U.	Tr	01.83	82	3	1	0

STALLARD, Mark
Derby, 24 October, 1974 (F)

League Club	Source	Date Signed	Seasons Played	Apps	Subs	Gls
Derby Co.	YT	11.91	91	2	1	0

STAMPER, Frank S.
Hartlepool, 22 February, 1926 (WH)

League Club	Source	Date Signed	Seasons Played	Apps	Subs	Gls
Hartlepool U.	Colchester U.	08.49	49-57	301	-	25

STAMPS, John D. (Jack)
Maltby, 2 December, 1918 Died 1991 (CF)

League Club	Source	Date Signed	Seasons Played	Apps	Subs	Gls
Mansfield T.	Silverwood Colly	10.37	37	1	-	0
New Brighton	Tr	08.38	38	12	-	5
Derby Co.	Tr	01.39	38-53	233	-	100
Shrewsbury T.	Tr	12.53	53	22	-	4

STANBRIDGE, George
Campsall, 28 March, 1920 (LB)

League Club	Source	Date Signed	Seasons Played	Apps	Subs	Gls
Rotherham U.		11.38	46-48	36	-	1
Aldershot	Tr	06.49	49	15	-	0

STANCLIFFE, Paul I.
Sheffield, 5 May, 1958 (CD)

League Club	Source	Date Signed	Seasons Played	Apps	Subs	Gls
Rotherham U.	App	03.76	75-82	285	0	8
Sheffield U.	Tr	08.83	83-90	278	0	12
Rotherham U.	L	09.90	90	5	0	0
Wolverhampton W.	Tr	11.90	90	17	0	0
York C.	Tr	07.91	91	16	2	1

STANDEN, James A.
Edmonton, 30 May, 1935 (G)

League Club	Source	Date Signed	Seasons Played	Apps	Subs	Gls
Arsenal	Rickmansworth	04.53	57-60	35	-	0
Luton T.	Tr	10.60	60-62	36	-	0
West Ham U.	Tr	11.62	62-67	179	0	0
Millwall	Detroit (USA)	10.68	68-69	8	0	0
Portsmouth	Tr	07.70	70-71	13	0	0

STANDING, John R.
Walberton, 3 September, 1943 (FB)

League Club	Source	Date Signed	Seasons Played	Apps	Subs	Gls
Brighton & H. A.	Bognor Regis T.	12.61	61-62	10	-	0

STANDLEY, Thomas L.
Poplar, 23 December, 1932 (WH)

League Club	Source	Date Signed	Seasons Played	Apps	Subs	Gls
Queens Park R.	Basildon	05.57	57	14	-	2
Bournemouth	Tr	11.58	58-64	159	-	5

STANIFORTH, David A.
Chesterfield, 6 October, 1950 (F)

League Club	Source	Date Signed	Seasons Played	Apps	Subs	Gls
Sheffield U.	App	05.68	68-73	22	4	3
Bristol Rov.	Tr	03.74	73-78	135	16	32
Bradford C.	Tr	06.79	79-81	107	8	25
Halifax T.	Tr	07.82	82-83	66	3	21

STANIFORTH, Gordon
Hull, 23 March, 1957 E Sch (F)

League Club	Source	Date Signed	Seasons Played	Apps	Subs	Gls
Hull C.	App	04.74	73-76	7	5	2
York C.	Tr	12.76	76-79	128	0	33
Carlisle U.	Tr	10.79	79-82	118	8	33
Plymouth Arg.	Tr	03.83	82-84	87	4	19
Newport Co.	Tr	08.85	85-86	84	3	13
York C. (N/C)		10.87	87	15	4	1

STANIFORTH, Ronald
Manchester, 13 April, 1924 E'B'-3/E-8 (FB)

League Club	Source	Date Signed	Seasons Played	Apps	Subs	Gls
Stockport Co.	Newton A.	10.46	46-51	223	-	1
Huddersfield T.	Tr	05.52	52-54	110	-	0
Sheffield Wed.	Tr	07.55	55-58	102	-	2
Barrow	Tr	10.59	59-60	38	-	0

STANISLAUS, Roger E. P.
Hammersmith, 2 November, 1968 (LB)

League Club	Source	Date Signed	Seasons Played	Apps	Subs	Gls
Arsenal	YT	07.86				
Brentford	Tr	09.87	87-89	109	2	4
Bury	Tre	07.90	90-91	76	8	5

STANLEY, Garry E.
Burton, 4 March, 1954 (M)

League Club	Source	Date Signed	Seasons Played	Apps	Subs	Gls
Chelsea	App	03.71	75-78	105	4	15
Everton	Tr	08.79	79-80	52	0	1
Swansea C.	Tr	10.81	81-83	60	12	4
Portsmouth	Tr	01.84	83-85	43	4	1
Bristol C.	Wichita (USA)	08.88	88	8	2	0

STANLEY, Graham
Sheffield, 27 January, 1938 (WH)

League Club	Source	Date Signed	Seasons Played	Apps	Subs	Gls
Bolton W.	Jnrs	10.55	56-63	141	-	3
Tranmere Rov.	Tr	07.65	65	0	1	1

STANLEY, Patrick J.
Dublin, 9 March, 1938 (FB)

League Club	Source	Date Signed	Seasons Played	Apps	Subs	Gls
Leeds U.	Jnrs	03.55				
Halifax T.	Tr	05.58	58-62	119	-	1

STANLEY, Terence J.
Brighton, 2 January, 1951 (M)

League Club	Source	Date Signed	Seasons Played	Apps	Subs	Gls
Brighton & H.A.	Lewes	11.69	69-70	16	6	0

STANLEY, Thomas
Hemsworth, 7 December, 1962 (M)

League Club	Source	Date Signed	Seasons Played	Apps	Subs	Gls
York C.	App	12.80	80-82	14	4	0

STANNARD, James D.
Harold Hill, 6 October, 1962 (G)

League Club	Source	Date Signed	Seasons Played	Apps	Subs	Gls
Fulham	Ford U.	06.80	80-84	41	0	0
Southend U.	L	09.84	84	6	0	0
Charlton Ath.	L	01.85	84	1	0	0
Southend U.	Tr	03.85	84-86	103	0	0
Fulham	Tr	08.87	87-91	223	0	1

STANNERS, Walter
Bo'ness, 2 January, 1921 (G)

League Club	Source	Date Signed	Seasons Played	Apps	Subs	Gls
Bournemouth	Bo'ness U.	07.47	47	3	-	0
Rochdale	Tr	08.49	49	5	-	0

STANSBRIDGE, Leonard E.
Southampton, 19 February, 1919 Died 1986 (G)

League Club	Source	Date Signed	Seasons Played	Apps	Subs	Gls
Southampton	Jnrs	08.36	37-51	48	-	0

STANSFIELD, Frederick
Cardiff, 12 December, 1917 W-1 (CH)

League Club	Source	Date Signed	Seasons Played	Apps	Subs	Gls
Cardiff C.	Grange A.	08.43	46-48	106	-	1
Newport Co.	Tr	09.49	49	21	-	0

STANT, Philip R.
Bolton, 13 October, 1962 (F)

League Club	Source	Date Signed	Seasons Played	Apps	Subs	Gls
Reading (N/C)	Army	08.82	82	3	1	2
Hereford U.	Army	11.86	86-88	83	6	38
Notts Co.	Tr	07.89	89	14	8	6
Blackpool	L	09.90	90	12	0	5
Lincoln C.	L	11.90	90	4	0	0
Huddersfield T.	L	01.91	90	5	0	1
Fulham	Tr	02.91	90	19	0	5
Mansfield T.	Tr	07.91	91	39	1	26

STANTON, Brian
Liverpool, 7 February, 1956 (M)

League Club	Source	Date Signed	Seasons Played	Apps	Subs	Gls
Bury	New Brighton	10.75	76-78	72	11	14
Huddersfield T.	Tr	09.79	79-85	199	10	45
Wrexham	L	03.86	85	8	0	0
Rochdale	Morecambe	12.86	86-87	42	7	4

STANTON, Sidney H.
Dudley, 16 June, 1923

League Club	Source	Date Signed	Seasons Played	Apps	Subs	Gls
Birmingham C.		03.46				
Northampton T.	Tr	07.46	47-48	7	-	0

STANTON, Thomas
Glasgow, 3 May, 1948 S Sch (FB)

League Club	Source	Date Signed	Seasons Played	Apps	Subs	Gls
Liverpool	Jnrs	05.65				
Arsenal	Tr	09.66				
Mansfield T.	Tr	09.67	67	37	0	1
Bristol Rov.	Tr	07.68	68-75	160	12	7

STAPLES, Leonard E.
Leicester, 23 January, 1926 E Sch (FB)

League Club	Source	Date Signed	Seasons Played	Apps	Subs	Gls
Leicester C.	Jnrs	07.47				
Newport Co.	Tr	08.49	49-56	164	-	2

STAPLETON, Francis A.
Dublin, 10 July, 1956 IR Yth/IR-70 (F)

League Club	Source	Date Signed	Seasons Played	Apps	Subs	Gls
Arsenal	App	09.73	74-80	223	2	75
Manchester U.	Tr	08.81	81-86	204	19	60
Derby Co.	Ajax (Neth)	03.88	87	10	0	1
Blackburn Rov.	Le Havre (Fr)	07.89	89-90	80	1	13
Aldershot (N/C)	Tr	09.91				
Huddersfield T. (N/C)	Tr	10.91	91	5	0	0
Bradford C.	Tr	12.91	91	25	2	0

Frank Stapleton (Arsenal, Manchester United, Ajax, Derby County, Le Havre, Blackburn Rovers, Aldershot, Huddersfield Town, Bradford City & Republic of Ireland)

STAPLETON, John R.
Manchester, 30 September, 1969 (LB)

League Club	Source	Date Signed	Seasons Played	Apps	Subs	Gls
Stockport Co.	West Bromwich A. (YT)	08.88	88	1	0	0

STAPLETON, Joseph F.
London, 27 June, 1928 (CH)

League Club	Source	Date Signed	Seasons Played	Apps	Subs	Gls
Fulham	Uxbridge T.	08.52	54-59	97	-	2

STAPLETON, Simon J.
Oxford, 10 December, 1968 (RB)

League Club	Source	Date Signed	Seasons Played	Apps	Subs	Gls
Portsmouth	App	12.86				
Bristol Rov.	Tr	07.88	88	4	1	0

STARBUCK, Philip M.
Nottingham, 24 November, 1968 (F)

League Club	Source	Date Signed	Seasons Played	Apps	Subs	Gls
Nottingham F.	App	08.86	86-90	9	27	2
Birmingham C.	L	03.88	87	3	0	0
Hereford U.	L	02.90	89	6	0	0
Blackburn Rov.	L	09.90	90	5	1	1
Huddersfield T.	Tr	08.91	91	42	2	14

STARK, Roy H.
Nottingham, 28 November, 1953 (CD)

League Club	Source	Date Signed	Seasons Played	Apps	Subs	Gls
Aston Villa	App	06.69	73	2	0	0

STARK, William R.
Glasgow, 27 May, 1937 (F)

League Club	Source	Date Signed	Seasons Played	Apps	Subs	Gls
Crewe Alex.	Glasgow Rangers	08.60	60-61	39	-	13
Carlisle U.	Tr	12.61	61-62	35	-	17
Colchester U.	Tr	11.62	62-65	95	0	32
Luton T.	Tr	09.65	65	8	2	4
Chesterfield	Tr	07.66	66	30	1	15
Newport Co.	Tr	07.67	67	11	1	2

STARKEY, Malcolm J.
Bulwell, 25 January, 1936 (IF/FB)

League Club	Source	Date Signed	Seasons Played	Apps	Subs	Gls
Blackpool		08.54	56-58	3	-	0
Shrewsbury T.	Tr	06.59	59-62	121	-	33
Chester C.	Tr	04.63	62-66	109	0	1

STARLING, Alan W.
Barking, 2 April, 1951 (G)

League Club	Source	Date Signed	Seasons Played	Apps	Subs	Gls
Luton T.	App	04.69	69-70	7	0	0
Torquay U.	L	02.71	70	1	0	0
Northampton T.	Tr	06.71	71-76	238	0	1
Huddersfield T.	Tr	03.77	76-79	112	0	0

STARLING, Ronald W.
Pelaw, 11 October, 1909 Died 1991 E-2 (IF)

League Club	Source	Date Signed	Seasons Played	Apps	Subs	Gls
Hull C.	Washington Colly	10.26	27-29	78	-	13
Newcastle U.	Tr	05.30	30-31	51	-	8
Sheffield Wed.	Tr	06.32	32-36	176	-	31
Aston Villa	Tr	01.37	36-46	88	-	11

STAROCSIK, Felix
Poland, 20 May, 1920 (W)

League Club	Source	Date Signed	Seasons Played	Apps	Subs	Gls
Northampton T.	Third Lanark	07.51	51-54	49	-	19

STATHAM, Brian
Zimbabwe, 21 May, 1969 Eu21-2 (FB)

League Club	Source	Date Signed	Seasons Played	Apps	Subs	Gls
Tottenham H.	YT	07.87	87-88	20	4	0
Reading	L	03.91	90	8	0	0
Bournemouth	L	11.91	91	2	0	0
Brentford	Tr	02.92	91	18	0	0

STATHAM, Derek J.
Wolverhampton, 24 March, 1959 E Yth/Eu21-6/E'B'/E-3 (LB)

League Club	Source	Date Signed	Seasons Played	Apps	Subs	Gls
West Bromwich A.	App	01.77	76-87	298	1	8
Southampton	Tr	08.87	87-88	64	0	2
Stoke C.	Tr	08.89	89-90	41	0	1
Walsall	Tr	08.91	91	29	0	0

STATHAM, Terence
Shirebrook, 11 March, 1940 (G)

League Club	Source	Date Signed	Seasons Played	Apps	Subs	Gls
Mansfield T.	Jnrs	03.57	56-59	26	-	0

STATON, Barry
Doncaster, 9 September, 1938 E Sch/E Yth (LB)

League Club	Source	Date Signed	Seasons Played	Apps	Subs	Gls
Doncaster Rov.	Jnrs	05.56	55-61	85	-	0
Norwich C.	Tr	07.62	62	23	-	1

STAUNTON, Stephen
Drogheda, 19 January, 1969 IRu21-2/IR-34 (LB/W)

League Club	Source	Date Signed	Seasons Played	Apps	Subs	Gls
Liverpool	Dundalk	09.86	88-90	55	10	0
Bradford C.	L	11.87	87	7	1	0
Aston Villa	Tr	08.91	91	37	0	4

STEAD, Kevin
West Ham, 2 October, 1958 (D)

League Club	Source	Date Signed	Seasons Played	Apps	Subs	Gls
Tottenham H.	App	04.76				
Arsenal	Tr	07.77	78	1	1	0

STEAD, Michael J.
West Ham, 28 February, 1957 (FB)

League Club	Source	Date Signed	Seasons Played	Apps	Subs	Gls
Tottenham H.	App	11.74	75-77	14	1	0
Swansea C.	L	02.77	76	5	0	1
Southend U.	Tr	09.78	78-85	296	1	5
Doncaster Rov.	Tr	11.85	85-87	83	2	0

STEANE, Nigel B.
Nottingham, 18 January, 1963 (F)

League Club	Source	Date Signed	Seasons Played	Apps	Subs	Gls
Sheffield U.	App	01.81	79	0	1	0

STEBBING, Gary S.
Croydon, 11 August, 1965 E Yth (M)

League Club	Source	Date Signed	Seasons Played	Apps	Subs	Gls
Crystal Palace	App	08.83	83-87	95	7	3
Southend U.	L	01.86	85	5	0	0
Maidstone U.	K.V. Ostend (Bel)	07.89	89-91	69	7	5

STEEDMAN, Alexander
Edinburgh, 13 May, 1938 (CF)

League Club	Source	Date Signed	Seasons Played	Apps	Subs	Gls
Barrow		09.64	64	9	-	1

Steve Staunton (Dundalk, Liverpool, Aston Villa & Republic of Ireland)

STEEDS, Cecil
Bristol, 11 January, 1929 (IF)

League Club	Source	Date Signed	Seasons Played	Apps	Subs	Gls
Bristol C.	Jnrs	03.47	49-51	9	-	0
Bristol Rov.	Tr	05.52	56	1	-	0

STEEL, Alfred
Glasgow, 15 August, 1925 (G)

League Club	Source	Date Signed	Seasons Played	Apps	Subs	Gls
Walsall	Petershill	10.47	48-49	2	-	0
Cardiff C.	Tr	01.50	49	10	-	0

STEEL, Gregory
Clevedon, 11 March, 1959 (FB)

League Club	Source	Date Signed	Seasons Played	Apps	Subs	Gls
Newport Co.	Clevedon T.	01.78	77	3	0	0

STEEL, W. James
Dumfries, 4 December, 1959 (F)

League Club	Source	Date Signed	Seasons Played	Apps	Subs	Gls
Oldham Ath.	App	12.77	78-82	101	7	24
Wigan Ath.	L	11.82	82	2	0	2
Wrexham	L	01.83	82	9	0	6
Port Vale	Tr	03.83	82-83	27	1	6
Wrexham	Tr	01.84	83-87	164	0	51
Tranmere Rov.	Tr	11.87	87-91	161	13	29

STEEL, Richard
Ferryhill, 13 March, 1930 (FB)

League Club	Source	Date Signed	Seasons Played	Apps	Subs	Gls
Bristol C.	Ferryhill Ath.	06.53	53-55	3	-	0
York C.	Tr	07.56	56-57	3	-	0

STEEL, Ronald
Newburn, 3 June, 1929 (OR)

League Club	Source	Date Signed	Seasons Played	Apps	Subs	Gls
Darlington	Bishop Auckland	01.50	49-51	66	-	5

STEEL, William
Denny, 1 May, 1923 Died 1982 SF Lge/S-30 (W)

League Club	Source	Date Signed	Seasons Played	Apps	Subs	Gls
Derby Co.	Morton	06.47	47-49	109	-	27

STEELE, Bennett J.
Seaton Delaval, 5 August, 1939 (OL)

League Club	Source	Date Signed	Seasons Played	Apps	Subs	Gls
Everton	Seaton Delaval	05.57				
Chesterfield	Tr	05.58	59	18	-	1
Gateshead	Tr	08.59	59	25	-	5

STEELE, Eric G.
Newcastle, 14 May, 1954 (G)

League Club	Source	Date Signed	Seasons Played	Apps	Subs	Gls
Newcastle U.	Jnrs	07.72				
Peterborough U.	Tr	12.73	73-76	124	0	0
Brighton & H. A.	Tr	02.77	76-79	87	0	0
Watford	Tr	10.79	79-83	51	0	0
Cardiff C.	L	03.83	82	7	0	0
Derby Co.	Tr	07.84	84-86	47	0	0
Southend U.	Tr	07.87	87	27	0	0
Mansfield T.	L	03.88	87	5	0	0

STEELE, Frederick C.
Stoke, 6 May, 1916 Died 1976 EF Lge/E-6 (CF)

League Club	Source	Date Signed	Seasons Played	Apps	Subs	Gls
Stoke C.	Downings	08.33	34-48	244	-	142
Mansfield T.	Tr	06.49	49-51	52	-	39
Port Vale	Tr	12.51	51-52	25	-	12

STEELE, Hedley
Barnsley, 3 February, 1954 (CD)

League Club	Source	Date Signed	Seasons Played	Apps	Subs	Gls
Exeter C.	Tiverton T.	07.74	74	6	1	1

STEELE, James
Edinburgh, 11 March, 1950 (CD)

League Club	Source	Date Signed	Seasons Played	Apps	Subs	Gls
Southampton	Dundee	01.72	71-76	160	1	2

STEELE, John
Glasgow, 24 November, 1916 (IL)

League Club	Source	Date Signed	Seasons Played	Apps	Subs	Gls
Barnsley	Ayr U.	06.38	38-48	48	-	21

STEELE, Joseph M.
Blackridge, 4 October, 1928 (OL)

League Club	Source	Date Signed	Seasons Played	Apps	Subs	Gls
Newcastle U.	Bellshill	12.48				
Bury	Tr	05.50	50	18	-	1
Leyton Orient	Tr	08.51				

STEELE, Percy E.
Liverpool, 26 December, 1923 (FB)

League Club	Source	Date Signed	Seasons Played	Apps	Subs	Gls
Tranmere Rov.		01.44	46-56	311	-	0

STEELE, Simon P.
Liverpool, 29 February, 1964 (G)

League Club	Source	Date Signed	Seasons Played	Apps	Subs	Gls
Everton	App	03.82				
Brighton & H. A.	Tr	06.83	83	1	0	0
Blackpool	L	09.83	83	3	0	0
Scunthorpe U. (N/C)	Tr	03.84	83	5	0	0

STEELE, Stanley F.
Stoke, 5 January, 1937 (IF)

League Club	Source	Date Signed	Seasons Played	Apps	Subs	Gls
Port Vale	Jnrs	05.55	56-60	185	-	67
West Bromwich A.	Tr	03.61	60	1	-	0
Port Vale	Tr	08.61	61-64	148	-	23
Port Vale	South Africa	01.68	67	2	0	0

STEELE, Timothy W.
Coventry, 1 December, 1967 (M)

League Club	Source	Date Signed	Seasons Played	Apps	Subs	Gls
Shrewsbury T.	App	12.85	85-88	41	20	5
Wolverhampton W.	Tr	02.89	88-91	52	19	6
Stoke C.	L	02.92	91	7	0	1

STEELE, William M.
Kirkmuirhill, 16 June, 1955 (M)

League Club	Source	Date Signed	Seasons Played	Apps	Subs	Gls
Norwich C.	App	06.73	73-76	56	12	3
Bournemouth	L	01.76	75	7	0	2

STEEN, Alan W.
Crewe, 26 June, 1922 (W)

League Club	Source	Date Signed	Seasons Played	Apps	Subs	Gls
Wolverhampton W.	Jnrs	03.39	38	1	-	1
Luton T.	Tr	05.46	46	10	-	0
Aldershot	Tr	06.49	49	10	-	0
Rochdale	Tr	06.50	50-51	45	-	8
Carlisle U.	Tr	12.51	51	16	-	2

STEEPLES, John
Doncaster, 28 April, 1959 (F)

League Club	Source	Date Signed	Seasons Played	Apps	Subs	Gls
Grimsby T.	Pilkington Rec.	05.80	80-81	4	3	0
Torquay U.	L	09.82	82	4	1	0

STEFFEN, William I.
Switzerland, 17 March, 1925 Swiss Int (FB)

League Club	Source	Date Signed	Seasons Played	Apps	Subs	Gls
Chelsea (Am)	Switzerland	11.46	46	15	-	0

STEGGLES, Kevin P.
Bungay, 19 March, 1961 (D)

League Club	Source	Date Signed	Seasons Played	Apps	Subs	Gls
Ipswich T.	App	12.78	80-85	49	1	1
Southend U.	L	02.84	83	3	0	0
Fulham	L	08.86	86	3	0	0
West Bromwich A.	Tr	02.87	86-87	14	0	0
Port Vale	Tr	11.87	87	20	0	0

STEIN, Brian
Cape Town (SA), 19 October, 1957 Eu21-3/E-1 (F)

League Club	Source	Date Signed	Seasons Played	Apps	Subs	Gls
Luton T.	Edgware T.	10.77	77-87	378	10	127
Luton T.	Annecy (Fr)	07.91	91	32	7	3

STEIN, Colin
Linlithgow, 10 May, 1947 Su23-1/SF Lge/S-21 (CF)

League Club	Source	Date Signed	Seasons Played	Apps	Subs	Gls
Coventry C.	Glasgow Rangers	10.72	72-74	83	0	22

STEIN, Edward
Cape Town (SA), 28 September, 1955 (M)

League Club	Source	Date Signed	Seasons Played	Apps	Subs	Gls
Barnet	Dagenham	07.82	91	0	1	0

STEIN, E. Mark S.
Cape Town (SA), 28 January, 1966 E Yth (F)

League Club	Source	Date Signed	Seasons Played	Apps	Subs	Gls
Luton T.	Jnrs	01.84	83-87	41	13	19
Aldershot	L	01.86	85	2	0	1
Queens Park R.	Tr	08.88	88-89	20	13	4
Oxford U.	Tr	09.89	89-91	72	10	18
Stoke C.	L	09.91	91	5	0	0
Stoke C.	Tr	11.91	91	31	0	16

STEINER, Geoffrey D.
Hackney, 8 June, 1928 (FB)

League Club	Source	Date Signed	Seasons Played	Apps	Subs	Gls
Watford	Barnet	11.50	51	3	-	0

STEJSKAL, Jan
Czechoslavakia, 15 January, 1962 Czech Int (G)

League Club	Source	Date Signed	Seasons Played	Apps	Subs	Gls
Queens Park R.	Sparta Prague (Cz)	10.90	90-91	67	0	0

STELL, Barry
Felling, 3 September, 1961 (M)

League Club	Source	Date Signed	Seasons Played	Apps	Subs	Gls
Sheffield Wed.	App	09.79				
Darlington	Tr	10.79	80	7	2	0

STELLING, John G. S. (Jack)
Washington, 23 May, 1924 (FB)

League Club	Source	Date Signed	Seasons Played	Apps	Subs	Gls
Sunderland	Usworth Colly	11.44	46-55	259	-	8

STEMP, Wayne D.
Epsom, 9 September, 1970 (FB)

League Club	Source	Date Signed	Seasons Played	Apps	Subs	Gls
Brighton & H. A.	YT	10.88	89-90	4	0	0

League Club	Source	Date Signed	Seasons Played	Career Record Apps	Subs	Gls
STENHOUSE, Alexander						
Stirling, 1 January, 1933						(OR)
Portsmouth	Dundee	02.57	56-57	4	-	1
Southend U.	Tr	11.58	58-60	84	-	7
STENNER, Arthur W. J.						
Yeovil, 7 January, 1934						(OL)
Bristol C.		08.54				
Plymouth Arg.	Tr	08.55	55	9	-	1
Norwich C.	Tr	08.56	56	6	-	0
Oldham Ath.	Exeter C. (Trial)	04.57	56	3	-	0
STENSON, Gerard P. (Ged)						
Bootle, 30 December, 1959						(M)
Port Vale	Everton (App)	08.78	78-79	11	1	0
STENSON, John A.						
Catford, 16 December, 1949 E SchE Yth						(M)
Charlton Ath.	App	12.66	67-68	3	8	0
Mansfield T.	Tr	06.69	69-71	103	4	21
Peterborough U.	L	01.72	71	2	0	0
Aldershot	Tr	07.72	72-73	34	11	4
STEPANOVIC, Dragoslav						
Yugoslavia, 30 August, 1948 Yugoslav Int						(D)
Manchester C.	Wormatia (Ger)	08.79	79-80	14	1	0
STEPHAN, Harold W.						
Farnworth, 24 February, 1924						(WH)
Blackburn Rov.		09.44	46-47	13	-	1
Accrington St.	Tr	09.48				
STEPHEN, George A.						
Ellon, 21 September, 1927						(FB)
Aldershot		08.48	48	2	-	0
STEPHEN, James F.						
Fettercairn, 23 August, 1922 S-2						(FB)
Bradford P. A.	Johnshaven	08.39	46-48	94	-	0
Portsmouth	Tr	11.49	49-53	100	-	0
STEPHENS, Alan						
Liverpool, 13 October, 1952						(FB)
Wolverhampton W.	App	10.70				
Crewe Alex.	Tr	07.72	72-73	30	3	0
STEPHENS, Alfred						
Cramlington, 13 June, 1919						(IF)
Leeds U.	Cramlington B.W.	09.38				
Swindon T.	Tr	08.46	46-47	16	-	2
STEPHENS, Archibald						
Liverpool, 19 May, 1954						(F)
Bristol Rov.	Melksham T.	08.81	81-84	100	27	40
Middlesbrough	Tr	03.85	84-87	87	5	24
Carlisle U.	Tr	12.87	87-88	20	4	3
Darlington	Tr	03.89	88	10	0	4
STEPHENS, Arnold E.						
Ross-on-Wye, 31 January, 1928 Died 1955						(W)
Wolverhampton W.	Jnrs	04.45				
Bournemouth	Tr	12.48	48-53	70	-	12
STEPHENS, Herbert J.						
Chatham, 13 May, 1909						(OL)
Brentford	Ealing Ass.	02.31	31-32	6	-	1
Brighton & H. A.	Tr	06.35	35-47	180	-	86
STEPHENS, John W.						
Cramlington, 13 June, 1919 Died 1974						(CF)
Leeds U.	Cramlington B.W.	09.38				
Swindon T.	Tr	07.46	46-47	47	-	26
West Ham U.	Tr	12.47	47-48	22	-	6
STEPHENS, W. John						
Cardiff, 26 June, 1935 Wu23-1						(OR)
Hull C.	Jnrs	08.53	52-57	94	-	20
Swindon T.	Tr	06.58	58-59	18	-	2
Coventry C.	Tr	02.60	59	14	-	0
STEPHENS, Kenneth J.						
Bristol, 14 November, 1946						(W)
West Bromwich A.	App	11.64	66-67	21	1	2
Walsall	Tr	12.68	68-69	5	2	0
Bristol Rov.	Tr	10.70	70-77	215	10	11
Hereford U.	Tr	10.77	77-79	56	4	2
STEPHENS, Kirk W.						
Coventry, 27 February, 1955						(RB)
Luton T.	Nuneaton Bor.	06.78	78-83	226	1	2
Coventry C.	Tr	08.84	84-85	33	1	2

League Club	Source	Date Signed	Seasons Played	Career Record Apps	Subs	Gls
STEPHENS, Lee M.						
Cardiff, 30 September, 1971						(F)
Cardiff C.	YT	07.90	90	1	2	0
STEPHENS, Malcolm K.						
Doncaster, 17 February, 1930						(IF)
Brighton & H. A.		07.54	54-56	29	-	14
Rotherham U.	Tr	07.57	57	12	-	3
Doncaster Rov.	Tr	07.58	58	11	-	2
STEPHENS, Terence G.						
Birkenhead, 5 November, 1935						(F)
Tranmere Rov.		08.55	55-56	15	-	5
STEPHENSON, Alan C.						
Cheshunt, 26 September, 1944 Eu23-7						(CH)
Crystal Palace	Jnrs	02.62	61-67	170	0	13
West Ham U.	Tr	03.68	67-71	106	2	0
Fulham	L	10.71	71	10	0	0
Portsmouth	Tr	05.72	72-74	98	0	1
STEPHENSON, Geoffrey						
Tynemouth, 28 April, 1970						(FB)
Grimsby T.	YT	07.88	88-89	19	2	0
STEPHENSON, Leonard R.						
Blackpool, 14 July, 1930						(CF)
Blackpool	Highfield Y.C.	11.48	50-54	24	-	10
Port Vale	Tr	03.55	54-56	62	-	16
Oldham Ath.	Tr	06.57	57	8	-	0
STEPHENSON, Paul						
Wallsend, 2 January, 1968 E Yth						(RW)
Newcastle U.	App	12.85	85-88	58	3	1
Millwall	Tr	11.88	88-91	81	12	6
STEPHENSON, Peter						
Ashington, 2 May, 1936						
Middlesbrough		08.55				
Gateshead	Ashington	09.59	59	35	-	6
STEPHENSON, G. Robert						
Derby, 19 November, 1942						(F)
Derby Co.	Jnrs	09.60	61-62	11	-	1
Shrewsbury T.	Tr	06.64	64	3	-	0
Rochdale	Tr	07.65	65-66	50	2	16
STEPHENSON, Ronald						
Barrow, 13 April, 1948						(WH)
Barrow	App	05.66	66-67	2	0	1
STEPHENSON, Roy A.						
Crook, 27 May, 1932						(OR)
Burnley	Jnrs	06.49	49-55	78	-	27
Rotherham U.	Tr	09.56	56-57	43	-	14
Blackburn Rov.	Tr	11.57	57-58	21	-	5
Leicester C.	Tr	03.59	58-59	12	-	0
Ipswich T.	Tr	07.60	60-64	144	-	21
STEPNEY, Alexander C.						
Mitcham, 18 September, 1942 Eu23-3/EF Lge/E-1						(G)
Millwall	Tooting & Mitcham	05.63	63-65	137	0	0
Chelsea	Tr	05.66	66	1	0	0
Manchester U.	Tr	09.66	66-77	433	0	2
STEPNEY, Robin E.						
Horsham, 26 February, 1936						(WH)
Aldershot	Redhill	09.58	58-64	213	-	35
STERLAND, Melvyn						
Sheffield, 1 October, 1961 Eu21-7/E-'B'/EF Lge/E-1						(RB)
Sheffield Wed.	App	10.79	78-88	271	8	37
Leeds U.	Glasgow Rangers	07.89	89-91	108	3	16
STERLING, Worrell R.						
Bethnal Green, 8 June, 1965						(W)
Watford	App	06.83	82-88	82	12	14
Peterborough U.	Tr	03.89	88-91	147	2	20
STEVEN, Trevor M.						
Berwick, 21 September, 1963 E Yth/Eu21-2/E-36						(RW)
Burnley	App	09.81	80-82	74	2	11
Everton	Tr	07.83	83-88	210	4	48
STEVENS, Arthur H.						
Battersea, 13 January, 1921						(OR)
Fulham	Sutton U.	12.43	46-58	386	-	110
STEVENS, Brian E.						
Andover, 13 November, 1933 Died 1980						(G)
Southampton	Andover O.B.	09.56	56-57	12	-	0

League Club	Source	Date Signed	Seasons Played	Career Record Apps	Subs	Gls
STEVENS, Dennis						
Dudley, 30 November, 1933 Eu23-2/EF Lge						(IF)
Bolton W.	Jnrs	12.50	53-61	273	-	90
Everton	Tr	03.62	61-65	120	0	20
Oldham Ath.	Tr	12.65	65-66	33	0	0
Tranmere Rov.	Tr	03.67	66-67	28	3	3
STEVENS, Gary A.						
Hillingdon, 30 March, 1962 Eu21-8/E-7						(RB/M)
Brighton & H. A.	App	10.79	79-82	120	13	2
Tottenham H.	Tr	06.83	83-89	140	7	6
Portsmouth	Tr	01.90	89-90	52	0	3
STEVENS, Gary M.						
Birmingham, 30 August, 1954						(F/CD)
Cardiff C.	Evesham	09.78	78-82	138	12	44
Shrewsbury T.	Tr	09.82	82-85	144	6	29
Brentford	Tr	07.86	86	29	3	10
Hereford U.	Tr	03.87	86-89	85	9	10
STEVENS, M. Gary						
Barrow, 27 March, 1963 Eu21-1/E-46						(RB)
Everton	App	03.81	81-87	207	1	9
STEVENS, Gregor						
Glasgow, 13 January, 1955 Su21-1						(CD)
Leicester C.	Motherwell	05.79	79	4	0	0
STEVENS, Ian D.						
Malta, 21 October, 1966						(F)
Preston N. E.	YT	11.84	84-85	9	2	2
Stockport Co. (N/C)	Lancaster C.	10.86	86	1	1	0
Bolton W.	Lancaster C.	03.87	86-90	26	21	7
Bury	Tr	07.91	91	44	1	17
STEVENS, John M.						
Hertford, 21 August, 1941						(CF)
Swindon T.	R.A.F.	06.62	62-63	22	-	10
STEVENS, Keith H.						
Merton, 21 June, 1964						(RB)
Millwall	App	06.81	80-91	308	7	4

Gary Stevens (Everton, Glasgow Rangers & England)

League Club	Source	Date Signed	Seasons Played	Career Record Apps	Subs	Gls
STEVENS, Leslie W. J.						
Croydon, 15 August, 1920 Died 1980						(OL)
Tottenham H.	Jnrs	01.40	46-48	54	-	5
Bradford P. A.	Tr	02.49	48-49	44	-	4
Crystal Palace	Tr	08.50	50	20	-	3
STEVENS, Mark A.						
Bristol, 31 January, 1963						(G)
Bristol C.	App	02.81				
Swindon T.	Tr	06.81	82	1	0	0
STEVENS, Norman J.						
Shoreham, 13 May, 1938						(FB)
Brighton & H. A.	Jnrs	10.55	58	1	-	0
STEVENS, Paul D.						
Bristol, 4 April, 1960						(RB)
Bristol C.	App	04.78	77-84	146	1	3
STEVENS, Samuel B.						
Rutherglen, 2 December, 1935						(WH)
Southampton	Airdrieonians	06.57	58	14	-	0
STEVENSON, Alan						
Staveley, 6 November, 1950						(G)
Chesterfield	Jnrs	10.69	69-71	104	0	0
Burnley	Tr	01.72	71-82	438	0	0
Rotherham U.	Tr	08.83	83	24	0	0
Hartlepool U.	Tr	09.84	84	35	0	0
STEVENSON, Alexander E.						
Dublin, 9 August, 1912 Died 1985 IR-7/NI-17						(IF)
Everton	Glasgow Rangers	01.34	33-48	255	-	82
STEVENSON, Andrew J.						
Scunthorpe, 29 September, 1967						(D)
Scunthorpe U.	Jnrs	01.86	85-91	53	25	1
Doncaster Rov.	L	01.92	91	1	0	0
STEVENSON, Arthur						
Lanchester, 2 March, 1924						(RB)
Doncaster Rov.	Denaby U.	11.44	47-48	14	-	0
STEVENSON, W. Byron						
Llanelli, 7 September, 1956 Wu21-3/W-15						(M)
Leeds U.	App	09.73	74-81	88	7	4
Birmingham C.	Tr	03.82	81-84	69	5	3
Bristol Rov.	Tr	07.85	85	30	1	3
STEVENSON, Ernest						
Rotherham, 28 December, 1923 Died 1970						(IF)
Wolverhampton W.	Jnrs	12.40	47-48	8	-	0
Cardiff C.	Tr	10.48	48-49	50	-	15
Southampton	Tr	02.50	49-50	24	-	8
Leeds U.	Tr	02.51	50-51	16	-	5
STEVENSON, W. Horace						
Derby, 26 June, 1923						(OR)
Nottingham F.		11.44				
Ipswich T.	Tr	02.48	47	3	-	0
STEVENSON, James						
Bellshill, 4 August, 1946 S Sch						(WH)
Southend U.	Hibernian	07.67	67	33	1	0
STEVENSON, Morris J.						
Tranent, 16 April, 1943						(IF)
Luton T.	Morton	11.68	68	1	0	0
STEVENSON, Nigel C. A.						
Swansea, 2 November, 1958 Wu21-2/W-4						(CD)
Swansea C.	App	11.76	75-86	247	12	15
Cardiff C.	L	10.85	85	14	0	0
Reading	L	03.86	85	3	0	0
Cardiff C.	Tr	08.87	87-88	66	2	2
STEVENSON, William						
Leith, 26 October, 1939 SF Lge						(WH)
Liverpool	Glasgow Rangers	10.62	62-67	188	0	15
Stoke C.	Tr	12.67	67-72	82	12	5
Tranmere Rov.	Tr	07.73	73	20	0	0
STEWART, Alan V.						
Newcastle, 24 July, 1922						(CH)
Huddersfield T.		04.40	46-48	14	-	0
York C.	Tr	08.49	49-56	208	-	1
STEWART, Andrew C.						
Letchworth, 29 October, 1956						(F)
Portsmouth	App	07.74	73-75	14	5	3

STEWART, Arthur
Ballymena, 13 January, 1942 NI-7 (WH)

League Club	Source	Date Signed	Seasons Played	Apps	Subs	Gls
Derby Co.	Glentoran	12.67	67-69	29	1	1

STEWART, David C.
Belfast, 20 May, 1958 NI-1 (W)

League Club	Source	Date Signed	Seasons Played	Apps	Subs	Gls
Hull C.	App	08.75	74-78	46	5	7
Chelsea	Tr	05.79				
Scunthorpe U.	Tr	11.79	79-81	88	9	19
Hartlepool U. (N/C)	Goole T.	03.83	82	6	2	0

STEWART, David S.
Glasgow, 11 March, 1947 Su23-7/S-1 (G)

League Club	Source	Date Signed	Seasons Played	Apps	Subs	Gls
Leeds U.	Ayr U.	10.73	73-78	55	0	0
West Bromwich A.	Tr	11.78				
Swansea C.	Tr	02.80	79-80	57	0	0

STEWART, Edward Mc.
Dundee, 15 November, 1934 (WH)

League Club	Source	Date Signed	Seasons Played	Apps	Subs	Gls
Norwich C.	Dundee U.	07.57	57	13	-	0

STEWART, George
Chirnside, 18 October, 1920 (F)

League Club	Source	Date Signed	Seasons Played	Apps	Subs	Gls
Brentford	Hamilton Acad.	08.46	46-47	24	-	3
Queens Park R.	Tr	03.48	47-52	38	-	4
Shrewsbury T.	Tr	01.53	52	10	-	2

STEWART, George S.
Larkhall, 16 November, 1932 (G)

League Club	Source	Date Signed	Seasons Played	Apps	Subs	Gls
Bradford C.	East Stirling	05.59	59-60	22	-	0

STEWART, George T. S.
Buckie, 17 February, 1927 (CF)

League Club	Source	Date Signed	Seasons Played	Apps	Subs	Gls
Accrington St.	St Mirren	09.54	54-58	182	-	136
Coventry C.	Tr	11.58	58-59	40	-	23
Carlisle U.	Tr	06.60	60	7	-	2

STEWART, Gerald
Dundee, 2 September, 1946 (G)

League Club	Source	Date Signed	Seasons Played	Apps	Subs	Gls
Preston N. E.	Jnrs	09.63	66-69	4	0	0
Barnsley	Tr	09.71	71-74	138	0	0

STEWART, J. Gordon
South Africa, 7 August, 1927 Died 1980 (IR)

League Club	Source	Date Signed	Seasons Played	Apps	Subs	Gls
Leeds U.	Parkhill (SA)	10.51	51-52	9	-	2

STEWART, Graham
Birkenhead, 8 March, 1938 (F)

League Club	Source	Date Signed	Seasons Played	Apps	Subs	Gls
Sheffield U.	Everton (Am)	08.58				
Chesterfield	Tr	05.59	59	5	-	2

STEWART, Henry
Wigan, 28 April, 1925 (LB)

League Club	Source	Date Signed	Seasons Played	Apps	Subs	Gls
Huddersfield T.	Thorne Colly	08.48	48-50	49	-	0

STEWART, Ian E.
Belfast, 10 September, 1961 NI Sch/NI-31 (LW)

League Club	Source	Date Signed	Seasons Played	Apps	Subs	Gls
Queens Park R.	Jnrs	05.80	80-84	55	12	2
Millwall	L	03.83	82	10	1	3
Newcastle U.	Tr	08.85	85-86	34	8	3
Portsmouth	Tr	07.87	87	0	1	0
Brentford	L	02.88	87	4	3	0
Aldershot	Tr	01.89	88-90	94	7	0

STEWART, James C.
Kilwinning, 9 March, 1954 Su21-3/Su23-5/S-2 (G)

League Club	Source	Date Signed	Seasons Played	Apps	Subs	Gls
Middlesbrough	Kilmarnock	06.78	78-80	34	0	0

STEWART, John
Armadale, 23 January, 1929

League Club	Source	Date Signed	Seasons Played	Apps	Subs	Gls
Walsall	East Fife	06.57	57	28	-	4

STEWART, John B.
Middlesbrough, 28 March, 1937 (OR)

League Club	Source	Date Signed	Seasons Played	Apps	Subs	Gls
York C.	Whitby T.	09.56	56	1	-	0
Darlington	Tr	12.57				

STEWART, John G.
Lochgelly, 4 September, 1921 (OR)

League Club	Source	Date Signed	Seasons Played	Apps	Subs	Gls
Birmingham C.	Raith Rov.	01.48	47-54	203	-	54

STEWART, W. Marcus P.
Bristol, 8 November, 1972 (F)

League Club	Source	Date Signed	Seasons Played	Apps	Subs	Gls
Bristol Rov.	YT	05.91	91	17	16	5

STEWART, Michael J.
Herne Hill, 16 September, 1932 E Amat (IF)

League Club	Source	Date Signed	Seasons Played	Apps	Subs	Gls
Charlton Ath.	Corinthian Casuals	10.56	56-58	9	-	3

STEWART, Paul A.
Manchester, 7 October, 1964 E Yth/Eu21-1/E-'B'/E-3 (F/M)

League Club	Source	Date Signed	Seasons Played	Apps	Subs	Gls
Blackpool	App	10.81	81-86	188	13	56
Manchester C.	Tr	03.87	86-87	51	0	27
Tottenham H.	Tr	06.88	88-91	126	5	28

STEWART, Raymond S. M.
Perth, 7 September, 1959 S Sch/Su21-12/S-10 (RB)

League Club	Source	Date Signed	Seasons Played	Apps	Subs	Gls
West Ham U.	Dundee U.	09.79	79-90	344	1	62

STEWART, Reginald P.
Sheffield, 30 October, 1925 (CH)

League Club	Source	Date Signed	Seasons Played	Apps	Subs	Gls
Sheffield Wed.	Sheffield Y.M.C.A.	09.44	46	6	-	0
Colchester U.	Tr	07.50	50-56	256	-	0

STEWART, Robert
Kirkcaldy, 4 December, 1933 S Sch

League Club	Source	Date Signed	Seasons Played	Apps	Subs	Gls
Crewe Alex.	St Mirren	08.55	55	22	-	3

STEWART, Robert A.
Broxburn, 14 June, 1971 (M)

League Club	Source	Date Signed	Seasons Played	Apps	Subs	Gls
Doncaster Rov. (YT)	YT	07.87	88	1	0	0

STEWART, William
Clydebank, 10 March, 1922 Died 1987 (IF)

League Club	Source	Date Signed	Seasons Played	Apps	Subs	Gls
Aldershot	St Mirren	06.51	51-53	25	-	3

STEWART, William I.
Liverpool, 1 January, 1965 (G)

League Club	Source	Date Signed	Seasons Played	Apps	Subs	Gls
Liverpool	App	01.83				
Wigan Ath.	Tr	07.84	84-85	14	0	0
Chester C.	Tr	08.86	86-91	223	0	0

STIFFLE, Nelson E.
India, 30 July, 1928 (OR)

League Club	Source	Date Signed	Seasons Played	Apps	Subs	Gls
Chester C.	Ashton U.	12.51	51	9	-	2
Chesterfield	Altrincham	03.54	54	38	-	9
Bournemouth	Tr	05.55	55-57	35	-	7
Exeter C.	Tr	03.58	57-59	94	-	17
Coventry C.	Tr	07.60	60	15	-	2

STILES, John C.
Manchester, 6 May, 1964 (M)

League Club	Source	Date Signed	Seasons Played	Apps	Subs	Gls
Leeds U.	Vancouver (USA)	05.84	84-88	49	16	2
Doncaster Rov.	Tr	08.89	89-91	88	1	2
Rochdale	L	03.92	91	2	2	0

STILES, Norbert P. (Nobby)
Manchester, 18 May, 1942 E Sch/E Yth/Eu23-3/EF Lge/E-28 (WH)

League Club	Source	Date Signed	Seasons Played	Apps	Subs	Gls
Manchester U.	Jnrs	06.59	60-70	311	0	17
Middlesbrough	Tr	05.71	71-72	57	0	2
Preston N.E.	Tr	08.73	73-74	44	2	1

STILL, John L.
West Ham, 24 April, 1950 (CH)

League Club	Source	Date Signed	Seasons Played	Apps	Subs	Gls
Leyton Orient (Am)	Jnrs	05.67	67	1	0	0

STILL, Robert A.
Chorley, 15 December, 1912 (WH)

League Club	Source	Date Signed	Seasons Played	Apps	Subs	Gls
Stockport Co.	Chorley	06.34	34-38	154	-	2
Crewe Alex.	Tr	08.39	46	1	-	0

STILL, Ronald G.
Aberdeen, 10 June, 1943 (CF)

League Club	Source	Date Signed	Seasons Played	Apps	Subs	Gls
Arsenal	Woodside B.C.	08.61				
Notts Co.	Tr	07.65	65-66	46	0	15
Brentford	Tr	07.67	67	1	0	0

STILLE, Giles K.
Westminster, 10 November, 1958 (M)

League Club	Source	Date Signed	Seasons Played	Apps	Subs	Gls
Brighton & H. A.	Kingstonian	05.79	79-83	20	7	4

STILLYARDS, George E. W.
Lincoln, 29 December, 1918 (WH)

League Club	Source	Date Signed	Seasons Played	Apps	Subs	Gls
Lincoln C.	Botolph U.	11.42	46-48	100	-	2

STIMPSON, Barrie G.
Billingham, 8 February, 1964 (LB)

League Club	Source	Date Signed	Seasons Played	Apps	Subs	Gls
Hartlepool U.	App	02.82	80-83	66	2	2
Chesterfield	Tr	11.83	83	27	0	0
Hartlepool U.	Tr	11.84	84	18	0	0

STIMSON, Mark
Plaistow, 27 December, 1967 (LB)

League Club	Source	Date Signed	Seasons Played	Apps	Subs	Gls
Tottenham H.	YT	07.85	86-88	1	1	0
Leyton Orient	L	03.88	87	10	0	0
Gillingham	L	01.89	88	18	0	0
Newcastle U.	Tr	06.89	89-91	81	3	2

STINSON, Hugh M. J.
Bacup, 18 May, 1937 (WH)

League Club	Source	Date Signed	Seasons Played	Apps	Subs	Gls
Accrington St.	Jnrs	05.55	58	3	-	0
Gillingham	Tr	07.59	59	1	-	0

STIRK, John
Consett, 5 September, 1955 E Yth (RB)

League Club	Source	Date Signed	Seasons Played	Apps	Subs	Gls
Ipswich T.	App	06.73	77	6	0	0
Watford	Tr	06.78	78	46	0	0
Chesterfield	Tr	03.80	79-82	54	2	0

STIRLAND, Cecil J.
Manchester, 15 July, 1921 (WH)

League Club	Source	Date Signed	Seasons Played	Apps	Subs	Gls
Doncaster Rov.	Jnrs	07.38	46-48	68	-	0
New Brighton	Tr	01.50	49-50	51	-	0
Scunthorpe U.	Tr	08.51	51	17	-	0

STIRLING, James R.
Airdrie, 23 July, 1925 (CH)

League Club	Source	Date Signed	Seasons Played	Apps	Subs	Gls
Bournemouth	Coltness U.	07.47	47-49	73	-	1
Birmingham C.	Tr	06.50				
Southend U.	Tr	12.50	50-59	218	-	1

STITFALL, Albert E.
Cardiff, 7 July, 1924 (FB)

League Club	Source	Date Signed	Seasons Played	Apps	Subs	Gls
Cardiff C.	Jnrs	11.48	48-51	9	-	1
Torquay U.	Tr	03.52	51-52	22	-	1

STITFALL, Ronald F.
Cardiff, 14 December, 1925 W-2 (FB)

League Club	Source	Date Signed	Seasons Played	Apps	Subs	Gls
Cardiff C.	Jnrs	09.47	47-63	402	-	8

STOBART, Barry H.
Doncaster, 6 June, 1938 (CF)

League Club	Source	Date Signed	Seasons Played	Apps	Subs	Gls
Wolverhampton W.	Jnrs	12.55	59-63	49	-	20
Manchester C.	Tr	08.64	64	14	-	1
Aston Villa	Tr	11.64	64-67	45	0	18
Shrewsbury T.	Tr	10.67	67-68	34	2	9

STOBART, Sean A.
Wolverhampton, 31 July, 1966 (F)

League Club	Source	Date Signed	Seasons Played	Apps	Subs	Gls
Scunthorpe U. (N/C)	Jnrs	07.84	85	0	2	1

STOBBART, George C.
Morpeth, 9 January, 1921 (IF)

League Club	Source	Date Signed	Seasons Played	Apps	Subs	Gls
Middlesbrough	Netherfield	11.45				
Newcastle U.	Tr	09.46	46-48	66	-	21
Luton T.	Tr	10.49	49-51	107	-	30
Millwall	Tr	08.52	52-53	68	-	27
Brentford	Tr	05.54	54-55	57	-	18

STOCK, Harold
Stockport, 31 July, 1918 (IF)

League Club	Source	Date Signed	Seasons Played	Apps	Subs	Gls
Stockport Co.		07.38	38-47	19	-	6
Oldham Ath.	Tr	07.48	48-50	35	-	10

STOCKIN, Ronald
Birmingham, 27 June, 1931 (IF)

League Club	Source	Date Signed	Seasons Played	Apps	Subs	Gls
Walsall	West Bromwich A. (Am)	01.52	51	6	-	3
Wolverhampton W.	Tr	02.52	52-53	21	-	7
Cardiff C.	Tr	06.54	54-56	57	-	16
Grimsby T.	Tr	06.57	57-59	49	-	14

STOCKLEY, Kenneth S.
Watford, 24 November, 1926 (IF)

League Club	Source	Date Signed	Seasons Played	Apps	Subs	Gls
Luton T.	Jnrs	02.44				
Watford	Tr	07.48	49	1	-	0

STOCKS, David H.
Dulwich, 20 April, 1943 (FB)

League Club	Source	Date Signed	Seasons Played	Apps	Subs	Gls
Charlton Ath.	Jnrs	01.62	61-64	26	-	0
Gillingham	Tr	05.65	65	45	0	0
Bournemouth	Tr	06.66	66-71	220	0	2
Torquay U.	Tr	01.72	71-76	150	0	3

STOCKS, Joseph R.
Hull, 27 November, 1941 (WH)

League Club	Source	Date Signed	Seasons Played	Apps	Subs	Gls
Hull C.	Jnrs	12.58	59-60	9	-	1
Millwall	Tr	08.61	61-63	30	-	1

STOCKWELL, Michael T.
Chelmsford, 14 February, 1965 (M)

League Club	Source	Date Signed	Seasons Played	Apps	Subs	Gls
Ipswich T.	App	12.82	85-91	205	14	15

STODDART, Terence
Newcastle, 28 November, 1931 (OR)

League Club	Source	Date Signed	Seasons Played	Apps	Subs	Gls
Newcastle U.	Jnrs	01.49				
Darlington	Tr	05.54	54-55	8	-	0
York C.	Tr	07.56	56	3	-	0

STOKER, Gareth
Bishop Auckland, 22 February, 1973 (M)

League Club	Source	Date Signed	Seasons Played	Apps	Subs	Gls
Hull C.	Leeds U. (YT)	09.91	91	19	5	2

STOKES, Albert W.
Sheffield, 26 January, 1933 (CF)

League Club	Source	Date Signed	Seasons Played	Apps	Subs	Gls
Grimsby T.	Hampton Sports	02.54	54-56	17	-	3
Scunthorpe U.	Tr	07.57	57	5	-	2
Southport	Tr	02.59	58	6	-	2

STOKES, Alfred F.
Hackney, 3 October, 1932 Eu23-1/EF Lge/E'B'-1 (IF)

League Club	Source	Date Signed	Seasons Played	Apps	Subs	Gls
Tottenham H.	Clapton	02.53	52-58	65	-	40
Fulham	Tr	07.59	59	15	-	6
Watford	Cambridge C.	04.61	61	14	-	2

STOKES, Derek
Normanton, 13 September, 1939 Eu23-4 (CF)

League Club	Source	Date Signed	Seasons Played	Apps	Subs	Gls
Bradford C.	Jnrs	04.57	57-59	94	-	44
Huddersfield T.	Tr	06.60	60-64	153	-	65
Bradford C.	Tr	01.66	65-66	31	1	11

STOKES, Robert W.
Portsmouth, 30 January, 1951 E Yth (F)

League Club	Source	Date Signed	Seasons Played	Apps	Subs	Gls
Southampton	App	02.68	68-76	194	22	40
Portsmouth	Tr	08.77	77	23	1	2

STOKES, Wayne D.
Wolverhampton, 16 February, 1965 (CD)

League Club	Source	Date Signed	Seasons Played	Apps	Subs	Gls
Gillingham	Coventry C. (App)	07.82	82-83	2	1	0
Stockport Co.	Gloucester C.	10.86	86	17	1	1
Hartlepool U.	Tr	07.87	87-89	62	0	2

STOKLE, David
Hartlepool, 1 December, 1969 (CD)

League Club	Source	Date Signed	Seasons Played	Apps	Subs	Gls
Hartlepool U.	YT	07.88	86-89	9	0	0

STOKOE, Dennis
Blyth, 6 June, 1925 (CH)

League Club	Source	Date Signed	Seasons Played	Apps	Subs	Gls
Chesterfield	North Shields	01.47				
Carlisle U.	Tr	07.48	48-53	148	-	2
Workington	Tr	10.53	53-55	107	-	2
Gateshead	Tr	08.56	56	13	-	0

STOKOE, Robert
Mickley, 21 September, 1930 (CH)

League Club	Source	Date Signed	Seasons Played	Apps	Subs	Gls
Newcastle U.	Jnrs	09.47	50-60	261	-	4
Bury	Tr	02.61	60-63	81	-	0

STONE, David K.
Bristol, 29 December, 1942 (HB)

League Club	Source	Date Signed	Seasons Played	Apps	Subs	Gls
Bristol Rov.	Jnrs	03.60	62-67	145	3	6
Southend U.	Tr	07.68	68	6	0	0

STONE, Edward L.
Gorleston, 5 January, 1942 (F)

League Club	Source	Date Signed	Seasons Played	Apps	Subs	Gls
Charlton Ath.	Jnrs	08.59				
Crystal Palace	Tr	05.61	61	1	-	0

STONE, Frederick W.
Bristol, 5 July, 1925 (FB)

League Club	Source	Date Signed	Seasons Played	Apps	Subs	Gls
Bristol C.		06.47	47-52	64	-	3

STONE, Geoffrey
Mansfield, 10 April, 1924 (CH)

League Club	Source	Date Signed	Seasons Played	Apps	Subs	Gls
Notts Co.	Beeston B.C.	09.48	48-49	4	-	0
Darlington	Tr	08.50	50-51	31	-	0

STONE, John G.
Saltburn, 3 March, 1953 (FB)

League Club	Source	Date Signed	Seasons Played	Apps	Subs	Gls
Middlesbrough	South Bank	07.70	71	2	0	0
York C.	Tr	07.72	72-75	86	0	5
Darlington	Tr	07.76	76-78	120	0	14
Grimsby T.	Tr	07.79	79-82	89	5	2
Rotherham U.	Tr	09.83	83	10	0	1

STONE, Michael
Hucknall, 23 May, 1938 (G)

League Club	Source	Date Signed	Seasons Played	Apps	Subs	Gls
Notts Co.	Linby Colly	07.58	58	7	-	0

STONE, Peter J.
Oxford, 8 October, 1922 (CH)

League Club	Source	Date Signed	Seasons Played	Apps	Subs	Gls
Luton T. (Am)	Oxford C.	12.51	51	1	-	0

STONE, Stephen B.
Gateshead, 20 August, 1971 (M)

League Club	Source	Date Signed	Seasons Played	Apps	Subs	Gls
Nottingham F.	YT	05.89	91	0	1	0

STONEHOUSE, Basil
Guisborough, 27 October, 1952 (D)

League Club	Source	Date Signed	Seasons Played	Apps	Subs	Gls
Middlesbrough	App	12.69				
Halifax T.	L	10.72	72	1	1	0

League Club	Source	Date Signed	Seasons Played	Apps	Subs	Gls
STONEHOUSE, Bernard						
Manchester, 23 December, 1934						(OL)
Rochdale	Crewe Alex. (Am)	08.55	55-56	19	-	1
STONEHOUSE, Derek						
Skelton, 18 November, 1932 E Yth						(FB)
Middlesbrough	Lingdale	05.51	53-61	174	-	0
Hartlepool U.	Tr	09.63	63-64	34	-	0
STONEHOUSE, Kevin						
Bishop Auckland, 20 September, 1959						(F/M)
Blackburn Rov.	Shildon	07.79	79-82	77	8	27
Huddersfield T.	Tr	03.83	82-83	20	2	4
Blackpool	Tr	03.84	83-85	53	2	19
Darlington	Tr	07.87	87-88	59	13	20
Carlisle U.	L	03.89	88	0	3	0
Rochdale	Tr	07.89	89	13	1	2
STONEMAN, Paul						
Tynemouth, 26 February, 1973						(D)
Blackpool	YT	07.91	91	17	2	1
STONES, Gordon						
Kearsley, 18 November, 1934						(CH)
Accrington St.	Bury (Am)	09.54	55-60	109	-	1
STOPFORD, Alan						
Sheffield, 20 November, 1946						(OR)
Chesterfield (Am)	Sheffield U. (Am)	01.67	66	2	0	0
STOPFORD, Leslie						
Manchester, 9 May, 1942						(F)
Chester C.	Jnrs	06.60	59-61	6	-	1
STORER, Peter R.						
Shoreditch, 14 February, 1935						(G)
Watford (Am)	Berkhamsted	03.59	58	9	-	0

League Club	Source	Date Signed	Seasons Played	Apps	Subs	Gls
STORER, Stuart J.						
Rugby, 16 January, 1967						(RW)
Mansfield T. (YT)	YT	08.83	83	0	1	0
Birmingham C.	V. S. Rugby	01.85	85-86	5	3	0
Everton	Tr	03.87				
Wigan Ath.	L	08.87	87	9	3	0
Bolton W.	Tr	12.87	87-91	94	26	12
STOREY, James						
Rowlands Gill, 30 December, 1929						(FB)
Newcastle U.	Spen Black & White	05.48				
Exeter C.	Tr	06.53	53	9	-	0
Bournemouth	Tr	07.54				
Rochdale	Tr	06.55	55-56	24	-	1
Darlington	Tr	06.57	57	6	-	0
STOREY, Luke D.						
Dawdon, 17 December, 1920						(OR)
Lincoln C.	Blackhall Colly	09.47	47-48	11	-	2
STOREY, Peter E.						
Farnham, 7 September, 1945 E Sch/EF Lge/E-19						(D)
Arsenal	App	10.62	65-76	387	4	9
Fulham	Tr	03.77	76-77	17	0	0
STOREY, Sydney						
Darfield, 25 December, 1919						(IF)
Huddersfield T.		09.43				
York C.	Wombwell	05.47	46-55	328	-	40
Barnsley	Tr	05.56	56	29	-	4
Accrington St.	Tr	10.57	57-58	30	-	2
Bradford P. A.	Tr	07.59	59	2	-	0
STOREY-MOORE, Ian						
Ipswich, 17 January, 1945 Eu23-2/EF Lge/E-1						(W)
Nottingham F.	Jnrs	05.62	63-71	235	1	105
Manchester U.	Tr	03.72	71-73	39	0	11

Ian Storey-Moore (Nottingham Forest, Manchester United & England)

STORF, David A.
Sheffield, 4 December, 1943 (OL)

League Club	Source	Date Signed	Seasons Played	Apps	Subs	Gls
Sheffield Wed.	Jnrs	12.60				
Rochdale	Tr	06.63	63-66	138	0	19
Barrow	Tr	07.67	67-71	154	4	26

STORRAR, David M.
Lochgelly, 16 January, 1933 (OL)

League Club	Source	Date Signed	Seasons Played	Apps	Subs	Gls
Sheffield Wed.		02.51	52	4	-	0

STORRIE, James
Kirkintilloch, 31 March, 1940 (CF)

League Club	Source	Date Signed	Seasons Played	Apps	Subs	Gls
Leeds U.	Airdrieonians	06.62	62-66	123	3	58
Rotherham U.	Aberdeen	12.67	67-69	70	1	19
Portsmouth	Tr	12.69	69-71	43	0	12
Aldershot	L	03.72	71	5	0	1

STORTON, Stanley E.
Keighley, 5 January, 1939 (FB)

League Club	Source	Date Signed	Seasons Played	Apps	Subs	Gls
Bradford C.	Huddersfield T. (Am)	07.57	59-63	111	-	5
Darlington	Tr	01.64	63	15	-	0
Hartlepool U.	Tr	07.64	64-65	72	0	0
Tranmere Rov.	Tr	07.66	66-69	113	7	2

STORTON, Trevor G.
Keighley, 26 November, 1949 (CD)

League Club	Source	Date Signed	Seasons Played	Apps	Subs	Gls
Tranmere Rov.	Jnrs	10.67	67-71	111	7	9
Liverpool	Tr	08.72	72-73	5	0	0
Chester C.	Tr	07.74	74-83	396	0	17

STOTT, Ian
Wallingford, 17 October, 1955 (CD)

League Club	Source	Date Signed	Seasons Played	Apps	Subs	Gls
Oxford U. (N/C)	West Ham U. (Am)	07.77	77-79	27	0	3

STOTT, Keith
Atherton, 12 March, 1944 (CD)

League Club	Source	Date Signed	Seasons Played	Apps	Subs	Gls
Crewe Alex.	Manchester C. (Am)	10.64	64-69	188	3	11
Chesterfield	Tr	07.70	70-74	140	1	4

STOUTT, Stephen P.
Halifax, 5 April, 1964 (D)

League Club	Source	Date Signed	Seasons Played	Apps	Subs	Gls
Huddersfield T. (N/C)	Bradley R.	01.84	83-84	6	0	0
Wolverhampton W.	Tr	04.85	85-87	91	3	5
Grimsby T.	Tr	07.88	88-89	3	0	1
Lincoln C.	Tr	12.89	89-90	36	10	1

STOWELL, Bruce
Bradford, 20 September, 1941 (WH)

League Club	Source	Date Signed	Seasons Played	Apps	Subs	Gls
Bradford C.	Jnrs	12.58	59-71	401	0	16
Rotherham U.	Tr	07.72	72	14	2	0

STOWELL, Michael
Preston, 19 April, 1965 (G)

League Club	Source	Date Signed	Seasons Played	Apps	Subs	Gls
Everton	Leyland Motors	12.85				
Chester C.	L	09.87	87	14	0	0
York C.	L	12.87	87	6	0	0
Manchester C.	L	01.88	87	14	0	0
Port Vale	L	10.88	88	7	0	0
Wolverhampton W.	L	03.89	88	7	0	0
Preston N. E.	L	02.90	89	2	0	0
Wolverhampton W.	Tr	06.90	90-91	85	0	0

STRACHAN, Gordon D.
Edinburgh, 9 February, 1957 S Yth/Su21-1/S-50 (RM)

League Club	Source	Date Signed	Seasons Played	Apps	Subs	Gls
Manchester U.	Aberdeen	08.84	84-88	155	5	33
Leeds U.	Tr	03.89	88-91	126	1	30

STRAIN, James H.
Chesham, 28 November, 1937 (CH)

League Club	Source	Date Signed	Seasons Played	Apps	Subs	Gls
Watford	Chesham U.	11.55	56	3	-	0
Millwall	Tr	09.58	58	5	-	0

STRATFORD, Paul
Northampton, 4 September, 1955 (F)

League Club	Source	Date Signed	Seasons Played	Apps	Subs	Gls
Northampton T.	App	10.72	72-77	169	3	58

STRATHIE, James W.
Beancross, 12 February, 1913 Died 1976 (CH)

League Club	Source	Date Signed	Seasons Played	Apps	Subs	Gls
Luton T.	St Bernards	05.37	37-38	2	-	0
Northampton T.	Tr	07.39	46	6	-	0

STRATTON, Reginald M.
Farnborough, 10 July, 1939 E Yth/E Amat (CF)

League Club	Source	Date Signed	Seasons Played	Apps	Subs	Gls
Fulham	Woking	05.59	59-64	21	-	1
Colchester U.	Tr	05.65	65-67	112	0	50

STRAUSS, William H.
South Africa, 6 January, 1916 Died 1987 (W)

League Club	Source	Date Signed	Seasons Played	Apps	Subs	Gls
Plymouth Arg.	Aberdeen	07.46	46-53	158	-	40

STRAW, Ian E.
Sheffield, 27 May, 1967 (M)

League Club	Source	Date Signed	Seasons Played	Apps	Subs	Gls
Grimsby T.	Southampton (App)	08.86	86	7	3	0

STRAW, Raymond
Ilkeston, 22 May, 1933 (CF)

League Club	Source	Date Signed	Seasons Played	Apps	Subs	Gls
Derby Co.	Ilkeston T.	10.51	51-57	94	-	57
Coventry C.	Tr	11.57	57-60	142	-	79
Mansfield T.	Tr	08.61	61-62	44	-	12

STREET, Jeffrey L.
Manchester, 20 April, 1948 (CH)

League Club	Source	Date Signed	Seasons Played	Apps	Subs	Gls
Manchester C.	Jnrs	08.65				
Southport	Tr	08.67	67	9	0	0
Barrow	Altrincham	07.69	69	11	0	1

STREET, John
Sheffield, 27 July, 1934 (OR)

League Club	Source	Date Signed	Seasons Played	Apps	Subs	Gls
Bradford C.	Jnrs	11.51	51	1	-	0

STREET, John
Liverpool, 30 May, 1928 (IF)

League Club	Source	Date Signed	Seasons Played	Apps	Subs	Gls
Sheffield Wed.	Liverpool (Am)	05.45				
Rotherham U.		07.47	47	2	-	0
Southport		01.49	48-49	7	-	1
Reading	Bootle	05.51				
Barrow	Tr	07.53	53-54	30	-	5

STREET, Terence E.
Poplar, 9 December, 1948 (WH)

League Club	Source	Date Signed	Seasons Played	Apps	Subs	Gls
Leyton Orient	Jnrs	12.66	66	1	0	0

STREETE, Floyd A.
Jamaica, 5 May, 1959 (CD)

League Club	Source	Date Signed	Seasons Played	Apps	Subs	Gls
Cambridge U.	Rivet Sports	07.76	76-82	111	14	19
Derby Co.	Utrecht (Neth)	10.84	84-85	35	0	0
Wolverhampton W.	Tr	10.85	85-89	157	2	6
Reading	Tr	07.90	90-91	38	0	0

STRETEN, Bernard R.
Gillingham, 14 January, 1921 E Amat/E-1 (G)

League Club	Source	Date Signed	Seasons Played	Apps	Subs	Gls
Luton T.	Shrewsbury T.	01.47	46-56	276	-	0

Gordon Strachan (Aberdeen, Manchester United, Leeds United & Scotland)

League Club	Source	Date Signed	Seasons Played	Career Record Apps	Subs	Gls
STRETTON, Donald						
Clowne, 4 September, 1920 Died 1978						(CF)
Halifax T.	Thorne Colly	07.47	47	10	-	5
STRICKLAND, Derek						
Stoneyburn, 7 November, 1959 S Sch						(F)
Leicester C.	Glasgow Rangers	09.79	79	4	3	2
STRIDE, David R.						
Lymington, 14 March, 1958						(LB)
Chelsea	App	01.76	78-79	35	0	0
Millwall	Memphis (USA)	01.83	82-83	55	0	3
Leyton Orient	Tr	07.84	84	29	0	0
STRINGER, David R.						
Great Yarmouth, 15 October, 1944 E Yth						(D)
Norwich C.	Gorleston Minors	05.63	64-75	417	2	18
Cambridge U.	Tr	09.76	76-80	153	4	1
STRINGER, Edmund						
Sheffield, 6 February, 1925						(IF)
Oldham Ath.	Norton Woodseats	07.49	49	1	-	0
STRINGFELLOW, Ian R.						
Nottingham, 8 May, 1969						(F)
Mansfield T.	App	04.86	85-91	73	50	20
STRINGFELLOW, Michael D.						
Kirkby-in-Ashfield, 27 January, 1943						(OL)
Mansfield T.	Jnrs	02.60	60-61	57	-	10
Leicester C.	Tr	01.62	61-74	292	23	82
STRINGFELLOW, Peter						
Walkden, 21 February, 1939						(IF)
Oldham Ath.	Walkden T.	12.58	58-60	54	-	16
Gillingham	Sankeys	12.62	62-63	35	-	2
Chesterfield	Tr	08.64	64	28	-	7
STRODDER, Colin J.						
Leeds, 23 December, 1941						(FB)
Huddersfield T.		04.60				
Halifax T.	Tr	07.61	61-62	20	-	0
STRODDER, Gary J.						
Cleckheaton, 1 April, 1965						(CD)
Lincoln C.	App	04.83	82-86	122	10	6
West Ham U.	Tr	03.87	86-89	59	6	2
West Bromwich A.	Tr	08.90	90-91	67	4	4
STRONACH, Peter						
Seaham, 1 September, 1956 E Sch						(W)
Sunderland	App	09.73	77	2	1	0
York C.	Tr	06.78	78-79	30	4	2
STRONG, Andrew F.						
Hartlepool, 17 September, 1966						(LB)
Middlesbrough	App	09.84	84	6	0	0
STRONG, Geoffrey H.						
Kirkheaton, 19 September, 1937						(IF)
Arsenal	Stanley U.	04.58	60-64	125	-	69
Liverpool	Tr	11.64	64-69	150	5	29
Coventry C.	Tr	07.70	70-71	33	0	0
STRONG, G. James						
Morpeth, 7 June, 1916 Died 1989						(G)
Hartlepool U.		02.34	33	1	-	0
Chesterfield	Tr	08.34	34	18	-	0
Portsmouth	Tr	03.35	34-37	59	-	0
Walsall		07.39				
Burnley	Tr	01.46	46-52	264	-	0
STRONG, Leslie						
Streatham, 3 July, 1953						(LB)
Fulham	App	06.71	72-82	370	3	5
Brentford	L	12.82	82	5	0	0
Crystal Palace (N/C)	Tr	08.83	83	7	0	0
Rochdale	U.S.A.	10.84	84	1	0	0
STRONG, Stephen						
Bristol, 17 April, 1962						(CD)
Hereford U.	App	02.80	78-80	16	0	0
STROUD, Derek N. L.						
Wimborne, 11 February, 1930						(OR)
Bournemouth	Poole T.	08.50	50-52	78	-	17
Grimsby T.	Tr	06.53	53-54	71	-	12
STROUD, Kenneth A.						
Fulham, 1 December, 1953						(M)
Swindon T.	App	03.71	71-81	302	9	16
Newport Co.	Tr	08.82	82-83	47	1	0
Bristol C.	Tr	10.83	83-84	68	1	4
STROUD, Roy						
Silvertown, 16 March, 1925 E Sch/E Amat						(OR)
West Ham U.	Hendon	04.52	51-56	13	-	4
STROUD, William J. A.						
Hammersmith, 7 July, 1919						(WH)
Southampton	Jnrs	02.40	46	29	-	4
Leyton Orient	Tr	06.47	47-49	65	-	1
Newport Co.	Tr	06.50	50-54	63	-	1
STRUTT, Brian						
Malta, 21 September, 1959						(F)
Sheffield Wed.	App	09.77	79	2	0	0
STUART, Edward A.						
South Africa, 12 May, 1931						(D)
Wolverhampton W.	Rangers (SA)	01.51	51-61	287	-	1
Stoke C.	Tr	07.62	62-63	63	-	2
Tranmere Rov.	Tr	08.64	64-65	83	0	2
Stockport Co.	Tr	07.66	66-67	77	0	1
STUART, Graham C.						
Tooting, 24 October, 1970 E Yth/Eu21-5						(F)
Chelsea	YT	06.89	89-91	39	9	5
STUART, Mark R. N.						
Chiswick, 15 December, 1966						(LW)
Charlton Ath.	Jnrs	07.84	84-88	89	18	28
Plymouth Arg.	Tr	11.88	88-89	55	2	11
Ipswich T.	L	03.90	89	5	0	2
Bradford C.	Tr	07.90	90-91	22	7	5
STUART, Robert W.						
Middlesbrough, 9 October, 1913 E Sch						(FB)
Middlesbrough	South Bank	01.31	31-47	247	-	2
Plymouth Arg.	Tr	10.47	47	20	-	0
STUBBINS, Albert						
Wallsend, 13 July, 1919 EF Lge						(CF)
Newcastle U.	Monkseaton	04.37	37-46	27	-	5
Liverpool	Tr	09.46	46-52	161	-	75
STUBBS, Alan						
Liverpool, 6 October, 1971						(CD)
Bolton W.	YT	07.90	90-91	42	13	1
STUBBS, Alfred T.						
West Ham, 18 April, 1922						(RH)
Crystal Palace		12.46	47-48	3	-	0
STUBBS, Brian H.						
Keyworth, 8 February, 1950						(CD)
Notts Co.	Loughborough U.	09.68	68-79	423	3	21
STUBBS, Charles F.						
West Ham, 22 January, 1920						(CF)
Darlington	Bamforths	01.44	46-47	41	-	17
STUBBS, Leslie L.						
Great Wakering, 18 February, 1929						(IF)
Southend U.	Great Wakering	05.48	49-52	84	-	40
Chelsea	Tr	11.52	52-58	112	-	34
Southend U.	Tr	11.58	58-59	22	-	3
STUBBS, Robin G.						
Birmingham, 22 April, 1941						(CF)
Birmingham C.	Jnrs	04.58	58-62	61	-	17
Torquay U.	Tr	08.63	63-68	214	3	121
Bristol Rov.	Tr	07.69	69-71	90	3	32
Torquay U.	Tr	02.72	71-72	19	2	1
STUBBS, William						
Hartlepool, 1 August, 1966						(F)
Nottingham F.	Seaham Red Star	04.87				
Doncaster Rov.	L	09.87	87	8	1	1
Grimsby T.	L	03.88	87	2	5	2
STUCKEY, Bruce G.						
Torquay, 19 February, 1947						(W)
Exeter C.	App	02.65	65-67	37	2	6
Sunderland	Tr	11.67	67-69	24	2	2
Torquay U.	Tr	02.71	70-73	70	18	6
Reading	Tr	11.73	73-76	92	5	7
Torquay U.	L	01.75	74	4	0	0
Bournemouth	L	03.77	76	5	0	0
STURRIDGE, Dean C.						
Birmingham, 26 July, 1973						(F)
Derby Co.	YT	07.91	91	1	0	0

STURRIDGE, Michael A.
Birmingham, 18 September, 1962 (F)

League Club	Source	Date Signed	Seasons Played	Apps	Subs	Gls
Birmingham C.	App	06.80				
Wrexham	L	12.83	83	3	1	0

STURRIDGE, Simon A.
Birmingham, 9 December, 1969 (F)

League Club	Source	Date Signed	Seasons Played	Apps	Subs	Gls
Birmingham C.	YT	07.88	88-91	114	16	29

STURROCK, David
Dundee, 22 February, 1938 (F)

League Club	Source	Date Signed	Seasons Played	Apps	Subs	Gls
Accrington St.	Dundee U.	07.60	60	17	-	5

STUTTARD, J. Ellis
Burnley, 24 April, 1920 Died 1984 (WH)

League Club	Source	Date Signed	Seasons Played	Apps	Subs	Gls
Plymouth Arg.	Burnley (Am)	09.38	38-46	29	-	1
Torquay U.	Tr	09.47	47-50	82	-	0

STYLES, Arthur
Liverpool, 3 September, 1949 E Sch/E Yth (LB)

League Club	Source	Date Signed	Seasons Played	Apps	Subs	Gls
Everton	App	08.67	72-73	22	1	0
Birmingham C.	Tr	02.74	73-77	71	3	4
Peterborough U.	Tr	07.78	78	32	0	1
Portsmouth	Tr	07.79	79	26	0	0

STYLES, Arthur J.
Smethwick, 29 October, 1939 (WH)

League Club	Source	Date Signed	Seasons Played	Apps	Subs	Gls
West Bromwich A.	Jnrs	11.56	59	1	-	0
Wrexham	Tr	03.60	59-60	16	-	0

SUART, Ronald
Kendal, 18 November, 1920 (CH)

League Club	Source	Date Signed	Seasons Played	Apps	Subs	Gls
Blackpool	Netherfield	01.39	46-49	104	-	0
Blackburn Rov.	Tr	09.49	49-54	176	-	0

SUCKLING, Perry J.
Leyton, 12 October, 1965 E Yth/Eu21-10 (G)

League Club	Source	Date Signed	Seasons Played	Apps	Subs	Gls
Coventry C.	App	10.83	82-83	27	0	0
Manchester C.	Tr	06.86	86-87	39	0	0
Crystal Palace	Tr	01.88	87-91	59	0	0
West Ham U.	L	12.89	89	6	0	0
Brentford	L	10.91	91	8	0	0

SUDDABY, Donald
Brighouse, 7 June, 1930

League Club	Source	Date Signed	Seasons Played	Apps	Subs	Gls
Halifax T.	Chelsea (Am)	08.51	51	5	-	0

SUDDABY, Peter
Stockport, 23 December, 1947 E Amat (CD)

League Club	Source	Date Signed	Seasons Played	Apps	Subs	Gls
Blackpool	Skelmersdale U.	05.70	70-79	331	1	9
Brighton & H. A.	Tr	11.79	79	21	2	0
Wimbledon	Tr	11.81	81	6	0	0

SUDDARDS, Jeffrey
Bradford, 17 January, 1929 (FB)

League Club	Source	Date Signed	Seasons Played	Apps	Subs	Gls
Bradford P. A.	Hull C. (Am)	03.49	49-58	327	-	0

SUDDICK, Alan
Chester-le-Street, 2 May, 1944 E Yth/Eu23-2 (M)

League Club	Source	Date Signed	Seasons Played	Apps	Subs	Gls
Newcastle U.	App	10.61	61-66	144	0	41
Blackpool	Tr	12.66	66-76	305	5	64
Stoke C.	Tr	12.76	76	9	0	1
Southport	L	08.77	77	6	0	0
Bury	Tr	09.77	77	30	4	2

SUGGETT, Colin
Washington, 30 December, 1948 E Sch/E Yth (M)

League Club	Source	Date Signed	Seasons Played	Apps	Subs	Gls
Sunderland	App	01.66	66-68	83	3	24
West Bromwich A.	Tr	07.69	69-72	123	5	20
Norwich C.	Tr	02.73	72-77	200	3	21
Newcastle U.	Tr	08.78	78	20	3	0

SUGRUE, Paul A.
Coventry, 6 November, 1960 (M)

League Club	Source	Date Signed	Seasons Played	Apps	Subs	Gls
Manchester C.	Nuneaton Bor.	02.80	79-80	5	1	0
Cardiff C.	Tr	08.81	81	2	3	0
Middlesbrough	Kansas C. (USA)	12.82	82-84	66	3	6
Portsmouth	Tr	12.84	84-85	2	2	0
Northampton T.	Tr	03.86	85	2	6	2
Newport Co.	Tr	08.86	86	1	1	0

SULLEY, Christopher S.
Camberwell, 3 December, 1959 (LB)

League Club	Source	Date Signed	Seasons Played	Apps	Subs	Gls
Chelsea	App	12.77				
Bournemouth	Tr	03.81	80-85	205	1	3
Blackburn Rov.	Dundee U.	03.87	86-91	134	0	3

SULLIVAN, Alan
Aberdare, 12 November, 1953 W Sch (W)

League Club	Source	Date Signed	Seasons Played	Apps	Subs	Gls
Swansea C.	App	08.71	70-71	7	1	1

SULLIVAN, Brian A. J.
Edmonton, 30 December, 1941 E Sch/E Yth (IF)

League Club	Source	Date Signed	Seasons Played	Apps	Subs	Gls
Fulham	Jnrs	05.59	59	2	-	1

SULLIVAN, Colin J.
Saltash, 24 June, 1951 E Yth/Eu23-2 (LB)

League Club	Source	Date Signed	Seasons Played	Apps	Subs	Gls
Plymouth Arg.	App	07.68	67-73	225	5	7
Norwich C.	Tr	06.74	74-78	154	3	3
Cardiff C.	Tr	02.79	78-81	61	2	1
Hereford U. (N/C)	Tr	12.81	81	8	0	0
Portsmouth	Tr	03.82	81-83	94	0	0
Swansea C.	Tr	03.85	84-85	53	0	0

SULLIVAN, Cornelius H. (Con)
Bristol, 22 August, 1928 (G)

League Club	Source	Date Signed	Seasons Played	Apps	Subs	Gls
Bristol C.	Horfield O.B.	05.49	50-52	73	-	0
Arsenal	Tr	02.54	53-57	28	-	0

SULLIVAN, Derek
Newport, 10 August, 1930 Died 1983 W-17 (WH)

League Club	Source	Date Signed	Seasons Played	Apps	Subs	Gls
Cardiff C.	Jnrs	09.47	47-60	276	-	18
Exeter C.	Tr	06.61	61	44	-	0
Newport Co.	Tr	07.62	62	23	-	0

SULLIVAN, Neil
Sutton, 24 February, 1970 (G)

League Club	Source	Date Signed	Seasons Played	Apps	Subs	Gls
Wimbledon	YT	07.88	90-91	2	0	0
Crystal Palace	L	05.92	91	1	0	0

SUMMERBEE, George M.
Winchester, 22 October, 1914 Died 1955 (FB)

League Club	Source	Date Signed	Seasons Played	Apps	Subs	Gls
Aldershot	Winchester C.	05.34	34	18	-	0
Preston N.E.	Tr	01.35	37-38	2	-	0
Chester C.	Tr	05.46	46	9	-	0
Barrow	Tr	06.47	47-49	122	-	0

SUMMERBEE, Michael G.
Cheltenham, 15 December, 1942 Eu23-1/EF Lge/E-8 (W)

League Club	Source	Date Signed	Seasons Played	Apps	Subs	Gls
Swindon T.	Cheltenham T.	03.60	59-64	218	-	39
Manchester C.	Tr	08.65	65-74	355	2	47
Burnley	Tr	06.75	75-76	51	0	0
Blackpool	Tr	12.76	76	3	0	0
Stockport Co.	Tr	08.77	77-79	86	1	6

SUMMERBEE, Nicholas J.
Altrincham, 26 August, 1971 (FB)

League Club	Source	Date Signed	Seasons Played	Apps	Subs	Gls
Swindon T.	YT	07.89	89-91	17	18	0

SUMMERFIELD, Kevin
Walsall, 7 January, 1959 E Yth (W)

League Club	Source	Date Signed	Seasons Played	Apps	Subs	Gls
West Bromwich A.	App	01.77	78-81	5	4	4
Birmingham C.	Tr	05.82	82	2	3	1
Walsall	Tr	12.82	82-83	42	12	17
Cardiff C.	Tr	07.84	84	10	0	1
Plymouth Arg.	Tr	12.84	84-90	118	21	26
Exeter C.	L	03.90	89	4	0	0
Shrewsbury T.	Tr	10.90	90-91	74	2	12

SUMMERHAYES, David M.
Cardiff, 21 March, 1947 Wu23-1 (WH)

League Club	Source	Date Signed	Seasons Played	Apps	Subs	Gls
Cardiff C.	App	03.65	65-67	7	6	0

SUMMERHAYES, Robert E.
Cardiff, 8 January, 1951 W Sch (M)

League Club	Source	Date Signed	Seasons Played	Apps	Subs	Gls
Cardiff C.	App	01.69				
Newport Co.	Tr	08.72	72-74	74	6	4

SUMMERHILL, Alan
Liss, 25 November, 1950 (D)

League Club	Source	Date Signed	Seasons Played	Apps	Subs	Gls
Bournemouth	Jnrs	07.68	69	28	0	0
Crewe Alex.	Tr	09.70	70-71	46	4	1

SUMMERILL, Philip E.
Birmingham, 20 November, 1947 E Yth (F)

League Club	Source	Date Signed	Seasons Played	Apps	Subs	Gls
Birmingham C.	App	12.64	66-72	108	10	46
Huddersfield T.	Tr	01.73	72-74	48	6	11
Millwall	Tr	11.74	74-77	83	4	20
Wimbledon	Tr	09.77	77-78	27	4	4

SUMMERS, Christopher
Cardiff, 6 January, 1972 W Yth (F)

League Club	Source	Date Signed	Seasons Played	Apps	Subs	Gls
Cardiff C.	YT	07.90	90	0	3	0

SUMMERS, George
Glasgow, 30 July, 1941 (F)

League Club	Source	Date Signed	Seasons Played	Apps	Subs	Gls
Brentford	Shawfield Jnrs	01.59	60-64	71	-	25

Mike Summerbee (Swindon Town, Manchester City, Burnley, Blackpool, Stockport County & England)

League Club	Source	Date Signed	Seasons Played	Apps	Subs	Gls
SUMMERS, Gerald T.						
Birmingham, 4 October, 1933						(WH)
West Bromwich A.	Jnrs	08.51	55-56	22	-	0
Sheffield U.	Tr	05.57	57-63	260	-	4
Hull C.	Tr	04.64	63-65	59	0	1
Walsall	Tr	10.65	65-66	39	2	1
SUMMERS, John H.						
Hammersmith, 10 September, 1927 Died 1962						(F)
Fulham	Jnrs	02.47	49	4	-	0
Norwich C.	Tr	06.50	50-53	71	-	33
Millwall	Tr	05.54	54-56	91	-	41
Charlton Ath.	Tr	11.56	56-60	171	-	100
SUMMERSBY, Roy D.						
Lambeth, 19 March, 1935						(WH/IF)
Millwall	Jnrs	03.52	51-58	87	-	13
Crystal Palace	Tr	12.58	58-62	176	-	59
Portsmouth	Tr	06.63	63-64	12	-	1
SUMMERSCALES, William C.						
Willesden, 4 January, 1949						(CD)
Port Vale	Leek T.	02.70	69-74	126	3	4
Rochdale	Tr	07.75	75-76	87	0	4
SUMNER, Alan						
Wrexham, 18 April, 1949						(M)
Stockport Co. (N/C)		06.78	78	3	2	0
SUMNER, Justin T.						
Harrogate, 19 October, 1970						(LW)
Doncaster Rov.	Leeds U. (YT)	08.89	89	2	0	0
SUMPNER, Richard A.						
Leeds, 12 April, 1947						(CF)
Bradford P. A.	Jnrs	01.67	66	2	0	1
SUNDERLAND, Alan						
Conisborough, 1 July, 1953 Eu21-1/Eu23-1/E-1						(F)
Wolverhampton W.	App	06.71	71-77	139	19	30
Arsenal	Tr	11.77	77-83	204	2	55
Ipswich T.	Tr	02.84	83-85	51	7	11
SUNLEY, David						
Skelton, 6 February, 1952						(F)
Sheffield Wed.	App	01.70	70-75	121	9	21
Nottingham F.	L	10.75	75	1	0	0
Hull C.	Tr	01.76	75-77	58	11	11
Lincoln C.	Tr	07.78	78-79	36	5	6
Stockport Co.	Tr	03.80	79-81	79	4	7
SUNLEY, Mark						
Guisborough, 11 August, 1972						(D)
Middlesbrough	YT	10.89				
Darlington	Tr	07.91	91	15	0	0
SURMAN, Leslie						
Tamworth, 23 November, 1947 Died 1978						(G)
Charlton Ath.	App	11.65	65	1	0	0
Rotherham U.	Tr	06.66	66	1	0	0
SURTEES, George H.						
Ryhope, 20 December, 1926						(G)
Southport	Murton Colly	08.46	46	3	-	0
SURTEES, Hubert						
Durham, 16 July, 1921						(W)
Watford	Bushey U.	07.46	47-48	14	-	1
Crystal Palace	Tr	08.49	49	5	-	0
SUSSEX, Andrew R.						
Enfield, 23 November, 1964						(W/F)
Leyton Orient	App	11.82	81-87	126	18	17
Crewe Alex.	Tr	06.88	88-90	86	16	24
Southend U.	Tr	07.91	91	12	3	3
SUTCH, Daryl						
Beccles, 11 September, 1971 E Yth/Eu21-3						(W)
Norwich C.	YT	07.90	90-91	7	6	0
SUTCLIFFE, Frederick						
Knottingley, 29 May, 1931						(LH)
Birmingham C.		09.51				
Chester C.	Tr	06.52	52-54	47	-	2
SUTCLIFFE, Frederick W. J.						
Fulham, 29 July, 1923						
Millwall		02.47	47-48	12	-	3
Walsall	Tr	07.50	50	5	-	0

League Club	Source	Date Signed	Seasons Played	Apps	Subs	Gls
SUTCLIFFE, Peter D.						
Manchester, 25 January, 1957 E Yth						(W)
Manchester U.	App	07.74				
Stockport Co.	Tr	12.75	75-76	19	8	2
Port Vale	Tr	03.77	76-78	44	6	6
Chester C.	Tr	12.78	78-81	103	6	8
Chester C. (N/C)	Bangor C.	11.83	83	11	0	0
Stockport Co. (N/C)	Tr	03.84	83	0	1	0
SUTHERLAND, George B.						
Glasgow, 11 September, 1923						(CF)
Leyton Orient	Partick Th.	08.49	49-50	42	-	22
SUTHERLAND, Harold R.						
Salford, 30 July, 1915						(CF)
Leeds U.	Sedgeley Park	07.38	38	3	-	1
Exeter C.	Tr	05.47	46-47	14	-	3
Bournemouth	Tr	07.48				
SUTHERLAND, James S.						
Armadale, 6 August, 1918 Died 1987						(LB)
Newport Co.	Forth W.	07.47	47-48	32	-	0
SUTHERLAND, John F.						
Cork (Ire), 10 February, 1932						(FB)
Everton	Evergreen	05.50	56	6	-	0
Chesterfield	Tr	06.57	57-58	47	-	0
Crewe Alex.	Tr	11.58	58-59	47	-	1
SUTTLE, Kenneth G.						
Hammersmith, 25 August, 1928						(W)
Chelsea	Worthing	08.48				
Brighton & H. A.	Tr	07.49	49	3	-	0
SUTTON, Brian						
Rochdale, 8 December, 1934						(G)
Rochdale	Norden Y.C.	10.52	52-55	13	-	0
SUTTON, Christopher R.						
Nottingham, 10 March, 1973						(CD/F)
Norwich C.	YT	07.91	90-91	16	7	2
SUTTON, David W.						
Tarleton (Lancs), 21 January, 1957						(CD)
Plymouth Arg.	App	07.74	73-77	60	1	0
Reading	L	11.77	77	9	0	0
Huddersfield T.	Tr	03.78	77-83	242	0	11
Bolton W.	Tr	06.85	85-87	98	0	4
Rochdale	Tr	08.88	88	28	0	2
SUTTON, David W.						
Leek, 15 December, 1966						(F)
Crewe Alex.	Stoke C. (YT)	07.86	86	0	1	1
SUTTON, Gary						
Folkestone, 2 February, 1962						(G)
Gillingham	App	02.80	80-81	11	0	0
SUTTON, James P.						
Glasgow, 6 September, 1949						(M)
Newcastle U.		06.69				
Mansfield T.	Tr	07.70	70	11	2	0
SUTTON, Melvyn C.						
Birmingham, 13 February, 1946						(M)
Cardiff C.	Aston Villa (Am)	12.67	68-71	135	3	5
Wrexham	Tr	07.72	72-80	355	5	21
Crewe Alex.	Tr	08.82	82	13	0	1
SUTTON, Michael J.						
Norwich, 5 October, 1944						(WH)
Norwich C.	Jnrs	09.62	62-66	46	5	3
Chester C.	Tr	05.67	67-69	136	1	9
Carlisle U.	Tr	06.70	70-71	51	2	1
SUTTON, Richard M.						
Gravesend, 21 August, 1965 E Yth						(D)
Peterborough (App)	App	08.81	82	1	0	0
SUTTON, Stephen J.						
Hartington, 16 April, 1961						(G)
Nottingham F.	App	04.79	80-89	199	0	0
Mansfield T.	L	03.81	80	8	0	0
Derby Co.	L	01.85	84	14	0	0
Coventry C.	L	02.91	90	1	0	0
Luton T.	L	11.91	91	14	0	0
Derby Co.	Tr	03.92	91	10	0	0

League Club	Source	Date Signed	Seasons Played	Apps	Subs	Gls

SVARC, Robert L.
Leicester, 8 February, 1946 (F)

League Club	Source	Date Signed	Seasons Played	Apps	Subs	Gls
Leicester C.	App	03.63	64-68	13	0	2
Lincoln C.	Tr	12.68	68-71	40	5	16
Barrow	L	09.70	70	15	0	3
Colchester U.	Boston U.	12.72	72-75	116	0	59
Blackburn Rov.	Tr	10.75	75-76	42	8	16
Watford	L	09.77	77	1	0	0

SWAIN, Kenneth J.
Cardiff, 31 December, 1954 W Sch (FB)

League Club	Source	Date Signed	Seasons Played	Apps	Subs	Gls
Newport Co.	App	12.72	71-73	7	1	0

SWAIN, Kenneth M.
Birkenhead, 28 January, 1952 (RB)

League Club	Source	Date Signed	Seasons Played	Apps	Subs	Gls
Chelsea	Wycombe W.	08.73	73-78	114	5	26
Aston Villa	Tr	12.78	78-82	148	0	4
Nottingham F.	Tr	10.82	82-84	112	0	2
Portsmouth	Tr	07.85	85-87	113	0	0
West Bromwich A.	L	02.88	87	7	0	1
Crewe Alex.	Tr	08.88	88-91	123	3	1

SWAIN, Malcolm
Windsor, 2 February, 1952 (M)

League Club	Source	Date Signed	Seasons Played	Apps	Subs	Gls
Reading	App	02.70	70-71	37	4	2

SWAIN, Robert
Ripon, 26 March, 1944 (W)

League Club	Source	Date Signed	Seasons Played	Apps	Subs	Gls
Bradford C.	Jnrs	09.61	62	7	-	0

SWAIN, Sidney
Liverpool, 14 October, 1927

League Club	Source	Date Signed	Seasons Played	Apps	Subs	Gls
Halifax T.		07.51	51	8	-	1

SWAINE, Mark A.
Hammersmith, 13 February, 1958 (W)

League Club	Source	Date Signed	Seasons Played	Apps	Subs	Gls
Gillingham (App)	App	07.74	74	1	0	0

SWALES, Stephen C.
Whitby, 26 December, 1973 (LB)

League Club	Source	Date Signed	Seasons Played	Apps	Subs	Gls
Scarborough (YT)	YT	07.90	91	4	0	0

SWALLOW, Barry E.
Doncaster, 2 July, 1942 (CH)

League Club	Source	Date Signed	Seasons Played	Apps	Subs	Gls
Doncaster Rov.	Jnrs	07.59	60-61	51	-	10
Crewe Alex.	Tr	08.62	62-63	14	-	0
Barnsley	Tr	07.64	64-66	97	-	2
Bradford C.	Tr	02.67	66-69	79	6	7
York C.	Tr	10.69	69-75	268	1	21

SWALLOW, Ernest
Wheatley Hill, 9 July, 1919 Died 1962 (FB)

League Club	Source	Date Signed	Seasons Played	Apps	Subs	Gls
Doncaster Rov.	Bentley Colly	11.41	46-47	50	-	0
Barnsley	Tr	01.48	47-49	35	-	0
Oldham Ath.	Tr	08.50	50	6	-	0

SWALLOW, Raymond
Southwark, 15 June, 1935 (W)

League Club	Source	Date Signed	Seasons Played	Apps	Subs	Gls
Arsenal	Jnrs	12.52	54-57	13	-	4
Derby Co.	Tr	09.58	58-63	118	-	21

SWAN, Carl
Sheffield, 12 December, 1957 (CD)

League Club	Source	Date Signed	Seasons Played	Apps	Subs	Gls
Doncaster Rov.	Burton A.	12.80	80-82	14	1	1
Rochdale	L	10.82	82	3	0	0

SWAN, Maurice M. G.
Dublin, 27 September, 1938 IR-1 (G)

League Club	Source	Date Signed	Seasons Played	Apps	Subs	Gls
Cardiff C.	Drumcondra	07.60	60-62	15	-	0
Hull C.	Tr	06.63	63-67	103	0	0

SWAN, Peter
South Elmsall, 8 October, 1936 E Yth/Eu23-3/EF Lge/E-19 (CH)

League Club	Source	Date Signed	Seasons Played	Apps	Subs	Gls
Sheffield Wed.	Jnrs	11.53	55-63	260	-	0
Sheffield Wed.	(Retired)	07.72	72	13	2	0
Bury	Tr	08.73	73	35	0	2

SWAN, Peter H.
Leeds, 28 September, 1966 (F/CD)

League Club	Source	Date Signed	Seasons Played	Apps	Subs	Gls
Leeds U.	YT	08.84	85-88	43	6	11
Hull C.	Tr	03.89	88-90	76	4	24
Port Vale	Tr	08.91	91	27	6	3

SWAN, Ronald M.
Stirling, 8 January, 1941 (G)

League Club	Source	Date Signed	Seasons Played	Apps	Subs	Gls
Oldham Ath.	East Stirling	05.64	64-66	64	0	0
Luton T.	Tr	01.67	66	13	0	0

SWANKIE, Robert B.
Arbroath, 25 February, 1932 (F)

League Club	Source	Date Signed	Seasons Played	Apps	Subs	Gls
Burnley	Arbroath Y.C.	07.50				
Darlington		01.54	53	1	-	0

SWANN, Gary
York, 11 April, 1962 (M/FB)

League Club	Source	Date Signed	Seasons Played	Apps	Subs	Gls
Hull C.	App	04.80	80-86	176	10	9
Preston N.E.	Tr	11.86	86-91	194	5	37

SWANN, Gordon
Maltby, 7 December, 1937 (F)

League Club	Source	Date Signed	Seasons Played	Apps	Subs	Gls
Rotherham U.		07.57	58-60	10	-	2
Barnsley	Tr	07.61	61	2	-	0

SWANNELL, John
Walton-on-Thames, 26 January, 1939 E Amat (G)

League Club	Source	Date Signed	Seasons Played	Apps	Subs	Gls
Stockport Co. (Am)	Corinthian Casuals	06.59	59	1	-	0

SWEENEY, Alan
Glasgow, 31 October, 1956 (RB)

League Club	Source	Date Signed	Seasons Played	Apps	Subs	Gls
Huddersfield T.	App	11.73	74-77	65	1	0
Hartlepool U.	Emley	09.79	79-81	97	0	2

SWEENEY, Andrew
Oldham, 15 October, 1951 (W)

League Club	Source	Date Signed	Seasons Played	Apps	Subs	Gls
Oldham Ath.	Jnrs	02.71	70-74	37	5	2
Bury	L	03.73	72	2	0	0
Rochdale	Tr	07.75	75	12	5	0

SWEENEY, Gerald
Glasgow, 10 July, 1945 (FB)

League Club	Source	Date Signed	Seasons Played	Apps	Subs	Gls
Bristol C.	Morton	08.71	71-81	396	10	22
York C.	Tr	02.82	81	12	0	0

SWEENEY, Paul M. F.
Glasgow, 10 January, 1965 (LB/W)

League Club	Source	Date Signed	Seasons Played	Apps	Subs	Gls
Newcastle U.	Raith Rov.	03.89	88-90	28	8	0

SWEENEY, Thomas J.
Luton, 4 November, 1951

League Club	Source	Date Signed	Seasons Played	Apps	Subs	Gls
Luton T. (App)	App	06.68	68	0	1	0

SWEENEY, William C.
St Andrews, 23 October, 1918 (G)

League Club	Source	Date Signed	Seasons Played	Apps	Subs	Gls
Carlisle U.	Clyde	01.48	47-48	37	-	0

SWEENIE, Thomas T.
Paisley, 15 July, 1945 (IF)

League Club	Source	Date Signed	Seasons Played	Apps	Subs	Gls
Leicester C.	Johnstone Burgh	06.63	63-66	50	1	11
York C.	Huddersfield T. (trial)	10.68	68	6	0	1

Peter Swan (Sheffield Wednesday, Bury & England)

SWEETZER, Gordon E. P.
Canada, 27 January, 1957 Canada Int (F)

League Club	Source	Date Signed	Seasons Played	Apps	Subs	Gls
Brentford		07.75	75-77	68	4	40
Cambridge U.	Tr	04.78	77-79	9	0	3
Brentford	Toronto (Can)	01.82	81	8	1	1

SWEETZER, James E.
Woking, 8 January, 1960 (F)

League Club	Source	Date Signed	Seasons Played	Apps	Subs	Gls
Oxford U.	App	02.77	78	0	8	1
Millwall	Tr	11.79	79	2	1	1

SWIFT, Colin
Barnsley, 23 December, 1933 (RB)

League Club	Source	Date Signed	Seasons Played	Apps	Subs	Gls
Barnsley	Jnrs	08.51	55-61	239	-	0

SWIFT, Frank V.
Blackpool, 26 December, 1913 Died 1958 EF Lge/E-19 (G)

League Club	Source	Date Signed	Seasons Played	Apps	Subs	Gls
Manchester C.	Fleetwood	10.32	32-49	338	-	0

SWIFT, Hugh M.
Sheffield, 22 January, 1921 E'B'-1 (FB)

League Club	Source	Date Signed	Seasons Played	Apps	Subs	Gls
Sheffield Wed.	Lopham Street Meths	09.42	46-50	181	-	0

SWIFT, John K.
Liverpool, 26 July, 1928 (F)

League Club	Source	Date Signed	Seasons Played	Apps	Subs	Gls
Liverpool	Jnrs	08.45				
Southport	Tr	07.51	51	5	-	0

SWIFT, Trevor
Rotherham, 14 September, 1948 (CD)

League Club	Source	Date Signed	Seasons Played	Apps	Subs	Gls
Rotherham U.	Jnrs	09.65	67-74	283	4	21

SWIGGS, Bradley
Plymouth, 12 October, 1959 (F)

League Club	Source	Date Signed	Seasons Played	Apps	Subs	Gls
Plymouth Arg.	Liskeard Ath.	03.84	83	1	1	0

SWIGGS, Robert
Plymouth, 30 March, 1930 (CF)

League Club	Source	Date Signed	Seasons Played	Apps	Subs	Gls
Plymouth Arg.	St Blazey	01.56	55-56	3	-	0

SWINBOURNE, Royston H.
Denaby, 25 August, 1929 E'B'-1 (CF)

League Club	Source	Date Signed	Seasons Played	Apps	Subs	Gls
Wolverhampton W.	Jnrs	09.46	49-55	211	-	107

SWINBURNE, Alan T. A.
Chester-le-Street, 18 May, 1946 (G)

League Club	Source	Date Signed	Seasons Played	Apps	Subs	Gls
Oldham Ath.	App	09.63	63	4	-	0

SWINBURNE, Thomas A.
Houghton-le-Spring, 9 August, 1915 (G)

League Club	Source	Date Signed	Seasons Played	Apps	Subs	Gls
Newcastle U.	Herrington Colly	04.34	34-46	77	-	0

SWINBURNE, Trevor
Houghton-le-Spring, 20 June, 1953 (G)

League Club	Source	Date Signed	Seasons Played	Apps	Subs	Gls
Sunderland	App	06.70	72-76	10	0	0
Carlisle U.	Tr	05.77	77-82	248	0	0
Brentford	Tr	08.83	83-84	45	0	0
Leeds U.	Tr	06.85	85	2	0	0
Doncaster Rov.	L	09.85	85	4	0	0
Lincoln C.	Tr	02.86	85-86	34	0	0

SWINDELLS, John (Jack)
Manchester, 12 April, 1937 E Yth (CF)

League Club	Source	Date Signed	Seasons Played	Apps	Subs	Gls
Blackburn Rov.	Manchester C. (Am)	11.57	57-59	9	-	1
Accrington St.	Tr	12.59	59-60	65	-	28
Barnsley	Tr	06.61	61	14	-	8
Workington	Tr	02.62	61-62	61	-	19
Torquay U.	Tr	07.63	63	18	-	6
Newport Co.	Tr	07.64	64	23	-	3

SWINDIN, George H.
Rotherham, 4 December, 1914 (G)

League Club	Source	Date Signed	Seasons Played	Apps	Subs	Gls
Bradford C.	Rotherham U. (Am)	02.33	34-35	26	-	0
Arsenal	Tr	04.36	36-53	271	-	0

SWINDLEHURST, David
Edgware, 6 January, 1956 E Yth/Eu21-1 (F)

League Club	Source	Date Signed	Seasons Played	Apps	Subs	Gls
Crystal Palace	App	01.73	73-79	221	16	73
Derby Co.	Tr	02.80	79-82	110	0	29
West Ham U.	Tr	03.83	82-84	52	9	16
Sunderland	Tr	08.85	85-86	59	0	11
Wimbledon (N/C)	Cyprus	03.88	87	2	0	0
Colchester U.	Tr	06.88	88	12	0	5
Peterborough U.	L	12.88	88	4	0	1

SWINFEN, Reginald
Battersea, 4 May, 1915 (OR)

League Club	Source	Date Signed	Seasons Played	Apps	Subs	Gls
Queens Park R.		03.36	36-46	26	-	5

SWINSCOE, Terence
Shirebrook, 31 August, 1934 (D)

League Club	Source	Date Signed	Seasons Played	Apps	Subs	Gls
Stockport Co.	Spalding U.	02.56				
Mansfield T.	Tr	11.56	56-58	14	-	0

SWINSCOE, Thomas W.
Mansfield, 16 October, 1919 (CF)

League Club	Source	Date Signed	Seasons Played	Apps	Subs	Gls
Chesterfield		03.46	46-47	43	-	12
Stockport Co.	Tr	02.48	47-49	73	-	30

SWORD, Alan
Newcastle, 5 July, 1934 (CF)

League Club	Source	Date Signed	Seasons Played	Apps	Subs	Gls
Newcastle U.	Jnrs	08.51				
Exeter C.	Tr	09.53	55	9	-	4

SWORD, Thomas W.
Newcastle, 12 November, 1957 (CD)

League Club	Source	Date Signed	Seasons Played	Apps	Subs	Gls
Stockport Co.	Bishop Auckland	11.79	79-85	236	2	51
Hartlepool U.	Tr	07.86	86	18	0	0
Halifax T.	L	02.87	86	8	0	2
Stockport Co.	Tr	03.87	86-87	6	1	1

SYDENHAM, John
Southampton, 15 September, 1939 E Yth/Eu23-2 (OL)

League Club	Source	Date Signed	Seasons Played	Apps	Subs	Gls
Southampton	Jnrs	04.57	56-69	341	2	36
Aldershot	Tr	03.70	69-71	53	5	4

SYKES, John
Huddersfield, 2 November, 1950 (IF)

League Club	Source	Date Signed	Seasons Played	Apps	Subs	Gls
Bradford P. A.	App	11.68	68	1	0	0
Wrexham	Tr	01.69	68	1	0	0

SYKES, Kenneth
Darlington, 29 January, 1926 (CF)

League Club	Source	Date Signed	Seasons Played	Apps	Subs	Gls
Darlington		05.46	46	6	-	2
Middlesbrough	Tr	06.47				
Hartlepool U.	Tr	09.49	49	1	-	0

SYKES, Norman A. J.
Bristol, 16 October, 1936 E Sch/E Yth (WH)

League Club	Source	Date Signed	Seasons Played	Apps	Subs	Gls
Bristol Rov.	Jnrs	10.53	56-63	214	-	5
Plymouth Arg.	Tr	09.64	64	3	-	0
Stockport Co.	Tr	09.65	65-66	52	0	8
Doncaster Rov.	Tr	02.67	66	15	0	0

SYME, Colin
Rosyth, 23 January, 1924 (OR)

League Club	Source	Date Signed	Seasons Played	Apps	Subs	Gls
Torquay U.	Dunfermline Ath.	12.46	46	1	-	0

SYMM, Colin
Gateshead, 26 November, 1946 (M)

League Club	Source	Date Signed	Seasons Played	Apps	Subs	Gls
Sheffield Wed.	Gateshead	05.65	66-68	16	3	1
Sunderland	Tr	06.69	69-71	9	5	0
Lincoln C.	Tr	06.72	72-74	60	9	7

SYMMONS, Iorwerth
Swansea, 3 February, 1930 (FB)

League Club	Source	Date Signed	Seasons Played	Apps	Subs	Gls
Swansea C.	Hafod	05.48	50-51	15	-	0

SYMONDS, Anthony
Wakefield, 10 November, 1944 (HB)

League Club	Source	Date Signed	Seasons Played	Apps	Subs	Gls
Bradford P.A.	Great Preston Jnrs	07.62	64-66	28	1	2

SYMONDS, Calvin R. C. H.
Bermuda, 29 March, 1932

League Club	Source	Date Signed	Seasons Played	Apps	Subs	Gls
Rochdale	Pembroke (Ber)	10.54	55	1	-	0

SYMONDS, Richard
Langham, 21 November, 1959 (FB)

League Club	Source	Date Signed	Seasons Played	Apps	Subs	Gls
Norwich C.	App	08.78	78-82	55	4	0

SYMONS, Christopher J. (Kit)
Basingstoke, 8 March, 1971 W Yth/Wu21-2/W-4 (CD)

League Club	Source	Date Signed	Seasons Played	Apps	Subs	Gls
Portsmouth	YT	12.88	88-91	50	0	1

SYRETT, David K.
Salisbury, 20 January, 1956 E Yth (F)

League Club	Source	Date Signed	Seasons Played	Apps	Subs	Gls
Swindon T.	App	11.73	73-76	110	12	30
Mansfield T.	Tr	08.77	77-78	65	0	20
Walsall	Tr	03.79	78	11	0	3
Peterborough U.	Tr	08.79	79-81	75	4	24
Northampton T.	Tr	06.82	82-83	42	2	13

SZABO, Tibor
Bradford, 28 October, 1959 (F)

League Club	Source	Date Signed	Seasons Played	Apps	Subs	Gls
Bradford C.	App	10.77	78	8	5	1

Colin Todd (Sunderland, Derby County, Everton, Birmingham City, Nottingham Forest, Oxford United, Luton Town & England)
The PFA "Player of the Year" in 1975 and a mainstay of Brian Clough's Championship winning sides

League Club	Source	Date Signed	Seasons Played	Career Record Apps	Subs	Gls

TADMAN, Maurice R.
Rainham, 28 June, 1921 (CF)

League Club	Source	Date Signed	Seasons Played	Apps	Subs	Gls
Charlton Ath.	Bexleyheath & Welling	06.38	46	3	-	0
Plymouth Arg.	Tr	08.47	47-54	240	-	109

TAFT, Douglas
Leicester, 9 March, 1926 Died 1987 (CF)

League Club	Source	Date Signed	Seasons Played	Apps	Subs	Gls
Derby Co.		11.47	48	6	-	1
Wolverhampton W.	Tr	07.49				

TAGG, Anthony P.
Epsom, 10 April, 1957 (CD)

League Club	Source	Date Signed	Seasons Played	Apps	Subs	Gls
Queens Park R.	App	03.75	75	4	0	0
Millwall	Tr	07.77	77-81	130	3	9
Wimbledon	Tr	07.82	82	14	0	0

TAGG, Ernest
Crewe, 15 September, 1917 (IF)

League Club	Source	Date Signed	Seasons Played	Apps	Subs	Gls
Crewe Alex.		10.37	37	19	-	7
Wolverhampton W.	Tr	05.38	38	1	-	0
Bournemouth	Tr	05.39	46-48	80	-	8
Carlisle U.	Tr	11.48	48	5	-	1

TAGGART, Gerald P.
Belfast, 18 October, 1970 NI Yth/NIu21-1/NI-13 (CD)

League Club	Source	Date Signed	Seasons Played	Apps	Subs	Gls
Manchester C.	YT	07.89	88-89	10	2	1
Barnsley	Tr	01.90	89-91	86	3	7

Ged Taggart (Manchester City, Barnsley & Northern Ireland)

TAGGART, Robert
Newmains (Lk), 10 March, 1927 (IF)

League Club	Source	Date Signed	Seasons Played	Apps	Subs	Gls
Cardiff C.	Coltness U.	05.49	49	2	-	0
Torquay U.	Tr	06.50	50	14	-	2
Aldershot	Tr	08.51	51	16	-	2

TAINTON, Trevor K.
Bristol, 8 June, 1948 E Sch (M)

League Club	Source	Date Signed	Seasons Played	Apps	Subs	Gls
Bristol C.	App	09.65	67-81	456	30	24
Torquay U.	Tr	02.82	81	19	0	1

TAIT, Alexander
Bedlington, 28 November, 1933 E Yth (CF)

League Club	Source	Date Signed	Seasons Played	Apps	Subs	Gls
Newcastle U.	Jnrs	09.52	54-59	32	-	8
Bristol C.	Tr	06.60	60-63	117	-	38
Doncaster Rov.	Tr	06.64	64	19	-	7

TAIT, Barry S.
York, 30 June, 1938 (IF)

League Club	Source	Date Signed	Seasons Played	Apps	Subs	Gls
York C.	Doncaster Rov. (Am)	09.58	58-60	15	-	5
Bradford C.	Peterborough U. (Trial)	11.61	61	20	-	10
Halifax T.	Tr	07.62	62-63	36	-	21
Crewe Alex.	Tr	09.63	63	9	-	2
Notts Co.	Tr	07.64	64	3	-	0

TAIT, Michael P.
Wallsend, 30 September, 1956 (M/D)

League Club	Source	Date Signed	Seasons Played	Apps	Subs	Gls
Oxford U.	App	09.74	74-76	61	3	23
Carlisle U.	Tr	01.77	76-79	101	5	20
Hull C.	Tr	09.79	79	29	4	3
Portsmouth	Tr	06.80	80-86	228	12	31
Reading	Tr	08.87	87-89	98	1	10
Darlington	Tr	07.90	90-91	79	0	2

TAIT, Paul R.
Sutton Coldfield, 31 July, 1971 (M)

League Club	Source	Date Signed	Seasons Played	Apps	Subs	Gls
Birmingham C.	YT	07.88	87-91	40	14	5

TAIT, Peter
York, 17 October, 1936 (CF)

League Club	Source	Date Signed	Seasons Played	Apps	Subs	Gls
York C. (Am)	Jnrs	08.55	55	3	-	1

TAIT, Robert J.
Edinburgh, 4 October, 1938 (IF)

League Club	Source	Date Signed	Seasons Played	Apps	Subs	Gls
Notts Co.	Aberdeen	07.62	62-63	60	-	11
Barrow	Tr	07.64	64-65	78	1	27
Chesterfield	Tr	07.66	66	27	1	2

TALBOT, Brian E.
Ipswich, 21 July, 1953 Eu21-1/E'B'/E-6 (M)

League Club	Source	Date Signed	Seasons Played	Apps	Subs	Gls
Ipswich T.	App	07.70	73-78	177	0	25
Arsenal	Tr	01.79	78-84	245	9	40
Watford	Tr	06.85	85-86	46	2	8
Stoke C.	Tr	10.86	86-87	51	3	5
West Bromwich A.	Tr	01.88	87-89	66	8	5
Fulham (N/C)	Tr	03.91	90	5	0	1
Aldershot (N/C)	Tr	03.91	90	10	0	0

TALBOT, Ernest
Workington, 13 November, 1932 (F)

League Club	Source	Date Signed	Seasons Played	Apps	Subs	Gls
Workington		08.51	52-57	19	-	7

TALBOT, Gary
Blackburn, 15 December, 1937 (CF)

League Club	Source	Date Signed	Seasons Played	Apps	Subs	Gls
Chester C.		09.63	63-66	110	1	61
Crewe Alex.	Tr	07.67	67	35	0	20
Chester C.	Tr	06.68	68	43	0	22

TALBOT, F. Leslie
Hednesford, 3 August, 1910 (IF)

League Club	Source	Date Signed	Seasons Played	Apps	Subs	Gls
Blackburn Rov.	Hednesford T.	10.30	30-35	90	-	20
Cardiff C.	Tr	06.36	36-38	104	-	21
Walsall	Tr	06.39	46	18	-	5

TALBUT, John
Oxford, 20 October, 1940 E Sch/Eu23-7 (CH)

League Club	Source	Date Signed	Seasons Played	Apps	Subs	Gls
Burnley	Jnrs	10.57	58-66	138	0	0
West Bromwich A.	Tr	12.66	66-70	143	1	0

TALKES, Wayne N.
Ealing, 2 June, 1952 (M)

League Club	Source	Date Signed	Seasons Played	Apps	Subs	Gls
Southampton	App	07.69	71-73	7	2	0
Doncaster Rov.	L	12.73	73	3	1	0
Bournemouth	Tr	07.74	74	5	0	0

TALLON, Darren J. B.
Plymouth, 1 June, 1972 (CD)

League Club	Source	Date Signed	Seasons Played	Apps	Subs	Gls
Plymouth Arg.	YT	10.90	90	1	0	0

TAMBLING, Robert V.
Storrington, 18 September, 1941 E Sch/Eu23-13/E-3 (F)

League Club	Source	Date Signed	Seasons Played	Apps	Subs	Gls
Chelsea	Jnrs	09.58	58-69	298	4	164
Crystal Palace	Tr	01.70	69-73	67	1	12

TANKARD, Allen J.
Fleet, 21 May, 1969 E Yth (LB)

League Club	Source	Date Signed	Seasons Played	Apps	Subs	Gls
Southampton	App	05.87	85-86	5	0	0
Wigan Ath.	Tr	07.88	88-91	166	2	3

TANNER, Graham G.
Bridgwater, 4 September, 1947 (CH)

League Club	Source	Date Signed	Seasons Played	Apps	Subs	Gls
Bristol C.	App	09.64				
Bradford P.A.	Tr	10.67	67-68	44	0	2

TANNER, John D. P.
Harrogate, 2 July, 1921 Died1987 E Amat (CF)

League Club	Source	Date Signed	Seasons Played	Apps	Subs	Gls
Huddersfield T.(Am)	Yorkshire Amats	08.48	48	1	-	1

TANNER, Michael W.
Bristol, 28 October, 1964 (M)

League Club	Source	Date Signed	Seasons Played	Apps	Subs	Gls
Bristol C.		07.85	85-87	16	3	1

TANNER, Nicholas
Kingswood, 24 May, 1965 (D)

League Club	Source	Date Signed	Seasons Played	Apps	Subs	Gls
Bristol Rov.	Mangotsfield	06.85	85-87	104	3	3
Liverpool	Tr	07.88	89-91	34	2	1
Norwich C.	L	03.90	89	6	0	0
Swindon T.	L	09.90	90	7	0	0

TANNER, Thomas W.
Devonport, 24 June, 1922 (IF)

League Club	Source	Date Signed	Seasons Played	Apps	Subs	Gls
Torquay U. (Am)	Plymouth U.	09.46	46	1	-	0

TANSEY, Gerard
Liverpool, 15 October, 1933 (F)

League Club	Source	Date Signed	Seasons Played	Apps	Subs	Gls
Everton	Jnrs	10.51				
Tranmere Rov.	Tr	07.55	55	3	-	1

TANSEY, James
Liverpool, 29 January, 1929 (FB)

League Club	Source	Date Signed	Seasons Played	Apps	Subs	Gls
Everton		05.48	52-59	133	-	0
Crewe Alex.	Tr	06.60	60	9	-	0

TAPKEN, Norman
Wallsend, 21 February, 1913 (G)

League Club	Source	Date Signed	Seasons Played	Apps	Subs	Gls
Newcastle U.	Wallsend	05.33	34-37	106	-	0
Manchester U.	Tr	12.38	38	14	-	0
Darlington	Tr	04.47	46-47	31	-	0

TAPLEY, Reginald
Nantwich, 2 November, 1932

League Club	Source	Date Signed	Seasons Played	Apps	Subs	Gls
Crewe Alex.		09.53				
Rochdale	Tr	10.56	56	1	-	0

TAPLEY, Steven
Camberwell, 3 October, 1963 (D)

League Club	Source	Date Signed	Seasons Played	Apps	Subs	Gls
Fulham	App	10.81	83-84	2	0	1
Rochdale	L	02.85	84	1	0	0

TAPPING, Frederick H.
Derby, 29 July, 1921 (RH)

League Club	Source	Date Signed	Seasons Played	Apps	Subs	Gls
Blackpool		10.43				
Chesterfield	Tr	11.47	47	1	-	0

TAPSCOTT, Derek J. R.
Barry, 30 June, 1932 W-14 (CF)

League Club	Source	Date Signed	Seasons Played	Apps	Subs	Gls
Arsenal	Barry T.	10.53	53-57	119	-	62
Cardiff C.	Tr	09.58	58-64	194	-	79
Newport Co.	Tr	07.65	65	12	1	1

TAPSCOTT, Eli J.
Plymouth, 29 April, 1928 (WH)

League Club	Source	Date Signed	Seasons Played	Apps	Subs	Gls
Leeds U.		03.50				
Wrexham	Tr	05.50	50-55	172	-	4

TARANTINI, Alberto
Argentina, 3 December, 1955 Argentine Int (D)

League Club	Source	Date Signed	Seasons Played	Apps	Subs	Gls
Birmingham C.	Boca Juniors (Arg)	10.78	78	23	0	1

TARBUCK, Alan D.
Liverpool, 10 October, 1948 (W)

League Club	Source	Date Signed	Seasons Played	Apps	Subs	Gls
Everton	App	08.66				
Crewe Alex.	Tr	06.67	67-69	80	5	18
Chester C.	Tr	10.69	69-71	69	0	23
Preston N.E.	Tr	09.71	71-72	42	6	17
Shrewsbury T.	Tr	03.73	72-75	107	17	17
Rochdale	Tr	07.76	76-77	48	0	1

TARGETT, Haydn R.
Shepton Mallet, 1 July, 1928 (FB)

League Club	Source	Date Signed	Seasons Played	Apps	Subs	Gls
Torquay U.		10.49	50	1	-	0

TARRANT, Brian L.
Stainforth, 22 July, 1938 (F)

League Club	Source	Date Signed	Seasons Played	Apps	Subs	Gls
Leeds U.	Jnrs	08.55				
Mansfield T.	Tr	07.60	60	3	-	0

TARRANT, J. Edward
Stainforth, 12 February, 1932 (WH)

League Club	Source	Date Signed	Seasons Played	Apps	Subs	Gls
Hull C.	Jnrs	02.49	50-53	30	-	2
Walsall	Tr	12.53	53-57	103	-	13

TARTT, Colin
Liverpool, 23 November, 1950 (D)

League Club	Source	Date Signed	Seasons Played	Apps	Subs	Gls
Port Vale	Alsager Colly	07.72	72-76	171	4	7
Chesterfield	Tr	03.77	76-81	185	1	7
Port Vale	Tr	10.81	81-84	111	6	9

TATE, Geoffrey M.
Leicester, 16 December, 1937 E Sch/E Yth (F)

League Club	Source	Date Signed	Seasons Played	Apps	Subs	Gls
Derby Co.	Jnrs	08.55	55	1	-	1

TATE, Jeffrey
Blyth, 11 May, 1959 (M)

League Club	Source	Date Signed	Seasons Played	Apps	Subs	Gls
Burnley	Jnrs	08.78	79	5	0	1

TAVENER, Colin R.
Trowbridge, 26 June, 1945 (M)

League Club	Source	Date Signed	Seasons Played	Apps	Subs	Gls
Hereford U.	Trowbridge T.	(N/L)	72-73	50	1	3

TAWSE, Brian
Ellon, 30 July, 1945 (W)

League Club	Source	Date Signed	Seasons Played	Apps	Subs	Gls
Arsenal	King Street A.	04.63	64	5	-	0
Brighton & H.A.	Tr	12.65	65-69	97	5	14
Brentford	Tr	02.70	69-70	19	2	1

TAYLOR, Alan
Thornton-Cleveleys, 17 May, 1943 (G)

League Club	Source	Date Signed	Seasons Played	Apps	Subs	Gls
Blackpool	Blackpool R.	10.63	65-70	94	0	0
Oldham Ath.	L	12.69	69	2	0	0
Stockport Co.	L	08.70	70	5	0	0
Southport	Tr	07.71	71-73	102	0	0

TAYLOR, Alan D.
Hinckley, 14 November, 1953 (F)

League Club	Source	Date Signed	Seasons Played	Apps	Subs	Gls
Rochdale	Morecambe	05.73	73-74	55	0	8
West Ham U.	Tr	11.74	74-78	88	10	25
Norwich C.	Tr	08.79	79	20	4	5
Cambridge U.	Vancouver (Can)	10.80	80-81	17	1	4
Hull C. (N/C)	Vancouver (Can)	01.84	83	13	1	3
Burnley	Tr	08.84	84-85	60	4	23
Bury	Tr	06.86	86-87	55	7	10
Norwich C.		09.88	88	1	3	1

Alberto Tarantini (Boca Juniors, Birmingham City & Argentina)

League Club	Source	Date Signed	Seasons Played	Apps	Subs	Gls
TAYLOR, Alan F.						
Derby, 7 March, 1954						(OL)
Chelsea	Alfreton T.	10.72				
Reading	Tr	05.74	74	13	8	4
TAYLOR, Albert H.						
Worksop, 2 May, 1924						(G)
Bury		10.45	46-47	4	-	0
Sheffield U.	Tr	05.48				
Halifax T.	Tr	07.51	51	8	-	0
TAYLOR, Alexander						
Menstrie, 25 December, 1916 Died 1982						(CH)
Carlisle U.	Stirling A.	06.38	38-46	24	-	0
TAYLOR, Alexander						
Glasgow, 13 June, 1962						(M)
Walsall	Hamilton Acad.	08.88	88-89	43	2	6
TAYLOR, Andrew						
Stratford-on-Avon, 4 April, 1963						(RB)
Northampton T.	Aston Villa (App)	06.81	81	17	0	0
TAYLOR, Andrew						
Rawmarsh, 19 January, 1973						(LB)
Rotherham U.	YT	06.91	90-91	11	0	0
TAYLOR, Andrew						
Chesterfield, 30 December, 1967						(F)
Chesterfield	YT	07.86	86-87	7	5	1
TAYLOR, Anthony						
Glasgow, 6 September, 1946						(LB)
Crystal Palace	Morton	11.68	68-73	192	3	8
Southend U.	Tr	08.74	74-75	56	0	1
Swindon T.	Tr	08.76	76	20	6	0
Bristol Rov.	Athlone T.	09.77	77	12	0	0
Portsmouth	Tr	02.78	77	17	0	0
Northampton T. (N/C)	Tr	07.79	79	4	0	0
TAYLOR, Archibald						
Glasgow, 4 October, 1918						(WH)
Reading		06.39	46-47	15	-	2
Leyton Orient	Tr	08.48	48-50	46	-	1
TAYLOR, Arthur A.						
Lisburn (NI), 5 April, 1931						
Luton T.	Glentoran	07.50	52-55	8	-	0
TAYLOR, Arthur M.						
Dunscroft, 7 November, 1939						(W)
Bristol C.	Doncaster Rov. (Am)	05.58	59-60	12	-	2
Barnsley	Tr	07.61	61	2	-	0
Hull C.	Goole T.	05.62	62	1	-	0
Halifax T.	Tr	07.63	63-67	173	0	18
Bradford C.	Tr	12.67	67	10	1	0
York C.	Tr	10.68	68-70	93	3	9
TAYLOR, Arthur S.						
Birmingham, 14 March, 1925						(CF)
West Bromwich A.	Handsworth Wood	03.42	47	4	-	5
TAYLOR, Ashley						
Conisborough, 11 December, 1959						(LB)
Rotherham U.	App	12.77	79-81	21	1	0
TAYLOR, G. Barry						
Sheffield, 3 December, 1939						(FB)
Sheffield U.	Jnrs	04.59				
Oldham Ath.	Tr	06.63	63	40	-	0
Chesterfield	Tr	08.64	64-65	35	0	2
TAYLOR, J. Brian						
Doncaster, 7 October, 1931						(G)
Doncaster Rov.	Sheffield Wed. (Am)	03.49				
Leeds U.	Worksop T.	05.51	51	11	-	0
Bradford P.A.	Kings Lynn	06.54	54-55	66	-	0
TAYLOR, Brian						
Manchester, 29 June, 1942						(WH)
Rochdale	Jnrs	03.62	63-67	130	1	7
TAYLOR, Brian						
Hammersmith, 2 July, 1944						(FB)
Queens Park R.	Jnrs	03.62	62-65	50	0	0

League Club	Source	Date Signed	Seasons Played	Apps	Subs	Gls
TAYLOR, Brian						
Whitwell, 12 February, 1954						(CD)
Middlesbrough	App	07.71	72-75	14	4	1
Doncaster Rov.	Tr	12.75	75-78	118	1	12
Rochdale	Tr	12.78	78-82	152	2	10
TAYLOR, Brian J.						
Walsall, 24 March, 1937						(OL)
Walsall	Jnrs	09.54	54-57	75	-	19
Birmingham C.	Tr	06.58	58-61	54	-	7
Rotherham U.	Tr	10.61	61-62	44	-	5
Shrewsbury T.	Tr	08.63	63-64	73	-	8
Port Vale	Tr	08.65	65-66	44	2	2
Barnsley	Tr	06.67	67	23	1	2
TAYLOR, Brian J.						
Gateshead, 2 July, 1949						(FB)
Coventry C.	Durham C.	02.68				
Walsall	Tr	05.71	71-77	204	12	25
Plymouth Arg.	Tr	10.77	77-78	34	1	5
Preston N.E.	Tr	10.78	78-81	93	6	1
Wigan Ath.	L	03.82	81	7	1	0
TAYLOR, Carl W.						
Kirkby Stephen, 20 January, 1937						(OR)
Middlesbrough	Penrith	01.56	57-59	11	-	1
Aldershot	Tr	06.60	60-62	78	-	13
Darlington	Tr	09.62	62	18	-	1
TAYLOR, Colin						
Stourbridge, 24 August, 1940						(OL)
Walsall	Stourbridge	02.58	58-62	213	-	93
Newcastle U.	Tr	06.63	63-64	33	-	7
Walsall	Tr	10.64	64-67	148	0	52
Crystal Palace	Tr	05.68	68	32	2	8
Walsall	Tr	09.69	69-72	86	11	24
TAYLOR, Colin D.						
Liverpool, 25 December, 1971 E Yth						(F)
Wolverhampton W.	YT	03.90	90-91	7	11	2
Wigan Ath.	L	01.92	91	7	0	2
TAYLOR, David						
Rochester, 17 September, 1940						(IF)
Gillingham	Jnrs	09.57	57-58	21	-	3
Portsmouth	Tr	06.59	59	2	-	0
TAYLOR, Derek M.						
Bradford, 6 June, 1927						(OR)
Halifax T. (Am)	Bradford P.A. (Am)	08.48	48	2	-	0
TAYLOR, Douglas						
Wolverhampton, 20 April, 1931						(CF)
Wolverhampton W.	West Bromwich A. (Am)	10.49	54	3	-	0
Walsall	Tr	11.55	55-56	38	-	8
TAYLOR, Edward K.						
Irvine, 17 May, 1956						(M)
Scunthorpe U.	Ipswich T. (App)	08.74	74	7	0	0
TAYLOR, Ernest						
Sunderland, 2 September, 1925 Died 1985 E'B'-1/E-1						(IF)
Newcastle U.	Hylton Colly	09.42	47-51	107	-	19
Blackpool	Tr	10.51	51-57	217	-	53
Manchester U.	Tr	02.58	57-58	22	-	2
Sunderland	Tr	12.58	58-60	68	-	11
TAYLOR, Francis G.						
Magherafelt (NI), 2 January, 1923						(OL)
Leeds U.	Bangor	07.49	49	3	-	0
TAYLOR, Frederick						
Burnley, 24 February, 1920 Died 1983						(OR)
Burnley	Jnrs	03.37	37-46	49	-	7
New Brighton	Tr	07.48	48-49	55	-	10
TAYLOR, Frederick R.						
Doncaster, 28 October, 1943						(OL)
Doncaster Rov.	Jnrs	07.61	61-64	34	-	2
TAYLOR, Gareth K.						
Weston-super-Mare, 25 February, 1973						(LB)
Bristol Rov.	Southampton (YT)	07.91	91	1	0	0

League Club	Source	Date Signed	Seasons Played	Career Record Apps	Subs	Gls

TAYLOR, Geoffrey A.
Henstead (Sk), 22 January, 1923 (W)

League Club	Source	Date Signed	Seasons Played	Apps	Subs	Gls
Norwich C.	C.N.S.O.B.U.	08.46	46	1	-	0
Reading	Tr	03.47	46	1	-	0
Lincoln C.	Tr	08.47	47	1	-	0
Brighton & H.A.	Tr	08.48	48	2	-	0
Bristol Rov.	Stade Rennais (Fr)	09.51	51	3	-	0
Queens Park R.		11.53	53	2	-	0

TAYLOR, George A.
Aberdeen, 9 June, 1913 Died 1982 (LH)

League Club	Source	Date Signed	Seasons Played	Apps	Subs	Gls
Plymouth Arg.	Aberdeen	08.48	48-49	48	-	2

TAYLOR, George E.
Wigan, 21 March, 1920 (G)

League Club	Source	Date Signed	Seasons Played	Apps	Subs	Gls
West Ham U.	Gainsborough Trin.	12.38	46-55	115	-	0

TAYLOR, George J.
Dundee, 23 October, 1948 (IF)

League Club	Source	Date Signed	Seasons Played	Apps	Subs	Gls
Grimsby T.	Jnrs	11.65	65	0	1	0

TAYLOR, George L.
Edinburgh, 11 May, 1926 (G)

League Club	Source	Date Signed	Seasons Played	Apps	Subs	Gls
Aldershot	Hamilton Acad.	06.53				
Hartlepool U.	Tr	11.53	53-54	34	-	0

TAYLOR, George Mc.
Edinburgh, 12 December, 1927 (OR)

League Club	Source	Date Signed	Seasons Played	Apps	Subs	Gls
Aldershot	Hamilton Acad.	07.52	52	8	-	2

TAYLOR, Gerald W.
Hull, 15 August, 1947 (FB)

League Club	Source	Date Signed	Seasons Played	Apps	Subs	Gls
Wolverhampton W.	Jnrs	11.64	66-75	151	3	1
Swindon T.	L	10.75	75	19	0	0

TAYLOR, Gordon
Ashton-u-Lyne, 28 December, 1944 (W)

League Club	Source	Date Signed	Seasons Played	Apps	Subs	Gls
Bolton W.	Curzon Ashton	01.62	62-70	253	5	41
Birmingham C.	Tr	12.70	70-75	156	10	9
Blackburn Rov.	Tr	03.76	75-77	62	2	3
Bury	Tr	06.78	78-79	58	2	2

TAYLOR, Gordon S.
Stanley, 10 June, 1936 (G)

League Club	Source	Date Signed	Seasons Played	Apps	Subs	Gls
Gateshead	West Stanley	02.57	57	3	-	0

TAYLOR, Graham
Worksop, 15 September, 1944 (FB)

League Club	Source	Date Signed	Seasons Played	Apps	Subs	Gls
Grimsby T.	Jnrs	07.62	63-67	189	0	2
Lincoln C.	Tr	07.68	68-72	150	2	1

TAYLOR, J. Harold
Ryton-on-Tyne, 6 October, 1935 (OR)

League Club	Source	Date Signed	Seasons Played	Apps	Subs	Gls
Newcastle U.	Jnrs	11.52	54-56	7	-	1
Fulham	L	02.57	57	4	-	0
Newcastle U.	Tr	11.57	58-59	21	-	4

TAYLOR, Ian
Doncaster, 25 November, 1967 (G)

League Club	Source	Date Signed	Seasons Played	Apps	Subs	Gls
Carlisle U.	Bridlington T.	08.90				
Scarborough (N/C)	Tr	02.92	91	1	0	0

TAYLOR, James
Alnwick, 7 April, 1925

League Club	Source	Date Signed	Seasons Played	Apps	Subs	Gls
Manchester C.		10.44				
Crewe Alex.	Tr	06.47	47-48	48	-	8

TAYLOR, James
Strood, 13 May, 1934 (IF)

League Club	Source	Date Signed	Seasons Played	Apps	Subs	Gls
Charlton Ath.	Tonbridge	08.54				
Gillingham	Tr	08.56	56-57	30	-	16
Watford	Tr	07.58				

TAYLOR, James G.
Hillingdon, 5 November, 1917 EF Lge/E-2 (CH)

League Club	Source	Date Signed	Seasons Played	Apps	Subs	Gls
Fulham	Hillingdon B.L.	03.38	46-52	261	-	5
Queens Park R.	Tr	04.53	53	41	-	0

TAYLOR, Jason S.
Wrexham, 29 August, 1970

League Club	Source	Date Signed	Seasons Played	Apps	Subs	Gls
Wrexham (YT)	YT	09.87	88	0	1	0

TAYLOR, Jeffrey N.
Huddersfield, 20 September, 1930 (CF)

League Club	Source	Date Signed	Seasons Played	Apps	Subs	Gls
Huddersfield T.	Jnrs	09.49	49-51	68	-	27
Fulham	Tr	11.51	51-53	33	-	14
Brentford	Tr	08.54	54-56	94	-	34

TAYLOR, John
Salford, 2 November, 1936 (W)

League Club	Source	Date Signed	Seasons Played	Apps	Subs	Gls
Bolton W.	Jnrs	12.54				
Southport	Tr	07.59	59	29	-	0

TAYLOR, John (Jack)
Barnsley, 15 February, 1914 Died 1978 (FB)

League Club	Source	Date Signed	Seasons Played	Apps	Subs	Gls
Wolverhampton W.	Worsboro' Bridge	01.34	35-37	78	-	0
Norwich C.	Tr	06.38	38-46	50	-	0
Hull C.	Tr	07.47	47-49	72	-	0

TAYLOR, John
Creswell, 11 January, 1939 (W)

League Club	Source	Date Signed	Seasons Played	Apps	Subs	Gls
Mansfield T.	Chesterfield (Jnrs)	05.57	59	5	-	2
Peterborough U.	Tr	07.60	60	1	-	0

TAYLOR, John
Bradford, 24 June, 1924 (IL)

League Club	Source	Date Signed	Seasons Played	Apps	Subs	Gls
Bradford C.	Kilmarnock	09.46	46	2	-	2

TAYLOR, John E.
Newcastle, 11 September, 1924 E'B'-1 (IF)

League Club	Source	Date Signed	Seasons Played	Apps	Subs	Gls
Luton T.	Stockton	02.49	48-51	85	-	29
Wolverhampton W.	Tr	06.52	52	10	-	1
Notts Co.	Tr	02.54	53-56	53	-	19
Bradford P.A.	Tr	07.57	57	12	-	6

TAYLOR, John J.
Manchester, 12 October, 1928 (OR)

League Club	Source	Date Signed	Seasons Played	Apps	Subs	Gls
Blackpool		09.49				
Accrington St.	Tr	07.52	52	16	-	0

TAYLOR, John L.
Birmingham, 25 June, 1949 (G)

League Club	Source	Date Signed	Seasons Played	Apps	Subs	Gls
Chester C.	Pwllheli	07.70	70-73	70	0	0
Rochdale	L	10.74	74	3	0	0
Stockport Co.	Bangor C.	11.75	75	1	0	0

TAYLOR, John P.
Norwich, 24 October, 1964 (F)

League Club	Source	Date Signed	Seasons Played	Apps	Subs	Gls
Colchester U.	Jnrs	12.82				
Cambridge U.	Sudbury T.	08.88	88-91	139	21	46
Bristol Rov.	Tr	03.92	91	8	0	8

TAYLOR, John W. R.
Durham, 10 July, 1926 (IF)

League Club	Source	Date Signed	Seasons Played	Apps	Subs	Gls
Crystal Palace Am	Leytonstone	05.48	48	1	-	0

TAYLOR, Kenneth
Huddersfield, 21 August, 1935 (CH)

League Club	Source	Date Signed	Seasons Played	Apps	Subs	Gls
Huddersfield T.	Jnrs	09.52	53-64	250	-	14
Bradford P.A.	Tr	02.65	64-66	51	0	1

TAYLOR, Kenneth
Portmadoc, 5 June, 1952 (FB)

League Club	Source	Date Signed	Seasons Played	Apps	Subs	Gls
Wrexham	Jnrs	05.70	70	1	-	0

TAYLOR, Kenneth G.
South Shields, 15 March, 1931 (FB)

League Club	Source	Date Signed	Seasons Played	Apps	Subs	Gls
Blackburn Rov.	North Shields	01.50	54-63	200	-	0

TAYLOR, Kenneth V.
Manchester, 18 June, 1936 (FB)

League Club	Source	Date Signed	Seasons Played	Apps	Subs	Gls
Manchester C.	Manchester Transport	08.54	57	1	-	0

TAYLOR, Kevin
Wakefield, 22 January, 1961 (M)

League Club	Source	Date Signed	Seasons Played	Apps	Subs	Gls
Sheffield Wed.	App	10.78	78-83	118	7	21
Derby Co.	Tr	07.84	84	22	0	2
Crystal Palace	Tr	03.85	84-87	85	2	14
Scunthorpe U.	Tr	10.87	87-90	149	8	25

TAYLOR, Lawrence D. (Larry)
Exeter, 23 November, 1947 (G)

League Club	Source	Date Signed	Seasons Played	Apps	Subs	Gls
Bristol Rov.	App	12.65	66-69	90	0	0

TAYLOR, Leslie
North Shields, 4 December, 1956 (M)

League Club	Source	Date Signed	Seasons Played	Apps	Subs	Gls
Oxford U.	App	12.74	74-80	219	0	15
Watford	Tr	11.80	80-85	167	5	13
Reading	Tr	10.86	86-88	69	6	3
Colchester U.	Tr	01.89	88-89	44	8	1

TAYLOR, Mark
Hartlepool, 5 December, 1962 (FB)

League Club	Source	Date Signed	Seasons Played	Apps	Subs	Gls
Hartlepool U. (N/C)	Henry Smiths B.C.	08.82	82	1	0	0

League Club	Source	Date Signed	Seasons Played	Career Record Apps	Subs	Gls
TAYLOR, P. Mark R.						
Hartlepool, 20 November, 1964						(LW)
Hartlepool U.		01.84	83-85	42	5	4
Crewe Alex.	L	12.85	85	3	0	0
Blackpool	Tr	08.86	86-91	104	15	43
Cardiff C.	L	12.90	90	6	0	3
Wrexham	Tr	03.92	91	6	3	0
TAYLOR, R. Mark						
Birmingham, 22 February, 1966						(FB/M)
Walsall	YT	07.84	84-88	100	13	4
Sheffield Wed.	Tr	06.89	89	8	1	0
Shrewsbury T.	L	02.91	90	19	0	3
Shrewsbury T.	Tr	09.91	91	29	0	2
TAYLOR, Martin J.						
Tamworth, 9 December, 1966						(G)
Derby Co.	Mile Oak Rov.	07.86	89-91	15	0	0
Carlisle U.	L	09.87	87	10	0	0
Scunthorpe U.	L	12.87	87	8	0	0
TAYLOR, Paul						
Leith, 20 December, 1966						(LB)
Mansfield T. (YT)	YT	10.83	83	3	0	0
TAYLOR, Paul A.						
Sheffield, 3 December, 1949						(M)
Sheffield Wed.		06.71	71-72	5	1	0
York C.	Tr	07.73	73	4	0	0
Hereford U.	L	01.74	73	0	1	0
Colchester U.	Tr	03.74	73	6	3	0
Southport	Tr	07.74	74-76	95	0	15
TAYLOR, Peter J.						
Southend, 3 January, 1953 E Semi-Pro/Eu23-4/E-4						(W)
Southend U.	App	01.71	70-73	57	18	12
Crystal Palace	Tr	10.73	73-76	122	0	33
Tottenham H.	Tr	09.76	76-80	116	7	31
Leyton Orient	Tr	11.80	80-82	49	7	11
Oldham Ath.	L	01.83	82	4	0	0
Exeter C. (N/C)	Maidstone U.	10.83	83	8	0	0
TAYLOR, Peter T.						
Nottingham, 2 July, 1928 Died 1990						(G)
Coventry C.	Nottingham F. (Am)	05.46	50-54	86	-	0
Middlesbrough	Tr	08.55	55-59	140	-	0
Port Vale	Tr	06.61	61	1	-	0
TAYLOR, Philip A.						
Sheffield, 11 July, 1958						(M)
York C.	App	07.76	74-77	14	7	1
Darlington	Tr	07.78	78-79	18	8	2
TAYLOR, Philip H.						
Bristol, 18 September, 1917 E Sch/EF Lge/E'B'-2/E-3						(WH)
Bristol Rov.	Jnrs	03.35	35	21	-	2
Liverpool	Tr	03.36	35-53	312	-	32
TAYLOR, Raymond J.						
Doncaster, 1 March, 1930						(OL)
Huddersfield T.	Wath W.	09.49	49	2	-	0
Southport	Tr	08.53	53-54	51	-	7
TAYLOR, Richard E.						
Wolverhampton, 9 April, 1918						(CH)
Grimsby T.	Jnrs	05.35	38-47	36	-	0
Scunthorpe U.	Tr	05.48	50-53	131	-	2
TAYLOR, Richard H.						
Huddersfield, 24 January, 1957 E Yth						(G)
Huddersfield T.	App	01.74	73-81	105	0	0
York C.	L	03.80	79	2	0	0
TAYLOR, Richard M.						
Oldham, 21 August, 1928						(G)
Everton		06.51				
Southport		08.54	54	1	-	0
TAYLOR, Richard W.						
Sunderland, 20 June, 1951						(OL)
Sunderland	App	10.68	71	0	1	0
York C.	Tr	07.72	72	26	2	2
TAYLOR, Robert						
Horden, 3 February, 1967						(F)
Leeds U.	Horden Colly	01.86	85-88	33	9	8
Bristol C.	Tr	03.89	88-91	96	10	50
West Bromwich A.	Tr	01.92	91	19	0	8

League Club	Source	Date Signed	Seasons Played	Career Record Apps	Subs	Gls
TAYLOR, Robert A.						
Norwich, 30 April, 1971						(F)
Norwich C.	YT	03.90				
Leyton Orient	L	03.91	90	0	3	1
Birmingham C.	Tr	08.91				
Leyton Orient	Tr	10.91	91	6	5	1
TAYLOR, Robert J.						
Croydon, 16 March, 1936						(WH)
Crystal Palace (Am)	Fulham (Am)	08.54	54	2	-	0
Gillingham	Tr	09.56	56-58	31	-	5
Millwall	Tr	08.59	59	2	-	1
TAYLOR, Robert S.						
Plymouth, 3 December, 1967						(F)
Portsmouth	YT	08.86				
Newport Co.	Tr	03.87	86-87	38	6	7
Torquay U.	Weymouth	09.89	89	11	7	1
TAYLOR, Robin G.						
Rinteln (WG), 14 January, 1971						(M)
Wigan Ath.	Leicester C. (N/C)	10.89	89	0	1	0
TAYLOR, Rodney V.						
Corfe Castle, 9 September, 1943						(WH)
Portsmouth	Jnrs	05.61				
Gillingham	Tr	07.63	63-65	9	2	0
Bournemouth	Tr	02.66	65-66	29	1	0
TAYLOR, Roy						
Hoyland, 2 April, 1933						(G)
Scunthorpe U.	Denaby U.	01.53	52	2	-	0
TAYLOR, Royston						
Blackpool, 28 September, 1956						(M)
Preston N.E.	App	10.74	75	3	0	0
Blackburn Rov.	Sunderland (N/C)	11.76	78	3	0	1

Bob Taylor (Leeds United, Bristol City & West Bromwich Albion)

League Club	Source	Date Signed	Seasons Played	Apps	Subs	Gls
TAYLOR, Samuel M.						
Glasgow, 23 September, 1933						(W)
Preston N.E.	Falkirk	06.55	55-60	149	-	40
Carlisle U.	Tr	06.61	61-63	93	-	12
Southport	Tr	07.64	64	36	-	3
TAYLOR, Scott D.						
Portsmouth, 28 November, 1970						(M)
Reading	YT	06.89	88-91	69	24	5
TAYLOR, Shaun						
Plymouth, 26 March, 1963						(CD)
Exeter C.	Bideford	12.86	86-90	200	0	17
Swindon T.	Tr	07.91	91	42	0	4
TAYLOR, Stanley						
Southport, 17 November, 1932						(OL)
Southport	Fleetwood Hesketh	02.56	55	2	-	0
TAYLOR, Steven J.						
Royton, 18 October, 1955						(F)
Bolton W.	App	10.73	74-77	34	6	16
Port Vale	L	10.75	75	4	0	2
Oldham Ath.	Tr	10.77	77-78	45	2	25
Luton T.	Tr	01.79	78	15	5	1
Mansfield T.	Tr	07.79	79	30	7	7
Burnley	Tr	07.80	80-82	80	6	37
Wigan Ath.	Tr	08.83	83	29	1	7
Stockport Co.	Tr	03.84	83-84	26	0	8
Rochdale	Tr	11.84	84-86	84	0	42
Preston N.E.	Tr	10.86	86	5	0	2
Burnley	Tr	08.87	87-88	38	7	6
Rochdale	Tr	03.89	88	16	1	4
TAYLOR, Stewart R.						
Owston Ferry, 6 April, 1946						(LB)
Scunthorpe U.		08.65	65-68	64	3	0
TAYLOR, Stuart						
Bristol, 18 April, 1947						(CD)
Bristol Rov.	Jnrs	01.66	65-79	546	0	28
TAYLOR, Thomas						
Barnsley, 29 January, 1932 Died 1958 E'B'-2/EF Lge/E-19						(CF)
Barnsley	Jnrs	07.49	50-52	44	-	26
Manchester U.	Tr	03.53	52-57	166	-	112
TAYLOR, Thomas F.						
Hornchurch, 26 September, 1951 E Sch/E Yth/Eu23-11						(CD)
Leyton Orient	App	10.68	67-70	112	2	4
West Ham U.	Tr	10.70	70-78	340	0	8
Leyton Orient	Tr	05.79	79-81	116	0	5
Charlton Ath.	Beerschot (Bel)	08.83				
TAYLOR, Thomas W.J.						
Wandsworth, 10 September, 1946						(IF)
Portsmouth		04.64				
Gillingham	Tr	05.65	65	19	1	0
Bournemouth	Tr	06.66	66-67	26	0	8
TAYLOR, Walter B.						
Kirton-in-Lindsey, 30 October, 1926						(FB)
Grimsby T.	Hibaldstow	08.44	49-50	21	-	0
Southport	Tr	07.51	51-57	269	-	1
Oldham Ath.	Tr	07.58	58-59	51	-	0
TAYLOR, William						
Edinburgh, 31 July, 1939 Died 1981						(M)
Leyton Orient	Bonnyrigg Rose	08.59	60-62	23	-	0
Nottingham F.	Tr	10.63	63-68	10	10	1
Lincoln C.	Tr	05.69	69-70	74	5	6
TAYLOR, William D.						
Keldholm, 3 June, 1938						(G)
Luton T.	Partick Th.	12.67	67-68	6	0	0
TEAGUE, William E.						
Gloucester, 26 September, 1937						(G)
Swindon T.	Gloucester C.	03.61	60-61	3	-	0
TEALE, Richard G.						
Millom, 27 February, 1952						(G)
Queens Park R.	Walton & Hersham	07.73	74	1	0	0
Fulham	Tr	08.76	76	5	0	0
Wimbledon	Tr	08.77	77	15	0	0

League Club	Source	Date Signed	Seasons Played	Apps	Subs	Gls
TEALE, Shaun						
Southport, 10 March, 1964 E Semi-Pro						(CD)
Bournemouth	Weymouth	01.89	88-90	99	1	4
Aston Villa	Tr	07.91	91	42	0	0
TEARSE, David J.						
Newcastle, 7 August, 1951						(F)
Leicester C.	North Kenton B.C.	10.69	69-70	7	1	1
Torquay U.	Tr	11.71	71-74	77	0	23
Reading	L	01.75	74	2	0	0
TEASDALE, John G. (Jack)						
Rossington, 15 March, 1929						(WH)
Doncaster Rov.		10.49	50-55	113	-	0
TEASDALE, John S.						
Glasgow, 15 October, 1962						(W)
Wolverhampton W.	Nairn Co.	12.80	80-81	6	2	0
Walsall	Tr	03.82	81-82	13	0	3
Hereford U. (N/C)	Tr	01.83	82	5	0	1
Blackpool (N/C)		11.84	84	1	6	1
TEASDALE, Thomas						
						(OL)
Hull C. (Am)		05.47	46	1	-	0
TEBBUTT, Robert S.						
Irchester, 10 November, 1934						(IF)
Northampton T.		10.56	56-59	56	-	21
TEDDS, William H.						
Bedworth, 27 July, 1943						(FB)
Coventry C.	Jnrs	09.60	61-64	8	-	0
TEDESCO, John J.						
Modbury, 7 March, 1949						(F)
Plymouth Arg.	App	05.66	66-69	34	8	4
TEECE, David A.						
Middleton, 1 September, 1927						(G)
Hull C.	Hyde U.	02.52	53-55	25	-	0
Oldham Ath.	Tr	06.56	56-58	91	-	0
TEER, Kevin P.						
Wood Green, 7 December, 1963						(D)
Brentford	App	12.81	80	0	1	0
TEES, Matthew						
Johnstone, 13 October, 1939						(CF)
Grimsby T.	Airdrieonians	07.63	63-66	113	0	51
Charlton Ath.	Tr	02.67	66-69	88	1	32
Luton T.	Tr	08.69	69-70	33	2	13
Grimsby T.	Tr	11.70	70-72	83	0	42
TELFER, George A.						
Liverpool, 6 July, 1955						(W)
Everton	App	08.72	73-80	81	18	20
Scunthorpe U.	San Diego (USA)	12.81	81-82	34	2	11
Preston N.E. (N/C)	Altrincham	08.83	83	0	2	0
TELFER, Paul N.						
Edinburgh, 21 October, 1971						(M)
Luton T.	YT	11.88	90-91	17	4	1
TELFORD, William A.						
Carlisle, 5 March, 1956						(CF)
Manchester C.	Tranmere. Rov. (App)	08.75	75	0	1	0
Peterborough U.	Tr	09.75	75	3	1	2
Colchester U.	L	01.76	75	1	1	1
TELLING, Maurice W.						
London, 5 August, 1919 Died 1973						(CF)
Millwall	Berkhamsted	10.46	46	1	-	0
TEMBY, William						
Dover, 16 September, 1934						(F)
Queens Park R.	Rhyl	02.55	55-56	6	-	3
TEMPEST, Dale M.						
Leeds, 30 December, 1963						(F)
Fulham	App	12.81	80-83	25	9	6
Huddersfield T.	Tr	08.84	84-85	63	2	27
Gillingham	L	03.86	85	9	0	4
Colchester U.	Lokeren (Bel)	08.87	87-88	69	8	18

League Club	Source	Date Signed	Seasons Played	Apps	Subs	Gls

TEMPLE, Derek W.
Liverpool, 13 November, 1938 E Sch/E Yth/EF Lge/E-1 (OL)

Everton	Jnrs	08.56	56-67	231	1	72
Preston N.E.	Tr	09.67	67-69	75	1	14

Derek Temple (Everton, Preston North End & England)

TEMPLE, William
Barlow, 12 December, 1915 (IF)

Aldershot		11.34	34-36	11	-	2
Carlisle U.	Tr	05.37	37	11	-	4
Grimsby T.	Tr	09.38	38	2	-	0
Gateshead	Tr	05.46	46	10	-	0

TEMPLEMAN, John H.
Yapton (Sx), 21 September, 1947 (FB)

Brighton & H.A.	Arundel T.	07.66	66-73	219	7	16
Exeter C.	Tr	05.74	74-78	205	1	7
Swindon T.	Tr	07.79	79-80	20	1	0

TENNANT, Albert E.
Ilkeston, 29 October, 1917 Died 1986 (WH)

Chelsea	Stanton Iron Wks	11.34	46-48	2	-	0

TENNANT, David
Ayr, 22 January, 1930 (W)

Ipswich T.	Annbank U.	07.52	52	4	-	0

TENNANT, David
Walsall, 13 June, 1945 (G)

Walsall	Jnrs	08.63	63-64	19	-	0
Lincoln C.	Worcester C.	09.66	66-68	40	0	0
Rochdale	Tr	08.69	70	16	0	0

TENNANT, Desmond W.
Cardiff, 17 October, 1925 (FB)

Cardiff C.	Jnrs	08.45				
Brighton & H.A.	Barry T.	07.48	48-58	400	-	40

TENNANT, John G.
Darlington, 1 August, 1939 (G)

Darlington		05.57	56-57	8	-	0
Chelsea	Tr	08.59				
Southend U.	Tr	10.59	60-62	2	-	0

TENNANT, S. D. Keith
Newport, 6 June, 1934 (WH)

Newport Co.	Jnrs	01.55	55-57	40	-	1

TENNANT, Roy F.
South Africa, 12 September, 1936 (CH)

Brighton & H.A.		08.57				
Workington	Tr	07.58	58-61	152	-	1

TERNENT, Raymond
Blyth, 9 September, 1948 (FB)

Burnley	App	09.65	66-70	13	0	0
Southend U.	Tr	06.71	71-72	82	0	1
Doncaster Rov.	Tr	08.73	73-76	78	6	3

TERNENT, F. Stanley
Gateshead, 16 June, 1946 (D)

Burnley	App	06.63	66-67	5	0	0
Carlisle U.	Tr	05.68	68-73	186	2	5

TERRIS, James
Chippenham, 25 July, 1933 (FB)

Bristol C.	Chippenham T.	10.55	56-57	4	-	0
Carlisle U.	Tr	04.59	59-60	28	-	1

TERRY, Patrick A.
Lambeth, 2 October, 1933 (CF)

Charlton Ath.	Eastbourne	03.54	53-54	4	-	1
Newport Co.	Tr	05.56	56-57	55	-	30
Swansea C.	Tr	02.58	57-58	17	-	9
Gillingham	Tr	10.58	58-60	109	-	62
Northampton T.	Tr	07.61	61	24	-	10
Millwall	Tr	02.62	61-63	97	-	41
Reading	Tr	08.64	64-66	99	0	41
Swindon T.	Tr	02.67	66-67	60	1	23
Brentford	Tr	06.68	68	29	0	12

TERRY, Peter E.
Enfield, 11 September, 1972 (CD)

Aldershot	YT	07.91	90	1	0	0

TERRY, Stephen G.
Clapton, 14 June, 1962 (CD)

Watford	App	01.80	79-87	160	0	14
Hull C.	Tr	06.88	88-89	62	0	4
Northampton T.	Tr	03.90	89-91	100	0	11

TESTER, Paul L.
Stroud, 10 March, 1959 (LW)

Shrewsbury T.	Cheltenham T.	07.83	83-87	86	12	12
Hereford U.	L	11.84	84	4	0	0
Hereford U.	Tr	08.88	88-90	105	9	14

TETHER, Colin
Halesowen, 11 August, 1938 E Yth (FB)

Wolverhampton W.	Jnrs	08.55	56	1	-	0
Oxford U.	Tr	07.60				

TEWLEY, Alan B.
Leicester, 22 January, 1945 (OR)

Leicester C.	App	03.62	66-68	15	3	5
Bradford P.A.	Tr	11.69	69	28	0	4
Crewe Alex.	Tr	10.70	70-72	57	11	13

THACKERAY, Andrew J.
Huddersfield, 13 February, 1968 (M/RB)

Manchester C.	Jnrs	02.86				
Huddersfield T.	Tr	07.86	86	2	0	0
Newport Co.	Tr	03.87	86-87	53	1	4
Wrexham	Tr	07.88	88-91	139	13	14

THARME, Derek
Brighton, 19 August, 1938 (FB)

Tottenham H.	Whitehaven	10.56				
Southend U.	Tr	05.62	62	7	-	0

THEAKER, Clarence A.
Spalding, 8 December, 1912 (G)

Grimsby T.		05.34	35-38	5	-	0
Newcastle U.	Tr	11.38	38-46	13	-	0
Hartlepool U.	Tr	06.47	47	14	-	0

THEAR, Anthony C.
Edmonton, 4 February, 1948 (CF)

Arsenal	Jnrs	02.65				
Luton T.	Tr	07.66	66	12	2	5
Gillingham	Tr	02.67	66-68	7	0	1

THEODOSIOU, Andrew
Stoke Newington, 30 October, 1970 (CD)

Norwich C.	Tottenham H. (YT)	07.89				
Hereford U.	Tr	07.91	91	33	0	1

THIJSSEN, Frans J.
Netherlands, 23 January, 1952 Dutch Int (M)

League Club	Source	Date Signed	Seasons Played	Apps	Subs	Gls
Ipswich T.	Twente Enschede (Neth)	02.79	78-82	123	2	10
Nottingham F.	Vancouver (Can)	10.83	83	17	0	3

THOM, Lewis M.
Stornaway, 10 April, 1944 (OL)

League Club	Source	Date Signed	Seasons Played	Apps	Subs	Gls
Shrewsbury T.	Dundee U.	09.65	65-66	48	1	5
Lincoln C.	Tr	05.67	66-68	45	2	4
Bradford P.A.	Tr	06.69	69	31	0	1

THOMAS, Andrew M.
Oxford, 16 December, 1962 (M)

League Club	Source	Date Signed	Seasons Played	Apps	Subs	Gls
Oxford U.	App	12.80	80-85	89	27	32
Fulham	L	12.82	82	3	1	2
Derby Co.	L	03.83	82	0	1	0
Newcastle U.	Tr	09.86	86-87	24	7	6
Bradford C.	Tr	06.88	88	15	8	5
Plymouth Arg.	Tr	07.89	89-90	47	3	19

THOMAS, Barrie
Merthyr Tydfil, 27 August, 1954 (M)

League Club	Source	Date Signed	Seasons Played	Apps	Subs	Gls
Swansea C. (Am)	Jnrs	08.71	71	2	0	0
Bournemouth	Merthyr Tydfil	08.79	79	3	0	0

THOMAS, Barrie E.
Measham, 19 May, 1937 E Yth (CF)

League Club	Source	Date Signed	Seasons Played	Apps	Subs	Gls
Leicester C.	Jnrs	07.54	54-55	7	-	3
Mansfield T.	Tr	06.57	57-59	72	-	48
Scunthorpe U.	Tr	09.59	59-61	88	-	67
Newcastle U.	Tr	01.62	61-64	73	-	48
Scunthorpe U.	Tr	11.64	64-66	52	0	26
Barnsley	Tr	11.66	66-67	43	0	18

THOMAS, Brian H.
Carmarthen, 28 June, 1944 (WH)

League Club	Source	Date Signed	Seasons Played	Apps	Subs	Gls
Swansea C.	Jnrs	06.62	64	4	-	0

THOMAS, Bryn
Coventry, 13 December, 1932 (CF)

League Club	Source	Date Signed	Seasons Played	Apps	Subs	Gls
Coventry C.	Longford Rov.	09.50	52-53	12	-	1

THOMAS, Cedric D.
Hebden Bridge, 19 September, 1936 (IF)

League Club	Source	Date Signed	Seasons Played	Apps	Subs	Gls
Halifax T.	Heptonstall	07.57	57-59	20	-	5
Southport	Tr	07.60				

THOMAS, Daniel J.
Worksop, 12 November, 1961 E Sch/Eu21-8/E-2 (FB)

League Club	Source	Date Signed	Seasons Played	Apps	Subs	Gls
Coventry C.	App	12.78	79-82	103	5	5
Tottenham H.	Tr	06.83	83-86	80	7	1

THOMAS, David
Kirkby-in-Ashfield, 5 October, 1950 E Yth/Eu23-11/E-8 (W)

League Club	Source	Date Signed	Seasons Played	Apps	Subs	Gls
Burnley	App	10.67	66-72	153	4	19
Queens Park R.	Tr	10.72	72-76	181	1	29
Everton	Tr	08.77	77-78	71	0	4
Wolverhampton W.	Tr	10.79	79	10	0	0
Middlesbrough	Vancouver (Can)	03.82	81	13	0	1
Portsmouth	Tr	07.82	82-84	24	6	0

THOMAS, David A. (Dai)
Port Talbot, 1 August, 1926 W-2 (FB)

League Club	Source	Date Signed	Seasons Played	Apps	Subs	Gls
Swansea C.	Abercregan	08.48	49-59	298	-	16
Newport Co.	Tr	07.61	61-62	58	-	1

THOMAS, David S. L.
Swansea, 19 September, 1920 W Sch (F)

League Club	Source	Date Signed	Seasons Played	Apps	Subs	Gls
Swansea C.		10.42				
Brighton & H.A.	Tr	06.47	47	13	-	4

THOMAS, David W. J.
Stepney, 6 July, 1917 (CF)

League Club	Source	Date Signed	Seasons Played	Apps	Subs	Gls
Plymouth Arg.	Romford	06.38	38-47	74	-	29
Watford	Tr	02.48	47-50	105	-	39
Gillingham	Tr	10.50	50-52	80	-	42

THOMAS, Dean R.
Bedworth, 19 December, 1961 (M/FB)

League Club	Source	Date Signed	Seasons Played	Apps	Subs	Gls
Wimbledon	Nuneaton Bor.	07.81	81-83	57	0	8
Northampton T.	Fortuna Dusseldorf (Ger)	08.88	88-89	74	0	11
Notts Co.	Tr	03.90	89-91	88	2	6

THOMAS, Dennis
Hebburn, 2 February, 1926 (OL)

League Club	Source	Date Signed	Seasons Played	Apps	Subs	Gls
Bury	Wardley Welfare	01.49	49	3	-	0
Accrington St.	Tr	07.50	50	34	-	5

THOMAS, Edward
Newton-le-Willows, 23 October, 1933 (IF)

League Club	Source	Date Signed	Seasons Played	Apps	Subs	Gls
Everton	Jnrs	10.51	56-59	86	-	39
Blackburn Rov.	Tr	02.60	59-61	37	-	9
Swansea C.	Tr	07.62	62-64	68	-	21
Derby Co.	Tr	08.64	64-67	102	3	43
Leyton Orient	Tr	09.67	67	11	0	2

THOMAS, Edwin H. C.
Swindon, 9 November, 1932 (G)

League Club	Source	Date Signed	Seasons Played	Apps	Subs	Gls
Southampton		05.51	51	8	-	0

THOMAS, Geoffrey
Swansea, 18 February, 1948 Wu23-3 (M)

League Club	Source	Date Signed	Seasons Played	Apps	Subs	Gls
Swansea C.	App	02.66	66-75	345	15	52

THOMAS, Geoffrey P.
Bradford, 12 March, 1946 (FB)

League Club	Source	Date Signed	Seasons Played	Apps	Subs	Gls
Bradford P.A.	App	03.63	63-65	53	0	0

THOMAS, Geoffrey R.
Manchester, 5 August, 1964 E'B'/E-9 (M)

League Club	Source	Date Signed	Seasons Played	Apps	Subs	Gls
Rochdale (N/C)	Littleborough	08.82	82-83	10	1	1
Crewe Alex.	Tr	03.84	83-86	120	5	21
Crystal Palace	Tr	06.87	87-91	164	2	24

THOMAS, Geoffrey S.
Derby, 21 February, 1926 (FB)

League Club	Source	Date Signed	Seasons Played	Apps	Subs	Gls
Nottingham F.	Jnrs	09.43	46-59	403	-	1

THOMAS, George V.
Cardiff, 25 June, 1930 (CH)

League Club	Source	Date Signed	Seasons Played	Apps	Subs	Gls
Cardiff C.	Cardiff Nomads	05.49				
Newport Co.	Tr	07.53	53-58	135	-	0

THOMAS, Glen A.
Hackney, 6 October, 1967 (D)

League Club	Source	Date Signed	Seasons Played	Apps	Subs	Gls
Fulham	App	10.85	86-91	159	5	6

THOMAS, D. Gwyn
Swansea, 26 September, 1957 W Sch/Wu21-2 (M)

League Club	Source	Date Signed	Seasons Played	Apps	Subs	Gls
Leeds U.	App	07.75	74-83	79	10	3
Barnsley	Tr	03.84	83-89	197	4	17
Hull C.	Tr	03.90	89-90	21	1	0
Carlisle U.	Tr	08.91	91	35	2	1

THOMAS, Jeffrey
Newport, 18 May, 1949 Wu23-1 (W)

League Club	Source	Date Signed	Seasons Played	Apps	Subs	Gls
Newport Co.	Jnrs	05.66	65-72	207	5	31

THOMAS, John
Poole, 28 May, 1936 (G)

League Club	Source	Date Signed	Seasons Played	Apps	Subs	Gls
Bournemouth	Poole T.	05.58	58	4	-	0

THOMAS, John C.
Great Houghton, 22 September, 1932 (FB)

League Club	Source	Date Signed	Seasons Played	Apps	Subs	Gls
Wolverhampton W.	Wath W.	08.51				
Barnsley	Tr	06.52	52-57	135	-	0
Mansfield T.	Tr	03.58	57-58	41	-	0
Chesterfield	Tr	07.59	59	6	-	0

THOMAS, John E.
Walsall, 15 July, 1922 (F)

League Club	Source	Date Signed	Seasons Played	Apps	Subs	Gls
Bournemouth		05.46				
West Bromwich A.	Tr	07.46				
Crystal Palace	Tr	10.48	48-51	53	-	17

THOMAS, John W.
Wednesbury, 5 August, 1958 (F)

League Club	Source	Date Signed	Seasons Played	Apps	Subs	Gls
Everton		07.77				
Tranmere Rov.	L	03.79	78	10	1	2
Halifax T.	L	10.79	79	5	0	0
Bolton W.	Tr	06.80	80-81	18	4	6
Chester C.	Tr	08.82	82	44	0	20
Lincoln C.	Tr	08.83	83-84	56	11	18
Preston N.E.	Tr	06.85	85-86	69	9	38
Bolton W.	Tr	07.87	87-88	71	2	31
West Bromwich A.	Tr	07.89	89	8	10	1
Preston N.E.	Tr	02.90	89-91	24	3	6
Hartlepool U.	Tr	03.92	91	5	2	1

THOMAS, John W.
Liverpool, 23 December, 1926 (W)

League Club	Source	Date Signed	Seasons Played	Apps	Subs	Gls
Everton		12.48				
Swindon T.	Tr	02.49	50-51	17	-	3
Chester C.	Headington U.	07.53	53	29	-	5
Stockport Co.	Tr	07.54	54	6	-	0

League Club	Source	Date Signed	Seasons Played	Apps	Subs	Gls
THOMAS, W. Keith						
Oswestry, 28 July, 1929						(OR)
Sheffield Wed.	Oswestry T.	09.50	50-51	10	-	1
Cardiff C.	Tr	07.52	52-53	9	-	4
Plymouth Arg.	Tr	11.53	53-55	35	-	8
Exeter C.	Tr	03.56	55-56	44	-	6
THOMAS, Kevin A.						
Prescot, 13 August, 1945						(G)
Blackpool	Prescot Cables	06.66	66-68	12	0	0
Tranmere Rov.	Tr	09.69	69-70	18	0	0
Oxford U.	Tr	07.71	72	5	0	0
Southport	Tr	07.74	74-75	67	0	0
THOMAS, Lee						
Tredegar, 1 November, 1970						(FB)
Hereford U.	Newport Co. (YT)	07.89	89	0	1	0
THOMAS, Martin R.						
Senghenydd, 28 November, 1959 W Yth/Wu21-2/W-1						(G)
Bristol Rov.	App	09.77	76-81	162	0	0
Cardiff C.	L	07.82	82	15	0	0
Southend U.	L	02.83	82	6	0	0
Newcastle U.	Tr	03.83	82-87	118	0	0
Middlesbrough	L	10.84	84	4	0	0
Birmingham C.	Tr	10.88	88-91	139	0	0
THOMAS, Michael L.						
Lambeth, 24 August, 1967 E Sch/E Yth/Eu21-12/E'B'/E-2						(M)
Arsenal	App	12.84	86-91	149	14	24
Portsmouth	L	12.86	86	3	0	0
Liverpool	Tr	12.91	91	16	1	3
THOMAS, Michael R.						
Newtown, 7 July, 1954 Wu23-2/W-51						(W/M)
Wrexham	Jnrs	05.72	71-78	217	13	33
Manchester U.	Tr	11.78	78-80	90	0	11
Everton	Tr	08.81	81	10	0	0
Brighton & H.A.	Tr	11.81	81	18	2	0
Stoke C.	Tr	08.82	82-83	57	0	14
Chelsea	Tr	01.84	83-84	43	1	9
West Bromwich A.	Tr	09.85	85	20	0	0
Derby Co.	L	03.86	85	9	0	0
Shrewsbury T.	Wichita (USA)	08.88	88	40	0	1
Leeds U.	Tr	06.89	89	3	0	0
Stoke C.	L	03.90	89	8	0	0
Stoke C.	Tr	08.90	90	32	6	7
Wrexham	Tr	07.91	91	26	0	1

Mickey Thomas (Wrexham, Manchester United, Everton, Brighton & Hove Albion, Stoke City, Chelsea, West Bromwich Albion, Shrewsbury Town, Leeds United, Stoke City, Wrexham & Wales)

League Club	Source	Date Signed	Seasons Played	Apps	Subs	Gls
THOMAS, Mitchell A.						
Luton, 2 October, 1964 E Yth/Eu21-3/E'B'						(FB/M)
Luton T.	App	08.82	82-85	106	1	1
Tottenham H.	Tr	07.86	86-90	136	21	6
West Ham U.	Tr	08.91	91	34	1	3
THOMAS, Patrick A.						
Sidmouth, 7 March, 1965						
Exeter C. (N/C)	Jnrs	06.82	82	0	1	0
THOMAS, Peter J.						
Cardiff, 18 October, 1932						(OR)
Cardiff C.		03.53	53	5	-	1
Exeter C.	Tr	12.54	54-55	29	-	4
Newport Co.	Tr	07.56	56-57	6	-	1
THOMAS, Peter J.						
Coventry, 20 November, 1944 IR-2						(G)
Coventry C.	Coventry G.E.C.	06.66	66	1	0	0
THOMAS, Philip L.						
Sherborne, 14 December, 1952						(M)
Bournemouth	App	07.71				
Colchester U.	Tr	05.72	72-75	103	5	8
THOMAS, Rees						
Aberdare, 3 January, 1934						(RB)
Cardiff C.	Jnrs	01.51				
Torquay U.	L	08.53	53	1	-	0
Brighton & H.A.	Tr	09.56	56-57	31	-	1
Bournemouth	Tr	01.58	57-58	48	-	0
Portsmouth	Tr	07.59	59-60	30	-	0
Aldershot	Tr	07.61	61-63	103	-	2
THOMAS, Robert A.						
Stepney, 2 August, 1919						(IF)
Brentford	Hendon	05.39				
Plymouth Arg.	Tr	04.46	46	41	-	17
Fulham	Tr	06.47	47-51	167	-	55
Crystal Palace	Tr	09.52	52-54	96	-	31
THOMAS, Roderick C.						
Brent, 10 October, 1970 E Sch/E Yth/Eu21-1						(RW)
Watford	YT	05.88	87-91	62	21	9
Gillingham	L	03.92	91	8	0	1
THOMAS, Roderick J.						
Glyncorrwg, 11 January, 1947 Wu23-6/W-47						(RB)
Swindon T.	Gloucester C.	07.64	65-73	296	0	5
Derby Co.	Tr	11.73	73-77	89	0	2
Cardiff C.	Tr	11.77	77-81	89	7	0
Newport Co. (N/C)	Gloucester C.	03.82	81	3	0	0
THOMAS, D. Sidney						
Machynlieth, 12 November, 1919 W-4						(W)
Fulham	Treharris	08.38	46-49	57	-	4
Bristol C.	Tr	06.50	50	13	-	1
THOMAS, Steven J.						
Batley, 29 January, 1957						(FB)
Swansea C. (Am)	Jnrs	08.73	73-74	10	0	0
THOMAS, Tony						
Liverpool, 12 July, 1971						(LB/W)
Tranmere Rov.	YT	02.89	88-91	113	1	10
THOMAS, Valmore N.						
Worksop, 30 April, 1958						(FB)
Coventry C.	App	03.76				
Hereford U.	Tr	03.79	78-80	31	1	1
THOMAS, William P.						
Glyn-Neath, 28 October, 1923						(OL)
Torquay U.	Merthyr Tydfil	09.47	47-54	90	-	17
THOMAS, Wilson G.						
Derby, 18 November, 1918						(IF)
Bristol C.	Matlock T.	10.44	46-49	77	-	18
THOMPSON, Alan						
Goole, 2 September, 1931						(FB)
Luton T.	Westpark Jnrs	12.49	56	1	-	0
THOMPSON, Alan						
Newcastle, 22 December, 1973						(M/LB)
Newcastle U.	YT	03.91	91	12	2	0

THOMPSON, Alexander
Sheffield, 8 December, 1917 (RB)

League Club	Source	Date Signed	Seasons Played	Apps	Subs	Gls
Sheffield Wed.		06.37				
Lincoln C.	Tr	06.39	46-47	34	-	1
Tranmere Rov.	Tr	06.48	48	2	-	0

THOMPSON, W. Allan
Liverpool, 20 January, 1952 (CD)

League Club	Source	Date Signed	Seasons Played	Apps	Subs	Gls
Sheffield Wed.	App	01.69	70-75	150	6	3
Stockport Co.	Tr	08.76	76-78	93	1	17
Bradford C.	Portland (USA)	01.80	79-81	31	0	0
Scunthorpe U.	Tr	03.82	81	11	0	0

THOMPSON, Andrew R.
Cannock, 9 November, 1967 (LB/W)

League Club	Source	Date Signed	Seasons Played	Apps	Subs	Gls
West Bromwich A.	App	11.85	85-86	18	6	1
Wolverhampton W.	Tr	11.86	86-91	204	7	23

THOMPSON, Arthur
Dewsbury, 15 June, 1922 (IF)

League Club	Source	Date Signed	Seasons Played	Apps	Subs	Gls
Huddersfield T.	Thornhill Edge	09.41	46-48	25	-	5

THOMPSON, Brian
Brierley Hill, 9 February, 1950 (M)

League Club	Source	Date Signed	Seasons Played	Apps	Subs	Gls
Wolverhampton W.	App	02.67				
Oxford U.	Tr	10.69	69-72	52	5	4
Torquay U.	L	03.73	72	9	0	1

THOMPSON, G. Brian
Ashington, 7 August, 1952 E Semi-Pro (RB)

League Club	Source	Date Signed	Seasons Played	Apps	Subs	Gls
Sunderland		06.71				
York C.	L	03.73	72	4	2	0
Mansfield T.	Yeovil T.	11.79	79	9	0	0

THOMPSON, Charles M.
Chesterfield, 19 July, 1920 (CF)

League Club	Source	Date Signed	Seasons Played	Apps	Subs	Gls
Sheffield U.	Bolsover Colly	07.37	46	17	-	3

THOMPSON, Christopher D.
Walsall, 24 January, 1960 E Yth (M)

League Club	Source	Date Signed	Seasons Played	Apps	Subs	Gls
Bolton W.	App	07.77	77-82	66	7	18
Lincoln C.	L	03.83	82	5	1	0
Blackburn Rov.	Tr	08.83	83-85	81	4	24
Wigan Ath.	Tr	07.86	86-87	67	7	12
Blackpool	Tr	07.88	88-89	27	12	8
Cardiff C.	Tr	03.90	89	1	1	0
Walsall (N/C)		02.91	90	3	0	0

THOMPSON, Cyril A.
Southend, 18 December, 1918 (CF)

League Club	Source	Date Signed	Seasons Played	Apps	Subs	Gls
Southend U.		07.45	46-47	67	-	35
Derby Co.	Tr	07.48	48-49	16	-	3
Brighton & H.A.	Tr	03.50	49-50	41	-	16
Watford	Tr	03.51	50-52	78	-	36

THOMPSON, David
Middlesbrough, 26 February, 1945 (CF)

League Club	Source	Date Signed	Seasons Played	Apps	Subs	Gls
Lincoln C.		06.64	64	3	-	1

THOMPSON, David G.
Ashington, 20 November, 1968 (CD)

League Club	Source	Date Signed	Seasons Played	Apps	Subs	Gls
Millwall	App	11.86	87-91	88	9	6

THOMPSON, David S.
Catterick Camp, 12 March, 1945 (OR)

League Club	Source	Date Signed	Seasons Played	Apps	Subs	Gls
Wolverhampton W.	Jnrs	04.62	64	8	-	1
Southampton	Tr	08.66	66-70	21	2	0
Mansfield T.	Tr	10.70	70-73	129	2	21
Chesterfield	Tr	12.73	73	14	0	3

THOMPSON, David S.
Manchester, 27 May, 1962 (RW)

League Club	Source	Date Signed	Seasons Played	Apps	Subs	Gls
Rochdale	Withington	09.81	81-85	147	8	13
Notts Co.	Tr	08.86	86-87	52	3	8
Wigan Ath.	Tr	10.87	87-89	107	1	16
Preston N.E.	Tr	07.90	90-91	39	7	4

THOMPSON, Dennis
Sheffield, 2 June, 1925 E Sch (OR)

League Club	Source	Date Signed	Seasons Played	Apps	Subs	Gls
Sheffield U.	Jnrs	08.42	46-50	96	-	20
Southend U.	Tr	07.51	51-53	49	-	11

THOMPSON, Dennis
Bolsover, 19 July, 1934 (OR)

League Club	Source	Date Signed	Seasons Played	Apps	Subs	Gls
Chesterfield	Jnrs	07.51	50-52	24	-	0
Scunthorpe U.	Tr	07.55	55	3	-	0

THOMPSON, Dennis
Whitburn, 10 April, 1924 (CF)

League Club	Source	Date Signed	Seasons Played	Apps	Subs	Gls
Hull C.	Whitburn Welfare	04.47	46-47	9	-	8

THOMPSON, Desmond
Southampton, 4 December, 1928 (G)

League Club	Source	Date Signed	Seasons Played	Apps	Subs	Gls
York C.	Gainsborough Trin.	01.51	50-52	80	-	0
Burnley	Tr	11.52	52-54	62	-	0
Sheffield U.	Tr	05.55	55-63	25	-	0

THOMPSON, R. Eric
Mexborough, 3 December, 1944 (CH)

League Club	Source	Date Signed	Seasons Played	Apps	Subs	Gls
Doncaster Rov.	Leeds U. (App)	07.62	62	9	-	0

THOMPSON, Frederick N.
Swindon, 24 November, 1937 (WH)

League Club	Source	Date Signed	Seasons Played	Apps	Subs	Gls
Swindon T.	Jnrs	09.55	54-60	21	-	1

THOMPSON, Garry L.
Birmingham, 7 October, 1959 Eu21-6 (F)

League Club	Source	Date Signed	Seasons Played	Apps	Subs	Gls
Coventry C.	App	06.77	77-82	127	7	38
West Bromwich A.	Tr	02.83	82-84	91	0	39
Sheffield Wed.	Tr	08.85	85	35	1	7
Aston Villa	Tr	06.86	86-88	56	4	17
Watford	Tr	12.88	88-89	24	10	8
Crystal Palace	Tr	03.90	89-90	17	3	3
Queens Park R.	Tr	08.91	91	10	5	1

THOMPSON, George
Sligo (Ire) (RB)

League Club	Source	Date Signed	Seasons Played	Apps	Subs	Gls
Huddersfield T.	Sligo Rov.	12.38				
Exeter C.	Tr	06.46	46-47	63	-	4
Rochdale	Tr	07.48				

THOMPSON, George H.
Maltby, 15 September, 1926 (G)

League Club	Source	Date Signed	Seasons Played	Apps	Subs	Gls
Chesterfield		06.47				
Scunthorpe U.	Tr	06.50	50-52	92	-	0
Preston N.E.	Tr	10.52	52-55	140	-	0
Manchester C.	Tr	06.56	56	2	-	0
Carlisle U.	Tr	06.57	57-61	202	-	0

THOMPSON, Harold
Mansfield, 29 April, 1915 (HB)

League Club	Source	Date Signed	Seasons Played	Apps	Subs	Gls
Mansfield T.		06.32				
Wolverhampton W.	Tr	06.33	35-38	69	-	16
Sunderland	Tr	12.38	38	11	-	1
York C.	Tr	12.45				
Northampton T.	Tr	11.46	46-48	38	-	2

THOMPSON, Henry
South Shields, 21 February, 1932 (F)

League Club	Source	Date Signed	Seasons Played	Apps	Subs	Gls
Gateshead		08.51	51-55	23	-	4

THOMPSON, Ian P.
Dartford, 8 June, 1958 (F)

League Club	Source	Date Signed	Seasons Played	Apps	Subs	Gls
Bournemouth	Salisbury	07.83	83-85	119	2	30

THOMPSON, James
Oldham, 26 November, 1935 (WH)

League Club	Source	Date Signed	Seasons Played	Apps	Subs	Gls
Oldham Ath.	Chadderton	01.54	53-58	110	-	19
Exeter C.	Tr	12.58	58-60	105	-	10
Rochdale	Tr	03.61	60-65	199	0	15
Bradford C.	Tr	12.65	65	23	1	1

THOMPSON, James B.
Gateshead, 7 January, 1943 (FB)

League Club	Source	Date Signed	Seasons Played	Apps	Subs	Gls
Grimsby T.	St. Mary's B.C.	09.61	62-66	156	0	2
Cambridge U.	Port Elizabeth (SA)	01.69	70-72	116	1	0

THOMPSON, John (Jack)
Cramlington, 21 March, 1915 (IF)

League Club	Source	Date Signed	Seasons Played	Apps	Subs	Gls
Sheffield Wed.	Blyth Spartans	06.33	33-38	36	-	9
Doncaster Rov.	Tr	05.46	46-47	59	-	17
Chesterfield	Tr	07.48	48-52	82	-	8

THOMPSON, John H.
Newcastle, 4 July, 1932 (G)

League Club	Source	Date Signed	Seasons Played	Apps	Subs	Gls
Newcastle U.	Jnrs	09.50	54-55	8	-	0
Lincoln C.	Tr	05.57	57-59	42	-	0

THOMPSON, Joseph P.
Seaham, 15 November, 1927 (FB)

League Club	Source	Date Signed	Seasons Played	Apps	Subs	Gls
Luton T.	Electrolux	05.46				
Shrewsbury T.	Tr	07.51	51	7	-	0

League Club	Source	Date Signed	Seasons Played	Apps	Subs	Gls
THOMPSON, Keith A.						
Birmingham, 24 April, 1965 E Yth						(W)
Coventry C.	App	01.83	82-83	9	3	0
Wimbledon	L	10.83	83	0	3	0
Northampton T.	L	03.85	84	10	0	1
Coventry C.	Real Oviedo (Sp)	09.88	88-90	2	9	1
THOMPSON, Kenneth H.						
Sunderland, 24 April, 1926						(RB)
Middlesbrough		11.44				
Gateshead	L	11.46	46	9	-	0
York C.	Tr	07.50	50-51	21	-	0
THOMPSON, Kenneth J.						
Ipswich, 1 March, 1945						(WH)
Ipswich T.	App	03.62	64-65	11	1	0
Exeter C.	Tr	06.66	66	38	1	1
THOMPSON, Kevin J.						
Middlesbrough, 8 September, 1948						(CF)
Hartlepool U. (Am)	Fred Halls B.C.	10.70	70	5	0	1
THOMPSON, Leslie A.						
Cleethorpes, 23 September, 1968						(LB)
Hull C.	YT	03.87	87-90	31	4	4
Scarborough	L	12.88	88	2	1	1
Maidstone U.	Tr	07.91	91	38	0	0
THOMPSON, Malcolm G.						
Beverley, 19 October, 1946						(CF)
Hartlepool U.	Goole T.	11.68	68-69	42	1	9
Gillingham	Tr	06.70				
THOMPSON, Maxwell S.						
Liverpool, 31 February, 1956						(CD)
Liverpool	App	01.74	73	1	0	0
Blackpool	Tr	12.77	77-80	92	7	6
Swansea C.	Tr	09.81	81-82	25	1	2
Bournemouth	Tr	08.83	83	9	0	0
Port Vale	L	11.83	83	2	0	0
THOMPSON, Neil						
Beverley, 2 October, 1963						(LB)
Hull C.	Nottingham F. (App)	11.81	81-82	29	2	0
Scarborough	Tr	08.83	87-88	87	0	15
Ipswich T.	Tr	06.89	89-91	122	6	15
THOMPSON, Nigel D.						
Leeds, 1 March, 1967						(M)
Leeds U.	App	12.84	83-86	6	1	0
Rochdale	L	08.87	87	3	2	0
Chesterfield	Tr	03.88	87-89	18	2	1
THOMPSON, Patrick A.						
Exeter, 11 February, 1932						
Brighton & H.A.	Topsham	01.51	50	1	-	0
THOMPSON, Peter						
Carlisle, 27 November, 1942 E Sch/Eu23-4/E-16						(W)
Preston N.E.	Jnrs	11.59	60-62	121	-	20
Liverpool	Tr	08.63	63-71	318	4	41
Bolton W.	Tr	11.73	73-77	111	6	2
THOMPSON, Peter						
Blackhall (Dm), 16 February, 1936 E Amat						(CF)
Wrexham (Am)	Blackhall Colly	11.55	55-57	42	-	21
Hartlepool U.	Tr	07.57	57-58	47	-	17
Derby Co.	Tr	11.58	58-61	52	-	19
Bournemouth	Tr	01.62	61-62	39	-	14
Hartlepool U.	Tr	09.63	63-65	91	0	34
THOMPSON, Peter C.						
Kenya, 25 July, 1942						(W)
Peterborough U.	Grantham	03.64	63-68	79	6	15
THOMPSON, Philip B.						
Liverpool, 21 January, 1954 E Yth/Eu23-1/EF Lge/E-42						(CD)
Liverpool	App	02.71	71-82	337	3	7
Sheffield U.	Tr	12.84	84-85	36	1	0
THOMPSON, Raymond						
Bishop Auckland, 21 October, 1925						(FB)
Sunderland		11.45				
Hartlepool U.	Tr	01.47	46-57	396	-	2

League Club	Source	Date Signed	Seasons Played	Apps	Subs	Gls
THOMPSON, Richard J.						
Bristol, 11 April, 1969						(F)
Newport Co.	Yate T.	01.87	87	10	3	2
Torquay U.	Tr	06.88	88	11	4	3
THOMPSON, Ronald						
Carlisle, 20 January, 1932						(WH)
Carlisle U.		07.51	51-63	374	-	12
THOMPSON, Ronald						
Sheffield, 24 December, 1921						(IF)
Sheffield Wed.	Wadsley C.F.C.	04.45				
Rotherham U.	Tr	05.47	47-48	30	-	11
York C.	Tr	06.49	49	8	-	0
THOMPSON, Sidney						
Bedlington, 14 July, 1928						(IF)
Nottingham F.		09.47	52-54	22	-	8
Scunthorpe U.	Tr	08.55				
THOMPSON, Simon L.						
Sheffield, 27 February, 1970						(W)
Rotherham U.	YT	06.88	88-90	12	16	0
Scarborough	Tr	12.91	91	22	1	3
THOMPSON, Stephen J.						
Plymouth, 12 January, 1963						(M)
Bristol C.	Jnrs	07.81	81-82	10	2	1
Torquay U. (N/C)	Tr	02.83	82	0	1	0
THOMPSON, Stephen J.						
Oldham, 2 November, 1964						(M)
Bolton W.	App	11.82	82-91	329	6	49
Luton T.	Tr	09.91	91	5	0	0
Leicester C.	Tr	10.91	91	31	3	3
THOMPSON, Steven A.						
Manchester, 17 February, 1972						(CD)
Gillingham (YT)	YT	07.88	89	1	1	0
THOMPSON, Steven P.						
Sheffield, 28 July, 1955						(CD)
Lincoln C.	Boston U.	04.80	80-84	153	1	8
Charlton Ath.	Tr	08.85	85-87	95	0	0
Leicester C.	Tr	07.88				
Sheffield U.	Tr	11.88	88	20	0	1
Lincoln C.	Tr	07.89	89	27	0	0

Peter Thompson (Preston North End, Liverpool, Bolton Wanderers & England)

THOMPSON, Stuart C.
Littleborough, 2 September, 1964 E Sch (F)

League Club	Source	Date Signed	Seasons Played	Apps	Subs	Gls
Rochdale	App	09.82	82-83	23	8	7

THOMPSON, Terence W.
Barleston (Lei), 25 December, 1946 (WH)

League Club	Source	Date Signed	Seasons Played	Apps	Subs	Gls
Wolverhampton W.	App	01.64				
Notts Co.	Tr	03.66	65-67	66	0	3

THOMPSON, Thomas
Houghton-le-Spring, 10 November, 1928 EF Lge/E'B'-1/E-2 (IF)

League Club	Source	Date Signed	Seasons Played	Apps	Subs	Gls
Newcastle U.	Lumley Y.M.C.A.	08.46	47-49	20	-	6
Aston Villa	Tr	08.50	50-54	149	-	67
Preston N.E.	Tr	07.55	55-60	188	-	117
Stoke C.	Tr	06.61	61-62	42	-	18
Barrow	Tr	03.63	62-63	44	-	16

THOMPSON, Thomas W.
Stockton, 9 March, 1938 E Amat (FB)

League Club	Source	Date Signed	Seasons Played	Apps	Subs	Gls
Blackpool	Stockton	08.61	61-68	154	1	1
York C.	Tr	07.70	70	4	0	0

THOMPSON, J. Trevor
North Shields, 21 May, 1955 (FB)

League Club	Source	Date Signed	Seasons Played	Apps	Subs	Gls
West Bromwich A.	App	01.74	73-75	20	0	0
Newport Co.	Washington (USA)	08.78	78-79	32	3	2
Lincoln C.	Tr	12.79	79-81	80	0	1

THOMPSON, William
Bedlington, 5 January, 1940 (CH)

League Club	Source	Date Signed	Seasons Played	Apps	Subs	Gls
Newcastle U.	Jnrs	01.57	60-66	79	1	1
Rotherham U.	Tr	06.67	67	8	0	0
Darlington	Tr	01.68	67-69	30	0	5

THOMPSON, William
Ashington, 23 December, 1921

League Club	Source	Date Signed	Seasons Played	Apps	Subs	Gls
Gateshead		09.45	46-47	3	-	0

THOMPSON, William
Berwick, 31 August, 1916 (G)

League Club	Source	Date Signed	Seasons Played	Apps	Subs	Gls
Leeds U.	Ashington	10.35				
Watford		08.46	46	9	-	0

THOMPSON, William G.
Glasgow, 10 August, 1921 (WH)

League Club	Source	Date Signed	Seasons Played	Apps	Subs	Gls
Portsmouth	Carnoustie	03.46	48-52	40	-	2
Bournemouth	Tr	01.53	52-53	45	-	0

THOMPSTONE, Ian P.
Bury, 17 July, 1971 (M)

League Club	Source	Date Signed	Seasons Played	Apps	Subs	Gls
Manchester C.	YT	07.89	87	0	1	1
Oldham Ath.	Tr	05.90				
Exeter C.	Tr	01.92	91	15	0	3

THOMSON, Arthur C.
Edinburgh, 2 September, 1948 Su23-3 (CD)

League Club	Source	Date Signed	Seasons Played	Apps	Subs	Gls
Oldham Ath.	Hearts	01.70	69-70	27	1	0

THOMSON, Bertram
Glasgow, 18 February, 1929 (HB)

League Club	Source	Date Signed	Seasons Played	Apps	Subs	Gls
Rochdale	Yeovil T.	06.58	58-59	55	-	1

THOMSON, Brian L.
Paisley, 1 March, 1959 (W)

League Club	Source	Date Signed	Seasons Played	Apps	Subs	Gls
West Ham U.	Morecambe	01.77				
Mansfield T.	Tr	08.79	79-81	54	9	1

THOMSON, Charles R. (Chick)
Perth, 2 March, 1930 (G)

League Club	Source	Date Signed	Seasons Played	Apps	Subs	Gls
Chelsea	Clyde	10.52	52-55	46	-	0
Nottingham F.	Tr	08.57	57-60	121	-	0

THOMSON, David L.
Bothkennar, 2 February, 1938 (IF)

League Club	Source	Date Signed	Seasons Played	Apps	Subs	Gls
Leicester C.	Dunfermline Ath.	08.61	61	1	-	1

THOMSON, George M.
Edinburgh, 19 October, 1936 SF Lge (FB)

League Club	Source	Date Signed	Seasons Played	Apps	Subs	Gls
Everton	Hearts	11.60	60-62	73	-	1
Brentford	Tr	11.63	63-67	160	2	5

THOMSON, Harold W.
Edinburgh, 25 August, 1940 (G)

League Club	Source	Date Signed	Seasons Played	Apps	Subs	Gls
Burnley	Bo'ness U.	08.59	64-68	117	0	0
Blackpool	Tr	07.69	69-70	59	0	0
Barrow	Tr	08.71	71	40	0	0

THOMSON, James A.
Glasgow, 28 June, 1948 (M)

League Club	Source	Date Signed	Seasons Played	Apps	Subs	Gls
Newcastle U.	Petershill	08.68	69	4	1	0
Barrow	L	12.70	70	2	0	0
Grimsby T.	Tr	07.71	71	23	3	4

THOMSON, James D.
Govan, 17 March, 1931 (IF)

League Club	Source	Date Signed	Seasons Played	Apps	Subs	Gls
Southend U.	Raith Rov.	05.56	56-58	40	-	10

THOMSON, James S.
Glasgow, 1 October, 1946 (D)

League Club	Source	Date Signed	Seasons Played	Apps	Subs	Gls
Chelsea	Provanside Hibs	01.65	65-67	33	6	1
Burnley	Tr	09.68	68-80	294	3	3

THOMSON, John
Newcastle, 3 December, 1954 (CD)

League Club	Source	Date Signed	Seasons Played	Apps	Subs	Gls
Newcastle U.	App	12.72				
Bury	Tr	11.73	73-77	92	11	8

THOMSON, John B.
Glasgow, 22 October, 1934 (FB)

League Club	Source	Date Signed	Seasons Played	Apps	Subs	Gls
Workington	Hearts	05.58	58	11	-	1

THOMSON, Kenneth G.
Aberdeen, 25 February, 1930 (CH)

League Club	Source	Date Signed	Seasons Played	Apps	Subs	Gls
Stoke C.	Aberdeen	09.52	52-59	278	-	6
Middlesbrough	Tr	12.59	59-62	84	-	1
Hartlepool U.	Tr	10.62	62	28	-	0

THOMSON, Lawrence J.
Menstrie, 26 August, 1936 (F)

League Club	Source	Date Signed	Seasons Played	Apps	Subs	Gls
Carlisle U.	Partick Th.	01.60	59	12	-	1

THOMSON, Richard B.
Edinburgh, 26 June, 1957 (F)

League Club	Source	Date Signed	Seasons Played	Apps	Subs	Gls
Preston N.E.	App	06.75	74-79	60	11	20

THOMSON, Robert
Glasgow, 21 March, 1955 (M)

League Club	Source	Date Signed	Seasons Played	Apps	Subs	Gls
Middlesbrough	Morton	09.81	81	18	2	2
Blackpool	Hibernian	09.85	85-86	50	2	6
Hartlepool U. (N/C)	Tr	08.87	87	2	1	0

THOMSON, Robert
Menstrie, 21 November, 1939 (FB)

League Club	Source	Date Signed	Seasons Played	Apps	Subs	Gls
Liverpool	Partick Th.	12.62	62-63	6	-	0
Luton T.	Tr	08.65	65-66	74	0	0

THOMSON, Robert A.
Smethwick, 5 December, 1943 Eu23-15/EF Lge/E-8 (LB)

League Club	Source	Date Signed	Seasons Played	Apps	Subs	Gls
Wolverhampton W.	App	07.61	61-68	277	1	2
Birmingham C.	Tr	03.69	68-70	63	0	0
Walsall	L	11.71	71	9	0	1
Luton T.	Tr	07.72	72-75	110	0	1
Port Vale	Hartford (USA)	10.76	76	18	0	0

THOMSON, Robert G. M.
Dundee, 21 March, 1937 (IF)

League Club	Source	Date Signed	Seasons Played	Apps	Subs	Gls
Wolverhampton W.	Airdrieonians	08.54	56	1	-	1
Aston Villa	Tr	06.59	59-63	140	-	56
Birmingham C.	Tr	09.63	63-67	109	5	23
Stockport Co.	Tr	12.67	67	16	1	0

THORBURN, James H. F.
Lanark, 10 March, 1938 (G)

League Club	Source	Date Signed	Seasons Played	Apps	Subs	Gls
Ipswich T.	Raith Rov.	06.63	63-64	24	-	0

THORLEY, Dennis
Stoke, 7 November, 1956 (D)

League Club	Source	Date Signed	Seasons Played	Apps	Subs	Gls
Stoke C.	Jnrs	07.76	76-80	9	4	0
Blackburn Rov.	L	03.80	79	2	2	0

THORN, Andrew C.
Carshalton, 12 November, 1966 Eu21-5 (CD)

League Club	Source	Date Signed	Seasons Played	Apps	Subs	Gls
Wimbledon	YT	11.84	84-87	106	1	2
Newcastle U.	Tr	08.88	88-89	36	0	2
Crystal Palace	Tr	12.89	89-91	84	0	2

THORNBER, Stephen J.
Dewsbury, 11 October, 1965 (M)

League Club	Source	Date Signed	Seasons Played	Apps	Subs	Gls
Halifax T.	Jnrs	01.83	83-87	94	10	4
Swansea C.	Tr	08.88	88-91	98	19	5

THORNE, Adrian E.
Brighton, 2 August, 1937 (OL)

League Club	Source	Date Signed	Seasons Played	Apps	Subs	Gls
Brighton & H.A.	Jnrs	08.54	57-60	76	-	38
Plymouth Arg.	Tr	06.61	61-63	11	-	2
Exeter C.	Tr	12.63	63-64	41	-	8
Leyton Orient	Tr	07.65	65	2	0	0

League Club	Source	Date Signed	Seasons Played	Career Record Apps	Subs	Gls
THORNE, Steven T.						
Hampstead, 15 September, 1968						(M)
Watford	YT	07.86				
Brentford	Tr	09.87	87	1	0	1
THORNE, Terence						
Kirton-in-Lindsey, 2 February, 1947						(HB)
Ipswich T.	Lincoln C. (Am)	08.64				
Notts Co.	Tr	06.66	66	2	0	0
THORNHILL, Dennis						
Draycott, 5 July, 1923						
Wolverhampton W.	Jnrs	07.40				
Southend U.	Tr	03.48	48-49	11	-	0
THORNHILL, Keith E.						
Crewe, 20 December, 1963						(F)
Crewe Alex. (N/C)	Nantwich T.	07.83	83	1	0	0
THORNHILL, Rodney D.						
Reading, 24 January, 1942						(WH)
Reading		05.63	63-69	188	4	19
THORNLEY, Barry E.						
Gravesend, 11 February, 1948						(OL)
Brentford	Gravesend & Nft	09.65	65	7	0	0
Oxford U.	Tr	07.67	67-68	22	1	4
THORNS, John W.						
Newcastle, 10 July, 1928 Died1975						(OR)
Darlington (Am)		08.49	49	1	-	0
THORPE, Adrian						
Chesterfield, 25 November, 1963						(LW)
Mansfield T. (N/C)	YT	08.82	82	0	2	1
Bradford C.	Heanor T.	08.85	85-87	9	8	1
Tranmere Rov.	L	11.86	86	4	1	3
Notts Co.	Tr	11.87	87-88	48	11	9
Walsall	Tr	08.89	89	24	3	1
Northampton T.	Tr	03.90	89-91	36	16	6
THORPE, Andrew						
Stockport, 15 September, 1960						(D)
Stockport Co.	Jnrs	08.78	77-85	312	2	3
Tranmere Rov.	Tr	07.86	86-87	51	2	0
Stockport Co.	Tr	01.88	87-91	172	3	0
THORPE, Arthur W.						
India, 31 July, 1939						(OL)
Scunthorpe U.	Ossett T.	09.60	60-62	27	-	4
Bradford C.	Tr	07.63	63-65	81	0	17
THORPE, Ian R.						
Blackheath, 3 September, 1953 E Amat						(G)
Gillingham	Charlton Ath. (Am)	09.73	73	5	0	0
THORPE, Jeffrey R.						
Cockermouth, 17 November, 1972						(LW)
Carlisle U.	YT	07.91	90-91	29	12	1
THORPE, Leonard						
Warsop, 7 June, 1924						(WH)
Mansfield T.	Nottingham F. (Am)	08.45	46	5	-	0
THORPE, Samuel						
Sheffield, 2 December, 1920						
Sheffield U.		04.45	47-48	2	-	0
THORSTVEDT, Erik						
Norway, 28 October, 1962 Norway Int						(G)
Tottenham H.	I.F.K. Goteborg (Swe)	12.88	88-91	113	0	0
THORUP, Borge						
Denmark, 4 October, 1943						(FB)
Crystal Palace	Morton	03.69	69	0	1	0
THREADGOLD, J. Harold						
Tattenhall, 6 November, 1924						(G)
Chester C.		10.47	50-51	83	-	0
Sunderland	Tr	07.52	52	35	-	0
Southend U.	Tr	07.53	53-62	319	-	0
TRELFALL, John						
Little Lever, 22 March, 1935						(FB)
Bolton W.		12.54	55-62	47	-	1
Bury	Tr	11.62	62-64	37	-	1
THRELFALL, J. Richard						
Ashton, 5 March, 1916						(FB)
Bolton W.		07.45	46	3	-	0
Halifax T.	Tr	10.47	47	30	-	0
THRESHER, T. Michael						
Cullompton, 9 March, 1931						(FB)
Bristol C.	Chard T.	01.54	54-64	379	-	1
THRIPPLETON, Allen						
Huddersfield, 16 June, 1928						(WH)
Millwall	Rainham T.	11.50	50-54	26	-	4
THROWER, Dennis						
Ipswich, 1 August, 1938						(WH)
Ipswich T.	Jnrs	08.55	56-64	27	-	2
THROWER, Nigel J.						
Nottingham, 12 March, 1962						(LB)
Nottingham F.	App	03.80				
Chesterfield	L	02.83	82	4	0	0
THURLOW, Alec C. E.						
Depwade, 24 February, 1922 Died 1956						(G)
Huddersfield T.		09.44				
Manchester C.	Tr	09.46	46-48	21	-	0
THURLOW, Brian A.						
Loddon (Nk), 6 June, 1936						(RB)
Norwich C.	Loddon	07.54	55-63	193	-	1
Bristol C.	Tr	07.64				
THURNHAM, Roy T.						
Macclesfield, 17 February, 1942						(CH)
Manchester C.	Jnrs	06.60				
Wrexham	Tr	06.61	62	2	-	0
THWAITES, Dennis						
Stockton, 14 December, 1944 E Sch/E Yth						(OL)
Birmingham C.	App	05.62	62-70	83	4	18

Erik Thorstvedt (EIK Tonsberg, Viking Stavanger, IFK Goteborg, Tottenham Hotspur & Norway)

League Club	Source	Date Signed	Seasons Played	Apps	Subs	Gls
THWAITES, Peter						
Batley, 21 August, 1936						(CF)
Halifax T. (Am)	Swillington	02.61	60	2	-	0
THYNE, Robert B.						
Glasgow, 9 January, 1920 Died 1986						(CH)
Darlington	Clydebank	10.43	46	7	-	0
TIBBOTT, Leslie						
Oswestry, 25 August, 1955 Wu21-2						(FB)
Ipswich T.	App	03.73	75-78	52	2	0
Sheffield U.	Tr	03.79	78-81	78	0	2
TICKELL, Brian G.						
Carlisle, 15 November, 1939						(CF)
Huddersfield T.	Jnrs	11.56	58	1	-	0
Carlisle U.	Tr	05.59	59	3	-	1
TICKELL, E. Roy						
Liverpool, 25 April, 1924						(OR)
Exeter C.	St Leonards	12.45				
Southport	Tr	05.47	47	6	-	1
TICKRIDGE, Sidney						
Stepney, 10 April, 1923 E Sch						(FB)
Tottenham H.	Jnrs	04.46	46-50	95	-	0
Chelsea	Tr	03.51	50-52	61	-	0
Brentford	Tr	07.55	55-56	62	-	0
TIDDY, Michael D.						
Helston, 4 April, 1929						(OR)
Torquay U.	Jnrs	11.46	46-50	5	-	0
Cardiff C.	Tr	11.50	50-54	145	-	19
Arsenal	Tr	09.55	55-57	48	-	8
Brighton & H.A.	Tr	10.58	58-61	134	-	11
TIERNEY, James M.						
Ayr, 2 May, 1940						(OR)
Bradford C.	Saltcoats Vic.	01.60	60	2	-	0
TIERNEY, Lawrence						
Leith, 4 April, 1959						(M)
Wigan Ath.	Hibernian	07.80	80	4	3	0
TIGHE, John						
Aghamore (Ire), 13 March, 1923						(G)
West Bromwich A.	Larkhall Th.	11.45	46	1	-	0
TIGHE, Terence W.						
Edinburgh, 12 August, 1934						(WH)
Accrington St.	Dunfermline Ath.	06.57	57-60	117	-	20
Crewe Alex.	Tr	12.60	60-62	86	-	5
Southport	Tr	08.63	63	36	-	3

Terry Tighe (Dunfermline Athletic, Accrington Stanley, Crewe Alexandra & Southport)

League Club	Source	Date Signed	Seasons Played	Apps	Subs	Gls
TILER, Brian						
Rotherham, 15 March, 1943 Died 1990						(CD)
Rotherham U.		07.62	62-68	212	0	27
Aston Villa	Tr	12.68	68-72	106	1	3
Carlisle U.	Tr	10.72	72-73	51	1	1
TILER, Carl						
Sheffield, 11 February, 1970 Eu21-13						(CD)
Barnsley	YT	07.88	87-90	67	4	4
Nottingham F.	Tr	06.91	91	24	2	1

Carl Tiler (Barnsley & Nottingham Forest)

League Club	Source	Date Signed	Seasons Played	Apps	Subs	Gls
TILER, Kenneth D.						
Sheffield, 23 May, 1950						(FB)
Chesterfield		09.70	70-74	138	1	1
Brighton & H.A.	Tr	11.74	74-78	130	0	0
Rotherham U.	Tr	07.79	79-80	45	1	1
TILLEY, Darren J.						
Bristol, 15 March, 1967						(M)
York C.	Yate T.	01.92	91	13	2	0
TILLEY, Kevin						
Feltham, 6 September, 1957						(FB)
Wimbledon	Queens Park R. (App)	09.75	77	11	2	0
TILLEY, Peter						
Lurgan (NI), 13 January, 1930						(WH)
Arsenal	Witton A.	05.52	53	1	-	0
Bury	Tr	11.53	53-57	86	-	12
Halifax T.	Tr	07.58	58-62	184	-	17
TILLEY, H. Rex						
Swindon, 16 February, 1929						(WH)
Plymouth Arg.	Chippenham T.	03.51	52-56	123	-	0
Swindon T.	Tr	08.58	58-59	31	-	0
TILLING, Harold K.						
Warrington, 6 January, 1918						(OL)
Oldham Ath.	Whitecross	09.42	47	3	-	0

League Club	Source	Date Signed	Seasons Played	Career Record Apps	Subs	Gls

TILLOTSON, Maurice
Silsden, 20 January, 1944 (FB)

Huddersfield T.	Jnrs	07.62				
Stockport Co.	Tr	10.64	64-65	35	0	0

TILLSON, Andrew
Huntingdon, 30 June, 1966 (CD)

Grimsby T.	Kettering T.	07.88	88-90	104	1	6
Queens Park R.	Tr	12.90	90-91	27	2	2

TILSED, Ronald W.
Weymouth, 6 August, 1952 E Yth (G)

Bournemouth	App	01.70	69	2	0	0
Chesterfield	Tr	02.72	71	16	0	0
Arsenal	Tr	09.72				
Portsmouth	Tr	03.73	72-73	14	0	0
Hereford U.	Tr	06.74				

TILSON, Stephen B.
Wickford, 27 July, 1966 (M)

Southend U.	Witham T.	02.89	88-91	103	13	17

TILSTON, Thomas A.
Chester, 19 February, 1926 (IF)

Chester C.	Jnrs	09.43	49-50	22	-	7
Tranmere Rov.	Tr	06.51	51	25	-	15
Wrexham	Tr	03.52	51-53	78	-	29
Crystal Palace	Tr	02.54	53-55	58	-	13

TILTMAN, Richard G.
Shoreham, 14 December, 1960 (F)

Brighton & H.A.	Maidstone U.	11.86	86-87	10	3	1

TIMMINS, Arnold
Whitehaven, 29 January, 1940 (IF)

Workington	Lowca	09.60	60-63	44	-	10

TIMMINS, Charles
Birmingham, 29 May, 1922 (FB)

Coventry C.	Jack Moulds Ath.	09.46	48-57	161	-	5

TIMMINS, John
Brierley Hill, 30 May, 1936 (FB)

Wolverhampton W.	Jnrs	06.53				
Plymouth Arg.	Tr	01.58	57	5	-	0
Bristol Rov.	Tr	09.58	58-59	4	-	0

TIMSON, David Y.
Leicester, 24 August, 1947 (G)

Leicester C.	App	09.64	63-66	3	0	0
Newport Co.	Tr	08.67	67	22	0	0

TINDALL, Michael C.
Birmingham, 5 April, 1941 E Yth (WH)

Aston Villa	Jnrs	04.58	59-67	118	2	8
Walsall	Tr	06.68	68	17	0	0

TINDALL, Ronald A. E.
Streatham, 23 September, 1935 EF Lge (CF)

Chelsea	Jnrs	04.53	55-61	160	-	68
West Ham U.	Tr	11.61	61	13	-	3
Reading	Tr	10.62	62-63	36	-	12
Portsmouth	Tr	09.64	64-69	159	2	7

TINDILL, Herbert
South Hiendley, 31 December, 1926 Died 1973 (IF)

Doncaster Rov.	South Hiendley	04.44	46-57	402	-	122
Bristol C.	Tr	02.58	57-58	56	-	29
Barnsley	Tr	03.59	59-61	98	-	26

TINGAY, Philip
Chesterfield, 2 May, 1950 (G)

Chesterfield	Chesterfield Tube Wks	07.72	71-80	181	0	0
Barnsley	L	03.73	72	8	0	0

TINKLER, John
Trimdon, 24 August, 1968 (M)

Hartlepool U.	Jnrs	12.86	86-91	153	17	7

TINKLER, Luke
Chester-le-Street, 4 December, 1923 (OL)

Plymouth Arg.	West Bromwich A.	10.45	46-47	23	-	4
Walsall	Tr	06.48	48	18	-	0

TINNEY, Hugh J.
Glasgow, 14 May, 1944 Su23-2 (RB)

Bury	Partick Th.	03.67	66-72	235	3	3

TINNION, Brian
Stanley, 23 February, 1968 (M/LB)

Newcastle U.	App	02.86	86-88	30	2	2
Bradford C.	Tr	03.89	88-91	113	5	19

TINNION, Brian
Workington, 11 June, 1948 E Yth (F)

Workington	Jnrs	03.66	65-68	93	5	24
Wrexham	Tr	01.69	68-75	265	14	54
Chester C.	L	12.71	71	3	0	0

TINSLEY, Alan
Fleetwood, 1 January, 1951 (M)

Preston N.E.	App	01.69	69	8	1	1
Bury	Tr	08.70	70-74	82	12	15

TINSLEY, Colin
Redcar, 24 October, 1935 (G)

Grimsby T.	Redcar B.C.	09.54	54-57	24	-	0
Darlington	Tr	08.58	58-60	79	-	0
Exeter C.	Tr	07.61	61-62	56	-	1
Luton T.	Tr	08.63	63-67	55	0	0

TIPPETT, Michael F.
Bristol, 11 June, 1930 (W)

Bristol Rov.		04.48	49-51	8	-	2

TIPPETT, Thomas J.
Gateshead, 4 August, 1924 (OL)

Southend U.		05.46	46-51	92	-	20
Bournemouth	Tr	09.51	51-52	37	-	10

TITTERTON, David S. J.
Warwick, 25 September, 1971 E Yth (M)

Coventry C.	YT	05.90	89-90	0	2	0
Hereford U.	Tr	09.91	91	20	5	1

TIVEY, Mark R.
Brent, 10 February, 1971 (W)

Charlton Ath.	YT	05.89	91	0	1	0

TOALE, Ian
Liverpool, 28 August, 1967 (FB)

Liverpool	App	05.85				
Grimsby T.	Tr	07.87	87	16	4	0

TOASE, Donald V.
Darlington, 31 December, 1929 E Yth (RB)

Newcastle U.	Portsmouth (Am)	06.48				
Darlington	Tr	08.51	51	7	-	0

TOBIN, Donald J.
Liverpool, 1 November, 1955 (M)

Rochdale	Everton (App)	08.73	73-75	46	2	5

TOBIN, Maurice
Airdrie, 30 July, 1920 (LB)

Norwich C.	Longriggend B.C.	09.38	46-50	102	-	0

TOBIN, Robert
Cardiff, 29 March, 1921 (IL)

Cardiff C.	Cardiff Corries	08.40	47	2	-	0
Newport Co.	Barry T.	10.49				

TOCKNELL, Brian T.
South Africa, 21 May, 1937 (WH)

Charlton Ath.	Berea Park (SA)	07.59	60-65	199	0	14

TODD, Alexander
South Shields, 7 November, 1929 (F)

Hartlepool U.		04.50	52-53	4	-	0

TODD, Colin
Chester-le-Street, 12 December, 1948 E Yth/Eu23-14/EF Lge/E-27 (CD)

Sunderland	App	12.66	66-70	170	3	3
Derby Co.	Tr	02.71	70-78	293	0	6
Everton	Tr	09.78	78-79	32	0	1
Birmingham C.	Tr	09.79	79-81	92	1	0
Nottingham F.	Tr	08.82	82-83	36	0	0
Oxford U.	Tr	02.84	83	12	0	0
Luton T.	Vancouver (Can)	10.84	84	2	0	0

TODD, James
Belfast, 19 March, 1921 (WH)

League Club	Source	Date Signed	Seasons Played	Apps	Subs	Gls
Blackpool		02.45				
Port Vale	Tr	10.46	46-52	147	-	0

TODD, Keith H.
Swansea, 2 March, 1941 Wu23-1 (CF)

League Club	Source	Date Signed	Seasons Played	Apps	Subs	Gls
Swansea C.	Clydach	09.59	60-67	196	3	76

TODD, Kenneth
Butterknowle (Dm), 24 August, 1957 (M)

League Club	Source	Date Signed	Seasons Played	Apps	Subs	Gls
Wolverhampton W.	App	08.75	76-77	4	1	1
Port Vale	Tr	08.78	78-79	42	2	9
Portsmouth	Tr	10.79	79	1	2	1

TODD, Kevin
Sunderland, 28 February, 1958 (F)

League Club	Source	Date Signed	Seasons Played	Apps	Subs	Gls
Newcastle U.	Ryhope Colly	08.81	81-82	5	2	3
Darlington	Tr	02.83	82-84	99	3	23

TODD, Lee
Hartlepool, 7 March, 1972 (LB/W)

League Club	Source	Date Signed	Seasons Played	Apps	Subs	Gls
Stockport Co.	Hartlepool U. (YT)	07.90	90-91	29	4	0

TODD, Mark K.
Belfast, 4 December, 1967 NIu23-1 (M)

League Club	Source	Date Signed	Seasons Played	Apps	Subs	Gls
Manchester U.	YT	08.85				
Sheffield U.	Tr	06.87	87-90	62	8	4
Wolverhampton W.	L	03.91	90	6	1	0
Rotherham U.	Tr	09.91	91	23	0	2

TODD, Paul R.
Middlesbrough, 8 May, 1920 (IL)

League Club	Source	Date Signed	Seasons Played	Apps	Subs	Gls
Doncaster Rov.		09.45	46-49	160	-	51
Blackburn Rov.	Tr	07.50	50-51	46	-	12
Hull C.	Tr	10.51	51-52	27	-	3

TODD, Robert C.
Goole, 11 September, 1949 (W)

League Club	Source	Date Signed	Seasons Played	Apps	Subs	Gls
Liverpool	Scunthorpe U. (App)	07.67				
Rotherham U.	Tr	03.68	68	2	4	0
Mansfield T.	Tr	11.68	68	3	1	0
Workington	Tr	07.69	69	10	6	0

TODD, Ronald
Bellshill, 4 October, 1935 (WH)

League Club	Source	Date Signed	Seasons Played	Apps	Subs	Gls
Accrington St.	Lesmahagow	02.56	59	5	-	0

TODD, Samuel J.
Belfast, 22 September, 1945 NIu23-4/NI-11 (D)

League Club	Source	Date Signed	Seasons Played	Apps	Subs	Gls
Burnley	Glentoran	09.62	63-69	108	8	1
Sheffield Wed.	Tr	05.70	70-72	22	2	1
Mansfield T.	L	02.74	73	6	0	0

TODD, Thomas B.
Stonehouse, 1 June, 1926 (CF)

League Club	Source	Date Signed	Seasons Played	Apps	Subs	Gls
Crewe Alex.	Hamilton Acad.	08.55	55	13	-	3
Derby Co.	Tr	11.55	55	4	-	3
Rochdale	Tr	05.56	56	5	-	1

TOLCHARD, Jeffrey G.
Torquay, 17 March, 1944 (W)

League Club	Source	Date Signed	Seasons Played	Apps	Subs	Gls
Torquay U.		03.64	63-64	11	-	4
Exeter C.	Tr	07.65	65	1	0	0

TOLLIDAY, Stanley A.
Hackney, 6 August, 1922 Died 1951 (G)

League Club	Source	Date Signed	Seasons Played	Apps	Subs	Gls
Leyton Orient		12.46	46-48	64	-	0
Walsall	Tr	06.50				

TOLMIE, James
Glasgow, 20 November, 1960 Su21-1 (LW)

League Club	Source	Date Signed	Seasons Played	Apps	Subs	Gls
Manchester C.	Lokeren (Bel)	08.83	83-85	46	15	15
Carlisle U.	L	03.86	85	7	1	1

TOLSON, Maxwell
Australia, 18 July, 1945 (CF)

League Club	Source	Date Signed	Seasons Played	Apps	Subs	Gls
Workington	South Coast U. (Aus)	02.66	65-66	29	2	6

TOLSON, Neil
Wordsley, 25 October, 1973 (F)

League Club	Source	Date Signed	Seasons Played	Apps	Subs	Gls
Walsall	YT	12.91	91	3	6	1
Oldham Ath.	Tr	03.92				

TOLSON, William
Rochdale, 29 March, 1931 (IF)

League Club	Source	Date Signed	Seasons Played	Apps	Subs	Gls
Rochdale	St Albans B.C.	10.53	53-54	10	-	0

TOM, Stephen E.
Ware, 5 February, 1951 (CD)

League Club	Source	Date Signed	Seasons Played	Apps	Subs	Gls
Queens Park R.	App	02.69				
Brentford	Tr	06.71	71	13	5	1

TOMAN, J. Andrew
Northallerton, 7 March, 1962 (W)

League Club	Source	Date Signed	Seasons Played	Apps	Subs	Gls
Lincoln C.	Bishop Auckland	08.85	85	21	3	4
Hartlepool U.	Bishop Auckland	01.87	86-88	112	0	28
Darlington	Tr	07.89	90-91	86	0	9

TOMKIN, Cyril J.
Barrow, 18 November, 1918 (CF)

League Club	Source	Date Signed	Seasons Played	Apps	Subs	Gls
Barrow	Dumbarton	03.48	46-47	3	-	0

TOMKINS, Leonard A.
Isleworth, 16 January, 1949 E Yth (M)

League Club	Source	Date Signed	Seasons Played	Apps	Subs	Gls
Crystal Palace	App	01.67	67-69	18	2	2

TOMKINSON, Derek
Stoke, 6 April, 1931 (IR)

League Club	Source	Date Signed	Seasons Played	Apps	Subs	Gls
Port Vale	Burton A.	12.52	52-54	29	-	5
Crewe Alex.		08.56	56	17	-	1

TOMKYS, Michael G.
Kensington, 14 December, 1932 E Yth (OR)

League Club	Source	Date Signed	Seasons Played	Apps	Subs	Gls
Queens Park R.	Fulham (Am)	11.51	51-58	91	-	15

TOMLEY, Frederick W.
Liverpool, 11 July, 1931 (CH)

League Club	Source	Date Signed	Seasons Played	Apps	Subs	Gls
Liverpool	Litherland	09.53	54	2	-	0
Chester C.	Tr	07.55	55	1	-	0

TOMLIN, David
Nuneaton, 9 February, 1953 (W)

League Club	Source	Date Signed	Seasons Played	Apps	Subs	Gls
Leicester C.	App	02.71	71-75	19	7	2
Torquay U.	Tr	04.77	76-77	37	1	2
Aldershot	Tr	08.78	78-80	24	6	2

TOMLINSON, Ashley D.
Doncaster, 28 September, 1966 (W)

League Club	Source	Date Signed	Seasons Played	Apps	Subs	Gls
Doncaster Rov. (YT)	YT	07.83	83	2	2	0

TOMLINSON, Charles C.
Sheffield, 2 December, 1919 (OL)

League Club	Source	Date Signed	Seasons Played	Apps	Subs	Gls
Bradford P.A.	Sheffield Wed. (Am)	04.39				
Sheffield Wed.	Tr	07.44	46-50	68	-	7
Rotherham U.	Tr	03.51	50-51	32	-	12

TOMLINSON, David I.
Rotherham, 13 December, 1968 (RW)

League Club	Source	Date Signed	Seasons Played	Apps	Subs	Gls
Sheffield Wed.	App	12.86	86	0	1	0
Rotherham U.	Tr	08.87	87	6	3	0
Barnet	Boston U.	12.90	91	0	3	0

TOMLINSON, Frank
Manchester, 5 January, 1926 (F)

League Club	Source	Date Signed	Seasons Played	Apps	Subs	Gls
Halifax T.	Stalybridge Celtic	11.50	50	14	-	4

TOMLINSON, Frank
Manchester, 23 October, 1925 (OR)

League Club	Source	Date Signed	Seasons Played	Apps	Subs	Gls
Oldham Ath.	Goslings	11.46	46-51	115	-	27
Rochdale	Tr	11.51	51	20	-	2
Chester C.	Tr	08.52	52	10	-	0

TOMLINSON, Harold
Plymouth, 26 October, 1922 (FB)

League Club	Source	Date Signed	Seasons Played	Apps	Subs	Gls
Doncaster Rov.		10.44	46-48	58	-	0

TOMLINSON, John
Birkenhead, 26 June, 1934 E Yth (W)

League Club	Source	Date Signed	Seasons Played	Apps	Subs	Gls
Everton	Jnrs	06.52	56	2	-	0
Chesterfield	Tr	06.57	57-58	47	-	5

TOMLINSON, Michael L.
Lambeth, 15 September, 1972 (W)

League Club	Source	Date Signed	Seasons Played	Apps	Subs	Gls
Leyton Orient	YT	07.91	90-91	0	2	1

TOMLINSON, Paul
Brierley Hill, 22 February, 1964 (G)

League Club	Source	Date Signed	Seasons Played	Apps	Subs	Gls
Sheffield U.	Middlewood R.	06.83	83-86	37	0	0
Birmingham C.	L	03.87	86	11	0	0
Bradford C.	Tr	06.87	87-91	209	0	0

TOMLINSON, Robert W.
Blackburn, 4 June, 1924 (FB)

League Club	Source	Date Signed	Seasons Played	Apps	Subs	Gls
Blackburn Rov.	Feniscowles	01.43	46-47	25	-	0
Halifax T.	Mossley	06.51	51	9	-	0

TOMPKIN, Maurice
Countesthorpe (Lei), 17 February, 1919 Died 1956 (IF)

League Club	Source	Date Signed	Seasons Played	Apps	Subs	Gls
Leicester C.		03.38	37	1	-	0
Bury		12.45				
Huddersfield T.	Tr	09.46	46	10	-	1

TONER, James
Glasgow, 23 August, 1924 (OR)

League Club	Source	Date Signed	Seasons Played	Apps	Subs	Gls
Leeds U.	Dundee	06.54	54	7	-	1

TONER, William
Glasgow, 18 December, 1929 SF Lge (CH)

League Club	Source	Date Signed	Seasons Played	Apps	Subs	Gls
Sheffield U.	Dundee	05.51	51-53	55	-	2

TONES, John D.
Silksworth, 3 December, 1950 (CD)

League Club	Source	Date Signed	Seasons Played	Apps	Subs	Gls
Sunderland	App	05.68	72	2	4	0
Arsenal	Tr	07.73				
Swansea C.	L	09.74	74	7	0	0
Mansfield T.	L	10.74	74	3	0	0

TONG, David J.
Blackpool, 21 September, 1955 (M)

League Club	Source	Date Signed	Seasons Played	Apps	Subs	Gls
Blackpool	App	09.73	74-78	70	8	7
Shrewsbury T.	Tr	09.78	78-81	156	4	8
Cardiff C.	Tr	08.82	82-85	119	1	3
Rochdale	L	09.85	85	0	2	0
Bristol C.	Tr	10.85	85	19	0	0
Gillingham	Tr	03.86	85	5	0	0
Cambridge U.	Tr	08.86	86	4	2	0

TONG, Raymond
Bolton, 3 February, 1942 (W)

League Club	Source	Date Signed	Seasons Played	Apps	Subs	Gls
Blackburn Rov.		07.62				
Bradford C.	Tr	06.63	63-64	20	-	2

TONGE, Alan J.
Bury, 25 February, 1972 (D)

League Club	Source	Date Signed	Seasons Played	Apps	Subs	Gls
Manchester U.	YT	07.90				
Exeter C.	Horwich R.M.I.	12.91	91	1	2	0

TONGE, Geoffrey
Manchester, 5 May, 1942 (F)

League Club	Source	Date Signed	Seasons Played	Apps	Subs	Gls
Bury	Droylsden	03.60	59	1	-	0

TONGE, Keith A.
Edmonton, 6 November, 1964 (F)

League Club	Source	Date Signed	Seasons Played	Apps	Subs	Gls
Brentford	App	11.82	81	0	1	0

TOON, Colin
New Houghton, 26 April, 1940 (FB)

League Club	Source	Date Signed	Seasons Played	Apps	Subs	Gls
Mansfield T.	Jnrs	07.57	57-65	213	0	1

TOOTILL, George A.
Walkden, 20 October, 1913 (CH)

League Club	Source	Date Signed	Seasons Played	Apps	Subs	Gls
Plymouth Arg.	Chorley	05.36	36-37	9	-	0
Sheffield U.	Tr	01.38	38	12	-	0
Hartlepool U.	Tr	07.47	47	18	-	0

TOOZE, Dennis G.
Swansea, 12 October, 1917 (FB)

League Club	Source	Date Signed	Seasons Played	Apps	Subs	Gls
Coventry C.	Redditch T.	05.37	46-48	36	-	0

TOOZE, Robert W.
Bristol, 19 December, 1946 (G)

League Club	Source	Date Signed	Seasons Played	Apps	Subs	Gls
Bristol C.	Jnrs	07.65				
Shrewsbury T.	Tr	03.69	68-72	73	0	0
Gillingham	L	03.72	71	7	0	0

TOPPING, Christopher
Selby, 6 March, 1951 (CD)

League Club	Source	Date Signed	Seasons Played	Apps	Subs	Gls
York C.	App	03.69	68-77	410	2	11
Huddersfield T.	Tr	05.78	78-80	43	0	1

TOPPING David
Shotts, 9 March, 1926 (FB)

League Club	Source	Date Signed	Seasons Played	Apps	Subs	Gls
Torquay U.	Clyde	05.48	48-52	151	-	3

TOPPING, Henry W.
Kearsley, 21 September, 1913 (FB)

League Club	Source	Date Signed	Seasons Played	Apps	Subs	Gls
Manchester U.		12.32	32-34	12	-	1
Barnsley	Tr	05.35	35	14	-	2
Exeter C.	Macclesfield T.	05.37	37	1	-	0
New Brighton	Tr	07.38	38-47	72	-	0

TORPEY, Stephen D. J.
Islington, 8 December, 1970 (F)

League Club	Source	Date Signed	Seasons Played	Apps	Subs	Gls
Millwall	YT	02.89	89	3	4	0
Bradford C.	Tr	11.90	90-91	69	3	17

Steve Torpey (Millwall & Bradford City)

TORRANCE, Andrew
Glasgow, 8 April, 1934 (W)

League Club	Source	Date Signed	Seasons Played	Apps	Subs	Gls
Barrow	Yeovil T.	05.58	58	29	-	2

TORRANCE, George C.
Rothesay, 17 September, 1957 (M)

League Club	Source	Date Signed	Seasons Played	Apps	Subs	Gls
Brentford	Wokingham T.	12.84	84-85	29	5	1

TORRANCE, George S.
Glasgow, 27 November, 1935 (G)

League Club	Source	Date Signed	Seasons Played	Apps	Subs	Gls
Leicester C.	Thorniewood Ath.	07.54				
Oldham Ath.	Tr	08.56	56	4	-	0
Rochdale	Tr	09.57	57	2	-	0

TOSELAND, Geoffrey V.
Kettering, 31 January, 1931 (OL)

League Club	Source	Date Signed	Seasons Played	Apps	Subs	Gls
Sunderland	Kettering T.	12.48	52	6	-	1

TOSER, Ernest W.
London, 30 November, 1913 E Sch (CH)

League Club	Source	Date Signed	Seasons Played	Apps	Subs	Gls
Millwall	Dulwich Hamlet	05.37	37	2	-	0
Notts Co.	Tr	09.46	46	2	-	0

TOSHACK, J. Cameron
Cardiff, 7 March, 1970 (F)

League Club	Source	Date Signed	Seasons Played	Apps	Subs	Gls
Swansea C.	Jnrs	09.88				
Bristol C.	Tr	11.89				
Cardiff C.	Tr	02.91	90-91	1	4	0

TOSHACK, John B.
Cardiff, 22 March, 1949 W Sch/Wu23-3/W-40 (F)

League Club	Source	Date Signed	Seasons Played	Apps	Subs	Gls
Cardiff C.	App	03.66	65-70	159	3	75
Liverpool	Tr	11.70	70-77	169	3	74
Swansea C.	Tr	03.78	77-83	58	5	24

John Toshack (Cardiff City, Liverpool, Swansea City & Wales)

TOTTOH, Melvyn D.
Manchester, 26 July, 1956 (W)

League Club	Source	Date Signed	Seasons Played	Apps	Subs	Gls
Preston N.E. (N/C)	Lytham	05.85	85	0	1	0

TOULOUSE, Cyril H.
Acton, 24 December, 1923 Died 1980 (WH)

League Club	Source	Date Signed	Seasons Played	Apps	Subs	Gls
Brentford		05.46	46-47	13	-	0
Tottenham H.	Tr	12.47	48	2	-	0

TOVEY, Ronald A.
Bristol, 24 September, 1930 (IF)

League Club	Source	Date Signed	Seasons Played	Apps	Subs	Gls
Bristol C.		01.53	52-53	12	-	3

TOVEY, William J.
Bristol, 18 October, 1931 (WH)

League Club	Source	Date Signed	Seasons Played	Apps	Subs	Gls
Bristol C.	Jnrs	12.48	48-52	57	-	2

TOWERS, M. Anthony
Manchester, 13 April, 1952 E Sch/E Yth/Eu23-8/E-3 (M)

League Club	Source	Date Signed	Seasons Played	Apps	Subs	Gls
Manchester C.	App	04.69	68-73	117	5	10
Sunderland	Tr	03.74	73-76	108	0	18
Birmingham C.	Tr	07.77	77-79	90	2	4
Rochdale (N/C)	Tacoma (USA)	02.85	84	1	1	0

TOWERS, Ian J.
Consett, 11 October, 1940 (F)

League Club	Source	Date Signed	Seasons Played	Apps	Subs	Gls
Burnley	Jnrs	10.57	60-65	43	1	12
Oldham Ath.	Tr	01.66	65-67	94	1	45
Bury	Tr	07.68	68-70	44	5	7

TOWERS, E. James
Shepherds Bush, 15 April, 1933 (CF)

League Club	Source	Date Signed	Seasons Played	Apps	Subs	Gls
Brentford	Jnrs	05.51	54-60	262	-	153
Queens Park R.	Tr	05.61	61	27	-	12
Millwall	Tr	08.62	62	19	-	7
Gillingham	Tr	01.63	62	8	-	6
Aldershot	Tr	07.63	63	28	-	11

TOWERS, John
Willington, 21 December, 1913 Died 1979 (WH)

League Club	Source	Date Signed	Seasons Played	Apps	Subs	Gls
Darlington (Am)	Willington	05.46	46	13	-	0

TOWERS, William H.
Leicester, 13 July, 1920 (WH)

League Club	Source	Date Signed	Seasons Played	Apps	Subs	Gls
Leicester C.		01.45	46	4	-	0
Torquay U.	Tr	10.46	46-55	274	-	0

TOWNEND, Gary A.
Kilburn, 1 April, 1940 (IF)

League Club	Source	Date Signed	Seasons Played	Apps	Subs	Gls
Millwall	Redhill	08.60	60-63	50	-	20

TOWNER Anthony J.
Brighton, 2 May, 1955 (W)

League Club	Source	Date Signed	Seasons Played	Apps	Subs	Gls
Brighton & H.A.	App	01.73	72-78	153	9	24
Millwall	Tr	10.78	78-79	68	0	13
Rotherham U.	Tr	08.80	80-82	108	0	12
Sheffield U.	L	03.83	82	9	1	1
Wolverhampton W.	Tr	08.83	83	25	6	2
Charlton Ath.	Tr	09.84	84-85	22	5	2
Rochdale (N/C)	Tr	11.85	85	4	1	0
Cambridge U. (N/C)	Tr	03.86	85-86	8	0	0

TOWNSEND, Andrew D.
Maidstone, 23 July, 1963 IR-31 (LM)

League Club	Source	Date Signed	Seasons Played	Apps	Subs	Gls
Southampton	Weymouth	01.85	84-87	77	6	5
Norwich C.	Tr	08.88	88-89	66	5	8
Chelsea	Tr	07.90	90-91	69	0	8

Andy Townsend (Southampton, Norwich City, Chelsea & Republic of Ireland)

TOWNSEND, Christopher G.
Abertillery, 30 March, 1966 W Sch/W Yth (F)

League Club	Source	Date Signed	Seasons Played	Apps	Subs	Gls
Cardiff C. (N/C)	Jnrs	07.83	83	2	3	0

TOWNSEND, Donald E.
Swindon, 17 September, 1930 (LB)

League Club	Source	Date Signed	Seasons Played	Apps	Subs	Gls
Charlton Ath.	Trowbridge T.	07.50	54-61	249	-	1
Crystal Palace	Tr	07.62	62-64	77	-	0

TOWNSEND, George E.
Ashton-u-Lyne, 29 July, 1957 (LB)

League Club	Source	Date Signed	Seasons Played	Apps	Subs	Gls
Rochdale	App	07.75	74-75	31	1	0

League Club	Source	Date Signed	Seasons Played	Career Record Apps	Subs	Gls
TOWNSEND, James						
Greenock, 2 February, 1945						(WH)
Middlesbrough	St Johnstone	02.64	63-65	65	2	6
TOWNSEND, Leonard F.						
Brentford, 31 August, 1917						(IF)
Brentford	Hayes	05.37	38-46	33	-	12
Bristol C.	Tr	06.47	47-48	74	-	45
Millwall	Tr	07.49	49	5	-	1
TOWNSEND, Martin V.						
Romford, 15 June, 1946						(G)
Fulham (App)	App	07.61	63	2	-	0
TOWNSEND, Neil R.						
Long Buckby, 1 February, 1950 E Yth						(CD)
Northampton T.	Jnrs	09.68	68-71	65	2	1
Southend U.	Bedford T.	07.73	73-78	156	1	7
Bournemouth	Weymouth	07.79	79-80	34	0	2
TOWNSEND, Russell N.						
Reading, 17 January, 1960						(M)
Northampton T.	Barnet	09.79	79	12	1	0
TOWNSEND, William						
Bedworth, 27 December, 1922 Died 1988						(G)
Derby Co.	Nuneaton Bor.	09.42	46-52	79	-	0
TOWSE, Gary T.						
Dover, 14 May, 1952						(G)
Crystal Palace	Folkestone T.	01.72				
Brentford	Tr	06.73	73	5	0	0
TOZE, Edward						
Manchester, 6 March, 1923						
Halifax T.		08.50	50	5	-	0
TRACEY, Michael G.						
Durham, 14 February, 1935 E Amat						(W)
Luton T.	Crook T.	11.59	59-60	24	-	3
Lincoln C.	Tr	07.61	61	21	-	5
TRACEY, Simon P.						
Woolwich, 9 December, 1967						(G)
Wimbledon	App	02.86	88	1	0	0
Sheffield U.	Tr	10.88	88-91	113	0	0

Simon Tracey (Wimbledon & Sheffield United)

League Club	Source	Date Signed	Seasons Played	Career Record Apps	Subs	Gls
TRAFFORD, Stanley J.						
Leek, 2 December, 1945						(W)
Port Vale	App	10.64	64	12	-	1
TRAIL, Derek J. F.						
Edinburgh, 2 January, 1946						(M)
Workington	Falkirk	07.67	67-68	39	5	5
Hartlepool U.	Tr	07.69	69	36	3	2
TRAILOR, Cyril H.						
Merthyr Tydfil, 15 May, 1919 W Sch						(WH)
Tottenham H.	Jnrs	10.38	46-47	11	-	0
Leyton Orient	Tr	08.49	49-50	39	-	0
TRAIN, Raymond						
Nuneaton, 10 February, 1951						(M)
Walsall	App	11.68	68-71	67	6	11
Carlisle U.	Tr	12.71	71-75	154	1	8
Sunderland	Tr	03.76	75-76	31	1	1
Bolton W.	Tr	03.77	76-78	49	2	0
Watford	Tr	11.78	78-80	91	1	3
Oxford U.	Tr	03.82	81-83	49	1	0
Bournemouth	L	11.83	83	7	0	0
Northampton T.	Tr	03.84	84	46	0	1
Tranmere Rov.	Tr	08.85	85	36	0	0
Walsall	Tr	08.86	86	16	0	0
TRAINER, John (Jack)						
Glasgow, 14 July, 1952						(CD)
Halifax T.	Cork Hibs	08.76	76-78	101	4	5
Bury	Hong Kong	09.80	80	1	0	1
Rochdale (N/C)	Waterford	08.82	82	7	0	0
TRAINOR, Daniel						
Belfast, 12 July, 1944 NI Amat/NIu23-1/NI-1						(CF)
Plymouth Arg.	Crusaders	08.68	68	16	1	3
TRAINOR, Peter						
Workington, 2 March, 1915 Died1979						(CH)
Preston N.E.		08.37				
Brighton & H.A.	Tr	05.38	38-47	71	-	4
TRANTER, George H.						
Birmingham, 11 September, 1915						(CH)
West Bromwich A.	Rover Wks	12.43	46	16	-	0
TRANTER, Wilfred						
Pendlebury, 5 March, 1945						(D)
Manchester U.	App	04.62	63	1	-	0
Brighton & H.A.	Tr	05.66	65-67	46	1	1
Fulham	Baltimore (USA)	01.69	68-71	20	3	0
TRAUTMANN, Bernhard C. (Bert)						
Germany, 22 October, 1923 EF Lge						(G)
Manchester C.	St Helens	11.49	49-63	508	-	0
TRAVERS, Michael J. P.						
Camberley, 23 June, 1942						(M)
Reading	Jnrs	10.60	60-66	156	2	34
Portsmouth	Tr	07.67	67-71	74	11	5
Aldershot	Tr	07.72	72	29	1	2
TRAVIS, David A.						
Doncaster, 4 July, 1964						(M)
Doncaster Rov. (N/C)	Hatfield Main Colly	08.84	84-85	10	2	0
Scunthorpe U. (N/C)	Tr	02.86	85-86	13	0	1
Chesterfield (N/C)	Tr	08.87	87	6	5	0
TRAVIS, Donald						
Manchester, 21 January, 1924						(IF)
West Ham U.	Blackpool (Am)	09.45	46-47	5	-	0
Southend U.	Tr	05.48	48	1	-	0
Accrington St.	Tr	12.48	48-50	71	-	36
Crewe Alex.	Tr	11.50	50-51	36	-	11
Oldham Ath.	Tr	10.51	51	5	-	1
Chester C.	Tr	02.52	51-53	99	-	46
Oldham Ath.	Tr	08.54	54-56	109	-	61
TRAYNOR, Thomas J.						
Dundalk (Ire), 22 July, 1933 IR-8						(LB)
Southampton	Dundalk	06.52	52-65	433	0	7
TREACY, Darren P.						
Lambeth, 6 September, 1970						(M)
Millwall	YT	02.89	88-89	7	0	0
Bradford C.	Tr	11.90	90	16	0	2

Bert Trautmann (Manchester City)

League Club	Source	Date Signed	Seasons Played	Apps	Subs	Gls
TREACY, Francis						
Glasgow, 14 July, 1939						(IF)
Ipswich T.	Johnstone Burgh	03.61	63-65	17	1	5
TREACY, Raymond C. P.						
Dublin, 18 June, 1946 IR-42						(F)
West Bromwich A.	App	06.64	66-67	2	3	1
Charlton Ath.	Tr	02.68	67-71	144	5	44
Swindon T.	Tr	06.72	72-73	55	0	16
Preston N.E.	Tr	12.73	73-75	54	4	11
Oldham Ath.	L	03.75	74	3	0	1
West Bromwich A.	Tr	08.76	76	20	1	6
TREBILCOCK, Michael						
Gunnislake, 29 November, 1944						(CF)
Plymouth Arg.	Tavistock	12.62	62-65	71	0	27
Everton	Tr	12.65	65-67	11	0	3
Portsmouth	Tr	01.68	67-71	99	10	33
Torquay U.	Tr	07.72	72	23	1	10
TREHARNE, Colin						
Bridgend, 30 July, 1937						(G)
Mansfield T.		12.60	61-65	191	0	0
Lincoln C.	Tr	07.66	66	19	0	0
TREHARNE, Cyril A.						
Wellington, 12 March, 1928						
Shrewsbury T.		11.50	50	4	-	1
TRENTER, Ronald H.						
Ipswich, 13 December, 1928						(OR)
Ipswich T.	Jnrs	12.45				
Ipswich T.	Clacton T.	06.51	51	2	-	0
TREVIS, Derek A.						
Birmingham, 9 September, 1942						(M)
Aston Villa		06.62				
Colchester U.	Tr	03.64	63-68	196	0	13
Walsall	Tr	09.68	68-69	63	2	6
Lincoln C.	Tr	07.70	70-72	100	8	18
Stockport Co.	Tr	09.73	73	33	2	2
TREVITT, Simon						
Dewsbury, 20 December, 1967						(RB)
Huddersfield T.	YT	06.86	86-91	161	12	2
TREWICK, Alan						
Blyth, 27 April, 1941						
Gateshead		09.59	59	10	-	1
TREWICK George						
Stakeford, 15 November, 1933						(HB)
Gateshead	West Sleekburn	04.53	56-59	111	-	0
TREWICK, John						
Bedlington, 3 June, 1957 E Sch/E Yth						(M)
West Bromwich A.	App	07.74	74-80	83	13	11
Newcastle U.	Tr	12.80	80-83	76	2	8
Oxford U.	L	01.84	83	3	0	0
Oxford U.	Tr	08.84	84-87	109	2	4
Birmingham C.	Tr	09.87	87-88	35	2	0
Hartlepool U. (N/C)	Bromsgrove Rov.	10.89	89	8	0	0
TRICK, Desmond						
Swansea, 7 November, 1969						(CD)
Swansea C.	YT	07.88	89-90	25	4	0
TRIGG, Cyril						
Measham, 8 April, 1917						(CF/RB)
Birmingham C.	Bedworth T.	08.35	35-53	268	-	67
TRIM, Reginald F.						
Portsmouth, 1 October, 1913 E Sch						(FB)
Bournemouth		04.31	30-32	20	-	0
Arsenal	Tr	04.33	34	1	-	0
Nottingham F.	Tr	07.37	37-38	70	-	0
Derby Co.	Tr	12.43				
Swindon T.	Tr	07.46	46	15	-	0
TRINER, Donald A.						
Sanford Hill, 21 August, 1919						(OR)
Port Vale	Downings	12.38	38-47	25	-	7
TRISE, Guy G.						
Portsmouth, 22 November, 1933						
Portsmouth	Jnrs	05.53				
Aldershot	Tr	08.54	54	1	-	0

League Club	Source	Date Signed	Seasons Played	Apps	Subs	Gls
TROLLOPE, N. John						
Wroughton, 14 June, 1943						(LB)
Swindon T.	Jnrs	07.60	60-80	767	3	21

John Trollope (Swindon Town)

League Club	Source	Date Signed	Seasons Played	Apps	Subs	Gls
TROLLOPE, Paul J.						
Swindon, 3 June, 1972						(W)
Swindon T.	YT	12.89				
Torquay U.	Tr	03.92	91	10	0	0
TROOPS, Harold						
Sheffield, 10 February, 1926 Died 1963						(OR)
Barnsley	Hadfield Wks	12.46	48	3	-	1
Lincoln C.	Tr	08.49	49-57	295	-	33
Carlisle U.	Tr	06.58	58-59	60	-	1
TROTTER, Michael						
Hartlepool, 27 October, 1969						(M)
Middlesbrough	YT	11.87				
Doncaster Rov.	L	11.88	88	3	0	0
Darlington	Tr	06.90	90-91	16	13	2
Leicester C.	Tr	12.91	91	0	2	0
TROUGHTON, Samuel E.						
Lisburn (NI), 27 March, 1964 NI Sch/NI Yth						(F)
Wolverhampton W.	Glentoran	12.83	83	17	0	2
TRUETT, Geoffrey F.						
High Wycombe, 23 May, 1935						(WH)
Crystal Palace	Wycombe W.	06.57	57-61	38	-	5
TRUSLER, John W.						
Shoreham, 7 June, 1934						
Brighton & H.A.	Shoreham	08.54	54	1	-	0
TRUSSON, Michael S.						
Northolt, 26 May, 1959						(M)
Plymouth Arg.	App	01.77	76-79	65	8	15
Sheffield U.	Tr	07.80	80-83	125	1	31
Rotherham U.	Tr	12.83	83-86	124	0	19
Brighton & H.A.	Tr	07.87	87-88	34	3	2
Gillingham	Tr	09.89	89-91	69	5	7
TUCK, Peter G.						
Plaistow, 14 May, 1932						(IF)
Chelsea	Jnrs	06.51	51	3	-	1

TUCKER, W. Barry
Swansea, 28 August, 1952 (FB)

League Club	Source	Date Signed	Seasons Played	Apps	Subs	Gls
Northampton T.	App	08.70	71-77	209	5	3
Brentford	Tr	02.78	77-82	168	1	5
Northampton T.	Tr	10.82	82-83	62	1	5

TUCKER, Gordon
Manchester, 5 January, 1968 (CD)

League Club	Source	Date Signed	Seasons Played	Apps	Subs	Gls
Huddersfield T.	Derby Co. (N/C)	07.87	87-88	30	5	0
Scunthorpe U.	Tr	07.89	89	14	1	1

TUCKER, Jason J.
Isleworth, 3 February, 1973 (LB)

League Club	Source	Date Signed	Seasons Played	Apps	Subs	Gls
Aldershot	YT	07.91	90	0	1	0

TUCKER, Keith
Deal, 25 November, 1936 (FB)

League Club	Source	Date Signed	Seasons Played	Apps	Subs	Gls
Charlton Ath.	Betteshanger Colly	02.54	54-60	3	-	0

TUCKER, Kenneth
Poplar, 2 October, 1925 (OL)

League Club	Source	Date Signed	Seasons Played	Apps	Subs	Gls
West Ham U.	Finchley	08.46	47-56	83	-	31
Notts Co.	Tr	03.57	56-57	28	-	5

TUCKER, Kenneth J.
Merthyr Tydfil, 15 July, 1935 (W)

League Club	Source	Date Signed	Seasons Played	Apps	Subs	Gls
Cardiff C.	Aston Villa (Am)	10.55	56-57	13	-	0
Shrewsbury T.	Tr	02.58	57-59	46	-	8
Northampton T.	Tr	03.60	59-60	9	-	3

TUCKER, Lee D.
Middlesbrough, 14 September, 1971 (W)

League Club	Source	Date Signed	Seasons Played	Apps	Subs	Gls
Middlesbrough	YT	10.89				
Darlington	Tr	07.91	91	0	5	0

TUCKER, Malcolm
Cramlington, 12 April, 1933 (CH)

League Club	Source	Date Signed	Seasons Played	Apps	Subs	Gls
Grimsby T.	Newcastle U. (Am)	11.50	53-57	40	-	0

TUCKER, Mark J.
Woking, 27 April, 1972 (RB)

League Club	Source	Date Signed	Seasons Played	Apps	Subs	Gls
Fulham	YT	07.90	91	1	1	0

TUCKER, William J.
Kidderminster, 17 May, 1948 (CD)

League Club	Source	Date Signed	Seasons Played	Apps	Subs	Gls
Hereford U.	Kidderminster Hrs	07.72	72-76	135	2	12
Bury	Tr	12.76	76-78	96	0	8
Swindon T.	Tr	06.79	79	35	0	4

TUDDENHAM, Anthony R.
Reepham (Nk), 28 September, 1956 (FB)

League Club	Source	Date Signed	Seasons Played	Apps	Subs	Gls
West Ham U.	App	09.74				
Cambridge U.	Tr	02.76	75-76	11	1	0

TUDOR, Edward T.
Neston, 15 March, 1935 (F)

League Club	Source	Date Signed	Seasons Played	Apps	Subs	Gls
Gillingham	Bolton W. (Am)	04.58	58	1	-	0

TUDOR, John A.
Ilkeston, 25 June, 1946 (F)

League Club	Source	Date Signed	Seasons Played	Apps	Subs	Gls
Coventry C.	Ilkeston T.	01.66	66-68	63	6	13
Sheffield U.	Tr	11.68	68-70	64	7	30
Newcastle U.	Tr	01.71	70-76	161	3	53
Stoke C.	Tr	09.76	76	28	2	3

TUDOR, William H.
Shotton, 14 February, 1918 Died 1955 W Sch (CH)

League Club	Source	Date Signed	Seasons Played	Apps	Subs	Gls
West Bromwich A.	Lavender	05.35	38	31	-	0
Wrexham	Tr	05.46	46-48	56	-	2

TUEART, Dennis
Newcastle, 27 November, 1949 Eu23-1/EF Lge/E-6 (W)

League Club	Source	Date Signed	Seasons Played	Apps	Subs	Gls
Sunderland	Jnrs	08.67	68-73	173	5	46
Manchester C.	Tr	03.74	73-77	139	1	59
Manchester C.	New York (USA)	02.80	79-82	77	7	27
Stoke C.	Tr	08.83	83	2	1	0
Burnley	Tr	12.83	83	8	7	5

TUGMAN, James
Workington, 14 March, 1945 (D)

League Club	Source	Date Signed	Seasons Played	Apps	Subs	Gls
Workington		07.64	65-67	32	12	0

TULIP, William E.
Gateshead, 3 May, 1933 (CF)

League Club	Source	Date Signed	Seasons Played	Apps	Subs	Gls
Newcastle U.		06.51				
Darlington	Tr	05.56	56-57	44	-	34

TULLOCH, Roland
South Africa, 15 July, 1932 (WH)

League Club	Source	Date Signed	Seasons Played	Apps	Subs	Gls
Hull C.	South Africa	12.53	54	3	-	0

TULLOCH, Ronald T.
Haddington, 5 June, 1933 (IF)

League Club	Source	Date Signed	Seasons Played	Apps	Subs	Gls
Southend U.	Hearts	05.56	56	11	-	4
Carlisle U.	Tr	07.57	57-59	73	-	22

TULLY, Kevin F.
Manchester, 18 December, 1952 (W)

League Club	Source	Date Signed	Seasons Played	Apps	Subs	Gls
Blackpool	Prestwich Heys	11.72	72-73	10	1	0
Cambridge U.	Tr	07.74	74-75	40	4	8
Crewe Alex.	Tr	01.76	75-78	81	5	4
Port Vale	Tr	10.78	78-79	7	6	2
Bury	Chorley	08.80	80	7	3	1

TUMBRIDGE, Raymond A.
Hampstead, 6 March, 1955 (LB)

League Club	Source	Date Signed	Seasons Played	Apps	Subs	Gls
Charlton Ath.	App	03.73	72-74	43	3	0
Northampton T.	L	02.75	74	11	0	0

TUNE, David B.
Reading, 1 November, 1938 (HB)

League Club	Source	Date Signed	Seasons Played	Apps	Subs	Gls
Reading	Jnrs	11.55	57	1	-	0

TUNE, Michael G.
Stoke, 28 February, 1962 (M)

League Club	Source	Date Signed	Seasons Played	Apps	Subs	Gls
Crewe Alex.	Stoke C. (App)	06.79	79	0	1	0

TUNKS, Roy W.
Worthing, 21 January, 1951 (G)

League Club	Source	Date Signed	Seasons Played	Apps	Subs	Gls
Rotherham U.	App	03.68	67-73	138	0	0
York C.	L	01.69	68	4	0	0
Preston N.E.	Tr	11.74	74-80	277	0	0
Wigan Ath.	Tr	11.81	81-87	245	0	0
Hartlepool U.	Tr	07.88	88	5	0	0
Preston N.E.	Tr	11.88	88-89	25	0	0

TUNNEY, Edward
Wirral, 23 September, 1915 (FB)

League Club	Source	Date Signed	Seasons Played	Apps	Subs	Gls
Everton		08.36				
Wrexham		09.37	37-51	222	-	0

TUNNICLIFFE, William F.
Stoke, 5 January, 1920 (OL)

League Club	Source	Date Signed	Seasons Played	Apps	Subs	Gls
Port Vale		01.37	36-37	3	-	0
Bournemouth	Tr	05.38	38-46	49	-	7
Wrexham	Tr	06.47	47-52	236	-	73
Bradford C.	Tr	01.53	52-54	89	-	20

TUNSTALL, Eric W.
Hartlepool, 21 November, 1950 (WH)

League Club	Source	Date Signed	Seasons Played	Apps	Subs	Gls
Hartlepool U.	App	11.68	68	2	1	0
Newcastle U.	Tr	01.69				

TUOHY, Liam
Dublin, 27 April, 1933 IR'B'-2/IR-8 (OL)

League Club	Source	Date Signed	Seasons Played	Apps	Subs	Gls
Newcastle U.	Shamrock Rov.	05.60	60-62	38	-	9

TUOHY, Michael P. F.
West Bromwich, 28 March, 1956 (F)

League Club	Source	Date Signed	Seasons Played	Apps	Subs	Gls
Southend U.	Redditch U.	06.79	79	20	1	4

TUPLING, Stephen
Wensleydale, 11 July, 1964 (M)

League Club	Source	Date Signed	Seasons Played	Apps	Subs	Gls
Middlesbrough	App	07.82				
Carlisle U. (N/C)	Tr	07.84	84	1	0	0
Darlington	Tr	10.84	84-86	105	6	8
Newport Co.	Tr	08.87	87	30	3	2
Cardiff C.	Tr	08.88	88-89	3	2	0
Torquay U.	L	09.88	88	1	2	0
Exeter C.	L	01.89	88	8	1	1
Hartlepool U.	Tr	12.89	89-91	83	6	3

TURBITT, Peter
Keighley, 1 July, 1951 E Yth (OR)

League Club	Source	Date Signed	Seasons Played	Apps	Subs	Gls
Bradford C.	Keighley C.Y.C.	08.69	69-70	5	3	0

TURLEY, John W.
Bebington, 26 January, 1939 (CF)

League Club	Source	Date Signed	Seasons Played	Apps	Subs	Gls
Sheffield U.	Ellesmere Port	05.56	57	5	-	3
Peterborough U.	Tr	07.61	61-63	32	-	14
Rochdale	Tr	05.64	64	22	-	5

League Club	Source	Date Signed	Seasons Played	Apps	Subs	Gls

TURLEY, Michael D.
Rotherham, 14 February, 1936 (WH)

League Club	Source	Date Signed	Seasons Played	Apps	Subs	Gls
Sheffield Wed.	Jnrs	03.53	54	3	-	0
Burnley	Tr	10.56				

TURNBULL, Frederick
Wallsend, 28 August, 1946 (CH)

League Club	Source	Date Signed	Seasons Played	Apps	Subs	Gls
Aston Villa	Centre 64	09.66	67-73	160	1	3
Halifax T.	L	10.69	69	7	0	0

TURNBULL, George F.
Gateshead, 4 February, 1927 (G)

League Club	Source	Date Signed	Seasons Played	Apps	Subs	Gls
Grimsby T.	Alnwick T.	08.50	50	2	-	0
Accrington St.	Tr	09.51	51	33	-	0
Gateshead	Tr	07.52	52	3	-	0

TURNBULL, Lee M.
Stockton, 27 September, 1967 (M/F)

League Club	Source	Date Signed	Seasons Played	Apps	Subs	Gls
Middlesbrough	YT	09.85	85-86	8	8	4
Aston Villa	Tr	08.87				
Doncaster Rov.	Tr	11.87	87-90	108	15	21
Chesterfield	Tr	02.91	90-91	45	1	16

TURNBULL, Ronald W.
Newbiggin, 18 July, 1922 Died 1966 (CF)

League Club	Source	Date Signed	Seasons Played	Apps	Subs	Gls
Sunderland	Dundee	11.47	47-48	40	-	16
Manchester C.	Tr	09.49	49-50	30	-	5
Swansea C.	Tr	01.51	50-52	67	-	35

TURNBULL, Roy
Edinburgh, 22 October, 1948 (IF)

League Club	Source	Date Signed	Seasons Played	Apps	Subs	Gls
Lincoln C.	Hearts	09.69	69	0	2	0

TURNBULL, Terence M.
Stockton, 18 October, 1945 (F)

League Club	Source	Date Signed	Seasons Played	Apps	Subs	Gls
Hartlepool U. (N/C)	Crook T.	08.76	76	13	0	3

TURNER, Adam E.
Glasgow, 13 March, 1934

League Club	Source	Date Signed	Seasons Played	Apps	Subs	Gls
Sheffield Wed.	Dunfermline Ath.	01.56				
Gateshead	Dunfermline Ath.	10.58	58	6	-	0

TURNER, Alan
Hull, 5 July, 1943 (IF)

League Club	Source	Date Signed	Seasons Played	Apps	Subs	Gls
Coventry C.	Scunthorpe U. (Am)	03.62	61-65	4	0	0
Shrewsbury T.	Tr	07.66	66	14	2	4
Bradford P.A.	Tr	05.67	67	30	2	4

TURNER, Alan
Sheffield, 22 September, 1935 (F)

League Club	Source	Date Signed	Seasons Played	Apps	Subs	Gls
Sheffield U.		09.57				
Halifax T.	Tr	07.58	58	7	-	0

TURNER, Alfred S.
USA, 26 December, 1929 (CF)

League Club	Source	Date Signed	Seasons Played	Apps	Subs	Gls
New Brighton (Am)	Port Sunlight	02.51	50	4	-	0

TURNER, Arthur A.
London, 22 January, 1922 (IF)

League Club	Source	Date Signed	Seasons Played	Apps	Subs	Gls
Colchester U.	Charlton Ath. (Am)	(N/L)	50-51	45	-	14

TURNER, Arthur
Newcastle-u-Lyme, 1 April, 1909 (CH)

League Club	Source	Date Signed	Seasons Played	Apps	Subs	Gls
Stoke C.	Woolstanton	11.30	30-38	291	-	17
Birmingham C.	Tr	01.39	38-46	39	-	0
Southport	Tr	02.48	47-48	28	-	0

TURNER, Brian
Whittlesey, 27 August, 1925 (CF)

League Club	Source	Date Signed	Seasons Played	Apps	Subs	Gls
Lincoln C. (Am)	March T.	11.47	47	5	-	0

TURNER, Brian
Salford, 23 July, 1936 (WH)

League Club	Source	Date Signed	Seasons Played	Apps	Subs	Gls
Bury	Bury Amats	02.57	57-69	451	3	24
Oldham Ath.	Tr	08.70	70	10	1	0

TURNER, Brian A.
New Zealand, 31 July, 1949 (M)

League Club	Source	Date Signed	Seasons Played	Apps	Subs	Gls
Chelsea	Eden (NZ)	05.68				
Portsmouth	Tr	06.69	69	3	1	0
Brentford	Tr	01.70	69-71	88	4	7

TURNER, Charles J.
Newport, 1 July, 1919 (G)

League Club	Source	Date Signed	Seasons Played	Apps	Subs	Gls
Newport Co.		05.38	38-47	37	-	0
Swansea C.	Tr	08.48	48	2	-	0

TURNER, Christopher J.
St Neots, 3 April, 1951 (CD)

League Club	Source	Date Signed	Seasons Played	Apps	Subs	Gls
Peterborough U.	Jnrs	11.69	69-77	308	6	37
Luton T.	Tr	07.78	78	30	0	5
Cambridge U.	New England (USA)	09.79	79	15	4	0
Swindon T.	New England (USA)	09.80	80	0	3	0
Cambridge U.	Tr	10.80	80-83	68	3	3
Southend U.	Tr	10.83	83	22	0	1

TURNER, Christopher R.
Sheffield, 15 September, 1958 E Yth (G)

League Club	Source	Date Signed	Seasons Played	Apps	Subs	Gls
Sheffield Wed.	App	08.76	76-78	91	0	0
Lincoln C.	L	10.78	78	5	0	0
Sunderland	Tr	07.79	79-84	195	0	0
Manchester U.	Tr	08.85	85-87	64	0	0
Sheffield Wed.	Tr	09.88	88-90	75	0	0
Leeds U.	L	11.89	89	2	0	0
Leyton Orient	Tr	10.91	91	34	0	0

Chris Turner (Sheffield Wednesday, Sunderland, Manchester United, Sheffield Wednesday & Leyton Orient)

TURNER, David
Derby, 26 December, 1948 (RB)

League Club	Source	Date Signed	Seasons Played	Apps	Subs	Gls
Everton	App	10.66	67	1	0	0
Southport	Tr	05.70	70-72	69	2	0

TURNER, David J.
Retford, 7 September, 1943 (WH)

League Club	Source	Date Signed	Seasons Played	Apps	Subs	Gls
Newcastle U.	App	10.60	61-62	2	-	0
Brighton & H.A.	Tr	12.63	63-71	292	8	28
Blackburn Rov.	Tr	08.72	72-73	23	2	0

TURNER, Eric
Huddersfield, 13 January, 1921

League Club	Source	Date Signed	Seasons Played	Apps	Subs	Gls
Halifax T.	Wooldale W.	04.46	46	7	-	0

TURNER, Frederick A.
Southampton, 28 February, 1930 Died 1955 (RB)

League Club	Source	Date Signed	Seasons Played	Apps	Subs	Gls
Southampton	Jnrs	02.50				
Torquay U.	Tr	08.51	51	1	-	0
Southampton	Tr	03.53	53-54	19	-	0

League Club	Source	Date Signed	Seasons Played	Apps	Subs	Gls

TURNER, Gordon R.
Hull, 7 June, 1930 Died 1976 EF Lge (CF)

League Club	Source	Date Signed	Seasons Played	Apps	Subs	Gls
Luton T.		03.50	50-63	406	-	243

TURNER, Graham J.
Ellesmere Port, 5 October, 1947 E Yth (CD/M)

League Club	Source	Date Signed	Seasons Played	Apps	Subs	Gls
Wrexham	Jnrs	07.65	64-67	77	0	0
Chester C.	Tr	01.68	67-72	215	3	5
Shrewsbury T.	Tr	01.73	72-83	342	13	22

TURNER, Herbert G.
Brithdir, 19 June, 1909 Died 1981 W-8 (FB)

League Club	Source	Date Signed	Seasons Played	Apps	Subs	Gls
Charlton Ath.	Brithdir	08.33	33-46	176	-	3

TURNER, Hugh
Middlesbrough, 12 May, 1917 (FB)

League Club	Source	Date Signed	Seasons Played	Apps	Subs	Gls
Middlesbrough		08.35				
Darlington	Tr	08.39	46	6	-	0

TURNER, Ian
Middlesbrough, 17 January, 1953 (G)

League Club	Source	Date Signed	Seasons Played	Apps	Subs	Gls
Huddersfield T.	South Bank	10.70				
Grimsby T.	Tr	01.72	71-73	26	0	0
Walsall	L	02.73	72	3	0	0
Southampton	Tr	03.74	73-77	77	0	0
Newport Co.	L	03.78	77	7	0	0
Lincoln C.	L	10.78	78	7	0	0
Walsall	Tr	01.79	78-80	39	0	0
Halifax T.	L	01.81	80	5	0	0

TURNER, John G. A.
Peterlee, 23 December, 1954 (G)

League Club	Source	Date Signed	Seasons Played	Apps	Subs	Gls
Derby Co.	App	12.72				
Doncaster Rov.	L	02.74	73	4	0	0
Huddersfield T.	L	03.75	74	1	0	0
Reading	Tr	05.75	75-77	31	0	0
Torquay U.	Tr	08.78	78-79	76	0	0
Chesterfield	Tr	02.80	79-82	132	0	0
Torquay U.	Tr	08.83	83	34	0	0
Burnley	Weymouth	08.84				
Peterborough U.	Tr	10.84	84-85	60	0	0

TURNER, Joseph
Barnsley, 21 March, 1931 (G)

League Club	Source	Date Signed	Seasons Played	Apps	Subs	Gls
Stockport Co.	Denaby U.	07.54	54-56	79	-	0
Darlington	Tr	12.57	57-59	68	-	0
Scunthorpe U.	Tr	06.60	60-61	22	-	0
Barnsley	Tr	11.61	61	7	-	0

TURNER, Keith J.
Coventry, 9 April, 1934 (IF)

League Club	Source	Date Signed	Seasons Played	Apps	Subs	Gls
Nottingham F.		06.54	54	1	-	0

TURNER, Kenneth
Great Houghton, 22 April, 1941 (FB)

League Club	Source	Date Signed	Seasons Played	Apps	Subs	Gls
Huddersfield T.	Jnrs	10.58	61	5	-	0
Shrewsbury T.	Tr	07.63	63-65	64	0	1
York C.	Tr	06.66	66-67	88	0	2

TURNER, Mark B.
Stockport, 19 September, 1956 (M)

League Club	Source	Date Signed	Seasons Played	Apps	Subs	Gls
Stockport Co.	Everton (App)	08.75	75	8	0	0

TURNER, Michael G. E.
Bridport, 20 September, 1938 E Yth (G)

League Club	Source	Date Signed	Seasons Played	Apps	Subs	Gls
Swindon T.	Dorchester T.	12.61	61-63	75	-	0
Torquay U.	Tr	07.64	64-65	14	0	0

TURNER, Neil S. T.
Blackpool, 15 March, 1942 (M)

League Club	Source	Date Signed	Seasons Played	Apps	Subs	Gls
Blackpool	Jnrs	12.59	63-66	10	1	1
Crewe Alex.	Tr	07.68	68-71	80	6	4

TURNER, Paul
Barnsley, 8 July, 1953 (RB)

League Club	Source	Date Signed	Seasons Played	Apps	Subs	Gls
Barnsley	App	07.71	70-74	27	8	1

TURNER, Paul E.
Cheshunt, 13 November, 1968 (M)

League Club	Source	Date Signed	Seasons Played	Apps	Subs	Gls
Arsenal	App	07.86				
Cambridge U.	Tr	09.87	87-88	28	9	0

TURNER, Peter A.
Leicester, 14 August, 1931

League Club	Source	Date Signed	Seasons Played	Apps	Subs	Gls
Crewe Alex.		03.54	54-55	23	-	4

TURNER, Philip
Sheffield, 12 February, 1962 (M)

League Club	Source	Date Signed	Seasons Played	Apps	Subs	Gls
Lincoln C.	App	02.80	79-85	239	2	19
Grimsby T.	Tr	08.86	86-87	62	0	9
Leicester C.	Tr	02.88	87-88	18	6	2
Notts Co.	Tr	03.89	88-91	117	10	10

Phil Turner (Lincoln City, Grimsby Town, Leicester City & Notts County)

TURNER, Philip S.
Chester, 20 February, 1927 (IF)

League Club	Source	Date Signed	Seasons Played	Apps	Subs	Gls
Chester C.	Jnrs	07.46	46-47	27	-	6
Carlisle U.	Tr	09.48	48-50	79	-	23
Bradford P.A.	Tr	06.51	51-53	55	-	24
Scunthorpe U.	Tr	06.54	54	5	-	2
Accrington St.	Tr	10.55	55-56	14	-	5
Chester C.	Tr	11.56	56	15	-	3

TURNER, Robert P.
Ripon, 18 September, 1966 (F)

League Club	Source	Date Signed	Seasons Played	Apps	Subs	Gls
Huddersfield T.	App	09.84	84	0	1	0
Cardiff C.	Tr	07.85	85-86	34	5	8
Hartlepool U.	L	10.86	86	7	0	1
Bristol Rov.	Tr	12.86	86-87	19	7	2
Wimbledon	Tr	12.87	87-88	2	8	0
Bristol C.	Tr	01.89	88-89	45	7	12
Plymouth Arg.	Tr	07.90	90-91	64	0	17

TURNER, Robin D.
Carlisle, 10 September, 1955 E Yth (F)

League Club	Source	Date Signed	Seasons Played	Apps	Subs	Gls
Ipswich T.	App	04.73	75-83	22	26	2
Swansea C.	Tr	03.85	84-85	20	0	8
Colchester U.	Tr	11.85	85	6	5	0

TURNER, Stanley F.
Wokingham, 31 May, 1941 (OR)

League Club	Source	Date Signed	Seasons Played	Apps	Subs	Gls
Reading	Jnrs	12.58	60	3	-	0

TURNER, Stanley S.
Hanley, 21 October, 1926 (FB)

League Club	Source	Date Signed	Seasons Played	Apps	Subs	Gls
Port Vale		03.49	50-56	227	-	0

TURNER, Wayne L.
Luton, 9 March, 1961 (M)

League Club	Source	Date Signed	Seasons Played	Apps	Subs	Gls
Luton T.	App	04.78	78-84	81	3	2
Lincoln C.	L	10.81	81	16	0	0
Coventry C.	Tr	07.85	85	14	1	1
Brentford	Tr	09.86	86-87	56	0	2

TURNEY, James A.
Cramlington, 8 July, 1922 (OR)

League Club	Source	Date Signed	Seasons Played	Apps	Subs	Gls
Darlington		08.48	48-49	40	-	3

TURPIE, Robert P.
Hampstead, 13 November, 1949 (M)

League Club	Source	Date Signed	Seasons Played	Apps	Subs	Gls
Queens Park R.	App	11.67	69	1	1	0
Peterborough U.	Tr	07.70	70-71	31	6	3

TURTON, Cyril
South Kirkby, 20 September, 1921 (CH)

League Club	Source	Date Signed	Seasons Played	Apps	Subs	Gls
Sheffield Wed.	Frickley Colly	11.44	46-53	146	-	0

TUTILL, Stephen A.
York, 1 October, 1969 (CD)

League Club	Source	Date Signed	Seasons Played	Apps	Subs	Gls
York C.	YT	01.88	87-91	164	2	2

TUTIN, Harold
Silksworth, 6 June, 1919

League Club	Source	Date Signed	Seasons Played	Apps	Subs	Gls
Southport (Am)		09.46	46	2	-	0

TUTT, Graham C.
Deptford, 27 August, 1956 (G)

League Club	Source	Date Signed	Seasons Played	Apps	Subs	Gls
Charlton Ath.	Jnrs	03.74	73-75	65	0	0
Workington	L	09.74	74	4	0	0

TUTTLE, David P.
Reading, 6 February, 1972 E Yth (CD)

League Club	Source	Date Signed	Seasons Played	Apps	Subs	Gls
Tottenham H.	YT	02.90	90-91	6	2	0

TUTTON, Alan
Bexley, 23 February, 1973 (F)

League Club	Source	Date Signed	Seasons Played	Apps	Subs	Gls
Maidstone U.	Alma Swanley	07.91	91	0	4	0

TUTTY, Paul
Manchester, 22 February, 1952 (CH)

League Club	Source	Date Signed	Seasons Played	Apps	Subs	Gls
Stockport Co. (Am)	Manchester U. (Am)	07.70	70	1	0	0

TUTTY, Wayne K.
Oxford, 18 June, 1963 (M)

League Club	Source	Date Signed	Seasons Played	Apps	Subs	Gls
Reading	Banbury U.	08.82	82-83	11	2	4

TWAMLEY, Bruce R.
Canada, 23 May, 1952 (FB)

League Club	Source	Date Signed	Seasons Played	Apps	Subs	Gls
Ipswich T.		10.69	73-74	2	0	0

TWEEDY, George J.
Willington, 8 January, 1913 Died 1987 E-1 (G)

League Club	Source	Date Signed	Seasons Played	Apps	Subs	Gls
Grimsby T.	Willington	08.31	32-52	347	-	0

TWELL, Terence K.
Doncaster, 21 February, 1947 (G)

League Club	Source	Date Signed	Seasons Played	Apps	Subs	Gls
Birmingham C.	Bourne T.	10.64	67	2	0	0

TWENTYMAN, Geoffrey
Liverpool, 10 March, 1959 (CD)

League Club	Source	Date Signed	Seasons Played	Apps	Subs	Gls
Preston N.E.	Chorley	08.83	83-85	95	3	4
Bristol Rov.	Tr	08.86	86-91	241	3	6

TWENTYMAN, Geoffrey
Carlisle, 19 January, 1930 (CH)

League Club	Source	Date Signed	Seasons Played	Apps	Subs	Gls
Carlisle U.	Jnrs	02.47	46-53	149	-	2
Liverpool	Tr	12.53	53-59	170	-	18
Carlisle U.	Ballymena U.	06.63	63	10	-	0

TWIDLE, Kenneth G.
Brigg, 10 October, 1931 (CF)

League Club	Source	Date Signed	Seasons Played	Apps	Subs	Gls
Rotherham U.	Retford T.	12.57	57-58	24	-	

TWIGG, Richard L.
Barry, 10 September, 1939 (G)

League Club	Source	Date Signed	Seasons Played	Apps	Subs	Gls
Notts Co.	Barry T.	11.57	58	3	-	0

TWISSELL, Charles H.
Singapore, 16 December, 1932 E Amat (W)

League Club	Source	Date Signed	Seasons Played	Apps	Subs	Gls
Plymouth Arg.		04.57	55-57	41	-	9
York C.	Tr	11.58	58-60	53	-	8

TWIST, Franklin
Liverpool, 2 November, 1940 E Yth (W)

League Club	Source	Date Signed	Seasons Played	Apps	Subs	Gls
Liverpool	Jnrs	08.58				
Bury	Prescot Cables	10.61	61-62	8	-	0
Halifax T.	Tr	07.63	63-64	64	-	11
Tranmere Rov.	Tr	07.65	65	7	0	3

TWITCHIN, Ian R.
Teignmouth, 22 January, 1952 E Yth (FB)

League Club	Source	Date Signed	Seasons Played	Apps	Subs	Gls
Torquay U.	Jnrs	01.70	69-80	374	29	14

TWOMEY, James F.
Newry (NI), 13 April, 1914 Died 1984 LOI/NI-2 (G)

League Club	Source	Date Signed	Seasons Played	Apps	Subs	Gls
Leeds U.	Newry T.	12.37	37-48	108	-	0

TYDEMAN, Richard
Chatham, 26 May, 1951 (M)

League Club	Source	Date Signed	Seasons Played	Apps	Subs	Gls
Gillingham	App	05.69	69-76	293	2	13
Charlton Ath.	Tr	12.76	76-80	158	0	7
Gillingham	Tr	08.81	81-83	75	1	2
Peterborough U.	Tr	10.83	83	29	0	0

TYLER, Dudley H. J.
Salisbury, 21 September, 1944 (W)

League Club	Source	Date Signed	Seasons Played	Apps	Subs	Gls
West Ham U.	Hereford U.	06.72	72-73	29	0	1
Hereford U.	Tr	11.73	73-76	97	5	10

TYLER, Leonard D. V.
Rotherhithe, 7 January, 1919 Died 1988 (LB)

League Club	Source	Date Signed	Seasons Played	Apps	Subs	Gls
Millwall	Redhill	03.43	46-49	90	-	0
Ipswich T.	Tr	07.50	50-51	73	-	0

TYLER, Simon
Pontypool, 1 May, 1962 (F)

League Club	Source	Date Signed	Seasons Played	Apps	Subs	Gls
Newport Co. (N/C)	Abergavenny	10.84	84-85	0	4	0

TYNAN, Paul
Whitehaven, 15 July, 1969 (M)

League Club	Source	Date Signed	Seasons Played	Apps	Subs	Gls
Carlisle U.	Ipswich T. (App)	08.87	87	2	3	0

TYNAN, Robert
Liverpool, 7 December, 1955 E Yth (M)

League Club	Source	Date Signed	Seasons Played	Apps	Subs	Gls
Tranmere Rov.	App	07.73	72-77	193	2	25
Blackpool	Tr	07.78				

TYNAN, Thomas E.
Liverpool, 17 November, 1955 (F)

League Club	Source	Date Signed	Seasons Played	Apps	Subs	Gls
Liverpool	App	11.72				
Swansea C.	L	10.75	75	6	0	2
Sheffield Wed.	Tr	09.76	76-78	89	2	31
Lincoln C.	Tr	10.78	78	9	0	1
Newport Co.	Tr	02.79	78-82	168	15	66
Plymouth Arg.	Tr	08.83	83-84	80	0	43
Rotherham U.	Tr	07.85	85-86	32	0	13
Plymouth Arg.	L	03.86	85	9	0	10
Plymouth Arg.	Tr	09.86	86-89	172	1	73
Torquay U.	Tr	05.90	90	34	1	13
Doncaster Rov.	Tr	07.91	91	5	6	1

TYRELL, Joseph J.
Stepney, 21 January, 1932 (IF)

League Club	Source	Date Signed	Seasons Played	Apps	Subs	Gls
Aston Villa	Bretforton O.B.	05.50	53-55	7	-	3
Millwall	Tr	03.56	55-56	37	-	18
Bournemouth	Tr	06.57	57-58	3	-	1

TYRER, Alan
Liverpool, 8 December, 1942 (M)

League Club	Source	Date Signed	Seasons Played	Apps	Subs	Gls
Everton	Jnrs	12.59	59-61	9	-	2
Mansfield T.	Tr	07.63	63-64	41	-	5
Arsenal	Tr	08.65				
Bury	Tr	08.67	67	2	0	0
Workington	Tr	07.68	68-75	228	15	18

TYRER, Arthur
Liverpool, 14 October, 1934 (F)

League Club	Source	Date Signed	Seasons Played	Apps	Subs	Gls
Crewe Alex.	St Helens	03.58	57	6	-	3

TYRER, Arthur S.
Manchester, 25 February, 1931 (WH)

League Club	Source	Date Signed	Seasons Played	Apps	Subs	Gls
Leeds U.	Mossley	09.50	51-53	39	-	4
Shrewsbury T.	Tr	06.55	55	24	-	3
Aldershot	Tr	06.56	56-63	235	-	9

TYSON, John
Barrow, 19 November, 1935 (F)

League Club	Source	Date Signed	Seasons Played	Apps	Subs	Gls
Barrow		04.54	53-56	8	-	0

Terry Venables (Chelsea, Tottenham Hotspur, Queens Park Rangers, Crystal Palace & England)
The only player ever to have won international honours at all levels, he now guides Tottenham Hotspur as its Chief Executive

UFTON, Derek G.
Crayford, 31 May, 1928 E-1 (CH)

League Club	Source	Date Signed	Seasons Played	Apps	Subs	Gls
Charlton Ath.	Bexleyheath & Welling	09.48	49-59	263	-	0

UGOLINI, Rolando
Italy, 4 June, 1924 (G)

League Club	Source	Date Signed	Seasons Played	Apps	Subs	Gls
Middlesbrough	Glasgow Celtic	05.48	48-55	320	-	0
Wrexham	Tr	06.57	57-59	83	-	0

ULLATHORNE, Robert
Wakefield, 11 October, 1971 E Yth (M/LB)

League Club	Source	Date Signed	Seasons Played	Apps	Subs	Gls
Norwich C.	YT	07.90	90-91	22	0	3

Robert Ullathorne (Norwich City)

UNDERHILL, Graham S.
Bristol, 10 April, 1968 (D)

League Club	Source	Date Signed	Seasons Played	Apps	Subs	Gls
Bristol C.	App	04.86	85	1	0	0

UNDERWOOD, E. David
Camden, 15 March, 1928 Died 1989 (G)

League Club	Source	Date Signed	Seasons Played	Apps	Subs	Gls
Queens Park R.	Edware T.	12.49	51	2	-	0
Watford	Tr	02.52	51-53	52	-	0
Liverpool	Tr	12.53	53-55	45	-	0
Watford	Tr	06.56	56	16	-	0
Watford	Dartford	04.60	60-62	108	-	0
Fulham	Tr	07.63	63-64	18	-	0

UNDERWOOD, George
Sheffield, 6 September, 1925

League Club	Source	Date Signed	Seasons Played	Apps	Subs	Gls
Sheffield U.		09.46	49-50	17	-	0
Sheffield Wed.	Tr	10.51				
Scunthorpe U.	Tr	06.53	53	8	-	0
Rochdale	Tr	06.54	54	19	-	0

UNDERWOOD, William K.
Brigg, 28 December, 1921 (OL)

League Club	Source	Date Signed	Seasons Played	Apps	Subs	Gls
Hartlepool U. (Am)		01.48	47	1	-	0

UNSWORTH, David G.
Chorley, 16 October, 1973 E Yth (LB)

League Club	Source	Date Signed	Seasons Played	Apps	Subs	Gls
Everton	YT	06.92	91	1	1	1

UNSWORTH, Jamie J.
Bury, 1 May, 1973 (RB)

League Club	Source	Date Signed	Seasons Played	Apps	Subs	Gls
Cardiff C.	YT	07.91	90-91	1	3	0

UPHILL, Dennis E.
Bath, 11 August, 1931 (IF)

League Club	Source	Date Signed	Seasons Played	Apps	Subs	Gls
Tottenham H.	Jnrs	09.49	50-52	6	-	2
Reading	Tr	02.53	52-55	92	-	43
Coventry C.	Tr	10.55	55-56	49	-	17
Mansfield T.	Tr	03.57	56-58	83	-	38
Watford	Tr	06.59	59-60	51	-	30
Crystal Palace	Tr	10.60	60-62	63	-	17

UPRICHARD, W. Norman
Moyraverty (NI), 20 April, 1928 NI-18 (G)

League Club	Source	Date Signed	Seasons Played	Apps	Subs	Gls
Arsenal	Distillery	06.48				
Swindon T.	Tr	11.49	49-52	73	-	0
Portsmouth	Tr	11.52	52-58	182	-	0
Southend U.	Tr	07.59	59	12	-	0

UPTON, Colin C.
Reading, 2 October, 1960 (F)

League Club	Source	Date Signed	Seasons Played	Apps	Subs	Gls
Plymouth Arg.	App	10.78	78	2	1	0

UPTON Frank
Nuneaton, 18 October, 1934 (WH)

League Club	Source	Date Signed	Seasons Played	Apps	Subs	Gls
Northampton T.	Nuneaton Bor.	03.53	52-53	17	-	1
Derby Co.	Tr	06.54	54-60	224	-	12
Chelsea	Tr	08.61	61-64	74	-	3
Derby Co.	Tr	09.65	65-66	35	0	5
Notts Co.	Tr	09.66	66	33	1	3
Workington	Worcester C.	01.68	67	6	1	0

UPTON, James E.
Coatbridge, 3 June, 1940 (FB)

League Club	Source	Date Signed	Seasons Played	Apps	Subs	Gls
Cardiff C.	Glasgow Celtic	08.63	63	5	-	0

UPTON, Robin P.
Lincoln, 9 November, 1942 (WH)

League Club	Source	Date Signed	Seasons Played	Apps	Subs	Gls
Brighton & H.A.	Jnrs	11.59	62-66	40	0	0

URE, John F. (Ian)
Ayr, 7 December, 1939 SF Lge/Su23-1/S-11 (CH)

League Club	Source	Date Signed	Seasons Played	Apps	Subs	Gls
Arsenal	Dundee	08.63	63-69	168	0	2
Manchester U.	Tr	08.69	69-70	47	0	1

Ian Ure (Dundee, Arsenal, Manchester United & Scotland)

URQUHART, George S. M.
Glasgow, 22 April, 1950 (M)

League Club	Source	Date Signed	Seasons Played	Apps	Subs	Gls
Wigan Ath.	Ross Co.	07.79	79-80	63	5	6

URQUHART, William M.
Inverness, 22 November, 1956 (F)

League Club	Source	Date Signed	Seasons Played	Apps	Subs	Gls
Wigan Ath.	Glasgow Rangers	11.80	80	5	5	2

URSEM, Loek A. J. M.
Netherlands, 7 January, 1958 (W)

League Club	Source	Date Signed	Seasons Played	Apps	Subs	Gls
Stoke C.	A.Z. Alkmaar (Neth)	07.79	79-82	32	8	7
Sunderland	L	03.82	81	0	4	0

URWIN, Graham E.
South Shields, 15 February, 1949 (OR)

League Club	Source	Date Signed	Seasons Played	Apps	Subs	Gls
Darlington		08.67	67	1	0	0

USHER, Brian
Durham, 11 March, 1944 Eu23-1 (OR)

League Club	Source	Date Signed	Seasons Played	Apps	Subs	Gls
Sunderland	Jnrs	03.61	63-64	61	-	5
Sheffield Wed.	Tr	06.65	65-67	55	1	2
Doncaster Rov.	Tr	06.68	68-72	164	6	6

USHER, John A. G.
Hexham, 6 September, 1918 (WH)

League Club	Source	Date Signed	Seasons Played	Apps	Subs	Gls
Watford		05.46	46-47	23	-	3

UYTENBOGARDT, Albert
South Africa, 5 March, 1930 (G)

League Club	Source	Date Signed	Seasons Played	Apps	Subs	Gls
Charlton Ath.	Cape Town Trams (SA)	10.48	48-52	6	-	0

Albert Uytenbogardt (Charlton Athletic)

UZELAC, Stephen
Doncaster, 12 March, 1953 (CD)

League Club	Source	Date Signed	Seasons Played	Apps	Subs	Gls
Doncaster Rov.	Jnrs	06.71	71-76	182	3	9
Mansfield T.	L	02.76	75	2	0	0
Preston N.E.	Tr	05.77	77-78	9	0	0
Stockport Co.	Tr	03.80	79-81	31	0	2

UZZELL, John E.
Plymouth, 31 March, 1959 (D)

League Club	Source	Date Signed	Seasons Played	Apps	Subs	Gls
Plymouth Arg.	App	03.77	77-88	292	10	6
Torquay U.	Tr	08.89	89-91	91	1	2

VAESSEN, Leon H.
New Cross, 8 November, 1940 E Sch (WH)

League Club	Source	Date Signed	Seasons Played	Apps	Subs	Gls
Millwall	Chelsea (Am)	01.58	57-60	26	-	2
Gillingham	Tr	08.61	61-62	29	-	0

VAESSEN, Paul L.
Gillingham, 16 October, 1961 (F)

League Club	Source	Date Signed	Seasons Played	Apps	Subs	Gls
Arsenal	App	07.79	78-81	23	9	6

VAFIADIS, Odysseus (Seth)
Hammersmith, 8 September, 1945 (W)

League Club	Source	Date Signed	Seasons Played	Apps	Subs	Gls
Queens Park R.	Chelsea (App)	11.62	63	15	-	4
Millwall	Tr	09.64	64	4	-	0

VAIREY, Roy H.
South Elmsall, 10 June, 1932 (G)

League Club	Source	Date Signed	Seasons Played	Apps	Subs	Gls
Stockport Co.		09.51	56	5	-	0

VALENTINE, Carl H.
Manchester, 4 July, 1958 Canadian Int (W)

League Club	Source	Date Signed	Seasons Played	Apps	Subs	Gls
Oldham Ath.	Jnrs	01.76	76-79	75	7	8
West Bromwich A.	Vancouver (Can)	10.84	84-85	44	0	6

VALENTINE, Peter
Huddersfield, 16 April, 1963 (CD)

League Club	Source	Date Signed	Seasons Played	Apps	Subs	Gls
Huddersfield T.	App	04.80	81-82	19	0	1
Bolton W.	Tr	07.83	83-84	66	2	1
Bury	Tr	07.85	85-91	279	4	13

VALLANCE, Thomas H. W.
Stoke, 28 March, 1924 (OL)

League Club	Source	Date Signed	Seasons Played	Apps	Subs	Gls
Arsenal	Torquay U. (Am)	07.47	48-49	15	-	2

VALLARD, Leonard G. H.
Sherborne, 6 July, 1940 (FB)

League Club	Source	Date Signed	Seasons Played	Apps	Subs	Gls
Reading	Yeovil T.	05.58	59-61	37	-	2

VAN BREUKELEN, Johannes (Hans)
Netherlands, 4 October, 1956 Dutch Int (G)

League Club	Source	Date Signed	Seasons Played	Apps	Subs	Gls
Nottingham F.	Utrecht (Neth)	09.82	82-83	61	0	0

Hans van Breukelen (Utrecht, Nottingham Forest & Holland)

VAN DEN HAUWE, Patrick W. R.
Belgium, 16 December, 1960 W-13 (FB)

League Club	Source	Date Signed	Seasons Played	Apps	Subs	Gls
Birmingham C.	App	08.78	78-84	119	4	1
Everton	Tr	09.84	84-88	134	1	2
Tottenham H.	Tr	08.89	89-91	97	1	0

VAN DER ELST, Francois
Belgium, 1 December, 1954 Belgian Int (M)

League Club	Source	Date Signed	Seasons Played	Apps	Subs	Gls
West Ham U.	New York (USA)	12.81	81-82	61	1	16

VAN DER LAAN, Robin
Schiedam (Neth), 5 September, 1968 (M)

League Club	Source	Date Signed	Seasons Played	Apps	Subs	Gls
Port Vale	Wageningen (Neth)	02.91	90-91	53	8	9

VAN GOOL, Roger
Belgium, 1 June, 1950 Belgian Int (W)

League Club	Source	Date Signed	Seasons Played	Apps	Subs	Gls
Coventry C.	F.C. Cologne (Ger)	03.80	79-80	17	0	0

VAN MIERLO, Anthony W. M.
Netherlands, 24 August, 1957 Dutch Int (W)

League Club	Source	Date Signed	Seasons Played	Apps	Subs	Gls
Birmingham C.	Willem Tilburg (Neth)	08.81	81-82	44	0	4

VAN ROSSUM, Johannes C. (Erik)
Nijmegen (Neth.), 27 March, 1963 (CD)

League Club	Source	Date Signed	Seasons Played	Apps	Subs	Gls
Plymouth Arg.	Twente Enschede (Neth)	01.92	91	9	0	0

VAN WIJK, Dennis J.
Netherlands, 16 February, 1962 (LB/M)

League Club	Source	Date Signed	Seasons Played	Apps	Subs	Gls
Norwich C.	Ajax (Neth)	10.82	82-85	109	9	3

VANDERMOTTEN, William
Glasgow, 26 August, 1930 Died 1979 (FB)

League Club	Source	Date Signed	Seasons Played	Apps	Subs	Gls
Bradford P.A.	Third Lanark	03.53	52	1	-	0

VANSITTART, Thomas
Merton, 23 January, 1950 (D)

League Club	Source	Date Signed	Seasons Played	Apps	Subs	Gls
Crystal Palace	App	04.67	67-69	10	1	2
Wrexham	Tr	02.70	69-74	86	2	1

VARADI, Imre
Paddington, 8 July, 1959 (F)

League Club	Source	Date Signed	Seasons Played	Apps	Subs	Gls
Sheffield U.	Letchworth G.C.	04.78	78	6	4	4
Everton	Tr	03.79	79-80	22	4	6
Newcastle U.	Tr	08.81	81-82	81	0	39
Sheffield Wed.	Tr	08.83	83-84	72	4	33
West Bromwich A.	Tr	07.85	85	30	2	9
Manchester C.	Tr	10.86	86-88	56	9	26
Sheffield Wed.	Tr	09.88	88-89	14	8	3
Leeds U.	Tr	02.90	89-91	19	3	4
Luton T.	L	03.92	91	5	1	1

VARNEY, John F.
Oxford, 27 November, 1929 (CF)

League Club	Source	Date Signed	Seasons Played	Apps	Subs	Gls
Hull C.	Oxford C.	12.49	50	9	-	0
Lincoln C.	Tr	05.51	51-52	20	-	4

VARTY, Thomas H.
Hetton-le-Hole, 2 December, 1921 (IF)

League Club	Source	Date Signed	Seasons Played	Apps	Subs	Gls
Darlington		08.45	46-49	162	-	31
Watford	Tr	09.50	50	34	-	5

VASPER, Peter J.
Bromley, 3 September, 1945 (G)

League Club	Source	Date Signed	Seasons Played	Apps	Subs	Gls
Leyton Orient		11.63				
Norwich C.	Guilford C.	02.68	67-69	31	0	0
Cambridge U.	Tr	09.70	70-73	136	0	0

VASS, Stephen
Leicester, 10 January, 1954 (FB)

League Club	Source	Date Signed	Seasons Played	Apps	Subs	Gls
Hartlepool U.		10.79	79	4	0	0
Huddersfield T.	Tr	01.81				

VASSALLO, Barrie E.
Newport, 3 March, 1956 W Sch (M)

League Club	Source	Date Signed	Seasons Played	Apps	Subs	Gls
Arsenal	App	05.73				
Plymouth Arg.	Tr	11.74	74-75	6	7	2
Torquay U.	Barnstaple	03.77	76-78	44	2	4

VAUGHAN, Charles J.
Bermondsey, 23 April, 1921 Died 1989 E Amat/E'B'-1 (CF)

League Club	Source	Date Signed	Seasons Played	Apps	Subs	Gls
Charlton Ath.	Sutton U.	01.47	46-52	227	-	91
Portsmouth	Tr	03.53	52-53	26	-	14

VAUGHAN, N. Glyn
Llanidloes, 25 August, 1921 (IF)

League Club	Source	Date Signed	Seasons Played	Apps	Subs	Gls
Exeter C.	Oldham Ath. (Am)	05.46	46-47	6	-	0

VAUGHAN, Ian
Sheffield, 3 July, 1961 (CD)

League Club	Source	Date Signed	Seasons Played	Apps	Subs	Gls
Rotherham U.	App	07.79	79-80	4	0	0
Stockport Co.	L	12.81	81	2	0	1

VAUGHAN, John
Isleworth, 26 June, 1964 (G)

League Club	Source	Date Signed	Seasons Played	Apps	Subs	Gls
West Ham U.	App	06.82				
Charlton Ath.	L	03.85	84	6	0	0
Bristol Rov.	L	09.85	85	6	0	0
Wrexham	L	10.85	85	4	0	0
Bristol C.	L	03.86	85	2	0	0
Fulham	Tr	08.86	86	44	0	0
Bristol C.	L	01.88	87	3	0	0
Cambridge U.	Tr	06.88	88-91	151	0	0

VAUGHAN, Nigel M.
Caerleon, 20 May, 1959 Wu21-2/W-10 (M)

League Club	Source	Date Signed	Seasons Played	Apps	Subs	Gls
Newport Co.	App	05.77	76-83	215	9	32
Cardiff C.	Tr	09.83	83-86	144	5	42
Reading	L	02.87	86	5	0	1
Wolverhampton W.	Tr	08.87	87-89	86	7	10
Hereford U.	Tr	08.90	90-91	9	4	1

VAUGHAN, Terence R.
Ebbw Vale, 22 April, 1938 (IF)

League Club	Source	Date Signed	Seasons Played	Apps	Subs	Gls
Mansfield T.		06.57	58	6	-	2

VEACOCK, James
Liverpool, 8 September, 1919 (CF)

League Club	Source	Date Signed	Seasons Played	Apps	Subs	Gls
Southport	Marine	11.47	47	10	-	0

VEALL, Raymond J.
Skegness, 16 March, 1943 (OL)

League Club	Source	Date Signed	Seasons Played	Apps	Subs	Gls
Doncaster Rov.	Skegness	03.61	60-61	19	-	6
Everton	Tr	09.61	62	11	-	1
Preston N.E.	Tr	05.65	65	11	0	0
Huddersfield T.	Tr	12.65	65-66	12	0	1

VEARNCOMBE, Graham
Cardiff, 28 March, 1934 W-2 (G)

League Club	Source	Date Signed	Seasons Played	Apps	Subs	Gls
Cardiff C.	Jnrs	02.52	52-63	208	-	0

VEART, Robert
Hartlepool, 11 August, 1944 E Amat (F)

League Club	Source	Date Signed	Seasons Played	Apps	Subs	Gls
Hartlepool U.	Whitby T.	07.70	70-72	58	12	11

VECK, Robert
Fareham, 1 April, 1920 (OL)

League Club	Source	Date Signed	Seasons Played	Apps	Subs	Gls
Southampton	Jnrs	09.45	46-49	23	-	2
Gillingham	Tr	07.50	50	36	-	12

VEITCH, George H.
Sunderland, 18 January, 1931 (WH)

League Club	Source	Date Signed	Seasons Played	Apps	Subs	Gls
Hull C.	Silkworth Colly	08.51				
Millwall	Tr	06.52	52-57	93	-	0

VEITCH, Thomas
Edinburgh, 16 October, 1949 (M)

League Club	Source	Date Signed	Seasons Played	Apps	Subs	Gls
Tranmere Rov.	Hearts	07.72	72-74	76	3	5
Halifax T.	Tr	08.75	75	20	2	0
Hartlepool U.	Tr	08.76	76	10	0	0

VENABLES, Terence F.
Bethnal Green, 6 January, 1943 E Sch/E Yth/E Amat/Eu21-4/EF Lge/E-2 (M)

League Club	Source	Date Signed	Seasons Played	Apps	Subs	Gls
Chelsea	Jnrs	08.60	59-65	202	0	26
Tottenham H.	Tr	05.66	65-68	114	1	5
Queens Park R.	Tr	06.69	69-74	178	1	19
Crystal Palace	Tr	09.74	74	14	0	0

VENISON, Barry
Consett, 16 August, 1964 E Yth/Eu21-10 (RB)

League Club	Source	Date Signed	Seasons Played	Apps	Subs	Gls
Sunderland	App	01.82	81-85	169	4	2
Liverpool	Tr	07.86	86-91	103	7	1

VENNARD, Walter
Belfast, 17 October, 1919 (CH)

League Club	Source	Date Signed	Seasons Played	Apps	Subs	Gls
Stockport Co.	Crusaders	09.47	47	5	-	0

VENTERS, Alexander
Cowdenbeath, 9 June, 1913 Died 1960 SF Lge/S-3 (IF)

League Club	Source	Date Signed	Seasons Played	Apps	Subs	Gls
Blackburn Rov.	Third Lanark	02.47	46-47	25	-	7

VENTOM, Eric G.
Hemsworth, 15 February, 1920 (LB)

League Club	Source	Date Signed	Seasons Played	Apps	Subs	Gls
Brentford		02.46	47	1	-	0

VENUS, Mark
Hartlepool, 6 April, 1967 (LB)

League Club	Source	Date Signed	Seasons Played	Apps	Subs	Gls
Hartlepool U. (N/C)	Jnrs	03.85	84	4	0	0
Leicester C.	Tr	09.85	85-87	58	3	1
Wolverhampton W.	Tr	03.88	87-91	131	4	3

League Club	Source	Date Signed	Seasons Played	Career Record Apps	Subs	Gls

VERDE, Pedro A.
Argentina, 12 March, 1952 (F)

League Club	Source	Date Signed	Seasons Played	Apps	Subs	Gls
Sheffield U.	Hercules Alicante (Sp)	08.79	79	9	1	3

VERITY, David A.
Halifax, 21 September, 1949 (M)

League Club	Source	Date Signed	Seasons Played	Apps	Subs	Gls
Scunthorpe U.	App	09.67	66-67	3	2	0
Halifax T.	Tr	09.68	69-72	64	14	5

VERITY, Kevin P.
Halifax, 16 March, 1940 (F)

League Club	Source	Date Signed	Seasons Played	Apps	Subs	Gls
Halifax T.	Jnrs	10.58	58-59	13	-	6

VERNON, John (Jack)
Belfast, 26 September, 1918 Died 1981 IR-2/NI-17 (CH)

League Club	Source	Date Signed	Seasons Played	Apps	Subs	Gls
West Bromwich A.	Belfast Celtic	02.47	46-51	190	-	1

VERNON, John E.
South Africa, 2 March, 1956 (W)

League Club	Source	Date Signed	Seasons Played	Apps	Subs	Gls
Stockport Co.	Jnrs	08.75	74-75	4	2	0

VERNON, T. Roy
Prestatyn, 14 April, 1937 Wu23-2/W-32 (IF)

League Club	Source	Date Signed	Seasons Played	Apps	Subs	Gls
Blackburn Rov.	Jnrs	03.55	55-59	131	-	49
Everton	Tr	02.60	59-64	176	-	101
Stoke C.	Tr	03.65	64-68	84	3	22
Halifax T.	L	01.70	69	4	0	0

Roy Vernon (Blackburn Rovers, Everton, Stoke City & Wales)

VERTANNES, Desmond M. S.
Hounslow, 25 April, 1972 (CD)

League Club	Source	Date Signed	Seasons Played	Apps	Subs	Gls
Fulham (YT)	YT	07.88	89	0	2	0
Aldershot	Chelsea (N/C)	08.90				

VERVEER, Etienne
Surinam, 22 September, 1967 (M)

League Club	Source	Date Signed	Seasons Played	Apps	Subs	Gls
Millwall	Chur (Swit)	12.91	91	24	1	2

VESEY, Kieron G.
Manchester, 24 November, 1965 (G)

League Club	Source	Date Signed	Seasons Played	Apps	Subs	Gls
Halifax T. (N/C)	Jnrs	02.83	83	2	0	0

VESSEY, Anthony W.
Derby, 28 November, 1961 (CD)

League Club	Source	Date Signed	Seasons Played	Apps	Subs	Gls
Brighton & H.A.	App	11.79	80	1	0	0

VEYSEY, Kenneth J.
Hackney, 8 June, 1967 (G)

League Club	Source	Date Signed	Seasons Played	Apps	Subs	Gls
Torquay U.	Dawlish	11.87	88-90	72	0	0
Oxford U.	Tr	10.90	90-91	57	0	0

VICKERS, Peter
Doncaster, 6 March, 1934 E Sch (IF)

League Club	Source	Date Signed	Seasons Played	Apps	Subs	Gls
Leeds U.	Jnrs	03.51	50-55	20	-	4
Northampton T.	Wisbech T.	02.60	59	2	-	0

VICKERS, Stephen H.
Bishop Auckland, 13 October, 1967 (CD)

League Club	Source	Date Signed	Seasons Played	Apps	Subs	Gls
Tranmere Rov.	Spennymoor U.	09.85	85-91	257	1	11

VICKERS, Wilfred
Wakefield, 3 August, 1924

League Club	Source	Date Signed	Seasons Played	Apps	Subs	Gls
Brighton & H.A.		09.47	47	5	-	1
West Bromwich A.	Tr	05.48				
Aldershot	Tr	06.49	49-51	14	-	1

VICKERY, Paul W.
Chelmsford, 20 May, 1953

League Club	Source	Date Signed	Seasons Played	Apps	Subs	Gls
Southend U. (App)	App	07.69	69	0	1	0

VILJOEN, Colin
South Africa, 20 June, 1948 E-2 (M)

League Club	Source	Date Signed	Seasons Played	Apps	Subs	Gls
Ipswich T.	South Africa	03.67	66-77	303	2	45
Manchester C.	Tr	08.78	78-79	25	2	0
Chelsea	Tr	03.80	79-81	19	1	0

VILLA, J. Ricardo (Ricki)
Argentina, 18 August, 1952 Argentina Int (M)

League Club	Source	Date Signed	Seasons Played	Apps	Subs	Gls
Tottenham H.	Racing Club (Arg)	07.78	78-82	124	9	18

Ricki Villa (Racing Club, Tottenham Hotspur & Argentina)

VILLARS, Anthony K.
Cwmbran, 24 January, 1952 Wu23-2/W-3 (W)

League Club	Source	Date Signed	Seasons Played	Apps	Subs	Gls
Cardiff C.	Cwmbran T.	06.71	71-75	66	7	4
Newport Co.	Tr	07.76	76	23	6	1

VILLAZAN, Rafael
Uruguay, 19 July, 1956 Uruguay Int (D)

League Club	Source	Date Signed	Seasons Played	Apps	Subs	Gls
Wolverhampton W.	Huelva (Sp)	05.80	80-81	20	3	0

VINALL, Albert
Birmingham, 6 March, 1922 (FB)

League Club	Source	Date Signed	Seasons Played	Apps	Subs	Gls
Aston Villa	Southampton (Am)	07.46	47-53	11	-	1
Walsall	Tr	08.54	54-55	79	-	0

VINALL, Edward J.
Birmingham, 16 December, 1910 (CF)

League Club	Source	Date Signed	Seasons Played	Apps	Subs	Gls
Sunderland	Folkestone	10.31	31-32	16	-	2
Norwich C.	Tr	06.33	33-37	168	-	72
Luton T.	Tr	10.37	37-38	44	-	18
Walsall	Tr	07.46	46	2	-	0

VINCENT, John V.
West Bromwich, 8 February, 1947 E Yth (M)

League Club	Source	Date Signed	Seasons Played	Apps	Subs	Gls
Birmingham C.	App	02.64	63-70	168	3	41
Middlesbrough	Tr	03.71	70-72	37	3	7
Cardiff C.	Tr	10.72	72-74	58	8	11

John Vincent (Birmingham City, Middlesbrough & Cardiff City)

VINCENT, Norman E. (Ned)
Prudhoe, 3 March, 1909 Died 1980 (FB)

League Club	Source	Date Signed	Seasons Played	Apps	Subs	Gls
Stockport Co.	Spennymoor U.	03.28	28-33	132	-	20
Grimsby T.	Tr	06.34	34-46	144	-	2

VINCENT, Robert
Leicester, 29 May, 1949 (F)

League Club	Source	Date Signed	Seasons Played	Apps	Subs	Gls
Notts Co. (Am)	Jnrs	01.66	65	1	0	0

VINCENT, Robert G.
Newcastle, 23 November, 1962 E Sch (M)

League Club	Source	Date Signed	Seasons Played	Apps	Subs	Gls
Sunderland	App	11.79	80	1	1	0
Leyton Orient	Tr	05.82	81-82	8	1	0

VINE, Peter W.
Southampton, 11 December, 1940 E Yth (F)

League Club	Source	Date Signed	Seasons Played	Apps	Subs	Gls
Southampton	Jnrs	12.57	58	1	-	0

VINEY, Keith B.
Portsmouth, 26 October, 1957 (LB)

League Club	Source	Date Signed	Seasons Played	Apps	Subs	Gls
Portsmouth	App	10.75	75-81	160	6	3
Exeter C.	Tr	08.82	82-88	270	0	8
Bristol Rov.	L	09.88	88	2	1	0

VINNICOMBE, Christopher
Exeter, 20 October, 1970 Eu21-12 (LB)

League Club	Source	Date Signed	Seasons Played	Apps	Subs	Gls
Exeter C.	YT	07.89	88-89	35	4	1

VINTER, Michael
Boston, 23 May, 1954 (F)

League Club	Source	Date Signed	Seasons Played	Apps	Subs	Gls
Notts Co.	Boston U.	03.72	72-78	135	31	53
Wrexham	Tr	06.79	79-81	90	12	25
Oxford U.	Tr	08.82	82-83	67	2	21
Mansfield T.	Tr	08.84	84-85	52	2	7
Newport Co.	Tr	08.86	86	30	2	7

VIOLLET, Dennis S.
Manchester, 20 September, 1933 E Sch/E-2 (CF)

League Club	Source	Date Signed	Seasons Played	Apps	Subs	Gls
Manchester U.	Jnrs	09.50	52-61	259	-	159
Stoke C.	Tr	01.62	61-66	181	1	59

VIPHAM, Peter
Rawtenstall, 9 September, 1942 (G)

League Club	Source	Date Signed	Seasons Played	Apps	Subs	Gls
Accrington St.	Jnrs	06.61	60	6	-	0

VIRGIN, Derek E.
Bristol, 10 February, 1934 (W)

League Club	Source	Date Signed	Seasons Played	Apps	Subs	Gls
Bristol C.		09.55	55-60	21	-	4

VITTY, John (Jack)
Chilton (Dm), 19 January, 1923 (FB)

League Club	Source	Date Signed	Seasons Played	Apps	Subs	Gls
Charlton Ath.	Boldon Villa	11.46	48	2	-	0
Brighton & H. A.	Tr	10.49	49-51	47	-	1
Workington	Tr	07.52	52-56	196	-	3

VITTY, Ronald
Chilton (Dm), 18 April, 1927

League Club	Source	Date Signed	Seasons Played	Apps	Subs	Gls
Charlton Ath.	Boldon Villa	09.47				
Hartlepool U.	Tr	08.49	49	7	-	0
Bradford C.	Tr	07.50				

VIVEASH, Adrian L.
Swindon, 30 September, 1969 (LB)

League Club	Source	Date Signed	Seasons Played	Apps	Subs	Gls
Swindon T.	YT	07.88	90-91	32	3	1

VIZARD, Colin J.
Newton-le-Willows, 18 June, 1933 (F)

League Club	Source	Date Signed	Seasons Played	Apps	Subs	Gls
Everton	Jnrs	09.51				
Rochdale	Tr	05.57	57-58	41	-	7

VONK, Michel C.
Netherlands, 28 October, 1968 (CD)

League Club	Source	Date Signed	Seasons Played	Apps	Subs	Gls
Manchester C.	S.V.V. Dordrecht (Neth)	03.92	91	8	1	0

VOWDEN, Geoffrey A.
Barnsley, 27 April, 1941 (F)

League Club	Source	Date Signed	Seasons Played	Apps	Subs	Gls
Nottingham F.	Jersey D.M.	01.60	59-64	90	-	40
Birmingham C.	Tr	10.64	64-70	213	8	79
Aston Villa	Tr	03.71	70-73	93	4	22

Geoff Vowden (Nottingham Forest, Birmingham City & Aston Villa)

Billy Wright (Wolverhampton Wanderers & England)
The first man to win 100 caps for England, many of them as team captain

WADDELL, Robert
Kirkcaldy, 5 September, 1939 (CF)

League Club	Source	Date Signed	Seasons Played	Apps	Subs	Gls
Blackpool	Dundee	03.65	64-66	28	0	6
Bradford P.A.	Tr	11.66	66	20	0	3

WADDELL, William
Denny, 16 April, 1950 (F)

League Club	Source	Date Signed	Seasons Played	Apps	Subs	Gls
Leeds U.	Jnrs	04.67				
Barnsley	Kilmarnock	05.71	71	17	1	3
Hartlepool U.	Tr	03.72	71-73	43	5	9
Workington	L	02.73	72	1	2	0

WADDINGTON, Anthony
Manchester, 9 November, 1924 (WH)

League Club	Source	Date Signed	Seasons Played	Apps	Subs	Gls
Crewe Alex.	Manchester U. (Am)	01.46	46-52	179	-	7

WADDINGTON, John
Darwen, 16 February, 1952 (CD)

League Club	Source	Date Signed	Seasons Played	Apps	Subs	Gls
Liverpool	Darwen	05.70				
Blackburn Rov.	Tr	08.73	73-78	139	9	18
Bury	Tr	08.79	79-80	46	1	0

WADDINGTON, D. Paul
Oldbury, 14 February, 1961 E Sch (M)

League Club	Source	Date Signed	Seasons Played	Apps	Subs	Gls
Walsall	App	11.78	78-81	14	5	1

WADDINGTON, Stephen F.
Crewe, 5 February, 1956 (M)

League Club	Source	Date Signed	Seasons Played	Apps	Subs	Gls
Stoke C.	App	06.73	76-78	49	3	5
Walsall	Tr	09.78	78-81	122	8	12
Port Vale	Tr	08.82	82	0	1	0
Chesterfield	Tr	07.83	83	14	4	1

WADDLE, Alan R.
Wallsend, 9 June, 1954 (F)

League Club	Source	Date Signed	Seasons Played	Apps	Subs	Gls
Halifax T.	Jnrs	11.71	71-72	33	6	4
Liverpool	Tr	06.73	73-74	11	5	1
Leicester C.	Tr	09.77	77	11	0	1
Swansea C.	Tr	05.78	78-80	83	7	34
Newport Co.	Tr	12.80	80-81	19	8	8
Mansfield T.	Tr	08.82	82	14	0	4
Hartlepool U.	Hong Kong	08.83	83	12	0	2
Peterborough U.	Tr	10.83	83-84	35	1	12
Hartlepool U. (N/C)	Tr	01.85	84	4	0	0
Swansea C.	Tr	03.85	84-85	39	1	10

WADDLE, Christopher R.
Felling, 14 December, 1960 Eu21-1/E-62 (W)

League Club	Source	Date Signed	Seasons Played	Apps	Subs	Gls
Newcastle U.	Tow Law T.	07.80	80-84	169	1	46
Tottenham H.	Tr	06.85	85-88	137	1	33

WADDOCK, Gary P.
Kingsbury, 17 March, 1962 IRu21-1/IR'B'/IR-20 (M)

League Club	Source	Date Signed	Seasons Played	Apps	Subs	Gls
Queens Park R.	App	07.79	79-86	191	12	8
Millwall	Charleroi (Bel)	08.89	89-90	51	7	2
Queens Park R.	Tr	12.91				
Swindon T.	L	03.92	91	5	1	0

WADE, Allen
Manchester, 19 July, 1926 (WH)

League Club	Source	Date Signed	Seasons Played	Apps	Subs	Gls
Notts Co.		07.52	52-55	10	-	0

WADE, Bryan A.
Bath, 25 June, 1963 (F)

League Club	Source	Date Signed	Seasons Played	Apps	Subs	Gls
Swindon T.	Trowbridge T.	05.85	85-87	48	12	18
Swansea C.	Tr	08.88	88-89	19	17	5
Brighton & H.A.	Tr	09.90	90-91	12	6	9

WADE, Donald G.
Tottenham, 5 June, 1926 (IF)

League Club	Source	Date Signed	Seasons Played	Apps	Subs	Gls
West Ham U.	Edgware T.	12.47	47-49	36	-	5

WADE, S. Joseph
Shoreditch, 7 July, 1921 EF Lge (FB)

League Club	Source	Date Signed	Seasons Played	Apps	Subs	Gls
Arsenal	Hoxton B.C.	09.45	46-54	86	-	0

WADE, P. Meshach
Bermuda, 23 January, 1973 (M)

League Club	Source	Date Signed	Seasons Played	Apps	Subs	Gls
Hereford U.	Pembroke (Ber)	08.91	91	10	0	0

WADSWORTH, Albert W.
Heywood, 22 March, 1925 (IF)

League Club	Source	Date Signed	Seasons Played	Apps	Subs	Gls
Oldham Ath.	Stalybridge Celtic	08.49	49-51	33	-	8

WADSWORTH, Ian J.
Huddersfield, 24 September, 1966 (F)

League Club	Source	Date Signed	Seasons Played	Apps	Subs	Gls
Huddersfield T.	App	09.84	84	0	1	0
Doncaster Rov. (N/C)	Tr	02.86	85	1	1	0

WADSWORTH, Michael
Barnsley, 3 November, 1950 (W)

League Club	Source	Date Signed	Seasons Played	Apps	Subs	Gls
Scunthorpe U.	Gainsborough Trin.	08.76	76	19	9	3

WAGSTAFF, Anthony
Wombwell, 19 February, 1944 (M)

League Club	Source	Date Signed	Seasons Played	Apps	Subs	Gls
Sheffield U.	App	03.61	60-68	140	3	19
Reading	Tr	07.69	69-73	164	7	6

WAGSTAFF, Barry
Wombwell, 28 November, 1945 (M)

League Club	Source	Date Signed	Seasons Played	Apps	Subs	Gls
Sheffield U.	App	06.63	64-68	105	10	5
Reading	Tr	07.69	69-74	198	6	23
Rotherham U.	Tr	03.75	74-76	42	3	1

WAGSTAFF, Kenneth
Langwith, 24 November, 1942 (CF)

League Club	Source	Date Signed	Seasons Played	Apps	Subs	Gls
Mansfield T.	Woodland Imp.	05.60	60-64	181	-	93
Hull C.	Tr	11.64	64-75	374	4	173

WAGSTAFFE, David
Manchester, 5 April, 1943 E Yth/EF Lge (W)

League Club	Source	Date Signed	Seasons Played	Apps	Subs	Gls
Manchester C.	Jnrs	05.60	60-64	144	-	8
Wolverhampton W.	Tr	12.64	64-75	324	0	27
Blackburn Rov.	Tr	01.76	75-77	72	3	7
Blackpool	Tr	08.78	78	17	2	1
Blackburn Rov.	Tr	03.79	78	2	0	0

WAIN, Leslie J.
Crewe, 2 August, 1954 E Sch (M)

League Club	Source	Date Signed	Seasons Played	Apps	Subs	Gls
Crewe Alex.	App	08.72	70-74	48	6	1
Southport	Tr	07.75	75	3	2	0

WAINMAN, W. Harold
Hull, 22 March, 1947 E Yth (G)

League Club	Source	Date Signed	Seasons Played	Apps	Subs	Gls
Grimsby T.	Hull C. (Am)	07.64	64-77	420	0	0
Rochdale	L	10.72	72	9	0	0

Chris Waddle (Newcastle United, Tottenham Hotspur, Marseille & England)

WAINWRIGHT, Edward F.
Southport, 22 June, 1924 EF Lge (IF)

League Club	Source	Date Signed	Seasons Played	Apps	Subs	Gls
Everton	Jnrs	03.44	46-55	207	-	68
Rochdale	Tr	06.56	56-58	100	-	27

WAINWRIGHT, Lewis
Kirton-in-Lindsey, 15 December, 1930 (HB)

League Club	Source	Date Signed	Seasons Played	Apps	Subs	Gls
Scunthorpe U.	Brigg T.	05.51	51-55	3	-	0

WAINWRIGHT, Robin K.
Luton, 9 March, 1951 (M)

League Club	Source	Date Signed	Seasons Played	Apps	Subs	Gls
Luton T.	App	12.68	71	15	1	3
Cambridge U.	L	03.71	70	1	0	0
Millwall	Tr	11.72	73	2	2	0
Northampton T.	Tr	02.74	73-74	23	9	5

WAITE, T. J. Aldwyn
Pontllanfraith, 3 August, 1928 (WH)

League Club	Source	Date Signed	Seasons Played	Apps	Subs	Gls
Newport Co.		12.51	51-53	57	-	1

WAITE, John A.
Grimsby, 16 January, 1942 E Yth (OR)

League Club	Source	Date Signed	Seasons Played	Apps	Subs	Gls
Grimsby T.	Jnrs	11.60	61-62	8	-	1

WAITE, William J.
Newport, 29 November, 1917 Died 1980 (CF)

League Club	Source	Date Signed	Seasons Played	Apps	Subs	Gls
Oldham Ath.		11.42	46	4	-	4

WAITERS, Anthony K.
Southport, 1 February, 1937 E Amat/EF Lge/E-5 (G)

League Club	Source	Date Signed	Seasons Played	Apps	Subs	Gls
Blackpool	Macclesfield T.	10.59	59-66	257	0	0
Burnley	(Retired)	07.70	70-71	38	0	0

WAITES, George E.
Stepney, 12 March, 1938 (W)

League Club	Source	Date Signed	Seasons Played	Apps	Subs	Gls
Leyton Orient	Harwich & Parkeston	12.58	58-60	43	-	9
Norwich C.	Tr	01.61	60-61	36	-	11
Leyton Orient	Tr	07.62	62	2	-	0
Brighton & H.A.	Tr	12.62	62-63	22	-	1

WAITES, Paul
Hull, 24 January, 1971 (M)

League Club	Source	Date Signed	Seasons Played	Apps	Subs	Gls
Hull C.	YT	07.89	89-90	11	0	0

WAITT, Michael H.
Hexham, 25 June, 1960 (F)

League Club	Source	Date Signed	Seasons Played	Apps	Subs	Gls
Notts Co.	Arnold Kingswell	12.84	84-86	71	11	27
Lincoln C.	Tr	06.87	89	7	1	1

WAKE, Geoffrey
Bristol, 25 February, 1954 (G)

League Club	Source	Date Signed	Seasons Played	Apps	Subs	Gls
Torquay U.	Barnstaple	12.77	77	9	0	0

WAKEFIELD, Albert J.
Pudsey, 19 November, 1921 (CF)

League Club	Source	Date Signed	Seasons Played	Apps	Subs	Gls
Leeds U.	Stanningley Wks	10.42	47-48	49	-	23
Southend U.	Tr	08.49	49-52	109	-	57

WAKEFIELD, David
South Shields, 15 January, 1965 (M)

League Club	Source	Date Signed	Seasons Played	Apps	Subs	Gls
Darlington	App	01.83	82-83	7	15	0
Torquay U.	Tr	03.84	83	10	0	1

WAKEHAM, Peter F.
Kingsbridge, 14 March, 1936 (G)

League Club	Source	Date Signed	Seasons Played	Apps	Subs	Gls
Torquay U.	Jnrs	10.53	53-58	56	-	0
Sunderland	Tr	09.58	58-61	134	-	0
Charlton Ath.	Tr	07.62	62-64	55	-	0
Lincoln C.	Tr	05.65	65	44	0	0

WAKEMAN, Alan D.
Walsall, 20 November, 1920 E Sch (G)

League Club	Source	Date Signed	Seasons Played	Apps	Subs	Gls
Aston Villa	Jnrs	12.38	38-49	12	-	0
Doncaster Rov.	Tr	07.50	50-51	5	-	0
Shrewsbury T.	Bloxwich Strollers	02.53	52-53	6	-	0

WAKENSHAW, Robert A.
Ponteland, 22 December, 1965 E Yth (W)

League Club	Source	Date Signed	Seasons Played	Apps	Subs	Gls
Everton	App	12.83	83-84	2	1	1
Carlisle U.	Tr	09.85	85	6	2	2
Doncaster Rov.	L	03.86	85	8	0	3
Rochdale	Tr	09.86	86	28	1	5
Crewe Alex.	Tr	06.87	87-88	18	4	1

WALDEN, Harold B.
Walgrave, 22 December, 1940 (W)

League Club	Source	Date Signed	Seasons Played	Apps	Subs	Gls
Luton T.	Kettering T.	01.61	60-63	96	-	11
Northampton T.	Tr	06.64	64-66	76	1	3

WALDEN, Richard F.
Hereford, 4 May, 1948 (FB)

League Club	Source	Date Signed	Seasons Played	Apps	Subs	Gls
Aldershot	App	05.65	64-75	401	4	16
Sheffield Wed.	Tr	01.76	75-77	100	0	1
Newport Co.	Tr	08.78	78-81	151	0	2

WALDOCK, Desmond H.
Northampton, 4 December, 1961 (CD)

League Club	Source	Date Signed	Seasons Played	Apps	Subs	Gls
Northampton T.	App	11.79	78-80	52	2	4

WALDOCK, Ronald
Heanor, 6 December, 1932 (IF)

League Club	Source	Date Signed	Seasons Played	Apps	Subs	Gls
Coventry C.	Loscoe Y.C.	02.50	52-53	27	-	8
Sheffield U.	Tr	05.54	54-56	52	-	10
Scunthorpe U.	Tr	02.57	56-59	97	-	45
Plymouth Arg.	Tr	09.59	59	18	-	6
Middlesbrough	Tr	01.60	59-61	34	-	7
Gillingham	Tr	10.61	61-63	66	-	14

WALDRON, Alan
Royton, 6 September, 1951 (M)

League Club	Source	Date Signed	Seasons Played	Apps	Subs	Gls
Bolton W.	App	09.69	70-77	127	14	6
Blackpool	Tr	12.77	77-78	22	1	1
Bury	Tr	06.79	79-80	34	0	0
York C.	Tr	09.81	81	3	0	1

WALDRON, Colin
Bristol, 22 June, 1948 (CD)

League Club	Source	Date Signed	Seasons Played	Apps	Subs	Gls
Bury	App	05.66	66	20	0	1
Chelsea	Tr	07.67	67	9	0	0
Burnley	Tr	10.67	67-75	308	0	16
Manchester U.	Tr	05.76	76	3	0	0
Sunderland	Tr	02.77	76-77	20	0	1
Rochdale	Atlanta (USA)	10.79	79	19	0	1

WALDRON, Ernest
Birmingham, 3 June, 1913 (F)

League Club	Source	Date Signed	Seasons Played	Apps	Subs	Gls
Crystal Palace	Bromsgrove Rov.	11.34	34-46	80	-	30

WALDRON, Malcolm
Emsworth, 6 September, 1956 E'B' (D)

League Club	Source	Date Signed	Seasons Played	Apps	Subs	Gls
Southampton	App	09.74	74-82	177	1	10
Burnley	Tr	09.83	83	16	0	0
Portsmouth	Tr	03.84	83-84	23	0	1

WALES, Anthony
Doncaster, 12 May, 1943 E Yth (FB)

League Club	Source	Date Signed	Seasons Played	Apps	Subs	Gls
Doncaster Rov.	Jnrs	05.60	60-62	25	-	0

WALFORD, Stephen J.
Highgate, 5 January, 1958 E Yth (D)

League Club	Source	Date Signed	Seasons Played	Apps	Subs	Gls
Tottenham H.	App	04.75	75	1	1	0
Arsenal	Tr	08.77	77-80	64	13	3
Norwich C.	Tr	03.81	80-82	93	0	2
West Ham U.	Tr	08.83	83-86	114	1	2
Huddersfield T.	L	10.87	87	12	0	0
Gillingham	L	12.88	88	4	0	0
West Bromwich A.	L	03.89	88	3	1	0

WALKDEN, Francis
Aberdeen, 21 June, 1921 (IF)

League Club	Source	Date Signed	Seasons Played	Apps	Subs	Gls
Rochdale (Am)	Bolton W. (Am)	11.46	46	1	-	0

WALKER, Alan
Mossley, 17 December, 1959 (CD)

League Club	Source	Date Signed	Seasons Played	Apps	Subs	Gls
Stockport Co.		08.78				
Lincoln C.	Telford U.	10.83	83-84	74	1	4
Millwall	Tr	07.85	85-87	92	0	8
Gillingham	Tr	03.88	87-91	150	1	7

WALKER, Andrew F.
Glasgow, 6 April, 1965 Su21-1/S-1 (F)

League Club	Source	Date Signed	Seasons Played	Apps	Subs	Gls
Newcastle U. (L)	Glasgow Celtic	09.91	91	2	0	0
Bolton W.	Glasgow Celtic	01.92	91	23	1	15

WALKER, Arnold
Haltwhistle, 23 December, 1932 (WH)

League Club	Source	Date Signed	Seasons Played	Apps	Subs	Gls
Grimsby T.	Jnrs	05.50	50-57	65	-	0
Walsall	Tr	05.58	58-59	7	-	0

WALKER, Bruce A.
Newbury, 27 August, 1946 (OL)

League Club	Source	Date Signed	Seasons Played	Apps	Subs	Gls
Swindon T.	Jnrs	12.63	65-67	26	3	5
Bradford C.	Tr	03.68	67-68	27	1	1
Exeter C.	Tr	06.69	69	21	3	2

WALKER, Clive
Oxford, 26 May, 1957 E Sch (LW)

League Club	Source	Date Signed	Seasons Played	Apps	Subs	Gls
Chelsea	App	04.75	76-83	168	30	60
Sunderland	Tr	07.84	84-85	48	2	10
Queens Park R.	Tr	12.85	85-86	16	5	1
Fulham	Tr	10.87	87-89	102	7	29
Brighton & H.A.	Tr	08.90	90-91	68	0	5

Clive Walker (Chelsea, Sunderland, Queens Park Rangers, Fulham & Brighton & Hove Albion)

WALKER, D. Clive A.
Watford, 24 October, 1945 E Sch (LB)

League Club	Source	Date Signed	Seasons Played	Apps	Subs	Gls
Leicester C.	App	10.62	63-65	17	0	0
Northampton T.	Tr	10.66	66-68	72	0	1
Mansfield T.	Tr	07.69	69-74	223	6	8

WALKER, Colin
Rotherham, 1 May, 1958 (F)

League Club	Source	Date Signed	Seasons Played	Apps	Subs	Gls
Barnsley	Gisborne C. (NZ)	11.80	80-82	21	3	11
Doncaster Rov.	L	02.83	82	12	0	5
Doncaster Rov. (N/C)	Gisborne C. (NZ)	11.85	85	3	2	0
Cambridge U. (N/C)	Tr	01.86	85	3	0	1
Sheffield Wed.	Harworth Colly	08.86	86	2	0	0
Darlington	L	12.86	86	6	1	0
Torquay U.	L	10.87	87	3	0	0

WALKER, Colin
Long Eaton, 7 July, 1929 (WH)

League Club	Source	Date Signed	Seasons Played	Apps	Subs	Gls
Derby Co.	Jnrs	10.46	48-54	25	-	0

WALKER, Cyril J.
Newport Pagnell, 24 February, 1914 (IF)

League Club	Source	Date Signed	Seasons Played	Apps	Subs	Gls
Watford		11.35				
Gillingham		06.37	37	10	-	0
Sheffield Wed.	Tr	10.37	37	4	-	0
Norwich C.	Shorts Sports	08.46	46	3	-	2

WALKER, David
Colne, 15 October, 1941 (CD)

League Club	Source	Date Signed	Seasons Played	Apps	Subs	Gls
Burnley	Jnrs	05.59	60-64	38	-	1
Southampton	Tr	05.65	65-73	189	8	1

WALKER, Dean
Newcastle, 18 May, 1962 (D)

League Club	Source	Date Signed	Seasons Played	Apps	Subs	Gls
Burnley	App	05.80				
Scunthorpe U. (N/C)	Tr	03.82	81	1	0	0

WALKER, Dennis A.
Northwich, 26 October, 1944 (M)

League Club	Source	Date Signed	Seasons Played	Apps	Subs	Gls
Manchester U.	App	11.61	62	1	-	0
York C.	Tr	04.64	64-67	149	5	19
Cambridge U.	Tr	07.68	70-72	48	8	4

WALKER, Dennis G.
Spennymoor, 5 July, 1948 (F)

League Club	Source	Date Signed	Seasons Played	Apps	Subs	Gls
West Ham U.	App	05.66				
Luton T.	Tr	08.67	67	0	1	0

WALKER, Derek W.
Perth, 24 November, 1964 (F)

League Club	Source	Date Signed	Seasons Played	Apps	Subs	Gls
Chesterfield	Kinnoull Jnrs	08.86	86-87	19	4	3

WALKER, Desmond S.
Enfield, 26 November, 1965 Eu21-7/E-47 (CD)

League Club	Source	Date Signed	Seasons Played	Apps	Subs	Gls
Nottingham F.	App	11.83	83-91	259	5	1

WALKER, Donald H.
Edinburgh, 10 September, 1935 (WH)

League Club	Source	Date Signed	Seasons Played	Apps	Subs	Gls
Leicester C.	Tranent Jnrs	11.55	57-58	32	-	1
Middlesbrough	Tr	10.59	59-61	23	-	1
Grimsby T.	Tr	09.63	63	15	-	1

WALKER, Frederick
Stirling, 7 April, 1929 (FB)

League Club	Source	Date Signed	Seasons Played	Apps	Subs	Gls
Southport		10.51	51-52	5	-	0

WALKER, Gary
Manchester, 11 October, 1963 (G)

League Club	Source	Date Signed	Seasons Played	Apps	Subs	Gls
Stockport Co.	Oldham T.	09.85	85-86	29	0	0

WALKER, R. Geoffrey
Bradford, 29 September, 1926 (OL)

League Club	Source	Date Signed	Seasons Played	Apps	Subs	Gls
Bradford P.A.	Jnrs	12.43				
Middlesbrough	Tr	06.46	46-54	240	-	50
Doncaster Rov.	Tr	12.54	54-56	84	-	15
Bradford C.	Tr	06.57	57	2	-	0

WALKER, George W.
Sunderland, 30 May, 1934 (IF)

League Club	Source	Date Signed	Seasons Played	Apps	Subs	Gls
Bristol C.	Chippenham T.	05.56	56-58	15	-	5
Carlisle U.	Tr	03.59	58-62	164	-	51

WALKER, Glenn P.
Warrington, 15 March, 1967 (M)

League Club	Source	Date Signed	Seasons Played	Apps	Subs	Gls
Crewe Alex.	Burnley (App)	03.85	84	1	1	0

WALKER, J. Gordon
Sheffield, 26 November, 1949 (F)

League Club	Source	Date Signed	Seasons Played	Apps	Subs	Gls
Grimsby T.	Stocksbridge Wks	11.68	68-69	25	2	5

WALKER, Greig G.
Dundee, 11 October, 1963 (F)

League Club	Source	Date Signed	Seasons Played	Apps	Subs	Gls
Chesterfield	Broughty Ath.	10.83	83	6	0	0

WALKER, G. Harold
Aysgarth, 20 May, 1916 Died 1976 (G)

League Club	Source	Date Signed	Seasons Played	Apps	Subs	Gls
Darlington		12.34	35-37	49	-	0
Portsmouth	Tr	03.38	37-46	49	-	0
Nottingham F.	Tr	04.47	46-54	293	-	0

WALKER, Ian M.
Watford, 31 October, 1971 E Yth/Eu21-4 (G)

League Club	Source	Date Signed	Seasons Played	Apps	Subs	Gls
Tottenham H.	YT	12.89	90-91	19	0	0
Oxford U.	L	09.90	90	2	0	0

WALKER, James
Aberdeen, 25 August, 1933 (FB)

League Club	Source	Date Signed	Seasons Played	Apps	Subs	Gls
Bradford P.A.	Aberdeen	05.59	59-63	144	-	2

WALKER, James
Belfast, 29 March, 1932 NI-1 (CF)

League Club	Source	Date Signed	Seasons Played	Apps	Subs	Gls
Doncaster Rov.	Linfield	05.54	54-56	46	-	14

WALKER, James F.
Sheffield, 1 July, 1931 (LB)

League Club	Source	Date Signed	Seasons Played	Apps	Subs	Gls
Sheffield U.	Jnrs	11.48	49-53	4	-	0
Huddersfield T.	Tr	08.55				
Peterborough U.	Tr	(N/L)	60-64	125	-	0

WALKER, James M.
Northwich, 10 June, 1947 (LB)

League Club	Source	Date Signed	Seasons Played	Apps	Subs	Gls
Derby Co.	Northwich Vic.	02.68	67-73	35	7	3
Hartlepool U.	L	03.70	69	10	0	0
Brighton & H.A.	Tr	09.74	74-75	24	4	4
Peterborough U.	Tr	10.75	75-76	20	11	1
Chester C.	Tr	11.76	76-80	171	1	4

WALKER, John
Southend, 10 December, 1958 (D)

League Club	Source	Date Signed	Seasons Played	Apps	Subs	Gls
Southend U.	App	12.76	77-82	38	13	0

WALKER, John H.
Glasgow, 17 December, 1928 (IF/WH)

League Club	Source	Date Signed	Seasons Played	Apps	Subs	Gls
Wolverhampton W.	Campsie B.W.	07.47	49-51	37	-	21
Southampton	Tr	10.52	52-57	172	-	48
Reading	Tr	12.57	57-64	287	-	24

WALKER, Keith C.
Edinburgh, 17 April, 1966 (M/CD)

League Club	Source	Date Signed	Seasons Played	Apps	Subs	Gls
Swansea C.	St Mirren	11.89	89-91	62	7	1

WALKER, Leonard
Darlington, 4 March, 1944 (D)

League Club	Source	Date Signed	Seasons Played	Apps	Subs	Gls
Newcastle U.	Spennymoor U.	05.63	63	1	-	0
Aldershot	Tr	07.64	64-75	440	10	23
Darlington (N/C)	Tr	08.76	76-77	10	0	0

WALKER, Michael
Mexborough, 8 March, 1952 (FB)

League Club	Source	Date Signed	Seasons Played	Apps	Subs	Gls
Bradford P.A.	App	03.70	68-69	2	2	0

WALKER, Michael J.
Harrogate, 10 April, 1945 (F)

League Club	Source	Date Signed	Seasons Played	Apps	Subs	Gls
Bradford C.	Bourne T.	10.64	64-65	19	1	1
Mansfield T.	Los Angeles (USA)	03.69	68	2	0	0
Stockport Co.	Altrincham	08.70	70	1	1	0
Chesterfield	Tr	09.70	70	1	0	0

WALKER, Michael S. G.
Colwyn Bay, 28 November, 1945 Wu23-4 (G)

League Club	Source	Date Signed	Seasons Played	Apps	Subs	Gls
Reading	Jnrs	01.63				
Shrewsbury T.	Tr	06.64	64-65	7	0	0
York C.	Tr	06.66	66-68	60	0	0
Watford	Tr	09.68	68-72	137	0	0
Charlton Ath.	L	03.73	72	1	0	0
Colchester U.	Tr	06.73	73-82	451	0	0

WALKER, J. Nicholas
Aberdeen, 29 September, 1962 (G)

League Club	Source	Date Signed	Seasons Played	Apps	Subs	Gls
Leicester C.	Elgin C.	08.80	81	6	0	0
Burnley (L)	Hearts	02.92	91	6	0	0

WALKER, Nigel S.
Gateshead, 7 April, 1959 (M)

League Club	Source	Date Signed	Seasons Played	Apps	Subs	Gls
Newcastle U.	Whickham	07.77	77-81	65	5	3
Crewe Alex. (N/C)	San Diego (USA)	01.83	82	20	0	5
Sunderland	Tr	07.83	83	0	1	0
Blackpool	L	03.84	83	8	2	3
Chester C.	Tr	07.84	84	41	0	9
Hartlepool U.	Tr	07.85	85-86	77	5	8

WALKER, Patrick J. A.
Carlow (Ire), 20 December, 1959 (W)

League Club	Source	Date Signed	Seasons Played	Apps	Subs	Gls
Gillingham	App	10.77	77-80	34	17	3

WALKER, Paul E.
Hetton-le-Hole, 26 February, 1958 E Semi-Pro (M)

League Club	Source	Date Signed	Seasons Played	Apps	Subs	Gls
Hull C.	Sunderland (App)	05.76				
Doncaster Rov.	L	12.76	76	4	0	0

WALKER, Paul G.
Bradford, 3 April, 1949 (M)

League Club	Source	Date Signed	Seasons Played	Apps	Subs	Gls
Wolverhampton W.	Bradford P.A. (Am)	10.66	68-71	17	9	0
Watford	L	12.71	71	2	1	0
Swindon T.	L	03.73	72	2	3	0
Peterborough U.	Tr	07.73	73-74	75	3	3
Barnsley	Tr	07.75	75	11	2	0
Huddersfield T.	Ottawa (Can)	11.76	76	1	0	0

WALKER, Paul J.
Wood Green, 17 December, 1960 E Sch (M)

League Club	Source	Date Signed	Seasons Played	Apps	Subs	Gls
Brentford	App	01.78	76-82	53	18	5

WALKER, Peter M.
Watford, 31 March, 1933 (IF)

League Club	Source	Date Signed	Seasons Played	Apps	Subs	Gls
Watford	Bushey U.	07.54	54-61	172	-	37

WALKER, Philip
Sheffield, 27 November, 1956 (IF)

League Club	Source	Date Signed	Seasons Played	Apps	Subs	Gls
Cambridge U.	Sheffield U. (App)	02.75	74-75	19	0	0
Rotherham U.	Tr	09.77				

WALKER, Philip A.
Kirkby-in-Ashfield, 27 January, 1957 (F)

League Club	Source	Date Signed	Seasons Played	Apps	Subs	Gls
Chesterfield	Mansfield Y.C.	12.77	77-82	151	15	38
Rotherham U.	Tr	12.82	82-83	20	5	3
Cardiff C.	L	09.83	83	2	0	0
Chesterfield	Tr	10.84	84-85	30	8	9
Scarborough	Tr	08.86	87	0	1	0

WALKER, Philip L.
Fulham, 29 August, 1954 (M)

League Club	Source	Date Signed	Seasons Played	Apps	Subs	Gls
Millwall	Epsom & Ewell	10.75	75-78	143	3	17
Charlton Ath.	Tr	07.79	79-82	80	9	15
Gillingham	L	11.82	82	1	1	0

WALKER, Raymond
North Shields, 28 September, 1963 E Yth (M)

League Club	Source	Date Signed	Seasons Played	Apps	Subs	Gls
Aston Villa	App	09.81	82-85	15	8	0
Port Vale	L	09.84	84	15	0	1
Port Vale	Tr	07.86	86-91	238	3	23

WALKER, Richard E. W.
Hackney, 22 July, 1913 Died 1988 (CH)

League Club	Source	Date Signed	Seasons Played	Apps	Subs	Gls
West Ham U.	Park Royal	05.34	34-52	292	-	2

WALKER, Richard P.
Northampton, 4 April, 1959 (FB)

League Club	Source	Date Signed	Seasons Played	Apps	Subs	Gls
Coventry C.	App	03.77				
Northampton T.	Tr	08.78	78-80	50	3	0

WALKER, Robert
Wallsend, 23 July, 1942 (FB)

League Club	Source	Date Signed	Seasons Played	Apps	Subs	Gls
Brighton & H.A.	Gateshead	05.62	62	12	-	1
Bournemouth	Margate	08.65	65-66	10	0	0
Colchester U.	Tr	07.67	67	13	4	0

WALKER, Robert M.
Glasgow, 15 January, 1935 (F)

League Club	Source	Date Signed	Seasons Played	Apps	Subs	Gls
Middlesbrough	Redcar	08.52				
Barrow	Tr	08.55	55	11	-	1

WALKER, Robert W.
Aberdeen, 21 May, 1922 (CF)

League Club	Source	Date Signed	Seasons Played	Apps	Subs	Gls
Bournemouth	Aberdeen	11.46	46	2	-	2
Wrexham	Tr	06.47	47	2	-	0

WALKER, Roger A.
Bolton, 15 November, 1966 (W)

League Club	Source	Date Signed	Seasons Played	Apps	Subs	Gls
Bolton W.	YT	07.85	84-85	7	5	1

WALKER Roger W.
Shrewsbury, 17 February, 1944 (W)

League Club	Source	Date Signed	Seasons Played	Apps	Subs	Gls
Shrewsbury T. (Am)	Jnrs	05.60	60	1	-	0

WALKER, Ronald
Swansea, 24 February, 1933

League Club	Source	Date Signed	Seasons Played	Apps	Subs	Gls
Shrewsbury T.		11.55	55	1	-	0

WALKER, Ronald
Sheffield, 4 February, 1932 (OL)

League Club	Source	Date Signed	Seasons Played	Apps	Subs	Gls
Doncaster Rov.	Sunderland (Am)	05.50	52-60	234	-	46

WALKER, Ronald L.
Wembley, 2 September, 1952 (CD)

League Club	Source	Date Signed	Seasons Played	Apps	Subs	Gls
Watford	App	08.70				
Workington	Tr	08.71	71-75	143	10	3
Newport Co.	Tr	08.76	76-78	88	1	5

WALKER, Ronald W.
Westminster, 10 April, 1930 (OL)

League Club	Source	Date Signed	Seasons Played	Apps	Subs	Gls
Watford	Walthamstow Ave.	04.54	54	3	-	0

WALKER, Samuel
Eccles, 22 April, 1922 (CH)

League Club	Source	Date Signed	Seasons Played	Apps	Subs	Gls
Oldham Ath.	Darwen	08.47	47	1	-	0

WALKER, Shane
Pontypool, 25 November, 1957 (M)

League Club	Source	Date Signed	Seasons Played	Apps	Subs	Gls
Hereford U.	Arsenal (App)	03.75	74-76	15	2	2
Newport Co.	Sligo Rov.	08.77	77	27	1	2

League Club	Source	Date Signed	Seasons Played	Apps	Subs	Gls
WALKER, Stephen						
Sheffield, 16 October, 1914						(HB)
Sheffield U.	Gainsborough Trin.	05.37				
Exeter C.	Tr	05.38	38-49	141	-	3
WALKER, Steven						
Ilkeston, 25 December, 1963						(M)
Halifax T.		01.82	81	0	1	0
WALKER, Stuart						
Tadcaster, 9 January, 1951						(G)
York C.	Tadcaster A.	08.75	76	2	0	0
WALKER, Terence						
Poppleton, 29 November, 1921						(F)
York C.		05.49	49	16	-	9
WALKER, Thomas						
Livingston, 26 May, 1915 S Sch/SF Lge/S-20						(IF)
Chelsea	Hearts	09.46	46-48	97	-	23
WALKER, Thomas J.						
Newcastle, 20 February, 1952						(M)
Stoke C.	App	07.69	71	2	0	0
WALKER, Thomas J.						
Cramlington, 14 November, 1923						(OR)
Newcastle U.	Netherton	10.41	46-53	184	-	35
Oldham Ath.	Tr	02.54	53-56	120	-	21
Chesterfield	Tr	02.57	56	14	-	1
Oldham Ath.	Tr	07.57	57-58	38	-	4
WALKER, Victor						
Kirkby-in-Ashfield, 14 April, 1922						(WH)
Nottingham F.		08.43				
Stockport Co.	Tr	06.46	46-49	94	-	10
WALL, Adrian A.						
Clowne, 25 November, 1949						(W)
Sheffield Wed.	App	05.67	67	3	0	0
Workington	Tr	08.69	69	21	3	2
WALL, T. Peter						
Westbury (Salop), 13 September, 1944						(FB)
Shrewsbury T.	App	09.62	63-64	18	-	0
Wrexham	Tr	11.65	65-66	15	7	1
Liverpool	Tr	10.66	67-69	31	0	0
Crystal Palace	Tr	06.70	70-77	167	10	4
Leyton Orient	L	12.72	72	10	0	0
WALL, William J.						
Taunton, 28 October, 1939						(W)
Chelsea	Jnrs	01.57				
Southend U.	Tr	03.60	59-62	57	-	5
WALLACE, Barry D.						
Plaistow, 17 April, 1959						(M)
Queens Park R.	Jnrs	08.76	77-79	17	8	0
WALLACE, Clive L.						
Kirriemuir, 6 January, 1932						(F)
Bury		03.59				
Stockport Co.	Tr	08.59	59	13	-	4
WALLACE, David L. (Danny)						
Greenwich, 21 January, 1964 E Yth/Eu21-14/E-1						(F)
Southampton	App	01.82	80-89	238	15	64
Manchester U.	Tr	09.89	89-90	36	9	6
WALLACE, George						
Aberdeen, 18 April, 1920						(F)
Scunthorpe U.		06.50	51-52	33	-	9
WALLACE, Gordon H.						
Lanark, 13 June, 1944						(M)
Liverpool	App	07.61	62-64	19	-	3
Crewe Alex.	Tr	10.67	67-71	91	3	20
WALLACE, Ian A.						
Glasgow, 23 May, 1956 Su21-1/S-3						(F)
Coventry C.	Dumbarton	08.76	76-79	128	2	58
Nottingham F.	Tr	07.80	80-83	128	6	36
Sunderland	Brest (Fr)	01.85	84-85	28	6	6

League Club	Source	Date Signed	Seasons Played	Apps	Subs	Gls
WALLACE, Ian R.						
Hedley, 12 September, 1948						(WH)
Wolverhampton W.	App	09.66	66	0	1	0
WALLACE, James						
Bebington, 13 December, 1937						(OL)
Stoke C.		10.55	58-59	8	-	1
Doncaster Rov.	Northwich Vic.	03.63	62	14	-	1
WALLACE, James						
Bridge of Allan, 9 June, 1954 Su23-1						(LB)
Aldershot	Dunfermline Ath.	07.75	75-76	53	3	0
WALLACE, James						
Kirkintilloch, 17 February, 1933						(CH)
Northampton T.	Aberdeen	05.55	55	1	-	0
WALLACE, John C.						
Glasgow, 11 January, 1936						(HB)
Rochdale	St Rochs	03.58	57-58	7	-	0
WALLACE, John M. (Jock)						
Deantown, 13 April, 1911 Died 1978						(G)
Blackpool	Raith Rov.	02.34	33-47	235	-	0
Derby Co.	Tr	02.48	47	16	-	0
WALLACE, John M.B. (Jock)						
Musselburgh, 6 September, 1935						(G)
Workington	Blackpool (Am)	09.52	52	5	-	0
West Bromwich A.	Airdrieonians	10.59	59-61	69	-	0
WALLACE, Joseph B.						
Glasgow, 28 December, 1933						(WH)
Shrewsbury T.	R.A.O.C. Donnington	03.54	54-62	337	-	3
Southport	Tr	10.62	62-64	78	-	0
WALLACE, Kenneth						
Frizington, 14 January, 1932						(FB)
Workington		07.51	51-52	48	-	1
WALLACE, Kenneth						
Workington, 5 January, 1953						(FB)
Workington (N/C)	Jnrs	02.74	73-76	6	1	0

Danny Wallace (Southampton, Manchester United & England)

League Club	Source	Date Signed	Seasons Played	Career Record Apps	Subs	Gls
WALLACE, Kenneth R.						
Islington, 8 June, 1952						(W)
West Ham U.	Jnrs	07.69				
Brentford	L	02.72	71	3	0	0
Hereford U.	Tr	07.72	72	26	6	4
Exeter C.	Tr	09.73	73	8	2	1
WALLACE, Raymond G.						
Greenwich, 2 October, 1969 Eu21-4						(RB)
Southampton	YT	04.88	88-89	33	2	0
Leeds U.	Tr	05.91				
Swansea C.	L	03.92	91	2	0	0
WALLACE, Robert A.						
Huddersfield, 14 February, 1948						(M)
Huddersfield T.	App	05.65	66	4	0	0
Halifax T.	Tr	03.67	66-71	190	11	16
Chester C.	Tr	06.72	72	41	0	9
Aldershot	Tr	07.73	73-76	70	6	1
WALLACE, Rodney S.						
Greenwich, 2 October, 1969 Eu21-11						(W)
Southampton	YT	04.88	87-90	111	17	44
Leeds U.	Tr	05.91	91	34	0	11

Rod Wallace (Southampton & Leeds United)

League Club	Source	Date Signed	Seasons Played	Career Record Apps	Subs	Gls
WALLACE, William B. S.						
Kirkintilloch, 23 June, 1941 SF Lge/S-7						(F)
Crystal Palace	Glasgow Celtic	10.71	71-72	36	3	4
WALLBANK, Bernard						
Preston, 11 November, 1943						(CF)
Southport		08.61	61	1	-	0
WALLBANKS, Harold						
Chopwell, 27 July, 1921						(RH)
Fulham		10.38	46-47	33	-	1
Southend U.	Tr	10.49	49-50	39	-	2
Workington	Tr	08.52	52	26	-	9
WALLBANKS W. Horace						
Chopwell, 4 September, 1918						(OR)
Grimsby T.	Aberdeen	11.46	46	9	-	1
Luton T.	Tr	05.47	46-47	4	-	1

League Club	Source	Date Signed	Seasons Played	Career Record Apps	Subs	Gls
WALLBANKS, James						
Wigan, 12 September, 1909 Died 1979						(CH)
Barnsley	Annfield Plain	03.29	29-30	11	-	0
Norwich C.	Tr	05.31	31	3	-	0
Northampton T.	Tr	08.32	32	2	-	0
Millwall	Wigan Ath.	06.34	34-38	88	-	0
Reading	Tr	10.38	38-46	47	-	1
WALLBRIDGE, Trevor						
Southampton, 8 February, 1959						(F)
Bournemouth (N/C)	Totton	01.78	77	0	1	0
WALLER, David H.						
Urmston, 20 December, 1963						(F)
Crewe Alex.		01.82	81-85	165	3	55
Shrewsbury T.	Tr	07.86	86	11	0	3
Chesterfield	Tr	03.87	87-89	117	2	53
WALLER, Henry						
Ashington, 20 August, 1917						(WH)
Arsenal	Ashington	10.37	46	8	-	0
Leyton Orient	Tr	07.47	47	17	-	0
WALLER, Philip						
Leeds, 12 April, 1943						(WH)
Derby Co.	Jnrs	05.61	61-67	102	2	5
Mansfield T.	Tr	03.68	67-71	153	6	1
WALLEY, Ernest						
Caernarfon, 19 April, 1933						(WH)
Tottenham H.	Jnrs	05.51	55-57	5	-	0
Middlesbrough	Tr	05.58	58	8	-	0
WALLEY, Keith J.						
Weymouth, 19 October, 1954						(M)
Crystal Palace	App	10.72	73	6	1	1
WALLEY, J. Thomas						
Caernarfon, 27 February, 1945 Wu23-4/W-1						(M)
Arsenal	Caernarfon	12.64	65-66	10	4	1
Watford	Tr	03.67	66-71	202	1	17
Leyton Orient	Tr	12.71	71-75	155	2	6
Watford	Tr	06.76	76	12	1	0
WALLING, Dean A.						
Leeds, 17 April, 1969						(F)
Rochdale	Leeds U. (App)	07.87	87-89	43	22	8
Carlisle U.	Guiseley	06.91	91	33	4	5
WALLINGTON, F. Mark						
Sleaford, 17 September, 1952 E Yth/Eu23-2						(G)
Walsall	Jnrs	10.71	71	11	0	0
Leicester C.	Tr	03.72	71-84	412	0	0
Derby Co.	Tr	07.85	85-86	67	0	0
Lincoln C.	Tr	08.88	88-90	87	0	0
WALLIS, Derek R.						
Hartlepool, 6 October, 1937						(CF)
Hartlepool U. (Am)		05.63	63	2	-	0
WALLS, Arthur J.						
Glasgow, 15 January, 1931						(F)
Tranmere Rov.	Airdrieonians	06.54	54-55	23	-	6
WALLS, David						
Leeds, 16 June, 1953						(W)
Lincoln C.	Leeds U. (App)	07.71	71-72	9	0	0
WALLS, James P.						
Dunfermline, 11 March, 1928						(CH)
Charlton Ath.	Crossgates	09.45	49-52	10	-	0
Ipswich T.	Tr	05.54	54	1	-	0
WALLS, John						
Seaham, 8 May, 1932						(G)
Barnsley	Jnrs	05.49	52	7	-	0
Peterborough U.	Tr	05.56	60-61	78	-	0
WALMSLEY, David G.						
Hull, 23 November, 1972						(F)
Hull C.	YT	07.91	90-91	5	5	4
WALMSLEY, Dennis						
Southport, 1 May, 1935						(W)
Southport (Am)	Crossens	05.54	54	4	-	1

League Club	Source	Date Signed	Seasons Played	Apps	Subs	Gls

WALSH, Alan
Hartlepool, 9 December, 1956 (F)

Middlesbrough	Horden Colly	12.76	77	0	3	0
Darlington	Tr	10.78	78-83	245	6	87
Bristol C.	Tr	08.84	84-88	215	3	77
Walsall (N/C)	Besiktas (Turkey)	10.91	91	4	0	0
Huddersfield T. (N/C)	Tr	12.91	91	0	4	0
Shrewsbury T. (N/C)	Tr	01.92	91	2	0	0
Cardiff C. (N/C)	Tr	03.92	91	1	0	0

WALSH, Andrew
Blackburn, 15 February, 1970 (CD)

Bury	Preston N.E. (N/C)	11.87	87	0	1	0

WALSH, J. Brian
Aldershot, 26 March, 1932 (W)

Arsenal	Jnrs	08.49	53-55	17	-	0
Cardiff C.	Tr	09.55	55-61	206	-	32
Newport Co.	Tr	11.61	61-62	27	-	3

Brian Walsh (Arsenal, Cardiff City & Newport County)

WALSH, Colin D.
Hamilton, 22 July, 1962 Su21-5 (LW)

Nottingham F.	App	08.79	80-85	115	24	32
Charlton Ath.	Tr	09.86	86-91	121	10	15
Peterborough U.	L	02.89	88	5	0	1
Middlesbrough	L	01.91	90	10	3	1

WALSH, David J.
Waterford (Ire), 28 April, 1923 IR-20/NI-9 (CF)

West Bromwich A.	Linfield	07.46	46-50	165	-	94
Aston Villa	Tr	12.50	50-54	108	-	37
Walsall	Tr	07.55	55	20	-	6

WALSH, Derek
Hamilton, 24 October, 1967 (M/RB)

Everton	App	10.84	84	1	0	0
Carlisle U.	Hamilton Acad.	08.88	88-91	88	9	6

WALSH, Francis
Wishaw, 15 September, 1923 (CF)

Southport	Glasgow Celtic	10.49	49	5	-	3

WALSH, Gary
Wigan, 21 March, 1968 Eu21-2 (G)

Manchester U.	App	04.85	86-91	37	0	0

League Club	Source	Date Signed	Seasons Played	Apps	Subs	Gls

WALSH, Ian P.
St Davids, 4 September, 1958 W Sch/Wu21-2/W-18 (F)

Crystal Palace	App	10.75	76-81	101	16	23
Swansea C.	Tr	02.82	81-83	32	5	11
Barnsley	Tr	07.84	84-85	45	4	15
Grimsby T.	Tr	08.86	86-87	36	5	13
Cardiff C.	Tr	01.88	87-88	5	12	4

WALSH, James
Glasgow, 3 December, 1930 Su23-1 (CF)

Leicester C.	Glasgow Celtic	11.56	56-62	176	-	79

WALSH, James T.P.
Paddington, 20 November, 1954 (FB)

Watford	App	11.72	73-77	60	5	0
York C.	Tr	06.78	78-80	91	8	2

WALSH, Kevin W.
Rochdale, 11 February, 1928 (WH)

Oldham Ath.	St Patricks O.B.	10.49	49-50	3	-	0
Southport	Tr	07.52	52-53	67	-	1
Bradford C.	Tr	07.54	54-55	25	-	3
Southport	Tr	08.56	56	3	-	0

WALSH, Mario M.
Paddington, 19 January, 1966 (F)

Portsmouth	App	01.84				
Torquay U.	Tr	01.85	84-86	89	11	18
Colchester U.	Tr	08.87	87-88	29	9	11
Southend U.	Tr	07.89	89	10	1	2

WALSH, Mark
Preston, 7 October, 1962 (M)

Preston N.E.	App	10.80	81-83	56	6	2
Exeter C. (N/C)	New Zealand	08.85	85	0	1	0

WALSH, Michael A.
Chorley, 13 August, 1954 IR-22 (F)

Blackpool	Chorley	11.71	73-77	172	8	72
Everton	Tr	08.78	78	18	3	1
Queens Park R.	Tr	03.79	78-80	13	5	3

WALSH, Michael T.
Manchester, 20 June, 1956 IR-5 (CD)

Bolton W.	Jnrs	07.74	74-80	169	8	4
Everton	Tr	08.81	81-82	20	0	0
Norwich C.	L	10.82	82	5	0	0
Burnley	L	12.82	82	3	0	0
Manchester C.	Fort Lauderdale (USA)	10.83	83	3	1	0
Blackpool	Tr	02.84	83-88	146	7	5
Bury	Tr	07.89				

WALSH, Paul A.M.
Plumstead, 1 October, 1962 E Yth/Eu21-4/E-2 (F)

Charlton Ath.	App	10.79	79-81	85	2	24
Luton T.	Tr	07.82	82-83	80	0	24
Liverpool	Tr	05.84	84-87	63	14	25
Tottenham H.	Tr	02.88	87-91	84	44	19
Queens Park R.	L	09.91	91	2	0	0

WALSH, Peter
Dublin, 18 October, 1922 IR F Lge (F)

Luton T.	Dundalk	08.49	49	8	-	2
Brighton & H.A.	Tr	08.50				

WALSH, Roy
Belfast, 25 November, 1955 (D)

Swindon T.	Glentoran	03.80	80	7	0	0

WALSH, Roy W.
Dedham (Sk), 15 January, 1947 (IF)

Ipswich T.	App	01.65	65	6	1	0

WALSH, Steven
Preston, 3 November, 1964 (CD)

Wigan Ath.	Jnrs	09.82	82-85	123	3	4
Leicester C.	Tr	06.86	86-91	194	1	22

WALSH, Wilfred
Pontlottyn, 29 July, 1917 Died 1977 (W)

Arsenal	Margate	05.36	38	3	-	0
Derby Co.	Tr	06.39	46	1	-	0
Walsall	Tr	03.47	46-47	33	-	4

WALSH, William
Easington, 4 December, 1923 (CH)

Sunderland	Horden Colly	09.46	46-52	98	-	1
Northampton T.	Tr	07.53	53	19	-	0
Darlington	Tr	06.54	54	28	-	4

WALSH, William
Dublin, 31 May, 1921 IR-9/NI-5 (WH)

League Club	Source	Date Signed	Seasons Played	Apps	Subs	Gls
Manchester C.	Manchester U. (Am)	06.38	46-49	109	-	1

WALSHAW, Kenneth
Tynemouth, 28 August, 1918 (IF)

League Club	Source	Date Signed	Seasons Played	Apps	Subs	Gls
Sunderland	Jnrs	08.44				
Lincoln C.	Tr	08.47	47	17	-	6
Carlisle U.	Tr	12.47	47-49	50	-	15
Bradford C.	Tr	08.50	50	9	-	3

WALSHAW, Lee
Sheffield, 20 January, 1967 (M)

League Club	Source	Date Signed	Seasons Played	Apps	Subs	Gls
Sheffield U.	App	01.85	84-86	8	1	1

WALSHAW, Philip D.
Leeds, 16 April, 1929 (OR)

League Club	Source	Date Signed	Seasons Played	Apps	Subs	Gls
Halifax T. (Am)	Jnrs	09.46	46	6	-	1

WALTER, David W.
Holsworthy, 3 September, 1961 (G)

League Club	Source	Date Signed	Seasons Played	Apps	Subs	Gls
Exeter C.	Bideford	11.88	88-89	44	0	0
Plymouth Arg.	Tr	07.90	90-91	15	0	0

WALTERS, George
Wolverhampton, 21 June, 1935 (RB)

League Club	Source	Date Signed	Seasons Played	Apps	Subs	Gls
Shrewsbury T.	Jenks & Cattell	02.57	56-62	246	-	3
Newport Co.	Tr	09.63	63-65	80	0	2

WALTERS, George A.
Glasgow, 30 March, 1939 (OL)

League Club	Source	Date Signed	Seasons Played	Apps	Subs	Gls
Oldham Ath.	Clyde	08.59	59	13	-	2

WALTERS, Henry
Rotherham, 15 March, 1925 (WH)

League Club	Source	Date Signed	Seasons Played	Apps	Subs	Gls
Wolverhampton W.		06.42				
Walsall	Tr	05.46	46-52	253	-	2
Barnsley	Tr	07.53	53-59	160	-	4

WALTERS, Mark E.
Birmingham, 2 June, 1964 E Sch/E Yth/Eu21-9/E'B'/E-1 (LW)

League Club	Source	Date Signed	Seasons Played	Apps	Subs	Gls
Aston Villa	App	05.82	81-87	168	13	39
Liverpool	Glasgow Rangers	08.91	91	18	7	3

Mark Walters (Aston Villa, Glasgow Rangers, Liverpool & England)

WALTERS, Michael
Banbury, 17 November, 1939 (WH)

League Club	Source	Date Signed	Seasons Played	Apps	Subs	Gls
Coventry C.	Jnrs	12.56	57	3	-	0
Bradford C.	Rugby T.	01.62	61-62	19	-	0

WALTERS, Peter L.
Whickham, 8 June, 1952 (G)

League Club	Source	Date Signed	Seasons Played	Apps	Subs	Gls
Hull C.		08.70	70-71	2	0	0
Darlington	L	03.72	71	16	0	0

WALTERS, Robert J.
Glasgow, 9 March, 1944 (CH)

League Club	Source	Date Signed	Seasons Played	Apps	Subs	Gls
Shrewsbury T.	Winsford U.	12.62	62	1	-	0

WALTERS, Steven P.
Plymouth, 9 January, 1972 E Sch/E Yth (M)

League Club	Source	Date Signed	Seasons Played	Apps	Subs	Gls
Crewe Alex.	YT	03.89	87-91	84	8	5

WALTERS, Trevor B.
Aberdare, 13 January, 1916 (CH)

League Club	Source	Date Signed	Seasons Played	Apps	Subs	Gls
Hull C.	Dundee	03.37				
Chester C.	Tr	05.37	37-48	156	-	5

WALTERS, William E. (Sonny)
Edmonton, 5 September, 1924 Died 1970 E'B'-1 (W)

League Club	Source	Date Signed	Seasons Played	Apps	Subs	Gls
Tottenham H.	Jnrs	08.44	46-55	210	-	66
Aldershot	Tr	07.57	57-58	66	-	11

WALTON, Frank H.
Southend, 9 April, 1918 (FB)

League Club	Source	Date Signed	Seasons Played	Apps	Subs	Gls
Southend U.		12.37	37-50	144	-	0

WALTON, Harold
Manchester, 1 April, 1924 (F)

League Club	Source	Date Signed	Seasons Played	Apps	Subs	Gls
Southend U.	Leicester C. (Am)	05.46	46	1	-	0

WALTON, Ian J.
Goole, 17 April, 1958 (M)

League Club	Source	Date Signed	Seasons Played	Apps	Subs	Gls
Grimsby T. (App)	App	08.74	75	2	0	1
Scunthorpe U.	Tr	03.76	76	1	0	0

WALTON, John A.
Horwich, 21 March, 1928 Died 1979 E Amat (IF)

League Club	Source	Date Signed	Seasons Played	Apps	Subs	Gls
Bury (Am)		05.49	49-50	26	-	4
Manchester U. (Am)	Tr	07.51	51	2	-	0
Bury (Am)	Tr	07.52	52-53	29	-	2
Burnley	Tr	02.54	54-55	18	-	2
Coventry C.	Tr	10.56	56-57	13	-	0
Chester C.	Kettering T.	07.59	59	1	-	0

WALTON, Joseph W.
Manchester, 5 June, 1925 EF Lge (FB)

League Club	Source	Date Signed	Seasons Played	Apps	Subs	Gls
Manchester U.	Jnrs	10.43	46-47	21	-	0
Preston N.E.	Tr	03.48	47-60	401	-	4
Accrington St.	Tr	02.61	60	18	-	0

WALTON, Mark A.
Merthyr Tydfil, 1 June, 1969 Wu21-1 (G)

League Club	Source	Date Signed	Seasons Played	Apps	Subs	Gls
Luton T.	Jnrs	02.87				
Colchester U.	Tr	11.87	87-88	40	0	0
Norwich C.	Tr	08.89	89-91	22	0	0

WALTON, Richard
Hull, 12 September, 1924 (FB)

League Club	Source	Date Signed	Seasons Played	Apps	Subs	Gls
Leicester C.		01.43				
Leyton Orient	Tr	07.48	48-51	63	-	4
Exeter C.	Tr	12.51	51-55	135	-	6

WALTON, Ronald P.
Newcastle, 12 October, 1945 (W)

League Club	Source	Date Signed	Seasons Played	Apps	Subs	Gls
Northampton T.	Rotherham U. (Am)	09.63	64	1	-	0
Crewe Alex.	Tr	10.65	65	2	0	0
Carlisle U.	Tr	01.66	65	1	0	0
Aldershot	Tr	08.66	66-71	190	5	41
Cambridge U.	Tr	11.71	71-72	62	0	9
Aldershot	Tr	07.73	73-76	108	5	14

WALTON, Roy
Crewe, 19 July, 1928 (HB)

League Club	Source	Date Signed	Seasons Played	Apps	Subs	Gls
Crewe Alex.		06.50	50-51	12	-	0

WALWYN, Keith I.
Jamaica, 17 February, 1956 (F)

League Club	Source	Date Signed	Seasons Played	Apps	Subs	Gls
Chesterfield	Winterton R.	11.79	80	3	0	2
York C.	Tr	07.81	81-86	245	0	119
Blackpool	Tr	06.87	87-88	51	18	16
Carlisle U.	Tr	07.89	89-90	59	3	15

League Club	Source	Date Signed	Seasons Played	Career Record Apps	Subs	Gls

WANDS, Alexander M. D.
Cowdenbeath, 5 December, 1922 (LH)

League Club	Source	Date Signed	Seasons Played	Apps	Subs	Gls
Sheffield Wed.	Gateshead (Am)	05.45	46	11	-	1
Doncaster Rov.	Tr	05.47	47	22	-	1

WANKLYN, E. Wayne
Hull, 21 January, 1960 (M)

League Club	Source	Date Signed	Seasons Played	Apps	Subs	Gls
Reading	App	01.78	77-80	47	7	3
Aldershot	Tr	08.81	81	15	3	2

WANLESS, Paul S.
Banbury, 14 December, 1973 (M)

League Club	Source	Date Signed	Seasons Played	Apps	Subs	Gls
Oxford U.	YT	12.91	91	3	3	0

WANN, Alexander H. (Sandy)
Perth, 20 December, 1940 (WH)

League Club	Source	Date Signed	Seasons Played	Apps	Subs	Gls
Manchester C.	Luncarty Jnrs	07.58				
Oldham Ath.	St Mirren	12.60	60	19	-	0

WANN, J. Dennis
Blackpool, 17 November, 1950 (W)

League Club	Source	Date Signed	Seasons Played	Apps	Subs	Gls
Blackpool	App	07.67	69-71	11	6	0
York C.	Tr	01.72	71-75	65	1	7
Chesterfield	L	11.75	75	3	0	0
Hartlepool U.	L	01.76	75	2	0	0
Darlington	Tr	07.76	76-78	119	2	13
Rochdale	Tr	06.79	79-80	66	1	7
Blackpool	Tr	10.81	81	13	6	0
Chester C. (N/C)	Workington	10.83	83	2	1	0

WANT, Anthony G.
Shoreditch, 13 December, 1948 E Yth (LB)

League Club	Source	Date Signed	Seasons Played	Apps	Subs	Gls
Tottenham H.	App	12.65	67-71	46	4	0
Birmingham C.	Tr	06.72	72-77	98	3	1

WARBOYS, Alan
Goldthorpe, 18 April, 1949 (F)

League Club	Source	Date Signed	Seasons Played	Apps	Subs	Gls
Doncaster Rov.	App	04.67	66-67	39	1	12
Sheffield Wed.	Tr	06.68	68-70	66	5	13
Cardiff C.	Tr	12.70	70-72	56	4	27
Sheffield U.	Tr	09.72	72	7	0	0
Bristol Rov.	Tr	03.73	72-76	141	3	53
Fulham	Tr	02.77	76-77	19	0	2
Hull C.	Tr	09.77	77-78	44	5	9
Doncaster Rov.	Tr	07.79	79-81	89	0	21

Alan Warboys (Doncaster Rovers, Sheffield Wednesday, Cardiff City, Sheffield United, Bristol Rovers, Fulham, Hull City & Doncaster Rovers)

WARBURTON, George
Brymbo, 13 September, 1934 (FB)

League Club	Source	Date Signed	Seasons Played	Apps	Subs	Gls
Wrexham		11.57	58-59	22	-	0
Barrow	Tr	06.60	60	14	-	0

WARBURTON, Ian T.
Haslingden, 22 March, 1952 (F)

League Club	Source	Date Signed	Seasons Played	Apps	Subs	Gls
Bury		11.72	72	6	0	2
Southport	Tr	07.74	74	5	2	1

WARBURTON Raymond
Rotherham, 7 October, 1967 (CD)

League Club	Source	Date Signed	Seasons Played	Apps	Subs	Gls
Rotherham U.	App	10.85	84-86	3	1	0
York C.	Tr	08.89	89-91	72	2	6

WARD, Anthony
Warrington, 4 April, 1970 (W)

League Club	Source	Date Signed	Seasons Played	Apps	Subs	Gls
Everton	YT	06.88				
Doncaster Rov.	L	12.88	88	4	0	0
Wigan Ath.	Tr	06.89	89	8	3	2

WARD, Ashley S.
Manchester, 24 November, 1970 (F)

League Club	Source	Date Signed	Seasons Played	Apps	Subs	Gls
Manchester C.	YT	07.89	89	0	1	0
Wrexham	L	01.91	90	4	0	2
Leicester C.	Tr	07.91	91	2	8	0

WARD, David (Dai)
Barry, 16 July, 1934 W-2 (IF)

League Club	Source	Date Signed	Seasons Played	Apps	Subs	Gls
Bristol Rov.	Barry T.	11.54	54-60	175	-	90
Cardiff C.	Tr	02.61	60-61	35	-	18
Watford	Tr	06.62	62-63	59	-	31
Brentford	Tr	10.63	63-64	47	-	11

WARD, David A.
Crewe, 8 March, 1941 (FB)

League Club	Source	Date Signed	Seasons Played	Apps	Subs	Gls
Swansea C.	Taunton T.	01.59	60-65	44	1	0

WARD, Dennis
Burton, 25 October, 1924 (G)

League Club	Source	Date Signed	Seasons Played	Apps	Subs	Gls
Nottingham F.		08.47	47	1	-	0
Stockport Co.	Tr	08.49	49-52	52	-	0
Bradford P.A.	Hastings U.	08.55	55-57	50	-	0

WARD, Derek
Stoke, 23 December, 1934 (W)

League Club	Source	Date Signed	Seasons Played	Apps	Subs	Gls
Stoke C.	Jnrs	08.52	52-60	54	-	8
Stockport Co.	Tr	07.61	61-63	81	-	21

WARD, Gavin J.
Sutton Coldfield, 30 June, 1970 (G)

League Club	Source	Date Signed	Seasons Played	Apps	Subs	Gls
Shrewsbury T.	Aston Villa (YT)	09.88				
Cardiff C.	West Bromwich A. (N/C)	09.89	89-91	26	1	0

WARD, Gerald
Stepney, 5 October, 1936 E Sch/E Yth/E Amat (WH)

League Club	Source	Date Signed	Seasons Played	Apps	Subs	Gls
Arsenal	Jnrs	10.53	53-62	81	-	10
Leyton Orient	Tr	07.63	63-64	44	-	2

WARD, James
Glasgow, 26 July, 1929

League Club	Source	Date Signed	Seasons Played	Apps	Subs	Gls
Crewe Alex. (Am)	Queens Park	08.56	56	11	-	0

WARD, John
Mansfield, 18 January, 1948 (FB)

League Club	Source	Date Signed	Seasons Played	Apps	Subs	Gls
Notts Co.	App	07.65	65	5	0	0

WARD, John P.
Lincoln, 7 April, 1951 (F)

League Club	Source	Date Signed	Seasons Played	Apps	Subs	Gls
Lincoln C.	Adelaide Park	03.71	70-78	223	17	91
Workington	L	09.72	72	9	2	3
Watford	Tr	07.79	79-80	22	5	6
Grimsby T.	Tr	06.81	81	2	1	0
Lincoln C.	Tr	03.82	81	1	0	0

WARD, John S.
Frodsham, 15 June, 1933

League Club	Source	Date Signed	Seasons Played	Apps	Subs	Gls
Crewe Alex. (Am)		12.56	56	2	-	0

WARD, Joseph
Glasgow, 25 November, 1954 (F)

League Club	Source	Date Signed	Seasons Played	Apps	Subs	Gls
Aston Villa	Clyde	12.78	78-79	2	1	0

WARD, Lawrence (Polly)
Halifax, 15 June, 1929 (IF)

League Club	Source	Date Signed	Seasons Played	Apps	Subs	Gls
Bradford C.	Ovenden	10.48	48-53	149	-	37
Bradford P.A.	Kings Lynn	07.55	55-58	108	-	31

WARD, Mark W.
Huyton, 10 October, 1962 E Semi-Pro (W)

League Club	Source	Date Signed	Seasons Played	Apps	Subs	Gls
Everton	App	09.80				
Oldham Ath.	Northwich Vic.	07.83	83-84	84	0	12
West Ham U.	Tr	08.85	85-89	163	2	12
Manchester C.	Tr	12.89	89-90	55	0	14
Everton	Tr	08.91	91	37	0	4

WARD, Michael H.
Nottingham, 30 August, 1920

League Club	Source	Date Signed	Seasons Played	Apps	Subs	Gls
Stockport Co.		10.48	48	1	-	0

WARD, Mitchum D.
Sheffield, 19 June, 1971 (F)

League Club	Source	Date Signed	Seasons Played	Apps	Subs	Gls
Sheffield U.	YT	07.89	90-91	7	3	2
Crewe Alex.	L	11.90	90	4	0	1

WARD, Noel G.
Derry (NI), 8 December, 1952 (CD)

League Club	Source	Date Signed	Seasons Played	Apps	Subs	Gls
Wigan Ath.	Aberdeen	(N/L)	78-79	47	1	4

WARD, Patrick
Dumbarton, 28 December, 1926 (WH)

League Club	Source	Date Signed	Seasons Played	Apps	Subs	Gls
Leicester C.	Hibernian	09.55	55-57	57	-	0
Crewe Alex.	Tr	06.58	58	31	-	1

WARD, Paul T.
Fishburn (Dm), 15 September, 1963 (M)

League Club	Source	Date Signed	Seasons Played	Apps	Subs	Gls
Chelsea	App	08.81				
Middlesbrough	Tr	09.82	82-85	69	7	1
Darlington	Tr	09.85	85-87	124	0	9
Leyton Orient	Tr	07.88	88-89	30	1	1
Scunthorpe U.	Tr	10.89	89-90	53	2	6
Lincoln C.	Tr	03.91	90-91	37	1	0

WARD, Peter
Rotherham, 20 October, 1954 (FB)

League Club	Source	Date Signed	Seasons Played	Apps	Subs	Gls
Sheffield U.	App	10.72				
Workington	Tr	07.74	74-75	39	4	2

WARD, Peter
Co Durham, 15 October, 1964 (M)

League Club	Source	Date Signed	Seasons Played	Apps	Subs	Gls
Huddersfield T.	Chester-le-Street	01.87	86-88	24	13	2
Rochdale	Tr	07.89	89-90	83	1	10
Stockport Co.	Tr	05.91	91	44	0	1

WARD, Peter D.
Derby, 27 July, 1955 Eu21-2/E-1 (F)

League Club	Source	Date Signed	Seasons Played	Apps	Subs	Gls
Brighton & H.A.	Burton A.	05.75	75-80	172	6	79
Nottingham F.	Tr	10.80	80-82	28	5	7
Brighton & H.A.	L	10.82	82	16	0	2

WARD, Ralph A.
Leicester, 5 February, 1911 E Sch (FB)

League Club	Source	Date Signed	Seasons Played	Apps	Subs	Gls
Bradford P.A.	Hinckley	11.29	30-35	129	-	0
Tottenham H.	Tr	03.36	35-38	115	-	10
Crewe Alex.	Tr	08.46	46-48	89	-	7

WARD, J. Richard
Scunthorpe, 16 September, 1940 E Amat (IF)

League Club	Source	Date Signed	Seasons Played	Apps	Subs	Gls
Scunthorpe U. (Am)	Jnrs	05.58	58	1	-	0
Northampton T. (Am)	Tr	06.59	59-61	7	-	0
Millwall	Tooting & Mitcham	07.62	62-63	13	-	3

WARD, Robert
Glasgow, 21 October, 1958 (M)

League Club	Source	Date Signed	Seasons Played	Apps	Subs	Gls
Newport Co.	Glasgow Celtic	01.80	79-80	2	1	0

WARD, Robert A.
West Bromwich, 4 August, 1953 (G)

League Club	Source	Date Signed	Seasons Played	Apps	Subs	Gls
West Bromwich A.	Imperial Star	03.73	74-76	9	0	0
Northampton T.	L	02.77	76	8	0	0
Blackpool	Tr	09.77	77-78	41	0	0
Wigan Ath.	Tr	07.79	80-81	46	0	0

WARD, Ronald
Killamarsh, 10 February, 1935 E Sch (G)

League Club	Source	Date Signed	Seasons Played	Apps	Subs	Gls
Chesterfield	Jnrs	02.52	51-52	8	-	0

WARD, Ronald
Altrincham, 17 October, 1932 (IF)

League Club	Source	Date Signed	Seasons Played	Apps	Subs	Gls
Stockport Co.		03.54	53-55	16	-	4

WARD, Ronald H.
Walthamstow, 29 March, 1932 (G)

League Club	Source	Date Signed	Seasons Played	Apps	Subs	Gls
Tottenham H.		05.50				
Darlington	Headington U.	08.56	56	26	-	0

WARD, Stephen
Chapeltown, 27 December, 1960 (FB)

League Club	Source	Date Signed	Seasons Played	Apps	Subs	Gls
Lincoln C.	App	12.78	79	2	0	0

WARD, Stephen C.
Derby, 21 July, 1959 (W)

League Club	Source	Date Signed	Seasons Played	Apps	Subs	Gls
Brighton & H.A.	App	10.76				
Northampton T.	Tr	08.79	79	13	2	2
Halifax T.	Tr	06.80	80-85	233	13	17

WARD, Sydney
Dewsbury, 26 November, 1923 (G)

League Club	Source	Date Signed	Seasons Played	Apps	Subs	Gls
Bradford C.	Upton Colly	09.47	47	2	-	0

WARD, Terence
Stoke, 10 December, 1939 (FB)

League Club	Source	Date Signed	Seasons Played	Apps	Subs	Gls
Stoke C.	Jnrs	03.58	59-62	43	-	0

WARD, Thomas A.
Tow Law, 6 August, 1917 (CF)

League Club	Source	Date Signed	Seasons Played	Apps	Subs	Gls
Sheffield Wed.	Crook T.	03.37	46-47	35	-	19
Darlington	Tr	08.48	48-53	119	-	32

WARD, Timothy V.
Cheltenham, 17 October, 1918 E-2 (WH)

League Club	Source	Date Signed	Seasons Played	Apps	Subs	Gls
Derby Co.	Cheltenham T.	04.37	37-50	238	-	4
Barnsley	Tr	03.51	50-52	33	-	0

WARD, Warren
Plympton, 25 May, 1962 (F)

League Club	Source	Date Signed	Seasons Played	Apps	Subs	Gls
York C. (N/C)	Guiseley	03.85	84	4	0	3
Lincoln C.	Tr	07.85	85	15	6	8
Exeter C.	L	02.86	85	14	0	3

WARD, Wayne W.
Colchester, 28 April, 1964 (FB)

League Club	Source	Date Signed	Seasons Played	Apps	Subs	Gls
Colchester U.	App	05.82	81-82	17	2	0

WARD, William
Chester-le-Street, 30 June, 1949 (W)

League Club	Source	Date Signed	Seasons Played	Apps	Subs	Gls
Hartlepool U.		01.72	71-74	87	8	9

WARDLE, Ernest
Consett, 13 June, 1930 (FB)

League Club	Source	Date Signed	Seasons Played	Apps	Subs	Gls
Middlesbrough	Billingham Synth.	05.48				
York C.	Tr	01.55	54-58	60	-	2

WARDLE, Geoffrey
Trimdon, 7 January, 1940 (WH)

League Club	Source	Date Signed	Seasons Played	Apps	Subs	Gls
Sunderland	Houghton Jnrs	01.58				
Lincoln C.	Tr	06.61	61	1	-	0

WARDLE, George
Kimblesworth (Dm), 24 September, 1919 (OR)

League Club	Source	Date Signed	Seasons Played	Apps	Subs	Gls
Middlesbrough		05.37	37	1	-	0
Exeter C.	Tr	06.39	46	38	-	6
Cardiff C.	Tr	05.47	46-48	40	-	11
Queens Park R.	Tr	01.49	48-50	53	-	3
Darlington	Tr	08.51	51-53	95	-	6

WARDLE, Ian S.
Doncaster, 27 March, 1970 (G)

League Club	Source	Date Signed	Seasons Played	Apps	Subs	Gls
Barnsley	Jnrs	05.88	89	9	0	0

WARDLE, Robert I.
Halifax, 5 March, 1955 (G)

League Club	Source	Date Signed	Seasons Played	Apps	Subs	Gls
Bristol C.	App	11.72				
Shrewsbury T.	Tr	07.74	77-81	131	0	0
Liverpool	Tr	08.82				
Wrexham	L	09.83	83	13	0	0

WARDLE, William
Hetton-le-Hole, 20 January, 1918 Died 1989 (OL)

League Club	Source	Date Signed	Seasons Played	Apps	Subs	Gls
Southport		12.36	36-37	14	-	0
Manchester C.	Tr	10.37	37	6	-	0
Grimsby T.	Tr	07.39	46-47	73	-	11
Blackpool	Tr	05.48	48-50	58	-	1
Birmingham C.	Tr	09.51	51-52	60	-	5
Barnsley	Tr	11.53	53-54	28	-	1

WARDROBE, Michael
Newcastle, 24 March, 1962 (F)

League Club	Source	Date Signed	Seasons Played	Apps	Subs	Gls
Burnley	App	03.80	80	0	1	0
Stockport Co.	Tr	08.81	81-82	19	8	2

WARE, Charles
York, 9 March, 1931 (OL)

League Club	Source	Date Signed	Seasons Played	Apps	Subs	Gls
York C.	Jnrs	12.48	53	9	-	0

WARE, Paul D.
Congleton, 7 November, 1970 (D/M)

League Club	Source	Date Signed	Seasons Played	Apps	Subs	Gls
Stoke C.	YT	11.88	87-91	70	16	6

WARHURST, Paul
Stockport, 26 September, 1969 Eu21-8 (D)

League Club	Source	Date Signed	Seasons Played	Apps	Subs	Gls
Manchester C.	YT	06.88				
Oldham Ath.	Tr	10.88	88-90	60	7	2
Sheffield Wed.	Tr	07.91	91	31	2	0

Paul Warhurst (Manchester City, Oldham Athletic & Sheffield Wednesday)

WARHURST, Roy
Sheffield, 18 September, 1926 (WH)

League Club	Source	Date Signed	Seasons Played	Apps	Subs	Gls
Sheffield U.	Huddersfield T. (Am)	09.44	46-49	17	-	2
Birmingham C.	Tr	03.50	49-56	213	-	10
Manchester C.	Tr	06.57	57-58	40	-	2
Crewe Alex.	Tr	03.59	58-59	51	-	1
Oldham Ath.	Tr	08.60	60	8	-	0

WARING, T. Alan
Preston, 3 August, 1929 (HB)

League Club	Source	Date Signed	Seasons Played	Apps	Subs	Gls
Burnley		08.48				
Halifax T.	Tr	07.54	54	12	-	0

WARK, John
Glasgow, 4 August, 1957 Su21-8/S-29 (M)

League Club	Source	Date Signed	Seasons Played	Apps	Subs	Gls
Ipswich T.	App	08.74	74-83	295	1	94
Liverpool	Tr	03.84	83-87	64	6	28
Ipswich T.	Tr	01.88	87-89	87	2	23
Middlesbrough	Tr	08.90	90	31	1	3
Ipswich T. (N/C)	Tr	08.91	91	36	1	3

WARMAN, Philip R.
Bromley, 18 December, 1950 E Yth (LB)

League Club	Source	Date Signed	Seasons Played	Apps	Subs	Gls
Charlton Ath.	Jnrs	03.68	69-80	313	3	19
Millwall	Tr	08.81	81	27	0	1

WARMINGTON, Peter
Birmingham, 8 April, 1934 (F)

League Club	Source	Date Signed	Seasons Played	Apps	Subs	Gls
Birmingham C.	Jnrs	12.51	54-56	8	-	3

WARN, Keith D.
Watford, 20 March, 1941 (G)

League Club	Source	Date Signed	Seasons Played	Apps	Subs	Gls
Watford	Croxley B.C.	04.59	59	3	-	0

WARNE, Raymond J.
Ipswich, 16 June, 1929 (CF)

League Club	Source	Date Signed	Seasons Played	Apps	Subs	Gls
Ipswich T.	Leiston	10.50	50-51	30	-	11

WARNER, Dennis P. A.
Rotherham, 6 December, 1930 (FB)

League Club	Source	Date Signed	Seasons Played	Apps	Subs	Gls
Rotherham U.	Spurley Hey O.B.	03.50	52-56	64	-	0
Chesterfield	Tr	05.57	57	8	-	0

WARNER, John
Ashington, 6 May, 1940 (F)

League Club	Source	Date Signed	Seasons Played	Apps	Subs	Gls
Luton T.		10.59	59	1	-	0

WARNER, John
Tonyrefail, 21 September, 1911 W-2 (WH)

League Club	Source	Date Signed	Seasons Played	Apps	Subs	Gls
Swansea C.	Trealaw	01.34	33-37	132	-	8
Manchester U.	Tr	06.38	38-49	102	-	1
Oldham Ath.	Tr	06.51	51	34	-	2
Rochdale	Tr	07.52	52	21	-	0

WARNER, John
Paddington, 20 November, 1961 (F)

League Club	Source	Date Signed	Seasons Played	Apps	Subs	Gls
Colchester U. (N/C)	Burnham Ramblers	02.89	88	7	8	3
Colchester U. (N/C)	Heybridge Swifts	12.89	89	1	1	0

WARNER, Leslie H.
Birmingham, 19 December, 1918 Died 1982 (OR)

League Club	Source	Date Signed	Seasons Played	Apps	Subs	Gls
Coventry C.	Jack Moulds Ath.	07.37	37-53	197	-	19

WARNER, Reginald O.
Anstey, 1 March, 1931 E Yth (HB)

League Club	Source	Date Signed	Seasons Played	Apps	Subs	Gls
Leicester C.	Jnrs	04.49	52-53	7	-	0
Mansfield T.	Tr	03.55	54-56	33	-	0

WARNES, George
Sheffield, 4 December, 1925 (G)

League Club	Source	Date Signed	Seasons Played	Apps	Subs	Gls
Rotherham U.	Dinnington Colly	12.44	46-49	98	-	0
Aldershot	Tr	06.50	50-51	32	-	0

John Wark (Ipswich Town, Liverpool, Ipswich Town, Middlesbrough, Ipswich Town & Scotland)

WARNOCK, Neil
Sheffield, 1 December, 1948 (W)

League Club	Source	Date Signed	Seasons Played	Apps	Subs	Gls
Chesterfield		07.68	67-68	20	4	2
Rotherham U.	Tr	06.69	69-70	46	8	5
Hartlepool U.	Tr	07.71	71-72	58	2	5
Scunthorpe U.	Tr	02.72	72-74	63	9	7
Aldershot	Tr	03.75	74-76	35	2	6
Barnsley	Tr	10.76	76-77	54	4	10
York C.	Tr	05.78	78	1	3	0
Crewe Alex.	Tr	12.78	78	20	1	1

WARREN, Derek B.
Colyton, 23 May, 1923 (RB)

League Club	Source	Date Signed	Seasons Played	Apps	Subs	Gls
Exeter C.	Axminster	01.48	48-51	55	-	0

WARREN, Lee A.
Manchester, 28 February, 1969 (D/M)

League Club	Source	Date Signed	Seasons Played	Apps	Subs	Gls
Leeds U.	YT	07.87				
Rochdale	Tr	10.87	87	31	0	1
Hull C.	Tr	08.88	88-91	78	6	1
Lincoln C.	L	09.90	90	2	1	1

WARREN, Mark W.
Clapton, 12 November, 1974 (F)

League Club	Source	Date Signed	Seasons Played	Apps	Subs	Gls
Leyton Orient (YT)	YT	07.91	91	0	1	0

WARREN, Raymond R.
Bristol, 23 June, 1918 Died 1988 (CH)

League Club	Source	Date Signed	Seasons Played	Apps	Subs	Gls
Bristol Rov.	Jnrs	11.35	35-55	450	-	28

WARREN, Robert E.
Devonport, 8 January, 1927 (CH)

League Club	Source	Date Signed	Seasons Played	Apps	Subs	Gls
Plymouth Arg.	Plymouth U.	02.46	46	3	-	0
Chelsea	Tr	07.48	48	1	-	0
Torquay U.	Tr	08.51	51	5	-	1

WARRENDER, Robert
Leven, 13 February, 1929 (F)

League Club	Source	Date Signed	Seasons Played	Apps	Subs	Gls
York C.	East Fife	05.52	52-53	24	-	5

WARRILOW, Thomas
Plumstead, 26 July, 1964 (D)

League Club	Source	Date Signed	Seasons Played	Apps	Subs	Gls
Torquay U. (N/C)	Gravesend & Nft	03.87	86	2	0	0

WARRINER, Stephen W.
Liverpool, 18 December, 1958 (FB)

League Club	Source	Date Signed	Seasons Played	Apps	Subs	Gls
Liverpool	App	12.76				
Newport Co.	Tr	07.78	78-80	28	8	2
Rochdale	Tr	08.81	81-82	11	1	1
Tranmere Rov.	Tr	02.83	82	5	4	0

WARRINGTON, Anthony
Ecclesfield, 12 February, 1934 (G)

League Club	Source	Date Signed	Seasons Played	Apps	Subs	Gls
Lincoln C.		03.54	53-55	2	-	0

WARSAP W. John B.
Leytonstone, 18 May, 1921 (W)

League Club	Source	Date Signed	Seasons Played	Apps	Subs	Gls
Gillingham		(N/L)	50-52	9	-	1

WARZYCHA, Robert
Wielun (Poland), 20 August, 1963 Polish Int (RW)

League Club	Source	Date Signed	Seasons Played	Apps	Subs	Gls
Everton	Gornik Zabrze (Pol)	03.91	90-91	33	12	5

WASILEWSKI, Adam
1925 Died 1956

League Club	Source	Date Signed	Seasons Played	Apps	Subs	Gls
Rochdale		07.53	53	4	-	1

WASS, William
Ryhope, 16 November, 1922 (OR)

League Club	Source	Date Signed	Seasons Played	Apps	Subs	Gls
Middlesbrough		02.45				
Bradford C.	Tr	07.46	46	7	-	1

WASSALL, Darren P. J.
Birmingham, 27 June, 1968 (CD)

League Club	Source	Date Signed	Seasons Played	Apps	Subs	Gls
Nottingham F.	App	06.86	87-91	17	10	0
Hereford U.	L	10.87	87	5	0	0
Bury	L	03.89	88	7	0	1

WASSALL, John C.
Birmingham, 9 June, 1933 Died 1987 (D)

League Club	Source	Date Signed	Seasons Played	Apps	Subs	Gls
Coventry C.	Jnrs	05.51	55-56	17	-	0
Southport	Tr	08.57	57	4	-	0

WASSALL, John V.
Shrewsbury, 11 February, 1917 (IF)

League Club	Source	Date Signed	Seasons Played	Apps	Subs	Gls
Manchester U.	Wellington T.	02.35	35-38	45	-	6
Stockport Co.	Tr	10.46	46-47	19	-	2

WASSALL, Kim D.
Wolverhampton, 9 June, 1957 (W/FB)

League Club	Source	Date Signed	Seasons Played	Apps	Subs	Gls
West Bromwich A.	App	06.75				
Northampton T.	Tr	09.77	77-78	13	7	0
Hull C. (N/C)	Australia	08.83	83	1	0	0
Swansea C. (N/C)		09.84	84	1	1	0
Wolverhampton W. (N/C)		10.85	85	2	0	0
Shrewsbury T. (N/C)	Finland	11.89	89	0	2	0

WATERHOUSE, Kenneth
Ormskirk, 23 January, 1930 (WH)

League Club	Source	Date Signed	Seasons Played	Apps	Subs	Gls
Preston N.E.	Burscough	12.48	53-56	22	-	5
Rotherham U.	Tr	05.58	58-62	115	-	11
Bristol C.	Tr	04.63	62-63	16	-	1
Darlington	Tr	08.64	64	1	-	0

WATERMAN, Derek
Guildford, 12 April, 1939 (WH)

League Club	Source	Date Signed	Seasons Played	Apps	Subs	Gls
Exeter C.	Guildford C.	06.57	57	4	-	0

WATERS, Graham J.
St. Austell, 5 November, 1971 (FB)

League Club	Source	Date Signed	Seasons Played	Apps	Subs	Gls
Oxford U.	YT	05.90				
Exeter C.	Tr	07.91	91	1	1	0

WATERS, Joseph W.
Limerick (Ire), 20 September, 1953 IR-2 (M)

League Club	Source	Date Signed	Seasons Played	Apps	Subs	Gls
Leicester C.	App	10.70	73-74	11	2	1
Grimsby T.	Tr	01.76	75-83	356	1	65

WATERS, Patrick M.
Dublin, 31 January, 1922 (WH)

League Club	Source	Date Signed	Seasons Played	Apps	Subs	Gls
Preston N.E.	Glentoran	06.47	47-49	64	-	0
Carlisle U.	Tr	12.50	50-57	261	-	0

WATERS, Richard E.
Gateshead, 18 May, 1945 (G)

League Club	Source	Date Signed	Seasons Played	Apps	Subs	Gls
Darlington (Am)	Blyth Spartans	03.65	64	2	-	0

WATERS, Samuel
Croy, 31 May, 1917 Died 1975 (OL)

League Club	Source	Date Signed	Seasons Played	Apps	Subs	Gls
Halifax T.	Third Lanark	07.46	46	26	-	9

WATERS, William A.
Swansea, 19 September, 1931 (G)

League Club	Source	Date Signed	Seasons Played	Apps	Subs	Gls
Blackpool		11.50				
Southend U.		11.53				
Swansea C.	Tr	08.54				
Wrexham	Tr	06.55	55-58	99	-	0
Millwall	Tr	07.60	60	5	-	0

WATFORD, Albert
Chesterfield, 12 February, 1917

League Club	Source	Date Signed	Seasons Played	Apps	Subs	Gls
Chesterfield		02.44				
Lincoln C.	Tr	09.46	46	14	-	0

WATKIN, Alan J.
Felling, 16 May, 1940 (OR)

League Club	Source	Date Signed	Seasons Played	Apps	Subs	Gls
Gateshead (Am)		08.59	59	3	-	0

WATKIN, Cyril
Stoke, 21 July, 1926 (FB)

League Club	Source	Date Signed	Seasons Played	Apps	Subs	Gls
Stoke C.	Jnrs	09.44	48-51	86	-	0
Bristol C.	Tr	07.52	52	3	-	0

WATKIN, George
Chopwell, 14 April, 1944 (CF)

League Club	Source	Date Signed	Seasons Played	Apps	Subs	Gls
Newcastle U.	App	04.62	62	1	-	0
Chesterfield	Kings Lynn	07.64	64	7	-	1

WATKIN, Stephen
Wrexham, 16 June, 1971 Wu21-1 (F)

League Club	Source	Date Signed	Seasons Played	Apps	Subs	Gls
Wrexham	Jnrs	07.89	90-91	33	4	9

WATKIN, T. William S.
Grimsby, 21 September, 1932 E Sch (F)

League Club	Source	Date Signed	Seasons Played	Apps	Subs	Gls
Grimsby T.	Jnrs	10.49				
Gateshead	Tr	12.52	52-53	38	-	12
Middlesbrough	Tr	03.54	53-54	11	-	2
Mansfield T.	Tr	06.55	55	25	-	4

WATKINS, Albert J. (Alan)
Usk, 21 April, 1922 (WH)

League Club	Source	Date Signed	Seasons Played	Apps	Subs	Gls
Plymouth Arg.		12.45	46	4	-	1
Cardiff C.	Tr	07.48				

WATKINS, R. Barry
Merthyr Tydfil, 30 November, 1921 (FB)

League Club	Source	Date Signed	Seasons Played	Apps	Subs	Gls
Bristol Rov.	B.A.C.	10.45	46-54	116	-	7

WATKINS, Charles
Glasgow, 14 January, 1921 (WH)

League Club	Source	Date Signed	Seasons Played	Apps	Subs	Gls
Luton T.	Glasgow Rangers	09.48	48-54	217	-	16

WATKINS, Dale A.
Peterborough, 4 November, 1971 (F)

League Club	Source	Date Signed	Seasons Played	Apps	Subs	Gls
Peterborough U.	Rotherham U. (YT)	03.90	89-90	5	5	0

WATKINS, John V.
Bristol, 9 April, 1933 E Yth (OL)

League Club	Source	Date Signed	Seasons Played	Apps	Subs	Gls
Bristol C.	Jnrs	06.51	53-58	95	-	19
Cardiff C.	Tr	06.59	59-60	65	-	17
Bristol Rov.	Tr	02.61	60-61	23	-	0

WATKINS, Philip J.
Caerphilly, 2 January, 1945 (WH)

League Club	Source	Date Signed	Seasons Played	Apps	Subs	Gls
Cardiff C.	Jnrs	09.62	63	1	-	0

WATKINS, Robert (Wally)
Bristol, 20 December, 1946 (OL)

League Club	Source	Date Signed	Seasons Played	Apps	Subs	Gls
Bristol Rov.	Bristol C. (Am)	07.65	65	1	0	0

WATKINSON, William W.
Prescot, 16 March, 1922 (CF)

League Club	Source	Date Signed	Seasons Played	Apps	Subs	Gls
Liverpool	Prescot Cables	02.46	46-49	24	-	2
Accrington St.	Tr	01.51	50-54	105	-	45
Halifax T.	Tr	09.54	54-55	60	-	24

WATKISS, Stuart P.
Wolverhampton, 8 May, 1966 (CD)

League Club	Source	Date Signed	Seasons Played	Apps	Subs	Gls
Wolverhampton W. (YT)		07.84	83	2	0	0
Crewe Alex. (N/C)		02.86	85	3	0	0

WATLING, Barry J.
Walthamstow, 16 July, 1946 (G)

League Club	Source	Date Signed	Seasons Played	Apps	Subs	Gls
Leyton Orient	App	07.64				
Bristol C.	Tr	07.65	67-68	2	0	0
Notts Co.	Tr	07.69	69-71	65	1	0
Hartlepool U.	Tr	07.72	72-75	139	0	0
Chester C.	L	09.75	75	5	0	0
Rotherham U.	L	12.75	75	5	0	0
Sheffield Wed.	Tr	01.76	75	1	0	0

WATLING, John D.
Bristol, 11 May, 1925 (OL)

League Club	Source	Date Signed	Seasons Played	Apps	Subs	Gls
Bristol Rov.	St Andrews B.C.	01.47	47-61	323	-	19

WATSON, Albert
Bolton-on-Dearne, 1 June, 1918 (LH)

League Club	Source	Date Signed	Seasons Played	Apps	Subs	Gls
Huddersfield T.		12.35	37-47	17	-	0
Oldham Ath.	Tr	07.48	48-49	42	-	0

WATSON, Alexander F.
Liverpool, 6 April, 1968 (CD)

League Club	Source	Date Signed	Seasons Played	Apps	Subs	Gls
Liverpool	App	05.85	87-88	3	1	0
Derby Co.	L	08.90	90	5	0	0
Bournemouth	Tr	01.91	90-91	38	0	3

WATSON, Andrew
Aberdeen, 3 September, 1959 Su21-4 (M)

League Club	Source	Date Signed	Seasons Played	Apps	Subs	Gls
Leeds U.	Aberdeen	06.83	83-84	37	1	7

WATSON, Andrew A.
Leeds, 1 April, 1967 (M)

League Club	Source	Date Signed	Seasons Played	Apps	Subs	Gls
Halifax T.	Harrogate T.	08.88	88-89	75	8	15
Swansea C.	Tr	07.90	90	9	5	1
Carlisle U.	Tr	09.91	91	34	1	14

WATSON, Andrew L.
Huddersfield, 3 April, 1967 (CD)

League Club	Source	Date Signed	Seasons Played	Apps	Subs	Gls
Huddersfield T.	App	04.85				
Exeter C.	Tr	07.86	86-87	41	1	1

WATSON, Arthur E.
South Hiendley, 12 July, 1913 (FB)

League Club	Source	Date Signed	Seasons Played	Apps	Subs	Gls
Lincoln C.	Monkton Colly	05.34	34-35	37	-	0
Chesterfield	Tr	06.36	36-38	10	-	0
Hull C.	Tr	06.39	46	35	-	2

WATSON, Charles R.
Newark, 10 March, 1949 (G)

League Club	Source	Date Signed	Seasons Played	Apps	Subs	Gls
Notts Co.		02.67	67	1	0	0

WATSON, David V.
Stapleford, 5 October, 1946 E-65 (CD)

League Club	Source	Date Signed	Seasons Played	Apps	Subs	Gls
Notts Co.		01.67	66-67	24	1	2
Rotherham U.	Tr	01.68	67-70	121	0	20
Sunderland	Tr	12.70	70-74	177	0	27
Manchester C.	Tr	06.75	75-78	146	0	4
Southampton	Werder Bremen (Ger)	10.79	79-81	73	0	7
Stoke C.	Tr	01.82	81-82	59	0	5
Derby Co.	Vancouver (Can)	09.83	83	34	0	1
Notts Co.	Vancouver (Can)	09.84	84	23	2	1

WATSON, David
Liverpool, 20 November, 1961 Eu21-7/E-12 (CD)

League Club	Source	Date Signed	Seasons Played	Apps	Subs	Gls
Liverpool	Jnrs	05.79				
Norwich C.	Tr	11.80	80-85	212	0	11
Everton	Tr	08.86	86-91	199	1	16

WATSON, Donald
Barnsley, 27 August, 1932 (F)

League Club	Source	Date Signed	Seasons Played	Apps	Subs	Gls
Sheffield Wed.	Worsboro' Bridge	09.54	54	8	-	1
Lincoln C.	Tr	12.56	56-57	14	-	2
Bury	Tr	11.57	57-61	172	-	65
Barnsley	Tr	01.62	61	9	-	1
Rochdale	Tr	07.62	62-63	58	-	15
Barrow	Tr	07.64	64	17	-	1

WATSON, Gary
Easington, 2 March, 1961 (LB)

League Club	Source	Date Signed	Seasons Played	Apps	Subs	Gls
Oxford U.	App	11.78	78-79	24	0	0
Carlisle U.	Tr	05.80	80	17	1	0

WATSON, Garry
Bradford, 7 October, 1955 (LB)

League Club	Source	Date Signed	Seasons Played	Apps	Subs	Gls
Bradford C.	App	10.73	72-83	246	17	28
Doncaster Rov.	L	10.82	82	13	0	0
Halifax T.	Tr	07.84	84	21	0	0

WATSON, Gordon W. G.
Sidcup, 20 March, 1971 Eu21-2 (F)

League Club	Source	Date Signed	Seasons Played	Apps	Subs	Gls
Charlton Ath.	YT	04.89	89-90	20	11	7
Sheffield Wed.	Tr	02.91	90-91	5	4	0

WATSON, T. Gordon
Wolsingham (Dm), 1 March, 1914 (LH)

League Club	Source	Date Signed	Seasons Played	Apps	Subs	Gls
Everton	Blyth Spartans	01.33	36-48	61	-	1

WATSON, Graham S.
Doncaster, 3 August, 1949 (M)

League Club	Source	Date Signed	Seasons Played	Apps	Subs	Gls
Doncaster Rov.	App	11.66	66-67	47	1	11
Rotherham U.	Tr	02.68	67-68	13	0	0
Doncaster Rov.	Tr	01.69	68-72	105	4	23
Cambridge U.	Tr	09.72	72-78	206	3	24
Lincoln C.	Tr	09.78	78-79	43	0	2
Cambridge U.	Tr	03.80	79	0	1	0

WATSON, Ian
North Shields, 5 February, 1960 (G)

League Club	Source	Date Signed	Seasons Played	Apps	Subs	Gls
Sunderland	App	02.78	78	1	0	0
Rochdale	L	08.79	79	33	0	0
Newport Co.	Tr	04.82				

WATSON, Ian L.
Hammersmith, 7 January, 1944 (FB)

League Club	Source	Date Signed	Seasons Played	Apps	Subs	Gls
Chelsea	Jnrs	02.62	62-64	5	-	1
Queens Park R.	Tr	07.65	65-73	197	6	1

WATSON, James
Cowie, 16 January, 1924 SF Lge/S-2 (IF)

League Club	Source	Date Signed	Seasons Played	Apps	Subs	Gls
Huddersfield T.	Motherwell	06.52	52-56	140	-	29

WATSON, James M.
Birmingham, 3 March, 1937

League Club	Source	Date Signed	Seasons Played	Apps	Subs	Gls
Walsall		05.55	55	1	-	0
Birmingham C.	Tr	08.57				

WATSON, John
Dewsbury, 10 April, 1959 (G)

League Club	Source	Date Signed	Seasons Played	Apps	Subs	Gls
Huddersfield T.	Jnrs	03.77				
Hartlepool U.	Tr	03.79	78-82	44	0	0

WATSON, John
Wrexham, 2 May, 1942 W Sch (FB)

League Club	Source	Date Signed	Seasons Played	Apps	Subs	Gls
Everton	Jnrs	05.59				
Chester C.	Tr	08.60	60-61	25	-	0

WATSON, John F.
Hamilton, 31 December, 1917 (CH)

League Club	Source	Date Signed	Seasons Played	Apps	Subs	Gls
Bury	Douglas Jnrs	06.36	38	6	-	0
Fulham	Tr	08.46	46-47	71	-	2
Crystal Palace	Real Madrid (Sp)	07.49	49-50	61	-	1

WATSON, John I.
South Shields, 14 April, 1974 (RB/F)

League Club	Source	Date Signed	Seasons Played	Apps	Subs	Gls
Newcastle U.	YT	04.92	90	0	1	0

WATSON, John M.
Edinburgh, 13 February, 1959 (F)

League Club	Source	Date Signed	Seasons Played	Apps	Subs	Gls
Fulham	Dunfermline Ath.	08.89	89	12	2	0

WATSON, Kenneth
Newcastle, 8 September, 1934 (HB)

League Club	Source	Date Signed	Seasons Played	Apps	Subs	Gls
Lincoln C.		05.52				
Aldershot	Tr	07.55	57-59	29	-	1

WATSON, Peter
Newcastle, 18 March, 1935 (CF)

League Club	Source	Date Signed	Seasons Played	Apps	Subs	Gls
Workington	North Shields	11.62	62-64	45	-	10

WATSON, Peter F.
Stapleford, 15 April, 1934 (CH)

League Club	Source	Date Signed	Seasons Played	Apps	Subs	Gls
Nottingham F.	Jnrs	05.55	55-58	13	-	0
Southend U.	Tr	07.59	59-65	249	0	3

WATSON, T. Sidney
Mansfield, 12 December, 1927 (WH)

League Club	Source	Date Signed	Seasons Played	Apps	Subs	Gls
Mansfield T.	Palterton Welfare	01.49	51-60	292	-	9

WATSON, Stanley
Darlington, 17 March, 1937 (HB)

League Club	Source	Date Signed	Seasons Played	Apps	Subs	Gls
Darlington		11.57	57-58	27	-	0

WATSON, Stephen C.
North Shields, 1 April, 1974 E Yth (M/RB)

League Club	Source	Date Signed	Seasons Played	Apps	Subs	Gls
Newcastle U.	YT	04.91	90-91	45	7	1

WATSON, Thomas
Lesmahagow, 23 August, 1943 (W)

League Club	Source	Date Signed	Seasons Played	Apps	Subs	Gls
Peterborough U.	Stevenage T.	05.65	65-67	75	0	20
Walsall	Tr	09.67	67-69	83	3	17
Gillingham	Tr	06.70	70-71	43	7	7

WATSON, Thomas D.
Boldon, 3 February, 1936 (OR)

League Club	Source	Date Signed	Seasons Played	Apps	Subs	Gls
West Bromwich A.	Boldon Colly	11.53				
Gateshead	Tr	06.57	57	21	-	5

WATSON, Thomas R.
Liverpool, 29 September, 1969 (RW)

League Club	Source	Date Signed	Seasons Played	Apps	Subs	Gls
Grimsby T.	YT	06.88	87-91	84	30	16

WATSON, Trevor P.
Great Yarmouth, 26 September, 1938 (W)

League Club	Source	Date Signed	Seasons Played	Apps	Subs	Gls
Fulham	Jnrs	07.56	56-63	17	-	1

WATSON, Vaughan
Mansfield, 5 November, 1931 (CF)

League Club	Source	Date Signed	Seasons Played	Apps	Subs	Gls
Mansfield T.		04.52	52-53	14	-	9
Chesterfield	Tr	05.54	54	13	-	5

WATSON, William
South Hiendley, 29 May, 1916 (RB)

League Club	Source	Date Signed	Seasons Played	Apps	Subs	Gls
Lincoln C.	Monkton Colly	02.35	34-35	9	-	0
Chesterfield	Tr	06.36	46-47	36	-	0
Rochdale	Tr	06.48	48-53	200	-	0

WATSON, William
Bolton-on-Dearne, 3 March, 1920 E'B'-3/E-4 (WH)

League Club	Source	Date Signed	Seasons Played	Apps	Subs	Gls
Huddersfield T.		10.37	38	11	-	0
Sunderland	Tr	04.46	46-53	211	-	15
Halifax T.	Tr	11.54	54-55	33	-	1

WATSON, William
Motherwell, 4 December, 1949 (RB)

League Club	Source	Date Signed	Seasons Played	Apps	Subs	Gls
Manchester U.	Jnrs	12.66	70-72	11	0	0

WATSON, William T.
Swansea, 11 June, 1918 Died 1978 (FB)

League Club	Source	Date Signed	Seasons Played	Apps	Subs	Gls
Preston N.E.		02.46	46	15	-	0
Cardiff C.	Tr	10.47	47	1	-	0

WATT, John
Kilmarnock, 17 June, 1943 (OR)

League Club	Source	Date Signed	Seasons Played	Apps	Subs	Gls
Blackpool	Jnrs	08.60	62	5	-	0
Stockport Co.	Tr	07.63	63-64	55	-	3
Southport	Tr	03.65	64-65	17	1	2

WATT, John G.
Airdrie, 23 November, 1954 (FB)

League Club	Source	Date Signed	Seasons Played	Apps	Subs	Gls
Watford	App	11.72	71	0	1	0

WATT, William D.
Aberdeen, 6 June, 1946 (OL)

League Club	Source	Date Signed	Seasons Played	Apps	Subs	Gls
Preston N.E.	Jnrs	06.63	62-65	7	1	0

WATTERS, John
Glasgow, 24 September, 1913 (OR)

League Club	Source	Date Signed	Seasons Played	Apps	Subs	Gls
New Brighton	Ayr U.	07.36	36	19	-	2
Stockport Co.	Cowdenbeath	08.47	47	5	-	1

WATTON, James
Wolverhampton, 1 November, 1936 (LB)

League Club	Source	Date Signed	Seasons Played	Apps	Subs	Gls
Port Vale	De Graafschap (Neth)	09.62	62	5	-	0
Doncaster Rov.	Tr	07.64	64-67	121	3	0

WATTS, Derek
Leicester, 30 June, 1952 (F)

League Club	Source	Date Signed	Seasons Played	Apps	Subs	Gls
Leicester C.	App	05.70				
Northampton T.	L	10.73	73	0	1	0

WATTS, James A.
Cowes (IOW), 25 October, 1933 (CF)

League Club	Source	Date Signed	Seasons Played	Apps	Subs	Gls
Gillingham (Am)		12.56	56	12	-	1

WATTS, John W.
Birmingham, 13 April, 1931 (WH)

League Club	Source	Date Signed	Seasons Played	Apps	Subs	Gls
Birmingham C.	Saltley O.B.	08.51	51-62	206	-	3

WATTS, Julian D.
Sheffield, 17 March, 1971 (CD)

League Club	Source	Date Signed	Seasons Played	Apps	Subs	Gls
Rotherham U.	Frecheville C.A.	07.90	90-91	17	3	1
Sheffield Wed.	Tr	03.92				

WATTS, Mark R.
Hatfield, 24 September, 1965 (F)

League Club	Source	Date Signed	Seasons Played	Apps	Subs	Gls
Luton T.	App	01.83	82	1	0	0

WAUGH, Keith
Sunderland, 27 October, 1956 (G)

League Club	Source	Date Signed	Seasons Played	Apps	Subs	Gls
Sunderland	App	07.74				
Peterborough U.	Tr	07.76	76-80	195	0	0
Sheffield U.	Tr	08.81	81-84	99	0	0
Cambridge U.	L	11.84	84	4	0	0
Bristol C.	L	12.84	84	3	0	0
Bristol C.	Tr	07.85	85-88	167	0	0
Coventry C.	Tr	08.89	89	1	0	0
Watford	Tr	01.91	91	3	0	0

WAUGH, Kenneth
Newcastle, 6 August, 1933 (FB)

League Club	Source	Date Signed	Seasons Played	Apps	Subs	Gls
Newcastle U.	Film Renters	08.52	55	7	-	0
Hartlepool U.	Tr	12.56	56-61	194	-	0

WAUGH, William L.
Edinburgh, 27 November, 1921 (OL)

League Club	Source	Date Signed	Seasons Played	Apps	Subs	Gls
Luton T.	Bathgate Th.	09.44	46-49	135	-	9
Queens Park R.	Tr	07.50	50-52	76	-	6
Bournemouth	Tr	07.53	53	18	-	3

WAY, Michael A.
Salisbury, 18 May, 1950 (FB)

League Club	Source	Date Signed	Seasons Played	Apps	Subs	Gls
Oxford U.	Thame U.	08.69	69-71	14	2	0

WAYMAN, Charles
Bishop Auckland, 16 May, 1922 (CF)

League Club	Source	Date Signed	Seasons Played	Apps	Subs	Gls
Newcastle U.	Spennymoor U.	09.41	46-47	47	-	32
Southampton	Tr	10.47	47-49	100	-	73
Preston N.E.	Tr	09.50	50-54	157	-	104
Middlesbrough	Tr	09.54	54-55	55	-	31
Darlington	Tr	12.56	56-57	23	-	14

WAYMAN, Frank
Bishop Auckland, 30 December, 1931 (OR)

League Club	Source	Date Signed	Seasons Played	Apps	Subs	Gls
Preston N.E.		09.53				
Chester C.	Tr	08.55	55	30	-	2
Darlington	Easington Colly	06.57	57	1	-	0

League Club	Source	Date Signed	Seasons Played	Apps	Subs	Gls
WEAKLEY, Bernard						
Rotherham, 20 December, 1932						
Rotherham U.		08.55	55	2	-	1
WEALANDS, Jeffrey A.						
Darlington, 26 August, 1951						(G)
Wolverhampton W.	App	10.68				
Darlington	Tr	07.70	71	28	0	0
Hull C.	Tr	03.72	71-78	240	0	0
Birmingham C.	Tr	07.79	79-81	102	0	0
Manchester U.	Tr	02.83	82-83	7	0	0
Oldham Ath.	L	03.84	84	10	0	0
Preston N.E.	L	12.84	84	4	0	0
WEALTHALL, Barry A.						
Nottingham, 1 May, 1942						(FB)
Nottingham F.	Jnrs	06.59	60	2	-	0
Grimsby T.	Tr	05.62	61-62	9	-	0
York C.	Tr	06.63	63-66	75	0	0
WEARE, A. John (Jack)						
Newport, 21 September, 1912						(G)
Wolverhampton W.	Lovells Ath.	05.33	33-36	42	-	0
West Ham U.	Tr	09.36	36-37	58	-	0
Bristol Rov.		11.45	46-49	141	-	0
WEARE, Leonard						
Newport, 23 July, 1934						(G)
Newport Co.		08.55	55-69	526	0	0
WEARMOUTH, Michael						
Barrow, 16 May, 1944						(CH)
Barrow	Jnrs	06.62	61-63	33	-	0
Preston N.E.	Tr	03.64	64-66	11	0	0
WEATHERALL, Leonard						
Middlesbrough, 21 May, 1936						(CF)
Grimsby T.	Redcar B.C.	04.55	54-55	10	-	1
WEATHERHEAD, Shaun						
Halifax, 3 September, 1970						(CD)
Huddersfield T.	YT	07.89				
York C.	Tr	09.90	90	6	2	0
WEATHERLY, C. Mark						
Ramsgate, 18 January, 1958						(CD)
Gillingham	App	12.75	74-88	408	49	47
WEATHERSPOON, Charles						
Newcastle, 3 October, 1929						(F)
Sunderland	Jnrs	08.47				
Sheffield U.	Annfield Plain	01.51	50	1	-	0
Hartlepool U.	Tr	08.52	52	3	-	2
WEAVER, Eric						
Rhymney, 1 July, 1943						(W)
Swindon T.	Trowbridge T.	12.61	61-66	55	0	6
Notts Co.	Tr	08.67	67	16	1	4
Northampton T.	Tr	12.67	67-69	61	3	9
WEAVER, John N.						
Wrexham, 26 November, 1924						
Wrexham	Jnrs	05.46	46	2	-	0
WEAVER, Samuel						
Pilsley (Dy), 8 February, 1909	*EF Lge/E-3*					(WH)
Hull C.	Sutton T.	03.28	28-29	48	-	5
Newcastle U.	Tr	11.29	29-35	204	-	41
Chelsea	Tr	08.36	36-38	116	-	4
Stockport Co.	Tr	12.45	46	2	-	0
WEBB, Alan R.						
Telford, 1 January, 1963						(D)
West Bromwich A.	App	01.80	81-83	23	1	0
Lincoln C.	L	03.84	83	11	0	0
Port Vale	Tr	08.84	84-91	187	3	2
WEBB, David J.						
Stratford, 9 April, 1946						(D)
Leyton Orient	West Ham U. (Am)	05.63	64-65	62	0	3
Southampton	Tr	03.66	65-67	75	0	2
Chelsea	Tr	02.68	67-73	230	0	21
Queens Park R.	Tr	07.74	74-77	116	0	7
Leicester C.	Tr	09.77	77-78	32	1	0
Derby Co.	Tr	12.78	78-79	25	1	1
Bournemouth	Tr	05.80	80-82	11	0	0
Torquay U. (N/C)	(Manager)	10.84	84	2	0	1

League Club	Source	Date Signed	Seasons Played	Apps	Subs	Gls
WEBB, Douglas J.						
Stokechurch, 10 March, 1939						(IF)
Reading		11.56	56-66	177	2	81
WEBB, James K.						
Warrington, 6 July, 1938						(F)
Shrewsbury T.	Lymm R.	04.56	55-56	2	-	1
WEBB, John						
Liverpool, 10 February, 1952						(RB)
Liverpool	App	02.69				
Plymouth Arg.	L	09.73	73	4	0	0
Tranmere Rov.	Tr	07.74	74	17	3	0
WEBB, Neil J.						
Reading, 30 July, 1963	*E Yth/Eu21-3/E'B'/E-26*					(M)
Reading	App	11.80	79-81	65	7	22
Portsmouth	Tr	07.82	82-84	123	0	34
Nottingham F.	Tr	06.85	85-88	146	0	47
Manchester U.	Tr	06.89	89-91	70	4	8

Neil Webb (Reading, Portsmouth, Nottingham Forest, Manchester United & England)

League Club	Source	Date Signed	Seasons Played	Apps	Subs	Gls
WEBB, Robert						
Altofts, 29 November, 1933						(OR)
Leeds U.	Jnrs	04.51	53-54	3	-	0
Walsall	Tr	03.55	54	9	-	3
Bradford C.	Tr	07.55	55-61	208	-	59
Torquay U.	Tr	07.62	62-63	49	-	12
WEBB, Ronald C. T.						
Brentford, 13 March, 1925						(WH)
Queens Park R.		10.44				
Crystal Palace	Tr	09.46	46	3	-	0
WEBB, Stanley J.						
Middlesbrough, 6 December, 1947						(F)
Middlesbrough		07.67	67-70	20	8	6
Carlisle U.	Tr	02.71	70-72	16	10	5
Brentford	Tr	10.72	72-73	37	2	8
Darlington	Tr	07.74	74-75	69	5	21
WEBB, William						
Mexborough, 7 March, 1932						(FB)
Leicester C.	Wath W.	06.51	51-56	47	-	0
Stockport Co.	Tr	06.57	57-62	243	-	0
WEBBER, Andrew J.						
Port Talbot, 15 March, 1963						(F)
Swansea C. (N/C)		11.84	84	0	1	0
Exeter C. (N/C)		09.85	85	1	0	0
WEBBER, Eric N.						
Hove, 22 December, 1919						(CH)
Southampton	Jnrs	03.46	46-50	182	-	0
Torquay U.	Tr	10.51	51-54	149	-	2
WEBBER, George M.						
Abercynon, 28 June, 1925						(G)
Torquay U.	Cardiff C. (Am)	06.50	50-53	118	-	0
Northampton T.	Tr	06.54	54	13	-	0
WEBBER, John V.						
Blackpool, 2 June, 1920						(CF)
Blackburn Rov.	Hyde U.	02.47	46-47	8	-	1

WEBBER, Keith J.
Cardiff, 5 January, 1943 Died 1983 (CF)

League Club	Source	Date Signed	Seasons Played	Apps	Subs	Gls
Everton	Barry T.	02.60	60-61	4	-	0
Brighton & H.A.	Tr	04.63	62-64	35	-	14
Wrexham	Tr	09.64	64-65	73	0	33
Doncaster Rov.	Tr	07.66	66-68	63	4	18
Chester C.	Tr	06.69	69-70	66	6	13
Stockport Co.	Tr	07.71	71	36	4	7

WEBBER, Trevor
Bovey Tracey, 5 September, 1968 (W)

League Club	Source	Date Signed	Seasons Played	Apps	Subs	Gls
Torquay U. (YT)	YT	02.86	85	5	0	0

WEBSTER, Alan J.
Melton Mowbray, 3 July, 1948 (WH)

League Club	Source	Date Signed	Seasons Played	Apps	Subs	Gls
Scunthorpe U.		07.66	66-67	4	1	0

WEBSTER, Andrew
Colne, 18 March, 1947 (CF)

League Club	Source	Date Signed	Seasons Played	Apps	Subs	Gls
Bradford C.	Clitheroe	07.65	65-66	10	2	1

WEBSTER, J. Barry
Sheffield, 3 March, 1935 (OR)

League Club	Source	Date Signed	Seasons Played	Apps	Subs	Gls
Rotherham U.	Gainsborough Trin.	05.56	56-61	180	-	37
Bradford C.	Tr	06.62	62-63	53	-	9

WEBSTER, Colin
Halifax, 5 March, 1930

League Club	Source	Date Signed	Seasons Played	Apps	Subs	Gls
Halifax T.		09.50	50	16	-	1

WEBSTER, Colin
Cardiff, 17 July, 1932 W-4 (CF)

League Club	Source	Date Signed	Seasons Played	Apps	Subs	Gls
Cardiff C.	Jnrs	05.50				
Manchester U.	Tr	05.52	53-58	65	-	26
Swansea C.	Tr	09.58	58-62	159	-	65
Newport Co.	Tr	03.63	62-63	31	-	3

WEBSTER, Eric
Manchester, 24 June, 1931 (WH)

League Club	Source	Date Signed	Seasons Played	Apps	Subs	Gls
Manchester C.		02.52	52	1	-	0

WEBSTER, Harold
Sheffield, 22 August, 1930 (IF)

League Club	Source	Date Signed	Seasons Played	Apps	Subs	Gls
Bolton W.	Jnrs	10.48	49-56	98	-	38
Chester C.	Tr	06.58	58-59	34	-	11

WEBSTER, Ian A.
Askern, 30 December, 1965 (CD)

League Club	Source	Date Signed	Seasons Played	Apps	Subs	Gls
Scunthorpe U.	YT	07.83	82-85	15	3	0

WEBSTER, Keith
Newcastle, 6 November, 1945 (W)

League Club	Source	Date Signed	Seasons Played	Apps	Subs	Gls
Newcastle U.	Stockton	12.62				
Darlington	Tr	11.66	66	8	1	0

WEBSTER, Malcolm W.
Rossington, 12 November, 1950 E Sch/E Yth (G)

League Club	Source	Date Signed	Seasons Played	Apps	Subs	Gls
Arsenal	App	01.68	69	3	0	0
Fulham	Tr	12.69	69-73	94	0	0
Southend U.	Tr	01.74	73-75	96	0	0
Cambridge U.	Tr	09.76	76-83	256	0	0

WEBSTER, Richard
Accrington, 6 August, 1919 Died 1979 (FB)

League Club	Source	Date Signed	Seasons Played	Apps	Subs	Gls
Accrington St.	Woodnook	11.37	37-38	41	-	0
Sheffield U.	Tr	01.39				
Accrington St.	Tr	08.45	46-50	186	-	3

WEBSTER, Ronald
Belper, 21 June, 1943 (RB)

League Club	Source	Date Signed	Seasons Played	Apps	Subs	Gls
Derby Co.	Jnrs	06.60	61-77	451	4	7

WEBSTER, Simon P.
Hinckley, 20 January, 1964 (CD)

League Club	Source	Date Signed	Seasons Played	Apps	Subs	Gls
Tottenham H.	App	12.81	82-83	2	1	0
Exeter C.	L	11.83	83	26	0	0
Huddersfield T.	Tr	02.85	84-87	118	0	4
Sheffield U.	Tr	03.88	87-89	26	11	3
Charlton Ath.	Tr	08.90	90-91	84	0	5

WEBSTER, Terence
Retford, 27 September, 1941 (WH)

League Club	Source	Date Signed	Seasons Played	Apps	Subs	Gls
Sheffield U.	Jnrs	10.58				
Accrington St.	Tr	11.59				
Barrow	Tr	07.60	60	4	-	0

WEBSTER, Terence C.
Doncaster, 9 July, 1930 (G)

League Club	Source	Date Signed	Seasons Played	Apps	Subs	Gls
Doncaster Rov.	Jnrs	06.48				
Derby Co.	Tr	10.48	48-57	172	-	0

WEDDLE, Derek K.
Newcastle, 27 December, 1935 (F)

League Club	Source	Date Signed	Seasons Played	Apps	Subs	Gls
Sunderland	Jnrs	05.53	55-56	2	-	0
Portsmouth	Tr	12.56	56-58	24	-	8
Middlesbrough	Cambridge C.	08.61	61	3	-	1
Darlington	Tr	06.62	62-63	36	-	10
York C.	Tr	07.64	64-65	44	0	13

WEDDLE, George D.
Ashington, 24 February, 1919

League Club	Source	Date Signed	Seasons Played	Apps	Subs	Gls
Gateshead		06.46	46-48	48	-	10

WEEKS, Graham J.
Exeter, 3 March, 1958 (M)

League Club	Source	Date Signed	Seasons Played	Apps	Subs	Gls
Exeter C.	App	03.76	76-77	49	4	1
Bournemouth	Tr	05.78	78	3	0	0

WEETMAN, Darren G.
Oswestry, 7 June, 1968 (W)

League Club	Source	Date Signed	Seasons Played	Apps	Subs	Gls
Wrexham (N/C)	Jnrs	06.85	85	1	0	0

WEGERLE, Roy C.
Johannesburg (SA), 19 March, 1964 USA Int (F)

League Club	Source	Date Signed	Seasons Played	Apps	Subs	Gls
Chelsea	Tampa Bay (USA)	06.86	86-87	15	8	3
Swindon T.	L	03.88	87	7	0	1
Luton T.	Tr	07.88	88-89	39	6	10
Queens Park R.	Tr	12.89	89-91	71	4	29
Blackburn Rov.	Tr	03.92	91	9	3	2

Roy Wegerle (Chelsea, Luton Town, Queens Park Rangers, Blackburn Rovers & USA)

WEIGH, Raymond E.
Flint, 23 June, 1928 (OR)

League Club	Source	Date Signed	Seasons Played	Apps	Subs	Gls
Bournemouth	Shrewsbury T.	03.49	49-50	28	-	8
Stockport Co.	Tr	07.51	51-53	75	-	31
Shrewsbury T.	Tr	06.54	54-56	107	-	43
Aldershot	Tr	07.57	57	11	-	1

League Club	Source	Date Signed	Seasons Played	Apps	Subs	Gls

WEIR, Alan
South Shields, 1 September, 1959 E Yth (D)

League Club	Source	Date Signed	Seasons Played	Apps	Subs	Gls
Sunderland	App	05.77	77	1	0	0
Rochdale	Tr	06.79	79-82	96	10	3
Hartlepool U.	Tr	08.83	83	9	1	0

WEIR, Alexander
Longridge, 20 October, 1916 (IF)

League Club	Source	Date Signed	Seasons Played	Apps	Subs	Gls
Preston N.E.		02.36				
Watford		12.45	46	1	-	0
Northampton T.	Tr	09.47				

WEIR, James (Jock)
Glasgow, 12 April, 1939 (OL)

League Club	Source	Date Signed	Seasons Played	Apps	Subs	Gls
Fulham	Clydebank	07.57	57	3	-	0
York C.	Tr	06.60	60-62	82	-	38
Mansfield T.	Tr	09.62	62	18	-	3
Luton T.	Tr	08.63	63	12	-	1
Tranmere Rov.	Tr	07.64	64	13	-	3

WEIR, John B.
Fauldhouse, 20 October, 1923 (CF)

League Club	Source	Date Signed	Seasons Played	Apps	Subs	Gls
Blackburn Rov.	Hibernian	01.47	46-47	23	-	7

WEIR, Michael G.
Edinburgh, 16 January, 1966 (W)

League Club	Source	Date Signed	Seasons Played	Apps	Subs	Gls
Luton T.	Hibernian	09.87	87	7	1	0

WEIR, Peter R.
Johnstone, 18 January, 1958 S-6 (LW)

League Club	Source	Date Signed	Seasons Played	Apps	Subs	Gls
Leicester C.	Aberdeen	01.88	87-88	26	2	2

WEIR, William H.
Glasgow, 11 April, 1968 (W)

League Club	Source	Date Signed	Seasons Played	Apps	Subs	Gls
Shrewsbury T.	Baillieston Jnrs	03.90	89-90	4	13	1

WELBOURNE, Donald
Scunthorpe, 12 March, 1949 (WH)

League Club	Source	Date Signed	Seasons Played	Apps	Subs	Gls
Scunthorpe U.	App	03.67	66-75	250	7	5

WELBOURNE, Duncan
Scunthorpe, 28 July, 1940 (D)

League Club	Source	Date Signed	Seasons Played	Apps	Subs	Gls
Grimsby T.	Scunthorpe U. (Am)	08.57	57-63	130	-	3
Watford	Tr	11.63	63-73	404	7	22
Southport	Tr	07.74	74-75	52	1	2

WELCH, Keith J.
Bolton, 3 October, 1968 (G)

League Club	Source	Date Signed	Seasons Played	Apps	Subs	Gls
Rochdale	Bolton W. (YT)	03.87	86-90	205	0	0
Bristol C.	Tr	08.91	91	26	0	0

WELCH, Michael A.
Barbados (WI), 21 May, 1958 (F)

League Club	Source	Date Signed	Seasons Played	Apps	Subs	Gls
Wimbledon (N/C)	Grays Ath.	11.84	84	2	2	0
Southend U. (N/C)	Grays Ath.	02.85	84	4	0	0

WELCH, Ronald
Chesterfield, 26 September, 1952 (M)

League Club	Source	Date Signed	Seasons Played	Apps	Subs	Gls
Burnley	App	10.69	70	1	0	0
Brighton & H.A.	Tr	12.73	73-74	35	1	4
Chesterfield	Tr	11.74	74-76	17	7	1

WELFORD, William
Newcastle, 14 April, 1934

League Club	Source	Date Signed	Seasons Played	Apps	Subs	Gls
Hartlepool U.		11.58	58	8	-	0

WELLER, Christopher W.
Reading, 25 December, 1939 (IF)

League Club	Source	Date Signed	Seasons Played	Apps	Subs	Gls
Bournemouth	Reading (Am)	09.59	60-64	70	-	17
Bristol Rov.	Tr	07.65	65	2	1	0
Bournemouth	Tr	01.66	65-66	39	2	9

WELLER, Keith
Islington, 11 June, 1946 EF Lge/E-4 (M)

League Club	Source	Date Signed	Seasons Played	Apps	Subs	Gls
Tottenham H.	Jnrs	01.64	64-66	19	2	1
Millwall	Tr	06.67	67-69	121	0	40
Chelsea	Tr	05.70	70-71	34	4	14
Leicester C.	Tr	09.71	71-78	260	2	37

WELLINGS, Barry
Liverpool, 10 June, 1958 (F)

League Club	Source	Date Signed	Seasons Played	Apps	Subs	Gls
Everton	App	06.76				
York C.	Tr	06.78	78-79	40	7	9
Rochdale	Tr	07.80	80-82	111	5	30
Tranmere Rov.	Tr	02.83	82	16	0	3
Tranmere Rov. (N/C)	Northwich Vic.	12.83	83	9	0	0
Swansea C. (N/C)		09.84	84	6	0	3

WELLS, Archibald
Clydebank, 4 October, 1920 (IF)

League Club	Source	Date Signed	Seasons Played	Apps	Subs	Gls
New Brighton	Hibernian	07.46	46-48	37	-	4

WELLS, W. David
Eccleston (Lancs), 16 December, 1940 (FB)

League Club	Source	Date Signed	Seasons Played	Apps	Subs	Gls
Blackburn Rov.	Jnrs	05.58				
Rochdale	Tr	07.63	63	8	-	0

WELLS, Ian M.
Wolverhampton, 27 October, 1964 (F)

League Club	Source	Date Signed	Seasons Played	Apps	Subs	Gls
Hereford U.	Harrisons	06.85	85-86	47	4	12

WELLS, Mark A.
Leicester, 15 October, 1971 (LW)

League Club	Source	Date Signed	Seasons Played	Apps	Subs	Gls
Notts Co.	YT	07.90	91	0	1	0

WELLS, Peter A.
Nottingham, 13 August, 1956 (G)

League Club	Source	Date Signed	Seasons Played	Apps	Subs	Gls
Nottingham F.	App	10.74	75-76	27	0	0
Southampton	Tr	12.76	76-82	141	0	0
Millwall	Tr	02.83	82-83	33	0	0
Leyton Orient	Tr	07.85	85-88	148	0	0

WELSH, Alan
Edinburgh, 9 July, 1947 (M)

League Club	Source	Date Signed	Seasons Played	Apps	Subs	Gls
Millwall	Bonnyrigg Rose	07.65	65-67	3	2	0
Torquay U.	Tr	11.67	67-71	140	8	45
Plymouth Arg.	Tr	07.72	72-73	64	2	14
Bournemouth	Tr	02.74	73-74	33	2	3
Millwall	Tr	08.75	75	5	4	1

WELSH, Andrew J.
Fleetwood, 20 November, 1962 (F)

League Club	Source	Date Signed	Seasons Played	Apps	Subs	Gls
Blackpool	App	08.80	80	1	0	0
Bury (N/C)		07.84	85	0	1	0

WELSH, Colin
Liverpool, 9 June, 1945 (OR)

League Club	Source	Date Signed	Seasons Played	Apps	Subs	Gls
Southport		10.63	64	1	-	0

WELSH, Donald
Manchester, 25 February, 1911 Died 1990 EF Lge/E-3 (IF)

League Club	Source	Date Signed	Seasons Played	Apps	Subs	Gls
Torquay U.	R.N. Devonport	07.34	32-34	80	-	4
Charlton Ath.	Tr	02.35	34-47	199	-	44

WELSH, Eric
Belfast, 1 May, 1942 NIu23-1/NI-4 (OR)

League Club	Source	Date Signed	Seasons Played	Apps	Subs	Gls
Exeter C.	Distillery	09.59	59-65	105	0	19
Carlisle U.	Tr	10.65	65-68	73	2	17
Torquay U.	Tr	06.69	69-70	38	2	12
Hartlepool U.	Tr	07.71	71	13	2	2

WELSH, James P.
Edinburgh, 21 December, 1923

League Club	Source	Date Signed	Seasons Played	Apps	Subs	Gls
Luton T.	Tranent Jnrs	09.46				
Aldershot	Tr	06.48	49	5	-	0

WELSH, Paul W.
Liverpool, 10 May, 1966 E Sch (CD)

League Club	Source	Date Signed	Seasons Played	Apps	Subs	Gls
Preston N.E.	Formby	05.84	84-85	13	7	1

WELSH, Peter M.
Coatbridge, 19 July, 1959 (D)

League Club	Source	Date Signed	Seasons Played	Apps	Subs	Gls
Leicester C.	App	08.76	76-81	24	17	4

WELSH, Stephen G.
Glasgow, 19 April, 1968 (D)

League Club	Source	Date Signed	Seasons Played	Apps	Subs	Gls
Cambridge U.	Wimborne T.	02.90	90	0	1	0
Peterborough U.	Tr	08.91	91	42	0	0

WELTON, R. Patrick
Eltham, 3 May, 1928 (G)

League Club	Source	Date Signed	Seasons Played	Apps	Subs	Gls
Leyton Orient	Chislehurst	05.49	49-57	263	-	0
Queens Park R.	Tr	03.58	58	3	-	0

WENT, Paul F.
Bromley-by-Bow, 12 October, 1949 E Sch/E Yth (CD)

League Club	Source	Date Signed	Seasons Played	Apps	Subs	Gls
Leyton Orient	App	10.66	65-66	48	2	5
Charlton Ath.	Tr	06.67	67-71	160	3	15
Fulham	Tr	07.72	72-73	58	0	3
Portsmouth	Tr	12.73	73-76	92	0	5
Cardiff C.	Tr	10.76	76-78	71	1	11
Leyton Orient	Tr	09.78	78-79	45	0	3

WERGE, Edward
Sidcup, 9 September, 1936 (W)

League Club	Source	Date Signed	Seasons Played	Apps	Subs	Gls
Charlton Ath.	Jnrs	05.55	57-60	44	-	19
Crystal Palace	Tr	05.61	61-64	82	-	6
Leyton Orient	Arcadia (SA)	11.66	66-67	30	3	0

WESSON, Robert W.
Thornaby, 15 October, 1940 (G)

League Club	Source	Date Signed	Seasons Played	Apps	Subs	Gls
Coventry C.	Thornaby B.B.	11.58	60-65	133	0	0
Walsall	Tr	09.66	66-72	191	0	0
Doncaster Rov.	L	02.70	69	5	0	0

WEST, Alan
Hyde, 18 December, 1951 Eu23-1 (M)

League Club	Source	Date Signed	Seasons Played	Apps	Subs	Gls
Burnley	App	12.68	69-72	41	4	3
Luton T.	Tr	10.73	73-80	272	13	16
Millwall	Tr	07.81	81-82	57	0	4

WEST, Colin
Wallsend, 13 November, 1962 (F)

League Club	Source	Date Signed	Seasons Played	Apps	Subs	Gls
Sunderland	App	07.80	81-84	88	14	21
Watford	Tr	03.85	84-85	45	0	20
Sheffield Wed.	Glasgow Rangers	09.87	87-88	40	5	8
West Bromwich A.	Tr	02.89	88-91	64	9	22
Port Vale	L	11.91	91	5	0	1

WEST, Colin W.
Middlesbrough, 19 September, 1967 E Yth (F)

League Club	Source	Date Signed	Seasons Played	Apps	Subs	Gls
Chelsea	App	09.85	86-87	8	8	4
Swansea C.	L	03.89	88	14	0	3

WEST, David C.
Dorchester, 16 November, 1964 (W)

League Club	Source	Date Signed	Seasons Played	Apps	Subs	Gls
Liverpool	Dorchester T.	03.83				
Torquay U.	Bristol C. (trial)	09.85	85	19	2	2

WEST, Dean
Morley, 5 December, 1972 (M)

League Club	Source	Date Signed	Seasons Played	Apps	Subs	Gls
Lincoln C.	YT	07.91	90-91	20	13	4

WEST, Edward
Parbold (Lancs), 4 November, 1930 (FB)

League Club	Source	Date Signed	Seasons Played	Apps	Subs	Gls
Doncaster Rov.	Eastbourne U.	02.53				
Gillingham	Tr	07.54	54-56	98	-	0
Oldham Ath.	Tr	07.57	57-60	117	-	0

WEST, Gary
Scunthorpe, 25 August, 1964 E Yth (CD)

League Club	Source	Date Signed	Seasons Played	Apps	Subs	Gls
Sheffield U.	App	08.82	82-84	75	0	1
Lincoln C.	Tr	08.85	85-86	83	0	4
Gillingham	Tr	07.87	87-88	51	1	3
Port Vale	Tr	02.89	88-89	14	3	1
Gillingham	L	11.90	90	1	0	0
Lincoln C.	L	01.91	90	3	0	0
Lincoln C.	Tr	08.91	91	14	4	1

WEST, Gordon
Barnsley, 24 April, 1943 Eu23-3/E-3 (G)

League Club	Source	Date Signed	Seasons Played	Apps	Subs	Gls
Blackpool	Jnrs	05.61	60-61	31	-	0
Everton	Tr	03.62	61-72	335	0	0
Tranmere Rov.	Tr	10.75	76-78	17	0	0

WEST, Thomas
Salford, 8 December, 1916 (F)

League Club	Source	Date Signed	Seasons Played	Apps	Subs	Gls
Stockport Co.		03.38	37-38	3	-	0
Oldham Ath.		10.45				
Rochdale	Tr	06.46	46	4	-	2

WEST, Trefor J.
Coventry, 14 December, 1944 (FB)

League Club	Source	Date Signed	Seasons Played	Apps	Subs	Gls
West Bromwich A.	App	05.62				
Walsall	Tr	05.64	64	12	-	0

WESTAWAY, Kevin D.
Bristol, 24 November, 1962 (FB)

League Club	Source	Date Signed	Seasons Played	Apps	Subs	Gls
Bristol Rov.	App	11.80	80-81	2	0	0

WESTBY, John L. (Jack)
Aintree, 20 May, 1916 (FB)

League Club	Source	Date Signed	Seasons Played	Apps	Subs	Gls
Liverpool		05.44				
Southport	Tr	08.47	47	13	-	0

WESTCOTT, Dennis
Wallasey, 2 July, 1917 Died 1960 EF Lge (CF)

League Club	Source	Date Signed	Seasons Played	Apps	Subs	Gls
New Brighton	Leasowe R.B.	01.36	35	18	-	10
Wolverhampton W.	Tr	07.36	36-47	128	-	105
Blackburn Rov.	Tr	04.48	48-49	63	-	37
Manchester C.	Tr	02.50	49-51	72	-	37
Chesterfield	Tr	06.52	52	40	-	21

WESTLAKE, Brian
Newcastle-u-Lyme, 19 September, 1943 (CF)

League Club	Source	Date Signed	Seasons Played	Apps	Subs	Gls
Stoke C.		09.61				
Doncaster Rov.	Tr	06.63	63	5	-	1
Halifax T.	Tr	01.64	63-66	100	0	27
Tranmere Rov.	Tr	09.66	66	13	1	3
Colchester U.	Tr	02.67	66	14	1	5

WESTLAKE, Francis A.
Bolton-on-Dearne, 11 August, 1915 (FB)

League Club	Source	Date Signed	Seasons Played	Apps	Subs	Gls
Sheffield Wed.	Thurnscoe Vic.	05.37	37-49	110	-	0
Halifax T.	Tr	06.50	50	2	-	0

WESTLAND, James
Aberdeen, 21 July, 1916 Died 1972 (IL)

League Club	Source	Date Signed	Seasons Played	Apps	Subs	Gls
Stoke C.	Aberdeen	09.35	35-38	60	-	16
Mansfield T.	Tr	11.46	46	10	-	0

WESTLEY, Graham N.
Hounslow, 4 March, 1968 E Yth (F)

League Club	Source	Date Signed	Seasons Played	Apps	Subs	Gls
Gillingham	Queens Park R. (App)	03.86	85-86	1	1	0

WESTLEY, Shane L. M.
Canterbury, 16 June, 1965 (CD)

League Club	Source	Date Signed	Seasons Played	Apps	Subs	Gls
Charlton Ath.	App	06.83	83	8	0	0
Southend U.	Tr	03.85	84-88	142	2	10
Wolverhampton W.	Tr	06.89	89-90	42	0	1

WESTMORLAND, Joseph E.
Carlisle, 30 June, 1937 (FB)

League Club	Source	Date Signed	Seasons Played	Apps	Subs	Gls
Carlisle U.		02.59	58	3	-	0

WESTON, Anthony D.
Yalding (Kt), 3 April, 1945 (FB)

League Club	Source	Date Signed	Seasons Played	Apps	Subs	Gls
Gillingham	Bromley	11.63	64-69	162	0	3

WESTON, Donald P.
Mansfield, 6 March, 1936 (IF)

League Club	Source	Date Signed	Seasons Played	Apps	Subs	Gls
Wrexham	Army	06.59	58-59	42	-	21
Birmingham C.	Tr	01.60	59-60	23	-	3
Rotherham U.	Tr	12.60	60-62	76	-	21
Leeds U.	Tr	12.62	62-65	68	0	24
Huddersfield T.	Tr	10.65	65-66	20	2	7
Wrexham	Tr	12.66	66-67	42	0	19
Chester C.	Tr	06.68	68	1	2	0

Gordon West (Blackpool, Everton, Tranmere Rovers & England)

WESTON, Ian P.
Bristol, 6 May, 1968 (M)

League Club	Source	Date Signed	Seasons Played	Apps	Subs	Gls
Bristol Rov.	App	05.86	86-87	13	3	0
Torquay U.	Tr	09.88	88-89	57	5	2

WESTON, James J.
Whiston, 16 September, 1955 (M)

League Club	Source	Date Signed	Seasons Played	Apps	Subs	Gls
Blackpool	Skelmersdale U.	01.74	75-79	97	8	8
Torquay U.	Tr	06.80	80-81	38	0	1
Wigan Ath.	Tr	09.81	81-82	63	3	2

WESTON, Reginald H.
Greenhithe, 16 January, 1918 (CH)

League Club	Source	Date Signed	Seasons Played	Apps	Subs	Gls
Swansea C.	Northfleet	03.45	46-51	227	-	1

WESTWELL, Simon
Clitheroe, 12 November, 1961 (FB)

League Club	Source	Date Signed	Seasons Played	Apps	Subs	Gls
Preston N.E.	App	10.79	80-82	63	0	1

WESTWOOD, Daniel
Dagenham, 25 July, 1953 (F)

League Club	Source	Date Signed	Seasons Played	Apps	Subs	Gls
Queens Park R.	Billericay T.	07.74	74	0	1	1
Gillingham	Tr	11.75	75-81	201	10	74

WESTWOOD, Eric
Manchester, 25 September, 1917 EF Lge/E-2 (LB)

League Club	Source	Date Signed	Seasons Played	Apps	Subs	Gls
Manchester C.	Manchester U. (Am)	11.37	37-52	248	-	3

WESTWOOD, Gary M.
Barrow, 3 April, 1964 E Yth (G)

League Club	Source	Date Signed	Seasons Played	Apps	Subs	Gls
Ipswich T.	App	04.81				
Reading	L	09.83	83	5	0	0
Reading	Tr	07.84	84-87	123	0	0

WESTWOOD, Raymond W.
Brierley Hill, 14 April, 1912 Died 1982 EF Lge/E-6 (IF)

League Club	Source	Date Signed	Seasons Played	Apps	Subs	Gls
Bolton W.	Brierley Hill Alliance	03.30	30-47	301	-	127
Chester C.	Tr	12.47	47-48	39	-	13

WETHERALL, David
Sheffield, 14 March, 1971 E Sch (CD)

League Club	Source	Date Signed	Seasons Played	Apps	Subs	Gls
Sheffield Wed.	YT	07.89				
Leeds U.	Tr	07.91	91	0	1	0

WETTON, Albert S.
Winlaton, 23 October, 1928 (CF)

League Club	Source	Date Signed	Seasons Played	Apps	Subs	Gls
Tottenham H.	Cheshunt	10.49				
Brighton & H.A.	Tr	06.51	51-52	3	-	0
Crewe Alex.	Tr	10.53	53	2	-	0

WETTON, Ralph
Winlaton, 6 June, 1927 (WH)

League Club	Source	Date Signed	Seasons Played	Apps	Subs	Gls
Tottenham H.	Cheshunt	08.50	51-54	45	-	0
Plymouth Arg.	Tr	06.55	55	36	-	1
Aldershot	Tr	11.56	56-57	49	-	1

WHALE, Raymond
West Bromwich, 23 February, 1937 (FB)

League Club	Source	Date Signed	Seasons Played	Apps	Subs	Gls
West Bromwich A.	West Bromwich C.A.	12.54				
Southend U.	Tr	04.59	59-60	29	-	0

WHALEY, George D.
Darlington, 30 July, 1920 (CF)

League Club	Source	Date Signed	Seasons Played	Apps	Subs	Gls
Gateshead	Hearts	09.46	46	6	-	0

WHALEY, Kenneth
Leeds, 22 June, 1935 (HB)

League Club	Source	Date Signed	Seasons Played	Apps	Subs	Gls
Bradford P.A.		06.57	58	1	-	0

WHALLEY, Harold
Nelson, 4 April, 1923 (OL)

League Club	Source	Date Signed	Seasons Played	Apps	Subs	Gls
Accrington St.	Barnoldswick T.	12.46	46	3	-	0

WHALLEY, Herbert
Ashton-u-Lyne, 6 August, 1912 Died 1958 (LH)

League Club	Source	Date Signed	Seasons Played	Apps	Subs	Gls
Manchester U.	Stalybridge Celtic	05.34	35-46	32	-	6

WHALLEY, Jeffrey H.
Rossendale, 8 February, 1952 (W)

League Club	Source	Date Signed	Seasons Played	Apps	Subs	Gls
Blackburn Rov.	App	02.70	69-70	2	0	0

WHALLEY, Selwyn D.
Stoke, 24 February, 1934 (FB)

League Club	Source	Date Signed	Seasons Played	Apps	Subs	Gls
Port Vale		08.53	56-65	178	0	22

WHARE, William
Guernsey, 14 May, 1924 (RB)

League Club	Source	Date Signed	Seasons Played	Apps	Subs	Gls
Nottingham F.		05.47	48-59	298	-	2

WHARTON, Andrew
Burnley, 21 December, 1961 (M)

League Club	Source	Date Signed	Seasons Played	Apps	Subs	Gls
Burnley	App	12.79	80-83	63	2	6
Torquay U.	L	11.83	83	10	0	0
Chester C.	Tr	02.84	83-84	19	4	2

WHARTON, Guy
Broomfield, 5 December, 1916 (WH)

League Club	Source	Date Signed	Seasons Played	Apps	Subs	Gls
Chester C.		05.34	35	12	-	5
Wolverhampton W.	Tr	05.36	36-37	29	-	2
Portsmouth	Tr	11.37	37-47	91	-	4
Darlington	Tr	07.48	48-49	39	-	2

WHARTON, John E. (Jackie)
Bolton, 18 June, 1920 (W)

League Club	Source	Date Signed	Seasons Played	Apps	Subs	Gls
Plymouth Arg.		06.37	38	11	-	2
Preston N.E.	Tr	07.39	46	25	-	7
Manchester C.	Tr	03.47	46-47	23	-	2
Blackburn Rov.	Tr	06.48	48-52	129	-	14
Newport Co.	Tr	02.53	52-54	74	-	10

WHARTON, Kenneth
Newcastle, 28 November, 1960 (LB/M)

League Club	Source	Date Signed	Seasons Played	Apps	Subs	Gls
Newcastle U.	Grainger Park B.C.	01.79	78-88	268	22	26
Carlisle U. (N/C)	Tr	08.89	89	1	0	0
Bradford C. (N/C)	Tr	08.89	89	5	0	0

WHARTON, Sean R.
Newport, 31 October, 1968 (F)

League Club	Source	Date Signed	Seasons Played	Apps	Subs	Gls
Sunderland	YT	07.87	88	1	0	0

WHARTON, Terence J.
Bolton, 1 July, 1942 (OR)

League Club	Source	Date Signed	Seasons Played	Apps	Subs	Gls
Wolverhampton W.	Jnrs	10.59	61-67	223	1	69
Bolton W.	Tr	11.67	67-70	101	1	28
Crystal Palace	Tr	01.71	70-71	19	1	1
Walsall	Durban C. (SA)	11.73	73	1	0	0

WHATLING, Keith R.
Worlingworth (Sk), 1 November, 1947 (OL)

League Club	Source	Date Signed	Seasons Played	Apps	Subs	Gls
Ipswich T.	Jnrs	03.66				
Exeter C.	Tr	07.67	67-68	19	3	3

WHATMORE, Neil
Ellesmere Port, 17 May, 1955 (F)

League Club	Source	Date Signed	Seasons Played	Apps	Subs	Gls
Bolton W.	App	05.73	72-80	262	15	102
Birmingham C.	Tr	08.81	81-82	24	2	6
Bolton W.	L	12.82	82	10	0	3
Oxford U.	Tr	02.83	82-83	33	3	15
Bolton W.	L	03.84	83	7	0	2
Burnley	Tr	08.84	84	8	0	1
Mansfield T.	Tr	11.84	84-86	71	1	20
Bolton W.	Tr	08.87				
Mansfield T. (N/C)	Tr	11.87	87	0	4	0

WHEAT, Arthur B.
Nottingham, 26 October, 1921 (IF)

League Club	Source	Date Signed	Seasons Played	Apps	Subs	Gls
Bradford P.A.	Montrose	12.49	50-51	22	-	3
York C.	Tr	08.52	52	4	-	0

WHEATLEY, Barry
Sandbach, 21 February, 1938 (IF)

League Club	Source	Date Signed	Seasons Played	Apps	Subs	Gls
Liverpool		03.56				
Crewe Alex.	Tr	07.57	57-65	242	0	49
Rochdale	Tr	07.66	66	13	0	4

WHEATLEY, H. Joseph
Eastham, 9 May, 1920

League Club	Source	Date Signed	Seasons Played	Apps	Subs	Gls
Port Vale		03.38	38	2	-	0
Shrewsbury T.	Tr	(N/L)	50	7	-	0

WHEATLEY, Roland
Nottingham, 20 June, 1924 (WH)

League Club	Source	Date Signed	Seasons Played	Apps	Subs	Gls
Nottingham F.	Beeston B.C.	06.46	47-48	6	-	0
Southampton	Tr	01.49	48-50	10	-	1
Grimsby T.	Tr	06.51	51	5	-	0

WHEATLEY, Stephen J.
Bishop Auckland, 12 April, 1959 (G)

League Club	Source	Date Signed	Seasons Played	Apps	Subs	Gls
Gillingham	App	04.77	76-77	4	0	0

WHEATLEY, Stephen P.
Hinckley, 26 December, 1929 (OR)

League Club	Source	Date Signed	Seasons Played	Apps	Subs	Gls
Derby Co.	Hinckley Ath.	12.50	51-52	4	-	0
Chesterfield	Boston U.	07.55	55	3	-	0

WHEATLEY, Thomas
Hebburn, 1 June, 1929 (G)

League Club	Source	Date Signed	Seasons Played	Apps	Subs	Gls
Leeds U.	Amble	04.53	53	6	-	0

WHEATLEY, William
Mansfield, 5 November, 1920 (OR)

League Club	Source	Date Signed	Seasons Played	Apps	Subs	Gls
Mansfield T.	Mansfield Colly	08.48	48-49	38	-	3

WHEATON, Gilbert J.
Newcastle, 1 November, 1941 (CH)

League Club	Source	Date Signed	Seasons Played	Apps	Subs	Gls
Grimsby T.	Mickley Colly	09.60	62	7	-	0
Chester C.	Tr	06.63	63	1	-	0

WHEELDON, Thomas E.
Prescot, 28 December, 1957 (W)

League Club	Source	Date Signed	Seasons Played	Apps	Subs	Gls
Torquay U. (N/C)	Runcorn	09.81	81	5	3	0
Torquay U. (N/C)	Falmouth	08.85	85	6	2	0

WHEELER, Alfred J.
Fareham, 6 April, 1922 (OR)

League Club	Source	Date Signed	Seasons Played	Apps	Subs	Gls
Blackburn Rov.	Portsmouth (Am)	04.47	47-48	21	-	5
Swindon T.	Tr	07.49	49-50	23	-	4

WHEELER, James
Reading, 21 December, 1933 (IF)

League Club	Source	Date Signed	Seasons Played	Apps	Subs	Gls
Reading		08.52	52-66	404	1	144

WHEELER, John E.
Liverpool, 26 July, 1928 EF Lge/E'B'-5/E-1 (WH)

League Club	Source	Date Signed	Seasons Played	Apps	Subs	Gls
Tranmere Rov.	Carlton	04.46	48-50	101	-	9
Bolton W.	Tr	02.51	50-55	189	-	18
Liverpool	Tr	09.56	56-61	164	-	21

WHEELER, W. John (Jack)
Evesham, 13 July, 1919 (G)

League Club	Source	Date Signed	Seasons Played	Apps	Subs	Gls
Birmingham C.	Cheltenham T.	03.38	38-47	12	-	0
Huddersfield T.	Tr	08.48	48-55	166	-	0

WHEELER, Paul
Caerphilly, 3 January, 1965 (F)

League Club	Source	Date Signed	Seasons Played	Apps	Subs	Gls
Bristol Rov.	App	01.83				
Cardiff C.	Aberaman	08.85	85-88	72	29	10
Hull C. (N/C)	Tr	10.89	89	0	5	0
Hereford U.	Tr	02.90	89-90	34	20	12
Stockport Co.	Tr	08.91	91	13	9	5

WHEELER, William H.
Carlisle, 27 September, 1920 (WH)

League Club	Source	Date Signed	Seasons Played	Apps	Subs	Gls
Carlisle U.		10.46	46	4	-	0

WHELAN, Anthony G.
Dublin, 23 November, 1959 IRu21-1 (FB)

League Club	Source	Date Signed	Seasons Played	Apps	Subs	Gls
Manchester U.	Bohemians	08.80	80	0	1	0

WHELAN, Anthony M.
Salford, 20 November, 1952 (F)

League Club	Source	Date Signed	Seasons Played	Apps	Subs	Gls
Manchester U.	App	12.69				
Manchester C.	Tr	03.73	72-73	3	3	0
Rochdale	Tr	07.74	74-76	124	0	20

WHELAN, David
Bradford, 24 November, 1936 (FB)

League Club	Source	Date Signed	Seasons Played	Apps	Subs	Gls
Blackburn Rov.	Wigan B.C.	12.53	56-59	78	-	3
Crewe Alex.	Tr	01.63	62-65	115	0	0

WHELAN, Philip J.
Stockport, 7 March, 1972 (CD)

League Club	Source	Date Signed	Seasons Played	Apps	Subs	Gls
Ipswich T.	Jnrs	07.90	91	8	0	2

WHELAN, Robert
Salford, 9 November, 1930 (RH)

League Club	Source	Date Signed	Seasons Played	Apps	Subs	Gls
Manchester C.	Salford Y.C.	04.50				
Oldham Ath.	Tr	07.52	52	1	-	0

WHELAN, Ronald A.
Dublin, 25 September, 1961 IRu21-1/IR-42 (M)

League Club	Source	Date Signed	Seasons Played	Apps	Subs	Gls
Liverpool	Home Farm	10.79	80-91	311	11	44

WHELAN, Spencer R. C.
Liverpool, 17 September, 1971 (FB)

League Club	Source	Date Signed	Seasons Played	Apps	Subs	Gls
Chester C.	Liverpool (YT)	04.90	90-91	39	4	0

WHELAN, William A.
Dublin, 1 April, 1935 Died 1958 IR-4 (IF)

League Club	Source	Date Signed	Seasons Played	Apps	Subs	Gls
Manchester U.	Home Farm	05.53	54-57	79	-	43

WHELLANS, Robert
Harrogate, 14 February, 1969 (F)

League Club	Source	Date Signed	Seasons Played	Apps	Subs	Gls
Bradford C.	YT	06.87				
Hartlepool U.	L	12.87	87	8	3	1
Rochdale	Tr	07.89	89	5	6	1

WHENT, John R.
Darlington, 3 May, 1920 (WH)

League Club	Source	Date Signed	Seasons Played	Apps	Subs	Gls
Brighton & H.A.		08.47	47-49	101	-	4
Luton T.	Tr	08.50	50	11	-	3

WHETTER, Gary
Middlesbrough, 6 September, 1963 (M)

League Club	Source	Date Signed	Seasons Played	Apps	Subs	Gls
Darlington (N/C)	Crook Town	09.86	86	3	2	1

WHIFFEN, Kingsley
Welshpool, 3 December, 1950 (G)

League Club	Source	Date Signed	Seasons Played	Apps	Subs	Gls
Chelsea (App)	App	08.66	66	1	0	0

WHIGHAM, William M.
Airdrie, 9 October, 1939 (G)

League Club	Source	Date Signed	Seasons Played	Apps	Subs	Gls
Middlesbrough	Falkirk	10.66	66-71	187	0	0
Darlington	Dumbarton	08.74	74	4	0	0

WHISTON, Donald
Stoke, 4 April, 1930 (FB)

League Club	Source	Date Signed	Seasons Played	Apps	Subs	Gls
Stoke C.	Jnrs	12.49	49-56	30	-	4
Crewe Alex.	Tr	02.57	56-57	52	-	9
Rochdale	Tr	05.58	58	14	-	0

WHISTON, Joseph R.
Stoke, 5 October, 1928

League Club	Source	Date Signed	Seasons Played	Apps	Subs	Gls
Crewe Alex.		09.51	51-52	9	-	2

WHISTON, Peter M.
Widnes, 4 January, 1968 (CD)

League Club	Source	Date Signed	Seasons Played	Apps	Subs	Gls
Plymouth Arg.		12.87	88-89	4	6	0
Torquay U.	Tr	03.90	89-91	39	1	1
Exeter C.	Tr	09.91	91	36	0	3

Ronnie Whelan (Home Farm, Liverpool & Republic of Ireland)

League Club	Source	Date Signed	Seasons Played	Apps	Subs	Gls
WHITAKER, Colin						
Leeds, 14 June, 1932						(OL)
Sheffield Wed.	Leeds U. (Jnr)	11.51	51	1	-	0
Bradford P.A.	Tr	06.53	53-55	49	-	10
Shrewsbury T.	Tr	06.56	56-60	152	-	59
Queens Park R.	Tr	02.61	60	8	-	0
Rochdale	Tr	05.61	61-62	54	-	11
Oldham Ath.	Tr	10.62	62-63	72	-	29
Barrow	Tr	08.64	64	12	-	0
WHITAKER, William						
Chesterfield, 7 October, 1923 EF Lge						(CH)
Chesterfield	Tapton S.O.B.	08.42	46	13	-	0
Middlesbrough	Tr	06.47	47-54	177	-	1
WHITBREAD, Adrian R.						
Epping, 22 October, 1971						(CD)
Leyton Orient	YT	11.89	89-91	89	0	1
WHITBY, Brian K.						
Luton, 21 February, 1939						(W)
Luton T.	Hitchin T.	05.57	57-58	7	-	1
WHITCHURCH, Charles H.						
Grays, 29 October, 1920 Died 1977 E Sch						(W)
West Ham U.	Portsmouth (Am)	05.45				
Tottenham H.	Tr	01.46	46	8	-	2
Southend U.	Tr	07.47	47	17	-	5
WHITE, Alexander						
Lasswade, 28 January, 1916						(RB)
Chelsea	Bonnyrigg Rose	02.37	46-47	17	-	0
Swindon T.	Tr	07.48	48-49	35	-	0
Southport	Tr	07.50	50	3	-	0
WHITE, Andrew C. J.						
Newport, 6 November, 1948						(OL)
Newport Co.	Caerleon	08.69	69-76	225	27	26
WHITE, Anthony J.						
Clacton, 3 November, 1966						(D)
Bournemouth (N/C)	Dorchester T.	07.85	85	1	0	0
WHITE, Archibald						
Dumbarton, 11 January, 1959						(M)
Oxford U.	App	01.76	76-79	10	14	1
WHITE, Arnold						
Bristol, 25 July, 1924						(IR)
Bristol C.	Soundwell	03.47	46-50	82	-	12
Millwall	Tr	08.51	51-52	14	-	0
WHITE, Barry J.						
Beverley, 30 July, 1950						(G)
Hull C.	App	08.68				
Halifax T.	Tr	11.70	71-74	23	0	0
WHITE, Christopher J.						
Chatham, 11 December, 1970						(D)
Portsmouth	YT	07.89				
Peterborough U.	Tr	05.91	91	7	1	0
WHITE, Dale						
Sunderland, 17 March, 1968 E Sch						(F)
Sunderland	App	03.86	85	2	2	0
Peterborough U.	L	12.87	87	14	0	4
WHITE, David						
Manchester, 30 October, 1967 E Yth/Eu21-6/E'B'						(F)
Manchester C.	YT	10.85	86-91	215	12	64
WHITE, Dean						
Hastings, 4 December, 1958						(M)
Gillingham	Chelsea (App)	07.78	78-82	108	8	26
Millwall	Tr	03.83	82-83	41	0	4
WHITE, Dennis						
Hartlepool, 10 November, 1948						(FB)
Hartlepool U.		11.67	67-72	55	2	0
WHITE, Devan W.						
Nottingham, 2 March, 1964						(F)
Lincoln C.	Arnold	12.84	84-85	21	8	4
Bristol Rov.	Shepshed Charterhouse	08.87	87-91	190	12	54
Cambridge U.	Tr	03.92	91	1	1	0
WHITE, Edward A.						
Crewe, 22 November, 1956						(F)
Crewe Alex. (N/C)		11.78	78	1	0	0

League Club	Source	Date Signed	Seasons Played	Apps	Subs	Gls
WHITE, Edward R.						
Musselburgh, 13 April, 1935						(CF)
Bradford C.	Falkirk	10.59	59	4	-	1
WHITE, Frederick						
Wolverhampton, 5 December, 1916						(G)
Everton		05.35				
Sheffield U.		05.37	47-49	44	-	0
Lincoln C.	Tr	06.50	50	42	-	0
WHITE, Gwilym D.						
Doncaster, 23 February, 1936						(FB)
Oldham Ath. (Am)	Plymouth Arg. (Am)	08.60	60	1	-	0
WHITE, Howard K.						
Timperley, 2 March, 1954						(D)
Manchester C.	App	05.71	70	1	0	0
WHITE, Ian S.						
Glasgow, 20 December, 1935						(WH)
Leicester C.	Glasgow Celtic	05.58	59-61	47	-	1
Southampton	Tr	06.62	62-66	60	1	5
WHITE, James						
Poole, 13 June, 1942 E Yth						(CH)
Bournemouth (Am)	Jnrs	04.58	57	1	-	0
Portsmouth	Jnrs	06.59	58-61	34	-	6
Gillingham	Tr	06.63	63-65	65	0	1
Bournemouth	Tr	07.66	66-69	176	0	7
Cambridge U.	Tr	12.70	70-71	28	2	2
WHITE, Jason G.						
Meriden, 19 October, 1971						(F)
Scunthorpe U.	Derby Co. (N/C)	09.91	91	15	7	11
WHITE, John (Jack)						
Doncaster, 17 March, 1924						(CH)
Aldershot		07.44	46-52	209	-	24
Bristol C.	Tr	10.52	52-57	216	-	11
WHITE, John A.						
Musselburgh, 28 April, 1937 Died 1964 Su23-1/SF Lge/EF Lge/S-22						(IF)
Tottenham H.	Falkirk	10.59	59-63	183	-	40

John White (Alloa Athletic, Falkirk, Tottenham Hotspur & Scotland)

League Club	Source	Date Signed	Seasons Played	Apps	Subs	Gls
WHITE, Kenneth						
Selby, 15 March, 1922						(RH)
Hull C.	Selby T.	12.47	48	1	-	0
WHITE, Kevin N.						
Poole, 26 June, 1948						(W)
Bournemouth	App	08.66	66-68	45	3	4
WHITE, Leonard R.						
Skellow, 23 March, 1930 EF Lge						(CF)
Rotherham U.	Upton Colly	05.48	50-52	43	-	14
Newcastle U.	Tr	02.53	52-61	244	-	142
Huddersfield T.	Tr	02.62	61-64	102	-	37
Stockport Co.	Tr	01.65	64-65	53	0	22
WHITE, Lewis						
Stoke, 2 August, 1927						
Port Vale		10.48	48	1	-	0
WHITE, Malcolm						
Sunderland, 24 April, 1941						(G)
Grimsby T.	Wolverhampton W. (Am)	08.58	58-62	65	-	0
Walsall	Tr	08.63	63	28	-	0
Lincoln C.	Tr	07.64	64	27	-	0
Bradford C.	Tr	07.65	65	9	0	0
Halifax T.	Tr	11.65	65-67	100	0	0
WHITE, Mark I.						
Sheffield, 26 October, 1958						(FB/M)
Reading	Sheffield U. (App)	03.77	77-87	265	13	11
WHITE, Maurice H.						
Keadby, 29 January, 1938						(FB)
Doncaster Rov.		04.56	57-60	56	-	0
WHITE, Philip G. J.						
Fulham, 29 December, 1930						(OR)
Leyton Orient	Wealdstone	07.53	53-63	217	-	28
WHITE, Raymond						
Brockley, 5 February, 1941						(WH)
Millwall	Jnrs	08.58	58	2	-	0
Stoke C.	Tr	07.60				
WHITE, Raymond S.						
Rochford, 14 January, 1948						(G)
Southend U.	App	01.66	63-67	10	0	0
Bristol Rov.	Tr	07.68	68	3	0	0
WHITE, Richard						
Scunthorpe, 18 August, 1931						(CH)
Scunthorpe U.	Scunthorpe S.C.	(N/L)	50-55	133	-	11
Liverpool	Tr	11.55	55-61	203	-	0
Doncaster Rov.	Tr	07.62	62-63	82	-	0
WHITE, Ronald T.						
Bethnal Green, 9 November, 1931						(IF)
Charlton Ath.	Maccabi Sports	03.54	53-61	165	-	8
WHITE, Roy B. W.						
Bootle, 13 August, 1918 Died 1988						(WH)
Bradford P.A.	Tottenham H. (Am)	05.46	46-50	151	-	3
WHITE, Stephen J.						
Chipping Sodbury, 2 January, 1959 E Sch						(F)
Bristol Rov.	Mangotsfield	07.77	77-79	46	4	20
Luton T.	Tr	12.79	79-81	63	9	25
Charlton Ath.	Tr	07.82	82	29	0	12
Lincoln C.	L	01.83	82	2	1	0
Luton T.	L	02.83	82	4	0	0
Bristol Rov.	Tr	08.83	83-85	89	12	24
Swindon T.	Tr	07.86	86-91	178	26	76
WHITE, Thomas						
Musselburgh, 12 August, 1939						(CF)
Crystal Palace	Aberdeen	06.66	66-67	37	2	13
Blackpool	Tr	03.68	67-69	34	0	9
Bury	Tr	06.70	70-71	46	2	13
Crewe Alex.	Tr	12.71	71	4	0	0
WHITE, Thomas						
High Hold, 10 November, 1924						(IF)
Sunderland	Chester Moor Jnrs	04.45	46	2	-	1
WHITE, William						
Clackmannan, 25 September, 1932						(G)
Accrington St.	Motherwell	08.53	53	18	-	0
Mansfield T.	Tr	05.54	54	3	-	0
Derby Co.	L	08.55	55	3	-	0
WHITE, William H.						
Liverpool, 13 October, 1936						(F)
Burnley		01.54	57-59	9	-	4
Wrexham	Tr	03.61	60	8	-	0
Chester C.	Tr	07.61	61	11	-	4
WHITE, E. Winston						
Leicester, 26 October, 1958						(RW)
Leicester C.	App	10.76	76-78	10	2	1
Hereford U.	Tr	03.79	78-82	169	6	21
Chesterfield (N/C)	Hong Kong	09.83	83	0	1	0
Port Vale (N/C)	Tr	10.83	83	0	1	0
Stockport Co. (N/C)	Tr	11.83	83	4	0	1
Bury	Tr	12.83	83-86	125	0	11
Rochdale	L	10.86	86	4	0	0
Colchester U.	Tr	02.87	86-88	64	1	8
Burnley	Tr	10.88	88-90	93	11	14
West Bromwich A.	Tr	03.91	90-91	13	3	1
WHITEAR, John M.						
Isleworth, 31 May, 1935 E Yth						(IF)
Aston Villa	Walton & Hersham	04.53				
Crystal Palace	Tr	05.56	56	5	-	1
WHITEFOOT, Jeffrey						
Cheadle, 31 December, 1933 E Sch/Eu23-1						(WH)
Manchester U.	Jnrs	12.51	49-55	93	-	0
Grimsby T.	Tr	11.57	57	26	-	5
Nottingham F.	Tr	07.58	58-67	255	0	5
WHITEHALL, Steven C.						
Bromborough, 8 December, 1966						(W)
Rochdale	Southport	07.91	91	20	14	7
WHITEHEAD, Alan						
Bury, 20 November, 1956						(CD)
Bury	Darwen	12.77	77-80	98	1	13
Brentford	Tr	08.81	81-83	101	1	4
Scunthorpe U.	Tr	01.84	83-86	106	2	8
York C.	Tr	10.86	86-87	40	1	1
Wigan Ath.	L	03.87	86	2	0	0
Halifax T.	Tr	08.88	88	10	1	1
WHITEHEAD, Alan J.						
Birmingham, 3 September, 1951						(CD)
Birmingham C.	App	07.69	71-72	4	0	0
WHITEHEAD, Barry						
Sheffield, 3 December, 1946						(IF)
Chesterfield		07.65	65	5	1	1
WHITEHEAD, Clive R.						
Birmingham, 24 November, 1955 E Yth						(M)
Bristol C.	Northfield Jnrs	08.73	73-81	209	20	10
West Bromwich A.	Tr	11.81	81-86	157	11	6
Wolverhampton W.	L	01.86	85	2	0	0
Portsmouth	Tr	06.87	87-88	57	8	2
Exeter C.	Tr	07.89	89-90	44	2	5
WHITEHEAD, Norman J.						
Liverpool, 22 April, 1948						(W)
Southport	Skelmersdale U.	12.67	67	7	1	0
Rochdale	Tr	07.68	68-71	154	2	11
Rotherham U.	Tr	03.72	71-72	29	4	2
Chester C.	Tr	08.73	73-75	66	8	5
Grimsby T.	Tr	08.76	76	3	1	0
WHITEHEAD, Philip M.						
Halifax, 17 December, 1969						(G)
Halifax T.	YT	06.88	86-89	42	0	0
Barnsley	Tr	03.90	91	3	0	0
Halifax T.	L	03.91	90	9	0	0
Scunthorpe U.	L	11.91	91	8	0	0
WHITEHEAD, Robert						
Ashington, 22 September, 1936						(FB)
Newcastle U.	Fatfield Ath.	12.54	57-59	20	-	0
Darlington	Cambridge C.	08.62	62-63	53	-	0
WHITEHEAD, Scott A.						
Doncaster, 20 April, 1974						(W)
Chesterfield	YT	07.92	91	3	2	0
WHITEHEAD, William G.						
Maltby, 6 February, 1920						(OL)
Queens Park R.	Maltby Colly	08.39				
Aldershot	Tr	08.47	47	6	-	1

WHITEHOUSE, Brian
West Bromwich, 8 September, 1935 (IF)

League Club	Source	Date Signed	Seasons Played	Apps	Subs	Gls
West Bromwich A.	Jnrs	10.52	55-59	37	-	13
Norwich C.	Tr	03.60	59-61	41	-	14
Wrexham	Tr	03.62	61-63	45	-	19
Crystal Palace	Tr	11.63	63-65	82	0	17
Charlton Ath.	Tr	03.66	65	13	0	1
Leyton Orient	Tr	07.66	66-67	52	0	6

WHITEHOUSE, Dane L.
Sheffield, 14 October, 1970 (LW)

League Club	Source	Date Signed	Seasons Played	Apps	Subs	Gls
Sheffield U.	YT	07.89	88-91	37	18	8

WHITEHOUSE, Dean
Mexborough, 3 October, 1963 (M)

League Club	Source	Date Signed	Seasons Played	Apps	Subs	Gls
Barnsley	App	10.81	83	1	1	0
Torquay U.	Tr	08.84	84	7	2	0

WHITEHOUSE, James A.
West Bromwich, 19 September, 1934 (IF)

League Club	Source	Date Signed	Seasons Played	Apps	Subs	Gls
West Bromwich A.	Jnrs	11.54				
Reading	Tr	06.56	56-61	203	-	61
Coventry C.	Tr	08.62	62-63	46	-	12
Millwall	Tr	03.64	63-64	38	-	13

WHITEHOUSE, James E.
West Bromwich, 19 September, 1924 (IF)

League Club	Source	Date Signed	Seasons Played	Apps	Subs	Gls
West Bromwich A.	Hawthorns	05.48				
Walsall	Tr	06.49	49	19	-	8
Rochdale	Tr	07.50	50-51	46	-	13
Carlisle U.	Tr	10.51	51-56	198	-	100

WHITEHOUSE, Philip
Wolverhampton, 23 March, 1971 (LB)

League Club	Source	Date Signed	Seasons Played	Apps	Subs	Gls
West Bromwich A.	YT	07.89				
Walsall	Tr	12.89	89-90	10	2	0

WHITEHURST, Walter
Manchester, 7 June, 1934 (WH)

League Club	Source	Date Signed	Seasons Played	Apps	Subs	Gls
Manchester U.		05.52	55	1	-	0
Chesterfield	Tr	11.56	56-59	91	-	2
Crewe Alex.	Tr	07.60	60	3	-	1

WHITEHURST, William
Thurnscoe, 10 June, 1959 (F)

League Club	Source	Date Signed	Seasons Played	Apps	Subs	Gls
Hull C.	Mexborough T.	10.80	80-85	176	17	47
Newcastle U.	Tr	12.85	85-86	28	0	7
Oxford U.	Tr	10.86	86-87	36	4	4
Reading	Tr	02.88	87-88	17	0	8
Sunderland	Tr	09.88	88	17	0	3
Hull C.	Tr	12.88	88-89	36	0	5
Sheffield U.	Tr	02.90	89-90	12	10	2
Stoke C.	L	11.90	90	3	0	0
Doncaster Rov.	Tr	02.91	90-91	22	0	1
Crewe Alex.	Tr	01.92	91	4	6	0

WHITELAW, George
Paisley, 1 January, 1937 S Amat (CF)

League Club	Source	Date Signed	Seasons Played	Apps	Subs	Gls
Sunderland	St Johnstone	02.58	57-58	5	-	0
Queens Park R.	Tr	03.59	58-59	26	-	10
Halifax T.	Tr	10.59	59-60	52	-	22
Carlisle U.	Tr	02.61	60-61	34	-	10
Stockport Co.	Tr	01.62	61-62	51	-	18
Barrow	Tr	08.63	63	7	-	0

WHITELEY, Albert
Sheffield, 13 July, 1932 (OL)

League Club	Source	Date Signed	Seasons Played	Apps	Subs	Gls
Leyton Orient	Sheffield Wed. (Am)	11.52	52-53	23	-	3

WHITELEY, Andrew M.
Sowerby Bridge, 1 August, 1961 (M)

League Club	Source	Date Signed	Seasons Played	Apps	Subs	Gls
Halifax T.		08.79	79-81	20	16	1

WHITELOCK, Arthur
Stockton, 31 July, 1931 (RB)

League Club	Source	Date Signed	Seasons Played	Apps	Subs	Gls
Hartlepool U.	South Bank	12.50	50	6	-	0

WHITELUM, Clifford
Farnworth, 2 December, 1919 (CF)

League Club	Source	Date Signed	Seasons Played	Apps	Subs	Gls
Sunderland	Bentley Colly	12.38	38-47	43	-	18
Sheffield Wed.	Tr	10.47	47-48	41	-	15

WHITESIDE, Arnold
Garstang, 6 November, 1911 (WH)

League Club	Source	Date Signed	Seasons Played	Apps	Subs	Gls
Blackburn Rov.	Wood Plumpton	01.33	32-48	218	-	3

WHITESIDE, Charles W.
Liverpool, 16 August, 1927 (IF)

League Club	Source	Date Signed	Seasons Played	Apps	Subs	Gls
Swindon T.		12.48	49	1	-	0

WHITESIDE, E. Kenneth
Liverpool, 11 December, 1929 (IF)

League Club	Source	Date Signed	Seasons Played	Apps	Subs	Gls
Preston N.E.	British Eckna	05.52				
Chesterfield	British Eckna	05.53	53	9	-	3
York C.	Tr	05.54	54	8	-	0
Bournemouth	Tr	07.55	55	1	-	0

WHITESIDE, Norman
Belfast, 7 May, 1965 NI Sch/NI-38 (F)

League Club	Source	Date Signed	Seasons Played	Apps	Subs	Gls
Manchester U.	App	07.82	81-88	193	13	47
Everton	Tr	07.89	89-90	27	2	9

WHITESIDE, William R.
Belfast, 24 September, 1935 (OR)

League Club	Source	Date Signed	Seasons Played	Apps	Subs	Gls
Exeter C.	Portadown	11.55	55	3	-	1
Scunthorpe U.	Portadown	08.56	56	2	-	0
Rotherham U.	Tr	12.56				

WHITFIELD, George A.
Penrith, 10 February, 1934 (FB)

League Club	Source	Date Signed	Seasons Played	Apps	Subs	Gls
Carlisle U.		11.55	55-56	2	-	0

WHITFIELD, James
Grimsby, 18 May, 1919 Died 1984 (IR)

League Club	Source	Date Signed	Seasons Played	Apps	Subs	Gls
Grimsby T.	Humber U.	05.46	46-48	29	-	7
Scunthorpe U.	Tr	04.49	50	16	-	6
Southport	Tr	08.51	51	12	-	0
Scunthorpe U.	Tr	02.52	51-54	103	-	20

WHITFIELD, John S.
Gateshead, 10 June, 1938 (FB)

League Club	Source	Date Signed	Seasons Played	Apps	Subs	Gls
Gateshead		07.59	59	1	-	1

WHITFIELD, Kenneth
Bishop Auckland, 24 March, 1930 (WH)

League Club	Source	Date Signed	Seasons Played	Apps	Subs	Gls
Wolverhampton W.	Shildon Colly	12.47	51-52	9	-	3
Manchester C.	Tr	03.53	52-53	13	-	3
Brighton & H.A.	Tr	07.54	54-58	175	-	4
Queens Park R.	Tr	07.59	59-60	19	-	3

WHITFIELD, Michael
Sunderland, 17 October, 1962 (CD)

League Club	Source	Date Signed	Seasons Played	Apps	Subs	Gls
Sunderland	App	10.80	82	3	0	0
Hartlepool U.	Tr	08.83	83	15	1	0

WHITFIELD, Robert
Bywell, 30 June, 1920

League Club	Source	Date Signed	Seasons Played	Apps	Subs	Gls
Charlton Ath.	Prudhoe	05.39				
Torquay U.	Tr	02.47	46-49	11	-	1

George Whitelaw (St Johnstone, Sunderland, Queens Park Rangers, Halifax Town, Carlisle United, Stockport County & Barrow)

Norman Whiteside (Manchester United, Everton & Northern Ireland)

WHITFIELD, Wilfred
Chesterfield, 17 November, 1916 (WH)

League Club	Source	Date Signed	Seasons Played	Apps	Subs	Gls
Bristol Rov.	Worksop T.	07.38	38-46	26	-	1
Torquay U.		08.49	49-50	37	-	1

WHITHAM, John (Jack)
Burnley, 8 December, 1946 Eu23-1 (F)

League Club	Source	Date Signed	Seasons Played	Apps	Subs	Gls
Sheffield Wed.		11.64	66-69	54	9	27
Liverpool	Tr	05.70	70-71	15	0	7
Cardiff C.	Tr	01.74	73-74	12	2	3
Reading	Tr	07.75	75	13	6	3

WHITHAM, Terence
Sheffield, 14 August, 1935 (WH)

League Club	Source	Date Signed	Seasons Played	Apps	Subs	Gls
Sheffield Wed.	Jnrs	09.52	56-58	4	-	0
Chesterfield	Tr	06.61	61-63	66	-	3

WHITLOCK, Mark
Portsmouth, 14 March, 1961 (CD)

League Club	Source	Date Signed	Seasons Played	Apps	Subs	Gls
Southampton	App	03.79	81-85	55	6	1
Grimsby T.	L	10.82	82	7	1	0
Aldershot	L	03.83	82	14	0	0
Bournemouth	Tr	07.86	86-88	98	1	1
Reading	Tr	12.88	88-89	26	1	0
Aldershot	Tr	08.90	90	28	1	2

WHITLOCK, Philip J.
Cardiff, 1 May, 1930 (WH)

League Club	Source	Date Signed	Seasons Played	Apps	Subs	Gls
Cardiff C.		02.49				
Chester C.	Tr	08.50	50-58	142	-	3

WHITLOW, Michael W.
Northwich, 13 January, 1968 (LB/W)

League Club	Source	Date Signed	Seasons Played	Apps	Subs	Gls
Leeds U.	Witton A.	11.88	88-91	62	15	4
Leicester C.	Tr	03.92	91	4	1	0

WHITNALL, Brian
Doncaster, 25 May, 1933 (FB)

League Club	Source	Date Signed	Seasons Played	Apps	Subs	Gls
Hull C.	Jnrs	06.50	54	2	-	0
Scunthorpe U.	Tr	05.56	56-57	2	-	0
Exeter C.	Tr	07.58	58-61	36	-	0

WHITTAKER, Frederick J.
Canada, 12 October, 1923 (CF)

League Club	Source	Date Signed	Seasons Played	Apps	Subs	Gls
Notts Co.	Vancouver (Can)	08.46	46	10	-	2

WHITTAKER, Raymond H.
Bow, 15 January, 1945 E Sch/E Yth (W)

League Club	Source	Date Signed	Seasons Played	Apps	Subs	Gls
Arsenal	Jnrs	05.62				
Luton T.	Tr	03.64	63-68	169	1	40
Colchester U.	Tr	07.69	69-70	41	2	6

WHITTAKER, Richard
Dublin, 10 October, 1934 IR'B'-1/IR-1 (FB)

League Club	Source	Date Signed	Seasons Played	Apps	Subs	Gls
Chelsea	St Mary's B.C.	05.52	55-59	48	-	0
Peterborough U.	Tr	09.60	60-62	82	-	0
Queens Park R.	Tr	07.63	63	17	-	0

WHITTAKER, William P.
Charlton, 20 December, 1922 Died 1977 E Sch (CH)

League Club	Source	Date Signed	Seasons Played	Apps	Subs	Gls
Charlton Ath.	Arsenal (Am)	02.40	46-48	28	-	0
Huddersfield T.	Tr	11.48	48-49	43	-	0
Crystal Palace	Tr	06.50	50	35	-	1

WHITTAM, Ernest A.
Wealdstone, 7 January, 1911 (IF)

League Club	Source	Date Signed	Seasons Played	Apps	Subs	Gls
Huddersfield T.	Jnrs	11.28	29-32	19	-	4
Chester C.	Tr	05.33	33-34	54	-	21
Wolverhampton W.	Tr	02.36	35	1	-	0
Bournemouth	Tr	05.36	36-38	107	-	28
Reading	Tr	06.39				
Rotherham U.	Tr	04.45	46	1	-	0

WHITTINGHAM, Alfred
Altofts, 19 June, 1914 (IF)

League Club	Source	Date Signed	Seasons Played	Apps	Subs	Gls
Bradford C.	Altofts	10.36	36-46	87	-	24
Huddersfield T.	Tr	02.47	46-48	67	-	17
Halifax T.	Tr	03.49	48-49	39	-	9

WHITTINGHAM, Guy
Evesham, 11 November, 1964 (F)

League Club	Source	Date Signed	Seasons Played	Apps	Subs	Gls
Portsmouth	Yeovil T.	06.89	89-91	103	11	46

WHITTINGHAM, Stephen
Birkenhead, 4 February, 1962 (F)

League Club	Source	Date Signed	Seasons Played	Apps	Subs	Gls
Tranmere Rov.	App	02.80	78-80	0	2	0

WHITTINGTON, Eric P.
Brighton, 18 September, 1946 E Yth (IF)

League Club	Source	Date Signed	Seasons Played	Apps	Subs	Gls
Brighton & H.A.	Chelsea (Am)	10.64	65-67	26	6	8

WHITTLE, Alan
Liverpool, 10 March, 1950 E Sch/E Yth/Eu23-1 (M)

League Club	Source	Date Signed	Seasons Played	Apps	Subs	Gls
Everton	App	07.65	67-72	72	2	21
Crystal Palace	Tr	12.72	72-75	103	5	19
Leyton Orient	Tr	09.76	76-79	47	3	6
Bournemouth (N/C)	Iran	01.81	80	8	1	0

WHITTLE, Ernest
Lanchester, 25 November, 1925 (IF)

League Club	Source	Date Signed	Seasons Played	Apps	Subs	Gls
Newcastle U.		11.44				
Lincoln C.	Seaham Colly	01.50	49-53	145	-	63
Workington	Tr	03.54	53-56	112	-	45
Chesterfield	Tr	11.56	56	15	-	4
Bradford P.A.	Tr	08.57	57	18	-	6

WHITTLE, Graham
Liverpool, 30 May, 1953 (F)

League Club	Source	Date Signed	Seasons Played	Apps	Subs	Gls
Wrexham	Jnrs	07.71	70-80	288	18	91

WHITTLE, James A.
Hamilton, 5 September, 1929 (CF)

League Club	Source	Date Signed	Seasons Played	Apps	Subs	Gls
Southampton (L)	Hearts	01.54	53	2	-	0

WHITTLE, Maurice
Wigan, 5 July, 1948 (LB)

League Club	Source	Date Signed	Seasons Played	Apps	Subs	Gls
Blackburn Rov.	App	07.66	68	5	2	0
Oldham Ath.	Tr	05.69	69-76	307	5	39
Wigan Ath.	Barrow	03.80	79-80	21	0	1

WHITTON, Stephen P.
East Ham, 4 December, 1960 (M/F)

League Club	Source	Date Signed	Seasons Played	Apps	Subs	Gls
Coventry C.	App	09.78	79-82	64	10	21
West Ham U.	Tr	07.83	83-84	35	4	6
Birmingham C.	L	01.86	85	8	0	2
Birmingham C.	Tr	08.86	86-88	94	1	28
Sheffield Wed.	Tr	03.89	88-90	22	10	4
Ipswich T.	Tr	01.91	90-91	53	0	11

WHITWORTH, George A.
Eckington, 22 September, 1927 (FB)

League Club	Source	Date Signed	Seasons Played	Apps	Subs	Gls
Liverpool	Stanton Iron Wks	03.50	51	9	-	0

WHITWORTH, Harold
Radcliffe, 1 December, 1920 (WH)

League Club	Source	Date Signed	Seasons Played	Apps	Subs	Gls
Bury		11.45	46-50	112	-	14
Rochdale	Tr	07.51	51-52	70	-	9
Southport	Northwich Vic.	09.53	53	33	-	6
Crewe Alex.	Tr	07.54	54	14	-	1

WHITWORTH, Neil A.
Wigan, 12 April, 1972 E Yth (CD)

League Club	Source	Date Signed	Seasons Played	Apps	Subs	Gls
Wigan Ath. (YT)	YT	07.88	89	1	1	0
Manchester U.	Tr	07.90	90	1	0	0
Preston N.E.	L	01.92	91	6	0	0
Barnsley	L	02.92	91	11	0	0

WHITWORTH, Stephen J.
Coalville, 20 March, 1952 E Sch/E Yth/Eu23-6/E-7 (RB)

League Club	Source	Date Signed	Seasons Played	Apps	Subs	Gls
Leicester C.	App	11.69	70-78	352	1	0
Sunderland	Tr	03.79	78-81	83	0	0
Bolton W.	Tr	10.81	81-82	67	0	0
Mansfield T.	Tr	08.83	83-84	80	0	2

WHYKE, Peter
Barnsley, 7 September, 1939 (W)

League Club	Source	Date Signed	Seasons Played	Apps	Subs	Gls
Barnsley	Smithies	01.58	57-60	27	-	1
Rochdale	Tr	07.61	61	5	-	0

WHYMARK, Trevor J.
Diss, 4 May, 1950 Eu23-6/E-1 (F)

League Club	Source	Date Signed	Seasons Played	Apps	Subs	Gls
Ipswich T.	Diss T.	05.69	69-78	249	11	74
Derby Co.	Sparta Rotterdam (Neth)	12.79	79	2	0	0
Grimsby T.	Vancouver (Can)	12.80	80-83	83	10	16
Southend U.	Tr	01.84	83-84	37	1	5
Peterborough U.	Tr	08.85	85	3	0	0
Colchester U. (N/C)	Tr	10.85	85	2	0	0

WHYTE, J. Archibald
Falkirk, 17 July, 1919 (CH)

League Club	Source	Date Signed	Seasons Played	Apps	Subs	Gls
Barnsley	Armadale Th.	05.38	46-49	91	-	2
Oldham Ath.	Tr	08.50	50-55	234	-	0

WHYTE, Christopher A.
Islington, 2 September, 1961 Eu21-4 (CD)

League Club	Source	Date Signed	Seasons Played	Apps	Subs	Gls
Arsenal	App	09.79	81-85	86	4	8
Crystal Palace	L	08.84	84	13	0	0
West Bromwich A.	Los Angeles (USA)	08.88	88-89	83	1	7
Leeds U.	Tr	06.90	90-91	79	0	4

Chris Whyte (Arsenal, West Bromwich Albion & Leeds United)

WHYTE, David
Dunfermline, 2 March, 1959 (D)

League Club	Source	Date Signed	Seasons Played	Apps	Subs	Gls
Leeds U.	App	03.77	76	1	1	0

WHYTE, David A.
Greenwich, 20 April, 1971 (F)

League Club	Source	Date Signed	Seasons Played	Apps	Subs	Gls
Crystal Palace	Greenwich Bor.	02.89	91	7	4	1
Charlton Ath.	L	03.92	91	7	1	2

WHYTE, Francis
Govan Hill, 18 April, 1929 (CH)

League Club	Source	Date Signed	Seasons Played	Apps	Subs	Gls
Swindon T.	Glasgow Celtic	06.56	56	7	-	0

WHYTE, James Mc.
Glasgow, 19 January, 1930 (IF)

League Club	Source	Date Signed	Seasons Played	Apps	Subs	Gls
Southend U.	Third Lanark	05.54	54-56	33	-	8

WHYTE, John N.
Calder, 7 May, 1921 (FB)

League Club	Source	Date Signed	Seasons Played	Apps	Subs	Gls
Bradford C.	Falkirk	08.50	50-56	236	-	2

WICKS, Alan H.
Henley, 8 February, 1933 (WH)

League Club	Source	Date Signed	Seasons Played	Apps	Subs	Gls
Reading		05.52	55	1	-	0

WICKS, Peter
Hemsworth, 14 May, 1948 E Yth (G)

League Club	Source	Date Signed	Seasons Played	Apps	Subs	Gls
Sheffield Wed.	App	05.65	64-69	13	0	0

WICKS, Roger C.
Darlington, 19 April, 1947 (M)

League Club	Source	Date Signed	Seasons Played	Apps	Subs	Gls
Darlington	Netherfield	02.81	80-82	31	10	4

WICKS, Stanley M.
Reading, 11 July, 1928 Died 1983 E'B'-1/EF Lge (CH)

League Club	Source	Date Signed	Seasons Played	Apps	Subs	Gls
Reading		08.48	49-53	168	-	1
Chelsea	Tr	01.54	54-56	71	-	1

WICKS, Stephen J.
Reading, 3 October, 1956 E Yth/Eu21-1 (CD)

League Club	Source	Date Signed	Seasons Played	Apps	Subs	Gls
Chelsea	App	06.74	74-78	117	1	5
Derby Co.	Tr	01.79	78-79	24	0	0
Queens Park R.	Tr	09.79	79-80	73	0	0
Crystal Palace	Tr	06.81	81	14	0	1
Queens Park R.	Tr	03.82	81-85	116	0	6
Chelsea	Tr	07.86	86-87	32	0	1

WIDDOP, Dennis
Keighley, 14 March, 1931 (OR)

League Club	Source	Date Signed	Seasons Played	Apps	Subs	Gls
Bradford C.	Portadown	08.54	54	1	-	0

WIDDOWSON, J. Robert
Loughborough, 12 September, 1941 (G)

League Club	Source	Date Signed	Seasons Played	Apps	Subs	Gls
Sheffield U.		07.59	61-67	7	0	0
York C.	Tr	06.68	68-69	30	0	0
Portsmouth	L	11.69	69	4	0	0

WIDDRINGTON, Thomas
Newcastle, 1 October, 1971 (M)

League Club	Source	Date Signed	Seasons Played	Apps	Subs	Gls
Southampton	YT	05.90	91	2	1	0
Wigan Ath.	L	09.91	91	5	1	0

WIFFILL, David P.
Bristol, 19 April, 1961 (M)

League Club	Source	Date Signed	Seasons Played	Apps	Subs	Gls
Manchester C.	Bath C.	04.80				
Bristol Rov. (N/C)	Hong Kong	08.87	87	2	0	0

WIGG, Ronald G.
Dunmow, 18 May, 1949 (F)

League Club	Source	Date Signed	Seasons Played	Apps	Subs	Gls
Ipswich T.	Leyton Orient (App)	04.67	67-69	35	2	14
Watford	Tr	06.70	70-72	91	6	20
Rotherham U.	Tr	03.73	72-74	65	0	22
Grimsby T.	Tr	01.75	74-76	51	12	12
Barnsley	Tr	03.77	76-77	14	4	5
Scunthorpe U.	Tr	10.77	77-78	48	2	6

WIGGAN, Trenton A.
West Indies, 20 September, 1962 E Sch (W)

League Club	Source	Date Signed	Seasons Played	Apps	Subs	Gls
Sheffield U.	App	08.80	79-81	20	4	3

WIGGETT, David J.
Sheffield, 25 May, 1957 Died 1978 (LB)

League Club	Source	Date Signed	Seasons Played	Apps	Subs	Gls
Lincoln C.	App	06.75	73-75	4	2	0
Hartlepool U.	Tr	10.76	76-77	54	0	1

WIGGIN, Raymond
Rushall, 13 September, 1942 (CF)

League Club	Source	Date Signed	Seasons Played	Apps	Subs	Gls
Walsall		09.62	62-63	19	-	6

WIGGINTON, Clive A.
Sheffield, 18 October, 1950 (CD)

League Club	Source	Date Signed	Seasons Played	Apps	Subs	Gls
Grimsby T.	App	10.68	68-74	164	9	6
Scunthorpe U.	Tr	07.75	75-76	88	0	7
Lincoln C.	Tr	09.77	77-78	60	0	6
Grimsby T.	Tr	03.79	78-81	122	0	2
Doncaster Rov.	L	03.82	81	13	0	1
Torquay U.	Tr	07.82	82	9	0	0
Doncaster Rov.	Tr	10.82	82	18	0	0

WIGHTMAN, John R.
Duns, 2 November, 1912 Died 1964 (WH)

League Club	Source	Date Signed	Seasons Played	Apps	Subs	Gls
York C.	Scarborough	08.33	33	5	-	0
Bradford P.A.	Tr	09.34	34	17	-	0
Huddersfield T.	Tr	01.35	34-36	64	-	0
Blackburn Rov.	Tr	01.37	36-46	66	-	2
Carlisle U.	Tr	08.47	47	36	-	0

WIGLEY, Steven
Ashton-u-Lyne, 15 October, 1961 (W)

League Club	Source	Date Signed	Seasons Played	Apps	Subs	Gls
Nottingham F.	Curzon Ashton	03.81	82-85	69	13	2
Sheffield U.	Tr	10.85	85-86	21	7	1
Birmingham C.	Tr	03.87	86-88	87	0	4
Portsmouth	Tr	03.89	88-91	103	17	12

WIGNALL, David A.
Liverpool, 3 April, 1959 (M)

League Club	Source	Date Signed	Seasons Played	Apps	Subs	Gls
Doncaster Rov.	App	07.76	75-77	35	6	1

WIGNALL, Frank
Chorley, 21 August, 1939 EF Lge/E-2 (CF)

League Club	Source	Date Signed	Seasons Played	Apps	Subs	Gls
Everton	Horwich R.M.I.	05.58	59-62	33	-	15
Nottingham F.	Tr	06.63	63-67	156	1	47
Wolverhampton W.	Tr	03.68	67-68	32	0	15
Derby Co.	Tr	02.69	68-71	29	16	15
Mansfield T.	Tr	11.71	71-72	50	6	15

WIGNALL, Mark
Preston, 6 December, 1962 (M)

League Club	Source	Date Signed	Seasons Played	Apps	Subs	Gls
Wigan Ath.	App	12.80	80-81	34	0	0

WIGNALL, Steven L.
Liverpool, 17 September, 1954 (CD)

League Club	Source	Date Signed	Seasons Played	Apps	Subs	Gls
Doncaster Rov.	Liverpool (Jnrs)	03.72	72-76	127	3	1
Colchester U.	Tr	09.77	77-83	279	2	22
Brentford	Tr	08.84	84-86	67	0	2
Aldershot	Tr	09.86	86-90	158	3	4

WILBERT, George N.
Dunston, 11 July, 1924 (CF)

League Club	Source	Date Signed	Seasons Played	Apps	Subs	Gls
Gateshead		08.42	47-54	268	-	92

WILBY, Edward
Rotherham, 18 May, 1922 (FB)

League Club	Source	Date Signed	Seasons Played	Apps	Subs	Gls
Wolverhampton W.		05.46				
Bradford C.	Tr	09.46	46	3	-	0

WILCOCK, Roderick W.
Middlesbrough, 28 February, 1956 (D)

League Club	Source	Date Signed	Seasons Played	Apps	Subs	Gls
Crewe Alex.	Southampton (Am)	08.74	74	2	2	0

WILCOCKSON, Harold
Sheffield, 23 July, 1943 (RB)

League Club	Source	Date Signed	Seasons Played	Apps	Subs	Gls
Rotherham U.		07.63	64-67	108	0	3
Doncaster Rov.	Tr	02.68	67-69	75	0	3
Sheffield Wed.	Tr	12.69	69-70	40	0	1
Doncaster Rov.	Tr	05.71	71-72	36	0	1

WILCOX, Alexander
Lossiemouth, 5 November, 1923 (CF)

League Club	Source	Date Signed	Seasons Played	Apps	Subs	Gls
Hartlepool U.	Cowdenbeath	07.51	51	6	-	0

WILCOX, Anthony
Rotherham, 13 June, 1944 (G)

League Club	Source	Date Signed	Seasons Played	Apps	Subs	Gls
Rotherham U.		10.62				
Barnsley	Tr	08.64	64	8	-	0

WILCOX, Caradoc
Merthyr Tydfil, 8 November, 1923 (HB)

League Club	Source	Date Signed	Seasons Played	Apps	Subs	Gls
Cardiff C.	Treharris	05.49				
Newport Co.	Tr	07.52	52-53	30	-	0

WILCOX, Edward E.
Blaengarw, 24 March, 1927 (CF)

League Club	Source	Date Signed	Seasons Played	Apps	Subs	Gls
West Bromwich A.	Oxford C.	05.48	48-50	12	-	3

WILCOX, Frederick H.
St Helens, 23 October, 1922 (RB)

League Club	Source	Date Signed	Seasons Played	Apps	Subs	Gls
Chester C.		07.47	47	16	-	0

WILCOX, George E.
Treeton, 23 August, 1917 (FB)

League Club	Source	Date Signed	Seasons Played	Apps	Subs	Gls
Derby Co.	Denaby U.	10.36	37-46	12	-	0
Rotherham U.	Tr	08.48	48	1	-	0

WILCOX, Jason M.
Farnworth, 15 March, 1971 (W)

League Club	Source	Date Signed	Seasons Played	Apps	Subs	Gls
Blackburn Rov.	YT	06.89	89-91	49	8	4

WILCOX, Raymond
Merthyr Tydfil, 12 April, 1921 (CH)

League Club	Source	Date Signed	Seasons Played	Apps	Subs	Gls
Newport Co.	Treharris	05.39	46-59	489	-	0

WILCOX, Russell
Hemsworth, 25 March, 1964 E Semi-Pro (CD)

League Club	Source	Date Signed	Seasons Played	Apps	Subs	Gls
Doncaster Rov. (App)	App	05.80	80	1	0	0
Northampton T.	Frickley Ath.	06.86	86-89	137	1	9
Hull C.	Tr	08.90	90-91	64	7	5

WILDER, Christopher J.
Stocksbridge, 23 September, 1967 (RB)

League Club	Source	Date Signed	Seasons Played	Apps	Subs	Gls
Southampton	App	09.85				
Sheffield U.	Tr	08.86	86-91	89	4	1
Walsall	L	11.89	89	4	0	0
Charlton Ath.	L	10.90	90	1	0	0
Charlton Ath.	L	11.91	91	2	0	0
Leyton Orient	L	02.92	91	16	0	1

WILDON, Leslie E.
Middlesbrough, 5 April, 1924 (CF)

League Club	Source	Date Signed	Seasons Played	Apps	Subs	Gls
Hartlepool U.		12.47	47-54	198	-	87

WILE, John D.
Sherburn (Dm), 9 March, 1947 (CD)

League Club	Source	Date Signed	Seasons Played	Apps	Subs	Gls
Sunderland	Durham C.	06.66				
Peterborough U.	Tr	07.67	67-70	116	2	7
West Bromwich A.	Tr	12.70	70-82	499	1	24
Peterborough U.	Tr	08.83	83-85	86	1	3

WILEMAN, Richard A.
Breedon (Leics), 4 October, 1947 (WH)

League Club	Source	Date Signed	Seasons Played	Apps	Subs	Gls
Notts Co.		07.66	66	2	0	0

WILKES, David A.
Barnsley, 10 March, 1964 (M)

League Club	Source	Date Signed	Seasons Played	Apps	Subs	Gls
Barnsley	App	03.82	81-83	14	3	2
Halifax T.	L	03.83	82	4	0	0
Stockport Co.	Hong Kong	08.86	86	8	0	0
Carlisle U. (N/C)	Bridlington T.	11.90	90-91	1	4	0

WILKES, Stephen B.
Preston, 30 June, 1967 (M)

League Club	Source	Date Signed	Seasons Played	Apps	Subs	Gls
Wigan Ath.	App	06.85				
Preston N.E.	Tr	08.86	87	1	2	0

WILKIE, Arthur W.
Woolwich, 7 October, 1942 (G)

League Club	Source	Date Signed	Seasons Played	Apps	Subs	Gls
Reading	Jnrs	10.59	61-67	169	0	2

WILKIE, Derrick
Browney, 27 July, 1939 (CH)

League Club	Source	Date Signed	Seasons Played	Apps	Subs	Gls
Middlesbrough	Jnrs	03.57	59-60	4	-	0
Hartlepool U.	Tr	09.61	61-63	74	-	0

WILKIE, John C.
Dundee, 1 July, 1947 (F)

League Club	Source	Date Signed	Seasons Played	Apps	Subs	Gls
Halifax T.	Ross Co.	02.73	72-73	29	8	8
Wigan Ath.	Elgin C.	(N/L)	78	3	1	0

WILKIE, Robert M.
Dundee, 7 October, 1935 (OL)

League Club	Source	Date Signed	Seasons Played	Apps	Subs	Gls
Tottenham H.	Lochee Harp	12.56	56	1	-	0

WILKIN, Kevin
Cambridge, 1 October, 1967 (F)

League Club	Source	Date Signed	Seasons Played	Apps	Subs	Gls
Northampton T.	Cambridge C.	08.90	90	7	2	2

WILKINS, Alan J.
Treherbert, 3 October, 1944 (IF)

League Club	Source	Date Signed	Seasons Played	Apps	Subs	Gls
Swansea C.		05.63	63-64	5	-	0

WILKINS, Dean M.
Hillingdon, 12 July, 1962 (M)

League Club	Source	Date Signed	Seasons Played	Apps	Subs	Gls
Queens Park R.	App	05.80	80-82	1	5	0
Brighton & H.A.	Tr	08.83	83	2	0	0
Leyton Orient	L	03.84	83	10	0	0
Brighton & H.A.	P.E.C. Zwolle (Neth)	07.87	87-91	201	4	18

WILKINS, George E.
Hackney, 27 October, 1917 (IF)

League Club	Source	Date Signed	Seasons Played	Apps	Subs	Gls
Brentford	Hayes	02.38	38-46	29	-	7
Bradford P.A.	Tr	02.47	46-47	27	-	6
Nottingham F.	Tr	12.47	47-48	24	-	6
Leeds U.	Tr	09.49	49	3	-	0

WILKINS, Graham G.
Hillingdon, 28 June, 1955 (FB)

League Club	Source	Date Signed	Seasons Played	Apps	Subs	Gls
Chelsea	App	07.72	72-81	136	1	1
Brentford	Tr	07.82	82-83	36	2	0
Southend U.	L	03.84	83	3	0	0

WILKINS, Kenneth
Salford, 24 October, 1928 (F)

League Club	Source	Date Signed	Seasons Played	Apps	Subs	Gls
Southampton		10.49	50	2	-	0
Exeter C.	Tr	10.51	51	3	-	0
Southampton	Tr	07.52	52	1	-	0
Fulham	Tr	07.53				

WILKINS, Leonard
Southampton, 20 September, 1925 (FB)

League Club	Source	Date Signed	Seasons Played	Apps	Subs	Gls
Southampton	Cunliffe-Owen	10.45	48-57	260	-	2

WILKINS, Leonard H. J.
Dublin, 12 August, 1920 (FB)

League Club	Source	Date Signed	Seasons Played	Apps	Subs	Gls
Brighton & H.A.	Guildford C.	10.48	48-50	44	-	2

WILKINS, Michael J.
Leeds, 6 May, 1942 (CF)

League Club	Source	Date Signed	Seasons Played	Apps	Subs	Gls
Bradford C.	Jnrs	09.59	59	1	-	0

WILKINS, Paul
Hackney, 20 March, 1964 (F)

League Club	Source	Date Signed	Seasons Played	Apps	Subs	Gls
Crystal Palace	Tottenham H. (App)	01.82	81-83	9	4	3
Preston N.E.	Tr	06.84	84	3	3	2

WILKINS, Raymond C.
Hillingdon, 14 September, 1956 E Sch/E Yth/Eu21-1/Eu23-2/E-84 (M)

League Club	Source	Date Signed	Seasons Played	Apps	Subs	Gls
Chelsea	App	10.73	73-78	176	3	30
Manchester U.	Tr	08.79	79-83	158	2	7
Queens Park R.	Glasgow Rangers	11.89	89-91	87	1	4

Ray Wilkins (Chelsea, Manchester United, AC Milan, Paris St Germain, Glasgow Rangers, Queens Park Rangers & England)

WILKINS, Raymond J. H.
Crossley, 16 August, 1928 (CF)

League Club	Source	Date Signed	Seasons Played	Apps	Subs	Gls
Derby Co.	Moira U.	01.50	49-53	30	-	11
Wrexham	Boston U.	05.57	57	3	-	1

WILKINS, Richard J.
Lambeth, 28 May, 1965 (M)

League Club	Source	Date Signed	Seasons Played	Apps	Subs	Gls
Colchester U.	Haverhill Rov.	11.86	86-89	150	2	24
Cambridge U.	Tr	07.90	90-91	71	2	7

WILKINS, Ronald
Treherbert, 21 December, 1923 (IL)

League Club	Source	Date Signed	Seasons Played	Apps	Subs	Gls
Newport Co.	Gwynfil B.C.	01.46	46	1	-	0

WILKINSON, Alan
Middlewich, 5 June, 1935 (IF)

League Club	Source	Date Signed	Seasons Played	Apps	Subs	Gls
Crewe Alex. (Am)	Middlewich	10.55	55	1	-	0

WILKINSON, Albert
Barnsley, 3 November, 1928 (W)

League Club	Source	Date Signed	Seasons Played	Apps	Subs	Gls
Bradford C. (Am)		03.51	50	2	-	0
Halifax T.	Denaby U.	07.52	52	14	-	2
Rotherham U.	Tr	07.53				
Chesterfield	Tr	06.54				

WILKINSON, G. Barry
Bishop Auckland, 16 June, 1935 E Yth (WH)

League Club	Source	Date Signed	Seasons Played	Apps	Subs	Gls
Liverpool	West Auckland	06.54	53-59	78	-	0
Tranmere Rov.	Bangor C.	08.63	63	3	-	0

WILKINSON, Barry J.
Lincoln, 19 July, 1942 (CF)

League Club	Source	Date Signed	Seasons Played	Apps	Subs	Gls
Lincoln C.	Ruston Sports	12.63	62-63	6	-	3

WILKINSON, David L.
Sunderland, 28 May, 1928 (OL)

League Club	Source	Date Signed	Seasons Played	Apps	Subs	Gls
Blackburn Rov.		07.48	48	1	-	0
Bournemouth	Tr	06.50	50-51	8	-	3

WILKINSON, Derek
Stalybridge, 4 June, 1935 EF Lge (OR)

League Club	Source	Date Signed	Seasons Played	Apps	Subs	Gls
Sheffield Wed.	Dukinfield	11.53	54-64	212	-	53

WILKINSON, Eric
Sheffield, 6 March, 1931 (WH)

League Club	Source	Date Signed	Seasons Played	Apps	Subs	Gls
Bradford C.		01.51				
Sheffield U.	Tr	08.53				
Bournemouth	Tr	07.55	55	4	-	0

WILKINSON, Eric
Stalybridge, 4 June, 1935 (F)

League Club	Source	Date Signed	Seasons Played	Apps	Subs	Gls
Sheffield Wed.	Dukinfield	03.58	58	1	-	0

WILKINSON, Ernest S.
Chesterfield, 13 February, 1947 (CH)

League Club	Source	Date Signed	Seasons Played	Apps	Subs	Gls
Arsenal	App	02.64				
Exeter C.	Tr	06.66	66-67	59	1	0
Rochdale	L	03.68	67	9	0	0

WILKINSON, Graham J.
Hull, 21 October, 1934 (FB)

League Club	Source	Date Signed	Seasons Played	Apps	Subs	Gls
Hull C.	Jnrs	09.52	58-59	3	-	0

WILKINSON, Harold S.
Sunderland, 20 March, 1926 (WH)

League Club	Source	Date Signed	Seasons Played	Apps	Subs	Gls
Chelsea		06.46				
Exeter C.	Tr	05.50	50	1	-	0
Colchester U.	Tr	08.51	52	1	-	0

WILKINSON, Herbert
Sunderland, 2 August, 1922

League Club	Source	Date Signed	Seasons Played	Apps	Subs	Gls
Lincoln C.		08.45	46-50	39	-	0

WILKINSON, Howard
Sheffield, 13 November, 1943 (W)

League Club	Source	Date Signed	Seasons Played	Apps	Subs	Gls
Sheffield Wed.	Sheffield U. (Am)	06.62	64-65	22	0	3
Brighton & H.A.	Tr	07.66	66-80	116	13	19

WILKINSON, John
Middlewich, 17 September, 1931 (CF)

League Club	Source	Date Signed	Seasons Played	Apps	Subs	Gls
Arsenal	Witton A.	10.53	54	1	-	0
Sheffield U.	Tr	03.56	55-56	29	-	16
Port Vale	Tr	06.57	57-59	83	-	38
Exeter C.	Poole T.	10.59	59-60	48	-	26

WILKINSON, John
Worksop, 1 April, 1949 (FB)

League Club	Source	Date Signed	Seasons Played	Apps	Subs	Gls
Grimsby T.	App	04.66	65-67	8	1	0

WILKINSON, Joseph
Seaham, 8 December, 1934 (G)

League Club	Source	Date Signed	Seasons Played	Apps	Subs	Gls
Burnley	West Auckland	12.55				
Bradford C.	Tr	03.59	58-59	17	-	0
Hartlepool U.	Tr	02.60	59-61	74	-	0

WILKINSON, Kenneth
Gateshead, 9 May, 1924

League Club	Source	Date Signed	Seasons Played	Apps	Subs	Gls
Huddersfield T.	Jnrs	05.42				
Hartlepool U.	Tr	04.47	46-48	53	-	5

WILKINSON, Neil
Blackburn, 16 February, 1955 (RB)

League Club	Source	Date Signed	Seasons Played	Apps	Subs	Gls
Blackburn Rov.	App	02.73	72-76	27	3	0
Port Vale	South Africa	07.78	78	7	0	0
Crewe Alex.	Tr	10.78	78-80	68	7	0

WILKINSON, Norman
Tantobie, 9 June, 1910 (G)

League Club	Source	Date Signed	Seasons Played	Apps	Subs	Gls
Huddersfield T.	Tanfield Lea	05.32				
Stoke C.		07.35	35-51	186	-	0

WILKINSON, Norman F.
Alnwick, 16 February, 1931 (CF)

League Club	Source	Date Signed	Seasons Played	Apps	Subs	Gls
Hull C. (Am)		11.52	53	8	-	3
York C.	Tr	05.54	54-65	354	0	127

League Club	Source	Date Signed	Seasons Played	Career Record Apps	Subs	Gls

WILKINSON, Paul
Louth, 30 October, 1964 Eu21-4 (F)

League Club	Source	Date Signed	Seasons Played	Apps	Subs	Gls
Grimsby T.	App	10.82	82-84	69	2	27
Everton	Tr	03.85	84-86	19	12	6
Nottingham F.	Tr	03.87	86-87	32	2	5
Watford	Tr	08.88	88-90	133	1	52
Middlesbrough	Tr	08.91	91	46	0	15

WILKINSON, Paul I.
Themelthorpe (Nk), 19 April, 1952 (M)

League Club	Source	Date Signed	Seasons Played	Apps	Subs	Gls
Norwich C.	App	04.70				
Plymouth Arg.	L	01.71	70	2	0	0

WILKINSON, Roy J.
Hiendley Green, 17 September, 1941 (WH)

League Club	Source	Date Signed	Seasons Played	Apps	Subs	Gls
Bolton W.	Jnrs	02.60	60-61	3	-	0

WILKINSON, Stephen J.
Lincoln, 1 September, 1968 (F)

League Club	Source	Date Signed	Seasons Played	Apps	Subs	Gls
Leicester C.	App	09.86	86-89	5	4	1
Crewe Alex.	L	09.88	88	3	2	2
Mansfield T.	Tr	10.89	89-91	102	4	40

WILKINSON, Stephen J.
Halifax, 6 August, 1946 (G)

League Club	Source	Date Signed	Seasons Played	Apps	Subs	Gls
Halifax T. (Am)	Jnrs	08.63	63	2	-	0

WILKINSON, Thomas
Blackhall (Dm), 8 May, 1931 (WH)

League Club	Source	Date Signed	Seasons Played	Apps	Subs	Gls
Hartlepool U.		09.52	53-57	22	-	0

WILKINSON, William
Stockton, 24 March, 1943 (M)

League Club	Source	Date Signed	Seasons Played	Apps	Subs	Gls
Hull C.	Middlesbrough (Am)	05.62	62-72	208	15	34
Rotherham U.	Tr	11.72	72-73	25	1	0
Southport (N/C)	Tacoma (USA)	10.76	76	10	0	0

WILKS, Alan
Slough, 5 October, 1946 (F)

League Club	Source	Date Signed	Seasons Played	Apps	Subs	Gls
Chelsea	App	08.64				
Queens Park R.	Tr	05.65	66-70	44	5	14
Gillingham	Tr	07.71	71-75	138	13	29

WILLARD, Cecil T.
Chichester, 16 January, 1924 (WH)

League Club	Source	Date Signed	Seasons Played	Apps	Subs	Gls
Brighton & H.A.	Chichester C.	11.46	46-52	190	-	23
Crystal Palace	Tr	07.53	53-54	46	-	5

WILLDER, Frederick
Lytham St Annes, 20 March, 1944 E Yth (IF)

League Club	Source	Date Signed	Seasons Played	Apps	Subs	Gls
Blackpool	Jnrs	05.62				
Chester C.	Preston N.E. (trial)	09.63	64-65	1	1	0

WILLDIG, Patrick G.
Stoke, 5 June, 1932 (F)

League Club	Source	Date Signed	Seasons Played	Apps	Subs	Gls
Port Vale	Stoke C. (Am)	05.50	55	2	-	0

WILLEMSE, Stanley B.
Brighton, 23 August, 1924 E Sch/EF Lge/E'B'-1 (LB)

League Club	Source	Date Signed	Seasons Played	Apps	Subs	Gls
Brighton & H.A.	Jnrs	06.46	46-48	91	-	3
Chelsea	Tr	07.49	49-55	198	-	2
Leyton Orient	Tr	06.56	56-57	59	-	2

WILLETT, Ernest
Burslem, 27 July, 1919 (CH)

League Club	Source	Date Signed	Seasons Played	Apps	Subs	Gls
Port Vale	Stoke C. (Am)	01.46	46	1	-	0

WILLETT, Leonard
Ruabon, 17 September, 1940 W Sch (HB)

League Club	Source	Date Signed	Seasons Played	Apps	Subs	Gls
Wrexham	Jnrs	05.58	59	1	-	0

WILLETTS, Joseph
Shotton (Dm), 12 July, 1924 (FB)

League Club	Source	Date Signed	Seasons Played	Apps	Subs	Gls
Hartlepool U.		09.43	46-55	239	-	20

WILLEY, Alan E.
Exeter, 16 September, 1941 (IF)

League Club	Source	Date Signed	Seasons Played	Apps	Subs	Gls
Oxford U.	Bridgwater T.	12.60	62-65	85	1	23
Millwall	Tr	03.66	65-66	9	1	0

WILLEY, Alan S.
Houghton-le-Spring, 18 October, 1956 (F)

League Club	Source	Date Signed	Seasons Played	Apps	Subs	Gls
Middlesbrough	App	09.74	74-77	27	22	7

WILLIAMS, Adrian
Reading, 16 August, 1971 (D)

League Club	Source	Date Signed	Seasons Played	Apps	Subs	Gls
Reading	YT	03.89	88-91	69	2	6

WILLIAMS, Alan
Bristol, 3 June, 1938 (CH)

League Club	Source	Date Signed	Seasons Played	Apps	Subs	Gls
Bristol C.	Jnrs	09.55	55-60	135	-	2
Oldham Ath.	Tr	06.61	61-64	172	-	9
Watford	Tr	07.65	65-66	43	0	4
Newport Co.	Tr	11.66	66-68	63	0	2
Swansea C.	Tr	10.68	68-71	141	4	7

WILLIAMS, Alan C.
Aberdare, 4 December, 1923 (RH)

League Club	Source	Date Signed	Seasons Played	Apps	Subs	Gls
Norwich C.	Fulham (Am)	01.47	46	1	-	0

WILLIAMS, Aled A.
Holywell, 14 June, 1933 (HB)

League Club	Source	Date Signed	Seasons Played	Apps	Subs	Gls
Burnley	Rhyl	10.52				
Chester C.	Tr	07.57	57	32	-	1

WILLIAMS, Alexander
Manchester, 13 November, 1961 E Yth (G)

League Club	Source	Date Signed	Seasons Played	Apps	Subs	Gls
Manchester C.	App	11.79	80-85	114	0	0
Port Vale	Tr	11.86	86-87	35	0	0

WILLIAMS, Alfred S.
South Africa, 1 May, 1919 (OL)

League Club	Source	Date Signed	Seasons Played	Apps	Subs	Gls
Plymouth Arg.	Aberdeen	08.49	49	35	-	4

WILLIAMS, Alvan
Anglesey, 21 November, 1932 (CH)

League Club	Source	Date Signed	Seasons Played	Apps	Subs	Gls
Bury	Stalybridge Celtic	12.54	55	2	-	1
Wrexham	Tr	06.56	56	13	-	6
Bradford P.A.	Tr	06.57	57-59	92	-	21
Exeter C.	Tr	08.60	60	19	-	1

WILLIAMS, Andrew
Birmingham, 29 July, 1962 (M)

League Club	Source	Date Signed	Seasons Played	Apps	Subs	Gls
Coventry C.	Solihull Bor.	07.85	85-86	3	6	0
Rotherham U.	Tr	10.86	86-88	87	0	13
Leeds U.	Tr	11.88	88-90	25	21	3
Port Vale	L	12.91	91	5	0	0
Notts Co.	Tr	02.92	91	14	1	1

WILLIAMS, Benjamin F.
Lincoln, 14 April, 1951 (W)

League Club	Source	Date Signed	Seasons Played	Apps	Subs	Gls
Grimsby T.	Lincoln U.	07.69	69	2	0	0

WILLIAMS, Bert F.
Bilston, 31 January, 1920 E'B'-1/EF Lge/E-24 (G)

League Club	Source	Date Signed	Seasons Played	Apps	Subs	Gls
Walsall		05.37	37-38	25	-	0
Wolverhampton W.	Tr	09.45	46-56	381	-	0

WILLIAMS, Brett
Dudley, 19 March, 1968 (LB)

League Club	Source	Date Signed	Seasons Played	Apps	Subs	Gls
Nottingham F.	App	12.85	85-91	34	0	0
Stockport Co.	L	03.87	86	2	0	0
Northampton T.	L	01.88	87	3	1	0
Hereford U.	L	09.89	89	14	0	0
Oxford U.	L	02.92	91	7	0	0

WILLIAMS, Brian
Salford, 5 November, 1955 (LB/W)

League Club	Source	Date Signed	Seasons Played	Apps	Subs	Gls
Bury	App	04.73	71-76	148	11	19
Queens Park R.	Tr	07.77	77	9	10	0
Swindon T.	Tr	06.78	78-80	89	10	8
Bristol Rov.	Tr	07.81	81-84	172	0	20
Bristol C.	Tr	07.85	85-86	77	0	3
Shrewsbury T.	Tr	07.87	87-88	62	3	1

WILLIAMS, R. Brian
Liverpool, 4 October, 1927 (WH)

League Club	Source	Date Signed	Seasons Played	Apps	Subs	Gls
Liverpool	South Liverpool	08.45	48-52	31	-	5
Crewe Alex.	Tr	05.54	54-57	144	-	5

WILLIAMS, Ceri
Tonyrefail, 16 October, 1965 W Yth (W)

League Club	Source	Date Signed	Seasons Played	Apps	Subs	Gls
Newport Co.	Jnrs	06.83	82-84	19	8	2

WILLIAMS, Charles A.
Barnsley, 23 December, 1928 (CH)

League Club	Source	Date Signed	Seasons Played	Apps	Subs	Gls
Doncaster Rov.	Upton Colly	10.48	49-58	158	-	1

WILLIAMS, Christopher R.
Brecon, 25 December, 1955 (F)

League Club	Source	Date Signed	Seasons Played	Apps	Subs	Gls
Cardiff C.	Talgarth	12.77	77	3	0	0

WILLIAMS, Clarence
Felling, 13 January, 1933 (G)

League Club	Source	Date Signed	Seasons Played	Apps	Subs	Gls
Grimsby T.	Doncaster Rov. (Am)	03.53	52-59	188	-	0
Barnsley	Tr	03.60	60-61	23	-	0

WILLIAMS, Cyril E.
Bristol, 17 November, 1921 Died 1980 (IF)

League Club	Source	Date Signed	Seasons Played	Apps	Subs	Gls
Bristol C.	Jnrs	05.39	46-47	78	-	27
West Bromwich A.	Tr	06.48	48-50	71	-	19
Bristol C.	Tr	08.51	51-57	218	-	42

WILLIAMS, Daniel T.
Rotherham, 20 November, 1924 (WH)

League Club	Source	Date Signed	Seasons Played	Apps	Subs	Gls
Rotherham U.	Silverwood Colly	10.43	46-59	459	-	19

WILLIAMS, Darren
Birmingham, 15 December, 1968 (M)

League Club	Source	Date Signed	Seasons Played	Apps	Subs	Gls
Leicester C.	App	12.86	88-89	7	3	2
Lincoln C.	L	11.89	89	2	0	0
Lincoln C.	L	03.90	89	5	2	0
Chesterfield	L	09.90	90	4	1	1

WILLIAMS, Darwell
Llanelli, 4 November, 1926 (WH)

League Club	Source	Date Signed	Seasons Played	Apps	Subs	Gls
Swansea C.	Loughor	05.46	50-54	130	-	4

WILLIAMS, David
Shafton, 25 February, 1946 (WH)

League Club	Source	Date Signed	Seasons Played	Apps	Subs	Gls
Doncaster Rov.		07.64	64	1	-	0

WILLIAMS, David
Sheffield, 7 October, 1931 (WH)

League Club	Source	Date Signed	Seasons Played	Apps	Subs	Gls
Grimsby T.	Beighton Colly	03.53	53	5	-	0

WILLIAMS, David M.
Cardiff, 11 March, 1955 W Yth/Wu21-1/W-5 (M)

League Club	Source	Date Signed	Seasons Played	Apps	Subs	Gls
Bristol Rov.	Clifton Ath.	08.75	75-84	342	10	66
Norwich C.	Tr	07.85	85-87	56	4	11

WILLIAMS, David P.
Liverpool, 18 September, 1968 (G)

League Club	Source	Date Signed	Seasons Played	Apps	Subs	Gls
Oldham Ath.	YT	08.87				
Burnley	Tr	03.88	88-91	22	0	0
Rochdale	L	09.91	91	6	0	0

WILLIAMS, David S.
Newport, 1 March, 1942 (RB)

League Club	Source	Date Signed	Seasons Played	Apps	Subs	Gls
Newport Co.	Nash U.	10.60	60-72	302	3	2

WILLIAMS, Dean
Lichfield, 5 January, 1972 (G)

League Club	Source	Date Signed	Seasons Played	Apps	Subs	Gls
Birmingham C.	YT	07.90	89-90	4	0	0

WILLIAMS, Dean A.
Hemel Hempstead, 14 November, 1970 (F)

League Club	Source	Date Signed	Seasons Played	Apps	Subs	Gls
Cambridge U. (YT)	YT	07.87	87	1	0	0

WILLIAMS, Derek
Mold, 15 June, 1934 W Amat (G)

League Club	Source	Date Signed	Seasons Played	Apps	Subs	Gls
Manchester C. (Am)	Mold Alex	05.51	51	1	-	0
Wrexham (Am)	Mold Alex	08.54	54	12	-	0
Oldham Ath.	Mold Alex	09.56	56	28	-	0

WILLIAMS, Derek
Felling, 28 January, 1937 (CF)

League Club	Source	Date Signed	Seasons Played	Apps	Subs	Gls
Grimsby T.	Doncaster Y.M.C.A.	01.57	56-61	44	-	19
Bradford P.A.	Tr	08.62	62	19	-	8

WILLIAMS, Derek H.
Ellesmere Port, 9 December, 1922 (HB)

League Club	Source	Date Signed	Seasons Played	Apps	Subs	Gls
Chester C.	Little Sutton	09.41	46	2	-	0

WILLIAMS, Derek O.
Chirk, 3 September, 1949 (G)

League Club	Source	Date Signed	Seasons Played	Apps	Subs	Gls
Shrewsbury T.	Oswestry T.	10.69	69	1	0	0

WILLIAMS, Edgar
Sheffield, 20 May, 1919 (G)

League Club	Source	Date Signed	Seasons Played	Apps	Subs	Gls
Rotherham U.		05.46				
Nottingham F.	Tr	05.47				
Northampton T.	Tr	06.48	48	3	-	0

WILLIAMS, Edward M. L.
Chester, 28 November, 1935

League Club	Source	Date Signed	Seasons Played	Apps	Subs	Gls
Aston Villa	Everton (Am)	08.53				
Wrexham	Tr	08.54	54	1	-	0

WILLIAMS, Elfyn
Barmouth, 25 September, 1939 (F)

League Club	Source	Date Signed	Seasons Played	Apps	Subs	Gls
Wrexham	Portmadoc	03.58	58	1	-	0
Crystal Palace	Tr	07.59				

WILLIAMS, Emlyn
Maesteg, 15 January, 1912 (FB)

League Club	Source	Date Signed	Seasons Played	Apps	Subs	Gls
Barnsley		10.36	36-38	88	-	0
Preston N.E.	Tr	06.39	46-47	62	-	0
Barnsley	Tr	04.48	47-48	17	-	0
Accrington St.	Tr	12.48	48	15	-	0

WILLIAMS, Eric
Manchester, 10 July, 1921 (FB)

League Club	Source	Date Signed	Seasons Played	Apps	Subs	Gls
Manchester C.	Brindle Heath L.C.	03.45	46-49	38	-	0
Halifax T.	Mossley	10.51	51-53	111	-	0

WILLIAMS, Evan M.
Swansea, 12 October, 1932 (LB)

League Club	Source	Date Signed	Seasons Played	Apps	Subs	Gls
Cardiff C.	Penllegaer	03.50				
Exeter C.	Tr	05.54	54	1	-	0
Aldershot	Tr	07.55				

WILLIAMS, Evan S.
Dumbarton, 15 July, 1943 (G)

League Club	Source	Date Signed	Seasons Played	Apps	Subs	Gls
Wolverhampton W.	Third Lanark	03.66	67	13	0	0
Aston Villa	L	08.69	69	12	0	0

WILLIAMS, A. Everton
Blackrod, 1 February, 1957 (F)

League Club	Source	Date Signed	Seasons Played	Apps	Subs	Gls
Wrexham	Jnrs	07.75	75	1	1	0

WILLIAMS, Frank
Halifax, 23 May, 1921 (OL)

League Club	Source	Date Signed	Seasons Played	Apps	Subs	Gls
Halifax T. (Am)	Boothstown	09.47	47	4	-	0

WILLIAMS, R. Frank
Overton, 12 March, 1917 Died 1978 (G)

League Club	Source	Date Signed	Seasons Played	Apps	Subs	Gls
Wrexham		08.46	46-47	35	-	0

WILLIAMS, Gareth C.
Hendon, 30 October, 1941 (M)

League Club	Source	Date Signed	Seasons Played	Apps	Subs	Gls
Cardiff C.	Jnrs	04.59	62-67	161	0	14
Bolton W.	Tr	10.67	67-70	108	1	11
Bury	Tr	10.71	71-72	39	3	4

WILLIAMS, Gareth J.
Cowes (IOW), 12 March, 1967 (FB)

League Club	Source	Date Signed	Seasons Played	Apps	Subs	Gls
Aston Villa	Gosport Bor.	01.88	87-89	6	6	0
Barnsley	Tr	08.91	91	15	2	0

WILLIAMS, Gary
Wolverhampton, 17 June, 1960 (FB)

League Club	Source	Date Signed	Seasons Played	Apps	Subs	Gls
Aston Villa	App	06.78	78-86	235	5	0
Walsall	L	03.80	79	9	0	0
Leeds U.	Tr	07.87	87-88	39	0	3
Watford	Tr	01.90	89-90	39	3	0
Bradford C.	Tr	12.91	91	22	0	0

WILLIAMS, Gary
Nantwich, 14 May, 1959 (M/FB)

League Club	Source	Date Signed	Seasons Played	Apps	Subs	Gls
Tranmere Rov. (N/C)	Jnrs	09.76	76	1	0	0
Blackpool	Djurgaardens (Swe)	08.80	80	30	1	2
Swindon T.	Tr	08.81	81	37	1	3
Tranmere Rov.	Tr	02.83	82-88	163	11	16

WILLIAMS, Gary A.
Bristol, 8 June, 1963 (M)

League Club	Source	Date Signed	Seasons Played	Apps	Subs	Gls
Bristol C.	App	08.80	80-83	98	2	1
Swansea C. (N/C)	Portsmouth (N/C)	01.85	84	6	0	0
Oldham Ath.	Bristol Rov. (N/C)	08.85	85-90	45	16	12

WILLIAMS, Gary P.
Liverpool, 8 March, 1954 (LB)

League Club	Source	Date Signed	Seasons Played	Apps	Subs	Gls
Preston N.E.	Marine	04.72	71-76	107	5	2
Brighton & H.A.	Tr	07.77	77-81	158	0	7
Crystal Palace	Tr	07.82	82	10	0	0

WILLIAMS, George
Ynysddu, 19 May, 1914 (FB)

League Club	Source	Date Signed	Seasons Played	Apps	Subs	Gls
Charlton Ath.		11.34				
Aldershot	Tr	05.36	36-38	69	-	0
Millwall	Tr	11.38	38-46	25	-	0

WILLIAMS, D. Geraint
Treorchy, 5 January, 1962 W Yth/Wu21-2/W-11 (M)

League Club	Source	Date Signed	Seasons Played	Apps	Subs	Gls
Bristol Rov.	App	01.80	80-84	138	3	8
Derby Co.	Tr	03.85	84-91	276	1	9

WILLIAMS, Gilbert
West Bromwich, 12 January, 1925 (WH)

League Club	Source	Date Signed	Seasons Played	Apps	Subs	Gls
West Bromwich A.	Harvills Hearts	02.44	47	7	-	0

WILLIAMS, Glyn J. J.
Maesteg, 3 November, 1918 W-1 (RB)

League Club	Source	Date Signed	Seasons Played	Apps	Subs	Gls
Cardiff C.	Caerau	08.46	46-52	144	-	0

WILLIAMS, Gordon
Newcastle, 22 February, 1929 (CF)

League Club	Source	Date Signed	Seasons Played	Apps	Subs	Gls
Sheffield U.		09.49	49	5	-	0
Darlington	Tr	06.50	50	5	-	1

WILLIAMS, Gordon G.
Swindon, 19 June, 1925 (OL)

League Club	Source	Date Signed	Seasons Played	Apps	Subs	Gls
Swindon T.		05.45	46-56	129	-	14

WILLIAMS, Graham E.
Denbigh, 2 April, 1938 Wu23-2/W-26 (LB)

League Club	Source	Date Signed	Seasons Played	Apps	Subs	Gls
West Bromwich A.	Rhyl	04.55	55-70	308	6	10

WILLIAMS, Graham G.
Wrexham, 31 December, 1936 W Sch/Wu23-1/W-5 (OL)

League Club	Source	Date Signed	Seasons Played	Apps	Subs	Gls
Bradford C.	Oswestry T.	08.55	55	9	-	2
Everton	Tr	03.56	55-58	31	-	6
Swansea C.	Tr	02.59	58-61	89	-	20
Wrexham	Tr	07.64	64	24	-	6
Tranmere Rov.	Wellington T.	08.66	66-67	73	0	12
Port Vale	Tr	07.68	68	21	2	1

WILLIAMS, Grenville R.
Swansea, 30 June, 1921 (WH)

League Club	Source	Date Signed	Seasons Played	Apps	Subs	Gls
Norwich C.	Waverley	06.46	46-47	40	-	0
Newport Co.	Tr	04.49	49	5	-	0

WILLIAMS, Harold T.
Briton Ferry, 17 June, 1924 W-4 (OR)

League Club	Source	Date Signed	Seasons Played	Apps	Subs	Gls
Newport Co.	Ferry Ath.	11.46	46-48	75	-	16
Leeds U.	Tr	06.49	49-55	211	-	32
Newport Co.	Tr	03.57	56	10	-	0
Bradford P.A.	Tr	07.57	57	15	-	0

WILLIAMS, Henry G.
Salford, 24 February, 1929 (IF)

League Club	Source	Date Signed	Seasons Played	Apps	Subs	Gls
Manchester U.		05.49				
West Ham U.	Witton A.	04.51	51	5	-	1
Bury	Tr	06.53	53	2	-	0
Swindon T.	Tr	06.54	54	14	-	7

WILLIAMS, Herbert J.
Swansea, 6 October, 1940 W Sch/Wu23-5/W-3 (M)

League Club	Source	Date Signed	Seasons Played	Apps	Subs	Gls
Swansea C.	Jnrs	05.58	58-74	492	21	104

WILLIAMS, Herbert J.
Cwmbran, 19 June, 1925 W Amat (OL)

League Club	Source	Date Signed	Seasons Played	Apps	Subs	Gls
Newport Co. (Am)	Westons	09.48	48	2	-	1

WILLIAMS, Horace O.
Laughton, 4 October, 1921 (CH)

League Club	Source	Date Signed	Seasons Played	Apps	Subs	Gls
Rotherham U.	Thurcroft Colly	01.43	46-53	210	-	12

WILLIAMS, Ivor
Scunthorpe, 29 May, 1935 (G)

League Club	Source	Date Signed	Seasons Played	Apps	Subs	Gls
Scunthorpe U.		08.59	59	8	-	0

WILLIAMS, James L.
Wolverhampton, 8 May, 1953 (F)

League Club	Source	Date Signed	Seasons Played	Apps	Subs	Gls
Walsall	Worcester C.	03.79	78-79	29	9	2

WILLIAMS, Jeffrey B.
Salford, 1 January, 1933 (IF)

League Club	Source	Date Signed	Seasons Played	Apps	Subs	Gls
Oldham Ath.		06.51	51	1	-	0

WILLIAMS, Jeremy S.
Didcot, 24 March, 1960 (M/D)

League Club	Source	Date Signed	Seasons Played	Apps	Subs	Gls
Reading	App	03.78	76-87	283	26	17
Gillingham	Tr	08.88	88	7	6	0
Aldershot	Tr	07.89	89-90	64	3	7

WILLIAMS, John
Greenock, 21 November, 1925

League Club	Source	Date Signed	Seasons Played	Apps	Subs	Gls
Blackburn Rov.		06.47				
Southport	Tr	07.48	48	2	-	0

WILLIAMS, John
Doncaster, 14 April, 1920 (RB)

League Club	Source	Date Signed	Seasons Played	Apps	Subs	Gls
Leeds U.	Denaby U.	12.48	48	1	-	0

WILLIAMS, John D.
Trelewis, 15 May, 1935 (F)

League Club	Source	Date Signed	Seasons Played	Apps	Subs	Gls
Everton		05.56				
Crewe Alex.	Tr	06.57	57	5	-	0

WILLIAMS, John D.
Pwllheli, 22 August, 1965

League Club	Source	Date Signed	Seasons Played	Apps	Subs	Gls
Wrexham (N/C)	Jnrs	08.82	82	0	1	0

WILLIAMS, John L.
Rhymney, 27 January, 1936 (WH)

League Club	Source	Date Signed	Seasons Played	Apps	Subs	Gls
Cardiff C.	Jnrs	05.53				
Plymouth Arg.	Tr	07.58	58-61	34	-	0
Torquay U.	Tr	06.62	62-64	43	-	0

WILLIAMS, John N.
Birmingham, 11 May, 1968 (W)

League Club	Source	Date Signed	Seasons Played	Apps	Subs	Gls
Swansea C.	Cradley T.	08.91	91	36	3	11

WILLIAMS, John R.
Tottenham, 26 March, 1947 (LB)

League Club	Source	Date Signed	Seasons Played	Apps	Subs	Gls
Watford	App	10.64	64-74	371	3	2
Colchester U.	Tr	07.75	75-77	107	1	1

WILLIAMS, John S. J.
Plymouth, 16 August, 1935 (WH)

League Club	Source	Date Signed	Seasons Played	Apps	Subs	Gls
Plymouth Arg.	Jnrs	10.52	55-65	411	1	48
Bristol Rov.	Tr	12.66	66-68	66	3	10

WILLIAMS, John W.

League Club	Source	Date Signed	Seasons Played	Apps	Subs	Gls
Tranmere Rov. (Am)		08.46	46	1	-	0

WILLIAMS, W. John
Liverpool, 3 October, 1960 (CD)

League Club	Source	Date Signed	Seasons Played	Apps	Subs	Gls
Tranmere Rov.	Jnrs	10.79	78-84	167	6	13
Port Vale	Tr	07.85	85-86	50	0	3
Bournemouth	Tr	12.86	86-89	115	2	9
Wigan Ath.	L	10.91	91	4	0	0
Cardiff C.	Tr	12.91	91	5	0	0

WILLIAMS, Keith D.
Burntwood, 12 April, 1957 (M/D)

League Club	Source	Date Signed	Seasons Played	Apps	Subs	Gls
Aston Villa	App	04.75				
Northampton T.	Tr	02.77	76-80	128	3	6
Bournemouth	Tr	08.81	81-86	99	3	1
Colchester U.	Bath C.	12.87	87	9	1	0

WILLIAMS, R. A. Keith
Eastham, 14 January, 1937 (IF)

League Club	Source	Date Signed	Seasons Played	Apps	Subs	Gls
Everton	Jnrs	03.54				
Tranmere Rov.	Tr	05.57	57-60	161	-	87
Plymouth Arg.	Tr	06.61	61	10	-	4
Bristol Rov.	Tr	01.62	61-62	49	-	18

WILLIAMS, Kenneth

League Club	Source	Date Signed	Seasons Played	Apps	Subs	Gls
Watford		01.47	46	2	-	0

WILLIAMS, Kenneth
Doncaster, 7 January, 1927 (WH)

League Club	Source	Date Signed	Seasons Played	Apps	Subs	Gls
Rotherham U.		09.48	49	3	-	0
York C.	Tr	07.51	53	1	-	0

WILLIAMS, Leslie
Thurcroft, 27 March, 1935 (G)

League Club	Source	Date Signed	Seasons Played	Apps	Subs	Gls
Sheffield Wed.		07.53	55-56	11	-	0
Swindon T.	Tr	01.57				
Rotherham U.	Tr	01.58				

WILLIAMS, Mark
Hereford, 17 September, 1957 (M)

League Club	Source	Date Signed	Seasons Played	Apps	Subs	Gls
Newport Co.	Bromsgrove Rov.	08.76	76-78	59	9	9

WILLIAMS, Mark
Bangor, 10 December, 1973 (F)

League Club	Source	Date Signed	Seasons Played	Apps	Subs	Gls
Shrewsbury T.	YT	07.92	91	0	1	0

WILLIAMS, Mark S.
Hyde, 28 September, 1970 (CD)

League Club	Source	Date Signed	Seasons Played	Apps	Subs	Gls
Shrewsbury T. (N/C)	Newtown	03.92	91	2	1	0

WILLIAMS, Martin K.
Luton, 12 July, 1973 (W)

League Club	Source	Date Signed	Seasons Played	Apps	Subs	Gls
Luton T.	Leicester C. (YT)	09.91	91	0	1	0

WILLIAMS, Michael
Bangor, 1 December, 1956 (M)

League Club	Source	Date Signed	Seasons Played	Apps	Subs	Gls
Wrexham	Jnrs	06.75	74-77	9	0	0

Geraint Williams (Bristol Rovers, Derby County & Wales)

League Club	Source	Date Signed	Seasons Played	Apps	Subs	Gls

WILLIAMS, Michael
Deeside, 6 February, 1965 W Yth (CD)

Chester C.	App	02.83	81-83	30	4	4
Wrexham	Tr	07.84	84-89	172	6	3

WILLIAMS, Michael J.
Hull, 23 October, 1944 (G)

Hull C.	App	10.62	62-65	88	0	0
Aldershot	Tr	07.66				
Workington	Tr	07.68	68-69	15	0	0
Scunthorpe U.	Tr	07.70	70-73	28	0	0

WILLIAMS, Mostyn
Cymfelinfach, 2 October, 1928 Died 1990 (RB)

Newport Co.	Ynysddu Welfare	12.49	49-51	28	-	0

WILLIAMS, Neil J. F.
Waltham Abbey, 23 October, 1964 (W/FB)

Watford	App	08.82				
Hull C.	Tr	07.84	84-87	75	16	9
Preston N.E.	Tr	07.88	88-91	109	12	6

WILLIAMS, Nigel J.
Canterbury, 29 July, 1954 (FB)

Wolverhampton W.	App	08.72	74-75	11	0	0
Gillingham	Tr	07.76	76-78	51	2	1

WILLIAMS, Oshor J.
Stockton, 21 April, 1958 (W)

Manchester U.	Middlesbrough (App)	08.76				
Southampton	Gateshead	03.78	78-79	4	2	0
Exeter C.	L	08.78	78	2	1	0
Stockport Co.	Tr	08.79	79-84	192	1	26
Port Vale	Tr	11.84	84-85	47	2	6
Preston N.E.	Tr	08.86	86-87	38	1	12

WILLIAMS, Paul A.
Sheffield, 8 September, 1963 NI Yth/NI-1 (CD/F)

Preston N.E.	Nuneaton Bor.	12.86	86	1	0	0
Newport Co.	Tr	08.87	87	26	0	3
Sheffield U.	Tr	03.88	87-88	6	2	0
Hartlepool U.		10.89	89	7	1	0
Stockport Co.	Tr	08.90	90	24	0	15
West Bromwich A.	Tr	03.91	90-91	26	18	5

WILLIAMS, Paul A.
Stratford, 16 August, 1965 Eu21-4 (F)

Charlton Ath.	Woodford T.	02.87	87-89	74	8	23
Brentford	L	10.87	87	7	0	3
Sheffield Wed.	Tr	08.90	90-91	71	15	24

WILLIAMS, Paul D.
Burton, 26 March, 1971 Eu21-6 (M)

Derby Co.	YT	07.89	89-91	67	3	17
Lincoln C.	L	11.89	89	3	0	0

WILLIAMS, Paul J.
Lambeth, 16 November, 1962 (D)

Chelsea	App	07.80	82	1	0	0

WILLIAMS, Paul L.
Liverpool, 25 September, 1970 (FB/W)

Sunderland	YT	07.89	88-91	6	4	0
Swansea C.	L	03.91	90	12	0	0

WILLIAMS, Paul R. C.
Leicester, 11 September, 1969 (W/LB)

Leicester C.	YT	06.88				
Stockport Co.	Tr	07.89	89-91	37	7	3

WILLIAMS, Paul S.
Newton Abbot, 20 February, 1964 (F)

Bristol C.	Ottery St Mary	03.83	82-83	16	3	1
Exeter C. (N/C)	Saltash U.	08.85	85-87	8	10	1

WILLIAMS, Peter J.
Nottingham, 21 October, 1931 (W)

Derby Co.	South Normanton	08.52	52	2	-	0
Chesterfield	Boston U.	07.55	55	13	-	4

WILLIAMS, Peter S. H.
Plymouth, 18 December, 1938 (WH)

Exeter C.	Plymouth Arg. (Am)	04.60	60	1	-	0

WILLIAMS, Peter W.
Wrexham, 17 May, 1960 (F)

Wrexham	Jnrs	07.78	78-80	4	1	1

League Club	Source	Date Signed	Seasons Played	Apps	Subs	Gls

WILLIAMS, Philip D.
Swansea, 24 November, 1966 (W)

Swansea C.	App	10.84	83-87	42	17	5

WILLIAMS, Philip J.
Swansea, 7 February, 1963 W Sch (M)

Blackpool	Arsenal (App)	11.80				
Crewe Alex.	Tr	08.81	81	39	0	3
Wigan Ath.	Tr	08.82	82-83	1	2	0
Chester C.	L	09.83	83	6	1	0
Crewe Alex.	Tr	12.83	83	14	6	3

WILLIAMS, Philip L.
Birkenhead, 5 April, 1958 (F)

Chester C.	Jnrs	07.76	76	1	0	0

WILLIAMS, Raymond
Wrexham, 1 May, 1931 (FB)

Wrexham	Holyhead	05.51	51	12	-	0

WILLIAMS, Raymond
Stoke, 30 August, 1946 (F)

Port Vale	Stafford Rangers	08.72	72-76	165	8	39

WILLIAMS, W. Raymond
Bebington, 30 December, 1930 (WH)

Tranmere Rov.		02.49	51-58	195	-	12

WILLIAMS, Reginald F.
Watford, 28 January, 1922 (IF)

Chelsea	Watford (Am)	10.45	46-51	58	-	13

WILLIAMS, G. Robert
Felling, 18 November, 1932 (WH)

Rotherham U.	Jnrs	07.50	53	4	-	2
Sheffield U.	Tr	05.54				
Bradford C.	Wisbech T.	05.56	56	6	-	0
Mansfield T.	Tr	07.57	57-61	154	-	5

WILLIAMS, Robert F.
Chester, 24 November, 1932 (IF)

New Brighton (Am)	Saltney Jnrs	08.49	49	1	-	0
Chester C.	South Liverpool	10.51	51-59	37	-	3

WILLIAMS, Robert G.
Bristol, 17 February, 1940 (IF)

Bristol C.	Jnrs	05.58	58-64	187	-	76
Rotherham U.	Tr	02.65	64-66	47	0	12
Bristol Rov.	Tr	03.67	66-68	28	1	5
Reading	Tr	08.69	69-70	60	4	20

WILLIAMS, Robert J.
Bridgend, 9 October, 1968 (FB)

Oxford U.	YT	08.87				
Hereford U.	Tr	08.88	88	5	0	0

WILLIAMS, Robert R.
Liverpool, 25 October, 1927

Liverpool	Jnrs	11.45				
Wrexham	Tr	06.51	51	7	-	0
Shrewsbury T.	Tr	10.51	51	5	-	0

WILLIAMS, Ronald A.
Swansea, 12 September, 1949 (F)

Swansea C.	Jnrs	09.68	67-68	8	2	1

WILLIAMS, D. Rowland (Roley)
Swansea, 10 July, 1927 (IF)

Cardiff C.	Milford U.	02.49	48-55	138	-	19
Northampton T.	Tr	03.56	55-56	15	-	0

WILLIAMS, Roy B.
Hereford, 3 March, 1932 (IF)

Southampton	Hereford U.	11.52	52-54	41	-	7

WILLIAMS, Sidney F.
Bristol, 21 December, 1919 (W)

Bristol C.		07.46	46-51	100	-	11

WILLIAMS, Stephen J.
Barry, 27 April, 1963 W Yth (F)

Bristol Rov.	App	04.81	80	8	0	1

WILLIAMS, Stephen M.
Swansea, 5 November, 1954 (OL)

Swansea C.		03.76	75	7	3	1

WILLIAMS, Steven B.
Mansfield, 18 July, 1970 (F/LB)

Mansfield T.	YT	07.88	86-88	4	7	0
Chesterfield	Tr	10.89	89-91	52	15	7

WILLIAMS, Steven C.
Hammersmith, 12 July, 1958 Eu21-14/E'B'/E-6 (M)

League Club	Source	Date Signed	Seasons Played	Apps	Subs	Gls
Southampton	App	07.76	75-84	277	1	18
Arsenal	Tr	12.84	84-87	93	2	4
Luton T.	Tr	08.88	88-90	39	1	1
Exeter C.	Tr	08.91	91	36	0	0

WILLIAMS, Stuart G.
Wrexham, 9 July, 1930 W-43 (FB)

League Club	Source	Date Signed	Seasons Played	Apps	Subs	Gls
Wrexham (Am)	Victoria Y.C.	06.47	47-49	6	-	0
West Bromwich A.	Tr	02.51	51-62	226	-	6
Southampton	Tr	09.62	62-65	148	2	3

WILLIAMS, Terence J.
Stoke, 23 October, 1966 (M)

League Club	Source	Date Signed	Seasons Played	Apps	Subs	Gls
Stoke C.	App	10.84	84-86	6	5	0

WILLIAMS, Thomas A.
Liverpool, 1 August, 1929 Died 1979 (WH)

League Club	Source	Date Signed	Seasons Played	Apps	Subs	Gls
Tranmere Rov.	Jnrs	11.48	46-56	53	-	2
Southport	Tr	08.58	58	17	-	0

WILLIAMS, Thomas E.
Winchburgh, 18 December, 1957 (D)

League Club	Source	Date Signed	Seasons Played	Apps	Subs	Gls
Leicester C.	App	12.75	77-85	236	5	10
Birmingham C.	Tr	08.86	86-87	62	0	1
Grimsby T.	Tr	07.88	88-89	19	1	0

WILLIAMS, Thomas J.
Battersea, 10 February, 1935 (W)

League Club	Source	Date Signed	Seasons Played	Apps	Subs	Gls
Colchester U.	Carshalton Ath.	09.56	56-60	151	-	30
Watford	Tr	06.61	61	12	-	6

WILLIAMS, Wayne
Telford, 17 November, 1963 (RB)

League Club	Source	Date Signed	Seasons Played	Apps	Subs	Gls
Shrewsbury T.	App	11.81	82-88	212	9	7
Northampton T.	L	11.88	88	3	0	1
Northampton T.	Tr	01.89	88-90	47	5	0
Walsall	Tr	08.91	91	42	0	0

WILLIAMS, William H. J.
Manchester, 24 September, 1925 (F)

League Club	Source	Date Signed	Seasons Played	Apps	Subs	Gls
Bury		01.47	46	1	-	0
Rochdale	Tr	08.49	49	8	-	3
Aldershot	Tr	06.50	50	6	-	4

WILLIAMS, William R.
Littleborough, 7 October, 1960 (CD)

League Club	Source	Date Signed	Seasons Played	Apps	Subs	Gls
Rochdale	Ashe Labs	08.81	81-84	89	6	2
Stockport Co.	Tr	07.85	85-88	104	0	1
Manchester C.	Tr	10.88	88	0	1	0
Stockport Co.	Tr	12.88	88-91	115	3	5

WILLIAMS, William T.
Esher, 23 August, 1942 E Sch/E Yth (CH)

League Club	Source	Date Signed	Seasons Played	Apps	Subs	Gls
Portsmouth	Jnrs	06.60	60	3	-	0
Queens Park R.	Tr	07.61	61-62	45	-	0
West Bromwich A.	Tr	06.63	64	1	-	0
Mansfield T.	Tr	01.66	65-67	47	2	0
Gillingham	Tr	09.67	67-71	169	2	8

WILLIAMSON, Arthur H.
Ardblae, 26 July, 1930 (FB)

League Club	Source	Date Signed	Seasons Played	Apps	Subs	Gls
Southend U.	Clyde	05.55	55-61	269	-	2

WILLIAMSON, Brian W.
Blyth, 6 October, 1939 (G)

League Club	Source	Date Signed	Seasons Played	Apps	Subs	Gls
Gateshead	Seaton Delaval	10.58	58-59	55	-	0
Crewe Alex.	Tr	07.60	60-62	55	-	0
Leeds U.	Tr	12.62	62-64	5	-	0
Nottingham F.	Tr	02.66	67-68	19	0	0
Leicester C.	L	08.67	67	6	0	0
Fulham	Tr	11.68	68-69	12	0	0

WILLIAMSON, Charles
Glasgow, 12 April, 1956 (FB)

League Club	Source	Date Signed	Seasons Played	Apps	Subs	Gls
Bristol C.	Jnrs	07.74				
Torquay U.	L	03.77	76	5	0	0

WILLIAMSON, Charles H.
Sheffield, 16 March, 1962 (LB)

League Club	Source	Date Signed	Seasons Played	Apps	Subs	Gls
Sheffield Wed.	App	02.80	79-83	61	1	1
Lincoln C.	L	01.84	83	5	0	0
Southend U.	L	03.85	84	10	0	0
Chesterfield	Tr	07.85	85-86	47	8	2

WILLIAMSON, Colin J.
Gretna , 25 October, 1957 (W)

League Club	Source	Date Signed	Seasons Played	Apps	Subs	Gls
Workington (N/C)	Liverpool (App)	08.76	76	11	4	2

WILLIAMSON, George
Newcastle, 13 September, 1925 (HB)

League Club	Source	Date Signed	Seasons Played	Apps	Subs	Gls
Middlesbrough		12.45				
Chester C.	Tr	07.47	47-49	76	-	4
Bradford C.	Tr	06.50	50-56	223	-	31

WILLIAMSON, Ian J.
Larbert, 14 March, 1939 (LH)

League Club	Source	Date Signed	Seasons Played	Apps	Subs	Gls
Norwich C.	Falkirk	05.58	58	10	-	1
Bradford P.A.	Tr	06.62	62	17	-	0

WILLIAMSON, John
Manchester, 8 May, 1929 (F)

League Club	Source	Date Signed	Seasons Played	Apps	Subs	Gls
Manchester C.	Newton Heath	08.49	49-54	59	-	18
Blackburn Rov.	Tr	03.56	55-56	9	-	3

WILLIAMSON, Kenneth
Stockton, 7 August, 1928 (IF)

League Club	Source	Date Signed	Seasons Played	Apps	Subs	Gls
Darlington (Am)	Bishop Auckland	08.52	52	13	-	3

WILLIAMSON, Michael
Ashbourne, 30 May, 1942 (OL)

League Club	Source	Date Signed	Seasons Played	Apps	Subs	Gls
Derby Co.	Ashbourne	08.61	61-63	12	-	0
Gillingham	Tr	07.64	65	1	0	0

WILLIAMSON, Philip J.
Macclesfield, 19 June, 1962 (D)

League Club	Source	Date Signed	Seasons Played	Apps	Subs	Gls
Blackburn Rov.	App	09.80	81	0	1	0

WILLIAMSON, Robert
Edinburgh, 6 December, 1933 (G)

League Club	Source	Date Signed	Seasons Played	Apps	Subs	Gls
Barnsley	St Mirren	08.63	63-64	46	-	0
Leeds U.	Tr	06.65				
Rochdale	Tr	07.66	66-67	36	0	0

WILLIAMSON, Robert
Glasgow, 13 August, 1961 (F)

League Club	Source	Date Signed	Seasons Played	Apps	Subs	Gls
West Bromwich A.	Glasgow Rangers	08.86	86-87	40	13	11
Rotherham U.	Tr	07.88	88-90	91	2	49

WILLIAMSON, Stuart H.
Wallasey, 7 April, 1926 (OL)

League Club	Source	Date Signed	Seasons Played	Apps	Subs	Gls
Tranmere Rov.		03.44	46-52	96	-	23
Swindon T.	Tr	06.53	53-54	17	-	0

WILLIAMSON, Thomas
Salford, 16 March, 1913 Died 1992 (CH)

League Club	Source	Date Signed	Seasons Played	Apps	Subs	Gls
Leeds U.	Pendlebury Wed.	09.32				
Oldham Ath.	Northwich Vic.	05.35	35-46	157	-	4

WILLINGHAM, C. Kenneth
Sheffield, 1 December, 1912 Died 1975 EF Lge/E-12 (CH)

League Club	Source	Date Signed	Seasons Played	Apps	Subs	Gls
Huddersfield T.	Worksop T.	11.30	32-38	247	-	4
Sunderland	Tr	12.45	46	14	-	0
Leeds U.	Tr	03.47	46-47	35	-	0

WILLIS, Arthur
Denaby, 2 February, 1920 E-1 (FB)

League Club	Source	Date Signed	Seasons Played	Apps	Subs	Gls
Tottenham H.	Finchley	01.44	46-53	144	-	1
Swansea C.	Tr	09.54	54-57	95	-	0

WILLIS, George
Newcastle, 9 November, 1926 (IR)

League Club	Source	Date Signed	Seasons Played	Apps	Subs	Gls
Wolverhampton W.		01.45				
Brighton & H.A.	Tr	02.48	47-48	28	-	12
Plymouth Arg.	Tr	05.49	49-55	56	-	14
Exeter C.	Tr	03.56	55-56	26	-	3

WILLIS, J. George
Shotton, 25 July, 1933 (OL)

League Club	Source	Date Signed	Seasons Played	Apps	Subs	Gls
Leeds U.	Evenwood T.	03.53	53	3	-	0
Hartlepool U.	Tr	11.54	54-58	25	-	6

WILLIS, Graham
Bradwell, 20 October, 1946 (FB)

League Club	Source	Date Signed	Seasons Played	Apps	Subs	Gls
Norwich C.	App	10.64	64	1	-	0

WILLIS, James A.
Liverpool, 12 July, 1968 (CD)

League Club	Source	Date Signed	Seasons Played	Apps	Subs	Gls
Halifax T.	Blackburn Rov. (YT)	08.86				
Stockport Co.	Tr	12.87	87	10	0	0
Darlington	Tr	03.88	87-91	90	0	6
Leicester C.	Tr	12.91	91	9	1	0
Bradford C.	L	03.92	91	9	0	1

WILLIS, John J.
Boldon, 28 May, 1934 (F)

League Club	Source	Date Signed	Seasons Played	Apps	Subs	Gls
Blackburn Rov.		08.54	55	1	-	0
Aston Villa	Mossley	08.58	58	1	-	0

WILLIS, Paul E.
Liverpool, 24 January, 1970 (M)

League Club	Source	Date Signed	Seasons Played	Apps	Subs	Gls
Halifax T.	YT	05.88	87-88	1	4	0
Darlington	Tr	03.89	88	1	1	1

WILLIS, Roger C.
Sheffield, 17 June, 1967 (F)

League Club	Source	Date Signed	Seasons Played	Apps	Subs	Gls
Grimsby T.	Dunkirk	07.89	89	1	8	0
Barnet	Tr	08.90	91	33	5	12

WILLIS, Ronald I.
Romford, 27 December, 1947 E Yth (G)

League Club	Source	Date Signed	Seasons Played	Apps	Subs	Gls
Leyton Orient	Coventry C. (Am)	01.66	66-67	45	0	0
Charlton Ath.	Tr	10.67	67	1	0	0
Brentford	L	09.68	68	1	0	0
Colchester U.	Tr	10.68	68-69	6	0	0

WILLMOTT, Ian M.
Bristol, 10 July, 1968 (FB)

League Club	Source	Date Signed	Seasons Played	Apps	Subs	Gls
Bristol Rov.	Weston-super-Mare	11.88	89-91	18	4	0

WILLS, Gordon F.
West Bromwich 24 April, 1934 (OL)

League Club	Source	Date Signed	Seasons Played	Apps	Subs	Gls
Wolverhampton W.	West Bromwich A. (Am)	12.51				
Notts Co.	Tr	08.53	53-57	154	-	47
Leicester C.	Tr	05.58	58-61	111	-	30
Walsall	Tr	06.62	62-63	35	-	1

WILLS, Leonard E.
Hackney, 8 November, 1927 (FB)

League Club	Source	Date Signed	Seasons Played	Apps	Subs	Gls
Arsenal	Eton Manor	10.49	53-60	195	-	4

WILLSHAW, George J.
Hackney, 18 October, 1912 (OL)

League Club	Source	Date Signed	Seasons Played	Apps	Subs	Gls
Southend U.	Walthamstow Ave.	02.36	35-37	28	-	6
Bristol C.	Tr	06.38	38	34	-	9
Leyton Orient	Tr	09.42	46	12	-	2

WILMOT, Rhys J.
Newport, 21 February, 1962 W Sch/Wu21-6 (G)

League Club	Source	Date Signed	Seasons Played	Apps	Subs	Gls
Arsenal	App	02.80	85-86	8	0	0
Hereford U.	L	03.83	82	9	0	0
Leyton Orient	L	05.84	84	46	0	0
Swansea C.	L	08.88	88	16	0	0
Plymouth Arg.	L	03.89	88	17	0	0
Plymouth Arg.	Tr	07.89	89-91	116	0	0

WILMOTT, Gordon A.
Brinsley, 26 May, 1929 (CH)

League Club	Source	Date Signed	Seasons Played	Apps	Subs	Gls
Birmingham C.		05.47				
Stockport Co.	Tr	06.48	48-58	206	-	1
Crewe Alex.	Tr	03.59	58-60	54	-	0

WILSHAW, Dennis
Stoke, 11 March, 1926 E'B'-2/E-12 (IF)

League Club	Source	Date Signed	Seasons Played	Apps	Subs	Gls
Wolverhampton W.	Packmoor B.C.	09.43	48-57	211	-	105
Walsall	L	05.46	46-48	74	-	27
Stoke C.	Tr	12.57	57-60	94	-	40

WILSHAW, Steven E.
Stoke, 11 January, 1959 (M)

League Club	Source	Date Signed	Seasons Played	Apps	Subs	Gls
Stoke C.	App	01.77				
Crewe Alex.	Tr	08.78	78	20	2	1

WILSHIRE, Peter J.
Bristol, 15 October, 1934 (CF)

League Club	Source	Date Signed	Seasons Played	Apps	Subs	Gls
Bristol Rov.	Jnrs	01.54	53	1	-	0
Bristol C.	Tr	06.55				

WILSON, Alan
Liverpool, 17 November, 1952 (M)

League Club	Source	Date Signed	Seasons Played	Apps	Subs	Gls
Everton	App	07.70	71-72	2	0	0
Southport	Tr	07.75	75-77	134	0	13
Torquay U.	Tr	06.78	78	38	4	2

WILSON, Alan A.
Bathgate, 10 January, 1945 (G)

League Club	Source	Date Signed	Seasons Played	Apps	Subs	Gls
Scunthorpe U.	Partick Th.	07.64				
Mansfield T.	Tr	08.66	66	5	0	0

WILSON, Albert
Rotherham, 28 January, 1915 (W)

League Club	Source	Date Signed	Seasons Played	Apps	Subs	Gls
Derby Co.	Stafford R.	05.36	36	1	-	0
Mansfield T.	Tr	07.38	38	20	-	2
Rotherham U.	Tr	06.46	46	38	-	19
Grimsby T.	Tr	07.47	47	17	-	1

WILSON, Alexander
Stenhousemuir, 3 July, 1938 (OR)

League Club	Source	Date Signed	Seasons Played	Apps	Subs	Gls
Rotherham U.	Clyde	07.61	61	5	-	0

WILSON, Alexander
Buckie, 29 October, 1933 S-1 (FB)

League Club	Source	Date Signed	Seasons Played	Apps	Subs	Gls
Portsmouth	Jnrs	11.50	51-66	348	3	4

WILSON, Alexander A.
Wishaw, 29 October, 1908 Died 1971 (G)

League Club	Source	Date Signed	Seasons Played	Apps	Subs	Gls
Arsenal	Morton	05.33	33-38	82	-	0
Brighton & H.A.	St Mirren	09.47	47	1	-	0

WILSON, Ambrose M.
Lurgan (NI), 10 October, 1924 (FB)

League Club	Source	Date Signed	Seasons Played	Apps	Subs	Gls
Swansea C.	Glenavon	09.50	50	1	-	0

WILSON, Andrew
Rotherham, 27 September, 1940 (W)

League Club	Source	Date Signed	Seasons Played	Apps	Subs	Gls
Sheffield U.		01.60	59-60	4	-	0
Scunthorpe U.	Tr	06.61	61-64	112	-	14
Doncaster Rov.	Tr	07.65	65	20	1	0
Chesterfield	Tr	07.66	66-67	70	2	13
Aldershot	Tr	07.68	68	19	1	1

WILSON, Andrew P.
Maltby, 13 October, 1947 (OR)

League Club	Source	Date Signed	Seasons Played	Apps	Subs	Gls
Rotherham U.		06.67	67	12	4	3
Notts Co.	L	08.68	68	1	0	0
Scunthorpe U.	Tr	09.68	68	23	1	4

WILSON, Andrew W.
Wigan, 7 January, 1965 (M)

League Club	Source	Date Signed	Seasons Played	Apps	Subs	Gls
Wigan Ath.	Skelmersdale U.	08.87	87-88	1	1	0

WILSON, Archibald
South Shields, 4 December, 1924 (G)

League Club	Source	Date Signed	Seasons Played	Apps	Subs	Gls
Gateshead		08.45	46	5	-	0
Lincoln C.	South Shields	04.51	50-51	4	-	0

WILSON, Beverley
Stockport, 11 April, 1953 (CD)

League Club	Source	Date Signed	Seasons Played	Apps	Subs	Gls
Stockport Co.	App	07.70	69-73	59	2	1

WILSON, Beverley A. M.
Eccles, 14 May, 1924 (CH)

League Club	Source	Date Signed	Seasons Played	Apps	Subs	Gls
Wrexham		06.47	47-50	98	-	0
Barrow	Tr	03.51	50-58	309	-	1

WILSON, Brian
Newcastle, 14 April, 1957 (D)

League Club	Source	Date Signed	Seasons Played	Apps	Subs	Gls
Blackpool	App	05.74	76-79	21	10	6
Torquay U.	Tr	11.79	79-82	129	2	6

WILSON, Carl A.
Consett, 8 May, 1940 (CF)

League Club	Source	Date Signed	Seasons Played	Apps	Subs	Gls
Newcastle U.	Jnrs	02.58	58	1	-	0
Gateshead	Tr	01.60	59	17	-	4
Doncaster Rov.	Tr	07.60	60	14	-	2
Millwall	Tr	07.61	61	5	-	1

WILSON, Clive A.
Manchester, 13 November, 1961 (LB/W)

League Club	Source	Date Signed	Seasons Played	Apps	Subs	Gls
Manchester C.	Jnrs	12.79	81-86	107	2	9
Chester C.	L	09.82	82	21	0	2
Chelsea	Tr	05.87	87-89	68	13	5
Queens Park R.	Tr	07.90	90-91	51	2	4

WILSON, Daniel J.
Wigan, 1 January, 1960 NI-24 (M)

League Club	Source	Date Signed	Seasons Played	Apps	Subs	Gls
Bury	Wigan Ath.	09.77	77-79	87	3	8
Chesterfield	Tr	07.80	80-82	100	0	13
Nottingham F.	Tr	01.83	82	9	1	1
Scunthorpe U.	L	10.83	83	6	0	3
Brighton & H.A.	Tr	11.83	83-86	132	3	33
Luton T.	Tr	07.87	87-89	110	0	24
Sheffield Wed.	Tr	08.90	90-91	70	2	9

WILSON, Darren A.
Manchester, 30 September, 1971 (FB)

League Club	Source	Date Signed	Seasons Played	Apps	Subs	Gls
Manchester C.	YT	07.90				
Bury	Tr	06.91	91	30	2	1

WILSON, David
Glasgow, 21 November, 1923

League Club	Source	Date Signed	Seasons Played	Apps	Subs	Gls
Manchester C.		07.47				
Bury	Tr	07.48	48	2	-	1

WILSON, David C.
Nelson, 24 December, 1942 E Sch/Eu23-7 (W)

League Club	Source	Date Signed	Seasons Played	Apps	Subs	Gls
Preston N.E.	Jnrs	04.60	60-66	168	2	31
Liverpool	Tr	02.67	66	0	1	0
Preston N.E.	Tr	06.68	68-73	99	12	10
Bradford C.	L	03.72	71	5	0	0
Southport	L	10.73	73	2	0	0

Dave Wilson (Preston North End, Liverpool & Preston North End)

WILSON, David E. J.
Wednesfield, 4 October, 1944 (F)

League Club	Source	Date Signed	Seasons Played	Apps	Subs	Gls
Nottingham F.	Jnrs	10.61	62-65	8	1	1
Carlisle U.	Tr	10.65	65-66	54	1	23
Grimsby T.	Tr	03.67	66-68	63	0	22
Walsall	Tr	09.68	68-69	34	2	9
Burnley	Tr	09.69	69-70	10	3	0
Chesterfield	Tr	06.71	71-74	125	3	22

WILSON, David G.
Todmorden, 20 March, 1969 (M)

League Club	Source	Date Signed	Seasons Played	Apps	Subs	Gls
Manchester U.	App	03.87	88	0	4	0
Lincoln C.	L	11.90	90	3	0	0
Charlton Ath.	L	03.91	90	6	1	2
Bristol Rov.	Tr	07.91	91	3	0	0

WILSON, Dennis
Bebington, 30 April, 1936 (FB)

League Club	Source	Date Signed	Seasons Played	Apps	Subs	Gls
Wrexham	Jnrs	07.54				
Stoke C.	Rhyl	08.59	59-60	14	-	0

WILSON, Dennis F.
Farnham, 6 September, 1929

League Club	Source	Date Signed	Seasons Played	Apps	Subs	Gls
Norwich C.	Jnrs	09.46				
Aldershot	Tr	06.50	50-51	5	-	0
Crewe Alex.		10.55	55	23	-	0

WILSON, Donald
Heywood, 4 June, 1930 (RB)

League Club	Source	Date Signed	Seasons Played	Apps	Subs	Gls
Bury		05.51	52-58	62	-	1

WILSON, Eugene
Sheffield, 11 September, 1932 (W)

League Club	Source	Date Signed	Seasons Played	Apps	Subs	Gls
Rotherham U.		05.53				
Stockport Co.	Tr	05.54	54-61	224	-	41

WILSON, Eugene A. (Gus)
Manchester, 11 April, 1963 (RB)

League Club	Source	Date Signed	Seasons Played	Apps	Subs	Gls
Crewe Alex.	Runcorn	07.91	91	41	0	0

WILSON, Frederick C.
Nottingham, 10 November, 1918 (CH)

League Club	Source	Date Signed	Seasons Played	Apps	Subs	Gls
Wolverhampton W.		05.36				
Bournemouth		05.37	38-50	98	-	0

WILSON, Glen E.
Newcastle, 2 July, 1929 (WH)

League Club	Source	Date Signed	Seasons Played	Apps	Subs	Gls
Brighton & H.A.	Newcastle U. (Am)	09.49	49-59	410	-	25
Exeter C.	Tr	06.60	60-61	36	-	2

WILSON, Harold
Hetton-le-Hole, 29 November, 1953 E Sch/E Yth (LB)

League Club	Source	Date Signed	Seasons Played	Apps	Subs	Gls
Burnley	App	12.70	71	12	0	0
Brighton & H.A.	Tr	12.73	73-76	130	0	4
Preston N.E.	Tr	07.77	77-79	38	4	0
Darlington	Tr	09.80	80-82	82	3	0
Hartlepool U.	Tr	08.83	83	16	0	0

WILSON, Ian W.
Aberdeen, 27 March, 1958 S-5 (LM)

League Club	Source	Date Signed	Seasons Played	Apps	Subs	Gls
Leicester C.	Elgin C.	04.79	79-87	276	9	17
Everton	Tr	09.87	87-88	24	10	1
Derby Co. (N/C)	Besiktas (Turkey)	02.91	90	11	0	0
Bury	Tr	08.91	91	21	3	1

WILSON, James
Newmains, 20 April, 1942 (OL)

League Club	Source	Date Signed	Seasons Played	Apps	Subs	Gls
Newcastle U.	Shotts B.A.	09.59	60-61	12	-	2

WILSON, James
Glasgow, 19 December, 1929 (OR)

League Club	Source	Date Signed	Seasons Played	Apps	Subs	Gls
Leicester C.	Alloa Ath.	07.54				
Mansfield T.	Tr	03.55	54-55	19	-	1

WILSON, James A.
Musselburgh, 28 June, 1922 (FB)

League Club	Source	Date Signed	Seasons Played	Apps	Subs	Gls
Luton T.	Peterborough U.	07.47	47-50	39	-	1
Northampton T.	Tr	07.51	51	23	-	0

WILSON, James M.
Saltcoats, 19 March, 1923 (IF)

League Club	Source	Date Signed	Seasons Played	Apps	Subs	Gls
Accrington St.	Dundalk	07.49	49	4	-	0

WILSON, James T.
Middlesbrough, 15 March, 1924 (IF)

League Club	Source	Date Signed	Seasons Played	Apps	Subs	Gls
Chelsea	Gravesend & Nft	06.47				
Watford	Leeds U. (trial)	11.50	50-56	49	-	12
Southend U.	Tr	07.57				

WILSON, Jeffrey H.
South Shields, 7 December, 1964 (D)

League Club	Source	Date Signed	Seasons Played	Apps	Subs	Gls
Darlington	App	12.82	82-83	10	1	0

WILSON, John
Airdrie, 29 October, 1916 (IF)

League Club	Source	Date Signed	Seasons Played	Apps	Subs	Gls
Chesterfield	Glasgow Celtic	05.39	46	16	-	3
Oldham Ath.	Tr	07.47	47-48	29	-	2
Accrington St.	Tr	10.48	48-49	27	-	1

WILSON, John A.
Jarrow, 11 April, 1952 (M)

League Club	Source	Date Signed	Seasons Played	Apps	Subs	Gls
Darlington	Consett	09.71	71-72	15	5	1

WILSON, John C.
Norwich, 28 October, 1934 (FB)

League Club	Source	Date Signed	Seasons Played	Apps	Subs	Gls
Norwich C.	Jnrs	08.53	53-58	47	-	0
Chesterfield	Tr	07.59	59	16	-	0

WILSON, John G. (Ian)
Kennoway (Fife), 11 February, 1923 (OL)

League Club	Source	Date Signed	Seasons Played	Apps	Subs	Gls
Preston N.E.	Forfar Ath.	11.46	46-47	16	-	6
Burnley	Tr	06.48	48-49	19	-	1
Leicester C.	Tr	03.50	49-50	12	-	2
Chesterfield	Tr	10.51	51-52	77	-	18
Rotherham U.	Tr	05.53	53-55	108	-	44

WILSON, Joseph
Workington, 6 July, 1937 (FB)

League Club	Source	Date Signed	Seasons Played	Apps	Subs	Gls
Workington	Jnrs	01.56	55-61	153	-	5
Nottingham F.	Tr	03.62	61-64	84	-	1
Wolverhampton W.	Tr	03.65	64-66	58	0	0
Newport Co.	Tr	05.67	67	42	1	0
Workington	Tr	09.68	68-72	168	1	4

WILSON, Joseph A.
Wylam (Nd), 23 March, 1909 Died 1984 (D)

League Club	Source	Date Signed	Seasons Played	Apps	Subs	Gls
Newcastle U.	Tanfield Lea	09.33	34-35	28	-	5
Brighton & H.A.	Tr	05.36	36-46	156	-	15

League Club	Source	Date Signed	Seasons Played	Apps	Subs	Gls
WILSON, Joseph H.						
Manchester, 17 May, 1925						(FB)
Manchester U.	Jnrs	09.44				
Accrington St.	Tr	10.46	46-50	109	-	4
WILSON, Joseph W.						
Newcastle, 10 September, 1911						(CH)
Newcastle U.	Jnrs	09.28	29	1	-	0
Southend U.	Tr	08.30	30-34	162	-	4
Brentford	Tr	07.35	35-38	60	-	2
Reading	Tr	08.39				
Barnsley	Tr	05.46	46	20	-	0
WILSON, Keith						
Wallington, 14 December, 1935						(IF)
Southampton	Andover	07.59				
Gillingham	Tr	07.61	61	5	-	2
WILSON, Kenneth M.						
Dumbarton, 15 September, 1946						(F)
Carlisle U.	Dumbarton	09.72	72	14	6	1
York C.	L	09.73	73	2	0	0
Workington	L	10.73	73	4	1	0
WILSON, Kevin J.						
Banbury, 18 April, 1961 NI-27						(F)
Derby Co.	Banbury U.	12.79	79-84	106	16	30
Ipswich T.	Tr	01.85	84-86	94	4	34
Chelsea	Tr	06.87	87-91	124	28	41
Notts Co.	Tr	03.92	91	8	0	1
WILSON, Leslie J.						
Manchester, 10 July, 1947						(RB)
Wolverhampton W.	Jnrs	09.64	65-71	90	11	7
Bristol C.	Tr	03.71	70-72	42	1	1
Norwich C.	Tr	09.73	73	6	0	0
WILSON, Paul A.						
Norwich, 19 June, 1956						(M)
Norwich C.	App	07.74	75	0	1	0
WILSON, Paul A.						
Bradford, 2 August, 1968						(LB)
Huddersfield T.	YT	06.86	85-86	15	0	0
Norwich C.	Tr	07.87				
Northampton T.	Tr	02.88	87-91	132	9	6
Halifax T.	Tr	12.91	91	23	0	5
WILSON, Paul R.						
Forest Gate, 26 September, 1964						(M)
Barnet (N/C)	Barking	03.88	91	23	2	1
WILSON, F. Peter						
Newcastle, 15 September, 1947						(FB)
Middlesbrough		04.66	67	1	0	0
WILSON, Philip						
Hemsworth, 16 October, 1960						(M)
Bolton W.	App	10.78	79-80	35	4	4
Huddersfield T.	Tr	08.81	81-86	229	4	16
York C.	Tr	08.87	87-88	38	8	2
Scarborough (N/C)	Macclesfield T.	12.89	89-90	39	4	1
WILSON, Philip M.						
Billingham, 5 February, 1972						(CD)
Hartlepool U. (YT)	YT	08.88	89	0	1	0
WILSON, Ramon (Ray)						
Shirebrook, 17 December, 1934 EF Lge/E-63						(LB)
Huddersfield T.	Langwith Jnrs	08.52	55-63	266	-	6
Everton	Tr	07.64	64-68	114	2	0
Oldham Ath.	Tr	07.69	69	25	0	0
Bradford C.	Tr	07.70	70	2	0	0
WILSON, Raymond T.						
Grangemouth, 8 April, 1947 Su23-1						(LB)
West Bromwich A.	Jnrs	05.64	65-75	230	2	3
WILSON, Richard						
Orpington, 8 May, 1960						(F)
Chelsea	App	08.78				
Charlton Ath.	Tr	08.79	79	16	1	1
WILSON, J. Robert						
Liverpool, 8 September, 1928						(RB)
Preston N.E.	Burscough	04.50	52-62	91	-	0
Tranmere Rov.	Tr	09.62	62-63	54	-	0
WILSON, Robert						
Motherwell						(LH)
Workington	Stirling A.	12.52	52	2	-	0
WILSON, Robert J.						
Birmingham, 23 May, 1943						(G)
Aston Villa	Jnrs	09.61	63	9	-	0
Cardiff C.	Tr	08.64	64-67	114	0	0
Bristol C.	L	10.69	69	1	0	0
Exeter C.	Tr	01.70	69-75	205	0	0
WILSON, Robert J.						
Kensington, 5 June, 1961						(M)
Fulham	App	06.79	79-84	168	7	34
Millwall	Tr	08.85	85	28	0	12
Luton T.	Tr	08.86	86-87	19	5	1
Fulham	Tr	09.87	87-88	43	4	4
Huddersfield T.	Tr	07.89	89-90	52	5	8
Rotherham U.	Tr	09.91	91	11	3	3
WILSON, Robert P.						
Chesterfield, 30 October, 1941 E Sch/S-2						(G)
Arsenal	Wolverhampton W. (Am)	03.64	63-73	234	0	0
WILSON, Robert S. W.						
Musselburgh, 29 June, 1934						(WH)
Norwich C.	Aberdeen	05.57	57-58	62	-	0
Gillingham	Tr	06.60	60	35	-	0
Accrington St.	Tr	07.61				
Chester C.	Tr	04.62	62	15	-	0
WILSON, Robert W.						
Oxford, 29 May, 1944						(CF)
Brentford (Am)	Feltham	04.67	66	1	0	1
WILSON, Ronald						
Edinburgh, 6 September, 1941						(LB)
Stoke C.	Musselburgh Ath.	08.59	59-63	11	-	0
Port Vale	Tr	11.63	63-70	261	3	5
WILSON, Ronald						
Ellesmere Port, 7 August, 1933						
Crewe Alex.		11.57	57	1	-	0
WILSON, Ronald G.						
Sale, 10 September, 1924						(WH)
West Ham U.		10.44	46-47	3	-	0
WILSON, Samuel						
Glasgow, 16 December, 1931						(IF)
Millwall	Glasgow Celtic	07.59	59	23	-	11
Northampton T.	Tr	07.60				
WILSON, Stephen L.						
Hull, 24 April, 1974						(G)
Hull C.	YT	07.92	90-91	5	0	0
WILSON, Terence						
Broxburn, 8 February, 1969 Su21-4						(M)
Nottingham F.	App	04.86	87-91	89	11	9
Newcastle U.	L	01.92	91	2	0	0
WILSON, Thomas						
Rosewell, 29 November, 1940						(CH)
Millwall	Falkirk	07.61	61-67	200	1	15
Hull C.	Tr	11.67	67-69	60	0	1
WILSON, Thomas						
Bedlington, 15 September, 1930 Died 1992						(CF)
Nottingham F.	Cinderhill	04.51	51-60	191	-	75
Walsall	Tr	11.60	60-61	53	-	19
WILSON, Thomas B.						
Ayr, 25 July, 1933						(OR)
Reading	Thornton Hibs	03.56	56	8	-	1
Exeter C.	Tr	07.57	57	22	-	2
WILSON, Thomas F.						
Southampton, 3 July, 1930						(FB)
Fulham	Southampton (Am)	08.50	52-56	45	-	0
Brentford	Tr	07.57	57-61	148	-	0
WILSON, Ulrich J.						
Netherlands, 5 May, 1964						(D)
Ipswich T. (L)	Twente Enschede (Neth)	12.87	87	5	1	0

WILSON, William
Seaton Delaval, 10 July, 1946 (FB)

League Club	Source	Date Signed	Seasons Played	Apps	Subs	Gls
Blackburn Rov.	Jnrs	09.63	64-71	246	1	0
Portsmouth	Tr	01.72	71-78	188	6	5

WILSON, William J. R.
Portadown, 23 September, 1936 NI'B'-2 (HB)

League Club	Source	Date Signed	Seasons Played	Apps	Subs	Gls
Burnley	Portadown	09.55	56-57	2	-	0

WILTON, Graham E.
Chesterfield, 19 October, 1942 (OR)

League Club	Source	Date Signed	Seasons Played	Apps	Subs	Gls
Chesterfield (Am)	Chesterfield T.W.	06.61	61	1	-	0

WILTSHIRE, David J.
Folkestone, 8 July, 1954 (RB)

League Club	Source	Date Signed	Seasons Played	Apps	Subs	Gls
Gillingham	Canterbury C.	01.74	73-75	54	8	2
Aldershot	Tr	07.76	76	5	0	0

WIMBLETON, Paul P.
Havant, 13 November, 1964 E Sch (M)

League Club	Source	Date Signed	Seasons Played	Apps	Subs	Gls
Portsmouth	App	02.82	81-83	5	5	0
Cardiff C.	Tr	08.86	86-88	118	1	17
Bristol C.	Tr	05.89	89	10	6	2
Shrewsbury T.	Tr	01.90	89-90	25	9	1
Maidstone U.	L	01.91	90	2	0	1
Exeter C.	Tr	09.91	91	35	1	4

WIMSHURST, Kenneth P.
South Shields, 23 March, 1938 (WH)

League Club	Source	Date Signed	Seasons Played	Apps	Subs	Gls
Newcastle U.	South Shields	07.57				
Gateshead	Tr	11.58	58-59	7	-	0
Wolverhampton W.	Tr	11.60				
Southampton	Tr	07.61	61-67	148	4	9
Bristol C.	Tr	10.67	67-71	146	3	9

WINDASS, Dean
Hull, 1 April, 1969 (M)

League Club	Source	Date Signed	Seasons Played	Apps	Subs	Gls
Hull C.	North Ferriby U.	10.91	91	31	1	6

WINDLE, Charles
Barnsley, 8 January, 1917 Died 1975 (OR)

League Club	Source	Date Signed	Seasons Played	Apps	Subs	Gls
Bury		09.38				
Exeter C.		07.39				
Bristol Rov.	Tr	12.46	46	7	-	1

WINDLE, William H.
Maltby, 9 July, 1920 (W)

League Club	Source	Date Signed	Seasons Played	Apps	Subs	Gls
Leeds U.	Denaby U.	10.47	47	2	-	0
Lincoln C.	Tr	02.48	47-51	91	-	22
Chester C.	Tr	10.51	51-54	128	-	20

WINDRIDGE, David H.
Atherstone, 7 December, 1961 (W)

League Club	Source	Date Signed	Seasons Played	Apps	Subs	Gls
Sheffield U.	Jnrs	01.79				
Chesterfield	Tr	03.80	80-82	66	12	14
Blackpool	Tr	08.83	83-86	87	14	18
Bury (N/C)	Turkey	11.88	88	1	0	0
Rochdale (N/C)	Tr	01.89	88	5	0	0

WINDROSS, Dennis
Gainsborough, 12 May, 1938 (WH)

League Club	Source	Date Signed	Seasons Played	Apps	Subs	Gls
Middlesbrough	Jnrs	05.56	59-60	4	-	1
Brighton & H.A.	Tr	11.60	60	18	-	2
Darlington	Tr	06.61	61	25	-	4
Doncaster Rov.	Tr	06.62	62-63	51	-	4

WINDSOR, Robert
Stoke, 31 January, 1926

League Club	Source	Date Signed	Seasons Played	Apps	Subs	Gls
Stoke C.	Jnrs	12.43				
Lincoln C.	Tr	02.49	48-49	11	-	1

WINFIELD, B. John
Draycott, 28 February, 1943 (LB)

League Club	Source	Date Signed	Seasons Played	Apps	Subs	Gls
Nottingham F.	Jnrs	05.60	61-73	353	2	4
Peterborough U.	Tr	07.74	74	11	0	0

WINFIELD, Philip
Denaby, 16 February, 1937 (HB)

League Club	Source	Date Signed	Seasons Played	Apps	Subs	Gls
Lincoln C.	Denaby U.	10.57	57	1	-	0

WINGATE, John
Budleigh Salterton, 19 December, 1948 (M)

League Club	Source	Date Signed	Seasons Played	Apps	Subs	Gls
Plymouth Arg. (Am)	Dawlish	12.68	68	1	0	0
Exeter C.	Dawlish	02.69	68-73	187	16	32
Bournemouth	Tr	07.74	74	30	3	3
Exeter C.	Tr	07.75	75	44	1	2

WINN, Stephen
Thornaby, 16 September, 1959 (F)

League Club	Source	Date Signed	Seasons Played	Apps	Subs	Gls
Rotherham U.		03.78	78-80	17	7	3
Torquay U.	Tr	01.82	81	12	2	2
Hartlepool U. (N/C)	Scunthorpe U. (N/C)	03.83	82	1	0	0

WINSPEAR, John (Jack)
Leeds, 24 December, 1946 (OR)

League Club	Source	Date Signed	Seasons Played	Apps	Subs	Gls
Leeds U.	Jnrs	10.64				
Cardiff C.	Tr	06.66	66	1	0	0
Rochdale	Tr	07.67	67	15	1	3

WINSTANLEY, Eric
Barnsley, 15 November, 1944 E Yth (CD)

League Club	Source	Date Signed	Seasons Played	Apps	Subs	Gls
Barnsley	Jnrs	05.62	61-72	409	0	35
Chesterfield	Tr	08.73	73-76	100	1	7

WINSTANLEY, Graham
Croxdale (Dm), 20 January, 1948 (CD)

League Club	Source	Date Signed	Seasons Played	Apps	Subs	Gls
Newcastle U.	App	12.68	66-68	5	2	0
Carlisle U.	Tr	08.69	69-74	165	1	8
Brighton & H.A.	Tr	10.74	74-78	63	1	4
Carlisle U.	Tr	07.79	79	32	1	1

WINSTANLEY, Mark A.
St Helens, 22 January, 1968 (CD)

League Club	Source	Date Signed	Seasons Played	Apps	Subs	Gls
Bolton W.	YT	07.86	85-91	169	1	2

WINTER, Daniel T.
Tonypandy, 14 June, 1918 (FB)

League Club	Source	Date Signed	Seasons Played	Apps	Subs	Gls
Bolton W.	Mais-y-hof	06.35	36-38	34	-	0
Chelsea	Tr	12.45	46-50	131	-	0

WINTER, John G. A.
Stoke Newington, 6 March, 1928 (CF)

League Club	Source	Date Signed	Seasons Played	Apps	Subs	Gls
Sheffield U.		11.48				
Walsall	Tr	01.51	50-51	42	-	12

WINTER, Julian
Huddersfield, 6 September, 1965 (M)

League Club	Source	Date Signed	Seasons Played	Apps	Subs	Gls
Huddersfield T.	App	09.83	84-88	89	4	5
Scunthorpe U.	L	08.88	88	4	0	0
Sheffield U.	Tr	07.89				

WINTER, Steven D.
Bristol, 26 October, 1973 (M)

League Club	Source	Date Signed	Seasons Played	Apps	Subs	Gls
Walsall	YT	03.92	91	13	3	0

WINTERBOTTOM, Dennis T.
Glossop, 23 October, 1928 (CH)

League Club	Source	Date Signed	Seasons Played	Apps	Subs	Gls
Accrington St.	Stalybridge Celtic	06.51	51	12	-	0

WINTERBURN, Nigel
Nuneaton, 11 December, 1963 E Yth/Eu21-1/E-1 (LB)

League Club	Source	Date Signed	Seasons Played	Apps	Subs	Gls
Birmingham C.	App	08.81				
Wimbledon	Tr	08.83	83-86	164	1	8
Arsenal	Tr	05.87	87-91	169	1	4

WINTERS, Frank
Johnstone, 30 October, 1923 (WH)

League Club	Source	Date Signed	Seasons Played	Apps	Subs	Gls
Torquay U.	Clyde	05.49	49-51	14	-	0

WINTERS, Herbert R.
Chipping Sodbury, 14 April, 1920 (CH)

League Club	Source	Date Signed	Seasons Played	Apps	Subs	Gls
Bristol Rov.		09.46	46-47	13	-	0

WINTERS, Ian A.
Renfrew, 8 February, 1921 (IF)

League Club	Source	Date Signed	Seasons Played	Apps	Subs	Gls
York C.	Earswick	08.45	46-47	27	-	10
Gateshead	Boston U.	12.48	48-52	152	-	49
Workington	Tr	07.53	53	30	-	3

WINTERS, John M.
Wisbech, 24 October, 1960 (RB)

League Club	Source	Date Signed	Seasons Played	Apps	Subs	Gls
Peterborough U.	App	10.78	80-82	60	0	3

WINTERSGILL, David
Northallerton, 19 September, 1965 (D/M)

League Club	Source	Date Signed	Seasons Played	Apps	Subs	Gls
Wolverhampton W.	App	06.83	82-83	3	1	0
Chester C.	L	03.84	83	6	0	0
Darlington	Finland	11.86	86	15	2	1

WINTLE, Frank J.
Stoke, 20 December, 1929 (FB)

League Club	Source	Date Signed	Seasons Played	Apps	Subs	Gls
Port Vale		05.49	56	1	-	0
Crewe Alex.	Tr	06.57				

WINTON, G. Douglas
Perth, 6 October, 1929 S'B'-1 (FB)

League Club	Source	Date Signed	Seasons Played	Apps	Subs	Gls
Burnley	Jeanfield Swifts	09.47	51-58	183	-	1
Aston Villa	Tr	01.59	58-60	37	-	0
Rochdale	Tr	06.61	61-63	119	-	0

WIPFLER, Charles J.
Trowbridge, 15 July, 1915 (IL)

League Club	Source	Date Signed	Seasons Played	Apps	Subs	Gls
Bristol Rov.		09.34	34	18	-	5
Watford	Hearts	06.37	37-46	35	-	8

WISE, Dennis F.
Kensington, 16 December, 1966 Eu21-1/E'B'/E-5 (W)

League Club	Source	Date Signed	Seasons Played	Apps	Subs	Gls
Wimbledon	Southampton (App)	03.85	84-89	127	8	26
Chelsea	Tr	07.90	90-91	70	1	20

Dennis Wise (Wimbledon, Chelsea & England)

WISEMAN, George
East Dereham, 23 May, 1921 (G)

League Club	Source	Date Signed	Seasons Played	Apps	Subs	Gls
Notts Co.		05.45				
Norwich C.	Tr	09.46	46	8	-	0

WITCOMB, Douglas F.
Ebbw Vale, 18 April, 1918 W-3 (WH)

League Club	Source	Date Signed	Seasons Played	Apps	Subs	Gls
West Bromwich A.	Enfield	10.37	38-46	55	-	3
Sheffield Wed.	Tr	03.47	46-52	224	-	12
Newport Co.	Tr	11.53	53	25	-	0

WITHAM, Richard
Bowburn (Dm), 4 May, 1915 (FB)

League Club	Source	Date Signed	Seasons Played	Apps	Subs	Gls
Huddersfield T.	Durham C.	01.34	33	4	-	0
Blackpool	Tr	02.34	33-37	149	-	0
Oldham Ath.		06.46	46	5	-	0

WITHE, Christopher
Liverpool, 25 September, 1962 (LB)

League Club	Source	Date Signed	Seasons Played	Apps	Subs	Gls
Newcastle U.	App	09.80	80	2	0	0
Bradford C.	Tr	06.83	83-87	141	2	2
Notts Co.	Tr	10.87	87-88	80	0	3
Bury	Tr	07.89	89	22	9	1
Chester C.	L	10.90	90	2	0	0
Mansfield T.	Tr	01.91	90-91	31	0	1

WITHE, Peter
Liverpool, 30 August, 1951 E-11 (F)

League Club	Source	Date Signed	Seasons Played	Apps	Subs	Gls
Southport	Smith Coggins	11.70	70-71	3	0	0
Barrow	Tr	12.71	71	1	0	0
Wolverhampton W.	Arcadia Shep. (SA)	11.73	73-74	12	5	3
Birmingham C.	Tr	08.75	75-76	35	0	9
Nottingham F.	Tr	09.76	76-78	74	1	28
Newcastle U.	Tr	08.78	78-79	76	0	25
Aston Villa	Tr	05.80	80-84	182	0	74
Sheffield U.	Tr	07.85	85-87	70	4	18
Birmingham C.	L	09.87	87	8	0	2
Huddersfield T. (N/C)	Tr	07.88	88-89	22	16	1

Peter Withe (Southport, Barrow, Wolverhampton Wanderers, Birmingham City, Nottingham Forest, Newcastle United, Aston Villa, Sheffield United, Huddersfield Town & England)

WITHEFORD, James D.
Sheffield, 16 April, 1930 (OR)

League Club	Source	Date Signed	Seasons Played	Apps	Subs	Gls
Chesterfield (Am)	Norton Woodseats	12.53	53	9	-	0

WITHERS, Alan
Nottingham, 20 October, 1930 (OL)

League Club	Source	Date Signed	Seasons Played	Apps	Subs	Gls
Blackpool		07.49	50-54	22	-	2
Lincoln C.	Tr	02.55	54-58	97	-	18
Notts Co.	Tr	01.59	58-62	121	-	22

WITHERS, Charles F.
Edmonton, 6 September, 1922 E'B'-1 (FB)

League Club	Source	Date Signed	Seasons Played	Apps	Subs	Gls
Tottenham H.	Jnrs	10.47	47-55	153	-	0

WITHERS, Colin C.
Birmingham, 21 March, 1940 E Sch (G)

League Club	Source	Date Signed	Seasons Played	Apps	Subs	Gls
Birmingham C.	West Bromwich A. (Am)	05.57	60-64	98	-	0
Aston Villa	Tr	11.64	64-68	146	0	0
Lincoln C.	Tr	06.69	69	1	0	0

WITHERS, David R.
Pontypridd, 28 April, 1967 (F)

League Club	Source	Date Signed	Seasons Played	Apps	Subs	Gls
Newport Co. (N/C)		10.86	86-87	7	4	1

WITHEY, Graham A.
Bristol, 11 June, 1960 (F)

League Club	Source	Date Signed	Seasons Played	Apps	Subs	Gls
Bristol Rov.	Bath C.	08.82	82	19	3	10
Coventry C.	Tr	08.83	83-84	11	11	4
Cardiff C.	Tr	12.84	84-85	27	0	7
Bristol C.	Bath C.	09.86	86	1	1	0
Exeter C.	Cheltenham T.	07.88	88	5	2	2

WITHINGTON, Richard
South Shields, 8 April, 1921 (OR)

League Club	Source	Date Signed	Seasons Played	Apps	Subs	Gls
Blackpool	Jnrs	05.38				
Rochdale	Tr	06.47	47	32	-	6
Chesterfield	Tr	06.48	48	6	-	0

WITTER, Anthony J.
London, 12 August, 1965 (CD)

League Club	Source	Date Signed	Seasons Played	Apps	Subs	Gls
Crystal Palace	Grays Ath.	10.90				
Queens Park R.	Tr	08.91				
Plymouth Arg.	L	01.92	91	3	0	1

WOAN, Alan E.
Liverpool, 8 February, 1931 (IF)

League Club	Source	Date Signed	Seasons Played	Apps	Subs	Gls
Norwich C.	New Brighton	12.53	53-55	21	-	7
Northampton T.	Tr	07.56	56-59	120	-	69
Crystal Palace	Tr	10.59	59-60	41	-	21
Aldershot	Tr	02.61	60-63	108	-	44

WOAN, Donald
Liverpool, 7 November, 1927 (W)

League Club	Source	Date Signed	Seasons Played	Apps	Subs	Gls
Liverpool	Bootle	10.50	50	2	-	0
Leyton Orient	Tr	11.51	51-52	25	-	5
Bradford C.	Tr	10.52	52-53	21	-	4
Tranmere Rov.	Tr	02.54	53-54	27	-	2

WOAN, Ian S.
Heswall, 14 December, 1967 (LM)

League Club	Source	Date Signed	Seasons Played	Apps	Subs	Gls
Nottingham F.	Runcorn	03.90	90-91	29	4	8

Ian Woan (Nottingham Forest)

WOFFINDEN, Colin R.
Hove, 6 August, 1947 (CF)

League Club	Source	Date Signed	Seasons Played	Apps	Subs	Gls
Brighton & H.A. (Am)	Lewes T.	11.70	70	0	2	0

WOJTCZAK, Edouard A.
Poland, 29 April, 1921 (G)

League Club	Source	Date Signed	Seasons Played	Apps	Subs	Gls
York C. (Am)	Polish Army	10.46	46	8	-	0

WOLLEN, Terence L.
Swindon, 30 July, 1943 (RB)

League Club	Source	Date Signed	Seasons Played	Apps	Subs	Gls
Swindon T.	Jnrs	08.60	60-64	84	-	0

WOLSTENHOLME, Ian A.
Bradford, 12 January, 1943 E Amat (G)

League Club	Source	Date Signed	Seasons Played	Apps	Subs	Gls
York C. (Am)	St Johns College	10.63	63	2	-	0

WOLSTENHOLME J. Trevor
Prestbury, 18 June, 1943 (WH)

League Club	Source	Date Signed	Seasons Played	Apps	Subs	Gls
Birmingham C.	Jnrs	09.60				
Torquay U.	Tr	08.63	63-65	82	0	2
York C.	Tr	07.66	66	11	0	0

WOMACK, Albert R. (Kim)
Denaby, 20 September, 1934 (W)

League Club	Source	Date Signed	Seasons Played	Apps	Subs	Gls
Derby Co.	Denaby U.	10.57	57	2	-	0
Southampton	Tr	05.59				
Workington	Tr	07.60	60	9	-	1

WOMBLE, Trevor
South Shields, 7 June, 1951 (M)

League Club	Source	Date Signed	Seasons Played	Apps	Subs	Gls
Rotherham U.	App	10.68	68-77	185	28	39
Crewe Alex.	L	11.71	71	4	0	1
Halifax T.	L	03.73	72	9	1	2

WOMERSLEY, Ernest H.
Hartshead, 28 August, 1932 (OR)

League Club	Source	Date Signed	Seasons Played	Apps	Subs	Gls
Huddersfield T.	Jnrs	09.49	50	1	-	0
Bradford C.	Tr	05.57				

WOOD, Alan E.
Gravesend, 1 December, 1954 (D)

League Club	Source	Date Signed	Seasons Played	Apps	Subs	Gls
Charlton Ath.	App	12.72	72	1	0	0

WOOD, Alan H.
Newport, 13 January, 1941 W Amat (CD)

League Club	Source	Date Signed	Seasons Played	Apps	Subs	Gls
Bristol Rov.	Lovells Ath.	10.62	62	1	-	0
Newport Co.	Merthyr Tydfil	05.65	65-72	149	7	5

WOOD, Alfred E. H.
Macclesfield, 25 October, 1945 E Yth (CD/F)

League Club	Source	Date Signed	Seasons Played	Apps	Subs	Gls
Manchester C.	App	06.63	62-65	24	1	0
Shrewsbury T.	Tr	06.66	66-71	257	1	64
Millwall	Tr	06.72	72-74	99	1	38
Hull C.	Tr	11.74	74-76	51	2	10
Middlesbrough	Tr	10.76	76	22	1	2
Walsall	Tr	07.77	77	26	3	2

WOOD, Alfred R.
Aldridge, 14 May, 1915 (G)

League Club	Source	Date Signed	Seasons Played	Apps	Subs	Gls
Coventry C.	Nuneaton T.	12.35	37-51	221	-	0
Northampton T.	Tr	12.51	51-54	139	-	0
Coventry C.	Tr	07.55	55-58	13	-	0

WOOD, Archibald
Leven, 18 March, 1926 (OL)

League Club	Source	Date Signed	Seasons Played	Apps	Subs	Gls
Tranmere Rov.	Bowhill	08.49	49	31	-	5

WOOD, Barrie W.
Doncaster, 5 December, 1936 (IF)

League Club	Source	Date Signed	Seasons Played	Apps	Subs	Gls
Doncaster Rov.	Wolverhampton W. (Am)	08.54	55	2	-	0
Scunthorpe U.	Tr	07.58	58	3	-	1
Barnsley	South Shields	03.61	60-61	5	-	2

WOOD, Brian T.
Poole, 8 December, 1940 (CH)

League Club	Source	Date Signed	Seasons Played	Apps	Subs	Gls
West Bromwich A.	Jnrs	01.58				
Crystal Palace	Tr	05.61	61-66	142	1	1
Leyton Orient	Tr	12.66	66-67	58	0	3
Colchester U.	Tr	08.68	68-69	71	0	1
Workington	Tr	07.70	70-75	202	2	9

WOOD, Charles
(CH)

League Club	Source	Date Signed	Seasons Played	Apps	Subs	Gls
Millwall (Am)		05.46	46	3	-	0

WOOD, Christopher C.
Penistone, 18 May, 1955 (G)

League Club	Source	Date Signed	Seasons Played	Apps	Subs	Gls
Huddersfield T.	App	05.72	72	7	0	0
Barnsley	L	02.73	72	1	0	0
Doncaster Rov.	L	07.74	74	4	0	0

WOOD, Darren
Derby, 22 October, 1968 (CD)

League Club	Source	Date Signed	Seasons Played	Apps	Subs	Gls
Chesterfield	YT	06.87	86-88	61	6	3
Reading	Tr	07.89	89	31	1	2
Northampton T.	Tr	08.90	90-91	3	0	1

WOOD, Darren T.
Scarborough, 9 June, 1964 E Sch (RB/M)

League Club	Source	Date Signed	Seasons Played	Apps	Subs	Gls
Middlesbrough	App	07.81	81-84	101	0	6
Chelsea	Tr	09.84	84-88	134	10	3
Sheffield Wed.	Tr	01.89	88-89	10	1	0

League Club	Source	Date Signed	Seasons Played	Apps	Subs	Gls
WOOD, Edward J.						
West Ham, 23 October, 1919 E Amat						(OL)
West Ham U.	Leytonstone	03.38	37-48	58	-	13
Leyton Orient	Tr	10.49	49	9	-	1
WOOD, Eric						
Bolton, 13 March, 1920						(WH)
Rochdale		08.43	46-50	148	-	15
WOOD, Frank						
Manchester, 17 August, 1924						(CH)
Bury	Hulme	10.48	50	1	-	0
Exeter C.	Shrewsbury T. (trial)	01.53	52	8	-	0
WOOD, Gary T.						
Corby, 2 December, 1955						(FB)
Notts Co.	Kettering T.	12.77	77-80	7	4	0
WOOD, George						
Douglas (Lk), 26 September, 1952 S-4						(G)
Blackpool	East Stirling	01.72	71-76	117	0	0
Everton	Tr	08.77	77-79	103	0	0
Arsenal	Tr	08.80	80-82	60	0	0
Crystal Palace	Tr	08.83	83-87	192	0	0
Cardiff C.	Tr	01.88	87-89	67	0	0
Blackpool	L	03.90	89	15	0	0
Hereford U.	Tr	08.90	90	41	0	0
WOOD, Graham						
Doncaster, 10 February, 1933						(CF)
Wolverhampton W.		09.50				
Halifax T.	Tr	06.53	53-54	19	-	3
WOOD, Harold						
Barrow, 31 December, 1911						
Barrow		02.33	32-48	21	-	2
WOOD, Henry						
Liverpool, 8 April, 1927						(OR)
Chesterfield	South Liverpool	07.53	53	9	-	1
WOOD, Hugh S.						
Bellshill, 16 November, 1960						(D)
Scunthorpe U.	Grantham	09.80	80	0	1	0
WOOD, Ian N.						
Kirkby-in-Ashfield, 24 May, 1958						(D)
Mansfield T.	App	06.76	75-81	135	14	9
Aldershot	Tr	08.82	82	14	0	1
WOOD, Ian T.						
Radcliffe, 15 Janaury, 1948						(FB)
Oldham Ath.	Park Lane Olympic	11.65	65-79	517	7	22
Burnley	Tr	05.80	80	14	3	0
WOOD, James H.						
New Brighton, 25 October, 1938						(G)
Southport	Burscough	04.58	57	1	-	0
WOOD, Jeffrey R.						
Islington, 4 February, 1954						(G)
Charlton Ath.	Harlow T.	11.75	75-80	147	0	0
Colchester U.	Denmark	09.81				
Exeter C.	Happy Valley (HK)	08.84	84	33	0	0
WOOD, John						
Royton, 12 February, 1931						(WH)
Aldershot		09.52	52-54	39	-	1
WOOD, John M.						
Walsall Wood, 9 September, 1948						(FB)
Wrexham	Jnrs	07.66	65-67	4	3	0
WOOD, Kevin						
Armthorpe, 3 November, 1929						(IF)
Doncaster Rov.		10.49				
Grimsby T.	Worksop T.	03.51	50-51	3	-	2
WOOD, T. Leslie						
Haslingden, 20 December, 1932						(G)
Huddersfield T.		04.52				
Barrow	Tr	08.55	55	32	-	0
Port Vale	Tr	06.56	56	2	-	0
Southport	Tr	01.58	57	1	-	0
WOOD, Mark						
Scarborough, 27 June, 1972						(M)
York C.	YT	07.90	90	0	1	0
WOOD, Michael A.						
Halifax, 9 March, 1962						(F)
Rochdale (N/C)	Guiseley	08.86	86	5	1	3
WOOD, Michael J.						
Bury, 3 July, 1952						(D)
Blackburn Rov.	App	02.70	69-77	140	8	2
Bradford C.	Tr	02.78	77-81	143	3	9
Halifax T.	Tr	08.82	82-83	80	1	2
WOOD, Nicholas A.						
Oldham, 6 January, 1966 E Yth						(F)
Manchester U.	App	06.83	85-86	2	1	0
WOOD, Norman						
Sunderland, 10 August, 1932						(WH)
Sunderland	Silksworth Jnrs	05.54	54	1	-	0
WOOD, Norman						
Chadderton, 20 October, 1921						(OR)
Oldham Ath. (Am)	Royton Amats	09.46	46	1	-	0
WOOD, Paul						
Oldham, 20 March, 1970						(M)
Sheffield U.	YT	09.88	87	0	1	0
Rochdale	L	11.88	88	2	3	0
WOOD, Paul A.						
Saltburn, 1 November, 1964						(RW)
Portsmouth	App	11.82	83-86	25	22	7
Brighton & H.A.	Tr	08.87	87-89	77	15	8
Sheffield U.	Tr	02.90	89-91	19	9	3
Bournemouth	L	02.91	90	20	1	0
Bournemouth	Tr	10.91	91	35	0	9
WOOD, Raymond E.						
Hebburn, 11 June, 1931 Eu23-1/E'B'-1/EF Lge/E-3						(G)
Darlington	Newcastle U. (Am)	09.49	49	12	-	0
Manchester U.	Tr	12.49	49-58	178	-	0
Huddersfield T.	Tr	12.58	58-64	207	-	0
Bradford C.	Toronto (Can)	10.65	65	32	0	0
Barnsley	Tr	08.66	66-67	30	0	0
WOOD, Robert						
Elphinstone, 15 February, 1930						(WH)
Barnsley	Hibernian	07.51	51-64	336	-	41
WOOD, Royden						
Wallasey, 16 October, 1930						(G)
Leeds U.	Clitheroe	05.52	53-59	196	-	0
WOOD, Stephen A.						
Bracknell, 2 February, 1963						(CD)
Reading	App	02.81	79-86	216	3	9
Millwall	Tr	06.87	87-91	108	2	0
Southampton	Tr	10.91	91	15	0	0
WOOD, Terence L.						
Newport, 3 September, 1920 W Sch						(WH)
Cardiff C. (Am)	Newport Docks	09.46	46	4	-	0
WOOD, Trevor J.						
Jersey, 3 November, 1968						(G)
Brighton & H.A.	App	11.86				
Port Vale	Tr	07.88	88-90	37	0	0
WOOD, William						
Barnsley, 28 December, 1927						(FB)
Sunderland	Spen. Jnrs	10.48	49	1	-	0
Hull C.	Tr	07.51				
Sheffield U.	Tr	06.52	52	5	-	0
WOOD, William R.						
Manchester, 11 November, 1925						(F)
Wrexham		11.49	49	16	-	5
WOODALL, Arthur J.						
Stoke, 4 June, 1930						(F)
Stoke C.	Jnrs	05.50	53	1	-	0
WOODALL, Brian H.						
Chester, 6 June, 1948						(W)
Sheffield Wed.	App	06.65	67-69	19	3	4
Oldham Ath.	L	02.70	69	3	1	1
Chester C.	Tr	06.70	70	11	2	2
Crewe Alex.	L	03.71	70	10	1	3

WOODALL, John B.
Goole, 16 January, 1949 (F)

League Club	Source	Date Signed	Seasons Played	Apps	Subs	Gls
York C.	Goole T.	02.67	67	2	0	0
Rotherham U.	Gainsborough Trin.	03.74	73-74	25	1	6

WOODBURN, James
Rutherglen, 29 January, 1917 (LH)

League Club	Source	Date Signed	Seasons Played	Apps	Subs	Gls
Newcastle U.	Coltness U.	02.38	38-47	44	-	4
Gateshead	Tr	09.48	48-51	132	-	10

WOODCOCK, Anthony S.
Eastwood, 6 December, 1955 Eu21-2/E-42 (F)

League Club	Source	Date Signed	Seasons Played	Apps	Subs	Gls
Nottingham F.	App	01.74	73-79	125	4	36
Lincoln C.	L	02.76	75	2	2	1
Doncaster Rov.	L	09.76	76	6	0	2
Arsenal	F.C. Köln (Ger)	07.82	82-85	129	2	56

WOODCOCK, David K.
Darlington, 13 October, 1966 (M)

League Club	Source	Date Signed	Seasons Played	Apps	Subs	Gls
Sunderland	App	10.84				
Darlington	Tr	08.85	85-86	14	13	2

WOODCOCK, Ernest
Salford, 14 May, 1925 (W)

League Club	Source	Date Signed	Seasons Played	Apps	Subs	Gls
Bury	Blackburn Rov. (Am)	01.47	46-47	18	-	3
Oldham Ath.	Tr	06.48	48-49	28	-	4

WOODCOCK, Harold
Darlington, 18 September, 1928 (RH)

League Club	Source	Date Signed	Seasons Played	Apps	Subs	Gls
Darlington		08.52	52-53	5	-	0

WOODCOCK, Thomas
Chorley, 19 March, 1926 (IF)

League Club	Source	Date Signed	Seasons Played	Apps	Subs	Gls
Southport (Am)	Preston N.E. (Am)	07.46	46	1	-	0

WOODFIELD, David
Leamington, 11 October, 1943 (CH)

League Club	Source	Date Signed	Seasons Played	Apps	Subs	Gls
Wolverhampton W.	Jnrs	10.60	61-69	247	3	13
Watford	Tr	09.71	71-73	14	1	0

WOODFIELD, Terence
Nottingham, 21 January, 1946 (WH)

League Club	Source	Date Signed	Seasons Played	Apps	Subs	Gls
Notts Co.	Jnrs	07.63	63	5	-	0

WOODFORD, Robert M.
Keyworth, 6 December, 1943 (WH)

League Club	Source	Date Signed	Seasons Played	Apps	Subs	Gls
Notts Co.	Jnrs	03.61	61	3	-	0

WOODGATE, Terence J.
West Ham, 11 December, 1919 Died 1985 (OL)

League Club	Source	Date Signed	Seasons Played	Apps	Subs	Gls
West Ham U.	Beckton	09.38	38-52	259	-	48

WOODHEAD, Andrew
Wallsend, 12 July, 1966 (M)

League Club	Source	Date Signed	Seasons Played	Apps	Subs	Gls
Gillingham (App)	App	07.82	83	1	1	0

WOODHEAD, Dennis
Sheffield, 12 June, 1925 (OL)

League Club	Source	Date Signed	Seasons Played	Apps	Subs	Gls
Sheffield Wed.	Hillsborough B.C.	04.45	46-54	213	-	73
Chesterfield	Tr	09.55	55	15	-	6
Derby Co.	Tr	01.56	55-58	94	-	24
Southport	L	02.59	58	4	-	1

WOODHEAD, Dennis
Huddersfield, 2 September, 1924 (OL)

League Club	Source	Date Signed	Seasons Played	Apps	Subs	Gls
Bradford C.		01.48				
Accrington St.	Tr	05.48	48	6	-	0

WOODHEAD, Simon C.
Dewsbury, 26 December, 1962 (M/FB)

League Club	Source	Date Signed	Seasons Played	Apps	Subs	Gls
Mansfield T.	Jnrs	09.80	80-84	108	14	6

WOODHOUSE, John
Middlesbrough, 5 April, 1937

League Club	Source	Date Signed	Seasons Played	Apps	Subs	Gls
Leeds U.	South Bank	06.55				
Gateshead	Tr	07.57	57	2	-	0

WOODIN, Stephen
Birkenhead, 6 January, 1955 (W)

League Club	Source	Date Signed	Seasons Played	Apps	Subs	Gls
Tranmere Rov.	Jnrs	02.75	74	1	2	0

WOODLEY, Derek G.
Isleworth, 2 March, 1942 E Sch/E Yth (W)

League Club	Source	Date Signed	Seasons Played	Apps	Subs	Gls
West Ham U.	Jnrs	04.59	59-61	12	-	3
Southend U.	Tr	08.62	62-66	159	2	23
Charlton Ath.	Tr	06.67	67	2	1	0
Southend U.	Tr	10.67	67	7	2	0
Gillingham	Tr	01.68	67-70	99	1	9

WOODLEY, Victor R.
Slough, 26 February, 1911 Died 1978 EF Lge/E-19 (G)

League Club	Source	Date Signed	Seasons Played	Apps	Subs	Gls
Chelsea	Windsor & Eton	05.31	31-38	252	-	0
Derby Co.	Bath C.	03.46	46	30	-	0

WOODROFFE, Lewis C.
Portsmouth, 29 October, 1921 (OR)

League Club	Source	Date Signed	Seasons Played	Apps	Subs	Gls
Manchester C.		10.45	46	9	-	1
Watford	Tr	08.47	47-50	63	-	6

WOODRUFF, Arthur
Barnsley, 12 April, 1913 Died 1983 EF Lge (CH)

League Club	Source	Date Signed	Seasons Played	Apps	Subs	Gls
Bradford C.		08.34				
Burnley	Tr	07.36	36-51	271	-	0
Workington	Tr	07.52	52	11	-	0

WOODRUFF, Robert J.
Wolverhampton, 11 March, 1965 (F)

League Club	Source	Date Signed	Seasons Played	Apps	Subs	Gls
Newport Co.	Cardiff C. (Jnrs)	08.83	83	9	1	0
Swindon T.	L	05.84	83	1	1	0

WOODRUFF, Robert W.
Highworth, 9 November, 1940 (M)

League Club	Source	Date Signed	Seasons Played	Apps	Subs	Gls
Swindon T.	Jnrs	05.58	58-63	180	-	20
Wolverhampton W.	Tr	03.64	63-65	63	0	18
Crystal Palace	Tr	06.66	66-69	123	2	48
Cardiff C.	Tr	11.69	69-73	141	9	22
Newport Co.	Tr	08.74	74-75	52	0	7

WOODS, Alan E.
Doncaster, 15 February, 1937 E Sch/E Yth (WH)

League Club	Source	Date Signed	Seasons Played	Apps	Subs	Gls
Tottenham H.	Jnrs	02.54	54	6	-	0
Swansea C.	Tr	12.56	57-59	31	-	0
York C.	Tr	07.60	60-65	227	1	4

WOODS, Charles M.P.
Whitehaven, 18 March, 1941 (IF)

League Club	Source	Date Signed	Seasons Played	Apps	Subs	Gls
Newcastle U.	Cleator Moor	05.59	60-61	26	-	7
Bournemouth	Tr	11.62	62-64	70	-	26
Crystal Palace	Tr	11.64	64-65	49	0	5
Ipswich T.	Tr	07.66	66-69	65	17	5
Watford	Tr	06.70	70-71	40	2	3
Colchester U.	L	11.71	71	3	0	0

WOODS, Christopher C. E.
Boston, 14 November, 1959 E Yth/Eu21-6/E-34 (G)

League Club	Source	Date Signed	Seasons Played	Apps	Subs	Gls
Nottingham F.	App	12.76				
Queens Park R.	Tr	07.79	79-80	63	0	0
Norwich C.	Tr	03.81	80-85	216	0	0
Sheffield Wed.	Glasgow Rangers	08.91	91	41	0	0

Chris Woods (Nottingham Forest, Queens Park Rangers, Norwich City, Glasgow Rangers, Sheffield Wednesday & England)

WOODS, Clive R.
Norwich, 18 December, 1947 (W)

League Club	Source	Date Signed	Seasons Played	Apps	Subs	Gls
Ipswich T.	Gothic	06.69	69-79	217	50	24
Norwich C.	Tr	03.80	79-81	29	3	4

WOODS, Dennis J.
Norwich, 12 December, 1936 (OR)

League Club	Source	Date Signed	Seasons Played	Apps	Subs	Gls
Watford	Cambridge U.	10.62	62	13	-	2

WOODS, Derek E.
Northampton, 23 March, 1941 E Amat (OR)

League Club	Source	Date Signed	Seasons Played	Apps	Subs	Gls
Northampton T. (Am)	Jnrs	06.59	61	6	-	2

WOODS, Edward
Ferndale, 29 July, 1951 (F)

League Club	Source	Date Signed	Seasons Played	Apps	Subs	Gls
Bristol C.	Ton Pentre	09.71	72	1	1	0
Scunthorpe U.	L	10.73	73	4	0	2
Newport Co.	Tr	09.74	74-78	149	2	54

WOODS, Jonathan P.
Blackwood, 5 October, 1966 (F)

League Club	Source	Date Signed	Seasons Played	Apps	Subs	Gls
Cardiff C. (N/C)	Jnrs	08.84	84	0	1	0

WOODS, Maurice (Matt)
Skelmersdale, 1 November, 1931 EF Lge (CH)

League Club	Source	Date Signed	Seasons Played	Apps	Subs	Gls
Everton	Burscough	11.49	52-56	8	-	1
Blackburn Rov.	Tr	11.56	56-62	260	-	2
Luton T.	Hellas (Aus)	07.65	65	34	0	0
Stockport Co.	Tr	07.66	66-67	85	0	2

WOODS, Neil S.
Bradford, 30 July, 1966 (F)

League Club	Source	Date Signed	Seasons Played	Apps	Subs	Gls
Doncaster Rov.	App	08.83	82-86	55	10	16
Ipswich T.	Glasgow Rangers	07.87	87-89	15	12	5
Bradford C.	Tr	03.90	89	13	1	2
Grimsby T.	Tr	08.90	90-91	72	9	20

WOODS, Patrick J.
Islington, 29 April, 1933 (FB)

League Club	Source	Date Signed	Seasons Played	Apps	Subs	Gls
Queens Park R.	Jnrs	06.50	52-60	304	-	16
Colchester U.	Australia	08.63	63	36	-	0

WOODS, Peter A.
Sale, 21 January, 1950 (FB)

League Club	Source	Date Signed	Seasons Played	Apps	Subs	Gls
Manchester U.	App	04.67				
Luton T.	Tr	04.70				
Southend U.	Tr	02.72	71-72	25	0	0
Doncaster Rov.	Tr	07.73	73-74	41	8	1

WOODS, Raymond
Peterborough, 27 April, 1930 (RH)

League Club	Source	Date Signed	Seasons Played	Apps	Subs	Gls
Southend U.	Peterborough U.	05.48	50-51	3	-	1
Crystal Palace	Tr	06.53	53-54	18	-	0

WOODS, Raymond G.
Birkenhead, 7 June, 1965 (RW)

League Club	Source	Date Signed	Seasons Played	Apps	Subs	Gls
Tranmere Rov.	App	06.83	82-84	9	5	2
Wigan Ath.	Colne Dynamoes	02.89	88-90	25	3	3
Coventry C.	Tr	01.91	90-91	21	0	1

WOODS, William
Farnworth, 12 March, 1926 (IF)

League Club	Source	Date Signed	Seasons Played	Apps	Subs	Gls
Rochdale	Moss Grove	04.45	46	15	-	1
Bradford P.A.	Tr	01.47	46	5	-	0
Rochdale	Tr	01.49	48-49	13	-	1
Barrow	Tr	11.49	49	16	-	4
Crewe Alex.	Tr	07.50				
Accrington St.	Tr	11.50	50	3	-	0

WOODTHORPE, Colin J.
Ellesmere Port, 13 January, 1969 (LB)

League Club	Source	Date Signed	Seasons Played	Apps	Subs	Gls
Chester C.	YT	08.86	86-89	154	1	6
Norwich C.	Tr	07.90	90-91	13	3	1

WOODWARD, Alan
Chapeltown, 7 September, 1946 E Yth/EF Lge (W)

League Club	Source	Date Signed	Seasons Played	Apps	Subs	Gls
Sheffield U.	App	09.63	63-78	537	2	158

WOODWARD, Alan
Stanton Hill, 19 June, 1947 (W)

League Club	Source	Date Signed	Seasons Played	Apps	Subs	Gls
Grimsby T.	Alfreton T.	07.70	70-71	54	0	13

WOODWARD, Brian
Leeds, 12 July, 1929 (CF)

League Club	Source	Date Signed	Seasons Played	Apps	Subs	Gls
Leeds U.	Jnrs	07.47				
York C.	Hereford U.	08.50	50	5	-	0

WOODWARD, Harold G.
Bromley, 29 August, 1919 (FB)

League Club	Source	Date Signed	Seasons Played	Apps	Subs	Gls
Southend U.		05.46	50-51	14	-	0

WOODWARD, Horace J.
Islington, 16 January, 1924 (CH)

League Club	Source	Date Signed	Seasons Played	Apps	Subs	Gls
Tottenham H.	Jnrs	05.46	46-48	63	-	1
Queens Park R.	Tr	06.49	49-50	57	-	0
Walsall	Tr	07.53	53	5	-	0

WOODWARD, John
Glasgow, 10 January, 1949 (M)

League Club	Source	Date Signed	Seasons Played	Apps	Subs	Gls
Arsenal	Possilpark Jnrs	01.66	66	2	1	0
York C.	Tr	07.71	71-77	152	15	7

WOODWARD, John
Stoke, 16 January, 1947 (F)

League Club	Source	Date Signed	Seasons Played	Apps	Subs	Gls
Stoke C.	App	03.64	64-66	10	1	1
Aston Villa	Tr	10.66	66-68	22	4	7
Walsall	Tr	05.69	69-72	116	10	23
Port Vale	Tr	02.73	72-74	88	11	30
Scunthorpe U.	Tr	07.75	75	16	3	5

WOODWARD, Kenneth R.
Battersea, 16 November, 1947 (IF)

League Club	Source	Date Signed	Seasons Played	Apps	Subs	Gls
Crystal Palace	App	12.65				
Leyton Orient	Tr	08.66	66	1	0	0

WOODWARD, Laurence (Dai)
Troedyrhiw, 5 July, 1918 (WH)

League Club	Source	Date Signed	Seasons Played	Apps	Subs	Gls
Wolverhampton W.		05.38				
Bournemouth		05.39	46-56	275	-	7

WOODWARD, T. Peter
Birmingham, 6 July, 1934 (G)

League Club	Source	Date Signed	Seasons Played	Apps	Subs	Gls
West Bromwich A.	Moor Green	09.54				
Walsall	Tr	08.58	58	13	-	0

WOODWARD, Thomas
Westhoughton, 8 December, 1917 (OR)

League Club	Source	Date Signed	Seasons Played	Apps	Subs	Gls
Bolton W.	White Horse Temp.	01.35	35-49	152	-	18
Middlesbrough	Tr	10.49	49-50	19	-	6

WOODWARD, Vivian
Troedyrhiw, 20 May, 1914 (IF)

League Club	Source	Date Signed	Seasons Played	Apps	Subs	Gls
Fulham	Folkestone T.	01.36	35-46	92	-	24
Millwall	Tr	02.47	46-47	42	-	13
Brentford	Tr	07.48	48-49	20	-	4
Aldershot	Tr	02.50	49-50	54	-	5

WOODWORTH, Anthony D.
Burnley, 5 March, 1968 (G)

League Club	Source	Date Signed	Seasons Played	Apps	Subs	Gls
Burnley	App	03.86	86	1	0	0

WOOF, Clifford E.
Liverpool, 20 September, 1956 (F)

League Club	Source	Date Signed	Seasons Played	Apps	Subs	Gls
Liverpool	Jnrs	05.76				
Southport (N/C)		12.77	77	1	0	0

WOOF, William
Gateshead, 16 August, 1956 (F)

League Club	Source	Date Signed	Seasons Played	Apps	Subs	Gls
Middlesbrough	App	08.74	74-81	30	16	5
Peterborough U.	L	03.77	76	2	1	0
Cardiff C. (N/C)	Blyth Spartans	09.82	82	1	0	1
Hull C.	Gateshead	02.83	82	9	2	3

WOOKEY, Kenneth G.
Newport, 30 December, 1946 (W)

League Club	Source	Date Signed	Seasons Played	Apps	Subs	Gls
Newport Co.	Jnrs	01.64	64-68	57	6	5
Port Vale	Tr	07.69	69	23	1	4
Workington	Tr	07.70	70	11	5	4

WOOKEY, Kenneth W.
Newport, 23 February, 1922 W Sch (OR)

League Club	Source	Date Signed	Seasons Played	Apps	Subs	Gls
Newport Co.	Jnrs	02.39	46	14	-	2
Bristol Rov.	Tr	12.46	46-48	54	-	9
Swansea C.	Tr	11.48	48-49	13	-	0
Ipswich T.	Hereford U.	10.50	50	15	-	1

WOOLCOTT, Roy A.
Leyton, 29 July, 1946 (CF)

League Club	Source	Date Signed	Seasons Played	Apps	Subs	Gls
Tottenham H.	Eton Manor	02.68	69	1	0	0
Gillingham	L	02.72	71	13	0	5

WOOLDRIDGE, James
Rossington, 28 September, 1918 (LB)

League Club	Source	Date Signed	Seasons Played	Apps	Subs	Gls
Doncaster Rov.	Benburb	12.40	46-47	30	-	0

WOOLDRIDGE, Stephen J.
Chiswick, 18 July, 1950 (RB)

League Club	Source	Date Signed	Seasons Played	Apps	Subs	Gls
Crystal Palace	App	07.67				
Plymouth Arg.	L	08.70	70	20	0	0
Colchester U.	Tr	06.72	72	3	0	0

League Club	Source	Date Signed	Seasons Played	Career Record Apps	Subs	Gls

WOOLER, Alan T.
Poole, 17 August, 1953 (LB)

Reading	Weymouth	11.71	71-72	38	0	0
West Ham U.	Tr	08.73	73-75	3	1	0
Aldershot	Tr	04.76	76-83	264	2	3

WOOLER, M. Graham
Huddersfield, 23 October, 1944 (CF)

Huddersfield T.		08.64				
Halifax T.	Tr	12.64	64-67	51	7	8

WOOLFALL, Alan F.
Liverpool, 30 November, 1956 (W)

Bury	Skelmersdale U.	10.74	74-78	46	11	11
Port Vale	Tr	08.79	79-80	13	5	3

WOOLFORD, Michael
Swindon, 29 September, 1939 (F)

Swindon T.	Swindon B.R.	12.59	59	3	-	0

WOOLGAR, Philip R. J.
Worthing, 24 September, 1948 (G)

Brighton & H.A. (Am)	Wigmore Ath.	06.66	66	1	0	0

WOOLGAR, J. Stuart
Chesterfield, 21 September, 1952 (M)

West Bromwich A.	App	10.69	72	2	2	0
Doncaster Rov.	Tr	07.74	74	2	5	1

WOOLLARD, Arnold J.
Bermuda, 24 August, 1930 (FB)

Northampton T.	Bermuda A.A. (Ber)	06.49	50	3	-	0
Newcastle U.	Tr	12.52	52-55	8	-	0
Bournemouth	Tr	06.56	56-61	161	-	0
Northampton T.	Tr	03.62	61-62	28	-	0

WOOLLETT, Alan H.
Wigston, 4 March, 1947 (D)

Leicester C.	App	08.64	66-77	213	15	0
Northampton T.	Tr	07.78	78	23	0	0

Alan Woollett (Leicester City & Northampton Town)

WOOLLETT, Charles
Seaham, 25 November, 1920 (OL)

Newcastle U.	Eppleton Colly	11.42				
Bradford C.	Tr	08.46	46-48	43	-	5
York C.	Tr	02.49	48	4	-	0

WOOLLEY, Robert A.
Nottingham, 29 December, 1947 Died 1971 (CF)

Notts Co.	App	07.65	63-65	9	0	2

WOOLMER, Anthony J.
Norwich, 25 March, 1946 (CF)

Norwich C.	Jnrs	12.65	66-67	4	1	1
Bradford P.A.	Tr	10.69	69	30	0	7
Scunthorpe U.	Tr	11.70	70-71	35	5	3

WOON, Andrew G.
Bognor Regis, 26 June, 1952 (CF)

Brentford	Bognor Regis T.	10.72	72-74	42	8	12

WOOSNAM, Philip A.
Caersws, 22 December, 1932 W Sch/W Amat/EF Lge/W-17 (IF)

Manchester C. (Am)	Bangor Univ.	06.52	52	1	-	0
Leyton Orient	Sutton U.	03.55	54-58	108	-	19
West Ham U.	Tr	11.58	58-62	138	-	26
Aston Villa	Tr	11.62	62-65	106	0	24

Phil Woosnam (Manchester City, Leyton Orient, West Ham United, Aston Villa & Wales)

WOOTTON, Leonard
Stoke, 13 June, 1925 (F)

Port Vale		08.45	46	10	-	1
Wrexham	Queen of South	08.51	51	20	-	2

WORBOYS, Gavin A.
Doncaster, 14 July, 1974 (F)

Doncaster Rov.	YT	04.92	91	6	1	2

WORDLEY, Edward H.
Stoke, 17 October, 1923

Stoke C.	Jnrs	10.41	46-49	11	-	0
Bury	Tr	06.50				

WORKMAN, Ian P.
Liverpool, 13 November, 1962 (M)

Chester C. (N/C)	Southport	01.83	82	3	0	0

WORLEY, Leonard F.
Amersham, 27 June, 1937 E Yth/E Amat (OL)

League Club	Source	Date Signed	Seasons Played	Apps	Subs	Gls
Charlton Ath. (Am)	Wycombe W.	10.56	56	1	-	0
Tottenham H. (Am)	Wycombe W.	05.59	59	1	-	0

WORMLEY, Paul
Leeds, 16 September, 1961 (F)

League Club	Source	Date Signed	Seasons Played	Apps	Subs	Gls
Barnsley	Yorkshire Amats	10.79	79	1	0	0

WORRALL, Frederick J.
Warrington, 8 September, 1910 Died 1979 E-2 (OR)

League Club	Source	Date Signed	Seasons Played	Apps	Subs	Gls
Oldham Ath.	Nantwich	12.28	28-31	105	-	21
Portsmouth	Tr	10.31	31-38	309	-	65
Crewe Alex.	Tr	04.46	46	7	-	1
Stockport Co.	Tr	09.46				

WORRALL, Gary G.
Salford, 4 November, 1961 (LW)

League Club	Source	Date Signed	Seasons Played	Apps	Subs	Gls
Manchester U.	App	11.78				
Peterborough U.	Tr	03.84	83-85	93	2	16
Carlisle U.	Tr	07.86	86	32	0	0

WORRALL, Harold
Northwich, 19 November, 1918 (FB)

League Club	Source	Date Signed	Seasons Played	Apps	Subs	Gls
Manchester U.	Winsford U.	10.37	46-47	6	-	0
Swindon T.	Tr	06.48				

WORRELL, Colin H.
Yarmouth, 29 August, 1943 (FB)

League Club	Source	Date Signed	Seasons Played	Apps	Subs	Gls
Norwich C.	Jnrs	11.61	62-64	9	-	0
Leyton Orient	Tr	09.64	64-65	51	0	0

WORSDALE, M. John
Stoke, 29 October, 1948 (W)

League Club	Source	Date Signed	Seasons Played	Apps	Subs	Gls
Stoke C.	App	11.65	68	4	0	0
Lincoln C.	Tr	05.71	71-73	55	12	9

WORSLEY, Graeme
Liverpool, 4 January, 1969 (RB)

League Club	Source	Date Signed	Seasons Played	Apps	Subs	Gls
Shrewsbury T.	Bootle	03.89	88-91	63	14	2

WORSMAN, Reginald H.
Bradford, 19 May, 1933 (IF)

League Club	Source	Date Signed	Seasons Played	Apps	Subs	Gls
Bradford P.A.	Jnrs	10.43	54-55	22	-	5
Bradford C.	Tr	06.56	56	1	-	0
Darlington	Nelson	06.60	60	4	-	1

WORSWICK, Michael A.
Preston, 14 March, 1945 E Amat (W)

League Club	Source	Date Signed	Seasons Played	Apps	Subs	Gls
Wigan Ath.	Chorley	(N/L)	78	0	1	0

WORTHINGTON, David
Halifax, 28 March, 1945 (RB)

League Club	Source	Date Signed	Seasons Played	Apps	Subs	Gls
Halifax T.	Jnrs	04.62	61-63	37	-	8
Barrow	Tr	07.64	64-65	60	1	7
Grimsby T.	Tr	06.66	66-72	292	1	14
Halifax T.	L	10.73	73	5	0	0
Southend U.	Tr	12.73	73-75	92	3	0

WORTHINGTON, Eric S.
Sheffield, 29 December, 1925 (IF)

League Club	Source	Date Signed	Seasons Played	Apps	Subs	Gls
Queens Park R.		09.47				
Watford	Tr	08.49	49-50	24	-	4
Bradford C.	Dover T.	09.53	53	2	-	1

WORTHINGTON, Frank S.
Halifax, 23 November, 1948 Eu23-2/EF Lge/E-8 (F)

League Club	Source	Date Signed	Seasons Played	Apps	Subs	Gls
Huddersfield T.	App	11.66	66-71	166	5	41
Leicester C.	Tr	08.72	72-77	209	1	72
Bolton W.	Tr	09.77	77-79	81	3	35
Birmingham C.	Tr	11.79	79-81	71	4	29
Leeds U.	Tr	03.82	81-82	32	0	14
Sunderland	Tr	12.82	82	18	1	2
Southampton	Tr	06.83	83	34	0	4
Brighton & H.A.	Tr	05.84	84	27	4	7
Tranmere Rov.	Tr	06.85	85-86	51	8	21
Preston N.E.	Tr	02.87	86-87	10	13	3
Stockport Co.	Tr	11.87	87	18	1	6

WORTHINGTON, Frederick
Manchester, 6 January, 1924 (IR)

League Club	Source	Date Signed	Seasons Played	Apps	Subs	Gls
Bury		07.47	47-50	69	-	14
Leicester C.	Tr	03.51	50-54	55	-	9
Exeter C.	Tr	07.55	55	16	-	1
Oldham Ath.	Tr	06.56	56	10	-	1

WORTHINGTON, Gary L.
Cleethorpes, 10 November, 1966 E Yth (F)

League Club	Source	Date Signed	Seasons Played	Apps	Subs	Gls
Manchester U.	App	11.84				
Huddersfield T.	Tr	07.86				
Darlington	Tr	07.87	87-88	31	9	15
Wrexham	Tr	06.89	89-90	68	4	18
Wigan Ath.	Tr	03.91	90-91	44	9	20

WORTHINGTON, Nigel
Ballymena (NI), 4 November, 1961 NI Yth/NI-37 (LB/W)

League Club	Source	Date Signed	Seasons Played	Apps	Subs	Gls
Notts Co.	Ballymena U.	07.81	81-83	62	5	4
Sheffield Wed.	Tr	02.84	83-91	264	3	10

WORTHINGTON, P. Robert
Halifax, 22 April, 1947 (LB)

League Club	Source	Date Signed	Seasons Played	Apps	Subs	Gls
Halifax T.	App	05.65	64	12	-	0
Middlesbrough	Tr	08.66	67	2	0	0
Notts Co.	Tr	09.68	68-73	230	2	1
Southend U.	Tr	08.74	74	20	0	1
Hartlepool U.	L	03.75	74	6	0	0

WOSAHLO, Roger F.
Cambridge, 11 September, 1947 E Sch (W)

League Club	Source	Date Signed	Seasons Played	Apps	Subs	Gls
Chelsea	App	12.64	66	0	1	0
Ipswich T.	Tr	07.67	67	1	0	0
Peterborough U.	Tr	07.68	68	13	2	1
Ipswich T.	Tr	07.69	69	0	1	0

WRAGG, Douglas
Nottingham, 12 September, 1934 E Sch (OR)

League Club	Source	Date Signed	Seasons Played	Apps	Subs	Gls
West Ham U.		06.53	56-59	16	-	0
Mansfield T.	Tr	03.60	59-60	46	-	13
Rochdale	Tr	07.61	61-63	103	-	15
Chesterfield	Tr	07.64	64	17	-	4

Frank Worthington (Huddersfield Town, Leicester City, Bolton Wanderers, Birmingham City, Leeds United, Sunderland, Southampton, Brighton & Hove Albion, Tranmere Rovers, Preston North End, Stockport County & England)

League Club	Source	Date Signed	Seasons Played	Apps	Subs	Gls
WRAGG, Peter						
Rotherham, 12 January, 1931						(IF)
Rotherham U.	Jnrs	05.48	48-52	31	-	4
Sheffield U.	Tr	01.53	52-54	56	-	17
York C.	Tr	08.56	56-62	264	-	78
Bradford C.	Tr	07.63	63-64	73	-	5
WRAITH, Robert						
Largs, 26 April, 1948						(G)
Southport	Glasgow Celtic	07.69	69-70	28	0	0
WRATTEN, Paul						
Middlesbrough, 29 November, 1970 E Yth						(M)
Manchester U.	YT	12.88	90	0	2	0
WRAY, John G.						
Mytholmyroyd, 7 July, 1941						(G)
Halifax T.	Stainland A.	11.64	64	7	-	0
WREN, John						
Bonnybridge, 26 April, 1936						(G)
Rotherham U.	Hibernian	08.60	60	1	-	0
WRENCH, Mark N.						
Warrington, 27 September, 1969						(FB)
Wrexham	YT	09.88	88-89	5	1	0
WRIGGLESWORTH, J. Lance						
Halifax, 4 July, 1924						(FB)
Halifax T.	Watford (Am)	07.46	46	10	-	1
WRIGGLESWORTH, William						
South Elmsall, 12 November, 1912						(OL)
Chesterfield	Frickley Colly	05.32	32-34	34	-	6
Wolverhampton W.	Tr	12.34	34-36	50	-	21
Manchester U.	Tr	02.37	36-46	27	-	7
Bolton W.	Tr	01.47	46-47	13	-	1
Southampton	Tr	10.47	47	12	-	4
Reading	Tr	06.48	48	5	-	0
WRIGHT, Alan G.						
Birmingham, 20 May, 1938						(F)
Walsall		05.58	58	1	-	1
WRIGHT, Alan G.						
Ashton-u-Lyne, 28 September, 1971 E Sch/E Yth						(LB)
Blackpool	YT	04.89	87-91	91	7	0
Blackburn Rov.	Tr	10.91	91	32	1	1

Alan Wright (Blackpool & Blackburn Rovers)

League Club	Source	Date Signed	Seasons Played	Apps	Subs	Gls
WRIGHT, Albert						
Lincoln C.		10.46	46	1	-	0
WRIGHT, Alexander, M.						
Kirkcaldy, 18 October, 1925						(IF)
Barnsley	Hibernian	08.47	47-50	83	-	30
Tottenham H.	Tr	09.50	50	2	-	1
Bradford P.A.	Tr	08.51	51-54	131	-	25
WRIGHT Archibald W.						
Glasgow, 23 November, 1924						(IR)
Blackburn Rov.	Falkirk	05.51	51-52	22	-	10
Grimsby T.	Tr	07.53	53	39	-	9
Accrington St.	Tr	06.54	54-56	80	-	27
WRIGHT, Arthur W. T.						
Burradon, 23 September, 1919 E Sch						(WH)
Sunderland	Jnrs	09.36	37-54	270	-	13
WRIGHT, Barrie						
Bradford, 6 November, 1945 E Sch/E Yth						(FB)
Leeds U.	App	11.62	62-63	5	-	0
Brighton & H.A.	New York R. (USA)	01.69	68-69	8	2	0
WRIGHT, Barry A.						
Wrexham, 23 July, 1939						(FB)
Wrexham	Jnrs	05.59	59-61	11	-	0
Chester C.	Tr	08.62	62	1	-	0
WRIGHT, Bernard A.						
Derry (NI), 8 June, 1940						(OR)
Port Vale	Sligo Rov.	09.62	62	14	-	2
WRIGHT, Bernard A. W.						
Walthamstow, 19 September, 1923						(G)
Notts Co.		02.46	46	3	-	0
WRIGHT, Bernard P.						
Birmingham, 17 September, 1952						(F)
Walsall	Birmingham C. (Am)	09.71	71	15	0	2
Everton	Tr	02.72	71-72	10	0	2
Walsall	Tr	01.73	72-76	145	7	38
Bradford C.	Tr	02.77	76-77	65	1	13
Port Vale	Tr	06.78	78-79	76	0	23
WRIGHT, G. Brian						
Sunderland, 16 September, 1939						(WH)
Newcastle U.	Jnrs	09.56	59-62	45	-	1
Peterborough U.	Tr	05.63	63-71	291	2	9
WRIGHT, Brian R.						
Leicester, 9 January, 1937 E Yth						(W)
Leicester C.	Jnrs	02.54				
Lincoln C.	Tr	01.59	58-60	22	-	3
WRIGHT, Charles G.						
Glasgow, 11 December, 1938						(G)
Workington	Glasgow Rangers	06.58	58-62	123	-	0
Grimsby T.	Tr	02.63	62-65	129	0	0
Charlton Ath.	Tr	03.66	65-70	195	0	0
Bolton W.	Tr	06.71	71-72	88	0	0
WRIGHT, G. Clifford						
Skelton, 18 October, 1944						(IF)
Middlesbrough	App	10.62				
Hartlepool U.	Tr	06.64	64-69	179	4	31
Darlington	Tr	02.70	69-70	16	0	4
WRIGHT, Darren J.						
West Bromwich, 14 March, 1968						(FB)
Wolverhampton W.	YT	07.85	85	1	0	0
Wrexham	Tr	08.86	86-89	105	5	4
WRIGHT, Dennis						
Chesterfield, 19 December, 1919						(G)
Mansfield T.	Clay Lane R.	03.39	46-56	379	-	0
WRIGHT, Dennis						
Royton, 9 January, 1930						(OL)
Oldham Ath. (Am)	Jnrs	05.46	46	3	-	0
Oldham Ath.	Glasgow Rangers	08.51	51	6	-	0
WRIGHT, Gary						
Torquay, 21 May, 1966						(RB)
Torquay U. (N/C)	Jnrs	08.84	84	2	0	0
Torquay U. (N/C)	Chard T.	08.87	87	1	1	0

League Club	Source	Date Signed	Seasons Played	Apps	Subs	Gls
WRIGHT, Gary J.						
Sunderland, 15 September, 1964						(G)
Hartlepool U. (N/C)	App	10.82	82	12	0	0
WRIGHT, Geoffrey D.						
Countesthorpe (Lei), 1 March, 1930						(CF)
Aston Villa		05.49				
Bournemouth	Tr	06.51				
Walsall	Rugby T.	03.52	52	16	-	1
WRIGHT, George A.						
Sheffield, 4 February, 1920						(IF)
Cardiff C.		03.42				
Hull C.	Tr	06.46	46	4	-	1
WRIGHT, George W.						
Ramsgate, 19 March, 1930						(FB)
West Ham U.	Margate	02.51	51-57	161	-	0
Leyton Orient	Tr	05.58	58-61	87	-	1
Gillingham	Tr	07.62	62	4	-	0
WRIGHT, George W.						
Plymouth, 10 October, 1919						(G)
Plymouth Arg.	Kitto Inst.	10.38	38-46	12	-	0
Colchester U.	Tr	07.49	50-54	151	-	0
WRIGHT, Glenn M.						
Liverpool, 27 May, 1956						(M)
Blackburn Rov. (App)	App	10.72	73	1	0	0
WRIGHT, Herbert M.						
Shirebrook, 29 May, 1931						(HB)
Leeds U.	Bolsover Colly	10.51				
Stockport Co.	Tr	06.53	53	1	-	0
Chester C.	Tr	07.54	54	21	-	4
WRIGHT, Ian E.						
Woolwich, 3 November, 1963 E'B'/E-5						(F)
Crystal Palace	Greenwich Bor.	08.85	85-91	206	19	90
Arsenal	Tr	09.91	91	30	0	24

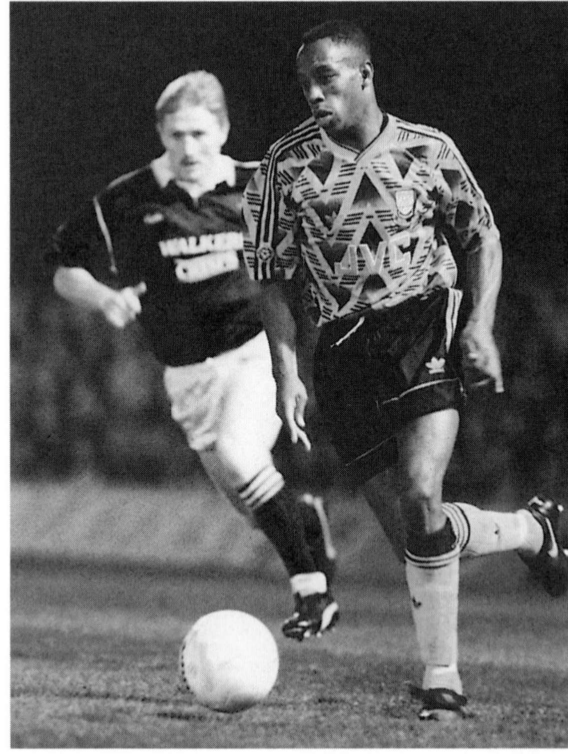

Ian Wright (Crystal Palace, Arsenal & England)

League Club	Source	Date Signed	Seasons Played	Apps	Subs	Gls
WRIGHT, Ian M.						
Lichfield, 10 March, 1972						(CD)
Stoke C.	YT	05.90	89-91	5	0	0
WRIGHT, James F.						
Whitefield, 19 February, 1924						(G)
Accrington St. (Am)	Bury Amats	09.47	47	1	-	0

League Club	Source	Date Signed	Seasons Played	Apps	Subs	Gls
WRIGHT, Jeffrey K.						
Alston, 23 June, 1952						(M)
Wigan Ath.	Netherfield	(N/L)	78-81	139	4	19
WRIGHT, John						
Blackhall (Dm), 30 January, 1925						(LH)
Darlington		01.47	46-48	17	-	0
WRIGHT, John						
Tyldesley, 11 August, 1926 E'B'-1						(FB)
Blackpool	Mossley	06.46	48-58	158	-	1
WRIGHT, John B.						
South Shields, 16 November, 1922						(CH)
Hull C.	Tyne Dock U.	09.47	47	1	-	0
WRIGHT, John D.						
Southend, 29 April, 1917 E-1						(WH)
Southend U.		08.36	36-37	30	-	2
Newcastle U.	Tr	05.38	38-46	72	-	1
Lincoln C.	Tr	12.48	48-54	233	-	2
WRIGHT, John F. D.						
Aldershot, 13 August, 1933						(G)
Colchester U.		11.54	54-60	5	-	0
WRIGHT, Kenneth L.						
Newmarket, 16 May, 1922						(F)
West Ham U.	Cambridge C.	05.46	46-49	51	-	20
WRIGHT, Mark						
Dorchester (Ox), 1 August, 1963 Eu21-4/E-42						(CD)
Oxford U.	Jnrs	08.80	81	8	2	0
Southampton	Tr	03.82	81-86	170	0	7
Derby Co.	Tr	08.87	87-90	144	0	10
Liverpool	Tr	07.91	91	21	0	0
WRIGHT, Mark A.						
Manchester, 29 January, 1970						(D)
Everton	YT	06.88	89	1	0	0
Blackpool	L	08.90	90	3	0	0
Huddersfield T.	Tr	03.91	90-91	14	4	1
WRIGHT, Martin H.						
Chesterfield, 1 April, 1950						(F)
Chesterfield	Alfreton T.	10.68	68-71	39	4	12
Torquay U.	Tr	07.72	72	8	5	3
WRIGHT, J. Michael						
Ellesmere Port, 25 September, 1946 E Yth						(RB)
Aston Villa	App	09.63	63-72	280	2	1
WRIGHT, Michael						
Darlington, 17 February, 1950						(D)
Darlington	Jnrs	06.68	68-72	82	7	0
WRIGHT, Michael E.						
Newmarket, 16 January, 1942						(IF)
Northampton T.	Newmarket	11.59	59-61	26	-	7
WRIGHT, Michael H.						
Winsford, 22 October, 1948						(F)
Shrewsbury T. (App)	App	03.64	65	0	1	0
Crewe Alex.	Tr	09.66				
WRIGHT, Patrick D. J.						
Oldbury, 17 November, 1940						(FB)
Birmingham C.	Brookfield	11.59	59-61	3	-	0
Shrewsbury T.	Tr	09.62	62-67	202	0	3
Derby Co.	Tr	10.67	67	12	1	0
Southend U.	L	03.70	69	11	0	0
Rotherham U.	Tr	09.70	70	1	0	0
WRIGHT, Paul H.						
East Kilbride, 17 August, 1967 S Yth/Su21-3						(F)
Queens Park R.	Aberdeen	07.89	89	9	6	5
WRIGHT, Peter B.						
Colchester, 26 January, 1934						(OL)
Colchester U.	Jnrs	11.51	51-53	426	-	89
WRIGHT, Ralph L.						
Newcastle, 3 August, 1947						(M)
Norwich C.	Spennymoor U.	07.68				
Bradford P.A.	Tr	10.69	69	13	1	1
Hartlepool U.	Tr	06.70	70	24	1	3
Stockport Co.	Tr	07.71	71	19	2	0
Bolton W.	Tr	02.72	71-72	25	7	5
Southport	Tr	12.72	72-73	40	3	5

Mark Wright (Oxford United, Southampton, Derby County, Liverpool & England)

League Club	Source	Date Signed	Seasons Played	Apps	Subs	Gls
WRIGHT, H. Raymond						
Pontefract, 6 September, 1918						(IF)
Wolverhampton W.		05.36	37-38	8	-	1
Exeter C.	Tr	03.46	46-47	56	-	11
WRIGHT, Richard						
Mexborough, 5 December, 1931						(G)
Leeds U.		05.49				
Chester C.	Tr	08.51	52-54	53	-	0
Bradford C.	Tr	03.55	55	1	-	0
WRIGHT, Robert C. A.						
Glasgow, 20 February, 1916						(LH)
Charlton Ath.	Horden Colly	05.37	38-46	28	-	0
WRIGHT, Ronald W.						
Glasgow, 6 December, 1940						(IF)
Leeds U.	Shettleston	06.59	60	1	-	0
WRIGHT, Stephen P.						
Clacton, 16 June, 1959						(D)
Colchester U.	Jnrs	06.77	77-81	112	5	2
Wrexham	H.J.K. Helsinki (Fin)	09.83	83-84	76	0	0
Torquay U.	Tr	07.85	85	33	0	0
Crewe Alex.	Tr	07.86	86-87	67	5	3
WRIGHT, Terence I.						
Newcastle, 22 June, 1939						(OL)
Barrow	Nuneaton Bor.	11.62	62-64	10	-	1
WRIGHT, Thomas						
Clackmannan, 20 January, 1928 S-3						(OR)
Sunderland	Partick Th.	03.49	48-54	170	-	52
Oldham Ath.	East Fife	03.57	56	7	-	2
WRIGHT, Thomas B.						
Glossop, 11 January, 1917						(OL)
Manchester C.	Droylsden	06.37				
Hull C.	Altrincham	07.47				
Accrington St.	Tr	10.47	47-48	20	-	4
WRIGHT, Thomas E.						
Dunfermline, 10 January, 1966 S Yth/Su21-1						(LW)
Leeds U.	App	01.83	82-85	73	8	24
Oldham Ath.	Tr	10.86	86-88	110	2	23
Leicester C.	Tr	08.89	89-91	122	7	22
WRIGHT, Thomas J.						
Liverpool, 21 October, 1944 Eu23-7/E-2						(FB)
Everton	Jnrs	03.63	64-72	307	1	4
WRIGHT, Thomas J.						
Belfast, 29 August, 1963 NIu21-1/NI-8						(G)
Newcastle U.	Linfield	01.88	88-91	56	0	0
Hull C.	L	02.91	90	6	0	0
WRIGHT, Thomas K.						
Stepps, 11 January, 1925						(F)
Aldershot	Dunfermline Ath.	07.52	52	17	-	1
WRIGHT, Vincent						
Bradford, 12 Aprl, 1931 E Yth						(W)
Derby Co.		09.51				
Mansfield T.	Tr	07.52	52	2	-	0
WRIGHT, J. William						
Blackpool, 4 March, 1931						(W)
Blackpool		05.50	51-54	15	-	2
Leicester C.	Tr	08.55	55-57	27	-	10
Newcastle U.	Tr	08.58	58	5	-	3
Plymouth Arg.	Tr	08.59	59-60	42	-	9
Millwall	Tr	08.61	61	15	-	0
WRIGHT, William						
Liverpool, 28 April, 1958 Eu21-6/E-'B'						(CD)
Everton	Jnrs	01.77	77-82	164	2	10
Birmingham C.	Tr	07.83	83-85	111	0	8
Chester C.	L	02.86	85	6	0	1
Carlisle U.	Tr	08.86	86-87	87	0	3
WRIGHT, William A.						
Ironbridge, 6 February, 1924 EF Lge/E-105						(CH)
Wolverhampton W.	Jnrs	02.41	46-58	490	-	13
WRIGHT, William H. R.						
Corbridge, 4 November, 1962						(F)
Burnley		01.81				
Crewe Alex.	L	11.82	82	3	0	1

League Club	Source	Date Signed	Seasons Played	Apps	Subs	Gls
WRIGHT, William S.						
Wordsley, 26 April, 1959						(D)
Birmingham C.	App	04.77				
Lincoln C.	Tr	07.78	78	3	0	0
WRIGHTSON, Jeffrey G.						
Newcastle, 18 May, 1968						(CD)
Newcastle U.	App	05.86	86	3	1	0
Preston N.E.	Tr	07.87	87-91	161	5	4
WRIGLEY, Wilfred						
Clitheroe, 4 October, 1949						(CH)
Burnley	Jnrs	07.68	68-69	6	0	1
WROE, Mark						
Manchester, 1 June, 1966						(M)
Stockport Co.	Jnrs	08.85	84-85	26	3	4
WYATT, George A.						
Whitechapel, 28 March, 1924 Died 1957						(LB)
Crystal Palace		11.47	48	7	-	0
WYATT, Reginald G.						
Plymouth, 18 September, 1932						(CH)
Plymouth Arg.	Astor Inst.	08.50	55-64	202	-	2
Torquay U.	Tr	10.64	64-66	80	0	6
WYER, Peter W.						
Coventry, 10 February, 1937						(IF)
Coventry C.		10.55	55	1	-	0
Derby Co.	Tr	06.56	56	2	-	1
Coventry C.	Tr	07.58	58	4	-	0
WYLDE, Rodger J.						
Sheffield, 8 March, 1954						(F)
Sheffield Wed.	App	07.71	72-79	157	11	54
Oldham Ath.	Tr	02.80	79-82	109	4	51
Sunderland	Sporting Lisbon (Port)	07.84	84	8	3	3
Barnsley	Tr	12.84	84-87	50	2	19
Rotherham U.	L	03.88	87	6	0	1
Stockport Co.	Tr	07.88	88	24	2	12
WYLDES, Robert J.						
Southport, 6 October, 1928						(OL)
Luton T.	Desborough	10.49	49-51	26	-	8
WYLES, Harold						
Melton Mowbray, 28 October, 1922						(FB)
Leicester C.		04.42				
Gateshead	Tr	03.48	47-53	235	-	7
WYLES, Thomas C.						
Bourne, 1 November, 1919 Died 1990						(CF)
Everton		02.38				
Bury	Tr	05.46	46	2	-	0
Southport	Tr	11.46	46-49	143	-	53
WYLIE, John E.						
Newcastle, 25 September, 1936						(WH)
Huddersfield T.		09.54				
Preston N.E.	Tr	05.57	58-62	91	-	1
Stockport Co.	Tr	11.62	62-63	68	-	2
Doncaster Rov.	Tr	08.64	64-67	123	1	2
WYLIE, Ronald M.						
Glasgow, 6 August, 1933 S Sch						(IF)
Notts Co.	Clydesdale Jnrs	09.50	51-58	227	-	33
Aston Villa	Tr	11.58	58-64	196	-	16
Birmingham C.	Tr	06.65	65-69	125	3	2
WYLLIE, James						
Saltcoats, 15 October, 1927						
Southport	Kilmarnock	07.50	50	15	-	1
Wrexham	Tr	12.50	50	20	-	4
WYLLIE, Robinson G. N. (Bob)						
Dundee, 4 April, 1929						(G)
Blackpool	Dundee U.	05.53	53-54	13	-	0
West Ham U.	Tr	05.56	56	13	-	0
Plymouth Arg.	Tr	07.58	58	5	-	0
Mansfield T.	Tr	10.59	59-61	92	-	0
WYNN, Ronald W.						
Wrexham, 2 November, 1923						(FB)
Wrexham		04.48	47-55	183	-	11
WYNNE, Darren L.						
St. Asaph, 12 October, 1970						(M)
Chester C.	YT	07.89	88-89	0	12	0

Ron Yeats (Dundee United, Liverpool, Tranmere Rovers & Scotland)
A driving force in Bill Shankley's Liverpool side that roared out of the Second Division, en-route to greater honours

YALLOP, Frank W.
Watford, 4 April, 1964 E Yth/Canadian Int (RB)

League Club	Source	Date Signed	Seasons Played	Apps	Subs	Gls
Ipswich T.	App	01.82	83-91	238	17	4

YANUSHEVSKI, Victor
Minsk (USSR), 23 January, 1960 (D)

League Club	Source	Date Signed	Seasons Played	Apps	Subs	Gls
Aldershot (N/C)	C.S.K. Moscow (USSR)	03.91	90	6	0	1

YARD, Ernest J.
Stranraer, 3 May, 1941 (CF/WH)

League Club	Source	Date Signed	Seasons Played	Apps	Subs	Gls
Bury	Partick Th.	12.63	63-64	45	-	13
Crystal Palace	Tr	05.65	65-66	35	2	3
Reading	Tr	11.66	66-68	101	3	6

YARDLEY, George
Kirkcaldy, 8 October, 1942 (CF)

League Club	Source	Date Signed	Seasons Played	Apps	Subs	Gls
Luton T.	Australia	10.66	66	1	0	0
Tranmere Rov.	Tr	11.66	66-70	123	0	69

YATES, David
Barnsley, 18 March, 1953 (FB)

League Club	Source	Date Signed	Seasons Played	Apps	Subs	Gls
Barnsley	App	03.71	72-77	104	0	2
Grimsby T.	L	03.77	76	10	0	0

YATES, Dean R.
Leicester, 26 October, 1967 Eu21-5 (CD)

League Club	Source	Date Signed	Seasons Played	Apps	Subs	Gls
Notts Co.	App	06.85	84-91	291	1	33

Dean Yates (Notts County)

YATES, Harold
Huddersfield, 28 September, 1925 (IF)

League Club	Source	Date Signed	Seasons Played	Apps	Subs	Gls
Huddersfield T.	Jnrs	10.43	49	1	-	0
Darlington	Tr	05.50	50-51	91	-	29

YATES, John
Rotherham, 18 November, 1929 (OR)

League Club	Source	Date Signed	Seasons Played	Apps	Subs	Gls
Sheffield U.		06.50				
Chester C.	Tr	08.51	51	2	-	0

YATES, Mark J.
Birmingham, 24 January, 1970 (M)

League Club	Source	Date Signed	Seasons Played	Apps	Subs	Gls
Birmingham C.	YT	07.88	87-91	38	16	6
Burnley	Tr	08.91	91	9	8	1

YATES, Richard
Queensferry, 6 June, 1921 (CF)

League Club	Source	Date Signed	Seasons Played	Apps	Subs	Gls
Chester C.		08.39	46-47	52	-	37
Wrexham	Tr	12.47	47-48	31	-	19
Carlisle U.	Tr	11.48	48	16	-	9
New Brighton	Tr	08.49	49-50	43	-	14

YATES, Stephen
Measham, 8 December, 1953 (LB)

League Club	Source	Date Signed	Seasons Played	Apps	Subs	Gls
Leicester C.	App	12.71	73-76	12	7	0
Southend U.	Tr	11.77	77-83	223	1	8
Doncaster Rov.	Tr	12.83	83-84	44	0	1
Darlington	L	01.85	84	4	0	0
Chesterfield	L	03.85	84	1	0	0
Stockport Co. (N/C)	Tr	08.85	85	2	0	0

YATES, Steven
Bristol, 29 January, 1970 (CD)

League Club	Source	Date Signed	Seasons Played	Apps	Subs	Gls
Bristol Rov.	YT	06.88	86-91	151	1	0

YEATS, Ronald
Aberdeen, 15 November, 1937 S Sch/S-2 (CH)

League Club	Source	Date Signed	Seasons Played	Apps	Subs	Gls
Liverpool	Dundee U.	07.61	61-70	357	1	13
Tranmere Rov.	Tr	12.71	71-73	96	1	5

YEATS, Thomas B.
Newcastle, 30 May, 1935 (F)

League Club	Source	Date Signed	Seasons Played	Apps	Subs	Gls
Sunderland	Jnrs	02.53				
Gateshead	Tr	08.54	54	1	-	0

YEATS, William
Hebburn, 4 February, 1951 (F)

League Club	Source	Date Signed	Seasons Played	Apps	Subs	Gls
Newcastle U.	North Shields	06.71				
York C.	Tr	03.72	71-72	8	1	0
Darlington	Tr	08.73	73-74	22	3	7

YEO, Brian G.
Worthing, 12 April, 1944 (F)

League Club	Source	Date Signed	Seasons Played	Apps	Subs	Gls
Portsmouth	Jnrs	05.61				
Gillingham	Tr	07.63	63-74	345	10	136

YEOMAN, Raymond I.
Perth, 13 May, 1934 (WH)

League Club	Source	Date Signed	Seasons Played	Apps	Subs	Gls
Northampton T.	St Johnstone	09.53	53-58	168	-	4
Middlesbrough	Tr	11.58	58-63	210	-	3
Darlington	Tr	06.64	64-66	103	0	2

YEOMANS, Kelvin
Nottingham, 25 August, 1947 (FB)

League Club	Source	Date Signed	Seasons Played	Apps	Subs	Gls
Notts Co. (Am)	Beeston	06.67	67	1	0	0

YEOMANSON, John
Margate, 3 March, 1920 (FB)

League Club	Source	Date Signed	Seasons Played	Apps	Subs	Gls
West Ham U.	Margate	02.47	47-50	106	-	1

YORATH, Terence C.
Cardiff, 27 March, 1950 W Sch/Wu23-7/W-59 (M)

League Club	Source	Date Signed	Seasons Played	Apps	Subs	Gls
Leeds U.	App	04.67	67-76	120	21	10
Coventry C.	Tr	08.76	76-78	99	0	3
Tottenham H.	Tr	08.79	79-80	44	4	1
Bradford C.	Vancouver (Can)	12.82	82-84	22	5	0
Swansea C.	(Manager)	10.86	86	1	0	0

YORK, Alan
Newcastle, 13 July, 1941 (FB)

League Club	Source	Date Signed	Seasons Played	Apps	Subs	Gls
Bradford C.	Gateshead	02.65	64-66	42	3	2
Lincoln C.	Tr	07.67				

YORKE, Dwight
Tobago, 3 November, 1971 Trinidad Int (F)

League Club	Source	Date Signed	Seasons Played	Apps	Subs	Gls
Aston Villa	Signal Hill (Tob.)	11.89	89-91	35	17	13

YOUDS, Edward P.
Liverpool, 3 May, 1970 (D)

League Club	Source	Date Signed	Seasons Played	Apps	Subs	Gls
Everton	YT	06.88	90	5	3	0
Cardiff C.	L	12.89	89	0	1	0
Wrexham	L	02.90	89	20	0	2
Ipswich T.	Tr	11.91	91	1	0	0

YOUELL, Jasper H.
Bilston, 23 March, 1925 (FB)

League Club	Source	Date Signed	Seasons Played	Apps	Subs	Gls
Portsmouth	West Bromwich A. (Am)	08.46	46-51	30	-	0
Barnsley	Tr	08.52	52	19	-	0

YOULDEN, Thomas F.
Islington, 8 July, 1949 E Sch (CD)

League Club	Source	Date Signed	Seasons Played	Apps	Subs	Gls
Arsenal	App	07.66				
Portsmouth	Tr	04.68	68-71	82	8	1
Reading	Tr	07.72	72-76	161	2	3
Aldershot	Tr	04.77	76-80	118	5	1

YOUNG, Alan F.
Kirkcaldy, 26 October, 1955 S Sch (F)

League Club	Source	Date Signed	Seasons Played	Apps	Subs	Gls
Oldham Ath.	Jnrs	07.74	74-78	107	15	30
Leicester C.	Tr	07.79	79-81	102	2	26
Sheffield U.	Tr	08.82	82	23	3	7
Brighton & H.A.	Tr	08.83	83	25	1	12
Notts Co.	Tr	09.84	84-85	39	4	13
Rochdale	Tr	08.86	86	19	9	2

YOUNG, Alan R.
Hornsey, 20 January, 1941 (CH)

League Club	Source	Date Signed	Seasons Played	Apps	Subs	Gls
Arsenal	Jnrs	04.59	60	4	-	0
Chelsea	Tr	11.61	61-66	20	0	0
Torquay U.	Tr	01.69	68-71	59	0	1

YOUNG, Albert E.
Caerleon, 11 September, 1917 (FB)

League Club	Source	Date Signed	Seasons Played	Apps	Subs	Gls
Arsenal		09.38				
Swindon T.	Tr	06.46	46-49	123	-	1

YOUNG, Alexander
Loanhead, 3 February, 1937 Su23-6/SF Lge/S-8 (F)

League Club	Source	Date Signed	Seasons Played	Apps	Subs	Gls
Everton	Hearts	11.60	60-67	227	1	77
Stockport Co.	Glentoran	11.68	68	23	0	5

Alex Young (Hearts, Everton, Glentoran, Stockport County & Scotland)

YOUNG, T. Anthony
Urmston, 24 December, 1952 (M)

League Club	Source	Date Signed	Seasons Played	Apps	Subs	Gls
Manchester U.	App	12.69	71-75	69	14	1
Charlton Ath.	Tr	01.76	75-76	20	0	1
York C.	Tr	09.76	76-78	76	2	2

YOUNG, Charles F.
Cyprus, 14 February, 1958 (CD)

League Club	Source	Date Signed	Seasons Played	Apps	Subs	Gls
Aston Villa	App	11.75	76	9	1	0
Gillingham	Tr	03.78	77-81	27	1	1

YOUNG, Charles S. R.
Falkirk, 23 August, 1929 (G)

League Club	Source	Date Signed	Seasons Played	Apps	Subs	Gls
Sheffield U.	Stalybridge Celtic	05.51	51	3	-	0

YOUNG, Clarence W.
Bow, 23 February, 1920 (OL)

League Club	Source	Date Signed	Seasons Played	Apps	Subs	Gls
Coventry C.	Margate	09.38	46	1	-	0

YOUNG, David
Newcastle, 12 November, 1945 (CD)

League Club	Source	Date Signed	Seasons Played	Apps	Subs	Gls
Newcastle U.	Jnrs	09.64	69-72	41	2	2
Sunderland	Tr	01.73	72-73	23	6	1
Charlton Ath.	Tr	08.74	74-76	76	1	0
Southend U.	Tr	09.76	76-77	56	4	0

YOUNG, David A.
Trimdon, 31 January, 1965 (LB)

League Club	Source	Date Signed	Seasons Played	Apps	Subs	Gls
Darlington	App	01.83	82-83	13	5	0

YOUNG, David J.
Birkenhead, 27 April, 1962 (M)

League Club	Source	Date Signed	Seasons Played	Apps	Subs	Gls
Wigan Ath. (N/C)	Mossley	03.83	82	3	0	0

YOUNG, Douglas H.
Croydon, 2 February, 1927 E Amat (FB)

League Club	Source	Date Signed	Seasons Played	Apps	Subs	Gls
Southend U.	Walthamstow Ave.	06.53	53-55	37	-	0

YOUNG, Eric
Singapore, 25 March, 1960 W-10 (CD)

League Club	Source	Date Signed	Seasons Played	Apps	Subs	Gls
Brighton & H.A.	Slough T.	11.82	83-86	126	0	10
Wimbledon	Tr	07.87	87-89	96	3	9
Crystal Palace	Tr	08.90	90-91	64	0	4

YOUNG, Eric R.
Stockton, 26 November, 1952 E Yth (M)

League Club	Source	Date Signed	Seasons Played	Apps	Subs	Gls
Manchester U.	App	12.69				
Peterborough U.	L	11.72	72	24	1	2
Walsall	L	10.73	73	8	0	0
Stockport Co.	Tr	01.74	73	16	0	0
Darlington	Tr	07.74	74-77	123	7	15

YOUNG, George
Dundee, 2 November, 1919 (IF)

League Club	Source	Date Signed	Seasons Played	Apps	Subs	Gls
Watford	Hibernian	07.46	46-48	43	-	5

YOUNG, George R.
Newport, 5 January, 1950 Wu23-1 (M)

League Club	Source	Date Signed	Seasons Played	Apps	Subs	Gls
Newport Co.	Cromwell Jnrs	07.67	67-71	90	15	6

YOUNG, Gerald M.
Jarrow, 1 October, 1936 E-1 (WH)

League Club	Source	Date Signed	Seasons Played	Apps	Subs	Gls
Sheffield Wed.	Hebburn Arg.	05.55	56-70	308	2	13

YOUNG, John D.
Hartlepool, 9 November, 1951 (OR)

League Club	Source	Date Signed	Seasons Played	Apps	Subs	Gls
Hartlepool U. (Am)	Newcastle U. (Am)	08.68	68	3	0	0

YOUNG, John R.
(G)

League Club	Source	Date Signed	Seasons Played	Apps	Subs	Gls
Gateshead (Am)		08.49	49	4	-	0

YOUNG, Kenneth
Halifax, 11 June, 1930

League Club	Source	Date Signed	Seasons Played	Apps	Subs	Gls
Halifax T.	Jnrs	11.49	49	1	-	0

YOUNG, Kevin
Sunderland, 12 August, 1961 (LW)

League Club	Source	Date Signed	Seasons Played	Apps	Subs	Gls
Burnley	App	05.79	78-83	114	6	11
Torquay U.	L	11.83	83	3	0	1
Port Vale	L	12.83	83	28	0	4
Bury	Tr	07.84	84-86	85	3	10

YOUNG, Leonard A.
East Ham, 23 February, 1912 (CH)

League Club	Source	Date Signed	Seasons Played	Apps	Subs	Gls
West Ham U.		04.34	33-37	12	-	0
Reading	Tr	11.37	37-47	83	-	0
Brighton & H.A.	Tr	02.48	47-48	8	-	0

YOUNG, Martin
Grimsby, 9 April, 1955 (D/M)

League Club	Source	Date Signed	Seasons Played	Apps	Subs	Gls
Grimsby T.	Jnrs	03.74	74-78	87	7	4

YOUNG, Michael S.
Chester-le-Street, 15 March, 1973 (W)

League Club	Source	Date Signed	Seasons Played	Apps	Subs	Gls
Middlesbrough	Newcastle U. (YT)	07.91	91	0	1	0

YOUNG, Neil J.
Manchester, 17 February, 1944 E Yth (F)

League Club	Source	Date Signed	Seasons Played	Apps	Subs	Gls
Manchester C.	App	02.61	61-71	332	2	86
Preston N.E.	Tr	01.72	71-73	67	1	16
Rochdale	Tr	07.74	74	8	5	4

League Club	Source	Date Signed	Seasons Played	Career Record Apps	Subs	Gls

YOUNG, Noel J.
Derry (NI), 22 December, 1932

Middlesbrough	Jnrs	04.50				
Doncaster Rov.		01.55	54	3	-	0

YOUNG, Quintin
Irvine, 19 September, 1947 Su23-1 (W)

Coventry C.	Ayr U.	07.71	71-72	25	1	2

YOUNG, G. Raymond
Derby, 14 March, 1934 E Sch (CH)

Derby Co.	Jnrs	03.51	53-65	253	1	5

YOUNG, Richard
Felling, 13 July, 1939 (CF)

Newcastle U.	Usworth Jnrs	07.57				
Grimsby T.	South Shields	03.62	62-64	33	-	13
Stockport Co.	Tr	05.65	65	27	0	5

YOUNG Richard A.
Nottingham, 18 October, 1968 (F)

Notts Co.	YT	08.86	86	18	17	5
Southend U.	Tr	08.87	87-88	5	4	0
Exeter C.	Tr	03.89	88-90	32	17	10

YOUNG, Richard H.
Gateshead, 17 April, 1918 Died 1989 (CH)

Sheffield U.	Wardley Colly	11.35	36-48	71	-	0
Lincoln C.	Tr	03.49	48-53	100	-	2

YOUNG, Robert G.
Bournemouth, 24 December, 1923 (FB)

Bournemouth	Jnrs	01.46	47	1	-	0
Crewe Alex.	Tr	06.48	48-51	144	-	2

YOUNG, C. Ronald
Bournemouth, 22 July, 1925 (HB)

Bournemouth		06.48	48-49	18	-	0

YOUNG, Ronald
Gateshead, 31 August, 1945 (W)

Hull C.		08.63	64-67	24	2	5
Hartlepool U.	Tr	09.68	68-72	176	10	40

YOUNG, Roy
Sheffield, 2 October, 1950 (FB)

Doncaster Rov.	Sheffield U. (Am)	07.70	70	6	1	0

YOUNG, Stuart R.
Hull, 16 December, 1972 (F)

Hull C.	Arsenal (YT)	07.91	91	7	8	2

YOUNG, Thomas
Glasgow, 24 December, 1947 (M)

Tranmere Rov.	Falkirk	06.72	72-76	170	2	27
Rotherham U.	Tr	07.77	77-78	11	4	1

YOUNG, William D.
Edinburgh, 25 November, 1951 Su23-5 (CD)

Tottenham H.	Aberdeen	09.75	75-76	54	0	3
Arsenal	Tr	03.77	76-81	170	0	11
Nottingham F.	Tr	12.81	81-82	59	0	5
Norwich C.	Tr	08.83	83	5	1	0
Brighton & H.A.	L	03.84	83	4	0	0
Darlington (N/C)	Tr	09.84	84	4	0	0

YOUNG, William J.
Glasgow, 24 February, 1956 (W)

Aston Villa	Arthurlie	07.78	78	3	0	0
Torquay U.	Tr	10.81	81-82	35	3	0

YOUNGER, Thomas
Edinburgh, 10 April, 1930 Died 1984 SF Lge/S-24 (G)

Liverpool	Hibernian	06.56	56-58	120	-	0
Stoke C.	Falkirk	03.60	59	10	-	0
Leeds U.	Toronto (Can)	09.61	61-62	37	-	0

YOUNGER, William
Whitley Bay, 22 March, 1940 (IF)

Nottingham F.	Whitley Bay	05.57	58-60	12	-	2
Lincoln C.	L	02.61	60	4	-	0
Walsall	Tr	06.61	61	7	-	5
Doncaster Rov.	Tr	12.61	61	18	-	1
Hartlepool U.	Tr	08.62	62	37	-	3

League Club	Source	Date Signed	Seasons Played	Career Record Apps	Subs	Gls

YOUNGMAN, Stuart T.
Beccles, 15 October, 1965

Colchester U.		07.84	84	0	1	0

ZELEM, Peter R.
Manchester, 13 February, 1962 (CD)

Chester C.	App	02.80	80-84	124	5	15
Wolverhampton W.	Tr	01.85	84-86	45	0	1
Preston N.E.	Tr	03.87	86	6	0	1
Burnley	Tr	08.87	87-88	17	2	2

ZENCHUK, Steven J.
Peterborough, 20 November, 1966 (G)

Peterborough U.	YT	08.83	83	1	0	0

ZONDERVAN, Romeo
Surinam, 4 March, 1959 Neth Int (M/FB)

West Bromwich A.	Twente Enschede (Neth)	03.82	81-83	82	2	5
Ipswich T.	Tr	03.84	83-91	270	4	13

Romeo Zondervan (Den Haag, Twente Enschede, West Bromwich Albion, Ipswich Town & Holland)

ZORICICH, Christopher V.
New Zealand, 3 May, 1970 (D)

Leyton Orient		02.90	90-91	43	7	0